Associate Justices (continued)

NAME	YEARS OF SERVICE	STATE APP'T FROM	APPOINTING PRESIDENT	AGE APP'T	POLITICAL AFFILIATION	EDUCATIONAL BACKGROUND
Johnson, William	1804-1834	South Carolina	Jefferson	33	Democratic-Republican	College of New Jersey (Princeton)
Livingston, Henry Brockholst	1807-1823	New York	Jefferson	50	Democratic-Republican	College of New Jersey (Princeton)
Todd, Thomas	1807-1826	Kentucky	Jefferson	42	Democratic-Republican	Liberty Hall (Washington and Lee University)
Duvall, Gabriel	1811-1835	Maryland	Madison	59	Democratic-Republican	Self-taught in law
Story, Joseph	1812-1845	Massachusetts	Madison	33	Democratic-Republican	Harvard
Thompson, Smith	1823-1843	New York	Monroe	55	Democratic-Republican	College of New Jersey (Princeton)
Trimble, Robert	1826-1828	Kentucky	Adams, J. Q.	50	Democratic-Republican	Kentucky Academy (Transylvania University)
McLean, John	1830-1861	Ohio	Jackson	45	Democrat	Read law under Arthur St. Clair, Jr.
Baldwin, Henry	1830-1844	Pennsylvania	Jackson	50	Democrat	Yale College
Wayne, James Moore	1835-1867	Georgia	Jackson	45	Democrat	Princeton
Barbour, Philip Pendleton	1836-1841	Virginia	Jackson	53	Democrat	Read on his own; attended one session at College of William and Mary
Catron, John	1837-1865	Tennessee	Van Buren	51	Democrat	Self-taught in law
McKinley, John	1838-1852	Alabama	Van Buren	58	Democrat	Self-taught in law
Daniel, Peter Vivian	1842-1860	Virginia	Van Buren	58	Democrat	Attended one year at Princeton
Nelson, Samuel	1845-1872	New York	Tyler	53	Democrat	Middlebury College
Woodbury, Levi	1845-1851	New Hampshire	Polk	56	Democrat	Dartmouth College; Tapping Reeve Law School
Grier, Robert Cooper	1846-1870	Pennsylvania	Polk	52	Democrat	Dickinson College
Curtis, Benjamin Robbins	1851-1857	Massachusetts	Fillmore	42	Whig	Harvard; Harvard Law School
Campbell, John Archibald	1853-1861	Alabama	Pierce	42	Democrat	Franklin College; U.S. Military Academy at West Point
Clifford, Nathan	1858-1881	Maine	Buchanan	55	Democrat	Read law in offices of Josiah Quincy
Swayne, Noah Haynes	1862-1881	Ohio	Lincoln	58	Republican	Read law privately
Miller, Samuel Freeman	1862-1890	Iowa	Lincoln	46	Republican	Transylvania University Medical School; read law privately
Davis, David	1862-1877	Illinois	Lincoln	47	Republican	Kenyon College; Yale Law School
Field, Stephen Johnson	1863-1897	California	Lincoln	47	Democrat	Williams College; read law privately
Strong, William	1870-1880	Pennsylvania	Grant	62	Republican	Yale College
Bradley, Joseph P.	1870-1892	New Jersey	Grant	57	Republican	Rutgers
Hunt, Ward	1873-1882	New York	Grant	63	Republican	Union College; read law privately
Harlan, John Marshall	1877-1911	Kentucky	Hayes	61	Republican	Centre College; studied law at Transylvania University
Woods, William Burnham	1881-1887	Georgia	Hayes	57	Republican	Yale
Matthews, Stanley	1881-1889	Ohio	Garfield	57	Republican	Kenyon College
Gray, Horace	1882-1902	Massachusetts	Arthur	54	Republican	Harvard College; Harvard Law School
Blatchford, Samuel	1882-1893	New York	Arthur	62	Republican	Columbia College

BUSINESS LAW TODAY

Text, Summarized Cases, Legal, Ethical, Regulatory and International Environment

Third Edition

The Three Versions of

Business Law Today, Third Edition

You now have a choice of three different versions of the third edition of *Business Law Today*, depending on your teaching needs.

Business Law Today: Text, Summarized Cases, Legal, Ethical, Regulatory and International Environment

- 36 Chapters
- Summarized cases
- All pedagogical features
- A full supplements package
- *Personal Law Handbook*

Business Law Today: Comprehensive Edition, Text, Cases, Legal, Ethical, Regulatory and International Environment

The ideal text for a complete two-semester course in business law and the legal environment. This version includes additional legal environment chapters and those chapters necessary for students taking the CPA exam.

- 42 Chapters
- Actual case excerpts in the words of the court
- All pedagogical features
- A full supplements package
- *Personal Law Handbook* (as a separate booklet)

Business Law Today: The Essentials, Text, Summarized Cases, Legal, Ethical, Regulatory, and International Environment

This shorter version is aimed at a one-semester introductory course in business law and the legal environment.

- 22 Chapters
- Paraphrased cases
- All pedagogical features
- A full supplements package
- *Personal Law Handbook*

BUSINESS LAW TODAY

Text, Summarized Cases, Legal, Ethical, Regulatory and International Environment

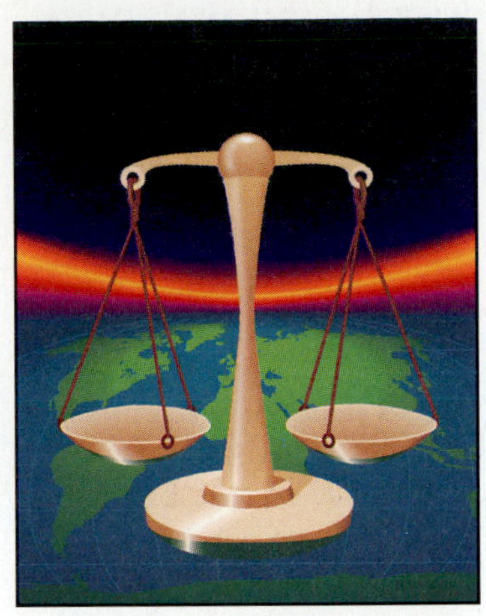

Third Edition

ROGER LeROY MILLER
School of Law
University of Miami

GAYLORD A. JENTZ
Herbert D. Kelleher
Professor in Business Law
Department of MSIS
University of Texas at Austin

WEST PUBLISHING COMPANY
St. Paul/Minneapolis New York Los Angeles San Francisco

WEST'S COMMITMENT TO THE ENVIRONMENT

In 1906, West Publishing Company began recycling materials left over from the production of books. This began a tradition of efficient and responsible use of resources. Today, up to 95 percent of our legal books and 70 percent of our college and school texts are printed on recycled, acid-free stock. West also recycles nearly 22 million pounds of scrap paper annually—the equivalent of 181.717 trees. Since the 1960s, West has devised ways to capture and recycle waste inks, solvents, oils, and vapors created in the printing process. We also recycle plastics of all kinds, wood, glass, corrugated cardboard, and batteries, and have eliminated the use of Styrofoam book packaging. We at West are proud of the longevity and the scope of our commitment to the environment.

Production, Prepress, Printing and Binding by West Publishing Company.

610 Opperman Drive
P.O. Box 64526
St. Paul, MN 55164-0526

Printed in the United States of America

01 00 99 98 97 96 95 8 7 6 5 4 3 2

Library of Congress Cataloging-in-Publication Data

Miller, Roger LeRoy.
Business law today / Roger LeRoy Miller, Gaylord A. Jentz.—3rd ed.
p. cm.

Includes index.
ISBN 0-314-02582-0 (hard)
1. Commercial law—United States—Cases. 2. Trade regulation——United States—Cases. I. Jentz, Gaylord A. II. Title.
KF888.M55 1994
346.73'07—dc20
(347.3067)

93-25927
CIP

7 From the Painting by Benjamin Ferrers in the National Portrait Gallery, UPI/Bettmann Archive; **10** Bettmann Archive; **23** West Publishing; **35** Will & Deni McIntyre, Photo Researchers, Inc.; **44** P. F. Gero, Sygma; **46** Michael Newman, PhotoEdit; **61** Reuters/Bettmann; **66 left** Jeffrey Markowitz, Sygma; **66 right** Collection of the Supreme Court of the United States; **70** Bettmann Archive; **72** Collection of the Supreme Court of the United States; **78** John Neubauer, PhotoEdit; **97** Michael Evans, Sygma; **103** Collection of the Supreme Court of the United States; **107** Frank Trapper, Sygma; **128** P. Hammerschmidt, Photo Researchers, Inc.; **135** David Butow, Black Star; **139** Bernard Asset, Photo Researchers, Inc.; **143** Jim Zipp, Photo Researchers, Inc.; **154** A. Tannenbaum, Sygma; **158** Will & Deni McIntyre, Photo Researchers, Inc.; **177 left** Richard Mims, Sygma; **177 right** Stephen Ferry, Gamma-Liaison; **182** Elena Rooraid, PhotoEdit; **184** Flip Schulke, Black Star; **205** Photo Researchers, Inc.; **206** Yale University Art Gallery, Gift of the Class of 1929 Law and friends of the Law School; **222** J. P. Laffont, Sygma; **232** Michael Newman, PhotoEdit; **246** Ken Lax, Photo Researchers, Inc.; **252** Bettmann Archive; **272** Ewing Galloway, Inc; **308** Stephen Feld Photography; **317** Dwight Cendrowski, FocuSing Group; **360** Dean Abramson, Stock Boston; **362** Michael Newman, PhotoEdit; **373** Leslye Borden, PhotoEdit; **405** Bart Richmond; **408** Jerry Mason/Science Photo Library, Photo Researchers, Inc.; **410** Steve Leonard, Black Star; **411** Collection of the Supreme Court of the United States; **487** Bart Richmond; **504** David Young-Wolff, PhotoEdit; **538** Tony Freeman, PhotoEdit; **559** Deborah Davis, PhotoEdit; **562** Myrleen Ferguson, PhotoEdit; **586** Phil Borden, PhotoEdit; **592** Bart Richmond; **627** Painting by Robert Burns, Hood Museum of Art; **631** Barth Falkenberg, Stock Boston, Inc.; **643** Joe McNally, Sygma; **666** Myrleen Ferguson, PhotoEdit; **679 left** David Young-Wolff, PhotoEdit; **680 right** David Young-Wolff, PhotoEdit; **705** Sygma; **734** Bart Richmond; **743** Bart Richmond; **747** PhotoEdit; **755** J. L. Atlan, Sygma; **756** Tom Prettyman, PhotoEdit; **771** Jim Corwin, Stock Boston, Inc.; **777** Lowell Georgia, Photo Researchers, Inc.; **779** Bob Daemmrich, Stock Boston, Inc.; **791** Painting by Charles Sidney Hopkinson; **803** B. Annebicque, Sygma; **813** Michael Newman, PhotoEdit; **817** Michael Newman, PhotoEdit; **830** Tony Freeman, PhotoEdit; **835** Tony Freeman, PhotoEdit; **878** Bill Bachman, PhotoEdit; **879** Stock Boston, Inc.; **889** P. Perrin, Sygma

Contents in Brief

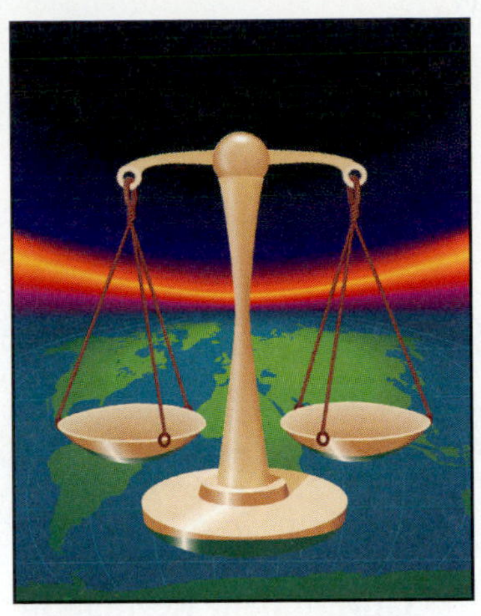

❖ *Unit Five* Government Regulation 715

❖ *Unit Six* Property and Its Protection 799

❖ *Unit Seven* The International Legal Environment 873

❖ Personal Law Handbook

❖ Appendices A-1

Contents

Preface to the Instructor

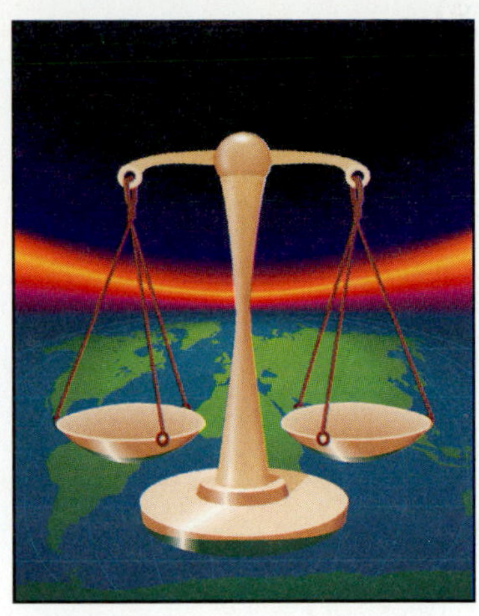

We have always felt that business law and the legal environment is an exciting, contemporary, and interesting course. *Business Law Today*, we believe, imparts this excitement to your students. They will find the study of business law and the legal environment accessible and fun. We spent a great deal of effort giving this book a visual appeal that would encourage learning the law. We know we have departed from the traditional presentation of the usual course materials, but up to this date, students and instructors who have used this text in its first two editions have found it extremely effective.

We believe that a thorough understanding of "black letter law" in the traditional business law topics—contracts, sales, torts, agency, business organizations, and the like—is important. Additionally, though, we strongly believe that students must learn these traditional topics within the context of the social, ethical, cultural, global, economic, technological, political, environmental, and practical context of the law.

❖ Key Features

Virtually all of the chapters in this text have one or more of the following special sections, which are designed both to instruct and to pique the interest of the business law student.

Landmark in the Law

In this edition, thirty-four chapters have a *Landmark in the Law*. For the most part, these *Landmarks* discuss important cases or statutes affecting business law. Among the *Landmarks* are the following:

- Courts of Equity and Equitable Maxims (Chapter 1).
- *Miranda v. Arizona* (1966) (Chapter 7).
- Plain-Language Laws (Chapter 8).
- The Statute of Frauds (Chapter 11).
- Limited Liability Company (LLC) Statutes (Chapter 24).
- Corporate Sentencing Guidelines (Chapter 27).
- Superfund (Chapter 31).
- The United Nations Convention on Contracts for the International Sale of Goods (CISG) (Chapter 36).

Business Law in Action

A special feature entitled *Business Law in Action* is included in thirty-four of the thirty-six chapters of this text. These features present practical and instructive examples of how the law affects people in the business and/or personal world. Some of these features are as follows:

- High Tech in the Courtroom (Chapter 3).
- Box Tops and the Battle of the Forms (Chapter 14).
- Scam Schools and Student Loans (Chapter 22).
- Who Owns "Works for Hire"? (Chapter 23).
- Interstate Water Pollution (Chapter 31).
- Teamwork—A Solution or a Problem? (Chapter 32).
- Who Owns Your Body Tissue? (Chapter 33).

Application

Nearly all of the chapters have an *Application* section, which presents the student with some practical advice on how to apply the law discussed in the chapter to real-world business problems. Each *Application* ends with a "Checklist" for the future businessperson on how to avoid legal problems. The following are some of the *Applications:*

- Law and the Businessperson—How to Choose and Use a Lawyer (Chapter 1).
- Law and the Employer—How to Create an Ethical Workplace (Chapter 2).
- Law and the Businessperson—Creating and Protecting Your Trademark (Chapter 6).
- Law and the Corporation—Developing a Document-Retention Policy (Chapter 27).
- Law and the Businessperson—Keeping Abreast of Environmental Laws (Chapter 31).
- Law and the Employer—A Rational Approach to Sexual Harassment in the Workplace (Chapter 32).

Ethical Perspective

Understanding ethics and the ethical dimensions of business and business law is undoubtedly a crucial factor in the business law student's education. In addition to a chapter on ethics, chapter-ending ethical questions, and the *Ethical Considerations* following many of the cases presented in this text, we have included a special feature entitled *Ethical Perspectives* in many of the chapters, including those listed below:

- No Duty to Rescue (Chapter 5).
- Lies, Trickery, and Justice (Chapter 7).
- The Equitable Remedy of Quasi Contract (Chapter 8).
- Ethics and Unconscionability (Chapter 10).
- Good Faith and Commercial Reasonableness (Chapter 14).
- Should Insider Trading Be Legal? (Chapter 29).
- Business and the Environment—The Valdez Principles (Chapter 31).
- The "Reasonable Woman" Standard (Chapter 32).

International Perspective

In an era of increasing global awareness, we felt that it was appropriate to add to this edition a special feature, entitled *International Perspectives*, which focuses on international dimensions of business law. The following topics are addressed in these *International Perspectives*:

- Should U.S. Drug Companies Sell Banned Drugs Overseas? (Chapter 2).
- European Privacy Laws (Chapter 4).
- Combating Foreign Product Counterfeiters (Chapter 6).
- Electronic Failure and Liability for Breach (Chapter 13).
- Product Liability Laws and Product Innovation (Chapter 17).
- The Growing Popularity of U.S. Antitrust Laws Overseas (Chapter 30).
- Comparative Product Liability Laws (Chapter 36).

Law in the Extreme

For the third edition of *Business Law Today*, we have added to many of the chapters a new feature entitled *Law in the Extreme*. As the title suggests, this feature discusses some of the more extreme applications of the law. Some examples of this feature are as follows:

- Warning: If You Fall, You Might Get Hurt (Chapter 2).
- The $10,600 Order of Toast (Chapter 5).
- When Ghosts Are Good Enough (Chapter 13).
- Chicken Enchiladas, Raw Oysters, and Other Perils (Chapter 17).
- How to Imprison a Corporation (Chapter 26).
- Are "Frozen Embryos" Property? (Chapter 33).

Profiles

A number of chapters in this edition include *Profiles* of important jurists and legal scholars. For each *Profile*, a photograph of the person being discussed is presented. Individuals featured in the *Profiles* are listed below:

- John Marshall (Chapter 3).
- Sandra Day O'Connor (Chapter 4).
- Arthur L. Corbin (Chapter 8).
- Benjamin Cardozo (Chapter 17).
- Oliver Wendell Holmes, Jr. (Chapter 32).

❖ Case Selection and Presentation

Much of the study of business law must involve an analysis of actual court cases. In each chapter, we present a number of cases (on average, about five per chapter) that have been selected to illustrate the principles of law discussed in the text. The cases are numbered sequentially for easy referencing in class discussions, homework assignments, and examinations. In choosing the cases to be included in this edition, our goal has been to achieve a balance between classic cases and recent cases from the 1990s.

A Special Case Format

Each case is paraphrased in a special format, which begins with the case and citation. The full citation includes the name of the court deciding the case, the date of the case, and the major parallel reporters in which the case can be found. For federal court or agency cases, the appropriate court or agency seal is also presented. For state court cases, the seal of the state is presented.

Historical and Social Settings A special section entitled *Historical and Social Setting* appears just following the case title and citation. Because business law now touches virtually every aspect of life, it is appropriate that the most recent curriculum pronouncements by the American Assembly of Collegiate Schools of Business (AACSB) should include a remarkably broad array of topics to be taught to today's business student. The *Historical and Social Settings* explicitly address the AACSB's curriculum requirements by focusing on the global, political, ethical, social, environmental, technological, or cultural diversity context of each case being presented. Depending on the specific focus, the title of the section varies. For example, for one case the section title might be *Historical and Social Setting;* for another, it may be *Historical and Political Setting* or *Historical and Cultural Setting.*

Basic Format Following the *Historical and Social Setting,* each case is summarized in the following four clearly labeled sections:

- *Facts*—The facts of the case are presented in paraphrased form in one paragraph.
- *Issue*—The issue before the court is briefly phrased in the form of a question.
- *Decision*—The court's decision is presented in one or two sentences.
- *Reason*—The reason for the decision is paraphrased in one paragraph. When appropriate, direct quotations from the court opinion are included to illustrate the court's reasoning.

Ethical Considerations A number of the cases presented in this text conclude with a section entitled *Ethical Considerations.* This section addresses the AACSB's curriculum requirements by focusing on the ethical aspects of the dispute being decided or the court's decision on the issue.

Finding and Analyzing Case Law

It is particularly important for students to know how to find case law. We have made sure that case citations are clear, accessible, and complete. We have presented a special section on this topic in Chapter 1, including an exhibit, to ensure that each student will understand the wide variety of legal citations.

We also go to great lengths to help the student learn how to analyze case law. At the end of Chapter 1, your students will find a fully annotated sample court case. The annotations are clearly marked in the margins with brackets pointing to the specific parts of the paraphrased case that are being explained. In addition, throughout the remainder of the text, any unfamiliar terms included in direct quotations from court opinions are defined in brackets within the quotation. A more fully annotated version of this case is presented at the beginning of Appendix A.

Case Briefing Assignments

Many professors prefer to have their students brief cases. To make these assignments more manageable for both students and professors, we provide in Appendix A a short explanation of how to brief a case, followed by several cases for briefing. Case briefing assignments, including questions that should be answered for each of the cases chosen for briefing, are found at the end of the problem sets in thirteen of the chapters in this text. Each case briefing assignment contains a reference to the specific case in Appendix A that is to be briefed. Sample answers to the questions listed in the case briefing assignments are found in *Answers to Questions and Case Problems,* which is free to adopters of *Business Law Today,* Third Edition.

Case Printouts

Some instructors like to see the entire set of court opinions for cases summarized within the chapters of *Business Law Today*. We have created a free book, called *Case Printouts for Business Law Today*, which contains the output from WESTLAW (without headnotes) for virtually every case that is included in each chapter. If the instructor wishes, the full set of opinions can be copied and handed out to students.

❖ Questions and Case Problems

Every chapter in this text ends with ten to fifteen questions and case problems. The first four or five of these are either review or hypothetical questions that are graded in difficulty, beginning with straightforward, review-type questions and advancing to more complex hypothetical situations. The remaining questions are based on actual case problems, many of which were decided in the 1990s. Each question or case problem is preceded by a boldfaced word or phrase indicating the point of law being addressed in the question or problem. In addition, full citations are given for the case problems.

Complete answers to the questions and case problems are given in a separate manual entitled *Answers to Questions and Case Problems to Accompany Business Law Today* (discussed later in this Preface), which is free to adopters. This manual can be placed on reserve in the library, if desired, for student reference.

A Question of Ethics and Social Responsibility

In every chapter of the Third Edition of *Business Law Today*, at the end of the *Questions and Case Problems* section, we have included A *Question of Ethics and Social Responsibility*. Following a brief summary of the legal dispute involved in a particular case and the court's decision, two or more questions are given for the student's consideration from an ethical point of view. Suggested answers are found in the *Answers Manual*.

Case Briefing Assignments

Thirteen of the chapters of *Business Law Today*, Third Edition, include a *Case-Briefing Assignment* (discussed earlier in this Preface).

For Critical Analysis

Each set of *Questions and Case Problems* in this edition concludes with a critical-thinking question concerning some aspect of the law covered in the chapter. Suggested answers are found in the *Answers Manual*.

Case-Problem Cases Available on Diskettes

For those instructors or students who wish to view the entire court opinion on which a case problem is based, we have included with this edition supplemental diskettes containing virtually all of the case-problem cases. Some of the cases on which the case problems are based can also be found in their entirety in the LEGAL CLERK Research Software System (discussed below).

❖ Other Special Pedagogical Features

We have included in *Business Law Today* a number of additional pedagogical devices, including those discussed below.

Unit Introductions

Each unit has a concise introduction indicating why a student should study the topics covered within that unit. The unit on contracts, for example, is introduced by a discussion of the function of contracts in the business world and the importance of understanding the nature of contractual relationships.

Margin Definitions

Legal terminology is often a major stumbling block in the study of business law. We have used an important pedagogical device—margin definitions—to help the student understand terminology. Whenever an important legal term is introduced, it is done so in boldface type. In the margin of the page, alongside the paragraph in which the boldfaced term appears, the term is defined. We have made every attempt to ensure that each important legal term is fully defined upon its first use by the authors.

At the end of each chapter, all terms that have been boldfaced within the chapter are listed in alphabetical order in a section entitled *Key Terms.* The page on which the term is defined is given after each term. Students can briefly examine the list to make sure that they understand all important terms introduced in the chapter and can immediately review terms that they do not completely understand by referring to the page number given. All boldfaced terms are again listed and defined in the *Glossary* at the end of the text. The *Glossary* for the Third Edition of *Business Law Today* contains over five hundred important legal terms.

Exhibits and Forms

When appropriate, exhibits illustrating important aspects of the law are presented. Each exhibit is accompanied by a complete explanation—alongside the exhibit itself—to ensure that the student fully understands the concept being illustrated. We think that these explanations will make the pedagogical exhibits more useful for students. Additionally, we have included a number of forms for the student's reference. In all, there are seventy-four exhibits and forms in the third edition of *Business Law Today*, including those listed below:

- How to Read Case Citations (Chapter 1).
- Exclusive and Concurrent Jurisdiction (Chapter 3).
- Major Steps in Processing a Criminal Case (Chapter 7).
- Third Party Rights in Contracts (Chapter 12).
- Major Differences between Contract Law and Sales Law (Chapter 14).
- Secured Transactions—Concept and Terminology (Chapter 21).
- Articles of Incorporation (Chapter 26).
- Federal Consumer Protection Statutes (Chapter 31).
- Sample International Purchase Order Form (Chapter 36).

Chapter Summaries

At the end of each chapter, we present in graphic form a thorough *Chapter Summary* designed to aid the student in reviewing the concepts covered in the chapter.

The *Chapter Summaries* can also be used as a reviewing device prior to examinations.

Quotations

Each chapter opens with a brief quotation that is relevant to the material under study. Often, two or three other quotations have been included in the margins of the pages in the chapter. For each quotation, we provide a brief biographical statement after the name of the person being quoted.

Photographs and Cartoons

We believe that appropriate and well-placed photographs and cartoons not only provide visual relief from the printed word but also help students to relate the material under study to the everyday world around them. We have included in this volume numerous photographs and several carefully selected cartoons. Many of the photographs are accompanied by captions that consist of critical-thinking questions.

❖ Personal Law Handbook

At the end of the regular text, your students will find a *Personal Law Handbook*. We view this as a practical guide to an application of the law to personal, financial, business, and consumer problems. Under no circumstances do we ever suggest that the student act as his or her own attorney. Indeed, the maxim that "he who acts as his own attorney has a fool for a client" is stressed at the beginning of the handbook. The topics we have chosen to cover in the personal law handbook are as follows:

- Renting a Home
- Family Law (including divorce settlements)
- Consumer Law
- Employment Law
- Owning and Operating Motor Vehicles (including automobile insurance and driving violations)
- Criminal Law
- Jury Duty

❖ Appendices

Because the majority of students keep their business law text as a reference source, we have included the following full set of appendices:

A. How to Brief a Case and Selected Cases.
B. The Constitution of the United States.
C. The Uniform Commercial Code (Excerpts) (fully updated excerpts, as discussed below).
D. The Uniform Partnership Act.
E. The Restatement (Second) of Torts (Excerpts).
F. The Sherman Antitrust Act of 1890 (Excerpts).
G. The Securities Act of 1933 (Excerpts).
H. The Securities Exchange Act of 1934 (Excerpts).
I. Title VII of the Civil Rights Act of 1964 (Excerpts).

J. The Americans with Disabilities Act of 1990 (Excerpts).
K. The Civil Rights Act of 1991 (Excerpts).
L. Spanish Equivalents for Important Legal Terms in English.

To make sure that you and your students have the latest information available, we have included all of the recently issued and revised articles of the Uniform Commercial Code in Appendix C. Specifically, we have included Article 2A on leases, the revised Articles 3 and 4 on commercial paper, Article 4A on fund transfers, and Article 6—Alternative B on bulk transfers.

❖ Supplemental Teaching Materials

This edition of *Business Law Today* is accompanied by a vastly expanded number of teaching and learning supplements. We understand that instructors face a difficult task in finding the time necessary to teach the material that they wish to cover during each term. Individually and in conjunction with a number of our colleagues, we have developed supplementary teaching materials that we believe are the best available today. Each component of the supplements package is described below.

An Instructor's Planning Guide

To simplify and make more efficient the work effort of the instructor using *Business Law Today*, we have developed a unique guide that integrates all of the printed, software, and video supplements. For each chapter in the text, you will find in the *Instructor's Course Planning Guide and Media Handbook* helpful suggestions about what parts of the complete learning/teaching package can be used in conjunction with that chapter.

Printed Supplements

The printed supplements for *Business Law Today* have a single goal in mind: to make the task of teaching and the task of learning more enjoyable and efficient.

Instructor's Manual The *Instructor's Manual* has been written by text author Roger LeRoy Miller, together with William Eric Hollowell. Having one of the co-authors of the main text write the *Instructor's Manual* has resulted in complete agreement between what is stressed in the text and what is fully outlined in the *Instructor's Manual*. Each chapter of the manual contains the following features:

- An introductory section, which highlights the main concepts and importance of the law covered in the chapter.
- A detailed, explanatory outline of the chapter contents, which is keyed very closely to the text.
- Synopses of all cases, often accompanied by additional notes and comments, as well as questions to ask in class and answers to these questions.
- Additional background on significant persons, statutes, and especially Restatements that are mentioned or referred to within the text.
- Teaching suggestions, including points to be stressed, hypothetical questions to elicit class discussion, and discussion questions keyed closely to the text and based on information contained within the text.
- Suggested activities and research assignments.
- Explanations of selected footnotes. Many of the cases, statutes, and other references cited in footnotes of the chapter are briefly summarized or explained so that the relationship between the footnote and the text is clear.

A computerized version of the *Instructor's Manual* is now also available (discussed below, under software supplements).

Study Guide For this edition of *Business Law Today*, a new study guide entitled *Study Guide to Accompany Business Law Today* has been prepared by text author Roger LeRoy Miller, together with William Eric Hollowell. This study guide contains an introductory study skills section, a guide to briefing cases, and a chapter-by-chapter review of *Business Law Today*. The chapter-by-chapter review offers the following pedagogical aids for each chapter of the text:

- Pre-study questions.
- Brief chapter introduction.
- Checklist of what each student should be able to do after finishing the chapter.
- Chapter outline (often including helpful mnemonics).
- A list of cases presented in the chapter.
- True-false questions.
- Fill-in questions.
- Multiple-choice questions.
- Short essay problems (with answers in the *Instructor's Manual*).
- Programmed review.

All answers to (1) pre-study questions, (2) true-false questions, (3) fill-in questions, and (4) multiple-choice questions are found at the back of this study guide.

A computerized version of this study guide—called *Microguide*—is also available (discussed below, under software supplements).

A Comprehensive Test Bank Again, to ensure consistency between the teaching materials and the text, one of the authors, Roger LeRoy Miller, has co-written the test bank. There are approximately 2000 multiple-choice questions with answers and over 1500 true-false questions with answers. These questions are available in booklet form or, as discussed below, on software.

Answers Manual A complete answers manual entitled *Answers to Questions and Case Problems* is available to all adopters. Each answer is presented in the following format:

- *Point of Law*—The point of law to which the problem relates is first stated in boldface.
- *Page Reference*—The point of law is followed by the page number or numbers indicating where the topic is discussed in the text.
- *Answer*—The specific answer to the question or problem is then given.

The answers manual also contains sample answers for the ethical and social responsibility questions, case briefing assignments, and questions for critical analysis that are included at the end of *Questions and Case Problems* sections in the text.

Case Printouts As mentioned earlier in this Preface, most of the cases in the main body of the text have been reprinted in their entirety in a separate booklet entitled *Case Printouts for Business Law Today*.

Handbook on Critical Thinking and Writing A booklet entitled *Handbook on Critical Thinking and Writing in Business Law*, written by text author Roger LeRoy Miller, provides students with an overview of techniques used in critical thinking. It illustrates how students can examine and analyze legal assumptions and arguments. The *Handbook* is tied to some of the examples given in the chapters of

Business Law Today, Third Edition. Additionally, the student is given twelve steps to effective writing. Copies are available to adopters and their students on request.

West's Advanced Topics and Contemporary Issues A specially prepared paperback text entitled *West's Advanced Topics and Contemporary Issues: Expanded Coverage* has been created by Frank B. Cross. This book adds a unique element to the total teaching/learning package for *Business Law Today*. The book is available to students free of charge at their instructor's option. *West's Advanced Topics*, for which a cross-referencing to the third edition of *Business Law Today* can be found in the beginning of the *Instructor's Manual*, provides supplemental detailed coverage of the most pressing legal issues confronting business today:

1. Business Ethics
2. International Business Law
3. Individual Employee Rights
4. Employment Discrimination Law
5. Occupational Safety and Workers' Compensation
6. Accounting and the Law
7. Securities Law and Regulation
8. Mergers and Acquisitions
9. Insurance Law
10. Real Estate Finance and Liability
11. Bank Regulation and Liability
12. Unfair Competition
13. Advertising Law
14. Environmental Liability
15. Health Care Law
16. Sports and Entertainment Law
17. Hospitality Management Law
18. Communications Law
19. Government Contracts
20. Legal Representation of Business

Revised Articles 3 and 4 of the Uniform Commercial Code A special handbook to accompany *Business Law Today* has been prepared by the text authors and William Eric Hollowell. This handbook, entitled *Revised Articles 3 and 4 of the Uniform Commercial Code*, summarizes the most significant ways in which the 1990 revision of Articles 3 and 4 of the Uniform Commercial Code changes the law governing commercial paper.

Instructor's Manuals for Software and Video Supplements Virtually all of the software and videos that are offered with *Business Law Today* have instructor's manuals. These manuals will be referred to later in this Preface when discussing the specific software and video supplements that the manuals accompany.

Transparency Acetates *Transparency Acetates*, covering all important exhibits, are available free to adopters.

West's Book of Forms *West's Book of Forms*, prepared by Robert McNutt, offers forty sample business forms. Professors can order this supplement for their students to purchase.

Regional Reporters West's regional reporters cover all state appellate court decisions. The following reporters are available to qualified adopters: Pacific, North Western, South Western, North Eastern, Atlantic, South Eastern, and Southern.

Software Supplements

Software supplements represent an increasingly significant portion of the *Business Law Today* teaching/learning package. We now offer for adopters and students a wide variety of software supplements.

LEGAL CLERK® Software The LEGAL CLERK Research Software System is a user-friendly, interactive software package that simultaneously introduces students to the rudiments of computer-aided legal research and reinforces the underlying concepts of business law and the legal environment. LEGAL CLERK provides a valuable learning tool to help your school meet AACSB recommendations for using microcomputers in business law courses.

To provide instructors with maximum flexibility, LEGAL CLERK covers three major subject areas of business law and the legal environment: (1) UCC/Article 2—Sales, (2) Government Regulation and the Legal Environment of Business, and (3) Contracts. Instructors may select one version or all three versions for their classes. Cases appearing in LEGAL CLERK are clearly identified in the text with a computer logo. The logos are color coded to help users easily identify which version of LEGAL CLERK contains specific cases:

 *Uniform Commercial Code/Article 2—Sales (Version 1.0).*

 *Government Regulation and the Legal Environment of Business (Version 1.0).*

 *Contracts (Version 1.0).*

A site license for all three versions of LEGAL CLERK is free to qualified adopters. Each version is accompanied by an *Instructor's Resource Guide* and, for student purchase, a *Student User's Guide.*

LEGAL REVIEW

Software This software allows students to review legal concepts found in all three LEGAL CLERK versions. LEGAL REVIEW runs on IBM PCs and compatible microcomputers and is available to qualified adopters. A *LEGAL REVIEW Student User's Manual* can be purchased by the student. The manual contains specific questions about the legal concepts covered in the software.

Computerized Instructor's Manual For those instructors who wish to modify the *Instructor's Manual* by adding their own notes, we provide a fully computerized version of the *Instructor's Manual.* You may order the manual in many formats.

This software allows the *Instructor's Manual* to be imported into any popular word-processing program, such as WordPerfect. Instructors wishing to obtain these diskettes may request them directly from their West sales representative.

Computerized Study Guide Your students can test their knowledge of chapter material with the computerized study guide called *Microguide.* Selected questions from the printed study guide described above are now on diskette, allowing your students to practice taking computerized tests. Multiple-choice and true-false questions are included. *Microguide* runs on IBM PCs and compatible microcomputers or Macintosh microcomputers (with Hypercard). *Microguide* is available free to qualified adopters of the text.

Computerized Test Bank The test bank is available on the latest version of WESTEST, a highly acclaimed computerized testing system, which is offered for IBM PCs and compatible microcomputers or the Macintosh family of microcomputers. WESTEST allows instructors to do the following:

- Import and export graphs.
- Add or edit questions, instructions, and answers.
- Select questions by previewing the question on the screen.
- Let the system select questions randomly.
- Select questions by question number.
- View summaries of the test or test-bank chapters.
- Set up the page layout for exams.
- Print exams in a variety of formats.

Interactive Software—Contracts and Sales For those students who have their own computers or who have access to computers through friends, libraries, or learning labs, we have developed unique interactive programs for the teaching and learning of contracts and sales. These programs use HyperText and allow for flexibility in learning the subject matter based on each user's level of understanding.

"You Be the Judge" This software provides case problems for ten topic areas. The user is supplied with the facts and is then asked how the issue should be decided. A word processing program integrated in the software allows the user to key in his or her response and print it. A glossary of key legal terms is also included.

Case-Problem Cases on Diskette As mentioned earlier in this Preface, nearly all of the case-problem cases are now included on diskettes for use by instructors or students. The cases are available in ASCII format and can be imported into any word-processing program, such as Microsoft Word or WordPerfect. The diskettes are available in many formats.

WESTLAW WESTLAW, the premiere computerized legal-research system, is renowned for its ability to help law professors, law students, attorneys, and paralegals do research in the law. Qualified adopters of *Business Law Today*, Third Edition, are allowed free hours of WESTLAW. WESTLAW now offers an easy-to-use natural language, WIN. Contact your West sales representative for details on how to obtain this service.

CD-ROM This new supplement will include cases, state statutes, and other appropriate legal materials.

Enhancing the Learning Experience: Videocassettes and Videodisc

Many instructors now find that the use of videocassettes and videodiscs can enhance the teaching/learning experience. We believe this to be true in many teaching situations. We are proud of our extensive videocassette library that is available for adopters of the third edition of *Business Law Today*. These instructional videos can help you in the teaching of business law in a variety of areas, including ethics and social responsibility, employment law, and others. Many of these instructional videos have specially prepared instructor's manuals, most of which were written by one of this text's authors.

The Drama of the Law Video Series West is proud to offer a ten-videocassette series entitled *The Drama of the Law*. This is the first law tele-series that uses humor and wit to teach important legal concepts to today's business law and legal environment students. The scripts were written by John Jay Osborn, Jr., author of *The Paper Chase* and *The Associates*. The ten videos are as follows:

1. Mistake
2. Offer and Acceptance

3. Negligence and Assumption of Risk
4. Conditions on a Promise
5. Risk of Loss
6. Third Party Beneficiaries
7. Breach and Remedies
8. Warranties
9. Agency and *Respondeat Superior*
10. Private Property and Bailments

Most of these videos are also available on *West's Business Law and Legal Environment Laser Videodisc* (discussed below).

John Jay Osborn, Jr. and text-author Roger LeRoy Miller have prepared a unique one-hundred-page *Instructor's Manual for the Drama of the Law* video series. For each chapter, there is a complete shooting script of the video with underlined and numbered sections. In the pages that follow each script, the authors refer to these numbered sections when discussing the video. The authors' discussion of each video includes the following sections:

- A text reference to page numbers in *Business Law Today* in which the point of law addressed by the video is discussed.
- A lead-in question for your students.
- One to fifteen points showing the legal implications of selected excerpts from the video script.
- An answer to the lead-in question.

This manual is presented in its entirety in the back of the *Instructor's Manual to Accompany Business Law Today.*

The Drama of the Law II Video Series Soon to be available.

Moot Court—*The Texaco/Pennzoil* Case Students at Stanford University demonstrate how moot court works. This is an effective learning device to show the elements of a trial and is of special interest to students because it was done by students.

The Making of a Case This is a specially prepared video hosted and narrated by *L.A. Law's* Richard Dysart. He takes the viewer on a tour of the process by which appellate decisions are published by West Publishing Company.

PBS Ethics in America Series Several of the highly acclaimed videos from PBS's series on ethics are now available for use in your business law courses. Included are videos on advertising and corporate takeovers. An *Instructor's Manual* is available for these videos.

Anatomy of a Trial—Contracts A series of videos on a hypothetical contract case prepared by the American Bar Association has been edited down to two videos. These videos show each aspect of a typical trial. Additionally, the videos contain much information on contract and sales law. There is an *Instructor's Manual.*

Anatomy of a Trial—A Product Liability Case This video again shows many of the aspects of a typical trial. It also brings out important points in product liability law. There is an *Instructor's Manual.*

The Law and Literature This video consists of a videotaped lecture given by John Jay Osborn, Jr., from the University of California School of Law, Berkeley (Boalt Hall). He has presented this lecture to business law students, law students, law professors, and state and federal judges. In this lecture Professor Osborn attempts to relate different legal theories to great dramatic works.

Equal Justice for All The PBS series *Equal Justice under Law* is available free to adopters of this text. The videos cover the following landmark cases:

- *Marbury v. Madison.*
- *McCulloch v. Maryland.*
- *Gibbons v. Ogden.*

West's Business Law and Legal Environment Laser Videodisc Technology has provided instructors of business law and the legal environment of business with yet another way to present teaching materials: the laser videodisc. We are making available for this text a videodisc that provides you with the latest method for presenting important topics to your students.

West's Business Law and Legal Environment Laser Videodisc includes the following:

- Most of the videos from *The Drama of the Law* video series.
- Excerpts from sample trials, ethics videos, and other videos.
- Hundreds of still-frame exhibits.

Those who use *West's Business Law and Legal Environment Laser Videodisc* will find that THE LECTURE BUILDER software allows for complete customization of each separate lecture. This software works with any Macintosh system and any IBM or IBM compatible using the WINDOWS operating system environment. THE LECTURE BUILDER permits the instructor to pick and choose the order of the still frames and the motion videos from any part of the videodisc. Also, the motion videos can be edited by the instructor in any fashion desired. THE LECTURE BUILDER also has a fully automated mode with programmable time segments. Ask your West sales representative for a demonstration.

❖ For Users of the Second Edition

We thought that those of you who have been using *Business Law Today* would like to know some of the major changes that have been made for the third edition. The book is basically the same, but we think that we have improved it greatly, thanks in part to the many letters, telephone calls, and reviews that we have received.

Organizational Changes

- Constitutional law is now presented as an entire chapter (Chapter 4) instead of in Chapter 1.
- The ethics chapter now appears earlier in the text, as Chapter 2.
- The chapter on agency relationships (Chapter 23) now appears as the first chapter in the unit on business organizations, rather than as the second chapter in that unit.
- Corporate financing has been moved from the chapter covering securities regulation and investor protection to the first chapter on corporations (Chapter 26).
- The coverage in the corporations chapters has been streamlined to prevent overlapping discussions of roles, rights, and responsibilities of directors, officers, and shareholders. The rights and duties of these corporate participants are now discussed in one chapter (Chapter 27).

● The chapter on international law (Chapter 36) now appears in a separate, final unit of the text.

New or Significantly Revised Chapters

● Chapter 1 (The Legal and International Environment)—Chapter 1 has been extensively revised for *Business Law Today*, Third Edition. An entire chapter is now devoted to constitutional law (Chapter 4, described below), and new sections have been added, including a new section on "Schools of Jurisprudential Thought," additional sections on sources of American law, and two sections on international law—"Law around the World" and "International Law." The discussion of administrative law and process has also been greatly expanded. The chapter now concludes with a new appendix entitled "Diagramming Case Problems" to help students interpret and analyze case problems.

● Chapter 2 (Ethics and Social Responsibility)—This chapter was moved up to appear earlier in the text as Chapter 2. Several new sections have been added, including sections discussing obstacles to ethical behavior and the derivation of ethical standards. The coverage of corporate social responsibility has been greatly expanded and now includes a discussion of the corporation's duty to employees, the "stakeholder view of corporate social responsibility," consumer boycotts, and other topics relevant to today's business world.

● Chapter 3 (Courts and Procedures)—Alternative dispute resolution is covered in greater detail generally and now includes negotiation and conciliation as methods of settling disputes outside the judicial process. The section on summary judgment has been expanded and is now illustrated with a case to make this procedure more understandable for students. We have created new exhibits for the state and federal court systems, and we have also added an exhibit illustrating exclusive and concurrent jurisdiction.

● Chapter 4 (Constitutional Law)—This new chapter opens with a discussion of the constitutional powers of government, including sections on the separation of powers, the commerce clause, the supremacy clause, and the taxing and spending powers of the national government. The remainder of the chapter discusses business and the Bill of Rights. Freedom of speech is treated in detail. Other sections discuss freedom of religion, self-incrimination, searches and seizures, due process, equal protection, and privacy rights.

● Chapter 5 (Torts)—Now contains an expanded discussion of the duty of care and a new section on special negligence doctrines and statutes.

● Chapter 6 (Business Torts and Intellectual Property)—This chapter now presents a clearer and fuller discussion of copyright and trademark law. Also included for this edition are sections on the torts of appropriation and the misappropriation of trade secrets.

● Chapter 7 (Criminal Law)—Now presents fuller coverage of the rights of the accused, including the right to counsel and other *Miranda* rights. We have also added sections covering the exclusionary rule and juvenile rights and procedures. Also included is a new exhibit illustrating the steps involved in criminal procedure. The section on white-collar crime has been extensively revised and now includes sections on money laundering and insider trading.

● Chapter 12 (Third Party Rights and Discharge)—This chapter has been reorganized and revised as needed to clarify for students the law as it relates to third party rights in contracts.

● Chapter 18 (Commercial Paper—Negotiability and Transferability)—In this chapter as well as in the subsequent chapters on commercial paper, we have added in footnotes the ways in which the 1990 revision of Articles 3 and 4 of the Uniform Commercial Code have changed the law governing commercial paper.

● Chapter 27 (Corporate Directors, Officers, and Shareholders)—This chapter has been rewritten as necessary to combine the material covered in the sections on corporate management (in Chapter 26 of the Second Edition) with the other rights and liabilities of directors, officers, and shareholders.

- Chapter 29 (Investor Protection)—Has been revised to include sections on the misappropriation theory and tipper/tippee theory of liability for insider trading and a new section on the expanding authority and powers of the Securities and Exchange Commission.
- Chapter 30 (Antitrust Law)—This chapter now offers more thorough and streamlined coverage of antitrust law, including expanded coverage of monopolization and market power.
- Chapter 32 (Employee and Labor Law)—This chapter has been virtually rewritten to provide thorough coverage of the types of employment discrimination prohibited under federal laws, including Title VII of the Civil Rights Act of 1964, as amended by the 1991 Civil Rights Act; the Americans with Disabilities Act of 1990; and other laws. A section on the employment-at-will doctrine and its exceptions, including those for whistleblowers, has been included, and the section on employee privacy rights has been updated.
- Chapter 36 (International Law in a Global Economy)—This chapter has been substantially rewritten and now includes sections on ways of doing business internationally (exporting, importing, and manufacturing abroad), expanded coverage of international sales contracts (including a *Landmark in the Law* on the Convention on Contracts for the International Sale of Goods), more detail on how payments are made on international contracts (including a discussion of foreign exchange markets, correspondent banking, and letters of credit), a section discussing the laws governing specific types of activities (including exporting, importing, investing, and the bribery of foreign officials), and a concluding section on the extraterritorial application of U.S. laws (including antitrust laws, patent laws, and discrimination laws).

What Else Is New?

In addition to the changes noted above, you will find a number of other items or features in *Business Law Today*, Third Edition, as listed below:

New Features in the Text The following new features appear (each feature has been discussed in greater detail in the preceding sections of this Preface):

- Two entirely new pedagogical features entitled *Law in the Extreme* and *International Perspective*, as well as twelve new *Landmarks in the Law*, thirty-four new or extensively revised *Business Law in Action* features, thirteen new *Applications*, and six new *Ethical Perspectives*.
- *Historical and Social Settings* introducing each of the cases presented in the text.
- *Ethical Considerations* following many of the cases presented in the text.
- *Key Terms* (with page reference) at the end of each chapter.
- Boldfaced points of law preceding each of the questions and case problems at the end of each chapter.
- A *Question of Ethics and Social Responsibility* in the problem sets at the end of each chapter.
- *For Critical Analysis* questions concluding each of the end-of-chapter problem sets.

New Exhibits To enhance the student's understanding of concepts presented in the text, we have modified exhibits contained in the second edition of *Business Law Today* whenever necessary to achieve greater clarity or accuracy. In addition, the following entirely new exhibits have been added for *Business Law Today*, Third Edition:

- Criminal and Civil Law (Exhibit 1–1).
- Exclusive and Concurrent Jurisdiction (Exhibit 3–4).
- Major Steps in Prosecuting a Criminal Case (Exhibit 7–2).
- Third Party Rights in Contracts (Exhibit 12–3).
- Void and Voidable Title (Exhibit 15–3).
- Converting Order Paper to Bearer Paper and Vice Versa (Exhibit 18–5).
- Taking for Value (Exhibit 19–1).
- IRS Factors for Determining Employee Status (Exhibit 23–1).
- Types of Corporate Bonds (Exhibit 26–2).
- A Sample International Purchase Order Form (Exhibit 36–1).

New Cases There are 102 new cases.

Case Problems There are 120 new ones.

Personal Law Handbook A 64-page handbook found at the back of the regular text.

New Appendices

- Appendix F [The Restatement (Second) of Torts (Excerpts)].
- Appendix G [The Securities Act of 1933 (Excerpts)].
- Appendix H [The Securities Exchange Act of 1934 (Excerpts)].
- Appendix I [Title VII of the Civil Rights Act of 1964 (Excerpts)].
- Appendix J [The Americans with Disabilities Act of 1990 (Excerpts)].
- Appendix K [The Civil Rights Act of 1991 (Excerpts)].

New Supplements—Printed

- *Study Guide to Accompany Business Law Today.*
- *Handbook on Critical Thinking and Writing.*
- *Instructor's Course Planning Guide and Media Handbook*
- *West's Advanced Topics and Contemporary Issues: Expanded Coverage*
- *Revised Articles 3 and 4 of the Uniform Commercial Code.*
- A completely new and revised *Instructor's Manual* now written by text author, Roger LeRoy Miller, with William Eric Hollowell.
- Completely new *Test Bank* that is now separate from the *Instructor's Manual.*

New Supplements—Software

- LEGAL REVIEW Software.
- Computerized Instructor's Manual.
- Computerized Study Guide (*Microguide*).
- Interactive Software—Contracts and Sales.
- "You Be the Judge."
- Case-Problem Cases on Diskette.
- CD-ROM

New Supplements—Video

- *The Drama of the Law* Video Series.
- *The Drama of the Law II* Video Series
- Moot Court—The *Texaco/Pennzoil* Case

- *The Making of a Case.*
- *PBS Ethics in America* Video Series.
- *Anatomy of a Trial—A Product Liability Case.*
- *The Law and Literature.*
- *West's Business Law and Legal Environment Laser Videodisc* (with LECTURE BUILDER Software).

❖ Acknowledgments

Numerous careful and conscientious users of *Business Law Today* were kind enough to help us revise the book. In addition, the staff at West Publishing Company went out of its way to make sure that this edition came out early and in accurate form. We wish to thank our project supervisor, John Orr, for designing and managing this edition. Also, the following individuals at West gave us their unending professional service: Shannon Richmond in production for handling the production coordination and Christine Henry for assistance in manuscript preparation. Lavina Leed Miller provided expert research, editing, and proofing services for this project. Additional proofing was done by Marie-Christine Loiseau. We must also thank William Eric Hollowell for his masterful research and proof-reading efforts. At many phases of the project we had the expert assistance of Karen Morris. And the work flowed smoothly through Austin due to the efforts of Kathleen Orillion. Finally, we continue to be in debt to our (apparently) life-long editor, Clyde Perlee, Jr., who guided us at all stages of this revision. Our developmental editor, Jan Lamar, deserves our thanks for her efforts in coordinating reviews and in guaranteeing the timely and accurate publication of all supplemental materials.

Reviewers of the First Edition

John J. Balek
Morton College, Illinois
Brad Botz
Garden City Community College, Kansas
Lee B. Burgunder
California Polytechnic University—San Luis Obispo
Dale Clark
Corning Community College, New York
Patricia L. DeFrain
Glendale College, California
Joe D. Dillsaver
Northeastern State University, Oklahoma
Larry R. Edwards
Tarrant County Junior College, South Campus, Texas
George E. Eigsti
Kansas City, Kansas, Community College
Jerry Furniss
University of Montana
Nancy L. Hart
Midland College, Texas
George Otto
Truman College, Illinois
William M. Rutledge
Macomb Community College, Michigan
Anne W. Schacherl
Madison Area Technical College, Wisconsin
Edward F. Shafer
Rochester Community College, Minnesota
Lou Ann Simpson
Drake University, Iowa
Janine S. Hiller
Virginia Polytechnic Institute & State University
Sarah Weiner Keidan
Oakland Community College, Michigan
Bradley T. Lutz
Hillsborough Community College, Florida
John D. Mallonee
Manatee Community College, Florida
James K. Miersma
Milwaukee Area Technical Institute, Wisconsin
Jim Lee Morgan
West Los Angeles College
Jack K. Morton
University of Montana

Solange North
Fox Valley Technical Institute, Wisconsin
Robert H. Orr
Florida Community College at Jacksonville
James E. Walsh, Jr.
Tidewater Community College, Virginia
Edward L. Welsh, Jr.
Phoenix College
Clark W. Wheeler
Santa Fe Community College, Florida
James L. Wittenbach
University of Notre Dame
Joseph Zavaglia, Jr.
Brookdale Community College, New Jersey

Reviewers of the Second Edition

Merlin Bauer
Mid State Technical College, Wisconsin
Fred Ittner
College of Alameda, California
Susan S. Jarvis
University of Texas, Pan American, Texas
Beverly McCormick
Morehead State University, Kentucky
Robert H. Orr
Florida Community College at Jacksonville
Donald L. Petote
Genessee Community College, New York
Anne W. Schacherl
Madison Area Technical College, Wisconsin

Reviewers of the Third Edition

Daryl Barton
Eastern Michigan University
Jere L. Crago
Delgado Community College
Tony Enerva
Lakeland Community College
Richard N. Kleeberg
Solano Community College
Darlene Mallick
Anne Arundel Community College
Susan J. Mitchell
Des Moines Area Community College
Thomas L. Palmer
Northern Arizona University
Francis D. Polk
Ocean County College

We know that we're not perfect. If you or your students find something you don't like or want us to change, write to us. That's how we can make *Business Law Today* an even better book in the future. We promise to answer every single letter that we receive.

Roger LeRoy Miller
Gaylord A. Jentz

DEDICATION

R.L.M. dedicates this book to
Lois and Richard;
for our many great
years together

Gaylord A. Jentz dedicates this
edition to his wife, JoAnn; his
children, Kathy, Gary, Lori,
and Rory; and his two grandaughters,
Erin Marie and Megan Kathleen

Unit One

The Legal Environment of Business

❖ Why We Study the Legal Environment of Business

Men and women in business today find themselves in an environment that is increasingly subject to laws and regulations. Virtually all activities of businesses are governed by rules enacted by a state legislature or Congress, issued by a local, state, or federal agency, or developed through the years in our judicial system. The rules govern all aspects of business—raising capital, hiring and firing personnel, marketing and advertising, repairing or replacing defective products, and so on. In a broad sense, the legal environment of business includes the topics in every chapter of this book. After all, any law that touches on business becomes part of the legal environment of business. Thus, the legal environment of business embraces contracts, sales, the formation of partnerships, corporation transactions, government regulations concerning the business environment, insurance policies on business properties, and employment, as well as most other transaction relationships. Anyone contemplating a career in the business world cannot escape the legal environment of business, and knowledge of that legal environment can only help the future businessperson become better at whatever job is undertaken.

In this unit, we discuss many of the laws and procedures affecting the legal environment of business. Chapter 1 introduces the unit with a survey of the nature and sources of law. Because ethical decision making is part of the legal environment, Chapter 2 addresses this important topic. In Chapter 3, courts and legal procedures are outlined. No businessperson can realistically assume that he or she will not at some time be exposed to the mechanics of a lawsuit. Chapter 4 covers *constitutional law*—law that is directly derived from the Constitution of the United States, particularly as applied to business. In Chapter 5, we examine torts, including business torts. Business torts involving intellectual property, such as copyrights and trademarks, and computers are discussed in Chapter 6, which also covers computer-related crimes. The unit concludes with Chapter 7, which focuses on criminal law.

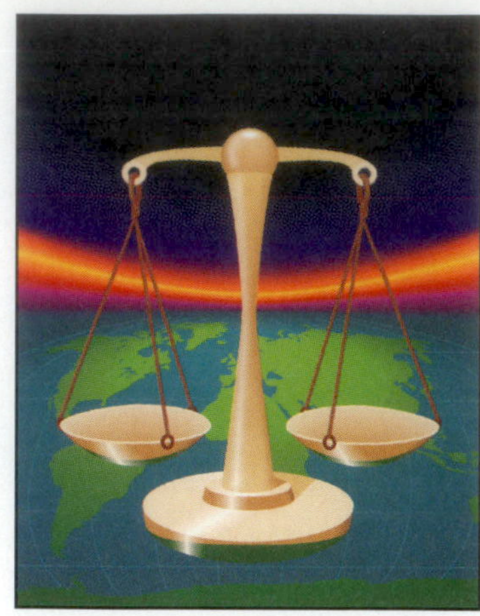

Chapter 1

The Legal and International Environment

"The law is of as much interest to the layman as it is to the lawyer."

Lord Balfour, 1848–1930
(British prime minister, 1902–1905)

Lord Balfour's assertion in the opening quotation emphasizes the underlying theme of every page in this book—that law is of interest to all persons, not just to lawyers. Those entering the world of business will find themselves subject to numerous laws and government regulations. An acquaintance with these laws and regulations is beneficial—if not essential—to anyone contemplating a successful career in the business world of today.

In this introductory chapter, we first look at the nature of law in general and at the history and sources—both domestic and international—of American law in particular. Then, because we cite statutes, regulations, and cases throughout this text, we explain how to read citations to these sources of law and how to find them. The chapter concludes with a section on how to read and understand case law, including an annotated sample court case.

❖ What Is Law?

There have been and will continue to be different definitions of law. The Greek philosopher Aristotle (384–322 B.C.) saw law as a "pledge that citizens of a state will do justice to one another." Aristotle's mentor, Plato (427–347 B.C.), believed law was a form of social control. The Roman orator and politician Cicero (106–43 B.C.) contended that law was the agreement of reason and nature, the distinction between the just and the unjust. The British jurist Sir William Blackstone (1723–1780) described law as "a rule of civil conduct prescribed by the supreme power in a state, commanding what is right, and prohibiting what is wrong." In America, the eminent jurist Oliver Wendell Holmes, Jr., (1841–1935) contended that law was a set of rules that allowed one to predict how a court would resolve a particular dispute—"the prophecies of what the courts will do in fact, and nothing more pretentious, are what I mean by the law."

LAW
A body of rules of conduct with legal force and effect, prescribed by the controlling authority (the government) of a society.

Although these definitions vary in their particulars, they all are based on the following general observation concerning the nature of **law**: *Law consists of enforceable rules governing relationships among individuals and between individuals and their society.* In the study of law, often referred to as **jurisprudence,** this very broad statement concerning the nature of law is the point of departure for all legal scholars and philosophers.

JURISPRUDENCE
The science or philosophy of law.

❖ Schools of Jurisprudential Thought

The court opinions in this book show that judges often refer to logic, history, custom, or philosophy in making their decisions. These opinions also show that when different judges—for example, a trial court judge and a reviewing court judge—examine the same case, they sometimes arrive at different conclusions about how the law should apply. That judges differ in their philosophies of law should come as no surprise to Americans. We frequently read or hear about the differences in legal philosophy among United States Supreme Court justices, especially when a significant, controversial case—such as one relating to abortion—is before the court. Part of the study of law, or jurisprudence, is discovering how different approaches to law affect judicial decision making.

Legal philosophers and scholars frequently disagree on what the proper function of law should be, and their disagreements have produced different schools of jurisprudence, or philosophies of law. The three most influential schools of legal thought are described below and then illustrated by a hypothetical court case.

The Natural Law School

The oldest and one of the most significant schools of jurisprudence is the **natural law school.** Those who adhere to the natural law school of thought believe that government and the legal system should reflect universal moral and ethical principles that are inherent in human nature.

The natural law school traces its origins to ancient Greece. The Greek philosopher Aristotle made the distinction between natural law and conventional law (**positive law**, or written law). He pointed out that natural law has the same force everywhere and is not a function of individual situations, cultures, or history. A law prohibiting murder, for example, does not reflect the values accepted by a particular society at a particular time but is based on a universally accepted precept that murder is wrong. To murder someone is thus a violation of natural law.

Because natural law is universal, it takes on a higher order than positive, or conventional, law. It was this higher law to which the international tribunal of judges at Nuremburg appealed when convicting Nazi war criminals of "crimes against humanity" at the end of World War II. Although these "criminals" may not have disobeyed any positive law of their country and may have been merely following their government's (Hitler's) orders, they were deemed by the tribunal to have violated a natural law that transcends any particular country's written laws. The natural law school of thought encourages individuals to disobey conventional, or written, laws if those individuals believe that the laws are in conflict with natural law. Protesters who felt that America's involvement in Vietnam (1963–1974) was wrong, for example, used natural law as their reason to violate written laws as they protested America's war effort.

At the basis of natural law is the concept that all persons have natural rights. John Locke, an English political philosopher, argued in a treatise written in 1689 that no one was born with an obligation to obey rulers. He contended that all individuals were born free, equal, and independent and that they had a natural right to life, liberty, and property. The purpose of government was to secure those rights. The authors of the Declaration of Independence relied heavily on Locke's notion of natural law. In the first paragraph of the Declaration of Independence, for example, we read that people have to assume the "separate and equal Station to which the Laws of Nature and of Nature's God entitle them." In the first paragraph are also listed the "unalienable rights" of "mankind," including the right to life, liberty, and the pursuit of happiness.

In essence, the natural law tradition presupposes that the legitimacy of conventional, or positive, law derives from natural law. Whenever it conflicts with natural law, conventional law loses its legitimacy and should be changed.

The Positivist School

At the other end of the spectrum is the **positivist school.** Those who adhere to this school believe that there can be no higher law than a nation's positive law—law created by a particular society at a particular point in time.

NATURAL LAW SCHOOL
The oldest and one of the most significant schools of legal thought. Adherents of the natural law school believe that government and the legal system should reflect universal moral and ethical principles that are inherent in human nature.

POSITIVE LAW
The objective laws legally created by a society, as opposed to natural law or the unwritten laws arising from social customs; also called *black-letter law.*

"The first requirement of a sound body of law is that it should correspond with the actual feelings and demands of the community, whether right or wrong."

Oliver Wendell Holmes, Jr., 1841–1935
(Associate justice of the United States Supreme Court, 1902–1932)

POSITIVIST SCHOOL
A school of legal thought that holds that there can be no higher law than a nation's positive law—law created by a particular society at a particular point in time. In contrast to the natural law school, the positivist school maintains that there are no "natural" rights; rights come into existence only when there is a sovereign power (government) to confer and enforce those rights.

Many view Thomas Hobbes, an English philosopher who lived from 1588 to 1679, as the founder of the positivist approach to law. Hobbes believed that in the original state of nature, humans were no better than monkeys killing each other to get at the few bananas on the banana tree. Therefore, he concluded that sovereign power was necessary for stability and peace—in fact, for survival. No rights existed prior to the creation of a sovereign power (government) that could make and enforce laws, and it was governmental authority—not nature or a deity—that conferred rights on individuals. In other words, individuals do not have any "natural" rights, only those acquired as a result of the existence of enforceable law. This is why, in the positivist view, the significance and finality of positive law are greater than in the natural law tradition. Essentially, from the positivist perspective, the law is the law and must be obeyed on pain of punishment. Whether a particular law is bad or good is irrelevant. The merits or demerits of a given law can be discussed, and laws can be changed—in an orderly manner through a legitimate lawmaking process—but as long as a law exists, it must be obeyed.

The Legal Realists

LEGAL REALISM
A school of legal thought of the 1920s and 1930s that challenged many existing jurisprudential assumptions, particularly the assumption that subjective elements played no part in judicial reasoning. The legal realists, as the term implies, generally advocated a less abstract and more realistic approach to the law, an approach that would take into account customary practices and the circumstances in which transactions take place. The school left a lasting imprint on American jurisprudence.

Legal realism, which was a popular school of legal thought in the 1920s and 1930s, left a strong imprint on American jurisprudence. The legal realists were in a sense rebels. They were rebelling against some of the common assumptions of the legal theorists and jurists of their time. One such assumption was that judges, at least ideally, apply the law impartially, logically, and uniformly. Thus, in theory at least, all cases involving similar circumstances and issues should have similar outcomes. But in fact, reality rarely demonstrated such consistency—issues involving identical facts would often be decided differently by different courts, even when the same legal principles were applied. Why was this? For the legal realists, different outcomes resulted from the fact that judges are human beings with unique personalities, value systems, and intellects. It would be impossible, given this obvious fact, for any two judges to engage in an identical reasoning process when evaluating the same case. In other words, it would be impossible for the law to be applied in a completely impartial, logical, and uniform manner. The task of jurists, from the legal realists' point of view, was to acknowledge this fact and become as objective as possible by becoming aware of, and clarifying, the ways in which their reasoning in particular cases was affected by their personal biases and values.

The legal realists further believed that, just as each judge is influenced by the beliefs and attitudes unique to his or her personality, so too is each case attended by a unique set of circumstances. That is, no two cases, no matter how similar, are ever exactly the same. Therefore, judges should tailor their decisions to take into account the specific circumstances of each case, rather than rely on some abstract rule that may not relate to those particular circumstances. Judges should also consider extra-legal sources, such as economic and sociological data, in making decisions, to the extent that such sources illuminate the circumstances and issues involved in specific cases.

United States Supreme Court Justice Oliver Wendell Holmes, Jr., was an influential proponent of legal realism. In one of his best-known works, *The Common Law,*[1] Holmes emphasized the practical nature of the law: "The life of law has not been logic; it has been experience." Another proponent of this legal school of thought was Karl Llewellyn, who lived from 1893 to 1962. He, too, viewed judges' decisions as being necessarily shaped by the judges' value judgments and their interpretations of the outcomes of previous cases. Llewellyn is best known for his dominant role in drafting the Uniform Commercial Code, a set of rules for commercial transactions that will be discussed later in this chapter. This code, which governs

1. Boston: Little, Brown, 1963 (originally published in 1881).

contracts for the sale of goods, reflects the influence of legal realism in its emphasis on practicality, flexibility, reasonability, and customary trade practices.

The Case of the Speluncean Explorers

To illustrate how philosophies of law affect judicial decisions, Lon Fuller, a professor of law at Harvard, devised a hypothetical court case entitled *The Case of the Speluncean Explorers.*[2]

The "facts" of this hypothetical case, briefly, are as follows. In May of the year 4299, five members of the Speluncean Society, a society of cave explorers, were exploring a deep cavern when a landslide blocked the entrance to the cave. When the men failed to return to their homes, a rescue effort was launched at the site, and for days the workers attempted to clear the entrance. Further landslides made the task extremely difficult and dangerous, and several members of the rescue team were killed during the rescue operation. Thirty-two days elapsed before the rescuers finally succeeded in clearing the entrance and reaching the men trapped inside. The rescue team then learned that the five men had cast lots by a throw of the dice, and the man who threw the losing number was put to death and eaten by the others.

The four survivors were given medical treatment, then indicted for murder, tried, and sentenced to death by the Court of General Instances of the County of Stowfield. The four men petitioned the Supreme Court of Newgarth to hear the case. The relevant statute stated, "Whoever shall willfully take the life of another shall be punished by death." The decisions reached by the judges were essentially as described below. As you read them, try to relate each judge's reasoning to one of the schools of legal thought discussed above.

Judge Truepenny held that the men should be sentenced to death, in accordance with the statute—which "permits of no exception"—but suggested that the court should also petition the Chief Executive of the state of Newgarth to commute the death sentence to life imprisonment or grant the defendants a pardon in recognition of the ordeal that the defendants had suffered.

Judge Foster held the men to be innocent of any crime for two reasons. First, the positive law of the state of Newgarth was inapplicable to the "state of nature" in which the men had lived. Moreover, even if the men's action violated the letter of the law of Newgarth, it did not violate the spirit of the law because self-defense is permitted by the law, and the men essentially had acted in self-defense—that is, they committed cannibalism so that they could survive.

Judge Tating withdrew from the decision because of his inability "to resolve the doubts that beset me about the law of this case."

Judge Keen, in agreeing with Judge Truepenny, argued that the motivations underlying the killing were irrelevant because the statute did not make an exception for intentional murders that might be justified.

Judge Handy concluded that the men were innocent of any crime and that the lower court's judgment should be reversed. Handy believed that the law should take into account the desperate conditions that the defendants faced in the cave. In Judge Handy's opinion, the issue before the court was "a question of practical wisdom, to be exercised in a context, not of abstract theory, but of human realities."

Because the court was evenly divided, the lower court's ruling remained unchanged, and the men were put to death.

Obviously, both Judge Truepenny and Judge Keen are legal positivists. Although they differ in some of their views, both stress that the law is the law, and no exceptions are to be made. Because the explorers violated the law by killing their companion, they must pay the consequences and be sentenced to death, as the law

2. 62 *Harvard Law Review* 616 (1949).

requires. Judge Foster believes that applying the law of the Commonwealth of Newgarth would be inappropriate because the deed occurred outside the bounds of civilized society. Given the extraordinary circumstances, the only law appropriate to the situation was natural law. From this perspective, the men's actions were reasonable and excusable, according to Judge Foster. Judge Handy's approach is that of the legal realist. If the court fails to take "human realities" into account, it will not serve the needs of society.

❖ Sources of American Law

A major source of American law is the *common law* tradition that originated in medieval England. Laws, or statutes, enacted by Congress and the state legislatures constitute another important source of American law, a source generally referred to as *statutory law.* Other sources of American law are *constitutional* law, which is based on the federal Constitution and state constitutions, and *administrative* law. The latter consists of the numerous regulations created by administrative agencies, such as the Food and Drug Administration. Each of these important sources of law will be described in the following pages.

The Common Law Tradition

Because of our colonial heritage, much of American law is based on the English legal system. A knowledge of this tradition is necessary to an understanding of the nature of our legal system today.

"After all, that is the beauty of common law; it is a maze and not a motorway."

L. J. Diplock, 1907–1985
(British jurist)

Early English Courts of Law In 1066, the Normans conquered England, and William the Conqueror and his successors began the process of unifying the country under their rule. One of the means they used to this end was the establishment of the king's courts, or *curia regis.* Before the Norman Conquest, disputes had been settled according to the local legal customs and traditions in various regions of the country. The king's courts sought to establish a uniform set of customs for the country as a whole. What evolved in these courts was the beginning of the **common law**—a body of general rules that prescribed social conduct and applied throughout the entire English realm.

COMMON LAW
That body of law developed from custom or judicial decisions in English and U.S. courts, not attributable to a legislature.

Courts developed the common law rules from the principles behind judges' decisions in actual legal controversies. Judges attempted to be consistent. When possible, they based their decisions on the principles suggested by earlier cases. They sought to decide similar cases in a similar way and considered new cases with care because they knew that their decisions would make new law. Each interpretation became part of the law on the subject and served as a legal **precedent**. Later cases that involved similar legal principles or facts could be decided with reference to that precedent. The courts were guided by traditions and customs that built up in the handling of case after case.

PRECEDENT
A court decision that furnishes an example or authority for deciding subsequent cases in which identical or similar facts are presented.

In the early years of the common law, there was no single place or publication in which legal opinions could be found. In the late thirteenth and early fourteenth centuries, however, decisions of each year were gathered together and recorded in *Year Books.* These books were informal, containing only notes of cases made by lawyers and law students, and were not organized according to different legal topics; they were not official reports, did not include every case, and sometimes did not report cases until two or three years after the cases had been decided. Nevertheless, the *Year Books* were useful to lawyers and judges. In the sixteenth century, the *Year Books* were discontinued, and other reports of cases became available.

Stare Decisis The practice of deciding new cases with reference to former decisions, or precedents, eventually became a cornerstone of the English and American

The Court of Chancery in the reign of George I. Early English court decisions formed the basis of what type of law?

judicial systems. It forms a doctrine called ***stare decisis***[3] ("to stand on decided cases"). Under this doctrine, judges are obligated to follow the precedents established within their jurisdictions.

STARE DECISIS
A flexible doctrine of the courts, recognizing the value of following prior decisions (precedents) in cases similar to the one before the court; the courts' practice of being consistent with prior decisions based on similar facts.

The doctrine of *stare decisis* performs many useful functions. It helps the courts to be more efficient because if other courts have carefully reasoned through a similar case, their legal reasoning and opinions can serve as guides. *Stare decisis* also makes the law more stable and predictable because if the law on a given subject is well settled, someone bringing a case to court can usually rely on the court to make a decision based on what the law has been.

Sometimes a court will depart from the rule of precedent if it decides that the precedent should no longer be followed. If a court decides that a ruling precedent is simply incorrect or that technological or social changes have rendered the precedent inapplicable, the court might rule contrary to the precedent. Cases that overturn precedent often receive a great deal of publicity. In *Brown v. Board of Education of Topeka,*[4] for example, the United States Supreme Court expressly overturned precedent when it concluded that separate educational facilities for whites and blacks, which had been upheld as constitutional in numerous previous cases,[5] were inherently unequal. The Supreme Court's departure from precedent in *Brown* received a tremendous amount of publicity as people began to realize the ramifications of this change in the law.

Sometimes there is no precedent on which to base a decision, or there are conflicting precedents. In these situations, courts may consider a number of factors, including legal principles and policies underlying previous court decisions or existing statutes, fairness, social values and customs, public policy, and data and concepts drawn from the social sciences. Which of these sources is chosen or receives the greatest emphasis will depend on the nature of the case being considered and the

3. Pronounced *ster*-ay dih-*si*-ses.
4. 347 U.S. 483, 74 S.Ct. 686, 98 L.Ed. 873 (1954). (Legal citations are explained later in this chapter.)
5. See *Plessy v. Ferguson,* 163 U.S. 537, 16 S.Ct. 1138, 41 L.Ed. 256 (1896).

Landmark in the Law

Courts of Equity and Equitable Maxims

In the early king's courts of England, the kinds of remedies that could be granted were severely restricted. If one person wronged another, the king's courts could award as compensation one or more of the following: (1) land, (2) items of value, or (3) money. These courts became known as *courts of law*, and the three remedies were called *remedies at law*. Even though this system introduced uniformity in the settling of disputes, when plaintiffs wanted a remedy other than economic compensation, the courts of law could do nothing, so "no remedy, no right."

Equity Courts

Equity is that branch of unwritten law, founded in justice and fair dealing, that seeks to supply a fairer and more adequate remedy than any remedy available at law. In medieval England, when individuals could not obtain an adequate remedy in a court of law because of strict technicalities, they petitioned the king for relief. Most of these petitions were decided by an adviser to the king called the *chancellor*. The chancellor was said to be the "keeper of the king's conscience." When the chancellor thought that the claim was a fair one, new and unique remedies were granted. In this way, a new body of rules and remedies came into being, and eventually formal *chancery courts*, or *courts of equity*, were established. The remedies granted by these courts were called *remedies in equity*. Thus, two distinct court systems were created, each having a different set of judges and a different set of remedies.

Plaintiffs had to specify whether they were bringing an "action at law" or an "action in equity," and they chose their courts accordingly. For example, a plaintiff might ask a court of equity to order a defendant to perform within the terms of a contract. A court of law could not issue such an order because its remedies were limited to payment of money or property as compensation for damages. A court of equity, however, could issue a decree for *specific performance*—an order to perform what was promised. A court of equity could also issue an *injunction*, directing that a party do or refrain from doing a particular act. In certain cases, when the legal remedy of the payment of money for damages was unavailable or inadequate, a court of equity could allow for the *rescission* (cancellation) of the contract so that the parties would be returned to the positions that they held prior to the contract's formation. Equitable remedies will be discussed in greater detail in Chapter 13.

Equitable Principles and Maxims

Courts of equity had the responsibility of using discretion in supplementing the common law. Even today, when the same court can award both legal and equitable remedies, such discretion is exercised. It is often guided by what are known as *equitable principles and maxims*. These principles and maxims are propositions or general statements of rules of equity that courts often invoke. Some of them are listed here.

1. Whoever seeks equity must do equity. (Anyone who wishes to be treated fairly must treat others fairly.)
2. Where there is equal equity, the law must prevail. (The law will determine the outcome of a controversy in which the merits of both sides are equal.)
3. One seeking the aid of an equity court must come to the court with clean hands. (Plaintiffs must have acted fairly and honestly.)
4. Equity will not suffer a wrong to be without a remedy. (Equitable relief will be awarded when there is a right to relief and there is no adequate remedy at law.)
5. Equity regards substance rather than form. (Equity is more concerned with fairness and justice than with legal technicalities.)
6. Equity aids the vigilant, not those who rest on their rights. (Equity will not help those who neglect their rights for an unreasonable period of time.)

The last maxim has become known as the *equitable doctrine of laches*. The doctrine arose to encourage people to bring lawsuits while the evidence was fresh; if they failed to do so, they would not be allowed to bring a lawsuit. What constitutes a reasonable time, of course, varies according to the circumstances of the case. Time periods for different types of cases are now usually fixed by *statutes of limitations*. After the time allowed under a statute of limitations has expired, no action can be brought, no matter how strong the case was originally.

The Merging of Law and Equity

Today, in most states, the courts of law and equity are merged, and thus the distinction between the two courts has largely disappeared. A plaintiff may now request both legal and equitable remedies in the same action, and the trial court judge may grant either form—or both forms—of relief. Yet the merging of law and equity does not diminish the importance of distinguishing legal remedies from equitable remedies. To request the proper remedy, one must know what remedies are available for specific kinds of harms suffered.

particular judge hearing the case. Although judges always strive to be free of subjectivity and personal bias in deciding cases, each judge has his or her own unique personality, set of values or philosophical leanings, and intellectual attributes—all of which necessarily frame the decision-making process.

The Common Law Today The body of law that was first developed in England and that is still used today in the United States consists of the rules of law announced in court decisions. These rules of law include interpretations of constitutional provisions, of statutes enacted by legislatures, and of regulations created by administrative agencies. Today, this body of law is referred to variously as the common law, judge-made law, or **case law.**

CASE LAW
Rules of law announced in court decisions. Case law includes the aggregate of reported cases that interpret judicial precedents, statutes, regulations, and constitutional provisions.

The common law governs all areas not covered by *statutory law,* which, as will be discussed shortly, generally consists of those laws enacted by state legislatures and, at the federal level, by Congress. The body of statutory law has expanded greatly since the beginning of this nation, and this expansion has resulted in a proportionate reduction in the scope and applicability of the common law. Nonetheless, the common law remains a significant source of legal authority. Even when legislation has been substituted for common law principles, courts often rely on the common law as a guide to interpreting the legislation, on the theory that the people who drafted the statute intended to codify an existing common law rule.

Restatements of the Law To summarize and clarify common law rules and principles, the American Law Institute (ALI) drafted and published compilations of the common law called Restatements of the Law. The ALI, which was formed in the 1920s, consists of practicing attorneys, legal scholars, and judges. There are Restatements of the Law in the areas of contracts, torts, agency, trusts, property, restitution, security, judgments, and conflict of laws. Many of the Restatements are now in their second edition. The *Restatement of the Law of Contracts,* for example, was first published in 1932. Thirty years later, a second edition was undertaken. It was completed in 1979 and is referred to as the *Restatement (Second) of the Law of Contracts* or, more simply, as the *Restatement (Second) of Contracts.*

The Restatements, which generally summarize the common law rules followed by most states, do not in themselves have the force of law but are an important secondary source of legal analysis and opinion on which judges often rely in making their decisions. We refer to the Restatements frequently in subsequent chapters of this text.

Constitutional Law

The federal government and the states have separate constitutions that set forth the general organization, powers, and limits of their respective governments. The U.S. Constitution is the supreme law of the land. A law in violation of the Constitution, no matter what its source, will be declared unconstitutional and will not be enforced. The Tenth Amendment to the U.S. Constitution, which defines the powers and limitations of the federal government, reserves all powers not granted to the federal government to the states. Unless they conflict with the U.S. Constitution, state constitutions are supreme within each state's respective borders.

The regulation of interstate commerce is one of the chief ways in which the U.S. Constitution affects business. The constitutional authority to regulate business and other aspects of constitutional law will be discussed in detail in Chapter 4. The complete text of the U.S. Constitution is presented in Appendix B.

Statutory Law

Statutes enacted by the Congress and the various state legislative bodies make up another source of law, which, as mentioned earlier, is generally referred to as

George Washington presiding at the Constitutional Convention in 1787.

STATUTORY LAW
Laws enacted by a legislative body (as opposed to constitutional law, administrative law, or case law).

statutory law. The statutory law of the United States also includes the ordinances passed by cities and counties, none of which can violate the U.S. Constitution or the relevant state constitution. Today, legislative bodies and regulatory agencies assume an ever-increasing share of lawmaking. Much of the work of modern courts consists of interpreting what the lawmakers meant when the law was passed and of applying that law to a present set of facts.

Uniform Laws No two states in the United States have identical statutes, constitutions, and case law. In other words, state laws differ from state to state. The differences among state laws were even more notable in the 1800s, when conflicting state statutes frequently made the rapidly developing trade and commerce among the states very difficult. To counter these problems, a group of legal scholars and lawyers formed the National Conference of Commissioners (NCC) on Uniform State Laws in 1892 to draft uniform statutes for adoption by the states. The NCC still exists today and continues to issue uniform statutes.

Adoption of a uniform law is a state matter, and a state may reject all or part of the statute or rewrite it as the state legislature wishes. Hence, even when a uniform law is said to have been adopted in many states, those states' laws may not be entirely "uniform." Once adopted by a state, a uniform act becomes a part of the statutory law of that state.

The earliest uniform law, the Uniform Negotiable Instruments Law, was completed by 1896 and was adopted in every state by the early 1920s (although not all states used exactly the same wording). Over the following decades, other acts were drawn up in a similar manner, including the Uniform Sales Act, the Uniform Warehouse Receipts Act, the Uniform Bills of Lading Act, the Uniform Partnership Act, the Model Business Corporation Act (drafted by the American Bar Association), the Uniform Stock Transfer Act, the Uniform Probate Code, and, more recently, the Uniform Status of Children of Assisted Conception Act (also known as the Uniform Surrogacy Act) and the Uniform Prenuptial Agreements Act. The most ambitious uniform act of all, however, was the Uniform Commercial Code.

The Uniform Commercial Code (UCC) The Uniform Commercial Code (UCC), which was created through the joint efforts of the NCC and the American

Law Institute, was first issued in 1952. The UCC has been adopted in all fifty states,[6] the District of Columbia, and the Virgin Islands. The UCC facilitates commerce among the states by providing a uniform, yet flexible, set of rules governing commercial transactions. The UCC assures businesspersons that their contracts, if validly entered into, normally will be enforced. Because of its importance in the area of commercial law, the UCC will be cited frequently in this text, particularly in Unit Three, which covers commercial transactions. The creation of the UCC is the subject of the *Landmark in the Law* in the opening chapter of that unit (Chapter 14). The entire text of the latest version of the UCC is presented in Appendix C.

Administrative Law

Administrative law consists of the rules, orders, and decisions of **administrative agencies**. Regulations issued by various administrative agencies affect virtually every aspect of a business's operation, including the firm's capital structure and financing, its hiring and firing procedures, its relations with employees and unions, and the way it manufactures and markets its products.

At the national level, numerous agencies exist within the executive departments. The Food and Drug Administration, for example, is within the Department of Health and Human Services. There are also major independent regulatory agencies at the federal level, such as the Federal Trade Commission, the Securities and Exchange Commission, and the Federal Communications Commission. There are administrative agencies at the state and local levels, as well, but because the rules of state and local agencies vary widely, we will focus here exclusively on federal administrative law.

Federal administrative agencies are created by Congress when it enacts **enabling legislation**, which specifies the name, composition, and powers of the agency being created. For example, the Federal Trade Commission (FTC) was created in 1914 by the Federal Trade Commission Act.[7] The act prohibits unfair and deceptive trade practices. It also describes the procedures the agency must follow to charge persons or organizations with violations of the act, and it provides for judicial review (review by the courts) of agency orders. Other portions of the act grant the agency powers to "make rules and regulations for the purpose of carrying out the Act," to conduct investigations of business practices, to obtain reports from interstate corporations concerning their business practices, to investigate possible violations of the act, to publish findings of its investigations, and to recommend new legislation. The act also empowers the FTC to hold trial-like hearings and to adjudicate certain kinds of trade disputes that involve FTC regulations.

Note that the FTC's grant of power incorporates functions associated with the legislative branch of government (rulemaking), the executive branch (investigation and enforcement), and the judicial branch (adjudication). Taken together, these functions constitute what has been termed **administrative process**, which is the administration of law by administrative agencies, in contrast to **judicial process,** which is the administration of law by the courts.

Rulemaking One of the major functions of an administrative agency is **rulemaking.** The most common rulemaking procedure involves the following steps: First, the agency must give public notice of the proposed rulemaking proceedings, where and when the proceedings will be held, the agency's legal authority for the proceedings, and the terms or subject matter of the proposed rule. Following this notice, the agency must allow ample time for persons to comment in writing on

ADMINISTRATIVE LAW
Body of law created by administrative agencies—such as the Securities and Exchange Commission and the Federal Trade Commission—in the form of rules, regulations, orders, and decisions in order to carry out their duties and responsibilities. This law can initially be enforced by these agencies outside the judicial process.

ADMINISTRATIVE AGENCY
A federal or state government agency established to perform a specific function. Administrative agencies are authorized by legislative acts to make and enforce rules relating to the purpose for which they were established.

ENABLING LEGISLATION
Statutes enacted by Congress that authorize the creation of an administrative agency and specify the name, composition, and powers of the agency being created.

ADMINISTRATIVE PROCESS
The procedure used by administrative agencies in the administration of law.

JUDICIAL PROCESS
The procedures relating to, or connected with, the administration of justice through the judicial system.

RULEMAKING
The actions undertaken by administrative agencies when formally adopting new regulations or amending old ones. Under the Administrative Procedures Act, rulemaking includes notifying the public of proposed rules or changes and receiving and considering the public's comments.

6. Louisiana has adopted only Articles 1, 3, 4, 5, 7, 8, and 9. All states have, of course, modified the UCC.
7. 15 U.S.C. Sections 45–58.

the proposed rule. After the comments have been received and reviewed, the agency takes them into consideration when drafting the final version of the regulation.

Investigation and Enforcement Agencies have both investigatory and prosecutorial powers. An agency can compel individuals or organizations to hand over specified books, papers, records, or other documents. In addition, agencies may conduct on-site inspections, although a search warrant is normally required for such inspections. Sometimes the search of a home, an office, or a factory is the only means of obtaining evidence needed to prove a regulatory violation. Agencies investigate a wide range of activities, including coal mining, automobile manufacturing, and the industrial discharge of pollutants into the environment.

After conducting its own investigation of a suspected rule violation, an agency may decide to take action against specific parties. The action may involve a trial-like hearing before an **administrative law judge (ALJ)**. The ALJ may compel the charged party to pay damages or may forbid the party to carry on some specified activity. Either side may appeal the ALJ's decision to the commission or board that governs the agency, and upon failure of the party to get relief here, appeal can be made to a federal court.

ADMINISTRATIVE LAW JUDGE
One who presides over an administrative agency hearing and who has the power to administer oaths, take testimony, rule on questions of evidence, and make determinations of fact.

Limitations on Agency Powers Combining what are essentially legislative, executive, and judicial functions into one governmental entity creates institutional flexibility, but it also concentrates a considerable amount of power in a single organization. The broad range of authority exercised by administrative agencies is at the heart of much of the controversy surrounding the regulatory process. Not only do agency regulations impose costly compliance requirements on business firms, but also agency rules can, on occasion, seem rather arbitrary or impractical. (See this chapter's *Law in the Extreme* for an example of the latter.)

Agency power is not unlimited, however. For one thing, agencies cannot exceed the power granted to them by Congress in its enabling legislation. Furthermore, Congress controls the purse strings. If it is dissatisfied with an agency's performance, it may refuse to allocate funds for the agency in the future. The fact that agency orders may be appealed to the courts may also act as a check on the arbitrary use of agency power. The executive branch can also exert control over administrative agencies, particularly through the president's power to appoint federal officers. Another significant limitation to agency power is the Administrative Procedure Act of 1946,[8] which imposes strict procedural requirements that agencies must meet when undertaking rulemaking or adjudication.

❖ Civil Law versus Criminal Law

The huge body of the law may be broken down according to several classification systems. An important classification system divides law into *civil law* and *criminal law*. **Civil law** spells out the duties that exist between persons or between citizens and their governments (*excluding* the duty not to commit crimes). Contract law, for example, is part of civil law. The whole body of tort law (see Chapters 5 and 6), which deals with the infringement by one person of the legally recognized rights of another, is also an area of civil law.

Criminal law, in contrast to civil law, has to do with a wrong committed against the public as a whole (see Chapter 7). Criminal acts are proscribed by local, state,

CIVIL LAW
The branch of law dealing with the definition and enforcement of all private or public rights, as opposed to criminal matters.

CRIMINAL LAW
Law that governs and defines those actions that are crimes and that subject the convicted offender to punishment imposed by the government.

8. 5 U.S.C. Sections 551–706.

Law in the Extreme

Is This Man a Criminal?

The policy of preserving wetlands to protect the wildlife and endangered species thereon is supported by a large and growing number of Americans. And in the last several years, federal administrative agencies charged with making and enforcing rules to implement this policy have made it clear that those who fill in wetlands without permission from the appropriate agencies may end up in court and possibly in prison. At times, however, the maze of administrative rules becomes so entangled and bewildering that even a law-abiding former wetlands regulator can end up in prison for violating the law. Consider, for example, the bizarre case of William Ellen.

After working for many years as a wetlands regulator for the state of Virginia, Ellen started his own nonprofit wildlife rescue center. In 1987, he was hired by a Maryland property owner to convert 103 acres of an estate into a wildlife sanctuary. Ellen, who was careful to abide by the rules, secured a number of permits from various agencies and went ahead with his work. He filled in some areas so that a gatehouse and some sheds could be built. In those areas that were dry and dusty, he created a number of duck ponds.

All went well until 1989, when the government redefined wetlands to include some of the areas that Ellen had already filled in and notified Ellen of this—as well as of the fact that Ellen had been filling in areas that were designated as wetlands under the previous rules. Ellen was ordered by the government to stop all work on the project, and he substantially complied with the request. Nonetheless, after a series of encounters and agreements with agency officials, Ellen was convicted in a federal court of having willfully filled in wetlands without a permit. He was sentenced to six months in prison and one year of supervised release.

On appeal,[a] Ellen argued, among other things, that it was unconstitutional to hold him liable for violating the regulations created in 1989 because they did not exist at the time the alleged violation took place. Ellen cited the "ex post facto" clause of Article I, Section 9, of the Constitution, which mandates that laws cannot be enacted that apply retroactively. Although the average layperson might be persuaded by the logic of Ellen's argument, the court was not moved. Why? Because the court deemed that the wetlands rule was not a law but merely an "interpretative rule." In contrast to "legislative rules," which have the force of law, interpretative rules serve merely as guidelines to assist agencies in interpreting statutes. Because the wetlands rule was not a "law," the Constitution's "ex post facto" clause did not apply.

Did it count for anything that Ellen's duck ponds had actually added forty-five more acres of wetlands to the property? No. The government claimed that the duck ponds were in fact harmful to the environment because ducks and geese would defecate in the water and thereby pollute the ponds. (To remedy this problem, the government used dynamite to blast a channel linking the ponds to ocean water.)

a. *United States v. Ellen*, 961 F.2d 462 (4th Cir. 1992).

or federal government statutes. In a criminal case, the government seeks to impose a penalty (a monetary fine, imprisonment, or both) on an allegedly guilty person. In a civil case, one party (sometimes the government) tries to make the other party comply with a duty or pay for the damage caused by failure to so comply. Exhibit 1–1 lists the areas of law classified as criminal law and civil law.

◆ **Exhibit 1–1**
Criminal and Civil Law
An important feature distinguishing criminal and civil law is the sanction imposed on the wrongdoer. Criminal sanctions may include imprisonment, while civil sanctions emphasize payment of money.

CRIMINAL LAW	CIVIL LAW
Administrative law	Agency
Antitrust law	Bailments
Constitutional law	Bankruptcy
Criminal law	Business organizations
Environmental law	Commercial paper
Labor law	Contracts
Securities law	Insurance
	Property
	Sales
	Secured transactions
	Torts
	Trusts and wills

❖ Law around the World

Earlier, we discussed one of the major legal systems of today's world—the common law system of England and the United States. Generally, those countries that were once colonies of Great Britain retained their English common law heritage after they achieved their independence. Today, common law systems exist in Ireland, Canada, Australia, New Zealand, and India.

In contrast to Great Britain and the common law countries, most of the other European nations base their legal systems on Roman civil law, or "code law." The term *civil law,* as used here, refers not to civil as opposed to criminal law but to *codified* law—an ordered grouping of legal principles enacted into law by a legislature or governing body. In a **civil law system,** the primary source of law is a statutory code, and case precedents are not judicially binding, as normally they are in a common law system. This is not to say that precedents are unimportant in a civil law system. On the contrary, judges in such systems commonly refer to previous decisions as sources of legal guidance. The difference is that judges in a civil law system are *not bound* by precedent; in other words, the doctrine of *stare decisis* does not apply.

CIVIL LAW SYSTEM
A system of law derived from that of the Roman Empire and based on a code rather than case law; the predominant system of law in the nations of continental Europe and the nations that were once their colonies. In the United States, Louisiana is the only state that has a civil law system.

Today, the civil law system is followed in most of the continental European countries, as well as in the Latin American, African, and Asian countries that were once colonies of the continental European nations. Japan and South Africa also have civil law systems. Ingredients of the civil law system are found in the Islamic courts of predominantly Muslim countries. In the United States, the state of Louisiana, because of its historical ties to France, has in part a civil law system. The legal systems of Puerto Rico, Québec, and Scotland are similarly characterized as having elements of the civil law system.

Despite the differences in the two systems, distinctions are beginning to blur. For example, judges in the civil law system frequently rely on precedents for legal guidance. And judges in the common law system have shown an increased willingness to emulate their civil law system counterparts by playing a more active role in court proceedings than they have in the past; for example, American law judges increasingly act to develop facts and issues during trial proceedings. Yet another trend in the coalescence of the two systems is the increasing importance of statutes and administrative rules in the common law system. Recent decades have witnessed a proliferation of statutes and administrative rules that have modified or wholly superseded the earlier common law. This is especially true with regard to commercial transactions subject to the statutory provisions of the Uniform Commercial Code and with regard to business activities subject to the administrative rules of numerous federal and state regulatory agencies.

Even though, as just discussed, broad similarities may exist in the legal systems of various countries, differences exist as well. The laws of nations differ because the legal system of each country reflects its own unique cultural, historical, economic, and political background. The law of a particular nation is referred to as **national law.**

NATIONAL LAW
Law that pertains to a particular nation (as opposed to international law).

Because business is becoming increasingly global in scope, numerous cases now brought before the courts involve issues concerning foreign parties or governments. The laws of the nations involved may affect the outcome of these cases. International doctrines, treaties, and other agreements relating to business are also sources of law that govern business transactions. The international environment of business is examined in detail in Chapter 36, but because many of the topics covered in this text have international dimensions, it is worthwhile at this point to summarize the major sources and characteristics of laws affecting international business dealings.

❖ International Law

International law can be defined as a body of written and unwritten laws observed by independent nations and governing the acts of individuals as well as governments. The key difference between national law and international law is the fact that national law can be enforced by government authorities. But what government can enforce international law? By definition, a *nation* is a sovereign entity, which means that there is no higher authority to which that nation must submit. If a nation violates an international law, the most that other countries or international organizations can do (if persuasive tactics fail) is resort to coercive actions against the violating nation. Coercive actions range from severance of diplomatic relations and boycotts to, at the last resort, war.

INTERNATIONAL LAW
The law that governs relations among nations. International customs and treaties are generally considered to be two of the most important sources of international law.

In essence, international law is the result of centuries-old attempts to reconcile the traditional need of each nation to be the final authority over its own affairs with the desire of nations to benefit economically from trade and harmonious relations with one another. Although no sovereign nation can be compelled to obey a law external to itself, nations can and do voluntarily agree to be governed in certain respects by international law for the purpose of facilitating international trade and commerce and civilized discourse.

"I asked Tom if countries always apologized when they had done wrong, and he says: 'Yes; the little ones does.' "

Samuel Clemens (Mark Twain), 1835–1910
(American author and humorist)

Sources of International Law

International law is an intermingling of rules and constraints derived from a variety of sources. The laws of individual nations are sources of international law, as are the customs that have evolved among nations in their relations with one another. Of increasing importance in regulating international activities, however, are treaties and international organizations.

Treaties A **treaty** is an agreement between two or more nations that creates rights and duties binding on the parties to the treaty, just as a private contract creates rights and duties binding on the parties to the contract. To give effect to a treaty, the supreme power of each nation that is a party to the treaty must ratify it. For example, the U.S. Constitution requires approval by two-thirds of the Senate before a treaty executed by the president will be binding on the U.S. government. Bilateral agreements, as the term implies, occur when only two nations form an agreement that will govern their commercial exchanges or other relations with one another. Multilateral agreements are those formed by several nations. The European Union (EU), for example, which regulates commercial activities among its European member nations, is the result of a multilateral trade agreement. Other multilateral agree-

TREATY
An agreement, or compact, formed between two independent nations.

ments have led to the formation of regional trade associations, such as the one recently being formed by Canada, Mexico, and the United States.

One treaty of particular significance to the international legal environment of business is the United Nations 1980 Convention on Contracts for the International Sale of Goods (CISG). Essentially, the CISG is to international sales contracts what the Uniform Commercial Code is to domestic sales contracts. The CISG governs the international sale of goods between firms or individuals located in different countries, providing that the countries involved have ratified the CISG. So far, thirty-four countries have ratified the CISG.[9] Although that number is small, it includes many of the world's leading economic powers, including the United States, and it is expected to grow rapidly.

International Organizations International organizations and conferences also play an important role in the international legal arena. International organizations and conferences adopt resolutions, declarations, and other types of standards that often require a particular behavior of nations. The General Assembly of the United Nations, for example, has adopted numerous resolutions and declarations that embody principles of international law and has sponsored conferences that have led to the formation of international agreements, such as the CISG. The United States is a member of more than one hundred multilateral and bilateral organizations, including at least twenty through the United Nations.

The World Court The International Court of Justice, commonly called the World Court, is a fifteen-member judicial tribunal whose jurisdiction is established in a statute annexed to the Charter of the United Nations. The World Court is the principal judicial arm of the United Nations. The fifteen judges are elected by the United Nations General Assembly and the United Nations Security Council for a term of nine years. All member nations of the United Nations automatically have *standing* (the right to bring a lawsuit) to bring disputes before the World Court, but no country may be compelled to submit to its jurisdiction. This lack of compulsory jurisdiction is a major institutional weakness of the court.

Despite the World Court's status as the judicial arm of the United Nations, the court has not played a decisive role in resolving international legal issues, particularly in the area of commercial activity, for several reasons. First, only nations can appear before the World Court, although sometimes governments have appeared as representatives of private parties to contest the actions of another government. Second, the World Court's decisions are binding only on the parties to a particular case; in other words, decisions of the World Court do not serve as precedents and thus cannot bind future actions of countries that did not participate directly in a proceeding. Third, as noted previously, nations are free to choose whether to subject themselves to the World Court's jurisidiction in any particular case. Finally, there is no effective power to enforce compliance with the World Court's decision. If a nation chooses not to abide by a decision (assuming it consented to the World Court's jurisdiction to begin with), there is no international police officer to enforce a penalty for the failure to comply.

Public and Private International Law

Most scholars of international law make a distinction between public and private international law. *Public international law* concerns rules that govern the actions of nations in their dealings with one another and, in some circumstances, the actions of nations in their dealings with individuals of a foreign country. The rules are based

9. As of March 1992.

on principles that are generally accepted as binding on nations as members of the international community. Nations rely on public international law in conducting diplomatic relations, negotiations, and policymaking. Public international law includes issues that relate to justifications and conduct in the use of military force. Other issues include how investments by foreigners and sales of foreign products should be treated by the host government. Most of these issues may be analyzed with reference to the various treaties, conventions, and domestic laws of a nation, as well as to the policies and regulations of international organizations.

In contrast to public international law, *private international law* concerns the rules that affect the dealings between individual citizens of one country and individual citizens of another country. To a certain extent, private international law overlaps with public international law, because individuals undertake international transactions that may be governed by a trade treaty or convention, such as the CISG, entered into by their respective governments.

Apart from international treaties and conventions, private international law with regard to business transactions centers on the right of private parties to choose the law that will govern their transactions. Within certain limits, parties can choose not only the law that will govern their transaction (for example, the law of California or the law of Nigeria) but also the *forum* in which future disputes will be decided (for example, a U.S. court or a Nigerian court). Also common in international agreements involving parties that speak different languages are clauses specifying the language that will be used in interpreting the terms of the agreement. Contractual clauses relating to these issues are discussed in greater detail in Chapter 36.

❖ Finding Statutory and Administrative Law

This text includes numerous citations to federal and state laws and regulations. When Congress passes laws, they are collected in a publication titled *United States Statutes at Large*. When state legislatures pass laws, they are collected in similar state publications. Most frequently, however, laws are referred to in their codified form—that is, the form in which they appear in the federal and state codes.

In these codes, laws are compiled by subject. The *United States Code* (U.S.C.) arranges all existing federal laws of a public and permanent nature by subject. Each of the fifty subjects into which the U.S.C. arranges the laws is given a title and a title number. For example, laws relating to commerce and trade are collected in Title 15, which is titled "Commerce and Trade." Titles are subdivided by sections. A citation to the U.S.C. includes title and section numbers. Thus, a reference to "15 U.S.C. Section 1" means that the statute can be found in Section 1 of Title 15. ("Section" may also be designated by the symbol §, and "Sections" by §§.)

Sometimes a citation includes the abbreviation *et seq.*—as in "15 U.S.C. Section 1 *et seq.*" The term is an abbreviated form of *et sequitur*, which in Latin means "and the following"; when used in a citation, it refers to sections that concern the same subject as the numbered section and follow it in sequence.

State codes follow the U.S.C. pattern of arranging law by subject. They may be called codes, revisions, compilations, consolidations, general statutes, or statutes, depending on the preference of the states. In some codes, subjects are designated by number. In others, they are designated by name. For example, "13 Pennsylvania Consolidated Statutes Section 1101" means the statute can be found in Title 13, Section 1101, of the Pennsylvania code. "California Commercial Code Section 1101" means the statute can be found under the subject heading "Commercial Code" of the California code in Section 1101. Abbreviations may be used. For example, "13 Pennsylvania Consolidated Statutes Section 1101" may be abbreviated "13 Pa. C.S. § 1101," and "California Commercial Code Section 1101" may be abbreviated "Cal. Com. Code § 1101."

Rules and regulations adopted by federal administrative agencies are compiled in the *Code of Federal Regulations* (C.F.R.). Like the U.S.C., the C.F.R. is divided into fifty titles. Rules within each title are assigned section numbers. A full citation to the C.F.R. includes title and section numbers. For example, a reference to "17 C.F.R. Section 230.504" means that the rule can be found in Section 230.504 of Title 17.

Commercial publications of these laws and regulations are available and are widely used. For example, West Publishing Company publishes the *United States Code Annotated* (U.S.C.A.). The U.S.C.A. contains the complete text of laws included in the U.S.C., as well as notes of court decisions that interpret and apply specific sections of the statutes, plus the text of presidential proclamations and executive orders. The U.S.C.A. also includes research aids, such as cross-references to related statutes, historical notes, and library references. A citation to the U.S.C.A. is similar to a citation to the U.S.C.: "15 U.S.C.A. Section 1."

❖ Finding Case Law

Laws pertaining to business consist of case law as well as statutory law. A substantial number of cases are presented in this text to provide you with concise, real-life illustrations of the interpretation and application of the law by the courts. Many other court decisions have been referenced in footnotes throughout the text. Because of the importance of knowing how to find these and other court opinions, this section offers a brief introduction to the case reporting system and to the legal "shorthand" employed in referencing court cases.

First, though, we need to look briefly at the court system. As will be discussed in detail in Chapter 3, there are two types of courts in the United States, federal courts and state courts. Both the federal and state court systems consist of several levels, or tiers, of courts. *Trial courts*, in which evidence is presented and testimony given, are on the bottom tier (which also includes lower courts handling specialized issues). Decisions from a trial court can be appealed to a higher court, which commonly would be an intermediate *court of appeals*, or an *appellate court*. Appellate courts are known as *reviewing courts* because they do not hear evidence or testimony, as trial courts do; rather, an appellate court reviews all of the records relating to a case to determine whether the trial court's decision was correct. Decisions from these intermediate courts of appeals may be appealed to an even higher court, such as a state supreme court or the United States Supreme Court.

State Court Decisions

Most state trial court decisions are not published. Except in New York and a few other states that publish selected opinions of their trial courts, decisions from the state trial courts are merely filed in the office of the clerk of the court, where they are available for public inspection.

Written decisions of the appellate, or reviewing, courts, however, are published and distributed. The reported appellate decisions are published in volumes called *Reports*, which are numbered consecutively. State appellate court decisions are found in the state reports of that particular state.

Additionally, state court opinions appear in regional units of the *National Reporter System*, published by West Publishing Company. Most lawyers and libraries have the West reporters because they report cases more quickly and are distributed more widely than the state-published reports. In fact, many states have eliminated their own reporters in favor of West's National Reporter System. The National Reporter System divides the states into the following geographical areas: *Atlantic* (A. or A.2d), *South Eastern* (S.E. or S.E.2d), *South Western* (S.W. or S.W.2d), *North Western* (N.W. or N.W.2d), *North Eastern* (N.E. or N.E.2d), *Southern* (So. or

So.2d), and *Pacific* (P. or P.2d). (The *2d* in the abbreviations refers to *Second Series.*) The states included in each of these regional divisions are indicated in Exhibit 1–2, which illustrates West's National Reporter System.

After appellate decisions have been published, they are normally referred to (cited) by the name of the case; the volume, name, and page of the state's official reporter (if different from West's National Reporter System); the volume, unit, and page number of the *National Reporter;* and the volume, name, and page number of any other selected reporter. This information is included in what is called the **citation.** (Citing a reporter by volume number, name, and page number, in that order, is common to all citations.) When more than one reporter is cited for the same case, each reference is called a *parallel citation.* For example, consider the following case: *Leasefirst v. Hartford Rexall Drugs,* 168 Wis.2d 83, 483 N.W.2d 585 (1992). We see that the opinion in this case may be found in Volume 168 of the official *Wisconsin Reports, Second Series,* on page 83. The parallel citation is to Volume 483 of the *North Western Reporter, Second Series,* page 585. In reprinting appellate opinions in this text, in addition to the reporter, we give the name of the court hearing the case and the year of the court's decision.

CITATION
A citation indicates where a particular constitutional provision, statute, reported case, or article may be found; also an order for a defendant to appear in court or indicating that a person has violated a legal rule.

A few of the states—including those with intermediate appellate courts, such as California, Illinois, and New York—have more than one reporter for opinions given by courts within their states. Sample citations from these courts, as well as others, are listed and explained in Exhibit 1–3.

Federal Court Decisions

Federal district court decisions are published unofficially in West's *Federal Supplement* (F.Supp.), and opinions from the circuit courts of appeals (federal reviewing courts) are reported unofficially in West's *Federal Reporter* (F. or F.2d). Cases concerning federal bankruptcy law are published unofficially in West's *Bankruptcy Reporter* (Bankr.). Opinions from the United States Supreme Court are reported in the *United States Reports* (U.S.), West's *Supreme Court Reporter* (S.Ct.), the *Lawyers' Edition of the Supreme Court Reports* (L.Ed. or L.Ed.2d), and other publications.

The *United States Reports* is the official edition of all decisions of the United States Supreme Court for which there are written opinions. Published by the federal government, the series includes reports of Supreme Court cases dating from the August term of 1791, although originally many of the decisions were not reported in the early volumes.

West's *Supreme Court Reporter* is an unofficial edition dating from the Court's term in October 1882. Preceding each of its case reports are a summary of the case and *headnotes* (brief editorial statements of the law involved in the case, numbered to correspond to numbers in the report). The headnotes are also given classification numbers that serve to cross-reference each headnote to other headnotes on similar points throughout the National Reporter System and other West publications. The numbers facilitate research of all relevant cases on a given point. This is important because, as may be evident from the discussion of *stare decisis,* a lawyer's goal in undertaking legal research is to find an authority that cannot be factually distinguished from his or her case.

The Lawyers Cooperative Publishing Company of Rochester, New York, publishes the *Lawyers' Edition of the Supreme Court Reports,* which is an unofficial edition of the entire series of the Supreme Court reports and contains many of the decisions not reported in the early official volumes. Also, among other editorial features, the *Lawyers' Edition,* in its second series, precedes the report of each case with a full summary, includes excerpts from the attorneys' notes on the cases, and discusses in detail selected cases of special interest to the legal profession.

Sample citations for federal court decisions are also listed and explained in Exhibit 1–3.

◆ **Exhibit 1–2**
National Reporter System—Regional/Federal

Regional Reporters	Coverage Beginning	Coverage
Atlantic Reporter (A. or A.2d)	1885	Connecticut, Delaware, Maine, Maryland, New Hampshire, New Jersey, Pennsylvania, Rhode Island, Vermont, and District of Columbia.
North Eastern Reporter (N.E. or N.E.2d)	1885	Illinois, Indiana, Massachusetts, New York, and Ohio.
North Western Reporter (N.W. or N.W.2d)	1879	Iowa, Michigan, Minnesota, Nebraska, North Dakota, South Dakota, and Wisconsin.
Pacific Reporter (P. or P.2d)	1883	Alaska, Arizona, California, Colorado, Hawaii, Idaho, Kansas, Montana, Nevada, New Mexico, Oklahoma, Oregon, Utah, Washington, and Wyoming.
South Eastern Reporter (S.E. or S.E.2d)	1887	Georgia, North Carolina, South Carolina, Virginia, and West Virginia.
South Western Reporter (S.W. or S.W.2d)	1886	Arkansas, Kentucky, Missouri, Tennessee, and Texas.
Southern Reporter (So. or So.2d)	1887	Alabama, Florida, Louisiana, and Mississippi.
Federal Reporters		
Federal Reporter (F., F.2d, or F.3d)	1880	U.S. Circuit Court from 1880 to 1912; U.S. Commerce Court from 1911 to 1913; U.S. District Courts from 1880 to 1932; U.S. Court of Claims (now called U.S. Court of Federal Claims) from 1929 to 1932 and since 1960; U.S. Court of Appeals since 1891; U.S. Court of Customs and Patent Appeals since 1929; U.S. Emergency Court of Appeals since 1943.
Federal Supplement (F.Supp.)	1932	U.S. Court of Claims from 1932 to 1960; U.S. District Courts since 1932; U.S. Customs Court since 1956.
Federal Rules Decisions (F.R.D.)	1939	U.S. District Courts involving the Federal Rules of Civil Procedure since 1939 and Federal Rules of Criminal Procedure since 1946.
Supreme Court Reporter (S.Ct.)	1882	U.S. Supreme Court since the October term of 1882.
Bankruptcy Reporter (Bankr.)	1960	Bankruptcy decisions of U.S. Bankruptcy Courts, U.S. District Courts, U.S. Courts of Appeals, and U.S. Supreme Court.
Military Justice Reporter (M.J.)	1978	U.S. Court of Military Appeals and Courts of Military Review for the Army, Navy, Air Force, and Coast Guard.

NATIONAL REPORTER SYSTEM MAP

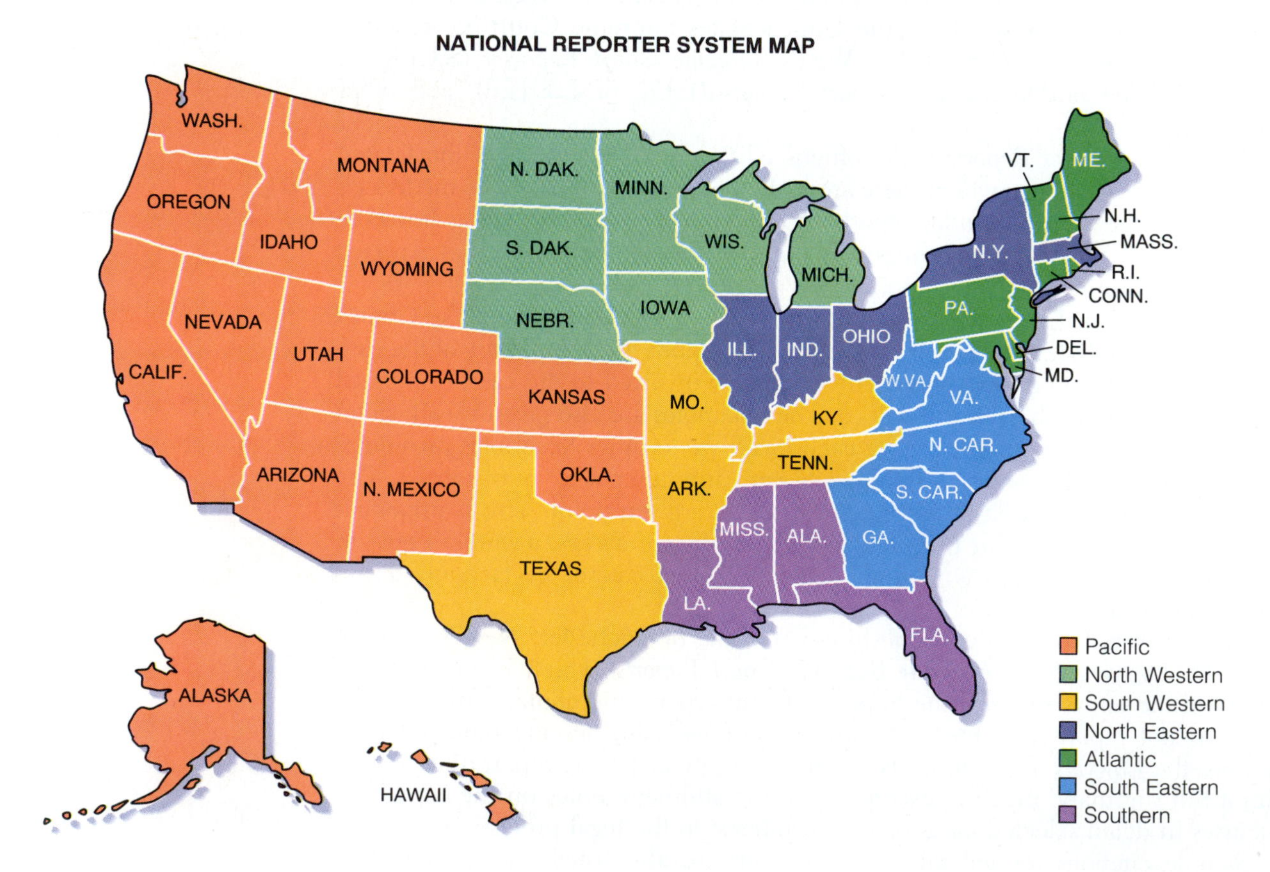

◆ **Exhibit 1–3**
How to Read Case Citations

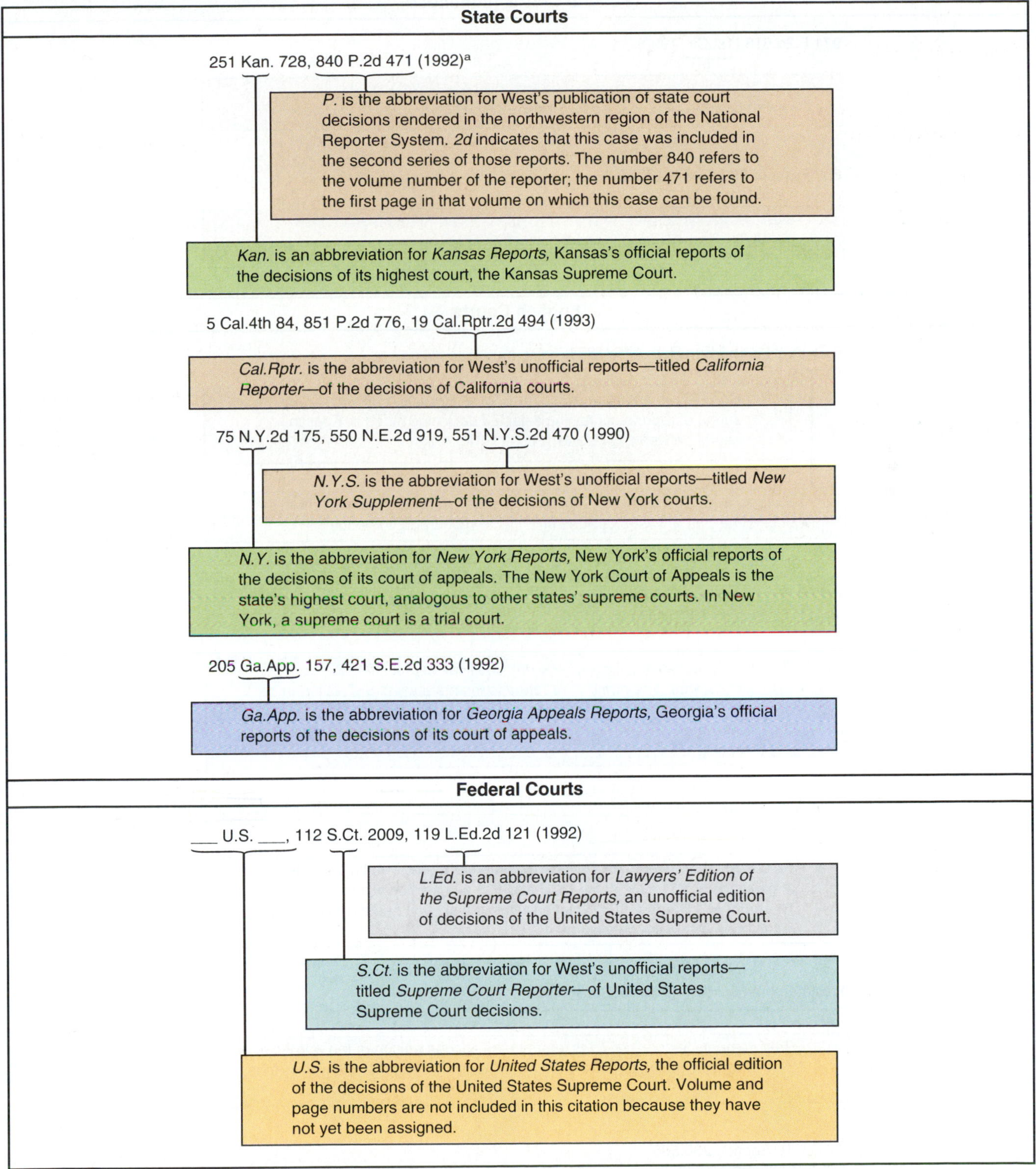

State Courts
251 Kan. 728, 840 P.2d 471 (1992)[a]
P. is the abbreviation for West's publication of state court decisions rendered in the northwestern region of the National Reporter System. 2d indicates that this case was included in the second series of those reports. The number 840 refers to the volume number of the reporter; the number 471 refers to the first page in that volume on which this case can be found.
Kan. is an abbreviation for Kansas Reports, Kansas's official reports of the decisions of its highest court, the Kansas Supreme Court.
5 Cal.4th 84, 851 P.2d 776, 19 Cal.Rptr.2d 494 (1993)
Cal.Rptr. is the abbreviation for West's unofficial reports—titled California Reporter—of the decisions of California courts.
75 N.Y.2d 175, 550 N.E.2d 919, 551 N.Y.S.2d 470 (1990)
N.Y.S. is the abbreviation for West's unofficial reports—titled New York Supplement—of the decisions of New York courts.
N.Y. is the abbreviation for New York Reports, New York's official reports of the decisions of its court of appeals. The New York Court of Appeals is the state's highest court, analogous to other states' supreme courts. In New York, a supreme court is a trial court.
205 Ga.App. 157, 421 S.E.2d 333 (1992)
Ga.App. is the abbreviation for Georgia Appeals Reports, Georgia's official reports of the decisions of its court of appeals.
Federal Courts
___ U.S. ___, 112 S.Ct. 2009, 119 L.Ed.2d 121 (1992)
L.Ed. is an abbreviation for Lawyers' Edition of the Supreme Court Reports, an unofficial edition of decisions of the United States Supreme Court.
S.Ct. is the abbreviation for West's unofficial reports—titled Supreme Court Reporter—of United States Supreme Court decisions.
U.S. is the abbreviation for United States Reports, the official edition of the decisions of the United States Supreme Court. Volume and page numbers are not included in this citation because they have not yet been assigned.

a. The case names have been deleted from these citations to emphasize the publications. It should be kept in mind, however, that the name of a case is as important as the specific page numbers in the volumes in which it is found. If a citation is incorrect, the correct citation may be found in a publication's index of case names. The date of a case is also important because, in addition to providing a check on error in citations, the value of a recent case as an authority is likely to be greater than that of earlier cases.

(Figure continued on next page)

◆ Exhibit 1–3 How to Read Case Citations—Continued

Federal Courts (continued)

971 F.2d 818 (1st Cir. 1990)

1st Cir. is an abbreviation denoting that this case was decided in the United States Court of Appeals for the First Circuit.

802 F.Supp. 680 (D.R.I. 1992))

D.R.I. is an abbreviation indicating that the United States District Court for the District of Rhode Island decided this case.

English Courts

9 Exch. 341, 156 Eng.Rep. 145 (1854)

Eng.Rep. is an abbreviation for *English Reports, Full Reprint,* a series of reports containing selected decisions made in English courts between 1378 and 1865.

Exch. is an abbreviation for *English Exchequer Reports,* which included the original reports of cases decided in England's Court of Exchequer.

Statutory and Other Citations

18 U.S.C. Section 1961(1)(A)

U.S.C. denotes *United States Code,* the codification of *United States Statutes at Large.* The number 18 refers to the statute's U.S.C. title number and 1961 to its section number within that title. The number 1 refers to a subsection within the section and the letter A to a subdivision within the subsection.

UCC 2–206(1)(b)

UCC is an abbreviation for *Uniform Commercial Code.* The first number 2 is a reference to an article of the UCC and 206 to a section within that article. The number 1 refers to a subsection within the section and the letter b to a subdivision within the subsection.

Restatement (Second) of Torts, Section 568

Restatement (Second) of Torts refers to the second edition of the American Law Institute's *Restatement of the Law of Torts.* The number 568 refers to a specific section.

17 C.F.R. Section 230.505

C.F.R. is an abbreviation for *Code of Federal Regulations,* a compilation of federal administrative regulations. The number 17 is a reference to the regulation's title number and 230.505 to a specific section within that title.

Old Case Law

On a few occasions, this text cites opinions from old, classic cases dating to the nineteenth century or earlier; some of these are from the English courts. The citations to these cases appear not to conform to the descriptions given above because the reporters in which they were published have since been replaced. A sample citation for an English reporter is included in Exhibit 1–3. Whenever citations to old reporters are made in this text, the citations will be explained as they are presented.

❖ Computerized Legal Research

One of the quickest ways to obtain information concerning statutory or case law is by accessing a computer data base. Although the days of the hunched-over, bespectacled law clerk searching through dusty tomes filled with ancient cases are not completely over, computers have streamlined the legal research techniques used by businesses, lawyers, and members of the judiciary. Today there are a number of data bases—collections of information useful to anyone doing legal research—that can be accessed through several high-speed data-delivery systems. The two most commonly used systems are WESTLAW and LEXIS. WESTLAW is a computer-assisted legal research service of West Publishing Company. LEXIS is a similar service provided by Mead Data Central, Inc. Each system has data-base-access software that makes it possible for the researcher to interact with the delivery system.

In the WESTLAW data-delivery system, data are stored at West's headquarters in Eagan, Minnesota. User interaction with the data-delivery system can be initiated from a computer terminal or a personal computer running a special WESTLAW access program literally anywhere in the world. The WESTLAW user sends a query, or message, to the computer. Queries can even be made in natural language called

WESTLAW is a widely used computerized data-search system that allows law students, lawyers, and legal scholars immediate access to cases, statutes, federal regulations, and legal treatises and law journal articles.

WIN (regular sentences). The query is then processed, and documents are identified that satisfy the search request. The information is transmitted back to the user, where it is seen on a video display terminal (VDT) and can be printed out as "hard copy" on paper. The documents displayed on the VDT can be stored on the user's storage equipment, such as a hard disk or diskettes.

In short, WESTLAW, LEXIS, and similar computerized data-search systems allow for access to virtually all statutes, federal regulations, and cases with a minimum of time delay and a minimum of physical effort. Often the latest cases can be retrieved via such a system before the printed editions are available.[10]

❖ Reading and Understanding Case Law

Case law is critical to decision making in the business context because businesses must operate within the boundaries established by law. It is thus essential that businesspersons understand the law as evidenced by adjudicated cases.

The cases in this text have been rewritten and condensed from the full text of the courts' opinions. For those wishing to review court cases for future research projects or to gain additional legal information, the following sections will provide useful insights into how to read and understand case law.

Case Titles and Terminology

The title of a case, such as *Adams v. Jones,* indicates the names of the parties to the lawsuit. The *v.* in the case title stands for *versus,* which means "against." In the trial court, Adams was the plaintiff—the person who filed the suit. Jones was the defendant. If the case is appealed, however, the appellate court will sometimes place the name of the party appealing the decision first, so that the case may be called *Jones v. Adams.* Because some reviewing courts retain the trial court order of names, it is often impossible to distinguish the plaintiff from the defendant in the title of a reported appellate court decision. You must carefully read the facts of each case to identify each party. Otherwise, the discussion by the appellate court will be difficult to understand.

The following terms and phrases are frequently encountered in court opinions and legal publications. Because it is important to understand what is meant by these terms and phrases, we define and discuss them here.

Plaintiffs and Defendants The **plaintiff** in a lawsuit is always the party that initiates the action. The **defendant** is the party against whom a lawsuit is brought. Lawsuits frequently involve more than one plaintiff and/or defendant.

Appellants and Appellees The **appellant** is the party that appeals a case to another court or jurisdiction from the court or jurisdiction in which the case was originally brought. Sometimes, an appellant that appeals from a judgment is referred to as the **petitioner.** The **appellee** is the party against whom the appeal is taken. Sometimes, an appellee is referred to as the **respondent.**

Judges and Justices The terms *judge* and *justice* are usually synonymous and represent two designations given to judges in various courts. All members of the United

PLAINTIFF
One who initiates a lawsuit.

DEFENDANT
One against whom a lawsuit is brought; the accused person in a criminal proceeding.

APPELLANT
The party who takes an appeal from one court to another; sometimes referred to as the petitioner.

PETITIONER
The party who presents a petition to a court, initiates an equity proceeding, or appeals from a judgment.

APPELLEE
The party against whom an appeal is taken—that is, the party who opposes setting aside or reversing the judgment; sometimes referred to as the respondent.

RESPONDENT
In equity practice, the party who answers a bill or other proceeding. In appellate practice, the party against whom an appeal is taken (sometimes referred to as the appellee).

10. The Computer Legal Research Key System (CLERK) supplementing this textbook is an example of how computers can be used to facilitate the teaching and learning of business law. By directly linking specific cases (indicated by a computer logo) within this text to a computerized data base, students and professors can quickly access the full court opinions.

States Supreme Court, for example, are referred to as justices. And justice is the formal title usually given to judges of appellate courts, although this is not always the case. In New York, a justice is a judge of the trial court (which is called the Supreme Court), and a member of the Court of Appeals (the state's highest court) is called a judge. The term *justice* is commonly abbreviated to J., and *justices* to JJ. A Supreme Court case might refer to Justice Kennedy as Kennedy, J., or to Chief Justice Rehnquist as Rehnquist, C.J.

Decisions and Opinions Most decisions reached by reviewing, or appellate, courts are explained in written **opinions.** The opinion contains the court's reasons for its decision, the rules of law that apply, and the judgment. There are four possible types of written opinions for any particular case decided by an appellate court. When all judges or justices unanimously agree on an opinion, the opinion is written for the entire court and can be deemed a *unanimous opinion.* When there is not a unanimous opinion, a *majority opinion* is written, outlining the views of the majority of the judges or justices deciding the case. Often, a judge or justice who feels strongly about making or emphasizing a point that was not made or emphasized in the unanimous or majority opinion will write a *concurring opinion.* That means the judge or justice agrees (concurs) with the judgment given in the unanimous or majority opinion but for different reasons. In other than unanimous opinions, a *dissenting opinion* is usually written by a judge or justice who does not agree with the majority. The dissenting opinion is important because it may form the basis of the arguments used years later in overruling the precedential majority opinion.

OPINION
A statement by the court expressing the reasons for its decision in a case.

A Note on Abbreviations In court opinions, as well as in other areas of this text, certain terms appearing in the names of firms or organizations will often be abbreviated. The terms *Company, Incorporated,* and *Limited,* for example, will frequently appear in their abbreviated forms as *Co., Inc.,* and *Ltd.,* respectively, and *Brothers* is commonly abbreviated to *Bros.* Certain organizations and legislative acts are also frequently referred to by their initials or acronyms. In all such cases, to prevent confusion we will give the complete name of the organization or act upon first mentioning it in a given section of the text.

A Sample Court Case

Knowing how to read and analyze a court opinion is an essential step in undertaking accurate legal research. A further step involves "briefing" the case. Legal researchers routinely brief cases by summarizing and reducing the texts of the opinions to their essential elements. Instructions on how to brief a case are given in Appendix A, which also includes selected cases for briefing.

The cases contained within the chapters of this text have already been analyzed and briefed by the authors, and the essential aspects of each case are presented in a convenient format consisting of four basic sections: *Facts, Issue, Decision,* and *Reason.* This basic format is illustrated in the sample court case below, which has also been annotated to illustrate the kind of information that is contained in each section. (Annotated excerpts from the actual court opinion for this case appear as the first case opinion in Appendix A.) In the remaining chapters of this book, the basic format is expanded to include a special introductory section entitled *Historical and Social Setting.*[11] In some instances, a final section—variously called *Ethical Considerations, International Considerations,* or otherwise—has also been added.

11. The word *Social* in the title of this section may be replaced by *Economic* or *Political* or some other term, depending on the nature of the case and the point of law being illustrated.

1 — **BUKOWSKI v. COOPERVISION, INC.**

2 — Supreme Court, Appellate Division, Third Department, 1993.

3 — 185 A.D.2d 31,

4 — 592 N.Y.S.2d 807

5 — **HISTORICAL AND ECONOMIC SETTING** *Health care is the biggest industry in the United States. In 1970, national expenditures on health care were approximately $75 billion. By the 1990s, health-care expenditures had risen to about $950 billion—about $3,000 for every person in the nation. According to the Health Care Financing Administration (an agency within the Department of Health and Human Services), these costs continue to rise. Large, well-known companies, such as Johnson & Johnson, have sold products to hospitals and doctors for more than one hundred years, but they represent only a small portion of the health-care industry expenditures. The biggest cost of the industry is hospital care, which accounts for about 40 percent of all health-care expenditures. Private doctors and small firms also make up a significant cost of the industry.*

6 — **FACTS** On April 18, 1984, Margaret Bukowski bought from George Roberts, a licensed optometrist, a pair of Permalens XL extended wear contact lenses manufactured by CooperVision, Inc. On July 4, Bukowski experienced "a lot of dry eye symptoms." On July 7, her eyes became irritated and she removed the lenses. When she awoke the following morning, her left eye was swollen shut. She was subsequently diagnosed with a pseudomonas corneal ulcer and abscess of the left eye, which she later claimed to have resulted in reduced visual acuity and psychological injury. Bukowski filed suits against CooperVision, Roberts, and others involved in the case, alleging that they should be held liable for her injuries on such grounds as negligence (which in this case required her to prove that they had a duty to warn her of the risks associated with the lenses). CooperVision moved for summary judgment (a pretrial motion granted only when no facts are disputed and the only question is what law should be applied). The trial court granted the motion in part, but refused to dismiss the negligence claim. CooperVision appealed, contending that it had no duty to warn Bukowski and that it should be absolved of liability under the informed intermediary doctrine. (Under this doctrine, a physician who prescribes a drug or, in some cases, a medical device for a patient acts as an "informed intermediary" between the product's manufacturer and the patient, assessing the risks and benefits and advising the patient.)

7 — **ISSUE** Was CooperVision absolved of liability either because it had no duty to warn Bukowski of the risks or because the informed intermediary doctrine applied?

8 — **DECISION** No. The appellate court affirmed the trial court's decision.

9 — **REASON** In its discussion of the first part of the issue, the court explained that a "manufacturer's duty extends to warning consumers of latent dangers resulting from the foreseeable use of its product of which the manufacturer knew or should have known." The law is clear on this point. Thus, it must be determined whether CooperVision knew of the risk. CooperVision offered unsubstantiated testimony that it either did not know of the risk of corneal ulceration or believed the risk to be insignificant before 1984. Bukowski countered with clinical reports and other evidence. The court concluded that the reports and evidence were enough "to raise a question of fact as to whether CooperVision knew or should have known of the risk" and this was a question to be answered at trial. In its discussion of the second part of the issue, the court outlined two reasons for not immediately applying the informed intermediary doctrine. First, it was unclear exactly what roles Bukowski and Roberts played in selecting the CooperVision lenses. Second, the doctrine requires "a medical professional with the knowledge and expertise to assimilate technical information and * * * the corresponding need for that profession-

al to assess the risks and benefits posed by the drug or device in light of the particular patient's medical history and treatment needs." In this case, there was no evidence that an optometrist is this sort of professional or that there was a need for him to assess the risks and benefits posed by the CooperVision lenses, given Bukowski's medical history — 9
and vision needs. The court also pointed out that even if the doctrine did apply, there was still the question of the sufficiency of the warnings.

Review of Sample Court Case

1. The name of the case is *Bukowski v. CooperVision, Inc.* Bukowski is the plaintiff; CooperVision and others not included in the case title are the defendants.
2. The court deciding this case was the Appellate Division of the Supreme Court of New York, an intermediate-level appellate court in the New York state court system.
3. This citation is to the New York state reporter and indicates that this case can be found in Volume 185 of the *Appellate Division Reports, Second Series,* on page 31.
4. This citation is a parallel citation to a West reporter and indicates that this case can also be found in Volume 592 of West's *New York Supplement, Second Series,* on page 807.
5. The *Historical and Economic Setting* section outlines the background of the health-care industry, of which the defendant is a member, at the time that this case was decided. In other cases, this section examines other aspects of the social, political, global, environmental, technological, ethical, or cultural background.
6. The *Facts* section identifies the plaintiff and the defendant, describes the events leading up to this lawsuit, the allegations made by the plaintiff, the defendant's response to these allegations, and (because this case is an appellate court decision) the trial court's decision and the party appealing that decision. The appealing party's contention on appeal is also included here.
7. The *Issue* section presents the central issue (or issues) to be decided by the court. In this case, the appellate court was faced with issues raised by the defendant (CooperVision) on appeal. Cases frequently will involve more than one issue.
8. The *Decision* section, as the term indicates, contains the court's decision on the issue or issues before the court. The decision reflects the opinion of the majority of the judges or justices hearing the case. Decisions by appellate courts are frequently phrased in reference to the lower court's decision. That is, the appellate court may "affirm" the lower court's ruling or "reverse" it. In this particular case, the decision by the appellate court affirmed the judgment of the lower court.
9. The *Reason* section indicates what relevant laws and judicial principles were applied in forming the particular conclusion arrived at in the case at bar ("before the court"). In this case, the lack of evidence in the record of the lower court's proceeding guided the court's reasoning.

*Application**

Law and the Businessperson—How to Choose and Use a Lawyer

If you are contemplating a career in the business world, sooner or later you will probably face the question, "Do I need a lawyer?" The answer to this question will likely be "Yes," at least at some time during your career. Even individuals who have gone on to law school and later entered into a business often hire an outside lawyer to help them with their legal problems. Today, it is virtually impossible for nonexperts to keep up with the myriad rules and regulations that govern the way in which business can be conducted in the United States. And it is increasingly possible for businesspersons to incur penalties for violating laws or regulations of which they were totally unaware. While lawyers may seem expensive—anywhere from $75 to $400 per hour—the cautious businessperson will make sure that he or she is not "penny wise and pound foolish." The consultation fee paid to an attorney may be a drop in the bucket compared with the potential liability facing a businessperson. Legal actions involving employment discrimination, improper incorporation, the violation of environmental or safety regulations, or the breach of a duty of care may end up costing millions of dollars in fines or damages.

Learn Some Law First

As you will discover in your study of business law and the legal environment, law has its own vocabulary and its own concepts. To communicate well with any attorney, you should have a minimal understanding of the terminology of the law and the theories that underlie the most important areas in commercial law. You are acquiring that knowledge as you read this text. But in addition, when you enter the business world, you will undoubtedly find that certain areas of the law are more important to you than others. If you know that you are going to be in charge of hiring and firing employees, for example, then you will need to know more about employment laws and regulations than about laws governing other aspects of commercial activity. The more you know about laws affecting the specific area of business in which you are involved, the better able you will be to decide when to obtain legal advice. You will also be better prepared to ask specific and relevant questions of your attorney.

It is possible to keep up with certain areas of the law by subscribing to newsletters and regular publications from specialized legal reporting services, but doing so is time consuming. It is often cheaper, in terms of resource costs, to hire an attorney who specializes in a particular area. It does not do you or your company any good to spend $10,000 worth of your time to avoid consulting with an attorney from whom you might receive a bill for $1,000.

In any event, you should consult a lawyer if you (1) are served with legal papers in a civil lawsuit; (2) are arrested for a crime; (3) are involved in a serious accident causing injury or damage; or (4) undergo a change in financial status, such as obtaining or losing real estate or other valuable assets or filing for bankruptcy.

Selecting an Attorney

In selecting an attorney, you can—as most individuals do—ask friends, relatives, or business associates to recommend someone. Or you can call the local or state bar association to obtain the names of several lawyers. You can also go to your local library to look at the *Martindale-Hubbell Law Directory*. This tome features professional biographies of most of the attorneys engaged in private practice throughout the country. It lists areas of concentration, as well as bank references and representative clients. Some legal aid programs have staff attorneys, and others may refer you to volunteers. There are also legal clinics and prepaid legal service plans that you might look into. In choosing an attorney, you might keep in mind that some lawyers concentrate their efforts in specific areas of law. Depending on your legal needs, you might want to retain a lawyer that specializes in a certain area.

Once you have selected an attorney, you need to make an initial appointment as soon as possible. Delaying may cost you or your company money if you need to pursue a legal action quickly. At your initial meeting with the attorney, disclose any relevant information about the problem at hand or what kind of legal assistance you need. (Remember that virtually everything you say to your attorney is protected by the attorney–client privilege of confidentiality. In other words, the lawyer is legally prohibited from talking about your case

*Remember that "He who is his own lawyer has a fool for a client." None of the *Applications* in this text are meant to substitute for the services of an attorney who is licensed to practice in your state.

Application —Continued

with anyone else except his or her assistants, who may be given information to the extent that they need it to work on your case.) Ask about fees. How are they charged? How much will be required to handle your situation? Can you pay the fee in installments? Will other legal professionals (such as attorneys in the same office, paralegals, and other assistants) be working with the lawyer on your case? If so, how are their fees determined? Be specific in questioning your attorney about fees, and ask for a written statement describing them.

Ask yourself the following questions after your first meeting: Did the attorney seem knowledgeable about what is needed to address your concerns? Did he or she seem willing to investigate the law and the facts further to ensure an accurate understanding of your legal situation? Did you communicate well with each other? Did the attorney perceive what issues were of foremost concern to you and address those issues to your satisfaction? Did the attorney "speak your language" when explaining the legal implications of those issues? Continue to evaluate the relationship as it continues. Ask yourself the following questions: Does your lawyer advise you of possible courses of action to take and then act according to your choice? Does the attorney keep you informed about developments in the law affecting your concerns?

For many businesspersons, relationships with attorneys last for decades. Make sure that your relationship with your attorney will be a fruitful one.

Checklist for Choosing and Using a Lawyer

☐ 1. Attorneys can advise you, but they cannot make your decisions. You must have a basic knowledge of business law to make sound decisions.

☐ 2. If you ever doubt that you need legal advice, you probably do. Check with an attorney.

☐ 3. When choosing an attorney, try to get recommendations from friends, relatives, or business associates who have had long-standing relationships with their attorneys. If that fails, check with your local or state bar association or with the *Martindale-Hubbell Law Directory*.

☐ 4. Do not hesitate to ask explicit questions about the fees that your attorney will charge for his or her services. Make sure that you understand how the fee will be determined, what the hourly rate is, who else will be working on your project and his or her hourly rates, and so on. Normally, it is best to ask for a detailed breakdown of your bill.

☐ 5. When you initially consult with an attorney, be sure to understand what advice he or she is giving you and what your legal options are. Do not worry about appearing "stupid." Ask direct and specific questions whenever you have the slightest doubt about what you are hearing.

❖ Key Terms

administrative agencies 11
administrative law 11
administrative law judge (ALJ) 12
administrative process 11
appellant 24
appellee 24
case law 9
citation 19
civil law 12
civil law system 14
common law 6
criminal law 12
defendant 24
enabling legislation 11
international law 15
judicial process 11
jurisprudence 2
law 2
legal realism 4
national law 15
natural law school 3
opinion 25
petitioner 24
plaintiff 24
positive law 3
positivist school 3
precedent 6
respondent 24
rulemaking 11
stare decisis 7
statutory law 10
treaty 15

❖ Chapter Summary: The Legal and International Environment

CLASSIFICATIONS	TYPES AND DEFINITIONS
Schools of Jurisprudential Thought	1. *Natural law school*—One of the oldest and most significant schools of jurisprudence. Adherents of this school hold that there is a universal law applicable to all human beings and that this law is of a higher order than positive, or conventional law. 2. *Positivist school*—A school of legal thought centered on the assumption that human rights come into existence only with the creation of a sovereign power (government) that can make and enforce laws. Therefore, there is no law higher than the laws created by the government. 3. *Legal realism*—A school of thought emphasizing that the purpose of the law is to serve society and society's interests, and therefore judges must take social realities into account when making legal determinations.
Sources of American Law	1. *Common law*—Originated in medieval England with the creation of the king's courts; consists of past judicial decisions and reasoning; involves the application of the doctrine of *stare decisis*—the rule of precedent—in deciding cases. Common law governs all areas not covered by statutory law. 2. *Constitutional law*—The law as expressed in the U.S. Constitution and the various state constitutions. The U.S. Constitution is the supreme law of the land. State constitutions are supreme within state borders to the extent that they do not violate a clause of the U.S. Constitution or a federal law. 3. *Statutory law*—Laws or ordinances created by federal, state, and local legislatures and governing bodies. None of these laws can violate the U.S. Constitution or the relevant state constitutions. Uniform statutes, when adopted by a state, become statutory law in that state. 4. *Administrative law*—The branch of law concerned with the power and actions of administrative agencies at all levels of government. Federal administrative agencies are created by enabling legislation enacted by the U.S. Congress. Agency functions include rulemaking, investigation and enforcement, and adjudication.
Civil Law versus Criminal Law	1. *Civil Law*—Law concerned with acts against persons for which the injured party seeks redress in the form of compensation and or other relief. 2. *Criminal law*—Law concerned with acts against society for which society seeks redress in the form of punishment.
Law around the World	1. *Common law system*—See the summary of common law under "Sources of American Law" above. Originating in England, the common law tradition has been adopted by the United States and other former colonies of Great Britain, including Ireland, Canada, Australia, New Zealand, and India. 2. *Civil law system*—A legal system in which the primary source of law is a statutory code, which is an ordered grouping of legal principles enacted into law by a legislature or governing body. Precedents are not binding in a civil law system. Most of the continental European countries have a civil law system, as do those African, Latin American, and Asian nations that were once colonies of the European countries. Japan and South Africa also have civil law systems.
International Law	A body of written and unwritten laws observed by independent nations and governing the acts of individuals as well as governments. Sources of international law include national laws, customs, treaties, and international organizations and conferences.

❖ Questions and Case Problems

1–1. Philosophy of Law. What are the three major schools of jurisprudential thought, and how do they differ from one another?

1–2. Legal Systems. What are the key differences between a common law system and a civil law system? Why do some countries have common law systems and others have civil law systems?

1–3. Reading Citations. Assume that you want to read the entire court opinion in the case of *United States v. Sun and Sand Imports, Ltd.*, 725 F.2d 184 (2d Cir. 1984). The case deals with the transportation, via interstate commerce, of flammable sleepwear for children in violation of the federal Flammable Fabrics Act. Explain specifically where you would find the court's opinion.

1–4. Sources of American Law. This chapter discussed a number of sources of American law. Which source of law takes priority in the following situations, and why?

(a) A federal statute conflicts with the U.S. Constitution.
(b) A federal statute conflicts with a state constitution.
(c) A state statute conflicts with the common law of that state.
(d) A state constitutional amendment conflicts with the U.S. Constitution.

1–5. *Stare Decisis*. In the text of this chapter, we stated that the doctrine of *stare decisis* "became a cornerstone of the English and American judicial systems." What does *stare decisis* mean, and why has this doctrine been so fundamental to the development of our legal tradition?

1–6. Court Opinions. What is the difference between a concurring opinion and a majority opinion? Between a concurring opinion and a dissenting opinion? Why do judges and justices write concurring and dissenting opinions, given the fact that these opinions will not affect the outcome of the case at hand, which has already been decided by majority vote?

1–7. Common Law versus Statutory Law. Courts are able to overturn precedents and thus can change the common law. Should judges have the same authority to overrule statutory law? Explain.

1–8. Philosophy of Law. In the middle of the last century, the United States declared war on Mexico and levied taxes to support the war effort. Henry David Thoreau (author of *Walden*), who felt that the war was unjust, refused to pay taxes to support it and was subsequently imprisoned for violating the law. Thoreau maintained that obeying the law in these circumstances would be unethical. Which of the schools of legal philosophy discussed in this chapter would be the most sympathetic toward Thoreau's views on law? Explain.

1–9. Statute of Limitations. The equitable principle "Equity aids the vigilant, not those who rest on their rights" means that courts will not aid those who do not pursue a cause of action while the evidence is fresh and while the true facts surrounding the issue can be discovered. State statutes of limitations are based on this principle. Under Article 2 of the Uniform Commercial Code, which has been adopted by virtually all of the states, the statute of limitations governing sales contracts states that parties must bring an action for the breach of a sales contract within four years, although the parties (the seller and the buyer) can reduce this period by agreement to only one year. Which party (the seller or the buyer) would benefit more by a one-year period, and which would benefit more by a four-year period? Discuss.

1–10. International Transactions. Assume that you own a business specializing in designing and constructing aircraft engines. You learn that a German firm manufactures some of the parts that you need for your engines and sells them at a good price. In your negotiations with the German firm, you want to make sure that you provide in your contract for any difficulties that might arise relating to the purchase. What are some of these difficulties? Are they different in nature from those that could arise under a contract with, say, a California firm? What clauses could you include in your contract with the German company to protect your interests?

A Question of Ethics and Social Responsibility

1–11. *On July 5, 1884, Dudley, Stephens, and Brooks—"all able-bodied English seamen"—and an English boy between seventeen and eighteen years of age were cast adrift in a lifeboat following a storm at sea that occurred when they were some sixteen hundred miles from the Cape of Good Hope. The lifeboat was not stocked with food and water, and all they had for sustenance were two one-pound tins of turnips. On July 24, Dudley proposed that one of the four in the lifeboat be sacrificed to save the others. Stephens agreed with Dudley, but Brooks refused to consent—and the boy was never asked for his opinion. On July 25, Dudley killed the boy, and the three men then fed upon the boy's body and blood. Four days later, the men were rescued by a passing vessel. They were taken to the port of Falmouth in England and committed for trial at Exeter for the murder of the boy. If the men had not fed upon the boy's body, they would probably have died of famine within the four-day period. The boy, who was in a much weaker condition, would likely have died before the rest.* [Regina v. Dudley and Stephens, *14 Q.B.D.[Queen's Bench Division, England] 273 (1884)*]

1. This problem is similar to *The Case of the Speluncean Explorers*, the hypothetical case discussed in this chapter. The basic question in that case, as here, is whether the survivors should be subject to penalties under the criminal law, given the men's unusual circumstances. You be the judge and decide the issue. Give the reasons for your decisions.
2. Should judges ever have the power to look beyond the written "letter of the law" in making their decisions? Why or why not?

For Critical Analysis

1–12. *Courts of equity tend to follow general rules or maxims rather than common law precedents, as courts of law do. Some of these maxims were listed in this chapter's* Landmark in the Law. *Why would equity courts give credence to such general maxims rather than a hard-and-fast body of law?*

Appendix to Chapter 1
Diagramming Case Problems

When briefing and analyzing a case problem in *Business Law Today*, you may find it helpful in attempting to understand the facts of the problem to diagram those facts. You might use a square for a plaintiff (the party who files a legal action) and a triangle for a defendant (the party against whom the action is brought), for example, and arrows to indicate who is suing whom. You might also find that it saves time to use symbols in your diagrams. There are many symbols that are commonly used among law students and lawyers. To indicate a reference to a plaintiff, for example, the pi symbol—π—is often used, and a defendant is noted by delta—Δ—a triangle.

Diagramming the facts helps to emphasize that the facts should be accepted as they are given. For example, under some circumstances, the manager of a store may have a duty to warn customers of the hazard presented by a wet floor by putting a sign near the hazard. If there is a statement in a case problem about the existence of a wet floor and the lack of a sign, it should be accepted that the floor was wet and there was no sign. Arguing with the statement ("Anyone can see when a floor is wet," "Maybe the floor was not too wet," "Maybe an employee was getting a sign to put up," "Maybe someone stole the sign") only diminishes your ability to learn. When you have learned what the principle is that the case problem involves, then you can ask, "What if the facts were different?"

In analyzing and diagramming case problems, you may find the following method helpful. First, before reading a problem, read the question. Does it ask you to evaluate the facts, the plaintiff's claim, the defendant's defense? The point is to gain an understanding of the answer toward which the problem is directed. Second, read the problem, paying special attention to the facts that are directed to the question. As you read, write down the names of the plaintiff and defendant and draw different shapes around them with an arrow to indicate who is bringing the action against whom. This illustrates the litigation and gives you a framework for answering the question.

For instance, consider the following case problem (Problem 17–7) from Chapter 17:

> George Nesselrode lost his life in an airplane crash. The plane had been manufactured by Beech Aircraft Corp. and sold to Executive Beechcraft, Inc. Shortly before the crash occurred, Executive Beechcraft had conducted a routine inspection of the plane and found that some of the parts needed to be replaced. The new parts were supplied by Beech Aircraft but installed by Executive Beechcraft. These particular parts could be installed backwards, and if they were, the plane would crash. In Nesselrode's case, the crash resulted from just such an incorrect installation of airplane parts. Nesselrode's wife Jane and three daughters sued Beech Aircraft, Executive Beechcraft, and Gerald Hultgren, the pilot who had flown the plane. Beech Aircraft claimed that it was not at fault because it had not installed the parts. Will Beech Aircraft be held liable for Nesselrode's death? [*Nesselrode. v. Executive Beechcraft, Inc.*, 707 S.W.2d 371 (Mo. 1986)]

Here is how the facts in this problem might be diagrammed.

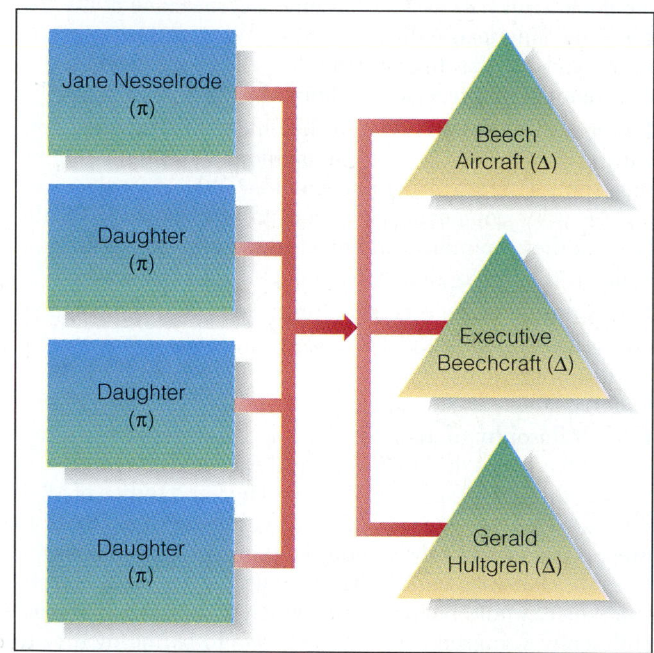

If, after diagramming the facts, you have trouble applying the principle that a problem asks you to discuss, reread the relevant section in the text. The diagramming method may also prove helpful when you are briefing and analyzing cases already analyzed and edited by the authors or assigned or researched separately.

Chapter 2

Ethics and Social Responsibility

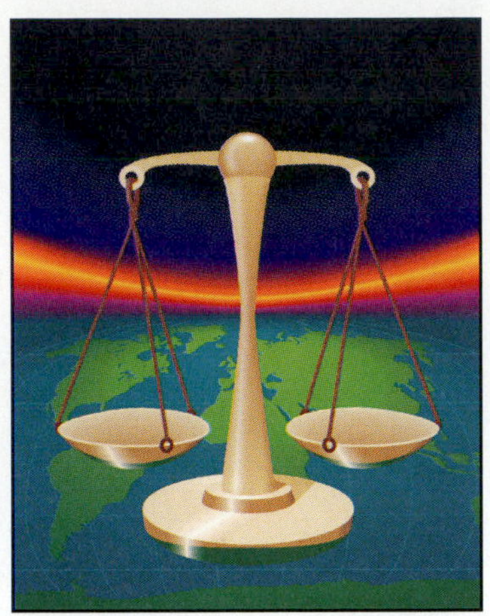

"It must be remembered that all trade is and must be in a sense selfish."

John Duke Coleridge, 1821–1892
(English jurist)

Business and ethics have never been a truly happy couple. This is because, as Coleridge indicated in the opening quotation, business "must be in a sense selfish." In fact, for most of Western history, the pursuit of profits was deemed to be inherently unethical. In the ancient world, the social status of merchants was about the same as that of slaves. In the medieval world, merchants were regarded as a kind of necessary evil. On the one hand, they provided useful and vitally needed products for the community; on the other hand, the profit motive and personal accumulation of wealth were seen as selfish and therefore anti-Christian. It was only in the eighteenth century that profit-making activities acquired ethical underpinnings. In 1776, Adam Smith, a Scottish economist and the so-called father of capitalism, published his *Wealth of Nations.* In this treatise, Smith demonstrated that individuals acting in their own self-interest generate the greatest social welfare for the greatest number of citizens. According to Smith, this is because an "invisible hand" (the forces of supply and demand) regulates the free market to ensure that only socially worthwhile enterprises survive. If people like what a firm produces, they will buy it, and the firm will prosper. If a firm markets goods or services that are not desired by society, it will not make profits and will have to either market a different product or close its doors.

Today, few would claim that it is unethical to seek profits. In fact, successful businesspersons often rank among the most admired individuals in our society. But there continues to be an underlying tension between the pursuit of profits and the welfare of those groups affected by this pursuit, which may include employees, shareholders, consumers, creditors, the community, and the global society as a whole. When a business firm concentrates on the "bottom line" at the expense of one or more of these groups, that firm may end up being targeted by the press as unethical and subject to sanctions, such as boycotts. In the long run, the firm may lose customers and therefore profits because its behavior is perceived to be unethical. In sum, businesspersons have to walk a fine line to ensure that their profit-making activities do not exceed the ethical boundaries established by society.

In preparing for a career in business, you will find that a background in business ethics and a commitment to ethical behavior is just as important as a knowledge of the specific laws that you will read about in this text. Furthermore, if you wish to truly understand the law, you need to be aware of the ethical framework within which it operates. In this chapter, we first examine the nature of business ethics and some of the sources of ethical standards that have guided others in their business decision making. We then look at some of the obstacles to ethical behavior faced by businesspersons. In the final section of the chapter, which deals with corporate social responsibility, we return to the important question raised in the preceding paragraph: How can businesspersons act in an ethically responsible manner and at the same time make profits for their firms or their firms' owners?

❖ The Nature of Business Ethics

ETHICS
Moral principles and values applied to social behavior.

Before we can talk about business ethics, we need to define what is meant by ethics generally. **Ethics** can be defined as the study of what constitutes right or wrong behavior. It is the branch of philosophy that focuses on morality and the way in which moral principles are applied to daily life. Ethics has to do with questions relating to the fairness, justness, rightness, or wrongness of an action. What is fair? What is just? What is the right thing to do in this situation?—these are essentially ethical questions.

Although the concept of ethics and ethical duties may seem abstract, in fact ethics plays an active role in our lives. Ethics affects and gives meaning to our everyday lives and the decisions we make. We constantly apply our values and moral convictions to our actions and decisions, frequently without even being aware that we are doing so. The clothes we buy, the music we prefer, the way we treat our friends and families, the books we choose to read—these and a thousand other everyday activities and decisions, if you analyze them carefully, ultimately relate to values and goals.

Defining Business Ethics

BUSINESS ETHICS
Ethics in a business context; a consensus of what constitutes right or wrong behavior in the world of business and the application of moral principles to situations that arise in a business setting.

Business ethics focuses on what constitutes right or wrong behavior in the world of business and on how moral principles are applied by businesspersons to situations that arise in their daily activities in the workplace. It is important to remember that business ethics is not a different *kind* of ethics. That is, businesspersons do not necessarily adopt one set of ethical principles to guide them in their business decisions and another set to guide them in their personal lives. The ethical standards that guide our behavior as, say, mothers, fathers, or students apply equally well to our activities as businesspersons. Business activities are just one part of the human enterprise, and business ethics is a subset of ethics that relates specifically to the kinds of situations that arise in the everyday world of business.

The Complexity of Business Ethics

Ethical decision making in the business world is somewhat more complicated than it is in our personal lives, however. First of all, a businessperson rarely has complete control over the decision-making process. In the corporate setting, for example, the ultimate decision makers are the members of the board of directors, who must make decisions as a group. No one individual (normally) can dictate policy or decide corporate issues. Corporate officers and managers, of course, also make decisions that affect the corporation, but their decision-making authority is usually limited to their departments or particular spheres of activity. Furthermore, their decisions must harmonize with the policies and decisions made by the directors and top management. If you are an employee of a large company, you will find that the decision as to what is right or wrong for the company is not yours to make, although your input may weigh in the decision.

TRADE-OFF
A desired result that one must sacrifice (trade off) to obtain another, equally desired result.

Second, business decision making often involves difficult **trade-offs** between two equally desirable goals. That is, in order for one desired goal to be obtained, some other desired goal may have to be traded off, or sacrificed. It is important to realize that the ethical trade-offs normally faced by businesspersons are not clear-cut trade-offs between "good" and "bad" alternatives. By definition, ethical dilemmas arise only when two or more *ethical* goals come into conflict. For example, assume that a corporate executive has to decide whether to approve the sale of a new product that would be beneficial for most consumers but that might have undesirable side effects for a small percentage of its users. In this situation, the trade-off becomes relatively obvious: expose an unknown but extremely small number of individuals to possible harm while allowing all other consumers to enjoy the benefits of the new product (and in the process, probably make higher profits for the shareholders) or protect that small number of individuals from possible harm and not allow all other consumers to enjoy the benefits of the new product.

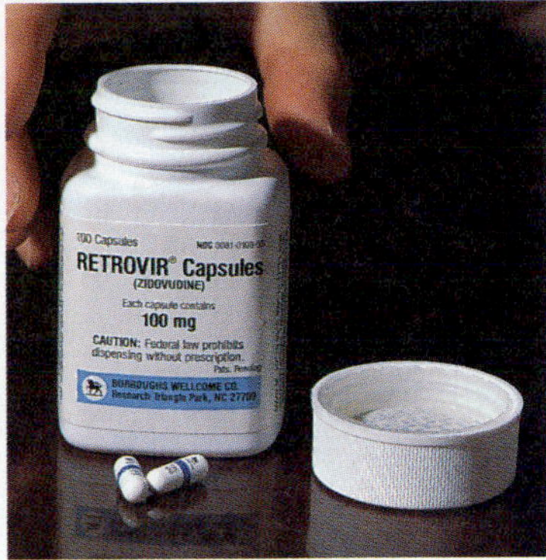

This AIDS drug may have negative side-effects, but what is the cost to society of not marketing it?

In statistics, this trade-off is known as a trade-off between *Type I* and *Type II errors.* A **Type I error** occurs because of the sin of *commission.* When a new product, such as a drug, is sold and there is an undesirable side effect—a customer becomes sick or is injured—this occurs because of the sin of commission. But if the product is not entered into the marketplace, a **Type II error** will occur. Type II errors result from the sin of *omission.* All of the benefits that people would have derived had the product been introduced do not exist if the product is not marketed.

Finally, decisions made by businesspersons normally have wider effects than private decisions do. Indeed, one business decision can have repercussions throughout the entire society. Therefore, as a businessperson, you need to be prepared to justify—to your superiors, to your colleagues or employees, to corporate shareholders, or even in a court of law—whatever decisions you make. It is not enough to say, as we might in our private lives, "I felt that it was the best decision under the circumstances" or "it seemed like the right thing to do at the time." You will need to demonstrate the rational basis for your decision and explain why, given the alternatives facing you, you concluded that your decision was the right one. In the business context, ethical behavior requires that you decide ethical issues on the basis of clearly defined ethical standards.

TYPE I ERROR
An error made as a result of a decision or an action.

TYPE II ERROR
An error made as a result of the failure to make a decision or take action.

❖ Sources of Ethical Standards

Despite our progressive and technologically advanced modern world, science and technology offer us little guidance when it comes to establishing ethical standards of behavior. In fact, science and technology sometimes create serious ethical dilemmas that did not exist previously. Medical technology is a good example. Organ transplants and life-sustaining medical equipment have created life-lengthening possibilities that did not even exist a decade or so ago. But these developments have also created difficult ethical issues, such as whether individuals should have the "right to die" and whether health care should be rationed. Technology cannot answer such questions because such questions relate to human values and beliefs that cannot be measured quantitatively.

This is not to say that there are no resources to which we can turn for ethical guidance. One important guiding source is business law itself. Other sources of ethical standards include religious beliefs and philosophically derived ethical values.

"Laws that do not embody public opinion can never be enforced."

Elbert Hubbard, 1856–1915
(American author and publisher)

Ethics and the Law

In all societies, ethics and the law go hand in hand. Law can never operate in a vacuum. It cannot be a series of rules that are imposed on society from without; rather, the law must reflect a society's customs and values and reinforce principles of behavior that society deems right and just.

Ethics and the Evolution of Law Law both affects and is affected by the society in which it functions. At times, the law is an active social force that helps to bring about changes within a society. For example, historical legal cases (such as those prohibiting segregation and discrimination) have been spearheads for social and political movements (such as those advocating civil rights and equal-opportunity legislation). At other times, the law represents a *response* to social changes, not a causal force that *brings about* those changes. For example, laws governing rights in computer software, computer crimes, electronic transfer systems, and the like represent a response to changes in business practices brought about by technological developments.

With respect to the law governing commercial transactions, law seems to be less an active social force than a response to social forces at work in our dynamic society. Throughout this text, we present a wide variety of landmark cases that, taken together, show the evolution of business law. For example, the underlying assumption, or watchword, used to be *caveat emptor* (let the buyer beware), but now it is *caveat venditor* (let the seller beware). This gradual change in the view of the courts and the legislatures can be seen as a result of changing social forces, the most important being the changing economic landscape of America. In the rural economy of early America, buyers and sellers had more equal bargaining power in the marketplace. In fact, buyers sometimes tended to be more sophisticated than sellers in the purchase and sale of commodities. This is because the sellers were often isolated farmers selling their crops. In such circumstances, *caveat emptor* was appropriate. The industrialization and urbanization of America, the growth of huge corporations, and the technological progress of the past century, however, have created a marketplace in which sellers have greater power than buyers. Because of these economic and social changes, *caveat venditor* is perceived to be more appropriate to today's world, and the consumer protection legislation of the past several decades was based on this conviction.

Business Law as a Guide to Ethical Behavior Laws governing business all reflect, directly or indirectly, the moral assumption that businesspersons should act ethically in their dealings with one another. Business law requires that people in business honor their contractual commitments, cooperate with one another in the performance of contracts, act reasonably and in good faith, and exercise due care and consideration for others in their undertakings. When studying business law, in essence you are studying particular applications of general ethical precepts held by society and expressed through statutes and court decisions. Although a law may seem arbitrary at first glance, if you look closely, you will often find the connection between that particular law and the broad, underlying ethical premise on which it ultimately rests. Insofar as is possible, we will help you see this connection by indicating, as we discuss particular laws in this text, how these laws relate to broad social policies and ethical principles.

UNCONSCIONABILITY
A doctrine under which courts may deny enforcement of a contract or clause on the basis of public policy, when one party, as a result of his or her disproportionate bargaining power, is forced to accept terms that are unfairly burdensome and that unfairly benefit the dominating party.

Often, you will find that this connection is very clear. For example, the legal doctrine of **unconscionability** rests on the clearly ethical assumption that one party to a contract should not take undue advantage of the other party. For example, if a contract is so one-sided or grossly unfair that it "shocks the conscience of the court," the court will not enforce it. This doctrine, which will be discussed at greater length in subsequent chapters, existed under the common law and is also explicitly stated in Section 2–302 of the Uniform Commercial Code. The following case illustrates one court's application of this doctrine.

Case 2.1
SHO-PRO OF INDIANA, INC. v. BROWN
Court of Appeals of Indiana, Third District, 1992.
585 N.E.2d 1357.

HISTORICAL AND ETHICAL SETTING *The concept of unconscionability has deep roots in the American legal system. Unconscionability has been said to underlie virtually the entire law of equity. Equitable principles forbid the enforcement of a contract unless it is fair and open, and the parties have communicated to each other all material matters of which they are aware. Before the creation and adoption of the Uniform Commercial Code, a court of law sometimes refused to enforce a contract on the ground that it was an agreement no one in their "senses and not under delusion" would make and no honest and fair person would accept. The drafters of the Uniform Commercial*

Case 2.1—Continued

Code wanted to combine these approaches to prevent "oppression and unfair surprise" in contracts for sales of goods. The primary beneficiaries of this application of the unconscionability doctrine have been consumers.

FACTS Roger Brown entered a contest to win a "house full of windows." As a result, sales representatives of Sho-Pro of Indiana, Inc., visited Brown at his home. After a sales pitch of more than four hours, the representatives had Brown sign a number of documents, which he did not read before signing. Three days later, Sho-Pro told Brown that he had bought four replacement windows for his home for $4,322. Brown protested that he had not bought any windows, that he could not afford $4,322, and that he did not even own the house in which he lived. No windows were delivered. Sho-Pro sued Brown to collect $4,322, plus attorneys' fees and interest. During the trial, it was revealed that the windows cost Sho-Pro $1,080.50. The rest of the contract price represented "lead costs" of $432.20, "sales management costs" of $600.61, "administrative costs" of $379.99, sales commissions of $648.30, profit of $648.30, and $532.10 to cover installation costs. The trial court concluded that the bargaining process and the contract price rendered the alleged contract unconscionable and therefore unenforceable. Sho-Pro appealed.

ISSUE Was the contract between Brown and Sho-Pro unconscionable, both as to the circumstances surrounding its signing and as to its price?

DECISION Yes.

REASON The appellate court pointed out that a contract may be declared unconscionable when there is "a great disparity in bargaining power which leads the party with the lesser power to sign a contract unwillingly or unaware of its terms." An Indiana statute provides that "a home improvement contract is unconscionable if an unreasonable difference exists between the fair market value of the services, materials, and work * * * and the * * * contract price." Another Indiana statute provides that "[i]f the court as a matter of law finds the contract * * * to have been unconscionable at the time it was made the court may refuse to enforce the contract." Thus, the appellate court concluded that if "the contract (if a contract existed) was unconscionable, the trial court could decline to enforce it."

> *"The law often permits what honor forbids."*
>
> **Bernard Joseph Saurin, 1706–1781**
> ***(French writer and poet)***

The Distinction between Ethics and the Law Because the law reflects and codifies a society's ethical values, many of our ethical decisions are made for us—by our laws. Nevertheless, simply obeying the law does not fulfill all ethical obligations. In the interest of preserving personal freedom, as well as for practical reasons, the law does not—and cannot—codify all ethical requirements. No law says, for example, that it is *illegal* to lie to one's family, but it may be *unethical* to do so. Likewise, in the business world, numerous actions might be unethical but not necessarily illegal. And even though it may be convenient for businesspersons to satisfy themselves by mere compliance with the law, such an approach may not always yield ethical outcomes.

Consider the following hypothetical example. The U.S. government has discovered that a child's toy is dangerous and has caused the deaths of some children. Consequently, the government has banned sales of the toy, leaving the manufacturer with a large unsold inventory. Although sales of the product are banned in the United States, it may be perfectly legal to export this purportedly dangerous toy to nations that have little consumer protection legislation. But would it be ethical to do so?

It is also possible that an individual may consider a particular law to be immoral. In such a situation, should the individual obey the law even if he or she thinks it would be unethical to do so? The pages of history are filled with stories of individuals—such as Mahatma Gandhi, Martin Luther King, Jr., and members of resistance movements in European countries that were controlled by Nazi Germany during World War II—who felt it would be immoral to comply with "unjust" laws.

In short, the law has its limits—it cannot make all our ethical decisions for us. When it does not, ethical standards must guide the decision-making process.

The Derivation of Ethical Standards

Religious and philosophical inquiry into the nature of "the good" is an age-old pursuit. Broadly speaking, though, ethical reasoning relating to business has traditionally been characterized by two fundamental approaches. One approach defines ethical behavior in terms of *duty*. The other approach determines what is ethical in terms of the *consequences* of any given action. We examine each of these approaches in the following sections.

Duty-Based Ethics Is it wrong to cheat on an examination, if nobody will ever know that you cheated and if it helps you get into law school so that you can eventually volunteer your legal services to the poor and needy? Is it wrong to lie to your parents if the lie harms nobody but helps to keep family relations congenial? These kinds of ethical questions implicitly weigh the "end" of an action against the "means" used to attain that end. If you believe that you have an ethical *duty* not to lie or cheat, then lying and cheating can never be justified by the consequences, no matter how benevolent or desirable those consequences may be.

In America, the dominant duty-based ethical standard derives from religious sources. Religious ethical standards are *absolute*. When an act is prohibited by religious teachings, it is unethical and should not be undertaken, regardless of its consequences. Religious ethical standards also involve an element of *compassion*. Therefore, even though it might be profitable for a firm to lay off a less productive employee, if that employee were to find it difficult to find employment elsewhere and his or her family were to suffer as a result, this potential suffering would be given substantial weight by the decision makers. Compassionate treatment of others is also mandated—to a certain extent, at least—by the Golden Rule of the ancients ("Do unto others as you would have them do unto you"), which has been adopted by most religions.

Ethical standards based on a concept of duty may also be derived solely from philosophical principles. Immanual Kant (1724–1804), for example, identified some general guiding principles for moral behavior based on what he believed to be the fundamental nature of human beings. Kant held that it is rational to assume that human beings are qualitatively different from other physical objects occupying space, such as CD players, sofas, and computers. Person are *moral* agents; that is, they are endowed with moral integrity and the capacity to reason and conduct their affairs rationally. Therefore, their thoughts and actions should be respected. When human beings are treated merely as a means to an end, they are being treated as the equivalent of objects and are being denied their basic humanity. A central postulate in Kantian ethics is that individuals should evaluate their actions in light of the consequences that would follow if *everyone* in society acted in the same way. This **categorial imperative** can be applied to any action. For example, say that you are deciding whether to cheat on an examination. If you have adopted Kant's categorical imperative, you will decide not to cheat because if everyone cheated, the examination would be meaningless.

CATEGORICAL IMPERATIVE
A concept developed by the philosopher Immanual Kant as an ethical guideline for behavior. In deciding whether an action is right or wrong, or desirable or undesirable, a person should evaluate the action in terms of what would happen if everybody else in the same situation, or category, acted the same way.

UTILITARIANISM
An approach to ethical reasoning in which ethically correct behavior is not related to any absolute ethical or moral values but to an evaluation of the consequences of a given action on those who will be affected by it. In utilitarian reasoning, a "good" decision is one that results in the greatest good for the greatest number of people affected by the decision.

Utilitarian Ethics "Thou shalt act so as to generate the greatest good for the greatest number." This is a paraphrase of the major premise of the utilitarian approach to ethics. **Utilitarianism** is a philosophical theory first developed by Jeremy Bentham (1748–1832) and then advanced, with some modifications, by John Stuart Mill (1806–1873)—both British philosophers. In contrast to duty-based ethics, utilitarianism is outcome oriented. It focuses on the consequences of an action, not on the nature of the action itself or on any set of preestablished moral values or religious beliefs.

Under a utilitarian model of ethics, an action is morally correct, or "right," when, among the people it affects, it produces the greatest amount of good for the greatest number. When an action affects the majority adversely, it is morally wrong.

Applying the utilitarian theory thus requires (1) a determination of which individuals will be affected by the action in question; (2) an assessment, or **cost-benefit analysis,** of the negative and positive effects of alternative actions on these individuals; and (3) a choice among alternative actions that will produce maximum societal utility (the greatest positive benefits for the greatest number of individuals).

COST-BENEFIT ANALYSIS
A way to reach decisions in which the costs of a given action are compared with the benefits of the action.

Utilitarianism is often criticized because its objective, calculated approach to problems tends to reduce the welfare of human beings to plus and minus signs on a cost-benefit worksheet and to "justify" human costs that many find totally unacceptable.

❖ Obstacles to Ethical Business Behavior

It cannot be denied that in the pursuit of self-interest, people sometimes behave unethically in the business context just as they do in their private lives. Some businesspersons knowingly engage in unethical behavior because they think that they can "get away with it"—that no one will ever learn of their unethical actions. Examples of this kind of unethical behavior include padding expense accounts, casting doubts on the integrity of a rival coworker to gain a job promotion, stealing company supplies or equipment, and so on. Obviously, these acts are unethical and, in most cases, illegal as well.

"Nothing is illegal if a hundred businessmen decide to do it."

Andrew Young, 1923–
(American politician)

In other situations, the distinction between ethical and unethical (and legal and illegal) behavior is not quite so clear-cut. For example, what if you wanted to use your employer's computer system for private purposes? Clearly, it would be wrong to do so if your employer's interests would be harmed as a result. But would they be? After all, you would not be stealing anything in the sense of physically "taking away" your employer's property. Similarly, would it be wrong to make a copy of your employer's software without permission? As in the previous example, the personal benefit is clear. You would avoid having to pay for the software. But would your employer suffer any detriment as a result of your actions? Would anyone suffer? (In the past decade or so, the laws governing the nature of ownership rights in technological property have been expanded by statutes and court decisions, and new laws have been created to cover these kinds of situations, as you will see in Chapter 6. But because these laws are relatively new, many people are unaware of them.) The point is, in these kinds of situations, it is easy to rationalize by telling yourself that because your behavior will not harm another, it is ethical. Even if you conclude that such behavior is wrong and perhaps illegal, you might be tempted to go ahead with it under the assumption that nobody will ever discover what you have done.

In the following case, a travel agent took advantage of her position to transfer unclaimed mileage credits to herself to gain, ultimately, free airline tickets. She claimed that she had not harmed the interests of the airline and therefore had not committed any wrongful or illegal action.

Case 2.2
UNITED STATES v. SCHREIER
United States Court of Appeals, Tenth Circuit, 1990.
908 F.2d 645.

HISTORICAL AND TECHNOLOGICAL SETTING *Before the electronic age, most business transactions were evidenced by paper. Schemes involving fraudulent fund transfers or forged documents were easier to trace because they were effected in person, usually involved signatures, and generally left a "paper trail" of evidence. Technological innovations in the past two decades have made it much easier to engage in unethical or illegal behavior and get away with it. Schemes carried out by computer, for example, are often difficult to detect. It may be some time before the scheme is discovered and even longer before the perpetrator is identified—if ever.*

Case 2.2—Continued

FACTS Gayle Schreier, who worked in a travel service office, had access to American Airlines' computer reservation system, which stores passengers' names and flight information. On a number of occasions, Schreier accessed the system to replace the names of actual passengers with "G. Johnson," a fictitious person whom Schreier enrolled as a member of American's Frequent Flyer AAdvantage Program, as well as the names of other fictitious passengers. The fictitious passenger received mileage credits, for which American issued coupons that were used to acquire tickets for American flights. Irwin Schreier, her husband, set up a number of mail drops, the addresses of which were provided to American as the addresses of fictitious AAdvantage members such as G. Johnson. The Schreiers were convicted in U.S. district court of wire fraud. On appeal, they argued that the proof against them was "fatally flawed" because it did not show that they had acquired property of American. The Schreiers contended that if the mileage they acquired was the property of anyone, it was the property of the passengers, none of whom complained.

ISSUE Did the Schreiers acquire property of American by accessing the airline's computer reservation system and replacing passengers' names with the name of a fictitious person to acquire mileage in the airline's frequent flyer program?

DECISION Yes.

REASON The court pointed out that mileage credited to AAdvantage members is considered a liability of the airline for accounting purposes. In acquiring mileage for a fictitious person, the Schreiers created a liability for American. Creating this liability was as much a misappropriation of property as would be the theft of an asset of an equal amount. When liability was created on American's books, through a transfer of mileage from passengers who did not claim the credits to an AAdvantage account in a fictitious name, the victim was American, because the airline thereby owed a liability that otherwise would not exist.

"When a man keeps hollering, 'It's the principle of the thing,' he's talking about the money."

Oliver Wendell Holmes, Jr., 1841–1935
(Associate justice of the United States Supreme Court, 1902–1932)

Ethics and Management

It is important to realize that much unethical business behavior occurs simply because it is not always clear what ethical standards and behaviors are appropriate or acceptable in a given business context. Although today, most firms issue ethical policies or codes of conduct, often these policies and codes are ineffective in indicating to employees what behavior is expected of them. Sometimes, the firm's ethical policies are not communicated clearly to employees or do not bear on the real ethical issues confronting decision makers. At other times, management may talk about ethics but in fact, by its own conduct, indicate that ethical considerations take second place. For example, if management makes no attempt to deter unethical behavior by reprimands or discharge, it will be clear to employees that management is not all that serious about ethics. Likewise, if a company rewards—for example, through promotions or salary increases—those who obviously engage in unethical tactics to increase the firm's profits, then employees who do not resort to unethical tactics will be at a disadvantage.

Of course, an even stronger deterrent to ethical behavior occurs when managers engage in blatantly unethical or illegal conduct and expect their employees to do likewise. Consider, for example, the case of Alan Russ, who worked as an accountant for TRW, Inc., a firm that did business with the government. Russ was told on several occasions to revise his figures to increase the man-hours allocated to the production of an item so as to support a higher selling price. Russ complained about this several times to both his immediate supervisor and the manager of the accounting division, but he was told that "everybody did it" and that he should just "do his job" and stop worrying about it. The ethical choice for Russ was clear: "do his job" as directed or follow his own conscience and be out of a job. Russ opted to do the former.[1] Many employees in this situation, however, have chosen to "blow the whis-

1. Russ later cooperated with an internal investigation conducted by the company, and for his efforts, the company fired Russ and gave his name to the federal government for possible criminal investigation and indictment. See *Russ v. TRW, Inc.*, 59 Ohio St.3d 42, 570 N.E.2d 1076 (1991).

"Have you noticed ethics creeping into some of these deals lately?"

Drawing by H. Martin, © 1992, The New Yorker Magazine

tle" on their employers and suffer the consequences (see Chapter 32). Employees who are required by their employers to participate in unethical or illegal practices face a particularly difficult ethical dilemma. The employee must weigh the duty of loyalty to the firm for which he or she works against the duty of loyalty to his or her conscience. If the employee's spouse and/or children rely on the employee's income for essential expenses, this further complicates the issue.

Ethics and the Corporate Structure

According to some, the corporate structure itself may promote unethical behavior because it tends to shield corporate actors from personal responsibility for their actions. For example, if a corporation markets a product that results in a consumer's death, the corporate officer who made the decision to market the product may not be deemed a "murderer." Nor would that officer, in all likelihood, condone the killing of others. In effect, corporate decision makers are often protected from the consequences of their decisions by the corporate entity—that is, they do not witness or deal directly with the harm or injuries generated by their decisions. To a certain extent, they are also often shielded from personal responsibility for their actions by the corporate collectivity. As mentioned earlier, normally, no *one* individual makes a corporate decision, and therefore no one individual normally ever has to assume total responsibility for a corporate action. In recent years, however, the courts have been increasingly willing to look behind the "corporate veil" and hold individual corporate actors liable for actions resulting in harm to others (see Chapter 27).

"You never expected justice from a company, did you? They have neither a soul to lose nor a body to kick."

Sydney Smith, 1771–1845
(English writer and clergyman)

❖ Corporate Social Responsibility

As already discussed, business decision making is often complicated by the necessity of making trade-offs. It is important to keep this trade-off concept in mind when evaluating the question of **corporate social responsibility**. This is because corpo-

CORPORATE SOCIAL RESPONSIBILITY
The concept that corporations can and should act ethically and be accountable to society for their actions.

rations are charged with a host of duties, and when these duties come into conflict, as they frequently do, difficult trade-offs must be made. We look now at some of the groups to which corporations are perceived to owe duties.

Duty to Shareholders

Because the owners of any corporate business firm are the shareholders, corporate directors and officers have a duty to act in the shareholders' interest. Corporate directors and decision makers are regarded as trustees of the shareholders' funds. Because of the nature of the relationship between corporate directors and officers and the shareholder-owners, the law holds directors and officers to a high standard of care in business decision making (see Chapter 27).

Traditionally, it was perceived that this duty to shareholders took precedence over all other corporate duties and that the primary goal of corporations should be profit maximization. Still today, some observers claim that maximizing profits for the shareholders is a corporation's primary duty. Milton Friedman, the Nobel-Prize-winning economist, effectively phrases this view:

> In a free enterprise, private property system, a corporate executive is an employee of the owners of the business [shareholders]. He [or she] has a direct responsibility to his [or her] employers. That responsibility is to conduct the business in accordance with their desires, which generally will be to make as much money as possible while conforming to the basic rules of society, both those embodied in law and those embodied in ethical custom.[2]

Those arguing for profit maximization as a corporate goal also point out that it would be inappropriate to use the power of the corporate business world to fashion society's goals. Determinations as to what exactly is in society's best interest are essentially political questions, and therefore the political process—not the corporate boardroom—is the appropriate forum for such decisions.

Duty to Employees

One of the primary concerns of every employer is the ability to control the workplace environment. After all, it is the employer who is responsible for making the business firm a success, and success requires qualified, competent, loyal employees and efficient operations. But employees also have concerns. They want to earn a fair wage; they want to work in an environment free of health-endangering hazards; they want to be treated fairly and equally by their employers; and, increasingly in recent years, they want employers to respect their personal integrity and privacy rights.

By law, employers are required to provide a safe workplace, to pay a minimum wage, and to provide equal employment opportunities for all potential and existing employees. But does an employer have ethical obligations to employees that go beyond those duties written into the law? And what if in fulfillment of one ethical (or legal) obligation, another duty must be violated? In the next section, we discuss some employment decisions facing employers in which various ethical or legal duties come into conflict. (See this chapter's *Business Law in Action* for another example of how these duties can sometimes collide.)

Employment Discrimination As will be discussed in Chapter 32, by law employers must offer equal employment opportunities to all job applicants and employees. Today's employers are prohibited from discriminating against existing or potential

2. Milton Friedman, "Does Business Have Social Responsibility?" *Bank Administration*, April 1971, pp. 13–14.

employees on the basis of race, color, national origin, sex, pregnancy, religion, or age. Discrimination against the handicapped is also prohibited. Many companies have adopted *affirmative action* policies to make up for past discriminatory practices against protected classes, such as minority groups or women. These policies occasionally result in what has been termed "reverse discrimination"—that is, discrimination against qualified members of the "majority" group. This means that employers must sometimes treat some actual and potential employees unfairly and unequally. Essentially, the ethical question here is whether it is fair to promote a less qualified employee to a position instead of a more qualified employee simply to correct for past discrimination. Some would say yes; others, no. But the question indicates how employers who are trying to fulfill a perceived ethical obligation to treat employees fairly and equally can sometimes find themselves in a no-win situation.

The following case is illustrative. Even though the employer went substantially beyond minimum legal compliance in attempting to provide a safe workplace for employees, the firm was nonetheless charged by some of its employees with having violated another ethical (and legal) duty—that of providing equal employment opportunities for women.

Case 2.3

UNITED AUTOMOBILE WORKERS v. JOHNSON CONTROLS, INC.

Supreme Court of the United States, 1991.
499 U.S. 187,
111 S.Ct. 1196,
113 L.Ed.2d 158.

HISTORICAL AND SOCIAL SETTING *With the Industrial Revolution of the nineteenth century came factories, assembly-line production, and a different way of life for workers. Those who had once worked (or had not found work) in rural areas moved to the cities to find jobs. Persons who prided themselves on the quality of their handmade goods, such as tailors, now faced competition from manufacturers producing lower-priced goods made by machines. In those days, employees had few rights and often worked long hours in conditions that today would be inconceivable. There was no minimum wage, and the concept of "overtime" pay was not yet born. Over the course of the twentieth century, numerous labor and employee laws were enacted to cure these problems. Today, employers who are insensitive to employee needs and working conditions may find themselves subject to lawsuits brought by the affected employees. In the interests of protecting female employees (and protecting the firm against potential liability), some firms have established fetal protection policies.*

FACTS Johnson Controls, Inc., created its Battery Division in 1978. In 1982, as part of an ongoing attempt to reduce the health hazards that might result from lead exposure, Johnson adopted a "fetal protection policy," under which women of childbearing age were prohibited from working in the Battery Division. This decision was reached after scientific studies indicated that a pregnant woman's exposure to high lead levels could harm the fetus. Johnson adopted this mandatory policy largely because its previous voluntary policy had failed to achieve the desired purpose: protecting pregnant women and their unborn children from dangerously high blood lead levels. Employees and their union, United Auto Workers, brought a suit against Johnson, claiming that the fetal protection policy violated Title VII of the Civil Rights Act of 1964, which prohibits discrimination in employment on the basis of sex. The trial court held for Johnson, and the unions and employees appealed. The appellate court affirmed the trial court's ruling. The case was then appealed to the United States Supreme Court.

ISSUE Did Johnson Controls' fetal protection policy constitute illegal discrimination on the basis of sex?

DECISION Yes. The Supreme Court reversed the judgment of the appellate court and remanded the case for further proceedings. Johnson Controls' fetal protection policy was discriminatory in violation of Title VII of the Civil Rights Act of 1964 and the Pregnancy Discrimination Act of 1978.

REASON The Court stated that employers may discriminate on the basis of "religion, sex, or national origin in those certain instances where religion, sex, or national origin is a bona fide occupational qualification [BFOQ] reasonably necessary to the normal operation of that particular business or enterprise." Therefore, the key issue to be decided was whether the BFOQ defense applied in this case.

Case 2.3—Continued

The Court held that it did not. In the eyes of the Court, neither gender nor pregnancy impaired an employee's ability to perform the job. In forming its decision, the Court looked to the Pregnancy Discrimination Act, an amendment to Title VII, which explicitly states that unless pregnant employees differ from others "in their ability or inability to work," they must be "treated the same" as other employees "for all employment-related purposes." The Court noted that "[f]ertile women, as far as [it] appears in the record, participate in the manufacture of batteries as efficiently as anyone else."

ETHICAL CONSIDERATIONS *The ruling in this case stunned those who believed that the Court should have shown more sensitivity to the unborn. But the Court believed that its ruling was "neither remarkable nor unprecedented. Concern for a woman's existing or potential offspring historically has been the excuse for denying women equal employment opportunities." The Court deemed it inappropriate for either the courts or employers "to decide whether a woman's reproductive role is more important to herself and her family than her economic role." Congress, by passing the Pregnancy Discrimination Act, "left this choice to the woman as hers to make."*

Profits and "Price Discrimination" In recent years, some firms have been criticized for firing highly paid employees who have worked for—and received annual raises from—the firms for years and then replacing those employees with younger, less experienced persons who are happy to accept lower salaries. Such actions are not necessarily illegal. If the fired employee cannot prove that the employer has breached an employment contract or violated the Age Discrimination in Employment Act (ADEA) of 1967, he or she will not have a **cause of action** (the right to seek legal redress or relief) against the employer. The ADEA prohibits discrimination against workers forty years old and older on the basis of their age, but employers can always say that lack of performance or ability, not age, was the deciding factor.

CAUSE OF ACTION
A situation or set of facts that entitles a party to sustain a legal action against another and gives the party the right to seek a judicial remedy on his or her behalf.

Increasingly, employers who want to shed older, highly paid employees are avoiding liability for age discrimination by offering the employees early retirement plans, financial incentives, and perhaps job-placement services—in return for a writ-

At what age are employees protected against discrimination on the basis of age?

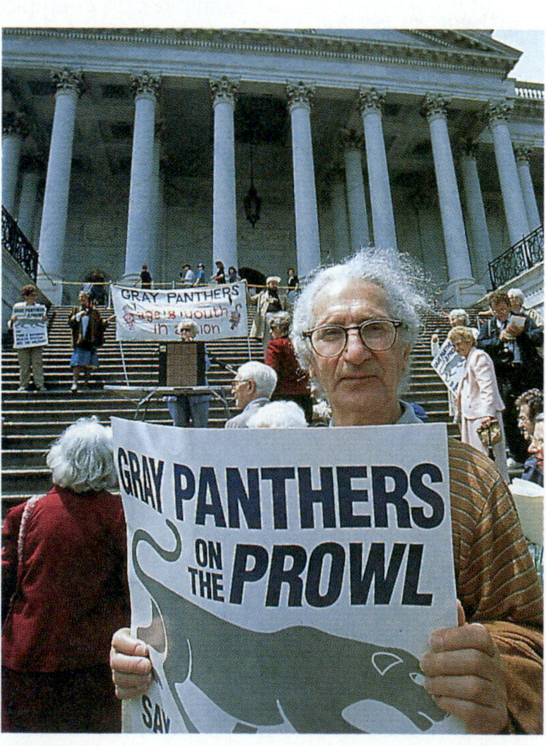

Business Law in Action

Sometimes, You Just Can't Win

Employers are finding it increasingly difficult to avoid liability for violating one or another duty to employees. In recent years; lawsuits for sexual harassment in the workplace have climbed dramatically in number. So have suits for wrongful discharge—firing an employee without good cause or for discriminatory reasons. And in some cases, those who have been fired for sexually harassing female coworkers have in turn claimed that they were wrongfully discharged—and won in court.

An obvious question presents itself: How can a court hold an employer liable for wrongful discharge when, in firing the employee, the employer was complying with a legal requirement? After all, federal law and the Equal Employment Opportunity Commission's guidelines require employers to take "immediate and appropriate corrective action" in response to an employee's complaint of sexual abuse. The answer to this question is that under some state laws and employment agreements, employers are prohibited from firing employees without a "just cause." And particular incidents of sexual harassment may or may not constitute just cause for firing the harasser.

Such a predicament faced Chrysler Corporation when one of its female employees informed management that she had been sexually assaulted by a male co-worker. Chrysler acted promptly. A brief investigation of the incident confirmed that Ronald Gallenbeck, a forklift operator, had indeed assaulted the woman. Gallenbeck had approached the woman from behind while she was inspecting a door panel, grabbed her breasts, then returned to the phone conversation he was having, and said, "Yup, they're real." Chrysler summarily discharged Gallenbeck for his actions. Gallenbeck claimed that his employment had been wrongfully terminated.

In accordance with a collective bargaining agreement, the dispute was heard eventually by an arbitrator. (In arbitration proceedings, the dispute is heard by an impartial third party, the arbitrator, who decides the issue. The arbitrator's decision is rarely appealed or overturned by the courts, however—see Chapter 3.) The collective bargaining agreement also stipulated that employees could only be discharged for a "just cause." The arbitrator concluded that one incident of sexual assault did not qualify as a "just cause" for summary discharge and that severe discipline—short of discharge—would have been adequate to deter Gallenbeck from further misconduct. Although Chrysler presented evidence of at least four other incidents in which Gallenbeck had grabbed or pinched female employees, the arbitrator refused to consider these incidents because Chrysler had learned of them *after* Gallenbeck's discharge. The arbitrator directed Chrysler to reinstate Gallenbeck with back pay, following a thirty-day suspension. A federal district court affirmed the arbitrator's decision. Chrysler did rehire Gallenbeck, as directed, but fired him the same day for the incidents of sexual harassment not considered by the arbitrator.

Chrysler also appealed the district court's decision to a federal appellate court.[a] Chrysler argued on appeal that the arbitrator's decision should be set aside on the ground that it was contrary to the public policy against sexual harassment in the workplace. The arbitrator had held that under the principle of just cause, "extremely serious offenses, such as stealing or striking a foreman[,] usually justify summary discharge without the necessity of prior warnings or attempts at corrective discipline. Less serious infractions call not for discharge for the first offense, but for some milder penalty aimed at correction." According to Chrysler, the arbitrator had created a "double standard" by holding that assaulting a male "foreman" justified summary discharge whereas sexual assault against a female did not. The appellate court, though noting the merits of Chrysler's arguments, affirmed the district court's ruling that the arbitrator's award should not be set aside.

Firms who fire employees for sexual harassment may find, as Chrysler did, that they have simply traded one set of problems for another. The question is, which set of problems is worse? The prevailing wisdom seems to be that risking a lawsuit for wrongful discharge may be the most reasonable course. This is because firing the harasser may prevent multiple sexual harassment lawsuits brought by other female employees who may be harassed by the same male worker.

a. *Chrysler Motors Corp. v. International Union, Allied Industrial Workers of America*, 959 F.2d 685 (7th Cir. 1992).

WAIVER
An intentional, knowing relinquishment of a legal right.

ten **waiver** (or relinquishment) of the right to sue the firm for age discrimination. To ensure that employees are fully cognizant of the rights they are waiving, the Older Workers Benefit Protection Act, which went into effect in 1990, requires that employees be given forty-five days to consider the waiver agreement and seven days to revoke the waiver after signing it. But from an ethical viewpoint, is it fair to long-time, loyal employees to force them to make a choice between early retirement and continuing on the job when the latter choice may involve a lower salary, a demotion to a less desirable position, or even eventual dismissal on the ground of some "manufactured" reason other than age?

In deciding this issue, remember that if employers fail to keep their eyes on their profit margins, they may place the financial well-being of the firm in jeopardy. Why should a firm retain highly paid employees if it can obtain essentially the same work output for a lower price by hiring cheaper labor? Does an employer or manager owe an ethical duty to employees who have served the firm loyally over a long period of time? Most people would say yes. Should this duty take precedence over, say, a corporate manager's duty to the firm's owners to maintain or increase the profitability of the firm? Would your answer be the same if the firm faced imminent bankruptcy if it could not lower its operational costs? What if long-time employees were willing to take a slight reduction in pay to help the firm through its financial difficulties? What if they were not?

Duty to Consumers

Many people believe that the corporation has an ethical duty to look beyond profit maximization to the welfare of consumers. To a certain extent, product liability laws, warranty laws, and other laws protecting consumers help to ensure that corporations will indeed market only products that are safe to use or consume. But there is a large "gray area" in which marketing a certain product may be legal but would be considered unethical. For example, suppose a corporation produces a type of baby food that babies like and mothers buy but that is not nutritionally satisfactory for babies because of a high MSG or sugar content. It would not be *illegal* to market the food, although it might be *unethical* to do so.

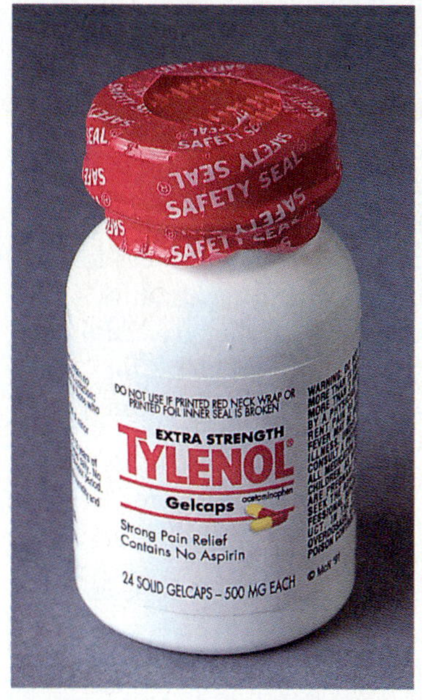

Duty to what group is met by the use of the tamper-proof seals on food and medication?

But what really is at issue here? Can the corporation willfully ignore the well-being of the consumer? Can the goal of profit maximization be met if the welfare of consumers is ignored? Some would argue that the ultimate control of the corporation actually lies in the hands of the consumer. After all, they argue, the consumer freely chooses to buy or not to buy a corporation's product. Even in the absence of effective competition, the consumer can purchase a smaller quantity of the product being offered. Thus, it is in the corporation's best interest to attempt to satisfy the consumer.

Even assuming that the consumer can exert control over corporate production decisions, however, an ethical question still remains. The process of competition takes time. Information is costly to obtain and is never perfect. If corporate leaders know or suspect that certain of their products may have deleterious long-run effects on the consumer, do not these corporate leaders have an ethical responsibility to either inform the consumer of those effects or simply withdraw the product from the market? For example, the manufacturer of a mechanical heart valve knew of the valve's propensity to fail but did not inform persons in whom the valve was surgically implanted of the valve's risks. Several lawsuits were brought against the manufacturer, Shiley, Inc., before the firm began warning valve recipients of the potential danger.[3]

3. See the *Business Law in Action* in Chapter 11 for a discussion of the liability facing Shiley, Inc., and its parent company, Pfizer, Inc., for failing to inform recipients of the valve's history of failure.

Although most people would probably agree that a corporation has an ethical duty to consumers, there is less agreement on how far that duty should extend. In other words, at what point does corporate responsibility for the safety of consumers end and consumer responsibility begin? If a consumer is harmed by a product because that consumer failed to exercise due care or did not use the product as directed by the manufacturer, who should bear the responsibility for that harm, the consumer or the manufacturer? This issue is addressed in the following case.

Case 2.4

CAMPBELL v. BIC CORP.

Supreme Court, Fulton County, 1992.
586 N.Y.S.2d 871.

HISTORICAL AND SOCIAL SETTING *As discussed earlier in this chapter, the prevailing watchword in the marketplace was once* caveat emptor *("let the buyer beware"). In other words, if a buyer purchased a faulty or defective product, the buyer had little recourse against the seller. In the last few decades, in the wake of a consumer movement seeking greater legal protection for consumers in the form of product safety laws and other consumer protection legislation, the watchword in the marketplace has become* caveat venditor *("let the seller beware"). In the interests of consumer protection, sellers are now subject to strict product liability laws. Today, to avoid liability, corporations must exercise great care in producing and distributing their products and must make sure that consumers are adequately warned of any possible harms that can result from the intended use (and sometimes the unintended but foreseeable use) of their products.*

FACTS Terry Campbell, a six-year-old boy, placed a cigarette lighter under his shirt and lit the lighter. His shirt caught on fire, causing him to suffer severe burns. Terry's mother, Mary Campbell, sued BIC Corporation, the manufacturer of the lighter, for damages. Mrs. Campbell contended that the corporation had the capacity to produce cigarette lighters with child-resistant qualities and that its failure to do so was a design defect that made its lighters unreasonably dangerous. (Under strict product liability laws—discussed in Chapter 17—if a design defect makes a product unreasonably dangerous, the manufacturer and seller of the product may be held liable for any resulting injuries.) BIC sought to dismiss the complaint, claiming that it did not have a duty to design and manufacture child-resistant lighters because the lighters it manufactured were intended only for adult use. BIC cited the Restatement (Second) of Torts, which holds that manufacturers are subject to liability for physical harm caused to consumers by the manufacturers' products only when the products are being used "for the purposes and in the manner normally intended." BIC further argued that the risks associated with a lighter are open and obvious and that the corporation therefore should not be held liable.

ISSUE Can BIC be held liable for Terry Campbell's injuries, even though the lighter was not being used as intended?

DECISION Yes. The court held that although Terry's use of the lighter was an unintended use, BIC should have known that harm caused by a child's use of its product was a foreseeable risk. Because BIC failed to design its product in such a way as to avoid this risk, it did not exercise reasonable care and was therefore liable for Terry's injuries.

REASON The court stated that because lighters such as those manufactured by BIC "are commonly used and kept about the home, it is reasonably foreseeable that children will have access to them and will try to use them." In response to BIC's argument under the Restatement (Second) of Torts, the court held that New York law is broader than that set forth in the Restatement. In New York, manufacturers have a duty to design a product so that it avoids an unreasonable risk of harm to anyone who is likely to be exposed to danger when the product is being used either as intended or in unintended but foreseeable ways. In response to BIC's claim that the risks associated with its lighter were "open and obvious," which in some situations is a defense to a claim of negligence, the court held that in New York that doctrine "is simply another factor that is considered in determining the reasonable care exercised by the parties."

Law in the Extreme

Warning: If You Fall, You Might Get Hurt

Today's manufacturers are plagued by product liability suits, many of which strain the limits of one's legal imagination. There is, after all, something called common sense, and most courts agree that consumers should expect to incur certain risks when they use particular products. For example, if a consumer is cut by a sharp knife, the manufacturer should not be held responsible for that injury because the risk was obvious and inherent in the nature of the product. Similarly (one would think), manufacturers of playground equipment should not have to bear responsibility for injuries sustained by children who fall off such equipment, providing the equipment itself is not faulty. But many consumers view the matter otherwise, and in recent years, a number of cases have come before the courts in which plaintiffs allege that manufacturers of playground equipment should be held liable for injuries sustained by children while playing on the equipment.

Although common sense sometimes gets lost in the thicket of a court's legal reasoning, at other times, it wins out, as it did in the case of *Cozzi v. North Palos Elementary School District No. 117.*[a] In this case, the father of an eleven-year-old child sued the manufacturer of a jungle gym because the manufacturer had failed to warn users of the equipment that they might fall off the gym and get hurt, as the boy did in this case. The father also claimed that the jungle gym was "unreasonably dangerous" because, as his son began to fall and reached frantically for a bar to grasp, there was no bar within reach. The father based his argument in part on a previous case involving a plaintiff who was injured as a result of somersaulting off a trampoline. In that case, the court had held that the trampoline's manufacturer was liable for the plaintiff's injuries because it had failed to warn of the trampoline's propensity to cause severe spinal cord injuries if it was used for somersaulting.[b]

But the court hearing the *Cozzi* case was not convinced by the father's arguments. Rather, the court held that certain risks, such as falling off a jungle gym, are so obvious that manufacturers need not warn of them. In its decision, the court applied an age-old common-sense principle: "If you fall, you might get hurt."

a. 232 Ill.App.3d 379, 597 N.E.2d 683, 173 Ill.Dec. 709 (1992).

b. *Pell v. Victor J. Andrew High School,* 123 Ill.App.3d 423, 462·N.E.2d 858, 78 Ill.Dec. 739 (1984).

STAKEHOLDER VIEW OF CORPORATE SOCIAL RESPONSIBILITY
A view of corporate social responsibility holding that corporations have duties to all individuals or groups who have a "stake" in the corporation, not just to shareholders, employees, and customers. In the stakeholder view of corporate social responsibility, corporations should also consider the needs of lenders, suppliers, the community, and others who will be affected by corporate decision making.

Duty to "Stakeholders"

In recent years, some business managers have advocated a **stakeholder view of corporate social responsibility.** From this perspective, the links established by a business firm with its employees, customers, suppliers, and local communities may balance or even outweigh the firm's duty to its shareholders. For example, when bad management or unethical behavior causes a firm to lose profits and eventually to go out of business, the shareholders will of course be affected; but so will the welfare of the other above-mentioned groups. Consider another example. A heavily indebted corporation is facing imminent bankruptcy. The shareholder-investors have little to lose in this situation because their stock is already next to worthless. The corporation's creditors will be first in line for any corporate assets remaining. Because in this situation it is the creditors who have the greatest "stake" in the corporation, under the stakeholder view, corporate directors and officers should give greater weight to the creditors' interests than to those of the shareholders.

Those who advocate a stakeholder view of corporate responsibility implicitly base their argument on a duty-based ethical standard: corporations have an ethical duty to consider the fate of these other groups, most of which are external to the corporation itself, when making decisions that significantly affect those groups.

Duty to Society

Most people concede that a corporation should be concerned not only with the welfare of its employees and the consumers of its products, but also with the welfare of the community in which it operates or society in general. But people have different ideas on how corporations can best enhance social welfare.

Profit Maximization, Revisited Those who contend that corporations should first and foremost attend to the goal of profit maximization would argue that it is by generating profits that a firm can best contribute to society. After all, profits are only realized when a firm markets products or services that are desired by society. These products and services enhance the standard of living, and the profits accumulated by successful business firms generate national wealth. Our laws and court decisions promoting trade and commerce reflect the public policy that the fruits of commerce (wealth) are desirable and good. Because wealth is valued by our society as an ethical goal, corporations, by contributing to that wealth, automatically are acting ethically. This argument—which was first posited by Adam Smith and touched on in this chapter's introduction—reflects the essential paradox of capitalism: that the self-interested pursuit of profits can result at the same time in greater social welfare.

"It is not from the benevolence of the butcher, the brewer, or the baker, that we expect our dinner, but from their regard to their own self-interest."

Adam Smith, 1723–1790
(Scottish economist)

Corporations as Trustees Many Americans believe that because so much of the wealth and power of this country is controlled by business, business in turn has a responsibility to society to use that wealth and power in socially beneficial ways. From this perspective, corporations are in a sense trustees or caretakers of society. Since the nineteenth century and the emergence of giant, wealthy business enterprises in America, corporations have generally recognized, at least implicitly, that they have an obligation to society to use some of their wealth to aid others. Corporations have generally been very responsive to social needs. Today, corporations routinely donate to hospitals, medical research, the arts, universities, and programs that benefit society.

For example, the Coca-Cola Company established the National Hispanic Business Agenda—a major program to expand ties with the Hispanic community. More recently, that firm contributed $50 million to support educational institutions and programs throughout the United States. As one of its many philanthropic projects, Levi Strauss & Company established an "AIDS Initiatives" program to fund public educational programs concerning AIDS and patient care for the victims of that disease. Indeed, today nearly every major corporation has a corporate branch or foundation that has been established specifically to screen charitable requests and to decide on and manage corporate charitable contributions and programs.

As caretakers of society, corporations are also charged with a host of other ethical duties. They should promote human rights, strive for equal treatment of minorities and women in the workplace, take care to preserve the environment, and generally not profit from activities that society has deemed unethical.

The Corporate Balancing Act

Clearly, it is impossible for corporations to be all things to all people at all times. Each corporate board of directors has to make numerous trade-offs in determining corporate goals. Directors do have an ethical duty to shareholders because they control the shareholders' wealth. They also have a legal duty to provide a workplace free of health hazards and discriminatory treatment for their employees and, in the eyes of many, an ethical duty to treat employees fairly and with integrity. Society has also deemed that corporate directors and officers have an ethical duty not to market defective or unreasonably dangerous products; this social ethic is written into warranty and product liability laws. Many people hold that corporations also owe a duty to other groups affected by their decisions, including society at large. But there are no laws or clear-cut guidelines for determining which of these duties should come first—or, more realistically, how much weight each duty should be given on the balancing scales beyond the minimum prescribed by law.

As the preceding sections have indicated, each of the major duties discussed—to shareholders, to employees, to consumers, and to stakeholders and society generally—involve not one duty to each group but a bundle of often conflicting duties. No matter what choice a corporate director or officer may make, it is possible that some ethical duty will necessarily have to be traded off, or sacrificed, in the process. The trade-offs are also complicated by the fact that corporate decision makers have to view both the short-run and long-run effects of their decisions and evaluate risks accordingly. For example, for a corporation to run smoothly and productively, it must recruit qualified personnel. To attract qualified personnel in a competitive marketplace, the firm must offer a competitive salary, a good benefits package, and desirable working conditions. If this is done and the corporation is well managed by the qualified personnel, ideally profits will increase and both shareholders and employees will benefit. But this ideal result is not a certainty. What is certain is that such additional expenses will mean reduced profits for shareholders in the short run. Similarly, corporate philanthropic activities that receive wide publicity may benefit shareholders in the long run—if the enhanced public image of the corporation entices more consumers to purchase its product—but such long-run possible benefits are difficult to calculate.

In sum, ethical decision making in the corporate context is not easy. Ideally, each corporate decision would provide equal benefits for all individuals affected by that decision—but this is rarely possible. When it is not, difficult trade-offs must be made.

Evaluating Corporate Social Responsibility

Now you can see why it is difficult to evaluate corporate social responsibility. First of all, because we live in a world of imperfect information, it is not always possible to acquire a sufficient amount of information about a given corporation's activities to make an informed decision as to whether that corporation is acting ethically or not. We might read in the paper, for example, that a certain firm has made generous contributions toward a worthy social cause and therefore assume the corporation has socially responsible goals. What we might not know, however, is that the same corporation is marketing a product that some corporate officers have reason to suspect may be harmful to many of those who purchase it.

Second, and perhaps more important, corporate social responsibility means different things to different persons, depending on their economic and moral convictions. What might be perceived as ethical behavior by one group might be considered unethical behavior by another. For example, a firm that makes a charitable contribution to an organization such as Planned Parenthood comes under fire from those groups opposed to birth control. Yet if the firm fails to make the contribution, or withdraws a pledge of support, it is attacked by birth-control advocates. Corporations and other business firms that strive to behave ethically face social mandates that are sometimes contradictory and sometimes representative of the interests of only a small but intensely committed and politically active interest group. Nonetheless, firms that fail to respond to these mandates often become targets of various sanctions, such as boycotts or the withdrawal of investors from the enterprise.

International Perspective

Should U.S. Drug Companies Sell Banned Drugs Overseas?

The production of a new pharmaceutical product is both expensive and time consuming. Because the adverse side effects of a particular drug cannot always be determined in laboratory experiments—especially when symptoms may not manifest themselves for many years—a pharmaceutical company can never be completely certain about the safety of its products when it first brings them to market. Further complicating the marketing strategies of these companies is the fact that certain drug products may be banned in the United States by the Food and Drug Administration. Because U.S. drug laws are among the toughest in the world, companies with such products will naturally look elsewhere for potential customers—particularly in developing countries that do not have such extensive restrictions on consumer products.

The marketing of banned drugs overseas has prompted charges that U.S. drug companies are selling potentially dangerous products to people who are often unable to appreciate the risks. Critics charge that these drugs, many of which are either unavailable in the United States or available only with a prescription, are often sold over-the-counter in poor countries and marketed by use of exaggerated or erroneous claims. Company spokespersons respond that these products are usually manufactured overseas and that it is the responsibility of the particular foreign government to determine whether a product is safe.

Among the most widely distributed of these banned drugs have been several antidiarrheal products produced by companies such as G. D. Searle, Johnson & Johnson, and Wyeth. Because diarrhea kills several million children in underdeveloped countries each year, the need for effective products is evident. The World Health Organization has said that an inexpensive mixture of sugar, salt, and water can help to rehydrate children much more effectively and safely than any of the drugs available for sale. Yet the lure of an estimated $500 million market has until recently proved irresistible to many companies.

After a scathing British documentary revealed that a number of infants in Pakistan had died after being given the antidiarrheal drug Immodium, Johnson & Johnson agreed to withdraw its product from all developing countries. Johnson & Johnson moved with considerably less speed, however, than in 1982, when it swiftly withdrew its complete stock of Tylenol from U.S. stores after several bottles were found to contain cyanide. Admittedly, marketing products in the developing world involves logistical and administrative problems not usually encountered in the United States. Still, it is possible that many U.S. pharmaceutical companies may be less concerned about selling potentially dangerous drugs overseas than they should be, at least in the eyes of some critics.

Consumer Boycotts Some consumer campaigns are underway nationwide against business firms that are deemed to be acting unethically. These firms have included many of the nation's leading corporations, such as General Electric (for its role in manufacturing nuclear weapons), Anheuser-Busch (for keeping whales in captivity), the Coca-Cola Company (for investing in South Africa), and Time Warner, Inc. (for marketing Ice-T's "Body Count" album). Indeed, some companies have become boycott veterans. Consider, for example, the boycott history of just one U.S. firm, Procter and Gamble (P&G). In the 1980s, in a rather bizarre controversy, P&G was boycotted by consumers who felt that its moon-and-stars logo was a satanic symbol. To end the controversy, P&G eventually redesigned its logo. In 1990, P&G was again boycotted when it was learned that the coffee beans in P&G's Folgers coffee came from El Salvador. A peace organization ran a commercial in which coffee cups were shown to be oozing with blood. The message was that P&G was "brewing misery and death" by purchasing coffee beans from a country torn by "death squads." More recently, P&G again became the recipient of consumer hostility when a number of ethically conscious consumers discovered that the company used animals in the testing of household products.

In view of the economic pressures that consumers can bring to bear on business firms, it is not surprising that many companies have decided that it pays to be ethical.

Ethical Investing Refusing to invest in corporations that are perceived to act unethically is yet another sanction that society can impose. In the last decade or so, several ethical investment funds have been established that allow individuals to make their investment decisions on the basis of corporate conduct. These funds evaluate how ethical a firm is according to any number of criteria, such as whether the firm uses animals in product research or testing, does business in or with countries whose governments are oppressive, produces environmentally safe products or has environmentally sound policies, has a specified percentage of women and minorities on its board of directors, participates in the construction or maintenance of nuclear plants, and so on. Some funds, such as Green Century Funds, invest only in companies that meet clearly stated environmental rules and goals for environmental improvement.

A few of these "ethical" funds have outperformed the stock market average, but most have not. For business firms, the message is becoming increasingly clear: it may pay to act ethically and to support socially desirable goals.

❖ The Ever-Changing Ethical Landscape

"The law is not the same morning and night."

George Herbert, 1593–1633
(English poet and clergyman)

It is important to remember that our sense of what is ethical—what is fair or just or right in a given situation—changes over time. Conduct that might have been considered ethical ten years ago might be considered unethical today. For example, the commercial bribery of foreign government officials has characterized international business transactions for centuries. Not until 1977, however, did the bribery of foreign officials become an ethical issue (see this chapter's *Landmark in the Law*). It took several scandals involving large payoffs to bring this issue to the forefront. Because enough groups concluded that this type of behavior was unethical, Congress was induced to pass a law prohibiting it. In short, the previous trade-off—looking the other way when it came to bribery of foreign officials in return for more profitable foreign contracts—was no longer acceptable to society.

Indeed, most of the ethical and social issues discussed in this chapter and elsewhere in this text either did not exist or were of little public concern at the turn of the twentieth century and, in some cases, even as recently as a decade ago. Technological innovations, the communications revolution, pressing environmental problems, and social movements resulting in greater rights for minorities, women, and consumers have all dramatically changed the society in which we live and, consequently, the business and ethical landscape of America.

Landmark in the Law

The Foreign Corrupt Practices Act of 1977

In the 1970s, the U.S. press, and government officials as well, uncovered a number of business scandals involving large *side payments* by American corporations—such as Lockheed Aircraft—to foreign representatives for the purpose of securing advantageous international trade contracts. In response to this unethical behavior, Congress passed the Foreign Corrupt Practices Act (FCPA) in 1977.[a]

Requirements of the Act

The act is divided into two major parts. The first part, which applies to all U.S. companies and their directors, officers, shareholders, employees, or agents, prohibits giving bribes (anything of value) to foreign government officials if the purpose of the payment is to obtain or retain business for the U.S. company. (The act does not prohibit so-called "grease payments" to minor officials to facilitate and speed up the performance of customary services.) The second part is directed toward accountants because bribes had often been concealed in corporate financial records. The act requires all companies to keep detailed records that "accurately and fairly" reflect the company's financial activities and to have an accounting system that provides "reasonable assurance" that all transactions entered into by the company are accounted for and legal. The act further prohibits any person in a U.S. company from making a false entry in any record or account.

Although these requirements are broad in scope, they seem to assist in detecting illegal foreign bribes. Any violation of the act results in fines of up to $1 million and the imprisonment of officers or directors of convicted companies for up to five years. Those officers and directors can also be fined up to $10,000, and the fine cannot be paid by the company.

Ethics versus Economic Reality

American corporations wishing to do business abroad, particularly in developing countries and in the Middle East, have probably always engaged in some sort of side-payment system to win contracts. In the United States, the majority of contracts are formed within the private sector; but in many foreign countries, decisions on most construction and manufacturing contracts are made by government officials because of extensive government regulation and control over trade and industry. Side payments to government officials in exchange for favorable business contracts are not unusual in such countries; nor are they considered to be unethical, as they are in the United States. By participating in this practice, U.S. corporations doing business in less-developed countries were largely following the dictum, "When in Rome, do as the Romans do."

The passage of the FCPA thus created an ethical dilemma for American business firms seeking to do business abroad. An employee of an American corporation has an ethical responsibility to do what is in the best interest of the corporation's shareholders. In many cases, that necessitates making some sort of side payment to a foreign official or officials to obtain a profitable contract abroad. But such offers of side payments are in violation of the FCPA. Since the passage of the act in 1977, American corporations have been at a competitive disadvantage *vis-à-vis* foreign corporations from countries that are not subject to any type of legislation governing side payments. In short, although the FCPA did not change international trade practices in other countries, it effectively tied the hands of American firms trying to secure foreign contracts.

This ethical dilemma did not escape the attention of the U.S. Congress, and beginning in 1982, some modifications to the FCPA were made. The rigorous accounting standards of the act are now relaxed somewhat, and corporations are now required only to ensure that "reasonable assurances" exist about the authorization and use of business enterprise funds.

a. 15 U.S.C. Sections 78m–78ff.

Application

Law and the Employer—How to Create an Ethical Workplace

Creating an ethical workplace requires, first of all, a commitment to ethical behavior on the part of top management. Second, if you are a manager, you should create a well-defined, written ethical code in which your firm's ethical goals and policies are clearly stated. Third, it is important that, as an employer, you make sure that your employees become well acquainted with this ethical code through employee training programs, ethics seminars, and the like. Finally, establish an ongoing ethics program through which ethical conduct can be monitored and employees can participate directly in ethical discussions and decision making.

The Role of Management

Surveys of business executives indicate that management's behavior, more than anything else, sets the ethical tone of a firm. If a chief executive officer (CEO), for example, routinely appears at the office at 10 or 11 A.M., takes long lunches, and so on, what does this behavior signal for employees who have to appear at 8:00 sharp every morning and take few breaks? Clearly, they may get the message that the CEO is not all that committed to the company or to working as a team toward a common goal. Similarly, if management itself behaves unethically, or tolerates clearly unethical behavior by one or more of its employees, it should surprise no one if the other employees do likewise.

If an employee persists in unethical behavior, you should consider discharging the employee as a clear example to other employees that unethical behavior will not be tolerated. While this may seem harsh, business managers have found that discharging even one employee for ethical reasons has had a tremendous impact as a deterrent to unethical behavior in the workplace.

Another important thing that management can do to ensure ethical behavior on the part of employees is to make sure that the firm's production or marketing goals are realistic. If a sales quota, for example, can only be met through high-pressure, unethical sales tactics, employees trying to act "in the interest of the firm" may think that management is implicitly asking them to behave unethically.

Create a Written Ethical Code

Most firms today create, print, and distribute among their employees an ethical code, which may be called a code of ethics, a code of conduct, a mission statement, a policy statement, or some other name. The code should be a clear, written statement of ethical goals and priorities. Some firms have lengthy, detailed codes; others have relatively brief mission statements. Generally, though, a code of ethics will make clear to employees how they are expected to relate to their supervisors or managers, to consumers, to suppliers, and to other employees.

Above all, it is important to state explicitly what your firm's ethical priorities are. For example, when Johnson & Johnson (J&J) was confronted with the Tylenol crisis in 1982 (Tylenol "spiked" with cyanide had caused the deaths of several persons in Chicago), top management at J&J was able to act swiftly and ethically because the company had made its goals clear in its ethical code. The code begins with the following words: "We believe that our first responsibility is to the doctors, nurses, and patients, to mothers and all others who use our products and services. In meeting their needs, everything we do must be of high quality." Although J&J could have chosen other alternatives in handling the crisis, the firm decided to withdraw thirty-one million bottles of Tylenol from the market, at a cost of about $100 million, in the interests of protecting the users of its products and preserving J&J's good reputation.

Communicate Ethical Standards to Employees

For an ethical code to be effective, its provisions must be clearly communicated to employees. A good way to do this is by implementing an ethics training program, in which management discusses with employees, face to face, the firm's policies and the importance of ethical conduct. Some firms hold periodic ethics seminars. These seminars allow employees to discuss openly any ethical problems that they may be experiencing and how the firm's ethical policies apply to those specific problems. Generally, the smaller the group, the more effective these discussions are.

Establish an Ongoing Ethics Program

A final element in implementing ethical standards in the workplace is the establishment of an ongoing ethics program. For example, you might arrange to hold pe-

Application—Continued

riodic seminars or meetings such as those described above. It is important that employees know that the ethical program is a "two-way street." That is, management must make it clear that feedback from employees and their ethical concerns are a top priority. Another effective technique is to evaluate periodically the ethical performance of each individual employee. One company, for example, hands out to its employees each week an ethical "checklist" to fill out and return to their supervisors. This practice serves two purposes: first, employees realize that ethics matters; and second, employees are given an opportunity to reflect on how well they have measured up in terms of ethical performance.

Checklist for Creating an Ethical Workplace

- ☐ 1. Make sure that management is committed to ethical behavior and sets an ethical example.
- ☐ 2. Create, print, and distribute an ethical code clearly stating your firm's ethical goals and priorities; the code should indicate to employees what behavior is expected of them in their areas of responsibility.
- ☐ 3. Implement an ethics training program to communicate your firm's ethical policies to employees.
- ☐ 4. Hold seminars or small group meetings in which ethical policies and performance can be discussed on an ongoing basis.
- ☐ 5. Devise a method, such as an ethical checklist, for evaluating the ethical performance of each individual employee.

❖ Key Terms

business ethics 34
categorical imperative 38
cause of action 44
corporate social responsibility 41
cost-benefit analysis 39
ethics 34
stakeholder view of corporate social responsibility 48
trade-off 34
Type I error 35
Type II error 35
unconscionability 36
utilitarianism 38
waiver 46

❖ Chapter Summary: Ethics and Social Responsibility

Ethics and Business Ethics	Ethics can be defined as the study of what constitutes right or wrong behavior. Business ethics focuses on how moral and ethical principles are applied in the business context. Ethical decision making in business is more complex than private ethical decision making for the following reasons: 1. Frequently, decision making in the business context is a collective process. 2. Business decisions often require difficult trade-offs between equally desired ethical goals. 3. Businesspersons, because their decisions may affect a broader number of people, must be prepared to provide a rational basis for those decisions and justify them from an ethical point of view.
Sources of Ethical Standards	1. Business law, which reflects society's convictions on what constitutes right or wrong behavior. 2. Professional codes of conduct or business ethical codes. 3. Religious beliefs (duty-based ethics). 4. Philosophical reasoning, such as that of Kant (duty-based ethics) or John Stuart Mill (utilitarian ethics).

❖ Chapter Summary: Ethics and Social Responsibility—Continued

Obstacles to Ethical Business Behavior	1. Unethical conduct by management. 2. Uncertainty on the part of employees as to what kind of behavior is expected of them. 3. The corporate structure, because it shields corporate actors from responsibility (normally, no one person is responsible for a corporate decision).
Corporate Social Responsibility	Most people agree that corporations should conduct their affairs in a socially responsible manner, but there is disagreement as to what constitutes socially responsible behavior. Corporations also frequently face conflicting duties and therefore must make trade-offs. Corporations are perceived to hold duties to the following groups: 1. *Duty to shareholders*—Because the shareholders are the owners of the corporation, directors and officers have a duty to act in the shareholders' interest (maximize profits). 2. *Duty to employees*—Employers have numerous legal duties to employees, including providing employees with a safe workplace and refraining from discriminating against employees on the basis of race, color, national origin, sex, pregnancy, religion, age, or handicap. These duties sometimes come into conflict. Many believe that employers hold ethical duties to their employees that go beyond those prescribed by law. 3. *Duty to consumers*—Corporate directors and officers have a legal duty to market safe products. Most people feel that corporations also have an ethical duty that goes beyond what the law requires. Controversy exists over the point at which corporate responsibility for consumer safety ends and consumer responsibility begins. 4. *Duty to stakeholders*—In recent years, it has been claimed that the foremost duty of corporations should be to "stakeholders"—those groups who have a "stake" in the enterprise. Under this theory, the duty to shareholders, for example, should be balanced against (or give way to) the interests of such groups as employees, consumers, suppliers, creditors, and the community. 5. *Duty to society*—Most people hold that a corporation has a duty to the community in which it operates or to society in general, but they differ in their ideas on how corporations can best fulfill this duty. One view is that corporations serve society's needs most effectively by maximizing profits because profits generally increase national wealth and social welfare. Another view holds that corporations, because they control so much of the country's wealth and power, are in a sense caretakers of society. They should use their wealth and power in socially beneficial ways and not engage in actions that society deems unethical; they should also contribute some of their wealth to charitable causes.
Evaluating Corporate Social Responsibility	1. It is difficult to evaluate corporate social responsibility because it is hard to obtain accurate information on corporate activities and because social responsibility means different things to different people. What might be deemed ethical by one group, for example, might not be deemed ethical by another. 2. Social sanctions against firms that are perceived to be acting unethically include boycotts against the firms and withdrawing investments from (or refusing to invest in) the firms.
Changing Ethical Standards	What is considered ethical in a society may change over time as social customs change and new developments alter our social and business environment. An example of changing ethical standards is the passage of the Foreign Corrupt Practices Act of 1977, which prohibits the bribery of foreign officials, in response to American society's changing ethical perceptions.

❖ Questions and Case Problems

2-1. Ethical Decision Making. How does ethical decision making in the business context differ from ethical decision making in private life?

2-2. Corporate Social Responsibility. Milton Friedman once wrote, "There is one and only one social responsibility of business . . . to increase its profits." What arguments could you raise in defense of this position? Against it?

2-3. Corporate Social Responsibility. Should the conservation of natural resources and other environmental considerations be ethical concerns of businesses? Discuss.

2-4. Ethical Reasoning. In the 1970s, the Nestlé Co. outraged a number of consumer groups by distributing its baby formula in developing countries even after it learned that the product was harming consumers. Mothers frequently mixed the infant formula with impure water or excessively diluted it to make it last longer. As a result, babies suffered from malnutrition, diarrhea, and in some cases even death. Other companies selling baby food in the same area pulled out of the market upon learning of this product misuse, but Nestlé did not. Nestlé justified its continued distribution of the product by stating that the social benefits of the formula outweighed the costs. The availability of the formula freed mothers from the task of breastfeeding and thus allowed them to earn money to help raise their income and standard of living. Besides, Nestlé claimed, mothers who drank impure water would pass on these impurities to the babies while breastfeeding anyway. What approach to ethical reasoning is reflected in Nestlé's argument? Do you agree with Nestlé's conclusion? If not, explain the ethical reasoning supporting your conclusion.

2-5. Ethical Decision Making. Shokun Steel Company owns many steel plants. One of its plants is much older than the others. Equipment at the old plant is outdated and inefficient, and the costs of production at that plant are now twice what they are at any of Shokun's other plants. The price of steel cannot be increased because of competition, both domestic and international. The plant is located in Twin Firs, Pennsylvania, which has a population of about forty-five thousand, and currently employs over a thousand workers. Shokun is contemplating whether to close the plant. What factors should the firm consider in making its decision? Will the firm violate any ethical duties if it closes the plant? Analyze these questions from the various perspectives on ethical reasoning and corporate responsibility discussed in this chapter.

2-6. Duty to Consumers. Two eight-year-old boys, Douglas Bratz and Bradley Baughn, were injured while riding a mini–trail bike manufactured by Honda Motor Co. Bratz, who was driving the bike while Baughn rode as a passenger behind him, ran three stop signs and then collided with a truck. Bratz did not see the truck because, at the time of the accident, he was looking behind him at a girl chasing them on another mini–trail bike. Bratz wore a helmet, but it flew off on impact because it was unfastened. Baughn was not wearing a helmet. The owner's manual for the mini–trail bike stated in bold print that the bike was intended for off-the-road use only and urged users to "Always Wear a Helmet." A prominent label on the bike itself also warned that the bike was for off-the-road use only and that it should not be used on public streets or highways. In addition, Bratz's father had repeatedly told the boy not to ride the bike in the street. The parents of the injured boys filed suit against Honda, alleging that the mini–trail bike was unreasonably dangerous. Honda claimed it had sufficiently warned consumers of potential dangers that could result if the bike was not used as directed. Should Honda be held responsible for the boys' injuries? Why or why not? [*Baughn v. Honda Motor Co.*, 107 Wash.2d 127, 727 P.2d 655 (1986)]

2-7. Duty to Employees. In 1984, General Telephone Co. of Illinois, Inc., (GTE) for reasons of efficiency, decided to consolidate its nationwide operations and eliminate unnecessary job positions. One of the positions eliminated was held by John Burnell, a fifty-two-year-old employee who had worked for GTE for thirty-four years and had always received "above average" performance ratings. GTE offered Burnell the choice of either accepting another position within the firm at the same salary or accepting early retirement with a salary continuation for a certain period of time. Burnell did not want to retire, but he was afraid that if he did accept the other position and if the other position was later eliminated, he might not then have the choice of early retirement with the same separation benefit. Because he received no assurances that the other job would be secure in the future, he accepted the early-retirement alternative. Burnell later alleged that he had been "constructively discharged" because GTE had made his working conditions so intolerable that he was forced to resign. Had GTE constructively discharged Burnell? Can GTE's actions toward Burnell be justified from an ethical standpoint? Discuss. [*Burnell v. General Telephone Co. of Illinois, Inc.*, 181 Ill.App.3d 533, 536 N.E.2d 1387, 130 Ill.Dec. 176 (1989)]

2-8. **Duty to Consumers.** Beverly Landrine's infant daughter died after the baby swallowed a balloon while playing with a doll known as "Bubble Yum Baby." When a balloon was inserted into the doll's mouth and the doll's arm was pumped, thereby inflating the balloon, the doll simulated the blowing of a bubble gum bubble. The balloon was made by Perfect Product Co. and distributed by Mego Corp. Landrine brought a suit against the manufacturer and distributor, alleging that the balloon was defectively made or inherently unsafe when used by children and that Perfect had failed to warn of the danger associated with the balloon's use. Discuss whether the producer and distributor of the balloon should be held liable for the harm caused by its product. [*Landrine v. Mego Corp.*, 95 A.D.2d 759, 464 N.Y.S.2d 516 (1983)]

2-9. Duty to Consumers. The Seven-Up Co., as part of a marketing scheme, placed two glass bottles of "Like" cola on the front entrance of the Gruenemeier residence. Russell Gruenemeier, a nine-year-old boy, began playing while holding one of the bottles. He tripped and fell, and the bottle broke, severely cutting his right eye and causing him to eventually lose his eyesight in the eye. Russell's mother brought an action against the Seven-Up Co. for damages, claiming that the cause of Russell's injury was Seven-Up's negligence. She claimed that the company was negligent because it placed potentially dangerous instrumentalities—glass bottles—within the reach of small children and that the firm should have used unbreakable bottles for its marketing scheme. Are glass bottles so potentially dangerous that the Seven-Up Co. should be held liable for the boy's harm? If you were the judge, how would you decide the issue? [*Gruenemeier v. Seven-Up Co.*, 229 Neb. 267, 426 N.W.2d 510 (1988)]

A Question of Ethics and Social Responsibility

2-10. *In 1986, the federal government required that all aspirin manufacturers include labels on their products warning consumers of the possible link between Reye's syndrome—a serious and often fatal disease—and aspirin ingestion by people with viral infections or chicken pox. Warnings in foreign languages were encouraged but not mandatory. Jorge Ramirez, a four-month-old California child, contracted Reye's syndrome* *after Rosa Rivera gave him St. Joseph Aspirin for Children (SJAC), manufactured by Plough, Inc. Rivera, who could speak and understand only Spanish, had not read the label, nor had she asked English-speaking members of her household to translate the label for her. Acting as guardian for Ramirez, Rivera sued Plough, alleging that Plough's failure to warn in the Spanish language constituted a breach of its duty of care to consumers. Plough contended that it had no duty to warn in a foreign language. In fact, because California had adopted English as its official language, Plough argued that to hold it liable would be counter to an explicitly stated public policy. The trial court granted summary judgment for Plough. (Summary judgment is a pretrial judgment that ends a case before it goes to trial.) Summary judgment will be granted when a dispute only concerns how the law should be applied and when no facts are disputed (see Chapter 3). On appeal, the state supreme court affirmed the summary judgment.* [Ramirez v. Plough, Inc., *6 Cal.4th 539, 863 P.2d 167, 25 Cal.Rptr.2d 97 (1993)*]

1. In view of the fact that Plough had complied with federal law and the fact that the California legislature had deemed that English should be the official language of that state, would it have been fair to hold Plough liable for Ramirez's injury? Would the fact that Plough advertised SJAC in the Spanish media affect your answer?
2. In defending against this lawsuit, Plough pointed to the fact that over 148 languages are spoken in the United States, and nearly twenty-three million Americans speak languages other than English in their homes. In view of this country's increasing cultural diversity, to hold manufacturers liable for failing to warn in foreign languages would create a "staggering" burden for business. Therefore, as a matter of law, firms should not be required to warn consumers in languages other than English. Do you agree with Plough's argument? Is there any "fair" solution to this problem?

FOR CRITICAL ANALYSIS

2-11. ***If a firm engages in "ethically responsible" behavior solely for the purpose of gaining profits from the goodwill it generates, the "ethical" behavior is essentially a means toward a self-serving end (profits and the accumulation of wealth). In this situation, is the firm acting unethically in any way? Should motive or conduct carry greater weight on the ethical scales in this situation?***

Chapter 3

Courts and Procedures

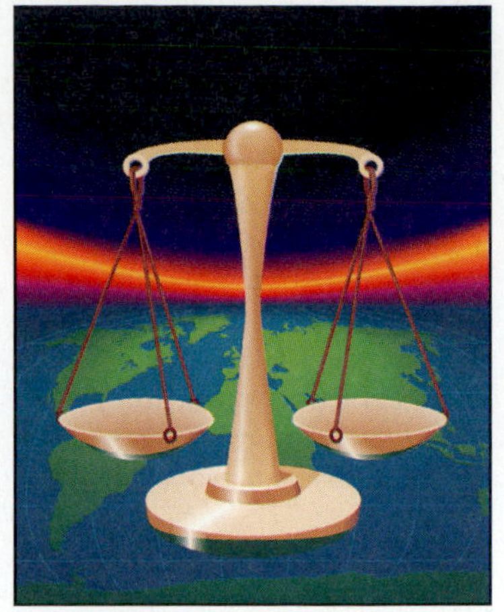

"Laws are a dead letter without courts to expound and define their true meaning and operation."

Alexander Hamilton, 1755–1804
(American statesman)

The body of law is vast and complex. As explained in Chapter 1, American law is based on numerous elements—the case decisions and reasoning that form common law; statutes passed by federal and state legislatures; federal and state constitutions; law codifications, such as the Uniform Commercial Code, that have been adopted by the various states; administrative law; and so on. But, as the opening quotation from Alexander Hamilton indicates, laws would be "a dead letter" without the courts to interpret and apply them.

Because businesspersons will likely face either a potential or an actual lawsuit at some time in their careers, it is important to anyone involved in business to have an understanding of American court systems, including the mechanics of lawsuits. Even though there are fifty-two court systems—one for each of the fifty states, one for the District of Columbia, plus a federal system—similarities abound. Keep in mind that the federal courts are not superior to the state courts; they are simply an independent system of courts, which derives its authority from Article III, Section 2, of the U.S. Constitution.

Both state and federal court systems are examined in this chapter, and to clarify judicial procedure we follow a typical case through a state court system. We also examine alternative methods of settling disputes.

❖ Jurisdiction

In Latin, *juris* means "law"; *diction* means "to speak." Thus, "the power to speak the law" is the literal meaning of the term **jurisdiction.** Jurisdiction refers either to the geographical area within which a court has the right and power to decide cases or to the right and power of a court to adjudicate matters concerning certain persons, property, or subject matter. Before any court can hear a case, it must have jurisdiction over the person against whom the suit is brought or over the property involved in the suit, and jurisdiction over the subject matter of the suit.

JURISDICTION
The authority of a court to hear and decide a specific action.

Jurisdiction over Persons and Property

Generally, a court's power is limited to the territorial boundaries of the state in which it is located. Thus, a court can exercise personal jurisdiction (*in personam* jurisdiction) over residents of the state and anyone who can be served with a *summons* (an order directing a party to a lawsuit to appear in court) within its boundaries. A court can also exercise jurisdiction over property (*in rem* jurisdiction, or "jurisdiction over the thing") located within its boundaries. For example, if a dispute arises over the ownership of a boat in dry dock in Fort Lauderdale, Florida, a Florida court can exercise jurisdiction.

LONG ARM STATUTE
A state statute that permits a state to obtain personal jurisdiction over nonresident individuals and corporations. Individuals or corporations, however, must have certain "minimum contacts" with that state for the statute to apply.

In some cases, a court can exercise personal jurisdiction over nonresidents under the authority of a long arm statute. A **long arm statute** is a state law permitting courts to exercise jurisdiction over nonresident defendants. Before a court can exercise jurisdiction over a nonresident under a long arm statute, though, it must be demonstrated that the nonresident had sufficient contacts (*minimum contacts*) with the state to justify the jurisdiction. For example, if an individual has committed a wrong within the state, such as causing an automobile injury or selling defective goods, a court can usually exercise jurisdiction even if the person or firm causing the harm is located in another state. In regard to corporations, the minimum-contacts requirement is usually met if the corporation does business within the state. The view that jurisdiction over out-of-state corporations is determined by a minimum-contacts standard was established in the following landmark case.

Case 3.1
INTERNATIONAL SHOE CO. v. STATE OF WASHINGTON
Supreme Court of the United States, 1945.
326 U.S. 310,
66 S.Ct. 154,
90 L.Ed. 95.

HISTORICAL AND SOCIAL SETTING *At one time, every state had exclusive jurisdiction over persons and property within its borders. A state could exercise jurisdiction over a nonresident defendant only if the defendant was subject to personal service within the state, appeared before the court voluntarily, or owned property that could be seized in the state. Problems with these rules developed as courts faced the economic reality that businesses carry on activities on regional and national scales.*

FACTS The state of Washington sought to collect unemployment contributions from the International Shoe Company based on commissions paid by the company to its sales representatives who lived in Washington. International Shoe asserted that its activities within the state of Washington were not sufficient to manifest its "presence" there, and thus the state courts could not constitutionally exercise jurisdiction over it. It argued that (1) it had no office in the state of Washington; (2) although it employed eleven to thirteen Washington sales representatives to market its product in Washington, no actual sales or purchase contracts were made in that state; and (3) it maintained no stock of merchandise in Washington. Consequently, it was a denial of due process for the state to subject it to suit. The Supreme Court of Washington held for the state, and International Shoe appealed to the United States Supreme Court.

ISSUE Does International Shoe have sufficient contacts with the state of Washington to enable the state of Washington to claim jurisdiction over International Shoe?

DECISION Yes. The United States Supreme Court affirmed the Supreme Court of Washington's decision and found that International Shoe had sufficient contacts with the state of Washington to allow the state to exercise jurisdiction constitutionally over the out-of-state corporation.

REASON The Court found that the activities of the Washington sales representatives were "systematic and continuous," resulting in a large volume of business for International Shoe. The company, by conducting its business within the state, received the benefits and protections of the laws of Washington and was entitled to have its rights enforced in Washington courts. Thus, International Shoe's operations established "sufficient contacts or ties with the state . . . to make it reasonable and just according to our traditional conception of fair play and substantial justice to permit the state to enforce the obligation" that the company incurred there.

Jurisdiction over Subject Matter

Subject matter jurisdiction is a limitation on the types of cases a court can hear. The distinction between courts of general jurisdiction and courts of special, or limited, jurisdiction lies in the subject matter of cases heard. Probate courts—courts that handle only matters relating to wills and estates—are a common example of limited subject matter jurisdiction. A court of general jurisdiction can decide virtually any type of case. The subject matter jurisdiction of a court is usually defined in the statute or constitution creating the court. A court's subject matter jurisdiction can be limited not only by the subject of the lawsuit, but also by the amount of money in controversy, by whether a case is a felony (a serious crime) or a misdemeanor, or by whether the proceeding is a trial or an appeal.

Original and Appellate Jurisdiction

The distinction between courts of original jurisdiction and courts of appellate jurisdiction normally lies in whether the case is being heard for the first time. Courts having *original jurisdiction* are courts of the first instance—that is, courts where the trial of a case begins. In contrast, courts having *appellate jurisdiction* act as reviewing courts. In general, cases can be brought to them only on appeal from an order or a judgment of a lower court.

❖ Venue

Jurisdiction has to do with whether a court has authority to hear a case involving specific persons, property, or subject matter. More than one court may possess potential jurisdiction over a case. **Venue** is concerned with the most appropriate location for a trial. The question of venue arises after a determination of jurisdiction. A particular court may have jurisdiction but not venue. The proper venue (location) for a lawsuit is defined by statute. Improper venue does not necessarily deprive the court of power to hear a case, but a party can request a change of venue if venue is not proper.

VENUE
The geographical district in which an action is tried and from which the jury is selected.

Basically, the concept of venue reflects the policy that a court trying a suit should be in the geographic neighborhood (usually the county) in which the incident leading to the suit occurred or in which the parties involved in the suit reside. Pretrial publicity or other factors, though, may require a change of venue to another community, especially in criminal cases in which the defendant's right to a fair and impartial jury is impaired. For example, in 1992, when the four Los Angeles police

Because of the extensive pretrial publicity, the defendants in the Rodney King case were granted a change of venue.

officers accused of beating up Rodney King were brought to trial in state court, the attorneys defending the police officers requested a change of venue from Los Angeles to Simi Valley, California. The attorneys argued that to try the case in a Los Angeles court would prejudice the police officers' right to a fair trial. The court agreed and granted the request. (The "not guilty" verdict entered by the Simi Valley jurors, however, was followed by several days of the most extensive and expensive inner-city rioting in the history of South Central Los Angeles—and of the United States.)

❖ The State Court System

"With all the law's faults, it had one great virtue. It was there."

Arthur Hailey, 1920– ***(English-born Canadian novelist)***

One can view the typical state court system as being made up of trial courts and appellate courts. Trial courts are exactly what their name implies—courts in which trials are held and testimony is taken. Appellate courts are courts of appeal and review.

As Exhibit 3–1 indicates, there are several levels, or tiers, of courts within state court systems: (1) state trial courts of limited jurisdiction, (2) state trial courts of general jurisdiction, (3) appellate courts, and (4) the state supreme court. Any person who is a party to a lawsuit typically has the opportunity to plead the case before a trial court and then, if he or she loses, before at least one level of appellate court. Finally, if a federal statute or constitutional issue is involved in the decision of the state supreme court, that decision may be further appealed to the United States Supreme Court.

Trial Courts

The state trial courts have either *general* or *limited* jurisdiction. Trial courts that have general jurisdiction as to subject matter may be called county, district, superior, or circuit courts.[1] The jurisdiction of these courts of general and original jurisdiction is often determined by the size of the county in which the court sits. Many important cases involving businesses originate in these general trial courts.

SMALL CLAIMS COURTS
Special courts in which parties may litigate small claims (usually, claims involving $2,500 or less). Attorneys are not required in small claims courts, and in many states, attorneys are not allowed to represent the parties.

Courts with limited jurisdiction as to subject matter are often called special inferior trial courts or minor judiciary courts. **Small claims courts** are inferior trial courts that hear only civil cases involving claims of less than a certain amount, usually $2,500. Most small claims involve less than $500. Suits brought in small claims courts are generally conducted informally, and lawyers are not required. In a minority of states, lawyers are not even allowed to represent people in small claims courts for most purposes. Decisions of small claims courts may be appealed to a state trial court of general jurisdiction.

Other courts of limited jurisdiction are domestic relations courts, which handle only divorce actions and child custody cases; local municipal courts, which mainly handle traffic cases; and probate courts, which handle the administration of wills and estate settlement problems.

Courts of Appeals

Although in some states, trial courts of general jurisdiction (such as county courts) also have limited jurisdiction to hear appeals from the minor judiciary—for example, small claims and traffic cases—when one discusses courts of review, or appellate courts, one usually means courts that are not trial courts.

Every state has at least one court of appeals, or reviewing court. About half of the states have intermediate appellate courts. The subject matter jurisdiction of these

1. The name in Ohio is Court of Common Pleas; the name in New York is Supreme Court.

◆ **Exhibit 3–1 State Court Systems**

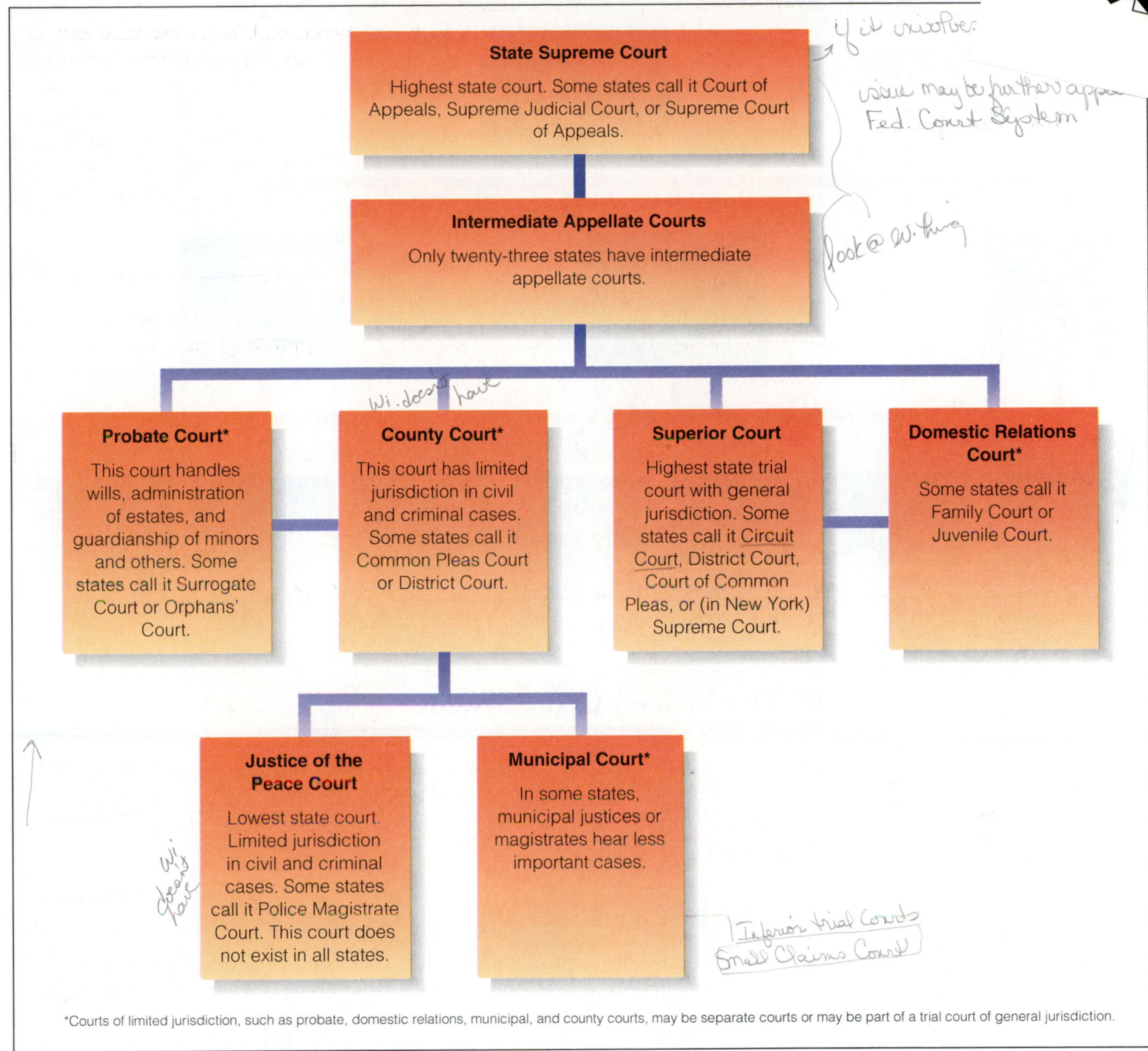
State Supreme Court
Highest state court. Some states call it Court of Appeals, Supreme Judicial Court, or Supreme Court of Appeals.
Intermediate Appellate Courts
Only twenty-three states have intermediate appellate courts.
Probate Court*
This court handles wills, administration of estates, and guardianship of minors and others. Some states call it Surrogate Court or Orphans' Court.
County Court*
This court has limited jurisdiction in civil and criminal cases. Some states call it Common Pleas Court or District Court.
Superior Court
Highest state trial court with general jurisdiction. Some states call it Circuit Court, District Court, Court of Common Pleas, or (in New York) Supreme Court.
Domestic Relations Court*
Some states call it Family Court or Juvenile Court.
Justice of the Peace Court
Lowest state court. Limited jurisdiction in civil and criminal cases. Some states call it Police Magistrate Court. This court does not exist in all states.
Municipal Court*
In some states, municipal justices or magistrates hear less important cases.

*Courts of limited jurisdiction, such as probate, domestic relations, municipal, and county courts, may be separate courts or may be part of a trial court of general jurisdiction.

courts of appeals, or reviewing courts, is substantially limited to hearing appeals. Appellate courts normally examine the record of the case on appeal and determine whether the trial court committed an error. They look at questions of law and procedure but usually not at questions of fact. An appellate court will tamper with a trial court's finding of fact when the finding is clearly erroneous (that is, when it is contrary to the evidence presented at trial) or when there is no evidence to support the finding. Realize, however, that the appeals court has liberal power to reverse a trial court's finding of fact when the case is a nonjury one.

The highest appellate court in a state is usually called the supreme court but may be called by some other name. For example, in both New York and Maryland, the highest state court is called the Court of Appeals. The decisions of each state's highest court on all questions of state law are final. Only when issues of federal law are involved can a state's highest court be overruled by the United States Supreme Court.

Exhibit 3–2 The Organization of the Federal Court System

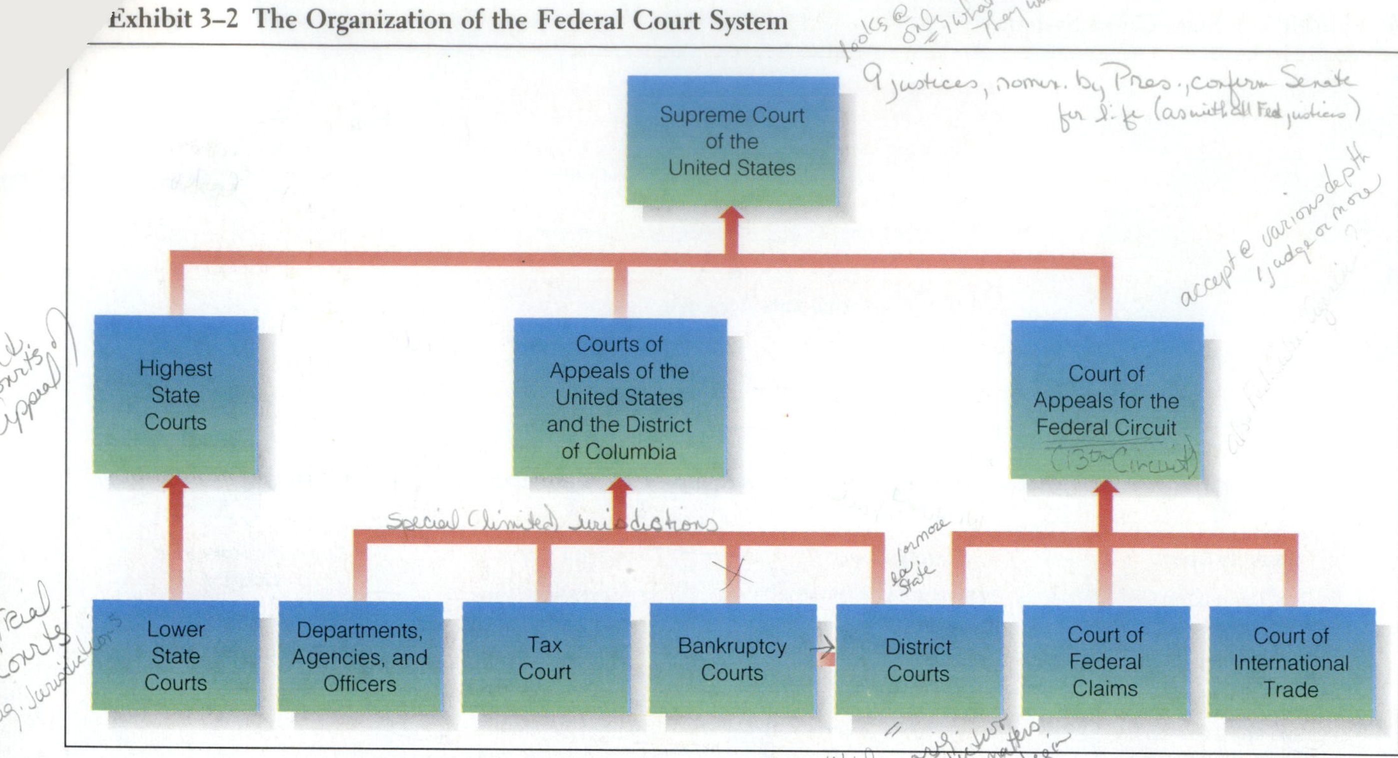

❖ The Federal Court System

The federal court system is similar in many ways to most state court systems. It is a three-tiered model consisting of (1) trial courts, (2) intermediate courts of appeals, and (3) the United States Supreme Court. Exhibit 3–2 shows the organization of the federal court system.

U.S. District Courts

At the federal level, the equivalent of a state trial court of general jurisdiction is the district court. There is at least one federal district court in every state. The number of judicial districts can vary over time, primarily owing to population changes and corresponding caseloads. The law now provides for 191 circuit court judgeships within the 13 circuits (including the federal circuit) and 629 district court judgeships within the 96 judicial districts.[2] U.S. district courts have original jurisdiction in federal matters. Federal cases originate in district courts. There are other trial courts with original, albeit special (or limited) jurisdiction, such as the U.S. Tax Court, the U.S. Bankruptcy Court, and the U.S. Court of Federal Claims.[3] Certain administrative agencies and departments with judicial power also have original jurisdiction.

U.S. Courts of Appeals

There are thirteen judicial circuits within the United States. The U.S. (circuit) courts of appeals for twelve of the circuits hear appeals from the federal district courts located within their respective judicial circuits. The court of appeals for the

2. See 28 U.S.C. Sections 44(a), 133.
3. Formerly the U.S. Claims Court.

◆ **Exhibit 3–3 U.S. Courts of Appeals and U.S. District Courts**

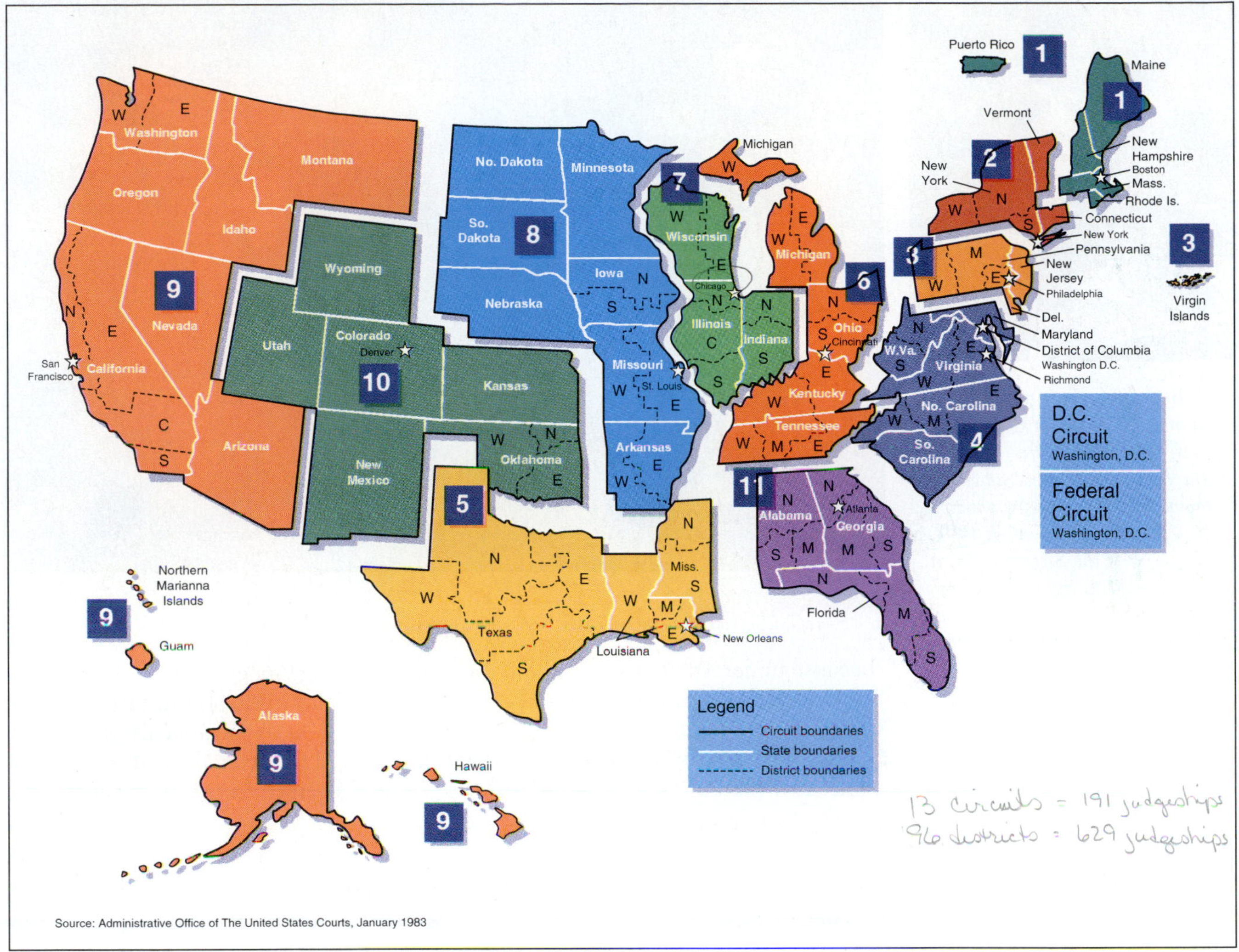

Source: Administrative Office of The United States Courts, January 1983

thirteenth circuit, called the federal circuit, has national jurisdiction over certain types of cases, such as those concerning customs law and patent law.

The decisions of the circuit courts of appeals are final in most cases, but appeal to the United States Supreme Court is possible. Appeals from federal administrative agencies, such as the Federal Trade Commission, are also made to the U.S. circuit courts of appeals. See Exhibit 3–3 for the geographical boundaries of U.S. district courts and U.S. courts of appeals.

The United States Supreme Court

The highest level of the three-tiered model of the federal court system is the United States Supreme Court. According to the language of Article III of the U.S. Constitution, there is only one national Supreme Court. All other courts in the federal system are considered "inferior." Congress is empowered to create other inferior courts as it deems necessary. The inferior courts that Congress has created include the second tier in our model—the U.S. courts of appeals—as well as the district courts and any other courts of limited, or specialized, jurisdiction.

The United States Supreme Court consists of nine justices; these justices are nominated by the president of the United States and confirmed by the Senate. They (as do all federal district and courts of appeals judges) receive lifetime appointments

Ruth Bader Ginsburg was appointed by President Clinton to replace Justice White. In the photo on the right, the United States Supreme Court is shown prior to Justice White's retirement in 1993. The Justices of the Supreme Court are, seated left to right, John Paul Stevens; Byron R. White; William H. Rehnquist, Chief Justice; Harry A. Blackmun; Sandra Day O'Connor. Standing are, from left to right, David H. Souter; Antonin Scalia; Anthony M. Kennedy; Clarence Thomas.

(because under Article III they "hold their offices during Good Behavior"). Although the United States Supreme Court has original, or trial, jurisdiction in rare instances (set forth in Article III, Section 2), most of its work is as an appeals court. The Supreme Court can review any case decided by any of the federal courts of appeals, and it also has appellate authority over some cases decided in the state courts.

❖ Jurisdiction of the Federal Courts

Because the federal government is a government of limited powers, the jurisdiction of the federal courts is limited. Article III of the U.S. Constitution established the boundaries of federal judicial power. Section I of Article III states that "[t]he judicial Power of the United States shall be vested in one supreme Court and in such inferior Courts as the Congress may from time to time ordain and establish." Section 2 of Article III states that "[t]he judicial Power shall extend to all Cases, in Law and Equity, arising under this Constitution, the Laws of the United States, and Treaties made, or which shall be made, under their Authority."

In line with the *checks and balances system* of the federal government (discussed in Chapter 4), Congress has the power to control the number and kind of inferior courts in the federal system. Except in those cases in which the Constitution gives the Supreme Court original jurisdiction (including cases involving ambassadors and controversies between states), Congress can also regulate the jurisdiction of the Supreme Court. Although the Constitution sets the outer limits of federal judicial power, Congress can set other limits on federal jurisdiction. Furthermore, the courts themselves can promulgate rules that further narrow the types of cases they will hear.

DIVERSITY OF CITIZENSHIP
Under Article III, Section 2, of the Constitution, a basis for federal court jurisdiction over a lawsuit between citizens of different states.

Diversity Jurisdiction

Federal district court jurisdiction also extends to cases involving **diversity of citizenship**. Such cases may arise between (1) citizens of different states; (2) a foreign country and citizens of a state or of different states; or (3) citizens of a state and citizens or subjects of a foreign country. The amount in controversy must be more than $50,000 before a federal court can take jurisdiction in such cases. For purposes of diversity-of-citizenship jurisdiction, a corporation is a citizen of the state in which it is incorporated and of the state in which its principal place of business is located. A case involving diversity of citizenship can commence in the appropriate federal district court, or, if the case starts in a state court, it can sometimes be transferred.

Diversity jurisdiction originated in 1789. The authors of the Constitution felt that a state might be biased in favor of its own citizens. Hence, the option of using the federal courts provided by the principle of diversity of citizenship is a means of protecting the out-of-state party. A large percentage of the more than seventy thousand cases filed in federal courts each year are based on diversity of citizenship.

Federal Questions

Whenever a plaintiff's cause of action is based, at least in part, on the U.S. Constitution, a treaty, or a federal law, then a **federal question** arises, and the case comes under the judicial power of the federal courts. Any lawsuit involving a federal question can originate in a federal court. People whose claims are based on rights granted by an act of Congress can sue in a federal court. People who claim that their constitutional rights have been violated can also begin their suits in a federal court.

When both federal and state courts have the power to hear a case, as is true in suits involving diversity of citizenship, **concurrent jurisdiction** exists. When cases can be tried only in federal courts or only in state courts, **exclusive jurisdiction** exists. Federal courts have exclusive jurisdiction in cases involving federal crimes, bankruptcy, patents, and copyrights; in suits against the United States; and in some areas of admiralty law. States also have exclusive jurisdiction in certain subject matters—for example, in divorce and adoptions. The concepts of concurrent and exclusive jurisdiction are illustrated in Exhibit 3–4.

FEDERAL QUESTION
A question that pertains to the U.S. Constitution, acts of Congress, or treaties. A federal question provides jurisdiction for federal courts. This jurisdiction arises from Article III, Section 2, of the Constitution.

CONCURRENT JURISDICTION
Jurisdiction that exists when two different courts have the power to hear a case. For example, some cases can be heard in a federal or state court.

EXCLUSIVE JURISDICTION
Jurisdiction that exists when a case can only be heard in a particular court.

❖ How Cases Reach the Supreme Court

Many people are surprised to learn that there is no absolute right of appeal to the United States Supreme Court. The Supreme Court is given original, or trial court, jurisdiction in a small number of situations. In all other cases, its jurisdiction is appellate "with such Exceptions, and under such Regulations as the Congress shall make." Thousands of cases are filed with the Supreme Court each year; yet it hears, on average, only about one hundred. To bring a case before the Supreme Court, a party requests that the Court issue a writ of *certiorari*.

A **writ of *certiorari*** is an order issued by the Supreme Court to a lower court requiring the latter to send it the record of the case for review. Parties can petition the Supreme Court to issue a writ of *certiorari*, but whether the Court will issue one is entirely within its discretion. In no instance is the Court required to issue a writ of *certiorari*.[4]

WRIT OF *CERTIORARI*
A writ from a higher court asking the lower court for the record of a case.

Below are some of the situations in which the Supreme Court may issue a writ of *certiorari*:

1. When a state court has decided a substantial federal question that has not been determined by the Supreme Court or when a state court has decided such a question

4. Between 1790 and 1891, Congress allowed the Supreme Court almost no discretion over which cases to decide. After 1925, the Court could choose in almost 95 percent of appealed cases whether to hear arguments and issue an opinion. Beginning with the term of October 1988, mandatory review was eliminated altogether.

◆ **Exhibit 3–4**
Exclusive and Concurrent Jurisdiction

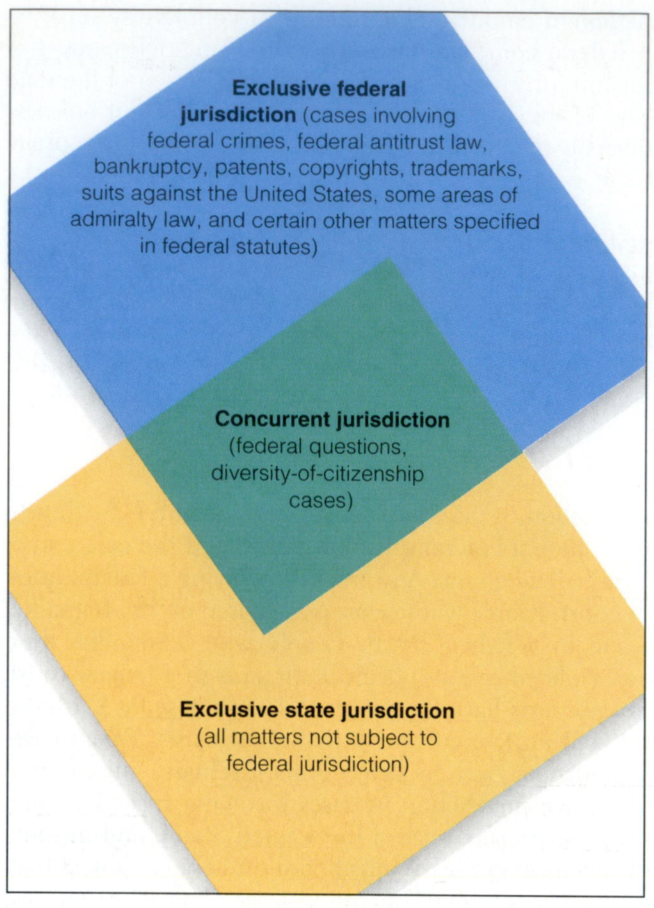

in a way that is probably in disagreement with the intent of Congress or with the trend of the Supreme Court's decisions.

2. When two or more federal courts of appeals are in disagreement with each other.

3. When a federal court of appeals has decided an important state question in conflict with state law, has decided an important federal question not yet addressed by the Court but which should be decided by the Court, has decided a federal question in conflict with applicable decisions of the Court, or has departed from the accepted and usual course of judicial proceedings.

4. When a federal court of appeals holds that a state statute is invalid because it violates federal law.

5. When the highest state court of appeals holds a federal law invalid or upholds a state law that has been challenged as violating federal law.

6. When a federal court holds an act of Congress unconstitutional and the federal government or one of its employees is a party.

Most petitions for writs of *certiorari* are denied. A denial is not a decision on the merits of a case, nor does it indicate agreement with the lower court's opinion. Denial of the writ also has no value as a precedent.[5] The Court will not issue a writ unless at least four justices approve of it. This is called the "rule of four." Typically, only the petitions that raise the possibility of important constitutional questions are granted.

---

5. *Singleton v. Commissioner of Internal Revenue,* 439 U.S. 940, 899 S.Ct. 335, 58 L.Ed. 335 (1978).

❖ Judicial Review

The problem often arises as to whether a law is contrary to the mandates of the Constitution. **Judicial review** is the process for making such a determination. It is the judicial branch of the national government that has the authority and power to determine whether a particular law violates the Constitution.

JUDICIAL REVIEW
The authority of a court to reexamine a previously considered dispute; the process by which a court decides on the constitutionality of legislative acts.

The power of judicial review was established in *Marbury v. Madison* (see this chapter's *Landmark in the Law*). In determining that the United States Supreme Court had the power to decide that a law passed by Congress violated the Constitution, the Court stated, "It is emphatically the province and duty of the Judicial Department to say what the law is. . . . If two laws conflict with each other, the courts must decide on the operation of each. . . . So if the law be in opposition to the Constitution . . . [t]he Court must determine which of these conflicting rules governs the case. This is the very essence of judicial duty."[6]

❖ Declaratory Judgment

All federal courts and virtually all state courts can make declaratory judgments. A **declaratory judgment** is a court's binding determination of the rights and status of the parties. It provides a method of determining the parties' legal rights before any wrongs have been committed so that they will know what they can legally do. A declaratory judgment is usually sought to test the constitutionality of a statute. It can also be requested by a party interested in, and in doubt concerning, any right, interpretation, or application of a contract or other document. For example, if the parties to a contract have a dispute concerning the meaning of the language in their contract, one of the parties can seek a declaratory judgment to resolve the dispute. A declaratory judgment can be granted whether or not any other form of relief is awarded, and in some circumstances, other relief can be sought later.

DECLARATORY JUDGMENT
A judgment rendered by a court that declares for the parties what their respective rights and duties are in regard to a specific controversy.

❖ Following a Case through the State Courts

American and English courts follow the *adversary system of justice*. In this system, the judge's role is viewed as nonbiased and mostly passive. The lawyer functions as the client's advocate, presenting the client's version of the facts in order to convince the judge or the jury (or both) that it is true. Judges are responsible for the appropriate application of the law. They do not have to accept the legal reasoning of the attorneys but, instead, can base a ruling and a decision on their own study of the law. Furthermore, judges do not have to be entirely passive; they sometimes ask questions of witnesses and even suggest types of evidence to be presented. For example, if an indigent defendant chooses to act as his or her own counsel, the judge will often play a role that is more supporting than passive, intervening during the trial proceedings to help the defendant.[7]

"The penalty for laughing in a courtroom is six months in jail."

H. L. Mencken, 1880–1956
(American editor and critic)

Court Procedure

Procedure involves the way in which disputes are handled in the courts. A large body of law—procedural law—establishes the rules and standards for determining disputes in courts. The rules are very complex, and they vary from court to court.

6. 5 U. S. (1 Cranch) 137, 2 L.Ed. 60 (1803).
7. See *Faretta v. California*, 422 U.S. 806, 95 S.Ct. 2525, 45 L. Ed. 2d 562 (1975).

Landmark in the Law

Marbury v. Madison (1803)

In the edifice of American law, the *Marbury v. Madison* decision in 1803 can be viewed as the keystone of the constitutional arch. The story is often told, and for a reason—it shows how seemingly insignificant cases can have important and enduring results.

Consider the facts behind *Marbury v. Madison.* John Adams had lost his bid for reelection to Thomas Jefferson in 1800. Adams, a Federalist, thought the Jeffersonian Republicans (the Anti-Federalists) would weaken the power of the national government by asserting states' rights. He also feared the Anti-Federalists' antipathy toward business. During the final hours of Adams's presidency, he worked feverishly to "pack" the judiciary with loyal Federalists by appointing what came to be called "midnight judges" just before Jefferson took office.

All of the judicial commissions had to be certified and delivered. The task of delivery fell on Adams's secretary of state, John Marshall. Out of fifty-nine midnight appointments, Marshall delivered only forty-two. He assumed that the remaining seventeen would be sent out by Jefferson's new secretary of state, James Madison. Of course, the new administration would not cooperate in packing the judiciary: Jefferson had Madison refuse to deliver the remaining commissions. William Marbury,

James Madison

along with three other Federalists to whom the commissions had not been delivered, decided to sue. The suit was brought directly to the Supreme Court. Marbury sought a writ of *mandamus* (an order directing a lower court or government official to fulfill a duty), as authorized by Section 13 of the Judiciary Act of 1789.

As fate would have it, the man who was in a sense responsible for the lawsuit, John Marshall, had stepped down as Adams's secretary of state only to become chief

---

There is a set of federal rules of procedure and various sets of rules for state courts. Procedural rules differ in criminal and civil cases.

We will now follow a hypothetical civil case through the state court system. The case involves an automobile accident in which Kevin Anderson, driving a Mercedes, struck Lisa Marconi, driving a Ford Taurus. The accident occurred at the intersection of Wilshire Boulevard and Rodeo Drive in Beverly Hills, California. Marconi suffered personal injuries, incurring medical and hospital expenses as well as lost wages for four months. Anderson and Marconi are unable to agree on a settlement, and Marconi sues Anderson. Marconi is the plaintiff and Anderson is the defendant. Both are represented by lawyers.

PLEADINGS
Statements by the plaintiff and the defendant that detail the facts, charges, and defenses. Modern rules simplify common law pleading, often requiring only the complaint, an answer, and sometimes a reply to the answer.

The Pleadings

The complaint and answer (and the counterclaim and reply)—all of which are discussed below—taken together are called the **pleadings.** The pleadings inform each party of the claims of the other and specify the issues (disputed questions) involved in the case. Pleadings remove the element of surprise from a case. They allow lawyers to gather the most persuasive evidence and to prepare better arguments, thus increasing the probability that a just and true result will be forthcoming from the trial.

justice of the Supreme Court. He was now in a position to decide the case for which he was responsible.[a] Marshall was faced with a dilemma: On the one hand, if he ordered the commissions delivered, the new secretary of state could simply refuse. The Court had no way to compel action because it had no police force. Also, Congress was controlled by the Jeffersonian Republicans (Anti-Federalists). It might impeach Marshall for such an action.[b] On the other hand, if Marshall simply allowed Secretary of State Madison to do as he wished, the Court's power would be severely eroded.

Marshall stated for the unanimous Court that Jefferson and Madison had acted incorrectly in refusing to deliver Marbury's commission. Marshall also stated, however, that the highest court did not have the power to issue a writ of *mandamus* in this particular case because the section of the law that gave it the power to do so was unconstitutional. The Judiciary Act of 1789 specified that the Supreme Court could issue writs of *mandamus* as part of its original jurisdiction, but Marshall pointed out that Article III of the Constitution, which spelled out the Supreme Court's original jurisdiction, did not mention writs of *mandamus*. In other words, Congress did not have the right to expand the Court's jurisdiction, so this section of the Judiciary Act of 1789 was unconstitutional and hence null and void.

The decision avoided a showdown between the Federalists and the Jeffersonian Republicans. The power of the Supreme Court was enlarged: "A law repugnant to the Constitution is void."

Was the Marshall Court's assumption of judicial review power justified by the Constitution? Whether it was or not, *Marbury v. Madison* confirmed a doctrine that was part of the legal tradition of the time. Indeed, judicial review was a major (although not articulated) premise upon which the movement to draft constitutions and bills of rights was ultimately based, and it was also part of the legal theory underlying the Revolution of 1776. During the decade before the adoption of the federal Constitution, cases in at least eight states involved the power of judicial review. Also, the Supreme Court had considered the constitutionality of an act of Congress in *Hylton v. United States*,[c] in which Congress's power to levy certain taxes was challenged. But because that particular act was ruled constitutional rather than unconstitutional, this first federal exercise of true judicial review was not clearly recognized as such.

In any event, because Marshall masterfully fashioned a decision that did not require anyone to do anything, there was no practical legal point to challenge. The decision still stands today as a judicial and political masterpiece.

a. Today, any justice who has been involved in the issue before the Court would probably disqualify himself or herself because of a conflict of interest.

b. In fact, Congress later did impeach Supreme Court Justice Samuel Chase, although he was not convicted. The charge was abusive behavior under the Sedition Act.

c. 3 U.S. (3 Dallas) 171, 1 L.Ed. 556 (1796).

Complaint and Summons Marconi's suit, or action, against Anderson commences when her lawyer files a **complaint** (sometimes called a petition or declaration) with the clerk of the trial court in the appropriate geographic area. In most states it will be a court having general jurisdiction; in others it may be a court having special jurisdiction with regard to subject matter. The complaint contains (1) a statement alleging the facts necessary for the court to take jurisdiction, (2) a short statement of the facts necessary to show that the plaintiff is entitled to a remedy, and (3) a statement of the remedy the plaintiff is seeking.

COMPLAINT
The pleading made by a plaintiff or a charge made by the state alleging wrongdoing on the part of the defendant.

The complaint in this case (shown in Exhibit 3–5) states that Marconi was driving her car through a green light at the specified intersection, exercising good driving habits and reasonable care, when Anderson carelessly drove his car through a red light and into the intersection from a cross street, striking Marconi and causing serious personal injury and property damage. The complaint goes on to state that she is entitled to $10,000 to cover medical bills, $9,000 to cover lost wages, and $5,000 to cover property damage to her car.[8]

8. For our purposes here, we will ignore the fact that, by California statute, this type of claim is now subject to mandatory arbitration.

Profile

John Marshall (1755–1835)

It is often said that John Marshall was probably the greatest chief justice ever to head the United States Supreme Court. During his thirty-four-year tenure as chief justice, he penned many decisions of lasting impact on American history and the American judicial system.

Marshall was born in 1755 in a log cabin on the Virginia frontier. He was the first of fifteen children born to Thomas Marshall, a descendant of Welsh immigrants, and his wife, who was the daughter of a Scottish clergyman. According to John Marshall, his father had only a "limited education," but in spite of this he educated his son as best he could in English literature and in Blackstone's *Commentaries on the Laws of England.* (The elder Marshall eventually became a member of the Virginia House of Burgesses and a landowner of some substance.) Apart from what he learned from his father, John Marshall's education was also limited—to two years of formal schooling. His legal education took even less time and consisted of six weeks of lectures given by George Wythe, America's first law professor, at the College of William and Mary. When he began practicing law six months after attending Wythe's lectures, Marshall's legal library consisted solely of notes he had taken while reading a borrowed copy of a legal text by Francis Bacon. Three years later he was elected to the Virginia legislature and eventually participated in Virginia's constitutional convention as one of the state's leading Federalists.

Chief Justice Marshall is most renowned for enunciating the doctrine of judicial review and for establishing the Supreme Court as the final arbiter and authority in matters concerning constitutional interpretation. Marshall first exercised the power of judicial review in *Marbury v. Madison*, discussed in this chapter's *Landmark in the Law*. This power was also expressed in later decisions by the Marshall Court, including *McCulloch v. Maryland* (1819),[a] which concerned the constitutionality of the Second National Bank of the United States. In this case, the central question before the Court was whether Congress had the power to establish a national bank, even though the Constitution did not specify any such power. In his decision, Marshall admitted that the power to establish a national bank was not expressed in the Constitution. In Article I, Section 8, of the Constitution, however, Congress was granted the general power "to make all laws which shall be necessary and proper" for carrying out "all other powers" vested in the national government. If establishing such a national bank aided the national government in the exercise of its designated powers, then the authority to set up such a bank was implied. To Marshall, the "necessary and proper" clause embraced "all means which are appropriate" to carry out "the legitimate ends" of the Constitution. The national bank was necessary to exercise governmental powers enumerated in the Constitution, and hence the Second Bank could not be declared unconstitutional. Marshall's decision was to have great significance for the American banking industry. Without it, the history of U.S. banking might have taken an entirely different course.

Other significant rulings by the Marshall Court include *Trustees of Dartmouth College v. Woodward* (see the *Landmark in the Law* in Chapter 26) and *Gibbons v. Ogden* (see the *Landmark in the Law* in Chapter 4). In these and other decisions, the Marshall Court, by refusing to hold the national government to the literal limits of its expressed powers, enabled the national government to grow and to meet problems that the framers of the Constitution could not have foreseen.

a. 17 U.S. (4 Wheat.) 316, 4 L.Ed. 579 (1819).

SUMMONS
A document informing a person that a legal action has been commenced against him or her and that he or she must appear in court on a certain date to respond.

After the complaint has been filed, the sheriff or a deputy of the county or other *process server* (one who delivers a complaint and summons) serves a **summons** and a copy of the complaint on defendant Anderson. The summons notifies Anderson that he is required to prepare an answer to the complaint and to file a copy of his answer with both the court and the plaintiff's attorney within a specified time period (usually twenty to thirty days after the summons has been served). The summons

◆ **Exhibit 3–5**
Example of a Typical Complaint

IN THE LOS ANGELES MUNICIPAL COURT
FOR THE LOS ANGELES JUDICIAL DISTRICT

CIVIL NO. 8–1026

Lisa Marconi
Plaintiff

v.

COMPLAINT

Kevin Anderson
Defendant

Comes now the plaintiff and for her cause of action against the defendant alleges and states as follows:

1. The jurisdiction of this court is based on Section 86 of the California Civil Code.

2. This action is between plaintiff, a California resident living at 1434 Palm Drive, Anaheim, California, and defendant, a California resident living at 6950 Garrison Avenue, Los Angeles, California.

3. On September 10, 1993, plaintiff, Lisa Marconi, was exercising good driving habits and reasonable care in driving her car through the intersection of Rodeo Drive and Wilshire Boulevard when defendant, Kevin Anderson, negligently drove his vehicle through a red light at the intersection and collided with plaintiff's vehicle. Defendant was negligent in the operation of the vehicle as to:

   a. Speed,
   b. Lookout,
   c. Management and control.

4. As a result of the collision plaintiff suffered severe physical injury that prevented her from working and property damage to her car. The costs she incurred included $10,000 in medical bills, $9,000 in lost wages, and $5,000 for automobile repairs.

WHEREFORE, plaintiff demands judgment against the defendant for the sum of $24,000 plus interest at the maximum legal rate and the costs of this action.

By ______________________________
Roger Harrington
Attorney for the Plaintiff
800 Orange Avenue
Anaheim, CA 91426

also informs Anderson that failure to answer will result in a **default judgment** for the plaintiff, meaning the plaintiff will be awarded the damages alleged in her complaint.

DEFAULT JUDGMENT
A judgment entered by a clerk or court against a party who has failed to appear in court to answer or defend against a claim that has been brought against him or her by another party.

Rules governing how a summons can be served vary, but usually the summons is handed to the defendant or is left at the defendant's residence or place of business. In a few states, a summons can be served by mail. When the defendant cannot be reached, special rules sometimes permit the summons to be left with a designated person, such as the secretary of state.

Choices Available after Receipt of the Summons and Complaint Once the defendant has been served with a copy of the summons and complaint, the defendant must respond by filing a pre-answer *motion to dismiss* or an *answer.* If a defendant does not respond, either by choice or for some other reason, the court may enter a default judgment against him or her.

MOTION TO DISMISS
A pleading in which a defendant admits the facts as alleged by the plaintiff but asserts that the plaintiff's claim fails to state a cause of action (that is, has no basis in law) or that there are other grounds on which a suit should be dismissed. Also called a demurrer.

Motion to Dismiss If the defendant challenges the sufficiency of the plaintiff's complaint, the defendant can present to the court a **motion to dismiss,** or *demurrer.* (The rules of civil procedure in many states do not use the term *demurrer;* they use only *motion to dismiss.*) The motion to dismiss is an allegation that even if the facts presented in the complaint are true, their legal consequences are such that there is no reason to go further with the suit and no need for the defendant to present an answer. It is a contention that the defendant is not legally liable even if the facts are as the plaintiff alleges. If, for example, Marconi's complaint alleges facts that exclude the possibility of negligence on Anderson's part, Anderson can move to dismiss. If his motion is granted, he will not be required to answer. By granting the motion to dismiss, the judge is saying that the plaintiff has failed to state a recognized cause of action. The plaintiff generally is given time to file an amended complaint. If the plaintiff does not file this amended complaint, a judgment will be entered against the plaintiff solely on the basis of the pleadings, and the plaintiff will not be allowed to bring suit on the matter again. If, however, the court denies the motion to dismiss, the judge is indicating that the plaintiff has stated a recognized cause of action, and the defendant is given an extension of time to file a further pleading. If the defendant does not do so, a judgment will normally be entered for the plaintiff.

In addition to a plaintiff's failure to state a claim on which relief can be granted, a defendant's pre-answer motion to dismiss may be based on the court's lack of subject matter or personal jurisdiction, improper venue, insufficiency of process or of service of process (delivery of the summons), and other specific reasons. The motion to dismiss is often used for purposes of delay.

If Marconi wishes to discontinue the suit because, for example, an out-of-court settlement has been reached, she can likewise move for dismissal. The court can also dismiss the case on its own motion.

ANSWER
Procedurally, a defendant's response to the complaint.

Answer and Counterclaim If the defendant has not chosen to file a motion to dismiss or has filed a motion to dismiss that has been denied, then he or she must file an **answer.** This document either admits the statements or allegations set forth in the complaint or denies them and outlines any defenses that the defendant may have. If Anderson admits to all of Marconi's allegations in his answer, the court will enter a judgment for Marconi. If Anderson denies Marconi's allegations, the matter will proceed to trial.

COUNTERCLAIM
A claim made by a defendant in a civil lawsuit that in effect sues the plaintiff; it can be based on entirely different grounds than those given in the plaintiff's complaint.

Anderson can deny Marconi's allegations and set forth his own claim that Marconi was in fact negligent and therefore owes him money for damages to his Mercedes. This is appropriately called a **counterclaim.** If Anderson files a counterclaim, Marconi will have to answer it with a pleading, normally called a **reply,** which has the same characteristics as an answer.

REPLY
Procedurally, a plaintiff's response to a defendant's answer.

AFFIRMATIVE DEFENSE
A response to a plaintiff's claim that does not deny the plaintiff's facts but attacks the plaintiff's legal right to bring an action. An example is the running of the statute of limitations.

Answer and Affirmative Defenses Anderson can also admit the truth of Marconi's complaint but raise new facts that may result in dismissal of the action. This is called raising an **affirmative defense.** For example, Anderson could admit that he was negligent but plead that the time period for raising the claim has passed and that Marconi's complaint must therefore be dismissed because it is barred by the statute of limitations (a statutory limit to the time during which one can raise a claim).

Dismissals and Judgments before Trial

There are numerous procedural avenues for disposing of a case without a trial. Many of them involve one or the other party's attempts to get the case dismissed through the use of pretrial motions. We have already mentioned the motion to dismiss, or demurrer. Other important pretrial motions are the motion for a judgment on the pleadings and the motion for summary judgment.

Motion for Judgment on the Pleadings After the pleadings are closed—after the complaint, answer, and any counterclaim and reply have been filed—either of the parties can file a *motion for a judgment on the pleadings*, or on the merits of the case. This motion may be used when no facts are disputed and, thus, only questions of law are at issue. The difference between this motion and a motion for summary judgment, discussed below, is that the party requesting the motion may support a motion for summary judgment with sworn statements and other materials; but on a motion for a judgment on the pleadings, a court may consider only those facts pleaded.

Motion for Summary Judgment A lawsuit can be shortened or a trial can be avoided if there are no disagreements about the facts in a case and the only question is which laws apply to those facts. Both sides can agree to the facts and ask the judge to apply the law to them. In this situation, it is appropriate for either party to move for **summary judgment.** When the court considers a motion for summary judgment, it can take into account evidence outside the pleadings. The evidence may consist of sworn statements (affidavits) by parties or witnesses, as well as documents, such as a contract. As mentioned, the use of this additional evidence distinguishes the motion for summary judgment from the motion to dismiss and from the motion for judgment on the pleadings.

SUMMARY JUDGMENT
A judgment entered by a trial court prior to trial that is based on the valid assertion by one of the parties that there are no disputed issues of fact that would necessitate a trial.

A motion for summary judgment will be granted only when there are no genuine *questions of fact* (which may be decided by a judge or jury) and the only question is a *question of law* (on which only a judge, not a jury, can rule). Motions for summary judgment can be made before or during a trial, but they will be granted only if it is clear that there are no factual disputes.

Judges sometimes disagree on what constitutes a question of fact and therefore on whether summary judgment is appropriate in a given case. The following case illustrates this point.

Case 3.2
PEOPLES RESTAURANT v. SABO

Supreme Court of Florida, 1991.
591 So.2d 907.

HISTORICAL AND SOCIAL SETTING *Motions to dismiss and motions for judgment on the pleadings existed before motions for summary judgment. In making a motion to dismiss or a motion for judgment on the pleadings, a party cannot introduce outside evidence. Thus, any challenge to the truth of a pleading in response to one of the motions can require a trial, even when there is no genuine dispute and it only appears from the pleadings that there is. In the nineteenth century, courts came to realize that they could save time if facts could be established without a trial. Different courts tried different rules to circumvent the prohibition against admitting outside evidence on a motion to dismiss or a motion for judgment on the pleadings. Over time, most jurisdictions adopted the motion for summary judgment to determine whether an issue included in the pleadings is really in dispute.*

FACTS Mary Sabo suffered injuries in an automobile accident caused by Daniel Hoag, an intoxicated driver. Hoag had just left Peoples Restaurant after having consumed a large number of drinks. Sabo sued Peoples for damages, alleging that the restaurant had violated a state statute that provided that any person who "knowingly serves" an individual who is "habitually addicted" to alcohol may be held liable for any injuries or damages caused by the intoxication of that individual. In spite of evidence indicating that for the two years prior to the accident, Hoag had gone to Peoples twice a week and on each occasion had drunk liquor until he was intoxicated, the trial court granted Peoples' motion for summary judgment. The court held that Sabo had failed to show that Peoples had knowledge that Hoag was an alcoholic and the bar had therefore not "knowingly" served an alcohol addict. Sabo appealed. The appellate court reversed the trial court's ruling, and Peoples appealed the case to the Supreme Court of Florida.

Case 3.2—Continued

ISSUE Was summary judgment for Peoples appropriate in this case?

DECISION No. The Florida Supreme Court affirmed the appellate court's decision. The evidence was sufficient to indicate that it was a question of fact whether the bar knew that Hoag was an alcoholic. Therefore, summary judgment was inappropriate, and the case should proceed to trial.

REASON The court's one-page opinion in this case was mostly a summary of Hoag's drinking habits. Hoag had testified that over the two-year period prior to the accident, he (1) normally consumed a case of beer during the day while on his construction job; (2) drank hard liquor every evening at various bars; (3) went to Peoples twice a week, becoming overtly intoxicated on each occasion (exhibiting slurred speech, red eyes, and unsteady appearance); and (4) was well known to the bartenders at Peoples, who never refused to serve him on any occasion. Hoag stated that on the night of the accident, he had been served the equivalent of twenty shots of hard liquor and was so intoxicated that he did not recall leaving the bar, eating dinner, or much about the accident. Given this record, the court concluded that "the circumstantial evidence adduced [pointed out] was sufficient to permit a jury to find that the employees of Peoples knew of Hoag's addiction, based on his repeated behavior and appearance."

Discovery

Before a trial begins, the parties can use a number of procedural devices to obtain information and gather evidence about the case. Marconi, for example, will want to know how fast Anderson was driving, whether he had been drinking, whether he saw the red light, and so on. The process of obtaining information from the opposing party or from other witnesses is known as **discovery.**

DISCOVERY
A method by which opposing parties may obtain information from each other to prepare for trial. Generally governed by rules of procedure, but may be controlled by the court.

The federal rules of civil procedure and similar rules in the states set forth the guidelines for discovery activity. Discovery includes gaining access to witnesses, documents, records, and other types of evidence. The rules governing discovery are designed to make sure that a witness or a party is not unduly harassed, that privileged material (communications that need not be presented in court) is safeguarded, and that only matters relevant to the case at hand are discoverable.

Discovery prevents surprises by giving parties access to evidence that might otherwise be hidden. This allows both parties to learn as much as they can about what to expect at a trial before they reach the courtroom. It also serves to narrow the issues so that trial time is spent on the main questions in the case. Currently, the trend is toward allowing more discovery and thus fewer surprises.

DEPOSITION
A generic term that refers to any evidence verified by oath. As a legal term, it is often limited to the testimony of a witness taken under oath before a trial, with the opportunity of cross-examination.

Depositions and Interrogatories Discovery can involve the use of depositions or interrogatories, or both. **Depositions** are sworn testimony by a party to the lawsuit or any witness, recorded by an authorized court official. The person deposed gives sworn testimony under oath and answers questions asked by the attorneys from both sides. The questions and answers are taken down, sworn to, and signed. These answers will, of course, help the attorneys prepare their cases. They can also be used in court to impeach a party or a witness who changes testimony at the trial. In addition, they can be used as testimony if the witness is not available at trial. Lawyers from both sides can prepare for depositions with written questions ahead of time.

INTERROGATORIES
A series of written questions for which written answers are prepared and then signed under oath by a party to a lawsuit (the plaintiff or the defendant).

Interrogatories are a series of written questions for which written answers are prepared and then signed under oath. The main difference between interrogatories and depositions with written questions is that interrogatories are directed to a party to the lawsuit (the plaintiff or the defendant), not to a witness, and the party can prepare answers with the aid of an attorney. The scope of interrogatories is broader because parties are obligated to answer questions, even if it means disclosing information from their records and files.

Other Information A party can serve a written request to the other party for an admission of the truth of matters relating to the trial. Any matter admitted under such a request is conclusively established for the trial. For example, Marconi can ask Anderson to admit that he was driving at a speed of forty-five miles an hour. A request for admission saves time at trial because parties will not have to spend time proving facts on which they already agree.

A party can also gain access to documents and other items not in his or her possession in order to inspect and examine them. Likewise, a party can gain "entry upon land" to inspect the premises. Anderson's attorney, for example, normally can gain permission to inspect and duplicate Marconi's repair bills.

When the physical or mental condition of one party is in question, the opposing party can ask the court to order a physical or mental examination. If the court is willing to make the order, the opposing party can obtain the results of the examination. It is important to note that the court will make such an order only when the need for the information outweighs the right to privacy of the person to be examined.

Compliance with Discovery Requests If a party refuses to cooperate with requests made by the opposing party during discovery, the court may compel the party to comply with the requests by a specific date. If the party still does not comply, he or she may be held in contempt of court and, as a consequence, may be fined or imprisoned and required to pay the opposing party's resulting expenses. If a party blatantly disregards the discovery process, the court might even enter a default judgment for the opposing party. The courts rarely use the latter sanction, however, because it would deprive a litigant of the right to be heard in court.

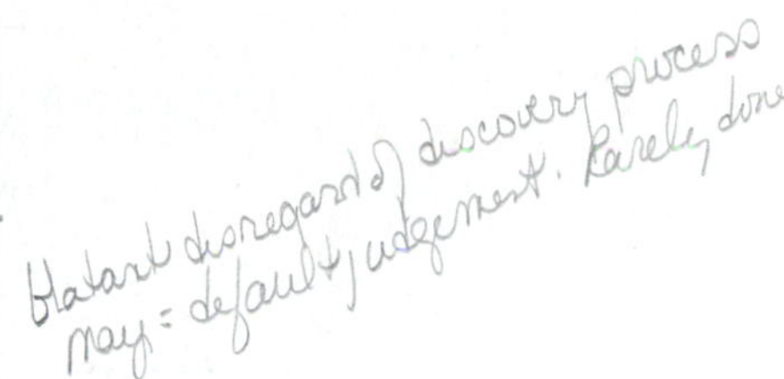

Pretrial Hearing

Either party or the court can request a pretrial conference, or hearing. Usually the hearing consists of an informal discussion between the judge and the opposing attorneys after discovery has taken place. The purpose of the hearing is to identify the matters that are in dispute and to plan the course of the trial. The pretrial hearing is not intended to compel the parties to settle their case before trial, although judges may encourage them to settle out of court if circumstances suggest that a trial would be a waste of time.

The Right to a Jury Trial

A trial can be held with or without a jury. If there is no jury, the judge determines the truth of the facts alleged in the case. The Seventh Amendment to the U.S. Constitution guarantees the right to a jury trial for cases at law in federal courts when the amount in controversy exceeds $20. Most states have similar guarantees in their own constitutions, although many states put a higher minimum-dollar-amount restriction on the guarantee. For example, Iowa requires the dollar amount of damages to be at least $1,000 before there is a right to a jury trial. The right to a trial by jury does not have to be exercised, and many cases are tried without a jury. In most states and in federal courts, one of the parties must request a jury or the right is presumed to be waived.

Note that there are two types of juries: the ordinary ("petit," or small) jury and the grand jury. The latter is called "grand" because it consists of a greater number of jurors than the ordinary trial jury. A grand jury does not determine the guilt or innocence of an accused party; rather, its function is to determine, after hearing the state's evidence, whether a reasonable basis, or **probable cause,** exists for supposing that a crime has been committed and whether a trial ought to be held. If the jury finds probable cause, it will return a "bill of indictment"; if no probable cause is found, it will return "no bill."

PROBABLE CAUSE
Reasonable grounds to believe the existence of facts warranting certain actions, such as the search or arrest of a person.

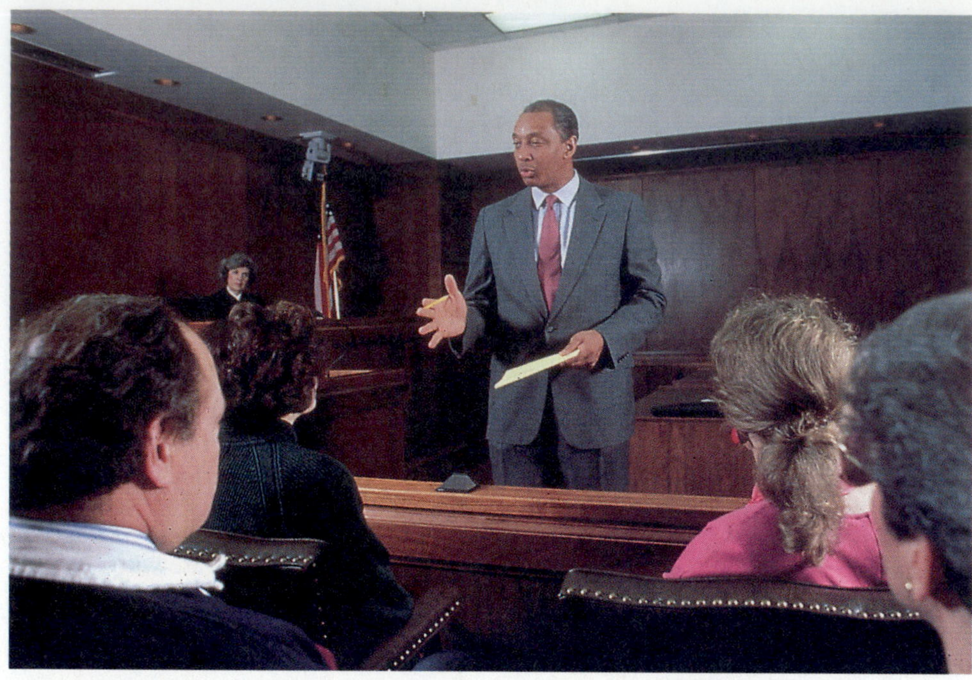

During which parts of a typical trial do attorneys address the jury?

Jury Selection

Prior to the commencement of any jury trial, a jury must be selected. The process by which the jury is selected is known as ***voir dire*** (a French phrase meaning "to speak the truth"). In most jurisdictions, the *voir dire* consists of oral questions that attorneys for the plaintiff and the defendant ask a group of prospective jurors (one at a time) to determine whether a potential jury member is biased or has any connection with a party to the action or with a prospective witness. Some trial attorneys go so far as to use psychologists to help them pick juries. During *voir dire*, a party may challenge a certain number of prospective jurors *peremptorily*—that is, ask that an individual not be sworn in as a juror without providing any reason. Alternatively, a party may challenge a prospective juror *for cause*—that is, provide a reason why an individual should not be sworn in as a juror. If the judge grants the challenge, the individual is asked to step down.

"A fox should not be of the jury at a goose's trial."

Proverb

VOIR DIRE
From the French, meaning "to speak the truth." A phrase denoting the preliminary questions that attorneys for the plaintiff and the defendant ask prospective jurors to determine whether potential jury members are biased or have any connection with a party to the action or with a prospective witness.

At the Trial

At the trial, both attorneys are allowed to make opening statements concerning the facts that they expect to prove during the trial, with the plaintiff's lawyer going first. Because Marconi is the plaintiff, she has the burden of proving that her case is correct. Marconi's attorney begins by calling the first witness for the plaintiff and examining (questioning) the witness. (For both attorneys, the type of question and the manner of asking are governed by the rules of evidence.) This questioning is called **direct examination.** After Marconi's attorney is finished, the witness is subject to **cross-examination** by Anderson's attorney. Then Marconi's attorney has another opportunity to question the witness in *redirect examination,* and Anderson's attorney can follow with *recross-examination.* When both attorneys have finished with the first witness, Marconi's attorney calls the succeeding witnesses in the plaintiff's case, each of whom is subject to cross-examination (and redirect and recross, if necessary).

At the conclusion of the plaintiff's case, the defendant's attorney has the opportunity to ask the judge to direct a verdict for the defendant on the ground that the plaintiff has presented no evidence that would justify the granting of the plaintiff's remedy. This is called a motion for a **directed verdict** (federal courts use the term *judgment as a matter of law* instead of *directed verdict*). In considering the motion, the judge looks at the evidence in the light most favorable to the plaintiff and grants

DIRECT EXAMINATION
The examination of a witness by the attorney who calls the witness to the stand to testify on behalf of the attorney's client.

CROSS-EXAMINATION
The questioning of an opposing witness during the trial.

DIRECTED VERDICT
A verdict in which the judge takes the decision out of the hands of the jury.

the motion only if there is insufficient evidence to raise an issue of fact. (Motions for directed verdicts at this stage of trial are seldom granted.)

The defendant's attorney then presents the evidence and witnesses for the defendant's case. Witnesses are called and examined (questioned) by the defendant's attorney. The plaintiff's attorney has the right to cross-examine them, and there is a redirect and a recross-examination, if necessary. At the end of the defendant's case, either attorney can move for a directed verdict, and the test again is whether the jury can, through any reasonable interpretation of the evidence, find for the party against whom the motion is made.

After the defendant's attorney has finished presenting evidence, the plaintiff's attorney can present a **rebuttal**, which includes additional evidence to refute the defendant's case. The defendant's attorney can meet that evidence in a **rejoinder.** After both sides have rested their cases, each attorney presents a **closing argument,** with the plaintiff's lawyer going first. In their closing arguments, the two opposing attorneys urge a verdict in favor of their respective clients. The judge instructs the jury (assuming it is a jury trial) in the law that applies to the case. The instructions to the jury are often called *charges.* Then the jury retires to the jury room to deliberate a verdict. In the Marconi-Anderson case, the jury will not only decide for the plaintiff or for the defendant but, if it finds for the plaintiff, will also decide on the amount of money to be paid to her.

"Proceed. You have my biased attention."

Learned Hand, 1872–1961
(American jurist)

REBUTTAL
The refutation of evidence introduced by an adverse party's attorney.

REJOINDER
The defendant's answer to the plaintiff's rebuttal.

CLOSING ARGUMENT
An argument made after the plaintiff and defendant have rested their cases. Closing arguments are made prior to the jury charges.

After the Trial

After the jury has rendered its verdict, either party may make a prejudgment or posttrial motion.

Motion for New Trial At the end of the trial, a motion can be made to set aside an adverse verdict and any judgment and to hold a new trial. The motion will be granted if the judge is convinced, after looking at all the evidence, that the jury was in error but does not feel it is appropriate to grant judgment for the other side. This will usually occur when the jury verdict is the obvious result of a misapplication of the law or misunderstanding of the evidence. A new trial can also be granted on the grounds of newly discovered evidence, misconduct by the participants or the jury[9] during the trial, or error by the judge. In the following case, a juror's inattentiveness to *voir dire* proceedings was held to constitute juror misconduct.

Case 3.3
HUMMEL v. GAINESVILLE RADIOLOGY GROUP, P.C.
Court of Appeals of Georgia, 1992.
205 Ga.App. 157,
421 S.E.2d 333.

HISTORICAL AND SOCIAL SETTING *The jury system used in our courts today originated in medieval England with the desire to take potentially oppressive power from the government and place it in the hands of the people. The right to a trial by jury has traditionally been held to be one of the most important constitutional rights of Americans, and the law makes it difficult to challenge a jury's decision. But jurors can sometimes err, and they sometimes engage in misconduct, knowingly or negligently. When a party to a lawsuit requests a new trial because of juror misconduct, it is up to the judge to decide whether the jurors' actions were improper or permissible.*

FACTS Ms. Hummel sued Dr. James Strittmatter and his professional corporation, the Gainesville Radiology Group, P.C. ("the Group"), for medical malpractice. Hummel alleged that the Group was negligent in failing to timely diagnose her breast cancer after a mammogram examination. During *voir dire,* jurors were asked if any of them had family members who had been diagnosed with breast can-

9. Recently, the loser in a medical malpractice suit filed a motion for a new trial on the ground that jurors were improperly influenced by an episode of the television show "L.A. Law" that aired the day before the jury decided the case.

Case 3.3—Continued

cer or other forms of cancer, how the cancer had been diagnosed, and whether there had been any recurrence. One juror made no response, but it was later discovered that the juror's wife had died of breast cancer some years before. When the trial court jury returned a verdict for the Group, Hummel moved for a new trial on the ground that the juror had violated his oath and failed to disclose pertinent information during *voir dire.* In opposing the motion, the Group submitted an affidavit signed by the juror in which the juror averred that he had not answered the question because he had not heard it and that the cause of his wife's death had not influenced his judgment in the case. The trial court denied the motion, holding that the juror's "inadvertent" failure to respond to a question during *voir dire* did not "rise to the level of juror misconduct which would require the grant of a new trial." Hummel appealed.

ISSUE Did the juror's failure to hear the question about cancer constitute juror misconduct to the extent that Hummel's motion for a new trial should have been granted?

DECISION Yes. The appellate court held that the juror's failure to hear the question violated the juror's duty to be attentive during *voir dire* proceedings. The trial court's decision was thus reversed.

REASON The court stressed how important it was for jurors to respond truthfully to questions asked of them during *voir dire*. If a litigant cannot depend on jurors to answer questions truthfully, "then he cannot be certain he is getting a fair, just, and impartial trial as guaranteed by the Constitution." The court went on to state that it is just as important for jurors to tell the truth as it is for trial witnesses to tell the truth and that a "failure to respond is tantamount to giving an untruthful answer." Noting that the *voir dire* questions regarding cancer filled sixteen pages of the trial transcript, the court concluded that "in view of all the conversation that transpired between counsel and the other jurors" on the issue of cancer, the juror's claim not to have heard the question "amounts to an admission that he was grossly inattentive to the whole *voir dire* process."

JUDGMENT N.O.V.
A judgment notwithstanding the verdict; may be entered by the court for the plaintiff (or the defendant) after there has been a jury verdict for the defendant (or the plaintiff).

Judgment N.O.V. If Marconi wins, and if Anderson's attorney has previously moved for a directed verdict, Anderson's attorney can now make a motion for a **judgment *n.o.v.*** (from the Latin, *non obstante veredicto,* "notwithstanding the verdict"; federal courts use the term *judgment as a matter of law* instead of *judgment n.o.v.*). The standards for granting a judgment *n.o.v.* are the same as those for granting a motion to dismiss or a motion for a directed verdict. Assume here that this motion is denied and that Anderson appeals the case. (If Marconi wins but receives a smaller money award than she sought, she can appeal also.) These events are illustrated in Exhibit 3–6.

The Appeal A notice of appeal must be filed with the clerk of the trial court within the prescribed time. Anderson then becomes the appellant, or petitioner. His attorney files in the reviewing court (usually an intermediate court of appeals) the record on appeal, which contains the following: (1) the pleadings, (2) a transcript of the trial testimony and copies of the exhibits, (3) the judge's rulings on motions made by the parties, (4) the arguments of counsel, (5) the instructions to the jury, (6) the verdict, (7) the posttrial or prejudgment motions, and (8) the judgment order from which the appeal is taken. Anderson may also be required to post a bond for the appeal.

BRIEF
A written summary or statement prepared by one side in a lawsuit to explain its case to the judge; a typical brief has a facts summary, a law summary, and an argument about how the law applies to the facts.

Anderson's attorney is required to prepare a condensation of the record, known as an abstract. The abstract and the **brief** are filed with the reviewing court. The brief contains (1) a short statement of the facts, (2) a statement of the issues, (3) the rulings by the trial court that Anderson contends are erroneous and prejudicial (biased in favor of one of the parties), (4) the grounds for reversal of the judgment, (5) a statement of the applicable law, and (6) arguments on Anderson's behalf, citing applicable statutes and relevant cases as precedents. The attorney for the appellee, or respondent, Marconi, usually files an answering brief. Anderson's attorney can file a reply, although it is not required. The reviewing court then considers the case.

A court of appeals does not hear any evidence. Its decision concerning a case is based on the abstracts, the record, and the briefs. The attorneys can present oral

Law in the Extreme

Confusion in the Court

In contrast to judges and lawyers, juries rarely come under the pen strokes of caustic caricaturists, cartoonists, or jokesters. In fact, jurors are generally the most respected participants in our legal system. They are not in court for monetary reasons (although they are nominally compensated for their time), nor will their careers be affected by the outcome of the case. They are in court merely to serve their legally required duty to society. Jurors also inject an element of "reality" into legal proceedings. They come from all walks of life, speak plain language, and usually apply common sense to the issues before them. But precisely because of these special and diverse qualities of jurors, communication problems between judges and jurors sometimes arise, which may lead to unpredictable responses. For example, in one case, a judge instructed the jurors that the "foreperson" should sign the jury form. In doing their best to comply with these instructions, "four persons" signed the form. (After this case, the progressive judge returned to his use of the term "foreman.")

More significant, though, are those cases in which the jurors return a verdict that is totally at odds with the law, which usually means that the case will be retried. Consider, for example, the verdict returned by a jury in a recent case.[a] The case involved a dispute between the buyer and the seller of some property located in West Palm Beach, Florida. The dispute apparently arose over mistaken assumptions about the nature of performance under the contract. The seller eventually sued the buyer, claiming that the buyer had breached the contract (not performed the contract as promised).

Recall from Chapter 1 that two types of remedies are granted by courts: remedies at law (damages) and remedies in equity (including rescission). A principle long followed by the courts is that an equitable remedy will be granted only if a plaintiff has no adequate remedy at law. For example, if a plaintiff is not awarded damages for breach of contract, or if money damages would not suffice to "cure" the problem, the court might grant the equitable remedy of rescission, which would involve returning the parties to the positions they held prior to the contract's formation. The seller, for example, would be required to return to the buyer all of the money received for the property, and so on. One of the grounds for rescinding a contract is the contract's failure to reflect the true intention of the parties because of mistaken assumptions about the nature of the performance called for under the contract. Keep this distinction between legal and equitable remedies in mind as you consider the jury verdict in the case discussed here.

Essentially, the questions put to the jury can be summarized as follows: First, did either party breach the contract, and if so, what amount of damages should be awarded to the nonbreaching party? Second, if neither party breached an essential term of the contract, should the contract simply be rescinded (canceled) on the basis of mistake? In responding to these questions, the jury first decided that the buyer had breached the contract and awarded the seller $17,000 in damages. But the jury did not stop there. It also held that the contract was rescinded, or canceled, on the basis of mistake. In short, the buyer breached a nonexistent contract!

a. *Chabad House–Lubavitch of Palm Beach County, Inc. v. Banks*, 602 So.2d 670 (Fla.App. 1992).

◆ Exhibit 3–6 A Typical Lawsuit

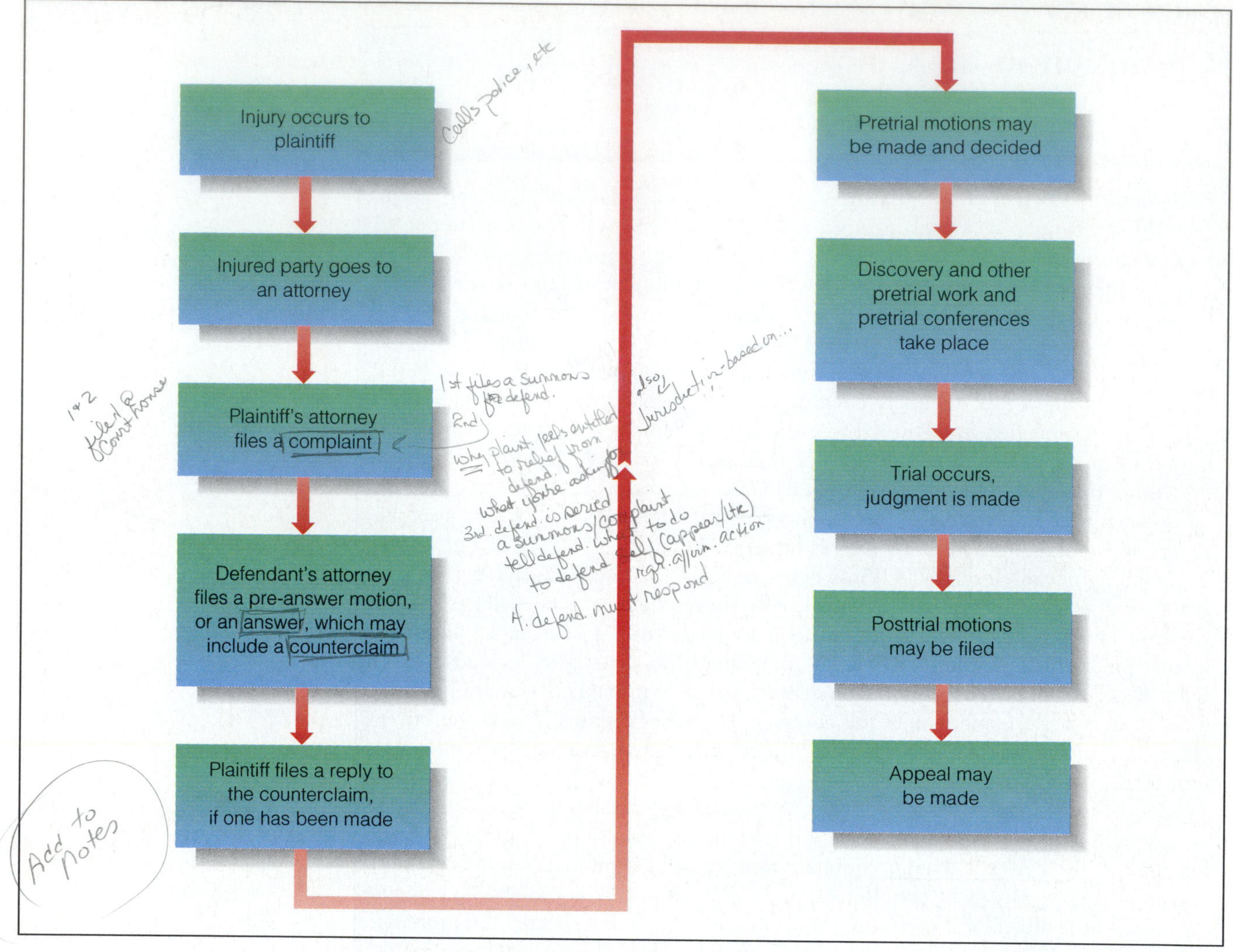

arguments, after which the case is taken under advisement. In general, the appellate courts do not reverse findings of fact unless the findings are unsupported or contradicted by the evidence. Rather, they review the record for errors of law. If the reviewing court believes that an error was committed during the trial or that the jury was improperly instructed, the judgment will be *reversed.* Sometimes the case will be *remanded* (sent back to the court that originally heard the case) for a new trial. In most cases, the judgment of the lower court is *affirmed,* resulting in the enforcement of the court's judgment or decree.

If the reviewing court is an intermediate appellate court, the losing party normally may appeal to the state supreme court. Such a petition corresponds to a petition for a writ of *certiorari* in the United States Supreme Court. If the petition is granted, new briefs must be filed before the state supreme court, and the attorneys may be allowed or requested to present oral arguments. Like the intermediate appellate courts, the supreme court may reverse or affirm the appellate court's decision or remand the case. At this point, unless a federal question is at issue, the case has reached its end.

It is important to note that most disputes are settled out of court, mainly because of the time and expense of trying a case. Of those cases that go to trial, about 97 percent are permanently resolved at the trial level, as relatively few trial court decisions are changed on appeal.

Business Law in Action

High Tech in the Courtroom

Imagine this courtroom scene: Computer beeps and the hum of electronic equipment fill the air. Connecting cables snake along the floor to connect a number of computers, videodisc monitors, and other video display equipment. While a witness is testifying, a lawyer directs arrow movement on a screen to focus the judge's and jury's attention on certain portions of a computerized display. Sections of images or text are magnified for clarity. The attorney later calls the court's attention to certain words or design elements on a monitor by highlighting those areas with a red dot of light. Counsel for the other party uses a laser videodisc system that features a menu of bar codes resembling those found on product labels. By waving a wand over the bar code for a desired display, the lawyer can call up the display on the screens.

This scene is not from a futuristic novel but from a federal courtroom in New Jersey in 1992. In a complicated trial featuring more than six thousand graphs, reports, and other exhibits, Honeywell, Inc., was trying to convince the court that Minolta Camera Company had infringed upon Honeywell's patent rights in lenses for autofocus cameras.[a] Clearly, today's courtrooms are entering the high-tech age.

"Before counsel make their final summations, we're going to take some calls from across the country."

Videotaped Trials

The courts took their first step into the video age when the United States Supreme Court acknowledged the right of state courts to experiment with courtroom cameras in its decision in *Chandler v. Florida* in 1981.[b]

Today, all but a few states allow video cameras to be used in their courtrooms, and in addition to television coverage of trials provided by the news networks, the new Court Television channel now offers its viewers gavel-to-gavel coverage of selected trials. In some courts, videotapes are used as the official trial reports. In most of the courts in Kentucky, for example, videotapes have replaced court-reporting services. Some federal courts are also creating official videotapes of their trials in an experiment closely monitored by federal judicial administrators.

The use of videotapes as official trial reports has some interesting implications. For one thing, videotapes of trials capture more accurately what transpired in the courtroom and sometimes record details that might have escaped notice during the trial itself. In one case, for example, the videotape recorded a conversation between a judge and a juror in which the juror revealed that she had discussed the substance of the trial with her husband, in violation of the juror's duty not to discuss the case with anyone but the other jurors. This exchange went unnoticed by the attorneys for both parties and was only discovered when the plaintiff's attorney was later reviewing the tape in the course of preparing for an appeal. The Kentucky Supreme Court ruled that the case be retried because of the juror's misconduct.[c]

a. *Honeywell, Inc. v. Minolta Camera Co.*, 1991 WL 50063 (D.N.J. 1991).

b. *Chandler v. Florida*, 449 U.S. 560, 101 S.Ct. 802, 66 L.Ed.2d 740 (1981).

c. *Deemer v. Finger*, 817 S.W.2d 435 (Ky. 1991).

Business Law in Action—Continued

Videotapes also allow appellate court judges to observe the "body language" of trial participants. The reviewing court is then in a position to evaluate not only the credibility of witnesses but also the trial judge's attitudes. A judge may express bias, for example, through gestures and other expressions that would not be evident in a written transcript. In one case, the video revealed that the trial court judge had left the bench when a witness was testifying. The attorney examining the witness did not notice this because his back was turned. So far, however, the use of official videotaped reports has not significantly altered the number of cases affirmed or reversed at the appellate level.

New Forms of Evidence

Video displays are also increasingly being used as evidence in the courtroom. A recent and controversial development is the use of "day in the life" videos—videos created by injured plaintiffs who want juries to know what it is like to live with a certain type of injury or disability. Defendants regard such tapes as little more than a "parade of horribles" manufactured to sway juries. Generally, courts have required plaintiffs to allow defendants to monitor the filming or editing of such tapes during discovery to ensure that the tapes do not exaggerate the plaintiffs' difficulties.[d] In addition to these types of videos, computer simulations and animations are used to visually recreate events. In some trials, these displays can almost make a case by themselves. For example, the defendants in one case presented a computer simulation of a hotel fire to "prove" their claim. The fire, which killed ninety-eight people and injured more than a hundred others, occurred in the DuPont Plaza Hotel in Puerto Rico in 1986.[e] A class-action suit was brought against a number of firms that had been involved in the hotel's construction, including the maker of some platforms that had been stored outside the ballroom in which the victims died. The simulation showed that the temperatures inside the rooms were so high that the outside platforms were of no significance.

d. In a controversial ruling, the Supreme Court of Illinois recently held that a video depicting a typical day in the life of a brain-damaged infant did not have to be subjected to more stringent discovery guidelines than other types of evidence [*Cisarik v. Palos Community Hospital*, 144 Ill.2d 339, 579 N.E.2d 873 (1992)].

e. See *In re San Juan DuPont Plaza Hotel Fire Litigation*, 907 F.2d 4 (1st Cir. 1990). See also William M. Bulkeley, "More Lawyers Use Animation to Sway Juries," *Wall Street Journal*, August 8, 1992, p. B1.

❖ Alternative Dispute Resolution

DOCKET
The list of cases entered on a court's calendar and thus scheduled to be heard by the court.

ALTERNATIVE DISPUTE RESOLUTION (ADR)
The resolution of disputes in ways other than those involved in the traditional judicial process. Mediation and arbitration are forms of ADR.

NEGOTIATION
A form of alternative dispute resolution by which the parties informally meet and by themselves resolve their dispute.

CONCILIATION
A form of alternative dispute resolution in which the parties reach an agreement themselves with the help of a neutral third party, called a conciliator, who facilitates the negotiations.

Because the number of court cases filling the **dockets** (court schedules listing the cases to be heard) grows every year and the cost of litigation continues to increase, more and more businesspersons, consumers, and others are turning to **alternative dispute resolution (ADR)** as an alternative to civil lawsuits. Methods of ADR range from neighbors sitting down over a cup of coffee to work out their differences to huge multinational corporations agreeing to resolve a dispute through a formal hearing before a panel of experts. In the following sections, we look at the numerous methods employed for settling disputes outside the court system.

Negotiation, Conciliation, and Mediation

Negotiation is one alternative means of resolving disputes. In the process of negotiation, the parties come together informally, with or without attorneys to represent them. Within this informal setting, the parties air their differences and try to reach a settlement or resolution without the involvement of independent third parties. Because no third parties are involved and because of the informal setting, negotiation is the simplest form of ADR.

Disputes may also be resolved in a friendly, nonantagonistic manner through **conciliation,** in which a third party assists the parties to a dispute in reconciling their differences. The conciliator helps to schedule negotiating sessions and carries offers back and forth between the parties when they refuse to face each other in direct negotiations. Technically, conciliators are not to recommend solutions. In practice, however, they often do. In contrast, a mediator is expected to propose solutions.

In the **mediation** process, the parties themselves must reach an agreement with the assistance of a mediator. The parties may select the mediator on the basis of expertise in a particular field or on the basis of the person's reputation for fairness and impartiality. The mediator may be a volunteer from the community and need not be a lawyer. Usually, a mediator will charge a fee for his or her services (which can be split between the parties).

MEDIATION
A method of settling disputes outside of court by using the services of a neutral third party, who acts as a communicating agent between the parties; a method of dispute settlement that is less formal than arbitration.

In mediation, the mediator talks face to face with the parties and allows them to discuss their disagreement in an informal atmosphere, such as a community center, church, or neighbor's home. There are few procedural rules, certainly fewer than in a courtroom. In fact, most mediation programs discourage lawyers from participating, and thus legal terminology is frequently avoided. Mediation often results in disputes being settled quickly. Initial meetings between the parties and the mediator often occur within several weeks after a voluntary request to mediate has been made by one or both parties.

Arbitration

A more formal method of alternative dispute resolution is **arbitration.** The key difference between arbitration and the forms of ADR just discussed is that in negotiation, conciliation, and mediation, the parties themselves settle their dispute, although a third party may assist them in doing so. In arbitration, the third party hearing the dispute normally makes a legally binding decision by which both parties must abide.[10] In a sense, the arbitrator becomes a private judge, even though the arbitrator does not have to be a lawyer. Frequently, a panel of experts arbitrates the dispute.

ARBITRATION
The settling of a dispute by submitting it to a disinterested third party (other than a court), who renders a legally binding decision.

Virtually any commercial matter can be submitted to arbitration. When a dispute arises, parties can agree to settle their differences through arbitration rather than through the court system. Frequently, however, disputes are arbitrated because of an **arbitration clause** in a contract entered into before the dispute arose. An arbitration clause provides that any disputes arising under the contract will be resolved by arbitration.

ARBITRATION CLAUSE
A clause in a contract that provides that, in case of a dispute, the parties will determine their rights by arbitration rather than through the judicial system.

The Arbitration Process The first step in the arbitration process is *submission*, which occurs when the parties agree to submit their dispute for arbitration. (If an arbitration clause is included in a contract, the clause itself is the submission to arbitration.) Most states require that an agreement to submit a dispute be in writing. The agreement typically identifies the parties, the nature of the dispute to be resolved, the monetary amounts involved in the dispute, the place of arbitration, and the powers that the arbitrator will exercise; frequently, the agreement includes a signed statement that the parties intend to be bound by the arbitrator's decision. The parties may agree to submit questions of fact, questions of law, or both to the arbitrator and may even agree to leave the interpretation of the arbitration agreement to the arbitrator.

The next step in the process is the *hearing*. The arbitrator may be given power at the beginning of the process to establish rules that will govern the proceedings. Typically, these rules are much less restrictive than those governing formal litigation. Regardless of who establishes the rules, the arbitrator will apply them during the course of the hearing. In the typical hearing format, the parties begin as they would

"Lawsuits consume time and money, and rest and friends."

George Herbert, 1593–1633 (English poet)

10. Depending on the parties' circumstances and preferences, the arbitrator's decision may also be nonbinding on the parties. In some situations, for example, the parties may submit their dispute to a third party but remain free to reject the third party's decision. Such nonbinding arbitration is more similar to conciliation or mediation than to binding arbitration. As will be discussed in the final section of this chapter, arbitration that is mandated by the courts is often not binding on the parties.

at a trial by presenting opening arguments to the arbitrator and stating what remedies should or should not be granted. After the opening statements have been made, evidence is presented. Witnesses may be called and examined by both sides. After all the evidence has been presented, the parties give their closing arguments. On completion of the closing arguments, the arbitrator closes the hearing.

After each side has had an opportunity to present evidence and to argue its case, the arbitrator will reach a decision. The final decision of the arbitrator is called an **award**, even if no money is conferred on a party as a result of the proceedings. Under most statutes, the arbitrator must render an award within thirty days of the close of the hearing.

AWARD
As a noun, the decision rendered by an arbitrator or other extrajudicial decider of a controversy. As a verb, to give or assign by sentence, judicial determination, or otherwise after a careful weighing of evidence, as when a jury awards damages.

Arbitration Statutes Most states have statutes (often based in part on the Uniform Arbitration Act of 1955) under which arbitration clauses will be enforced, and some state statutes compel arbitration of certain types of disputes, such as those involving public employees.

At the federal level, the Federal Arbitration Act (FAA), enacted in 1925, enforces arbitration clauses in contracts involving maritime activity or interstate commerce and can preempt state coverage in these areas in the event of conflict between a state statute and the federal act. Even business activities that have only remote or minimal effects on commerce between two or more states are regarded as interstate commerce. Thus, arbitration agreements involving transactions only slightly connected to the flow of interstate commerce may fall under the FAA. The FAA does not establish a set arbitration procedure. The parties themselves must agree on the manner of resolving their disputes. The FAA provides the means for enforcing the arbitration procedure that the parties establish for themselves.

It is important to note that if parties enter into a contract containing an arbitration clause, it is likely that a state or federal statute will compel them to arbitrate any dispute arising under the contract—providing there are no reasons against arbitrating the dispute.

Enforcement of Arbitration Agreements The role of the courts in the arbitration process is limited. One important role is played at the prearbitration stage. When a dispute arises as to whether or not the parties have agreed in an arbitration clause to submit a particular matter to arbitration, one party may file suit to compel arbitration. The court before which the suit is brought will not decide the basic controversy but must decide the issue of arbitrability—that is, whether the matter is one that must be resolved through arbitration. The arbitrability of a dispute is at issue in the following case.

Case 3.4 

SHEARSON/AMERICAN EXPRESS, INC. v. McMAHON
Supreme Court of the United States, 1987.
482 U.S. 220,
107 S.Ct. 2332,
96 L.Ed.2d 185.

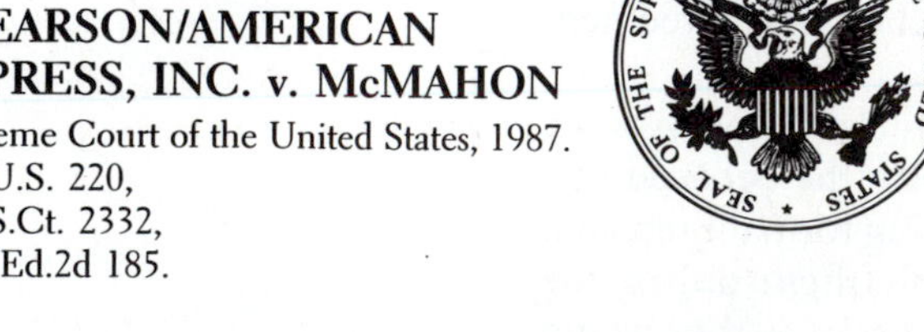

HISTORICAL AND SOCIAL SETTING *In the nineteenth century, some judges would give little respect to the decisions of private arbitrators. Perhaps these judges did not want competition for the power to decide cases. In 1925, Congress had to order federal courts to respect the decisions of arbitrators. In general, courts now will enforce arbitration judgments without reexamining their correctness. At times, though, it may not be clear whether a certain dispute is arbitrable. For example, Congress passed the Securities Exchange Act of 1934 (see Chapter 29) specifically to prevent fraudulent practices in the buying and selling of securities and thus protect a certain class of people—investors. Whether arbitration clauses should be enforced in cases involving alleged violations of federal legislation enacted specifically to protect the rights of certain classes of people (in this case, investors) has posed a significant policy question for the courts. In some cases, for example, an arbitration clause specifies that a dispute must be arbitrated before an industry-sponsored arbitration board. The complaining party may contend that his or her*

Case 3.4—Continued

chances of success would be better if the dispute were decided by a more impartial third party, such as a court judge or jury.

FACTS In October 1984, Eugene and Julia McMahon filed a complaint in a federal district court against Shearson/American Express, Inc., a brokerage firm registered with the Securities and Exchange Commission, and Mary Ann McNulty, the broker who handled the McMahons' account with Shearson. The complaint alleged, among other things, that with Shearson's knowledge McNulty had violated Section 10(b) of the Securities Exchange Act of 1934 by engaging in fraudulent excessive trading on the McMahons' accounts and by making false statements. Relying on two customer agreements signed by Julia McMahon that provided for the arbitration of any controversy relating to the McMahons' accounts with Shearson, McNulty and Shearson moved to compel arbitration of the McMahons' claim pursuant to the Federal Arbitration Act. The district court found that the McMahons' Section 10(b) claims were arbitrable under the terms of the agreement. The court of appeals reversed the decision. The United States Supreme Court granted *certiorari* to resolve the issue.

ISSUE Are Section 10(b) claims arbitrable under the Federal Arbitration Act?

DECISION Yes. The United States Supreme Court reversed the decision of the court of appeals.

REASON The Court cited the Federal Arbitration Act, which provides that arbitration agreements "shall be valid, irrevocable, and enforceable, save upon grounds as exist at law or in equity for the revocation of any contract." The "federal policy favoring arbitration" established by the act could be overridden, however, by a contrary congressional command. The Court pointed out that the burden is on the party opposing arbitration to prove "that Congress intended to preclude a waiver of judicial remedies for statutory rights." The Court found that the McMahons failed to establish that Congress intended to make an exception to the Federal Arbitration Act for claims arising under the Securities Exchange Act. Accordingly, "having made the bargain to arbitrate," the McMahons were held to their bargain.

ETHICAL CONSIDERATIONS *The decision to compel arbitration in this case may seem to contradict the public policy enunciated by the federal legislation passed to protect investors. But in making their decisions, courts must weigh this public policy against two other policies: (1) freedom of contract, which means that the courts are reluctant to interfere with contracts (and arbitration clauses contained therein) voluntarily formed, and (2) the policy favoring alternative methods of dispute settlement to reduce the heavy caseload of the courts.*

Setting Aside an Arbitration Award Courts also may play an important role at the postarbitration stage. If the arbitration has produced an award, one of the parties may appeal the award or may seek a court order compelling the other party to comply with the award. In determining whether an award should be enforced, a court conducts a review that is much more restricted in scope than an appellate court's review of a trial court decision. The general view is that because the parties were free to frame the issues and set the powers of the arbitrator at the outset, they cannot complain about the result.

An arbitration award may be set aside, though, in certain circumstances. An arbitrator's award may be set aside if the award resulted from the arbitrator's misconduct or "bad faith." For example, if the arbitrator exhibited bias or corruption, refused to hear pertinent evidence, or acted in any way that substantially prejudiced the rights of one of the parties, the award may be set aside. Another basis for setting aside an award exists if the arbitrator exceeded his or her powers in arbitrating the dispute. An arbitrator is empowered to resolve only those issues that are covered by the agreement to submit to arbitration. As mentioned, if the arbitrability of a dispute is in question, the courts must decide that issue, not the arbitrator.

In keeping with contract law principles, no award will be enforced if compliance with the award would result in the commission of a crime or would conflict with some greater social policy mandated by statute. A court will not overturn an award, however, simply because the arbitrator was called on to resolve a dispute involving a matter of important public concern. For an award to be set aside, it must call for some action by the parties that would conflict with or in some way undermine public policy. In the following case, the court refused to enforce an arbitrator's award on the ground that its enforcement would be contrary to a significant and explicitly enunciated public policy.

Case 3.5
STATE v. COUNCIL 4, AFSCME

Appellate Court of Connecticut, 1992.
27 Conn.App. 635,
608 A.2d 718.

HISTORICAL AND SOCIAL SETTING *Traditionally, in regard to employment contracts, the common law held that employment was "at will." Employers could discharge employees at any time for any reason. Today, employers' rights are much more restricted. In many states, the employment-at-will doctrine has been superseded by statutes governing employment relationships. Even in states in which the at-will doctrine still controls, employer-employee contracts or employer-union contracts may limit the conditions under which an employee may be fired. Federal laws regulating employment relationships further restrict an employer's ability to discharge employees. For example, federal laws prohibiting discriminatory practices now require employers to reasonably accommodate the needs of employees or potential employees who are mentally or physically handicapped.*

FACTS Phillip Beaudry, who suffered from mental illness, worked in the Department of Income Maintenance for the state of Connecticut. Between November 1989 and March 1990, Beaudry misappropriated approximately $1,640 in state funds, which was a ground for dismissal under state personnel regulations. After he was fired from his job, Beaudry filed a complaint with his union, Council 4 of the American Federation of State, County, and Municipal Employees. Eventually the dispute was submitted to an arbitrator. The arbitrator concluded that Beaudry had been dismissed without "just cause" because Beaudry's acts were caused by his mental illness and "were not willful or volitional or within his capacity to control." Because Beaudry was disabled, the employer was required, under state law, to transfer him to a position that he was competent to hold. The arbitrator awarded Beaudry reinstatement, back pay, seniority, and other benefits. The state appealed the decision to a state court, which vacated (canceled or nullified) the award on the ground that it was contrary to the public policy of not rewarding state employees who knowingly misappropriate state funds. The union appealed.

ISSUE Did the public policy of not rewarding state officials and employees who misappropriated state funds outweigh the public policy of discouraging discrimination against mentally ill persons?

DECISION Yes. The court affirmed the trial court's decision, holding that the arbitrator's award had been properly vacated.

REASON The court emphasized that the "public policy exception to arbitral authority should be narrowly construed." Courts can refuse to enforce an arbitrator's decision only if the decision's enforcement "would violate some explicit public policy that is well defined and dominant" and that can "be ascertained by reference to the laws and legal precedents and not from general considerations of supposed public interests." The court pointed out that the state of Connecticut's public policy of not tolerating the knowing misappropriation of state funds by state officials or employees was explicitly articulated in the state's statutory law. The court further noted that the "public policy of discouraging fraud generally is firmly rooted in our common law." The court agreed with the trial court that "the arbitral award's contribution to the policy of minimizing discrimination against the mentally ill did not outweigh the damaging consequences to the concomitant policy goal of refusing to countenance the knowing misappropriation of state moneys."

AMERICAN ARBITRATION ASSOCIATION (AAA)
The major organization offering arbitration services in the United States.

Arbitration Services Arbitration services are provided by both government agencies and private organizations. The major source of arbitration services is the **American Arbitration Association (AAA).** Most of the largest law firms in the nation are members of this association. Founded in 1926, the AAA now settles more than fifty-five thousand disputes a year in its numerous offices around the country. Settlements usually are effected quickly and, at times, in informal settings, such as a conference room or even a hotel room. Cases brought before the AAA are heard by an expert or a panel of experts in the area relating to the dispute. Generally, about half of the panel members are lawyers.

To cover its costs, the nonprofit organization charges a fee, paid by the party filing the claim. In addition, each party to the dispute pays a specified amount for each hearing day, as well as a special additional fee in cases involving personal injuries or property loss.

❖ Court-Mandated ADR

Increasingly, the courts are requiring that parties attempt to settle their differences through some form of ADR before proceeding to trial. Usually, the claims involved must fall under a certain threshold amount. Since 1984, federal courts in several districts have been experimenting with court-sponsored, nonbinding arbitration for cases involving up to $100,000. Because of the success of this program (less than 10 percent of the cases referred for arbitration go to trial), federal courts will continue to use this method. State courts are also increasingly turning to alternative dispute resolution programs as a means of relieving their burgeoning caseloads. Hawaii, for example, has a program of mandatory, nonbinding arbitration for disputes involving less than $150,000, and Colorado initiated a program that required all civil actions involving damages of less than $50,000 to be arbitrated as part of a pilot project embracing eight judicial districts in the state.

In the federal courts and in many state courts, when cases are referred for arbitration, the arbitrator's decision is not binding. If either party rejects the award, the case proceeds to trial, and the court reconsiders all of the evidence and legal questions pertaining to the dispute.

South Carolina became the first state to institute a voluntary arbitration program at the appellate court level. Litigants under the South Carolina system must waive the court hearing when requesting arbitration, and all decisions by the arbitrators are final. To date, arbitration programs of some kind have been adopted in at least twenty states.

❖ Other Forms of ADR

A form of ADR that has been successfully employed in the federal system is the **summary jury trial (SJT)**. In an SJT, the litigants present their arguments and evidence, and the jury then renders a verdict. The jury's verdict is not binding, but it does act as a guide to both sides in reaching an agreement during the mandatory negotiations that immediately follow the trial. Because no witnesses are called, the SJT is much speedier than a regular trial, and frequently the parties are able to settle their dispute without resorting to an actual trial. If no settlement is reached, both sides have the right to a full trial later. Summary jury trials are now held by approximately sixty-five federal judges.

SUMMARY JURY TRIAL (SJT)
A relatively recent method of settling disputes in which a trial is held, but the jury's verdict is not binding. The verdict only acts as a guide to both sides in reaching an agreement during the mandatory negotiations that immediately follow the trial. If a settlement is not reached, both sides have the right to a full trial later.

Another development in the area of ADR is the use of mini-trials to facilitate dispute settlement. A **mini-trial** is a private proceeding in which each party's attorney briefly argues the party's case before the other party. Often, a neutral third party, who acts as an adviser, is also present. If the parties fail to reach an agreement, the adviser renders an opinion as to how a court would likely decide the issue.

MINI-TRIAL
A private proceeding that assists disputing parties in determining whether to take their case to court. During the proceeding, each party's attorney briefly argues the party's case before the other party and (usually) a neutral third party, who acts as an adviser. If the parties fail to reach an agreement, the adviser renders an opinion as to how a court would likely decide the issue.

❖ The Privatization of Justice

Given the popularity of alternatives to traditional court proceedings, it is not surprising that the private enterprise system would respond to the growing demand for more efficient, less costly forums for settling disputes. One such response is the so-called rent-a-judge system. The rent-a-judge option began in 1976 in California, the state that still handles about half of the cases submitted to hired judges for decision. Under a California state statute,[11] litigants can bypass the formal court system by having their cases heard before former judges of the California courts. Under the statute, cases can be "tried before a referee selected and paid by the litigants and empowered by the statute to enter decisions having the finality of trial court judgments." In California, and in the dozen or so other states with similar statutes, jurors can be selected from the public jury rolls, and verdicts can be appealed to a state appellate court. Private courts are a boon to those who do not wish to wait for years to go to trial. In Los Angeles County, for example, litigants must wait from three to eight years (the national average is eighteen months) to be heard in a public court.

The private system of justice spread quickly, and now hundreds of firms throughout the country offer dispute-resolution services by hired judges. Procedures in these private courts are fashioned to meet the desires of the clients seeking their services. For example, the parties usually can decide on the date of the hearing, the presiding judge, whether the judge's decision will be legally binding, and the site of the hearing—which could be a conference room, a law-school office, or a leased courtroom. The judges follow procedures similar to those of the federal courts and use similar rules. Normally, each party to the dispute pays a filing fee and a designated fee for a hearing session or conference. Although rent-a-judge courts first became popular in settling contract and employment disputes, in recent years they have been frequently used to settle disputes relating to family law and personal injuries as well.

Many are concerned, understandably, that the entry of justice into the marketplace may herald abuses. Already, the rent-a-judge system has been hailed as "Cadillac justice" because those who can afford it have access to simpler and more efficient justice than the poorer groups in society who must wait their turn in the public courts. Another concern is that private courts may lure the best jurists away from the public court benches, because judges can earn more income by hiring out their services to private clients. Still another criticism is that hearings in private courts are not open to the public or press, and this means that corporations and other parties can shield their activities from the public eye. Finally, some observers feel that the alternative, private system of justice is making needed reforms in the public system less likely.

11. California Civil Procedure Code Sections 638–645.

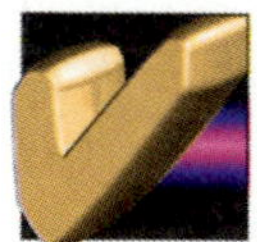

Application

Law and the Businessperson—to Sue or Not to Sue

Wrongs are committed every minute of every day in the United States. These wrongs may be committed inadvertently or on purpose. Sometimes businesspersons believe that wrongs have been committed against them by other businesspersons, consumers, or by local, state, or federal government. There are many issues to consider when deciding whether or not to sue for a wrong that has been committed against you or your business.

The Question of Cost

Competent legal advice is not inexpensive. Good commercial business law attorneys charge $75 to $400 an

Application—Continued

hour, plus expenses. It is almost always worthwhile to make an initial visit to an attorney who has skills in the area in which you are going to sue to get an estimate of the expected costs of pursuing a redress for your grievance. You may be charged for the initial visit as well.

Note also that less than 10 percent of all corporate lawsuits end up in trial—the rest are settled beforehand. You may end up settling for far less than you thought you were "owed" simply because of the length of time it takes your attorney to bring your case to trial and to finish the trial. And then you might not win, anyway!

Basically, then, you must do a cost-benefit analysis to determine whether you should sue. Your attorney can give you the costs, and you can "guesstimate" the benefits. You do this by multiplying the probable size of the award by the probability of obtaining that award.

The Alternatives before You

Another method of settling your grievance is by alternative dispute resolution (ADR). Negotiation, mediation, and arbitration are all forms of ADR, and they are becoming increasingly attractive alternatives to court litigation because you can usually get quick results at a comparatively low cost. Labor disputes, commercial contract disputes, and insurance claims can be arbitrated through the American Arbitration Association (AAA), and there are numerous other ADR centers as well. You can obtain information on ADR by writing to the Special Committee on Dispute Resolution, American Bar Association, 1800 M Street N.W., Washington, DC 20036. The Yellow Pages in large metropolitan areas usually list agencies and firms that could help you settle your dispute out of court; look under "Mediation" or "Social Service Agencies."

Checklist for Deciding Whether to Sue

- ☐ 1. Are you prepared to pay for going to court? Make this decision only after you have consulted an attorney to get an estimate of the costs of preparing the lawsuit.
- ☐ 2. Do you have the patience to follow a court case through the judicial system, even if it takes several years?
- ☐ 3. Is there a way for you to settle your grievance without going to court? Even if the settlement is less than you think you are owed, in net terms corrected for future expenses, time waiting, time lost, and frustration, you may be better off settling now for the smaller figure.
- ☐ 4. Can you use some form of alternative dispute resolution? Before you say no, investigate these alternatives—they are usually cheaper and quicker to use than the standard judicial process.
- ☐ 5. In all cases, only make your decision based on the advice of a competent legal professional. Remember the old adage, "He who does his own legal work has a fool for a client."

❖ Key Terms

affirmative defense 74
alternative dispute resolution (ADR) 84
American Arbitration Association (AAA) 88
answer 74
arbitration 85
arbitration clause 85
award 86
brief 80
closing argument 79
complaint 71
conciliation 84
concurrent jurisdiction 67
counterclaim 74
cross-examination 78
declaratory judgment 69
default judgment 73
depositions 76
direct examination 78
directed verdict 78
discovery 76
diversity of citizenship 66
docket 84
exclusive jurisdiction 67
federal question 67
interrogatories 76
judgment *n.o.v.* 80
judicial review 69
jurisdiction 59
long arm statute 60
mediation 85
mini-trial 89
motion to dismiss 74
negotiation 84
pleadings 70
probable cause 77
rebuttal 79
rejoinder 79
reply 74
small claims court 62
summary judgment 75
summary jury trial (SJT) 89
summons 72
venue 61
voir dire 78
writ of *certiorari* 67

❖ Chapter Summary: Courts and Procedures

Types of Jurisdiction	1. *Jurisdiction over persons/property*—Territorial boundaries within which a court has the right and power to decide cases concerning a defendant or a defendant's property. 2. *Jurisdiction over subject matter*—Restriction limiting a court to hearing a particular type of case. a. Limited jurisdiction—Exists when a court is limited to a specific subject matter, such as probate or divorce. b. General jurisdiction—Exists when a court can hear any kind of case. 3. *Original jurisdiction*—Exists with courts that have authority to hear a case for the first time (trial courts). 4. *Appellate jurisdiction*—Exists with courts of appeal and review; generally, appellate courts do not have original jurisdiction. 5. *Federal jurisdiction*—Arises in the following situations: a. When a federal question is involved (when the plaintiff's cause of action is based at least in part on the U.S. Constitution, a treaty, or a federal law). b. In diversity of citizenship cases between (1) citizens of different states, (2) a foreign country and citizens of a state or different states, or (3) citizens of a state and citizens or subjects of a foreign country. The amount in controversy must exceed $50,000. 6. *Concurrent jurisdiction*—Exists when two different courts have authority to hear the same case. 7. *Exclusive jurisdiction*—Exists when only state courts or only federal courts have authority to hear a case.
Judicial Review	The process by which the judicial branch determines whether a law is contrary to the mandates of the Constitution. The doctrine of judicial review was first enunciated by the United States Supreme Court in John Marshall's decision in *Marbury v. Madison* in 1803.
Types of Courts	1. *Trial courts*—Courts of original jurisdiction, where an action is initiated. a. State—Courts of general jurisdiction can hear any case; courts of limited jurisdiction include divorce courts, probate courts, traffic courts, small claims courts, etc. b. Federal—The federal district court is the equivalent of the state trial court. Federal courts of limited jurisdiction include the U.S. Tax Court, the U.S. Bankruptcy Court, and the U.S. Court of Federal Claims. 2. *Intermediate appellate courts*—Courts of appeal and review, generally without original jurisdiction. Many states have an intermediate appellate court; in the federal court system, the U.S. circuit courts of appeals are the intermediate appellate courts. 3. *Supreme court*—The highest court. Each state has a supreme court, although it may be called by some other name, from which appeal to the United States Supreme Court is only possible if a federal question is involved. The United States Supreme Court is the highest court in the federal court system and the final arbiter of the Constitution and federal law.
Rules of Procedure	Rules of procedure prescribe the way in which disputes are handled in the courts. Rules differ from court to court, and separate sets of rules exist for federal and state courts, as well as for criminal and civil cases. A sample civil court procedure in a state court would involve the following steps: 1. *The pleadings:* a. Complaint or petition—A statement of the cause of action and parties involved, filed with the court by the plaintiff's attorney. A summons and a copy of the complaint are delivered to the defendant. b. Pre-answer motion—Such as a motion to dismiss for failure to state a claim on which relief can be granted. c. Answer—Can take the form of (1) a motion to dismiss, (2) an affirmative defense, (3) a counterclaim, or (4) an answer denying allegations, which could contain an admission, an affirmative defense, and a counterclaim. 2. *Dismissal/judgment before trial:* a. Motion for judgment on the pleadings—May be made by either party; will be granted if no cause of action exists or if the defendant fails to answer.

❖ Chapter Summary: Courts and Procedures—Continued

Rules of Procedure—Continued	b. Motion for summary judgment—May be made by either party; will be granted if the parties agree on the facts. Judge applies law in rendering judgment. 3. *Discovery*—The process of gathering evidence concerning the case; involves *depositions* (sworn testimony by a party to the lawsuit or any witness) and *interrogatories* (written answers to questions made by parties to the action with the aid of their attorneys). 4. *Pretrial hearing*—Either party or the court can request a pretrial hearing to identify the matters in dispute after discovery has taken place and to plan the course of the trial. 5. *Trial*—Involves opening statements from both parties' attorneys and then: a. Plaintiff's introduction and direct examination of witnesses and cross-examination by defendant's attorney; possible redirect by plaintiff's attorney and recross-examination by defendant's attorney. b. Defendant's introduction and direct examination of witnesses and cross-examination by plaintiff's attorney; possible redirect by defendant's attorney and recross-examination by plaintiff's attorney. c. Possible rebuttal of defendant's argument by plaintiff's attorney, who presents more evidence. d. Possible rejoinder by defendant's attorney to meet that evidence. e. Closing arguments by both plaintiff's and defendant's attorneys in favor of their respective clients. f. Judge's instructions to the jury. g. Jury verdict. 6. *Posttrial and prejudgment options:* a. Motion for a new trial—Will be granted if the judge is convinced that the jury was in error. Can also be granted on the grounds of newly discovered evidence, misconduct by the participants during the trial, or error by the judge. b. Motion for judgment *n.o.v.* (notwithstanding the verdict)—A second chance to move for directed verdict; will be granted if the judge is convinced that the jury was in error. c. Appeal—Either party can appeal the trial court's judgment to an appropriate court of appeals. After posting of bond(s), briefs are filed, a hearing is held, and the court renders a written opinion.
Alternative Dispute Resolution (ADR)	ADR is a less costly, less time-consuming, and an increasingly attractive alternative to litigation in the courts. Forms of ADR include the following: 1. *Negotiation*—The parties come together, with or without attorneys to represent them, and try to reach a settlement without the involvement of a third party. 2. *Conciliation*—A third party, called a conciliator, assists the parties in a dispute in reconciling their differences. 3. *Mediation*—The parties themselves reach an agreement with the help of a third party, called a mediator, who proposes solutions. 4. *Arbitration*—A more formal method of ADR in which the parties submit their dispute to a neutral third party, the arbitrator, who renders a decision, which may or may not be legally binding, depending on the circumstances. Some courts refer certain cases for arbitration before allowing the cases to proceed to trial; in most cases, this kind of arbitration is nonbinding on the parties. 5. *Summary jury trial (SJT)*—A kind of trial employed by some federal courts in which litigants present their arguments and evidence and the jury renders a nonbinding verdict. The SJT acts as a guide to both parties in reaching an agreement during the mandatory negotiations that immediately follow the trial. 6. *Mini-trial*—A private proceeding in which each party's attorney argues the party's case before the other party. Often, a neutral third party acts as an adviser and renders an opinion on how a court would likely decide the issue. 7. *Rent-a-judge courts*—The parties rent a judge to hear their case and render a verdict to which the parties agree to be bound. Several firms now provide for this kind of private justice.

❖ Questions and Case Problems

3-1. Jurisdiction. Before a court can hear a case, it must have jurisdiction. Over what must it have jurisdiction?

3-2. Appellate Process. If a judge enters a judgment on the pleadings, the losing party can usually appeal but cannot present evidence to the appellate court. Does this seem fair? Explain.

3-3. Arbitration. In an arbitration proceeding, the arbitrator need not be a judge or even a lawyer. How, then, can the arbitrator's decision have the force of law and be binding on the parties involved?

3-4. Appellate Process. Sometimes on appeal there are questions concerning whether the facts presented in the trial court support the conclusion reached by the judge or the jury. The appellate court will reverse on the basis of the facts only when so little evidence was presented at trial that no reasonable person could have reached the conclusion that the judge or jury reached. Appellate courts normally defer to a judge's decision with regard to the facts. Can you see any reason for this?

3-5. Jurisdiction. Marya Callais, a citizen of Florida, was walking near a busy street in Tallahassee, Florida, one day when a large crate flew off a passing truck and hit her, resulting in numerous injuries to Callais. She incurred a great deal of pain and suffering plus numerous medical expenses, and she could not work for six months. She wished to sue the trucking firm for $300,000 in damages. The firm's headquarters were in Georgia, although the company did business in Florida. In what court may Marya bring suit—a Florida state court, a Georgia state court, or a federal court? What factors might influence her decision?

3-6. Arbitration. Gates worked for Arizona Brewing Co. and was a member of the International Union of United Brewers, Flour, Cereal, and Soft Drink Workers of America. A contract between Gates's employer and the union stated that the employer and the union were to try to settle their differences but if the parties could not reach a settlement, the matter was to be decided by arbitration. Claiming that the arbitration clause was void under an Arizona arbitration statute, Gates brought a lawsuit against Arizona Brewing Co. to recover wages. Gates had not made any attempt to submit the dispute between him and the employer to arbitration. The employer argued that Gates could not bring a lawsuit until after arbitration had occurred. A provision in the Arizona arbitration statute, which generally enforced arbitration clauses in contracts, stated that "this act shall not apply to collective [bargained] contracts between employers and . . . associations of employ[ees]." Must Gates undergo arbitration before bringing a lawsuit? Explain. [*Gates v. Arizona Brewing Co.*, 54 Ariz. 266, 95 P.2d 49 (1939)]

3-7. Arbitration. When Roger and Susan Faherty divorced, they entered into a property settlement agreement that was incorporated into the final divorce degree. The property settlement agreement contained a clause that mandated arbitration of any dispute arising out of the agreement. Roger failed to make several alimony and child support payments, and Susan sought court enforcement of the property settlement agreement. Roger's consequent motion to have the court compel arbitration was granted by the court, and the dispute was arbitrated. The arbitrator's decision required Roger to pay Susan $37,648 for back alimony payments and $12,284 for overdue child support. Roger, although he had been the one to petition the court for arbitration, now challenged the validity of the arbitration clause in alimony and child support matters. He claimed that as a matter of public policy, such matters should be settled by the courts, not by arbitration. Will the court agree with Roger? Discuss. [*Faherty v. Faherty*, 97 N.J. 99, 477 A.2d 1257 (1984)]

3-8. Discovery. Joseph Stout, while on the job as a construction worker, fell from a beam that he was attempting to secure to a steel column. As a result of the fall, Stout sustained injuries that rendered him a paraplegic. Stout brought suit against his employer, A. M. Sunrise Construction Co., and Central Rent-A-Crane, Inc., for damages. Prior to the trial, a number of discovery motions were filed by the defendants, who sought detailed information on the nature of the accident and the injuries incurred. Stout repeatedly failed to respond to these requests, even when the trial court ordered him to do so. Finally, the trial court dismissed the action because of Stout's failure to respond. Stout appealed the dismissal. On appeal, Stout claimed that the trial court had abused its discretion by dismissing his action against the defendants, thus depriving him of his right to be heard in court. What will the appellate court decide? [*Stout v. A. M. Sunrise Construction Co.*, 505 N.E.2d 500 (Ind.App. 1987)]

3-9. Arbitration. Colorado's Mandatory Arbitration Act, which went into effect in January 1988, required that all civil lawsuits involving damages of less than $50,000 be arbitrated rather than tried in court. The statutory scheme, which was a pilot project to continue until July 1, 1990, affected eight judicial districts in the state. It provided for a court trial for any party dissatisfied with an arbitrator's decision. It also provided that if the trial did not result in an improvement of more than 10 percent in the position of the party who demanded the trial, that party had to pay the costs of the arbitration proceeding. The constitutionality of the act was challenged by a plaintiff who maintained in part that it violated litigants' rights of access to the courts and to trial by jury. What will the court decide? Explain your answer. [*Firelock, Inc. v. District Court, 20th Judicial District*, 776 P.2d 1090 (Colo. 1989)]

3-10. Arbitration. Robert Gilmer was hired by Interstate/Johnson Lane Corp. in 1981 as a financial manager. As a condition of his employment, Gilmer was required to register as a securities representative with the New York Stock Exchange. Gilmer's application for the securities registration contained an arbitration clause under which Gilmer agreed to the arbitration of any disputes between himself and his employer arising out of his employment. When Gilmer's employment was terminated in 1987, he sued Interstate, alleging that his termination violated the Age Discrimination in Employment Act (ADEA) of 1967. Interstate filed a motion to compel arbitration in accordance with the contract. The trial court denied the motion, but on appeal, the trial court's judgment was reversed. How would you argue in support of the trial court's decision that the dispute should not be submitted to arbitration? How would you argue in support of the appellate court's conclusion that the dispute should be arbitrated? [*Gilmer v. Interstate/Johnson Lane Corp.*, ___ U.S. ___, 111 S.Ct. 1647, 114 L.Ed.2d 26 (1991)]

3-11. Arbitration. A few years ago, New York State revised its New Car Lemon Law to allow consumers who complained of purchasing a "lemon" to have their disputes arbitrated before a professional arbitrator appointed by the New York attorney general. Before it was revised, the Lemon Law allowed for the arbitration of disputes, but the forum in which arbitration took place was sponsored by trade associations within the automobile industry, and consumers often complained of unfair awards. The revised law also provided that consumers were not required to arbitrate and, if they wished, could sue a manufacturer in court. Manufacturers, however, were *compelled* to arbitrate claims if a consumer chose to do so and could not resort to the courts. Trade associations representing automobile manufacturers and importers brought an action seeking a declaration that the alternative arbitration mechanism of the Lemon Law was unconstitutional because it deprived them of their right to trial by jury. How will the court decide? Discuss. [*Motor Vehicle Manufacturers Association of the United States v. State*, 551 N.Y.S.2d 470, 550 N.E.2d 919, 75 N.Y.2d 175 (1990)]

3-12. Jurisdiction. Alex Sutton, a professional golfer living in Middleburg, Florida, entered into a sponsorship agreement with ARS & Associates, a Michigan partnership. Among other things, the agreement provided that (1) ARS would sponsor Sutton on a Professional Golfing Association (PGA) tour, (2) ARS would pay all of Sutton's expenses, (3) ARS and Sutton would split the proceeds (whatever remained after ARS had been reimbursed for expenses) fifty-fifty, and (4) ARS would provide health insurance for Sutton. Preliminary negotiations were carried out mostly over the phone. ARS drew up the agreement in Michigan and sent it to Sutton in Florida, who signed and returned the contract to ARS. ARS then signed the agreement and sent a copy of it to Sutton. Sutton subsequently participated in several senior PGA events, including two tournaments in Florida. While playing golf in a senior PGA tournament in Palm Springs, California, Sutton suffered a heart attack and, as a result, later incurred costs of more than $100,000 for open-heart surgery and related medical expenses. Because ARS had not obtained health-insurance coverage for Sutton, Sutton sued ARS in a Florida state court for breach of the agreement. ARS moved to dismiss the action for lack of personal jurisdiction. Can the Florida court, under its long arm statute, exercise personal jurisdiction over the Michigan defendant in this case? Discuss. [*Sutton v. Smith*, 603 So.2d 693 (Fla.App. 1992)]

A Question of Ethics and Social Responsibility

3-13. *Linda Bender brought a complaint in federal court, alleging sexual harassment by her supervisor, John Donovan, at A. G. Edwards & Sons, Inc., a stock-brokerage firm (the defendants). She sought relief under state statutes as well as under Title VII of the Civil Rights Act of 1964, which prohibits employment discrimination on the basis of race, color, religion, national origin, or sex. In her application for registration as a stockbroker, Bender had agreed to submit any disputes with her employer to an arbitrator for resolution. The defendants moved for a stay (an order to stop a legal action) of Bender's claims pending arbitration. The district judge denied the motion, holding that the arbitration clause could not be enforced because Bender could not waive her right to a federal adjudication of Title VII claims. On appeal, the Eleventh Circuit Court of Appeals reversed the trial court's decision, holding that Title VII claims are arbitrable. The court held that compelling Bender to submit her claim for arbitration did not deprive her of the right to a judicial forum because if the arbitration proceedings were somehow legally deficient, she could still take her case to a federal court for review.* [Bender v. A. G. Edwards & Sons, Inc., *971 F.2d 698 (11th Cir. 1992)*]

1. Does the right to a postarbitration judicial forum equate to the right to initial access to a judicial forum in employment disputes?
2. Should the fact that reviewing courts rarely set aside arbitrators' awards have any bearing on the arbitrability of certain types of claims, such as those brought under Title VII?
3. In negotiating employment contracts, employers normally have greater bargaining power than job applicants. A contract may be presented to a job seeker on a "take it or leave it" basis, and the applicant is often powerless to alter the terms of the proposed contract. Given this situation, is it fair to enforce such clauses in disputes relating to laws that were enacted specifically to protect employees against discriminatory practices on the part of employers?

Case Briefing Assignment

3-14. *Examine Case* A.2 [Goeller v. Liberty Mutual Insurance Co., *568 A.2d 176 (Pa. 1990)*] *in Appendix A. The case has been excerpted there in great detail. Review and then brief the case, making sure that you include answers to the following questions in your brief.*

1. The Pennsylvania Supreme Court acknowledged that a strong presumption exists in favor of an arbitration panel's award. What must occur before that presumption is applied?
2. What statutory authority guided the court in its deliberations?
3. What two reasons underlie the court's decision that the arbitration panel's award was a nullity?

For Critical Analysis

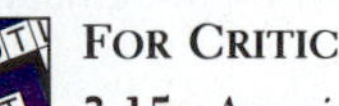

3-15. *American courts are forums for adversarial justice, in which attorneys defend the interests of their respective clients before the court. This means an attorney may end up claiming before a court that his or her client is innocent, even though the attorney knows that the client acted wrongfully. Is it ethical for attorneys to try to "deceive" the court in these situations? Can the adversarial system of justice really lead to "truth"?*

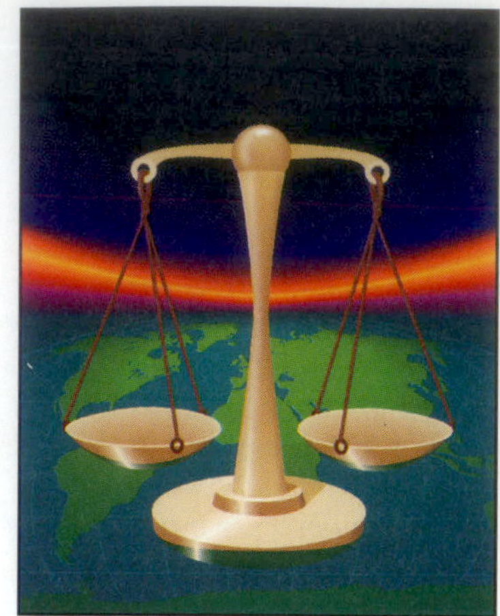

Chapter 4

Constitutional Law

"While the Declaration [of Independence] was directed against an excess of authority, the Constitution was directed against anarchy."

Robert H. Jackson, 1892–1954
(Associate justice of the United States Supreme Court, 1941–1954)

AMEND
To change and improve through a formal procedure.

Jackson's statement above summarizes the dilemma faced by the founders of this nation—how to create a national government that was at once too weak to squash the colonists' newfound liberties and strong enough to prevent anarchy. The first experiment in national government took the form of a *confederation.* The Articles of Confederation, ratified in 1778, established a confederation of independent states and a central government with very limited powers. The central government could handle only those matters of common concern expressly delegated to it by the member states, and the national congress had no ability to make laws directly applicable to individuals unless the member states explicitly supported such laws. In short, the *sovereign power* to govern rested essentially with the states.[1] The Articles of Confederation clearly reflected the central tenet of the American Revolution—that a government should not have unlimited power.

After the Revolutionary War, however, the states began to pass laws that hampered national commerce and foreign trade by preventing the free movement of goods and services. Consequently, in 1787, the Constitutional Convention convened to **amend** the Articles of Confederation to give the national government the power to address the country's commercial problems. Instead of amending the Articles of Confederation, the convention created the Constitution and a completely new government, based on a federal system, which they believed was much better equipped than its predecessor to resolve the problems of the nation.

The Constitution, because it provides the legal basis for both state and federal (national) powers, is the supreme law in this country.[2] Neither Congress nor any state may pass a law that conflicts with the Constitution. Laws that govern business have their origin in the lawmaking authority granted by this document. In this chapter, we first look at some basic constitutional concepts and clauses and their significance for business. Then we examine how certain fundamental freedoms guaranteed by the *Bill of Rights* (the first ten amendments to the Constitution) affect businesspersons and the workplace.

❖ The Constitutional Powers of Government

The federal form of government established by the Constitution reflects the compromise made between those delegates to the Constitutional Convention who de-

1. *Sovereign power* refers to that supreme power to which no other person or authority is superior or equal.
2. See Appendix B for the full text of the U.S. Constitution.

How does the Constitution balance the powers of government between the states and the national government? How does the Constitution prevent the national government's arbitrary use of power?

sired a strong national government and those delegates who believed that the states should hold sovereign power. A federal form of government is one in which the states form a union and the sovereign power is divided between a central governing authority and the member states. The Constitution delegates certain powers to the national government, and the states retain all other powers. The relationship between the national government and the state governments is a partnership—neither partner is superior to the other except within the particular area of exclusive authority granted to it under the Constitution. Hence, the concept of **federalism** recognizes that society may be best served by a distribution of functions among local governments and the national government on the basis of which government is better equipped to perform these functions.

FEDERALISM
A system of government in which power is divided by a written constitution between a central government and regional, or subdivisional, governments. Each level must have some domain in which its policies are dominant and some genuine political or constitutional guarantee of its authority. The United States has a federal government in which power is shared between the central government and the state governments.

Separation of Powers

To prevent the possibility that the national government may use its power arbitrarily, the Constitution provided for three branches of government, each of which performs a different government function. The legislative branch makes the laws, the executive branch enforces the laws, and the judicial branch interprets the laws. Each branch performs a separate function, and no branch may exercise the authority of another branch. Each branch, however, has some power to limit the actions of the other two branches. Congress, for example, has power over spending and commerce, but the president can veto that legislation. The executive branch is responsible for foreign affairs, but treaties with foreign governments require the advice and consent of members of the Senate. Although Congress determines the jurisdiction of the federal courts, the United States Supreme Court has the power to hold acts of the other branches of the federal government unconstitutional.[3] Thus, with this system of **checks and balances,** no one branch of government can accumulate too much power.

CHECKS AND BALANCES The national government is composed of three separate branches: the executive, the legislative, and the judicial. Each branch of the government exercises a check upon the actions of the others.

COMMERCE CLAUSE The provision in Article I, Section 8, of the U.S. Constitution that gives Congress exclusive powers over interstate commerce.

"We are under a Constitution, but the Constitution is what judges say it is."

Charles Evans Hughes, 1862–1948
(American jurist)

The Commerce Clause

Article I, Section 8, of the United States Constitution expressly permits Congress "[t]o regulate Commerce with foreign Nations, and among the several States, and with the Indian Tribes." This clause, referred to as the **commerce clause,** has had a greater impact on business than any other provision in the Constitution. This power was delegated to the federal government to ensure the uniformity of rules governing the movement of goods through the states.

The Regulatory Power of the National Government For some time, the commerce power was interpreted as being limited to *interstate* commerce and not applicable to *intrastate* commerce. In 1824, however, the United States Supreme Court held that commerce within states could also be regulated by the national government as long as the commerce concerned more than one state (see this chapter's *Landmark in the Law*). Over time, the Supreme Court further extended the power of the national government to regulate commerce. In a 1942 case,[4] for example, the Court held that wheat production of an individual farmer intended wholly for consumption on his own farm was subject to federal regulation. The Court reasoned that the home consumption of wheat reduced the demand for wheat and thus could have a substantial effect on interstate commerce. In *McLain v. Real Estate Board of New Orleans, Inc.*, a 1980 case, the Supreme Court acknowledged that the commerce clause had "long been interpreted to extend beyond activities actually in interstate commerce to reach other activities, while wholly local in nature, which nevertheless substantially affect interstate commerce."[5] Today, at least theoretically, the power over commerce authorizes the national government to regulate every commercial enterprise in the United States.

The breadth of the commerce clause permits the national government to legislate in areas in which there is no explicit grant of power to Congress. The following case is illustrative. The case specifically demonstrates the United States Supreme Court's use of the commerce clause to affirm the power of Congress to pass the Civil Rights Act of 1964.

Case 4.1 

HEART OF ATLANTA MOTEL v. UNITED STATES

Supreme Court of the United States, 1964.
379 U.S. 241,
85 S.Ct. 348,
13 L.Ed. 2d 258.

HISTORICAL AND SOCIAL SETTING *In the first half of the twentieth century, state governments sanctioned segregation on the basis of race. In 1954, the United States Supreme Court decided that racially segregated school systems violated the Constitution. In the following decade, the Court ordered an end to racial segregation imposed by the states in other public facilities, such as beaches, golf courses, buses, parks, auditoriums, and courtroom seating. Privately owned facilities that excluded or segregated*

3. See the *Landmark in the Law* in Chapter 3 on *Marbury v. Madison*, 5 U.S. (1 Cranch) 137, 2 L.Ed. 60 (1803), a case in which the doctrine of judicial review was clearly enunciated by Chief Justice John Marshall.

4. See *Wickard v. Filburn*, 317 U.S. 111, 63 S.Ct. 82, 87 L.Ed. 122 (1942).

5. 444 U.S. 232, 100 S.Ct. 502, 62 L.Ed.2d 441 (1980).

Case 4.1—Continued

African Americans and others on the basis of race were not subject to the same constitutional restrictions, however. Congress passed the Civil Rights Act of 1964 to prohibit racial discrimination in "establishments affecting interstate commerce." These facilities included "places of public accommodation."

FACTS The owner of the Heart of Atlanta Motel refused to rent rooms to African Americans in violation of the Civil Rights Act of 1964. The motel owner brought an action to have the act declared unconstitutional. The owner alleged that Congress had exceeded its power to regulate commerce by enacting the 1964 act. The owner argued that his motel was not engaged in interstate commerce but was "of a purely local character." The motel, however, was accessible to state and interstate highways. The owner advertised nationally, maintained billboards throughout the state, and accepted convention trade from outside the state (75 percent of the guests were residents of other states). The court sustained the constitutionality of the act and enjoined (prohibited) the owner from discriminating on the basis of race. The owner appealed. The case ultimately went to the United States Supreme Court.

ISSUE Did Congress exceed its constitutional power to regulate interstate commerce by enacting legislation that could halt discriminatory practices in local operations, such as the Heart of Atlanta Motel?

DECISION No. The United States Supreme Court upheld the constitutionality of the Civil Rights Act of 1964. The power of Congress to regulate interstate commerce permitted the enactment of legislation that could halt local discriminatory practices.

REASON The Court noted that the act was passed to correct "the deprivation of personal dignity" accompanying the denial of equal access to "public establishments." Testimony before Congress leading to the passage of the act indicated that African Americans in particular experienced substantial discrimination in attempting to secure lodging while traveling. This discrimination impeded interstate travel and thus impeded interstate commerce. As for the owner's argument that his motel was "of a purely local character," the Court said that even if this was true, "if it is interstate commerce that feels the pinch, it does not matter how local the operation that applies the squeeze." Therefore, under the commerce clause, "the power of Congress to promote interstate commerce also includes the power to regulate the local incidents thereof, including local activities."

The Regulatory Powers of the States A problem that frequently arises under the commerce clause concerns a state's ability to regulate matters within its own borders. The U.S. Constitution does not expressly exclude state regulation of commerce, and there is no doubt that states have a strong interest in regulating activities within their borders. As part of their inherent sovereignty, states possess **police powers.** The term does not relate solely to criminal law enforcement but also to the right of state governments to regulate private activities to protect or promote the public order, health, safety, morals, and general welfare. Fire and building codes, antidiscrimination laws, parking regulations, zoning restrictions, licensing requirements, and thousands of other state statutes covering virtually every aspect of life have been enacted under the state police power.

POLICE POWERS
Powers possessed by states as part of their inherent sovereignty. These powers may be exercised to protect or promote public health, safety, or morals, or the general welfare.

When state regulations impinge on interstate commerce, courts must balance the state's interest in the merits and purposes of the regulation against the burden placed on interstate commerce.[6] Generally, state laws enacted pursuant to a state's police powers carry a strong presumption of validity. But if state laws substantially interfere with interstate commerce, they will be held to violate the commerce clause of the Constitution. In *Raymond Motor Transportation, Inc. v. Rice*, for example, the United States Supreme Court invalidated Wisconsin administrative regulations limiting the length of trucks traveling on its highways. The Court weighed the burden on interstate commerce against the benefits of the regulations and concluded that the challenged regulations "place a substantial burden on interstate commerce

6. See, for example, *Maine v. Taylor*, 477 U.S. 131, 106 S.Ct. 2440, 91 L.Ed.2d 110 (1986).

and they cannot be said to make more than the most speculative contribution to highway safety."[7]

Because courts balance the interests involved, it is extremely difficult to predict the outcome in a particular case. The following case concerns an issue that has elicited much controversy in recent years: whether states have the power to discriminate against shipments of out-of-state waste to intrastate disposal facilities.

Case 4.2

CHEMICAL WASTE MANAGEMENT, INC. v. HUNT

Supreme Court of the United States, 1992.
___ U.S. ___,
112 S.Ct. 2009,
119 L.Ed.2d 121.

HISTORICAL AND SOCIAL SETTING *The treatment and disposal of hazardous waste is a major industry. Annually, more than 240 million tons of hazardous waste are generated by nearly 80,000 different sources. Under federal law, the waste can be disposed of at licensed facilities only. Nearly 4,700 facilities are licensed, but these facilities are located in only sixteen states. Thus, large quantities of hazardous waste move in interstate commerce every day. Increasing regulation of the facilities has forced many of them to close. Many other sites are running out of space. The largest facility in the country is in Emelle, Alabama, where the presence of a unique geologic feature will prevent landfill from polluting the local water supply for at least 300 years.*

FACTS Chemical Waste Management, Inc., operates the hazardous waste disposal facility in Emelle, Alabama. The facility receives waste from sources in Alabama and from sources outside the state. Concerned about the volume of waste entering the facility and its effect on the environment and on the public's health and safety, Alabama imposed a fee on all of the waste that the facility received, with a higher fee imposed on waste that was generated outside the state. Chemical Waste filed a suit against the state in an Alabama court, seeking an injunction against enforcement of the higher fee. The court declared that the higher fee violated the commerce clause, and the state appealed. The Alabama Supreme Court reversed the decision of the trial court. Chemical Waste appealed to the United States Supreme Court.

ISSUE Did the higher fee imposed by Alabama on hazardous waste generated outside the state violate the commerce clause?

DECISION Yes. The Supreme Court held that Alabama's different treatment of out-of-state waste discriminated against interstate commerce in violation of the commerce clause.

REASON The Supreme Court explained that Alabama's fee scale "facially discriminates against hazardous waste generated in States other than Alabama" and "plainly discouraged" the full operation of Chemical Waste's facility. "Such burdensome taxes imposed on interstate commerce * * * are generally forbidden" and "typically struck down." Addressing Alabama's concerns about harm to the environment and the public, the Court reasoned that the volume of waste entering the Chemical Waste facility could be alleviated by means that did not discriminate as much against interstate commerce. For example, the state could impose a higher fee on *all* waste disposed of in Alabama, a tax on *all* vehicles transporting waste across state roads, or a "cap on the total tonnage landfilled at Emelle." The Court pointed out that the effect of the waste on the environment and on the public is no different because the waste is generated outside the state.

ETHICAL CONSIDERATIONS *As the effects of hazardous waste on the environment and public health have become more widely known, some of the states have tried to restrict the amount of hazardous waste disposed of within their borders. Yet the holding in the* Chemical Waste *case precludes states from discouraging, through discriminatory pricing tactics, the disposal of out-of-state wastes within their borders in an attempt to control this pressing environmental problem. Although the Court based its ruling on the well-established principle that no state should be allowed to isolate itself from a problem common to all the states, there are those who believe that environmental concerns are sufficiently pressing that the Court should allow the states (Alabama, in this case) to exercise control over hazardous waste disposal.*

---

7. 434 U.S. 429, 98 S.Ct. 787, 54 L.Ed.2d 664 (1978).

Landmark in the Law

Gibbons v. Ogden (1824)

Article I, Section 8, of the U.S. Constitution gives Congress the power "to regulate Commerce with foreign Nations, and among the several States, and with the Indian Tribes." What exactly does "to regulate commerce" mean? What does "commerce" entail? These questions came before the United States Supreme Court in 1824 in the case of *Gibbons v. Ogden*.[a]

The background of the case was as follows. Robert Fulton, inventor of the steamboat, and Robert Livingston, who was then American minister to France, secured a monopoly on steam navigation on the waters in New York State from the New York legislature in 1803. Fulton and Livingston licensed Aaron Ogden, a former governor of New Jersey and a U.S. senator, to operate steam-powered ferryboats between New York and New Jersey. Thomas Gibbons, a wealthy southern planter, decided to compete with Ogden, but he did so without New York's permission. Ogden sued Gibbons. The New York state courts granted Ogden an injunction, prohibiting Gibbons from operating in New York waters. Gibbons appealed the decision to the United States Supreme Court.

Sitting as chief justice on the Supreme Court was John Marshall, an advocate of a strong national government. In his decision, Marshall defined the word "commerce" as used in the commerce clause to mean all commercial intercourse—that is, all business dealings. The Court ruled against Ogden's monopoly, reversing the injunction against Gibbons. Marshall used this opportunity not only to expand the definition of commerce but also to validate and increase the power of the national legislature to regulate commerce. Said Marshall, "What is this power? It is the power * * * to prescribe the rule by which commerce is to be governed. This power, like all others vested in Congress, is complete in itself." In other words, the power of the national government to regulate commerce has no limitations other than those specifically found in the Constitution.

As a result of Marshall's decision, the commerce clause allowed the national government to exercise increasing authority over all areas of economic affairs throughout the land. Today, few areas of economic activity remain outside the regulatory power of the national legislature.

a. 22 U.S. (9 Wheat.) 1, 6 L.Ed. 23 (1824).

The Supremacy Clause

Article VI of the Constitution provides that the Constitution, laws, and treaties of the United States are "the supreme Law of the Land." This article, commonly referred to as the **supremacy clause**, is important in the ordering of state and federal relationships. When there is a direct conflict between a federal law and a state law, the state law is rendered invalid. But because some powers are concurrent—that is, they are shared by the federal government and the states—it is necessary to determine which law governs in a particular circumstance.

SUPREMACY CLAUSE
The provision in Article VI of the Constitution that provides that the Constitution, laws, and treaties of the United States are "the supreme Law of the Land." Under this clause, state laws that directly conflict with federal law will be rendered invalid.

When Congress chooses to act exclusively in a concurrent area, it is said to have *preempted* the area. In this circumstance, a valid federal statute or regulation will take precedence over a conflicting state or local law or regulation on the same general subject. Congress, however, rarely makes clear its intent to preempt an entire subject area against state regulation; consequently, the courts must determine whether Congress intended to exercise exclusive dominion over a given area. Consideration of **preemption** often occurs in the commerce clause context.

PREEMPTION
A doctrine under which certain federal laws preempt, or take precedence over, state or local laws.

No single factor is decisive as to whether a court will find preemption. Generally, congressional intent to preempt will be found if the federal law is so pervasive, comprehensive, or detailed that the states have no room to supplement it. Also, when a federal statute creates an agency—such as the National Labor Relations Board—to enforce the law, matters that may come within the agency's jurisdiction will likely preempt state laws.

In the following case, the court had to determine whether a federal law preempted a state statute.

Case 4.3
GREENWOOD TRUST CO. v. COMMONWEALTH OF MASSACHUSETTS
United States Court of Appeals, First Circuit, 1992.
971 F.2d 818.

HISTORICAL AND ECONOMIC SETTING *At the end of the 1970s, interest rates were high. Lending institutions that were chartered in certain states were constrained in the maximum interest rate and other fees that they could charge, however. Such restrictions often made loans uneconomical from the lender's point of view. Banks that were chartered at the federal level could charge higher rates and fees under the National Bank Act of 1864. In 1980, Congress enacted the Depository Institutions Deregulation and Monetary Control Act (DIDMA) to allow "competitive equity" among lending institutions. Among other things, the DIDMA permits state-chartered banks to charge higher rates and fees. The DIDMA also provides that a bank can use the laws of its home state in setting rates and fees in certain transactions with out-of-state borrowers.*

FACTS Greenwood Trust Company is a banking corporation chartered in Delaware. Greenwood offers a credit card (the Discover Card) to customers nationwide. Under the terms of the Discover Card, a late charge may be imposed for failing to make a minimum monthly payment on or before a designated due date. More than 100,000 cardholders live in Massachusetts. In 1989, the Commonwealth of Massachusetts advised Greenwood that its imposition of late charges violated state law. Massachusetts threatened to take legal action. Greenwood filed a complaint in the United States District Court for the District of Massachusetts, claiming that the DIDMA preempted the state prohibition against the imposition of late fees. The court held that Greenwood could not charge its Massachusetts customers late fees. Greenwood appealed.

ISSUE Does the DIDMA preempt state law, so that a bank chartered in Delaware can charge its Massachusetts credit-card customers a late fee on delinquent accounts, notwithstanding a Massachusetts statute prohibiting the practice?

DECISION Yes.

REASON The appellate court acknowledged that under Massachusetts law, late charges could not be imposed on delinquent credit-card accounts. Under the DIDMA, however, a credit-card issuer can impose charges in some circumstances according to (among other figures) amounts allowed by the law of the state in which the issuer is chartered. The DIDMA expressly preempts any state law that otherwise restricts those charges. Greenwood is a bank chartered in the state of Delaware. Greenwood can, therefore, impose charges according to the law of Delaware. Under the law of Delaware, credit-card issuers can impose late charges on delinquent credit-card accounts.

The Taxing Power

Article I, Section 8, further provides that Congress has the "Power to lay and collect Taxes, Duties, Imposts, and Excises * * * ; but all Duties, Imposts and Excises shall be uniform throughout the United States." The requirement of uniformity refers to uniformity among the states, and thus Congress may not tax some states while exempting others.

Traditionally, in reviewing cases related to the taxing power, the courts examined whether Congress was actually attempting to regulate indirectly, by taxation, an area in which it had no authority to regulate directly. If the regulatory effect could have been achieved directly by Congress, then the tax would not be stricken as an invalid, disguised regulation. If Congress was attempting to regulate an area over which it had no authority, however, the tax would be invalidated.

Over time, the United States Supreme Court has come to focus less on the motives of Congress and more on whether the tax can be sustained as a valid exercise of federal regulation. The Court has upheld taxes on dealers in firearms,[8] on the transfer of marijuana,[9] and on persons engaged in the business of accepting wagers.[10] If Congress does not have the power to regulate the activity being taxed, the tax

8. *Sonzinsky v. United States,* 300 U.S. 506, 57 S.Ct. 554, 81 L.Ed. 772 (1937).
9. *United States v. Sanchez,* 340 U.S. 42, 71 S.Ct. 108, 95 L.Ed. 47 (1950).
10. *United States v. Kahriger,* 345 U.S. 22, 73 S.Ct. 510, 97 L.Ed. 754 (1953).

Profile

Sandra Day O'Connor (1930–)

On September 21, 1981, history was made when the U.S. Senate unanimously confirmed the nomination of Sandra Day O'Connor as the first woman justice of the United States Supreme Court. Born in El Paso, Texas, she was raised on her grandfather's 162,000-acre Lazy B Ranch near Duncan, Arizona. O'Connor graduated *magna cum laude* from Stanford University with a B.A. degree in economics in 1950. Two years later, in 1952, she earned her LL.B. law degree from Stanford University Law School, where she was an editor of the *Stanford Law Review* and a member of the Order of the Coif, an honorary society. Also in 1952, she married John Jay O'Connor. In law school, she was a classmate of one of her future colleagues on the United States Supreme Court, William H. Rehnquist.

As was common for women professionals in the early 1950s, O'Connor had some difficulty finding employment where she could use her legal training. After serving briefly as deputy county attorney for San Mateo County, California, from 1952 to 1953, she accompanied her husband to Germany during his military service and worked as a civilian attorney for the army. Following a several-year interruption in her career to raise three sons—during which she worked part-time in the law—she became an assistant attorney general for the state of Arizona in 1965.

In 1969, she was appointed to fill a vacancy in the Arizona senate and retained the seat in the next year's election. She was chosen senate majority leader as a Republican in 1972—the first woman majority leader in history. Active in Republican politics, O'Connor also co-chaired the Arizona Committee to Re-Elect the President (Nixon) in 1972. In 1974, she was elected to the Superior Court for Maricopa County, and five years later she was appointed to the Arizona Court of Appeals. On August 19, 1981, President Ronald Reagan nominated her as an associate justice of the United States Supreme Court to replace Potter Stewart, who had retired. Her years on the Court have marked her as a conservative justice, but she is not doctrinaire or rigid in her approach to the law. Indeed, in some recent cases,[a] she has taken the liberal position. Generally, because she is less conservative than more recent appointments to the Court, she has come to occupy the Court's "middle," often casting the deciding vote in controversial cases.

a. See, for example, *United Automobile Workers v. Johnson Controls*, 499 U.S. 187, 111 S.Ct. 1196, 113 L.Ed.2d 158 (1991). In this case, which was presented as Case 2.3 in Chapter 2, Justice O'Connor found with the majority that fetal protection policies (banning fertile women from jobs that could result in harm to an unborn child) violate the Pregnancy Discrimination Act of 1978.

will still be upheld if it is a valid revenue-raising measure. If a tax measure bears some reasonable relationship to revenue production, it is generally held to be within the national taxing power. Moreover, the expansive interpretation of the commerce clause almost always provides a basis for sustaining a federal tax.

The Spending Power

Under Article I, Section 8, Congress has the power "to pay the Debts and provide for the common Defence and general welfare of the United States." Through the spending power, Congress disposes of the revenues accumulated from the taxing power. This power necessarily involves policy choices, with which taxpayers may disagree.

The requirement of **standing** makes it difficult for taxpayers to use the judicial system to object to government spending, and consequently, the spending power is seldom challenged. The doctrine of standing to sue requires that a litigant must have a sufficient stake in a controversy before the litigant can bring a lawsuit. The

STANDING
The requirement that an individual must have a sufficient stake in a controversy before he or she can bring a lawsuit. The plaintiff must demonstrate that he or she either has been injured or threatened with injury.

plaintiff must demonstrate that he or she has suffered *a direct and immediate personal injury* caused by the challenged action. Thus, a litigant must show that the injury suffered can be fairly traced to the challenged action and will be redressed by the judicial relief sought.[11] Communicating directly with members of Congress has proved to be a more efficient route to curbing or increasing federal allocations.

Congress can spend revenues not only to carry out its enumerated powers but also to promote any objective it deems worthwhile, so long as it does not violate the Bill of Rights. For example, Congress could not condition welfare payments on the recipients' agreements not to criticize government policies.

❖ Business and the Bill of Rights

BILL OF RIGHTS
The first ten amendments to the Constitution.

The importance of a written declaration of the rights of individuals eventually caused the first Congress of the United States to submit twelve amendments to the Constitution to the states for approval. Ten of these amendments, commonly known as the **Bill of Rights,** were adopted in 1791 and embody a series of protections for the individual against various types of interference by the federal government.[12] Some constitutional protections apply to business entities as well. For example, corporations exist as separate legal entities, or *legal persons*, and enjoy many of the same rights and privileges as *natural persons* do. Summarized here are the protections guaranteed by these ten amendments.[13] The *due process clause* of the Fourteenth Amendment applies many of the rights guaranteed by these first ten amendments to the states.

1. The First Amendment guarantees the freedoms of religion, speech, and the press and the rights to assemble peaceably and to petition the government.
2. The Second Amendment guarantees the right to keep and bear arms.
3. The Third Amendment prohibits, in peacetime, the lodging of soldiers in any house without the owner's consent.
4. The Fourth Amendment prohibits unreasonable searches and seizures of persons or property.
5. The Fifth Amendment guarantees the rights to indictment by grand jury, to due process of law, and to fair payment when private property is taken for public use. The Fifth Amendment also prohibits compulsory self-incrimination and double jeopardy (trial for the same crime twice).
6. The Sixth Amendment guarantees the accused in a criminal case the right to a speedy and public trial by an impartial jury and with counsel. The accused has the right to cross-examine witnesses against him or her and to solicit testimony from witnesses in his or her favor.
7. The Seventh Amendment guarantees the right to a trial by jury in a civil case involving at least twenty dollars.[14]
8. The Eighth Amendment prohibits excessive bail and fines, as well as cruel and unusual punishment.
9. The Ninth Amendment establishes that the people have rights in addition to those specified in the Constitution.
10. The Tenth Amendment establishes that those powers neither delegated to the federal government nor denied to the states are reserved for the states.

---

11. *Sierra Club v. Morton*, 405 U.S. 727, 92 S.Ct. 1361, 31 L.Ed.2d 636 (1972).
12. One of these proposed amendments was ratified 203 years later (in 1992) and became the Twenty-seventh Amendment to the Constitution. See Appendix B.
13. See the Constitution in Appendix B for the complete text of each amendment.
14. Twenty dollars was forty days' pay for the average person when the Bill of Rights was written.

It is important to realize that the rights secured by the Bill of Rights are not absolute. The principles enunciated in the Constitution are given form and substance by the government. Ultimately, it is the United States Supreme Court, as the interpreter of the Constitution, that both gives meaning to these constitutional rights and determines their boundaries.

Freedom of Speech

The First Amendment freedoms of religion, speech, press, assembly, and petition have all been applied to the states through the due process clause of the Fourteenth Amendment (discussed later in this chapter). As mentioned, however, none of these freedoms confers an absolute right.

"Free speech is not to be regulated like diseased cattle and impure butter. The audience . . . that hissed yesterday may applaud today, even for the same performance."

William O. Douglas, 1898–1980
(Associate justice of the United States Supreme Court, 1939–1975)

Unprotected Speech In interpreting the meaning of the First Amendment's guarantee of free speech, the United States Supreme Court has made it clear that certain types of speech will not be protected. Speech that harms the good reputation of another, for example, will not be protected under the First Amendment. Such speech can take the form of *libel* (if it is in writing) or *slander* (if it is made orally). Libel and slander are both forms of *defamatory* speech, as will be discussed in Chapter 5.

Lewd and obscene speech is another class of speech that is unprotected by the Constitution. Numerous state and federal statutes make it a crime to disseminate obscene materials. The United States Supreme Court has grappled from time to time with the problem of trying to establish an operationally effective definition of obscene speech, but frequently this determination is left to state and local authorities. Generally, obscenity is still a constitutionally unsettled area, whether it deals with speech or printed or filmed materials. In the interest of protecting against the abuse of children, however, the Supreme Court has upheld state laws prohibiting the sale and possession of child pornography;[15] and in the interest of protecting

15. See *Osborne v. Ohio*, 495 U.S. 103, 110 S.Ct. 1691, 109 L.Ed.2d 98 (1990).

Law in the Extreme

Are Erotic Messages Protected Speech?

Conflicts often arise between the First Amendment's protection of freedom of speech and the state's desire to regulate public behavior in the interest of protecting the health, safety, and morals of society. Nowhere is this conflict more evident than when the subject matter involves sexually explicit expression, whether it be in videos and movies, in books and magazines, or in erotic dancing. When an Indiana public indecency statute was enforced against totally nude dancing, several affected establishments sued, asserting that the statute violated the First Amendment. The United States District Court for the Northern District of Indiana agreed and permanently enjoined enforcement of the statute.[a] The Court of Appeals for the Seventh Circuit, however, did not agree.[b] In a new trial, the district court found that nude dancing was not protected by the First Amendment.[c] On appeal, this decision was also reversed.[d] The district court asked for a rehearing, which it got. The court of appeals reversed again.[e]

The case then went to the United States Supreme Court.[f] The Court was divided five to four on the issue. In the majority opinion, the Court held that enforcement of a public indecency statute that requires dancers at adult entertainment establishments to wear pasties and a G-string does not violate the First Amendment. The Court held that the law furthers a substantial government interest in protecting societal order and morality. Public indecency statutes reflect society's moral disapproval of people's appearing in the nude among strangers in public places. The Court said that erotic performances may be presented without any state interference as long as the performers wear a scant amount of clothing, however. The Court further argued that the state's interest in this case was unrelated to the suppression of free expression because the effects of the state statute are merely associated with nude dancing establishments and are not the result of the expression inherent in nude dancing. The Court stated that pasties and a G-string moderate expression to a minor degree when measured against the dancers'remaining capacity and opportunity to express an erotic message through their dancing.

a. *Glen Theater, Inc. v. Civil City of South Bend*, 726 F.Supp. 728 (N.D.Ind. 1985).
b. *Glen Theater, Inc. v. Pearson*, 802 F.2d 287 (7th Cir. 1986).
c. *Civil City of South Bend v. Miller*, 695 F.Supp. 414 (N.D.Ind. 1988).
d. *Miller v. Civil City of South Bend*, 887 F.2d 826 (7th Cir. 1989).
e. *Miller v. Civil City of South Bend*, 904 F.2d 1081 (7th Cir. 1990).
f. *Barnes v. Glen Theatre, Inc.*, ____U.S.____, 111 S.Ct. 2456, 115 L.Ed.2d 504 (1991).

women against sexual harassment in the workplace, at least one court has banned lewd speech and pornographic pinups in the workplace.[16] In recent years, obscenity issues have also arisen in relation to television shows, movies, the lyrics and covers of record albums, and the content of monologues by "shock" comedians.

Other unprotected speech includes "fighting words," or words that are likely to incite others to respond violently. Many people think that the hateful words ("hate speech") exchanged between members of different ethnic groups on college campuses should be included in the category of "fighting words." Courts, however, have

16. *Robinson v. Jacksonville Shipyards, Inc.*, 760 F.Supp. 1486 (M.D.Fla. 1991); see also the *Law in the Extreme* in Chapter 32, which discusses another case concerning this issue.

Why is symbolic speech—conduct that expresses opinions about a subject, such as the wearing of red ribbons to call attention to the AIDS epidemic—protected under the First Amendment to the Constitution?

been reluctant to uphold university "hate speech codes" banning such speech. In one case, for example, a federal court enjoined (prohibited) the University of Wisconsin from enforcing its hate speech code. The court held that the code was unconstitutional because it went too far in restricting the free speech of students.[17]

Symbolic Speech Not all expression is in words or in writing. Nonverbal expressions, such as gestures, movements, articles of clothing, and so on may, under certain circumstances, be considered **symbolic speech.** Such speech is given substantial protection today by our courts. For example, in 1969, the United States Supreme Court held that an Iowa school district's regulation prohibiting students from wearing black arm bands to school, as a gesture of protest against the Vietnam War (1964–1973), violated the First Amendment.[18] In 1989, in *Texas v. Johnson,* the Supreme Court ruled that state laws that prohibited the burning of the American flag as part of a peaceful protest also violated the freedom of expression protected by the First Amendment.[19] More recently, the Supreme Court ruled that a city statute banning bias-motivated disorderly conduct (including, in this case, the placing of a burning cross in another's front yard as a gesture of hate) was an unconstitutional restriction of speech.[20]

SYMBOLIC SPEECH
Nonverbal conduct that expresses opinions or thoughts about a subject. Symbolic speech is protected under the First Amendment's guarantee of freedom of speech.

Commercial Speech—Advertising A distinction is often made between "normal" speech and "commercial" speech. Commercial speech and communications, which

17. *The UWM Post v. Board of Regents of the University of Wisconsin System,* 774 F.Supp. 1163 (E.D.Wis. 1991).
18. *Tinker v. Des Moines School District,* 393 U.S. 503, 89 S.Ct. 733, 21 L.Ed.2d 731 (1969).
19. 491 U.S. 397, 109 S.Ct. 2533, 105 L.Ed.2d 89 (1989).
20. *R.A.V. v. City of St. Paul, Minnesota,* ___ U.S. ___, 112 S.Ct. 2538, 120 L.Ed.2d 305 (1992).

is speech by business firms, includes advertising and political contributions. Although commercial speech is protected by the First Amendment, its protection is not so extensive as that afforded to noncommercial speech. A state may restrict certain kinds of advertising, for example, in the interest of protecting consumers from being misled by the advertising practices. States also have a legitimate interest in the beautification of roadsides, and this interest allows states to place restraints on billboard advertising. Generally, a restriction on commercial speech will be considered valid as long as it (1) seeks to implement a substantial government interest, (2) directly advances that interest, and (3) goes no further than necessary to accomplish its objective.

Political Speech Speech that otherwise would be within the protection of the First Amendment does not lose that protection simply because its source is a corporation. For example, in *First National Bank of Boston v. Bellotti*, national banking associations and business corporations sought United States Supreme Court review of a Massachusetts statute that prohibited corporations from making political contributions or expenditures that individuals were permitted to make. The Court ruled that the Massachusetts law was unconstitutional because it violated the right of corporations to freedom of speech.[21] Similarly, the Court has held that a law forbidding a corporation from using bill inserts to express its views on controversial issues also violates the First Amendment.[22]

In the following case, decided by a more conservative Supreme Court, this trend was reversed.

Case 4.4

AUSTIN v. MICHIGAN CHAMBER OF COMMERCE

United States Supreme Court, 1990.
494 U.S. 652,
110 S.Ct. 1391,
108 L.Ed.2d 652.

HISTORICAL AND POLITICAL SETTING *In the 1970s, as one consequence of the scandals surrounding the events collectively known as Watergate, an effort was begun to limit the influence of wealth and corporate power on U.S. politics. This resulted in the restructuring of the federal and state election processes. At the federal level, amendments to the Federal Election Campaign Act of 1971 imposed more stringent limitations on funds spent by candidates for federal office. In a case involving a suit that challenged those amendments, the United States Supreme Court upheld the law on the ground that the government has an important interest in stopping corruption, or the appearance of corruption, that may result from large political campaign contributions. This government interest was sufficiently important to justify the law.*[a] *In many states, a number of laws that impose similar restrictions at the state level have also been enacted. Of course, none of these laws may violate the First Amendment.*

a. *Buckley v. Valeo,* 424 U.S. 1, 96 S.Ct. 612, 46 L.Ed.2d 659 (1976).

FACTS In June 1985, Michigan scheduled a special election to fill a vacancy in the state house of representatives. The Michigan State Chamber of Commerce, a Michigan corporation, sought to use its general corporate funds to place a newspaper advertisement supporting a specific candidate. Under the Michigan Campaign Finance Act, this is a felony. The act prohibits corporations from using general corporate funds for independent expenditures in state political campaigns. The act allows corporations to make expenditures through separate funds used solely for political purposes. The chamber filed a suit against the state in federal district court for an injunction against enforcement of the act, arguing in part that this restriction on expenditures is unconstitutional because it violates the First Amendment. The district court upheld the statute, and the chamber appealed. The court of appeals reversed the decision, reasoning that the act violated the First Amendment. The state, through Richard Austin, Michigan's secretary of state, appealed to the United States Supreme Court.

ISSUE Does the Michigan Campaign Finance Act violate the First Amendment?

---

21. 435 U.S. 765, 98 S.Ct. 1407, 55 L.Ed.2d 707 (1978).

22. *Consolidated Edison Co. v. Public Service Commission,* 447 U.S. 530, 100 S.Ct. 2326, 65 L.Ed.2d 319 (1980).

Case 4.4—Continued

DECISION No. The Supreme Court held that the act does not violate the First Amendment and reversed the decision of the court of appeals.

REASON The Supreme Court acknowledged that independent corporate spending to support a political candidate is political speech "at the core * * * of the First Amendment freedoms." Thus, any law that restricts such spending must be "narrowly tailored to serve a compelling state interest." The compelling state interest that justifies the Michigan act is preserving the fairness of political debate. State law grants corporations advantages that enable some of them to amass wealth. The Michigan act ensures that this wealth does not "unfairly influence elections when it is deployed in the form of independent expenditures." The act is "sufficiently narrowly tailored to achieve its goal" because it does not ban all forms of corporate political spending. Corporations can make independent expenditures through separate funds dedicated solely to political purposes.

Freedom of Religion

The First Amendment states that the government may neither establish any religion nor prohibit the free exercise of religious practices. This constitutional provision is referred to as either the **establishment clause** or the **free exercise clause.** Government action, both federal and state, must be consistent with this constitutional mandate.

ESTABLISHMENT CLAUSE
The provision in the First Amendment to the Constitution that prohibits Congress from creating any law "respecting an establishment of religion"

FREE EXERCISE CLAUSE
The provision in the First Amendment to the Constitution that prohibits Congress from making any law "prohibiting the free exercise" of religion.

Federal or state regulation that does not promote or place a significant burden on religion is constitutional even if it has some impact on religion. "Sunday closing laws," for example, make the performance of some commercial activities on Sunday illegal. These statutes, also known as "blue laws," have been upheld on the ground that it is a legitimate function of government to provide a day of rest. The United States Supreme Court has held that the closing laws, although originally of a religious character, have taken on the secular purpose of promoting the health and welfare of workers.[23] Even though closing laws admittedly make it easier for Christians to attend religious services, the Court has viewed this effect as an incidental, not a primary, purpose of Sunday closing laws.

The First Amendment does not require a complete separation of church and state. On the contrary, it affirmatively mandates *accommodation* of all religions and forbids hostility toward any.[24] The courts do not have an easy task in determining the extent to which governments can accommodate a religion without appearing to promote that religion and thus violate the establishment clause (see the *Business Law in Action* in this chapter).

For business firms, an important issue involves the accommodation that businesses must make for the religious beliefs of their employees. Title VII of the Civil Rights Act of 1964 prohibits government employers, private employers, and unions from discriminating against persons because of their religions. The Equal Employment Opportunity Commission—the regulatory agency that interprets and applies Title VII—has required that private employers "reasonably accommodate" the religious practices of their employees, unless to do so would cause undue hardship to the employer's business. For example, if an employee's religion prohibits him or her from working on a certain day of the week or at a certain type of job, the employer must make a reasonable attempt to accommodate these religious requirements. Employers must reasonably accommodate an employee's religious belief even if the belief is not based on the tenets or dogma of a particular church, sect, or denomination. The only requirement is that the belief be sincerely held by the employee.[25]

23. *McGowan v. Maryland*, 366 U.S. 420, 81 S.Ct. 1101, 6 L.Ed.2d 393 (1961).
24. *Zorach v. Clauson*, 343 U.S. 306, 72 S.Ct. 679, 96 L.Ed. 954 (1952).
25. *Frazee v. Illinois Department of Employment Security*, 489 U.S. 829, 109 S.Ct. 1514, 103 L.Ed.2d 914 (1989).

In the following case, the sacramental use of peyote by two employees violated both an employment policy and state law. When the employees were discharged for "misconduct," the state refused to grant them unemployment benefits. Ultimately, the United States Supreme Court had to determine whether a state law prohibiting the use of peyote violated the religious rights of members of the Native American Church whose religion required the sacramental use of this drug.

Case 4.5

EMPLOYMENT DIVISION, DEPARTMENT OF HUMAN RESOURCES OF THE STATE OF OREGON v. SMITH

Supreme Court of the United States, 1990.
494 U.S. 872,
110 S.Ct. 1595,
108 L.Ed.2d 876.

HISTORICAL AND CULTURAL DIVERSITY SETTING *The First Amendment protects persons from being punished for their religious beliefs. Thus, a law cannot make it a crime to hold a certain religious belief. To be protected under the First Amendment against a law that discriminates against a person's religious beliefs, the person must first prove that obeying the specific law would interfere with his or her sincerely held religious beliefs. The courts then balance three factors to determine whether to grant the person relief: (1) the severity of the burden of the law on the person, (2) the strength of the state interest behind the law, and (3) any alternative means that the legislature could employ to achieve the same objective. Before 1960, it was assumed that laws prohibiting the use of certain drugs could be applied to those who wished to use the drugs as part of their religions. After the development of the balancing test in the 1960s and 1970s, however, it seemed that a new approach to the problem might be needed.*

FACTS Smith and Black, both members of the Native American Church, worked as drug and alcohol abuse rehabilitation counselors. They were discharged by their employer for ingesting peyote, a hallucinogenic drug, for sacramental purposes during a religious ceremony of the Native American Church. When Smith and Black applied for state unemployment compensation, their applications were denied under an Oregon statute disqualifying employees who were discharged for work-connected misconduct. Smith and Black appealed the Employment Division's decision to the courts, claiming that the sacramental use of peyote did not constitute "misconduct" and that the state's denial of unemployment benefits violated their religious rights under the free exercise clause of the First Amendment. The Supreme Court of Oregon ruled in their favor, notwithstanding the fact that the use of peyote was illegal under Oregon law. According to the Supreme Court of Oregon, the law prohibiting the sacramental use of peyote was itself in violation of the First Amendment. The United States Supreme Court then addressed the issue of the statute's constitutionality.

ISSUE Did the Oregon law prohibiting the sacramental use of peyote violate the First Amendment?

DECISION No. The United States Supreme Court reversed the Oregon court's ruling. The Oregon statute prohibiting the ingestion of peyote did not violate the First Amendment, and the denial of unemployment benefits to Smith and Black—whose employment dismissal resulted from the use of this drug—did not violate their rights under the free exercise clause.

REASON The Court stated that "an individual's religious beliefs [do not] excuse him from compliance with an otherwise valid law prohibiting conduct that the State is free to regulate." Otherwise, the government's ability to enforce prohibitions of socially harmful conduct would be inhibited. "To make an individual's obligation to obey such a law contingent upon the law's coincidence with his religious beliefs" would contradict "both constitutional tradition and common sense." The Court acknowledged that less common religious practices might be at a disadvantage, "but that unavoidable consequence of democratic government must be preferred to a system in which each conscience is a law unto itself or in which judges weigh the social importance of all laws against the centrality of all religious beliefs."

Self-Incrimination

The Fifth Amendment guarantees that no person "shall be compelled in any criminal case to be a witness against himself." Thus, in any federal proceeding, an accused person cannot be compelled to give testimony that might subject him or her to any criminal prosecution. Nor can an accused person be forced to testify

Business Law in Action

Religious Symbols Go to Court

Retailers in America know the importance of the Christmas season. Some major retailers obtain 40 percent of their annual sales revenues during the Christmas season. Merchants begin decorating their stores for Christmas as early as October. Municipalities also spend tax dollars to decorate streets and government offices. Most of these decorations are not religious and apparently offend few individuals. Candy canes and pictures of Santa Claus abound.

But what about blatantly religious scenes? Does any government in the United States have the legal right to use public monies for the display of religious scenes or to permit the display of religious symbols on government (public) property? At issue here is the establishment clause of the First Amendment to the U.S. Constitution: "Congress shall make no law respecting an establishment of religion."

A major test of a municipality's ability to spend public funds on religious scenes during the Christmas season occurred in 1984. The city of Pawtucket in Rhode Island included a crèche—a model depicting Mary, Joseph, and others around the crib of Jesus in the stable at Bethlehem—in a larger, nonreligious Christmas display, which included reindeer, candy-striped poles, and a Christmas tree. The entire display was in a private park in a shopping district, rather than on government property. It was the city's official display, however, and had been both erected and maintained by city employees. This case, known as *Lynch v. Donnelly*,[a] was decided in favor of the municipal government. The crèche could be included as long as it was just one part of a holiday display. The presence of the crèche was deemed constitutional; it did not violate the establishment clause.

What about the simultaneous display by local governments of objects that are symbols from various religions? The American Civil Liberties Union (ACLU) sued Allegheny County, where Pittsburgh, Pennsylvania, is located, because of what the ACLU claimed were "frankly religious displays." Allegheny County annually erects a crèche in its county courthouse. Since 1982, Pittsburgh has also displayed a menorah (a nine-branched candelabrum used in celebrating Chanukah) near the annual Christmas tree on the steps of its city-county building. Although the county displays nonreligious holiday symbols in the courthouse, they are not displayed alongside the crèche, as they were in the *Lynch* case. Therefore, the Supreme Court held that the prescence of the crèche was unconstitutional.[b] Displaying the menorah, however, did not violate the First Amendment's prohibition against the establishment of religion, because it was situated in close proximity to the forty-five-foot-high Christmas tree.

By allowing the menorah to be positioned near the Christmas tree, the city of Pittsburgh had hoped to allay any fears that it was "endorsing" any one religion. During oral arguments, Justice Antonin Scalia asked the attorney representing the ACLU, "How can you possibly be endorsing either Christianity or Judaism when you have symbols of both?" The attorney answered, "You are endorsing Judeo-Christian symbols with an appalling lack of consideration for those who don't adhere to the Judeo-Christian tradition." Justice Scalia asked the attorney representing the city of Pittsburgh what the city did for Muslims. The attorney answered, "Nothing," and noted that a Muslim witness in the case had testified that the Muslim faith does not use outward symbols. Justice Scalia continued his queries with the general question: "[M]ustn't the city do something for every religion in order to avoid appearing to endorse one religion over another?" But, Justice John Paul Stevens wondered where does one draw the line? Should a religion with only three or four adherents also be represented?

Although the Supreme Court has had a respite in the last few years from decisions relating to Christmas displays, menorahs, and the like, other federal courts continue to face such questions. In 1992, for example, a federal district court in Cincinnati had to settle a conflict between the city of Cincinnati and two groups who wanted to display religious symbols on Cincinnati's Fountain Square. The issue arose after the Sixth Circuit Court of Appeals enjoined the city of Cincinnati from prohibiting the display of an eighteen-foot-high menorah in the public square during the eight days of Chanukah in 1991.[c] The Ku Klux Klan responded to the menorah display with a decision to erect a ten-foot-high cross in the square during the 1992 Chanukah season to "represent Jesus." The city of Cincinnati tried to foil the plans of both groups by approving the displays for 1992 but requiring that they be removed for the nighttime hours, from 10 P.M. to 6 A.M. Because of the time required to erect and remove these displays, in effect, the

a. 465 U.S. 668, 104 S.Ct. 1355, 79 L.Ed.2d 604 (1984).

b. *County of Allegheny v. American Civil Liberties Union*, 492 U.S. 573, 109 S.Ct. 3086, 106 L.Ed.2d 472 (1989).

c. *Congregation Lubavitch v. City of Cincinnati*, 923 F.2d 458 (6th Cir. 1991).

Business Law in Action—Continued

city's order made the displays impossible to be shown. The issue was again brought before a federal court. In deciding the issue, Judge Rubin emphasized not the establishment clause but the rights of the two groups to free speech and to the free expression of their religious beliefs. The city, by requiring the removal of the displays at night, had unconstitutionally restricted the groups' rights to free speech.[d]

d. *Congregation Lubavitch v. City of Cincinnati*, 807 F.Supp. 1353 (S.D.Ohio 1992).

Clearly, court judges and justices do not have an easy job. In addition to their other duties, they periodically have to function as a kind of "theology board," as Justice Kennedy put it, and must decide questions that would defy even the theological wizardry of a St. Thomas Aquinas.

against himself or herself in state courts because the due process clause of the Fourteenth Amendment incorporates the Fifth Amendment provision against self-incrimination.

The Fifth Amendment's guarantee against self-incrimination extends only to natural persons. Because a corporation is a legal entity and not a natural person, the privilege against self-incrimination is inapplicable to it. Similarly, the business records of a partnership do not receive Fifth Amendment protection.[26] When it is required that records of such organizations be produced, the information must be given even if it incriminates the persons who constitute the business entity. Sole proprietors and sole practitioners (those who fully own their businesses) who have not incorporated cannot be compelled to produce their business records. These individuals have full protection against self-incrimination because they function in only one capacity: there is no separate business entity.

Searches and Seizures

The Fourth Amendment protects the "right of the people to be secure in their persons, houses, papers, and effects." Federal, state, and local governments must obtain search warrants before searching or seizing private property. To obtain a **warrant,** law enforcement officers must convince a judge that they have reasonable grounds, or **probable cause,** to believe a search will reveal a specific illegality. Probable cause requires law enforcement officials to have trustworthy evidence that would convince a reasonable person that the proposed search or seizure is more likely justified than not. Furthermore, the Fourth Amendment prohibits *general* warrants. It requires a particular description of that which is to be searched or seized. General searches through a person's belongings are impermissible. The search cannot extend beyond what is described in the warrant.

WARRANT
An order granted by a public authority. An arrest warrant authorizes law-enforcement personnel to arrest a particular suspect; a search warrant authorizes law-enforcement personnel to search particular premises or property.

PROBABLE CAUSE
Reasonable grounds to believe the existence of facts warranting certain actions, such as the search or arrest of a person.

There are exceptions to the requirement of a search warrant, as when it is likely that the items sought will be removed before a warrant can be obtained. For example, if a police officer has probable cause to believe an automobile contains evidence of a crime and it is likely that the vehicle will be unavailable by the time a warrant is obtained, the officer can search the vehicle without a warrant.

Constitutional protection against unreasonable searches and seizures is important to businesses and professionals. As federal and state regulation of commercial activities increased, frequent and unannounced government inspections were conducted to ensure compliance with the regulations. Such inspections were at times extremely disruptive. In *Marshall v. Barlow's, Inc.*,[27] the United States Supreme Court held that government inspectors do not have the right to enter business premises without a warrant, although the standard of probable cause is not the same as

26. The privilege has been applied to some small family partnerships. See *United States v. Slutsky*, 352 F.Supp. 1005 (S.D.N.Y. 1972).
27. 436 U.S. 307, 98 S.Ct. 1816, 56 L.Ed.2d 305 (1978).

that required in nonbusiness contexts. The existence of a general and neutral enforcement plan will justify issuance of the warrant. Lawyers and accountants frequently possess the business records of their clients, and inspecting these documents while they are out of the hands of their true owners also requires a warrant. No warrant is required, however, for seizures of spoiled or contaminated food. Nor are warrants required for searches of businesses in such highly regulated industries as liquor, guns, and strip mining. General manufacturing is not considered to be one of these highly regulated industries.

Of increasing concern to many employers is how to maintain a safe and efficient workplace without jeopardizing the Fourth Amendment rights of employees "to be secure in their persons." Requiring employees to undergo random drug tests, for example, may be held to violate the Fourth Amendment. Fourth Amendment issues in the employment context, as well as employee privacy rights in general, will be discussed in Chapter 32.

❖ Other Constitutional Protections

Two other constitutional guarantees of great significance to Americans are mandated by the *due process clauses* of the Fifth and Fourteenth Amendments and the *equal protection clause* of the Fourteenth Amendment.

Due Process

Both the Fifth and the Fourteenth Amendments provide that no person shall be deprived "of life, liberty, or property, without due process of law." The **due process clause** of these constitutional amendments has two aspects—procedural and substantive. *Procedural* due process requires that any government decision to take life, liberty, or property must be made fairly, and thus fair procedures must be used in determining whether a person will be subjected to punishment or have some burden imposed on him or her. Fair procedure has been interpreted as requiring that the person have at least an opportunity to object to a proposed action before a fair, neutral decision maker (which need not be a judge). Thus, for example, if a driver's license is construed as a property interest, some sort of opportunity to object to its suspension or termination by the state must be provided.

DUE PROCESS CLAUSE
The provisions of the Fifth and Fourteenth Amendments to the Constitution provide that no person shall be deprived of life, liberty, or property without due process of law (fair and just reason and procedure). Similar clauses are found in most state constitutions.

Substantive due process focuses on the content, or substance, of legislation. In general, a law that is not compatible with the Constitution violates substantive due process. If a law or other governmental action limits a *fundamental right*, it will be held to violate substantive due process unless it promotes a *compelling or overriding state interest*. Fundamental rights include interstate travel, privacy, voting, and all First Amendment rights. Compelling interests could include, for example, the public's safety. Thus, laws designating speed limits may be upheld even though they affect interstate travel, if they are shown to reduce highway fatalities, because the state has a compelling interest in protecting the lives of its citizens.

In all other situations, a law or action does not violate substantive due process if it rationally relates to any legitimate governmental end. It is almost impossible for a law or action to fail the "rationality" test. Under this test, virtually any business regulation will be upheld as reasonable—the United States Supreme Court has sustained insurance regulations, price and wage controls, banking controls, and controls of unfair competition and trade practices against substantive due process challenges.

To illustrate, if a state legislature enacted a law imposing a fifteen-year term of imprisonment without a trial on all businesspersons who appeared in their own television commercials, the law would be unconstitutional on both substantive and procedural grounds. Substantive review would invalidate the legislation because it abridges freedom of speech. Procedurally, the law is unfair because it imposes the penalty without giving the accused a chance to defend his or her actions. The lack of procedural due process will cause a court to invalidate any statute or prior court decision. Similarly, a denial of substantive due process requires courts to overrule any state or federal law that violates the Constitution.

Equal Protection

EQUAL PROTECTION CLAUSE
The provision in the Fourteenth Amendment to the Constitution that guarantees that no state will "deny to any person within its jurisdiction the equal protection of the laws." This clause mandates that the state governments treat similarly situated individuals in a similar manner.

Under the Fourteenth Amendment, a state may not "deny to any person within its jurisdiction the equal protection of the laws." The United States Supreme Court has used the due process clause of the Fifth Amendment to make the **equal protection clause** applicable to the federal government. Equal protection means that the government must treat similarly situated individuals in a similar manner.

Both substantive due process and equal protection require review of the substance of the law or other governmental action rather than the procedures used. When a law or action limits the liberty of all persons to do something, it may violate substantive due process; when a law or action limits the liberty of some persons but not others, it may violate the equal protection clause. Thus, for example, if a law prohibits all persons from buying contraceptive devices, it raises a substantive due process question; if it prohibits only unmarried persons from buying the same devices, it raises an equal protection issue.

Basically, in determining whether a law or action violates the equal protection clause, a court will consider questions similar to those previously noted as applicable in a substantive due process review. Under an equal protection inquiry, when a law or action distinguishes between or among individuals, the basis for the distinction—that is, the *classification*—is examined. If the law or action inhibits some persons' exercise of a fundamental right, the classification must be necessary to promote a compelling state interest. Also, if the classification is based on a *suspect* trait—such as race, national origin, or citizenship status—the classification must be necessary to promote a compelling state interest. Compelling state interests include remedying past unconstitutional or illegal discrimination but do not include correcting the general effects of "society's" discrimination. Thus, for example, if a city gives preference to minority applicants in awarding construction contracts, the city normally must identify the past unconstitutional or illegal discrimination against minority construction firms that it is attempting to correct.

In matters of economic or social welfare, the classification will be considered valid if there is any conceivable *rational basis* on which the classification might relate to any legitimate government interest. Again, it is almost impossible for a law or action to fail the rational basis test. Thus, for example, a city ordinance that in effect prohibits all pushcart vendors except a specific few from operating in a particular area of the city will be upheld if the city proffers a rational basis—perhaps regulation and reduction of traffic in the particular area—for the ordinance. In contrast, a law that provides unemployment benefits only to people over six feet tall would violate the guarantee of equal protection. There is no rational basis for determining the distribution of unemployment compensation on the basis of height. Such a distinction could not further any legitimate government objective.

Another approach is applied in cases involving discrimination based on gender or legitimacy. Laws using these classifications must be *substantially related to important government objectives*. For example, an important government objective is preventing illegitimate teenage pregnancies. Because males and females are not similarly situated in this circumstance—only females can become pregnant—a law that punishes men but not women for statutory rape will be upheld. But a state law requiring illegitimate children to bring paternity suits within six years of their births will be struck down if legitimate children are allowed to seek support from their parents at any time. An important objective behind statutes of limitations is to prevent persons from bringing stale or fraudulent claims, but distinguishing between support claims on the basis of legitimacy has no relation to this objective.

The following case illustrates a court's application of the rational basis test in determining the validity of a state statute requiring motorcyclists to wear helmets.

Case 4.6
ROBOTHAM v. STATE
Supreme Court of Nebraska, 1992.
241 Neb. 379,
488 N.W.2d 533.

HISTORICAL AND SOCIAL SETTING *The history of state laws that require motorcycle riders to wear helmets demonstrates that the laws have dedicated proponents and equally dedicated opponents. Since the first mandatory helmet statute was enacted, the courts have been confronted with challenges to the laws. Normally, the question before the courts is not what a legislature should do as regards motorcycle riders but what a legislature can do. The general issue is whether the law violates the constitutional rights of individuals.*

FACTS In 1988, the Nebraska legislature enacted a statute that requires any motorcycle operator or passenger on Nebraska's highways to wear a "protective helmet." Eugene Robotham, a licensed motorcycle operator, sued the state of Nebraska to block enforcement of the law. Robotham asserted, among other things, that the statute violated the equal protection clause because it placed requirements on motorcyclists that were not imposed on other motorists. The court concluded that the law was constitutional. Robotham appealed.

ISSUE Does a statute that requires a person riding a motorcycle to wear a helmet violate the equal protection clause?

DECISION No. The Nebraska Supreme Court affirmed the lower court's decision regarding this part of Robotham's challenge to the mandatory helmet law.

REASON First, the Nebraska Supreme Court determined that the mandatory helmet law did not impinge on any fundamental constitutional rights and that motorcycle ridership is not a classification based on a suspect trait, gender, or illegitimacy. Thus, the rational basis test was applicable to determine whether the law violated the equal protection clause. The court identified the government interests in enacting the statute to be "[t]he protection of motorcycle riders from serious injury and the * * * protection of society from the repercussions of such injuries" and held that these are "legitimate legislative aim[s]." Finally, pointing out that mandatory helmet laws have been upheld by the United States Supreme Court, the Nebraska Supreme Court concluded that "the helmet law is a rational means to those ends."

Privacy Rights

Today, virtually all institutions with which an individual has dealings—including schools, doctors and dentists, insurance companies, mail-order houses, banking institutions, credit-card companies, and mortgage firms—obtain information about that individual and store it in their computer files. In addition, numerous government agencies, such as the Census Bureau, the Social Security Administration, and the Internal Revenue Service, collect and store data concerning individuals' incomes, expenses, marital status, and other personal history and habits. Any time an individual applies for a driver's license, a credit card, or even telephone service, information concerning that individual is gathered and stored. Frequently, this personal information finds its way to credit bureaus, marketing departments and firms, or other organizations without the permission or even the knowledge of the individuals concerned.

A personal right to privacy is held to be so fundamental as to be applicable at both the state and the federal level. Although there is no specific guarantee of a right to privacy in the Constitution, such a right has been derived from guarantees found in the First, Third, Fourth, Fifth, and Ninth Amendments. Invasion of another's privacy is also a civil wrong (see Chapter 5), and over the last several decades legislation has been passed at the federal level to protect the privacy of individuals in several areas of concern (see Exhibit 4–1). The privacy rights of individuals will be examined further, in the employment context, in Chapter 32.

♦ **Exhibit 4–1 Federal Legislation Relating to Privacy**

TITLE	PROVISIONS CONCERNING PRIVACY
Freedom of Information Act (1966)	Provides that individuals have a right to obtain access to information about them collected in government files.
Fair Credit Reporting Act (1970)	Provides that consumers have the right to be informed of the nature and scope of a credit investigation, the kind of information that is being compiled, and the names of the firms or individuals who will be receiving the report.
Crime Control Act (1973)	Safeguards the confidentiality of information amassed for certain state criminal systems.
Family Educational Rights and Privacy Act (1974)	Limits access to computer-stored records of education-related evaluations and grades in private and public colleges and universities.
Privacy Act (1974)	Protects the privacy of individuals about whom the federal government has information. Specifically, the act provides that: 1. Agencies originating, using, disclosing, or otherwise manipulating personal information must ensure the reliability of the information and provide safeguards against its misuse. 2. Information compiled for one purpose cannot be used for another without the concerned individual's permission. 3. Individuals must be able to find out what data concerning them are being compiled and how the data will be used. 4. Individuals must be given a means by which to correct inaccurate data.
Tax Reform Act (1976)	Preserves the privacy of personal financial information.
Right to Financial Privacy Act (1978)	Prohibits financial institutions from providing the federal government with access to a customer's records unless the customer authorizes the disclosure.
Electronic Fund Transfer Act (1978)	Requires financial institutions to notify an individual if a third party gains access to the individual's account.
Counterfeit Access Device and Computer Fraud and Abuse Act (1984)	Prohibits the use of a computer without authorization to retrieve data in a financial institution's or consumer reporting agency's files.
Cable Communications Policy Act (1984)	Regulates access to information collected by cable service operators on subscribers to cable services.
Electronic Communications Privacy Act (1986)	Prohibits the interception of information communicated by electronic means.

International Perspective

European Privacy Laws

As the nations of western Europe continue to integrate their economies, the difficulties of unifying into a single continental economy so many nations with varying political, social, economic, and cultural characteristics have become even more apparent. The European Commission has proposed to standardize the hodgepodge of privacy laws now in effect in some European states by passing a comprehensive privacy code known as the Privacy Directive. This initiative—though perhaps inspired by earlier American laws that prohibit certain intrusive actions by government—goes much further than American law because it requires firms to obtain the consent of the profiled persons before disseminating *any* personal data to third parties.

Proponents of the Privacy Directive see it as a powerful tool that could greatly change many business practices. Credit-card companies would have to obtain the permission of cardholders before they could sell their membership lists to direct-mail operations. Banks and credit agencies would find their access to the credit histories of individuals severely curtailed. In addition, consumers could withdraw their consent at any time and sue companies that continued to use their names. The Privacy Directive would also ban the dissemination of individual consumer spending profiles and prohibit the transmission of data to countries that do not have similarly strict privacy laws. Because the Privacy Directive represents the most comprehensive attempt to restrict the ability of companies to use data about particular individuals without their permission, the data transfer problems that could arise—especially for companies that operate throughout the world—are potentially staggering.

Many American businesses view the prior-consent aspect of the Privacy Directive as unworkable, because it would, in theory, require that a European subsidiary of an American company obtain the permission of each employee before it could ship copies of its employees' personnel records back to the United States. Direct-marketing companies, in particular, argue that the need to obtain the consent of every person on a mailing list would render such advertising prohibitively expensive. Multinational companies fear that the costs of business will skyrocket and that any company files remotely related to company personnel could be subject to inspection by the European Commission.

Despite fears that the Privacy Directive will further complicate doing business in the international arena, it has enormous appeal to consumers who are concerned about the uncontrolled dissemination of data about their personal lives. The Privacy Directive has already attracted the attention of civil libertarians and consumer advocates in the United States, because the leading federal law, the Privacy Act of 1974, applies only to government agencies—not to private businesses. If an Americanized version of the Privacy Directive is proposed in Congress, it may prove politically irresistible for most legislators.

Application

Law and the Publisher—How to Avoid Liability for Discriminatory Advertising

Advertising, as a form of commercial speech, receives a certain degree of protection under the First Amendment. But a law prohibiting certain forms of advertising will be deemed valid if, as mentioned in the text of this chapter, it seeks to implement a substantial government interest, directly advances that interest, and goes no further than necessary to accomplish its objective. Laws that prohibit misleading or discriminatory advertising usually meet these criteria for constitutional validity.

What this means for owners of newspapers and other media in which advertisements are placed is that they must take precautionary steps to avoid liability for unlawful advertising. Sex-based classifications in advertising, for example, such as "Help Wanted—Female" or "Males only need apply," are illegal because they violate laws prohibiting discrimination based on gender. Similarly, ads for the rental or sale of real estate that have racially discriminatory messages may be illegal and may subject the advertising media owner to liability.

Not only the wording of advertisements but also the illustrations must be monitored. In a recent case, for example, the Open Housing Center, Inc., and several African Americans in New York City brought suit against the New York Times Company (the Times), alleging that certain real estate ads in the *New York Times* communicated a "whites only" message to potential buyers of the real estate. The message was not conveyed by the words in the ads but by the illustrations, in which African Americans were depicted as being subservient to whites.[a] The Times claimed that the suit should be dismissed because it would be unconstitutional to require newspapers to monitor their ads. The federal trial court hearing the case did not agree with the Times (nor did the appellate court when the case was appealed). The court pointed out that the Times routinely monitors ads to avoid publishing ads that do not meet its "Standards of Advertising Acceptability." These standards provide, among other things, that the Times will not accept ads that fail to comply with antidiscrimination laws. The appellate court concluded that "it strains the credibility beyond the breaking point to assert that monitoring ads for racial messages imposes an unconstitutional burden [on the Times]."

The outcome in this case was significant for owners of newspapers and other media that accept advertisements because the suit was brought not against the real estate agency that placed the ads but against the Times, which published them. Holding publishers liable for ads that offend certain groups of readers may seem unfair, as it did to the Times, but the court viewed the matter otherwise.

a. *Ragin v. New York Times Co.*, 923 F.2d 995 (2d Cir. 1991).

Checklist for the Publisher

- ☐ 1. Do not assume that you cannot be liable for illegal ads placed in your newspaper (or other medium) simply because you were unaware that they were illegal.
- ☐ 2. Become familiar with federal and state laws regulating advertising.
- ☐ 3. Establish a policy of monitoring both the words and illustrations in ads to ensure that they do not violate any law.

❖ Key Terms

amend 96
Bill of Rights 104
checks and balances 98
commerce clause 98
due process clause 113
equal protection clause 114
establishment clause 109
federalism 97
free exercise clause 109
police powers 99
preemption 101
probable cause 112
standing 203
supremacy clause 101
symbolic speech 107
warrant 112

❖ Chapter Summary: Constitutional Law

Constitutional Powers of Government	The U.S. Constitution established a federal form of government in which government powers are shared by the national government and the state governments. At the national level, government powers are divided among the legislative, executive, and judicial branches.
Commerce Clause	1. *The regulatory power of the national government*—The commerce clause expressly permits Congress to regulate commerce. Over time, courts expansively interpreted the national regulatory power of Congress under the commerce clause, and today that power authorizes the national government, at least theoretically, to regulate every commercial enterprise in the United States. 2. *The regulatory power of the states*—Under their police powers, state governments may regulate private activities to protect or promote the public order, health, safety, morals, and general welfare. If state regulations substantially interfere with interstate commerce, they will be held to violate the commerce clause of the Constitution.
Supremacy Clause	The U.S. Constitution provides that the Constitution, laws, and treaties of the United States are "the supreme Law of the Land." Whenever a state law directly conflicts with a federal law, the state law is rendered invalid.
The Taxing Power	The U.S. Constitution gives Congress the power to impose taxes throughout the United States, but such taxes must be uniformly imposed; that is, Congress may not tax some states while exempting others.
The Spending Power	The U.S. Constitution gives Congress the power to spend revenues accumulated from the taxing power. Congress can spend revenues to promote any objective it deems worthwhile, so long as it does not violate the Bill of Rights.
Business and the Bill of Rights	The Bill of Rights consists of the first ten amendments to the U.S. Constitution. The amendments were adopted in 1791 and embody a series of protections for individuals—and in some cases, business entities—against various types of interference by the federal government. The Fourteenth Amendment applied most of these protections to the states. One of the freedoms guaranteed by the Bill of Rights that affect businesses is the following: *Freedom of speech*—Freedom of speech is guaranteed by the First Amendment. Symbolic speech, which consists of nonverbal expressions, gestures, clothing, and so on, is also given substantial protection by the courts. Commercial speech, such as advertising, falls under the protection of the First Amendment, but such speech is not protected to the degree that noncommercial speech is. Political speech, such as campaign contributions by corporations, also receives a certain degree of constitutional protection. There are certain classes of speech, however, such as defamatory speech and lewd and obscene speech, that the courts have held are not protected under the First Amendment.
Other Constitutional Protections	1. *Due process*—Both the Fifth and the Fourteenth Amendments provide that no person shall be deprived of "life, liberty, or property, without due process of law." Procedural due process requires that any government decision to take life, liberty, or property must be made fairly, using fair procedures. Substantive due process focuses on the content of legislation. Generally, a law that is not compatible with the Constitution violates substantive due process unless the law promotes a compelling state interest, such as public safety. 2. *Equal protection*—Under the Fourteenth Amendment, a state may not "deny to any person within its jurisdiction the equal protection of the laws." A law or action that limits the liberty of some persons but not others may violate the equal protection clause. Such a law may be deemed valid, however, if there is a rational basis for the discriminatory treatment of a given group or if the law substantially relates to an important government objective.

❖ Questions and Case Problems

4-1. Government Structure. What is the basic structure of the American national government?

4-2. Government Powers. The framers of the Constitution feared the twin evils of tyranny and anarchy. Discuss how specific provisions of the Constitution and the Bill of Rights reflect these fears and protect against both of these extremes.

4-3. Commercial Speech. A mayoral election is about to be held in a large U.S. city. One of the candidates is Luis Delgado, and his campaign supporters wish to post campaign signs on lampposts and utility posts throughout the city. A city ordinance, however, prohibits the posting of any signs on public property. Delgado's supporters contend that the city ordinance is unconstitutional because it violates their rights to free speech. Do you agree? In your answer, discuss what factors a court might consider in determining the constitutionality of the ordinance.

4-4. Commerce Clause. Suppose that Georgia enacts a law requiring the use of contoured rear-fender mudguards on trucks and trailers operating within its state lines. The statute further makes it illegal for trucks and trailers to use straight mudguards. In thirty-five other states, straight mudguards are legal. Moreover, in the neighboring state of Florida, straight mudguards are explicitly required by law. There is some evidence suggesting that contoured mudguards might be a little safer than straight mudguards. Discuss whether this Georgia statute would violate the commerce clause of the U.S. Constitution.

4-5. Freedom of Religion. A business has a backlog of orders, and to meet its deadlines, management decides to run the firm seven days a week, eight hours a day. One of the employees, Marjorie Tollens, refuses to work on Saturday on religious grounds. Her refusal to work means that the firm may not meet its production deadlines and may therefore suffer a loss of future business. The firm fires Tollens and replaces her with an employee who is willing to work seven days a week. Tollens claims that her employer, in terminating her employment, violated her constitutional right to the free exercise of her religion. Do you agree? Why or why not?

4-6. Freedom of Religion. Thomas worked in the nonmilitary operations of a large firm. The company discontinued the production of nonmilitary goods and transferred Thomas to a plant producing war materials. Thomas left his job, claiming that it violated his religious principles to participate in the manufacture of materials to be used in destroying life. In effect, he argued, the transfer to the war-materials plant forced him to quit his job. He was denied unemployment compensation by the state, which maintained that Thomas had not been effectively "discharged" by the employer but had voluntarily terminated his employment. Does the state's denial of unemployment compensation to Thomas violate the free exercise clause of the First Amendment? [*Thomas v. Review Board of the Indiana Employment Security Division*, 450 U.S. 707, 101 S.Ct. 1425, 67 L.Ed.2d 624 (1981)]

4-7. Freedom of Religion. A 1988 Minnesota statute required all operators of slow-moving vehicles to display on their vehicles a fluorescent orange-red triangular emblem or, as an alternative, a dull black triangle with a white reflective border plus seventy-two square inches of permanent red reflective tape. A vehicle operator who chose the alternative emblem still had to carry a regular orange-red emblem in the vehicle and display it externally during times of darkness or low visibility. When Hershberger and other members of the Amish religion (the defendants) refused to comply with the statute, the state brought charges against them. The defendants claimed that the statute violated their freedom of religion under the First Amendment because displaying the "loud" colors and "worldly symbols" on their slow-moving vehicles (black, boxlike buggies) compromised their religious belief that they should remain separate and apart from the modern world. The defendants stated that they would not object to displaying a sign similar to the alternative symbol if they could use silver, instead of red, reflective tape and if they did not have to display the "regular" emblem at night. The state argued that, although the silver tape was as effective as the red in terms of visibility, the red tape was customarily associated with slow-moving vehicles and therefore the Amish should comply with the statute as written. What will the court hold? Discuss. [*State v. Hershberger*, 444 N.W.2d 282 (Minn. 1989)]

4-8. Commercial Speech. In 1982, Philip Zauderer, an attorney practicing in Columbus, Ohio, placed a series of newspaper ads directed at women who had used the Dalkon Shield intrauterine device (IUD). In his ads, Zauderer included a drawing of the Dalkon Shield and informed women that they could still sue for any injuries or other harm to their health sustained by its use, even though the IUD was no longer being marketed. As a result of these ads, Zauderer filed lawsuits for 106 women. The Ohio Supreme Court deemed such advertisements unethical, and Zauderer was reprimanded by the court for his actions. He was further reprimanded for not having disclosed in his ads that, although his clients would owe no legal fees if they lost, they might still be faced with other costs involved in litigation. Zauderer appealed, claiming the ads were protected under the First Amendment as commercial speech and that failure to disclose other costs was not deceptive. Discuss the probable success of Zauderer's appeal. [*Zauderer v. Office of Disciplinary Counsel*, 471 U.S. 626, 105 S.Ct. 2265, 85 L.Ed.2d 652 (1985)]

4-9. Commerce Clause. Taylor owned a bait business in Maine and arranged to have live baitfish imported into the state. The importation of the baitfish violated a Maine statute. Taylor was indicted under a federal statute that makes it a federal crime to transport fish in interstate commerce in violation of state law. Taylor moved to dismiss the indictment on the ground that the Maine statute unconstitutionally burdened interstate commerce. Maine intervened to defend the validity of its statute, arguing that the law legitimately protected the state's fisheries from parasites and nonnative species that might be included in shipments of live baitfish. Were Maine's interests in protecting its fisheries from parasites and nonnative species sufficient to justify the burden placed on interstate commerce by the Maine statute? Discuss. [*Maine v. Taylor*, 477 U.S. 131, 106 S.Ct. 2440, 91 L.Ed.2d 110 (1986)]

4-10. Freedom of Speech. In 1988, as a result of a general election, Arizona added Article XXVIII to its constitution. Article XXVIII provided that English was to be the official language of the state and required all state officials and employees to use only the English language during the performance of government business. Maria-Kelly Yniguez, an employee of the Arizona Department of Administration, frequently spoke in Spanish to Spanish-speaking persons with whom she dealt in the course of her work. Yniguez claimed that Article XXVIII violated constitutionally protected free speech rights and brought an action in federal court against the state governor, Rose Mofford, and other state officials. Does Article XXVIII violate the freedom of speech guaranteed by the First Amendment to the U.S. Constitution? Why or why not? [*Yniguez v. Mofford*, 730 F.Supp. 309 (D.Ariz. 1990)]

4-11. Equal Protection. Adela Izquierdo Prieto, age forty-two, had worked for a government-owned and -operated radio and television station in Puerto Rico for over a decade when, without any prior notice, she was suddenly transferred from her television program to a position in radio. Her replacement in the television program was a twenty-eight-year-old woman with less experience. Agustin Mercado Rosa, the administrator of the television channel, explained to a newspaper reporter that Izquierdo was removed because "we need new faces" and because Izquierdo's replacement "is young, attractive and refreshing." Izquierdo sued Mercado, alleging in part that the transfer discriminated against her on the basis of age and therefore violated her rights under the equal protection clause. Mercado claimed that the transfer was rationally related to furthering a legitimate state interest in maximizing viewership for the public television channel and therefore was a permissible action. Will the court agree with Mercado? (In forming your answer, disregard the fact that Izquierdo could have sued Mercado under a federal law prohibiting age discrimination in employment. She did not do so but based her claim only on the equal protection clause, and therefore the court did not address that issue. The sole issue here is whether the state's interest was sufficient to justify replacing Izquierdo.) [*Izquierdo Prieto v. Mercado Rosa*, 8942 F.2d 467 (1st Cir. 1990)]

4-12. Equal Protection. In response to rapidly rising property taxes, California voters approved a statewide ballot initiative, Proposition 13, that added Article XIIIA to the state constitution. Among other things, Article XIIIA embodied an "acquisition value" system of taxation, whereby property was reassessed up to current appraised value on new construction or a change in ownership. Exemptions from the reassessment existed for two types of transfers: (1) exchanges of principal residences by persons over the age of fifty-five and (2) transfers between parents and children. Over time, the acquisition-value system created dramatic disparities in the taxes paid by persons owning similar parcels of property. Long-term owners paid lower taxes reflecting historic property values, while new owners paid higher taxes reflecting more recent values. Faced with such a disparity, Stephanie Nordlinger, who had recently bought a house in Los Angeles County, sued the county and Kenneth Hahn, the county tax assessor, claiming that Article XIIIA's reassessment scheme violated the equal protection clause. The complaint was dismissed, and ultimately Nordlinger appealed to the United States Supreme Court. Will the Court hold that the California property tax system violates the equal protection clause? [*Nordlinger v. Hahn*, ___U.S.___, 112 S.Ct. 2326, 120 L.Ed.2d 1 (1992)]

A Question of Ethics and Social Responsibility

4-13. *Agnes and John Donahue refused to rent an apartment to an unmarried couple, Verna Terry and Robert Wilder. The Donahues were devout Roman Catholics and firmly believed, in accordance with the church's teachings, that engaging in sexual relations outside of marriage was a mortal sin. Agnes Donahue also believed that it would be sinful for her to aid another person in the commission of a sin. Renting an apartment to an unmarried couple would, in Agnes Donahue's mind, be aiding the couple in the commission of a sin, and therefore she refused to rent the apartment to Terry and Wilder. Terry and Wilder filed a complaint with the California Fair Employment and Housing Commission, alleging that the Donahues' refusal to rent them an apartment violated a state statute prohibiting discrimination on the basis of marital status. Eventually, the case was heard by a California appellate court. The question before the court was whether the state's interest in prohibiting discrimination based on marital status outweighed the Donahues' constitutional right to the free exercise of their religion.* [Donahue v. Fair Employment and Housing Commission, 7 *Cal.App.4th* 1498, 2 *Cal.Rptr.2d* 32 *(1991)*]

1. In your opinion, should the court make an exception to the state statute's applicability in the Donahues' case? Why or why not?
2. Review Case 4.5, which involved a conflict between a state statute and the right to the free exercise of religion. How did the court decide the issue in that case? Should the same principle be applied to the Donahues' actions?

Case Briefing Assignment

4-14. *Examine Case A.2* [Austin v. Berryman, 878 F.2d 786 *(4th Cir. 1989)*] *in Appendix A. The case has been excerpted there in great detail. Review and then brief the case, making sure that you include answers to the following questions in your brief.*

1. Who were the plaintiff and defendant in this action?
2. Why did Austin claim that she had been forced to leave her job?
3. Why was she refused state unemployment benefits?
4. Did the state's refusal to give her unemployment compensation violate her rights under the free exercise clause of the First Amendment?
5. What logic or reasoning did the court employ in arriving at its conclusion?

For Critical Analysis

4-15. *Look at the Constitution in Appendix B. Explain why this document, which was written well over two hundred years ago, can still function today as the "supreme Law of the Land."*

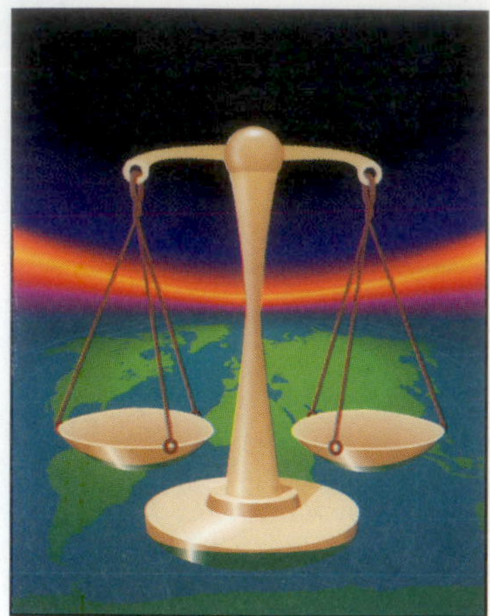

Chapter 5

Torts

"You cannot do wrong without suffering wrong."

Ralph Waldo Emerson, 1803–1882
(American author)

TORTS
Civil (as opposed to criminal) wrongs not arising from a breach of contract. A breach of a legal duty owed by the defendant to the plaintiff; the breach must be the proximate cause of harm to the plaintiff.

PROTECTED INTERESTS
All interests protected by law. Protected interests include civil rights and liberties, freedom from harms resulting from intentional or unintentional torts, harms caused by criminal actions, and so on.

Emerson's statement expresses the principle underlying the law governing **torts** (wrongful conduct).[1] Through tort law, society compensates those who have suffered injuries for such wrongful conduct. Although some torts, such as assault and trespass, originated in the English common law, the field of tort law continues to expand as new ways to commit wrongs are discovered and new conceptions of what is right and wrong in a social or business context emerge.

Tort law covers a wide variety of injuries. Society recognizes an interest in personal physical safety, and tort law provides remedies for acts that cause physical injury or that interfere with physical security and freedom of movement. Society recognizes an interest in protecting personal property, and tort law provides remedies for acts that cause destruction or damage to property. Society also recognizes an interest in protecting certain intangible interests, such as personal privacy, family relations, reputation, and dignity, and tort law provides remedies for invasion of these **protected interests.**

Torts also occur in the business context. This important area of tort law will be treated in Chapter 6.

❖ The Basis of Tort Law

Two notions serve as the basis of all torts: wrongs and compensation. Tort law recognizes that some acts are wrong because they cause injuries to others. Of course, a tort is not the only type of wrong that exists in the law; crimes also involve wrongs. A crime, however, is an act so reprehensible that it is considered a wrong against the state or against society as a whole, as well as against the individual victim. Therefore, the *state* prosecutes a person committing a criminal act. A tort action, however, is a *civil* action in which one person brings a personal suit against another.

In some cases, such as *assault and battery* (explained in a following section), a basis could exist for a criminal prosecution as well as a tort action. For example, Joe is walking down the street, minding his own business, when suddenly he is attacked by someone. In the ensuing struggle, Joe is punched in the nose, breaking it. The wrongdoer is restrained and arrested by a police officer. In this situation, the attacker may be subject both to criminal prosecution by the state and to a tort lawsuit brought by Joe for **damages** to compensate him for his injury.

DAMAGES
Money sought as a remedy for a breach of contract or for a tortious act.

1. The term *tort* is French for "wrong."

❖ Intentional Torts against Persons

An **intentional tort**, as the term implies, requires *intent.* The **tortfeasor** (the one committing the tort) must intend to commit an act, the consequences of which interfere with the personal or business interests of another in a way not permitted by law. An evil or harmful motive is not required—in fact, the actor may even have a beneficial motive for committing what turns out to be a tortious act. In tort law, intent only means that the actor intended the consequences of her or his act or knew with substantial certainty that certain consequences would result from the act. The law generally assumes that individuals intend the *normal* consequences of their actions. Thus, forcefully pushing another—even if done in jest and without any evil motive—is an intentional tort (if injury results) because the object of a strong push can ordinarily be expected to go flying. A light pat on the shoulder, in contrast, is not an intentional tort, even though, in drawing away suddenly, the person touched may be injured.

INTENTIONAL TORT
A wrongful act knowingly committed.

TORTFEASOR
One who commits a tort.

This section discusses intentional torts against persons, which include assault and battery, false imprisonment, infliction of emotional distress, defamation, invasion of the right to privacy, and misrepresentation.

Assault and Battery

Any intentional, unexcused act that creates in another person a reasonable apprehension or fear of immediate harmful or offensive contact is an **assault**. Note that apprehension is not the same as fear. If a contact is such that a reasonable person would want to avoid it, and if there is a reasonable basis for believing that the contact will occur, then the plaintiff suffers apprehension whether or not he or she is afraid. The interest protected by tort law concerning assault is the freedom from having to expect harmful or offensive contact. The occurrence of apprehension is enough to justify compensation.

ASSAULT
Any word or action intended to make another person fearful of immediate physical harm; a reasonably believable threat.

The *completion* of the act that caused the apprehension, if it results in harm to the plaintiff, is a **battery,** which is defined as an unexcused and harmful or offensive physical contact *intentionally* performed. For example, Ivan threatens Jean with a gun, then shoots her. The pointing of the gun at Jean is an assault; the firing of the gun (if the bullet hits Jean) is a battery. The interest protected by tort law concerning battery is the right to personal security and safety. The contact can be harmful, or it can be merely offensive (such as an unwelcome kiss). Physical injury need not occur. The contact can involve any part of the body or anything attached to it—for example, a hat or other item of clothing, a purse, or a chair or an automobile in which one is sitting. Whether the contact is offensive or not is determined by the *reasonable person* standard.[2] The contact can be made by the defendant or by some force the defendant sets in motion—for example, a rock thrown, food poisoned, or a stick swung.

BATTERY
The unprivileged, intentional touching of another.

If the plaintiff shows that there was contact, and the jury agrees that the contact was offensive, the plaintiff has a right to compensation. There is no need to show that the defendant acted out of malice; the person could have been joking or playing or could even have had some benevolent motive. The underlying motive does not matter, only the intent to bring about the harmful or offensive contact to the plaintiff. In fact, proving a motive is never necessary (but is sometimes relevant). A plaintiff may be compensated for the emotional harm or loss of reputation resulting from a battery, as well as for physical harm.

---

2. The reasonable person standard is an objective test of how a reasonable person would have acted under the same circumstances. See "The Duty of Care and Its Breach" later in this chapter.

DEFENSE
That which a defendant offers and alleges in an action or suit as a reason why the plaintiff should not recover or establish what he or she seeks.

LIABILITY
Any actual or potential legal obligation, duty, debt, or responsibility.

A number of legally recognized **defenses** can be raised by a defendant who is sued for assault or battery, or both:

1. *Consent.* When a person consents to the act that damages him or her, there is generally no **liability** for the damage done.
2. *Self-defense.* An individual who is defending his or her life or physical well-being can claim self-defense. In situations of both *real* and *apparent* danger, a person is privileged to use whatever force is *reasonably* necessary to prevent harmful contact.
3. *Defense of others.* An individual can act in a reasonable manner to protect others who are in real or apparent danger.
4. *Defense of property.* Reasonable force may be used in attempting to remove intruders from one's home, although force that is likely to cause death or great bodily injury can never be used just to protect property.

False Imprisonment

False imprisonment is defined as the intentional confinement or restraint of another person's activities without justification. It involves interference with the freedom to move without restraint. The confinement can be accomplished through the use of physical barriers, physical restraint, or threats of physical force. Moral pressure or future threats do not constitute false imprisonment. It is essential that the person being restrained not comply with the restraint willingly.

Businesspersons are often confronted with suits for false imprisonment after they have attempted to confine a suspected shoplifter for questioning. Under the privilege to detain granted to merchants in some states, a merchant can use the defense of *probable cause* to justify delaying a suspected shoplifter. Probable cause exists when the evidence to support the belief that a person is guilty outweighs the evidence against that belief. The detention, however, must be conducted in a *reasonable* manner and for only a *reasonable* length of time.

Infliction of Emotional Distress

The tort of *infliction of emotional distress* can be defined as an intentional act that amounts to extreme and outrageous conduct resulting in severe emotional distress to another.[3] For example, a prankster telephones an individual and says that the individual's spouse has just been in a horrible accident. As a result, the individual suffers intense mental pain or anxiety. The caller's behavior is deemed to be extreme and outrageous conduct that exceeds the bounds of decency accepted by society and is therefore **actionable** (capable of serving as the ground for a lawsuit).

ACTIONABLE
Capable of serving as the basis of a lawsuit. An actionable claim can be pursued in a lawsuit or other court action.

Because infliction of emotional distress is a relatively new tort, it poses some problems. It is difficult to prove the existence of emotional suffering, and so a few states require that the emotional disturbance be evidenced by some physical illness. In the following case, the court looks at some of the requirements that plaintiffs must meet in establishing an emotional distress claim.

Case 5.1
FUDGE v. PENTHOUSE INTERNATIONAL, LTD.
United States Court of Appeals, First Circuit, 1988.
840 F.2d 1012.

HISTORICAL AND SOCIAL SETTING *Intentional infliction of emotional distress is a relatively new tort. The law's reluctance to protect freedom from emotional distress as a separate interest may be due to a fear of false claims and a mistrust of the proof that plaintiffs sometimes offer to support their claims for damages for emotional distress. Whatever the reasons may be, the ultimate limits of the tort*

3. Restatement (Second) of Torts, Section 46, Comment d. The Restatement (Second) of Torts is a compilation of the law of torts by the American Law Institute.

Case 5.1—Continued

*have not yet been determined. Generally, in the words of the Restatement (Second) of Torts, Section 46, Comment d, liability has not been found in cases involving "mere insults, indignities, threats, annoyances, petty oppressions, or other trivialities. * * * [People] must necessarily be expected and required to be hardened to a certain amount of rough language, and to occasional acts that are inconsiderate and unkind. There is no occasion for the law to intervene in every case where someone's feelings are hurt."*

FACTS Leslie Fudge was a student at the Oakland Beach Elementary School in Warwick, Rhode Island. In the fall of 1985, because of apparent conflicts between some of the school's male and female students, the school's principal decided to segregate the sexes during recess periods. A Providence, Rhode Island, newspaper ran an item on the story, along with a photograph showing Leslie Fudge and other girls giving the thumbs-down sign to show their disapproval of the principal's decision. The story and the picture were eventually picked up by *Penthouse* magazine, which printed a one-paragraph story about the girls, along with a slightly cropped version of the photograph that had appeared in the Providence newspaper. The story was headlined "Little Amazons Attack Boys" and appeared in a section of the magazine entitled "Hard Times: A compendium of bizarre, idiotic, lurid, and ofttimes witless driblets of information culled from the nation's press." The brief item told how the Warwick school had segregated the sexes to protect the boys from the girls who "kick them in the shins, pull their hair, and kick them, well, in various painful places." It concluded: "In the battle of the sexes, we'd certainly score this round for the girls." Four of the girls in the picture and their parents brought an action against the owners of *Penthouse* magazine, Penthouse International, Ltd., alleging, among other things, that the publication of the photograph of the girls in a sexually explicit men's magazine constituted the intentional infliction of emotional distress. Penthouse moved for summary judgment, which the district court granted. The plaintiffs—the girls and their parents—appealed.

ISSUE Does the publication of the photograph of the girls in *Penthouse* magazine constitute the tort of intentional infliction of emotional distress?

DECISION No. The First Circuit Court of Appeals agreed with the district court that the plaintiffs had failed to state an emotional distress claim. The decision to grant Penthouse's motion for summary judgment against the plaintiffs was affirmed.

REASON In determining whether summary judgment should have been granted in this case, the court looked to the Restatement (Second) of Torts, Section 46, Comment h, which states as follows: "It is for the court to determine, in the first instance, whether the defendant's conduct may reasonably be regarded as so extreme and outrageous as to permit recovery * * *. Where reasonable men may differ, it is for the jury, subject to the control of the court, to determine whether, in the particular case, the conduct has been sufficiently extreme and outrageous to result in liability." The court went on to say that the "extreme and outrageous" standard is a difficult one to meet. Citing Comment d of the same section of the Restatement (Second) of Torts, the court said, "Liability has been found only where the conduct has been so outrageous in character, and so extreme in degree, as to go beyond all possible bounds of decency, and to be regarded as atrocious, and utterly intolerable in a civilized community." The court could find nothing in the plaintiffs' allegations that was "sufficiently extreme and outrageous to warrant the imposition of liability." There was nothing shocking about the photograph itself; what the plaintiffs objected to was the fact that it had been published in *Penthouse* magazine. But, stated the court, "Magazines such as *Penthouse* are sufficiently a part of the contemporary scene that their reprinting of relatively innocuous news items or photographs that have already appeared in other media simply cannot be characterized as exceeding all possible bounds of decency, atrocious, or utterly intolerable in a civilized society."

Defamation

Defamation of character involves wrongfully hurting a person's good reputation. The law has imposed a general duty on all persons to refrain from making false, defamatory statements about others. Breaching this duty orally involves the tort of *slander;* breaching it in writing involves the tort of *libel.* The tort of defamation also arises when a false statement is made about a person's product, business, or title to property. These torts will be dealt with in the following chapter.

DEFAMATION
Anything published or publicly spoken that causes injury to another's good name, reputation, or character.

The Publication Requirement The basis of the tort of defamation is the *publication* of a statement or statements that hold an individual up to contempt, ridicule,

"Reputation, reputation, reputation! O, I have lost my reputation! I have lost the immortal part of myself, and what remains is bestial."

William Shakespeare, 1564–1616
(English dramatist and poet)

or hatred. *Publication* here means that the defamatory statements are communicated to persons other than the defamed party. If Thompson writes Andrews a private letter accusing him of embezzling funds, the action does not constitute libel. If Peters calls Gordon dishonest, unattractive, and incompetent when no one else is around, the action does not constitute slander. In neither case was the message communicated to a third party. The courts have generally held that even dictating a letter to a secretary constitutes publication, although the publication may be *privileged* (as explained in the following section). Moreover, if a third party overhears defamatory statements by chance, the courts usually hold that this also constitutes publication. Note further that any individual who republishes or repeats defamatory statements is liable even if that person reveals the source of such statements.

The common law defines four types of false utterances that are considered torts *per se* (meaning no proof of injury or harm is required for these false utterances to be actionable):

1. A statement that another has a loathsome communicable disease.
2. A statement that another has committed improprieties while engaging in a profession or trade.
3. A statement that another has committed or has been imprisoned for a serious crime.
4. A statement that an unmarried woman is unchaste.

PRIVILEGE
In tort law, the ability to act contrary to another person's right without being liable for the consequences.

Defenses against Defamation Truth is normally an *absolute* defense against a defamation charge. Furthermore, there may be a **privilege** involved in certain communications. For example, statements made by attorneys and judges during a trial are privileged and therefore cannot be the basis for a defamation charge. Members of Congress making statements on the floor of Congress have an absolute privilege. Legislators have complete immunity from liability for false statements made in debate, even if they make such statements maliciously—that is, knowing them to be untrue. In general, false and defamatory statements that are made about public figures and that are published in the press are privileged if they are made without **actual malice.**[4] To be made with actual malice, a statement must be made *with either knowledge of falsity or a reckless disregard of the truth.*

ACTUAL MALACE
Real and demonstrable evil intent. In a defamation suit, a statement made about a public figure normally must be made with actual malice (with either knowledge of its falsity or a reckless disregard of the truth) for liability to be incurred.

Notice here the difference between *private individuals* and *public figures.* Public figures include public officers and employees who exercise substantial governmental power and any persons in the public limelight. Statements made about public figures, especially when they are made via a public medium, are usually related to matters of general public interest; they are made about people who substantially affect all of us. Furthermore, public figures generally have some access to a public medium for answering disparaging falsehoods about themselves; private individuals do not. For these reasons, public figures have a greater burden of proof in defamation cases than do private individuals. A public figure must prove that a defamatory statement was made with actual malice in order to recover damages.

Invasion of the Right to Privacy

A person has a right to solitude and freedom from prying public eyes—in other words, to privacy. Four acts qualify as an invasion of that privacy:

1. The use of a person's name or picture for commercial purposes without permission.
2. Intrusion upon an individual's affairs or seclusion.
3. Publication of information that places a person in a false light. This could be

4. *New York Times Co. v. Sullivan,* 376 U.S. 254, 84 S.Ct. 710, 11 L.Ed.2d 686 (1964).

a story attributing to the person ideas not held or actions not taken by the person. (Publishing such a story could involve the tort of defamation as well.)
4. Public disclosure of private facts about an individual that an ordinary person would find objectionable.

"Truth is generally the best vindication against slander."

Abraham Lincoln, 1809–1865
(Sixteenth president of the United States, 1861–1865)

Misrepresentation—Fraud (Deceit)

The tort of **misrepresentation** as fraud involves intentional deceit for personal gain. It includes several elements:

MISREPRESENTATION
A false representation created by one party—by a misstatement of facts, by a failure to mention a material fact, or by conduct—deceiving another and on which the other reasonably relies to his or her detriment.

1. Misrepresentation of facts or conditions with knowledge that they are false or with reckless disregard for the truth.
2. Intent to induce another to rely on the misrepresentation.
3. Justifiable reliance by the deceived party.
4. Damages suffered as a result of reliance.
5. Causal connection between the misrepresentation and the injury suffered.

A misrepresentation leads another to believe in a condition that is different from the one that actually exists. This is often accomplished through a false or an incorrect statement. Misrepresentations may be innocently made by someone who is unaware of the existing facts, but a misrepresentation is fraudulent when it is made by a person who knows the facts to be false and intends to mislead another.

For **fraud** to occur, more than mere **puffery,** or *seller's talk,* must be involved. Fraud exists only when a person represents as a fact something he or she knows is untrue. For example, it is fraud to claim that a building does not leak when one knows it does. Facts are objectively ascertainable, whereas seller's talk is not. "I am the best accountant in town" is seller's talk. The speaker is not trying to represent something as fact because the term *best* is a subjective, not an objective, term.

FRAUD
Any misrepresentation, either by misstatement or omission of a material fact, knowingly made with the intention of deceiving another and on which a reasonable person would and does rely to his or her detriment.

Normally, the tort of misrepresentation or fraud occurs only when there is reliance upon a *statement of fact.* Sometimes, however, reliance on a *statement of opinion* may involve the tort of misrepresentation if the individual making the statement of opinion has a superior knowledge of the subject matter. For example, when a lawyer makes a statement of opinion about the law, a court would construe reliance on such a statement to be equivalent to reliance on a statement of fact. Fraudulent and nonfraudulent misrepresentation will be examined further in Chapter 11, in the context of contract law.

PUFFERY
A salesperson's often exaggerated claims concerning the quality of the goods offered for sale. Such claims involve opinions rather than facts and are not considered to be legally binding promises or warranties.

❖ Intentional Torts against Property

Intentional torts against property include (1) trespass to land and (2) trespass to personal property and conversion. Here, the wrong is committed against the individual who has legally recognized rights with regard to land or personal property. The law distinguishes real property from personal property (see Chapters 33 and 34). *Real property* is land and things "permanently" attached thereto. *Personal property* consists of all other items, which are basically movable. Thus, a house and lot are real property, whereas the furniture inside a house is personal property. Money and securities are also personal property.

Trespass to Land

TRESPASS TO LAND
Passing over another's land uninvited. Most courts require that to constitute trespass, an intrusion must be intentional, negligent, or the result of an "abnormally dangerous activity."

Any time a person, without permission, enters onto, above, or below the surface of land that is owned by another, or causes anything to enter onto the land, or remains on the land, or permits anything to remain on it, such action constitutes the civil tort called a **trespass to land.** Note that actual harm to the land is not an essential

Do "Private Property" or "No Trespassing" signs have to be posted for trespass to occur?

NOMINAL DAMAGES
A small monetary award (often one dollar) granted to a plaintiff when no actual damage was suffered.

element of this tort because the tort is designed to protect the right of an owner to exclusive possession. Usually, however, if no harm is done, only **nominal damages** (such as $1) can be recovered by the landowner. Common types of trespass to land include walking or driving on the land, shooting a gun over the land, throwing rocks or spraying water on a building that belongs to someone else, building a dam across a river that causes water to back up on someone else's land, and placing part of one's building on an adjoining landowner's property.

Trespass Criteria, Rights, and Duties Before a person can be a trespasser, the real property owner (or other person in actual and exclusive possession of the property) must establish that person as a trespasser. For example, "posted" trespass signs expressly establish as a trespasser a person who ignores these signs and enters onto the property. A guest in your home is not a trespasser—unless he or she has been asked to leave but refuses. Any person who enters onto your property to commit an illegal act (such as a thief entering a lumberyard at night to steal lumber) is established impliedly as a trespasser, without posted signs. At common law, a trespasser is liable for damages caused to the property and generally cannot hold the owner liable for injuries sustained on the premises. This common law rule is being abandoned in many jurisdictions in favor of a "reasonable duty" rule that varies depending on the status of the parties; for example, a landowner may have a duty to post a notice that the property is patrolled by guard dogs. Trespassers normally can be removed from the premises through the use of reasonable force without the owner's being liable for assault and battery.

Defenses against Trespass to Land Trespass to land involves wrongful interference with another person's real property rights. But if it can be shown that the trespass was warranted, as when a trespasser enters to assist someone in danger, a defense exists. Another defense is to show that the purported owner did not actually have the right to possess the land in question.

Trespass to Personal Property and Conversion

Whenever any individual unlawfully harms the personal property of another or otherwise interferes with the personal property owner's right to exclusive possession

Law in the Extreme

The $10,600 Order of Toast

Malcolm Stroud went to a Denny's Restaurant early one morning to have breakfast. Stroud ordered sausage, eggs, hash browns, and toast. The menu indicated that the toast was topped with melted butter. When the breakfast arrived, however, the toast did not have melted butter on it. Instead, a refrigerated patty of butter was placed on the toast. Stroud complained to the waitress about the butter, and the waitress took the toast back to the kitchen. When the toast was returned to Stroud, however, the butter was unchanged. After finishing his breakfast, Stroud paid for the meal but deducted twenty-five cents for the unsatisfactory toast.

Clearly, Stroud liked melted butter on his toast. And just as clearly, he was a man of principle. If a menu says the toast has melted butter on it, the toast should have melted butter on it. If it does not, well, then the customer should not have to pay for it. One would assume that most restaurants, when faced with a determined non-payer such as Stroud, would simply drop the matter and forgo the twenty-five cents—particularly when "the law" is on the customer's side (after all, the restaurant had misrepresented its product). But not this restaurant. As a result, in a tort lawsuit that was eventually decided by the Supreme Court of Oregon, Denny's had to pay Stroud $10,600 in damages!

How is it possible that a dispute over twenty-five cents could result in a lawsuit involving thousands of dollars? The answer is short, if not simple: tort law. Stroud's refusal to pay for the toast, of course, started the chain of events that terminated in the Oregon Supreme Court. But it was largely the response to Stroud's refusal that created the problem. The cook at Denny's shouted to the cashier that Stroud had to pay. Stroud refused, and a restaurant employee called the police. When the police arrived and refused to arrest Stroud, the cook took matters into his own hands and performed a citizen's arrest.

Stroud, in response to the cook's action, brought a suit for *malicious prosecution* against the restaurant. The tort of malicious prosecution occurs when a defendant in a frivolous or unwarranted legal action (in this case, Stroud) in turn sues the party bringing the action (in this case, Denny's Restaurant). Although the restaurant claimed that it could not be responsible for its employee's unauthorized action, the trial court held otherwise[a] and awarded a total of $10,600 in damages to Stroud. Neither the trial court's ruling nor the award of damages was upset on appeal.[b]

a. Under agency-employment law, an employer may be held liable for the tortious actions of an employee if the employee was acting "in the course of employment" at the time of the action (see Chapter 23).

b. *Stroud v. Denny's Restaurant, Inc.*, 271 Or. 430, 532 P.2d 790 (1975).

and enjoyment of that property, **trespass to personal property**—also called *trespass to personalty*—occurs. If a student takes another student's business law book as a practical joke and hides it so that the owner is unable to find it for several days prior to a final examination, the student has engaged in a trespass to personal property.

TRESPASS TO PERSONALTY
Any wrongful transgression or offense against the personal property of another.

If it can be shown that trespass to personal property was warranted, then a complete defense exists. Most states, for example, allow automobile repair shops to hold a customer's car (under what is called an *artisan's lien*, discussed in Chapter 22) when the customer refuses to pay for repairs already completed.

CONVERSION
The wrongful taking or retaining possession of personal property that belongs to another.

Whenever personal property is wrongfully taken from its rightful owner or possessor and placed in the service of another, the act of **conversion** occurs. Conversion is defined as any act depriving an owner of personal property without that owner's permission and without just cause. Conversion is the civil side of crimes related to theft. A store clerk who steals merchandise from the store commits a crime and engages in the tort of conversion at the same time. When conversion occurs, the lesser offense of trespass to personal property usually occurs as well. If the initial taking of the property was unlawful, there is trespass; retention of that property is conversion. If the initial taking of the property was permitted by the owner or for some other reason is not a trespass, failure to return it may still be conversion.

Even if a person mistakenly believed that he or she was entitled to the goods, a tort of conversion may occur. In other words, good intentions are not a defense against conversion; in fact, conversion can be an entirely innocent act. Someone who buys stolen goods, for example, is guilty of conversion even if he or she did not know the goods were stolen. If the true owner brings a tort action against the buyer, the buyer must either return the property to the owner or pay the owner the full value of the property, despite having already paid money to the thief.

A successful defense against the charge of conversion is that the purported owner does not in fact own the property or does not have a right to possess it that is superior to the right of the holder. Necessity is another possible defense against conversion. If Abrams takes Mendoza's cat, Abrams is guilty of conversion. If Mendoza sues Abrams, Abrams must return the cat or pay damages. If, however, the cat has rabies and Abrams took the cat to protect the public, Abrams has a valid defense—necessity (and perhaps even self-defense, if he can prove that he was in danger because of the cat).

❖ Unintentional Torts (Negligence)

NEGLIGENCE
The failure to exercise the standard of care that a reasonable person would exercise in similar circumstances.

In contrast to intentional torts, in torts involving **negligence**, the tortfeasor neither wishes to bring about the consequences of the act nor believes that they will occur. The actor's conduct merely creates a *risk* of such consequences. If no risk is created,

"I fell out of your birdhouse and hurt my wing, and this is my lawyer. . ."

Business Law in Action

The High Cost of Tort Litigation

Americans like to sue, or at least that's what it looks like if you examine the number of lawsuits occurring in this country. We have more than 750,000 lawyers in the United States. Both totally and on a per capita basis, that is more lawyers than most other nations on earth can claim. Also, the percentage of total national income devoted to tort costs is higher in the United States than anywhere else on earth. It is five times what it is in Canada, France, Germany, Britain, or Japan. And while tort costs in other nations have remained relatively stable, they have been on the rise in the United States. In the United States, the number of multimillion-dollar damage awards in tort cases grew from just one in 1970 to more than six hundred in 1992.

Not surprisingly, if you are in the business world, you have to be insured against the possibility of tort litigation. Businesspersons and professionals are potentially subject to a wide array of tort lawsuits brought by business invitees, clients, consumers, and others. The cost of high damage awards and insurance protection against them is borne not just by business but by society in general. This is because those costs are passed on to customers, clients, and consumers in the form of higher prices. Manufacturers and sellers, for example, are frequently the targets of *product liability* lawsuits—that is, lawsuits brought by consumers who are harmed by a faulty or defective product. To protect against having to pay millions of dollars in damages, manufacturers and sellers purchase liability insurance. The cost of this insurance is factored into the price of the product. Today, fully 20 percent of the cost of a $35 stepladder goes to insurance.

Businesses are not the only entities being sued. So, too, are federal, state, and local governments. When a disabled weather buoy off the coast of Massachusetts failed to send a storm warning, several fishermen lost their lives. The federal government had to pay their families $1.2 million. When a speeder in California hit a light pole, an injured passenger argued that the pole should have broken on impact. The state was ordered to pay a $400,000 settlement. Litigation costs for cities and counties rose at least 13 percent from 1990 to 1993. The problem has become so severe that many local jurisdictions are routinely settling out of court.

Tort lawsuits are brought not just for defective products, but also for saying the wrong thing. Indeed, whenever individuals in either the private or the public sector are criticized, they seem increasingly to want to sue their critics. In one case, the head of a protection organization for primates wrote to a professional journal protesting the plans of an Australian firm to use chimpanzees in hepatitis research. A year later, the research firm sued the letter writer for $4 million, accusing the critic of harming its "standing, prestige, reputation, and credibility." An insurance company settled the case for $100,000. In Northglenn, Colorado, conservative Christian parents complained that a teacher talked to students favorably about "occult religious practices," such as walking on hot coals. The teacher sued the parents, claiming that she had been subjected to reckless charges based on innocuous classroom remarks, and won $110,000 in damages. Many observers of this particular type of litigation contend that, if it continues, it will have a chilling effect on valid criticism in our society and place in jeopardy our First Amendment right to free speech.

Much tort litigation in recent years has resulted in high damage awards, particularly for punitive damages. *Punitive damages* are awarded in civil cases as a means of deterring a defendant's action. They are assessed in addition to *compensatory damages*, which are intended to reimburse a plaintiff for actual losses—to make the plaintiff whole. High punitive damages awards, which in some cases have been more than one hundred times the compensatory damages awarded to a plaintiff, have led some defendants to claim that these awards violate the Eighth Amendment's prohibition against excessive fines or their constitutional rights to due process. To date, the United States Supreme Court has not held that excessively high punitive damages awards are unconstitutional.[a] In a 1991 case,[b] however, the Court stated that a ratio of more than four to one between actual and punitive damages "may be close to the line" in terms of constitutionality and suggested that punitive damages awards should bear an "understandable relationship to compensatory damages." The Court declined, however, to draw "a mathematical bright line between the constitutionally acceptable and the constitutionally unacceptable" in regard to punitive damages awards,

a. See, for example, *Browning-Ferris Industries of Vermont, Inc., v. Kelco Disposal, Inc.*, 492 U.S. 257, 109 S.Ct. 2909, 106 L.Ed.2d 219 (1989), in which the Supreme Court held that the excessive-fines clause of the Eighth Amendment does not apply to awards of punitive damages in cases between private parties.

b. *Pacific Mutual Life Insurance Co. v. Haslip*, ____U.S.____, 111 S.Ct. 1032, 113 L.Ed.2d 1 (1991).

Business Law in Action—Continued

and many courts have since held that excessively high punitive damages do not violate defendants' constitutional rights.[c]

Attempts at reducing the number and size of damage awards fall under the rubric of tort reform. Efforts at tort reform in many states are aimed at capping, or putting a ceiling on, high awards. Some states limit the size of punitive awards. New Jersey requires a finding of actual malice or wanton and willful disregard of rights before granting punitive damages. Some members of Congress have sponsored bills to set national punitive-award standards in product liability cases. Some states have limited awards for such noneconomic harm as emotional distress.

Some tort reform advocates recommend that all product liability cases at the state court level be reviewed by federal judges. Occasionally, during the reviewing process, the federal judiciary could proclaim a broad new principle or correct a particularly bad state decision. One tort reform proponent suggests that manufacturers be allowed to disclaim liability in certain states. If a manufacturer doesn't want to take a chance in a state notorious for its high product liability awards, it could stamp on its product "not for sale or use in ________" (with the blank filled in with the appropriate state name). If passed at the federal level, such tort reform legislation would allow manufacturers to escape state laws.

c. See, for example, *Southern Life and Health Insurance Co. v. Turner*, 586 So.2d 854 (Ala. 1991), a case decided five months after *Haslip*, in which the plaintiff was awarded punitive damages 499 times the amount of compensatory damages awarded.

there is no negligence. Moreover, the risk must be foreseeable; that is, it must be such that a reasonable person engaging in the same activity would anticipate the risk and guard against it. In determining what is reasonable conduct, courts consider the nature of the possible harm. A very slight risk of a dangerous explosion might be unreasonable, whereas a distinct possibility of burning one's fingers on a stove might be reasonable.

Many of the actions discussed in the section on intentional torts constitute negligence if the element of intent is missing. For example, if Juarez intentionally shoves Natsuyo, who falls and breaks an arm as a result, Juarez will have committed an intentional tort. If Juarez carelessly bumps into Natsuyo, however, and she falls and breaks an arm as a result, Juarez's action will constitute negligence. In either situation, Juarez has committed a tort. In a sense, then, negligence is a *way of committing* a tort rather than a distinct *category* of torts.

The tort of negligence occurs when someone suffers injury because of another's failure to live up to a required *duty of care*. In examining a question of negligence, one should ask four questions:

1. Did the defendant owe a duty of care to the plaintiff?
2. Did the defendant breach that duty?
3. Did the plaintiff suffer a legally recognizable injury as a result of the defendant's breach of the duty of care?
4. Did the defendant's breach cause the plaintiff's injury?

Each of these elements of neligence is discussed below.

DUTY OF CARE
The duty of all persons, as established by tort law, to exercise a reasonable amount of care in their dealings with others. Failure to exercise due care, which is normally determined by the "reasonable person standard," constitutes the tort of negligence.

The Duty of Care and Its Breach

The concept of a **duty of care** arises from the notion that if we are to live in society with other people, some actions can be tolerated and some cannot; some actions are right and some are wrong; and some actions are reasonable and some are not.

The basic principle underlying the duty of care is that people are free to act as they please so long as their actions do not infringe on the interests of others.

When someone fails to comply with the duty of exercising reasonable care, a potentially tortious act may have been committed. Failure to live up to a standard of care may be an act (setting fire to a building) or an omission (neglecting to put out a fire). It may be an intentional act, a careless act, or a carefully performed but nevertheless dangerous act that results in injury. Courts consider the nature of the act (whether it is outrageous or commonplace), the manner in which the act is performed (cautiously versus heedlessly), and the nature of the injury (whether it is serious or slight) in determining whether the duty of care has been breached.

"Liberty means responsibility. That is why most men dread it."

George Bernard Shaw, 1856–1950
(English writer and socialist)

The Reasonable Person Standard Tort law measures duty by the **reasonable person standard.** In determining whether a duty of care has been breached, the courts ask how a reasonable person would have acted in the same circumstances. The reasonable person standard is said to be (though in an absolute sense it cannot be) objective. It is not necessarily how a particular person would act. It is society's judgment on how people should act. If the so-called reasonable person existed, he or she would be careful, conscientious, even tempered, and honest. This hypothetical "reasonable person" is frequently used by the courts in decisions relating to other areas of law as well.

REASONABLE PERSON STANDARD
The standard of behavior expected of a hypothetical "reasonable person." The standard against which negligence is measured and that must be observed to avoid liability for negligence.

That individuals are required to exercise a reasonable standard of care in their activities is a pervasive concept in business law, and many of the issues dealt with in subsequent chapters of this text have to do with this duty. What constitutes reasonable care varies, of course, with the circumstances.

Duty of Landowners Landowners are expected to exercise reasonable care to protect persons coming onto their property from harm. As mentioned earlier, in some jurisdictions, landowners are held to owe a duty to protect even trespassers against certain risks. Landowners who rent or lease premises to tenants are expected to exercise reasonable care to ensure that the tenants and their guests are not harmed in common areas, such as stairways, entryways, laundry rooms, and the like (see Chapter 34).

Retailers and other firms that explicitly or implicitly invite persons to come onto their premises are usually charged with a duty to exercise reasonable care to protect their **business invitees.** For example, if you entered a supermarket, slipped on a wet floor, and sustained injuries as a result, the owner of the supermarket would be liable for damages if when you slipped there was no sign warning that the floor was wet. A court would hold that the business owner was negligent because the owner failed to exercise a reasonable degree of care in protecting the store's customers against foreseeable risks that the owner knew or *should have known* about. That a patron might slip on the the wet floor and be injured as a result was a foreseeable risk, and the owner should have taken care to avoid this risk or warn the customer of it.

BUSINESS INVITEES
Those people, such as customers or clients, who are invited onto business premises by the owner of those premises for business purposes.

Some risks, of course, are so obvious that the owner need not warn of them. For example, a business owner does not need to warn customers to open a door before attempting to walk through it. But other risks, even though they may seem obvious to a business owner, may not be so in the eyes of another, such as a child. For example, a hardware store owner may not think it is necessary to warn customers that a stepladder leaning against the back wall of the store could fall down and harm them. Yet it is possible that a child could tip the ladder over and be hurt as a result and that the store could be held liable.

In the following case, the court has to decide whether a restaurant owner should be held liable for a customer's injuries on the premises.

Case 5.2
BRAY v. KATE
Supreme Court of Nebraska, 1990.
235 Neb. 315,
454 N.W.2d 698.

HISTORICAL AND SOCIAL SETTING *The rule regarding the liability of owners or occupiers of land to their business invitees was established in the mid–nineteenth century. Over the next hundred years, the courts held that "business invitees" included customers and patrons of restaurants, bars, banks, theaters, beaches, fairs, amusement parks, sports events, gas stations, funeral homes, utility companies, and colleges. To qualify as a business invitee, is it required that an individual be on the premises for the purpose of buying something? Not necessarily. Business invitees have been held to include persons who are only window-shopping, as well as those who are on the premises only to use a telephone, to use a bathroom, or to get change. Business invitees have also been held to include drivers picking up or delivering goods, independent contractors working on the property, and the employees of those independent contractors.*

FACTS Lowell Bray was about to open the door of a restaurant owned by Kate, Inc., when he slipped on some ice and fell, injuring his shoulder. He stated that he could not see the ice but felt it when he slipped. Bray sued Kate, Inc., for damages, alleging that Kate, Inc., by failing to remove the ice from in front of its restaurant door, had breached its duty of care to Bray and was thus negligent. The trial court held for Bray, and Kate, Inc., appealed.

ISSUE Had Kate, Inc., breached its duty of care to Bray by failing to remove the ice from the area in front of the restaurant?

DECISION Yes. The Supreme Court of Nebraska affirmed the lower court's judgment for Bray. Kate, Inc., owed a duty to its patron, Bray, and because it had breached that duty, it was liable to Bray for damages.

REASON The court held that under Nebraska law, "A possessor of land is subject to liability for injury caused to a business invitee by a condition on the land if (1) the possessor defendant either created the condition, knew of the condition, or by the exercise of reasonable care would have discovered the condition; (2) the defendant should have realized the condition involved an unreasonable risk of harm to a business invitee; (3) the defendant should have expected that a business invitee such as the plaintiff, either (a) would not discover or realize the danger, or (b) would fail to protect himself or herself against the danger; (4) the defendant failed to use reasonable care to protect the plaintiff invitee against the danger; and (5) the condition was a proximate cause of damage to the plaintiff." The trial court jury had found that the restaurant owed a duty to Bray, the restaurant breached its duty, Bray's injury resulted from the restaurant's breach of its duty, and the restaurant should therefore be held liable to Bray for damages. The Supreme Court of Nebraska concluded that "a clear factual issue was presented and resolved by the jury verdict."

ETHICAL CONSIDERATIONS *It is not uncommon for a court to hold a business owner liable when a customer is harmed by what may seem to be an obvious risk. To a certain extent, such decisions rest on the public policy that business owners are in a better position both to protect against the risks and to bear the costs associated with customers' injuries. Many, however, question whether it is fair to hold businesspersons responsible in these situations. (See the* Question of Ethics and Social Responsibility *at the end of this chapter for a further inquiry into this issue.)*

Duty of Professionals If an individual has knowledge, skill, or intelligence superior to that of an ordinary person, the individual's conduct must be consistent with that status. Professionals—including doctors, dentists, psychiatrists, architects, engineers, accountants, lawyers, and others—are required to have a standard minimum level of special knowledge and ability. Therefore, in determining what constitutes reasonable care in the case of professionals, their training and expertise is taken into account. In other words, an accountant cannot defend against a lawsuit for negligence by stating, "But I was not familiar with that principle of accounting."

MALPRACTICE
Professional misconduct or the lack of the requisite degree of skill as a professional or the negligence—the failure to exercise due care—on the part of a professional, such as a physician, is commonly referred to as malpractice.

If a professional violates his or her duty of care toward a client, the professional may be sued for **malpractice.** For example, a patient might sue a physician for *medical malpractice.* A client might sue an attorney for *legal malpractice.*

The Injury Requirement and Damages

For a tort to have been committed, the plaintiff must have suffered a *legally recognizable* injury. To recover damages (receive compensation), the plaintiff must

Any professional is assumed to have special knowledge and ability. How does this affect a professional's standard of care?

have suffered some loss, harm, wrong, or invasion of a protected interest. Essentially, the purpose of tort law is to compensate for legally recognized injuries resulting from wrongful acts. If no harm or injury results from a given negligent action, there is nothing to compensate—and no tort exists. For example, if you carelessly bump into a passerby, who stumbles and falls as a result, you may be liable in tort if the passerby is injured in the fall. If the person is unharmed, however, there could be no suit for damages because no injury was suffered. Although the passerby might be angry and suffer emotional distress, few courts recognize negligently inflicted emotional distress as a tort unless it results in physical injury.

"There's no limit to how complicated things can get, on account of one thing always leading to another."

E. B. White, 1899–1985
(American author)

It is important to stress that the purpose of tort law is not to punish people for tortious acts but to compensate the injured parties for damages suffered. Because society wants to discourage some torts, however, occasionally the injured person may be given extra compensation in the form of **punitive damages** (discussed in this chapter's *Business Law in Action*). But few negligent acts are so reprehensible that punitive damages are available.

PUNITIVE (EXEMPLARY) DAMAGES
Compensation in excess of actual or consequential damages. They are awarded in order to punish the wrongdoer and usually will be awarded only in cases involving willful or malicious misconduct.

Causation

Another element necessary to a tort is *causation*. If a person fails in a duty of care and someone suffers injury, the wrongful activity must have caused the harm for a tort to have been committed.

CAUSATION IN FACT
An act or omission without which an event would not have occurred.

Causation in Fact and Proximate Cause In deciding whether there is causation, the court must address two questions:

1. Is there **causation in fact?** Did the injury occur because of the defendant's act, or would it have occurred anyway? If an injury would not have occurred without the defendant's act, then there is causation in fact. Causation in fact can usually be determined by the use of the *but for* test: "but for" the wrongful act, the injury would not have occurred.
2. Was the act the **proximate cause** of the injury? How far should a defendant's liability extend for a wrongful act that was a substantial factor in causing injury? For example: Ackerman carelessly leaves a campfire burning. The fire not only burns

PROXIMATE CAUSE
The "next" or "substantial" cause; in tort law, a concept used to determine whether a plaintiff's injury was the natural and continuous result of a defendant's negligent act. If the negligent act of a defendant was the sole cause or a substantial cause of injuries to a plaintiff, the defendant will be liable.

Ethical Perspective

No Duty to Rescue

Generally, the law requires individuals to act reasonably and responsibly in their relations with others. Reckless or carelessly performed actions, if they result in harm to another, may allow the injured person to bring an action in tort for negligence. And yet, if a person fails to come to the aid of a stranger in peril, that person will not be considered negligent under tort law. For example, assume that you are walking down a city street and notice that a pedestrian is about to step directly in front of an oncoming bus. You realize that the person has not seen the bus and is unaware of the danger. Do you have a legal duty to warn that individual? No. Although most people would probably concede that in this situation, the observer has an *ethical* duty to warn the other, tort law does not impose a general duty to rescue others in peril.

People involved in special relationships, however, have been held to have a duty to rescue other parties within the relationship. A married person, for example, has a duty to rescue his or her child or spouse if either is in danger. Other special relationships, such as those between teachers and students or hiking and hunting partners, may also give rise to a duty to rescue. In addition, if a person who has no duty to rescue undertakes to rescue another, then the rescuer is charged with a duty to follow through with due care on the rescue attempt. The law also will hold that a duty to rescue exists on the part of a person who places another in peril. For example, business owners who invite the public onto their premises must make sure that the premises are safe. If a customer is endangered by an unsafe condition, then a business owner has a duty to rescue the person because the owner was responsible for the danger.

What if a person chokes on a piece of food in a restaurant? Does the restaurant owner have a duty to rescue the choking diner? This issue recently came before an Illinois court[a] when a diner, Ernesto Parra, choked to death on a piece of food while eating at a restaurant. The administrator of Parra's estate sued the restaurant, claiming, among other things, that the restaurant breached its duty to rescue Parra while he was choking. The court stressed that under the common law, there is no general duty to aid a person in peril: "A mere bystander incurs no liability where he fails to take any action, however negligently or even intentionally[,] to rescue another in distress." If Parra had been injured by a dangerous condition in the restaurant, such as a slippery floor, then the restaurant would have had a duty to come to Parra's assistance and ensure that he received any medical treatment necessary. But in the circumstances of the case before the court, the restaurant had not been responsible for placing Parra in danger; the fact that Parra choked was totally personal to Parra. According to the court, "As a general rule, a restaurateur is not an insurer of his customers' safety against all personal injuries. He has no duty as to 'conditions or risks which are ordinary and are, or should be, known or obvious to the patrons.' "

When discussing the distinction between legal and ethical duties in Chapter 2, we pointed out that ethical duties exist beyond the scope of the law. In regard to the duty to rescue, the distinction is clearly evident. Although the law might not require a passerby to save a drowning toddler in a wading pool, society expects that people will aid others who are in danger and cannot help themselves.

a. *Parra v. Tarasco, Inc.*, 230 Ill.App.3d 819, 595 N.E.2d 1186, 172 Ill.Dec. 516 (1992).

down the forest, but also sets off an explosion in a nearby chemical plant that spills chemicals into a river, killing all the fish for a hundred miles downstream and ruining the economy of a tourist resort. Should Ackerman be liable to the resort owners? To the tourists whose vacations were ruined? These are questions of proximate cause (sometimes called legal cause). Proximate cause is not a question of fact but a question of law and policy. The question is whether the connection between an act and an injury is strong enough to justify imposing liability.

Probably the most cited case on proximate cause is the *Palsgraf* case. The question before the court is as follows: Does the defendant's duty of care extend only to those who may be injured as a result of a foreseeable risk, or does it extend also to a person whose injury could not reasonably be foreseen?

Case 5.3
PALSGRAF v. LONG ISLAND RAILROAD CO.

Court of Appeals of New York, 1928.
248 N.Y. 339,
162 N.E. 99.

HISTORICAL AND ECONOMIC SETTING *In the nineteenth century, railroads spread across the American countryside. The success of these railroads was due in no small part to the absence of strict liability rules, which made it difficult for injured workers and other victims to sue the railroads for their injuries. As the toll of injuries mounted, early twentieth-century courts eased the rules for recovering from the railroads. This provoked more litigation against railroads, which were among the "deepest financial pockets" of their day.*

FACTS The plaintiff, Palsgraf, was waiting for a train on a station platform. A man carrying a package was rushing to catch a train that was moving away from a platform across the tracks from Palsgraf. As the man attempted to jump aboard the moving train, he seemed unsteady and about to fall. A railroad guard on the car reached forward to grab him, and another guard on the platform pushed him from behind to help him board the train. In the process, the man's package fell on the railroad tracks and exploded because it contained fireworks. There was nothing about the package to indicate its contents. The repercussions of the explosion caused scales at the other end of the train platform to fall on Palsgraf, causing injuries for which she sued the railroad company. At the trial, the jury found that the railroad guards were negligent in their conduct.

ISSUE Was the conduct of the railroad guards the proximate cause of Palsgraf's injuries? (That is, did the guards' duty of care extend to Palsgraf, who was outside the zone of danger and whose injury could not reasonably have been foreseen?)

DECISION No. The railroad guards were not negligent with respect to Palsgraf, and the railroad was thus not liable for the injuries that Palsgraf suffered.

REASON The question of whether the guards were negligent with respect to Palsgraf has to do with whether her injury was reasonably foreseeable to the railroad. It is true that the guards may have acted negligently in helping the man board the train and that this conduct may have resulted in injury to that man. This, however, has no bearing on the question of their negligence with respect to Palsgraf. This is not a situation in which a person commits an act so potentially harmful (for example, firing a gun at a building) that he or she would be held responsible for any harm that resulted. According to the court, "Here, by concession, there was nothing in the situation to suggest to the most cautious mind that the parcel wrapped in newspaper would spread wreckage through the station."

Foreseeability Since the *Palsgraf* case, the courts have used *foreseeability* as the test for proximate cause. The railroad guards were negligent, but the railroad's duty of care did not extend to Palsgraf because she was an unforeseeable plaintiff. If the consequences of the harm done or the victim of the harm are unforeseeable, there is no proximate cause. Of course, it is foreseeable that people will stand on railroad platforms and that objects attached to the platforms will fall as the result of explosions nearby—however, this is not a chain of events that a reasonable person would usually guard against. It is difficult to predict when a court will say that something is foreseeable and when it will say that something is not. How far a court stretches foreseeability is determined in part by the extent to which the court is willing to stretch the defendant's duty of care.

Superseding Intervening Forces A superseding intervening force may break the connection between a wrongful act and an injury to another. If so, it cancels out the wrongful act. For example, keeping a can of gasoline in the trunk of one's car creates a foreseeable risk and is thus a negligent act. If lightning strikes the car, exploding the gas tank *and* the car, injuring passing pedestrians, the lightning supersedes the original negligence as a cause of the damage, because it was not foreseeable.

In negligence cases, the negligent party will often attempt to show that some act has intervened after his or her action and that this second act was the proximate cause of injury. Typically, in cases in which an individual takes a defensive action, such as swerving to avoid an oncoming car, the original wrongdoer will not be relieved of liability even if the injury actually resulted from the attempt to escape harm. The same is true under the "danger invites rescue" doctrine. Under this doctrine, if Ludlam commits an act that endangers Schwaller, and Yokem sustains an injury trying to protect Schwaller, then Ludlam will be liable for Yokem's injury, as well as for any injuries Schwaller may sustain. Rescuers can injure themselves, or the person rescued, or even a stranger, but the original wrongdoer will still be liable.

In the following case, the defendant asserted that a superseding intervening force precluded the defendant's liability for the plaintiffs' injuries.

Case 5.4
CLAY v. FERRELLGAS, INC.
Court of Appeals of New Mexico, 1992.
838 P.2d 487.

HISTORICAL AND SOCIAL SETTING *In the mid-nineteenth century and early twentieth century, the courts tended to ask the following question regarding superseding intervening forces: "Why should a person be held liable for an injury brought about by something for which the person is not wholly responsible?" The question was asked after the cause in fact of an injury was established. Thus, it was not primarily a question of causation but one of policy. Today, the issue of liability may still turn on questions of policy, but the question regarding superseding intervening forces has changed. Now, the courts tend to ask, "Why should a person be relieved of liability for something as to which the person's conduct is one cause, along with other causes?"*

FACTS Stella Snider received a car as a present from a friend, Boyd Clement. Clement contracted with Ferrellgas, Inc., to alter the car's fuel system so that the car could run on liquid propane as well as gasoline. Ferrellgas installed a used propane tank in the automobile but did not complete the job because of an inability to get parts. Ferrellgas did not vent the tank, made no adjustments to allow for remote filling, and did not install a vapor barrier between the trunk and the passenger compartment. The car was then taken to Gary Roybal, a mechanic, to complete the conversion. Roybal leak-tested only the parts of the conversion system that he installed. When he received the car, Roybal noticed that there was propane in the tank. Roybal did not check the tank for leaks, nor did he check to see if a vapor barrier had been installed—he assumed that one had been installed based on the fact that propane was already in the tank. After Roybal returned the car to Snider, it was never run on propane, nor was the tank ever filled, because Clement still intended to have the tank adapted for remote filling. Later, the propane gas leaked from a faulty valve on the tank, migrated into the passenger compartment, and ignited a fire when Snider started the car, injuring both Snider and a passenger, Royce Clay. Snider and Clay sued Ferrellgas for damages, and the trial court awarded them $595,000 in compensatory damages and $375,000 in punitive damages. Ferrellgas appealed, contending that Roybal's negligence was the proximate cause of the accident.

ISSUE Can Ferrellgas be held liable for the plaintiffs' injuries, even though Roybal had worked on the automobile after Ferrellgas?

DECISION Yes. The trial court's verdict in favor of the plaintiffs was affirmed.

REASON Ferrellgas contended that it could not be responsible for the accident because its work on the car was not the proximate cause of the plaintiffs' injuries. The appellate court ruled, however, that proximate cause "need not be [the] last act * * * but may be one which actually aided in producing injury" and that proximate cause "need not be the sole cause but merely a concurring cause." The cause of the injury was in dispute in this case. There was expert testimony suggesting that Ferrellgas was negligent in failing to provide a vapor barrier and venting for the tank, but there was also evidence suggesting that Roybal should have inspected the car more thoroughly before returning it to Clement. The key question in the case revolved around the issue of residual propane gas in the tank. Ferrellgas denied leaving gas in the tank, and both Snider and Clement denied putting propane in the tank. Roybal indicated that there was propane in the tank when he received the car, which was his reason for assuming a vapor barrier had been installed. The court concluded that "a reasonable jury could have found that Ferrellgas left propane in the tank, thereby leading Roybal to believe that the vapor barrier was in place. Under these circumstances, Roybal's work would not necessarily be an intervening cause as a matter of law."

A driver entering a race knows there is a risk of being killed or injured in a crash. Does this mean that the driver has assumed the risk of death or injury?

Defenses to Negligence

The basic defenses in negligence cases are (1) assumption of risk and (2) contributory and comparative negligence.

Assumption of Risk A plaintiff who voluntarily enters into a risky situation, knowing the risk involved, will not be allowed to recover. This is the defense of **assumption of risk.** For example, a driver entering a race knows there is a risk of being killed or injured in a crash. The driver has assumed the risk of injury. The requirements of this defense are (1) knowledge of the risk and (2) voluntary assumption of the risk.

ASSUMPTION OF RISK
A doctrine whereby a plaintiff may not recover for injuries or damages suffered from risks he or she knows of and assents to. A defense against negligence that can be used when the plaintiff has knowledge of and appreciates a danger and voluntarily exposes himself or herself to the danger.

The risk can be assumed by express agreement, or the assumption of risk can be implied by the plaintiff's knowledge of the risk and subsequent conduct. Of course, the plaintiff does not assume a risk different from or greater than the risk normally carried by the activity. In our example, the race driver assumes the risk of being injured in the race but not the risk that the banking in the curves of the racetrack will give way during the race because of a construction defect.

Risks are not deemed to be assumed in situations involving emergencies. Neither are they assumed when a statute protects a class of people from harm and a member of the class is injured by the harm. For example, employees are protected by statute from harmful working conditions and therefore do not assume the risks associated with the workplace. If an employee is injured, he or she will generally be compensated regardless of fault. In the following case, the defendant successfully asserted the defense of assumption of risk in defending against a lawsuit for negligence.

Case 5.5
SCHROYER v. McNEAL
Court of Appeals of Maryland, 1991.
592 A.2d 1119,
323 Md. 275.

HISTORICAL AND SOCIAL SETTING *Assumption of risk developed as a defense against charges of negligence in the late eighteenth and early nineteenth centuries. At one time, the defense was used by employers to restrict recoveries by employees in dangerous occupations. Today, state workers' compensation statutes compensate workers for on-the-job injuries. In some jurisdictions, implied assumption of risk has been abolished by statute or by court decisions. Where it has not been abolished, the effect of the defense varies from state to state.*

Case 5.5—Continued

FACTS Shortly after checking in at a Holiday Inn in Maryland, Frances McNeal slipped and fell on some ice in the hotel parking area. McNeal had requested a room near an entrance because she had a great deal of luggage. To accommodate McNeal's request, she was given a room near the west entrance, in spite of the hotel's policy of not assigning rooms near that entrance in inclement weather. Also contrary to policy, McNeal was not advised that she should not use the west entrance, and no warnings were posted by that door. McNeal noticed that the parking lot and the sidewalk by the west entrance were covered with snow and ice and were slippery. She made one trip into the hotel without mishap, walking carefully because of the hazardous conditions, but she fell on the second trip. McNeal sustained a broken ankle in the incident and subsequently sued Thomas and Patricia Schroyer, the hotel owners, for negligence. McNeal alleged that the Schroyers had failed to maintain the parking lot, to warn guests of the slippery conditions, and to post warning signs. The jury found in McNeal's favor, and the Schroyers appealed. The appellate court affirmed the trial court's judgment, and the case was appealed to Maryland's highest court.

ISSUE Did McNeal, because she knew of the hazardous conditions, assume the risk of injury therefrom?

DECISION Yes. In reversing the judgment of the lower courts, the highest state court held that McNeal was well aware of the risk she was taking and voluntarily assumed it.

REASON The court stated that the rationale underlying the doctrine of assumption of risk "rests upon the plaintiff's consent to relieve the defendant of an obligation of conduct toward him, and to take his chances of harm from a particular risk. Such consent may be found: * * * by implication from the conduct of the parties. When the plaintiff enters voluntarily into a relation or situation involving obvious danger, he may be taken to assume the risk, and to relieve the defendant of responsibility. Such implied assumption of risk requires knowledge and appreciation of the risk, and a voluntary choice to encounter it." In McNeal's case, the court noted that she had testified as to her awareness of the dangerous condition of the parking area near the hotel's west entrance. Nonetheless, she "took a chance" and walked over the ice and snow because "she did not think that it was 'that' slippery." The court concluded that "McNeal took an informed chance. * * * [I]t cannot be [denied] that she intentionally exposed herself to a known risk. With full knowledge that the parking lot and sidewalk were ice and snow covered and aware that the ice and snow were slippery, McNeal voluntarily chose to park on the parking lot and to walk across it and the sidewalk, thus indicating her willingness to accept the risk and relieving the Schroyers of responsibility for her safety."

Contributory and Comparative Negligence All individuals are expected to exercise a reasonable degree of care in looking out for themselves. In some jurisdictions, recovery for injury resulting from negligence is prevented by failure of the injured person to exercise such care over himself or herself. This is the defense of **contributory negligence,** in which both parties have been negligent, and their combined negligence has contributed to cause the injury.

CONTRIBUTORY NEGLIGENCE
A theory in tort law under which a complaining party's own negligence contributed to or caused his or her injuries. Contributory negligence is an absolute bar to recovery in a minority of jurisdictions.

COMPARATIVE NEGLIGENCE
A theory in tort law under which the liability for injuries resulting from negligent acts is shared by all persons who were guilty of negligence (including the injured party), on the basis of each person's proportionate carelessness.

The trend is to narrow the scope of the defense of contributory negligence. Instead of allowing contributory negligence to negate a cause of action completely, a majority of states allow recovery based on the doctrine of **comparative negligence.** This doctrine enables both the plaintiff's and the defendant's negligence to be computed and the liability for damages distributed accordingly. Some jurisdictions have adopted a "pure" form of comparative negligence that allows the plaintiff to recover, even if the extent of his or her fault is greater than that of the defendant. For example, if the plaintiff was 80 percent at fault and the defendant 20 percent at fault, the plaintiff may recover 20 percent of his or her damages. Many states' comparative negligence statutes, however, contain a "50 percent" rule by which the plaintiff recovers nothing if he or she was more than 50 percent at fault.

A comparative negligence rule may be established by state statute or by a state supreme court's ruling, which becomes a precedent that all courts within the state must follow. In the following case, the Tennessee Supreme Court overturned precedent by abandoning the contributory negligence doctrine and adopting a comparative negligence standard.

Case 5.6
McINTYRE v. BALENTINE
Supreme Court of Tennessee, 1992.
833 S.W.2d 52.

HISTORICAL AND SOCIAL SETTING *Contributory negligence developed as a defense against negligence suits in the early nineteenth century. The hardship of the doctrine on a plaintiff is obvious: it places on one party the entire burden of a loss for which at least two parties may be responsible. Thus, in the twentieth century, dissatisfaction with the doctrine increased, and there were a number of attempts to find a method of dealing with cases in which there is negligence on the part of both the plaintiff and the defendant. The doctrine of comparative negligence is the most widely applied alternative. It has been adopted by statute in about half the states. At one time, in the absence of legislative action, courts were reluctant to apply the doctrine, perhaps because it represents a fundamental change in the law and affects thousands of cases every year. Since 1973, however, in at least ten additional states the courts have adopted the doctrine.*

FACTS In the early morning hours of November 2, 1986, Harry McIntyre's pickup truck was struck by a vehicle driven by Clifford Balentine in Savannah, Tennessee. Balentine was driving south on Highway 69 when McIntyre entered the highway from a truck stop area. Both men had consumed alcohol the evening of the accident. Evidence suggested that Balentine was also speeding. McIntyre sued Balentine for negligence. Balentine asserted that McIntyre was also negligent, in part because he was operating his vehicle while intoxicated. The court ruled in favor of Balentine; however, the court found that McIntyre was equally at fault in the accident. Under the doctrine of contributory negligence, which was still controlling in Tennessee courts, the fact that McIntyre was also negligent completely barred recovery. McIntyre appealed, alleging, among other things, that the trial court erred by refusing to instruct the jury regarding the doctrine of comparative negligence. Eventually, the case reached the Supreme Court of Tennessee.

ISSUE The central issue to be decided by the court in this case was whether the state of Tennessee should adopt the doctrine of comparative negligence, in which case Balentine's liability would be retried under this doctrine.

DECISION The court adopted a modified comparative fault system, under which a plaintiff can recover only if the plaintiff's own negligence does not exceed 49 percent. Holding that the trial court jury's verdict that the parties were equally at fault was not sufficiently trustworthy to form the basis of a final determination (because the jury had not been instructed in comparative fault), the court remanded the case for a new trial.

REASON The court stated that fifteen years before, when the court had been asked to adopt a system of comparative fault, it had responded as follows: "[W]e do not deem it appropriate to consider making such a change unless and until a case reaches us wherein the pleadings and proof present an issue of contributory negligence accompanied by advocacy that the ends of justice will be served by adopting the rule of comparative negligence." The court went on to state that "[s]uch a case is now before us." Noting that a majority of other states had adopted either a "pure" or a "modified" comparative fault system, the court held that "it is time to abandon the outmoded and unjust common law doctrine of contributory negligence and adopt in its place a system of comparative fault." Nonetheless, the court did not want to abandon entirely the fault-based tort system. Therefore, it adopted the modified form of comparative fault, under which a plaintiff cannot recover damages if he or she is more than 49 percent at fault. The court rejected the pure form of comparative fault because it did "not agree that a party should necessarily be able to recover in tort even though he may be 80, 90, or 95 percent at fault."

Last Clear Chance *Last clear chance* is a doctrine that can excuse the effect of a plaintiff's contributory negligence. If applicable, the last clear chance rule allows the plaintiff to recover full damages despite failure to exercise care. This rule operates when, through his or her own negligence, the plaintiff is endangered (or his or her property is endangered) by a defendant who has an opportunity to avoid causing damage. For example, if Murphy walks across the street against the light, and Lewis, a motorist, sees her in time to avoid hitting her but hits her anyway, Lewis (the defendant) is not permitted to use Murphy's (the plaintiff's) prior negligence as a defense. The defendant negligently missed the opportunity to avoid injuring the plaintiff. (The adoption of the comparative negligence rule has effectively abolished the last clear chance doctrine in many jurisdictions.)

Special Negligence Doctrines and Statutes

There are a number of special doctrines and statutes relating to negligence. We examine a few of them here.

Res Ipsa Loquitur Generally, in lawsuits involving negligence, the plaintiff has the burden of proving that the defendant was negligent. In certain situations, when negligence is very difficult or impossible to prove, the courts may infer that negligence has occurred, in which case the burden of proof rests on the defendant—to prove he or she was *not* negligent. The inference of the defendant's negligence is known as the doctrine of ***res ipsa loquitur***, which translates as "the facts speak for themselves." This doctrine is applied only when the event creating the damage or injury is one that ordinarily does not occur in the absence of negligence. *Res ipsa loquitur* has been applied to such events as trains derailing, wheels falling off moving vehicles, elevators falling, and bricks or windowpanes falling from a defendant's premises. For the doctrine to apply, the event must have been caused by an agency or instrumentality within the exclusive control of the defendant, and it must not have been due to any voluntary action or contribution on the part of the plaintiff. Some courts will add still another condition—that the evidence available to explain the event be more accessible to the defendant than to the plaintiff.

RES IPSA LOQUITUR
A doctrine under which negligence may be inferred simply because an event occurred, if it is the type of event that would not occur absent negligence. Literally, the term means *the thing speaks for itself.*

Negligence *Per Se* Certain conduct, whether it consists of an action or a failure to act, may be treated as **negligence *per se*** ("in or of itself"). Negligence *per se* may occur if an individual violates a statute or an ordinance providing for a criminal penalty and that violation causes another to be injured. The injured person must prove (1) that the statute clearly sets out what standard of conduct is expected, when and where it is expected, and of whom it is expected; (2) that he or she is in the class intended to be protected by the statute; and (3) that the statute was designed to prevent the type of injury that he or she suffered. The standard of conduct required by the statute is the duty that the defendant owes to the plaintiff, and a violation of the statute is the breach of that duty.

NEGLIGENCE *PER SE*
An action or failure to act in violation of a statutory requirement.

For example, a statute may require a landowner to keep a building in a safe condition and subject the owner to a criminal penalty, such as a fine, if the building is not kept safe. The statute is meant to protect those who are rightfully in the building. Thus, if the owner, without a sufficient excuse, violates the statute and a tenant is thereby injured, then a majority of courts will hold that the owner's unexcused violation of the statute conclusively establishes negligence—that is, that the owner's violation is negligence *per se*.

Special Negligence Statutes A number of states have enacted statutes prescribing duties and responsibilities in certain circumstances, the violation of which will impose civil liability. For example, many states have passed **dram shop acts** under which a tavern owner or bartender may be held liable for injuries caused by a person who became intoxicated while drinking at the bar or who was already intoxicated when served by the bartender.[5] In some states, statutes impose liability on *social hosts* (persons hosting parties) for injuries caused by guests who became intoxicated at the hosts' homes. Under these statutes, it is unnecessary to prove that the tavern owner, bartender, or social host was negligent.

DRAM SHOP ACTS
State statutes that impose liability on the owners of bars and taverns, as well as those who serve alcoholic drinks to the public, for injuries resulting from accidents caused by intoxicated persons when the sellers or servers of alcoholic drinks contributed to the intoxication.

Most states now also have what are called **Good Samaritan statutes.** Under these statutes, persons who are aided voluntarily by others cannot turn around and sue the "Good Samaritans" for negligence. These laws were passed largely to protect physicians and medical personnel who voluntarily render their services in emergency situations to those in need, such as individuals hurt in car accidents.

GOOD SAMARITAN STATUTES
State statutes that provide that persons who provide emergency services to, or rescue, others in peril—unless they do so recklessly, thus causing further harm—cannot be sued for negligence.

5. See Case 3.2 in Chapter 3 for an application of a Florida dram shop statute.

❖ Strict Liability

STRICT LIABILITY
Liability regardless of fault. In tort law, strict liability is imposed on a merchant who introduces into commerce a good that is unreasonably dangerous when in a defective condition.

Another category of torts is called **strict liability,** or *liability without fault.* Intentional torts and torts of negligence involve acts that depart from a reasonable standard of care and cause injuries. Under the doctrine of strict liability, liability for injury is imposed for reasons other than fault. Strict liability for damages proximately caused by an abnormally dangerous or exceptional activity is one application of this doctrine. Strict liability is applied in such cases because of the extreme risk of the activity. For example, even if blasting with dynamite is performed with all reasonable care, there is still a risk of injury. Balancing that risk against the potential for harm, it is fair to ask the person engaged in the activity to pay for injury caused by that activity. Although there is no fault, there is still responsibility because of the dangerous nature of the undertaking.

Courts will take into consideration the circumstances surrounding the activity—such as when and where it is occurring—in determining whether strict liability should be applied. In an early application of the strict liability principle, for example, the owner of a water reservoir that leaked and flooded adjacent areas was held strictly liable for damages. Strict liability was applied not because a water reservoir is in itself dangerous or exceptional but because this reservoir was located in a coal-mining area. It was the location of the reservoir that created risk. (See this chapter's *Landmark in the Law.*)

There are other applications of the strict liability principle. Persons who keep dangerous animals, for example, are strictly liable for any harm inflicted by the animals. A significant application of strict liability is in the area of *product liability*—liability of manufacturers and sellers for harmful or defective products. Liability here is a matter of social policy and is based on two factors: (1) the manufacturing company can better bear the cost of injury because it can spread the cost throughout society by increasing prices of goods and services, and (2) the manufacturing company is making a profit from its activities and therefore should bear the cost of injury as an operating expense. Product liability will be discussed in greater detail in Chapter 17.

For what reason is strict liability imposed on those who engage in abnormally dangerous acts?

The following case illustrates an application of the doctrine of strict liability.

Case 5.7
OLD ISLAND FUMIGATION, INC. v. BARBEE
District Court of Appeal of Florida, Third District, 1992.
604 So.2d 1246.

HISTORICAL AND SOCIAL SETTING *The early law of torts was not primarily concerned with whether a wrongdoer was at fault. It was concerned primarily with keeping the peace—with providing a remedy in lieu of private vengeance. At that time, a person who hurt another by accident, or even in self-defense, was required to pay for the injury or damage. The rule was "he who breaks must pay." Gradually, the law came to recognize fault as the basis for imposing liability, and it was suggested that there should be no liability without fault. In the late nineteenth century, however, the law began to accept that in some cases, a defendant may be liable not only in the absence of fault but even if he or she has followed a standard of reasonable care. In the context of abnormally dangerous activities, the courts recognized a new doctrine: in the event of harm for which no one is at fault, the party who can best bear the loss will be held liable.*

FACTS Old Island Fumigation, Inc., fumigated buildings A and B of a condominium complex. Residents in buildings A and B were evacuated during the procedure, but occupants of building C were not. Shortly after the fumigation, which involved the use of Vikane gas, several residents of building C became ill and were treated for sulfuryl fluoride poisoning. Sulfuryl fluoride is the active ingredient of Vikane gas. Several months later, an architect discovered that the fire wall between buildings B and C was defective and contained a four-foot-by-eighteen-inch open space through which the gas had entered building C. The defect was visible only from within the crawl space, and thus it had been missed by various building inspectors as well as by the fumigating company. Residents of building C sued Old Island, alleging that fumigation was an ultrahazardous activity and that Old Island was therefore strictly liable for their injuries. The company asserted that it should not be responsible for injuries caused by the negligence of others—the original architect and contractors for the condominiums, who had failed to note and repair the defect in the fire wall. The trial court granted the plaintiffs' motion for summary judgment against Old Island, and Old Island Fumigation appealed.

ISSUE The issue in this case is twofold: (1) Is fumigation an ultrahazardous activity? (2) Even if fumigation is an ultrahazardous activity, can Old Island be held liable for damages when the negligence of others (including the building contractors) made the injuries possible?

DECISION Yes, to both questions. The trial court's judgment was affirmed.

REASON Citing another case, the court stated that the factors to be considered in determining whether an activity is ultrahazardous are "whether [the] activity involves [a] high degree of risk of harm to property of others; whether [the] potential harm is likely to be great; whether [the] risk can be eliminated by exercise of reasonable care; whether [the] activity is [a] matter of common usage; whether [the] activity is appropriate to [the] place where [the activity is] conducted [and] whether [the] activity has substantial value to [the] community." The court held that fumigation is an ultrahazardous activity because it "necessarily involves a risk of serious harm * * * which cannot be eliminated by the exercise of the utmost care, and is not a matter of common usage." Old Island was thus liable regardless of how careful it had been in fumigating the buildings. The court also emphasized that the fact that a third party had also been negligent did not relieve Old Island from liability for a hazard created by the company for its own profit.

Landmark in the Law

Rylands v. Fletcher (1866)

The modern concept of strict liability traces its origins, in part, to the English case of *Rylands v. Fletcher,* which was decided in 1866. In the coal-mining area of Lancashire, England, the Rylands, who were mill owners, had constructed a reservoir on their land. Water from the reservoir broke through a filled-in shaft of an abandoned coal mine nearby and flooded the connecting passageways in an active coal mine owned by Fletcher. At trial, the court found that the defendants were ignorant of the abandoned mine shaft and therefore free of negligence. The case was decided in their favor.[a]

On appeal, the decision was reversed. The defendants were held liable, even though the circumstances did not fit within existing tort liability theories. After all, there was no trespass, because the flooding was not direct or immediate. Further, there was no nuisance, because there was nothing offensive to the senses and the damage was not continuous or recurring.[b] In justifying the appellate decision, Justice Blackburn compared the situation to the trespass of dangerous animals: "the true rule of law is, that the person who for his own purposes brings on his land and collects and keeps there anything likely to do mischief if it escapes, must keep it at his peril, and, if he does not do so, is *prima facie* answerable for all the damage which is the natural consequence of its escape."[c]

The Rylands appealed to the House of Lords. The House of Lords had to decide whether one is responsible for the consequences of any extraordinary or dangerous process, even if one is as careful as possible—that is, as careful as "the reasonable person." The House of Lords affirmed the ruling of the lower reviewing court but limited the ruling to apply only to the "nonnatural" use of the defendants' land.[d] In this case, the emphasis was placed on the abnormal and inappropriate character of a reservoir in coal-mining country, rather than on the mere tendency of water to "escape."

The rule from *Rylands v. Fletcher* can be seen in the strict liability rule for dangerous activities such as blasting: "[a] defendant will be liable when he damages another by a thing or activity unduly dangerous and inappropriate to the place where it is maintained, in the light of the character of the place and its surroundings."[e] Clearly, the primary basis of liability is the creation of an extraordinary risk. In subsequent American cases, though, water reservoirs in arid western states have not been considered inappropriate.

The doctrine that emerged from *Rylands v. Fletcher* was liberally applied by British courts with some important exceptions. In the United States, few courts accepted the doctrine, presumably because the courts were worried about the doctrine's effect on the expansion of American businesses. As New Hampshire's Chief Justice Charles Doe once said, the doctrine would "impose a penalty upon efforts, made in a reasonable, skillful, and careful manner, to rise above a condition of barbarism."[f] In other words, even dangerous enterprises were considered indispensable to the industrial and commercial development of this nation. Today, however, the doctrine of strict liability is the norm rather than the exception.

a. *Fletcher v. Rylands,* 3 H.&C. 774, 159 Eng.Rep. 737 (1865).

b. At the time of *Fletcher v. Rylands,* nuisances (a *nuisance* is a type of tort) included activities that substantially interfered with others' use or enjoyment of their land. Such things as foul odors and noxious gases constituted nuisances. It was thought, however, that a single occurrence was not sufficient—the interference had to be continuous or recurring.

c. *Fletcher v. Rylands,* L.R. 1 Ex. 265, 279–280 (1866).

d. *Rylands v. Fletcher,* L.R. 3 H.L. 330, 338 (1868).

e. W. Page Keeton et al., *Prosser and Keeton on Torts,* 5th ed. (St. Paul: West Publishing Co., 1984), pp. 547–548.

f. *Brown v. Collins,* 53 N.H. 442 (1873).

Application

Law and the Retailer

Retailers are faced with potential legal problems every day. They face a potential lawsuit not only every time a customer steps onto their property but also whenever a customer purchases a product from them. Here we consider only a few areas in which knowledge of the law can help a retailer prevent a legal problem.

Negligence

Negligence is an important area in tort law. Any retail business firm, whether a shoe store or a hamburger stand, must take reasonable care—not be negligent—in providing a safe environment in which the customer can examine products or purchase goods and services. The courts tend to conclude that "the customer is always right." Therefore, if you are a retailer, to assume that your customers will take reasonable care in their behavior or in the management of their small children while on your premises is to invite disaster. In contrast, if you assume that any person on the premises may show a complete lack of common sense, you are going a long way toward preventing a lawsuit for negligence. For example, even though it might be obvious that an employee is washing a section of the salesroom floor, there should be signs posted that warn the customer what the employee is doing. Also, if your premises include a parking lot used by customers, the parking lot should be periodically inspected to make sure that there are no hazards, such as potholes, that might cause a customer to be injured. Again, even if a risk appears "obvious," the retailer should take steps to remove the risk.

Handling Shoplifters

To what extent can you, the businessperson, detain a suspected shoplifter without being successfully sued for false imprisonment, invasion of privacy, or some other charge, such as defamation or infliction of emotional distress? Suspected shoplifters can be accosted, accused, and temporarily detained if certain reasonable procedures are used. These procedures differ, depending on the jurisdiction. The word to remember is *reasonable.* Keeping a suspected shoplifter in a locked storeroom for two hours because the manager has not yet got around to contacting the police would usually not be considered reasonable if the individual in question sued for false imprisonment.

When apprehending and questioning a suspected shoplifter, choose your words carefully. Using abusive or accusatory words or otherwise subjecting the person to indignity may result in a lawsuit. In one case, for example, the words "a big fat woman like you" served as the basis for the tort of infliction of emotional distress.[a] If you think someone has shoplifted, act on your suspicion before the suspect leaves the store. Usually, the courts will allow detention only if the suspected shoplifter is still on your premises. This is not always the case, however. In *Bonkowski v. Arlan's Department Store,*[b] for example, the court allowed detention after the suspect had left the store but was still in the immediate vicinity.

Checklist for the Retailer

- ☐ 1. Obtain adequate liability insurance coverage, if possible.
- ☐ 2. Always assume that the worst can happen; post warnings near all potential hazards no matter how obvious they may seem.
- ☐ 3. Always provide immediate medical care to an individual injured while on your premises.
- ☐ 4. Even for the most minor negligence lawsuit, hire an attorney and be willing to consider an out-of-court settlement (even if you believe that the customer was 100 percent at fault).
- ☐ 5. Employees who handle shoplifters should be appropriately trained in the proper procedure for apprehending and detaining someone suspected of shoplifting. Print out a short list of rules and have it checked by a local attorney familiar with recent court decisions in your area.

a. *Haile v. New Orleans Railway & Light Co.,* 135 La. 229, 65 So. 225 (1914). According to tort scholar William Prosser, this is the mildest insult for which recovery on the grounds of infliction of emotional distress has been allowed. See W. Page Keeton et al., *Prosser and Keeton on Torts,* 5th ed. (St. Paul: West Publishing Co., 1984), p. 58.

b. 383 Mich. 90, 174 N.W.2d 765 (1970).

❖ Key Terms

actionable 124
actual malice 126
assault 123
assumption of risk 139
battery 123
business invitee 133
causation in fact 135
comparative negligence 140
contributory negligence 140
conversion 130
damages 122
defamation 125
defense 124
dram shop act 142
duty of care 132
fraud 127
Good Samaritan statute 142
intentional tort 123
liability 127
malpractice 134
misrepresentation 127
negligence 130
negligence *per se* 142
nominal damages 128
privilege 126
protected interest 122
proximate cause 135
puffery 127
punitive damages 135
reasonable person standard 133
res ipsa loquitur 142
strict liability 143
tort 122
tortfeasor 123
trespass to land 127
trespass to personal property 129

❖ Chapter Summary: Torts

Intentional Torts against Persons	1. *Assault and battery*—An unexcused and intentional act that causes another person to be apprehensive of immediate harm is assault. Assault resulting in physical contact is battery. 2. *False imprisonment*—Intentional confinement or restraint of another person's movement without justification. 3. *Infliction of emotional distress*—An intentional act that amounts to extreme and outrageous conduct resulting in severe emotional distress to another. 4. *Defamation (libel or slander)*—A false statement of fact, not made under privilege, that is communicated to a third person and that causes damage to a person's reputation. For public figures, the plaintiff must also prove malice. 5. *Invasion of the right to privacy*—Use of a person's name or likeness for commercial purposes without permission, wrongful intrusion into a person's private activities, publication of information that places a person in a false light, or disclosure of private facts that an ordinary person would find objectionable. 6. *Misrepresentation—fraud (deceit)*—A false representation made by one party, through misstatement of facts or through conduct, with the intention of deceiving another and on which the other reasonably relies to his or her detriment.
Intentional Torts against Property	1. *Trespass to land*—Invasion of another's real property without consent or privilege. Specific rights and duties apply once a person is expressly or impliedly established as a trespasser. 2. *Trespass to personal property*—Unlawfully damaging or interfering with the owner's right to use, possess, or enjoy his or her personal property. 3. *Conversion*—A wrongful act in which personal property is taken from its rightful owner or possessor and placed in the service of another.
Unintentional Torts—Negligence	1. *Negligence*—The careless performance of a legally required duty or the failure to perform a legally required act. Elements that must be proved are that a legal duty exists, that the defendant breached that duty, and that the breach caused damage or injury to another. 2. *Defenses to negligence*—The basic defenses in negligence cases are (a) assumption of risk, and (b) contributory and comparative negligence.
Special Negligence Doctrines and Statutes	1. *Res ipsa loquitur*—A doctrine under which a plaintiff need not prove negligence on the part of the defendant because "the facts speak for themselves." *Res ipsa loquitur* has been applied to such events as trains derailing, wheels falling off moving vehicles, and elevators falling. 2. *Negligence per se*—A type of negligence that may occur if a person violates a statute or an ordinance providing for a criminal penalty and the violation causes another to be injured.

❖ Chapter Summary: Torts—Continued

Special Negligence Doctrines and Statutes—Continued	3. *Special negligence statutes*—State statutes that prescribe duties and responsibilities in certain circumstances, the violation of which will impose civil liability. Dram Shop acts and Good Samaritan statutes are examples of special negligence statutes.
Unintentional Torts—Strict Liability	Under the doctrine of strict liability, a person may be held liable, regardless of the degree of care exercised, for damages or injuries caused by his or her product or activity. Strict liability includes liability for defective products (product liability) and liability for abnormally dangerous activities.

❖ Questions and Case Problems

5-1. Function of Tort Law. What is the function of tort law? How does tort law differ from criminal law?

5-2. Liability to Business Invitees. Kim went to Ling's Market to pick up a few items for dinner. It was a rainy, windy day, and the wind had blown water through the door of Ling's Market each time the door opened. As Kim entered through the door, she slipped and fell in the approximately one-half inch of rain water that had accumulated on the floor. The manager knew of the weather conditions but had not posted any sign to warn customers of the water hazard. Kim injured her back as a result of the fall and sued Ling's for damages. Can Ling's be held liable for negligence in this situation? Discuss.

5-3. Negligence. In which of the following situations will the acting party be liable for the tort of negligence? Explain fully.

(a) Mary goes to the golf course on Sunday morning, eager to try out a new set of golf clubs she has just purchased. As she tees off on the first hole, the head of her club flies off and injures a nearby golfer.

(b) Mary's doctor gives her some pain medication and tells her not to drive after she takes it, as the medication induces drowsiness. In spite of the doctor's warning, Mary decides to drive to the store while on the medication. Owing to her lack of alertness, she fails to stop at a traffic light and crashes into another vehicle, in which a passenger is injured.

5-4. Causation. Ruth carelessly parks her car on a steep hill, leaving the car in neutral and failing to engage the parking brake. The car rolls down the hill, knocking down an electric line. The sparks from the broken line ignite a grass fire. The fire spreads until it reaches a barn one mile away. The barn houses dynamite, and the burning barn explodes, causing part of the roof to fall on and injure a passing motorist, Jim. Can Jim recover from Ruth? Why or why not?

5-5. Trespass to Land. During a severe snowstorm, Yoshiko parked his car in a privately owned parking lot. The car was later towed from the lot, and Yoshiko had to pay $100 to the towing company to recover his car. Yoshiko sued the owner of the parking lot, Icy Holdings, Inc., to get back the $100 he had paid. Icy Holdings claimed that, notwithstanding the severe snowstorm, Yoshiko's parking of his car on its property constituted trespass and therefore Icy Holdings did not act wrongfully in having the car towed off the lot. Discuss whether Yoshiko can recover his $100.

5-6. Emotional Distress. Jim Meads had a VISA credit-card account with Citibank, a subsidiary of Citicorp. Meads fell behind in his payments on the $5,000 owing on the account, and in July 1986 Citibank closed Meads's account and notified him that the account would be referred to the Collection Group of Citicorp Credit Services, Inc. (CCSI), for collection. Thereafter, Meads wrote to CCSI explaining that owing to medical problems and related medical expenses, he was unable to meet the minimum-payment requirements but would make partial payments on the account. Meads's attorney also wrote to CCSI, requesting that CCSI not contact Meads again about the account and instead direct all future inquiries to the attorney's office. Nevertheless, CCSI continued to contact Meads, by telephone and letter, at frequent intervals (at times more often than once per week) over a four-month period. Calls were made not only to Meads's home but to his place of work. Meads alleged that the callers were so abusive as to reduce his wife to tears. Meads finally sued CCSI for intentional infliction of emotional distress. Although Meads did not deny the validity of his debt to Citicorp, he felt that the collection attempts were abusive and stated that both he and his wife had suffered verifiable emotional and physical complaints as a direct result of the actions of CCSI. Was CCSI's conduct sufficiently outrageous to warrant an emotional distress claim? [*Meads v. Citicorp Credit Services, Inc.*, 686 F.Supp. 330 (S.D.Ga. 1988)]

5-7. **Strict Liability.** The Yommers operated a gasoline station. In December 1967 their neighbors, the McKenzies, noticed a smell in their well water, which proved to be caused by gasoline in the water. McKenzie complained to the Yommers, who arranged to have one of their underground storage tanks replaced. Nevertheless, the McKenzies were unable to use their water for cooking or bathing until they had a filter and water softener installed. At the time of the trial, in December 1968, they were still bringing in drinking water from an outside source. The McKenzies sued the Yommers for damages. The Yommers claimed that the McKenzies had not proved that there was any intentional wrongdoing or negligence on their part and therefore they should not be held liable. Under what theory might the McKenzies recover damages even in the absence of any negligence on the Yommers' part? Explain. [*Yommer v. McKenzie*, 255 Md. 220, 257 A.2d 138 (1969)]

5-8. Contributory Negligence. George Giles was staying at a Detroit hotel owned by the Pick Hotels Corp. While a hotel employee was removing luggage from the back seat of Giles's car, Giles reached into the front seat to remove his briefcase. As he did so, he supported himself by placing his left hand on the center pillar to which the rear door was hinged, with his fingers in a position to be injured if the rear door was closed. The hotel employee closed the rear door, and a part of Giles's left index finger was amputated. Giles sued the hotel for damages. The hotel claimed that it was not liable because Giles, by placing his hand on the car as he did, contributed to the injury. (Under state law, contributory negligence was an absolute defense to liability.) Discuss whether the hotel will succeed in its defense. [*Giles v. Pick Hotels Corp.*, 232 F.2d 887 (6th Cir. 1956)]

5-9. Liability to Business Invitees. While Charles and Esther Kveragas were in a rented motel room at the Scottish Inns in Knoxville, Tennessee, three intruders kicked open the door, shot Charles, and injured Esther. The intruders also took $3,000 belonging to the Kveragases. The Kveragases brought an action against the motel owners, claiming that the owners had been negligent in failing to provide adequately for the safety of the motel's guests. At trial, the evidence showed that the door had a hollow core and that it fit poorly into the door frame. There was no deadbolt lock on the door although such locks were easily available and commonly used in motels. The only lock on the door was one fitted into the door handle, which was described as a grade three lock, although a security chain was attached to the door. The Kveragases had both locked and chained the door, but still a single kick on the part of the intruders was all that was necessary to open it. Evidence at trial also indicated that a deadbolt lock would have withstood the force that was applied to the door. Did the motel owners have a duty to protect their guests from criminal acts on the motel premises, and if so, did the owners breach that duty of care by failing to provide more secure locks on the doors of the motel rooms? [*Kveragas v. Scottish Inns, Inc.*, 733 F.2d 409 (6th Cir. 1984)]

5-10. Emotional Distress. Lofton Johnson, a police officer employed by the West Virginia University Security Police, was called to the emergency room of the university's hospital to help subdue an unruly patient. Prior to Johnson's arrival, the patient had informed the doctors and nurses in the emergency room that he was infected with acquired immune deficiency syndrome (AIDS). While Johnson assisted medical personnel in restraining the patient, the patient bit Johnson on the forearm. The patient had previously bitten himself, and his blood was in and around his mouth when he bit Johnson. On previous occasions, the officer had assisted in restraining AIDS patients, but it was always the hospital's procedure to inform him that these patients were infected with AIDS so that proper precautions could be taken. Although Johnson tested negative for AIDS on several subsequent occasions, he claimed that he suffered severe emotional distress as a result of the AIDS exposure—he was shunned by his family and coworkers and generally felt like a social outcast with an uncertain future. In his suit against the hospital to recover for emotional distress, what will the court decide? Explain. [*Johnson v. West Virginia University Hospitals, Inc.*, 186 W.Va. 648, 413 S.E.2d 889 (1991)]

5-11. Strict Liability. Danny and Marion Klein were injured when an aerial shell at a public fireworks exhibit went astray and exploded near them. They sued the Pyrodyne Corp., the pyrotechnic company that was hired to set up and discharge the fireworks, alleging, among other things, that the company should be strictly liable for damages caused by the fireworks display. Will the court agree with the Kleins? What factors will the court consider in making its decision? Discuss fully. [*Klein v. Pyrodyne Corp.*, 117 Wash.2d 1, 810 P.2d 917 (1991)]

A Question of Ethics and Social Responsibility

5-12. *George Ward entered a K Mart department store in Champaign, Illinois, through a service entrance near the home improvements department. After purchasing a large mirror, Ward left the store through the same door. On his way out the door, carrying the large mirror in front and somewhat to the side of him, he collided with a concrete pole located just outside the door about a foot and a half from the outside wall. The mirror broke, and the broken glass cut his right cheek and eye, resulting in reduced vision in that eye. He later stated that he had not seen the pole, had not realized what was happening, and only knew that he felt "a bad pain, and then saw stars." Ward sued K Mart Corp. for damages, alleging that the store was negligent. The Supreme Court of Illinois ultimately decided in Ward's favor and upheld the jury's award of $68,000 in damages. The court held that the store had failed its duty to its patrons by not maintaining the premises in a reasonably safe condition. The store should have foreseen the risk to its customers posed by the poles and guarded against it.* [Ward v. K Mart Corp., *136 Ill.2d 132, 554 N.E.2d 223, 143 Ill.Dec. 288 (1990)*]

1. What ethical principle underlies the common law doctrine that business owners have a duty of care toward their customers?
2. K Mart argued that the pole was such an obvious obstacle that it did not pose any risk and therefore no warning to customers was needed. Do you agree with this argument? Why or why not?
3. Can you think of any reasons for the court's conclusion that K Mart should have foreseen the possibility that a customer could be injured because of the presence of the pole?
4. Does the duty of care unfairly burden business owners? Discuss.

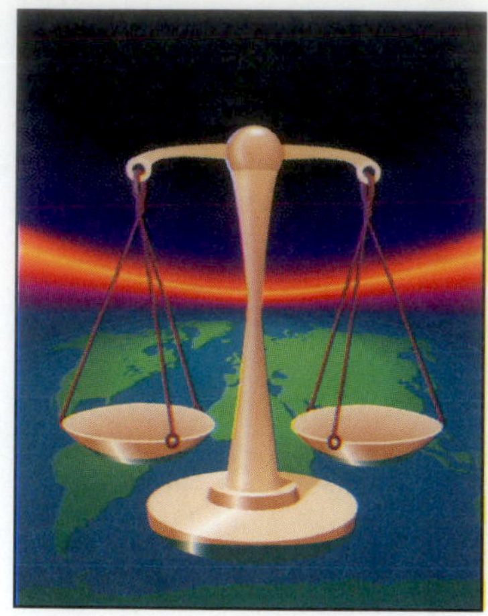

Chapter 6

Business Torts and Intellectual Property

"The language of the law must not be foreign to the ears of those who are to obey it."

Learned Hand, 1872–1961
(American jurist)

BUSINESS TORT
A tort occurring within the business context; typical business torts are wrongful interference with the business or contractual relationships of others and unfair competition.

Our economic system of free enterprise is predicated on the ability of persons, acting either as individuals or as business firms, to compete for customers and for sales. Unfettered competitive behavior has been shown to lead to economic efficiency and economic progress. Yet overly enthusiastic competitive efforts sometimes fall into the realm of intentional torts and crimes. Businesses may, generally speaking, engage in whatever is *reasonably* necessary to obtain a fair share of a market or to recapture a share that has been lost. But they are not allowed to use the motive of complete elimination of competition to justify certain business activities. Thus, an entire area of what is called business torts has arisen.

Business torts are defined as wrongful interference with another's business rights. Included in business torts are such vaguely worded common law concepts as *unfair competition* and *interfering with the business relations of others*. Those who enter into business should be acquainted with the point at which zealous competition might be construed by a court of law to cross over into tortious interference with the business rights of others. As the opening quotation indicates, businesspersons need to know what the law is if they are to obey it.

Of significant concern to businesspersons is the protection available for *intellectual property* rights. Although it is an abstract term for an abstract concept, intellectual property is nonetheless wholly familiar to virtually everyone. *Trademarks, copyrights,* and *patents* are all forms of intellectual property. The book you are reading is copyrighted. Undoubtedly, the personal computer you use at home is trademarked. Some of the resident software within that computer might be copyrighted. You see advertisements for trademarked items every day—Xerox, Macintosh, and the like. The study of intellectual property law is important because intellectual property has taken on an increasing importance not only in the United States but globally as well. Much of what is sold abroad, including popular American television series, computer programs, and blockbuster films, consists of intellectual property.

Because the field of business torts is so broad, the discussion here will be limited to the following causes of action:

1. Wrongful interference with contractual or business relationships.
2. Wrongfully entering into business.
3. Appropriation of another's name without permission.
4. Defamation in a business context.
5. Disparagement of business property or reputation.
6. Infringement of rights in intellectual property, such as trademarks, patents, and copyrights.
7. Misappropriation of trade secrets.

Following our discussion of these torts, we consider the application of the Racketeer Influenced and Corrupt Organizations Act (known more popularly as RICO) to fraudulent business activities.

"If you've a good case, try to compromise; if a bad one, take it to court."

(French proverb)

❖ Wrongful Interference

Business torts involving wrongful interference are generally divided into two categories: wrongful interference with a contractual relationship and wrongful interference with a business relationship.

Wrongful Interference with a Contractual Relationship

Tort law relating to *intentional interference with a contractual relationship* has expanded greatly in recent years. A landmark case involved an opera singer, Joanna Wagner, who was under contract to sing for a man named Lumley for a specified period of years.[1] A man named Gye, who knew of this contract, nonetheless "enticed" Wagner to refuse to carry out the agreement, and Wagner began to sing for Gye. Gye's action constituted a tort because it interfered with the contractual relationship between Wagner and Lumley. (Wagner's refusal to carry out the agreement also entitled Lumley to sue for breach of contract.)

Three elements are necessary for a wrongful interference with a contractual relationship to occur:

1. A valid, enforceable contract must exist between two parties.
2. A third party must *know* that this contract exists.
3. The third party must *intentionally* cause either of the two parties to break the contract.

The contract may be between a firm and its employees or a firm and its customers. Sometimes a competitor of a firm draws away one of the firm's key employees. If the original employer can show that the competitor induced the breach—that is, that the former employee would not otherwise have broken the contract—damages can be recovered from the competitor.

The following, highly publicized case illustrates the requirements for the tort of wrongful interference with a contractual relationship.

Case 6.1 

TEXACO, INC. v. PENNZOIL CO.

Court of Appeals of Texas, Houston (First District), 1987.
729 S.W.2d 768.

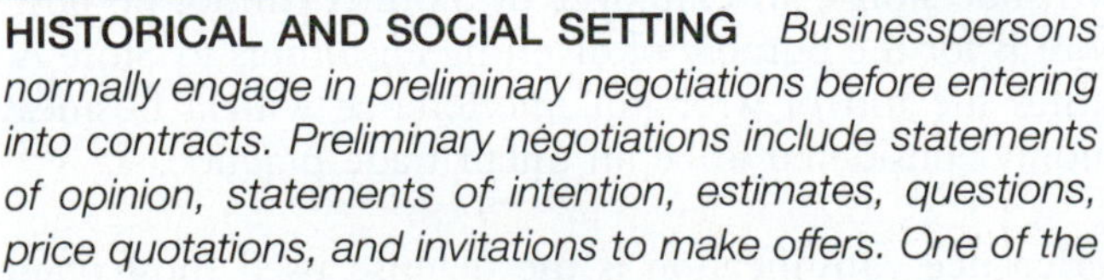

HISTORICAL AND SOCIAL SETTING *Businesspersons normally engage in preliminary negotiations before entering into contracts. Preliminary negotiations include statements of opinion, statements of intention, estimates, questions, price quotations, and invitations to make offers. One of the requirements of a contract is that one of the parties make an offer to contract. At what point does a preliminary negotiation become an offer to contract? The answer is not always clear. The test is whether a reasonable person in the position of the party who claims that an offer was made would conclude that the other party had made a commitment. Under this test, there have been differences of opinion as to the correct result in particular cases. In determining whether an offer has been made, one of the important factors to consider is whether it is clear that the party who is charged with making the offer has ceased dealing with others with respect to the same subject matter.*

1. *Lumley v. Gye,* 118 Eng.Rep. 749 (1853).

Case 6.1—Continued

FACTS Pennzoil made an offer to buy control of Getty Oil and negotiated the offer with the major stockholders, Gordon Getty and the Getty Museum. A memorandum of agreement was made subject to the agreement of Getty's board of directors. The board declined to approve the arrangement and made a counteroffer; the board also began looking for other potential bidders. Although some details of the agreement remained unsettled, Pennzoil eventually accepted one of Getty's counteroffers. The news was announced by both companies and reported widely in newspapers, including the *Wall Street Journal,* on January 5, 1984. While the lawyers from each company were negotiating a formal and specific written document, Getty's investment banker continued to look for another bidder. Texaco made a bid that Getty's board promptly accepted on January 6. Pennzoil subsequently sued Texaco, alleging tortious interference with its contract with Getty Oil. The trial court held that Texaco had wrongfully interfered with the Pennzoil–Getty Oil agreement and awarded Pennzoil $7.53 billion in actual damages and $3 billion in punitive damages. Texaco appealed.

ISSUE Had Texaco committed the tort of wrongful interference with a contractual relationship?

DECISION Yes. The appellate court affirmed the lower court's decision.

REASON In evaluating Pennzoil's claim, the appellate court had to address the following three questions: (1) Did Pennzoil and Getty actually have a contract? (2) Did Texaco know that a contract existed between Pennzoil and Getty? (3) Did Texaco's actions interfere with this contract? As to whether a contract existed, the appellate court found that there was sufficient evidence to support the trial court jury's conclusion that the Getty entities "intended to bind themselves to an agreement with Pennzoil at the end of the Getty Oil board meeting." The court also held that the evidence was sufficient to support the jury's inference that Texaco knew about the contract. The evidence reviewed by the appellate court included (1) documents setting out Texaco's strategy to defeat Pennzoil's deal, which contained such phrases as "stop the train" and "stop the signing"; (2) the notice of a contract given in a *Wall Street Journal* article; (3) the request by major Getty stockholders for full indemnity (a guaranty of payment) from Texaco against any claims by Pennzoil arising out of the memorandum of agreement; and (4) the Getty Museum's demand that if the Texaco deal fell through, the museum would be guaranteed the price that Pennzoil had agreed to pay for the museum's shares. As to whether Texaco acted to interfere with the contract between Getty and Pennzoil, the court stated that merely entering into a contract with a party with knowledge of that party's contractual obligations to someone else is not the same as inducing a breach. For liability to arise, it must be shown that there was some act of interference or of persuading the party to breach. Texaco argued that its offer was merely in response to a campaign of active solicitation by the Getty entities, who were dissatisfied with the terms of Pennzoil's offer. After reviewing the events and testimony, however, the court concluded that the record contained sufficient evidence from which the jury could infer that Texaco actively induced the breach of the Pennzoil–Getty Oil agreement.[a]

a. On Texaco's subsequent appeal, the Texas Supreme Court found no reversible errors. Other issues in the case were appealed as high as the United States Supreme Court. In 1988, the case was settled for $3 billion.

Wrongful Interference with a Business Relationship

Businesspersons devise countless schemes to attract customers, but they are forbidden by the courts to interfere unreasonably with another's business in their attempts to gain a share of the market. There is a difference between *competition* and *predatory behavior.* The distinction usually depends on whether a business is attempting to attract customers in general or to solicit only those customers who have shown an interest in a similar product or service of a specific competitor. If a shopping center contains two shoe stores, an employee of Store A cannot be positioned at the entrance of Store B for the purpose of diverting customers to Store A. This type of activity constitutes the tort of wrongful interference with a business relationship, which is commonly considered to be an unfair trade practice.

"Anyone can win unless there happens to be a second entry."

George Ade, 1866–1944
(American humorist)

Defenses to Wrongful Interference Justification is the defense used most often against the accusation of the tort of wrongful interference with a contractual or business relationship. For example, bona fide competitive behavior is not a wrongful interference even if it results in the breaking of a contract. If Antonio's Meats advertises so effectively that it induces Alex's Restaurant Chain to break its contract with Alvarez Meat Company, Alvarez Meat Company will be unable to recover against Antonio's Meats on a wrongful interference theory. After all, the public policy that favors free competition in advertising outweighs any possible instability that such competitive activity might cause in contractual relations.

❖ Wrongfully Entering into Business

In a freely competitive society it is usually true that any person can enter into any business to compete for the customers of existing businesses. Two situations in which this notion of free competition does not hold, however, are (1) when entering into business is a violation of the law and (2) when competitive behavior is predatory.

Any business or profession not subject to regulatory agencies or occupational licensing standards is open to an individual. No one can open a business for the sole purpose of driving another firm out of business, however; such a predatory motive is considered to be *simulated competition.* What the courts consider normal competitive activity is not always easy to ascertain—where does the normal desire to compete and obtain profits end and the tortious action begin? The following landmark case illustrates how a Minnesota court grappled with the question of malicious injury to business.

Case 6.2 

TUTTLE v. BUCK

Supreme Court of Minnesota, 1909.
107 Minn. 145,
119 N.W. 946.

HISTORICAL AND ETHICAL SETTING *We often think of traditional common law as stable, stretching unchanged back in time to old England. This is often contrasted with modern "activist" judicial rulings that allegedly lack respect for precedent. Yet the strength of the common law has always been its flexibility to adapt to new sets of circumstances. Even decades ago, courts would create new torts and expand common law precedents in light of contemporary standards of ethics and justice.*

FACTS The plaintiff, Edward Tuttle, a barber, filed suit against the defendant, Cassius Buck, for malicious interference with his business. The plaintiff had owned and operated a barbershop for the past ten years and had been able to support himself and his family comfortably from the income of the business. The defendant was a banker in the same community. During the previous twelve months, the defendant had "maliciously" established a competitive barbershop, employed a barber to carry on the business, and used his personal influence to attract customers from the plaintiff's barbershop. Apparently, the defendant had circulated false and malicious reports and accusations about the plaintiff and had personally solicited, urged, threatened, and otherwise persuaded many of the plaintiff's patrons to stop using the plaintiff's services and to use the defendant's shop instead. The plaintiff charged that the defendant undertook this entire plan with the sole design of injuring the plaintiff and destroying his business and not to serve any legitimate business interest or to practice fair competition.

ISSUE Did the defendant's activities constitute malicious interference with the plaintiff's business?

DECISION Yes. The defendant was guilty of maliciously interfering with the plaintiff's business.

REASON Based on the facts presented, the court determined that the defendant's sole purpose in establishing the competing barbershop was to deprive the plaintiff of his livelihood. The court was bound by precedent to preserve competition in the marketplace, but at the same time it was supposed to guard against abusive practices. When a person starts a competing business to drive a competitor out of business rather than to earn profits, that person is guilty of a tort and must answer for the harm done. "To call such conduct competition is a perversion of terms. It is simply the application of force without legal justification, which in its moral quality may be no better than highway robbery."

❖ Appropriation

APPROPRIATION
In tort law, the act of making a thing one's own or exercising or making use of an object to subserve one's own interest. When the act is wrongful, a tort is committed.

The use of one person's name or likeness by another, without permission and for the benefit of the user, constitutes the tort of **appropriation.** Under the law, an individual's right to privacy includes the right to the exclusive use of his or her identity. A number of cases have arisen concerning the use of a famous person's name for the benefit of the user. One case involved the use of "Here's Johnny"—the opening line of the former Johnny Carson show. A Michigan corporation that rented and sold portable toilets advertised them as "Here's Johnny" toilets. Carson brought suit, claiming that the Michigan corporation had violated his right to privacy by publicly appropriating his celebrity status for the corporation's commercial benefit. Even though the corporation had not used Carson's name or picture, the court held that the use of "Here's Johnny" was an appropriation of Carson's identity because the phrase was so strongly associated with Carson's public personality.[2]

Other cases have involved the unauthorized use of "The Greatest"—the appellation of former world heavyweight boxing champion Muhammad Ali—to describe a nude male model[3] and of "Crazylegs"—the moniker of professional football wide receiver Elroy Hirsch—as the name of a shaving gel.[4] In the following case, Vanna White sued a company for appropriating her celebrity status in one of its advertisements.

Case 6.3
WHITE v. SAMSUNG ELECTRONICS AMERICA, INC.
United States Court of Appeals, Ninth Circuit, 1992.
971 F.2d 1395.

HISTORICAL AND SOCIAL SETTING *One of the earliest discussions of the tort of appropriation appeared in a law review (a law school publication) in an article by William Prosser, a well-known legal educator and scholar in the field of torts.[a] Prosser recognized that up to the time the article appeared, in 1960, appropriation cases had involved one of two basic sets of facts: name appropriation and appropriation of a picture or other likeness. In his article, Prosser concluded, however, that "[i]t is not impossible that there might be appropriation of * * * identity, as by impersonation, without the use of either * * * name or * * * likeness." Prosser also noted that "[n]o such case appears to have arisen." Since 1960, case law has borne out his insight that the tort of appropriation is not limited to the appropriation of name or likeness. For example, in a case involving a Ford Motor Company television commercial in which a Bette Midler "sound-alike" sang a song that Midler had made famous, the court held that Ford "for their own profit in selling their product did appropriate part of her identity.[b]*

a. William Prosser, "Privacy," 48 *California Law Review* 383 (1960).

b. *Midler v. Ford Motor Co.,* 849 F.2d 460 (9th Cir. 1988).

FACTS Vanna White is the hostess of "Wheel of Fortune," one of the most popular game shows in the history of television. Capitalizing on her fame to enhance her fortune, White markets her identity to advertisers. Without White's permission, Samsung Electronics America, Inc., also attempted to capitalize on White's fame to enhance its fortune. An advertisement for Samsung VCRs depicted

2. *Carson v. Here's Johnny Portable Toilets,* 698 F.2d 831 (6th Cir. 1983).
3. *Ali v. Playgirl, Inc.,* 447 F.Supp. 723 (S.D.N.Y. 1978).
4. *Hirsch v. S. C. Johnson & Son, Inc.,* 90 Wis.2d 379, 280 N.W.2d 129 (1979).

Case 6.3—Continued

a robot, dressed in a wig, gown, and jewelry and posed next to a game board that resembled the "Wheel of Fortune" set, in a stance for which White is famous. The robot's hair, dress, and accessories were selected to resemble White's. White sued Samsung in federal district court, alleging, among other things, that Samsung had appropriated her celebrity status. The district court granted a motion for summary judgment against White, reasoning in part that because the robot ad did not use White's name or likeness, Samsung had not appropriated her celebrity status. White appealed.

ISSUE Does the tort of appropriation require the use of a celebrity's name or likeness?

DECISION No. The appellate court held that it is not important how a celebrity's identity is appropriated. The trial court's judgment on this issue was reversed, and the case was remanded for further proceedings.

REASON The appellate court ruled that "the specific means of appropriation are relevant only for determining whether the defendant has in fact appropriated the plaintiff's identity." The court reasoned that "[i]f the celebrity's identity is commercially exploited, there has been an invasion of his right whether or not his 'name or likeness' is used." The court explained that the tort of appropriation "has developed to protect the commercial interest of celebrities in their identities. The theory * * * is that a celebrity's identity can be valuable in the promotion of products, and the celebrity has an interest that may be protected from the unauthorized commercial exploitation of that identity." The court pointed out that Samsung's robot ad left "little doubt" as to the identity of the celebrity that the ad was meant to depict.

❖ Defamation in the Business Context

The tort of *defamation* occurs when an individual makes a false statement that injures another's reputation (see Chapter 5). Defamation may take the form of libel (defamatory statements in written or printed form) or slander (defamatory statements made orally). Defamation becomes a business tort when the defamatory matter injures someone in a profession, business, or trade or when it adversely affects a business entity in its credit rating and other dealings. Recently, questions have arisen about the potential liability of on-line computer information services, such as CompuServe and PRODIGY, for defamatory statements made in sources included in their data bases. The following case addresses this issue.

"Hurl your calumnies boldly; something is sure to stick."

Francis Bacon, 1561–1626
(English philosopher and statesman)

Case 6.4
CUBBY, INC. v. COMPUSERVE, INC.
United States District Court, Southern District of New York, 1991.
776 F. Supp. 135.

HISTORICAL AND SOCIAL SETTING *Traditional notions of freedom of expression have always conflicted with the law of defamation. Following the oppression of political publications on grounds of defamation in the seventeenth and eighteenth centuries, a tide of sentiment in favor of freedom of speech and of the press led to cases in which liability for defamation was limited. Among those who came to be protected by the First Amendment's guaranties of freedom of speech and of the press were libraries, bookstores, newsstands, and other distributors of books and periodicals. The courts ruled that a distributor has no duty to monitor, for example, each issue of every periodical it distributes. As the United States Supreme Court has held, this would be an unreasonable demand on the seller and a restriction on the public's access to reading matter.*[a] *If the contents of bookstores and newsstands were restricted to materials that the proprietors had read, they might be nearly empty.*

FACTS CompuServe, Inc., offers subscribers CompuServe Information Service (CIS), to which access is gained through the use of phone lines, modems, and computers. Among CIS's thousands of information sources, including electronic bulletin boards and topical data bases, is the Journalism Forum, which is controlled by Cameron Com-

a. *Smith v. California*, 361 U.S. 147, 80 S.Ct. 215, 4 L.Ed.2d 205 (1959).

Case 6.4—Continued

munications, Inc., an organization independent of CompuServe. The Journalism Forum includes *Rumorville USA,* a newsletter that reports on the broadcast journalism industry. CompuServe has no opportunity to review *Rumorville's* contents before it is uploaded into CIS, from which it is immediately available to subscribers. In 1990, Cubby, Inc., and Robert Blanchard developed Skuttlebut, a computer data base designed to focus on news and gossip in the television news and radio industries. In April 1990, *Rumorville* suggested that Skuttlebut had gained access to information first published in *Rumorville* "through some back door." *Rumorville* also stated that Blanchard had been "bounced" from his previous employment, and described Skuttlebut as a "new start-up scam." Cubby and Blanchard filed suit against CompuServe in federal district court, alleging in part libel based on these statements. CompuServe filed a motion for summary judgment, denying that it knew or had reason to know of the statements.

ISSUE Could CompuServe be held liable for defamatory statements made in publications that it distributed in the absence of proof that it knew or had reason to know of the statements?

DECISION No. The court held that CompuServe was only a distributor of information and thus could not be held liable for defamatory statements made in publications that it distributed unless there was a showing that it knew or had reason to know of the statements.

REASON The court acknowledged that normally, "one who repeats or otherwise republishes defamatory matter is subject to liability as if he had originally published it." But the court pointed out that "New York courts have long held that vendors and distributors of defamatory publications are not liable if they neither know nor have reason to know of the defamation." Recognizing that "[t]echnology is rapidly transforming the information industry," the court compared a computerized data base to a news vendor. "Given the relevant First Amendment considerations," the court held that the appropriate standard of liability to be applied to CompuServe was whether it knew or had reason to know of the allegedly defamatory statements. CompuServe denied that it knew of the statements, and Cubby and Blanchard offered no facts indicating otherwise. Thus, the court granted CompuServe's motion for summary judgment.

❖ Disparagement of Property

DISPARAGEMENT OF PROPERTY
Economically injurious falsehoods made about another's product or property. A general term for torts that are more specifically referred to as slander of quality or slander of title.

SLANDER OF QUALITY
Publication of false information about another's product, alleging it is not what its seller claims; also referred to as trade libel.

Disparagement of property occurs when economically injurious falsehoods are made not about another's reputation but about another's *product* or *property*. Disparagement of property is a general term for torts that can be more specifically referred to as *slander of quality* or *slander of title.*

Slander of Quality Publication of false information about another's product, alleging that it is not what its seller claims, constitutes a tort of **slander of quality.** This tort has also been given the name trade libel. The plaintiff must prove that actual damages proximately resulted from the slander of quality. That is, it must be shown not only that a third person refrained from dealing with the plaintiff because of the improper publication, but also that there were associated damages. The economic calculation of such damages—they are, after all, conjectural—is often extremely difficult.

It is possible for an improper publication to be both a slander of quality and a defamation. For example, a statement that disparages the quality of an article may also, by implication, disparage the character of the person who would sell such a product. In one case, for instance, claiming that a product that was marketed as a sleeping aid contained "habit-forming drugs" was held to constitute defamation.[5]

Trademark law (to be discussed shortly) has, to some extent, made it easier for companies to sue other companies on the basis of purported false advertising. In the past, courts often ruled that companies could be liable for false advertising only

5. *Harwood Pharmacal Co. v. National Broadcasting Co.*, 9 N.Y.2d 460, 174 N.E.2d 602, 214 N.Y.S.2d 725 (1961).

when they misrepresented their own products. It mattered little what such companies claimed about their competitors' brands, particularly in so-called comparative advertisements. Today, false or misleading statements about another firm's products are actionable.

Slander of Title When a publication denies or casts doubt on another's legal ownership of any property, and when this results in financial loss to that property's owner, the tort of **slander of title** may exist. Usually, this is an intentional tort in which someone knowingly publishes an untrue statement about property with the intent of discouraging a third person from dealing with the person slandered. For example, it would be difficult for a car dealer to attract customers after competitors published a notice that the dealer's stock consisted of stolen autos.

SLANDER OF TITLE
The publication of a statement that denies or casts doubt upon another's legal ownership of any property, causing financial loss to that property's owner.

❖ Trademark, Patent, and Copyright Infringement

The need to protect creative works was voiced by the framers of the U.S. Constitution over two hundred years ago: Article I, Section 8, of the Constitution authorized Congress "[t]o promote the Progress of Science and useful Arts, by securing for limited Times to Authors and Inventors the exclusive Right to their respective Writings and Discoveries." Laws protecting patents, trademarks, and copyrights are explicitly designed to protect and reward inventive and artistic creativity.

Trademarks and Related Property

A **trademark** is a distinctive mark, motto, device, or implement that a manufacturer stamps, prints, or otherwise affixes to the goods it produces so that they may be identified on the market and their origin vouched for. At common law, the person who used a symbol or mark to identify a business or product was protected in the use of that trademark. Clearly, if one used the trademark of another, it would lead consumers to believe that one's goods were made by the other. The law seeks to avoid this kind of confusion.

TRADEMARK
A word or symbol that has become sufficiently associated with a good (at common law) or has been registered with a government agency. Once a trademark is established, the owner has exclusive use of it and has the right to bring a legal action against those who infringe upon the protection given the trademark.

Distinctiveness of Mark Generally, the more distinctive a trademark is, the less likely it is that it will be confused with other trademarks. Therefore, the extent to which the law protects a trademark is normally determined by how distinctive the trademark is. Fanciful, arbitrary, or suggestive trademarks are inherently distinctive (that is, they need no proof of their distinctiveness) and are protected by law. Fanciful trademarks include invented words, such as Xerox for one manufacturer's copiers and Kodak for another company's photographic products. Arbitrary trademarks include actual words used with products that have no literal connection to the words, such as "English Leather" used as a name for an after-shave lotion (and not for leather processed in England). Suggestive trademarks are those that suggest something about a product without describing the product directly. For example, "Dairy Queen" suggests an association between its products and milk, but it does not directly describe ice cream.

Descriptive terms, geographic terms, and personal names are not inherently distinctive and do not receive protection under the law until they acquire a secondary meaning. A secondary meaning may arise when customers begin to associate a specific trademark with the source of the trademarked product. For example, the name Calvin Klein is a strong trademark because consumers associate that name with goods marketed by Calvin Klein or licensed distributors of Calvin Klein products. Whether a secondary meaning becomes attached to a term or name usually depends on how extensively the product is advertised, the market for the product, the number of sales, and other factors. Once a secondary meaning is attached to a term or name, a trademark is considered distinctive and is protected. Of course, geographic terms and personal names used in fanciful or arbitrary ways are inherently distinctive. Generic terms, such as *bicycle* or *computer*, receive no protection, even if they acquire secondary meanings.

Trademarks may be registered with the state or with the federal government. Once a trademark has been registered, a firm is entitled to its exclusive use for marketing purposes. Whenever that trademark is copied to a substantial degree or used in its entirety by another, intentionally or unintentionally, the trademark has been infringed. The owner of the trademark need not register it to obtain protection from the tort of trademark infringement, but registration does furnish proof of the date of inception of its use. Moreover, registration may prolong the life of the trademark. Registration is renewable between the fifth and sixth years after the initial registration and every twenty years thereafter, as long as the mark remains distinctive and is used.

A particularly thorny problem arises when a trademark acquires generic use. For example, *aspirin* and *thermos* were originally trademarked products but today the words are used generically. Other examples are *escalator, trampoline, raisin bran, dry ice, lanolin, linoleum, nylon,* and *corn flakes*. Even so, the courts will not allow another firm to use those marks in such a way as to deceive a potential consumer. Consider, for example, the following famous case concerning Coca-Cola, which was decided by the United States Supreme Court.

Case 6.5 

THE COCA-COLA CO. v. KOKE CO. OF AMERICA

Supreme Court of the United States, 1920.
254 U.S. 143,
41 S.Ct. 113,
65 L.Ed. 189.

HISTORICAL AND SOCIAL SETTING *Trademarks can be valuable aspects of intellectual property, carrying substantial goodwill with consumers. This is evident from the numerous trademarks that have persisted unchanged for decades. Today's trademark may be the same as a company's 1920 trademark, but today's product may be quite different from the 1920 product. The trademark that described the 1920 product, therefore, may not be so descriptive of today's product.*

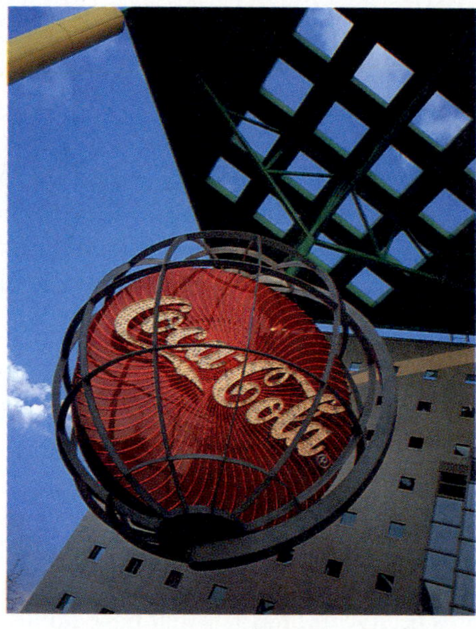

FACTS The Coca-Cola Company sought to enjoin other beverage companies from using the words Koke and Dope for the defendants' products. The defendants contended that the Coca-Cola trademark was a fraudulent representation and that Coca-Cola was therefore not entitled to any help from the courts. By use of the Coca-Cola name, the defendants alleged, the Coca-Cola Company represented that the beverage contained cocaine (from coca leaves).

ISSUE Did the marketing of products called Koke and Dope by the Koke Company and other firms constitute an infringement on Coca-Cola's trademark?

DECISION Yes for Koke, but no for Dope. The competing beverage companies were enjoined from calling their products Koke, but the Court did not prevent them from calling their products Dope.

REASON Justice Holmes noted that, to be sure, prior to 1900 the Coca-Cola beverage had contained a small amount of cocaine, but this ingredient had been deleted from the formula by 1906 at the latest, and the Coca-Cola Company had advertised to the public that no cocaine was present in its drink. Coca-Cola was a widely popular drink

Case 6.5—Continued

"to be had at almost any soda fountain." Because of the public's widespread familiarity with Coca-Cola, the retention of the name of the beverage (referring to coca leaves and cola nuts) was not misleading. "It hardly would be too much to say that the drink characterizes the name as much as the name the drink. In other words Coca-Cola probably means to most persons the plaintiff's familiar product to be had everywhere rather than a compound of particular substances." The name Coke was found to be so common a term for the trademarked product Coca-Cola that the defendants' use of the similar-sounding Koke as a name for their beverages was disallowed. The Court could find no reason to restrain the defendant from using the name Dope, however.

The Trademark Revision Act In 1988, the Trademark Revision Act was passed by Congress. This act, which took effect on November 16, 1989, significantly altered the prior registration scheme. That scheme required that the mark be used before an application could be filed. The 1988 act, in contrast, allows an applicant to file on the basis either of use or of the bona fide intention to use the mark in commerce. This is the so-called "intent to use" provision, which requires that the mark be put into commerce within six months after filing with the U.S. Patent and Trademark Office. At the end of the six months, the applicant must provide proof that the mark was put into commerce and that the application was not opposed.

Under extenuating circumstances, the six-month period can be extended by thirty months, giving the applicant a total of three years from the date of notice of trademark approval to make use of the mark and file the required use statement. Registration under the 1988 act is postponed until actual use of the mark. Nonetheless, during this waiting period, any applicant can legally protect his or her trademark against a third party who previously has neither used the mark nor filed an application for it.

Service, Certification, and Collective Marks A **service mark** is similar to a trademark but is used to distinguish the services of one person or company from those of another. For example, each airline has a particular mark or symbol associated with its name. Titles and character names used in radio and television are frequently registered as service marks.

SERVICE MARK
A mark used in the sale or the advertising of services, such as to distinguish the services of one person from the services of others. Titles, character names, and other distinctive features of radio and television programs may be registered as service marks.

Other marks protected by law include certification marks and collective marks. A *certification mark* is used by one or more persons other than the owner to certify the region, materials, mode of manufacture, quality, or accuracy of the owner's goods or services. When used by members of a cooperative, association, or other organization, it is referred to as a *collective mark*. Examples of certification marks are the "Good Housekeeping Seal of Approval" and "UL Tested." Collective marks appear at the ends of the credits of movies to indicate the various associations and organizations that participated in the making of the films. The union marks found on the tags of certain products are also collective marks.

Trade Names Trademarks apply to *products*. The term **trade name** is used to indicate part or all of a business's name, whether the business is a sole proprietorship, a partnership, or a corporation. Generally, a trade name is directly related to a business and its goodwill. Trade names may be protected as trademarks if the trade name is the same as the company's trademarked product—for example, Coca-Cola. Unless also used as a trademark or service mark, a trade name cannot be registered with the federal government. Trade names are protected under the common law, however. As with trademarks, words must be unusual or fancifully used if they are to be protected as trade names. The word *Safeway* was held by the courts to be sufficiently fanciful to obtain protection as a trade name for a foodstore chain.[6]

TRADE NAME
A name used in commercial activity to designate a particular business, a place at which a business is located, or a class of goods. Trade names can be exclusive or nonexclusive. Examples of trade names are Sears, Safeway, and Firestone.

6. *Safeway Stores v. Suburban Foods,* 130 F.Supp. 249 (E.D.Va. 1955).

Law in the Extreme

A Grim Solution to the Passing-Off Problem

Perhaps the central tort in unfair competition at common law is what is known as *passing off*, which is falsely inducing buyers to believe that one product is another, usually because the other product is well known or has a reputation for high quality. Recent examples abound: jeans, perfume, cameras, and a variety of other consumer goods have been passed off through reputable merchants. Commonly, passing off involves the infringement of a trademark, a trade name, a patent, or a copyright. The basic question is whether the ordinary customer, paying the usual amount of attention, would be deceived.

In the United States, a business firm that infringes on the trademark, trade name, patent, or copyright of another may end up paying costly damages. Recently, for example, the Johnson & Johnson Company paid $129 million to settle a patent infringement suit brought by the Minnesota Mining & Manufacturing Company. Yet even million-dollar settlements pale in significance when compared with the penalty recently levied on a Chinese liquor factory manager, Luo Leming, for passing off ordinary white wine as *maotai*, which is reputed to be China's best alcoholic beverage. Using fake *maotai* labels, Luo relabeled bottles of inexpensive white wine and pocketed the profits. In one year alone, his profits from this practice amounted to $375,900. Unfortunately for Luo and his family, he was not given the "opportunity" to pay damages to the maker of *maotai* wine. The Chinese government sentenced him to death and executed him in late 1992. (Apparently, this was the first time the Chinese government had sentenced anyone to the death penalty for passing off fake goods.)

Patents

PATENT
A government grant that gives an inventor the exclusive right or privilege to make, use, or sell his or her invention for a limited time period. The word *patent* usually refers to some invention and designates either the instrument by which patent rights are evidenced or the patent itself.

A **patent** is a grant from the government that conveys to and secures for an inventor the exclusive right to make, use, and sell an invention for a period of seventeen years. Patents for a lesser period are given for designs, as opposed to inventions. For either a regular patent or a design patent, the applicant must demonstrate to the satisfaction of the patent office that the invention, discovery, or design is genuine, novel, useful, and not obvious in light of current technology. A patent holder gives notice to all that an article or design is patented by placing on it the word "Patent" or "Pat." plus the patent number.

Patent Infringement If a firm makes, uses, or sells another's patented design, product, or process without the patent owner's permission, it commits the tort of patent infringement. Patent infringement may exist even though not all features or parts of an invention are copied. (With respect to a patented process, however, all steps or their equivalent must be copied for infringement to exist.) Often, litigation for patent infringement is so costly that the patent holder will instead offer to sell to the infringer a license to use the patented design, product, or process. Indeed, in many cases the costs of detection, prosecution, and monitoring are so high that patents are valueless to their owners, because the owners cannot afford to protect them.

Patents for Computer Software At one time, it was difficult for developers and manufacturers of software to obtain patent protection because many software products simply automate procedures that can be performed manually. In other words, the computer programs do not meet the "novel" and "not obvious" requirements previously mentioned. Also, the basis for software is often a mathematical equation or formula, which is not patentable. In 1981, the United States Supreme Court held that it is possible, however, to obtain a patent for a *process* that incorporates a computer program—providing, of course, that the process itself is patentable.[7] Subsequently, many patents have been issued for software-related inventions. Some critics believe that patents are being issued too readily for software that is not novel or that represents merely an obvious change of another's computer program.

Another obstacle to obtaining patent protection for software is the procedure of obtaining patents. The process can be expensive and slow. The time element is a particularly important consideration for someone wishing to obtain a patent on software. In light of the rapid changes and improvements in computer technology, the delay could undercut the product's success in the marketplace.

Despite these difficulties, patent protection is used in the computer industry. If a patent is infringed, the patent holder may sue for an injunction, damages, and the destruction of all infringing copies, as well as attorneys' fees and court costs.

Copyrights

A **copyright** is an intangible right granted by statute to the author or originator of certain literary or artistic productions. Works created after January 1, 1978, are automatically given statutory copyright protection for the life of the author plus fifty years. For copyrights owned by publishing houses, the copyright expires seventy-five years from the date of publication or one hundred years from the date of creation, whichever is first. For works by more than one author, the copyright expires fifty years after the death of the last surviving author. A copyright owner no longer needs to place a © or R on the work to have the work protected against infringement.[8] Chances are that if somebody created it, somebody owns it.

COPYRIGHT
The exclusive right of "authors" to publish, print, or sell an intellectual production for a statutory period of time. A copyright has the same monopolistic nature as a patent or trademark, but it differs in that it applies exclusively to works of art, literature, and other works of authorship (including computer programs).

What Is Protected Expression? Works that are copyrightable include books, records, films, artworks, architectural plans, menus, music videos, and product packaging. To obtain protection under the Copyright Act, a work must be original and fall into one of the following categories: (1) literary works; (2) musical works; (3) dramatic works; (4) pantomimes and choreographic works; (5) pictorial, graphic, and sculptural works; (6) films and other audiovisual works; and (7) sound recordings. In recent years, the Copyright Act has been amended to include protection for computer software (this topic is discussed later in this chapter, as well as in the *Landmark in the Law*) and architectural plans. To be protected, a work must be "fixed in a durable medium" from which it can be perceived, reproduced, or communicated. Protection is automatic. Registration is not required.

Section 102 of the Copyright Act specifically excludes copyright protection for any "idea, procedure, process, system, method of operation, concept, principle, or

---

7. *Diamond v. Diehr*, 450 U.S. 175, 101 S.Ct. 1048, 67 L.Ed.2d 155 (1981).

8. This is also true under an international copyright treaty, the Berne Convention. Copyright notice is not needed to protect works published after March 1, 1989. If, for example, an American writes a book, the American author's copyright in the book must be recognized by every other country that has signed the Berne Convention. (Also, if a citizen of a country that has not signed the convention first publishes a book in a country that has, all other countries that have signed the convention must recognize that author's copyright.)

discovery, regardless of the form in which it is described, explained, illustrated, or embodied." Note that it is not possible to copyright an *idea.* The underlying ideas embodied in a work may be freely used by others. What is copyrightable is the particular way in which an idea is *expressed.* Whenever an idea and an expression are inseparable, the expression cannot be copyrighted.

Generally, anything that is not an original expression will not qualify for copyright protection. Facts widely known to the public are not copyrightable. Page numbers are not copyrightable because they follow a sequence known to everyone. Mathematical calculations are not copyrightable. *Compilations* of facts, however, are copyrightable. Section 103 of the Copyright Act defines a compilation as "a work formed by the collection and assembling of preexisting materials of data that are selected, coordinated, or arranged in such a way that the resulting work as a whole constitutes an original work of authorship."

Does the compilation of "facts" (names, addresses, and telephone numbers) listed in the white pages of a telephone directory qualify for copyright protection? This issue was raised in the following case.

Case 6.6 FEIST PUBLICATIONS, INC. v. RURAL TELEPHONE SERVICE CO.

Supreme Court of the United States, 1991.
499 U.S. 340,
111 S.Ct. 1282,
113 L.Ed.2d 358.

HISTORICAL AND SOCIAL BACKGROUND *Some types of works are relatively new or difficult to fit into the traditional framework of copyright law. Copyright protection for these works may be controversial in some way. Computer software, for example, does not seem to fit easily into the traditional framework. Compilations, such as telephone directories, also pose problems in terms of copyrightability. Yet both of these types of works play an important role in business. A compilation results from a process of selecting, bringing together, organizing, and arranging existing materials of all kinds, even if the individual items have previously been, or could have been, subject to copyright. Compilations are expressly mentioned in the Copyright Act. But the extent to which particular types of compilations are protected by copyright has been left to the courts to determine.*

FACTS The Rural Telephone Service Company provides telephone service to several communities in Kansas. Rural publishes a typical telephone directory, consisting of white pages and yellow pages. Data for the directory are obtained from Rural's subscribers, who must provide their names and addresses to obtain telephone service. Feist Publications, Inc., is a publishing company that specializes in area-wide telephone directories covering a geographic range much larger than that covered by directories such as Rural's. To obtain white-pages listings for its area-wide directory, Feist approached each of the eleven telephone companies operating in northwest Kansas and offered to pay for the right to use its white-pages listings. Rural was the only company that refused to license its listings to Feist. Rural's refusal created a problem for Feist because omitting Rural's listings would leave an unacceptable "gap" in its area-wide directory, rendering it less attractive to potential yellow-pages advertisers. To overcome this problem, Feist used the listings without Rural's consent. Rural sued Feist for copyright infringement. The trial court granted summary judgment to Rural, holding that telephone directories are copyrightable, and the appellate court affirmed the decision. The United States Supreme Court granted *certiorari.*

ISSUE Did Feist's use of Rural's white-pages listings constitute copyright infringement?

DECISION No. The United States Supreme Court reversed the decision of the appellate court. Feist's use of Rural's white-pages listings did not constitute copyright infringement.

REASON The Supreme Court explained that "[n]ot all copying * * * is copyright infringement. To establish infringement, two elements must be proven: (1) ownership of a valid copyright, and (2) copying of constituent elements of the work that are original." The first element was not at issue—Rural's directory had copyright protection because it contained some original text and some original material in its yellow-pages advertisements. As for the second element, the Court discussed whether Feist copied anything that was "original" to Rural's directory. Names, towns, and telephone numbers are "uncopyrightable facts; they ex-

Case 6.6—Continued

isted before Rural reported them and would have continued to exist if Rural had never published a telephone directory." Thus, the only question was whether Rural "selected, coordinated, or arranged these uncopyrightable facts in an original way." The Court noted that "Rural's selection of listings could not be more obvious: it publishes the most basic information—name, town, and telephone number—about each person who applies to it for telephone service. * * * Nor can Rural claim originality in its coordination and arrangement of facts. * * * [T]here is nothing remotely creative about arranging names alphabetically in a white pages directory." The Court concluded that Rural's directory lacked "the modicum of creativity necessary to transform mere selection into copyrightable expression."

ETHICAL CONSIDERATIONS *This case raises an obvious ethical question: Is it fair that Feist should be able to reap the fruits of Rural's labors without any penalty? In addressing just this question, the Court at one point in its opinion pointed out that the "primary objective of copyright is not to reward the labor of authors, but '[t]o promote the Progress of Science and useful Arts.' To this end, copyright assures authors the right to their original expression, but encourages others to build freely upon the ideas and information conveyed by a work. This principle, known as the idea/expression or fact/expression dichotomy, applies to all works of authorship. As applied to a factual compilation, assuming the absence of original written expression, only the compiler's selection and arrangement may be protected; the raw facts may be copied at will. This result is neither unfair nor unfortunate. It is the means by which copyright advances the progress of science and art."*

Copyright Infringement Whenever the form or expression of an idea is copied, an infringement of copyright occurs. The reproduction does not have to be exactly the same as the original, nor does it have to reproduce the original in its entirety.

Penalties or remedies can be imposed on those who infringe copyrights. These range from actual damages (damages based on the actual harm caused to the copyright holder by the infringement) or statutory damages (damages provided for under the Copyright Act, not to exceed $100,000), imposed at the court's discretion, to criminal proceedings for willful violations (which may result in fines and/or imprisonment).

An exception to liability for copyright infringement is made under the "fair use" doctrine. In certain circumstances, a person or organization can reproduce copyrighted material without paying royalties (fees paid to the copyright holder for the privilege of reproducing the copyrighted material). Section 107 of the Copyright Act provides as follows:

> [T]he fair use of a copyrighted work, including such use by reproduction in copies or phonorecords or by any other means specified by [Section 106 of the Copyright Act,] for purposes such as criticism, comment, news reporting, teaching (including multiple copies for classroom use), scholarship, or research, is not an infringement of copyright. In determining whether the use made of a work in any particular case is a fair use the factors to be considered shall include—
>
> (1) the purpose and character of the use, including whether such use is of a commercial nature or is for nonprofit educational purposes;
>
> (2) the nature of the copyrighted work;
>
> (3) the amount and substantiality of the portion used in relation to the copyrighted work as a whole; and
>
> (4) the effect of the use upon the potential market for or value of the copyrighted work.

Because these guidelines are very broad, the courts determine whether a particular use is fair on a case-by-case basis. Thus, anyone reproducing copyrighted material may still be subject to a violation (see this chapter's *Business Law in Action*).

The following case discusses whether recording television broadcasts on home videotape recorders constitutes copyright infringement or qualifies as a "fair use."

Case 6.7
SONY CORP. OF AMERICA v. UNIVERSAL CITY STUDIOS, INC.

Supreme Court of the United States, 1984.
464 U.S. 417,
104 S.Ct. 774,
78 L.Ed.2d 574.

HISTORICAL AND TECHNOLOGICAL SETTING *Technology does not necessarily cooperate with the law. The law gives rights to the producers of television programs, enabling them to sell their programs and make a profit. When videocassette recorders became affordable and were purchased by many households, individuals could tape the programs from their televisions and thus avoid buying official copies of the programs and compensating the performers and producers for their efforts. The courts were faced with the problem of adapting the law governing rights in intellectual property to new possible copying uses without stifling the development of valuable technologies.*

FACTS Universal City Studios, Inc., alleged that the general public used Betamax videocassette recorders (VCRs), manufactured and marketed by Sony, to record TV broadcasts of Universal's copyrighted television programs, thereby infringing on Universal's copyrights. Claiming that Sony was vicariously liable because it sold the equipment knowing that its customers would use Betamax VCRs to make unauthorized copies of copyrighted material, Universal sought money damages, an accounting for profits, and an injunction against the manufacture and marketing of the VCRs. The district court denied relief, but the court of appeals held Sony liable for contributory infringement. Sony appealed to the United States Supreme Court.

ISSUE Should Sony be held liable for contributory infringement of Universal's copyright?

DECISION No. The Supreme Court concluded that because a substantial number of television broadcast copyright holders would not object to having their broadcasts recorded, and because Universal failed to show that such recording would cause more than minimal harm to the market for or value of its copyrighted works, such uses of the Betamax VCRs were noninfringing. Therefore, Sony was not liable for contributory infringement.

REASON Copyright protection does not "accord the copyright owner absolute control over all possible uses of his work." Rather, Section 106 of the Copyright Act grants the copyright holder certain exclusive rights while Section 107, conversely, allows a noncopyright holder certain "fair uses" of the work. The sale of the VCR "does not constitute contributory infringement if the product is widely used for legitimate purposes, or is even capable of substantial noninfringing uses." Moreover, unless the unauthorized use conflicts with one of the exclusive rights granted under Section 106, the use is not infringing. The Court concluded that to challenge a noncommercial use of a copyrighted work, proof is required that either (1) the particular use is harmful or (2) if such a use should become widespread, it would adversely affect the market for the copyrighted work. Balancing these factors, the Court found that home taping of the copyrighted programs is a "fair use."

Copyright Protection for Computer Software The Computer Software Act of 1980 extended copyright protection to computer software, but because of the unique nature of computer programs, the courts have had many problems in applying and interpreting the act. Generally, determinations as to what elements of a program will be protected by copyright have been made by the courts on a case-by-case basis. (See this chapter's *Landmark in the Law.*)

Computer software companies face a problem similar to that faced by other generators of intellectual property, such as videotapes or musical recordings—the ease with which intellectual property can be duplicated. The home viewer need only hook a videotape recorder up to a television set receiving the broadcast to make a copy of the broadcast itself. Moreover, the cost of duplication is insignificant. Record companies also claim to lose billions of dollars in sales each year due to private taping. In regard to software, the same issue of lost sales must be addressed. Software companies have complained that would-be customers are often able to obtain copies of programs from friends or computer bulletin boards and thereby avoid paying anything to the owners of the programs. We will return to this subject in Chapter 7 in the section on *software piracy.*

MASK WORK
A series of images related to the pattern formed by the many layers of a semiconductor chip product.

The Semiconductor Chip Protection Act **Mask works,** which are defined as a series of images related to the pattern formed by the many layers of a semiconductor

Business Law in Action

It Used to Be So Simple . . .

It would be hard to imagine life without photocopiers. Pages of textbooks, articles from journals, memos, and an endless variety of textual and illustrative material can be copied quickly and at relatively low cost for a myriad of purposes. While the ease and low cost of making photocopies may be a boon for those making and using the photocopies, it can cost publishers whose copyrighted works are copied millions of dollars in lost revenues. Because of this, some publishers have recently taken aim at those who make copies of their copyright-protected works without permission.

In 1989, for example, Basic Books and seven other major New York publishers sued Kinko's, the national chain of copy stores, for violating copyright laws by producing unauthorized course anthologies for students. For many years, professors on college campuses have assembled excerpts from relevant articles or textbooks into a packet, which would then be copied and bound by a local copy shop and sold to students at modest prices. The problem is that few professors and even fewer copy shops ever bother to contact the copyright holders of the excerpted pages from copyrighted works to secure permission to reproduce the materials. In defending against the publishers' claim of copyright infringement, Kinko's admitted that it had not obtained permission from the copyright holders but argued that its anthologies were protected under the "fair use" doctrine because the materials were for educational use. The court thought otherwise. Noting that the profit motive for producing the anthologies was of primary importance to Kinko's, the court ordered Kinko's to pay the publishers over one million dollars in damages and legal expenses.[a] The court's decision has convinced copy shops to begin demanding proof of authorization before agreeing to reproduce anthologies for university courses.

Other recent cases have been brought by publishers of journals or newsletters against clients who make multiple copies of journal articles or newsletters for purposes of internal circulation without the publishers' permission and without paying additional fees to the publishers. In 1991, for example, Washington Business Information, Inc. (WBII), the publisher of a product liability safety newsletter, settled a dispute with the Washington law firm of Coller, Shannon, and Scott regarding the firm's allegedly unauthorized duplication of its newsletter. According to David Swit, the head of WBII, the law firm made the copies to avoid paying $590 for two additional subscriptions. The *New York Times* reported that this practice may have ended up costing the law firm an estimated one million dollars in legal fees.[b]

In a similar case, a U.S. District Court held that Texaco, Inc., infringed on the copyrights held by a number of publishers of scientific journals by allowing its employees to make photocopies of scientific journals to which Texaco subscribed. Texaco argued that the unauthorized photocopying constituted a fair use because it was necessary for the advancement of scientific research. According to the court, however, profit-making companies, such as Texaco, cannot make copies of copyrighted journal articles without obtaining permission from and compensating the copyright holders.[c]

a. *Basic Books, Inc. v. Kinko's Graphics Corp.*, 758 F.Supp. 1522 (S.D.N.Y. 1991).

b. December 6, 1991, p. B10.

c. *American Geophysical Union v. Texaco, Inc.*, 802 F.Supp. 1 (S.D.N.Y. 1992).

chip product, are protected under the Semiconductor Chip Protection Act of 1984. A mask work must be fixed in the product to qualify for the protection, and within two years of initially taking commercial advantage of the mask work, the owner must register it with the U.S. Copyright Office. On registration, the owner of the protected mask work obtains the exclusive right, for ten years, to reproduce, import, or distribute the work or a semiconductor chip product that contains it.

❖ Misappropriation of Trade Secrets

Some business processes and information that are not, or cannot be, patented, copyrighted, or trademarked are nevertheless protected against appropriation by a competitor as **trade secrets.** Customer lists, plans, research and development, pricing information, marketing techniques, production techniques, and generally anything

TRADE SECRETS
Information or processes that give a business an advantage over competitors who do not know the information or processes.

Landmark in the Law

The Computer Software Copyright Act of 1980

In 1980 Congress passed the Computer Software Copyright Act, which amended the Copyright Act of 1976 to include computer programs in the list of creative works covered by copyright law. The 1980 statute defines a computer program as a "set of statements or instructions to be used directly or indirectly in a computer in order to bring about a certain result."

Problems for the Courts

The 1980 act has posed some difficult problems for the courts. The first has to do with the fact that computer programs, unlike literary works, interact with machines and are "readable" by machines. Should copyright protection be limited to those parts of a computer program that can be read by humans, such as the high-level language of a source code? Or should it extend to the binary-language object code of a computer program, which is readable only by the computer?

In a 1982 case, a program's source code was held to be copyrightable.[a] In an important 1983 decision, *Apple Computer, Inc. v. Franklin Computer Corp.*, copyright protection was extended to include the binary object code of a computer program.[b] In this decision, the Court of Appeals for the Third Circuit held that "as source code instructions must be translated into object code before the computer can act upon them, only instructions expressed in object code can be used 'directly' by the computer. Thus, a computer program, whether in object code or source code . . . is protected from unauthorized copying, whether from its object or source code version."

Program Structure, Sequence, and Organization

By 1983, it was thus fairly well established—particularly by the *Apple Computer* decision just mentioned—that a program's computer codes were copyrightable. But should copyright protection cover other elements of computer software, such as the overall structure, sequence, and organization of a program? This issue was addressed in a significant 1986 case, *Whelan Associates, Inc. v. Jaslow Dental Laboratory, Inc.*[c] In *Whelan*, the court noted that copyrights of other literary works can be infringed upon even when there is no substantial similarity between the works' literal elements. The copyright of a play or a book, for example, can be infringed upon by copying of its plot or plot devices. The court applied the same principle to computer programs, which are classified as "literary works" in the Copyright Act, and held that the structure, sequence, and organization of computer programs were copyrightable.

Idea versus the Expression of an Idea

In forming its decision, the court had to deal with the

a. *Stern Electronics, Inc. v. Kaufman*, 669 F.2d 852 (2d Cir. 1982).

b. 714 F.2d 1240 (3d Cir. 1983).

c. 797 F.2d 1222 (3d Cir. 1986).

that makes an individual company unique and that would have value to a competitor constitute trade secrets.

Virtually all law with respect to trade secrets is common law. Identical types of information reviewed by different courts in similar factual settings have been classified differently. In an effort to reduce the unpredictability of common law with respect to trade secrets, a model act, the Uniform Trade Secrets Act, was presented to the states in 1979 for adoption. Parts of it have been adopted in over twenty states. Typically, a state that has adopted parts of the act has adopted only those parts that encompass its own existing common law.

Unlike copyright and trademark protection, protection of trade secrets extends both to ideas and to their expression. (For this reason, and because a trade secret involves no registration or filing requirements, trade secret protection may be well suited for software.) Of course, the secret formula, method, or other information must be disclosed to some persons, particularly to key employees. Businesses generally attempt to protect their trade secrets by having all employees who use the process or information agree in their contracts never to divulge it. Theft of confidential business data by industrial espionage, as when a business taps into a competitor's computer, is a theft of trade secrets without any contractual violation and is actionable in itself.

distinction between an "idea," which is not copyrightable, and the "expression of an idea," which is copyrightable. In *Whelan*, the defendant alleged that the structure and organization of the program were the idea, not the expression of the idea. The court responded by saying that the particular structure of the program (designed to aid the business operations of dental laboratories) was not essential to that idea, because other programs on the market perform the same functions but are expressed through different structures and design. The court held that the detailed structure of the plaintiff's program was part of the expression of the idea, not the idea itself.

"Look and Feel" Protection

An issue addressed in *Whelan* has evolved into what is now generally called program "look and feel" protection. Should the "look and feel"—the general appearance, command structure, video images, menus, windows, and other screen displays—of computer programs also be protected by copyright? This question has been at issue in several recent cases brought before the courts, and the answer is not yet entirely clear. In a case brought by Lotus Development Corporation against Paperback Software International and its Canadian development partner, Stephenson Software, Ltd.,[d] Lotus claimed that Paperback Software had infringed its copyright by adapting its Lotus 1-2-3 spreadsheet format design and the keystroke sequences used in manipulating information. The court held that Lotus's menu command structure—including the choice of command terms, the structure and order of those terms, their presentation on the screen, and the long prompts—was copyrightable and that Paperback Software had infringed Lotus's copyright.

Recently, however, it would seem that the courts are narrowing their view of which software elements are protectable. For example, a federal district court in 1992 held that the user interface of Apple's Macintosh computer is not protectable under a "look and feel" theory and that Apple's use of windows, icons, and menus, and generally the series of images that Apple calls a "desktop metaphor," are unprotectable "ideas."[e] This decision concluded Apple's four-year-long legal struggle with Microsoft Corporation and the Hewlett-Packard Company. Apple had claimed that the other two firms had imitated the "look and feel" of the Macintosh user interface. In another 1992 decision that many feel is significant for the software industry, *Computer Associates International v. Altai, Inc.*,[f] the Court of Appeals for the Second Circuit adopted a test to be used in determining copyright infringement issues relating to computer programs. The test requires a court to divide a program into its component parts and then determine whether each individual component is (1) protectable as an expression of an idea or (2) unprotectable because it is an idea or a technique dictated by utilitarian considerations.

d. *Lotus Development Corp. v. Paperback Software International, Ltd.*, 740 F.Supp. 37 (D.Mass. 1990).

e. *Apple Computer, Inc. v. Microsoft Corp.*, 799 F.Supp. 1006 (N.D.Cal. 1992).

f. *Computer Associates International v. Altai, Inc.*, 982 F.2d 693 (2d Cir. 1992).

❖ RICO

Increasingly in recent years, businesses have been sued for fraudulent or other tortious activities under the Racketeer Influenced and Corrupt Organizations Act.[9] The act, which is commonly known as RICO, was passed by Congress in 1970 as part of the Organized Crime Control Act. The purpose of the act was to curb the apparently increasing entry of organized crime into the legitimate business world. Under RICO, it is a federal crime (1) to use income obtained from racketeering activity to purchase any interest in an enterprise, (2) to acquire or maintain an interest in an enterprise through racketeering activity, (3) to conduct or participate in the affairs of an enterprise through racketeering activity, or (4) to conspire to do any of the preceding.

Racketeering activity is not a new type of substantive crime created by RICO; rather, RICO incorporates by reference twenty-six separate types of federal crimes and nine types of state felonies[10] and states that if a person commits two of these

9. 18 U.S.C. Sections 1961–1968.
10. See 18 U.S.C. Section 1961(1)(A).

International Perspective

Combating Foreign Product Counterfeiters

The word *counterfeiter* may evoke the image of a small-time thief with ink-stained sleeves huddled over a printing press that is spewing out sheets of fake currency. Times have changed, though, and so have the tastes of counterfeiters. Although currency counterfeiting operations are occasionally uncovered by police, many counterfeiters today are involved in the production of phony products, ranging from pharmaceutical drugs to computer software. Because the raw materials and equipment costs are minimal, many such counterfeiters are able to earn profits fifteen to twenty times greater than their costs. The huge economic incentive to manufacture counterfeit products has meant that many developing countries are deluged with counterfeit products, some of which are useless or dangerous.

The growing trade in counterfeit drugs has not appreciably benefited consumers in developing countries, because such products may consist of inert or even harmful chemicals. The death in 1990 of more than a hundred children in Nigeria after they were given a counterfeit medicine that contained an industrial solvent is just one of the more obvious examples of the dangers posed by these products. Unfortunately, drug counterfeiters are so skilled at duplicating the packaging of the legitimate products that a chemical analysis of the product itself is often necessary to uncover the fraud. Although U.S. pharmaceutical companies are losing billions of dollars in revenue each year to the counterfeiters, they have been reluctant to acknowledge that such a problem even exists. Moreover, many developing countries do not offer any form of legal protection for drugs patented in the United States, further complicating efforts to stop the production and sale of phony drugs.

The entertainment industry, like the pharmaceutical industry, is one of America's most dynamic business sectors. It, too, has been plagued by counterfeiters, particularly those operating in the Pacific Rim countries. Although counterfeit recordings and movies admittedly pose less danger than phony drugs, the theft of such properties is even more widespread, especially in Japan, Indonesia, China, and Thailand, where there has traditionally been little concern with protecting intellectual property rights.[a] Until recently, it was difficult to find authorized versions of hit movies or records in many of these countries, because counterfeiting was so pervasive. Only after the United States began threatening to impose trade restrictions did the governments of these countries take active steps to close down many of the counterfeiting operations and thus spur demand for authorized versions of these products. Unfortunately, the ease with which movies and recordings can be duplicated makes it unlikely that the problem will ever be stamped out entirely.

Software programs are yet another favorite of foreign counterfeiters. Unlike drugs and videocassettes, software has been stolen from American companies by some of the world's most prominent foreign corporations. Thousands of hours of labor must be expended by highly skilled programmers to create a commercially successful software program that in turn is sold to purchasers. Each copy of the program may sell for hundreds of dollars. Consequently, there is a tremendous incentive for companies to purchase a single copy of the program and then make as many duplicates as it needs. The popularity of such practices in companies throughout Europe and Asia has proved particularly annoying and costly to U.S. software manufacturers. The ease with which software programs can be duplicated leaves U.S. companies with little choice except to pursue aggressively any available legal remedies in the courts.

a. Federal criminal provisions relating to record piracy and copyright infringement are found in 18 U.S.C. Sections 2318–2319.

offenses, he or she is guilty of "racketeering activity." Recently, the statute has been rigorously enforced, and the penalties for violations are harsh. The act provides for both criminal liability (to be discussed in the following chapter) and civil liability.

In the event of a violation, the RICO statute permits the government to seek civil penalties, including the divestiture of a defendant's interest in a business or the dissolution of the business. Perhaps the most controversial aspect of RICO is that, in some cases, private individuals are allowed to recover three times their actual losses (treble damages), plus attorneys' fees, for business injuries caused by a violation of the statute.

The broad language of RICO has allowed it to be applied in cases that have little or nothing to do with organized crime, and an aggressive prosecuting attorney may attempt to show that any business fraud constitutes "racketeering activity." Plaintiffs have used the RICO statute in numerous commercial fraud cases because of the inviting prospect of being awarded treble damages if they win. The most frequent targets of civil RICO lawsuits are insurance companies, employment agencies, commercial banks, and stock brokerage firms.

In the next case, a plaintiff brought suit against a business firm, claiming that the firm's fraudulent business activities violated RICO. By interpreting RICO provisions very broadly, the United States Supreme Court set a significant precedent for subsequent applications of RICO. The broad application of RICO in recent years has been strongly criticized, however, and as a result Congress is considering legislation to restrict the use of RICO in civil actions. Several states have already toned down their versions of RICO.

Case 6.8

SEDIMA, S.P.R.L. v. IMREX CO.

Supreme Court of the United States, 1985.
473 U.S. 479,
105 S.Ct. 3275,
87 L.Ed.2d 346.

HISTORICAL AND SOCIAL SETTING *Organized crime is as old as America. The modern organized crime that served as the impetus for RICO had its roots in prohibition in the 1920s, when liquor manufacturing, distribution, and sales were illegal and crime became organized out of necessity. In the 1930s, when liquor became legal again, organized crime infiltrated businesses related to its formerly illegal liquor operations. Eventually, organized crime spread into businesses involved in garment manufacturing, construction, food supply, garbage collection, trucking, and banking, as well as trade unions. RICO was intended to attack this infiltration of legitimate businesses from all directions. Designed to strip racketeers of their financial bases, the civil side of RICO was ignored for almost a decade. Finally, in the late 1970s, the civil side of RICO was recognized as a powerful litigation weapon. RICO lawsuits began to be brought against "legitimate" businesses, including major corporations. Federal district courts often dismissed the suits, reasoning that RICO was not intended to punish these types of defendants, but the dismissals were often reversed on appeal.*

FACTS In 1979, a Belgian corporation, Sedima, S.P.R.L., entered into a contract with another Belgian firm to supply the latter with electronic components. Sedima also formed a joint venture with a U.S. firm, Imrex Company, whereby Imrex would ship the components to Europe and share the proceeds jointly with Sedima. Approximately $8 million in orders had been shipped by Imrex when Sedima concluded that Imrex was fraudulently claiming extra expenses and inflating its bills—in order to get more than its fair portion of the proceeds. Sedima brought suit against Imrex, alleging, in part, that Imrex had violated Section 1962(c) of RICO. Section 1962(c) requires that a private suit under RICO must be based on an injury brought about by the (1) conduct (2) of an enterprise (3) through a pattern (4) of racketeering activity. Sedima claimed an injury of at least $175,000 (the amount of alleged overbilling) and asked for treble damages. Sedima's RICO claims were dismissed by the district court on the ground that Sedima failed to demonstrate it had suffered any "racketeering injury." The appellate court affirmed, and Sedima appealed to the United States Supreme Court.

ISSUE Is it necessary to prove that a "racketeering injury" occurred for the plaintiff to recover under RICO?

DECISION No. The judgment of the appellate court was reversed. Sedima could recover.

REASON The United States Supreme Court stated that RICO "is to be read broadly." Justice White wrote that "we perceive no distinct 'racketeering injury' requirement. Given that 'racketeering activity' consists of no more and no less than commission of a predicate act, we are initially doubtful about a requirement of a 'racketeering injury' separate from the harm from the predicate acts. . . . Underlying the Court of Appeals' holding was its distress at the 'extraordinary, if not outrageous' uses to which civil RICO has been put. Instead of being used against mobsters and organized criminals, it has become a tool for everyday fraud cases brought against 'respected and legitimate enterprises.' Yet Congress wanted to reach both 'legitimate' and 'illegitimate' enterprises. The former enjoy neither an inherent incapacity for criminal activity nor immunity from its consequences."

Application

Law and the Businessperson—Creating and Protecting Your Trademark

Imagine the following scenario: You have decided to turn your hobby of recording rap music into a bona fide business. You pick a name for your company—Cruising—and incorporate the company in your state. The secretary of state approves the name because no one else in your state has incorporated under that name or one that could be confused with it. You open for business, and the name Cruising appears in your ads and brochures and in the Yellow Pages. You put out your first CD using the Cruising label. Then you receive a letter in the mail from Tom Cruise's attorneys informing you that Cruising is a federally registered trademark used for all of Tom Cruise's enterprises and in fact he may someday have a CD label. If you attempt to fight Tom Cruise's attorneys, you will probably lose.

A Trademark Is Not the Same as a Trade Name

When you incorporated in your state, the secretary of state only approved your company's name, Cruising, as a trade name—the formal name for your business that you can use on checks, invoices, and letterhead stationery. You have permission to use Cruising as a trade name only in your state. A trademark (or a service mark) is the word, phrase, slogan, design, or symbol that identifies a specific product brand that you use to market products. If you decide to use your business (trade) name as a trademark, then you need to follow the principles of trademark law. The general rule is that you cannot use a trademark that might lead a customer to think that your product was produced by someone else.

Who Owns a Trademark?

Generally, the first business to use a trademark owns it. The way to qualify as a first user is to be the first company to actually use the trademark in the marketplace or to register the trademark with the U.S. Patent and Trademark Office.

First use sometimes takes precedence over federal registration. If Tom Cruise had not registered Cruising as a trademark until two years after you started selling Cruising-labeled CDs throughout the United States, you would probably win your trademark dispute.

Doing a Trademark Search

After you have decided on a trademark, you need to do a search to find out if the trademark is confusingly similar to existing trademarks. You can look at the federal trademark register as well as the trademark register in your state. You can examine the Yellow Pages in your area of business. You can also go to your library to look at *Gale's List of Tradenames.* It is also possible to do a computer search. Finally, you can hire a trademark search firm to do the search for you.

Once you have done an appropriate trademark search and you have not found another trademark that would be confusingly similar to yours, you are probably entitled to register the mark with the U.S. Patent and Trademark Office. Normally, you have to start using the trademark within six months within your state or across state, international, or territorial lines.

Checklist for the Businessperson

- ☐ 1. Remember that a trade name authorized for use by a secretary of state is not the same as a trademark.
- ☐ 2. When deciding on a trademark, be sure that it is not confusingly similar to an existing trademark.
- ☐ 3. There are two ways to own a trademark—being the first to use a trademark or registering the trademark with the U.S. Patent and Trademark Office.
- ☐ 4. Remember that in trademark disputes, first use of a trademark sometimes takes precedence over federal registration.

❖ Key Terms

appropriation 154
business tort 150
copyright 161
disparagement of property 156
mask work 164
patent 160
service mark 159
slander of quality 156
slander of title 157
trade name 159
trade secret 165
trademark 157

❖ Chapter Summary: Business Torts and Intellectual Property

Wrongful Interference	1. *Wrongful interference with a contractual relationship*—The intentional interference with a valid, enforceable contract by a third party. 2. *Wrongful interference with a business relationship*—The unreasonable interference by one party with another's business relationship.
Wrongfully Entering into Business	Entering into business in violation of the law or for the purpose of engaging in predatory behavior.
Appropriation	The use of one person's name, likeness, or celebrity status by another, without permission and for the benefit of the user.
Defamation in the Business Context	A false statement that injures someone in a profession, business, or trade or that adversely affects a business entity in its credit rating and other dealings.
Disparagement of Property	Slanderous or libelous statements made about another's product or property; more specifically referred to as slander of quality or slander of title.
Trademark, Patent, and Copyright Infringement	1. *Trademark infringement and infringement of related property*—Occurs when one uses the protected trademark, trade name, or service mark of another without permission when marketing goods or services. 2. *Patent infringement*—Occurs when one uses or sells another's patented design, product, or process without the patent owner's permission. 3. *Copyright infringement*—Occurs whenever the form or expression of an idea is copied without the permission of the copyright holder.
Misappropriation of Trade Secrets	Trade secrets—such as customer lists, plans, research and development, pricing information, and so on—are protected under the common law against misappropriation by competitors.
RICO	The Racketeer Influenced and Corrupt Organizations Act (RICO) of 1970 makes it a federal crime (1) to use income obtained from racketeering activity to purchase any interest in an enterprise, (2) to acquire or maintain an interest in an enterprise through racketeering activity, (3) to conduct or participate in the affairs of an enterprise through racketeering activity, or (4) to conspire to do any of the preceding. The broad language of RICO has allowed it to be applied in cases that have little or nothing to do with organized crime.

❖ Questions and Case Problems

6-1. Wrongful Interference. Under what circumstances will a person who interferes with a business relationship of another not be considered liable for the tort of wrongful interference?

6-2. Copyright Infringement. Max plots a new Batman adventure and carefully and skillfully imitates DC Comics' art to create an authentic-looking Batman comic. Max is not affiliated with the owners of the copyright to Batman. Can Max publish the comic without infringing on the owners' copyright?

6-3. Copyright Infringement. In which of the following situations would a court likely hold Maruta liable for copyright infringement?

(a) Maruta photocopies ten pages from a scholarly journal at the library relating to a topic on which she is writing a term paper.

(b) Maruta makes leather handbags and sells them in her small leather shop. She advertises her handbags as "Vutton handbags," hoping that customers might mistakenly assume that they were made by Vuitton, the well-known maker of high-quality luggage and handbags.

(c) Maruta owns a video store. She purchases the latest videos from various video manufacturers but buys only one copy of each video. Then, using blank videotapes, she makes copies to rent or sell to her customers.

(d) Maruta teaches Latin American history at a small university. She has a VCR and frequently tapes television programs relating to Latin America and then takes the videos to her classroom so that her students can watch them.

6-4. Wrongful Interference. Jennings owns a bakery shop. He has been trying to obtain a long-term contract with the owner of Julie's Tea Salon for some time. Jennings starts a local advertising campaign on radio and television and in the newspaper. The campaign is so persuasive that Julie decides to break the contract she has had for some time with Orley's Bakery so that she can patronize Jennings's bakery. Is Jennings liable to Orley's Bakery for the tort of wrongful interference with a contractual relationship? Is Julie liable for this tort? For anything?

6-5. Patent Infringement. John and Andrew Doney invented a hard-bearing device for balancing rotors. Although they registered their invention with the patent office, it was never used as an automobile wheel balancer. Some time later, Exetron Corp. produced an automobile wheel balancer that used a hard-bearing device with a support plate similar to that of the Doneys. Given the fact that the Doneys had not used their device for automobile wheel balancing, does Exetron's use of a similar hard-bearing device infringe upon the Doneys' patent?

6-6. Copyright Infringement. West Publishing Co. brought a copyright infringement action against Mead Data Central, Inc., owners of LEXIS, a computer-assisted legal research system. At issue was a plan for a "star pagination" feature that Mead had developed for use on LEXIS. This feature would incorporate page numbers from West's case reporters into the opinions available on LEXIS and would allow LEXIS users to learn the precise page breaks in a West reporter without ever physically having to refer to a West volume. West claimed that Mead Data's proposed star pagination system would constitute a copyright infringement of its reporting format. Mead Data contended that "mere page numbers" cannot be copyrighted. Can the use of page numbers, which cannot in themselves be copyrighted, fall under copyright protection in this case? [*West Publishing Co. v. Mead Data Central, Inc.*, 799 F.2d 1219 (8th Cir. 1986)]

6-7. Fair Use Doctrine. Vault Corp. produces computer diskettes, under the registered trademark PROLOK, that are designed to prevent the unauthorized copying of programs placed on the diskettes by software computer companies, Vault's customers. A program placed on a PROLOK diskette can be copied onto another diskette, but the computer will not read the program from the copy unless the original PROLOK diskette is also in one of the computer's disk drives. Quaid Software, Ltd., markets the CopyWrite diskette. Quaid's diskette contains a feature called RAMKEY, which unlocks the PROLOK protective device. Individuals who purchase the CopyWrite diskette can therefore make fully functional copies of any programs placed on PROLOK diskettes. Vault alleged that Quaid's RAMKEY feature contributed to the infringement of Vault's copyright and Vault's customers' copyrights in violation of the Copyright Act. Quaid claimed that because the RAMKEY feature is capable of substantial noninfringing uses—including the making of archival copies of PROLOK diskettes to be used if the original PROLOK diskettes are damaged—Quaid should not be held responsible for any infringing uses of RAMKEY made by those who purchase the CopyWrite diskette. Review *Sony Corp. v. Universal City Studios* (Case 6.7) and discuss the merits of Quaid's claim in light of that decision. [*Vault Corp. v. Quaid Software, Ltd.*, 847 F.2d 255 (5th Cir. 1988)]

6-8. Fair Use Doctrine. Jonathan Caven-Atack had been a member of the Church of Scientology for nine years when he decided that the church was a dangerous cult and its leader, L. Ron Hubbard, a vindictive and profoundly disturbed man. Caven-Atack spent the next several years investigating, and then writing a book about, Hubbard and the church. Caven-Atack's purpose was to expose what he believed was the pernicious nature of the church and the deceit upon which its teachings were based. Approximately 3 percent of Caven-Atack's book consisted of quotations from Hubbard's published works. When New Era Publications International, which held exclusive copyright rights in all of Hubbard's works, learned that the Carol Publishing Group planned to publish Caven-Atack's book, it sued Carol Publishing for copyright infringement. Carol Publishing claimed that Caven-Atack's use of Hubbard's works was a "fair use" of the copyrighted materials. What factors must the court consider in making its decision? What will its decision be? Discuss. [*New Era Publications International, ApS v. Carol Publishing Group*, 904 F.2d 152 (2d Cir. 1990)]

6-9. Wrongful Interference. DBI Services, Inc., provided oil-field trucking services, brine water, and drilling mud to oil producers in the Seminole area of Texas. From 1983 to 1986, the major oil producer in the area, Amerada Hess Corp. (AH), regularly contracted with DBI for its services. AH learned in a 1986 audit of its contractors that DBI had engaged in lavish entertainment of certain AH employees who were responsible for awarding job contracts. Disturbed by this discovery, AH thereafter refused to deal with DBI. AH also refused to accept contract bids from any firms that planned to subcontract work out to DBI, even if the firms had submitted the lowest bids for the contracts. DBI sued AH for tortious interference with its contractual relationships with these other firms. AH claimed that it was not obligated to accept the lowest bids for contracts and that it had a right to determine with whom it would do business. How will the court decide the issue? Discuss. [*DBI Services, Inc. v. Amerada Hess Corp.*, 907 F.2d 506 (5th Cir. 1990)]

6-10. Fair Use Doctrine. Original Appalachian Artworks, Inc. (OAA), makes and distributes the very successful product called Cabbage Patch Kids—soft, sculptured dolls that were in great demand in the early 1980s. The dolls are unique in appearance, and the name is registered as a trademark to OAA. The design, too, is protected under a copyright registration. The testimony at trial indicated that in 1986 Topps Chewing Gum, Inc., had an artist copy many of the features of the dolls for Topps's new product—stickers that depicted obnoxious cartoon characters called Garbage Pail Kids. The stickers, and the other product line that Topps developed, proved very lucrative; in fact, Topps expanded the product line to include T-shirts, balloons, and school notebooks. Topps claimed that its product was actually a satire of OAA's product and therefore a fair use of a protected work. Did Topps's use of OAA's product constitute a fair use of the product, or did it constitute trademark and copyright infringement? [*Original Appalachian Artworks, Inc. v. Topps Chewing Gum, Inc.*, 642 F.Supp. 1031 (N.D.Ga. 1986)]

6-11. Trademark Infringement. On September 21, 1987, Quality Inns International, Inc., announced a new chain of economy hotels to be marketed under the name "McSleep Inns." The response of the owners of McDonald's Corp., the fast-food chain, was immediate. McDonald's wrote Quality Inns a letter stating that the use of "McSleep Inns" infringed upon the McDonald's family of trademarks characterized by the prefix "Mc" attached to a generic term. Five days later, Quality Inns filed an action seeking a declaratory judgment from the court that the mark "McSleep Inns" did not infringe on McDonald's federally registered trademarks or common law rights to its marks and would not constitute an unfair trade practice. McDonald's counterclaimed, alleging trademark infringement and unfair competition. McDonald's argued that the use of "McSleep Inns" by Quality Inns would confuse and mislead the public and allow Quality Inns to trade on the goodwill and reputation of McDonald's. Quality Inns claimed that "Mc" had come into generic use as a prefix and therefore McDonald's had no trademark rights to the prefix itself. Quality Inns further claimed that its use of the prefix for lodging accommodations would not be confusing to the public because McDonald's products were fast foods. Does the use of the prefix "Mc" by Quality Inns for its new "McSleep" chain of economy motels infringe on McDonald's trademark rights? [*Quality Inns International, Inc. v. McDonald's Corp.*, 695 F.Supp. 198 (D.Md. 1988)]

A Question of Ethics and Social Responsibility

6-12. *Peter Bonyhard, a physicist, had developed disk-drive heads for International Business Machines Corp. (IBM) for five years when he was hired away from IBM by Seagate Technology, Inc. Bonyhard's assignment was to develop at Seagate the same new type of disk-drive head, called a magnetoresistive (MR) head, that he had been working on for IBM. IBM sued Seagate and Bonyhard, alleging that Seagate had hired Bonyhard for the purpose of stealing its secret formula for the MR heads. IBM, without any evidence that Bonyhard had actually disclosed any trade secrets, sought to have the court enjoin Bonyhard from working for Seagate on the ground that it would be simply impossible for Bonyhard to work for Seagate without disclosing IBM information. A district court granted the injunction, but on appeal, the injunction was vacated. The appellate court held that the terms of the injunction were too vague and not based on any specific evidence for what IBM claimed were confidential information and trade secrets.* [Seagate Technology, Inc. v. International Business Machines Corp., *962 F.2d 12 (8th Cir. 1992)*]

1. Do you agree with IBM that it would be simply impossible for Bonyhard to work for Seagate without disclosing IBM trade secrets? If so, do you agree with the district court that Bonyhard should be enjoined from continuing to work for Seagate? Why or why not?
2. The issue raised in this case is a significant one for high-tech industries that capitalize on state-of-the-art technology in producing and distributing new electronic products. Talented employees who are well versed in certain technology, as Bonyhard was in this case, are frequently sought after by competing firms. What two broad public policies, or ethical precepts, are at issue in this kind of situation?
3. Many firms require employees to sign "covenants not to compete" as a way to protect their interests and trade secrets. (Covenants not to compete, discussed in Chapter 10, are agreements in which the employees promise not to work for any competitor of the firm in a given geographic area for a given period of time.) But courts scrutinize such agreements closely and are often reluctant to enforce them. Can you think of alternative ways in which employers might protect themselves against the divulgence of their trade secrets by former employees?
4. Assuming that an employee is violating no law when he or she responds to an enticing offer from another firm, is it ethical for that employee to use his or her skill and talents to the detriment of a former employer?

For Critical Analysis

6-13. *Patent protection in the United States is granted to the first person to invent a given product or process, even though another person might be the first to file for a patent on the same product or process. What are the advantages of this patenting procedure? Can you think of any disadvantages? Explain.*

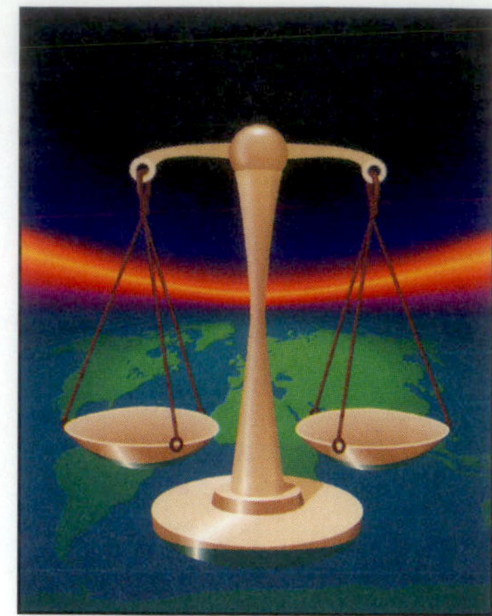

Chapter 7

Criminal Law

"No state shall make or enforce any law which shall abridge the privileges or immunities of citizens of the United States; nor shall any state deprive any person of life, liberty or property without due process of law, nor deny to any person within its jurisdiction the equal protection of the laws."

Fourteenth Amendment to the U.S. Constitution, July 28, 1868

Civil law spells out the duties that exist between persons or between citizens and their governments, excluding the duty not to commit crimes. Contract law, for example, is part of civil law. The whole body of tort law, which deals with the infringement by one person on the legally recognized rights of another, is also an area of civil law. The right of people engaged in business to compete and flourish is sustained by the civil law, which imposes damages for various types of tortious conduct (as discussed in the preceding chapters) and damages for breach of contract (to be discussed in Chapter 13). Society also demands certain business conduct. As a result, a *criminal law element* exists in the legal environment of business. The prerequisites of *fault* or *guilt* in this area are different from those in the civil law, as are the sanctions and penalties.

Criminal law has to do with crimes, which are different from other wrongful acts (torts) in a number of ways:

1. Crimes are *offenses against society as a whole* and thus are prosecuted by a public official, not by victims.
2. Those who commit crimes are punished. Tort remedies—remedies for civil wrongs—usually compensate the injured (except when punitive damages are assessed), whereas criminal law punishes (and, ideally, rehabilitates) the wrongdoer.
3. The source of criminal law is now primarily statutory, although common law was once the main body of criminal law.

CRIME
A broad term for violations of law that are punishable by the state and are codified by legislatures. The objective of criminal law is to protect the public.

Both crimes and punishments are very specifically set out in statutes. A **crime** can thus be defined as a wrong against society proclaimed in a statute and, if committed, punishable by society.

❖ Classification of Crimes

Depending on their degree of seriousness, crimes are classified as felonies or misdemeanors.

FELONY
A crime—such as arson, murder, rape, or robbery—that carries the most severe sanctions, usually ranging from one year in a state or federal prison to the forfeiture of one's life.

Felonies

Felonies are serious crimes punishable by death or by imprisonment in a federal or state penitentiary for more than a year. The Model Penal Code[1] provides for four degrees of felony: (1) capital offenses, for which the maximum penalty is death; (2) first-degree felonies, punishable by a maximum penalty of life imprisonment;

(3) second-degree felonies, punishable by a maximum of ten years' imprisonment; and (4) third-degree felonies, punishable by up to five years' imprisonment.

Misdemeanors and Petty Offenses

Under federal law and in most states, any crime that is not a felony is considered a **misdemeanor.** Misdemeanors are crimes punishable by a fine or by confinement for up to a year. If incarcerated (imprisoned), the guilty party goes to a local jail instead of a penitentiary. Disorderly conduct and trespass are common misdemeanors. Some states have different classes of misdemeanors. For example, in Illinois misdemeanors are either Class A (confinement for up to a year), Class B (not more than six months), or Class C (not more than thirty days). Whether a crime is a felony or a misdemeanor can also determine whether the case is tried in a magistrate's court (for example, by a justice of the peace) or a general trial court.

MISDEMEANORS
Lesser crimes than felonies, punishable by a fine or imprisonment for up to one year in other than a state or federal penitentiary.

In most jurisdictions, **petty offenses** are considered to be a subset of misdemeanors. Petty offenses are minor violations, such as violations of building codes. Even for petty offenses, however, a guilty party can be put in jail for a few days or fined, or both, depending on state law.

PETTY OFFENSES
In criminal law, the least serious kind of wrong, such as a traffic or building-code violation. (Not classified as a crime in some states.)

❖ What Constitutes Criminal Liability?

Two elements must exist simultaneously for a person to be convicted of a crime: (1) the performance of a prohibited act and (2) a specified state of mind or intent on the part of the actor. Even if both elements exist, there are defenses that the law deems sufficient to excuse such actions. These defenses will also be discussed subsequently.

"A man may have as bad a heart as he chooses, if his conduct is within the rules."

Oliver Wendell Holmes,
1841–1935
(Associate justice of the United States Supreme Court, 1902–1932)

The Criminal Act

Every criminal statute prohibits certain behavior. Most crimes require an act of *commission;* that is, a person must *do* something in order to be accused of a crime.[2] In some cases, an act of *omission* can be a crime, but only when a person has a legal duty to perform the omitted act. Failure to file a tax return is an example of an omission that is a crime.

The *guilty act* requirement is based on one of the premises of criminal law—that a person is punished for *harm done* to society. Thinking about killing someone or about stealing a car may be wrong, but the thoughts do no harm until they are translated into action. Of course, a person can be punished for attempting murder or robbery, but normally only if substantial steps toward the criminal objective have been taken.

Intent to Commit a Crime

A wrongful mental state[3] is as necessary as a wrongful act in establishing criminal liability. What constitutes such a mental state varies according to the wrongful ac-

1. The American Law Institute issued the Official Draft of the Model Penal Code in 1962. The Model Penal Code is not a uniform code. Uniformity of criminal law among the states is not as important as uniformity in other areas of the law. Crime varies with local circumstances, and it is appropriate that punishments vary accordingly. The Model Penal Code contains four parts: (1) general provisions, (2) definitions of special crimes, (3) provisions concerning treatment and corrections, and (4) provisions on the organization of correction.
2. Called the *actus reus* (pronounced *ak*-tuhs *ray*-uhs), or guilty act.
3. Called the *mens rea* (pronounced mehns *ray*-uh), or evil intent.

tion. For murder, the act is the taking of a life, and the mental state is the intent to take life. For theft, the guilty act is the taking of another person's property, and the mental state involves both the knowledge that the property belongs to another and the intent to deprive the owner of it. Without the mental state required by law for a particular crime, there is no crime, as the following case illustrates.

Case 7.1
JOHNSON v. STATE
Supreme Court of Florida, 1992.
597 So.2d 798.

HISTORICAL AND SOCIAL SETTING *During the early days of the development of crimes at common law, judges often held an act to be criminal even if the perpetrator had no criminal intent. After the year 1600, judges began to require, in addition to the commission of a criminal act, some sort of criminal intent. Today, although most crimes are statutory crimes, criminal liability still generally requires criminal intent.*

FACTS Raymond Johnson allegedly snatched a purse left in an unattended car at a gas station. Because the purse contained both money and a firearm, among other items, the trial court convicted and sentenced Johnson for burglary of a conveyance (vehicle), grand theft of property (cash and payroll checks), and grand theft of a firearm. On appeal, Johnson claimed that he could not be guilty of grand theft of a firearm because he did not know that the purse contained a firearm. In other words, intent to commit the latter crime was lacking, and therefore that crime had not been committed.

ISSUE Can Johnson be convicted and sentenced for the crime of grand theft of a firearm even though he did not know that the firearm was in the purse?

DECISION No. There can be only one conviction for grand theft in this case.

REASON The court held that Johnson had committed the crime of theft and that it was grand theft because of the value of property contained in the purse, including the value of the firearm. But only one crime of theft had occurred. The court stated that "a separate crime occurs only when there are separate distinct acts of seizing the property of another." In this case, the crime occurred "in one swift motion." Johnson saw the purse and snatched it without knowing what it contained: "there was one intent and one act * * *."

❖ Defenses to Criminal Liability

DEFENSE
That which a defendant offers and alleges in an action or suit as a reason why the plaintiff should not recover or establish what he or she seeks.

The law recognizes certain conditions that relieve a defendant of criminal liability. These conditions are called **defenses,** and among the important ones are infancy, intoxication, insanity, mistake, consent, duress, justifiable use of force, entrapment, and the statute of limitations.

Infancy

The term *infant,* as used in the law, refers to any person who has not yet reached the age of majority (see Chapter 10). Under the common law, children up to age seven were considered incapable of committing a crime because they did not have the moral sense to understand that they were doing wrong. Children between the ages of seven and fourteen were presumed to be incapable of committing a crime, but this presumption could be rebutted if it could be shown that the child understood the wrongful nature of the act (see Exhibit 7–1).

In all states, certain courts handle cases involving children who are alleged to have violated the law. In some states, juvenile courts handle children's cases exclusively. In most states, however, courts that handle children's cases also have jurisdiction over other matters, such as traffic offenses. Originally, juvenile court hearings were informal and lawyers were rarely present. Since 1967, when the United States Supreme Court ordered that a child charged with delinquency must be allowed to

Exhibit 7–1
Responsibility of Infants for Criminal Acts under the Common Law

Age 0–7	Absolute presumption of incompetence.
Age 7–14	Presumption of incompetence, but government may oppose.
Age 14+	Presumption of competence, but infant may oppose.

consult with an attorney before being committed to a state institution,[4] juvenile court hearings have become more formal. In some states, a child will be treated as an adult and tried in a regular court if he or she is above a certain age (usually fourteen) and is guilty of a felony such as rape or murder.

Intoxication

The law recognizes two types of intoxication, whether from drugs or from alcohol: *involuntary* and *voluntary*. Involuntary intoxication occurs when a person either is physically forced to ingest or inject an intoxicating substance or is unaware that a substance contains drugs or alcohol. Involuntary intoxication is a defense to a crime if its effect was to make a person incapable of understanding that the act committed was wrong or incapable of obeying the law.

Using voluntary drug or alcohol intoxication as a defense is based on the theory that extreme levels of intoxication may negate the state of mind that a crime requires. Many courts are reluctant to allow voluntary intoxication as a defense to a crime, however. After all, the defendant, by definition, voluntarily chose to put himself or herself into an intoxicated state. Voluntary intoxication as a defense may be effective in cases in which the defendant was *extremely* intoxicated when committing the wrong.

"Insanity is often the logic of an accurate mind overtaxed."

Oliver Wendell Holmes, Jr., 1841–1935
(Associate justice of the United States Supreme Court, 1902–1932)

Insanity

Just as a child is often judged incapable of the state of mind required to commit a crime, so also may be someone suffering from a mental illness. Thus, insanity may be a defense to a criminal charge. The courts have had difficulty deciding what the

One of the most famous insanity defenses involved John Hinckley who wounded President Ronald Reagan. Hinckley said he was attempting to get actress Jodi Foster's attention. What are the legal tests for insanity?

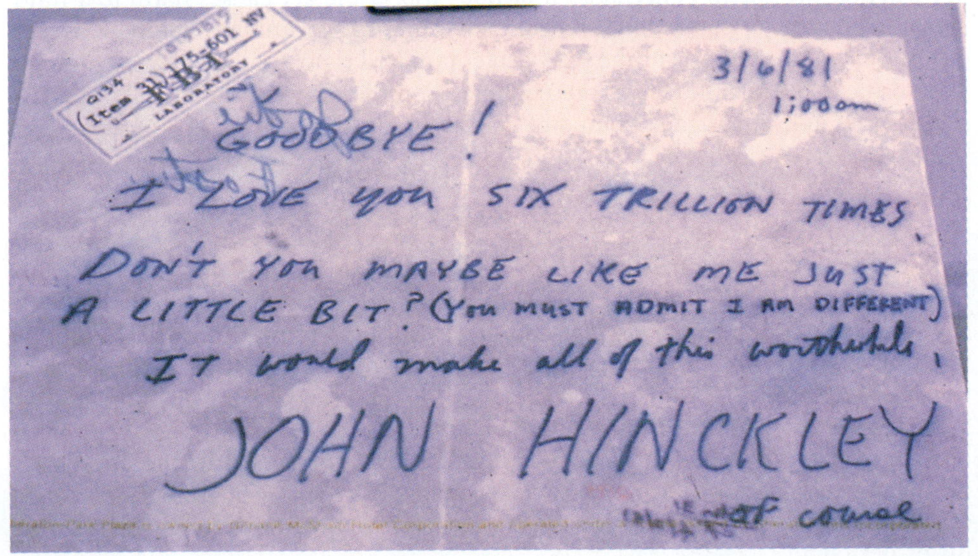

FBI LABORATORY

3/6/81
1:00am

GOODBYE!
I LOVE YOU SIX TRILLION TIMES.
DON'T YOU MAYBE LIKE ME JUST A LITTLE BIT? (YOU MUST ADMIT I AM DIFFERENT)
IT would make all of this worthwhile.
JOHN HINCKLEY

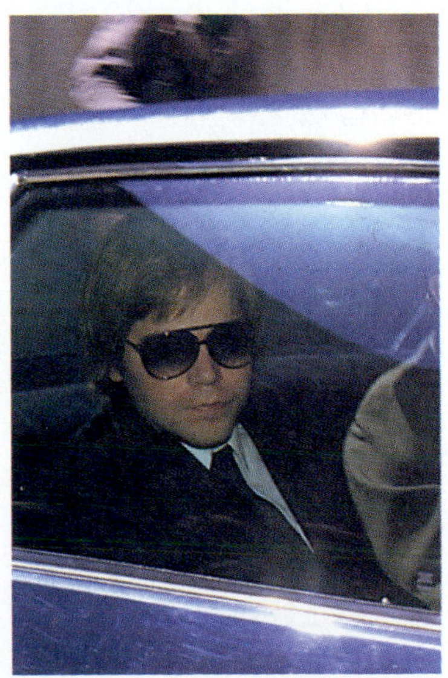

4. *In re Gault,* 387 U.S.1 87 S.Ct. 1428, 18 L.Ed.2d 527 (1967).

test for legal insanity should be, and psychiatrists as well as lawyers are critical of the tests used. Almost all federal courts and some states use the relatively liberal standard set forth in the Model Penal Code:

> A person is not responsible for criminal conduct if at the time of such conduct as a result of mental disease or defect he lacks substantial capacity either to appreciate the wrongfulness of his conduct or to conform his conduct to the requirements of the law.

Some states use the *M'Naghten* test,[5] under which a criminal defendant is not responsible if, at the time of the offense, he or she did not know the nature and quality of the act or did not know that the act was wrong. Other states use the irresistible-impulse test. A person operating under an irresistible impulse may know an act is wrong but cannot refrain from doing it.

Mistake

Everyone has heard the saying, "ignorance of the law is no excuse." Ordinarily, ignorance of the law or a mistaken idea about what the law requires is not a valid defense. In some states, however, that rule has been modified. A person who claims that he or she honestly did not know that a law was being broken may have a valid defense if (1) the law was not published or reasonably made known to the public or (2) the person relied on an official statement of the law that was erroneous.

A *mistake of fact*, as opposed to a *mistake of law*, operates as a defense if it negates the mental state necessary to commit a crime. If, for example, Oliver Wheaton mistakenly drives off in Julie Tyson's car because he thinks it is his, there is no theft. Theft requires knowledge that the property belongs to another.

Consent

CONSENT
Voluntary agreement to a proposition or an act of another. A concurrence of wills.

What if a victim consents to a crime or even encourages the person intending a criminal act to commit it? The law allows **consent** as a defense if the consent cancels the harm that the law is designed to prevent. In each case, the question is whether the law forbids an act that was committed against the victim's will or forbids the act without regard to the victim's wish. The law forbids murder, prostitution, and drug use whether the victim consents to it or not. Also, if the act causes harm to a third person who has not consented, there is no escape from criminal liability. Consent or forgiveness given after a crime has been committed is not really a defense, though it can affect the likelihood of prosecution. Consent operates as a defense most successfully in crimes against property.

Duress

DURESS
Unlawful pressure brought to bear on a person, overcoming that person's free will and causing him or her to do (or refrain from doing) what he or she otherwise would not (or would) have done.

Duress exists when the *wrongful threat* of one person induces another person to perform an act that he or she would not otherwise perform. In such a situation, duress is said to negate the mental state necessary to commit a crime. For duress to qualify as a defense, the following requirements must be met:

1. The threat must be of serious bodily harm or death.
2. The harm threatened must be greater than the harm caused by the crime.
3. The threat must be immediate and inescapable.
4. The defendant must have been involved in the situation through no fault of his or her own.

"An act against my will is not my act."

(Legal maxim)

5. A rule derived from *M'Naghten's Case*, 8 Eng. Rep. 718 (1843).

One crime that cannot be excused by duress is murder. It is difficult to justify taking a life even if one's own life is threatened.

Justifiable Use of Force

Probably the most well-known defense to criminal liability is **self-defense.** But there are other situations that justify the use of force: the defense of one's dwelling, the defense of other property, and the prevention of a crime. In all of these situations, it is important to distinguish between the use of deadly and nondeadly force. Deadly force is likely to result in death or serious bodily harm. Nondeadly force is force that reasonably appears necessary to prevent the imminent use of criminal force.

SELF-DEFENSE
The legally recognized privilege to protect one's self or property against injury by another. The privilege of self-defense only protects acts that are reasonably necessary to protect one's self or property.

Generally speaking, people can use the amount of nondeadly force that seems necessary to protect themselves, their dwellings, or other property or to prevent the commission of a crime. Deadly force can be used in self-defense if there is a *reasonable belief* that imminent death or grievous bodily harm will otherwise result, if the attacker is using unlawful force (an example of lawful force is that exerted by a police officer), and if the defender has not initiated or provoked the attack. Deadly force can be used to defend a dwelling only if the unlawful entry is violent and the person believes deadly force is necessary to prevent imminent death or great bodily harm or—in some jurisdictions—if the person believes deadly force is necessary to prevent the commission of a felony in the dwelling.

What if deadly force results from a mechnical device, such as a gun rigged to go off when a trespasser enters through a doorway? A leading case on this issue is presented next.

Case 7.2
KATCO v. BRINEY
Supreme Court of Iowa, 1971.
183 N.W.2d 657.

HISTORICAL AND SOCIAL SETTING *In the nineteenth century, some courts reasoned that the defense of a home was as important as the defense of a life. These courts permitted a homeowner to use deadly force if it reasonably appeared necessary to prevent forcible entry against the owner's will after a warning had been issued to the intruder not to enter and not to use force. In the twentieth century, this view was generally rejected as being too broad. Today, the states have different answers to the question of when deadly force may be used in the defense of property against a trespasser or a thief. The Model Penal Code takes the view that a deadly trap is never justifiable as a protection against trespass or theft. Under the Model Penal Code, to protect property, an owner may use nondeadly devices, such as spiked fences.*

FACTS In 1957, Bertha Briney inherited her parents' farm. Over the next ten years, the unoccupied farmhouse was broken into a number of times, resulting in the loss of some household items, in broken windows, and in the "messing up of the property in general." In June 1967, the Brineys set a shotgun trap in one of the bedrooms. Wire was rigged from the gun's trigger to the doorknob so that the gun would fire when the door was opened. On the night of July 16, Marvin Katco and Marvin McDonough broke into the house looking for antique bottles and jars. When Katco opened the bedroom door, he detonated the shotgun and was hit in the right leg above the ankle bone. Much of his leg, including part of the tibia, was blown away. He spent forty days in the hospital, a year on crutches, and a year in a special brace. He pleaded guilty to criminal charges of larceny, paid a $50 fine, and was paroled during good behavior from a sixty-day jail sentence. Katco sued the Brineys for damages. The trial court instructed the jury that "one may use reasonable force in the protection of his property, but * * * one may not use such means of force as will take human life or inflict great bodily injury." The jury returned a verdict for Katco for $30,000. The Brineys appealed.

ISSUE Can a property owner lawfully use a spring-fired gun in an unoccupied dwelling to prevent the unlawful entry of a thief?

DECISION No. The Supreme Court of Iowa affirmed the trial court's decision.

REASON The supreme court concluded that "[t]he overwhelming weight of authority, both textbook and case law, supports the trial court's statement of the applicable prin-

Case 7.2—Continued

ciples of law." The court quoted from the Restatement of Torts, Section 85: "A possessor of land cannot do indirectly and by a mechanical device that which, were he present, he could not do immediately and in person." The court pointed out that in a previous case it had held a "vineyard owner liable for damages resulting from a spring gun shot although plaintiff was a trespasser and there to steal grapes. * * * [A] mere trespass against property * * * is not a sufficient justification to authorize the use of a deadly weapon by the owner in its defense." Also, the court noted that "[i]n addition to civil liability many jurisdictions hold a landowner criminally liable for serious injuries or homicide caused by spring guns or other set devices."

ETHICAL CONSIDERATIONS *In the first case involving a spring-fired gun, in England in 1820, a property owner was held not liable to the injured trespasser. The public reaction was so intense that in a subsequent case, the court allowed an injured trespasser to sue a property owner for damages, and Parliament enacted a law prohibiting the use of spring-fired guns. The ethical consideration reflected in the public's reaction is that the life and physical integrity of a human being is more valuable than property. This is also the ethical value behind the holding in the* Katco *case, which received an enormous amount of publicity.*

Entrapment

ENTRAPMENT
In criminal law, a defense in which the defendant claims that he or she was induced by a public official—usually an undercover agent or police officer—to commit a crime that he or she would otherwise not have committed.

Entrapment is a defense designed to prevent police officers or other government agents from encouraging crimes in order to apprehend persons wanted for criminal acts. In the typical entrapment case, an undercover agent *suggests* that a crime be committed and somehow pressures or induces an individual to commit it. The agent then arrests the individual for the crime. For entrapment to be considered a defense, both the suggestion and the inducement must take place. The defense is intended not to prevent law enforcement agents from setting a trap for an unwary criminal but rather to prevent them from pushing the individual into it. The crucial issue is whether a person who committed a crime was predisposed to commit the crime or did so because the agent induced it. The following case is illustrative in this respect.

Case 7.3
JACOBSON v. UNITED STATES

Supreme Court of the United States, 1992.
___U.S.___,
112 S.Ct. 1535,
118 L.Ed.2d 174.

HISTORICAL AND SOCIAL SETTING *At one time there were no legal limits to the degree of temptation to which law enforcement officers could subject persons who were under investigation. The courts did "not look to see who held out the bait, but who took it." At least one court cited Genesis 3:13, in which Eve, who was charged with consuming forbidden fruit, offered the defense that she was tempted by the serpent. The court noted that this "defense was overruled by the great Lawgiver."* [a] *In the late nineteenth century, the defense of entrapment began to develop in the state courts. In 1932, the federal courts took over its development. The defense of entrapment has been asserted in cases involving a variety of criminal charges, including prostitution, counterfeiting, alcohol and drug offenses, and bribery of public officials. As noted in a comment to the Model Penal Code, the "purpose of the defense is to deter misconduct in enforcing the law."*

FACTS Prior to the passage of the Child Protection Act of 1984, which makes it a crime to knowingly receive through the mails sexually explicit depictions of children, Keith Jacobson had ordered and received from a bookstore two *Bare Boys* magazines containing photographs of nude preteen and teenage boys. After the 1984 act was passed, government agents found Jacobson's name on the bookstore's mailing list. To test Jacobson's willingness to break the law, government agencies sent mail to him through five fictitious organizations and a bogus pen pal. Many of these "organizations" claimed that they had been founded to protect and promote sexual freedom and freedom of choice and that they promoted lobbying efforts through catalog sales and other publications. The agencies continued to send mailings to Jacobson for two-and-a-half years. Jacobson responded to some of the correspondence and finally, in response to a letter decrying international censorship, ordered a magazine. He testified at trial

a. *Board of Commissioners v. Backus,* 29 How.Pr. 33 (N.Y.Sup. 1864).

Case 7.3—Continued

that he ordered the magazine because he was curious about "all the trouble and the hysteria over pornography and I wanted to see what the material was." When the magazine was delivered, he was arrested and subsequently convicted of violating the 1984 act. Johnson appealed, claiming entrapment. The appellate court upheld the conviction, and Johnson appealed to the United States Supreme Court.

ISSUE Did the government's actions over two-and-a-half years constitute entrapment?

DECISION Yes. The appellate court's decision was reversed.

REASON To prevail against Jacobson's claim of entrapment, the government would have had to have proven that Jacobson had a prior disposition to break the law, which in this case meant that the government would have had to have proven that Jacobson had a prior disposition to receive through the mail sexually explicit material depicting children. If government agents had merely offered the defendant the opportunity to break the law, and Jacobson had done so because he had a prior disposition to receive such materials, there could be no consideration of entrapment. Government agents, however, "may not * * * implant in an innocent person's mind the disposition to commit a criminal act, and then induce commission of the crime so that the Government may prosecute." Jacobson ordered the magazine that led to his arrest only after he had been the target of repeated government mailings over two-and-a-half years. The government failed to prove that Jacobson, if left to his own devices, would have broken the law.

ETHICAL CONSIDERATIONS *Undercover police operations raise a number of ethical questions. Like the psychiatrist who stepped hard on a catatonic's foot (and elicited a response from the catatonic, which a number of other psychiatrists treating the patient had been unable to do), undercover law enforcement officials often resort to unprofessional tactics to bring about a desired result. The assumption is that the end (justice) justifies the means (deception) in these cases. But does it? Many would contend that it is never ethical to deceive others, particularly if the person undertaking the deception has taken an oath to uphold the law.*

Statute of Limitations

An individual can be excused from criminal liability by a **statute of limitations.** Such a statute provides that the state has only a certain amount of time—which varies from state to state and from crime to crime—within which to prosecute a crime. If the state does not prosecute within the allotted time, it loses its opportunity, and the suspect is free from prosecution. The idea behind such statutes is that people should not have to live under the threat of criminal prosecution indefinitely. Also, if prosecution is delayed too long, it becomes difficult to discover the truth because witnesses die or disappear and evidence is destroyed. Most statutes of limitations do not apply to murder and do not run while the defendant is out of the jurisdiction or in hiding.

STATUTE OF LIMITATIONS
A federal or state statute setting the maximum time period during which a certain action can be brought or rights enforced. After the time period set out in the applicable statute of limitations has run, no legal action can be brought.

Immunity

At times, the state may wish to obtain information from a person accused of a crime. Accused persons are understandably reluctant to give information if it will be used to prosecute them, and they cannot be forced to do so. The privilege against self-incrimination is granted by the Fifth Amendment to the Constitution, which reads, in part, "nor shall [any person] be compelled in any criminal case to be a witness against himself." In cases in which the state wishes to obtain information from a person accused of a crime, the state can grant *immunity* from prosecution or agree to prosecute for a less serious offense in exchange for the information. Once immunity is given, the person can no longer refuse to testify on Fifth Amendment grounds, because he or she now has an absolute privilege against self-incrimination. Often a grant of immunity from prosecution for a serious crime is part of the **plea bargaining** between the defending and prosecuting attorneys. The defendant may

PLEA BARGAINING
The process by which the accused and the prosecutor in a criminal case work out a mutually satisfactory disposition of the case, subject to court approval. Usually involves the defendant's pleading guilty to a lesser offense in return for a lighter sentence.

Landmark in the Law

Miranda v. Arizona (1966)

In regard to criminal procedure, one of the questions facing many courts in the 1950s and 1960s was not whether suspects had constitutional rights—that was not in doubt—but how and when those rights could be exercised. For example, the Fifth Amendment to the Constitution guarantees the privilege against compulsory self-incrimination. That amendment states, among other things, that no person "shall be compelled in any criminal case to be a witness against himself." But could this right be exercised during pretrial interrogation proceedings, or only during the trial? Were confessions obtained from suspects admissible in court if the suspects had not been advised of their right to remain silent and other constitutional rights? To clarify these issues, the United States Supreme Court issued a landmark decision in 1966 in the case of *Miranda v. Arizona.*[a]

The case involved Ernesto Miranda, a man described by the court as "a seriously disturbed individual with pronounced sexual fantasies." On March 13, 1963, Miranda was arrested at his home for the kidnapping and rape of an eighteen-year-old woman. Miranda was taken to a Phoenix, Arizona, police station and questioned by two police officers. Two hours later, the officers emerged from the interrogation room with a written confession signed by Miranda. A paragraph at the top of the confession stated that the confession had been made voluntarily, without threats or promises of immunity, and "with full knowledge of my legal rights, understanding any statement I make may be used against me." Miranda was at no time advised that he had a right to remain silent and a right to have a lawyer present. The confession was admitted into evidence at the trial, and Miranda was convicted and sentenced to prison for twenty to thirty years.

a. 384 U.S. 436, 86 S.Ct. 1602, 16 L.Ed.2d 694 (1966).

What are the rights a suspect must be informed of under the Miranda *rule?*

Miranda appealed the decision, claiming that he had not been informed of his constitutional rights. He did not claim that he was innocent of the crime or that his confession was false or made under duress. He only claimed that he would not have confessed to the crime if he had been advised of his right to remain silent and

be convicted of a lesser offense, while the state uses the defendant's testimony to prosecute accomplices for serious crimes carrying heavy penalties.

❖ Procedure in Criminal Law

"It is better that ten guilty persons escape than that one innocent suffer."

William Blackstone, 1723–1780
(*English jurist and educator*)

Our criminal justice system operates on the premise that it is far worse for an innocent person to be punished than for a guilty person to go free. A person is innocent until proved guilty, and guilt must be proved *beyond a reasonable doubt.* The procedure of the criminal legal system is designed to protect the rights of the individual and to preserve the presumption of innocence.

Constitutional Safeguards

Criminal law brings the force of the state, with all its resources, to bear against the individual. Specific safeguards are provided in the Constitution for those accused of crimes. The United States Supreme Court has ruled that most of these safeguards to have an attorney. Nonetheless, the Supreme Court of Arizona held that Miranda's constitutional rights had not been violated and affirmed his conviction. In forming its decision, the court emphasized the fact that Miranda had not specifically requested an attorney. The *Miranda* case was subsequently consolidated with three other cases involving similar issues and reviewed by the United States Supreme Court.

In its decision, written by Chief Justice Earl Warren, the Court stated as follows:

> [W]hen an individual is taken into custody or otherwise deprived of his freedom by the authorities in any significant way and is subjected to questioning, the privilege against self-incrimination is jeopardized. Procedural safeguards must be employed to protect the privilege and unless other fully effective means are adopted to notify the person of his right of silence and to assure that the exercise of the right will be scrupulously honored, the following measures are required. He must be warned prior to any questioning that he has the right to remain silent, that anything he says can be used against him in a court of law, that he has the right to the presence of an attorney, and that if he cannot afford an attorney one will be appointed for him prior to any questioning if he so desires. Opportunity to exercise these rights must be afforded to him throughout the interrogation. After such warnings have been given, and such opportunity afforded him, the individual may knowingly and intelligently waive these rights and agree to answer questions or make a statement. But unless and until such warnings and waiver are demonstrated by the prosecution at trial, no evidence obtained as a result of interrogation can be used against him.

The Supreme Court held in Miranda's favor. Miranda could not be convicted of the crime on the basis of his confession because his confession was inadmissible as evidence. For any statement made by a defendant to be admissible, the defendant must be informed of the constitutional rights enumerated by Justice Warren prior to police interrogation. If the accused waives his or her rights to remain silent and to have counsel present, the government must be able to demonstrate that the waiver was made knowingly and intelligently.

The Supreme Court and lower courts have enforced the rules hundreds of times since the *Miranda* decision, and the protection afforded accused persons by the *Miranda* case was recently strengthened by a case decided by the Supreme Court in 1990. In *Minnick v. Mississippi*,[b] the Court held that once a defendant has requested counsel, the police cannot question the defendant unless the defendant's attorney is present.

The *Miranda* decision has not only been cited in more court decisions than any other case in the history of American law but, through television shows and other media, has also become familiar to most of America's adult population. Today, both on television and in the real world, police officers routinely advise suspects of their "*Miranda* rights" upon arrest. When Ernesto Miranda himself was later murdered, the suspected murderer was "read his *Miranda* rights."

b. 498 U.S. 146, 111 S.Ct. 486, 112 L.Ed.2d 489 (1990).

apply not only in federal but also in state courts by virtue of the due process clause of the Fourteenth Amendment. The safeguards include the following:

1. The Fourth Amendment protection from unreasonable searches and seizures.
2. The Fourth Amendment requirement that no warrants for a search or an arrest can be issued without probable cause.
3. The Fifth Amendment requirement that no one can be deprived of "life, liberty, or property without due process of law."
4. The Fifth Amendment prohibition against double jeopardy (trying someone twice for the same criminal offense).
5. The Sixth Amendment guaranties of a speedy trial, trial by jury, a public trial, the right to confront witnesses, and the right to a lawyer at various stages in some proceedings.
6. The Eighth Amendment prohibitions against excessive bails and fines and cruel and unusual punishment.

The Exclusionary Rule In recent decades, the United States Supreme Court has been active in interpreting the constitutional rights of accused persons. Under what is known as the **exclusionary rule,** all evidence obtained in violation of the consti-

EXCLUSIONARY RULE
In criminal procedure, a rule under which any evidence that is obtained in violation of the accused's constitutional rights guaranteed by the Fourth, Fifth, and Sixth Amendments, as well as any evidence derived from illegally obtained evidence, will not be admissible in court.

tutional rights spelled out in the Fourth, Fifth, and Sixth Amendments normally must be excluded, as well as all evidence derived from the illegally obtained evidence. Illegally obtained evidence is known as the "fruit of the poisonous tree." For example, if a confession is obtained after an illegal arrest, the arrest would be "the poisonous tree" and the confession, if "tainted" by the arrest, would be the "fruit."

Miranda v. Arizona, which is the subject of this chapter's *Landmark in the Law*, established the rule that individuals who are arrested must be informed of certain constitutional rights, including their right to remain silent and their right to counsel, before any statements they make can be admissible in court.

The Right to Counsel The Sixth Amendment to the U.S. Constitution provides that "in all criminal prosecutions, the accused shall enjoy the right * * * to have the assistance of counsel for his defense." By the passage of the Fourteenth Amendment in 1868, following the Civil War, this and other rights and privileges contained in the Bill of Rights were to be secured for all U.S. citizens, and no state was to "deprive any person of life, liberty, or property, without due process of law." Nearly a century passed, however, before the right to counsel was made available to accused persons in state criminal proceedings. Even as late as 1942, the United States Supreme Court held, in *Betts v. Brady*, that criminal defendants were not automatically guaranteed the right to have a lawyer present when they were tried in court except in capital cases.[6]

In 1963, however, the *Betts v. Brady* precedent was overturned by the decision in *Gideon v. Wainwright*, which became a landmark case in securing the right to counsel for criminal defendants.

6. 316 U.S. 455, 62 S.Ct. 1252, 86 L.Ed. 1595 (1942).

Case 7.4
GIDEON v. WAINWRIGHT
Supreme Court of the United States, 1963.
372 U.S. 335,
83 S.Ct. 792,
9 L.Ed.2d 799.

HISTORICAL AND SOCIAL SETTING *The Sixth Amendment guarantees a defendant the right to have the assistance of counsel for his or her defense. This means that people accused of crimes have the right to hire lawyers to represent their cases in court. If an accused person cannot afford to hire a lawyer, the court will appoint one. Even lawyers taken to court hire other lawyers to represent them. The Sixth Amendment assures the right to counsel in federal courts, but as mentioned in the text, until relatively recently, people who were tried in state courts did not have this right. Not until 1963, in the* Gideon *decision, did the United States Supreme Court extend that right to everyone accused of a crime.*

What change in criminal procedure resulted from Clarence Earl Gideon's prison-based legal research?

FACTS Clarence Earl Gideon was charged with robbing a pool hall in Florida by stealing change from a vending machine. He did not have any money to hire a lawyer, so he asked the court to appoint one for him, but his request was denied. He was convicted of the crime and sentenced to five years in prison. Later, he appealed to the state supreme court, alleging that the trial court's refusal to provide counsel violated rights guaranteed him by the Constitution and the Bill of Rights. The state supreme court upheld the trial court's conviction. The United States Supreme Court granted *certiorari* because the question of a defendant's federal constitutional right to counsel in state courts had been an ongoing source of controversy.

Case 7.4—Continued

ISSUE Can a state deny an indigent defendant the right to counsel in certain cases?

DECISION No. The Supreme Court ruled that the right to legal representation is a necessity, not a luxury.

REASON In 1942, the Court decided in *Betts v. Brady* that state courts could refuse to appoint lawyers in certain cases. Betts's situation in that case was similar to Gideon's: Betts was indicted for robbery and asked the court to appoint an attorney. The court refused to appoint one because it was not the practice of the courts to appoint counsel except in murder and rape cases. The Supreme Court in *Betts* concluded that "appointment of counsel is not a fundamental right, essential to a fair trial." The *Betts* ruling, however, made an abrupt break with precedent. In its ruling on Gideon's claim, the Court found that the "right of one charged with a crime to counsel may not be deemed fundamental and essential to fair trials in some countries, but it is in ours. * * * From the very beginning, our state and national constitutions and laws have laid great emphasis on procedural and substantive safeguards designed to assure fair trials before impartial tribunals in which every defendant stands equal before the law. This noble ideal cannot be realized if the poor man charged with a crime has to face his accusers without a lawyer to assist him."

Criminal Process

A criminal prosecution differs significantly from a civil case in several respects. These differences reflect the desire to safeguard the rights of the individual against the state. Exhibit 7–2 summarizes the major steps in processing a criminal case. We discuss below in more detail three phases of the criminal process—arrest, indictment, and trial.

Arrest Before a warrant for arrest can be issued, there must be probable cause for believing that the individual in question has committed a crime. *Probable cause* can be defined as a substantial likelihood that the person has committed or is about to commit a crime. Note that probable cause involves a likelihood, not just a possibility. Arrests may sometimes be made without a warrant if there is no time to get one, but the action of the arresting officer is still judged by the standard of probable cause.

Indictment Individuals must be formally charged with having committed specific crimes before they can be brought to trial. This charge is called an **indictment** if issued by a grand jury and an **information** if issued by a prosecutor. Before a charge can be issued, the grand jury or the magistrate must determine that there is sufficient evidence to justify bringing the individual to trial. The standard used to make this determination varies from jurisdiction to jurisdiction. Some courts use the *probable cause standard.* Others use the *preponderance of evidence standard,* which is a belief, based on evidence provided by both sides, that it is more likely than not that the individual committed the crime. Still other courts use the *prima facie case standard,* which is a belief, based on only the prosecution's evidence, that the individual is guilty.

Trial At the trial, the accused person does not have to prove anything; the entire burden of proof is on the prosecutor (the state). Guilt is judged on the basis of the **reasonable doubt** test. The prosecution must show that, based on all the evidence, the defendant's guilt is established beyond all reasonable doubt. Giving a verdict of "not guilty" is not the same as stating that the defendant is innocent. A "not guilty" verdict merely means that not enough evidence was properly presented to the court to prove guilt beyond all reasonable doubt. Courts have complex rules about what types of evidence may be presented and how the evidence may be brought out,

INDICTMENT
A charge or written accusation, issued by a grand jury, that a named person has committed a crime.

INFORMATION
A formal accusation or complaint (without an indictment) issued in certain types of actions by a prosecuting attorney or other law officer, such as a magistrate. The types of actions are set forth in the rules of states or in the Federal Rules of Criminal Procedure.

REASONABLE DOUBT
The standard used to determine the guilt or innocence of a person charged with a criminal offense. To be guilty of a crime, one must be proved guilty "beyond and to the exclusion of every reasonable doubt." A reasonable doubt is one that would cause prudent or "reasonable" persons to hesitate before acting in matters important to them.

◆ **Exhibit 7–2 Major Steps in Processing a Criminal Case**

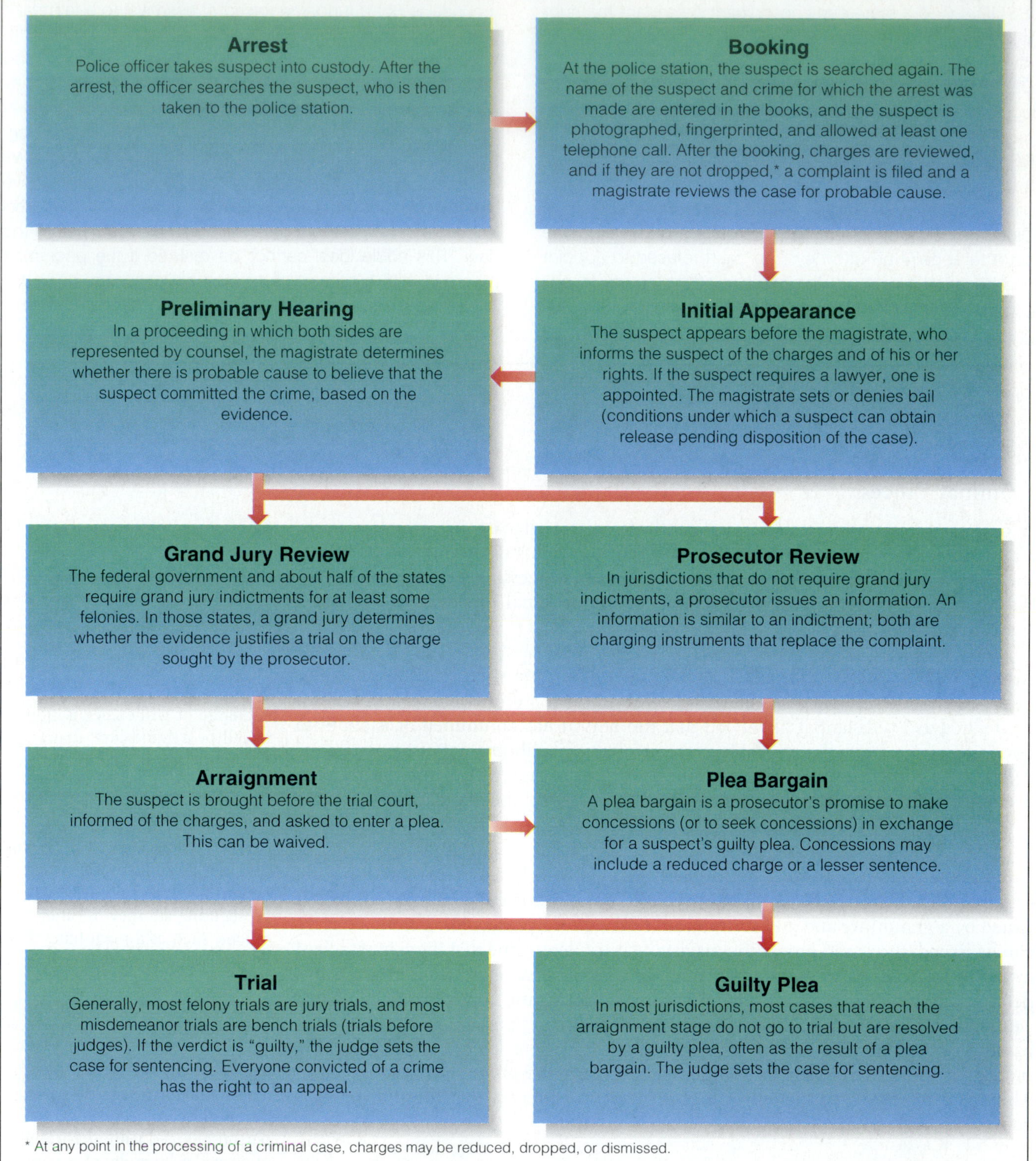

Arrest
Police officer takes suspect into custody. After the arrest, the officer searches the suspect, who is then taken to the police station.
Booking
At the police station, the suspect is searched again. The name of the suspect and crime for which the arrest was made are entered in the books, and the suspect is photographed, fingerprinted, and allowed at least one telephone call. After the booking, charges are reviewed, and if they are not dropped,* a complaint is filed and a magistrate reviews the case for probable cause.
Preliminary Hearing
In a proceeding in which both sides are represented by counsel, the magistrate determines whether there is probable cause to believe that the suspect committed the crime, based on the evidence.
Initial Appearance
The suspect appears before the magistrate, who informs the suspect of the charges and of his or her rights. If the suspect requires a lawyer, one is appointed. The magistrate sets or denies bail (conditions under which a suspect can obtain release pending disposition of the case).
Grand Jury Review
The federal government and about half of the states require grand jury indictments for at least some felonies. In those states, a grand jury determines whether the evidence justifies a trial on the charge sought by the prosecutor.
Prosecutor Review
In jurisdictions that do not require grand jury indictments, a prosecutor issues an information. An information is similar to an indictment; both are charging instruments that replace the complaint.
Arraignment
The suspect is brought before the trial court, informed of the charges, and asked to enter a plea. This can be waived.
Plea Bargain
A plea bargain is a prosecutor's promise to make concessions (or to seek concessions) in exchange for a suspect's guilty plea. Concessions may include a reduced charge or a lesser sentence.
Trial
Generally, most felony trials are jury trials, and most misdemeanor trials are bench trials (trials before judges). If the verdict is "guilty," the judge sets the case for sentencing. Everyone convicted of a crime has the right to an appeal.
Guilty Plea
In most jurisdictions, most cases that reach the arraignment stage do not go to trial but are resolved by a guilty plea, often as the result of a plea bargain. The judge sets the case for sentencing.

* At any point in the processing of a criminal case, charges may be reduced, dropped, or dismissed.

especially in jury trials. These rules are designed to ensure that evidence in trials is relevant, reliable, and not prejudicial against the defendant. The defense attorney cross-examines the witnesses who present evidence against his or her client and attempts to show that their evidence is not reliable. The state may cross-examine any witnesses presented by the defendant.

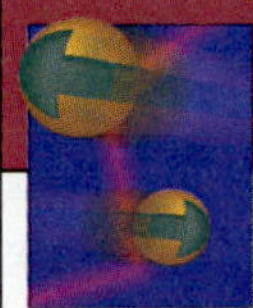

Ethical Perspective

Lies, Trickery, and Justice

Whenever an individual is taken into custody, the suspect must be informed of his or her constitutional rights, or "*Miranda* rights" (see this chapter's *Landmark in the Law*). Otherwise, any statement the suspect makes will not be admissible as evidence. The *Miranda* rights may be waived, but the waiver must be made voluntarily; and "any evidence that the accused was threatened, tricked, or cajoled into a waiver will * * * show that the defendant did not voluntarily waive his privilege." But what about tricking a suspect *after* the accused person has waived his or her rights? What if a police officer's lie to a suspect induces the suspect to confess to a crime? Will that confession be admissible in court?

This ethically disturbing question recently faced a Minnesota court. A man was assaulted and stabbed multiple times with a knife before he managed to wrest the knife from the attacker, who then fled. The police were informed that the attacker was Michael Barner, who was then arrested, read his *Miranda* rights, and taken to the police station for questioning. Barner, who had waived his rights upon arrest, freely discussed the crime and denied that he had committed it. But when one of the police officers told Barner that his fingerprints had been found on the knife (which was not true), Barner confessed to the crime. The trial court held that the evidence was inadmissible, but the Minnesota Court of Appeals reversed that decision, holding that the police officer's lie did not make it necessary to suppress the confession.[a]

a. *State v. Barner*, 486 N.W.2d 1 (Minn.App. 1992).

Lying to criminal suspects to induce them to confess to crimes is not all that uncommon. In one case, for example, a suspect was told that a co-defendant had said something that, in fact, the co-defendant had not said.[b] In another case, an interrogating officer told a defendant that the police had both blood tests and witnesses to prove that the defendant had committed the crime.[c] In both of these cases, the courts held that the confessions induced by the lies were admissible. Coercion was not involved, no threats of harm were made, no bribes tendered, and generally the defendants' will was not "overcome" by the police. The central question remains, however: Where does society draw the line between trickery and coercion?

Other kinds of police actions, such as "reverse sting" operations carried out by undercover agents, raise similar ethical questions. Society's willingness to tolerate such seemingly unethical behavior on the part of law enforcement personnel is reflected in court decisions, such as those discussed above. Obviously, there are trade-offs to consider, the primary one being the safety of society versus the rights of the accused.

b. *Frazier v. Cupp*, 394 U.S. 731, 89 S.Ct. 1420, 22 L.Ed.2d 684 (1969).

c. *State v. C.J.M.*, 409 N.W.2d 857 (Minn.App. 1987).

❖ Crimes Affecting Business

Crimes occur in the business world, just as they do elsewhere. Numerous forms of crime occur in a business context. In this section, we focus on some of the important crimes affecting business. Many of the crimes discussed in the following pages are popularly referred to as **white-collar crimes.** Although there is no official definition of white-collar crime, the term is popularly used to mean an illegal act or series of acts committed by an individual or business entity using some nonviolent means to obtain a personal or business advantage. Usually, this kind of crime is committed in the course of a legitimate occupation. So-called white-collar crimes cost the public billions of dollars each year.

WHITE-COLLAR CRIME
Nonviolent crime committed by corporations and individuals. Embezzlement and commercial bribery are two examples of white-collar crime.

Corporate crimes, which are not treated here, also fall under the category of white-collar crimes. The liability of corporations and corporate personnel for criminal actions will be discussed in detail in Chapter 26 and Chapter 27.

Forgery

FORGERY
The false or unauthorized signature of a document, or the false making of a document, with the intent to defraud.

The fraudulent making or altering of any writing in a way that changes the legal rights and liabilities of another is **forgery.** If, without authorization, Pollocka signs Bennett's name to the back of a check made out to Bennett, Pollocka is committing forgery. Forgery also includes changing trademarks, falsifying public records, counterfeiting, and altering a legal document.

Robbery

ROBBERY
Theft from a person, accompanied by force or fear of force.

At common law, **robbery** was defined as forcefully and unlawfully taking personal property of any value from another. The use of force or intimidation is usually necessary for an act of theft to be considered a robbery. Thus, picking pockets is not robbery, because the action is unknown to the victim. Typically, states have more severe penalties for *aggravated* robbery—robbery with the use of a deadly weapon.

Burglary

BURGLARY
The unlawful entry into a building with the intent to commit a felony. (Some state statutes expand this to include the intent to commit any crime.)

At common law, **burglary** was defined as breaking and entering the dwelling of another at night with the intent to commit a felony. Originally, the definition was aimed at protecting an individual's home and its occupants. Most state statutes have eliminated some of the requirements found in the common law definition. The time at which the breaking and entering occurs, for example, is usually immaterial. State statutes frequently omit the element of breaking, and some states do not require that the building be a dwelling. Aggravated burglary, which is defined as burglary with the use of a deadly weapon or burglary of a dwelling, or both, incurs a greater penalty.

Larceny

LARCENY
The act of taking another person's personal property unlawfully. Some states classify larceny as either grand or petit, depending on the property's value.

Any person who wrongfully or fraudulently takes and carries away another person's personal property is guilty of **larceny.** Larceny includes the fraudulent intent to deprive an owner permanently of property. Many business-related larcenies entail fraudulent conduct.

The place from which physical property is taken is generally immaterial. Statutes usually prescribe a stiffer sentence for taking property from buildings such as banks or warehouses, however. Whereas robbery involves force or fear, larceny does not. Therefore, picking pockets is larceny, not robbery.

As society becomes more complex, the question often arises as to what is property (see, for example, this chapter's *Law in the Extreme*). In most states, the definition of property that is subject to larceny statutes has expanded. Stealing computer programs may constitute larceny even though the "property" consists of magnetic impulses. Stealing computer time can also constitute larceny. Trade secrets can be subject to larceny statutes. Stealing the use of telephone wires through the device known as a blue box is subject to larceny statutes. So, too, is the theft of natural gas. These types of larceny are covered by "theft of services" statutes in many jurisdictions.

The common law distinction between grand and petit larceny depends on the value of the property taken. Many states have abolished this distinction, but in those that have not, grand larceny is a felony and petit larceny a misdemeanor.

Obtaining Goods by False Pretenses

It is a criminal act to obtain goods by means of false pretenses—for example, buying groceries with a check, knowing that one has insufficient funds to cover it. Statutes dealing with such illegal activities vary widely from state to state.

Law in the Extreme

Sometimes "Theft" Isn't a Crime

Recently, a New York state court judge faced the following question: If a video store owner makes unauthorized copies of videos for rent or sale to the store's customers, can the owner be indicted for the "criminal possession of stolen property"? Although the question sounds relatively straightforward and simple, the answer is not, and the judge's reasoning in the case illustrates how challenging it can sometimes be to apply the law to situations involving technological property.

The question arose in the case of *People v. Borriello*.[a] Ralph Borriello owned three video stores and routinely made unauthorized copies of videos to sell or rent to his customers. In all, he had between eight hundred and nine hundred unauthorized video recordings in his stores. Borriello was indicted by a grand jury for, among other crimes, the criminal possession of stolen property. The judge had little difficulty with the jury's indictment for the other crimes, but he took issue with the charge of criminal possession of stolen property.

First, what exactly had been stolen? Under state law, for a theft to occur, there must be a taking from an owner. But had Borriello taken anything? Borriello was the lawful owner of both the videos he had copied and the blank cartridges onto which the videos had been transferred. The only possible thing Borriello could have stolen, then, was a series of magnetic patterns that ultimately produce video images.

Second, state law defined an owner as "any person who has a right to possession thereof superior to that of the taker, obtainer or withholder." But did anyone have possessory rights in the videos that were superior to Borriello's rights? Copyright owners have rights in their works, of course, and these rights include the right to a share of the income received on the sale or transfer of their works. But copyright holders do not have the right to "possess" unauthorized copies of their works. Moreover, state law defined "possession" as the act of having physical possession or otherwise exercising dominion or control over tangible property. But the magnetic patterns on videotapes are not tangible property.

Third, state law did not define the possession of unauthorized recordings as a crime. Although state penal law had been amended to include computer data, software, and other computer intangibles as "property" and their theft as a crime, this was not the case with video recordings.

Finally, the judge considered the policy implications of finding Borriello guilty of the criminal possession of stolen property. If Borriello were guilty of this crime, the judge stated, so would be any person who rented or purchased the videos from Borriello and who had reason to know that the recordings were unauthorized. The judge concluded that it would be counter to both state law and public policy to indict Borriello for the "criminal possession of stolen property." He dismissed the indictment for this crime.

a. 154 Misc.2d 529, 587 N.Y.S.2d 518 (1992).

Receiving Stolen Goods

It is a crime to receive stolen goods. The recipient of such goods need not know the true identity of the owner or the thief. All that is necessary is that the recipient knows or should have known that the goods are stolen, which implies an intent to deprive the owner of those goods.

Embezzlement

EMBEZZLEMENT
The fraudulent appropriation of money or other property by a person to whom the money or property has been entrusted.

When a person entrusted with another person's property or money fraudulently appropriates it, **embezzlement** occurs. Typically, embezzlement involves an employee who steals money. Banks face this problem, and so do a number of businesses in which corporate officers or accountants "jimmy" the books to cover up the fraudulent conversion of money for their own benefit. Embezzlement is not larceny because the wrongdoer does not physically take the property from the possession of another, and it is not robbery because force or fear is not used.

It does not matter whether the accused takes the money from the victim or from a third person. If, as the comptroller of a large corporation, Saunders pockets a certain number of checks from third parties that were given to her to deposit into the corporate account, she is embezzling.

Ordinarily, an embezzler who returns what has been taken will not be prosecuted because the owner usually will not take the time to make a complaint, give depositions, and appear in court. That the accused intended eventually to return the embezzled property, however, does not constitute a sufficient defense to the crime of embezzlement. The role of intention in establishing whether embezzlement has occurred is emphasized in the following case.

Case 7.5 

UNITED STATES v. FAULKNER

United States Court of Appeals, Ninth Circuit, 1981.
638 F.2d 129.

HISTORICAL AND SOCIAL SETTING *At one time, the law generally divided theft into three separate crimes—larceny, false pretenses, and embezzlement. Statutes prohibiting embezzlement often listed the kinds of persons who might have lawful possession of another's property (store clerks, bank employees, merchants, and so on) and provided that any such person who fraudulently converted the property was guilty of embezzlement. Today, in those jurisdictions that have enacted new criminal codes, the three separate crimes have been replaced with a single crime. With regard to the once-separate crime of embezzlement, these statutes may simply provide that one who is in lawful possession of another's property and intends to convert it to his or her own use is guilty.*

FACTS Faulkner, a truck driver, was hauling a load of refrigerators from San Diego to New York for the trucking company that employed him. He departed from his assigned route and stopped in Las Vegas, where he attempted to display and sell some of the refrigerators to a firm. Although the refrigerators never left the truck, to display them he had to break the truck's seals, enter the cargo department, and open two refrigerator cartons. The store owner refused to purchase the appliances, and when Faulkner left the store, he was arrested. He was later convicted under federal law for the embezzlement of an interstate shipment. Faulkner appealed, claiming that there were no grounds for the charge since he had never removed any equipment from the truck.

ISSUE Does the charge of embezzlement apply when the property has not been physically removed from the owner's possession?

DECISION Yes. The judgment of the lower court was affirmed.

REASON If a person has possession and control over the property of another and has the *intent* of converting the goods to his or her own use, then embezzlement occurs. By leaving his assigned route in order to sell the refrigerators and keep the proceeds, Faulkner exercised control over the property, with the intent to convert it to his own use.

ARSON
The malicious burning of another's dwelling. Some statutes have expanded this to include any real property regardless of ownership and the destruction of property by other means—for example, by explosion.

Arson

The willful and malicious burning of a building (and in some states, personal property) owned by another is the crime of **arson.** At common law, arson applied only to burning down another person's house. The law was designed to protect human life. Today, arson statutes have been extended to cover the destruction of any building, regardless of ownership, by fire or explosion.

Every state has a special statute that covers a person's burning a building for the purpose of collecting insurance. If Smith owns an insured apartment building that is falling apart and sets fire to it himself or pays someone else to do so, he is guilty not only of arson but also of defrauding insurers, which is an attempted larceny. Of course, the insurer need not pay the claim when insurance fraud is proved.

"A large number of houses deserve to be burnt."

H. G. Wells, 1866–1946
(English author)

Mail Fraud

One of the most potent weapons against white-collar criminals is the Wire and Mail Fraud Act of 1988.[7] Under this act, it is a federal crime to use the mails to defraud the public. Illegal use of the mails must involve (1) mailing or causing someone else to mail a writing—something written, printed, or photocopied—for the purpose of executing a scheme to defraud and (2) a contemplated or an organized scheme to defraud by false pretenses. If, for example, Johnson advertises by mail the sale of a cure for cancer that he knows to be fraudulent because it has no medical validity, he can be prosecuted for fraudulent use of the mails. Federal law also makes it a crime to use a telegram to defraud. Violators may be fined up to $1,000, imprisoned for up to five years, or both. If the violation affects a financial institution, the fine may be up to $1 million and the imprisonment up to twenty years, or both.

Computer Crime

The American Bar Association defines **computer crime** as any act that is directed against computers and computer parts, that uses computers as instruments of crime, or that involves computers and constitutes abuse. Frequently our laws are inadequate to deal with the various types of computer crimes that are committed. As mentioned earlier, larceny statutes were originally passed to prohibit the taking and carrying away of property belonging to another. Computer crimes, however, particularly those involving the theft of computer data or services, frequently do not require a physical "taking and carrying away" of another's property. While some states have expanded their definitions of property to allow computer crimes to fall within their larceny statutes, in other states prosecutors have to rely on other criminal statutes. Computer crimes often result in lenient punishments, which has led lawmakers to put forth various proposals to deal with this relatively new type of crime.

COMPUTER CRIME
Any wrongful act that is directed against computers and computer parts, or wrongful use or abuse of computers or software.

Types of Computer Crime A variety of different types of crime can be committed with or against computers. In this section, we look at some of the ways in which computers have been involved in criminal activity.

Financial Crimes Many computer crimes fall into the broad category of financial crimes. In addition to using computers for information storage and retrieval, businesses increasingly use computers to conduct financial transactions. This is equally true of the government, which handles virtually all of its transactions via computer. These circumstances provide opportunities for employees and others to commit crimes that can involve serious economic losses. For example, employees of accounting and computer departments can transfer monies among accounts with little effort and without the risk involved in transactions evidenced by paperwork. Thus, not only is the potential for crime in the area of financial transactions great, but most monetary losses from computer crime are suffered in this area.

7. 18 U.S.C. Section 1341.

Software Piracy For the average consumer, software is expensive. It is also costly to produce. Often, considerable sums are invested in the research and development necessary to create new, innovative software programs. And once marketed, new software requires that user support be provided during its life on the market.

Given the expense of software, many individuals and businesses have been tempted to steal software by decoding and making unauthorized copies of software programs. This is known as *software piracy*. It has been estimated that the annual loss to developers from this practice is more than $500 million.

"Any sufficiently advanced technology is indistinguishable from magic."

Arthur C. Clarke, 1917–
(English writer)

Under most state laws, the theft of software is now classified as a crime. At the federal level, existing laws protecting intellectual property (such as patent and copyright laws) have been amended in recent years to extend coverage to computer programs, as was discussed in Chapter 6. In 1990, in an attempt to further control the unauthorized copying of computer programs, the federal government passed a law that prohibits, with some exceptions, the renting, leasing, or lending of computer software without the express permission of the copyright holder.

Property Theft Computer crimes can also involve property theft. One type is the theft of computer equipment (hardware), which has become easier in recent years as computer components have become smaller and more readily transportable. Another type is the theft of computer-related property, which may involve taking goods that are controlled and accounted for by means of a computer applications program. For example, an employee in a company's accounting department could manipulate inventory records to conceal unauthorized shipments of goods. The theft of computer equipment and the theft of goods with the aid of computers are subject to the same criminal and tort laws as thefts of other physical property.

Vandalism and Destructive Programming On occasion, political activists, terrorists, and disgruntled employees have physically damaged computer hardware or ruined computer software. These acts have included such conduct as smashing computer equipment with a crowbar, shooting it with a pistol, and—in an attempt to make a political point—pouring blood over a computer. In one instance, an individual erased a company's records merely by walking past computer storage banks with an electromagnet. Other destructive acts have required greater technical awareness and facility. A knowledgeable individual can do a considerable amount of damage. For example, a computer program (referred to popularly as a *virus*) can be designed to rearrange, replace, or destroy data.

Theft of Data or Services Many people would agree that when an individual uses another's computer or computer information system without authorization, the individual is stealing. For example, an employee who used a computer system or data stored in a computer system for private gain and without the employer's authorization would likely be considered a thief, as would a politician who used a government computer to send out campaign brochures. Under an increasing number of revised criminal codes and broad judicial interpretations of existing statutes, the unauthorized use of computer data or services is considered larceny.

Detecting and Prosecuting Computer Crime One of the challenges presented by computer crime is its relative invisibility. Such crime is often difficult to detect, and if the crime is cleverly executed and no accounting discrepancy is immediately apparent, it may go undetected for some time. In some cases, victimized companies, and even the government, have discovered multimillion-dollar thefts only after a considerable lapse of time. Even when it is apparent that a computer crime has occurred, tracing the crime to the individual who committed it can be difficult because the individual's identity is "hidden" by the anonymous nature of the computer system. In the employment context, often no one with enough expertise to discover a crime is overseeing the perpetrator's activities. Even when computer crimes are detected and reported, the complexities of the computer systems involved have often frustrated the attempts of attorneys, police officers, jurors, and others to comprehend the offenses and prosecute the offenders successfully.

In attempting to control computer crime, governments at both the federal and state levels have undertaken protective measures. The Counterfeit Access Device and Computer Fraud and Abuse Act of 1984, as amended, prohibits unauthorized access to certain types of information, such as restricted government information, information contained in a financial institution's financial records, and information contained in a consumer reporting agency's files on consumers. In 1990, Robert Morris, Jr., a Cornell University student, was convicted of violating this act by writing a program (virus) that paralyzed a nationwide computer research network involving six thousand computers. Penalties for violations include up to five years' imprisonment and a fine of up to $250,000 or twice the amount that was gained by the thief or lost by the victim as a result of the crime. Several states have also passed legislation specifically addressing the problem of computer crime.

One of the major problems in attempting to control computer crime is that it cannot be prosecuted if it is not reported. And it seems clear to many people that the reason many computer crimes go unreported is because business firms are reluctant to disclose the vulnerability of their systems. Companies adversely affected by such crime do not want to publicize the fact because they are afraid customers will doubt the accuracy and security of computer-generated material. Cases involving computer crimes are thus often settled out of court to avoid publicity.

Bribery

Basically, three types of bribery are considered crimes: bribery of public officials, commercial bribery, and bribery of foreign officials.

"[It is] very much better to bribe a person than kill him. . . ."

Sir Winston Churchill, 1874–1965
(British prime minister, 1940–1945, 1951–1955)

Bribery of Public Officials The attempt to influence a public official to act in a way that serves a private interest is a crime. As an element of this crime, intent must be present and proved. The bribe can be anything the recipient considers to be valuable. It is important to realize that *the commission of the crime of bribery occurs when the bribe is offered.* The recipient does not have to agree to perform whatever action is desired by the person offering the bribe, nor does the recipient have to accept the bribe, for the crime of bribery to occur.

Commercial Bribery Typically, people make commercial bribes to obtain proprietary information, cover up an inferior product, or secure new business. Industrial espionage sometimes involves commercial bribes. For example, a person in one firm may offer an employee in a competing firm some type of payoff in exchange for trade secrets and pricing schedules. So-called kickbacks or payoffs for special favors or services are a form of commercial bribery in some situations.

Bribery of Foreign Officials Bribing foreign officials to obtain favorable business contracts is a crime. This crime and the Foreign Corrupt Practices Act of 1977, which was passed to curb the practice of bribery by American businesspersons in securing foreign contracts, are discussed in detail in the *Landmark in the Law* in Chapter 2.

Bankruptcy Fraud

When a business finds itself with an oppressive amount of debt, its creditors may seek to have the court adjudge it a bankrupt company, or it may seek voluntary bankruptcy. Today, individuals or businesses can be relieved of oppressive debt by federal law under the Bankruptcy Reform Act of 1978 as amended (see Chapter 22). In short, the act requires that the debtor disclose all assets. Typically, a *trustee* then

Business Law in Action

The High Cost of Crime

In 1988, a young free-lance photographer checked into a Motel 6 in Forth Worth, Texas. Two men forced their way into the woman's room, raped her, and beat her up. The woman, claiming that the experience had made it impossible for her to work, later sued Motel 6 for negligent failure to ensure the safety of motel guests. The motel eventually paid $10 million to settle the suit.

Tort litigation initiated by business guests or employees who are victimized by crimes on business premises is just one example of the numerous types of costs imposed on businesses as a result of criminal activity. Losses incurred as a result of burglaries and robberies total nearly $12 billion annually, while employee theft, embezzlement, and kickbacks cost an estimated $27 billion. And, as mentioned in the text, businesses suffer increasingly from computer fraud and high-tech crimes, including fraud involving automated teller machines (ATMs), other unauthorized electronic fund transfers, the illegal use of telephone access numbers, the electronic filing of fraudulent tax returns, and so on.

An even higher cost is that paid for security measures, estimated to be $36 billion a year. Depending on the type of business, security measures may involve surveillance cameras, security guards, locks, alarm systems, employee escorts (in high-crime areas), computer experts to devise techniques to deter unauthorized access to computer data, and other security equipment or personnel. In the case of Motel 6, management ended up paying more than $8 million to provide better security at its motels, in the form of deadbolt locks and safety latches for its room doors, better lighting and fencing on motel premises, and training programs for security personnel. Security measures by banking firms are particularly costly. Just to combat ATM fraud, U.S. banks spend more than $650 million on security systems.

In all, business costs resulting from crime and the expensive security measures necessary for its prevention are estimated to be $130 billion per year. Ultimately, however, it is not business firms but consumers who foot the crime bill. This is because costs relating to criminal activity normally are built into the prices charged by business firms for their goods and services. According to one source, the annual "crime tax" paid by each American household is, on average, $1,376.[a]

a. See Terri Thompson, David Hage, and Robert F. Black, "Crime and the Bottom Line," *U.S. News & World Report*, April 13, 1992, pp. 55–58.

takes possession of the assets and follows certain rules and procedures in distributing them to creditors.

Numerous white-collar crimes may be committed during the many phases of a bankruptcy proceeding. A creditor, for example, may file a false claim against the debtor, which is a crime. Also, a debtor may fraudulently transfer assets to favored parties before or after the petition for bankruptcy is filed. For example, a company-owned automobile may be "sold" at a bargain price to a trusted friend or relative. Closely related to the crime of fraudulent transfer of property is the crime of fraudulent concealment of property, such as hiding gold coins.

In a *scam bankruptcy*, a bankruptcy is planned in advance. The perpetrators buy a legitimate business that sells goods that can be sold rapidly, such as jewelry or electronic home-entertainment equipment. They next purchase numerous items on credit and pay off the creditors within a relatively short period of time. This activity continues until the creditors are willing to offer the new owners larger and larger amounts of credit. Finally, the new owners order a very large amount of merchandise on credit, sell it at whatever price is necessary to unload it quickly for cash, and then close down the business. Of course, the creditors file an involuntary petition in bankruptcy against the business. The amount the creditors recover, however, is usually very small, and the scam operators are nowhere to be found.

Money Laundering

The profits from illegal activities amount to billions of dollars a year, particularly the profits from illegal drug transactions and, to a lesser extent, from racketeering, prostitution, and gambling. Under federal law, banks, savings and loan associations, and other financial institutions are required to report currency transactions of over $10,000. Consequently, those who engage in illegal activities face difficulties in placing their cash profits from illegal transactions. Until 1977, Switzerland was a haven for such "flight money." In that year, however, a treaty gave the United States access to Swiss bank-deposit information relating to certain white-collar crimes. Panama City then became a leading shelter for such money.

As an alternative to simply placing cash from illegal transactions in bank deposits, wrongdoers and racketeers have invented ways to launder "dirty" money to make it "clean." This **money laundering** is done through legitimate businesses. For example, a successful drug dealer might become partners with a restaurateur. Little by little, the restaurant shows an increasing profit. As a shareholder or partner in the restaurant, the wrongdoer is able to report the "profits" of the restaurant as legitimate income on which federal and state taxes are paid. The wrongdoer can then spend those monies without worrying about whether his or her lifestyle exceeds the level possible with his or her reported income. The Federal Bureau of Investigation estimates that organized crime alone has invested tens of billions of dollars in as many as a hundred thousand business establishments in the United States.

MONEY LAUNDERING
Falsely reporting income that has been obtained through criminal activity as income obtained through a legitimate business enterprise—in effect, "laundering" the "dirty money."

Insider Trading

An individual who obtains "inside information" about the plans of large corporations can often make staggering profits by using such information to guide decisions relating to the purchase or sale of corporate securities. An *insider* is an individual who has inside information—that is, information not available to the general public—about a publicly traded corporation. **Insider trading** is a violation of securities law and will be considered more fully in Chapter 29. At this point, it may be said that one who possesses inside information and who has a duty not to disclose it to outsiders may not profit from the purchase or sale of securities based on that information until the information is available to the public.

INSIDER TRADING
Purchasing or selling securities on the basis of information that has not been made available to the public.

Criminal RICO Violations

The Racketeer Influenced and Corrupt Organizations Act (RICO) was passed in an attempt to prevent the use of legitimate business enterprises as shields for racketeering activity and to prohibit the purchase of any legitimate business interest with illegally obtained funds (see the discussion of RICO in Chapter 6).

Most of the criminal RICO offenses have little, if anything, to do with normal business activities, for they involve gambling, arson, and extortion. But securities fraud (involving the sale of stocks and bonds) and mail fraud are also criminal RICO violations, and RICO has become an effective tool in attacking these white-collar crimes in recent years. Under criminal provisions of RICO, any individual found guilty of a violation is subject to a fine of up to $25,000 per violation or imprisonment for up to twenty years, or both.

Application

Law and the Businessperson—Protecting against Computer and Other Crimes

A major concern of any business owner is the protection of business property.

Protecting Your Business Premises

Obviously, business premises should be insured to protect against theft, fire, vandalism, and other crimes or hazards. But what else should the business owner do to protect business premises against trespassers (that is, thieves)? The law of trespass may seem clear to the businessperson who has invested his or her life savings in starting a small retail store. But to the courts, the law of trespass and, more specifically, the protection of property against trespassers are not so clear. The usual methods of protecting property against trespassers, such as hiring police protection services and installing alarm systems, are frequently used and acceptable methods of protecting business property. Other methods of protection may not be legally acceptable, however. For example, business owners cannot devise "mantraps" to protect themselves against thieves. As indicated in *Katco v. Briney* (see Case 7.2), courts will hold that landowners cannot do mechanically what they cannot do in person—that is, use deadly force without sufficient justification.

Rare exceptions to this principle have been made, however. For example, in 1986, a Dade County, Florida, grand jury refused to hold a shopkeeper liable for a death resulting from an electrified wire grid the shopkeeper, Prentice Rasheed, had constructed to deter potential burglars. Rasheed's store, which was located in an area of Miami noted for its high crime rate, had been burglarized seven times and, according to Rasheed, had received little police protection—although he stated he had "begged" the city to provide it. Rasheed testified that he had created the grid only to "shock"—not to kill—potential intruders and was "deeply sorry" that death had resulted from his device.[a]

Protecting Your Intangible Property

In addition to protecting physical property, businesspersons today also are concerned about protecting their intangible property—such as computer data or files—from outside access. One way to prevent unauthorized access to computer data or files is to restrict access to information in a computer system through the use of various security measures. For example, the data might be made available only to those with special security clearances. Establishing a system of security clearances may involve organizing data in specific categories. The category to which an individual is given access is related to the information the individual needs to perform his or her job. For example, the names of account holders can be kept separate from the accounts' balances. In this way, a party who needs to work with the balances can be prevented from learning the holders' identities.

Passwords may be attached to a system or to a portion of the data within a system to preclude unauthorized access. Considering the relative ease with which unauthorized individuals have discovered passwords in the past, however, it is advisable to change the passwords frequently.

Another means of limiting access to computer information is to encrypt (translate into a secret code) the data contained within the system. Data can be encoded before they are stored or communicated to another party. The data can be decoded when they are taken from storage or when the other party receives them.

As a further protective measure, a copy of the data can be stored outside the facilities in which a company's computer system is located. Then, if some of the information kept in the system is destroyed or lost, it can be reproduced.

Checklist for the Businessperson

- ☐ 1. Obtain insurance coverage for your business premises.
- ☐ 2. Do not resort to self-made devices, such as "mantraps," to deter potential burglars.
- ☐ 3. Limit employees' access to computer data and files through the establishment of a system of security clearances.
- ☐ 4. If passwords are used to access data, make sure the passwords are changed frequently.
- ☐ 5. Consider encrypting (encoding) computer data before storage or communication of the data to another party.
- ☐ 6. Store a copy of computer files in outside facilities to ensure against destruction or loss of data.

a. See the *Miami Herald*, February 10, 1987, p. 2.

❖ Key Terms

arson 190
burglary 188
computer crime 191
consent 178
crime 174
defense 176
duress 178
embezzlement 190
entrapment 180
exclusionary rule 183
felony 174
forgery 188
indictment 185
information 185
insider trading 195
larceny 188
misdemeanor 175
money laundering 195
petty offense 175
plea bargaining 181
reasonable doubt 185
robbery 188
self-defense 179
statute of limitations 181
white-collar crime 187

❖ Chapter Summary: Criminal Law

Classification of Crimes	1. *Felonies*—Serious crimes punishable by death or by imprisonment in a penitentiary for more than a year. 2. *Misdemeanors*—Under federal law and in most states, any crime that is not a felony.
Elements of Criminal Liability	1. *Guilty act*—In general, some form of harmful act must be committed for a crime to exist. 2. *Intent*—An intent to commit a crime, or a wrongful mental state, is required for a crime to exist.
Defenses to Criminal Liability	1. *Infancy.* 2. *Intoxication.* 3. *Insanity.* 4. *Mistake.* 5. *Consent.* 6. *Duress.* 7. *Justifiable use of force.* 8. *Entrapment.* 9. *Statute of limitations.* 10. *Immunity.*
Procedure in Criminal Law	1. *Constitutional safeguards*—The rights of accused persons are protected under the Constitution, particularly by the Fourth, Fifth, Sixth, and Eighth Amendments. In *Miranda v. Arizona,* the United States Supreme Court ruled that individuals must be informed of their constitutional rights (such as their rights to counsel and to remain silent) upon being taken into custody. Under the exclusionary rule, evidence obtained in violation of the constitutional rights of the accused will not be admissible in court. 2. *Criminal process*—Procedures governing arrest, indictment, and trial for a crime are designed to safeguard the rights of the individual against the state.
Crimes Affecting Business	1. *Forgery*—The fraudulent making or altering of any writing in a way that changes the legal rights and liabilities of another. 2. *Robbery*—The forceful and unlawful taking of personal property of any value from another. 3. *Burglary*—At common law, defined as breaking and entering the dwelling of another at night with the intent to commit a felony. State statutes now vary in their definitions of burglary. 4. *Larceny*—The wrongful or fraudulent taking and carrying away of another's personal property with the intent to deprive the owner permanently of the property. 5. *Obtaining goods by false pretenses*—Such as cashing a check knowing that there are insufficient funds in the bank to cover it. 6. *Receiving stolen goods*—A crime if the recipient knew or should have known that the goods were stolen. 7. *Embezzlement*—The fraudulent appropriation of another person's property or money by a person to whom the property or money was entrusted. 8. *Arson*—The willful and malicious burning of a building or (in some states) personal property owned by another. 9. *Mail fraud*—Using the mails to defraud the public.

❖ Chapter Summary: Criminal Law—Continued

Crimes Affecting Business—Continued	10. *Computer crime*—Any act that is directed against computers and computer parts, that uses computers as instruments of crime, or that involves computers and constitutes abuse. Computer crime includes financial crimes that involve computers; theft of computer equipment, software, data, or services; and vandalism and destructive programming of computers. 11. *Bribery*—Includes bribery of public officials, commercial bribery, and bribery of foreign officials. The crime of bribery is committed when the bribe is tendered. 12. *Bankruptcy fraud*—Includes false claims of creditors, fraudulent transfer of assets by the debtor before or after the bankruptcy petition is filed, and scam bankruptcies—bankruptcies that are planned for the purpose of defrauding creditors. 13. *Money laundering*—Establishing legitimate enterprises through which "dirty" money (obtained through criminal activities) can be "laundered." 14. *Insider trading*—The buying or selling of corporate securities by a person in possession of material nonpublic information in violation of securities laws. 15. *Criminal RICO violations*—Include the use of legitimate business enterprises to shield racketeering activity, securities fraud, and mail fraud.

❖ Questions and Case Problems

7-1. Crimes versus Torts. What distinguishes crimes from other wrongful acts, such as torts?

7-2. Types of Crimes. Determine from the facts below what type of crime (larceny, burglary, embezzlement, arson, etc.) has been committed in each case.

(a) Carlos is walking through an amusement park when his wallet, with $2,000 in it, is "picked" from his pocket.

(b) Carlos walks into a camera shop. Without force and without the owner noticing, Carlos walks out of the store with a camera.

7-3. Types of Crimes. The following situations are similar (all involve the theft of Makoto's television set), yet they represent three different crimes. Identify the three crimes, noting the differences among them.

(a) While passing Makoto's house one night, Sarah sees a portable television set left unattended on Makoto's lawn. Sarah takes the television set, carries it home, and tells everyone she owns it.

(b) While passing Makoto's house one night, Sarah sees Makoto outside with a portable television set. Holding Makoto at gunpoint, Sarah forces him to give up the set. Then Sarah runs away with it.

(c) While passing Makoto's house one night, Sarah sees a portable television set in a window. Sarah breaks the front-door lock, enters, and leaves with the set.

7-4. Types of Crimes. Which, if any, of the following crimes necessarily involve illegal activity on the part of more than one person?

(a) Bribery
(b) Forgery
(c) Embezzlement
(d) Larceny
(e) Receiving stolen property

7-5. Receiving Stolen Property. Rafael stops Laura on a busy street and offers to sell her an expensive wristwatch for a fraction of its value. After some questioning by Laura, Rafael admits that the watch is stolen property, although he says he was not the thief. Laura pays for and receives the wristwatch. Has Laura committed any crime? Has Rafael? Explain.

7-6. Criminal Intent. In 1965, Rybicki failed to pay the federal government the total amount of income tax he owed. Attempts by the Internal Revenue Service (IRS) to collect the tax proved fruitless. Therefore, the IRS obtained (through lawful means) a tax lien on Rybicki's personal property, which included his truck. In February 1967, Rybicki's wife, upon hearing the truck's motor, awakened her sleeping husband. Wielding a shotgun, Rybicki went to his front door and told the two men who were attempting to take his truck to stop. Rybicki claimed that he did not know the two men were IRS agents. Subsequently, the federal government indicted Rybicki for obstructing justice. Can Rybicki be held criminally liable if he did not know that the men were IRS agents performing their duty? [*United States v. Rybicki*, 403 F.2d 599 (6th Cir. 1968)]

7-7. Criminal Act. Khoury went to a department store, spent some time shopping, and eventually filled a large, empty chandelier box with approximately $900 worth of tools. When he went to the check-out counter, the cashier indicated she wanted to look inside the box before accepting Khoury's payment for the chandelier. Khoury then pushed the cart back into the store and departed from the premises. Khoury was convicted of grand larceny by the trial court. On appeal, Khoury alleged that because he had not actually removed any goods from the store, he had not committed larceny. Is Khoury correct? [*People v. Khoury*, 108 Cal.App.3d, 166 Cal.Rptr. 705 (1980)]

7-8. Embezzlement. Slemmer, who had been a successful options trader, gave lectures to small groups about stock options. Several persons who attended his lectures decided to invest in stock options and have Slemmer advise them. They formed an investment club called Profit Design Group (PDG). Slemmer set up an account for PDG with a brokerage firm. Slemmer had control of the PDG account and could make decisions on which stock options to buy or sell. He was not authorized to withdraw money from the account for his own benefit. Nonetheless, he withdrew money from the PDG account to make payments on real estate that he owned. Slemmer made false representations to the members of PDG, and he eventually lost all the money in their account. A jury found him guilty of first degree theft by embezzlement. Slemmer objected to the trial court's failure to instruct the jury that an intent to permanently deprive was an element of the crime charged. Is intent to permanently deprive another of property a required element for the crime of embezzlement? [*State v. Slemmer*, 48 Wash.App. 48, 738 P.2d 281 (1987)]

7-9. Self-defense. Bernardy came to the defense of his friend Harrison in a fight with Wilson. Wilson started the fight, and after Harrison knocked him down, Bernardy (who was wearing tennis shoes) kicked Wilson several times in the head. Bernardy stated that he did so because he believed an onlooker, Gowens, would join forces with Wilson against Harrison. Bernardy maintained that his use of force was justifiable because he was protecting another (Harrison) from injury. Discuss whether Bernardy's use of force to protect Harrison from harm was justified. [*State v. Bernardy*, 605 P.2d 791(1980)]

7-10. Criminal Intent. While at a grocery store, Moses Raquemore stuffed two packages of meat into his pants and was just pulling his shirt down over them when he noticed that the store manager and a security guard were watching him. He returned the meat to the counter, but he was arrested for shoplifting anyway. Had Racquemore committed a criminal act? Were Racquemore's actions in the store sufficient to prove the element of intent? Discuss. [*Racquemore v. State*, 204 Ga.App. 88, 418 S.E.2d 448 (1992)]

7-11. Criminal Liability. In January 1988, David Ludvigson was hired as chief executive officer of Leopard Enterprises, a group of companies that owned funeral homes and cemeteries in Iowa and sold "pre-need" funeral contracts. Under Iowa law, 80 percent of monies obtained under such a contract must be set aside in trust until the death of the person for whose benefit the funds were paid. Shortly after Ludvigson was hired, the firm began having financial difficulties. Ludvigson used money from these contracts to pay operating expenses until the company went bankrupt and was placed in receivership. Ludvigson was charged and found guilty on five counts of second degree theft stemming from the misappropriation of these funds. He appealed, alleging, among other things, that because none of the victims whose trust funds were used to cover operating expenses was denied services, no injury was done. Will the court agree with Ludvigson? Explain. [*State v. Ludvigson*, 482 N.W.2d 419 (Iowa 1992)]

A Question of Ethics and Social Responsibility

7-12. *A troublesome issue concerning the constitutional privilege against self-incrimination has to do with "jail plants"—that is, placing undercover police officers in cells with criminal suspects to gain information from the suspects. For example, in one case the police placed an undercover agent, Parisi, in a jail cellblock with Lloyd Perkins, who had been imprisoned on charges unrelated to the murder that Parisi was investigating. When Parisi asked Perkins if he had ever killed anyone, Perkins made statements implicating himself in the murder. Perkins was then charged with the murder.* [Illinois v. Perkins, *496 U.S. 914, 110 S.Ct. 2394, 110 L.Ed.2d 243 (1990)*]

1. Review the discussion of *Miranda v. Arizona* in this chapter's *Landmark in the Law.* Should Perkins's statements be suppressed—that is, not be treated as admissible evidence at trial—because he was not "read his rights," as required by the *Miranda* decision, prior to making his self-incriminating statements? Does *Miranda* apply to Perkins's situation?
2. Do you think that it is fair for the police to resort to trickery and deception to bring those who have committed crimes to justice? Why or why not? What rights or public policies must be balanced in deciding this issue?

For Critical Analysis

7-13. *Do you think that criminal procedure in this country is weighted too heavily in favor of accused persons? Can you think of a fairer way to balance the constitutional rights of accused persons against the right of society to be protected against criminal violence? Explain.*

Unit Two

Contracts

❖ Why We Study Contract Law

The noted legal scholar Roscoe Pound once said that "[t]he social order rests upon the stability and predictability of conduct, of which keeping promises is a large item."[1] Contract law deals with, among other things, the formation and keeping of promises (in Latin, *pacta sunt servanda*—"agreements shall be kept"). The law encourages competent parties to form contracts for lawful objectives. No aspect of modern life is entirely free of contractual relationships. Indeed, even the ordinary consumer in his or her daily activities acquires rights and obligations based on contract law. You acquire rights and obligations, for example, when you borrow money to make a purchase or when you buy a stereo or a house. Contract law is designed to provide stability and predictability, as well as certainty, for both buyers and sellers in the marketplace.

Why do we study contract law? Simply because it is the framework for all commercial law. The law described in the chapters within this unit is the basis for much of the law in more specialized areas, such as the sale of goods. You will learn that transactions governed by statutes, such as the Uniform Commercial Code, can nonetheless be changed by express terms in a contract between parties. In Chapter 8, you will be introduced to the nature and terminology of contracts. As you will see, there are many types of contracts. There are also basic requirements that must be met before a valid and enforceable contract comes into existence. These requirements are discussed in detail in Chapters 9 through 11. Sometimes, a third party (one who is not a direct party to the contract) acquires rights under the contract. Third party rights are covered in Chapter 12, as are the various ways in which duties under a contract can be fulfilled, or discharged. Finally, in Chapter 13, you will learn what remedies are available to the nonbreaching party when the other party breaches the contract.

The Uniform Commercial Code (UCC), which governs contracts and other transactions relating to the sale of goods, occasionally departs from common law contract rules. Generally, the different treatment of contracts falling under the UCC stems from the general policy of encouraging commerce. The ways in which the UCC changes common law contract rules will be discussed extensively in Unit Three. In this unit, we will only indicate briefly or in footnotes which common law rules have been altered by the UCC for sales contracts.

1. R. Pound, *Jurisprudence*, Vol. 3 (St. Paul: West Publishing Co., 1959), p. 162.

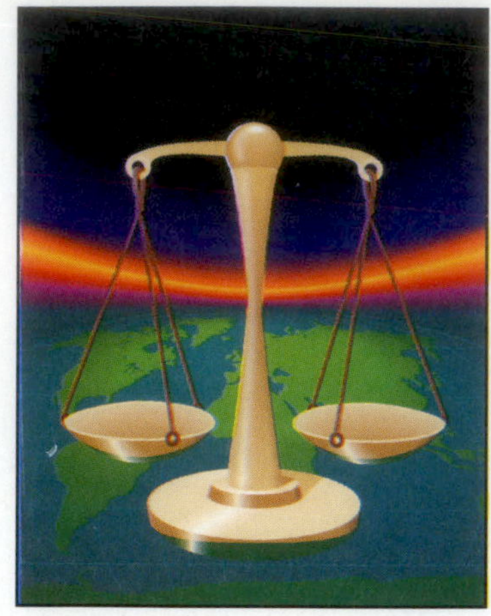

Chapter 8

Nature and Classification

"Life marches on, with new conditions and new interests, causing constant judicial development."

Arthur L. Corbin, 1874–1967
(American legal scholar and educator)

As Arthur Corbin—an eminent scholar in the field of contract law and the subject of this chapter's *Profile*—observed, "new conditions and new interests" continually fashion the law. Like other types of law, contract law reflects our social values, interests, and expectations at a given point in time. It shows, for example, to what extent our society allows people to make promises or commitments that are legally binding. It shows what excuses our society accepts for breaking such promises. And it shows what promises are considered to be contrary to public policy and therefore legally void. If a promise goes against the interests of society as a whole, it will be invalidated. Also, if it was made by a child or a mentally incompetent person, or on the basis of false information, a question will arise as to whether the promise should be enforced. Resolving such questions is the essence of contract law.

In the legal environment of business, questions and disputes concerning contracts arise daily. Although aspects of contract law vary from state to state, much of it is based on common law. In 1932, the American Law Institute compiled the Restatement of the Law of Contracts. This work is a nonstatutory, authoritative exposition of the present law on the subject of contracts. The Restatement is presently in its second edition and will be referred to throughout the following chapters on contracts.

❖ The Function of Contracts

PROMISE
A declaration that binds the person who makes it (promisor) to do or not to do a certain act. The person to whom the promise is made (promisee) has a right to expect or demand the performance of some particular thing.

PROMISEE
A person to whom a promise is made.

PROMISOR
A person who makes a promise.

Contract law assures the parties to private agreements that the **promises** they make will be enforceable. A promise is a declaration that something either will or will not happen in the future. Sometimes the promises exchanged create *moral* rather than *legal* obligations. Failure to perform a moral obligation, such as an agreement to take a friend to lunch, does not usually create a legal liability. Some promises may create both a moral and a legal obligation, such as a father's promise to pay for his daughter's college education.

Clearly, many promises are kept because of a sense of duty or because keeping them is in the mutual self-interest of the parties involved, not because the **promisor** (the person making the promise) or the **promisee** (the person to whom the promise is made) is conscious of the rules of contract law. Nevertheless, the rules of contract law are often followed in business agreements to avoid potential problems.

By supplying procedures for enforcing private agreements, contract law provides an essential condition for the existence of a market economy. Without a legal framework of reasonably assured expectations within which to plan and venture, businesspersons would be able to rely only on the good faith of others. Duty and good faith are usually sufficient, but when price changes or adverse economic factors make it costly to comply with a promise, these elements may not be enough. Contract law is necessary to ensure compliance with a promise or to entitle the innocent party to some form of relief.

"A promise made is a debt unpaid."

Robert William Service, 1874–1958
(Canadian writer and poet)

❖ Definition of a Contract

A **contract** is an agreement that can be enforced in a court of law or equity. It is formed by two or more parties who agree to perform or refrain from performing some act now or in the future. Generally, contract disputes arise when there is a promise of future performance. If the contractual promise is not fulfilled, the party who made it is subject to the sanctions of a court of law or equity (see Chapter 13). That party may be required to pay money damages for failing to perform; in limited instances, the party may be required to perform the promised act.

In determining whether a contract has been formed, the element of intent is of prime importance. In contract law, intent is determined by what is called the **objective theory of contracts,** not by the personal or subjective intent, or belief, of a party. The theory is that a party's intention to enter into a contract is judged by outward, objective facts as interpreted by a *reasonable* person, rather than by the party's own secret, subjective intentions. Objective facts include (1) what the party said when entering into the contract, (2) how the party acted or appeared, and (3) the circumstances surrounding the transaction. As will be discussed later in this chapter, in the section on express versus implied contracts, intent to form a contract may be manifested not only in words, oral or written, but also by conduct.

CONTRACT
A set of promises constituting an agreement between parties, giving each a legal duty to the other and also the right to seek a remedy for the breach of the promises/duties owed to each. The elements of an enforceable contract are competent parties, a proper or legal purpose, consideration (an exchange of promises/duties), and mutuality of agreement and of obligation.

OBJECTIVE THEORY OF CONTRACTS
The view taken by American law that contracting parties shall only be bound by terms that can actually be inferred from promises made. Contract law does not examine a contracting party's subjective intent or underlying motive.

❖ The Basic Requirements of a Contract

The following list describes the requirements of a contract. Each item will be explained more fully in the chapter indicated. Although we pair these requirements in subsequent chapters (for example, agreement and consideration are treated in Chapter 9), it is important to stress that each requirement is separate and independent. They are paired merely for reasons of space.

1. *Agreement.* An agreement includes an *offer* and an *acceptance.* One party must offer to enter into a legal agreement, and another party must accept the terms of the offer (Chapter 9).
2. *Consideration.* Any promises made by parties must be supported by legally sufficient and bargained-for *consideration* (something of value received or promised, to convince a person to make a deal) (Chapter 9).
3. *Contractual capacity.* Both parties entering into the contract must have the contractual *capacity* to do so; the law must recognize them as possessing characteristics that qualify them as competent parties (Chapter 10).
4. *Legality.* The contract's purpose must be to accomplish some goal that is *legal* and not against public policy (Chapter 10).
5. *Genuineness of assent.* The apparent consent of both parties must be *genuine* (Chapter 11).
6. *Form.* The contract must be in whatever *form* the law requires; for example, some contracts must be in writing to be enforceable (Chapter 11).

The first four items in this list are formally known as the *elements of a contract.* The last two are possible *defenses to the formation or the enforcement of a contract.*

Business Law in Action

Freedom of Contract

Cathy mails an offer to Lyle. Without opening the envelope and with no idea that the envelope contains an offer, Lyle mails to Cathy a letter that states, "I accept." Do they have a contract? Yes. Cathy could reasonably believe that Lyle had agreed to the offer, and under the objective theory of contracts, a party is bound by the reasonable impression that he or she creates. This example also illustrates that a party may be bound by something that he or she has not read. The basis for this rule is that no one could rely on a signed contract if the other party could avoid the transaction by arguing that he or she had not read the document.

Of course, as in other areas of the law, there are many exceptions to this rule. For example, if a document is illegible, it is easy to conclude that the party to whom it was offered could not have agreed to it. In many cases, parties have been held not to be bound by "fine print" on the ground that it was illegible. Even when a document is legible, some clause may be included in a way that makes it unlikely to come to the attention of the parties. In some cases, for example, parties have been held not to be bound by a contractual clause that was included as part of a letterhead or on the back of a document. Standard form contracts are also sometimes excepted from the rule. When a standard form contract is involved, a court will sometimes consider the fairness of the terms in determining whether the parties truly agreed to what the document says. Despite these and other exceptions, however, freedom of contract is a highly valued principle in American law. Thus, as a general rule, courts are reluctant to interfere with contracts that have been *voluntarily negotiated* between the parties.

In accordance with this principle, just as a failure to read a contract is often no defense to its enforcement, a failure to investigate the possible ramifications of a contract will receive little sympathy from judges. Consider the fate of John Beasley and Laverne Kintop. These two individuals purchased $33,333 worth of stock in a small corporation from Leone Medin based on Medin's oral representations of the corporation's worth and a one-page tax return. Beasley and Kintop later discovered that the corporation owed a number of debts, including back taxes, of which they had been unaware. They further learned that a bookkeeper had embezzled approximately $40,000 from the corporation. In short, they had entered into a bargain that was not what it seemed to be. When Beasley and Kintop sought to have the contract rescinded (canceled), however, the court refused. The court noted that both Beasley and Kintop were educated persons who should have had the foresight to investigate the corporation's accounts and financial status. The court held that "rescission is inappropriate in the absence of a reasonable investigation of the facts."[a]

In a sense, the precepts underlying contract law are similar to those involved in all areas of the law that you will read about in this book: people are expected to be responsible in their actions. In regard to contracts, this means that parties to contracts are expected to look after their own interests, and if they fail to do so, courts often may not lend a sympathetic ear to their pleadings.

a. *Beasley v. Medin*, 479 N.W.2d 95 (Minn.App. 1992).

❖ Types of Contracts

There are numerous types of contracts. The categories into which contracts are placed involve legal distinctions as to formation, enforceability, or performance. The best method of explaining each type of contract is to compare one type with another.

Bilateral versus Unilateral Contracts

OFFEROR
A person who makes an offer.

OFFEREE
A person to whom an offer is made.

BILATERAL CONTRACT
A contract that includes the exchange of a promise for a promise.

Every contract involves at least two parties. The **offeror** is the party making the offer. The **offeree** is the party to whom the offer is made. The offeror always promises to do or not to do something and thus is also a promisor. Whether the contract is classified as *unilateral* or *bilateral* depends on what the offeree must do to accept the offer and to bind the offeror to a contract.

If to accept the offer the offeree must only *promise* to perform, the contract is a **bilateral contract.** Hence, a bilateral contract is a "promise for a promise." No performance, such as the payment of money or delivery of goods, need take place

At what moment does a bilateral contract come into existence?

for a bilateral contract to be formed. The contract comes into existence at the moment the promises are exchanged. If the offer is phrased so that the offeree can accept only by completing the contract performance, the contract is a **unilateral contract.** Hence, a unilateral contract is a "promise for an act."

UNILATERAL CONTRACT
A contract that includes the exchange of a promise for an act (completion of the contract performance).

A classic example of a unilateral contract is as follows: Joe says to Celia, "If you walk across the Brooklyn Bridge, I'll give you $10." Joe promises to pay only if Celia walks the entire span of the bridge. Only upon Celia's complete crossing does she fully accept Joe's offer to pay $10. If she chooses not to undertake the walk, there are no legal consequences. Contests, lotteries, and other prize-winning competitions are also examples of offers for unilateral contracts. If a person complies with the rules of the contest—such as by submitting the right lottery number at the right place and time—a unilateral contract is formed, binding the organization offering the prize to a contract to perform as promised in the offer.

A problem arises in unilateral contracts when the promisor attempts to *revoke* (cancel) the offer after the promisee has begun performance but before the act has been completed. The promisee can accept the offer only upon full performance, and offers are normally *revocable* (capable of being taken back, or canceled) until accepted. The modern-day view, however, is that the offer becomes irrevocable once performance has begun. Thus, even though the offer has not yet been accepted, the offeror is prohibited from revoking it for a reasonable time period.

Suppose Roberta offers to buy Ed's sailboat, moored in San Francisco, upon delivery of the boat to Roberta's dock in Newport Beach, three hundred miles south of San Francisco. Ed rigs the boat and sets sail. Shortly before his arrival at Newport Beach, Ed receives a radio message from Roberta withdrawing her offer. Roberta's offer is part of a unilateral contract, and only Ed's delivery of the sailboat at her dock is an acceptance. Ordinarily, her revocation would terminate the offer, but because Ed had undertaken performance and sailed almost three hundred miles, under the modern-day view her offer is irrevocable. Ed can deliver the boat and bind Roberta to the contract.

Profile

Arthur L. Corbin (1874–1967)

Arthur Linton Corbin was born in 1874 in Cripple Creek, Colorado; he died in 1967 in New Haven, Connecticut. During the course of his long and productive career, Corbin became a preeminent scholar and leading authority in the field of American contract law. The fact that "Corbin on Contracts"—Corbin's treatise on contracts—is now a byword in the halls of law schools throughout the country testifies to his influence.

For nearly fifty years, Corbin was associated with the law school at Yale, first as a student and then as a member of the law faculty. During his many years there, he became widely respected not only for his superb teaching and scholarly abilities but also for the reforms he implemented to improve Yale's law school. He is credited with introducing the case method of teaching law, as well as creating a full-time law faculty and initiating new recruitment procedures to ensure a better-trained and more mature student body at Yale.

Throughout his life, Corbin fully embraced the view that legal principles, if they were to be appropriate and effective, should be flexible enough to adjust to a changing social context. Corbin didn't abandon legal rules (or *standards*, as he preferred to call them), but he believed that such standards should not be regarded as inflexible. Corbin stressed that although the formation and application of general principles are essential to the law, such principles can only be "tentative, working rules, the value of which depends upon the industry and the intelligence of the men who made them, and upon the changes in time and circumstance since they were made."[a]

Corbin's legal pragmatism, or practical approach to the law, is evident in his approach to contract law. The purpose of contract law, according to Corbin, is the "realization of reasonable expectations that have been induced by the making of a promise." What constitutes "reasonable expectations" necessarily depends on the prevailing customs in the society in which the promise was made. For this reason, Corbin felt that when faced with contractual disputes, judges should place the contract in question within its social context and should then look at the intention of the parties within that context before deciding whether a contract exists or has been breached. This "contextualization" of the law—emphasizing what is a reasonable action or expectation in a given set of circumstances—is at the heart of Corbin's methodology. The influence of this approach to contract law is evident in the first and second Restatements of the Law of Contracts and in Article 2 of the Uniform Commercial Code, projects on which he worked in an advisory capacity and that bear his imprint.

Corbin authored numerous treatises and books on contract law, the most outstanding and widely known being his six-volume treatise on the law of contracts. First published in 1950 and since revised, this opus has become a landmark in the development of American contract law.

a. Arthur L. Corbin, "Principles of Law and Their Evolution," 64 *Yale Law Journal* 8 (1954).

The problem of substantial performance in unilateral contracts often arises in the sale of real estate. A broker, for example, may invest substantial effort in finding a buyer for someone who has listed his or her property for sale and then learn that the seller is canceling the brokerage agreement.

Express versus Implied Contracts

EXPRESS CONTRACT
A contract that is oral and/or written (as opposed to an implied contract).

An **express contract** is one in which the terms of the agreement are fully and explicitly stated in words, oral or written. A signed lease for an apartment or a house is an express written contract. If a classmate calls you on the phone and agrees to buy your textbooks from last semester for $50, an express oral contract has been made.

A contract that is implied from the conduct of the parties is called an **implied-in-fact contract** or an implied contract. This type of contract differs from an express contract in that the *conduct* of the parties, rather than their words, creates and defines the terms of the contract. For example, suppose you need a tax consultant or an accountant to fill out your tax return this year. You look through the Yellow Pages and find both an accountant and a tax consultant at an office in your neighborhood, so you drop by to see them. You go into the office and explain your problem, and they tell you what their fees are. The next day you return, giving the secretary all the necessary information and documents, such as canceled checks, W-2 forms, and so on. You say nothing expressly to the secretary; rather, you walk out the door. Nonetheless, you have entered into an implied-in-fact contract to pay the tax consultant and accountant the usual and reasonable fees for their services. The contract is implied by your conduct and by their conduct. They expect to be paid for completing your tax return. By bringing in the records they will need to do the work, you have implied an intent to pay them.

IMPLIED-IN-FACT CONTRACT
A contract formed in whole or in part from the conduct of the parties (as opposed to an express contract).

The following three steps establish an implied-in-fact contract:

1. The plaintiff furnished some service or property.
2. The plaintiff expected to be paid for that service or property, and the defendant knew or should have known that payment was expected (by using the objective-theory-of-contracts test, discussed previously).
3. The defendant had a chance to reject the services or property and did not.

"Outward actions are a clue to hidden secrets."

(Legal maxim)

The court emphasizes in the following case that a contract can be implied by conduct as well as by express agreement.

Case 8.1
WELLER v. SPRING CREEK RESORT, INC.
Supreme Court of South Dakota, 1991.
477 N.W.2d 839.

HISTORICAL AND SOCIAL SETTING *At one time, when a plaintiff wanted to sue, he or she had to phrase the complaint very carefully, because if the facts as alleged did not fit a particular predefined* cause of action *(a situation or state of facts that entitles a party to judicial relief), the case would be thrown out of court. Sometimes, this strict requirement kept a plaintiff from obtaining any relief. Over time, the old causes of action were changed, and new causes of action were developed, to provide avenues for such plaintiffs to obtain relief. For example, in the early seventeenth century, when a buyer, at his or her request, received goods or services without expressly agreeing to the price, and he or she did not pay for the goods, there was no cause of action into which the seller could fit a complaint. A remedy for this problem developed later in the century when courts began to imply in these circumstances a promise to pay a* reasonable price. *This came to be known as a contract implied in fact.*

FACTS Richard and Darolyn Weller leased a marina mooring space for their houseboat at the Spring Creek Resort in 1988 and again in 1989, in which year Weller made improvements to the space. At the end of the 1989 season, Weller informed John Brakss, manager of Spring Creek Resort, that he wished to reserve the same mooring space for 1990. In January 1990, Weller learned that others who leased mooring spaces at Spring Creek had been informed that rent for the 1990 season should be paid by February 1, 1990. Weller then sent a check for the full amount of the rent to Brakss, who returned the check approximately two months later with the explanation that low water levels made it impossible to accommodate the Wellers' boat in 1990. The Wellers sued for damages, alleging, among other things, that Spring Creek Resort had breached an implied contract. The trial court dismissed the Wellers' complaint, on the ground that they had failed to state a claim. The Wellers appealed.

ISSUE Did the Wellers allege facts that could establish an implied-in-fact contract?

DECISION Yes. The Supreme Court of South Dakota determined that the trial court had erred in dismissing the implied-contract claim.

REASON The court pointed out that contracts can be either express—oral or written—or implied. The court defined an implied contract as a contract that is "manifested by conduct * * * [which] can be both acts and words.

Case 8.1—Continued

By its very nature, an implicit agreement is not as detailed as a written agreement formally negotiated." The court stated that a "contract is implied in fact where the intention as to it is not manifested by direct or explicit words by the parties, but is to be gathered by implication or proper deduction from the conduct of the parties, language used, or acts done by them." Although the Wellers had no express contract with Spring Creek Resort, the court concluded that the question of whether an implied contract existed was one that should be resolved at a trial or by summary judgment.

Quasi Contracts—Contracts Implied in Law

QUASI CONTRACT
An obligation or contract imposed by law, in the absence of agreement, to prevent unjust enrichment. Sometimes referred to as an implied-in-law contract (a legal fiction) to distinguish it from an implied-in-fact contract.

Quasi contracts, or contracts *implied in law,* are wholly different from actual contracts. Express contracts and implied-in-fact contracts are actual, or true, contracts. Quasi contracts, as their name suggests, are not true contracts. They do not arise from any agreement, express or implied, between the parties themselves. Rather, quasi contracts are fictional contracts imposed on parties by courts in the interests of fairness and justice. Quasi contracts are therefore equitable, rather than contractual, in nature. Usually, quasi contracts are imposed to avoid the *unjust enrichment* of one party at the expense of another.

Examples of Quasi Contracts Suppose Larrissa enters into a contract with Pavel, agreeing to work for Pavel for one year. At the end of the year, Larrissa is to be paid $18,000. Larrissa works for ten months and then leaves voluntarily, without cause. Pavel refuses to pay her for the ten months she worked, so Larrissa sues in quasi contract for the value of services rendered. Will the court allow Larrissa to recover her salary for the ten months worked? Very likely, yes—minus any damages caused to Pavel by her early departure.[1]

"A legal fiction is always consistent with equity."

(Legal maxim)

In another example, a vacationing doctor is driving down the highway and comes upon Emerson lying unconscious on the side of the road. The doctor renders medical aid that saves Emerson's life. Although the injured, unconscious Emerson did not solicit the medical aid and was not aware that the aid had been rendered, Emerson received a valuable benefit, and the requirements for a quasi contract were fulfilled. In such a situation, the law will impose a quasi contract, and Emerson will have to pay the doctor for the reasonable value of the medical services rendered. The following case emphasizes the function of quasi contracts in preventing unjust enrichment.

Case 8.2
DRS. LAVES, SAREWITZ AND WALKO v. BRIGGS
Superior Court of New Jersey, 1992.
259 N.J.Super. 368,
613 A.2d 506.

HISTORICAL AND SOCIAL SETTING *In many situations, there is no doubt that a party has been unjustly enriched, but it is difficult or impossible to find a promise. Such situations resemble those in which there is contractual liability, but in the early years of the law, there was no cause of action to fit obligations arising from situations of this kind. As the law developed, courts began to allow a plaintiff who alleged such an obligation to file a claim that included a fictional promise. By this means, a noncontractual obligation came to be treated as if it were a contract. Such contracts came to be known as contracts implied in law, or quasi contracts.*

FACTS Garris Briggs died on October 11, 1990, leaving $782 in unpaid medical bills. Following his death, insurance checks in the amount of $676.72, payable to Briggs, were sent to his widow, Beatrice Briggs. The Briggses had been living apart for the previous five years and during that time had not had any financial connections. Under state law, a surviving spouse, upon the execution of an affidavit before

1. *Britton v. Turner,* 6 N.H. 481 (1834).

Case 8.2—Continued

the appropriate county official, was entitled to all of the estate's assets without administration, and the assets of the estate up to $5,000 were free from all debts of the decedent. Garris Briggs's estate was worth less than $5,000, so Beatrice Briggs signed the necessary affidavit, cashed the checks, and deposited the funds. The physicians who had provided medical services for Garris Briggs sued the widow to recover the insurance proceeds. The widow claimed that because she had not lived with her husband for five years, she should not be liable for his debts.

ISSUE Should the physicians be allowed to recover the insurance proceeds from Beatrice Briggs?

DECISION Yes. The court held that to allow the widow to keep the funds, which were intended to cover the husband's medical expenses, would constitute unjust enrichment.

REASON The court first expressed its view that the state legislature, when drafting the law exempting the first $5,000 of a decedent's estate from the satisfaction of the decedent's debts, did not intend insurance proceeds paid with a specific purpose in mind to be included as "assets of the estate." Because the insurance proceeds were issued as a direct result of the services provided to Briggs by the physicians, the court held that "it is only just and fair that they be used for their intended purpose; that result is mandated by good conscience and fairness." The court pointed out that the doctrine of unjust enrichment, on which quasi-contractual obligations are frequently based, "rests on the equitable principle that a person shall not be allowed to enrich himself unjustly at the expense of another." In this case, the judge concluded that it was "disingenuous for defendant to have claimed that she is not liable because the marriage was not viable, and at the same time claim to be entitled to the proceeds of the insurance because she was the widow in fact of decedent. It is certain to me that she should have used these funds for the purpose for which they were issued. Otherwise, she will have been unjustly enriched, at the expense of plaintiffs, by an interpretation of a statute that I find the legislature did not contemplate."

ETHICAL CONSIDERATIONS *A question that goes to the heart of the doctrine of quasi contracts could be phrased as follows: "Of all the benefits that people confer, for which ones should the law allow recovery, and why?" Is the mere fact that a person confers a benefit on another enough to require the other to pay? For example, a property owner who improves her property benefits her neighbors to some extent, but should she be entitled to payment from them? Ordinarily, to obtain relief under the doctrine of quasi contract, there must be a type of trade-off—a benefit to one party and a loss to the other.*

A Limitation on Quasi Contracts Although quasi contracts exist to prevent unjust enrichment, situations exist in which the party obtaining the unjust enrichment is not liable. Basically, the quasi-contractual principle cannot be invoked by the party who has conferred a benefit on someone else unnecessarily or as a result of misconduct or negligence. Consider the following example. You take your car to the local car wash and ask to have it run through the washer and to have the gas tank filled. While it is being washed, you go to a nearby shopping center for two hours. In the meantime, one of the workers at the car wash has mistakenly believed that your car is the one that he is supposed to hand wax. When you come back, you are presented with a bill for a full tank of gas, a wash job, and a hand wax. Clearly, a benefit has been conferred on you. But this benefit has been conferred because of a mistake by the car wash employee. You have not been *unjustly* enriched under these circumstances. People cannot normally be forced to pay for benefits "thrust" upon them.

The doctrine of quasi contract generally cannot be used when there is an actual contract that covers the area in controversy. For example, Martinez contracts with Stevenson to deliver a furnace to a building project owned by Richards. Martinez delivers the furnace, but Stevenson never pays Martinez. Stevenson has been unjustly enriched in this situation, to be sure. But Martinez cannot collect from Richards in quasi contract because Martinez had an existing contract with Stevenson. Martinez already has a remedy—he can sue for breach of contract to recover the price of the furnace from Stevenson. No quasi contract need be imposed by the court in this instance to achieve justice.

In the following case, the court refused to allow recovery in quasi contract because an express contract covering the area in controversy already existed.

Case 8.3 

INDUSTRIAL LIFT TRUCK SERVICE CORP. v. MITSUBISHI INTERNATIONAL CORP.

Appellate Court of Illinois,
First District, Fourth Division, 1982.
104 Ill.App.3d 357,
432 N.E.2d 999,
60 Ill.Dec. 100.

HISTORICAL AND SOCIAL BACKGROUND *Quasi contracts have sometimes been applied in contractual contexts. But these contexts usually involve valid contracts that are unenforceable. Of course, an agreement may be unenforceable because its terms are too indefinite, because each party has a different reasonable understanding of the agreement, or because the agreement is illegal. A contract, however, may be unenforceable because it is not in the correct form; because it involves fraud, duress, mistake, or incapacity; or because of other circumstances that allow a contract to be avoided. In none of the situations in which the doctrine of quasi contract is applied, however, is there an enforceable contract covering the area in controversy.*

FACTS In 1973 and again in 1976, an agreement was executed between Industrial Lift Truck Service Corporation (IL) and Mitsubishi International Corporation calling for IL to purchase forklift trucks from Mitsubishi and to use its best efforts to service and sell the trucks. The agreement also allowed Mitsubishi to terminate the agreement without just cause by giving ninety days' notice. From 1973 to 1977, IL allegedly became the nation's largest dealer of Mitsubishi forklift trucks. During this period, IL made design changes in the trucks to better suit the American market, design changes that Mitsubishi did not request but later incorporated into the trucks it sold to other dealers. In 1978, Mitsubishi terminated the agreement. IL sued under quasi-contract principles to recover the benefits conferred upon Mitsubishi by the design changes. The suit was dismissed, and IL appealed.

ISSUE Could IL's quasi-contractual claim overcome the written contract attesting to the companies' relationship?

DECISION No. The appellate court affirmed the lower court's dismissal, holding that the written contract between the parties defined their entire relationship.

REASON The court reasoned that, in the absence of a valid amendment to the agreement, Mitsubishi had a right to assume that it did not have to compensate IL for any acts performed in relation to the subject matter of the contract except in accordance with the express provisions of the contract. The court characterized a contract implied in law (a quasi contract) as "fictitious and arising by implication of law wholly apart from the usual rules" of contract formation. At times, the court said, when one party confers a benefit on another party and the other party accepts the benefit, the law will impose a duty on the benefited party to pay for the services—provided the benefit was not intended as a gift. But when there is already a written contract concerning the same subject matter, the usual rule is that no quasi-contractual claim can arise. In this case, IL understood the terms of the existing contract, and it knew the risks involved in initiating the design changes it made. The court found that IL, by suing, attempted to unilaterally circumvent the contract it had freely entered into. The contract controlled the relationship between the parties, and the suit had to be dismissed.

ETHICAL CONSIDERATIONS *This case clearly illustrates a basic principle of contract law: courts generally hold parties to their contractual promises, even though one of the parties may feel that being held to the terms of a contract in some situations is unfair. As mentioned in this chapter's* Business Law in Action, *exceptions to this principle are sometimes made, but it is important to realize that such exceptions are rare.*

FORMAL CONTRACTS
Agreement or contract that by law requires for its validity a specific form, such as executed under seal.

Formal versus Informal Contracts

Formal contracts require a special form or method of creation (formation) to be enforceable. They include (1) contracts under seal, (2) recognizances, (3) negotiable instruments, and (4) letters of credit.[2] *Contracts under seal* are formalized writings

2. Restatement (Second) of Contracts, Section 6.

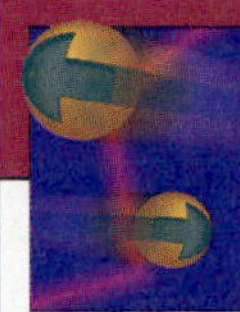

Ethical Perspective

The Equitable Remedy of Quasi Contract

Quasi contracts, often referred to as contracts implied in law, arise to establish justice and fairness. The term *quasi contract* is misleading because a quasi contract is not really a contract at all. It does not arise from any agreement between two individuals. Rather, a court imposes a quasi contract on the parties when justice so requires. Quasi contracts are used to prevent unjust enrichment. The doctrine of unjust enrichment is based on the theory that individuals should not be allowed to profit or enrich themselves inequitably at the expense of others. This belief is fundamental in our society and is clearly inspired by ethical considerations.

A typical situation in which a court, as a matter of judicial policy, may impose a quasi contract on the parties arises when one person who normally renders emergency services for a fee provides those services to another person without first entering into a contract. In these circumstances, courts generally allow the person who renders the emergency services to recover in quasi contract the reasonable fee for his or her services. This recovery is allowed even though the parties never entered into a contract.

We have said previously in this text that ethical issues generally involve a trade-off in one form or another. What trade-off is involved here? Obviously, by imposing contractual obligations on persons who did not freely enter into those obligations, the government, by way of the courts, is interfering with the personal freedom of individuals to contract as they wish and to be responsible for *only* those obligations that they freely undertake. To a certain extent, when quasi-contractual remedies are granted, this freedom is sacrificed to attain greater justice and fairness by preventing unjust enrichment by one person at the expense of others.

with a special seal attached.[3] The significance of the seal has lessened, although about ten states require no consideration when a contract is under seal. A *recognizance* is an acknowledgment in court by a person that he or she will perform some specified obligation, or pay a certain sum if he or she fails to perform. One form of recognizance is the surety bond.[4] Another is the personal recognizance bond used as bail in a criminal matter. Negotiable instruments and letters of credit are special methods of payment designed for use in many commercial settings (they are discussed at length in subsequent chapters). *Negotiable instruments* include checks, notes, drafts, and certificates of deposit. *Letters of credit* are agreements to pay contingent on the purchaser's receipt of invoices and bills of lading (documents evidencing receipt of, and title to, goods shipped).

Informal contracts (also called *simple contracts*) include all other contracts. No special form is required (except for certain types of contracts that must be in writing), as the contracts are usually based on their substance rather than on their form.

INFORMAL CONTRACTS
Contracts that do not require a specified form or formality for validity.

Executed versus Executory Contracts

EXECUTED CONTRACT
A contract that has been completely performed by both parties.

Contracts are also classified according to their state of performance. A contract that has been fully performed on both sides is called an **executed contract.** A contract that has not been fully performed on either side is called an **executory contract.** If one party has fully performed but the other has not, the contract is said to be executed on the one side and executory on the other, but the contract is still clas-

EXECUTORY CONTRACT
A contract that has not as yet been fully performed.

3. A seal may be actual (made of wax or some other durable substance) or impressed on the paper or indicated simply by the word *seal* or the letters *L.S.* at the end of the document. *L.S.* stands for *locus sigilli* and means "the place for the seal."

4. An obligation of a party guaranteeing that a second party will be paid if a third party does not perform.

Landmark in the Law

Plain-Language Laws

Compare the following sentence from a Citibank loan agreement:

> In the event of default in the payment of this or any other Obligation or the performance or observance of any term or covenant contained herein or in any note or other contract or agreement evidencing or relating to any Obligation or any Collateral on the Borrower's part to be performed or observed, or the undersigned Borrower shall die; or any of the undersigned become insolvent or make an assignment for the benefit of creditors; or a petition shall be filed by or against any of the undersigned under any provision of the Bankruptcy Act; or any money, securities, or property of the undersigned now or hereafter on deposit with or in the possession or under the control of the Bank shall be attached or become subject to distraint proceedings or any order or process of any court, or the Bank shall deem itself to be insecure, then . . .

with this:

> Default
> 1. If I don't pay an installment on time; or
> 2. If any other creditor tries by legal process to take any money of mine in your possession . . .[a]

The difference is obvious: one statement is in "legalese" and the other is in "plain English." Citibank's use of the plain-language version in loan agreements has led to fewer *defaults* (failures to pay) by borrowers.

Plain language is increasingly being required in contracts and for good reason: parties to contracts cannot genuinely assent to contractual terms that they do not understand. By 1980, the federal government and at least half the states were attempting to regulate legal writing through statutes and administrative regulations. In the last decade or so, plain-language laws have been introduced at the state level to enable the average consumer to read and understand the terms of form contracts and the like without having to obtain professional assistance. These bills and laws deal with private contracts in their entirety and attempt to reach a broad variety of consumer agreements relating to personal, family, and household matters, including residential leases.

The New York and Connecticut plain-language statutes, which have strongly influenced the plain-language laws adopted by other states, illustrate how such statutes address the language problem. In New York, an agreement must be (1) "written in a clear and coherent manner using words with common and everyday meanings" and (2) "appropriately divided and captioned by its various sections."[b] Minnesota, West Virginia, and the Virgin Islands all have similar statutes. In Connecticut, an agreement must be "written in plain language." The test of

a. As quoted in Scott J. Burnham, "The Hazards of Using Plain English: A New Look at Contracts," *The Compleat Lawyer*, Summer 1991, pp. 46–47.

b. N.Y. Gen. Oblig. Law, Section 5–702.

sified as executory. For example, assume you agree to buy ten tons of coal from the Western Coal Company. Further assume that Western has delivered the coal to your steel mill, where it is now being burned. At this point, the contract is executed on the part of Western and executory on your part. After you pay Western for the coal, the contract will be executed on both sides.

Valid, Void, Voidable, and Unenforceable Contracts

VALID CONTRACT
A properly constituted contract having legal strength or force.

VOID CONTRACT
A contract having no legal force or binding effect.

VOIDABLE CONTRACT
A contract that may be legally annulled at the option of one of the parties.

A **valid contract** has the elements necessary to entitle at least one of the parties to enforce it in court. Those elements consist of (1) an offer and an acceptance (2) supported by legally sufficient consideration (3) for a legal purpose and (4) made by parties who have the legal capacity to enter into the contract. Each element is discussed in detail in the following chapters.

A **void contract** is no contract at all. The terms *void* and *contract* are contradictory. A void contract produces no legal obligations on the part of any of the parties. For example, a contract can be void because one of the parties was adjudged by a court to be legally insane or because the purpose of the contract was illegal.

A **voidable contract** is a *valid* contract, but one that can be avoided at the option of one or both of the parties. The party having the option can elect either to avoid any duty to perform or to *ratify* (make valid) the contract. If the contract is avoided, plain language is as follows: Does the agreement contain everyday words that are "written and organized in a clear and coherent manner," use "short sentences and paragraphs," employ "simple and active verb forms," and refer to parties in the contract by "personal pronouns, the . . . names of the parties . . . or both" (but not as "parties")? If so, then the language has met the statutory test.

What if a party—say, an insurance company—violates a plain-language statute? Is the contract void? Not necessarily, particularly if the defendant has made a good faith effort to comply with the statute. Indeed, in Minnesota and New Jersey, the statutes allow proposed contracts to be submitted to the state attorney general, whose approval then eliminates any liability for damages because of supposed violation of the plain-language statute.

There is little doubt that the use of plain language in contracts is beneficial. But it is also possible that some of the meaning and clarity of a traditional legal phrase may be lost in the translation from legalese to plain language. A good example of this problem arose in a recent case when a borrower, Linda Wetzel, pledged her new Nissan 300ZX as security for a $20,000 loan from a credit union. The car also secured a prior loan and two later loans. As will be discussed in Chapter 21, it is not uncommon for a creditor to secure several loans, including loans to be made in the future, with the same collateral (in this case, Wetzel's car) and with just one writing covering the agreement. Traditional wording in such agreements states that the borrower promises to pay "all obligations now existing and hereafter incurred." The credit union in this case, however, had substituted plainer language for those terms. Its agreement stated that Wetzel's car would serve as security "to make sure I pay back this loan and meet all of my obligations to you at any time."

Later, a bankruptcy court declared that the agreement only secured the $20,000 loan, and because that loan was nearly paid, the credit union was not allowed to foreclose on (take possession of and sell) the car to satisfy the debt. The court held that the writing was not "clear and unambiguous," as security agreements were required to be under state law, because it was not clear from the agreement whether the car secured any other loans. The problem would not have existed if the traditional phrase ("all obligations now existing and hereafter incurred") had been used.[c]

c. *In re Wetzel,* 134 Bankr. 718 (Bankr. W.D.N.Y. 1992).

both parties are released from it. If it is ratified, both parties must fully perform their respective legal obligations.

As a general rule, but subject to exceptions, contracts made by minors are voidable at the option of the minor (see Chapter 10). Contracts entered into under fraudulent conditions are voidable at the option of the defrauded party. In addition, contracts entered into under legally defined duress or undue influence are voidable (see Chapter 11).

UNENFORCEABLE CONTRACT
A valid contract having no legal effect or force in a court action.

An **unenforceable contract** is one that cannot be enforced because of certain legal defenses against it. It is not unenforceable because a party failed to satisfy a legal requirement of the contract; rather, it is a valid contract rendered unenforceable by some statute or law. For example, certain contracts must be in writing (see Chapter 11), and if they are not, they will not be enforceable except in certain exceptional circumstances.

❖ Interpretation of Contracts

Common law rules of contract interpretation have evolved over time to provide the courts with guidelines for determining the meaning of, and giving effect to, contracts.

The Plain Meaning Rule

When the writing is clear and unequivocal, a court will enforce it according to its plain terms, and there is no need for the court to interpret the language of the contract. The meaning of the terms must be determined from *the face of the instrument*—from the written document alone. This is sometimes referred to as the *plain meaning rule.* Under this rule, if a contract's words appear to be clear and unambiguous, a court cannot consider *extrinsic evidence,* which is any evidence not contained in the document itself. Admissibility of such evidence can significantly affect how a court may interpret ambiguous contractual provisions and thus the outcome of litigation.

Other Rules of Interpretation

When the writing contains ambiguous or unclear terms, a court will interpret the language to give effect to the parties' intent *as expressed in their contract.* This is the primary purpose of the rules of interpretation—to determine the parties' intent from the language used in their agreement and to give effect to that intent. A court normally will not make or remake a contract, nor will it normally interpret the language according to what the parties *claim* their intent was when they made it. The following rules are used by the courts in interpreting ambiguous contractual terms:

1. Insofar as possible, a reasonable, lawful, and effective meaning will be given to all of a contract's terms.
2. A contract will be interpreted as a whole; individual, specific clauses will be considered subordinate to the contract's general intent. All writings that are a part of the same transaction will be interpreted together.
3. Terms that were the subject of separate negotiation will be given greater consideration than standardized terms and terms that were not negotiated separately.
4. A word will be given its ordinary, commonly accepted meaning, and a technical word or term will be given its technical meaning, unless the parties clearly intended something else.
5. Specific and exact wording will be given greater consideration than general language.
6. Written or typewritten terms prevail over preprinted ones.
7. Because a contract should be drafted in clear and unambiguous language, a party who uses ambiguous expressions is held to be responsible for the ambiguities. Thus, when the language has more than one meaning, it will be interpreted against the party who drafted the contract.
8. Evidence of trade usage, prior dealing, and course of performance may be admitted to clarify the meaning of an ambiguously worded contract. (These terms are defined and discussed in Chapter 14.) In such cases, what each of the parties does in pursuance of the contract will be interpreted as consistent with what the other does and with any relevant usage of trade and course of dealing or performance. In these circumstances, express terms are given the greatest weight, followed by course of performance, course of dealing, and usage of trade—in that order. When considering custom and usage, a court will look at the trade customs and usage common to the particular business or industry and to the locale in which the contract was made or is to be performed.

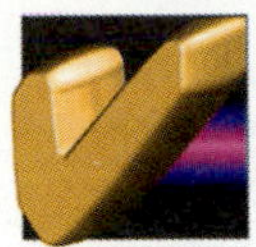

Application

Law and the Employer—Avoiding Unintended Employment Contracts

Employers have learned many lessons from court decisions. In recent years, for example, the message is becoming clear that promises made in an employment manual may create an implied-in-fact employment contract. If an employment handbook contains a statement that employees will be fired only for specific causes, the employer may be held to that "promise." Even if, by state law, employment is "at will"—that is, the employer is allowed to hire and fire employees at will, with or without cause—the at-will doctrine will not apply if the terms of employment are subject to a contract between the employer and employee. If a court holds that an implied employment contract exists, on the basis of promises made in an employment manual in effect, the employment is no longer at will. The employer will be bound by the contract and liable for damages for breaching the contract.

Employers who wish to avoid potential liability for breaching unintended employment contracts should therefore make it clear to employees that the policies expressed in an employment manual are not to be interpreted as contractual promises. One way to do this is to inform employees, when initially giving them the handbook or discussing its contents with them, that it is not intended as a contract. Even more effective in warding off potential contractual liability is the inclusion of a disclaimer to that effect in the employment application. The disclaimer might read as follows: "I understand and agree that, if hired, my employment is for no definite period and may be terminated at any time without any prior notice." Care should be taken to make the disclaimer clear and prominent so that the applicant cannot later claim that it was the employer's fault that he or she did not see the disclaimer. A disclaimer will be clear and prominent if it is set off from the surrounding text by the use of larger type, a different color, all capital letters, or some other device that calls the reader's attention to it.

In the handbook, the employer should avoid making definite promises that employees will be fired only for cause, or that they will not be fired after they have worked for a certain length of time except for certain reasons, or the like. A clear and prominent disclaimer of contractual liability for the contents of the handbook should also be included within the handbook itself.

Checklist for the Employer

- ☐ 1. Inform new employees that statements in an employment handbook are not intended as contractual terms.
- ☐ 2. Include a clear and prominent disclaimer to this effect in employment applications.
- ☐ 3. Avoid including in the handbook any definite promises relating to job security.
- ☐ 4. Include in the handbook a clear and prominent disclaimer of contractual liability for any statements made within it.
- ☐ 5. Last but not least: check with your attorney concerning your state's employment laws.

❖ Key Terms

bilateral contract 204
contract 203
executed contract 211
executory contract 211
express contract 206
formal contract 210
implied-in-fact contract 207
informal contract 211
objective theory of contracts 203
offeree 204
offeror 204
promise 202
promisee 202
promisor 202
quasi contract 208
unenforceable contract 213
unilateral contract 205
valid contract 212
void contract 212
voidable contract 212

❖ Chapter Summary: Nature and Classification

Contract Requirements	1. *Agreement.* 2. *Consideration.* 3. *Contractual capacity.* 4. *Legality.* — *Elements of a contract.* 5. *Genuineness of assent.* 6. *Form.* — *Possible defenses to the enforcement of a contract.*
Contract Formation	1. *Bilateral*—A promise for a promise. 2. *Unilateral*—A promise for an act (acceptance is the completed performance of the act). 3. *Express*—Formed by words (oral, written, or a combination). 4. *Implied in fact*—Formed by the conduct of the parties. 5. *Quasi contract* (implied in law)—Imposed by law to prevent unjust enrichment. 6. *Formal*—Requires a special form for creation. 7. *Informal*—Requires no special form for creation.
Performance	1. *Executed*—A fully performed contract. 2. *Executory*—A contract not fully performed.
Enforceability	1. *Valid*—The contract has the necessary contractual elements of offer and acceptance, consideration, parties with legal capacity, and it is made for a legal purpose. 2. *Void*—No contract exists or there is a contract without legal obligations. 3. *Voidable*—One party has the option of avoiding or enforcing the contractual obligation. 4. *Unenforceable*—A contract exists, but it cannot be enforced because of a legal defense.
Interpretation of Contracts	When the terms of a contract are unambiguous, a court will enforce the contract according to its plain terms, the meaning of which must be determined from the written document alone. When the terms of a contract are ambiguous, the following rules are used by the courts in interpreting the terms: 1. A reasonable, lawful, and effective meaning will be given to all contract terms. 2. A contract will be interpreted as a whole, specific clauses will be considered subordinate to the contract's general intent, and all writings that are a part of the same transaction will be interpreted together. 3. Terms that were negotiated separately will be given greater consideration than standardized terms and terms not negotiated separately. 4. Words will be given their commonly accepted meaning and technical words their technical meaning, unless the parties clearly intended otherwise. 5. Specific wording will be given greater consideration than general language. 6. Written or typewritten terms prevail over preprinted terms. 7. A party who uses ambiguous expressions is held to be responsible for the ambiguities. 8. Evidence of prior dealing, course of performance, or usage of trade is admissible to clarify an ambiguously worded contract. In these circumstances, express terms are given the greatest weight, followed by course of performance, course of dealing, and usage of trade—in that order.

❖ Questions and Case Problems

8-1. Contract Requirements. What are the basic elements necessary to the formation of a contract?

8-2. Implied Contracts. What is the difference between a contract implied in fact and a contract implied in law?

8-3. Contractual Promises. Rosalie, a wealthy widow, invited an acquaintance, Jonathan, to her home for dinner. Jonathan accepted the offer and, eager to please her, spent lavishly preparing for the evening. His purchases included a new blazer, new shoes, an expensive floral arrangement, and champagne. On the appointed evening, Jonathan arrived at Rosalie's house only to find that she had left for the evening. Jonathan wants to sue Rosalie to recover some of his expenses. Can he? Why or why not?

8-4. Contract Classification. Jennifer says to her neighbor, Gordon, "If you mow my lawn, I'll pay you $25." Gordon orally accepts her offer. Is there a contract? Is it a bilateral or unilateral contract? What is the legal significance of the distinction?

8-5. Contract Classification. High-Flying Advertising, Inc., contracted with Big Burger Restaurants to fly an advertisement above the Connecticut beaches. The advertisement offered $5,000 to any person who could swim from the Connecticut beaches to Long Island across Long Island Sound in less than a day. McElfresh saw the streamer and accepted the challenge. He started his marathon swim that same day at 10 A.M. After he had been swimming for four hours and was about halfway across the sound, McElfresh saw another plane pulling a streamer that read: "Big Burger revokes." Is there a contract between McElfresh and Big Burger? If there is a contract, what type(s) of contract is (are) formed?

8-6. Enforceable versus Unenforceable Contracts. Financial & Real Estate Consulting Co. (Financial) contracted with Regional Properties, Inc. (Regional), to sell to investors limited partnership interests (ownership interests) in some ventures being undertaken by Regional. Regional promised to pay Financial for its brokerage services. Financial sold a number of partnership interests and had been paid the stipulated fee for some (but not all) of the sales. Regional later discovered that Financial was not registered with the Securities and Exchange Commission as a broker-dealer, as required by law. Regional brought an action before the court to rescind (cancel) the contract with Financial. Financial counterclaimed for the unpaid fees. Is the contract between Financial and Regional enforceable? Why or why not? [*Regional Properties, Inc. v. Financial & Real Estate Consulting Co.*, 678 F.2d 552 (5th Cir. 1982)]

8-7. Equitable Doctrines. Ashton Co., which was engaged in a construction project, leased a crane from Artukovich & Sons, Inc., and hired the Reliance Truck Co. to deliver the crane to the construction site. Reliance, while the crane was in its possession and without permission from either Ashton or Artukovich, used the crane to install a transformer for a utility company, which paid Reliance for the job. Reliance then delivered the crane to the Ashton construction site at the appointed time of delivery. When Artukovich learned of the unauthorized use of the crane by Reliance, it sued Reliance for damages. What equitable doctrine could be used as a basis for awarding damages to Artukovich? [*Artukovich & Sons, Inc. v. Reliance Truck Co.*, 126 Ariz. 246, 614 P.2d 327 (1980)]

8-8. Bilateral versus Unilateral Contracts. William Greene began working for Grant Building, Inc., in 1959. Greene allegedly agreed to work at a pay rate below union scale in exchange for a promise that Grant would employ him "for life." In 1975, Oliver Realty, Inc., took over the management of Grant Building. Oliver Realty's president assured former Grant employees that existing employment contracts would be honored. During that same year, Greene explained the terms of his agreement to an Oliver Realty supervisor. The supervisor stated that he would look into the matter but never got back to Greene. After twenty-four years of service, Greene was fired by the new owners of the business. Greene sued Oliver Realty for breach of a unilateral contract. Discuss fully whether Greene and Oliver Realty had a unilateral contract. [*Greene v. Oliver Realty, Inc.*, 363 Pa.Super. 534, 526 A.2d 1192 (1987)]

8-9. Equitable Doctrines. Sosa Crisan, an eighty-seven-year-old widow, collapsed while shopping at a local grocery store. The Detroit police took her to the Detroit city hospital by ambulance. She was admitted, and she remained there fourteen days. Then she was transferred to another hospital, at which she died some eleven months later. Crisan had never regained consciousness after her collapse at the grocery store. After she died, the city of Detroit sued her estate to recover the expenses of both the ambulance that took her to the Detroit city hospital and the expenses of her Detroit city hospital stay. Is there a contract between Sosa Crisan and the Detroit city hospital? If so, how much can the hospital recover? [*In re Estate of Crisan*, 362 Mich. 569, 107 N.W.2d 907 (1961)]

8-10. Bilateral versus Unilateral Contracts. Nichols is the principal owner of Samuel Nichols, Inc., a real estate firm. Nichols signed an exclusive brokerage agreement with Molway to find a purchaser for Molway's property within ninety days. This type of agreement entitles the broker to a commission if the property is sold to any purchaser to whom the property is shown during the ninety-day period. Molway tried to cancel the brokerage agreement before the ninety-day term had expired. Nichols had already advertised the property, put up a "for sale" sign, and shown the property to prospective buyers. Molway claimed that the brokerage contract was unilateral and that she could cancel at any time before Nichols found a buyer. Nichols claimed the contract was bilateral and that Molway's cancellation breached the contract. Discuss who should prevail at trial. [*Samuel Nichols, Inc. v. Molway*, 25 Mass.App. 913, 515 N.E.2d 598 (1987)]

8-11. Implied Contracts. Weichert Co. Realtors sought damages from Thomas Ryan and his partner because they refused to pay a commission to William Tackaberry, one of Weichert's agents, for work done on a sale of property. Tackaberry had contacted Ryan about the property and subsequently met with him to discuss the sale. At that time and during subsequent discussions, Tackaberry informed Ryan that his commission was to be 10 percent of the purchase price of the property, payable at closing. Despite Tackaberry's continued efforts to get Ryan to sign a letter that spelled out the terms of the commission, Ryan refused to sign it. Ryan offered several times to negotiate with Tackaberry the amount and terms of the commission, but Tackaberry insisted that his commission must be 10 percent of the final price and that it was due at closing. When the deal was finalized, Weichert sent Ryan and his partner a bill for Tackaberry's commission. When the bill remained unpaid, Weichert filed suit for breach of an implied-in-fact contract or, failing that, for quasi-contractual recovery. Did an implied-in-fact contract exist between Tackaberry and Ryan? If not, could Weichert recover in quasi contract for the value of Tackaberry's services? What should the court decide? [*Weichert v. Ryan*, 128 N.J. 427, 608 A.2d 280 (1992)]

A QUESTION OF ETHICS AND SOCIAL RESPONSIBILITY

8-12. *In 1982, in the closing days of Minnesota's gubernatorial campaign, Dan Cohen offered a reporter from the* Minneapolis Star and Tribune *some "documents which may or may not relate to a candidate in the upcoming election." Cohen, who was actively promoting one of the gubernatorial candidates, agreed to give the reporter the documents—copies of two public court records of a rival party's candidate for lieutenant governor—if the reporter promised not to reveal the source of the information. The reporter promised to keep the source confidential. The editor of the* Tribune, *however, in spite of the reporter's objections, decided to name Cohen as the source of the information so as not to mislead the public into thinking that the information came from an unbiased source. On the day the newspaper article was published, Cohen was fired by his employer. Cohen sued the newspaper's owner, Cowles Media Co., for breach of contract. Given these facts, discuss the following questions.* [Cohen v. Cowles Media Co., *501 U.S. 663, 111 S.Ct. 2513, 115 L.Ed.2d 586 (1991).*]

1. Do you think that the editor's ethical duty to provide the reading public with unbiased news coverage should have overridden the editor's ethical duty to honor the reporter's promise to Cohen?
2. Did the reporter's promise to keep Cohen's identity confidential create solely an ethical obligation or a contract enforceable in a court of law?
3. If the court decides that an enforceable contract was formed between Cohen and the reporter, would the decision be counter to society's valuation—as expressed in the First Amendment to the Constitution—that freedom of the press should not be constrained?

FOR CRITICAL ANALYSIS

8-13. *Review the list of basic requirements for contract formation given at the beginning of this chapter. In view of those requirements, analyze the relationship entered into when a student enrolls in a college or university. Has a contract been formed? If so, is it a bilateral contract or a unilateral contract? Discuss.*

Chapter 9

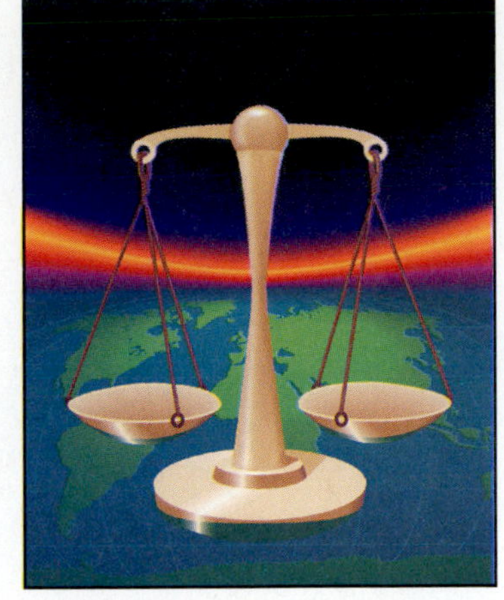

Agreement and Consideration

"It is necessity that makes laws, and force that makes them observed."

Voltaire (1749–1832)
(French writer)

Voltaire's statement that it is "necessity that makes laws" is certainly true in regard to contracts. In the introduction to this unit, we pointed out that life as we know it would be unthinkable without contracts. This is because promises and agreements, and the knowledge that certain of those promises and agreements will be legally enforced, are essential to civilized society. The homes we live in, the food we eat, the clothes we wear, the cars we drive, the books we read, the recordings we listen to—all of these have been purchased through contractual agreements that we have made with sellers. Contract law developed over time, through the common law tradition, to meet society's need to know with certainty the kinds of promises, or contracts, that will be enforced and the point at which a valid and binding contract is formed.

For a contract to be considered valid and enforceable, the four requirements listed in Chapter 8 must be met. In this chapter, we look closely at two of these requirements, *agreement* and *consideration.*

❖ Agreement

Essential to any contract is that the parties agree on the terms of the contract. **Agreement** exists when an offer made by one party is accepted or assented to by the other. Ordinarily, agreement is evidenced by an **offer** and an **acceptance.** One party offers a certain bargain to another party, who then accepts that bargain. Because words often fail to convey the precise meaning intended, the law of contracts generally adheres to the *objective theory of contracts,* as discussed in Chapter 8. Under this theory, a party's words and conduct are held to mean whatever a reasonable person in the offeree's position would think they meant. The court will give words their usual meaning even if "it were proved by twenty bishops that [the] party . . . intended something else."[1]

AGREEMENT
A meeting of two or more minds; often used as a synonym for a contract.

OFFER
An offeror's proposal to do something, which creates in the offeree accepting the offer a legal power to bind the offeror to the terms of the proposal by accepting the offer.

ACCEPTANCE
(1) In contract law, the offeree's notification to the offeror that the offeree agrees to be bound by the terms of the offeror's proposal. Although historically the terms of acceptance had to be the mirror image of the terms of the offer, the UCC provides that even modified terms of the offer in a definite expression of acceptance constitute a contract. (2) In commercial paper law, the drawee's signed agreement to pay a draft when presented.

Requirements of the Offer

An *offer* is a promise or commitment to perform or refrain from performing some specified act in the future. As discussed in Chapter 8, the party making an offer is called the *offeror,* and the party to whom the offer is made is called the *offeree.*

1. Judge Learned Hand in *Hotchkiss v. National City Bank of New York,* 200 F. 287 (2d Cir. 1911), aff'd 231 U.S. 50, 34 S.Ct. 20, 58 L.Ed. 115 (1913). (The term *aff'd* is an abbreviation for *affirmed;* an appellate court can affirm a lower court's judgment, decree, or order, thereby declaring that it is valid and must stand as rendered.)

Three elements are necessary for an offer to be effective:

1. There must be a *serious, objective intention* by the offeror.
2. The terms of the offer must be reasonably *certain*, or *definite*, so that the parties and the court can ascertain the terms of the contract.
3. The offer must be communicated to the offeree.

Once an effective offer has been made, the offeree has the power to accept the offer. If the offeree accepts, the offer is translated into an agreement (and into a contract, if other essential elements are present).

"We can judge the intent of parties only by their words."

Sir John Powell, 1635–1713
(English jurist)

Intention The first requirement for an effective offer to exist is a serious, objective intention on the part of the offeror. Intent is not determined by the *subjective* intentions, beliefs, or assumptions of the offeror. It is determined by what a reasonable person in the offeree's position would conclude the offeror's words and actions meant. Offers made in obvious anger, jest, or undue excitement do not meet the serious-and-objective-intent test. Because these offers are not effective, an offeree's acceptance does not create an agreement.

For example, you and three classmates ride to school each day in Julio's new automobile, which has a market value of $8,000. One cold morning the four of you get into the car, but Julio cannot get it started. He yells in anger, "I'll sell this car to anyone for $500!" You drop $500 in his lap. A reasonable person, taking into consideration Julio's frustration and the obvious difference in value between the car's market price and the purchase price, would declare that his offer was not made with serious and objective intent and that you do not have an agreement. The concept of intention can be further explained by distinctions between offers and nonoffers.

Expressions of Opinion An expression of opinion is not an offer. It does not evidence an intention to enter into a binding agreement. In *Hawkins v. McGee,* for example, Hawkins took his son to McGee, a doctor, and asked McGee to operate on the son's hand. McGee said the boy would be in the hospital three or four days and that the hand would *probably* heal a few days later. The son's hand did not heal for a month, but the father did not win a suit for breach of contract. The court held that McGee did not make an offer to heal the son's hand in three or four days. He merely expressed an opinion as to when the hand would heal.[2]

Statements of Intention If Arif says "I *plan* to sell my stock in Novation, Inc., for $150 per share," a contract is not created if John "accepts" and tenders the $150 per share for the stock. Arif has merely expressed his intention to enter into a future contract for the sale of the stock. If John accepts and tenders the $150 per share, no contract is formed because a reasonable person would conclude that Arif was only *thinking about* selling his stock, not promising to sell.

Preliminary Negotiations A request or invitation to negotiate is not an offer; it only expresses a willingness to discuss the possibility of entering into a contract. Examples are statements such as "Will you sell Forest Acres?" and "I wouldn't sell my car for less than $1,000." A reasonable person in the offeree's position would not conclude that such a statement evidenced an intention to enter into a binding obligation. Likewise, when the government and private firms need to have construction work done, contractors are invited to submit bids. The *invitation* to submit bids is not an offer, and a contractor does not bind the government or private firm by

2. *Hawkins v. McGee,* 84 N.H. 114, 146 A. 641 (1929).

submitting a bid. (The bids that the contractors submit are offers, however, and the government or private firm can bind the contractor by accepting the bid.)

In the following case, the court addressed the question of whether a letter informing several people that a cottage was for sale was an offer or merely a preliminary negotiation.

Case 9.1 

MELLEN v. JOHNSON

Supreme Judicial Court of Massachusetts, 1948.
322 Mass. 236,
76 N.E.2d 658.

HISTORICAL AND SOCIAL SETTING *Generally, courts hold that a price quotation is an invitation to the buyer to offer to buy at that price, rather than an offer to sell at that price. One important factor is whether it is disclosed that the quotation is addressed to many people. When a person wants to sell a piece of real property, for example, he or she is likely to negotiate with more than one potential buyer. If a person who communicates a proposal to sell also indicates in some way that the same proposal has been addressed to others, the proposal cannot reasonably be understood as an offer. Instead, it should be looked at as a simple price quotation or as an invitation to make an offer. In cases involving real property, courts are reluctant to interpret a communication as an offer unless it is clear that a promise has been made. This may be, in part, because once a contract has been made, courts are reluctant to interfere.*

FACTS Johnson, who owned a small cottage, sent a letter to Mellen saying that he was putting the cottage on the market. Earlier, Mellen had expressed an interest in purchasing it. The letter indicated that several other people, who had also expressed an interest in purchasing the property, were being informed by letter of its availability at the same time. Mellen, interpreting the letter as an offer, promptly accepted. Johnson sold the property to a higher bidder, and Mellen sued.

ISSUE Was Johnson's letter to Mellen an offer?

DECISION No. The court found that the letter was not an offer.

REASON The court held that the letter merely expressed Johnson's desire to sell the property and thus was not an offer but instead an attempt to negotiate. Because the letter announced that Johnson was sending the same letter to other people, Mellen "could not reasonably understand this to be more than an attempt at negotiation. It was a mere request or suggestion that an offer be made to the defendant [Johnson]."

Advertisements, Catalogues, and Circulars In general, mail-order catalogues, price lists, and circular letters (meant for the general public) are treated not as offers to contract but as invitations to negotiate.[3] Suppose that Tartop & Company advertises a used paving machine. The ad is mailed to hundreds of firms and reads, "Used Case Construction Co. paving machine. Builds curbs and finishes cement work all in one process. Price $11,250." If General Paving, Inc., calls Tartop and says, "We accept your offer," no contract is formed. A reasonable person must conclude that Tartop was not promising to sell the paving machine but rather was soliciting offers to purchase it, because the seller never has an unlimited supply of goods. If advertisements were offers, then everyone who "accepted" after the retailer's supply was exhausted could sue for breach of contract.

Suppose that you put an ad in the classified section of your local newspaper offering to sell your guitar for $75. Suppose also that seven people called and "accepted" your "offer" before you could remove the ad from the newspaper. If the ad were truly an offer, you would be bound by seven contracts to sell your guitar. But because *initial* advertisements are treated as *invitations* to make offers rather than offers, you would have seven offers to choose from, and you could accept the best

3. Restatement (Second) of Contracts, Section 26, Comment b.

one without incurring any liability for the six you rejected. There are occasions, however, when an advertisement contains such definite terms that it can be construed as an offer. (One such occasion is discussed in this chapter's *Business Law in Action.*)

Price lists are another form of invitation to negotiate or trade. A seller's price list is not an offer to sell at that price; it merely invites the buyer to offer to buy at that price. In fact, the seller usually puts "prices subject to change" on the price list. Only in rare circumstances will a price quotation be construed as an offer.[4]

Auctions In an auction, a seller "offers" goods for sale through an auctioneer. This is not, however, an offer for purposes of contract. The seller is really only expressing a willingness to sell. Unless the terms of the auction are explicitly stated to be *without reserve,* the seller (through the auctioneer) may withdraw the goods at any time before the auctioneer closes the sale by announcement or by fall of the hammer. The seller's right to withdraw the goods characterizes an auction *with reserve;* all auctions are assumed to be of this type unless a clear statement to the contrary is made.[5] At auctions "without reserve," the goods cannot be withdrawn and must be sold to the highest bidder.

In an auction with reserve, there is no obligation to sell, and the seller may refuse the highest bid. The bidder is actually the offeror. Before the auctioneer strikes the hammer, which constitutes acceptance of the bid, a bidder may revoke his or her bid, or the auctioneer may reject that bid or all bids. Typically, an auctioneer will reject a bid that is below the price the seller is willing to accept. When the auctioneer accepts a higher bid, he or she rejects all previous bids. Because rejection terminates an offer (as will be pointed out later), those bids represent offers that have been terminated. Thus, if the highest bidder withdraws his or her bid before the hammer falls, none of the previous bids is reinstated. If the bid is not withdrawn or rejected, the contract is formed when the auctioneer announces "Going once, going twice, sold" (or something similar) and lets the hammer fall.

In an auction, who is the offeror and who is the offeree?

4. See, for example, *Fairmount Glass Works v. Grunden-Martin Woodenware Co.,* 106 Ky. 659, 51 S.W. 196 (1899).
5. See UCC 2–328.

In auctions with reserve, the seller may reserve the right to confirm or reject the sale even after the "hammer has fallen." In this situation, the seller is obligated to notify those attending the auction that sales of goods made during the auction are not final until confirmed by the seller. The following case illustrates this point.

Case 9.2
LAWRENCE PAPER CO. v. ROSEN & CO.
United States Court of Appeals, Sixth Circuit, 1991.
939 F.2d 376.

HISTORICAL AND SOCIAL SETTING *More than two hundred years ago, it was established at common law that when an auctioneer says, "What am I bid?" the auctioneer is not making an offer to sell but is inviting offers to buy, which the auctioneer is free to accept or reject. More than one hundred years ago, it was established that, in some cases, even if an auctioneer announces, "I will sell to the highest bidder," the statement still does not constitute an offer. These common law rules relating to auctions plus auctions "without reserve" were adopted by the Uniform Commercial Code, which has governed most sales of goods for more than thirty years. It is also generally held that when a seller reserves the right to refuse to accept a bid, a binding sale is not made until the seller accepts the bid.*

FACTS This dispute arose from an auction of equipment used to make corrugated cardboard boxes. The equipment, which had served as collateral for a loan obtained by North Coast Corrugator Company from Ameritrust Company, was to be sold at auction to satisfy the debt, in accordance with a court judgment. (Collateral is security for a loan, which a lender can use to satisfy the debt if the borrower does not pay.) Ameritrust Company employed Rosen & Company to conduct the sale. Included in Rosen's extensive advertisements of the sale was the announcement that the sale was subject to confirmation by Ameritrust. The auctioneer made a similar announcement at the time of the sale. Sixty bidders attended the auction, including Alpine Company (a defendant), Lawrence Paper Company (a plaintiff), and American Corrugated Machine Corporation (ACMC) (a plaintiff). The auctioneer first offered the equipment in bulk, but only one bid—from Alpine for $50,000—was received. Then the equipment was offered piecemeal, and total bids of $139,000 were received. Two bids from Lawrence and ACMC were accepted, and both companies submitted checks for 25 percent of their bid totals, as requested. After the auction, Alpine offered $175,000 for the equipment, and Ameritrust sold the entire lot to Alpine. Lawrence and ACMC sued for breach of contract. The trial judge dismissed the suit, and the plaintiffs appealed.

ISSUE Did a contract exist between the plaintiffs and Rosen as a result of the auctioneer's acceptance of the plaintiffs' bids?

DECISION No. The trial court's decision was affirmed.

REASON The trial court judge had found that the auction was clearly "with reserve" and therefore there was "no acceptance of the bid, because the sale was not confirmed by the secured party." The appellate court agreed, finding that "there was no binding contract and the sellers were free to accept the subsequent offer." The court found that "where a sale is with reserve and subject to 'confirmation' by the seller, the bids are subject to rejection after the sale, even though accepted by the auctioneer."

Agreements to Agree Traditionally, agreements to agree—that is, agreements to agree to a material term of a contract at some future date—were not considered to be binding contracts. More recent cases illustrate the view that agreements to agree serve valid commercial purposes and can be enforced if the parties clearly intended to be bound by such agreements. For example, suppose Zahn Consulting leases office space from Leon Properties, Inc. Their lease agreement includes a clause permitting Zahn to extend the lease at an amount of rent to be agreed on when the lease is extended. Under the traditional rule, because the amount of rent was not specified in the lease clause itself, the clause would be too indefinite in its terms to be enforced. Under the modern view, a court could hold that the parties intended the future rent to be a reasonable amount and could enforce the clause.[6]

6. Restatement (Second) of Contracts, Section 33. See also UCC 2–204, 2–305.

In other words, under the modern view, the emphasis is on the parties' intent rather than on form. For example, when the Pennzoil Company discussed with the Getty Oil Company the possible purchase of Getty's stock, a memorandum of agreement was drafted to reflect the terms of the conversations. After more negotiations over the price, both companies issued press releases announcing an agreement in principle on the terms of the memorandum. The next day, Texaco, Inc., offered to buy all Getty's stock at a higher price. The day after that, Getty's board of directors voted to accept Texaco's offer, and Texaco and Getty signed a merger agreement. When Pennzoil sued Texaco for tortious interference with its "contractual" relationship with Getty, a jury concluded that Getty and Pennzoil had intended a binding contract before Texaco made its offer, with only the details left to be worked out. Texaco was held liable for wrongfully interfering with this contract.[7]

Definiteness The second requirement for an effective offer involves the definiteness of its terms. An offer must have reasonably definite terms so that a court can determine if a breach has occurred and give an appropriate remedy.[8]

An offer may invite an acceptance to be worded in such specific terms that the contract is made definite. For example, assume Marcus Business Machines contacts your corporation and offers to sell "from one to ten MacCool copying machines for $1,600 each; state number desired in acceptance." Your corporation agrees to buy two copiers. Because the quantity is specified in the acceptance, the terms are definite, and the contract is enforceable.

Communication A third requirement for an effective offer is communication, resulting in the offeree's knowledge of the offer. Suppose that Tolson advertises a reward for the return of her lost cat. Dirlik, not knowing of the reward, finds the cat and returns it to Tolson. Ordinarily, Dirlik cannot recover the reward, because an essential element of a reward contract is that the one who claims the reward must have known it was offered. A few states would allow recovery of the reward, but not on contract principles—Dirlik would be allowed to recover on the basis that it would be unfair to deny him the reward just because he did not know about it.

The following case is one of the classic reward suits in common law.

Case 9.3

GLOVER v. JEWISH WAR VETERANS OF THE UNITED STATES, POST NO. 58

Municipal Court of Appeals for the District of Columbia, 1949.
68 A.2d 233.

HISTORICAL AND SOCIAL SETTING *Rewards have been offered for the capture of criminals since the days of the Old West. Such rewards gave rise to the bounty hunters who tried to make a living by finding alleged criminals. After World War II, which ended in 1945, the professional bounty-hunting business had died, but some rewards continued to be given. The purpose of these rewards remained the same as in the Old West—to provide incentives for persons to make an extra effort to find those accused of committing crimes.*

FACTS The Jewish War Veterans of the United States placed in the newspaper an offer of a reward of $500 "to the person or persons furnishing information resulting in the apprehension and conviction of the persons guilty of the murder of Maurice L. Bernstein." Mrs. Glover gave police information that led to the arrest and conviction of the murderers, not knowing that a reward had been offered and not learning of it until several days afterward.

ISSUE Does a contract between Mrs. Glover and the Jewish War Veterans exist, given the fact that Mrs. Glover did not know of the reward when she delivered the requested information?

7. *Texaco, Inc. v. Pennzoil Co.*, 729 S.W.2d 768 (Tex.App—Houston [1st Dist.] 1987, writ ref'd n.r.e.). This case is presented in Chapter 6 as Case 6.1.

8. Restatement (Second) of Contracts, Section 33.

Case 9.3—Continued

DECISION No. Mrs. Glover's act did not constitute an acceptance because she did not act in response to the offer.

REASON Mrs. Glover was not entitled to the $500 reward because she was not aware of the nongovernmental offer when she gave the police the information. The Restatement of the Law of Contracts says: "It is impossible that there should be an acceptance unless the offeree knows of the existence of the offer."

ETHICAL CONSIDERATIONS *In regard to government rewards, should rewards be given regardless of whether a claimant knew about the reward when he or she gave the information? After all, the public good is served in either case. One could argue that the public can be assumed to have knowledge of government actions and therefore should receive the rewards without further proof of knowledge.*

Termination of the Offer

The communication of an effective offer to an offeree gives the offeree the power to transform the offer into a binding, legal obligation (a contract) by an acceptance. This power of acceptance, however, does not continue forever. It can be terminated by *action of the parties* or by *operation of law.*

Termination by Action of the Parties An offer can be terminated by the action of the parties in any of three ways: by revocation, by rejection, or by counteroffer.

Revocation of the Offer The offeror's act of withdrawing an offer is called **revocation.** Unless an offer is irrevocable, the offeror usually can revoke the offer (even if he or she has promised to keep the offer open), as long as the revocation is communicated to the offeree before the offeree accepts. Revocation may be accomplished by express repudiation of the offer (for example, with a statement such as "I withdraw my previous offer of October 17") or by performance of acts inconsistent with the existence of the offer, which are made known to the offeree. For example, Geraldine offers to sell some land to Gary. A week passes, and Gary, who has not yet accepted the offer, learns from his friend Konstantine that Geraldine has in the meantime sold the property to Fenwick. Gary's knowledge of Geraldine's sale of the land to Fenwick, even though Gary learned of it through a third party, effectively revokes her offer to sell the land to Gary. Geraldine's sale of the land to Fenwick is inconsistent with the continued existence of the offer to Gary, and thus the offer to Gary is revoked.

REVOCATION
In contract law, the withdrawal of an offer by an offeror; unless the offer is irrevocable, it can be revoked at any time prior to acceptance without liability.

The general rule followed by most states is that a revocation becomes effective when the offeree or offeree's agent (a person who acts on behalf of another) actually receives it. Therefore, a letter of revocation mailed on April 1 and delivered at the offeree's residence or place of business on April 3 becomes effective on April 3.

An offer made to the general public can be revoked in the same manner the offer was originally communicated. Suppose that a department store offers a $10,000 reward to anyone giving information leading to the apprehension of the persons who burglarized its downtown store. The offer is published in three local papers and four papers in neighboring communities. To revoke the offer, the store must publish the revocation in all seven papers for the same number of days it published the offer. The revocation is then accessible to the general public even if some particular offeree does not know about it.

Although most offers are revocable, some can be made irrevocable. Increasingly, courts refuse to allow an offeror to revoke an offer when the offeree has changed position because of justifiable reliance on the offer (under the doctrine of detrimental reliance, or promissory estoppel, discussed later in the chapter). In some circumstances, offers made by merchants may also be considered irrevocable. These so-called "firm offers" are discussed in Chapter 14.

Business Law in Action

When Is an Ad an Offer?

Although most advertisements are treated as invitations to negotiate, this does not mean that an advertisement can never be an offer. If the ad makes a promise so definite in character that it is apparent that the offeror is binding himself or herself to the terms stated, then the ad is treated as an offer. Such was the situation in *Lefkowitz v. Great Minneapolis Surplus Store, Inc.*,[a] a case brought before the Supreme Court of Minnesota in 1957. The case arose when a merchant refused to sell to a customer a fur stole for $1, as promised in a newspaper advertisement. The customer, Lefkowitz, had read the following ad on April 13, 1956, in a Minneapolis newspaper:

"Saturday 9 A.M.
2 Brand New Pastel
Mink 3-Skin Scarfs
Selling for $89.50
Out they go
Saturday. Each . . . $1.00
1 Black Lapin Stole
Beautiful,
worth $139.50 . . . $1.00
First Come
First Served"

Lefkowitz was the first to appear at the appropriate counter on the Saturday morning of the sale. He was told, however, that according to a "house rule," the offer was intended for women only and that men could not make the purchase.

Lefkowitz then sued the store for breach of contract, and the trial court awarded him damages. The store appealed the decision, contending that no contract existed because no offer had been made. The advertisement was solely an invitation to customers to make offers to buy the goods on the terms given in the ad—offers that, when forthcoming, could be accepted or rejected by the store.

In evaluating the claim, the court held for Lefkowitz. The court stated that "where the offer is clear, definite, and explicit, and leaves nothing open for negotiation, it constitutes an offer, acceptance of which will complete the contract. . . . We are of the view on the facts before us that the offer by the defendant of the sale of the Lapin fur was clear, definite, and explicit, and left nothing open for negotiation. The plaintiff having successfully managed to be the first one to appear at the seller's place of business to be served, as requested by the advertisement, and having offered the stated purchase price of the article, was entitled to performance on the part of the defendant." As to the "house rule," the court stated that the defendant did "not have the right, after acceptance, to impose new or arbitrary conditions not contained in the published offer."

In short, the advertisement in this case was sufficiently definite to create an offer. The quantity was specified (one fur stole), as were the price ($1), the value ($139.50), and the person who could accept (first come, first served).[b]

a. 251 Minn. 188, 86 N.W.2d 689 (1957).

b. Note that today, the surplus store could have been charged with violating Federal Trade Commission rules that prohibit deceptive advertising (see Chapter 31).

OPTION CONTRACT
A contract (with consideration) whereby the offeror agrees not to withdraw an offer for a period of time as specified in the contract, or if no time period is specified, for a reasonable period.

Another form of irrevocable offer is an **option contract.** An option contract is created when an offeror promises to hold an offer open for a specified period of time in return for a payment (consideration) given by the offeree. An option contract takes away the offeror's power to revoke an offer for the period of time specified in the option. If no time is specified, then a reasonable period of time is implied. For example, assume that you are in the business of writing movie scripts. Your agent contacts the head of development at New Line Cinema and offers to sell New Line your new movie script. New Line likes your script and agrees to pay you $5,000 for a six-month option. In this situation, you (through your agent) are the offeror, and New Line is the offeree. You cannot revoke your offer to sell New Line your script for the next six months. If after six months no contract has been formed, however, New Line loses the $5,000, and you are free to sell the script to another firm.

Option contracts are also frequently used in conjunction with the sale of real estate. For example, you might agree with a landowner to lease a home and include in the lease contract a clause stating that you will pay $2,000 for an option to purchase the home within a specified period of time. If you decide not to purchase the home after the specified period has lapsed, you forfeit the $2,000, and the landlord is free to sell the property to another buyer.

Rejection of the Offer by the Offeree The offer may be rejected by the offeree, in which case the offer is terminated. Any subsequent attempt by the offeree to accept will be construed as a new offer, giving the original offeror (now the offeree) the power of acceptance. A rejection is ordinarily accomplished by words or by conduct evidencing an intent not to accept the offer.

As with revocation, rejection of an offer is effective only when it is actually received by the offeror or the offeror's agent. Suppose Growgood Farms mailed a letter to Campbell's Soup Company offering to sell carrots at ten cents a pound. Campbell's Soup Company could reject the offer by writing or telephoning Growgood Farms, expressly rejecting the offer, or by mailing the offer back to Growgood, evidencing an intent to reject it. Or Campbell's could offer to buy the carrots at eight cents per pound (a counteroffer), necessarily rejecting the original offer.

Merely inquiring about the offer does not constitute rejection. For example, a friend offers to buy your stereo for $100. You respond, "Is this your best offer?" or "Will you pay me $175 for it?" A reasonable person would conclude that you did not reject the offer but merely made an inquiry for further consideration of the offer. You can still accept and bind your friend to the $100 purchase price. When the offeree merely inquires as to the firmness of the offer, there is no reason to presume that he or she intends to reject it.

Counteroffer by the Offeree A **counteroffer** is a rejection of the original offer and the simultaneous making of a new offer. Suppose that Burke offers to sell his home to Lang for $170,000. Lang responds, "Your price is too high. I'll offer to purchase your house for $165,000." Lang's response is termed a counteroffer because it rejects Burke's offer to sell at $170,000 and creates a new offer by Lang to purchase at $165,000. At common law, the **mirror image rule** requires that the offeree's acceptance match the offeror's offer exactly. In other words, the terms of the acceptance must "mirror" those of the offer. If the acceptance materially changes or adds to the terms of the original offer, it will be considered not an acceptance but a counteroffer—which, of course, need not be accepted. The original offeror can, however, accept the terms of the counteroffer and create a valid contract.[9]

COUNTEROFFER
An offeree's response to an offer in which the offeree rejects the original offer and at the same time makes a new offer.

MIRROR IMAGE RULE
A common law rule that requires, for a valid contractual agreement, that the terms of the offeree's acceptance adhere exactly to the terms of the offeror's offer.

Termination by Operation of the Law The offeree's power to transform an offer into a binding, legal obligation can be terminated by the operation of the law if any of four conditions occur: lapse of time, destruction of the subject matter, death or incompetence of the offeror or offeree, or supervening illegality of the proposed contract.

Lapse of Time An offer terminates automatically by law when the period of time specified in the offer has passed. For example, suppose Jane offers to sell her boat to Jonah if he accepts within twenty days. Jonah must accept within the twenty-day period, or the offer will lapse (terminate). The time period specified in an offer normally begins to run when the offer is actually received by the offeree, not when it is drawn up or sent. When the offer is delayed (through the misdelivery of mail, for example), the period begins to run from the date the offeree would have received the offer, but only if the offeree knows or should know that the offer is delayed.[10] For example, if Jane used improper postage when mailing the offer to Jonah and Jonah knew about the improper mailing, the offer would lapse twenty days after the day Jonah would ordinarily have received the offer had Jane used proper postage.

9. The mirror image rule has been greatly modified in regard to sales contracts. Section 2–207 of the UCC provides that a contract is formed if the offeree makes a definite expression of acceptance (such as signing the form in the appropriate location), even though the terms of the acceptance modify or add to the terms of the original offer (see Chapter 14).

10. Restatement (Second) of Contracts, Section 49.

If no time for acceptance is specified in the offer, the offer terminates at the end of a *reasonable* period of time. A reasonable period of time is determined by the subject matter of the contract, business and market conditions, and other relevant circumstances. An offer to sell farm produce, for example, will terminate sooner than an offer to sell farm equipment because farm produce is perishable and subject to greater fluctuations in market value.

Destruction of the Subject Matter An offer is automatically terminated if the specific subject matter of the offer is destroyed before the offer is accepted. For example, if Bekins offers to sell his cow to Yatsen, but the cow dies before Yatsen can accept, the offer is automatically terminated.

Death or Incompetence of the Offeror or Offeree An offeree's power of acceptance is terminated when the offeror or offeree dies or is deprived of legal capacity to enter into the proposed contract, unless the offer is irrevocable.[11] An offer is personal to both parties and normally cannot pass to the decedent's heirs, guardian, or estate. This rule applies whether or not the one party had notice of the death or incompetence of the other party.

Supervening Illegality of the Proposed Contract A statute or court decision that makes an offer illegal will automatically terminate the offer. If Eva offers to lend Jack $20,000 at 15 percent annually and a usury statute is enacted prohibiting loans at interest rates greater than 12 percent before Jack can accept, the offer is automatically terminated. (If the statute is enacted after Jack accepts the offer, a valid contract is formed, but the contract may still be unenforceable.)

Acceptance

Acceptance is a voluntary act (which may consist of words or conduct) by the offeree that shows assent (agreement) to the terms of an offer. The acceptance must be unequivocal and must be communicated to the offeror.

Who Can Accept? Generally, a third person cannot substitute for the offeree and effectively accept the offer. After all, the identity of the offeree is as much a condition of a bargaining offer as any other term contained therein. Thus, except in special circumstances, only the person to whom the offer is made or that person's agent can accept the offer and create a binding contract. For example, Lotte makes an offer to Paul. Paul is not interested, but Paul's friend, José, accepts the offer. No contract is formed.

Unequivocal Acceptance To exercise the power of acceptance effectively, the offeree must accept unequivocally. This is the *mirror image rule* previously discussed. If the acceptance is subject to new conditions or if the terms of the acceptance materially change the original offer, the acceptance may be deemed a counteroffer that implicitly rejects the original offer. An acceptance may be unequivocal even though the offeree expresses dissatisfaction with the contract. For example, "I accept the offer, but I wish I could have gotten a better price" is an effective acceptance. So, too, is "I accept, but can you shave the price?" In contrast, the statement "I accept the offer but only if I can pay on ninety days' credit" is not an unequivocal acceptance and operates as a counteroffer, rejecting the original offer.

Certain terms when added to an acceptance will not qualify the acceptance sufficiently to constitute rejection of the offer. Suppose that in response to a person

11. Restatement (Second) of Contracts, Section 48. If the offer is irrevocable, it is not terminated when the offeror dies. Also, if the offer is such that it can be accepted by the performance of a series of acts, and those acts began before the offeror died, the offeree's power of acceptance is not terminated.

offering to sell a piano, the offeree replies, "I accept; please send a written contract." The offeree is requesting a written contract but is not making it a condition for acceptance. Therefore, the acceptance is effective without the written contract. If the offeree replies, "I accept if you send a written contract," however, the acceptance is expressly conditioned on the request for a writing, and the statement is not an acceptance but a counteroffer. (Notice how important each word is!)[12]

In the following case, the offeree accepted an offer but also returned to the offeror a separate document entitled "Acceptance and Counteroffer" that stipulated certain conditions of sale not contained in the offeror's offer. In this situation, has the offeree accepted the offer or made a counteroffer?

Case 9.4

CHOSNYKA v. MEYER

Appellate Court of Illinois,
Fifth District, 1992.
223 Ill.App.3d 493,
585 N.E.2d 204,
165 Ill.Dec. 808.

HISTORICAL AND SOCIAL SETTING *To be valid, a contract for the sale of land must describe the property in writing. Typically, the contract does this by defining a series of boundary lines. The earliest descriptions relied heavily on natural features, such as "the great oak tree" or "the banks of Elm Creek." These descriptions sometimes caused problems for later buyers if the tree was removed or the creek changed course. Thomas Jefferson devised a system of land description and measurement that Congress adopted in 1785 for use throughout most of the United States. This system is based on "principal meridians" and intersecting "base lines." Land descriptions can be long and complicated and mistakes are easily made. Over the years, in hundreds of cases, the courts have developed a list of priorities to resolve inconsistencies. The last item to receive consideration if there is an inconsistency is a description of land as constituting a certain number of acres.*

FACTS Dominic Meyer, after seeing a "For Sale 95 Acres" sign on plaintiffs' property and conducting a title search, offered to pay $250,000 for the property. Meyer's offer read, in part, as follows: "Seller has ten (10) days from the date hereof to accept the offer." The plaintiffs (including the estate of Bernice Chosnyka) returned a signed copy the agreement to Meyer the next day. Along with the signed offer, they returned to Meyer a document entitled "Acceptance and Counteroffer," which stated that their acceptance included these conditions: (1) the closing date was to be no later than sixty days from the date of acceptance and (2) although the legal description of the property was accurate, the true number of acres had not been ascertained. Partly because the land was not warranted to be exactly ninety-five acres, Meyer told the real estate broker that he was withdrawing his offer. The plaintiffs, alleging that a contract of sale had been formed between them and Meyer, sued Meyer for $50,000 in damages, the difference between the contract price and the eventual selling price of the property. The trial court found for the plaintiffs, and Meyer appealed.

ISSUE Did a valid contract exist between the buyer (Meyer) and the sellers?

DECISION Yes. The appellate court affirmed the trial court's ruling.

REASON Meyer claimed that the conditions set forth in the document "Acceptance and Counteroffer" constituted a counteroffer that he never accepted. The court held, however, that the document was irrelevant. The plaintiffs had effectively accepted Meyer's offer to buy the property by signing and returning Meyer's offer within the specified ten-day period. Meyer also claimed that because the property was not "warranted to be 95 acres, mutual assent was destroyed." The court disagreed. Under Illinois law, the boundaries specified in a legal description "will control as to the quantity of acres * * *. The mention of acres * * * has no legal effect." Unless the discrepancy in acres affects the use of the property, there can be no remedy. Such was not the case here.

ETHICAL CONSIDERATIONS *Meyer testified that the day after he received the signed offer, he went to the property and discovered, for the first time, a marker indicating an underground pressurized gas line. There was conflicting testimony about whether he knew about the gas line before he made his offer, however, and the court decided against him on the issue. The presence of a gas line can reduce the value of property considerably. The plaintiffs' quick re-*

12. As noted in footnote 9, in regard to sales contracts, the UCC provides that an acceptance may still be valid even if some terms are added. The new terms are simply treated as proposals for additions to the contract.

Case 9.4—Continued

ply to his offer and the subsequent selling price of the property could indicate that the value was much less than he offered. If he did not know about the gas line before making his offer, was it fair to require him to pay damages?

Silence as Acceptance Ordinarily, silence cannot constitute acceptance, even if the offeror states, "By your silence and inaction, you will be deemed to have accepted this offer." This general rule applies because an offeree should not be put under a burden of liability to act affirmatively in order to reject an offer. No consideration—nothing of value—has passed to the offeree to impose such a liability.

In some instances, however, the offeree does have a duty to speak, in which case his or her silence or inaction will operate as an acceptance. For example, silence may be an acceptance when an offeree takes the benefit of offered services even though he or she had an opportunity to reject them and knew that they were offered with the expectation of compensation. Suppose Jameson watches while a stranger mows her lawn, even though the stranger has not been asked to mow the lawn. Jameson knows the stranger expects to be paid and does nothing to stop him. Here, her silence constitutes an acceptance, and an implied-in-fact contract is created. She is bound to pay a reasonable value for the stranger's work. This rule normally applies only when the offeree has received a benefit from the goods or services.

Silence can also operate as acceptance when the offeree has had prior dealings with the offeror. If a merchant, for example, routinely receives shipments from a supplier and in the past has always notified the supplier of rejection of defective goods, then silence constitutes acceptance. Also, if a person solicits an offer specifying that certain terms and conditions are acceptable, and the offeror makes the offer in response to the solicitation, the offeree has a duty to reject—that is, a duty to tell the offeror that the offer is not acceptable. Failure to reject (silence) would operate as an acceptance. The following case illustrates a situation in which the silence of the offeree operated as an acceptance.

Case 9.5

FEIST & FEIST REALTY CORP. v. DOCKSIDE URBAN RENEWAL CORP.

Superior Court of New Jersey, 1992.
255 N.J.Super. 100,
604 A.2d 653.

HISTORICAL AND SOCIAL SETTING *A broker's function is to arrange contracts involving property in which he or she has no personal interest or concern. A broker may be an intermediary in the contracting of any type of bargain. Real estate brokers, for example, are hired to transact the buying, selling, or leasing of real property. Their compensation is a commission based on the value of the property in the sale or the amount of rent in the lease. Generally, a commission is earned when negotiations between the parties to the sale or lease are completed and an agreement is reached. Real estate brokers sometimes make fabulous commissions for what appears to be only a little effort. A single commission can represent months of uncompensated work, however.*

FACTS Feist & Feist Realty Corporation sought rental premises for a tenant, the New York Bronze Powder Company. Feist introduced New York Bronze to a location in Newark owned by Dockside Urban Renewal Corporation. After showing the premises to New York Bronze, Feist sent the owner of Dockside a letter on December 18, 1985, by certified mail, advising the owner that if Dockside succeeded in leasing its property to New York Bronze, Feist would be entitled to a commission equal to 5 percent of the gross rental. Dockside acknowledged the receipt of the letter on December 19, 1985, and began negotiating with New York Bronze. Eventually, a lease was formed between Dockside and New York Bronze on April 28, 1986. The total amount of the rent was $12,941,250 for a ten-year period, and the lease acknowledged that Feist had been "instrumental in consummating this lease." The lease further stated that Dockside would "satisfy any commissions due to Feist & Feist by a separate agreement." After the lease was signed, Feist demanded payment of its commission of $647,062 (5 percent of $12,941,250). When Dockside failed to respond to this letter and subsequent demands for payment, Feist sued. Dockside claimed that

Case 9.5—Continued

it had never contracted with Feist to pay Feist a commission.

ISSUE Was Dockside contractually obligated to pay Feist the commission?

DECISION Yes. The court held that a contract had been formed, and Dockside was obligated to pay Feist the commission.

REASON The court stated that it is a "well established principle that when a broker is engaged by an owner of property to find a purchaser, the broker earns a commission when the broker produces a ready, willing and able purchaser who enters into a contract with the owner and the transaction is completed by a closing of title." The same principle applies when a lease (rather than a sale) of property is involved. Even though the lease provided that any commission to the broker would be satisfied by way of "a separate agreement," the court found that the phrase in fact referred to Feist's certified letter to Dockside, which clearly spelled out the terms of Feist's offer of a tenant in return for a broker's commission. Dockside acknowledged its receipt of Feist's letter and never repudiated the agreement, even though it had more than four months to do so before negotiating the lease. The court stated that under both case law and the Restatement (Second) of Contracts, Section 69(1), the rule is that "where a party fails to repudiate an offer or remains silent and then accepts the benefit of the offer, the party may be deemed to have accepted the contract terms."

ETHICAL CONSIDERATIONS *Although courts are reluctant to construe silence as acceptance, this case illustrates how such a construction may be necessary to avoid injustice. Clearly, it would have been unfair for Dockside to take advantage of Feist's services and not pay for them on the ground that it had never accepted Feist's offer in writing.*

Communication of Acceptance Whether the offeror must be notified of the acceptance depends on the nature of the contract. In a bilateral contract, communication of acceptance is necessary, because acceptance is in the form of a promise (not performance) and the contract is formed when the promise is made (rather than when the act is performed). The offeree must communicate the acceptance to the offeror. Communication of acceptance is not necessary, however, if the offer dispenses with the requirement. Also, if the offer can be accepted by silence, no communication is necessary.[13]

Because in a unilateral contract the full performance of some act is called for, acceptance is usually evident, and notification is therefore unnecessary. Exceptions do exist, however. When the offeror requests notice of acceptance or has no adequate means of determining whether the requested act has been performed, or when the law requires such notice of acceptance, then notice is necessary.[14]

Mode and Timeliness of Acceptance The general rule is that acceptance in a bilateral contract is timely if it is effected within the duration of the offer. Problems arise, however, when the parties involved are not dealing face to face. In such cases, the offeree may use an authorized mode of communication. Acceptance takes effect, thus completing formation of the contract, at the time the communication is sent via the mode expressly or impliedly authorized by the offeror. This is the so-called **mailbox rule,** also called the "deposited acceptance rule," which the majority of courts uphold. Under this rule, if the authorized mode of communication is via the mail, then an acceptance becomes valid when it is dispatched—not when it is received by the offeror. The mailbox rule was formed to prevent the confusion that arises when an offeror sends a letter of revocation but, before this letter is received by the offeree, the offeree sends a letter of acceptance. Thus, whereas a revocation becomes effective only when it is *received* by the offeree, an acceptance becomes

MAILBOX RULE
A rule providing that an acceptance of an offer becomes effective upon dispatch (upon being placed in a mailbox), if mail is, expressly or impliedly, an authorized means of communication of acceptance to the offeror.

13. Under the UCC, an order or other offer to buy goods that are to be promptly shipped may be treated as either a bilateral or a unilateral offer and can be accepted by a promise to ship or by actual shipment.

14. UCC 2–206(2).

effective upon *dispatch* (even if it is never received), providing that *authorized* means of communication are used.

Authorized means can be either expressly authorized—that is, expressly stipulated in the offer—or impliedly authorized by facts or law.[15] When an offeror specifies how acceptance should be made (for example, by first-class mail or express delivery), *express authorization* is said to exist, and no contract is formed unless the offeree uses that mode of acceptance. Moreover, both the offeror and the offeree are bound in contract the moment that such means of acceptance are employed.

Most offerors do not specify expressly the means by which the offeree is to accept. Thus, the common law recognizes the following implied authorized means of acceptance:[16]

1. The choice of a particular means by the offeror in making the offer implies that the offeree is authorized to use the *same* or *faster* means for acceptance.
2. When two parties are at a distance, *mailing* is impliedly authorized.

There are three basic exceptions to the rule that a contract is formed when acceptance is sent by authorized means:

1. If the acceptance is not properly dispatched (if a letter is incorrectly addressed, for example, or is without the proper postage), in most states it will not be effective until it is received by the offeror.
2. The offeror can specifically condition his or her offer upon the receipt of an acceptance by a certain time, in which case, to be effective, the acceptance must be received prior to the end of the time period.
3. Sometimes an offeree sends a rejection first, then later changes his or her mind and sends an acceptance. Obviously, this chain of events could cause confusion and

If an offeror expressly authorizes acceptance of his or her offer by first-class mail or express delivery, can the offeree accept by a faster means, such as a fax?

15. Restatement (Second) of Contracts, Section 30, provides that an offer invites acceptance "by any medium reasonable in the circumstances," unless the offer is specific about the means of acceptance. Under Section 65, a medium is reasonable if it is one used by the offeror or one customary in similar transactions, unless the offeree knows of circumstances that would argue against the reasonableness of a particular medium (the need for speed because of rapid price changes, for example).
16. Note that under the UCC, acceptance of an offer for the sale of goods can be made by any *medium* that is *reasonable* under the circumstances.

even detriment to the offeror, depending on whether the rejection or the acceptance arrived first. In such cases, the law cancels the rule of acceptance upon dispatch, and the first communication received by the offeror determines whether a contract is formed. If the rejection comes first, there is no contract.[17]

An acceptance given by means not expressly or impliedly authorized is not effective until it is received by the offeror. The following case illustrates the principle that, when the means of acceptance is not expressly authorized by the offeror, the same or a *faster* means is impliedly the authorized means of acceptance.

Case 9.6
DEFEO v. AMFARMS ASSOCIATES
Supreme Court of New York, Appellate Division, Third Department, 1990.
161 A.D.2d 904,
557 N.Y.S.2d 469.

HISTORICAL AND ECONOMIC SETTING *In the mid-1980s, some rural communities throughout the United States were experiencing an economic depression. Foreign grain exporters were underselling U.S. grain exporters. This contributed to a $14.2 billion U.S. trade deficit (an excess of imports over exports) in May 1986, which included the first agricultural deficit in twenty years.*

FACTS On September 5, 1987, Ralph Defeo and others offered to purchase a farm that Amfarms Associates had listed for sale in 1986. Amfarms made a counteroffer in which certain conditions in the Defeo offer were deleted. A month later, Defeo and the others submitted another offer that included the previously deleted conditions. On October 9, Amfarms, using the same form, counteroffered by again deleting the conditions. Amfarms added that the offer would be valid only until 5 P.M. on October 17. Amfarms's attorney sent the offer to Defeo's attorney via Federal Express. On October 16, Defeo and the others sent their acceptance to Amfarms's October 9 offer by certified mail to Amfarms's real estate broker. Amfarms received the acceptance on October 19. On October 16, however, Amfarms had accepted an offer from another party. Defeo and the others sued in a New York state court, claiming that their acceptance on October 16 was effective on the day that it was sent. The trial court dismissed the complaint, holding that because the offer had been transmitted by Federal Express overnight delivery, the impliedly authorized means of acceptance was by the same or a faster delivery service. Therefore, the acceptance sent by certified mail was ineffective. Defeo and the others appealed.

ISSUE Was the acceptance ineffective because it was sent via certified mail rather than via overnight delivery by Federal Express or another delivery service?

DECISION Yes. The trial court's decision was affirmed.

REASON The acceptance was not effective on dispatch because it was not transmitted by the impliedly authorized means of acceptance. The appellate court explained that "[t]he reasonableness of the manner in which an offer is accepted must be viewed under the circumstances in which the offer had been made, with speed and reliability being relevant factors." Federal Express overnight delivery is faster than certified mail, and Amfarms had emphasized time. The receipt of the acceptance two days after the acceptance deadline "was not operative."

❖ Consideration and Its Requirements

In every legal system, there are promises that will be enforced and promises that will not be enforced. The simple fact that a party has made a promise, then, does not mean the promise is enforceable. Under the common law, a primary basis for the enforcement of promises is **consideration.** At a minimum, requiring consideration makes the distinction between gratuitous promises and those that are part of a bargained-for exchange. Therefore, consideration is used to distinguish contracts from gifts.

CONSIDERATION
That which motivates the exchange of promises or performance in a contractual agreement. The consideration, which must be present to make the contract legally binding, must result in a detriment to the promisee (something of legal value, legally sufficient, and bargained for) or a benefit to the promisor.

17. Restatement (Second) of Contracts, Section 40.

Consideration is usually defined as the value (such as money) given in return for a promise (such as the promise to sell a stereo upon receipt of payment). Often, consideration is broken down into two parts: (1) something of *legal value* must be given in exchange for the promise, and (2) there must be a *bargained-for* exchange. The "something of legal value" may consist of a return promise that is bargained for. If it consists of performance, that performance may be (1) an act (other than a promise); (2) a forbearance (a refraining from action); or (3) the creation, modification, or destruction of a legal relation.[18]

For example, Jerry says to his son, "When you finish painting the garage, I will pay you $100." Jerry's son paints the garage. The act of painting the garage is the consideration that creates the contractual obligation of Jerry to pay his son $100. Suppose, however, that Jerry says to his son, "In consideration of the fact that you are not as wealthy as your brothers, I will pay you $500." This promise is not enforceable because Jerry's son has not given any consideration for the $500 promised.[19] Jerry has simply stated his motive for giving his son a gift. The fact that the word *consideration* is used does not, alone, mean that consideration has been given.

Legal Sufficiency of Consideration

For a binding contract to be created, consideration not only must exist but must also be legally sufficient. To be *legally sufficient,* consideration for a promise must be legally *detrimental to the promisee* or *beneficial to the promisor.* Note that *legal* detriment is not synonymous with actual (economic) detriment. A person can incur legal detriment in either of two ways: (1) by doing or promising to do something that he or she had no prior legal duty to do or (2) by refraining from, or promising to refrain from, doing something that he or she had no prior legal duty to refrain from doing (that is, by forbearance).

Adequacy of Consideration

Legal sufficiency of consideration involves the requirement that consideration be something of value in the eyes of the law. Adequacy of consideration involves "how much" consideration is given. Essentially, adequacy of consideration concerns the fairness of the bargain. On the surface, fairness would appear to be an issue when the values of items exchanged are unequal. In general, however, courts do not question the adequacy of consideration if the consideration is legally sufficient. Under the doctrine of freedom of contract, parties are usually free to bargain as they wish. If people could sue merely because they had entered into an unwise contract, the courts would be overloaded with frivolous suits. In extreme cases, a court of law may look to the amount or value (the adequacy) of the consideration because apparently inadequate consideration can indicate fraud, duress (unlawful pressure causing someone to do something he or she would not otherwise have done), or undue influence. In cases in which the consideration is grossly inadequate, the courts may declare the contract unenforceable on the ground that it is *unconscionable*[20]—that is, generally speaking, it is so one-sided under the circumstances as to be overly unfair. (Unconscionability is discussed further in Chapter 10.)

Preexisting Duty

Under most circumstances, a promise to do what one already has a legal duty to do does not constitute legally sufficient consideration because no legal detriment or

18. Restatement (Second) of Contracts, Section 71.
19. See *Fink v. Cox,* 18 Johns. 145, 9 Am.Dec. 191 (N.Y. 1820).
20. Pronounced un-*kon*-shun-uh-bul.

Landmark in the Law

Hamer v. Sidway (1891)

If, in return for a promise to pay, a person forbears to pursue harmful habits, such as the use of tobacco and alcohol, does such forbearance represent a legal "detriment to the promisee" and thus create consideration for the contract? This was the issue before the court in the landmark case of *Hamer v. Sidway*.[a]

The contract in question was created in 1869 when William Story, Sr., promised his nephew, William Story II, that if the nephew refrained from drinking alcohol, using tobacco, and playing billiards and cards for money until he reached the age of twenty-one, he would pay him $5,000. The nephew, who indulged occasionally in all of these "vices," agreed to refrain from them and did so for the next six years. Following his twenty-first birthday in 1875, the nephew wrote to his uncle that he had performed his part of the bargain and was thus entitled to the promised $5,000. A few days later, the uncle responded with the following letter:

> Buffalo, Feb. 6, 1875
>
> W. E. Story, Jr:
>
> DEAR NEPHEW—Your letter of the 31st ult, came to hand all right, saying that you had lived up to the promise made to me several years ago. I have no doubt but you have, for which you shall have five thousand dollars, as I promised you. I had the money in the bank the day you was 21 years old that I intend for you, and you shall have the money certain. Now, Willie, I do not intend to interfere with this money in any way till I think you are capable of taking care of it, and the sooner that time comes the better it will please me. . . . This money you have earned much easier than I did besides acquiring good habits at the same time and you are quite welcome to the money; hope you will make good use of it. I was ten long years getting this together after I was your age.
>
> Truly yours,
> W. E. Story
>
> P.S.—You can consider this money on interest.

The nephew agreed to the terms and conditions and left the money in the care of his uncle, who held it for the next twelve years. When the uncle died in 1887, however, the executor of the uncle's estate refused to pay the $5,000 claim brought by Hamer, a third party to whom the promise had been *assigned*. (The law allows parties to assign, or transfer, rights in contracts to third parties; see Chapter 12.) The executor, Sidway, contended that the contract was invalid because there was insufficient consideration to support it. He argued that neither a benefit to the promisor (the uncle) nor a detriment to the promisee (the nephew) existed in this case. The uncle had received nothing, and the nephew had actually benefited by fulfilling the uncle's wishes. Therefore, no contract existed.

Although a lower court upheld Sidway's position, the New York Court of Appeals reversed and ruled in favor of the plaintiff, Hamer. "The promisee used tobacco, occasionally drank liquor, and he had a legal right to do so," the court stated. "That right he abandoned for a period of years upon the strength of the promise of the testator [one who makes a will] that for such forbearance he would give him $5,000. We need not speculate on the effort which may have been required to give up the use of those stimulants. It is sufficient that he restricted his lawful freedom of action within certain prescribed limits upon the faith of his uncle's agreement."

a. 124 N.Y. 538, 27 N.E. 256 (1891).

benefit has been incurred.[21] The preexisting legal duty may be imposed by law or may arise out of a previous contract. A sheriff, for example, cannot collect a reward for information leading to the capture of a criminal if the sheriff already has a legal duty to capture the criminal. Likewise, if a party is already bound by contract to perform a certain duty, that duty cannot serve as consideration for a second contract. For example, suppose that Bauman-Bache, Inc., begins construction on a seven-story office building and after three months demands an extra $75,000 on its contract. If the extra $75,000 is not paid, it will stop working. The owner of the land, having no one else to complete construction, agrees to pay the extra $75,000. The agreement is not enforceable, because it is not supported by legally sufficient consideration; Bauman-Bache was under a preexisting contract to complete the building.

21. See *Foakes v. Beer*, 9 App.Cas. 605 (1884).

Unforeseen Difficulties The rule regarding preexisting duty is meant to prevent extortion and the so-called hold-up game. But what happens when an honest contractor, who has contracted with a landowner to build a house, runs into extraordinary difficulties that were totally unforeseen at the time the contract was formed? In the interests of fairness and equity, the courts sometimes allow exceptions to the preexisting duty rule. In the example just mentioned, if the landowner agrees to pay extra compensation to the contractor for overcoming these unforeseen difficulties, the court may refrain from applying the preexisting duty rule and enforce the agreement. But when the "unforeseen difficulties" that give rise to a contract modification are the types of risks ordinarily assumed in business, the courts will usually assert the preexisting duty rule.[22]

Rescission and New Contract The law recognizes that two parties can mutually agree to rescind their contract, at least to the extent that it is executory (still to be carried out). **Rescission** is defined as the unmaking of a contract so as to return the parties to the positions they occupied before the contract was made. When rescission and the making of a new contract take place at the same time, the courts frequently are given a choice (as in the earlier Bauman-Bache example) of applying the preexisting duty rule or allowing rescission and letting the new contract stand.

RESCISSION
A remedy whereby a contract is terminated and the parties are returned to the positions they occupied before the contract was made; may be effected through the mutual consent of the parties, by their conduct, or by the decree of a court of equity.

Past Consideration

Promises made in return for actions or events that have already taken place are unenforceable. These promises lack consideration in that the element of bargained-for exchange is missing. In short, you can bargain for something to take place now or in the future but not for something that has already taken place. Therefore, **past consideration** is no consideration.

PAST CONSIDERATION
An act done before the contract is made, which ordinarily, by itself, cannot be consideration for a later promise to pay for the act.

Suppose that Elsie, a real estate agent, does her friend Judy a favor by selling Judy's house and not charging any commission. Later, Judy says to Elsie, "In return for your generous act, I will pay you $3,000." This promise is made in return for past consideration and is thus unenforceable; in effect, Judy is stating her intention to give Elsie a gift. As a further example, assume that Ellen, a nurse, spent many years living with and looking after her parents. Shortly after her parents died, her brother told her, in the presence of several other people, that he was so grateful to her for the care she gave their parents that he would take care of her for the rest of her life. When her brother fails to keep his promise, Ellen brings an action to have the promise enforced. Will the court hold that a contract exists? Not likely, because Ellen had already provided the services to her parents before her brother's promise was made. Therefore, Ellen's consideration for her brother's promise was not a promise to do something in the future. Instead, it was something she had done in the past. Because past consideration is no consideration, Ellen cannot enforce the contract because no contract exists. (Note, however, that if Ellen materially changes her position in reliance on the promised future income, a court might assert the existence of a contract under the doctrine of *promissory estoppel*, discussed later in this chapter).

Problems Concerning Consideration

Problems concerning consideration usually fall into one of the following categories:

1. Promises exchanged when total performance by the parties is uncertain.

22. Note that under the Uniform Commercial Code, any agreement modifying a contract within Article 2 on Sales needs no consideration to be binding. See UCC 2–209(1).

2. Settlement of claims.
3. Certain promises enforceable without consideration (under the doctrine of *promissory estoppel*).

The courts' solutions to these types of problems can give you insight into how the law views the complex concept of consideration.

Uncertain Performance If the terms of the contract express such uncertainty of performance that the promisor has not definitely promised to do anything, the promise is said to be *illusory*—without consideration and unenforceable. For example, suppose that the president of Tuscan Corporation says to his employees, "All of you have worked hard, and if profits continue to remain high, a 10 percent bonus at the end of the year will be given—if management thinks it is warranted." The employees continue to work hard, and profits remain high, but no bonus is given. This is an *illusory promise*, or no promise at all, because performance depends solely on the discretion of the president (the management). There is no bargained-for consideration. The statement declares merely that the management may or may not do something in the future. The president is not obligated (incurs no detriment) now or in the future.

Option-to-cancel clauses in contracts sometimes present problems in regard to consideration. For example, suppose that I contract to hire you for one year at $5,000 per month, reserving the right to cancel the contract at any time. On close examination of these words, you can see that I have not actually agreed to hire you, as I could cancel without liability before you started performance. I have not given up the opportunity of hiring someone else. This contract is therefore illusory. Now suppose that I contract to hire you for a one-year period at $5,000 per month, reserving the right to cancel the contract at any time after you have begun performance by giving you thirty days' notice. By saying that I will give you thirty days' notice, I am relinquishing the opportunity (legal right) to hire someone else instead of you for a thirty-day period. If you work for one month, at the end of which I give you thirty days' notice, you have a valid and enforceable contractual claim for $10,000 in salary.

Settlement of Claims There are several ways in which businesspersons or others can settle legal claims, and it is important to understand the nature of consideration given in these kinds of settlement agreements, or contracts. A common means of settling a claim is through an *accord and satisfaction*, in which a debtor offers to pay a lesser amount than the creditor purports to be owed. We will discuss the concept of accord and satisfaction in Chapter 12 in the context of discharging contractual obligations. Here we look at two other methods that are commonly used to settle claims, the release and the covenant not to sue.

Release A **release** bars any further recovery beyond the terms stated in the release. For example, suppose that you are involved in an automobile accident caused by Raoul's negligence. Raoul offers to give you $1,000 if you will release him from further liability resulting from the accident. You believe that this amount will cover your damages, so you agree to the release. Later you discover that it will cost $1,200 to repair your car. Can you collect the balance from Raoul? The answer is normally no; you are limited to the $1,000 in the release. Why? Because a valid contract existed. You and Raoul both assented to the bargain (hence, agreement existed), and sufficient consideration was present. The consideration was the legal detriment you suffered (by releasing Raoul from liability, you forfeited your right to sue to recover damages, should they be more than $1,000). Clearly, you are better off if you know the extent of your injuries or damages before signing a release. Releases

RELEASE
The relinquishment, concession, or giving up of a right, claim, or privilege, by the person in whom it exists or to whom it accrues, to the person against whom it might have been enforced or demanded.

will generally be binding if they are (1) given in good faith, (2) stated in a signed writing (required by many states), and (3) accompanied by consideration.[23]

COVENANT NOT TO SUE
An agreement to substitute a contractual obligation for some other type of action.

Covenant Not to Sue A **covenant not to sue,** unlike a release, does not always bar further recovery. The parties simply substitute a contractual obligation for some other type of legal action based on a valid claim. Suppose (following the earlier example) that you agreed with Raoul not to sue for damages in a tort action if he will pay for the damage to your car. If Raoul fails to pay, you can bring an action for breach of contract.

PROMISSORY ESTOPPEL
A doctrine that applies when a promisor reasonably expects a promise to induce definite and substantial action or forbearance by the promisee, and that does induce such action or forbearance in reliance thereon; such a promise is binding if injustice can be avoided only by enforcing the promise. *See also* Estoppel.

Promissory Estoppel Sometimes individuals rely on promises, and such reliance may form a basis for contract rights and duties. Under the doctrine of **promissory estoppel** (also called *detrimental reliance*), a person who has reasonably relied on the promise of another can often hope to obtain some measure of recovery. For the doctrine of promissory estoppel to be applied, a number of elements are required:

1. There must be a promise.
2. The promisee must justifiably rely on the promise.
3. The reliance normally must be of a substantial and definite character.
4. Justice will be better served by the enforcement of the promise.

Consider some examples. Your uncle tells you, "I'll pay you $150 a week so you won't have to work anymore." You quit your job, but your uncle refuses to pay you. Under the doctrine of promissory estoppel, you may be able to enforce such a promise.[24] Now your uncle makes a promise to give you $10,000 with which to buy a car. If you buy the car and he does not pay you, you may once again be able to enforce the promise under this doctrine. The promisor (the offeror) is **estopped** (barred, or impeded) from revoking the promise.

ESTOPPED
Barred, impeded, or precluded.

Application

Law and the Offeror or Offeree—The Mailbox Rule Doesn't Matter

The world of offer and acceptance has changed in recent years. To a certain extent, this change has been brought about by the emergence of express delivery services. To save valuable time, businesses now frequently send important documents via Federal Express (Fed Ex), the U.S. Postal Service's Express Mail, United Parcel Service (UPS), Airborne Express, and other carriers to be delivered the next day or two days later. When an offer is sent via Federal Express (or some other overnight service), is express delivery the impliedly authorized means of acceptance? This question was raised in Case 9.6, and the court held that the answer was yes. The "mailbox rule," which states that an acceptance is effective on dispatch, did not come into play, because certified mail was not an impliedly authorized means of acceptance.

Electronic communications systems have even more significantly altered the ways in which offers and acceptances are exchanged by businesspersons. Consider, for example, what happens when an offer or acceptance is transmitted via a fax machine. In effect, because of the nearly instantaneous sending and receiving of faxes, the mailbox rule becomes irrelevant. Another legal issue

23. Under the UCC, a written, signed waiver or renunciation by an aggrieved party discharges any further liability for a breach, even without consideration.

24. *Ricketts v. Scothorn,* 57 Neb. 51, 77 N.W. 365 (1898).

Application—Continued

raised by the use of faxes is whether faxed documents are valid in light of the fact that faxed signatures are not "original." To date, courts that have addressed this issue have generally held that signatures on faxed documents are legally binding unless an "original" signature is specifically required.

What happens when an acceptance is faxed to the offeror's office but for some reason is not received by the offeror in a timely fashion or is lost? This is similar to a situation in which a letter goes astray because of an incorrect address. Recall from the chapter text that in such a situation, the mailbox rule that an acceptance is "effective on dispatch" does not apply, and the acceptance will not be effective until received by the offeror. Very likely, if a fax transmitted to the offeror failed to reach the offeror for some reason, a court would look closely at the circumstances. For example, if the offeror did not receive the fax because her fax machine was out of paper, and the offeree had reason to suspect or know that the offeror did not receive the fax, then the court might hold that the faxed acceptance was not effective.

Whether an offer is made via fax, express delivery, or mail, it is important to remember that the offeror controls the offer. In other words, the offeror is free to state how and when the offer is to be effective. To avoid the kinds of problems to which faxed acceptances may give rise, the offeror should exercise caution when phrasing the terms of the offer. If you make an offer and want the acceptance to be faxed to you, you should clearly indicate that the acceptance must be faxed to you at a given fax number by a specific time or it will not be effective.

Checklist for the Offeror or Offeree

☐ 1. Remember that if an offer is sent via an overnight express delivery service, the same or a faster means of communication will be the impliedly authorized means of acceptance.

☐ 2. Offers and acceptances transmitted and received by fax machines will probably be legally binding unless an "original" signature is specifically required.

☐ 3. To avoid potential difficulties with faxed offers and acceptances, the offeror should clearly indicate in the offer to what fax number and by what time the acceptance must be transmitted if it is to be effective.

❖ Key Terms

acceptance 219
agreement 219
consideration 233
counteroffer 227
covenant not to sue 238
estopped 238
mailbox rule 231
mirror image rule 227
offer 219
option contract 226
past consideration 236
promissory estoppel 238
release 237
rescission 236
revocation 225

❖ Chapter Summary: Agreement and Consideration

AGREEMENT	
Offer—Requirements	1. *Intent*—There must be a serious, objective intention by the offeror to become bound by the offer. Nonoffer situations include (a) expressions of opinion, (b) statements of intention, (c) preliminary negotiations, (d) generally, advertisements, catalogues, and circulars, (e) solicitations for bids made by an auctioneer, and (f) agreements to agree in the future. 2. *Definiteness*—The terms of the offer must be sufficiently definite to be ascertainable by the parties or by a court. 3. *Communication*—The offer must be communicated to the offeree.
Offer—Termination	1. *By action of the parties*— a. Revocation—Unless the offer is irrevocable, it can be revoked at any time before acceptance without liability. Revocation is not effective until *received* by the offeree or the offeree's agent. Some offers, such as the merchant's firm offer and option contracts, are irrevocable.

❖ Chapter Summary: Agreement and Consideration—Continued

Offer—Termination Continued	b. Rejection—Accomplished by words or actions that demonstrate a clear intent not to accept the offer; not effective until *received* by the offeror or offeror's agent. c. Counteroffer—A rejection of the original offer and the making of a new offer. 2. *By operation of law*— a. Lapse of time—The offer terminates (a) at the end of the time period specified in the offer or (b) if no time period is stated in the offer, at the end of a reasonable time period. b. Destruction of the specific subject matter of the offer—Automatically terminates the offer. c. Death or incompetence—Terminates the offer unless the offer is irrevocable. d. Illegality—Supervening illegality terminates the offer.
Acceptance	1. Can be made only by the offeree or the offeree's agent. 2. Must be unequivocal. Under the common law (mirror image rule), if new terms or conditions are added to the acceptance, it will be considered a counteroffer. 3. Acceptance of a bilateral offer can be communicated by the offeree by any authorized mode of communication and is effective upon dispatch. Unless the mode of communication is expressly specified by the offeror, the following methods are impliedly authorized: a. The same mode used by the offeror or a faster mode. b. Mail, when the two parties are at a distance. 4. Acceptance of a unilateral offer is effective upon full performance of the requested act. Generally, no communication is necessary.
	CONSIDERATION
Legal Sufficiency of Consideration	To be legally sufficient, consideration must involve a legal detriment to the promisee or a legal benefit to the promisor, or both. One incurs a legal detriment by doing (or refraining from doing) something that one had no prior legal duty to do (or refrain from doing). Consideration is not legally sufficient if one is either by law or by contract under a *preexisting duty* to perform the action being offered as consideration for a new contract. *Past consideration* (actions or events that have already taken place) is not legally sufficient consideration.
Adequacy of Consideration	Adequacy of consideration relates to "how much" consideration is given and whether a fair bargain was reached. Courts will inquire into the adequacy of consideration (if the consideration is legally sufficient) only when fraud, undue influence, duress, or unconscionability may be involved.
Problems Concerning Consideration	1. *Uncertain performance*—When the nature or extent of performance is too uncertain, the promise is rendered illusory (without consideration) and unenforceable. 2. *Settlement of claims*— a. Release—An agreement by which, for consideration, a party is barred from further recovery beyond the terms specified in the release. b. Covenant not to sue—An agreement not to sue on a present, valid claim. 3. *Promissory estoppel*—An equitable doctrine that applies when a promisor reasonably expects a promise to induce definite and substantial action or forbearance by the promisee, and the promisee does act in reliance thereon; such a promise is binding if injustice can be avoided only by enforcement of the promise. Also known as the doctrine of detrimental reliance.

❖ Questions and Case Problems

9-1. Offers versus Nonoffers. What elements are necessary for an offer to be effective? What are some examples of nonoffers?

9-2. Offers versus Nonoffers. On June 1, Jason placed an ad in a local newpaper, to be run on the following Sunday, June 5, offering a reward of $100 to anyone who found his wallet. When his wallet had not been returned by June 12, he purchased another one and took steps to obtain duplicates of his driver's license, credit cards, and other items that he had lost. On June 15, Sharith, who had seen Jason's ad in the paper, found Jason's wallet, returned it to Jason, and asked for the $100. Is Jason obligated to pay Sharith the $100? Why or why not?

9-3. Offer and Acceptance. Carrie offered to sell her set of legal encyclopedias to Antonio for $300. Antonio said that he would think about her offer and let her know the next day what he decided. Norvel, who had overheard the conversation between Carrie and Antonio, said to Carrie, "I accept your offer" and gave her $300. Carrie gave Norvel the books. The next day, Antonio, who had no idea that Carrie had already sold the books to Norvel, told Carrie that he accepted her offer. Has Carrie breached a valid contract with Antonio? Explain.

9-4. Consideration. Ben hired Lewis to drive his racing car in a race. Tuan, a friend of Lewis, promised to pay Lewis $3,000 if he won the race. Lewis won the race, but Tuan refused to pay the $3,000. Tuan contended that no legally binding contract had been formed because he had received no consideration from Lewis for his promise to pay the $3,000. Lewis sued Tuan for breach of contract, arguing that winning the race was the consideration given in exchange for Tuan's promise to pay the $3,000. What rule of law discussed in this chapter supports Tuan's claim?

9-5. Acceptance. On Saturday, Arthur mailed Tanya an offer to sell his car to her for $2,000. On Monday, having changed his mind and not having heard from Tanya, Arthur sent her a letter revoking his offer. On Wednesday, before she had received Arthur's letter of revocation, Tanya mailed a letter of acceptance to Arthur. When Tanya demanded that Arthur sell his car to her as promised, Arthur claimed that no contract existed because he had revoked his offer prior to Tanya's acceptance. Is Arthur correct? Explain.

9-6. Detrimental Reliance. Red Owl Stores, Inc., induced the Hoffmans to give up their current business and run a Red Owl franchise. Although no contract was ever signed, the Hoffmans incurred numerous expenses in reliance upon Red Owl's representations. When the deal ultimately fell through because of Red Owl's failure to keep its promise concerning the operation of the franchise agency store, the Hoffmans brought suit to recover their losses. Will the Hoffmans succeed? [*Hoffman v. Red Owl Stores, Inc.*, 26 Wis.2d 683, 133 N.W.2d 267 (1965)]

9-7. Offers versus Nonoffers. John H. Surratt was one of John Wilkes Booth's alleged accomplices in the murder of President Lincoln. On April 20, 1865, the secretary of war issued and caused to be published in newspapers the following proclamation: "$25,000 reward for the apprehension of John H. Surratt and liberal rewards for any information that leads to the arrest of John H. Surratt." On November 24, 1865, President Johnson revoked the reward and published the revocation in the newspapers. Henry B. St. Marie learned of the reward but left for Rome prior to its revocation. In Rome, St. Marie discovered Surratt's whereabouts. In April 1866, unaware that the reward had been revoked, he reported this information to U.S. officials. Based on this information, the officials were able to arrest Surratt. Should St. Marie have received the reward? If so, was he entitled to the full $25,000? [*Shuey v. United States*, 92 U.S. (2 Otto) 73, 23 L.Ed. 697 (1875)]

9-8. Offers versus Nonoffers. The Olivers were planning to sell some of their ranch land and mentioned this fact to Southworth, a neighbor. Southworth expressed interest in purchasing the property and later notified the Olivers that he had the money available to buy it. The Olivers told Southworth they would let him know shortly about the details concerning the sale. The Olivers later sent a letter to Southworth—and (unknown to Southworth) to several other neighbors—giving information about the sale, including the price, the location of the property, and the amount of acreage involved. When Southworth received the letter, he sent a letter to the Olivers "accepting" their offer. The Olivers stated that the information letter had not been intended as an "offer" but merely as a starting point for negotiations. Southworth brought suit against the Olivers to enforce the "contract." Did a contract exist? [*Southworth v. Oliver*, 284 Or. 361, 587 P.2d 994 (1978)]

9-9. Consideration. Ellen and Gabriel Fineman held MasterCards issued by Citibank. Holders of these cards paid an annual $15 fee. The issuance and use of the cards were governed by a retail installment credit agreement, which contained the following statement: "We can change this Agreement including the *finance charge* and the *annual percentage rate* at any time." The agreement did provide for thirty days' notice of any such changes, and the cardholder had a right to reject the changes in writing and return the credit card. Two months before the expiration of the Finemans' cards, Citibank notified them that it was increasing its annual fee to $20; however, Citibank was also providing its cardholders with extra services and benefits, such as "$100,000 common carrier travel insurance." The Finemans did not object in writing, nor did they return the cards. Citibank added 83 cents to the Finemans' next bill, the prorated portion of the increase for the two months remaining on their cards. The Finemans filed suit (a class-action suit on behalf of all cardholders) to recover the increased charges. Among other claims, the Finemans argued that the modification failed because (1) the travel insurance was not adequate consideration for the modification because they never received any benefits from the insurance and (2) its cost to Citibank was negligible. Was there adequate and legally sufficient consideration for Citibank's modification of the annual credit-card fee? [*Fineman v. Citicorp USA, Inc.*, 137 Ill.App.3d 1055, 485 N.E. 2d 591, 92 Ill.Dec. 780 (1985)]

9-10. Serious Intent of Offeror. Treece, a vice president of Vend-A-Win, Inc., was testifying before the Washington State Gambling Commission concerning an application his firm had made for a temporary license to distribute punch boards (gambling devices). The Gambling Commission was conducting an investigation into gambling practices, and Treece's testimony was given during a televised hearing. Treece made the following statement at the hearing: "I'll pay a hundred thousand dollars to anyone to find a crooked board. If they find it, I'll pay it." The audience laughed, and Treece thought no more about the offer until he received a telephone call from Barnes. Barnes had watched Treece's television appearance and later read about Treece's statement in a newspaper. Barnes asked Treece if Treece had been serious when he made the statement, and Treece affirmed that he had been serious. Barnes then brought a crooked board into Vend-A-Win's offices and delivered another crooked board to the Gambling Commission. When Vend-A-Win and Treece refused to pay Barnes $100,000, Barnes sued them for the promised amount, claiming that Treece had made an offer for a unilateral contract. What will the court decide? [*Barnes v. Treece*, 15 Wash.App. 437, 549 P.2d 11252 (1976)]

9-11. Offer and Acceptance. James sent invitations to a number of potential buyers to submit bids for some timber James wanted to sell. Two bids were received as a result, the highest one submitted by Eames. James changed his mind about selling the timber and did not accept Eames's bid. Eames claimed that a contract for sale existed and sued James for breach. Did a contract exist? [*Eames v. James*, 452 So.2d 384 (La.App., 3d Cir 1984)]

9-12. Offers versus Nonoffers. Chia and Shin Chang read First Colonial Bank's advertisement about the bank's saving certificates, which stated that a depositor could deposit $14,000, receive a gift immediately, and collect $20,136.12 in three and a half years when the certificate matured. The Changs, in reliance on the ad, deposited $14,000 at First Colonial and received a color television and a certificate of deposit. When they cashed in the certificate upon its maturity, however, they received only $18,823.93 instead of the promised $20,136.12. First Colonial informed the Changs that the advertisement had contained a typographical error and that they would have had to deposit $15,000, not $14,000, to receive $20,136.12. The Changs filed suit to recover $1,312.19, the difference between the amount they received and the amount they had expected. Did the newspaper advertisement constitute an offer that, when accepted, created a legally enforceable contract? Explain. [*Chang v. First Colonial Savings Bank*, 242 Va. 388, 410 S.E.2d 928 (1991)]

A Question of Ethics and Social Responsibility

9-13. *Widener and Mozumder were employed as geophysicists by Arco Oil and Gas Co. On March 31, 1986, both employees were notified by letter that they were being placed on "surplus" status—which meant that if they were not placed in another position in the company during the next sixty days, their employment would be terminated. On termination, they would become eligible for benefits, including lump-sum allowance payments, under either of two company termination and retirement programs. To be eligible for payments under either plan, the employees were required to sign release documents. The employees were given informational packets outlining each plan in detail and advising the employees to contact the company's benefits specialist, Barbara Hough, about which plan they wished to elect. The employees went to Hough's office and signed various documents, among which was a general release that read, in part: "I release and discharge the Company * * * from all claims, liabilities, demands, and causes of action known or unknown, fixed or contingent, which I may have or claim to have against the Company as a result of this termination and do hereby covenant not to file a lawsuit to assert such claims." After signing the release, each employee received a lump-sum payment. When the employees later sued Arco, alleging wrongful discharge on the basis of age discrimination, Arco claimed that the release documents signed by the employees released it from any liability. The employees contended that they had not voluntarily and knowingly given the releases. The release document was confusing because it was not entitled a release, and Hough had never informed them of the significance of what they were signing. She had told them only that they had to sign the various documents before they left. The court held that the releases were valid and granted Arco's motion for summary judgment.* [Widener v. Arco Oil and Gas Co., *717 F.Supp. 1211 (N.D.Tex. 1989)*]

1. Widener and Mozumder were apparently genuinely surprised to learn that one of the documents that they had each signed was a release. In view of their apparent "innocence" in this regard, is it fair that they should be held to what they promised in the release documents?
2. If the two employees had not been highly educated men, would your answer to the above question be different?
3. A recurring problem in the area of contract law is that innocent parties sometimes suffer harmful consequences because they failed to read what they were signing. A general ethical principle underlying the law is that people should be held responsible for their own actions. But the law also seeks to prevent one party from taking undue advantage of another. How well do you think the court balanced these two fundamental ethical policies in its decision in this case? Would you have held differently if you had been the judge? Why?
4. Companies seeking to reduce or replace personnel frequently offer special retirement or termination benefits to induce employees to retire early or voluntarily terminate their employment. A company frequently will also request—as Arco did in this case—that the departing employees, in consideration for termination benefits received, sign release forms in which they promise not to hold the company liable for any future claims that the employees may have against the company. Is this practice in any way unethical?

For Critical Analysis

9-14. *Discuss the implications of the use of fax machines, which are nearly ubiquitous in business offices today, for the communication requirements relating to offers and acceptances.*

Chapter 10

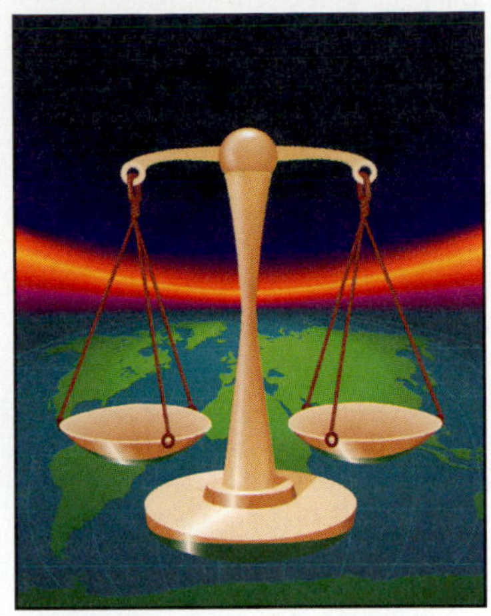

Capacity and Legality

"The state . . . has the power to prevent the individual from making certain kinds of contracts, and in regard to them the Federal Constitution offers no protection."

Rufus W. Peckham,
1838–1909
(Associate justice of the United States Supreme Court, 1896–1909)

Courts generally want contracts to be enforceable, and much of the law is made to aid in the enforceability of contracts. Nonetheless, as indicated in the opening quotation, the state can prevent the making of certain kinds of contracts—that is, not all people can make legally binding contracts at all times. Contracts entered into by persons lacking the *contractual capacity* to do so may not be enforced. Similarly, contracts calling for the performance of an illegal act are *illegal* and thus void—they are not contracts at all. In this chapter, we examine contractual capacity and some aspects of illegal bargains.

❖ Contractual Capacity

Although the parties to a contract must assume certain risks, the law indicates that neither party should be allowed to benefit from the other party's lack of **contractual capacity**—the legal ability to enter into a contractual relationship. Courts generally presume the existence of contractual capacity, but there are some situations in which capacity is lacking or may be questionable. A person *adjudged by a court* to be mentally incompetent, for example, cannot form a legally binding contract with another party. In other situations, a party may have the capacity to enter into a valid contract but also have the right to avoid liability under it. For example, minors usually are not legally bound by contracts. In this section, we look at the effect of youth, mental incompetence, and intoxication on contractual capacity. There are other factors that may affect the capacity to form an enforceable contract, but the question of legal capacity most often involves minors, intoxicated persons, or mentally incompetent persons.

CONTRACTUAL CAPACITY
The mental capacity required by the law for a party who enters into a contract to be bound by that contract.

Minors

Under the common law, a minor was defined as a male who had not attained the age of twenty-one or a female who was not yet eighteen. Today, in most states, the *age of majority* (when a person is no longer a minor) for contractual purposes is eighteen years for both sexes.[1] In addition, some states provide for the termination

1. The age of majority may still be twenty-one for other purposes, such as the purchase and consumption of alcohol. The word *infant* is usually used synonymously with the word *minor.*

of minority upon marriage. Subject to certain exceptions, the contracts entered into by a minor are voidable at the option of that minor. The minor has the option of *disaffirming* (renouncing) the contract and setting aside the contract and all legal obligations arising from it. An adult who enters into a contract with a minor, however, cannot avoid his or her contractual duties on the ground that the minor can do so. Unless the minor exercises the option to disaffirm the contract (to be discussed shortly), the adult party is bound by it.

Disaffirmance The general rule is that a minor can enter into any contract an adult can, provided that the contract is not one prohibited by law for minors (for example, the sale of alcoholic beverages). Although minors have the right to disaffirm their contracts, there are exceptions (to be discussed later).

DISAFFIRMANCE
The repudiation of an obligation.

Disaffirmance in General For a minor to exercise the option to avoid a contract, he or she need only manifest an intention not to be bound by it. The minor "avoids" the contract by "disaffirming" it. The technical definition of **disaffirmance** is the legal avoidance, or setting aside, of a contractual obligation. Words or conduct may serve to express this intent. The contract can ordinarily be disaffirmed at any time during minority or for a reasonable time after the minor comes of age. In some states, however, when there is a contract for the sale of land by a minor, the minor cannot disaffirm the contract until he or she reaches the age of majority.

It is important that disaffirmance be timely. If, for example, an individual wishes to disaffirm an executed contract made as a minor but fails to do so until two years after he or she has reached the age of majority, a court will likely hold that the contract has been ratified (see the discussion of ratification below).

Duty of Restitution When a contract has been executed, a minor cannot disaffirm it without returning whatever goods he or she may have received or without paying for their reasonable use. The majority of courts hold that the minor need only return the goods (or other consideration), provided such goods are in the minor's possession or control. Suppose that Jim Garrison, a seventeen-year-old, purchases a computer from Radio Shack. While transporting the computer to his home, Garrison negligently drops it, breaking the plastic casing. The next day, he returns the computer to Radio Shack and disaffirms the contract. Under the majority view, this return fulfills Garrison's duty even though the computer is now damaged.

RESTITUTION
An equitable remedy under which a person is restored to his or her original position prior to loss or injury, or placed in the position he or she would have been in had the breach not occurred.

A few states, however, either by statute or by court decision, place an additional duty on the minor—the duty of **restitution.** This rule recognizes the legitimate interests of those who deal with minors. The theory is that the adult should be returned to the position he or she held before the contract was made. In the example just given, Garrison would be required not only to return the computer but also to pay Radio Shack for damages to the computer.

If a minor disaffirms a contract, he or she must disaffirm the *entire* contract. The minor cannot decide to keep part of the goods contracted for and return the remainder. When a minor disaffirms, all property that he or she has transferred to the adult as consideration can be recovered, even if it is then in the possession of a third party.[2] In the following case, a minor's father brought an action on behalf of his son to disaffirm the minor's purchase of an automobile and to recover the money paid for the car from a seller who knew that the purchaser was a minor when the contract was made.

2. The Uniform Commercial Code allows an exception if the third party is a "good faith purchaser for value." See UCC 2–403(1).

Case 10.1
QUALITY MOTORS, INC. v. HAYS

Supreme Court of Arkansas, 1949.
216 Ark. 264,
225 S.W.2d 326.

HISTORICAL AND ECONOMIC SETTING *In 1949, a business recession produced a decline in the cost of living. United Automobile Workers at General Motors plants accepted a slight wage cut, after they had obtained a wage increase the year before. Unemployment jumped more than two percentage points, while stock prices fell more than 10 percent. The cost of housing and health care rose, while other consumer prices fell. A gallon of gasoline cost 21 cents. A new Cadillac cost $5,000. The average steel worker, after taxes, made $3,000, and the average high school teacher made $4,700. The typical car salesperson made, after taxes, $8,000.*

FACTS Johnny Hays, a sixteen-year-old minor, went to Quality Motors, Inc., seeking to purchase a car. The salesperson refused to sell the car unless the purchase was made by an adult. Shortly thereafter, Johnny returned with a young man of twenty-three whom Johnny had met that day for the first time. The sales agent then accepted Hays's cashier's check (a check drawn by a bank on itself), and a bill of sale was made out to the twenty-three-year-old. The salesperson recommended a notary public who could prepare the necessary papers to transfer title from the young man to Johnny and then drove the two boys into town for this purpose. The young man transferred title to Johnny, and the salesperson delivered the car to Johnny. Johnny's father attempted to return the car to Quality Motors for a full refund, but Quality Motors refused it. The car was stored while Johnny's father sought to get Quality Motors to take it back, but Johnny found the keys and wrecked the car in an accident. Johnny, through his father, brought suit to disaffirm the contract and recover the purchase price. The trial court ordered the purchase price to be refunded to Hays on his return of the car to Quality Motors. Quality Motors appealed.

ISSUE Can Johnny disaffirm this contract although it was nominally made by an adult?

DECISION Yes. Johnny was able to disaffirm the contract and return the car. He was not held liable for any damages.

REASON The court reasoned that because the salesperson knew that Johnny was a minor, aided Johnny in obtaining the car by selling it to an adult, and assisted in the transfer of title to Johnny, the sale was essentially made to Johnny. When goods—other than *necessaries* (food, clothing, and so on, as will be discussed shortly)—are sold to a minor, the minor can disaffirm the contract of sale. The loss that Quality Motors suffered was the result of its own act of not accepting the undamaged car when it could have. The presiding justice quoted the law as follows: "The law is well settled * * * that an infant may disaffirm his contracts, except those made for necessaries, without being required to return the consideration received, except such part as may remain in specie in his hands."

Misrepresentation of Age Suppose that a minor tells a seller she is twenty-one years old when she is really seventeen. Ordinarily, the minor can disaffirm the contract even though she has misrepresented her age. Moreover, the minor is not liable in certain jurisdictions for the tort of deceit for such misrepresentation, the rationale being that such a tort judgment might indirectly force the minor to perform the contract.

Many jurisdictions, however, do find circumstances under which a minor can be bound by a contract when age has been misrepresented. First, several states have enacted statutes for precisely this purpose. In these states, misrepresentation of age is enough to prohibit disaffirmance. Other statutes prohibit disaffirmance by a minor who has engaged in business as an adult.

Second, some courts refuse to allow minors to disaffirm executed (fully performed) contracts unless they can return the consideration received. The combination of the minors' misrepresentation and their unjust enrichment has persuaded these courts to *estop* (prevent) minors from asserting contractual incapacity.

Third, some courts allow a misrepresenting minor to disaffirm the contract, but they hold the minor liable for damages in tort. Here, the defrauded party may sue the minor for misrepresentation or fraud. A split in authority exists on this point,

Can a minor who induces a sale by misrepresenting his or her age nevertheless avoid any obligation under the resulting contract by disaffirming it?

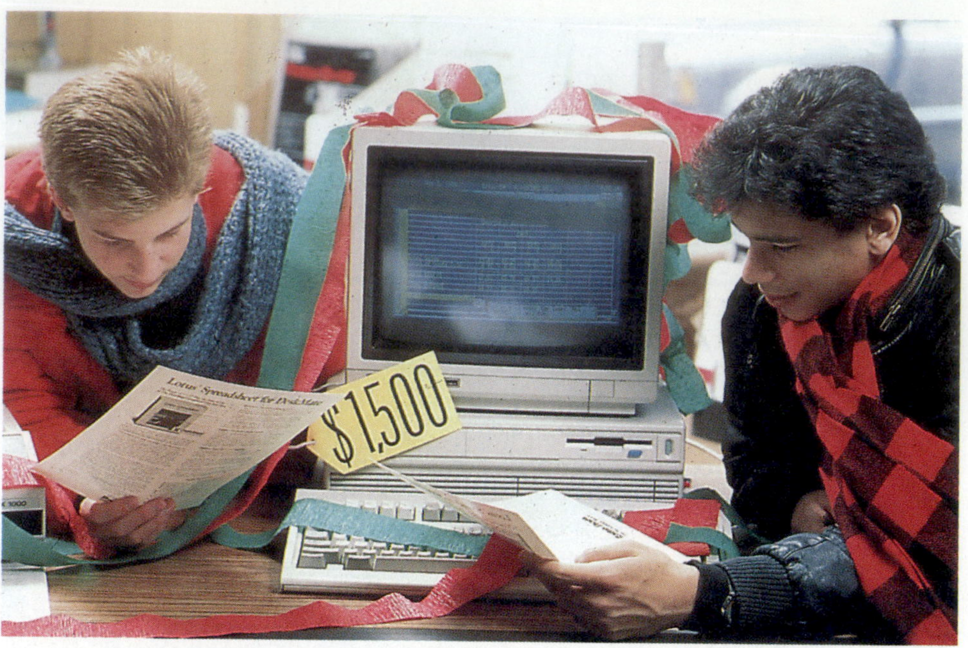

because some courts, as previously noted, have recognized that allowing a suit in tort is equivalent to the indirect enforcement of the minor's contract.

Basically, a minor's ability to avoid a contractual obligation is allowed by the law as a shield for the minor's defense, not as a sword for his or her unjust enrichment. In the following case, an Ohio appellate court had to deal with a contract involving a minor's false representation of age. The age of majority in Ohio at the time this case was decided was twenty-one.

Case 10.2 

HAYDOCY PONTIAC, INC. v. LEE

Court of Appeals of Ohio, Franklin County, 1969. 19 Ohio App.2d 217, 250 N.E.2d 898.

HISTORICAL AND ECONOMIC SETTING *In 1969, the U.S. economy was booming. Unemployment fell to its lowest level in fifteen years, and a record number of workers were employed. Stock prices were higher than they had ever been. The largest oil field outside the Middle East was discovered beneath the North Sea. U.S. automobile manufacturers produced approximately nine million automobiles. The wholesale price for the average American-made car was $2,280, compared with $1,880 ten years before.*

FACTS Jennifer Lee was twenty years old when she contracted to purchase an automobile from Haydocy Pontiac, Inc., but she told the salesperson that she was twenty-one years old. Lee financed most of the purchase price. Immediately following delivery of the automobile, she turned the car over to a third person and never thereafter had possession. She made no further payments on the contract and attempted to rescind (cancel) it. She made no offer to return the automobile. Haydocy sued for the balance owed. The trial court held for Lee on the rule that permits a minor to avoid a transaction without being required to restore the consideration received if the minor does not possess it.

ISSUE Could Haydocy recover the balance still owed on the car, given the fact that the purchaser was a minor?

DECISION Yes. Haydocy was allowed to recover the fair market value of the automobile from Lee on equitable grounds, although the fair market value could not exceed the original purchase price of the automobile. Lee was estopped from rescinding the contract on the ground that she was a minor because she had induced the sale by misrepresenting her age.

REASON The court reasoned that under the particular circumstances of this case, the disaffirmance of the contract should be determined on the basis of equitable principles. In the words of the presiding judge, "Where [an] infant * * * through falsehood and deceit enters into a

Case 10.2—Continued

contract with another who enters therein in honesty and good faith and, thereafter, the infant seeks to disaffirm the contract without tendering back the consideration, no right or interest of the infant exists which needs protection. The privilege given the infant thereupon becomes a weapon of injustice."

Liability for Necessaries, Insurance, and Loans A minor who enters into a contract for **necessaries** may disaffirm the contract but remains liable for the reasonable value of the goods. The legal duty to pay a reasonable value does not arise from the contract itself but is imposed by law under a theory of quasi contract. One theory is that the minor should not be unjustly enriched and should therefore be liable for purchases that fulfill basic needs, such as food, clothing, and shelter. Another theory is that the minor's right to disaffirm a contract has economic ramifications in that a seller is likely to refuse to deal with minors because of it. If minors can at least be held liable for the reasonable value of the goods, a seller's reluctance to enter into contracts with minors may be offset. This theory explains why the courts narrow the subject matter to necessaries—without such a rule, minors might be denied the opportunity to purchase even necessary goods.

NECESSARIES
Necessities required for life, such as food, shelter, clothing, and medical attention; normally, necessaries are also considered to include items or services appropriate to an individual's circumstances and condition in life.

Traditionally, insurance has not been viewed as a necessary, so minors can ordinarily disaffirm their contracts and recover all premiums paid. Some jurisdictions, however, prohibit the right to disaffirm such contracts—for example, when minors contract for life insurance on their own lives.

Financial loans are seldom considered to be necessaries, even if the minor spends the money borrowed on necessaries. If, however, a lender makes a loan to a minor for the express purpose of enabling the minor to purchase necessaries, and the lender personally makes sure the money is so spent, the minor normally is obligated to repay the loan.

Ratification In contract law, **ratification** is the act of accepting and giving legal force to an obligation that previously was not enforceable. A minor who has reached the age of majority can ratify a contract in three ways—by express ratification, by conduct, or by a failure to disaffirm an executed contract within a reasonable period of time. Express ratification takes place when the minor, upon reaching the age of majority, states orally or in writing that he or she intends to be bound by the contract. If a minor, on reaching the age of majority, manifests an intent to ratify the contract by conduct (by enjoying the benefits of the contract, for example), this may also constitute ratification, particularly if the adult party to the contract has performed his or her part of the bargain. A minor's failure to disaffirm a contract within a reasonable time after reaching the age of majority may also be deemed by the courts to constitute ratification when the contract is executed (performed by both parties). If the contract is still executory (not yet performed or only partially performed), however, failure to disaffirm the contract will not necessarily imply ratification. Generally, the courts base their determination on whether the minor, after reaching the age of majority, has had ample opportunity to consider the nature of the contractual obligations he or she entered into as a minor and the extent to which the adult party to the contract has performed.

RATIFICATION
The approval or validation of a previous action. In contract law, the confirmation of a voidable act (that is, an act that without ratification would not be an enforceable contractual obligation). In agency law, the confirmation by one person of an act or contract performed or entered into on his or her behalf by another, who assumed, without authority, to act as his or her agent.

Parents' Liability As a general rule, parents are not liable for the contracts made by minor children acting on their own. This is why businesses ordinarily require parents to sign any contract made with a minor. The parents then become personally obligated under the contract to perform the conditions of the contract, even if their child avoids liability.

Generally, a minor is held personally liable for the torts he or she commits. Therefore, minors cannot disaffirm their liability for their tortious conduct. The parents of the minor can *also* be held liable under certain circumstances. For example, if the minor commits a tort under the direction of a parent or while performing an act requested by a parent, the injured party can hold the parent liable. In addition, parents are liable in many states up to a statutory amount for malicious torts committed by a minor child living in their home.

EMANCIPATION
In regard to minors, the act of being freed from parental control. The emancipation of a minor by his or her parents involves the parents' surrender of the right to the care, custody, and earnings of the minor as well as a renunciation of parental duties.

Emancipation The release of a minor by his or her parents is known as **emancipation.** Emancipation involves completely relinquishing the right to the minor's control, care, custody, and earnings. It is a repudiation of parental obligations. Emancipation may be express or implied, absolute or conditional, total or partial. Several jurisdictions permit minors to petition a court for emancipation themselves. For business purposes, a minor may petition a court to be treated as an adult. If the court grants the minor's request, it removes the minor's lack of contractual capacity and right of disaffirmance for those contracts entered into in conducting the business.

Intoxicated Persons

A contract entered into by an intoxicated person can be either voidable or valid. If the person was sufficiently intoxicated to lack mental capacity, the transaction is voidable at the option of the intoxicated person, even if the intoxication was purely voluntary. For the contract to be voidable, it must be proved that the intoxicated person's reason and judgment were impaired to the extent that he or she did not comprehend the legal consequences of entering into the contract. If the person was intoxicated but understood these legal consequences, the contract is enforceable. Simply because the terms of the contract are foolish or are obviously favorable to the other party does not mean the contract is voidable (unless the other party fraudulently induced the person to become intoxicated). Problems often arise in determining whether a party was sufficiently intoxicated to avoid legal duties. Many courts prefer looking at objective indications rather than assessing the intoxicated party's mental state.

The following case shows an unusual business transaction in which boasts and dares "after a few drinks" resulted in a binding sale and purchase transaction. It should be noted that avoidance on the ground of intoxication is rare.

Case 10.3 

LUCY v. ZEHMER

Supreme Court of Appeals of Virginia, 1954.
196 Va. 493,
84 S.E.2d 516.

HISTORICAL AND SOCIAL SETTING *In part because intoxication is usually self-induced, the emphasis in cases that concern lack of capacity on the ground of intoxication is sometimes different from the emphasis in cases that concern lack of capacity on other grounds. Particularly in older cases, there is often a discussion of the parties' morals. It has been suggested that the motivation for enforcing a contract made by an intoxicated person is not that the person was sober enough to understand what he or she was doing. Instead, the issue is whether the law will allow the person to get intoxicated and avoid the consequences of his or her behavior. Sometimes, it may appear that what is being judged is not the extent of a person's intoxication but his or her attitude. At least one court at the turn of the century held that intoxication is never a defense.*[a]

FACTS Lucy and Zehmer had known each other for fifteen or twenty years. For the last eight years or so, Lucy had been wanting to buy Zehmer's farm. Zehmer had always told Lucy that he was not interested in selling. One night, Lucy stopped in to visit with the Zehmers at a restaurant they operated. Lucy said to Zehmer, "I bet you wouldn't take $50,000 for that place." Zehmer replied, "Yes, I would, too; you wouldn't give fifty." Throughout the evening the conversation returned to the sale of the farm. At the same time, the parties were drinking whiskey. Eventually, Lucy convinced Zehmer to write up an agreement for the sale of the farm. Zehmer wrote the agreement on the back of a restaurant check and asked his wife to sign it. She did. When Lucy subsequently tried to enforce the agreement, Zehmer argued that he had been "high as a

a. *Cook v. Bagnell Timber Co.*, 78 Ark. 47, 94 S.W. 695 (1906).

Case 10.3—Continued

Georgia pine" at the time and that the offer had been made in jest: "two doggoned drunks bluffing to see who could talk the biggest and say the most." Lucy said that although he had felt the drinks, he had not been intoxicated and, from the way Zehmer handled the transaction, did not think he had been intoxicated either. The trial court ruled in favor of the Zehmers, and Lucy appealed.

ISSUE Can the Lucy-Zehmer agreement be avoided on the basis of mental incapacity resulting from intoxication?

DECISION No. The agreement to sell the farm was binding, and the Zehmers could not rescind (cancel) the contract.

REASON The opinion of the court was that the evidence given about the nature of the conversation, the appearance and completeness of the agreement, and the signing all tended to show that a serious business transaction and not a casual jest was intended. The court had to look into the objective meaning of the words and acts of the Zehmers. "An agreement or mutual assent is of course essential to a valid contract, but the law imputes to a person an intention corresponding to the reasonable meaning of his words and acts. If his words and acts, judged by a reasonable standard, manifest an intention to agree, it is immaterial what may be the real but unexpressed state of mind."

Mentally Incompetent Persons

Contracts made by mentally incompetent persons can be either void, voidable, or valid. If a person has been adjudged mentally incompetent by a court of law and a guardian has been appointed, any contract made by the mentally incompetent person is *void*—no contract exists. Only the guardian can enter into a binding legal duty on behalf of the mentally incompetent person.

If a mentally incompetent person not previously so adjudged by a court enters into a contract, the contract may be *voidable* if the person does not know he or she is entering into the contract or lacks the mental capacity to comprehend its nature, purpose, and consequences. In such situations, the contract is voidable at the option of the mentally incompetent person but not the other party. Whenever there is no prior adjudication of mental incompetence, most courts examine whether the party was able to understand the nature, purpose, and consequences of his or her act at the time of the transaction. The contract may then be disaffirmed or ratified. Ratification must occur after the person is mentally competent or after a guardian is appointed and ratifies the contract. Like minors and intoxicated persons, mentally incompetent persons are liable (in quasi contract) for the reasonable value of any necessaries they receive.

A contract entered into by a mentally incompetent person may also be *valid*. A person can understand the nature and effect of entering into a certain contract yet simultaneously lack capacity to engage in other activities. In such cases, the contract is valid, because the person is not legally mentally incompetent for contractual purposes. Modern courts no longer require that a person be completely irrational to disaffirm contracts on grounds of mental incompetency. A contract may be voidable if, by reason of a mental illness or defect, an individual was unable to act reasonably with respect to the transaction and the other party had reason to know of this condition.[3]

❖ Legality

To this point, we have discussed three of the requirements for a valid contract to exist—agreement, consideration, and contractual capacity. Now we examine a

3. See *Ortelere v. Teachers' Retirement Board,* 25 N.Y. 2d 196, 250 N.E.2d 460, 303 N.Y.S.2d 362 (1969). The court determines what tests for mental incompetence are used.

fourth—legality. For a contract to be valid and enforceable, it must be formed for a legal purpose. A contract to do something that is prohibited by federal or state statutory law is illegal and, as such, void from the outset and thus unenforceable. Also, a contract that is tortious or calls for an action contrary to public policy is illegal and unenforceable. Note that a contract, or a clause in a contract, may be illegal even in the absence of a specific statute prohibiting the action promised by the contract.

Contracts Contrary to Statute

"Death and dice level all distinctions."

Samuel Foote, 1720–1777
(English dramatist)

Statutes often prescribe the terms of contracts. In some instances, the laws are specific, even providing for the inclusion of certain clauses and their wording. Other statutes prohibit certain contracts on the basis of their subject matter, the time at which they are entered into, or the status of the contracting parties. In this section, we examine several ways in which contracts may be contrary to a statute and thus illegal.

Gambling In general, wagers and games of chance are illegal. All states have statutes that regulate gambling—defined as any scheme that involves distribution of property by chance among persons who have paid a valuable consideration for the opportunity (chance) to receive the property.[4] Gambling is the creation of risk for the purpose of assuming it. A few states do permit gambling, and a number of states have recognized the substantial revenues that can be obtained from legal, state-operated lotteries.

Sometimes it is difficult to distinguish a gambling contract from the risk sharing inherent in almost all contracts. Suppose that Isaacson takes out a life insurance policy on Donohue, naming himself as beneficiary under the policy. At first glance, this may seem entirely legal; but further examination shows that Isaacson is simply gambling on how long Donohue will live. To prevent that type of practice, insurance contracts can be entered into only by someone with an *insurable interest* (see Chapters 15 and 35).

Futures contracts, or contracts for the future purchase or sale of commodities (such as corn and wheat), are not illegal gambling contracts—although it might appear that a person selling or buying a futures contract is essentially gambling on the future price of the commodity. Because the seller of the futures contract either already has a property interest in the commodity or can purchase the commodity elsewhere and deliver the commodity as required in the futures contract, courts have upheld the legality of such contracts.

Sabbath (Sunday) Laws Statutes called Sabbath (Sunday) laws prohibit the formation or performance of certain contracts on a Sunday. Under the common law, such contracts are legal in the absence of this statutory prohibition. Under some state statutes, all contracts entered into on a Sunday are illegal. Statutes in other states prohibit only the sale of merchandise, particularly alcoholic beverages, on a Sunday. These statutes, which date back to colonial times, are often called **blue laws.** Blue laws get their name from the blue paper on which New Haven, Connecticut, printed its new town ordinance in 1781. The ordinance prohibited all work on Sunday and required all shops to close on the "Lord's Day." A number of states enacted laws forbidding the carrying on of "all secular labor and business on The Lord's Day." Exceptions to Sunday laws permit contracts for necessities (such as food) and works of charity. A fully performed (executed) contract that was entered into on a Sunday cannot be rescinded (canceled).

BLUE LAWS
State or local laws that make the performance of commercial activities on Sunday illegal.

4. See *Wishing Well Club v. Akron,* 66 Ohio Law Abs. 406, 112 N.E.2d 41 (1951).

Business Law in Action

The Gambler versus the Bank

Casinos make it easy for gamblers. Often, casinos will allow their patrons to cash personal checks or will otherwise accommodate them by extending credit or having automated teller machines (ATMs) on their premises so that money can be easily obtained for gambling. Some casinos now even have ATMs in their gambling "pits" that allow customers to obtain gambling tokens with their credit cards. Customers enjoy this convenience, casinos profit from it, and so do banks—but not always. It is just possible, as a Connecticut bank found out, that advances made to credit cardholders at these ATMs may not be legally collectible.

The bank in this case was the Connecticut National Bank of Hartford, a subsidiary of Shawmut National Corporation. The credit cardholder was Richard Kommit, to whom the Connecticut bank had issued a MasterCard. Kommit used his MasterCard to obtain $5,500 in gambling tokens from an ATM located in the gambling pit of a casino in Atlantic City, New Jersey. When the bank later tried to collect the $5,500 from Kommit, however, Kommit refused to pay it on the ground that it was a gambling debt and therefore uncollectible.

The situation was complicated by the fact that Kommit lived in Massachusetts, the bank was located in Connecticut, and the casino was located in New Jersey. Which law applied in this situation? The question was significant to the parties because the laws of the states differ in regard to gambling debts. In New Jersey, under that state's Casino Control Act, loans made for casino gambling in Atlantic City are legal and enforceable. In Massachusetts and Connecticut, however, gambling debts are void—but only if the bank knew or should have known that the money was borrowed for gambling. The bank argued, understandably, that New Jersey law should be applied. The lower courts agreed and granted summary judgment for the bank.

On appeal, however, the court noted that the contract between the Connecticut bank and Kommit expressly stated that "[t]his agreement and the use of your account [are] governed by Connecticut Law." The court applied Connecticut law in view of the fact that the parties had chosen that law to govern the contract. Because a question of fact existed as to the bank's knowledge that the loan was for gambling, summary judgment for the bank was inappropriate. The appellate court thus reversed the judgment.[a] Given that the ATM was located in a casino gambling area and dispensed gambling chits instead of cash, it is hard to imagine that the bank did not have knowledge that the funds were being used for gambling. In short, Kommit was able to "have his cake and eat it, too," while the bank was left holding the proverbial bag. But this particular bank will not have to face losses like this in the future—it has since sold its credit-card business.

a. *Connecticut National Bank of Hartford v. Kommit,* 31 Mass.App. 348, 577 N.E.2d 639 (1991).

Many states do not enforce Sunday laws, and some of these laws have been held to be unconstitutional on the ground that they are contrary to the freedom of religion.

Licensing Statutes All states require that members of certain professions or callings obtain licenses allowing them to practice. Doctors, lawyers, real estate brokers, architects, electricians, and stockbrokers are but a few of the people who must be licensed. Some licenses are obtained only after extensive schooling and examinations, which indicate to the public that a special skill has been acquired. Others require only that the particular person be of good moral character.

Generally, business licenses provide a means of regulating and taxing certain businesses and protecting the public against actions that could threaten the general welfare. For example, in nearly all states, a stockbroker must be licensed and must file a bond with the state to protect the public from fraudulent transactions in stock. Similarly, a plumber must be licensed and bonded to protect the public against incompetent plumbers and to protect the public health. Only persons or businesses possessing the qualifications and complying with the conditions required by statute are entitled to licenses. Typically, for example, an owner of a saloon or tavern is required to sell food as a condition of obtaining a license to sell liquor for consumption on the premises.

> *"Liberty of contract is not an absolute concept. It is relative to many conditions of time and place and circumstance."*
>
> **Benjamin Cardozo, 1870–1938**
> ***(Associate justice of the United States Supreme Court, 1932–1938)***

When a person enters into a contract with an unlicensed individual, the contract may still be enforceable depending on the nature of the licensing statute. Some states expressly provide that the lack of a license in certain occupations bars the enforcement of work-related contracts. If the statute does not expressly state this, one must look to the underlying purpose of the licensing requirements for a particular occupation. If the purpose is to protect the public from unauthorized practitioners, a contract involving an unlicensed individual is illegal and unenforceable. If, however, the underlying purpose of the statute is to raise government revenues, a contract entered into with an unlicensed practitioner is enforceable—although the unlicensed person is usually fined.

Contracts Contrary to Public Policy

Although contracts involve private parties, some are not enforceable because of the negative impact they would have on society. These contracts are said to be *contrary to public policy*. Examples include a contract to commit an immoral act and a contract that prohibits marriage. For example, suppose Everett offers a young man $500 if he refrains from marrying Everett's daughter. If the young man accepts, no contract is formed (the contract is void). Thus, if he marries Everett's daughter, Everett cannot sue him for breach of contract.

In recent years, lawsuits involving "surrogate-parenting" contracts have posed perplexing policy issues for the courts. Should these contracts be enforced? Or is it counter to public policy to allow what some people regard as "baby selling" to be legitimized under the principle of freedom of contract? A highly publicized lawsuit decided in 1987 involved a surrogate-parenting contract between William and Elizabeth Stern, who could not have children, and Mary Beth Whitehead. Mrs. Whitehead agreed to be artificially inseminated with Mr. Stern's sperm and to give the baby to the Sterns when it was born. When the baby was born, however, Mrs. Whitehead decided to keep the child and refused to perform her part of the bargain. Although the court decided it was in the best interests of the child that she be raised by the Sterns, Mrs. Whitehead, as the natural mother, was allowed visitation rights.[5] More recently, a court faced a perhaps even more challenging issue that arose from a surrogate-parenting contract (see this chapter's *Landmark in the Law*).

Mary Beth Whitehead, biological mother of Baby M. Whose interests are of chief importance in surrogate parenting situations?

5. *In re Baby M*, 217 N.J.Super. 313, 525 A.2d 1128 (1987).

Landmark in the Law

Anna J. v. Mark C. (1991)

In 1991, the California Court of Appeal for the Fourth District was faced with a question of "first impression"—that is, a question that the California courts had never before faced. (Indeed, no court had decided such an issue.) Was a so-called surrogate mother in whose womb a fertilized embryo had been implanted the "natural mother" of the child upon the child's birth? Or was the "natural mother" the woman whose egg had been fertilized and implanted in the surrogate's womb? Normally, even in surrogate-parenting contracts, the natural mother is the woman who bears and gives birth to the child. But in every previous case, the woman who gave birth to the child was also genetically linked to that child. Not so in this case.

The situation came about as a result of a contract formed on January 15, 1990, between a husband and wife (Mark and Crispina) and a woman (Anna). Anna agreed to have an embryo, created by Mark's sperm and Crispina's egg, implanted within her and to relinquish "all parental rights" to the child in favor of Mark and Crispina upon the child's birth. In return, Mark and Crispina would pay Anna $10,000 in a series of installments, the last to be six weeks after the child's birth. They were also to pay for a $200,000 insurance policy on Anna's life.

The embryo was implanted, and about a month later an ultrasound test confirmed that Anna was pregnant. Relations between the couple and Anna deteriorated over the following months. In July, Anna sent Mark and Crispina a letter stating how much she needed money and requesting the balance of the $10,000 right away. She also threatened to refuse to give up the child if they did not do as she requested. Mark and Crispina then brought suit, seeking a declaration from the court that they were the legal parents of the unborn child. Anna filed her own action to be declared the mother of the child, and the cases were eventually consolidated.

In the meantime, on September 19, the baby was born. Blood test results excluded Anna as the "genetic mother" of the child. The trial court ruled that Mark and Crispina were the child's "genetic, biological and natural" father and mother. It also ruled that Anna had no "parental" rights to the child, that the contract was legal and enforceable against Anna's claims, and that Anna's visitation rights were to be terminated. Anna appealed.

The appellate court could think of only one other case in which two women claimed to be the "natural mother" of the same child. In that case, the court had proposed that the matter be settled by cutting the baby in half.[a] Even though it was journeying "through uncharted territory," the court noted that the California legislature, by enacting the Uniform Parentage Act in 1975, had left a few "signs and markers" for the courts to follow.

And so, after a journey through the Uniform Parentage Act and a series of deductions based on the act's various provisions, the court agreed with the trial court that the natural mother was the woman whose egg was fertilized and the natural father was the man whose sperm fertilized the egg. The woman who gave birth to the child was not the natural mother and had, as a result, no legal rights as a mother.[b]

The court lamented the fact that the legislature had not sufficiently addressed the problems that may attend surrogate-parenting contracts—not only the kind of problem raised in this case but other potential problems. For example, what happens if the surrogate mother decides to abort the fetus? What if the surrogate's life is endangered by the pregnancy, and a decision must be made regarding the safety of the mother versus that of the fetus? What if the mother abuses drugs, and this affects the health of the baby? What if the baby is born deformed?—and so on. Public policy relating to these kinds of decisions—in the eyes of this court, anyway—should not be left to the courts to decide.

a. The court was referring to the biblical story recounted in 3 Kings 3:16–28. Ultimately, the court gave the child to the woman who showed the greater concern for the child's welfare by her requesting that the judge give the baby to the other woman so that its life would be spared.

b. *Anna J. v. Mark C.*, 12 Cal.App.4th 977, 286 Cal.Rptr. 369 (1991). This judgment was affirmed by the California Supreme Court in *Johnson v. Calvert*, 5 Cal.4th 84, 851 P.2d 776, 19 Cal.Rptr.2d 494 (1993).

Contracts in Restraint of Trade Contracts in restraint of trade (anticompetitive agreements) usually adversely affect the public (which favors competition in the economy) and typically violate one or more federal or state statutes.[6] An exception is recognized when the restraint is reasonable and an integral part of a contract.

6. Such as the Sherman Antitrust Act, the Clayton Act, and the Federal Trade Commission Act (see Chapter 30).

Many such exceptions involve a type of restraint called a *covenant not to compete*, or a restrictive covenant.

Covenants not to compete are often contained in contracts concerning the sale of an ongoing business. A covenant not to compete is created when a seller agrees not to open a new store in a certain geographical area surrounding the old store. Such agreements enable the seller to sell, and the purchaser to buy, the "goodwill" and "reputation" of an ongoing business. If, for example, a well-known merchant sells his or her store and opens a competing business a block away, many of the merchant's customers will likely do business at the new store. This, in turn, renders valueless the good name and reputation sold to the new merchant for a price. If a covenant not to compete was not accompanied by a sales agreement, however, it would be void because it unreasonably restrains trade and is contrary to public policy.

Agreements not to compete can also be contained in employment contracts. It is common for many people in middle-level and upper-level management positions to agree not to work for competitors or not to start a competing business for a specified period of time after terminating employment. Such agreements are legal so long as the specified period of time is not excessive in duration and the geographic restriction is reasonable. Basically, the restriction on competition must be reasonable—that is, not any greater than necessary to protect a legitimate business interest. The following case illustrates this point.

Case 10.4

BAXTER INTERNATIONAL, INC. v. MORRIS

United States Court of Appeals, Eighth Circuit, 1992.
976 F.2d 1189.

HISTORICAL AND SOCIAL SETTING *At one time, if a court concluded that a covenant not to compete was unreasonable, the court would cut the entire covenant from the contract. Over time, courts adopted the "blue pencil" rule. Under this rule, if it was grammatically possible, a court would cut only those words from the covenant that made it unreasonable. For example, when an employee agreed not to compete against a former employer in forty-six specific counties, a court concluded that this was unreasonable and reduced the list of counties to thirty-one.*[a] *More recently, courts have become more flexible. If a court concludes that a covenant is too broad, regardless of what cutting is grammatically possible, the court may issue an injunction that limits the restrictions of the covenant to make it reasonable. Under any of these approaches, a court may hold that a covenant is unenforceable if there is no protection for the interests of the employee.*

FACTS In 1988, Dr. Roger Morris, a research scientist holding a Ph.D. in physical biochemistry, signed an employment contract with Microscan, a subsidiary of Baxter International, Inc. The contract indicated that Microscan would be entrusting Morris, as an employee, with confidential information and included a covenant not to compete that read as follows: "I [Morris] will not render services, directly or indirectly, for a period of one year after the termination of my employment with [Baxter] to any Competing Organization in connection with any Competing Product within such geographic limits as [Baxter] and said Competing Organization are, or would be, in actual competition." In January 1992, Morris resigned his employment with Microscan and accepted a position with bioMerieux Vitek, Inc. (Vitek), which was essentially Microscan's only competitor in the research, development, manufacture, and sale of diagnostic equipment for use in microbiological laboratories. Baxter brought suit against Morris to enforce the clause containing the covenant not to compete. The district court entered a judgment restraining Morris from revealing trade secrets for a period of one year but refused to enforce the covenant not to compete on the grounds that it was overbroad, unreasonably burdensome, and unnecessary for Baxter's protection. Baxter appealed.

ISSUE Was the covenant not to compete overbroad, unreasonably burdensome, and unnecessary for Baxter's protection?

DECISION Yes. The appellate court affirmed the lower court's ruling.

a. *Thomas v. Coastal Industries Services, Inc.*, 214 Ga. 832, 108 S.E.2d 328 (1959).

Case 10.4—Continued

REASON The court stated that "restrictive covenants in employment agreements are enforceable only if reasonably necessary to protect a legitimate business interest of the employer." Whether a restrictive covenant will be deemed "reasonably necessary" is determined by the covenant's "impact on the parties, including its hardship on the employee." In this case, the district court had concluded that it was possible for Morris to work at Vitek without divulging Microscan's trade secrets. Evidence presented at trial had indicated that Vitek had not hired Morris to obtain confidential information from him and in fact had no need of such information. Therefore, by enjoining Morris from divulging confidential information to Vitek for a period of one year, the district court had adequately protected Microscan's interest. Further, to enforce the covenant would work an undue hardship on Morris; in his field of employment, job opportunities were scarce, and Vitek represented one of those opportunities for Morris. A year's absence from his position with Vitek could seriously harm Morris's relationship with his new employer. In view of these circumstances, the appellate court agreed with the trial court that the covenant not to compete was overbroad, unreasonably burdensome, and unnecessary for Baxter's protection.

Unconscionable Contracts or Clauses Ordinarily, a court does not look at the fairness or equity of a contract; in other words, it does not inquire into the adequacy of consideration. Persons are assumed to be reasonably intelligent, and the court does not come to their aid just because they have made unwise or foolish bargains. In certain circumstances, however, bargains are so oppressive that the courts relieve innocent parties of part or all of their duties. Such a bargain is called an **unconscionable contract or clause.** Both the Uniform Commercial Code and the Uniform Consumer Credit Code embody the unconscionability concept—the former with regard to the sale of goods and the latter with regard to consumer loans and the waiver of rights.[7]

UNCONSCIONABLE CONTRACT OR CLAUSE
A contract or clause that is void on the basis of public policy because one party, as a result of his or her disproportionate bargaining power, is forced to accept terms that are unfairly burdensome and that unfairly benefit the dominating party.

Recent court decisions have distinguished between procedural and substantive unconscionability. The former has to do with how a term becomes part of a contract and relates to factors bearing on a party's lack of knowledge or understanding of the contract terms because of inconspicuous print, unintelligible language ("legalese"), lack of opportunity to read the contract, lack of opportunity to ask questions about its meaning, and other factors. Procedural unconscionability sometimes relates to purported lack of voluntariness because of a disparity in bargaining power between the two parties. Contracts entered into because of one party's vastly superior bargaining power may be deemed unconscionable. These situations usually involve an **adhesion contract,** which is a contract drafted by the dominant party and then presented to the other—the adhering party—on a "take it or leave it" basis.[8]

ADHESION CONTRACT
A contract, such as one drafted by a large retailer on a standard form for a consumer's signature, in which the stronger party (retailer) dictates the terms.

Substantive unconscionability characterizes those contracts, or portions of contracts, that are oppressive or overly harsh. Courts generally focus on provisions that deprive one party of the benefits of the agreement or leave that party without remedy for nonperformance by the other. For example, suppose a welfare recipient with a fourth-grade education agrees to purchase a refrigerator for $2,000, signing a two-year installment contract. The same type of refrigerator usually sells for $400 on the market. Some courts have held this type of contract to be unconscionable, despite the general rule that the courts will not inquire into the adequacy of the consideration, simply because the contract terms are so oppressive as to "shock the conscience" of the court.[9] The following case illustrates some of the factors that courts will consider in determining whether a contract is unconscionable.

---

7. See, for example, UCC Sections 2–302 and 2–719 and UCCC Sections 5.108 and 1.107.
8. See, for example, *Henningsen v. Bloomfield Motors, Inc.*, 32 N.J. 358, 161 A.2d 69 (1960).
9. See, for example, *Jones v. Star Credit Corp.*, 59 Misc.2d 189, 298 N.Y.S.2d 264 (1969). This case is presented in Chapter 14 as Case 14.5.

Case 10.5
WATERS v. MIN, LTD.
Supreme Judicial Court of Massachusetts,
1992.
412 Mass. 64,
587 N.E.2d 231.

HISTORICAL AND ETHICAL SETTING *The concept of unconscionability has roots in the common law system in both law and equity, but chiefly in equity. It has been said that unconscionability underlies practically the whole of equity. Through the centuries, equity has applied the concept of unconscionability in a variety of circumstances, refusing to enforce a contract unless it is "fair and open, and in regard to which all material matters known to each [party] have been communicated to the other [party]."*[a] *Among the many cases in which unconscionability has been held to apply are cases involving home-improvement contracts, equipment leases, a contract to build an asphalt plant, a lease of an apartment building, a lease of a gasoline station, a lease of a hall for a Bar Mitzvah, and a contract opening a checking account.*

FACTS The plaintiff, Gail Waters, purchased an annuity policy[b] at age eighteen with insurance funds received as a result of a childhood accident. At the age of twenty-one, she became involved with Thomas Beauchemin, an ex-convict, who, among other things, persuaded her to sell her annuity policy, worth $189,000, to the defendants (Min, Ltd., and others with whom Beauchemin had dealings) for $50,000. The defendants had legal counsel during the contract negotiations, but the plaintiff did not. The defendants made an initial payment of $25,000 to Waters but deducted from the payment $7,000 that Beauchemin owed them. Later, Waters brought suit to rescind the contract. The court held that the contract was unconscionable and ordered the defendants to return the annuity to Waters upon Waters's repayment of the $18,000 that she had received from them. The defendants appealed.

ISSUE Was the contract between Waters and the defendants unconscionable and therefore void?

DECISION Yes. The appellate court affirmed the lower court's ruling.

REASON Several factors have been noted as features of unconscionable contracts, including high-pressure tactics, undue influence, and grossly inadequate consideration. The judge noted that "Beauchemin introduced the plaintiff to drugs, exhausted her credit card accounts to the sum of $6,000, unduly influenced her, suggested that [she] sell her annuity contract, initiated the contract negotiations, was the agent of the defendants, and benefited from the contract between the plaintiff and the defendants." The court particularly emphasized that "[g]ross disparity in the values exchanged is an important factor to be considered in determining whether a contract is unconscionable." In this case, the court found the disparity of interests in the contract to be "so gross that the court cannot resist the inference that [the contract] was improperly obtained and is unconscionable."

a. *Rothmiller v. Stein,* 143 N.Y. 581, 38 N.E. 718 (1894).
b. An annuity policy is an investment, such as a life insurance policy, that allows the holder to receive fixed, periodic payments commencing at a specified time in the future.

EXCULPATORY CLAUSE
A clause that releases a party (to a contract) from liability for his or her wrongful acts.

Exculpatory Clauses Often closely related to the concept of unconscionability are **exculpatory clauses,** defined as clauses that release a party from liability in the event of monetary or physical injury, *no matter who is at fault.* Indeed, some courts refer to such clauses in terms of unconscionability.

Exculpatory clauses that relieve a party from liability for harm caused by simple negligence normally are unenforceable when they are asserted by an employer against an employee. Suppose, for example, that Madison Manufacturing Company hires a laborer and has him sign a contract stating:

> Said employee hereby agrees with employer, in consideration of such employment, that he will take upon himself all risks incident to his position and will in no case hold the company liable for any injury or damage he may sustain, in his person or otherwise, by accidents or injuries in the factory, or which may result from defective machinery or carelessness or misconduct of himself or any other employee in service of the employer.

This contract provision attempts to remove Madison's potential liability for injuries occurring to the employee, and it would usually be held contrary to public

Ethical Perspective

Ethics and Unconscionability

The doctrine of unconscionability represents a good example of how the law attempts to enforce ethical behavior. This doctrine suggests that some contracts may be so unfair to one party as to be unenforceable, even though that party originally agreed to the contract's terms.

Section 2–302 of the Uniform Commercial Code (UCC) provides that a court will consider the fairness of contracts and may deem a contract or any clause of a contract to have been unconscionable at the time it was made. If so, the court may refuse to enforce the contract, or it may enforce the contract without the unconscionable clause, or it may limit the application of the clause so as to avoid an unconscionable result.

The UCC does not define the term *unconscionability*. The drafters of the UCC added explanatory comments to the relevant sections of the UCC, however, and these comments serve as guidelines to the UCC's application. Comment 1 to Section 2–302 suggests that the basic test for unconscionability is whether, under the circumstances existing at the time of the making of the contract, the clause in question was so one-sided as to be unconscionable. This test is to be applied against the general commercial background of the contract. Obviously, this test provides only general guidance.

Unconscionable action, like unethical action, is incapable of precise definition. Information about the particular facts and specific circumstances surrounding the contract is essential. For example, a contract with a marginally literate consumer might be seen as unfair and unenforceable, whereas the same contract with a major business firm would be upheld by the courts.

Courts are reluctant to hold a contract or contractual clause unconscionable except in the most extreme situations, as when the contract or clause is so one-sided as to "shock the conscience" of the court. This is because a trade-off is made whenever a contract is deemed unconscionable and thus unenforceable. What is traded off is the enforceability of the contract. The requirement that contracts be performed as promised is one of the cornerstones of society, and the courts do not forgo this requirement lightly. On the contrary, the courts will do all they can to save contracts rather than render them unenforceable.

policy.[10] Also, exculpatory clauses asserted by a public utility, such as a railroad or an electric company, regarding a harm caused during the public utility's function are usually unenforceable. A railroad, for example, cannot use an exculpatory clause to avoid liability for the negligent maintenance of its trains.

In general, the courts have shown a mixed response to exculpatory clauses used by landlords (regarding a landlord's liability for defective premises), by amusement parks, and by horse-rental and golf-cart concessions.

The Effect of Illegality

In general, an illegal contract is void: the contract is deemed never to have existed, and the courts will not aid either party. In most illegal contracts, both parties are considered to be equally at fault—*in pari delicto*. If the contract is executory (not yet fulfilled), neither party can enforce it. If it is executed, there can be neither contractual nor quasi-contractual recovery.

That one wrongdoer in an illegal contract is unjustly enriched at the expense of the other is of no concern to the law—except under certain circumstances (to be discussed shortly). The major justification for this hands-off attitude is that it is improper to place the machinery of justice at the disposal of a plaintiff who has

10. For a case with similar facts, see *Little Rock & Fort Smith Railway Co. v. Eubanks*, 48 Ark. 460, 3 S.W. 808 (1887). In such a case, the clause may also be illegal on the basis of a violation of a state workers' compensation law.

broken the law by entering into an illegal bargain. Another justification is the hoped-for deterrent effect of this general rule. A plaintiff who suffers a loss because of an illegal bargain should presumably be deterred from entering into similar illegal bargains in the future.

Some persons are excepted from the general rule that neither party to an illegal bargain can sue for breach and neither can recover for performance rendered.

Justifiable Ignorance of the Facts When one of the parties to a contract is relatively innocent (has no knowledge or any reason to know that the contract is illegal), that party can often obtain restitution or recovery of benefits conferred in a partially executed contract. The courts do not enforce the contract but do allow the parties to return to their original positions.

It is also possible for an innocent party who has fully performed under the contract to enforce the contract against the guilty party. For example, Debbie contracts with Tucker to purchase ten crates of goods that cannot legally be bought or sold. Tucker hires a trucking firm to deliver the shipment to Debbie and agrees to pay the firm the normal fee of $500. Although the law specifies that the shipment, use, and sale of the goods were illegal, the carrier, being an innocent party, can legally collect the $500 from Tucker.

Members of Protected Classes When a statute protects a certain class of people, a member of that class can enforce an illegal contract even though the other party cannot. For example, there are statutes that prohibit certain employees (such as flight attendants) from working more than a specified number of hours per month. These employees thus constitute a class protected by statute. An employee who is required to work more than the maximum can recover for those extra hours of service.

BLUE SKY LAWS
State laws that regulate the offer and sale of securities.

Another example of statutes designed to protect a particular class of people are **blue sky laws,** which are state laws that regulate and supervise investment companies for the protection of the public. Such laws are intended to stop the sale of stock in fly-by-night concerns, such as visionary oil wells and distant gold mines. Investors are protected as a class and can sue to recover the purchase price of stock issued in violation of such laws.

Most states also have statutes regulating the sale of insurance. If an insurance company violates a statute when selling insurance, the purchaser can nevertheless enforce the policy and recover from the insurer.

Withdrawal from an Illegal Agreement If the illegal part of a bargain has not yet been performed, the party tendering performance can withdraw from the bargain and recover the performance or its value. For example, suppose Martha and Andy decide to wager (illegally) on the outcome of a boxing match. Each deposits money with a stakeholder, who agrees to pay the winner of the bet. At this point, each party has performed part of the agreement, but the illegal part of the agreement will not occur until the money is paid to the winner. Before such payment occurs, either party is entitled to withdraw from the agreement by giving notice to the stakeholder of his or her withdrawal.

Contract Illegal through Fraud, Duress, or Undue Influence Whenever a plaintiff has been induced to enter into an illegal bargain as a result of fraud, duress, or undue influence, he or she can either enforce the contract or recover for its value.

Reformation of an Illegal Covenant Not to Compete On occasion, when a covenant not to compete is unreasonable in its essential terms, the court may *reform* the covenant, converting its terms into reasonable ones. Instead of declaring the covenant illegal and unenforceable, the court applies the rule of reasonableness and changes the contract so that its basic, original intent can be enforced. This presents a problem, however, in that the judge becomes a party to the contract. Consequently, contract **reformation** is usually carried out by a court only when necessary to prevent undue burdens or hardships.

REFORMATION
A court-ordered correction of a written contract so that it reflects the true intentions of the parties.

Application

Law and the Salesperson

Sales personnel, particularly those who are paid on a commission basis, are often eager to make contracts. But sometimes these salespersons must deal with minors and intoxicated persons, both of whom have limited contractual capacity upon entering into such contracts. Therefore, if you are a retailer, you should make sure that your employees are acquainted with the law governing minors and intoxicated persons.

If in your business you sell consumer durables, such as console televisions or automobiles, your sales personnel must be careful in forming contracts with minors and should heed the adage, "When in doubt, check." Remember that a contract signed by a minor (unless it is for necessaries) normally is voidable, and the minor may exercise the option to disaffirm the contract. You and your salespersons should know the legal age of majority in your state. Proof of legal age should be required of a customer when there is any doubt concerning his or her age.

In addition, because the law governing minors' rights varies substantially from state to state, you should check with your attorney concerning the laws governing disaffirmance and restitution in your state. You and those you hire to sell your products should know, for example, what the consequences will be if a minor has misrepresented his or her age when forming a sales contract. Similarly, you need to find out whether and in what circumstances restitution can be required.

Little need be said about a salesperson's dealings with obviously intoxicated persons. If the customer, despite intoxication, understands the legal consequences of the contract being signed, it is enforceable. Nonetheless, it is difficult to establish that the intoxicated customer understood the contract if he or she disputes it. Therefore, the best advice is, "When in doubt, don't." In other words, if you suspect a customer may be intoxicated, do not sign a contract with him or her.

Checklist for the Salesperson

- ☐ 1. Determine the legal age of majority in your state.
- ☐ 2. When in doubt about the age of a customer to whom you are about to sell major consumer durable goods or anything other than necessities, require legal proof of age. If such proof is not forthcoming, require that a parent or guardian sign the contract.
- ☐ 3. Check with an attorney about the laws governing minors' contracts in your state.
- ☐ 4. Do not sign contracts with intoxicated customers.

❖ Key Terms

adhesion contract 255
blue law 250
blue sky law 258
contractual capacity 243
disaffirmance 244
emancipation 248
exculpatory clause 256
necessaries 247
ratification 247
reformation 259
restitution 244
unconscionable contract or clause 255

❖ Chapter Summary: Capacity and Legality

<table>
<tr><th colspan="2">CONTRACTUAL CAPACITY</th></tr>
<tr><td>Minors</td><td>A minor is a person who has not yet reached the age of majority. In most states, the age of majority is eighteen for contract purposes. Contracts with minors are voidable at the option of the minor.
1. Disaffirmance—
a. Can take place (in most states) at any time during minority and within a reasonable time after the minor has reached the age of majority.
b. When disaffirming executed contracts, the minor has a duty of restitution to return received goods if they are still in the minor's control or (in some states) to pay their reasonable value.
c. If a minor disaffirms a contract, the entire contract must be disaffirmed.
d. A minor may disaffirm a contract for necessaries but remains liable for the reasonable value of the goods.
e. A minor who has committed an act of fraud (such as misrepresentation of age) will be denied the right to disaffirm by some courts.
2. Ratification—May be express or implied.
a. Express—Exists when the minor, through a writing or an oral agreement, explicitly assumes the obligations imposed by the contract.
b. Implied—Exists when the conduct of the minor is inconsistent with disaffirmance or when the minor fails to disaffirm an executed contract within a reasonable time after reaching the age of majority.
3. Parents' liability—Generally, parents are not liable for the contracts made by minor children acting on their own, nor are parents liable for minors' torts except in certain circumstances.
4. Emancipation—Occurs when parents completely relinquish the right to the minor's control, care, custody, and earnings. Emancipation may be express or implied, absolute or conditional, total or partial. In some jurisdictions, minors are permitted to petition for emancipation themselves.</td></tr>
<tr><td>Intoxicated Persons</td><td>1. A contract entered into by an intoxicated person is voidable at the option of the intoxicated person if the person was sufficiently intoxicated to lack mental capacity, even if the intoxication was voluntary.
2. A contract with an intoxicated person is enforceable if, despite being intoxicated, the person understood the legal consequences of entering into the contract.</td></tr>
<tr><td>Mentally Incompetent Persons</td><td>1. A contract made by a person adjudged by a court to be mentally incompetent is void.
2. A contract made by a mentally incompetent person not adjudged by a court to be mentally incompetent is voidable at the option of the mentally incompetent person.</td></tr>
<tr><th colspan="2">LEGALITY</th></tr>
<tr><td>Contracts Contrary to Statute</td><td>1. Gambling—Gambling contracts that contravene (go against) state statutes are deemed illegal and thus void.
2. Sabbath (Sunday) laws—Laws prohibiting the formation or the performance of certain contracts on Sunday. Such laws vary widely from state to state, and many states do not enforce them.
3. Licensing statutes—Contracts entered into by persons who do not have a license, when one is required by statute, will not be enforceable unless the underlying purpose of the statute is to raise government revenues (and not to protect the public from unauthorized practitioners).</td></tr>
<tr><td>Contracts Contrary to Public Policy</td><td>1. Contracts in restraint of trade—Contracts to reduce or restrain free competition are illegal. Most such contracts are now prohibited by statutes. An exception is a covenant not to compete. It is usually enforced by the courts if the terms are ancillary and are reasonable as to time and area of restraint, especially when the covenant is part of a contract for the sale of a business and the goodwill and reputation of the firm are essential to the contract. Courts tend to scrutinize a covenant not to compete closely when it is part of an employment contract. If the covenant is unreasonable as to time or area, courts may reform the covenant to fall within reasonable constraints and then enforce the reformed contract.</td></tr>
</table>

❖ Chapter Summary: Capacity and Legality—Continued

Contracts—Continued	2. *Unconscionable contracts and clauses*—When a contract or contract clause is so unfair that it is oppressive to one party, it can be deemed unconscionable by society; as such, it is illegal and cannot be enforced.
Effect of Illegality	1. In general, an illegal contract is void, and the courts will aid neither party when both parties are considered to be equally at fault *(in pari delicto)*. If the contract is executory, neither party can enforce it. If the contract is executed, there can be neither contractual nor quasi-contractual recovery. 2. Exceptions (i.e., situations in which recovery is allowed): a. When one party to the contract is relatively innocent. b. When one party to the contract is a member of a group of persons protected by statute. c. When one party was induced to enter into an illegal bargain through fraud, duress, or undue influence.

❖ Questions and Case Problems

10-1. Contracts by Minors. Generally, a minor can disaffirm any contract. What are some of the exceptions to this rule—that is, what are some contracts that minors cannot avoid?

10-2. Covenants Not to Compete. Joseph, who owns the only pizza parlor in Middletown, learns that Giovanni is about to open a competing pizza parlor in the same small town, just a few blocks from Joseph's restaurant. Joseph offers Giovanni $10,000 in return for Giovanni's promise not to open a pizza parlor in the Middletown area. Giovanni accepts the $10,000 but goes ahead with his plans, in spite of the agreement. When Giovanni opens his restaurant for business, Joseph sues to enjoin Giovanni's continued operation of his restaurant or to recover the $10,000. The court denies recovery. On what basis?

10-3. Intoxication. After Katie has several drinks one night, she sells Emily a valuable fur stole for ten dollars. The next day, Katie offers the ten dollars to Emily and requests the return of her stole. Emily refuses, claiming that they had a valid contract of sale. Katie explains that she was intoxicated at the time the bargain was made and thus the contract is voidable at her option. Who is right? Explain.

10-4. Mental Incompetence. Jermal has been the owner of a car dealership for a number of years. One day, Jermal sold one of his most expensive cars to Kessler. At the time of the sale, Jermal thought Kessler acted in a peculiar manner, but he gave the matter no further thought until four months later, when Kessler's court-appointed guardian appeared at his office, tendered back the car, and demanded Kessler's money back. The guardian informed Jermal that Kessler had been adjudicated mentally incompetent two months previously by a proper court.

(a) Discuss the rights of the parties.

(b) If Kessler had been adjudicated mentally incompetent before the contract was formed, what would be the legal effect of the contract?

10-5. Licensing Statutes. State X requires that persons be licensed who prepare and serve liquor in the form of drinks at commercial establishments. The only requirement for obtaining a yearly license is that the person be at least eighteen years old. Mickey, age thirty-five, is hired as a bartender for the Southtown Restaurant. Gerald, a staunch alumnus of a nearby university, brings twenty of his friends to the restaurant to celebrate a football victory one afternoon. Gerald orders four rounds of drinks, and the bill is nearly $200. Gerald learns that Mickey has failed to renew his bartender's license, and Gerald refuses to pay, claiming that the contract is unenforceable. Discuss whether Gerald is correct.

10-6. **Contracts by Minors.** In 1982, Webster Street Partnership, Ltd. (Webster), entered into a lease agreement with Matthew Sheridan and Pat Wilwerding. Webster was aware that both Sheridan and Wilwerding were minors. Both tenants were living away from home, apparently with the understanding that they could return home at any time. Sheridan and Wilwerding paid the first month's rent but then failed to pay the rent for the next month and vacated the apartment. Webster sued them for breach of contract. They claimed that the lease agreement was voidable because they were minors. Who will win, and why? [*Webster Street Partnership, Ltd. v. Sheridan*, 220 Neb. 9, 368 N.W.2d 439 (1985)]

10-7. **Contracts by Minors.** Smith purchased a car on credit from Bobby Floars Toyota, Inc., a month before his eighteenth birthday. Smith made regular monthly payments for eleven months but then returned the car to the dealer and made no further payments on it. The dealer sold the car and sued Smith to recover the difference between the amount obtained by the sale of the car and the money Smith still owed to the dealer. Smith refused to pay on the ground that he had been a minor at the time of purchase and had disaffirmed the contract after he had reached the age of majority. Will the car dealer succeed in its claim that the ten monthly payments made after Smith turned eighteen constituted a ratification of the purchase contract? Discuss. [*Bobby Floars Toyota, Inc. v. Smith*, 48 N.C.App. 580, 269 S.E.2d 320 (1980)]

10-8. **Unconscionability.** Carolyn Murphy was a welfare recipient with four minor children. Brian McNamara was in the business of renting and selling television and stereo sets. After seeing McNamara's advertisement for "rent to own" televisions, Murphy signed a lease agreement with McNamara for a twenty-five-inch Philco color TV at $16 per week. The lease payments were to run for seventy-eight weeks, after which she would become the owner. At no time did McNamara tell Murphy that the total lease payments amounted to $1,268, including the delivery charge. The retail sale price of the set was $499. Murphy had paid about $436 when she read a newspaper article criticizing the lease plan. When she learned that she was required to pay $1,268, Murphy stopped making payments. McNamara's employees attempted to take possession and made threats through telephone and written communications. Murphy filed suit, alleging, among other things, that the contract terms were unconscionable. Discuss her allegation and whether a court might find the contract unconscionable. [*Murphy v. McNamara*, 36 Conn.Supp. 183, 416 A.2d 170 (1979)]

10-9. Contracts by Minors. April Iverson's uncle, John Polachek, obtained a life insurance policy through his employer, Scholl, Inc. The policy, issued by Bankers Life and Casualty, named April as the sole beneficiary. April was eleven years old when her uncle died and when Bankers mailed the $10,000 death-benefit check to her. The check was made out in her name because Scholl had not informed Bankers that April was a minor. Subsequently, April's father misappropriated the funds by having April sign (indorse) the check. Later, April sued Bankers and Scholl for the $10,000. Bankers claimed that her indorsement discharged its obligation to her. April claimed that as a minor she did not have the capacity to discharge this contractual obligation. What will the court decide? [*Iverson v. Scholl, Inc.*, 136 Ill.App.3d 962, 483 N.E.2d 893, 91 Ill.Dec. 407 (1985)]

10-10. Licensing Statutes. Paris was a real estate broker licensed under the laws of the state of Georgia. After learning that certain Gulf County, Florida, acreage owned by Hilton & Associates was on the market, Paris contacted Cooper, a Florida resident who was interested in purchasing the property. Paris visited the property in Florida, helped prepare Cooper's written offer of purchase, worked with Cooper's attorney on the sales contract, and attended the closing of the sale in Panama City, Florida. As a result of this sale, Paris received a $315,070 commission. Cooper signed two promissory notes to Paris, one for $215,070 and one for $75,000, and gave Paris a check for $25,000. Cooper subsequently defaulted on his payments to both Hilton & Associates and Paris. When Hilton & Associates initiated foreclosure proceedings in circuit court, Paris filed suit against Cooper seeking recovery under the promissory notes. Cooper, in turn, filed suit against Paris, seeking to have Paris's conduct declared to be that of an unlicensed real estate broker, which would invalidate the promissory notes held by Paris. Cooper also sought to recover the sums he had already paid to Paris, $25,000 plus $12,904 that he had paid on one of the notes. Was the Paris-Cooper contract unenforceable on the ground that Paris was not licensed to conduct real estate transactions in Florida? Explain. [*Cooper v. Paris*, 413 So.2d 772 (Fla.App., 1st Dist. 1982)]

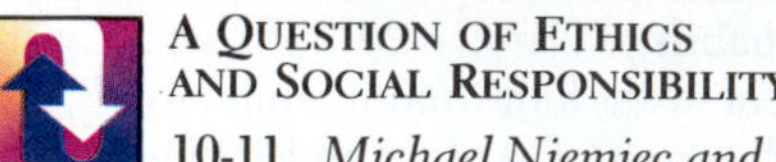

A Question of Ethics and Social Responsibility

10-11. *Michael Niemiec and Judith Polek (the plaintiffs) joined a buyer's club after they had been invited via telephone to visit the club's premises. A club salesperson told them that in exchange for a $1,160 membership fee, members would receive access to a number of catalogues from which they could order merchandise at supposedly low prices. The plaintiffs were told that they had to either sign the contract then and there or forgo the "once in a lifetime opportunity" to join the club. They signed the contract. Three days later, having some misgivings about what they had done, they sought to cancel the contract but learned that they could not do so. The contract specified that no dues were refundable, even on a member's death. The contract also stated that a membership could not be transferred for any reason, merchandise could not be returned once accepted (members were warned in bold type not to accept merchandise until after they had examined it), and orders for merchandise could not be canceled even prior to shipment. Further, although members were to rely on warranties of the supplier for all merchandise, they were forbidden to make any "contact with the suppliers of merchandise." The plaintiffs then sought relief in court. The court held that the contract was unconscionable.* [Niemiec v. Kellmark Corp., *153 Misc.2d 347, 581 N.Y.S.2d 569 (N.Y. City 1992)*]

1. Courts will sometimes hold contracts unconscionable because of gross inadequacy of consideration. Is that a possibility here? What, for example, did the club offer as consideration for the contract?
2. What might be some other possible reasons for the court's conclusion that this contract was unconscionable?
3. The defendant club argued that the plaintiffs in this case were neither poor (they earned over $50,000 a year and owned their own home) nor illiterate. Therefore, the club argued, they should be held to their bargain even if they found it unsatisfactory. Do you agree with this reasoning? Why or why not?

Case Briefing Assignment

10-12. *Examine Case A.4* [Mann v. Wetter, *100 Or.App. 184, 785 P.2d 1064 (1990)*] *in Appendix A. The case has been excerpted there in great detail. Review and then brief the case, making sure that you include answers to the following questions in your brief.*

1. What were the plaintiff's contentions on appeal?
2. Why did the appellate court conclude that the release signed by Virkler, which exempted the defendant from liability, did not violate public policy?
3. Why did the appellate court declare that the release agreement was ambiguous as to whether Wetter was among those released from liability under the agreement?

For Critical Analysis

10-13. *Do you think that contracts made by voluntarily intoxicated persons should ever be voidable? Why or why not?*

Chapter 11

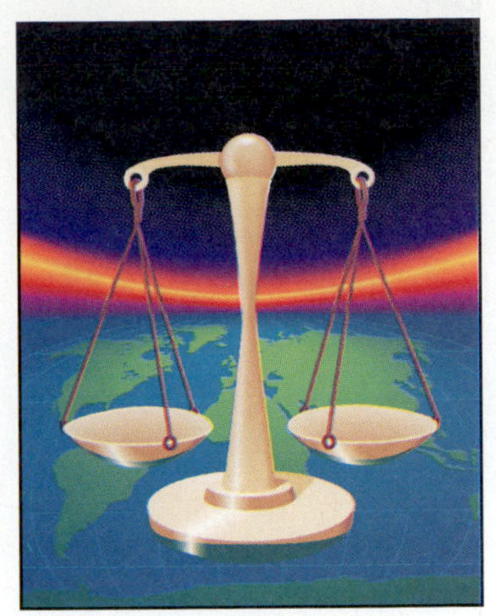

Assent and Form

A contract has been entered into by two parties, each with full legal capacity and for a legal purpose. The contract is also supported by consideration. Nonetheless, the contract may be unenforceable if the parties have not genuinely assented to the terms. Lack of genuine assent is a defense to the enforcement of a contract. As Aristotle stated, the law seeks to ensure that "the citizens of a state will do justice to one another." If the law were to enforce contracts not genuinely assented to by the contracting parties, injustice would result. The first part of this chapter focuses on what kinds of factors indicate that genuineness of assent to a contract may be lacking.

"Law is a pledge that the citizens of a state will do justice to one another."

Aristotle, 384–322 B.C.
(Greek philosopher)

A contract that is otherwise valid may also be unenforceable if it is not in the proper **form.** For example, certain types of contracts are required to be in writing. If a contract is required by law to be in writing and there is no written evidence of the contract, it may not be enforceable. In the second part of this chapter, we examine the kinds of contracts that require a writing under what is called the *Statute of Frauds.* The chapter concludes with a discussion of the *parol evidence rule,* under which courts determine the admissibility at trial of evidence extraneous (external) to written contracts.

FORM
The technical manner or order to be observed in creating legal agreements, as opposed to the substance of the agreements.

❖ Genuineness of Assent

Genuineness of assent may be lacking because of mistake, fraudulent misrepresentation, undue influence, or duress.

"Mistakes are the inevitable lot of mankind."

Sir George Jessel, 1824–1883
(English jurist)

Mistakes

We all make mistakes, and it is not surprising that mistakes are made when contracts are created. In certain circumstances, contract law allows a contract to be avoided on the basis of mistake. Realize, though, that the concept of mistake in contract law has to do with mistaken assumptions relating to contract formation. For example, if you send an installment payment due under a loan contract with your local bank to your plumber "by mistake," that is a kind of mistake totally different from the kind of mistake that we are discussing here. In contract law, a mistake may be a defense to the enforcement of a contract if it can be proved that the parties entered into the contract under different assumptions relating to the subject matter of the contract.

Courts have considerable difficulty in specifying the circumstances that justify allowing a mistake to invalidate a contract. Thus, the results in cases with similar facts can be different, and finding clearly defined rules governing the effects of mistakes can be difficult. Generally, though, courts distinguish between *mistakes as to judgment of market value or conditions* and *mistakes as to fact*. Only the latter have legal significance. Suppose, for example, that Jud Wheeler contracts to purchase ten acres of land in Idaho. Jud believes that the land is owned by the Mittens, but it actually belongs to the Krauses. A court may allow this contract to be avoided because Jud has made a mistake of fact. Suppose, however, that Jud contracts to buy ten acres of land because he believes that he can resell the land at a profit to Bart. Can Jud escape his contractual obligations if it later turns out that he was mistaken? Not likely. Jud's overestimation of the value of the land or of Bart's interest in it is an ordinary risk of business for which a court will not normally provide relief.

In contract formation, mistakes can occur in two forms—*unilateral* and *bilateral (mutual)*. A unilateral mistake is made by only one of the contracting parties; a mutual mistake is made by both.

Unilateral Mistakes A unilateral mistake involves some *material fact*—that is, a fact important to the subject matter of the contract. In general, a unilateral mistake does not afford the mistaken party any right to relief from the contract. In other words, the contract normally is enforceable.[1] For example, Ellen intends to sell her stereo for $550. When she learns that Chin is interested in buying a used stereo, she writes a letter to him and offers to sell her stereo, but she mistakenly types in the price of $500. Chin immediately writes back, accepting Ellen's offer. Even though Ellen intended to sell her stereo for $550, she has made a unilateral mistake and is bound by contract to sell the stereo to Chin for $500.

There are at least two exceptions. The contract may not be enforceable (1) if the *other* party to the contract knows or should have known that a mistake was made or (2) if the error was due to a mathematical mistake in addition, subtraction, division, or multiplication and was done inadvertently and without gross negligence. Of course, the mistake must still involve some *material* fact.

Consider the following situation. Odell Construction Company made a bid to install the plumbing in an apartment building. When Herbert Odell, the president, added up his costs, his secretary forgot to give him the figures for the pipe fittings. Because of the omission, Odell's bid was $6,500 below that of the other bidders. The prime contractor, Sunspan, Inc., accepted and relied on Odell's bid. If Sunspan was not aware of Odell's mistake and could not reasonably have been aware of it, the contract will be enforceable, and Odell will be required to install the plumbing at the bid price. If, however, it can be shown that Odell's secretary mentioned her error to Sunspan, or if Odell's bid was so far below the others that, as a contractor, Sunspan should reasonably have known the bid was a mistake, the contract can be rescinded. Sunspan would not be allowed to accept the offer knowing it was made by mistake.[2] The law of contracts protects only *reasonable* expectations.

In the following case, a unilateral mistake was made when a typist erroneously transformed $500 to $500,000 in a settlement offer.

Case 11.1
WHITAKER v. ASSOCIATED CREDIT SERVICES, INC.
United States Court of Appeals,
Sixth Circuit, 1991.
946 F.2d 1222.

HISTORICAL AND ETHICAL SETTING *At one time, courts of law generally enforced all contracts without regard to the equity of the circumstances in a particular case. It was at this time that the law regarding mistakes developed in the courts of equity. Today, although the law regarding mistakes is part of the law of contracts, it is still applied and interpreted as a matter of equity. Thus, when deciding an issue concerning a mistake, a court may make*

1. The Restatement (Second) of Contracts, Section 153, liberalizes this rule to take into account the modern trend of allowing avoidance although only one party has been mistaken.
2. *Peerless Glass Co. v. Pacific Crockery Co.*, 121 Cal. 641, 54 P. 101 (1898).

Case 11.1—Continued

use of the concepts of fault, good faith, unconscionability, unjust enrichment, and fairness. In other words, the basic rules of the law concerning mistakes are subject, in a particular case, to considerations of what is fair under the circumstances.

FACTS Kenneth and Linda Whitaker had filed an action against Trans Union Corporation and others, alleging violations of the Fair Credit Reporting Act. The lawyer for Trans Union drafted an offer of settlement and presented it to the Whitakers' attorney. The amount of the settlement was supposed to be $500, but the first draft contained a typographical error showing the amount as $500,000. The error went undetected, and the $500,000 figure was typed into the second draft, which was forwarded to Linda Gosnell, Trans Union's attorney, who also did not detect the mistake. Gosnell filed the offer with the clerk of the court and mailed a copy to the Whitakers' lawyer. The Whitakers filed an acceptance of the settlement and forwarded it to Gosnell, who at that time noticed the typing error. The Whitakers refused a substitute offer, and Trans Union filed a motion to set aside the settlement. The district court found for Trans Union, and the Whitakers appealed.

ISSUE Could the settlement be set aside on the basis of mistake, notwithstanding the fact that the mistake was unilateral?

DECISION Yes. The court of appeals affirmed the district court's ruling.

REASON In this case, a clerical error was indisputably the cause of the mistake. The court stated that "any reasonable person would have been shocked by the offer in light of the circumstances of this case * * * that before they filed their action, plaintiffs had made no demands for monetary damages; * * * that plaintiffs in their complaint had specified only $3,600 in actual damages caused by Trans Union's conduct; and that the purported $500,000 offer was the first offer of any kind that plaintiffs had received from defendants." If the offer was allowed to stand, it would result in unjust enrichment. The court found that there was, in fact, no "meeting of the minds" because the Whitakers were aware of the outrageousness of the $500,000 offer.

ETHICAL CONSIDERATIONS *We all know that typographical and clerical errors can happen and that occasionally they result in grossly disproportionate benefits to beneficiaries. For example, the Internal Revenue Service might send a tax refund for $50,000 when in fact the refund should have been only $5,000. There is a tendency to think that if the government or some "big business" firm made a mistake, it is okay to retain the benefits. As some beneficiaries have said, it's like "winning the lottery." Little need be said about the ethics of these assumptions, just as little need be said about the ethics of the Whitakers, who tried to enforce the settlement agreement under which they were the beneficiaries of a gross financial error of which they were obviously aware.*

Mutual Mistakes When both parties are mistaken about the same material fact, the contract can be rescinded by either party.[3] Note that, as with unilateral mistakes, the mistake must be about a *material fact* (one that is important and central to the contract). If, instead, a mutual mistake concerns the later *market value* or *quality* of the object of the contract, the contract normally can be enforced by either party. This rule is based on the theory that both parties assume certain risks when they enter into a contract. Without this rule, almost any party who did not receive what he or she considered a fair bargain could argue bilateral mistake. In essence, this would make adequacy of consideration a factor in determining whether a contract existed; and as discussed previously, the courts normally do not inquire into the adequacy of the consideration.

A word or term in a contract may be subject to more than one reasonable interpretation. In that situation, if the parties to the contract attach materially different meanings to the term, their mutual misunderstanding may allow the contract to be rescinded. The classic case on mutual misunderstanding involved a ship named *Peerless* that was to sail from Bombay with certain cotton goods on board. More than one ship named *Peerless* sailed from Bombay that winter, however.

3. Restatement (Second) of Contracts, Section 152.

Case 11.2
RAFFLES v. WICHELHAUS
Court of Exchequer, England, 1864.
159 Eng.Rep. 375.

HISTORICAL AND POLITICAL SETTING *Before the Civil War, the states in the southern United States were largely agricultural. By the mid–nineteenth century, the staple of this agricultural area had become cotton. Cotton was important to the economy of the South and to the economy of the European textile industry, which by 1860 was booming. In the 1860s, when the southern states seceded from the United States to form the Confederate States, the United States announced a blockade of southern ports. The states of the Confederacy knew that cotton was important to the European economy, and they were confident that Europe would exert pressure on the United States to lift the blockade. Instead, to obtain cotton, European merchants turned to other sources, including India.*

FACTS Wichelhaus purchased a shipment of cotton from Raffles "to arrive ex 'Peerless' from Bombay." Wichelhaus meant a ship called the *Peerless* sailing from Bombay in October; Raffles meant another ship called the *Peerless* sailing from Bombay in December. When the goods arrived on the December *Peerless,* Raffles delivered them to Wichelhaus. By that time, however, Wichelhaus was no longer willing to accept them.

ISSUE Was there a bilateral mistake of fact, which would release Wichelhaus from the contract?

DECISION Yes. The court adjudged that a bilateral mistake of fact had occurred, and hence there was no contract.

REASON When both parties contract under the mistaken, but reasonable, belief that a certain fact is true from an objective viewpoint, neither one is bound by the contract. The British court hearing the case stated, "There is nothing on the face of the contract to show that any particular ship called the 'Peerless' was meant; but the moment it appears that two ships called the 'Peerless' were about to sail from Bombay there is a latent ambiguity. * * * That being so, there was no consensus * * * and therefore no binding contract."

"It was beautiful and simple as all truly great swindles are."

O. Henry, 1862–1910
(American short story writer)

Fraudulent Misrepresentation

Although fraud is a tort, the presence of fraud also affects the genuineness of the innocent party's consent to the contract. Thus, the transaction is not voluntary in the sense required by "mutual assent." When an innocent party consents to a contract with fraudulent terms, the contract usually can be voided, because he or she has not *voluntarily* consented.[4] Normally, the innocent party can either rescind (cancel) the contract and be restored to the original position or enforce the contract and seek damages for injuries resulting from the fraud.

Typically, there are three elements of fraud:

1. A misrepresentation of a material fact must occur.
2. There must be an intent to deceive.
3. The innocent party must justifiably rely on the misrepresentation.

To collect damages, a party must also have been injured.

Misrepresentation Must Occur The first element of proving fraud is to show that misrepresentation of a material fact has occurred. This misrepresentation can take the form of words or actions. For example, an art gallery owner's statement "This painting is a Picasso" is a misrepresentation of fact if the painting was done by another artist.

A statement of opinion is generally not subject to a claim of fraud. For example, claims such as "this computer will never break down" and "this car will last for years and years" are statements of opinion, not fact, and contracting parties should recognize them as such and not rely on them. A fact is objective and verifiable; an opinion is usually subject to debate. Therefore, a seller is allowed to "huff and puff

4. Restatement (Second) of Contracts, Sections 163 and 164.

his wares" without being liable for fraud. In certain cases, however, particularly when a naïve purchaser relies on a so-called expert's opinion, the innocent party may be entitled to rescission or reformation (an equitable remedy granted by a court in which the terms of a contract are altered to reflect the true intentions of the parties). This occurred in the following case.

Case 11.3 

VOKES v. ARTHUR MURRAY, INC.

District Court of Appeal of Florida, Second District, 1968.
212 So.2d 906.

HISTORICAL AND SOCIAL SETTING *In the seventeenth century, in some of the new American colonies, the law prohibited professional performances of music. By the time of the Revolutionary War, however, the bans had generally been lifted, and the nineteenth century saw the founding of opera companies, city orchestras, and music schools. In the South, gospel music gave birth to the blues, which in turn gave birth to ragtime and jazz. With the development of radio and the recording industries in the first decades of the twentieth century, music became available to an ever-growing American audience, and social dancing became increasingly popular. Dancing skills often led to popularity on the dance floor and—because dancing was popular—to social popularity, especially for the generations that came of age in the 1920s, 1930s, and 1940s. With the popularity of social dance came dancing schools.*

FACTS Audrey Vokes was a fifty-one-year-old widow. While she was attending a dance party at Davenport's School of Dancing, an Arthur Murray dancing school, an instructor sold her eight half-hour dance lessons for the sum of $14.50. Thereafter, over a period of less than sixteen months, she was sold a total of fourteen dance courses, which amounted to 2,302 hours of dancing lessons for a total cash outlay of $31,090.45. All of these lessons were sold to her by salespersons who continually assured her that she was very talented, that she was progressing in her lessons, that she had great dance potential, and that they were "developing her into a beautiful dancer." Vokes contended that, in fact, she was not progressing in her dancing ability, had no "dance aptitude," and had difficulty even "hearing the musical beat." She filed suit against the school, alleging fraudulent misrepresentation. When the trial court dismissed her complaint, she appealed.

ISSUE Could Vokes's contract be rescinded because the salespersons misrepresented her dancing ability?

DECISION Yes. The appellate court reinstated Vokes's complaint and remanded the case to the trial court to allow Vokes to prove her case.

REASON The court held that Vokes could avoid the contract because it was procured by false representations that she had a promising career in dancing. The court acknowledged that ordinarily, to be grounds for rescission, a misrepresentation must be one of fact rather than of opinion. The court concluded that "[a] statement of a party having * * * superior knowledge may be regarded as a statement of fact although it would be considered as opinion if the parties were dealing on equal terms. It could be reasonably supposed here that defendants [the dance studio] had 'superior knowledge' as to whether plaintiff had 'dance potential.' "

ETHICAL CONSIDERATIONS *The job of salespersons is to sell their wares or services. Salespersons working at the Arthur Murray studios are no different. After all, their income is determined by how many dance lessons they can sell to the extent that they receive "commissions" for selling dance lessons to customers. The law recognizes that salespersons "huff and puff their wares" and will not hold salespersons liable for statements that are essentially "puffery." Yet even puffery has its limits. In the* Vokes *case, clearly Audrey Vokes did not have the "dance potential" that the Arthur Murray representatives claimed she had. Obviously, there is a point at which ethics has to frame the claims made by salespersons. The court's decision in the* Vokes *case clearly illustrates this ethical precept.*

Misrepresentation by Conduct Misrepresentation need not be expressly made through words or writings. It can also occur by conduct. For example, if a seller, by his or her actions, prevents a buyer from learning of some fact that is material to the contract, such an action constitutes misrepresentation by conduct. Suppose that Cummings contracts to purchase a racehorse from Garner. The horse is blind in one eye, but when Garner shows the horse, he skillfully conceals this fact by keeping the horse's head turned so that Cummings does not see the defect. The

Law in the Extreme

In Search of Wisdom

In 1959, a case involving alleged misrepresentation came before the appellate division of the Superior Court of New Jersey: *Trustees of Columbia University v. Jacobsen.*[a] After attending Dartmouth for his freshman year, Roy Jacobsen attended Columbia from 1951 to 1954, but he failed to graduate because of poor scholastic standing. When Columbia sued Jacobsen for $1,000 in tuition still owed by him, Jacobsen countered with the allegation that the august institution of higher learning had failed to impart the wisdom promised—by its motto, its brochures, the inscriptions over its buildings, in its presidential addresses, and so on. Because Columbia had promised something it could not deliver, it was guilty of misrepresentation and deceit and should return to Jacobsen all the tuition he had paid—$7,016.

Jacobsen's counterclaim consisted of fifty counts, which alleged that Columbia had promised to teach him "wisdom, truth, character, enlightenment, understanding, justice, liberty, honesty, courage, beauty, and similar virtues and qualities; that it would develop the whole man, maturity, well-roundedness, objective thinking, and the like." At the heart of these fifty counts was a single complaint, according to Jacobsen:

> I have really only one charge against Columbia: that it does not teach Wisdom as it claims to do. From this charge ensues an endless number of charges, of which I have selected fifty at random . . . though the central issue is that of Columbia's pretense of teaching Wisdom.

The court delved into the problem with proper judicial rigor. After commenting on the "inartistic" character of the defendant's counterclaim, the court noted that Jacobsen cited no legal authority for his position. Also, during his years at Columbia, Jacobsen had been a difficult student and had become increasingly critical of his professors. He had shifted his academic interests a number of times—from physics to social work to creative writing and other areas. In his last year, he had attended classes only as he chose, and he had rejected the university's regimen requiring examinations and term papers. "I want to learn," Jacobsen had said in a letter to the dean of students, "but I must do it my own way. I realize my behavior is non-conforming, but in these times when there are so many forces that demand conformity I hope I will find Columbia willing to grant some freedom to a student who wants to be a literary artist."

The court's heartstrings were largely untouched by the claims of the defendant—who acted as his own counsel during the trial. The court found no cause of action. The judges felt that Jacobsen simply "chose to judge Columbia's educational system by the shifting standards of his own fancy, and now seeks to place his failure at Columbia's door on the theory that it had deliberately misrepresented that it taught wisdom." The court concluded that if the defendant's "pleadings, affidavit and exhibits demonstrate anything, it is indeed the validity of what Pope said in his *Moral Essays:* 'A little learning is a dangerous thing.' "

a. 53 N.J.Super. 574, 148 A.2d 63 (1959); aff'd 31 N.J. 121, 156 A.2d 251 (1959).

concealment constitutes fraud.[5] Another example of misrepresentation by conduct is the false denial of knowledge or information concerning facts that are material to the contract when such knowledge or information is requested.

Misrepresentation of Law Misrepresentation of law does not *ordinarily* entitle the party to be relieved of a contract. For example, Debbie has a parcel of property that she is trying to sell to Barry. Debbie knows that a local ordinance prohibits building anything higher than three stories on the property. Nonetheless, she tells Barry, "You can build a condominium fifty stories high if you want to." Barry buys the land and later discovers that Debbie's statement is false. Normally, Barry cannot avoid the contract because under the common law people are assumed to know state and local laws. Exceptions to this rule occur, however, when the misrepresenting party is in a profession known to require greater knowledge of the law than the average citizen possesses.

"You can fool some of the people all of the time, and all of the people some of the time, but you cannot fool all of the people all of the time."

Abraham Lincoln, 1809–1865
(Sixteenth president of the United States, 1861–1865)

Misrepresentation by Silence Ordinarily, neither party to a contract has a duty to come forward and disclose facts, and a contract normally will not be set aside because certain pertinent information has not been volunteered. For example, suppose you are selling a car that has been in an accident and has been repaired. You do not need to volunteer this information to a potential buyer. If, however, the purchaser asks you if the car has had extensive body work and you lie, you have committed a fraudulent misrepresentation. Generally, if a *serious* defect or a *serious* potential problem is known to the seller but cannot reasonably be suspected by the buyer, the seller may have a duty to speak. For example, if a city fails to disclose to bidders subsoil conditions that will cause great expense in constructing a sewer, the city is guilty of fraud.[6] Also, when the parties are in a fiduciary relationship (one of trust, such as partners, doctor and patient, and attorney and client), there is a duty to disclose material facts; failure to do so may constitute fraud.

Intent to Deceive The second element of fraud is knowledge on the part of the misrepresenting party that facts have been falsely represented. This element, normally called ***scienter***,[7] or "guilty knowledge," generally signifies that there was an *intent to deceive. Scienter* clearly exists if a party knows a fact is not as stated. *Scienter* also exists if a party makes a statement that he or she believes not to be true or makes a statement recklessly, without regard to whether it is true or false. Finally, this element is met if a party says or implies that a statement is made on some basis, such as personal knowledge or personal investigation, when it is not.

SCIENTER
Knowledge by the misrepresenting party that material facts have been falsely represented or omitted with an intent to deceive.

For example, suppose that Rolando, when selling a house to Cariton, tells Cariton that the plumbing includes pipe of a certain quality. Rolando knows nothing about the quality of the pipe but does not believe it to be as she is representing it to be (and in fact it is not as she says it is). Rolando's statement induces Cariton to buy the house. Rolando's statement is a misrepresentation because Rolando does not believe that what she says is true and because she knows that she does not have any basis for making the statement. Cariton can avoid the contract.

Reliance on the Misrepresentation The third element of fraud is *justifiable reliance* on the misrepresentation of fact. The deceived party must have a justifiable reason for relying on the misrepresentation, and the misrepresentation must be an important factor (but not necessarily the sole factor) in inducing the party to enter into the contract.

5. Restatement (Second) of Contracts, Section 160.

6. *City of Salinas v. Souza & McCue Construction Co.*, 66 Cal. 2d 217, 424 P.2d 921, 57 Cal.Rptr. 337 (1967). Normally, the seller must disclose only "latent" defects—that is, defects that would not readily be discovered. Thus, termites in a house would not be a latent defect, because a buyer could normally discover their presence.

7. Pronounced sy-*en*-ter.

Reliance is not justified if the innocent party knows the true facts or relies on obviously extravagant statements. Suppose a used-car dealer tells you, "This old Cadillac will get sixty miles to the gallon." You would not normally be justified in relying on this statement. But suppose Merkel, a bank director, induces O'Connell, a co-director, to sign a statement that the bank's assets will satisfy its liabilities by stating, "We have plenty of assets to satisfy our creditors." If O'Connell knows the true facts, he is not justified in relying on Merkel's statement. If O'Connell does not know the true facts, however, *and has no way of finding them out,* he may be justified in relying on the statement. The same rule applies to defects in property sold. If the defects are obvious, the buyer cannot justifiably rely on the seller's representations. If the defects are hidden or latent (that is, not apparent on examination), the buyer is justified in relying on the seller's statements.

Injury to the Innocent Party Most courts do not require a showing of injury when the action is to *rescind* the contract—these courts hold that because rescission returns the parties to the positions they held before the contract was made, a showing of injury to the innocent party is unnecessary.[8]

For a person to recover damages caused by fraud, proof of an injury is universally required. The measure of damages is ordinarily equal to the property's value had it been delivered as represented, less the actual price paid for the property. In actions based on fraud, courts often award *punitive,* or *exemplary, damages*—which are granted to a plaintiff over and above the proved, actual compensation for the loss. Punitive damages are based on the public-policy consideration of punishing the defendant or setting an example for similar wrongdoers.

Undue Influence

Undue influence arises from relationships in which one party can greatly influence another party, thus overcoming that party's free will. Minors and elderly people, for example, are often under the influence of guardians. If a guardian induces a young or elderly *ward* (a person placed by a court under the care of a guardian) to enter into a contract that benefits the guardian, undue influence may have been exerted. Undue influence can arise from a number of confidential relationships or relationships founded on trust, including attorney-client, doctor-patient, guardian-ward, parent-child, husband-wife, and trustee-beneficiary relationships. The essential feature of undue influence is that the party being taken advantage of does not, in reality, exercise free will in entering into a contract. A contract entered into under excessive or undue influence lacks genuine assent and is therefore voidable.[9]

Duress

Assent to the terms of a contract is not genuine if one of the parties is *forced* into the agreement. Recognizing this, the courts allow that party to rescind the contract. Forcing a party to enter into a contract under the fear of threats is legally defined as *duress.*[10] In addition, blackmail or extortion to induce consent to a contract constitutes duress. Duress is both a defense to the enforcement of a contract and a ground for rescission, or cancellation, of a contract. Therefore, the party upon whom the duress is exerted can choose to carry out the contract or to avoid the entire transaction. (The wronged party usually has this choice in cases in which assent is not real or genuine.)

8. See, for example, *Kaufman v. Jaffe,* 244 App.Div. 344, 279 N.Y.S. 392(1935).
9. Restatement (Second) of Contracts, Section 177.
10. Restatement (Second) of Contracts, Sections 174 and 175.

Business Law in Action

Matters of the Heart

In the last several decades, in the wake of the consumer protection movement, legislatures and the courts have virtually turned on its head the traditional concept of *caveat emptor* ("let the buyer beware"). Starting in the 1970s, it was the seller who had to be wary—of lawsuits based on negligence, warranty theories, or product liability laws. Manufacturers and sellers of products today must take great care to ensure that their products will not harm consumers when used as intended (or, in some cases, when used in unintended ways). But for a consumer to find refuge under these laws, he or she must be able to demonstrate, among other things, that a given product is in fact defective.

This represented a major stumbling block for Judy Khan. Khan had a Bjork-Shiley mechanical heart valve implanted in her heart to replace a diseased valve after having been told that she would die without the implant. Khan later stated that she had been thoroughly advised of the risks associated with mechanical heart valves, including possible blood clotting, the possible rejection of the valve by her body, and the fact that she would always have to take blood-thinner medication. She had never been told, however, that there was a risk that the valve might fracture. A little over two years after the valve was implanted, Khan learned from her surgeon that the implanted valve was in a group of valves being recalled because of numerous reports that the valves were "falling apart and malfunctioning without notice resulting in death to the patients." The surgeon also told Khan that the risk of open-heart surgery to remove the valve was even greater than the risk of a malfunction.

Khan and her husband brought suit against the valve's manufacturer, Shiley, Inc., and its parent company, Pfizer, Inc., alleging a number of claims under product liability and warranty theories (see Chapter 17), as well as fraud and misrepresentation. The Khans met with little success in the trial court, however. That court entered summary judgment for Shiley on the ground that Khan's valve had not yet malfunctioned and she could not demonstrate that it was defective. On appeal, however, the court held that even though Khan could not recover under product liability or warranty theories, she had stated a cause of action for fraud. Evidence indicated that Shiley had not disclosed the risks attending the use of its heart valve, of which it was well aware.[a]

Pfizer has paid—and is paying—dearly for its failure to disclose these risks. It is estimated that between 1979 and 1986, Shiley produced somewhere between 50,000 and 100,000 of these valves, that approximately 60,000 valves are implanted in persons around the world, that about 450 of the valves have fractured, and that about 300 persons have died as a result of fractured valves. Since the Khan suit, Shiley and Pfizer have been sued by hundreds of individuals in whom the defective valves are implanted. In 1992, Pfizer agreed to settle a class-action suit that had been brought by plaintiff-users of the valve.[b] Pfizer agreed to establish a fund of up to $250 million, to be replenished each year, for the purpose of providing valve-replacement surgery, counseling, and other services to individuals using the valve and suffering the distress of knowing that their valves could rupture at any moment.

a. *Khan v. Shiley, Inc.*, 217 Cal.App.3d 848, 266 Cal.Rptr. 106 (1990).
b. *Bowling v. Pfizer, Inc.*, 143 F.R.D. 141 (S.D.Ohio 1992). F.R.D. is the abbreviation for the West reporter entitled *Federal Rules Decisions.*

Economic need is generally not sufficient to constitute duress, even when one party exacts a very high price for an item the other party needs. If the party exacting the price also creates the need, however, economic duress may be found. For example, the Internal Revenue Service (IRS) assessed a large tax and penalty against Weller. Weller retained Eyman to resist the assessment. Two days before the deadline for filing a reply with the IRS, Eyman declined to represent Weller unless Weller agreed to pay a very high fee for Eyman's services. The agreement was unenforceable.[11] Although Eyman had threatened only to withdraw his services, something that he was legally entitled to do, he was responsible for delaying his withdrawal until the last days. Because it would have been impossible at that late date to obtain adequate representation elsewhere, Weller was forced into either signing the contract or losing his right to challenge the IRS assessment.

11. *Thompson Crane & Trucking Co. v. Eyman*, 123 Cal.App.2d 904, 267 P.2d 1043 (1954).

Landmark in the Law

The Statute of Frauds

King Charles II

On April 12, 1677, the English Parliament passed "An Act for the Prevention of Frauds and Perjuries." Four days later, the act was signed by King Charles II and became the law of the land. The act contained twenty-five sections and required that certain types of contracts, if they were to be enforceable by the courts, would henceforth have to be in writing or evidenced by a written memorandum.[a]

The intention of the act was to prevent harm to innocent parties by requiring written evidence of agreements concerning important transactions. Although it was acknowledged that the requirements of the act would render commercial transactions more cumbersome, it was felt that the benefits would far outweigh the costs. Today, in the United States, nearly every state has a Statute of Frauds modeled after the British act. Some of the statute's provisions have also been incorporated into the Uniform Commercial Code.

The British act was created specifically to prevent further perpetration of the many frauds that had been brought about through the perjured testimony of witnesses in cases involving breached oral agreements, for which no written evidence existed. Although in the early history of common law in England, oral contracts were generally not enforced by the courts, they began to be enforced in the fourteenth century in certain *assumpsit* actions.[b] These actions, to which the origins of modern contract law are traced, allowed a party to sue and obtain relief in cases in which a promise or contract had been breached. Enforcement of oral promises in actions in *assumpsit* became a common practice in the king's court during the next two centuries.

Because courts enforced oral contracts on the strength of oral testimony by witnesses, it was not too difficult to evade justice by alleging that a contract had been breached and then procuring "convincing" witnesses to support the claim. The possibility of fraud in such actions was enhanced by the fact that in seventeenth-century England, courts did not allow oral testimony to be given by the parties to a lawsuit—or by any parties with an interest in the litigation, such as husbands or wives. Defense against breach of contract actions was thus limited to written evidence and the testimony given by third parties.

Essentially, the Statute of Frauds offers a defense against oral contracts that fall under the statute. If a contract is oral when it is required to be in writing, it will not, as a rule, be enforced by the courts. Since its inception three hundred years ago, the statute has been criticized by some because, although it was created to protect the innocent, it can also be used as a technical defense by a party breaching a genuine oral contract—if the contract falls within the Statute of Frauds. For this reason, some legal scholars believe the act has caused more fraud than it has prevented. Thus, at times, the courts are slow to apply the Statute of Frauds if its application will result in obvious injustice. In some instances, this has required a good deal of inventiveness on the part of the courts.[c]

a. These contracts are discussed in the text of this chapter.

b. *Assumpsit* is Latin for *he undertook* or *he promised*. The emergence of remedies given on the basis of breached promises dates to these actions. One of the earliest occurred in 1370, when the court allowed an individual to sue a person who, in trying to cure the plaintiff's horse, had acted so negligently that the horse died. Another such action was permitted in 1375, when a plaintiff obtained relief for having been maimed by a surgeon hired to cure him.

c. See, for example, *Bader v. Hiscox*, 188 Iowa 986, 174 N.W. 565 (1919). According to Arthur Corbin (see the *Profile* in Chapter 8), the court "worked indefatigably [tirelessly] to prevent the defendant from using the statute to defeat the enforcement of his promise." See *Corbin on Contracts* (St. Paul: West Publishing Co., 1952), Section 275, footnote 2.

❖ The Statute of Frauds—Requirement of a Writing

"Ignorance of the law is no excuse in any country. If it were, the laws would lose their effect, because ignorance can always be pretended."

Thomas Jefferson, 1743–1826
(Third president of the United States, 1801–1809)

The actual name of the **Statute of Frauds** is misleading, because it neither applies to fraud nor invalidates any type of contract (see this chapter's *Landmark in the Law*). Rather, it denies enforceability to certain contracts that do not comply with its requirements. The primary purpose of the act is to ensure that there is reliable evidence of the existence and terms of certain classes of contracts deemed historically to be important or complex. Although the statutes vary slightly from state to state, all require the following types of contracts to be in writing or evidenced by a written memorandum.

1. Contracts involving interests in land.
2. Contracts that cannot *by their terms* be performed within one year from the date of formation.
3. Collateral contracts, such as promises to answer for the debt or duty of another.
4. Promises made in consideration of marriage.
5. Contracts for the sale of goods priced at $500 or more.

STATUTE OF FRAUDS
A state statute under which certain types of contracts must be in a signed writing to be enforceable.

Certain exceptions are made to the applicability of the Statute of Frauds in some circumstances. These exceptions are discussed later in this section.

Contracts Involving Interests in Land

Under the Statute of Frauds, a contract involving an interest in land must be attested to by a writing. Land is real property and includes all physical objects that are permanently attached to the soil, such as buildings, plants, trees, and the soil itself. A contract calling for the sale of land is not enforceable unless it is in writing or evidenced by a written memorandum.[12] If Carol, for example, contracts orally to sell Seaside Shelter to Axel but later decides not to sell, Axel cannot enforce the contract. Likewise, if Axel refuses to close the deal, Carol cannot force Axel to pay for the land by bringing a lawsuit. The Statute of Frauds is a *defense* to the enforcement of this type of oral contract.

A contract for the sale of land ordinarily involves the entire interest in the real property, including buildings, growing crops, vegetation, minerals, timber, and anything else affixed to the land. Therefore, a **fixture** (personal property so affixed or so used as to become a part of the realty) is treated as real property.

FIXTURE
A thing that was once personal property but that has become attached to real property in such a way that it takes on the characteristics of real property and becomes part of that real property.

The Statute of Frauds requires written contracts not just for the sale of land, but also for the transfer of other interests in land, such as mortgages and leases. These other interests are described in Chapter 34.

The One-Year Rule

Contracts that cannot, *by their own terms*, be performed within one year from the day after the contract is formed must be in writing to be enforceable. Because disputes over such contracts are unlikely to occur until some time after the contracts are made, resolution of these disputes is difficult unless the contract terms have been put in writing. The idea behind this rule is that a witness's memory is not to be trusted for longer than a year. The one-year period begins to run *the day after the contract is made.*[13]

The test for determining whether an oral contract is enforceable under the one-year rule of the statute is not whether the agreement is *likely* to be performed within

12. In some states, the contract will be enforced, however, if each party admits to the existence of the oral contract in court or admits to its existence during discovery before trial (see Chapter 3).
13. Arthur Corbin, *Corbin on Contracts* (St. Paul: West Publishing Co., 1952), Section 444.

♦ **Exhibit 11–1 The One-Year Rule**

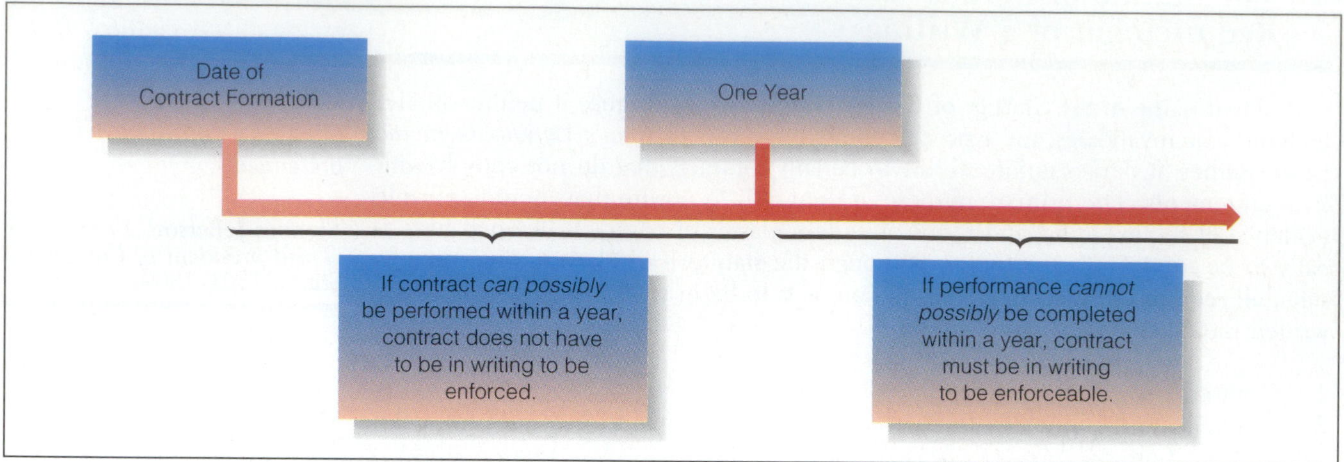

one year from the date of contract formation, but whether performance within a year is *possible*. Conversely, when performance of a contract is impossible during the one-year period, this provision of the Statute of Frauds will bar recovery on an oral contract. Exhibit 11–1 illustrates the one-year rule.

Collateral Promises

COLLATERAL PROMISE
A secondary promise that is ancillary to a principal transaction or primary contractual relationship, such as a promise made by one person to pay the debts or discharge the duties of another if the latter fails to perform. A collateral promise normally must be in writing to be enforceable.

A **collateral promise,** or secondary promise, is one that is ancillary to a principal transaction or primary contractual relationship. In other words, a collateral promise is one made by a third party to assume the debts or obligations of a primary party to a contract if that party does not perform. Any collateral promise of this nature falls under the Statute of Frauds and therefore must be in writing to be enforceable. To understand this concept, it is important to distinguish between primary and secondary promises and obligations.

Primary versus Secondary Obligations Suppose that Kenneth orally contracts with Joanne's Floral Boutique to send his mother a dozen roses for Mother's Day. Kenneth's oral contract with Joanne's Floral Boutique provides that he will pay for the roses when he receives the bill for the flowers. Kenneth is a direct party to this contract and has incurred a *primary* obligation under the contract. Because he is a party to the contract and has a primary obligation to Joanne's Floral Boutique, this contract does *not* fall under the Statute of Frauds and does not have to be in writing to be enforceable. If Kenneth fails to pay the florist and the florist sues him for payment, Kenneth cannot raise the Statute of Frauds as a defense. He cannot claim that the contract is unenforceable because it was not in writing.

Now suppose that Kenneth's mother borrows $1,000 from the Medford Trust Company on a promissory note payable six months later. Kenneth promises the bank officer handling the loan that he will pay the $1,000 *if his mother does not pay the loan on time.* Kenneth, in this situation, becomes what is known as a *guarantor* on the loan. That is, he is guaranteeing to the bank that he will pay back the loan if his mother fails to do so. This kind of collateral promise, in which the guarantor states that he or she will become responsible *only* if the primary party does not perform, must be in writing to be enforceable.

We will return to the concept of guaranty and the distinction between primary and secondary obligations in Chapter 22, in the context of creditors' rights.

An Exception—the "Main Purpose" Rule An oral promise to answer for the debt of another is covered by the Statute of Frauds *unless* the guarantor's main purpose in accepting secondary liability is to secure a personal benefit. This type of contract need not be in writing.[14] The assumption is that a court can infer from the circumstances of a case whether the "leading objective" of the promisor was to secure a personal benefit and thus, in effect, to answer for his or her own debt.

Consider an example. Oswald contracts with Machine Manufacturing Company to have some machines custom-made for Oswald's factory. She promises Allrite Materials Supply Company, Machine Manufacturing's supplier, that if Allrite continues to deliver materials to Machine Manufacturing, she will guarantee payment. This promise need not be in writing, even though the effect may be to pay the debt of another, because Oswald's main purpose is to secure a benefit for herself.[15]

Another typical application of the so-called main purpose doctrine is the situation in which one creditor guarantees the debtor's debt to another creditor to forestall litigation. This allows the debtor to remain in business long enough to generate profits sufficient to pay *both* creditors.

Promises Made in Consideration of Marriage

A unilateral promise to pay a sum of money or to give property in consideration of a promise to marry must be in writing. If Mr. Baumann promises to pay Joe Villard $10,000 if Villard promises to marry Baumann's daughter, the promise must be in writing. The same rule applies to **prenuptial agreements.** These agreements, which are also sometimes called *antenuptial agreements*, are agreements made before marriage that define each partner's ownership rights in the other partner's property. For example, a prospective wife may wish to limit the amount her prospective husband could obtain if the marriage ended in divorce. Prenuptial agreements made in consideration of marriage must be in writing to be enforceable.

PRENUPTIAL AGREEMENT
An agreement entered into in contemplation of marriage that specifies the rights and ownership of property brought into the marriage and, where permitted, property acquired during the marriage.

Generally, courts tend to give more credence to prenuptial agreements that are accompanied by consideration. For example, assume that Maureen, who has little money, marries Kaiser, who has a net worth of $300 million. Kaiser has several children, and he wants them to receive most of his wealth upon his death. Prior to their marriage, Maureen and Kaiser draft and sign a prenuptial agreement in which Kaiser promises to give Maureen $100,000 per year for the rest of her life should they divorce. As consideration for her consenting to this amount, Kaiser offers Maureen $200,000. If Maureen consents to the agreement and accepts the $200,000, very likely a court would hold this to be a valid prenuptial agreement should the agreement ever be contested.

To add certainty to the enforceability of prenuptial agreements, the National Conference of Commissioners on Uniform State Laws issued the Uniform Prenuptial Agreements Act (UPAA) in 1983. In the preface to the UPAA, it was recognized that "[t]he number of marriages between persons previously married and the number of marriages between persons each of whom is intending to continue to pursue a career is steadily increasing. For these and other reasons, it is becoming more and more common for persons contemplating marriage to seek to resolve by agreement certain issues presented by the forthcoming marriage." The act provides that prenuptial agreements must be in writing to be enforceable and that the agreements become effective when the parties marry. Under the UPAA, in some circumstances, a prenuptial agreement is not enforceable even if it is in writing. For example, an agreement is not enforceable if the party against whom enforcement is sought proves that he or she did not execute the agreement voluntarily.

Contracts for the Sale of Goods

The Uniform Commercial Code (UCC) contains several Statute of Frauds provisions that require written evidence of a contract. Section 2–201 contains the major

14. Restatement (Second) of Contracts, Section 116.
15. See *Kampman v. Pittsburgh Contracting and Engineering Co.*, 316 Pa. 502, 175 A. 396 (1934).

provision, which generally requires a writing or memorandum for the sale of goods priced at $500 or more. A writing that will satisfy the UCC requirement need only state the quantity term; other terms agreed upon need not be stated "accurately" in the writing, as long as they adequately reflect both parties' intentions. The contract will not be enforceable, however, for any quantity greater than that set forth in the writing. In addition, the writing must be signed by the person to be charged—that is, by the person who refuses to perform or the one being sued. The writing need not designate the buyer or the seller, the terms of payment, or the price.

Exceptions to the Statute of Frauds

Exceptions to the applicability of the Statute of Frauds are made in the following situations.

Partial Performance In cases involving contracts relating to the transfer of interests in land, if the purchaser has paid part of the price, taken possession, and made permanent improvements to the property and the parties cannot be returned to the positions they held before their contract, a court may grant *specific performance* (performance of the contract according to its precise terms). Whether the courts will enforce an oral contract for an interest in land when partial performance has taken place is usually determined by the degree of injury that would be suffered if the court chose not to enforce the oral contract. In some states, mere reliance on an oral contract is enough to remove it from the Statute of Frauds.

Under the UCC, an oral contract is enforceable to the extent that a seller accepts payment or a buyer accepts delivery of the goods.[16] For example, if Ajax Corporation ordered by telephone twenty crates of bleach from Cloney, Inc., and repudiated the contract after ten crates had been delivered and accepted, Cloney could enforce the contract to the extent of the ten crates accepted by Ajax.

Admissions In some states, if a party against whom enforcement of an oral contract is sought "admits" in pleadings, testimony, or otherwise in court that a contract for sale was made, the contract will be enforceable.[17] A contract subject to the UCC will be enforceable but only to the extent of the quantity admitted.[18] Thus, if the president of Ajax Corporation admits under oath that an oral agreement was made with Cloney, Inc., for twenty crates of bleach, the agreement will be enforceable to that extent.

Promissory Estoppel In some states, an oral contract that would otherwise be unenforceable under the Statute of Frauds may be enforced under the doctrine of promissory estoppel, or detrimental reliance. Recall from Chapter 9 that if a promisor makes a promise on which the promisee justifiably relies to his or her detriment, a court may *estop* (prevent) the promisor from denying that a contract exists. Section 139 of the Restatement (Second) of Contracts provides that in these circumstances, an oral promise can be enforceable notwithstanding the Statute of Frauds if the reliance was foreseeable to the person making the promise and if injustice can be avoided only by enforcing the promise. Using promissory estoppel in these circumstances is intended to prevent the Statute of Frauds—which was created to prevent injustice—from being used to promote injustice. Nevertheless, this use of the doctrine is controversial. Enforcing an oral contract on the basis of a party's reliance arguably undercuts the essence of the statute.

---

16. UCC 2–201(3)(c).
17. Restatement (Second) of Contracts, Section 133.
18. UCC 2–201(3)(b).

Special Exceptions under the UCC Special exceptions to the applicability of the Statute of Frauds apply to sales contracts. These exceptions, which deal with oral contracts between merchants, customized goods, admissions in court proceedings, and partial contract performance, will be examined in detail in the discussion of the UCC provisions regarding the Statute of Frauds in Chapter 14.

❖ The Statute of Frauds—Sufficiency of the Writing

To be safe, all contracts should fully set forth the terms in a writing signed by all the parties. This assures that if any problems arise concerning performance of the contract, a written agreement fully specifying the performance promised by each party can be introduced into court. For contracts covered by the Statute of Frauds, the law requires either a written contract or a *written memorandum* signed by the party against whom enforcement is sought.[19]

A written memorandum can consist of any confirmation, invoice, sales slip, check, or fax; or such items in combination may constitute a writing that satisfies the Statute of Frauds. The writing need not consist of a single document to constitute an enforceable contract. One document may incorporate another document by expressly referring to it. Several documents may form a single contract if they are physically attached, by staple, paper clip, or glue. Several documents may form a single contract even if they are only placed in the same envelope. The signature need not be placed at the end of the document but can be anywhere in the writing; it can even be initials rather than the full name. For example, Sam orally agrees to sell Terry some land next to a shopping mall. Sam gives Terry an unsigned memo that contains a legal description of the property, and Terry gives Sam an unsigned first draft of their contract. Sam writes a signed letter to Terry that refers to the memo and to the first and final drafts of the contract. Terry sends Sam an unsigned copy of the final draft of the contract with a signed check stapled to it. Together, the documents can constitute a writing sufficient to satisfy the Statute of Frauds and bind both parties to the terms of the contract.

A memorandum evidencing the oral contract need only contain the essential terms of the contract. Under the UCC, for the sale of goods the writing need only name the quantity term and be signed by the party being charged. Under most provisions of the Statute of Frauds, the writing must name the parties, subject matter, consideration, and quantity. Contracts for the sale of land, in some states, require that the memorandum also state the essential terms of the contract, such as location and price, with sufficient clarity to allow the terms to be determined from the memo itself, without reference to any outside sources.[20]

Only the party against whom enforcement is sought need have signed the writing. Therefore, a contract may be enforceable by one of its parties but not by the other. Suppose Devlin and Rock contract for the sale of Devlin's lake house and lot for $150,000. Devlin writes Rock a letter confirming the sale by identifying the parties and the essential terms of the sales contract—price, method of payment, and legal address—and signs the letter. Devlin has made a written memorandum of the oral land contract. Because she signed the letter, she normally can be held to the oral contract by Rock. Rock, however, because he has not signed or entered into a written contract or memorandum, can plead the Statute of Frauds as a defense, and Devlin cannot enforce the contract against him. The following classic case illustrates what may be considered a "signed writing" by the court.

19. Under the UCC Statute of Frauds, a writing is only required for contracts for the sale of goods priced at $500 or more.

20. *Rhodes v. Wilkins*, 83 N.M. 782, 498 P.2d 311 (1972).

Case 11.4
DRURY v. YOUNG
Court of Appeals of Maryland, 1882.
58 Md. 546.

HISTORICAL AND ECONOMIC SETTING *A contract to buy a product can prove most profitable to the buyer if the contract is signed when the product is plentiful and the price is good but the goods are delivered at a time when the product is scarce in the market and the price is high. Prices for food and other products that depend on agricultural output can fluctuate from year to year. The amount of agricultural output can depend on the weather. Changes in the weather have affected U.S. harvests dramatically. In 1880, U.S. wheat production was up more than 200 percent over production a dozen years before. Due in part to this greater quantity of wheat on the market, the price was down nearly 30 percent. Corn production was so high, and prices so low, that many corn farmers burned corn for fuel because it was cheaper than shipping the crop to market. The next year, drought struck the United States and harvests were poor. This caused prices to rise in 1882. At the time, one popular dish was sliced tomatoes with sugar and vinegar.*

FACTS The plaintiff, Young, formed an oral agreement with the defendant, Drury, to buy several carloads of tomatoes. Afterward, Drury wrote a memorandum concerning the agreement and all its terms for his own records and put it in his safe. The memo, which Drury did not sign, was created on Drury's letterhead (which is a sufficient signing in the eyes of the court) and contained Young's name in the text. Subsequently, Drury wrote a letter to Young stating he was not going to sell Young the tomatoes as agreed. On the date of the scheduled delivery, however, Young tendered payment and requested that Drury keep his part of the bargain—but Drury again refused to sell. When Young sued Drury for breach of contract, Drury used the Statute of Frauds as a defense, alleging that because his memo had never been delivered to Young, no written confirmation of the oral contract existed. The trial court held in Young's favor, claiming that Drury's memo (even if it was never delivered to Young) combined with the subsequent letter satisfied the writing requirement of the Statute of Frauds. Drury appealed.

ISSUE Does the memo written by Drury satisfy the writing requirement under the Statute of Frauds?

DECISION Yes. The judgment of the trial court was affirmed.

REASON The court stated that the Statute of Frauds is not concerned with whether or not a writing has been delivered, or with the custody of a writing, but just with the *existence* of a writing evidencing the agreement. Drury's memo with the terms of the agreement, kept in his own safe, in conjunction with the subsequent letter to Young denying delivery, provided sufficient evidence to the court that the Statute of Frauds had been satisfied.

❖ The Parol Evidence Rule

PAROL EVIDENCE RULE
A substantive rule of contracts under which a court will not receive into evidence prior statements or contemporaneous oral statements that contradict a written agreement when the court finds that the written agreement was intended by the parties to be a final, complete, and unambiguous expression of their agreement.

The **parol evidence rule** prohibits the introduction at trial of evidence of the parties' prior negotiations or agreements or contemporaneous oral agreements that contradicts or varies the terms of written contracts.[21] The written contract is ordinarily assumed to be the complete embodiment of the parties' agreement. Because of the rigidity of the parol evidence rule, however, courts make several exceptions.

1. Evidence of *subsequent modification* of a written contract can be introduced into court. Keep in mind that the oral modifications may not be enforceable if they come under the Statute of Frauds—for example, if they increase the price of the goods for sale to $500 or more or increase the term for performance to more than one year. Also, oral modifications will not be enforceable if the original contract provides that any modification must be in writing.[22]
2. Oral evidence can be introduced in all cases to show that the contract was voidable or void (for example, induced by mistake, fraud, or misrepresentation). In

21. Restatement (Second) of Contracts, Section 213.
22. UCC 2–209(2), (3).

this case, if deception led one of the parties to agree to the terms of a written contract, oral evidence attesting to fraud should not be excluded. Courts frown upon bad faith and are quick to allow such evidence when it establishes fraud.

3. When the terms of a written contract are ambiguous, evidence is admissible to show the meaning of the terms.

4. Evidence is admissible when the written contract is incomplete in that it lacks one or more of the essential terms. The courts allow evidence to "fill in the gaps."

5. Under the UCC, evidence can be introduced to explain or supplement a written contract by showing a prior dealing, course of performance, or usage of trade.[23] These terms will be discussed in further detail in Chapter 14, in the context of sales contracts. Here, it is sufficient to say that when buyers and sellers deal with each other over extended periods of time, certain customary practices develop. These practices are often overlooked in the writing of the contract, so courts allow the introduction of evidence to show how the parties have acted in the past.

6. The parol evidence rule does not apply if the existence of the entire written contract is subject to an orally agreed-upon condition. Proof of the condition does not *alter* or *modify* the written terms but involves the *enforceability* of the written contract. Suppose, for example, you agree with your friend Amy to buy her car for $4,000, but only if your brother, Frank, inspects it and approves of your purchase. Amy agrees to this condition, but because she is leaving town for the weekend and you want to use the car (if you buy it) before she returns, you write up a contract of sale, and both of you sign it. Frank does not approve of the purchase, and when you do not buy the car, Amy sues you, alleging that you breached the contract. In this case, your oral agreement did not alter or modify the terms of your written agreement but concerned whether or not the contract would exist at all.

7. When an *obvious* or *gross* clerical (or typographical) error exists that clearly would not represent the agreement of the parties, parol evidence is admissible to correct the error. For example, Sharon agrees to lease 1,000 square feet of office space at the current monthly rate of $3 per square foot from Stone Enterprises. The signed written lease provides for a monthly lease payment of $30 rather than the $3,000 agreed to by the parties. Because the error is obvious, Stone Enterprises would be allowed to admit parol evidence to correct the mistake.

The key in determining whether evidence will be allowed basically depends on whether the written contract is intended to be a complete and final embodiment of the terms of the agreement. If it is so intended, it is referred to as an **integrated contract,** and extraneous evidence is excluded. If it is only partially integrated, evidence of consistent additional terms is admissible to supplement the written agreement.[24] In the following case, a shipper claimed that an oral understanding as to the insurance value placed on shipped goods superseded a written contract.

INTEGRATED CONTRACT A written contract that constitutes the final expression of the parties' agreement. If a contract is integrated, evidence extraneous to the contract that contradicts or alters the meaning of the contract in any way is inadmissible.

Case 11.5
CHAFETZ v. UNITED PARCEL SERVICE, INC.
Massachusetts Appellate Division, District Court, 1992.
1992 Mass.App.Div. 67.

HISTORICAL AND ECONOMIC SETTING *A common carrier is a business that is customarily employed to transport people or property from one location to another. Common carriers include railroads, airlines, trucking companies, buses, taxis, and express delivery companies. Common carriers engaged in interstate transportation are regulated by federal law. Federal law requires a carrier to give a shipper of goods a shipping receipt, commonly a bill of lading (or other document that serves as a receipt). This receipt can serve as a contract between the carrier and the shipper. Terms in this contract can restrict the dollar amount of the carrier's liability for the loss of, or damage to, the*

23. UCC 1–205, 2–202.
24. Restatement (Second) of Contracts, Section 216.

Case 11.5—Continued

shipper's goods, as long as the terms are clear and the receipt is accepted and signed by the shipper. Otherwise, with some exceptions, the carrier is absolutely liable.

FACTS On November 11, 1988, Roberta Chafetz telephoned a United Parcel Service (UPS) office to inquire about shipping two packages containing diamonds from her home to New York City. She told the UPS representative that each package would need to be insured for $25,000. Arrangements were made to pick up the packages, and three days later, a UPS driver called at Chafetz's home, presented her with the standard "pick-up record" form, and requested payment of $6.65. Chafetz paid the charge and signed the pick-up agreement form without reading it and without filling in the blank on the form that provided for extra insurance coverage. Subsequently, one of the two packages was lost or stolen during shipment. UPS claimed its liability was limited to $100—the standard package insurance specified on the shipping agreement that Chafetz signed. The trial court found for Chafetz, and UPS appealed.

ISSUE Can Chafetz modify the written shipping agreement with UPS on the basis of UPS's prior oral statements?

DECISION No. The appellate court found that the parol evidence rule bars oral evidence that contradicts the terms of a written contract.

REASON The appellate court held that implicit in the trial court's finding was the assumption that parol evidence (of the prior oral statements) could be admitted on the basis that the contract was induced by fraud or deceit. It was claimed that Chafetz was an "unsophisticated shipper" who relied to her detriment on the telephone conversation with the UPS representative. The facts, however, seemed otherwise to the appellate court. As part of her business, which she conducted out of her home, Chafetz routinely shipped diamonds via other common carriers; furthermore, any "reasonable person" would have questioned the charge of $6.65 as payment for shipment plus insurance coverage of $50,000. The terms of the written agreement were clear and unambiguous, and under federal law, "obligations of a carrier and the amount of any recovery by a shipper for lost or damaged goods are ordinarily determined solely from the provisions of their written contract." A shipper is normally bound by such a written agreement even if he or she has not read the contract. Someone who signs a contract in the absence of fraud or deceit cannot avoid it simply because he or she did not read it or took "someone else's word as to what it contained."

Application

Law and the Businessperson—The Problem with Oral Contracts

As a general rule, most business contracts should be in writing even when these fall outside the Statute of Frauds requirement. Oral contracts are frequently made over the telephone, however, particularly when the parties have done business with each other in the past.

Any time an oral contract is made, it is advisable for one of the parties to send either a written memorandum or a confirmation of the oral agreement by fax to the other party. Two purposes are accomplished by this: (1) it demonstrates a party's clear intention to form a contract, and (2) it provides the terms that at least one of the parties believes were agreed upon. If the party receiving the memorandum or confirmation then disagrees with the terms or the intent, the issue can be addressed before performance begins.

What about the sale of goods between merchants? Under the UCC, written confirmation received by one merchant removes the Statute of Frauds requirement of a writing unless the merchant receiving the confirmation objects in writing within ten days of its receipt. This law points out clearly the need for the merchant receiv-

Application—Continued

ing the confirmation to review it carefully to ascertain that the confirmation conforms to the oral contract. If the writing does not so conform, the merchant can object in writing (the Statute of Frauds still applies), and the parties can resolve misunderstandings without legal liability. If the merchant fails to object, the written confirmation can be used as evidence to prove the terms of the oral contract. Note, however, that this ten-day rule does not apply to contracts for interests in realty or for services.

Checklist for Oral Contracts

- ☐ 1. When feasible, use written contracts.
- ☐ 2. If you enter into an oral contract over the telephone, fax a written confirmation outlining your understanding of the oral contract.
- ☐ 3. If you receive the other party's written or faxed confirmation, read it carefully to make sure that its terms agree with what you believed was already agreed on in the oral contract.
- ☐ 4. If you have any objections, put them in writing within ten days.

❖ Key Terms

collateral promise 274
fixture 273
form 263
integrated contract 279
parol evidence rule 278
prenuptial agreement 275
scienter 269
Statute of Frauds 273

❖ Chapter Summary: Assent and Form

GENUINENESS OF ASSENT	
Mistakes	1. *Unilateral*—Generally, the mistaken party is bound by the contract *unless* (a) the other party knows or should have known of the mistake or (b) the mistake is an inadvertent mathematical error—such as an error in addition or subtraction—committed without gross negligence. 2. *Bilateral*—When both parties are mistaken about the same material fact, such as identity, either party can avoid the contract. If the mistake concerns value or quality, either party can enforce the contract.
Misrepresentation	1. *Fraudulent misrepresentation*—When fraud occurs, usually the innocent party can enforce or avoid the contract. The elements necessary to establish fraud are as follows: a. A misrepresentation of a material fact must occur. b. There must be an intent to deceive. c. The innocent party must justifiably rely on the misrepresentation. For damages, the innocent party must suffer an injury. 2. *Other types of misrepresentation*—Intent to deceive need not be proved. Usually, the innocent party can rescind the contract but cannot seek damages unless he or she has suffered an injury due to the misrepresentation. A misrepresentation of law generally does not permit a person to avoid the contract.
Undue Influence	Undue influence arises from special relationships, such as fiduciary or confidential relationships, in which one party's free will has been overcome by the undue influence exerted by the other party. Usually, the contract is voidable.
Duress	Duress is defined as forcing a party to enter a contract under the fear of a threat—for example, the threat of violence or serious economic loss. The party forced to enter the contract can rescind the contract.

❖ Chapter Summary: Assent and Form—Continued

FORM	
Contracts Subject to the Statute of Frauds	*Applicability*—The following types of contracts fall under the Statute of Frauds and must be in writing to be enforceable: 1. *Contracts involving interests in land*—Statute applies to any contract for an interest in realty, such as a sale, a lease, or a mortgage. 2. *Contracts whose terms cannot be performed within one year*—Statute applies only to contracts objectively impossible to perform fully within one year from (the day after) the contract's formation. 3. *Collateral promises*—Statute applies only to express contracts made between the guarantor and the creditor whose terms make the guarantor secondarily liable. Exception: main purpose rule. 4. *Promises made in consideration of marriage*—Statute applies to promises to pay money or give property in consideration of a promise to marry and to prenuptial agreements made in consideration of marriage. 5. *Contracts for the sale of goods priced at $500 or more*—Under UCC Statute of Frauds provision in UCC 2–201(1). *Exceptions*—Partial performance; admissions; promissory estoppel.
Sufficiency of the Writing	To constitute an enforceable contract under the Statute of Frauds, a writing must be signed by the party against whom enforcement is sought, must name the parties, must identify the subject matter, and must state with reasonable certainty the essential terms. In a sale of land, the price and a description of the property may need to be stated with sufficient clarity to be determined without reference to outside sources. Under the UCC, a contract for a sale of goods is not enforceable beyond the quantity of goods shown.
Parol Evidence Rule	The parol evidence rule prohibits the introduction at trial of evidence of the parties' prior negotiations or agreements or contemporaneous oral agreements that contradicts or varies the terms of written contracts. The written contract is assumed to be the complete embodiment of the parties' agreement. Exceptions are made in the following circumstances: 1. To show that the contract was subsequently modified. 2. To show that the contract was voidable or void. 3. To clarify the meaning of ambiguous terms. 4. To clarify the terms of the contract when the written contract lacks one or more of its essential terms. 5. Under the UCC, to explain the meaning of contract terms in light of a prior dealing, course of performance, or usage of trade. 6. To show that the entire contract is subject to an orally agreed-upon condition. 7. When an obvious clerical or typographical error was made.

❖ Questions and Case Problems

11-1. Genuineness of Assent. What kinds of actions or events might cause a court to conclude that genuineness of assent is lacking and therefore the contract should not be enforced?

11-2. Collateral Promises. You promise a local hardware store that you will pay for a lawnmower your brother is purchasing on credit if your brother fails to pay the debt. Must this promise be in writing to be enforceable? Why or why not?

11-3. One-Year Rule. On January 1, Dominic, for consideration, orally promised to pay Francis $300 a month for as long as Francis lived, with the payments to be made on the first day of every month. Dominic made the payments regularly for nine months and then made no further payments. Francis claimed that Dominic had breached the oral contract and sued Dominic for damages. Dominic contended that the contract was unenforceable because, under the Statute of Frauds, contracts that cannot be performed within one year must be in writing. Discuss whether Dominic will succeed in this defense.

11-4. Fraudulent Misrepresentation. Larry offered to sell Stanley his car and told Stanley that the car had been driven only 25,000 miles and had never been in an accident. Stanley hired Cohen, a mechanic, to appraise the condition of the car, and Cohen said that the car probably had at least 50,000 miles on it and probably had been in an accident. In spite of this information, Stanley still thought the car would be a good buy for the price, so he purchased it. Later, when the car developed numerous mechanical problems, Stanley sought to rescind the contract on the basis of Larry's fraudulent misrepresentation of the auto's condition. Will Stanley be able to rescind his contract? Discuss.

11-5. Collateral Promises. Jeffrey took his mother on a special holiday to Mountain Air Resort. Jeffrey was a frequent patron of the resort and well known by its manager. The resort required of each of its patrons a large deposit to ensure payment of the room rental. Jeffrey asked the manager to waive the requirement for his mother and told the manager that if his mother for any reason failed to pay the resort for her stay there, he would cover the bill. Relying on Jeffrey's promise, the manager waived the deposit requirement for Jeffrey's mother. After she returned home from her holiday, Jeffrey's mother refused to pay the resort bill. The resort manager tried to collect the sum from Jeffrey, but Jeffrey also refused to pay, stating that his promise was not enforceable under the Statute of Frauds. Is Jeffrey correct? Explain.

11-6. Fraudulent Misrepresentation. Division West Chinchilla Ranch made numerous television advertisements that induced listeners to go into the business of raising chinchillas. The advertisements stated that, in return for a payment of $2,150, Division would send one male and six female chinchillas and—for an additional sum—cages, feed, and supplies. Division's representations were that "chinchilla ranching can be done in the basement [and] spare rooms . . . with minor modifications" and that chinchillas were "odorless and practically noiseless" and "a profitable pastime that can explode into a FIVE FIGURE INCOME." All statements would lead one to believe that no special skill was needed in the raising of chinchillas. Based on these representations, Adolph Fischer and others (the plaintiffs) purchased chinchillas from Division. None of the plaintiffs was a sophisticated businessperson or highly educated. It soon became apparent that greater skill than that advertised by Division was required to raise chinchillas and that certain statements made by Division's sales representatives as to the value of the pelts were untrue. None of the plaintiffs had financial success with their growing (ranching) of chinchillas over a three-year period. Claiming fraud on the part of Division, the plaintiffs sought to rescind the contracts to get their money back. Discuss whether Division's statements constituted fraud. [*Fischer v. Division West Chinchilla Ranch*, 310 F.Supp. 424 (D.Minn. 1970)]

11-7. Mistake. Steven Lanci was involved in an automobile accident with an uninsured motorist. Lanci was insured with Metropolitan Insurance Co., although he did not have a copy of the insurance policy. Lanci and Metropolitan entered settlement negotiations, during which Lanci told Metropolitan that he did not have a copy of his policy. Ultimately, Lanci agreed to settle all claims for $15,000, noting in a letter to Metropolitan that $15,000 was the "sum you have represented to be the . . . policy limits applicable to this claim." After signing a release, Lanci learned that the policy limits were actually $250,000, and he refused to accept the settlement proceeds. When Metropolitan sued to enforce the settlement agreement, Lanci argued that the release was signed as the result of a mistake and was void. Should the court enforce the contract or void it? [*Lanci v. Metropolitan Insurance Co.*, 388 Pa.Super. 1, 564 A.2d 972 (1989)]

11-8. Fraudulent Misrepresentation. The plaintiff publishes a directory entitled *New York Yellow Pages*, which is strikingly similar in color and format to the *New York Telephone Company Yellow Pages* but which in fact is part of an independent business enterprise. In addition, the *New York Yellow Pages* has on its cover the legend "Let your fingers do the walking!"—along with the familiar logo of walking fingers that appears on the *New York Telephone Company Yellow Pages.* The plaintiff's representative, stating that this publication would replace the bulkier *New York Telephone Company Yellow Pages,* sold advertising space to Grossman for $1,492.80. Grossman made a down payment of $118.40 and one installment payment of $65.20 and thereafter refused to make any more payments. The plaintiff sued. Grossman claimed that the plaintiff had fraudulently induced him to enter into the contract by leading him to believe that the plaintiff's book was a new, improved version of the *New York Telephone Company Yellow Pages.* Can Grossman rescind the contract on grounds of fraudulent misrepresentation? [*New York Yellow Pages, Inc. v. Growth Personnel Agency, Inc.*, 98 Misc.2d 541, 414 N.Y.S.2d 260 (Civ.Ct. 1979)]

11-9. Statute of Frauds/Land Sales Contracts. The plaintiffs—the Nicols, Hoerrs, Turners, and Andersons—purchased subdivision lots from Ken Nelson. The lots bordered an undeveloped tract and offered scenic views of an adjacent lake. When Nelson and his partners began taking steps to develop the previously undeveloped tract, the plaintiffs sued. The trial court found that the plaintiffs had purchased their lots only after receiving oral assurances from Nelson that (1) the tract would remain undeveloped open space, (2) the property was owned by a company that had no plans to build on the land, (3) he held an option to purchase the property if it became available, and (4) he would not develop the land if it came under his ownership. Concluding that the plaintiffs had reasonably relied on Nelson's oral promise, the trial court enjoined Nelson's development of the property. Nelson appealed, arguing that the Statute of Frauds, which requires that contracts involving interests in real property be in writing, barred enforcement of his oral promise. Will the appellate court affirm the trial court's judgment? [*Nicol v. Nelson*, 776 P.2d 1144 (Colo.App. 1989)]

11-10. Fraudulent Misrepresentation. Nosrat, a citizen of Iran, owned a hardware store with his brother-in-law, Edwin. Edwin induced Nosrat to sign a promissory note for $11,400, payable to a third party, telling Nosrat that the document was a credit application for the hardware store. Although Nosrat could read and write English, he failed to read the note or to notice that the document was clearly entitled "PROMISSORY NOTE (SECURED) and Security Agreement." The money received from the third party in exchange for the note was spent by Edwin and others. When the third party sued for payment, Nosrat sought to void the note on the basis of Edwin's fraudulent inducement. Will Nosrat succeed in his attempt? [*Waldrep v. Nosrat*, 426 So.2d 822 (Ala. 1983)]

11-11. One-Year Rule. Fernandez orally promised Pando that if Pando helped her win the New York state lottery, she would share the proceeds equally with him. Pando agreed to purchase the tickets in Fernandez's name, select the lottery numbers, and pray for the divine intervention of a saint to help them win. Fernandez won $2.8 million in the lottery, which was to be paid over a ten-year period. When Fernandez failed to share the winnings equally, Pando sued for breach of her contractual obligation. Fernandez countered that their contract was unenforceable under the Statute of Frauds, because the contract could not be performed within one year. Could the contract be performed within one year? [*Pando by Pando v. Fernandez,* 127 Misc.2d 224, 485 N.Y.S.2d 162 (1984)]

11-12. Parol Evidence Rule. Butler Brothers, Inc., was the main contractor for a highway construction project near Minneapolis. Butler hired another contractor, Ganley Brothers Building Co., to perform some of the highway construction work. At the time the contract was formed, Butler made several false representations orally to Ganley. If Ganley had known Butler's statements were fraudulent, Ganley would never have entered into the contract. The written contract between Butler and Ganley included the following clause: "The contractor [Ganley] has examined the said contracts . . . and is not relying upon any statement made by the company in respect thereto." In light of this clause, can Ganley introduce evidence of Butler's fraudulent misstatements at trial? [*Ganley Brothers, Inc. v. Butler Brothers Building Co.,* 170 Minn. 373, 212 N.W. 602 (1927)]

11-13. One-Year Rule. Carol Mann and Gerald Harris worked for Helmsley-Spear, Inc. (HSI), as account managers for various HSI properties. In 1983, each received a bonus of $50,000 for their work in converting an HSI apartment complex, known as Windsor Park, into a cooperative housing unit. The conversion had taken several years to complete. After they had finished the Windsor Park conversion, they were asked to work on another cooperative conversion of two HSI apartment buildings known as Park West Village. Mann and Harris were orally promised compensation, over and above their base salaries, on the basis of a formula similar to the one that had been orally agreed upon with regard to the Windsor Park conversion. In 1987, after they had completed the conversion of Park West Village, they were fired, and HSI refused to pay them the additional compensation. Among other things, HSI contended that their oral agreement concerning the extra compensation was unenforceable under the Statute of Frauds. How should the court rule on this issue, and why? [*Mann v. Helmsley-Spear, Inc.,* 177 A.D.2d 147, 581 N.Y.S.2d 16 (1992)]

A Question of Ethics and Social Responsibility

11-14. *In July 1987, Mark and Kathryn Van Wagoner attended a real estate "open house" held by Carol Klas, who was selling the property for her former husband, John Klas. Mark Van Wagoner, an attorney experienced in real estate transactions, subsequently prepared and delivered to Carol Klas a written offer to purchase the property for $175,000. John Klas accepted the offer, and the Van Wagoners signed the agreement on August 11, 1987. Prior to signing the agreement, the Van Wagoners asked Carol Klas if there had been any appraisals of the property. She replied that there had been several appraisals, ranging from $175,000 to $192,000. At trial, Carol claimed that she understood the term "appraisal" to mean any opinion as to the market value of the house. The Van Wagoners did not request a written appraisal of the property until after signing the agreement. Carol Klas then provided them with a written appraisal, older than the others referred to by her, that listed the house's value as $165,000. The Van Wagoners subsequently refused to purchase the house, and John Klas brought suit to recover the difference between the agreement price and the price the house was later sold for. In view of these facts, answer the following questions.* [Klas v. Van Wagoner, *829 P.2d 135 (Utah App.1992)*]

1. The Van Wagoners claimed that the contract should be rescinded on the basis of their mistaken assumption as to the value of the house. What kind of mistake was made in this situation (bilateral or unilateral, mistake of value or mistake of fact)? How should the court rule on this issue?
2. Mark Van Wagoner was an attorney experienced in real estate transactions. Should the court take this fact into consideration when making its decision? If this had been the Van Wagoners' first experience in purchasing real estate, would the legal result be any different? Should it?
3. Generally, what ethical principles, as expressed in public policies, are in conflict here and in similar situations in which parties enter into a contract with mistaken assumptions?

Case Briefing Assignment

11-15. *Examine Case A.5* [Wilkin v. 1st Source Bank, *548 N.E.2d 170 (Ind.App. 1990)*] *in Appendix A. The case has been excerpted there in great detail. Review and then brief the case, making sure that you include answers to the following questions in your brief.*

1. Why did the probate court rule that no contract existed as to the purchase or sale of the Mestrovic paintings and sculpture?
2. In its discussion, the court pointed out several similarities between the present case and *Sherwood v. Walker,* a classic case on mutual assent. What are these similarities?

For Critical Analysis

11-16. *As stated in this chapter's* Landmark in the Law, *some legal scholars and jurists maintain that the Statute of Frauds results in more injustice than justice. Do you agree? Why? How would you argue in defense of the Statute of Frauds?*

Chapter 12

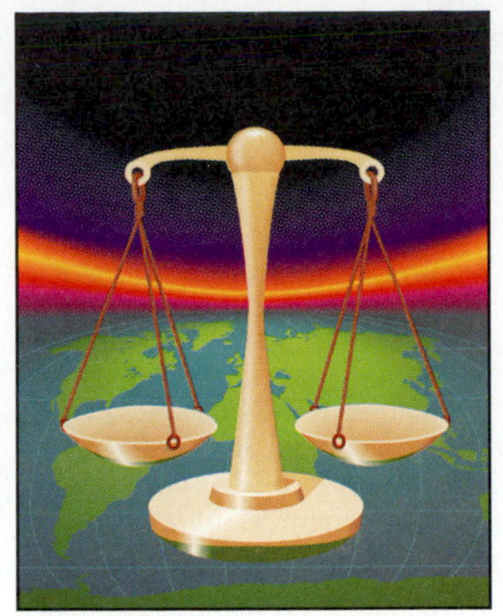

Third Party Rights and Discharge

"A fruitful parent of injustice is the tyranny of concepts."

Benjamin Cardozo, 1870–1938
(Associate justice of the United States Supreme Court, 1932–1938)

Once it has been determined that a valid and legally enforceable contract exists, attention can turn to the rights and duties of the parties to the contract. Because a contract is a private agreement between the parties who have entered into it, it is fitting that these parties alone should have rights and liabilities under the contract. This is referred to as **privity of contract**, and it establishes the basic concept that third parties have no rights in contracts to which they are not parties.

PRIVITY OF CONTRACT
The relationship that exists between the promisor and the promisee of a contract.

Suppose I offer to sell you my watch for $100, and you accept. Later, I refuse to deliver the watch to you, even though you tender the $100. You decide to overlook my breach, but your close friend, Ann, is unhappy with my action and files suit. Can she receive a judgment? The answer is no, as she was not a party to the contract. You, as a party, have rights under the contract and could file a successful suit, but Ann has no *standing to sue* (right to sue).

You are probably convinced by now that for every rule of contract law there is an exception. Exceptions exist to prevent the "tyranny of concepts" referred to by Justice Cardozo in the opening quotation. When justice cannot be served by adherence to a rule of law, exceptions to the rule must be made. There are two exceptions to the rule of privity of contract. One exception allows a party to a contract to transfer the rights arising from the contract to another or to free himself or herself from the duties of a contract by having another person perform them. Legally, the first of these actions is referred to as an *assignment of rights* and the second as a *delegation of duties*. A second exception to the rule of privity of contract involves a *third party beneficiary* contract. Here, the rights of a third party against the promisor arise from the original contract, as the parties to the original contract normally make it with the intent to benefit the third party. The law relating to assignments, delegations, and third party beneficiary contracts is discussed in the first half of this chapter.

At some point, parties to the contract must know when their duties are at an end. In other words, when is a contract terminated? The second part of this chapter deals with the *discharge* of a contract, which is normally accomplished when both parties have performed the acts promised in the contract. We will look at the degree of performance required and at some other ways in which discharge can occur, such as by agreement or by impossibility of performance.

❖ Assignments and Delegations

When third parties acquire rights or assume duties arising from contracts to which they were not parties, the rights are transferred to them by *assignment* and the duties

◆ **Exhibit 12–1**
Assignment Relationships
In the assignment relationship illustrated here, Alessio assigns her *rights* under a contract that she made with Bren to a third party, Cabrera. Alessio thus becomes the *assignor* and Cabrera the *assignee* of the contractual rights. Bren, the *obligor* (the party owing performance under the contract), now owes performance to Cabrera instead of Alessio. Alessio's original contract rights are extinguished after assignment.

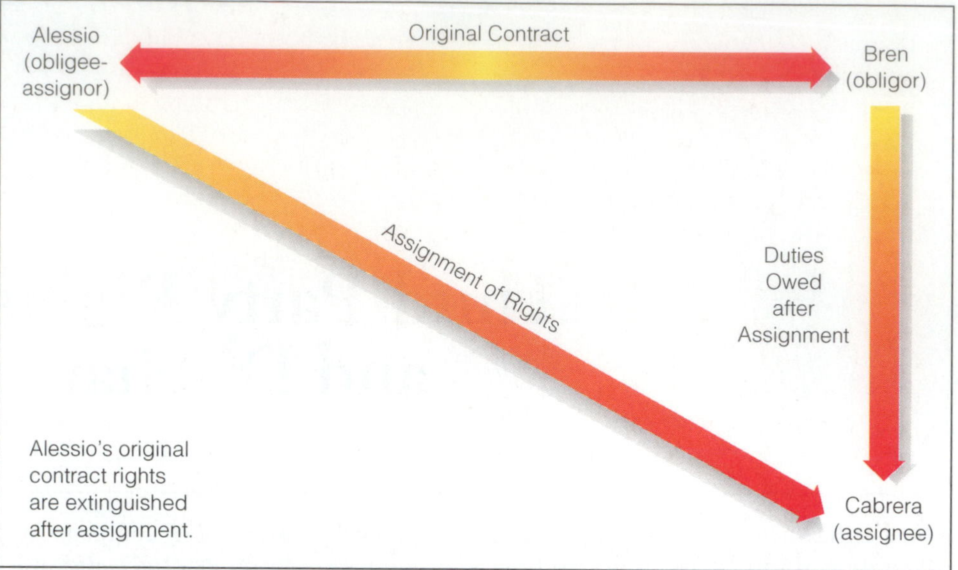

are transferred by *delegation.* Assignment and delegation occur *after* the original contract is made, when one of the parties transfers to another party an interest or duty in the contract.

Assignments

ASSIGNMENT
The act of transferring to another all or part of one's rights arising under a contract.

In a bilateral contract, the two parties have corresponding rights and duties. One party has a *right* to require the other to perform some task, and the other has a *duty* to perform it. The transfer of *rights* to a third person is known as an **assignment.** When rights under a contract are assigned unconditionally, the rights of the *assignor* (the party making the assignment) are extinguished.[1] The third party (the *assignee,* or party receiving the assignment) has a right to demand performance from the other original party to the contract (the *obligor*). These relationships are illustrated in Exhibit 12–1.

Once Alessio has assigned to Cabrera her rights under the original contract with Bren, as shown in the exhibit, Cabrera can enforce the contract against Bren if Bren fails to perform. The assignee takes only those rights that the assignor originally had. For example, suppose Bren owes Alessio $50, and Alessio assigns to Cabrera the right to receive the $50. Here, a valid assignment of a debt exists. Cabrera is entitled to enforce payment in a court of law if Bren does not pay her the $50.

Furthermore, the assignee's rights are subject to the defenses that the obligor has against the assignor. Suppose that Bren leases her apartment to Alessio for one year. The lease provides that the monthly rent payment is $400 and that if Alessio fails to pay the rent, she can be evicted. After Alessio has lived in the apartment for six months, she gives Bren a worthless check for the seventh month's rent. The next day, Alessio assigns her rights under the lease contract to Cabrera. On discovering the worthlessness of the check, Bren has a legal right to enforce the lease and evict Alessio. Because Cabrera's (the assignee's) rights are subject to this same defense, Cabrera may also be evicted, even though she is an innocent party to these events.

Assignments are important because they are involved in much business financing. Probably the most common contractual right that is assigned is the right to the payment of money. For example, Wayne is in the business of selling video equipment—camcorders, VCRs, and television sets. To prepare for the holiday sales sea-

1. Restatement (Second) of Contracts, Section 317.

son, Wayne needs to buy more inventory. Because he sells on credit to most of his customers (who make small monthly payments), he does not have enough funds on hand, but he does have the *right* to receive the monthly payments from his customers. To obtain funds, Wayne assigns the right to those payments to a financing agency, which then gives him cash. The agency may purchase those rights or only lend money to Wayne based on the accounts. The agency may insist that Wayne's customers make their payments directly to the agency, or it may have nothing to do with the accounts unless Wayne fails to repay.

Similarly, banks frequently assign the rights to receive payments under their loan contracts to other firms, which pay for those rights. For example, if you obtain a student loan from your local bank, you might later receive in the mail a notice from your bank stating that it has transferred (assigned) its rights to receive payments on the loan to another firm and that, when the time comes to repay your loan, you must make the payments to that other firm. Banks that make *mortgage loans* to allow prospective home buyers to purchase a house (see Chapter 34) often assign their rights to collect the mortgage payments to a third party, such as GMAC Mortgage Corporation, and the home buyers are notified that they must in the future make payments not to the bank that loaned them the funds but to the third party. Millions of dollars change hands daily in the business world in the form of assignments of rights in contracts. If it were not possible to transfer (assign) contractual rights, many businesses could not continue to operate.

Rights That Cannot Be Assigned As a general rule, all rights can be assigned, except in the following special circumstances.

1. If a statute expressly prohibits assignment, the particular right in question cannot be assigned. Suppose Marn is a new employee of Computer Future, Inc. Computer is an employer under workers' compensation statutes in this state, and thus Marn is a covered employee. Marn has a relatively high-risk job. In need of a loan, Marn borrows some money from Stark, assigning to Stark all workers' compensation benefits due her should she be injured on the job. The assignment of *future* workers' compensation benefits is prohibited by state statute, and thus such rights cannot be assigned.
2. When a contract is *personal* in nature, the rights under the contract cannot be assigned unless all that remains is a money payment.[2] Suppose Bren signs a contract to be a tutor for Alessio's children. Alessio then attempts to assign to Cabrera her right to Bren's services. Cabrera cannot enforce the contract against Bren. Cabrera's children may be more difficult to tutor than Alessio's; thus, if Alessio could assign her rights to Bren's services to Cabrera, it would change the nature of Bren's obligation. Because personal services are unique to the person rendering them, rights to receive personal services are likewise unique and cannot be assigned.
3. A right cannot be assigned if assignment will materially increase or alter the risk or duties of the obligor.[3] Assume Alessio has a hotel and to insure it she takes out a policy with Northwest Insurance. The policy insures against fire, theft, floods, and vandalism. Alessio attempts to assign the insurance policy to Cabrera, who also owns a hotel. The assignment is ineffective because it substantially alters Northwest Insurance's *duty of performance*. An insurance company evaluates the particular risk of a certain party and tailors its policy to fit that risk. If the policy is assigned to a third party, the insurance risk is materially altered. Therefore, the assignment will not operate to give Cabrera any rights against Northwest Insurance.
4. If a contract stipulates that the right cannot be assigned, then *ordinarily* it cannot be assigned. For example, suppose that Bren agrees to build a house for Alessio.

2. Restatement (Second) of Contracts, Sections 317 and 318.
3. See UCC 2–210(2).

The contract between Bren and Alessio states, "The contract cannot be assigned by Alessio. Any assignment renders this contract void, and all rights hereunder will thereupon terminate." Alessio then attempts to assign her rights to Cabrera. Cabrera cannot enforce the contract against Bren.

ALIENATION
A term used to define the process of transferring land out of one's ownership (thus "alienating" the land from oneself).

There are several exceptions to this fourth rule. First, a contract cannot prevent an assignment of the right to receive money. This exception exists to encourage the free flow of money and credit in modern business settings. Second, the assignment of rights in real estate often cannot be prohibited because such a prohibition is contrary to public policy. Prohibitions of this kind are called restraints against **alienation** (transfer of land ownership). Third, the assignment of *negotiable instruments* (see Chapter 18) cannot be prohibited. Fourth, in a contract for the sale of goods, the right to receive damages for breach of contract or for payment of an account owed may be assigned even though the sales contract prohibits such assignment.[4] In the following case, the central issue was whether a covenant not to compete contained in an employment contract could be assigned.

Case 12.1
PINO v. SPANISH BROADCASTING SYSTEM OF FLORIDA, INC.
District Court of Appeal of Florida, Third District, 1990.
564 So.2d 186.

HISTORICAL AND CULTURAL DIVERSITY SETTING *Owing to waves of immigration from Latin American countries in the 1960s and 1980s, more than half of the population of Dade County, Florida, is of Hispanic ancestry. In more than half of the households of this group, the language spoken at home is Spanish. Spanish-language radio and television stations are integral parts of the local entertainment spectrum, and therefore Spanish-speaking radio announcers and disc jockeys are in demand. Employment contracts between these stations and Spanish-speaking announcers or disc jockeys may contain covenants not to compete.*

FACTS In October 1985, Beatriz Pino signed a five-year employment contract as a radio announcer and disc jockey with two radio stations. The contract provided that Pino would not "engage directly or indirectly in the broadcasting business * * * in Dade or Broward Counties, Florida, for a period of twelve (12) months after the termination of her employment by the stations." The contract also provided that it was assignable. In December 1986, the stations sold their assets to Spanish Broadcasting System of Florida, Inc. (SBS), and as part of the sale, Pino's contract was assigned to SBS. In October 1989, Pino contracted with Viva, a broadcasting competitor of SBS, to begin working for Viva when her SBS contract terminated in March 1990. SBS asked a Florida state court to grant a temporary injunction to enforce the agreement not to compete. Pino contended that the assignment of the clause containing the covenant not to compete was invalid. Although a Florida statute provided that covenants not to compete could be enforced, it said nothing about such covenants' being assignable. The trial court held for SBS, and Pino appealed.

ISSUE Was the covenant not to compete assignable?

DECISION Yes. The trial court's ruling was affirmed.

REASON The appellate court held that because the contract contained a provision permitting its assignment, the covenant not to compete was assignable. The court explained that its holding "conform[ed] with the policy of preserving the sanctity of contract and providing uniformity and certainty in commercial transactions."

Notice of Assignment Once a valid assignment of rights has been made to a third party, the third party should notify the obligor of the assignment (for example, in Exhibit 12–1, Cabrera should notify Bren). Giving notice is not legally necessary to establish the validity of the assignment because an assignment is effective immedi-

4. UCC 2–210(2).

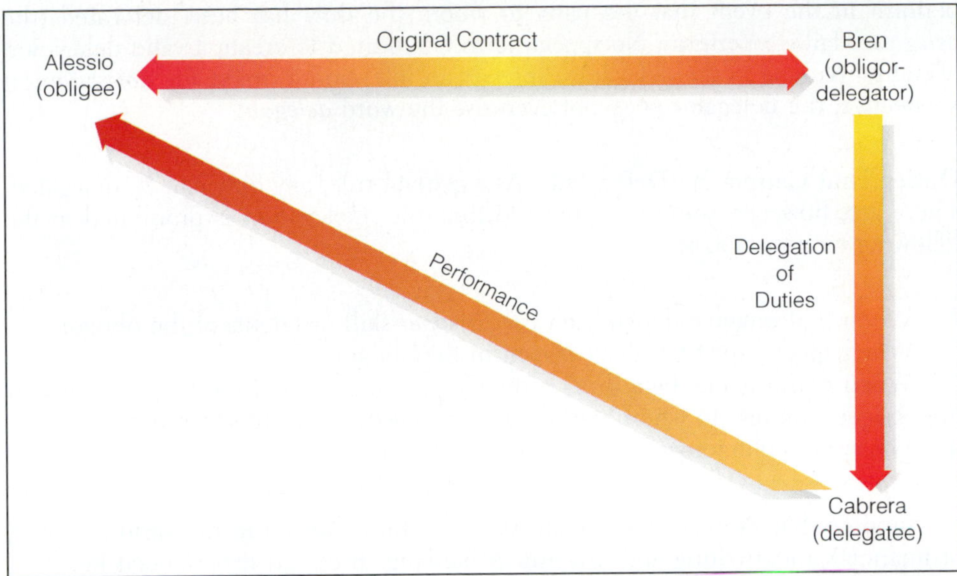

◆ **Exhibit 12–2**
Delegation Relationships
In the delegation relationship illustrated here, Bren delegates her *duties* under a contract that she made with Alessio to a third party, Cabrera. Bren thus becomes the *delegator* and Cabrera the *delegatee* of the contractual duties. Cabrera now owes performance of the contractual duties to Alessio. Note that a delegation of duties does not normally relieve the delegator of liability if the delegatee fails to perform the contractual duties.

ately, whether or not notice is given. Two major problems arise, however, when notice of the assignment is not given to the obligor:

1. If the assignor assigns the same right to two different persons, the question arises as to which one has priority—that is, which one has the right to the performance by the obligor. Although the rule most often observed in the United States is that the first assignment in time is the first in right, some states follow the English rule, which basically gives priority to the first assignee who gives notice. For example, suppose that Bren owes Alessio $1,000 on a contractual obligation. On May 1, Alessio assigns this monetary claim to Cabrera. No notice of assignment is given to Bren. On June 1, for services Dorman has rendered to Alessio, Alessio assigns the same monetary claim from Bren to Dorman. Dorman immediately notifies Bren of the assignment. In the majority of states, Cabrera would have priority because Cabrera's assignment was first in time. In some states, however, Dorman would have priority because Dorman gave first notice.
2. Until the obligor has notice of assignment, the obligor can discharge his or her obligation by performance to the assignor, and performance by the obligor to the assignor constitutes a discharge to the assignee. Once the obligor receives proper notice, only performance to the assignee can discharge the obligor's obligations.

To illustrate, suppose that Bren owes Alessio $1,000 on a contractual obligation. Alessio assigns this monetary claim to Cabrera. No notice of assignment is given to Bren. Bren pays Alessio the $1,000. Although the assignment was valid, Bren's payment to Alessio was a discharge of the debt, and Cabrera's failure to give notice to Bren of the assignment caused Cabrera to lose the right to collect the money from Bren. If Cabrera had given Bren notice of the assignment, Bren's payment to Alessio would not have discharged the debt, and Cabrera would have had a legal right to require payment from Bren.

Delegations

Just as a party can transfer rights through an assignment, a party can also transfer duties. Duties are not assigned, however; they are *delegated*. Delegation relationships are graphically illustrated in Exhibit 12–2. Normally, a **delegation of duties** does not relieve the party making the delegation (the *delegator*) of the obligation to

DELEGATION OF DUTIES
The act of transferring to another all or part of one's duties arising under a contract.

perform in the event that the party to whom the duty has been delegated (the *delegatee*) fails to perform. No special form is required to create a valid delegation of duties. As long as the delegator expresses an intention to make the delegation, it is effective; the delegator need not even use the word *delegate.*

Duties That Cannot Be Delegated As a general rule, any duty can be delegated. There are, however, some exceptions to this rule. Delegation is prohibited in the following circumstances:

1. When performance depends on the *personal* skill or talents of the obligor.
2. When special trust has been placed in the obligor.
3. When performance by a third party will vary materially from that expected by the obligee (the one to whom performance is owed) under the contract.
4. When the contract expressly prohibits delegation.

Suppose that Bren contracts with Alessio to tutor Alessio in the various aspects of financial underwriting and investment banking. Bren, an experienced businessperson known for her expertise in finance, wants to delegate her duties to a third party, Cabrera. This delegation is ineffective because Bren contracted to render a service that is founded on Bren's *expertise.* The delegation would change Alessio's expectancy under the contract. Therefore, Cabrera cannot perform Bren's duties.

Suppose that Bren, the son of Alessio's neighbor, contracts with Alessio *personally* to mow Alessio's lawn during June, July, and August. Then Bren decides that he would rather spend the summer at the beach. Bren delegates his lawn-mowing duties to Cabrera, who is in the business of mowing lawns and doing other landscaping work to earn money to pay for college. The delegation is not effective, no matter how competent Cabrera is, without Alessio's consent. The contract was for *personal* performance.

Assume that Bren contracts with Alessio to pick up and deliver heavy construction machinery to Alessio's property. Bren delegates this duty to Cabrera, who is in the business of delivering heavy machinery. The delegation is effective. The performance required is of a *routine* and *nonpersonal* nature, and the delegation does not change Alessio's expectancy under the contract.

Effect of a Delegation If a delegation of duties is enforceable, the *obligee* (the one to whom performance is owed) must accept performance from the delegatee. The obligee can legally refuse performance from the delegatee only if the duty is one that cannot be delegated. A valid delegation of duties does not relieve the delegator of obligations under the contract.[5] If the delegatee fails to perform, the delegator is still liable to the obligee.

Liability of the Delegatee If the delegatee fails to perform, whether the obligee can hold the delegatee liable comes into issue. If the delegatee has made a promise of performance that will directly benefit the obligee, there is an "assumption of duty." Breach of this duty makes the delegatee liable to the obligee.

Suppose, for example, that Bren contracts to build Alessio a house according to Alessio's blueprint. Bren becomes seriously ill and contracts to have Cabrera build the house for Alessio (the obligee). Cabrera fails to build the house. Because the delegatee, Cabrera, contracted with Bren (the obligor) to build the house for the benefit of Alessio (the obligee), Alessio can sue Bren, or Cabrera, or both. Although there are many exceptions, the general rule today is that the obligee can sue both the delegatee and the obligor-delegator.

---

5. *Crane Ice Cream Co. v. Terminal Freezing & Heating Co.,* 147 Md. 588, 128 A. 280 (1925).

Assignment of "All Rights"

When a contract provides for an "assignment of all rights," this wording may also be treated as an "assumption of duties." The traditional view was that under this type of assignment, the assignee did not assume any duties. This view was based on the theory that the assignee's agreement to accept the benefits of the contract was not sufficient to imply a promise to assume the duties of the contract.

Modern authorities, however, take the view that the probable intent in using such general words is to create both an assignment of rights and an assumption of duties.[6] Therefore, when general words are used (for example, "I assign the contract" or "all my rights under the contract"), the contract is construed as implying both an assignment of rights and an assumption of duties.

❖ Third Party Beneficiaries

To have contractual rights, a person normally must be a party to the contract. As mentioned earlier in this chapter, an exception exists when the original parties to the contract intend at the time of contracting that the contract performance directly benefit a third person. In this situation, the third person becomes a *beneficiary* of the contract and has legal rights.

The law distinguishes between two types of **third party beneficiaries:** *intended* beneficiaries and *incidental* beneficiaries. It is important to realize that only intended beneficiaries acquire legal rights in a contract.

THIRD PARTY BENEFICIARY
One for whose benefit a promise is made in a contract but who is not a party to the contract.

Intended Beneficiaries

An **intended beneficiary** is one for whose benefit the contract was made and who can thus sue the promisor directly for breach of the contract. But who is the promisor? In bilateral contracts, both parties to the contract are promisors because they both make promises that can be enforced. In third party beneficiary contracts, courts will determine the identity of the promisor by asking which party made the promise that benefits the third party—that person is the promisor. Allowing a third party to sue the promisor directly in effect circumvents the "middle person" (the promisee) and thus reduces the burden on the courts. Otherwise, a third party would sue the promisee, who would then sue the promisor.

INTENDED BENEFICIARY
A third party for whose benefit a contract is formed; intended beneficiaries can sue the promisor if such a contract is breached.

Types of Intended Beneficiaries A *creditor beneficiary* can sue the promisor directly. A creditor beneficiary is one who benefits from a contract in which one party (the promisor) promises another party (the promisee) to pay a debt that the promisee owes to a third party (the creditor beneficiary). The creditor beneficiary, although not a party to the contract between the debtor and the other person, becomes the *intended beneficiary* and can thus enforce the promisor's promise to pay the debt (see this chapter's *Landmark in the Law* on page 295).

When a contract is made for the express purpose of giving a *gift* to a third party, the third party can sue the promisor directly to enforce the promise.[7] In this situation, the third party is called a *donee beneficiary*. A donee beneficiary can enforce the promise of a promisor just as a creditor beneficiary can. Suppose Alessio goes to her attorney, Bren, and enters into a contract in which Bren promises to draft a will naming Alessio's son, John, as an heir. John is a donee beneficiary, and if Bren does not prepare the will properly, John can sue Bren.[8] Or suppose Alessio offers to put in a swimming pool in Bren's backyard if Bren pays $2,000 to John, Alessio's

6. See UCC 2–210(1), (4); Restatement (Second) of Contracts, Section 328.
7. *Seaver v. Ransom*, 224 N.Y. 233, 120 N.E. 639 (1918).
8. *Lucas v. Hamm*, 56 Cal.2d 583, 364 P.2d 685, 15 Cal.Rptr. 821 (1961).

son. Alessio wants to give the money to John as a gift. John is a donee beneficiary and can enforce Bren's promise to pay the $2,000.

The most common donee beneficiary contract is a life insurance contract. In a typical contract, Alessio (the promisee) pays premiums to Standard Life, a life insurance company, and Standard Life (the promisor) promises to pay a certain amount of money on Alessio's death to anyone Alessio designates as a beneficiary. The designated beneficiary, John, is a donee beneficiary under the life insurance policy and can enforce the promise made by the insurance company to pay John on Alessio's death.

As the law concerning third party beneficiaries evolved, numerous cases arose in which the third party beneficiary did not fit readily into either category—creditor beneficiary or donee beneficiary. Thus, the modern view, and the one adopted by the Restatement (Second) of Contracts, does not draw such clear lines and distinguishes only between intended beneficiaries (who can sue to enforce contracts made for their benefit) and incidental beneficiaries (who cannot sue, as will be discussed in the next section). In the following case, the issue before the court was whether an adult child was an intended beneficiary under her parents' divorce agreement.

Case 12.2
ORR v. ORR

Appellate Court of Illinois,
First District, 1992.
228 Ill.App.3d 234,
592 N.E.2d 553,
170 Ill.Dec. 117.

HISTORICAL AND ECONOMIC SETTING *The amount of child support awarded in divorce actions is usually inadequate to provide for the children involved. Even when a family has enjoyed a substantial income, the amount of a child-support order rarely covers all of the expenses of feeding, clothing, and educating a child. Whatever the amount of the order, it is of no value if it is not paid. Studies in the 1980s revealed that payments are made to less than 75 percent of those entitled to receive child support and less than half of all child-support orders are ever paid in full.*

FACTS When Charles and Judy Orr were divorced in 1970, their divorce agreement included a provision that Charles would pay for the college or professional school education of the couple's two children, then minors. In 1990, Jennifer Orr, Charles's daughter, filed a petition to compel her father to pay her college expenses. The trial court dismissed the action on the ground that Jennifer, as an adult child of the involved parties, did not have standing to seek the relief asked for in the petition because she was not a party to her parents' divorce agreement. Jennifer appealed the ruling.

ISSUE Is Jennifer an intended third party beneficiary of her parents' divorce agreement?

DECISION Yes. The appeals court reversed the trial court's decision and remanded the case for further action.

REASON The critical issue before the court was whether the criteria necessary to confer third party status in the contract had been met. The court noted that an Illinois appellate court had previously held, in a similar case, that three factors were controlling: "(1) it must be clear from the contract that the parties to the contract intended the third party to benefit; (2) the benefit to the agreement is direct to the third party and the liability of the promisor affirmatively appears from the language of the agreement; and (3) the third party must have relied on the father's promise in the agreement to pay his college expenses." The court determined that "[t]he rule is well established that where a person makes a promise to another, based upon a valid consideration, for the benefit of a third person, such third person may maintain an action on the contract. Moreover, children who are beneficiaries under a contract entered into by their parents' have standing to bring suit against their [parents] to compel" compliance with the terms of the contract. The appellate court found that Jennifer was a direct beneficiary of her parents' divorce settlement and that she relied upon the promised benefits by enrolling in college.

ETHICAL CONSIDERATIONS *The parent taking custody of a child after a divorce frequently bears the burden of paying for the child's college educational expenses. Even if the noncustodial parent agreed to help cover these expenses during divorce proceedings, by the time the child is grown, the noncustodial parent may have changed his or her mind and may try to avoid performance under the agreement, or contract. Allowing children to sue as third party beneficiaries increases the chances that such agreements will be enforced.*

When the Rights of an Intended Beneficiary Vest An intended third party beneficiary cannot enforce a contract against the original parties until the rights of the third party have *vested*, which means the rights have taken effect and cannot be taken away. Until these rights have vested, the original parties to the contract—the promisor and the promisee—can modify or rescind the contract without the consent of the third party. When do the rights of third parties vest? Generally, the rights of an intended beneficiary vest when either of the following occurs:

1. When the third party demonstrates *manifest assent* to the contract, such as sending a letter or note acknowledging awareness of and consent to a contract formed for his or her benefit.
2. When the third party materially alters his or her position in *detrimental reliance* on the contract.

If the contract expressly reserves to the contracting parties the right to cancel, rescind, or modify the contract, the rights of the third party beneficiary are subject to any changes that result. In such a case, the vesting of the third party's rights does not terminate the power of the original contracting parties to alter their legal relationships.[9] This is particularly true in most life insurance contracts, in which the right to change the beneficiary is reserved to the policyholder.

Exhibit 12–3 summarizes the third party rights in contracts generally, including when the rights of an intended third party beneficiary vest.

Incidental Beneficiaries

The benefit that an **incidental beneficiary** receives from a contract between two parties is unintentional. Therefore, an incidental beneficiary cannot enforce a contract to which he or she is not a party. In determining whether a third party beneficiary is an intended or an incidental beneficiary, the courts generally use the *reasonable person* test. That is, a beneficiary will be considered an intended beneficiary if a reasonable person in the position of the beneficiary would believe that the promisee *intended* to confer upon the beneficiary the right to bring suit to enforce the contract. Several other factors must also be examined to determine whether a party is an intended or an incidental beneficiary. The presence of one or more of the following factors strongly indicates an *intended* (rather than an incidental) benefit to a third party:

INCIDENTAL BENEFICIARY
A third party who incidentally benefits from a contract but whose benefit was not the reason the contract was formed; incidental beneficiaries have no rights in a contract and cannot sue the promisor if the contract is breached.

1. Performance is rendered directly to the third party.
2. The third party has the right to control the details of performance.
3. The third party is expressly designated as beneficiary in the contract.

In contrast, the following are examples of *incidental* beneficiaries. The third party has no rights in the contract and cannot enforce it against the promisor.

1. Jules contracts with Vivian to build a cottage on Vivian's land. Jules's plans specify that Super Insulation Company's insulation materials must be used in constructing the house. Super Insulation Company is an incidental beneficiary and cannot enforce the contract against Jules by attempting to require that Jules purchase its insulation materials.
2. Ed contracts with Ona to build a recreational facility on Ona's land. Once the facility is constructed, it will greatly enhance the property values in the neighborhood. If Ed subsequently refuses to build the facility, Tandy, Ona's neighbor, cannot enforce the contract against Ed by attempting to require that Ed build the facility.

9. Defenses raised against third party beneficiaries are given in Restatement (Second) of Contracts, Section 309.

◆ **Exhibit 12–3 Third Party Rights in Contracts**

	THIRD PARTY BENEFICIARY CONTRACT	ASSIGNMENT	DELEGATION
Is a third party contemplated in the original contract?	Purpose of original contract is to benefit third party. If purpose is: 1. To discharge a duty or debt owed, third party is *creditor* beneficiary. 2. To confer a gift, third party is *donee* beneficiary.	Third party not contemplated in original contract. After contract formation, rights are assigned to third party.	Third party not contemplated in original contract. After contract formation, duties are delegated to third party.
Is the third party beneficiary contract, assignment, or delegation effective?	For a third party beneficiary contract to be effective, rights under the contract must vest by: 1. Third party manifesting assent to the contract. 2. Third party materially altering position in detrimental reliance.	To be effective, an assignment cannot involve: 1. Rights that a statute expressly prohibits from being assigned. 2. Rights to performance by personal service. 3. Rights the assignment of which will materially increase or alter the obligor's duties. 4. Rights that the contract stipulates cannot be assigned, except: a. Rights to receive money. b. Rights to damages for breach of contract or for payment of an account. c. Rights to negotiable instruments (see Chapter 18). d. Rights in real property (see Chapter 34).	To be effective, a delegation cannot involve: 1. Duties that depend on personal skill or talent of the obligor. 2. Duties that involve special trust placed in the obligor. 3. Duties the delegation of which will materially increase or alter the performance expected by the obligee. 4. Duties that the contract stipulates cannot be delegated.

DISCHARGE
The termination of one's obligation. In contract law, discharge occurs when the parties have fully performed their contractual obligations or when events, conduct of the parties, or operation of the law releases the parties from further performance.

PERFORMANCE
In contract law, the fulfillment of one's duties arising under a contract with another; the normal way of discharging one's contractual obligations.

❖ Contract Discharge

The most common way to **discharge**, or terminate, one's contractual duties is by **performance** of those duties. The duty to perform under a contract may be *conditioned* on the occurrence or nonoccurrence of a certain event, or the duty may be *absolute*. In addition to performance, there are numerous other ways in which a contract can be discharged, including discharge by agreement of the parties and discharge based on impossibility of performance.

Conditions of Performance

In most contracts, promises of performance are not *expressly* conditioned or qualified. Instead, they are *absolute promises*. They must be performed, or the party

Landmark in the Law

Lawrence v. Fox (1859)

In 1859, a landmark decision was handed down by the New York Court of Appeals in *Lawrence v. Fox*.[a] The decision held that a third party beneficiary to a contract could sue the promisor to enforce the contract. At the time, this was a novel idea and represented a radical departure from contract law. Prior to that time, contractual liability had always been limited to the parties to the contract.

As one might suspect, given the exceptional outcome of this case, the circumstances surrounding it were also somewhat novel. In its simplest outline, the background to *Lawrence v. Fox* was as follows: On or about November 15, 1854, Holly borrowed $300 from Lawrence. Shortly thereafter, Holly loaned $300 to Fox, who in return promised Holly that he would pay Holly's debt to Lawrence on the following day. Lawrence therefore was the creditor beneficiary of the contract between Holly and Fox. When Lawrence failed to obtain the $300 from Fox after several attempts, he brought suit against Fox to recover the money. The trial court held for Lawrence, as did, ultimately, the New York Court of Appeals (the highest court in the New York state system).

The case is puzzling for two reasons. First, given the large sum of money involved (about a year's wages back then), why wasn't a promissory note of some kind created and indorsed over to Lawrence by Fox as a means of repayment of the debt, in accordance with the commercial practice of the times? And second, why didn't Lawrence sue Holly directly, rather than pursue the highly unusual and more circuitous route of suing Fox, whereby his chances at recovery were much slimmer? The answers to both questions have to do with the apparent fact[b] that the "Holly" in this case was one Merwin Spencer Hawley, a prominent Buffalo, New York, merchant and president of the Buffalo Board of Trade, of which the defendant, Arthur Wellesley Fox, was also a member. Evidence at trial suggested that the debt Hawley owed Lawrence was a gambling debt. Because gambling was illegal under New York law, Lawrence could not recover from Hawley directly in court, as the contract would have been deemed illegal and thus void.

Although citing numerous precedents, the Court of Appeals based its decision ultimately on equitable grounds: it was manifestly "just" to allow Lawrence to recover the money from Fox. The principle of law enunciated was that "[in the case of] a promise made for the benefit of another, he for whose benefit it is made may bring an action for its breach." The dissenting justices vigorously opposed the ruling and expressed their concern about privity of contract and the ability of the promisor and the promisee to rescind or modify a contract. They stressed that Lawrence had had nothing to do with the contract. "It was not made to him, nor did the consideration proceed from him. If Lawrence can maintain the suit, it is because an anomaly has formed its way into the law on this subject."

The third party beneficiary rule is unique to this country. In all other common law countries, privity of contract is required before a party can sue to have a contract enforced—unless a statutory exception exists to counter common law. This legal precedent of 1859 went largely unnoted in the courts for more than fifty years, and privity of contract remained the guiding principle until after the turn of the century. In *MacPherson v. Buick Motor Co.* (1916)[c] and in *Seaver v. Ransom* (1918),[d] the New York Court of Appeals cited *Lawrence v. Fox* in justifying its departure from the privity of contract principle. Since then, the third party beneficiary rule has been continuously expanded in scope, and today any "intended beneficiary" to a contract will likely be entitled to sue to have the contract enforced.

a. 20 N.Y. 268 (1859).

b. See Antony Jon Waters, "The Property in the Promise: A Study of the Third Party Beneficiary Rule," 98 *Harvard Law Review* 1109, 1168 (1985).

c. 217 N.Y. 382, 111 N.E. 1050 (1916). This case is discussed in the *Landmark in the Law* in Chapter 17.

d. 224 N.Y. 233, 120 N.E. 639 (1918).

promising the act will be in breach of contract. For example, I contract to sell you my radio for fifty dollars. Our promises are unconditional: my transfer of the radio to you and your payment of fifty dollars to me. The payment does not have to be made if the radio is not transferred.

In some cases, however, performance may be beneficial only if a certain event either does or does not occur. Therefore, a *condition* is inserted into the contract, either expressly by the parties or impliedly by the courts. If this condition is not satisfied, the obligations of the parties are discharged. Suppose that I offer to purchase a tract of your land on the condition that your neighbor to the south agrees to sell me her land. You accept my offer. Our obligations (promises) are conditioned upon your neighbor's willingness to sell her land. Should this condition not be satisfied (for example, if your neighbor refuses to sell), our obligations to each other are discharged and cannot be enforced.

CONDITION
A qualification, provision, or clause in a contractual agreement, the occurrence of which creates, suspends, or terminates the obligations of the contracting parties.

Thus, a **condition** is a possible future event, the occurrence or nonoccurrence of which will trigger the performance of a legal obligation or terminate an existing obligation under a contract. Three types of conditions can be present in any given contract: conditions precedent, conditions subsequent, and concurrent conditions.

CONDITION PRECEDENT
In a contractual agreement, a condition that must be met before the other party's obligations arise.

Conditions Precedent A condition that must be fulfilled before a party's promise becomes absolute is called a **condition precedent.**[10] The condition precedes the absolute duty to perform. For example, James promises to contribute $2,000 to Friends Church if Jonathan completes college. James's promise is subject to the (express) condition precedent that Jonathan complete college. Until the condition is fulfilled, James's promise to donate $2,000 to the church is not absolute. Insurance contracts frequently specify that certain conditions must be met before the insurance company will be obligated to perform under the contract. The following case is illustrative in this respect.

Case 12.3

McLANAHAN v. FARMERS INSURANCE CO. OF WASHINGTON

Court of Appeals of Washington, 1992.
66 Wash.App. 36,
831 P.2d 160.

HISTORICAL AND SOCIAL SETTING *In September 1981, the television show "Miami Vice" debuted. The popular series, a highly stylized drama about undercover police officers in Miami, Florida, featured as a prominent character Detective Sonny Crockett. Playing Crockett, the actor Don Johnson wore shoes without socks and linen suits without shirts and with the sleeves of the suit jackets rolled up. For a short time, Johnson's character's style became fashionable. In the show, Johnson's character also drove a very expensive automobile—a Lamborghini.*

FACTS Larry McLanahan's 1985 Lamborghini was stolen, and by the time McLanahan recovered the car, it had been extensively damaged. The car was insured by Farmers Insurance Company of Washington under a policy providing comprehensive coverage, including theft. A provision in the policy stated that the coverage for theft damages was subject to certain terms and conditions, including the condition that any person claiming coverage under the policy must allow Farmers "to inspect and appraise the damaged vehicle before its repair or disposal." Farmers agreed to pay for damages resulting from the theft and requested that McLanahan make the car available to certain mechanics for inspection and appraisal. McLanahan, however, without notifying Farmers and without giving Farmers an opportunity to inspect the vehicle, sold the car to a wholesale car dealer. Farmers then denied coverage, and McLanahan brought suit to recover for the damages caused to his car by the theft. The trial court dismissed McLanahan's claim, and he appealed.

ISSUE Did McLanahan have a valid claim against the insurance company?

DECISION No. The trial court's decision was affirmed.

REASON The court stated that the "unchallenged findings, which are verities on appeal, establish that Mr. McLanahan knew of, and agreed to abide by, the requirement under the policy that Farmers be allowed to inspect the damaged Lamborghini as a condition precedent to recovery for damage due to theft. Instead, he sold the vehicle. Accordingly, the [trial] court's findings support its conclusion that Mr. McLanahan breached the contract, thus relieving Farmers of any obligation to pay."

ETHICAL CONSIDERATIONS *Insurance companies frequently include conditions in their policies. If the insured*

---

10. The difference between conditions precedent and conditions subsequent is relatively unimportant from a substantive point of view but very important procedurally. Usually, the plaintiff must prove conditions precedent because usually it is he or she who claims there is a duty to be performed. Similarly, the defendant must usually prove conditions subsequent because usually it is he or she who claims a duty no longer exists.

Case 12.3—Continued

person fails to meet one of these conditions, the company will raise that failure as a defense against payment. Because insurance contracts are adhesion (one-sided) contracts in the sense that an insurance applicant has little to say about the terms of the contract, courts generally will give the benefit of the doubt to the insured person when a policy is ambiguous. In McLanahan's case, though, the policy was not at all ambiguous in regard to the condition at issue, and it would have been unfair to require the insurance company to pay McLanahan's claim in this situation.

Conditions Subsequent When a condition operates to terminate a party's absolute promise to perform, it is called a **condition subsequent.** The condition follows, or is subsequent to, the absolute duty to perform. If the condition occurs, the party need not perform any further. For example, imagine that a law firm hires Darby, a recent law school graduate and a newly licensed atto rney. Their contract provides that the firm's obligation to continue employing Darby is discharged if Darby fails to maintain her license to practice law. This is a condition subsequent, because a failure to maintain the license would discharge a duty that has already arisen.

CONDITION SUBSEQUENT
A condition in a contract that, if not met, discharges an existing obligation of the other party.

Generally, conditions precedent are common; conditions subsequent are rare. The Restatement (Second) of Contracts deletes the terms *condition subsequent* and *condition precedent* and refers to both simply as "conditions."[11]

Concurrent Conditions When each party's absolute duty to perform is conditioned on the other party's absolute duty to perform, there are **concurrent conditions.** These conditions exist only when the parties expressly or impliedly are to perform their respective duties *simultaneously*. For example, if a buyer promises to pay for goods when they are delivered by the seller, each party's absolute duty to perform is conditioned upon the other party's absolute duty to perform. The buyer's duty to pay for the goods does not become absolute until the seller either delivers or attempts to deliver the goods. Likewise, the seller's duty to deliver the goods does not become absolute until the buyer tenders or actually makes payment. Therefore, neither can recover from the other for breach without first tendering performance.

CONCURRENT CONDITIONS
Conditions that must occur or be performed at the same time; they are mutually dependent. No obligations arise until these conditions are simultaneously performed.

Discharge by Performance

The contract comes to an end when both parties fulfill their respective duties by performance of the acts they have promised. Performance can also be accomplished by tender. **Tender** is an unconditional offer to perform by a person who is ready, willing, and able to do so. Therefore, a seller who places goods at the disposal of a buyer has tendered delivery and can demand payment according to the terms of the agreement. A buyer who offers to pay for goods has tendered payment and can demand delivery of the goods. Once performance has been tendered, the party making the tender has done everything possible to carry out the terms of the contract. If the other party then refuses to perform, the party making the tender can consider the duty discharged and sue for breach of contract.

"The law is not exact upon the subject, but leaves it open to a good man's judgment."

Hugo Grotius, 1583–1645
(Dutch jurist, statesman, and theologian)

Complete versus Substantial Performance It is important to distinguish between *complete performance* and *substantial performance.* Normally, conditions expressly stated in the contract must fully occur in all aspects for complete (or strict) performance to take place. Any deviation breaches the contract and discharges the other party's obligations to perform. Although in most contracts the parties fully discharge their obligations by complete performance, sometimes a party fails to fulfill all of

TENDER
A timely offer or expression of willingness to pay a debt or perform an obligation.

11. Restatement (Second) of Contracts, Section 224.

the duties or completes the duties in a manner contrary to the terms of the contract. The issue then arises as to whether the performance was nonetheless sufficiently substantial to discharge the contractual obligations.

To qualify as substantial, the performance must not vary greatly from the performance promised in the contract, and it must create substantially the same benefits as those promised in the contract. If performance is substantial, the other party's duty to perform remains absolute (less damages, if any, for the minor deviations).

For example, a couple contracts with a construction company to build a house. The contract specifies that Brand X plasterboard be used for the walls. The builder cannot obtain Brand X plasterboard, and the buyers are on holiday in France and virtually unreachable. The builder decides to install Brand Y instead, which he knows is identical in quality and durability to Brand X plasterboard. All other aspects of construction conform to the contract. Does this deviation constitute a breach of contract? Can the buyers avoid their contractual obligation to pay the builder because Brand Y plasterboard was used instead of Brand X? Very likely, a court would hold that the builder had substantially performed his end of the bargain and the couple is therefore obligated to pay the builder.[12]

What if the plasterboard substituted for Brand X had been inferior in quality to Brand X, reducing the value of the house by $1,000? Again, a court would likely have held that the contract was substantially performed and that the contractor should be paid the price agreed on in the contract, less that $1,000.

Performance to the Satisfaction of Another Contracts often state that completed work must personally satisfy one of the parties or a third person. The question arises as to whether this satisfaction becomes a condition precedent, requiring actual personal satisfaction or approval for discharge, or whether the test of satisfaction is an absolute promise requiring such performance as would satisfy a *reasonable person* (substantial performance).

"Men do less than they ought, unless they do all that they can."

Thomas Carlyle, 1795–1881
(Scottish historian and essayist)

When the subject matter of the contract is personal, a contract to be performed to the satisfaction of one of the parties is conditioned, and performance must actually satisfy that party. For example, contracts for portraits, works of art, medical or dental work, and tailoring are considered personal. Therefore, only the personal satisfaction of the party fulfills the condition—unless a jury finds the party is expressing dissatisfaction only to avoid payment or otherwise is not acting in good faith.

Contracts that involve mechanical fitness, utility, or marketability need only be performed to the satisfaction of a reasonable person unless they *expressly state otherwise.* When such contracts require performance to the satisfaction of a third party (for example, "to the satisfaction of Robert Ames, the supervising engineer"), the courts are divided. A majority of courts require the work to be satisfactory to a reasonable person, but some courts hold that the personal satisfaction of the third party (Robert Ames) must be met. Again, the personal judgment must be made honestly, or the condition will be excused.

BREACH OF CONTRACT
The failure, without legal excuse, of a promisor to perform the obligations of a contract.

Material Breach of Contract A **breach of contract** is the nonperformance of a contractual duty. When the breach is *material*[13]—that is, when performance is not deemed substantial—the nonbreaching party is excused from the performance of contractual duties and has a cause of action to sue for damages caused by the breach. If the breach is *minor* (not material), the nonbreaching party's duty to perform can sometimes be suspended until the breach is remedied, but the duty is not entirely excused. Once the minor breach is cured, the nonbreaching party must resume

12. For a classic case on substantial performance, see *Jacobs & Young, Inc. v. Kent,* 230 N.Y. 239, 129 N.E. 889 (1921).

13. Restatement (Second) of Contracts, Section 241.

performance of the contractual obligations undertaken. A breach entitles the nonbreaching party to sue for damages, but only a material breach discharges the nonbreaching party from the contract. The policy underlying these rules allows contracts to go forward when only minor problems occur but permits contracts to be terminated if major problems arise.[14]

The difference between substantial performance and performance so inferior as to constitute a material breach of contract is illustrated in the following case.

Case 12.4 

BUTKOVICH & SONS, INC. v. STATE BANK OF ST. CHARLES

Appellate Court of Illinois,
Second District, 1978.
62 Ill.App.3d 810,
379 N.E.2d 837,
20 Ill.Dec. 4.

HISTORICAL AND ECONOMIC SETTING *In the late 1960s, the condition of the U.S. economy was excellent. In 1968, the average price of an existing single-family home was $20,000. By 1969, a record number of workers were employed, unemployment was lower than it had been in fifteen years, the dollar was strong in world markets, and average stock prices on Wall Street were higher than they had ever been. The next year, stock prices fell and unemployment rose. In 1971, because of increasing inflation, President Nixon imposed a ninety-day freeze on U.S. wages and prices. The same year, the United States experienced its first trade deficit since 1888. As the 1970s progressed, prices increased at a rapid pace. By 1973, the median price of an existing single-family house was $28,900; by 1976, the price was $38,100. By the end of the decade, the annual inflation rate was double digit, compared with an average annual inflation rate of 2.4 percent between 1948 and 1972.*

FACTS In May 1969, Hubert Grane, a homeowner, contracted with George Butkovich & Sons, Inc., to enlarge Grane's basement and build a new room over the new basement area. Butkovich was also to lay a new garage floor and construct a patio area. The parties agreed to a price of $19,290 for the work. When the construction was completed, Grane refused to pay the contractor the $9,290 balance he still owed, claiming that Butkovich had failed to install water stops and reinforcing wire in one concrete floor as Grane had specified and that the main floor of the addition was 8⅞ inches lower than the plans had called for. Butkovich filed suit. As a mortgage holder on the property, the State Bank of St. Charles was named co-defendant, as its interests would be affected by a judgment against Grane if the latter could not pay. The trial court ruled that, notwithstanding the defects, Butkovich had substantially performed the contract. Grane and the bank appealed.

ISSUE Had the contract been substantially performed by Butkovich, notwithstanding the deviations from the specifications made by Grane?

DECISION No. The appellate court reversed the trial court's judgment and ruled that the contract had not been substantially performed. The case was remanded to the trial court for further proceedings.

REASON The appellate court concluded that the trial court had been in error when it accepted Butkovich's argument that the plans did not call for the water stops or the reinforcing wire. Both had been specifically indicated by the plans drawn up by Grane and submitted to the trial court as evidence. Because these plans constituted express conditions of performance, and because the main floor was 8⅞ inches lower than the plans called for, it was clear that plaintiff had *not* substantially performed the contract.

Anticipatory Repudiation of Contract Before either party to a contract has a duty to perform, one of the parties may refuse to perform his or her contractual obligations. This is called **anticipatory repudiation.**[15] When anticipatory repudiation occurs, it is treated as a material breach of contract, and the nonbreaching party is

ANTICIPATORY REPUDIATION
An assertion or action by a party indicating that he or she will not perform an obligation that the party is contractually obligated to perform at a future time.

14. See UCC 2-612 dealing with installment contracts for the sale of goods.
15. Restatement (Second) of Contracts, Section 253, and UCC 2-610.

permitted to bring an action for damages immediately, even though the scheduled time for performance under the contract may still be in the future.[16]

There are two reasons for treating an anticipatory repudiation as a present, material breach:

1. The nonbreaching party should not be required to remain ready and willing to perform when the other party has already repudiated the contract.
2. The nonbreaching party should have the opportunity to seek a similar contract elsewhere and should have the duty to do so to minimize his or her loss.

"Agreement makes law."

(Legal maxim)

It is important to note that, until the nonbreaching party treats this early repudiation as a breach, the breaching party can retract his or her anticipatory repudiation by proper notice and restore the parties to their original obligations.[17]

Quite often, an anticipatory repudiation occurs when a sharp fluctuation in market prices creates a situation in which performance of the contract would be extremely unfavorable to one of the parties. For example, Shasta Manufacturing Company contracts to manufacture and sell 100,000 personal computers to New Age, Inc., a computer retailer with 500 outlet stores. Delivery is to be made eight months from the date of the contract. The contract price is based on the seller's immediate costs of acquiring inventory parts purchased from others. One month later, three parts suppliers raise their prices to Shasta. Based on the prices of these parts, if Shasta manufactures and sells the computers to New Age at the contract price, Shasta stands to lose $500,000. Shasta immediately writes a letter to New Age stating that Shasta cannot deliver the 100,000 computers at the agreed-upon contract price. Even though you might feel sorry for Shasta, its letter is an anticipatory repudiation of the contract, allowing New Age the option of treating the repudiation as a material breach and proceeding immediately to pursue remedies, even though the actual contract delivery date is still seven months away.[18]

Discharge by Agreement

Any contract can be discharged by the agreement of the parties. The agreement can be contained in the original contract, or the parties can form a new contract for the express purpose of discharging the original contract.

RESCISSION
A remedy whereby a contract is terminated and the parties are returned to the positions they occupied before the contract was made; may be effected through the mutual consent of the parties, by their conduct, or by the decree of a court of equity.

Discharge by Rescission **Rescission** is the process in which the parties cancel the contract and are returned to the positions they occupied prior to the contract's formation. For *mutual rescission* to take place, the parties must make another agreement that also satisfies the legal requirements for a contract—there must be an *offer*, an *acceptance*, and *consideration*. Ordinarily, if the parties agree to rescind the original contract, their promises *not* to perform those acts promised in the original contract will be legal consideration for the second contract. Mutual recission can occur in this manner when the original contract is executory on *both* sides (that is, neither party has completed performance). The agreement to rescind an executory contract is generally enforceable, even if it is made orally and even if the original agreement was in writing. There are two basic exceptions. One applies to transfers

16. The doctrine of anticipatory repudiation first arose in the landmark case of *Hochster v. De La Tour*, 2 Ellis and Blackburn Reports 678 (1853), when the English court recognized the delay and expense inherent in a rule requiring a nonbreaching party to wait until the time of performance before suing on an anticipatory repudiation. This case is discussed in the *Landmark in the Law* in Chapter 16.
17. See UCC 2–611.
18. Another illustration can be found in *Reliance Cooperage Corp. v. Treat*, 195 F.2d 977 (8th Cir. 1952).

of realty, and the other has to do with the sale of goods under the UCC, when the sales contract requires written rescission.[19]

When one party has fully performed, however, an agreement to rescind the original contract is not usually enforceable. Because the performing party has received no consideration for the promise to call off the original bargain, additional consideration is necessary.

Generally, then, contracts that are *executory* on *both* sides can be rescinded solely by agreement.[20] But contracts that are *executed* on *one* side (that is, one party has performed) can be rescinded only if the party who has performed receives consideration for the promise to call off the deal.[21]

Discharge by Novation The process of **novation** substitutes a third party for one of the original parties. Essentially, the parties to the original contract and one or more new parties all get together and agree to the substitution. The requirements of a novation are as follows:

1. The existence of a previous, valid obligation.
2. Agreement by all the parties to a new contract.
3. The extinguishing of the old obligation (discharge of the prior party).
4. A new, valid contract.

NOVATION
The substitution, by agreement, of a new contract for an old one, with the rights under the old one being terminated. Typically, there is a substitution of a new person who is responsible for the contract and the removal of the original party's rights and duties under the contract.

An important distinction between an assignment or delegation and a novation is that a novation involves a new contract and an assignment or delegation involves the old contract.

Suppose that you contract with A. Logan Enterprises to sell it your office-equipment business. Logan later learns that it should not expand at this time but knows of another party, MBI Corporation, interested in purchasing your business. All three of you get together and agree to a novation. As long as the new contract is supported by consideration, the novation discharges the original contract between you and Logan and replaces it with the new contract between you and MBI Corporation. Logan prefers the novation to an assignment because it discharges all the contract liabilities stemming from its contract with you. For example, if an installment sales contract had been involved, requiring twelve monthly payments, and Logan had merely assigned the contract to MBI Corporation, Logan would have remained liable to you for the payments if MBI Corporation defaulted.

Discharge by Accord and Satisfaction In an **accord and satisfaction,** the parties agree to accept performance different from the performance originally promised. An *accord* is defined as an executory contract (one that has not yet been performed) to perform some act in order to satisfy an existing contractual duty that is not yet discharged.[22] A *satisfaction* is the performance of the accord agreement. An *accord* and its *satisfaction* discharge the original contractual obligation.

"Law is a practical matter."

Roscoe Pound, 1870–1964
(American jurist)

Once the accord has been made, the original obligation is merely suspended unless the accord agreement is breached. Thus, the obligor can discharge the original obligation by performing the obligation agreed to in the accord; and if the obligor refuses to perform the accord, the obligee can bring action on the original obligation.

ACCORD AND SATISFACTION
An agreement between the parties to allow discharge of a contract by a performance different from the performance originally contracted.

19. UCC 2–209(2), (4).

20. Note that certain contracts made by a consumer in his or her home can be rescinded by the consumer within three days for no reason at all. This three-day "cooling-off" period is designed to aid consumers who are susceptible to high-pressure door-to-door sales tactics. See 15 U.S.C. Section 1635(a).

21. Under UCC 2–209(1), however, no consideration is needed to modify a contract for a sale of goods. See Chapter 14. Also see UCC 1–107.

22. Restatement (Second) of Contracts, Section 281.

Suppose that Shea obtains a judgment against Marla for $4,000. Later, both parties agree that the judgment can be satisfied by Marla's transfer of her automobile to Shea. This agreement to accept the auto in lieu of $4,000 in cash is the accord. If Marla transfers her automobile to Shea, the accord agreement is fully performed, and the $4,000 debt is discharged. If Marla refuses to transfer her car, the accord is breached. Because the original obligation is merely suspended, Shea can bring an action to enforce the judgment for $4,000 in cash.

When Performance Is Impossible

IMPOSSIBILITY OF PERFORMANCE
A doctrine under which a party to a contract is relieved of his or her duty to perform when performance becomes impossible or totally impracticable (through no fault of either party).

After a contract has been made, performance may become impossible in an objective sense. This is known as **impossibility of performance** and may discharge a contract.[23] This *objective impossibility* ("It can't be done") must be distinguished from *subjective impossibility* ("I simply can't do it"). Examples of subjective impossibility include contracts in which goods cannot be delivered on time because of freight car shortages[24] and contracts in which money cannot be paid on time because the bank is closed.[25] In effect, the party in these cases is saying "It is impossible for *me* to perform," not "It is impossible for *anyone* to perform." Accordingly, such excuses do not discharge a contract, and the nonperforming party is normally held in breach of contract.

Objective Impossibility Four basic types of situations will generally qualify as grounds for the discharge of contractual obligations based on impossibility of performance:[26]

1. When one of the parties to a personal contract *dies or becomes incapacitated prior to performance.* For example, Fred, a famous dancer, contracts with Ethereal Dancing Guild to play a leading role in its new ballet. Before the ballet can be performed, Fred becomes ill and dies. His personal performance was essential to the completion of the contract. Thus, his death discharges the contract and his estate's liability for his nonperformance.
2. When the *specific* subject matter of the contract is destroyed. For example, A-1 Farm Equipment agrees to sell Gudgel the green tractor on its lot and promises to have it ready for Gudgel to pick up on Saturday. On Friday night, however, a truck veers off the nearby highway and smashes into the tractor, destroying it beyond repair. Because the contract was for this specific tractor, A-1's performance is rendered impossible owing to the accident.
3. When a change in *law* renders performance illegal. An example is a contract to build an apartment building, when the zoning laws are changed to prohibit the construction of residential rental property at this location. This change renders the contract impossible to perform.
4. When performance becomes *commercially impracticable.* The inclusion of this type of "impossibility" as a basis for contract discharge results from a growing trend to allow parties to discharge contracts in which the originally contemplated performance turns out to be much more difficult or expensive than anticipated. In such situations, courts may excuse parties from their performance obligations under the doctrine of **commercial impracticability.** For example, in one case, a court held that a contract was discharged because a party would have to pay ten times more than the original estimate to excavate a certain amount of gravel.[27]

COMMERCIAL IMPRACTICABILITY
A doctrine under which a seller may be excused from performing a contract when (1) a contingency occurs, (2) the contingency's occurrence makes performance impracticable, and (3) the nonoccurrence of the contingency was a basic assumption on which the contract was made. Despite the fact that UCC 2–615 expressly frees only sellers under this doctrine, courts have not distinguished between buyers and sellers in applying it.

23. Restatement (Second) of Contracts, Section 261.
24. *Minneapolis v. Republic Creosoting Co.*, 161 Minn. 178, 201 N.W. 414 (1924).
25. *Ingham Lumber Co. v. Ingersoll & Co.*, 93 Ark. 447, 125 S.W. 139 (1910).
26. Restatement (Second) of Contracts, Sections 262–266, and UCC 2–615.
27. *Mineral Park Land Co. v. Howard*, 172 Cal. 289, 156 P. 458 (1916).

Caution should be used in invoking the doctrine of commercial impracticability. The added burden of performing must be *extreme* and must *not* be within the cognizance of the parties at the time the contract is made. The element of foreseeability is emphasized in the following case.

Case 12.5
SYROVY v. ALPINE RESOURCES, INC.
Court of Appeals of Washington, 1992.
841 P.2d 1279.

HISTORICAL AND SOCIAL SETTING *Contract performance is absolute, or, as a Latin maxim expresses it,* pacta sunt servanda *(contracts are to be kept). In the early years of the common law, courts made exceptions to this rule and excused parties from fulfilling contractual duties when performance became impossible owing to the first three situations outlined in the preceding text. In early cases, however, a supervening event that made performance more difficult or more costly or that made the contract less profitable or even unprofitable did not excuse performance. The general rule was that commercial impracticability was not sufficient to excuse performance, because excuse of performance required impossibility. As the law developed through the centuries, this rule changed. Courts came to release parties from their contractual obligations when performance was highly impracticable, even though it might not have been impossible in the strictest sense of the word.*

FACTS The George Syrovy Trust (Syrovy) agreed to sell Alpine Resources, Inc., all of the timber from Syrovy's property that Alpine could harvest over a two-year period for $140,000. Over the next two years, Alpine harvested some timber and paid Syrovy $50,000. When Syrovy sued for the contract balance of $90,000, Alpine claimed that it should be released from its obligation to pay the remainder of the contract price on the ground of commercial impracticability. Alpine claimed that bad weather conditions during both winters and the fact that Alpine could not engage in logging operations during the hunting season made it impossible to harvest the quantity of timber it had planned to harvest when the contract was formed. The trial court granted Syrovy's motion for summary judgment, and Alpine appealed.

ISSUE Can Alpine avoid its contractual obligations on the ground of commercial impracticability?

DECISION No. The trial court's decision was affirmed.

REASON The court first pointed out that it is usually the seller of goods who is responsible for production, but that here the buyer was responsible for "production" in the sense that it was up to Alpine to engage in the logging operations necessary to harvest the timber. Nevertheless, the court determined that the "operative term" was "impracticability," regardless of whether it was the buyer or the seller who was responsible for production. The court stated that nonperformance may be excused if an unforeseen contingency occurs, and the nonoccurrence of that contingency was a basic assumption made by the parties to the contract. The court noted that Ken Reoh, who negotiated the contract for Alpine, was "a logger with considerable experience in purchasing timber. It would be unreasonable to suggest that weather conditions were an unforeseeable event." In regard to the difficulties caused, according to Alpine, by the hunting season, the court held that such "problems were also foreseeable."

ETHICAL CONSIDERATIONS *Although courts generally hold that contractual parties must abide by their promises, exceptions to this rule are sometimes made in the interests of fairness and justice. The doctrine of commercial impracticability is one of these exceptions. Yet the courts will not excuse parties from their contractual obligations just because an event occurred that made performance more difficult than expected. If the event should have been foreseeable at the time the contract was formed, then courts will assume that the possibility of that event's occurrence is one of the risks attending the contract. Businesses are allowed to profit from risk taking and therefore should be held to their bargains when they incur losses.*

Temporary Impossibility An occurrence or event that makes performance temporarily impossible operates to *suspend* performance until the impossibility ceases. Then, ordinarily, the parties must perform the contract as originally planned. If, however, the lapse of time and the change in circumstances surrounding the contract make it substantially more burdensome for the parties to perform the promised acts, the contract is discharged.

The leading case on the subject, *Autry v. Republic Productions*, involved an actor who was drafted into the army in 1942.[28] Being drafted rendered the actor's contract temporarily impossible to perform, and it was suspended until the end of the war. When the actor got out of the army, the value of the dollar had so changed that performance of the contract would have been substantially burdensome to him. Therefore, the contract was discharged.

❖ Key Terms

accord and satisfaction 301
alienation 288
anticipatory repudiation 299
assignment 286
breach of contract 298
commercial impracticability 302
concurrent condition 297
condition 296
condition precedent 296
condition subsequent 297
delegation of duties 289
discharge 294
impossibility of performance 302
incidental beneficiary 293
intended beneficiary 291
novation 301
performance 294
privity of contract 285
rescission 300
tender 297
third party beneficiary 291

❖ Chapter Summary: Third Party Rights and Discharge

THIRD PARTY RIGHTS	
Assignment	1. An assignment is the transfer of rights under a contract to a third party whereby the *rights* of the assignor (the person making the assignment, who is also the obligee) may be extinguished and the assignee (the person to whom the rights are assigned) has a right to demand performance from the other original party to the contract (the obligor). 2. Generally, all rights can be assigned, except in the following circumstances: a. When assignment is expressly prohibited by statute (e.g., workers' compensation benefits). b. When a contract calls for the performance of personal services. c. When the assignment will materially increase or alter the risks or duties of the obligor. d. When the contract itself stipulates that the rights cannot be assigned (except a money claim). 3. Notice of the assignment should be given by the assignee to the obligor. a. If the assignor assigns the same right to two different persons, generally the first assignment in time is the first in right, although in some states the first assignee to give notice takes priority. b. Until the obligor is notified of the assignment, the obligor can tender performance to the assignor; and if performance is accepted by the assignor, the obligor's duties under the contract are discharged without benefit to the assignee.
Delegation	1. A delegation is the transfer of duties under a contract to a third party whereby the delegatee (the third party) assumes the obligation of performing the contractual duties previously held by the delegator (the one making the delegation). 2. As a general rule, any duty can be delegated, except in the following circumstances: a. When performance depends on the personal skill or talents of the obligor. b. When special trust has been placed in the obligor. c. When performance by a third party will vary materially from that expected by the obligee (the one to whom the duty is owed) under the contract. d. When the contract expressly prohibits delegation. 3. A valid delegation of duties does not relieve the delegator of obligations under the contract. If the delegatee fails to perform, the delegator is still liable to the obligee. 4. An "assignment of all rights" or an "assignment of contract" is often construed to mean that both the rights and duties arising under the contract are transferred to a third party.

28. 30 Cal.2d 144, 180 P.2d 888 (1947).

❖ Chapter Summary: Third Party Rights and Discharge—Continued

Third Party Beneficiary Contract	A third party beneficiary contract is one made for the purpose of benefiting a third party. 1. *Intended beneficiary*—one for whose benefit a contract is created. When the promisor (the one making the contractual promise that benefits a third party) fails to perform as promised, the third party can sue the promisor directly. Examples of third party beneficiaries are creditor and donee beneficiaries. 2. *Incidental beneficiary*—A third party who indirectly (incidentally) benefits from a contract but for whose benefit the contract was not specifically intended. Incidental beneficiaries have no rights to the benefits received and cannot sue the promisor to have them enforced.
WAYS TO DISCHARGE A CONTRACT	
1. *Conditions of performance*—Contract obligations may be subject to (a) a condition precedent (a condition that must be fulfilled before a party's promise becomes absolute), (b) a condition subsequent (a condition that operates to terminate a party's absolute promise to perform), or (c) concurrent conditions (in which case each party's absolute duty to perform is conditioned on the other party's absolute duty to perform). 2. *Discharge by performance*—A contract may be discharged by complete (strict) or substantial performance. In some cases, performance must be to the satisfaction of another. Totally inadequate performance constitutes a material breach of contract. Anticipatory repudiation of contract allows the other party to sue immediately for breach of contract. 3. *Discharge by agreement of the parties*—Parties may agree to discharge their contractual obligations in several ways: (a) by mutually agreeing to rescind (cancel) the contract, (b) by novation, in which a new party is substituted for one of the primary parties to a contract, and (c) by accord and satisfaction, in which the parties agree to render performance different from that originally agreed upon. 4. *Discharge by objective impossibility of performance owing to one of the following:* a. The death or incapacity of a person whose performance is essential to the completion of the contract. b. The destruction of the specific subject matter of the contract prior to transfer. c. A change in the law that renders the performance called for by the contract illegal. d. Commercial impracticability of performance.	

❖ Questions and Case Problems

12-1. Third Party Beneficiaries. What factors indicate that a third party beneficiary is an intended beneficiary?

12-2. Third Party Beneficiaries. Wilken owes Rivera $2,000. Howie promises Wilken to pay Rivera the $2,000 in return for Wilken's promise to give Howie's children guitar lessons. Is Rivera an intended beneficiary of the Howie-Wilken contract? Explain.

12-3. Substantial Performance. Complete performance is strict performance according to the terms of a contract. What is substantial performance?

12-4. Novation versus Accord and Satisfaction. Doug owes creditor Cartwright $1,000, which is due and payable on June 1. Doug has a car accident, misses several months of work, and consequently does not have the money on June 1. Doug's father, Bert, offers to pay Cartwright $1,100 in four equal installments if Cartwright will discharge Doug from any further liability on the debt. Cartwright accepts. In view of these events, answer the following questions.

(a) Is the transaction a novation, or is it an accord and satisfaction? Explain.

(b) Does the contract between Bert and Cartwright have to be in writing to be enforceable? (Review the Statute of Frauds.) Explain.

12-5. Impossibility of Performance. Millie contracted to sell Frank 1,000 bushels of corn to be grown on Millie's farm. Owing to drought conditions during the growing season, Millie's yield was much less than anticipated, and she could deliver only 250 bushels to Frank. Frank accepted the lesser amount but sued Millie for breach of contract. Can Millie defend successfully on the basis of objective impossibility of performance? Explain.

12-6. Third Party Beneficiaries. Rensselaer Water Co. was under contract to the city of Rensselaer, New York, to provide water to the city, including water at fire hydrants. A warehouse owned by H. R. Moch Co. was totally destroyed by a fire that could not be extinguished because of inadequate water pressure at the fire hydrants. Moch brought suit against Rensselaer Water Co. for damages, claiming that Moch was a third party beneficiary to the city's contract with the water company. Will Moch be able to recover damages from the water company on the basis that the water company breached its contract with the city? Explain. [*H. R. Moch Co. v. Rensselaer Water Co.*, 247 N.Y. 160, 159 N.E. 896 (1928)]

12-7. Third Party Beneficiaries. Owens, a federal prisoner, was transferred from federal prison to the Nassau County Jail pursuant to a contract between the U.S. Bureau of Prisons and the county. The contract included a policy statement that required the receiving prison to provide for the safekeeping and protection of transferred federal prisoners. While in the Nassau County Jail, Owens was beaten severely by prison officials and suffered lacerations, bruises, and a lasting impairment that caused blackouts. Can Owens, as a third party beneficiary, sue the county for breach of its agreement with the U.S. Bureau of Prisons? [*Owens v. Haas*, 601 F.2d 1242 (2d Cir. 1979)]

12-8. Impossibility of Performance. John Agosta and his brother Salvatore had formed a corporation, but disagreements between the two brothers caused John to petition for voluntary dissolution of the corporation. According to the dissolution agreement, the total assets of the corporation, which included a warehouse and inventory, would be split between the brothers by Salvatore's selling his stock to John for $500,000. This agreement was approved, but shortly before the payment was made, a fire totally destroyed the warehouse and inventory, which were the major assets of the corporation. John refused to pay Salvatore the $500,000, and Salvatore brought suit for breach of contract. Discuss whether the destruction of the major assets of the corporation affects John's required performance. [*In the Matter of Fontana v. D'Oro Foods, Inc.*, 122 Misc.2d 1091, 472 N.Y.S.2d 528 (1983)]

12-9. Assignments. Abby's Cakes on Dixie, Inc., agreed in a lease contract to lease space in a shopping center from Colonial Palms Plaza, Inc. The contract included a provision in which Colonial agreed to pay Abby's a construction allowance of up to $11,250 after Abby's had satisfactorily completed certain improvements to the rented premises. The contract also contained a clause stating that Abby's agreed "not to assign, mortgage, pledge, or encumber this Lease" without first obtaining the written consent of Colonial and that any such "assignment, encumbrance or subletting without such consent shall be void." Prior to the completion of the improvements, Abby's assigned its right to receive the first $8,000 of the construction allowance to Robert Aldana (without first obtaining Colonial's consent). In return, Aldana loaned Abby's $8,000 to finance the construction. Aldana notified Colonial of the assignment by certified mail. After Abby's had completed the improvements to the rented premises, Colonial ignored the assignment and paid Abby's the construction allowance. In Aldana's suit against Colonial for the $8,000 due him pursuant to the assignment, Colonial claimed that the assignment was prohibited by the contract provision and therefore void. Who will win, and why? [*Aldana v. Colonial Palms Plaza, Ltd.*, 591 So.2d 953 (Fla.App. 1992)]

12-10. Conditions Precedent. Edgar and Peggy Stacy owned a 588-acre farm in Mississippi County, Arkansas. In June 1985, the Williams family agreed to purchase the Stacys' farm for $882,000. The Stacys' real estate agent inserted into a preprinted contract (just after the provision stating the purchase price) the following typewritten statement: "Buyers to pledge approximately 900 acres of land in Tallahatchie County in Mississippi together with lands herein described for loan to pay purchase price." The Williams family failed to obtain financing for the property, in part because the farm in Tallahatchie County was subject to a long-term lease and because the value of the lands they held turned out to be less than they had assumed. The Williams family notified the Stacys' real estate broker of these facts, and the family also wrote a letter to Edgar Stacy stating that they wanted to rescind the contract for these reasons. Several months later, the Stacys sold the farm to another party for $630,000 and sued the Williams family for breach of contract, seeking $252,000, which represented the difference between the $882,000 purchase price offered by the Williams family and the $630,000 paid by the purchaser of the property. The issue before the court is whether the ability of the Williamses to obtain financing was a condition precedent to the Williamses' obligation to perform under the contract. Assuming that parol evidence is admissible (you may want to review the parol evidence rule, discussed in Chapter 11), how should the court rule? Discuss. [*Stacy v. Williams*, 38 Ark.App. 192, 834 S.W.2d 156 (1992)]

A Question of Ethics and Social Responsibility

12-11. *Sharon Russell's weight varied between 280 and 305 pounds while she was enrolled in a nursing program at Salve Regina College in Newport, Rhode Island. Her weight was never an issue until her sophomore year, at which time she began to be the target of cruel remarks by school officials. In her junior year, she received a failing grade in a clinical nursing course—not on the basis of her performance, but simply because she was obese. The normal consequence of failing a clinical nursing course was expulsion from the college, but Russell was offered a deal: if she signed a "contract" in which she promised to attend Weight Watchers regularly and to submit proof of her attendance, and if she steadily managed to lose two pounds a week, she would remain in good standing. Russell attended Weight Watchers regularly but failed to lose the required two pounds a week, and the following year the college requested that she withdraw from the nursing program. Russell sued the college for damages for breach of contract. The jury found that Russell's relationship to the college was essentially a contractual one in which she was required to abide by disciplinary rules, pay tuition, and maintain a good academic record (which she did—except for the course that she failed because of her obesity) and the college was required to provide her with an education until graduation. The jury also found that Russell had "substantially performed" her side of the bargain and that the college's actions prevented Russell from rendering complete performance and constituted a breach.* [Russell v. Salve Regina College, *890 F.2d 484 (1st Cir. 1989)*]

1. The college contended that it was inappropriate to apply the principle of substantial performance to contracts between a college and its students. From an ethical point of view, what arguments could you make in support of the college's contention? That is, what would be some of the negative ethical ramifications of permitting such flexibility in the relationship between student and college?
2. Do the circumstances of Russell's situation justify the application of the principle of substantial performance in this case?

For Critical Analysis

12-12. *The concept of substantial performance permits parties to be discharged from their contracts even though they have breached (albeit in minor ways) those contracts. Is this fair? What policy interests are at issue here?*

Chapter 13

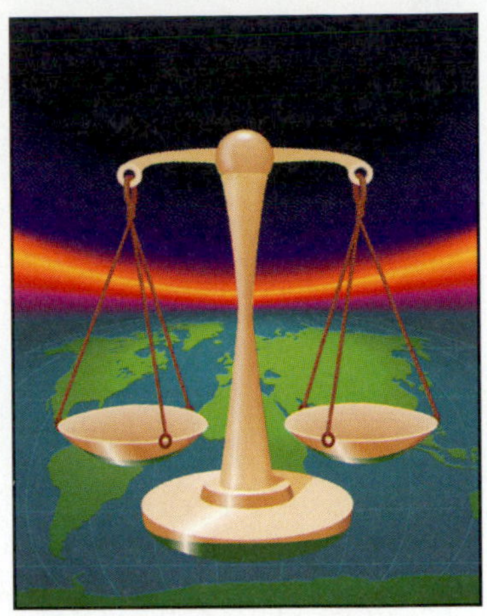

Breach and Remedies

"Men keep their engagements when it is to the advantage of both not to break them."

Solon, sixth century B.C.
(Athenian legal reformer)

Normally, the reason a person enters into a contract with another is to secure benefits. And normally, as the Greek lawgiver Solon instructed centuries ago, a contract will not be broken so long as "it is to the advantage of both" parties not to break it. When it is no longer advantageous for a party to fulfill his or her contractual obligations, breach of contract may result. As discussed in Chapter 12, a *breach of contract* occurs when a party fails to perform part or all of the required duties under a contract.[1] Once a party fails to perform or performs inadequately, the other party—the nonbreaching party—can choose one or more of several remedies. A **remedy** is the relief provided for an innocent party when the other party has breached the contract. It is the means employed to enforce a right or to redress an injury. The most common remedies available to a nonbreaching party are *damages, rescission and restitution, specific performance,* and *reformation.*

REMEDY
The relief given to innocent parties, by law or by contract, to enforce a right or to prevent or compensate for the violation of a right.

Recall from the *Landmark in the Law* in Chapter 1 that in the past, a distinction was made between *remedies at law* and *remedies in equity.* Although this distinction is now mostly only of historical significance, the distinction is still drawn by the courts and is therefore important. Generally, remedies in equity (including rescission and restitution, specific performance, and reformation) will not be granted unless the remedy at law (money damages) is inadequate.

❖ Damages

A breach of contract entitles the nonbreaching party to sue for money damages. **Damages** are designed to compensate the nonbreaching party for the loss of the bargain. Often, courts say that innocent parties are to be placed in the position they would have occupied had the contract been fully performed.[2]

DAMAGES
Money sought as a remedy for a breach of contract or for a tortious act.

Types of Damages

There are basically four kinds of damages: compensatory, consequential, punitive, and nominal.

Compensatory Damages Damages to compensate the nonbreaching party for the *loss* of the bargain are known as **compensatory damages.** These damages compen-

COMPENSATORY DAMAGES
A money award equivalent to the actual value of injuries or damages sustained by the aggrieved party.

1. Restatement (Second) of Contracts, Section 235(2).
2. Restatement (Second) of Contracts, Section 347, and UCC 1–106(1).

sate the injured party only for injuries actually sustained and proved to have arisen directly from the loss of the bargain caused by the breach of contract. They simply replace the loss caused by the wrong or injury. The amount of compensatory damages is the difference between the value of the breaching party's promised performance and the value of his or her actual performance. This amount is reduced by any loss that the injured party has avoided, however.

Suppose you contract with Marinot Industries to perform certain services exclusively for Marinot during August for a payment of $3,000. Marinot cancels the contract and is in breach. You are able to find another job during August but can only earn $500. You can sue Marinot for breach and recover $2,500 as compensatory damages. You may also recover from Marinot the amount you spent to find the other job. Expenses or costs that are caused directly by a breach of contract—such as those incurred to obtain performance from another source—are *incidental damages.*

The measurement of compensatory damages varies by type of contract. Certain types of contracts deserve special mention—contracts for the sale of goods, contracts for the sale of land, and construction contracts.

Sale of Goods In a contract for the sale of goods, the usual measure of compensatory damages is an amount equal to the difference between the contract price and the market price.[3] Suppose MediQuick Laboratories contracts with Cal Computer Industries to purchase ten Model X-15 computer work stations for $8,000 each. If Cal Computer fails to deliver the ten work stations, and the current market price of the work stations is $8,150, MediQuick's measure of damages is $1,500 (10 x

What factors influence the measure of damages on the breach of a construction contract?

3. That is, the difference between the contract price and the market price at the time and place at which the goods were to be delivered or tendered. See UCC 2–708 and 2–713.

PARTY IN BREACH	TIME OF BREACH	MEASUREMENT OF DAMAGES
Owner	Before construction begins	Profits (contract price less cost of materials and labor)
Owner	After construction begins	Profits plus costs incurred up to time of breach
Owner	After construction is completed	Contract price
Contractor	Before construction is completed	Generally, all costs incurred by owner to complete construction

♦ **Exhibit 13–1 Measurement of Damages—Breach of Construction Contracts**

$150). In cases in which the buyer breaches and the seller has not yet produced the goods, compensatory damages normally equal the lost profits on the sale, not the difference between the contract price and the market price.

Sale of Land The measure of damages in a contract for the sale of land is ordinarily the same as it is for contracts involving the sale of goods—that is, the difference between the contract price and the market price of the land. The majority of states follow this rule regardless of whether it is the buyer or the seller who breaches the contract. A minority of states, however, follow a different rule when the seller breaches the contract and the breach is not deliberate. An example of a nondeliberate breach of a contract to sell land occurs when a previously unknown easement (a right of use over the property of another) comes to light and renders title to the land unmarketable. (In real property law, *title* means the right to own property or the evidence of that right.) In such a case, these states allow the prospective purchaser to recover any down payment plus any expenses incurred (such as fees for title searches or attorneys). This minority rule effectively places a purchaser in the position that he or she occupied prior to the contract of sale.

Construction Contracts With construction contracts, the measure of damages often varies depending on which party breaches and at what stage the breach occurs. See Exhibit 13–1 for illustrations. In the following case, the issue centers on the proper measure of damages in a breached construction contract.

Case 13.1
CASTRICONE v. MICHAUD

Appellate Court of Illinois,
Third District, 1991.
223 Ill.App.3d 138,
583 N.E.2d 1184,
164 Ill.Dec. 862.

HISTORICAL AND ECONOMIC SETTING *There are two measures of damages that may be applied when a construction contract is breached by the contractor. When a contractor fails to complete the construction, the usual measure of damages is the cost to the owner of completing the work. If the quality of the work is poor, the usual measure of damages is the cost of repairing the defects. Awarding an owner the cost of completion or repair has been called the "cost" rule. Sometimes, a different rule is applied when a contractor falls short in only a minor way. This may occur when a defect causes only a minor loss in the value of a building, and the cost of repairing the defect is disproportionately high. For example, in one case, the contract to build a house called for plumbing supplies manufactured by a specific company, but the contractor used supplies manufactured by a different company. The supplies were of equal quality, and rectifying the defect would have required tearing down much of the house. The court awarded the owner the difference between the value of the house as it was built and the value that it would have had*

Case 13.1—Continued

if it had been built to the specifications.[a] *This has been called the "value" rule. The cost rule has been applied in many cases and is generally preferred. It gives the owner money equal to what he or she bargained for by giving him or her the cost of getting the work done.*

FACTS Frank Michaud, a building contractor, contracted with Quentin and Marcia Castricone to build the Castricones a home for a price of $89,000. As construction proceeded, disputes arose over the quality of the work being done and the contract specifications. Michaud stopped working on the project, and the Castricones, who had already paid Michaud a total of $76,400, had to pay an additional $29,280.87 to tear down and redo some of the work Michaud had done and to complete the project. The Castricones sued Michaud for, among other things, breach of contract. Michaud counterclaimed for the unpaid portion of the contract price. The trial court stated that "it had never seen such poor workmanship" and found that Michaud had breached the contract. The court found that the $76,400 already paid to Michaud was sufficient to compensate Michaud for the work he had done and awarded the Castricones $29,280.87—the amount they had paid to complete and repair the house—in damages. Michaud appealed the damage award, contending that the damage award to the Castricones should have been offset by the amount remaining unpaid on the contract. In other words, the damage award should have been the amount the Castricones paid above and beyond the $89,000 contract price, not above and beyond the $76,400 they had paid to Michaud.

a. *Jacobs & Young, Inc. v. Kent,* 230 N.Y. 239, 129 N.E. 889 (1921).

ISSUE Did the trial court properly calculate the amount of the Castricones' damages?

DECISION No. The trial court's decision as to Michaud's breach of contract was affirmed, but the damage award was reduced.

REASON According to the appellate court, the proper measure of damages was the difference between the $89,000 contract price and the total amount paid by the Castricones ($76,400 to Michaud and $29,280.87 to repair and complete the house). The court stated that "[a]s a general rule, damages for breach of contract should place an aggrieved party in the position they would have been in had the contract been performed." The Castricones had contracted for an $89,000 home, and the proper measure of damages was the amount in excess of $89,000 that they had to pay to complete the home.

CONSEQUENTIAL DAMAGES Special damages that compensate for a loss that is not direct or immediate (for example, lost profits). The special damages must have been reasonably foreseeable at the time the breach or injury occurred in order for the plaintiff to collect them.

Consequential Damages **Consequential damages,** which are also referred to as *special damages,* are foreseeable damages that result from a party's breach of contract. They differ from compensatory damages in that they are caused by special circumstances beyond the contract itself. When a seller does not deliver goods, knowing that a buyer is planning to resell those goods immediately, consequential damages are awarded for the loss of profits from the planned resale. For a nonbreaching party to recover consequential damages, the breaching party must know (or have reason to know) that special circumstances will cause the nonbreaching party to suffer an additional loss[4] (see this chapter's *Landmark in the Law*).

For example, Gilmore contracts to have a specific item shipped to her—one that she desperately needs to repair her printing press. In contracting with the shipper, Gilmore tells him that she must receive it by Monday or she will not be able to print her paper and will lose $750. If the shipper is late, Gilmore can recover the consequential damages caused by the delay (that is, the $750 in losses).

Likewise, when a bank wrongfully dishonors a check, the drawer of the check (who is a customer of the bank) may recover consequential damages (such as those resulting from slander of credit or reputation) if he or she is arrested or prosecuted.[5] Another example of consequential damages used to occur when an ice company

4. See UCC 2–715(2).

5. *Weaver v. Bank of America,* 59 Cal.2d 428, 380 P.2d 644, 30 Cal.Rptr. 4 (1963). A checking account is a contractual arrangement; see UCC 4–402.

Landmark in the Law

Hadley v. Baxendale (1854)

A landmark case in establishing the rule that notice of special ("consequential") circumstances must be given if consequential damages are to be recovered is *Hadley v. Baxendale*,[a] decided in 1854. This case involved a broken crankshaft used in a flour mill run by the Hadley family in Gloucester, England. The crankshaft attached to the steam engine in the mill broke, and the shaft had to be sent to a foundry located in Greenwich so that a new shaft could be made to fit the other parts of the engine. The Hadleys hired Baxendale, a common carrier, to transport the shaft from Gloucester to Greenwich. Baxendale received payment in advance and promised to deliver the shaft the following day. It was not delivered for several days, however. As a consequence, the mill was closed during those days because the Hadleys had no extra crankshaft on hand to use. The Hadleys sued Baxendale to recover the profits they lost during that time. Baxendale contended that the loss of profits was "too remote."

In the mid-1800s, it was normal for large mills, such as that run by the Hadleys, to have more than one crankshaft in case the main one broke and had to be repaired, as it did in this case. Also, in those days it was common knowledge that flour mills did indeed carry spares. It is against this background that the parties argued their respective positions on whether the damages resulting from loss of profits while the crankshaft was out for repair were "too remote" to be recoverable.

The trial court held that the lost profits were recoverable by the Hadleys, but the appellate court viewed the matter differently. According to the appellate court, the crucial issue was whether the Hadleys had informed Baxendale of the special circumstances surrounding the crankshaft's repair, particularly of the fact that the mill would have to shut down while the crankshaft was being repaired. If Baxendale had been notified of this circumstance at the time the contract was formed, then the damages for breaching the contract would have been the amount of injury that would reasonably follow from the breach—including the Hadleys' lost profits. But in the appellate court's opinion, the only circumstances communicated by the Hadleys to Baxendale at the time the contract was made were that the item to be transported was a broken crankshaft of a mill and that the Hadleys were the owners and operators of that mill. The court concluded that these circumstances did not reasonably indicate that the mill would have to stop operations if the delivery of the crankshaft was delayed.

In this case, the delay in delivery was, in fact, the reason for the mill's stoppage and the consequent loss of profits. But, said the court, "in the great multitude of cases of millers sending off broken shafts to third persons by a carrier under ordinary circumstances, such consequences would not, in all probability, have occurred; and these special circumstances were here never communicated by the plaintiffs to [Baxendale]."

The court enunciated the rule that for a plaintiff to recover for lost profits, the defendant must be notified at the time the contract is formed of special circumstances that will result from the defendant's breach. Today, this rule still applies. When damages are awarded, compensation is given only for those injuries that the defendant could reasonably have foreseen as a probable result of the usual course of events following a breach. If the injury complained of is outside the usual and foreseeable course of events, it must be shown specifically that the defendant had reason to know the facts and foresee the injury.

a. 9 Exch. 341, 156 Eng.Rep. 145 (1854).

failed to deliver ice to keep a butcher's meat cold. The ice company could be held liable for meat spoilage if it did not deliver the ice on time.

In summary, the amount of damages an injured party may recover from a breaching party in a breach of contract action is calculated as follows. Imagine that Bill sells a pizza oven to Tino's Pizza, promising that the oven will bake forty pizzas per hour. The price of the oven is $10,000. Tino gives Bill $8,000, promising to pay the rest of the price in monthly installments. Before Tino makes any installment payments, he discovers that the oven will bake only twenty pizzas per hour. Tino spends $400 in search costs to locate a second oven that will bake twenty pizzas an hour (so that together the ovens will perform as Bill had promised Bill's oven would). He has to pay $5,000 for this second oven. Tino loses $4,000 in profits before installing the second oven.

As promised, Bill's oven would have been worth $10,000, but as it is, the oven is worth only $5,000 because it can only bake twenty, not forty, pizzas in an hour. In this situation, Tino may recover $5,000 in damages—the value of the promised oven ($10,000) less the value of the actual oven ($5,000). Tino's recovery will be reduced by the loss that he avoided by not having to perform his part of the contract. Tino paid $8,000 towards the price of the oven, and thus, his recovery will be reduced by the amount of the payments that he did not make ($2,000). Tino's recovery will be increased, however, by $400 in incidental damages (the amount that he had to pay to find the second oven) and $4,000 in consequential damages (his lost profits). In total, Tino may recover $7,400 in damages.

PUNITIVE (EXEMPLARY) DAMAGES
Compensation in excess of actual or consequential damages. They are awarded in order to punish the wrongdoer and usually will be awarded only in cases involving willful or malicious misconduct.

Punitive Damages **Punitive damages,** which are also known as *exemplary damages,* are generally not recoverable in a breach of contract action. Punitive damages are designed to punish and make an example of a guilty party for the purpose of deterring similar conduct in the future. Such damages have no legitimate place in contract law because they are, in essence, penalties, and a breach of contract is not unlawful in a criminal sense. A contract is simply a civil relationship between the parties. The law may compensate one party for the loss of the bargain—no more and no less.

In a few situations, a person's actions can cause both a breach of contract and a tort. For example, the parties can establish by contract a certain reasonable standard or duty of care. Failure to live up to that standard is a breach of contract, and the act itself may constitute negligence.

A review of Chapter 5, dealing with torts, indicates that an intentional tort (such as fraud) may also be tied to a breach of contract. In such a case, it is possible for the nonbreaching party to recover punitive damages for the tort in addition to compensatory and consequential damages for the breach of contract.

"Nominal damages are, in effect, only a peg to hang costs on."

Sir William Henry Maule, 1788–1858
(British jurist)

Nominal Damages **Nominal damages** are awarded to an innocent party when only a technical injury is involved and no actual damage (no financial loss) has been suffered. Nominal damage awards are often small, such as a dollar, but they do establish that the defendant acted wrongfully. For example, suppose that Parrott contracts to buy potatoes at 50 cents a pound from Lentz. Lentz breaches the contract and does not deliver the potatoes. Meanwhile, the price of potatoes falls. Parrott is able to buy them in the open market at half the price he agreed to pay Lentz. He is clearly better off because of Lentz's breach. Thus, in a breach of contract suit, Parrott may be awarded only nominal damages for the technical injury he sustained, as no monetary loss was involved. Most lawsuits for nominal damages are brought as a matter of principle under the theory that a breach has occurred and some damages must be imposed regardless of actual loss.

NOMINAL DAMAGES
A small monetary award (often one dollar) granted to a plaintiff when no actual damage was suffered.

Mitigation of Damages

MITIGATION OF DAMAGES
The rule requiring the party suing to have done whatever was reasonable to minimize the damages caused by the defendant.

In most situations, when a breach of contract occurs, the injured party is held to a duty to mitigate, or reduce, the damages that he or she suffers. Under this doctrine of **mitigation of damages,** the required action depends on the nature of the situation. For example, in the majority of states, wrongfully terminated employees owe the duty to mitigate damages suffered by their employers' breach. The damages they will be awarded are their salaries less the incomes they would have received in similar jobs obtained by reasonable means. It is the employers' burden to prove the existence of such jobs and to prove that the employees could have been hired. An employee is, of course, under no duty to take a job that is not of the same type and rank. This is illustrated in the following case.

Case 13.2
PARKER v. TWENTIETH CENTURY-FOX FILM CORP.
Supreme Court of California, 1970.
3 Cal.3d 176,
474 P.2d 689,
89 Cal.Rptr. 737.

HISTORICAL AND SOCIAL SETTING *In some instances, when an employer has breached an employment contract, to mitigate damages, the employer may offer to make a new contract that is less advantageous to the employee than the first contract. Courts are divided as to whether the mitigation doctrine requires the employee to agree to the second contract if it will have the effect of minimizing damages resulting from the breach. Generally, courts do not require employees to accept positions that are demeaning or beneath their dignity. Courts look at such factors as the geographic location of the new position, any danger posed by the nature of the employment, the impact of the new position on the employee's future employment and career, and any other factors that indicate whether the new position is a reasonable alternative for this employee.*

FACTS Twentieth Century-Fox Film Corporation planned to produce a musical, *Bloomer Girl,* and contracted with Shirley MacLaine Parker to play the leading female role. According to the contract, Fox was to pay Parker $53,571.42 per week for fourteen weeks, for a total of $750,000. Fox later decided not to produce *Bloomer Girl* and tried to substitute for the existing contract another contract. Under the terms of this second contract, Parker would play the leading role in a western movie for the same amount of money guaranteed by the first contract. Fox gave Parker one week in which to accept the new contract. Parker filed suit against Fox to recover the amount of compensation guaranteed in the first contract because, she maintained, the two roles were not at all equivalent. The *Bloomer Girl* production was a musical, to be filmed in California, and could not be compared with a "western-type" production that Fox tentatively planned to produce in Australia. When the trial court held for Parker, Fox appealed.

ISSUE May Fox's substitute offer of the western movie contract be used in mitigating the damages ensuing from the breach of the first contract?

DECISION No. The judgment for Parker was affirmed.

REASON The court noted that the "measure of recovery by a wrongfully discharged employee is the amount of salary agreed upon for the period of service, less the amount which the employer affirmatively proves the employee has earned or with reasonable effort might have earned from other employment. Before projected earnings from other employment opportunities not sought or accepted by the discharged employee can be applied in mitigation, however, the employer must show that the other employment was comparable, or substantially similar, to that of which the employee has been deprived." The court held that the two roles were substantially dissimilar—that is, one called for Parker's dancing and acting abilities, and the other was simply an acting role in a western movie. The court asserted that "by no stretch of the imagination" could the latter "be considered the equivalent of or substantially similar to the lead in a song-and-dance production."

Liquidated Damages versus Penalties

A **liquidated damages** provision in a contract specifies a certain amount of money to be paid in the event of a future default or breach of contract. (*Liquidated* means determined, settled, or fixed.) Liquidated damages differ from penalties. A **penalty** specifies a certain amount to be paid in the event of a default or breach of contract and is *designed to penalize* the breaching party. Liquidated damages provisions normally are enforceable; penalty provisions are not.[6]

To determine whether a particular provision is for liquidated damages or for a penalty, the court must answer two questions: First, at the time the contract was formed, was it difficult to estimate the potential damages that would be incurred if the contract was not performed on time? Second, was the amount set as damages a reasonable estimate of those potential damages and not excessive?[7] If both answers are yes, the provision will be enforced. If either answer is no, the provision will normally not be enforced.

LIQUIDATED DAMAGES
An amount, stipulated in the contract, that the parties to a contract believe to be a reasonable estimation of the damages that will occur in the event of a breach.

PENALTY
A sum inserted into a contract, not as a measure of compensation for its breach but rather as punishment for a default. The agreement as to the amount will not be enforced, and recovery will be limited to actual damages.

6. See UCC 2–718(1).
7. Restatement (Second) of Contracts, Section 356(1).

Business Law in Action

Do Contaminated Water and Liquidated Damages Mix?

One of the most contested areas in contract law involves the distinction between liquidated damages and penalties. Only the former are enforceable. When Mary and George Rivera signed a standard-form, conditional real estate sales contract for some ranch property in Montana, the contract contained a "liquidated damages" clause. The clause stated that if either party failed to complete the transaction, that party would be required to pay the other party 10 percent of the purchase price—in this case, that amounted to $43,000. The Riveras had a water test done, and the results showed that the water was contaminated. Consequently, they failed to close on the contract on the specified date. The owners of the ranch, Brien and Gayle Weber, sued the Riveras for breach of contract and sought to enforce the liquidated damages clause.

The case ultimately reached the Supreme Court of Montana. The court stated that two requirements had to be met before liquidated damages clauses in contracts would be enforced. First, the damages must have been difficult to ascertain at the time of contract formation. Second, the amount of damages stipulated in the clause had to be a reasonable estimate of probable damages or reasonably proportionate to the actual damages sustained at the time of the breach. The court concluded that the first requirement for enforcing a liquidated damages clause had been met. Clearly, it was difficult at the time of contract formation to determine what damages might be incurred as a result of this contract's breach. If the buyers breached, for example, the Webers might sell the rangeland to someone else the next day, or the next week, or the next year. The court held, however, that the second requirement had not been met. Because in this case the liquidated damages clause was part of a standard-form contract, there clearly had been no attempt on the part of the parties to estimate what a reasonable amount of damages might be in the event of a breach of their specific contract. "The fact that the liquidated damage provision in this case *may* approximate the actual damages suffered is insufficient by itself to create a valid liquidated damages provision" (emphasis added). The court concluded that the provision was simply a penalty clause and as such was "void under Montana law."[a]

a. *Weber v. Rivera*, 841 P.2d 534 (Mont. 1992).

In a construction contract, it is difficult to estimate the amount of damages that might be caused by a delay in completing construction, so liquidated damages clauses are often used. See this chapter's *Business Law in Action* for a further discussion of the concept of liquidated damages.

❖ Rescission and Restitution

RESTITUTION
An equitable remedy under which a person is restored to his or her original position prior to loss or injury, or placed in the position he or she would have been in had the breach not occurred.

As discussed in Chapter 12, *rescission* is essentially an action to undo, or cancel, a contract—to return nonbreaching parties to the positions that they occupied prior to the transaction.[8] When fraud, mistake, duress, or failure of consideration is present, rescission is available. The failure of one party to perform entitles the other party to rescind the contract. The rescinding party must give prompt notice to the breaching party. Furthermore, to rescind a contract, both parties must make **restitution** to each other by returning goods, property, or money previously conveyed.[9] If the goods or property can be restored *in specie*—that is, if they can be returned—they must be. If the goods or property have been consumed, restitution must be made in an equivalent amount of money.

8. The rescission discussed here refers to *unilateral* rescission, in which only one party wants to undo the contract. In *mutual* rescission, both parties agree to undo the contract. Mutual rescission discharges the contract; unilateral rescission is generally available as a remedy for breach of contract.

9. Restatement (Second) of Contracts, Section 370.

Essentially, restitution refers to the recapture of a benefit conferred on the defendant through which the defendant has been unjustly enriched. For example, Andrea pays $10,000 to Miles in return for Miles's promise to design a house for her. The next day Miles calls Andrea and tells her that he has taken a position with a large architectural firm in another state and cannot design the house. Andrea decides to hire another architect that afternoon. Andrea can get restitution of $10,000 because an unjust benefit of $10,000 was conferred on Miles.

The following case illustrates a situation in which the equitable remedy of rescission and restitution was deemed an appropriate remedy by the court.

"Laws are made to protect the trusting as well as the suspicious."

Hugo L. Black, 1886–1971
(Associate justice of the United States Supreme Court, 1937–1971)

Case 13.3
RACICKY v. SIMON
Supreme Court of Wyoming, 1992.
831 P.2d 241.

HISTORICAL AND ECONOMIC SETTING *When a seller breaches a contract to transfer land and it is impossible for the seller to perform, the buyer's normal remedy at law is damages consisting of the amount of the loss of the bargain, plus consequential damages. Usually, the amount awarded as damages for the loss of the bargain is the difference between the contract price and the market value of the land on the date of the breach. But suppose the seller's breach is unintentional (as it would be if, for example, it turned out that someone else had certain rights in the property that were unknown to the seller at the time the contract was formed). In that case, in some states, the buyer can recover only the amount paid on the purchase price. This rule, which is sometimes called the "restitutionary" rule, originated in 1776 in the English case of* Flureau v. Thornhill.[a] *Imagine that you sign a contract to buy some land and make payments on the price. Before the sale is complete, it becomes impossible for the seller to perform. Meanwhile, the market value of the land has decreased. Would you to prefer to recover money damages in the amount of the loss of the bargain (which in this case would be a net loss), or would you prefer to have the contract rescinded and recover the amount that you paid toward the purchase price?*

FACTS In January 1980, Bud Racicky entered into a contract to sell 320 acres of land to Dorothy Simon for $144,000, to be paid in three installments. Simon made the payments on time, and the contract price was fully paid by January 30, 1982. At the time the contract was formed, Racicky was in the process of buying the land he was going to convey to Simon from another party. In the fall of 1985, before he completed the contract with the other party, Racicky sought bankruptcy relief. As a consequence of these events, it was impossible for Racicky to perform his contract with Simon. Simon died, and her personal representative brought an action against Racicky, seeking rescission of the contract and restitution of the full amount of the payments that Simon had made to Racicky. The trial court ordered rescission of the contract and restitution in the amount of the payments received, together with interest at 10 percent, which was calculated from the time that Racicky's performance became impossible. The total restitution awarded was $212,267.33. Racicky appealed the decision. Racicky asserted that the market value of the land was considerably less than the contract price and contended that money damages (of a much lower amount than the restitution award) constituted an adequate remedy at law for his breach of contract.

ISSUE Is the equitable remedy of rescission and restitution, instead of money damages, appropriate on the breach of a contract for a sale of land?

DECISION Yes. The trial court's decision was affirmed.

REASON The court recognized that "the payment of money damages generally is considered an adequate remedy for a breach of contract, but this general rule does not control a situation in which the contract is one for the sale of land." In contracts for the sale of land, "the legal presumption is that equitable concepts will control the resolution of the dispute. The rationale underlying this presumption is that the unique character of each individual parcel of land renders the remedy of money damages inadequate." In this case, the parties could not be returned to the status quo at the time the contract was made by awarding money damages, and the remedy of restitution and rescission was properly granted.

a. 96 Eng.Rep. 635 (C.P. 1776).

Law in the Extreme

When Ghosts Are Good Enough

While everybody knows that some people believe in ghosts, courts typically take a jaundiced view of parties who seek to rescind their contracts for supernatural reasons. One court, nonetheless, allowed a buyer to rescind an otherwise valid real estate contract because the buyer learned, after the purchase, that the house was rumored to be possessed by poltergeists. The buyer, Jeffrey Stambovsky, was a resident of New York City. While looking at houses in the village of Nyack, New York, Stambovsky had come across a riverfront Victorian house that he liked. He purchased it only to discover later that the house had a local reputation for being haunted. The seller, Helen Ackley, had promoted this reputation herself by reporting to *Readers' Digest* in 1977 and to the local press in 1982 that the house was haunted. By 1989, the house was included in a five-home walking tour of Nyack because of the purported presence of ghosts in the house. There was even a newspaper article describing it as "a riverfront Victorian (with ghost)."

Stambovsky brought an action to rescind the contract, contending that the house's reputation for being haunted impaired the value of the property. The Supreme Court in New York County dismissed the suit. On appeal, the court viewed the poltergeist issue more favorably. The court noted that under New York law, the real estate broker, as an agent of the seller, was under no duty to disclose the phantasmal reputation of the property, and thus Stambovsky did not have a "ghost of a chance" to pursue a remedy for fraudulent misrepresentation on the seller's part. But, the court held, it was a different matter when a condition that materially impaired the value of the contract had been created by the seller and was unlikely to be discovered by a prudent purchaser exercising due care. Ackley had chosen to inform the public at large, with whom she had no legal relationship, about the poltergeists. Yet she did not disclose this information to Stambovsky, who was obviously not a "local" and therefore would not likely know about the house's reputation. The court, concluding that to enforce the contract in these circumstances would be offensive to equity, allowed Stambovsky to rescind the contract.[a]

a. *Stambovsky v. Ackley*, 169 A.D.2d 254, 572 N.Y.S.2d 672 (1991).

❖ Specific Performance

SPECIFIC PERFORMANCE An equitable remedy requiring *exactly* the performance that was specified in a contract. Usually granted only when money damages would be an inadequate remedy and the subject matter of the contract is unique (for example, real property).

The equitable remedy of **specific performance** calls for the performance of the act promised in the contract. This remedy is quite attractive to the nonbreaching party because it provides the exact bargain promised in the contract. It also avoids some of the problems inherent in a suit for money damages. First, the nonbreaching party need not worry about collecting the judgment.[10] Second, the nonbreaching party need not look around for another contract. Third, the actual performance may be more valuable than the money damages. Although the equitable remedy of specific performance is often preferable to other remedies, it is not granted unless the party's legal remedy (money damages) is inadequate.[11]

10. As final dispositions of cases, courts enter judgments, which must then be collected. Collection, however, poses problems—such as when the judgment debtor is insolvent or has only a small net worth.
11. Restatement (Second) of Contracts, Section 359.

For example, contracts for the sale of goods that are readily available on the market rarely qualify for specific performance. Money damages ordinarily are adequate in such situations because substantially identical goods can be bought or sold in the market. If the goods are unique, however, a court of equity will decree specific performance. For example, paintings, sculptures, and rare books and coins are so unique that money damages will not enable a buyer to obtain substantially identical substitutes in the market. The same principle applies to contracts relating to sales of land or interests in land, as each parcel of land is unique.

Courts of equity normally refuse to grant specific performance of personal-service contracts. Sometimes the remedy at law may be adequate if substantially identical service is available from other persons (as with lawn-mowing services). Even for individually tailored personal-service contracts, courts are very hesitant to order specific performance by a party, because public policy strongly discourages involuntary servitude.[12] Moreover, the courts do not want to monitor a personal-service contract. For example, if you contract with a brain surgeon to perform brain surgery on you, and the surgeon refuses to perform, the court would not compel (and you certainly would not want) the surgeon to perform under these circumstances. There is no way the court can assure meaningful performance in such a situation.[13]

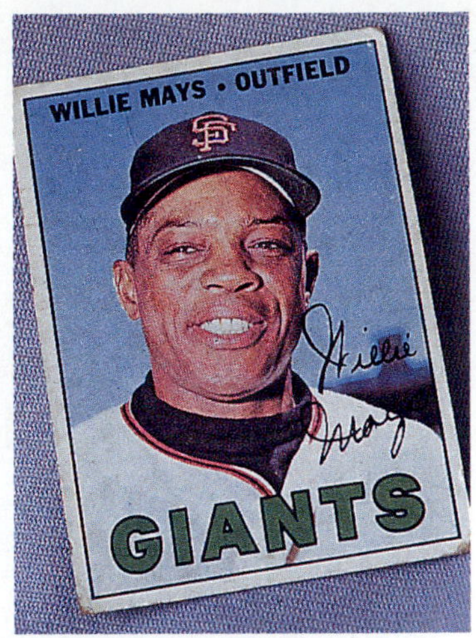

If the seller refuses to deliver this baseball card, would the buyer's remedies include specific performance?

❖ Reformation

Reformation is an equitable remedy used when the parties have *imperfectly* expressed their agreement in writing. Reformation allows the contract to be rewritten to reflect the parties' true intentions. It applies most often when fraud or mutual mistake (for example, a clerical error) has occurred. If Keshkekian contracts to buy a certain piece of equipment from Shelley, but the written contract refers to a different piece of equipment, a mutual mistake has occurred. Accordingly, a court of equity could reform the contract so that the writing conforms to Keshkekian and Shelley's original intention as to which piece of equipment is being sold.

Two other examples deserve mention. The first involves two parties who have made a binding oral contract. They further agree to reduce the oral contract to writing, but in doing so, they make an error in stating the terms. Universally, the courts allow into evidence the correct terms of the oral contract, thereby reforming the written contract.

The second example has to do with written agreements (covenants) not to compete (see Chapter 10). If the covenant is for a valid and legitimate purpose (such as the sale of a business), but the area or time restraints of the covenant are unreasonable, some courts reform the restraints by making them reasonable and enforce the entire contract as reformed. Other courts throw the entire restrictive covenant out as illegal.

"Specific performance is a remedy of grace and not a matter of right, and the test of whether or not it should be granted depends on the particular circumstances of each case."

George Bushnell, 1887–1965
(American jurist)

❖ Recovery Based on Quasi Contract

As stated in Chapter 8, a quasi contract is not a true contract but a fictional contract that is *imposed* on the parties to obtain justice and prevent unjust enrichment. Hence, a quasi contract becomes an equitable basis for relief. The legal obligation,

12. The Thirteenth Amendment to the U.S. Constitution prohibits involuntary servitude, but negative injunctions (that is, prohibiting rather than ordering certain conduct) are possible. Thus, you may not be able to compel a person to perform under a personal-service contract, but you may be able to restrain that person from engaging in similar contracts for a period of time.

13. Similarly, courts often refuse to order specific performance of construction contracts because courts are not set up to operate as construction supervisors or engineers.

or duty, arises because the law *implies* a promise on the part of one who has received a benefit to pay for the benefit received. Generally, when one party confers a benefit on another, justice requires that the party receiving the benefit pay a reasonable value for it so as not to be unjustly enriched at the other party's expense.

Quasi-contractual recovery is useful when one party has *partially* performed under a contract that is unenforceable. It can be an alternative to suing for damages and allows the party to recover the reasonable value of the partial performance.

For quasi-contractual recovery to occur, the party seeking recovery must show the following:

1. A benefit was conferred on the other party.
2. The party conferring the benefit did so with the expectation of being paid.
3. The party seeking recovery did not act as a volunteer in conferring the benefit.
4. Retaining the benefit without paying for it would result in an unjust enrichment of the party receiving the benefit.

For example, suppose Ericson contracts to build two oil derricks for Petro Industries. The derricks are to be built over a period of three years, but the parties do not make a written contract. Enforcement of the contract will therefore be barred by the Statute of Frauds.[14] Ericson completes one derrick, and then Petro Industries informs him that it will not pay for the derrick. Ericson can sue in quasi contract because (1) a benefit has been conferred on Petro Industries because one oil derrick has been built; (2) Ericson built the derrick (conferred the benefit) expecting to be paid; (3) Ericson did not volunteer to build the derrick but built it under an unenforceable oral contract; and (4) allowing Petro Industries to retain the derrick without paying would enrich the company unjustly. Therefore, Ericson should be able to recover the reasonable value of the oil derrick (under the theory of *quantum meruit*[15]—"as much as he deserves"). The reasonable value is ordinarily equal to the fair market value.

❖ Election of Remedies

In many cases, a nonbreaching party has several remedies available, but they may be inconsistent with each other. The common law of contract requires the party to choose which remedy to pursue. This is called *election of remedies*. For example, a person who buys a fraudulently represented car can either cancel (rescind) the sales contract or sue to recover damages. Obviously, these remedies are inconsistent. An action to rescind undoes the contract; an action for damages affirms it.

The purpose of the election-of-remedies doctrine is to prevent double recovery. Suppose that Jefferson agrees to sell his land to Adams. Then Jefferson changes his mind and repudiates the contract. Adams can sue for compensatory damages or for specific performance. If she receives damages as a result of the breach, she should not also be granted specific performance of the sales contract because that would mean she would end up with both the land *and* damages, which would be unfair. If Adams could seek compensatory damages in addition to specific performance, she would recover twice for the same breach of contract. The doctrine of election of remedies requires that Adams choose the remedy she wants, and it eliminates any possibility of double recovery.

---

14. Contracts that by their terms cannot be performed within one year must be in writing to be enforceable. See Chapter 11.

15. Pronounced *kwahn*-tuhm *mehr*-oo-wuht.

International Perspective

Electronic Failure and Liability for Breach

The world's financial markets are tied together by gigantic electronic networks that make it possible for traders in Tokyo to trade foreign currencies with other traders in London or New York almost instantaneously. Although improving technologies have made it possible for traders to handle increasingly large transactions, these enormously complicated systems may be more vulnerable to breakdown. Because large orders may disappear when a computer system "crashes," computer traders may not know for some time whether a particular purchase or sale of currencies, stocks, or commodities was completed. Substantial amounts of money are often involved in such transactions. The parties who suffer financial losses when the system fails to complete a transaction may seek money damages from the traders or even the manufacturers and operators of the trading system itself.[a]

The potential problems inherent in such trading systems have become apparent to the British information company Reuters, which developed an electronic network to be used by currency traders. Reuters was forced to delay the network's introduction because of growing concerns within the company about offers it had made to prospective purchasers to assume liability for any trades not completed as a result of technical malfunctions. Reuters has since decided that it would be more prudent to encourage the traders themselves to take responsibility for the system's breakdowns; the traders, not surprisingly, have not been very sympathetic to this plan. In any event, Reuters's concern is understandable, given that traders exchange more than $500 billion worth of currency every day. Even an occasional system breakdown could subject Reuters to potentially unlimited liability.

This specter of massive liability convinced Reuters to begin pressing traders to consider the merits of a more interactive approach in which they would communicate directly with one another and work out any trading problems by themselves, without resorting to an electronic go-between. Such an approach not only would reduce the traders' dependence on the system itself but also would enable individual traders to take actions to mitigate the possible consequences of a system failure. Because the planned Reuters system would operate by matching up purchase and sales offers electronically, traders would not know the identities of the parties with whom they were transacting business before the transaction itself was completed. This lack of contact could make it more difficult to complete trades when systems crashed. Although Reuters's originally offered guaranties were undoubtedly prompted by marketing considerations, they were still somewhat surprising, because trading system operators do not usually assume any liability for trades that fail owing to system malfunctions.

a. The amount of damages awarded would probably be based on the fair value of what the innocent party would have received in the absence of a system breakdown. See, for example, *Randall v. Loftsgaarden*, 478 U.S. 647, 106 S.Ct. 3143, 92 L.Ed.2d 525 (1986).

Unfortunately, the doctrine has been applied in a rigid and technical manner, leading to some harsh results. For example, in a Wisconsin case, a man named Carpenter was fraudulently induced to buy a piece of land for $100.[16] He spent $140 moving onto the land and then discovered the fraud. Instead of suing for damages, Carpenter sued to rescind the contract. The court denied recovery of the $140 because the seller, Mason, had not received the $140 and was therefore not required to reimburse Carpenter for his moving expenses. So Carpenter suffered a net loss of $140 on the transaction. If Carpenter had sued for damages, he could have recovered the $100 purchase price and the $140.[17]

In the following case, the plaintiff filed a complaint for damages and/or rescission. In such a situation, can the court elect the appropriate remedy?

16. See *Carpenter v. Mason*, 181 Wis. 114, 193 N.W. 973 (1923).

17. Because of the harsh results of the doctrine, the Uniform Commercial Code expressly rejects it. Remedies under the UCC (see UCC 2–703 and 2–711) are essentially *cumulative* in nature.

Case 13.4
STRYKEN v. PANELL
Court of Appeals of Washington, 1992.
66 Wash.App. 566,
832 P.2d 890.

HISTORICAL AND SOCIAL SETTING *At one time, it was required that a party make his or her election of remedies in the pleadings (see Chapter 3). Today, the time at which an election must be made is different in different jurisdictions and under different circumstances, but generally an election does not have to be made in the pleadings. Some jurisdictions allow a plaintiff to plead alternative remedies and then elect one as the trial proceeds. Even in those jurisdictions, in cases not subject to the Uniform Commercial Code, an election must still be made before a case is submitted to the jury.*

FACTS Paul Stryken bought a house from Norman and Ruth Panell for $38,000. A septic tank served the property, and the Panells warranted in the sales contract that the tank was in good condition and that they had "no knowledge of any needed repairs" to the tank. The Panells pointed out a couple of problems with the house but told Stryken that there were no other problems. Stryken later learned of a number of problems: the septic tank did not function properly, and sewage was backing up whenever it rained; the roof leaked; and there were electrical problems. Stryken paid nearly $4,800 to put a new roof on the house, repair the electrical system, and pump the septic tank on three occasions. Eventually, Stryken filed a complaint against the Panells that read, in part, as follows: "1. For judgment against Defendants * * * for damages in a manner and amount to be proven at trial; 2. For rescission of the contract of sale and restitution of all funds paid to date toward the purchase of the subject real property [or for repairs]." The trial court ordered rescission, based on its finding of mutual mistake regarding the septic tank. To return the parties to their status quo prior to the contract, the court ordered the Panells to return to Stryken the down payment he had made to the Panells plus the amount he had paid for the new roof and repairs. Stryken appealed, arguing that the trial court erred in granting rescission and restitution rather than awarding damages.

ISSUE Is it appropriate for a court to elect a remedy for a plaintiff who pleads alternative remedies?

DECISION Yes. The appellate court confirmed the trial court's decision, holding that the trial court properly chose which remedy to grant.

REASON Stryken contended that the trial court erred in granting an equitable remedy because "[e]quity does not intervene when there is a complete and adequate remedy at law." In response to this contention, the appellate court stated as follows: "What Stryken fails to note is that the plaintiff has a right to seek an equitable remedy if he so chooses, and is not confined to the legal remedy of damages. When an executory contract for the sale of real estate has been breached by the seller, the purchaser has the option to institute an action for specific performance of the contract or for damages resulting from the breach, or to seek only rescission of the contract by returning possession of the property contracted for and recovering only the amount of his down payment." The court also stated that when a party asks for inconsistent remedies in the alternative and the court renders a final judgment, "the court's choice becomes the pleading party's choice. Because Stryken elected to plead for an equitable remedy as well as a legal remedy, he is now bound by the trial court's election between the remedies."

ETHICAL CONSIDERATIONS *In the* Stryken *case, it is apparent that if Stryken wanted damages instead of rescission and restitution, his complaint should have been phrased so as to state his election clearly. This illustrates that legal pleadings should be written as carefully as, for example, the clauses in a contract. While it may seem unfair to hold a party to what later appears to have been poorly drafted pleadings, it might be equally unfair to the other party to change the pleadings after the verdict is in.*

❖ Provisions Limiting Remedies

A contract may include provisions stating that no damages can be recovered for certain types of breaches or that damages must be limited to a maximum amount. The contract may also provide that the only remedy for breach is replacement, repair, or refund of the purchase price. Provisions stating that no damages can be recovered are called *exculpatory clauses* (see Chapter 11). Provisions that affect the availability of certain remedies are called *limitation-of-liability clauses.*

Whether these contract provisions and clauses will be enforced depends on the type of breach that is excused by the provision. For example, a provision excluding liability for fraudulent or intentional injury will not be enforced. Likewise, a clause excluding liability for illegal acts or violations of law will not be enforced. A clause excluding liability for negligence may be enforced in some cases. When an exculpatory clause for negligence is contained in a contract made between parties who have roughly equal bargaining positions, the clause usually will be enforced.

The UCC provides that in a contract for the sale of goods, remedies can be limited. We will examine the UCC provisions on limited remedies in Chapter 16, in the context of the remedies available upon the breach of a sales contract.

Application

Law and the Contractor—Who Cannot Perform

Not every contract can be performed. If you are a contractor, you may take on a job that, for one reason or another, you cannot or do not wish to perform. Simply walking away from the job and hoping for the best is not normally the best way to avoid litigation—which can be costly, time consuming, and emotionally draining. Instead, avoidance of litigation through *compromise* should usually be considered.

For example, suppose you are a building contractor who signs a contract to custom-build a home for the Andersons. Performance is to begin on June 15. On June 1, Central Enterprises offers you a position that will yield you two-and-a-half times the amount of net income you could earn as an independent builder. To take the job, you have to start on June 15. You cannot be in two places at the same time, so to accept the new position you must breach the contract with the Andersons.

What to do? One option is to subcontract the work to another builder and oversee the work yourself to make sure it conforms to the contract. Another option is to negotiate with the Andersons for a *release*. You can offer to find another qualified builder who will build a house of the same quality at the same price. Or you can offer to pay any additional costs if another builder takes the job and is more expensive. In any event, this additional cost would be the measure of damages that a court would impose on you if you were sued by the Andersons for breach of contract and the Andersons prevailed. Thus, by making the offer, you might be able to avoid the expense of litigation—if the Andersons accept your offer.

Often, parties are reluctant to propose compromise settlements because they fear that what they say will be used against them in court if litigation ensues. The general rule, however, is that offers for settlement cannot be used in court to prove that you are liable for a breach of contract.

Checklist for the Contractor Who Cannot Perform

- ☐ 1. Consider a compromise.
- ☐ 2. Subcontract out the work and oversee it.
- ☐ 3. Offer to find an alternative contractor to fulfill your obligation.
- ☐ 4. Make a cash offer to "buy" a release from your contract. If anything other than an insignificant amount of money is involved, however, work with an attorney in making the offer.

❖ Key Terms

❖ Chapter Summary: Breach and Remedies

COMMON REMEDIES AVAILABLE TO NONBREACHING PARTY	
Damages	A legal remedy designed to compensate the nonbreaching party for the loss of the bargain. By awarding money damages, the court tries to place the parties in the positions that they would have occupied had the contract been fully performed. The nonbreaching party frequently has a duty to *mitigate* (lessen or reduce) the damages incurred as a result of the contract's breach. There are five broad categories of damages: 1. *Compensatory damages*—Damages that compensate the nonbreaching party for injuries actually sustained and proved to have arisen directly from the loss of the bargain resulting from the breach of contract. a. In breached contracts for the sale of goods, the usual measure of compensatory damages is an amount equal to the difference between the contract price and the market price. b. In breached contracts for the sale of land, the measure of damages is ordinarily the same as in contracts for the sale of goods. c. In breached construction contracts, the measure of damages depends on which party breaches and at what stage of construction the breach occurs. 2. *Consequential damages*—Damages resulting from special circumstances beyond the contract itself; they flow only from the consequences of a breach. For a party to recover consequential damages, the damages must be the foreseeable result of a breach of contract, and the breaching party must have known at the time the contract was formed that special circumstances existed and that the nonbreaching party would incur additional loss upon breach of the contract. Also called *special* damages. 3. *Punitive damages*—Damages awarded to punish the breaching party. Usually not awarded in a breach of contract action unless a tort is involved. 4. *Nominal damages*—Damages small in amount (such as one dollar) that are awarded when a breach has occurred but no actual damages have been suffered. Awarded only to establish that the defendant acted wrongfully. 5. *Liquidated damages*—Damages that may be specified in a contract as the amount to be paid to the nonbreaching party in the event the contract is breached. Liquidated damages clauses are enforced if the damages were difficult to estimate at the time the contract was formed and if the amount stipulated is reasonable. If construed to be a penalty, the clause cannot be enforced.
Rescission and Restitution	1. *Recission*—An action by prompt notice to cancel the contract and return the parties to the positions that they occupied prior to the transaction. Available when fraud, a mistake, duress, or failure of consideration is present. 2. *Restitution*—When a contract is rescinded, both parties must make restitution to each other by returning the goods, property, or money previously conveyed. Restitution prevents the unjust enrichment of the defendant.
Specific Performance	An equitable remedy calling for the performance of the act promised in the contract. Only available in special situations—such as those involving contracts for the sale of unique goods or land—and when monetary damages would be an inadequate remedy. Specific performance is not available as a remedy in breached contracts for personal services.
Reformation	An equitable remedy allowing a contract to be "reformed" or rewritten to reflect the parties' true intentions. Available when an agreement is imperfectly expressed in writing.

❖ Chapter Summary: Breach and Remedies—Continued

Quasi-Contractual Recovery	An equitable theory imposed by the courts to obtain justice and prevent unjust enrichment in a situation in which no enforceable contract exists. The party seeking recovery must show the following: 1. A benefit was conferred on the other party. 2. The party conferring the benefit did so with the expectation of being paid. 3. The benefit was not volunteered. 4. Retaining the benefit without paying for it would result in the unjust enrichment of the party receiving the benefit.
ELECTION OF REMEDIES, WAIVER OF BREACH, AND CONTRACT PROVISIONS LIMITING REMEDIES	
Election of Remedies	1. *Under the common law*—A nonbreaching party must choose one remedy from those available. This election-of-remedies doctrine prevents double recovery. 2. *Under the UCC*—In contracts for the sale of goods, the doctrine of election of remedies has been eliminated; remedies are cumulative.
Waiver of Breach	A waiver is a knowing relinquishment of a legal right. If a party repeatedly accepts defective performance from the other party to the contract, this pattern of conduct operates as a waiver of the right to full performance—unless notice is given that full performance is expected in the future. The waiver prevents the nonbreaching party from calling the contract to an end or rescinding the contract, but the nonbreaching party can recover damages caused by defective performance.
Limitation of Remedies	A contract may provide that no damages (or only a limited amount of damages) can be recovered in the event the contract is breached. Clauses excluding liability for fraudulent or intentional injury or for illegal acts cannot be enforced. Clauses excluding liability for negligence may be enforced if both parties hold roughly equal bargaining power. Under the UCC, in contracts for the sale of goods, contract provisions may be included that limit the nonbreaching party to a sole or exclusive remedy (such as repair and/or replacement of parts). Such clauses are normally enforceable.

❖ Questions and Case Problems

13-1. Rescission. What is the difference between mutual rescission and unilateral rescission? In what kinds of situations will the remedy of rescission and restitution be granted?

13-2. Election of Remedies. What is the rationale underlying the doctrine of election of remedies? Why does the doctrine sometimes result in harsh effects? Does the UCC accept or reject the doctrine?

13-3. Specific Performance. Discuss fully which of the following breach of contract situations warrant specific performance as a remedy.

(a) Tarrington contracts to sell her house and lot to Rainier. Then, on finding another buyer willing to pay a higher purchase price, she refuses to deed the property to Rainier.

(b) Marita contracts to sing and dance in Horace's nightclub for one month, beginning June 1. She then refuses to perform.

(c) Juan contracts to purchase a rare coin owned by Edmund, as Edmund is breaking up his coin collection. At the last minute, Edmund decides to keep his coin collection intact and refuses to deliver the coin to Juan.

(d) There are three shareholders of Astro Computer Corp.: Coase, who owns 48 percent of the stock; De Valle, who owns 48 percent; and Cary, who owns 4 percent. Cary contracts to sell his 4 percent to De Valle but later refuses to transfer the shares to him.

13-4. Measure of Damages. Johnson contracted to lease a house to Fox for $700 a month, beginning October 1. Fox stipulated in the contract that before he moved in, the interior of the house had to be completely repainted. On September 9, Johnson hired Keever to do the required painting for $1,000. He told Keever that the painting had to be finished by October 1 but did not explain why. On September 28, Keever quit for no reason, having completed approximately 80 percent of the work. Johnson then paid Sam $300 to finish the painting, but Sam did not finish until October 4. Fox, when the painting had not been completed as stipulated in his contract with Johnson, leased another home. Johnson found another tenant who would lease the property at $700 a month, beginning October 15. Johnson then sued Keever for breach of contract, claiming damages of $650. This amount included the $300 Johnson paid Sam to finish the painting and $350 for rent for the first half of October, which Johnson had lost as a result of Keever's breach. Johnson had not yet paid Keever anything for Keever's work. Can Johnson collect the $650 from Keever? Explain.

13-5. Measure of Damages. Ben owns and operates a famous candy store. He makes most of the candy sold in the store, and business is particularly heavy during the Christmas season. Ben contracts with Sweet, Inc., to purchase 10,000 pounds of sugar, to be delivered on or before November 15. Ben informs Sweet that this particular order is to be used for the Christmas season business. Because of production problems, the sugar is not tendered to Ben until December 10, at which time Ben refuses the order because it is so late. Ben has been unable to purchase the quantity of sugar needed to meet the Christmas orders and has had to turn down numerous regular customers, some of whom have indicated that they will purchase candy elsewhere in the future. The sugar that Ben has been able to purchase has cost him 10 cents per pound above Sweet's price. Ben sues Sweet for breach of contract, claiming as damages the higher price paid for the sugar from others, lost profits from this year's lost Christmas sales, future lost profits from customers who have indicated that they will discontinue doing business with him, and punitive damages for failure to meet the contracted-for delivery date. Sweet claims Ben is limited to compensatory damages only. Discuss who is correct and why.

13-6. Mitigation of Damages. Ballard was working for El Dorado Tire Co. He was discharged, and he sued El Dorado for breach of the employment contract. The trial court awarded damages to Ballard, and El Dorado appealed. In the appeal, El Dorado claimed that the trial court had failed to reduce Ballard's damages by the amount that he might have earned in other employment during the remainder of the period covered by the breached contract. El Dorado introduced as evidence the fact that there was an extremely low rate of unemployment for professional technicians and managers with Ballard's qualifications. The implication was that Ballard had not taken advantage of the opportunity to mitigate his damages. Was El Dorado correct? Explain. [*Ballard v. El Dorado Tire Co.*, 512 F.2d 901 (5th Cir. 1975)]

13-7. Consequential Damages. Kerr Steamship Co. delivered to RCA a twenty-nine-word, coded message to be sent to Kerr's agent in Manila. The message included instructions on loading cargo onto one of Kerr's vessels. Kerr's profits on the carriage of the cargo were to be about $6,600. RCA mislaid the coded message, and it was never sent. Kerr sued RCA for the $6,600 in profits that it lost because RCA failed to send the message. Can Kerr recover? Explain. [*Kerr Steamship Co. v. Radio Corp. of America*, 245 N.Y. 284, 157 N.E. 140 (1927)]

13-8. Liquidated Damages versus Penalties. Dewerff was a teacher and basketball coach for Unified School District No. 315. The employment contract included a clause that read, in part: "Penalty for breaking contracts: . . . In all cases where a teacher under contract fails to honor the full term of his or her contract, a lump sum of $400 is to be collected if the contract is broken before August 1." Dewerff resigned on June 28, 1978, and he was told that the school would accept his resignation upon his payment of the $400 stipulated in the contract. When Dewerff refused to make the $400 payment, the school district sued for $400 as "liquidated damages" on the basis of the contract clause. Dewerff argued that the contract provision was a "penalty" clause and unenforceable in this situation. Is Dewerff correct? Discuss. [*Unified School District No. 315, Thomas County v. Dewerff*, 6 Kan.App.2d 77, 626 P.2d 1206 (1981)]

13-9. Limitation of Liability. Westinghouse Electric Corp. entered into a contract with New Jersey Electric to manufacture and install a turbine generator for producing electricity. The contract price was over $10 million. The parties engaged in three years of negotiations and bargaining before they agreed on a suitable contract. The ultimate contract provided, among other things, that Westinghouse would not be liable for any injuries to the property belonging to the utility or to its customers or employees. Westinghouse warranted only that it would repair any defects in workmanship and materials appearing within one year of installation. After installation, part of New Jersey Electric's plant was damaged and several of its employees were injured because of a defect in the turbine. New Jersey Electric sued Westinghouse, claiming that Westinghouse was liable for the damages because the exculpatory provisions in the contract were unconscionable. What was the result? [*Royal Indemnity Co. v. Westinghouse Electric Corp.*, 385 F.Supp. 520 (S.D.N.Y. 1974)]

13-10. **Liquidated Damages.** Vrgora, a general contractor, entered into a contract with the Los Angeles Unified School District (LAUSD) to construct an "automotive service shed" and an enclosed room outfitted with an electronic vehicle performance tester. The contract specified a price of $167,195.09, a completion time of 250 days from commencement, and a liquidated damages clause of $100 per day for late completion. Vrgora began construction on January 31, 1977, with an expected completion date of July 29, 1977. Delays in the project arose when the manufacturer of the tester did not receive approval for the tester until September 23, 1977 (a delay of over six months). The tester arrived on November 15, 1977, but because of a conflict over its payment, the manufacturer removed the tester. Upon payment, the manufacturer redelivered the tester on December 2, 1977, and Vrgora completed the project on May 2, 1978. LAUSD assessed $20,700 as liquidated damages and eventually brought an action against Vrgora to collect the assessed damages, which Vrgora refused to pay. Given the circumstances of this case, will the court require Vrgora to pay the liquidated damages demanded by LAUSD? [*Vrgora v. Los Angeles Unified School District*, 152 Cal.App.3d 1178, 200 Cal.Rptr. 130 (1984)]

13-11. Limitation of Liability. Patricia Elsken leased an apartment in a large apartment complex. She signed a "Residential Alarm Security Agreement" in which she agreed to have security services provided by Network Multi-Family Security Corp. The contract contained a clause limiting Network's liability to $250 for any injury or damage caused by a failure of the alarm service or by Network's negligent performance. The agreement stated, in capital letters, that Network was not an insurer and that "resident assumes all responsibility for obtaining insurance to cover losses of all types." The agreement also provided that "[r]esident may obtain from Network increased liability by paying an additional charge directly to Network." Network received an alarm signal indicating intrusion into Elsken's apartment at 10:33 A.M. on April 11, 1988. Network called Elsken's apartment and, receiving no answer, called the apartment manager instead of going to Elsken's apartment. The manager told Network to disregard the alarm.

Later that day, Elsken was found dead in her apartment, the victim of an apparent homicide. The administrator of Elsken's estate brought an action for damages against Network, alleging negligence. Will the court hold that the contractual limitation of liability for personal injury is valid and enforceable? Discuss. [*Elsken v. Network Multi-Family Security Corp.*, 838 P.2d 1007 (Okla. 1992)]

A QUESTION OF ETHICS AND SOCIAL RESPONSIBILITY

13-12. *Robert Ryan, a widower with a ninth-grade education, fell behind in his mortgage payments and in April 1984 faced foreclosure. In May 1984, Norman Weiner, whom Ryan had never met, called on Ryan at his home and told Ryan that he could loan him money to help him keep his house if Ryan signed over the deed to the house as "security" for the loan. When he left, he took Ryan's deed to the property with him for "safekeeping." The next day, Weiner drove Ryan to a lawyer's office, where Ryan signed several papers. Ryan signed the papers without reading them, believing that he was signing loan documents, because he trusted Weiner. In fact, he had signed documents that conveyed ownership of his house to Weiner. Weiner brought the mortgage payments up to date and continued to make the payments on the house. Weiner also paid for electricity and other utilities and services necessary to maintain the house. Ryan continued to live in the house and made monthly payments to Weiner. The payments steadily increased from $100 to $310 a month. During that time, the mortgage payments increased also, from $93 in 1984 to $120 in 1991. In May 1991, Ryan concluded that he had paid off his mortgage and also his "loan" from Weiner and refused to make further payments. When Weiner initiated legal proceedings to evict Ryan, Ryan sought to rescind his transfer of the deed to Weiner. Based on these facts, answer the following questions.* [Ryan v. Weiner, *610 A.2d 1377 (Del. 1992)*]

1. In view of the fact that Ryan voluntarily signed a document (contract) conveying his property to Weiner, should he be allowed to rescind that contract? What public policies are in conflict here?
2. When the equitable remedy of rescission and restitution is granted, the parties are restored to their status quo prior to the contract's formation. Is it possible to restore the parties to their status quo as of May 1984 in this case? Discuss.

CASE BRIEFING ASSIGNMENT

13-13. *Examine Case* A.6 [Potter v. Oster, *426 N.W.2d 148 (Iowa 1988)*] *in Appendix* A. *The case has been excerpted there in great detail. Review and then brief the case, making sure that you include answers to the following questions in your brief.*

1. Why was Oster appealing the trial court's decision?
2. Why did Oster assert that allowing the remedy of rescission and restitution in this case would lead to an inequitable result?
3. According to the court, what three requirements must be met before rescission will be granted?
4. Did the Potters meet these three requirements, and if so, why?
5. What reasons did the court give for its conclusion that remedies at law were inadequate in this case?
6. Why are remedies at law presumed inadequate for breach of real estate contracts?

FOR CRITICAL ANALYSIS

13-14. *Review the discussion of "Election of Remedies" in this chapter. Do you think that it is fair to an innocent (nonbreaching) party to a contract that he or she can only pursue one remedy? What are some of the advantages and disadvantages of this doctrine?*

Unit Three

Commercial Transactions

❖ Why We Study the Uniform Commercial Code

This unit deals primarily with the Uniform Commercial Code (UCC), the official text of which (with comments) is more than seven hundred pages long. It is probably the most sweeping in scope of any law codification in the United States. As you will read in the *Landmark in the Law* in Chapter 14, the UCC contains rules that deal with all of the phases that ordinarily arise in the handling of a commercial transaction. An understanding of the fundamental rules governing such transactions is imperative for anyone contemplating a career in business. Because the UCC is the general and inclusive group of laws adopted by virtually all the states, it is impossible for a person to be in the business world without coming into contact with some aspect of the UCC.

Chapter 14 opens the unit with a discussion of the requirements of sales contracts and how they are formed. The sometimes sticky concept of when title passes and who bears the risk of loss for goods in the process of being sold—for example, goods en route from the seller to the buyer—is examined in Chapter 15. The performance and obligations required under sales contracts are then discussed in Chapter 16, as well as the remedies available to a buyer or seller when a sales contract is breached. A sale of goods usually carries with it at least one type of warranty. Additionally, the manufacture and sale of products may subject the manufacturers and sellers to liability. These topics—sales warranties and product liability—are covered in Chapter 17. Chapters 18 and 19 discuss the rights and liabilities of parties to commercial paper, including checks, drafts, promissory notes, and certificates of deposits. In Chapter 20, we look closely at checks and the banking system, as well as at the rights and duties of banks and their customers in regard to electronic fund transfers. Few creditors would loan money without some kind of assurance of repayment. For this reason, lenders frequently require loan applicants to pledge some form of collateral, or security, for loans. Secured transactions are the focus of Chapter 21. The unit concludes with Chapter 22, which examines the rights of debtors and creditors both under the common law and under the Bankruptcy Code.

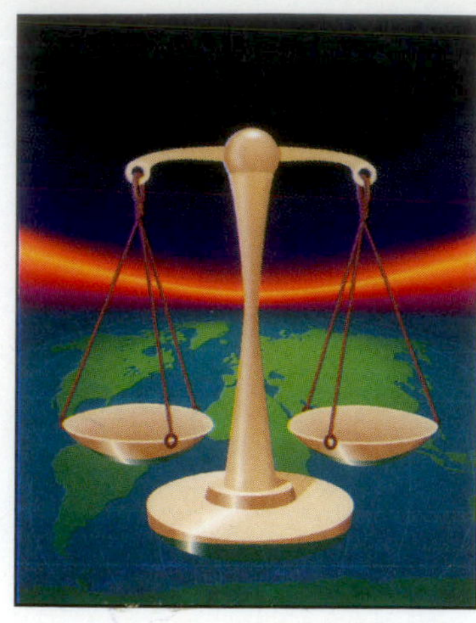

Chapter 14

The Formation of Sales Contracts

"The great object of the law is to encourage commerce."

J. Chambre, 1739–1823
(British jurist)

When we focus on sales contracts, we move away from common law principles and into the area of statutory law. As discussed in the unit introduction, state statutory law governing sales transactions is based on the Uniform Commercial Code (UCC). It qualifies as one of the most voluminous legal codifications ever created in this nation. The opening quotation states that the object of the law is to encourage commerce. This is particularly the case with the UCC. Despite its great volume, the UCC does not hinder commercial transactions but rather facilitates them by making the laws governing the purchase and sale of goods clearer, simpler, and more readily applicable to the numerous difficulties that can arise during such transactions. Because of its importance in the discussion of sales contracts that follows, excerpts from the most recent version of the Uniform Commercial Code have been included as Appendix C in this text. It is also the subject of this chapter's *Landmark in the Law.*

❖ The Sale of Goods—Article 2

SALES CONTRACT
A contract by means of which the ownership of goods is transferred from a seller to a buyer for a fixed price in money, paid or agreed to be paid by the buyer.

No body of law operates in a vacuum. A **sales contract** is governed by the common law principles applicable to all contracts—offer, acceptance, consideration, capacity, and legality—and you should reexamine these principles when studying sales. The law of sales is based both on Article 2 of the UCC and on the relevant common law that has not been modified by the UCC.

Keep in mind two things. First, Article 2 deals with the sale of *goods;* it does not deal with real property (real estate), services, or intangible property such as stocks and bonds. Second, in some cases, the rules may vary quite a bit, depending on whether the buyer or the seller is a *merchant.*

It is always a good idea to note the subject matter of a dispute and the kind of parties involved. If the subject is goods, the UCC governs. If it is real estate or services, common law applies. The relationship between general contract law and the law governing sales of goods is illustrated in Exhibit 14–1.

What Is a Sale?

Section 2–102 of the UCC states that Article 2 "applies to transactions in goods." This implies a broad scope—covering leases, gifts, bailments (temporary deliveries of personal property), and purchases of goods. In this chapter, however, we treat Article 2 as being applicable only to an actual sale (as would most authorities and

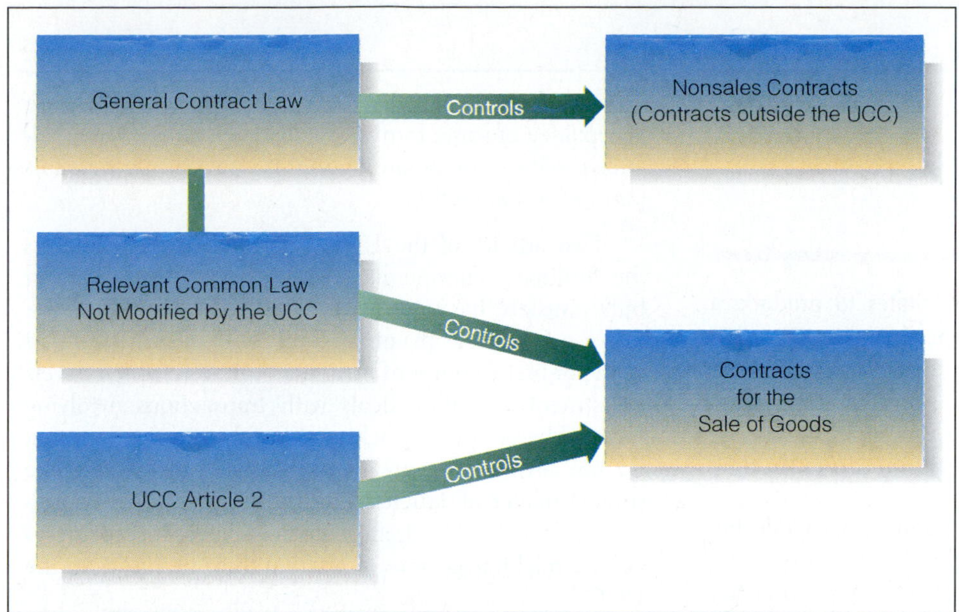

◆ **Exhibit 14–1**
Law Governing Contracts
This exhibit graphically illustrates the relationship between general contract law and the law governing sales of goods contracts. Sales contracts are not governed exclusively by Article 2 of the Uniform Commercial Code but also by general contract law whenever it is relevant and has not been modified by the UCC.

courts).[1] A **sale** is officially defined as "the passing of title from the seller to the buyer for a price," where title refers to the formal right of ownership of property [UCC 2–106(1)]. The price may be payable in money or in other goods, services, or realty (real estate).

SALE
The passing of title from the seller to the buyer for a price.

What Are Goods?

To be characterized as a *good*, the item of property must be *tangible*, and it must be *movable*. **Tangible property** has physical existence—it can be touched or seen. Intangible property—such as corporate stocks and bonds, patents and copyrights, and ordinary contract rights—have only conceptual existence and thus do not come under Article 2. A *movable* item can be carried from place to place. Hence, real estate is excluded from Article 2.

TANGIBLE PROPERTY
Property that has physical existence and can be distinguished by the senses of touch, sight, and so on. A car is tangible property; a patent right is intangible property.

Two areas of dispute arise in determining whether the object of the contract is goods and thus whether Article 2 is applicable. One problem concerns *goods associated with realty*, such as crops or timber, and the other concerns contracts involving a combination of *goods and services*.

Goods associated with real estate often fall within the scope of Article 2. Section 2–107 provides the following rules:

1. A contract for the sale of minerals or the like (including oil and gas) or a structure (such as a building) is a contract for the sale of goods *if severance, or separation, is to be made by the seller.* If the *buyer* is to sever (separate) the minerals or structures from the land, the contract is considered to be a sale of real estate governed by the principles of real property law, not the UCC.
2. A sale of growing crops or timber to be cut is a contract for the sale of goods *regardless of who severs them.*
3. Other "things attached" to realty but capable of severance without material harm to the land are considered goods *regardless of who severs them.*[2] Examples of

1. Recently, a codification of the law with respect to leases of goods has been incorporated into the UCC as Article 2A.
2. The Code avoids the term *fixtures* here because of the numerous definitions of the word. A fixture is anything so firmly or permanently attached to land or to a building as to become a part of it. Once personal property becomes a fixture, it is governed by real estate law. See Chapter 34.

Landmark in the Law

The Uniform Commercial Code

Of all the attempts in the United States to produce a uniform body of laws relating to commercial transactions, none has been as comprehensive or successful as the Uniform Commercial Code (UCC). The Code was the brainchild of William A. Schnader, president of the National Conference of Commissioners on Uniform State Laws (NCC).

The drafting of the Uniform Commercial Code began in 1945. The most significant individual involved in the project was its chief editor, Karl N. Llewellyn of the Columbia University Law School. Llewellyn's intellect, continuous efforts, and ability to compromise made the first draft of the UCC (1949) a legal landmark. Over the next several years, the UCC was reviewed and substantially accepted by every state in the Union (except Louisiana, which accepted only parts of it).

The UCC attempts to provide a consistent and integrated framework of rules to deal with all phases *ordinarily arising* in a commercial sales transaction from start to finish. Consider, for example, the following events, all of which may be involved in a single sales transaction.

1. A commercial transaction might involve a contract for the sale of goods followed by the actual sale. Article 2 of the UCC examines all the facets of this transaction.
2. The transaction might also involve a check given in payment of all or part of the purchase price of the goods. The check will be negotiated and will pass through one or more banks for collection. Article 3, on commercial paper, and Article 4, on bank deposits and collections, cover this part of the transaction.
3. Suppose that the goods purchased are shipped or stored. Then they may be covered by a warehouse receipt. Article 7, on documents of title, deals with this subject.
4. Suppose further that the transaction involves the acceptance of some form of security for a remaining balance owed. Article 9, on secured transactions, covers this part of the transaction.

Two articles of the UCC seemingly do not address the "ordinary" commercial sales transaction. Article 6, on bulk transfers, has to do with merchants who sell off the major part of their inventory. Such bulk sales are not part of the ordinary course of business. Article 8, which covers investment securities, deals with transactions involving negotiable securities (stocks and bonds), transactions that do not involve the sale of or payment for *goods*. The subject matter of Articles 6 and 8, however, was considered by the UCC's drafters to be related *sufficiently* to commercial transactions to warrant their inclusion in the UCC.

Various sections and articles of the UCC are periodically changed or supplemented to clarify certain rules or to establish new rules when changes in business customs render the existing UCC provisions inapplicable. Because of the importance of leases of goods in the commercial context, Article 2A, governing leases, was added to the UCC. To clarify the rights of parties to commercial fund transfers, particularly electronic fund transfers, Article 4A was issued. Articles 3 and 4, on commercial paper, recently underwent a significant revision. Because of other changes in business and in the law, the NCC has recommended the repeal of Article 6, offering a revised Article 6 to those states that prefer not to repeal it. These new and revised articles are all included in Appendix C, which presents the excerpts from the UCC. At present, a revision of Article 2, on sales transactions, is in its initial stages. Since its promulgation as part of the UCC over three decades ago, Article 2 has remained virtually unchanged. Yet business practices have not—electronic communications systems have significantly changed commercial practices in regard to sales transactions. The revised Article 2 will clarify the law in regard to these new business practices.

"things attached" that are severable without harm to realty are a heater, a window air conditioner in a house, and counters and stools in a restaurant. Thus, removal of one of these things would be considered a sale of goods. The test is whether removal will cause substantial harm to the real property to which the item is attached.

In cases in which goods and services are combined, courts disagree. For example, is the blood furnished to a patient during an operation a "sale of goods" or the "performance of a medical service"? Some courts say it is a good; others say it is a service. Because the UCC does not provide the answer, the courts try to determine which factor is predominant—the good or the service.

The UCC does stipulate, however, that serving food or drink to be consumed either on or off restaurant premises is a "sale of goods," at least for the purpose of an implied warranty of merchantability (to be explained in Chapter 17) [UCC 2–314(1)]. Other special cases are also explicitly characterized as goods by the UCC, including unborn animals and rare coins. Whether the transaction in question involves the sale of goods or services is important because the majority of courts treat services as being excluded by the UCC, in which case the implied warranties of the UCC would not apply. In the following case, the key issue before the court was whether computer programs should be classified as goods or services.

Case 14.1
ADVENT SYSTEMS, LTD. v. UNISYS CORP.
United States Court of Appeals, Third Circuit, 1991.
925 F.2d 670.

HISTORICAL AND TECHNOLOGICAL SETTING *Computer systems consist of hardware and software. Hardware includes a computer's monitor, electronic circuitry, and items such as keyboards and printers. Hardware is a good. Software refers, in part, to the medium that stores computer data, such as a computer diskette or magnetic tape. Software also refers to computer programs, which are codes that tell a computer to perform certain functions. When a program is transposed onto a medium compatible with a computer, it becomes software. In the last fifteen years, the increasing number of cases involving computer products has led to controversy over whether software is a good within the meaning of the UCC. The UCC does not mention software, but the law was designed "to be developed by the courts in the light of unforeseen and new circumstances and practices."[a] Thus, when the UCC is silent on an issue, courts usually interpret it in light of commercial and technological developments. The question as to whether software is a good has stimulated the publication of many law review articles, most of them expressing the view that software is within the UCC's definition of a "good."*

FACTS Advent Systems, Ltd., a software producer, developed an electronic document management system through which engineering drawings and similar documents could be transformed into a computer data base. In June 1987, Unisys Corporation agreed with Advent to market the document system in the United States. The agreement, which was to continue for two years, provided that Advent would supply sales and marketing material and personnel, as well as technical personnel to work with Unisys employees in building and installing the document systems. In December 1987, Unisys changed its plans and told Advent that their arrangement had ended. Advent filed a complaint against Unisys, alleging, among other things, breach of contract. As part of its defense, Unisys contended that the agreement involved primarily a sale of goods. Advent argued that software is not a good and that thus the contract was primarily one for services. The trial court agreed with Advent on this issue. Because the court found for Unisys on another issue, both parties appealed.

a. UCC 1–102, Comment 1.

ISSUE Is software a good within the meaning of the UCC?

DECISION Yes. The appellate court reversed the judgment in favor of Advent and remanded the case for a new trial.

REASON The court reasoned that "computer programs are the product of an intellectual process, but once implanted in a medium are widely distributed to computer owners. An analogy can be drawn to a compact disc recording of an orchestral rendition. The music is produced by the artistry of musicians and in itself is not a 'good' but when transferred to a laser-readable disc becomes a readily merchantable commodity." Similarly, a computer program, once transferred to a diskette, is "tangible, moveable and available in the marketplace." The court also reasoned that "applying the UCC to computer software transactions offers substantial benefits to litigants and the courts" and that the importance of computer software to the business world favors its inclusion under the UCC.

Who Is a Merchant?

MERCHANT
Under the UCC, a person who deals in goods of the kind involved in the sales contract. (For additional definitions, see UCC 2–104.)

Article 2 governs the sale of goods in general. It applies to sales transactions between all buyers and sellers. In a limited number of instances, however, the UCC presumes that in certain phases of sales transactions involving **merchants,** special business standards ought to be imposed because of the merchants' relatively high degree of commercial expertise.[3] Such standards do not apply to the casual or inexperienced seller or buyer ("consumer"). Section 2–104 defines three ways in which *merchant* status can arise:

1. A merchant is a person who *deals in goods of the kind* involved in the sales contract. Thus, a retailer, a wholesaler, or a manufacturer is a merchant of those goods sold in the business. A merchant for one type of goods is not necessarily a merchant for another type. For example, a sporting-equipment retailer is a merchant when selling tennis equipment but not when selling stereo equipment.
2. A merchant is a person who, by occupation, *holds himself or herself out as having knowledge and skill unique to the practices or goods involved in the transaction.* This broad definition may include banks or universities as merchants.
3. A person who *employs a merchant as a broker, agent, or other intermediary* has the status of merchant in that transaction. Hence, if a "gentleman farmer" who ordinarily does not run the farm hires a broker to purchase or sell livestock, the farmer is considered a merchant in the transaction.

In summary, a person is a merchant when he or she, acting in a mercantile capacity, possesses or uses an expertise specifically related to the goods being sold. This basic distinction is not always clear-cut. For example, courts in some states have determined that farmers may be merchants, while courts in other states have determined that it was not within the contemplation of the drafters of the UCC to include farmers as merchants.

Whether a farmer is a merchant is at issue in the following case. The question is significant because if the farmer is deemed a merchant, then an oral contract for the sale of corn will be subject to the "between merchants" provisions of the UCC. As will be discussed later in this chapter, in sales contracts between merchants, a memorandum confirming an oral contract will suffice as a writing under the UCC Statute of Frauds if the merchant receiving the memorandum fails to object to its provisions, in writing, within ten days.

Case 14.2

COLORADO-KANSAS GRAIN CO. v. REIFSCHNEIDER

Colorado Court of Appeals, 1991.
817 P.2d 637.

HISTORICAL AND SOCIAL SETTING *In Alabama, Arkansas, Iowa, Kansas, South Dakota, and Utah, the courts have held that the drafters of the UCC did not contemplate that a farmer would be considered a "merchant." The courts in Indiana, Michigan, Missouri, Nebraska, Ohio, Illinois, and Texas have determined that a farmer may be a merchant. In those states, however, not all farmers have been considered merchants in all circumstances. In deciding the issue, the courts consider the following and other relevant factors: (1) the length of time the farmer has been engaged in the practice of selling the particular product to the marketers of the product; (2) the degree of business acumen shown by the farmer in dealings with other parties; (3) the farmer's awareness of the operation and existence of farm markets; and (4) the farmer's past experience with, or knowledge of, the customs and practices that are unique to the particular marketing of the product. A farmer does not need to have grown and sold a particular crop in the past to be considered a merchant regarding that crop. In one case, for example, a farmer who conceded that he was a merchant as to corn claimed that his lack of experience in growing and selling soybeans precluded a finding that he was a merchant in soybeans. The court disagreed, reasoning that both are grains and may be considered "goods of the same kind."*[a]

a. *Continental Grain Co. v. Harbach*, 400 F.Supp. 695 (N.D.Ill. 1975).

---

3. The provisions that apply only to merchants deal principally with the Statute of Frauds, firm offers, confirmatory memoranda, warranties, and contract modification. These special rules reflect expedient business practices commonly known to merchants in the commercial setting. They will be discussed later in this chapter.

Case 14.2—Continued

FACTS Albert Reifschneider was raised on a farm and had been in the business of selling corn and in the business of selling other crops under futures contracts (contracts for goods to be harvested in the future) for twenty years. In April 1988, Reifschneider orally agreed to sell Colorado-Kansas Grain Company 12,500 bushels of corn after the harvest in the fall. The company sent Reifschneider a written confirmation of the agreement with instructions to sign it and return it. In June, Reifschneider told the company that he would not sign the confirmation and that no contract existed between the parties. The company demanded that Reifschneider deliver the corn, but the demand was to no avail. The company sued Reifschneider for breach of contract. The trial court held for the company, based in part on the court's conclusion that Reifschneider was a "merchant" within the meaning of the UCC. Reifschneider appealed.

ISSUE Should Reifschneider be considered a merchant under the UCC?

DECISION Yes. The appellate court affirmed the trial court's decision that Reifschneider was a merchant.

REASON The court noted that whether a farmer has merchant status under the UCC is a question that has divided the courts. The court also noted that "the cases which hold that farmers may be merchants reflect on the fact that today's farmer is involved in far more than simply planting and harvesting crops. Indeed, many farmers possess an extensive knowledge and sophistication regarding the purchase and sale of crops on the various agricultural markets. Often, they are more aptly described as agri-businessmen." In the court's opinion, Reifschneider met the UCC's criteria for merchant status. His long experience in selling corn established that he was a "person who deals in goods of the kind." Furthermore, his extensive experience in selling other crops under futures contracts supported the trial court's finding that Reifschneider, "by his occupation [held] himself out as having knowledge or skill peculiar to the practices or goods involved in the transaction."

❖ The Sales Contract

The policy of the UCC is to recognize that the law of sales is part of the general law of contracts. The UCC often restates general principles. In situations not covered by the UCC, the common law of contracts and applicable state statutes govern. The following sections summarize the ways that UCC provisions *change* the effect of the general law of contracts. It is important to remember that parties to sales contracts are free to establish whatever terms they wish. The UCC comes into play when the parties have not, in their contract, provided for a contingency that later gives rise to a dispute. The UCC makes this very clear time and again by its use of phrases such as "Unless the parties otherwise agree" or "Absent a contrary agreement by the parties."

The Offer

In general contract law, the moment a definite offer is met by an unqualified acceptance, a binding contract is formed. In commercial sales transactions, the verbal exchanges, the correspondence, and the actions of the parties may not reveal exactly when a binding contractual obligation arises. The UCC states that an agreement sufficient to constitute a contract can exist even if the moment of its making is undetermined [UCC 2–204(2)].

Open Terms According to contract law, an offer must be definite enough for the parties (and the courts) to ascertain its essential terms when it is accepted. The UCC states that a sales contract will not fail for indefiniteness even if one or more terms are left open as long as (1) the parties intended to make a contract and (2) there is a reasonably certain basis for the court to grant an appropriate remedy [UCC 2–204(3)].

Although the UCC has radically lessened the requirements for definiteness of essentials in contracts of sale, it has not removed the common law requirement that the contract be at least definite enough for the court to identify the agreement, so as to enforce the contract or award appropriate damages in the event of breach.

Keep in mind that the more terms left open, the less likely the courts will find that the parties intended to form a contract.

Open Price Term If the parties have not agreed on a price, the court will determine a "reasonable price *at the time for delivery*" [UCC 2–305(1)]. If either the buyer or the seller is to determine the price, the price is to be fixed in good faith [UCC 2–305(2)].

Sometimes the price fails to be fixed through the fault of one of the parties. In that case, the other party can treat the contract as canceled or fix a reasonable price. For example, Johnson and Merrick enter into a contract for the sale of goods and agree that Johnson will fix the price. Johnson refuses to fix the price. Merrick can either treat the contract as canceled or set a reasonable price [UCC 2–305(3)].

Open Payment Term When parties do not specify payment terms, payment is due at the time and place at which the buyer is to receive the goods [UCC 2–310(a)]. The buyer can tender payment using any commercially normal or acceptable means, such as a check or credit card. If the seller demands payment in cash, however, the buyer must be given a reasonable time to obtain it [UCC 2–511(2)]. This is especially important when a definite and final time for performance is stated in the contract.

Open Delivery Term When no delivery terms are specified, the buyer normally takes delivery at the seller's place of business [UCC 2–308(a)]. If the seller has no place of business, the seller's residence is used. When goods are located in some other place and both parties know it, delivery is made there. If the time for shipment or delivery is not clearly specified in the sales contract, the court infers a "reasonable" time for performance [UCC 2–309(1)].

Duration of an Ongoing Contract A single contract might specify successive performances but not indicate how long the parties are required to deal with one another. Although either party may terminate the ongoing contractual relationship, principles of good faith and sound commercial practice call for reasonable notification before termination so as to give the other party reasonable time to seek a substitute arrangement [UCC 2–309(2), (3)].

Options and Cooperation Regarding Performance When specific shipping arrangements have not been made but the contract contemplates shipment of the goods, the *seller* has the right to make these arrangements in good faith, using commercial reasonableness in the situation [UCC 2–311]. (Good faith and commercial reasonableness are discussed in this chapter's *Ethical Perspective.*)

When terms relating to the assortment of goods are omitted from a sales contract, the *buyer* can specify the assortment. For example, Marconi's Dental Supply and Powers contract for the sale of 1,000 toothbrushes. The toothbrushes come in a variety of colors, but the contract does not specify color. Powers, the buyer, has the right to take 600 blue toothbrushes and 400 green ones if he wishes. Powers must make the selection in good faith and use commercial reasonability [UCC 2–311].

REQUIREMENTS CONTRACT
An agreement under which a promisor promises to supply the promisee with all the goods and/or services the promisee might require from period to period.

Open Quantity Term Normally, if the parties do not specify a quantity, a court will have no basis for determining a remedy. The UCC recognizes two exceptions in requirements and output contracts [UCC 2–306(1)]. In a **requirements contract,** the buyer agrees to purchase and the seller agrees to sell all or up to a stated amount of what the buyer *needs* or *requires.* There is implicit consideration in a requirements contract, for the buyer gives up the right to buy from any other seller, and this forfeited right creates a legal detriment. Requirements contracts are common in the business world and are normally enforceable. If, however, the buyer promises to purchase only if the buyer *wishes* to do so, or if the buyer reserves the right to buy the goods from someone other than the seller, the promise is illusory (without consideration), and the promise is unenforceable by either party.

In an **output contract,** the seller agrees to sell and the buyer agrees to buy all or up to a stated amount of what the seller *produces*. Again, because the seller essentially forfeits the right to sell goods to another buyer, there is implicit consideration in an output contract.

OUTPUT CONTRACT
A binding agreement in which a seller agrees to deliver/sell the seller's output of a good (an unspecified amount at the time of agreement) to a buyer, and the buyer agrees to buy all the goods supplied.

The UCC imposes a *good faith limitation* on requirements and output contracts. The quantity under such contracts is the amount of requirements or the amount of output that occurs during a *normal* production year. The actual quantity purchased or sold cannot be unreasonably disproportionate to normal or comparable prior requirements or output [UCC 2–306].

Merchant's Firm Offer The **firm offer** is in the category of rules applicable only to merchants. Under regular contract principles, an offer can be revoked at any time before acceptance. The major common law exception is an *option contract* (discussed in Chapter 9), in which the offeree pays consideration for the offeror's irrevocable promise to keep the offer open for a stated period.

FIRM OFFER
An offer (by a merchant) that is irrevocable without consideration for a period of time (not longer than three months). A firm offer by a merchant must be in writing and must be signed by the offeror.

The UCC creates another exception, which applies only to firm offers for the sale of goods made by a merchant (regardless of whether or not the offeree is a merchant). If the merchant-offeror gives *assurances* in a *signed writing* that the offer will remain open, the merchant's firm offer is irrevocable without the necessity of consideration[4] for the stated period or, if no definite period is stated, a reasonable period (neither to exceed three months) [UCC 2–205].

It is necessary that the offer be both *written* and *signed* by the offeror.[5] When a firm offer is contained in a form contract prepared by the offeree, a *separate* firm offer assurance must be signed also. The purpose of the merchant's firm offer rule is to give effect to a merchant's deliberate intent to be bound to a firm offer. If the firm offer is buried amid copious language in one of the pages of the offeree's form contract, the offeror might inadvertently sign the contract without realizing that there is a firm offer, thus defeating the purpose of the rule.

Acceptance

The following sections examine the UCC's provisions governing acceptance. As you will see, acceptance of an offer to buy or sell goods generally may be made in any reasonable manner and by any reasonable means.

Methods of Acceptance The general common law rule is that an offeror can specify, or authorize, a particular means of acceptance, making that means the only one effective for contract formation. The rule has been altered recently, however, so that even unauthorized means of communication are effective as long as the acceptance is received by the specified deadline. For example, suppose the offer states, "Answer by fax within five days." If the offeree sends a letter, and the offeror receives it within five days, a valid contract is formed. (For a review of the requirements relating to mode and timeliness of acceptance, see Chapter 9.)

No consid. pd. for firm offer

4. If the offeree pays consideration, then an option contract (not a merchant's firm offer) is formed.
5. "Signed" includes any symbol executed or adopted by a party with a present intention to authenticate a writing [UCC 1–201(39)]. A complete signature is not required. Therefore initials, a thumbprint, a trade name, or any mark used in lieu of a written signature will suffice, regardless of its location on the document.

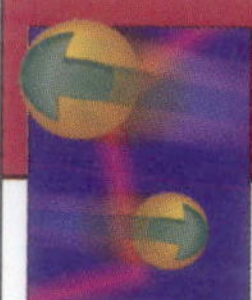

Ethical Perspective

Good Faith and Commercial Reasonableness

The concepts of *good faith* and *commercial reasonableness* permeate the Uniform Commercial Code. Good faith and commercial reasonableness are read into every contract and impose certain duties on all parties. The concept of good faith implies that one party will not take advantage of another party by manipulating contract terms. Good faith means that honesty in fact is a condition *precedent* to a contract, and good faith exists if a party can meet the subjective test of innocence—sometimes called the "pure heart and empty head" test—when entering into the contract. Merchants are also held to an objective standard of observing reasonable commercial practices, and good faith in the case of a merchant means honesty in fact *and* the observance of reasonable commercial standards of fair dealing in the trade [UCC 2–103(1)(b)].

The obligation of good faith is particularly important in requirements and output contracts. Requirements contracts often provide that the buyer purchase all of his or her needs for a specific good from the seller. An output contract often provides that the buyer purchase the seller's entire output. Without the obligation of good faith, it is clear that the potential for abuse would be tremendous. If, for example, the cost of producing the good that is the subject of a requirements contract suddenly increases and the market price of the good unexpectedly quadruples, the buyer could claim that his or her needs are now equivalent to the entire output of the seller. Then, after buying all the seller's output at a price that is substantially below the market price, the buyer could turn around and resell the goods that are not needed for his or her own use at the new, higher market price.

Under the UCC, this type of unethical behavior is prohibited. Even though contracts that call for the buyer to purchase all of his or her needs from the seller are explicitly authorized under the UCC, such contracts are construed to involve actual requirements that may occur in good faith. Under UCC 2–306(1), no quantity "unreasonably disproportionate to any stated estimate or in the absence of a stated estimate to any normal or otherwise comparable prior output or requirements may be tendered or demanded." Thus, the UCC reflects ethical considerations in prohibiting the abuse of such contracts.

The concept of commercial reasonableness means not only that sellers and buyers are expected to perform contracts in a reasonable manner but also that performance may be excused when circumstances render performance unreasonable or impracticable. The doctrine of commercial impracticability, discussed in Chapters 12 and 16, relies on a theory of reasonability. The fact that the word *reasonable* appears about ninety times in Article 2 of the UCC demonstrates the UCC's opposition to imposing undue hardship upon merchants and upon those with whom they deal. A merchant is expected to act in a reasonable manner according to reasonable commercial customs.

Any Reasonable Means When the offeror does not specify a means of acceptance, the UCC provides that acceptance can be made by any means of communication reasonable under the circumstances [UCC 2–206(1)]. For example, Anodyne Corporation writes Bethlehem Industries a letter offering to sell $1,000 worth of goods. The offer states that Anodyne will keep the offer open for only ten days from the date of the letter. Before the ten days have lapsed, Bethlehem sends Anodyne an acceptance by fax. The fax is misdirected by someone at Anodyne's offices and does not reach the right person at Anodyne until after the ten-day deadline has passed. Is a valid contract formed? The answer is probably yes, because acceptance by fax appears to be a commercially reasonable medium of acceptance under the circumstances. Acceptance would be effective upon Bethlehem's transmission of the fax, which occurred before the offer lapsed.

Promise to Ship or Prompt Shipment The UCC permits acceptance of an offer to buy goods for current or prompt shipment by either a *promise* to ship or *prompt shipment* of the goods to the buyer [UCC 2–206(1)(b)]. This provision of the Code retains the common law means of acceptance of an offer (performance by delivery of conforming goods to the carrier) and adds as another means of acceptance the commercial practice of sellers who send promises to ship conforming goods. These promises are effective when sent if they are sent by a medium that is commercially reasonable under the circumstances.

The UCC goes one step further and provides that if the seller does not promise to ship conforming goods but instead ships *nonconforming goods*, this shipment constitutes both an *acceptance* (a contract) and a *breach*. This rule does not apply if the seller seasonably (within a reasonable amount of time) notifies the buyer that the nonconforming shipment is offered only as an accommodation, or as a favor. The notice of accommodation must clearly indicate to the buyer that the shipment does not constitute an acceptance and that, therefore, no contract has been formed.

For example, McIntosh orders 5,000 *blue* widgets from Halderson. Halderson ships 5,000 *black* widgets to McIntosh, notifying McIntosh that, as Halderson only has black widgets in stock, these are sent as an accommodation. The shipment of black widgets is not an acceptance but an offer (usually a counteroffer), and a contract will be formed only if McIntosh accepts the black widgets.

If Halderson ships 5,000 black widgets instead of blue widgets *without* notifying McIntosh that the goods are being shipped *as an accommodation*, Halderson's shipment acts as both an acceptance of McIntosh's offer and a *breach* of the resulting contract. McIntosh may sue Halderson for any appropriate damages.

Notice of Acceptance Under the common law, because a unilateral offer invites acceptance by a performance, the offeree need not notify the offeror of performance unless the offeror would not otherwise know about it. The UCC is more stringent than common law, stating that "[w]here the beginning of requested performance is a reasonable mode of acceptance[,] an offeror who is not notified of acceptance within a reasonable time may treat the offer as having lapsed before acceptance" [UCC 2–206(2)].

For example, Lee writes to Pickwick Book Store on Monday, "Please send me a copy of *West's Best Law Text* for $45, C.O.D.," and signs it, "Lee." Pickwick receives the request on Tuesday and immediately prepares the book for shipment—but does not ship it for four weeks. When the book arrives, Lee rejects it, claiming that it has arrived too late to be of value. In this case, because Lee heard nothing from Pickwick for a month, he was justified in assuming that the store did not intend to deliver *West's Best Law Text*. Lee could consider that the offer had lapsed because of the length of time.

Additional Terms Under the common law, if Alderman makes an offer to Beale, and Beale in turn accepts but adds some slight modification, there is no contract. The so-called *mirror image rule* (which requires that the terms of the acceptance exactly match those of the offer—see Chapter 9) makes Beale's action a rejection of—and a counteroffer to—Alderman's offer.

Variations in terms between the offer and the offeree's acceptance, which violate the mirror image rule, have caused considerable problems in commercial transactions. This is particularly true in contracts involving the sale of goods when different standardized purchase forms of the seller and buyer are exchanged in the process of offer and acceptance. Seldom do the terms of the purchase forms match each other exactly, but often this fact goes unnoticed until problems arise. Say, for example, that a buyer contracts with a seller over the phone to purchase a certain piece of equipment. The parties agree to all of the terms of the sale. The buyer then enters the terms of the agreement on the appropriate form and sends it to the seller. The seller does likewise. Because the parties presume that they have reached an oral agreement on the telephone, discrepancies on their respective forms may go unnoticed. The buyer, for example, may not notice that the seller's form says nothing about a warranty—which is a condition of purchase on the buyer's form. Exhibit 14–2 indicates the kinds of terms and conditions that may be included in a standard purchase order form.

◆ **Exhibit 14–2 An Example of a Purchase Order (Front)**

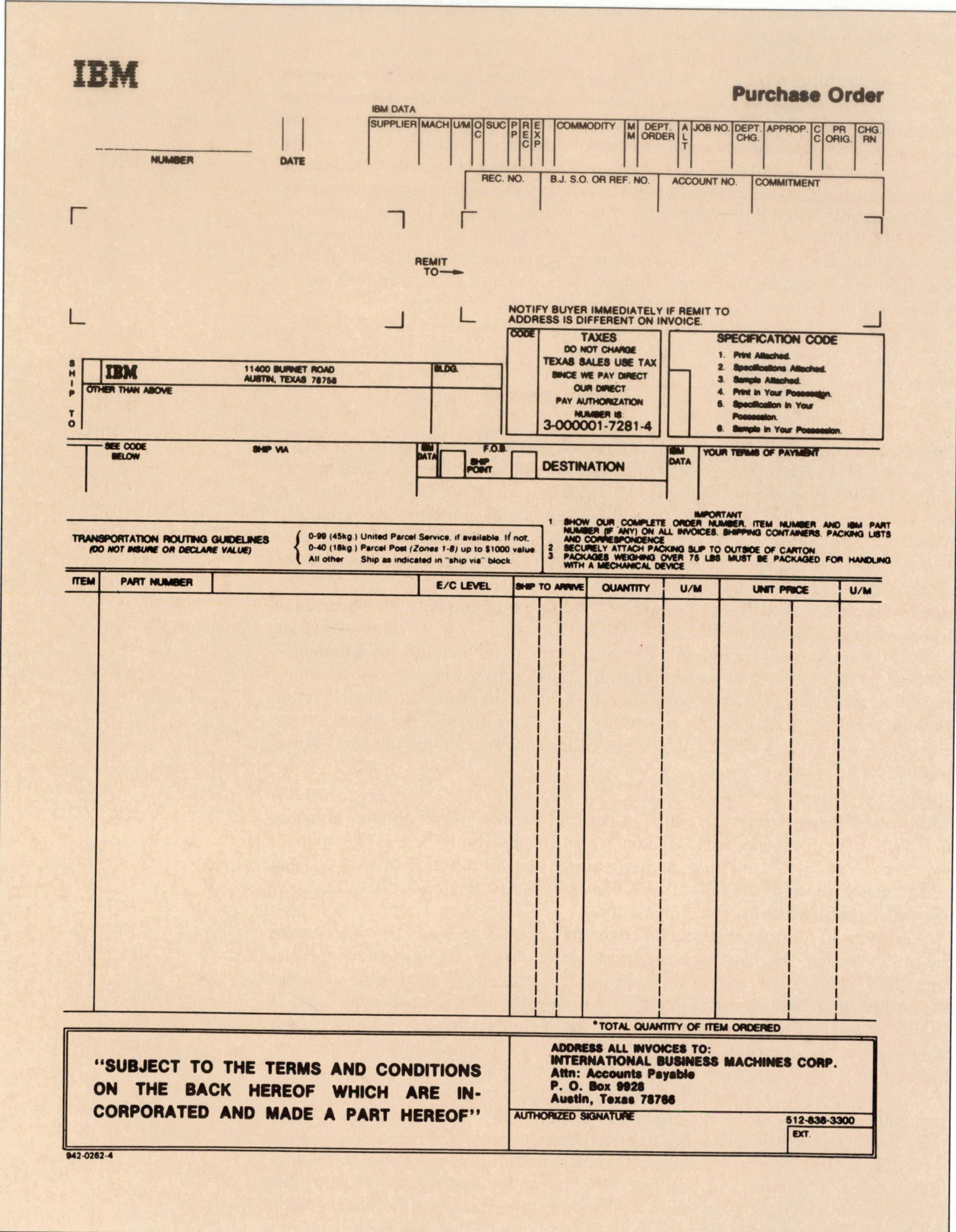

IBM

Purchase Order

IBM DATA

SUPPLIER	MACH	U/M	OC	SUC	PP	REC	EXP	COMMODITY	MM	DEPT. ORDER	ALT	JOB NO.	DEPT. CHG.	APPROP.	CC	PR ORIG.	CHG. RN

NUMBER DATE

REC. NO.	B.J. S.O. OR REF. NO.	ACCOUNT NO.	COMMITMENT

REMIT TO→

NOTIFY BUYER IMMEDIATELY IF REMIT TO ADDRESS IS DIFFERENT ON INVOICE.

SHIP TO: IBM 11400 BURNET ROAD AUSTIN, TEXAS 78758 BLDG.
OTHER THAN ABOVE

CODE | TAXES
DO NOT CHARGE TEXAS SALES USE TAX SINCE WE PAY DIRECT OUR DIRECT PAY AUTHORIZATION NUMBER IS: 3-000001-7281-4

SPECIFICATION CODE
1. Print Attached.
2. Specifications Attached.
3. Sample Attached.
4. Print in Your Possession.
5. Specification in Your Possession.
6. Sample in Your Possession.

SEE CODE BELOW | SHIP VIA | IBM DATA | F.O.B. SHIP POINT | DESTINATION | IBM DATA | YOUR TERMS OF PAYMENT

TRANSPORTATION ROUTING GUIDELINES
(DO NOT INSURE OR DECLARE VALUE)
0-99 (45kg.) United Parcel Service, if available. If not,
0-40 (18kg.) Parcel Post *(Zones 1-8)* up to $1000 value
All other Ship as indicated in "ship via" block.

IMPORTANT
1. SHOW OUR COMPLETE ORDER NUMBER, ITEM NUMBER AND IBM PART NUMBER (IF ANY) ON ALL INVOICES, SHIPPING CONTAINERS, PACKING LISTS AND CORRESPONDENCE
2. SECURELY ATTACH PACKING SLIP TO OUTSIDE OF CARTON
3. PACKAGES WEIGHING OVER 75 LBS MUST BE PACKAGED FOR HANDLING WITH A MECHANICAL DEVICE

ITEM	PART NUMBER		E/C LEVEL	SHIP TO ARRIVE	QUANTITY	U/M	UNIT PRICE	U/M

*TOTAL QUANTITY OF ITEM ORDERED

"SUBJECT TO THE TERMS AND CONDITIONS ON THE BACK HEREOF WHICH ARE INCORPORATED AND MADE A PART HEREOF"

ADDRESS ALL INVOICES TO:
INTERNATIONAL BUSINESS MACHINES CORP.
Attn: Accounts Payable
P. O. Box 9928
Austin, Texas 78766

AUTHORIZED SIGNATURE 512-838-3300 EXT.

942-0262-4

(Continued on next page)

◆ **Exhibit 14–2 (Continued) An Example of a Purchase Order (Back)**

STANDARD TERMS AND CONDITIONS

IBM EXPRESSLY LIMITS ACCEPTANCE TO THE TERMS SET FORTH ON THE FACE AND REVERSE SIDE OF THIS PURCHASE ORDER AND ANY ATTACHMENTS HERETO:

PURCHASE ORDER CONSTITUTES COMPLETE AGREEMENT This Purchase order, including the terms and conditions on the face and reverse side hereof and any attachments hereto, contains the complete and final agreement between International Business Machines Corporation (IBM) and Seller. Reference to Seller's bids or proposals, if noted on this order, shall not affect terms and conditions hereof, unless specifically provided to the contrary herein, and no other agreement or quotation in any way modifying any of said terms and conditions will be binding upon IBM unless made in writing and signed by IBM's authorized representative.

ADVERTISING Seller shall not, without first obtaining the written consent of IBM, in any manner advertise, publish or otherwise disclose the fact that Seller has furnished, or contracted to furnish to IBM, the material and/or services ordered hereunder.

APPLICABLE LAW The agreement arising pursuant to this order shall be governed by the laws of the State of New York. No rights, remedies and warranties available to IBM under this contract or by operation of law are waived or modified unless expressly waived or modified by IBM in writing.

CASH DISCOUNT OR NET PAYMENT PERIOD Calculations will be from the date an acceptable invoice is received by IBM. Any other arrangements agreed upon must appear on this order and on the invoice.

CONFIDENTIAL INFORMATION Seller shall not disclose to any person outside of its employ, or use for any purpose other than to fulfill its obligations under this order, any information received from IBM pursuant to this order, which has been disclosed to Seller by IBM in confidence, except such information which is otherwise publicly available or is publicly disclosed by IBM subsequent to Seller's receipt of such information or is rightfully received by Seller from a third party. Upon termination of this order, Seller shall return to IBM upon request all drawings, blueprints, descriptions or other material received from IBM and all materials containing said confidential information. Also, Seller shall not disclose to IBM any information which Seller deems to be confidential, and it is understood that any information received by IBM, including all manuals, drawings and documents will not be of a confidential nature or restrict, in any manner, the use of such information by IBM. Seller agrees that any legend or other notice on any information supplied by Seller, which is inconsistent with the provisions of this article, does not create any obligation on the part of IBM.

GIFTS Seller shall not make or offer gifts or gratuities of any type to IBM employees or members of their families. Such gifts or offerings may be construed as Seller's attempt to improperly influence our relationship.

IBM PARTS All parts and components bailed by IBM to Seller for incorporation in work being performed for IBM shall be used solely for such purposes.

OFF-SPECIFICATION Seller shall obtain from IBM written approval of all off-specification work.

PACKAGES Packages must bear IBM's order number and show gross, tare and net weights and/or quantity.

PATENTS Seller will settle or defend, at Seller's expense (and pay any damages, costs or fines resulting from), all proceedings or claims against IBM, its subsidiaries and affiliates and their respective customers, for infringement, or alleged infringement, by the goods furnished under this order, or any part or use thereof of patents (including utility models and registered designs) now or hereafter granted in the United States or in any country where Seller, its subsidiaries or affiliates, heretofore has furnished similar goods. Seller will, at IBM's request, identify the countries in which Seller, its subsidiaries or affiliates, heretofore has furnished similar goods.

PRICE If price is not stated on this order, Seller shall invoice at lowest prevailing market price.

QUALITY Material is subject to IBM's inspection and approval within a reasonable time after delivery. If specifications are not met, material may be returned at Seller's expense and risk for all damages incidental to the rejection. Payment shall not constitute an acceptance of the material nor impair IBM's right to inspect or any of its remedies.

SHIPMENT Shipment must be made within the time stated on this order, failing which IBM reserves the right to purchase elsewhere and charges Seller with any loss incurred, unless delay in making shipment is due to unforeseeable causes beyond the control and without the fault or negligence of Seller.

SUBCONTRACTS Seller shall not subcontract or delegate its obligations under this order without the written consent of IBM. Purchases of parts and materials normally purchased by Seller or required by this order shall not be construed as subcontracts or delegations.

(NON-U.S. LOCATIONS ONLY) Seller further agrees that during the process of bidding or production of goods and services hereunder, it will not re-export or divert to others any IBM specification, drawing or other data, or any product of such data.

TAXES Unless otherwise directed, Seller shall pay all sales and use taxes imposed by law upon or on account of this order. Where appropriate, IBM will reimburse Seller for this expense.

TOOLS IBM owned tools held by Seller are to be used only for making parts for IBM. Tools of any kind held by Seller for making IBM's parts must be repaired and renewed by Seller at Seller's expense.

TRANSPORTATION
<u>Routing</u>—As indicated in transportation routing guidelines on face of this order.
<u>F.O.B.</u>—Unless otherwise specified, ship collect, F.O.B. origin.
<u>Prepaid Transportation (when specified)</u>—Charges must be supported by a paid freight bill or equivalent.
<u>Cartage</u>) No charge allowed
<u>Premium Transportation</u>) unless authorized
<u>Insurance</u>) by IBM.
<u>Consolidation</u>—Unless otherwise instructed, consolidate all daily shipments to one destination on one bill of lading.

COMPLIANCE WITH LAWS AND REGULATIONS Seller shall at all times comply with all applicable Federal, State and local laws, rules and regulations.

EQUAL EMPLOYMENT OPPORTUNITY There are incorporated in this order the provisions of Executive Order 11246 (as amended) of the President of the United States on Equal Employment Opportunity and the rules and regulations issued pursuant thereto with which the Seller represents that he will comply, unless exempt.

EMPLOYMENT AND PROCUREMENT PROGRAMS There are incorporated in this order the following provisions as they apply to performing work under Government procurement contracts: Utilization of Small Business Concerns (if in excess of $10,000) (Federal Procurement Regulation (FPR) 1-1.710-3(a)); Small Business Subcontracting Program (if in excess of $500,000) (FPR 1-1.710-3 (b)); Utilization of Labor Surplus Area Concerns (if in excess of $10,000) (FPR 1-1.805-3(a)); Labor Surplus Area Subcontracting Program (if in excess of $500,000) (FPR 1-1.805-3 (b)); Utilization of Minority Enterprises (if in excess of $10,000) (FPR 1-1.1310-2 (a)); Minority Business Enterprises Subcontracting Program (if in excess of $50,000) (FPR 1-1.1310-2(b)); Affirmative Action for Handicapped Workers (if $2,500 or more) (41 CFR 60-741.4); Affirmative Action for Disabled Veterans and Veterans of the Vietnam Era (if $10,000 or more) (41 CFR 60-250.4); Utilization of Small Business Concerns and Small Business Concerns Owned and Controlled by Socially and Economically Disadvantaged Individuals (if in excess of $10,000) (44 Fed. Reg. 23610 (April 20, 1979)); Small Business and Small Disadvantaged Business Subcontracting Plan (if in excess of $500,000) (44 Fed. Reg. 23610 (April 20, 1979)).

WAGES AND HOURS Seller warrants that in the performance of this order Seller has complied with all of the provisions of the Fair Labor Standards Act of 1938 of the United States as amended.

WORKERS' COMPENSATION, EMPLOYERS' LIABILITY INSURANCE If Seller does not have Workers' Compensation or Employer's Liability Insurance, Seller shall indemnify IBM against all damages sustained by IBM resulting from Seller's failure to have such insurance.

This problem has led to the so-called *battle of the forms*, in which each party claims that his or her form represents the true terms of the agreement. Under the common law, the courts tended to resolve this difficulty by holding that the last form to be sent was the final counteroffer. To avoid the battle of the forms, the UCC dispenses with the mirror image rule. Section 2–207(1) of the UCC provides that a contract is formed if the offeree makes a definite expression of acceptance (such as signing the form in the appropriate location), even though the terms of the acceptance modify or add to the terms of the original offer. What happens to these new terms? The answer depends on whether the parties are nonmerchants or merchants.

One or Both Parties Are Nonmerchants If one (or both) of the parties is a *nonmerchant*, the contract is formed according to the terms of the original offer submitted by the original offeror and not according to the additional terms of the acceptance. For example, Tolsen offers in writing to sell his personal computer to Valdez for $1,500. Valdez faxes a reply to Tolsen in which Valdez states, "I accept your offer to purchase your computer for $1,500. I *would like* a box of computer paper and ten diskettes to be included in the purchase price." Valdez has given Tolsen a definite expression of acceptance (creating a contract) even though Valdez's acceptance also suggests an added term for the offer. Because Tolsen is not a merchant, the additional term is merely a proposal (suggestion), and Tolsen is not legally obligated to comply with that term.

Both Parties Are Merchants In contracts *between merchants* (that is, when both parties to the contract are merchants), the additional terms automatically become part of the contract unless (1) the original offer expressly required acceptance of its terms, (2) the new or changed terms materially alter the contract, or (3) the offeror objects to the new or changed terms within a reasonable period of time.

Conditioned on Offeror's Assent Regardless of merchant status, the UCC provides that the offeree's expression cannot be construed as an acceptance if the modifications are subject to (conditioned on) the offeror's "assent" [UCC 2–207(1)]. For example, Philips offers to sell Hundert 650 pounds of turkey thighs at a specified price and with specified delivery terms. Hundert responds, "I accept your offer for 650 pounds of turkey thighs, *as evidenced by a city scale weight certificate*, at the price and delivery terms stated in your offer." Hundert's response constitutes a contract even though the acceptance adds the words "as evidenced by a city scale weight certificate." If, however, Hundert says, "I accept your offer for 650 pounds of turkey thighs *on the condition* that the weight be evidenced by a city scale weight certificate," Hundert's response will be construed not as an acceptance but as a counteroffer, which Philips may or may not accept. The following case illustrates this point.

Case 14.3
PROVIDENCE & WORCESTER RAILROAD CO. v. SARGENT & GREENLEAF, INC.

United States District Court,
District of Rhode Island, 1992.
802 F.Supp. 680.

HISTORICAL AND SOCIAL SETTING *UCC 2–207 was designed in large measure to enforce a contract against a party who would take advantage of a technicality to avoid keeping his or her end of the bargain. For instance, under the mirror image rule, if forms sent by a buyer and a seller to each other were identical except in one minor respect, a party who wanted to back out of the deal might use the minor difference to effectively avoid the contract. Over time, however, the courts have had to use UCC 2–207 to decide not whether there is a contract but what the contract's terms are. This poses different and more difficult questions. For example, what effect does UCC 2–207 have when a buyer and a seller send forms to each other, and a term is found in the second form that was not in the first? In one well-known case, the buyer sent a purchase order form to*

Case 14.3—Continued

the seller, who responded with an acknowledgment form that contained a disclaimer.[a] *The court concluded that the acknowledgment was a counteroffer, which the buyer accepted on receiving and using the goods. Thus, the seller's disclaimer was part of the contract. The case has been widely criticized, in part because it seems to favor the party who happened to send the second document. If the buyer had sent the second form, the result might have been different. The case has been cited, however, to support the proposition that its result might have been different if the buyer had objected to the disclaimer in the acknowledgment form.*

FACTS The Providence & Worcester Railroad Company (P&W), by a printed form purchase order dated November 1986, purchased 198 switchlocks from Sargent & Greenleaf, Inc. (S&G). The front side of S&G's acknowledgment form contained the printed words "acceptance subject to terms and revisions on reverse side." On the reverse side, listed under the title "CONDITIONS GOVERNING THE ACCEPTANCE OF ALL ORDERS," were a number of provisions, including one disclaiming all warranties and limiting the buyer's remedies to the repair, replacement, or repayment of the purchase price of defective goods. In 1990, a vandal picked one of the S&G locks in less than two minutes and "threw" the switch secured by it, which resulted in the derailment of a freight train the next day. Although no persons were injured, the derailment caused nearly $1 million in property damage. In making the initial decision to purchase the S&G switchlocks, P&W had relied on statements made in various S&G advertising materials, including a statement that even after 10,000 operating cycles an S&G switchlock could not be picked by an amateur in less than four minutes. P&W sued S&G for, among other things, breach of the express warranties made by S&G in its advertising materials. S&G claimed that it was not liable because it had specifically disclaimed all warranties on its acceptance (acknowledgment form).

ISSUE Did S&G's form constitute an acceptance or a counteroffer?

DECISION The court held that S&G's form, because it expressly conditioned its acceptance on the offeror's agreement to its terms, was not an acceptance but a counteroffer.

REASON In determining whether S&G's form was an acceptance or a counteroffer, the court looked to UCC 2–207(1). Under that provision, an acknowledgment form may constitute a definite acceptance even though it contains additional terms. But UCC 2–207(1) also includes an exception to the acceptance rule that applies when "acceptance is expressly made conditional on assent to the additional or different terms." The court found that S&G's form had expressly conditioned the contract on P&W's assent to the additional terms and therefore the form constituted not an acceptance but a counteroffer. The court stated that P&W "had the opportunity to accept or reject this counteroffer or make its own counteroffer." P&W never objected to the additional terms but instead accepted, paid for, and used the locks. The court held that by its conduct, P&W had accepted S&G's counteroffer and was bound in contract. The court then addressed the other issues involved in this case, including whether S&G's limitation of the buyer's remedy to repair, replacement, or repayment of the purchase price of defective goods was effective. The court held that it was effective, and for this and other reasons, P&W's recovery was limited to repair, replacement, or repayment of the purchase price of the lock.

ETHICAL CONSIDERATIONS *In support of its decision that the clause limiting P&W's recovery to repair, replacement, or repayment of the purchase price of the faulty lock was "perfectly fair and equitable," the court mentioned several points. The court noted first that "[m]erchants are free to allocate risks among themselves." (See UCC 2–719.) The court also found "absolutely no evidence of unequal bargaining power" between the two merchants in this case: "[t]he transaction * * * involved two sophisticated businesses." Finally, the court emphasized that P&W sought to hold S&G liable for nearly $1 million in property damage based on the "alleged failure of a lock that cost about twenty dollars, out of a total shipment worth $4,237.67." The court agreed with S&G that "prohibiting manufacturers from limiting their liability * * * would surely discourage them from producing products such as this."*

a. *Roto-Lith, Ltd. v. F. P. Bartlet & Co.*, 297 F.2d 497 (1st Cir. 1962).

Consideration

The UCC radically changes the common law rule that contract modification must be supported by new consideration. Section 2–209(1) states that "an agreement modifying a contract needs no consideration to be binding."

Business Law in Action

Box Tops and the Battle of the Forms

The "forms" in the so-called "battle of the forms" come in various shapes, colors, and sizes. In striking a bargain, a buyer and a seller may communicate numerous times by phone and follow up these phone conversations with written memoranda confirming their oral agreements. Letters, faxes, and other written communications relating to the terms of the bargain may be exchanged. Once the deal is struck, the buyer normally sends to the seller a purchase order, which may contain terms that were never discussed by the parties. The seller, in turn, may acknowledge the purchase order by an acceptance (acknowledgment) form, which might contain still other terms or conditions that were not agreed on during the contract negotiations. If, after all this, the contract fails—if the contract is breached—then comes the problem of wading through this mountain of forms to decide just exactly what terms were actually agreed on by the buyer and seller.

To further complicate this task, yet another "form" recently entered the battle: a box-top license on a computer software package. A software package marketed by The Software Link, Inc. (TSL), specifically conditioned the sale of the software on the buyer's agreement to the terms and conditions spelled out on the top of the box in a "Limited Use License Agreement." Among these terms and conditions were the following: (1) TSL disclaimed all express and implied warranties except for a warranty that the disks in the box were free from defects, and (2) the terms and conditions in the box-top license represented the final and complete expression of the terms of the parties' agreement. The box-top license also stated that opening the package constituted agreement to the box-top terms: "Opening this package indicates your acceptance of these terms and conditions. If you do not agree with them, you should promptly return the package unopened to the person from whom you purchased it within fifteen days from the date of purchase and your money will be refunded to you by that person."

What was the legal effect of these terms? This question came before the Third Circuit Court of Appeals in 1991[a] when a company that had purchased a number of the programs found that the programs were not performing as promised. When the company sued TSL for breach of warranties, TSL defended on the basis of the box-top warranty disclaimers. The court had to decide whether the box-top terms had become part of the parties' contract. The court held that the terms and conditions in the box-top license were additional terms in an acceptance. Because both parties to the contract were merchants, UCC 2–207(2) governed. Among other things, that section states that additional terms in an acceptance become part of the contract unless the terms materially alter the contract. The court concluded that the terms materially altered the contract and therefore, in accordance with the provisions of UCC 2–207(2), did not become part of the contract.

The court emphasized that it was merely "following the well-established distinction between conspicuous disclaimers made available before the contract is formed and disclaimers made available only after the contract is formed." Disclaimers that are expressed only after a contract is formed are subject to the provisions of UCC 2–207. "If TSL wants relief for its business operations from this well-established rule," said the court, "their arguments are better addressed to a legislature than a court."

a. *Step-Saver Data Systems, Inc. v. Wyse Technology*, 939 F.2d 91 (3d Cir. 1991).

Modifications Must Be Made in Good Faith Of course, contract modification must be sought in good faith [UCC 1–203]. For example, Jim agrees to manufacture and sell certain goods to Louise for a stated price. Subsequently, a sudden shift in the market makes it difficult for Jim to sell the items to Louise at the given price without suffering a loss. Jim tells Louise of the situation, and Louise agrees to pay an additional sum for the goods. Later Louise reconsiders and refuses to pay more than the original price. Under Section 2–209(1) of the UCC, Louise's promise to modify the contract needs no consideration to be binding. Hence, Louise is bound by the modified contract.

In this example, a shift in the market is a *good faith* reason for contract modification. In fact, Section 1–203 states, "Every contract or duty within this act imposes an obligation of good faith in its performance or enforcement." Good faith in the case of a merchant is defined to mean honesty in fact and the observance of reasonable commercial standards of fair dealing in the trade [UCC 2–103(1)(b)]. But

"'Then Jack traded his cow for five magic beans.' Here's a copy of the contract, the accounting summary, the insurance waiver, the shareholders' briefing, and the receipt."

Drawing by Cheney, *The New Yorker Magazine*

what if there really was no shift in the market, and Jim knew that Louise needed the goods immediately but refused to deliver them unless Louise agreed to pay an additional sum of money? This sort of extortion of a modification without a legitimate commercial reason would be ineffective because it would violate the duty of good faith. Jim would not be permitted to enforce the higher price.

When Modification without Consideration Requires a Writing In some situations, modification without consideration must be written to be enforceable. For example, the contract itself may prohibit any changes to the contract unless they are in a signed writing. Therefore, only those changes agreed to in the signed writing are enforceable [UCC 2–209(2)]. If a consumer (nonmerchant buyer) is dealing with a merchant *and* the merchant supplies the form that contains a prohibition against oral modification, the consumer must sign a separate acknowledgment of such a clause.

Also, any modification that brings the contract under the Statute of Frauds must usually be in writing to be enforceable. Thus, if an oral contract for the sale of goods priced at $400 is modified so that the contract goods are now priced at $600, the modification must be in writing to be enforceable [UCC 2–209(3)]. If, however, the buyer accepts delivery of the goods after the modification, he or she is bound to the $600 price [UCC 2–201(3)(c)].

Statute of Frauds

Section 2–201(1) of the UCC contains a Statute of Frauds provision that applies to contracts for the sale of goods. The provision requires that if the price is $500 or more, there must be a writing in order for the contract to be enforceable. The parties can have an initial oral agreement, however, and satisfy the Statute of Frauds by having a subsequent written memorandum of their oral agreement. In each case, the writing must be signed by the party against whom enforcement is sought.

Sufficiency of the Writing The UCC has greatly relaxed the requirements for the sufficiency of a writing to satisfy the Statute of Frauds. A writing or a memorandum will be sufficient as long as it indicates that the parties intended to form a contract and as long as it is signed by the party (or agent of the party) against whom enforcement is sought. The contract will not be enforceable beyond the quantity of goods shown in the writing, however (except in the case of output and requirements contracts). All other terms can be proved in court by oral testimony. Often, terms that are not agreed on can be supplied by the open term provisions of Article 2.

Written Confirmation between Merchants Once again the UCC provides a special rule for a contract for the sale of goods between merchants. Merchants can

"When there's no law, there's no bread."

Benjamin Franklin, 1706–1790
(American diplomat, author, and scientist)

satisfy the requirements of a writing for the Statute of Frauds if, after the parties have agreed orally, one of the merchants sends a signed written confirmation to the other merchant. The communication must indicate the terms of the agreement, and the merchant receiving the confirmation must have reason to know of its contents. Unless the merchant who receives the confirmation gives written notice of objection to its contents within ten days after receipt, the writing is sufficient against the receiving merchant, even though he or she has not signed anything.

For example, Alfonso is a merchant buyer in Cleveland. He contracts over the telephone to purchase $4,000 worth of goods from Goldstein, a New York City merchant seller. Two days later, Goldstein sends written confirmation detailing the terms of the oral contract, and Alfonso subsequently receives it. If Alfonso does not give Goldstein written notice of objection to the contents of the written confirmation within ten days of receipt, Alfonso cannot raise the Statute of Frauds as a defense against the enforcement of the oral contract.

Exceptions Section 2–201 defines three exceptions to the Statute of Frauds requirement of a writing. An oral contract for the sale of goods priced at $500 or more will be enforceable despite the absence of a writing in the following circumstances. These exceptions and other ways in which sales law differs from general contract law are summarized in Exhibit 14–3.

Specially Manufactured Goods An oral contract is enforceable if it is for (a) specially manufactured goods for a particular buyer, (b) these goods are not suitable for resale to others in the ordinary course of the seller's business, and (c) the seller has substantially started to manufacture the goods or made commitments for the manufacture of the goods. In this situation, once the seller has taken action, the buyer cannot repudiate the agreement claiming the Statute of Frauds as a defense.

For example, suppose Womach orders custom-made draperies for her new boutique. The price is $1,000, and the contract is oral. When the merchant seller finishes the draperies and tenders delivery to Womach, Womach refuses to pay for them even though the job has been completed on time. Womach claims that she is not liable because the contract was oral. Clearly, if the unique style of the draperies makes it improbable that the seller can find another buyer, Womach is liable to the seller. Note that the seller must have made a substantial beginning in manufacturing the specialized item prior to the buyer's repudiation. (Here, the drapery manufacture was completed.) Of course, the court must still be convinced by evidence of the terms of the oral contract.

Admissions An oral contract is enforceable if the party against whom enforcement of a contract is sought admits in pleadings (written answers), testimony, or other court proceedings that a contract for sale was made. In this case, the contract will be enforceable even though it was oral, but enforceability will be limited to the quantity of goods admitted.

For example, Lane and Sugg negotiate an agreement over the telephone. During the negotiations, Lane requests a delivery price for 500 gallons of gasoline and a separate price for 700 gallons of gasoline. Sugg replies that the price would be the same, $1.10 per gallon. Lane orally orders 500 gallons. Sugg honestly believes that Lane ordered 700 gallons and tenders that amount. Lane refuses the shipment of 700 gallons, and Sugg sues for breach. In his answer and testimony, Lane admits that an oral contract was made but only for 500 gallons. Because Lane admits the existence of the oral contract, Lane cannot plead the Statute of Frauds as a defense. The contract is enforceable, however, only to the extent of the quantity admitted (500 gallons).

Partial Performance An oral contract is enforceable if payment has been made and accepted or goods have been received and accepted. This is the "partial per-

♦ Exhibit 14–3
Major Differences between Contract Law and Sales Law

	CONTRACT LAW	SALES LAW
Contract Terms	Contract must contain all material terms.	Open terms acceptable, if parties intended to form a contract, but contract not enforceable beyond quantity term.
Acceptance	Mirror image rule applies. If additional terms are added in acceptance, counteroffer is created.	Additional terms will not negate acceptance unless acceptance is made expressly conditional on assent to the additional terms.
Contract Modification	Requires consideration.	Does not require consideration.
Irrevocable Offers	Option contracts (with consideration).	Merchants' firm offers (without consideration).
Statute of Frauds Requirements	All material terms must be included in the writing.	Writing required only in sale of goods of $500 or more but not enforceable beyond quantity specified. *Between merchants:* Contract is enforceable if merchant fails to object in writing to confirming memorandum within ten days. *Exceptions:* 1. Contracts for specially manufactured goods. 2. Contracts admitted to under oath by party against whom enforcement is sought. 3. Contracts will be enforced to extent goods delivered or paid for.

formance" exception. The oral contract will be enforced at least to the extent that performance *actually* took place.

Suppose that Allan orally contracts to sell Opus ten chairs at $100 each. Before delivery, Opus sends Allan a check for $600, which Allan cashes. Later, when Allan attempts to deliver the chairs, Opus refuses delivery, claiming the Statute of Frauds as a defense, and demands the return of his $600. Under the UCC's partial performance rule, Allan can enforce the oral contract by tender of delivery of six chairs for the $600 accepted. Similarly, if Opus had made no payment but had accepted the delivery of six chairs from Allan, the oral contract would have been enforceable against Opus for $600, the price of the six chairs delivered.

Parol Evidence

If the parties to a contract set forth its terms in a confirmatory memorandum (a writing expressing offer and acceptance of the deal) or in a writing intended as their final expression, the terms of the contract cannot be contradicted by evidence of

"Merchants know perfectly well what they mean when they express themselves, not in the language of lawyers, but in the language of courteous mercantile communication."

Lord Cairn, 1819–1885 ***(British jurist)***

any prior agreements or contemporaneous oral agreements. The terms of the contract may, however, be explained or supplemented by *consistent additional terms* or by *course of dealing, usage of trade,* or *course of performance* [UCC 2–202].

Consistent Additional Terms If the court finds an ambiguity in a writing that is supposed to be a complete and exclusive statement of the agreement between the parties, it may accept evidence of consistent additional terms to clarify or remove the ambiguity. The court will not, however, accept evidence of contradictory terms. This is the rule under both the UCC and the common law of contracts.

COURSE OF DEALING
A sequence of previous conduct between the parties to a particular transaction that establishes a common basis for their understanding.

Course of Dealing and Usage of Trade The UCC has determined that the meaning of any agreement, evidenced by the language of the parties and by their actions, must be interpreted in light of commercial practices and other surrounding circumstances. In interpreting a commercial agreement, the court will assume that the *course of prior dealing* between the parties and the *usage of trade* were taken into account when the agreement was phrased [UCC 2–202 and 1–201(3)]. A **course of dealing** is a sequence of previous actions and communications between the parties to a particular transaction that establishes a common basis for their understanding [UCC 1–205(1)]. A course of dealing is restricted to the sequence of actions and communications between the parties that has occurred prior to the agreement in question. The UCC states, "A course of dealing between the parties and any usage of trade in the vocation or trade in which they are engaged or of which they are or should be aware give particular meaning to [the terms of the agreement] and supplement or qualify the terms of [the] agreement" [UCC 1–205(3)].

USAGE OF TRADE
Any practice or method of dealing having such regularity of observance in a place, vocation, or trade as to justify an expectation that it will be observed with respect to the transaction in question.

Usage of trade is defined as any practice or method of dealing having such regularity of observance in a place, vocation, or trade as to justify an expectation that it will be observed with respect to the transaction in question [UCC 1–205(2)]. Further, the express terms of an agreement and an applicable course of dealing or usage of trade will be construed to be consistent with each other whenever reasonable. When such a construction is *unreasonable,* however, the express terms in the agreement will prevail [UCC 1–205(4)]. In the following case, the court permitted the introduction of evidence of usage and custom in the trade to explain the meaning of the quantity figures specified by the parties when the contract was formed.

Case 14.4 

HEGGBLADE-MARGULEAS-TENNECO, INC. v. SUNSHINE BISCUIT, INC.

Court of Appeal of California, Fifth District, 1976.
59 Cal.App.3d 948,
131 Cal.Rptr. 183.

HISTORICAL AND SOCIAL SETTING *The common law prohibited the introduction of extrinsic evidence to explain a written contract unless the written terms were ambiguous. The UCC changed this rule—extrinsic evidence of usage of trade can be introduced to explain a written contract whether or not the written terms are ambiguous. For example, in 1966 a buyer and seller contracted for the sale of a specific quantity of phosphate at a certain price. When prices in the phosphate market fell, the buyer refused to buy unless the seller would reduce the price, which the seller refused to do. In the seller's suit, the buyer defended its action under the UCC on the ground that usage in the phosphate trade imposed no duty to accept the specified quantity of phosphate at the price set in the contract. In a decision issued in 1971, the court agreed, pointing out that "[t]he contract is silent about adjusting prices and quantities to reflect a declining market. * * * [T]his neutrality provides a fitting occasion for recourse to usage of trade * * * to * * * explain its terms."*[a]

FACTS In 1970, Heggblade-Marguleas-Tenneco, Inc. (HMT), contracted with Sunshine Biscuit, Inc., to supply potatoes to be used in the 1971 production of snack foods. HMT had never marketed processing potatoes before. The quantity mentioned in its contract negotiations was 100,000 sacks of potatoes. The parties agreed that the amount of potatoes to be supplied would vary somewhat

a. *Columbia Nitrogen Corp. v. Royster Co.,* 451 F.2d 3 (4th Cir. 1971).

Case 14.4—Continued

with Sunshine Biscuit's needs. Subsequently, a decline in demand for Sunshine Biscuit's products severely reduced its need for potatoes, and it prorated the reduced demand among its suppliers, including HMT, as fairly as possible. Sunshine Biscuit was able to take only 60,105 sacks out of the 100,000 previously estimated. In HMT's suit for breach of contract, Sunshine Biscuit attempted to introduce evidence that it is customary in the potato-processing industry for the number of potatoes specified in sales contracts to be reasonable estimates rather than exact numbers that a buyer intends to purchase. The trial court held for Sunshine Biscuit, and HMT appealed.

ISSUE Could evidence of custom in the potato-processing trade be admissible?

DECISION Yes. The trial court's ruling was affirmed.

REASON UCC Section 2–202 states that even though evidence of prior agreements or contemporaneous oral agreements that contradict a written contract is inadmissible, evidence of a course of dealing or of trade usage is admissible to explain or supplement a written contract. The fact that specific numbers were used to designate what quantities of potatoes Sunshine Biscuit thought it would need does not dispose of the issue. In its statement that evidence of trade usage was admissible, the court quoted an official comment to the UCC: "[I]n order that the true understanding of the parties as to the agreement may be [reached, such] writings are to be read on the assumption that * * * the usages of trade were taken for granted when the document was phrased. Unless carefully negated they have become an element of the meaning of the words used." HMT was held to have sufficient knowledge of the "trade custom."

Course of Performance A **course of performance** is the conduct that occurs under the terms of a particular agreement. Presumably, the parties themselves know best what they meant by their words, and the course of performance actually undertaken under their agreement is the best indication of what they meant [UCC 2–208].

COURSE OF PERFORMANCE
The conduct that occurs under the terms of a particular agreement; such conduct indicates what the parties to an agreement intended it to mean.

For example, suppose Janson's Lumber Company contracts with Barrymore to sell Barrymore a specified number of "2-by-4s." The lumber in fact does not measure 2 inches by 4 inches but rather 1⅞ inches by 3¾ inches. Janson's agrees to deliver the lumber in five deliveries, and Barrymore without objection accepts the lumber in the first three deliveries. At the fourth delivery, however, Barrymore objects that the 2-by-4s do not measure 2 inches by 4 inches. The course of performance in this transaction—that is, the fact that three deliveries were accepted without objection under the agreement—is relevant in determining that here the words "2 by 4" actually mean "1⅞-by-3¾."

Janson's can also prove that 2-by-4s need not be exactly 2 inches by 4 inches by applying usage of trade or course of prior dealing or both. Janson's can, for example, show that in previous transactions, Barrymore took 1⅞-inch by 3¾-inch lumber without objection. In addition, Janson's can show that in the trade, 2-by-4s are commonly 1⅞ inches by 3¾ inches.

Rules of Construction The UCC provides *rules of construction* for interpreting contracts. Express terms, course of performance, course of dealing, and usage of trade are to be construed together when they do not contradict one another. When such a construction is unreasonable, however, the following order of priority controls: (1) express terms, (2) course of performance, (3) course of dealing, and (4) usage of trade [UCC 1–205(4) and 2–208(2)].

Unconscionability

As discussed in Chapter 10, an unconscionable contract is one that is so unfair and one-sided that it would be unreasonable to enforce it. Section 2–302 of the UCC allows the court to evaluate a contract or any clause in a contract, and if the court deems it to have been unconscionable *at the time it was made,* the court can (1) refuse to enforce the contract, (2) enforce the remainder of the contract without the unconscionable clause, or (3) limit the application of any unconscionable clauses to avoid an unconscionable result.

The inclusion of Section 2–302 in the UCC reflects an increased sensitivity to certain realities of modern commercial activities. Classical contract theory holds that a contract is a bargain in which the terms have been worked out *freely* between parties that are equals. In many modern commercial transactions, this premise is invalid. Standard-form contracts are often signed by consumer-buyers who understand few of the terms used and who often do not even read them. Virtually all the terms are advantageous to the party supplying the standard-form contract. With Section 2–302, the courts have a powerful weapon for policing such transactions, as the next case illustrates.

Case 14.5 

JONES v. STAR CREDIT CORP.

Supreme Court of New York, Nassau County, 1969.
59 Misc. 2d 189,
298 N.Y.S.2d 264.

HISTORICAL AND ECONOMIC SETTING *In the sixth century, under Roman civil law, the rescission of a contract was allowed when the court determined that the market value of the goods that were the subject of the contract equaled less than half the contract price. This same ratio has appeared over the last thirty years in many cases in which courts have found contract clauses to be unconscionable under UCC 2–302 on the ground that the price was excessive. In a Connecticut case, for example, the court held that a contract requiring a welfare recipient to make payments totaling $1,248 for a television set that retailed for $499 was unconscionable.*[a] *The seller had not told the buyer the full purchase price. Most of the litigants who have used UCC 2–302 successfully have been consumers who are poor or otherwise at a disadvantage. In one New York case, for example, the court held that a contract requiring a Spanish-speaking consumer to make payments totaling nearly $1,150 for a freezer that wholesaled for less than $350 was unconscionable.*[b] *The contract was in English, and the salesperson did not translate or explain it.*

a. *Murphy v. McNamara,* 36 Conn.Supp. 183, 416 A.2d 170 (1979).
b. *Frostifresh Corp. v. Reynoso,* 52 Misc.2d 26, 274 N.Y.S.2d 757 (Dist. 1966); rev'd on issue of relief, 54 Misc.2d 119, 281 N.Y.S.2d 946 (Sup. 1967).

FACTS The Joneses, the plaintiffs, were welfare recipients who agreed to purchase a freezer for $900 as the result of a salesperson's visit to their home. Tax and financing charges raised the total price to $1,234.80. At trial, the freezer was found to have a maximum retail value of approximately $300. The plaintiffs, who had made payments totaling $619.88, sued to have the purchase contract declared unconscionable under the UCC.

ISSUE Can this contract be denied enforcement on the ground of unconscionability?

DECISION Yes. The court held that the contract was not enforceable as it stood, and the contract was "reformed" so that no further payments were required.

REASON The court relied on UCC 2–302(1), which states that if "the court as a matter of law finds the contract or any clause of the contract to have been unconscionable at the time it was made the court may * * * so limit the application of any unconscionable clause as to avoid any unconscionable result." The court then examined the disparity between the $900 purchase price and the $300 retail value, as well as the fact that the credit charges alone exceeded the retail value. These excessive charges were exacted despite the seller's knowledge of the plaintiffs' limited resources. The court reformed the contract so that the plaintiffs' payments, amounting to more than $600, were regarded as payment in full.

❖ Key Terms

course of dealing 346
course of performance 347
firm offer 335
merchant 331
output contract 335
requirements contract 334
sale 329
sales contract 328
tangible property 329
usage of trade 346

❖ Chapter Summary: The Formation of Sales Contracts

Offer and Acceptance	1. Not all terms have to be included for a contract to be formed [UCC 2–204]. 2. The price does not have to be included for a contract to be formed [UCC 2–305]. 3. Particulars of performance can be left open [UCC 2–311(1)]. 4. A firm written offer by a *merchant*, covering a period of three months or less, cannot be revoked [UCC 2–205]. 5. Acceptance may be made by any reasonable means of communication; it is effective when dispatched [UCC 2–206(1)(a)]. 6. The acceptance of a unilateral offer can be made by a promise to ship or by shipment of conforming goods [UCC 2–206(1)(b)]. 7. Acceptance by performance requires notice within a reasonable time; otherwise, the offer can be treated as lapsed [UCC 2–206(2)]. 8. Variations in terms between the offer and the acceptance may not be a rejection but may be an acceptance [UCC 2–207].
Consideration	A modification of a contract for the sale of goods does not require consideration [UCC 2–209(1)].
Requirements under the Statute of Frauds	1. All contracts for the sale of goods priced at $500 or more must be in writing. A writing is sufficient so long as it indicates a contract between the parties and is signed by the party against whom enforcement is sought. A contract is not enforceable beyond the quantity shown in the writing [UCC 2–201(1)]. 2. When written confirmation of an oral contract *between merchants* is not objected to in writing by the receiver within ten days, the contract is enforceable [UCC 2–201(2)]. 3. Exceptions to the requirement of a writing exist in the following situations: a. When the oral contract is for specially manufactured goods not suitable for resale to others, and the seller has substantially started to manufacture the goods [UCC 2–201(3)(a)]. b. When the defendant admits in pleadings, testimony, or other court proceedings that an oral contract for the sale of goods was made. In this case, the contract will be enforceable to the extent of the quantity of goods admitted [UCC 2–201(3)(b)]. c. The oral agreement will be enforceable to the extent that such payment has been received and accepted or to the extent that goods have been received and accepted [UCC 2–201(3)(c)].
Parol Evidence Rule	1. The terms of a clearly and completely worded written contract cannot be contradicted by evidence of prior agreements or contemporaneous oral agreements. 2. Evidence is admissible to clarify the terms of a writing in the following situations: a. If the contract terms are ambiguous. b. If evidence of course of dealing, usage of trade, or course of performance is necessary to learn or to clarify the intentions of the parties to the contract.
Unconscionability	An unconscionable contract is one that is so unfair and one-sided that it would be unreasonable to enforce it. If the court deems a contract to have been unconscionable at the time it was made, the court can (1) refuse to enforce the contract, (2) refuse to enforce the unconscionable clause of the contract, or (3) limit the application of any unconscionable clauses to avoid an unconscionable result [UCC 2–302].

❖ Questions and Case Problems

14-1. Terms of the Offer. The UCC changes the effect of the common law of contracts in several ways. For instance, at common law, an offer must be definite enough for the parties to ascertain its essential terms when it is accepted. What happens under the UCC if some of an offer's terms—the price term, for example—are left open? What if the quantity term is left open?

14-2. Statute of Frauds. Section 2–201 of the UCC defines exceptions to the Statute of Frauds requirement of a writing. What are these exceptions?

14-3. Statute of Frauds. Fresher Foods, Inc., orally agreed to purchase from Dale Vernon, a farmer, 1,000 bushels of corn for $1.25 per bushel. Fresher Foods paid $125 down and agreed to pay the remainder of the purchase price upon delivery, which was scheduled for one week later. When Fresher Foods tendered the balance of $1,125 on the scheduled day of delivery and requested the corn, Vernon refused to deliver it. Fresher Foods sued Vernon for damages, claiming that Vernon had breached their oral contract. Can Fresher Foods recover? If so, to what extent?

14-4. Merchant's Firm Offer. On September 1, Jennings, a used-car dealer, wrote a letter to Wheeler in which he stated: "I have a 1955 Thunderbird convertible in mint condition which I will sell you for $13,500 at any time before October 9. [signed] Peter Jennings." By September 15, having heard nothing from Wheeler, Jennings sold the Thunderbird to another party. On September 29, Wheeler accepted Jennings's offer and tendered the $13,500. When Jennings told Wheeler he had sold the car to another party, Wheeler claimed Jennings had breached their contract. Is Jennings in breach? Explain.

14–5. Accommodation Shipments. M. M. Salinger, Inc., a retailer of television sets, orders 100 Model Color-X sets from manufacturer Fulsom. The order specifies the price and that the television sets are to be shipped via Interamerican Freightways on or before October 30. The order is received by Fulsom on October 5. On October 8, Fulsom writes Salinger a letter indicating that the order has been received and that the sets will be shipped as directed, at the specified price. This letter is received by Salinger on October 10. On October 28, Fulsom, in preparing the shipment, discovers it has only 90 Color-X sets in stock. Fulsom ships the 90 Color-X sets and 10 television sets of a different model, stating clearly on the invoice that the 10 are being shipped only as an accommodation. Salinger claims that Fulsom is in breach of contract. Fulsom claims that the shipment was not an acceptance and therefore no contract was formed. Explain who is correct and why.

14-6. Statute of Frauds. Loeb & Co. entered into an oral agreement with Schreiner, a farmer, in which Schreiner agreed to sell Loeb 150 bales of cotton, each weighing 480 pounds. Shortly thereafter, Loeb sent Schreiner a letter confirming the terms of the oral contract. Schreiner neither acknowledged receipt of the letter nor objected to its terms. When delivery came due, Schreiner ignored the oral agreement and sold his cotton on the open market because the price of cotton had more than doubled (from 37 cents to 80 cents per pound) after the oral agreement was made. In the lawsuit by Loeb & Co. against Schreiner, did Loeb recover? Explain. [*Loeb & Co. v. Schreiner*, 294 Ala. 722, 321 So.2d 199 (1975)]

14-7. Statute of Frauds. Ingram Meyers, a B. F. Goodrich Co. employee and agent, made an oral agreement with James Thomson of Thomson Printing Machinery Co. to sell Thomson some surplus printing machinery. Four days later, Thomson sent a "writing in confirmation" to Goodrich. The writing consisted of (1) a purchase order, which contained Thomson Printing's name, address, telephone number, and some details concerning the purchase of the machinery, and (2) a check that, by its notations, was specifically connected with the purchase order. Several weeks later, when Thomson called Goodrich about the machinery, it was revealed that the machinery had been sold to someone else. Thomson then brought suit against Goodrich to enforce the oral contract. Goodrich contended that the oral contract was not enforceable because the "writing" sent to Goodrich by Thomson had never been received by Ingram Meyers. Thus, Goodrich could not be held liable for the contract because it could not repudiate a writing that it had not received. Goodrich alleged that the written confirmation had never been received by its agent/seller because the envelope had not been properly sent to the attention of Meyers or to the surplus equipment department in which Meyers worked. Goodrich further contended that it made several attempts to "find a home" for the purchase order and check by sending copies of its contents to various divisions. Meyers stated that he did not learn of the purchase order until several weeks later, when Thomson called to arrange for the removal of the machines. Does the writing (the purchase order and check) sent by Thomson to Goodrich and received in Goodrich's mailroom satisfy the writing requirements of the Statute of Frauds, thus making the oral contract enforceable? Discuss. [*Thomson Printing Machinery Co. v. B. F. Goodrich Co.*, 714 F.2d 744 (7th Cir. 1983)]

14-8. Additional Terms in Acceptance. The Carpet Mart, a carpet dealer, telephoned an order (offer) for carpet to Collins & Aikman Corp., a carpet manufacturer. Collins & Aikman then sent Carpet Mart an acknowledgment form (acceptance), which specified the quantity and price agreed to in the telephone conversation. The reverse side of the printed acknowledgment form stated that Collins & Aikman's acceptance was subject to the buyer's agreement to submit all disputes to arbitration. Collins & Aikman shipped the carpet to Carpet Mart, which received the acknowledgment form and shipment without objection. Later, a dispute arose, and Carpet Mart brought a civil suit against Collins & Aikman, claiming misrepresentation as to the quality of the carpet. Collins & Aikman filed a motion to stay (cease all action on) the civil suit and to enforce the arbitration clause. Will the court enforce the arbitration clause? Discuss. [*Dorton v. Collins & Aikman Corp.*, 453 F.2d 1161 (6th Cir. 1972)]

14-9. Statute of Frauds. Peggy Holloway was a real estate broker who guaranteed payment for shipment of over $11,000 worth of mozzarella cheese sold by Cudahy Foods Co. to Pizza Pride in Jamestown, North Carolina. The entire arrangement was made orally. Cudahy mailed to Holloway an invoice for the order, and Holloway did not object in writing to the invoice within ten days of receipt. Later, when Cudahy demanded payment from Holloway, Holloway denied ever having guaranteed payment for the cheese and raised the Statute of Frauds [UCC 2–201] as a defense. Cudahy claimed that the Statute of Frauds could not be used as a defense, as both Cudahy and Holloway were merchants and Holloway failed to object within ten days to Cudahy's invoice. Discuss Cudahy's argument. [*Cudahy Foods Co. v. Holloway*, 286 S.E.2d 606 (N.C.App. 1982)]

14-10. Statute of Frauds. Harry Starr orally contracted to purchase a new automobile from Freeport Dodge, Inc. Starr signed an order form describing the car and made a down payment of $25. The dealer did not sign the form, and the form stated that "this order is not valid unless signed and accepted by the dealer." The dealer deposited the $25, and that was noted on the order form. On the day scheduled for delivery, a sales representative for the dealer told Starr that an error had been made in determining the price and that Starr would be required to pay an additional $175 above the price on the order form. Starr refused to pay the additional amount and sued for breach of contract. Freeport Dodge claimed that the contract fell under the Statute of Frauds and that because Freeport Dodge had not signed the contract, the oral contract was not enforceable. Discuss Freeport Dodge's contention. [*Starr v. Freeport Dodge, Inc.*, 54 Misc.2d 271, 282 N.Y.S.2d 58 (Dist. 1967)]

14-11. Statute of Frauds. R-P Packaging, Inc., is a manufacturer of cellophane wrapping material. The plant manager for Flowers Baking Company decided to improve its packaging of cookies. The plant manager contacted R-P Packaging for the possible purchase of cellophane wrap imprinted with designed "artwork." R-P took measurements to determine the appropriate size of the wrap and submitted to Flowers a sample size with the artwork to be imprinted. After agreeing that the artwork was satisfactory, Flower gave a verbal order to R-P for the designed cellophane wrap at a price of $13,000. When the wrap was tendered, although it conformed to the measurements and design, Flowers complained that the wrap was too short and the design off-center. Flowers rejected the shipment. R-P sued. Flowers contended that the oral contract was unenforceable under the Statute of Frauds. Discuss this contention. [*Flowers Baking Co. v. R-P Packaging, Inc.*, 229 Va. 370, 329 S.E.2d 462 (1985)]

14-12. Statute of Frauds. Monetti, S.P.A., is an Italian firm that makes decorative plastic trays and related products for the food services industry. In 1981, Monetti set up a wholly owned subsidiary, Melform U.S.A., to market its products in the United States. In 1984, after orally agreeing with Anchor Hocking Corp. (Anchor) that Anchor would become the exclusive U.S. distributor of Monetti products, Monetti terminated all of Melform's current distributors and informed all of Melform's customers that Anchor would be the exclusive distributor of its products in the future. Relations between Monetti and Anchor deteriorated over the next several months, and eventually Monetti sued for breach of contract. Anchor contended that their contract was unenforceable under the Statute of Frauds. Although their agreement had never been reduced to a writing, at one point Raymond Davis, the marketing director of Anchor, summarized the terms of the agreement on a memorandum on Anchor's letterhead that was sent to Anchor's law department. The memo included some handwritten notes by Davis, which, Davis stated, represented "more clearly our current position regarding the agreement." Will the memorandum signed by Davis constitute a sufficient writing under the UCC Statute of Frauds provisions? Discuss. [*Monetti, S.P.A. v. Anchor Hocking Corp.*, 931 F.2d 1178 (7th Cir. 1991)]

A QUESTION OF ETHICS AND SOCIAL RESPONSIBILITY

14-13. *John Schwanbeck entered into negotiations with Federal-Mogul Corp. to purchase Federal-Mogul's Vellumoid Division. The two parties drew up a letter of intent stating that "[n]o further obligation will arise until a definitive agreement is reduced to writing" and that it was the parties' intention "to proceed in good faith in the negotiation of such binding definitive agreement." At another place in the letter of intent were the words, "Of course, this letter is not intended to create, nor do you or we presently have any binding legal obligation whatever in any way relating to such sale and purchase." Federal-Mogul eventually sold the Vellumoid Division to another party. Schwanbeck sued Federal-Mogul, alleging, among other things, that Federal-Mogul had breached an agreement to negotiate in good faith the proposed contract with Schwanbeck. Given these facts, consider the following questions.* [Schwanbeck v. Federal-Mogul Corp., *412 Mass. 703, 592 N.E.2d 1289 (1992)*]

1. Did the letter of intent create a legally binding obligation, or was the letter merely an "agreement to agree" in the future? (You may wish to review the section on "Agreements to Agree" in Chapter 9 before you answer this question.)
2. As discussed in the *Ethical Perspective* in this chapter, the UCC requires that all parties to commercial contracts exercise good faith and commercial reasonableness in their dealings with one another. In your opinion, did Federal-Mogul breach this duty when it sold its Vellumoid Division to a third party?
3. Regardless of its legal duties under the UCC, did Federal-Mogul have an ethical duty to proceed in negotiating a contract with Schwanbeck? Discuss.

CASE BRIEFING ASSIGNMENT

14-14. *Examine Case A.7* [Goldkist, Inc. v. Brownlee, *182 Ga.App. 287, 355 S.E.2d 733 (1987)*] *in Appendix A. The case has been excerpted there in great detail. Review and then brief the case, making sure that you include answers to the following questions in your brief.*

1. What defense did the Brownlees raise against Goldkist's claim that the Brownlees had formed a contract with Goldkist for the sale of goods?
2. Why is the question as to whether the Brownlees were merchants significant?
3. Summarize the court's reasons for reversing the trial court's summary judgment for the Brownlees.

FOR CRITICAL ANALYSIS

14-15. *Why is the designation "merchant" or "nonmerchant" important?*

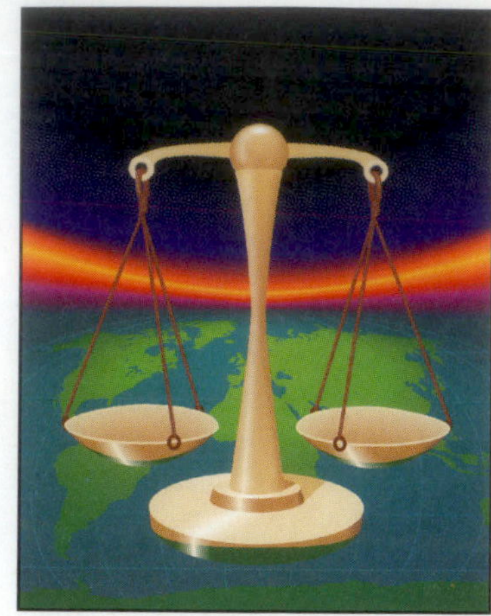

Chapter 15

Title and Risk of Loss

"Now, it is of great moment that well-drawn laws should themselves define all the points they possibly can and leave as few as may be to the decision of the judges."

Aristotle, 384–322 B.C.
(Greek philosopher)

The sale of goods transfers ownership (title) from the seller to the buyer. Often, a sales contract is signed before the actual goods are available. For example, a sales contract for oranges might be signed in May, but the oranges may not be ready for picking and shipment until October. Any number of things can happen between the time the sales contract is signed and the time the goods are actually transferred to the buyer's possession. For example, fire, flood, or frost may destroy the orange groves, or the oranges may be lost or damaged in transit. Because of these possibilities, it is important to know the rights and liabilities of the parties between the time the contract is formed and the time the goods are actually received by the buyer.

Before the creation of the Uniform Commercial Code (UCC), *title*—the right of ownership—was the central concept in sales law, controlling all issues of rights and remedies of the parties to a sales contract. There were numerous problems attending this concept. For example, frequently it was difficult to determine when title actually passed from seller to buyer, and therefore it was also difficult to predict which party a court would decide had title at the time of a loss. Because of such problems, the UCC divorced the question of title as completely as possible from the question of the rights and obligations of buyers, sellers, and third parties (such as subsequent purchasers, creditors, or the tax collector).

In some situations, title is still relevant under the UCC, and the UCC has special rules for locating title. These rules will be discussed in the sections that follow. In most situations, however, the UCC has replaced the concept of title with three other concepts: (1) identification, (2) risk of loss, and (3) insurable interest. By breaking down the transfer of ownership into these three components, the drafters of the UCC have essentially followed Aristotle's advice quoted above and created greater precision in the law governing sales—leaving as few points of law as possible "to the decision of the judges."

❖ Identification

Before any interest in specific goods can pass from the seller to the buyer, two conditions must prevail: (1) the goods must be in existence, and (2) they must be identified as the specific goods designated in the contract. (This second condition is commonly referred to as *identification to the contract.*) If either condition is lacking, only a *contract to sell* (not a sale) exists [UCC 2–105(2)]. Goods that are not both existing and identified to the contract are called *future goods.* For example, a contract to purchase next year's crop of hay would be a contract for future goods, a crop yet to be grown. For title to pass, the goods must be identified in a way that will distinguish them from all other similar goods.

Identification is a designation of goods as the subject matter of the sales contract. In many cases, identification is simply a matter of specific designation. For example, you contract to purchase a fleet of five cars by the serial numbers listed for the cars, or you agree to purchase all the wheat in a specific bin at a stated price per bushel. Usually, problems only occur when a quantity of goods is purchased from a larger mass, such as 1,000 cases of beans from a 10,000-case lot.

IDENTIFICATION
Proof that a thing is what it is purported or represented to be. In the sale of goods, the express designation of the goods provided for in the contract.

There is a general rule that when a purchaser buys a quantity of goods to be taken from a larger mass, identification can be made only by separation of the contract goods from the mass. Therefore, until the seller separates the 1,000 cases of beans from the 10,000-case lot, title and risk of loss remain with the seller.

A few exceptions exist. For example, a seller owns approximately 55,000 chickens (hens and roosters). A buyer agrees to purchase all the hen chickens at a stated price. Most courts would hold that "all the hen chickens" is a sufficient identification, and title and risk can pass to the buyer without a physical separation of the goods identified in the contract from the other goods (the hens from the roosters). The reasoning is that the contract identification serves as sufficient separation.

The most common exception deals with fungible goods [UCC 1–201(17)]. **Fungible goods** are goods that are alike naturally or by agreement or trade usage. Typical examples are wheat, oil, and wine. If these goods are held or intended to be held by owners in common (owners having shares undivided from the entire mass), a seller-owner can pass title and risk of loss to the buyer without an actual separation. The buyer replaces the seller as an owner in common [UCC 2–105(4)].

FUNGIBLE GOODS
Goods that are alike by physical nature, by agreement, or by trade usage. Examples of fungible goods are wheat, oil, and wine that are identical in type and quality.

For example, Anselm, Braudel, and Carpenter are farmers. They deposit, respectively, 5,000 bushels, 3,000 bushels, and 2,000 bushels of grain of the same grade and quality in a bin. The three become owners in common, with Anselm owning 50 percent of the 10,000 bushels, Braudel 30 percent, and Carpenter 20 percent. Anselm could contract to sell 5,000 bushels of grain to Tareyton and, because the goods are fungible, pass title and risk of loss to Tareyton without physically separating 5,000 bushels. Tareyton now becomes an owner in common with Braudel and Carpenter.

Identification is significant because it gives the buyer the right to obtain insurance on (an insurable interest in) the goods and the right to recover from third parties who damage the goods. In certain circumstances, identification allows the buyer to take the goods from the seller.

In their contract, parties can agree on when identification will take place. But if they do not so specify, the following additional rules apply [UCC 2–501(1)]:

1. Identification takes place at the time the contract is made *if the contract calls for the sale of specific and ascertained goods already existing.*
2. If the sale involves unborn animals that are conceived and will be born within twelve months from the time of the contract, or if it involves crops that are planted or growing and are to be harvested within twelve months (or the next harvest season occurring after contracting, whichever is longer), identification has taken place at the time of contract formation.
3. In other cases, identification takes place when the goods are marked, shipped, or somehow designated by the seller as the particular goods to pass under the contract. The seller can delegate the right to identify goods to the buyer.

"The worse the society, the more law there will be. In Hell there will be nothing but law."

Grant Gilmore, 1910–
(American legal scholar)

❖ Passage of Title

Once goods exist and are identified, the provisions of UCC 2–401 apply to the passage of title. In virtually all subsections of UCC 2–401, the words "unless otherwise explicitly agreed" appear, meaning that any explicit understanding between the buyer and the seller determines when title passes. Unless an agreement is explicitly made, title passes to the buyer at the time and the place the seller performs the *physical* delivery of the goods [UCC 2–401(2)]. The delivery arrangements determine when this occurs.

Shipment and Destination Contracts

SHIPMENT CONTRACT
A contract for the sale of goods in which the buyer assumes liability for any losses or damage to the goods on the seller's delivery of the goods to a carrier.

DESTINATION CONTRACT
A contract for the sale of goods in which the seller assumes liability for any losses or damage to the goods until they are tendered at the destination specified in the contract.

In a **shipment contract,** the seller is required or authorized to ship goods by carrier, such as a trucking company. Under a shipment contract, the seller is required only to deliver the goods into the hands of a carrier, and title passes to the buyer at the time and place of shipment [UCC 2–401(2)(a)].

In a **destination contract,** the seller is required to deliver the goods to a particular destination, usually directly to the buyer, but sometimes the buyer designates that the goods should be delivered to another party. Title passes to the buyer when the goods are *tendered* at that destination [UCC 2–401(2)(b)]. A tender of delivery is the seller's placing or holding of conforming goods at the buyer's disposition (with any necessary notice), enabling the buyer to take delivery [UCC 2–503(1)].

It is important to realize that generally, *all contracts are assumed to be shipment contracts if nothing to the contrary is stated in the contract.*

Delivery without Movement of the Goods

DOCUMENTS OF TITLE
Paper exchanged in the regular course of business that evidences the right to possession of goods (for example, a bill of lading or warehouse receipt).

When the contract of sale does not call for the seller's shipment or delivery of the goods (when the buyer is to pick up the goods), the passage of title depends on whether the seller must deliver a **document of title,** such as a bill of lading or a warehouse receipt, to the buyer. A *bill of lading* is a receipt for goods that is signed by a carrier and that serves as a contract for the transportation of the goods. A *warehouse receipt* is a receipt issued by a warehouser for goods stored in a warehouse. (See Exhibits 15–1 and 15–2.) When a document of title is required, title passes to the buyer *when and where the document is delivered.* Thus, if the goods are stored in a warehouse, title passes to the buyer when the appropriate documents are delivered to the buyer. The goods never move. In fact, the buyer can choose to leave the goods at the same warehouse for a period of time, and the buyer's title to those goods will be unaffected.

When no documents of title are required, and delivery is made without moving the goods, title passes at the time and place the sales contract is made, if the goods have already been identified. If the goods have not been identified, title does not pass until identification occurs. Consider an example. Rogers sells lumber to Boudakian. It is agreed that Boudakian will pick up the lumber at the yard. If the lumber has been identified (segregated, marked, or in any other way distinguished from all other lumber), title passes to Boudakian when the contract is signed. If the lumber is still in storage bins at the mill, title does not pass to Boudakian until the particular pieces of lumber to be sold under this contract are identified [UCC 2–401(3)].

Sales by Nonowners

Problems relating to passage of title also occur when persons who acquire goods with imperfect titles attempt to resell them. Sections 2–402 and 2–403 of the UCC deal with the rights of two parties who lay claim to the same goods, sold with imperfect titles. Generally, a buyer acquires at least whatever title the seller has to the goods sold.

Void Title A buyer may unknowingly purchase goods from a seller who is not the owner of the goods. If the seller is a thief, the seller's title is *void*—legally, no title

◆ **Exhibit 15–1 A Sample Negotiable Bill of Lading**

1st Sheet

UNIFORM MOTOR CARRIER ORDER BILL OF LADING

Original—Domestic

Shipper's No. ______

Agent's No. ______

CENTRAL FREIGHT LINES INC.

RECEIVED, subject to the classifications and tariffs in effect on the date of the issue of this Bill of Lading,

From ______ , Date ______ 19

At ______ Street, ______ City, ______ County, ______ State

the property described below, in apparent good order, except as noted (contents and condition of contents of packages unknown) marked, consigned and destined as shown below, which said company (the word company being understood throughout this contract as meaning any person or corporation in possession of the property under the contract) agrees to carry to its usual place of delivery at said destination, if within the scope of its lawful operations, otherwise to deliver to another carrier on the route to said destination. It is mutually agreed, as to each carrier of all or any of said property over all or any portion of said route to destination, and as to each party at any time interested in all or any of said property, that every service to be performed hereunder shall be subject to all the conditions not prohibited by law, whether printed or written, herein contained, including the conditions on back hereof, which are hereby agreed to by the shipper and accepted for himself and his assigns.

The surrender of this Original ORDER Bill of Lading properly indorsed shall be required before the delivery of the property. Inspection of property covered by this bill of lading will not be permitted unless provided by law or unless permission is indorsed on this original Bill of lading or given in writing by the shipper.

Consigned to Order of ______

Destination ______ Street, ______ City, ______ County, ______ State

Notify ______

At ______ Street, ______ City, ______ County, ______ State

I. C. C. No. ______ Vehicle No. ______

Routing ______

No. Packages	Description of Articles, Special Marks, and Exceptions	*Weight (Subject to Correction)	Class or Rate	Check Column
	SAMPLE			

Subject to Section 7 of Conditions, if this shipment is to be delivered to the consignee without recourse on the consignor, the consignor shall sign the following statement:

The carrier shall not make delivery of this shipment without payment of freight and all other lawful charges.

______ (Signature of consignor.)

If charges are to be prepaid write or stamp here, "To be Prepaid."

Received $______ to apply in prepayment of the charges on the property described hereon.

______ Agent or Cashier.

Per______ (The signature here acknowledges only the amount prepaid.)

Charges advanced:

$______

*If the shipment moves between two ports by a carrier by water, the law requires that the bill of lading shall state whether it is "carrier's or shipper's weight."

Note—Where the rate is dependent on value, shippers are required to state specifically in writing the agreed or declared value of the property.

The agreed or declared value of the property is hereby specifically stated by the shipper to be not exceeding

______ per ______

______ Shipper ______ Agent.

Per ______ Per ______

Permanent address of Shipper ______ Street, ______ City, ______ State

MOORE BUSINESS FORMS, INC., WACO, TEX. M

Source: Reprinted with permission of Central Freight Lines, Inc. © 1985 Central Freight Lines, Inc.
Note: The back of the form permits negotiation by indorsement.

◆ **Exhibit 15–2 A Sample Nonnegotiable Warehouse Receipt**

HART

Warehouse Receipt–Not Negotiable

Agreement No. ________ Vault No. ________ ________ ________ ________ ________

Service Order ________ ________ ________ ________ ________ ________
Receipt and
Lot Number________

Date of Issue________________19____

Received for the account of and deliverable to •________________________

whose latest known address is ________________________________

SAMPLE

________________________ the goods enumerated on the inside or attached schedule to be

stored in Company warehouse, located at ________________________________
which goods are accepted only upon the following conditions set forth below:

READ CAREFULLY ☛ That the value of all goods stored, including the contents of any container, and all goods hereafter stored for Depositor's account to be not over $ per pound † per article unless a higher value is noted in the schedule, for which an additional monthly storage charge of ________¢ on each $________ valuation in excess of $ per pound † per article or fraction thereof will be made.

If there are any items enumerated in this receipt valued in excess of the above limitations per pound per article and not so noted in the schedule, return this receipt within 10 days with proper values so indicated in writing in order that the receipt may be re-issued and proper higher storage rates assessed.

OWNERSHIP. The Customer, Shipper, Depositor, or Agent represents and warrants that he is lawfully possessed of goods to be stored and/or has the authority to store or ship said goods. (If the goods are mortgaged, notify the Company the name and address of the mortgagee.)

PAYMENT OF CHARGES. Storage bills are payable monthly in advance for each month's storage or fraction thereof. Labor charges, cartage and other services rendered are payable upon completion of work. All charges shall be paid at the warehouse location shown hereon, and if delinquent, shall incur interest monthly at the rate of per cent ( ) per year.

The Depositor will pay reasonable attorney's fee incurred by The Company in collecting delinquent accounts.

LIABILITY OF COMPANY. The company shall be liable for any loss or injury to the goods caused by its failure to exercise such care as a reasonably careful man would exercise under like circumstances. The company will not be liable for loss or damage to fragile articles not packed, or articles packed or unpacked by other than employees of this company. Depositor specifically agrees that the warehouse will not be liable for contamination of or for insect damage to articles placed in drawers of furniture by the depositor. Periodic spraying of the warehouse premises shall constitute ordinary and proper care, unless the depositor requests in writing and pays for anti-infestation treatment of articles in drawers and compartments of stored furniture.

CHANGE OF ADDRESS. Notice of change of address must be given the Company in writing, and acknowledged in writing by the Company.

TRANSFER OR WITHDRAWAL OF GOODS. The warehouse receipt is not negotiable and shall be produced and all charges must be paid before delivery to the Depositor, or transfer of goods to another person; however, a written direction to the Company to transfer the goods to another person or deliver the goods may be accepted by the Company at its option without requiring tender of the warehouse receipt.

ACCESS TO STORAGE. PARTIAL WITHDRAWAL. A signed order from the person in whose name the receipt is issued is required to enable others to remove or have access to goods. A charge is made for stacking and unstacking, and for access to stored goods.

BUILDING–FIRE–WATCHMAN. The Company does not represent or warrant that its building cannot be destroyed by fire or that the contents of said buildings including the said property cannot be destroyed by fire. The Company shall not be required to maintain a watchman or sprinkler system and its failure to do so shall not constitute negligence.

CLAIMS OR ERRORS. All claims for non-delivery of any article or articles and for damage, breakage, etc., must be made in writing within ninety (90) days from delivery of goods stored or they are waived. Failure to return the warehouse receipt for correction within ( ) days after receipt thereof by the depositor will be conclusive that it is correct and delivery will be made only in accordance therewith.

FUTURE SERVICE. This Contract shall extend and apply to future services rendered to the Depositor by the Company and to any additional goods deposited with the Company by the Depositor.

WAREHOUSEMAN'S LIEN. The Company reserves the right to sell the goods stored, in accordance with the provisions of the Uniform Commercial Code (Business and Commerce Code if stored in Texas), for all lawful charges in arrears.

TERMINATION OF STORAGE. The Company reserves the right to terminate the storage of the goods at any time by giving to the Depositor thirty (30) days' written notice of its intention so to do, and, unless the Depositor removes such goods within that period, the Company is hereby empowered to have the same removed at the cost and expense of the Depositor, or the Company may sell them at auction in accordance with state law.

DEPOSITOR WILL PAY REASONABLE LEGAL FEES INCURRED BY WAREHOUSE IN COLLECTING DELINQUENT CHARGES.

THIS DOCUMENT CONTAINS THE WHOLE CONTRACT BETWEEN THE PARTIES AND THERE ARE NO OTHER TERMS, WARRANTIES, REPRESENTATIONS, OR AGREEMENTS OF EITHER DEPOSITOR OR COMPANY NOT HEREIN CONTAINED.

Storage per month or fraction thereof	$________
Warehouse labor	$________
Cartage	$________
Packing at residence . . .	$________
Wrapping and preparing for storage	$________
Charges advanced	$________
________________	$________
________________	$________

By________________________

•Insert "Mr. and/or Mrs." or, if military personnel, appropriate rank or grade.
†Delete the words "per pound" if the declared value is per article.
For goods stored for military personnel under PL 245, the contractor's liability for care of goods is as provided in Basic Agreement with U.S. Government.

THIS PROPERTY HAS NOT BEEN INSURED BY THIS COMPANY FOR FIRE OR ANY OTHER CASUALTY
SCHEDULE OF GOODS ON FOLLOWING PAGE OR ATTACHED

H-1 (9/81) Approved by SH WT4 ©

Re-order from Hart Graphics, Austin, Texas

Source: Reprinted with permission of Hart Graphics, Inc. of Austin, Texas. © 1985 Hart Graphics, Inc.

◆ Exhibit 15–3 Void and Voidable Title

If goods are transferred from their owner to another by theft, the thief acquires no ownership rights. Because the thief's title is *void,* a later buyer can acquire no title, and the owner can recover the goods. If the transfer occurs by fraud, the transferee acquires a *voidable* title. A later good faith purchaser for value can acquire good title, and the original owner cannot recover the goods. If the buyer is aware of circumstances that would make a person of ordinary prudence ask about the seller's title to the goods, however, the owner can recover them.

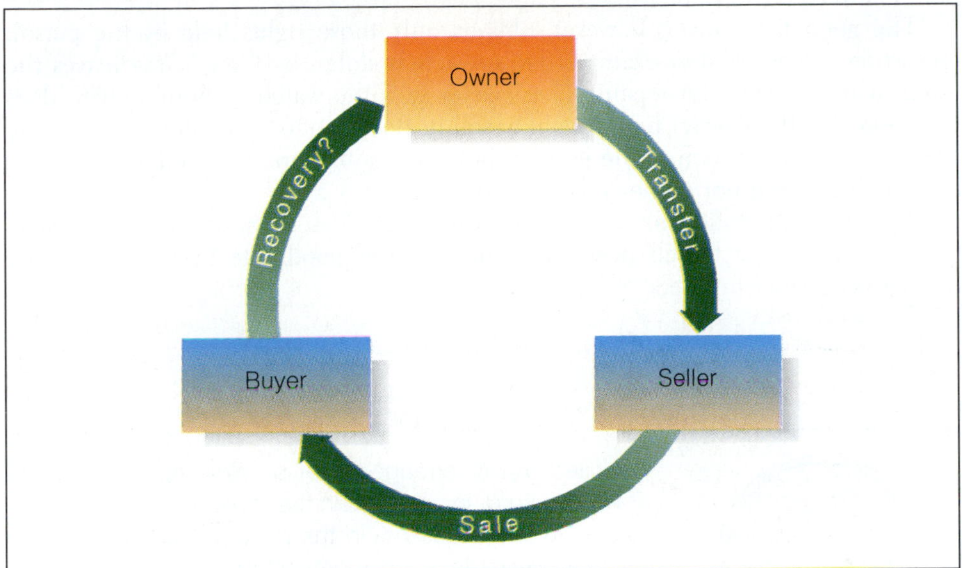

exists. Thus, the buyer acquires no title, and the real owner can reclaim the goods from the buyer.

For example, if Jim steals goods owned by Margaret, Jim has a *void title* to those goods. If Jim sells the goods to Sandra, Margaret can reclaim them from Sandra even though Sandra acted in good faith and honestly was not aware that the goods were stolen.

Voidable Title A seller has a *voidable title* if the goods that he or she is selling were obtained by fraud, paid for with a check that is later dishonored, purchased from a minor, or purchased on credit when the seller was **insolvent.** (Under the UCC, a person is insolvent when that person ceases to pay "his debts in the ordinary course of business or cannot pay his debts as they become due or is insolvent within the meaning of federal bankruptcy law" [UCC 1–201(23)].) In contrast to a seller with *void* title, a seller with *voidable title* has the power to transfer a good title to a good faith purchaser for value. A **good faith purchaser** is one who buys without knowledge of circumstances that would make a person of ordinary prudence inquire about the validity of the seller's title to the goods. One who purchases **for value** gives legally sufficient consideration (value) for the goods purchased. The real owner cannot recover goods from a good faith purchaser for value [UCC 2–403(1)]. If the buyer of the goods is not a good faith purchaser for value, then the actual owner of the goods can reclaim them from the buyer (or from the seller, if the goods are still in the seller's possession). Exhibit 15–3 illustrates these concepts.

The Entrustment Rule According to Section 2–403(2), entrusting goods to a merchant *who deals in goods of that kind* gives the merchant the power to transfer all rights to a *buyer in the ordinary course of business.* Entrusting includes both delivering the goods to the merchant and leaving the purchased goods with the merchant for later delivery or pickup [UCC 2–403(3)]. A buyer in the ordinary course of

INSOLVENT
A term describing a person whose liabilities exceed the value of owned assets *or* a person who "either has ceased to pay his debts in the ordinary course of business or cannot pay his debts as they come due" [UCC 1–201(23)].

GOOD FAITH PURCHASER
A purchaser who buys without notice of any circumstance that would put a person of ordinary prudence on inquiry as to whether the seller has valid title to the goods being sold.

FOR VALUE
In a sale of goods, legally sufficient consideration (such as a money payment).

business is a person who, in good faith and without knowledge that the sale violates the ownership rights or security interest of a third party, buys in ordinary course from a person (other than a pawnbroker) in the business of selling goods of that kind [UCC 1–201(9)].

For example, Jan leaves her watch with a jeweler to be repaired. The jeweler sells both new and used watches. The jeweler sells Jan's watch to Kim, a customer, who does not know that the jeweler has no right to sell it. Kim gets good title against Jan's claim of ownership.

The good faith buyer, however, obtains only those rights held by the person entrusting the goods. For example, Jan's watch is stolen by Greg. Greg leaves the watch with a jeweler for repairs. The jeweler sells the watch to Bonnie, who does not know that the jeweler has no right to sell it. Bonnie gets good title against Greg, who entrusted the watch to the jeweler, but not against Jan, who neither entrusted the watch to Greg nor authorized Greg to entrust it.

At issue in the following case was whether a car dealer that did not have a state government license to sell new cars could transfer good title to a buyer in the ordinary course of business.

Case 15.1

PERIMETER FORD, INC. v. EDWARDS

Court of Appeals of Georgia, 1990.
197 Ga.App. 747,
399 S.E.2d 520.

HISTORICAL AND SOCIAL SETTING *Merchant status is based on specialized knowledge of business practices, goods, or both. The UCC has special provisions that apply to merchants. One group of special provisions deals with the UCC's Statute of Frauds, firm offers, confirmatory memoranda, and contract modifications. These provisions are based on normal business practices that are familiar to any businessperson—answering business correspondence, for example. Under these provisions, almost any person in business with the requisite "knowledge or skill peculiar to the practices" could be deemed a merchant. A second group of provisions applies only to persons with professional status as to particular kinds of goods. These provisions include UCC 2–403, which is concerned only with a merchant "who deals in goods of that kind." Essentially, this distinction is based on appearances. An individual who buys something from a seller who appears to deal in the goods expects to get good title. For example, a buyer who buys a new car from an automobile dealership expects to get good title. Similarly, a buyer knows that a warehouse company selling goods to recover storage costs is dealing with the goods of someone else.*

FACTS In the summer of 1988, Gary Edwards contacted United Car & Truck Leasing (United) about purchasing a new Ford Escort. Edwards had been told that United sold cars at a lower markup than franchise dealers. Jay Kafka, a United agent, arranged with a sales representative of Perimeter Ford, Inc., to obtain the model Edwards wanted. On numerous occasions in the past, Kafka had arranged with the Perimeter Ford representative for United to purchase cars on credit from Perimeter. Then, when the car was leased or sold by United, Perimeter would be repaid. Kafka picked up the Ford Escort in August 1988 from Perimeter Ford, delivered it to United's parking lot, and replaced Perimeter Ford's dealer tag with a United tag. Two days later, Edwards signed a sales agreement for the Escort at United's office. Subsequently, Edwards received title to the car through the bank that financed the purchase. When United failed to pay Perimeter for the car, Perimeter brought suit to recover the car from Edwards, claiming that United was not a licensed new car dealer and therefore could not transfer ownership rights in the vehicle to Edwards. The trial court dismissed Perimeter's motion for summary judgment, holding that the Ford Escort had been properly entrusted to United and that Edwards, as a buyer in the ordinary course of business, had received ownership rights to the car. Perimeter appealed.

ISSUE Had the Ford Escort been properly entrusted to United, in which case United could transfer ownership rights in the car to a buyer in the ordinary course of business?

DECISION Yes. The appeals court upheld the trial court's ruling.

REASON The court noted that if United was a "merchant" as defined by the UCC and if Perimeter "entrusted" the possession of the car within the meaning of UCC 2–403(3), "then United had the authority to transfer [Perimeter's] ownership interest in the car" to Edwards—if

Case 15.1—Continued

Edwards was a "buyer in the ordinary course of business." The court held that United met the criteria for merchant status under the UCC, even though it did not have a state-government-issued license to sell new cars. The court stated that the purpose of the licensing statute in this case was to raise government revenues. Because of that, transactions conducted by United were not void (as they would have been had the purpose of the licensing requirement been to protect the public safety, for example—see Chapter 10). Furthermore, although United was primarily in the business of leasing cars, not selling them, approximately one-third of its revenues came from car sales. Having concluded that United was a merchant, the court then focused on whether Edwards was a "buyer in the ordinary course of business." The court concluded that he was. Edwards had no reason to believe that he was violating the ownership interests or rights of another party when he purchased the car from United. Indeed, the first knowledge he had of Perimeter's claim to the car was when he received a demand letter from Perimeter's attorney shortly before this suit was filed. The court found that Edwards was a buyer in the ordinary course of business and as such had received all ownership rights to the car.

ETHICAL CONSIDERATIONS *It may seem unethical to allow a buyer, who is presumed to act in good faith, to qualify as a "buyer in the ordinary course of business" without checking on the seller's title. If a buyer could not expect good title from an apparent dealer in the goods, however, the free flow of commerce would be slowed, or it could be blocked. In the* Edwards *case, for example, Perimeter would not have released the title to the Escort until United had paid the total price, and United could not have paid the total price until it had received funds from Edwards, who could not have borrowed the money from the bank without Perimeter's release of the title. The parties would have been at an impasse.*

❖ Risk of Loss

Under the UCC, risk of loss does not necessarily pass with title. The question of who suffers a financial risk if goods are damaged, destroyed, or lost is resolved primarily under Sections 2–509 and 2–319. Risk of loss may depend on whether a sales contract has been breached at the time of loss [UCC 2–510].

Risk of loss can be determined through an agreement by the parties, preferably in writing. In this way, the parties can generally control the exact moment that risk of loss passes from the seller to the buyer. Of course, at that moment, the goods must be in existence and identified to the contract for this contract provision to be enforceable.

Buyers and sellers commonly guard against risk of loss by obtaining insurance coverage on the goods. The point at which a buyer or a seller has a sufficient interest in contract goods to obtain insurance coverage will be discussed later in this chapter.

Delivery with Movement of the Goods—Carrier Cases

When there is no specification in the agreement, the following rules apply to cases involving movement of the goods (carrier cases).

Shipment Contracts In a shipment contract, if the seller is required or authorized to ship goods by carrier (but not required to deliver them to a particular destination), risk of loss passes to the buyer when the goods are duly delivered to the carrier [UCC 2–509(1)(b)].

For example, a seller in Texas sells 500 cases of grapefruit to a buyer in New York, F.O.B. Houston (free on board in Houston—that is, the buyer pays the transportation charges from Houston). The contract authorizes a shipment by carrier; it does not require that the seller tender the grapefruit in New York. Risk passes to the buyer when conforming goods are properly placed in the possession of the carrier. If the goods are damaged in transit, the loss is the buyer's. (Actually, buyers

If the goods on board this train were damaged, what determines who bears the risk?

have recourse against carriers, subject to certain limitations, and they usually insure the goods from the time the goods leave the seller.)

Destination Contracts In a destination contract, the risk of loss passes to the buyer when the goods are tendered to the buyer at the specified destination. In the preceding example, if the contract had been F.O.B. New York, risk of loss during transit to New York would have been the seller's.

Contract Terms Specific terms in the contract help determine when risk of loss passes to the buyer. These terms, which are listed and defined in Exhibit 15–4, relate generally to the determination of which party will bear the costs of delivery.

In the following case, the court reviewed UCC 2–509(1) as it relates to passage of risk of loss. Under the UCC, an F.O.B. term indicates whether the contract is a shipment contract or a destination contract, with the risk of loss passing at a different time with each. The F.O.B. terminology controls. In this case, a shipment contract shifted the risk of loss to the buyer when the goods were delivered to a carrier.

♦ **Exhibit 15–4 Contract Terms—Definitions**

F.O.B. (free on board)—Indicates that the selling price of goods includes transportation costs (and that the seller carries risk of loss) to the specific F.O.B. place named in the contract. The place can be either the place of shipment (for example, seller's city or place of business) or the place of destination (for example, buyer's city or place of business) [UCC 2–319(1)].
F.A.S. (free alongside vessel)—Requires that the seller at his or her own expense and risk deliver the goods alongside the vessel before risk passes to the buyer [UCC 2–319(2)].
C.I.F. or **C.&F.** (cost, insurance, and freight, or just cost and freight)—Requires, among other things, that the seller "put the goods in possession of a carrier" before risk passes to the buyer [UCC 2–320(2)]. (These are basically pricing terms and remain shipment contracts, not destination contracts.)
Delivery ex-ship (delivery from the carrying vessel)—Means that risk of loss does not pass to the buyer until the goods leave the ship or are otherwise properly unloaded [UCC 2–322].

Case 15.2 

PESTANA v. KARINOL CORP.
District Court of Appeal of Florida,
Third District, 1979.
367 So.2d 1096.

HISTORICAL AND SOCIAL SETTING *Before the UCC, risk-of-loss problems were governed by the Uniform Sales Act. Under that act, a contract term that required a seller to pay the cost of transporting the goods was considered an agreement to deliver the goods to a destination. Thus, a contract "to ship" was considered a destination contract. The drafters of the UCC omitted this rule "with the specific intention of negating" it, so that "the 'shipment' contract is regarded as the normal one."*[a] *Thus, the parties must expressly agree to a destination contract, or their contract will be considered a shipment contract.*

FACTS Karinol Corporation contracted "to ship" watches to Pestana in Chetumal, Mexico. The contract contained no delivery terms, such as F.O.B., nor did it contain any specific terms for allocation of loss while the goods were in transit. Pestana made a deposit, and the watches were shipped by Karinol, but they were lost in transit. Pestana sought a refund for the deposit, claiming that the risk of loss was the seller's. Karinol claimed that Pestana suffered the risk of loss and owed the balance of the purchase price. The trial court held for Karinol and ruled that Pestana was liable for the loss. Pestana appealed.

ISSUE Who should bear the risk of loss when no provision concerning risk allocation or delivery terms is included in the sales contract?

DECISION The buyer—in this case, Pestana. The appellate court upheld the trial court's decision.

REASON After discussing risk of loss under both shipment and destination contracts, the court held that when the contract has "(a) no explicit provisions allocating the risk of loss while the goods are in the possession of the carrier and (b) no delivery terms such as F.O.B. place of destination, * * * [s]uch a contract, without more, constitutes a shipment contract wherein the risk of loss passes to the buyer when the seller duly delivers the goods to the carrier." Thus, "where the risk of loss falls on the buyer at the time the goods are lost or destroyed, the buyer is liable to the seller for the purchase price of the goods sold."

a. UCC 2–503, Comment 2.

Delivery without Movement of the Goods

The UCC also addresses situations in which the seller is required neither to ship nor to deliver the goods. Frequently, the buyer is to pick up the goods from the seller, or the goods are held by a **bailee.** Under the UCC, a bailee is a party who, by a bill of lading, warehouse receipt, or other document of title, acknowledges possession of goods and contracts to deliver them. A warehousing company, for example, or a trucking company that normally issues documents of title for goods it receives is a bailee. (Bailments are discussed in detail in Chapter 33.)

BAILEE
One to whom goods are entrusted by a bailor.

Goods Held by the Seller If the goods are held by the seller, a document of title is usually not used. If the seller is a merchant, risk of loss to goods held by the seller passes to the buyer when the buyer *actually takes physical possession of the goods* [UCC 2–509(3)]. If the seller is not a merchant, the risk of loss to goods held by the seller passes to the buyer upon *tender of delivery* [UCC 2–509(3)].

Goods Held by a Bailee When a bailee is holding goods for a person who has contracted to sell them and the goods are to be delivered without being moved, the goods are usually represented by a negotiable or nonnegotiable document of title (a bill of lading or a warehouse receipt—see Exhibits 15–1 and 15–2). Risk of loss passes to the buyer when (1) the buyer receives a negotiable document of title for the goods, or (2) the bailee acknowledges the buyer's right to possess the goods, or (3) the buyer receives a nonnegotiable document of title *and* has had a *reasonable time* to present the document to the bailee and demand the goods. Obviously, if the bailee refuses to honor the document, the risk of loss remains with the seller [UCC 2–509(2) and 2–503(4)(b)].

Conditional Sales

Buyers and sellers sometimes form sales contracts that are conditioned either on the buyer's approval of the goods or on the buyer's resale of the goods. Under such contracts, the buyer is in possession of the goods, but sometimes problems arise as to whether the buyer or seller should bear the loss if, for example, the goods are damaged or stolen while in the possession of the buyer.

SALE ON APPROVAL
A type of conditional sale that becomes absolute only when the buyer approves or is satisfied with the good(s) sold. Besides express approval of goods, approval may be inferred if the buyer keeps the goods beyond a reasonable time or uses the goods in any way that is inconsistent with the seller's ownership.

Sale on Approval When a seller offers to sell goods to a buyer and permits the buyer to take the goods on a trial basis, a **sale on approval** is usually made. The term *sale* here is a misnomer, as only an *offer* to sell has been made, along with a *bailment* created by the buyer's possession. (A bailment is a temporary delivery of personal property into the care of another—see Chapter 33.)

Therefore, title and risk of loss (from causes beyond the buyer's control) remain with the seller until the buyer accepts (approves) the offer. Acceptance can be made expressly, by any act inconsistent with the *trial* purpose or the seller's ownership, or by the buyer's election not to return the goods within the trial period. If the buyer does not wish to accept, the buyer may notify the seller of that fact within the trial period, and the return is made at the seller's expense and risk [UCC 2–327(1)]. Goods held on approval are not subject to the claims of the buyer's creditors until acceptance.

SALE OR RETURN
A type of conditional sale wherein title and possession pass from the seller to the buyer; however, the buyer retains the option to rescind or return the goods during a specified period even though the goods conform to the contract.

Sale or Return A **sale or return** (sometimes called a *sale and return*) is a species of contract by which the seller delivers a quantity of goods to the buyer on the understanding that if the buyer wishes to retain any portion of those goods (for use or resale), the buyer will consider the portion retained as having been sold to him or her and will pay accordingly. The balance will be returned to the seller. When the buyer receives possession at the time of sale, the title and risk of loss pass to the buyer. Both remain with the buyer until the buyer returns the goods to the seller within the time period specified. If the buyer fails to return the goods within this time period, the sale is finalized. The return of the goods is made at the buyer's risk and expense. Goods held under a sale-or-return contract are subject to the claims of the buyer's creditors while they are in the buyer's possession.

Who holds title to consigned goods on display?

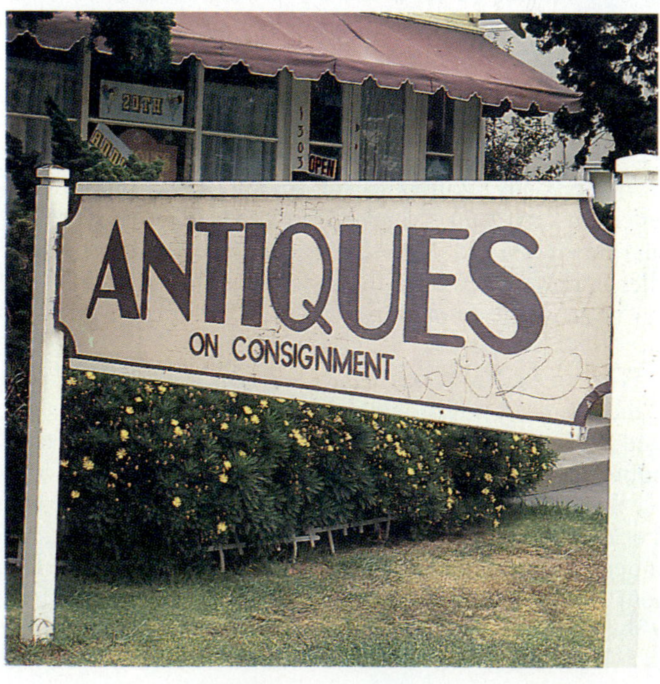

It is often difficult to determine from a particular transaction which exists—a contract for sale on approval or a contract for sale or return. The UCC states that (unless otherwise agreed) if the goods are primarily for the buyer to use, the transaction is a sale on approval; if the goods are primarily for the buyer to resell, the transaction is a sale or return [UCC 2–326(1)].

The UCC treats a **consignment** as a sale or return. Under a consignment, the owner of goods (the *consignor*) delivers them to another (the *consignee*) for the consignee to sell. If the consignee sells the goods, she or he must pay the consignor for them. If the goods are not sold, they may simply be returned to the consignor. While the goods are in the possession of the consignee, the consignee holds title to them, and creditors of the consignee will prevail over the consignor in any action to repossess the goods [UCC 2–326(3)].

CONSIGNMENT
A transaction in which an owner of goods (the consignor) delivers the goods to another (the consignee) for the consignee to sell. The consignee pays the consignor for the goods sold and returns unsold goods to the consignor.

Risk of Loss When a Sales Contract Is Breached

There are many ways to breach a sales contract, and the transfer of risk operates differently depending on whether the seller or the buyer breaches. Generally, the party in breach bears the risk of loss.

When the Seller Breaches If the goods are so nonconforming that the buyer has the right to reject them, the risk of loss does not pass to the buyer until the defects are **cured** (that is, until the goods are repaired, replaced, or discounted in price by the seller) or until the buyer accepts the goods in spite of their defects (thus waiving the right to reject). For example, a buyer orders blue widgets from a seller, F.O.B. seller's plant. The seller ships black widgets instead. The widgets are damaged in transit. The risk of loss falls on the seller (although the risk would have fallen on the buyer if blue widgets had been shipped) [UCC 2–510(2)].

CURE
The right of a party who tenders nonconforming performance to correct his or her performance within the contract period [UCC 3–508].

If a buyer accepts a shipment of goods and later discovers a defect, acceptance can be revoked. Revocation allows the buyer to pass the risk of loss back to the seller, at least to the extent that the buyer's insurance does not cover the loss [UCC 2–510(2)]. This situation is illustrated in the following case.

Case 15.3 

GRAYBAR ELECTRIC CO. v. SHOOK

Supreme Court of North Carolina, 1973.
283 N.C. 213,
195 S.E.2d 514.

HISTORICAL AND SOCIAL SETTING *Under the Uniform Sales Act, risk of loss was placed in some circumstances on the party who breached the contract. The UCC clearly provides that a party who breaches a contract bears the risk of loss. There have been relatively few cases arising under this provision of the UCC. This is in part because it seems reasonable that, for example, a seller should bear the risk when he or she has delivered goods that are nonconforming or clearly defective.*

FACTS Harold Shook agreed with Graybar Electric Company to purchase three reels of burial cable for use in Shook's construction work. When the reels were delivered, each carton was marked "burial cable," but two of the reels were in fact aerial cable. Shook accepted the conforming reel of cable and notified Graybar that he was rejecting the two reels of aerial cable. Because of a truckers' strike, Shook was unsuccessful in arranging for the return of the reels to Graybar and stored the reels in a well-lighted space near a grocery store owner's dwelling, which was close to Shook's work site. About four months later, Shook noticed that one of the reels had been stolen. On the following day, he notified Graybar of the loss and, worried about the safety of the second reel, arranged to have it transported to a garage for storage. Before the second reel was transferred, however, it was also stolen, and Shook notified Graybar of the second theft. Graybar sued Shook for the purchase price, claiming that Shook had agreed to return to Graybar the nonconforming reels and had failed to do so. Shook contended that he had agreed only to contact a trucking company to return the reels and, because he had contacted three trucking firms to no avail (owing to the strike), his obligation had been fulfilled. The trial court ruled for Shook, and Graybar appealed.

Case 15.3—Continued

ISSUE Who should bear the risk of loss for the reels?

DECISION Graybar. The Supreme Court of North Carolina affirmed the lower court's judgment in Shook's favor.

REASON The court relied on UCC 2–510(1), which states, "Where tender or delivery of goods so fails to conform to the contract as to give a right of rejection the risk of their loss remains on the seller until cure or acceptance." The court held that Shook had formed no contract with Graybar to return the nonconforming goods, although Shook had attempted to facilitate the aerial cable's return at the owner's request. Graybar, however, "with full notice of the place of storage which was at the place of delivery did nothing but sleep on its rights for more than three months." Thus, Graybar had evidenced neither promptness of action nor good faith.

"When the praying does no good, insurance does help."

Bertolt Brecht, 1898–1956
(German playwright and poet)

When the Buyer Breaches The general rule is that when a buyer breaches a contract, the risk of loss *immediately* shifts to the buyer. There are three important limitations to this rule:

1. The seller must already have identified the contract goods.
2. The buyer bears the risk for only a *commercially reasonable time* after the seller has learned of the breach.
3. The buyer is liable only to the extent of any *deficiency* in the seller's insurance coverage [UCC 2–510(3)].

❖ Insurable Interest

Buyers and sellers often obtain insurance coverage to protect against damage, loss, or destruction of goods. But any party purchasing insurance must have a sufficient interest in the insured item to obtain a valid policy. Insurance laws—not the UCC—determine sufficiency. The UCC is helpful, however, because it contains certain rules regarding the buyer's and seller's insurable interests in goods.

Buyer's Insurable Interest

INSURABLE INTEREST
An interest either in a person's life or well-being or in property that is sufficiently substantial that insuring against injury to the person or damage to the property does not amount to a mere wagering (betting) contract.

Buyers have an **insurable interest** in *identified* goods. The moment the contract goods are identified by the seller, the buyer has a special property interest that allows the buyer to obtain necessary insurance coverage for those goods even before the risk of loss has passed [UCC 2–501(1)].

Consider an example: In March, a farmer sells a cotton crop he hopes to harvest in October. After the crop is planted, the buyer insures it against hail damage. In September, a hailstorm ruins the crop. When the buyer files a claim under her insurance policy, the insurer refuses to pay the claim, asserting that the buyer has no insurable interest in the crop. The insurer is not correct. The buyer acquired an insurable interest in the crop when it was planted, because she had a contract to buy it. The rule in UCC 2–501(1)(c) states that such buyers obtain an insurable interest in crops by identification, which occurs "when the crops are planted or otherwise become growing crops * * * if the contract is * * * for the sale of crops to be harvested within twelve months or the next normal harvest season after contracting, whichever is longer."

Seller's Insurable Interest

A seller has an insurable interest in goods as long as he or she retains title to the goods. Even after title passes to a buyer, however, a seller who has a security interest

Business Law in Action

The Case of the Missing Art Dealer

The struggling artist has a hard enough life without also having to worry about shady art dealers. Usually, the struggling artist can look to the law for assistance if he or she suffers harm as a result of an art dealer's dishonesty or fraud. This was not so in the case of Jois Shuttie, an artist in Miami, Florida.

Shuttie, along with others in Miami's artistic community, came in contact with John Guggenheim, who had started the Guggenheim Gallery (later renamed the Guggenheim Collection) in the mid-1980s. Guggenheim led all concerned to believe that he was a member of the famous New York Guggenheim family of art patrons. On several occasions, Shuttie consigned to Guggenheim a number of paintings for display in Guggenheim's gallery. Unbeknownst to Shuttie, Guggenheim placed sixteen of Shuttie's paintings in a trendy Miami restaurant, called the Festa Restaurant. Guggenheim told the owner of the restaurant that the paintings were from his private collection. Guggenheim also placed a few more of Shuttie's paintings in another restaurant on Miami Beach.

When Shuttie discovered that his paintings were being displayed in the restaurants, he wrote Guggenheim and requested the return of all his paintings. When Guggenheim did not respond, Shuttie sent him another letter. In the meantime, Guggenheim convinced the owner of the Festa Restaurant to loan him $25,000 and to use the Shuttie paintings as security for the debt. Guggenheim also sent three paintings to New York for another loan of $30,000 from an unrelated party. A little while later, Guggenheim returned a few of Shuttie's paintings to Shuttie's apartment and then disappeared.

The normal arrangement between an artist and an art dealer or an owner of an art gallery is one of consignment. The artist consigns his or her paintings to the gallery, thereby giving the gallery owner the authority to sell the consigned artwork to whomever the art dealer chooses. In return, of course, the artist receives a percentage—normally between 40 and 70 percent—of the sales price. The sale to a third party ends the artist's ownership. During the time before a sale is made and the artist receives his or her share of the sales price, the artist can be at risk. The dealer's creditors may try to lay claim to the "consigned" works. That is exactly what happened to Shuttie.

Shuttie sued the Festa Restaurant to recover his paintings, but to no avail. Both the trial court and the appellate court held for the restaurant.[a] Why? Shuttie had failed to comply with the requirements of a Florida statute covering consignments of artwork. Therefore, the consignment was treated as a sale-or-return contract. Recall from the text that in a sale-or-return contract, the buyer has title to the goods sold as long as they are in the buyer's possession (that is, until they are returned to the seller when the buyer has been unable to resell them). Creditors of the buyer can thus lay claim to the goods if the buyer defaults on loans or other credit arrangements [UCC 2–326(3)]. Under the Florida statute, all an artist has to do to protect his or her interests when consigning artworks to a dealer is to affix to each work a sign or tag indicating that the artwork is being sold subject to a contract of consignment. If an artist complies with this requirement, then the statute accords "a priority in favor of the artist over claims, liens, or security interest of the creditors of the art dealer, notwithstanding any provisions of the UCC." Unfortunately for Shuttie, he did not comply with the statute, and the restaurant owner had the superior claim to the paintings.

a. *Shuttie v. Festa Restaurant, Inc.*, 556 So.2d 554 (Fla.App.3d 1990).

in the goods (a right to secure payment) still has an insurable interest and can insure the goods [UCC 2–501(2)].

Hence, both a buyer and a seller can have an insurable interest in identical goods at the same time. In all cases, they must sustain an actual loss to have the right to recover from an insurance company.

❖ Bulk Transfers

Special problems arise when a major portion of a business's assets are transferred. This is the subject matter of UCC Article 6, on bulk transfers. A *bulk transfer* is defined as any transfer of a major part of the transferor's material, supplies, merchandise, or other inventory *not made in the ordinary course of the transferor's business* [UCC 6–102(1)]. Difficulties may occur, for example, when a business that owes debts to numerous creditors sells a substantial part of its equipment and inventories to a buyer. The business should use the proceeds to pay off the debts. But what if the merchant instead spends the money on a trip, leaving the creditors without payment? Can the creditors lay any claim to the goods that were transferred in bulk to the buyer?

To prevent this situation, UCC 6–104 and 6–105 establish certain requirements for bulk transfers. All four of the following steps must be undertaken in order for the statutory requirements to be met:

1. The seller must furnish to the buyer a sworn list of his or her existing creditors. The list must include those whose claims are disputed and must state names, business addresses, and amounts due.
2. The buyer and the seller must prepare a schedule of the property to be transferred.
3. The buyer must preserve the list of creditors and the schedule of property for six months and permit inspection of the list by any creditor of the seller or must file the list and the schedule of property in a designated public office.
4. The buyer must give notice of the proposed bulk transfer to each of the seller's creditors at least ten days before the buyer takes possession of the goods or makes payments for them, whichever happens first.

If these requirements are met, the buyer acquires title to the goods free of all claims by the seller's creditors. If the requirements are not met, goods in the possession of the buyer continue to be subject to the claims of the unpaid creditors of the seller for six months [UCC 6–111].

Recently, the National Conference of Commissioners on Uniform State Laws recommended that those states that have adopted Article 6 repeal it, because changes in the business and legal contexts in which bulk sales are conducted have made their regulation unnecessary. For states disinclined to do so, Article 6 has been revised to provide creditors with better protection while reducing the burden imposed on good faith purchasers.

The revised Article 6 limits its application to bulk sales by sellers whose principal business is the sale of inventory from bulk stock. It does not apply to transactions involving property valued at less than $10,000 or more than $25 million. If a seller has more than two hundred creditors, rather than having to send individual notice to each creditor, a buyer can give notice by public filing (for example, in the office of a state's secretary of state). The notice period is increased from ten to forty-five days. The statute of limitations is extended from six months to one year.

Application

Law and the Shipper or Buyer—Who Bears the Risk of Loss?

A major aspect of commercial transactions involves the shipment of goods. Many issues arise when the unforeseen occurs, such as fire, theft, or other forms of damage to goods in transit.

The UCC uses a three-part checklist to determine risk of loss:

1. If the contract includes terms allocating risk of loss, those terms are binding and must be applied.
2. If the contract is silent as to risk, and either party breaches the contract, the breaching party is liable for risk of loss.
3. When a contract makes no reference to risk and neither party breaches, risk of loss is borne by the party having control over the goods.

If you are a seller of goods to be shipped, realize that as long as you have control over the goods, you are liable for any loss unless there is an explicit agreement to the contrary in the contract or a breach on the buyer's part.

When there is no explicit agreement, the UCC uses the delivery terms in your contract as a basis for determining control. Thus, "F.O.B. buyer's business" is a destination-delivery term, and risk of loss for goods shipped under those terms does not pass to the buyer until there is a tender of delivery at the point of destination. Any loss or damage in transit falls on the seller, because the seller has control until proper tender has been made.

From the buyer's point of view, it is important to remember that most sellers prefer "F.O.B. seller's business" delivery terms. Under these terms, once the goods are delivered to the carrier, the buyer bears the risk of loss. Thus, if conforming goods are completely destroyed or lost in transit, the buyer not only suffers the loss but is obligated to pay the seller the contract price.

At the time of contract negotiation, both the seller and the buyer should determine the importance of risk of loss. In some cases, risk is relatively unimportant (such as when ten boxes of mimeograph paper are being sold), and the delivery terms should simply reflect costs and price. In other cases, risk is extremely important (such as when a fragile piece of equipment is being sold), and the parties will need an express agreement as to the moment risk is to pass so that they can insure accordingly. The important point is that risk should be considered before the loss occurs, not after.

A major consideration relating to risk is when to insure goods against possible losses. Buyers and sellers should determine the point at which they have an insurable interest in the goods and obtain insurance coverage to protect them against loss from that point.

Checklist for the Shipment of Goods

- ☐ 1. Prior to entering a contract, determine the importance of risk of loss for a given sale.
- ☐ 2. If risk is extremely important, the contract should expressly state the moment risk of loss will pass from the seller to the buyer. This clause could even provide that risk will not pass until the goods are "delivered, installed, inspected, and tested (or in running order for a period of time)."
- ☐ 3. If an express clause is not agreed upon, delivery terms determine passage of risk of loss.
- ☐ 4. When appropriate, either or both parties should consider the need to procure insurance.

❖ Key Terms

❖ Chapter Summary: Title and Risk of Loss

Shipment Contracts	In the absence of an agreement, title and risk pass upon the seller's delivery of conforming goods to the carrier [UCC 2–401(2)(a), UCC 2–509(1)(a)].
Destination Contracts	In the absence of an agreement, title and risk pass upon the seller's *tender* of delivery of conforming goods to the buyer at the point of destination [UCC 2–401(2)(b), UCC 2–509(1)(b)].
Delivery without Movement of the Goods	1. In the absence of an agreement, if the goods are not represented by a document of title: a. Title passes upon the formation of the contract [UCC 2–401(3)(b)]. b. Risk passes to the buyer, if the seller is a merchant, upon the buyer's receipt of the goods or, if the seller is a nonmerchant, upon the seller's *tender* of delivery of the goods [UCC 2–509(3)]. 2. In the absence of an agreement, if the goods are represented by a document of title: a. If the document is negotiable, and the goods are held by a bailee, title and risk pass upon the buyer's *receipt* of the document [UCC 2–401(3)(a), UCC 2–509(2)(a)]. b. If the document is nonnegotiable, and the goods are held by a bailee, title passes upon the buyer's receipt of the document, but risk does *not* pass until the buyer, after receipt of the document, has had a reasonable time to present the document to demand the goods [UCC 2–401(3)(a), UCC 2–509(2)(c), UCC 2–503(4)(b)]. 3. In the absence of an agreement, if the goods are held by a bailee and no document of title is transferred, risk passes to the buyer when the bailee acknowledges the buyer's right to the possession of the goods [UCC 2–509(2)(b)].
Sales by Nonowners	Between the owner and a good faith purchaser: 1. Void title—owner prevails [UCC 2–403(1)]. 2. Voidable title—buyer prevails [UCC 2–403(1)]. 3. Entrusting to a merchant—buyer prevails [UCC 2–403(2), (3)].
Sale-on-Approval Contracts	Title and risk of loss (from causes beyond the buyer's control) remain with the seller until the buyer approves (accepts) the offer [UCC 2–327(1)].
Sale-or-Return Contracts	When the buyer receives possession of the goods, title and risk of loss pass to the buyer, with the buyer's option to return to the seller the goods, title, and risk [UCC 2–327(2)].
Passage of Risk of Loss When a Sales Contract Is Breached	1. If the seller breaches by tendering nonconforming goods that are rejected by the buyer, the risk of loss does not pass to the buyer until the defects are cured (unless the buyer accepts the goods in spite of their defects, thus waiving the right to reject) [UCC 2–510(1)]. 2. If the buyer breaches the contract, the risk of loss to identified goods immediately shifts to the buyer. Limitations to this rule are as follows: a. The seller must already have identified the contract goods. b. The buyer bears the risk for only a commercially reasonable time after the seller has learned of the breach. c. The buyer is liable only to the extent of any deficiency in the seller's insurance coverage [UCC 2–510(3)].
Buyer's Insurable Interest	Buyers have an insurable interest in goods the moment the goods are identified to the contract by the seller [UCC 2–510(3)].
Seller's Insurable Interest	Sellers have an insurable interest in goods as long as they have (1) title to the goods or (2) a security interest in the goods [UCC 2–501(2)].
Bulk Transfers	In a bulk transfer of assets, the buyer acquires title to the goods free of all claims of the seller's creditors if the following statutory requirements are met: 1. The transferor (seller) furnishes to the transferee (buyer) a sworn list of existing creditors, listing their names, business addresses, amounts due, and any disputed claims [UCC 6–104(1)(a)]. 2. The buyer and seller prepare a schedule of the property to be transferred [UCC 6–104(1)(b)]. 3. The buyer preserves the list of creditors and the schedule of property for six months, allowing any creditors of the seller to inspect it, or files the list and schedule of property in a designated public office [UCC 6–104(1)(c)]. 4. Notice of the proposed bulk transfer is given by the buyer to each creditor of the seller at least ten days before the buyer takes possession of the goods or pays for them, whichever happens first [UCC 6–105].

❖ Questions and Case Problems

15-1. Identification. What is the significance of identifying goods to a contract?

15-2. Risk of Loss. When will risk of loss pass from the seller to the buyer under each of the following contracts, assuming the parties have not expressly agreed on when risk of loss would pass?

(a) A New York seller contracts with a San Francisco buyer to ship goods to the buyer F.O.B. San Francisco.
(b) A New York seller contracts with a San Francisco buyer to ship goods to the buyer in San Francisco. There is no indication as to whether the shipment will be F.O.B. New York or San Francisco.
(c) A seller contracts with a buyer to sell goods located on the seller's premises. The buyer pays for the goods and makes arrangements to pick them up the next week at the seller's place of business.
(d) A seller contracts with a buyer to sell goods located in a warehouse.

15-3. Sales by Nonowners. Julian Makepeace, who had been declared mentally incompetent by a court, sold his diamond ring to Golding for value. Golding later sold the ring to Carmichael for value. Neither Golding nor Carmichael knew that Makepeace had been adjudged mentally incompetent by a court. Farrel, who had been appointed as Makepeace's guardian, subsequently learned that the diamond ring was in Carmichael's possession and demanded its return from Carmichael. Who has legal ownership of the ring? Why?

15-4. Risk of Loss. Alberto's Food Stores contracts to purchase from Giant Food Distributors, Inc., 100 cases of Golden Rod corn to be shipped F.O.B. seller's warehouse by Janson Truck Lines. Giant Food Distributors, by mistake, delivers 100 cases of Gold Giant corn to Janson Truck Lines. While in transit, the Gold Giant corn is stolen. Between Alberto's and Giant Food Distributors, who suffers the loss? Explain.

15-5. Sale on Approval. Chi Moy, a student, contracted to buy a television set from Ted's Electronics. Under the terms of the contract, Moy was to try out the set for thirty days, and if he liked it, he was to pay for the set at the end of the thirty-day period. If he did not want to purchase the set after thirty days, he could return the TV to Ted's Electronics with no obligation. Ten days after Moy took the set home, the set was stolen from Moy's apartment, although Moy had not been negligent in his care of the set in any way. Ted's Electronics claimed that Moy had to pay for the stolen set. Moy argued that the risk of loss fell on Ted's Electronics. Which party will prevail?

15-6. Sales by Nonowners. Tony Mangum contracted to purchase a 580C Case backhoe and loader from Liles Brothers & Son on November 25, 1977. The sales price was $20,561. Mangum wrote two checks in payment for the machine, one for $3,000 dated November 25 and one for $17,561 postdated to December 2. Liles checked with Mangum's bank and learned that there were sufficient funds to cover the $3,000 check, and Mangum assured Liles that by December 2 there would be sufficient funds in his account to cover the second check. Three days later, Mangum, posing as a heavy-equipment sales representative, sold the equipment for $11,000 to Carl Wright, who operated a septic-tank service. Wright had been looking for a backhoe and knew the market price for this equipment was around $20,000. Wright paid for the equipment with a certified check. On December 2, Liles learned that Mangum did not have funds in his bank account to cover the check dated December 2 and that Mangum was in jail. When Liles discovered that the backhoe was in Wright's possession, he sought the return of the backhoe from Wright. Does Wright have valid title to the backhoe? Explain. [*Liles Bros. & Son v. Wright*, 638 S.W.2d 383 (Tenn. 1982)]

15-7. **Entrustment Rule.** Samuel Porter was the owner of a Maurice Utrillo painting entitled "Chateau de Lion-sur Mer." Harold Von Maker, who called himself Peter Wertz, bought a different painting from Porter, paying $50,000 cash and giving Porter ten promissory notes for $10,000 each. At the same time, Wertz talked Porter into allowing Wertz to hang the Utrillo painting in Wertz's home while he decided whether to buy it. When the first promissory note was not paid, Porter learned that he was dealing with Von Maker, a man with a history of arrests and judgments against him. Von Maker told Porter that the Utrillo painting was on consignment and would be returned or Porter would receive $30,000. Actually, the painting had already been sold to the Feigen Gallery, which had in turn sold it to Irwin Brenner, trading under the name Irwin Brenner Gallery. At the time of this lawsuit, the painting was in Venezuela. Porter filed suit against Wertz, the Feigen Gallery, and Irwin Brenner to recover either possession of the painting or its value. The Feigen Gallery and Irwin Brenner claimed that they had good title under UCC 2–403 and that Porter was estopped from repossessing the painting or its value. Discuss whether Porter was entitled to repossession or the value of the Utrillo painting. [*Porter v. Wertz*, 68 A.D.2d 141, 416 N.Y.S.2d 254 (1979)]

15-8. Risk of Loss. Isis Foods, Inc., located in St. Louis, wanted to purchase a shipment of food from Pocasset Food Sales, Inc. The sale of food was initiated by a purchase order from Isis stating that the shipment was to be made "F.O.B. St. Louis." Pocasset made the shipment by delivery of the goods to the carrier. Pocasset's invoices contained a provision stating "Our liability ceases upon delivery of merchandise to carrier." The shipment of food was destroyed before reaching St. Louis. Discuss which party bears the risk of loss and why. [*In re Isis Foods, Inc.*, 38 Bankr. 48 (Bankr.W.D.Mo. 1983)]

15-9. **Sales by Nonowners.** A new car owned by a New Jersey car-rental agency was stolen in 1967. The agency collected the full price of the car from its insurance company, Home Indemnity Co., and assigned all its interest in the automobile to the insurer. Subsequently, the thief sold the car to an automobile wholesaler, who in turn sold it to a retail car dealer. Schrier purchased the car from the dealer without knowledge of the theft. Home Indemnity sued Schrier to recover the car. Can Home Indemnity recover? [*Schrier v. Home Indemnity Co.*, 273 A.2d 248 (D.C. 1971)]

15-10. **Sales by Nonowners.** Fred Lane was the owner of Lane's Outboard and was engaged in the business of selling boats, motors, and trailers. He sold a new boat, motor, and trailer to a person who called himself John

Willis. Willis took possession of the goods and paid for them with a check for $6,285. The check was later dishonored. About six months later, Jimmy Honeycutt bought the boat, motor, and trailer from a man identified as "Garrett," who was renting a summer beach house to the Honeycutts that year and whom Honeycutt had known for several years. Honeycutt paid $2,500 for the boating equipment and did not receive an official certificate of title. Lane sought to recover the boat, motor, and trailer from Honeycutt. Honeycutt's sole defense was that he was a good faith purchaser and therefore Lane should not be able to recover from him. Discuss whether Honeycutt will succeed in his defense. [*Lane v. Honeycutt*, 14 N.C.App. 436, 188 S.E.2d 604 (1972)]

15-11. Sale or Return. Hargo Woolen Mills had purchased bales of surplus wool fibers, which Hargo used in its manufacture of woolen cloth, from Shabry Trading Co. for many years. On one occasion, however, Shabry shipped twenty-four bales to Hargo without an order. Rather than pay for reshipment, both parties decided that Hargo would retain possession of the bales and pay for what it used. Hargo kept the bales separate inside its warehouse and eventually used, and was billed for, eight bales. The remaining sixteen bales were still kept separate by Hargo. Hargo went bankrupt, and everything in its warehouse was taken by the receiver, Meinhard-Commercial Corp. Shabry claimed that it was the owner and title holder of the bales and requested their return, but Meinhard-Commercial refused to return them. Should Shabry be able to retake possession of the bales? [*Meinhard-Commercial Corp. v. Hargo Woolen Mills*, 112 N.H.500, 300 A.2d 321 (1972)]

15-12. Risk of Loss. Donald Hayward agreed to buy a thirty-foot Revel Craft Playmate Yacht from Herbert F. Postma, a yacht dealer, on February 7, 1967. The boat was to be delivered to a slip on Lake Macatawa during April 1967. Hayward signed a security agreement on March 1, 1967, and gave a promissory note for $13,095.60 to Postma's dealership. The note was subsequently assigned to a bank. The security agreement contained clauses requiring the buyer to keep the boat in first-class order or repair and to keep the boat fully insured at all times. After Hayward had made some payments but before the boat was delivered to Hayward, it was destroyed by fire. Neither Postma nor Hayward had insured the boat, and Hayward requested that Postma pay off the note or reimburse him for payments made. Postma refused, and Hayward sued. Discuss whether Hayward or Postma bears the risk of loss as to the boat destroyed in the fire. [*Hayward v. Postma*, 31 Mich.App. 720, 188 N.W.2d 31 (1971)]

15-13. Entrustment Rule. Bobby Locke, the principal stockholder and chief executive officer (CEO) of Worthco Farm Center, Inc., hired a Mr. Hobby as the company's manager. Subsequently, it was discovered that during the approximately thirteen months of Locke's tenure as CEO, Hobby had sold corn stored with Worthco to Arabi Grain & Elevator Co. and pocketed the proceeds. When Locke brought an action against Arabi to recover the corn, Arabi alleged, among other things, that Locke had entrusted the corn to Hobby and that because Arabi was a purchaser in the ordinary course of business, Hobby had transferred ownership rights in the corn to Arabi. Assuming that Arabi was a buyer in the ordinary course of business, how should the court rule? Discuss. [*Locke v. Arabi Grain & Elevator Co.*, 197 Ga.App. 854, 399 S.E.2d 705 (1991)]

A Question of Ethics and Social Responsibility

15-14. *When Toby and Rita Kahr donated some used clothing to Goodwill Industries, Inc., they were not aware that a small bag containing their sterling silver had been accidentally included in one of the bags of donated clothing. The silverware, which was valued at over $3,500, had been given to them twenty-seven years earlier by Rita's father as a wedding present and had great sentimental value for them. The Kahrs realized what had happened shortly after Toby returned from Goodwill, but when Toby called Goodwill, he was told that the silver had immediately been sold to a customer, Karon Markland, for $15. Although Goodwill called Markland and asked her to return the silver, Markland refused to return it. The Kahrs then brought an action against Markland to regain the silver, claiming that Markland did not have good title to it. In view of these circumstances, discuss the following issues.* [Kahr v. Markland, *187 Ill.App.3d 603, 543 N.E.2d 579, 135 Ill.Dec. 196 (1989)*]

1. The basic issue in this case is whether the silver was "lost property" (defined as property unintentionally separated from its owner) or property entrusted to a merchant, Goodwill Industries. If the court decides that the silver was lost, the party in possession of the property will have good title against all parties except the true owner—in which case, the Kahrs will be able to recover the silver from Markland. If the court decides that the Kahrs entrusted the silver to Goodwill, then the entrustment rule will be applied—in which case, the Kahrs will be unable to recover the silver from Markland, a good faith purchaser. If you were the judge, how would you decide the issue? Why?
2. The entrustment rule can sometimes result in unfair treatment of the entrustor, because the entrustor cannot recover the property from a good faith purchaser (although the entrustor can recover the *value* of the property from the merchant who wrongfully sold the entrusted property). Given this potential for unfair treatment, how can the entrustment rule be justified from an ethical point of view?
3. Did Karon Markland act wrongfully in any way by not returning the silver to Goodwill when requested to do so? What would you have done in her position?
4. Goodwill argued that the entrustment rule should apply. Is this ethical behavior on the part of Goodwill? Why or why not? How might Goodwill justify its argument from an ethical point of view?

For Critical Analysis

15-15. *Under the UCC, passage of title does not always occur simultaneously with passage of risk of loss. Why is this? Give some examples of what might result if risk of loss and title always passed from the buyer to the seller at the same time.*

Chapter 16

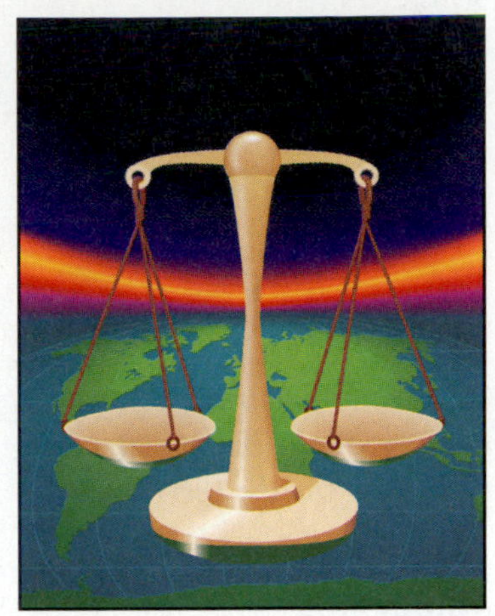

Performance and Breach

> *"It has been uniformly laid down . . . , as far back as we can remember, that good faith is the basis of all mercantile transactions."*
>
> **J. Buller, 1746–1800**
> ***(British jurist)***

Most sales contracts involve virtually no problems. Billions of such contracts are carried out every year in the United States without any difficulties. This is because most people are aware of, and try to fulfill, their contractual obligations.

To understand the performance that is required of a seller and a buyer under a sales contract, it is necessary to know the duties and obligations each party has assumed under the terms of the contract. Keep in mind that "duties and obligations" under the terms of the contract here include those specified by the agreement, by custom, and by the Uniform Commercial Code (UCC). In this chapter, after first looking at the general requirement of good faith, we will examine the basic performance obligations of the buyer and the seller under a sales contract.

Sometimes circumstances make it difficult for a person to carry out the promised performance, in which case the contract may be breached. When breach occurs, the aggrieved party looks for remedies—which are dealt with in the second half of the chapter.

❖ Good Faith and Commercial Reasonableness

Sometimes the sales contract leaves open some particulars of performance and permits one of the parties to specify them. Here, as elsewhere, the obligations of "good faith" and "commercial reasonableness" come into play. Indeed, these obligations underlie every sales contract within the UCC. They are obligations that can form the basis for a breach of contract suit later on. As discussed in the *Ethical Perspective* in Chapter 14 and stressed in the opening quotation to this chapter, these standards are read into every contract, and they provide a framework in which the parties can specify particulars of performance. "Any such specification must be made in good faith and within limits set by commercial reasonableness" [UCC 2–311(1)].

Thus, when one party delays specifying particulars of performance for an unreasonable period of time or fails to cooperate with the other party, the innocent party is excused from any resulting delay in performance. In addition, the innocent party can proceed to perform in any reasonable manner. If the innocent party has performed as far as is reasonably possible under the circumstances, the other party's failure to specify particulars or to cooperate can be treated as a breach of contract. Good faith is a question of fact for the jury.

❖ Performance of a Sales Contract

In the performance of a sales contract, a seller has the basic obligation to *transfer and deliver conforming goods.* The buyer has the basic obligation to *accept and pay for conforming goods* in accordance with the contract [UCC 2–301]. Overall performance of a sales contract is controlled by the agreement between the buyer and the seller. When the contract is unclear and disputes arise, the courts look to the UCC.

"It is only when merchants dispute about their own rules that they invoke the law."

J. Brett, 1815–1899
(British jurist)

❖ Obligations of the Seller

The seller's major obligation under a sales contract is to *tender* conforming goods to the buyer.

Tender of Delivery

TENDER OF DELIVERY
A seller's holding out conforming goods in a reasonable manner with notice to enable the buyer to take delivery.

Tender of delivery requires that the seller have and hold *conforming* goods at the buyer's disposal and give the buyer whatever notification is reasonably necessary to enable the buyer to take delivery [UCC 2–503(1)].

Tender must occur at a *reasonable hour* and in a *reasonable manner.* In other words, a seller cannot call the buyer at 2:00 A.M. and say, "The goods are ready. I'll give you twenty minutes to get them." Unless the parties have agreed otherwise, the goods must be tendered for delivery at a reasonable time and kept available for a reasonable period of time to enable the buyer to take possession of them [UCC 2–503(1)(a)].

All goods called for by a contract must be tendered in a single delivery unless the parties agree otherwise [UCC 2–612] or the circumstances are such that either party can rightfully request delivery in lots [UCC 2–307]. Hence, an order for 1,000 shirts cannot be delivered 2 shirts at a time. If, however, the seller and the buyer contemplate that the shirts will be delivered in four orders of 250 each, as they are produced (for summer, winter, fall, and spring stock), and the price can be apportioned accordingly, it may be commercially reasonable to deliver the shirts in this way.

Place of Delivery

The UCC provides for the place of delivery pursuant to a contract if the contract does not. Of course, the parties may agree on a particular destination, or their contract's terms or the circumstances may indicate the place.

Noncarrier Cases If the contract does not designate the place of delivery for the goods, and the buyer is expected to pick them up, the place of delivery is the *seller's place of business* or, if the seller has none, the *seller's residence* [UCC 2–308]. If the contract involves the sale of *identified goods,* and the parties know when they enter into the contract that these goods are located somewhere other than at the seller's place of business (such as at a warehouse), then the *location of the goods* is the place for their delivery [UCC 2–308].

For example, Rogers and Aguirre live in San Francisco. In San Francisco, Rogers contracts to sell Aguirre five used trucks, which both parties know are located in Chicago. If nothing more is specified in the contract, the place of delivery for the trucks is Chicago. Assume further that the trucks are stored in a warehouse and that Aguirre will need some type of document to show the bailee (the warehouser to

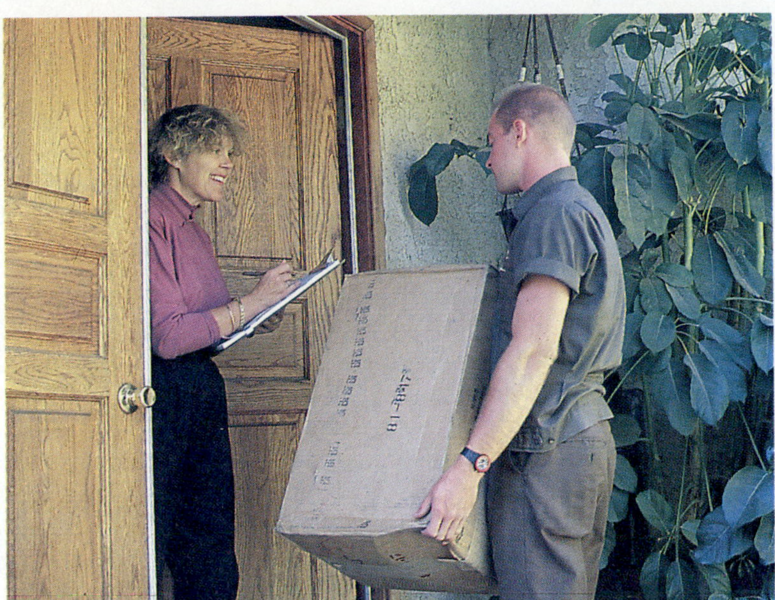

Under what circumstances can a buyer reject goods without breaching the sales contract?

whom the goods are entrusted) in Chicago that Aguirre is entitled to take possession of the five trucks. The seller "tenders delivery" without moving the goods. The seller may "deliver" by either giving the buyer a *negotiable or nonnegotiable document of title* or obtaining the *bailee's (warehouser's) acknowledgment* that the buyer is entitled to possession.[1]

Carrier Cases In many instances, attendant circumstances or delivery terms in the contract make it apparent that the parties intend that a carrier be used to move the goods. There are two ways a seller can complete performance of the obligation to deliver the goods in carrier cases—through a shipment contract and through a destination contract.

Shipment Contracts Recall from Chapter 15 that a *shipment contract* requires or authorizes the seller to ship goods by a carrier. The contract does not require that the seller deliver the goods at a particular destination [UCC 2–509 and 2–319]. Unless otherwise agreed, the seller must do the following:

1. Put the goods into the hands of the carrier.
2. Make a contract for their transportation that is reasonable according to the nature of the goods and their value. (For example, certain types of goods need refrigeration in transit.)
3. Obtain and promptly deliver or tender to the buyer any documents necessary to enable the buyer to obtain possession of the goods from the carrier.
4. Promptly notify the buyer that shipment has been made [UCC 2–504].

If the seller fails to notify the buyer that shipment has been made or fails to make a proper contract for transportation, and a *material loss* of the goods or a significant *delay* results, the buyer can reject the shipment. Of course, the parties can agree that a lesser amount of loss or any delay will be grounds for rejection.

---

1. If the seller delivers a nonnegotiable document of title or merely writes instructions to the bailee to release the goods to the buyer without the bailee's *acknowledgment* of the buyer's rights, this is also a sufficient tender, unless the buyer objects [UCC 2–503(4)]. But risk of loss does not pass until the buyer has a reasonable amount of time in which to present the document or the instructions.

Destination Contracts Under a *destination contract,* the seller agrees to see that conforming goods will be duly tendered to the buyer at a particular destination. The goods must be tendered at a reasonable hour and held at the buyer's disposal for a reasonable length of time. The seller must also give the buyer appropriate notice. In addition, the seller must provide the buyer with any documents of title necessary to enable the buyer to obtain delivery from the carrier. This is often done by tendering the documents through ordinary banking channels [UCC 2–503].

The Perfect Tender Rule

"It is the duty of a judge to inquire not only into the matter but into the circumstances of the matter."

Ovid, 43 B.C.–17 A.D.
(Roman poet)

As previously noted, the seller has an obligation to ship or tender *conforming goods,* and this entitles the seller to acceptance by and payment from the buyer according to the terms of the contract. Under the common law, the seller was obligated to deliver goods in conformity with the terms of the contract in every detail. This was called the *perfect tender* doctrine. The UCC (in Section 2–601) preserves the perfect tender doctrine by stating that "if goods or tender of delivery fail *in any respect* to conform to the contract" (emphasis added), the buyer has the right to accept the goods, reject the entire shipment, or accept part and reject part.

For example, a buyer contracts to purchase 200 cases of Brand X canned carrots to be delivered at the buyer's place of business on or before October 1. On September 28, the seller discovers that there are only 180 cases of Brand X in inventory, but there will be another 500 cases within the next two weeks. So the seller tenders delivery of the 180 cases of Brand X on October 1, with the promise that the other cases will be delivered within three weeks. Because the seller failed to make a perfect tender of 200 cases of Brand X, the buyer has the right to reject the entire shipment and hold the seller in breach.

Exceptions to the Perfect Tender Rule

Because of the rigidity of the perfect tender rule, several exceptions to the rule have been created, some of which are discussed here.

Agreement of the Parties Exceptions to the perfect tender rule may be established by agreement. If the parties have agreed, for example, that defective goods or parts will not be rejected if the seller is able to repair or replace them within a reasonable period of time, the perfect tender rule does not apply.

Cure The term cure is not specifically defined in the UCC, but it refers to the seller's right to repair, adjust, or replace defective or nonconforming goods [UCC 2–508]. When any tender or delivery is rejected because of nonconforming goods and the time for performance has not yet expired, the seller can notify the buyer promptly of the intention to cure and can then do so *within the contract time for performance* [UCC 2–508(1)]. Once the time for performance under the contract has expired, the seller can still exercise the right to cure if the seller had *reasonable grounds to believe that the nonconforming tender would be acceptable to the buyer* [UCC 2–508(2)].

Frequently, a seller will tender nonconforming goods with some type of price allowance. The allowance serves as the "reasonable grounds" for the seller to believe the nonconforming tender will be acceptable to the buyer. Other reasons might also serve as the basis for a seller's assumption that a buyer will accept a nonconforming tender. For example, if in the past a buyer frequently accepted a particular substitute for a good when the good ordered was not available, the seller has reasonable grounds to believe the buyer will again accept such a substitute. If the buyer rejects the substitute good on a particular occasion, the seller nonetheless had reasonable grounds to believe that the substitute would be acceptable. Therefore, the seller can cure within a reasonable time, even though conforming delivery will occur after the time limit for performance allowed under the contract.

The seller's right to cure substantially restricts the buyer's right to reject. If the buyer refuses a tender of goods as nonconforming but does not disclose the nature of the defect to the seller, the buyer cannot later assert the defect as a defense if the defect is one that the seller could have cured. The buyer must act in good faith and state specific reasons for refusing to accept the goods [UCC 2–605].

Substitution of Carriers When an agreed manner of delivery (such as which carrier will be used to transport the goods) becomes impracticable or unavailable through no fault of either party, but a commercially reasonable substitute is available, this substitute performance is sufficient tender to the buyer [UCC 2–614(1)].

For example, a sales contract calls for the delivery of a large piece of machinery to be shipped by Roadway Trucking Corporation on or before June 1. The contract terms clearly state the importance of the delivery date. The employees of Roadway Trucking go on strike. The seller will be entitled to make a reasonable substitute tender, perhaps by rail. Note that the seller here is responsible for any additional shipping costs, unless contrary arrangements have been made in the sales contract.

Installment Contracts An **installment contract** is a single contract that requires or authorizes delivery in two or more separate lots to be accepted and paid for separately. In an installment contract, a buyer can reject an installment *only if the nonconformity substantially impairs the value* of the installment and cannot be cured [UCC 2–612(2) and 2–307].

INSTALLMENT CONTRACT
A contract in which payments due are made periodically. Also may allow for delivery of goods in separate lots with payment made for each.

The entire installment contract is breached only when one or more nonconforming installments *substantially* impair the value of the *whole contract.* If the buyer subsequently accepts a nonconforming installment and fails to notify the seller of cancellation, however, the contract is reinstated [UCC 2–612(3)].

A major issue to be determined is what constitutes substantial impairment of the "value of the whole contract." For example, consider an installment contract for the sale of twenty carloads of plywood. The first carload does not conform to the contract because 9 percent of the plywood deviates from the thickness specifications. The buyer cancels the contract, and immediately thereafter the second and third carloads of plywood arrive at the buyer's place of business. If a lawsuit ensued, the court would have to grapple with the question of whether the 9 percent of nonconforming plywood substantially impaired the value of the whole.[2]

The point to remember is that the UCC substantially alters the right of a buyer to reject the entire contract if the contract requires delivery to be made in several installments. Such contracts are broadly defined in the UCC, which strictly limits rejection to cases of substantial nonconformity.

Commercial Impracticability Occurrences unforeseen by either party when the contract was made may make performance commercially impracticable. When this is the case, the rule of perfect tender no longer holds. According to UCC 2–615(a), delay in delivery or nondelivery in whole or in part is not a breach when performance has been made impracticable "by the occurrence of a contingency the nonoccurrence of which was a basic assumption on which the contract was made." The seller must, however, notify the buyer as soon as practicable that there will be a delay or nondelivery.

"Inability suspends the law."

(Legal maxim)

The notion of commercial impracticability is derived from contract law theories relating to impossibility of performance (see Chapter 12). An increase in cost re-

2. *Continental Forest Products, Inc. v. White Lumber Sales, Inc.*, 256 Or. 466, 474 P.2d 1 (1970). The court held that the deviation did not substantially impair the value of the whole contract. Additionally, the court stated that the nonconformity could be cured by an adjustment in the price.

sulting from inflation does not in and of itself excuse performance, as this kind of risk is ordinarily assumed by a seller conducting business. The unforeseen contingency must be one that would have been impossible to contemplate in a given business situation.

For example, a major oil company that receives its supplies from the Middle East has a contract to supply a buyer with 100,000 gallons of oil. Because of an oil embargo by the Organization of Petroleum Exporting Countries (OPEC), the seller is prevented from securing oil supplies to meet the terms of the contract. Because of the same embargo, the seller cannot secure oil from any other source. This situation comes fully under the commercial-impracticability exception to the perfect tender doctrine.

Sometimes the unforeseen event only *partially* affects the seller's capacity to perform, and the seller is thus able to fulfill the contract *partially* but cannot tender total performance. In this event, the seller is required to allocate in a fair and reasonable manner any remaining production and deliveries among contracted and regular customers. The buyer must receive notice of the allocation, with the obvious right to accept or reject the allocation.

For example, a Florida orange grower, Best Citrus, Inc., contracts to sell this season's production to a number of customers, including Martin's grocery chain. Martin's contracts to purchase 2,000 crates of oranges. Best Citrus has sprayed *some* of its orange groves with a chemical called Karmoxin. The Department of Agriculture discovers that persons who eat products sprayed with Karmoxin may develop cancer. An order prohibiting the sale of these products is effected. Best Citrus picks all the oranges not sprayed with Karmoxin, but the quantity does not fully meet all the contracted-for deliveries. In this case, Best Citrus is required to allocate its production, notifying Martin's that it cannot deliver the full quantity agreed upon in the contract and specifying the amount it will be able to deliver under the circumstances. Martin's can either accept or reject the allocation, but Best has no further contractual liability.

Can unanticipated increases in a seller's costs, which make performance "impracticable," constitute a valid defense to performance on the basis of commercial impracticability? The court deals with this question in the following case.

Case 16.1 

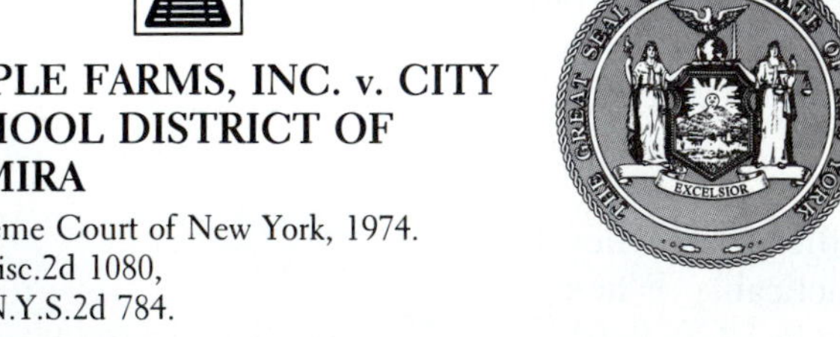

MAPLE FARMS, INC. v. CITY SCHOOL DISTRICT OF ELMIRA

Supreme Court of New York, 1974.
76 Misc.2d 1080,
352 N.Y.S.2d 784.

HISTORICAL AND ECONOMIC SETTING *In 1972, the former Soviet Union (now fifteen independent republics) suffered its worst drought in ten years, forcing it to buy American grain, including 25 percent of the U.S. wheat crop. This led to higher U.S. grain prices, which consequently forced up the prices of other food, including dairy products. In response, U.S. farmers planted more grain. Nevertheless, food prices continued to rise. Consumers organized boycotts in protest. On June 13, 1973, President Richard Nixon ordered a temporary freeze on all retail food prices. On June 27, Nixon ordered a temporary embargo on soybean exports. The embargo shocked foreign buyers. Although the embargo was lifted after five days, amounts due under previous contracts were cut 40 to 50 percent. Fearing further controls would be applied, foreign buyers doubled their purchases of U.S. grain. In response, U.S. farmers held back their crops as prices were bid up.*

FACTS On June 15, 1973, Maple Farms, Inc., formed an agreement with the city school district of Elmira, New York, to supply the school district with milk for the 1973–1974 school year. The agreement was in the form of a requirements contract, under which Maple Farms would sell to the school district all the milk the district required at a fixed price—which was the June market price of milk. By December of 1973, the price of raw milk had increased by 23 percent over the price specified in the contract. This meant that if the terms of the contract were fulfilled, Maple Farms would lose $7,350. Because it had similar contracts with other school districts, Maple Farms stood to lose a great deal if it was held to the price stated in the contracts. When the school district would not agree to release Maple Farms from its contract, Maple Farms brought an action for a de-

Case 16.1—Continued

claratory judgment (a determination of the parties' rights under a contract). It contended that the substantial increase in the price of raw milk was an event not contemplated by the parties when the contract was formed and that, given the increased price, performance of the contract was commercially impracticable.

ISSUE Can Maple Farms be released from the contract on the grounds of commercial impracticability?

DECISION No. The court ruled that performance in this case was not impracticable.

REASON The court reasoned that commercial impracticability arises when an event occurs that is totally unexpected and unforeseeable by the parties. The increased price of raw milk was not totally unexpected, given the facts that in the previous year the price of milk had risen 10 percent and that the price of milk had traditionally varied. Also, the general inflation of prices in the United States should have been anticipated. Maple Farms had reason to know these facts and could have placed a clause in its contract with the school district to protect itself from its present situation. The court also noted that the primary purpose of the contract, on the part of the school district, was to protect itself (for budgeting purposes) against price fluctuations.

Destruction of Identified Goods The UCC provides that when an unexpected event, such as a fire, totally destroys *goods identified* at the time the contract is formed through no fault of either party and *before risk passes to the buyer*, the seller and buyer are excused from performance [UCC 2–613(a)]. If the goods are only partially destroyed, however, the buyer can inspect them and either treat the contract as void or accept the damaged goods with a reduction of the contract price.

Consider an example. Atlas Appliances has on display six Model X dishwashers, a model that has been discontinued. Five are white, and one is black. No others of that model are available. Rivers, who is not a merchant, clearly specifies that she needs the black dishwasher because it fits her kitchen's color scheme, and she buys it. Before Atlas can deliver the dishwasher, it is destroyed by a fire. In such a case, under Section 2–613 of the UCC, Atlas Appliances is not liable to Rivers for failing to deliver the black dishwasher. The goods were destroyed, through no fault of either party, before the risk of loss passed to the buyer. The loss was total, so the contract is avoided. Clearly, Atlas has no obligation to tender that dishwasher, and Rivers has no obligation to pay for it.

❖ Obligations of the Buyer

Once the seller has adequately tendered delivery, the buyer is obligated to accept the goods and pay for them according to the terms of the contract. In the absence of any specific agreements, the buyer must do the following:

1. Furnish facilities reasonably suited for receipt of the goods [UCC 2–503(1)(b)].
2. Make payment at the time and place the buyer *receives* the goods, even if the place of shipment is the place of delivery [UCC 2–310(a)].

Payment

When a sale is made on credit, the buyer is obliged to pay according to the specified credit terms (for example, 60, 90, or 120 days), *not* when the goods are received. The credit period usually begins on the *date of shipment* [UCC 2–310(d)].

Payment can be made by any means agreed upon between the parties—cash or any other method generally acceptable in the commercial world. If the seller de-

Business Law in Action

Look before You Leap (to Conclusions)

The doctrine of commercial impracticability, by allowing buyers and sellers to be excused from performance of their contracts in certain situations, is one of the exceptions to the rule that contracts freely entered into will be enforced. But as mentioned in this chapter's text, courts will not normally excuse performance under this doctrine unless performance becomes *extremely* impracticable or objectively impossible. While a party to a sales contract may assume that a certain event has rendered performance impracticable and repudiate a contract for this reason, a court may not agree with the assessment. As a result, the buyer or seller may end up paying damages for anticipatory breach of contract. This is exactly what happened to a buyer, Medcon Enterprises, Inc., when President Bush imposed a freeze on all Iraqi assets in the United States in the fall of 1990.

Medcon had contracted with Engel Industries, Inc., to purchase from Engel certain heavy machinery, which Medcon would then sell to a purchaser in Iraq. The financing was to be handled through First American Bank.

The bank was to pay Engel 10 percent of the amount ($27,210) upon the completion of general assembly drawings of the machinery. The bank would pay Engel the remainder of the contract price when Engel submitted documents proving that the machinery was crated, labeled, and ready for shipment to Iraq, which was to be no later than August 24, 1990.

The transaction did not go as planned, however, because on August 2, 1990, the president ordered a freeze on all Iraqi assets in the United States. On August 8, Medcon wrote Engel a letter stating that because of the president's order, Medcon "must and hereby does withdraw, cancel and rescind" its purchase order for the machinery. On August 14, First American wrote Engel a letter stating that it was prohibited by the president's order from making payment. But by this time, Engel had already substantially completed its performance under the contract. The only things left to be done were the painting and crating of the equipment. In an effort to mitigate its damages, Engel sold some of the machinery over the next few months but was unable to recoup its losses, which totaled $148,000. Eventually, Engel sued Medcon and First American.

The essential question before the court was, of course, whether the president's order had in fact rendered it impossible (illegal) for Medcon and First American to perform their obligations. The court held to the contrary.

In forming this conclusion, the court relied on an opinion it had requested from the federal Office of Foreign Assets Control (OFAC) regarding the legal effect of the freeze on contracts, specifically the Medcon-Engel contract. According to the court, OFAC stated that to be effective, a freeze must create "the broadest possible embargo," but that this sweeping interpretation "may then be fine-tuned by interpretations, specific and general licenses when the nature and relative importance of various types of Iraqi property and transactions with Iraq have been assessed." OFAC stated that the freeze did not prevent the bank's payment to Engel. "First American always retained the option of applying for a specific license from OFAC so that it could pay Engel. OFAC concluded that under the current regulations: OFAC would treat the financing agreement for the Medcon-Engel contract as incidental to a domestic transaction * * *, and would permit payment by First American upon a court finding that all * * * conditions to payment by First American were complied with."

Accepting OFAC's opinion on the matter, the court found that both Medcon and First American had committed an anticipatory breach of contract when they wrote to Engel stating that they would not perform their obligations. Neither party retracted its anticipatory repudiation. Therefore, Engel, which had exercised its right under the UCC to complete its performance and resell the goods, was entitled to damages.[a]

The moral of this story is that buyers and sellers should not leap to the conclusion that performance is impossible without investigating the matter fully. Implicit in the court's judgment in this case is that Medcon and First American, upon learning of the president's order, should have done as the court itself did: request information from an appropriate government agency on how the freeze would affect their contractual obligations. Had they done so, they would have learned, as the court did, that performance under their contract was not impossible after all.

a. *Engel Industries, Inc. v. First American Bank, N.A.*, 798 F.Supp. 9 (D.C. 1992).

mands cash when the buyer offers a check, credit card, or the like, the seller must permit the buyer reasonable time to obtain legal tender [UCC 2–511].

Right of Inspection

Unless otherwise agreed, or for C.O.D. (collect on delivery) goods, the buyer's right to inspect the goods is absolute. This right allows the buyer to verify, before making payment, that the goods tendered or delivered are what were contracted for or ordered. If the goods are not what the buyer ordered, the buyer has no duty to pay. *An opportunity for inspection is therefore a condition precedent to the seller's right to enforce payment* [UCC 2–513(1)].

Unless otherwise agreed, inspection can take place at any reasonable place and time and in any reasonable manner. Generally, what is reasonable is determined by custom of the trade, past practices of the parties, and the like. Costs of inspecting conforming goods are borne by the buyer unless otherwise agreed [UCC 2–513(2)].

C.O.D. Shipments If a seller ships goods to a buyer C.O.D. (or under similar terms) and the buyer has not agreed to a C.O.D. shipment in the contract, the buyer can rightfully *reject* them. This is because a C.O.D. shipment does not permit inspection before payment, which is a denial of the buyer's right of inspection. But when the buyer has agreed to a C.O.D. shipment in the contract or has agreed to pay for the goods upon the presentation of a bill of lading, no right of inspection exists because it was negated by the agreement [UCC 2–513(3)].

Payment Due—Documents of Title Under certain contracts, payment is due upon the receipt of the required documents of title even though the goods themselves may not have arrived at their destination. With C.I.F. and C.&F. contracts (see Exhibit 15–4 in Chapter 15), payment is required upon receipt of the documents unless the parties have agreed otherwise. Thus, payment is required prior to inspection, and it must be made unless the buyer knows that the goods are nonconforming [UCC 2–310(b) and 2–513(3)].

Acceptance

The buyer can manifest assent to the delivered goods in the following three ways, each of which constitutes acceptance.

1. The buyer can expressly accept the shipment by words or conduct. For example, there is an acceptance if the buyer, after having had a reasonable opportunity to inspect the goods, signifies agreement to the seller that the goods are either conforming or are acceptable despite their nonconformity [UCC 2–606(1)(a)].
2. Acceptance is presumed if the buyer has had a reasonable opportunity to inspect the goods and has failed to reject them within a reasonable period of time [UCC 2–606(1)(b) and 2–602(1)].
3. The buyer accepts the goods by performing any act inconsistent with the seller's ownership. For example, any use or resale of the goods generally constitutes an acceptance. Limited use for the sole purpose of testing or inspecting the goods is not an acceptance, however [UCC 2–606(1)(c)].

Revocation of Acceptance

Acceptance of the goods by the buyer precludes the buyer from exercising the right of rejection. Acceptance does not in and of itself impair the right of the buyer to pursue remedies (discussed later in this chapter). But if the buyer accepts the nonconforming goods and fails to notify the seller of the breach when it is discovered (or when it should have been discovered), the buyer is barred from pursuing any remedy against the seller. In other words, the buyer must inform the seller of the breach within a reasonable time. The burden is on the buyer to establish the existence of a breach of contract once the goods have been accepted [UCC 2–607(3)].

After a buyer has accepted a lot or a commercial unit, any return of the goods must be carried out by *revocation of acceptance*. Acceptance can be revoked if the nonconformity *substantially* impairs the value of the unit or lot and if one of the following factors is present:

1. If acceptance was predicated on the reasonable assumption that the nonconformity would be cured and it has not been cured within a reasonable period of time [UCC 2–608(1)(a)].
2. If the buyer did not discover the nonconformity before acceptance, either because it was difficult to discover before acceptance or because the seller's assurance that the goods were conforming kept the buyer from inspecting the goods [UCC 2–608(1)(b)].

Revocation of acceptance is not effective until notice is given to the seller, which must occur within a reasonable time after the buyer either discovers *or should have discovered* the grounds for revocation. Also, revocation must occur before the goods have undergone any substantial change (such as spoilage) not caused by their own defects [UCC 2–608(2)].

If some of the goods delivered do not conform to the contract, and the seller has failed to cure, the buyer can make a *partial* acceptance [UCC 2–601(c)]. The same is true if the nonconformity was not reasonably discoverable before acceptance. A buyer cannot accept less than a single commercial unit, however. According to Section 2–105 of the UCC, a *commercial unit* is a unit of goods that, by commercial usage, is viewed as a "single whole" for purposes of sale, division of which would materially impair the character of the unit, its market value, or its use. A commercial unit can be a single article (such as a machine), or a set of articles (such as a suite of furniture or an assortment of sizes), or a quantity (such as a bale, a gross, or a carload), or any other unit treated in the trade as a single whole. The requirements for revocation of acceptance are summarized in the following case.

Case 16.2
INNISS v. METHOT BUICK-OPEL, INC.

Supreme Judicial Court of Maine, 1986.
506 A.2d 212.

HISTORICAL AND ECONOMIC SETTING *In the late 1970s, gasoline prices nearly doubled. Although prices in the United States were still less than half the prices in most other countries, Americans sought greater fuel efficiency in their vehicles, which generally meant smaller cars. Automobile manufacturers retooled their manufacturing plants and introduced fuel-efficient models in the early 1980s. Nonetheless, in 1981, sales of U.S.-made automobiles fell to the lowest level in twenty years, and production declined 30 percent. Meanwhile, automobile production by Japanese manufacturers rose 10 percent and overtook U.S. production. This angered U.S. automobile manufacturers. To placate U.S. automakers, Japanese manufacturers agreed to limit exports to the United States. Despite these voluntary quotas, by 1982 Japanese automakers held nearly a fourth of the U.S. market, and Honda began manufacturing cars in the United States. At the time, Japanese-made automobiles had a reputation for greater quality, which meant less maintenance and fewer problems.*

FACTS In September of 1982, Kathleen Inniss purchased a 1982 Buick Skylark from Methot Buick-Opel, Inc. The car, which was a demonstrator, had nearly 6,000 miles on it but was accompanied by a new-car, twelve-month or 12,000-mile warranty. It also had a history of significant mechanical and electrical problems, which Methot failed to mention to Inniss. Shortly after Inniss took possession, she experienced problems with the car. Between September and December of 1982, she took the car back to Methot eight times for repairs. The horn, rear window defogger, throttle, and brakes were repaired, but by the end of the warranty period, several other problems had not been. The

Case 16.2—Continued

temperature gauge continued to malfunction, the car intermittently would not start, it would vibrate in the front end, and the directional indicators would intermittently flash incorrectly when in use. In addition, although the purchase agreement had provided that the car would be rustproofed, much of it had not been. The state of Maine did not have a "lemon law."[a] Before the twelve-month warranty had lapsed, Inniss sought to revoke her acceptance of the contract and asked for her money back. The trial court held for Inniss, and the dealer appealed.

ISSUE Can Inniss revoke her acceptance of the purchase contract and recover the purchase price of the automobile?

DECISION Yes. Inniss had sufficient grounds to revoke acceptance in this case.

REASON The court held that before revocation could be permitted, Inniss would have to show (1) that the goods were so nonconforming (fell so far short of the contract specifications) as to impair substantially their value to her, (2) that it was difficult to discover the nonconformity before acceptance took place, (3) that she revoked within a reasonable period of time, (4) that the revocation took place prior to any substantial change in the condition of the car not caused by its own defects, and (5) that she had given notification of her revocation to Methot. The court reasoned that the history of Inniss's experience with the car was evidence enough that its value to her was substantially impaired. Further, she had met all the other criteria necessary to permit revocation. She was thus entitled to recover the purchase price of the car, plus damages for breach of express warranty and other damages.

a. Lemon laws will be discussed in Chapter 17.

❖ Anticipatory Repudiation

What if, before the time for contract performance, one party clearly communicates to the other the intention not to perform? Such an action is a breach of the contract by *anticipatory repudiation.* When anticipatory repudiation occurs, the nonbreaching party has a choice of two responses. He or she can treat the repudiation as a final breach by pursuing a remedy; or he or she can wait, hoping that the repudiating party will decide to honor the obligations required by the contract despite the avowed intention to renege [UCC 2–610].

Should the latter course be pursued, the UCC permits the breaching party (subject to some limitations) to "retract" his or her repudiation. This can be done by any method that clearly indicates an intent to perform. Once retraction is made, the rights of the repudiating party under the contract are reinstated [UCC 2–611].

❖ Remedies of the Seller

There are numerous remedies available to a seller when the buyer is in breach under the UCC, many of which are discussed here.

"Consequences cannot alter statutes, but may help to fix their meaning."

Benjamin N. Cardozo, 1870–1938
(American jurist)

The Right to Withhold Delivery

In general, sellers can withhold or discontinue performance of their obligations under a sales contract when buyers are in breach. If the breach results from the buyer's insolvency, the seller can refuse to deliver the goods unless the buyer pays in cash [UCC 2–702(1)]. If a buyer has wrongfully rejected or revoked acceptance of contract goods, failed to make proper and timely payment, or repudiated a part of the contract, the seller can withhold delivery of the goods in question. Furthermore, the seller can withhold the entire undelivered balance of the goods if the buyer's breach is material [UCC 2–703].

The Right to Stop Delivery of Goods in Transit

If the seller has delivered the goods to a carrier or a bailee, but the buyer has not as yet received them, the goods are said to be *in transit.* If the seller learns of the buyer's insolvency while the goods are in transit, the seller can stop the carrier or bailee from delivering the goods to the buyer on the basis of the buyer's insolvency, regardless of the quantity shipped.

If the buyer is not insolvent but repudiates the contract or gives the seller some other right to withhold or reclaim the goods, the seller can stop the goods in transit only if the quantity shipped is at least a carload, a truckload, a planeload, or a larger shipment [UCC 2–705(1)]. To stop delivery, the seller must *timely notify* the carrier or other bailee that the goods are to be returned or held for the seller. If the carrier has sufficient time to stop delivery, the goods must be held and delivered according to the instructions of the seller, who is liable to the carrier for any additional costs incurred [UCC 2–705(3)].

The right of the seller to stop delivery of goods in transit is lost when:

1. The buyer obtains possession of the goods.
2. The carrier acknowledges the buyer's rights by reshipping or storing the goods for the buyer.
3. A bailee of the goods other than a carrier acknowledges that he or she is holding the goods for the buyer.
4. A document of title covering the goods has been negotiated (properly transferred, giving the buyer ownership rights in the goods) to the buyer [UCC 2–705(2)].

The Right to Reclaim Goods

If a seller discovers that the buyer has received goods on credit and is insolvent, the seller can demand return of the goods, if the demand is made within ten days of the buyer's receipt of the goods. The seller can demand and reclaim the goods at any time if the buyer misrepresented his or her solvency in writing within three months prior to the delivery of the goods [UCC 2–702(2)]. The seller's right to reclaim, however, is subject to the rights of a good faith purchaser or other buyer in the ordinary course of business who purchases the goods from the buyer before the seller reclaims.

Under the UCC, a seller seeking to exercise the right to reclaim goods receives preferential treatment over the buyer's other creditors—the seller need only demand the return of the goods within ten days after the buyer has received them.[3] Because of this preferential treatment, the UCC provides that reclamation *bars* the seller from pursuing any other remedy as to these goods [UCC 2–702(3)].

The Right to Resell the Goods

Sometimes a buyer breaches or repudiates a sales contract while the seller is still in possession of the goods. In this event, the seller can resell the goods, holding the buyer liable for any loss [UCC 2–704 and 2–706(1)].

When the goods contracted for are unfinished at the time of breach, the seller can do one of two things: (1) cease manufacturing the goods and resell them for scrap or salvage value or (2) complete the manufacture and resell them, holding the buyer liable for any deficiency. In choosing between these two alternatives, the seller must exercise reasonable commercial judgment in order to mitigate the loss and obtain maximum value from the unfinished goods [UCC 2–704(2)].

---

3. This remedy is extremely important should the buyer go through bankruptcy. The 1978 Bankruptcy Reform Act as amended provides that the rights of the trustee are "subject to any statutory right or common law right of a seller * * * if the debtor has received such goods while insolvent."

When a seller possesses or controls the goods at the time of the buyer's breach, or rightfully reacquires the goods by stopping them in transit, the seller has the right to resell the goods. The resale must be made in good faith and in a commercially reasonable manner. The seller can recover any deficiency between the resale price and the contract price, along with **incidental damages,** defined as those costs to the seller resulting from the breach [UCC 2–706(1) and 2–710].

INCIDENTAL DAMAGES
Damages resulting from a breach of contract, including all reasonable expenses incurred because of the breach.

The resale can be private or public, and the goods can be sold as a unit or in parcels. The seller must give the original buyer reasonable notice of the resale, unless the goods are perishable or will rapidly decline in value [UCC 2–706(2) and 2–706(3)]. In the latter case, the seller has a duty to resell the goods as rapidly as possible to mitigate damages. A **bona fide purchaser** in a resale takes the goods free of any of the rights of the original buyer, even if the seller fails to comply with these requirements of the UCC [UCC 2–706(5)].

BONA FIDE PURCHASER
A buyer who purchases in good faith for value without notice of any defects in the title of the seller.

The Right to Recover the Purchase Price

Before the UCC was adopted, a seller could not sue for the purchase price (the price of the goods as stated in the contract) of the goods unless title had passed to the buyer. Under the UCC, however, an unpaid seller can bring an action to recover the purchase price and incidental damages in any of the following circumstances:

1. When the buyer has accepted the goods and has not revoked acceptance, in which case title has passed to the buyer.
2. When conforming goods have been lost or damaged after the risk of loss has passed to the buyer.
3. When the buyer has breached the contract after the contract goods have been identified and the seller is unable to resell the goods [UCC 2–709(1)].

If a seller sues for the contract price of goods that he or she has been unable to resell, the goods must be held for the buyer. The seller can resell at any time prior to collection (of the judgment) from the buyer, but the net proceeds from the sale must be credited to the buyer. This is an example of the duty to mitigate damages.

For example, suppose Southern Realty contracts with Gem Point, Inc., to purchase 1,000 pens with Southern Realty's name inscribed on them. Gem Point delivers the 1,000 pens, but Southern Realty refuses to pay. Or suppose Gem Point tenders the 1,000 pens to Southern Realty, but Southern Realty refuses to accept them. In either case, Gem Point has, as a proper remedy, an action for the purchase price. In the first situation, Southern Realty accepted conforming goods, but because it failed to pay, it is in breach. In the second case, it is obvious that Gem Point could not sell to anyone else the pens inscribed with the buyer's business name. Thus, both situations fall under UCC 2–709.

In the following case, the court had to determine whether a seller was entitled to recover the purchase price of specially manufactured goods after the buyer had breached the sales contract.

Case 16.3
ROYAL JONES & ASSOCIATES, INC. v. FIRST THERMAL SYSTEMS, INC.
District Court of Appeal of Florida, 1990.
566 So.2d 853.

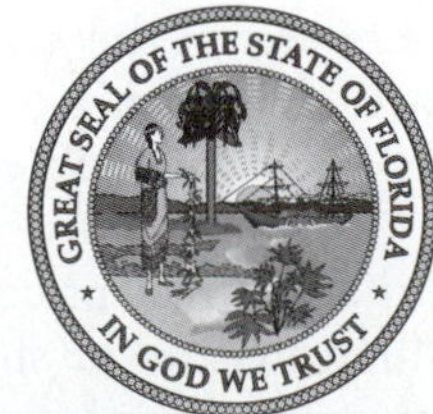

HISTORICAL AND SOCIAL SETTING *In a case decided soon after the enactment of the UCC in Massachusetts, a buyer refused to accept a "petite" mink jacket that had been altered at the buyer's request to be smaller in the neck and shoulders. Although the seller was "ready and willing to sell the coat at any time" for a "good offer," the coat remained unsold. In the seller's suit against the buyer, the court held that the seller could recover the price from*

Case 16.3—Continued

the buyer.[a] *In a case decided a few years later, a court held that a seller could recover from a buyer the price of cloth woven into a specific knit that was "no longer acceptable in the market."*[b] *In other cases, sellers recovered the prices of several "tailor-made" rolling steel doors and custom-made backing for insulation board. The courts held that the goods were generally unmarketable at the prices that the buyers had originally agreed to pay.*[c]

FACTS Royal Jones & Associates, Inc., ordered three steel rendering tanks from First Thermal Systems, Inc., for use in its business of constructing rendering plants (factories that process livestock carcasses into hides, fertilizer, and so on). The contract provided that First Thermal would manufacture the tanks according to Royal Jones's specifications for a price of $64,350. When the manufacture of the tanks was completed, Royal Jones refused to accept or pay for the tanks. First Thermal brought an action for the contract price of the tanks. The trial court, finding that Royal Jones had breached the contract and that the specially manufactured goods were not suitable for sale in the ordinary course of First Thermal's business, awarded First Thermal the full contract price as damages. Royal Jones appealed.

ISSUE Is First Thermal entitled to the full contract price as damages?

DECISION Yes. The trial court's ruling was affirmed.

REASON The appellate court held that First Thermal was entitled to the full contract price of the specially manufactured tanks as damages because the evidence showed that efforts to resell the tanks would be useless. The court pointed to evidence that the rendering tanks "were the only ones First Thermal ever made, the tanks were manufactured according to Royal Jones's specifications, First Thermal had no other customers to which it could resell the tanks," First Thermal did not know how to market the tanks for resale, and the "tanks were built without needed internal components and to a special size" and "could not be used as rendering tanks without special engineering to which First Thermal had no access." The court also noted that the scrap value of the tanks to First Thermal was only about $700.

ETHICAL CONSIDERATIONS *Basically, the court's decision in this case reflects the ethical principle—expressed in UCC 2–709(1)—that it would be unfair not to allow the seller to recover the purchase price for goods that were custom-made for the buyer and of no use to anyone else. Note, though, that allowing a seller to recover the purchase price for specially manufactured goods may not always achieve a fair or ethical result. In a case decided in Pennsylvania, for example, a court held that a seller could not recover the price of furniture that had been upholstered in unusual colors. The court stated that the seller had not proved that the furniture could not be sold at "reasonably marked-down prices." Because the buyer was dead, the buyer's heirs would have been liable for the price. It has been suggested that the court was unwilling to allow the seller "to reap the benefits of a decedent's profligacy out of the heirs' legacies," although this was not stated in the court's opinion.*[d] *The point to remember is that circumstances vary from case to case, and while applying a given law to one case might achieve a fair or ethical result, applying it to another might not.*

a. *Ludwig v. Tobey,* 28 Mass.App.Dec. 6 (1964).

b. *Jacobson v. Donnkenny, Inc.,* 4 U.C.C. Rep. 480 (N.Y.Sup. 1967).

c. *Walter Balfour & Co. v. Lizza & Sons, Inc.,* 6 U.C.C. Rep. 649 (N.Y.Sup. 1969) and *FMI, Inc. v. RMAX, Inc.,* 286 S.C. 343, 333 S.E.2d 360 (App. 1985).

d. James J. White and Robert S. Summers, *Uniform Commercial Code,* 3d ed. (St. Paul: West Publishing Co., 1988), p. 299.

The Right to Recover Damages

If a buyer repudiates a contract or wrongfully refuses to accept the goods, a seller can maintain an action to recover the damages that were sustained. Ordinarily, the amount of damages equals the difference between the contract price and the market price (at the time and place of tender of the goods) plus incidental damages [UCC 2–708(1)]. The time and place of tender are frequently given by such terms as F.O.B., F.A.S., C.I.F., and the like, which determine whether there is a shipment or destination contract.

If the difference between the contract price and the market price is too small to place the seller in the position that he or she would have been in if the buyer had fully performed, the proper measure of damages is the seller's lost profits, including a reasonable allowance for overhead and other expenses [UCC 2–708(2)].

The Right to Cancel the Sales Contract

A seller can cancel a contract if the buyer wrongfully rejects or revokes acceptance of conforming goods, fails to make proper payment, or repudiates the contract in part or in whole. The contract can be canceled with respect to the goods directly involved, or the entire contract can be canceled if the breach is material.

The seller must *notify* the buyer of the cancellation, and at that point all remaining obligations of the seller are discharged. The buyer is not discharged from all remaining obligations but is in breach and can be sued under any of the subsections mentioned in UCC 2–703 and UCC 2–106(4).

❖ Remedies of the Buyer

Under the UCC, there are numerous remedies available to the buyer. We treat many of them here.

"The buyer needs a hundred eyes, the seller not one."

George Herbert, 1593–1633
(English poet)

The Right to Reject

If either the goods or the seller's tender of the goods fails to conform to the contract *in any respect*, the buyer can reject the goods. If some of the goods conform to the contract, the buyer can keep the conforming goods and reject the rest [UCC 2–601].

Timeliness and Reason for Rejection Required Goods must be rejected within a reasonable amount of time, and the seller must be notified **seasonably**—that is, in a timely fashion or at the proper time [UCC 2–602]. Furthermore, the buyer must designate defects that would have been apparent to the seller on reasonable inspection. Failure to do so precludes the buyer from using such defects to justify rejection or to establish breach when the seller could have cured the defects if they had been stated seasonably [UCC 2–605].

SEASONABLY
Within a specified time period, or if no period is specified, within a reasonable time.

Merchant Buyer's Duties When Goods Are Rejected If a *merchant buyer* rightfully rejects goods, and the seller has no agent or business at the place of rejection, the buyer is required to follow any reasonable instructions received from the seller with respect to the goods controlled by the buyer. The buyer is entitled to reimbursement for the care and cost entailed in following the instructions [UCC 2–603]. The same requirements hold if the buyer rightfully revokes his or her acceptance of the goods at some later time [UCC 2–608(3)].

If no instructions are forthcoming and the goods are perishable or threaten to decline in value quickly, the buyer can resell the goods in good faith, taking the appropriate reimbursement from the proceeds [UCC 2–603(1)]. If the goods are not perishable, the buyer may store them for the seller's account or reship them to the seller [UCC 2–604].

The Right to Recover

If a buyer has made a partial or full payment for goods that remain in the possession of the seller, the buyer can recover the goods if the seller becomes insolvent within ten days after receiving the first payment and if the goods are identified to the contract. To exercise this right, the buyer must tender to the seller any unpaid balance of the purchase price [UCC 2–502].

The Right to Obtain Specific Performance

A buyer can obtain specific performance when the goods are unique or when the buyer's remedy at law is inadequate [UCC 2–716(1)]. Ordinarily, a suit for money damages is sufficient to place a buyer in the position he or she would have occupied if the seller had fully performed. When the contract is for the purchase of a particular work of art or a similarly unique item, however, money damages may not be sufficient. Under these circumstances, equity will require that the seller perform exactly by delivering the particular goods identified to the contract (a remedy of specific performance).

The Right of Cover

COVER
Under the UCC, a remedy of the buyer that allows the buyer, on the seller's breach, to purchase the goods from another seller and substitute them for the goods due under the contract. If the cost of cover exceeds the cost of the contract goods, the breaching seller will be liable to the buyer for the difference, plus incidental and consequential damages.

In certain situations, buyers can protect themselves by obtaining **cover**—that is, by substituting goods for those that were due under the sales contract. This option is available to a buyer who has rightfully rejected goods or revoked acceptance. It is also available when the seller repudiates the contract or fails to deliver the goods. In obtaining cover, the buyer must act in good faith and without unreasonable delay [UCC 2–712]. After purchasing substitute goods, the buyer can recover from the seller the difference between the cost of cover and the contract price, plus incidental and consequential damages, less the expenses (such as delivery costs) that were saved as a result of the seller's breach [UCC 2–712 and 2–715]. Consequential damages are any losses suffered by the buyer that the seller could have foreseen (had reason to know about) at the time of contract and any injury to the buyer's person or property proximately resulting from the contract's breach [UCC 2–715(2)].

Buyers are not required to cover, and failure to do so will not bar them from using any other remedies available under the UCC [UCC 2–712(3)]. But a buyer who fails to cover may *not* be able to collect consequential damages that could have been avoided had he or she purchased substitute goods [UCC 2–715(2)(a)].

The Right to Replevy Goods

REPLEVIN
An action brought to recover the possession of personal property unlawfully held by another.

Replevin is an action to recover specific goods in the hands of a party who is unlawfully withholding them from the other party. Outside the UCC, the term *replevin* refers to a prejudgment process (a proceeding that takes place prior to a court's judgment) that permits the seizure of specific personal property in which a party claims a right or an interest. For example, when a buyer defaults on installment payments under a contract for the purchase of an automobile, the seller might make use of replevin to obtain possession of the vehicle. Under the UCC, the buyer can replevy goods subject to the contract if the seller has repudiated or breached the contract. *Additionally,* buyers must usually show that they are unable to cover for the goods after a reasonable effort [UCC 2–716(3)].

Consider the following example. On July 1, Woods contracts to sell her tomato crop to Creighton, with delivery and payment due on August 10. By August 1, it is clear that the local tomato crop will be bad and that the price of tomatoes is going to rise. Woods contracts to sell her tomato crop to De Valle for a higher price and then informs Creighton that she will not deliver on August 10 as agreed. Creighton indicates that cover is unavailable and that he is therefore going to bring a replevin action against Woods to force her to deliver the tomatoes to Creighton on August 10.

This replevin action normally will succeed. Although a tomato crop is not unique, a buyer of scarce goods for which no cover is available has a right to replevin. In a more typical season (when tomato crops thrive), cover would probably have been available and Creighton would have been limited to an action for damages.

The Right to Retain and Enforce a Security Interest in the Goods

Buyers who rightfully reject goods or who justifiably revoke acceptance of goods that remain in their possession or control have a *security interest* in the goods (basically, a legal claim to the goods to the extent necessary to recover expenses, costs, and the like). The security interest encompasses any payments the buyer has made for the goods as well as any expenses incurred with regard to inspection, receipt, transportation, care, and custody of the goods [UCC 2–711(3)]. A buyer with a security interest in the goods is a "person in the position of a seller." This gives the buyer the same rights as an unpaid seller. Thus, the buyer can resell, withhold delivery, or stop delivery of the goods. A buyer who chooses to resell must account to the seller for any amounts received in excess of the security interest [UCC 2–711 and 2–706(6)].

The Right to Cancel the Contract

When a seller fails to make proper delivery or repudiates the contract, the buyer can cancel or rescind the contract. In addition, a buyer who has rightfully rejected or revoked acceptance of the goods can cancel or rescind that portion of the contract directly involved in the breach. If the seller's breach is material and substantially impairs the value of the whole contract, the buyer can cancel or rescind the whole contract. Upon notice of cancellation, the buyer is relieved of any further obligations under the contract but retains all rights to other remedies against the seller.

The Right to Recover Damages for Nondelivery or Repudiation

If a seller repudiates the sales contract or fails to deliver the goods, the buyer can sue for damages. The measure of recovery is the difference between the contract price and the market price of the goods at the time the buyer *learned* of the breach. The market price is determined at the place where the seller was supposed to deliver the goods. The buyer can also recover incidental and consequential damages less the expenses that were saved as a result of the seller's breach [UCC 2–713].

Consider an example. Schilling orders 10,000 bushels of wheat from Valdone for $5 a bushel, with delivery due on June 14 and payment due on June 20. Valdone does not deliver on June 14. On June 14, the market price of wheat is $5.50 per bushel. Schilling chooses to do without the wheat. He sues Valdone for damages for nondelivery. Schilling can recover $0.50 x 10,000, or $5,000, plus any expenses the breach may have caused him. The measure of damages is the market price less the contract price on the day Schilling was to have received delivery. (Any expenses Schilling saved by the breach would be deducted from the damages.)

In the following case, the question at issue was whether the measure of a buyer's damages in a contract breached by the seller should be the buyer's actual losses caused by the breach (as suggested by UCC 1–106) or the difference between the contract price and the market price of the goods at the time the buyer learned of the breach (as provided by UCC 2–713).

Case 16.4
TONGISH v. THOMAS
Supreme Court of Kansas, 1992.
251 Kan. 728,
840 P.2d 471.

HISTORICAL AND SOCIAL SETTING *Throughout the twentieth century, courts have been divided as to the appropriate measure of a buyer's damages on breach of a contract for a sale of goods. Most courts award the difference between the contract price and the market price. In some cases, however, courts award the buyer's actual loss. For example, in a California case, a buyer contracted to buy 375,000 pounds of raisins at a 4 percent discount and contracted to resell the raisins to another party at the full price. The buyer's expected profit was the amount of the discount. Heavy rains destroyed the raisin crop and led to a doubling of the market price for raisins. The seller was unable to deliver. The buyer was awarded the expected profit instead of the difference between the contract price*

Case 16.4—Continued

and the market price.[a] *The result in this case has been criticized for several reasons. One reason is that if this measure of damages were applied in all cases, sellers would be encouraged to breach contracts when market prices fluctuated to their advantage. Would the result in the case have been different if the crop had not been destroyed by heavy rains?*

FACTS In April 1988, Denis Tongish agreed to sell sunflower seeds grown on certain acres to the Decatur Cooperative Association (the co-op). One-third of the seeds were to be delivered by December 31, 1988, one-third on March 31, 1989, and one-third on May 31, 1989. The co-op then entered into a contract to sell the seeds, when they had been delivered by Tongish, to Bambino Bean & Seed, Inc., for the same price plus a handling charge of 55 cents per hundredweight. Tongish delivered seeds to the co-op in October and November 1988. A smaller-than-normal crop, bad weather, and other factors caused the market price of sunflower seeds to double that winter from what it had been in April, and in January 1989, Tongish notified the co-op that he would not deliver any more seeds. Tongish then sold 82,820 pounds of sunflower seeds to Danny Thomas for $14,714.89, which was $5,153.13 more than the co-op contract price. Thomas failed to pay the entire purchase price of the seeds, and Tongish sued him. The co-op intervened in the action, seeking damages for Tongish's breach of their contract. The district court, finding that Tongish had breached the contract, awarded damages to the co-op in the amount of $455.51—the co-op's actual losses (the handling charges) resulting from the breach. The co-op appealed, contending that the damage award should have been the difference between the contract price of the seeds and the market price of the seeds at the time of the contract's breach. The appellate court agreed with the co-op and reversed the trial court's decision. Ultimately, the case was reviewed by the Supreme Court of Kansas.

a. *Allied Canners & Packers, Inc. v. Victor Packing Co.*, 162 Cal.App.3d 905, 209 Cal.Rptr. 60 (1984).

ISSUE Should the amount of the co-op's damages be the actual losses it sustained or the difference between the market price of the seeds and the contract price of the seeds at the time of the breach?

DECISION The Supreme Court of Kansas affirmed the appellate court's decision. The appropriate remedy for the co-op for Tongish's breach was the difference between the contract price of the seeds and the market price of the seeds at the time of breach.

REASON This case brought two UCC provisions into conflict. The trial court's ruling that the co-op was only entitled to damages in the amount of its actual losses was based on UCC 1–106(1), which states as follows: "The remedies provided by this Act shall be liberally administered to the end that the aggrieved party may be put in as good a position as if the other party had fully performed but neither consequential or special nor penal damages may be had except as specifically provided in this Act or by other rule of law." But the appellate court had held that the measure of damages under UCC 2–713(1) should apply. That section provides that "the measure of damages for nondelivery or repudiation by the seller is the difference between the market price at the time when the buyer learned of the breach and the contract price together with any incidental and consequential damages provided in this article." The Supreme Court of Kansas noted that while both sections of the UCC related to damages for breach of contract, UCC 1–106(1) was a general statement concerning the application of remedies under the UCC while UCC 2–713(1) provided a specific remedy for a specific situation. According to the court, "General and special statutes should be read together and harmonized whenever possible, but to the extent a conflict between them exists, the special statute will prevail."

The Right to Recover Damages for Breach in Regard to Accepted Goods

A buyer who has accepted nonconforming goods must notify the seller of the breach within a reasonable time after the defect was or should have been discovered. Otherwise, the buyer cannot complain about defects in the goods [UCC 2–607(3)]. In addition, the parties to a sales contract can insert a provision requiring that the buyer give notice of any defects in the goods within a prescribed period.

When the seller breaches a warranty, the measure of damages equals the difference between the value of the goods as accepted and their value if they had been delivered as warranted. For this and other types of breaches in which the buyer has accepted the goods, the buyer is entitled to recover for any loss "resulting in the ordinary course of events * * * as determined in any manner which is reasonable" [UCC 2–714(1)]. The UCC also permits the buyer, with proper notice to the seller, to deduct all or any part of the damages from the price still due and payable to the seller [UCC 2–717]. The requirement that a buyer who has accepted nonconforming goods must notify the seller of the breach within a reasonable time after the breach was discovered is emphasized in the following case.

Case 16.5
HAPAG-LLOYD, A.G. v. MARINE INDEMNITY INSURANCE CO. OF AMERICA
District Court of Appeal of Florida, Third District, 1991.
576 So.2d 1330.

HISTORICAL AND ETHICAL SETTING *The issue that arises most frequently under UCC 2–607(3)(a) is the question as to what constitutes a "reasonable time" within which a buyer should discover a breach and notify the seller. What constitutes a "reasonable time" appears to be different in nearly every case. For example, in a case involving a leaking underground gas tank, fourteen months was held to be reasonable;*[a] *in a case involving toys for a Christmas season, two months was held to be unreasonable.*[b] *Despite the different interpretations, there are reasons for requiring the buyer to notify the seller that can serve as a basis for a court to hold that a particular time period is reasonable. For instance, one reason for requiring notice is to enable a seller to make adjustments, supply replacements, or suggest opportunities to resolve a situation so as to minimize the buyer's loss and reduce the seller's liability. Thus, for example, the buyer of a truck should tell the seller immediately of any defects. Based on the reason for the notice requirement, a court may hold that the buyer is not entitled to relief if the buyer lets the truck sit in a parking lot for a year before notifying the seller. Comment 4 to UCC 2–607 refers to such conduct by a buyer as "commercial bad faith."*

a. *Larrance Tank Corp. v. Burrough,* 476 P.2d 346 (Okla. 1970).
b. *Hays Merchandise, Inc. v. Dewey,* 78 Wash.2d 343, 474 P.2d 270 (1970).

FACTS Marine Indemnity Insurance Company of America purchased a "toploader" (a piece of ship-loading equipment) from Hapag-Lloyd, A.G. Marine Indemnity was aware of the fact that the wiring in the toploader's engine was defective but nevertheless used the equipment in its defective state without notifying the seller. After Marine Indemnity had used the toploader for about four weeks, the wiring caused an explosion in the engine, which severely damaged the equipment. After the accident, Marine Indemnity brought an action against Hapag-Lloyd for breach of express warranty. The trial court held for Marine Indemnity. Hapag-Lloyd appealed, contending that Marine Indemnity's failure to give timely notice of the breach barred it from pursuing any remedy.

ISSUE Was Marine Indemnity barred from pursuing any remedy because of its failure to give Hapag-Lloyd timely notice of the breach?

DECISION Yes. The trial court's judgment was reversed.

REASON The court stated that under Florida law—the state's equivalent of UCC 2–607(3)(a)—a buyer is required to give notice to the seller of an alleged breach "within a reasonable time after [the buyer discovered] or should have discovered any breach." In this case, timely notice of breach had not been given. The court concluded that Marine Indemnity's "failure to afford the seller reasonable notice of an already-discovered defect until after the loss caused by the breach of warranty had already occurred—when, as clearly appears, the seller could have remedied the defect and prevented the loss—requires a conclusion that, as the statute provides, the buyer is 'barred from any remedy.' "

❖ Statute of Limitations

An action brought by a buyer or seller for breach of contract must be commenced under the UCC *within four years after the cause of action accrues*—that is, within four years after the breach occurs. In addition to filing suit within the four-year period, an aggrieved party usually must notify the breaching party of the breach to goods accepted by the buyer within a reasonable time or the buyer is barred from pursuing any remedy [UCC 2–607(3)(a)]. By agreement in the contract, the parties can reduce this period to not less than one year but cannot extend it beyond four years [UCC 2–725(1)]. A cause of action accrues for breach of warranty when the seller makes *tender* of delivery. This is the rule even if the aggrieved party is unaware that the cause of action has accrued [UCC 2–725(2)].

❖ Limitation of Remedies

The parties to a sales contract can vary their respective rights and obligations by contractual agreement. For example, a seller and buyer can expressly provide for remedies in addition to those provided in the UCC. They can also provide remedies in lieu of those provided in the UCC, or they can change the measure of damages. The seller can provide that the buyer's only remedy upon breach of warranty be repair or replacement of the item, or the seller can limit the buyer's remedy to return of the goods and refund of the purchase price. An agreed-upon remedy is in addition to those provided in the UCC unless the parties expressly agree that the remedy is exclusive of all others [UCC 2–719(1)].

If the parties state that a remedy is exclusive, then it is the sole remedy. But when circumstances cause an exclusive remedy to fail in its essential purpose, it is no longer exclusive [UCC 2–719(2)]. For example, a sales contract that limits the buyer's remedy to repair or replacement fails in its essential purpose if the item cannot be repaired and no replacements are available.

A contract can limit or exclude consequential damages, provided the limitation is not unconscionable. When the buyer is a consumer, the limitation of consequential damages for personal injuries resulting from a breach of warranty is *prima facie* unconscionable. The limitation of consequential damages is not necessarily unconscionable when the loss is commercial in nature—for example, lost profits and property damage [UCC 2–719(3)]. Most sellers' forms limit a buyer's right to receive consequential damages.

❖ Key Terms

bona fide purchaser 383
cover 386
incidental damages 383
installment contract 375
replevin 386
seasonably 385
tender of delivery 372

❖ Chapter Summary: Performance and Breach

REQUIREMENTS OF PERFORMANCE	
Seller's Obligations	1. The seller must ship or tender *conforming* goods to the buyer. Tender must take place at a *reasonable hour* and in a *reasonable manner.* Under the perfect tender doctrine, the seller must tender goods that exactly conform to the terms of the contract [UCC 2–301, UCC 2–503(1), UCC 2–601]. 2. If the seller tenders nonconforming goods and the buyer rejects them, the seller may *cure* (repair or replace the goods) within the contract time for performance [UCC 2–508(1)]. 3. If the seller tenders nonconforming goods, but the seller has reasonable grounds to believe the buyer would accept them, upon the buyer's rejection the seller has a reasonable time to substitute conforming goods without liability [UCC 2–508(2)].

❖ Chapter Summary: Performance and Breach—Continued

Seller's Obligations —Continued	4. If the agreed means of delivery becomes impracticable or unavailable, the seller must substitute an alternative means (such as a different carrier) if such is available [UCC 2–614(1)]. 5. If a seller tenders nonconforming goods in any one installment under an installment contract, the buyer may reject the installment only if its value is substantially impaired and cannot be cured. The entire installment contract is breached when one or more installments *substantially* impair the value of the *whole* contract [UCC 2–612]. 6. When performance becomes commercially impracticable owing to circumstances unforeseen when the contract was formed, the perfect tender rule no longer holds [UCC 2–615(a)].
Buyer's Obligations	1. Upon tender of delivery by the seller, the buyer must furnish facilities reasonably suited for receipt of the goods [UCC 2–503(1)(b)]. 2. The buyer must pay for the goods at the time and place the buyer *receives* the goods, even if the place of shipment is the place of delivery, unless the sale is made on credit. Payment may be made by any method generally acceptable in the commercial world [UCC 2–310, UCC 2–511]. 3. Unless otherwise agreed, the buyer has an absolute right to inspect the goods before acceptance [UCC 2–513(1)]. 4. The buyer can manifest acceptance of delivered goods expressly in words or by conduct; by failing to reject the goods after a reasonable period of time following inspection or after having had a reasonable opportunity to inspect them; or by performing any act inconsistent with the seller's ownership [UCC 2–606(1)]. 5. Following acceptance of delivered goods, the buyer may revoke acceptance only if the nonconformity *substantially* impairs the value of the unit or lot and if one of the following factors is present: a. Acceptance was predicated on the reasonable assumption that the nonconformity would be cured and it was not cured within a reasonable time [UCC 2–608(1)(a)]. b. The buyer did not discover the nonconformity before acceptance, either because it was difficult to discover before acceptance or because the seller's assurance that the goods were conforming kept the buyer from inspecting the goods [UCC 2–608(1)(b)].
Anticipatory Repudiation	If, before the time for performance, either party clearly indicates to the other an intention not to perform, under UCC 2–610 the aggrieved party may do the following: 1. Await performance by the repudiating party for a commercially reasonable time. 2. Resort to any remedy for breach. 3. In either case, *suspend performance.*
REMEDIES FOR BREACH OF CONTRACT	
Seller's Remedies for Buyer's Breach	1. If the goods are in the seller's possession, the seller may do the following: a. Withhold delivery [UCC 2–703(a)]. b. Identify goods to the contract [UCC 2–704]. c. Resell the goods [UCC 2–706]. d. Sue for breach of contract [UCC 2–708]. e. Cancel (rescind) the contract [UCC 2–703]. 2. If the goods are in transit, the seller may stop the carrier or bailee from delivering the goods [UCC 2–705]. 3. If the goods are in the buyer's possession, the seller may do the following: a. Sue for the purchase price [UCC 2–709]. b. Reclaim goods received by an insolvent buyer if the demand is made within ten days of receipt (excludes all other remedies on reclamation) [UCC 2–702].
Buyer's Remedies for Seller's Breach	1. If the seller refuses to deliver or the seller tenders nonconforming goods and the buyer rejects them, the buyer may do the following: a. Cancel (rescind), with notice [UCC 2–711]. b. Cover [UCC 2–712]. c. Sue for breach of contract [UCC 2–713].

❖ Chapter Summary: Performance and Breach—Continued

Buyer's Remedies for Seller's Breach—Continued	2. If the seller tenders nonconforming goods and the buyer accepts them, the buyer, with notice, may do the following: a. Sue for ordinary damages [UCC 2–714(1)]. b. Sue for breach of warranty [UCC 2–714(2)]. c. Deduct damages from the price of the goods [UCC 2–717]. 3. If the seller refuses delivery and the buyer wants the goods, the buyer may do the following: a. Sue for specific performance [UCC 2–716(1)]. b. Replevy the goods [UCC 2–716(3)]. c. Recover goods from the seller on the seller's insolvency within ten days, if the buyer has paid part or all of the purchase price [UCC 2–502].
Statute of Limitations	The UCC has a four-year statute of limitations for breach of contract actions. By agreement, the parties to a sales contract can reduce this period to not less than one year, but they cannot extend it beyond four years [UCC 2–725(1)].
Limitation of Remedies	Remedies may be limited in sales contracts by agreement of the parties. If the contract states that a remedy is exclusive, then that is the sole remedy—unless the remedy fails in its essential purpose. Sellers can also limit buyers' rights to consequential damages—unless the limitation is unconscionable.

❖ Questions and Case Problems

16-1. Anticipatory Repudiation. What remedies are available to a seller if a buyer repudiates a contract prior to the time for contractual performance?

16-2. Revocation of Acceptance. What events or circumstances must occur before a buyer can rightfully revoke his or her acceptance of a sales contract?

16-3. Buyer's Right of Inspection. Cummings ordered two Model-X Super Fidelity speakers from Jamestown Wholesale Electronics, Inc. Jamestown shipped the speakers via United Parcel Service, C.O.D. (collect on delivery), although Cummings had not requested or agreed to a C.O.D. shipment of the goods. When the speakers were delivered, Cummings refused to accept them because he would not be able to inspect them before payment. Jamestown claimed that Cummings had breached their contract, because Jamestown had shipped conforming goods. Had Cummings breached the contract? Explain.

16-4. Anticipatory Repudiation. Moore contracted in writing to sell her 1992 Olds Ciera to Hammer for $8,500. Moore agreed to deliver the car on Wednesday, and Hammer promised to pay the $8,500 on the following Friday. On Tuesday, Hammer informed Moore that he would not be buying the car after all. By Friday, Hammer had changed his mind again and tendered $8,500 to Moore. Moore, although she had not sold the car to another party, refused the tender and refused to deliver. Hammer claimed that Moore had breached their contract. Moore contended that Hammer's repudiation released her from her duty to perform under the contract. Who is correct, and why?

16-5. Remedies of the Buyer. Rodriguez is an antique car collector. He contracts to purchase spare parts for a 1938 engine from Gerrard. These parts are not made anymore and are scarce. To get the contract with Gerrard, Rodriguez has to pay 50 percent of the purchase price in advance. On May 1, Rodriguez sends the payment, which is received on May 2. On May 3, Gerrard, having found another buyer willing to pay substantially more for the parts, informs Rodriguez that he will not deliver as contracted. That same day, Rodriguez learns that Gerrard is insolvent. Gerrard has the parts, and Rodriguez wants them. Discuss fully any available remedies that would allow Rodriguez to obtain these car parts.

16-6. Commercial Impracticability. In November of 1975, Sun Maid Raisin Growers of California contracted to purchase 1,900 tons of raisins from Victor Packing Co. The first 100 tons were priced at 39 cents per pound and the remainder at 40 cents per pound. No delivery date was specified in the contract. On August 10, 1976, Victor informed Sun Maid that it would not complete performance, as it was unable to deliver the last 610 tons. Sun Maid was able to purchase 200 tons of raisins at 43 cents per pound from another supplier. In September of 1976, heavy rains damaged the new crop of raisins, causing the price of raisins to increase dramatically. Sun Maid sued Victor for damages, including lost profits (consequential damages). Victor claimed it should not be liable for lost profits because the disastrous rain was not foreseeable. Discuss Victor's claim. [*Sun Maid Raisin Growers of California v. Victor Packing Co.*, 146 Cal.App.3d 787, 194 Cal.Rptr. 612 (1983)]

16-7. Seller's Right to Cure. Wilson purchased a new television set from Scampoli in 1965. When the set was delivered, Wilson found that it did not work properly; the color was defective. Scampoli's repairperson could not correct the problem, and Wilson refused to allow the repairperson to dismantle the set and take it back to the shop to determine the cause of the difficulty. Instead, Wilson demanded that Scampoli deliver a new television set or return the purchase price. Scampoli refused to refund Wilson's money and insisted that he receive the opportunity to correct the malfunctioning of Wilson's set before replacing it or issuing a refund. Discuss whether Scampoli has the right to attempt to cure the product according to UCC 2–508. [*Wilson v. Scampoli*, 228 A.2d 848 (D.C.App. 1967)]

16-8. **Measure of Damages.** Bigelow-Sanford, Inc., entered into a contract to buy 100,000 yards of jute (a strong, coarse fiber used for sacking and cordage) at $0.64 per yard from Gunny Corp. Gunny delivered 22,228 yards to Bigelow but informed the company that no more would be delivered. Several other suppliers to Bigelow defaulted, and Bigelow was forced to go into the market one month later to purchase a total of 164,503 yards of jute for $1.21 per yard. Bigelow sued Gunny for the difference between the market price and the contract price of the amount of jute that Gunny had not delivered. Discuss whether Bigelow could recover this amount from Gunny. [*Bigelow-Sanford, Inc. v. Gunny Corp.*, 649 F.2d 1060 (5th Cir. 1981)]

16-9. Remedies of the Seller. Lupofresh, Inc., contracted to sell a quantity of hops to the defendant, Pabst Brewing Co. Lupofresh processed the hops and notified Pabst that the hops were ready for shipment. Pabst responded with a letter indicating acceptance of the hops but later refused to issue shipping orders, claiming that the price determination violated antitrust laws. Lupofresh sued for the full purchase price under UCC 2–709(1)(a). Pabst claimed that the goods had not been accepted but merely identified to the contract and that Lupofresh was required to attempt to resell the hops before it was entitled to recover the purchase price. Discuss fully who was correct. [*Lupofresh, Inc. v. Pabst Brewing Co.*, 505 A.2d 37 (Del.Super. 1985)]

16-10. Limited Remedies. In 1968, Canal Electric Co. purchased a steam turbine generator from Westinghouse Corp. In 1983, Canal purchased some new rotating blades from Westinghouse to use in the generator. The contract covering the 1983 sale of the blades warranted that Westinghouse would repair or replace any defective parts for a one-year period and limited Westinghouse's total liability under the contract to the purchase price of the blades, which was $40,750. Liability for incidental and consequential damages was specifically disclaimed. A few months later, the blades developed cracks, and Canal had to shut down operations for 124 days while the blades were being replaced. As a result, Canal incurred costs (which were significantly higher than the purchase price of the blades) to obtain replacement power during this period. Ultimately, Canal sued Westinghouse for breach of warranty and negligence. Westinghouse claimed that its liability to Canal was limited to the purchase price of the blades, $40,750. Will the court enforce the limitation-of-liability clause? What factors will the court consider in deciding the issue? Discuss fully. [*Canal Electric Co. v. Westinghouse Electric Corp.*, 756 F.Supp. 620 (D.Mass. 1991)]

A Question of Ethics and Social Responsibility

16-11. *In March 1985, Bruce Young purchased from Hessel Tractor & Equipment Co., a John Deere equipment dealer, a machine to shear trees in his logging business. The only warranty in the contract was a one-year warranty against defects in the equipment with an exclusive remedy of repair and replacement for any defect in material or workmanship. All other warranties were expressly and conspicuously disclaimed. Young began to have serious problems with the equipment after less than a month of use. After over a year of continuing unsuccessful attempts at repair and after the one-year warranty had expired, Hessel stopped repairing the machine. Given these facts, consider the following questions.* [Young v. Hessel Tractor & Equipment Co., *782 P.2d 164 (Or.App. 1989)*]

1. Do you think that it is fair for a seller to limit available remedies under a sales contract to just one exclusive remedy, such as repair and replacement of parts? Is there anything unethical about this practice?
2. When an exclusive remedy leads to unfair results, as in this case, what, if anything, can be done about it?
3. What UCC provisions might Young cite to persuade the court that he is entitled to revoke his acceptance of the machine and recover the purchase price? How do these provisions reflect the UCC's attempt to balance freedom of contract against the need for fairness and justice in commercial transactions?

Case Briefing Assignment

16-12. *Examine Case A.8* [Triad Systems Corp. v. Alsip, *880 F.2d 247 (10th Cir. 1989)*] *in Appendix A. The case has been excerpted there in great detail. Review and then brief the case, making sure that you include answers to the following questions in your brief.*

1. Why did Alsip seek to revoke his acceptance of the computer system?
2. How did the district court rule on the matter of evidence regarding statements made to Alsip by Triad's employees prior to the contract's execution?
3. Why did Triad Systems Corp. contend on appeal that Alsip's attempt to revoke acceptance was ineffective as a matter of law?
4. What other arguments did Triad Systems raise on appeal, and how did the court respond to them?

For Critical Analysis

16-13. *Review this chapter's* Business Law in Action. *Do you agree with the court's conclusion in regard to the Medcon-Engel contract? Why or why not?*

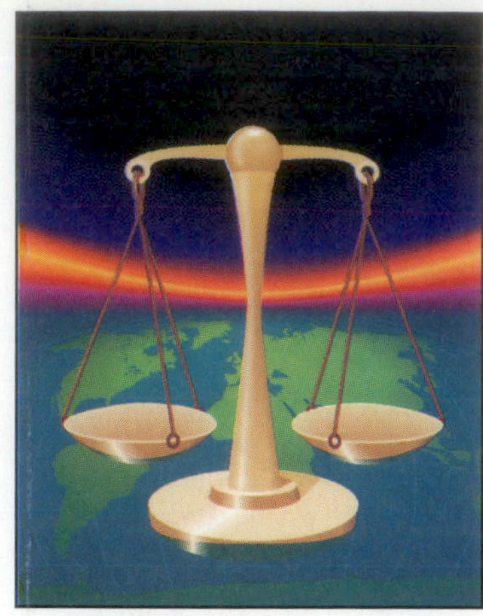

Chapter 17

Warranties and Product Liability

"I'll warrant him heart-whole."

William Shakespeare, 1564–1616
(English dramatist and poet)

Warranty is an age-old concept. In sales law, a warranty is an assurance by one party of the existence of a fact upon which the other party can rely. Just as Shakespeare's character warranted his friend "heart-whole" in the play *As You Like It,* so sellers warrant to buyers that their goods are as represented or will be as promised.

The Uniform Commercial Code (UCC) has numerous rules governing the concept of product warranty as it occurs in a sales contract. That will be the subject matter of the first part of this chapter. A natural addition to the discussion is *product liability:* who is liable to consumers, users, and bystanders for physical harm and property damage caused by a particular good or the use thereof? Product liability encompasses the contract theory of warranty, as well as the tort theories of negligence and strict liability (discussed in Chapter 5).

❖ Warranties

Article 2 of the UCC designates several types of warranties that can arise in a sales contract, including warranties of title, express warranties, and implied warranties. Note that warranties do not expressly apply to leased goods under Article 2, which governs only sales transactions. In the past, the fact that Article 2 did not cover leased goods posed many problems to those injured by a defective leased product, such as a car. To rectify these kinds of problems, Article 2A of the UCC was promulgated in 1987. Essentially, Article 2A is a repetition of Article 2, but the provisions vary to reflect the differences between leases and sales.

Warranties of Title

Title warranty arises automatically in most sales contracts. UCC 2–312 imposes three types of warranties of title.

Good Title In most cases, sellers warrant that they have good and valid title to the goods sold and that transfer of the title is rightful [UCC 2–312(1)(a)]. For example, Sharith steals goods from Miguel and sells them to Carrie, who does not know that the goods are stolen. If Miguel discovers that Carrie has the goods, Miguel has the right to reclaim them from her. Under this UCC provision, however, Carrie can then sue Sharith for breach of warranty, because a thief has no title to stolen goods and thus cannot give good title in a subsequent sale. When Sharith sold Carrie the goods, Sharith *automatically* warranted to her that the title conveyed was valid and that its transfer was rightful. Because this was not in fact the case, Sharith breached the warranty of title imposed by UCC 2–312(1)(a) and became liable to the buyer for the appropriate damages.

No Liens A second warranty of title provided by the Code protects buyers who are *unaware* of any encumbrances (claims, charges, or liabilities—usually called **liens**) against goods at the time the contract was made [UCC 2–312(1)(b)]. This warranty protects buyers who, for example, unknowingly purchase goods that are subject to a creditor's security interest (see Chapter 21). If a creditor legally repossesses the goods from a buyer who *had no actual knowledge of the security interest,* the buyer can recover from the seller for breach of warranty. For example, Harvey buys a used color television set from Suarez, his next door neighbor, for cash. A month later, Roper repossesses the set from Harvey, proving that she, Roper, has a valid security interest in the set. She proves that Suarez is in default, having missed five payments. Harvey demands his money back from Suarez. Under Section 2–312(1)(b), Harvey can recover because the seller of goods warrants that the goods shall be delivered free from any security interest or other lien of which the buyer has no knowledge.

LIEN
An encumbrance upon a property to satisfy or protect a claim for payment of a debt.

No Infringements A merchant is also deemed to warrant that the goods delivered are free from any patent, trademark, or copyright claims of a third person[1] [UCC 2–312(3)]. If this warranty is breached and the buyer is sued by the claim holder, the buyer *must notify the seller* of litigation within a reasonable time to enable the seller to decide whether to defend the lawsuit. If the seller states in writing that he or she has decided to defend and agrees to bear all expenses, including that of an adverse judgment, then the buyer must let the seller undertake litigation; otherwise, the buyer loses all rights against the seller if any infringement liability is established [UCC 2–607(3)(b) and (5)(b)].

For example, Gleason buys a machine from Baker, a manufacturer of such machines, for use in his factory. Three years later, Parker sues Gleason for damages for patent infringement. Parker claims that he has a patent on the machine and that it cannot be used without his permission. At once, Gleason informs Baker of this suit and demands that Baker take over the defense. Baker refuses to do so, claiming that Parker has no case. Gleason goes to court and loses. Parker obtains a judgment against Gleason, which Gleason pays. Gleason now demands that Baker reimburse him for this amount. Baker normally must reimburse Gleason, because merchant sellers of goods warrant to buyers that the goods they regularly sell are free of infringement claims by third parties.

Disclaimer of Title Warranty In an ordinary sales transaction, the title warranty can be disclaimed or modified only by *specific language* in the contract. For example, sellers can assert that they are transferring only such rights, title, and interest as they have in the goods. In certain cases, the circumstances of the sale are sufficient to indicate clearly to a buyer that no assurances as to title are being made. The classic example is a sheriff's sale. At a sheriff's sale, buyers know that the goods have been seized to satisfy debts, and it is apparent that the goods are not the property of the person conducting the sale [UCC 2–312(2)].

"Cheat me in the price, but not in the goods."

Thomas Fuller, 1608–1661
(English clergyman and writer)

Express Warranties

A seller can create an **express warranty** by making representations concerning the quality, condition, description, or performance potential of the goods. Under UCC 2–313, express warranties arise when a seller indicates any of the following:

EXPRESS WARRANTY
A promise, ancillary to an underlying sales agreement, that is included in the written or oral terms of the sales agreement under which the promisor assures the quality, description, or performance of the goods.

1. Recall from Chapter 14 that a *merchant* is defined in UCC 2–104(1) as a person who deals in goods of the kind involved in the sales contract or who, by occupation, presents himself or herself as having knowledge or skill peculiar to the goods involved in the transaction.

1. That the goods conform to any *affirmation or promise* of fact that the seller makes to the buyer about the goods. Such affirmations or promises are usually made during the bargaining process. Statements such as "these drill bits will *easily* penetrate stainless steel—and without dulling" are express warranties.
2. That the goods conform to any *description* of them. For example, a label that reads "Crate contains one 150-horsepower diesel engine" or a contract that calls for the delivery of a "camel's-hair coat" creates an express warranty.
3. That the goods conform to any *sample or model* of the goods shown to the buyer.

Basis of the Bargain The UCC requires that for an express warranty to be created, the affirmation, promise, description, or sample must become part of the "basis of the bargain." Just what constitutes the basis of the bargain is hard to say. The UCC does not define the concept, and it is a question of fact in each case whether a representation was made at such a time and in such a way that it induced the buyer to enter the contract.

Statements of Opinion According to Section 2–313(2), "It is not necessary to the creation of an express warranty that the seller use formal words such as 'warrant' or 'guarantee' or that he have a specific intention to make a warranty." It is necessary only that a reasonable buyer would regard the representation as part of the basis of the bargain.

If the seller merely makes a statement that relates to the value or worth of the goods, or makes a statement of opinion or recommendation about the goods, however, the seller is not creating an express warranty [UCC 2–313(2)]. For example, a seller claims that "this is the best used car to come along in years; it has four new tires and a 350-horsepower engine just rebuilt this year." The seller has made several *affirmations of fact* that can create a warranty: the automobile has an engine; it has a 350-horsepower engine; it was rebuilt this year; there are four tires on the automobile; and the tires are new. But the seller's *opinion* that the vehicle is "the best used car to come along in years" is known as "puffing" and creates no warranty. (Puffing is the expression of a seller's opinion that is not made as a representation of fact.) A statement relating to the value of the goods, such as "it's worth a fortune" or "anywhere else you'd pay $10,000 for it," does not usually create a warranty. If the seller is an expert and gives an opinion as an expert, however, then a warranty can be created.

It is not always easy to determine what constitutes an express warranty and what constitutes puffing. The reasonableness of the buyer's reliance appears to be the controlling criterion in many cases. For example, a salesperson's statements that a ladder "will never break" and will "last a lifetime" are so clearly improbable that no reasonable buyer should rely on them. Also, the context within which a statement is made might be relevant in determining the reasonableness of the buyer's reliance. For example, a reasonable person is more likely to rely on a written statement made in an advertisement than on a statement made orally by a salesperson.

Implied Warranties

IMPLIED WARRANTY
A warranty that the law implies through either the situation of the parties or the nature of the transaction.

An **implied warranty** is one that *the law derives* by implication or inference from the nature of the transaction or the relative situation or circumstances of the parties.

For example, Joplin buys an axe at Gershwin's Hardware Store. No express warranties are made. The first time she chops wood with it, the axe handle breaks, and she is injured. She immediately notifies Gershwin. Examination shows that the wood in the handle was rotten but that the rottenness could not have been noticed by either Gershwin or Joplin. Nonetheless, Joplin notifies Gershwin that she will hold him responsible for the medical bills. Gershwin is responsible because a merchant seller of goods warrants that the goods he or she sells are fit for normal use.

Implied Warranty of Merchantability An **implied warranty of merchantability** automatically arises in every sale of goods made *by a merchant* who deals in goods of the kind sold [UCC 2–314]. Thus, a retailer of ski equipment makes an implied warranty of merchantability every time the retailer sells a pair of skis, but a neighbor selling his or her skis at a garage sale does not.

IMPLIED WARRANTY OF MERCHANTABILITY
A presumed promise by a merchant seller of goods that the goods are reasonably fit for the general purpose for which they are sold, are properly packaged and labeled, and are of proper quality.

Goods that are *merchantable* are "reasonably fit for the ordinary purposes for which such goods are used." They must be of at least average, fair, or medium-grade quality. The quality must be comparable to quality that will pass without objection in the trade or market for goods of the same description. To be merchantable, the goods must also be adequately packaged and labeled as provided by the agreement, and they must conform to the promises or affirmations of fact made on the container or label, if any.

An implied warranty of merchantability also imposes on the merchant liability for the safe performance of the product. It makes no difference whether the merchant knew of or could have discovered a defect that makes the product unsafe—he or she is liable in either case. Of course, merchants are not absolute insurers against *all* accidents arising in connection with the goods. For example, a bar of soap is not unmerchantable merely because a user could slip and fall by stepping on it. In an action based on breach of implied warranty, it is necessary to show:

1. The existence of the implied warranty.
2. That the warranty was broken.
3. That the breach of warranty was the proximate cause of the damage sustained.

The serving of food or drink to be consumed on or off the premises is recognized as a sale of goods subject to the implied warranty of merchantability [UCC 2–314(1)]. "Merchantable" food means food that is fit to eat. What is food that is fit to eat? It might be argued that food that contains cholesterol is nonmerchantable because cholesterol may contribute to heart disease. But if that food is exactly like all other food of the particular brand and virtually the same as other brands on the market, it is unlikely that a court would agree. In such cases, consumers could reasonably expect the product to contain cholesterol. Similarly, the courts assume that consumers should reasonably expect to find on occasion bones in fish fillets, cherry pits in cherry pie, a nut shell in a package of shelled nuts, and so on—because such substances are natural incidents of the food. Cases in which courts have found breaches of the implied warranty of merchantability have involved food containing substances that are not natural to the food product; for example, consumers would not reasonably expect to find an inchworm in a can of peas or a piece of glass in a soft drink. (This foreign-natural distinction is explored further in this chapter's *Law in the Extreme.*)

In the following classic case, the court had to determine whether a fish bone was a substance that one should reasonably expect to find in fish chowder.

Case 17.1 

WEBSTER v. BLUE SHIP TEA ROOM, INC.

Supreme Judicial Court of Massachusetts, 1964.
347 Mass. 421,
198 N.E.2d 309.

HISTORICAL AND SOCIAL SETTING *Chowder, a soup or stew made with fresh fish, possibly originated in the fishing villages of Brittany and was probably carried to Canada and New England by Breton fishermen. In the nineteenth century and earlier, recipes for chowder did not call for the removal of the fish bones. Chowder recipes in the first half of the twentieth century remained as they had in previous centuries, sometimes specifying that the fish head, tail, and backbone were to be broken in pieces and boiled, with the "liquor thus produced * * * added to the balance of the chowder."*[a] *By the mid–twentieth century, there was a considerable body of case law involving implied warranties*

a. Fannie Farmer, *The Boston Cooking School Cook Book* (Boston: Little Brown Co., 1937), p. 166.

Case 17.1—Continued

and foreign and natural substances in food. It was perhaps inevitable that sooner or later, a consumer injured by a fish bone in chowder would challenge the merchantability of chowder containing fish bones.

FACTS Blue Ship Tea Room, Inc., was located in Boston in an old building overlooking the ocean. Webster, who had been born and raised in New England, went to the restaurant and ordered fish chowder. The chowder was milky in color. After three or four spoonfuls, she felt something lodged in her throat. As a result, she underwent two esophagoscopies; in the second, a fish bone was found and removed. Webster brought suit against the restaurant for breach of implied warranty of merchantability. The jury rendered a verdict for Webster, and the restaurant appealed.

ISSUE Does serving fish chowder that contains a bone constitute the breach of an implied warranty of merchantability on the part of the restaurant?

DECISION No. Webster could not recover against Blue Ship Tea Room, because no breach of warranty had occurred.

REASON The court, citing UCC Section 2–314, stated that "a warranty that goods shall be merchantable is implied in a contract for their sale if the seller is a merchant with respect to goods of that kind. Under this section the serving for value of food or drink to be consumed either on the premises or elsewhere is a sale. * * * Goods to be merchantable must at least be * * * fit for the ordinary purposes for which such goods are used." The question here is whether a fish bone made the chowder unfit for eating. In the judge's opinion, "the joys of life in New England include the ready availability of fresh fish chowder. We should be prepared to cope with the hazards of fish bones, the occasional presence of which in chowders is, it seems to us, to be anticipated, and which, in the light of a hallowed tradition, do not impair their fitness or merchantability."

Implied Warranty of Fitness for a Particular Purpose The implied warranty of fitness for a particular purpose arises when *any seller* (merchant or nonmerchant) knows the particular purpose for which a buyer will use the goods *and* knows that the buyer is relying on the seller's skill and judgment to select suitable goods [UCC 2–315].

A "particular purpose of the buyer" differs from the "ordinary purpose for which goods are used" (merchantability). Goods can be merchantable but unfit for a buyer's particular purpose. Say, for example, that you need a gallon of paint to match the color of your living room walls—a light shade somewhere between coral and peach. You take a sample to your local hardware store and request a gallon of paint of that color. Instead, you are given a gallon of bright blue paint. Here, the salesperson has not breached any warranty of implied merchantability—the bright blue paint is of high quality and suitable for interior walls—but he or she has breached an implied warranty of fitness for a particular purpose.

A seller does not need to have actual knowledge of the buyer's particular purpose. It is sufficient if a seller "has reason to know" the purpose. The buyer, however, must have *relied* on the seller's skill or judgment in selecting or furnishing suitable goods for an implied warranty to be created.

For example, Bloomberg buys a shortwave radio from Radio Shop, telling the salesperson that she wants a set strong enough to pick up Radio Luxembourg, which is 8,000 miles away. Radio Shop sells Bloomberg a Model X set. The set works, but it does not pick up Radio Luxembourg. Bloomberg wants her money back. Here, as Radio Shop has breached the implied warranty of fitness for a particular purpose, Bloomberg normally will be able to recover. The salesperson knew specifically that she wanted a set that would pick up Radio Luxembourg. Furthermore, Bloomberg relied on the salesperson to furnish a radio that would fulfill this purpose. Because Radio Shop did not do so, the warranty was breached.

Other Implied Warranties The UCC recognizes in Section 2–314(3) that implied warranties can arise (or be excluded or modified) as a result of course of dealing, course of performance, or usage of trade. In the absence of evidence to the contrary,

Law in the Extreme

Chicken Enchiladas, Raw Oysters, and Other Perils

As mentioned in this chapter, in determining whether food is "merchantable" (fit for human consumption), courts frequently distinguish between whether the substance causing a plaintiff's injury is "natural" to the food product (such as a chicken bone in chicken soup) or a "foreign" substance (such as a rock in the chicken soup). Although this foreign-natural distinction may be helpful in some situations, in others it can become problematic. For example, should a chicken enchilada that contains a one-inch chicken bone be deemed "merchantable" simply because the bone is natural to the product?[a] Is a hamburger that contains a bone fragment large enough to break a consumer's tooth merchantable because the bone is a "natural" substance in cows?[b] And what about raw oysters that are tainted with a health-harming bacteria? Are the bacteria "natural" or "foreign" to the oysters?[c]

Questions such as these led the California Supreme Court to establish some guidelines on the issue. It did so in its review of the case concerning the chicken enchilada, *Mexicali Rose v. Superior Court.*[d] The court stated that the foreign-natural distinction should be retained. In other words, if the injury-causing substance is "natural" to the food product, the food is considered merchantable, and a consumer does not have a cause of action for breach of the implied warranty of merchantability. The consumer can, however, pursue an action for negligence in the preparation of the food. If the injury-causing substance is "foreign" to the food product, then a consumer can bring an action for breach of the implied warranty of merchantability. It will then be up to a jury to decide whether a consumer would reasonably expect to find the substance in the food and whether the substance rendered the food unfit or defective.

Three dissenting justices declared, in two separate dissents, that the distinction was just a little ambiguous and not too helpful: "What exactly do we mean when we say an object is 'foreign to' or 'natural to' a dish? 'Natural to' surely cannot include all natural material. Salmonella is natural and feces are natural, but their presence in food surely makes the food unfit for consumption. What about a hamburger made out of chopped rat flesh?" The second dissent suggested that a cow's eye in a hamburger is natural to the product. Does that, it asked, mean that the hamburger is "merchantable"? To these questions, the majority answered: "The term 'natural' refers to bones and other substances natural to the product served, and does not encompass substances such as mold, botulinus bacteria or other substances (like rat flesh or cow eyes) not natural to the preparation of the product served." One dissenting justice found this explanation insufficient. In particular, the justice could not understand how the majority had arrived at the conclusion that while a chicken bone is "natural to the preparation" of a chicken enchilada, a cow's eye was not "natural to the preparation" of a hamburger.

a. *Mexicali Rose v. Superior Court,* 214 Cal.App.3d 238, 262 Cal.Rptr. 750 (1989). The court held that the food was merchantable because the bone was "natural" to the food served.

b. *Evart v. Suli,* 211 Cal.App.3d 605, 259 Cal.Rptr. 535 (1989). The court held that a jury might find that a hamburger containing a bone fragment large enough to break a consumer's tooth was not merchantable because consumers do not reasonably expect to find bone fragments of such a size within ground meat.

c. *Kilpatrick v. Superior Court,* 8 Cal.App.4th 1717, 11 Cal.Rptr.2d 323 (1992). In this case, which was stayed until the California Supreme Court rendered its decision in *Mexicali Rose v. Superior Court,* the court decided that the bacteria in the oysters were "foreign" to the oysters.

d. 1 Cal.4th 617, 4 Cal.Rptr.2d 145, 822 P.2d 1292 (1992).

when both parties to a sales contract have knowledge of a well-recognized trade custom, the courts will infer that they both intended for that custom to apply to their contract. For example, if an industry wide custom is to lubricate a new car before it is delivered and a dealer fails to do so, the dealer can be held liable to a buyer for resulting damages, under breach of implied warranty. This, of course, would also be negligence on the part of the dealer.

Overlapping Warranties

Sometimes two or more warranties are made in a single transaction. An implied warranty of merchantability or fitness for a particular purpose, or both, can exist in addition to an express warranty. For example, when a sales contract for a new car states that "this car engine is warranted to be free from defects for 36,000 miles or thirty-six months, whichever occurs first," there is an express warranty against all defects and an implied warranty that the car will be fit for normal use.

The rule of UCC 2–317 is that express and implied warranties are construed as *cumulative* if they are consistent with one another. If the warranties are *inconsistent*, the courts usually hold as follows:

1. *Express* warranties displace inconsistent *implied* warranties, except implied warranties of fitness for a particular purpose.
2. Samples take precedence over inconsistent general descriptions.
3. Technical specifications displace inconsistent samples or general descriptions.

Suppose that when Bloomberg buys the shortwave radio at Radio Shop, as described earlier, the contract expressly warrants radio receivership to a maximum range of 4,000 miles. She tries to pick up Radio Luxembourg—the stated purpose of her purchase—which is 8,000 miles away. The set cannot perform that well. Bloomberg claims that Radio Shop has breached the implied warranty of fitness for a particular purpose. Here, the express warranty takes precedence over any implied warranty of merchantability that a shortwave set should pick up a station anywhere in the world. Bloomberg does have a good claim for the breach of implied warranty of fitness for a particular purpose, however, because she made it clear that she was buying the set to pick up Radio Luxembourg. In cases of inconsistency between an express warranty and an implied warranty of fitness for a particular purpose, the implied warranty of fitness for the buyer's purpose normally prevails [UCC 2–317(c)].

Third Party Beneficiaries of Warranties

One of the general principles of contract law is that unless you are one of the parties to a contract, you have no rights under the contract. (Notable exceptions are assignments and third party beneficiary contracts, discussed in Chapter 12.) In short, common law established that *privity* must exist between a plaintiff and a defendant before any action based on a contract could be maintained.

For example, I purchase a ham from retailer Bill. I invite you to my house that evening. I prepare the ham properly. You eat the ham and become severely ill because the ham is spoiled. Can you sue retailer Bill for breach of the implied warranty of merchantability? Because warranty is based on a contract for the sale of goods, under the common law, you would normally have warranty rights only if you were a party to the purchase of the ham. Therefore, the warranty would extend only to me, the purchaser.

In the past, this hardship was sometimes resolved by court decisions removing privity as a requirement so that manufacturers and sellers could be held liable for certain defective products (notably food, drugs, and cosmetics) that were sold. The UCC, reflecting some of these decisions, has addressed the problem of privity, at least to the extent of including optional, alternative provisions eliminating the requirement of privity in various circumstances.

There is sharp disagreement over how far warranty liability should extend. To satisfy opposing views of the various states, the drafters of the UCC proposed three alternatives for liability under UCC 2–318. All three alternatives are intended to eliminate the privity requirement with respect to certain enumerated types of injuries (personal versus property) for certain beneficiaries (for example, household members or bystanders). The following case involves a third party who suffered injuries as a result of a faulty lock on the door of a walk-in freezer, which was located in a church. The issue is whether the seller's express and implied warranties extended to the third party.

Case 17.2

CREWS v. W. A. BROWN & SON, INC.

Court of Appeals of North Carolina, 1992.
106 N.C.App. 324,
416 S.E.2d 924.

HISTORICAL AND SOCIAL SETTING *In most states, personal injury claims that do not meet the privity requirement can be brought on the ground of strict liability (discussed in Chapter 5 and also later in this chapter). Lack of privity is no defense to a suit brought on this ground by a product's user or consumer. (Courts also allow parties who are not "users or consumers" to recover on this ground.) If a state does not recognize strict liability or the case is brought under a warranty claim, however, an injured party may look to UCC 2–318. UCC 2–318, as it was drafted in 1962 ("Alternative A" of the current version), extends warranty liability to "any natural person who is in the family or household of [the] buyer or who is a guest in his home" and who could reasonably be expected to use, consume, or be affected by the goods. In a state that has adopted this version of UCC 2–318, whether other individuals can recover for personal injuries depends on developments in the state's case law. In North Carolina, the official comment to UCC 2–318 states that the section "does not abolish North Carolina's requirement of privity with reference to strangers to the contract."*

FACTS Thirteen-year-old Vickie Crews was working as a volunteer at Calvary Baptist Church in Winston-Salem, North Carolina, on the evening of July 2, 1985. At about 8:45 P.M., Vickie went to the church's kitchen and thought she heard a noise in the walk-in freezer. Crews, barefoot and wearing shorts, stepped inside the freezer, and the door closed behind her. She pushed the red emergency release button on the inside of the door, but the door did not open. At approximately 10:00 P.M., someone discovered Crews, and she was taken to a hospital and treated for severe frostbite. During the next two months, she endured five separate operations and the amputation of most of her toes. Crews and her mother (the plaintiffs) sued W. A. Brown & Son, Inc. (the manufacturer of the freezer), Foodcraft Equipment Company (the firm that had assembled and installed the freezer and sold it to the church), and the church. The plaintiffs alleged, among other things, breach of express and implied warranties. The court granted Foodcraft's motion for summary judgment, holding that the plaintiffs' claims were barred by a lack of privity with Foodcraft. The plaintiffs appealed.

ISSUE Were the plaintiffs' breach of warranty claims barred by a lack of privity with Foodcraft?

DECISION Yes. The appellate court affirmed the trial court's decision.

REASON The court stated that under North Carolina law, the ultimate purchaser of a product may sue a seller for breach of express or implied warranties. Additionally, "any natural person who is in the family or household of [the] buyer or who is a guest in his home if it is reasonable to expect that such person may use, consume or be affected by the goods and who is injured in person by breach of the warranty" has standing to sue a seller for breach of warranty. The court stressed that the statute did not extend warranty coverage to persons beyond those specifically enumerated and Vickie Crews was not among them. "Because a church does not have a 'family' or a 'household' in the ordinary meanings of those terms, Crews cannot be classified as a member of Church's 'family' or 'household.' " And because "a church is not a 'home,' * * * she was not a guest in the buyer's 'home.' "

Warranty Disclaimers

Because each type of warranty is created in a special way, the manner in which warranties can be disclaimed or qualified by the seller varies from type to type.

Express Warranties Any affirmation of fact or promise, description of the goods, or use of samples or models by a seller creates an express warranty. Obviously, then, express warranties can be excluded if the seller carefully refrains from making any promise or affirmation of fact relating to the goods, describing the goods, or using a sample or model [UCC 2–313].

The UCC does permit express warranties to be negated or limited by specific and unambiguous language, provided that this is done in a manner that protects the buyer from surprise. Therefore, a written disclaimer in language that is clear and conspicuous, and called to a buyer's attention, could negate all oral express warranties not included in the written sales contract. This allows the seller to avoid false allegations that oral warranties were made, and it ensures that only representations by properly authorized individuals are included in the bargain.

Note, however, that a buyer must be made aware of any warranty disclaimers or modifications *at the time the sales contract is formed.* In other words, any oral or written warranties—or disclaimers—made during the bargaining process cannot be modified at a later time by the seller.

Implied Warranties Generally speaking, unless circumstances indicate otherwise, implied warranties (of merchantability and fitness) are disclaimed by the expressions "as is," "with all faults," and other similar expressions that in common understanding for *both* parties call the buyer's attention to the fact that there are no implied warranties [UCC 2–316(3)(a)].

The UCC also permits a seller to specifically disclaim an implied warranty either of fitness or of merchantability [UCC 2–316(2)]. To disclaim an implied warranty of fitness for a particular purpose, the disclaimer *must* be in writing and conspicuous. The word *fitness* does not have to be mentioned in the writing; it is sufficient if, for example, the disclaimer states, **"THERE ARE NO WARRANTIES THAT EXTEND BEYOND THE DESCRIPTION ON THE FACE HEREOF."**

A merchantability disclaimer must be more specific; it must mention *merchantability*. It need not be written; but if it is, the writing must be conspicuous. According to UCC 1–201(10),

> A term or clause is conspicuous when it is so written that a reasonable person against whom it is to operate ought to have noticed it. A printed heading in capitals * * * is conspicuous. Language in the body of a form is conspicuous if it is in larger or other contrasting type or color.

For example, Forbes, a merchant, sells Maves a particular lawnmower selected by Forbes with the characteristics clearly requested by Maves. At the time of the sale, Forbes orally tells Maves that he does not warrant the merchantability of the mower, as it is last year's model. The mower proves to be defective and does not work. Maves wants to hold Forbes liable for breach of the implied warranties of merchantability and fitness for a particular purpose.

Maves can hold Forbes liable for breach of the warranty of fitness for a particular purpose but not for breach of the warranty of merchantability. Forbes's oral disclaimer mentioning the word *merchantability* is a proper disclaimer. But for Forbes to have disclaimed the implied warranty of fitness for a particular purpose, a conspicuous writing would have been required. As no written disclaimer was made, Forbes can still be held liable.

Buyer's Refusal to Inspect If a buyer actually examines the goods (or a sample or model) as fully as desired before entering into a contract, or if the buyer refuses to examine the goods, *there is no implied warranty with respect to defects that a reasonable examination would reveal or defects that are accidentally found.* Note that *failing* to examine the goods is not a *refusal* to examine them; a refusal occurs only when the seller *demands* that the buyer examine the goods.

Suppose, in the illustration concerning Joplin's purchase of an axe from Gershwin's hardware store, the defect in Joplin's axe could have been spotted easily by normal inspection. Joplin, even after Gershwin asks, refuses to inspect the axe before buying it. After being hurt by the defective axe, she normally cannot hold Gershwin liable for breach of warranty of merchantability because she could have spotted the defect during an inspection [UCC 2–316(3)(b)].

The seller remains liable for any latent (hidden) defects that ordinary inspection would not reveal. What the examination ought to reveal depends on a buyer's skill and method of examination. For example, an auto mechanic purchasing a car should be responsible for discovering defects that a nonexpert would not be expected to find. The circumstances of each case determine what defects a so-called reasonable inspection should reveal.

Warranty Disclaimers and Unconscionability The UCC sections dealing with warranty disclaimers do not refer specifically to unconscionability as a factor. Ultimately, however, the courts will test warranty disclaimers with reference to the unconscionability standards of Section 2–302. Such things as lack of bargaining position, "take-it-or-leave-it" choices, and a buyer's failure to understand or know of a warranty-disclaimer provision will become relevant to the issue of unconscionability. In the following landmark decision, which was decided before the UCC was effective in New Jersey, a consumer's lack of bargaining power with respect to a large auto manufacturer was given significant weight by the court in determining whether a warranty disclaimer was unconscionable.

Case 17.3

HENNINGSEN v. BLOOMFIELD MOTORS, INC.

Supreme Court of New Jersey, 1960.
32 N.J. 358,
161 A.2d 69.

HISTORICAL AND SOCIAL SETTING *The Uniform Sales Act of 1906 liberalized the common law of sales. To lessen the harshness of the doctrine of* caveat emptor *("let the buyer beware"), the act imposed obligations on sellers by operation of law, rather than depending on the express agreement of the parties. Of particular significance was the act's recognition of the right to sue on the basis of personal injury arising from a breach of warranty. The Uniform Sales Act also provided, however, that a warranty could be varied by express agreement. Through trade associations, manufacturers and sellers drafted standardized contracts with broad disclaimer clauses. For example, a uniform warranty disclaimer was standard with the members of the Automobile Manufacturers Association, which represented almost 94 percent of automobile production in the United States in 1958. Disclaimers of warranties that normally accompanied a sale were not favored, especially by the New Jersey courts.*

FACTS Henningsen purchased a new Chrysler from Bloomfield Motors, Inc., for his wife. Subsequently, his wife suffered severe injuries as a result of an apparent defect in the steering wheel mechanism. The standard-form purchase order used in the transaction contained an express ninety-day/4,000-mile warranty. In addition, the purchase order contained a disclaimer, in fine print, of any and all other express or implied warranties. Thus, Bloomfield Motors and Chrysler Corporation refused to pay for Mrs. Henningsen's injuries, asserting that the sales contract, which warranted that Bloomfield would repair defects at no charge, disclaimed warranty liabilities for injuries suffered. A lawsuit followed, based in part on breach of the implied warranty of merchantability. The trial court held for the Henningsens, and Bloomfield appealed.

ISSUE Can the Henningsens recover from Bloomfield Motors and Chrysler despite the disclaimer contained in the sales contract?

DECISION Yes. The trial court's judgment was affirmed.

REASON The liability of Bloomfield Motors and Chrysler Corporation was based on an implied warranty of merchantability contained in the Uniform Sales Act (now included in the UCC) for the sale of goods. The court stated

Case 17.3—Continued

that the implied warranty of merchantability is "a general incident of sale of an automobile by description. The warranty does not depend upon the affirmative intention of the parties" or a finding of fault. The legislature's purpose in implying a warranty in the sale of goods was to protect buyers and "not to limit the liability of the seller or manufacturer." In the opinion of the court, "[t]he disclaimer of the implied warranty and exclusion of all obligations except those specifically assumed by the express warranty signify a studied effort to frustrate the protection. True, the [Uniform] Sales Act authorizes agreements between buyer and seller qualifying the warranty obligations. But quite obviously the Legislature contemplated lawful stipulations [which are determined by the circumstances of a particular case] arrived at freely by parties of relatively equal bargaining strength. The lawmakers did not authorize the automobile manufacturer to use its grossly disproportionate bargaining power [and the unfair surprise of fine print] to relieve itself from liability and to impose on the ordinary buyer, who in effect has no real freedom of choice, the grave danger of injury to himself and others that attends the sale of such a dangerous instrumentality as a defectively made automobile. In the framework of this case, illustrated as it is by the facts and the many decisions noted, we are of the opinion that Chrysler's [and Bloomfield's] attempted disclaimer of an implied warranty of merchantability and of the obligations arising therefrom is so inimical to the public good as to compel an adjudication of its invalidity."

Magnuson-Moss Warranty Act

The Magnuson-Moss Warranty Act of 1975 was designed to prevent deception in warranties by making them easier to understand.[2] The act is mainly enforced by the Federal Trade Commission (FTC). Additionally, the attorney general or a consumer who has been injured can enforce the act if informal procedures for settling disputes prove to be ineffective. The act modifies UCC warranty rules to some extent when *consumer* sales transactions are involved. The UCC, however, remains the primary codification of warranty rules for industrial and commercial transactions.

No seller is *required* to give a written warranty for consumer goods sold under the Magnuson-Moss Act. But if a seller chooses to make an express written warranty, and the cost of the consumer goods is more than $10, the warranty must be labeled as "full" or "limited." In addition, if the cost of the goods is more than $15, by FTC regulation, the warrantor must make certain disclosures fully and conspicuously in a single document in "readily understood language." This disclosure states the names and addresses of the warrantor(s), what specifically is warranted, procedures for enforcement of the warranty, any limitations on warranty relief, and that the buyer has legal rights.

Although a *full warranty* may not cover every aspect of the consumer product sold, what it covers ensures some type of buyer satisfaction in case the product is defective. A full warranty requires free repair or replacement of any defective part; if the product cannot be repaired within a reasonable time, the consumer has the choice of either a refund or a replacement without charge. The full warranty frequently does not have a time limit on it. Any limitation on consequential damages must be *conspicuously* stated. Also, the warrantor need not perform warranty services if the problem with the product was caused by damage to the product or unreasonable use by the consumer.

A *limited warranty* arises when the written warranty fails to meet one of the minimum requirements of a full warranty. The fact that a seller is giving only a limited warranty must be conspicuously designated. If it is only a time limitation that distinguishes a limited warranty from a full warranty, the Magnuson-Moss Warranty Act allows the seller to identify the warranty as a full warranty by such language as "full twelve-month warranty."

Implied warranties are not covered under the Magnuson-Moss Warranty Act; they continue to be created according to UCC provisions. When an express warranty

2. 15 U.S.C. Sections 2301–2312.

Lemon laws were enacted in response to the frustrations of the buyers of defective automobiles. What does a lemon law provide for a frustrated buyer?

is made in a sales contract or a combined sales and service contract (when the service contract is undertaken within ninety days of the sale), the Magnuson-Moss Warranty Act prevents sellers from disclaiming or modifying the implied warranties of merchantability and fitness for a particular purpose. Sellers can impose a time limit on the duration of an implied warranty, but it has to correspond to the duration of the express warranty.[3]

"The biggest corporation, like the humblest private citizen, must be held to strict compliance with the will of the people."

Theodore Roosevelt, 1858–1919
(Twenty-sixth president of the United States, 1901–1909)

❖ Lemon Laws

Some purchasers of defective automobiles—called "lemons"—found that the remedies provided by the UCC, after limitations had been imposed by the seller, were inadequate. In response to the frustrations of these buyers, the majority of states have enacted *lemon laws.* Basically, lemon laws provide that if an automobile under warranty possesses a defect that significantly affects the vehicle's value or use, and the defect has not been remedied by the seller within a specified number of opportunities (usually four), the buyer is entitled to a new car, replacement of defective parts, or return of all consideration paid.

In most states, lemon laws require an aggrieved new-car owner to notify the dealer or manufacturer of the problem and provide the dealer or manufacturer with an opportunity to solve it. If the problem remains, the owner must then submit complaints to the arbitration program specified in the manufacturer's warranty before taking the case to court. Decisions by arbitration panels are binding on the manufacturer (that is, cannot be appealed by the manufacturer to the courts) but are not usually binding on the purchaser.

Most major automobile companies use their own arbitration panels. Ford and Chrysler, for example, have the Ford Consumer Appeals Board and the Chrysler Customer Arbitration Board, to which lemon-law disputes are submitted. Some companies, however, such as General Motors, subscribe to independent arbitration ser-

3. The time limit on an implied warranty occurring by virtue of the seller's express warranty must, of course, be reasonable, conscionable, and set forth in clear and conspicuous language on the face of the warranty.

Landmark in the Law

MacPherson v. Buick Motor Co. (1916)

Today, product liability laws allow any person who is injured by a defective product to sue the manufacturer of the product for damages. That was not always the case. In fact, in the long history of the common law, product liability is a relatively recent development, dating to the early part of the twentieth century. Prior to that time, with few exceptions, only those persons in privity of contract with the manufacturer could sue the manufacturer for negligence or breach of warranty. In the landmark case of *MacPherson v. Buick Motor Co.*,[a] the New York Court of Appeals—New York's highest court—dealt with the liability of a manufacturer that failed to exercise reasonable care in manufacturing a finished product.

The case was brought by Donald MacPherson, who suffered injuries while riding in a Buick automobile that suddenly collapsed because one of the wheels was made of defective wood. The spokes crumbled into fragments, throwing MacPherson out of the vehicle and injuring him. MacPherson had purchased the car from a Buick dealer, but he brought suit against the manufacturer, Buick Motor Company. The wheel itself had not been made by Buick; it had been bought from another manufacturer. There was evidence, though, that the defects could have been discovered by reasonable inspection and that no such inspection had taken place. Although there was no charge that Buick knew of the defect and willfully concealed it, MacPherson charged Buick with negligence for putting a human life in imminent danger.

The major issue before the court was whether Buick owed a duty of care to anyone but the immediate purchaser of the car (that is, the Buick dealer). In deciding the issue, the court referred to an earlier case in which an exception to the privity requirement was made. That case involved a poison that had been falsely labeled when it was sold to a druggist, who in turn sold it to a customer. The customer was allowed to recover damages from the seller who affixed the label on the ground that the defendant's negligence had "put human life in imminent danger." The principle enunciated in that case was that if a danger is foreseeable, then a duty arises to avoid the danger.

In *MacPherson*, Justice Benjamin Cardozo (see the *Profile* in this chapter) applied the same principle. The court stated that "[i]f the nature of a thing is such that it is reasonably certain to place life and limb in peril when negligently made, it is then a thing of danger. Its nature gives warning of the consequences to be expected. If to the element of danger there is added knowledge that the thing will be used by persons other than the purchaser, and used without new tests, then, irrespective of contract, the manufacturer of this thing of danger is under a duty to make it carefully." The court concluded that "[b]eyond all question, the nature of an automobile gives warning of probable danger if its construction is defective. This automobile was designed to go 50 miles an hour. Unless its wheels were sound and strong, injury was almost certain."

Although Buick had not manufactured the wheel itself, the court held that Buick had a duty to inspect the wheels and that Buick "was responsible for the finished product. * * * The obligation to inspect must vary with the nature of the thing to be inspected. The more probable the danger, the greater the need of caution." Based on this reasoning, the court held that Buick was liable to MacPherson for the injuries he sustained when he was thrown from the car.

a. 217 N.Y. 382, 111 N.E. 1050 (1916).

vices, such as those provided by the Better Business Bureau. Although arbitration boards must meet state and/or federal standards of impartiality, industry-sponsored arbitration boards have been criticized for not being truly impartial in their decisions. In response to this criticism, some states have established mandatory, government-sponsored arbitration programs for lemon-law disputes.

PRODUCT LIABILITY
The legal liability of manufacturers and sellers to buyers, users, and bystanders for injuries or damages suffered because of defects in goods. Liability arises when a product has a defective condition that makes it unreasonably dangerous and the product causes damage or injury.

❖ Product Liability

Manufacturers and sellers of goods can be held liable to consumers, users, and bystanders for physical harm or property damage that is caused by the goods. This is called **product liability.** Product liability may be based on the warranty theories just discussed, as well as on the theories of *negligence, misrepresentation*, and *strict liability*.

Negligence

Chapter 5 defined *negligence* as failure to use the degree of care that a reasonable, prudent person would have used under the circumstances. If a seller fails to exercise such reasonable care and an injury results, he or she may be sued for negligence. Thus, a manufacturer must exercise "due care" to make a product safe. Due care must be exercised in designing the product, in selecting the materials, in using the appropriate production process, in assembling and testing the product, and in placing adequate warnings on the label informing the user of dangers of which an ordinary person might not be aware. The duty of care also extends to the inspection and testing of any purchased products that are used in the final product sold by the manufacturer. The failure to exercise due care is negligence.

"Negligence is the omission to do something which a reasonable man . . . would do, or doing something which a prudent and reasonable man would not do."

B. Alderson
(in *Hadley v. Baxendale*, 1854)

An action based on negligence does not require privity of contract between the injured plaintiff and the negligent defendant-manufacturer. Section 395 of the Restatement (Second) of Torts states as follows:

> A manufacturer who fails to exercise reasonable care in the manufacture of a chattel [movable good] which, unless carefully made, he should recognize as involving an unreasonable risk of causing physical harm to those who lawfully use it for a purpose for which the manufacturer should expect it to be used and to those whom he should expect to be endangered by its probable use, is subject to liability for physical harm caused to them by its lawful use in a manner and for a purpose for which it is supplied.

More simply stated, a manufacturer is liable for its failure to exercise due care to any person who sustained an injury proximately caused by a negligently made (defective) product, regardless of whether there was a sale or a contract to sell.

Misrepresentation

When a fraudulent misrepresentation has been made to a user or consumer, and that misrepresentation ultimately results in an injury, the basis of liability may be the tort of fraud. Examples are the intentional mislabeling of packaged cosmetics and the intentional concealment of a product's defects.

A more interesting basis of liability is nonfraudulent misrepresentation, which occurs when a merchant *innocently* misrepresents the character or quality of goods. A famous example involved a drug manufacturer and a person who became addicted to a prescription medication called Talwin. The manufacturer, Winthrop Laboratories, a division of Sterling Drug, Inc., innocently indicated to the medical profession that the drug was not physically addictive. Using this information, a physician prescribed the drug for his patient, who developed an addiction that turned out to be fatal. Even though the addiction was a highly unusual reaction resulting from the victim's highly unusual susceptibility to this product, the drug company was still held liable.[4]

Strict Liability

A fairly recent development in tort law is the revival of the doctrine of strict liability. Under this doctrine, people are liable for the results of their acts regardless of their intentions or their exercise of reasonable care. The Restatement (Second) of Torts designates how the doctrine of strict liability should be applied. It is a precise and widely accepted statement of the liabilities of sellers of goods (including manufac-

4. *Crocker v. Winthrop Laboratories, Division of Sterling Drug, Inc.*, 514 S.W.2d 429 (Tex. 1974).

Business Law in Action

Limitations on Liability—Blood-Shield Statutes

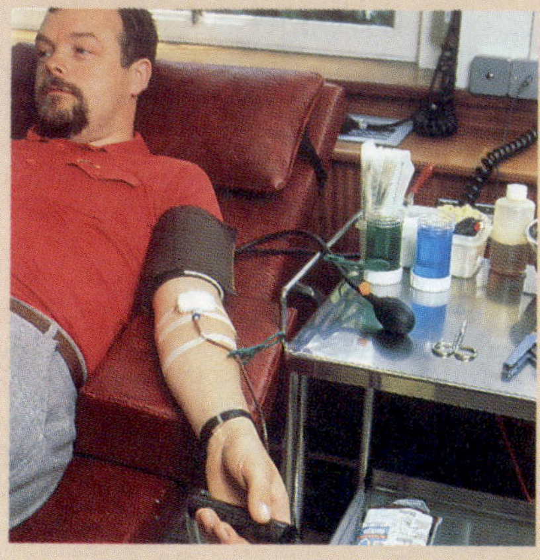

If you are ever in a serious accident or have an operation, you may need a blood transfusion. Blood transfusions can mean the difference between life and death. In a tiny fraction of cases, however, the blood used for transfusions has been contaminated. Particularly serious consequences have resulted when transfused blood contains the AIDS virus. In this situation, recipients of the blood are infected with a debilitating disease that is physically, emotionally, and financially devastating. Because there is no known cure for AIDS, some of the patients who have been infected with the virus after receiving contaminated blood have tried to sue their hospitals, doctors, and blood banks.

To a great extent, warranty liability for bad blood is precluded by so-called *blood-shield statutes,* which many states have passed. These laws insulate hospitals and other blood suppliers from warranty liability in the event that the recipient of transfused blood suffers sickness or death as a result. In effect, blood-shield statutes prevent plaintiffs from bringing lawsuits based on a warranty theory of liability. Infected patients have also unsuccessfully argued that doctors, hospitals, and blood banks should be held strictly liable for any harm resulting from transfusions of contaminated blood.[a]

Unable to recover under warranty or strict liability theories, many plaintiffs are now attempting to hold blood banks or suppliers liable under negligence theory (see Chapter 5). More than three hundred bad-blood lawsuits have been filed by infected patients in the past few years. Before 1990, such suits rarely resulted in the plaintiffs' being awarded damages. More recently, though, a handful of plaintiffs have won judgments with substantial money awards. The most successful plaintiffs have been those who could prove that the transfusions were unnecessary, that the blood donors were inadequately screened and examined, or that the blood itself was improperly tested or labeled by the hospital or blood bank.

Two recent court decisions also have far-reaching implications for suppliers of blood or blood components. In a case heard by the Colorado Supreme Court in 1992, the plaintiff had received a blood transfusion in which the blood was contaminated by the AIDS virus. The transfusion occurred prior to 1985, when the first reliable blood test for AIDS became available. Most courts have ruled that blood banks are not liable for AIDS-contaminated blood supplied before that time on the ground that the blood banks met the professional standards of the time and should not be expected to have done more. The Colorado court held otherwise. It concluded that it should be left to the jury to decide whether the professional standards were in fact adequate, given the knowledge of the medical community and blood banks about the importance of using strict screening procedures when collecting blood from donors.[b]

In another case, the Supreme Court of Hawaii held that the state's blood-shield statute did not preclude a plaintiff from bringing a negligence claim against manufacturers of a blood protein known as antihemophiliac factor concentrate (AHF). The plaintiff, a hemophiliac who had received AHF injections in 1983 and 1984, later tested positive for the AIDS virus and alleged that he had been exposed to the virus through the AHF injections. The AHF had been dispensed by an army hospital in Hawaii that obtained AHF from several manufacturers. Because it was not known which manufacturer was responsible for the particular AHF received by the plaintiff, the court held that all of the manufacturers of AHF could be held liable under a market-share theory of liability (see the discussion of liability sharing in this chapter). In justifying its decision to apply the market-share theory, the court stated that "the problem calls for adopting new rules of causation, for otherwise innocent plaintiffs would be left without a remedy."[c]

a. *Kozup v. Georgetown University,* 663 F.Supp. 1048 (D.D.C. 1987).

b. *United Blood Services v. Quintana,* 827 P.2d 509 (Colo. 1992).

c. *Smith v. Cutter Biological, Inc.,* 72 Haw. 416, 823 P.2d 717 (1991).

turers, processors, assemblers, packagers, bottlers, wholesalers, distributors, and retailers) and deserves close attention. Section 402A of the Restatement (Second) of Torts states as follows:

> (1) One who sells any product in a defective condition unreasonably dangerous to the user or consumer or to his property is subject to liability for physical harm thereby caused to the ultimate user or consumer or to his property, if
> (a) the seller is engaged in the business of selling such a product, and
> (b) it is expected to and does reach the user or consumer without substantial change in the condition in which it is sold.
> (2) The rule stated in Subsection (1) applies although
> (a) the seller has exercised all possible care in the preparation and sale of his product, and
> (b) the user or consumer has not bought the product from or entered into any contractual relation with the seller.

"One may smile, and smile, and be a villain."

William Shakespeare, 1564–1616
(English dramatist and poet)

Under this doctrine, liability does not depend on privity of contract. The injured party does not have to be the buyer or a third party beneficiary, as required under contract warranty theory [UCC 2–318]. Indeed, this type of liability in law is not governed by the provisions of the UCC. Under this doctrine, liability does not depend on proof of negligence. If the requirements discussed in the following section are met, the manufacturer's liability to an injured party may be virtually unlimited.[5]

Strict liability is imposed by law as a matter of public policy. This public policy rests on the threefold assumption that (1) consumers should be protected against unsafe products, (2) manufacturers and distributors should not escape liability for faulty products simply because they are not in privity of contract with the ultimate user of those products, and (3) manufacturers and sellers of products are in a better position to bear the costs associated with injuries caused by their products—costs that they can ultimately pass on to all consumers in the form of higher prices.

California was the first state to impose strict liability in tort on manufacturers. In the landmark decision that follows, the California Supreme Court sets out the reasons for applying tort law rather than contract law to cases in which consumers are injured by defective products.

Case 17.4 

GREENMAN v. YUBA POWER PRODUCTS, INC.

Supreme Court of California, 1962.
59 Cal.2d 57,
377 P.2d 897,
27 Cal.Rptr. 697.

HISTORICAL AND SOCIAL SETTING *The English courts accepted the doctrine of strict liability for many years. Often persons whose conduct resulted in the injury of another were held liable for damages, even if they had not intended to injure anyone and had exercised reasonable care. This approach was abandoned around 1800 in favor of the fault approach, in which an action was considered tortious only if it was wrongful or blameworthy in some respect. Strict liability was reapplied to manufactured goods in several landmark cases in the 1960s. During the 1960s, many other traditional assumptions were also called into question. The concept of tradition lost much of its appeal, and people began to reexamine the reasons for certain traditions. The most pronounced example of this changing attitude toward tradition is the civil rights legislation of the early 1960s, which rejected decades-old concepts of racial segregation. Courts of the time also reexamined other traditional legal doctrines under new conceptions of fairness.*

5. Some states have enacted what are called *statutes of repose.* Basically, these statutes provide that after a specific statutory period of time from the date of manufacture or sale, a plaintiff is precluded from pursuing a cause of action for injuries or damages sustained from a product, even though the product is defective. The states of Illinois, Indiana, Alabama, Tennessee, Florida, Texas, and Nebraska are illustrative.

Case 17.4—Continued

FACTS The plaintiff, Greenman, wanted a Shopsmith—a combination power tool that could be used as a saw, drill, and wood lathe—after seeing a Shopsmith demonstrated by a retailer and studying a brochure prepared by the manufacturer. The plaintiff's wife bought and gave him one for Christmas. More than a year later, a piece of wood flew out of the lathe attachment of the Shopsmith while the plaintiff was using it, inflicting serious injuries on him. About ten and a half months later, the plaintiff sued both the retailer and the manufacturer for breach of warranties and negligence. The trial court jury found for the plaintiff. The case was ultimately appealed to the California Supreme Court.

ISSUE Can the manufacturer and retailer be held liable for the plaintiff's injuries?

DECISION Yes. The verdict for the plaintiff was upheld.

REASON The plaintiff had successfully proved that the design and construction of the Shopsmith were defective, that statements in the manufacturer's brochure constituted express warranties and were untrue, and that the plaintiff's injuries were caused by their breach. The manufacturer argued that the plaintiff had waited too long to give notice of the breach of warranty, but the court, in imposing strict liability upon the manufacturer, held that it was not necessary for the plaintiff to establish an express warranty or a breach thereof. The court stated that "a manufacturer is strictly liable in tort when an article he places on the market, knowing that it is to be used without inspection for defects, proves to have a defect that causes injury to a human being." The court stated that the "purpose of such liability is to insure that the costs of injuries resulting from defective products are borne by the manufacturers * * * rather than by the injured persons who are powerless to protect themselves."

Requirements of Strict Product Liability Just because a person is injured by a product does not mean he or she will have a cause of action against the manufacturer of the product. A cause of action will exist only if the following six basic requirements of strict product liability are met:

1. The product must be in a defective condition when the defendant sells it.
2. The defendant must normally be engaged in the business of selling that product.
3. The product must be unreasonably dangerous to the user or consumer because of its defective condition (in most states).
4. The plaintiff must incur physical harm to self or property by use or consumption of the product.
5. The defective condition must be the proximate cause of the injury or damage.
6. The goods must not have been substantially changed from the time the product was sold to the time the injury was sustained.

If a child is injured by a toy, does he or she have a cause of action against the manufacturer?

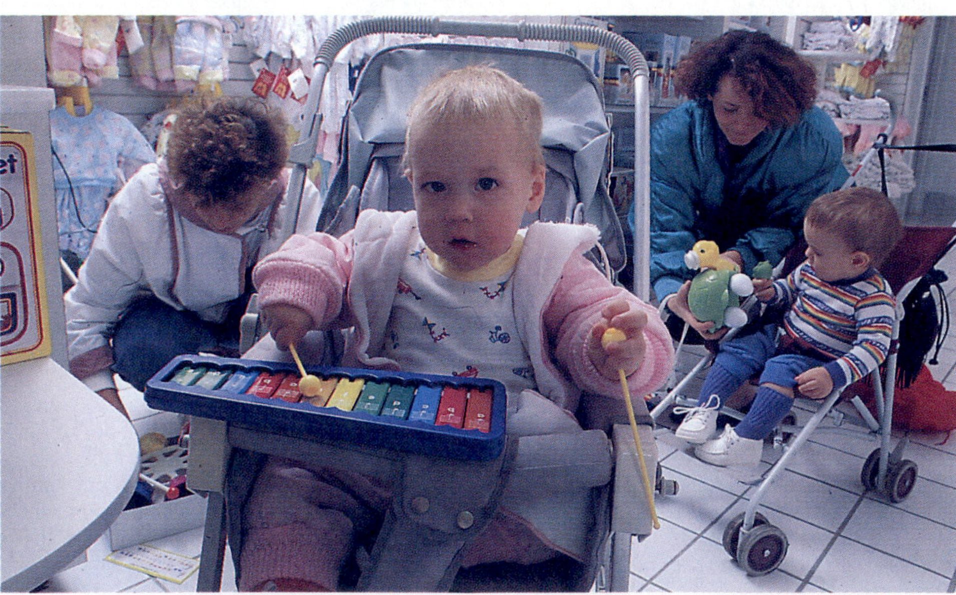

Profile

Benjamin Cardozo (1870–1938)

Benjamin Nathan Cardozo, one of the most notable liberal jurists of the twentieth century and an eminent legal scholar, was born in New York City on May 24, 1870. His productive career began with legal studies at Columbia University Law School, after which he entered private practice in New York. Over the next twenty years, Cardozo's skill as an attorney and his legal knowledge became well known to the legal community—eventually leading United States Supreme Court Chief Justice Charles Evans Hughes to refer to him as "a walking encyclopedia of the law."

During his nearly twenty years on the bench of the New York Court of Appeals and later as a United States Supreme Court justice, Cardozo's opinions had a profound effect on American jurisprudence. One of his most significant and far-reaching decisions was *MacPherson v. Buick Motor Co.* This case, which is discussed in the *Landmark in the Law* in this chapter, laid the foundation for the product liability law accepted by the courts today.

Generally, Cardozo sided with the liberal voices of the Court (such as Louis Brandeis and Harlan Stone) in his decisions. He believed that the Constitution was flexible enough to allow the government considerable latitude in matters relating to the public welfare. Indeed, Cardozo made clear on several occasions his conviction that the law should change to meet changing circumstances. "What is critical and urgent changes with the times," he maintained in *Helvering v. Davis.*[a] "Needs that were narrow or parochial a century ago may be interwoven in our day with the well-being of the nation."

The conviction that legal principles must be flexible and must change over time permeates all of Cardozo's writing. In *The Nature of the Judicial Process* (1921), one of his most influential and widely read works, he wrote of the "uncertainty" that such flexibility must ultimately lend to the law and, consequent upon this uncertainty, the creative nature of the judicial process.

Cardozo advised judges and lawmakers to look beyond the specific principles, precedents, and policies of American jurisprudence to the delicate, integrating web of justice that holds them all together. Those who do so, Cardozo suggests, will find, as he did, that ultimately the judicial process involves more creation than discovery.

a. 301 U.S. 619, 57 S.Ct. 904, 81 L.Ed. 1307 (1937).

Thus, in any action against a manufacturer or seller, the plaintiff does not have to show why or in what manner the product became defective. The plaintiff does, however, have to show that at the time the injury was sustained, the condition of the product was essentially the same as when it left the hands of the defendant manufacturer or seller.

The plaintiff normally must also show that the product was so defective as to be **unreasonably dangerous.** A court may consider a product so defective as to be unreasonably dangerous if either (1) the product was dangerous beyond the expectation of the ordinary consumer or (2) a less dangerous alternative was economically feasible for the manufacturer, but the manufacturer failed to produce it.

UNREASONABLY DANGEROUS
In product liability, defective to the point of threatening a consumer's health and safety. A product will be considered unreasonably dangerous if it is dangerous beyond the expectation of the ordinary consumer or if a less dangerous alternative was economically feasible for the manufacturer, but the manufacturer failed to produce it.

When determining whether a less dangerous alternative was economically feasible for the manufacturer, courts will consider a number of factors, including the following:

1. A product's utility and desirability.
2. The availability of other, safer products.

3. The dangers that have been identified prior to an injured user's suit.
4. The obviousness of the dangers.
5. The normal expectation of danger, particularly for established products.
6. The probability of injury and its likely seriousness.
7. The avoidability of injury by care in the product's use, including the contribution of instructions and warnings.
8. The viability of eliminating the danger without appreciably impairing the product's function or making the product too expensive.

People often cut themselves on knives. But because there is no way to avoid injuries without making the product useless and the danger is obvious to users, a court normally would not find a knife to be unreasonably dangerous and would not hold a supplier of knives liable. In contrast, a court may consider a snowblower without a safety guard over the opening through which the snow is blown to be in a condition that is unreasonably dangerous, even if it carries warnings to stay clear of the opening. The danger may be within the users' expectations, but the court will also consider the likelihood of injury and its probable seriousness, as well as the cost of putting a guard over the opening and the guard's effect on the blower's operation.

Some products are safe when used as their manufacturers and distributors intend but not safe when used in other ways. Suppliers are generally required to expect reasonably foreseeable misuses and to design products that are either safe when misused or marketed with some protective device—for example, a childproof cap.

In product liability cases, the courts are frequently left to decide what the expectations of the "ordinary consumer" should be in relation to the product in question. Should a manufacturer of a windshield sun screen have to warn a consumer not to drive his or her car without first removing the sun screen? Should a manufacturer of swimming pools have to warn swimmers not to dive into the shallow end of the pool? Should the manufacturer of a plastic tobogganlike sled be required to warn of the dangers inherent in sledding? The court looks closely at the last question in the following case.

Case 17.5
JORDON v. K-MART CORP.

Superior Court of Pennsylvania, 1992.
611 A.2d 1328.

HISTORICAL AND SOCIAL SETTING *The first case in which strict liability was imposed on a seller of goods without the requirement of privity involved bad food. Over the next forty-five years, courts made strict liability an established rule in cases of food, drink, animal food, and cosmetics. In 1958, a court found a warranty without privity as to the building materials in a home,*[a] *and in 1960 came the decision in* Henningsen v. Bloomfield Motors, Inc. *(Case 17.4). There followed "the most rapid and almost spectacular overturn of an established rule in the entire history of the law of torts."*[b] *In a large number of cases, courts began to dispense with the requirement of privity and find implied warranties in a variety of products (and in many cases, disclaimers were held to be invalid). Strict liability based on warranty concepts created problems, however, because of warranty's roots in the law of contracts. The American Law Institute drafted Section 402A of the Restatement (Second) of Torts, adopting a principle of strict liability in tort as a more realistic theory of recovery when defectively dangerous products are involved.* Greenman v. Yuba Power Products, Inc., *(Case 17.4), was the first general application of the tort theory, and that decision and Section 402A swept the country as* Henningsen *and the warranty theory had a few years before. Over the next thirty years, in some dramatic cases, recoveries soared into the millions of dollars. Statistically, these cases were not common, but they contributed to a sense that some lawsuits resulted less in justice than in financial windfalls for a lucky few. It sometimes appeared that many persons were eager to play what has been referred to colloquially as "lawsuit lottery."*

a. *Spence v. Three Rivers Builders & Masonry Supply, Inc.*, 353 Mich. 120, 90 N.W.2d 873 (1958). The opinion in this case was written by Justice John Voelker, author of the best-selling novel *Anatomy of a Murder* (New York: St. Martin's Press, 1957), which was made into a popular motion picture.

b. W. Page Keeton et al., *Prosser and Keeton on Torts* (St. Paul: West Publishing Co., 1986), p. 690.

Case 17.5—Continued

FACTS On February 16, 1986, David Jordon, a ten-year-old boy, lost control of his sled, hit a tree, and was injured. The sled was a plastic tobogganlike sled that had been purchased from K-Mart. David's parents brought suit against K-Mart, alleging negligence, strict liability, and breach of implied warranties. The Jordons claimed that the sled was defective and unreasonably dangerous for two reasons: (1) The sled contained design defects—the molded runners on the sled rendered the sled unsteerable, and the sled lacked any independent steering or braking mechanisms. (2) There were no warnings of the dangers inherent in the use of the sled. The trial court found that the sled was not unreasonably dangerous and granted K-Mart's motion for summary judgment. The Jordons appealed.

ISSUE Was the sled unreasonably dangerous because of design defects and because there were no warnings of the dangers inherent in the sled's use?

DECISION No. The trial court's ruling was affirmed.

REASON In response to the Jordons' argument that the sled was defectively designed, the court found that "like most recreational activities, sledding involves a degree of risk and even changing the design to require brakes or steering would not remove the inherent risk in the activity." In response to the Jordons' argument that the manufacturer should have warned of the dangers inherent in the sled's use, the court found that the danger of sledding is one that an ordinary ten-year-old boy would recognize. The danger is not latent. Indeed, it is common knowledge that sleds are difficult to steer, are hard to stop, and should not be used in areas where there are rocks, trees, or other obstacles. Furthermore, the record showed that David had used the same sled the day before without injury or accident and that he had made seven sledding runs down the same hill in the same location without incident on the day of the accident. He described in court how he steered the sled by holding the handles and leaning to the right or left. The court concluded that the product in question was not one that required warnings as to its danger.

ETHICAL CONSIDERATIONS *This case illustrates an ethical problem discussed in Chapter 2 in regard to the corporation's duty to consumers. The question raised there had to do with the point at which a seller's responsibility for injuries associated with its products should end and the consumer's responsibility for the injuries begin. There is no clear-cut answer to this question, and often common sense seems to give way to the principle that consumers should be warned of all foreseeable harms associated with products, even if those harms are obvious. When this happens, other plaintiffs are encouraged to bring suits for injuries for which, at least in the minds of many, the sellers should not be held responsible.*

Liability Sharing Generally, in all cases involving product liability, a plaintiff must prove that the defective product that caused his or her injury was the product of a specific defendant. Recently, in cases in which plaintiffs could not prove which of many distributors of a harmful product supplied the particular product that caused the plaintiffs' injuries, courts have dropped this requirement. This has occurred in several cases involving DES (diethylstilbestrol), a drug administered in the past to prevent miscarriages. DES's harmful character was not realized until, a generation later, daughters of the women who had taken DES developed health problems, including vaginal carcinoma, that were linked to the drug. Partly because of the passage of time, a plaintiff-daughter often could not prove which pharmaceutical company—out of as many as 300—had marketed the DES her mother had ingested. In these cases, some courts applied *industry-wide liability*, holding that all firms that manufactured and distributed DES during the period in question were liable for the plaintiffs' injuries in proportion to the firms' respective shares of the market.[6] The New York Court of Appeals recently went even further and held that even if a firm can prove that it did not manufacture the particular product that caused injuries to the plaintiff, the firm can be held liable based on its share of the national market.[7]

As discussed in this chapter's *Business Law in Action*, in a controversial decision, the Hawaii Supreme Court recently allowed this market-share theory of liability to

6. See, for example, *Martin v. Abbott Laboratories*, 102 Wash.2d 581, 689 P.2d 368 (1984).

7. *Hymowitz v. Eli Lilly and Co.*, 73 N.Y.2d 487, 539 N.E.2d 1069, 541 N.Y.S.2d 941 (1989).

be applied to manufacturers of a blood component when it could not be determined which of several manufacturers had marketed the particular unit that infected a recipient with the AIDS virus.

Strict Liability to Bystanders All courts extend the strict liability of manufacturers and other sellers to injured bystanders, although the drafters of the Restatement (Second) of Torts, Section 402A, did not take a position on bystanders. For example, in one case, an automobile manufacturer was held liable for injuries caused by the explosion of a car's motor. A cloud of steam that resulted from the explosion caused multiple collisions because other drivers could not see well.[8]

Other Applications of Strict Liability Under the rule of strict liability in tort, the basis of liability has been expanded to include suppliers of component parts. Thus, if General Motors buys brake pads from a subcontractor and puts them in Chevrolets without changing their composition, and those pads are defective, both the supplier of the brake pads and General Motors will be held strictly liable for the damages caused by the defects.

Liability for personal injuries caused by defective goods extends also to those who lease such goods. Section 408 of the Restatement (Second) of Torts states the following:

> One who leases a chattel [movable good] as safe for immediate use is subject to liability to those whom he should expect to use the chattel, or to be endangered by its probable use, for physical harm caused by its use in a manner for which and by a person for whose use it is leased, if the lessor fails to exercise reasonable care to make it safe for such use or to disclose its actual condition to those who may be expected to use it.

Some courts have held that a leasing agreement gives rise to a contractual implied warranty that the leased goods will be fit for the duration of the lease. Under this view, if Hertz Rent-a-Car leases a Chevrolet that has been improperly maintained, and a passenger is injured in an accident, the passenger can sue Hertz for breach of implied warranty.

Defenses to Product Liability

Frequently, damage or injury is caused by negligent misconduct or misuse of a product by the harmed person or a third party, coupled with the product's defect. A plaintiff's misconduct or misuse of the product may be a defense to reduce the claimant's recovery or bar it altogether.

Assumption of Risk Assumption of risk can sometimes be used as a defense in an action based on strict liability in tort. For such a defense to be established, the defendant must show the following:

1. The plaintiff voluntarily engaged in the risk while realizing the potential danger.
2. The plaintiff knew and appreciated the risk created by the defect in the product.
3. The plaintiff's decision to undertake the known risk was unreasonable.

Product Misuse Similar to the defense of voluntary assumption of risk is that of misuse of the product. Here the injured party does not know that the product is dangerous for a particular use, but that use is not the one for which the product was designed. (Contrast this with assumption of risk.) This defense has been severely limited by the courts, however. Even if the injured party does not know about the

8. *Giberson v. Ford Motor Co.*, 504 S.W.2d 8 (Mo. 1974).

International Perspective

Product Liability Laws and Product Innovation

Americans are among the most litigious people in the world. A black-and-blue mark, a sprained ankle, or even a sense of mental distress can form the basis for a lawsuit in this country. Manufacturers have discovered that just about anything they produce can result in a lawsuit, even if the consumer has used the product incorrectly or in violation of the manufacturer's printed instructions. In most instances, the manufacturer of a defective product may be held strictly liable—that is, liable without regard to fault—for any physical injury that results from use of the product. At one time in the United States, it was believed that to hold developing industries responsible for all injuries that resulted from their development would inhibit progress. The current theory behind imposing strict liability is that certain activities, including marketing defective products, present an undue risk of harm to members of the community. When something goes wrong, even innocently, and someone is injured, the party who presented the risk is considered to be in the best position to pay for the injury.

The fear of huge liability lawsuits may have discouraged many companies from engaging in the kind of research and development necessary to be internationally competitive in certain markets thought to have high legal risks. Some manufacturers feel that they cannot afford to produce any product that is not completely risk free, because they may face potentially unlimited legal liability. Although other industrialized countries are developing more stringent consumer product laws and thus affording injured parties greater opportunities to sue manufacturers for injuries caused by defective products, most of these countries do not hold their manufacturers to standards of strict liability. Consequently, foreign companies are able to undertake research programs and produce products that American companies, fearful of potential liability, may not consider economically justifiable. Of course, foreign producers that sell their products in the United States must abide by U.S. liability rules and still manage to thrive.

inherent danger of using the product in a wrong way, if the misuse is foreseeable, the seller must take measures to guard against it.

Comparative Negligence Developments in the area of comparative negligence (discussed in Chapter 5) are affecting the doctrine of strict liability. Whereas previously the plaintiff's conduct was not a defense to strict liability, today a growing number of jurisdictions consider the negligent or intentional actions of the plaintiff in the apportionment of liability and damages. This "comparing" of the plaintiff's conduct with the defendant's strict liability results in an application of the doctrine of comparative negligence.

Application

Law and the Salesperson—the Creation of Warranties

Warranties are important in both commercial and consumer purchase transactions. There are three types of product warranties: express warranties, implied warranties of merchantability, and implied warranties of fitness for a particular purpose. If you are a seller of products, you can make or create any one of these warranties, which are available to both consumers and commercial purchasers.

First and foremost, sellers and buyers need to know whether warranties have been created. Express warran-

Application—Continued

ties do not have to be labeled as such, but statements of simple opinion generally do not constitute express warranties. Express warranties can be made by descriptions of the goods. Express warranties can be found in a seller's advertisement, brochure, or promotional materials or can be made orally or in an express writing. A sales representative should use care in describing the merits of a product; otherwise the seller could be held to an express warranty. If an express warranty is not intended, the sales pitch should not promise too much.

In most sales, because the seller is a merchant, the purchased goods carry the implied warranty of merchantability. If you are a seller, you must also be aware of the importance of the implied warranty of fitness for a particular purpose. Assume a customer comes to your sales representative, describes the job to be done in detail, and says, "I really need something that can do the job." Your sales representative replies, "This product will do the job." An implied warranty that the product is fit for that particular purpose has been created.

Many sellers, particularly in commercial sales, try to limit or disclaim warranties. The Uniform Commercial Code permits all warranties, including express warranties, to be excluded or negated. Conspicuous statements—such as "THERE ARE NO WARRANTIES WHICH EXTEND BEYOND THE DESCRIPTION ON THE FACE HEREOF" or "THERE ARE NO IMPLIED WARRANTIES OF FITNESS FOR A PARTICULAR PURPOSE NOR MERCHANTABILITY WHICH ACCOMPANY THIS SALE"—can be used to disclaim the implied warranties of fitness and merchantability. Used goods are sometimes sold "as is" or "with all faults" so that implied warranties of fitness and merchantability are disclaimed. Whenever these warranties are disclaimed, a purchaser should be aware that his or her expectations of even an average-quality product will not be enforced.

Checklist for the Salesperson

☐ 1. If you wish to limit warranties, do so by means of a carefully worded and prominently placed written or printed provision that a reasonable person would understand and accept.

☐ 2. As a seller, you might wish to have the buyer sign a statement certifying that he or she has read all of your warranty disclaimer provisions.

☐ 3. If you do not intend to make an express warranty, do not make a promise or an affirmation of fact concerning the performance or quality of a product you are selling.

❖ Key Terms

express warranty 395
implied warranty 396
implied warranty of merchantability 397
lien 395
product liability 406
unreasonably dangerous 411

❖ Chapter Summary: Warranties and Product Liability

WARRANTIES		
TYPE	**HOW CREATED**	**POSSIBLE DEFENSES**
Warranty of Title [UCC 2–312]	Upon transfer of title, the seller warrants— 1. The right to pass good and rightful title. 2. That the goods are free from unstated liens or encumbrances. 3. If a merchant, that the goods are free from infringement claims.	Exclusion or modification only by specific language or circumstances [UCC 2–312(2)].
Express Warranty [UCC 2–313]	As part of a sale or bargain— 1. An affirmation or promise of fact. 2. A description of the goods.	1. Opinion (puffing). 2. Exclusion or limitation [UCC 2–316(1)] 3. No statement by seller.

❖ Chapter Summary: Warranties and Product Liability—Continued

<table>
<tr><td>Express Warranty [UCC 2–313]—Continued</td><td>3. A sample shown as conforming to the contract goods.

Under the Magnuson-Moss Warranty Act, express written warranties covering consumer goods priced at more than $10, if made, must be labeled as one of the following—
1. Full warranty—free repair or replacement of defective parts; refund or replacement for goods if they cannot be repaired in a reasonable time.
2. Limited warranty—when less than full warranty is being offered.</td><td></td></tr>
<tr><td>Implied Warranty of Merchantability [UCC 2–314]</td><td>When the seller is a merchant who deals in goods of the kind sold, the seller warrants that the goods sold are properly packaged and labeled, are of proper quality, and are reasonably fit for the ordinary purposes for which such goods are used.</td><td>1. Specific disclaimer—can be oral or in writing but must mention merchantability and if in writing must be conspicuous [UCC 2–316(2)].
2. Sales stated "as is" or "with all faults" [UCC 2–316(3)(a)].
3. If there is an examination by the buyer, the buyer is bound by all defects that are found or that should have been found; if the buyer refuses to examine, the buyer is bound by obvious defects [UCC 2–316(3)(b)].</td></tr>
<tr><td>Implied Warranty of Fitness for a Particular Purpose [UCC 2–315]</td><td>Arises when—
1. The buyer's purpose or use is expressly or impliedly known by the seller, and
2. The buyer purchases in reliance on the seller's selection.</td><td>1. Specific disclaimer—must be in writing and conspicuous. For example, "There are no warranties which extend beyond the description on the face hereof" [UCC 2–316(2)].
2. Same as merchantability above (numbers 2 through 4).</td></tr>
<tr><td>Implied Warranty Arising from Course of Dealing or Trade Usage [UCC 2–314(3)]</td><td>By prior dealings and/or usage of trade.</td><td>Exclusion by specific language or as provided under UCC 2–316.</td></tr>
<tr><td colspan="3">PRODUCT LIABILITY</td></tr>
<tr><td>Liability Based on Negligence or Fraud</td><td colspan="2">1. Due care must be used by the manufacturer in designing the product, selecting materials, using the appropriate production process, assembling and testing the product, and placing adequate warnings on the label or product.
2. Privity of contract is not required. A manufacturer is liable for failure to exercise due care to any person who sustains an injury proximately caused by a negligently made (defective) product.
3. Fraudulent misrepresentation of a product may result in the tort of fraud. A manufacturer may also be liable for nonfraudulent (innocent) misrepresentation of a product to a user.</td></tr>
<tr><td>Requirements of Strict Product Liability</td><td colspan="2">1. The defendant must sell the product in a defective condition.
2. The defendant must normally be engaged in the business of selling that product.
3. The product must be unreasonably dangerous to the user or consumer because of its defective condition (in most states).
4. The plaintiff must incur physical harm to self or property by use or consumption of the product. (Courts will also extend strict liability to include injured bystanders.)
5. The defective condition must be the proximate cause of the injury or damage.</td></tr>
</table>

❖ Chapter Summary: Warranties and Product Liability—Continued

Requirements—Continued	6. The goods must not have been substantially changed from the time the product was sold to the time the injury was sustained.
Liability Sharing	In cases in which plaintiffs cannot prove which of many distributors of a harmful product supplied the particular product that caused the plaintiffs' injuries, some courts have applied industrywide liability. All firms that manufactured and distributed the harmful product during the period in question are then held liable for the plaintiffs' injuries in proportion to their respective shares of the market as directed by the court.
Possible Defenses to Product Liability	1. Assumption of risk on the part of the user or consumer. 2. Misuse of the product by the user or consumer in a way unforeseeable by the manufacturer. 3. Contributory negligence on the part of the user-consumer. If allowed, liability may be distributed between plaintiff and defendant under the doctrine of comparative negligence.

❖ Questions and Case Problems

17-1. What factors will a court consider when determining whether a seller's statement is an express warranty or mere "puffing"?

17-2. Under what contract theory can a seller be held liable to a consumer for physical harm or property damage that is caused by the goods sold? Under what tort theories can the seller be held liable?

17-3. Implied Warranties. Corinna purchased 1,000 baby chickens from Evanston's Poultry Farm with the intention of starting a chicken business. After the chickens were delivered, Corinna discovered that they were afflicted by avian leukosis, a type of cancer. Corinna sued Evanston's Poultry for breach of the implied warranties of merchantability and fitness for a particular purpose. Evanston's Poultry claimed that the cancerous disease that afflicted the chickens was impossible to discover in baby chicks and therefore it should not be held liable for the defect. What will the court decide? Discuss.

17-4. Warranty Disclaimers. Naoko Yajima purchased a washing machine from Marshall Appliances. The sales contract included a provision explicitly disclaiming all express or implied warranties, including the implied warranty of merchantability. The disclaimer was printed in the same size and color as the rest of the contract. The machine turned out to be a "lemon" and never functioned properly. Yajima sought a refund of the purchase price, claiming that Marshall had breached the implied warranty of merchantability. Can Yajima recover her money, notwithstanding the warranty disclaimer in the contract? Explain.

17-5. Implied Warranties. Sam, a farmer, needs to place a 2,000-pound piece of equipment in his barn. The equipment must be lifted thirty feet into a hayloft. Sam goes to Durham Hardware and tells Durham that he needs some heavy-duty rope to be used on his farm. Durham recommends a one-inch-thick nylon rope, and Sam purchases 200 feet of it. Sam ties the rope around the piece of equipment, puts it through a pulley, and with the aid of a tractor lifts the equipment off the ground. Suddenly the rope breaks. In the crash to the ground, the equipment is severely damaged. Sam files suit against Durham for breach of the implied warranty of fitness for a particular purpose. Discuss how successful Sam will be with his suit.

17-6. Express Warranties. Myrtle Carpenter purchased hair dye from a drugstore. The use of the dye caused an adverse skin reaction. She sued the local drugstore and the manufacturer of the dye, Alberto Culver Co. She claimed that a sales clerk had indicated that several of Myrtle's friends had used the product and that their hair had come out "very nice." The clerk purportedly had also told Myrtle that she would get very fine results. On the package, there were cautionary instructions telling the user to make a preliminary skin test to determine if the user was susceptible in any unusual way to the product. Myrtle stated that she had not made the preliminary skin test. Did the seller make an express warranty about the hair dye? [*Carpenter v. Alberto Culver Co.*, 28 Mich.App. 399, 184 N.W.2d 547 (1970)]

17-7. Product Liability. George Nesselrode lost his life in an airplane crash. The plane had been manufactured by Beech Aircraft Corp. and sold to Executive Beechcraft, Inc. Shortly before the crash occurred, Executive Beechcraft had conducted a routine inspection of the plane and found that some of the parts needed to be replaced. The new parts were supplied by Beech Aircraft but installed by Executive Beechcraft. These particular airplane parts could be installed backwards, and if they were, the plane would crash. In Nesselrode's case, the crash resulted from just such an incorrect installation of the airplane parts. Nesselrode's wife Jane and three daughters sued Executive Beechcraft, Beech Aircraft, and Gerald Hultgren, the pilot who had flown the plane, for damages. Beech Aircraft claimed that it was not at fault because it had not installed the parts. Will Beech Aircraft be held liable for Nesselrode's death? Discuss. [*Nesselrode v. Executive Beechcraft, Inc.*, 707 S.W.2d 371 (Mo. 1986)]

17-8. Strict Liability. Embs was buying some groceries at Stamper's Cash Market. Unnoticed by her, a carton of 7-Up was sitting on the floor at the edge of the produce counter about one foot from where she was standing. Several of the 7-Up bottles exploded. Embs's leg was injured severely enough that Embs had to be taken to the hospital by a managing agent of the store. Embs sued the manufacturer of 7-Up, Pepsi-Cola Bottling Co. of Lexington, Kentucky, Inc., claiming that the manufacturer should be held strictly liable for the harm caused by its products. The trial court dismissed her claim. On appeal, what will the court decide? [*Embs v. Pepsi-Cola Bottling Co. of Lexington, Kentucky, Inc.*, 528 S.W.2d 703 (Ky.App. 1975)]

17-9. Product Liability. William Mackowick, who had worked as an electrician for thirty years, was installing high-voltage capacitors in a switchgear room in a hospital when he noticed that a fellow electrician had removed the cover from an existing capacitor manufactured by Westinghouse Electric Corp. A warning label placed by Westinghouse inside the cover of the metal box containing the capacitor instructed users to ground the electricity before handling. Nothing was said on the label about the propensity of electricity to arc. (Arcing occurs when electricity grounds itself by "jumping" to a nearby object or instrument.) Mackowick walked over to warn the other electrician of the danger associated with the exposed capacitor. While talking, he pointed his screwdriver toward the capacitor box. The electricity flowing through the fuses arced to the screwdriver and sent a high-voltage electric current through Mackowick's body. As a result, he sustained severe burns and was unable to return to work for three months. Should Westinghouse be held liable because it failed to warn users of arcing—a principle of electricity? Discuss. [*Mackowick v. Westinghouse Electric Corp.*, 575 A.2d 100 (Pa. 1990)]

17-10. Implied Warranties. Robert Levondosky was a patron at Harrah's Marina Hotel Casino, an Atlantic City casino owned by Marina Associates. While playing at one of the casino's tables, he ordered a cocktail, which was served free of charge—it was the casino's custom to give complimentary drinks to patrons at the gambling tables. According to Levondosky, he swallowed a few thin chips of glass from the rim of the glass in which the drink was served and, as a result, suffered internal injuries. Levondosky sued the casino, contending that the casino had breached an implied warranty of merchantability. In evaluating this claim, the court had to determine (1) whether a "sale" had in fact occurred, which is prerequisite to the creation of an implied warranty of merchantability, and (2) whether the casino gave an implied warranty as to the glass as well as the drink within it. Review UCC 2–314 and discuss how the court should rule on both issues. [*Levondosky v. Marina Associates*, 731 F.Supp. 1210 (D.N.J. 1990)]

17-11. Implied Warranties. In March 1986, Donald Laird discussed the purchase of corn with the manager of Scribner Cooperative, Inc., Gary Ruwe, whom Laird had trained for his job as manager. Ruwe told Laird that the co-op was having some heating problems in its corn storage bins, but Laird said that he would take four loads (about 1,300 bushels) of corn if Ruwe would "pull out the center and pull out all the damaged corn and get the fines [the fine bits of corn kernel knocked off during handling of the grain] out of the center." On inspecting the corn after it was delivered, Laird noticed damaged corn and a silage odor (which is the result of a fermentation process caused by heating). Although Laird was dissatisfied with the corn, he did not reject it. After Laird began feeding his hogs the corn, the hogs became ill. Eventually, it was concluded that the problem might be in the corn. In October 1986, Laird asked the University of Nebraska to test the corn, and traces of a toxic substance called vomitoxin were found in the corn. The veterinarian tending Laird's hogs testified that their symptoms were the direct result of feed containing vomitoxin. Laird sued the co-op for breach of the implied warranties of merchantability and fitness for a particular purpose. How should the court rule? Discuss. [*Laird v. Scribner Coop, Inc.*, 237 Neb. 532, 466 N.W. 2d 798 (1991)]

A Question of Ethics and Social Responsibility

17-12. *Arvo Lake, a retired seventy-one-year-old man, bought an air conditioner in May 1986. The unit was installed and operated according to the manufacturer's instructions. Unbeknownst to Lake, the unit contained a hole in the refrigeration system that allowed Freon, the coolant, to escape from the unit. By August, the unit had ceased cooling, and Lake's residence reached a temperature of at least 96 degrees Fahrenheit. The heat caused Lake to suffer from hyperthermia, which caused circulatory failure and death. The executor of Lake's estate, David Garavalia, sued the manufacturer of the air conditioner for damages. The circuit court dismissed the suit, and Garavalia appealed. The appellate court found for the plaintiff, alleging that the risk of death from an air conditioner that failed to operate properly was foreseeable, given Lake's age and the climate in southern Illinois in the summer.* [Garavalia v. Heat Controller, Inc., *212 Ill.App.3d 380, 570 N.E.2d 1227, 156 Ill.Dec. 505 (1991)*]

1. For a manufacturer to be liable for consequential damages caused by a breach of warranty, the consequential damages must be foreseeable to the manufacturer. Do you agree with the court that Lake's death was a foreseeable consequence of the air conditioner's failure to operate properly?
2. In determining whether Lake's death was a foreseeable result of the malfunctioning air conditioner, the court considered such circumstances as the heat of the Illinois summer, Lake's age, and the high crime rate in Lake's neighborhood. Should these factors have any bearing on whether the manufacturer should be held liable for Lake's death? Why or why not?
3. One of the judges in this case dissented, stating that "[f]oreseeability means that which is objectively reasonable to expect, not merely what might conceivably occur." He went on to state that an air conditioner is "a rather benign machine" and that the manufacturer of such an appliance could not *reasonably* foresee that an air conditioner's failure to cool would result in death. Do you agree with this analysis? Discuss.

For Critical Analysis

17-13. *From a policy viewpoint, how do blood-shield statutes serve the public interest? What would result if blood banks and other suppliers of blood were not shielded from warranty and strict liability suits for health problems caused by contaminated blood?*

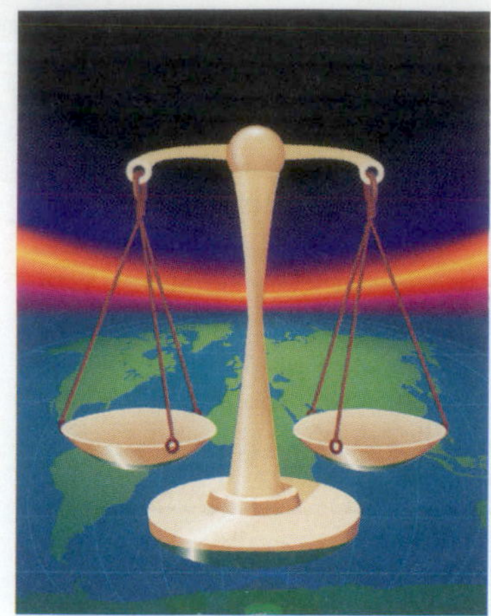

Chapter 18

Commercial Paper—Negotiability and Transferability

"Convenience is the basis of mercantile law."

Lord Mansfield, 1705–1793
(British jurist)

The vast number of commercial transactions that take place daily in the modern business world would be inconceivable without commercial paper. **Commercial paper** is any written promise or order to pay a sum of money. Drafts, checks, and promissory notes are typical examples. Commercial paper is transferred more readily than ordinary contract rights, and persons who acquire it are normally subject to less risk than the ordinary assignee of a contract right.

COMMERCIAL PAPER
Under UCC Article 3, negotiable instruments, including drafts, promissory notes, certificates of deposit, and checks.

In the opening quotation, Lord Mansfield stresses the element of convenience in the evolution of mercantile law, and the law governing commercial paper did indeed grow out of commercial necessity. As early as the thirteenth century, merchants dealing in foreign trade were using commercial paper to finance and conduct their affairs. Problems in transportation and in the safekeeping of gold or coins had prompted this practice. Because the king's courts of those times did not recognize the validity of commercial paper, the merchants had to develop their own rules governing its use, and these rules were enforced by "fair" or "borough" courts. Eventually, these decisions became a distinct set of laws known as the *Lex Mercatoria* (Law Merchant).

By the end of the seventeenth century, the principles of the Law Merchant were widely accepted and quite naturally became a part of the common law. Later, the Law Merchant was codified in England in the Bills of Exchange Act of 1882. In 1896, in the United States, the National Conference of Commissioners on Uniform State Laws drafted the Uniform Negotiable Instruments Law. This law was reviewed by the states, and by 1920 all the states had adopted it. The Uniform Negotiable Instruments Law was the forerunner of Article 3 of the Uniform Commercial Code (UCC).

❖ Article 3 and Its Revision

NEGOTIABLE INSTRUMENT
A written and signed unconditional promise or order to pay a specified sum of money on demand or at a definite time to order (to a specific person or entity) or to bearer.

Both Article 3 and Article 4 of the UCC apply to transactions involving commercial paper. To understand the applicability of Article 3 to commercial paper, it is necessary to distinguish between *negotiable* and *nonnegotiable* paper. To qualify as a **negotiable instrument,** commercial paper must meet special requirements relating to form and content. These requirements, which are imposed by UCC 3–104, will be discussed at length in this chapter. When an instrument is negotiable, its transfer from one person to another is governed by Article 3 of the UCC. Indeed, UCC 3–102(e) defines *instrument* as a "negotiable instrument." For that reason, whenever the term *instrument* is used in this book, it refers to a negotiable instrument. Transfers of nonnegotiable commercial paper are governed by rules of assignment of contract rights (see Chapter 12). Article 4 of the UCC governs bank deposits and collections.

In 1990, a revised version of Article 3 was promulgated for adoption by the states. As of this writing, approximately one-half of the states have adopted the revised article. Many of the changes to Article 3 simply clarify old sections; some significantly alter the existing UCC Article 3 provisions. Because the unrevised Article 3 is still the law in the majority of the states and because most of the case law concerning negotiable instruments refers to the unrevised Article 3, we have retained the unrevised version as the basis for our text in this and the following chapters on commercial paper. Whenever a point of law is significantly changed by the revised article, however, we will indicate this either in the text or in a footnote. All references to sections of the revised article will be preceded by RUCC instead of UCC. Article 4 was also revised in 1990, in part to reflect changes in Article 3 that affect Article 4 provisions.

❖ The Functions of Commercial Paper

Commercial paper may represent an extension of credit or be a substitute for money. When a buyer gives a seller a promissory note, the terms of which provide that it is payable within sixty days, the seller has essentially extended sixty days of credit to the buyer. The credit aspect of commercial paper was developed in the Middle Ages soon after bills of exchange began to be used as substitutes for money. Merchants were able to give to sellers bills of exchange that were not payable until a future date. Because the seller would wait until a maturity date to collect, this was a form of extending credit to the buyer.

For commercial paper to operate *practically* as either a substitute for money or a credit device, or both, it is essential that the paper be easily transferable without danger of being uncollectible. This is the function that characterizes *negotiable* commercial paper. Each rule described in the following pages can be examined in light of this function.

❖ Types of Negotiable Instruments

The UCC specifies four types of negotiable instruments: *drafts, checks, promissory notes,* and *certificates of deposit (CDs).* These instruments are frequently divided into the two classifications that we will discuss in the following sections: *orders to pay* (drafts and checks) and *promises to pay* (promissory notes and CDs).

Negotiable instruments may also be classified as either *demand instruments* or *time instruments.* A demand instrument is payable on demand; that is, a demand instrument is payable immediately after it is issued. (Instruments payable on demand include those payable at sight, or on **presentment,** and those in which no time for payment is stated [UCC 3–108].) All checks are demand instruments because, by definition, they must be payable on demand; therefore, checking accounts are sometimes called **demand deposits.** Time instruments are payable at a future date.

Drafts and Checks (Orders to Pay)

A **draft** (bill of exchange) is an unconditional written order that involves *three parties.* The party creating it (the **drawer**) orders another party (the **drawee**) to pay money, usually to a third party (the **payee**). Exhibit 18–1 shows a typical draft. The drawee must be obligated to the drawer either by agreement or through a debtor-creditor relationship for the drawee to be obligated to the drawer to honor the order. A *time draft* is payable at a definite future time. A *sight draft* (or demand draft) is

PRESENTMENT
Occurs when the holder of a negotiable instrument presents it to the maker, acceptor, drawee, or other payor for acceptance or payment.

DEMAND DEPOSIT
Funds (accepted by a bank) subject to immediate withdrawal, in contrast to a time deposit, which requires that a depositor wait a specific time before withdrawing or pay a penalty for early withdrawal.

DRAFT
Any instrument drawn on a drawee (such as a bank) that orders the drawee to pay a certain sum of money.

DRAWER
A person who initiates a draft (including a check), thereby ordering the drawee to pay.

DRAWEE
The person who is ordered to pay a draft or check. With a check, a financial institution is always the drawee.

PAYEE
A person to whom an instrument is made payable.

◆ **Exhibit 18–1 A Typical Time Draft**

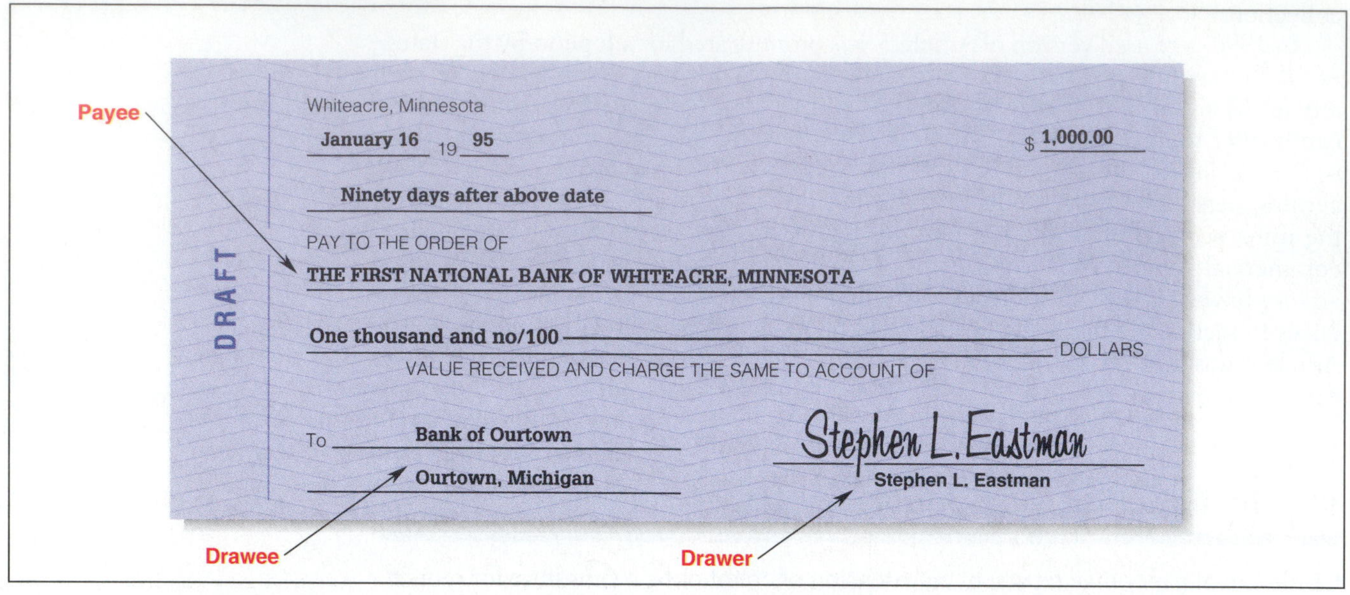

payable on sight—that is, when it is presented for payment.[1] A draft can be both a time and a sight draft; such a draft is one payable at a stated time after sight.

TRADE ACCEPTANCE
A draft drawn by the seller of goods on the purchaser and accepted by the purchaser's written promise to pay the draft. Once accepted, the purchaser becomes primarily liable to pay the draft.

A **trade acceptance** is a draft frequently used in the sale of goods. The seller is both the drawer and the payee on this draft. Essentially, the draft orders the buyer to pay a specified sum of money to the seller, usually at a stated time in the future. For example, Jackson River Fabrics sells $50,000 worth of fabric to Comfort Creations, Inc., each fall on terms requiring payment to be made in ninety days. One year Jackson River needs cash, so it draws a *trade acceptance* that orders Comfort Creations to pay $50,000 to the order of Jackson River Fabrics ninety days hence. Jackson River presents the paper to Comfort Creations. Comfort Creations *accepts* by signing the face of the paper and returns it to Jackson River Fabrics. Comfort Creations' acceptance creates an enforceable promise to pay the draft when it comes due in ninety days. Jackson River can sell the trade acceptance in the commercial money market more easily than it can assign the $50,000 account receivable. Trade acceptances are the standard credit instruments in sales transactions (see Exhibit 18–2).

CHECK
A draft drawn by a drawer ordering the drawee bank or financial institution to pay a certain amount of money to the holder on demand.

The most commonly used type of draft is a **check.** The writer of the check is the drawer, the bank upon which the check is drawn is the drawee, and the person to whom the check is payable is the payee. As mentioned earlier, checks, because they are payable on demand, are demand instruments.

Checks will be discussed more fully in Chapter 20, but it should be noted here that with certain types of checks, such as *cashier's checks*, the bank is both the drawer and the drawee. The bank customer purchases a cashier's check from the bank—that is, pays the bank the amount of the check—and indicates to whom the check should be made payable. The bank, not the customer, is the drawer of the check (as well as the drawee).

---

1. A sight draft may be payable on acceptance. Acceptance is the drawee's written promise to pay the draft when it comes due. The usual manner of accepting is by writing the word *accepted* across the face of the instrument, followed by the date of acceptance and the signature of the drawee. Under the revised Article 3, a bank draft (a draft drawn by one bank on another bank) is now referred to as a "teller's check" [RUCC 3–104(h)]. (Recall from this chapter's introductory remarks that RUCC refers to the revised UCC; in this case, we are referring to Section 3–104(h) of the revised Article 3.)

◆ **Exhibit 18–2 A Typical Trade Acceptance**

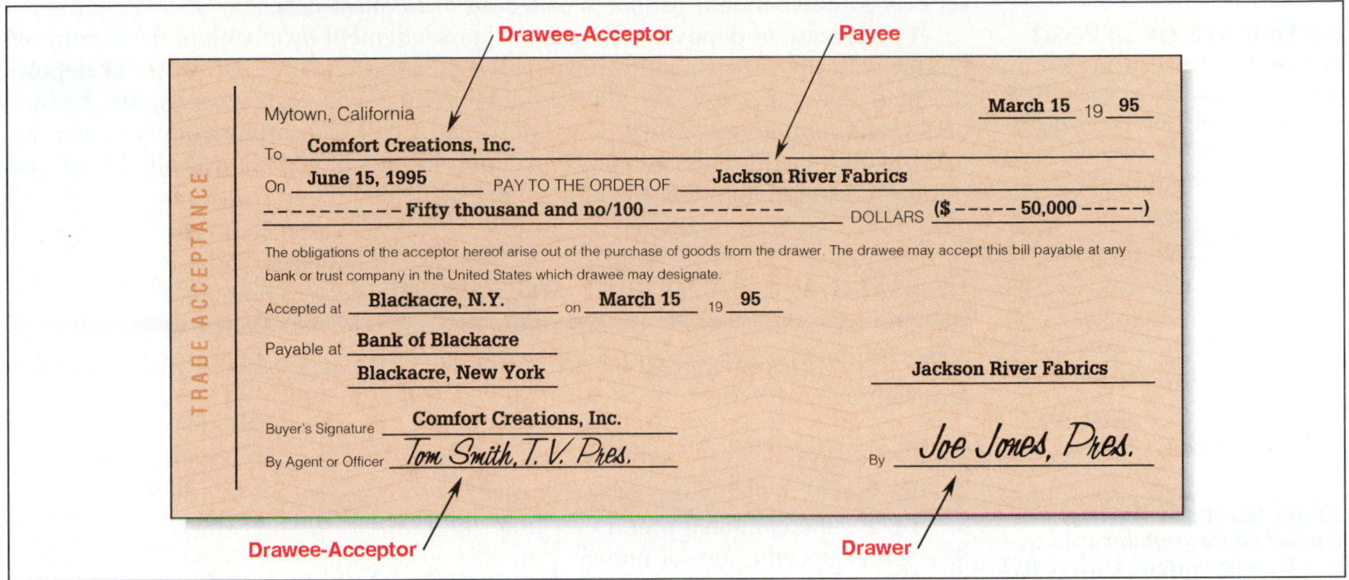

Promissory Notes and CDs (Promises to Pay)

The **promissory note** is a written promise between *two parties.* One party is the **maker** of the promise to pay, and the other is the payee, or the one to whom the promise is made. A promissory note, which is often referred to simply as a *note*, can be made payable at a definite time or on demand. It can name a specific payee or merely be payable to bearer. A typical promissory note is shown in Exhibit 18–3.

Notes are used in a variety of credit transactions and often carry the name of the transaction involved. For example, in real estate transactions, a promissory note for the unpaid balance on a house, secured by a mortgage on the property, is called a *mortgage note.* A note that is secured by personal property is called a *collateral note* because the property pledged as security for the satisfaction of the debt is called

PROMISSORY NOTE
A written instrument signed by a maker unconditionally promising to pay a certain sum in money to a payee or a holder on demand or on a specified date.

MAKER
One who issues a promissory note or certificate of deposit (that is, one who promises to pay a certain sum to the holder of the note or CD).

◆ **Exhibit 18–3 A Typical Promissory Note**

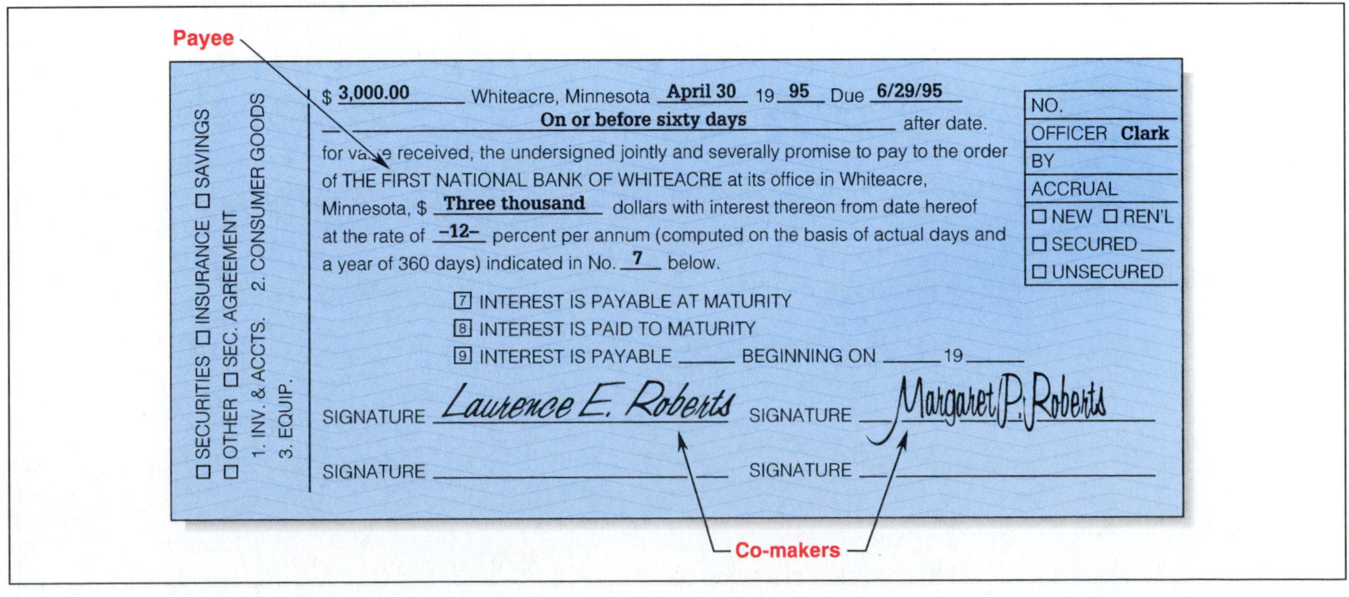

collateral. And a note payable in installments, such as for payment for a television set over a twelve-month period, is called an *installment note*.

CERTIFICATE OF DEPOSIT An instrument evidencing a promissory acknowledgment by a bank of a receipt of money with an engagement to repay it.

A **certificate of deposit (CD)** is an acknowledgment by a bank of the receipt of money with an engagement to repay it [UCC 3–104(2)(c)]. Certificates of deposit in small denominations are often sold by savings and loan associations, savings banks, and commercial banks. They are called small CDs and are for amounts up to $100,000. Certificates of deposit for amounts over $100,000 are called large (or jumbo) CDs. Exhibit 18–4 shows a typical small CD.

❖ What Is a Negotiable Instrument?

"Money has little value to its possessor unless it also has value to others."

Leland Stanford, 1824–1893 ***(United States senator and founder of Stanford University)***

UCC 3–104(1) specifies that for an instrument to be negotiable, it must meet the following requirements:

1. Be in writing.
2. Be signed by the maker or the drawer.
3. Be an unconditional promise or order to pay.
4. State a specific sum of money.
5. Be payable on demand or at a definite time.
6. Be payable to order or to bearer.

Written Form

Negotiable instruments must be in written form. Clearly, an oral promise can create the danger of fraud or make it difficult to determine liability. Negotiable instruments must possess the quality of certainty that only formal, written expression can give.

There are certain practical limitations concerning the writing and the substance on which it is placed:

1. The writing must be on material that lends itself to *permanence*. Instruments carved in blocks of ice or recorded on other impermanent surfaces would not qualify as negotiable instruments. Suppose Suzanne writes in the sand, "I promise to pay $500 to the order of Jack." This is not a negotiable instrument because, although it is in writing, it lacks permanence.

♦ **Exhibit 18–4 A Typical Small CD**

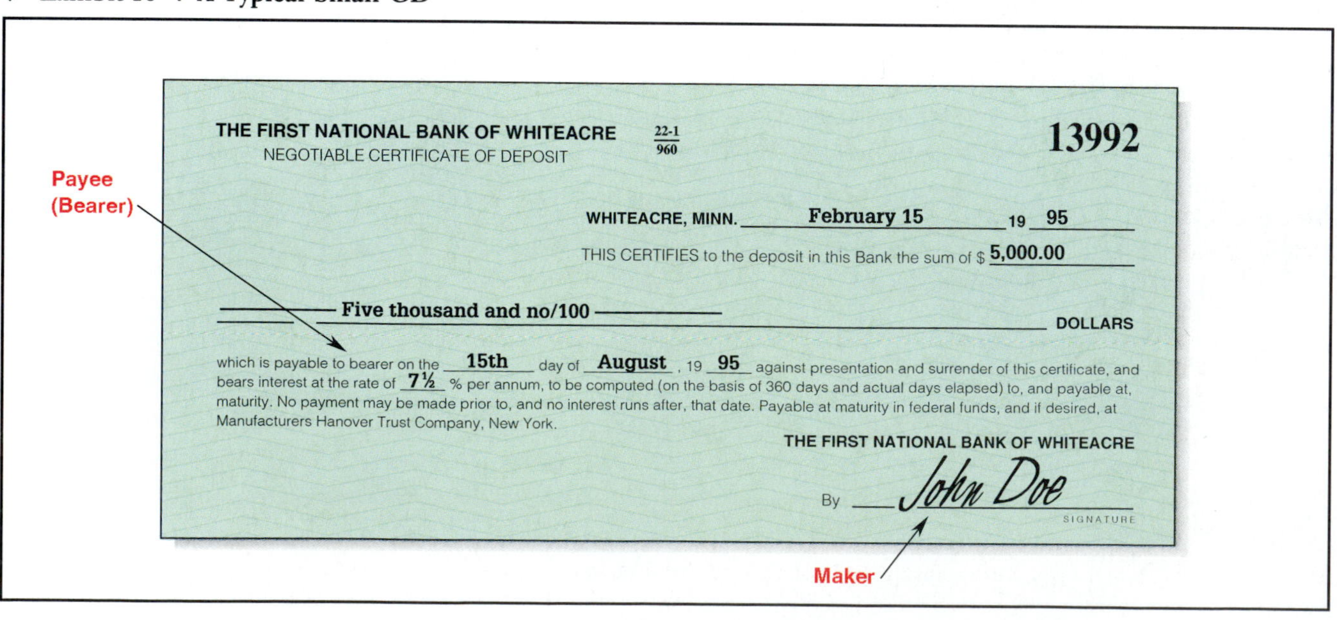
THE FIRST NATIONAL BANK OF WHITEACRE 22-1/960 13992
NEGOTIABLE CERTIFICATE OF DEPOSIT

WHITEACRE, MINN. February 15 19 95
THIS CERTIFIES to the deposit in this Bank the sum of $ 5,000.00
Five thousand and no/100 DOLLARS
which is payable to bearer on the 15th day of August, 19 95 against presentation and surrender of this certificate, and bears interest at the rate of 7½ % per annum, to be computed (on the basis of 360 days and actual days elapsed) to, and payable at, maturity. No payment may be made prior to, and no interest runs after, that date. Payable at maturity in federal funds, and if desired, at Manufacturers Hanover Trust Company, New York.
THE FIRST NATIONAL BANK OF WHITEACRE
By John Doe SIGNATURE

2. The writing must have *portability*. Though this is not a spelled-out legal requirement, if an instrument is not movable, it obviously cannot meet the requirement that it be freely transferable. For example, Charles writes on the side of a cow, "I promise to pay Paul $500." Technically, this meets the requirements of a negotiable instrument, but as a cow cannot easily be transferred in the ordinary course of business, the "instrument" is nonnegotiable. (See this chapter's *Law in the Extreme* for a discussion of the various types of materials on which "negotiable instruments" have been written.)

Signatures

For an instrument to be negotiable, it must be signed by (1) the maker if it is a note or a certificate of deposit or (2) the drawer if it is a draft or a check [UCC 3–104(1)(a)]. If a person signs an instrument as the *agent* for the maker or drawer, the maker or drawer has effectively signed the instrument, provided the agent has the appropriate authority. (Agents' signatures will be discussed in the next chapter.)

Extreme latitude is granted in determining what constitutes a **signature.** UCC 1–201(39) defines the word *signed* as "[including] any symbol executed or adopted by a party with present intention to authenticate a writing." Section 3–401(2) of the UCC expands on this: "A signature is made by use of any name, including any trade or assumed name, upon an instrument, or by any word or mark used in lieu of a written signature." Thus, initials, an X, or a thumbprint will suffice. A trade name or an assumed name is sufficient even if it is false. A rubber stamp bearing a person's signature is permitted and frequently used in the business world. If necessary, parol evidence (discussed in Chapter 11) is admissible in identifying the signer. When the signer is identified, the signature becomes effective.

SIGNATURE
The name or mark of a person, written by that person or at his or her direction. In commercial law, any name, word, or mark used with the intention to authenticate a writing constitutes a signature.

The location of the signature on the document is unimportant, although unless the instrument clearly indicates that it is the signature of a drawer or a maker, it is construed as an indorsement [UCC 3–402]. The usual place is the lower right-hand corner. A *handwritten* statement on the body of the instrument, such as "I, Yasuko Maruta, promise to pay John Grant," is sufficient to act as a signature.

There are virtually no limitations on the manner in which a signature can be made, but one should be careful about receiving an instrument that has been signed in an unusual way. Furthermore, an unusual signature clearly decreases the *marketability* of an instrument, because it creates uncertainty.

Unconditional Promise or Order to Pay

The terms of the promise or order must be included in the writing on the face of a negotiable instrument. These terms must not be conditioned upon the occurrence or nonoccurrence of some other event or agreement or state that the instrument is to be paid only out of a particular fund [UCC 3–105(2)].[2]

Promise or Order For an instrument to be negotiable, it must contain an express order or promise to pay. A mere acknowledgment of the debt, which might logically *imply* a promise, is not sufficient under the UCC, because the promise must be an *affirmative* undertaking [UCC 3–102(1)(c)]. For example, the traditional I.O.U. is only an acknowledgment of indebtedness. Although the I.O.U. might logically *imply* a promise, it is not a negotiable instrument, because it does not contain an express promise to repay the debt. But if such words as "to be paid on demand" or "due on demand" are added to the I.O.U., the need for an affirmative promise is satisfied. Thus, if a buyer executes a promissory note using the words "I promise to pay $1,000

2. Under the revised Article 3, a promise that states that an instrument is to be paid only out of a particular fund or source is not generally conditional [RUCC 3–106(b)].

to the order of the seller for the purchase of goods X," then the requirement for a negotiable instrument is satisfied. A certificate of deposit is exceptional in this respect. No express promise is required in a CD because the bank's acknowledgment of the deposit and the other terms of the instrument clearly indicate a promise.

An order is associated with three-party instruments, such as trade acceptances, checks, and drafts. An order directs a third party to pay the instrument as drawn. In the typical check, for example, the word "pay" (to the order of a payee) is a command to the drawee bank to pay the check when presented, and thus it is an order. The order is mandatory even if it is written in a courteous form with words like "Please pay" or "Kindly pay." Generally, precise language must be used. An order stating, "I wish you would pay," does not fulfill the requirement of precision.

In addition to being precise, an effective order must specifically identify the drawee (the person who must pay) [UCC 3–102(1)(b)]. A bank's name printed on the face of a check, for example, sufficiently designates the bank as drawee.

Unconditionality of Promise or Order A negotiable instrument's utility as a substitute for money or as a credit device would be dramatically reduced if it had conditional promises attached to it. It would be expensive and time consuming to investigate conditional promises, and therefore the transferability of the instrument would be greatly restricted. Substantial administrative costs would be required to process conditional promises. Also, the payee or any **holder** of the instrument would risk the possibility that the condition would not occur. The term *holder* includes any person in the possession of an instrument drawn, issued, or indorsed to him or her or to his or her order or to bearer or in blank [see UCC 1–201(20)]. The terms *indorse, bearer,* and *in blank* are explained later in this chapter.

HOLDER
A person "who is in possession of a document of title or negotiable instrument or a certificated investment security drawn, issued, or indorsed to him or his order or to bearer or in blank" [UCC 1–201(20)].

Suppose Andrew promises in a note to pay Frances $10,000 only if a certain ship reaches port. No one could safely purchase the promissory note without first investigating whether the ship had arrived. Even then, the facts disclosed by the investigation might be incorrect. To avoid such problems, the UCC provides that only unconditional promises or orders can be negotiable [UCC 3–104(1)(b)].

The UCC expands the definition of *unconditional,* however, to prevent certain necessary conditions commonly used in business transactions from rendering an otherwise negotiable instrument nonnegotiable. These conditions, resolved by UCC 3–105, are discussed here.

Statements of Consideration Many instruments state the terms of the underlying agreement or refer to the consideration paid for the instrument as a matter of standard business practice. Somewhere on its face, such an instrument refers to the transaction or agreement for which it is being used in payment. Because the policy of the UCC is to integrate standard trade usages into its provisions, such references are not considered conditions and do not affect negotiability. For example, the words "as per contract" or "This debt arises from the sale of goods X and Y" do not render an instrument nonnegotiable.

References to Other Agreements The UCC provides that mere reference to another agreement does not affect negotiability. If, however, the instrument is made subject to the other agreement, it is rendered nonnegotiable [UCC 3–105(2)(a)]. A reference to another agreement is normally inserted for the purpose of keeping a record or giving information to anyone who may be interested. Notes frequently refer to separate agreements that give special rights to a creditor for an acceleration of payment or to a debtor for prepayment. References to these rights do not destroy the negotiability of the instrument. For example, the statement that an instrument's payment is secured by collateral will not render an otherwise negotiable instrument nonnegotiable. This statement adds to the salability and marketability of the instrument.

Payments out of a Particular Fund UCC 3–105(2)(b) states that if the terms of an instrument provide that payment can be made only out of a particular fund or source, such terms render the instrument nonnegotiable. Thus, for example, terms in a note that include the condition that payment will be made out of next year's cotton crop will make the note nonnegotiable. There is an exception for certain entities and organizations because such a rule would operate as a hardship for them. Hence, the UCC specifically states that government entities can issue negotiable instruments, even if payment is to come only from a particular fund or source [UCC 3–105(1)(g)]. Also, partnerships, unincorporated associations, and trusts or estates can issue negotiable instruments, even though payment is to come from the entire assets of the organization or the estate [UCC 3–105(1)(h)].[3]

Secured by a Mortgage A simple statement in an otherwise negotiable note indicating that the note is secured by a mortgage does not destroy its negotiability. Actually, such a statement might make the note even more acceptable in commerce. Realize, though, that the statement that a note is secured by a mortgage must not stipulate that the maker's promise to pay is *subject* to the terms and conditions of the mortgage. The following case illustrates this point.

Case 18.1

HOLLY HILL ACRES, LTD. v. CHARTER BANK OF GAINESVILLE

District Court of Appeal of Florida, Second District, 1975.
314 So.2d 209.

HISTORICAL AND SOCIAL SETTING *Before the UCC was drafted, it was generally accepted that when an instrument contained such language as "subject to the terms of a contract between the maker and payee," the instrument was not negotiable. In Florida, before the state adopted the UCC in 1965, the law provided that a promissory note incorporating by reference the terms of another agreement did not contain an unconditional promise to pay. In a case decided in 1932, for example, the Florida Supreme Court held that certain bonds that were "to be received and held subject to" a certain mortgage were nonnegotiable.*[a]

FACTS Holly Hill Acres was the maker of a promissory note that named Rogers and Blythe as payees. Holly Hill Acres gave the note to Rogers and Blythe as payment for certain property, and they retained a mortgage (lien) on the property. The note stated in part: "This note is secured by a mortgage on real estate. * * * The terms of said mortgage are by this reference made part hereof." Subsequently, Rogers and Blythe assigned the promissory note and the mortgage to Charter Bank of Gainesville. Holly Hill Acres defaulted on the note, and when the bank sued to recover, Holly Hill Acres claimed that Rogers and Blythe had fraudulently induced the company to purchase the land. Holly Hill Acres refused to pay on the note. The bank argued that it was a special type of assignee called a *holder in due course*[b] because the promissory note was a negotiable instrument. This being so, the bank claimed an unhampered right to recover on the note despite any underlying disputes between Holly Hill Acres and Rogers and Blythe. (A holder in due course takes a negotiable instrument free of most claims of other parties, including defenses against payment on it. This is the rule only when a negotiable instrument is involved.) The trial court held that the promissory note was negotiable and that the bank, as a holder in due course, could recover. Holly Hill Acres appealed, claiming that because the note was made subject to the mortgage agreement, the note was rendered nonnegotiable.

ISSUE Does the fact that the note was made subject to the mortgage agreement render the note nonnegotiable?

DECISION Yes. The appellate court reversed the trial court's decision and held the note to be nonnegotiable.

REASON For the note to be negotiable, the "[m]ere reference to a note being secured by mortgage * * * does not impede the negotiability of the note." The court held, however, that when the instrument provides that the terms

a. *Brown v. Marion Mortgage Co.,* 107 Fla. 727, 145 So. 413 (1932).

b. A holder in due course is a holder who acquires special status by taking an instrument in good faith, among other things. See Chapter 19.

3. See footnote 2.

Case 18.1—Continued

of a mortgage are by reference made a part thereof, the note is conditional, being governed by the mortgage, and "the note is rendered nonnegotiable." Because the note was nonnegotiable, the bank was not a holder in due course, and Holly Hill Acres could assert fraud as a defense.

Sum Certain in Money

Negotiable instruments must state the amount to be paid in a *sum certain in money*, a requirement that promises clarity and certainty in determining the value of the instrument [UCC 3–104(1)(b)]. The UCC mandates that negotiable commercial paper be paid wholly in money. A promissory note that provides for payment in diamonds, or in 1,000 hours of services, would not be payable in money and thus would be nonnegotiable.

Sum Certain The term *sum certain* means an amount that is ascertainable from the instrument itself without reference to an outside source.[4] A demand note payable with 12 percent interest meets the requirement of sum certain because its amount can be determined at the time it is payable [UCC 3–106(1)]. Instruments that provide simply for payment of interest at prevailing bank rates are generally nonnegotiable because bank rates fluctuate. A mortgage note tied to a variable rate of interest that fluctuates as a result of market conditions is not negotiable.[5] When, however, an instrument is payable at the *legal rate of interest* (a rate of interest fixed by statute), at a *judgment rate of interest* (a rate of interest fixed by statute that is applied to a monetary judgment awarded by a court until the judgment is paid or terminated), or as fixed by state law, the instrument is negotiable—if it meets the other criteria for negotiability.

Money and No Other Promise Section 3–104(1)(b) of the UCC provides that a sum certain is to be payable in "money and no other promise." The UCC defines money as "a medium of exchange authorized or adopted by a domestic or foreign government as a part of its currency" [UCC 1–201(24)].

Suppose that the maker of a note promises "to pay on demand $1,000 in U.S. gold." Because gold is not a medium of exchange adopted by the U.S. government, the note is not payable in money. The same result would occur if the maker promises "to pay $1,000 and fifty liters of 1964 Chateau Lafite-Rothschild wine," as the instrument is not payable *entirely* in money. An instrument payable in government bonds or in shares of IBM stock is not negotiable because neither is a medium of exchange recognized by the U.S. government.

The statement "Payable in $1,000 U.S. currency or an equivalent value in gold" would render the instrument nonnegotiable if the maker reserved the option of paying in money or gold. If the option were left to the payee, some legal scholars argue that the instrument would be negotiable.

If an instrument is payable in a foreign currency, the UCC has a special provision [UCC 3–107(2)]. Any instrument payable in the United States with a face amount stated in a foreign currency can be paid in the equivalent in U.S. dollars at the due date, unless the paper expressly requires payment in the foreign currency.

---

4. Under the revised Article 3, the amount or rate of interest may be determined with reference to information not contained in the instrument [RUCC 3–112(b)].

5. Variable-rate loans have become popular because lenders are protected when rates rise and borrowers benefit when rates decline. Some states have amended UCC 3–106 to make these notes negotiable. Under the revised Article 3, a variable-interest-rate note can be negotiable. The requirement that to be negotiable a writing must contain a promise or order to pay a fixed sum applies only to the principal. Interest may be stated as a variable amount [RUCC 3–112].

Payable on Demand or at a Definite Time

UCC 3–104(1)(c) requires that a negotiable instrument "be payable on demand or at a definite time." Clearly, to ascertain the value of a negotiable instrument, it is necessary to know when the maker, drawee, or acceptor is required to pay. It is also necessary to know when the obligations of secondary parties will arise. Furthermore, it is necessary to know when an instrument is due in order to calculate when the statute of limitations may apply. And finally, with an interest-bearing instrument, it is necessary to know the exact interval during which the interest will accrue to determine the present value of the instrument.

Payable on Demand Instruments that are payable on demand include those that contain the words "Payable at sight" or "Payable upon presentment" and those that say nothing about when payment is due. The very nature of the instrument may indicate that it is payable on demand. For example, a check, by definition, is payable on demand [UCC 3–104(2)(b)]. If no time for payment is specified, and if the person responsible for payment must pay upon the instrument's presentment, the instrument is payable on demand [UCC 3–108].

Payable at a Definite Time If an instrument is not payable on demand, to be negotiable it must be payable at a definite time specified on the face of the instrument. The maker or drawee is under no obligation to pay until the specified time.

Often, instruments contain additional terms that seem to conflict with the definite-time requirement. UCC 3–109 attempts to clear up some of these potential problems as follows:

> (1) An instrument is payable at a definite time if by its terms it is payable
> (a) on or before a stated date or at a fixed period after a stated date; or
> (b) at a fixed period after sight; or
> (c) at a definite time subject to any acceleration; or
> (d) at a definite time subject to extension at the option of the holder, or to extension to a further definite time at the option of the maker or acceptor, or automatically upon or after a specified act or event.
>
> (2) An instrument which by its terms is otherwise payable only upon an act or event uncertain as to time of occurrence is not payable at a definite time even though the act or event has occurred.

Suppose that an instrument dated June 1, 1994, states, "One year after the death of my grandfather, Henry Adams, I promise to pay to the order of James Harmon $500. [Signed] Jacqueline Wells." This instrument is nonnegotiable. Because the date of the grandfather's death is uncertain, the maturity date is uncertain, even though the event is bound to occur or has already occurred.

When an instrument is payable on or before a stated date, it is clearly payable at a definite time, although the maker has the option of paying before the stated maturity date. This uncertainty does not violate the definite-time requirement. Suppose Levine gives Hirsch an instrument dated May 1, 1994, that indicates on its face that it is payable on or before May 1, 1995. This instrument satisfies the requirement. In contrast, an instrument that is undated and made payable "one month after date" is clearly nonnegotiable. There is no way to determine the maturity date from the face of the instrument.

ACCELERATION CLAUSE
A clause in an installment contract that provides for all future payments to become due immediately upon the failure to tender timely payments or upon the occurrence of a specified event.

Acceleration Clause An **acceleration clause** allows a payee or other holder of a time instrument to demand payment of the entire amount due, with interest, if a certain event occurs, such as a default in payment of an installment when due. There must be, of course, a good faith belief that payment will not be made for an acceleration clause to be invoked.

Assume that Martin lends $1,000 to Ruth. Ruth makes a negotiable note promising to pay $100 per month for eleven months. The note may contain an acceleration provision that permits Martin or any holder to demand at once all the payments plus the interest owed to date if Ruth fails to pay an installment in any given month. If, for example, Ruth fails to make the third payment, the note will be due and payable in full. If Martin accelerates the unpaid balance, Ruth will owe Martin the remaining principal plus any unpaid interest.

Under UCC 3–109(1)(c), instruments that include acceleration clauses are negotiable because (1) the exact value of the instrument can be ascertained and (2) the instrument will be payable on a fixed date if the event allowing acceleration does not occur. Thus, the fixed date is the outside limit used to determine the value of the instrument.

EXTENSION CLAUSE
A clause in a time instrument extending the instrument's date of maturity. An extension clause is the reverse of an acceleration clause.

Extension Clause The reverse of an acceleration clause is an **extension clause,** which allows the date of maturity to be extended into the future. To keep the instrument negotiable, the interval of the extension must be specified if the right to extend is given to the maker of the instrument. If, however, the holder of the instrument can extend it, the extended maturity date does not have to be specified.

Suppose a note reads, "The maker [obligor] has the right to postpone the time of payment of this note beyond its definite maturity date of January 1, 1994. This extension, however, shall be for no more than a reasonable time." A note with this language is not negotiable, because it does not satisfy the definite-time requirement. The right to extend is the maker's, and the maker has not indicated when the note will become due after the extension.

In contrast, if a note reads, "The holder of this note at the date of maturity, January 1, 1994, can extend the time of payment until the following June 1 or later, if the holder so wishes," it is a negotiable instrument. The length of the extension does not have to be specified, because the option to extend is solely that of the holder. After January 1, 1994, the note is, in effect, a demand instrument.

Payable to Order or to Bearer

Because one of the functions of a negotiable instrument is to serve as a substitute for money, freedom to transfer is an essential requirement. To assure a proper transfer, the instrument must be "payable to order or to bearer" [UCC 3–104(1)(d)].[6] These words indicate that at the time of issuance it is expected that future unknown persons—not just the immediate party—will eventually be the owners. If an instrument is neither order nor bearer paper, the instrument is nonnegotiable and therefore only assignable and governed by contract law.

ORDER INSTRUMENT
A negotiable instrument that is payable to the order of a specific person.

Order Instruments UCC 3–110(1) defines an instrument as an order to pay "when by its terms it is payable to the order * * * of any person therein specified with reasonable certainty." This section goes on to state that an **order instrument** can be payable to the order of

(a) the maker or drawer; or
(b) the drawee; or
(c) a payee who is not maker, drawer, or drawee; or
(d) two or more payees together or in the alternative; or
(e) the representative of an estate, trust, or fund, or [the representative's] successor; or
(f) an office or officer by title [such as a tax assessor]; or
(g) a partnership or unincorporated association.

6. Under the revised Article 3, a check that does not include the words "to the order of" is negotiable [RUCC 3–104(c)].

The purpose of order paper is to allow the maker or drawer to transfer the instrument to a specific person. This in turn allows that person to transfer the instrument to whomever he or she wishes. Thus, the maker or drawer is agreeing to pay either the person specified or whomever that person might designate. In this way, the instrument retains its transferability.

Suppose an instrument states, "Payable to the order of Rocky Reed" or "Pay to Rocky Reed or order." Clearly, the maker or drawer has indicated that a payment will be made to Reed or to whomever Reed designates. The instrument is negotiable.

If, however, the instrument states, "Payable to Rocky Reed" or "Pay to Rocky Reed only," the instrument loses its negotiability. The maker or drawer indicates only that Reed will be paid. (An instrument that is *indorsed* in such a manner, however, does not lose its negotiability, as will be discussed later in this chapter.)

In addition, except for bearer paper (explained in the following paragraph), the person specified must be named with *certainty*, because the transfer of an order instrument requires an **indorsement.**[7] (An indorsement is a signature placed on an instrument, such as on the back of a check, for the purpose of transferring one's ownership rights in the instrument.) If an instrument states, "Payable to the order of my kissing cousin," the instrument is nonnegotiable, as a holder could not be sure which cousin was intended to indorse and properly transfer the instrument.

INDORSEMENT
A signature placed on an instrument or a document of title for the purpose of transferring one's ownership in the instrument or document of title.

Bearer Instruments UCC 3–111 defines a **bearer instrument** as one that does not designate a specific payee. The term **bearer** refers to a person in possession of an instrument that is payable to bearer or indorsed in blank (with a signature only, as will be discussed shortly) [UCC 1–201(5)]. This means that the maker or drawer agrees to pay anyone who presents the instrument for payment. Any instrument containing the following terms is a bearer instrument:

BEARER INSTRUMENT
In the law of commercial paper, any instrument that is not payable to a specific person, including instruments payable to the bearer or to "cash."

BEARER
A person in the possession of an instrument payable to bearer or indorsed in blank.

- "Payable to the order of bearer."
- "Payable to Rocky Reed or bearer."
- "Payable to bearer."
- "Pay cash."
- "Pay to the order of cash."

In addition, an instrument that contains "any other indication which does not purport to designate a specific payee" is bearer paper [UCC 3–111(c)]. An instrument "payable to the order of a bucket of milk," for example, would not designate a specific payee, and the instrument would be a bearer instrument. The use of such designations can cause problems, however, and should be avoided.

Suppose an instrument is made payable both to order and to bearer. If the bearer words are handwritten or typewritten, the instrument is a bearer instrument. But if the bearer words are in a preprinted form, it is an order instrument [UCC 3–110(3)].

The following case illustrates the requirements that must be met for an instrument to be classified as a bearer instrument.

Case 18.2
DAVIS v. DAVIS
Court of Appeals of Kentucky, 1992.
838 S.W.2d 415.

HISTORICAL AND SOCIAL SETTING *In a case decided in 1920, the Kentucky Court of Appeals (Kentucky's highest state court until 1976) stated that "the rule is well settled that the name of the payee may be left blank, which makes the instrument payable in effect to the bearer."*[a] *Under the UCC, which Kentucky adopted in 1958, this rule was*

a. *Finley v. Rose*, 189 Ky. 359, 224 S.W. 1059 (1920).

7. We should note here that because the UCC uses the spelling *indorse* (*indorsement*, etc.), rather than *endorse* (and so on), we adopt that spelling here and in other chapters in the text.

Case 18.2—Continued

superseded. Comment 2 to UCC 3–111 explains that the drafters of the UCC took parts of Section 9 of the Uniform Negotiable Instruments Law of 1896, which preceded the UCC, and reworded them in drafting UCC 3–111 "to remove any possible implication that 'Pay to the order of ____' makes the instrument payable to bearer. It is an incomplete order instrument, and falls under Section 3–115."

FACTS Aubrey and Jessie Davis were married in 1984. Aubrey's mother, Eva Davis, lived with them after the marriage. In 1985, Aubrey allegedly gave Eva a promissory note for $12,000 as payment for some property she was transferring to Aubrey. Aubrey died in 1987, and Eva died in 1988. After Eva's death, her grandson, Darrell Davis (Aubrey's son by a previous marriage), claimed that before she died Eva had given him the note to collect for her. The note had been written on a preprinted bank form, but the bank's name had been scratched out, as had the town. The note had been dated and signed by Aubrey, but no payee was indicated—the note stated that "the undersigned maker(s) promise to pay to the order of: ____." Darrell sought payment on the note from Jessie, alleging that he was the holder of a bearer instrument. Jessie refused to pay, claiming that Darrell had no ownership rights in the note. She further claimed that the note could not be enforced because it had been materially altered. The trial court held that the note was a bearer instrument and granted summary judgment for Darrell. Jessie appealed.

ISSUE Is the promissory note signed by Aubrey a bearer instrument?

DECISION No. The appellate court reversed the trial court's decision on this issue.

REASON UCC 3–111 describes bearer paper as follows: "An instrument is payable to bearer when by its terms it is payable to (a) bearer or the order of bearer; or (b) a specified person or bearer; or (c) 'cash' or the order of 'cash,' or any other indication which does not purport to designate a specific payee." The court concluded that the note at issue was not a bearer instrument under any of these statutory definitions. The court held that the instrument was an incomplete instrument that could not be enforced until it was completed. Because there was no indication that Aubrey had authorized anyone to complete the note, the note was unenforceable.

❖ Factors Not Affecting Negotiability

Certain ambiguities or omissions will not affect the negotiability of an instrument. The UCC's rules for clearing up ambiguous terms include the following:

1. Unless the date of an instrument is necessary to determine a definite time for payment, the fact that an instrument is undated does not affect its negotiability. A typical example is an undated check [UCC 3–114(1)].
2. Postdating or antedating an instrument does not affect negotiability [UCC 3–114(1)].
3. Handwritten terms outweigh typewritten and printed terms [UCC 3–118(b)]. For example, if your check is printed, "Pay to the order of," and in handwriting you insert in the blank, "Anita Delgado or bearer," the check is a bearer instrument.
4. Words outweigh figures unless the words are ambiguous [UCC 3–118(c)]. This is important when the numerical amount and written amount on a check differ.
5. When a particular interest rate is not specified but the instrument simply states "with interest," the interest rate is the judgment rate [UCC 3–118(d)].

❖ Transfer by Assignment or Negotiation

Once issued, a negotiable instrument can be transferred by *assignment* or by *negotiation.*

Transfer by Assignment

Recall from Chapter 12 that an assignment is a transfer of rights under a contract. Under general contract principles, a transfer by assignment to an assignee gives the assignee only those rights that the assignor possessed. Any defenses that can be raised against an assignor can normally be raised against the assignee. Article 3 applies only to negotiable instruments; obviously, there can be no negotiation of a nonnegotiable instrument. Furthermore, when a transfer fails to qualify as a negotiation, it becomes an assignment. The transferee is then an *assignee* rather than a *holder.*

Transfer by Negotiation

Negotiation is the transfer of an instrument in such form that the transferee (the person to whom the instrument is transferred) becomes a holder [UCC 3–202(1)]. Under UCC principles, a transfer by negotiation creates a holder who, at the very least, receives the rights of the previous possessor [UCC 3–201(1)]. Unlike an assignment, a transfer by negotiation can make it possible for a holder to receive more rights in the instrument than the prior possessor [UCC 3–305]. (A holder who receives greater rights is known as a *holder in due course.* See Chapter 19.) There are two methods of negotiating an instrument so that the receiver becomes a holder. The method used depends on whether the instrument is order paper or bearer paper.

NEGOTIATION
The transferring of a negotiable instrument to another in such form that the transferee becomes a holder.

Negotiating Order Paper *Order paper* contains the name of a payee capable of indorsing, as in "Pay to the order of Lloyd Sorenson." Order paper is also paper that has as its last or only indorsement a *special* indorsement, as in "Pay to Sorenson. [Signed] Adams." (Special indorsements are discussed in more detail later in this chapter.) If the instrument is order paper, it is negotiated by delivery with any necessary indorsements. For example, National Express Corporation issues a payroll check "to the order of Lloyd Sorenson." Sorenson takes the check to the supermarket, signs his name on the back (an indorsement), gives it to the cashier (a delivery), and receives cash. Sorenson has negotiated the check to the supermarket [UCC 3–202(1)]. In the following case, a party intended to assign to another party her rights in a promissory note payable to her. Because she indorsed the note with a special indorsement, however, the court held that the note had been not assigned but negotiated to the other party.

Case 18.3 

ALVES v. BALDAIA
Court of Appeals of Ohio,
Third District, 1984.
14 Ohio App.3d 187,
470 N.E.2d 459.

HISTORICAL AND SOCIAL SETTING *Checks and promissory notes have been in use for centuries. Nearly everyone can identify a check, and most people can explain its general legal effect. Most people can also explain the general obligation of a promissory note, particularly when it is pointed out that a note is usually an instrument that is signed when money is borrowed. Despite this familiarity with checks and notes, most people are not aware of some of the most important consequences of dealing with negotiable instruments.*

FACTS In January of 1973, Keith and Joyce Alves loaned Joyce Alves's parents, Beatrice and William Baldaia, $15,000. In return, the Baldaias executed a promissory note payable to Joyce Alves. In February of 1978, Keith and Joyce Alves divorced. The separation agreement contained the following provision: "Wife agrees to assign to Husband any and all right, title, and interest she may have in a certain note, executed by her parents, dated January 3, 1973 on or before date of final hearing." Joyce Alves later wrote on the promissory note, "Pay to the order of Keith R. Alves. [Signed] Joyce Ann Alves." Some time later, Keith Alves tried to collect payment on the note from the Baldaias, who refused to pay it. Alves then sought payment from his former wife, who had since remarried and taken the name of Schaller. Schaller claimed that her transfer of the promissory note to Alves, pursuant to the separation agreement, constituted an "assignment" of her rights and interests in the note and not a formal "negotiation" of the

Case 18.3—Continued

note. The trial court held that Schaller's signature on the note operated as an indorsement. Schaller and her parents, the Baldaias, then appealed the decision, claiming that the trial court had been in error by dismissing their motion for summary judgment.

ISSUE Was the transfer of the promissory note an assignment or a negotiation?

DECISION The appellate court confirmed the trial court's judgment that the transfer had been a negotiation and, hence, Schaller was secondarily liable (liable in the event that her parents failed to pay the note).

REASON The court reasoned that if Schaller had wished only to "assign" the note, she should not have indorsed it. As it stood, the indorsement of the note technically gave Keith Alves the rights of a holder. Although the divorce agreement made it clear that Joyce Alves had intended an assignment of the note, as a matter of law such collateral evidence could not be used to determine the intent of the parties. The decision had to rest on what the *instrument itself* stated or reflected, and parol evidence was inadmissible in this case. The court stated that an "indorser may disclaim his liability on the contract of indorsement, *but only if the indorsement itself so specifies.* * * * *The customary manner of disclaiming the indorser's liability is* * * * *to indorse 'without recourse.'* " Because no disclaimer was written on the instrument, Schaller's signature on the note meant that "she contracted to pay the instrument, according to its tenor [its exact words], to the holder thereof if the maker dishonored the note at maturity."

ETHICAL CONSIDERATIONS *Sometimes, the application of negotiable instruments law has seemingly unfair results, as in this case. After all, Schaller had intended to assign the note, not accept secondary liability for its payment. Yet negotiable instrument law gives little weight to subjective intentions. Rather, a court will decide liability on the basis of what is specifically contained within the "four corners" of an instrument. Overall, the public benefits from this rule, because it promotes the negotiability of commercial paper. If subjective intentions were to be considered in determining whether a note is negotiable or nonnegotiable, the commercial world would come to a standstill.*

Negotiating Bearer Paper If an instrument is payable to bearer, it is negotiated by delivery—that is, by transfer into another person's possession. Indorsement is not necessary [UCC 3–202(1)]. The use of *bearer paper* involves more risk through loss or theft than the use of order paper.

Assume Richard Kraychek writes a check "payable to cash" and hands it to Jessie Arnold (a delivery). Kraychek has issued the check (a bearer instrument) to Arnold. Arnold places the check in her wallet, which is subsequently stolen. The thief has possession of the check. At this point, negotiation has not occurred, because delivery must be voluntary on the part of the transferor. If the thief "delivers" the check to an innocent third person, however, negotiation will be complete. All rights to the check will be passed *absolutely* to that third person, and Arnold will lose all right to recover the proceeds of the check from him or her [UCC 3–305]. Of course, she can recover her money from the thief if the thief can be found.

Converting Order Paper to Bearer Paper and Vice Versa The method used for negotiation depends on the character of the instrument at the time the negotiation takes place. For example, a check originally payable to "cash" but subsequently indorsed with the words "Pay to Arnold" must be negotiated as order paper (by indorsement and delivery), even though it was previously bearer paper [UCC 3–204(1)].

An instrument payable to the order of a named payee and indorsed in blank (by the holder's signature only, as will be discussed subsequently) becomes a bearer instrument [UCC 3–204(2)]. To illustrate, a check made payable to the order of Jessie Arnold is issued to Arnold, and Arnold indorses it by signing her name on the back. The instrument can now be negotiated by delivery without indorsement. Arnold can negotiate the check to whomever she wishes by delivery, and that person can negotiate by delivery without indorsement. If Arnold, after such indorsement, loses the check, then a finder can negotiate it further. How indorsements can convert order paper to bearer paper and vice versa is illustrated in Exhibit 18–5.

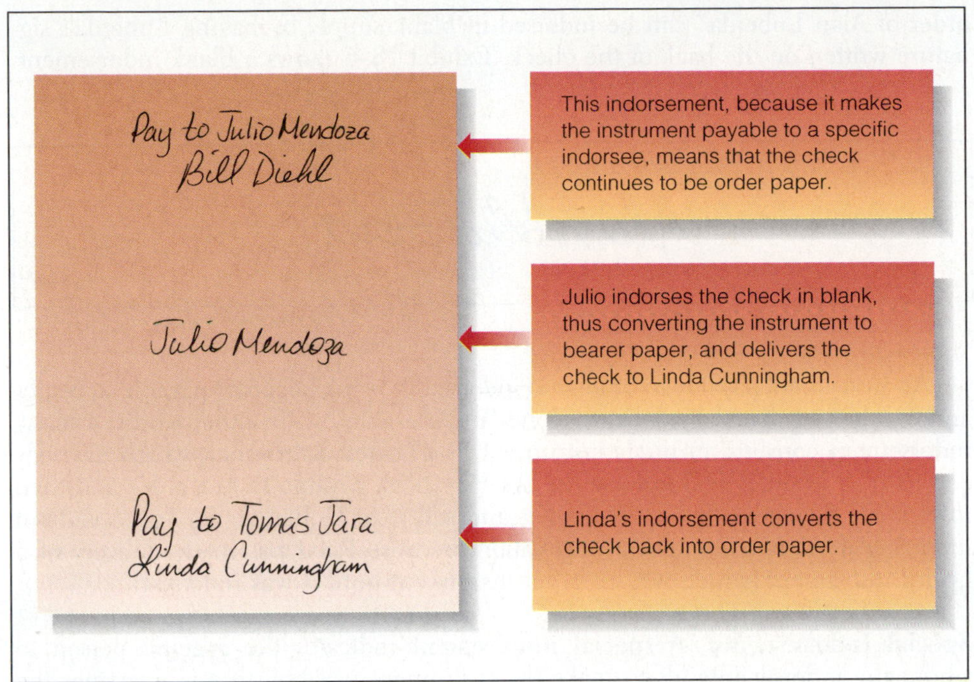

◆ **Exhibit 18–5 Converting Order Paper to Bearer Paper and Vice Versa**

❖ Indorsements

Indorsements are required whenever the instrument being negotiated is classified as an order instrument. (Many transferees of bearer paper require indorsement for identification purposes, even though the UCC does not require it.) An *indorsement* is a signature with or without additional words or statements. It is most often written on the back of the instrument itself. If there is no room on the instrument, indorsements can be written on a separate piece of paper called an **allonge.** The allonge must be "so firmly affixed [to the instrument] as to become a part thereof" [UCC 3–202(2)]. Pins or paper clips will not suffice. Most courts hold that staples are sufficient.

ALLONGE
A piece of paper firmly attached to a negotiable instrument, upon which transferees can make indorsements if there is no room left on the instrument itself.

A person who transfers a note or a draft by signing (indorsing) it and delivering it to another person is an **indorser.** For example, Martha receives a graduation check for $100. She can transfer the check to her mother (or to anyone) by signing it on the back. Martha is an indorser. If Martha indorses the check by writing "Pay to Mary Grimes," Mary Grimes is the **indorsee.**

INDORSER
One who, being the payee or holder of a negotiable instrument, signs his or her name on the back of it.

INDORSEE
The one to whom a negotiable instrument is transferred by indorsement.

One purpose of an indorsement is to effect the negotiation of order paper. Sometimes the transferee of bearer paper will request the holder-transferor to indorse. This is done to impose liability on the indorser. The liability of indorsers will be discussed in Chapter 19. Once an instrument qualifies as a negotiable instrument, the form of indorsement will have no effect on the character of the underlying instrument. Indorsement relates to the right of the holder to negotiate the paper and the manner in which it must be done.

Types of Indorsements

We will examine four categories of indorsements: blank, special, qualified, and restrictive.

BLANK INDORSEMENT
An indorsement made by the mere writing of the indorser's name on the back of an instrument. Such indorsement causes an instrument, otherwise payable to order, to become payable to bearer and negotiated only by delivery.

Blank Indorsements A **blank indorsement** specifies no particular indorsee and can consist of a mere signature [UCC 3–204(2)]. Hence, a check payable "to the order of Alan Luberda" can be indorsed in blank simply by having Luberda's signature written on the back of the check. Exhibit 18–6 shows a blank indorsement.

♦ **Exhibit 18–6**
A Blank Indorsement

Alan Luberda

An instrument payable to order and indorsed in blank becomes payable to bearer and can be negotiated by delivery alone [UCC 3–204(2)]. In other words, a blank indorsement converts an order instrument to a bearer instrument, which anybody can cash. If Jennifer Hill indorses in blank a check payable to her order and then loses it on the street, Reed can find it and sell it to Hollander for value without indorsing it. This constitutes a negotiation, because Reed has made delivery of a bearer instrument (which was an order instrument until it was indorsed).

SPECIAL INDORSEMENT
An indorsement on an instrument that specifies a specific person to whom or to whose order the instrument is payable.

Special Indorsements A **special indorsement** indicates the specific person to whom the indorser intends to make the instrument payable; that is, it names the indorsee [UCC 3–204(1)]. No special words of negotiation are needed. Words such as "Pay to the order of Storr" or "Pay to Storr" followed by the signature of the indorser are sufficient. When an instrument is indorsed in this way, it is order paper. Had the words "Pay to Storr" been used on the face of the instrument to indicate the payee, the instrument would not have been negotiable.

To avoid the risk of loss from theft, one may convert a blank indorsement to a special indorsement. This changes the bearer paper back to order paper. UCC 3–204(3) allows a holder to "convert a blank indorsement into a special indorsement by writing over the signature of the indorser in blank any contract consistent with the character of the indorsement."

QUALIFIED INDORSEMENT
An indorsement on a negotiable instrument under which the indorser disclaims to subsequent holders secondary liability on the instrument; the most common qualified indorsement is "without recourse."

For example, a check is made payable to Arthur Rabe. He indorses his name by blank indorsement on the back of the check and negotiates the check to Anthony Alfono. Anthony, not wishing to cash the check immediately, wants to avoid any risk should he lose the check. He therefore writes "Pay to Anthony Alfono" above Arthur's blank indorsement. In this manner, Anthony has converted Arthur's blank indorsement into a special indorsement. Further negotiation now requires Anthony Alfono's indorsement plus delivery. (See Exhibit 18–7.)

♦ **Exhibit 18–7**
A Special Indorsement

Pay to Anthony Alfono
Arthur Rabe

Qualified Indorsements Generally, an indorser, *merely by indorsing,* impliedly promises to pay the holder, or any subsequent indorser, the amount of the instrument in the event that the drawer or maker defaults on the payment [UCC 3–414(1)]. A **qualified indorsement** is used by an indorser to disclaim this contract liability on the instrument. The notation "without recourse" is commonly used. Such an indorsement is shown in Exhibit 18–8.

Pay to Elvie Lang without recourse
Bridgett Cage

◆ **Exhibit 18–8**
A Qualified Indorsement

Qualified indorsements are often used by persons acting in a representative capacity. For instance, insurance agents sometimes receive checks payable to them that are really intended as payment to the insurance company. The agent is merely indorsing the payment through to the insurance company and should not be required to make good on the check if it is later dishonored. The "without recourse" indorsement absolves the agent. If the instrument is dishonored, the holder cannot obtain recovery from the agent who indorsed "without recourse" unless the indorser has breached one of the warranties listed in UCC 3–417(2) and (3), which relate to good title, authorized signature, no material alteration, and so forth.

Usually, then, blank and special indorsements are *unqualified indorsements*. That is, the blank or special indorser is guaranteeing payment of the instrument in addition to transferring title to it. The qualified indorser is not guaranteeing payment. Nonetheless, the qualified indorsement ("without recourse") still transfers title to the indorsee; an instrument bearing a qualified indorsement can be negotiated.

A qualified indorsement is accompanied by either a special or a blank indorsement that determines further negotiation. Accordingly, a special qualified indorsement makes the instrument an order instrument, and it requires an indorsement plus delivery for negotiation. A blank qualified indorsement makes the instrument a bearer instrument, and only delivery is required for negotiation.

Assume that a check is made payable to the order of Bridgett Cage and that Bridgett wants to negotiate the check specifically to Elvie Ling with a qualified indorsement. Bridgett would indorse the check as follows: "Pay to Elvie Ling, without recourse. [Signed] Bridgett Cage." For Elvie to negotiate the check further to Chau Nguyen, Elvie would have to indorse and deliver the check to Chau.

Restrictive Indorsements The **restrictive indorsement** requires indorsees to comply with certain instructions regarding the funds involved. Restrictive indorsements come in many forms. UCC 3–205 describes four separate categories, which are discussed here.

RESTRICTIVE INDORSEMENT
Any indorsement of a negotiable instrument that purports to condition or prohibit further transfer of the instrument. As against payor and intermediary banks, such indorsements are usually ineffective. A restrictive indorsement does not prohibit further transfer or negotiation of the instrument.

Conditional Indorsements When payment depends on the occurrence of some event specified in the indorsement, (for example, "Pay to Lars Johansen if he completes the renovation of my kitchen by June 1, 1995"), the instrument has a conditional indorsement [UCC 3–205(a)]. Except against intermediary banks (defined in Chapter 20), the indorsement is enforceable, and neither the indorsee nor any subsequent holder has the right to enforce payment against that indorser on the instrument before the condition is met [UCC 3–206(3)].[8]

It is important to note that a conditional indorsement does not prevent further negotiation of the instrument. If conditional language appears on the face of an instrument, however, the instrument is not negotiable because it does not meet the requirement that it contain an unconditional promise to pay.

8. Revised Article 3 states that an indorsement conditioning the right to receive payment "does not affect the right of the indorsee to enforce the instrument." A person paying or taking for value an instrument can disregard the condition without liability [RUCC 3–206(b)].

Indorsements Prohibiting Further Indorsement An indorsement such as "Pay to Makoto Ing only. [Signed] Jerome Edelman" does not destroy transfer by negotiation. Ing can negotiate the instrument to a holder just as if it had read "Pay to Makoto Ing. [Signed] Jerome Edelman" [UCC 3–206(1)]. If the holder gives value, this type of restrictive indorsement has the same legal effect as a special indorsement. It is rarely used [UCC 3–205(b)].

Indorsements for Deposit or Collection A common type of restrictive indorsement is one that makes the indorsee (almost always a bank) a collecting agent of the indorser. Exhibit 18–9 illustrates this type of indorsement on a check payable and issued to Stephanie Mallak. In particular, a "Pay any bank or banker" or "For deposit only" indorsement has the effect of locking the instrument into the bank collection process. A bank's liability for payment of an instrument with a restrictive indorsement of this kind is discussed in Chapter 20.

◆ **Exhibit 18–9**
For Deposit/For Collection Indorsements

For deposit
Stephanie Mallak

or

For collection only
Stephanie Mallak

TRUST INDORSEMENT
An indorsement for the benefit of the indorser or a third person; also known as an agency indorsement. The indorsement results in legal title vesting in the original indorsee.

Trust Indorsements Indorsements by persons who are to hold or use the funds for the benefit of the indorser or a third party are called **trust indorsements** (also known as agency indorsements). For example, assume that Ramon Martinez asks his accountant, Ada Alvarez, to pay some bills for him while he is out of the country. He indorses a check to Ada Alvarez "as agent for Ramon Martinez." This agency indorsement obligates Alvarez to use the funds only for the benefit of Martinez. Sample trust and agency indorsements are shown in Exhibit 18–10.

◆ **Exhibit 18–10**
Trust Indorsements

Pay to Ada Alvarez in trust
for José Martinez
Ramon Martinez

or

Pay to Ada Alvarez as Agent
for Ramon Martinez
Ramon Martinez

The result of a trust indorsement is that legal rights in the instrument are transferred to the original indorsee. To the extent that the original indorsee pays or applies the proceeds consistently with the indorsement (for example, "In trust for José Martinez"), the indorsee is a holder and can become a holder in due course (described in Chapter 19) [UCC 3–205(d) and 3–206(4)].

The fiduciary restrictions (restrictions mandated by a relationship involving trust and loyalty) on the instrument do not reach beyond the original indorsee.[9] Any subsequent purchaser can qualify as a holder in due course unless he or she has actual notice that the instrument was negotiated in breach of the fiduciary duty.[10]

Miscellaneous Indorsement Problems

Of course, a significant problem in relation to indorsements occurs when an indorsement is forged or unauthorized. The UCC rules concerning unauthorized or forged signatures and indorsements will be discussed in Chapter 19 in the context of signature liability and again in Chapter 20 in the context of the bank's liability for payment of an instrument over an unauthorized signature. Here we look at two other problems that may arise with indorsements.

Correction of Name An indorsement should be identical to the name that appears on the instrument. The payee or indorsee whose name is misspelled can indorse with the misspelled name or the correct name, or both [UCC 3–203]. For example, if Sheryl Kruger receives a check payable to the order of Sherrill Krooger, she can indorse the check either "Sheryl Kruger" or "Sherrill Krooger." The usual practice is to indorse the name as it appears on the instrument and follow it by the correct name.[11]

Multiple Payees An instrument payable to two or more persons *in the alternative* (for example, "Pay to the order of Tuan or Johnson") requires the indorsement of only one of the payees [UCC 3–116(a)]. If, however, an instrument is made payable to two or more persons *jointly* (for example, "Pay to the order of Sharrie and Bob Covington" or "Pay to the order of Sharrie Covington, Bob Covington"), all of the payees' indorsements are necessary for negotiation [UCC 3–116(b)]. (See this chapter's *Business Law in Action* for a discussion of an unusual situation in which two payees' names were separated by a slash mark.) The following case raises some interesting questions concerning checks payable to two persons jointly.

9. Compare this with the rule governing conditional indorsements. A conditional indorsement obligates all subsequent indorsers (except certain banks) and primary parties to see that the money is applied consistently with the condition. Agency, or trust, indorsements limit this responsibility to the original indorsee.

10. See *In re Quantum Development Corp.*, 397 F.Supp. 329 (D.V.I. 1975).

11. *Watertown Federal Savings and Loan v. Spanks*, 346 Mass. 398, 193 N.E.2d 333 (1963).

Case 18.4 GENERAL MOTORS ACCEPTANCE CORP. v. ABINGTON CASUALTY INSURANCE CO.

Supreme Judicial Court of Massachusetts, 1992.
413 Mass. 583,
602 N.E.2d 1085.

HISTORICAL AND SOCIAL SETTING *Before the adoption of the UCC, the common law rule was that any joint obligee had the power to discharge the promisor by receipt of the promised performance. For example, if Ann promised to pay $100 to Burt and Clint, she could ordinarily discharge her obligation by paying either Burt or Clint. This rule complicated matters when applied to negotiable instruments. For instance, an unpaid co-payee could not collect from the drawer of an instrument because the instrument was considered discharged, but the unpaid co-payee could sue the drawee for conversion of funds. UCC 3–116 simplified the issue by stating that an instrument is discharged only when every joint payee has indorsed it. The Restatement (Second) of Contracts expressly recognizes this exception to the common law rule.*[a]

FACTS Abington Casualty Insurance Company issued an insurance policy to Robert Azevedo. The policy covered Azevedo's 1984 Jeep. General Motors Acceptance Corporation (GMAC) held a security interest in the vehicle, and the insurance policy named GMAC as the beneficiary. In other words, if the Jeep was damaged and a claim submitted, Abington was to pay GMAC for the amount of appraised damages. The Jeep was later damaged, and Abington appraised the loss and issued a check payable jointly "to the order of Robert A. Azevedo and G.M.A.C." The check was delivered to Azevedo, who then indorsed the check and presented it to the bank. The bank accepted the check, which had not been indorsed by GMAC, and Azevedo received full payment. GMAC never received the funds. GMAC sued the drawer of the check, Abington, to recover the insurance payment it should have received. The trial court dismissed the action, and GMAC appealed.

ISSUE As the court stated, this case presents two "novel issues": (1) Does the delivery of a negotiable instrument to one joint payee operate as a delivery to all joint payees? (2) Is the drawer's underlying obligation to joint payees discharged when one joint payee cashes a check without the indorsement of the other?

DECISION Yes, to the first question; no, to the second.

REASON The court noted that Massachusetts courts had never addressed the issue of whether delivery to one joint payee operates as delivery to all joint payees. Courts in other states, however, had dealt with the issue and concluded that delivery to one joint payee constituted delivery to all joint payees. The court reasoned that because state law required that every payee had to indorse an instrument before it could be negotiated, transferred, or discharged, "delivery of the instrument to one payee does not jeopardize the rights of the other payees." Abington's delivery of the check to Azevedo therefore was held to constitute delivery to both payees. As to the second issue before the court—whether Abington's obligations to GMAC were discharged when the check was cashed by Azevedo—the court held that "a negotiable instrument cannot be discharged by the actions of only one payee. Section 3–116(b) expressly prohibits the discharge of an instrument except by all the payees." The court stated that if it were not for this rule, "there would be no assurance that all the joint payees would receive payment." Because GMAC, as a joint payee, had not received payment, Abington had not discharged its obligation to GMAC.

ETHICAL CONSIDERATIONS *It may seem unfair that Abington, having paid the insurance proceeds once, now must pay them again to GMAC. But Abington can, in turn, recover the funds from the bank, which improperly paid the instrument without GMAC's indorsement. (The court noted that ideally, GMAC would have sued the bank in the first place, instead of Abington, to avoid this "circuitous litigation.") Ultimately, it is the bank that will bear the loss, which accords with the general principle in negotiable instruments law that the loss should fall on the party in the best position to prevent it.*

a. Restatement (Second) of Contracts, Section 299.

Business Law in Action

The Case of the Deceptive Virgule

In negotiable instruments law, little things can mean a lot. Consider a check containing a special indorsement to two indorsees whose names are separated by a virgule, or slash mark. Does the virgule in this case mean "and," or does it mean "or"?

While this question may sound academic, in Jan Mumma's case, it was not. Mumma's investment advisor, James Liddell, who was doing business under the corporate name of JHL & Associates, Inc., agreed to invest Mumma's funds in Fidelity, a nationally traded mutual fund management company. Mumma indorsed a cashier's check for $13,904.48 to "Fidelity/JHL & Associates." Liddell indorsed the check with JHL's indorsement stamp and deposited the check, without Fidelity's indorsement, into JHL's bank account at Rainier National Bank. Liddell never invested the funds in Fidelity. Mumma was unable to recover her money from JHL, which had become insolvent, or from Liddell, who was serving a jail sentence for fraud stemming from this incident and others like it. Mumma then attempted to recover from Rainier National Bank, claiming that she had intended and expected that Fidelity as well as JHL would have to indorse the check. Mumma alleged that the bank, by failing to require the indorsements of both parties, was negligent in its handling of the check.

The resolution of the case depended on whether the slash mark used by Mumma in indorsing her check should be interpreted to mean "and" or "or." Rainier contended that the common meaning of the slash mark is "or,"and thus the check was payable in the alternative either to Fidelity or JHL. Mumma claimed the the slash mark is often used to mean something other than "or." In "miles/hour," for example, the slash mark means "per." In dates, such as "7/20/90," the slash mark separates the day, month, and year. In fractions, such as "3/4," the slash has yet another meaning. She also pointed out that "M/M" is commonly used in the travel industry to mean "Mr. and Mrs." Mumma's basic contention was that because the slash mark can have many different meanings, depending on its context, the symbol is ambiguous and should not be read to mean "in the alternative."

The court did not agree. In the opinion of the court, Mumma disregarded "the plain meaning of the slash symbol, which two federal courts and courts in two other states have unanimously held to mean 'or' in the same context presented here." The court pointed out that in each case, the court's decision rested on various dictionaries' definitions of the term *virgule*, all of which suggested a "disjunctive, or alternative, construction." While it was true that the virgule was used in many different situations and had different meanings, the only use of the symbol to mean "and" (among the many uses Mumma had cited) was the usage of the travel industry. "We are not inclined," the court stated, "to transport the peculiarities of a particular business usage into the code of commercial law. In the absence of a more general showing that the virgule means 'and' in common usage, we choose to put our own law in accordance with previously decided cases on the same issue."

The court also found that Mumma's cause was not assisted by looking to the intent of the parties responsible for the language in question: "It is difficult to accept at face value Mumma's assertion that she endorsed her check intending that both Fidelity and JHL would have to provide their endorsements. It was Liddell who instructed Mumma to endorse the check as she did, and Liddell obviously intended that only one endorsement would be required."[a]

a. *Mumma v. Rainier National Bank,* 60 Wash.App. 937, 808 P.2d 767 (1991).

❖ Key Terms

acceleration clause 429
allonge 435
bearer 431
bearer instrument 431
blank indorsement 435
certificate of deposit (CD) 424
check 422
commercial paper 420
demand deposit 421
draft 421
drawee 421
drawer 421
extension clause 430
holder 426
indorsee 435
indorsement 431
indorser 435
maker 423
negotiable instrument 420
negotiation 433
order instrument 430
payee 421
presentment 421
promissory note 423
qualified indorsement 436
restrictive indorsement 437
signature 425
special indorsement 436
trade acceptance 422
trust indorsement 438

❖ Chapter Summary: Commercial Paper—Negotiability and Transferability

Law Governing Commercial Paper	Articles 3 and 4 of the Uniform Commercial Code govern commercial paper. Article 3 governs the negotiability and transferability of commercial paper; Article 4 governs bank deposit and collection procedures.
Functions of Commercial Paper	Commercial paper functions in two ways: 1. As a substitute for money. 2. As a credit device.
Types of Negotiable Instruments	Negotiable instruments may be classified by either of the following schemes: 1. *Demand instruments versus time instruments*—A demand instrument is payable on demand (when the holder presents it to the maker or drawer). A time instrument is payable at a future date. 2. *Orders to pay versus promises to pay*—Checks and drafts are *orders* to pay. Promissory notes and certificates of deposit (CDs) are *promises* to pay.
Requirements for Negotiable Instruments	1. Must be in writing [UCC 3–104(1)]. 2. Must be signed by the maker or drawer [UCC 3–104(1)(a), 1–201(39), 3–401]. 3. Must be an unconditional promise or order [UCC 3–104(1)(b), 3–105]. 4. Must state a sum certain in money [UCC 3–104(1)(b), 3–106, 3–107]. 5. Must be payable on demand or at a definite time [UCC 3–104(1)(c), 3–108, 3–109]. 6. Must be payable to order or bearer [UCC 3–104(1)(d), 3–110, 3–111].
Types of Indorsements	1. Blank (e.g., "Alan Luberda"). 2. Special (e.g., "Pay to Anthony Alfono. [Signed] Arthur Rabe"). 3. Qualified (e.g., "Without recourse. [Signed] Bridgett Cage"). 4. Restrictive (e.g., "Pay to Makoto Ing only. [Signed] Alan Luberda" or "For Deposit Only. [Signed] Stephanie Mallak" or "Pay to Ada Alvarez in trust for José Martinez. [Signed] Ramon Martinez").

❖ Questions and Case Problems

18-1. Article 3 of the UCC. What are the four types of commercial paper with which Article 3 of the UCC is concerned? Which of these are *orders* to pay, and which are *promises* to pay?

18-2. Parties to Negotiable Instruments. A note has two original parties. Who are they? A check has three original parties. Who are they?

18-3. Requirements of Negotiable Instruments. The following note is written by Muriel Evans on the back of an envelope: "I, Muriel Evans, promise to pay Karen Marvin or bearer $100 on demand." Is this a negotiable instrument? Discuss fully.

18-4. Requirements of Negotiable Instruments. The following instrument was written on a sheet of paper by Jeff Nolan: "I, the undersigned, do hereby acknowledge that I owe Stephanie Craig one thousand dollars, with interest, payable out of the proceeds of the sale of my horse, Swiftfoot, next month. Payment is to be made on or before six months from date." Discuss specifically why this instrument is nonnegotiable.

18-5. Indorsements. A check drawn by David for $500 is made payable to the order of Matthew and issued to Matthew. Matthew owes his landlord $500 in rent and transfers the check to his landlord with the following indorsement: "For rent paid. [Signed] Matthew." Matthew's landlord has contracted to have Juarez do some landscaping on the property. When Juarez insists on immediate payment, the landlord transfers the check to Juarez without indorsement. Later, to pay for some palm trees purchased from Green's Nursery, Juarez transfers the check with the following indorsement: "Pay to Green's Nursery, without recourse. [Signed] Juarez." Green's Nursery sends the check to its bank indorsed "For deposit only. [Signed] Green's Nursery."

(a) Classify each of these indorsements.

(b) Was the transfer from Matthew's landlord to Juarez, without indorsement, an assignment or a negotiation? Explain.

18-6. Negotiable versus Nonnegotiable Instruments. Briggs signed a note that read in part: "Ninety days after date, I, we, or either of us, promise to pay to the order of Three Thousand Four Hundred Ninety-Eight and 45/100 - - -Dollars." The words and symbols underlined in this quotation were typed, and the remainder of the words were preprinted. No blanks had been left on the face of the instrument; unused space had been filled in with hyphens. The note contained several clauses that permitted acceleration in the event the holder deemed itself insecure. When the note was not paid at maturity, Broadway Management Corp. brought suit on the note for full payment, claiming that it (Broadway) was a holder. Is this note order paper or bearer paper? What changes, if any, would have to be made on the note for it to be a negotiable instrument? [*Broadway Management Corp. v. Briggs*, 30 Ill.App.3d 403, 332 N.E.2d 131 (1975)]

18-7. Requirements for Negotiation. Dynamics Corp. and Marine Midland Bank had a long-standing agreement under which Marine Midland received checks payable to Dynamics and indorsed and deposited them into Dynamics's account. Dynamics never saw the checks. They were made out to the order of Dynamics and delivered directly to Marine Midland. Marine Midland stamped the backs of the checks with Dynamics's name and insignia and transferred them. Within the meaning of the UCC, is the act of sending checks to Marine Midland Bank a negotiation? If Marine Midland transfers the checks to other parties, is this a negotiation? [*Marine Midland Bank–New York v. Graybar Electric Co.*, 41 N.Y.2d 703, 363 N.E.2d 1139, 395 N.Y.S.2d 403 (1977)]

18-8. Undated Instruments. During a three-year period, Appliances, Inc., performed electrical heating and plumbing work for Yost Construction worth approximately $7,000. Yost never paid Appliances for any of these jobs. Yost, in both his capacity as president of the construction company and his individual capacity, signed an undated ninety-day promissory note in favor of Appliances to reduce Yost Construction's debt and to have Appliances perform services for Yost as an individual. Neither Yost in his individual capacity nor Yost Construction paid the note, and Appliances filed suit. The trial court held that the undated note was totally unenforceable. Should Appliances prevail on appeal by arguing that the note was negotiable? [*Appliances, Inc. v. Yost*, 181 Conn. 207, 435 A.2d 1 (1980)]

18-9. Bearer Instruments. Gilbert Ramirez claimed that he had purchased a winning lottery ticket, the prize for which was approximately $1.5 million. Unfortunately, Ramirez had lost the ticket itself and therefore could not claim the prize. Even though the evidence indicated that he very likely was indeed the purchaser of the winning ticket, under the state lottery rules, he could not claim the prize unless he produced the winning ticket. In a legal action brought by Ramirez against the state lottery bureau, Ramirez claimed, among other things, that the lottery ticket was a negotiable instrument because on the back of each lottery ticket were the following words: "THIS TICKET IS A BEARER INSTRUMENT SO TREAT IT AS IF IT WERE CASH." Because under UCC 3–804 the owner of a lost negotiable instrument can collect on the instrument if certain requirements are met—such as establishing proof of ownership, the terms of the instrument, and so on—Ramirez argued that he should be allowed to claim the prize if he could meet these requirements. Discuss fully whether Ramirez succeeded in his claim that the lottery ticket was a negotiable instrument. [*Ramirez v. Bureau of State Lottery*, 186 Mich.App. 275, 463 N.W.2d 245 (1990)]

18-10. Words Versus Figures. Eugene Kindy, a seller of diesel engine parts, agreed to buy four diesel engines from Tony Hicks for $13,000. Kindy transferred $6,500 by wire and issued a check for the remainder. Kindy placed two different amounts on the check because he did not want the check honored until Hicks had delivered the engine parts. Using a check-imprinting machine, Kindy imprinted $5,550 on the check in the space where the dollar amount is normally written in words, but he wrote $6,550 in figures in the box usually reserved for numbers. An employee of Galatia Community State Bank, noticing the discrepancy, altered the figures to read "$5,550," initialed the change, and accepted the check. The check was returned to Galatia by First National Bank at Kindy's request because Hicks had not delivered the engine parts. In the litigation that followed, a key issue was whether the machine-imprinted figure took precedence over the handwritten figure. What should the court decide on this issue? Discuss. [*Galatia Community State Bank v. Kindy*, 807 Ark. 467, 821 S.W.2d 765 (1991)]

A Question of Ethics and Social Responsibility

18-11. *Richard Caliendo, an accountant, prepared tax returns for various clients. To satisfy their tax liabilities, the clients issued checks payable to various state taxing entities and gave them to Caliendo. Between 1977 and 1979, Caliendo forged indorsements on these checks, deposited them in his own bank account, and subsequently withdrew the proceeds. In 1983, after learning of these events and after Caliendo's death, the state brought this action against Barclays Bank of New York, N.A., the successor to Caliendo's bank, to recover the amount of the checks. Barclays moved for dismissal on the ground that because the checks had never been delivered to the state, the state never acquired the status of holder and therefore never acquired any rights in the instruments. The trial court held for the state, but the appellate court reversed. The state then appealed the case to the state's highest court. That court ruled that the state could not recover the amount of the checks from the bank because, although it was the named payee on the checks, the checks had never been delivered to the payee.* [State v. Barclays Bank of New York, N.A., *561 N.Y.2d 533, 563 N.E.2d 11, 561 N.Y.S.2d 697 (1990)*]

1. If you were deciding this case, would you make an exception to the rule and let the state collect the funds from Barclays Bank? Why or why not? What ethical trade-offs are involved in this situation?
2. Under agency law, which will be discussed in Chapter 23, delivery to the agent of a given individual or entity constitutes delivery to that person or entity. The court deemed that Caliendo was not an agent of the state but an agent of the taxpayers. Does it matter that the taxpayers may not have known this principle of agency law and might have thought that, by delivering their checks to Caliendo, they were delivering them to the state?

For Critical Analysis

18-12. *The UCC requirements for negotiable instruments are generally strict. But in regard to what constitutes a signature on an instrument, the UCC grants extreme latitude—X marks, initials, and rubber-stamped signatures are all permitted. Given the potential for forgery of these kinds of signatures, why does the UCC permit them?*

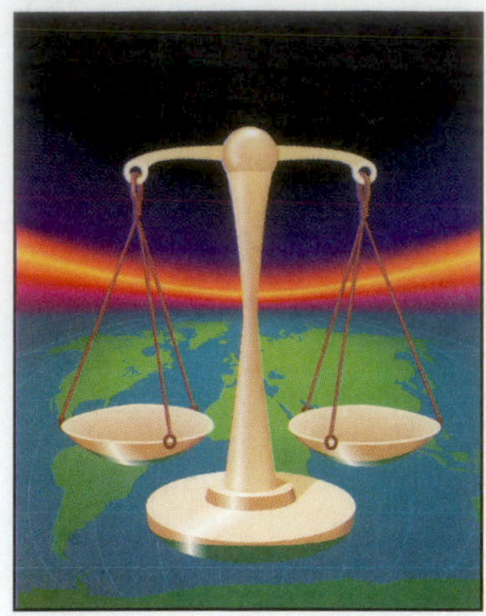

Chapter 19

Commercial Paper—Holder in Due Course, Liability, and Defenses

"However gradual may be the growth of confidence, that of credit requires still more time to arrive at maturity."

Benjamin Disraeli, 1804–1881
(Prime minister of Great Britain, 1878–1880)

Although it is used as a substitute for money, commercial paper is also, as mentioned in the last chapter, a form of credit. Any note promising to pay another creates a debtor (the one promising) and a creditor (the one to be paid). As the eminent British politician Disraeli indicated in the opening quotation, for credit to "arrive at maturity" is a long and gradual historical process. The extensive exchange of commercial paper that takes place daily in the United States is predicated, ultimately, on the existence of commercial paper law and a government capable of enforcing that law.

Issues of litigation concerning commercial paper usually turn on which party can obtain payment on an instrument when it is due or on whether a defense can be asserted to discharge or to cancel liability on an instrument. For these reasons, a person seeking payment prefers to have the rights of a *holder in due course (HDC)*—one who takes a negotiable instrument free of all claims and most defenses of other parties. The holder in due course has the right to collect payment on that instrument, and this right will take priority over the claims of other parties.

The first part of this chapter deals exclusively with the issue of the holder in due course. The chapter then discusses the liability associated with negotiable instruments. The remainder of the chapter considers the defenses available to prevent liability and, briefly, the ways in which a person can be discharged from an obligation on a negotiable instrument.

❖ Holder versus Holder in Due Course (HDC)

As pointed out in Chapter 18, the Uniform Commercial Code (UCC) defines a *holder* as a person who possesses a negotiable instrument "drawn, issued, or indorsed to him or his order or to bearer or in blank" [UCC 1–201(20)]. In other words, the holder is the person who, by the terms of the instrument, is legally entitled to payment. The holder of an instrument need not be its owner to transfer it, negotiate it, discharge it, or enforce payment of it in his or her own name [UCC 3–301].

HOLDER IN DUE COURSE (HDC)
Any holder who acquires a negotiable instrument for value; in good faith; and without notice that the instrument is overdue, that it has been dishonored, or that any defense or claim to it exists on the part of any person.

A holder has the status of an assignee of a contract right. A transferee of a negotiable instrument who is characterized merely as a holder obtains only those rights that the predecessor-transferor had in the instrument. In the event that there is a conflicting, superior claim to or defense against the instrument, an ordinary holder will not be able to collect payment.

In contrast, a **holder in due course (HDC)** is a special-status transferee of a negotiable instrument who, by meeting certain acquisition requirements, takes the instrument *free* of most defenses against or adverse claims to it. Stated another way, an HDC can normally acquire a higher level of immunity than an ordinary holder in regard to defenses against payment on the instrument or claims of ownership to the instrument by other parties.

❖ Requirements for HDC Status

The basic requirements for attaining HDC status are set forth in UCC 3–302. An HDC must first be a holder of a negotiable instrument and must take the instrument (1) for value, (2) in good faith, and (3) without notice that it is overdue, that it has been dishonored, or that any person has a defense against it or a claim to it.

The underlying requirement of "due course" status is that a person must first be a holder on that instrument. Regardless of other circumstances surrounding acquisition, only a holder has a chance to become an HDC.

Taking for Value

An HDC must have given *value* for the instrument [UCC 3–303]. A person who receives an instrument as a gift or who inherits it has not met the requirement of value. In these situations, the person becomes an ordinary holder and does not possess the rights of an HDC.[1]

The concept of *value* in the law of negotiable instruments is not the same as the concept of *consideration* in the law of contracts. An *executory promise* (a promise to give value in the future) is a clearly valid consideration to support a contract [UCC 1–201(44)]. It does not, however, normally constitute value sufficient to make one an HDC. UCC 3–303 provides that a holder takes the instrument for value only to the extent that the agreed-upon consideration has been performed. Therefore, if the holder plans to pay for the instrument later or plans to perform the required services at some future date, the holder has not yet given value. In that case, the holder is not yet a holder in due course.

Suppose Marcia Morrison draws a $500 note payable to Reinhold Niebuhr in payment for goods. Niebuhr negotiates the note to Judy Larson, who promises to pay Niebuhr for it in thirty days. During the next month, Larson learns that Niebuhr has breached the contract by delivering defective goods and that Morrison will not honor the $500 note. Niebuhr has left town. Whether Larson can hold Morrison liable on the note depends on whether Larson is a holder in due course.

Because Larson had given no value at the time that she learned of Morrison's defense (breach of contract), Larson is a mere holder, not a holder in due course. Thus, Morrison's defense is valid not only against Niebuhr but also against Larson. If Larson had paid Niebuhr for the note at the time of transfer (which would mean the agreed-upon consideration had been performed), she would be a holder in due course and could hold Morrison liable on the note even though Morrison has a valid defense against Niebuhr on the basis of breach of contract or breach of warranty. Exhibit 19–1 illustrates these concepts.

The UCC provides that a holder can take the instrument for value in one of three ways:

1. To the extent that the agreed-upon consideration has been paid or a security interest or lien acquired.
2. By taking an instrument in payment of or as security for an antecedent debt.
3. By giving a negotiable instrument or irrevocable commitment as payment.

---

1. There is one way an ordinary holder who fails to meet the value requirement can have the rights of a holder in due course. The shelter provision of the UCC allows an ordinary holder to succeed to HDC status if any prior holder was an HDC. This exception is discussed later in the chapter [UCC 3–201(1)].

◆ **Exhibit 19–1 Taking for Value**
By exchanging defective goods for the note, Niebuhr breached his contract with Morrison. Morrison could assert this defense if Niebuhr presented the note to her for payment. Niebuhr exchanged the note for Larson's promise to pay in thirty days, however. Because Larson did not take the note for value (as defined in UCC 3–303), she is not a holder in due course. Thus, Morrison can assert the defense of Niebuhr's breach against Larson when Larson submits the note to Morrison for payment. If Larson had taken the note for value, Morrison could not assert that defense and would be liable to pay the note.

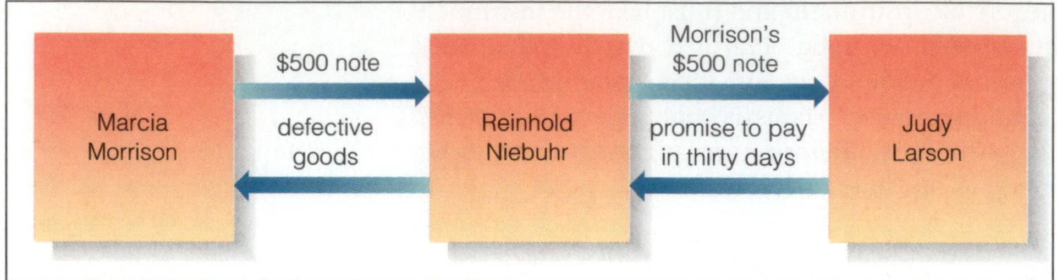

Taking in Good Faith

The second requirement for HDC status is that the holder take the instrument in *good faith* [UCC 3–302(1)(b)]. This means that the purchaser-holder must have acted honestly in the process of acquiring the instrument. As discussed earlier in this text, the UCC defines *good faith* as "honesty in fact in the conduct or transaction concerned."[2] The good faith requirement *applies only to the holder*. It is immaterial whether the transferor acted in good faith. Thus, a person who in good faith takes a negotiable instrument from a thief may become an HDC.

Because of the good faith requirement, one must ask whether the purchaser, when acquiring the instrument, honestly believed that the instrument was not defective. If a person purchases a $10,000 note for $100 from a stranger on a street corner, the issue of good faith can be raised on the grounds of the suspicious circumstances *as well as* the grossly inadequate consideration. The UCC does not provide clear guidelines to determine good faith, so each situation must be examined separately.

Taking without Notice

The third requirement for HDC status involves *notice* [UCC 3–304]. A person will not be afforded HDC protection if he or she acquires an instrument knowing, or having reason to know, that it is defective in any one of the following ways [UCC 3–302(1)(c)]:

1. It has been dishonored.
2. There is a claim to or a defense against it.
3. It is overdue.

What Constitutes Notice? The main provisions of UCC 3–304 spell out the common circumstances that, as a matter of law, constitute notice of a claim or defense and notice of an overdue instrument. Notice of a defective instrument is given whenever the holder has (1) actual knowledge of the defect, (2) receipt of a notice

2. Under the revised Article 3 (described in Chapter 18), good faith is defined as "honesty in fact and the observance of reasonable commercial standards of fair dealing" [RUCC 3–103(a)(4)].

about a defect, or (3) reason to know that a defect exists, given all the facts and circumstances known at the time in question. UCC 3–304(4) specifies, however, that certain facts that a purchaser might know about an instrument do not constitute notice that the instrument is defective.

Overdue Instruments Any negotiable instrument is either payable at a definite time (*a time instrument*) or payable on demand (*a demand instrument*). What constitutes notice that an instrument is overdue will vary depending on whether it is a time or a demand instrument.

Time Instruments A holder of a time instrument who takes the paper the day after its expressed due date is *on notice* that it is overdue. Nonpayment by the due date should indicate to any purchaser who is obligated to pay that the primary party has a defense to payment. Thus, a promissory note due on May 15 must be acquired before midnight on May 15. If it is purchased on May 16, the purchaser will be an ordinary holder, not an HDC. Sometimes instruments read, "Payable in thirty days." A note dated December 1 that is payable in thirty days is due by midnight on December 31. If the payment date falls on a Sunday or holiday, the instrument is payable on the next business day.

In the case of an installment note, notice that the maker has defaulted on any installment of principal (but not interest) payments will prevent a purchaser from becoming an HDC [UCC 3–304(3)(a)]. Also, when a series of notes, each with successive maturity dates, is issued at the same time for a single indebtedness, a default on any one note of the series will constitute overdue notice for the entire series. In this way, prospective purchasers know that they cannot qualify as HDCs.

Suppose that a note reads, "Payable May 15, but may be accelerated if the holder feels insecure." A purchaser, unaware that a prior holder has elected to accelerate the due date on the instrument, buys the instrument before May 15. UCC 3–304(3)(b) provides that such a purchaser can be an HDC unless he or she has reason to know that the acceleration has occurred.

Demand Instruments A purchaser has notice that a demand instrument is overdue if he or she takes the instrument knowing that demand has been made or takes it an unreasonable length of time after its issue. "A reasonable time for a check drawn and payable within the states and territories of the United States and the District of Columbia is *presumed* to be 30 days" (emphasis added) [UCC 3–304(3)(c)].[3]

Payee as HDC

Under certain circumstances, a payee may qualify as an HDC; the payee must exercise good faith, give value, and take the instrument without notice of a defense against it or claim to it [UCC 3–302(2)].

To illustrate, Manfred Rubens is an attorney for Don Adams. Rubens recently had minor outpatient surgery performed by Dr. Paulson in his office, and owes Dr. Paulson $500. Rubens has agreed to draft a land-sale contract for Adams next week, on the condition that Adams issue a check payable to Dr. Paulson for $500. Adams sends the check to Dr. Paulson with a note: "In payment of medical services rendered to Manfred Rubens." Rubens leaves town and never performs the legal services for Adams. Adams stops payment on the check. Can Dr. Paulson enforce payment as an HDC? The answer is yes. Dr. Paulson gave value (medical services), took the check in good faith, and took it without notice of dishonor, defense, or claim or notice that the check was overdue.

3. The revised Article 3 extends the thirty-day period to "90 days after its date" [RUCC 3–304(a)(2)].

Business Law in Action

Imposters and Impersonation: A Closer Look

If someone asked you to define the word *impersonate,* you would probably respond with one or more of the definitions commonly found in a dictionary, such as "play the part of," "personify," or "embody." On closer questioning, you might conclude, as others have, that impersonation has to be "in person." That is, to be an impersonator, or an "imposter," one must actually "play the part of another," whether over the phone or in a face-to-face encounter. For most of us, how the term is defined is of little significance. For banks, though, it may be a different story. In a recent case, for example, whether a defendant bank could be held liable for payment of a $25,000 check over a forged indorsement hinged on how the court defined the word *impersonate.*

The alleged impersonation took place totally via the telephone and the mails. Edward Bauerband contacted Minster State Bank by phone and requested a $25,000 loan, purportedly on behalf of himself and his wife, Michelle. The Bauerbands had a long-standing relationship with the bank, and the request was not so unusual as to put the bank on notice. The bank mailed a promissory note to Edward to be signed by both him and his wife. Edward forged his wife's signature on the note, signed it himself, and returned the note and other loan documents to the bank. On its receipt of the documents, the bank issued a cashier's check in the amount of $25,000, payable to Edward and Michelle jointly, and mailed the check to the Bauerbands' home. Edward indorsed the check in his name, forged his wife's indorsement, and deposited the check in his business account at another bank, Baybank Middlesex. Michelle knew nothing about the loan transaction or the check.

Ultimately, the forgery was discovered, and Minster State Bank sued Baybank Middlesex to recover the funds. Baybank contended that it was precluded from liability under the "imposter rule" of UCC 3–405(1)(a). That section provides that an indorsement made "by any person in the name of a named payee" will be considered effective if "an imposter by use of the mails or otherwise has induced the maker or drawer to issue the instrument to him or his confederate in the name of the payee." Minster argued that no impersonation had taken place because Edward never "impersonated" Michelle on the phone, nor did he impersonate Michelle at the bank—indeed, he had never appeared at the bank in person during the course of the transaction. In Minster's view, "this case entails nothing more than an ordinary forged endorsement."

To be an imposter, one must somehow "impersonate" another. But had Edward really impersonated his wife, Michelle? This brings us back to the question of whether impersonation has to be "in person." Minster pointed to several other cases involving similar husband-and-wife swindles in which the courts had held that the imposter rule did not apply because no "actual impersonation" of the wife had occurred. The court in this case viewed the matter otherwise. It stated that UCC 3–405(1)(a), by including the phrase "by use of the mails or otherwise," made it clear that impersonation need not occur in person. The court also cited the official comment to UCC 3–405(1)(a), which states that this section "rejects decisions which distinguish between face-to-face imposture and imposture by mail." According to the court, the "essential flaw" in Minster's position was that Minster equated the "absence of a physical imposter with a lack of the kind of impersonation cognizable under the 'imposter rule.' " The court held that Edward had impersonated his wife and the imposter rule therefore applied: Baybank was not liable for paying the check over the forged indorsement.[a]

No doubt, Minster State Bank is still puzzling over this definition of the word *impersonate.* No doubt, others are, too.

a. *Minster State Bank v. Bauerband,* 1992 Mass.App.Div. 61 (1992).

❖ Holder through an HDC

A person who does not qualify as an HDC but who derives his or her title through an HDC can acquire the rights and privileges of an HDC. According to UCC 3–201(1)

> Transfer of an instrument vests in the transferee such rights as the transferor has therein, except that a transferee who has himself been a party to any fraud or illegality affecting the instrument or who as a prior holder had notice of a defense or claim against it cannot improve his position by taking from a later holder in due course.

This rule, sometimes called the **shelter principle,** seems counter to the basic HDC philosophy. It is, however, in line with the concept of marketability and free transferability of commercial paper, as well as with contract law, which provides that assignees acquire the rights of assignors. The shelter principle extends the HDC benefits, and it is designed to aid the HDC in readily disposing of the instrument.

SHELTER PRINCIPLE
The principle that the holder of a negotiable instrument who cannot qualify as a holder in due course (HDC), but who derives his or her title through an HDC, acquires the rights of an HDC.

Anyone, no matter how far removed from an HDC, who can trace his or her title ultimately back to an HDC comes within the shelter principle. Normally, a person who acquires an instrument from an HDC or from someone with HDC rights receives HDC rights on the principle that the transferee of an instrument receives at least the rights that the transferor had.

There are, however, limitations on the shelter principle. UCC 3–201(1) explicitly indicates that certain persons who formerly held instruments cannot improve their positions by later reacquiring them from HDCs. Thus, if a holder was a party to fraud or illegality affecting the instrument or if, as a prior holder, he or she had notice of a claim or defense against an instrument, that holder is not allowed to improve his or her status by repurchasing from a later HDC. In other words, a person is not allowed to "launder" the paper by passing it into the hands of an HDC and then buying it back.

Suppose Barry and Sheila collaborate to defraud Helen. Helen is induced to give Sheila a negotiable note payable to Sheila's order. Sheila then specially indorses the note for value to Joseph, an HDC. Barry and Sheila split the proceeds. Joseph negotiates the note to Paul, another HDC. Paul then negotiates the note for value to Barry. Barry, even though he got the note through an HDC, is not a holder through an HDC, for he participated in the original fraud and can never acquire HDC rights in this note.

❖ Signature Liability of Parties to Commercial Paper

The key to liability on a negotiable instrument is a *signature,* which is defined in UCC 3–401(2) as "any name, including any trade or assumed name, upon an instrument, or * * * any word or mark used in lieu of a written signature." A signature can be handwritten, typed, or printed; or it can be made by mark, by thumbprint, or in virtually any other manner. According to UCC 1–201(39), "signed" means any symbol executed or adopted by a party with the "present intention to authenticate a writing."

"Most men are admirers of justice—when justice happens to be on their side."

Richard Whately, 1787–1863
(English theologian and logician)

The requirement of a signature has its origin in the Law Merchant (discussed in Chapter 18) and is based simply on the need to know whose obligation the instrument represents. The critical element with any signature is a "present intention to authenticate a writing." Parol evidence can be used to identify the signer, and once that person is identified, the signature is effective against him or her no matter how it is made. UCC 3–401(1) states the general rule: "No person is liable on an instrument unless his [or her] signature appears thereon." The following sections discuss the types of signature liability that exist in relation to negotiable instruments and the conditions that must be met before this liability can arise.

Primary and Secondary Liability

Every party, except a qualified indorser,[4] who signs a negotiable instrument is either primarily or secondarily liable for payment of that instrument when it comes due.

4. A qualified indorser—one who indorses "without recourse"—undertakes no contractual obligation to pay. A qualified indorser merely assumes warranty liability, which is discussed later in this chapter.

Primary Liability A person who is primarily liable on a negotiable instrument is absolutely required to pay the instrument, subject to certain defenses [UCC 3–305]. Primary liability is unconditional. The primary party's liability is immediate when the instrument becomes due. No action by the holder of the instrument is required. Only *makers* and *acceptors* are primarily liable [UCC 3–413(1)]. (Recall from Chapter 18 that one who signs a promissory note is called a *maker,* whereas one who signs a check or draft is referred to as a *drawer.*)

The maker of a promissory note promises to pay the note. It is the maker's promise to pay that makes the note a negotiable instrument. The words "I promise to pay" embody the maker's obligation to pay the instrument according to the terms as written at the time of the signing. If the instrument is incomplete when the maker signs it, then the maker's obligation is to pay it to a holder in due course according to the terms written when it is completed [UCC 3–413(1) and 3–115].

A maker guarantees that certain facts are true by signing a promissory note. In particular, UCC 3–413(3) specifies that a maker admits to all subsequent parties that the payee in fact exists and that the payee has current capacity to indorse the note (for example, that the payee is not a minor at the time the note is signed).

The drawee-acceptor of a draft or check is in virtually the same position as the maker of a promissory note [UCC 3–413(1), (3)]. A drawee's acceptance of a draft, which it makes by signing the draft, guarantees that the drawee will pay the draft when it is presented later for payment. When the drawee accepts the draft, the drawee becomes an **acceptor** and is primarily liable to all subsequent holders. A drawee that refuses to accept such a draft has dishonored the instrument.

ACCEPTOR
A drawee who accepts a draft and who engages to be primarily responsible for its payment.

There are three situations under which a holder must present the instrument to a drawee for acceptance:

1. When the instrument requires such presentation (as with trade acceptances, discussed in Chapter 18).
2. When the draft is to be payable at an address different from that of the drawee.
3. When the draft's payment date is dependent on such presentment [UCC 3–501(1)(a)]—for example, when the draft is payable thirty days after acceptance or sight.

A check is a special type of draft that is drawn on a bank and is payable on demand. Acceptance of a check is called *certification* (discussed in Chapter 20). Certification is not necessary on checks, and a bank is under no obligation to certify. Upon certification, however, the drawee bank occupies the position of an acceptor and is primarily liable on the check to holders [UCC 3–411].

Secondary Liability Secondary liability on a negotiable instrument is similar to that of a guarantor in a simple contract (described in Chapter 12). Drawers and indorsers have secondary liability. Secondary liability is *contingent liability.* In the case of notes, an indorser's secondary liability does not arise until the maker, who is primarily liable, has defaulted on the instrument [UCC 3–413(1) and 3–414]. With regard to drafts and checks, a drawer's secondary liability does not arise until the drawee fails to pay or to accept the instrument, whichever is required.

Dishonor of an instrument triggers the liability of parties who are secondarily liable on the instrument—that is, the drawer and unqualified indorsers. Parties who are secondarily liable on a negotiable instrument promise to pay on that instrument only if the following events occur:

1. The instrument is properly and timely presented.
2. The instrument is dishonored.
3. Timely notice of dishonor is given to the secondarily liable party.

These requirements are necessary for a secondarily liable party to have signature liability on a negotiable instrument, but they are not necessary for a secondarily liable party to have warranty liability (to be discussed later) [UCC 3–414, 3–501, and 3–502].[5]

UCC 3–413(2) provides that "upon dishonor of the draft and any necessary notice of dishonor * * * [the drawer] will pay the amount of the draft to the holder or to any indorser who takes it up." For example, Nina Lee writes a check on her account at Universal Bank payable to the order of Stephen Miller. If Universal Bank does not pay the check when Miller presents it for payment, then Nina is liable to Stephen on the basis of her secondary liability. Drawers are secondarily liable on drafts unless they disclaim their liability by drawing the instruments "without recourse" [UCC 3–413(2)].

Because drawers are secondarily liable, their liability does not arise until presentment and notice of dishonor have been made *properly* and in a *timely* way. If a draft (or check) is payable at a bank, improper presentment or notice relieves the drawer from secondary liability only when the drawee bank is insolvent.

An unqualified indorser promises that in the event of presentment, dishonor, and notice of dishonor, the indorser will pay the instrument. Thus, the liability of an indorser is much like that of a drawer, with one major exception: indorsers are relieved of their contractual liability to the holder of the instrument by (1) improper (late) presentment or (2) late notice or failure to notify of dishonor [UCC 3–414, 3–501, and 3–502].

Proper Presentment The UCC spells out what constitutes a proper presentment. Basically, presentment by a holder must be made to the proper person, must be made in a proper manner, and must be timely [UCC 3–503 and 3–504].

The party to whom the instrument must be presented depends on what type of instrument is involved. A note or certificate of deposit (CD) must be presented to the maker for payment. A draft is presented by the holder to the drawee for acceptance or payment, or both, whichever is required. A check is presented to the drawee for payment [UCC 3–504].

Presentment also depends on the type of instrument involved [UCC 3–504(2)]. Presentment can be properly made in any one of the following three ways:

1. By mail (but presentment is not effective until receipt of the mail).
2. Through a clearinghouse procedure used by banks, such as for deposited checks.
3. At the place specified in the instrument for acceptance or payment—or if the instrument is silent as to place, at the place of business or the residence of the person required to accept or pay.

One of the most crucial criteria for proper presentment is timeliness [UCC 3–503]. Failure to present on time is the most prevalent reason for improper presentment and consequent discharge of unqualified indorsers from secondary liability. See Exhibit 19–2, bearing in mind that its contents are oversimplified.

Proper Notice Once an instrument has been dishonored, proper notice must be given for secondary parties to be held liable. The rules of proper notice are basically as follows [UCC 3–508]:

1. Notice operates for the benefit of all parties who have rights on an instrument against the party notified [UCC 3–508(8)]. For example, assume that there are four indorsers on a note that its maker dishonors, and the holder gives timely notice to

5. An instrument can be drafted to provide a waiver of the presentment, dishonor, and notice of dishonor requirements. Presume for simplicity's sake that such waivers have not been incorporated into the instruments described in this chapter.

◆ **Exhibit 19–2 Time for Proper Presentment [UCC 3–503]**

TYPE OF INSTRUMENT	FOR ACCEPTANCE	FOR PAYMENT
Time	On or before due date	On due date
Demand	Within a reasonable time (after date or issue or after secondary party becomes liable thereon)	
Check (domestic)	Not applicable	Presumed to be:[a] Within thirty days (of date or issue, whichever is later) to hold drawer secondarily liable; Within seven days (of indorsement) to hold indorser secondarily liable

a. In the case of a domestic, uncertified check, these are the time periods within which to present for payment or to initiate the check-collection process.

indorsers one and four. If the holder collects payment from indorser four, indorser four does not have to give notice to indorser one again to collect from indorser one. It is important to remember that if more than one indorsement appears on an instrument, each indorser is liable for the full amount to any later indorser or to any holder.

2. Except for dishonor of foreign drafts, notice may be given in any reasonable manner. This includes oral or written notice and notice written or stamped on the instrument itself [UCC 3–508(3)]. To give notice of dishonor of a foreign draft (a draft drawn in one country and payable in another country), a formal notice called a *protest* is required [UCC 3–509].

3. Any necessary notice must be given by a bank before its midnight deadline (midnight of the next banking day after receipt) [UCC 4–104(1)(h)]. Notice by any party other than a bank must be given before midnight of the third business day after either dishonor or receipt of notice of dishonor [UCC 3–508(2)]. Written notice is effective when transmitted or sent, even though it is never received.

4. Notice to a partner is notice to a partnership. Similarly, when a party is deceased, incompetent, or bankrupt, notice may be given to that party's representative [UCC 3–508(6) and (7)].

Accommodation Parties

ACCOMMODATION PARTY
A person who signs an instrument for the purpose of lending his or her credit to another party on the instrument.

An **accommodation party** is one who signs an instrument for the purpose of lending his or her name as credit to another party on the instrument [UCC 3–415(1)]. Accommodation parties are one form of security against nonpayment on a negotiable instrument. For example, a bank about to lend money, a seller taking a large order for goods, or a creditor about to extend credit to a prospective debtor all want some reasonable assurance that the debts will be paid. A party's uncertain financial condition or the fact that the parties to a transaction are complete strangers can make a creditor reluctant to rely solely on the prospective debtor's ability to pay. To reduce the risk of nonpayment, the creditor can require the joining of a third person as an accommodation party on the instrument.

If the accommodation party signs on behalf of the *maker,* he or she is an *accommodation maker* and is primarily liable on the instrument. If the accommodation party signs on behalf of a *payee or other holder* (usually to make the instrument more marketable), he or she is an *accommodation indorser* and is secondarily liable.

AGENT
A person authorized by another to act for or in place of him or her.

PRINCIPAL
In agency law, a person who, by agreement or otherwise, authorizes an agent to act on his or her behalf in such a way that the acts of the agent become binding on the principal.

Agents' Signatures

The general law of agency, covered in Chapter 23, applies to negotiable instruments. An **agent** is a person who agrees to represent or act for another, called the **principal.**

Agents can sign negotiable instruments and thereby bind their principals [UCC 3–403(1)]. Without such a rule, all corporate commercial business would stop—as every corporation can and must act through its agents.

Generally, an authorized agent does not bind a principal on an instrument unless the agent *clearly names* the principal in his or her signature (by writing, mark, or some symbol). The agent may or may not add his or her own name.[6]

For example, any of the following signatures by Collingsworth as agent for Peterson would bind Peterson on the instrument:

1. Peterson, by Collingsworth, agent.
2. Peterson.
3. Peterson, Collingsworth. (This signature would bind Peterson only by parol evidence, as will be discussed shortly.)

If the authorized agent (Collingsworth, in this case) signed just his or her own name, however, the principal would not be bound on the instrument. The agent would be personally liable. In these situations, form prevails over intent. Under UCC 3–403(2)(a), this holds true even when the parties know of the agency relationship. In addition, the parol evidence rule (discussed in Chapter 11) precludes the introduction of extrinsic evidence to establish that the signature was made for a principal.

Under UCC 3–403(2)(b), two other situations in which an agent is held personally liable on a negotiable instrument can arise. If the instrument is signed in both the agent's name and the principal's name—"John Collingsworth, Bob Peterson" or "Peterson, Collingsworth"—but nothing on the instrument indicates the agency relationship (so the agent cannot be distinguished from the principal), the signature binds the agent (and it can also bind the principal). Because inclusion of both the agent's and the principal's names without an indication of their relationship is ambiguous, parol evidence is admissible *as between the original parties* (between the agent signing the instrument and the payee of the instrument) to prove the agency relationship.

Also, when an agent indicates agency status in signing a negotiable instrument but fails to name the principal (for example, "John Collingsworth, agent"), the agent is personally liable to any subsequent holder, and the unnamed principal cannot be held liable on the instrument. But because the indication of agency status in these cases is ambiguous, parol evidence is admissible *as between the original parties* (for example, the drawer and payee of a check) to prove the agency relationship and to establish the liability of the unnamed principal [UCC 3–403(2)(b)].[7]

When a negotiable instrument is signed in the name of an organization, and the organization's name is preceded or followed by the name and office of an authorized individual, the organization is bound; the individual who has signed the instrument in the representative capacity is not bound [UCC 3–403(3)].[8]

If the agent had no authority to sign the principal's name, the "unauthorized signature is wholly inoperative as that of the person whose name is signed" [UCC 3–404(1)]. Assume that Maria Ortega is the principal and Justin Cohen is her agent. Cohen, without authority, signs a promissory note as follows: "Maria Ortega, by

---

6. If the agent signs the principal's name, the UCC presumes that the signature is authorized and genuine [UCC 3–307(1)(b)].

7. Under the revised Article 3, the personal liability of the agent is the same as under the present UCC when a holder in due course is involved. For others, however, the agent can escape liability if the agent can prove that the original parties did not intend the agent to be liable on the instrument [RUCC 3–402(b)(2)].

8. Under the revised Article 3, if an organization requires more than one signature on a check, the signature of the organization is considered unauthorized if one of the required signatures is lacking [RUCC 3–403(b)].

Law in the Extreme

Hot Dog Bun, Anyone?

Business ventures can be risky, as every businessperson knows—including Fred Dowie. Dowie was the president and sole stockholder of Fred Dowie Enterprises, Inc., a catering corporation in Des Moines, Iowa. Dowie thought that he had been presented with a golden opportunity to make profits when he learned that the Pope would be visiting the Living History Farms in Des Moines, Iowa, in 1979. Dowie made arrangements to operate concession stands at the site and, with high expectations, purchased 325,000 hot dog buns from the Colonial Baking Company. Dowie paid for the buns with a postdated corporate check, which was imprinted with his corporation's name, in the amount of $28,640. Unfortunately for Dowie, his expectations were not realized. For whatever reasons, those coming to see the Pope were not eager to purchase hot dogs. In all, Dowie sold only about 300 of the buns purchased from Colonial.

Colonial Baking apparently was not interested in taking back the buns, and a dispute arose between Dowie and the baking company, culminating in Dowie's order to his bank to stop payment on his check. Colonial Baking then brought suit against Dowie personally for payment on the check. Dowie claimed that he was not personally liable on the check because he had signed in a representative capacity, as the president of his corporation. Dowie contended that the check was imprinted with the name of his corporation and this was sufficient to indicate that he had signed in a representative capacity and did not intend to assume personal liability for the check. The court looked to the UCC, specifically UCC 3–403 and case law interpreting that provision. The court held that because Dowie did not indicate on the check that he was signing in a representative capacity, he was personally liable on the check he gave to Colonial. In the end, Dowie had to pay for over 324,000 unused hot dog buns![a]

a. *Colonial Baking Co. of Des Moines v. Dowie,* 330 N.W.2d 279 (Iowa 1983).

Justin Cohen, agent." Because Maria Ortega's "signature" is unauthorized, she cannot be held liable on the note, but Cohen is liable. This would be true even if Cohen had merely signed the note "Maria Ortega," without indicating any agency. In either case, the unauthorized signer, Cohen, is liable on the instrument.

Unauthorized Signatures

People are not normally liable to pay on negotiable instruments unless their signatures appear on the instruments. Hence, an unauthorized signature is wholly inoperative and will not bind the person whose name is forged.[9] Assume, for example, that Parra finds Dolby's checkbook lying on the street, writes out a check to himself, and forges Dolby's signature. If a bank fails to ascertain that Dolby's signature is not genuine and cashes the check for Parra, the bank will generally be

9. In contrast, a drawee is charged with knowledge of the drawer's signature. The drawee cannot recover money it pays out to a holder in due course on a negotiable instrument bearing a forged drawer's signature. See UCC 3–418.

liable to Dolby for the amount. (The liability of banks for paying over forged signatures is discussed further in Chapter 20.) There are two exceptions to this rule:

1. Any unauthorized signature is wholly inoperative unless the person whose name is signed ratifies (affirms) it or is precluded from denying it [UCC 3–404(1)]. For example, Richard Eutsler was held to have ratified his brother's forgery of Richard's signature on checks cashed at a bank when Richard asked the bank not to prosecute, entered into a repayment agreement with his brother, and did not sue the bank until his brother disappeared six months later.[10] Moreover, a person who writes and signs a check, leaving blank the amount and the name of the payee, and who then leaves the check in a place available to the public can be estopped (prevented), on the basis of negligence, from denying liability for its payment [UCC 3–115, 3–406, and 4–401(2)(b)].
2. An unauthorized signature operates as the signature of the unauthorized signer in favor of an HDC. For example, a person who forges a check can be held personally liable by an HDC [UCC 3–404 and 3–401(2)].

In the following case, an employee, without authorization, indorsed checks payable to his employer and deposited them into his personal bank account. The question before the court is whether the employer's negligence should preclude liability on the part of the banks for paying the checks over an unauthorized indorsement.

Case 19.1
HUSKER NEWS CO. v. SOUTH OTTUMWA SAVINGS BANK
Supreme Court of Iowa, 1992.
482 N.W.2d 404.

HISTORICAL AND SOCIAL SETTING *In a case decided in England at the beginning of the nineteenth century, the court held that a drawer who draws an instrument so negligently as to facilitate its material alteration is liable to a drawee who pays the altered instrument in good faith.*[a] *Although this rule was not part of the Uniform Negotiable Instruments Law of 1896, the drafters of the UCC incorporated it into UCC 3–406. In Comment 7 to UCC 3–406, the drafters point out that "the section applies the same rule to negligence which contributes to a forgery or other unauthorized signature." The drafters also note that "no attempt is made to specify what is negligence, and the question is one for the court or the jury [to decide based] on the facts of the particular case."*

FACTS Husker News Company, a wholesale distributor of magazines and books, employed Walter Hopf to deliver magazines and books to retail stores. Hopf's duties included delivering the magazines to Husker's customers, returning magazines not sold by the customers to Husker for credit on the customers' accounts, delivering bills to Husker's customers, and collecting payments on those bills. Husker allowed Hopf to deposit customers' cash payments into his personal bank account and to reimburse Husker for the cash deposited with personal checks written by Hopf. All checks received by Hopf, however, from his customers on their accounts were to be delivered by Hopf to Husker. Hopf developed elaborate plots to appropriate funds from his customers' accounts. Among other things, he deposited checks payable to Husker into his personal account. Hopf indorsed the checks "Husker News by Walter Hopf" and told the teller at his bank that he was authorized to indorse the checks. The bank then stamped "P.E.G." (prior endorsement guaranteed) onto the checks, which meant that the bank assumed responsibility for the validity of the checks' indorsements. Between 1982 and 1988, several customers notified Husker of possible wrongdoings by Hopf, but Husker never did anything about it. Finally, in 1988, Husker fired Hopf. Husker then sued the customers' banks that had paid on the checks over Hopf's unauthorized indorsements to recover the funds. The trial court found for the defendant banks. Husker appealed.

a. *Young v. Grote*, 4 Bingham's C.P. Rep. 253 (1827).

ISSUE Can Husker recover the funds misappropriated by Hopf on the ground that Hopf's indorsement was unauthorized?

DECISION No. The Supreme Court of Iowa held that Husker, because of its negligence, was precluded from denying Hopf's authority to indorse the checks.

10. *Eutsler v. First National Bank, Pawhuska*, 639 P.2d 1245 (Okla. 1982).

Case 19.1—Continued

REASON The court noted that Husker was "correct in asserting that an unauthorized signature generally will prevent subsequent takers of an instrument from being holders, and therefore holders in due course. This is because a forger's signature does not constitute an endorsement, a requirement to qualify as a holder in due course." But the court noted that under UCC 3–406, a person whose negligence substantially contributed to the making of an unauthorized signature is "precluded from asserting the * * * lack of authority * * * against a drawee or other payor who pays the instrument in good faith and in accordance with the reasonable commercial standards of the drawee's or the payor's business." Hopf had worked for Husker for twenty years, and during that period of time, Husker had never inspected Hopf's checking account or audited Hopf's customer accounts, in spite of customer complaints that Hopf was "manipulating the records of Husker's credits with its customers." The court found that "these matters clearly amounted to negligence on Husker's part which substantially contributed to Hopf's false signatures on the checks." According to the court, the banks had acted in good faith in accepting the checks indorsed by Hopf. Hopf had told the teller at his bank that he was authorized to indorse the checks. "The evidence was that there was no practical way to check further, and it was therefore necessary to rely on the P.E.G. stamp. The procedure was eminently reasonable in view of the obvious fact that Husker acquiesced in [went along with] it for a period of years."

ETHICAL CONSIDERATIONS *Did the customers serviced by Hopf have an obligation to do more to prevent Hopf's misconduct? The law does not recognize a Good Samaritan obligation to prevent the perpetration of a tort by another on a third party. The general common law rule is that a person has no duty to prevent a third party from causing harm to another. Thus, there is no legal reason to impose a duty on an outsider to protect an employer from its own employee. It might be argued, however, that the customers had an ethical duty to monitor Hopf, once they suspected misconduct, to prevent as much of his wrongdoing as arose from their dealings with him.*

Special Rules for Unauthorized Indorsements

Generally, when there is a forged or unauthorized indorsement, the burden of loss falls on the first party to take the instrument with the forged indorsement. Two situations are possible, however, in which the loss falls on the maker or drawer:

1. When an imposter induces the maker or drawer of an instrument to issue it to the imposter.
2. When a person signs as or on behalf of a maker or drawer, intending that the payee will have no interest in the instrument, or when an agent or employee of the maker or drawer has supplied him or her with the name of the payee, also *intending* the payee to have no such interest [UCC 3–405(1)]. Such a situation often involves an employee who wishes to swindle an employer by padding bills or payrolls.

"Life is unfair."

Milton Friedman, 1912–
(American economist)

Imposters An **imposter** is one who, by use of the mails, telephone, or personal appearance, induces a maker or drawer to issue an instrument in the name of an impersonated payee. If the maker or drawer believes the imposter to be the named payee at the time of issue, the indorsement by the imposter is not treated as unauthorized when the instrument is transferred to an innocent party. This is because the maker or drawer *intended* the imposter to receive the instrument.

IMPOSTER
One who, with the intent to deceive, pretends to be somebody else.

In these situations, the unauthorized indorsement of a payee's name can be as effective as if the real payee had signed. The *imposter rule* of UCC 3–405 provides that an imposter's indorsement will be effective—that is, not considered a forgery—insofar as the drawer goes.

For example, a man walks into Harry Marsh's paint store and purports to be Jerry Lewis soliciting contributions for his annual fund-raising for muscular dystrophy. Marsh has heard of the Lewis Telethon but has never met or seen Jerry Lewis. Wishing to support a worthy cause, Marsh writes out a check for $250 payable to Jerry Lewis and hands it to the imposter. The imposter forges the signature of Jerry Lewis and negotiates the check to a Stop and Shop convenience store. Marsh discovers the fraud and stops payment on the check, claiming that the payee's signature is forged. Because the imposter rule is in effect, Marsh cannot claim a forgery against Stop and Shop but must seek redress from the imposter instead. If Marsh had sent the check to the real Jerry Lewis, but the check had been stolen and negotiated to the store by a forged indorsement, the imposter rule would not apply, and Stop and Shop would have to seek redress against the forger.

Fictitious Payees The so-called **fictitious payee** rule deals with the intent of the maker or drawer to issue an instrument to a payee who has *no interest* in the instrument. This most often takes place when (1) a dishonest employee deceives the employer into signing an instrument payable to a party with no right to receive the instrument or (2) a dishonest employee or agent has the authority to issue an instrument on behalf of the employer. In these situations, the payee's indorsement is not treated as a forgery, and the employer can be held liable on the instrument by an innocent holder.

FICTITIOUS PAYEE
A payee on a negotiable instrument whom the maker or drawer does not intend to have an interest in the instrument. Indorsements by fictitious payees are not forgeries under negotiable instruments law.

Assume that Flair Industries, Inc., gives its bookkeeper, Axel Ford, general authority to issue checks in the company name drawn on First State Bank so that Ford can pay employees' wages and other corporate bills. Ford decides to cheat Flair Industries out of $10,000 by issuing a check payable to Erica Nied, an old acquaintance of his. Neither Flair nor Ford intends Nied to receive any of the money, and Nied is not an employee or creditor of the company. Ford indorses the check in Nied's name, naming himself as indorsee. He then cashes the check with a local bank, which collects payment from the drawee bank, First State Bank. First State Bank charges Flair Industries' account $10,000. Flair Industries discovers the fraud and demands that the account be recredited.

Who bears the loss? The rule of UCC 3–405 provides the answer. Neither the local bank that first accepted the check nor First State Bank is liable. Because Ford's indorsement in the name of a payee with no interest in the instrument is "effective," there is no "forgery." Hence, the collecting bank is protected in paying on the check, and the drawee bank is protected in charging Flair's account. It is the employer-drawer, Flair Industries, that bears the loss.[11] Whether a dishonest employee actually signs the check or merely supplies his or her employer with names of fictitious creditors (or with true names of creditors having fictitious debts), the UCC makes no distinction in result. Assume that Nathan Knudson draws up the payroll list from which employees' salary checks are written. He fraudulently adds the name Sally Slight (a fictitious person) to the payroll, thus causing checks to be issued to her. Again, it is the employer-drawer who bears the loss.

In the following case, the court must determine whether a bank should bear the loss for forged indorsements on checks payable to fictitious payees.

Case 19.2

RETAIL SHOE HEALTH COMMISSION v. MANUFACTURERS HANOVER TRUST CO.

Supreme Court of New York, Appellate Division, First Department, 1990.
160 A.D.2d 47,
558 N.Y.S.2d 949.

HISTORICAL AND SOCIAL SETTING *The drafters of the UCC based UCC 3–405 on Section 9(3) of the Uniform Negotiable Instruments Law of 1896. They enlarged the original subsection, however, to include situations that it had not originally been held to cover. UCC 3–405(1)(c) was new. The section was added to extend the original subsection to include padded payroll cases. In a padded payroll case, the drawer's employee, for example, prepares a check for signing in the name of a fictitious payee. When the employee later indorses the check in the name of the payee, the employee commits forgery. Under the basic indorsement rules, the drawer would be able to obtain a recredit from its bank on the ground that the check had been paid over a forged indorsement. Under UCC 3–405(1)(c), however, the drawer must accept the forged indorsement*

11. *May Department Stores Co. v. Pittsburgh National Bank,* 374 F.2d 109 (3d Cir. 1967).

Case 19.2—Continued

as valid. Thus, a drawer cannot use the basic forgery rules to shift padded payroll losses to its bank.

FACTS Jerome Simon was the administrator of the Retail Shoe Health Commission, a jointly administered employee welfare fund ("the Fund"). Simon, who was an authorized signatory to the Fund's checking account at Manufacturers Hanover Trust Company, over a period of eight years embezzled approximately $675,000 from the Fund by preparing duplicate vouchers and signing checks payable to fictitious payees for medical benefit claims submitted by the Fund's beneficiaries. Simon then indorsed the fictitious payees' names on the backs of the checks and deposited the checks primarily into a bank account at Bankers Trust Company. Simon's scheme was not discovered until after his death, when various discrepancies in check vouchers surfaced. After discovering the embezzlement, the Fund's insurer sued Manufacturers Hanover and Bankers Trust to recover the full amount of the checks on the ground of forged indorsements. The trial court denied the banks' motion for summary judgment, and the banks appealed.

ISSUE Are the banks liable to the Fund for the checks?

DECISION No. The appellate court reversed the lower court's ruling. Summary judgment for the banks was appropriate, because the unauthorized indorsements fell under the fictitious payee rule of UCC 3–405(1) and hence the banks were not liable.

REASON The court noted that the principle underlying the fictitious payee rule rests on a fundamental public policy determination that losses arising from unauthorized checks payable to fictitious payees are "more business risks than banking risks." As a general rule, the employer—in this case, the Fund—is in a better position to prevent such forgeries by reasonable care in the selection and supervision of its employees. Furthermore, employers often obtain insurance (called fidelity insurance) to cover losses sustained as a result of the malfeasance (wrongdoing) of employees entrusted with the handling of funds. The court said, "[T]he Fund admits that Simon was its administrator and, in such capacity, prepared duplicate claims vouchers and supplied the Fund with the names of the payees of the checks intending that such payees have no interest in them. Thus, Simon's endorsements of those checks in the names of the payees were 'effective,' and appellant banks have no liability to the Fund. Recovery by the Fund against the banks is barred by U.C.C. [Section] 3–405(1)(c), known as the 'fictitious payee' or 'padded payroll' rule."

❖ Warranty Liability of Parties to Commercial Paper

In addition to the signature liability discussed in the preceding sections, transferors make certain implied warranties regarding the instruments that they are negotiating. Liability under these warranties is not subject to the conditions of proper presentment, dishonor, and notice of dishonor. These warranties arise even when a transferor does not indorse the instrument (as in delivery of bearer paper) [UCC 3–417]. Warranties fall into two categories, those that arise from the *transfer* of a negotiable instrument and those that arise upon *presentment*.[12]

TRANSFER WARRANTIES Warranties made by the indorser and transferor of a negotiable instrument who receives consideration to subsequent transferees and holders who take the instrument in good faith that (1) the transferor has good title to the instrument or is otherwise authorized to obtain payment or acceptance on behalf of one who does have good title; (2) all signatures are genuine or authorized; (3) the instrument has not been materially altered; (4) no defense of any party is good against the transferor; and (5) the transferor has no knowledge of any insolvency proceedings against the maker, the acceptor, or the drawer of an unaccepted instrument.

Transfer Warranties

Five **transfer warranties** are described in UCC 3–417(2). They provide that any person who indorses an instrument and *receives consideration* warrants the following to all subsequent transferees and holders who take the instrument in good faith:

1. The transferor has good title to the instrument or is otherwise authorized to obtain payment or acceptance on behalf of one who does have good title.

12. The revised Article 3 deals with these two warranties in two sections [RUCC 3–416 and 3–417]. The warranties cannot be disclaimed with respect to checks, and any claim for breach must be made on the warrantor "within thirty days" after the claimant has reason to know of the breach and the identity of the warrantor. Failure to give notice discharges the warrantor "to the extent of any loss caused by the delay" [RUCC 3–416(c) and 3–417(e)].

2. All signatures are genuine or authorized.
3. The instrument has not been materially altered.
4. No defense of any party is good against the transferor.
5. The transferor has no knowledge of any insolvency proceedings against the maker, the acceptor, or the drawer of an instrument.

A qualified indorser who indorses an instrument "without recourse" limits the fourth warranty to a warranty that he or she has "no knowledge" of such a defense rather than that there is no defense [UCC 3–417(3)].

The manner of transfer and the negotiation that is used determine how far and to whom a transfer warranty will run. Transfer by indorsement and delivery of order paper extends warranty liability to any subsequent holder who takes the instrument in good faith. The warranties of a person who transfers without indorsement (by delivery of bearer paper), however, will extend only to the immediate transferee [UCC 3–417(2)]. The indorser or transferor must receive consideration, however, before any warranties flow to any subsequent transferees.

Suppose that Abrams forges Peter's name as a maker of a promissory note. The note is made payable to Abrams. Abrams indorses the note in blank and negotiates it to Carla, then leaves the country. Carla, without indorsement, delivers the note to Bob. Bob, in turn without indorsement, delivers the note to Shirley. Upon Shirley's presentment of the note to Peter, the forgery is discovered. Shirley can hold Bob (the immediate transferor) liable for breach of warranty that all signatures are genuine. Shirley cannot hold Carla liable, because Carla is not Shirley's immediate transferor but is a prior nonindorsing transferor. This example shows the importance of the distinction between (1) transfer by indorsement and delivery of order paper and (2) transfer by delivery of bearer paper without indorsement.

Presentment Warranties

Any person who seeks payment or acceptance of a negotiable instrument impliedly warrants to any other person who in good faith pays or accepts the instrument that:

1. The party presenting has good title to the instrument or is authorized to obtain payment or acceptance on behalf of a person who has good title.
2. The party presenting has no knowledge that the signature of the maker or the drawer is unauthorized.
3. The instrument has not been materially altered.

These warranties exist under UCC 3–417(1) and are often referred to as **presentment warranties** because they protect the person to whom the instrument is presented. The second and third warranties in the preceding list do not apply in certain cases (to certain persons) in which the presenter is a holder in due course. It is assumed, for example, that a drawer or a maker will recognize his or her own signature and that a maker or an acceptor will recognize whether an instrument has been materially altered. Both transfer and presentment warranties attempt to shift liability back to a wrongdoer or to the person who dealt face to face with the wrongdoer and thus was in the best position to prevent the wrongdoing.

PRESENTMENT WARRANTIES
Implied warranties, made by any person who seeks payment or acceptance of a negotiable instrument to any person who in good faith pays or accepts the instrument, that the party presenting the instrument has good title to the instrument or is authorized to obtain payment or acceptance on behalf of a person who has good title, has no knowledge that the signature of the maker or the drawer is unauthorized, and has no knowledge that the instrument has been materially altered.

❖ Defenses

Depending upon whether a holder or an HDC (or a holder through an HDC) makes the demand for payment, certain defenses can bar collection from persons who would otherwise be primarily or secondarily liable or have warranty liability on the instrument. There are two general categories of defenses—*universal defenses* and *personal defenses*.

Universal Defenses

UNIVERSAL DEFENSES
Defenses that can be used to avoid payment to all holders of a negotiable instrument, including a holder in due course (HDC) or (under the shelter principle) a holder through an HDC. Also called *real defenses.*

Universal defenses (or real defenses) are valid against all holders, including HDCs and holders who take through an HDC. Universal defenses include those described in the following subsections.

Forgery

Forgery of a maker's or drawer's signature cannot bind the person whose name is used (unless that person ratifies the signature or is precluded from denying it) [UCC 3–401 and 3–404(1)]. Thus, when a person forges an instrument, the person whose name is used has no liability to pay any holder or any HDC the value of the forged instrument. In addition, a principal can assert the defense of unauthorized signature against any holder or HDC when an agent exceeds his or her authority to sign negotiable paper on behalf of the principal [UCC 3–403].

Fraud in the Execution If a person is deceived into signing a negotiable instrument, believing that he or she is signing something other than a negotiable instrument (such as a receipt), *fraud in the execution,* or inception, is committed against the signer. For example, a consumer unfamiliar with the English language signs a paper presented by a salesperson. The saleperson says the paper is a request for an estimate, but in fact it is a promissory note. Even if the note is negotiated to an HDC, the consumer has a valid defense against payment. This defense cannot be raised, however, if a reasonable inquiry would have revealed the nature and terms of the instrument.[13] Thus, the signer's age, experience, and intelligence are relevant, because they frequently determine whether the signer should have known the nature of the transaction before signing. The following case concerns a farmer who signed a negotiable instrument under the mistaken assumption that he was signing a receipt for funds received. As you read the case, try to determine what the outcome might have been had the plaintiff been an ordinary holder instead of a holder in due course.

Case 19.3
FEDERAL DEPOSIT INSURANCE CORP. v. CULVER
United States District Court, District of Kansas, 1986.
640 F.Supp. 725.

HISTORICAL AND SOCIAL SETTING *Cases decided under the Uniform Negotiable Instruments Law of 1896 recognized that the defense of fraud in the execution was effective against an HDC. The drafters of the UCC incorporated these holdings into UCC 3–305(1)(c). Fraud in the execution is more serious than other types of fraud. As the drafters explained in Comment 7 to UCC 3–305, "[t]he common illustration is that of the maker who is tricked into signing a note in the belief that it is merely a receipt or some other document." The drafters emphasized that "[t]he party must not only have been in ignorance, but must also have had no reasonable opportunity to obtain knowledge."*

FACTS Gary Culver, a Missouri farmer, made a business arrangement in 1984 with Nasib Ed Kalliel. Kalliel was to manage the business end of the farming enterprise, while Culver did the actual farming. Culver was to receive a salary and a percentage of the profits. In the summer of 1984, Culver notified Kalliel that he urgently needed money to prevent foreclosure. One week later, Culver received $30,000 from the Rexford State Bank of Rexford, Kansas. Culver thought that the money had come from Kalliel and that Kalliel was responsible for repayment. About a week later, a representative from the Rexford Bank, Jerry Gilbert, approached Culver and requested Culver's signature on a blank promissory note form, stating that "Rexford State Bank wanted to know where the $30,000.00 went, * * * for their records." Apparently, Gilbert led Culver to believe that the document was merely a receipt for the $30,000. The maturity date, interest rate, and amount of the promissory note were later filled in; but the amount read $50,000 instead of $30,000. It was later verified that $50,000 had been deposited into Kalliel's Rexford Bank account, from which the $30,000 sent to Culver had been drawn. Sub-

13. *Burchett v. Allied Concord Financial Corp.,* 74 N.M. 575, 396 P.2d 186 (1964).

Case 19.3—Continued

sequent to these events, the Rexford Bank became insolvent, and the Federal Deposit Insurance Corporation (FDIC) purchased the bank's outstanding notes, including the one signed by Culver. The FDIC sought recovery on the note because the note had matured and no money had ever been paid on it, and moved for summary judgment against Culver. Culver claimed that he should not be liable on the note because Gilbert's misrepresentations of the nature of the note constituted fraud in the execution.

ISSUE Can Culver successfully raise the universal defense of fraud in the execution to avoid liability on the note?

DECISION No. The court granted the FDIC's request for summary judgment against Culver.

REASON The court had little difficulty in establishing that the FDIC was a holder in due course in this instance. The FDIC had purchased Culver's note, along with others, in good faith, for value, and without notice that it was defective. Under the UCC, a holder in due course "takes the instrument free from * * * all defenses of any party to the instrument with whom the holder has not dealt except . . . such misrepresentation as has induced the party to sign the instrument *with neither knowledge nor reasonable opportunity to obtain knowledge of its character or its essential terms*" (emphasis added) [UCC 3–305(2)(c)]. The court found that, because Culver could read and understand English, he had had a "reasonable opportunity" to discover the "character" of the note. Culver argued that, while this may have been so, there was no way he could have had a reasonable opportunity to learn the "essential terms" of the note, as they were not included on the form when he signed it. In response to this argument, the court ruled that Culver's negligence in signing a blank promissory note was inexcusable and precluded him from asserting fraud as a universal defense against the claim of a holder in due course. Culver had, in effect, signed a "blank check" that could be enforced under UCC 3–407(3) by any subsequent holder in due course according to any terms added by an intervening holder.

Material Alteration An alteration is material if it changes the contract terms between any two parties in any way. Examples of material alterations follow [UCC 3–407(1)]:

1. Changing the number or relations of the parties.
2. Completing an instrument in an unauthorized manner.
3. Adding to the writing as signed or removing any part of it.

Thus, cutting off part of the paper of a negotiable instrument, adding clauses, or making any change in the amount, the date, or the rate of interest—even if the change is only one penny, one day, or 1 percent—is material. But it is not a material alteration to correct the maker's address, to have a red line drawn across the instrument to indicate that an auditor has checked it, or to correct the total final payment due when a mathematical error is discovered in the original computation. If the alteration is not material, any holder is entitled to enforce the instrument according to its terms.

Material alteration is a *complete defense* against an ordinary holder. An ordinary holder can recover nothing on an instrument if it has been materially altered [UCC 3–407(2)]. Material alteration is at best, however, only a *partial defense* against an HDC. When the holder is an HDC, if an original term, such as the monetary amount payable, has been altered, the HDC can enforce the instrument against the maker or drawer according to the original terms but not for the altered amount. If the instrument was originally incomplete and was later completed in an unauthorized manner, alteration no longer can be claimed as a defense against an HDC, and the HDC can enforce the instrument as completed [UCC 3–407(2) and (3)]. This is because the drawer or maker of the instrument, by issuing an incomplete instrument, will normally be held responsible for the alteration, which could have been avoided by the exercise of greater care. If the alteration is readily apparent, then obviously the holder has notice of some defect or defense and therefore cannot be an HDC [UCC 3–302(1)(c) and 3–304(1)(a)].

Discharge in Bankruptcy Discharge in bankruptcy is an absolute defense on any instrument regardless of the status of the holder because the purpose of bankruptcy is to settle finally all of the insolvent party's debts [UCC 3–305(2)(d)].

Minority Minority, or infancy, is a universal defense only to the extent that state law recognizes it as a defense to a simple contract. Because state laws on minority vary, so do determinations of whether minority is a universal defense against an HDC [UCC 3–305(2)(a)].

Illegality When the law declares that an instrument is void because it has been executed in connection with illegal conduct, then the defense is universal—that is, absolute against both an ordinary holder and an HDC. If the law merely makes the instrument voidable, as in the personal (rather than universal) defense of illegality, discussed later, then it is still a defense against a holder, but not against an HDC. The courts are sometimes prone to treat the word *void* in a statute as meaning *voidable* to protect a holder in due course [UCC 3–305(2)(b)]. Whether a contract was void or merely voidable is at issue in the following case.

Case 19.4
KEDZIE & 103RD STREET CURRENCY EXCHANGE, INC. v. HODGE
Appellate Court of Illinois, First District, Fourth Division, 1992.
234 Ill.App.3d 1017,
601 N.E.2d 803,
176 Ill.Dec. 105.

HISTORICAL AND SOCIAL SETTING *There was no section in the Uniform Negotiable Instruments Law of 1896 corresponding to the subsection of UCC 3–305(2) that validates the defense of illegality against payment on an instrument to an HDC. Under the UCC, as the drafters explained in Comment 6, illegality "may arise in many * * * forms under a great variety of statutes." The statutes "are primarily a matter of local concern and local policy. All such matters are * * * left to the local law." If under local law the effect of the illegality is to make the obligation void, the defense is good. For example, in a state in which gambling is illegal and gambling contracts are void, a check drawn to pay a gambling debt is unenforceable, even against an HDC. Similarly, when contracts in violation of trade or professional licensing laws are void, checks drawn to pay unlicensed contractors are unenforceable.*

FACTS Beula Hodge made out a check to Fred Fentress for $500 as a partial payment in advance for plumbing services at her home. When Fentress failed to appear on the date work was to begin, Hodge ordered her bank to stop payment on the check. Fentress, however, had already cashed the check at the Kedzie & 103rd Street Currency Exchange (Kedzie). When the check was returned to Kedzie marked "payment stopped," Kedzie filed suit against Hodge for payment on the check. In the meantime, Hodge had discovered that Fentress was not a licensed plumber and that under state law, engaging in the plumbing trade without a license constituted a criminal offense. Hodge moved to dismiss Kedzie's claim on the ground that the plumbing contract was illegal and void. The trial court granted Hodge's motion, ruling that the instrument was void because the underlying contract was illegal. Kedzie appealed, contending that the contract was not necessarily void and, even if it was, the instrument itself was not necessarily void.

ISSUE Is the check void?

DECISION Yes. The appeals court affirmed the trial court's ruling.

REASON The court stated that "the Illinois legislature, by adopting section 3–305 of the UCC, has expressly declared that illegality is an available defense against a holder in due course, as long as the effect of the illegality is to render the obligation sued upon null and void." In examining the question of whether the contract itself was void, the court noted that under state law, "one who attempts to practice plumbing without a license may suffer substantial penalties, including criminal prosecution and fines. By judicial construction, the unlicensed plumber also forfeits his right to compensation for (illegal) services rendered." The court ruled that a "contract made in violation of the plumbing licensing statute could [not] be specifically performed or ratified. * * * Consequently, the contract made in violation of the Act must be viewed as a legal nullity."[a]

a. On appeal to the Illinois Supreme Court, this judgment was reversed. See *Kedzie & 103rd Street Currency Exchange, Inc. v. Hodge,* 156 Ill.2d 112, 619 N.E.2d 732, 189 Ill.Dec. 31 (1993).

Mental Incapacity If a person is adjudicated mentally incompetent by state proceedings, then any instrument issued by that person thereafter is null and void. The instrument is *void ab initio* (from the beginning) and unenforceable by any holder or any HDC [UCC 3–305(2)(b)]. Instruments issued by a mentally incompetent person before being declared so by a court are voidable.

Extreme Duress When a person signs and issues a negotiable instrument under such extreme duress as an immediate threat of force or violence (for example, at gunpoint), the instrument is void and unenforceable by any holder or HDC [UCC 3–305(2)(b)]. (Ordinary duress is a personal, not a universal, defense.)

Personal Defenses

Personal defenses, such as those described here, are used to avoid payment to an ordinary holder of a negotiable instrument.

PERSONAL DEFENSES
Defenses that can be used to avoid payment to an ordinary holder of a negotiable instrument. Personal defenses cannot be used to avoid payment to a holder in due course (HDC) or (under the shelter principle) to a holder through an HDC.

Breach of Contract or Breach of Warranty When there is a breach of the underlying contract for which the negotiable instrument was issued, the maker of a note can refuse to pay it or the drawer of a check can stop payment. Breach of warranty can also be claimed as a defense to liability on the instrument. For example, Rhodes purchases several sets of imported china from Livingston. The china is to be delivered in four weeks. Rhodes gives Livingston a promissory note for $1,000, which is the price of the china. The china arrives, but many of the pieces are broken, and several others are chipped or cracked. Rhodes refuses to pay the note on the basis of breach of contract and breach of warranty. (Under sales law, a seller impliedly promises that the goods are at least merchantable; see Chapter 17.) If the note is no longer in the hands of the payee-seller but is presented for payment by an HDC, the maker-buyer will not be able to plead breach of contract or warranty as a defense against liability on the note.

Fraud in the Inducement A person who issues a negotiable instrument based on false statements by the other party will be able to avoid payment on that instrument, unless the holder is an HDC. To illustrate, Jerry agrees to purchase Howard's used tractor for $24,500. Howard, knowing his statements to be false, tells Jerry that the tractor is in good working order and that it has been used for only one harvest. In addition, he tells Jerry that he owns the tractor free and clear of all claims. Jerry pays Howard $4,500 in cash and issues a negotiable promissory note for the balance. As it turns out, Howard still owes the original seller $10,000 on the purchase of the tractor, and the tractor is subject to a filed security interest (discussed in Chapter 21). In addition, the tractor is three years old and has been used in three harvests. Jerry can refuse to pay the note if it is held by an ordinary holder, but if Howard has negotiated the note to an HDC, Jerry must pay the HDC. Of course, Jerry can then sue Howard.

Illegality Certain types of illegality constitute personal defenses. Other types, as mentioned, constitute universal defenses. The difference lies in the state statutes or ordinances that make the transactions illegal. If a statute provides that an illegal transaction is voidable, the defense is personal. If a statute makes an illegal transaction void, the defense is universal and can be successfully asserted against an HDC. For example, a state may make gambling contracts illegal and void but be silent on payments of gambling debts. Thus, the payment of a gambling debt becomes voidable and is a personal defense. Whether a contract and the negotiable instrument paid under the contract are void is at issue in the following case.

Case 19.5 

NEW JERSEY MORTGAGE & INVESTMENT CORP. v. BERENYI

Superior Court of New Jersey,
Appellate Division, 1976.
140 N.J.Super 406,
356 A.2d 421.

HISTORICAL AND SOCIAL SETTING *The fact that a defense is personal may render it ineffective against an HDC, but the party who has the defense may pursue his or her claim for damages, or any other relief, against the party involved in the transaction that gave rise to the defense. For example, a consumer buys house siding and signs a promissory note for the price. The seller negotiates the note to a third-party lender who qualifies as an HDC. The siding proves to be shoddy, but the lender insists on full payment. Because the lender is an HDC, the consumer cannot raise her personal defense and will have to pay the note. The consumer can, however, sue the seller. Of course, if the seller has gone out of business, the consumer may have no satisfactory recourse. With this set of circumstances in mind, most states have enacted laws that restrict the HDC doctrine in consumer transactions. Generally, these laws were passed after the events described in this case.*[a]

FACTS On May 25, 1964, Kroyden Industries, Inc., a New Jersey corporation, was prohibited by court order from making certain representations to its customers in connection with the sale of carpeting. In August of 1964, in violation of this order, one of Kroyden's employees offered to give Anna Berenyi and her husband carpeting free of charge if they referred prospective buyers to Kroyden Industries. Mr. and Mrs. Berenyi agreed to this condition, and relying on the employee's offer, Anna Berenyi signed a promissory note for $1,521, from which "finder's fees" would be deducted when prospective buyers were referred to Kroyden Industries. Kroyden subsequently negotiated the note to the plaintiff in this case, New Jersey Mortgage & Investment Corporation. When Berenyi refused to pay the note, the plaintiff brought this legal action against her to recover the debt. Berenyi claimed that she was not liable on the note because the contract with Kroyden was illegal, having been prohibited by court order. The trial court held for the plaintiff, and Berenyi appealed.

ISSUE Can Berenyi avoid her obligations on the note on the basis of illegality?

DECISION No. The appellate court affirmed the trial court's judgment.

REASON In addressing the question of Berenyi's liability on the note, the court stated that the "controlling issue presented is whether the defense here asserted is a ['universal'] defense or a 'personal' defense. [Universal] defenses are available against even a holder in due course of a negotiable instrument; personal defenses are not available against such a holder." It was undisputed that the plaintiff was a holder in due course. The New Jersey Mortgage & Investment Corporation had taken the note in good faith, for value, and with no notice of the court order against Kroyden or of its violation by Kroyden's employee. Under New Jersey law, "a holder in due course takes free and clear of the defense of illegality, unless the statute which declares the act illegal also indicates that payment thereunder is void." The court concluded that, because no New Jersey statute ordained "that a note obtained in violation of an injunction is void and unenforceable," the illegality involved did not qualify as a universal defense but only as a personal defense. As such, it was ineffective against the claim of a holder in due course.

a. The federal government (Federal Trade Commission) has also stated that personal defenses in a *consumer credit* transaction are valid even against a holder in due course. See this chapter's *Landmark in the Law.*

Mental Incapacity There are various types and degrees of mental incapacity. Ordinarily, it is only a personal defense; but if a maker or drawer is so extremely incapacitated (requiring a court to appoint a guardian) that the transaction becomes a nullity, then the instrument is void. In that case, the defense becomes universal, and it is good against an HDC as well as an ordinary holder [UCC 3–305(2)(b)]. If the maker drafts a negotiable instrument while mentally incompetent but before a formal court hearing has declared (adjudicated) him or her to be so, courts declare the obligation on the instrument to be voidable. If, however, the maker has been declared by a court to be mentally incompetent and a guardian has been appointed before the note is written, courts hold the obligation to be null and void.

Landmark in the Law

The FTC Rule of 1976

On May 14, 1976, the Federal Trade Commission (FTC) issued a rule[a] that has severely limited the preferential position enjoyed by holders in due course in certain circumstances. This FTC rule limits the rights of an HDC in an instrument that evidences a debt arising out of a *consumer credit* transaction. The rule, entitled "Preservation of Consumers' Claims and Defenses," is an attempt to prevent a situation in which a consumer is required to make payment for a defective product to a third party who is a holder in due course of a promissory note that formed part of the contract with the dealer who sold the defective good.

To illustrate, a consumer purchases a used car under express warranty from an automobile dealer, paying $1,000 down and signing a promissory note to the dealer for the remaining $4,000 due on the car. The dealer sells the bank this promissory note, which is a negotiable instrument, and the bank then becomes the creditor, to whom the consumer makes payments. The car does not perform as warranted, and the consumer returns the car, requesting return of the down payment and cancellation of the contract. Even if the dealer refunded the $1,000, however, under the traditional HDC rule, the consumer would normally still owe the remaining $4,000 because the consumer's claim of breach of warranty is a personal defense and the bank is a holder in due course. Thus, the traditional HDC rule leaves consumers who have purchased defective products liable to the holder.

The FTC rule requires that any seller or lessor of goods or services who takes or receives a consumer credit contract or who accepts as full or partial payment for a sale or lease the proceeds of any purchase money loan made in connection with any consumer credit contract include in the contract the following provision:

NOTICE

ANY HOLDER OF THIS CONSUMER CREDIT CONTRACT IS SUBJECT TO ALL CLAIMS AND DEFENSES WHICH THE DEBTOR COULD ASSERT AGAINST THE SELLER OF GOODS OR SERVICES OBTAINED PURSUANT HERETO OR WITH THE PROCEEDS HEREOF. RECOVERY HEREUNDER BY THE DEBTOR SHALL NOT EXCEED AMOUNTS PAID BY THE DEBTOR HEREUNDER.

A consumer who is party to a consumer credit transaction can now bring any defense he or she has against the seller of a product against a subsequent holder as well. In essence, the FTC rule places a holder in due course of the negotiable instrument in the position of a contract assignee. The rule makes the buyer's duty to pay conditional on the seller's full performance of the contract. It also makes both the seller and the creditor responsible for the seller's misconduct. Finally, it clearly reduces the degree of transferability of commercial paper resulting from consumer credit contracts.[b]

Problems can arise, however, if the seller fails, for whatever reason, to include the notice in a promissory note and then sells the note to a third party, such as a bank. While the seller has violated the rule, the bank has not. The FTC rule does not prohibit third parties from purchasing notes or credit contracts that do *not* contain the required rule. Therefore, if the FTC rule is not contained in the note, the bank does not become subject to the buyer's defenses against the seller. The FTC apparently recognized this shortcoming because the same day that it officially promulgated the rule, it proposed an amendment that would have made it an unfair or deceptive practice for either the seller or a third party to take or receive a credit contract without the required notice. The proposed amendment was never promulgated, however, and some consumers have suffered as a result.

a. 16 C.F.R. Section 433.2. The rule was enacted pursuant to the FTC's authority under the Federal Trade Commission Act, 15 U.S.C. Sections 41–58.

b. Revised Article 3 provides that a negotiable instrument that contains this notice or a similar statement required by law may remain negotiable [RUCC 3–106(d)], but the new section adds that there cannot be an HDC of such an instrument.

Other Personal Defenses Other personal defenses can be used to avoid payment to an ordinary holder of a negotiable instrument, including the following:

1. Discharge by payment or cancellation [UCC 3–601(1)(a) and 3–602].
2. Unauthorized completion of an incomplete instrument [UCC 3–115, 3–407, 3–304(4)(d), and 4–401(2)(b)].

3. Nondelivery [UCC 1–201(14), 3–305, and 3–306(c)].
4. Ordinary duress or undue influence [UCC 3–305].

❖ Discharge

Discharge from liability on an instrument can occur in several ways. The liability of all parties to an instrument is discharged when the party primarily liable on it pays to a holder the amount due in full [UCC 3–601 and 3–603]. Payment by any other party discharges only the liability of that party and subsequent parties.

Cancellation of an instrument discharges the liability of all parties [UCC 3–605]. Writing "Paid" across the face of an instrument cancels it. Tearing it up cancels it. If a holder crosses out a party's signature, that party's liability and the liability of subsequent indorsers who have already indorsed the instrument are discharged. Materially altering an instrument may discharge the liability of all parties [UCC 3–407]. (An HDC may be able to enforce the instrument against its maker or drawer according to its original terms. Material alteration was discussed previously.)

Discharge of liability can also occur when a party's right of recourse is impaired [UCC 3–606]. A right of recourse is a right to seek reimbursement. Ordinarily, when a holder collects the amount of an instrument from an indorser, the indorser has a right of recourse against prior indorsers, the maker or drawer, and so on. If the holder has adversely affected the indorser's right to seek reimbursement from these other parties, however, the indorser is not liable on the instrument. This occurs when, for example, the holder releases or agrees not to sue a party against whom the indorser has a right of recourse.

❖ Key Terms

acceptor 450
accommodation party 452
agent 452
fictitious payee 457
holder in due course (HDC) 444
imposter 456
personal defense 463
presentment warranty 459
principal 452
shelter principle 449
transfer warranty 458
universal defense 460

❖ Chapter Summary: Commercial Paper—Holder in Due Course, Liability, and Defenses

REQUIREMENTS FOR HOLDER-IN-DUE-COURSE STATUS	
Must Be a Holder	A holder is a person who possesses an instrument "drawn, issued, or indorsed to him or his order or to bearer or in blank" [UCC 1–201(20)].
Must Take for Value	A holder gives value: 1. To the extent that the agreed-upon consideration has been paid or a security interest or lien acquired, or 2. By taking an instrument in payment of or as security for an antecedent debt, or 3. By giving a negotiable instrument or irrevocable commitment as payment [UCC 3–303].

❖ Chapter Summary: Commercial Paper— Holder in Due Course, Liability, and Defenses—Continued

Must Take in Good Faith	Good faith is "honesty in fact in the conduct or transaction concerned" [UCC 1–201(19)].
Must Take without Notice	1. *That the instrument has been dishonored*—Knowledge of facts that would lead a person to suspect the instrument has been dishonored is required [UCC 3–302(1)(c)]. 2. *That a claim or a defense exists*—Actual knowledge is required. The instrument must be so incomplete, bear such visible evidence of forgery or alteration, or be so irregular that a reasonable person would be put on notice from examination or from facts surrounding the transaction [UCC 3–304(1)]. 3. *That the instrument is overdue:* a. Time instruments are overdue the day after the due date for payment. b. Demand instruments are overdue after demand has been made or a reasonable time has lapsed from issue. c. Domestic checks are *presumed* to be overdue after thirty days from issue [UCC 3–304].
The Shelter Principle (Holder through a Holder in Due Course)	A holder who cannot qualify as a holder in due course has the *rights* of a holder in due course if he or she derives title through a holder in due course [UCC 3–201].
SIGNATURE LIABILITY OF PARTIES TO COMMERCIAL PAPER	
Primary Liability	1. The maker or acceptor is obligated to pay a negotiable instrument according to "its tenor at the time of his engagement" or as completed [UCC 3–413(1)]. 2. The drawee is primarily liable to the drawer to pay a negotiable instrument in accordance with the drawer's orders but owes no duty to the payee or any holder.
Secondary Liability	Parties other than the maker who can be secondarily liable on a negotiable instrument are the drawer and unqualified indorsers. These parties promise to pay on the instrument only under the following circumstances [UCC 3–413(2), 3–414]: 1. The instrument is properly and timely presented. 2. The instrument is dishonored. 3. Timely notice of dishonor is given to the secondarily liable party.
Liability for Agents' Signatures	An agent can sign negotiable instruments and thereby bind the principal if the agent indicates that he or she is signing on behalf of a clearly named and identified principal or if he or she signs the principal's name (and is authorized by the principal to do so) [UCC 3–403(1), (2)].
Unauthorized Signatures	An unauthorized signature will not bind the person whose name is forged. Exceptions: a. The person whose unauthorized signature was used will be bound by the signature if he or she ratifies the signature or is in some way precluded from denying it [UCC 3–404, 3–406]. b. An unauthorized signature will operate as "the signature of the unauthorized signer in favor of any person who in good faith pays the instrument or takes it for value" [UCC 3–404(1)].
Special Rules for Unauthorized Indorsements	In cases of forged or unauthorized indorsements, the burden of loss falls on the first party to take the forged instrument, *except* in the following situations, in which the resulting loss falls on the drawer or maker: a. When an imposter induces the maker or drawer of an instrument to issue it to the imposter. b. When a person signs as or on behalf of a maker or drawer, intending that the payee will have no interest in the instrument, or when an agent or employee of the maker or drawer has supplied him or her with the name of the payee, also intending the payee to have no such interest (fictitious payee rule) [UCC 3–405(1)].
WARRANTY LIABILITY OF PARTIES TO COMMERCIAL PAPER	
Transfer Warranties	1. *General indorsers*—The following five transfer warranties extend to all subsequent holders: a. The transferor has good title or is otherwise authorized to obtain payment or acceptance on behalf of one who does have good title. b. All signatures are genuine or authorized.

❖ Chapter Summary: Commercial Paper—Holder in Due Course, Liability, and Defenses—Continued

Transfer Warranties—Continued	c. The instrument has not been materially altered. d. No defense of any party is good against the transferor. e. The transferor has no knowledge of insolvency proceedings against the maker, acceptor, or drawer of an unaccepted instrument [UCC 3–417(2)]. 2. *Nonindorsers*—The same five transfer warranties as for the general indorser, but *warranties extend only to the immediate transferee* [UCC 3–417(2)]. 3. *Qualified indorsers*—The same five transfer warranties as for the general indorser except that a qualified indorsement ("without recourse") limits the fourth warranty to a warranty of no knowledge of such a defense (as opposed to no defense). These warranties extend to all subsequent holders [UCC 3–417(2), (3)].
Presentment Warranties	The following *presentment warranties* are impliedly made by any person who seeks payment or acceptance of a negotiable instrument to any other person who in good faith pays or accepts the instrument: 1. The party presenting has good title to the instrument or is authorized to obtain payment or acceptance on behalf of a person who has good title. 2. The party presenting has no knowledge that the signature of the maker or the drawer is unauthorized. 3. The instrument has not been materially altered.
VALID DEFENSES AGAINST HOLDERS OF NEGOTIABLE INSTRUMENTS AND DISCHARGE	
Universal (Real) Defenses [UCC 3–305] **(Valid against all holders, including HDCs or holders with the rights of HDCs.)**	1. Forgery. 2. Fraud in the execution. 3. Material alteration. 4. Discharge in bankruptcy. 5. Minority—depending on state law. 6. Illegality, mental incapacity, or extreme duress—if the contract is void.
Personal Defenses [UCC 3–306] **(Valid against mere holders; not valid against HDCs or holders with rights of HDCs.)**	1. Breach of contract or breach of warranty. 2. Fraud in the inducement. 3. Illegality, ordinary duress or undue influence, and mental incapacity—if the contract is voidable. 4. Previous payment of the instrument. 5. Unauthorized completion of the instrument. 6. Nondelivery of the instrument.
Discharge [UCC 3–601]	All parties to a negotiable instrument will be discharged when the party primarily liable on it pays to a holder the amount due in full. Discharge can also occur in other circumstances (if the instrument has been canceled, materially altered, reacquired, etc.).

❖ Questions and Case Problems

19-1. Requirements for HDC Status. What are the requirements for attaining HDC status, besides the requirement of being a holder? How can a person who does not qualify as an HDC acquire the rights and privileges of an HDC?

19-2. Unauthorized Indorsements. What are the exceptions to the rule that a bank will be liable for paying a check over an unauthorized indorsement?

19-3. Defenses. Jules sold Alfred a small motorboat for $1,500, maintaining to Alfred that the boat was in excellent condition. Alfred gave Jules a check for $1,500, which Jules indorsed and gave to Sherry for value. When Alfred took the boat for a trial run, he discovered that the boat leaked, needed to be painted, and needed a new motor. Alfred stopped payment on his check, which had not yet been cashed. Jules has disappeared. Can Sherry recover from Alfred as a holder in due course? Discuss.

19-4. Defenses. Fox purchased a used car from Emerson for $1,000. Fox paid for the car with a check, written in pencil, payable to Emerson for $1,000. Emerson, through careful erasures and alterations, changed the amount on the check to read $10,000 and negotiated the check to Sanderson. Sanderson took the check for value, in good faith, and without notice of the alteration and thus met the UCC requirements for holder-in-due-course status. Can Fox successfully raise the real defense of material alteration to avoid payment on the check? Explain.

19-5. Signature Liability. Marion makes out a negotiable promissory note payable to the order of Perry. Perry indorses the note by writing "without recourse, Perry" and transfers the note for value to Steven. Steven, in need of cash, negotiates the note to Harriet by indorsing it with the words, "Pay to Harriet, Steven." On the due date, Harriet presents the note to Marion for payment, only to learn that Marion has filed for bankruptcy and will have all debts (including the note) discharged in bankruptcy. Discuss fully whether Harriet can hold Marion, Perry, or Steven liable on the note.

19-6. Defenses. One day, while Ort, a farmer, was working alone in his field, a stranger approached him. The stranger said he was the state agent for a manufacturer of iron posts and wire fence. The two men conversed for some time, and eventually the stranger persuaded the farmer to accept a township wide agency for the same manufacturer. The stranger then completed two documents for Ort to sign, telling Ort that they were identical copies of an agency agreement. Because the farmer did not have his glasses with him and could read only with great difficulty, he asked the stranger to read what the document said. The stranger then purported to read the document to Ort, not mentioning that it was a promissory note. Both men signed each document, the farmer assuming that he was signing a document of agency. The stranger later negotiated the promissory note that he had fraudulently obtained from Ort to an HDC. When the HDC brought suit against the farmer, the farmer attempted to defend on the basis of fraud in the execution. Did Ort succeed in the real defense of fraud? Explain. [*Ort v. Fowler*, 31 Kan. 478, 2 P. 580 (1884)]

19-7. HDC Status. An employee of Epicycle Corp. cashed a payroll check at Money Mart Check Cashing Center. Money Mart deposited the check, with others, into its bank account. When the check was returned marked "Payment stopped," Money Mart sought to recover from Epicycle for the value of the check. Money Mart claimed that it was a holder in due course on the instrument because it had accepted the check for value, in good faith, and without notice that a stop-payment order had been made. Epicycle argued that Money Mart was not a holder in due course, because it had failed to verify that the check was good before it cashed the check. Did Money Mart's failure to inquire into the validity of the check preclude it from being a holder in due course? Explain. [*Money Mart Check Cashing Center, Inc. v. Epicycle Corp.*, 667 P.2d 1372 (Colo. 1983)]

19-8. Agents' Signatures. Griffin issued three checks to Ellinger, drawn on the account of the Greenway Building Co. Griffin, the president of the company, signed his name to the checks without revealing his representative capacity. The name of the company was on the face of each check, and Griffin was authorized to sign checks as president of the company. At the time the checks were issued, neither Ellinger (the payee) nor Griffin discussed who was responsible for paying the checks. The drawee bank refused to honor the checks because of insufficient funds in the Greenway account, and Ellinger sought recovery from Griffin personally. The trial court held for Ellinger, and Griffin appealed. Can Griffin be held personally liable for the debt to Ellinger? Explain. [*Griffin v. Ellinger*, 538 S.W.2d 97 (Tex. 1976)]

19-9. Defenses. James Balkus died without leaving a will. A few days later, Ann Vesely, his sister, discovered in his personal effects two promissory notes made payable to her in the amount of $6,000. She presented the notes to the Security First National Bank of Sheboygan Trust Department, the personal representative for the estate of Balkus, for payment. The personal representative refused to pay the notes, claiming that Vesely was not a holder in due course and that nondelivery of the notes to her was a proper defense. The trial court upheld the personal representative's claim, and Vesely appealed. Discuss whether nondelivery is a proper defense against Vesely. [*Vesely v. Security First National Bank of Sheboygan Trust Department*, 128 Wis.2d 246, 381 N.W.2d 593 (1985)]

19-10. Unauthorized Indorsements. Mowatt worked as a bookkeeper for the law firm of McCarthy, Kenney & Reidy, P.C., which had several branch offices in the Boston area. Part of Mowatt's job involved preparing checks payable to the partners in other offices for the authorized signature of a partner of the firm. On numerous occasions, Mowatt wrote such checks with no intention of transmitting them to the payee-partners. Instead, after they had been signed by an authorized partner, Mowatt forged indorsements on the checks and then either cashed them or deposited them in one of three bank accounts that he had opened for this purpose. The fraudulent scheme went on for a year and a half, and when the forgeries were finally discovered, the law firm demanded that the bank credit its account with the full amount of loss that it had sustained as a result of the forgeries. The bank refused to do so, and the law firm brought an action against the bank. Which party had to bear the loss arising from the forgeries, the law firm or the drawee bank? Discuss. [*McCarthy, Kenney & Reidy, P.C. v. First National Bank of Boston*, 402 Mass. 630, 524 N.E.2d 390 (1988)]

19-11. Unauthorized Indorsements. James Liddell, the president of JHL & Associates, Inc., persuaded Clifford Marston and his wife to invest in Fidelity, a company that Liddell said he represented. To execute the transaction, Liddell had the Marstons issue a check for $15,000 payable to Seattle-First National Bank (Sea-First) for the purpose of obtaining cashier's checks, which would then be sent to Fidelity. Liddell, in Clifford Marston's presence, obtained three cashier's checks payable to "JHL & Associates, Trust." Liddell did not send the checks to Fidelity but rather indorsed them to different individuals as part of a fraudulent Ponzi scheme (a scheme in which the perpetrator uses funds of recent investors to pay previous investors—often referred to as pyramiding), signing the indorsements "JHL & Associates." Eventually, the Marstons sued Sea-First to recover their money, alleging that the bank was liable for the loss because the checks were indorsed by entities other than the named payee (JHL & Associates, Trust). Discuss fully whether Liddell's indorsements were ineffective and whether the bank should be liable to the Marstons. [*Marston Enterprises, Inc. v. Seattle-First National Bank*, 57 Wash.App. 662, 789 P.2d 784 (1990)]

19-12. HDC Status. Pamela Haas, an employee of Trail Leasing, Inc., had access to her employer's blank checks. Over a period of about two and a half years, Haas used the firm's checks to fraudulently obtain cash from the firm's bank, Drovers First American Bank. She carried out her scheme by writing checks payable to Drovers First, having the checks signed by an authorized officer of Trail Leasing, and then taking the checks to the bank. There she would fill out a "change order form"—a form used by bank customers to specify the coins and bill denominations in which they wished to take cash for business operations—and pocket the cash that she received. By the time the scheme was discovered (through a discrepancy in one of the change orders), Haas had negotiated fifty-five checks for a total of nearly $40,000. Trail Leasing sued the bank to recover the funds paid to Haas without its authorization, and the issue turned on whether the bank was a holder in due course of the checks delivered to it by Haas. The court had no trouble deciding that the bank took the checks in good faith and without notice of any claim. The issue thus became whether the bank met the remaining requirement for HDC status—taking for value. Trail Leasing argued that because the bank essentially paid Haas from Trail Leasing's funds (by debiting Trail Leasing's bank account), the bank had not given value for the instruments and therefore could not be an HDC. Will the court concur in this argument? Discuss. [*Trail Leasing, Inc. v. Drovers First American Bank*, 447 N.W.2d 190 (Minn. 1989)]

19-13. Unauthorized Indorsements. While Wanda Snow was married to Cary Byron, Byron established an account with Shearson Lehman Hutton, Inc.—a securities brokerage firm—for Wanda's son by a previous marriage. Wanda was designated as the account custodian. After Wanda and Cary had separated but before their divorce became final, Byron wrote a letter to Shearson instructing Shearson to close the account and send the proceeds (about $44,000) to a Florida bank account. Byron forged Wanda's signature on the letter. Later, Byron called Shearson, identified himself, and asked that the proceeds be sent instead to Wanda Snow in care of Byron's cousin in Connecticut. Byron obtained the check, forged Wanda's indorsement on it, and deposited the check into his bank account, later applying the proceeds to his personal use. Wanda sued Byron, Shearson, and the bank to recover the funds. In her claim against the bank, Wanda alleged that the bank was liable for paying the check over a forged indorsement. The bank raised the "imposter rule" as a defense. Is the imposter rule applicable to these circumstances? Why or why not? [*Snow v. Byron*, 580 So.2d 238 (Fla.App.1st 1991)]

A QUESTION OF ETHICS AND SOCIAL RESPONSIBILITY

19-14. *Kirkman was involved in the horse business. He formed a business arrangement with an acquaintance, John Roundtree, who worked as a loan officer for American Federal Bank. Under the arrangement, Kirkman would locate buyers for horses, and the buyers could seek financing from American Federal. Roundtree gave Kirkman blank promissory notes and security agreements from American Federal, and Kirkman was to locate potential purchasers, take care of the paperwork, and bring the documents to the bank for approval of the purchaser's loan. Eventually, Kirkman entered into a purchase agreement with Gene Parker, a horse dealer. Parker agreed with Kirkman that they would jointly purchase a certain horse for $35,000. Parker signed a blank American Federal promissory note, with the understanding that Kirkman would cosign the note and complete the details of the transaction with the bank. Parker also signed a form authorizing the bank to release the funds to the seller of the collateral (the horse). Kirkman did not cosign the note and completed it for $85,000 instead of $35,000. He then took the note and authorization form to Roundtree, told Roundtree that he was the seller, and received from Roundtree checks totaling $85,000. After paying the actual seller of the horse the agreed-on $35,000 and seeing to it that Parker received the horse, Kirkman skipped town with the remaining $50,000. Parker paid American Federal $35,000 but refused to pay any more, claiming that he had agreed to pay only $35,000 and that the other $50,000 was unauthorized by him. In the subsequent action brought by the bank to collect the $50,000, the bank prevailed. The court found that the bank was a holder in due course of the promissory note and had not been negligent in the way it handled the transaction.* [American Federal Bank, FSB v. Parker, 392 *S.E.2d* 798 *(S.C. 1990)*]

1. Parker contended that the bank was negligent because it did not contact him to make sure that everything was correct before disbursing the proceeds of the loan to Kirkman. Do you agree with the court's finding that the bank was not negligent in this regard? Even if the bank had been negligent, would its negligence have outweighed Parker's negligence in signing a blank promissory note?
2. Because the bank was deemed a holder in due course and Parker had signed an incomplete instrument, Parker was prohibited under UCC 3–407(3) from asserting successfully the universal defense of material alteration. What ethical premise underlies this rule?
3. Overall, from an ethical point of view, do you think that the court's holding in this case was fair? Would it have been fairer to hold the bank liable for the loss instead of Parker? If you were the judge, how would you decide the issue?

FOR CRITICAL ANALYSIS

19-15. *How does the concept of holder in due course further Article 3's general goal of encouraging the negotiability of commercial paper? How does it further Article 3's goal of balancing the rights of parties to negotiable instruments?*

Chapter 20

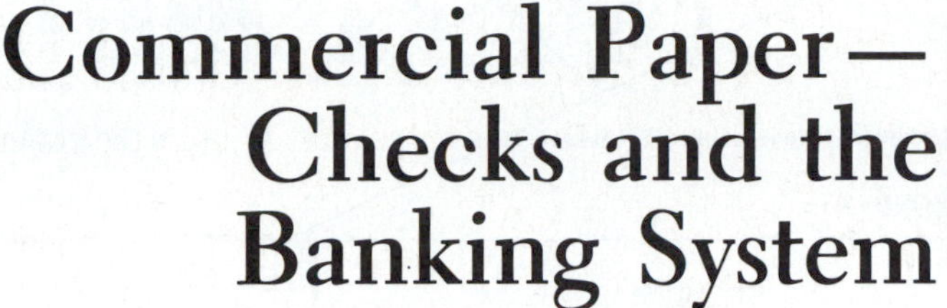

Commercial Paper—Checks and the Banking System

Most larger transactions for goods and services today involve payment by means of checks, credit cards, and charge accounts, which are rapidly replacing currency as a means of payment in most transactions for goods and services. Checks are the most common form of commercial paper regulated by the Uniform Commercial Code (UCC). It is estimated that approximately sixty billion personal and commercial checks are written each year in the United States. Checks are more than a daily convenience; they are an integral part of the American economic system.

"Money is power, freedom, a cushion, the root of all evil, the sum of all blessings."

Carl Sandburg, 1878–1967
(American poet and biographer)

Article 3 of the UCC, which deals with the use of commercial paper, sets forth the requirements for negotiable instruments. The extent to which any party is either charged with or discharged from liability on a check is established according to the provisions of this article. Article 4 of the UCC is a statement of the principles and rules of modern bank deposit and collection procedures. It governs the relationships of banks with one another as they process checks for payment, and it establishes a framework for deposit and checking agreements between a bank and its customers.[1]

This chapter will identify the legal characteristics of checks and the legal duties and liabilities that arise when a check is issued. Then it will consider the check deposit and collection process—that is, the actual procedure by which the checks deposited into bank accounts move through banking channels, causing the underlying cash dollars to be shifted from one bank account to another.

❖ Checks

A **check** is a special type of draft that is drawn on a bank, ordering it to pay a sum of money on demand [UCC 3–104(2)(b)]. A check does not, in and of itself, operate as an assignment of funds [UCC 3–409(1)]. It does not show an intention to make immediate transfer of the right to the specified sum. Thus, the drawee bank[2] is not liable to a payee or holder who presents the check for payment, even though the drawer has sufficient funds to pay the check. The payee's, or holder's, only recourse is against the drawer. (The drawer, however, may subsequently hold the bank liable for its wrongful refusal to pay.) We now look at some special types of checks.

CHECK
A draft drawn by a drawer ordering the drawee bank or financial institution to pay a certain amount of money to the holder on demand.

1. As mentioned in Chapter 18, revised versions of both Article 3 and Article 4 were promulgated in 1990. The text of the revised versions is included in Appendix C. The revised Article 4 defines the term *bank* as "a person engaged in the business of banking, including a savings bank, savings and loan association, credit union or trust company" [RUCC 4–105(1)].
2. See Chapter 18 for definitions of the parties to commercial paper, such as drawee, drawer, and payee.

◆ Exhibit 20–1
A Cashier's Check

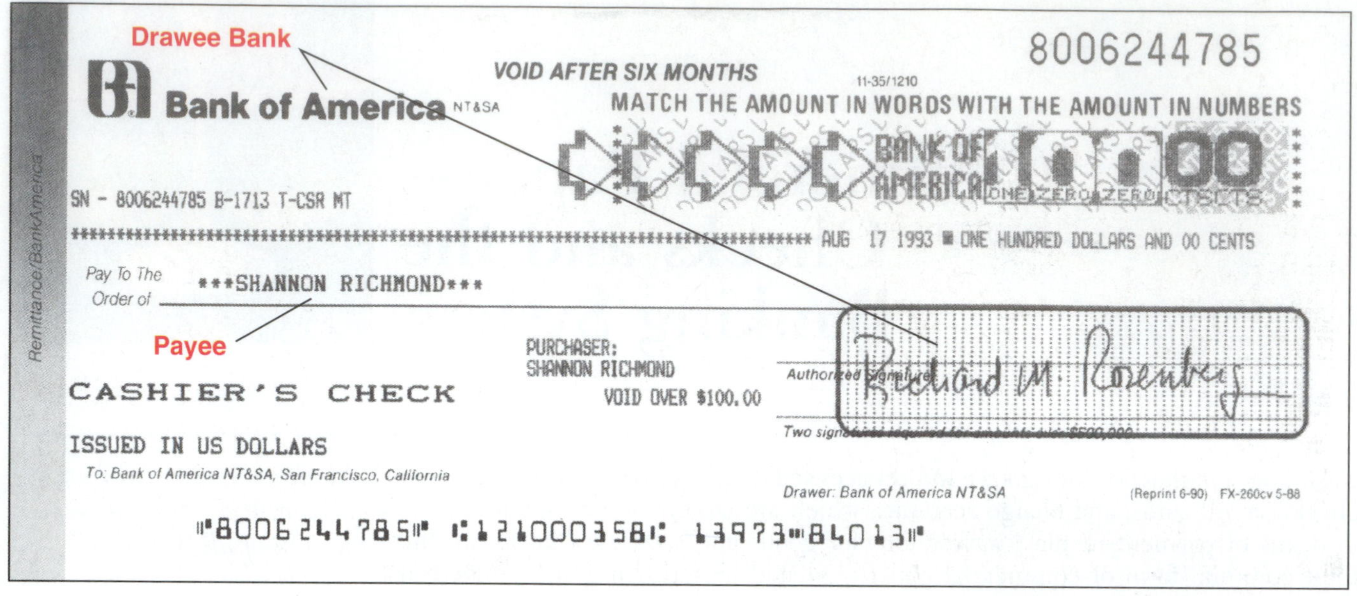

Cashier's Check

CASHIER'S CHECK
A draft drawn by a bank on itself.

Checks are usually three-party instruments, but on certain types of checks, the bank can serve as both the drawer and the drawee. For example, when a bank draws a check upon itself, the check is called a **cashier's check** and is a negotiable instrument upon issue (see Exhibit 20–1). In effect, with a cashier's check, the bank lends its credit to the purchaser of the check, thus making it available for immediate use in banking circles. A cashier's check is therefore an acknowledgment of a debt drawn by the bank upon itself.

Traveler's Check

TRAVELER'S CHECK
An instrument purchased from a bank, express company, or the like, in various denominations, that can be used as cash upon a second signature by the purchaser. It has the characteristics of a cashier's check.

A **traveler's check** has the characteristics of a cashier's check. It is an instrument on which a financial institution is both the drawer and the drawee. The institution is directly obligated to accept and pay its traveler's check according to the check's terms. The purchaser is required to sign the check at the time it is bought and again at the time it is used. Exhibit 20–2 shows an example of a traveler's check.

Certified Check

CERTIFIED CHECK
A check drawn by an individual on his or her own account but bearing a signature guaranty (acceptance) by a bank that the bank will pay the check at the time the check is presented.

A **certified check** is sometimes used to ensure against dishonor for insufficient funds. When a drawee bank agrees to certify a check, it immediately charges the drawer's account with the amount of the check and transfers those funds to its own certified check account. In effect, the bank is agreeing in advance to accept that check when it is presented for payment and to make payment from those funds reserved in the certified check account [UCC 3–411(1)]. Essentially, certification prevents the bank from denying liability. It is a promise that sufficient funds are on deposit and *have been set aside* to cover the check. A drawee bank is not obligated to certify a check, and failure to do so is not a dishonor of the check [UCC 3–411(2)]. Sometimes, certified checks (or cashier's checks) are the required form of payment under state law—for example, in purchases at a sheriff's sale. Exhibit 20–3 illustrates a sample certified check.

Certification can be requested by a holder, as well as the drawer. The legal liability of the drawer varies on the basis of whether the certification is requested by the drawer or the holder. The drawer who obtains certification remains *second-*

◆ **Exhibit 20–2**
A Traveler's Check

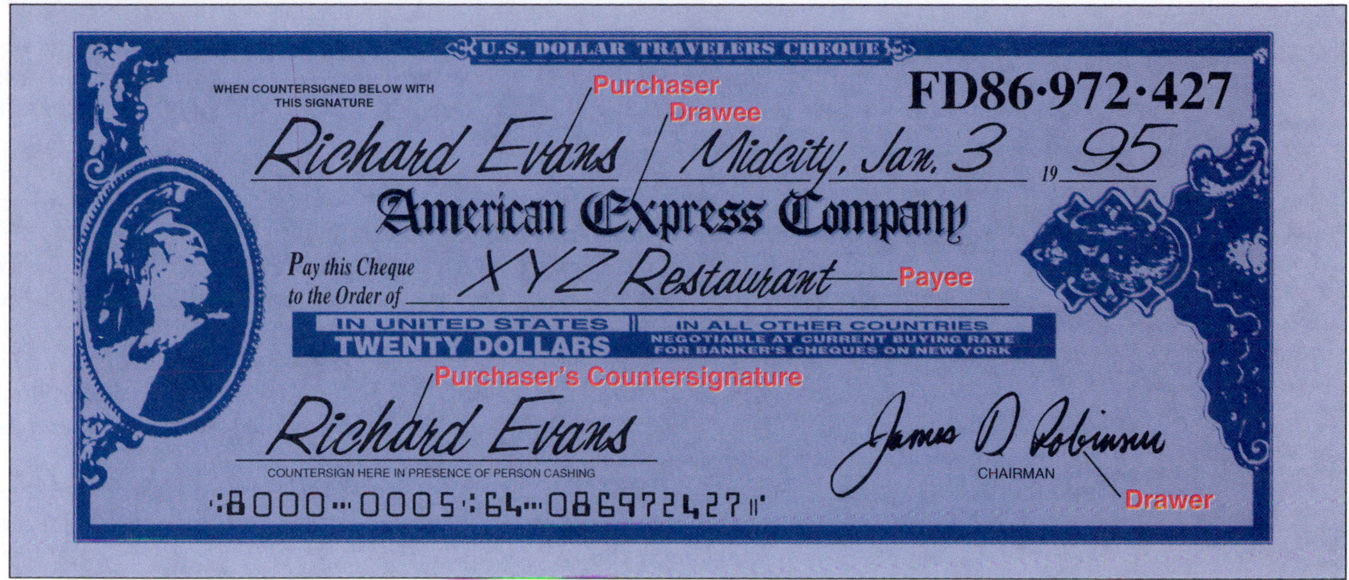

◆ **Exhibit 20–3**
A Certified Check

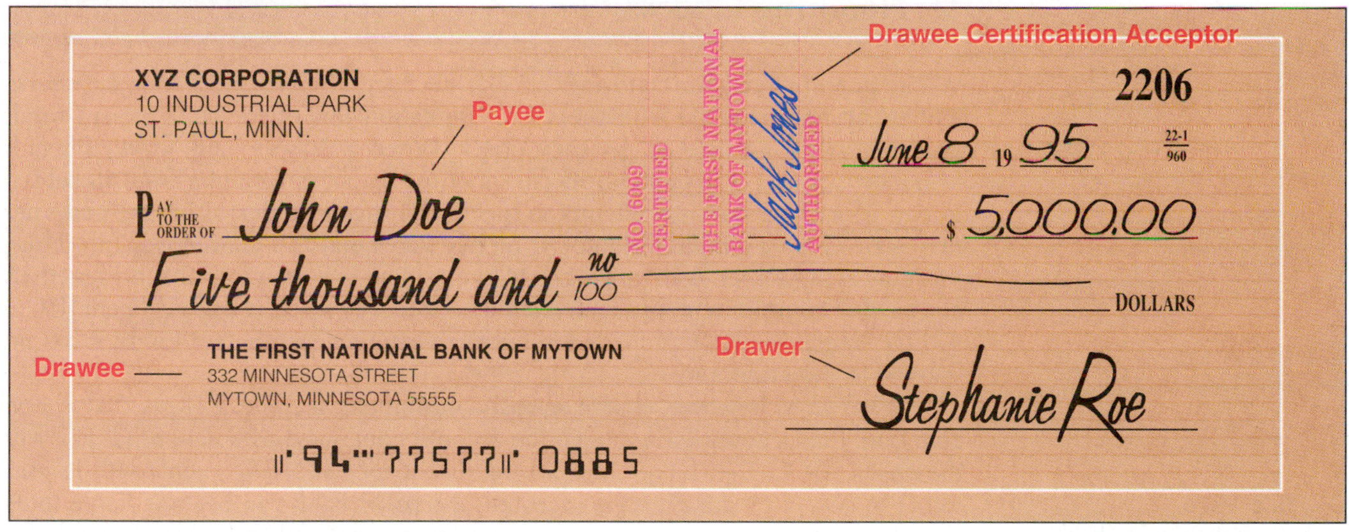

arily liable on the instrument if for some reason the certifying bank cannot or does not honor the check when it is presented for payment. If the check is certified at the request of the holder, then the drawer and anyone who indorsed the check prior to certification are completely discharged. A holder's request for certification is viewed as a choice of the bank's promise to pay over the drawer's and any indorser's promises. In this situation, the holder can look only to the bank for payment.[3]

3. A number of legal issues have arisen over cashier's, teller's, and certified checks that are lost, stolen, or destroyed and the liability of a drawee who wrongfully refuses to make payment. (A *teller's check* is usually drawn by a bank on another bank; when drawn on a nonbank, it is payable at or through a bank [see RUCC 3–104(h)].) The revised Article 3 addresses some of the issues in RUCC 3–312 and 3–411.

❖ The Bank-Customer Relationship

The bank-customer relationship begins when the customer opens a checking account and deposits money that will be used to pay for checks written. The rights and duties of the bank and the customer are contractual and depend on the nature of the transaction.

A creditor–debtor relationship is created between a customer and a bank when, for example, the customer makes cash deposits into a checking account or when final payment is received for checks drawn on other banks.

An agency relationship underlies the check-collection process. A check does not operate as an immediate legal assignment of funds between the drawer and the payee [UCC 3–409]. The money in the bank represented by that check does not immediately move from the drawer's account to the payee's account; nor is any underlying debt discharged until the drawee bank honors the check and makes final payment. To transfer checkbook dollars among different banks, each bank acts as the agent of collection for its customer [UCC 4–201(1)].

Whenever a bank–customer relationship is established, certain rights and duties arise. The respective rights and duties of banks and their customers are discussed in detail in the following sections.

❖ Honoring Checks

When a commercial bank provides checking services, it agrees to honor the checks written by its customers with the usual stipulation that there be sufficient funds available in the account to pay each check. When a drawee bank *wrongfully* fails to honor a check, it is liable to its customer for damages resulting from its refusal to pay. The UCC does not attempt to specify the theory under which the customer may recover for wrongful dishonor; it merely states that the drawee is liable. Thus, the drawer customer does not have to prove that the drawee bank breached its contractual commitment, or slandered the customer's credit, or was negligent [UCC 4–402]. When the bank properly dishonors a check for insufficient funds, it has no liability to the customer.

A bank may, however, charge against a customer's account a check that is payable from that account even though the account contains insufficient funds to cover the check [UCC 4–401(1)]. Once a bank makes special arrangements with its customer to accept **overdrafts** on an account, the payor bank can become liable to its customer for damages proximately caused by its wrongful dishonor of overdrafts. The charging of overdrafts will be discussed later in this chapter.

OVERDRAFT
A check written on a checking account in which there are insufficient funds to cover the check.

The customer's agreement with the bank includes a general obligation to keep sufficient money on deposit to cover all checks written. The customer is liable to the payee or to the holder of a check in a civil suit if a check is not honored. If intent to defraud can be proved, the customer can also be subject to criminal prosecution for writing a bad check.

Stale Checks

STALE CHECK
A check, other than a certified check, that is presented for payment more than six months after its date.

The bank's responsibility to honor its customers' checks is not absolute. A bank is not obliged to pay an uncertified check presented more than six months from its date [UCC 4–404]. Commercial banking practice regards a check presented for payment more than six months from its date as a **stale check.** UCC 4–404 gives a bank the option of paying or not paying on such a check without liability. The

Business Law in Action

What Is a Credit Reputation Worth?

Writing bad checks is not taken lightly in our society. Indeed, if a person writes a check that "bounces," that person's credit reputation and general trustworthiness may be seriously harmed, depending on the situation. Because of the adverse consequences that might result from a bounced check, the UCC provides that when a bank wrongfully dishonors a check, the bank will be liable to the customer for damages, including damages proximately caused by the dishonor. The difficulty in cases involving a bank's wrongful dishonor of a check is that often the harm caused by the dishonor is not quantifiable. A firm's credit reputation in a community can be a great asset, and a dishonored check can affect that reputation. But how does one measure the damage?

For example, assume that a bank wrongfully dishonors a business firm's check for $4,000 to a local supplier. The rumor spreads that the firm is having financial difficulties. Soon, the firm is unable to purchase goods on credit, and its business suffers as a result. Clearly, the bank is liable to the firm for any damages caused by the wrongful dishonor. But how do you measure the bank's liability for the firm's inability to obtain credit from other suppliers? How can the firm prove that this inability was proximately caused by the wrongful dishonor? Because of the difficulty of assessing damages, banks have sometimes been held liable for damages that seem disproportionately large relative to the amount of the check that was dishonored.

Consider what happened to the American Bank of Waco, Texas, when it wrongfully dishonored checks written by one of its customers. The customer was Waco Airmotive, Inc., a small corporation formed in 1976 to repair and maintain aircraft. Waco had procured a number of loans from American Bank over the years, and by 1980 it owed the bank approximately $18,000. Waco was also seven months behind in its payments on a Small Business Administration (SBA) loan that it had obtained through the bank in 1979. Waco had over $31,000 in its checking account and had written checks totaling $15,132.50 on those funds. The bank dishonored the checks and applied the account funds to Waco's loan balances.

In the lawsuit that followed, Waco claimed that the bank had wrongfully "offset" its account by the loan amounts and alleged damages to its credit reputation in the amount of $25,000. Even though Waco could not "prove" these damages, it did submit evidence that some of its business relationships had been harmed. For example, a fuel supply credit contract had been canceled after Waco's check to the supplier was dishonored, and as a result, the supplier would serve Waco only on a cash-on-delivery basis. The trial court held for Waco Airmotive. Although the court acknowledged that banks are allowed to "offset" customer accounts under certain conditions, these conditions had not been met by American Bank, and thus the offset and the dishonor of the checks was wrongful. The jury awarded Waco not only $25,000 in actual damages but also $500,000 in punitive damages!

The appellate court affirmed the award of *actual* damages, stating that "[u]nless an award of such damages is flagrantly outrageous, extravagant, and so excessive as to shock the judicial conscience, it should not be disturbed." What about the punitive damages award? Section 4–402 of the UCC, which deals with the bank's liability to a customer for wrongful dishonor, says nothing about punitive damages, and generally the UCC prohibits them: "penal damages may not be had except as specifically provided in this Act or by other rule of law." The court decided to create a rule of law: "We hold that a finding that a bank acted with malice or in reckless disregard of the rights of its depositor will support a depositor's recovery of exemplary [punitive] damages for wrongful dishonor of its checks under [Section] 4–402."

Whether the recovery of $500,000 in punitive damages was supported was another matter, but because the case was being remanded for other reasons, the amount of punitive damages would also be reconsidered at the trial court level. "In view of our remand," the court stated, "we deem it unnecessary, if not improper, to express our opinion on the matter of excessiveness of the award of exemplary damages or the propriety of the ratio of the award of exemplary damages to the actual damages found by the jury."[a] Doubtless, American Bank's spirits were cheered by the fact that it had another chance to avoid the punitive damages—or at least have them reduced.

Note that if the bank had wrongfully dishonored Waco's check by *mistake*, damages would have been limited to actual damages: "When the dishonor occurs through mistake liability is limited to actual damages proved. If so proximately caused and proved damages may include damages for an arrest or prosecution of the customer or other consequential damages. Whether any

a. *American Bank of Waco v. Waco Airmotive, Inc.*, 818 S.W.2d 163 (Tex.App.—Waco 1991); rehearing denied, 1991.

Business Law in Action—Continued

consequential damages are proximately caused by the wrongful dishonor is a question of fact to be determined in each case" [UCC 4–402]. Interestingly enough, in the revised version of Article 4, the wording of UCC 4–402 has been changed. Among other things, the phrase "When the dishonor occurs through mistake" has been deleted, meaning that in those states that adopt the revised Article 4, damages for a bank's wrongful dishonor of checks should be limited to actual damages regardless of whether the dishonor was intentional or inadvertent. Because the statute is not specific, however, whether a customer can recover punitive damages for a willful and malicious dishonor may still be left up to the courts.

usual banking practice is to consult the customer, but if a bank pays in good faith without consulting the customer, it has the right to charge the customer's account for the amount of the check.

Missing Indorsements

Banks and other institutions that accept checks for deposit are allowed to supply any necessary indorsements of a customer. This rule does not apply if the item expressly requires the payee's indorsement. The depositary bank places a statement on the item to the effect that it was deposited by a customer or credited to that customer's account [UCC 4–205(1)].

Death or Incompetence of a Customer

UCC 4–405 provides that if, at the time a check is issued or its collection has been undertaken, a bank does not know of an adjudication of incompetence or of the death of its customer, an item can be paid and the bank will not incur liability. Neither death nor incompetence revokes the bank's authority to pay an item until the bank knows of the situation and has had reasonable time to act. Even when a bank knows of the death of its customer, for ten days after the date of death, it can pay or certify checks drawn on or before the date of death—unless a person claiming an interest in that account, such as an heir or an executor of the estate, orders the bank to stop payment. Without this provision, banks would constantly be required to verify the continued life and competence of their drawers.

Stop-Payment Orders

Only a customer can order his or her bank to pay a check, and only a customer can order payment of a check to be stopped. This right does not extend to holders—that is, payees or indorsees—because the drawee bank's contract is not with them, but only with its drawers. A customer has no right to stop payment on a check that has been certified or accepted by a bank, however. Also, a **stop-payment order** must be received within a reasonable time and in a reasonable manner to permit the bank to act on it [UCC 4–403(1)].

STOP-PAYMENT ORDER
An order by the drawer of a draft or check directing the drawer's bank not to pay the check or draft.

Although a stop-payment order can be given orally, usually by phone, it is binding on the bank for only fourteen calendar days unless confirmed in writing.[4] A written stop-payment order (see Exhibit 20–4) or an oral order confirmed in writing

4. Some states do not recognize oral stop-payment orders; they must be in writing.

◆ **Exhibit 20–4**
A Stop-Payment Order

Bank of America

Checking Account
Stop Payment Order

To: Bank of America NT&SA
I want to stop payment on the following check(s).

ACCOUNT NUMBER: ____ – ____

SPECIFIC STOP

*ENTER DOLLAR AMOUNT: ____ *CHECK NUMBER: ____

THE CHECK WAS SIGNED BY: ____

THE CHECK IS PAYABLE TO: ____

THE REASON FOR THIS STOP PAYMENT IS: ____

STOP RANGE (Use for lost or stolen check(s) only.)

DOLLAR AMOUNT: 000

*ENTER STARTING CHECK NUMBER: ____ *END CHECK NUMBER: ____

THE REASON FOR THIS STOP PAYMENT IS: ____

I agree that this order (1) is effective only if the above check(s) has (have) not yet been cashed or paid against my account, (2) will end six months from the date it is delivered to you unless I renew it in writing, and (3) is not valid if the check(s) was (were) accepted on the strength of my Bank of America courtesy-check guarantee card by a merchant participating in that program. I also agree (1) to notify you immediately to cancel this order if the reason for the stop apyment no laonger exists or (2) that closing the account on which the check(s) is (are) drawn automatically cancels this order.

IF ANOTHER BRANCH OF THIS BANK OR ANOTHER PERSON OR ENTITY BECOMES A "HOLDER IN DUE COURSE" OF THE ABOVE CHECK, I UNDERSTAND THAT PAYMENT MAY BE ENFORCED AGINST THE CHECK'S MAKER (SIGNER).

*I CERTIFY THE AMOUNT AND CHECK NUMBER(S) ABOVE ARE CORRECT.

☐ I have written a replacement check (number and date of check).

(Optional—please circle one: Mr., Ms., Mrs., Miss) CUSTOMER'S SIGNATURE **X** ____ DATE ____

BANK USE ONLY

TRANCODE:

☐ 21—ENTER STOP PAYMENT (SEE OTHER SIDE TO REMOVE)

NON READS: ____
UNPROC. STMT HIST: ____
PRIOR STMT CYCLE: ____
HOLDS ON COOLS: ____
REJECTED CHKS: ____
LARGE ITEMS: ____
FEE COLLECTED: ____
DATE ACCEPTED: ____
TIME ACCEPTED: ____

is effective for six months, at which time it must be renewed in writing [UCC 4–403(2)]. If the drawee bank pays the check over the customer's properly instituted stop-payment order, the bank will be obligated to recredit the account of the drawer-customer. The bank, however, is liable for no more than the actual loss suffered by the drawer because of the wrongful payment.

Assume that Arlene Drury orders six bamboo palms from Waverly's Nursery at $50 each. Drury pays in advance for the trees with her check for $300. Later that day, Waverly's Nursery tells Drury that it will not deliver the palms as arranged. Drury immediately calls her bank and stops payment on the check. Two days later, in spite of this stop-payment order, the bank inadvertently honors Drury's check to Waverly's Nursery for the undelivered palms. The bank will be liable to Drury for the full $300. The result would be different if Waverly's had delivered five palms. Because Drury would have owed Waverly's $250 for the goods delivered, she would have been able to establish actual losses of only $50 resulting from the bank's payment over her stop-payment order. Consequently, the bank would be liable to Drury for only $50.

A stop-payment order has its risks for a customer. The drawer must have a *valid legal ground* for issuing such an order; otherwise, the holder can sue the drawer for payment. Moreover, defenses sufficient to refuse payment against a payee may not be valid grounds to prevent payment against a subsequent holder in due course [UCC 3–305]. A person who wrongfully stops payment on a check will not only be liable to the payee for the amount of the check but might also be liable for special damages resulting from the wrongful order. These special damages must be separately pleaded and proved at trial.

Cashier's checks, which were defined earlier in this chapter, are sometimes used in the business community as nearly the equivalent of cash. Except in very limited circumstances, payment will not be stopped on a cashier's check. Once it has been issued by a bank, the bank must honor it when it is presented for payment.[5]

5. The revised Article 3 considerably increases the acceptability of cashier's, certified, and teller's checks by allowing a holder to recover from a bank for wrongful dishonor all expenses incurred, interest, and consequential damages [RUCC 3–411].

The following case confirms the bank's duty to honor a customer's stop-payment order in a timely fashion.

Case 20.1
THOMAS v. MARINE MIDLAND TINKERS NATIONAL BANK
Civil Court of the City of New York, 1976.
86 Misc.2d 284,
381 N.Y.S.2d 797.

HISTORICAL AND SOCIAL SETTING *Before the UCC was adopted, there were no uniform laws governing stop-payment orders. The drafters of the UCC recognized that stop-payment orders constitute a service that bank depositors expect and should receive, "notwithstanding its difficulty, inconvenience and expense. The inevitable occasional losses through failure to stop should be borne by the banks as a cost of the business of banking." With this in mind, the drafters promulgated UCC 4–403.*

FACTS On December 8, 1973, the plaintiff (Thomas) gave Ralph Gallo a check for $2,500 as a down payment on two rugs that Thomas was purchasing from Gallo. The check was postdated December 10 and drawn on the Marine Midland Tinkers National Bank. Having changed his mind about the purchase, Thomas went to the Marine Midland bank on the morning of December 10 and arranged with a bank officer whom he knew to have a stop-payment order placed on the check. Thomas gave the bank officer all the required information but described the check as #22 instead of #221, the correct number. On the afternoon of the following day, the check was presented for payment at the same bank, and the bank cashed it and debited the plaintiff's account in the amount of the $2,500. When Thomas called Gallo, demanding the return of the $2,500, Gallo refused to pay and threatened to enforce the purchase agreement. Thomas then brought an action against the bank for wrongful payment. The bank moved for dismissal of the charge on the basis of the incorrect information (the erroneous check number) given by Thomas on the stop-payment order.

ISSUE Can Thomas recover the $2,500 from the bank?

DECISION Yes. The bank was held responsible for its act of improperly making payment on the check.

REASON The court held that "[a] day and a half is more than reasonable notice to enforce a stop order on a check presented at the very same branch, and payment of the item by the bank thereafter constitutes a breach of its obligations to honor the stop order. The normal problem of reasonable computer lag when dealing with a great number of other branches of a large bank has no relevancy to the facts at bar [the facts in this case], where all transactions occurred in a single branch." As to the error regarding the check number, the court stated, "The single digital mistake in describing the check in the stop order is deemed trivial, and insignificant. Enough information was supplied to the bank to reasonably provide it with sufficient information to comply with the stop payment order. The bank is therefore held responsible for its act of improperly making payment upon the check."

Overdrafts

When the bank receives an item properly payable from its customer's checking account, but there are insufficient funds in the account to cover the amount of the check, the bank can either dishonor the item or pay the item and charge the customer's account, creating an overdraft [UCC 4–401(1)].[6] The bank can subtract the difference from the customer's next deposit because the check carries with it an enforceable implied promise to reimburse the bank. When a check "bounces," a holder can resubmit the check, hoping that at a later date sufficient funds will be

6. The revised Article 4 permits a bank to make a payment creating an overdraft only if the customer has authorized the payment and the payment does not violate any bank-customer agreement [RUCC 4–401(a)]. Also, if there is a joint account, the bank cannot hold any joint-account customer liable for payment of an overdraft unless the customer has signed the item or has benefited from the proceeds of the item [RUCC 4–401(b)]. Lastly, a bank can pay a postdated check without liability unless the customer has properly notified the bank not to do so until the stated date. This is necessary because the automated check-collection system cannot accommodate the postdating of checks [RUCC 4–401(c)].

available to pay it. The holder must notify any indorsers on the check of the first dishonor; otherwise, they will be discharged from their signature liability.

Payment on Forged Signature of Drawer

When a bank pays a check on which the drawer's signature is forged, generally the bank is liable. An exception to this rule is made, however, if it can be shown that the customer's negligence contributed to the forgery.

The General Rule A forged signature on a check has no legal effect as the signature of a drawer [UCC 3–404(1)]. Banks require signature cards from each customer who opens a checking account. The bank is responsible for determining whether the signature on a customer's check is genuine. The general rule, illustrated in the following case, is that the bank must recredit the customer's account when it pays on a forged signature.

Case 20.2 

SCCI, INC. v. UNITED STATES NATIONAL BANK OF OREGON

Court of Appeals of Oregon, 1986.
78 Or.App. 176,
714 P.2d 1113.

HISTORICAL AND SOCIAL SETTING *The drafters of the UCC based UCC 3–404 on Section 23 of the Uniform Negotiable Instruments Law of 1896. The section was reworded and new provisions were added to alleviate some uncertainties. UCC 3–404(1) begins, "Any unauthorized signature is wholly inoperative as that of the person whose name is signed unless he ratifies it or is precluded from denying it." The words "or is precluded from denying it" appeared in the older law. They were retained in the UCC, as the drafters explained in Comment 4 to UCC 3–404, in part "to recognize the negligence which precludes a denial of the signature."*[a]

FACTS Susan Wolf, who was employed as a secretary and bookkeeper for SCCI, Inc., a construction contractor, forged her employer's name on more than ninety checks drawn on SCCI's account at the U.S. National Bank of Oregon. The bank cashed the checks and debited SCCI's account, and Susan Wolf wrongfully received a total of approximately $22,600. The plaintiff, SCCI, brought a criminal action against Wolf when the forgeries were discovered but later dropped the charges and settled out of court. SCCI also demanded that the bank credit its account for the $22,600 worth of forged checks. The bank, however, refused to credit SCCI's account for the amount of the forged checks, claiming that the out-of-court settlement between SCCI and Wolf would undermine its ability to collect from Wolf (which, of course, it would attempt to do if it credited SCCI's account). SCCI argued that it was the bank's duty, under its contractual responsibilities to SCCI, to cash checks only when they were authorized by SCCI. The trial court granted the bank's request for summary judgment, and SCCI appealed the decision.

ISSUE Can the bank be held liable for cashing the forged checks?

DECISION Yes. The trial court's ruling was reversed and the case remanded to the trial court.

REASON The court reasoned that because there was no evidence that "plaintiff's [SCCI's] negligence substantially contributed to the forgery, plaintiff was not obligated for the forged checks that the bank had honored * * * and the bank lacked authority to debit plaintiff's account for the checks. Plaintiff was entitled to have the bank credit its account."

ETHICAL CONSIDERATIONS *One of the general principles underlying the UCC's provisions governing commercial paper is that, between two innocent parties, the one in the better position to prevent the loss should bear the burden of the loss. In this case, the bank was held liable for the loss because it wrongfully paid the checks over the forged signatures. The bank could only have avoided liability by proving that SCCI's negligence contributed to the forgeries, but the court found that there was no evidence that SCCI had been negligent in this respect. One might speculate, however, that SCCI, through careful screening of job applicants and attentive supervision of its employees*

a. The words "or is precluded from denying it" were removed from the section as it appears in revised Article 3. Under RUCC 3–406, however, a party whose negligence contributes to a forgery or alteration of an instrument may still be "precluded from asserting the alteration or the forgery against a person who, in good faith, pays the instrument or takes it for value or for collection."

Case 20.2—Continued

and check-writing procedures, might have prevented the forgeries. In other words, in this situation, one might conclude that SCCI, and not the bank, was in the better position to prevent the loss and that therefore, from an ethical point of view at least, it was unfair to hold the bank liable for the $22,600.

Customer Negligence Section 3–406 of the UCC provides that when the customer's negligence substantially contributes to the forgery, the bank will not normally be obliged to recredit the customer's account for the amount of the check. Comment 2 to this section of the UCC states that the purpose of the section is to impose liability on the party whose negligence allows a forgery or alteration to be "set afloat upon a sea of strangers." Suppose, for example, that Gemco Corporation uses a mechanical check-writing machine to write its payroll and business checks. Gemco discovers that one of its employees used the machine to write himself a check for $10,000 and that the bank subsequently honored it. Gemco requests the bank to recredit $10,000 to its account for incorrectly paying on a forged check. If the bank can show that Gemco failed to take reasonable care in controlling access to the check-writing equipment, Gemco cannot require the bank to recredit its account for the amount of the forged check.[7]

Timely Examination Required A customer has an *affirmative duty* to examine monthly statements and canceled checks promptly and with reasonable care and to report any forged signatures promptly [UCC 4–406(1)].[8] This includes forged signatures of indorsers, to be discussed later [UCC 4–406]. Failure to so examine and report, or any carelessness that results in a loss to the bank, makes the customer liable for the loss [UCC 4–406(2)(a)]. Even if the customer can prove that reasonable care was taken against forgeries, the UCC provides that discovery of such forgeries and notice to the bank must take place within specific time frames in order for the customer to require the bank to recredit his or her account.

When a series of forgeries by the same wrongdoer has taken place, the UCC provides that the customer, to recover for all the forged items, must have discovered and reported the first forged check to the bank within fourteen calendar days of the receipt of the bank statement and canceled checks [UCC 4–406(2)(b)].[9] Failure to notify the bank within this period of time discharges the bank's liability for all forged checks that it pays prior to notification.

For example, Jamestown Bank sends out monthly statements and canceled checks on the last day of each month. Barker, the owner of a small store, unknowingly has had a number of his blank checks stolen by employee Sam. On April 20, Sam forges Barker's signature and cashes check #1. On April 22, Sam forges and cashes check #2. The checks canceled in April (including the forged ones) and the April statement from the Jamestown Bank are received on May 1. Barker sets aside the statement and does not reconcile his checking account. On May 20, Sam forges and cashes check #3. The checks canceled in May and the May statement are received by Barker on June 1. On June 2, Barker examines both statements, discovers the forgeries, and reports them to the bank. On June 4, Sam forges and cashes check #4.

---

7. Under the revised Article 3, this liability may be reduced by any amount of loss caused by negligence on the part of a person paying the instrument or taking it for value or for collection [RUCC 3–406(b)].

8. The revised Article 4 recognizes modern automated check-clearing procedures, which involve "truncation" (presentment by electronic means). All that is required is that either the items (canceled checks) be returned or the bank provide the customer with information to reasonably identify the items paid (item number, amount, date of payment) and maintain the ability to furnish legible copies of the items upon the request of the customer for a period of seven years [RUCC 4–406(a), (b)].

9. The revised Article 4 extends the fourteen-day requirement for examining and reporting to *thirty* days [RUCC 4–406(d)(2)].

Can Barker demand that the bank recredit his account for all forged checks? The answer is no (unless Barker can prove that the bank was *also* negligent, as will be discussed shortly). A series of forgeries by the same wrongdoer has been committed. Barker is liable for checks #1, 2, and 3 because he failed to notify the bank promptly (within the fourteen-day period following the receipt of his statement and canceled checks) of the April forgeries. The bank is liable for check #4 because it paid the check after Barker had notified the bank of the forgeries.

Had Barker examined his April statement immediately upon receipt and reported the two April forgeries, the bank would have been obligated to recredit Barker's account in full. If the bank could have proved that Barker's carelessness in permitting the blank checks to be stolen substantially contributed to the forgery, however, Barker, not the bank, would have been liable [UCC 3–406 and 4–406].

When the Bank Is Also Negligent There is one situation in which a bank customer can escape liability for failing to notify the bank of forged or altered checks within the required fourteen-day period. If the customer can prove that the bank was also negligent—that is, that the bank failed to exercise ordinary care—then the bank will be liable [UCC 4–406(3)].[10] In other words, even though a customer may have been negligent, the bank may still have to recredit the customer's account if the bank itself was negligent.

In recent years, a controversial question has been whether a bank is exercising ordinary care when it fails to examine every signature on every check. Because of the large volume of checks processed by banks, it has become customary in the banking industry to manually examine signatures only on checks written for amounts over a certain threshold amount, such as $1,000. The rationale behind this practice is that the time and money that banks save by using it outweigh the liability the banks might incur for paying checks in smaller amounts that have forged signatures or indorsements. Some courts have held that banks do not breach their duty of care by establishing and adhering to a policy that is cost-effective and customary within the industry. Other courts have held that because banks are supposed to verify all signatures on all checks, they are not exercising ordinary care when they fail to do so.[11]

Regardless of the degree of care exercised by the customer or the bank, the UCC has placed an absolute time limit on the liability of a bank for forged customer signatures. UCC 4–406(4) provides that a customer who fails to report his or her forged signature within one year from the date that the statement and canceled checks were made available for inspection loses the legal right to have the bank recredit his or her account.

Payment on Forged Indorsement

A bank that pays a customer's check bearing a forged indorsement must recredit the customer's account or be liable to the customer-drawer for breach of contract. Suppose that Brian issues a $50 check "to the order of Antonio." Jimmy steals the check, forges Antonio's indorsement, and cashes the check. When the check reaches Brian's bank, the bank pays it and debits Brian's account. Under UCC 4–401, the bank

10. Under the revised Article 4, when the customer failed to report promptly and the bank failed to exercise ordinary care in paying the check(s), allocation for the loss will be based on comparative negligence [RUCC 4–406(e)].

11. The revised Articles 3 and 4 define *ordinary care* to mean the "observance of reasonable commercial standards, prevailing in the area in which [a] person is located, with respect to the business in which that person is engaged" [RUCC 3–103(a)(7) and 4–104(c)]. In the case of a bank, reasonable commercial standards do not require the bank to examine all customers' checks if the failure to examine does not violate the bank's prescribed procedures and the procedures do not vary unreasonably from general banking usage.

must recredit Brian's account $50 because it failed to carry out Brian's order to pay "to the order of Antonio" [UCC 4–207(1)(a)]. (Brian's bank will in turn recover—under breach of warranty principles—from the bank that cashed the check.)

By comparison, the bank has no right to recover from a holder who, without knowledge, cashes a check bearing a forged *drawer's* signature. The holder merely guarantees that he or she has no knowledge that the signature of the drawer is unauthorized. Unless the bank can prove such knowledge, its only recourse is against the forger [UCC 3–418 and 4–207(1)(b)]. The customer, however, has a duty to examine the returned checks and statements received from the bank and to report forged indorsements promptly upon discovery or notice. Failure to report forged indorsements within a three-year period after the forged items have been made available to the customer relieves the bank of liability [UCC 4–406(4)].[12]

Payment on Altered Check

The customer's instruction to the bank is to pay the exact amount on the face of the check to the holder. The bank must examine each check before making final payment. If it fails to detect an alteration, it is liable to its customer for the loss because it did not pay as the drawer-customer ordered. The loss is the difference between the original amount of the check and the amount actually paid. Suppose that a check written for $11 is raised to $111. The customer's account will be charged $11 (the amount the customer ordered the bank to pay). The bank will normally be responsible for the $100 [UCC 4–401(2)(a)].

The bank is entitled to recover the amount of loss from the transferor, who, by presenting the check for payment, warrants that the check has not been materially altered. If the bank is the drawer (as it is on a cashier's check), however, it cannot recover on this ground from the presenting party if the party is an HDC acting in good faith [UCC 3–417(1)(c) and 4–207(1)(c)]. The reason is that an instrument's drawer is in a better position than an HDC to know whether the instrument has been altered. Similarly, an HDC, acting in good faith in presenting a certified check for payment, does not warrant to the check's certifier that the check was not altered before the HDC acquired it [UCC 3–417(1)(c) and 4–207(1)(c)]. For example, Selling, the drawer, draws a check for $500 payable to Deffen, the payee. Deffen alters the amount to $5,000. The First National Bank of Whiteacre, the drawee, certifies the check for $5,000. Deffen negotiates the check to Evans, an HDC. The drawee bank pays Evans $5,000. On discovering the mistake, the bank cannot recover from Evans the $4,500 paid by mistake, even though the bank was not in a superior position to detect the alteration. This is in accord with the purpose of certification, which is to obtain the definite obligation of a bank to honor a definite instrument.

A customer's negligence can shift the risk of loss. A common example occurs when a person carelessly writes a check, leaving large gaps around the numbers and words so that additional numbers and words can be inserted (see Exhibit 20–5).

Similarly, a person who signs a check and leaves the dollar amount for someone else to fill in is barred from protesting when the bank unknowingly and in good faith pays whatever amount is shown [UCC 4–401(2)(b)]. Finally, if the bank can trace its loss on successive altered checks to the customer's failure to discover the initial alteration, then the bank can reduce its liability for reimbursing the customer's

12. The revised Article 4 deletes the three-year limitation for reporting unauthorized indorsements [RUCC 4–406] but adds a new section called "Statute of Limitations" [RUCC 4–111], which provides that "[a]n action to enforce an obligation, duty, or right arising under this Article must be commenced within three years after the [cause of action] accrues." Thus, the drawer or customer still has a three-year period to seek credit for an instrument bearing an unauthorized indorsement that was paid by the bank.

◆ **Exhibit 20–5**
A Poorly Filled-Out Check

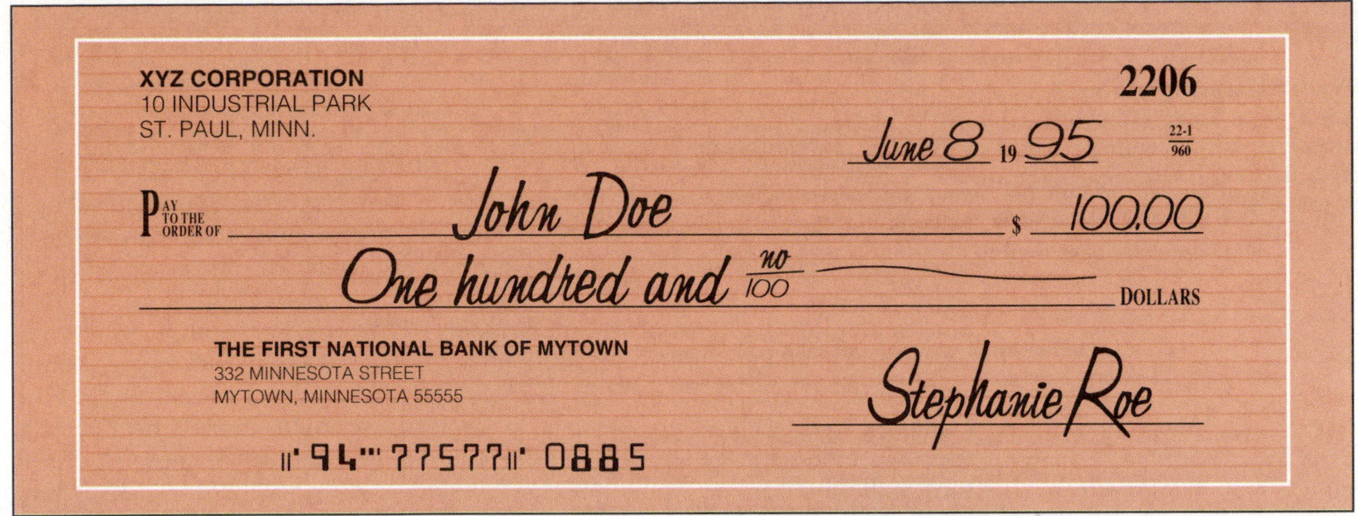

account [UCC 4–406].[13] The law governing the customer's duty to examine monthly statements and canceled checks, and to discover and report alterations to the drawee bank, is the same as that applied to forged customer signatures.

In every situation involving a forged drawer's signature or alteration, a bank must observe reasonable commercial standards of care in paying on a customer's checks [UCC 4–406(3)]. The customer's contributory negligence can be asserted only if the bank has exercised ordinary care.

❖ Bank's Duty to Accept Deposits

A second fundamental service a bank provides for its checking-account customers is that of accepting deposits of cash and checks. Cash deposits made in U.S. currency are received into the customer's account without being subject to further collection procedures. This section will focus on the check after it has been deposited. In most cases, deposited checks involve parties who do business at different banks, but sometimes checks are written between customers of the same bank. Either situation brings into play the bank collection process as it operates within the statutory framework of Article 4 of the UCC.

The Collection Process

The first bank to receive a check for payment is the **depositary bank.**[14] For example, when a person deposits an IRS tax-refund check into a personal checking account at the local bank, that bank is the depositary bank. The bank on which a check is drawn (the drawee bank) is called the **payor bank.** Any bank except the payor bank

DEPOSITORY BANK
The first bank to which an item is transferred for collection, even though it may also be the payor bank.

PAYOR BANK
A bank on which an item is payable as drawn (or is payable as accepted).

13. The bank's defense is the same whether the successive payments were made on forged drawers' signatures or on altered checks. The bank must prove that prompt notice would have prevented its loss. For example, notification might have alerted the bank to stop paying further items or might have enabled it to catch the forger.

14. All definitions in this section are found in UCC 4–105 and RUCC 4–105. The terms *depositary* and *depository* have different meanings in the banking context. A depository bank refers to a physical place (a bank or other institution) in which deposits or funds are held or stored.

COLLECTING BANK
Any bank handling an item for collection, except the payor bank.

INTERMEDIARY BANK
Any bank to which an item is transferred in the course of collection, except the depositary or payor bank.

that handles a check during some phase of the collection process is a **collecting bank.** Any bank except the payor bank or the depositary bank to which an item is transferred in the course of this collection process is called an **intermediary bank.**

During the collection process, any bank can take on one or more of the various roles of depositary, payor, collecting, and intermediary bank. To illustrate, a buyer in New York writes a check on her New York bank and sends it to a seller in San Francisco. The seller deposits the check in her San Francisco bank account. The seller's bank is both a *depositary bank* and a *collecting bank.* The buyer's bank in New York is the *payor bank.* As the check travels from San Francisco to New York, any collecting bank handling the item in the collection process (other than the ones acting as a depositary bank and a payor bank) is also called an *intermediary bank.*

Bank's Liability for Restrictive Indorsements Only the first bank to which the item is presented for collection must pay in a manner consistent with any restrictive indorsement [UCC 3–206(3)]. To illustrate, Charles writes a check on his San Francisco bank account and sends it to Leota. Leota indorses the check with a restrictive indorsement that reads, "For deposit into Account #4012 only." A Dallas bank is the first bank to which this check is presented for payment (the depositary bank), and it must act consistently with the terms of the restrictive indorsement. Therefore, it must credit account #4012 with the money or be liable to Leota for conversion. Charles's check leaves the Dallas bank indorsed "For collection." As the check moves through the collection network of intermediary banks to Charles's San Francisco bank for payment, each intermediary bank is bound only by the preceding bank's indorsement to collect.

The division of responsibility between types of banks is necessary. Collecting banks process huge numbers of commercial instruments, and there is no practical way for them to examine and comply with the effect of each restrictive indorsement. Therefore, the only reasonable alternative is to charge the depositary bank with the responsibility of examining and complying with any restrictive indorsements.

Check Collection between Customers of the Same Bank An item that is payable by the depositary bank (also the payor bank) that receives it is called an "on-us item." If the bank does not dishonor the check by the opening of the second banking day following its receipt, it is considered paid [UCC 4–213(4)(b)]. For example, Williams and Merkowitz both have checking accounts at State Bank. On Monday morning, Merkowitz deposits into his own checking account a $300 check from Williams. That same day, State Bank issues Merkowitz a "provisional credit" for $300. When the bank opens on Wednesday, Williams's check is considered honored, and Merkowitz's provisional credit becomes a final payment.

Check Collection between Customers of Different Banks Millions of checks circulate throughout the United States each day, and every check must be physically transported to its payor bank before final payment is made. Once a depositary bank receives a check, it must arrange to present it either directly or through intermediary banks to the appropriate payor bank. Each bank in the collection chain must pass the check on before midnight of the next banking day following its receipt [UCC 4–202(2)]. Thus, for example, a collecting bank that receives a check on Monday must forward it to the next collection bank before midnight on Tuesday. Unless the payor bank dishonors the check or returns it by midnight on the next banking day following receipt, the payor bank is accountable for the face amount of the check [UCC 4–302].[15]

15. The revised Article 4 recognizes that most checks are cleared by a computerized process and that communication and computer facilities may fail because of weather, equipment malfunction, or other conditions. If such conditions arise and a bank fails to meet its midnight deadline, the bank is "excused" from liability if the bank has exercised "such diligence as the circumstances require" [RUCC 4–109(d)].

Because of this and because of banks' need to maintain an even work flow in the many items they handle daily, the UCC permits what is called *deferred posting*, or delayed return, in which the posting (entering on the bank's records) of checks received after a certain time (say, 2:00 P.M.) can be deferred until the next day. Thus, a check received by a payor bank at 3:00 P.M. on Monday would be deferred for posting until Tuesday. In this case, the payor bank's deadline would be midnight Wednesday [UCC 4–301(1)].

The bank has a duty to use ordinary care in performing its collection functions [UCC 4–202(1)]. This duty requires banks to conform to general banking usage as established in the Uniform Commercial Code, Federal Reserve regulations, clearinghouse rules, and so on [UCC 4–103(1)].[16] Banks also have a duty to act seasonably, meaning that they should take appropriate action before the midnight deadline following the receipt of a check, a notice, or a payment [UCC 4–202(2)].

How the Federal Reserve System Clears Checks The **Federal Reserve System** has greatly simplified the clearing of checks—that is, the method by which checks deposited in one bank are transferred to the banks on which they were written—by acting as a **clearinghouse** for checks. Suppose that Pamela Moy of Philadelphia writes a check to Jeanne Sutton in San Francisco. When Jeanne receives the check in the mail, she deposits it in her bank. Her bank then deposits the check in the Federal Reserve Bank of San Francisco, which transfers it to the Federal Reserve Bank of Philadelphia. That Federal Reserve Bank then sends the check to Moy's bank, which deducts the amount of the check from Moy's account. Exhibit 20–6 illustrates this process.

FEDERAL RESERVE SYSTEM
A network of twelve central banks headed by a board of governors, with the advice of the Federal Advisory Council and the Federal Open Market Committee, to give the United States an elastic currency, supervise and regulate banking activities, and facilitate the flow and discounting of commercial paper. All national banks and state-chartered banks that voluntarily join the system are members.

CLEARINGHOUSE
A system or a place where banks exchange checks and drafts drawn on each other and settle daily balances.

Expedited Funds Availability Act

Congress recently passed an act to improve the check-processing system and to shorten the period between the time funds are deposited and the time the deposited funds are made available to a customer. The major problem Congress addressed in this legislation was the practice by which depository institutions (depositary banks) placed a "hold" on deposited checks—that is, did not allow depositors to draw on these funds (either as cash or by check) until the checks had been honored (paid) by the payor banks. Many "hold" periods were lengthy, and many institutions even placed a hold on deposited government checks for a week or longer.

The act, known as the Expedited Funds Availability Act of 1987,[17] requires that any local check deposited must be available for withdrawal by check or as cash within one business day from the date of deposit. A check is classified as a local check if the depositary and payor banks are located in the same "check-processing regions." (These regions have been designated by the Federal Reserve Board of Governors.) Nonlocal checks must be available for withdrawal within not more than five business days. In addition, the act requires the following:

1. That funds be available on the *next business day* for cash deposits and wire transfers, government checks, the first $100 of a day's check deposit, cashier's checks, certified checks, and checks for which the depositary and payor banks are branches of the same institution.
2. That, for cash withdrawals, the first $100 of any deposit be available on the opening of the next business day after deposit. If a local check is deposited, the next

16. The UCC is explicit that "the obligations of good faith, diligence, reasonableness and care * * * may not be disclaimed" [UCC 1–102(3)].
17. 12 U.S.C. Sections 4001–4010.

◆ **Exhibit 20–6**
How a Check Is Cleared

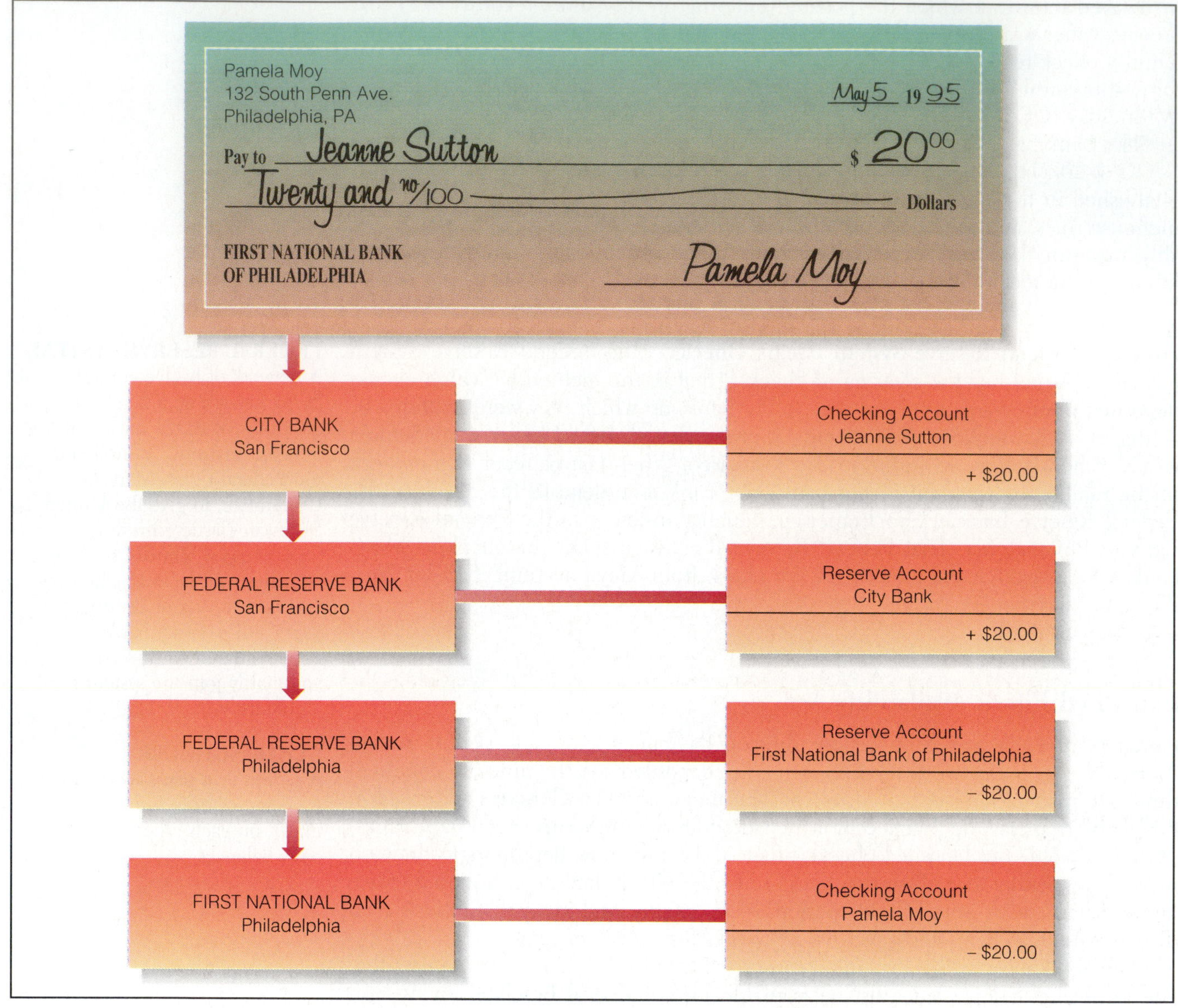

$400 will be available for withdrawal by no later than 5:00 P.M. the next business day. If, for example, you deposit a local check for $500 on Monday, you can withdraw $100 in cash at the opening of the business day on Tuesday, and an additional $400 must be available for withdrawal by no later than 5:00 P.M. on Wednesday.

A different availability schedule applies to deposits made at *nonproprietary* automated teller machines (ATMs). These are ATMs that are not owned or operated by the depository institution. Basically, a five-day hold is permitted on all deposits, including cash deposits, made at nonproprietary ATMs.

Other exceptions also exist. A depository institution has eight days to make funds available in new accounts (those open less than thirty days). It has an extra four days on deposits over $5,000 (except deposits of government and cashier's checks), on accounts with repeated overdrafts, and on checks of questionable collectibility (if the institution tells the depositor it suspects fraud or insolvency).

❖ Electronic Fund Transfer Systems

The present basis of the payment-collection process is the check, but banks are finding it increasingly difficult to cope with the trillions of pieces of paper that evidence funds. New systems of automatic payment and direct deposits, known as *electronic fund transfer (EFT) systems,* promise to rid banks of the burden of having to move mountains of paper in order to transfer money.

The benefits of EFT systems are obvious. Transferring funds electronically enormously reduces the task of handling masses of information. Not surprisingly, it also poses difficulties on occasion, including the following:

1. It is difficult to issue stop-payment orders.
2. Fewer records are available.
3. The possibilities for tampering (with a resulting decrease in privacy) are increased.
4. The time between the writing of a check and its deduction from an account (*float* time) is lost.

Funds can be transferred electronically by (1) automated teller machines, (2) point-of-sale systems, (3) systems handling direct deposits and withdrawals, and (4) pay-by-telephone systems. These and other aspects of electronic transfer systems are discussed here.

Automated Teller Machines

Automated teller machines (ATMs), which are also called *customer bank communications terminals* or *remote service units,* are located either on the bank's premises or at convenient locations such as supermarkets, drugstores and other stores, airports, and shopping centers. Automated teller machines receive deposits, dispense funds from checking or savings accounts, make credit-card advances, and receive payments. The devices are connected on-line to the bank's computers. Customers usu-

The advantages of using an automated teller machine are obvious. What are some of the disadvantages?

ally have a *debit card,* or *access card,* which is a plastic card that allows a customer to use a computer banking system. To make a withdrawal from an ATM, the customer uses his or her access card in addition to punching in a *personal identification number (PIN).* The PIN protects the customer from someone else's use of a lost or stolen access card.

Point-of-Sale Systems

Point-of-sale systems allow the consumer to transfer funds to merchants to pay for purchases. On-line terminals are located at checkout counters in the merchant's store. When a purchase is made, the customer's card is inserted into the terminal, which reads the data encoded on it. The computer at the customer's bank verifies that the card and identification code are valid and that there is enough money in the customer's account. After the purchase is made, the customer's account is debited for the amount of the purchase.

Direct Deposits and Withdrawals

A direct deposit may be made to a customer's account through an electronic terminal when the customer has authorized the deposit in advance. The federal government often uses this type of EFT to deposit Social Security payments directly into beneficiaries' accounts. Similarly, an employer may agree to make payroll and pension payments directly into an employee's account at specified intervals.

A customer may also authorize the bank (or other financial institution at which the customer's funds are on deposit) to make automatic payments at regular, recurrent intervals to a third party. For example, insurance premiums, utility bills, and automobile installment loan payments may sometimes be made automatically.

Pay-by-Telephone Systems

When it is undesirable to arrange in advance for an automatic payment—as, for example, when the amount of a regular payment varies—some financial institutions permit their customers to pay bills through a pay-by-telephone system. This allows the customer to access the institution's computer system by telephone and direct a transfer of funds. Utility bills frequently are paid directly by customers using pay-by-telephone systems. Customers may also be permitted to transfer funds between accounts—for example, to withdraw funds from a savings account and make a deposit in a checking account—in this way.

❖ Consumer Fund Transfers

Consumer fund transfers are governed by the Electronic Fund Transfer Act (EFTA) of 1978. This act and the rights and liabilities of banks and bank customers under the act are discussed in this chapter's *Landmark in the Law.* In this section, we look more closely at the act's coverage and its provisions concerning unauthorized transfers and error resolution.

Coverage of the EFTA

The EFTA governs financial institutions that offer electronic fund transfers involving customer accounts. The types of accounts covered include checking accounts, sav-

Landmark in the Law

The Electronic Fund Transfer Act (1978)

Congress stated in 1978 that the use of electronic systems to transfer funds promised to provide substantial benefits for consumers. But Congress also concluded that, given the unique characteristics of EFT systems, existing consumer protection legislation governing the rights and obligations of consumers, financial institutions, and intermediaries was inadequate with respect to the types of fund transfers occurring by means of EFT systems. Thus, in 1978, Congress passed the Electronic Fund Transfer Act (EFTA)[a] "to provide a basic framework establishing the rights, liabilities, and responsibilities of participants in electronic fund transfers." The EFTA is essentially a disclosure law benefiting consumers; it requires financial institutions to inform consumers of their rights with respect to EFT systems. The EFTA is not concerned with commercial electronic fund transfers—transfers between businesses or between businesses and financial institutions.

In addition to providing a basic framework for the rights, liabilities, and responsibilities of users of EFT systems, the act gave the Federal Reserve Board authority to issue rules and regulations to help implement the act's provisions. The Federal Reserve Board's implemental regulation is called Regulation E—Electronic Funds Transfers. The following are some of the major rules that apply to the use of EFT systems:

1. If a customer's debit card is lost or stolen and used without his or her permission, the customer may be required to pay no more than $50. The customer, however, must notify the bank of the loss or theft within two days of learning about it. Otherwise, the liability increases to $500. The customer may be liable for more than $500 if the unauthorized use is not reported within sixty days after it appears on the customer's statement. (Even the $50 limit does not apply if the customer gives his or her card to someone who uses it improperly or if fraud is committed.)
2. Any error on the monthly statement must be discovered by the customer within sixty days, and the bank must be notified. The bank then has ten days to investigate and must report its conclusions to the customer in writing. If the bank takes longer than ten days, it must return the disputed amount of money to the customer's account until the error is found. If there is no error, the customer has to give the money back to the bank.
3. The bank must furnish receipts for transactions made through computer terminals, but it is not obliged to do so for telephone transfers.
4. A monthly statement must be made for every month in which there is an electronic transfer of funds. Otherwise, statements must be made every quarter. The statement must show the amount and date of the transfer, the names of the retailers or other third parties involved, the location or identification of the terminal, and the fees. Additionally, the statement must give an address and a phone number for inquiries and error notices.
5. Any authorized prepayment for utility bills and insurance premiums can be stopped three days before the scheduled transfer.

All of the preceding information must be given to the customer who opens an EFTS account.

a. 15 U.S.C. Sections 1693–1693r.

ings accounts, and any other asset accounts established for personal, family, or household purposes. Note that telephone transfers are covered by the EFTA only if they are made in accordance with a prearranged plan under which periodic or recurring transfers are contemplated. Therefore, if an imposter, posing as an account holder, calls a bank official and requests a transfer of funds, the true account holder cannot hold the bank liable under the EFTA. The account holder may be able to recover the fraudulently transferred funds in a tort or contract lawsuit, but the action will not be covered under the EFTA.[18] In the following case, the court examines the purposes of the EFTA and stresses the fact that the act covers only electronic fund transfers made by *consumers*. Transfers between financial institutions are not covered by the act.

18. *Kashanchi v. Texas Commerce Medical Bank, N.A.*, 703 F.2d 936 (5th Cir. 1983).

Case 20.3
SHAWMUT WORCESTER COUNTY BANK v. FIRST AMERICAN BANK & TRUST
United States District Court,
District of Massachusetts, 1990.
731 F.Supp. 57.

HISTORICAL AND POLITICAL SETTING *Legal developments since the late 1960s have included important federal laws to protect consumers of banking and credit services. The enactment of these laws has been motivated in part by a concern that injustice results too frequently when professionals in the financial field do business with consumers who are uninformed, unsophisticated, and economically disadvantaged, relative to the professionals. In 1968, the Truth-in-Lending Act imposed disclosure requirements on consumer loans and retail credit transactions. Additional consumer safeguards concerning credit cards were enacted in 1970. In 1974, regulations were imposed on consumer credit reporting services, and Congress prohibited discrimination on the basis of gender or marital status in granting access to credit. In 1976, Congress extended the prohibition on discrimination to include race, religion, national origin, age, and receipt of public assistance. In 1978, the Electronic Fund Transfer Act defined rights, liabilities, and responsibilities with regard to debit cards and electronic fund transfers to protect consumers, whom the act defined as "natural persons."*[a]

FACTS Shawmut Worcester County Bank, a Massachusetts bank, transferred $10,000 to First American Bank & Trust of Palm Beach, Florida, through an EFTS system known as Fedwire. Shawmut's payment order stated that the beneficiary of the transfer was Fernando Degan and that First American should credit account number 100 205 001 633. It turned out that the First American account under that number was held jointly by Degan and Joseph Merle. When Shawmut discovered its error 106 days after the mistaken transfer, it credited the account of its customer who had requested the transfer with the $10,000 and then asked First American to "reverse" the transfer. First American asked Merle, its customer, if he would authorize the reversal. Merle refused. Accordingly, First American told Shawmut it would not reverse the transfer. Shawmut then sued First American to recover the $10,000, alleging, among other claims, that the transaction fell under the EFTA, which prescribes specific requirements that must be followed in the event of error in a funds transaction. First American moved for summary judgment in its favor.

a. 15 U.S.C. Section 1693a.

ISSUE Was the transfer between the two financial institutions covered by the EFTA?

DECISION No. The court granted First American's motion for summary judgment on Shawmut's claim alleging a cause of action under the EFTA. The transfer between the two financial institutions was not covered by the act.

REASON The court noted that although the EFTA does provide "a basic framework establishing the rights, liabilities and responsibilities of participants in [electronic fund transfer] systems," the act was created to benefit consumers and is aimed at providing "a framework of law regulating the rights of consumers as against financial institutions in electronic funds transfers." In this case, the dispute was between two financial institutions. There was no evidence that a financial institution–consumer relationship, which would be covered under the act, existed between First American and Shawmut. "In the absence of such evidence, it is evident that this sort of funds transfer—a garden-variety wire transfer between financial institutions—is specifically excepted from the Transfer Act coverage by the provisions of section 1693a(6)(B)."

Unauthorized Transfers

Unauthorized transfers of funds by means of EFT systems are one of the hazards of electronic banking. A paper check leaves visible evidence of a transaction, and a customer can easily detect a forgery or an altered check with ordinary vigilance. But the evidence of an electronic transfer is in many cases only an entry in a computer printout of the various debits and credits made to a particular account during a specified time period.

Because of the vulnerability of EFT systems to fraudulent activities, the EFTA of 1978 clearly defined what constitutes an unauthorized transfer. Under the act, a transfer is unauthorized if (1) it is initiated by a person other than the consumer who has no actual authority to initiate the transfer; (2) the consumer receives no benefit from it; and (3) the consumer did not furnish the person "with the card, code, or other means of access" to his or her account.

Law in the Extreme

Machines Don't Lie—or Do They?

Automated teller machines (ATMs) hold potential perils for consumers, as well as for banks. In one case, for example, a bank customer learned that certain withdrawals had been made from her account via an ATM, and she knew that she had not made them. Nor had she given her ATM card to anyone or divulged her PIN number (which she had memorized and never written down). Yet how could she argue against the ATM printout that showed that $800 had been withdrawn from her account at a certain time on a certain date? Clearly, it was her word against that of the machine. The judge decided that for once, he was going to depart from the tradition of taking the "machine's word" for it, and he held for the woman, who had offered proof at trial that she was at work when the withdrawals were made and whom the judge described as a "credible witness."[a]

More recently, another bizarre situation arose when Melanie Curde went to the ATM at her bank, checked her account balance, withdrew some funds, and attempted to deposit a $200 check that she had just received. She inserted the check and a deposit slip into the ATM slot labeled "Deposit." The check and deposit slip disappeared into the machine—and did not surface until months later. Curde's bank statements never reflected the deposit, and the bank claimed it had never been made. The ATM printout showed that Curde had checked her account balance on that date, made a withdrawal, and attempted a third transaction that resulted in an error and was canceled by the customer. Several months later, when the front covering of the ATM was removed for servicing, Curde's check and deposit slip were found between the covering and the machine itself, in an area near the bottom of the machine away from the deposit slot. Curde sued the bank for damages, alleging, among other things, that the bank had violated the EFTA. The bank contended that it could not be liable under the EFTA because that act governs electronic fund transfers, and no "transfer" of Curde's funds had ever in fact occurred.

The trial court agreed with the bank. No transfer had occurred, and therefore the EFTA did not cover this transaction. The trial court also held that because the EFTA governs *electronic* transfers of funds, Curde's transaction, which involved an attempted transfer of a paper check, was not covered by the act. The appellate court viewed the matter differently. It held that the transactions covered by the EFTA include deposits of paper checks at ATM machines and that Curde's transaction was therefore governed by the act. But this news was of little avail to Melanie Curde, because the court also held that the bank faced no liability under the EFTA. Why? Because the ATM printout showed that Curde had canceled the transaction![b]

a. *Judd v. Citibank,* 107 Misc.2d 526, 435 N.Y.S.2d 210 (1980).
b. *Curde v. Tri-City Bank & Trust Co.,* 826 S.W.2d 911 (Tenn. 1992).

In the following case, the court had to determine whether an account holder had authorized an imposter to withdraw funds from the customer's account. The first two parts of the definition of an unauthorized transfer just cited were obviously not relevant—the customer had not initiated or authorized the transfer, nor had he benefited from it. He had, however, unwittingly furnished the imposter with his EFT card and bank code. The case contains a lesson for all ATM users.

Case 20.4
OGNIBENE v. CITIBANK, N.A.
Civil Court of New York City, 1981.
112 Misc.2d 219,
446 N.Y.S.2d 845.

HISTORICAL AND ECONOMIC SETTING *Automated teller machines (ATMs) are often located outside banks. Many bank customers avoid these ATMs because they feel that the machines are impersonal and perhaps unsafe. At an outside ATM, criminals are more apt to practice fraud or theft on the young or elderly. At some ATM sites, mugging has been a frequent occurrence. Some of the problems may be resolved by sophisticated security devices. Such innovations are expensive, however, and banks are reluctant to spend more on ATMs, considering that, as a system, ATMs have not resulted in significant cost savings. There is also evidence that customers, as well as street criminals, practice fraud in connection with ATMs. Some customers claim that their bank statements reflect withdrawals that they never made. The banking industry estiimates that 10 percent of its losses from ATMs are from customer fraud.*

FACTS On August 16, 1981, Frederick Ognibene stopped at a Citibank automated teller machine located outside the bank to make a $20 withdrawal from his checking account. There were two ATMs located close together, and in between them was a customer service telephone. While Ognibene made his withdrawal, a man was talking on the phone and appeared to be telling the bank's customer service department that one of the machines was not working. The man, who Ognibene assumed was a bank employee, then turned to Ognibene and said that the bank's customer service department had asked if he might try Ognibene's card in the malfunctioning machine to see if it would activate it. Ognibene, the Good Samaritan in this case, complied and watched the man insert his card in the ATM in question. The man then punched in a personal identification number (which, unbeknownst to Ognibene, was Ognibene's own PIN, which the other man had observed when Ognibene made his $20 withdrawal a few seconds earlier) and continued talking on the telephone, supposedly to bank personnel. The man reinserted Ognibene's card and reported to the fictitious person on the other end of the phone line that the machine was now functioning. He then hung up, thanked Ognibene, took his cash, and left. Later, when Ognibene realized $400 had been withdrawn from his account at that same time of that same day, he brought an action against the bank to recover the $400.

ISSUE At issue was whether the stranger's withdrawal from Ognibene's account had been "authorized" by Ognibene. Ognibene had permitted the stranger to use his card and had allowed, albeit unwittingly, the stranger to view his personal identification code number as he punched it in for his $20 withdrawal. Thus, although Ognibene contended that he in no way had authorized the stranger to withdraw cash from his account, the bank argued that technically Ognibene had given that authority by his negligent actions.

DECISION The court held for Ognibene and ordered the bank to reinstate the $400 into Ognibene's account.

REASON Under the Electronic Fund Transfer Act (EFTA), a consumer's liability is limited in cases in which "unauthorized" access to his or her account was obtained. It was undisputed that the first two requirements for an unauthorized transfer under the EFTA had been met. Ognibene had clearly not initiated the transfer himself and had not given "actual authority" to the imposter to use his card, nor had he benefited from the transaction. As to the third requirement, the fact that Ognibene had handed the stranger his access card, even though he did it voluntarily, did not mean that Ognibene intended to authorize the stranger's withdrawal of funds from his account. Nor was Ognibene's act negligent—he innocently believed he was assisting a bank employee. When a fraud is committed, a court will often determine liability on the basis of which party was in the best position to prevent the fraud. In this case, evidence at trial indicated that the bank had received several reports of fraudulent withdrawals conducted by imposters posing as bank employees and gaining access to accounts in the same manner as in the Ognibene case. The court held that because "the bank had knowledge of the scam and its operational details (including the central role of the customer service telephone), it was negligent in failing to provide plaintiff-customer with information sufficient to alert him to the danger." The court thus concluded that "the responsibility for the fact that plaintiff's code, one of the two necessary components of the 'access device' * * * to his account, was observed and utilized as it was must rest with the bank."

ETHICAL CONSIDERATIONS *Clearly, the scam artist was acting unethically, as well as illegally. The ethical question here is whether the bank was in fact in a better position than the customer to protect against the fraud. As the court indicated, the bank could have taken steps to warn customers against the scam, but some responsibility must also rest with ATM users to protect their PIN numbers from unauthorized use. Although the court's decision in the Ognibene case sent a message to banks to be more careful, no message was sent to bank customers to exercise greater care when using ATMs.*

Error Resolution and Damages

The error-resolution procedures prescribed by the EFTA and described briefly in the *Landmark in the Law* must be followed strictly by a bank. If the bank fails to investigate the error and report its conclusion promptly to the customer, in the specific manner designated by the EFTA, it will be in violation of the act and subject to civil liability. Its liability extends to any actual damages sustained by a customer and to all the costs of a successful action brought against the bank by a customer, including attorneys' fees. In addition, the bank may be liable for punitive damages ranging from $100 to $1,000 in an individual action. Even when a customer has sustained no actual damage, the bank may be liable for legal costs and punitive damages if it fails to follow the proper procedures outlined by the EFTA in regard to error resolution. This point is illustrated clearly by the following case.

Case 20.5
BISBEY v. D.C. NATIONAL BANK
United States Court of Appeals, District of Columbia, 1986.
253 U.S.App.D.C. 244,
793 F.2d 315.

HISTORICAL AND TECHNOLOGICAL SETTING *Automatic fund transfers are mechanisms for handling recurring debits and credits without the paper exchange of checks. Automatic fund transfers can be conducted through an automated clearinghouse, which substitutes electronic, computerized information for paper. This exchange of funds can be quicker and less expensive than issuing and collecting checks, which may involve postal delays, occasional losses, or fraud. To initiate automatic fund transfers to pay insurance premiums, for example, the insurance company obtains the customer's authorization. Periodically, the company tells its bank to notify the automated clearinghouse, which debits and credits the accounts of the banks involved in the payment. In turn, the banks credit and debit the accounts of the company and the customer who authorized the payment. The efficiency of the system is enhanced by the fact that virtually the entire matter can be handled by computer input over telephone lines.*

FACTS Sandra Bisbey opened a checking account with the District of Columbia National Bank in January of 1981. Subsequently, she authorized the bank to debit her checking account for fund transfer directives submitted monthly by the New York Life Insurance Company (NYLIC) for payment of her insurance premiums. In September of 1981, Bisbey's account lacked sufficient funds to cover the NYLIC payment, and no transfer was made. In October, the September request was resubmitted by NYLIC, in addition to the October directive. Although Bisbey's account still lacked sufficient funds to cover the requests, the bank honored them anyway and sent Bisbey two overdraft notices, each in the amount of her monthly insurance premium. Bisbey, having forgotten her nonpayment of the September premium, believed that the bank had erroneously made two payments in October. She thus wrote a letter to the bank, requesting the bank to look into the matter. Approximately ten days later, a bank official telephoned Bisbey and explained that there had been no improper duplication of her premium payments. Bisbey, still convinced that there had been an error, filed suit against the bank for damages on the ground that the bank had not met the requirements of the Electronic Fund Transfer Act (EFTA), which requires a bank to give a *written* explanation of the results of its investigations of customers' complaints. The district court held that, although the bank had violated the EFTA in its resolution of Bisbey's inquiry about her account, the EFTA did not contemplate a finding of civil liability for this type of procedural mistake. Bisbey appealed.

ISSUE Can the bank be held liable for a violation of the EFTA, even though the bank's customer incurred no damage as a result of this violation?

DECISION Yes. The lower court's judgment was reversed and the case remanded for a determination of civil liability and attorneys' fees.

REASON The court noted the seeming injustice that the bank should be held "liable for a transaction that benefited the plaintiff. Ms. Bisbey's account contained insufficient funds to cover either of the premium requests submitted by NYLIC. Though she had no overdraft agreement, the bank did not charge an overdraft fee. Thus, the effect of the bank's payments was to provide her, at no cost, with insurance coverage she would not have had otherwise." The only error on the part of the bank was that it had failed to notify its customer in writing of its conclusions, using the telephone instead. Nonetheless, the bank clearly did fail to comply with the requirements of the EFTA, "and the statute compels a finding that the Bank is liable."

ETHICAL CONSIDERATIONS *Although it may seem unfair that Bisbey should succeed in her suit against the bank—given that she in fact benefited from the bank's*

Case 20.4—Continued

error—the reasoning behind holding banks to strict compliance with the requirements of the EFTA is clear: overall, strict compliance will ensure more fairness to consumers. As with any consumer protection statute, there will be occasional consumers who take unfair advantage of the letter of the law for personal gain.

❖ Commercial Transfers

The transfer of funds "by wire" between commercial parties is another way in which funds are transferred electronically. In fact, the dollar volume of payments by wire transfer is more than $1 trillion a day—an amount that far exceeds the dollar volume of payments made by other means. The two major wire payment systems are the Federal Reserve wire transfer network (Fedwire) and the New York Clearing House Interbank Payments Systems (CHIPS).

Unauthorized wire transfers are obviously possible and, indeed, have become a problem. If an imposter, for example, succeeds in having funds wired from another's account, the other party will bear the loss (unless he or she can recover from the imposter). In the past, any disputes arising as a result of unauthorized or incorrectly made transfers were settled by the courts under the common law principles of tort law or contract law. To clarify the rights and liabilities of parties involved in fund transfers not subject to the EFTA or other federal or state statutes, Article 4A of the UCC was promulgated in 1989. Most states have adopted this article.

The type of fund transfer covered by Article 4A is illustrated in the following example. Jellux, Inc., owes $5 million to Perot Corporation. Instead of sending Perot a check or some other instrument that would enable Perot to obtain payment, Jellux tells its bank, East Bank, to credit $5 million to Perot's account in West Bank. East Bank instructs West Bank to credit $5 million to Perot's account. In more complex transactions, additional banks would be involved.

In these and similar circumstances, ordinarily a financial institution's instruction is transmitted electronically. Any means may be used, however, including first class mail. To reflect this fact, Article 4A uses the term *funds transfer* rather than *wire transfer* to describe the overall payment transaction. The full text of Article 4A is presented in Appendix C, following Article 4 of the Uniform Commercial Code.

Application

Law and the Bank Customer—Stop-Payment Orders

For a variety of reasons, stop-payment orders should not be misused by a drawer. One reason is monetary: the bank's charges for stop-payment orders (which usually range between $10 and $20) are not small in relation to checks written for small amounts. Another reason is the risk attached to the issuing of a stop-payment order for any drawer-customer. The bank is entitled to take a reasonable amount of time to enforce your stop order before it has liability for improper payment. Hence, the payee or another holder may be able to cash the check despite your stop order if he or she acts quickly. Indeed, you could be writing out a stop order in the bank lobby while the payee or holder cashes the check in the drive-in facility next door. In addition, even if a bank pays over your proper stop-payment order, the bank is only liable to the drawer-customer for the amount of loss the drawer suffers from the improper payment.

Remember that a drawer must have a legal reason for issuing a stop-payment order. You cannot stop payment on a check simply because you have had a change

Application—Continued

of heart about the wisdom of your purchase. Generally, you can safely stop payment if you clearly did not get what you paid for or were fraudulently induced to make a purchase. You can also stop payment if a "cooling-off" law governs the transaction—that is, if you legally have a few days in which to change your mind about a purchase. Any wrongful stop order subjects the *drawer* to liability to the payee or a holder, and this liability may include special damages that resulted from the order. When all is considered, it may be unwise to order a stop payment hastily on a check because of a minor dispute with the payee.

Checklist for Stop-Payment Orders

☐ 1. Compare the stop-payment fee with the disputed sum to make sure it is worthwhile to issue a stop-payment order.

☐ 2. Make sure that your stop-payment order will be honored by your bank prior to the payee's cashing the check.

☐ 3. Make sure that you have a legal reason for issuing the stop-payment order.

❖ Key Terms

cashier's check 472
certified check 472
check 471
clearinghouse 485
collecting bank 484
depositary bank 483
Federal Reserve System 485
intermediary bank 484
overdraft 474
payor bank 483
stale check 474
stop-payment order 476
traveler's check 472

❖ Chapter Summary: Commercial Paper—Checks and the Banking System

CHECKS—DEFINITIONS	
Check	A special type of draft that is drawn on a *bank*, ordering the bank to pay a sum of money on *demand*. The maker of the check is the *drawer*, the bank is the *drawee*, and the person to whom the check is payable is the *payee*.
Cashier's Check	A check drawn by a bank on itself (the bank is both the drawer and the drawee) and purchased by a customer. In effect, the bank lends its credit to the purchaser of the check, thus making the funds available for immediate use in banking circles.
Traveler's Check	An instrument on which a financial institution is both the drawer and the drawee. The purchaser must provide his or her signature for a traveler's check to become a negotiable instrument.
Certified Check	A check for which the drawee bank certifies that it will set aside funds in the drawer's account to ensure payment of the check upon presentation. 1. When certification is requested by the drawer, the drawer remains secondarily liable on the instrument if the bank dishonors the check. 2. When certification is requested by a holder, the drawer and all prior indorsers are completely discharged from liability on the check.
HONORING CHECKS	
Bank's Charge against Customer's Account [UCC 4–401]	The bank has the right to charge a customer's account for any item properly payable, even if the charge results in an overdraft.
Wrongful Dishonor [UCC 4–402]	The bank is liable to its customer for actual damages proved to be due to wrongful dishonor. Damages can include those proximately caused for arrest or prosecution, or other consequential damages.
Stale Checks [UCC 4–404]	The bank is not obligated to pay an uncertified check presented more than six months after its date, but it may do so in good faith without liability.

❖ Chapter Summary: Checks and the Banking System—Continued

Death or Incompetence of a Customer [UCC 4–405]	So long as the bank does not know of the death or incompetence of a customer, the bank can pay an item without liability to the customer's estate. Even with knowledge of a customer's death, a bank can honor or certify checks (in the absence of a stop-payment order) for ten days after the date of the customer's death.
Stop-Payment Orders [UCC 4–403]	The customer must make a stop-payment order in time for the bank to have a reasonable opportunity to act. Oral orders are binding for only fourteen days unless they are confirmed in writing. Written orders are effective for only six months unless renewed in writing. The bank is liable for wrongful payment over a timely stop-payment order, but only to the extent of the loss suffered by the drawer-customer.
Unauthorized Signature or Alteration [UCC 4–406]	The customer has a duty to examine account statements with reasonable care upon receipt and to notify the bank promptly of any unauthorized signatures or alterations. On a series of unauthorized signatures or alterations by the same wrongdoer, examination and report must occur within fourteen calendar days of receipt of the statement. Failure to comply releases the bank from any liability unless the bank failed to exercise reasonable care. Regardless of care or lack of care, the customer is estopped from holding the bank liable after one year for unauthorized customer signatures or alterations and after three years for unauthorized indorsements.
BANK'S DUTY TO ACCEPT DEPOSITS	
Definitions [UCC 4–105]	1. *Depositary bank*—The bank accepting a check for deposit into a customer's account. 2. *Payor bank*—The bank on which a check is drawn. 2. *Collecting bank*—Any bank except the payor bank that handles a check during the collecting process. 4. *Intermediary bank*—Any bank except the payor bank or the depositary bank to which an item is transferred in the course of the collection process.
The Collection Process	1. *Liability for restrictive indorsements*—Only the depositary bank must pay in a manner consistent with any restrictive indorsement [UCC 3–206(3)]. 2. *Check collection between customers of the same bank*—A check payable by the depositary bank that receives it is an "on-us" item; if the bank does not dishonor the check by the opening of the second banking day following its receipt, the check is considered paid [UCC 4–213(4)(b)]. 3. *Check collection between customers of different banks*—Each bank in the collection process must pass the check on to the next appropriate bank before midnight of the next banking day following its receipt [UCC 4–202(2)]. 4. *The role of the Federal Reserve System*—The Federal Reserve System facilitates the check-clearing process by serving as a clearinghouse for checks.
ELECTRONIC FUND TRANSFER SYSTEMS	
Rights and Liabilities under the EFTA	1. If a customer's debit card is lost or stolen and used without his or her permission, the maximum amount the customer has to pay is $50, as long as the loss or theft is reported to the bank within two days. Otherwise, the customer's liability increases to $500. If the loss or theft is not reported within sixty days, the customer may be liable for more than $500. 2. Any error on the monthly statement must be reported to the bank within sixty days. The bank then has ten days to investigate. If the bank's investigation requires more time, the bank must return the disputed amount to the customer's account until the dispute is resolved. 3. The bank must furnish receipts for transactions made through computer terminals, but it is not required to do so for telephone transfers. 4. A monthly statement must be made for every month in which there is an electronic transfer of funds. Otherwise, statements must be made every quarter. 5. Any authorized direct prepayment from the customer's account made by the bank (such as for utility bills or insurance premiums) can be stopped three days before the scheduled transfer.
Unauthorized Transfers under the EFTA	Under the EFTA, a transfer is unauthorized if (1) it is initiated by a person other than the consumer who has no actual authority to initiate the transfer; (2) the consumer receives no benefit from it; and (3) the consumer did not furnish the person with the card, code, or other means of access to his or her account.

❖ Chapter Summary: Checks and the Banking System—Continued

Error Resolution and Damages under the EFTA	If a bank fails to follow the error-resolution procedures prescribed by the EFTA, it will be in violation of the act and subject to civil liability—including actual damages and legal costs incurred by the customer.
Commercial Wire Transfers	Disputes arising as a result of unauthorized or incorrectly made wire transfers are not covered under the EFTA and traditionally have been subject to common law principles of tort law and contract law. The newly drafted Article 4A of the UCC, which has been adopted by the majority of the states, now governs fund transfers not subject to the EFTA or other federal or state statutes.

❖ Questions and Case Problems

20-1. Types of Checks. Checks are usually three-party instruments. On what type of check, however, does a bank serve as both the drawer and the drawee? What type of check does a bank agree in advance to accept when the check is presented for payment?

20-2. Electronic Fund Transfers. Under the Electronic Fund Transfer Act, under what conditions will a bank be liable for an unauthorized fund transfer? When will the consumer be liable?

20-3. Missing Indorsements. Marco owed Joshua $300 and wrote a check payable to Joshua in this amount, drawn on First Bank. Joshua deposited the check into his account with Midland State Bank but failed to indorse the check. Midland State Bank supplied an indorsement stating that the funds were to be credited to Joshua's account and sent the check to First Bank for payment. First Bank honored the check. When Marco learned this, he claimed that the bank had wrongfully honored the check because Joshua had not indorsed it. Is Marco correct? Explain.

20-4. Forged Signatures. Gary goes grocery shopping and carelessly leaves his checkbook in his shopping cart. His checkbook, with two blank checks remaining, is stolen by Dolores. On May 5, Dolores forges Gary's name on a check for $10 and cashes the check at Gary's bank, Citizens Bank of Middletown. Gary has not reported the theft of his blank checks to his bank. On June 1, Gary receives his monthly bank statement and canceled checks from Citizens Bank, including the forged check, but he does not examine the canceled checks. On June 20, Dolores forges Gary's last check. This check is for $1,000 and is cashed at Eastern City Bank, a bank with which Dolores has previously done business. Eastern City Bank puts the check through the collection process, and Citizens Bank honors it. On July 1, upon receipt of his bank statement and canceled checks, Gary discovers both forgeries and immediately notifies Citizens Bank. Dolores cannot be found. Gary claims that Citizens Bank must recredit his account for both checks, as his signature was forged. Discuss fully Gary's claim.

20-5. Death of Bank Customer/Stale Checks. On January 5, Brian drafts a check for $3,000 drawn on the Southern Marine Bank and payable to his assistant, Shanta. Brian puts last year's date on the check by mistake. On January 7, before Shanta has had a chance to go to the bank, Brian is killed in an automobile accident. The Southern Marine Bank is aware of Brian's death. On January 10, Shanta presents the check to the bank, and the bank honors the check by payment to Shanta. Brian's widow, Joyce, claims that the bank wrongfully paid Shanta, because it knew of Brian's death and also paid a check that was by date over one year old. Joyce, as executor of Brian's estate and sole heir by his will, demands that Southern Marine Bank recredit Brian's estate for the check paid to Shanta. Discuss fully Southern Marine's liability in light of Joyce's demand.

20-6. Overdrafts. In September of 1976, Edward and Christine McSweeney opened a joint checking account with the United States Trust Co. of New York. Between April of 1978 and July of 1978, 195 checks totaling $99,063 were written. In July of 1978, activity in the account ceased. Ninety-five of the 195 checks, totaling $16,811, were written by Christine, and the rest of the checks were written by Edward. After deposits were credited for that period, the checks created a cumulative overdraft of $75,983. Can a bank knowingly honor a check when payment creates an overdraft, or must the bank dishonor the check? If the bank pays a check and thereby creates an overdraft, can the bank collect the amount of the overdraft from its customer? [*United States Trust Co. of New York v. McSweeney*, 91 A.D.2d 7, 457 N.Y.S.2d 276 (1982)]

20-7. Unauthorized Indorsements. Frank Quinn drew a check for $30,000 payable to Limetree Beach Associates, Ltd., a limited partnership formed for the purpose of investing in real estate. The check was delivered to Dan Wey, who served as the only general partner for the firm (in a limited partnership, general partners manage the firm, and those who invest in the firm are called limited partners). Wey was listed as an authorized signer for the partnership on its checking account with the American State Bank. Wey indorsed the check in his own name for deposit to his own personal account, which was also at American State. American State sent the check for collection to the drawee bank, National Bank, which paid the check. Quinn subsequently demanded that National Bank recredit his account for the amount of the check because the check had been improperly paid under UCC 4–401(1). Will the court agree with Quinn? [*National Bank v. Quinn*, 126 Ill.2d 129, 533 N.E.2d 846, 127 Ill.Dec. 764 (1988)]

20-8. Overdrafts. MJZ Corp. had a checking account with Gulfstream First Bank & Trust. MJZ was unaware of the bank's policy of honoring checks for thirty days after a checking account had been closed. The policy was formed to prevent embarrassment on the part of customers, whose checks would otherwise bounce if they were presented to the bank after the accounts had been closed. MJZ closed its checking account on April 2, 1980, and later that month, two outstanding checks written by the corporation were presented to the bank for payment. The bank paid the checks and requested reimbursement for the amounts from MJZ. When MJZ refused to reimburse the bank, the bank sued for recovery of the amounts. Should the bank be able to recover from MJZ for the amounts of the checks paid after MJZ's account had been closed? [*MJZ Corp. v. Gulfstream First Bank & Trust*, 420 So.2d 396 (Fla.App. 1982)]

20-9. Wrongfully Dishonored Checks. Robert Parrett was the principal shareholder, president, and chief operating officer of P & P Machinery, Inc., a farm machinery business located in Nebraska. On March 1, 1984, Parrett signed and delivered a check from P & P Machinery to a South Dakota firm. The check was dishonored by the bank even though P & P Machinery had sufficient funds in its account to cover the check. In addition, Parrett had a long-standing relationship with the bank as personal guarantor of corporate obligations to the bank and had never had any previous problems with the bank. As a result of the dishonored check, Parrett was charged with felony theft in South Dakota and extradited for trial in South Dakota. On learning that the bank had dishonored the check erroneously, the trial court dismissed the charge against Parrett. Parrett sued the bank for damages. The trial court held that Parrett had no standing to sue the bank because he was not the bank's "customer"—the corporation was. Will the appellate court agree that Parrett lacked standing to sue the bank? Discuss fully. [*Parrett v. Platte Valley State Bank & Trust Co.*, 236 Neb. 139, 459 N.W.2d 371 (1990)]

20-10. Unauthorized Fund Transfers. Lawrence Kruser and his wife maintained a joint checking account with the Bank of America. The bank issued to each of them a "Versatel" card and separate personal identification numbers so that they could access funds in their account from automated teller machines (ATMs). The Krusers believed that Mr. Kruser's card had been destroyed in September 1986. The December 1986 account statement mailed to the Krusers by the bank, however, reflected a $20 withdrawal of funds by someone using Mr. Kruser's card at an ATM. Mrs. Kruser underwent surgery in December 1986 and was in the hospital for eleven days. She spent the following months recuperating from the surgery. She therefore failed to examine the December bank statement promptly and did not discover the unauthorized December withdrawal until August or September of 1987, at which time she reported it to the bank. In September 1987, the Krusers received bank statements for July and August of 1987, which reflected forty-seven unauthorized withdrawals, totaling $9,020, made from an ATM by someone using Mr. Kruser's card. They notified the bank of these withdrawals within a few days of receiving the statements. Is the bank liable to the Krusers for the unauthorized withdrawals? Discuss. [*Kruser v. Bank of America NT & SA*, 230 Cal.App.3d 741, 281 Cal.Rptr. 463 (1991)]

A QUESTION OF ETHICS AND SOCIAL RESPONSIBILITY

20-11. *Wilder Binding Co. opened a checking account with Oak Park Trust and Savings Bank in 1981. The president and vice president of the company were the only ones authorized to sign checks on the account. In December 1983, the firm hired Lorine Daniels as bookkeeper. Among her other responsibilities, Daniels was entrusted with reconciling the bank statements with the firm's checkbook. Daniels forged signatures on forty-two checks, which she made payable to herself, and over a six-month period she embezzled a total of $25,254.78 in this way. Each of the forty-two checks was made out for less than $1,000. When the forgeries were discovered in July 1984, Wilder immediately notified the bank and demanded reimbursement of the total amount of the checks. In the lawsuit that followed, a key issue was whether the bank had breached its duty of care. Wilder alleged that the bank's use of automated check-sorting equipment and its automatic payment of checks drawn for less than $1,000, without manual verification of signatures on those checks, constituted a breach of the bank's duty to exercise reasonable care. The bank testified that such policies and procedures were customary and routine and that its adherence to the policies and procedures therefore did not violate its duty of care. Given these facts, how would you answer the following questions?* [Wilder Binding Co. v. Oak Park Trust and Savings Bank, *135 Ill.2d 121, 552 N.E.2d 783, 142 Ill.Dec. 1192 (1990)*]

1. As mentioned in the text of this chapter, automated check-sorting procedures have elicited substantial controversy in regard to a bank's duty to exercise due care in verifying signatures on checks. In this case, Wilder stands to lose more than $25,000 if the court holds that the bank's adherence to "customary" procedures in regard to check verification constitutes reasonable care. If you were the judge, how would you decide this issue?
2. What general social policies and legal precepts are brought into conflict by the issue in this case?
3. As stated in footnote 11 of this chapter, the revised version of Article 3 clarifies the standard of care required of banks. If a bank has an established procedure for checking signatures and the procedure is generally the standard used by the banking community in the area, the bank's failure to examine a signature on an item that it pays does not constitute bad faith or a breach of its duty for ordinary care, so long as the failure to examine the signature does not violate the established procedure. Evaluate the fairness of this standard. Is it fair to bank customers? Is it weighted too heavily in favor of banks?

FOR CRITICAL ANALYSIS

20-12. *Under the revised Article 4, banks are allowed to send their customers only a monthly itemized checking-account statement containing the check numbers, amounts, dates, and so on; banks may include the canceled checks, but if the checks are not returned, the banks must have them available for a period of seven years should a customer wish to examine them [RUCC 4–406(a), (b)]. What implications does this provision have for bank customers in terms of liability for unauthorized signatures and indorsements?*

Chapter 21

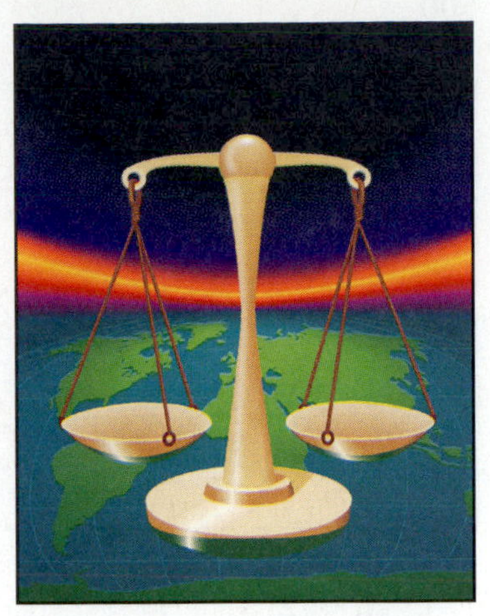

Secured Transactions

Whenever the payment of a debt is guaranteed, or *secured*, by personal property owned by the debtor or in which the debtor has a legal interest, the transaction becomes known as a **secured transaction.** The concept of the secured transaction is as basic to modern business practice as the concept of credit. Few purchasers (manufacturers, wholesalers, retailers, or consumers) have the resources to pay cash for goods being purchased, yet lenders are reluctant to lend money to a debtor solely on the debtor's promise to repay the debt. Logically, sellers and lenders do not want to risk nonpayment, so they will not sell goods or lend money unless the promise of payment is somehow guaranteed.

The importance of being a secured creditor cannot be overemphasized. Secured creditors are generally not hampered by state laws favorable to debtors, and if their security interest is perfected, they have a favored position should the debtor become bankrupt. Indeed, business as we know it could not exist without secured-transaction law.

The significance of Article 9 of the UCC, which governs secured transactions, is related in this chapter's *Landmark in the Law* (see page 305). As will become evident, the law of secured transactions tends to favor the rights of creditors; but to a lesser extent, it offers debtors some protection, too.

"Article 9 is clearly the most novel and probably the most important article of the Code . . . and covers the entire range of transactions in which the debts are secured by personal property."

Walter D. Malcolm, 1904–1979
(President of the National Conference of Commissioners on Uniform State Laws, 1963–1966)

SECURED TRANSACTION
Any debt transaction which creates a security interest in personal property or fixtures, including goods, documents, and other intangibles, guaranteeing payment of the debt.

❖ The Terminology of Secured Transactions

The UCC's terminology is now uniformly adopted in all documents used in situations involving secured transactions. A brief summary of the UCC's definitions of terms relating to secured transactions follows.

1. A **security interest** is any interest "in personal property or fixtures which secures payment or performance of an obligation" [UCC 1–201(37)].
2. A **secured party** is a lender, a seller, or any person in whose favor there is a security interest, including a person to whom accounts or *chattel paper* (any writing evidencing a debt secured by personal property) have been sold [UCC 9–105(1)(m)]. The terms *secured party* and *secured creditor* are used interchangeably.
3. A **debtor** is the party who owes payment or performance of the secured obligation, whether or not that party actually owns or has rights in the collateral. When the debtor and the owner of collateral are not the same person, the term *debtor* may

SECURITY INTEREST
Every interest "in *personal property or fixtures* [emphasis added] that secures payment or performance of an obligation" [UCC 1–201(37)].

SECURED PARTY
A lender, seller, or any other person in whose favor there is a security interest, including a person to whom accounts or chattel paper has been sold.

DEBTOR
A person who owes a sum of money or other obligations to another.

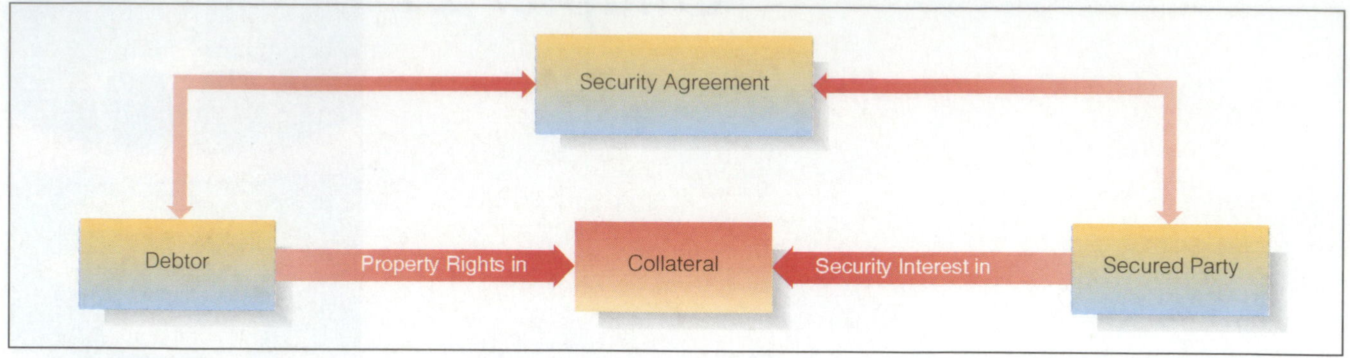

◆ **Exhibit 21–1**
Secured Transactions—Concept and Terminology
In a security agreement, a debtor and creditor agree that the creditor will have a security interest in collateral in which the debtor has rights. In essence, the collateral secures the loan and ensures the creditor of payment should the debtor default.

SECURITY AGREEMENT
The agreement that creates or provides for a security interest between the debtor and a secured party.

COLLATERAL
Any property used as security for a loan. Under the UCC, property of a debtor in which a creditor has an interest.

ATTACHMENT
(1) In a secured transaction, the process by which a security interest in the property of another becomes enforceable. (2) The legal process of seizing another's property in accordance with a writ or judicial order for the purpose of securing satisfaction of a judgment yet to be rendered.

refer to the actual owner of the collateral or the obligor on an obligation or both, depending on the context in which the term is used [UCC 9–105(1)(d)].
4. A **security agreement** is the agreement that creates or provides for a security interest between the debtor and a secured party [UCC 9–105(1)(l)].
5. **Collateral** is the property subject to a security interest, including accounts and chattel paper that have been sold [UCC 9–105(1)(c)].

These basic definitions form the concept under which a debtor-creditor relationship becomes a secured transaction relationship (see Exhibit 21–1).

❖ Creating a Security Interest

Before a creditor can become a secured party, the creditor must have a security interest in the collateral of the debtor. Three requirements must be met for a creditor to have an enforceable security interest:

1. Either (a) the collateral must be in the possession of the secured party in accordance with an agreement, or (b) there must be a written security agreement describing the collateral and signed by the debtor.
2. The secured party must give value.
3. The debtor must have rights in the collateral.

Once these requirements have been met, the creditor's rights are said to *attach* to the collateral. This means that the creditor has a security interest against the debtor that is enforceable. **Attachment** ensures that the security interest between the debtor and the secured party is effective [UCC 9–203].

Written Security Agreement

When the collateral is not in the possession of the secured party, a security agreement must be in writing to be enforceable. To be effective, (1) the security agreement must be signed by the debtor, (2) it must contain a description of the collateral, and (3) the description must reasonably identify the collateral [UCC 9–203(1) and 9–110]. See Exhibit 21–2 for a detailed sample security agreement.

At issue in the following case was whether a security agreement had reasonably identified the collateral and had, in fact, been signed by the debtor.

◆ **Exhibit 21–2 A Sample Security Agreement**

____
Date

____
Name No. and Street City County State

(hereinafter called "Debtor") hereby grants to _______________
Name

____
No. and Street City County State

(hereinafter called "Secured Party") a security interest in the following property (hereinafter called the "Collateral"): _______________

to secure payment and performance of obligations identified or set out as follows (hereinafter called the "Obligations"): _______________

Default in payment or performance of any of the Obligations or default under any agreement evidencing any of the Obligations is a default under this agreement. Upon such default Secured Party may declare all Obligations immediately due and payable and shall have the remedies of a secured party under the _______ Uniform Commercial Code.

Signed in (duplicate) triplicate.

_______________	_______________
Debtor	Secured Party
By _______________	By _______________

Case 21.1
IN RE ZILUCK[a]
United States District Court, Southern District of Florida, 1992. 139 Bankr. 44.

HISTORICAL AND SOCIAL SETTING *UCC 9–110 provides that a description of collateral is sufficient "whether or not it is specific if it reasonably identifies what is described." In cases decided before Article 9 of the UCC was adopted, courts often held that descriptions were insufficient unless they were "of the most exact and detailed nature, the so-called 'serial number' test."*[b] *In the Comment to UCC 9–110, the drafters of the UCC recognized that a description is sufficient if it does "the job assigned to it—that it make possible the identification of the thing described." Of course, in some cases, reasonably identifying what is described may be achieved only with a specific description. In holding that a description is too general, a court may believe that it is protecting a debtor against a clause that would otherwise subject much of his or her property to the claim of a single creditor.*

FACTS David Ziluck applied for a Radio Shack credit card. The front of the application contained blanks for various personal and employment information and a space for the applicant to sign. Above the signature line was the following statement: "I have read the Radio Shack Credit Account and Security Agreement, including the notice provisions in the last paragraph, and it contains no blanks or blank spaces. I agree to the terms of the Agreement and acknowledge a copy of the agreement." The back of the application contained a "Radio Shack Credit Account and Security Agreement," which stated in part, "We retain a security interest under the Uniform Commercial Code in all merchandise charged to your Account. If you do not make payments on your Account as agreed, the security interest allows us to repossess only the merchandise that has not

a. *In re* means in the matter of, concerning, or regarding. The use of *in re* is the usual method of entitling a judicial proceeding in which judicial action is to be taken on some matter, such as a debtor's estate in bankruptcy, in which there are no adversary parties. *In re, Matter of,* and *Estate of,* or some combination of these phrases (such as *In re Estate of*), are all commonly used in the titles of cases involving actions of the kind just mentioned.
b. UCC 9–110, Comment.

Case 21.1—Continued

been paid in full." When Ziluck later filed for bankruptcy protection, the bankruptcy court had to decide whether the application form constituted a valid security agreement. The court concluded that it did *not,* for two reasons. First, Ziluck's signature was not effective because it was not on the back side of the form, which stated the terms of the security agreement. Second, the security agreement's description of the collateral ("all merchandise charged to your Account") was not sufficiently descriptive. The bankruptcy court's decision was appealed.

ISSUE The issue in this case is twofold: (1) Had Ziluck effectively signed the security agreement? (2) Was the security agreement's description of the collateral sufficient?

DECISION Yes, to both questions.

REASON As to whether Ziluck had signed the security agreement, the court found that the language on the front of the credit-card application, above the signature line, made it clear that Ziluck was signing a security agreement. As to whether the collateral had been adequately described, the court stated that under UCC 9–110, "any description of personal property * * * is sufficient whether or not it is specific if it reasonably identifies what is described." In the court's view, the words "all merchandise charged to your Account" reasonably identified "the property subject to the security interest—namely any property purchased with the subject credit card."

"Nothing so cements and holds together all the parts of society as faith or credit, which can never be kept up unless men are under some force or necessity of honestly paying what they owe."

Cicero, 106–43 B.C.
(Roman statesman and philosopher)

Secured Party Must Give Value

The secured party must give value, which, according to UCC 1–201(44), is any consideration that supports a simple contract. In addition, value can be security given for a preexisting (antecedent) obligation or any binding commitment to extend credit. Normally, the value given by a secured party is in the form of a direct loan, or it involves a commitment to sell goods on credit.

Debtor Must Have Rights in the Collateral

The debtor must have rights in the collateral; that is, the debtor must have some ownership interest or right to obtain possession of that collateral. The debtor's rights can represent either a current or a future legal interest in the collateral. For example, a retail seller-debtor can give a secured party a security interest not only in existing inventory owned by the retailer but also in future inventory to be acquired by the retailer.

In the following case, a creditor held a security interest in a pharmacist's accounts receivable (payments yet to be made to the pharmacist by his customers). Among these receivables were Medicaid payments—payments to be made to the pharmacist by the government for services rendered to customers who received government assistance through the Medicaid program. Federal and state laws prohibit the assignment of Medicaid payments. Did this mean that the pharmacist had insufficient rights in these accounts to use them as collateral for a loan?

Case 21.2
ESTATE OF ANGIULLI
Surrogate's Court, Oneida County, 1990.
148 Misc.2d 796,
561 N.Y.S.2d 626.

HISTORICAL AND SOCIAL SETTING *In the early 1980s, much of the northeastern United States was experiencing an economic recession. At the same time, in many small communities, hometown businesses found themselves in competition with regional or national retail companies, which could open stores in or near small communities at comparatively low cost and undersell hometown competitors. Meanwhile, health-care costs were soaring. In 1986, Congress passed a law making it illegal for hospitals to turn away patients who could not afford to pay. Nearly a third of U.S. citizens, particularly those who were unemployed or living in depressed areas, had inadequate health insurance or none at all. To pay for providing medical care to those whose incomes fell below a certain*

Case 21.2—Continued

level, the Medicaid program used government funds. Many physicians avoided taking Medicaid patients, however, because the payments were considered too low.

FACTS When Frank Angiulli died in 1988, the pharmacy he owned in Utica, New York, was insolvent. At the time of his death, Angiulli owed H. K. Hineline Company, a supplier of pharmaceutical supplies, $34,469.63. The administrator of Angiulli's estate collected funds from several accounts due, including Medicaid payments, and used the monies to pay funeral and administrative costs. Hineline objected to this use of the funds, contending that Hineline's security interest in the accounts receivable entitled it to receive the payments. When the issue came before a New York state court, the administrator moved to dismiss Hineline's objections. The administrator argued that because Medicaid payments are not assignable under either federal or state law, Angiulli never acquired sufficient rights in those accounts to use them as collateral. Therefore, Hineline's security interest in the Medicaid accounts was not valid because it had never attached to the collateral.

ISSUE Did Hineline have a valid security interest in the Medicaid accounts receivable?

DECISION Yes. The court denied the administrator's motion to dismiss Hineline's objection.

REASON The court acknowledged that under both federal and state law, Medicaid payments were not assignable. In other words, the New York State Department of Social Services, the agency that issued Medicaid payments, could not issue them to anyone other than the provider of the services that were being paid for by the Medicaid payments. The administrator had argued that in view of this law, it necessarily followed that the Medicaid receivables could not have served as collateral for a security interest. The court disagreed. The court found that the reason behind the law prohibiting assignments of Medicaid payments was "to enable the social services district to pay the supplier regardless of any assignment and to relieve the district from the potential liability and increased administrative burdens involved in such assignments." The law did not prohibit the recipient of the payments from assigning them to another party once the funds had been disbursed by the relevant government agency, however. The court therefore concluded that "Hineline's security interest in the Medicaid Receivable attached once the Department approved decedent's claim and authorized payment." Hineline's security interest was therefore effective, and the payments "could not properly be used to pay funeral and administrative expenses."

❖ Purchase-Money Security Interest

Often, sellers of consumer durable goods, such as stereos and television sets, agree to extend credit for part or all of the purchase price of those goods. Also, lenders not necessarily in the business of selling such goods often agree to lend much of the purchase price for them. There is a special name for the security interest that the seller or the lender obtains when such a transaction occurs. It is called a **purchase-money security interest (PMSI).** Formally, such an interest exists when one or the other of the following conditions arises:

PURCHASE-MONEY SECURITY INTEREST (PMSI)
A security interest to the extent that it is (1) taken or retained by a seller of the collateral to secure all or part of the price of the collateral or (2) taken by a creditor who, by making advances or incurring an obligation, gives value to enable the debtor to acquire rights in, or use of, the collateral, if such value is in fact so used.

1. A security interest is retained in, or taken by the seller of, the collateral to secure part or all of its price.
2. A security interest is taken by a person who, by making advances or incurring an obligation, gives something of value that enables the debtor to acquire rights in the collateral or to use it [UCC 9–107].

In either case, a lender or seller has essentially provided a buyer with the "purchase money" to buy goods. Suppose Jamie wants to purchase a combination color television–stereo set from ABC Appliances. The purchase price is $900. Not being able to pay cash, Jamie signs a purchase agreement to pay $100 down and $50 per month until the balance plus interest is fully paid. ABC Appliances is to retain a security interest in the purchased set until full payment has been made. Because the security interest was created as part of the purchase agreement, it is a PMSI.

What do car dealers selling on credit have to do to perfect their security interests?

❖ Perfecting a Security Interest

DEFAULT
The failure to observe a promise or discharge an obligation. The term is commonly used to mean the failure to pay a debt when it is due.

A creditor has two main concerns if the debtor **defaults** (fails to pay the debt as promised): (1) satisfaction of the debt through possession of the collateral and (2) priority over any other creditors who may have rights in the same collateral. The concept of *attachment*, which establishes the criteria for creating an enforceable security interest, deals with the former; the concept of *perfection* deals with the latter.

PERFECTION
The method by which a secured party obtains a priority by notice that his or her security interest in the debtor's collateral is effective against the debtor's subsequent creditors. Usually accomplished by filing a financing statement at a location set out in the state statute.

Even though a security interest has attached, the secured party must nevertheless take steps to protect its claim to the collateral over claims that third parties may have. Third parties may be other secured creditors, general creditors, trustees in bankruptcy, or purchasers of the collateral that is the subject matter of the security agreement. **Perfection** represents the legal process by which secured parties protect themselves against the claims of third parties who may wish to have their debts satisfied out of the same collateral. In some circumstances, a security interest becomes perfected without the filing of a financing statement. Usually, however, perfection is accomplished by the filing of a financing statement with the appropriate government official.

Perfection Without Filing

In two types of situations, security interests can be perfected without filing a financing statement. First, when the collateral is transferred into the possession of the creditor, the creditor's security interest in the collateral is perfected. Second, a PMSI in consumer goods is perfected automatically.

PLEDGE
The bailment of personal property to a creditor as security for the payment of a debt.

Perfection by Possession Under the common law, one of the most common means of obtaining financing was to **pledge** certain collateral as security for the debt and transfer the collateral into the creditor's possession. When the debt was paid, the collateral would be returned to the debtor. Usually, the transfer of collateral was accompanied by a written security agreement, but the agreement did not have to be in writing. In other words, an oral security agreement was effective as long as the creditor possessed the collateral. Article 9 of the UCC retained the common law pledge and the principle that the security agreement need not be in writing to be enforceable if the collateral is transferred to the creditor [UCC 9–203(1)(a)].

Certain items, such as stocks, bonds, and jewelry, are commonly transferred into the creditor's possession when they are used as collateral for loans. For most collat-

Landmark in the Law

Article 9 Security Interest

Prior to the drafting and adoption by the states of Article 9 of the Uniform Commercial Code, secured transactions were governed by a patchwork of security devices replete with variations that many said made no logical sense. Each of these security devices had its own jargon. Depending on the device used, for example, a debtor could be called variously a pledgor, a mortgagor, a conditional vendee, an assignor, or a borrower.

One of the earliest security devices, historically, is the pledge. A *pledge* is a possessory security interest in which the secured party acquires or holds possession of the property involved, called the *collateral*, to secure the payment or performance of the secured obligation. The pledge has existed since at least Roman times. One security device that developed from the pledge concept involved obtaining a security interest in goods that could not be conveniently moved from the debtor's property. In such a case, the creditor would have an independent warehouseperson establish a warehouse on the debtor's premises to obtain possession of the goods. This was called a field warehouse and dates from about 1900. Other security devices included trust receipts, conditional sales contracts, chattel mortgages, and assignments of accounts receivable.

Despite the great number of security devices, many of which we haven't mentioned, creditors still faced several legal problems. For example, in many states, a security interest could not be taken in inventory or a stock in trade, such as cars for a dealer to sell or chocolate for a candy manufacturer. Sometimes, highly technical limitations were placed on the use of a particular device. If a court determined that a particular device was not appropriate for a given transaction, it might void the security interest.

The drafters of Article 9 concluded that the two elements common to all security devices were (1) the objective of conferring on a creditor or secured party priority in certain property (the collateral) against the risk of the debtor's nonpayment of the debt or the debtor's insolvency or bankruptcy and (2) a means of notifying other creditors of this interest. With these two elements in mind, the drafters created a new, simplified security device with a single set of terms to cover all cases. What, you might ask, is the official name for this device? The answer is that it is simply called an Article 9 security interest.

Those drafting Article 9 also wanted to create a uniform and simplified means of notifying other creditors of a security interest. They sought a more rational filing system that would replace the system in which different files were maintained for each security device that was subject to filing requirements. Article 9 supplanted the numerous, independent notice systems that existed for the previous types of security devices. But the drafters were politically astute; they knew that to encourage unanimous acceptance of Article 9, they had to provide for alternative filing systems. In particular, they had to give local-minded businesses and municipal politicians the option of local filing. Today, the development of inexpensive computer storage facilities and local information retrieval terminals obviates the need for local filing, and many states require central filing with the state government for most security interests.

Although the law of secured transactions still remains far from simple, as readers of this chapter will quickly note, it is now—thanks to the drafters of Article 9—far more rational and uniform than it was in the days prior to the UCC.

eral, possession by the secured party is impractical because it denies the debtor the right to use or derive income from the property to pay off the debt. For example, if a farmer took out a loan to finance the purchase of a piece of heavy farm equipment, using the equipment as collateral, the purpose of the purchase would be defeated if the farmer transferred the collateral into the creditor's possession.

Note that with respect to negotiable instruments and certain securities (such as stocks and bonds), with a few exceptions, the *only* way to properly perfect a security interest is through possession by the secured party. If a secured party is in possession of the collateral, he or she must use reasonable care in preserving it. Otherwise, the secured party is liable to the debtor [UCC 9–207(1) and 9–207(3)].

Purchase-Money Security Interest In certain circumstances, a security interest can be perfected automatically at the time of a credit sale—that is, at the time that a PMSI is created under a written security agreement. Note that this automatic-perfection rule with regard to PMSIs applies only to tangible collateral when the goods are consumer goods (defined as goods bought or used by the debtor primarily for personal, family, or household purposes). The seller in this situation need do nothing more to protect his or her interest. There are exceptions to this rule, however, that cover security interests in fixtures and in motor vehicles [UCC 9–302(1)(d)]. In the state that has not adopted the 1972 UCC amendments[1] and in states that have decided to retain certain pre-1972 sections, a PMSI in farm equipment under a certain statutory value is also automatically perfected by attachment.

Perfection by Filing

FINANCING STATEMENT
A document prepared by a secured creditor, and filed with the appropriate state or local official, to give notice to the public that the creditor claims an interest in collateral belonging to the debtor named in the statement. The financing statement must be signed by the debtor, contain the addresses of both the debtor and the creditor, and describe the collateral by type or item.

A creditor whose security interest is not automatically perfected can perfect the security interest by filing a **financing statement** with the appropriate state or local official. A sample financing statement is shown in Exhibit 21–3. The UCC requires a financing statement to contain (1) the signature of the debtor, (2) the addresses of both the debtor and the creditor, and (3) a description of the collateral by type or item [UCC 9–402(1)].[2] Filing is the most common means of perfection to use.

Both the security agreement and the financing statement must contain a description of the collateral in which the secured party has a security interest. The UCC requires that the security agreement include a description of the collateral because no security interest in goods can exist unless the parties agree on which goods are subject to the security interest and then describe these goods in writing. The purpose of describing collateral in the financing statement is to put persons who might later wish to lend to the debtor or buy the collateral on notice that certain goods in the debtor's possession are already subject to a security interest.

Sometimes, the descriptions in the two documents vary, with the description in the security agreement being more precise and the description in the financing statement more general. For example, a security agreement for a commercial loan to a manufacturer may list all the manufacturer's equipment subject to the loan by serial number, whereas the financing statement may simply state "all equipment owned or hereafter acquired." To avoid problems arising from such variations in descriptions, a secured party may repeat exactly the security agreement's description in the financing statement or file the security agreement itself as a financing statement (assuming the security agreement meets the previously discussed criteria). Alternatively, where permitted, the creditor might file a combination security agreement–financing statement form. If the financing statement is too general or vague, a court may find it insufficient to perfect a security interest.

Where to File Depending on the classification of collateral, filing is done either centrally with the secretary of state or locally with the county clerk or other official, or both, according to state law. According to UCC 9–401, a state may choose one of three alternatives.[3] In general, financing statements for consumer goods should be filed with the county clerk.[4] Other kinds of collateral require filing with the

---

1. Vermont is the only state that has not adopted the 1972 amendments.

2. Certain types of collateral—crops, timber to be cut, minerals, accounts, or goods that are to become fixtures—require more than mere description; a description of the real estate concerned may also be required [UCC 9–402(1), (5); 9–103(5); and 9–313].

3. See UCC 9–401 in Appendix C for these three alternatives. Approximately half the states have adopted the second alternative. Filing fees range from as low as $3 to as high as $25.

4. In the Food Security Act of 1985 are provisions that protect a purchaser in the ordinary course of business of farm products from a prior perfected security interest, unless the secured party has perfected a special form called an effective financing statement (EFS) centrally or the buyer has received proper notice. Prior to this act, most states required local filing for perfection of security interests in farm-related collateral.

◆ **Exhibit 21–3**
A Sample Financing Statement

This FINANCING STATEMENT is presented for filing pursuant to the California Uniform Commercial Code.

1. DEBTOR (LAST NAME FIRST—IF AN INDIVIDUAL)		1A. SOCIAL SECURITY OR FEDERAL TAX NO.
1B. MAILING ADDRESS	1C. CITY, STATE	1D. ZIP CODE
2. ADDITIONAL DEBTOR (IF ANY) (LAST NAME FIRST—IF AN INDIVIDUAL)		2A. SOCIAL SECURITY OR FEDERAL TAX NO.
2B. MAILING ADDRESS	2C. CITY, STATE	2D. ZIP CODE
3. DEBTOR'S TRADE NAMES OR STYLES (IF ANY)		3A. FEDERAL TAX NUMBER
4. SECURED PARTY NAME MAILING ADDRESS CITY STATE ZIP CODE		4A. SOCIAL SECURITY NO., FEDERAL TAX NO. OR BANK TRANSIT AND A.B.A. NO.
5. ASSIGNEE OF SECURED PARTY (IF ANY) NAME MAILING ADDRESS CITY STATE ZIP CODE		5A. SOCIAL SECURITY NO., FEDERAL TAX NO. OR BANK TRANSIT AND A.B.A. NO.

6. This FINANCING STATEMENT covers the following types or items of property **(include description of real property on which located and owner of record when required by instruction 4).**
As security for and in consideration of all present and any future advances or other obligations debtor hereby grants United California Bank a security interest in all of the following types or items of property ("Collateral" herein) in which the debtor now has or hereafter acquires any right, title, or interest, or rights present and future, wheresoever located and whether in the possession of the debtor, a warehouseman, bailee, trustee or any other person, and all increases, therein and replacements, products, and proceeds thereof. Proceeds include but are not limited to inventory, returned merchandise, accounts, chattel paper, general intangibles, insurance proceeds, documents, money, goods, equipment, instruments, and any other tangible or intangible property arising under the sale, lease or other disposition of collateral:

7. CHECK IF APPLICABLE ☒ | 7A. ☐ PRODUCTS OF COLLATERAL ARE ALSO COVERED | 7B. DEBTOR(S) SIGNATURE NOT REQUIRED IN ACCORDANCE WITH INSTRUCTION 5(c) ITEM: ☐ (1) ☐ (2) ☐ (3) ☐ (4)

8. CHECK IF APPLICABLE ☒ | ☐ DEBTOR IS A "TRANSMITTING UTILITY" IN ACCORDANCE WITH UCC § 9105 (1) (n)

9. DATE:

▶ SIGNATURE(S) of DEBTOR(S)

TYPE OR PRINT NAME(S) OF DEBTOR(S)

▶ SIGNATURE(S) OF SECURED PARTY(IES)

TYPE OR PRINT NAME(S) OF SECURED PARTY(IES)

11. *Return copy to:*

NAME
ADDRESS
CITY
STATE
ZIP CODE

CODE 1 2 3 4 5 6 7 8 9 0

10. THIS SPACE FOR USE OF FILING OFFICER (DATE, TIME, FILE NUMBER AND FILING OFFICER)

(1) FILING OFFICER COPY

FORM UCC-1—FILING FEE $3.00
Approved by the Secretary of State

MS-336 10-78

♦ Exhibit 21–4
Types of Collateral and Methods of Perfection

TYPE OF COLLATERAL	DEFINITIONS	PERFECTION METHOD	UCC SECTIONS
Tangible	All things that are *movable* at the time the security interest attaches or that are *fixtures* [UCC 9–105(1)(h)]. This includes timber to be cut, growing crops, and unborn animals.		
1. Consumer Goods	Goods used or bought primarily for personal, family, or household purposes—for example, household furniture [UCC 9–109(1)].	For purchase-money security interest, attachment is sufficient; for boats, motor vehicles, and trailers, there is a requirement of filing or compliance with a certificate of title statute; for other consumer goods, general rules of filing or possession apply.	9–302(1)(d); 9-302(3); 9-302(4); 9–305
2. Equipment	Goods bought for or used primarily in business—for example, a delivery truck [UCC 9–109(2)].	Filing or possession by secured party.	9–302(1); 9–305
3. Farm Products	Crops, livestock, and supplies used or produced in a farming operation in the possession of a farmer debtor. This includes products of crops or livestock—for example, milk, eggs, maple syrup, and ginned cotton [UCC 9–109(3)].	Filing or possession by secured party.	9–302(1); 9–305
4. Inventory	Goods held for sale or lease and materials used or consumed in the course of business—for example, raw materials or floor stock of a retailer [UCC 9–109(4)].	Filing or possession by secured party.	9–302(1); 9–305
5. Fixtures	Goods that become so affixed to realty that an interest in them arises under real estate law—for example, a central air-conditioning unit [UCC 9–313(1)(a)].	Filing only.	9–313(1)

secretary of state [UCC 9–401]. An improper filing reduces a secured party's claim in bankruptcy to that of an unsecured creditor.

Classification by Collateral The classification of collateral is also important in determining whether filing is necessary. Exhibit 21–4 summarizes the various classifications of collateral and the methods of perfecting a security interest in them.

Exceptions to Perfection

There are sources of law other than Article 9 that deal with the perfection of security interests. The three most important sources are federal law, such as the Federal Aviation Act; UCC Article 8, which deals with investment securities; and state certificate-of-title laws that deal with motor vehicles.

◆ **Exhibit 21–4**
Types of Collateral and Methods of Perfection—Continued

TYPE OF COLLATERAL	DEFINITIONS	PERFECTION METHOD	UCC SECTIONS
Intangible	Nonphysical property that exists only in connection with something else.		
1. Chattel Paper	Any writing that evidences both a *monetary obligation and a security interest*—for example, a thirty-six-month-payment retail security agreement signed by a buyer to purchase a car [UCC 9–105(1)(b)].	Filing or possession by secured party.	9–304(1); 9–305
2. Documents of Title	Papers that entitle the person in possession to hold, receive, or dispose of the paper or goods the documents cover—for example, bills of lading, warehouse receipts, and dock warrants [UCC 9–105(1)(f), 1–201(15), 7–201].	Filing or possession by secured party.	9–304(1), (3); 9–305
3. Instruments	Any writing that evidences a right to payment of money that is not a security agreement or lease, and any negotiable instrument or certificated security that in the ordinary course of business is transferred by delivery with any necessary indorsement or assignment—for example, stock certificates, promissory notes, and certificates of deposit [UCC 9–105(1)(i), 3–104, 8–102(1)(a)].	Except for temporary perfected status, possession only.	9–304(1), (4), (5); 9–305
4. Accounts	Any right to payment for goods sold or leased or services *rendered* that is not evidenced by an instrument or chattel paper—for example, accounts receivable and contract right payments [UCC 9–106].	Filing required (with exceptions).	9–302(1)(e), (g)
5. General Intangibles	Any personal property other than that defined above—for example, a patent, a copyright, goodwill, or a trademark [UCC 9–106].	Filing only.	9–302(1)

Most states require a certificate of title for any motor vehicle, boat, or motor home. The normal methods described above for perfection of a security interest typically do not apply to such vehicles. Rather, perfection of a security interest only occurs when a notation of such an interest appears on the certificate of title that covers the vehicle. As an example, suppose that your commercial bank lends you 80 percent of the money necessary to purchase a new BMW. You live in a state that requires certificates of title for all automobiles. If your bank fails to have its security interest noted on the certificate of title, its interest is not perfected. That means that a good faith purchaser of your BMW would take it free of the bank's interest. In most states, purchasers of motor vehicles can either buy or extend credit on those vehicles with the confidence that no security interest exists that is not disclosed on the certificate of title.[5]

5. In the few states that do not require title registration of motor vehicles, one must examine the appropriate statutes to determine the priority of conflicting security interests.

Collateral Moved to Another Jurisdiction

Obviously, collateral may be moved by the debtor from one jurisdiction (state) to another. In general, a properly perfected security interest in collateral moved into a new jurisdiction continues to be perfected in the new jurisdiction for priority purposes for a period of up to four months from the date it was moved or for the period of time remaining under the perfection in the original jurisdiction, whichever expires first [UCC 9–103(1)(d) and 9–103(3)(e)]. Collateral moved from county to county within a state (if local filing is required), rather than from one state to another, however, may not have a four-month limitation [UCC 9–403(3)].

To illustrate, suppose that on January 1, Wheeler secures a loan from a Nebraska bank by putting up all his wheat-threshing equipment as security. The Nebraska bank files the security interest centrally with the secretary of state. In June, Wheeler has an opportunity to harvest wheat crops in South Dakota and moves his equipment into that state on June 15. The law just mentioned means that the Nebraska bank's perfection remains effective in South Dakota for a period of four months from June 15. If the Nebraska bank wishes to retain its perfection priority, the bank must perfect properly in South Dakota during this four-month period. Should the bank fail to do so, its perfection would be lost after four months, and subsequent perfected security interests in the same collateral in South Dakota would prevail.

Among mobile goods, automobiles pose one of the biggest problems. If the original jurisdiction does not require a certificate of title as part of its perfection process for an automobile, perfection automatically ends four months after the automobile is moved into another jurisdiction. When a security interest exists on an automobile in a state in which title registration is required, and when the security interest is noted on the certificate of title, the perfection of the security interest continues after the automobile is moved to another state requiring a certificate of title until the automobile is registered in the new state [UCC 9–103(2)]. This rule protects the secured party against anyone purchasing the car in the new state prior to the new registration. Moreover, because each title state requires that the old certificate of title be surrendered to obtain a new one, and because the secured party typically holds the certificate, the secured party usually is able to ensure that the security interest is noted on the new certificate of title.

CONTINUATION STATEMENT
A statement that, if filed within six months prior to the expiration date of the original financing statement, continues the effectiveness of the original statement for another five years. The effectiveness of a financing statement can be continued in the same manner indefinitely.

Effective Time of Perfection

A financing statement is effective for five years from the date of filing [UCC 9–403(2)]. If a **continuation statement** is filed *within six months* prior to the expiration date, the effectiveness of the original statement is continued for another five years, starting with the expiration date of the first five-year period [UCC 9–403(3)]. The effectiveness of the statement can be continued in the same manner indefinitely.

❖ The Scope of a Security Interest

PROCEEDS
In secured transactions law, whatever is received when the collateral is sold, exchanged, collected, or otherwise disposed of, such as insurance payments for destroyed or lost collateral. Money, checks, and the like are *cash proceeds*, whereas all other proceeds received are *noncash proceeds*.

A security agreement can cover various types of property in addition to collateral already in the debtor's possession—the proceeds of the sale of collateral, after-acquired property, and future advances.

Proceeds

Proceeds include whatever is received when collateral is sold, exchanged, collected, or disposed of. A secured party has an interest in the proceeds of the sale of collateral. For example, suppose a bank has a perfected security interest in the inventory of a retail seller of heavy farm machinery. The retailer sells a tractor out of this inventory

Business Law in Action

Has Anyone Seen the Proceeds?

One of the ways in which the legal system protects creditors is by making it possible for a creditor to have not only a security interest in collateral but also an interest in the proceeds from the sale of the collateral. If a debtor sells to a third party equipment in which a creditor has a security interest, the payment received by the debtor in that sale will be proceeds of the collateral. Even if the goods in which there is a security interest are mixed with other goods and cannot be identified, the security interest still continues in the mass of mixed-up goods, such as wheat.

What happens when flour is the collateral and it is turned into bread? Obviously, the flour does not exist anymore, but the bread does, so the security interest persists in the bread.

What about cattle or hog feed? If there is a security interest in the feed and it is fed to animals, does the security interest continue in the animals? If we based our logic on the flour example above, the answer would have to be yes. At least one court, however, has come up with the opposite conclusion. In *Farmers Cooperative Elevator Co. v. Union State Bank*,[a] the issue was hog feed and hogs. The bank argued that the hogs were a form of proceeds. Because the UCC allows that a security interest continues in collateral "and also continues in any identifiable proceeds," the hogs were subject to a security interest as proceeds. The court said no. Fattened hogs as proceeds are unacceptable. The court reasoned that some end product or mass from the biological transformation of the feed had to exist for the UCC to be operative. The hogs were the same before and after feeding, and therefore there were "no traceable proceeds." The feed was ingested, rather than manufactured, processed, or assembled. Through the process of biological transformation, the feed had been transformed into the animals. At that point, according to the court, the feed (and the State Union Bank's security interest) ceased to exist.

As another example, what happens if the proceeds of secured collateral are real estate, which is not subject to Article 9? This was the situation in a case in which a creditor had a perfected security interest in the debtor's accounts receivable. One of the debtor's customers paid an account by transferring to the debtor a parcel of real estate. The debtor failed to record the property transfer in accordance with state statutory requirements. When the debtor later entered bankruptcy proceedings, the property was sold and the proceeds of the sale became part of the estate in bankruptcy. Because the creditor's unrecorded interest in property was not binding on a subsequent purchaser in good faith, the bankruptcy trustee (as the good faith purchaser) prevailed over the creditor.[b]

In the case of the hog feed, no doubt, Union State Bank is still wondering what the difference is between flour made into bread and feed used to fatten hogs. And creditors facing similar problems of "disappearing" proceeds are probably also wondering about why they are left empty-handed even though they had a perfected security interest in the proceeds.

a. 409 N.W.2d 178 (Iowa 1987).

b. *In re Seaway Express Corp.*, 912 F.2d 1125 (9th Cir. 1990).

to a farmer, a buyer in the ordinary course of business. The farmer agrees, in a retail security agreement, to pay monthly payments for a period of twenty-four months. If the retailer should go into default on the loan from the bank, the bank is entitled to the remaining payments the farmer owes to the retailer as proceeds.

A security interest in proceeds perfects automatically upon perfection of the secured party's security interest and remains perfected for ten days after receipt of the proceeds by the debtor. One way to extend the ten-day automatic period is to provide for such extended coverage in the original security agreement. This is typically done when the collateral is the type that is likely to be sold, such as a retailer's inventory.

The UCC provides that in the following circumstances the security interest in proceeds remains perfected for longer than ten days after the receipt of the proceeds by the debtor:

1. When a filed financing statement covers the original collateral and the proceeds are collateral in which a security interest may be perfected by a filing in the office

or offices with which the financing statement has been filed. Furthermore, a secured creditor's interest automatically perfects in property that the debtor acquires with cash proceeds, if the original filing would have been effective as to that property and the financing statement indicates that type of property [UCC 9–306(3)(a)]. Thus, in the farm-equipment example above, if the retailer used the farmer's monthly payments to acquire additional inventory, the bank would be entitled to that inventory, providing that the bank's original filing was effective as to that property and the financing statement indicated that type of property.
2. Whenever there is a filed financing statement that covers the original collateral and the proceeds are identifiable cash proceeds [UCC 9–306(3)(b)].
3. Whenever the security interest in the proceeds is perfected before the expiration of the ten-day period [UCC 9–306(3)(c)].

After-Acquired Property

AFTER-ACQUIRED PROPERTY
Property of the debtor that is acquired after a secured creditor's interest in the debtor's property has been created.

After-acquired property of the debtor is property acquired after the execution of the security agreement. The security agreement itself may provide for coverage of after-acquired property [UCC 9–204(1)]. This is particularly useful for inventory financing arrangements because a secured party whose security interest is in existing inventory knows that the debtor will sell that inventory, thereby reducing the collateral subject to the security interest. Generally, the debtor will purchase new inventory to replace the inventory sold. The secured party wants this newly acquired inventory to be subject to the original security interest. Thus, the after-acquired property clause continues the secured party's claim to any inventory acquired thereafter. This is not to say that the original security interest will be superior to the rights of all other creditors with regard to this after-acquired inventory, as will be discussed later.

Consider a typical example. Amato buys factory equipment from Bronson on credit, giving as security an interest in all of her equipment—both what she is buying and what she already owns. The security interest with Bronson contains an after-acquired property clause. Six months later, Amato pays cash to another seller for more equipment. Six months after that, Amato goes out of business before she has paid off her debt to Bronson. Bronson has a security interest in all of Amato's equipment, even the equipment bought from the other seller.

Future Advances

Often, a debtor will arrange with a bank to have a continuing *line of credit* under which the debtor can borrow funds intermittently. Advances against lines of credit can be subject to a properly perfected security interest in certain collateral. The security agreement may provide that any future advances made against that line of credit are also subject to the security interest in the same collateral. For example, Stroh is the owner of a small manufacturing plant with equipment valued at $1 million. He has an immediate need for $50,000 of working capital, so he secures a loan from Midwestern Bank and signs a security agreement, putting up all his equipment as security. The security agreement provides that Stroh can borrow up to $500,000 in the future, using the same equipment as collateral for any future advances. In such cases, it is not necessary to execute a new security agreement and perfect a security interest in the collateral each time an advance is made to the debtor [UCC 9–204(3)].

The Floating-Lien Concept

A security agreement may provide for the creation of a security interest in proceeds of the sale of the collateral that was the subject matter of the secured transaction—after-acquired property or future advances, or both. Such an agreement is referred to as a **floating lien.** The term **lien** is derived from the Latin word *ligare*, which means "to bind." When a creditor places a lien on a debtor's property, the creditor's rights are bound (attached) to the property, and the creditor acquires the right to sell or hold the property of a debtor as security or payment for a debt (see Chapter 22 for a further discussion of liens). Floating liens commonly arise in the financing of inventories. A creditor is not interested in specific pieces of inventory, because they are constantly changing, so the lien "floats" from one item to another, as the inventory changes.

FLOATING LIEN
A security interest retained in collateral even when the collateral changes in character, classification, or location.

LIEN
An encumbrance upon a property to satisfy or protect a claim for payment of a debt.

For example, suppose that Cascade Sports, Inc., a cross-country ski dealer, has a line of credit with Portland First Bank to finance an inventory of cross-country skis. Cascade and Portland First enter into a security agreement that provides for coverage of proceeds, after-acquired inventory, present inventory, and future advances. This security interest in inventory is perfected by filing centrally (with the secretary of state). One day, Cascade sells a new pair of the latest cross-country skis, for which it receives a used pair in trade. That same day, it purchases two new pairs of skis from a local manufacturer with an additional amount of money obtained from Portland First. Portland First gets a perfected security interest in the used pair of skis under the proceeds clause, has a perfected security interest in the two new pairs of skis purchased from the local manufacturer under the after-acquired property clause, and has the new amount of money advanced to Cascade secured by the future-advances clause. All of this is accomplished under the original perfected security agreement. The various items in the inventory have changed, but Portland First still has a perfected security interest in Cascade's inventory, and hence it has a floating lien on the inventory.

The concept of the floating lien can also apply to a shifting stock of goods. Under Section 9–205, the lien can start with raw materials and follow them as they become finished goods and inventories and as they are sold, turning into accounts receivable, chattel paper, or cash.

❖ Priorities among Security Interests

Whether a creditor's security interest is perfected or unperfected may have serious consequences for the creditor if the debtor defaults on the debt or files for bankruptcy. What if, for example, the debtor has borrowed money from two different creditors, using the same property as collateral for both loans? If the debtor defaults on both loans, which of the two creditors has first rights to the collateral? In this situation, the creditor with a perfected security interest will prevail. Generally, the following UCC rules apply when more than one party, or creditor, claims rights in the same collateral:

1. *Conflicting perfected security interests.* When two or more secured parties have perfected security interests in the same collateral, generally the first to perfect (file or take possession of collateral) has priority [UCC 9–312(5)(a)].
2. *Conflicting unperfected security interests.* When two conflicting security interests are unperfected, the first to attach has priority [UCC 9–312(5)(b)].
3. *Conflicting perfected security interests in commingled or processed goods.* When goods to which two or more perfected security interests attach are so manufactured or commingled that they lose their identities into a product or mass, the perfected parties' security interests attach to the new product or mass "according to the ratio that the cost of goods to which each interest originally attached bears to the cost of the total product or mass" [UCC 9–315(2)].

Under certain circumstances, upon the debtor's default, the perfection of a security interest will not protect a secured party against certain other third parties

◆ Exhibit 21–5
Priority of Claims to a Debtor's Collateral

PARTIES	PRIORITY
Unperfected Secured Party	Prevails over unsecured creditors and creditors who have obtained judgments against the debtor but who have not begun the legal process to collect on those judgments [UCC 9–301].
Purchaser of Debtor's Collateral	1. Goods purchased in the ordinary course of the seller's business—Purchaser prevails over a secured party's security interest, even if perfected and even if the purchaser knows of the security interest [UCC 9–307(1)]. 2. Consumer goods purchased out of the ordinary course of business—Purchaser prevails over a secured party's interest, even if perfected, providing purchaser purchased: a. For value. b. Without actual knowledge of the security interest. c. For use as a consumer good. d. Prior to secured party's perfection by *filing* [UCC 9–307(2)].
Perfected Secured Parties to Same Collateral	Between two perfected secured parties in the same collateral, the general rule is that first in time of perfection is first in right to the collateral [UCC 9–312(5)]. Exceptions are: 1. Crops—New value to produce crops given within three months of planting has priority over prior six-month perfected interest [UCC 9–312(2)]. 2. Purchase-money security interest—Even if second in time of perfection, it has priority providing the following: a. Inventory—PMSI is perfected and proper written notice is given to the other security-interest holder *on* or *before* the time that debtor takes possession [UCC 9–312(3)]. b. Other collateral—PMSI has priority providing it is perfected within ten days after debtor receives possession [UCC 9–312(4)].

having claims to the collateral. For example, the UCC provides that under certain conditions a PMSI, properly perfected, will prevail over another security interest in after-acquired collateral, even though the other was perfected first [UCC 9–312].

Because buyers should not be required to find out if there is an outstanding security interest in, for example, a merchant's inventory, the UCC also provides that a person who buys "in the ordinary course of business" will take the goods free from any security interest created by the seller in the purchased collateral. This is so even if the security interest is perfected and *even if the buyer knows of its existence* [UCC 9–307(1)]. A *buyer in the ordinary course of business* is defined as any person who in good faith, and without knowledge that the sale is in violation of the ownership rights or security interest of a third party in the goods, buys in ordinary course from a person in the business of selling goods of that kind [UCC 1–201(9)]. Under the Food Security Act of 1985, buyers in the ordinary course of business include buyers of farm products from a farmer. Under this act, these buyers are protected from prior perfected security interests unless the secured parties perfected centrally by a special form called an effective financing statement (EFS) or the buyers received proper notice. The priority of claims to a debtor's collateral is detailed in Exhibit 21–5.

"Let us live in a small circle as we will, we are either debtors or creditors before we have had time to look round."

Johann Wolfgang von Goethe, 1749–1832
(German poet and dramatist)

❖ Rights and Duties of Debtor and Creditor

The security agreement itself determines most of the rights and duties of the debtor and creditor. The UCC, however, imposes some rights and duties that are applicable in the absence of a security agreement to the contrary.

Information Request by Creditors

Under UCC 9–407(1), a secured creditor has the option, when making the filing, of asking the filing officer to make a note of the file number, the date, and the hour of the original filing on a copy of the financing statement. The filing officer must send this copy to the person making the request. Under UCC 9–407(2), a filing officer must also give information to a person who is contemplating obtaining a security interest from a prospective debtor. The filing officer must give a certificate that provides information on possible perfected financing statements with respect to the named debtor. The filing officer will charge a fee for the certification and for any information copies provided.

Assignment, Amendment, and Release

Whenever desired, a secured party of record can release part or all of the collateral described in a filed financing statement. This ends his or her security interest in the collateral [UCC 9–406]. A secured party can assign part or all of the security interest to another, called the assignee. That assignee becomes the secured party of record if, for example, he or she either makes a notation of the assignment somewhere on the financing statement or files a written statement of assignment [UCC 9–405(2)].

It is also possible to amend a financing statement that has already been filed. *The amendment must be signed by both parties.* The debtor signs the security agreement, the original financing statement, and the amendments [UCC 9–402]. All other secured transaction documents, such as releases, assignments, continuations of perfection, perfections of collateral moved into another jurisdiction, and termination statements, need only be signed by the secured party.

The Status of the Debt

During the time that the secured debt is outstanding, the debtor may wish to know the status of the debt. If so, the debtor need only sign a statement that indicates the aggregate amount of the unpaid debt at a specific date (and perhaps a list of the collateral covered by the security agreement). The secured party must then approve or correct this statement in writing. The creditor must comply with the request within two weeks of receipt; otherwise, the creditor is liable for any loss caused to the debtor by the failure to do so [UCC 9–208(2)]. One such request is allowed without charge every six months. For each additional request, the secured party can require a fee not exceeding $10 per request [UCC 9–208(3)].

Termination Statement

When a secured debt is paid, the secured party generally must send a termination statement to the debtor or file such a statement with the filing officer to whom the original financing statement was given. If the financing statement covers consumer goods, the termination statement must be filed by the secured party within one month after the debt is paid, or—if the debtor requests the termination statement in writing—it must be filed within ten days of receipt of such request after the debt is paid, whichever is earlier [UCC 9–404(1)]. In all other cases, the termination statement must be filed or furnished to the debtor within ten days after a written request is made by the debtor. If the affected secured party fails to file such a termination statement, as required by UCC 9–404(1), or fails to send the termination statement within ten days after proper demand, the secured party will be liable to the debtor for $100. Additionally, the secured party will be liable for any loss caused to the debtor.

❖ Default

"Thou canst not fly high with borrowed wings."

Proverb

Article 9 defines the rights, duties, and remedies of a secured party and of the debtor upon the debtor's default. Should the secured party fail to comply with his or her duties, the debtor is afforded particular rights and remedies.

The topic of default is one of great concern to secured lenders and to the lawyers who draft security agreements. What constitutes default is not always clear. In fact, Article 9 does not define the term. Consequently, parties are encouraged in practice and by the UCC to include in their security agreements certain standards to be applied should default occur. In so doing, parties can stipulate the conditions that will constitute a default [UCC 9–501(1)]. Typically, because of the disparity in bargaining position between a debtor and a creditor, these critical terms are shaped by the creditor in an attempt to provide the maximum protection possible. The ultimate terms, however, are not allowed to go beyond the limitations imposed by the good faith requirement of UCC 1–203 and the unconscionability doctrine.

Although any breach of the terms of the security agreement can constitute default, default occurs most commonly when the debtor fails to meet the scheduled payments that the parties have agreed on or when the debtor becomes bankrupt. If the security agreement covers equipment, however, the debtor may have warranted that he or she is the owner of the equipment or that no liens or other security interests are pending on that equipment. Breach of any of these representations can result in default.

Basic Remedies

A secured party's remedies can be divided into two basic categories:

EXECUTION
An action to carry into effect the directions in a decree or judgment; otherwise stated, an official carrying out of a court's order or judgment.

LEVY
The obtaining of money by legal process through the seizure and sale of property, usually done after a writ of execution has been issued.

1. A secured party can relinquish a security interest and proceed to judgment on the underlying debt, followed by execution and levy. **Execution** is an action to carry into effect the directions in a court decree or judgment. **Levy** is the obtaining of money by legal process through the seizure and sale of property, usually done after an execution has been issued. Execution and levy are rarely done unless the value of the secured collateral has been reduced greatly below the amount of the debt and the debtor has other nonexempt assets available to satisfy the debt [UCC 9–501(1)].
2. A secured party can take possession of the collateral covered by the security agreement [UCC 9–503]. Upon taking possession, the secured party can retain the collateral for satisfaction of the debt [UCC 9–505(2)] or can resell the goods and apply the proceeds toward the debt [UCC 9–504].

The rights and remedies under UCC 9–501(1) are *cumulative*. Therefore, if a creditor is unsuccessful in enforcing rights by one method, another method can be pursued.[6]

When a security agreement covers both real and personal property, the secured party can proceed against the personal property in accordance with the remedies of Article 9. Alternatively, the secured party can proceed against the entire collateral under procedures set down by local real estate law, in which case the UCC does not apply [UCC 9–501(4)]. Determining whether particular collateral is personal or real property can prove difficult, especially in dealing with fixtures—things affixed to real property. Under certain circumstances, the UCC allows the removal of fixtures upon default; such removal, however, is subject to the provisions of Article 9 [UCC 9–313].

6. See James J. White and Robert S. Summers, *Uniform Commercial Code,* 3d ed. (St. Paul: West Publishing Co., 1988), pp. 1197–1198.

Secured Party's Right to Take Possession

UCC 9–503 states that "[u]nless otherwise agreed, a secured party has on default the right to take possession of the collateral. In taking possession, a secured party may proceed without judicial process if this can be done without a breach of the peace." The underlying rationale for this "self-help" provision of Article 9 is that it simplifies the process of repossession for creditors and reduces the burden on the courts. Because the UCC does not define *breach of the peace,* however, it is not always easy to predict what will or will not constitute a breach of the peace.

Generally, the creditor or the creditor's agent cannot enter a debtor's home, garage, or place of business without permission. Consider a situation in which an automobile is collateral. If the repossessing party walks onto the debtor's premises, proceeds up the driveway, enters the vehicle without entering the garage, and drives off, it probably will not amount to a breach of the peace. In some states, however, an action for wrongful trespass could start a cause of action for breach of the peace or other tortious action (see, for example, this chapter's *Law in the Extreme*).

Disposition of Collateral

Once default has occurred and the secured party has obtained possession of the collateral, the secured party may sell, lease, or otherwise dispose of the collateral in any commercially reasonable manner [UCC 9–504(1)]. Any sale is always subject to procedures established by state law.

Retention of Collateral by Secured Party The UCC recognizes that parties are sometimes better off if they do not sell the collateral. Therefore, a secured party can retain collateral, but this general right is subject to several conditions. The secured party must send written notice of the proposal to the debtor if the debtor has not signed a statement renouncing or modifying his or her rights after default. In the case of consumer goods, no other notice need be given. In all other cases, notice must also be sent to any other secured party from whom the secured party has received written notice of a claim of interest in the collateral in question.

If within twenty-one days after the notice is sent, the secured party receives an objection in writing from a person entitled to receive notification, then the secured party must sell or otherwise dispose of the collateral in accordance with the provisions of UCC 9–504 (disposition procedures under UCC 9–504 will be discussed shortly). If no such written objection is forthcoming, the secured party can retain the collateral in full satisfaction of the debtor's obligation [UCC 9–505(2)].

Consumer Goods When the collateral is consumer goods with a PMSI, and the debtor has paid 60 percent or more of the cash price, or loan, then the secured party must sell or otherwise dispose of the collateral in accordance with the provisions of UCC 9–504 within ninety days. Failure to comply opens the secured party to an action for conversion or other liability under UCC 9–507(1) unless the consumer-debtor signed a written statement *after default* renouncing or modifying the right to demand the sale of the goods [UCC 9–505(1)].

Disposition Procedures A secured party who does not choose to retain the collateral must resort to the disposition procedures prescribed under UCC 9–504. The UCC allows a great deal of flexibility with regard to disposition. The only real limitation is that it must be accomplished in a commercially reasonable manner. UCC 9–507(2) supplies some examples of what does or does not meet the standard of commercial reasonableness.

A secured party is not compelled to resort to public sale to dispose of the collateral. The party is given latitude under the UCC to seek out the best terms possible

Law in the Extreme

All This for $370!

As mentioned in the text, the "self-help" provision of Article 9 allows creditors to repossess collateral themselves, without resort to judicial process, so long as they do not "breach the peace" while doing so. Often, to avoid confrontation with the debtor and any potential violence or breach of the peace, creditors will repossess collateral during the night or in the early morning hours when the repossession effort is least likely to be observed. And yet it is just at these times that the presence of strangers on a debtor's property could justifiably alarm the debtor. If violence results and the debtor is harmed, the creditor could face liability for damages that far exceeds the debt secured by the collateral. Repossession can thus be an extremely risky business.

For example, consider the case of *McCall v. Owens.*[a] The debtor, Boyce McCall, purchased a new Ford Pinto from a Ford dealer in May 1979, financing the purchase through a loan from the United American Bank. The installment sales contract stipulated that McCall would purchase and maintain insurance coverage on the Pinto and if he did not, the bank would purchase the insurance and charge McCall for the premiums. McCall, however, opted to "self-insure" the car and refused to obtain the required coverage. The bank subsequently purchased insurance and charged McCall for the premiums, which McCall persistently refused to pay. Eventually, United American assigned the contract to First Tennessee Bank.

When McCall finished paying for the car, he still owed the bank $370 for insurance premiums and continued in his refusal to pay them. First Tennessee Bank decided to repossess the car and hired Ron Beverly of East Tennessee Auto Recovery to undertake the repossession. To tow the car, Beverly arranged to use a wrecker owned by Ted Owens and his son, Ted Douglas Owens, who jointly operated Ted's Chevron Service Station. Thus it was that in the middle of a November night in 1983, McCall and his wife heard someone "stealing their car." Mrs. McCall phoned the police, while her husband got dressed and ran out to confront Ron Beverly and another man, who were about to tow the car from the property. The men were in such a hurry to tow the car that the wrecker ran over McCall's foot and knocked him to the ground. As a result of the affair, McCall required medical attention and six to eight weeks of bed rest. He also experienced embarrassment.

Ultimately, McCall paid the disputed premium, regained possession of his car, hired a lawyer, and sued all of the parties involved in the repossession—First Tennessee Bank, East Tennessee Auto Recovery, Ron Beverly, Ted's Chevron, Ted Owens, and Ted D. Owens. McCall sought damages for a long list of wrongful acts: wrongful repossession, trespass to realty, chattel conversion (some personal property had been taken from the car), assault and battery, outrageous conduct, and defamation (based on the bank's report to a credit bureau about the repossession).

The court found that although the bank had a right to repossess the car to recover the $370, it had wrongfully breached the peace and could therefore be held liable for damages. The jury awarded a total $115,000 in actual damages and $385,000 in punitive damages. The case had to be remanded because the jury's verdict contained inconsistencies (for example, it found Beverly liable but not Beverly's employer, East Tennessee Auto Recovery). Nevertheless, when all is said and done, this will be a very expensive repossession, indeed—and all to recover a $370 debt!

a. 820 S.W.2d 748 (Tenn.App. 1991).

in a private sale. Generally, no specific time requirements must be met; however, the time must ultimately meet the standard of commercial reasonableness.

Notice of any sale must be sent by the secured party to the debtor if the debtor has not signed a statement renouncing or modifying the right to notification of sale after default. For consumer goods, no other notification need be sent. In all other cases, notification must be sent to any other secured party from whom the secured party has received written notice of a claim of interest in the collateral [UCC 9–504(3)]. Such notice is not necessary, however, when the collateral is perishable or threatens to decline speedily in value or when it is of a type customarily sold on a recognized market. Generally, notice of the place, time, and manner of the sale is required if the sale is to be classified as a sale conducted in a commercially reasonable manner. At issue in the following case is whether a sale of collateral was conducted in a commercially reasonable manner.

Case 21.3

IN RE WHATLEY

United States Bankruptcy Court,
Northern District of Mississippi, 1991.
126 Bankr. 231.

HISTORICAL AND SOCIAL SETTING *Before the UCC, when a debtor defaulted, the property that had served as the collateral for the debt was sometimes literally sold on the courthouse steps. It was intended that the sale be conducted publicly with the posting of notices and a variety of other restrictions to protect the interests of the debtor. As practiced, however, these sales often resulted in a low price for the property—less than would have been received under normal selling conditions. The UCC replaced this approach with two fundamental requirements: the debtor and others are to be notified of the sale of the property, and "every aspect of the disposition * * * must be commercially reasonable."*[a]

FACTS Guaranty Bank and Trust Company, a secured creditor in John Whatley's bankruptcy proceedings, was authorized to take possession of the collateral—Whatley's farm equipment—securing a debt that Whatley owed to Guaranty Bank. The proceeds from the sale of the collateral were to be put into an *escrow account* (a bank account held by a third party) pending an appellate court's decision as to whether Guaranty Bank's security interest took priority over that of the Small Business Administration (SBA), which also held a security interest in the farm equipment. Guaranty Bank posted public notices of its foreclosure sale and sent copies of the notice to local equipment dealers, Whatley's attorney, and the attorney representing the SBA. The notice was received by the SBA on September 2, 1987, and the foreclosure sale was to be conducted by the bank on September 10. Before the sale, Guaranty Bank had the equipment appraised by Yokley and Lundy Auction Company, which indicated that the total value was between $40,312.50 and $42,000. By subtracting expenses and other amounts from this value, Guaranty Bank calculated that it would bid $25,000 for the equipment at the foreclosure sale. At the sale, Guaranty Bank was the only bidder, and it purchased the equipment for $25,000. In accordance with the court order, this amount was deposited into the escrow account. The following day, Guaranty Bank sold the goods at auction for a net amount (after expenses of the sale) of $39,748.29. The SBA filed a motion to compel Guaranty Bank to pay SBA the difference between the $25,000 the bank had paid for the equipment at the foreclosure sale and the $39,748.29 that it had received on selling the equipment at the auction. Among other things, the SBA contended that the first sale—the foreclosure sale—had not been conducted in a commercially reasonable manner.

ISSUE Had Guaranty Bank conducted the foreclosure sale in a commercially reasonable manner?

DECISION Yes. The foreclosure sale had been conducted in a commercially reasonable manner, and Guaranty Bank was allowed to retain the profits it realized on the resale of the equipment.

REASON The court noted that Guaranty Bank had based its foreclosure bid on the appraisal that it received from Yokley and Lundy, which "indicated a total value for the equipment of between $40,312.50 and $42,000.00." Guaranty Bank's estimate of the commission and other expenses was almost identical to the amount of the actual commission and expenses ($6,500.00 compared with $6,454.21). The court pointed out that " [t]he sale was noticed in keeping with customary standards of practice" and with the requirements of the UCC. The SBA was advised of the sale in a timely manner but elected not to attend the sale or bid on the equipment. The court added, "The fact that the auction sale enabled Guaranty Bank to

a. UCC 9–504(3).

Case 21.3—Continued

receive an excess of $14,748.29, over and above the price it paid at the foreclosure sale, is not conclusive that the foreclosure sale was not conducted in a commercially reasonable manner."

ETHICAL CONSIDERATIONS *In this case, it almost appears as if Guaranty Bank successfully orchestrated a scheme to profit at the expense of the SBA. After all, one day Guaranty Bank, with the apparent collusion of the appraisers and auctioneers, bid $25,000 for equipment that sold the next day for nearly $40,000. The SBA argued that "equity" required Guaranty Bank to pay its "excess profit" to the SBA. The auction had been conducted "without reservation," however. That meant that the equipment had to sell for whatever price it brought. Guaranty Bank was simply fortunate to receive more than it had paid.*

Proceeds from Disposition Proceeds from the disposition must be applied in the following order:

1. Reasonable expenses stemming from the retaking, holding, or preparing for sale are paid first. When authorized by law and if provided for in the agreement, these can include reasonable attorneys' fees and legal expenses.
2. Satisfaction of the balance of the debt owed to the secured party is then made.
3. Creditors with subordinate security interests whose written demands have been received prior to the completion of distribution of the proceeds are then entitled to receive the remaining proceeds from the sale [UCC 9–504(1)].
4. Any surplus generally goes to the debtor.

Deficiency Judgment Often, after proper disposition of the collateral, the secured party has not collected all that is still owed by the debtor. Unless otherwise agreed, the debtor is liable for any deficiency. Note, however, that if the underlying transaction was a sale of accounts or of chattel paper, the secured party can collect a **deficiency judgment** only if the security agreement so provides [UCC 9–504(2)].

DEFICIENCY JUDGMENT
A judgment against a debtor for the amount of a debt remaining unpaid after collateral has been repossessed and sold or after foreclosure proceedings.

Redemption Rights Any time before the secured party disposes of the collateral or enters into a contract for its disposition, or before the debtor's obligation has been discharged through the secured party's retention of the collateral, the debtor or any other secured party can exercise the right of *redemption* of the collateral. The debtor or other secured party can do this by tendering performance of all obligations secured by the collateral and by paying the expenses reasonably incurred by the secured party, in retaking and maintaining the collateral [UCC 9–506].

❖ Key Terms

after-acquired property 512
attachment 500
collateral 500
continuation statement 510
debtor 499
default 504
deficiency judgment 520
execution 516
financing statement 506
floating lien 513
levy 516
lien 513
perfection 504
pledge 504
proceeds 510
purchase-money security interest (PMSI) 503
secured party 499
secured transaction 499
security agreement 500
security interest 499

❖ Chapter Summary: Secured Transactions

Requirements for a Security Interest under Article 9	1. Unless the creditor has possession of the collateral, there must be an agreement in writing, signed by the debtor, describing and reasonably identifying the collateral. 2. The secured party must give value to the debtor. 3. The debtor must have rights in the collateral—some ownership interest or rights to obtain possession of the specified collateral.
Property That May Be Secured by a Creditor	1. *Collateral* in the present possession of the debtor. 2. *Proceeds* from a sale, exchange, or disposition of secured collateral. 3. *After-acquired property*—A security agreement may provide that property acquired after the execution of the security agreement will also be secured by the agreement. This provision often accompanies security agreements covering a debtor's inventory. 4. *Future advances*—A security agreement may provide that any future advances made against a line of credit will be subject to the security interest in the same collateral.
Methods of Perfecting a Security Interest	1. *By transfer of collateral*—The debtor can transfer possession of the collateral itself to the secured party. This type of transfer is called a *pledge*. 2. *By attachment of a purchase-money security interest in consumer goods*—If the secured party has a purchase-money security interest in consumer goods (goods bought or used by the debtor for personal, family, or household purposes), the secured party's security interest is perfected automatically. Exceptions: security interests in fixtures or motor vehicles. 3. *By filing*—The most common method of perfection is by filing a financing statement containing the names and addresses of the secured party and the debtor and describing the collateral by type or item. The financing statement must be signed by the debtor. a. State laws determine where the financing statement is to be filed—with the secretary of state, county clerk (or other local official), or both. b. Classification of collateral determines whether filing is necessary (see Exhibit 21–4).
Priorities among Parties with Claims to the Same Collateral	See Exhibit 21–5.
Rights and Duties of Creditors and Debtors under the UCC	1. *Information request by creditors*—Upon request by any person, the filing officer must send a statement listing the file number, the date, and the hour of original filing of financing statements covering collateral of a particular debtor. A fee is charged. 2. *Reasonable care of collateral*—If a secured party is in possession of the collateral, he or she must use reasonable care in preserving it and (unless the collateral is fungible) in maintaining its identifiable condition. The debtor must pay all reasonable charges incurred by the secured party in doing so. 3. *The status of the debt*—If a debtor wishes to know the status of a secured debt, he or she may sign a descriptive statement of the amount of the unpaid debt (and may include a list of the covered collateral) as of a specific date. The creditor must then approve or correct this statement in writing within two weeks of receipt or be liable for any loss caused to the debtor by failure to do so. Only one request without charge is permitted per six-month period.
Remedies of the Secured Party upon the Debtor's Default	1. Relinquish the security interest and proceed to judgment on the underlying debt, followed by execution and levy on the nonexempt assets of the debtor. This remedy is rarely pursued. 2. Take possession (peacefully or by court order) of the collateral covered by the security agreement and then pursue one of two alternatives: a. Retain the collateral (unless the secured party has a purchase-money security interest in consumer goods and the debtor has paid 60 percent or more of the selling price or loan), in which case the creditor— (1) Must give written notice to the debtor if the debtor has not signed a statement renouncing or modifying his or her rights after default. With consumer goods, no other notice is necessary.

❖ Chapter Summary: Secured Transactions—Continued

Remedies of the Secured Party upon the Debtor's Default —Continued	(2) Must send notice to any other secured party with an interest in the same collateral. If an objection is received from the debtor or any other secured party within twenty-one days, in writing, the creditor must dispose of the collateral according to the requirements of UCC 9–504. Otherwise, the creditor may retain the collateral in full satisfaction of the debt. b. Sell the collateral, in which case the creditor— (1) Must notify the debtor and (except in sales of consumer goods) other secured parties having claims to the collateral of the sale (unless the collateral is perishable or will decline rapidly in value). (2) Must sell the goods in a commercially reasonable manner at a public or private sale. (3) Must apply the proceeds in the following order: (a) Expenses incurred by the sale (which may include reasonable attorneys' fees and other legal expenses). (b) Balance of the debt owed to the secured party. (c) Subordinate security interests of creditors whose written demands have been received prior to the completion of the distribution of the proceeds. (d) Surplus to the debtor.
Termination Statement	When a debt is paid, the secured party generally must send to the debtor or file with the filing officer to whom the original financing statement was given a *termination statement.* Failure to comply results in the secured party's liability to the debtor for $100 plus any loss caused to the debtor. 1. If the financing statement covers consumer goods, the termination statement must be *filed* by the secured party within one month after the debt is paid, or, if the debtor requests the termination statement in writing, it must be filed within ten days of the request after the debt is paid—whichever is earlier. 2. In all other cases, the termination statement must be *filed* or *furnished to the debtor* within ten days after a written request is made by the debtor.

❖ Questions and Case Problems

21-1. Security Interest. What is a security interest? What are the three requirements that must be met for a security interest to be enforceable?

21-2. Oral Security Agreements. Marsh has a prize horse named Arabian Knight. Marsh is in need of working capital. She borrows $5,000 from Mendez, with Mendez taking possession of Arabian Knight as security for the loan. No written agreement is signed. Discuss whether, in the absence of a written agreement, Mendez has a security interest in Arabian Knight. If Mendez does have a security interest, is it a perfected security interest?

21-3. Default. Delgado is a retail seller of television sets. He sells a color television set to Cummings for $600. Cummings cannot pay cash, so she signs a security agreement, paying $100 down and agreeing to pay the balance in twelve equal installments of $50 each. The security agreement gives Delgado a security interest in the television set sold. Cummings makes six payments on time; then she goes into default because of unexpected financial problems. Delgado repossesses the set and wants to keep it in full satisfaction of the debt. Discuss Delgado's rights and duties in this matter.

21-4. Oral Security Agreements. Frank agreed to purchase Janet's used computer from Janet for $450. He paid $200 down and promised to pay the balance of the purchase price within thirty days. Both parties orally agreed that if Frank failed to pay, Janet could repossess the computer. Two months later, when Frank still had not paid the remaining $250, Janet threatened to repossess the computer. Frank claimed that she had no security interest in the computer because their entire agreement had been oral. Is Frank correct? Explain.

21-5. The Scope of a Security Interest. Edward owned a retail sporting-goods shop. A new ski resort was being created in his area, and to take advantage of the potential business, Edward decided to expand his operations. He borrowed a large sum of money from his bank, which took a security interest in his present inventory and any after-acquired inventory as collateral for the loan. The bank properly perfected the security interest by filing a financing statement. A year later, just a few months after the ski resort had opened, an avalanche destroyed the ski slope and lodge. Edward's business consequently took a turn for the worse, and he defaulted on his debt to the bank. The bank sought possession of his entire inventory, even though the inventory was now twice as large as it had been when the loan was made. Edward claimed that the bank only had rights to half his inventory. Is Edward correct? Explain.

21-6. Sale of Collateral. In 1969, Jones and Percell executed a promissory note and a security agreement covering a converted military aircraft built in the 1950s. Upon their default, the Bank of Nevada repossessed the aircraft. After providing the required notice to Jones and Percell, the bank placed advertisements in several trade journals as well as in major newspapers in several large cities. In addition, the bank sent 2,000 brochures to 240 sales organizations. A sales representative was hired to market the aircraft. The plane was later sold for $71,000 to an aircraft broker, who in turn resold it for $123,000 after spending $33,000 on modifications. Because the price obtained on the sale of the plane was about $75,000 less than the amount Jones and Percell owed the bank, the bank initiated a lawsuit to obtain the amount of the deficiency. Can Jones and Percell object to the bank's manner of resale? Why or why not? [*Jones v. Bank of Nevada*, 91 Nev. 368, 535 P.2d 1279 (1975)]

21-7. Priority Disputes. In 1977, the Marcuses sold their drugstore business to Mistura, Inc. Mistura made a down payment on the purchase price, and the Marcuses took a security interest in the fixtures and personal property of the business for the unpaid portion of the debt. Arizona law requires that financing statements relating to security interests in personal property be filed with the secretary of state. Because the Marcuses had filed their statement with the Maricopa County Recorder, only their security interest in the fixtures was properly perfected. Mistura later obtained a loan from McKesson, using the same property secured by the Marcuse transaction as collateral. McKesson properly perfected a security interest in this collateral by filing with the secretary of state. McKesson had actual knowledge at the time of the loan that the Marcuses had not properly perfected their security interest in the personal property of Mistura's business. A few days after McKesson's filing, the Marcuses filed a financing statement with the secretary of state. Which party had a superior security interest in the collateral, McKesson or the Marcuses? Explain. [*In re Mistura, Inc.*, 705 F.2d 1496 (9th Cir. 1983)]

21-8. Priority Disputes. In July of 1978, Dr. Jose B. Namer executed to Citizens & Southern National Bank a note in the amount of $35,000 with an accompanying security agreement covering the following property: "All equipment of the debtor of every description used or useful in the conduct of the debtor's business, now or hereafter existing or acquired. . . . The listed assets held for collateral are presently located at 4385 Hugh Howell Rd, Tucker, Ga." In July of 1980, Dr. Namer moved some of his equipment to a new office owned by Hudson Properties, Inc., in Fairburn, Georgia. To finance this move, Dr. Namer procured a loan from a Fairburn bank, and Hudson cosigned the note. The Fairburn bank prepared a security agreement covering the same equipment as the 1978 security agreement. In September of 1980, Dr. Namer defaulted on the first note and absconded with the equipment from the Fairburn office. Hudson received an insurance payment as cash proceeds for the missing equipment. Citizens & Southern National Bank claimed priority rights to the missing equipment or the insurance proceeds even though the equipment had been moved to Fairburn. Did Citizens & Southern National Bank recover this insurance money from Hudson? [*Hudson Properties, Inc. v. Citizens & Southern National Bank*, 168 Ga.App. 331, 308 S.E.2d 708 (1983)]

21-9. Sale of Collateral. Calcote obtained an automobile loan from Citizens & Southern National Bank, with the bank maintaining a security interest in the car. On March 28, 1984, after Calcote had defaulted on the loan, the bank repossessed the vehicle. On the following day, the bank sent a certified letter, return receipt requested, to Calcote informing her of the repossession, of the bank's plans to sell the auto at a private sale in May of 1984, and of her right to demand a public sale of the vehicle. Although the letter was sent to the address on the bank's records and at which the bank had repossessed the car, Calcote never received the letter. On April 19, 1984, it was returned to the bank stamped "unclaimed." On May 11, 1984, the car was sold at a private sale to which over 150 dealers had been invited. When Calcote learned that the car had been sold, she brought an action against the bank, claiming that she had not been properly notified of the repossession and sale and that the private sale was not a commercially reasonable method of disposition. Was sufficient notice given to Calcote, and was the private sale commercially reasonable? [*Calcote v. Citizens & Southern National Bank*, 179 Ga.App. 132, 345 S.E.2d 616 (1986)]

21-10. Priority Disputes. For several years, Hugh Meyer had financial dealings with the First National Bank of Midland. On one occasion, Meyer delivered some stock certificates to the bank as security for a loan. The security agreement defined the collateral to include any "profits, interest and income from the listed property." Although the securities were in the bank's possession, the bank never registered the stock in its name, nor did it take other steps to ensure that any stock dividends would be sent to the bank instead of to Meyer. Meyer eventually received a stock dividend of $500,000 and turned over the dividend to his law firm as security for a debt he owed to the firm for legal services. Meyer went bankrupt, and the bank's successor, the Federal Deposit Insurance Corp., laid claim to the $500,000 as a perfected secured creditor. The law firm claimed that it, and not the bank, had a perfected security interest in the dividend because the dividend was in the law firm's possession. Which party had a perfected security interest in the $500,000 dividend? [*Federal Deposit Insurance Corp. v. W. Hugh Meyer & Associates, Inc.*, 864 F.2d 371 (5th Cir. 1989)]

21-11. Conflicting Claims to Proceeds. The First National Bank of North Dakota loaned Freddie Mutschler, a prominent farmer in Jamestown, North Dakota, $3 million. Mutschler gave the bank a lien on his crops as partial security for the loan. The loan agreement provided that when Mutschler sold his grain, he would be obligated to turn over the proceeds to cover the indebtedness. Mutschler was also the owner, but not the manager, of the Jamestown Farmers Elevator, which bought and sold grain from various farmers. In the fall of 1982, Mutschler sold his crop to the Jamestown Farmers Elevator but did not apply the proceeds to the debt at the bank. The elevator in turn sold some of the grain to the Pillsbury Co., which knew of the bank's security interest but did not know the terms of the security agreement. The bank did not discover these events until Mutschler and the Jamestown Farmers Elevator filed for bankruptcy in early 1983. The bank sued Pillsbury for conversion of the collateral. Which party prevailed? [*First Bank of North Dakota v. Pillsbury Co.*, 801 F.2d 1036 (8th Cir. 1986)]

21-12. Oral Security Agreements. John and Melody Fish bought various pieces of expensive jewelry, including a diamond ring, a diamond necklace, and a wedding band, from Odom's Jewelers. The Fishes agreed to make monthly installment payments to Odom's until the purchase price was paid in full. In 1988, the Fishes fell behind in their monthly payments on the account. The Fishes and Odom's orally agreed that the Fishes would return the jewelry to Odom's and that Odom's would hold the items for the Fishes until the account was paid. In 1991, the Fishes filed for bankruptcy protection. The jewelry was still in the possession of Odom's. One of the issues before the bankruptcy court was whether Odom's had a security interest in the jewelry. Did it? Explain. [*In re Fish*, 128 Bankr. 468 (N.D.Okla. 1991)]

A QUESTION OF ETHICS AND SOCIAL RESPONSIBILITY

21-13. *Raymond and Joan Massengill borrowed money from Indiana National Bank (INB) to purchase a van. Toward the end of the loan period, the Massengills were notified by mail that they were delinquent on their last two loan payments. Joan called INB on a Saturday and said that she did not agree with the amount that INB said was due. It was arranged that the Massengills would go to the bank the following Monday morning and take care of the matter. In the meantime, INB had made arrangements for the van to be repossessed. At 1:30 A.M. Sunday morning, two men appeared at the Massengills' driveway and began to hook up the van to a tow truck. Raymond, assuming that the van was being stolen, went outside to intervene and did so vociferously. During the course of events, Massengill became entangled in machinery at the rear of the tow truck and was dragged down the street and then run over by his towed van. The "repo men"—those hired by INB to repossess the van—knew of Raymond's plight but sped away. The trial court granted summary judgment for the bank, ruling that the bank was not liable for the injuries caused by the repossession company. On appeal, however, the court ruled that the bank could be liable for the acts of the repossession company and remanded the case for the determination of damages.* [Massengill v. Indiana National Bank, 550 N.E.2d 97 (*Ind.App.1st Dist. 1990*)]

1. Frequently, courts must decide, as in this case, whether the creditor should be held liable for the wrongful acts of persons hired by the creditor to undertake the actual repossession effort. Is it fair to hold the creditor liable for acts that the creditor did not commit? Why or why not?
2. Given the potential for violence during repossession efforts, why do you think Article 9 permits creditors to resort to "self-help" repossessions?
3. Should repossession companies be prohibited from taking collateral from debtors' property during the middle of the night, when debtors are more likely to conclude that the activity is wrongful?

FOR CRITICAL ANALYSIS

21-14. *Review the three requirements for an enforceable security interest. Why is each necessary?*

Chapter 22

Creditors' Rights and Bankruptcy

America's font of practical wisdom, Ben Franklin, observed a truth known to all debtors—that creditors do observe "set days and times" and will expect to recover their money at the agreed-upon time. Normally, creditors have no problem collecting the debts owed to them. But when disputes arise over the amount owed, or when the debtor simply cannot or will not pay, what happens? What remedies are available to creditors when debtors default? We have already looked at the remedies available to secured creditors under Article 9 of the UCC (see Chapter 21). In the first part of this chapter, we focus on the various rights and remedies available under other statutory laws, the common law, and contract law to assist the debtor and creditor in resolving their disputes without the debtor having to resort to bankruptcy. The second part of this chapter discusses bankruptcy as a last resort in resolving debtor-creditor problems.

"Creditors are . . . great observers of set days and times."

Benjamin Franklin, 1706–1790
(American diplomat, author, and scientist)

❖ Laws Assisting Creditors

Numerous laws create rights and remedies for creditors. We discuss some of them in this section.

"Creditor: One of a tribe of savages dwelling beyond the Financial Straits and dreaded for their desolating incursions."

Ambrose Bierce, 1842–1914
(American writer)

Mechanic's Lien

When a person contracts for labor, services, or material to be furnished for the purpose of making improvements on real property but does not immediately pay for the improvements, the creditor can place a **mechanic's lien** on the property. This creates a special type of debtor-creditor relationship in which the real estate itself becomes security for the debt.

MECHANIC'S LIEN
A statutory lien upon the real property of another, created to ensure payment for work performed and materials furnished in erecting or repairing a building or other structure.

For example, a painter agrees to paint a house for a homeowner for an agreed price to cover labor and materials. If the homeowner cannot pay or pays only a portion of the charges, a mechanic's lien against the property can be created. The painter is the lienholder, and the real property is encumbered with a mechanic's lien for the amount owed. If the homeowner does not pay the lien, the property can be sold to satisfy the debt. Notice of the foreclosure and sale must be given to the debtor in advance, however. Note that state law governs mechanic's liens. The time period within which a mechanic's lien must be filed is usually 60 to 120 days from the last date labor or materials were provided.

Artisan's Lien

'S LIEN
ssory lien given to a n who has made provements and added value another person's personal property as security for payment for services performed.

An **artisan's lien** is a security device created at common law through which a creditor can recover payment from a debtor for labor and materials furnished in the repair of personal property. For example, Cindy leaves her diamond ring at the jeweler's to be repaired and to have her initials engraved on the band. In the absence of an agreement, the jeweler can keep the ring until Cindy pays for the services that the jeweler provides. Should Cindy fail to pay, the jeweler has a lien on Cindy's ring for the amount of the bill and can sell the ring in satisfaction of the lien.

In contrast to a mechanic's lien, an artisan's lien is *possessory*. The lienholder ordinarily must have retained possession of the property and have expressly or impliedly agreed to provide the services on a cash, not a credit, basis. Usually, the lienholder retains possession of the property. When this occurs, the lien remains in existence as long as the lienholder maintains possession and is terminated once possession is voluntarily surrendered—unless the surrender is only temporary. If it is a temporary surrender, there must be an agreement that the property will be returned to the lienholder. Even with such an agreement, if a third party obtains rights in that property while it is out of the possession of the lienholder, the lien is lost. The only way that a lienholder can protect a lien and surrender possession at the same time is to record notice of the lien in accordance with state lien and recording statutes.

Modern statutes permit the holder of an artisan's lien to foreclose and sell the property subject to the lien to satisfy payment of the debt. As with the mechanic's lien, the lienholder is required to give notice to the owner of the property prior to foreclosure and selling. The sale proceeds are used to pay the debt and the costs of the legal proceedings, and the surplus, if any, is paid to the former owner.

In the following case, a creditor with a purchase-money security interest (PMSI) in an automobile tried to repossess the property but failed to do so because an artisan's lien had also been placed on the car.

Case 22.1

NATIONAL BANK OF JOLIET v. BERGERON CADILLAC, INC.

Appellate Court of Illinois, 1977.
66 Ill.2d 140,
361 N.E.2d 116,
5 Ill.Dec. 588.

HISTORICAL AND SOCIAL SETTING *Before the UCC, there was generally no specific statutory rule concerning the priority of artisan's or mechanic's liens over other security interests (except for Section 11 of the Uniform Trust Receipts Act of 1933). Under the case law existing at that time, some courts ruled that the priority of the liens turned on whether the secured party had "title."*[a] *The drafters of the UCC clarified the law in respect to the priority of liens. UCC 9–310 provides that liens securing claims that arise from work intended to enhance or preserve the value of collateral take priority over earlier security interests, even if the earlier interests have been perfected. The work must have been performed in the ordinary course of the lienor's business, and the lienor must possess the collateral. Of course, another state statute may make the lien subordinate to an earlier, perfected security interest. If there is a state statute creating artisan's or mechanic's liens but the statute is silent regarding priorities, UCC 9–310 provides that an artisan's or mechanic's lien takes priority.*

FACTS In February of 1973, Gladys Schmidt borrowed $4,120 from the National Bank of Joliet to finance the purchase of a Cadillac. The bank held a security interest in the automobile and had perfected this interest by filing in the office of the secretary of state. In August of 1973, Schmidt took the car to Bergeron Cadillac for repairs, which cost approximately $2,000. When Schmidt failed to pay for the repairs, Bergeron Cadillac retained possession of the car and placed an artisan's lien on it. In September, Schmidt defaulted on her payments to the bank, and the bank later filed an action to gain possession of the Cadillac from Bergeron. The trial court held for Bergeron Cadillac, and the bank appealed.

ISSUE Which party has a right to possession of the vehicle—Bergeron Cadillac or the National Bank?

a. UCC 9–310, Comment 2.

Case 22.1—Continued

DECISION Bergeron Cadillac. The judgment of the trial court was affirmed.

REASON The court looked to both the common law and the UCC in its determination: "The plain language of Section 9–310 gives the lien of persons furnishing services or materials upon goods in their possession priority over a perfected security interest unless the lien is created by statute and the statute expressly provides otherwise." In response to the bank's contention that the common law possessory lien had been superseded in Illinois by two statutes providing for artisan's liens, the court ruled that in both cases "the statutes expressly provide that the liens created shall be in addition to, and shall not exclude, any lien existing by virtue of the common law."

Innkeeper's Lien

An **innkeeper's lien** is another security device created at common law. An innkeeper's lien is placed on the baggage of guests for the agreed-on hotel charges that remain unpaid. If no express agreement has been made on the amount of those charges, then the lien will be for the reasonable value of the accommodations furnished. The innkeeper's lien is terminated either by the guest's payment of the hotel charges or by the innkeeper's surrender of the baggage to the guest, unless the surrender is temporary. Also, the lien is terminated by conversion of the guest's baggage by the innkeeper. Although state statutes permit such conversion by means of a public sale, there is a trend toward requiring that the guest first be given an impartial judicial hearing.[1]

INNKEEPER'S LIEN
A possessory or statutory lien allowing the innkeeper to take the personal property of a guest, brought into the hotel, as security for nonpayment of the guest's bill (debt).

Judicial Liens

A debt must be past due before a creditor can commence legal action against a debtor. Once legal action is brought, the debtor's property may be seized to satisfy the debt. If the property is seized prior to trial proceedings, the seizure is referred to as an *attachment* of the property. The seizure may also occur following a court judgment in the creditor's favor. In that case, the court's order to seize the property is referred to as a *writ of execution*.

Attachment **Attachment** is a court-ordered seizure and taking into custody of property prior to the securing of a judgment for a past-due debt.[2] Attachment rights are created by state statutes. Attachment is a *prejudgment* remedy because it occurs either at the time of or immediately after the commencement of a lawsuit and before the entry of a final judgment. By statute, the restrictions and requirements for a creditor to attach before judgment are specific and limited. The due process clause of the Fourteenth Amendment to the Constitution limits the courts' power to authorize seizure of a debtor's property without notice to the debtor or a hearing on the facts. In recent years, a number of state attachment laws have been held to be unconstitutional.

ATTACHMENT
(1) In a secured transaction, the process by which a security interest in the property of another becomes enforceable. (2) The legal process of seizing another's property in accordance with a writ or judicial order for the purpose of securing satisfaction of a judgment yet to be rendered.

To use attachment as a remedy, the creditor must have an enforceable right to payment of the debt under law, and the creditor must follow certain procedures. Otherwise, the creditor can be liable for damages for wrongful attachment. He or she must file with the court an **affidavit** (a written or printed statement, made under

AFFIDAVIT
A written or printed voluntary statement of facts, confirmed by the oath or affirmation of the party making it and made before a person having the authority to administer the oath or affirmation.

1. *Klim v. Jones*, 315 F.Supp. 109 (N.D.Cal. 1970).
2. Attachment under the UCC's Article 9, as discussed in Chapter 21, is the process through which a security interest becomes enforceable against a debtor with respect to the debt's collateral [UCC 9–203]. In the present context, attachment is the process through which a debtor's property is seized to secure the debt or a creditor's claim prior to a judgment. In many cases, the creditor seeks attachment of the latter kind to assure that there will be some assets of the debtor against which to execute the judgment, should the court rule in the creditor's favor.

oath or sworn to) stating that the debtor is in default and stating the statutory grounds under which attachment is sought. A bond must be posted by the creditor to cover at least court costs, the value of the loss of use of the good suffered by the debtor, and the value of the property attached. When the court is satisfied that all the requirements have been met, it issues a **writ of attachment,** which is similar to a writ of execution in that it directs the sheriff or other officer to seize nonexempt property. If the creditor prevails at trial, the seized property can be sold to satisfy the judgment.

WRIT OF ATTACHMENT
A writ employed to enforce obedience to an order or judgment of the court. The writ may take the form of taking or seizing property to bring it under the control of the court.

Writ of Execution If a creditor is successful in a legal action against a debtor, the court awards the creditor a judgment against the debtor (usually for the amount of the debt plus any interest and legal costs incurred in obtaining the judgment). Frequently, however, the creditor finds it easy to secure a judgment against the debtor but nevertheless fails to collect the awarded amount. If the debtor will not or cannot pay the judgment, the creditor is entitled to go back to the court and obtain a **writ of execution,** which is an order, usually issued by the clerk of the court, directing the sheriff to seize (levy) and sell any of the debtor's nonexempt real or personal property that is within the court's geographic jurisdiction (usually the county in which the courthouse is located). The proceeds of the sale are used to pay off the judgment and the costs of the sale. Any excess is paid to the debtor. The debtor can pay the judgment and redeem the nonexempt property any time before the sale takes place. Because of exemption laws and bankruptcy laws, however, many judgments are virtually uncollectible.

WRIT OF EXECUTION
A writ that puts in force a court's decree or judgment.

Garnishment

Garnishment occurs when a creditor is permitted to collect a debt by seizing property of the debtor (such as wages or money in a bank account) that is being held by a third party (such as an employer or a bank). Typically, a garnishment judgment is served on a debtor's employer so that part of the debtor's usual paycheck will be paid to the creditor.

GARNISHMENT
A legal process whereby a creditor appropriates the debtor's property or wages that are in the hands of a third party.

The legal proceeding for a garnishment action is governed by state law. As a result of a garnishment proceeding, the debtor's employer is ordered by the court to turn over a portion of the debtor's wages to pay the debt. Garnishment operates differently from state to state, however. According to the laws in some states, the judgment creditor needs to obtain only one order of garnishment, which will then continuously apply to the judgment debtor's weekly wages until the entire debt is paid. In other states, the judgment creditor must go back to court for a separate order of garnishment for each pay period.

"If one wants to know the real value of money, he needs but to borrow some from his friends."

Confucius, 551–497 B.C.
(Chinese philosopher)

Both federal laws and state laws limit the amount of money that can be garnished from a debtor's weekly take-home pay.[3] Federal law provides a minimal framework to protect debtors from losing all their income in order to pay judgment debts.[4] State laws also provide dollar exemptions, and these amounts are often larger than those provided by federal law. State and federal statutes can be applied together to create a pool of funds to enable a debtor to continue to provide for family needs while reducing the amount of the judgment debt in a reasonable way.

Under federal law, garnishment of an employee's wages for any one indebtedness cannot be grounds for dismissal of an employee. But what if the employee is dis-

3. Some states (for example, Texas) do not permit garnishment of wages by private parties except under a child-support order.

4. For example, the federal Consumer Credit Protection Act of 1968, 15 U.S.C. Sections 1601–1693r, provides that a debtor can retain either 75 percent of the disposable earnings per week or the sum equivalent to thirty hours of work paid at federal minimum wage rates, whichever is greater.

missed after the employer learns of the garnishment proceeding but before any wages are actually garnished? The court addresses this issue in the following case.

Case 22.2 JOHNSON v. TOWN OF TRAIL CREEK

United States District Court,
Northern District of Indiana, 1991.
771 F.Supp. 271.

HISTORICAL AND POLITICAL SETTING *The federal law that limits the garnishment of wages is Title III of the Consumer Credit Protection Act (CCPA) of 1968.*[a] *In passing Title III, Congress intended to limit the effects of unrestricted garnishment of wages. For example, there were 18,000 personal bankruptcies in 1950, but the number had swelled to 208,000 by 1967. The number of personal bankruptcies was considerably higher in states that allowed virtually unrestricted garnishment than in states that did not allow garnishment of wages. Congress wanted to protect "honest debtors driven by economic desperation from plunging into bankruptcy in order to preserve their employment and insure a continued means of support for themselves and their families."*[b] *Of course, if an employer discharges an employee whose wages have been garnished, the employee also loses his or her means of support.*

FACTS John Johnson worked for the street department of the town of Trail Creek. In August 1989, Trail Creek received notice from a court that one of Johnson's creditors had received a court judgment against Johnson for an unpaid debt. The notice also stated that Johnson's wages would be subject to garnishment, pending a determination of whether Trail Creek owed any obligations or credits (for example, wages) to Johnson that could be garnished. Johnson was fired two days after this notice was received. Johnson brought an action against the town, the president of the town council, and the superintendent of the town's street department (the defendants), alleging, among other things, that the defendants had violated federal law because he was dismissed as a result of the notice of possible garnishment. The defendants moved to dismiss Johnson's complaint on the ground that they could not have violated the law because Johnson's wages were not actually being withheld at the time of his discharge—in other words, no garnishment proceeding had yet occurred.

a. The Consumer Credit Protection Act begins at 15 U.S.C. Section 1601. Title III begins at 15 U.S.C. Section 1673.
b. House of Representatives Report No. 1040, 90th Congress, 2d Session (1968).

ISSUE Must wages actually be withheld before a garnishment proceeding can be held to have occurred?

DECISION No. Trail Creek's motion to dismiss the complaint was denied.

REASON Federal law provides that "[n]o employer may discharge any employee by reason of the fact that his earnings have been subjected to garnishment for any one indebtedness" [15 U.S.C. Section 1674(a)]. The law also defines *garnishment* as meaning "any legal or equitable procedure through which the earnings of any individual are required to be withheld for payment of any debt" [15 U.S.C. Section 1672(c)]. To determine whether "any legal or equitable procedure" had occurred prior to Johnson's dismissal, the court turned to the Indiana procedure for garnishment of wages, which involves two steps: First, the employer is notified of a judgment against its employee, after which the employer must attend a court proceeding to determine whether the employer has "an obligation owing to the judgment debtor." Second, if the employer is found to have such an obligation, "the court may order the payment of obligation to the judgment-creditor." The court concluded that the notice received by Trail Creek was part of a "legal procedure" that required Johnson's earnings to be withheld for a debt. Therefore, if Johnson could prove that he had been discharged because of the notice of possible garnishment, Trail Creek would be liable for violating 15 U.S.C. Section 1674(a).

ETHICAL CONSIDERATIONS *Clearly, the defendants' defense to Johnson's claim was a technical defense that violated the "spirit" (as well as the "letter") of 15 U.S.C. Section 1674(a). But before judging too harshly the defendants' attempts to evade the law, consider the effect of garnishment proceedings on employers. Compliance by employers with garnishment procedures (appearing at a court hearing, filing the appropriate documents, establishing and maintaining records relating to the garnishment, and so on) requires time. For employers, time is a costly resource, and garnishment proceedings are burdensome for employers because they are not compensated for these time costs. When considering these costs and the fact that an employer is an innocent third party caught in the middle of a creditor-debtor dispute, it should come as no surprise that the employer would want to avoid the hassle of garnishment if at all possible.*

Creditors' Composition Agreements

CREDITORS' COMPOSITION AGREEMENT
An agreement formed between a debtor and his or her creditors in which the creditors agree to accept a lesser sum than that owed by the debtor in full satisfaction of the debt.

Creditors may contract with the debtor for discharge of the debtor's liquidated debts (debts that are definite, or fixed, in amount) upon payment of a sum less than that owed. These agreements are called *composition agreements* or **creditors' composition agreements** and are usually held to be enforceable.

Mortgage Foreclosure

MORTGAGEE
The creditor who takes the security interest under the mortgage agreement.

MORTGAGOR
The debtor who pledges collateral in a mortgage agreement.

Mortgage holders have the right to *foreclose* on mortgaged property in the event of a debtor's default. The usual method of foreclosure is by judicial sale of the property, although the statutory methods of foreclosure vary from state to state. If the proceeds of the foreclosure sale are sufficient to cover both the costs of the foreclosure and the mortgaged debt, any surplus is received by the debtor. If the sale proceeds are insufficient to cover the foreclosure costs and the mortgaged debt, however, the **mortgagee** (the creditor-lender) can seek to recover the difference from the **mortgagor** (the debtor) by obtaining a *deficiency judgment* representing the difference between the mortgaged debt and the amount actually received from the proceeds of the foreclosure sale. A deficiency judgment is obtained in a separate legal action that is pursued subsequent to the foreclosure action. It entitles the creditor to recover from other property owned by the debtor.

Suretyship and Guaranty

SURETYSHIP
A contract in which a third party to a debtor-creditor relationship (the surety) promises that the third party will be primarily responsible for the debtor's obligation.

SURETY
One who agrees to be primarily responsible for the debt of another, such as a cosigner on a note.

When a third person promises to pay a debt owed by another in the event the debtor does not pay, either a *suretyship* or a *guaranty* relationship is created. Exhibit 22–1 illustrates these relationships. The third person's credit becomes the security for the debt owed.

Surety A contract of strict **suretyship** is a promise made by a third person to be responsible for the debtor's obligation. It is an express contract between the **surety** and the creditor. The surety in the strictest sense is *primarily* liable for the debt of the principal. The creditor can demand payment from the surety from the moment that the debt is due. A suretyship contract is not a form of indemnity; that is, it is

◆ **Exhibit 22–1**
Suretyship and Guaranty Parties
In a suretyship or guaranty arrangement, a third party promises to be responsible for a debtor's obligations. A third party who agrees to be responsible for the debt even if the primary debtor does not default is known as a surety; a third party who agrees to be *secondarily* responsible for the debt only if the primary debtor defaults is known as a guarantor. As noted in Chapter 11, normally a promise of guaranty (a collateral, or secondary, promise) must be in writing to be enforceable.

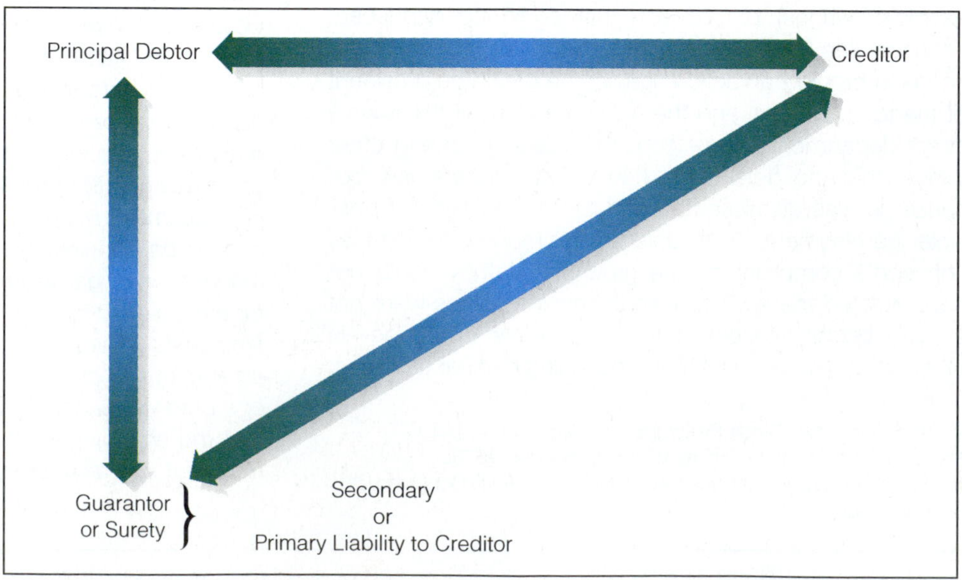

not merely a promise to make good any loss that a creditor may incur as a result of the debtor's failure to pay. The creditor need not exhaust all legal remedies against the principal debtor before holding the surety responsible for payment.

For example, Robert Delmar wants to borrow money from the bank to buy a used car. Because Robert is still in college, the bank will not lend him the money unless his father, Joseph Delmar, who has dealt with the bank before, will **cosign** (add his signature to the note, thereby becoming jointly liable for payment of the debt). When Mr. Delmar cosigns the note, he becomes primarily liable to the bank. On the note's due date, the bank has the option of seeking payment from either Robert or Joseph Delmar, or both jointly.

COSIGN
The act of signing a document (such as a note promising to pay another in return for a loan or other benefit) jointly with another person and thereby assuming liability for performing what was promised in the document.

Guaranty A guaranty contract is similar to a suretyship contract in that it includes a promise to answer for the debt or default of another. With a suretyship arrangement, however, the surety is primarily liable for the debtor's obligation. With a guaranty arrangement, the **guarantor**—the third person making the guaranty—is *secondarily* liable. The guarantor can be required to pay the obligation only after the principal debtor defaults, and default usually only takes place after the creditor has made an attempt to collect from the debtor.

GUARANTOR
One who agrees to satisfy the debt of another (the debtor) *only* if and when the debtor fails to pay the debt. A guarantor's liability is thus secondary.

For example, a closely held corporation, BX Enterprises, needs to borrow money to meet its payroll. The bank is skeptical about the creditworthiness of BX and requires Dawson, its president, who is a wealthy businessperson and owner of 70 percent of BX Enterprises, to sign an agreement making himself personally liable for payment if BX does not pay off the loan. As a guarantor of the loan, Dawson cannot be held liable until BX Enterprises is in default.

The Statute of Frauds requires that a guaranty contract between the guarantor and the creditor must be in writing to be enforceable unless the *main-purpose* exception applies. Briefly, this exception provides that if the main purpose of the guaranty agreement is to benefit the guarantor, then the contract need not be in writing to be enforceable. (See Chapter 11 for a more detailed discussion of this exception.)

The guaranty contract terms determine the extent and time of the guarantor's liability. For example, the guaranty can be *continuing*, designed to cover a series of transactions by the debtor. Also, the guaranty can be *unlimited* or *limited* as to time and amount. In addition, the guaranty can be *absolute*, in which case the guarantor becomes liable immediately upon the debtor's default, or *conditional*, in which case the guarantor becomes liable only upon the happening of a certain event.

Defenses of the Surety and the Guarantor The defenses of the surety and the guarantor are basically the same. Therefore, the following discussion applies to both, although it refers only to the surety. Certain actions will release the surety from the obligation. For example, making any material change in the terms of the original contract between the principal debtor and the creditor, including the awarding of a binding extension of time for making payment, without first obtaining the consent of the surety will discharge the surety either completely or to the extent that the surety suffers a loss.

Naturally, if the principal obligation is paid by the debtor or by another person on behalf of the debtor, the surety is discharged from the obligation. Similarly, if valid tender of payment is made, and the creditor rejects it with knowledge of the surety's existence, then the surety is released from any obligation on the debt.

Generally, any defenses available to a principal debtor can be used by the surety to avoid liability on the obligation to the creditor. Defenses available to the principal debtor that the surety *cannot* use include the principal debtor's incapacity or bankruptcy and the statute of limitations. The ability of the surety to assert any defenses the debtor may have against the creditor is the most important concept in suretyship because most of the defenses available to the surety are also those of the debtor.

Obviously, a surety may also have his or her own defenses—for example, incapacity or bankruptcy. If the creditor fraudulently induced the surety to guarantee the debt of the debtor, the surety can assert fraud as a defense. In most states, the creditor has a legal duty to inform the surety, prior to the formation of the suretyship contract, of material facts known by the creditor that would substantially increase the surety's risk. Failure to so inform is fraud and makes the suretyship obligation voidable. In addition, if a creditor surrenders or impairs the debtor's collateral while knowing of the surety and without the surety's consent, the surety is released to the extent of any loss suffered from the creditor's actions. The primary reason for this is to protect the surety who agreed to become obligated only because the debtor's collateral was in the possession of the creditor.

Rights of the Surety and the Guarantor The rights of the surety and the guarantor are basically the same. Therefore, again, the following discussion applies to both. When the surety pays the debt owed to the creditor, the surety is entitled to certain rights. First, the surety has the legal **right of subrogation.** Simply stated, this means that any right the creditor had against the debtor now becomes the right of the surety. Included are creditor rights in bankruptcy, rights to collateral possessed by the creditor, and rights to judgments secured by the creditor. In short, the surety now stands in the shoes of the creditor and may pursue any remedies that were available to the creditor against the debtor.

RIGHT OF SUBROGATION
The right of a person to stand in the place of (be substituted for) another, giving the substituted party the same legal rights that the original party had.

Second, the surety has the **right of reimbursement** from the debtor. This right may stem either from the suretyship contract or from equity. Basically, the surety is entitled to receive from the debtor all outlays made on behalf of the suretyship arrangement. Such outlays can include expenses incurred as well as the actual amount of the debt paid to the creditor.

RIGHT OF REIMBURSEMENT
The legal right of a person to be restored, repaid, or indemnified for costs, expenses, or losses incurred or expended on behalf of another.

Third, in the case of **co-sureties** (two or more sureties on the same obligation owed by the debtor), a surety who pays more than his or her proportionate share upon a debtor's default is entitled to recover from the co-sureties the amount paid above the surety's obligation. This is the **right of contribution.** Generally, a co-surety's liability either is determined by agreement or, in the absence of agreement, is set at the maximum liability under the suretyship contract.

CO-SURETY
A joint surety. One who assumes liability jointly with another surety for the payment of an obligation.

RIGHT OF CONTRIBUTION
The right of a co-surety who pays more than his or her proportionate share upon a debtor's default to recover the excess paid from other co-sureties.

For example, assume that two co-sureties are obligated under a suretyship contract to guarantee the debt of a debtor. Together, the sureties' maximum liability is $25,000. Surety A's maximum liability is $15,000, and surety B's is $10,000. The debtor owes $10,000 and is in default. Surety A pays the creditor the entire $10,000. In the absence of agreement, surety A can recover $4,000 from surety B ($10,000/$25,000 × $10,000 = $4,000, this co-surety's obligation).

❖ Protection for Debtors

The law protects debtors as well as creditors. Certain property of the debtor, for example, is exempt from creditors' actions. Consumer protection statutes also protect debtors' rights. Of course, bankruptcy laws, which will be discussed in the next section, are designed specifically to assist debtors in need of help.

Exemptions

HOMESTEAD EXEMPTION
A law allowing an owner to designate his or her home and adjoining land as a homestead and thus exempt it from liability for his or her general debt.

In most states, certain types of real and personal property are exempt from levy of execution or attachment. Probably the most familiar of these exemptions is the **homestead exemption.** Each state permits the debtor to retain the family home, either in its entirety or up to a specified dollar amount, free from the claims of unsecured creditors or trustees in bankruptcy. The purpose is to ensure that the debtor will retain some form of shelter.

Suppose that Van Cleave owes Acosta $40,000. The debt is the subject of a lawsuit, and the court awards Acosta a judgment of $40,000 against Van Cleave. The homestead of Van Cleave is valued at $50,000. There are no outstanding mortgages or other liens on his homestead. To satisfy the judgment debt, Van Cleave's family home is sold at public auction for $45,000. Assuming that the homestead exemption is $25,000, the proceeds of the sale are distributed as follows:

1. Van Cleave is given $25,000 as his homestead exemption.
2. Acosta is paid $20,000 toward the judgment debt, leaving a $20,000 deficiency judgment (that is, "leftover debt") that can be satisfied from any other nonexempt property (personal or real) that Van Cleave may have, if allowed by state law.

In a few states, statutes permit the homestead exemption only if the judgment debtor has a family. The policy behind this type of statute is to protect the family. If a judgment debtor does not have a family, a creditor may be entitled to collect the full amount realized from the sale of the debtor's home.

State exemption statutes usually include both real and personal property. Personal property that is most often exempt from satisfaction of judgment debts includes the following:

1. Household furniture up to a specified dollar amount.
2. Clothing and certain personal possessions, such as family pictures or a Bible.
3. A vehicle (or vehicles) for transportation (at least up to a specified dollar amount).
4. Certain classified animals, usually livestock but including pets.
5. Equipment that the debtor uses in a business or trade, such as tools or professional instruments, up to a specified dollar amount.

Special Protection for Consumer Debtors

Numerous consumer protection statutes and rules apply to the debtor-creditor relationship. We have already discussed the Federal Trade Commission's rule limiting the rights of a holder in due course (HDC) who holds a negotiable promissory note executed by a debtor-buyer as part of a consumer transaction. This rule, discussed in the *Landmark in the Law* in Chapter 19, provides basically that any personal defenses that the buyer can assert against the seller can also be asserted against an HDC. The seller must disclose this information clearly on the sales agreement.

Other laws regulating debtor-creditor relationships include the Truth-in-Lending Act, which protects consumers by requiring creditors to disclose specific types of information when making loans to consumers. This act, along with other consumer protection statutes, will be discussed in Chapter 31.

❖ Bankruptcy and Reorganization

Bankruptcy law in the United States has two goals—to protect a debtor by giving him or her a fresh start, free from creditors' claims, and to ensure equitable treatment to creditors who are competing for a debtor's assets. Bankruptcy law is federal law, as discussed in the *Landmark in the Law*, but state laws on secured transactions, liens, judgments, and exemptions also play a role in federal bankruptcy proceedings.

"Bankruptcy is one of those words like 'war' that you have heard all your life and think that you understand until you actually become involved with the process the word is intended to identify."

Jerome Weidman, 1913–
(Novelist and playwright)

Business Law in Action

Scam Schools and Student Loans

Most students are familiar with government-guaranteed student loans. Students receiving these loans know that after they graduate or leave school, they must begin to pay back the loans after a certain grace period, such as six months. Usually, a student can take up to ten years to repay the loan in full. In certain limited circumstances, the loan payments may be deferred. If a former student becomes disabled, is unemployed, is on parental leave, or enters a voluntary federal program such as the Peace Corps, for example, payments on the loan will be suspended.

If a former student fails to repay the loan, the lending institution, the government, or the college may initiate legal proceedings to collect the debt. Because of the high number of defaults on student loans, collection efforts have been stepped up. But what about students who refuse to pay their loans because they were defrauded by the school to which they paid tuition? Must they pay the loans? This issue is particularly relevant for students who receive government-guaranteed loans while attending trade schools or technical institutes. On many occasions, these schools fail to deliver on their promises and close their doors before students can recover for the fraud. The students are left without skills and without jobs, yet they still have to repay their government-guaranteed loans.

For example, consider the fate of Kerry Veal and other students who attended the Adelphi Business College in Gary, Indiana. These students claimed that Adelphi had fraudulently induced them to enroll at the school, made arrangements for them to obtain guaranteed student loans through various lenders, and then failed to provide them with an education. The students contended that Adelphi's public relations representatives would go into the streets of Gary and recruit candidates for enrollment. The story told by one of the students, Paul Graham, is representative of the other students' experiences. Graham was approached on the street by an Adelphi recruiter who promised the availability of "high-technology" job opportunities upon graduation. Shortly thereafter, Graham applied to Adelphi, took a ten-minute "entrance examination," and signed a promissory note for $2,500. He also applied for a government loan. After Graham completed the "bookkeeping" course, he attempted to enroll in a computer course, only to learn that Adelphi, despite its promises of "high-technology training," had neither a computer course nor a computer. Graham did not receive any diploma or certificate for the courses he completed, nor was he provided with any job-placement assistance prior to 1987, when Adelphi closed its doors and entered bankruptcy proceedings.

Kerry Veal and the other students filed an action against the lending institutions, seeking rescission of their loan contracts. The students contended that because of the close connection between the school and the lenders, their fraud defense against the school could also be raised against the banks that had loaned the money. Unfortunately for the students, the court did not agree. The fraud defense could be raised only against the school, not against the banks that had loaned the funds or the government as the guarantor of the loans.[a] In effect, the students were left without any remedy against Adelphi's fraudulent practices.

In response to this kind of fraud, the government no longer allows government-guaranteed loans to be made to students attending trade schools and technical institutes. But many former students are still being sued for defaulting on loans that they received in the past. Whether the students can succeed in raising the defense of fraud depends on how a particular court views the matter. Although the Adelphi students met with little success in the courtroom, in another case, the court held that the students could raise the fraud defense against the bank that had made the loans and also noted that any defense against the bank could be raised against the government as guarantor of the loans.[b]

a. *Veal v. First American Savings Bank*, 914 F.2d 909 (7th Cir. 1990).

b. *Tipton v. Secretary of Education of the United States*, 768 F.Supp. 540 (S.D.W.Va. 1991).

Bankruptcy proceedings are held in bankruptcy courts. A bankruptcy court's primary function is to hold *core proceedings*[5] dealing with the procedures required to administer the estate of the debtor in bankruptcy. Bankruptcy courts are under the authority of U.S. district courts (see the exhibit on the federal court system in

5. Core proceedings are procedural functions, such as allowance of claims, decisions on preferences, automatic stay proceedings, confirmation of bankruptcy plans, discharge of debts, and so on. These terms and procedures are defined and discussed in the following sections of this chapter.

Chapter 3), and rulings from bankruptcy courts can be appealed to the district courts. Fundamentally, a bankruptcy court fulfills the role of an administrative court for the district court concerning matters in bankruptcy.

The remaining sections in this chapter deal with the most frequently used bankruptcy plans: Chapter 7 liquidations, Chapter 11 reorganizations, and Chapter 12 and Chapter 13 plans. The latter three chapters are sometimes referred to as *rehabilitation chapters*. As you read the following sections on bankruptcy, be sure to keep in mind that references to Chapter 7, Chapter 11, Chapter 12, and Chapter 13 are references to chapters contained in the Bankruptcy Code (hereinafter referred to simply as the Code), not references to chapters within this textbook.

❖ Chapter 7 Liquidations

Liquidation is the most familiar type of bankruptcy proceeding and is often referred to as an *ordinary*, or *straight, bankruptcy*. Put simply, debtors in straight bankruptcies state their debts and turn their assets over to trustees. The trustees sell the assets and distribute the proceeds to creditors. With certain exceptions, the remaining debts are then discharged (extinguished), and the debtors are relieved of the obligation to pay the debts. Any "person"—defined as including individuals, partnerships, and corporations[6]—may be a debtor under Chapter 7. Railroads, insurance companies, banks, savings and loan associations, investment companies licensed by the Small Business Administration, and credit unions cannot be Chapter 7 debtors. Other chapters of the Code or other federal or state statutes apply to them.

Filing the Petition

A straight bankruptcy may be commenced by the filing of either a voluntary or an involuntary petition.

Voluntary Bankruptcy A voluntary petition is brought by the debtor, who files official forms designated for that purpose in the bankruptcy court. A consumer-debtor who has selected Chapter 7 must state in the petition, at the time of filing, that he or she understands the relief available under other chapters and has chosen to proceed under Chapter 7. If the consumer-debtor is represented by an attorney, the attorney must file an affidavit stating that the attorney has informed the debtor of the relief available under each chapter. Any debtor who is liable on a claim held by a creditor can file a voluntary petition. The debtor does not even have to be insolvent to do so. Insolvency exists when debts exceed the fair market value of assets, exclusive of exempt property. The voluntary petition contains the following schedules:

1. A list of both secured and unsecured creditors, their addresses, and the amount of debt owed to each.
2. A statement of the financial affairs of the debtor.
3. A list of all property owned by the debtor, including property claimed by the debtor to be exempt.
4. A listing of current income and expenses. This schedule provides creditors and the court with relevant information on the debtor's ability to pay creditors a reasonable amount from future income. This information could possibly lead a court, on its own motion, to dismiss a consumer-debtor's Chapter 7 petition after a hearing and encourage the debtor to file a Chapter 13 petition when that would result in a

6. The definition of *corporation* includes unincorporated companies and associations. It also covers labor unions.

Landmark in the Law

The Bankruptcy Reform Act of 1978 and Its Amendments

The U.S. Constitution, Article I, Section 8, states, "The Congress shall have the power * * * to establish * * * uniform Laws on the subject of Bankruptcies throughout the United States." The inclusion of this clause in the Constitution reflects the early conviction of our nation's leaders that debtors should be given a second chance and should not have to spend months, and sometimes years, in debtors' prisons—the fate of many a debtor at the time the Constitution was written.

Congress first exercised this power in 1800, when the first bankruptcy law was enacted as a result of the business crisis created by restraints imposed on American trade by the British and French. In 1803, the law was repealed, and during the rest of the century—always in response to some crisis—Congress periodically enacted (and later repealed) other bankruptcy legislation. The National Bankruptcy Act of 1898, however, was not repealed, and since that time the United States has had ongoing federal statutory laws concerning bankruptcy. The 1898 act allowed only for **liquidation** in bankruptcy proceedings (which occurs when the debtor's assets are sold and the proceeds distributed to creditors). Some relief through reorganization was first allowed by amendments to the 1898 act in the 1930s.

Modern bankruptcy law is based on the Bankruptcy Reform Act of 1978, which repealed the 1898 act as amended and represented a major overhaul of federal bankruptcy law. A major organizational change in the 1978 act was the establishment of a new system of bankruptcy courts, in which each federal judicial district would have an adjunct bankruptcy court with exclusive jurisdiction over bankruptcy cases. The act also specified that, in contrast to the lifetime terms of judges in other federal courts, bankruptcy court judges would have a fourteen-year term. The 1978 act was amended in 1984 by the passage of the Bankruptcy Amendments and Federal Judgeship Act. These amendments created 232 bankruptcy judgeships in various judicial districts throughout the United States. The 1984 amendments also placed bankruptcy court judges under the authority of the U.S. district courts.

The Bankruptcy Act of 1978 was further amended in 1986 by the Bankruptcy Judges, United States Trustees, and Family Farmer Bankruptcy Act. This amendment created fifty-two additional bankruptcy judgeships, extended the bankruptcy trustee system nationally, granted more power to bankruptcy trustees in the handling of bankruptcy matters, and created a new chapter in bankruptcy (Chapter 12) to aid financially troubled farmers.

The Bankruptcy Reform Act of 1978, as amended, is the basis for the description in this chapter of existing bankruptcy law. The Bankruptcy Code is contained in the U.S. Code as Title 11. Chapters 1, 3, and 5 of the Code include general definitional provisions and provisions governing case administration and procedures, creditors, the debtor,[a] and the estate. These three chapters apply generally to all types of bankruptcies. Chapters 7, 9, 11, 12, and 13 set forth the different types of relief that debtors may seek. Chapter 7 provides for liquidations. Chapter 9 governs the adjustment of the debts of municipalities. Chapter 11 governs reorganizations. Chapter 12 (for family farmers) and Chapter 13 (for individuals) provide for adjustment of the debts of parties with regular income. Chapter 15 sets up a U.S. trustee system.

The most significant changes to bankruptcy law since the enactment of the Bankruptcy Code in 1978 were made by the Bankruptcy Reform Act of 1994. Among the many important changes of the 1994 act was the creation of a "fast-track" procedure for small-business debtors (those not involved in owning or managing real estate and with debts of less than $2 million) under Chapter 11.

a. It is noteworthy that the term *bankrupt* no longer exists under the Bankruptcy Code. Those who were formerly bankrupts under the old Bankruptcy Act are now merely *debtors*.

substantial improvement in a creditor's receipt of payment. (Chapter 13 does not involve liquidation of the debtor's assets but provides for the adjustment of the amount owed to creditors and a plan for paying the adjusted amount over a specified period of years.)[7]

The official forms must be completed accurately, sworn to under oath, and signed by the debtor. To conceal assets or knowingly supply false information on

7. Note, however, that the law generally gives the debtor a presumption in favor of granting an order for relief for whatever chapter in the Bankruptcy Code the debtor requests.

these schedules is a crime under the bankruptcy laws. If the voluntary petition for bankruptcy is found to be proper, the filing of the petition will itself constitute an *order for relief.* This order relieves the debtor of the obligation to pay the debts listed in the petition. Once a consumer-debtor's voluntary petition has been filed, the clerk of the court (or person directed) must mail to the trustee and creditors notice of the order for relief not more than twenty days after the entry of the order.

As mentioned previously, debtors do not have to be insolvent to file for voluntary bankruptcy. Debtors do not have unfettered access to Chapter 7 bankruptcy proceedings, however, as the following case illustrates.

Case 22.3
IN RE WALTON
United States Court of Appeals, Eighth Circuit, 1989.
866 F.2d 981.

HISTORICAL AND POLITICAL SETTING *Before 1984, the Bankruptcy Code provided for the dismissal of Chapter 7 cases in only a few circumstances (nonpayment of court fees, for example). Alarmed at the dramatic rise in the number of personal bankruptcy cases being filed every year, a congressional committee proposed limiting the access of debtors to Chapter 7 relief. The committee drafted an amendment to the Code to require debtors to pass a future-income test, reasoning that "if a debtor can meet his debts without difficulty as they come due, use of Chapter 7 would represent a substantial abuse."*[a] *Congress agreed to limit the access of debtors who had no need to declare bankruptcy but replaced the future-income test with the undefined term "substantial abuse." Thus, in 1984, Congress amended Chapter 7 to allow a court to "dismiss a case filed by an individual debtor * * * whose debts are primarily consumer debts if it finds that the granting of relief would be a substantial abuse of the provisions of this chapter."*[b]

FACTS In 1985, Ronald Walton voluntarily petitioned for Chapter 7 bankruptcy. The bankruptcy court ordered a hearing at which it was determined that Walton's monthly income exceeded his monthly expenses by an amount sufficient to pay off at least a substantial portion of his debts under a sixty-month Chapter 13 reorganization plan. Therefore, the court concluded that granting Walton relief under Chapter 7 would constitute substantial abuse of Chapter 7 and dismissed his petition. Walton argued on appeal, among other things, that Congress intended "substantial abuse" to mean nothing more than "bad faith." According to Walton, because he had brought the petition in good faith, he was not abusing Chapter 7 bankruptcy provisions.

a. Senate Report No. 65, 98th Congress, 1st Session (1983).
b. 11 U.S.C. Section 707(b).

ISSUE Did Walton's petition for Chapter 7 bankruptcy constitute substantial abuse of Chapter 7, in view of the fact that his monthly income exceeded his monthly expenses?

DECISION Yes. The appellate court affirmed the lower court's ruling.

REASON The appellate court stressed that most bankruptcy commentators agree that "[t]he primary factor that may indicate substantial abuse is the ability of the debtor to repay the debts out of future disposable income." In this case, Walton's total unsecured debt was $26,484. Because Walton's monthly income exceeded his monthly expenses by an estimated $497, the court reasoned that Walton would very likely be able to pay his debts over a five-year period under Chapter 13. The court dismissed Walton's contention that Congress intended substantial abuse to mean nothing more than bad faith by stating that "the cramped interpretation * * * that Walton advances would drastically reduce the bankruptcy courts' ability to dismiss cases filed by debtors who are not dishonest, but who also are not needy."

ETHICAL CONSIDERATIONS *As mentioned in the* Ethical Perspective *in this chapter, the number of debtors petitioning for bankruptcy relief has increased substantially in recent years. The added burden on the bankruptcy courts is a social cost borne by the public, which pays (through taxes) the salaries of bankruptcy court judges, the overhead expenses of the courts, and so on. Debtors who resort to bankruptcy as a form of "default" rather than because they are truly needy do so at the expense of others in society who may be just as strapped financially but manage to pay their bills.*

On what basis might a court enter an order for relief in an involuntary bankruptcy proceeding?

Involuntary Bankruptcy An involuntary bankruptcy occurs when the debtor's creditors force the debtor into bankruptcy proceedings. Such a case cannot be commenced against a farmer[8] or a charitable institution, however. Nor can it be filed unless the following requirements are met:

1. If the debtor has twelve or more creditors, three or more of those having unsecured claims aggregating at least $10,000 must join in the petition.
2. If the debtor has fewer than twelve creditors, one or more creditors having an unsecured claim of $10,000 may file.

If the debtor challenges the involuntary petition, a hearing will be held, and the bankruptcy court will enter an order for relief if it finds either of the following:

1. That the debtor is generally not paying debts as they become due.[9]
2. That a custodian or assignee was appointed to take charge, or took possession, of substantially all of the debtor's property within 120 days before the filing of the petition.

If the court grants an order for relief, the debtor will be required to supply the bankruptcy schedules discussed previously.

An involuntary petition should not be used as an everyday debt-collection device, and the Code provides penalties for the filing of frivolous (unjustified) petitions against debtors. Judgment may be granted against the petitioning creditors for the

8. *Farmers* are defined as persons who receive more than 80 percent of their gross income from farming operations, such as tilling the soil, dairy farming, ranching, or the production or raising of crops, poultry, or livestock. Corporations and partnerships, as well as individuals, can be farmers.

9. The inability to pay debts as they become due is known as *equitable* insolvency. A *balance-sheet* insolvency, which exists when a debtor's liabilities exceed assets, is not the test. Thus, it is possible for debtors to be thrown into involuntary bankruptcy even though their assets far exceed their liabilities. This situation may occur when a debtor's cash-flow problems become severe.

costs and attorneys' fees incurred by the debtor in defending against an involuntary petition that is dismissed by the court. If the petition is filed in bad faith, damages can be awarded for injury to the debtor's reputation. Punitive damages may also be awarded.

Automatic Stay

The filing of a petition, either voluntary or involuntary, operates as an **automatic stay** on (suspension of) virtually all litigation and other action by creditors against the debtor or the debtor's property. In other words, once a petition is filed, creditors cannot commence or continue most legal actions against the debtor to recover claims. Nor can creditors take any action to repossess property in the hands of the debtor. A secured creditor, however, may petition the bankruptcy court for relief from the automatic stay in certain circumstances.

AUTOMATIC STAY
A suspension of all judicial proceedings upon the occurrence of an independent event. Under the Bankruptcy Code, the moment a petition to commence bankruptcy proceedings is filed, all litigation and other actions by creditors against a debtor and the debtor's property is suspended.

Underlying the Code's automatic-stay provision is a concept known as *adequate protection,* which holds, among other things, that secured creditors are protected from losing their security as a result of the automatic stay. The bankruptcy court can provide adequate protection by requiring the debtor or trustee to make periodic cash payments or a one-time cash payment (or provide additional collateral or liens) to the extent that the stay causes the value of the property involved to decrease. Or the court may grant other relief that is the equivalent of the secured party's interest in the property, such as a guaranty by a solvent third party to cover losses suffered by the secured party as a result of the stay.

For example, G&M Trucking owns two trucks in which Middleton Bank has a security interest. G&M Trucking has failed to make its monthly payments for two months. It files a petition in bankruptcy, and the automatic stay prevents Middleton Bank from repossessing the trucks. Meanwhile, the trucks (whose collective value is already less than the balance due) are depreciating at a rate of several hundred dollars a month. Thus, Middleton Bank's inability to repossess and immediately resell the trucks is harming the bank to the extent of several hundred dollars per month. The bankruptcy court may prevent Middleton Bank from being harmed by requiring G&M Trucking to make a one-time cash payment or periodic cash payments (or provide additional collateral or liens) to the extent that the trucks are depreciating in value. If the debtor is unable to provide adequate protection, the court may vacate the stay and allow Middleton Bank to repossess the trucks.

A creditor's failure to abide by an automatic stay imposed by the filing of a petition could be costly. If a creditor *knowingly* violates the automatic-stay provision (a willful violation), any party injured is entitled to recover actual damages, costs, and attorneys' fees and may also be entitled to recover punitive damages.

The Trustee

Promptly after the order for relief has been entered, an interim, or provisional, trustee is appointed to preside over the debtor's property until the first meeting of creditors.[10] At this first meeting, either a permanent trustee is elected or the interim trustee becomes the permanent trustee. As will be discussed later in this chapter, the trustee's principal duties are to collect and reduce to money the "property of the estate" for which he or she serves and to close up the estate as expeditiously as is compatible with the best interests of the parties. Trustees are entitled to compensation for services rendered, plus reimbursement for expenses.

---

10. The Bankruptcy Judges, United States Trustees, and Family Farmer Bankruptcy Act of 1986 provides for a national trustee system. Trustees can now be assigned to preside over the debtor's property and administer the debtor's estate, essentially performing tasks that the bankruptcy judge otherwise would perform. A U.S. trustee can act as a trustee in certain cases but is not intended as a substitute for private bankruptcy trustees. The U.S. trustee is more of a substitute for the bankruptcy judge.

Creditors' Meeting

Within a reasonable time after the order of relief is granted (not less than ten days or more than thirty days), the bankruptcy court must call a meeting of creditors listed in the schedules filed by the debtor. The bankruptcy judge does not attend this meeting. A permanent trustee[11] may be elected (by 20 percent or more of the unsecured creditors with fixed claims), in which case the interim trustee's duties are discharged. More typically, in the absence of election, the interim trustee becomes the permanent trustee. The debtor must attend this meeting (unless excused by the court) and submit to an examination under oath. Failing to appear or making false statements may result in the debtor's being denied a discharge. At the meeting, the trustee ensures that the debtor is advised of the potential consequences of bankruptcy and of his or her ability to file under a different chapter. Proof of claims by creditors must normally be filed within ninety days of this meeting.

Property of the Estate

Upon the commencement of a Chapter 7 proceeding, an *estate in property* is created. The estate consists of all the debtor's legal and equitable interests in property presently held, wherever located, together with certain jointly owned property, property transferred in transactions voidable by the trustee, proceeds and profits from the property of the estate, and certain after-acquired property. Interests in certain property—such as gifts, inheritances, property settlements (resulting from divorce), or life insurance death proceeds—to which the debtor becomes entitled *within 180 days after filing* may also become part of the estate. Thus, the filing of a bankruptcy petition generally fixes a dividing line: property acquired prior to the filing becomes property of the estate, and property acquired after the filing, except as just noted, remains the debtor's.

Exemptions

Any individual debtor is entitled to exempt certain property from the property of the estate. Prior to the enactment of the Code, state law exclusively governed the extent of the exemptions. The Code, however, establishes a federal exemption scheme under which the following property is exempt:

1. Up to $15,000 in equity in the debtor's residence and burial plot.
2. Interest in a motor vehicle up to $2,400.
3. Interest, up to $400 for any particular item or $8,000 for all items together, in household goods and furnishings, wearing apparel, appliances, books, animals, crops, or musical instruments.
4. Interest in jewelry up to $1,000.
5. Any other property worth up to $800, plus any unused part of the $15,000 homestead exemption up to an amount of $7,500.[12]
6. Interest in any tools of the debtor's trade, up to $1,500.
7. Any unmatured life insurance contract owned by the debtor.
8. Certain interests in accrued dividends or interest under life insurance contracts owned by the debtor.
9. Professionally prescribed health aids.
10. The right to receive Social Security and certain welfare benefits, alimony and support payments, and certain pension benefits.
11. The right to receive certain personal injury and other awards, up to $15,000.

11. See the discussion of U.S. trustees in footnote 10.
12. The Code places a cap of $7,500 on the unused part of the homestead exemption to prevent some debtors from receiving a complete $15,000 windfall.

Individual states are given the power to pass legislation to preclude the use of the federal exemptions by debtors in their states. A majority of the states have done this. In those states, debtors may use only state (not federal) exemptions. In the rest of the states, an individual debtor (or husband and wife who file jointly) may choose between the exemptions provided under state law and the federal exemptions.

Trustee's Powers

The basic duty of the trustee is to collect the debtor's available estate and reduce it to money for distribution, preserving the interests of both the debtor and unsecured creditors. In other words, the trustee is accountable for administering the debtor's estate. To enable the trustee to accomplish this duty, the Code gives him or her certain powers, stated in both general and specific terms.

The trustee has general powers by virtue of the fact that the trustee occupies a position *equivalent* in rights to that of other parties. For example, in some situations, the trustee has the same rights as creditors and can obtain a judicial lien or levy execution on the debtor's property. This means that a trustee has priority over an unperfected secured party to the debtor's property. The trustee also has the power to require persons holding the debtor's property at the time the petition is filed to deliver the property to the trustee.

In addition, the trustee has the power to avoid (cancel) certain types of transactions, including those transactions that the debtor could rightfully avoid, *preferences*, certain statutory *liens*, and *fraudulent transfers* by the debtor. Avoidance powers must be exercised within two years of the order for relief (the period runs even if a trustee has not been appointed). These powers are discussed in more detail in the following subsections.

Voidable Rights A trustee steps into the shoes of the debtor. Thus, any reason that a debtor can use to obtain the return of his or her property can be used by the trustee as well. These grounds (for recovery) include fraud, duress, incapacity, and mutual mistake.

For example, Rob sells his boat to Inga. Inga gives Rob a check, knowing that there are insufficient funds in her bank account to cover the check. Inga has committed fraud. Rob has the right to avoid that transfer and recover the boat from Inga. Once an order for relief has been entered for Rob, the trustee can exercise the same right to recover the boat from Inga.

If the trustee does not take action to enforce one of his or her rights (for example, to recover a preference), the debtor in a Chapter 7 bankruptcy will nevertheless be able to enforce that right.[13]

Preferences A debtor should not be permitted to transfer property or to make a payment in a way that favors one creditor over others. Thus, the trustee is allowed to recover such property or payments.

Transfers within Ninety Days of Filing For a transfer to constitute a preferential transfer that can be recovered, an *insolvent* debtor generally (though not always, as exceptions exist) must have made the transfer to cover a *preexisting* debt within ninety days of filing the petition in bankruptcy. The transfer must give the creditor more than would have been received in the normal course of a Chapter 7 liquidation proceeding. The trustee does not have to prove insolvency, as the Code provides that the debtor is presumed to be insolvent during this ninety-day period. If a preferred creditor has sold the property to an innocent third party, the property cannot be recovered from the innocent party, but in such circumstances, the creditor generally can be held accountable for the value of the property.

13. Under Chapter 11 (to be discussed later), for which no trustee generally exists, the debtor has the same avoiding powers as a trustee under Chapter 7. Under Chapters 12 and 13 (also to be discussed later), a trustee must be appointed.

Transfers to Insiders Sometimes the creditor receiving the preference is an *insider*—an individual, a partner, or an officer or director of a corporation (or relative of these) who has a close relationship with the debtor. If that is the case, the avoidance power of the trustee is extended from transfer preferences made within ninety days to those made within one year of the filing; however, the presumption of insolvency is confined to the ninety-day period, so the trustee must prove insolvency before that period.

Transfers in the Ordinary Course of Business Only those transfers involving something other than current consideration constitute preferences. Therefore, it is generally assumed by most courts that payments for services rendered within ten to fifteen days prior to the payment of the current consideration are not preferences. If a creditor receives payment in the ordinary course of business, such as payment of last month's telephone bill, the payment cannot be recovered by the trustee in bankruptcy. To be recoverable, a preference must be a transfer for an antecedent debt, such as a year-old telephone bill. In addition, a consumer-debtor may transfer any property to a creditor up to a total value of $600 without the transfer's constituting a preference. Recently, a federal court of appeals held that interest payments made on long-term loans during the ninety-day period were preferences and not payments in the ordinary course of business.

Liens on Debtor's Property The trustee is permitted to avoid the fixing of certain statutory liens, such as a mechanic's lien, on property of the debtor. Liens that first become effective at the time of the bankruptcy or insolvency of the debtor are voidable by the trustee. Liens that are not perfected or enforceable against a bona fide purchaser on the date of the petition are also voidable.

Fraudulent Transfers The trustee may avoid fraudulent transfers or obligations if they were made within one year of the filing of the petition or if they were made with actual intent to hinder, delay, or defraud a creditor. Transfers made for less than a reasonably equivalent consideration are also vulnerable if the debtor thereby became insolvent, was left engaged in business with an unreasonably small amount of capital, or intended to incur debts that would be beyond his or her ability to pay.

Claims of Creditors

Generally, any legal obligation of the debtor is a claim. In the case of disputed or unliquidated claims, the bankruptcy court will estimate the value of the claim. Any creditor holding a debtor's obligation can file a claim against the debtor's estate.

These claims are automatically allowed unless contested by the trustee, the debtor, or another creditor. The Code, however, does not allow claims for breach of employment contracts or real estate leases for terms longer than one year. Such claims are limited to one year's rent or wages, despite the remaining length of either contract in breach.

"By no means run in debt: take thine own measure. Who cannot live on twenty pounds a year, cannot on forty."

George Herbert, 1593–1633
(English poet)

Property Distribution

Creditors are either secured or unsecured. The rights of perfected secured creditors were discussed in Chapter 21. A *secured* creditor has a security interest in collateral that secures the debt. In the past, perfected secured parties were frequently put on hold for months concerning the disposition of the secured collateral held by the debtor because of the automatic-stay provisions. Today, the law provides that a consumer-debtor, within thirty days of the filing of a Chapter 7 petition or before the date of the first meeting of the creditors (whichever is first), must file with the clerk a statement of intention with respect to the secured collateral. The statement must indicate whether the debtor will retain the collateral or surrender it to the secured party.[14]

The trustee is obligated to enforce the debtor's statement within forty-five days after the statement is filed. If the secured collateral is surrendered to the perfected secured party, the secured creditor can enforce the security interest either by accepting the property in full satisfaction of the debt or by foreclosing on the collateral and using the proceeds to pay off the debt. In this way, the secured party has priority over unsecured parties to the proceeds from the disposition of the secured collateral. Indeed, the Code provides that if the value of the secured collateral exceeds the secured party's claim, the secured party also has priority to the proceeds in an amount that will cover reasonable fees and costs incurred because of the debtor's default. Any excess over this amount is used by the trustee to satisfy the claims of unsecured creditors. Should the secured collateral be insufficient to cover the secured debt owed, the secured creditor becomes an unsecured creditor for the difference.

Bankruptcy law establishes an order or priority for classes of debts owed to *unsecured* creditors, and they are paid in the order of their priority. Each class of debt must be fully paid before the next class is entitled to any of the proceeds—if there are sufficient funds to pay the entire class. If not, the proceeds are distributed *proportionately* to each creditor in a class, and all classes lower in priority on the list receive nothing. The order of priority is as follows:

1. All costs and expenses for preserving and administering the estate, including such items as court costs and trustees' and attorneys' fees and costs incurred by the trustee during the administration of the estate, such as rental fees and appraisal fees.
2. Unsecured claims in an involuntary proceeding arising in the ordinary course of the debtor's business after commencement of the case but before the appointment of a trustee or issuance of an order for relief.
3. Claims for wages, salaries, and commissions up to an amount of $4,000 per claimant, provided that they were earned within ninety days of the filing of the petition in bankruptcy. Any claims in excess of $4,000 are treated as "claims of general creditors" (number 8 in this list).
4. Unsecured claims for contributions to employee benefit plans arising under services rendered within 180 days before the filing of the petition and limited to the number of employees covered by the plan multiplied by $4,000.
5. Claims of farm producers and fishermen, up to $4,000, against debtors who own or operate grain-storage facilities or fish-storage or fish-processing facilities.
6. Unsecured claims for money (up to $1,800) deposited with the debtor before the filing of the petition in connection with the purchase, lease, or rental of property or services that were not delivered or provided. Any claims in excess of $1,800 are treated as "claims of general creditors" (number 8 in this list).
7. Certain taxes and penalties legally due and owed to various government units (rules vary depending on type of tax owed).
8. Claims of general creditors. These debts have the lowest priority and are paid on a pro rata basis if, and only if, funds remain after all the debts having priority have been paid in full.
9. Any remaining balance is returned to the debtor.

---

14. Also, if applicable, the debtor must specify whether the collateral will be claimed as exempt property and whether the debtor intends to redeem the property or reaffirm the debt secured by the collateral.

Discharge

From the debtor's point of view, the primary purpose of a Chapter 7 liquidation is to obtain a fresh start through the discharge of debts.[15] The primary effect of a discharge is to void any judgment on a discharged debt and enjoin any action to collect it. In certain circumstances, however, a claim will not be discharged, either because of the nature of the claim or because of the conduct of the debtor.

Exceptions to Discharge Claims that are not dischargeable under Chapter 7 include the following:

1. Claims for back taxes accruing within three years prior to bankruptcy (and claims for amounts borrowed to pay federal taxes).
2. Claims against property or money obtained by the debtor under false pretenses or by false representations.
3. Unscheduled claims (claims by creditors who were not notified of the bankruptcy; these claims did not appear on the schedules that the debtor was required to file).
4. Claims based on the debtor's fraud or misuse of funds while the debtor was acting in a fiduciary capacity or claims involving the debtor's embezzlement or larceny.
5. Alimony and child support.
6. Claims based on willful or malicious injury by the debtor to another or to the property of another.
7. Certain fines and penalties payable to government units.
8. Certain student loans, unless payment of the loans imposes an undue hardship on the debtor and the debtor's dependents.
9. Consumer debts of more than $1,000 for luxury goods or services owed to a single creditor and incurred within sixty days of the order of relief. This denial of discharge is a rebuttable presumption (that is, it can be disputed by the debtor), and any debts reasonably acquired to support or maintain the debtor or dependents are not classified as debts for luxury goods or services.
10. Cash advances totaling more than $1,000 as an extension of open-end consumer credit obtained by the debtor within sixty days of the order of relief. This is also a rebuttable presumption.
11. Judgments or consent decrees awarded against a debtor for liability incurred as a result of the debtor's operation of a motor vehicle while legally intoxicated.

The following case concerns the question of the discharge of a student loan.

Case 22.4
IN RE BAKER
United States Bankruptcy Court,
Eastern District of Tennessee, 1981.
10 Bankr. 870.

HISTORICAL AND SOCIAL SETTING *In 1980, about 53 percent of married women in the United States were working, compared with about 41 percent ten years earlier. More than 60 percent of wives who were separated from their husbands worked outside the home in 1980, compared with about 52 percent in 1970; for divorced women, the figures were about 74 percent and 72 percent. On average, however, in 1980, women earned only 62 cents for every dollar that men earned. In American families, husbands averaged nearly $21,000 in earnings, wives $8,600. At the same time, of mothers who were entitled to child support, less than 75 percent actually received any payments. Of mothers living below the poverty line, more than 60 percent received nothing at all.*

15. Discharges are granted only to "individuals" who are debtors under Chapter 7, not to corporations or partnerships. The latter may use Chapter 11 or (when appropriate) Chapter 12, or they may be liquidated under state law. Also note that a discharge does not affect the liability of a co-debtor.

Case 22.4—Continued

FACTS Mary Lou Baker attended three different institutions of higher learning. At these three schools, she received educational loans totaling $6,635. After graduation, she was employed, but her monthly take-home pay was less than $650. Monthly expenses for herself and her three children were approximately $925. Her husband had left town and provided no child or other financial support. She received no public aid and had no other income. In January 1981, just prior to this action, Baker's church paid her gas bill so that she and her children could have heat in their home. One child had reading difficulty, and another required expensive shoes. Baker had not been well and had been unable to pay her medical bills. She filed for bankruptcy. In her petition, she sought a discharge of her educational loans based on the hardship provision.

ISSUE Would paying the debt pose an undue hardship for Baker?

DECISION Yes. The student loans were discharged.

REASON The purpose of the prohibition against discharge was "to remedy an abuse by students who, immediately upon graduation, would file bankruptcy to secure a discharge of educational loans." In this case, Baker did not file bankruptcy to secure a discharge only from her educational loans. The bankruptcy court found that Baker could reduce her expenses somewhat but that her reasonable expenses each month far exceeded her income. Given Baker's circumstances, the court found that forcing payment of Baker's debts would create an undue hardship and that the Bankruptcy Code was drafted to provide a fresh start for those such as Baker "who have truly fallen on hard times."

Objections to Discharge In addition to the exceptions to discharge previously listed, the following circumstances (relating to the debtor's *conduct* and not the debt) will cause a discharge to be denied.

1. The debtor's concealment or destruction of property with the intent to hinder or delay or defraud a creditor.
2. The debtor's fraudulent concealment or destruction of records, or failure to keep adequate records, of his or her financial condition.
3. The debtor's refusal to obey a lawful order of a bankruptcy court.
4. The debtor's failure to explain the loss of assets satisfactorily.
5. The granting of a discharge to the debtor within six years of the filing of the petition.[16]
6. The debtor's written waiver of discharge, approved by the court.

When a discharge is denied under these circumstances, the assets of the debtor are still distributed to the creditors, but the debtor remains liable for the unpaid portions of all claims.

Revocation of Discharge The Code provides that a debtor may lose his or her bankruptcy discharge by *revocation.* The bankruptcy court may within one year revoke the discharge decree if it is discovered that the debtor was fraudulent or dishonest during the bankruptcy proceedings. The revocation renders the discharge null and void, allowing creditors not satisfied by the distribution of the debtor's estate to proceed with their claims against the debtor.

Reaffirmation of Debt A debtor may voluntarily agree to pay off a dischargeable debt. This is called a *reaffirmation* of the debt. To be enforceable, reaffirmation agreements must be made before a debtor is granted a discharge, and they must be filed with the court. If the debtor is represented by an attorney, court approval is

16. A discharge under Chapter 13 of the Code within six years of the filing of the petition does not bar a subsequent Chapter 7 discharge when a good faith Chapter 13 plan paid at least 70 percent of all allowed unsecured claims and was the debtor's "best effort."

not required if the attorney files a declaration or affidavit stating that (1) the debtor has been fully informed of the consequences of the agreement (and a default under the agreement), (2) the agreement is made voluntarily, and (3) the agreement does not impose a hardship on the debtor or the debtor's dependents. If the debtor is not represented by an attorney, court approval is required, and the agreement will be approved only if the court finds that the agreement will result in no undue hardship to the debtor and is in the best interest of the debtor. In addition, the debtor has the ability to rescind the agreement at any time prior to discharge or within sixty days of filing the agreement, whichever is later. This rescission period must be stated *clearly* and *conspicuously* in the reaffirmation agreement.

❖ Chapter 11 Reorganizations

In a Chapter 11 reorganization, the creditors and the debtor formulate a plan under which the debtor pays a portion of his or her debts and is discharged of the remainder. Then the debtor is allowed to continue in business. Although this type of bankruptcy is commonly a corporate reorganization, any debtor who is eligible for Chapter 7 relief is eligible for Chapter 11 relief. Railroads are also eligible for Chapter 11 relief. The same principles that govern the filing of a Chapter 7 petition apply to Chapter 11 proceedings.

WORKOUT
A common law or bankruptcy out-of-court negotiation with creditors in which a debtor enters into an agreement with a creditor or creditors for a payment or plan to discharge the debtor's debt(s).

In some instances, creditors may prefer private, negotiated adjustments of creditor-debtor relations, known as **workouts,** to bankruptcy proceedings. Quite frequently, these out-of-court workouts are much more flexible and thus more conducive to a speedy settlement. Speed is critical, because delay is one of the most costly elements in any bankruptcy proceeding.

Another advantage of workouts is that they avoid the various administrative costs of bankruptcy proceedings. Under Section 305(a) of the Bankruptcy Code, a court, after notice and a hearing, may dismiss or suspend all proceedings in a case at any time if such a dismissal or suspension would better serve the interests of the creditors. Another part of the Code, Section 1112, allows a court, at the request of a creditor or other party affected by the proceedings, and after notice and a hearing, to dismiss a case under Chapter 11 for cause. *Cause* includes the absence of a reasonable likelihood of rehabilitation, the inability to effectuate a plan, and an unreasonable delay by the debtor that is harmful to the interests of creditors.[17] In the following case, creditors of Johns-Manville Corporation sought to dismiss, under Section 1112, a voluntary Chapter 11 petition filed by Manville.

Case 22.5
IN RE JOHNS-MANVILLE CORP.
United States Bankruptcy Court, Southern District of New York, 1984. 36 Bankr. 727.

HISTORICAL AND ENVIRONMENTAL SETTING *In the late 1970s and early 1980s, the number of claims for injuries caused by asbestos in the products manufactured and sold by the Johns-Manville Corporation was mounting. Manville began to analyze its financial situation. Studies projected runaway asbestos-related health costs for the company within the foreseeable future. The accounting firm of Price Waterhouse advised the company that at least $1.9 billion would be needed as a reserve fund to meet those costs. This figure took into account only the moderate to severe asbestos disease cases, assumed that Manville's insurance companies would pay many of the costs, and did not include punitive damages. As the number of claims accelerated, Manville's insurance companies disavowed their liability. Asbestos-related property damage claims began to present another source of liability. Schools sought damages for their unknowing use of asbestos products in ceilings, walls, piping, ductwork, and boilers in school buildings. Two class action suits were filed in federal district court on behalf of every public school district and*

17. See 11 U.S.C. Section 1112(b).

Case 22.5—Continued

private school in the United States to seek redress for the school asbestos problem. Individual schools and school districts also filed suits. Manville estimated that it could need another $500 million to $1.4 billion to cover this liability. In addition, Manville had debts in the amount of approximately $700 million not related to the asbestos problem.

FACTS On August 26, 1982, Johns-Manville Corporation, a highly successful industrial enterprise, filed for protection under Chapter 11 of the Bankruptcy Code. This filing came as a surprise to some of Manville's creditors, as well as to some of the other corporations that were also being sued, along with Manville, for injuries caused by asbestos exposure. Manville asserted that the approximately 16,000 lawsuits pending as of the filing date and the potential lawsuits of people who had been exposed but who would not manifest the asbestos-related diseases until sometime in the future necessitated its filing. The creditors of Manville, on motion to the bankruptcy court, contended that Manville did not file in good faith, that Manville was not insolvent, and that therefore the voluntary Chapter 11 petition should be dismissed under Section 1112.

ISSUE Was Manville eligible to file a voluntary petition for Chapter 11 reorganization under the Bankruptcy Code?

DECISION Yes. The court held that bankruptcy proceedings were appropriate in this situation and denied the motions to dismiss Manville's petition.

REASON With respect to voluntary petitions, the court noted that "it is no longer necessary for a petitioner for reorganization to allege or show insolvency or inability to pay debts as they mature." Manville clearly met all of the threshold eligibility requirements for filing a voluntary petition. Furthermore, in determining whether to dismiss under Section 1112(b), a court is not necessarily required to consider the debtor's good faith in filing because "good faith" is not specifically necessary for filing under the Code. Rather, good faith emerges as a requirement for confirmation of the plan; that is, good faith is required to come out of Chapter 11, but not to get into it. A "principal goal" of the Code is to provide open and easy access to the bankruptcy process. Here, liquidation would be inefficient and wasteful, destroying the utility of Manville's assets as well as jobs. More importantly, liquidation would preclude compensation of future asbestos claimants. Ultimately, the court concluded that Manville needed the protection of the Bankruptcy Code and should not be required to wait until its economic picture deteriorated beyond salvation to file for reorganization.

ETHICAL CONSIDERATIONS *The court's decision in this case has been the target of much controversy. Many critics have argued that Manville, as a solvent corporation, was not deserving of the "fresh start" it achieved through Chapter 11 proceedings.*

Debtor in Possession

Upon entry of the order for relief, the debtor generally continues to operate his or her business as a **debtor in possession (DIP).** The court, however, may appoint a trustee (often referred to as a *receiver*) to operate the debtor's business if gross mismanagement of the business is shown or if appointing a trustee is in the best interests of the estate.

DEBTOR IN POSSESSION (DIP)
In Chapter 11 bankruptcy proceedings, a debtor who is allowed to continue in possession of the estate in bankruptcy (the business) and to continue business operations.

The DIP's role is similar to that of a trustee in a Chapter 7 liquidation. The DIP is entitled to avoid prepetition preferential payments made to creditors and prepetition fraudulent transfers of assets. The DIP has the power to decide whether to cancel or assume prepetition executory contracts (those that are not yet performed) or unexpired leases. Under the "strong-arm clause"[18] of the Bankruptcy Code, a DIP can avoid any obligation or any transfer of property of the debtor that could be avoided by certain parties. These parties include (1) a creditor who extended credit to the debtor at the time of bankruptcy and who consequently obtained a lien on the debtor's property; (2) a creditor who extended credit to the debtor at the time of bankruptcy and who consequently obtained a writ of execution against the debtor that was returned unsatisfied; and (3) a bona fide purchaser of real property from the debtor, if at the time of the bankruptcy the transfer was perfected.

18. 11 U.S.C. Section 544(a).

The DIP has the powers that these parties would have, even if these parties do not actually exist. For example, Scott loans Francesca $10,000, secured by a mortgage on Francesca's real property. Scott fails to record the mortgage with the proper authorities. If Francesca were to sell the property to Doug, a bona fide purchaser, Doug would take the property free of the mortgage. Imagine, instead, that Francesca does not sell the property to anyone but files for bankruptcy. Under the strong-arm clause, Francesca's trustee can assert the rights of a hypothetical bona fide purchaser and take the property free of the mortgage.

Creditors' Committees

As soon as practicable after the entry of the order for relief, a creditors' committee of unsecured creditors is appointed. The committee may consult with the trustee or the DIP concerning the administration of the case or the formulation of the plan. Additional creditors' committees may be appointed to represent special-interest creditors. Orders affecting the estate generally will not be entered without (1) the consent of the committee or (2) a hearing by the judge of the position of the committee. Businesses with debts of less than $2 million that do not own or manage real estate can avoid creditors' committees. In these cases, orders can be entered without a committee's consent.

The Chapter 11 Plan

A Chapter 11 plan of rehabilitation is a plan to conserve and administer the debtor's assets in the hope of an eventual return to successful operation and solvency. The plan must be "fair and equitable" and must do the following:

1. Designate classes of claims and interests under the plan.
2. Specify the treatment to be afforded the classes. Also, the plan must provide the same treatment for each claim in a particular class.
3. Provide an adequate means for the plan's execution.

Filing the Plan Only the debtor may file a plan within the first 120 days after the date of the order for relief. If the debtor does not meet the 120-day deadline, however, or if the debtor fails to obtain the required creditor consent within 180 days, any party may propose a plan. If a small-business debtor chooses to avoid creditors' committees, the time for the debtor's filing is shortened to 100 days, and any other party's plan must be filed within 160 days.

Acceptance of the Plan Once the plan has been developed, it is submitted to each class of claims for acceptance. A class of claims has accepted the plan when a majority of the number of creditors in the class, representing two-thirds of the amount of the total claim, vote to approve it.

Confirmation of the Plan Each plan submitted is almost a case history in itself, and each plan is unique. The plan must be "in the best interests of the creditors." Even when all classes of claims accept the plan, the court may refuse to confirm it if it fails to meet this requirement. The plan is binding upon confirmation. Upon confirmation, the debtor is given a Chapter 11 discharge from all claims not protected under the plan. This discharge, however, does not apply to any claims that would be denied discharge under Chapter 7 (as previously discussed).

Even if only one class of claims has accepted the plan, the court may still confirm it under the Code's so-called *cram-down* provision. In other words, the court may confirm the plan over the objections of creditors. Before the court can exercise this right, it must be demonstrated that the plan "does not discriminate unfairly" against any creditors and that the plan is "fair and equitable."

❖ Chapter 13 Plans

Chapter 13 of the Bankruptcy Code provides for "Adjustment of Debts of an Individual with Regular Income." Individuals (not partnerships or corporations) with regular income who owe fixed, unsecured debts of less than $250,000 or fixed, secured debts of less than $750,000 may take advantage of Chapter 13. Individual proprietors and individuals living on welfare, Social Security, fixed pensions, or investment income are included. There are several advantages in filing a Chapter 13 plan when eligible. One of these advantages is that it is less expensive and less complicated than a Chapter 11 proceeding or a Chapter 7 liquidation.

Filing the Petition

A Chapter 13 case can be initiated only by the filing of a voluntary petition by the debtor. Certain Chapter 7 and Chapter 11 cases may be converted to Chapter 13 cases with the consent of the debtor. A trustee must be appointed.

Automatic Stay

Upon the filing of a Chapter 13 petition, the automatic stay previously discussed takes effect. It enjoins creditors from taking action against the debtor's co-obligors (those who owe a debt jointly with the debtor). Although it applies to all or part of a consumer debt, it does not apply to any business debt incurred by the debtor. A creditor has the right to seek relief from the automatic stay. To save the creditor time and money in seeking court approval to vacate (set aside) the stay and recover from the co-obligor, the law provides that upon the creditor's request to vacate the stay against the co-obligor, unless written objection is filed, twenty days later the stay against the co-obligor is automatically terminated without a hearing.

The Chapter 13 Plan

A Chapter 13 plan must do the following:

1. Provide for the turnover of such future earnings or income of the debtor to the trustee as is necessary for execution of the plan.
2. Provide for full payment in deferred cash payments of all claims entitled to priority.
3. Provide for the same treatment of each claim within a particular class. The debtor may list co-debtors, such as guarantors or sureties, as a separate class.

The time for payment under the plan may not exceed three years unless the court approves an extension. The term, with extension, may not exceed five years.

Filing the Plan Only the debtor may file a plan under Chapter 13. This plan must be filed within ninety days after the order for relief and may provide either for the payment of all obligations in full or for payment of an amount less than 100 percent. The Code requires the debtor to make "timely" payments, and the trustee is required to ensure that the debtor commences these payments. The debtor must begin making payments under the proposed plan within thirty days after the plan has been *filed*. If the plan has not been confirmed, the trustee is instructed to retain the payments until the plan is confirmed and then distribute them accordingly. If the plan is denied, the trustee will return the payments to the debtor, less any costs. Failure of the debtor to make timely payments or to begin making payments within the thirty-day period will allow the court to convert the case to a Chapter 7 bankruptcy or to dismiss the petition.

Confirmation of the Plan After the plan is filed, the court holds a confirmation hearing at which interested parties may object to the plan. The court will confirm a plan with respect to each claim of a secured creditor under any of the following circumstances:

1. If the secured creditors have accepted the plan.
2. If the plan provides that creditors retain their liens and if the value of the property to be distributed to them under the plan is not less than the secured portion of their claims.
3. If the debtor surrenders the property securing the claims to the creditors.

Objection to the Plan Unsecured creditors do not have a vote to confirm a Chapter 13 plan. The court can approve a plan over the objection of the trustee or any unsecured creditor in either of the following situations:

1. The value of the property to be distributed under the plan is at least equal to the amount of the claims.
2. All the debtor's projected disposable income to be received during the three-year period will be applied to making payments. Disposable income is all income received *less* amounts needed to support the debtor and dependents or amounts needed to meet ordinary expenses to continue the operation of a business.

Modification of the Plan Prior to completion of payments, the plan may be modified upon the request of the debtor, the trustee, or an unsecured creditor. If any interested party objects to the modification, the court must hold a hearing to determine approval or disapproval of the modified plan.

Discharge

After the debtor's completion of all payments under a Chapter 13 plan, the court grants a discharge of all debts provided for by the plan. Except for claims constituting priority debts and except for alimony and child support, all other debts are dischargeable. Priority debts must be paid because the priority claims are a minimum requirement of what must be included in a plan. A Chapter 13 discharge is sometimes referred to as a "super-discharge" because debts dischargeable under Chapter 13 include fraudulently incurred debts and claims resulting from malicious or willful injury. Therefore, a Chapter 13 discharge is much more beneficial to some debtors than a Chapter 7 discharge. Even if the debtor does not complete the plan, a "hardship" discharge may be granted if the debtor failed to complete the plan because of circumstances beyond his or her control and if the property distributed with the plan was of greater value than would have been paid in a Chapter 7 liquidation. A discharge can be revoked within one year if it was obtained by fraud.

❖ Chapter 12 Plans

In 1986, to help relieve economic pressure on small farmers, Congress created a new chapter in the Bankruptcy Code called the Family Farmer Bankruptcy Act—Chapter 12. This law defines a family farmer as one whose gross income is at least 50 percent farm dependent and whose debts are at least 80 percent farm related. The total debt must not exceed $1,500,000. A partnership or closely held corporation (at least 50 percent owned by the "farm family") can also take advantage of this law.

A Chapter 12 filing is very similar in procedure to a Chapter 13 filing. The farmer-debtor must file a plan not later than ninety days after the order of relief. The filing of the petition acts as an automatic stay against creditors and co-obligor actions against the estate. The content of the plan is basically the same as a Chapter 13 filing. The plan can be modified by the farmer-debtor but, except for cause, must be confirmed or denied within forty-five days of the filing of the plan.

Court confirmation of the plan is the same as for a Chapter 13 plan. In summary, the plan must provide for payment of secured debts at the fair market value of the collateral. If the secured debt exceeds the value of the collateral, the remaining debt is unsecured. For unsecured debtors, the plan must be confirmed if either (1) the value of the property to be distributed under the plan equals the amount of the claim or (2) if the plan provides that all of the farmer-debtor's disposable income received in a three-year period (longer by court approval) will be applied to making payments. Disposable income is all income received less amounts needed to support the farmer-debtor and family and continue the farming operation. Completion of payments under the plan is a discharge of all debts provided for by the plan.

The law also allows a farmer who has already filed under Chapter 11 or Chapter 13 to convert to Chapter 12. Chapter 12, like Chapters 11 and 13, allows for the farmer-debtor to convert to liquidation under Chapter 7.

Application

Law and the Small Business Owner—Preparing for Bankruptcy

Chapter 11 of the Bankruptcy Code expresses the broad public policy of encouraging commerce. To this end, Chapter 11 allows financially troubled business firms to petition for reorganization in bankruptcy even while they are still solvent, so that the firms' business can continue. But the problem is, small businesses do not fare very well under Chapter 11. According to one study, although many megacorporations entering Chapter 11 emerge as functioning entities, fewer than 20 percent of smaller companies survive the process. The reason is that Chapter 11 proceedings are prolonged and extremely costly, and whether a firm survives is largely a matter of size. The greater the firm's assets, the greater the likelihood it will emerge from Chapter 11 intact.

If you ever are a small business owner contemplating Chapter 11 reorganization, you can improve your chances of being among the survivors by planning ahead. You should take action before, not after, entering bankruptcy proceedings to ensure the greatest possibility of success. Your first step, of course, should be to do everything possible to avoid having to resort to Chapter 11. Discuss your financial troubles openly and cooperatively with creditors to see if a workout or some other arrangement can be made.

If it appears you have no choice but to file for Chapter 11 protection, try to interest a lender in loaning you funds to see you through the bankruptcy. If your business is a small corporation, you might try to negotiate a favorable deal with a major investor. For example, you could offer to transfer stock ownership to the investor in return for a loan to pay the costs of the bankruptcy proceedings and an option to repurchase the stock when the firm becomes profitable again.

Most importantly, you should form a Chapter 11 plan prior to entering bankruptcy proceedings. Consult with creditors in advance to see what kind of a plan would be acceptable to them, and prepare your plan accordingly. Having an acceptable plan prepared before you file will help to expedite the proceedings and thereby save substantially on costs.

Checklist for the Small Business Owner

- ☐ 1. Try to negotiate workouts with creditors to avoid costly Chapter 11 proceedings.
- ☐ 2. If your business is a small corporation, see if a major investor will loan you funds to help you pay bankruptcy costs in return for stock ownership.
- ☐ 3. Consult with creditors in advance and have an acceptable Chapter 11 plan prepared before filing to expedite bankruptcy proceedings and save on costs.

❖ Key Terms

❖ Chapter Summary: Creditors' Rights and Bankruptcy

REMEDIES AVAILABLE TO CREDITORS	
Mechanic's Lien	A nonpossessory, filed lien on an owner's real estate for labor, services, or materials furnished to or made on the realty.
Artisan's Lien	A possessory lien on an owner's personal property for labor performed or value added.
Innkeeper's Lien	A possessory lien on a hotel guest's baggage for hotel charges that remain unpaid.
Attachment	A court-ordered seizure of property prior to a court's final determination of the creditor's rights to the property. Attachment is available only upon the creditor's posting of a bond and in strict compliance with the applicable state statutes.
Writ of Execution	A court order directing the sheriff to seize (levy) and sell a debtor's nonexempt real or personal property to satisfy a court judgment in the creditor's favor.
Garnishment	A collection remedy that allows the creditor to attach a debtor's money (such as wages owed or bank accounts) and property that are held by a third person.
Creditors' Composition Agreement	A contract between a debtor and his or her creditors by which the debtor's debts are discharged by payment of a sum less than that owed in the original debt.
Mortgage Foreclosure	Upon the debtor's default, the entire mortgage debt is due and payable, allowing the creditor to foreclose on the realty by selling it or taking title to it to satisfy the debt.
Suretyship or Guaranty	Under contract, a third person agrees to be primarily or secondarily liable for the debt owed by the principal debtor. A creditor can turn to this third person for satisfaction of the debt.
LAWS ASSISTING DEBTORS	
Exemption Laws	State laws exempting certain types of real and personal property from levy of execution or attachment. 1. *Real property*—Each state permits a debtor to retain the family home, either in its entirety or up to a specified dollar amount, free from the claims of unsecured creditors or trustees in bankruptcy (homestead exemption). 2. *Personal property*—Personal property that is most often exempt from satisfaction of judgment debts includes: a. Household furniture up to a specified dollar amount. b. Clothing and certain personal possessions. c. Transportation vehicles up to a specified dollar amount. d. Certain classified animals, such as livestock and pets.
Other Laws	Numerous consumer protection laws, including the Federal Trade Commission rule limiting the rights of a holder in due course and the Truth-in-Lending Act, protect the rights of debtors.

❖ Chapter Summary: Creditors' Rights and Bankruptcy—Continued

BANKRUPTCY—A COMPARISON OF CHAPTERS 7, 11, 12, AND 13			
Issues	**Chapter 7**	**Chapter 11**	**Chapters 12 and 13**
Purpose	Liquidation.	Reorganization.	Adjustment.
Who Can Petition	Debtor (voluntary) or creditors (involuntary).	Debtor (voluntary) or creditors (involuntary).	Debtor (voluntary) only.
Who Can Be a Debtor	Any "person" (including partnerships and corporations) except railroads, insurance companies, banks, savings and loan institutions, investment companies licensed by the Small Business Administration, and credit unions. Farmers and charitable institutions cannot be involunt[illegible]	Any debtor eligible for Chapter 7 relief, except that railroads are also eligible.	*Chapter 12*—Any family farmer whose gross income is at least 50 percent farm dependent and whose debts are at least 80 percent farm related, or any partnership or closely held corporation at least 50 percent owned by a farm family, when total debt does not exceed $1,500,000. *Chapter 13*—Any individual (not partnerships or corporations) with regular income who owes fixed unsecured debts of less than $250,000 and secured debts of less than $750,000.
Procedure Leading to Discharge	Nonexempt property sold with proceeds to be distributed (in order) to prioritized groups. Dischargeable debts are terminated.	Plan is submitted and, if approved, debts are discharged if plan is followed.	Plan is submitted (must be approved if debtor turns over disposable income for three-year period); upon approval, all debts are discharged if plan is followed.
Advantages	Upon liquidation and distribution, most debts are discharged, and debtor has opportunity for fresh start.	Debtor continues in business, and creditors can either accept plan, or it can be "crammed down" on them. Plan allows for reorganization and liquidation of debts over plan period.	Debtor continues in business or possession of assets. If plan is approved, most debts are discharged after a three-year pay-out period.

❖ Questions and Case Problems

22-1. Creditors' Remedies. In what circumstances would a creditor resort to each of the following remedies when trying to collect on a debt?

(a) Mechanic's lien.
(b) Artisan's lien.
(c) Innkeeper's lien.
(d) Writ of attachment.
(e) Writ of execution.
(f) Garnishment.

22-2. Trustee's Powers. What is a trustee, and what powers does a trustee have in bankruptcy proceedings?

22-3. Rights of the Surety. Meredith, a farmer, borrowed $5,000 from Farmer's Bank and gave the bank $4,000 in bearer bonds to hold as collateral for the loan. Meredith's neighbor, Peterson, who had known Meredith for years, signed as surety on the note. Because of a drought, Meredith's harvest that year was only a fraction of what it normally was, and he was forced to default on his payments to Farmer's

Bank. The bank did not immediately sell the bonds but instead requested $5,000 from Peterson. Peterson paid the $5,000 and then demanded that the bank give him the $4,000 in securities. Can Peterson enforce this demand? Explain.

22-4. Rights of the Guarantor. Sabrina is a student at Sunnyside University. In need of funds to pay for tuition and books, she attempts to secure a short-term loan from University Bank. The bank agrees to make a loan if Sabrina will have someone financially responsible guarantee the loan payments. Abigail, a well-known businessperson and a friend of Sabrina's family, calls the bank and agrees to pay the loan if Sabrina cannot. Because of Abigail's reputation, the loan is made. Sabrina makes several payments on the loan, but because of illness she is not able to work for one month. She requests that University Bank extend the loan for three months. The bank agrees, raising the interest rate for the extended period. Abigail has not been notified of the extension (and therefore has not consented to it). One month later, Sabrina drops out of school. All attempts to collect from Sabrina have failed. University Bank wants to hold Abigail liable. Will the bank succeed? Explain.

22-5. Distribution of Property. Runyan voluntarily petitions for bankruptcy. He has three major claims against his estate. One is by Calvin, a friend who holds Runyan's negotiable promissory note for $2,500; one is by Kohak, an employee who is owed three months' back wages of $4,500; and one is by the First Bank of Sunny Acres on an unsecured loan of $5,000. In addition, Martinez, an accountant retained by the trustee, is owed $500, and property taxes of $1,000 are owed to Micanopa County. Runyan's nonexempt property has been liquidated, with the proceeds totaling $5,000. Discuss fully what amount each party will receive and why.

22-6. Objections to Discharge. On July 6, 1982, Henry Wilson filed a voluntary petition for Chapter 7 bankruptcy. In October of that year, one of Wilson's creditors, John Milam, filed a complaint with the bankruptcy court objecting to the discharge of a debt owed to him by Wilson. The debt had been incurred in 1978 when Wilson purchased Milam's accounting practice. Wilson made a down payment, and under the terms of their written agreement, Wilson was obligated to make monthly payments to Milam until the balance of the debt was paid. When Wilson failed to make the June 1978 payment, Milam brought suit against Wilson and, as a result of the suit, was awarded a judgment against Wilson in the amount of $57,569. This was one of the debts that Wilson sought to discharge in bankruptcy. Milam contended that the debt should not be discharged because Wilson had failed to keep adequate records on the accounting business from which the financial condition of the business could be ascertained. Wilson admitted that the only business record he maintained for the accounting practice for 1980, 1981, and 1982 was a single checking account from which both business and personal expenses were paid. Will Wilson's debt to Milam be discharged by the bankruptcy court? Explain. [*Matter of Wilson*, 33 Bankr. 689 (Bankr.M.D.Ga. 1983)]

22-7. Chapter 11 Reorganization. Tracey Service Co. filed a petition for a Chapter 11 reorganization. Acar Supply Co., one of Tracey's creditors, filed a motion to convert the case to a Chapter 7 liquidation. The court found that the debtor corporation had no place of business, no inventory, no equipment, no employees, and no business phone. Should Tracey Service be permitted to reorganize under Chapter 11? Discuss. [*In re Tracey Service Co.*, 17 Bankr. 405 (Bankr.E.D.Pa. 1982)]

22-8. Automatic Stay. Max McNeely owed Western States Petroleum, Inc., over $130,000. Western sought and received writs of attachment on all of McNeely's real and personal property. Western also caused a writ of garnishment to be directed to McNeely's bank accounts. Because McNeely's total assets amounted to less than $75,000, McNeely sought protection from Western's collection attempts by filing for Chapter 7 bankruptcy. Because of the bankruptcy filing, Western was unable to execute the writs by having McNeely's property seized and sold in satisfaction of the debt. Western petitioned the bankruptcy court to vacate the automatic stay as to the property subject to the writs on the ground that the writs created a valid lien against the property, giving Western the status of a secured creditor. Should the automatic stay be removed in this case? Explain. [*In Re McNeely*, 51 Bankr. 816 (Bankr.D.Utah 1985)]

22-9. Writ of Attachment. Topjian Plumbing and Heating, Inc., the plaintiff, sought prejudgment writs of attachment to satisfy an anticipated judgment in a contract action against Bruce Topjian, Inc., the defendant. The plaintiff did not petition the court for permission to effect the attachments but merely completed the forms, served them on the defendant and on the Fencers (the owners of a parcel of land that had previously belonged to the defendant), and recorded them at the registry of deeds. On what grounds might the court invalidate the attachments? [*Topjian Plumbing and Heating, Inc. v. Bruce Topjian, Inc.*, 129 N.H. 481, 529 A.2d 391 (1987)]

22-10. Rights of the Guarantor. Hallmark Cards, Inc., sued Edward Peevy, who had guaranteed an obligation owed to Hallmark by Garry Peevy. At the time of Edward Peevy's guaranty, Hallmark had in its possession property pledged as security by Garry Peevy. Before suit was filed, Hallmark sold the pledged property without notice to Edward Peevy. Because the property sold did not cover the loan balance, Hallmark sued for the balance, seeking a deficiency judgment. Edward Peevy contended that because Hallmark had sold the property pledged by Garry Peevy as security for the obligation without notifying him, Hallmark was not entitled to a deficiency judgment against him. Hallmark contended that Edward Peevy was not entitled to notice of the sale of the collateral and was not required to give consent. Which party will prevail in court? Discuss. [*Hallmark Cards, Inc. v. Peevy*, 293 Ark. 594, 739 S.W.2d 691 (1987)]

22-11. Chapter 7 Liquidations. In 1987, Bank South repossessed and sold Jamie Lee Busbin's 1979 Ford LTD automobile. The price that the automobile brought at the sale was $1,450 short of the amount Busbin owed Bank South. Bank South obtained a deficiency judgment for the $1,450 and garnished Busbin's wages, collecting $896.46. Busbin filed a voluntary petition for a Chapter 7 bankruptcy discharge, listing Bank South's claim for $1,450 as his sole debt. Busbin told the court that he intended to file a complaint to recover the $896.46 Bank South had already collected on the ground that the sale had not been conducted so as to obtain the highest price for the car, but he offered no evidence to support his contention. Busbin showed that he had a monthly net income of $1,150, expenses of $970, and disposable income of $130, and that he expected an income tax refund of $500. A motion to dismiss Busbin's petition was filed, alleging that he had a present ability to pay his outstanding debts and that granting a discharge would be a substantial abuse of the provisions of Chapter 7. Will the court dismiss Busbin's petition? Explain. [*In re Busbin*, 95 Bankr. 240 (Bankr.N.D.Ga. 1989)]

22-12. Right of Subrogation. Levinson and Johnson, who had both signed a promissory note, did not pay the note when it was due. Instead, American Thermex, Inc., a corporation in which Johnson had a controlling interest, voluntarily paid the note. American Thermex later brought suit against Levinson, seeking reimbursement for the payment. American Thermex argued, among other things, that because it had paid the note, it had the legal right of subrogation against the note's co-maker, Levinson. Will the court agree that American Thermex has a legal right of subrogation? Why or why not? [*Levinson v. American Thermex, Inc.*, 196 Ga.App. 291, 396 S.E.2d 252 (1990)]

22-13. Preferences. Fred Currey purchased cattle from Itano Farms, Inc. As payment for the cattle, Currey gave Itano Farms worthless checks in the amount of $50,250. Currey was later convicted of passing bad checks, and the state criminal court ordered him to pay Itano Farms restitution in the amount of $50,250. About four months after this court order, Currey and his wife filed for Chapter 7 bankruptcy protection. During the ninety days prior to the filing of the petition, Currey had made three restitution payments to Itano, totaling $14,821. The Curreys sought to recover these payments as preferences. What should the court decide? Explain. [*In re Currey*, 144 Bankr. 490 (D.Ida. 1992)]

A Question of Ethics and Social Responsibility

22-14. *In September 1986, Edward and Debora Davenport pleaded guilty in a Pennsylvania court to welfare fraud and were sentenced to probation for one year. As a condition of their probation, the Davenports were ordered to make monthly restitution payments to the county probation department, which would forward the payments to the Pennsylvania Department of Public Welfare, the victim of the Davenports' fraud. In May 1987, the Davenports filed a petition for Chapter 13 relief and listed the restitution payments among their debts. The bankruptcy court held that the restitution obligation was a dischargeable debt. On appeal, the district court reversed, holding that state-imposed criminal restitution obligations cannot be discharged in a Chapter 13 bankruptcy. The Court of Appeals for the Third Circuit reversed the district court's decision, concluding that "the plain language of the chapter" demonstrated that restitution orders are debt within the meaning of the Code and hence dischargeable in proceedings under Chapter 13. Ultimately, the case was reviewed by the United States Supreme Court, which affirmed the Third Circuit's ruling. The Court noted that under the Bankruptcy Code a debt is defined as a liability on a claim and a claim is defined as a right to payment. Because the restitution obligations clearly constituted a right to payment, the Court held that the obligations were dischargeable in bankruptcy.* [Pennsylvania Department of Public Welfare v. Davenport, *495 U.S. 552, 110 S.Ct. 2126, 109 L.Ed.2d 588 (1990)*]

1. Critics of this decision contend that the Court adhered to the letter, but not the spirit, of bankruptcy law in arriving at its conclusion. In what way, if any, did the Court not abide by the "spirit" of bankruptcy law?
2. Do you think that Chapter 13 plans, which allow nearly all types of debts to be discharged, tip the scales of justice too far in favor of debtors?

For Critical Analysis

22-15. *In recent years, Chapter 11 bankruptcy proceedings have become the target of substantial criticism. One of the arguments against Chapter 11 is that it allows the very managers who "bankrupted" a firm to continue to manage the firm as debtors in possession while the firm is in Chapter 11 proceedings. How would you argue in defense of Chapter 11? How would you argue against it?*

Unit Four

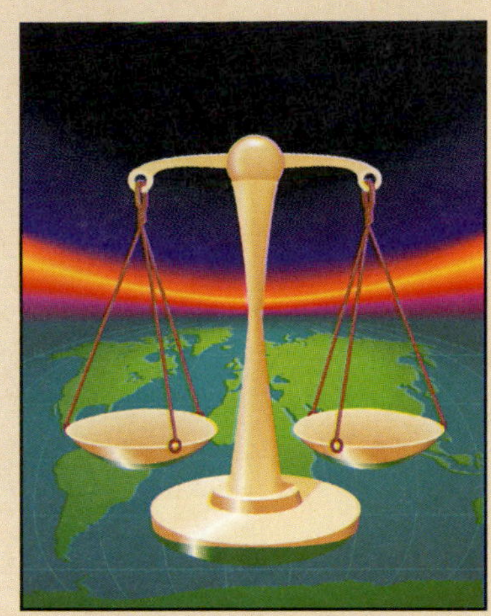

Business Organizations

❖ Why We Study Business Organizations

Every business activity involves—implicitly or explicitly—a form of business organization, whether it be a sole proprietorship, a partnership, a corporation, or some hybrid form. Each form provides different degrees of flexibility and different rights and liabilities, and it is important to be aware of these differences when choosing and structuring one's business organization.

Because agency law applies to relationships that exist within partnerships and corporations, we open this unit with Chapter 23, on agency relationships. An agent is a person authorized by another (called the principal) to act for him or her, and the law of agency governs that relationship. In Chapter 24, we introduce the various forms of business organizations available to entrepreneurs (those who risk going into business for themselves). A description of partnerships, including limited partnerships, is offered in Chapter 25, and Chapters 26 through 29 deal with corporations, including the financial regulation of corporations in the United States.

The goal of this unit is to provide a fundamental understanding of those laws that affect the most important business entities existing in the United States. The corporation is emphasized because the modern corporation is perhaps the most important form of business organization in the history of the world. Some even argue that without it, the tremendous economic growth of the Western world in the past several centuries would have been impossible.

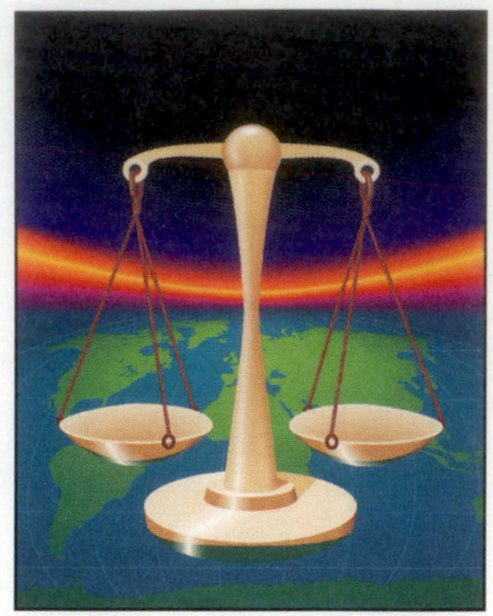

Chapter 23

Agency Relationships in Business

"[It] is a universal principle in the law of agency, that the powers of the agent are to be exercised for the benefit of the principal only, and not of the agent or of third parties."

Joseph Story, 1779–1845
(Associate justice of the United States Supreme Court, 1811–1844)

One of the most common, important, and pervasive legal relationships is that of **agency.** In an agency relationship between two parties, one of the parties, called the **agent,** agrees to represent or act for the other, called the **principal.** The principal has the right to control the agent's conduct in matters entrusted to the agent. By using agents, a principal can conduct multiple business operations simultaneously in various locations. Thus, for example, contracts that bind the principal can be made at different places with different persons at the same time. A familiar example of an agent is a corporate officer who serves in a representative capacity for the owners of the corporation. In this capacity, the officer has the authority to bind the principal (the corporation) to a contract. Indeed, agency law is essential to the existence and operation of a corporate entity, because only through its agents can a corporation function and enter into contracts.

A business world without agents is hard to imagine. Picture Henry Ford trying to sell all of the cars that Ford Motor Company manufactured. Obviously, other people must be appointed to fill in—act as agents—for the owner of a large company (the principal). Because agency relationships permeate the business world, an understanding of the law of agency is crucial to understanding business law.

AGENCY
A relationship between two persons in which, by agreement or otherwise, one is bound by the words and acts of the other. The former is a *principal;* the latter is an *agent.*

AGENT
A person authorized by another to act for or in place of him or her.

PRINCIPAL
In agency law, a person who, by agreement or otherwise, authorizes an agent to act on his or her behalf in such a way that the acts of the agent become binding on the principal.

FIDUCIARY
As a noun, a person having a duty created by his or her undertaking to act primarily for another's benefit in matters connected with the undertaking. As an adjective, a relationship founded upon trust and confidence.

❖ Agency Relationships

The Restatement (Second) of Agency[1] defines *agency* as "the fiduciary relation which results from the manifestation of consent by one person to another that the other shall act in his behalf and subject to his control, and consent by the other so to act." The term **fiduciary** is at the heart of agency law. The term can be used both as a noun and as an adjective. When used as a noun, it refers to a person having a duty created by his or her undertaking to act primarily for another's benefit in matters connected with the undertaking. When used as an adjective, as in "fiduciary relationship," it means that the relationship involves trust and confidence.

In a principal-agent relationship, the parties have agreed that the agent will act *on behalf and instead of* the principal in negotiating and transacting business with third persons. An agent is empowered to perform legal acts that are binding on the principal and can bind a principal in a contract with a third person. For example, Bruce is hired as a booking agent for a rock group—The Crash. As the group's

1. Restatement (Second) of Agency, Section 1(1). The Restatement is an authoritative summary of the law of agency and is often referred to by jurists in decisions and opinions.

Under what circumstances does the relationship between an employer and an independent contractor involve an agency relationship?

agent, Bruce can negotiate and sign contracts for the rock group to appear at concerts. The contracts will be binding and thus legally enforceable against the group.

Agency relationships commonly exist between employers and employees and sometimes between employers and independent contractors who are hired to perform special tasks or services.

Employer-Employee Relationships

Normally, all employees who deal with third parties are deemed to be agents. All employment laws (state and federal) apply only to the employer-employee relationship. Statutes governing Social Security, withholding taxes, workers' compensation, unemployment compensation, workplace safety laws, and the like (see Chapter 32) are applicable only if there is an employer-employee status. *These laws do not apply to the independent contractor.*

Employer–Independent Contractor Relationships

Independent contractors are not employees because those who hire them have no control over the details of their physical performance. The Restatement (Second) of Agency, Section 2, defines an **independent contractor** as follows:

INDEPENDENT CONTRACTOR
One who works for, and receives payment from, an employer but whose working conditions and methods are not controlled by the employer. An independent contractor is not an employee but may be an agent.

> a person who contracts with another to do something for him but who is not controlled by the other nor subject to the other's right to control with respect to his physical conduct in the performance of the undertaking. He may or may not be an agent.

Building contractors and subcontractors are independent contractors, and a property owner does not control the acts of either of these professionals. Truck drivers who own their equipment and hire out on a per-job basis are independent contractors; but truck drivers who drive company trucks on a regular basis are usually employees.

The relationship between a principal and an independent contractor may or may not involve an agency relationship. To illustrate: An owner of real estate who hires a real estate broker to negotiate a sale of his or her property has not only contracted with an independent contractor (the real estate broker) but has also established an agency relationship for the specific purpose of assisting in the sale of

◆ **Exhibit 23–1**
IRS Factors for Determining Employee Status

Generally, a worker will be classified by the Internal Revenue Service as an employee if the answers to the following questions are "yes":

☐ Yes	☐ No	1. *Does the worker receive training from the employer?*
☐ Yes	☐ No	2. *Is the worker given detailed instructions about performing particular tasks?*
☐ Yes	☐ No	3. *Does the worker provide services that must be rendered personally?*
☐ Yes	☐ No	4. *Does the worker maintain a continuous working relationship with the employer?*
☐ Yes	☐ No	5. *Does the worker abide by the employer's work schedule?*
☐ Yes	☐ No	6. *Does the worker work primarily at the employer's office or plant?*
☐ Yes	☐ No	7. *Does the worker receive regular payments at periodic intervals?*
☐ Yes	☐ No	8. *Does the worker use the employer's tools to perform work-related tasks?*
☐ Yes	☐ No	9. *Does the worker work for only one employer at a time?*
☐ Yes	☐ No	10. *Is the worker unable to offer work-related services to the general public?*
☐ Yes	☐ No	11. *May the worker be fired by the employer?*

the property. Another example is an insurance agent, who is both an independent contractor and an agent of the insurance company for which he or she sells policies.

A question frequently faced by the courts in determining liability under agency law is whether a person hired by another to do a job is an employee or an independent contractor. Because employers are normally held liable as principals for the actions made by their employee-agents within the scope of employment (as will be discussed later in this chapter), the court's decision as to employee versus independent-contractor status can be significant for the parties. In making this determination, courts often consider the following questions:

1. How much control can the employer exercise over the details of the work?
2. Is the employed person engaged in an occupation or business distinct from that of the employer?
3. Is the work usually done under the employer's direction or by a specialist without supervision?
4. Does the employer supply the tools at the place of work?
5. For how long is the person employed?
6. What is the method of payment—by time period or at the completion of the job?
7. What degree of skill is required of the person employed?

Generally, the greater the employer's control over the work, the more likely it is that the worker will be considered an employee. Another key factor is whether the employer withholds taxes from payments made to the worker and pays unemployment and Social Security taxes covering the worker.

How does the Internal Revenue Service (IRS) decide whether a person is an employee or an independent contractor for tax purposes? There is no precise test. Instead, the IRS takes into account any number of the twenty factors contained in its Revenue Ruling 87–41 to determine whether an alleged independent contractor should be deemed an employee. The IRS will compare the relative importance of these factors in making a final determination. If the IRS decides to classify the worker as an employee, then the employer will be responsible for paying any applicable Social Security, withholding, and unemployment taxes. Exhibit 23–1 lists eleven of the key factors that will be evaluated by the IRS in making its decision.

In some cases, it is advantageous to have independent-contractor status (see, for example, this chapter's *Business Law in Action*). In others, employee status may confer desirable benefits on the worker. In the following case, for example, an insurance agent who lost his job wanted to take advantage of the protection offered to older employees by the Age Discrimination in Employment Act of 1967. Because that act governs only employer-employee relationships, the agent tried to convince the court that he was an employee rather than an independent contractor.

Case 23.1
OESTMAN v. NATIONAL FARMERS UNION INSURANCE CO.
United States Court of Appeals, Tenth Circuit, 1992.
958 F.2d 303.

HISTORICAL AND POLITICAL SETTING *During congressional debates on the Civil Rights Act of 1964, amendments were proposed to include age along with race, color, religion, sex, and national origin as a characteristic that should not be allowed to serve as a basis for discrimination. Congress rejected the proposals but directed the secretary of labor to study the issue. Finding that older workers are often discriminated against, the secretary proposed a law prohibiting discrimination on the basis of age. Congress passed the Age Discrimination in Employment Act (ADEA) in 1967. Borrowing the language of the Civil Rights Act of 1964, the ADEA simply substituted "age" for "race, color, religion, sex, or national origin." The ADEA prohibits discrimination only in employment relationships. It does not generally regulate school-student relationships or the selection, compensation, and termination of military personnel, high-level government policymakers, or independent contractors.*

FACTS Elmer Oestman was an insurance agent for National Farmers Union Insurance Company. Their contract, called a "local agent agreement," provided—among other things—that the "[l]ocal agent, acting solely as an independent contractor, is hereby authorized to solicit and submit written applications for insurance policies and other contracts of insurer strictly in accordance with the instructions and direction of insurer." The contract specifically stated that "[n]othing contained herein shall be construed as creating the relationship of employer and employee between the local agent and insurer." Oestman was paid on a commission basis, and no Social Security or income taxes were paid or withheld for him by the company. He filed taxes as a self-employed individual. He set his own and his staff's working hours, had complete discretion over hiring and firing his staff, bore all expenses incurred in selling insurance, and provided his own transportation and office equipment. When his "employment" was terminated, Oestman sued the company, alleging violation of the Age Discrimination in Employment Act (ADEA) of 1967. The trial court found that Oestman was an independent contractor and therefore, because the ADEA governs only employer-employee relationships, had no cause of action under the ADEA. Oestman appealed.

ISSUE Was Oestman's status that of an employee or an independent contractor?

DECISION The appellate court affirmed the trial court's decision. Oestman was an independent contractor and thus had no cause of action under the ADEA.

REASON The court noted that the "question of whether an insurance agent is an employee or an independent contractor under ADEA is one of first impression in this circuit." The court therefore looked to the reasoning of other courts that had dealt with the issue. The court found that in cases dealing with Title VII laws (which prohibit discrimination in employment), a major factor in the decision as to whether a person was an employee or an independent contractor was whether the employer had a right to control the "means and manner" of the worker's performance. In Oestman's case, the court found that, taken as a whole, the facts "lead us to the conclusion that Mr. Oestman was an independent contractor." The court noted that there were "some elements of the working relationships between the parties that when looked at alone seem to indicate an employer/employee relationship. However, on balance, the relationship is more accurately characterized as employer/independent contractor."

ETHICAL CONSIDERATIONS *Clearly, independent contractors enjoy benefits that are not allowed to employees. For example, independent contractors are usually free to establish their own time schedules and work without any direct supervision by their "employers." Yet employees, in contrast, normally have benefits that are not accorded to independent contractors, including employee benefit plans, taxation benefits (the employer pays half of the employee's Social Security taxes, for example), and standing to sue under laws passed specifically to protect employees. In essence, those who opt for independent-contractor status trade off the rights and benefits that they could obtain as employees. Therefore, when independent contractors allege employee status to benefit from laws governing employer-employee relationships, courts will normally hold that those benefiting from independent-contractor status cannot, as the old adage phrases it, "have their cake and eat it, too."*

Business Law in Action

Who Owns "Works for Hire"?

Under copyright law, any copyrighted work created by an *employee* during the scope of his or her employment at the request of the employer is called a "work for hire." The employer owns and holds the copyright to a such a work. But what about free-lance artists, writers, computer programmers, and other workers who are not really employees in the usual sense but more like independent contractors?

Under the Copyright Act of 1976, the free-lancer who is commissioned to do a work will be the owner of the work created *unless* the parties agree in writing that the work is "for hire" *and* the work falls into one of nine categories stipulated by the act, such as audiovisual works, translations, supplementary works, and others.

Frequently, it takes a while for the business world to adjust to new laws governing its practices. In the case of the provisions of the Copyright Act of 1976 concerning commissioned works, not until June 1989 did the United States Supreme Court face the task of definitively interpreting the 1976 act in this respect and setting guidelines for determining who owns the copyright to a commissioned work done by a free-lancer. The case before the Court[a] involved a copyright dispute over a sculpture created by James Earl Reid for the Community for Creative Non-Violence (CCNV), a Washington, D.C., organization dedicated to eliminating homelessness. CCNV paid Reid $15,000 to cover the actual expenses Reid incurred in creating the statue. Reid donated his services. There was no written contract, and the question of copyright or ownership rights had not been discussed.

Who owns the copyright on commissioned art?

The crucial issue before the Court as it decided the case was whether Reid was an "employee" for purposes of the work-for-hire doctrine. Because the Copyright Act does not define the term, the Court concluded that to "determine whether a work is for hire under the Act, a court first should ascertain, using principles of the general common law of agency, whether the work was prepared by an employee or an independent contractor." The court then listed the factors to be used in making the determination: "In determining whether a hired party is an employee under the general common law of agency, we consider the hiring party's right to control the manner and means by which the product is accomplished. Among the other factors relevant to this inquiry are the skill required; the source of the instrumentalities and tools; the location of the work; the duration of the relationship between the parties, whether the hiring party has the right to assign additional projects to the hired party; the extent of the hired party's discretion over when and how long to work; the method of payment; the hired party's role in hiring and paying assistants; whether the work is part of the regular business of the hiring party; whether the hiring party is in business; the provision of employee benefits, and the tax treatment of the hired party." Applying these criteria to Reid's situation, the Court concluded that Reid was not an employee but an independent contractor. As such, because there was no written agreement to the contrary, Reid held the copyright in the statue.[b]

Since the *Reid* decision, this multifactored test of employee versus independent-contractor status has been used in a number of other cases relating to ownership rights in commissioned works.[c]

a. *Community for Creative Non-Violence v. Reid*, 490 U.S. 730, 109 S.Ct. 2166, 104 L.Ed.2d 811 (1989).

b. The Court indicated, however, that CCNV may still be considered a co-owner of the sculpture, and thus hold copyright jointly with Reid, if on remand the lower court determines that CCNV and Reid prepared the work "with the intention that their contributions be merged into inseparable or independent parts of a unitary whole."

c. See, for example *MacLean Associates, Inc. v. William M. Mercer-Meidinger-Hansen, Inc.*, 952 F.2d 769 (3d Cir. 1991); *Marco v. Accent Publishing Co.*, 969 F.2d 1547 (3d Cir. 1992); and *Johannsen v. Brown*, 797 F.Supp. 835 (D.Or. 1992).

❖ Agency Formation

The following discussions will emphasize the usual form taken by agency relationships. Such relationships are *consensual;* that is, they come about by voluntary consent and agreement between the parties. Generally, the agreement need not be in writing,[2] and consideration is not required.

A principal must have legal capacity to enter into contracts. A person who cannot legally enter into contracts directly should not be allowed to do so indirectly through an agent. Because an agent derives the authority to enter into contracts from the principal, and a contract made by an agent is legally viewed as a contract of the principal, it is immaterial whether the agent personally has the legal capacity to make that contract. Thus, a minor can be an agent but in some states cannot be a principal appointing an agent.[3] When a minor is permitted to be a principal, however, any resulting contracts will be voidable by the minor principal but not by the adult third party. In sum, any person can be an agent, regardless of whether he or she has the capacity to contract. Even a person who is legally incompetent can be appointed an agent.

An agency relationship can be created for any legal purpose. One created for an illegal purpose or contrary to public policy is unenforceable. If Sharp (as principal) contracts with Blesh (as agent) to sell illegal narcotics, the agency relationship is unenforceable, because selling illegal narcotics is a felony and is contrary to public policy. It is also illegal for medical doctors and other licensed professionals to employ unlicensed agents to perform professional actions. Generally, no formalities are required to create an agency. The agency relationship can arise by acts of the parties in one of the four ways discussed in the following sections.

Agency by Agreement

Because agency is a consensual relationship, normally it must be based on an express or implied agreement that the agent will act for the principal and the principal agrees to have the agent so act. An agency agreement can take the form of an express written contract. For example, Renato enters into a written agreement with Troy, a realtor, to sell Renato's house. An agency relationship exists between Renato and Troy for the sale of the house and is detailed in a document that both parties sign.

Many express agency agreements are oral. If Renato asks Cary, a gardener, to contract with others for the care of his lawn on a regular basis, and Cary agrees, an agency relationship exists between Renato and Cary for the lawn care.

An agency agreement can also be implied by conduct. For example, a hotel expressly allows only Boris Tcheperin to park cars, but Boris has no employment contract there. The hotel's manager tells Boris when to work and where and how to park the cars. The hotel's conduct amounts to a manifestation of its willingness to have Boris park its customers' cars, and Boris can infer from the hotel's conduct that he has authority to act as a parking valet. It can be inferred that he is an agent for the hotel, his purpose being to provide valet parking services for hotel guests.

Agency by Ratification

On occasion, a person who is in fact not an agent (or who is an agent acting outside the scope of his or her authority) may make a contract on behalf of another (a

2. There are two main exceptions to the statement that agency agreements need not be in writing: (1) Whenever agency authority empowers the agent to enter into a contract that the Statute of Frauds requires to be in writing, then the agent's authority from the principal must likewise be in writing (this is called the *equal dignity rule,* to be discussed later in this chapter). (2) A power of attorney, which confers authority to an agent, must be in writing.

3. Some courts have granted exceptions to allow a minor to appoint an agent for the limited purpose of contracting for the minor's necessities of life. See *Casey v. Kastel,* 237 N.Y. 305, 142 N.E. 671 (1924).

RATIFICATION
The approval or validation of a previous action. In contract law, the confirmation of a voidable act (that is, an act that without ratification would not be an enforceable contractual obligation). In agency law, the confirmation by one person of an act or contract performed or entered into on his or her behalf by another, who assumed, without authority, to act as his or her agent.

principal). If the principal approves or affirms that contract by word or by action, an agency relationship is created by **ratification.** Ratification is a question of intent, and intent can be expressed by either words or conduct. The basic requirements for ratification are discussed later in this chapter.

Agency by Estoppel

When a principal causes a third person to believe that another person is his or her agent, and the third person deals with the supposed agent, the principal is "estopped to deny" the agency relationship. In such a situation, the principal's actions create the *appearance* of an agency that does not in fact exist.

Suppose Andrew accompanies Charles, a seed sales representative, to call on a customer, Steve, the proprietor of the General Seed Store. Andrew has done sales work but is not employed by Charles at this time. Charles boasts to Steve that he wishes he had three more assistants "just like Andrew." Steve has reason to believe from Charles's statements that Andrew is an agent for Charles. Steve then places seed orders with Andrew. If Charles does not correct the impression that Andrew is an agent, Charles will be bound to fill the orders just as if Andrew were really Charles's agent. Charles's representation to Steve created the impression that Andrew was Charles's agent and had authority to solicit orders.

Agency by estoppel does not extend to all acts under all circumstances. For example, the acts or declarations of the purported agent in and of themselves do not create an agency by estoppel. It is the deeds or statements of the principal, not the agent, that create an agency. Suppose Olivia walks into Dru's Dress Boutique and claims to be a sales agent for an exclusive Paris dress designer, Pierre Dumont. Dru has never had business relations with Pierre Dumont. Based on Olivia's claim, however, Dru gives Olivia an order and prepays 15 percent of the sales price. Olivia is not an agent, and the dresses are never delivered. Dru cannot hold Pierre Dumont liable. Olivia's acts and declarations do not create an agency by estoppel.

In addition, to assert the creation of an agency by estoppel, the third person must prove that he or she *reasonably* believed that an agency relationship existed and that the agent had authority. Facts and circumstances must show that an ordinary, prudent person familiar with business practice and custom would have been justified in concluding that the agent had authority.

Agency by Operation of Law

In some cases, the courts have found it desirable to find an agency relationship in the absence of a formal agreement. This may occur in family relationships. For example, suppose one spouse purchases certain basic necessaries and charges them to the other spouse's charge account. The courts will often rule that the latter is liable for payment of the necessaries, either because of a social policy of promoting the general welfare of the spouse or because of a legal duty to supply necessaries to family members. Agency by operation of law may also occur in emergency situations, when the agent's failure to act outside the scope of his or her authority would cause the principal substantial loss. If the agent is unable to contact the principal, the courts will often grant this emergency power.

❖ Rights and Duties in Agency Relationships

Once the principal-agent relationship has been created, both parties have duties that govern their conduct. As discussed previously, the principal-agent relationship is *fiduciary*—one of trust. In a fiduciary relationship, each party owes the other the duty to act with the utmost good faith.

In this section, we examine closely the various duties of agents and principals. In general, for every duty of the principal, the agent has a corresponding right, and vice versa. When one party to the agency relationship violates his or her duty to the other party, the remedies available to the party not in breach arise out of contract and tort law. These remedies include monetary damages, termination of the agency relationship, injunction, and required accountings.

Agent's Duties

The duties that an agent owes to a principal are set forth in the agency agreement or arise by operation of law. They are implied from the agency relationship *whether or not the identity of the principal is disclosed to a third party*. When an agent employs or appoints a *subagent*, a fiduciary duty exists between the subagent and the principal as well as between the subagent and the agent. Subagents owe the same duties to agents and to principals as agents owe to principals. Generally, the agent owes the principal five duties—performance, notification, loyalty, obedience, and accounting.

Performance An implied condition in every agency contract is the agent's agreement to use reasonable diligence and skill in performing the work. When an agent fails to perform his or her duties entirely, liability for breach of contract generally will result. The degree of skill or care required of an agent is usually that expected of a reasonable person under similar circumstances. In most cases, this is interpreted to mean ordinary care. An agent may, however, have represented himself or herself as possessing special skills (such as those that an accountant or attorney possesses). In these situations, the agent is expected to exercise the skill or skills claimed. Failure to do so constitutes a breach of the agent's duty.

Not all agency relationships are based on contract. In some situations, an agent acts gratuitously—that is, not for money. A gratuitous agent cannot be liable for breach of contract, as there is no contract; he or she is subject only to tort liability. Once a gratuitous agent has begun to act in an agency capacity, he or she has the duty to continue to perform in that capacity in an acceptable manner and is subject to the same standards of care and duty to perform as other agents. Consider an example: Peterson's friend, Stendhof, is a real estate broker. Stendhof gratuitously offers to sell Peterson's farm. If Stendhof never attempts to sell the farm, Peterson has no legal cause of action to force Stendhof to do so. If Stendhof does find a buyer and keeps promising a sales contract, but fails to provide one within a reasonable period of time, causing the buyer to seek other property, then Peterson has a cause of action in tort for negligence. The following case raises an interesting question: Did an agent breach his duty to perform by failing to procure a life insurance policy notwithstanding the fact that no life insurance company would have insured the principal—because he used drugs?

Case 23.2
BIAS v. ADVANTAGE INTERNATIONAL, INC.
United States Court of Appeals, District of Columbia Circuit, 1990.
905 F.2d 1558.

HISTORICAL AND SOCIAL SETTING *In 1976, less than twenty metric tons of cocaine were smuggled into the United States. In 1983, drug traffickers on islands in the Caribbean developed crack. Crack is cocaine that has been crystallized so that it can be smoked to produce an intense high. The drug is apparently highly addictive. Its introduction into the United States the same year led to increasing crime rates and health emergencies. To combat drug use, Nancy Reagan, the wife of President Ronald Reagan, sponsored the slogan "Just Say No." By 1986, traffickers were smuggling nearly seventy-five metric tons of cocaine into the United States annually, and drug cartels based in Colombia were netting billions of dollars per week.*

Case 23.2—Continued

FACTS Leonard Bias, a basketball player, entered into an agency agreement with Advantage International, Inc., under which Advantage agreed to advise and represent Bias in his affairs. On June 17, 1986, Bias was picked by the Boston Celtics in the first round of the National Basketball Association draft. On the morning of June 19, 1986, Bias died of cocaine intoxication. Bias's estate sued Advantage, alleging, among other things, that Advantage had failed to procure a $1 million ("jumbo") life insurance policy on Bias, as it had been directed to do. Bias's parents maintained that Advantage had represented to Bias and to them that it had secured such a policy, and in reliance on these assurances, Bias's parents had not independently sought to buy an insurance policy on Bias's life. The trial court granted summary judgment for Advantage, holding that, in effect, the estate had not suffered any damage from Advantage's failure to obtain life insurance for Bias because even if Advantage had tried to obtain the life insurance policy, it would not have been able to do so because of Bias's cocaine use. The estate appealed, arguing that the questions of whether Bias was a drug user and was uninsurable were triable issues of fact and should have gone to the jury.

ISSUE Was summary judgment for Advantage properly granted in this case?

DECISION Yes. The appellate court affirmed the trial court's judgment.

REASON The appellate court stated that the testimony of Bias's former teammates "clearly tends to show that Bias was a cocaine user." The court pointed out that the estate did not attempt to impeach or counter the teammates' testimony. Although Bias's parents testified that they did not know Bias to be a drug user, their testimony did not rebut the testimony about Bias's drug use on particular occasions. Similarly, drug tests showing that Bias had no cocaine in his system indicated only that Bias had abstained from drug use during the periods preceding the tests. The court concluded that the estate was "not entitled to reach the jury merely on the supposition that the jury might not believe the defendants' witnesses." The court also pointed out that the estate "failed to name a single particular company or provide other evidence that a single company existed which would have issued a jumbo policy in 1986 without inquiring about the applicant's drug use." Thus, there was "no genuine issue of material fact as to the insurability of a drug user."

Notification It is a maxim in agency law that all that the agent knows, the principal knows. Thus, it is only logical that the agent be required to notify the principal of all matters that come to his or her attention concerning the subject matter of the agency. This is the duty of notification. What the agent actually tells the principal is not relevant; what the agent *should have told* the principal is crucial. Under the law of agency, notice to the agent is notice to the principal.

Loyalty Loyalty is one of the most fundamental duties in a fiduciary relationship. Basically stated, the agent has the duty to act solely for the benefit of his or her principal and not in the interest of the agent or a third party. For example, an agent cannot represent two principals in the same transaction unless both know of the dual capacity and consent to it. Thus, a real estate agent cannot represent both the seller and the buyer in a transaction, unless the seller and the buyer so agree. The duty of loyalty also means that any information or knowledge acquired through the agency relationship is considered confidential. It would be a breach of loyalty to disclose such information either during the agency relationship or after its termination. Typical examples of confidential information are trade secrets and customer lists compiled by the principal.

Furthermore, an agent employed by a principal to buy cannot buy from himself or herself, and an agent employed to sell cannot become the purchaser without the principal's consent. In short, the agent's loyalty must be undivided. The agent's actions must be strictly for the benefit of the principal and must not result in any secret profit for the agent.

Obedience When an agent is acting on behalf of the principal, a duty is imposed on that agent to follow all lawful and clearly stated instructions of the principal.

Any deviation from such instructions is a violation of this duty. During emergency situations, however, when the principal cannot be consulted, the agent may deviate from such instructions without violating this duty if the circumstances so warrant. Whenever instructions are not clearly stated, the agent can fulfill the duty of obedience by acting in good faith and in a manner reasonable under the circumstances.

Accounting Unless an agent and a principal agree otherwise, the agent has the duty to keep and make available to the principal an account of all property and money received and paid out on behalf of the principal. This includes gifts from third persons in connection with the agency. For example, a gift from a customer to a salesperson for prompt deliveries made by the salesperson's firm belongs to the firm. The agent has a duty to maintain separate accounts for the principal's funds and for the agent's personal funds, and no intermingling of these accounts is allowed. Whenever a licensed professional (such as an attorney) violates this duty to account, he or she may be subject to disciplinary proceedings carried out by the appropriate regulatory institution (such as the state bar association) in addition to being liable to the principal for failure to account.

Principal's Duties

The principal also has certain duties to the agent, either expressed or implied by law. The principal owes the agent four duties—compensation, reimbursement and indemnification, cooperation, and safe working conditions.

Compensation In general, when a principal requests certain services from an agent, the agent reasonably expects payment. A duty is therefore implied for the principal to pay the agent for services rendered. For example, when an accountant or an attorney is asked to act as an agent, an agreement to compensate the agent for such service is implied. The principal also has the duty to pay that compensation in a timely manner. Except in a gratuitous agency relationship, in which an agent does not act for money, the principal must pay the agreed-on value for an agent's services. If no amount has been expressly agreed on, then the principal owes the agent the customary compensation for such services.

Reimbursement and Indemnification Whenever an agent disburses sums of money at the request of the principal, and whenever the agent disburses sums of money to pay for necessary expenses in the course of a reasonable performance of his or her agency duties, the principal has the duty to reimburse the agent for these payments. Agents cannot recover for expenses incurred by their own misconduct or negligence, however.

Subject to the terms of the agency agreement, the principal has the duty to *indemnify* (compensate) an agent for liabilities incurred because of authorized and lawful acts and transactions. For example, if the agent, on the principal's behalf, forms a contract with a third party and the principal fails to perform the contract, the third party may sue the agent for damages. In this situation, the principal is obligated to compensate the agent for any costs incurred by the agent as a result of the principal's failure to perform the contract. Additionally, the principal must indemnify (pay) the agent for the value of benefits that the agent confers upon the principal. The amount of indemnification is usually specified in the agency contract. If it is not, the courts will look to the nature of the business and the type of loss to determine the amount.

Cooperation A principal has a duty both to cooperate with and to assist an agent in performing his or her duties. The principal must do nothing to prevent such performance. For example, when a principal grants an agent an exclusive territory, creating an *exclusive agency*, the principal cannot compete with the agent or appoint or allow another agent to so compete in violation of the exclusive agency. Such competition would expose the principal to liability for the agent's lost sales or profits.

Safe Working Conditions The common law requires the principal to provide safe working premises, equipment, and conditions for all agents and employees. The principal has a duty to inspect working conditions and to warn agents and employees about any unsafe areas. When the agency is one of employment, the employer's liability is frequently covered by workers' compensation insurance, which is the primary remedy for an employee's injury on the job (see Chapter 32).

❖ Scope of Agent's Authority

An agent's authority to act can be either *actual* (express or implied) or *apparent.* If an agent contracts outside the scope of his or her authority, the principal may still become liable by ratifying the contract.

Express Authority

EQUAL DIGNITY RULE
In most states, a rule stating that express authority given to an agent must be in writing if the contract to be made on behalf of the principal is required to be in writing.

Express authority is embodied in that which the principal has engaged the agent to do. It can be given orally or in writing. The **equal dignity rule** in most states requires that if the contract being executed is or must be in writing, then the agent's authority must also be in writing.[4] Failure to comply with the equal dignity rule can make a contract voidable *at the option of the principal.* The law regards the contract at that point as a mere offer. If the principal decides to accept the offer, acceptance must be ratified in writing. Assume that Gedsiri (the principal) orally asks Parkinson (the agent) to sell a ranch that Gedsiri owns. Parkinson finds a buyer and signs a sales contract (a contract for an interest in realty must be in writing) on behalf of Gedsiri to sell the ranch. The buyer cannot enforce the contract unless Gedsiri subsequently ratifies Parkinson's agency status *in writing.* Once the contract is ratified, either party can enforce rights under the contract.

The equal dignity rule does not apply when an agent acts in the presence of a principal or when the agent's act of signing is merely perfunctory. Thus, if Dickens (the principal) negotiates a contract but is called out of town the day it is to be signed and orally authorizes Suhartono to sign, the oral authorization is sufficient.

POWER OF ATTORNEY
A document or instrument authorizing another to act as one's agent or attorney.

NOTARY PUBLIC
A person authorized by a state government or the federal government to administer oaths and to attest to the authenticity of signatures.

Giving an agent a **power of attorney** confers express authority.[5] The power of attorney normally is a written document and is usually notarized. (A document is notarized when a **notary public**—a public official authorized to attest to the authenticity of signatures—signs and dates the document and imprints it with his or her seal of authority.) A power of attorney can be special—permitting the agent to do specified acts only—or it can be general—permitting the agent to transact all business for the principal. A sample power of attorney is shown in Exhibit 23–2. An ordinary power of attorney terminates on the incapacity of the person giving the power. A *durable* power of attorney, however, provides an agent with very broad powers to act and make decisions for the principal and specifies that it is not affected

4. An exception to the equal dignity rule exists in modern business practice. An executive officer of a corporation, when acting for the corporation in an ordinary business situation, is not required to obtain written authority from the corporation.

5. An agent who holds the power of attorney is called an *attorney-in-fact* for the principal. The holder does not have to be an attorney-at-law (and often is not).

◆ Exhibit 23–2
Power of Attorney

POWER OF ATTORNEY

GENERAL

Know All Men by These Presents: That I, ______________________________

____

the undersigned (jointly and severally, if more than one) hereby make, constitute and appoint ______________

____

as a true and lawful Attorney for me and in my name, place and stead and for my use and benefit:

(a) To ask, demand, sue for, recover, collect and receive each and every sum of money, debt, account, legacy, bequest, interest, dividend, annuity and demand (which now is or hereafter shall become due, owing or payable) belonging to or claimed by me, and to use and take any lawful means for the recovery thereof by legal process or otherwise, and to execute and deliver a satisfaction or release therefor, together with the right and power to compromise or compound any claim or demand;

(b) To exercise any or all of the following powers as to real property, any interest therein and/or any building thereon: To contract for, purchase, receive and take possession thereof and of evidence of title thereto; to lease the same for any term or purpose, including leases for business, residence, and oil and/or mineral development; to sell, exchange, grant or convey the same with or without warranty; and to mortgage, transfer in trust, or otherwise encumber or hypothecate the same to secure payment of a negotiable or non-negotiable note or performance of any obligation or agreement;

(c) To exercise any or all of the following powers as to all kinds of personal property and goods, wares and merchandise, choses in action and other property in possession or in action: To contract for, buy, sell, exchange, transfer and in any legal manner deal in and with the same; and to mortgage, transfer in trust, or otherwise encumber or hypothecate the same to secure payment of a negotiable or non-negotiable note or performance of any obligation or agreement;

(d) To borrow money and to execute and deliver negotiable or non-negotiable notes therefor with or without security; and to loan money and receive negotiable or non-negotiable notes therefor with such security as he shall deem proper;

(e) To create, amend, supplement and terminate any trust and to instruct and advise the trustee of any trust wherein I am or may be trustor or beneficiary; to represent and vote stock, exercise stock rights, accept and deal with any dividend, distribution or bonus, join in any corporate financing, reorganization, merger, liquidation, consolidation or other action and the extension, compromise, conversion, adjustment, enforcement or foreclosure, singly or in conjunction with others of any corporate stock, bond, note, debenture or other security; to compound, compromise, adjust, settle and satisfy any obligation, secured or unsecured, owing by or to me and to give or accept any property and/or money whether or not equal to or less in value than the amount owing in payment, settlement or satisfaction thereof;

(f) To transact business of any kind or class and as my act and deed to sign, execute, acknowledge and deliver any deed, lease, assignment of lease, covenant, indenture, indemnity, agreement, mortgage, deed of trust, assignment of mortgage or of the beneficial interest under deed of trust, extension or renewal of any obligation, subordination or waiver of priority, hypothecation, bottomry, charter-party, bill of lading, bill of sale, bill, bond, note, whether negotiable or non-negotiable, receipt, evidence of debt, full or partial release or satisfaction of mortgage, judgment and other debt, request for partial or full reconveyance of deed of trust and such other instruments in writing of any kind or class as may be necessary or proper in the premises.

Giving and Granting unto my said Attorney full power and authority to do and perform all and every act and thing whatsoever requisite, necessary or appropriate to be done in and about the premises as fully to all intents and purposes as I might or could do if personally present, hereby ratifying all that my said Attorney shall lawfully do or cause to be done by virtue of these presents. The powers and authority hereby conferred upon my said Attorney shall be applicable to all real and personal property or interests therein now owned or hereafter acquired by me and wherever situate.

My said Attorney is empowered hereby to determine in his sole discretion the time when, purpose for and manner in which any power herein conferred upon him shall be exercised, and the conditions, provisions and covenants of any instrument or document which may be executed by him pursuant hereto; and in the acquisition or disposition of real or personal property, my said Attorney shall have exclusive power to fix the terms thereof for cash, credit and/or property, and if on credit with or without security.

The undersigned, if a married woman, hereby further authorizes and empowers my said Attorney, as my duly authorized agent, to join in my behalf, in the execution of any instrument by which any community real property or any interest therein, now owned or hereafter acquired by my spouse and myself, or either of us, is sold, leased, encumbered, or conveyed.

When the contest so requires, the masculine gender includes the feminine and/or neuter, and the singular number includes the plural.

WITNESS my hand this ____________ day of ______________________, 19____

______________________________ ______________________________

______________________________ ______________________________

State of California, } ss.
County of ______________________

On ______________________________, before me, the undersigned, a Notary Public in and for said State, personally appeared ______________________________

____

known to me to be the person ____________ whose name ______________________ subscribed to the within instrument and acknowledged that ______________________ executed the same.

Witness my hand and official seal. (Seal) ______________________________
Notary Public in and for said State.

by the principal's incapacity. An elderly person, for example, might grant a durable power of attorney to provide for the handling of property and investments should she or he become incompetent. An agent holding a power of attorney for a client is authorized to act *only* on the principal's behalf when exercising that power.

Implied Authority

Implied authority can be (1) conferred by custom, (2) inferred from the position the agent occupies, or (3) inferred as being reasonably necessary to carry out express authority. For example, Mueller is employed by Al's Grocery to manage one of its stores. Al has not expressly stated that Mueller has authority to contract with third persons. In this situation, however, authority to manage a business implies authority to do what is reasonably required (as is customary or can be inferred from a manager's position) to operate the business. Such actions include creating contracts to hire employees, to buy merchandise and equipment, and even to arrange for advertising the products sold in the store.

Apparent Authority and Estoppel

"The law is not a series of calculating machines where definitions and answers come tumbling out when the right levers are pushed."

William O. Douglas, 1898–1980
(Associate justice of the United States Supreme Court, 1939–1975)

Actual authority arises from what the principal manifests *to the agent.* Apparent authority exists when the principal, by either word or action, causes a *third party* reasonably to believe that an agent has authority to act, even though the agent has no express or implied authority. If the third party changes his or her position in reliance on the principal's representations, the principal may be *estopped* from denying that the agent had authority.

To illustrate, suppose a traveling salesperson (the agent) has no express authority to collect payments for orders solicited from customers. Because the salesperson neither possesses the goods ordered nor delivers them, she also has no implied authority to collect. A customer, Huerta, pays this salesperson, Anderson, for a solicited order. Anderson then takes the payment to the principal's accounting department, and an accountant accepts the payment and sends Huerta a receipt. This procedure is thereafter followed for other orders solicited and paid for by Huerta.

Later, Anderson solicits an order, and Huerta pays her as before. This time, however, Anderson absconds with the money. Can Huerta claim that the payment to the agent was authorized and thus, in effect, a payment to the principal? The answer is normally yes, because the principal's *repeated* acts of accepting Huerta's payment led Huerta reasonably to expect that Anderson had authority to receive payments for goods solicited. Although Anderson did not have express or implied authority, the principal's conduct gave her *apparent* authority to collect. The principal cannot claim that the agent had no authority to collect in this particular case; the principal would be estopped from making such a claim. The next case illustrates the issue of whether there is apparent authority to bind a principal when the principal allows the agent to use the principal's corporate name as part of the agent's corporate name and in the agent's advertising.

Case 23.3

CITY OF DELTA JUNCTION v. MACK TRUCKS, INC.

Supreme Court of Alaska, 1983.
670 P.2d 1128.

HISTORICAL AND SOCIAL SETTING *Generally, each state authorizes its cities to acquire goods and services through a bidding process. The first step in the process is to advertise for bids. In some circumstances, a city will have the authority to reject all bids—for example, if none of the bids prove satisfactory. Usually, the city will reserve this right in its advertisement for bids. The advertisement must also include any specifications to which the bids and the ultimate contract must conform. Bids are submitted, opened, and read. In awarding a contract, a city may decide to select a higher bidder that is deemed more qualified than the lowest bidder. Sometimes, a state government offers to grant to a city funds to obtain goods or services on the condition that the city will spend the money within a certain period of time. If the city cannot make the deadline, it loses the funds. In that situation, when problems arise in the bidding process or with a project's specifications, the city may be hard-pressed to meet the deadline.*

Case 23.3—Continued

FACTS Under a grant from the state of Alaska, the city of Delta Junction decided to buy a fire tanker and sought bids from several truck manufacturers throughout the United States. When the responses proved inadequate, the city revised the specifications. The new specifications were sent only to manufacturers in Alaska in an attempt to speed the process so as to meet the state's deadline. The city eventually purchased a truck from Alaska Mack, Inc., a dealer in Fairbanks, on the basis of the reputation of Mack trucks, even though Alaska Mack's bid was the highest bid received. Alaska Mack modified a Mack chassis to carry a 5,000-gallon tank, but the truck exceeded the manufacturer's specified weight limits and was dangerously unbalanced and difficult to drive. When subsequent modifications failed to remedy these problems, the city brought suit for breach of warranty against Alaska Mack. It also brought suit against Mack Trucks, Inc., of Allentown, Pennsylvania, as principal under the theory of apparent agency (authority). Mack Trucks, Inc., the manufacturer of Mack trucks, claimed that Alaska Mack was not its agent and that it was not responsible for any actions undertaken by Alaska Mack. Delta Junction argued that Alaska Mack was listed in trade journals and the Fairbanks telephone directory under the heading "Mack Trucks" and that its advertisements carried the familiar Mack bulldog trademark. On the basis of these representations, both the mayor and the fire chief, at the time of the purchase, believed that Alaska Mack was an agent for the manufacturer of Mack trucks. Alaska Mack's bid was accepted by the city council, even though it was the highest bid received for the truck, because of the manufacturer's reputation. The trial court granted a directed verdict for Mack Trucks, Inc., and Delta Junction appealed.

ISSUE Did an apparent agency exist between Alaska Mack and Mack Trucks, Inc.?

DECISION The Alaska Supreme Court remanded the case to the trial court for the jury to decide whether an apparent agency existed in this case.

REASON The court stated that apparent authority for an act exists when the written or spoken words or other conduct of the principal, reasonably interpreted, cause a third person to believe that the principal consents to have the act done on his or her behalf by the person purporting to act for the principal. In this case, the mayor, the fire chief, and the city council of Delta Junction all assumed they were dealing with Mack Trucks, Inc. The court further noted that the Mack trademark and name have become "part of the American scene." In the words of the court: "The average citizen, who couldn't name five vice-presidents to save himself from eternal damnation, will recognize a Mack advertisement as far as the eye can see." The court believed it could be reasonably inferred from the evidence that Alaska Mack used the name and trademark with Mack Trucks, Inc.'s, knowledge and approval, but whether its acquiescence was sufficient to bind Mack Trucks, Inc., under Delta's theory of apparent authority was a question for a jury to decide.

Ratification

As already mentioned in this chapter, ratification is the affirmation of a previously unauthorized contract. Ratification can be either express or implied. If the principal does not ratify, there is no contract binding on the principal, and the third party's agreement with the agent is viewed merely as an unaccepted offer. In the case of repudiation, the unauthorized contract remains an offer. Because the third party's agreement is treated as an unaccepted offer, the third party can revoke it at any time prior to the principal's ratification without liability. Death or incapacity of the third party before ratification will void an unauthorized contract.

The requirements for ratification can be summarized as follows:

1. The purported agent must have acted on behalf of a principal who subsequently ratified the action.
2. The principal must know of all material facts involved in the transaction.
3. The agent's act must be affirmed in its entirety by the principal.
4. The principal must have the legal capacity to authorize the transaction at the time the agent engages in the act and at the time the principal ratifies.
5. The principal's affirmance must occur prior to the withdrawal of the third party from the transaction.

6. The principal must observe the same formalities when he or she approves the act purportedly done by the agent on his or her behalf as would have been required to authorize it initially.

❖ Liability in Agency Relationships

Frequently, the issue arises as to which party, the principal or the agent, should be held liable for the contracts formed by the agent or the torts or crimes committed by the agent. We look here at this aspect of agency law.

Liability for Agent's Contracts

An important consideration in determining liability for a contract formed by an agent is whether the identity of the principal was known to the third party at the time the contract was made. The Restatement (Second) of Agency, Section 4, classifies principals as disclosed, partially disclosed, or undisclosed.

DISCLOSED PRINCIPAL
A principal whose identity and existence as a principal is known by a third person at the time a transaction is conducted by an agent.

PARTIALLY DISCLOSED PRINCIPAL
A principal whose identity is unknown by a third person, but the third person knows that the agent is or may be acting for a principal at the time the contract is made.

UNDISCLOSED PRINCIPAL
A principal whose identity is unknown by a third person, and the third person has no knowledge that the agent is acting in an agency capacity at the time the contract is made.

A **disclosed principal** is one whose identity is known by the third party at the time the contract is made by the agent. For example, a purchasing agent signing a contract for the purchase of office supplies will probably sign his or her name as purchasing agent for a specific company (for which he or she works) whose identity is well known to the office-supply store owner.

The identity of a **partially disclosed principal** is not known by the third party, but the third party knows that the agent is or may be acting for a principal at the time the contract is made. For example, a seller of real estate may wish to keep his or her identity a secret, yet the agent with whom the seller has contracted can make it perfectly clear to the purchaser of the real estate that the agent is acting in an agency capacity for a principal.

The identity of an **undisclosed principal** is totally unknown to the third party, and furthermore the third party has no knowledge that the agent is acting in an agency capacity at the time the contract is made. For example, Albright agrees to sell two truckloads of apples to Zimmer. Zimmer believes that he is buying the apples from Albright; but actually Albright is the agent for Henderson, who legally owns the apples. In this situation, Henderson is an undisclosed principal.

A disclosed or partially disclosed principal is liable to a third party for a contract made by an agent who is acting within the scope of his or her authority. Ordinarily, if the principal is disclosed, the agent has no contractual liability for the nonperformance of the principal or the third party. But if the agent exceeds the scope of authority, and the principal fails to ratify the contract, the principal cannot be held liable in the contract by the third party. Hence, the agent is generally liable in such situations unless the third party knew of the agent's lack of authority.

When neither the fact of agency nor the identity of the principal is disclosed, a third party is deemed to be dealing with the agent personally, and the agent is liable as a party to the contract. If an agent has acted within the scope of his or her authority, the undisclosed principal is also liable as a party to the contract, just as if the principal had been fully disclosed at the time the contract was made. Conversely, the undisclosed principal can hold the third party to the contract, unless (1) the undisclosed principal was expressly excluded as a party in the contract, (2) the contract is a negotiable instrument signed by the agent with no indication of signing in a representative capacity, or (3) the performance of the agent is personal to the contract, allowing the third party to refuse the principal's performance.

In the following case, the issue was whether an agent, through a written agreement, could assume liability for a contract with a third party when the identity of the principal was fully disclosed to the third party.

Case 23.4
FAIRCHILD PUBLICATIONS DIVISION OF CAPITAL CITIES MEDIA, INC. v. ROSSTON, KREMER & SLAWTER, INC.

Supreme Court, New York County, 1992.
584 N.Y.S.2d 389.

HISTORICAL AND SOCIAL SETTING *The American Association of Advertising Agencies, Inc. (AAAA), represents approximately 750 advertising agencies. These agencies place ads that account for 80 percent of all national advertising revenues. For the use of its members in placing ads with the media, the AAAA has adopted form contracts. Clauses in the contracts impose sole liability on the advertising agencies for the cost of the ads. These clauses reflect what has been the custom and practice of the print media advertising industry for more than forty years. One reason for the practice is that in accepting ads, publications customarily rely on the credit ratings of the agencies, not the advertisers, in assessing whether to extend credit. Sometimes, in a particular instance, changes are made to a contract to ensure that an advertiser is solely liable.*

FACTS Fabrican, Inc., a home furnishings manufacturer, hired an advertising agency, Rosston, Kremer & Slawter, Inc. (RKS), to advertise Fabrican's products in national magazines. In early 1989, RKS arranged for Fabrican's ads to be placed in two magazines published by Fairchild Publications Division of Capital Cities Media, Inc. Daniel Kremer of RKS signed two contracts covering the advertising arrangement, both of which clearly designated Fabrican as the "advertiser." Both contracts, which consisted of preprinted forms containing filled-in blanks and typed and handwritten additions, provided that Fairchild agreed to publish the ads subject to the terms of advertising contracts adopted by the American Association of Advertising Agencies, Inc., "which terms are hereby incorporated herein and made part of this contract." The attached AAAA form stated that the advertising agency and the publisher agreed that the publisher would hold the advertising agency solely liable for payment. Fairchild published Fabrican's ads and sent invoices to RKS totaling $85,157. Neither Fabrican (which had since filed for bankruptcy) nor RKS paid the invoices, and Fairchild Publications sued RKS to recover the price of the ads. Kremer argued that RKS could not be liable because (1) he was unaware of the AAAA term holding the advertising agency solely liable for payment and (2) RKS was acting as an agent for a disclosed principal.

ISSUE Can RKS be held liable for payment of the price of the ads?

DECISION Yes.

REASON The court stated that "in order to prevail, Fairchild must prove either that RKS agreed to be liable for Fabrican's debts or that custom and usage rendered RKS liable." The court concluded that based on the evidence, Fairchild "met its burden of proof on both grounds." Even though Kremer was unaware that the AAAA terms regarding agency liability were incorporated by reference into the contracts, Kremer's lack of awareness "does not affect their validity. Under these terms, RKS is liable for payment." Furthermore, the court found that when the contracts were formed, RKS had been placing ads in Fairchild publications for more than forty years and, as a regular customer of Fairchild, knew or should have known of Fairchild's policy of holding advertising agencies solely liable for payment of the ads. "RKS acknowledged familiarity with the concept of sole agency liability, and did not dispute its liability, despite receiving regular bills, invoices, and dunning letters, until a number of months after executing the Contracts. All these factors combine to estop RKS from denying liability."

ETHICAL CONSIDERATIONS *If RKS had never contracted with Fairchild before for the placement of ads for a third party, the court might have viewed the matter differently. In such circumstances, Kremer's contention that he was unaware of the AAAA term specifying that the agency would be solely liable might have carried more weight. In view of RKS's forty-year history of placing ads in Fairchild Publications, Kremer's argument that he was unaware of his agency's liability for the price of the ads was weak.*

Liability for Agent's Torts

A principal becomes liable for an agent's torts if the torts are committed within the scope of the agency or the scope of employment. The theory of liability used here involves the doctrine of ***respondeat superior***,[6] a Latin term meaning "let the master

RESPONDEAT SUPERIOR
In Latin, "Let the master respond." A principle of law whereby a principal or an employer is held liable for the wrongful acts committed by agents or employees while acting within the scope of their agency or employment.

6. Pronounced ree-*spahn*-dee-uht soo-*peer*-ee-your. The doctrine of *respondeat superior* applies not only to employer-employee relationships but also to principal-agent relationships as long as the principal has the right of control over the agent.

Landmark in the Law

The Doctrine of *Respondeat Superior*

The idea that a master must respond to third persons for losses negligently caused by the master's servant first appeared in Lord Holt's opinion in *Jones* v. *Hart* (1698).[a] By the early nineteenth century, this maxim had been adopted by most courts and was referred to as the doctrine of *respondeat superior*—Latin for "let the master respond" or "let the master serve."

The vicarious (indirect) liability of the master for the acts of the servant has been supported primarily by two theories. The first rests on the issue of *control*, or *fault*: the master has control over the acts of the servant and is thus responsible for injuries arising out of such service. The second theory is economic in nature: because the master takes the benefits or profits of the servant's service, he or she should also suffer the losses; moreover, the master is better able than the servant to absorb such losses.

The *control* theory is clearly recognized in the Restatement (Second) of Agency, in which the master is defined as "a principal who employs an agent to perform service in his affairs and who controls, or has the right to control, the physical conduct of the other in the performance of the service." Accordingly, a servant is defined as "an agent employed by a master to perform service in his affairs whose physical conduct in his performance of the service is controlled, or is subject to control, by the master."

It is important to note that there are limitations on the master's liability for the acts of the servant. An employer (master) is only responsible for the wrongful conduct of an employee (servant) that occurs in "the scope of the employment." The criteria used by the courts in determining whether an employee is acting within the scope of employment are stated in the Restatement (Second) of Agency and discussed elsewhere in this chapter. Generally, the act must be of a kind the servant was employed to do, must have occurred within "authorized time and space limits," and must have been "activated, at least in part, by a purpose to serve the master."

A useful insight into the "scope of employment" concept may be gained from Baron Parke's classic distinction between a "detour" and a "frolic" in the case of *Joel* v. *Morison* (1834):

> If the servants, being on their master's business took a *detour* * * *, the master will be responsible. * * * The master is only liable where the servant is acting in the course of his employment. If he was going out of his way, against his master's implied commands, when driving on his master's business, he will make his master liable; but if he was going on a *frolic of his own*, without being at all on his master's business, the master will not be liable.[b]

The doctrine of *respondeat superior* has been accepted by the courts for nearly two centuries. This theory of vicarious liability is laden with practical implications in all situations in which a principal-agent (master-servant, employer-employee) relationship exists. The small-town grocer with one clerk and the multinational corporation with thousands of employees are equally subject to the doctrinal demand of "let the master respond."

a. Holt, K.B. 642, 90 Eng. Reprint 1255.

b. 6 Car. & P. 501, 172 Eng. Reprint 1338 (1834).

respond." This doctrine, which is discussed in this chapter's *Landmark in the Law*, is similar to the theory of strict liability discussed in Chapter 5. The doctrine imposes vicarious liability on the employer without regard to the personal fault of the employer for torts committed by an employee in the course or scope of employment.

Scope of Employment The Restatement (Second) of Agency, Section 229, indicates the factors that courts will consider in determining whether or not a particular act occurred within the course and scope of employment. They are as follows:

1. Whether the act was authorized by the employer.
2. The time, place, and purpose of the act.
3. Whether the act was one commonly performed by employees on behalf of their employers.
4. The extent to which the employer's interest was advanced by the act.
5. The extent to which the private interests of the employee were involved.
6. Whether the employer furnished the means or instrumentality (for example, a truck or a machine) by which the injury was inflicted.

7. Whether the employer had reason to know that the employee would do the act in question and whether the employee had ever done it before.
8. Whether the act involved the commission of a serious crime.

Misrepresentation A principal is exposed to tort liability whenever a third person sustains a loss due to the agent's misrepresentation. The principal's liability depends on whether or not the agent was actually or apparently authorized to make representations and whether such representations were made within the scope of the agency. The principal is always directly responsible for an agent's misrepresentation made within the scope of the agent's authority, whether the misrepresentation was made fraudulently or simply by the agent's mistake or oversight.

Liability for Independent Contractor's Torts

Generally, the principal is not liable for physical harm caused to a third person by the negligent act of an independent contractor in the performance of the contract because in this situation, the employer does not have the *right to control* the details of performance. An exception to this doctrine prevails when exceptionally hazardous activities are involved, such as blasting operations, the transportation of highly volatile chemicals, or the use of poisonous gases. In these cases, a principal cannot be shielded from liability merely by using an independent contractor. Strict liability is imposed on the principal as a matter of law and, in some states, by statute. In the following case, one of the issues before the court was whether the "self-help" repossession of collateral is an inherently dangerous activity, in which case the secured creditor could be held liable for damages caused by the independent contractor's tortious actions.

Case 23.5
SANCHEZ v. MBANK OF EL PASO
Court of Appeals of Texas—
El Paso, 1990.
792 S.W.2d 530.

HISTORICAL AND SOCIAL SETTING *Under uniform laws that predated the Uniform Commercial Code (UCC), a secured party could take possession of collateral on a debtor's default without judicial process. The drafters of the UCC followed these provisions in UCC 9–503. Taking possession of collateral on default must be done without a breach of the peace, however. Among the acts that have been considered to be peaceable, in connection with repossession, is the removal of an automobile from the debtor's driveway without the debtor's knowledge. Acts that have been considered to constitute a breach of the peace, in connection with repossession, include the removal of an automobile over the debtor's objection and the removal of an automobile after a threat of violence.*

FACTS MBank of El Paso contracted with El Paso Recovery Service (El Paso) to have El Paso repossess Yvonne Sanchez's 1978 Pontiac Trans Am, which had been purchased through MBank financing. Two men hired by El Paso went to Sanchez's home with a tow truck and proceeded to hook the tow truck to the car, which was in the driveway. Sanchez, who was in the yard cutting the grass at the time, asked them their purpose and demanded that they cease their attempt to take the automobile and leave the premises. When they ignored her, she entered and locked herself in the car in an effort to stall them until the police or her husband could arrive. It was only after they got the automobile in the street that they identified their purpose and told her to get out of the car, which she refused to do. They then took the vehicle with Sanchez locked in it on a high-speed ride from her home to the repossession lot and parked the car in a fenced and locked yard with a loose guard dog. She was rescued some time later by her husband and the police. Sanchez filed suit against MBank for damages, alleging that El Paso and its employees were MBank's agents and that they had willfully breached the peace in violation of UCC 9–503. The trial court granted the bank's motion for summary judgment, holding that the bank could not be liable because El Paso was an independent contractor and not an employee or agent of MBank. Sanchez appealed.

ISSUE Can MBank be held liable for the tortious actions of El Paso, notwithstanding the fact that El Paso was an independent contractor?

Case 23.5—Continued

DECISION Yes. The appellate court reversed the trial court's decision and remanded the case for trial.

REASON The appellate court pointed out that two situations represent exceptions to the general rule that an employer is not liable for the tortious acts of an independent contractor: "(1) where the employer is by the statute * * * under a duty to provide specific safeguards for the safety of others" and "(2) where the employer employs an independent contractor to do work involving a special or inherent danger to others." The court concluded that MBank had a nondelegable duty under UCC 9–503 to avoid breaching the peace when repossessing collateral and thus could be liable to Sanchez for a breach of the peace by El Paso. The court also concluded that self-help repossession—"[a]lways bordering on the edge of illegality if not carried out carefully"—is an inherently dangerous activity.

Liability for Agent's Crimes

Obviously, an agent is liable for his or her own crimes. A principal or employer is not liable for an agent's or employee's crime simply because the agent or employee committed the crime while otherwise acting within the scope of authority or employment, unless the principal or employer participated by conspiracy or other action. In some jurisdictions, under specific statutes, a principal may be liable for an agent's violating, in the course and scope of employment, such regulations as those governing sanitation, prices, weights, and the sale of liquor.

❖ Termination of Agency

Agency law is similar to contract law in that both an agency and a contract can terminate by an act of the parties or by operation of law. Once the relationship between the principal and the agent has ended, the agent no longer has the right to bind the principal. For an agent's apparent authority to be terminated, third persons may also need to be notified when the agency has been terminated.

Termination by Act of the Parties

An agency may be terminated by act of the parties in several ways, as discussed in the next sections.

Lapse of Time An agency agreement may specify the time period during which the agency relationship will exist. If so, the agency ends when that time period expires. Thus, if Allen signs an agreement of agency with Proust "beginning January 1, 1994, and ending December 31, 1996," the agency is automatically terminated on December 31, 1996. Of course, the parties can agree to continue the relationship, in which case the same terms will apply. If no definite time is stated, then the agency continues for a reasonable time and can be terminated at will by either party. What constitutes a "reasonable time" depends on the circumstances and the nature of the agency relationship.

Purpose Achieved An agent can be employed to accomplish a particular objective, such as the purchase of stock for a cattle rancher. In that case, the agency automatically ends after the cattle have been purchased. If more than one agent is employed to accomplish the same purpose, such as the sale of real estate, the first agent to complete the sale automatically terminates the agency relationship for all the others.

Occurrence of a Specific Event An agency can be created to terminate upon the happening of a certain event. If Proust appoints Rubik to handle his business affairs while he is away, the agency automatically terminates when Proust returns.

Sometimes, one aspect of the agent's authority terminates on the occurrence of a particular event, but the agency relationship itself does not terminate. Suppose

Proust, a banker, permits Rubik, the bank's credit manager, to grant a credit line of $2,000 to certain depositors who maintain $2,000 in a savings account. If any customer's savings account falls below $2,000, Rubik can no longer continue making the credit line available to that customer. But Rubik's right to extend credit to the other customers maintaining the minimum balance will continue.

Mutual Agreement Recall from basic contract law that parties can cancel (rescind) a contract by mutually agreeing to terminate the contractual relationship. The same holds true in agency law regardless of whether the agency contract is in writing or whether it is for a specific duration.

Termination by One Party As a general rule, either party can terminate the agency relationship. The agent's act is called a *renunciation of authority*. The principal's act is referred to as a *revocation of authority*. But although both parties may have the *power* to terminate, they may not possess the *right*. Wrongful termination can subject the canceling party to a suit for damages. For example, Rubik has a one-year employment contract with Proust to act as an agent in return for $35,000. Proust can discharge Rubik before the contract period expires (Proust has the *power* to breach the contract); however, Proust will be liable to Rubik for money damages, because Proust has no *right* to breach the contract.

Termination by Operation of Law

Termination of an agency by operation of law occurs in the following circumstances.

Death or Insanity The general rule is that the death or mental incompetence of either the principal or the agent automatically and immediately terminates the ordinary agency relationship. Knowledge of the death is not required.[7] Suppose Proust sends Rubik to the Far East to purchase a rare book. Before Rubik makes the purchase, Proust dies. Rubik's agent status is terminated at the moment of Proust's death, even though Rubik does not know that Proust has died. Some states, however, have changed this common law rule by statute.

An agent's transactions that occur after the death of the principal are not binding on the principal's estate.[8] Assume that Rubik is hired by Proust to collect a debt from Thomas (a third party). Proust dies, but Rubik, not knowing of Proust's death, still collects the money from Thomas. Thomas's payment to Rubik is no longer legally sufficient to discharge Thomas's debt to Proust because Rubik no longer has Proust's authority to collect the money. If Rubik absconds with the money, Thomas must again pay the debt to Proust's estate.

Impossibility When the specific subject matter of an agency is destroyed or lost, the agency terminates. If Proust employs Rubik to sell Proust's house but prior to the sale the premises are destroyed by fire, then Rubik's agency and authority to sell Proust's house terminate. When it is impossible for the agent to perform the agency lawfully, the agency terminates.

Changed Circumstances When an event occurs that has such an unusual effect on the subject matter of the agency that the agent can reasonably infer that the principal will not want the agency to continue, the agency terminates. For example, Proust hires Rubik to sell a tract of land for $20,000. Subsequently, Rubik learns that there is oil under the land and that the land is therefore worth $1 million. The agency and Rubik's authority to sell the land for $20,000 are terminated.

---

7. An exception to termination rules occurs in an agency coupled with an interest, which is not automatically terminated by death or incapacity.

8. There is an exception to this rule in bankng under which the bank as the agent can continue to exercise specific types of authority even after the customer's death or mental incompetence unless it has knowledge of the death or incompetence [UCC 4–405]. Even with knowledge of the customer's death, the bank has authority for ten days following the customer's death to honor checks in the absence of a stop-payment order.

Bankruptcy Bankruptcy of the principal or the agent usually terminates the agency relationship (although insolvency will not necessarily terminate the relationship). Some situations, such as a serious financial loss, might indicate that future contracts with third parties should not be made.

War When the principal's country and the agent's country are at war with each other, the agency is terminated or at least suspended.

Notice of Termination Required

When an agency terminates by operation of law because of the preceding reasons or some other unforeseen circumstance, there is no duty to notify third persons, unless the agent's authority is coupled with an interest. If the parties themselves have terminated the agency, however, it is the principal's duty to inform any third parties who know of the existence of the agency that it has been terminated (although notice may be given by others).

An agent's authority continues until the agent receives some notice of termination. Notice to third parties follows the general rule that an agent's *apparent* authority continues until the third person receives notice (from any source of information) that such authority has been terminated. The principal is expected to notify directly any third person who the principal knows has dealt with the agent. For third persons who have heard about the agency but have not dealt with the agent, *constructive notice* is sufficient.[9]

No particular form is required for notice of agency termination to be effective. The principal can actually notify the agent, or the agent can learn of the termination through some other means. For example, Manning bids on a shipment of steel, and Stone is hired as an agent to arrange transportation of the shipment. When Stone learns that Manning has lost the bid, Stone's authority to make the transportation arrangement terminates.

If the agent's authority is written, it must be revoked in writing, and the writing must be shown to all people who saw the original writing that established the agency relationship. Sometimes, a written authorization (like that granting power of attorney) contains an expiration date. The passage of the expiration date is sufficient notice of termination for third parties.

Agency Coupled with an Interest An agency *coupled with an interest* is a relationship created for the benefit of the agent. The agent actually acquires a beneficial interest in the subject matter of the agency. Under these circumstances, it is not equitable to permit a principal to terminate the relationship at will. Hence, a principal cannot revoke this type of agency.

Because, in an agency coupled with an interest, the interest is not created for the benefit of the principal, it is not really an agency in the usual sense. Therefore, any attempt by the principal to revoke an agency coupled with an interest normally has no legal force or effect, and the agency is not terminated by the death of either the principal or the agent.

9. Constructive notice is information or knowledge of a fact imputed by law to a person if he or she could have discovered the fact by proper diligence. Constructive notice is often accomplished pursuant to a statute by newspaper publication.

Application

Law and the Employer— Using Independent Contractors

As an employer, you may at some time consider hiring an independent contractor. One reason for using an independent contractor is that it may reduce your susceptibility to tort liability. If, however, an independent contractor's words or conduct lead another party to believe that he or she is your employee, you may not escape liability for the worker's tort. To minimize the possibility of your being legally liable for negligence on the part of an independent contractor, you should, prior to hiring that contractor, inquire about his or her qualifications. The degree to which you should investigate depends, of course, on the nature of the work. A more thorough investigation is necessary when there is a potential danger to the public from the contractor's activities (as in delivering explosives). Generally, it is a good idea to have the independent contractor assume, in a written contract, liability for harms caused to third parties by the independent contractor's negligence. You should also require the independent contractor to purchase liability insurance to cover the costs of potential lawsuits for harms caused to third persons by the independent contractor's hazardous activities or negligence.

Another reason for hiring an independent contractor is that you need not pay or deduct Social Security and unemployment taxes on behalf of such individuals. The independent contractor is the party responsible for paying these taxes. Additionally, the independent contractor is not eligible for any retirement or medical plans or other fringe benefits that you have for yourself and your employees, and this is a cost saving to you.

A word of caution, though: simply designating a person as an independent contractor does not make him or her one. Under Internal Revenue Service (IRS) rules, an individual will be treated as an employee if he or she is "in fact" an employee, regardless of any classification that you might have made. For example, a secretary will not be treated by the IRS as an independent contractor simply because you designate him or her as such. If, however, you contract with a secretarial service, the secretary is an employee of the service and not your employee directly. In this case, even though you are utilizing an independent contractor (the secretarial service), you still retain the right to supervise and inspect work to make sure that it meets your contract specifications. The fact that you utilize this right does not change the worker's status from independent contractor to employee. If you improperly designate an employee as an independent contractor, the penalty may be high. Usually, you will be liable for back Social Security and unemployment taxes, plus interest and penalty. When in doubt, seek professional assistance in such matters.

Checklist for Using Independent Contractors

☐ 1. Check the qualifications of any independent contractor you plan to use to reduce the potential for negligent actions.

☐ 2. It is best to require in any contract with an independent contractor that the contractor assume liability for harm to a third person caused by the contractor's negligence.

☐ 3. Require that independent contractors working for you carry liability insurance. Examine the policy to make sure that it is current, particularly when actions that are more than normally hazardous to the public are going to be undertaken by the contractor.

☐ 4. Make sure that independent contractors do not represent themselves as your employees to the rest of the world.

☐ 5. Regularly inspect the work of the independent contractor to make sure that it is being performed in accordance with contract specifications. Such supervision on your part will not change the worker's status as an independent contractor.

❖ Key Terms

agency 558
agent 558
disclosed principal 572
equal dignity rule 568
fiduciary 558
independent contractor 559
notary public 568
partially disclosed principal 572
power of attorney 568
principal 558
ratification 564
respondeat superior 573
undisclosed principal 572

❖ Chapter Summary: Agency Relationships in Business

Types of Agency Relationships	In a *principal-agent* relationship, an agent acts on behalf of and instead of the principal, using a certain degree of his or her own discretion. An employee who deals with third parties is normally an agent. An independent contractor is not an employee, and the employer has no control over the details of physical performance. The independent contractor is not usually an agent.
Agency Formation	1. *By agreement*—Through express consent (oral or written) or implied by conduct. 2. *By ratification*—Principal either by act or agreement ratifies the conduct of an agent who acted outside the scope of authority or the conduct of a person who is in fact not an agent. 3. *By estoppel*—When the principal causes a third person to believe that another person is his or her agent, and the third person deals with the supposed agent, the principal is "estopped to deny" the agency relationship. 4. *By operation of law*—Based on a social duty (such as the need to support family members) or created in emergency situations when the agent is unable to contact the principal.
Duties of Agents and Principals	1. *Duties of the agent:* a. Performance—The agent must use reasonable diligence and skill in performing his or her duties. b. Notification—The agent is required to notify the principal of all matters that come to his or her attention concerning the subject matter of the agency. c. Loyalty—The agent has a duty to act solely for the benefit of his or her principal and not in the interest of the agent or a third party. d. Obedience—The agent must follow all lawful and clearly stated instructions of the principal. e. Accounting—The agent has a duty to make available to the principal records of all property and money received and paid out on behalf of the principal. 2. *Duties of the principal:* a. Compensation—Except in a gratuitous agency relationship, the principal must pay the agreed-on value (or reasonable value) for an agent's services. b. Reimbursement and indemnification—The principal must reimburse the agent for all sums of money disbursed at the request of the principal and for all sums of money the agent disburses for necessary expenses in the course of reasonable performance of his or her agency duties. c. Cooperation—A principal must cooperate with and assist an agent in performing his or her duties. d. Safe working conditions—A principal must provide safe working conditions for the agent-employee.
Scope of Agent's Authority	1. *Express authority*—Can be oral or in writing. Authorization must be in writing if the agent is to execute a contract that must be in writing (Statute of Frauds). 2. *Implied authority*—Authority customarily associated with the position of the agent or authority that is deemed necessary for the agent to carry out expressly authorized tasks. 3. *Apparent authority and agency by estoppel*—Exists when the principal, by word or action, causes a third party reasonably to believe that an agent has authority to act, even though the agent has no express or implied authority. 4. *Ratification*—The affirmation by the principal of an agent's unauthorized action or promise. For the ratification to be effective, the principal must be aware of all material facts.
Liability for Contracts	1. *Disclosed principals and partially disclosed principals*—Principal is liable to a third party for a contract made by the agent, if the agent acted within the scope of his or her authority. 2. *Undisclosed principals*—Agent is liable to a third party for a contract made by the agent. If the agent acted within the scope of authority, the principal is fully bound by the contract.
Liability for Agent's Torts	Under the doctrine of *respondeat superior,* the principal is liable for any harm caused to another through the agent's negligence if the agent was acting within the scope of his or her employment at the time the harmful act occurred.
Liability for Independent Contractor's Torts	A principal is not liable for harm caused by an independent contractor's negligence. If hazardous activities are involved, the principal is strictly liable for any resulting harm.

❖ Chapter Summary: Agency Relationships in Business—Continued

Liability for Agent's Crimes	An agent is responsible for his or her own crimes, even if he or she committed such a crime while acting within the scope of authority or employment. A principal will be liable for an agent's crime only if the principal participated by conspiracy or other action or (in some jurisdictions) if the agent violated certain government regulations in the course of employment.
Termination of an Agency	1. *By act of the parties:* a. Lapse of time (when a definite time for the duration of the agency was agreed on when the agency was established). b. Purpose achieved. c. Occurrence of a specific event. d. Mutual rescission (requires mutual consent of principal and agent). e. Termination by act of either the principal (revocation) or the agent (renunciation). (But a principal cannot revoke an agency coupled with an interest.) 2. *By operation of law:* a. Death or mental incompetence of either the principal or the agent (except in an agency coupled with an interest). b. Impossibility (when the purpose of the agency cannot be achieved because of an event beyond the parties' control). c. Changed circumstances (in which it would be inequitable to require that the agency be continued). d. Bankruptcy (but not insolvency) of the principal or the agent. e. War between the principal's and agent's countries. 3. *Notification of termination:* a. When an agency is terminated by act of the parties, all third persons who have previously dealt with the agency must be directly notified; constructive notice will suffice for all other third parties. b. When an agency is terminated by operation of law, no notice to third parties is required.

❖ Questions and Case Problems

23-1. Duties of Principals and Agents. What is the general nature of the duties that agents and principals owe each other? What specific duties does an agent owe to his or her principal?

23-2. Authority of Agent. A principal's liability for an agent's act starts with the formation of the agency relationship. What are the two types of authority that an agent possesses? If an agent acts outside the scope of his or her authority, how might a principal still be held liable for the agent's act?

23-3. Ratification of Agent's Unauthorized Acts. Springer was a political candidate running for congressional office. He was operating on a tight budget and instructed his campaign staff not to purchase any campaign materials without his explicit authorization. In spite of these instructions, one of his campaign workers ordered Dubychek Printing Co. to print some promotional materials for Springer's campaign. When the printed materials were received, Springer did not return them but instead used them during his campaign. When Dubychek failed to obtain payment from Springer for the materials, he sued for recovery of the price. Springer contended that he was not liable on the sales contract because he had not authorized his agent to purchase the printing services. Dubychek argued that Springer's use of the materials constituted ratification of his agent's unauthorized purchase. Is Dubychek correct? Explain.

23-4. Agent's Duties to Principal. Iliana is a traveling sales agent. Iliana not only solicits orders but also delivers the goods and collects payments from her customers. Iliana places all payments in her private checking account and at the end of each month draws sufficient cash from her bank to cover the payments made. Giberson Corp., Iliana's employer, is totally unaware of this procedure. Because of a slowdown in the economy, Giberson tells all its salespeople to offer 20 percent discounts on orders. Iliana solicits orders, but she offers only 15 percent discounts, pocketing the extra 5 percent paid by customers. Iliana has not lost any orders by this practice, and she is rated as one of Giberson's top salespersons. Giberson now learns of Iliana's actions. Discuss fully Giberson's rights in this matter.

23-5. Liability for Agent's Contracts. Miguel Mireles is a purchasing agent–employee for Suharto Coal Supply, a partnership. Mireles has authority to purchase the coal needed by Suharto to satisfy the needs of its customers. While Mireles is leaving a coal mine from which he has just purchased a large quantity of coal, his car breaks down. He walks into a small roadside grocery store for help. While there, he runs into Wiley, who owns 360 acres back in the mountains with all mineral rights. Wiley, in need of money, offers to sell Mireles the property at $1,500 per acre. Upon inspection, Mireles believes the subsurface contains valuable coal deposits. Mireles contracts to purchase the property for Suharto, signing the contract, "Suharto Coal Supply, Miguel Mireles, agent." The closing date is set for August 1. Mireles takes the contract to the partnership. The managing partner is furious, as Suharto is not in the property business. Later, just before August 1, both Wiley and the partnership learn that the value of the land is at least $15,000 per acre. Discuss the rights of Suharto and Wiley concerning the land contract.

23-6. Agent's Duties to Principal. Sam Kademenos was about to sell a $1 million life insurance policy to a prospective customer when he resigned from his position with Equitable Life Assurance Society. Before resigning from the company, he had expended substantial amounts of company money and had utilized Equitable's medical examiners to procure the $1 million sale. After resigning, Kademenos joined a competing insurance firm, Jefferson Life Insurance Co., and made the sale through it. Has he breached any duty to Equitable? [*Kademenos v. Equitable Life Assurance Society*, 513 F.2d 1073 (3d Cir. 1975)]

23-7. *Respondeat Superior*. Richard Lanno worked for the Thermal Equipment Corp. as a project engineer. Lanno was allowed to keep a company van and tools at his home because he routinely drove to work sites directly from his home and because he was often needed for unanticipated trips during his off hours. The arrangement had been made for the convenience of Thermal Equipment, even though Lanno's managers permitted him to make personal use of the van. Lanno was involved in a collision with Lazar while driving the van home from work one day. At the time of the accident, Lanno had taken a detour in order to stop at a store—he had intended to purchase a few items and then go home. Lazar sued Thermal Equipment, claiming that Lanno had acted within the scope of his employment. Discuss whether Lazar was able to recover from Thermal Equipment. Can employees act on behalf of their employers and themselves at the same time? [*Lazar v. Thermal Equipment Corp.*, 148 Cal.App.3d 458, 195 Cal.Rptr. 890 (1983)]

23-8. Authority of Agent. The Federal Land Bank (FLB) filed an action to foreclose a mortgage on Tom and Judith Sullivan's real estate. Before the trial, FLB's attorney wrote to the Sullivans' attorney inviting settlement offers. A copy of the letter was sent to Wayne Williamson, an FLB vice-president. Nine days later, on September 3, the Sullivans' attorney wrote to FLB's attorney expressing interest in settling the case. A copy of this letter was sent to Williamson. On September 11, FLB's attorney replied with an offer that "[m]y client has authorized me to extend * * * to you." The Sullivans accepted the offer. Three weeks later, FLB's attorney wrote the following to the Sullivans' attorney: "Any compromises regarding Federal Land Bank loans must be cleared through [FLB's] Omaha [office]. The proposed compromise was not approved and therefore we have been requested to proceed through the foreclosure process." The case went to trial and FLB obtained a judgment of foreclosure. The trial court found that FLB was not bound by the offer made by its attorney. The Sullivans appealed, arguing that the attorney had or appeared to have authority to settle the case. What should the appellate court decide? [*Federal Land Bank v. Sullivan*, 430 N.W.2d 700 (S.Dak. 1988)]

23-9. Disclosure of Principal's Identity. Port Ship Service, Inc., a water taxi service, ferried crew members, customs agents, supplies, and the like between ships and the shore at the port of New Orleans. Norton, Lilly & Co. acted as an agent for various ships entering the harbor that required water taxi services. Ships needing water taxi services would call Norton, and Norton would communicate the names of the vessels needing such services to Port Ship. Although Norton never informed Port Ship of the names of the vessels' owners, such information was readily available to Port Ship in publications commonly used by port authorities, and in addition, Norton maintained a twenty-four-hour telephone service through which Port Ship could have ascertained the identities of any of the ship owners. Port Ship sought to hold Norton liable for unpaid taxi services, and the issue turned on whether the ship owners were fully disclosed principals (in which case Norton could not be held liable) or only partially disclosed principals (in which case Norton could be held liable). The Court stated that the Restatement (Second) of Agency, Section 4, "makes * * * clear" that "it is the agent's duty to disclose the principal's identity, and not a third party's duty to ascertain that identity." Had Norton disclosed the principals' identities by giving Port Ship the names of the vessels? Discuss fully. [*Port Ship Service, Inc. v. Norton, Lilly & Co.*, 883 F.2d 23 (5th Cir. 1989)]

23-10. Apparent Authority. Red River Commodities, Inc. (RRC), entered into a contract with Kelby Eidsness under which RRC agreed to purchase 250,000 pounds of sunflowers. Because of a drought, Kelby was only able to deliver 75,084 pounds. The contract contained a clause stating that if Kelby could not deliver the promised 250,000 pounds because of an event unanticipated at the time the contract was formed, Kelby would be excused from performance only if he seasonably notifed RRC of his inability to perform. Kelby orally notified RRC's contracting representative, Richard Frith, who Kelby assumed was RRC's agent, about his poor crop in September before the harvest. RRC insisted that Frith was not a contracting agent and had no authority to bind RRC in any way. The RRC-Kelby contract included the following statement: "The contracting representative identified below [Frith] does not have the authority to alter or vary the terms of this agreement. He is not an agent of RRC." Nevertheless, after contracts were made, Frith frequently contacted growers for RRC to help with their production problems. Frith talked to growers, inspected fields, and reported to RRC. RRC's manager testified that Frith was his "go between" with growers such as Kelby. Kelby assumed that Frith was an agent of RRC and therefore that notice to Frith of the drought and Kelby's inability to perform the contract completely would suffice as notice to RRC. In RRC's suit against Kelby for breach of contract, will the court find Frith to be RRC's agent? Discuss. [*Red River Commodities, Inc. v. Eidsness*, 459 N.W.2d 805 (N.Dak. 1990)]

23-11. Employee versus Independent Contractor. Clifford Aymes was hired by Jonathan Bonelli of Sun Island Sales, Inc., to create a computer program for Sun Island to use in maintaining records of its cash receipts, inventory, sales figures, and other data. No agreement was reached as to ownership rights in the program that Aymes developed, called CSALIB. Aymes did most of his programming at the Sun Island office. Although Bonelli gave Aymes frequent instructions as to what he wanted from the program, Aymes generally worked alone and enjoyed considerable autonomy in his work. He worked fairly regular hours, but he was not always paid by the hour—occasionally, he submitted bills (invoices) to Sun Island for his work. Aymes never received any employee benefits, such as health insurance, and Sun Island never withheld federal and state taxes from Aymes's paycheck; nor did it pay any Social Security taxes on Aymes's earnings. When Bonelli unilaterally cut Aymes's hours in violation of an alleged oral agreement, Aymes left Sun Island and demanded compensation for Sun Island's use of CSALIB. Bonelli refused to pay Aymes for the program's use and also stated that he would not pay Aymes $14,560 in back wages unless Aymes signed a form releasing all rights in CSALIB. Aymes then sued Bonelli and Sun Island for copyright infringement, and the court had to decide who owned the copyright in the program. Central to the determination of this issue was whether Aymes was an employee of Sun Island or an independent contractor. What should the court decide, and why? [*Aymes v. Bonelli*, 980 F.2d 857 (2d Cir. 1992)]

A QUESTION OF ETHICS AND SOCIAL RESPONSIBILITY

23-12. *Erwin Ernst was the sole shareholder and chief executive officer of Matchmaker Real Estate Sales Center, Inc., located in Chicago. During 1987 and 1988, the Leadership Council for Metropolitan Open Communities, a nonprofit corporation, conducted a series of tests to see if Matchmaker sales agents engaged in "racial steering"—that is, directing white home buyers to homes in white neighborhoods and black home buyers to homes in black or mixed neighborhoods. In each test, one white couple and one black couple, evenly matched with regard to financial qualifications and housing needs, were sent to Matchmaker and told Matchmaker that they were looking for homes in southwest Chicago. Matchmaker agents consistently directed the white couples to higher-priced homes in white neighborhoods and the black couples to lower-priced homes in black or racially mixed neighborhoods. The city of Chicago, the Leadership Council, and the individual testers (the plaintiffs) all sued Matchmaker for violations of federal laws prohibiting racial discrimination and discrimination in housing. The court found the real estate agents to be employees, not independent contractors, and both Ernst and his corporation, Matchmaker, were held liable for compensatory damages under the doctrine of* respondeat superior. *The agents were held liable for both compensatory and punitive damages.* [Chicago v. Matchmaker Real Estate Sales Center, Inc., 982 *F.2d 1086 (7th Cir. 1992)*]

1. In view of the fact that Ernst had specifically instructed his agents not to engage in discriminatory practices, is it fair to hold Ernst and Matchmaker liable for damages? Why or why not?
2. The court concluded that Ernst and Matchmaker should not be held liable for punitive damages in this case. Do you agree with this conclusion? Why or why not?
3. Ernst argued that the plaintiffs had no standing to sue because they had sustained no injury. The court, however, held that each of the plaintiffs had standing to bring suit. How might you justify the court's conclusion that the plaintiffs had met the injury requirement for standing to sue?

CASE BRIEFING ASSIGNMENT

23-13. *Examine Case A.9* [Green v. Shell Oil Co., *181 Mich.App. 439, 450 N.W.2d 50 (1989)*] *in Appendix A. The case is excerpted there in great detail. Review and then brief the case, making sure that you include answers to the following questions in your brief.*

1. Green sued Shell and Lanford on two grounds. What are they?
2. Why did the court hold that summary judgment on the issue of Lanford's agency status was inappropriate?
3. Why did the court hold that the service station attendant was not acting within the scope of employment while he was participating in the assault and battery?

FOR CRITICAL ANALYSIS

23-14. *When a worker is injured on the job, normally the sole remedy is provided through state workers' compensation statutes, regardless of fault or the employer's negligence. On average, recoveries under these statutes are less than half what recoveries in tort lawsuits would be. In view of the law's increasing concern with compensating injured parties, why are these statutes retained? What policy considerations underlie their retention?*

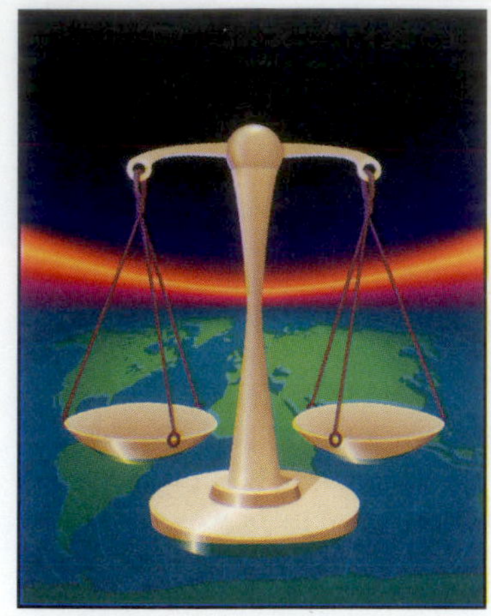

Chapter 24

The Entrepreneur's Options

"It is a socialist idea that making profits is a vice. I consider the real vice is making losses."

Sir Winston Churchill, 1874–1965
(British prime minister, 1940–1945, 1951–1955)

Many Americans would agree with Churchill that it is not profits but losses that are to be avoided. And yet, every entrepreneur risks taking a loss. An **entrepreneur** is by definition one who initiates and *assumes the financial risks* of a new enterprise and undertakes to provide or control its management.

One of the questions faced by any entrepreneur who wishes to start up a business is what form of business organization she or he should choose for the business endeavor. In this chapter, we will examine the basic features of the three major business forms—sole proprietorships, partnerships, and corporations. We will also touch on joint ventures, syndicates, joint stock companies, business trusts, and cooperatives. A discussion of private franchises concludes the chapter.

ENTREPRENEUR
One who initiates and assumes the financial risks of a new enterprise and who undertakes to provide or control its management.

SOLE PROPRIETORSHIP
The simplest form of business, in which the owner is the business; thus, anyone who does business without creating a formal business entity has a sole proprietorship. The owner of a sole proprietorship reports business income on his or her personal income tax return and is legally responsible for all debts and obligations incurred by the business.

❖ Sole Proprietorships

The simplest form of business is a **sole proprietorship.** In this form, the owner is the business; thus, anyone who does business without creating an organization has a sole proprietorship. Sole proprietorships are very common and constitute over two-thirds of all American businesses. They are also usually small enterprises—less than 1 percent of the sole proprietorships existing in the United States earn over $1 million per year. Sole proprietors can own and manage any type of business from an informal, home-office undertaking to a large restaurant or construction firm.

Advantages of Sole Proprietorships

A major advantage of the sole proprietorship is that the proprietor receives all the profits (because he or she takes all the risk). In addition, it is often easier and less costly to start a sole proprietorship than to start any other kind of business, as few legal forms are involved. This type of business organization also entails more flexibility than does a partnership or a corporation. The sole proprietor is free to make any decision she or he wishes to concerning the business—whom to hire, when to take a vacation, what kind of business to pursue, and so on. A sole proprietor pays only personal income taxes on profits. Sole proprietors are also allowed to establish tax-exempt retirement accounts in the form of Keogh plans.

Disadvantages of Sole Proprietorships

The major disadvantage of the sole proprietorship is that, as sole owner, the proprietor alone bears the burden of any losses or liabilities incurred by the business enterprise. In other words, the sole proprietor has unlimited liability, or legal responsibility, for all obligations incurred in doing business. This unlimited liability is a major factor to be considered in choosing a business form. Another disadvantage is that the proprietor's opportunity to raise capital is limited to personal funds and the funds of those who are willing to make loans. The sole proprietorship also has the disadvantage of lacking continuity upon the death of the proprietor. When the owner dies, so does the business—it is automatically dissolved. If the business is transferred to family members or other heirs, a new proprietorship is created.

❖ Partnerships

Partnerships can be either general partnerships or limited partnerships. The two forms of partnership differ considerably in regard to legal requirements and the rights and liabilities of partners.

General Partnerships

A **partnership** arises from an agreement, express or implied, between two or more persons to carry on a business for profit. Partners are co-owners of a business and have joint control over its operation and the right to share in its profits. No particular form of partnership agreement is necessary for the creation of a partnership, but it is desirable that the agreement be in writing. Both partnerships and sole proprietorships are creatures of common law rather than of statute, although the Uniform Partnership Act (UPA), adopted in forty-nine states,[1] governs the operation of partnerships in the absence of express agreements. Basically, the partners may agree to almost any terms when establishing the partnership so long as they are not illegal or contrary to public policy. The UPA comes into play only if the partners have neglected to include a necessary term. In a sense, then, the UPA is a gap filler rather than a code that must be followed to create the legal entity called a partnership.

Moreover, a partnership is a legal entity only for limited purposes, such as the partnership name and title of ownership and property. The personal net worth of the partners is subject to partnership obligations. The partnership itself is not subject to levy for federal income taxes, although an information return must be filed with the Internal Revenue Service (IRS). A partner's profit from the partnership (whether distributed or not) is taxed as individual income to the individual partner.

Limited Partnerships

A special and quite popular form of partnership is the **limited partnership,** which consists of at least one general partner and one or more limited partners. A limited partnership does not come into existence until a *certificate of partnership* is filed. Therefore, it is a creature of statute. A **general partner** assumes responsibility for the management of the partnership and liability for all partnership debts. A **limited partner** has no right to participate in the management or operation of the partnership and assumes no liability for partnership debts beyond the amount of capital he or she has contributed. Thus, one of the major benefits of becoming a limited partner is this limitation on liability, both with respect to lawsuits brought against the partnership and money at risk. (Limited partnerships are discussed in more detail in Chapter 25.)

1. Only the state of Louisiana has not adopted the UPA. Guam, the District of Columbia, and the Virgin Islands have also adopted the UPA. See Appendix D for the complete text of the UPA.

PARTNERSHIP
An association of two or more persons to carry on, as co-owners, a business for profit.

LIMITED PARTNERSHIP
A partnership consisting of one or more general partners (who manage the business and are liable to the full extent of their personal assets for debts of the partnership) and of one or more limited partners (who contribute only assets and are liable only up to the amount contributed by them).

GENERAL PARTNER
In a limited partnership, a partner who assumes responsibility for the management of the partnership and liability for all partnership debts.

LIMITED PARTNER
In a limited partnership, a partner who contributes capital to the partnership but has no right to participate in the management and operation of the business. The limited partner assumes no liability for partnership debts beyond the capital contributed.

"A man may be reputed an able man this year, and yet be a beggar the next: it is a misfortune that happens to many men, and his former reputation will signify nothing."

Sir John Holt, 1642–1710
(English jurist)

❖ Corporations

CORPORATION
A legal entity created under the authority of the laws of a state or the federal government. The entity is distinct from its shareholders/owners.

The most important form of business organization is the **corporation.** A corporation comes into existence by an act of the state, and it is therefore a legal entity. It typically has perpetual existence. One of the key features of a corporation is that the liability of its owners is limited to their investments. Their personal estates are usually not liable for the obligations of the corporation.

Corporations consist of *shareholders,* who are the owners of the business. A *board of directors,* elected by the shareholders, manages the business. The board of directors normally employs *officers* to oversee day-to-day operations.

❖ Major Business Forms Compared

Exhibit 24–1 lists the essential advantages and disadvantages of each of the three major forms of business. We select for further discussion here three important concerns for anyone starting up a business—the liability of the owners, tax features, and the need for capital.

What are the advantages of doing business as a sole proprietorship?

Liability of Owners

The form of the organization does not always in and of itself determine the liability of the owners. Generally, though, sole proprietors and general partners have personal liability, while the liability of limited partners and shareholders of corporations is limited to their investments. The issue of liability is an important one for creditors in deciding whether to extend credit to a business. For example, a bank may be unwilling to lend money to a corporation that is relatively small and has only a few shareholders. The fact that the business is a corporation does not guarantee that it is a better credit risk than, say, a sole proprietorship. Typically, in corporations with relatively few shareholders, the shareholders must personally sign for any loans made to the corporation. That is, the shareholders agree to become personally liable for the loan if the corporation goes under or cannot meet its debts. In essence, the shareholders become guarantors for the corporation's debt. Hence, the corporate form of business does not prevent them from having personal liability in such a case, because they have assumed the liability voluntarily.

Tax Considerations

Various tax considerations must be taken into account when one decides how best to organize a business. As discussed earlier, taxes on income earned by a sole proprietor are simply taxed as personal income. Tax aspects of partnerships and corporations are summarized in Exhibit 24–2.

Need for Capital

One of the most common reasons for changing from a sole proprietorship to a partnership or a corporation is the need for additional capital to finance expansion. A sole proprietor can seek partners who will bring capital with them. The partnership might be able to secure more funds from potential lenders than could the sole proprietor. But when a firm wants to expand greatly, simply increasing the number of partners can lead to too many partners and make it difficult for the firm to operate effectively. Therefore, incorporation might be the best choice for an expanding business organization. There are many possibilities for obtaining more capital by issuing shares of stock. The original owners will find that, although their proportion of ownership of the company is reduced, they are able to expand much more rapidly by selling shares in the company.

"Thou shalt not covet; but tradition approves all forms of competition."

A. H. Clough, 1819–1861
(English poet)

◆ **Exhibit 24–1**
Major Business Forms Compared

CHARACTERISTIC	SOLE PROPRIETORSHIP	PARTNERSHIP	CORPORATION
1. Method of Creation	Created at will by owner.	Created by agreement of the parties.	Charter issued by state—created by statutory authorization.
2. Legal Position	Not a separate entity; owner is the business.	Not a separate legal entity in many states.	Always a legal entity separate and distinct from its owners—a legal fiction for the purposes of owning property and being a party to litigation.
3. Liability	Unlimited liability.	Unlimited liability (except for limited partners in a limited partnership).	Limited liability of shareholders—shareholders are not liable for the debts of the corporation.
4. Duration	Determined by owner; automatically dissolved on owner's death.	Terminated by agreement of the partners, by the death of one or more of the partners, by withdrawal of a partner, by bankruptcy, etc.	Can have perpetual existence.
5. Transferability of Interest	Interest can be transferred, but individual's proprietorship then ends.	Although partnership interest can be assigned, assignee does not have full rights of a partner.	Share of stock can be transferred.
6. Management	Completely at owner's discretion.	Each general partner has a direct and equal voice in management unless expressly agreed otherwise in the partnership agreement. (Limited partner has no rights in management in a limited partnership.)	Shareholders elect directors, who set policy and appoint officers.
7. Taxation	Owner pays personal taxes on business income.	Each partner pays pro rata share of income taxes on net profits, whether or not they are distributed.	Double taxation—corporation pays income tax on net profits, with no deduction for dividends, and shareholders pay income tax on disbursed dividends they receive.
8. Organizational Fees, Annual License Fees, and Annual Reports	None.	None.	All required.
9. Transaction of Business in Other States	Generally no limitation.	Generally no limitation.[a]	Normally must qualify to do business and obtain certificate of authority.

[a]A few states have enacted statutes requiring that foreign partnerships qualify to do business there—for example, 3 N.H.Rev.Stat.Ann. Chapter 305-A in New Hampshire.

◆ Exhibit 24–2
Tax Aspects of Partnerships and Corporations

TAX ASPECT	PARTNERSHIP	CORPORATION
1. Federal Income Tax	Partners are taxed on proportionate shares of partnership income, even if not distributed; the partnership files information returns only.	Income of the corporation is taxed; stockholders are also taxed on distributed dividends. The corporation files corporate income tax forms.
2. Accumulation	Partners are taxed on accumulated as well as distributed earnings.	Corporate stockholders are not taxed on accumulated earnings. There is, however, a penalty tax, in some instances, that the corporation must pay for unreasonable accumulations of income.
3. Capital Gains	Partners are taxed on their proportionate shares of capital gains, which are taxed at ordinary income rate.	The corporation is taxed on capital gains and losses.
4. Exempt Income	Partners are not taxed on exempt income received from the firm.	Any exempt income distributed by a corporation is fully taxable income to the stockholders.
5. Pension Plan	Partners can adopt a Keogh plan, an Individual Retirement Account (IRA), or a 401-K plan.	Employees and officers who are also stockholders can be beneficiaries of a pension trust. The corporation can deduct its payments to the trust.
6. Social Security	Partners must pay a self-employment tax (15.3 percent in 1993).	All compensation to officers and employee stockholders is subject to Social Security taxation up to the maximum.
7. Death Benefits (excluding those provided by insurance)	There is no exemption for payments to partners' beneficiaries.	Benefits up to $5,000 can be received tax free by employee's beneficiaries.
8. State Taxes	The partnership is not subject to taxes. State income taxes are paid by each partner.	The corporation is subject to state income taxes (although these taxes can be deducted on federal returns).

❖ Other Organizational Forms

A business venture does not have to be organized as a sole proprietorship, a partnership, or a corporation. Several other organizational forms exist, although for the most part, they are hybrid organizations—that is, they have characteristics similar to those of partnerships or corporations or combine features of both. We look at several of these forms here.

Joint Venture

When two or more persons or entities combine their interests in a particular business enterprise and agree to share in losses or profits jointly or in proportion to their contributions, they are engaged in a *joint venture.* The joint venture is treated much like a partnership, but it differs in that it is created is contemplation of a limited activity or a single transaction.

Members of a joint venture usually have limited powers to bind their coventurers. A joint venture is normally not a legal entity and therefore cannot be sued as such, but its members can be sued individually. Usually, joint ventures are taxed like partnerships. They range in size from very small activities to huge, multimillion-dollar joint actions engaged in by some of the world's largest corporations.

Syndicate

A group of individuals getting together to finance a particular project, such as the building of a shopping center or the purchase of a professional basketball franchise, is called a *syndicate* or an *investment group*. The form of such groups varies considerably. A syndicate may exist as a corporation or as a general or limited partnership. In some cases, the members merely own property jointly and have no legally recognized business arrangement.

Joint Stock Company

A *joint stock company* or *association* is a true hybrid of a partnership and a corporation. It has many characteristics of a corporation in that (1) its ownership is represented by transferable shares of stock, (2) it is usually managed by directors and officers of the company or association, and (3) it can have a perpetual existence. Most of its other features, however, are more characteristic of a partnership, and it is usually treated like a partnership. As with a partnership, it is formed by agreement (not statute), property is usually held in the names of the members, shareholders have personal liability, and generally the company is not treated as a legal entity for purposes of a lawsuit. In a joint stock company, however, shareholders are not considered to be agents of each other, as would be the case if the company were a true partnership.

Business Trust

A *business trust* is created by a written trust agreement that sets forth the interests of the beneficiaries and the obligations and powers of the trustees. With a business trust, legal ownership and management of the property of the business stay with one or more of the trustees, and the profits are distributed to the beneficiaries.

The business trust was started in Massachusetts in an attempt to obtain the limited-liability advantage of corporate status while avoiding certain restrictions on a corporation's ownership and development of real property. The business trust resembles a corporation in many respects. Death or bankruptcy of a beneficiary, for example, does not terminate the trust, and beneficiaries are not personally responsible for the debts or obligations of the business trust. In fact, in a number of states, business trusts must pay corporate taxes.

Cooperative

A *cooperative* is an association, either incorporated or not, that is organized to provide an economic service without profit to its members (or shareholders). An incorporated cooperative is subject to state laws governing nonprofit corporations. It will make distributions of dividends, or profits, to its owners on the basis of their transactions with the cooperative rather than on the basis of the amount of capital they contributed.

Cooperatives that are unincorporated are often treated like partnerships. The members have joint liability for the cooperative's acts. This form of business is generally adopted by groups of individuals who wish to pool their resources to gain some advantage in the marketplace. Consumer purchasing co-ops are formed to obtain lower prices through quantity discounts. Seller marketing co-ops are formed to control the market and thereby obtain higher sale prices from consumers. Often

Landmark in the Law

Limited Liability Company (LLC) Statutes

The two most common forms of business organization selected by two or more persons entering into business together are the partnership and the corporation. As explained in the chapter text and summarized in Exhibits 24–1 and 24–2, each form has distinct advantages and disadvantages. Corporations, for example, offer the advantage of limited liability for shareholders. But a disadvantage of the corporate form is that income received by corporations is taxed twice—both when it is received by the company as corporate income and when the same income is distributed to shareholders. Partnerships offer tax advantages to their members because all income is "passed through" the partnership entity to the partners themselves, who are taxed only as individuals. But in contrast to the limited liability of corporate shareholders, the liability of partners in ordinary partnerships is unlimited. For many entrepreneurs and investors, the ideal business form would combine the tax advantages of the partnership form of business with the limited-liability feature of the corporate enterprise.

Two types of existing U.S. business forms partially address these needs. One of them is the limited partnership. Limited partners enjoy both the tax benefits of the partnership *and* limited liability. Yet the limited liability of limited partners is conditional: limited liability exists only so long as the limited partner does not participate in management. The other business form is an S corporation. As will be discussed in Chapter 26, the S corporation is a special corporate form of enterprise that emerged in the early 1980s to allow small corporations to avoid the double-taxation feature of corporations. Like partnerships, S corporations are "pass-through" entities with regard to taxes. S corporation shareholders pay taxes personally on their respective shares of the profits, and the corporation itself is not taxed. The problem with S corporations is that only small corporations (those with thirty-five or fewer shareholders) may acquire S corporation status. Furthermore, with few exceptions, only *individuals* may be shareholders in an S corporation; partnerships and corporations cannot be shareholders. Finally, no nonresident alien can be a shareholder in an S corporation. This means that, say, a European investor cannot purchase shares in an S corporation.

LLC Statutes

In 1977, the state of Wyoming passed legislation authorizing the creation of a limited liability company (LLC), which is a hybrid form of business enterprise that combines the pass-through tax benefits of S corporations and partnerships with the limited liability of limited partners and corporate shareholders. Interest in LLCs mushroomed after a 1988 ruling by the Internal Revenue Service that Wyoming LLCs would be taxed as partnerships instead of as corporations. Before that ruling, the only other state to enact a statute authorizing LLCs was Florida, in 1982. By the beginning of 1993, sixteen other states[a] had enacted LLC statutes, and it is estimated that

a. Arizona, Colorado, Delaware, Illinois, Iowa, Kansas, Louisiana, Maryland, Minnesota, Nevada, Oklahoma, Rhode Island, Texas, Utah, Virginia, and West Virginia.

cooperatives are exempt from certain federal laws—for example, *antitrust* statutes (see Chapter 30)—because of their special status.

LIMITED LIABILITY COMPANY (LLC)
A hybrid form of business organization or enterprise authorized by a state in which its members have limited liability and taxes on profits are passed through the entity to its members.

Limited Liability Company (LLC)

Since 1977, an increasing number of states have authorized a new form of business organization called the **limited liability company (LLC).** The LLC is a hybrid form of business enterprise that offers the limited liability of the corporation but the tax advantages of a partnership. The origins and characteristics of this increasingly significant form of business organization are discussed in this chapter's *Landmark in the Law.*

FRANCHISE
A written agreement whereby an owner of a trademark, trade name, or copyright licenses another to use that trademark, trade name, or copyright, under specified conditions in the selling of goods and services.

❖ Private Franchises

Times have changed dramatically since Ray Kroc, the late founder of McDonald's, launched the franchising boom more than thirty years ago. Today, over a third of by the beginning of 1994, at least forty states will permit this form of enterprise. The various state LLC statutes are far from uniform, but generally they are based on the Wyoming act's provisions, with variations based on the corporate and partnership laws of whatever state is enacting the LLC statute.

Advantages of the LLC

A major advantage of the LLC is that it is taxed as a partnership: profits are passed through the LLC entity, and taxes are paid personally by the members of the company. Another advantage is that the liability of members is limited to the amount of their investments. Furthermore, unlike limited partnerships, the LLC does not grant limited liability on the condition that the members refrain from active participation in the management of the company. In an LLC, members are allowed to participate fully in management activities, and under at least one state's statute, the firm's managers need not even be members of the LLC. Yet another advantage is that corporations and partnerships, as well as foreign investors, can be LLC members, whereas these entities cannot be shareholders in S corporations. Also, in contrast to S corporations, there is no limit on the number of shareholder-members of the LLC.

Disadvantages of the LLC

The disadvantages of the LLC are relatively few. Perhaps the greatest disadvantage is that until LLC statutes are adopted by all the states, or most of the states, any firm engaged in multistate operations may face difficulties. For example, members of an LLC formed in one state may have limited liability in that state but face unlimited liability in another state. Another disadvantage is the fact that because the LLC is a relatively new form of enterprise, little general or case law exists in regard to LLCs. In some situations, the restrictions placed by statute on the transfer of ownership interests in LLCs may be a disadvantage also.

LLCs and International Business

Although LLCs emerged in the United States only in 1977, with the passage of the Wyoming LLC statute, they have been in existence for over a century in other areas. They were first allowed in Germany, which passed legislation in 1892 providing for a form of business called a *Gesellschaft mit beschranker Haftung* (GmbH), or "company with limited liability." Over the next few decades, the LLC form of enterprise spread to Portugal (1901), Panama (1917), Brazil (1919), Chile (1923), France (1925), Turkey (1926), Cuba (1929), Argentina (1932), Mexico (1934), Belgium (1935), Switzerland (1936), and Italy (1936).

Part of the impetus behind creating LLCs in this country is that it allows foreign investors to become LLC members. Moreover, many potential foreign investors are familiar with the LLC form and feel comfortable with it. Generally, in an era increasingly characterized by global business efforts and investments, the LLC offers U.S. firms and potential investors from other countries opportunities and flexibility greater than those available through partnerships or corporations.[b]

b. For further details on the history and development of LLCs, see Philip P. Whynott and William D. Bagley, *The Limited Liability Company: The Better Alternative* (Cheyenne, Wyo.: Pioneer Printing, 1992).

all retail sales and an increasing part of the gross national product of the United States are generated by private franchises. A **franchise** is any arrangement in which the owner of a trademark, a trade name, or a copyright licenses others to use the trademark, trade name, or copyright in the selling of goods or services. As a **franchisee** (a purchaser of a franchise), you are generally legally independent, but at the same time you are economically dependent on the integrated business system of the **franchisor** (the seller of the franchise). In other words, you can operate as an independent businessperson but still obtain the advantages of a regional or national organization. Well-known franchises include McDonald's, KFC, and Burger King.

FRANCHISEE
One receiving a license to use another's (the franchisor's) trademark, trade name, or copyright in the sale of goods and services.

FRANCHISOR
One licensing another (the franchisee) to use his or her trademark, trade name, or copyright in the sale of goods or services.

Types of Franchises

Franchises can take the form of distributorships, chain-style business operations, or manufacturing or processing-plant arrangements. We briefly describe these here.

Distributorship A *distributorship* occurs when a manufacturing concern (franchisor) licenses a dealer (franchisee) to sell its product. Often, a distributorship covers an exclusive territory. An example of this franchise is an automobile dealership.

Chain-Style Business Operation A *chain-style business operation* exists when a franchise operates under a franchisor's trade name and is identified as a member of a select group of dealers that engages in the franchisor's business. The franchisee is generally required to follow standardized or prescribed methods of operations. Often, the franchisor requires that the franchisee maintain certain standards of operation. In addition, sometimes the franchisee is obligated to deal exclusively with the franchisor to obtain materials and supplies. Examples of this type of franchise are McDonald's and most other fast-food chains.

Manufacturing or Processing-Plant Arrangement A *manufacturing or processing-plant arrangement* occurs when the franchisor transmits to the franchisee the essential ingredients or formula to make a particular product. The franchisee then markets it either at wholesale or at retail in accordance with the franchisor's standards. Examples of this franchise are Coca-Cola and other soft-drink bottling companies.

Franchise Agreement

The franchise relationship is defined by a contract between the franchisor and the franchisee. Each franchise relationship and each industry has its own characteristics, so it is difficult to describe the broad range of details a franchising contract may include. The following sections, however, will define the essential characteristics of the franchise relationship.

Entering the Franchise Relationship Prospective franchisees must initially decide on the type of business they wish to undertake. Then they must obtain information about the business from the franchisor. Usually, franchisors have numerous statistics and market studies available for prospective franchisees to examine. Of course, people who acquire franchised businesses vary greatly in their degrees of business knowledge. Some are experienced businesspersons with a firm grasp of the economic realities of how to operate a franchise. Others have no business experience. Obviously, the inexperienced franchisee must rely heavily on the franchisor in evaluating and setting up the initial business organization.

What type of franchise is McDonald's and most other fast food chains?

Paying for the Franchise The franchisee ordinarily pays an initial fee or lump-sum price for the franchise license (the privilege of being granted a franchise). This fee is separate from the various products that the franchisee purchases from or through the franchisor. In some industries, the franchisor relies heavily on the initial sale of the franchise for realizing a profit. In other industries, the continued dealing between the parties brings profit to both. In most situations, the franchisor will receive a stated percentage of the annual sales or annual volume of business done by the franchisee. The franchise agreement may also require the franchisee to pay a percentage of advertising costs and certain administrative expenses.

Location and Business Organization of the Franchise Typically, the franchisor will determine the territory to be served. The franchise agreement may specify whether the premises for the business must be leased or purchased outright. In some cases, construction of a building is necessary to meet the terms of the agreement.

Certainly the agreement will specify whether the franchisor supplies equipment and furnishings for the premises or whether this is the responsibility of the franchisee. When the franchise is a service operation, such as a motel, the contract often provides that the franchisor will establish certain standards for the facility and will make inspections to ensure that the standards are being maintained in order to protect the franchise's name and reputation.

The business organization of the franchisee is of great concern to the franchisor. Depending on the terms of the franchise agreement, the franchisor may specify particular requirements for the form and capital structure of the business. The franchise agreement can provide that standards of operation—relating to such aspects of the business as sales quotas, quality, and record keeping—be met by the franchisee. Furthermore, a franchisor may wish to retain stringent control over the training of personnel involved in the operation and over administrative aspects of the business. Although the day-to-day operation of the franchise business is normally left up to the franchisee, the franchise agreement may provide for whatever amount of supervision and control the parties agree on.

One area of franchises that causes a great deal of conflict is the territorial exclusivity of the franchise. Many franchise agreements, while they do define the territory allotted to a particular franchise, specifically state that the franchise is nonexclusive. As discussed in this chapter's *Business Law in Action*, the ramifications of nonexclusivity can be severe, because nonexclusivity allows the franchisor to establish additional franchises in the territory of an existing franchisee. The following case illustrates this problem.

Case 24.1 

IMPERIAL MOTORS, INC. v. CHRYSLER CORP.

United States District Court,
District of Massachusetts, 1983.
559 F.Supp. 1312.

HISTORICAL AND SOCIAL SETTING *The first gasoline-driven automobile was built in Europe in 1886. Within a decade, Henry Ford and others had built automobiles powered by internal combustion engines. By 1920, there were more than eighty automobile manufacturers, including Ford Motor Company, General Motors Corporation, and Willys-Overland Motors Company. Mass-production techniques made automobiles affordable for persons at all income levels. The low prices, combined with improvements in the roads, stimulated demand and hence production. New business opportunities emerged on a wide scale. The automobile industry created new jobs and fueled the development of other products, including rubber, oil, steel, textiles, paint, and machinery. By 1925, Willys-Overland had evolved into Chrysler Corporation. By the end of the decade, Ford, General Motors, and Chrysler were the leaders of the automobile industry, which had become the largest industry in the United States. Sales of automobiles continued to rise, which delighted the members of a new profession—the automobile dealer. By the late 1970s, however, Chrysler was in financial trouble.*

Case 24.1—Continued

FACTS In 1976, Imperial Motors, Inc., entered into direct-dealer agreements for Chrysler and Plymouth dealerships with the Chrysler Corporation. The written agreements explicitly provided that Imperial would *not* have the right to an exclusive dealership for a four-town area of South Carolina. The Chrysler district manager orally assured Imperial, however, that Imperial's Chrysler-Plymouth dealership would be the only one in these four towns. In August of 1976, Chrysler allowed another Chrysler-Plymouth dealer, Carroll Motors, to move to a new showroom seven miles from Imperial's location. Imperial claimed that Chrysler, by approving the relocation of Carroll Motors, had violated the Automobile Dealers' Franchise Act of 1956. This federal statute gives to an auto dealer a federal cause of action against an automobile manufacturer who fails to act in good faith in complying with the terms and provisions of the franchise or in terminating the franchise. Chrysler moved for summary judgment, claiming that the Automobile Dealers' Franchise Act covered written franchise agreements only.

ISSUE Had Chrysler violated the Automobile Dealers' Franchise Act by disregarding its oral promise to Imperial?

DECISION No. The court upheld Chrysler's motion for summary judgment and ruled that Chrysler, by allowing a franchise to Carroll in the same area, had not violated the Automobile Dealers' Franchise Act.

REASON The court noted that the Automobile Dealers' Franchise Act covers only those actions of a franchisor that amount to a "failure * * * to act in good faith in performing or complying with any of the terms or provisions of the franchise, or in terminating, cancelling, or not renewing the franchise with a dealer." Good faith is narrowly defined as "the duty of each party * * * to act in a fair and equitable manner toward each other so as to guaranty the other party freedom from coercion, intimidation, or threats of coercion or intimidation by the other party." The court said the act explicitly defines a franchise as a "written agreement," and thus oral promises are not part of a franchise agreement and do not form the basis of a claim of bad faith. Thus, Imperial was left unprotected by the franchise agreement as far as territorial exclusivity was concerned.

Price and Quality Controls of the Franchise Franchises provide the franchisor with an outlet for the firm's goods and services. Depending on the nature of the business, the franchisor may require the franchisee to purchase certain supplies from the franchisor at an established price.[2] A franchisor cannot, however, set the prices at which the franchisee will resell the goods, because this is a violation of state or federal antitrust laws, or both. A franchisor can suggest retail prices but cannot insist on them. As a general rule, the validity of a provision permitting the franchisor to enforce certain quality standards is unquestioned. Because the franchisor has a legitimate interest in maintaining the quality of the product or service to protect its name and reputation, it can exercise greater control in this area than would otherwise be tolerated.

Termination of the Franchise Arrangement The duration of the franchise is a matter to be determined between the parties. Generally, a franchise will start out for a short period, such as a year, so that the franchisee and the franchisor can determine whether they want to stay in business with one another. Usually, the franchise agreement will specify that termination must be "for cause," such as death or disability of the franchisee, insolvency of the franchisee, breach of the franchise agreement, or failure to meet specified sales quotas. Most franchise contracts provide that notice of termination must be given. If no set time for termination is specified, then a reasonable time, with notice, will be implied. A franchisee must be given reasonable time to wind up the business—that is, to do the accounting and return the copyright or trademark or any other property of the franchisor.

2. Although a franchisor can require franchisees to purchase supplies from it, requiring a franchisee to purchase exclusively from the franchisor may violate federal antitrust laws (see Chapter 30). For two landmark cases in these areas, see *United States v. Arnold, Schwinn & Co.*, 388 U.S. 365, 87 S.Ct. 1856, 18 L.Ed.2d 1249 (1967), and *Fortner Enterprises, Inc. v. U.S. Steel. Corp.*, 394 U.S. 495, 89 S.Ct. 1252, 22 L.Ed.2d 495 (1969).

Business Law in Action

A Case of Territorial Encroachment

C. R. Weaver purchased franchises from Burger King Corporation (BKC) between 1976 and 1988 to operate two Burger King restaurants in the Great Falls, Montana, area and one in a nearby town. Weaver not only paid for the franchises but also paid for furniture, fixtures, and land to be used as a drive-through area and a playground for one of the restaurants, as well as various other construction and remodeling expenses. In all, according to Weaver, he spent over a million dollars on behalf of the three restaurants that he operated.

Business was profitable for Weaver until 1989, but in that year a competing BKC franchise opened on Malmstrom Air Force Base, which is situated on the outskirts of Great Falls. BKC had granted to the Army and Air Force Exchange Service (AAFES) the right to operate a Burger King restaurant on the base in accordance with a worldwide contract entered into between the AAFES and BKC in 1984. That agreement allowed the AAFES to unilaterally choose the sites or bases on which to place Burger King restaurants. The new franchise at Malmstrom caused profits to decline at both of Weaver's Great Falls restaurants. Concluding that BKC had breached their franchise agreements, Weaver refused to pay BKC the customary rents, fees, and related charges. When BKC sued Weaver for breach of the franchise agreements, Weaver counterclaimed that BKC had, among other things, breached the covenant of good faith and fair dealing.

In deciding whether to grant BKC's motion for summary judgment, the court looked closely at the two franchise agreements for the Great Falls restaurants. One agreement made no specific mention of either party's "territorial rights." The other did mention these rights, providing that "[t]his franchise is for the specified location only and does not in any way grant or imply any area, market or territorial rights proprietary to franchisee." Relying on this language, BKC argued that it had "specifically contracted for the right to place a franchise at any location, regardless of the cannibalization effect on another BKC franchisee." BKC further maintained that had Weaver "desired an 'exclusive territory' upon which BKC could not encroach," then Weaver "should have negotiated for such a term." Finally, BKC contended that the court "should not overstep its bounds and 'rewrite' the franchise agreements to include terms not agreed to at the time the contracts were signed."

Courts are sometimes quick to perceive unfairness, and in this case, the court's sympathies were clearly on Weaver's side. In response to BKC's seemingly correct arguments, the court stated that even though the agreements specifically denied territorial rights to Weaver, this did not mean that the agreements "expressly authorize BKC to place a Burger King restaurant at any location it wishes." The court emphasized that "to construe the franchise agreements in such a fashion would run afoul of the principle that a contract contains such implied conditions as are necessary to make sense of the contract. Taken to its logical extreme, BKC's construction of the franchise agreements would entitle it to set up a competing franchise next door to an existing franchise the day after the existing franchise had opened for business. If that were the plain and intended meaning of the 'territorial rights' language contained in the two franchise agreements, this Court entertains serious doubts about whether a rational franchisee would ever enter into a franchise agreement with BKC." The court denied BKC's motion for summary judgment, holding that Weaver had a cause of action based on the implied covenant of good faith and fair dealing and that the case should therefore go to trial.[a]

a. *Burger King Corporation v. Weaver,* 798 F.Supp. 684 (S.D.Fla. 1992).

The growth in franchise operations has outdistanced the law of franchising, and it is in the area of franchise termination that the lack of statutory law and case law is felt most keenly by the franchisee. Some federal protection is given to franchisees, however, under the Automobile Dealers' Franchise Act of 1956 and the Petroleum Marketing Practices Act of 1979; and increasingly, states are enacting laws governing various aspects of franchise relationships. Courts have also developed a growing body of case law to guide them in deciding issues involving allegedly wrongful franchise terminations. Generally, both statutory and case law emphasize the importance of good faith in terminating a franchise relationship. In determining whether a franchisor has acted in good faith when terminating a franchise agreement, the courts need to balance the rights of both parties. The following case illustrates this point.

Case 24.2
CAROLINA TRUCK & BODY CO. v. GENERAL MOTORS CORP.

Court of Appeals of North Carolina, 1991.
102 N.C.App. 262,
402 S.E.2d 135.

HISTORICAL AND SOCIAL SETTING *In the first decades of the twentieth century, motor vehicles manufactured by Ford Motor Company were the best-selling vehicles. Ford's methods were copied by its competitors, including General Motors Corporation (GMC), and by the mid-1920s, GMC began to surpass Ford. Ford's genius lay in technology and the application of mass-production techniques. GMC's genius lay in organization and marketing. Over the years, GMC acquired subsidiaries and entered into joint ventures or otherwise combined with other firms, including foreign manufacturers. By the 1950s, GMC had become the largest manufacturer of motor vehicles in the world and was enjoying higher profits than any other U.S. corporation. In the next decades, automobile production in the United States remained higher than that in any other nation, but truck production did not. In 1968, for example, U.S. manufacturers produced 8.8 million automobiles and nearly 2 million buses and trucks. In contrast, Japanese manufacturers produced less than 25 percent as many automobiles but the same number of trucks.*

FACTS Carolina Truck & Body Company (Carolina) had been a General Motors Corporation (GMC) franchisee since 1950, selling light-duty and medium-duty GMC trucks. In 1985, as an addendum to a renewal of their franchise agreement, Carolina and GMC agreed that Carolina would have the right to purchase and sell, for a period of five years, new heavy-duty GMC trucks. The addendum also stated that the addendum would remain in effect "until cancelled." Because of its declining share in the heavy-duty truck market, GMC decided to enter into a joint venture with Volvo Truck Corporation in the area of heavy-duty truck manufacturing. GMC notified Carolina and its other heavy-duty–truck franchise dealers in late 1986 that the heavy-duty–truck addendum would be canceled in December 1987 owing to GMC's plans to cease manufacturing heavy-duty trucks. Carolina unsuccessfully sought to obtain a franchise from Volvo GM (the new joint venture) for heavy-duty trucks. Carolina sued GMC for wrongful termination of the franchise. GMC claimed that it was losing money in the manufacture of heavy-duty trucks, had no control over Volvo GM decisions about franchises, and had not terminated the franchise in bad faith. The trial court entered a judgment in GMC's favor, and Carolina Truck appealed.

ISSUE Had GMC terminated the addendum to the franchise agreement in good faith?

DECISION Yes. The appellate court affirmed the trial court's judgment.

REASON The court noted that the state franchise statute provided "that a manufacturer may cancel a franchise if discontinuing the sale of the product line and that this action is for 'good cause.'" In the eyes of the court, GMC met the "good cause" requirement. "We cannot conceive," stated the court, "that the Legislature would enact a statute prohibiting a manufacturer from cancelling a franchise agreement if it determined to stop manufacturing that product because it was unprofitable. * * * Clearly, the Legislature does not require a manufacturer to continue on a road to certain bankruptcy by requiring the manufacturer to continue to make and sell unprofitable models of cars or trucks." The court concluded that GMC had also met the requirement of "good faith," which was defined by state statute as "honesty in fact and the observation of reasonable commercial standards of fair dealing in the trade." GMC had good cause to terminate the arrangement, treated Carolina no differently than its other dealers selling GMC heavy-duty trucks, and had fully complied with the franchise statute's notice requirements for termination.

ETHICAL CONSIDERATIONS *Often, we tend to sympathize with the franchisee when a franchise arrangement is terminated unilaterally by the franchisor. We tend to assume that the cancellation of a franchise agreement for "good cause" can only occur if the franchisee has substantially violated the franchise agreement. This case offers us a view from the other side—that of the franchisor facing declining profits and taking action, in a commercially reasonable manner, to reduce the adverse effects of an unprofitable undertaking. By defining "good cause" to include declining profits, the court acknowledged the economic realities facing the franchisor.*

Application

Law and the Franchisee

A franchise arrangement appeals to many prospective businesspersons who want independence and yet feel more comfortable with an established product or service and a management network that is regional or national in scope and that has been in place for some time. Franchises also have a high survival rate (90 percent)—at least relative to that of small businesses (20 percent). Franchise operations may, nonetheless, lead to difficulties, as well as financial loss to the franchisee.

Consider the franchise fee. Virtually all franchise contracts require a franchise fee payable up front or in installments. Some franchise arrangements hide franchise-fee payments as part of the price charged to the franchisee for goods or services that have to be purchased from the franchisor. In other words, if you as a franchisee are required to purchase paper napkins with a logo from the franchisor at a 20 percent premium over the wholesale price, then you are implicitly paying a franchise fee. Additionally, your required contribution to advertising monies administered by the franchisor may be in excess of the benefits that your franchise operation receives from the advertising. The difference again is an implicit franchise fee.

A major economic consequence, usually of a negative nature, will occur if your franchise agreement is terminated by the franchisor. The courts have not made a clear statement as to what a franchisee's rights are upon termination. Some courts, for example, have held that if a franchise investment is substantial and the relationship between the parties has been established, it cannot be terminated until a reasonable period of time has elapsed. What is considered to be a reasonable time period depends on the circumstances in each case, such as the amount of preliminary promotional expenditures made, the length of time in operation, the prospects of forfeiting profits, and the actual profitability of the franchise during its operation.

To avoid many economic, as well as legal, problems, it is imperative that you, as a potential franchisee—before paying for the franchise—obtain all of the relevant details of the business and of the franchise agreement.

Checklist for the Franchisee

- ☐ 1. Find out all you can about the franchisor: How long has the franchisor been in business? How profitable is the business? Is there a healthy market for the product?
- ☐ 2. Obtain the most recent financial statement from the franchisor and a complete description of the business.
- ☐ 3. Obtain a clear and complete statement of all fees that you will be required to pay.
- ☐ 4. Will the franchisor help you in training management and employees? With promotion and advertising? By supplying capital or credit? In finding a good location for your business?
- ☐ 5. Visit other franchisees in the same business. Ask them about their experiences with the product, the market, and the franchisor.
- ☐ 6. Evaluate your training and experience in the business upon which you are about to embark. Are they sufficient to ensure success as a franchisee?
- ☐ 7. Carefully examine the franchise contract provisions relating to termination of the franchise agreement. Are they specific enough to allow you to sue for breach of contract in the event the franchisor wrongfully terminates the contract? Find out how many franchises have been terminated in the past several years.
- ☐ 8. Have an attorney familiar with franchise law examine the contract before you sign it.
- ☐ 9. Will you be required to open additional outlets according to a fixed schedule?
- ☐ 10. Will you have an exclusive geographical territory and, if so, for how many years?
- ☐ 11. Finally, what can the franchisor do for you that you cannot do for yourself?

❖ Key Terms

corporation 586
entrepreneur 584
franchise 591
franchisee 591
franchisor 591
general partner 585
limited liability company (LLC) 590
limited partner 585
limited partnership 585
partnership 585
sole proprietorship 584

❖ Chapter Summary: The Entrepreneur's Options

FORM	ESSENTIAL CHARACTERISTICS
Sole Proprietorship	1. The simplest form of business; used by anyone who does business without creating an organization. The owner is the business. 2. The owner pays personal income taxes on all profits. 3. The owner is personally liable for all business debts.
General Partnership	1. Created by agreement of the parties. 2. Not treated as an entity except for limited purposes. 3. Partners have unlimited liability for partnership debts. 4. Each partner has an equal voice in management, unless otherwise provided for in the partnership agreement. 5. Capital contribution of each partner is determined by agreement. 6. Each partner pays a pro rata share of income taxes on the net profits of the partnership, whether or not they are distributed; the partnership files an information return only. 7. Terminated by agreement, action of partner (e.g., withdrawal), operation of law (e.g., death or bankruptcy), or court decree.
Limited Partnership	1. Must be formed in compliance with statutory requirements. 2. Consists of one or more general partners and one or more limited partners. 3. Only general partners can participate in management. Limited partners have no voice in management. 4. General partners have unlimited liability for partnership losses; limited partners are liable only to the extent of their contributions.
Corporation	1. Created by state-issued charter. 2. Legal entity separate and distinct from its owners. 3. Shareholders have limited liability—that is, they are not personally liable for the debts of the corporation. 4. Shareholders elect directors, who set policy and appoint officers to manage corporate affairs. 5. The corporation pays income tax on net profits; shareholders pay income tax on disbursed dividends. 6. Can have perpetual existence.
Other Business Forms	1. *Joint venture*—An organization created by two or more persons in contemplation of a limited activity or a single transaction. Otherwise, similar to a partnership. 2. *Syndicate*—An investment group that undertakes to finance a particular project; may exist as a corporation or as a general or limited partnership. 3. *Joint stock company*—A business form similar to a corporation in some respects (perpetual existence, transferable shares of stock, management by directors and officers) but otherwise resembling a partnership. 4. *Business trust*—Created by a written trust agreement that sets forth the interests of the beneficiaries and obligations and powers of the trustee(s). Similar to a corporation in many respects. Beneficiaries are not personally liable for the debts or obligations of the business trust.

❖ Chapter Summary: The Entrepreneur's Options—Continued

Other Business Forms—Continued	5. *Cooperative*—An association organized to provide an economic service, without profit, to its members. May take the form of a corporation or a partnership. 6. *Limited liability company (LLC)*—A hybrid form of business organization that has the limited-liability feature of corporations but the tax benefits of partnerships. Unlike limited partners, LLC members participate in management. Unlike shareholders in S corporations, members of LLCs may be corporations or partnerships, are not restricted in number, and may be nonresident aliens.
Private Franchises	1. *Types of franchises:* a. Distributorship (e.g., automobile dealerships). b. Chain-style operation (e.g., fast-food chains). c. Manufacturing/processing-plant arrangement (e.g., soft-drink bottling companies such as Coca-Cola). 2. *The franchise agreement:* a. Ordinarily requires the franchisee (purchaser) to pay a price for the franchise license. b. Specifies the territory to be served by the franchisee's firm. c. May require the franchisee to purchase certain supplies from the franchisor at an established price. d. May require the franchisee to abide by certain standards of quality relating to product or service offered but cannot set retail resale price. e. Usually provides for the date and/or conditions of termination of the franchise arrangement.

❖ Questions and Case Problems

24-1. Characteristics of Forms of Business Organizations. Which form of business organization is the simplest? Which form arises from an agreement between two or more persons to carry on a business for profit? Which form consists of shareholders and is managed by officers appointed by a board of directors?

24-2. Characteristics of Forms of Business Organizations Generally, the liability of a limited partner or a corporate shareholder is limited to the amount of his or her investment. Under what circumstances might a limited partner or a shareholder be held liable for the obligations of his or her partnership or corporation?

24-3. Characteristics of Forms of Business Organizations. In each of the following situations, determine whether Georgio's Fashions is a sole proprietorship, a partnership, or a corporation.

(a) Georgio's defaults on a payment to supplier Dee Creations. Dee sues Georgio's and each of the owners of Georgio's personally for payment of the debt.

(b) Georgio's raises $200,000 through the sale of shares of its stock.

(c) At tax time, Georgio's files an information return to the Internal Revenue Service (IRS) declaring the tax liability of the owners of the business but does not pay taxes directly to the IRS on the business profits.

(d) At tax time, Georgio's files a tax return with the IRS and pays taxes on the net profits of the firm.

24-4. Choice of Business Form. Suppose Jorge, Marta, and Jocelyn are college graduates, and Jorge has come up with an idea for a new product that he believes could make the three of them very rich. His idea is to manufacture beer dispensers for home use and market them to consumers throughout the Midwest. Jorge's personal experience qualifies him to be both first-line supervisor and general manager of the new firm. Marta is a born salesperson. Jocelyn has little interest in sales or management but would like to invest a large sum of money that she has inherited from her aunt. What factors should Jorge, Marta, and Jocelyn consider in deciding which form of business organization to adopt?

24-5. Business Forms and Liability. Assume that Faraway Corp. is considering entering into two contracts, one with a joint stock company that distributes home products east of the Mississippi River and the other with a business trust formed by a number of sole proprietors who are sellers of home products on the West Coast. Both contracts involve large capital outlays for Faraway, which will supply each business with beer dispensers. In both business organizations, at least two shareholders or beneficiaries are personally wealthy, but each business organization has limited financial resources. The owner-managers of Faraway are not familiar with either form of business organization. Because each form resembles a corporation, they are concerned about whether they will be able to collect payments from the wealthy members of the business organizations in the event that either business organization breaches the contract by failing to make the deferred payments. Discuss fully Faraway's concern.

24-6. Franchise Termination. The H. C. Blackwell Co. was a truck dealership owned by the Blackwell family. In 1961, they had purchased a franchise from Kenworth Truck Co. to sell Kenworth trucks, and the franchise agreement had been renewed several times. In November of 1975, the Blackwells began negotiations with Kenworth to renew the recently expired franchise, and disagreements arose concerning the franchise. On February 4, 1976, Kenworth wrote to Blackwell that the franchise would be terminated in ninety days unless Blackwell met twelve specific demands made by Kenworth. In trying to meet these demands—which included increased sales and capital improvements at the dealership—Blackwell spent approximately $90,000. By the end of the ninety-day period, however, the demands had not been met, so Kenworth terminated the franchise. Blackwell sued Kenworth for damages on the ground that Kenworth had wrongfully terminated the franchise agreement and, in so doing, had violated the Automobile Dealers' Franchise Act. During the trial, Kenworth's regional sales manager stated that the demands imposed by Kenworth upon Blackwell would have taken at least a year to meet. Did Kenworth wrongfully terminate the franchise under the Automobile Dealers' Franchise Act? [*H. C. Blackwell Co., Inc. v. Kenworth Truck Co.*, 620 F.2d 104 (5th Cir. 1980)]

24-7. Franchise Termination. In 1981, the Huangs entered into a franchise agreement with Holiday Inns, Inc., under which the Huangs agreed to adhere to the quality standards established by Holiday Inns and to comply in every respect with the Holiday Inns standards manual. In November of 1983, the district director of Holiday Inns made a courtesy inspection that revealed cracked windows, damaged and discolored walls, inoperative smoke detectors, and numerous other indications that the Huangs were not maintaining the established Holiday Inn quality standards in accordance with the franchise agreement. A formal inspection in February of 1984 revealed no significant improvement in quality standards, and the hotel was given an official rating of "unacceptable." The Huangs, who had been given detailed reports concerning the findings of both inspections, were advised that if the noted deficiencies were not remedied within sixty days, Holiday Inns would have grounds to terminate the franchise. When an inspection in April of 1984 revealed that the deficiencies had not been cured, Holiday Inns notified the Huangs that the franchise would be terminated on July 30 unless the deficiencies were remedied by June 28. The Huangs, who in May had begun renovations on the hotel costing $55,000, requested a ninety-day extension to the June 28 deadline, which Holiday Inns refused to grant. The Huangs then petitioned the court for a preliminary injunction against Holiday Inns' termination of the franchise, claiming that Holiday Inns had acted "capriciously and arbitrarily" by (1) not stating precisely the nature of the deficiencies and what was required to make repairs and improvements and (2) not giving the Huangs a reasonable time in which to remedy the deficiencies. Discuss fully whether Holiday Inns should be enjoined from terminating the franchise, given these circumstances. [*Huang v. Holiday Inns, Inc.*, 594 F.Supp. 352 (C.D.Cal.1984)]

24-8. Franchise Termination. In 1953, Atlantic Richfield Co. (ARCO) and Razumic signed a printed form titled "Dealer Lease." The agreement, which referred to the parties as lessor and lessee, authorized Razumic to operate an ARCO service station and provided, among other things, for ARCO's signs and trade name to be prominently displayed at the service station and for ARCO gasoline and other related products to be sold. The agreement detailed other aspects of the parties' business relationship, including Razumic's obligation to operate the service station in such a manner as to reflect favorably on Atlantic's goodwill. These basic terms were in all renewal agreements made by the parties over the years. In 1973, ARCO notified Razumic that the agreement was being terminated and gave him thirty days to vacate the premises. Razumic refused, and ARCO filed suit to force termination of the agreement. Did the "Dealer Lease" constitute a franchise agreement? If so—as the Petroleum Marketing Practices Act had not yet been passed when this case was decided—on what grounds might the court hold that ARCO could not terminate the franchise at will? [*Atlantic Richfield Co. v. Razumic*, 480 Pa. 366, 390 A.2d 736 (1978)]

24-9. Joint Ventures. Gustave Peterson contacted his family doctor, Leland Reichelt, complaining of abdominal pain. The doctor recommended gallbladder surgery. Dr. George Fortier performed the surgery, and Dr. Reichelt assisted. It was Dr. Reichelt's normal practice to refer patients to Dr. Fortier for surgery, and each doctor charged the patient separately for his services. During the operation, a metal clip was inadvertently left inside Peterson's abdominal cavity. It eventually formed a stone, which later caused Peterson chest and gastric pain. Peterson repeatedly complained to Dr. Reichelt, who diagnosed the problem as related to either a hernia or stress. Peterson finally sought the advice of another physician, who, upon performing surgery, discovered the metal clip. Peterson filed suit against both Dr. Reichelt and Dr. Fortier for malpractice under the theory that Fortier and Reichelt were engaged in a joint enterprise (joint venture). Discuss whether the two doctors were joint venturers. [*Peterson v. Fortier*, 406 N.W.2d 563 (Minn.App. 1987)]

24-10. Good Faith in Franchising Relationships. Ernst and Barbara Larese entered into a ten-year franchise agreement with Creamland Dairies, Inc. The agreement provided that the franchisee "shall not assign, transfer or sublet this franchise, or any of [the] rights under this agreement, without the prior written consent of Area Franchisor [Creamland] and Baskin Robbins, any such authorized assignment, transfer or subletting being null and without effect." The Lareses attempted to sell their franchise rights in February and August of 1979, but Creamland refused to consent to the sales. The Lareses brought suit, alleging that Creamland had interfered with their contractual relations with the prospective buyers by unreasonably withholding its consent; they claimed that Creamland had a duty to act in good faith and in a commercially reasonable manner when a franchisee sought to transfer its rights under the franchise agreement. Creamland contended that the contract gave it an unqualified right to refuse to consent to proposed sales of the franchise rights. Which party prevailed? Explain. [*Larese v. Creamland Dairies, Inc.*, 767 F.2d 716 (10th Cir. 1985)]

24-11. Franchise Termination. AB & B, Inc., sold wines produced by Banfi Products, Inc., under a distributorship agreement. In 1986, AB & B experienced a severe decline in the demand for one of Banfi's wines, Riunite, mostly because of a recall of that wine resulting from contamination problems in the fall of 1985. Because of decreasing sales, Banfi sent a letter to AB & B, which stated as follows: "You are aware that

Banfi's corporate policy requires our distributors to maintain no less than a 60-day inventory of products. Not only are you out of stock on most items in our line, but our records indicate that the last activity on your account was a credit in January of 1986, and your last purchase was in April of 1985. Your lack of interest in and support of the Banfi line leaves us no alternative but to terminate our distributorship relationship with you, effective sixty (60) days from your receipt of this notice." In fact, AB & B held, on average, a ninety-six-day inventory of Banfi wines. In support of its allegation that AB & B showed a "lack of interest in and support of the Banfi line," Banfi had indicated that AB & B routinely failed to send a representative to Banfi's sales meetings. Yet there was no evidence that those meetings were mandatory, and AB & B always received notebooks from Banfi containing the information from those meetings. Although AB & B requested a meeting with Banfi to discuss these issues, Banfi terminated the franchise relationship without responding to AB & B's request. In AB & B's lawsuit against Banfi for wrongful termination of the franchise relationship, what should the court decide? Discuss. [*AB & B, Inc. v. Banfi Products, Inc.*, 71 Ohio App.3d 650, 594 N.E.2d 1151 (1991)]

A QUESTION OF ETHICS AND SOCIAL RESPONSIBILITY

24-12. *Eugene Anderson, an attorney, had been a partner of a law firm in Burlington, Iowa, for thirteen years when he decided to withdraw from the firm and establish his own tax law practice. Many of the firm's clients, as well as one of his associates and two secretaries, chose to follow Anderson. Relations were fairly congenial during Anderson's departure, but tension later arose over the buy-out price of Anderson's partnership interest, which the partnership determined to be worth $114,243.99. Of that amount, $38,743 represented the cash Anderson had initially invested in the firm (his net purchase price), and the remainder signified the growth in the value of his partnership interest. Under the terms of the partnership agreement in effect at the time of Anderson's departure, the firm was obligated to pay a departing partner the net purchase price but could reduce (or eliminate entirely) payment for the growth value of the partner's partnership interest if the remaining partners determined that the withdrawing partner had "committed an act which is detrimental to the partnership which affects the value of the remaining partners' interest in the partnership." After his departure, the firm paid Anderson $38,743 but refused to pay him for his interest in the firm above the net purchase price on the grounds that Anderson had committed acts detrimental to the partnership. The detrimental acts cited were Anderson's continued practice in Burlington in competition with the firm, his taking of an associate and two secretaries with him, and the substantial number of clients retained by Anderson and the resulting loss to the firm. Given these facts, consider the following questions.* [Anderson v. Aspelmeier, Fisch, Power, Warner & Engberg, *461 N.W.2d 598 (Iowa 1990)*]

1. In Anderson's lawsuit against the firm to recover the remainder of his partnership interest, the trial court held that the "detriment" clause of the partnership agreement was in effect a covenant not to compete (see Chapter 10). Do you agree with this conclusion?
2. The Iowa Code of Professional Responsibility (an ethical code of conduct by which attorneys must abide) prohibits the inclusion of covenants not to compete in partnership or employment agreements. The purpose of this rule is to protect the client's freedom to choose or replace a lawyer at will. Apparently, the law firm in this case attempted to "punish" Anderson by refusing to pay him the full value of his partnership interest, because he continued to practice law in the same city and the clients chose to follow him to his new practice. Does this attempt counter the policy that clients should have freedom of choice?
3. Do you think that it is fair to law partnerships not to allow them to include covenants not to compete in their partnership agreements? How can a law partnership protect itself against the losses that are incurred when a partner, such as Anderson in this case, withdraws from the partnership and is followed by a significant number of the firm's clients? How would you argue in favor of the law firm in this case? What social or ethical considerations, if any, are being traded off to ensure freedom of choice on the part of clients?

FOR CRITICAL ANALYSIS

24-13. *As indicated in this chapter, the law permits individuals the option of organizing their business enterprises in many different forms. What policy interests are served by granting entrepreneurs these options? Would it be better if the law required that everyone organize his or her business in the same form? Discuss.*

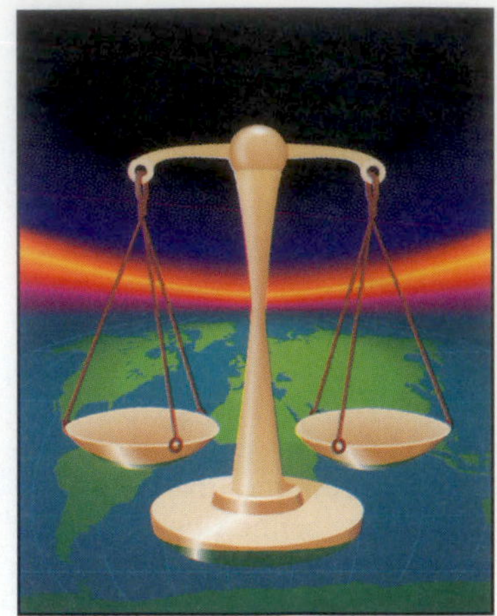

Chapter 25

Partnerships

"Many forms of conduct permissible in a workaday world for those acting at arm's length, are forbidden to those bound by fiduciary ties."

Benjamin Cardozo, 1870–1938
(Associate justice of the United States Supreme Court, 1932–1938)

As we pointed out in the introduction to this unit, agency law governs relationships arising in both partnerships and corporations. Partnership law derives from agency law because each partner is considered an agent of every other partner. Therefore, the agency concepts outlined in Chapter 23 apply—specifically, the imputation of knowledge of, and responsibility for, acts done within the scope of the partnership relationship. Like agents, in their relationship to one another, partners are bound by the "fiduciary ties" referred to by Justice Cardozo in the opening quotation.

In one important way, however, partnership law is distinct from agency law. A partnership is based on a voluntary contract between two or more competent persons who agree to place money, labor, and skill in a business with the understanding that profits and losses will be proportionately shared. In a nonpartnership agency relationship, the agent usually does not have an ownership interest in the business, nor is she or he obliged to bear a portion of the ordinary business losses.

The Uniform Partnership Act (UPA) governs the operation of partnerships *in the absence of express agreement* and has done much to reduce controversies in the law relating to partnerships. Except for Louisiana, all of the states, as well as the District of Columbia, have adopted the UPA. The UPA is now in the process of being revised. The revised UPA significantly changes the rules governing partnership termination by providing that a partnership no longer terminates every time a partner withdraws from the partnership. The entire text of the UPA is presented in Appendix D of this book.

A special type of partnership, called a *limited partnership* (examined in the latter part of this chapter), involves one or more *general partners* who assume the management of the partnership and also therefore assume full liability for all debts of the partnership. In addition, there are *limited partners*, who may contribute cash or other property and own an interest in the firm but are not allowed to involve themselves in management responsibilities. The limited partners are not personally liable for partnership debts beyond the amount that they have agreed to invest. An early form of the limited partnership, the *commenda* of the Middle Ages, is the subject of this chapter's *Landmark in the Law.*

❖ Definition of Partnership

Conflicts commonly arise over whether a business enterprise is legally a partnership, especially in the absence of a formal, written partnership agreement. Under the UPA, a *partnership* is defined as "an association of two or more persons to carry on as co-owners a business for profit" [UPA 6(1)]. In resolving disputes over whether

Landmark in the Law

The Medieval *Commenda*

It goes without saying that all businesses require capital. But often those individuals who have capital may not wish to assume responsibility for the management of a business or for business liabilities that extend beyond the amount of their original investments. The need for an organization allowing such individuals to share in the profits without management responsibilities and with limited liability for losses was felt keenly in the later Middle Ages, when trade and commerce were expanding and merchants were accumulating capital.

During the twelfth and thirteenth centuries, most commerce was undertaken by individual merchants who traveled from market to market or from fair to fair. But as the scope of commerce widened and the volume of transactions increased, more complex forms of business arose. One of these was the *commenda*, a partnership normally involving a short-term agreement between a merchant with capital and a traveler trading overseas. In this arrangement, the resident merchant would supply capital but no management, and the traveling party would supply management but no capital. In this partnership, in practice if not in theory, liability to the resident was usually limited to the amount of the investment, as it is in modern limited partnerships. It was by means of *commenda* agreements that many merchants, particularly in northern Italy, accumulated vast profits and the excess capital that eventually led to the creation of banking firms. The problem with the *commenda* partnership was its short-term nature. Usually the contract would only cover one voyage, as merchants were apparently reluctant to invest funds on a longer-term basis.

The *commenda* was included as a form of business organization in the French Commercial Code of 1807, in Sections 23–25. Shortly thereafter, the first limited partnership acts were adopted in New York (in 1822) and in Connecticut and Pennsylvania (in 1836). In 1916, the Uniform Limited Partnership Act was issued, and it was eventually adopted by most of the states. Limited liability and lack of management responsibility for limited partners remain the essential features of limited partnership law today.

partnership status exists, courts will usually look for the following three essential elements of partnership implicit in this definition:

1. A sharing of profits and losses.
2. A joint ownership of the business.
3. An equal right in the management of the business.

A problem arises when evidence is insufficient to establish all three factors. The UPA provides a set of guidelines to be used in this event. For example, the sharing of profits and losses from a business is considered *prima facie* ("on the face of it") evidence that a partnership has been created. No such inference is made, however, if the profits were received as payment of any of the following:

"The partner of my partner is not my partner."

Roman legal maxim

1. A debt by installments or interest on a loan.
2. Wages of an employee.
3. Rent to a landlord.
4. An annuity to a widow or representative of a deceased partner.
5. A sale of goodwill of a business or property [UPA 7(4)].

Joint ownership of property, obviously, does not in and of itself create a partnership. Therefore, the fact that Ablat and Burke own real property as joint tenants or as tenants in common (forms of joint ownership, to be discussed in Chapter 33) does not establish a partnership. In fact, the sharing of gross returns and even profits from such ownership is usually not enough to create a partnership [UPA 7(2), (3)]. Thus, if Ablat and Burke jointly own a piece of rural property and lease the land to a farmer, the sharing of the profits from the farming operation conducted by the farmer in lieu of set rental payments would ordinarily not make Ablat, Burke, and the farmer partners. In sum, the sharing of profits in itself does not prove the existence of a partnership, but sharing both profits and losses usually does.

The *intent* to associate is a key element of a partnership, and one cannot join a partnership unless all other partners consent [UPA 18(g)]. In the following case, a key factor in deciding whether a partnership existed was whether the partners ever intended to associate as partners.

Case 25.1
PAOLLELA v. PAOLLELA
Superior Court of Connecticut,
Judicial District of New Haven, 1991.
42 Conn.Supp. 184,
612 A.2d 145.

HISTORICAL AND SOCIAL SETTING *One of the most important reasons for choosing to do business in the partnership form, rather than as a corporation or a sole proprietorship, concerns tax liability. Corporate profits are taxed twice—once as income realized by the corporation and once as income realized by the individuals to whom the profits are distributed. Profits from a partnership are not realized, for tax purposes, at the partnership level but flow through the partnership to the individual partners. Similarly, a sole proprietor declares all of his or her business income as personal income. But partners pay taxes only on as much of the business income as each partner is allocated according to the terms of their partnership agreement. In other words, the business income is split between two or more partners before taxes are paid. In any case, the Internal Revenue Service (and state tax authorities) must be told of the form in which a business is being operated.*

FACTS John and Linda Paollela married in November 1987. It was the second marriage for both of them. In 1988, they purchased a restaurant business and took out a loan to cover the purchase price. Both Linda and John signed the note, but the loan was secured by a house that Linda had owned prior to her marriage to John. Although the couple jointly operated the restaurant and shared in the profits, they never formed a written partnership agreement. Also, the business was listed as a sole proprietorship on the tax returns filed by the couple. Later, when John and Linda divorced, Linda claimed full ownership of the business as a sole proprietor. John argued that he and Linda had entered into a partnership and therefore he was entitled to a one-half interest in the business.

ISSUE Had John and Linda entered into a partnership?

DECISION No. The court held that the requirements for partnership status had not been met.

REASON The court could find no evidence that the parties ever truly intended to enter into a partnership. Although they shared equally in the profits, the court held that this could be attributed to the husband-wife relationship. More significant in the eyes of the court was the fact that the business was listed, for tax purposes, as a sole proprietorship instead of a partnership. Also significant was the fact that, while both parties had signed the note with the lending institution to cover the purchase price of the restaurant, it was Linda's property that secured the note. The court found yet another reason for denying John's claim that he was a partner. During the trial, John had testified that the business was not put in his name "because of the concern that his former wife would learn of it and seek alimony or support due her. It would be contrary to public policy to reward him now for this intent to evade his legal responsibilities."

❖ Partnership Characteristics

A partnership is sometimes called a *firm* or a *company*, terms that connote an entity separate and apart from its aggregate members. Sometimes the law of partnership recognizes a partnership as an *independent entity*, but for certain other purposes, the law treats it as an *aggregate of the individual partners*. At common law, a partnership was never treated as a separate legal entity. Thus, at common law a suit could never be brought by or against the firm in its own name; each individual partner had to sue or be sued. Today, most states provide specifically that the partnership can be treated as an entity for certain purposes. For example, a partnership can usually sue or be sued, collect judgments, and have all accounting procedures in the name of the partnership entity. In addition, the UPA recognizes that partnership property may be held in the name of the partnership rather than in the names of the individual partners. Finally, federal procedural laws frequently permit the partnership to be treated as an entity in such matters as suits in federal courts, bankruptcy proceedings, and informational federal tax returns.

When the partnership is not regarded as a separate legal entity, it is treated as an aggregate of the individual partners. For example, as discussed in Chapter 24, for federal income tax purposes, a partnership is not a tax-paying entity. The income and losses it incurs are passed through the partnership framework and attributed to the partners on their individual tax returns.

"Mr. Morgan buys his partners; I grow my own."

Andrew Carnegie, 1835–1918
(American industrialist and philanthropist)

❖ Partnership Formation

A partnership is ordinarily formed by an explicit agreement among the parties, although the law recognizes another form of partnership—*partnership by estoppel*—which arises when persons who are not partners represent themselves as partners when dealing with third parties. This section will describe the requirements for the creation of a partnership, including references to the liability of alleged partners.

Formalities of Partnership Formation

As a general rule, agreements to form a partnership can be oral, written, or implied by conduct. Some partnership agreements, however, must be in writing to be legally enforceable within the Statute of Frauds (discussed in Chapter 11). For example, a partnership agreement that, by its terms, is to continue for more than one year must be evidenced by a sufficient writing. Practically speaking, the provisions of any partnership agreement should always be in writing. One disadvantage of an oral agreement is that its terms are difficult to prove because a court hearing such a case must evaluate oral testimony given by persons with an interest in the eventual decision. In addition, potential problems that would have been detected in the course of drafting a written agreement may go unnoticed in an oral agreement.

To illustrate, Terrence and Xiong plan to enter into a partnership agreement to sell tires. Among the provisions to be included is that Terrence will provide two-thirds of the capital to start up the business and receive two-thirds of the profits in return. The agreement is made orally. Terrence now sues because Xiong claims that one-half of the profits should be his. Without a writing, Terrence may have a hard time overcoming the presumption that he is entitled to only one-half of the profits of a two-person partnership.[1] This problem could have been avoided by the creation of a written partnership agreement that specified how the profits would be shared. A partnership agreement, called **articles of partnership,** usually specifies each partner's share of the profits and is binding regardless of how uneven the distribution appears to be. A sample partnership agreement is shown in Exhibit 25–1.

ARTICLES OF PARTNERSHIP
A written agreement that sets forth each partner's rights in, and obligations to, the partnership.

Partnership Duration

The partnership agreement can specify the duration of the partnership in terms of a date or the completion of a particular project. A partnership that is specifically limited in duration is called a *partnership for a term.* A dissolution without the consent of all the partners prior to the expiration of the partnership term constitutes a breach of the agreement, and the responsible partner can be liable for any losses resulting from it. If no fixed duration is specified, the partnership is a *partnership at will.* This type of partnership can be dissolved at any time by any partner without

1. The law assumes that members of a partnership share profits and losses equally unless a partnership agreement provides otherwise [UPA 18(a)].

♦ Exhibit 25–1 A Sample Partnership Agreement

PARTNERSHIP AGREEMENT

This agreement, made and entered into as of the __________, by and among __________ __________________ (hereinafter collectively sometimes referred to as "Partners").

WITNESSETH:

Whereas, the Parties hereto desire to form a General Partnership (hereinafter referred to as the "Partnership"), for the term and upon the conditions hereinafter set forth;

Now, therefore, in consideration of the mutual covenants hereinafter contained, it is agreed by and among the Parties hereto as follows:

Article I
BASIC STRUCTURE

Form. The Parties hereby form a General Partnership pursuant to the Laws of __________ __________.

Name. The business of the Partnership shall be conducted under the name of __________ __________.

Place of Business. The principal office and place of business of the Partnership shall be located at __________________, or such other place as the Partners may from time to time designate.

Term. The Partnership shall commence on __________, and shall continue for _____years, unless earlier terminated in the following manner: (a) By the completion of the purpose intended, or (b) Pursuant to this Agreement, or (c) By applicable ______________law, or (d) By death, insanity, bankruptcy, retirement, withdrawal, resignation, expulsion, or disability of all of the then Partners.

Purpose—General. The purpose for which the Partnership is organized is __________ ____

Article II
FINANCIAL ARRANGEMENTS

Each Partner has contributed to the initial capital of the Partnership property in the amount and form indicated on Schedule A attached hereto and made a part hereof. Capital contributions to the Partnership shall not earn interest. An individual capital account shall be maintained for each Partner. If at any time during the existence of the Partnership it shall become necessary to increase the capital with which the said Partnership is doing business, then (upon the vote of the Managing Partner(s)): each party to this Agreement shall contribute to the capital of this Partnership within _ days notice of such need in an amount according to his then Percentage Share of Capital as called for by the Managing Partner(s).

The Percentage Share of Profits and Capital of each Partner shall be (unless otherwise modified by the terms of this Agreement) as follows:

Names	Initial Percentage Share of Profits and Capital

No interest shall be paid on any contribution to the capital of the Partnership. No Partner shall have the right to demand the return of his capital contributions except as herein provided. Except as herein provided, the individual Partners shall have no right to any priority over each other as to the return of capital contributions except as herein provided.

Distributions to the Partners of net operating profits of the Partnership, as hereinafter defined, shall be made at __________________________. Such distributions shall be made to the Partners simultaneously.

For the purpose of this Agreement, net operating profit for any accounting period shall mean the gross receipts of the Partnership for such period, less the sum of all cash expenses of operation of the Partnership, and such sums as may be necessary to establish a reserve for operating expenses. In determining net operating profit, deductions for depreciation, amortization, or other similar charges not requiring actual current expenditures of cash shall *not* be taken into account in accordance with generally accepted accounting principles.

violating the agreement and without incurring liability for losses to other partners resulting from the termination.

The Corporation as Partner

General partners are personally liable for the debts incurred by the partnership. But if one of the general partners is a corporation, then what does personal liability mean? Basically, the capacity of corporations to contract is a question of corporation

◆ **Exhibit 25–1 A Sample Partnership Agreement—Continued**

No Partner shall be entitled to receive any compensation from the Partnership, nor shall any Partner receive any drawing account from the Partnership.

Article III
MANAGEMENT

The Managing Partner(s) shall be ______________________.

The Managing Partner(s) shall have the right to vote as to the management and conduct of the business of the Partnership as follows:

Names	Vote

Article IV
DISSOLUTION

In the event that the Partnership shall hereafter be dissolved for any reason whatsoever, a full and general account of its assets, liabilities and transactions shall at once be taken. Such assets may be sold and turned into cash as soon as possible and all debts and other amounts due the Partnership collected. The proceeds thereof shall thereupon be applied as follows:

(a) To discharge the debts and liabilities of the Partnership and the expenses of liquidation.

(b) To pay each Partner or his legal representative any unpaid salary, drawing account, interest or profits to which he shall then be entitled and in addition, to repay to any Partner his capital contributions in excess of his original capital contribution.

(c) To divide the surplus, if any, among the Partners or their representatives as follows: (1) First (to the extent of each Partner's then capital account) in proportion to their then capital accounts. (2) Then according to each Partner's then Percentage Share of [*Capital/Income*].

No Partner shall have the right to demand and receive property in kind for his distribution.

Article V
MISCELLANEOUS

The Partnership's fiscal year shall commence on January 1st of each year and shall end on December 31st of each year. Full and accurate books of account shall be kept at such place as the Managing Partner(s) may from time to time designate, showing the condition of the business and finances of the Partnership; and each Partner shall have access to such books of account and shall be entitled to examine them at any time during ordinary business hours. At the end of each year, the Managing Partner(s) shall cause the Partnership's accountant to prepare a balance sheet setting forth the financial position of the Partnership as of the end of that year and a statement of operations (income and expenses) for that year. A copy of the balance sheet and statement of operations shall be delivered to each Partner as soon as it is available.

Each Partner shall be deemed to have waived all objections to any transaction or other facts about the operation of the Partnership disclosed in such balance sheet and/or statement of operations unless he shall have notified the Managing Partner(s) in writing of his objectives within thirty (30) days of the date on which such statement is mailed.

The Partnership shall maintain a bank account or bank accounts in the Partnership's name in a national or state bank in the State of ______________. Checks and drafts shall be drawn on the Partnership's bank account for Partnership purposes only and shall be signed by the Managing Partner(s) or their designated agent.

Any controversy or claim arising out of or relating to this Agreement shall only be settled by arbitration in accordance with the rules of the American Arbitration Association, one Arbitrator, and shall be enforceable in any court having competent jurisdiction.

Witnesses	Partners
______________________	______________________
______________________	______________________

Dated: __________

law. The Revised Model Business Corporation Act allows corporations generally to make contracts and incur liabilities. The UPA specifically permits a corporation to be a partner. By definition, "a partnership is an association of two or more persons," and the UPA defines *person* as including corporations [UPA 2].

Many states have restrictions on corporations becoming partners, though such restrictions have become less common over the years. Many decisions in jurisdictions that do not permit corporations to be partners nevertheless validate the arrangements by characterizing them as joint ventures rather than partnerships.

Partnership by Estoppel

Parties who are not partners sometimes represent themselves as such and cause third persons to rely on their representations. The law of partnership does not confer any partnership rights on these persons, but it may impose liability on them. This is also true when a partner represents, expressly or impliedly, that a nonpartner is a member of the firm. When this occurs, the nonpartner is regarded as an agent whose acts are binding on the partnership. In such cases, *partnership by estoppel* is deemed to exist, provided a third person has reasonably and detrimentally relied on the representation that a nonpartner was part of the partnership. This theory is applied in the following case.

Case 25.2 

PARAMOUNT PETROLEUM CORP. v. TAYLOR RENTAL CENTER

Court of Appeals of Texas—
Houston (14th District), 1986.
712 S.W.2d 534.

HISTORICAL AND SOCIAL SETTING *The principle of partnership by estoppel was a rule of the common law before the Uniform Partnership Act (UPA) was drafted. The drafters recognized the rule by including it in the UPA. The principle is important because of another significant legal principle relating to partnerships: each partner is liable for all partnership debts and obligations. One partner can obligate the other partners, whether or not they authorized him or her to do so. Those with whom an alleged partner does business are entitled to rely on the alleged partner's representations, according to the customs of the particular trade or business.*

FACTS During June and July of 1981, Taylor Rental Center rented pumps and sandblasting equipment for use on the *M/V Courtney D,* a seagoing vessel. Apparently, the vessel was owned by Paramount Petroleum Corporation. When the request for rental was submitted, Taylor checked the authorization to rent by telephoning the number given. The phone was answered by a business calling itself "Paramount," and Taylor was instructed by phone to send invoices for the rental charges to the Houston post office box of the company. The identification of the employees picking up the equipment was also checked by Taylor. A second request to rent equipment was made by a captain claiming to represent Paramount Steamship Company. Because the equipment was to be used on the *Courtney D,* and because the invoices were to be sent to the same address as in the earlier rental, Taylor assumed that the two Paramount firms were a single enterprise or a partnership. The invoices went unpaid, and Taylor learned that Paramount Steamship had apparently gone out of business. Taylor then sought payment from Paramount Petroleum, claiming that it was liable for the bill and, if it was not the same corporation as Paramount Steamship, it was at least its partner. When the trial court held for Taylor, Paramount Petroleum appealed.

ISSUE Was a partnership between Paramount Petroleum and Paramount Steamship implied by the fact that they shared telephone facilities and a post office box and were both involved in operations on the *Courtney D?*

DECISION Yes. The appellate court affirmed the trial court's judgment that a partnership by estoppel existed.

REASON A finding of partnership by estoppel requires (1) a representation that a person is a member of a partnership when in fact that person is not a partner and (2) reliance on that person's status as a partner by the one to whom the representation was made. Thus, when the employees of Paramount Steamship rented the equipment from Taylor, Taylor reasonably assumed that they were also employees of Paramount Petroleum, because all indications led to that conclusion. Taylor relied in good faith on a partnership relationship between the two firms.

❖ Rights among Partners

The rights and duties of partners are governed largely by the specific terms of their partnership agreement. In the absence of provisions to the contrary in the partnership agreement, the law imposes the rights and duties discussed in this and the following section. The character and nature of the partnership business generally influence the application of these rights and duties.

Management of the Partnership

Under the UPA, all partners have equal rights in managing the partnership [UPA 18(e)]. Each partner in an ordinary partnership has one vote in management matters *regardless of the proportional size of his or her interest in the firm.*[2] Often, in a large partnership, partners will agree to delegate daily management responsibilities to a management committee made up of one or more of the partners.

The majority rule controls decisions in ordinary matters connected with partnership business, unless otherwise specified in the agreement. Unanimous consent of the partners is required, however, to bind the firm in any of the following actions, all of which significantly affect the nature of the partnership:

1. To alter the essential nature of the firm's business as expressed in the partnership agreement or to alter the capital structure of the partnership.
2. To admit new partners or to enter a wholly new business [UPA 18(g), (h)].
3. To assign partnership property into a trust for the benefit of creditors.
4. To dispose of the partnership's goodwill.
5. To confess judgment against the partnership or to submit partnership claims to arbitration. (A **confession of judgment** is the act of a debtor in permitting a judgment to be entered against him or her by a creditor, for an agreed sum, without the institution of legal proceedings.)
6. To undertake any act that would make further conduct of partnership business impossible [UPA 9(3)].
7. To amend the articles of the partnership agreement.

CONFESSION OF JUDGMENT
A judgment entered against a debtor by a creditor, with the debtor's permission and for an agreed sum, without the use of legal proceedings.

Interest in the Partnership

Each partner is entitled to the proportion of business profits and losses designated in the partnership agreement. If the agreement does not apportion profits or losses, the UPA provides that *profits shall be shared equally* and *losses shall be shared in the same ratio as profits* [UPA 18(a)].

To illustrate, the partnership agreement for Ponce and Brent provides for capital contributions of $6,000 from Ponce and $4,000 from Brent, but it is silent as to how Ponce and Brent will share profits or losses. In this case, Ponce and Brent will share both profits and losses equally. But if the partnership agreement provided for profits to be shared in the same ratio as capital contributions, the profits would be shared 60 percent for Ponce and 40 percent for Brent; and if in addition it was silent as to losses, losses would be shared in the same ratio as profits (60 percent to 40 percent).

"All partners have equal rights in the management and conduct of the partnership business."

Uniform Partnership Act, Section 18(e)

Compensation from the Partnership

A partner has a duty to expend time, skill, and energy on behalf of the partnership business, and such services are generally not compensable. Partners can, of course, agree otherwise. For example, the managing partner of a law firm often receives a salary in addition to his or her share of profits for performing special administrative duties in office and personnel management. When a partnership must be terminated because a partner dies, a surviving partner is entitled to reasonable compensation for services relating to the final settlement of partnership affairs (and reimbursement for expenses incurred in the process) above and apart from his or her share in the partnership profits [UPA 18(f)].

2. Compare the management rights of partners in ordinary partnerships with those of partners in limited partnerships, discussed later in this chapter. The absence of management responsibility and the concomitant liability limitations are distinguishing characteristics of limited partnerships.

Business Law in Action

What's in a Word?

The word *partner* has various shades of meaning. Legally, of course, the term has a specific meaning, and the relationship among partners carries with it special legal rights and duties. But in the common language, the word *partner* is often used simply to indicate a person with whom one is associated in a common activity. This activity may be marriage (marriage partners), dancing (dance partners), a game of bridge (bridge partners), a game of tennis (tennis partners), and so on. The dictionary lists such words as *ally, associate, colleague, and confederate* as being synonyms for *partner.*

The point is that when the word *partner* is used, it may be interpreted by different persons to mean different things. For example, what if you introduced someone who assisted you in your business affairs as a "partner" to a third party? While you might have used the word in a casual sense to mean something like *colleague,* the third party might assume that you and your associate had indeed entered into a business partnership. If the third party relied to his or her detriment on the apparent partnership, a court might find that a partnership by estoppel existed. You and your "partner" would be estopped (prevented) from denying the existence of a partnership and the consequent liability of partners. Clearly, it is important for businesspersons to exercise some caution when using the term *partner.*

Donald Gosch learned this lesson the hard way when a court deemed that he and another man, Jesse Bach, were estopped from denying that they were engaged in a business partnership. The lawsuit was brought against Bach and Gosch by B&D Shrimp, Inc., a firm from which Bach had purchased a shrimp boat. The sales contract for the boat provided that Bach would take marketable title to the shrimp boat after paying B&D $5,000 down and 15 percent of the cash proceeds generated from the daily shrimp catches for the next calendar year. As part of the deal, Bach was also to transfer a cabin cruiser to B&D. Bill McDonald, who as B&D's president had negotiated the sale, delivered a signed bill of sale to Bach as an indication of good faith. Bach then mortgaged the boat for a $6,000 loan from Gosch, without B&D's authority and in violation of the sales contract. When Bach failed to repay the loan, Gosch foreclosed and took possession of the boat. B&D then sued Gosch, alleging that Bach had represented Gosch as his partner and that B&D had relied on the partnership status when it sold the boat to Bach.

Bill McDonald claimed that at one point when he and Bach were discussing the sale, Bosch drove up, and Bach said, "Here is my partner." He introduced McDonald to Gosch, saying that "[t]his is the man that's going to be giving me the money, that's going in partners with me on this Shrimp boat." McDonald testified that Gosch never denied the partnership and that he was present when the exchange was initially negotiated. McDonald also testified that Gosch was present with Bach when it was explained that the title would not pass until all conditions of the agreement were met. Another witness for B&D stated that Bach introduced Gosch as his partner and that Gosch never denied the partnership. Gosch testified that he was not present during the negotiations for the purchase of the shrimp boat. He also stated that he was not a partner of Bach and had never been introduced as one.

We will probably never know the full truth of what transpired between the parties prior to McDonald's sale of the shrimp boat to Bach. If, as B&D claimed, Gosch had been introduced as a partner, perhaps he did not deny that he was a partner because it was true—perhaps he and Bach were, in fact, partners or about to enter into a partnership. Yet perhaps, as Gosch claimed under oath, he and Bach were not business partners, and Gosch failed to deny partnership status simply because he did not think it important to do so. Whatever the reason for Gosch's silence, the court decided in B&D's favor, holding that a partnership by estoppel existed and that Gosch was liable, as Bach's partner, for Bach's fraudulent activities.[a] If, as Gosch alleged, he and Bach were not partners, Gosch's failure to make that fact clear to B&D was costly indeed. Not only was Gosch out the $6,000 that he had loaned to Bach, but he also had to assume liability to B&D Shrimp, Inc., for Bach's failure to perform the conditions of the sales contract.

a. *Gosch v. B&D Shrimp, Inc.,* 830 S.W.2d 652 (Tex.App.—Houston [1st Dist.] 1992).

Each partner impliedly promises to subordinate his or her interests to those of the partnership. Assume that Hall, Banks, and Porter enter into a partnership. Porter undertakes independent consulting for an outside firm without the consent of Hall and Banks. Porter's compensation from the outside firm is considered partnership income [UPA 21]. A partner cannot engage in any independent competitive business that involves the partnership's time unless expressly agreed on by the partnership.

Inspection of Partnership Books

Partnership books and records must be kept accessible to all partners. Each partner has the right to receive (and each partner has the corresponding duty to produce) full and complete information concerning the conduct of all aspects of partnership business [UPA 20]. Each firm retains books in which to record and secure such information. Partners contribute the information, and a bookkeeper or an accountant typically has the duty to preserve it. The books must be kept at the firm's principal business office and cannot be removed without the consent of all the partners [UPA 19]. Every partner, whether active or inactive, is entitled to inspect all books and records upon demand and can make copies of the materials. The personal representative of a deceased partner's estate has the same right of access to partnership books and records that the decedent would have had.

Accounting of Partnership Assets

An accounting of partnership assets or profits is required to determine the value of each partner's share in the partnership. An accounting can be performed voluntarily, or it can be compelled by the order of a court in equity.[3] Formal accounting occurs by right in connection with *dissolution* proceedings (discussed later in this chapter), but under UPA 22, a partner also has the right to a formal accounting in the following situations:

1. When the partnership agreement provides for a formal accounting.
2. When a partner is wrongfully excluded from the business, from access to the books, or both.
3. When any partner is withholding profits or benefits belonging to the partnership in breach of the fiduciary duty.
4. When circumstances "render it just and reasonable."

Property Rights in Partnership

A partner has the following three basic property rights:

1. An interest in the partnership.
2. A right in specific partnership property.
3. A right to participate in the management of the partnership, as previously discussed [UPA 24].

Partner's Interest in the Firm A partner's interest in the firm is a personal asset consisting of a proportionate share of the profits earned [UPA 26] and a return of capital after the partnership is terminated. A partner's interest is susceptible to assignment or to a judgment creditor's lien (described in Chapter 22). Judgment creditors can attach a partner's interest by petitioning the court that entered the judgment to grant the creditors a **charging order.** This order entitles the creditors to profits of the partner and to any assets available to the partner upon the firm's dissolution [UPA 28]. Neither an assignment nor a court's charging order entitling

CHARGING ORDER
In partnership law, an order granted by a court to a judgment creditor that entitles the creditor to attach profits or assets of a partner upon dissolution of the partnership.

3. The principal remedy of a partner against co-partners is an equity suit for dissolution, an accounting, or both. With minor exceptions, a partner cannot maintain an action against other firm members for damages until partnership affairs are settled and an accounting is done. This rule is necessary because legal disputes between partners invariably involve conflicting claims to shares in the partnership. Logically, the value of each partner's share must first be determined by an accounting.

a creditor to receive a share of the partner's money will cause dissolution of the partnership [UPA 27].

Partnership Property UPA 8(1) provides that "all property originally brought into the partnership's stock or subsequently acquired, by purchase or otherwise, on account of the partnership, is partnership property." For example, in the formation of a partnership, a partner may bring into the partnership property he or she owns as a part of his or her capital contribution. This property becomes partnership property even though title to it may still be in the name of the contributing partner. Indications that the assets were acquired with the intention that they be partnership assets is the heart of the phrase "on account of the partnership." Thus, the more closely an asset is associated with the business operations of the partnership, the more likely it is to be a partnership asset.

Partners are *tenants in partnership* of all firm property [UPA 25(1)]. Tenancy in partnership has several important effects. If a partner dies, the surviving partners, not the heirs of the deceased partner, have the right of survivorship to the specific property. Although surviving partners are entitled to possession, they have a duty to account to the decedent's estate for the *value* of the deceased partner's interest in the property [UPA 25(2)(d), (e)].

A partner has no right to sell, assign, or in any way deal with a particular item of partnership property as an exclusive owner [UPA 25(2)(a), (b)]. Nor is a partner's personal credit related to partnership property; therefore, creditors cannot use partnership property to satisfy the personal debts of a partner. Partnership property is available only to satisfy partnership debts, to enhance the firm's credit, or to achieve other business purposes of the partnership.

Every partner is a co-owner with all other partners of specific partnership property, such as office equipment, paper supplies, and vehicles. Each partner has equal rights to possess partnership property for business purposes or in satisfaction of firm debts, but not for any other purpose without the consent of all the other partners.

❖ Duties and Liabilities of Partners

"Of legal knowledge I acquired such a grip, that they took me into the partnership."

William S. Gilbert, 1836–1911
(English playwright; Arthur Sullivan's collaborator in comic opera)

The duties and liabilities of partners are basically derived from agency law. Each partner is an agent of every other partner and acts as both a principal and an agent in any business transaction within the scope of the partnership agreement. Each partner is a general agent of the partnership in carrying out the usual business of the firm. Thus, every act of a partner concerning partnership business and every contract signed in the partnership name bind the firm [UPA 9(1)]. The UPA affirms general principles of agency law that pertain to the authority of a partner to bind a partnership in contract or tort. In this section, we examine the fiduciary duties of partners, the authority of partners, the joint and several liability that characterizes partnerships, and the limitations of liability for incoming partners.

Fiduciary Duties

Partners stand in a fiduciary relationship to one another just as principals and agents do (see Chapter 23). It is a relationship of extraordinary trust and loyalty. The fiduciary duty imposes a responsibility upon each partner to act in good faith for the benefit of the partnership. It requires that each partner subordinate his or her personal interests in the event of conflict to the mutual welfare of the partners.

This fiduciary duty underlies the entire body of law pertaining to partnership and agency. From it, certain other duties are commonly implied. Thus, a partner must account to the partnership for personal profits or benefits derived from any partnership transaction that is undertaken without the consent of all of the partners.[4] The following case illustrates this underlying principle of partnership law.

Case 25.3
MURPHY v. CANION
Court of Appeals of Texas—
Houston (14th District), 1990.
797 S.W.2d 944.

HISTORICAL AND SOCIAL SETTING *In an opinion written nearly seventy years ago, Justice Cardozo stated, in words that are often quoted in cases, textbooks, treatises, and legal publications of all kinds, that partners "owe to one another, while the enterprise continues, the duty of the finest loyalty. Many forms of conduct permissible in a workaday world for those acting at arm's length, are forbidden to those bound by fiduciary ties. A trustee is held to something stricter than the morals of the market place. Not honesty alone, but the punctilio* [fine point, meticulous observation of a duty] *of an honor the most sensitive, is then the standard of behavior. As to this there has developed a tradition that is unbending and inveterate* [of long standing]. *Uncompromising rigidity has been the attitude of courts of equity when petitioned to undermine the rule of undivided loyalty by the 'disintegrating erosion' of particular exceptions. Only thus has the level of conduct for fiduciaries been kept at a level higher than that trodden by the crowd."*[a]

FACTS David Murphy and James Canion formed a partnership to conduct real estate business. A provision in their partnership agreement provided that all personal earnings from personal services would be included as partnership income and that any real estate or other partnership business conducted by either partner during the term of the partnership agreement should be for the joint account of the partnership. Through his business associates and contacts, Canion learned of several profitable real estate opportunities. Canion never informed Murphy of these opportunities but instead secretly took advantage of them for his own gain. When Murphy found out about Canion's activities, he told Canion that he was canceling the partnership under a clause in the partnership agreement that allowed termination by a partner with ninety days' notice. In the lawsuit that followed, Murphy alleged that Canion had breached the partnership agreement and his fiduciary duty to the partnership. The trial court agreed with Murphy and awarded him, as damages, half of the profits made by Canion from certain real estate sales made by Canion without Murphy's knowledge. On appeal, Canion contended, among other things, that because he received income from those sales only after the partnership had been terminated, Murphy had no claim to that income.

a. *Meinhard v. Salmon,* 249 N.Y. 458, 164 N.E. 545 (1928).

ISSUE Is Murphy entitled to his share of the income received by Canion after the partnership's termination?

DECISION Yes. The appellate court affirmed the trial court's ruling that Murphy had a right to his share of the income, even though it was received by Canion after the partnership had ended.

REASON The appellate court concluded, as had the trial court, that the income Canion received after the partnership's dissolution resulted from efforts undertaken during the life of the partnership. By these efforts, Canion had taken advantage of partnership opportunities secretly, for his self-gain, in breach of his fiduciary duty to Murphy. Therefore, Murphy had a right to his share of the profits from Canion's usurpation of partnership opportunities.

ETHICAL CONSIDERATIONS *Society imposes an ethical duty on all persons, including partners, to abide by their agreements. In the context of partnership law, this ethical duty becomes a legal duty, in the interest of protecting the partnership form of enterprise. Obviously, the primary reason for establishing a business firm of any kind is to realize profits. To the extent that profits might be reduced by a partner's usurpation of partnership business opportunities or competing business activities, so, too, would the value of partnership as a business form be reduced.*

Authority of Partners

Agency concepts relating to apparent authority, actual and implied authority, and ratification are also applicable to partnerships. The extent of implied authority is generally broader for partners than for ordinary agents. The character and scope of

4. In this sense, to account to the partnership means not only to divulge the information but also to determine the value of any benefits or profits derived and to hold that money or property in trust on behalf of the partnership.

the partnership business and the customary nature of the particular business operation determine the scope of implied powers. For example, the usual course of business in a trading partnership involves the purchase and sale of commodities. Consequently, each partner in a trading partnership has a wide range of implied powers such as to manage the business by borrowing in the firm's name and extending the firm's credit in issuing or indorsing negotiable instruments.

In an ordinary partnership, firm members can exercise all implied powers reasonably necessary and customary to carry on that particular business. Some customarily implied powers include the authority to make warranties on goods in the sales business, the power to convey real property in the firm's name when such conveyances are part of the ordinary course of partnership business, the power to enter into contracts consistent with the firm's regular course of business, and the power to make admissions and representations concerning partnership affairs [UPA 11].

When a partner acts within the scope of authority, the partnership is bound to third parties by these acts. For example, a partner's authority to sell partnership products carries with it the implied authority to transfer title and to make the usual warranties. Hence, in a partnership that operates a retail tire store, any partner negotiating a contract with a customer for the sale of a set of tires can warrant that "each tire will be warranted for normal wear for 40,000 miles."

This same partner, however, does not have the authority to sell office equipment, fixtures, or the partnership office building without the consent of all of the other partners. In addition, because partnerships are formed to create profits, a partner does not generally have the authority to make charitable contributions without the consent of the other partners. Such actions are not binding on the partnership unless they are ratified by all of the other partners.

As in the law of agency, the law of partnership imputes one partner's knowledge to all other partners because members of a partnership stand in a fiduciary relationship to one another. This relationship implies that each partner will fully disclose to every other partner all information pertaining to the business of the partnership.

JOINT LIABILITY
Shared liability. In partnership law, partners incur joint liability for partnership obligations and debts. For example, if a third party sues a partner on a partnership debt, the partner has the right to insist that the other partners be sued with him or her.

JOINT AND SEVERAL LIABILITY
A doctrine under which a plaintiff may sue, and collect a judgment from, any of several jointly liable defendants, regardless of that particular defendant's degree of fault. In partnership law, joint and several liability means a third party may sue one or more of the partners separately or all of them together, at his or her option. This is true even if the partner did not participate in, ratify, or know about whatever it was that gave rise to the cause of action.

Joint Liability

In most states, partners are subject to joint liability on partnership debts and contracts [UPA 15(b)]. **Joint liability** means that if a third party sues a partner on, for example, a partnership debt, the partner has the right to insist that the other partners be sued with him or her. If the third party does not sue all of the partners, the partners sued cannot be required to pay a judgment, and the assets of the partnership cannot be used to satisfy the judgment. (Similarly, a release of one partner releases all.) In other words, to bring a successful claim against a partnership on a debt or contract, a plaintiff must name all the partners as defendants.

To simplify this rule, some states, such as California, have enacted statutes providing that a partnership may be sued in its own name and a judgment will bind the partnership's and the individual partners' property even though not all the partners are named in the complaint. If the third party is successful, he or she may collect on the judgment against the assets of one or more of the partners. Otherwise stated, each partner is liable and may be required to pay the entire amount of the judgment. When one partner pays the entire amount, the partnership is required to indemnify that partner [UPA 18(b)]. If the partnership cannot do so, the obligation falls on the other partners.

Joint and Several Liability

In some states, partners are both jointly liable and severally, or individually, liable for partnership debts and contracts. In all states, partners are jointly and severally liable for torts and breaches of trust [UPA 15(a)]. **Joint and several liability** means a third party may sue any one or more of the partners without suing all of them or the partnership itself. (That is, a third party may sue one or more of the partners separately or all of them together, at his or her option.) This is true even if the partner being sued did not participate in, ratify, or know about whatever it was that gave rise to the cause of action.

A judgment against one partner on his or her several liability does not extinguish the others' liability. (Similarly, a release of one partner discharges the partners' joint but not several liability.) Thus, those not sued in the first action may be sued subsequently. The first action, however, may have been conclusive on the question of liability. If, for example, in an action against one partner, the court held that the partnership was in no way liable, the third party cannot bring an action against another partner and succeed on the issue of the partnership's liability.

If the third party is successful, he or she may collect on the judgment only against the assets of those partners named as defendants. The partner who committed the tort is required to indemnify the partnership for any damages it pays.

Liability of Incoming Partner

A newly admitted partner to an existing partnership normally has limited liability for whatever debts and obligations the partnership incurred prior to the new partner's admission. The new partner's liability can be satisfied only from partnership assets [UPA 17]. This means that the new partner usually has no personal liability for these debts and obligations, but any capital contribution made by him or her is subject to these debts.

❖ Partnership Termination

Any change in the relations of the partners that demonstrates unwillingness or inability to carry on partnership business dissolves the partnership, resulting in termination [UPA 29]. If one of the partners wishes to continue the business, he or she is free to reorganize into a new partnership with the remaining members.

The termination of a partnership has two stages, both of which must take place before termination is complete. The first stage, **dissolution,** occurs when any partner (or partners) indicates an intention to disassociate from the partnership. The second stage, **winding up,**[5] is the actual process of collecting and distributing the partnership assets. Dissolution of a partnership can be brought about by the acts of the partners, by the operation of law, and by judicial decree. Each of these events will be discussed here.

DISSOLUTION
The formal disbanding of a partnership or a corporation. It can take place by (1) agreement of the parties or the shareholders and board of directors, (2) the death of a partner, (3) the expiration of a time period stated in a partnership agreement or a certificate of incorporation, or (4) court order.

WINDING UP
The second of two stages involved in the dissolution of a partnership or corporation. Once the firm is dissolved, it continues to exist legally until the process of winding up all business affairs (collecting and distributing the firm's assets) is complete.

Dissolution by Acts of Partners

Dissolution of a partnership may come about through the acts of the partners in several ways. First, the partnership can be dissolved by the partners' agreement. For example, when a partnership agreement expresses a fixed term or a particular business objective to be accomplished, the passing of the date or the accomplishment of the objective dissolves the partnership.

Second, because a partnership is a voluntary association, a partner has the power to disassociate himself or herself from the partnership at any time and thus dissolve the partnership. Any change in the partnership, whether by the withdrawal of a partner or by the admission of a new partner, results in dissolution. In practice, this is modified by the provision that the remaining or new partners may continue in

5. Although "winding down" would seem to describe more accurately the process of settling accounts and liquidating the assets of a partnership, "winding up" has been traditionally used in English and U.S. statutory and case law to denote this final stage of a partnership's existence.

the firm's business. Nonetheless, a new partnership arises. Creditors of the prior partnership become creditors of the new partnership [UPA 41].[6]

Finally, the UPA provides that neither a voluntary transfer of a partner's interest nor an involuntary sale of a partner's interest for the benefit of creditors [UPA 28] by itself dissolves the partnership. (A transferee acquires the right to the transferring partner's profits but does not become a partner; thus, a transferee has no say in the management of the partnership affairs and no right to inspect the partnership books.) Either occurrence, however, can ultimately lead to judicial dissolution of the partnership (judicial dissolution will be discussed shortly).

Dissolution by Operation of Law

If one of the partners dies, the partnership is dissolved by operation of law, even if the partnership agreement provides for carrying on the business with the executor of the decedent's estate. Any change in the composition among partners results in a new partnership. The bankruptcy of a partner will also dissolve a partnership, and naturally, the bankruptcy of the firm itself will result in dissolution. Additionally, any event that makes it unlawful for the partnership to continue its business or for any partner to carry on in the partnership will result in dissolution. Note, however, that even if the illegality of the partnership business is a cause for dissolution, the partners can decide to change the nature of their business and continue in the partnership. When the illegality applies to an individual partner, then dissolution is mandatory. For example, suppose the state legislature passes a law making it illegal for judges to engage in the practice of law. If an attorney in a law firm is appointed a judge, the attorney must leave the law firm and the partnership must be dissolved.

Dissolution by Judicial Decree

For dissolution of a partnership by judicial decree to occur, an application or petition must be made in an appropriate court. The court then either denies the petition or grants a decree of dissolution. UPA 32 cites situations in which a court can dissolve a partnership. One situation occurs when a partner is adjudicated mentally incompetent or is shown to be of unsound mind. Another situation arises when a partner appears incapable of performing his or her duties under the partnership agreement. If the incapacity is likely to be permanent and to affect substantially the partner's ability to discharge his or her duties to the firm, a court will dissolve the partnership by decree. Dissolution may also be ordered by a court when it becomes obviously impractical for the firm to continue—for example, if the business can only be operated at a loss. Additionally, a partner's impropriety involving partnership business (for example, fraud perpetrated on the other partners) or improper behavior reflecting unfavorably on the firm may provide grounds for a judicial decree of dissolution. Finally, if dissension between partners becomes so persistent and harmful as to undermine the confidence and cooperation necessary to carry on the firm's business, dissolution may also be granted.

Notice of Dissolution

The intent to dissolve or to withdraw from a firm must be communicated clearly to each partner. This notice of intent can be expressed by either actions or words. All partners will share liability for the acts of any partner who continues conducting business for the firm without knowing that the partnership has been dissolved.

Dissolution of a partnership by the act of a partner requires notice to all affected third persons as well. Any third person who has extended credit to the firm must receive *actual notice* (notice given to the party directly and personally). For all

6. As mentioned in this chapter's introduction, the UPA is currently undergoing revision. One of the significant changes in the revised form is that the partnership does not automatically dissolve upon the withdrawal of a partner.

others, *constructive notice* (a newspaper announcement or similar public notice) is sufficient. Dissolution resulting from operation of law generally requires no notice to third parties.[7]

Winding Up and Distribution of Assets

Once dissolution occurs and the partners have been notified, the partners cannot create new obligations on behalf of the partnership. Their only authority is to complete transactions begun but not finished at the time of dissolution and to wind up the business of the partnership. *Winding up* includes collecting and preserving partnership assets, discharging liabilities (paying debts), and accounting to each partner for the value of his or her interest in the partnership.

Both creditors of the partnership and creditors of the individual partners can make claims on the partnership's assets. In general, creditors of the partnership have priority over creditors of individual partners in the distribution of partnership assets; the converse priority is usually followed in the distribution of individual partner assets, except under bankruptcy law. The priorities in the distribution of a partnership's assets are as follows:

1. Payment of third party debts.
2. Refund of advances (loans) made to or for the firm by a partner.
3. Return of capital contribution to a partner.
4. Distribution of the balance, if any, to partners in accordance with their respective shares in the profits.

Partners continue in their fiduciary relationship until the winding-up process is completed.

❖ Limited Partnerships

In many ways, *limited partnerships* are like general partnerships, but they also differ from general partnerships in several ways. Because of this, they are sometimes referred to as *special partnerships*. Limited partnerships consist of at least one *general partner* and one or more *limited partners*. The general partner (or partners) assumes management responsibility for the partnership and so has full responsibility for the partnership and for all debts of the partnership. The limited partner (or partners) contributes cash (or other property) and owns an interest in the firm but does not undertake any management responsibilities and is not personally liable for partnership debts beyond the amount of his or her investment. A limited partner can forfeit limited liability by taking part in the management of the business. A comparison of the basic characteristics of partnerships appears in Exhibit 25–2.

Until 1976, the law governing limited partnerships in all states except Louisiana was the Uniform Limited Partnership Act (ULPA) of 1916. In 1976, the ULPA was revised, and most states and the District of Columbia have adopted its revision, which is known as the Revised Uniform Limited Partnership Act (RULPA). Because the RULPA is the dominant law governing limited partnerships in the United States, references within this section will be to the RULPA.

Formation of a Limited Partnership

Compared with the informal, private, and voluntary agreement that usually suffices for a general partnership, the formation of a limited partnership is a public and formal proceeding that must follow statutory requirements. A limited partnership must have at least one general partner and one limited partner, as mentioned pre-

7. *Childers v. United States*, 442 F.2d 1299 (5th Cir. 1971).

◆ **Exhibit 25–2**
A Basic Comparison of Types of Partnerships

CHARACTERISTIC	GENERAL PARTNERSHIP (UPA)	LIMITED PARTNERSHIP (RULPA)
Creation	By agreement of two or more persons to carry on a business as co-owners for profit.	By agreement of two or more persons to carry on a business as co-owners for profit. Must include one or more general partners and one or more limited partners. Filing of certificate with secretary of state is required.
Sharing of Profits and Losses	By agreement, or in the absence thereof, profits are shared equally by partners, and losses are shared in the same ratio as profits.	Profits are shared as required in certificate agreement, and losses are shared likewise, up to the amount of the limited partners' capital contributions. In the absence of provision in certificate agreement, profits and losses are shared on the basis of percentages of capital contributions.
Liability	Unlimited personal liability of all partners.	Unlimited personal liability of all general partners; limited partners liable only to extent of capital contributions.
Capital Contribution	No minimal or mandatory amount; set by agreement.	Set by agreement; may be cash, property, services, or any obligation.
Management	By agreement, or in the absence thereof, all partners have an equal voice.	General partners by agreement, or else each has an equal voice. Limited partners have no voice or else are subject to liability as general partners (but *only* if a third party has knowledge of such involvement). Limited partner may act as agent or employee of the partnership and vote on amending certificate or sale or dissolution of the partnership.
Duration	By agreement, or can be dissolved by action of partner (withdrawal), operation of law (death or bankruptcy), or court decree.	By agreement in certification or by withdrawal, death, or mental incompetence of general partner in absence of right of other general partners to continue the partnership. Death of a limited partner, unless he or she is the only remaining limited partner, does not terminate the partnership.
Assignment	Interest can be assigned, although assignee does not have rights of substituted partner without consent of other partners.	Same as general partnership; if partners consent to assignee's becoming a partner, certificate must be amended. Upon assignment of all interest, the partner ceases to be a partner.
Priorities (order) upon Liquidation	1. Outside creditors. 2. Partner creditors. 3. Partners, according to capital contributions. 4. Partners, according to profits.	1. Outside creditors and partner creditors. 2. Partners and former partners entitled to distributions before withdrawal under the agreement or RULPA. 3. Partners, according to capital contributions. 4. Partners, according to profits.

viously, and the partners must sign a **certificate of limited partnership**, which requires information similar to that found in a corporate charter. The certificate must be filed with the designated state official—under RULPA, the secretary of state. The certificate is usually open to public inspection. In essence, the content of the certificate and the method of filing are similar to those of the corporate charter.

CERTIFICATE OF LIMITED PARTNERSHIP
The basic document filed with a designated state official by which a limited partnership is formed.

Rights and Liabilities of Partners in a Limited Partnership

General partners, unlike limited partners, are personally liable to the partnership's creditors; thus, at least one general partner is necessary in a limited partnership so that someone has personal liability. This policy can be circumvented in states that allow a corporation to be the general partner in a partnership. Because the corporation has limited liability by virtue of corporate laws, no one in the limited partnership in this case has personal liability.

Rights of Limited Partners Subject to the limitations that will be discussed here, limited partners have essentially the same rights as general partners, including the right of access to partnership books and the right to other information regarding partnership business. Upon dissolution, they are entitled to a return of their contributions in accordance with the partnership certificate [RULPA 201(a)(10)]. They can also assign their interests subject to the certificate [RULPA 702, 704].

The RULPA provides a limited partner with the right to sue an outside party on behalf of the firm if the general partners with authority to do so have refused to file suit [RULPA 1001]. In addition, investor protection legislation, such as securities laws (discussed in Chapter 29), may give some protection to limited partners.

Liabilities of Limited Partners In contrast to the virtually unlimited liability of a general partner for partnership indebtedness, the liability of a limited partner is limited to the capital that he or she contributes or agrees to contribute to the partnership [RULPA 502]. If the firm is organized in an improper manner and the limited partner fails to renunciate (withdraw from the partnership) on the discovery of the defect, however, the partner can be held personally liable by the firm's creditors. Liability for false statements in a partnership certificate runs in favor of persons relying on the false statements and against members who sign the certificate knowing of the falsity [RULPA 207]. A limited partnership is formed by good faith compliance with the requirements for signing and filing the certificate, even if it is incomplete or defective. When a limited partner discovers a defect in the formation of the limited partnership, he or she can avoid future liability by causing an appropriate amendment or certificate to be filed or by renouncing an interest in the profits of the partnership [RULPA 304].

Limited Partners and Management The limited partners' exemptions from personal liability rest on their not participating in management [RULPA 303]. The surname of a limited partner, for example, cannot be included in the partnership name [RULPA 102]. A violation of this provision renders the limited partner just as liable as a general partner to any creditor who does not know that he or she is a limited partner. Note that *no* law expressly bars the participation of limited partners in the management of the partnership. Rather, the threat of personal liability normally deters their participation. Under the RULPA, a limited partner will be liable as a general partner only to a third party who had knowledge of the limited partner's management activities [RULPA 303]. How much actual review and advisement a limited partner can engage in before being exposed to liability is an unsettled question.[8] In the following case, a limited partner was alleged to have participated in the control of the business by interceding on the partnership's behalf to secure credit.

8. It is an unsettled question partly because there are differences among the laws in different states. Factors to be considered under RULPA are listed in RULPA 303(b), (c).

Case 25.4
PITMAN v. FLANAGAN LUMBER CO.
Supreme Court of Alabama, 1990.
567 So.2d 1335.

HISTORICAL AND INTERNATIONAL SETTING *Limited partnerships were first used in Pisa and Florence, Italy, in the twelfth century. The limited partnership spread to France and was brought to America by French explorers and settlers in Louisiana and Florida. Known as a* société en commandite, *the French limited partnership served as the idea for the drafters of the original statutes in the United States. The first limited partnership act was adopted by New York in 1822. By 1850, most of the other states had adopted similar statutes. Since the introduction of these early statutes, an important question has been the degree to which a limited partner can participate in the conduct of the business without becoming liable, beyond the extent of his or her investment, for its obligations.*

FACTS Robert Pitman was one of two limited partners in Ramsey Homebuilders, a limited partnership that engaged in the business of residential construction. Michael Ramsey was the sole general partner in the partnership. Because Ramsey had a poor credit history, he was unable to borrow the money or obtain the credit needed to sustain the partnership's business. Pitman, who had a personal account with Flanagan Lumber Company, contacted Flanagan's credit manager and secured an account in the partnership's name. After the partnership failed to pay the account, Flanagan sued Pitman, alleging that although Pitman was a limited partner in Ramsey Homebuilders, he was responsible for the partnership's debt under RULPA 303. Pitman argued that, if anything, he was operating within the waters of the "safe harbor" provided by RULPA 303(b)(3), which states that a limited partner does not participate in the control of the partnership solely by acting as a surety or guarantor for any liabilities incurred by the partnership. The trial court found that Pitman had participated in the control of the business by securing credit for the partnership, that Flanagan had reasonably relied on that participation in extending credit, and that Pitman was therefore liable to Flanagan for the debt subsequently incurred by the partnership. Pitman appealed.

ISSUE Can Pitman be held liable for the partnership's debt to Flanagan?

DECISION Yes. The trial court's judgment was affirmed.

REASON The Supreme Court of Alabama ruled that in securing credit that was vitally necessary to the partnership, Pitman had exercised a degree of "control" over partnership affairs sufficient to justify his being held liable as a general partner for the debt to Flanagan. The court held that control is defined as "the [p]ower or authority to manage, direct, superintend, restrict, regulate, govern, administer, or oversee." The court pointed out that "[t]he trial court could have found * * * that Pitman participated in the 'control' of the partnership's business by securing one of the things that the partnership needed to survive—a source of building materials that would be provided on credit." Moreover, the court found that Flanagan reasonably relied on Pitman's participation in the partnership's business in deciding to extend credit to the partnership.

Dissolution of a Limited Partnership

A limited partnership is dissolved in much the same way as an ordinary partnership. The retirement, death, or mental incompetence of a general partner can dissolve the partnership, but not if the business can be continued by one or more of the other general partners in accordance with their certificate or by consent of all members [RULPA 801]. The death or assignment of interest of a limited partner does not dissolve the limited partnership [RULPA 702, 704, 705]. A limited partnership can be dissolved by court decree [RULPA 802].

Bankruptcy or the withdrawal of a general partner dissolves a limited partnership. Bankruptcy of a limited partner, however, does not dissolves the partnership unless it causes the bankruptcy of the firm. The retirement of a general partner causes a dissolution unless the members consent to a continuation by the remaining general partners or unless this contingency is provided for in the certificate.

Upon dissolution, creditors' rights, including those of partners who are creditors, take first priority. Then partners and former partners receive unpaid distributions of partnership assets and, except as otherwise agreed, amounts representing returns on their contributions and amounts proportionate to their shares of the distributions [RULPA 804].

❖ Key Terms

articles of partnership 605	**charging order 611**	**joint and several liability 614**
certificate of limited partnership 614	**confession of judgment 609**	**joint liability 614**
	dissolution 615	**winding up 615**

❖ Chapter Summary: Partnerships

General Partnership	1. Created by agreement of the parties. 2. Not treated as an entity except for limited purposes. 3. Partners have unlimited liability for partnership debts. 4. Each partner has an equal voice in management unless otherwise provided for in the partnership agreement. 5. The capital contribution of each partner is determined by agreement. 6. Each partner pays a pro rata share of income taxes on the net profits of the partnership, whether or not they are distributed; the partnership files only an information return with the Internal Revenue Service. 7. Terminated by agreement or can be dissolved by action of partner (withdrawal), operation of law (death or bankruptcy), or court decree.
Limited Partnership	1. Must be formed in compliance with statutory requirements. 2. Consists of one or more general partners and one or more limited partners. 3. Only general partners can participate in management. Limited partners have no voice in management; if they do participate in management activities, they risk having general-partner liability. 4. General partners have unlimited liability for partnership losses; limited partners are liable only to the extent of their contributions.

❖ Questions and Case Problems

25-1. Indications of Partnership Status. What are the essential indications of partnership status? In other words, what factors does a court consider when determining whether a partnership exists?

25-2. General versus Limited Partners. What are the essential differences between the rights and liabilities of general partners and those of limited partners? Are the rights of general partners in a limited partnership the same as those of general partners in a general partnership?

25-3. Partnership Dissolution. Giuseppi, Bright, Romanovski, and Palance were partners in a small publishing enterprise. They had a written partnership agreement specifying that the partnership would endure for five years. For the first two years, the business ran smoothly, and the firm was profitable. In the third year, however, disagreements among the partners arose concerning a potential investment in a new printing process. Giuseppi and Bright were opposed to the investment as it would place the firm heavily in debt. Romanovski and Palance believed that if the investment was not made, the firm would lose profits in the long run. Eventually, the disagreement escalated into bitter hostility between the two factions, and it became difficult to perform the necessary day-to-day tasks of the business. Giuseppi wanted to withdraw from the partnership, but the other partners would not consent to his withdrawal. Discuss Giuseppi's options.

25-4. Partnership Property. Schwartz and Zenov were partners in an accounting firm. Because business was booming and profits were better than ever, they decided to invest some of the firm's profits in Munificent Corp. stock. The investment turned out to be a good one, as the stock continued to increase in value. On Schwartz's death several years later, Zenov assumed full ownership of the business, including the Munificent Corp. stock, a partnership asset. Schwartz's daughter Rosalie, however, claimed a 50 percent ownership interest in the Munificent Corp. stock as Schwartz's sole heir. Can Rosalie enforce her claim? Explain.

25-5. Partner's Property Rights. Maruta, Samms, and Ortega were partners in a business firm. The firm's business equipment included several expensive computers. One day, Maruta borrowed one of the computers for use in his home, but he never bothered to return it. When the other partners asked him about it, Maruta claimed that because the computer represented less than one-third of the computers owned by the partnership, and because he owned one-third of the business, he had a right to keep the equipment. Was he right? Explain.

25-6. Partnership by Estoppel. Alvin and Carol Volkman negotiated with David McNamee, a construction contractor, to have a house built. McNamee informed the Volkmans that he was going into business with Phillip Carroll. On several occasions when the Volkmans went to McNamee's offices, Carroll was present, and by all indications he was a partner in the decisions concerning the construction of their house. On one occasion, when McNamee had to make a decision about which contractor's form to use, McNamee left the room, stating, "I will ask Phil." On another occasion, Carroll made the following statement to the Volkmans: "I hope we'll be working together." Correspondence to the Volkmans from McNamee was written on stationery carrying the letterhead "DP Associates," and the Volkmans assumed the "DP" represented David and Phillip. When the construction contract was not performed as agreed, the Volkmans brought suit against DP Associates, McNamee, and Carroll. Carroll petitioned the trial court to dismiss the suit against him, as he was not a partner in DP Associates. Will the court find Carroll to be a partner by estoppel? Explain. [*Volkman v. DP Associates*, 48 N.C.App. 155, 268 S.E.2d 265 (1980)]

25-7. Rights among Partners. Jebeles and Costellos were partners in "Dino's Hot Dogs," doing business on the Montgomery Highway in Alabama. From the outset, Costellos worked at the business full-time, while Jebeles involved himself only to a small extent in the actual running of the business. Jebeles was married to Costellos's sister, and when marital difficulties developed between Jebeles and his wife, Costellos barred Jebeles from the premises. Jebeles sued for an accounting of the partnership's profits and for dissolution of the partnership, claiming a partnership at will and that the relationship between the partners made it impossible to conduct partnership business. Will the court grant the petition? Explain. [*Jebeles v. Costellos*, 391 So.2d 1024 (Ala. 1980)]

25-8. Partnership Dissolution. In 1964, Alex Gershunoff and Lawrence Silk formed a partnership to syndicate and manage apartment houses. Jacob Oliker served the partnership as legal counsel. In 1969, Oliker joined the partnership, known as Alex Co., as an equal partner. Oliker paid $5,000 to the partnership and gave up his legal practice as consideration for entering the partnership, but there was never a written partnership agreement. The partnership functioned smoothly from 1969 until 1974. The partnership bought apartment houses and called itself a "development company." In March 1974, Oliker withdrew from the partnership. After Oliker's withdrawal, the value of the property owned by the partnership greatly appreciated. For two and a half years, the parties failed to agree on the amount of Oliker's interest. In November 1976, Gershunoff and Silk sent Oliker a "final accounting," which Oliker rejected. Oliker filed suit, requesting a formal accounting and a court-supervised winding up of affairs, with his interest to be determined on the basis of its value at the time of the court-ordered accounting. Discuss whether Oliker was entitled to an equal share in the increased value of partnership assets. [*Oliker v. Gershunoff*, 195 Cal.App.3d 1288, 241 Cal.Rptr. 415 (1987)]

25-9. Liability of General Partners. Pat McGowan, Val Somers, and Brent Roberson were general partners in Vermont Place, a limited partnership formed to construct duplexes on a tract of land in Fort Smith, Arkansas. In 1984, the partnership mortgaged the property so that it could build there. McGowan owned a separate company, Advance Development Corp., that was hired by the partnership to develop the project. On September 3, 1984, Somers and Roberson discovered that McGowan had not been paying the suppliers to the project, including National Lumber Co., and had not been making the mortgage payments. The suppliers and the bank sued the partnership and the general partners individually. Discuss whether Somers and Roberson could be held individually liable for the debts incurred by McGowan. [*National Lumber Co. v. Advance Development Corp.*, 293 Ark. 1, 732 S.W.2d 840 (1987)]

25-10. Liability of Limited Partners. Combat Associates was formed as a limited partnership to promote an exhibition boxing match between Lyle Alzado (a professional football player) and Muhammad Ali. Alzado and others had formed Combat Promotions, and this organization was to be the general partner in Combat Associates. Blinder, Robinson & Co. (Blinder) was to be the limited partner. The general partner's contribution consisted of assigning all contracts pertaining to the match, and the limited partner's contribution was a $250,000 letter of credit to ensure Ali's compensation. Alzado personally guaranteed to repay Blinder for any amount of loss if the proceeds of the match were less than $250,000. In preparation for the match, at Alzado's request, Blinder's president participated in interviews and a promotional rally, and the company sponsored parties and allowed its local office to be used as a ticket sales outlet. The proceeds of the match were insufficient, and Blinder sued Alzado on his guaranty. Alzado counterclaimed that Blinder had taken an active role in the control and management of Combat Associates and thus should be held liable as a general partner. How did the court rule on Alzado's counterclaim? [*Blinder, Robinson & Co. v. Alzado*, 713 P.2d 1314 (Colo.App. 1985)]

25-11. Partnership Dissolution. In January 1987, Westbrook Pharmacy and Surgical Supply (doing business as Canter's Pharmacy, Inc.), Orrie Rockwell, Jr., and another business entity entered into a partnership agreement for the purpose of operating a personal care facility in Elizabeth, Pennsylvania. The partnership agreement provided that any disputes among the partners were to be submitted to arbitration. Two years later, the partnership sued Westbrook to recover capital contributions allegedly owed by Westbrook to the partnership. Westbrook filed a counterclaim against the partnership, seeking an accounting and a dissolution of the partnership. Subsequently, Westbrook brought a separate action alleging various breaches of the partnership agreement. The trial court granted Westbrook's petition to consolidate the actions. The partnership filed a motion to stay the consolidated proceedings pending arbitration in accordance with an arbitration provision in the partnership agreement. The trial court granted the partnership's motion, and Westbrook appealed. The question on appeal was whether the arbitration provision—or any provision of the partnership agreement—was enforceable, given the fact that Westbrook had sought an accounting and dissolution of the firm. Did Westbrook's action dissolve the partnership, thus rendering the provisions of the partnership—

including the arbitration provision—ineffective? Discuss fully. [*Canter's Pharmacy, Inc. v. Elizabeth Associates,* 396 Pa.Super. 505, 578 A.2d 1326 (1990)]

25-12. Partnership Property. Two brothers, Eugene and Marlowe Mehl, operated their family farm as a partnership. Property held by the partnership consisted primarily of farming equipment and machinery. The partnership did not own any real property but leased land from the family and other people. The brothers had agreed to split all profits on an equal basis, but there had never been a written partnership agreement. In 1973, Eugene withdrew $7,200 from the partnership bank account and bought the Dagmar Bar, located in Dagmar, Montana. The warranty deed and the liquor license to the bar were held in the names of Eugene Mehl and his wife, Bonnie. In 1980, Eugene and Bonnie were divorced, and Bonnie received the bar and liquor license as part of the property settlement. In 1983, Marlowe gave written notice to Eugene that he was dissolving the partnership. Eventually, a district court in Montana distributed the assets of the partnership. The court concluded that the Dagmar Bar was a partnership asset. On appeal, Eugene contended that the bar was not partnership property and entered into evidence a number of documents that tended to indicate that he had owned the bar, which then was transferred to Bonnie in the property settlement following the divorce. What should the appellate court decide? Discuss fully. [*Mehl v. Mehl,* 241 Mont. 310, 786 P.2d 1173 (1990)]

25-13. Indications of Partnership Status. Carmen Allen and Sandy Newsome, in accordance with a written agreement dated March 11, 1987, conducted a carpet and wallcovering business under the name of Newsome Carpets. The agreement provided that Allen would invest $5,000 cash in the business and that Newsome would invest carpet stock, fixtures, and equipment equal in value to $5,000. On November 4, 1987, Allen and Newsome executed a document entitled "Partnership Agreement" that established the name, place, nature, and duration of the business and outlined the operating procedures of the firm and the rights and responsibilities of the parties. The document referred to Newsome Carpets as their partnership and to Allen and Newsome as partners, each of whom received 50 percent ownership in the firm in return for their capital investment. The next day, on November 5, articles of incorporation designating Newsome and Allen as directors of Newsome Carpets, Inc., were filed in the office of the secretary of state. Evidence at trial indicated that Allen shared profits, rendered business advice, and signed documents as a general partner of Newsome Carpets. When the corporation was subsequently dissolved, one of the creditors, Orders Distributing Co., sued Allen and Newsome as partners to recover an outstanding debt. Allen (Newsome's whereabouts were unknown when the suit was brought) claimed that the business was a corporation, not a partnership, and that she therefore could not be held personally liable for the debt. Will the court hold that Newsome Carpets was a partnership and not a corporation? Discuss. [*Orders Distributing Co. v. Newsome Carpets & Wallcovering,* 418 S.E.2d 550 (S.C. 1992)]

A Question of Ethics and Social Responsibility

25-14. *Mt. Hood Meadows Oregon, Ltd., was a limited partnership established to carry on the business of constructing and operating a winter sports development in the Hood River area of Oregon. Elizabeth Brooke and two of the other limited partners were dissatisfied because, for all the years in which profits were earned after 1974, the general partner distributed only 50 percent of the limited partners' taxable profits. The remaining profits were retained and reinvested in the business. Each of the limited partners was taxed on his or her distributable share of the profits, however, regardless of whether the cash was actually distributed. Brooke and the others brought an action to compel the general partner to distribute all of the limited partnership's profits. The court held that, in the absence of a limited partnership agreement concerning the distribution of profits, the decision to reinvest profits was strictly a managerial one. Unless the limited partners could prove that the general partner's conduct was inappropriate or violated a fiduciary duty, the decision of the general partner was binding on the limited partners.* [Brooke v. Mt. Hood Meadows Oregon, Ltd., *81 Or.App. 387, 725 P.2d 925 (1986)*]

1. The major attraction of limited partnerships is that the investors, as limited partners, are not liable for partnership obligations beyond the amount that they have invested. The "price" paid for this limited liability, however, is that limited partners have no say in management—as is well illustrated by the case described here. What ethical considerations are expressed in the rule that limited partners cannot participate in management? Do you think such a rule is fair?
2. This case also illustrates how relatively helpless the limited partners are when faced with a general partner whose actions do not correspond to the limited partners' wishes. Apart from selling their partnership shares to others (and at times, buyers are hard to find) or participating in management (and losing their limited liability as a result), limited partners have little recourse against the decisions of general partners so long as the general partners have not violated their fiduciary duties or the partnership agreement. Do you think that, because limited partners cannot participate in management, general partners have ethical duties to limited partners that go beyond those prescribed by law? If not, why not? If so, how would you describe or define such duties?

For Critical Analysis

25-15. *Are there any advantages of partnership status that offset the unlimited personal liability of partners for partnership obligations? In other words, why would any two or more persons opt to form a partnership (in which personal liability is unlimited) rather than a corporation (in which personal liability is limited to the amount of capital invested)?*

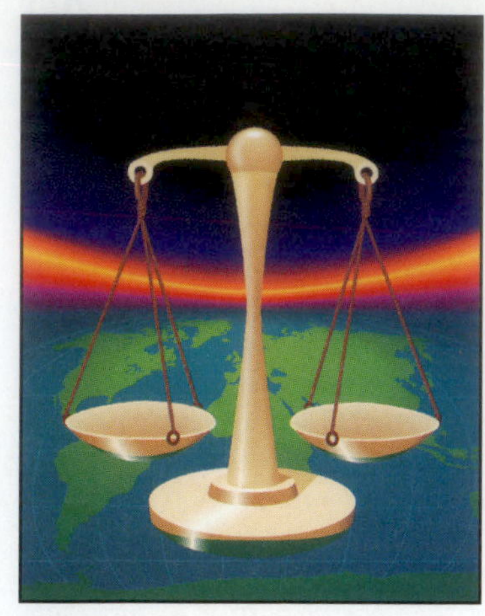

Chapter 26

Corporate Formation and Financing

"A corporation is an artificial being, invisible, intangible, and existing only in contemplation of law."

John Marshall, 1755–1835
(Chief justice of the United States Supreme Court, 1801–1835)

The corporation is a creature of statute. A corporation is an artificial being, existing in law only and neither tangible nor visible. Its existence depends generally on state law, although some corporations, especially public organizations, can be created under federal law. Each state has its own body of corporate law, and these laws are not entirely uniform. The Model Business Corporation Act (MBCA) is a codification of modern corporation law that has been influential in the drafting and revision of state corporation statutes. Today, the majority of state statutes are guided by the revised version of the MBCA, known as the Revised Model Business Corporation Act (RMBCA). You should keep in mind, however, that there is considerable variation among the statutes of the states that have used the MBCA or the RMBCA as a basis for their statutes, and several states do not follow either act. Because of this, individual state corporation laws should be relied on rather than the MBCA or RMBCA.

❖ The Nature of the Corporation

A *corporation* is a legal entity created and recognized by state law. It can consist of one or more *natural* persons (as opposed to the artificial "person" of the corporation) identified under a common name. (See this chapter's *Landmark in the Law* for a leading case in the early development of private corporations in the United States.)

A corporation is recognized under state and federal law as a "person," and it enjoys many of the same rights and privileges that U.S. citizens enjoy. The Bill of Rights guarantees a person, as a citizen, certain protections; and corporations are considered persons in most instances. Accordingly, a corporation has the same right as a natural person to equal protection of the laws under the Fourteenth Amendment. It has the right of access to the courts as an entity that can sue or be sued. It also has the right of due process before denial of life, liberty, or property, as well as freedom from unreasonable searches and seizures and from double jeopardy.

Under the First Amendment, corporations are entitled to freedom of speech, but commercial speech (such as advertising) and political speech (such as contributions to political causes or candidates) receive significantly less protection than noncommercial speech (see Chapter 4 for a fuller discussion of commercial and political speech).

Only the corporation's individual officers and employees possess the Fifth Amendment right against self-incrimination.[1] And the privileges and immunities

1. *In re Grand Jury No. 86–3 (Will Roberts Corp.)*, 816 F.2d 569 (11th Cir. 1987).

clause of the Constitution (Article IV, Section 2) does not protect corporations, nor does it protect an unincorporated association.[2] This clause requires each state to treat citizens of other states equally with respect to access to courts, travel rights, and so forth.

An unsettled area of corporation law has to do with the criminal acts of a corporation. Because obviously a corporation cannot be sent to prison—even though, under law, it is a person—most courts hold a corporation that has violated a criminal statute liable for fines. When criminal conduct can be attributed to corporate officers or agents, those individuals, as *natural* persons, are held liable and can be imprisoned for their acts.

Characteristics of the Corporate Entity

A corporation is an artificial person, with its own corporate name, owned by individual shareholders. It is a legal entity with rights and responsibilities. The corporation substitutes itself for its shareholders in conducting corporate business and in incurring liability, yet its authority to act and the liability for its actions are separate and apart from the individuals who own it. (In certain limited situations, the "corporate veil" can be pierced; that is, liability for the corporation's obligations can be extended to shareholders, a topic to be discussed later in this chapter.) Responsibility for the overall management of the corporation is entrusted to a board of directors, which is elected by the shareholders. Corporate officers and other employees are hired by the board of directors to run the daily business operations of the corporation.

"Corporation: An ingenious device for obtaining individual profit without individual responsibility."

Ambrose Bierce, 1842–1914
(American writer)

When an individual purchases a share of stock in a corporation, that person becomes a shareholder and an owner of the corporation. Unlike the members in a partnership, the body of shareholders can change constantly without affecting the continued existence of the corporation. A shareholder can sue the corporation, and the corporation can sue a shareholder. Also, under certain circumstances, a shareholder can sue on behalf of a corporation. The rights and duties of all corporate personnel will be examined in Chapter 27.

As a corporation is a separate legal entity, corporate profits are taxed by state and federal governments. Corporations can do one of two things with corporate profits—retain them or pass them on to shareholders in the form of dividends. The corporation receives no tax deduction for dividends distributed to shareholders. Dividends are again taxable (except when they represent distributions of capital) as ordinary income to the shareholder receiving them. This double-taxation feature of the corporation is one of its major disadvantages. Profits not distributed are retained by the corporation. **Retained earnings,** if invested properly, will yield higher corporate profits in the future and thus cause the price of the company's stock to rise. Individual shareholders can then reap the benefits of these retained earnings in the gains they receive when they sell their shares.

RETAINED EARNINGS
The portion of a corporation's profits that has not been paid out as dividends to shareholders.

Torts and Criminal Acts

A corporation is liable for the torts committed by its agents or officers within the course and scope of their employment. This principle applies to a corporation exactly as it applies to the ordinary agency relationships discussed in Chapter 23. It follows the doctrine of *respondeat superior.*

A criminal act requires intent. Under modern criminal law, a corporation can sometimes be held liable for the criminal acts of its agents and employees, provided the punishment is one that can be applied to the corporation. Obviously, corporations cannot be imprisoned (although at least one judge has held to the contrary—

"Did you expect a corporation to have a conscience, when it has no soul to be damned and no body to be kicked?"

Edward Thurlow, 1731–1806
(English jurist)

2. *W. C. M. Window Co. v. Bernardi,* 730 F.2d 486 (7th Cir. 1984).

Landmark in the Law

The *Dartmouth College* Case (1819)

In 1819, the United States Supreme Court heard the case of *The Trustees of Dartmouth College v. Woodward*.[a] The decision by the Court in that case determined not only the continued private existence of the small college in New Hampshire but also the continued existence of private corporations in the United States.

Dartmouth College, named in honor of one of its wealthy patrons, the Earl of Dartmouth, had been founded by the Reverend Eleazar Wheelock, a young Connecticut minister who sought to establish a school to train both missionaries and Native Americans. In 1769, a corporate charter was obtained from the royal governor of New Hampshire. The charter made Wheelock and his English patrons who had donated capital to the college a self-perpetuating board of trustees for the project. When Wheelock died, his son became president of the college. Under the new, less experienced leadership, many disputes arose over the running of the institution, and the participants eventually divided along the prevailing political party lines of New Hampshire.

The Republican group[b] believed that the college ought to be under the control of the state and become a public rather than a sectarian institution. The Republicans persuaded the Republican-controlled New Hampshire Congress to pass legislation that significantly altered the composition of the board of trustees and added a board of overseers that had virtual authority to control the college. The Federalist[c] board of trustees wanted to preserve the conservative, congregational character of the school and wanted to continue to govern the college without interference. They brought suit against William Woodward, the secretary-treasurer of the state-appointed board of overseers, alleging that the legislation violated the college's original charter. The trustees argued that the original grant of the charter, with its self-perpetuating board of trustees, was effectively a contract between the king and the board. Thus, the U.S. Constitution, which in Article I, Section 10, forbids states to pass legislation that would impair the obligation of contracts, prohibited the state from legislating changes in the self-governing structure of the board. The New Hampshire legislature was, therefore, without power to add trustees to the board, to create a board of overseers, or to alter the original charter in any manner.

Chief Justice Marshall delivered the opinion of the Court. He stated that the grant of the charter was a contract regarding private property within the meaning of Article I, Section 10, and that the legislative acts of New Hampshire, passed without the trustees' assent, were not binding upon them. Justice Story, in a separate opinion, distinguished between public and private corporations.

a. 17 U.S. (4 Wheaton) 518, 4 L.Ed. 629 (1819).
b. The forerunner of the modern-day Democratic party.
c. The Federalists were an early political group, or party, that advocated a strong national government.

see this chapter's *Law in the Extreme*), but they can be fined. (Of course, corporate directors and officers can be imprisoned, and in recent years, many have faced criminal penalties for their own actions or for the actions of employees under their supervision. The liability of corporate directors and officers is examined in Chapter 27.)

Corporate criminal liability is vicarious. That is, one person is punished for the act or acts of another. Thus, the corporation that is found to be criminally responsible for an act committed by an employee can be fined for that offense. Through the fine, stockholders and other employees suffer because of the vicarious liability of the corporation. The justification for such criminal liability involves a showing that the corporation could have exercised control and precluded the act or that there was authorization, consent, or knowledge of the act by persons in supervisory positions within the corporation.

❖ Corporate Powers

Under modern law, except as limited by charters, statutes, or constitutions, *a corporation can engage in all acts and enter into any contract available to a natural*

He stated that if the shareholders of a corporation were municipal or other public officials, then the corporation was a public corporation and therefore subject to continual public regulation. If the shareholders were private individuals, however, quite a contrary situation prevailed. The corporation was private, regardless of whether it served some public interest. The private corporation was consequently bound only by the terms of its original charter. Had the state reserved regulatory rights in the original grant of the charter, then the college would be subject to such control. In the absence of such reservations, the state of New Hampshire's legislative acts clearly impaired the original charter and thus violated the U.S. Constitution.

Story's opinion opened an avenue for the future regulation of new corporations, while at the same time creating vested rights in "private" corporations. Marshall and Story both made it clear that the United States Supreme Court would afford the property rights of private corporations the same protection afforded to other forms of property.

"THIS, SIR, IS MY CASE! IT IS THE CASE NOT MERE-
LY OF THAT HUMBLE INSTITUTION, IT IS THE CASE
OF EVERY COLLEGE IN OUR LAND!...IT IS, SIR, AS
I HAVE SAID, A SMALL COLLEGE. AND YET..."

Daniel Webster (standing) argues the Dartmouth *case before the Supreme Court. How did the outcome of this case affect the state regulation of corporations?*

person in order to accomplish the purposes for which it was created. When a corporation is created, the express and implied powers necessary to achieve its purpose also come into existence.

Express and Implied Powers

The express powers of a corporation are found in its **articles of incorporation** (a document containing information about the corporation, including its organization and functions), in the law of the state of incorporation, and in the state and federal constitutions. Corporate **bylaws** (rules of management adopted by the corporation at its first organizational meeting) and the resolutions of the corporation's board of directors also grant or restrict certain powers. The following order of priority is used when conflicts arise among documents involving corporations:

1. The U.S. Constitution.
2. State constitutions.
3. State statutes.
4. The articles of incorporation.

ARTICLES OF INCORPORATION
The document filed with the appropriate governmental agency, usually the secretary of state, when a business is incorporated; state statutes usually prescribe what kind of information must be contained in the articles of incorporation.

BYLAWS
A set of governing rules or regulations adopted by a corporation or other association.

Law in the Extreme

How to Imprison a Corporation

Individuals who commit crimes may be sent to prison. But, as everybody knows, corporations are a different matter. How can you imprison a corporation? Traditionally, judges have not even toyed with the idea, resorting instead to other types of criminal penalties—such as the imposition of fines. But at least one judge has concluded that it is possible to imprison a corporation. On August 30, 1988, in a case heard by the United States District Court for the Eastern District of Virginia, Judge Doumar sentenced a corporation to a three-year term of imprisonment and a $1 million fine.[a] The sentence was imposed on Allegheny Bottling Company (formerly Allegheny Pepsi-Cola Bottling Company) after that firm had been convicted of conspiring with a Coca-Cola distributor to fix prices in violation of the Sherman Antitrust Act of 1890.[b]

In his decision, Judge Doumar took issue with the common assumption that a corporation cannot be imprisoned. That assumption "was made by judges, and not by Congress" and "has lingered in the legal system unexamined and without support." The judge pointed out that Webster's dictionary defines imprisonment not in terms of stone walls and iron bars but as a "constraint of a person either by force or by such other coercion as restrains him within limits against his will." Judge Doumar also noted that cases involving false imprisonment do not entail confinement in a jail or prison but rather a forceful restraint of a person against that person's will. Therefore, concluded the judge, corporate imprisonment would require only that a court restrain or immobilize the corporation. Restraints (such as the seizure of corporate assets) are commonly placed on corporations in bankruptcy. Why not effectively "imprison" corporations that commit crimes by applying similar restraints?

After all, the judge reasoned, why should corporations escape imprisonment for criminal offenses when individuals cannot? In no case had any court cited an authority for the proposition that corporations cannot be imprisoned, and no court had ever—to the judge's knowledge—actually held that corporate imprisonment was illegal, unconstitutional, or impossible. The judge maintained that "considerable confusion" attends the concept of corporate imprisonment only because courts mistakenly think that imprisonment "necessarily involves incarceration in jail."

The judge fashioned his sentence so that, insofar as possible, the punishment would fit the crime. After the sentencing, the judge suspended all of the imprisonment and $50,000 of the fine and placed Allegheny on probation for three years. As special conditions of the probation, Allegheny would not be allowed to "dispose of any of its franchises, capital assets or plants or facilities in the Norfolk, Richmond or Baltimore areas, without specific permission of this Court through the probation officer."

"Stone walls do not a prison make, nor iron bars a cage"—so said Richard Lovelace, an English poet who lived from 1618 to 1658. Obviously, Judge Doumar agrees with Lovelace's sentiment—and, very possibly, so might Allegheny Bottling Company.

a. *United States v. Allegheny Bottling Co.*, 695 F.Supp. 856 (E.D.Va. 1988).

b. Price fixing and the Sherman Antitrust Act will be discussed in Chapter 30.

5. Bylaws.
6. Resolutions of the board of directors.

Certain implied powers attach when a corporation is created. Barring express constitutional, statutory, or charter prohibitions, the corporation has the implied power to perform all acts reasonably appropriate and necessary to accomplish its corporate purposes. For this reason, a corporation has the implied power to borrow money within certain limits, to lend money or to extend credit to those with whom it has a legal or contractual relationship, and to make charitable contributions.[3]

To borrow money, the corporation acts through its board of directors to authorize the loan. Most often, the president or chief executive officer of the corporation will execute the necessary papers on behalf of the corporation. In so doing, corporate officers have the implied power to bind the corporation in matters directly connected with the *ordinary* business affairs of the enterprise. A corporate officer does not have the authority to bind the corporation in matters of great significance to the corporate purpose or undertaking, however, as the following case illustrates.

Case 26.1 

BOSTON ATHLETIC ASSOCIATION v. INTERNATIONAL MARATHONS, INC.

Supreme Judicial Court of Massachusetts, 1984.
392 Mass. 356,
467 N.E.2d 58.

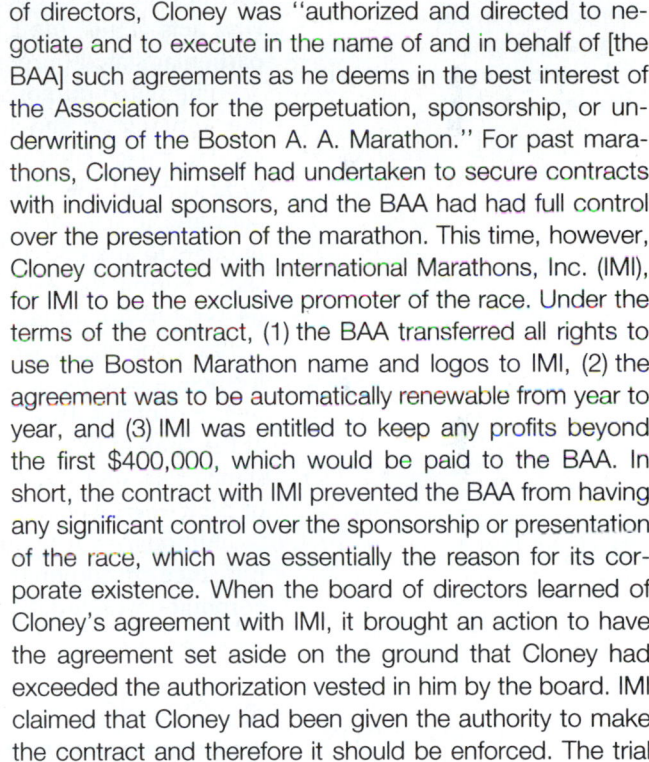

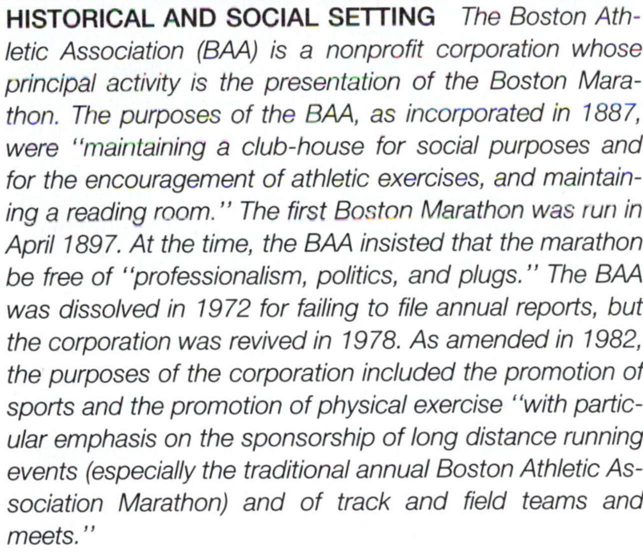
HISTORICAL AND SOCIAL SETTING *The Boston Athletic Association (BAA) is a nonprofit corporation whose principal activity is the presentation of the Boston Marathon. The purposes of the BAA, as incorporated in 1887, were "maintaining a club-house for social purposes and for the encouragement of athletic exercises, and maintaining a reading room." The first Boston Marathon was run in April 1897. At the time, the BAA insisted that the marathon be free of "professionalism, politics, and plugs." The BAA was dissolved in 1972 for failing to file annual reports, but the corporation was revived in 1978. As amended in 1982, the purposes of the corporation included the promotion of sports and the promotion of physical exercise "with particular emphasis on the sponsorship of long distance running events (especially the traditional annual Boston Athletic Association Marathon) and of track and field teams and meets."*

FACTS William T. Cloney was the president of the Boston Athletic Association. At a 1981 meeting of the BAA board of directors, Cloney was "authorized and directed to negotiate and to execute in the name of and in behalf of [the BAA] such agreements as he deems in the best interest of the Association for the perpetuation, sponsorship, or underwriting of the Boston A. A. Marathon." For past marathons, Cloney himself had undertaken to secure contracts with individual sponsors, and the BAA had had full control over the presentation of the marathon. This time, however, Cloney contracted with International Marathons, Inc. (IMI), for IMI to be the exclusive promoter of the race. Under the terms of the contract, (1) the BAA transferred all rights to use the Boston Marathon name and logos to IMI, (2) the agreement was to be automatically renewable from year to year, and (3) IMI was entitled to keep any profits beyond the first $400,000, which would be paid to the BAA. In short, the contract with IMI prevented the BAA from having any significant control over the sponsorship or presentation of the race, which was essentially the reason for its corporate existence. When the board of directors learned of Cloney's agreement with IMI, it brought an action to have the agreement set aside on the ground that Cloney had exceeded the authorization vested in him by the board. IMI claimed that Cloney had been given the authority to make the contract and therefore it should be enforced. The trial court held for the BAA, and IMI appealed.

ISSUE Had Cloney exceeded his authority by granting IMI excessive, and perpetual, control over the Boston Marathon?

DECISION Yes. The trial court's judgment was affirmed.

3. A corporation is prohibited from making political contributions in federal elections by the Federal Elections Campaign Act of 1974 (18 U.S.C. Section 321). Early law held that a corporation had no implied authority to make charitable contributions because charitable activities were contrary to the primary purpose of the corporation to make a profit. Modern law, by statutes and court decisions, holds that a corporation has such implied authority.

Case 26.1—Continued

REASON The Supreme Judicial Court of Massachusetts stated that under "the traditional principles of corporate governance, the board of governors of the BAA does not have the power to delegate to an individual officer authority to enter into a contract which so totally encumbers the most significant purpose of the BAA, the presentation of the Marathon. * * * It is the obligation of the board of governors to oversee the presentation of the Marathon, not to surrender virtually complete control of the event to another organization." The court also concluded that the contract was inconsistent with the nonprofit nature of the BAA because IMI's primary goal in promoting the marathon was to secure profits for itself from the promoting activities. For these reasons, the court deemed that Cloney was not empowered to make the contract with IMI, and the contract was thus unenforceable.

Ultra Vires Doctrine

ULTRA VIRES
A Latin term meaning *beyond the powers.* Activities of a corporation's managers that are outside the scope of the power granted them by the corporation's charter or the laws of the state of incorporation are *ultra vires* acts.

The term ***ultra vires*** means "beyond the powers." In corporate law, acts of a corporation that are beyond the authority given to it under its charter or under the statutes by which it was incorporated are *ultra vires* acts. In other words, acts in furtherance of the corporation's expressed purposes are within the corporate power; acts beyond the scope of corporate business as described in the charter are *ultra vires* acts. Thus, *ultra vires* acts can be understood only within the context of the particular stated purposes for which the corporation was organized.

The stated purposes in the articles of incorporation set the limits of the activities the corporation can legally pursue. Any time the corporation takes on activities outside these stated purposes, the corporation can be charged with committing an *ultra vires* act. Because of this, corporations are increasingly aware of the benefit of adopting a statement of purpose in their articles of incorporation that is broad enough to include virtually all conceivable activities. Corporate statutes in many states permit the expression "any lawful purpose" to be a legally sufficient stated purpose in the articles of incorporation.

In some states, when a contract is entirely executory, neither party having performed, a defense of *ultra vires* can be used by either party to prevent enforcement of the contract. In cases in which an *ultra vires* contract is only partially executed at the time of challenge, courts may nevertheless enforce the contract if the circumstances are such that it would be inequitable to allow a party to assert the defense of *ultra vires.* Today, executed contracts are usually held valid.

Although still of some importance, the *ultra vires* doctrine is of declining significance in corporate law, because courts have held that any legal action that a corporation undertakes to profit its shareholders is allowable and proper.

❖ Classification of Corporations

The classification of a corporation depends on its purpose, ownership characteristics, and location.

Domestic, Foreign, and Alien Corporations

DOMESTIC CORPORATION
In a given state, a corporation that does business in, and is organized under the laws of, that state.

FOREIGN CORPORATION
In a given state, a corporation that does business in the state without being incorporated therein.

ALIEN CORPORATION
A designation in the United States for a corporation formed in another country but doing business in the United States.

A corporation is referred to as a **domestic corporation** by its home state (the state in which it incorporates). A corporation formed in one state but doing business in another is referred to in that other state as a **foreign corporation.** A corporation formed in another country—say, Mexico—but doing business in the United States is referred to in the United States as an **alien corporation.**

A corporation does not have an automatic right to do business in a state other than its state of incorporation. It normally must obtain a *certificate of authority* in any state in which it plans to do business. Once the certificate has been issued, the

Honda Motor Company manufactures automobiles in factories in the United States, although Honda is an alien corporation. What is the difference between an alien corporation and a foreign corporation?

powers conferred upon a corporation by its home state generally can be exercised in the other state.

As discussed in Chapter 3, before a state court can hear a dispute in which a foreign corporation is the defendant, the state court must have *jurisdiction* over the defendant; and this requires that the foreign corporation have sufficient *contacts* with the state. A foreign corporation that has its home office in the state or has manufacturing plants in the state generally meets this *minimum-contacts* requirement. A foreign corporation whose only contact with the state is the fact that one of its directors resides there usually does not have sufficient contacts with the state for the state court to exercise jurisdiction over it. What about a Japanese corporation whose only contact with a state is through its wholly owned subsidiary? Can a state exercise jurisdiction over the Japanese corporation in these circumstances? This issue is raised in the following case, in which the court bases its decision on a "stream of commerce" theory of minimum contacts.

Case 26.2
LORAL FAIRCHILD CORP. v. VICTOR COMPANY OF JAPAN, LTD.
United States District Court,
Eastern District of New York, 1992.
803 F.Supp. 626.

HISTORICAL AND SOCIAL SETTING *Historically, a state court had jurisdiction over a party to an action only if the person or thing involved was in the state or if the party consented. In the middle of the twentieth century, the United States Supreme Court adopted a new, flexible standard for asserting personal jurisdiction on the basis of a party's relation to the state.*[a] *Today, each state has a statute that provides for the exercise of personal jurisdiction over nonresidents (which include foreign or alien corporations) for causes of action arising from certain specified grounds. For example, Virginia grants personal jurisdiction over a nonresident for any cause of action arising from the nonresident's "[c]ausing tortious injury in this Commonwealth by an act or omission outside this Commonwealth."*[b] *Under the Supreme Court's application of the due process clause of the Fourteenth Amendment, a court can exercise personal jurisdiction over a nonresident who has purposefully established minimum contacts with the state. A business is considered to establish minimum contacts with a state when the business places goods in the stream of commerce with the intent that the goods be sold in the state.*

FACTS In 1991, Loral Fairchild Corporation brought suit in a federal court against Victor Company of Japan, Ltd., and a number of other Japanese firms for patent infringement. One of the firms, Murata Machinery, Ltd. (Murata-Japan), manufactured facsimile (fax) machines that were distributed in the state of Virginia through its wholly owned

a. *International Shoe Co. v. State of Washington*, 326 U.S. 310, 66 S.Ct. 154, 90 L.Ed. 95 (1945). This case is presented in Chapter 3 as Case 3.1.

b. Va. Code Ann. Section 8.01–328.1.

Case 26.2—Continued

subsidiary, Murata Business Systems, Inc. (Murata-America). Loral, which also sold fax machines in Virginia, alleged that Murata-Japan's fax machines used a device that had been patented by Loral. Murata-Japan moved to dismiss the complaint for lack of personal jurisdiction, and the issue in this case centered on whether Murata-Japan had sufficient contacts with Virginia to justify jurisdiction over Murata-Japan by a U.S. court. The evidence indicated that Murata-Japan itself did not sell products or services in Virginia, had no offices or bank accounts in Virginia, and shipped its goods to ports in states other than Virginia. All advertising, marketing, and distribution of Murata-Japan fax machines in Virginia were controlled solely by Murata-America. In short, Murata-Japan's sole "contacts" with Virginia existed by virtue of the fact that its subsidiary served the Virginia market and that its products allegedly caused tortious injury (to Loral) in Virginia.

ISSUE Does Murata-Japan have sufficient contacts with the state of Virginia to justify the state's exercise of personal jurisdiction over that company?

DECISION Yes. The court held that by placing its machines in the stream of commerce and purposefully directing them toward the Virginia marketplace, Murata-Japan had satisfied the minimum-contacts requirement for personal jurisdiction.

REASON The court, citing a United States Supreme Court decision in a similar case, held that a state "does not exceed its powers * * * if it asserts personal jurisdiction over a corporation that delivers its products into the stream of commerce with the expectation that they will be purchased by consumers in the * * * State." The one qualification is that a "defendant's conduct and connection with the forum state" must be such that the defendant "should 'reasonably anticipate' being haled into court there." The court found that Murata-Japan had a substantial connection to Virginia through its subsidiary, Murata-America. First, Murata-Japan owned "not 96 percent but 100 percent" of Murata-America's stock. Second, four of Murata-America's seven directors were Murata-Japan representatives. Third, Murata-Japan derived significant economic benefits from Murata-America's marketing and distributing of its products in Virginia. In view of these circumstances, the court concluded that "Murata-Japan knew it had indirectly established contacts with the forum and intended such a result. Stated differently, Murata-Japan could have anticipated this lawsuit from its manufacture of infringing products sold by its distributor in Virginia."

ETHICAL CONSIDERATIONS *Murata-Japan argued, among other things, that being "haled into court" in the United States would impose an extreme burden on it, because its employees would be required to travel from Japan to the United States. In response to this argument, the court stated that "[a]ny inconvenience that Murata-Japan may suffer must be weighed against a public policy which favors providing a forum for an injured resident to bring an action against a non-resident manufacturer." The court concluded that this public policy outweighed "any inconvenience to Murata-Japan in defending this lawsuit."*

Public and Private Corporations

A public corporation is one formed by the government to meet some political or governmental purpose. Cities and towns that incorporate are common examples. In addition, many federal government organizations, such as the U.S. Postal Service, the Tennessee Valley Authority, and AMTRAK, are public corporations. Private corporations, however, are created either wholly or in part for private benefit. Most corporations are private. Although they may serve a public purpose, as a public utility does, they are owned by private persons rather than by the government.

Nonprofit Corporations

Corporations formed without a profit-making purpose are called *nonprofit, not-for-profit,* or *eleemosynary* (charitable) corporations. Private hospitals, educational institutions, charities, religious organizations, and the like are frequently organized as nonprofit corporations. The nonprofit corporation is a convenient form of organization that allows various groups to own property and to form contracts without the individual members' being personally exposed to liability.

Close Corporations

A **close corporation** is one whose shares are held by members of a family or by relatively few persons. Close corporations are also referred to as *closely held, family,* or *privately held* corporations. Usually, the members of the small group constituting a close corporation are personally known to each other. Because the number of shareholders is so small, there is no trading market for the shares. In practice, a close corporation is often operated like a partnership. A few states recognize this in special statutory provisions that cover close corporations.

CLOSE CORPORATION
A corporation whose shareholders are limited to a small group of persons, often including only family members. The rights of shareholders of a close corporation usually are restricted regarding the transfer of shares to others.

Statutes for Close Corporations To be eligible for close corporation status, a corporation has to have a limited number of shareholders, the transfer of corporation stock must be subject to certain restrictions, and the corporation must not make any public offering of its securities.[4] Close corporation statutes provide greater flexibility by expressly permitting close corporations to depart significantly from certain formalities required by traditional corporation law.[5]

Management of Close Corporations The close corporation has a single shareholder or a closely knit group of shareholders, who usually hold the positions of directors and officers. Management of a close corporation resembles that of a sole proprietorship or a partnership. As a corporation, however, the firm must meet the same legal requirements as other corporations, unless special statutes have been enacted, as mentioned previously.

To prevent a majority shareholder from dominating a close corporation, the corporation may require that action can be taken by the board only on approval of more than a simple majority of the directors. Typically, this would not be required for ordinary business decisions but only for extraordinary actions, such as changing the amount of dividends or dismissing an employee-shareholder.

Transfer of Shares in Close Corporations Because, by definition, a close corporation has a small number of shareholders, the transfer of one shareholder's shares to someone else can cause serious management problems. The other shareholders may find themselves required to share control with someone they do not know or like. To avoid this problem, it is usually advisable for the close corporation with several shareholders to specify restrictions on the transferability of stock in its articles of incorporation. A few states have statutes under which close corporation shares cannot be transferred unless certain persons—including shareholders, family members, and the corporation—are first given the opportunity to purchase the shares for the same price.

Consider an example. Three brothers, Terry, Damon, and Henry Johnson, are the only shareholders of Johnson's Car Wash, Inc. Terry and Damon do not want Henry to sell his shares to an unknown third person. The articles of incorporation might therefore restrict the transferability of shares to outside persons by stipulating that shareholders offer their shares to the corporation or other shareholders before selling them to an outside purchaser.

Another way that control of a close corporation can be stabilized is through the use of a shareholder agreement. Agreements among shareholders to vote their stock in a particular way are generally upheld.[6] Shareholder agreements can also provide

4. See, for example, 8 Del. Code Ann. Section 342, which provides that close corporations can have no more than thirty shareholders.

5. For example, in some states (such as Maryland), the close corporation need not have a board of directors.

6. An important case upholding the validity of shareholder agreements is *Ringling Bros.–Barnum and Bailey Combined Shows v. Ringling,* 29 Del.Ch. 610, 53 A.2d 441 (1947).

that when one of the original shareholders dies, his or her shares of stock in the corporation will be divided in such a way that the proportionate holdings of the survivors, and thus their proportionate control, will be maintained. (See this chapter's *Business Law in Action* for further discussion of shareholder agreements.)

S Corporations

S CORPORATION
A close business corporation that has met certain requirements as set out by the Internal Revenue Code and thus qualifies for special income-tax treatment. Essentially, an S corporation is taxed the same as a partnership, but its owners enjoy the privilege of limited liability.

In 1982, Congress enacted the Subchapter S Revision Act. The purpose of the act was "to minimize the effect of federal income taxes on choices of the form of business organizations and to permit the incorporation and operation of certain small businesses without the incidence of income taxation at both the corporate and shareholder level."[7] Additionally, Congress divided corporations into two groups: **S corporations,** which have elected Subchapter S treatment, and *C corporations,* which are all other corporations. Certain close corporations can choose to qualify under Subchapter S of the Internal Revenue Code to avoid the imposition of income taxes at the corporate level while retaining many of the advantages of a corporation, particularly limited liability.

Qualification Requirements for S Corporations Among the numerous requirements for S-corporation status, the following are the most important:

1. The corporation must be a domestic corporation.
2. The corporation must not be a member of an affiliated group of corporations.
3. The shareholders of the corporation must be individuals, estates, or certain trusts. Corporations, partnerships, and nonqualifying trusts cannot be shareholders.
4. The corporation must have thirty-five or fewer shareholders.
5. The corporation must have only one class of stock, although not all shareholders need have the same voting rights.
6. No shareholder of the corporation may be a nonresident alien.

Benefits of S Corporations At times, it is beneficial for a regular corporation to elect S-corporation status. Benefits include the following:

1. When the corporation has losses, the S election allows the shareholders to use the losses to offset other income.
2. When the stockholder's tax bracket is lower than the corporation's tax bracket, the S election causes the corporation's entire income to be taxed in the shareholder's bracket, whether or not it is distributed. This is particularly attractive when the corporation wants to accumulate earnings for some future business purpose.
3. As mentioned, a single tax on corporate income is imposed at individual income tax rates at the shareholder level. (The income is taxable to shareholders whether or not it is actually distributed.)

Professional Corporations

In the past, professional persons such as physicians, lawyers, dentists, and accountants could not incorporate. Today they can, and their corporations are typically identified by the letters S.C. (service corporation), P.C. (professional corporation), or P.A. (professional association). In general, the laws governing professional corporations are similar to those governing ordinary business corporations, but three basic areas of liability deserve special attention. First, a court might, for liability purposes, regard the professional corporation as a partnership in which each partner can be held liable for whatever malpractice liability is incurred by the others within

7. Senate Report No. 640, 97th Congress, 1st Session (1981).

Business Law in Action

The Sanctity of Shareholder Agreements

Courts are generally reluctant to interfere with private agreements, including shareholder agreements. In fact, according to a dissenting justice in *Rosiny v. Schmidt*,[a] the majority on the court was a little too reluctant to interfere. The dissenting justice held that a shareholder agreement that the court found enforceable should have been declared unconscionable. The case involved a shareholder agreement formed in 1981 among four shareholders, each of whom held 25 percent of the corporation's shares. The agreement provided that the shareholders would not, during their lifetimes, sell, assign, or transfer their stock unless it was first offered to the other shareholders. The agreement further stipulated that "[t]he price at which said stock shall be offered for sale shall be the book value thereof as of the last day of the month immediately preceding the date of the said offer or $200 per share, whichever amount is greater." In the event of a shareholder's death, the surviving shareholders could buy the decedent's shares "at the same price applicable to transfers during their lifetime."

Two of the shareholders, Allen and Frank Rosiny, were relatively young but well-educated and experienced attorneys. The other two shareholders, Charles McGuire and and at the time the 1981 agreement was signed, Priddy was preoccupied with the death of her husband and McGuire's mental condition was described by his family as "not good." When the 1981 agreement was formed, the book value of the corporation was negative (given depreciation on the premises, as recorded in the corporate books), but the market value was $4,225 per share and rising. Both Priddy and McGuire died in 1988, and at the time of their deaths, although the book value remained a negative figure, the market value had increased to $41,500 per share. In sum, the younger shareholders stood to gain a windfall on Priddy's and McGuire's deaths. According to the terms of the 1981 agreement, they were entitled to buy the decedents' shares at $200 per share.

The heirs of McGuire and Priddy claimed that there had been no "meeting of the minds" when the 1981 agreement was formed and therefore the agreement was unenforceable. The heirs further argued that the agreement was unconscionable because the younger shareholders, knowing that neither McGuire nor Priddy was aware of what they were signing, took advantage of this fact for their personal gain. The court did not agree with the heirs' arguments. The court pointed out that McGuire and Priddy had signed several shareholder agreements in the past and that, in a 1971 shareholder agreement, they had consciously and intentionally consented to the use of book value to measure the value of corporate shares. The court therefore reasoned that the 1981 agreement, which contained virtually the same provision, reflected McGuire's and Priddy's intentions.

The dissenting justice pointed to the fact that although McGuire and Priddy might have agreed in 1971 to a valuation based on book value, that was an insufficient basis for assuming that they had also agreed to the 1981 agreement. Also, the dissenting justice emphasized that shareholders in a close corporation are obligated, as are partners in a partnership, "to exercise fidelity and good faith in their dealings with each other." In the dissent's view, it was clear that the younger shareholders had not fulfilled this fiduciary obligation.

The younger shareholders' failure to point out to McGuire and Priddy the adverse effects of signing the agreement is, perhaps, unconscionable in the minds of many. But the majority on the court declared that "[w]hile it is true that in a close corporation, shareholders must deal in good faith in the conduct of the affairs of the corporation, we are unaware of any dictate requiring one shareholder to explain a provision of a shareholders' agreement to another, particularly when the latter signed previous agreements containing the identical provision in question." This conclusion was reached in spite of testimony by the Rosinys that they would never advise a client in McGuire's or Priddy's position to sign such an agreement.

a. 185 A.D.2d 727, 587 N.Y.S.2d 929 (1992).

the scope of the partnership. Second, a shareholder in a professional corporation is protected from the liability imposed because of torts (unrelated to malpractice) committed by other members. Third, many professional corporation statutes retain personal liability of professional persons for their acts and the professional acts performed under their supervision. In the following case, a law partnership incorporated as a professional corporation in 1977 primarily for the purpose of obtaining certain tax benefits. In fact, however, the firm continued to operate as a partnership. A central question before the court was whether the firm should be governed by partnership law or corporation law.

Case 26.3
BOYD, PAYNE, GATES & FARTHING, P.C. v. PAYNE, GATES, FARTHING & RADD, P.C.
Supreme Court of Virginia, 1992.
422 S.E.2d 784.

HISTORICAL AND SOCIAL SETTING *Professional corporations or associations are authorized by the statutes of all states and the District of Columbia. To be treated as a corporation, however, a professional corporation must act as a corporation, just as any individuals coming together to conduct business as a corporation must act as a corporation. This is not a new proposition. The principle applied to ordinary corporations before professional corporations were common. For example, in the late 1920s, two businesspersons entered into a partnership to manufacture and sell radio cabinets. They formed a corporation to carry out the purpose, but no stock was issued and no capital was invested. In a suit to determine what amounts creditors should receive from the funds of the company, the court held that although the company "became technically a corporate entity," the two businesspersons dealt with it as if it were a partnership. Consequently, the court decided that in settling the company's accounts, it should be treated as a partnership.*[a]

FACTS In 1977, Robert Boyd, Charles Payne, Ronald Gates, and Philip Farthing, who practiced law together as a partnership, formed a professional corporation known as Boyd, Payne, Gates & Farthing, P.C. (referred to here as Boyd P.C.). In a letter sent to its clients and the legal community, Boyd P.C. stated that the "partnership" would continue to practice under the new firm name. Corporate stock was issued to the four partners in the same percentages as their profit percentages (the percentage of the firm's profits resulting from each lawyer's work). Changes in the profit percentages occurred over time, but the stock ratio remained the same. In 1983, when Anthony Radd joined the practice, he received no stock but began receiving 5 percent of the profits. No partnership assets were ever transferred to the corporation. The members of the firm continued to refer to each other as "partners" and to Boyd as the "managing partner." "Partner meetings" were held to discuss the firm's business matters. In 1987, Payne, Gates, Farthing, and Radd left Boyd P.C. and formed their own professional corporation under the name of Payne, Gates, Farthing & Radd, P.C. (Payne P.C.). A dispute arose over the ownership of Boyd P.C.'s assets, including accounts receivable, and the trial court found that Boyd P.C. was in fact a partnership and that the former partners were entitled to an accounting and a distribution of the partnership's assets. The court ordered Boyd P.C. to pay Payne and the others their respective percentages of the value of the partnership (in all, over $550,000). Boyd P.C. appealed this decision, contending that the trial court erred in applying partnership law to its corporation.

a. *Deeds v. Gilmer,* 162 Va. 157, 174 S.E. 37 (1934).

ISSUE Was the trial court justified in applying partnership law to Boyd P.C.?

DECISION Yes. The trial court's judgment was affirmed.

REASON The Supreme Court of Virginia found, as the trial court had, that Boyd P.C. was merely a corporate "shell" formed to gain tax advantages. The evidence sufficiently indicated that the firm continued to operate as a partnership. The court also found it significant that after the corporation had been formed, the partners "executed an agreement dealing with the possibility of a tax audit" in which it was provided that if the firm was audited, each partner's tax liability would be based on the percentage of profits that the partner received in that particular year. This agreement effectively indicated that "tax liability was apportioned on the basis of partnership percentages, not stock ownership." The court cited a previous case in which partnership law was applied to a corporation because members of the corporation "utterly disregarded [the] corporate entity, and dealt with its rights, property and business as if they belonged to a partnership." The court concluded that "[b]ecause Boyd P.C. was a close corporation and its shareholders validly conducted the internal affairs of their law practice as a partnership, we hold that the trial court properly settled their rights and liabilities according to partnership law."

❖ Corporate Formation

The formation of a corporation involves two steps: (1) preliminary organizational and promotional undertakings—particularly obtaining capital for the future corporation—and (2) the legal process of incorporation.

Promotional Activities

Before a corporation becomes a reality, people invest in the proposed corporation as subscribers. Contracts are frequently made by **promoters** on behalf of the future corporation. Promoters are those who, for themselves or others, take the preliminary steps in organizing a corporation. One of the tasks of the promoter is to issue a **prospectus,** which is a document required by federal or state securities laws that describes the financial operations of the corporation, thus allowing investors to make informed decisions. (Securities laws are discussed in Chapter 29.) The promoter also secures the *corporate charter.* As will be discussed in the section on incorporation procedures, the corporate charter is a document issued by a state agency or authority—usually the secretary of state—that grants a corporation legal existence and the right to function.

"A man to carry on a successful business must have imagination. He must see things as in a vision, a dream of the whole thing."

Charles M. Schwab, 1862–1939
(American industrialist)

PROMOTER
An entrepreneur who participates in the organization of a corporation in its formative stage, usually by issuing a prospectus, procuring subscriptions to the stock, making contract purchases, securing a charter, and the like.

PROSPECTUS
A document that contains all material facts about a company and its operations so that those who wish to purchase stock (invest) in the corporation have the basis for making an informed decision.

Promoter's Liability It is not unusual for a promoter to purchase or lease property with a view to selling it to the corporation when the corporation is formed. A promoter may enter into contracts with attorneys, accountants, architects, or other professionals whose services will be needed in planning for the proposed corporation. Finally, a promoter induces people to purchase stock in the corporation.

As a general rule, a promoter is held personally liable on preincorporation contracts. Courts simply hold that promoters are not agents when a corporation has yet to come into existence. If, however, the promoter secures the contracting party's agreement to hold only the corporation (not the promoter) liable on the contract, the promoter will not be liable in the event of any breach of contract.

Basically, the personal liability of the promoter continues even after incorporation unless the third party *releases* the promoter. In most states, this rule is applied whether or not the promoter made the agreement in the name of, or with reference to, the proposed corporation.

Once the corporation is formed (the charter issued), the promoter remains personally liable until the corporation assumes the preincorporation contract by *novation* (discussed in Chapter 12). Novation releases the promoter and makes the corporation liable for performing the contractual obligations. In some cases, the corporation *adopts* the promoter's contract by undertaking to perform it. Most courts hold that adoption in and of itself does not discharge the promoter from contractual liability. A corporation cannot normally *ratify* a preincorporation contract, as no principal was in existence at the time the contract was made.

Subscribers and Subscriptions Prior to the actual formation of the corporation, the promoter can contact potential individual investors, and they can agree to purchase capital stock in the future corporation. This agreement is often called a *subscription agreement,* and the potential investor is called a *subscriber.* Depending on state law, subscribers become shareholders as soon as the corporation is formed or as soon as the corporation accepts the agreement. This way, if Corporation X becomes insolvent, the trustee in bankruptcy (discussed in Chapter 22) can collect the consideration for any unpaid stock from a preincorporation subscriber.

Most courts view preincorporation subscriptions as continuing offers to purchase corporate stock. On or after its formation, the corporation can choose to accept the offer to purchase stock. Many courts also treat a subscription as a contract between the subscribers, making it irrevocable except with the consent of all of the subscribers. A subscription is irrevocable for a period of six months unless otherwise provided in the subscription agreement or unless all the subscribers agree to the revocation of the subscription [RMBCA 6.20]. In some courts and jurisdictions, the preincorporation subscriber can revoke the offer to purchase before acceptance without liability, however.

"The laws of a nation suit its life."

Walter Bagehot, 1826–1877
(English economist and journalist)

Incorporation Procedures

Exact procedures for incorporation differ among states, but the basic requirements are similar.

State Chartering The first step in the incorporation procedure is to select a state in which to incorporate. Because state incorporation laws differ, individuals have found some advantage in looking for the states that offer the most advantageous tax or incorporation provisions. Delaware has historically had the least restrictive laws. Consequently, many corporations, including a number of the largest, have incorporated there. Delaware's statutes permit firms to incorporate in Delaware and carry out business and locate operating headquarters elsewhere. (Most other states now permit this.) Closely held corporations, however, particularly those of a professional nature, generally incorporate in the state in which their principal stockholders live and work.

Articles of Incorporation The primary document needed to begin the incorporation process is called the *articles of incorporation* (see Exhibit 26–1). The articles include basic information about the corporation and serve as a primary source of authority for its future organization and business functions. The person or persons who execute the articles are called *incorporators*. Generally, the elements discussed in the following sections should be included in the articles of incorporation.

Corporate Name The choice of a corporate name is subject to state approval to ensure against duplication or deception. State statutes usually require that the secretary of state run a check on the proposed name in the state of incorporation. Some states require that the incorporators, at their own expense, run a check on the proposed name for the newly formed corporation. Once cleared, a name can be reserved for a short time, for a fee, pending the completion of the articles of incorporation. All corporate statutes require the corporation name to include the word *Corporation*, *Incorporated*, *Company*, or *Limited*, or abbreviations of these terms.

A corporate name is prohibited from being the same as, or deceptively similar to, the name of an existing corporation doing business within the state. For example, if an existing corporation is named General Dynamics, Inc., the state will not allow another corporation to be called General Dynamic, Inc., because that name is deceptively similar to the first, and it impliedly transfers a part of the goodwill established by the first corporate user to the second corporation.

Duration A corporation can have perpetual existence under most state corporate statutes. A few states, however, prescribe a maximum duration, after which the corporation must formally renew its existence.

Nature and Purpose The intended business activities of the corporation must be specified in the articles, and, naturally, they must be lawful. A general statement of corporate purpose is usually sufficient to give rise to all of the powers necessary or convenient to the purpose of the organization. The corporate charter can state, for example, that the corporation is organized "to engage in the production and sale of agricultural products." As stated before, there is a trend toward allowing corporate charters to state that the corporation is organized for "any legal business," with no mention of specifics, to avoid unnecessary future amendments to the corporate charter.

Capital Structure The capital structure of the corporation is generally set forth in the articles. A few state statutes require a relatively small capital investment (for example, $1,000) for ordinary business corporations but a greater capital investment for those engaged in insurance or banking. The number of shares of stock authorized

◆ **Exhibit 26–1**
Articles of Incorporation

ARTICLE ONE

The name of the corporation is ______________________________.

ARTICLE TWO

The period of its duration is perpetual (may be a number of years or until a certain date).

ARTICLE THREE

The purpose (or purposes) for which the corporation is organized is (are) ______________________________
______________________________.

ARTICLE FOUR

The aggregate number of shares that the corporation shall have authority to issue is ________ of the par value of ________dollar(s) each (or without par value).

ARTICLE FIVE

The corporation will not commence business until it has received for the issuance of its shares consideration of the value of $1,000 (can be any sum not less than $1,000).

ARTICLE SIX

The address of the corporation's registered office is ______________________________, New Pacum, and the name of its registered agent at such address is ______________________________
______________________________.

(Use the street or building or rural route address of the registered office, not a post office box number.)

ARTICLE SEVEN

The number of initial directors is ____________________, and the names and addresses of the directors are ______________________________
______________________________.

ARTICLE EIGHT

The name and address of the incorporator is ______________________________
______________________________.

(signed) ______________________________
Incorporator

Sworn to on ____________________ by the above-named incorporator.
(date)

____
Notary Public ________ County, New Pacum

(Notary Seal)

for issuance, their valuation, the various types or classes of stock authorized for issuance, and other relevant information concerning equity, capital, and credit must be outlined in the articles.

Internal Organization Whatever the internal management structure of the corporation, it should be described in the articles, although it can be included in bylaws adopted after the corporation is formed. The articles of incorporation commence the corporation; the bylaws are formed after commencement by the board of directors. Bylaws are subject to and cannot conflict with the incorporation statute or the corporation's charter [RMBCA 2.06]. Under the RMBCA, shareholders may amend or repeal bylaws. The board of directors may also amend or repeal bylaws unless the articles of incorporation or provisions of the incorporation statute reserve the power to shareholders exclusively [RMBCA 10.20]. Typical bylaw provisions describe the quorum and voting requirements for shareholders, the election of the board of directors, the methods of replacing directors, and the manner and time of scheduling shareholder and board meetings.

Registered Office and Agent The corporation must indicate the location and address of its registered office within the state. Usually, the registered office is also the principal office of the corporation. The corporation must give the name and address of a specific person who has been designated as an *agent* and who can receive legal documents (such as orders to appear in court) on behalf of the corporation.

Incorporators Each incorporator must be listed by name and must indicate an address. An incorporator is a person—often, the corporate promoter—who applies to the state on behalf of the corporation to obtain its corporate charter. The incorporator need not be a subscriber and need not have any interest at all in the corporation. Many states do not impose residency or age requirements for incorporators. States vary on the required number of incorporators; it can be as few as one or as many as three. Incorporators are required to sign the articles of incorporation when they are submitted to the state; often this is their only duty. In some states, they participate at the first organizational meeting of the corporation.

Certificate of Incorporation Once the articles of incorporation have been prepared, signed, and authenticated by the incorporators, they are sent to the appropriate state official, usually the secretary of state, along with the appropriate filing fee. In many states, the secretary of state then issues a **certificate of incorporation** representing the state's authorization for the corporation to conduct business. (This may be called the **corporate charter.**) The certificate and a copy of the articles are returned to the incorporators.

CERTIFICATE OF INCORPORATION
The primary document that evidences corporate existence (referred to as articles of incorporation in some states).

CORPORATE CHARTER
The document issued by a state official (usually the secretary of state) granting a corporation legal existence and the right to function.

First Organizational Meeting The first organizational meeting is provided for in the articles of incorporation but is held after the charter has actually been granted. At this meeting, the incorporators elect the first board of directors and complete the routine business of incorporation (pass bylaws, issue stock, and so forth). Sometimes, the meeting is held after the election of the board, and the business transacted depends on the requirements of the state's incorporation statute, the nature of the business, the provisions made in the articles, and the desires of the promoters. Adoption of bylaws—the internal rules of management for the corporation—is probably the most important function of the meeting. The shareholders, directors, and officers must abide by the bylaws in conducting corporate business.

❖ Corporate Status

The procedures for incorporation are very specific. If they are not followed precisely, others may be able to challenge the existence of the corporation.

Improper Incorporation

Errors in the incorporation procedures can become important when, for example, a third person who is attempting to enforce a contract or bring suit for a tort injury learns of them. On the basis of improper incorporation, the plaintiff could seek to make the would-be shareholders personally liable. Also, when the corporation seeks to enforce a contract against a defaulting party, if the defaulting party learns of a defect in the incorporation procedure, he or she may be able to avoid liability on that ground. To prevent injustice, courts will sometimes attribute corporate status to an improperly formed corporation by holding it to be a *de jure* corporation or a *de facto* corporation, as discussed in the next section. In some cases, a corporation may be held to exist by estoppel.

De Jure and *De Facto* Corporations

In the event of substantial compliance with all conditions precedent to incorporation, the corporation is said to have *de jure* (rightful and lawful) existence. In most states and under the RMBCA, the certificate of incorporation is viewed as evidence that all mandatory statutory provisions have been met. This means that the corporation is properly formed, and neither the state nor a third party can attack its existence. If, for example, an incorporator's address was incorrectly listed, this would technically mean that the corporation was improperly formed; but the law does not regard such inconsequential procedural defects as detracting from substantial compliance, and courts will uphold the *de jure* status of the corporate entity.

Sometimes, there is a defect in complying with statutory mandates—for example, the corporation charter may have expired. Under these circumstances, the corporation may have *de facto* (actual) status, meaning that the corporation in fact exists, even if not rightfully or lawfully. A corporation with *de facto* status cannot be challenged by third persons (except for the state). The following elements are required for *de facto* status:

1. There must be a state statute under which the corporation can be validly incorporated.
2. The parties must have made a good faith attempt to comply with the statute.
3. The enterprise must already have undertaken to do business as a corporation.

Corporation by Estoppel

If an association that is neither an actual corporation nor a *de facto* or *de jure* corporation holds itself out as being a corporation, it will be estopped from denying corporate status in a lawsuit by a third party. This usually occurs when a third party contracts with an association that claims to be a corporation but does not hold a certificate of incorporation. When the third party brings suit naming the so-called corporation as the defendant, the association may not escape from liability on the ground that no corporation exists. When justice requires, the courts treat an alleged corporation as if it were an actual corporation for the purpose of determining the rights and liabilities involved in a particular situation. Corporation by estoppel is thus determined by the situation. It does not extend recognition of corporate status beyond the resolution of the problem at hand.

Disregarding the Corporate Entity

In some unusual situations, a corporate entity is used by its owners to perpetuate a fraud, circumvent the law, or in some other way accomplish an illegitimate objective. In these cases, the court will ignore the corporate structure by "piercing the corporate veil," exposing the shareholders to personal liability. The following are some of the factors that frequently cause the courts to pierce the corporate veil:

1. A party is tricked or misled into dealing with the corporation rather than the individual.
2. The corporation is set up never to make a profit or always to be insolvent, or it is too "thinly" capitalized—that is, it has insufficient capital at the time of formation to meet its prospective debts or potential liabilities.

3. Statutory corporate formalities, such as holding required corporation meetings, are not followed.
4. Personal and corporate interests are **commingled** (mixed together) to the extent that the corporation has no separate identity.

COMMINGLE
To put funds or goods together into one mass so that the funds or goods are so mixed that they no longer have separate identities.

To elaborate on the fourth factor in the preceding list, consider a close corporation that is formed according to law by a single person or by a few family members. In such a case, the separate status of the corporate entity and the sole stockholder (or family-member stockholders) must be carefully preserved. Certain practices invite trouble for the one-person or family-owned corporation: the commingling of corporate and personal funds, the failure to hold and record minutes of board of directors' meetings, or the shareholders' continuous personal use of corporate property (for example, vehicles). When the corporate privilege is abused for personal benefit and the corporate business is treated in such a careless manner that the corporation and the shareholder in control are no longer separate entities, the court usually will require an owner to assume personal liability to creditors for the corporation's debts. In short, when the facts show that great injustice would result from the use of a corporation to avoid individual responsibility, a court of equity will look behind the corporate structure to the individual stockholder.

General corporation law does not specifically prohibit a stockholder from lawfully lending money to his or her corporation. When an officer or director lends the corporation money and takes back security in the form of corporate assets, however, the courts will scrutinize the transaction closely. Any such transaction must be made in good faith and for fair value.

The following case raises a novel question: May a court pierce the corporate veil to impose personal liability on a *nonshareholder* by deeming the nonshareholder an "equitable owner" of the corporation?

Case 26.4
MORRIS v. NEW YORK STATE DEPARTMENT OF TAXATION AND FINANCE
Supreme Court, Appellate Division, Third Department, 1992.
183 A.D.2d 5,
588 N.Y.S.2d 927.

HISTORICAL AND SOCIAL SETTING *Courts will normally refuse to allow the existence of a corporation to further the perpetration of a fraud or the commission of some other injustice. A number of terms have been used to describe a technically correct corporation whose operations further injustice or are so commingled with the shareholders' personal activities that it has no separate and distinct existence. These terms have included "mere adjunct," "alias," "alter ego," "branch," "buffer," "cloak," "coat," "corporate double," "cover," "creature," "delusion," "dry shell," "dummy," "fiction," "fraud on the law," "mouthpiece," "nominal identity," "puppet," "screen," "sham," "stooge," "subterfuge," and "tool." As Judge Cardozo explained, "All this is well enough if the picturesqueness of the epithets does not lead us to forget that the essential term to be defined is the act of operation. Dominion [control] may be so complete, and interference so obtrusive," that the corporation is no more than an agent of those who operate it.*[a]

FACTS Sunshine Developers, Inc., was a New Jersey close corporation that was formed to purchase, own, and operate boats. Robert Morris and his son, Drew, were the only shareholders. Joseph Morris, Robert's brother, although not a shareholder, was a member of the board of directors. Robert and Drew knew very little of Sunshine's operations or of the acquisition by Joseph of two boats from a New York dealer in 1981 and 1984. Joseph took delivery of both boats and used at least one of them for his personal enjoyment. In 1985, the New York State Department of Taxation and Finance demanded payment of sales and use taxes on the boats in the amount of $76,390. Sunshine and the Morrises challenged the demand. A tax tribunal found, among other things, that Sunshine was merely a "dummy corporation." Sunshine had never conducted any type of business, had held very few board of directors' meetings, and could produce no meeting notes. Moreover, neither Joseph nor Robert could recall the details of Sunshine's incorporation, where the corporation

a. *Berkey v. Third Avenue Railway,* 244 N.Y. 84, 155 N.E. 914 (1927).

Case 26.4—Continued

had its bank account, or the name of the carrier supplying the insurance on the boats. The tribunal found Joseph Morris to be the "equitable owner" of the corporation—because he possessed the only corporate property (the boats)—and held that Joseph was personally liable for the taxes. Joseph appealed the tribunal's decision.

ISSUE The issue in this case is essentially twofold: (1) May the court pierce the corporate veil to impose personal liability on Sunshine's shareholders? (2) If so, can Joseph, as a nonshareholder, be held personally liable for the taxes?

DECISION Yes, to both questions. The tribunal's ruling was affirmed.

REASON The court had little difficulty determining the first issue, stating that "it is well established that a controlling shareholder may be held responsible for the corporation's obligations 'where [the] corporation is being operated by [that] individual in such a manner as to render the corporate form a fiction.' " The court found that there was "ample evidence to support the Tribunal's determination that Sunshine was nothing more than a 'dummy' corporation." As to the second issue, the court noted that the purpose of piercing the corporate veil is to achieve equity, and therefore "we should be concerned with 'reality and not form.' " In reality, Joseph controlled the corporate transactions leading to the tax liability and enjoyed possession of the boats. The court concluded that "there is substantial evidence to support the Tribunal's decision to impute equitable ownership, and the resulting liability for the tax assessed, to [Joseph]."

ETHICAL CONSIDERATIONS *The courts rarely will pierce the corporate veil and hold shareholders personally liable. Even more rarely will they impose equitable ownership of a corporation on a nonshareholder and then hold that person liable for alleged corporate obligations. Clearly, the only reason the latter was done in this case was to avoid the injustice that would have occurred if Robert and Drew, the shareholders of record, had been held liable while Joseph, the major corporate actor, had escaped liability simply because he was not a shareholder of record.*

❖ Corporate Financing

Corporations are financed by the issuance and sale of corporate securities—stocks and bonds. **Securities** evidence the obligation to pay money or of the right to participate in earnings and the distribution of corporate property. **Stocks,** or *equity*

SECURITIES
Stock certificates, bonds, notes, debentures, warrants, or other documents given as evidence of an ownership interest in the corporation or as a promise of repayment by the corporation.

STOCK
An equity or ownership interest in a corporation, measured in units of shares.

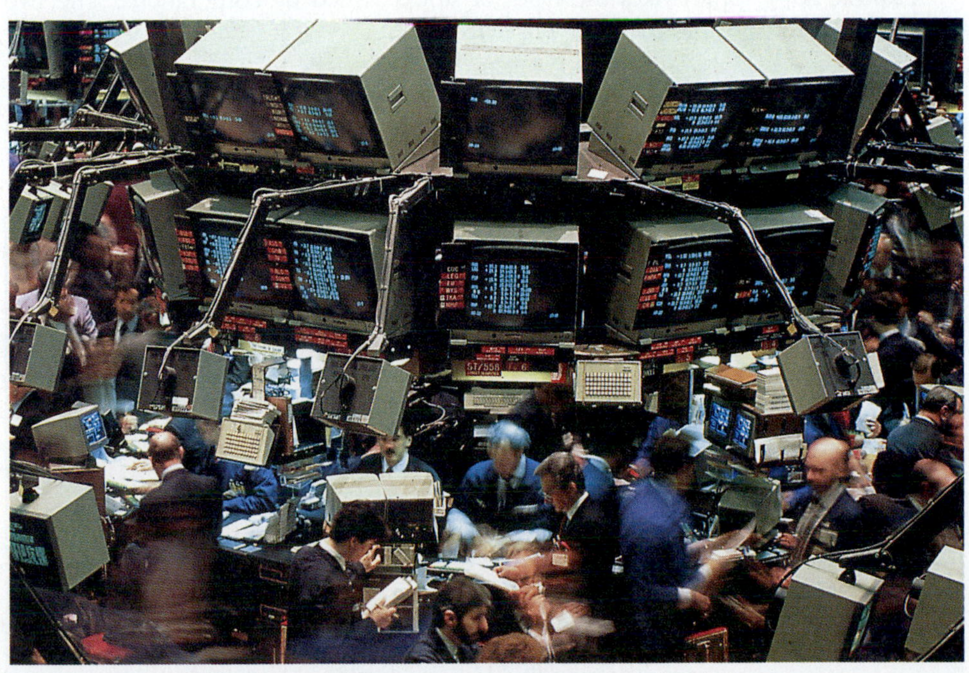

Corporations are financed by the issuance and sale of securities, which are bought and sold in such places as the New York Stock Exchange. What are securities, and what do they represent?

BOND
A certificate that evidences a corporate debt. It is a security that involves no ownership interest in the issuing corporation.

securities, represent the purchase of ownership in the business firm. **Bonds** (debentures), or *debt securities*, represent the borrowing of money by firms (and governments). Of course, not all debt is in the form of debt securities. For example, some debt is in the form of accounts payable and notes payable. Accounts and notes payable are typically short-term debts. Bonds are simply a way for the corporation to split up its long-term debt so that it can market it more easily.

Bonds

Bonds are issued by business firms and by governments at all levels as evidence of the funds they are borrowing from investors. Bonds almost always have a designated *maturity date*—the date when the principal, or face, amount of the bond is returned to the investor. They are sometimes referred to as *fixed-income securities* because their owners receive fixed-dollar interest payments during the period of time prior to maturity, usually semiannually.

BOND INDENTURE
A contract between the issuer of a bond and the bondholder.

Because debt financing represents a legal obligation on the part of the corporation, various features and terms of a particular bond issue are specified in a lending agreement called a **bond indenture.** A corporate trustee, often a commercial bank trust department, represents the collective well-being of all bondholders in ensuring that the terms of the bond issue are met by the corporation. The bond indenture specifies the maturity date of the bond and the pattern of interest payments until maturity. The different types of corporate bonds are described in Exhibit 26–2.

"There are two times in a man's life when he should not speculate: when he can't afford it and when he can."

Mark Twain (Samuel Clemens), 1835–1910
(American author and humorist)

Stocks

Issuing stocks is another way that corporations can obtain financing. The ways in which stocks differ from bonds are summarized in Exhibit 26–3. Basically, as mentioned, stocks represent ownership in a business firm, whereas bonds represent borrowing by the firm. The most important characteristics of stockholders are as follows:

1. They need not be paid back.
2. The stockholder receives dividends only when so voted by the directors.
3. Stockholders are the last investors to be paid off upon dissolution.
4. Stockholders vote for management and on major issues.

COMMON STOCK
Shares of ownership in a corporation that are lowest in priority with respect to payment of dividends and distribution of the corporation's assets upon dissolution.

Exhibit 26–4 summarizes the types of stocks issued by corporations. The two major types are *common stock* and *preferred stock*.

Common Stock **Common stock** represents the true ownership of a corporation. It provides a proportionate interest in the corporation with regard to (1) control, (2)

◆ **Exhibit 26–2**
Types of Corporate Bonds

Debenture Bonds	Bonds for which no specific assets of the corporation are pledged as backing. Rather, they are backed by the general credit rating of the corporation, plus any assets that can be seized if the corporation allows the debentures to go into default.
Mortgage Bonds	Bonds that pledge specific property. If the corporation defaults on the bonds, the bondholders can take the property.
Convertible Bonds	Bonds that can be exchanged for a specified number of shares of common stock under certain conditions.
Callable Bonds	Bonds that may be called in and the principal repaid at specified times or under conditions specified in the bond when it is issued.

◆ **Exhibit 26–3**
How Do Stocks and Bonds Differ?

STOCKS	BONDS
1. Stocks represent ownership.	1. Bonds represent debt.
2. Stocks (common) do not have a fixed dividend rate.	2. Interest on bonds must always be paid, whether or not any profit is earned.
3. Stockholders can elect a board of directors, which controls the corporation.	3. Bondholders usually have no voice in or control over management of the corporation.
4. Stocks do not have a maturity date; the corporation does not usually repay the stockholder.	4. Bonds have a maturity date when the bondholder is to be repaid the face value of the bond.
5. All corporations issue or offer to sell stocks. This is the usual definition of a corporation.	5. Corporations do not necessarily issue bonds.
6. Stockholders have a claim against the property and income of a corporation after all creditors' claims have been met.	6. Bondholders have a claim against the property and income of a corporation that must be met before the claims of stockholders.

earning capacity, and (3) net assets. A shareholder's interest is generally in proportion to the number of shares he or she owns out of the total number of shares issued.

Voting rights in a corporation apply to the election of the firm's board of directors and to any proposed changes in the ownership structure of the firm.[8] For example, a holder of common stock generally has the right to vote in a decision on a proposed merger, as mergers can change the proportion of ownership.

Firms are not obligated to return a principal amount per share to each holder of common stock because no firm can ensure that the market price per share of its common stock will not decline over time. Nor does the issuing firm have to guarantee a dividend; indeed, some corporations never pay dividends.

Holders of common stock are a group of investors who assume a *residual* position in the overall financial structure of a business. In terms of receiving payment for their investments, they are last in line. The earnings to which they are entitled are those left after preferred stockholders, bondholders, suppliers, employees, and other groups have been paid. Once those groups are paid, however, the owners of com-

◆ **Exhibit 26–4**
Types of Stocks

TYPES	DEFINITIONS
Common Stock	Voting shares that represent ownership interest in a corporation. Common stock has the lowest priority with respect to payment of dividends and distribution of assets upon the corporation's dissolution.
Preferred Stock	Shares of stock that have priority over common-stock shares as to payment of dividends and distribution of assets upon dissolution. Dividend payments are usually a fixed percentage of the face value of the share.
Cumulative Preferred Stock	Required dividends not paid in a given year must be paid in a subsequent year before any common-stock dividends are paid.
Participating Preferred Stock	The owner is entitled to receive the preferred-stock dividend and additional dividends after payment of dividends on common stock.
Convertible Preferred Stock	Preferred shareholders with the option to convert their shares into a specified number of common shares either in the issuing corporation or, sometimes, in another corporation.
Redeemable, or Callable, Preferred Stock	Preferred shares issued with the express condition that the issuing corporation has the right to repurchase the shares as specified.

8. State corporation law specifies the types of actions for which shareholder approval must be obtained.

◆ Exhibit 26–5
Cumulative Convertible Preferred-Stock Certificate

MORE THAN 100 SHARES
Number
640–0000

$1.75 CUMULATIVE CONVERTIBLE PREFERENCE STOCK

INCORPORATED UNDER THE LAWS OF THE STATE OF DELAWARE

GENERAL MILLS, INC.
THIS CERTIFICATE IS TRANSFERABLE IN COLUMBUS, GA. OR IN NEW YORK, N.Y.

See reverse for certain definitions

This Certifies that SPECIMEN is the owner of

FULL-PAID AND NON-ASSESSABLE SHARES, OF THE $1.75 CUMULATIVE CONVERTIBLE PREFERENCE STOCK, WITHOUT PAR VALUE, OF General Mills, Inc., transferable on the books of the Corporation by the holder hereof in person or by duly authorized attorney upon surrender of this Certificate properly endorsed. This Certificate and the shares represented hereby are issued and shall be held subject to all the provisions of the Certificate of Incorporation and By-Laws of the Corporation and all amendments thereof (copies of which are on file with the Corporation and with the Transfer Agent) to all of which the holder by acceptance hereof assents.

This Certificate is not valid until countersigned by the Transfer Agent or Transfer Clerk and registered by the Registrar.

In Witness Whereof the Corporation has caused this Certificate to be signed by its duly authorized officers and its Corporate Seal to be hereto affixed.

Dated

REGISTERED:
THE CHASE MANHATTAN BANK (NATIONAL ASSOCIATION), REGISTRAR
By
AUTHORIZED SIGNATURE

COUNTERSIGNED:
FIRST NATIONAL CITY BANK, TRANSFER AGENT
By
AUTHORIZED OFFICER.

PRESIDENT

SECRETARY

GENERAL MILLS INC.
DELAWARE
1928

mon stock may be entitled to *all* the remaining earnings as dividends. (But the board of directors is not normally under any duty to declare the remaining earnings as dividends.)

Preferred Stock **Preferred stock** is stock with *preferences*. Usually, this means that holders of preferred stock have priority over holders of common stock as to dividends and as to payment upon dissolution of the corporation. Holders of preferred stock may or may not have the right to vote.

PREFERRED STOCK
Classes of stock that have priority over common stock both as to payment of dividends and distribution of assets upon the corporation's dissolution.

Preferred stock is not included among the liabilities of a business because it is equity. Like other equity securities, preferred shares have no fixed maturity date on which they must be retired by the firm. Although occasionally firms retire preferred stock, they are not legally obligated to do so. A sample cumulative convertible preferred-stock certificate is shown in Exhibit 26–5.

Holders of preferred stock are investors who have assumed a rather cautious position in their relationship to the corporation. They have a stronger position than common shareholders with respect to dividends and claims on assets but as a result, they will not share in the full prosperity of the firm if it grows successfully over time. Preferred stockholders do receive fixed dividends periodically, however; and they may benefit from changes in the market price of the shares.

The return and the risk for preferred stock lie somewhere between those for bonds and those for common stock. Preferred stock is more similar to bonds than to common stock, even though preferred stock appears in the ownership section of the firm's balance sheet. As a result, preferred stock is often categorized with corporate bonds as a fixed-income security, even though the legal status is not the same.

Application

Law and the Entrepreneur—How to Incorporate

Incorporation generally involves a very modest investment in legal fees and filing fees. Indeed, just about anybody can form a corporation for any lawful purpose in any state in the Union. The requirements differ from state to state. But you do not have to form your corporation in the state in which you live or the state in which you are doing business. In fact, many individuals obtain their corporate charters from the state of Delaware because it has the fewest legal restrictions on corporate formation and operation. Recently, Delaware also limited the liability of directors, so a number of large companies are moving their charters into that state.

Delaware is also the state most often chosen for "mail-order incorporation." Perhaps you have even seen the ads—"You too, can incorporate"—in various national and regional magazines. Those ads are usually generated by organizations in Delaware that have preprinted incorporation forms for you to fill out and send back with a small fee. The employees of these organizations send or take your forms to the appropriate state office in Delaware to obtain your certificate of incorporation. Such "do-it-yourself" incorporating may be sufficient for those who are interested in starting small businesses but who have no serious aspirations that the companies will grow much larger. If you believe that the business in which you are going to engage has growth potential and may require significant financing in the future, though, you are best advised to contact a local lawyer to take you through the necessary steps in incorporating your business.

Checklist of Factors to Discuss with an Attorney Concerning Incorporation

- ☐ 1. Tax considerations.
- ☐ 2. The initial cost of incorporation and any continuing costs.
- ☐ 3. The formalities that are necessary.
- ☐ 4. The amount of record keeping that will be required.
- ☐ 5. What should be included in the bylaws.

❖ Key Terms

alien corporation 630
articles of incorporation 627
bond 644
bond indenture 644
bylaws 627
certificate of incorporation 640
close corporation 633
commingle 642
common stock 644
corporate charter 640
domestic corporation 630
foreign corporation 630
preferred stock 647
promoter 637
prospectus 637
retained earnings 625
S corporation 634
security 643
stock 643
ultra vires 630

❖ Chapter Summary: Corporate Formation and Financing

The Nature of the Corporation	1. Formal statutory requirements must be followed in forming a corporation. Corporate law varies from state to state, but statutory incorporation requirements that have been adopted to some degree in every state are embodied in the Model Business Corporation Act (MBCA) and the revised MBCA (RMBCA). 2. The corporation is a legal entity distinct from its owners. 3. The shareholders own the corporation. They elect a board of directors to govern the corporation. The board of directors hires corporate officers and other employees to run the daily business of the firm. 4. The corporation pays income tax on net profits; shareholders pay income tax on the disbursed dividends that they receive from the corporation (double-taxation feature). 5. The corporation can have perpetual existence or be chartered for a specific period of time. 6. The corporation is liable for the torts committed by its agents or officers within the course and scope of their employment (under the doctrine of *respondeat superior*). In some cases, a corporation can be held liable (and be fined) for the criminal acts of its agents and employees. Also, in certain circumstances, corporate officers may be held personally liable for corporate crimes.
Corporate Powers	1. *Express powers*—The express powers of a corporation are granted by the following laws and documents (listed according to their priority): federal constitution, state constitutions, state statutes, articles of incorporation, bylaws, and resolutions of the board of directors. 2. *Implied powers*—Barring express constitutional, statutory, or charter prohibitions, the corporation has the implied power to do all acts reasonably appropriate and necessary to accomplish its corporate purposes. 3. Ultra vires *doctrine*—Any act of a corporation that is beyond the authority given to it under its charter or under the statutes by which it was incorporated is an *ultra vires* act ("beyond the powers" of the corporation). a. *Ultra vires* contracts may or may not be enforced by the courts, depending on whether the contract is executed or executory and on whether its enforcement would lead to an inequitable result. b. In certain cases, shareholders, on behalf of the corporation, have the right to recover damages for *ultra vires* acts of corporate officers or directors. In addition, the state attorney general may bring an action either to institute an injunction against the transaction or to institute dissolution proceedings against the corporation for *ultra vires* acts.
Classification of Corporations	1. *Domestic, foreign, and alien corporations*—A corporation is referred to as a *domestic corporation* within its home state (the state in which it incorporates). A corporation is referred to as a *foreign corporation* by any state that is not its home state. A corporation is referred to as an *alien corporation* if it originates in another country but does business in the United States. 2. *Public and private corporations*—A public corporation is one formed by government (e.g., cities, towns, and public projects). A private corporation is one formed wholly or in part for private benefit. Most corporations are private.

❖ Chapter Summary: Corporate Formation and Financing—Continued

Classification of Corporations—Continued	3. *Nonprofit corporations*—Corporations formed without a profit-making purpose (e.g., charitable, educational, and religious organizations and hospitals). 4. *Close corporations*—Corporations owned by a family or a relatively small number of individuals; transfer of shares is usually restricted, and the corporation cannot make a public offering of its securities. 5. *S corporations*—Small domestic corporations (must have thirty-five or fewer shareholders as members) that, under Subchapter S of the Internal Revenue Code, are given special tax treatment. These corporations allow shareholders to enjoy the limited legal liability of the corporate form but avoid its double-taxation feature (taxes are paid by shareholders as personal income, and the S corporation is not taxed separately). 6. *Professional corporations*—Corporations formed by professionals (e.g., doctors, lawyers) to obtain the benefits of incorporation (pension plans, tax benefits, limited liability). In most cases, the professional corporation is treated like other corporations, but sometimes the courts will disregard the corporate form and treat the shareholders as partners.
Corporate Formation	1. *Promoter*—One who takes the preliminary steps in organizing a corporation (issues prospectus, secures charter, interests investors in the purchase of corporate stock, forms subscription agreements, etc.). 2. *Incorporation procedures:* a. Selection of a state in which to incorporate. b. Preparation and filing of the articles of incorporation. The articles generally should include the following information concerning the corporation: name, nature and purpose, duration, capital structure, internal organization, registered office and agent, and incorporators. c. Certificate of incorporation—Charter received from appropriate state office (usually the secretary of state) after articles of incorporation have been filed. Authorizes the corporation to conduct business. d. First organizational meeting—Provided for in the articles of incorporation but held after the charter is granted. Board of directors are elected and other business is completed (bylaws passed, stock issued, etc.).
Corporate Status	1. *Improper incorporation*—If a corporation has been improperly incorporated, courts will sometimes impute corporate status to the firm by holding that the firm is a *de jure* corporation (cannot be challenged by the state or third persons) or a *de facto* corporation (can be challenged by the state but not by third persons). If a firm is neither a *de jure* nor *de facto* corporation but represents itself to be a corporation and is sued as such by a third party, it may be held to be a corporation by estoppel. 2. *Disregarding the corporate entity*—To avoid injustice, courts may "pierce the corporate veil" and hold a shareholder or shareholders personally liable for a judgment against the corporation. This usually occurs only when the corporation was established to circumvent the law, or when it is used for an illegitimate or fraudulent purpose, or when the controlling shareholder commingles his or her own interests with those of the corporation to such an extent that the corporation no longer has a separate identity.
Corporate Financing—Bonds	Corporate bonds are securities representing *corporate debt*—money borrowed by a corporation. Types of corporate bonds include: 1. *Debenture bonds*—Bonds backed by the general credit rating of the corporation; no corporate assets are pledged as security. 2. *Mortgage bonds*—Bonds pledging as security specific corporate property. 3. *Convertible bonds*—Bonds that can be exchanged for a specified number of shares of common stock at the option of the bondholder. 4. *Callable bonds*—Bonds that may be called in and the principal repaid at specified times or under specified conditions.

❖ Chapter Summary: Corporate Formation and Financing—Continued

Corporate Financing—Stocks	Equity securities issued by a corporation that represent the purchase of ownership in the business firm. 1. *Important characteristics of stockholders:* a. They need not be paid back. b. The stockholder receives dividends only when so voted by the directors. c. Stockholders are the last investors to be paid upon dissolution. d. Stockholders vote for management and on major issues. 2. *Types of stock (see Exhibit 26–4 for details):* a. Common stock—Represents the true ownership of the firm. Holders of common stock share in the control, earning capacity, and net assets of the corporation. Common stockholders carry more risk than preferred stockholders but, if the corporation is successful, are compensated for this risk by greater returns on their investments. b. Preferred stock—Stock whose holders have a preferred status. Preferred stockholders have a stronger position than common shareholders with respect to dividends and claims on assets, but as a result, they will not share in the full prosperity of the firm if it grows successfully over time. The return and risk for preferred stock lie somewhere between those for bonds and common stock.

❖ Questions and Case Problems

26-1. Liability of Shareholders. Generally, shareholders are not personally liable for corporate obligations. In what circumstances might a court disregard the corporate entity ("pierce the corporate veil") and hold shareholders personally liable for corporate actions or obligations?

26-2. Corporate Formation. What are the steps for bringing a corporation into existence? Who is liable for preincorporation contracts? In what circumstances might an association that is not an actual corporation be treated as a corporation by a court?

26-3. Corporate Status. Three brothers inherited a small paper-supply business from their father, who had operated the business as a sole proprietorship. The brothers decided to incorporate under the name of Gomez Corp. and retained an attorney to draw up the necessary documents. The attorney drew up the papers and had the brothers sign them but neglected to send the application for a corporate charter to the secretary of state's office. The brothers assumed that all necessary legal work had been taken care of, and they proceeded to do business as Gomez Corp. One day, a Gomez Corp. employee was delivering a carton of paper supplies to one of Gomez's customers. On the way to the customer's office, the employee negligently ran a red light and caused a car accident. Baxter, the driver of the other vehicle, was injured as a result and sued Gomez Corp. for damages. Baxter then learned that no state charter had ever been issued to Gomez Corp., so he sued each of the brothers personally for damages. Can the brothers avoid personal liability for the tort of their employee? Explain.

26-4. Liability for Preincorporation Contracts. Christy, Briggs, and Dobbs are recent college graduates who want to form a corporation to manufacture and sell personal computers. Perez tells them that he will set in motion the formation of their corporation. Perez first makes a contract with Oliver for the purchase of a parcel of land for $25,000. Oliver does not know of the prospective corporate formation at the time the contract is signed. Perez then makes a contract with Kovac to build a small plant on the property being purchased. Kovac's contract is conditional on the corporation's formation. Perez secures all necessary subscription agreements and capitalization, and he files the articles of incorporation. A charter is issued.

(a) Discuss whether the newly formed corporation or Perez or both are liable on the contracts with Oliver and Kovac.

(b) Discuss whether the corporation, upon coming into legal existence, is automatically liable to Kovac.

26-5. Corporate Powers. Kora Nayenga and two business associates formed a corporation called Nayenga Corp. for the purpose of selling computer services. Kora, who owned 50 percent of the corporate shares, served as the corporation's president. Kora wished to obtain a personal loan from his bank for $250,000, but the bank required the note to be cosigned by a third party. Kora cosigned the note in the name of the corporation. Later, Kora defaulted on the note, and the bank sued the corporation for payment. The corporation asserted, as a defense, that Kora had exceeded his authority when he cosigned the note. Had he? Explain.

26-6. Constitutional Rights of Corporations. Leslie R. Barth was the president of five corporations. During the course of an investigation for failure to file corporate and personal income tax returns, the Internal Revenue Service (IRS) served an administrative summons for Barth to turn over prescribed corporate records. Barth only partially complied, and the IRS took him to court. The court ordered the corporations to furnish the requested information and to designate an agent to testify for the corporations "without revoking their personal privileges against self-incrimination." Barth appealed the order, claiming that such an order violated the "agent's" (his) constitutional right against self-incrimination and that Fifth Amendment protection against self-incrimination extended to the corporations. Discuss whether the corporations did possess Fifth Amendment privileges against self-incrimination and whether Barth's privilege against self-incrimination, as an individual officer, was denied by the district court's order. [*United States v. Barth*, 745 F.2d 184 (2d Cir. 1984)]

26-7. **Liability of Shareholders.** Charles Wolfe was the sole shareholder and president of Wolfe & Co., a firm that leased tractor-trailers. The corporation had no separate bank account. Banking transactions were conducted through Wolfe's personal accounts, and employees were paid from them. Wolfe never consulted with any other corporate directors. During the tax years 1974–1976, the corporation incurred $114,472.91 in federal tax liabilities. The government held Wolfe personally liable for the taxes. Wolfe paid the tax bill and then brought an action against the government for disregarding his corporate entity. Discuss whether the government can "pierce the corporate veil" in Wolfe's case and hold Wolfe personally liable for corporate taxes. [*Wolfe v. United States*, 798 F.2d 124 (9th Cir. 1961)]

26-8. ***Ultra Vires* Acts.** Hamfab Credit Union (HCU) borrowed, in a series of loans, a total of $550,000 from the Ohio Central Credit Union, Inc. (OCCU). This amount exceeded 25 percent of HCU's capital and surplus, which was in violation of Ohio state law. The statute in question provided that "[a] credit union may not borrow money in excess of twenty-five per cent of its unimpaired capital and surplus, without prior specific authorization by the supervisor." HCU had not received any such authorization. When HCU became insolvent, Wagner was appointed as the liquidator (a person who winds up the financial affairs of a dissolved corporation). Wagner refused to pay the full amount of the debt owed to OCCU, claiming that some of the loans had been made in violation of state law and therefore OCCU had acted *ultra vires* in making the loans. Did Wagner succeed in this defense? Explain. [*Ohio Central Credit Union, Inc. v. Wagner*, 67 Ohio App.2d 138, 426 N.E.2d 198 (1980)]

26-9. **Liability for Preincorporation Contracts.** Skandinavia, Inc., manufactured and sold polypropylene underwear. Following two years of poor sales, Skandinavia entered into negotiations to sell the business to Odilon Cormier, an individual who was an experienced textile manufacturer. Skandinavia and Cormier agreed that Cormier would take Skandinavia's underwear inventory and use it in a new corporation, which would be called Polypro, Inc. In return, Skandinavia would receive a commission on future sales from Polypro, Inc. Polypro was subsequently established and began selling the underwear. Skandinavia, however, never received any commissions from the sales. It therefore brought suit against Polypro and Cormier to recover its promised commissions. The claim against Polypro was dismissed by the trial court, but the trial court found Cormier to be personally liable for the commissions owed. Cormier appealed to the Supreme Court of New Hampshire. Is Cormier personally liable for the contract he signed in the course of setting up a new corporation? Discuss. [*Skandinavia, Inc. v. Cormier*, 128 N.H. 215, 214 A.2d 1250 (1986)]

26-10. **Professional Corporations.** Cohen, Stracher & Bloom, P.C., a law firm organized as a professional corporation under New York law, entered into an agreement with We're Associates Co. for the lease of office space located in Lake Success, New York. The lease was signed for We're Associates by one of the partners of that company and for the professional corporation by Paul J. Bloom, as vice president. Bloom, Cohen, and Stracher were the sole officers, directors, and shareholders of the professional corporation. The corporation became delinquent in paying its rent, and We're Associates brought an action to recover rents and other charges of approximately $9,000 alleged to be due under the lease. The complaint was filed against the professional corporation and each individual shareholder of the corporation. The individual shareholders moved to dismiss the action against them individually. Will the court grant their motion? Discuss. [*We're Associates Co. v. Cohen, Stracher & Bloom, P.C.*, 103 A.D.2d 130, 478 N.Y.S.2d 670 (1984)]

26-11. ***Ultra Vires* Acts.** The Midtown Club, Inc., was a nonprofit corporation whose certificate of incorporation stated that the sole purpose of the club was "to provide facilities for the serving of luncheon or other meals to members." Samuel Cross, a member of the club, brought a female guest to lunch at the club, but he and his friend were both refused seating. On several occasions, Cross made applications on behalf of females for their admission to the club, but the club ignored or rejected them. Cross brought an action against the club, alleging that its actions were *ultra vires*. Did he succeed? Explain. [*Cross v. Midtown Club, Inc.*, 33 Conn.Supp. 150, 365 A.2d 127 (1976)]

26-12. **Corporate Status.** Pat Daniels, John Daniels, and Bill Mandell (the defendants) planned to purchase a tavern and restaurant business in St. Charles, Illinois, and to organize their business in the form of a corporation under the name of D&M, Inc. The defendants negotiated with Howard Realty Group to lease the premises on which the tavern and restaurant were located. While the sale of the business and the negotiation of the lease were proceeding, neither the seller of the business nor Howard contemplated requiring personal guarantees from the defendants. On January 18, 1987, although D&M had not yet been incorporated, the lease was signed in the name of D&M, Inc., by Pat Daniels and Bill Mandell, in their capacities as president and secretary, respectively, of the future corporation. On February 11, 1987, the defendants filed the articles of incorporation for D&M with the secretary of state. The articles were returned by the secretary of state's office because the name D&M, Inc. was already in use by another Illinois corporation. The defendants then decided to file the articles of incorporation under the name of The Lodge at Tin Cup Pass, Inc. (the Lodge). They first checked with the landlord to see if they could use that name because it was similar to the name of the property, Tin Cup Pass. The Lodge was duly incorporated on March 5, 1987. In late 1988, when the Lodge defaulted on its lease payments, Tin Cup Pass Limited Partnership, to whom Howard had assigned the lease, sued the defendants personally to recover the lease payments due, alleging that the defendants should be held liable as corporate promoters for D&M, Inc., a corporation that was never formed. What will result in court? Discuss fully. [*Tin Cup Pass Limited Partnership v. Daniels*, 195 Ill.App.3d 847, 553 N.E.2d 82, 142 Ill.Dec. 732 (1990)]

26-13. **Liability of Shareholders.** In the early 1950s, Mary Emmons opened an account at M&M Wholesale Florist, Inc., to purchase flowers and florist supplies for her flower shop, called Bay Minette Flower Shop, which she operated as a sole proprietorship. In 1973, the flower shop was incorporated as Bay Minette Flower Shop, Inc. Emmons continued to order supplies from M&M, as did her son when he began to manage the day-to-day operations of the shop during the 1980s. M&M, which had no knowledge that Bay Minette was now a corporation, sued Emmons and her son personally to recover a balance owing on the Bay Minette account (for purchases made after Bay Minette had incorporated). Is the fact that M&M was never informed of the incorporation of Bay Minette Flower Shop a sufficient ground for piercing the corporate veil and holding Emmons and her son personally liable for the debt? Explain. [*M&M Wholesale Florist, Inc. v. Emmons*, 600 So.2d 998 (Ala. 1992)]

A QUESTION OF ETHICS AND SOCIAL RESPONSIBILITY

26-14. *On November 3, 1981, Garry Fox met with a representative of Coopers & Lybrand (Coopers), a national accounting firm, to obtain tax advice and other accounting services on behalf of a corporation Fox was in the process of forming. Coopers agreed to perform the services. The new corporation, G. Fox and Partners, Inc., was incorporated on December 4, 1981. Coopers had completed its work by mid-December and billed G. Fox and Partners for $10,827 for its accounting services. When neither the new corporation nor Fox paid the bill, Coopers sued Garry Fox personally for the amount. Coopers claimed that Fox had breached express and implied contracts and that, as a corporate promoter, Fox was liable for the unpaid debt. Fox argued that Coopers had agreed to look solely to the corporation for payment. The trial court found that there was no agreement, either express or implied, that would obligate Fox individually to pay Coopers's fee because Coopers failed to prove the existence of any such agreement. On appeal, however, the trial court's judgment was reversed. Fox was held liable as a corporate promoter for the unpaid debt.* [Coopers & Lybrand v. Fox, *758 P.2d 683 (Colo. 1988)*]

1. In view of the fact that Coopers & Lybrand knew that Fox was acting on behalf of a future corporation, do you think that it is fair that Fox should be held personally liable for the contract?
2. Undertaking preliminary organization and promotion is an essential step in the process of corporate formation. Do you think that imposing risks on promoters by holding them personally liable for preincorporation contracts counters the public policy of promoting business enterprises?
3. What might result if corporate promoters could never be held personally liable for preincorporation contracts? Would such a law also pose a barrier to commerce by increasing the difficulty in obtaining necessary preincorporation contracts, such as for office space, equipment, credit, and so on?

FOR CRITICAL ANALYSIS

26-15. *What are some of the ways in which the limited liability of corporate shareholders serves the public interest? Can you think of any ways in which this limited liability is harmful to the public interest? Explain.*

Chapter 27

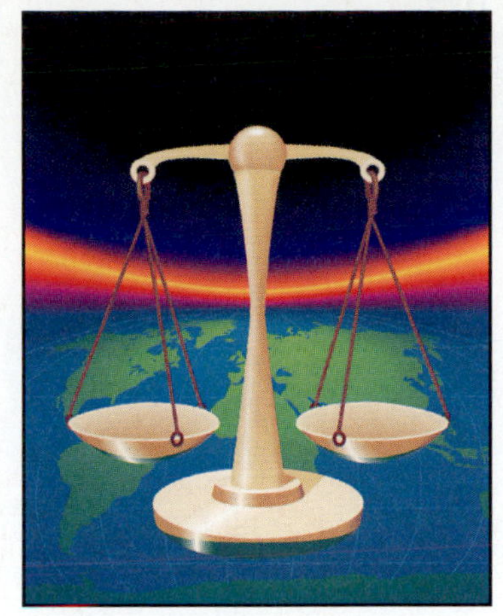

Corporate Directors, Officers, and Shareholders

"They [corporations] cannot commit treason, nor be outlawed nor excommunicated, because they have no soul."

Sir Edward Coke, 1552–1634
(British jurist and legal scholar)

Sir Edward Coke's observation that a corporation has no "soul" is based on the fact that a corporation is not a "natural" person but a legal fiction, a creature of statute, and no one individual shareholder or director bears sole responsibility for the corporation and its actions. Rather, a corporation joins the efforts and resources of a large number of individuals for the purpose of producing returns greater than the returns those persons could have obtained individually.

Sometimes, actions that benefit the corporation as a whole do not coincide with the separate interests of the individuals making up the corporation. In such situations, it is important to know the rights and duties of all participants in the corporate enterprise. This chapter focuses on the rights and duties of directors, managers, and shareholders and the ways in which conflicts among them are resolved.

❖ Role of Directors

Every corporation is governed by a board of directors. A director occupies a position of responsibility unlike that of other corporate personnel. Directors are sometimes inappropriately characterized as *agents* because they act for and on behalf of the corporation. No *individual* director, however, can act as an agent to bind the corporation; and as a group, directors collectively control the corporation in a way that no agent is able to control a principal. Directors are often incorrectly characterized as *trustees* because they occupy positions of trust and control over the corporation. Unlike trustees, however, they do not own or hold title to property for the use and benefit of others.

Election of Directors

Subject to statutory limitations, the number of directors is set forth in the corporation's articles or bylaws. Historically, the minimum number of directors has been three, but today many states permit fewer. Indeed, the Revised Model Business Corporation Act (RMBCA), in Section 8.01, permits corporations with fewer than fifty shareholders to eliminate the board of directors.

The first board of directors is normally appointed by the incorporators upon the creation of the corporation, or directors are named by the corporation itself in the articles. The first board serves until the first annual shareholders' meeting. Subsequent directors are elected by a majority vote of the shareholders.

The term of office for a director is usually one year—from annual meeting to annual meeting. Longer and staggered terms are permissible under most state statutes. A common practice is to elect one-third of the board members each year for a three-year term. In this way, there is greater management continuity.

A director can be removed *for cause* (that is, for failing to perform a required duty), either as specified in the articles or bylaws or by shareholder action. Even the board of directors itself may be given power to remove a director for cause, subject to shareholder review. In most states, unless the shareholders have reserved the right at the time of election, a director cannot be removed without cause.

When vacancies occur on the board of directors owing to death or resignation, or when a new position is created through amendment of the articles or bylaws, either the shareholders or the board itself can fill the position, depending on state law or on the provisions of the bylaws.

Directors' Qualifications and Compensation

Few legal requirements exist for directors' qualifications. Only a handful of states impose minimum age and residency requirements. A director is sometimes a shareholder, but this is not a necessary qualification—unless, of course, statutory provisions or corporate articles or bylaws require ownership.

Compensation for directors is ordinarily specified in the corporate articles or bylaws. Because directors have a fiduciary relationship to the shareholders and to the corporation, an express agreement or provision for compensation is necessary for them to receive money from the funds that they control and for which they have responsibilities.

Board of Directors' Forum

The board of directors conducts business by holding formal meetings with recorded minutes. The date on which regular meetings are held is usually established in the articles and bylaws or by board resolution, and no further notice is customarily required. Special meetings can be called, with notice sent to all directors.

QUORUM
The number of members of a decision-making body that must be present before business may be transacted.

Quorum requirements can vary among jurisdictions. Many states leave the decision to the corporate articles or bylaws. (A **quorum** is the minimum number of members of a body of officials or other group that must be present in order for business to be validly transacted.) In the absence of specific state statutes, most states provide that a quorum is a majority of the number of directors authorized in the articles or bylaws. Voting is done in person (unlike voting at shareholders' meetings, which can be done by proxy, as discussed later in this chapter).[1] The rule is one vote per director. Ordinary matters generally require a simple majority vote; certain extraordinary issues may require a greater-than-majority vote.

Rights of Directors

A director of a corporation has a number of rights, including the rights of participation, inspection, indemnification, and compensation.

Participation and Inspection A corporate director must have certain rights to function properly in that position. The main right is one of participation—meaning that the director must be notified of board of directors' meetings so as to participate in them. As pointed out earlier in this chapter, regular board meetings are usually established by the bylaws or by board resolution, and no notice of these meetings is required. If special meetings are called, however, notice is required unless waived

1. Except in Louisiana, which allows a director to vote by proxy under certain circumstances. Some states, such as Michigan and Texas, and Section 8.20 of the RMBCA permit telephone conferences for board of directors' meetings.

by the director. A director must have access to all corporate books and records to make decisions and to exercise the necessary supervision over corporate officers and employees. This right is virtually absolute and cannot be restricted.

Compensation and Indemnification Historically, directors have had no inherent right to compensation for their services as directors. Nominal sums are often paid as honoraria to directors, however. In many cases, directors are also chief corporate officers (president or chief executive officer, for example) and receive compensation in their managerial positions. Most directors, however, gain through indirect benefits, such as business contacts, prestige, and other rewards. There is a trend toward providing more than nominal compensation for directors, especially in large corporations in which directorships can be enormous burdens in terms of time, work, effort, and risk. Many states permit the corporate articles or bylaws to authorize compensation for directors, and in some cases the board can set its own compensation unless the articles or bylaws provide otherwise.

It is not unusual for corporate directors to become involved in lawsuits by virtue of their positions and their actions as directors. Most states (and RMBCA 8.51) permit a corporation to indemnify (guarantee reimbursement to) a director for legal costs, fees, and judgments involved in defending corporation-related suits. Many states specifically permit a corporation to purchase liability insurance for the directors and officers to cover indemnification. When the statutes are silent on this matter, the power to purchase such insurance is usually considered to be part of the corporation's implied power.

Directors' Management Responsibilities

Directors have responsibility for all policymaking decisions necessary to the management of all corporate affairs. Just as shareholders cannot act individually to bind the corporation, the directors must act as a body in carrying out routine corporate business. One director has one vote, and generally the majority rules. The general areas of responsibility of the board of directors include the following:

1. Declaration and payment of corporate dividends to shareholders.
2. Authorization for major corporate policy decisions—for example, the initiation of proceedings for the sale or lease of corporate assets outside the regular course of business, the determination of new product lines, and the overseeing of major contract negotiations and major management-labor negotiations.
3. Appointment, supervision, and removal of corporate officers and other managerial employees and the determination of their compensation.
4. Financial decisions such as the declaration and payment of dividends to shareholders and the issuance of authorized shares and bonds.

The board of directors can delegate some of its functions to an executive committee or to corporate officers. In doing so, the board is not relieved of its overall responsibility for directing the affairs of the corporation, but corporate officers and managerial personnel are empowered to make decisions relating to ordinary, daily corporate affairs within well-defined guidelines.

❖ Role of Corporate Officers and Executives

The officers and other executive employees are hired by the board of directors or, in rare instances, by the shareholders. In addition to carrying out the duties articulated in the bylaws, corporate and managerial officers act as agents of the corporation, and the ordinary rules of agency (discussed in Chapter 23) apply or have been applied to their employment. (In contrast, the board of directors' powers are conferred by the state.) Qualifications are determined at the discretion of the corporation and are included in the articles or bylaws. In most states, a person can hold more than one office and can be both an officer and a director of the corporation.

The rights of corporate officers and other high-level managers are defined by employment contracts because they are employees of the company. Corporate officers normally can be removed by the board of directors at any time with or without cause and regardless of the terms of the employment contracts, however—although in that case, the corporation may be liable for breach of contract. The duties of corporate officers are the same as those of directors, because their respective corporate positions involve both groups in decision making and place them in similar positions of control. Hence, officers are viewed as having the same fiduciary duties of care and loyalty in their conduct of corporate affairs as directors have, a subject to which we now turn.

❖ Duties of Directors and Officers

Directors and officers are deemed *fiduciaries* of the corporation, because their relationship with the corporation and its shareholders is one of trust and confidence. The fiduciary duties of the directors and officers include the duty of care and the duty of loyalty.

Duty of Care

"It is not the crook in modern business that we fear but the honest man who does not know what he is doing."

Owen D. Young, 1874–1962
(American corporate executive and public official)

Directors and officers are obligated to be honest and to use prudent business judgment in the conduct of corporate affairs. Directors must exercise the same degree of care that reasonably prudent people use in the conduct of their own personal affairs.

Directors can be held answerable to the corporation and to the shareholders for breach of their duty of care. When directors delegate work to corporate officers and employees, they are expected to use a reasonable amount of supervision. Otherwise, they will be held liable for negligence or mismanagement of corporate personnel. For example, assume that a corporate bank director failed to attend any board of directors' meetings in five and one-half years, never inspected any of the corporate books or records, and generally failed to supervise the efforts of the bank president and the loan committee. Meanwhile, a corporate officer, the bank president, made various improper loans and permitted large overdrafts. In this situation, the corporate director may be held liable to the corporation for losses resulting from the unsupervised actions of the bank president and the loan committee.

The standard of *due care* has been variously described and codified in many corporation codes and by judicial decisions.[2] The impact of the standard is to require that directors and officers carry out their responsibilities in an informed, businesslike manner.

Depending on the nature of the business, directors and officers are often expected to act in accordance with their own knowledge and training. Most states and the RMBCA [RMBCA 8.30], however, allow a director to make decisions in reliance on information furnished by competent officers or employees, professionals such as attorneys and accountants, or even an executive committee of the board without being accused of acting in bad faith or failing to exercise due care if such information turns out to be faulty.

2. See, for example, RMBCA 8.30(a).

Directors are expected to attend board of directors' meetings, and their votes should be entered into the minutes of corporate meetings. Unless a dissent is entered, the director is presumed to have assented. Directors who dissent are rarely held individually liable for mismanagement of the corporation. For this reason, a director who is absent from a given meeting sometimes registers with the secretary of the board a dissent to actions taken at the meeting.

Directors are expected to be informed on corporate matters and to understand legal and other professional advice rendered to the board. In *Smith v. Van Gorkom*,[3] for example, directors were held liable for accepting an offer for the purchase of a corporation because they purportedly failed to investigate the value of the business and whether a higher price could have been obtained. A director who is unable to carry out such responsibilities must resign. When the required duty of care has not been exercised, directors and officers are liable for the damages caused to the corporation by their negligence.

"It is not within the lawful powers of a board of directors to shape and conduct the affairs of a corporation for the merely incidental benefit of the shareholders."

Russell C. Ostrander,
1851–1919
(Michigan jurist)

Duty of Loyalty

One can define *loyalty* as faithfulness to one's obligations and duties. The essence of the fiduciary duty requires the subordination of self-interest to the interest of the entity to which the duty is owed. It presumes constant loyalty to the corporation on the part of the directors and officers. In general, the duty of loyalty prohibits directors from using corporate funds or confidential corporate information for personal advantage. It requires officers and directors to disclose fully to the board of directors any possible conflict of interest that might occur in conducting corporate transactions. Cases dealing with fiduciary duty typically involve one or more of the following:

1. Competing with the corporation.
2. Usurping a corporate opportunity.
3. Having an interest that conflicts with the interest of the corporation.
4. Engaging in insider trading (using information that is not public to make a profit trading securities, as discussed in Chapter 29).
5. Authorizing a corporate transaction that is detrimental to minority shareholders.
6. Selling control over the corporation.

Conflicts of Interest

Corporate directors often have many business affiliations, and they may even sit on the board of more than one corporation. Of course, they are precluded from entering into or supporting any business that operates in direct competition with the corporation. The fiduciary duty requires them to make a full disclosure of any potential conflicts of interest that might arise in any corporate transaction.

Sometimes, a corporation enters into a contract or engages in a transaction in which an officer or director has a material interest. The director or officer must make a *full disclosure* of that interest and must abstain from voting on the proposed transaction. For example, Sunwood Corporation needs office space. Lambert Alden, one of its five directors, owns the building adjoining the corporation's main office building. He negotiates a lease with Sunwood for the space, making a full disclosure to Sunwood and the other four board directors. The lease arrangement is fair and reasonable, and it is unanimously approved by the corporation's board of directors. In such a case, the contract is valid. The rule is one of reason. If it were otherwise, directors would be prevented from ever giving financial assistance to the corporations they serve. The various state statutes contain different standards, but a contract will

3. 488 A.2d 858 (Del. 1985).

generally not be voidable if it was fair and reasonable to the corporation at the time it was made, if there was a full disclosure of the interest of the officers or directors involved in the transaction, and if the contract was approved by a majority of the disinterested directors or shareholders.

Often, contracts are negotiated between corporations whose boards have some members in common. Such transactions require great care, as they are closely scrutinized by the courts. (As will be discussed in Chapter 30, in certain circumstances—if two large corporations are competing with each other, for example—it may constitute a violation of antitrust laws if the same director sits on the boards of both companies.) The following case involves a contract that was formed by corporations having common directors. It illustrates how the duty of loyalty can become cloudy in situations in which directors have conflicting interests.

Case 27.1
GRIES SPORTS ENTERPRISES, INC. v. CLEVELAND BROWNS FOOTBALL CO.
Supreme Court of Ohio, 1986.
26 Ohio St.3d 15,
496 N.E.2d 959.

HISTORICAL AND ETHICAL SETTING *At the end of the nineteenth century, courts began attempting to enforce fiduciary obligations against the officers and directors of corporations. In one case, for example, officers and directors of the Arkansas Valley Agricultural Society sold stock in the company to themselves for $5 per share when the stock was worth at least $50 per share because of a recent sale of company assets. The court refused to allow the majority shareholders to secure for themselves an advantage not common to all shareholders.*[a] *A century later, some directors and officers still believe that they can serve more than one master.*

FACTS Arthur Modell was the president and an 80 percent shareholder of the Cleveland Stadium Corporation (CSC). Modell also served on the board of directors of the Cleveland Browns Football Company and owned 53 percent of its stock. Aside from Modell, several other members of the board of directors of the Browns also served on the CSC board. At a March 16, 1982, meeting of the Browns' board of directors, the board voted to purchase all of the stock of CSC for $6,000,000. The one person who did not stand to benefit from the purchase of CSC by the Browns was Robert Gries. Gries, jointly with his business firm, Gries Sports Enterprises, Inc., owned 43 percent of the Browns and was also a director on the board. Gries felt the purchase price was far too high, based on other appraisals that valued CSC at no more than $2,000,000. Gries contended that to pay $6,000,000 for the stock would increase the debt load of the Browns more than necessary. Additionally, the sale of CSC directly—and, according to Gries, unfairly—benefited Modell. Gries objected to the purchase at the March meeting of the Browns' board but was outvoted by the other directors. Gries then filed a shareholder's derivative action (an action on behalf of the corporation) seeking rescission of the CSC purchase. The trial court ruled in Gries's favor, and the corporation (the Browns) appealed. When the appellate court reversed the trial court's decision, Gries appealed to the Supreme Court of Ohio.

ISSUE Had Modell breached his fiduciary duty, as a director of the Browns, to the other shareholders, including Gries?

DECISION Yes. The Supreme Court of Ohio reversed the appellate court's judgment and reinstated the trial court's decision.

REASON The Supreme Court of Ohio agreed with Gries that the Browns had purchased CSC at an inflated price to the detriment of the Browns' financial position and to the direct benefit of Modell. The court stated that "[r]ather than serving the best interests of the Browns and all of the Browns' stockholders, the effect of this transaction was to benefit the majority stockholder of the Browns [Modell] * * * at the expense of the principal minority shareholders [Gries]." Modell had thus breached his fiduciary duty of loyalty to the Browns' shareholders, and therefore the trial court's granting of Gries's petition for rescission of the purchase contract was properly granted.

a. *Arkansas Valley Agricultural Society v. Eichholtz*, 45 Kans. 164, 25 P. 613 (1891).

❖ Liability of Directors and Officers

"All business proceeds on beliefs, or judgments of probabilities, and not on certainties."

Charles Eliot, 1834–1936 ***(American educator and editor)***

Directors and officers are exposed to liability on many fronts. Shareholders may perceive that the corporate directors are not acting in the best interests of the corporation and may sue the directors, in what is called a *shareholder's derivative suit,* on behalf of the corporation. This type of action is discussed later in this chapter, in the context of the rights of shareholders. In this section, we first examine the so-called *business judgment rule,* under which a corporate director or officer may be able to avoid liability for poor business judgments. We then look at the liability of corporate directors and officers for torts and crimes committed either by themselves or by corporate employees under their supervision.

The Business Judgment Rule

Directors and officers are expected to use their best judgment in guiding corporate management, but they are not insurers of business success. Honest mistakes of judgment and poor business decisions on their part do not make them liable to the corporation for resulting damages. This is the **business judgment rule.** The rule immunizes directors—and officers—from liability for the consequences of a decision that is within managerial authority, as long as the decision complies with management's fiduciary duties and as long as acting on the decision is within the powers of the corporation. Consequently, if there is a reasonable basis for a business decision, it is unlikely that the court will interfere with that decision, even if the corporation suffers thereby.

BUSINESS JUDGMENT RULE
A rule that immunizes corporate management from liability for actions that are undertaken in good faith, when the actions are within both the power of the corporation and the authority of management to make.

To benefit from the rule, directors and officers must act in good faith, in what they consider to be the best interests of the corporation, and with the care that an ordinarily prudent person in a similar position would exercise in similar circumstances. This requires an informed decision, with a rational basis, and with no conflict between the decision maker's personal interest and the interest of the corporation. To be informed, the director or officer must do what is necessary to become informed: attend presentations, ask for information from those who have it, read reports, review other written materials such as contracts—in other words, carefully study a situation and its alternatives. To be free of conflicting interests, the director must not engage in self-dealing. For instance, a director should not oppose a *tender offer* (an offer to purchase shares in the company made by another company directly to the shareholders) that is in the corporation's best interest simply because its acceptance may cost the director her or his position. For a decision to have an apparently rational basis, the decision itself must appear to have been made reasonably. For example, a director should not accept a tender offer with only a moment's consideration based solely on the market price of the corporation's shares.

Liability for Torts and Crimes

As mentioned in previous chapters, the corporation as an entity is liable for the torts and crimes that are committed by corporate agents and employees when they are acting within the scope of their employment. This liability for the actions of corporate officers, directors, employees, and other agents is imputed to the corporation (the principal) under agency law. Directors, officers, and corporate employees are also personally liable for the torts and crimes that they commit within the scope of their employment. In other words, even though the corporation as an entity may assume liability for, say, a corporate agent's tort, that does not mean that the agent can avoid personal liability for the tort.

Corporate officers may also be held personally liable for the torts and crimes committed by corporate personnel under their direct supervision. Normally, the

Landmark in the Law

Corporate Sentencing Guidelines

Traditionally, persons committing the same crime might have received very different sentences, depending on the judge hearing the case, the jurisdiction in which it was heard, and many other factors. Many critics of this disparity in sentencing became quite vocal in the early 1980s, and in response to this criticism, Congress created in 1984 a seven-member U.S. Sentencing Commission. The commission was charged with the task of standardizing sentences for federal crimes. The argument in favor of such standardization was that if individuals have an idea of the penalties they will receive if convicted of a particular crime, it will help deter criminal acts. The commission not only fulfilled its task of creating uniform sentences for federal crimes, but it also went further: it formulated specific guidelines for the punishment of crimes committed by corporate employees. It is clear that the new federal sentencing guidelines for corporate crimes have changed the way corporations will deal with potential wrongdoing for years to come.

Tougher Sentences for Corporate Employees

The commission established sentencing guidelines for thirty-two levels of offenses. The punishment for each offense depends on such things as the seriousness of the charge, the amount of money involved, and the extent to which top company executives are involved. Under the new sentencing guidelines, corporate lawbreakers face sanctions and fines that can be as high as hundreds of millions of dollars. But the guidelines allow judges to ease up on penalties when companies have taken substantial steps to prevent, investigate, and punish wrongdoing. Additionally, if companies cooperate with government investigators, the sentences may be less severe. Nonetheless, the net effect of the guidelines in the last few years has been a fivefold to tenfold increase in criminal penalties for crimes committed by corporate employees.

The new guidelines cover violations of federal laws in the following areas:

- Antitrust (see Chapter 30).
- Securities (see Chapter 29).
- Employment laws (see Chapter 32).
- Mail and wire fraud (see Chapter 7).
- Commercial bribery (see Chapter 7).
- Kickbacks and money laundering (see Chapter 7).

Thousands of businesses are therefore covered by the federal sentencing guidelines. These include brokerage houses, law firms, banks, and a host of large and small businesses.

How to Prevent or Reduce Criminal Sanctions

The guidelines present judges with a complicated formula for sentencing businesses based on the seriousness of the offense and the degree of the company's guilt. The so-called *culpability score* of a company depends on what role senior management had in the alleged wrongdoing as well as the company's history of past violations and the extent of management's cooperation with federal investigators. Additionally, the effectiveness of the company's compliance program is important. Firms can establish "credits" against potential penalties if they have undertaken the measures listed below.

- The firm must establish and put in writing crime-prevention standards and procedures for all employees and agents, and these standards must be communicated to all employees and agents in writing, training programs, or both.
- The standards must be enforced by high-level employees.
- When an employee has demonstrated an apparent propensity to engage in criminal activities, the company must prevent that employee from exercising discretionary authority.
- All anticrime standards of the company must include methods of detecting as well as preventing crimes.
- Whistleblowers must be protected from reprisals.

court must show that the wrongful actions were committed at the officer's direction or with his or her permission. In some instances, however, liability may be imposed on the officer for his or her negligent failure to supervise the employees. In *United States v. Park,*[4] for example, the chief executive officer of a national supermarket chain was held personally liable for sanitation violations in corporate warehouses in which food was exposed to contamination by rodents. The officer admitted that as

4. 421 U.S. 658, 95 S.Ct. 1903, 44 L.Ed.2d 489 (1975).

president he was responsible for the entire operation of the company, including providing sanitary conditions. He testified that he had no choice but to delegate duties, including those concerning sanitation, to subordinates. He said that he had no reason to suspect that these subordinates were violating the law, and that when violations came to light, he requested his subordinates to do everything possible to correct the unsanitary conditions. Evidence of earlier violations at another warehouse was introduced, however, to show that he was on notice that he could not rely on these subordinates to prevent or correct unsanitary conditions. The court concluded that he was not justified in relying on the subordinates to handle sanitation matters. On appeal, the United States Supreme Court upheld the conviction.

Note that in *Park*, the court imposed personal liability on the corporate officer not because he intended the crime[5] or even knew about it. Rather, liability was imposed because the officer was in a "responsible relationship" to the corporation and had the power to prevent the violation. Since the *Park* decision, other courts have held corporate officers liable for their employees' statutory violations under this doctrine. The following case illustrates a recent application of the doctrine.

Case 27.2

IN THE MATTER OF THE AMENDED ADMINISTRATIVE PENALTY ORDER ISSUED TO PAUL S. DOUGHERTY III

Court of Appeals of Minnesota, 1992.
482 N.W.2d 485.

HISTORICAL AND SOCIAL SETTING *Some statutes impose criminal liability for what is termed "public welfare" offenses. A public welfare offense occurs under a statute that is intended to improve the public welfare. A violation of such a statute does not require intent; rather, strict liability is imposed. Environmental statutes, particularly hazardous waste laws, have been held to constitute public welfare statutes. Hazardous waste laws regulate activities that threaten human health and safety, as well as the environment, and violations often do not require "wilfulness" or "intent."*[a]

FACTS Paul Dougherty III was the president and principal shareholder of MCM Industries, Inc., which operated a metal galvanizing business in Minneapolis. As part of its operations, MCM galvanized steel with zinc, a process involving the use of large quantities of sulfuric acid. The company also used hazardous materials in conducting a commercial painting operation. Dougherty was ultimately in charge of all operations at the facility. In 1990, the Minnesota Pollution Control Agency (MPCA) issued an order stating that MCM and Dougherty had violated Minnesota statutes regulating hazardous waste disposal. Pools of sulfuric acid accumulated on the floor of one of the rooms in the plant, and this acid was routinely swept outside by employees. Other violations included the failure to label a hazardous waste container and the failure to update a hazardous waste emergency contingency plan. The MPCA imposed a $10,000 penalty, which was later reduced to $7,075, on MCM and Dougherty. Dougherty sought court review of the decision, contending that he could not be held personally liable for the penalty because he had not directly participated in the alleged violations, nor had he directed MCM employees to sweep hazardous materials outside the building or ignore environmental regulations.

a. *United States v. Hayes International Corp.*, 786 F.2d 1499 (11th Cir. 1986); *United States v. Liviola*, 605 F.Supp. 96 (N.D. Ohio 1985).

ISSUE Can Dougherty be held personally liable for the statutory violations committed by MCM employees under his control?

DECISION Yes. The court affirmed the agency's order and held that Dougherty could be held personally liable, as a responsible corporate officer, for failure to adequately supervise the actions of his employees.

REASON The court agreed with Dougherty that there was no evidence that he had participated in the alleged violations, had directed his employees to violate environmental laws, or had personally placed hazardous materials into the environment. But because he was ultimately in charge of plant operations, personal liability could be premised on his actions or inactions as a "responsible corporate officer." The court reviewed the three elements that must be satisfied for a corporate officer to be liable under this doctrine: "(1) the individual must be in a position of re-

5. Recall from Chapter 7 that two elements must be present for a crime to exist: a criminal act and criminal intent. In *Park*, the court dispensed with the latter requirement.

Case 27.2—Continued

sponsibility which allows the person to influence corporate policies or activities; (2) there must be a nexus [connection] between the individual's position and the violation in question such that the individual could have influenced the corporate actions which constituted the violations; and (3) the individual's actions or inactions facilitated the violations." The court held that Dougherty "satisfied all three elements of the doctrine" and therefore could be held personally liable for the violations.

ETHICAL CONSIDERATIONS *The court emphasized that imposing liability under the "responsible corporate officer" doctrine is particularly appropriate in the context of environmental laws because "[i]mposing liability upon only the corporation, but not those corporate officers and employees who actually make corporate decisions, would be inconsistent with [the legislature's] intent to impose liability upon the persons who are involved in the handling and disposal of hazardous substances."*

❖ Role of Shareholders

The acquisition of a share of stock makes a person an owner and shareholder in a corporation. Shareholders thus own the corporation. Although they have no legal title to corporate property, such as buildings and equipment, they do have an *equitable* (ownership) interest in the firm.

As a general rule, shareholders have no responsibility for the daily management of the corporation, although they are ultimately responsible for choosing the board of directors, which does have such control. Ordinarily, corporate officers and other employees owe no direct duty to individual stockholders. Their duty is to the corporation as a whole. A director, however, is in a fiduciary relationship to the corporation and therefore serves the interests of the shareholders as a whole. Generally, there is no legal relationship between shareholders and creditors of the corporation. Shareholders can, in fact, be creditors of the corporation and have the same rights of recovery against the corporation as any other creditor.

In this section, we look at the powers, rights, and liabilities of shareholders, which are generally established in the articles of incorporation and under the state's general incorporation law.

Shareholders' Powers

Shareholders must approve fundamental changes affecting the corporation before the changes can be effected. Hence, shareholders are empowered to amend the articles of incorporation (charter) and bylaws, approve a merger or the dissolution of the corporation, and approve the sale of all or substantially all of the corporation's assets. Some of these powers are subject to prior board approval.

Election and removal of the board of directors are accomplished by a vote of the shareholders. The first board of directors is either named in the articles of incorporation or chosen by the incorporators to serve until the first shareholders' meeting. From that time on, selection and retention of directors are exclusively shareholder functions.

Directors usually serve their full terms; if they are unsatisfactory, they are simply not reelected. Shareholders have the inherent power, however, to remove a director from office *for cause* (breach of duty or misconduct) by a majority vote.[6] Some state statutes even permit removal of directors *without cause* by the vote of a majority of the holders of outstanding shares entitled to vote.[7] Some corporate charters expressly

6. A director can often demand court review of removal for cause.

7. Most states allow *cumulative voting* (which will be discussed shortly) for directors, meaning that no individual director can be removed if the number of votes cast against his or her removal would be sufficient to elect that director if cumulatively voted at an election of the entire board of directors. See, for example, California Corporate Code Section 303A. Also see Section 8.08(c) of the RMBCA.

Business Law in Action

The Expanding Liability of Corporate Directors and Officers

Traditionally, corporate officers could only be held personally liable for the crimes of their employees if the officers directly participated in the crimes or directed employees to commit the wrongful acts. As indicated in this chapter, today, under what has become known as the "responsible corporate officer" doctrine, a court may impose criminal liability on a corporate officer regardless of whether he or she participated in, directed, or even knew about a given criminal violation.

In one case, yet another basis for imposing personal liability on a corporate officer was enunciated. In *United States v. Cusack*,[a] a court held that a corporate officer's control over corporate operations was so pervasive that, in effect, the officer was not only a corporate agent but also a principal-employer. Therefore, as an employer, the officer could be subject to liability for the statutory violations of corporate employees.

The defendant in the case, John Cusack, was the president and only officer of Quality Steel, Inc., and one of its two directors. The other director, Lawrence Karpinsky, had supplied the capital for the small corporation but played no role in corporate management. Cusack alone was in charge of all corporate operations. He made all company decisions, had unlimited access to corporate funds, hired and fired all employees, determined their salaries as well as his own, made all the bids for construction jobs, directed all work activities, and generally had unrestricted discretion to run the company as he saw fit.

At one point, Quality Steel was retained to erect the structural steel frame for a warehouse to be constructed in Riverdale, New Jersey. Cusack, who supervised and directed the operation, allegedly violated safety standards required by the Occupational Safety and Health Act of 1970 relating to the installation of steel joists. As a result, the building collapsed and caused the death of an employee.

Cusack was indicted for knowingly and willfully violating Section 666(e) of the act. That section provides that an "employer" convicted of a willful violation of standards required under the act that results in an employee's death may be fined up to $10,000 or imprisoned for up to six months, or both. Cusack moved to dismiss the indictment on the ground that Section 666(e) imposes liability only on employers and he, as a corporate officer, was an employee, not an employer.

The court held otherwise. In the eyes of the court, "an officer's or director's role in a corporate entity (particularly a small one) may be so pervasive and total that the officer or director is in fact the corporation and is therefore an employer under [Section] 666(e). To conclude that such a person cannot be held liable under the [Occupational Safety and Health Act's] criminal provisions would strip [Section] 666(e) of much of its force when applied to closely held corporations where, as in the present case, the owner and principal officer is also the person actively supervising the work in which [the act's] regulations were violated. In such a case it would seem that Congress' intent is implemented by recognizing the reality of the situation and treating the officer and director as the employer."

a. 806 F.Supp. 47 (D.N.J. 1992).

provide that shareholders, by majority vote, can remove a director at any time without cause.

Shareholders' Forum

Shareholders' meetings must occur at least annually, and in addition, special meetings can be called to take care of urgent matters. Because it is usually not practical for owners of only a few shares of stock of publicly traded corporations to attend shareholders' meetings, such stockholders normally give third parties written authorization to vote their shares at the meeting. This authorization is called a **proxy** (from the Latin *procurare*, "to manage, take care of"). Proxies are often solicited by management, as will be discussed later in this chapter.

PROXY
In corporation law, a written agreement between a stockholder and another under which the stockholder authorizes the other to vote the stockholder's shares in a certain manner.

Notice of Meetings Before a shareholders' meeting, each shareholder must receive written notice of the meeting, including the place where it will be held and the day and the hour on which it will be held.[8] Notice of a special meeting must include a statement of the purpose of the meeting; business transacted at a special meeting is limited to that purpose.

Shareholder Voting Shareholders exercise ownership control through the power of their votes. Each shareholder is entitled to one vote per share, although the voting techniques discussed below all enhance the power of the shareholder's vote. The articles of incorporation can exclude or limit voting rights, particularly to certain classes of shares. For example, owners of preferred shares are usually denied the right to vote.

For shareholders to act, a *quorum* (a minimum number of shareholders, in terms of the number of shares held) must be present at a meeting. Generally, a quorum exists when shareholders holding more than 50 percent of the outstanding shares are present. Corporate business matters are presented in the form of *resolutions*, which shareholders vote to approve or disapprove. Some state statutes have set forth specific voting requirements, and corporations' articles or bylaws must abide by these statutory requirements. Some states provide that the unanimous written consent of shareholders is a permissible alternative to holding a shareholders' meeting.

Once a quorum is present, a majority vote of the shares represented at the meeting is usually required to pass resolutions. Assume that Novo Pictures, Inc., has 10,000 outstanding shares of voting stock. Its articles of incorporation set the quorum at 50 percent of outstanding shares and provide that a majority vote of the shares present is necessary to pass on ordinary matters. Therefore, for this firm, at the shareholders' meeting, a quorum of stockholders representing 5,000 outstanding shares must be present to conduct business. If exactly 5,000 shares are represented at the meeting, a vote of at least 2,501 of those shares is needed to pass a resolution. If 6,000 shares are represented, a vote of 3,001 will be required, and so on.

At times, a larger-than-majority vote will be required either by statute or by corporate charter. Extraordinary corporate matters, such as a merger, consolidation, or dissolution of the corporation (see Chapter 28), require a higher percentage of the representatives of all corporate shares entitled to vote, not just a majority of those present at that particular meeting.

Voting Lists Voting lists are prepared by the corporation prior to each shareholders' meeting. Persons whose names appear on the corporation's stockholder records as owners are the ones ordinarily entitled to vote.[9] The voting list contains the name and address of each shareholder as shown on the corporate records on a given cut-off date, or record date. (Under RMBCA 7.07, the record date may be as much as seventy days before the meeting.) It also includes the number of voting shares held by each owner. The list is usually kept at the corporate headquarters and is available for shareholder inspection.

Cumulative Voting Most states permit or require shareholders to elect directors by *cumulative voting*, a method of voting designed to allow minority shareholders

---

8. The shareholder can waive the requirement of written notice by signing a waiver form. In some states, a shareholder who does not receive written notice, but who learns of the meeting and attends without protesting the lack of notice, is said to have waived notice by such conduct. State statutes and corporate bylaws typically set forth the time within which notice must be sent, what methods can be used, and what the notice must contain.

9. When the legal owner is deceased, bankrupt, incompetent, or in some other way under a legal disability, his or her vote can be cast by a person designated by law to control and manage the owner's property.

◆ **Exhibit 27–1**
Results of Cumulative Voting
This exhibit illustrates how cumulative voting gives minority shareholders a greater chance of electing a director of their choice. By casting all of their 9,000 votes for one candidate (Drake), the minority shareholders will succeed in electing Drake to the board of directors.

BALLOT	MAJORITY SHAREHOLDERS' VOTES			MINORITY SHAREHOLDERS' VOTES	DIRECTORS ELECTED
	Acevedo	Barkley	Craycik	Drake	
1	10,000	10,000	1,000	9,000	Acevedo/BarkleyDrake
2	9,001	9,000	2,999	9,000	Acevedo/Barkley/Drake
3	6,000	7,000	8,000	9,000	Barkley/Craycik/Drake

representation on the board of directors.[10] When cumulative voting is allowed or required, the number of members of the board to be elected is multiplied by the total number of voting shares. The result equals the number of votes a shareholder has, and this total can be cast for one or more nominees for director. All nominees stand for election at the same time. When cumulative voting is not required either by statute or under the articles, the entire board can be elected by a simple majority of shares at a shareholders' meeting.

Suppose, for example, that a corporation has 10,000 shares issued and outstanding. One group of shareholders (the minority shareholders) holds only 3,000 shares, and the other group of shareholders (the majority shareholders) holds the other 7,000 shares. Three members of the board are to be elected. The majority shareholders' nominees are Acevedo, Barkley, and Craycik. The minority shareholders' nominee is Drake. Can Drake be elected by the minority shareholders?

If cumulative voting is allowed, the answer is yes. The minority shareholders have 9,000 votes among them (the number of directors to be elected times the number of shares held by the minority shareholders equals 3 times 3,000, which equals 9,000 votes). All of these votes can be cast to elect Drake. The majority shareholders have 21,000 votes (3 times 7,000 equals 21,000 votes), but these votes have to be distributed among their three nominees. The principle of cumulative voting is that no matter how the majority shareholders cast their 21,000 votes, they will not be able to elect all three directors if the minority shareholders cast all of their 9,000 votes for Drake, as illustrated in Exhibit 27–1.

Other Voting Techniques A group of shareholders can agree in writing prior to a shareholders' meeting to vote their shares together in a specified manner. Such *shareholder voting agreements* are usually held to be valid and enforceable. A shareholder can also appoint a voting agent and vote by proxy. As mentioned, a proxy is a written authorization to cast the shareholder's vote, and a person can solicit proxies from a number of shareholders in an attempt to concentrate voting power.

Another technique is for shareholders to enter into a **voting trust,** which is an agreement (a trust contract) under which legal title (record ownership on the corporate books) is transferred to a trustee who is responsible for voting the shares. The agreement can specify how the trustee is to vote, or it can allow the trustee to use his or her discretion. The trustee takes physical possession of the stock certificate and in return gives the shareholder a *voting trust certificate.* The shareholder retains all of the rights of ownership (for example, the right to receive dividend payments) except for the power to vote the shares.

VOTING TRUST
The transfer of title by stockholders of shares of a corporation to a trustee who is authorized to vote the shares on their behalf.

10. See, for example, California Corporate Code Section 708. Under RMBCA 7.28, however, no cumulative voting rights exist unless the articles of incorporation so provide.

❖ Rights of Shareholders

Shareholders possess numerous rights. A significant right—the right to vote their shares—has already been discussed. In addition to voting rights, a shareholder has the rights discussed in the following subsections.

Stock Certificates

STOCK CERTIFICATE
A certificate issued by a corporation evidencing the ownership of a specified number of shares in the corporation.

A **stock certificate** is a certificate issued by a corporation that evidences ownership of a specified number of shares in the corporation. In jurisdictions that require the issuance of stock certificates, shareholders have the right to demand that the corporation issue certificates. In most states (and under RMBCA 6.26), boards of directors may provide that shares of stock be uncertificated (that is, that physical stock certificates need not be issued). In that circumstance, it may be required that the corporation send the holders of uncertificated shares letters or some other form of notice containing the same information as that included on stock certificates.

Stock is intangible personal property, and the ownership right exists independently of the certificate itself. A stock certificate may be lost or destroyed, but ownership is not destroyed with it. A new certificate can be issued to replace one that has been lost or destroyed.[11] Notice of shareholders' meetings, dividends, and operational and financial reports are all distributed according to the recorded ownership listed in the corporation's books, not on the basis of possession of the certificate.

PREEMPTIVE RIGHTS
Rights held by shareholders that entitle them to purchase newly issued shares of a corporation's stock, equal in percentage to shares presently held, before the stock is offered to any outside buyers. Preemptive rights enable shareholders to maintain their proportionate ownership and voice in the corporation.

Preemptive Rights

A **preemptive right** is a common law concept under which a preference is given to shareholders over all other purchasers to subscribe to or purchase shares of a new issue of stock in proportion to the percentage of total shares they already hold. This allows each shareholder to maintain his or her portion of control, voting power, or

Why does a corporation issue stock certificates?

11. For a lost or destroyed certificate to be reissued, a shareholder normally must furnish an indemnity bond to protect the corporation against potential loss should the original certificate reappear at some future time in the hands of a bona fide purchaser [UCC 8–302, 8–405(2)].

financial interest in the corporation. Most statutes either (1) grant preemptive rights but allow them to be negated in the corporation's articles or (2) deny preemptive rights except to the extent that they are granted in the articles. The result is that the articles of incorporation determine the existence and scope of preemptive rights. Generally, preemptive rights apply only to additional, newly issued stock sold for cash and must be exercised within a specified time period (usually thirty days).

For example, Detering Corporation authorizes and issues 1,000 shares of stock, and Callie Lebo purchases 100 shares, making her the owner of 10 percent of the company's stock. Subsequently, Detering, by vote of its shareholders, authorizes the issuance of another 1,000 shares (amending the articles of incorporation). This increases its capital stock to a total of 2,000 shares. If preemptive rights have been provided, Lebo can purchase one additional share of the new stock being issued for each share she currently owns—or 100 additional shares. Thus, she can own 200 of the 2,000 shares outstanding, and her relative position as a shareholder will be maintained. If preemptive rights are not reserved, her proportionate control and voting power may be diluted from that of a 10 percent shareholder to that of a 5 percent shareholder because of the issuance of the additional 1,000 shares.

Preemptive rights are far more significant in a close corporation because of the relatively small number of shares and the substantial interest that each shareholder controls.

Stock Warrants

Usually, when preemptive rights exist and a corporation is issuing additional shares, each shareholder is given **stock warrants,** which are transferable options to acquire a given number of shares from the corporation at a stated price. Warrants are often publicly traded on securities exchanges. When the option to purchase is in effect for a short period of time, the stock warrants are usually referred to as *rights.*

STOCK WARRANT
A certificate that grants the owner the option to buy a given number of shares of stock, usually within a set time period.

Dividends

A **dividend** is a distribution of corporate profits or income *ordered by the directors* and paid to the shareholders in proportion to their respective shares in the corporation. Dividends can be paid in cash, property, stock of the corporation that is paying the dividends, or stock of other corporations.[12]

DIVIDEND
A distribution to corporate shareholders of corporate profits or income, disbursed in proportion to the number of shares held.

State laws vary, but every state determines the general circumstances and legal requirements under which dividends are paid. State laws also control the sources of revenue to be used; only certain funds are legally available for paying dividends. Under statutes that limit the sources of funds from which dividends may be paid, prescribed sources include the following:

1. *Retained earnings.* All state statutes allow dividends to be paid from the undistributed net profits earned by the corporation, including capital gains from the sale of fixed assets. The undistributed net profits are called *retained earnings.*
2. *Net profits.* A few state statutes allow dividends to be issued from current net profits without regard to deficits in prior years.
3. *Surplus.* A number of statutes allow dividends to be paid out of any surplus.

Illegal Dividends A dividend paid while the corporation is insolvent is automatically an illegal dividend, and shareholders may be liable for returning the payment to the corporation or its creditors. Furthermore, as just discussed, dividends are

12. Technically, dividends paid in stock are not dividends. They maintain each shareholder's proportional interest in the corporation. On one occasion, a distillery declared and paid a "dividend" in bonded whiskey.

generally required by statute to be distributed only from certain authorized corporate accounts. Sometimes dividends are improperly paid from an unauthorized account, or their payment causes the corporation to become insolvent. Generally, in such cases, shareholders must return illegal dividends only if they knew that the dividends were illegal when they received them. In all cases of illegal and improper dividends, the board of directors can be held personally liable for the amount of the payment. When directors can show that a shareholder knew a dividend was illegal when it was received, however, the directors are entitled to reimbursement from the shareholder.

Directors' Failure to Declare a Dividend When directors fail to declare a dividend, shareholders can ask a court of equity for an injunction to compel the directors to meet and to declare a dividend. For the injunction to be granted, it must be shown that the directors have acted so unreasonably in withholding the dividend that their conduct is an abuse of their discretion.

Often, large money reserves are accumulated for a bona fide purpose, such as expansion, research, or other legitimate corporate goals. The mere fact that sufficient corporate earnings or surplus are available to pay a dividend is not enough to compel directors to distribute funds that, in the board's opinion, should not be paid. The courts are circumspect about interfering with corporate operations and will not compel directors to declare dividends unless abuse of discretion is clearly shown. A striking exception to this rule was made in the following classic case.

Case 27.3
DODGE v. FORD MOTOR CO.
Supreme Court of Michigan, 1919.
204 Mich. 459,
170 N.W. 668.

HISTORICAL AND SOCIAL SETTING *Corporations are owned by shareholders but run by directors and officers. Practical and ethical problems are inevitable. Directors are supposed to act in the best interests of the corporation, which is presumed to be the same as the best interests of the shareholders. Directors and shareholders may have different views about the corporation's best interests, however. Directors may want to invest profits in the firm, looking toward long-term growth and future profitability. Shareholders may be more interested in receiving those profits as dividends.*

FACTS Henry Ford was the president and major shareholder of Ford Motor Company. In the company's early years, business expanded rapidly, and in addition to regular quarterly dividends, special dividends were often paid. By 1916, surplus above capital was still $111,960,907. That year, however, Henry Ford declared that the company would no longer pay special dividends but would put back into the business all the earnings of the company above the regular dividend of 5 percent. The court quoted Ford: "My ambition," declared Mr. Ford, "is to employ still more men, to spread the benefits of this industrial system to the greatest possible number, to help them build up their lives and their homes. To do this, we are putting the greatest share of our profits back into the business." The minority shareholders of Ford (who owned 10 percent of the stock) brought a suit to force the declaration of a dividend.

ISSUE Was Ford's refusal to pay a dividend an abuse of managerial discretion?

DECISION Yes. Because of the special circumstances of this case, the court compelled Ford to pay a dividend.

REASON The undisputed facts were that Ford had a surplus of $112 million—approximately $54 million in cash on hand. It had made profits of $59 million in the past year and expected to make $60 million in the coming year. The board of directors gave no reason to justify withholding a dividend. Thus, in doing so, it violated the stated purpose of the corporation's existence. "Courts of equity will not interfere in the management of the directors unless it is clearly made to appear that they are guilty of fraud or misappropriation of the corporate funds, or refuse to declare a dividend when the corporation has a surplus of net profits which it can, without detriment to its business, divide among its stockholders, and when a refusal to do so would amount to such an abuse of discretion as would constitute a fraud, or breach of that good faith which they are bound to exercise towards the stockholders."

Inspection Rights Shareholders in a corporation enjoy both common law and statutory inspection rights.[13] The shareholder's right of inspection is limited, however, to the inspection and copying of corporate books and records for a *proper purpose,* provided the request is made in advance. The shareholder can inspect in person, or an attorney, agent, accountant, or other type of assistant can do so. The RMBCA requires the corporation to maintain an alphabetical voting list of shareholders with addresses and number of shares owned; this list must be kept open at the annual meeting for inspection by any shareholder of record [RMBCA 7.20].

The power of inspection is fraught with potential abuses, and the corporation is allowed to protect itself from them. For example, a shareholder can properly be denied access to corporate records to prevent harassment or to protect trade secrets or other confidential corporate information. Some states require that a shareholder must have held his or her shares for a minimum period of time immediately preceding the demand to inspect or must hold a minimum number of outstanding shares. The RMBCA provides that every shareholder is entitled to examine specified corporate records [RMBCA 16.02].

Transfer of Shares Although stock certificates are negotiable and freely transferable by indorsement and delivery, transfer of stock in closely held corporations is generally restricted by the bylaws, by a restriction stamped on the stock certificate, or by a shareholder agreement (shareholder agreements are discussed in Chapter 26). The existence of any restrictions on transferability must always be noted on the face of the stock certificate, and these restrictions must be reasonable.

Sometimes, corporations or their shareholders restrict transferability by reserving the option to purchase any shares offered for resale by a shareholder. This **right of first refusal** remains with the corporation or the shareholders for only a specified time or a reasonable time. Variations on the purchase option are possible. For example, a shareholder might be required to offer the shares to other shareholders first or to the corporation first.

RIGHT OF FIRST REFUSAL
The right to purchase personal or real property—such as corporate shares or real estate—before the property is offered for sale to others.

When shares are transferred, a new entry is made in the corporate stock book to indicate the new owner. Until the corporation is notified and the entry is complete, voting rights, notice of shareholders' meetings, dividend distribution, and so forth are all held by the current record owner.

Corporate Dissolution

When a corporation is dissolved and its outstanding debts and the claims of its creditors have been satisfied, the remaining assets are distributed to the shareholders in proportion to the percentage of shares owned by each shareholder. Certain classes of preferred stock can be given priority. If no preferences to distribution of assets upon liquidation are given to any class of stock, then the stockholders share the remaining assets.

In some circumstances, shareholders may petition a court to have the corporation dissolved. Suppose, for example, that a minority shareholder knows that the board of directors is mishandling corporate assets. The minority shareholder is not powerless to intervene. He or she can petition a court to appoint a receiver and to liquidate the business assets of the corporation.

The RMBCA permits any shareholder to initiate such an action in any of the following circumstances [RMBCA 14.30]:

1. The directors are deadlocked in the management of corporate affairs. Shareholders are unable to break that deadlock, and irreparable injury to the corporation is being suffered or threatened.

13. See, for example, *Schwartzman v. Schwartzman Packing Co.,* 99 N.M. 436, 659 P.2d 888 (1983).

2. The acts of the directors or those in control of the corporation are illegal, oppressive, or fraudulent.
3. Corporate assets are being misapplied or wasted.
4. The shareholders are deadlocked in voting power and have failed, for a specified period (usually two annual meetings), to elect successors to directors whose terms have expired or would have expired with the election of successors.

Shareholder's Derivative Suit

SHAREHOLDER'S DERIVATIVE SUIT
A suit by a shareholder to enforce a corporate cause of action for a wrong suffered by the corporation committed by a third person.

When those in control of a corporation—the corporate directors—fail to sue in the corporate name to redress a wrong suffered by the corporation, shareholders are permitted to do so "derivatively" in what is known as a **shareholder's derivative suit.** Some wrong must have been done to the corporation, and any damages recovered by the suit usually go into the corporation's treasury. The right of shareholders to bring a derivative action is especially important when the wrong suffered by the corporation results from the actions of corporate directors or officers. The shareholder's derivative suit is singular in that those suing are not pursuing rights or benefits for themselves personally but are acting as guardians of the corporate entity. The derivative nature of this type of lawsuit is stressed in the following case.

Case 27.4
GLENN v. HOTELTRON SYSTEMS, INC.
Court of Appeals of New York, 1989.
74 N.Y.2d 386,
547 N.E.2d 71,
547 N.Y.S.2d 816.

HISTORICAL AND SOCIAL SETTING *The right of shareholders to sue derivatively on the behalf of their corporation was indicated as early as the 1830s. In 1855, the United States Supreme Court upheld a shareholder's right to sue on behalf of a corporation whose officer had paid a tax that the shareholder claimed was unconstitutional.*[a] *The derivative suit developed more fully in the second half of the nineteenth century. Procedural restrictions on derivative suits also developed in the federal courts late in the nineteenth century and in the state courts in the first half of the twentieth century. During the 1970s, according to at least one study, there was only a slight increase in the amount of shareholder derivative litigation.*[b] *During the 1980s, however, the amount of shareholder derivative litigation for alleged breaches of management duties increased dramatically.*

FACTS Jacob Schachter and Herbert Kulik, the founders of Ketek Electric Corporation, each owned 50 percent of the corporation's shares and served as the corporation's only officers. Arnold Glenn, as trustee, and Kulik brought a shareholder's derivative suit against Schachter, alleging that Schachter had diverted Ketek assets and opportunities to Hoteltron Systems, Inc., a corporation wholly owned by Schachter. The trial court initially held that neither Schachter nor Kulik had proved a breach of duty by the other. The appellate court reversed this decision, and the trial court later determined damages and also decided that the damages should be paid to Kulik, not to Ketek Corporation. Schachter appealed, and the appellate court ruled that the damages should be awarded to the injured corporation, Ketek, rather than to the innocent shareholder, Kulik. Kulik argued that awarding damages to the corporation was inequitable because Schachter, as a shareholder of Ketek, would ultimately share in the proceeds of the award. Eventually, the case was heard by the New York Court of Appeals.

ISSUE Given the fact that Schachter is a 50 percent shareholder in Ketek Corporation, should the damages be paid to Ketek Corporation or to Kulik?

DECISION The New York Court of Appeals affirmed the appellate court's ruling that damages should be paid to Ketek Corporation and not to Kulik.

REASON The court stressed that the injury Kulik suffered was secondary to the corporate injury: "In this case, the diversion of Ketek's corporate assets by Schachter for his own profit resulted in a corporate injury because it deprived Ketek of those profits. Kulik, the innocent shareholder, was injured only to the extent that he was entitled to share in those profits. His injury was real, but it was derivative, not direct." The court acknowledged that the prospect of an inequitable result exists "in any successful derivative action

a. *Dodge v. Woolsey,* 59 U.S. 331, 15 L.Ed. 401 (1855).
b. Jones, "An Empirical Examination of the Incidence of Shareholder Derivative and Class Action Lawsuits, 1971–1978," 60 *Boston University Law Review* 306 (1980).

Case 27.4—Continued

in which the wrongdoer is a shareholder of the corporation." But, the court pointed out, if exceptions were made because of that prospect, the general rule that damages for a corporate injury should be awarded to the corporation would effectively be nullified. The court stated that "[w]hile awarding damages directly to the innocent shareholder may seem equitable with respect to the parties before the court," there were other interests to consider—particularly those of the corporation's creditors, whose claims might be superior to those of innocent shareholders.

❖ Liability of Shareholders

One of the hallmarks of the corporate organization is that shareholders are not personally liable for the debts of the corporation. If the corporation fails, shareholders can lose their investment, but that is generally the limit of their liability. As discussed in Chapter 26, in certain instances of fraud, undercapitalization, or careless observance of corporate formalities, a court will pierce the corporate veil (disregard the corporate entity) and hold the shareholders individually liable. But these situations are the exception, not the rule. Although rare, there are certain other instances where a shareholder can be personally liable. One relates to illegal dividends, which were discussed previously. Two others relate to *stock subscriptions* and *watered stock,* which will be discussed here.

Stock Subscriptions

Sometimes stock-subscription agreements—written contracts by which one agrees to buy capital stock of a corporation—exist prior to incorporation. Normally, these agreements are treated as continuing offers and are irrevocable (for up to six months under RMBCA 6.20). Once the corporation has been formed, it can sell shares to shareholder investors. In either case, once the subscription agreement or stock offer is accepted, a binding contract is formed. Any refusal to pay constitutes a breach resulting in the personal liability of the shareholder.

Watered Stock

Shares of stock can be paid for by property or by services rendered instead of cash. They cannot be purchased with promissory notes, however. The general rule is that for **par-value shares** (that is, shares that have a specific face value, or formal cash-in value, written on them, such as one penny or one dollar), the corporation must receive a value at least equal to the par-value amount. For **no-par shares** (shares that have no face value—no specific amount printed on their face), the corporation must receive the value of the shares as determined by the board or the shareholders. When shares are issued by the corporation for less than these stated values, the shares are referred to as **watered stock.** In most cases, the shareholder who receives watered stock must pay the difference to the corporation (the shareholder is personally liable). In some states, the shareholder who receives watered stock may be liable to creditors of the corporation for unpaid corporate debts.

To illustrate the concept of watered stock, suppose that during the formation of a corporation, Gomez, one of the incorporators, transfers his property, Sunset Beach, to the corporation for 10,000 shares of stock at a par value of $100 per share for a total price of $1 million. After the property is transferred and the shares are issued, Sunset Beach is carried on the corporate books at a value of $1 million. Upon appraisal, it is discovered that the market value of the property at the time of transfer was only $500,000. The shares issued to Gomez are therefore watered stock, and he is liable to the corporation for the difference.

PAR-VALUE SHARES
Corporate shares that have a specific face value, or formal cash-in value, written on them, such as one dollar.

NO-PAR SHARES
Corporate shares that have no face value—that is, no specific dollar amount is printed on their face.

WATERED STOCK
Stock issued by a corporation as if fully paid for, when in fact less than par value has been paid.

❖ Duties of Majority Shareholders

In some cases, a majority shareholder is regarded as having a fiduciary duty to the corporation and to the minority shareholders. This occurs when a single shareholder (or a few shareholders acting in concert) owns a sufficient number of shares to exercise *de facto* control over the corporation. In these situations, majority shareholders owe a fiduciary duty to the minority shareholders when they sell their shares, because such a sale would be, in fact, a transfer of control of the corporation.

Whether the controlling majority of shareholders owed a fiduciary duty to a minority shareholder was at issue in the following case.

Case 27.5
PEDRO v. PEDRO
Court of Appeals of Minnesota, 1992.
489 N.W.2d 798.

HISTORICAL AND SOCIAL SETTING *The purchase of a minority shareholder's shares in a corporation by the majority shareholders is termed a "buy-out." In litigation, when fashioning relief involving the buy-out of shareholders in a close corporation, trial courts have broad equitable powers. For example, Minnesota Statutes Section 302A.751(3a) provides that "[i]n determining whether to order equitable relief, dissolution, or a buy-out, the court shall take into consideration the duty which all shareholders in a closely held corporation owe one another to act in an honest, fair and reasonable manner in the operation of the corporation and the reasonable expectations of the shareholders as they exist at the inception and develop during the course of the shareholders' relationship with the corporation and with each other." This statute allows courts to look to a shareholder's reasonable expectations when awarding damages. Besides the shareholder's ownership interest in the corporation, "[t]he reasonable expectations of such a shareholder are a job, salary, a significant place in management, and economic security for his family."*[a]

FACTS Alfred, Carl, and Eugene Pedro each owned a one-third interest in The Pedro Companies (TPC), a close corporation that manufactured and sold luggage and leather products. All of the brothers had worked for the corporation for most of their adult lives. The relationship between Alfred and the other two brothers began to deteriorate in 1987 after Alfred discovered a discrepancy between the internal accounting records and the TPC checking account. Alfred was very concerned and insisted that an independent accountant be retained to locate the source of the discrepancy. Subsequently, two different accountants examined the records, but neither could identify the source of a $140,000 discrepancy, and one accountant said that he was denied access to numerous documents during the investigation. Alfred testified that during this time, Eugene would interfere with his area of responsibility in the TPC plant and undermine his management authority. Alfred also stated that his brothers told him that if he did not forget about the discrepancy, they would fire him—which they did in December 1987. Employees were told that Alfred had had a nervous breakdown, which was not true. At the time he was fired, Alfred was sixty-two years old and had worked for TPC for forty-five years. Alfred sued the brothers for breach of fiduciary duty and wrongful discharge. The trial court held for Alfred and awarded him over $1.8 million in damages, plus interest, for the value of his shares, lost wages, and attorneys' fees. The brothers appealed.

a. Joseph Olson, "A Statutory Elixir for the Oppression Malady," 36 *Mercer Law Review* 627 (1985).

ISSUE Had the brothers breached their fiduciary duty to Alfred by terminating his employment with TPC?

DECISION Yes. The trial court's judgment was affirmed.

REASON The court emphasized that the relationship among shareholders in closely held corporations is "analogous to that of partners" and that they owe one another a fiduciary duty. "Owing a fiduciary duty," stated the court, "includes dealing 'openly, honestly and fairly with other shareholders.' " The court found that the brothers had not acted openly, honestly, and fairly with Alfred. Furthermore, the court found that Alfred justifiably assumed that he had an implied contract with the corporation for lifetime employment, a contract that the brothers breached when they fired him. Given the fact that Alfred's father had worked for the company until his death and that Eugene, who had worked for TPC for over fifty years, testified that he intended to always work for the company, Alfred's expectation of a lifetime job was reasonable. The court concluded that "[b]ased upon this evidence it was reasonable for the trial court to determine that the parties did in fact have a contract that was not terminable at will."

ETHICAL CONSIDERATIONS *Carl and Eugene argued that because there was no diminution in the value of the*

Case 27.5—Continued

corporation or the value of Alfred's shares in the company, they had not breached their fiduciary duty. The court pointed out, however, that depleting corporate value is not the only method of breaching fiduciary duties. Carl and Eugene had made no payments to Alfred for the value of his shares (as determined by the trial court), had interfered with his responsibilities in TPC, had hired a private investigator to follow him when he was not in the office, had fabricated accusations of neglect and malfeasance, had told employees that he had had a nervous breakdown, and had threatened to fire him. Finally, Carl and Eugene had admitted that they acted "in a manner unfairly prejudicial" toward Alfred. "This admission," the court concluded, "supports a finding of breach of fiduciary duty."

Application

Law and the Corporation—Developing a Document-Retention Policy

If a corporation becomes the target of a civil lawsuit or criminal investigation, the company may be required to turn over any documents in its files relating to the dispute during the discovery stage of litigation. These documents might consist of legal documents, contracts, faxes, letters, interoffice memoranda, notebooks, diaries, and other materials, even if they are kept in personal files in the homes of directors or officers. While certain documents or letters might free a company of any liability arising from a claim, others might serve to substantiate a civil claim or criminal charge. It is also possible that information in a document—an interoffice memo, for example—could be used to convince a jury that the company or its directors or officers condoned a certain action when they deny it. To be fully prepared in the event of a lawsuit or criminal investigation, many companies today have created document-retention policies to determine what documents to keep. Such policies have also been necessitated by the rising costs of storing the huge volume of documents produced by company employees in a given year.

How does a company decide which documents should be retained and which should be destroyed? By law, corporations are required to keep certain types of documents, such as those specified in the Code of Federal Regulations and in regulations issued by government agencies, such as the Occupational Safety and Health Administration. Generally, any records that the company is not legally required to keep or that the company is sure it will have no legal need for should be removed from the files and destroyed. A joint venture agreement, for example, should be kept. But the memo about last year's company picnic obviously is just taking up storage space. Interoffice memos relating to corporate decisions, if they are no longer necessary, should be destroyed. As mentioned above, information in such files might be used to the disadvantage of the corporation.

If the company becomes the target of an investigation, then it usually must modify its document-retention policy until the investigation has been completed. John Schmutz, general counsel for E. I. du Pont de Nemours & Company, has suggested that company officers, after receiving a subpoena to produce specific types of documents, should instruct the appropriate employees not to destroy relevant papers that would otherwise be disposed of as part of the company's normal document-retention program. Generally, company officials must always exercise good faith in deciding what documents should or should not be destroyed when attempting to comply with a subpoena to avoid being charged with the obstruction of justice. The specter of criminal prosecution would appear to encourage the retention of even those documents that are only remotely related to the dispute—at least until it has been resolved.

Checklist for a Document-Retention Policy

- ☐ 1. Find out which documents must be retained under the Code of Federal Regulations and under other government agency regulations to which your corporation is subject.
- ☐ 2. Retain other documents only if the retention is in the corporation's interest.
- ☐ 3. If certain corporate documents are subpoenaed, modify your document-retention policy to retain any document that is even remotely related to the dispute until the legal action has been resolved.

❖ Key Terms

business judgment rule 659
dividend 667
no-par share 671
par-value share 671
preemptive right 666
proxy 663
quorum 654
right of first refusal 669
shareholder's derivative suit 670
stock certificate 666
stock warrant 667
watered stock 671
voting trust 665

❖ Chapter Summary: Corporate Directors, Officers, and Shareholders

DIRECTORS AND OFFICERS	
Election of Directors	The first board of directors is usually appointed by the incorporators; thereafter, directors are elected by the shareholders. Directors usually serve a one-year term, although the term can be longer.
Directors' Qualifications and Compensation	Few qualifications are required; a director can be a shareholder but is not required to be. Compensation is usually specified in the corporate articles or bylaws.
Board of Directors' Forum	The board of directors conducts business by holding formal meetings with recorded minutes. The date of regular meetings is usually established in the corporate articles or bylaws; special meetings can be called, with notice sent to all directors. Quorum requirements vary from state to state; usually, a quorum is the majority of the corporate directors. Voting must usually be done in person, and in ordinary matters only a majority vote is required.
Rights of Directors	Included are the rights of participation, inspection, indemnification, and agreed to compensation.
Directors' Management Responsibilities	1. Directors' management responsibilities include the following: a. Declaration and payment of corporate dividends to shareholders; issuance of authorized shares and bonds. b. Authorization for major corporate decisions. c. Appointment, supervision, and removal of corporate officers and other managerial employees; determination of employees' compensation. d. Financial decisions necessary to the management of corporate affairs. 2. Directors may delegate some of their responsibilities to executive committees and daily management operations to corporate officers and executives.
Duties of Directors and Officers	1. *Duty of care*—Directors are obligated to be honest and to use prudent business judgment in the conduct of corporate affairs. If a director fails to exercise this duty of care, he or she can be answerable to the corporation and to the shareholders for breaching the duty. 2. *Duty of loyalty*—Directors have a fiduciary duty to subordinate their own interests to those of the corporation in matters relating to the corporation. Loyalty to the corporation and its interests is required of all directors. They must make full disclosure of any potential conflicts of interest between their personal interests and those of the corporation.
Liability of Directors and Officers	1. *Business judgment rule*—Immunizes a director from liability in a corporate transaction as long as the transaction was within the powers of the corporation and the authority of the director and as long as due care was exercised by the director. 2. *Torts and crimes*—Corporate directors and officers may be held personally liable for the torts and crimes committed by corporate personnel under their direct supervision.
SHAREHOLDERS	
Shareholders' Powers	Shareholders' powers include approval of all fundamental changes affecting the corporation and election of the board of directors.

❖ Chapter Summary: Corporate Directors, Officers, and Shareholders—Continued

Shareholders' Forum	Shareholders' meetings must occur at least annually; special meetings can be called when necessary. Notice of the time and place of the meeting (and its purpose if it is specially called) must be sent to shareholders. Voting requirements and procedures are as follows: 1. A minimum number of shareholders (a quorum—generally, more than 50 percent of shares held) must be present at a meeting for business to be conducted; resolutions are passed (usually) by simple majority vote. 2. Voting lists of shareholders on record must be prepared by the corporation prior to each shareholders' meeting. 3. Cumulative voting may or may not be required or permitted. Cumulative voting gives minority shareholders a better chance to be represented on the board of directors. 4. Shareholders' voting agreements (agreements to vote their shares together) are usually held to be valid and enforceable. 5. A shareholder may appoint a proxy (substitute) to vote his or her shares. 6. A shareholder may enter into a voting trust agreement by which title (record ownership) of his or her shares is given to a trustee, and the trustee votes the shares in accordance with the trust agreement.
Rights of Shareholders	Shareholders have numerous rights, which may include the following: 1. The right to a stock certificate, preemptive rights, and the right to stock warrants (depending on the corporate charter). 2. The right to obtain a dividend (at the discretion of the directors). 3. Voting rights. 4. The right to inspect the corporate records. 5. The right to transfer shares (this right may be restricted in close corporations). 6. The right to a share of corporate assets when the corporation is dissolved. 7. The right to sue on behalf of the corporation (bring a shareholder's derivative suit) when the directors fail to do so.
Liability of Shareholders	Shareholders may be liable for the retention of illegal dividends, for breach of a stock-subscription agreement, and for the value of watered stock. In certain situations, majority shareholders may be regarded as having a fiduciary duty to minority shareholders and will be liable if that duty is breached.

❖ Questions and Case Problems

27-1. Business Judgment Rule. Directors are expected to use their best judgment in managing the corporation. What must directors do to avoid liability for honest mistakes of judgment and poor business decisions?

27-2. Rights of Shareholders. If a group of shareholders perceives that the corporation has suffered a wrong and the directors refuse to take action, can the shareholders compel the directors to act? If so, how?

27-3. Rights of Shareholders. Dmitri has acquired one share of common stock of a multimillion-dollar corporation with over 500,000 shareholders. Dmitri's ownership is so small that he is questioning what his rights are as a shareholder. For example, he wants to know whether this one share entitles him to attend and vote at shareholders' meetings, inspect the corporate books, and receive yearly dividends. Discuss Dmitri's rights in these matters.

27-4. Voting Techniques. Algonquin Corp. has issued and has outstanding 100,000 shares of common stock. Four stockholders own 60,000 of these shares, and for the past six years they have nominated a slate of people for membership on the board, all of whom have been elected. Sergio and twenty other shareholders, owning 20,000 shares, are dissatisfied with corporate management and want a representative on the board who shares their views. Explain under what circumstances Sergio and the minority shareholders can elect their representative to the board.

27-5. Liability of Shareholders. Mallard has made a preincorporation subscription agreement to purchase 500 shares of a newly formed corporation. The shares have a par value of $100 per share. The corporation is formed, and Mallard's subscription is accepted by the corporation. Mallard transfers a piece of land he owns to the corporation as payment for 250 of the shares, and the corporation issues 250 shares for it. Mallard pays for the other 250 shares with cash. One year later, with the corporation in serious financial difficulty, the board declares and pays a $5-per-share dividend. It is now learned that the land transferred by Mallard had a market value of $18,000. Discuss any liability that shareholder Mallard has to the corporation or to the creditors of the corporation.

27-6. **Rights of Shareholders.** Air Engineered Systems and Services, Inc., a Louisiana corporation, had three shareholders, Naquin, Dubois, and Hoffpauir. Each of the shareholders owned one-third of the corporation's outstanding shares. Naquin was fired after he had worked six years as an employee of the firm, but he retained his shares in the corporation. He then formed a competing business, hired away one of Air Engineered's employees, tried to hire another, and obtained a job for his own business that he had originally solicited for Air Engineered. Under Louisiana law, any shareholder who is also a business competitor is entitled to inspect the corporate records if she or he owns 25 percent of the outstanding shares for six months prior to the demand. When Naquin requested Air Engineered to allow him to inspect the corporate records, however, Air Engineered denied his request, because Naquin refused to sign an indemnity agreement protecting Air Engineered from any damages it might suffer as a result of Naquin's use of the information contained in the corporate records. Shortly thereafter, Dubois and Hoffpauir voted to increase the capital stock of the corporation, and then they each purchased additional shares. This had the effect of reducing Naquin's percentage to less than 25 percent—which meant that Naquin was not entitled under Louisiana law to inspect Air Engineered's records. Naquin filed suit to require the corporation to permit him to inspect the books, because at the time his request was made, he owned more than 25 percent of the outstanding shares of Air Engineered. What was the result? [*Naquin v. Air Engineered Systems and Services, Inc.*, 463 So.2d 992 (La.App. 1985)]

27-7. **Duties of Directors.** Midwest Management Corp. was looking for investment opportunities. Morris Stephens, one of Midwest's directors and the chairman of the investment committee, proposed that Midwest provide financing for Stephens's son and his business colleagues, who were in need of financing to open a broker-dealer business. Midwest agreed to propose to the shareholders for their approval an investment of $250,000 in the new business on the condition that Stephens would manage the business and would purchase 100,000 shares of stock in the new firm. At each of two shareholders' meetings, the directors informed the shareholders that Stephens had agreed to the condition. Stephens was present at both meetings and did not deny that he had agreed to purchase the 100,000 shares of stock and manage the new corporation. Upon the shareholders' approval, the $250,000 investment was made, and later another $150,000 was invested when the new business suffered losses. About a year after it had opened, the business closed, and Midwest ended up losing over $325,000. Midwest then learned that Stephens had not kept his agreement to purchase stock in and manage the corporation. Midwest sued Stephens for breaching his fiduciary duties and asked for compensatory and punitive damages. Did Midwest succeed? Explain. [*Midwest Management Corp. v. Stephens*, 353 N.W.2d 76 (Iowa 1984)]

27-8. **Duties of Directors and Officers.** Klinicki and Lundgren formed Berlinair, a closely held Oregon corporation, to provide air transportation out of West Germany. Klinicki, who owned 33 percent of the company stock, was the vice president and a director. Lundgren, who also owned 33 percent of the stock, was the president and a director. Lelco, Inc., a corporation owned by Lundgren and his family, owned 33 percent of Berlinair, and Berlinair's attorney owned the last 1 percent of stock. One of the goals of Berlinair was to obtain a contract with BFR, a West German consortium of travel agents, to provide BFR with air charter service. Later, Lundgren learned that the BFR contract might become available. Lundgren then incorporated Air Berlin Charter Co., of which he was the sole owner, and bid for the BFR contract. Lundgren won the BFR contract for Air Berlin while using Berlinair working time, staff, money, and facilities without the knowledge of Klinicki. When Klinicki learned of the BFR contract, he filed a derivative suit, as a minority stockholder, against Air Berlin for usurping a corporate opportunity. Did Klinicki recover against Air Berlin? If so, what was Klinicki awarded as damages? [*Klinicki v. Lundgren*, 67 Or.App. 160, 678 P.2d 1250 (1984)]

27-9. **Liability of Directors and Officers.** Dighton Grain, Inc., was a newly formed corporation operating a grain elevator business. Walter Gormley, the manager of the corporation, wrote $87,000 in corporate checks to himself during the first year of the firm's operation, kept inadequate records concerning grain shipments, and kept too short an inventory of grain. An auditor's report recommended that the directors have more frequent meetings, that Gormley discontinue his unauthorized use of the corporation's funds, and that new procedures be instituted by the corporation, such as requiring two signatures on corporate checks. None of these recommendations was followed, and Gormley continued to make personal use of corporate funds. After it had been in operation for two years, the firm went out of business, owing $400,000 to unsecured creditors. Gormley was convicted for misappropriating the firm's funds. One of the firm's creditors, Speer, brought a suit against the directors and officers of the corporation, alleging that they had been negligent in their duties and were thus personally liable for the debt to Speer. Did Speer succeed? [*Speer v. Dighton Grain, Inc.*, 229 Kan. 272, 624 P.2d 952 (1981)]

27-10. **Rights of Shareholders.** Frederick Valerino and his family owned 50 percent of the stock in Electrical-Mechanical of America, Inc. (EMA), and the remaining 50 percent was owned by Charles Little. Both Valerino and Little participated actively in operating the corporation until 1979, when a dispute arose, resulting in a stalemate. For two years, no shareholders' meeting was held, and no board of directors could be elected. Little held a shareholders' meeting in 1981 and sent a telegram to Valerino stating that the purpose of the meeting was "[f]or the sale and purchase of the Capital Stock of EMA." Valerino did not attend and sent a reply letter indicating that he did not wish to sell any of his stock. Actually, Little held the meeting with the intention of issuing more stock to himself and his family, thus reducing Valerino's ownership to 25 percent. Valerino sued to enforce his preemptive rights in the corporation and to set aside the new stock issuance because of fraud. Discuss whether Valerino should succeed in his claim. [*Valerino v. Little*, 62 Md.App. 588, 490 A.2d 756 (1985)]

27-11. Liability of Directors and Officers. Abe Schultz, Sol Schultz, and Lawrence Newfeld were the managing directors and officers of Chemical Dynamics, Inc., a close corporation. In 1967, the corporation leased a building in which to house its offices and operations. Included in the lease agreement was a provision giving Chemical Dynamics an option to purchase the property for $300,000. In 1970, because the corporation was experiencing financial problems and could not pay its rent, it assigned the lease and the purchase option to Newfeld in return for Newfeld's loan to the corporation of approximately $21,500. In 1973, Newfeld purchased the property. Eventually, when the corporation's financial situation had improved and its debts were paid, Abe Schultz sued Newfeld on behalf of the corporation, claiming that Newfeld had breached his fiduciary duty by usurping a corporate opportunity to purchase the property. Evaluate Schultz's claim. [*Chemical Dynamics, Inc. v. Newfeld*, 728 S.W.2d 590 (Mo.App. 1987)]

27-12. Rights of Shareholders. A group of stockholders of Ono Development Co. and Ono East, Inc., brought suit—both on behalf of themselves and the other stockholders of the corporations and derivatively, on behalf of the corporations—against Pannell Kerr Forster, an accounting firm, and two of its employees (the defendants). The suit was brought to recover damages for breach of contract and fraud. The stockholders alleged that the defendants had failed to disclose in annual audits of the corporations' books that certain commissions were being improperly paid to and by three of the corporation's principal officers and directors. As a result, the corporations had been deprived of the use of large sums of money over a period of approximately ten years. While the action was pending, the plaintiff stockholders all sold their stock back to the corporations. The defendants then argued that the stockholders lacked standing to sue the corporations either on their own behalf or on behalf of the corporations. What should the court decide, and why? [*McLaughlin v. Pannell Kerr Forster*, 589 So.2d 143 (Ala. 1991)]

A Question of Ethics and Social Responsibility

27-13. *McQuade was the manager of the New York Giants baseball team. McQuade and John McGraw purchased shares in the National Exhibition Co., the corporation that owned the Giants, from Charles Stoneham, who owned a majority of National Exhibition's stock. As part of the transaction, each of the three agreed to use his best efforts to ensure that the others continued as directors and officers of the organization. Stoneham and McGraw, however, subsequently failed to use their best efforts to ensure that McQuade continued as the treasurer and a director of the corporation, and McQuade sued to compel specific performance of the agreement. A court reviewing the matter noted that McQuade had been "shabbily" treated by the others but refused to grant specific performance on the ground that the agreement was void because it interfered with the duty of the others as directors to do what was best for all the shareholders. Although shareholders may join to elect corporate directors, they may not join to limit the directors' discretion in managing the business affairs of an organization; the directors must retain their independent judgment. Consider the implications of the case and address the following questions.* [McQuade v. Stoneham, 263 N.Y. 323, *189 N.E. 234 (1934)*]

1. Given that even the court sympathized with McQuade, was it ethical to put the business judgment of the directors ahead of an otherwise valid promise they had made?
2. Are there practical considerations that support the court's decision? How can directors perform the tasks dictated to them if their judgment is constrained by earlier agreements with some of the shareholders?
3. Can you think of any circumstances in which it would be fair to the shareholders, as a group, to interfere with the directors' business judgment by holding some of the directors to a similar prior agreement with some or all of the other directors?

Case Briefing Assignment

27-14. *Examine Case A.10* [Maschmeier v. Southside Press, Ltd., 435 *N.W.2d* 377 *(Iowa App. 1989)*] *in Appendix A. The case has been excerpted there in great detail. Review and then brief the case, making sure that you include answers to the following questions in your brief.*

1. What was the primary reason for this lawsuit?
2. What restriction did the corporate bylaws place on the transfer of corporate shares? Upon transfer, how was the price of shares to be determined?
3. How did the majority shareholders (the parents) effectively "freeze out" or "squeeze out" the minority shareholders (the sons)?
4. Why was it necessary for the court to determine the fair value of shares, as the shareholders had agreed in the bylaws on a method for accomplishing this?
5. Why was it necessary to establish that the majority shareholders had acted oppressively toward the minority shareholders or wasted corporate assets before the court could fashion its particular remedy in this case?

For Critical Analysis

27-15. *In recent years, courts have held corporate officers personally liable for corporate employees' violations of environmental and safety regulations in the workplace solely on the ground that the officers were in a position to prevent the violations. From a policy point of view, evaluate the public interests that are traded off in predicating liability on this basis.*

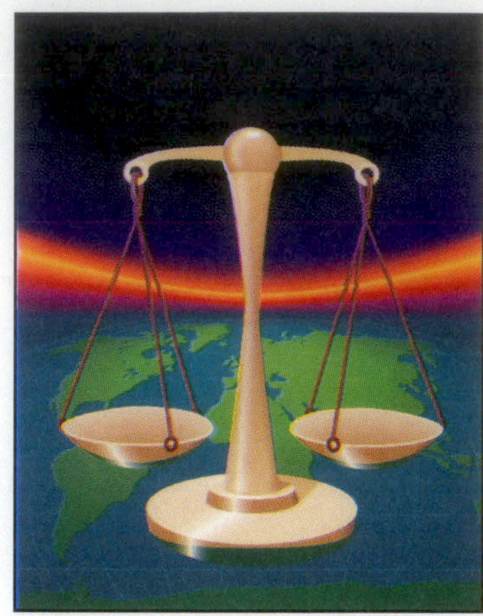

Chapter 28

Corporate Merger, Consolidation, and Termination

"Business is a combination of war and sport."

André Maurois, 1885–1967
(French author and historian)

Corporations increase the size of their operations for a number of reasons. They may wish to enlarge their physical plants, increase their property or investment holdings, or acquire the assets, know-how, or goodwill of another corporation. Sometimes, acquisition of another company is motivated by a desire to eliminate a competitor, to accomplish diversification, or to ensure adequate resources and markets for the acquiring corporation's product. Whatever the reason, during the 1980s, the acquisition of corporations by other corporations became a common phenomenon, and corporate takeovers continue in the 1990s. Observers of the numerous corporate takeovers occurring in the business world today might well conclude, as Maurois did, that business is indeed a "combination of war and sport."

A corporation typically extends its operations by combining with another corporation through a merger, a consolidation, a purchase of assets, or a purchase of a controlling interest in the other corporation. This chapter will examine these four types of corporate expansion.

Dissolution and liquidation are the combined processes by which a corporation terminates its existence. The last part of this chapter will discuss the typical reasons for, and methods used in, terminating a corporation.

❖ Merger and Consolidation

The terms *merger* and *consolidation* are often used interchangeably, but they refer to two legally distinct proceedings. The rights and liabilities of the corporation, its shareholders, and its creditors are the same for both, however.

Merger

MERGER
A contractual process by which one corporation (the surviving corporation) acquires all the assets and liabilities of another corporation (the merged corporation). The shareholders of the merged corporation receive either payment for their shares or shares in the surviving corporation.

A **merger** involves the legal combination of two or more corporations in such a way that only one of the corporations continues to exist. For example, Corporation A and Corporation B decide to merge. It is agreed that A will absorb B, so upon merger, B ceases to exist as a separate entity and A continues as the *surviving corporation.* This process is illustrated graphically in Exhibit 28–1.

After the merger, A is recognized as a single corporation, possessing all the rights, privileges, and powers of itself and B. It automatically acquires all of B's property and assets without the necessity of formal transfer. Also, A becomes liable for all of B's debts and obligations. Finally, A's articles of incorporation are deemed *amended*

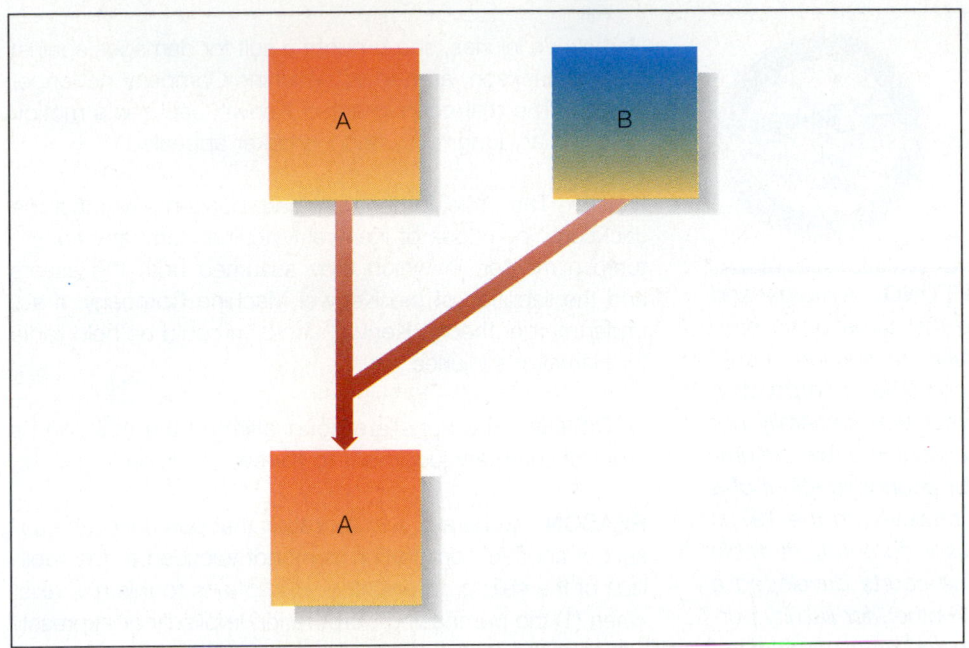

◆ **Exhibit 28–1**
Merger
In this illustration, Corporation A and Corporation B decide to merge. They agree that A will absorb B, so after the merger, B no longer exists as a separate entity, and A continues as the surviving corporation.

to include any changes that are stated in the *articles of merger* (the document setting forth the terms and conditions of the merger that is filed with the secretary of state).

In a merger, the surviving corporation is vested with the disappearing corporation's preexisting legal rights and obligations. For example, if the disappearing corporation had a right of action against a third party, the surviving corporation can bring suit after the merger to recover the disappearing corporation's damages.

The corporation statutes of many states provide that a successor (surviving) corporation inherits a **chose in action** (a right to sue for a debt or sum of money) from a merging corporation as a matter of law. So, too, the common law rule recognizes that a chose in action to enforce a property right upon merger will vest with the successor (surviving) corporation, and no right of action will remain with the disappearing corporation. In the following case, the issue arose as to whether a business transaction constituted a sale or a merger.

CHOSE IN ACTION
A right that can be enforced in court to recover a debt or to obtain damages.

In 1992, Bank of America merged with financially troubled Security Pacific. Why, in a merger, is the surviving corporation vested with the disappearing corporation's preexisting legal rights and obligations?

Case 28.1 

HAMAKER v. KENWEL-JACKSON MACHINE CO.

Supreme Court of South Dakota, 1986.
387 N.W.2d 515.

HISTORICAL AND ECONOMIC SETTING *A merger and a purchase of assets can produce the same basic economic result. Which form a particular transaction should take is a complicated question. At one time, a corporation that purchased the assets of another was generally not held liable for the other's liabilities, except in a few circumstances. Based in part on the similar economic effect of a merger and a purchase of assets, however, in the 1970s some courts began to hold successor corporations liable for their predecessors' liabilities. The courts developed a number of factors for determining whether, for liability purposes, the acquisition was to be treated as a purchase of assets or a merger. Of course, under these circumstances, proper business planning can be difficult, if not impossible.*

FACTS On March 6, 1981, Carolyn Hamaker lost three fingers on her left hand while operating a notcher machine (a lathe) at her place of employment in South Dakota, Pallets and Wood Products. The notching machine had been manufactured by Kenwel Machine Company. On December 31, 1975, Kenwel had sold its assets to John and Rosemary Jackson, who had created a new company called Kenwel-Jackson Machine Company. The original Kenwel Machine Company had terminated its existence in August of 1977. Kenwel-Jackson Machine Company continued to manufacture notchers, but it made several design changes and was in fact producing a machine different from the one that injured Carolyn Hamaker. As a result of Hamaker's injuries, she brought a suit for damages against Kenwel-Jackson, as Kenwel Machine Company no longer existed. The trial court granted Kenwel-Jackson's motion for summary judgment, and Hamaker appealed.

ISSUE The issue, in pertinent part, concerns whether the Jacksons' purchase of Kenwel Machine Company constituted a merger, in which they assumed both the assets and the liabilities of the Kenwel Machine Company. If so, under merger theory, Kenwel-Jackson could be held liable for Hamaker's injuries.

DECISION The appellate court affirmed the trial court's grant of summary judgment to Kenwel-Jackson.

REASON Generally, a corporation that purchases the assets of another corporation does not succeed to the liabilities of the selling corporation. Exceptions to this rule exist when (1) the purchasing corporation impliedly or expressly assumes the seller's liabilities; (2) the sale is really a merger, in which one corporation absorbs another, assuming both the assets and the liabilities of the other, and in which the other loses its existence as a separate entity; (3) the purchaser continues the seller's corporation and retains the same personnel; or (4) the sale is fraudulently executed to escape liability. Here, the Jacksons accepted none of the liabilities of Kenwel Machine Company but only purchased its assets. Also, the Jacksons did not make any express or implied agreement to accept Kenwel Machine Company's liabilities. Finally, the personnel of the former corporation were not retained. Accordingly, the court concluded that Kenwel-Jackson was immune from any liability claims against Kenwel Machine Company.

Consolidation

CONSOLIDATION
A contractual and statutory process whereby two or more corporations join to become a completely new corporation. The original corporations cease to exist, and the new corporation acquires all their assets and liabilities.

In the case of a **consolidation,** two or more corporations combine in such a way that each corporation ceases to exist and a new one emerges. For example, Corporation A and Corporation B consolidate to form an entirely new organization, Corporation C. In the process, A and B both terminate, and C comes into existence as an entirely new entity. This process is illustrated graphically in Exhibit 28–2.

As a result of the consolidation, C is recognized as a new corporation and a single entity; A and B cease to exist. C accedes to all the rights, privileges, and powers previously held by A and B. Title to any property and assets owned by A and B passes to C without formal transfer. C assumes liability for all debts and obligations owed by A and B. The terms and conditions of the consolidation are set forth in the *articles of consolidation,* which are filed with the secretary of state. These articles *take the place of* A's and B's original corporate articles and are thereafter regarded as C's corporate articles.

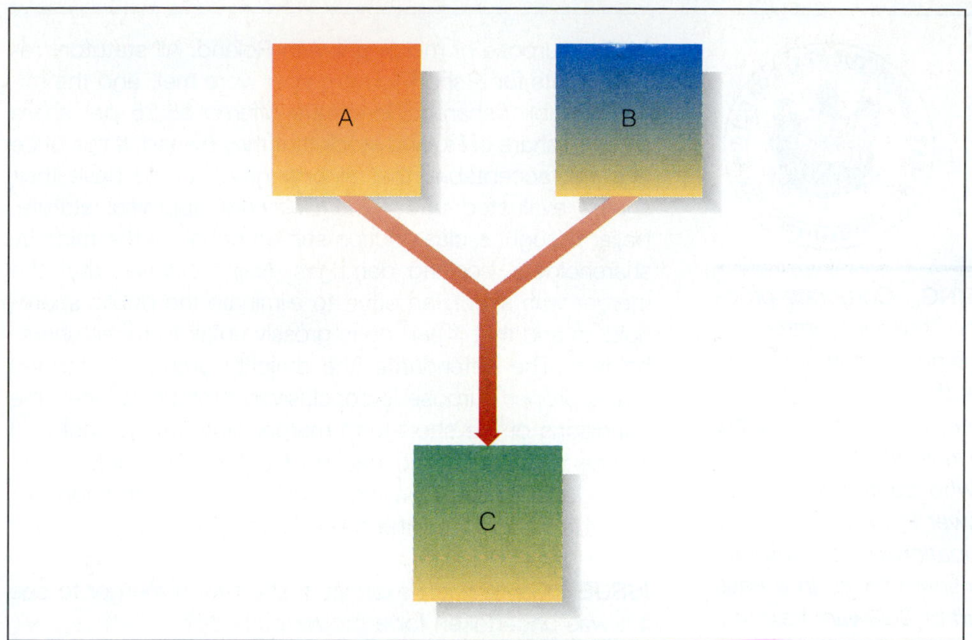

◆ **Exhibit 28–2**
Consolidation
In this illustration, Corporation A and Corporation B consolidate to form an entirely new organization, Corporation C. In the process, A and B terminate, and C comes into existence as an entirely new entity.

Procedure for Merger or Consolidation

All states have statutes authorizing mergers and consolidations for domestic corporations, and most states allow the combination of domestic (in-state) and foreign (out-of-state) corporations. Although the procedures vary somewhat among jurisdictions, in each case the basic requirements are as follows:

1. The board of directors of each corporation involved must approve a merger or consolidation plan.
2. The shareholders of each corporation must vote approval of the plan at a shareholders' meeting. Most state statutes require the approval of two-thirds of the outstanding shares of voting stock, although some states require only a simple majority and others require a four-fifths vote. Frequently, statutes require that each class of stock approve the merger; thus, the holders of nonvoting stock must also approve. A corporation's bylaws can dictate a stricter requirement.
3. Once approved by all the directors and the shareholders, the plan (articles of merger or consolidation) is filed, usually with the secretary of state.
4. When state formalities are satisfied, the state issues a certificate of merger to the surviving corporation or a certificate of consolidation to the newly consolidated corporation.

The RMBCA provides a simplified procedure for the merger of a substantially owned subsidiary corporation into its parent corporation. Under these provisions, a **short-form merger** can be accomplished *without the approval of the shareholders* of either corporation. The short-form merger can be utilized only when the parent corporation owns at least 90 percent of the outstanding shares of each class of stock of the subsidiary corporation. The simplified procedure requires that a plan for the merger be approved by the board of directors of the parent corporation before it is filed with the state. A copy of the merger plan must be sent to each shareholder of record of the subsidiary corporation. In the following case, a minority group of shareholders objected to a short-form merger undertaken to "cash out" public shareholders (including the plaintiffs in this case).

SHORT-FORM MERGER
A merger between a subsidiary corporation and a parent corporation that owns at least 90 percent of the outstanding shares of each class of stock issued by the subsidiary corporation. Short-form mergers can be accomplished without the approval of the shareholders of either corporation.

Case 28.2
ROLAND INTERNATIONAL CORP. v. NAJJAR
Supreme Court of Delaware, 1979.
407 A.2d 1032.

HISTORICAL AND SOCIAL SETTING *Corporate property belongs to all shareholders, and those in control of a corporation are accountable to all owners of the corporate property. These concepts underlie the rule that majority shareholders—who have the power to control corporate property—owe a fiduciary duty to minority shareholders. This duty is violated when those who control a corporation's voting machinery use that power to exclude minority shareholders from continued participation in the corporate life for no reason other than to eliminate them. In a case decided in 1977, the Supreme Court of Delaware held that "when a freeze-out of minority stockholders on a cash-out basis is alleged to be [a merger's] sole purpose," and it is alleged that "the purpose is improper," a court must consider the allegation, "because of the fiduciary obligation owed to the minority."*[a] *The case involved a long-form merger. Undecided at that time was whether the same rule applied to a short-form merger.*

FACTS Roland International Corporation was 97.6 percent owned by Hyatt Corporation and others. This controlling group of shareholders created Landro Corporation for the purpose of merging it with Roland. All statutory requirements for a short-form merger were met, and the minority (public) shareholders were offered $5.25 per share for each share of Roland stock that they owned. If this price was not acceptable, the minority group could have their shares evaluated under the Delaware appraisal statute. Najjar brought a class-action suit on behalf of the minority shareholders, seeking damages. Najjar claimed that the merger was simply an effort to eliminate the public shareholders and that it had been grossly unfair to those shareholders. The defendants (the majority group) contended that a proper purpose is conclusively presumed when the conditions of the short-form merger statutes are met and so the plaintiff had no cause of action. The defendants moved for dismissal on these grounds. The trial court denied the motion, and the defendants appealed.

ISSUE May a court examine a short-form merger to see if it was undertaken for a proper purpose?

DECISION Yes. The Supreme Court of Delaware affirmed the trial court's denial of the defendants' motion to dismiss.

REASON The court held that the short-form merger statute does not create a presumption that the merger serves a valid purpose. The court may examine such mergers to determine whether the majority shareholders have met their fiduciary duty to the minority. When a merger is undertaken with the sole purpose of eliminating the minority shareholders, it constitutes a breach of that duty. The plaintiff thus had a cause of action, and the defendants' motion to dismiss was properly denied.

a. *Singer v. Magnavox Co.*, 380 A.2d 969 (Del.Sup. 1977).

Appraisal Rights

"The greatest of all gifts is the power to estimate things at their true worth."

François la Rochefoucauld, 1613–1680
(French writer and moralist)

APPRAISAL RIGHT
A dissenting shareholder's right, if he or she objects to an extraordinary transaction of the corporation (such as a merger or consolidation), to have his or her shares appraised and to be paid the fair market value of his or her shares by the corporation.

What if a shareholder disapproves of the merger or consolidation but is outvoted by the other shareholders? The law recognizes that a dissenting shareholder should not be forced to become an unwilling shareholder in a corporation that is new or different from the one in which the shareholder originally invested. The shareholder has the right to dissent and may be entitled to be paid the *fair value* for the number of shares held on the date of the merger or consolidation. This right is referred to as the shareholder's **appraisal right.** It is available only when a state statute specifically provides for it. It is normally extended to regular mergers, consolidations, short-form mergers, sales of substantially all of the corporate assets not in the ordinary course of business, and in certain states, adverse amendments to the articles of incorporation. The appraisal right may be lost if the elaborate statutory procedures are not followed precisely. Whenever the right is lost, the dissenting shareholder must go along with the transaction despite his or her objections.

One of the basic procedures usually followed requires that a written notice of dissent be filed by dissenting shareholders prior to the vote of the shareholders on the proposed transaction. This notice of dissent is also basically a notice to all shareholders of costs that may be imposed by dissenting shareholders should the merger or consolidation be approved. In addition, after approval, the dissenting shareholders must make a written demand for payment and for fair value.

Valuation of shares is often a point of contention between the dissenting shareholder and the corporation. RMBCA 13.01 provides that the "fair value of shares" is the value on the day prior to the date on which the vote was taken.[1] The corporation must make a *written* offer to purchase a dissenting shareholder's stock, accompanying the offer with a current balance sheet and income statement for the corporation. If the shareholder and the corporation do not agree on the fair value, a court will determine it.

Once a dissenting shareholder elects appraisal rights under a statute, in some jurisdictions, the shareholder loses his or her shareholder status. Without that status, a shareholder cannot vote, receive dividends, or sue to enjoin whatever action prompted his or her dissent. In some of those jurisdictions, statutes provide or courts have held that shareholder status may be reinstated during the appraisal process (for example, if the shareholder decides to withdraw from the process and the corporation approves). In other jurisdictions, shareholder status may not be reinstated until the appraisal is concluded. Even if an individual's shareholder status is lost, courts may allow the individual to sue on grounds of fraud or other illegal conduct associated with the merger.

"Lots of folks confuse bad management with destiny."

Kin (F. McKinney) Hubbard, 1868–1930
(American humorist and journalist)

Shareholder Approval

Shareholders invest in a corporate enterprise with the expectation that the board of directors will manage the enterprise and will approve ordinary business matters. Actions taken on extraordinary matters must be authorized by the board of directors and the shareholders. Often, modern statutes require that certain types of extraordinary matters—such as the sale, lease, or exchange of all or substantially all corporate assets outside of the corporation's regular course of business—be approved by the shareholders. Other examples of matters requiring shareholder approval include amendments to the articles of incorporation, transactions concerning merger or consolidation, and dissolution.

Hence, when any extraordinary matter arises, the corporation must proceed as authorized by law to obtain the approval of the shareholders and the board of directors. Sometimes, a transaction can be characterized in such a way as not to require shareholder approval, but in that event, a court will use its equity powers to require such approval. To determine the nature of the transaction, the courts will look not only to the details of the transaction but also to its consequences.

❖ Purchase of Assets

When a corporation acquires all or substantially all of the assets of another corporation by direct purchase, the purchasing, or *acquiring*, corporation simply extends its ownership and control over more physical assets. Because no change in the legal entity occurs, the acquiring corporation is not required to obtain shareholder approval for the purchase.[2]

Although the acquiring corporation may not be required to obtain shareholder approval for such an acquisition, the U.S. Department of Justice and the Federal Trade Commission have issued guidelines that significantly constrain and often prohibit mergers that could result from a purchase of assets, including takeover bids. These guidelines are discussed later, in Chapter 30, in relation to federal antitrust laws.

1. Any appreciation or depreciation of the stock in anticipation of the approval is excluded.
2. If the acquiring corporation plans to pay for the assets with its own corporate stock and not enough authorized unissued shares are available, the shareholders must vote to approve issuance of additional shares by amendment of the corporate articles. Also, acquiring corporations whose stock is traded in a national stock exchange can be required to obtain their own shareholders' approval if they plan to issue a significant number of shares, such as a number equal to 20 percent or more of the outstanding shares.

Note that the corporation that is selling all its assets is substantially changing its business position and perhaps its ability to carry out its corporate purposes. For that reason, the corporation whose assets are acquired must obtain the approval of both the board of directors and the shareholders. In most states and under the RMBCA, a dissenting shareholder of the selling corporation can demand appraisal rights.

Generally, a corporation that purchases the assets of another corporation is not responsible for the liabilities of the selling corporation. As indicated in Case 28.1, exceptions to this rule are made in the following circumstances:

1. When the purchasing corporation impliedly or expressly assumes the seller's liabilities.
2. When the sale amounts to what in fact is a merger or consolidation.
3. When the purchaser continues the seller's business and retains the same personnel (same shareholders, directors, and officers).
4. When the sale is fraudulently executed to escape liability.

In any of these situations, the acquiring corporation will be held to have assumed both the assets and the liabilities of the selling corporation.

The following case addresses the issue of whether liability for punitive damages can be imposed on a successor corporation based on the conduct of its predecessor.

Case 28.3
DAVIS v. CELOTEX CORP.
Supreme Court of Appeals of West Virginia, 1992.
187 W.Va. 566,
420 S.E.2d 557.

HISTORICAL AND SOCIAL SETTING *Philip Carey Manufacturing Company was incorporated in Ohio in 1888. Philip Carey manufactured building products that contained asbestos. The dangers of asbestos were documented as early as 1918 in American medical literature. During the 1930s, there was considerable publicity on the risk of breathing asbestos dust. For example, in 1930, an article published in the asbestos-industry magazine* Asbestos *concluded that fifteen cases of pulmonary fibrosis among factory workers had been caused by asbestos dust. By 1942, there were enough cases of lung cancer associated with asbestos to be included in a medical textbook on occupational cancer. After several employees filed workers' compensation claims alleging that they suffered from work-related asbestosis, in 1962 Philip Carey hired a consultant to advise it on protecting its workers from asbestosis. The consultant discussed the risks associated with exposure to asbestos, recommended steps to protect workers, and outlined what the company should do to limit its future legal liability. The company did not act on the recommendations. In 1967, Philip Carey merged with the Glen Alden Corporation. Philip Carey transferred all of its assets, subject to liabilities, to Glen Alden and became its subsidiary. In 1969, this new corporation merged with another Glen Alden subsidiary, the Briggs Manufacturing Company. The surviving company was named the Panacon Corporation. In 1972, Celotex Corporation purchased the assets of Panacon and expressly assumed all liabilities and duties of Panacon.*

FACTS From 1965 to 1974, Jennings Davis was employed as a plumber and pipefitter by several electric power generating plants. During his employment, Davis was exposed to asbestos-containing products manufactured by numerous companies. As a purported result, Davis developed asbestosis and lung cancer and died from lung cancer in 1987. One of the companies supplying asbestos to the power plants for which Davis had worked was Panacon Corporation. On Davis's death, his son, Ronald Davis, sued Celotex Corporation for damages, alleging that Celotex had assumed Panacon's liability for health hazards associated with its products. The trial court found for Davis and awarded both compensatory and punitive damages. On appeal, Celotex claimed that although it continued to manufacture and market asbestos products, it placed warning labels on its products and therefore was not "engaged in the sort of egregious conduct that warrants punitive damages." According to Celotex, it was guilty only of acquiring a company that had knowingly concealed the dangers of asbestos.

ISSUE Can Celotex be held liable for punitive damages in these circumstances?

DECISION Yes. The trial court's judgment was affirmed. Celotex could be held liable, as a successor corporation, for both compensatory and punitive damages.

REASON The court acknowledged the general rule that a corporation that purchases the assets of another cor-

Case 28.3—Continued

poration is not liable for the debts and obligations of the predecessor corporation. An exception to this rule is made, however, when there is an express or implied assumption of liability. In this case, Celotex had expressly assumed the liabilities and obligations of Panacon when it purchased Panacon's assets. As to whether the liabilities assumed by Celotex should include liability for punitive damages, the court stated that while not "every acquisition or merger will automatically result in punitive damage liability," in the case of Celotex, such liability could be imposed. According to the court, "when a corporation acquires or merges with a company manufacturing a product that is known to create serious health hazards, and the successor corporation continues to produce the same product in the same manner, it may be found liable for punitive damages for liabilities incurred by the predecessor company in its manufacture of such product."

ETHICAL CONSIDERATIONS *Clearly, the court was not impressed with Celotex's argument that because it placed warning labels on its asbestos-containing products, it should therefore not be subject to punitive damages for harms caused by the same product manufactured by its predecessor. Citing another case, the court stated that "corporations are in a very real sense, 'molders of their own destinies' in acquisition transactions, with the full panoply of corporate transformations at their disposal." When a corporation such as Celotex voluntarily acquires another, it assumes the "bad will" as well as the "good will" of its predecessor. "We will not allow such an acquiring corporation to 'jettison inchoate [in an early stage, not yet formed] liabilities into a never-never land of transcorporate limbo.' "*

❖ Purchase of Stock

An alternative to the purchase of another corporation's assets is the purchase of a substantial number of the voting shares of its stock. This enables the acquiring corporation to control the acquired corporation. The acquiring corporation deals directly with the shareholders in seeking to purchase the shares they hold. It does this by making a **tender offer** to all shareholders of the **target corporation.** The tender offer is publicly advertised and addressed to all shareholders of the target company. The price of the stock in the tender offer is generally higher than the market price of the target stock prior to the announcement of the tender offer. The higher price induces shareholders to tender their shares to the acquiring firm.

TENDER OFFER
An offer to purchase shares made by one company directly to the shareholders of another company; often referred to more simply as a "take-over bid."

The tender offer can be conditional upon the receipt of a specified number of outstanding shares by a specified date. The offering corporation can make an *exchange tender offer* in which it offers target stockholders its own securities in exchange for their target stock. In a *cash tender offer,* the offering corporation offers the target stockholders cash in exchange for their target stock.

TARGET CORPORATION
The corporation to be acquired in a corporate takeover; a corporation to whose shareholders a tender offer is submitted.

Federal securities laws strictly control the terms, duration, and circumstances under which most tender offers are made. In addition, over thirty states have passed takeover statutes that impose additional regulations on tender offers. The use of the tender offer as a method of gaining corporate control began in the mid-1960s. Highly contested legal battles and enormous expenses involved in complying with federal and state regulations have worked in some situations to discourage the use of tender offers as a vehicle for obtaining control of a corporation through stock purchase.

A firm may respond to a tender offer in numerous ways. The colorful and imaginative vocabulary that has been devised to describe target companies' responses to takeover bids is the topic of this chapter's *Business Law in Action.*

❖ Termination

Termination of a corporate life has two phases. **Dissolution** is the legal death of the artificial "person" of the corporation. **Liquidation** is the process by which corporate assets are converted into cash and distributed among creditors and shareholders according to specific rules of preference. These rules of preference are discussed in more detail in Chapter 26.

DISSOLUTION
The formal disbanding of a partnership or a corporation. It can take place by (1) agreement of the parties or the shareholders and board of directors, (2) the death of a partner, (3) the expiration of a time period stated in a partnership agreement or a certificate of incorporation, or (4) court order.

LIQUIDATION
The sale of the assets of a business or an individual for cash and the distribution of the cash received to creditors, with the balance going to the owner(s).

Business Law in Action

The Terminology of Takeover Defenses

As discussed in Chapter 27, the directors of a corporation owe a fiduciary duty to the shareholders. In the context of a tender offer, this requires that, after full consideration, the directors of the target firm make a good faith decision as to whether the shareholders' acceptance or rejection of the offer would be most beneficial. In making any recommendation, the directors must fully disclose all *material facts.* A fact is material if there is a substantial likelihood that a reasonable shareholder would consider it important in deciding how to vote.

Sometimes, a target firm's board of directors will see a tender offer as favorable and recommend to the shareholders that they accept it. Alternatively, to resist a takeover, a target company may make a *self-tender,* which is an offer to acquire stock from its own shareholders and thereby retain corporate control.

To resist a takeover, a target company may solicit a merger with a third party, which then, of course, makes a better (often simply a higher) tender offer to the target's shareholders. This third party has been called a *white knight.* A white knight that interferes once the acquiring and target companies have agreed to merge may be held to have wrongfully interfered with a contractual relationship. This was the determination in the case involving Pennzoil's suit against Texaco in 1987. Texaco's acquisition of Getty Oil after Getty had agreed to merge with Pennzoil prompted a trial court to award $10.5 billion to Pennzoil—although on appeal this amount was reduced.[a]

Alternatively, the target company may attempt its own takeover of the acquiring corporation. This has been called the *Pac-Man defense.* Because the self-tender, the white knight defense, and the Pac-Man defense use tender offers, they are subject to the same federal and state laws as the tender offers that prompted their use.

Other oppositional strategies include the target company's making itself less financially attractive to the acquiring corporation. The target may implement *scorched earth* tactics, by which it sells off assets or divisions or takes out loans that it agrees to repay in the event of a takeover. To make a takeover more difficult, a target company may change its articles of incorporation or bylaws. For example, the bylaws may be amended to require that a large number of shareholders approve the firm's combination. This tactic has been described as *shark repellent,* as it casts an acquiring corporation in the role of a shark.

a. *Texaco, Inc. v. Pennzoil Co.,* 729 S.W.2d 768 (Tex.App.—Houston [1st Dist.] 1987). This case was presented in Chapter 6 as Case 6.1.

When the *poison pill* tactic is used, the target corporation issues to its stockholders shares that can be turned in for cash if a takeover is successful. This makes the takeover undesirably or even prohibitively expensive for the acquiring corporation. In response, parties intent on taking over a particular target have sometimes grouped together to enhance their financial position and make group bids.

An acquiring corporation may challenge its target's defensive tactics as violations of the target management's fiduciary duties to maximize the interests of the target's shareholders.

When a takeover is successful, top management is usually changed. With this in mind, many top executives have secured *golden parachutes,* which guarantee them certain attractive payments if they are discharged or demoted because of a takeover.

Even if a takeover attempt does not succeed, it may still be lucrative to the acquiring corporation. To regain control, the target company may pay an exceptional price to repurchase the stock that the acquiring corporation bought. Indeed, when a takeover is attempted through a gradual accumulation of target stock rather than a tender offer, the intent may be to get the target company to buy back the accumulated shares. This has been called *greenmail.*

Dissolution

Dissolution of a corporation can be brought about in any of the following ways:

1. An act of a legislature in the state of incorporation.
2. Expiration of the time provided in the certificate of incorporation.
3. Voluntary approval of the shareholders and the board of directors.
4. Unanimous action by all shareholders.
5. Court decree brought about by the attorney general of the state of incorporation for any of the following reasons: (a) the failure to comply with administrative re-

quirements (for example, failure to pay annual franchise taxes or to submit an annual report or to have a designated registered agent); (b) the procurement of a corporation charter through fraud or misrepresentation upon the state; (c) the abuse of corporate powers (*ultra vires* acts); (d) the violation of the state criminal code after the demand to discontinue has been made by the secretary of state; (e) the failure to commence business operations; or (f) the abandonment of operations before starting up [RMBCA 14.20].

Sometimes an *involuntary* dissolution of a corporation is necessary. For example, the board of directors may be deadlocked. Courts hesitate to order involuntary dissolution in such circumstances unless there is specific statutory authorization to do so, but if the deadlock cannot be resolved by the shareholders, and if it will irreparably injure the corporation, the court will proceed with an involuntary dissolution. Courts can also dissolve a corporation for mismanagement [RMBCA 14.30].

In the following case, two of the shareholders in a close corporation petitioned for the dissolution of a corporation after they were fired as employees.

Case 28.4

GUNZBERG v. ART-LLOYD METAL PRODUCTS CORP.

New York Supreme Court, Appellate Division, Second Department, 1985. 112 A.D.2d 423, 492 N.Y.S.2d 83.

HISTORICAL AND SOCIAL SETTING *A court may prevent a dissolution that is unduly oppressive for minority shareholders, particularly when the dissolution is effected to freeze out the minority. A court may also order a dissolution when it would be unduly oppressive for minority shareholders to continue the corporation. When the minority shareholders actively participate in the management of the corporation over a long period, they may have a reasonable expectation of continued employment by the company and continued input into its management. Oppression occurs if these expectations are not realized—if, for example, the minority shareholders are discharged. This is especially true in the case of a close corporation because the major part of the earnings of a close corporation are distributed in the form of salaries, bonuses, and retirement benefits.*

FACTS In 1946, Fred Gunzberg helped his father form Art-Lloyd Metal Products Corporation, and together they built it into a successful company. In 1955, Fred's brother Lloyd joined the business, and the two brothers were responsible for the day-to-day running of the firm—although the father had the final say in business matters until a stroke incapacitated him. In 1961, another brother, Arthur, joined the firm. A lawsuit arose as a result of a falling out among the brothers in 1979, when Arthur was elected president of the corporation and another brother and sister were elected as officers on the board of directors. After the election, Fred and Lloyd were fired as employees. They then sought judicial dissolution of the corporation based on the majority faction's oppression. The trial court ordered the dissolution, and the corporation appealed.

ISSUE Should dissolution be permitted?

DECISION Yes. The trial court's decision was affirmed by the appellate court.

REASON The New York court noted that, under New York corporate law, a petition for judicial dissolution may be presented by "the holders of twenty percent or more of all outstanding shares of a corporation * * * who are entitled to vote in an election of directors." In this case, Fred and Lloyd jointly owned 41 percent of the corporate shares that had been issued. The court quoted the New York Court of Appeals, which had held that when a petitioner has "set forth a prima facie case of oppressive conduct, it should be incumbent upon the parties seeking to forestall dissolution to demonstrate to the court the existence of an adequate, alternative remedy." In this case, the corporation had failed to suggest any alternative remedy—adequate or otherwise. Further quoting the New York Court of Appeals, the court stated that a "court has broad latitude in fashioning alternative relief, but when fulfillment of the oppressed petitioner's expectations by these means is doubtful, such as when there has been a complete deterioration of relations between the parties, a court should not hesitate to order dissolution."

Liquidation

When dissolution takes place by voluntary action, the members of the board of directors act as trustees of the corporate assets. As trustees, they are responsible for winding up the affairs of the corporation for the benefit of corporate creditors and shareholders. This makes the board members personally liable for any breach of their fiduciary trustee duties.

RECEIVER
A court-appointed person who receives, preserves, and manages a business or other property that is involved in bankruptcy proceedings.

Liquidation can be accomplished without court supervision unless the members of the board do not wish to act in this capacity, or unless shareholders or creditors can show cause to the court why the board should not be permitted to assume the trustee function. In either case, the court will appoint a **receiver** to wind up the corporate affairs and liquidate corporate assets. A receiver is always appointed by the court if the dissolution is involuntary.

❖ Key Terms

appraisal right 682
chose in action 679
consolidation 680
dissolution 685
liquidation 685
merger 678
short-form merger 681
target corporation 685
tender offer 685

❖ Chapter Summary: Corporate Merger, Consolidation, and Termination

Merger and Consolidation	1. *Merger*—The legal combination of two or more corporations, the result of which is that the surviving corporation acquires all the assets and obligations of the other corporation, which then ceases to exist. 2. *Consolidation*—The legal combination of two or more corporations, the result of which is that each corporation ceases to exist and a new one emerges. The new corporation assumes all the assets and obligations of the former corporations. 3. *Procedure*—Determined by state statutes. Basic requirements are: a. The board of directors of each corporation involved must approve the merger or consolidation plan. b. The shareholders of each corporation must approve the merger or consolidation plan at a shareholders' meeting. c. Articles of merger or consolidation (the plan) must be filed, usually with the secretary of state. d. The state issues a certificate of merger (or consolidation) to the surviving (or newly consolidated) corporation. 4. *Short-form merger (parent-subsidiary merger)*—Possible when the parent corporation owns at least 90 percent of the outstanding shares of each class of stock of the subsidiary corporation. a. Shareholder approval is not required. b. The merger must be approved only by the board of directors of the parent corporation. c. A copy of the merger plan must be sent to each shareholder of record. d. The merger plan must be filed with the state. 5. *Appraisal rights*—Rights of shareholders (given by state statute) to receive the *fair value* for their shares when a merger or consolidation takes place. If the shareholder and the corporation do not agree on the fair value, a court will determine it. 6. *Purchase of assets*—The acquisition by a corporation of all or substantially all of the assets of another corporation.

❖ Chapter Summary: Corporate Merger, Consolidation, and Termination—Continued

Merger and Consolidation—Continued	a. The acquiring corporation is not required to obtain shareholder approval; the corporation is merely increasing its assets, and no fundamental business change occurs. b. The acquired corporation is required to obtain the approval of both its directors and its shareholders for the sale of its assets, because this creates a substantial change in its business position. 7. *Purchase of stock*—The acquisition by a corporation of a substantial number of the voting shares of the stock of another (target) corporation. a. Tender offer—A public offer to all shareholders of the target corporation to purchase its stock at a price generally higher than the market price of the target stock prior to the announcement of the tender offer. Federal and state securities laws strictly control the terms, duration, and circumstances under which most tender offers are made. b. Target responses—Ways in which target corporations respond to takeover bids. These include self-tender (the target firm's offer to acquire its own shareholders' stock), the Pac-Man defense (the target firm's takeover of the acquiring corporation), and numerous other strategies (shark repellent, poison pill, etc.).
Termination	The termination of a corporation involves the following two phases: 1. *Dissolution*—The legal death of the artificial "person" of the corporation. Dissolution can be brought about in any of the following ways: a. An act of a legislature in the state of incorporation. b. Expiration of the time provided in the corporate charter. c. Voluntary approval of the shareholders and the board of directors. d. Unanimous action by all shareholders. e. Court decree. 2. *Liquidation*—The process by which corporate assets are converted into cash and distributed to creditors and shareholders according to specified rules of preference. May be supervised by members of the board of directors (when dissolution is voluntary) or by a receiver appointed by the court to wind up corporate affairs.

❖ Questions and Case Problems

28-1. Purchase of Assets. Under what circumstances is a corporation that buys the assets of another corporation responsible for the liabilities of the selling corporation?

28-2. Consolidations. Determine which of the following situations describes a consolidation:

(a) Arkon Corp. purchases all of the assets of Botrek Co.

(b) Arkon Corp. and Botrek Co. combine their firms, with Arkon Corp. being the surviving corporation.

(c) Arkon Corp. and Botrek Co. agree to combine their assets, dissolve their old corporations, and form a new corporation under a new name.

(d) Arkon Corp. agrees to sell all its accounts receivable to Botrek Co.

28-3. Corporate Combinations. Jolson is chairman of the board of directors of Artel, Inc., and Douglas is chairman of the board of directors of Fox Express, Inc. Artel is a manufacturing corporation, and Fox Express is a transportation corporation. Jolson and Douglas meet to consider the possibility of combining their corporations and activities into a single corporate entity. They consider two alternative courses of action: Artel could acquire all of the stock and assets of Fox Express, or the corporations could combine to form a new corporation, called A&F Enterprises, Inc. Both chairmen are concerned about the necessity of a formal transfer of property, liability for existing debts, and the problem of amending the articles of incorporation. Discuss what the two proposed combinations are called and the legal effect each has on the transfer of property, the liabilities of the combined corporations, and the need to amend the articles of incorporation.

28-4. Mergers. Tally Ho Co. was merged into Perfecto Corp., Perfecto being the surviving corporation in the merger. Hanjo, a creditor of Tally Ho, brought suit against Perfecto Corp. for payment of the debt. The directors of Perfecto refused to pay, stating that Tally Ho no longer existed and that Perfecto had never agreed to assume any of Tally Ho's liabilities. Discuss fully whether Hanjo will be able to recover from Perfecto.

28-5. Purchase of Assets. Fuju Enterprises, Inc., purchased all the assets of Grosmont Corp. The directors of both corporations approved of the sale, and 80 percent of Grosmont's shareholders approved. The shareholders of Fuju Enterprises, however, were never consulted. Some of these shareholders claimed that the purchase was invalid. Are they correct?

28-6. Sale of Assets. Mike and Peter Schwadel were major shareholders in HJU Sales & Investments, Inc. Over several years, the assets of the corporation had been sold off until only one asset remained—a restaurant called "The Place for Steak." The Schwadels sued the president and third major shareholder of the corporation, Hy Uchitel, when he entered into a contract to sell this remaining asset. Florida state law prohibits the sale of all or substantially all of a corporation's assets without shareholder approval. The Schwadels sought an injunction to prevent the sale of the restaurant. Will the court grant the injunction? [*Schwadel v. Uchitel*, 455 So.2d 401 (Fla.App. 1984)]

28-7. Corporate Dissolution. In 1984, Elmer Balvik and Thomas Sylvester decided to turn their partnership into a corporation because of the tax benefits that would result. The new Weldon Corp. carried on the partnership's old business of electrical contracting. Sylvester received 70 percent of the stock of the new corporation and Balvik the remaining 30 percent, in proportion to the capital that each contributed. Both took positions as directors and officers of the corporation, and each was entitled to one vote per share of stock. Balvik was at all times a minority voice in the company. Although Sylvester and Balvik had had no problems during their years as partners, difficulties emerged soon after incorporation. Sylvester believed that excess profits should be reinvested in the corporation, while Balvik wanted them withdrawn and paid out as bonuses or dividends. Balvik was fired from his job, allegedly because of poor performance, and he began working for another company. Balvik was unable to take any of his capital contribution in the corporation with him and no longer received a salary from the corporation. Balvik sued to have the corporation dissolved under North Dakota law, which allows dissolution for illegal, oppressive, or fraudulent acts by corporate directors or those in control of the corporation toward minority shareholders. Will the court order dissolution of the corporation in these circumstances? [*Balvik v. Sylvester*, 411 N.W.2d 383 (N.D. 1987)]

28-8. Corporate Dissolution. Two brothers, Albert and Raymond Martin, each owned 50 percent of the stock in Martin's News Service, Inc. Albert and Raymond had difficulty working together and communicated only through their accountant. For ten years, there were no corporate meetings, elections to the board of directors, or other corporate formalities. During that time, Raymond operated the business much as a sole proprietorship, failing to consult Albert on any matter and making all of the decisions himself. The corporation, however, was a viable concern that had grown successfully through the years. Albert sued to have the corporation dissolved. Should he succeed? Discuss. [*Martin v. Martin's News Service, Inc.*, 9 Conn.App. 304, 518 A.2d 951 (1986)]

28-9. Corporate Dissolution. I. Burack, Inc., was a family-operated close corporation that sold plumbing supplies in New York. The founder, Israel Burack, transferred his shares in the corporation to other family members, and when Israel died in 1974, the position of president passed to his son, Robert Burack. Robert held a one-third interest in the company, and the remainder was divided among Israel's other children and grandchildren. All shareholders participated in the corporation as employees or officers and thus relied on salaries and bonuses, rather than dividends, for distribution of the corporation's earnings. In 1976, several of the family-member employees requested a salary increase from Robert, who claimed that company earnings were not sufficient to warrant any employee salary increases. Shortly thereafter, a shareholders' meeting was held (the first in the company's fifty-year history), and Robert was removed from his position as president and denied the right to participate in any way in the corporation. Robert sued to have the company dissolved because he had been "frozen out" of the business by the allegedly oppressive tactics of the other shareholders. Discuss whether Robert should succeed in his suit or whether the court would choose another alternative. [*Burack v. I. Burack, Inc.*, 137 A.D.2d 523, 524 N.Y.S.2d 457 (1988)]

28-10. Mergers and Consolidations. Edward Antar and William Markowitz were the sole stockholders and directors of E.B.M., Inc., a corporation formed for the purpose of buying and managing real estate. Antar and Markowitz were also the controlling shareholders and directors of Acousti-Phase, Inc., a corporation that manufactured and sold stereo speakers. In 1982, Acousti-Phase was effectively shut down when a fire destroyed the manufacturing and storage facility that it was renting from E.B.M. Shortly after the fire, E.B.M. contracted with a New York firm to assemble the speakers, affix the Acousti-Phase name, and sell the final product, primarily to former customers of Acousti-Phase. At the time of the fire, Acousti-Phase owed $26,470 to Cab-Tek, Inc., a corporation that supplied it with cabinet housings for its stereo speakers. In 1985, Cab-Tek sued E.B.M. to recover the debt owed by Acousti-Phase. Discuss fully whether E.B.M. can be held liable for Acousti-Phase's debt. [*Cab-Tek, Inc. v. E.B.M., Inc.*, 153 Vt. 432, 571 A.2d 671 (1990)]

28-11. Purchase of Assets. In January 1981, Frederick Brandt purchased a Tredex treadmill from Atlantic Fitness Products. The treadmill was manufactured by American Tredex Corporation. In July 1981, Nissen Corp. purchased all of the assets of American Tredex, as well as its goodwill and the name American Tredex. The contract for the purchase of assets expressly excluded assumption of liability for injuries arising from any product previously sold by American Tredex. Although Nissen did not continue to manufacture and sell the treadmills, it did continue to sell replacement parts for equipment that had been sold by American Tredex before the sale of its assets. After Nissen's purchase of American Tredex's assets, Brandt obtained replacement parts for his treadmill from Nissen. In the fall of 1986, Brandt was injured when he caught one of his fingers in the treadmill's operating mechanism while adjusting the treadmill. Brandt and his wife sued Nissen and Atlantic Fitness to recover damages, alleging, among other things, negligence and breach of warranty. Nissen moved for summary judgment, contending that it was not responsible for any injuries involving equipment sold or manufactured by American Tredex prior to the date of the asset purchase agreement (July 1981). Should the court grant Nissen's motion? Why or why not? [*Nissen Corp. v. Miller*, 323 Md. 613, 594 A.2d 564 (1991)]

28-12. Purchase of Assets. In 1987, William Myers sustained injuries to his hand while operating a concrete cement pump that had been designed and manufactured by Thomsen Equipment Co. and purchased from Thomsen in 1981. Myers alleged that the pump was unreasonably dangerous because it had an "unguarded nip point in a flapper valve." Putzmeister, Inc., had purchased Thomsen's assets in 1982. Assuming that Myers has a valid product liability claim, what factors will the court consider in determining whether Putzmeister, as a successor corporation, can be held liable for injuries caused by Thomsen's product? [*Myers v. Putzmeister, Inc.*, 232 Ill.App.3d 419, 596 N.E.2d 754, 173 Ill.Dec. 130 (1992)]

A Question of Ethics and Social Responsibility

28-13. *The Natomas Corp. merged with the Diamond Shamrock Corp. Under the terms of the merger, Diamond Shamrock retained its corporate identity, and the Natomas Corp. was absorbed into the former's corporate hierarchy. As part of the merger agreement, five inside directors (directors who are also officers of the corporation) of Natomas were offered golden parachutes. The terms of the parachute agreements provided that each of the five individuals would receive a payment equal to three years' compensation in the event that they left their positions at Natomas at any time for any reason other than termination for just cause. Three of the five voluntarily left their positions after three years. Under the terms of their parachute agreements, they collected over ten million dollars. A suit challenging the golden parachutes was brought by Gaillard, a shareholder of Natomas. A trial court granted the defendants' motion for summary judgment, sustaining the golden parachutes on the ground that the directors were protected by the business judgment rule in effecting the agreement. The appellate court held that the business judgment rule does not apply in a review of the conduct of inside directors and remanded the case for trial.* [Gaillard v. Natomas, *208 Cal.App.3d 1250, 256 Cal.Rptr. 702 (1989)*]

1. Regardless of the legal issues, are golden parachutes ethical in a general sense? Discuss.
2. What practical considerations would lead a corporation to *want* to grant its top management such seemingly one-sided agreements?
3. In *Gaillard*, how would your views be affected by evidence showing that the golden parachutes had been developed and presented to the board by the very individuals who were the beneficiaries of the agreements—that is, by the five inside directors?

Case Briefing Assignment

28-14. *Examine Case A.11* [Greenlee v. Sherman, *142 A.D.2d 472, 536 N.Y.S.2d 877 (1989)*] *in Appendix A. The case has been excerpted there in great detail. Review and then brief the case, making sure that you include answers to the following questions in your brief.*

1. What issue was raised on appeal in this case?
2. The appellate court held that the successor liability theory did not apply in this case for two basic reasons. What were they?

For Critical Analysis

28-15. *At one time, a corporation that bought the assets of another corporation was not liable for the liabilities of the predecessor corporation—unless the successor corporation assumed the liabilities, fraud was involved, or the transaction was actually a merger or merely a change of name. Why have some courts expanded the liability of successor corporations to include liability for the defective products of their predecessors?*

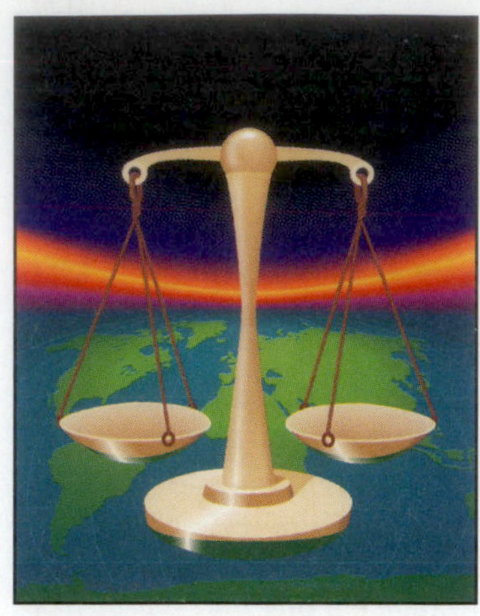

Chapter 29

Investor Protection

"It shall be unlawful for any person in the offer or sale of any security . . . to engage in any transaction, practice, or course of business which operates or would operate as a fraud or deceit upon the purchaser."

Securities Act of 1933, Section 17

After the great stock market crash of 1929, various studies showed a need for regulating securities markets. Basically, legislation for such regulation was enacted to provide investors with more information to help them make buying and selling decisions about **securities**—generally defined as any documents evidencing corporate ownership (stock) or debts (bonds)—and to prohibit deceptive, unfair, and manipulative practices. Today, the sale and transfer of securities are heavily regulated by federal and state statutes and by government agencies. This chapter will discuss the nature of federal securities regulations and their effects on the business world.

❖ Securities Act of 1933

SECURITIES
Stock certificates, bonds, notes, debentures, warrants, or other documents, certificates, or interests given as evidence of an ownership interest in the corporation or as a promise of repayment by the corporation.

The Securities Act of 1933[1] was designed to prohibit various forms of fraud and to stabilize the securities industry by requiring that all essential information concerning the issuance of securities be made available to the investing public. Essentially, the purpose of this act is to require disclosure. Under Section 2(1) of the Securities Act, securities include

> any note, stock, treasury stock, bond, debenture, evidence of indebtedness, certificate of interest or participation in any profit-sharing agreement, collateral-trust certificate, preorganization certificate or subscription, transferable share, investment contract, voting-trust certificate, certificate of deposit for a security, fractional undivided interest in oil, gas, or other mineral rights, or, in general, any interest or instrument commonly known as a "security," or any certificate of interest or participation in, temporary or interim certificate for, receipt for, guarantee of, or warrant or right to subscribe to or purchase, any of the foregoing.[2]

Basically, the courts have interpreted this definition to mean that a security exists in any transaction in which a person (1) invests (2) in a common enterprise (3) reasonably expecting profits (4) derived *primarily* or *substantially* from others' managerial or entrepreneurial efforts.[3]

For our purposes, it is probably most convenient to think of securities in their most common forms—stocks and bonds issued by corporations. Bear in mind that

1. 15 U.S.C. Sections 77–77aa.
2. 15 U.S.C. Section 77b(1). The 1982 amendments added stock options.
3. *SEC v. W. J. Howey Co.*, 328 U.S. 293, 66 S.Ct. 1100, 90 L.Ed. 1244 (1946).

securities can take many forms and have been held to include whiskey, cosmetics, worms, beavers, boats, vacuum cleaners, muskrats, and cemetery lots, as well as investment contracts in condominiums, franchises, limited partnerships, oil or gas or other mineral rights, and farm animals accompanied by care agreements.

Registration Statement

Section 5 of the Securities Act of 1933 broadly provides that if a security does not qualify for an exemption, that security must be *registered* before it is offered to the public either through the mails or through any facility of interstate commerce, including securities exchanges. Issuing corporations must file a *registration statement* with the Securities and Exchange Commission (SEC). (The creation and significance of the SEC is discussed in this chapter's *Landmark in the Law.*) Investors must be provided with a *prospectus* that describes the security being sold, the issuing corporation, and the investment or risk attaching to the security. In principle, the registration statement and the prospectus supply sufficient information to enable unsophisticated investors to evaluate the financial risk involved.

"Then words came like a fall of winter snow."

Homer, *circa* ninth century B.C.
(Greek epic poet)

Contents of the Registration Statement The registration statement must include the following:

1. A description of the significant provisions of the security offered for sale, including the relationship between that security and the other capital securities of the registrant. Also, the corporation must disclose how it intends to use the proceeds of the sale.
2. A description of the registrant's properties and business.
3. A description of the management of the registrant and its security holdings, remuneration, and other benefits, including pensions and stock options. Any interests of directors or officers in any material transactions with the corporation must be disclosed.
4. A financial statement certified by an independent public accounting firm.
5. A description of pending lawsuits.

Other Requirements Before filing the registration statement and the prospectus with the SEC, the corporation is allowed to obtain an *underwriter*—a person who agrees to purchase the new issue of securities for resale to the public. There is a twenty-day waiting period (which can be accelerated by the SEC) after registration before the sale can take place. During this period, oral offers between interested investors and the issuing corporation concerning the purchase and sale of the proposed securities may take place; very limited written advertising is allowed. At this time, the so-called **red herring prospectus** may be distributed. It gets its name from the red legend printed across it stating that the registration has been filed but has not become effective.

RED HERRING PROSPECTUS
A prospectus permitted to be distributed by an issuing corporation after a registration statement is filed and before the sale of securities can take place (during the twenty-day waiting period). The prospectus must have a red legend or mark on it.

After the waiting period, the registered securities can be legally bought and sold. Written advertising is allowed in the form of a **tombstone ad,** so named because the format resembles a tombstone. Such ads simply tell the investor where and how to obtain a prospectus. Normally, any other type of advertising is prohibited.

Violations Registration violations of the 1933 act are not treated lightly. In the following case, the BarChris Construction Corporation was sued by the purchasers of the corporation's debentures (discussed in Chapter 26) under Section 11 of the Securities Act of 1933. Section 11 imposes liability when a registration statement or a prospectus contains material false statements or material omissions.

TOMBSTONE AD
An advertisement announcing a sale of securities and informing the prospective investor where and how to obtain a prospectus.

Case 29.1
ESCOTT v. BARCHRIS CONSTRUCTION CORP.
United States District Court,
Southern District of New York, 1968.
283 F.Supp. 643.

HISTORICAL AND TECHNOLOGICAL SETTING *Before the 1950s, bowling alleys employed persons to reset bowling pins after each bowler took his or her turn. In 1946, an automatic pinsetting machine was displayed at a national bowling tournament in Buffalo, New York. Automatic pinsetting equipment was made widely available to the owners of bowling alleys in the early 1950s. Owing in part to the speed and accuracy with which an automatic pinsetter could reset the pins, bowling increased in popularity in bowling alleys that used the new equipment, and bowling became the leading U.S. indoor sport. Consequently, business was good for manufacturers and installers of automatic pinsetters. Not all lanes in all bowling alleys could accommodate the new equipment, however. Thus, business was also good for those who constructed and sold bowling alleys built to accommodate the new pinsetters. Because the buyers of the new bowling alleys could not always pay cash, the builders would sometimes finance the sale, accepting a small down payment and a promissory note for the remainder of the price. Ordinarily, however, the builders' suppliers would not accept promises to pay in the future but insisted on cash. For these reasons, the builders of the new bowling alleys were often in need of additional capital to expand their businesses.*

FACTS BarChris Construction Corporation was an expanding company that built bowling alleys and was in constant need of cash to finance its operations. In 1961, BarChris Construction Corporation issued securities after filing the appropriate registration statement with the Securities and Exchange Commission. By early 1962, the company's financial difficulties had become insurmountable, and BarChris defaulted on the interest due on the debentures one month after petitioning for bankruptcy. Purchasers of the BarChris bonds brought a lawsuit under Section 11 of the Securities Act of 1933. The plaintiffs challenged the accuracy of the registration statement filed with the Securities and Exchange Commission and charged that the text of the prospectus was false and that material information had been omitted. There were three categories of defendants: BarChris and all of the signers of the registration statement, the underwriters, and BarChris's auditors.

ISSUE Had BarChris violated the 1933 Securities Act requirements concerning the registration statement and prospectus accompanying its bond issue?

DECISION Yes. BarChris and all of the signers of the registration statement for the debentures, the underwriters, and the corporation's auditors were held liable.

REASON The court found that the registration statement contained false statements of fact and omitted other facts that should have been included to prevent the statement from being misleading. The misstatements included overstatement of sales and gross profits, understatement of contingent liabilities, overstatement of orders on hand, and failure to disclose true facts with respect to officers' loans, customers' delinquencies, application of proceeds, and the prospective operation of several bowling alleys. The facts that were falsely stated or omitted were "material" within the meaning of the Securities Act of 1933. The court found that "[t]he average prudent investor is not concerned with minor inaccuracies or with errors as to matters which are of no interest to him. The facts which tend to deter him from purchasing a security are facts which have an important bearing upon the nature or condition of the issuing corporation or its business. Judged by this test, there is no doubt that many of the misstatements and omissions in this prospectus were material."

Exemptions

A corporation can avoid the high cost and complicated procedures associated with registration by taking advantage of certain exemptions. SEC regulations provide that the following offerings are exempt:

1. Noninvestment company offerings up to $1,000,000 in any one year are exempt.[4]
2. Offerings up to $500,000 in any one year by so-called "blank check" companies—companies with no specific business plans except to locate and acquire

4. SEC Regulation D, 17 C.F.R. Section 230.504.

Landmark in the Law

The Securities and Exchange Commission

The creation of the Securities and Exchange Commission (SEC) was a direct result of the stock market crash of October 29, 1929. The crash and ensuing economic depression caused the public to focus on the importance of securities markets for the economic well-being of the nation. The feverish trading in securities during the preceding decade became the subject of widespread attention, and numerous reports were circulated concerning the speculative, manipulative, and at times unscrupulous trading that occurred in the stock markets.

As a result, in 1931, the Senate passed a resolution calling for an extensive investigation of securities trading. The investigation led, ultimately, to the passage by Congress of the Securities Act of 1933, which is also known as the *truth-in-securities* bill. In the following year, the Securities Exchange Act was passed by Congress. This 1934 act created the Securities and Exchange Commission as an independent regulatory agency whose function was to administer the 1933 and 1934 acts. Its major responsibilities in this respect are as follows:

1. Requiring disclosure of facts concerning offerings of securities listed on national securities exchanges and of certain securities traded over the counter (OTC).
2. Regulating the trade in securities on the thirteen national and regional securities exchanges and in the over-the-counter markets.
3. Investigating securities frauds.
4. Regulating the activities of securities brokers, dealers, and investment advisers and requiring their registration.
5. Supervising the activities of mutual funds.
6. Recommending administrative sanctions, injunctive remedies, and criminal prosecution against those who violate securities laws.

In the early years of its existence, during Franklin Roosevelt's administration, the SEC was headed successively by Joseph P. Kennedy, James M. Landis, and William O. Douglas—all of whom contributed their leadership abilities to strengthening the powers of the commission. Douglas, who was chairman from 1937 until he was appointed to the United States Supreme Court in 1939, was particularly effective in transforming the New York Stock Exchange from what was often characterized as a "men's club" into a public institution.

From the time of its creation until the present, the SEC's regulatory functions have gradually been increased by legislation granting it authority in different areas. In recent years, the SEC has been active in promoting stiffer penalties for insider trading. It has also promoted regulatory changes addressing the problem of hostile takeovers and corporate-control contests, in which outsiders attempt to wrest control of the corporation from its current board of directors. Another current major concern of the SEC is to effect fundamental changes in the basic regulatory framework applying to the financial services industry. Under the Securities Enforcement Remedies Act of 1990, for example, the SEC was granted substantial new powers, which increased the enforcement options and penalties available to the commission.

presently unknown businesses or opportunities—are exempt if no general solicitation or advertising is used, the SEC is notified of the sales, and precaution is taken against nonexempt, unregistered resales.[5] The limits on advertising and unregistered resales do not apply if the offering is made solely in states that provide for registration and disclosure and the securities are sold in compliance with those provisions.[6]

3. Private, noninvestment company offerings up to $5,000,000 in any twelve-month period are exempt, regardless of the number of **accredited investors** (banks, insurance companies, investment companies, the issuer's executive officers and directors, and persons whose income or net worth exceeds certain limits), so long as there are no more than thirty-five nonaccredited investors, no general solicitation or advertising is used, the SEC is notified of the sales, and precaution is taken against nonexempt, unregistered resales. If the sale involves *any* nonaccredited inves-

ACCREDITED INVESTORS In the context of securities offerings, "sophisticated" investors, such as banks, insurance companies, investment companies, the issuer's executive officers and directors, and persons whose income or net worth exceeds certain limits.

5. Precautions to be taken against nonexempt, unregistered resales include asking the investor whether he or she is buying the securities for others; before the sale, disclosing to each purchaser in writing that the securities are unregistered and thus cannot be resold, except in an exempt transaction, without first being registered; and indicating on the certificates that the securities are unregistered and restricted.

6. SEC Regulation D, 17 C.F.R. Section 230.504a.

tors, *all* investors must be given material information about the offering company, its business, and the securities before the sale. The issuer is not required to believe that each nonaccredited investor "has such knowledge and experience in financial and business matters that he is capable of evaluating the merits and the risks of the prospective investment." [7]

4. Private, noninvestment company offerings in unlimited amounts that are not generally solicited or advertised are exempt if the SEC is notified of the sales, precaution is taken against nonexempt, unregistered resales, and the issuer believes that each nonaccredited investor has sufficient knowledge or experience in financial matters to be capable of evaluating the investment's merits and risks. There may be no more than thirty-five nonaccredited investors, although there may be an unlimited number of accredited investors. If there are *any* nonaccredited investors, the issuer must provide to *all* purchasers material information about itself, its business, and the securities before the sale.[8]

This last exemption is perhaps the most important one to firms that want to raise funds through the sale of securities without registering them. It is often referred to as the *private placement* exemption, because it exempts "transactions not involving any public offering."[9] This provision applies to private offerings made to a limited number of persons who are sufficiently sophisticated and in a sufficiently strong bargaining position so as to be able to assume the risk of the investment (and who thus have no need for federal registration protection) and to private offerings made to similarly situated institutional investors.

5. Also exempt are intrastate transactions involving purely local offerings.[10] This exemption applies to offerings restricted to residents of the state in which the issuing company is organized and doing business. The exemption requires that 80 percent of the issuer's assets be located in the state of issue, 80 percent of the issuer's gross revenue be from business conducted within the state, and 80 percent of the net income from the sale of the issue be used in the state. Also, for nine months after the last sale, no resale may be made to a nonresident, and precautions must be taken against this possibility. (Precautions include obtaining a statement of residence in writing from each investor, as well as indicating on the securities certificates that they are unregistered and subject to resale only to state residents.) These offerings remain subject to applicable laws in the state of issue.

6. Among securities exempt from the registration requirement because of the "small amount involved,"[11] other than those mentioned previously, is an issuer's offer of up to $5,000,000 in securities in any twelve-month period (including no more than $1,500,000 million in nonissuer resales). Under the SEC's Regulation A,[12] the issuer must file with the SEC a notice of the issue and an offering circular, which must also be provided to investors before the sale; but this is a much simpler and less expensive process than the procedures associated with registration, and companies are allowed to "test the waters" for potential interest before having to prepare the required offering circular. To *test the waters* means to determine potential interest without actually selling any securities or requiring any commitment on the part of those who are interested. The SEC has also adopted a new, integrated registration and reporting system for small business issuers. Small business issuers are companies with less than $25,000,000 in annual revenues and less than $25,000,000 in outstanding voting stock. The new system uses simpler forms.

7. Also, an offer made *solely* to accredited investors is exempt if its amount is not more than $5,000,000. Any number of accredited investors may participate, but no

---

7. SEC Regulation D, 17 C.F.R. Section 230.505.
8. SEC Regulation D, 17 C.F.R. Section 230.506.
9. 15 U.S.C. Section 77d(2).
10. 15 U.S.C. Section 77c(a)(11).
11. 15 U.S.C. Section 77c(b).
12. 17 C.F.R. Sections 230.251–230.263.

nonaccredited investors may do so. No general solicitation or advertising may be used, the SEC must be notified of all sales, and precaution must be taken against nonexempt, unregistered resales (because these are restricted securities and may be resold only by registration or in an exempt transaction).[13]

These exemptions under the Securities Act of 1933 and SEC regulations are summarized in Exhibit 29–1.

Additional Exempt Securities

Other exempt securities are the following:[14]

1. All bank securities sold prior to July 27, 1933.
2. Commercial paper if the maturity date does not exceed nine months.
3. Securities of charitable organizations.
4. Securities resulting from a corporate reorganization issued for exchange with the issuer's existing security holders and certificates issued by trustees, receivers, or debtors in possession under the bankruptcy laws.
5. Securities issued exclusively for exchange with the issuer's existing security holders, provided no commission is paid (for example, stock dividends and stock splits).
6. Securities issued to finance the acquisition of railroad equipment.
7. Any insurance, endowment, or annuity contract issued by a state-regulated insurance company.
8. Government-issued securities.
9. Securities issued by banks, savings and loan associations, farmers' cooperatives, and similar institutions subject to supervision by governmental authorities.

❖ Securities Exchange Act of 1934

The Securities Exchange Act of 1934 provides for the regulation and registration of securities exchanges, brokers, dealers, and national securities associations, such as the National Association of Securities Dealers (NASD). It regulates the markets in which securities are traded by maintaining a continuous disclosure system for all corporations with securities on the securities exchanges and for those companies that have assets in excess of $5,000,000 and 500 or more shareholders. These corporations are referred to as Section 12 companies because they are required to register their securities under Section 12 of the 1934 act. The act regulates proxy solicitation for voting (discussed in Chapter 27), and it allows the SEC to engage in market surveillance to regulate undesirable market practices such as fraud, market manipulation, misrepresentation, and stabilization. (*Stabilization* is a market-manipulating technique by which securities underwriters bid for securities to stabilize their prices during their issuance.)

Section 10(b), Rule 10b-5, and Insider Trading

Section 10(b) is one of the most important sections of the Securities Exchange Act of 1934. This section proscribes the use of "any manipulative or deceptive device or contrivance in contravention of such rules and regulations as the [SEC] may prescribe." Among the rules that the SEC has prescribed is **Rule 10b-5,** which prohibits the commission of fraud in connection with the purchase or sale of any security.

RULE 10b-5
A rule of the Securities and Exchange Commission that makes it unlawful, in connection with the purchase or sale of any security, to make any untrue statement of a material fact or to omit a material fact if such omission causes the statement to be misleading.

13. 15 U.S.C. Section 77d(6).
14. 15 U.S.C. Section 77c.

◆ **Exhibit 29–1 Exemptions under the 1933 Act for Securities Offerings by Businesses**

TYPE OF OFFERING	REQUIRED CONDITIONS
Noninvestment company offerings up to $1,000,000 in any twelve-month period	1. No prohibition on general solicitation. 2. No disclosure required. 3. Investors can freely transfer their securities.
Offerings up to $500,000 in any one year by "blank-check" companies.	1. No general solicitation or advertising. 2. SEC is notified of sales. 3. Precaution is taken against nonexempt, unregistered resales.
Private, noninvestment company offerings up to $5,000,000 in any twelve-month period	1. Unlimited number of accredited investors. 2. No more than thirty-five nonaccredited investors. 3. If there are *any* nonaccredited investors, material information about offering firm must be disclosed. 4. No general solicitation or advertising. 5. SEC is notified of sales. 6. Precaution is taken against nonexempt, unregistered resales.
Private, noninvestment company offerings in unlimited amounts that are generally not solicited or advertised	1. Unlimited number of accredited investors. 2. No more than thirty-five nonaccredited investors. 3. If there are *any* nonaccredited investors, (a) material information about offering firm must be disclosed, and (b) issuer must reasonably believe that each nonaccredited investor is experienced in financial matters and capable of evaluating risks involved in investment. 4. SEC is notified of sales. 5. Precaution is taken against nonexempt, unregistered resales.
Intrastate transactions (offerings restricted to residents of the state in which issuing company is organized and doing business)	1. 80 percent of issuer's assets are located in the state of issue. 2. 80 percent of issuer's gross revenue is from business conducted within the state. 3. 80 percent of net income from the sale of the issue is used in the state. 4. No resale is made to a nonresident for nine months after last sale, and precautions are taken to prevent such resale.
Offerings up to $5,000,000 in any twelve-month period (under SEC Regulation A)	1. Notice of the issue and an offering circular are filed with SEC and provided to investors.
Offerings up to $5,000,000 in any twelve-month period	1. Unlimited number of accredited investors. 2. No nonaccredited investors. 3. No general solicitation or advertising. 4. SEC is notified of sales. 5. Precaution is taken against nonexempt, unregistered resales.

INSIDER TRADING
Purchasing or selling securities on the basis of information that has not been made available to the public.

One of the most important purposes of Section 10(b) and Rule 10b-5 relates to so-called **insider trading.** Because of their positions, corporate directors and officers often obtain advance inside information that can affect the future market value of the corporate stock. Obviously, their positions can give them a trading advantage over the general public and shareholders. The 1934 Securities Exchange Act defines inside information and extends liability to officers and directors for taking advantage of such information in their personal transactions when they know that it is unavailable to the public. In addition, to deter the use of inside information, the 1934 act requires officers, directors, and certain large shareholders (those holding 10 percent or more of the issued stock) to turn over to the corporation all profits realized by them on any purchase and sale or sale and purchase of the corporation's stock within any six-month period.

Section 10(b) of the 1934 act and SEC Rule 10b-5 cover not only corporate officers, directors, and majority shareholders but also any persons having access to or receiving information of a nonpublic nature on which trading is based.

In the following case, a shareholder alleged that a corporate officer and a corporate director breached their fiduciary duties by trading corporate shares on the basis of nonpublic information.

Case 29.2 

DIAMOND v. OREAMUNO

Court of Appeals of New York, 1969.
24 N.Y.2d 494,
248 N.E.2d 910,
301 N.Y.S.2d 78.

HISTORICAL AND SOCIAL SETTING *Officers and directors owe a fiduciary duty to their corporation and its shareholders with respect to corporate business and property. Shares in the corporation are private property, however, and trading in those shares is not usually a corporate transaction. Thus, at common law a century ago, directors and officers were considered to owe no fiduciary duty when they traded in the shares of their corporations. Directors or officers with inside information could trade with impunity without disclosing the information (as long as they avoided outright fraud). Although this rule is sometimes stated to be the "majority rule," it has been applied in only a few cases over the last ninety years. Instead, the courts have developed a number of "exceptions." Some state courts have developed an agency law theory. According to agency law, an agent may not profit from using the property of his or her principal. It is reasoned by analogy that a director or officer may not profit from using inside information belonging to the corporation. In other words, under this reasoning, officers and directors owe a fiduciary duty to their corporation not to engage in the trading of shares in the corporation on the basis of inside information.*

FACTS The defendants in this case were the chairman of the board (Oreamuno) and president (Gonzalez) of MAI (Management Assistance, Inc.), a corporation that bought and leased computers, with maintenance services being provided by IBM. The defendants learned that IBM was going to increase its maintenance prices dramatically, to such an extent that it would cut MAI's profits by 75 percent per month. Just before the IBM maintenance price increase was announced, the defendants sold their MAI stock for $28 per share. After IBM publicly announced its price increase, MAI stock fell to $11 per share. The plaintiff (Diamond) brought a derivative action on behalf of MAI to recover the difference in profits. The trial court granted the defendants' motion to dismiss, and the plaintiff appealed.

ISSUE When corporate fiduciaries have breached their duty to the corporation by the use of nonpublic information, may a derivative action be brought by a shareholder to recover any profit resulting from the breach of duty?

DECISION Yes. The appellate court ruled that those whose relationship with the corporation is such that they are privy to "inside information" may not use such knowledge for their own personal gain.

REASON The court pointed out that SEC Rule 10b-5 specifically renders it unlawful to engage in a variety of acts considered to be fraudulent. When the defendants sold their shares, they were guilty of withholding material information from the purchasers. Therefore, the activities of the defendants constituted a violation of Rule 10b-5. Any individual purchaser who could prove an injury as a result of this Rule 10b-5 violation could bring his or her own action, but in cases in which securities are bought and sold in large public markets through anonymous transactions handled by brokers, it is virtually impossible to match the ultimate buyer with the ultimate seller. Thus, it would be difficult if not impossible for an individual to recover successfully under Rule 10b-5. Therefore, the court reasoned that it was possible to use an effective common law remedy against Oreamuno and Gonzalez. The court held that a shareholder could enforce proper behavior on the part of corporate officials through the medium of the derivative action brought in the name of the corporation. Even if the corporation had suffered no harm from the defendants' activities, the defendants' profits resulting from their use of inside information might still be recovered on behalf of the corporation.

Disclosure under Rule 10b-5 Any material omission or misrepresentation of material facts in connection with the purchase or sale of a security may violate Section 10(b) and Rule 10b-5. The key to liability (which can be civil or criminal) under this rule is whether the insider's information is *material.* The following are some examples of material facts calling for a disclosure under the rule:

1. A new ore discovery.
2. Fraudulent trading in the company stock by a broker-dealer.
3. A dividend change (whether up or down).
4. A contract for the sale of corporate assets.
5. A new discovery (process or product).
6. A significant change in the firm's financial condition.

Courts have struggled with the problem of when information becomes public knowledge. Clearly, when inside information becomes public knowledge, all insiders should be allowed to trade without disclosure. The courts have suggested that insiders should refrain from trading for a "reasonable waiting period" when the news is not readily translatable into investment action. Presumably, this gives the news time to filter down to and to be evaluated by the investing public.

The following is one of the landmark cases interpreting Rule 10b-5. The SEC sued Texas Gulf Sulphur for issuing a misleading press release. The release underestimated the magnitude and the value of a mineral discovery. The SEC also sued several of Texas Gulf Sulphur's directors, officers, and employees under Rule 10b-5 for purchasing large amounts of the corporate stock prior to the announcement of the corporation's rich ore discovery.

Case 29.3
SEC v. TEXAS GULF SULPHUR CO.
United States Court of Appeals, Second Circuit, 1968.
401 F.2d 833.

HISTORICAL AND SOCIAL SETTING *No court has ever held that every buyer or seller is entitled to all of the information relating to all of the circumstances in every stock transaction. But by the mid-1950s, significant understatement of the value of the assets of a company had been held to be materially misleading.*[a] *In 1957, the Texas Gulf Sulphur Company began exploring for minerals in eastern Canada. In March 1959, aerial geophysical surveys were conducted over more than 15,000 square miles of the area. The operations revealed numerous and extraordinary variations in the conductivity of the rock, which indicated a remarkable concentration of commercially exploitable minerals. One site of such variations was near Timmins, Ontario. On October 29 and 30, 1963, a ground survey of the site near Timmins indicated a need to drill for further evaluation.*

FACTS The Texas Gulf Sulphur Company (TGS) drilled a hole on November 12, 1963, that appeared to yield a core with an exceedingly high mineral content. TGS kept secret the results of the core sample. Officers and employees of the company made substantial purchases of TGS's stock or accepted stock options after learning of the ore discovery, even though further drilling was necessary to establish whether there was enough ore to be mined commercially. On April 11, 1964, an unauthorized report of the mineral find appeared in the newspapers. On the following day, April 12, TGS issued a press release that played down the discovery and stated that it was too early to tell whether the ore finding would be a significant one. Later on, TGS announced a strike of at least 25 million tons of ore, substantially driving up the price of TGS stock. The SEC brought suit against the officers and employees of TGS for violating the insider-trading prohibition of Rule 10b-5. The officers and employees argued that the prohibition did not apply because the information on which they had traded was not material as the mine had not been commercially proved. The trial court held that most of the defendants had not violated Rule 10b-5, and the SEC appealed.

a. *Speed v. Transamerica Corp.*, 99 F.Supp. 808 (D.Del. 1951).

ISSUE Had the officers and employees of TGS violated Rule 10b-5 by purchasing the stock, even though they did not know the full extent and profit potential of the mine at the time they purchased the stock?

DECISION Yes. The court of appeals reversed and remanded the case to the trial court, holding that the employees and officers violated Rule 10b-5's prohibition against insider trading.

Case 29.3—Continued

REASON For Rule 10b-5, the test of materiality is whether the information would affect the judgment of reasonable investors. Reasonable investors include speculative as well as conservative investors. "[A] major factor in determining whether the * * * discovery [of the ore] was a material fact is the importance attached to the drilling results by those who knew about it. * * * [T]he timing by those who knew of it of their stock purchases and their purchases of short-term calls [rights to buy shares at a specified price within a specified time period]—purchases in some cases by individuals who had never before purchased calls or even TGS stock—virtually compels the inference that the insiders were influenced by the drilling results. * * * We hold, therefore, that all transactions in TGS stock or calls by individuals apprised of the drilling results * * * were made in violation of Rule 10b–5."

Applicability of Rule 10b-5 Rule 10b-5 applies in virtually all cases concerning the trading of securities, whether on organized exchanges, in over-the-counter markets, or in private transactions. The rule covers notes, bonds, certificates of interest and participation in any profit-sharing agreement, agreements to form a corporation, and joint-venture agreements; in short, it covers just about any form of security. It is immaterial whether a firm has securities registered under the 1933 act for the 1934 act to apply.

Although Rule 10b-5 is applicable only when the requisites of federal jurisdiction, such as the use of the mails, of stock exchange facilities, or of any instrumentality of interstate commerce, are present, virtually no commercial transaction can be completed without such contact. In addition, the states have corporate securities laws, many of which include provisions similar to Rule 10b-5.

In the following case, the United States Supreme Court examined the liability of a person who had received material nonpublic information from insiders in a corporation with which he had no connection.

Case 29.4
DIRKS v. SEC

Supreme Court of the United States, 1983.
463 U.S. 646,
103 S.Ct. 3255,
77 L.Ed.2d 911.

HISTORICAL AND ECONOMIC SETTING *Market analysts uncover and analyze information concerning corporations, often by meeting with and questioning officers and other corporate insiders. The information that an analyst obtains may form the basis for judgments as to the market value of corporate securities. An analyst makes this judgment available in newsletters or otherwise to his or her clients. Because of the nature of the information and the nature of the market, the information cannot be made simultaneously available to all of a corporation's shareholders or the general public. Nevertheless, the entire market benefits from analysts' efforts, which are reflected in the prices of corporate securities. It is not always entirely clear, however, how analysts are to obtain information from corporate management to fill in the gaps in their analyses. When legal requirements are imprecise, parties find it difficult to comply. Thus, without some guidance as to the line between permissible and impermissible disclosures and uses, neither corporate insiders nor market analysts could be sure when the line was crossed.*

FACTS Dirks was an officer of a New York broker-dealer firm. Dirks specialized in providing investment analyses of insurance company securities to institutional investors. In March 1973, Dirks received information from Ronald Secrist, a former officer of Equity Funding of America, who alleged that the assets of Equity Funding were vastly overstated as a result of fraudulent corporate practices. Secrist urged Dirks to verify the fraud and to disclose it publicly. Dirks decided to investigate the allegations, and throughout his investigation he openly discussed the information he had obtained with a number of clients and investors. The Securities and Exchange Commission subsequently filed a complaint against Equity Funding. It also found that Dirks had aided and abetted violations of Section 17(a) of the Securities Act of 1933, Section 10(b) of the Securities Exchange Act of 1934, and SEC Rule 10b-5 by repeating the allegations of fraud to members of the investment community, who later sold their Equity stock. Dirks sought review in the court of appeals, which entered a judgment against him. The United States Supreme Court granted *certiorari.*

ISSUE Did Dirks have a duty to refrain from using the

Case 29.4—Continued

inside information that he had acquired during his investigation of Equity Funding?

DECISION No. The decision of the court of appeals was reversed. The Supreme Court held that Dirks, under the circumstances, had no duty to refrain from using the inside information that he had acquired.

REASON The SEC claimed that a breach of the common law duty to disclose that is imposed on corporate insiders—particularly officers, directors, and controlling stockholders—also established a violation of Rule 10b-5. Therefore, under the SEC's position, individuals (as tippees) other than corporate insiders could be obligated under Rule 10b-5 either to disclose material nonpublic information before trading or to abstain from trading altogether. In response, the Court stated that there can be no duty to disclose if the individual who has traded on inside information "was not [the corporation's] agent, * * * was not a fiduciary, [or] was not a person in whom the sellers [of the securities] had placed their trust and confidence." Concluding that recipients of inside information do not invariably acquire a duty to disclose or abstain, the Court nonetheless stated that such tippees are not always free to trade on the information. In determining whether a tippee has a duty to disclose or abstain, it is necessary "to determine whether the insider's 'tip' constituted a breach of the insider's fiduciary duty. * * * Thus, the test is whether the insider personally will benefit, directly or indirectly, from his disclosure. Absent some personal gain, there has been no breach of duty to stockholders. And absent a breach by the insider, there is no derivative breach." Therefore, because Dirks had no preexisting fiduciary duty to Equity Funding's shareholders, and because the insiders did not breach their common law duty in disclosing nonpublic information to Dirks, he did not violate Rule 10b-5 by passing on the inside information he had acquired.

Outsiders and Rule 10b-5 The traditional insider-trading case involves true insiders—corporate officers, directors, and majority shareholders who have access to, and trade on, inside information. Increasingly, liability under Section 10(b) of the 1934 act and SEC Rule 10b-5 has been extended to include certain "outsiders"—those who trade on inside information acquired *indirectly*. Two theories have been developed in recent years under which outsiders may be held liable for insider trading: the *tipper/tippee theory* and the *misappropriation theory*.

TIPPEES
Persons who receive inside information from an insider or another tippee.

Tipper/Tippee Theory Anyone who acquires inside information as a result of a corporate insider's breach of his or her fiduciary duty can be liable under Rule 10b-5. This liability extends to **tippees** (those who receive "tips" from insiders) and even remote tippees (tippees of tippees). The key to liability under this theory is that inside information be obtained as a result of someone's breach of a fiduciary duty to the corporation whose shares are involved in the trading. Unless there is a breach of a duty not to disclose inside information, the disclosure was in exchange for personal benefit, and the tippee knows of this breach (or should know of it) and benefits from it, there is no liability under this theory.

For example, in *Chiarella v. United States*,[15] the United States Supreme Court considered the role Rule 10b-5 plays when there is no breach of duty and no use of interstate commerce, the mails, or any of the facilities of any national securities exchange. Chiarella was a printer who worked at a New York composing room and handled announcements of corporate takeover bids. Even though the documents that were delivered to the printer concealed the identities of the target corporations by blank spaces and false names, Chiarella was able to deduce the names of the target companies. Without disclosing his knowledge, he purchased stock in the target companies and sold the shares immediately after the takeover attempts were made public. He realized a gain of over $30,000 in the course of fourteen months.

In 1978, Chiarella was indicted on seventeen counts of violating Section 10(b) of the Securities Exchange Act of 1934 and SEC Rule 10b-5. The trial court con-

15. 445 U.S. 222, 100 S.Ct. 1108, 63 L.Ed. 348 (1980).

victed him on all counts, and the court of appeals affirmed that conviction. The United States Supreme Court, however, reversed the trial court's decision. The Supreme Court held that Chiarella could not be convicted for his failure to disclose his knowledge to stockholders or to target companies because he was under no duty to disclose his knowledge. Chiarella was under no duty to disclose because he had no prior dealing with the stockholders and was not their agent, nor was he a person in whom sellers had placed their trust and confidence. Thus, the Court held that Chiarella was not liable as a tippee.[16]

Misappropriation Theory Liability for insider trading may also be established under the misappropriation theory. This theory of liability holds that if an individual wrongfully obtains—misappropriates—inside information and trades on it for his or her personal gain, then the individual should be held liable, because in essence, he or she stole information rightfully belonging to another. This theory has significantly extended the reach of Rule 10b-5 to outsiders who would not ordinarily be deemed fiduciaries of the corporations in whose stock they trade. Courts will normally hold, however, that some fiduciary duty to some lawful possessor of material nonpublic information must have been violated and some harm to the defrauded party must have occurred for liability to exist.

The following case raises the question of whether an individual continued to have a fiduciary duty to his employer after his employment was terminated.

Case 29.5
SEC v. CHERIF
United States Court of Appeals,
Seventh Circuit, 1991.
933 F.2d 403.

HISTORICAL AND ETHICAL SETTING *Although the misappropriation theory has been adopted by the courts in at least five of the twelve geographical circuits into which the federal district courts are organized, most of the cases have arisen in the second circuit. Because the second circuit includes New York City, where Wall Street is located, perhaps it is only logical that this should be so. In one famous case arising in New York City, R. Foster Winans, a columnist for the* Wall Street Journal, *gave two stockbrokers advance information about the contents of his column, which often affected the prices of stock discussed in the column. The brokers bought or sold stock based on the anticipated impact of the column on the market and shared the profits. In broadly affirming the brokers' convictions for the misappropriation of information from the* Journal *and other crimes, the Second Circuit Court of Appeals rejected their defense that they "would have to have breached a duty to the corporations or shareholders * * * whose stock they purchased or sold" to be found guilty.*[a]

FACTS Danny Cherif was employed by the First National Bank of Chicago in its International Financial Institutions Department from 1979 until 1987, when Cherif's position was eliminated because of an internal reorganization. Cherif, through a forged memo to the bank's security department, caused his magnetic identification (ID) card—which he had received as an employee to allow him to enter the bank building—to remain activated after his employment was terminated. Cherif used his ID card to enter the building at night to obtain confidential financial information from the bank's Specialized Finance Department regarding extraordinary business transactions, such as tender offers. During 1988 and 1989, Cherif made substantial profits by using this information in securities trading. Eventually, Cherif's activities were investigated by the SEC, and Cherif was charged with violating Section 10(b) and Rule 10b-5 by misappropriating and trading on inside information in violation of his fiduciary duties to his former employer. The district court issued an injunction prohibiting Cherif from further trading and freezing his accounts until

a. *United States v. Carpenter*, 791 F.2d 1024 (2d Cir. 1986).

---

16. Note, though, that under the misappropriation theory discussed in the next section, it could be argued that Chiarella violated his duty of loyalty to his employer, the printing firm, by engaging in actions that could foreseeably be harmful to the printing firm's reputation. Note also that after *Chiarella*, the SEC adopted Rule 14e-3 (17 C.F.R. Section 240.14e-3), which makes it unlawful for a person who acquires advance knowledge of a tender offer to use that information in securities transactions.

Case 29.5—Continued

Cherif could prove that the account funds had not been obtained in violation of securities laws. Cherif appealed. On appeal, Cherif's central argument was that the SEC had wrongfully applied the misappropriation theory to his activities because, as a former employee, he no longer had a fiduciary duty to the bank.

ISSUE Does the misappropriation theory of insider trading apply to Cherif's activities?

DECISION Yes. The appellate court affirmed the trial court's decision. Cherif had misappropriated inside information in violation of his fiduciary duty to his former employer.

REASON The court observed that although the United States Supreme Court has not explicitly approved the misappropriation theory, numerous circuit and district courts have adhered to the theory. The court "join[ed] these courts in holding that a person violates Rule 10b-5 and Section 10(b) of the Securities Exchange Act of 1934 by misappropriating and trading upon material information entrusted to him by virtue of a fiduciary relationship such as employment." In response to Cherif's contention that he no longer owed a fiduciary duty to the bank because he was no longer a bank employee, the court held that Cherif's duty to the bank was not restricted only to the term of his employment. "Notwithstanding the contractual agreement," said the court, "Cherif was bound by a broader common law duty. This common law duty obligates an employee to protect any confidential information entrusted to him by his employer during his employment. In addition, an employee is obligated to continue to protect such information after his termination." The court went on to say that "Cherif betrayed a trust in a way that a mere thief does not. He used property and information belonging to First Chicago, and made available to him only through his fiduciary relationship, against the bank's own interests."

Insider Reporting and Trading—Section 16(b)

Officers, directors, and certain large stockholders[17] of Section 12 corporations are required to file reports with the SEC concerning their ownership and trading of the corporations' securities.[18] To discourage such insiders from using nonpublic information about their companies for their personal benefit in the stock market, Section 16(b) of the 1934 act provides for the recapture by the corporation of all profits realized by an insider on any purchase and sale or sale and purchase of the corporation's stock within any six-month period.[19] It is irrelevant whether the insider actually uses inside information; all such *short-swing* profits must be returned to the corporation. Section 16(b) applies not only to stock but to warrants, options, and securities convertible into stock. In addition, the courts have fashioned complex rules for determining profits. Corporate insiders are wise to seek competent counsel prior to trading in the corporation's stock. Exhibit 29–2 compares the effects of Rule 10b-5 and Section 16(b).

Insider-Trading Sanctions

The Insider Trading Sanctions Act of 1984 permits the SEC to bring suit in a federal district court against anyone violating or aiding in a violation of the 1934 act or SEC rules by purchasing or selling a security while in the possession of material nonpublic information.[20] The violation must occur on or through the facilities of a national securities exchange or through a broker or dealer. Transactions connected with a public offering by an issuer of securities are excepted.

17. Those stockholders owning 10 percent of the class of equity securities registered under Section 12 of the 1934 act.
18. 15 U.S.C. Section 78*l*.
19. When a decline is predicted in the market for a particular stock, one can realize profits by "selling short"—selling at a high price and repurchasing later at a lower price to cover the "short sale." The short seller typically has to borrow the stock in the meantime (and pay interest on the borrowed stock).
20. 15 U.S.C. Section 78u–1(a)(1).

The film "Wall Street" looked at insider trading. Who can take action against those who violate insider-trading laws, and what are the sanctions?

The court may assess as a penalty as much as triple the profits gained or the loss avoided by the guilty party. For purposes of the act, profit or loss is defined as "the difference between the purchase or sale price of the security and the value of that security as measured by the trading price of the security at a reasonable period of time after public dissemination of the nonpublic information."[21]

The Insider Trading and Securities Fraud Enforcement Act of 1988 extended the class of persons who may be subject to civil liability for insider-trading violations, gave the SEC authority to award **bounty payments** (rewards given by government officials for acts beneficial to the state) to persons providing information leading to the prosecution of insider-trading violations, gave the SEC rulemaking authority to require specific policies and procedures to prevent insider trading, and increased the criminal penalties for violations. Maximum jail terms were increased from five to ten years, and fines were increased to $1,000,000 for individuals and $2,500,000 for partnerships and corporations.[22] Neither act has any effect on other actions the SEC or private investors may take.

BOUNTY PAYMENT
A reward (payment) given to a person or persons who perform a certain service—such as informing legal authorities of illegal actions.

Proxy Statements

Section 14(a) of the Securities Exchange Act of 1934 regulates the solicitation of proxies from shareholders of Section 12 companies. The SEC regulates the content of proxy statements, which (as discussed in Chapter 27) are statements sent to shareholders by corporate officials who are requesting authority to vote on behalf of the shareholders in a particular election on specified issues. Whoever solicits a proxy must fully and accurately disclose in the proxy statement all of the facts that are pertinent to the matter on which the shareholders are to vote. SEC Rule 14a-9 is similar to the antifraud provisions of Rule 10b-5. Remedies for violation are extensive, ranging from injunctions that prevent a vote from being taken to monetary damages.

21. 15 U.S.C. Section 78u–1(d)(5)(f).
22. 15 U.S.C. Section 78ff(a).

◆ Exhibit 29–2 Comparison of Coverage, Application, and Liabilities under Rule 10b-5 and Section 16(b)

	RULE 10b-5	SECTION 16(b)
1. Subject matter of transaction.	Any security (does not have to be registered).	Any security (does not have to be registered).
2. Transactions covered.	Purchase or sale.	Short-swing purchase and sale or short-swing sale and purchase.
3. Who is subject to liability?	Virtually anyone with inside information under a duty to disclose—including officers, directors, controlling stockholders, and tippees.	Officers, directors, and certain 10 percent stockholders.
4. Is omission or misrepresentation necessary for liability?	Yes.	No.
5. Any exempt transactions?	No.	Yes, there are a variety of exemptions.
6. Is direct dealing with the party necessary?	No.	No.
7. Who may bring an action?	A person transacting with an insider, the SEC, or a purchaser or seller damaged by a wrongful act.	Corporation and shareholder by derivative action.

❖ The Expanding Powers of the SEC

In the 1980s, insider-trading scandals rocked Wall Street and led to jail sentences for some of the world's most successful traders, including Ivan Boesky and Michael Milken. These scandals prompted Congress to strengthen the powers of the SEC to prosecute insider-trading cases. With the Insider Trading and Securities Fraud Enforcement Act of 1988, Congress sent a strong message to Wall Street traders who believed that they could engage in insider trading with relative impunity and receive, at best, suspended sentences. As already noted, the law increased the maximum prison sentence for insider-trading activities to ten years and doubled the maximum fine for individuals to $1,000,000. It also authorized the payment of fixed percentages of any assessed penalties to informants and authorized private litigants to sue insider-trading violators to recover the amount of profits resulting from the illegal transaction. More ominously, the new law imposed joint and several liability on all persons who trade on the same inside information. This means that a so-called remote tippee who realizes a $10,000 profit on a transaction that ultimately nets a group of remote tippees $100,000 may be held liable for the entire $100,000.

The SEC's powers were further broadened in 1990 with the passage of the Securities Enforcement Remedies and Penny Stock Reform Act, which amended existing securities laws to greatly expand the types of securities violation cases that SEC administrative law judges can hear. This expanded jurisdictional authority promises to bolster the SEC's conviction rate for insider-trading violators because the conviction rate has tended to be much higher in administrative proceedings than in the courts. The expansion may also boost the number of cases brought by the SEC, as the new rules are intended to reduce the amount of time needed to prosecute a case.

Business Law in Action

Spouses and Inside Information

Are spouses in a fiduciary relationship with each other? If a husband delivers to his stockbroker inside information told to him in confidence by his wife, has he breached a fiduciary duty to his wife? The Second Circuit Court of Appeals recently faced this question in deciding whether a stockbroker should be liable as a tippee for violating securities laws.

The stockbroker was Robert Chestman, who was given information by Keith Loeb about a tender offer about to be made to a corporation owned by his wife's family. Loeb's wife was Susan Waldbaum, a niece of the president and controlling shareholder of Waldbaum, Inc. Susan's mother (the president's sister) told Susan that the company was going to be sold at a favorable price and that a tender offer was soon to be made. She told Susan not to tell anyone except her husband about the sale. The next day, Susan told her husband of the sale and cautioned him not to tell anyone because "it could possibly ruin the sale." The day after he learned of the sale, Loeb called Chestman, his broker, and told him that he "had some accurate information" that the company was about to be sold at a "substantially higher" price than the market value of its stock. That day, Chestman purchased shares of the company for himself as well as for Loeb. Chestman was later convicted by a jury of, among other things, trading on misappropriated inside information in violation of Rule 10b-5.[a]

On appeal, the central question in regard to liability under the misappropriation theory was whether Chestman had acquired the inside information about the Waldbaum company as a result of an insider's breach of a fiduciary duty. Essentially, the inquiry focused on whether Loeb owed a fiduciary duty to his wife's family or to his wife to keep the information confidential. The court found that Loeb owed a fiduciary duty to neither the family nor his wife.

"We have little trouble," said the court, "finding the evidence insufficient to establish a fiduciary relationship or its functional equivalent between Keith Loeb and the Waldbaum family. * * * Kinship alone does not create the necessary relationship." The court emphasized that Loeb had not been brought into the family's inner circle, in which family members discussed confidential business information, nor was Loeb an employee of the company.

As to whether Loeb's relationship with his wife was a fiduciary relationship, the court stated that "Keith's status as Susan's husband could not itself establish fiduciary status." Neither did the words "don't tell" establish a fiduciary relationship "absent a pre-existing fiduciary relation or an express agreement of confidentiality."

The court concluded that "because Keith owed neither Susan nor the Waldbaum family a fiduciary duty or its functional equivalent, he did not defraud them by disclosing news of the pending tender offer to Chestman. Absent a predicate act of fraud by Keith Loeb, the alleged misappropriator, Chestman could not be derivatively liable as Loeb's tippee." Furthermore, the court held that even if Loeb had breached a fiduciary duty, Chestman could not be held liable as a tippee unless the government could prove that Chestman not only knew that the information was material and nonpublic but also knew that Loeb had acquired it in confidence and had agreed not to disclose it.

For the past decade or so, the trend has been to extend the reach of liability under Rule 10b-5 ever further. The court's decision in this case—and in several other cases decided by the Second Circuit Court of Appeals[b]—significantly departs from this trend and, according to some observers, marks the beginning of a trend toward "lightening up" on liability under Rule 10b-5.

a. *United States v. Chestman*, 947 F.2d 551 (2d Cir. 1991).

b. See, for example, *United States v. Mulheren*, 938 F.2d 364 (2d Cir. 1991), and *United States v. GAF Corp.*, 928 F.2d 1253 (2d Cir. 1991).

❖ Regulation of Investment Companies

INVESTMENT COMPANY A company that acts on behalf of many smaller shareholders/owners by buying a large portfolio of securities and managing that portfolio professionally.

Investment companies, and mutual funds in particular, grew rapidly after World War II. **Investment companies** act on behalf of many smaller shareholders by buying a large portfolio of securities and managing that portfolio professionally. A

Ethical Perspective

Should Insider Trading Be Legal?

What sort of harm is caused by insider trading? Because insiders have access to certain information that will affect the price of stocks, they are able to make advantageous trading decisions and realize profits at the expense of investors buying or selling those same stocks without benefit of that information. News of insider-trading practices may deter many small investors from participating in the stock market, because they do not believe that they can get a "fair" break. Their nonparticipation presumably deprives American companies of access to capital that could be used to increase investment in such things as research and development, as well as in plants and equipment.

Should insider trading be legal? Would the legalization of insider trading bring certain benefits that merit consideration? To see how legalized insider trading might work, let us return to the case of *SEC v. Texas Gulf Sulphur Co.* (Case 29.3 in this chapter). A very promising mineral sample was found by the company while it was engaged in exploratory drilling in Canada. The company ordered its crews not to talk about the find. At the same time, the company began to acquire surrounding parcels of property in the expectation that it would expand its drilling operations. Several corporate officers and directors also purchased large quantities of company stock. To put an end to rumors surrounding the company's drilling activities, the company issued a press release on April 12, 1964, downplaying the extent of the find. Four days later, a more accurate estimate of the value of the discovery was released to the public. Soon after, the SEC charged several company directors and officers with violating the securities laws.

How might legalized insider trading have altered this scenario? The discovery of the sample would probably have set off a mad rush by many company officers, directors, and employees to purchase stock, because there would have been no legal penalty for such conduct. Consequently, the price of Texas Gulf stock would have increased fairly quickly, depending on the amount of stock purchased. These increases presumably would have attracted the attention of outside investors, particularly those who had contemplated selling or purchasing that stock. Those who might otherwise have sold Texas Gulf stock probably would have held onto it longer to see how high the price might go. Those who were contemplating buying that stock might have been persuaded to buy the stock sooner, in anticipation of quicker profits. Similarly, stockbrokers tracking the number of purchases of company stock by insiders would probably have recommended the stock to some of their customers, thus helping to increase the number of investors purchasing the stock. In short, the absence of legal penalties would have encouraged Texas Gulf insiders to purchase as much stock as possible as quickly as possible. The higher demand for the stock would have more quickly translated into higher prices for the stock and hence a more efficient capital market. In this way, more outside investors would have learned sooner that something positive had happened to the company and would thus have had the opportunity to purchase the stock.[a]

Although legalizing insider trading would arguably assist in the creation of more efficient capital markets, it is unlikely to happen anytime soon. Congress does not want to fuel public suspicions that it hears only the voices of the rich and powerful.

a. For a complete analysis of this point of view, see Henry Manne, *Insider Trading* (New York: Free Press, 1966).

MUTUAL FUND
A specific type of investment company that continually buys or sells to investors shares of ownership in a portfolio.

mutual fund is a specific type of investment company that continually buys or sells to investors shares of ownership in a portfolio. Such companies are regulated by the Investment Company Act of 1940,[23] which provides for SEC regulation of their activities. The act was expanded by the 1970 amendments to the Investment Company Act. Further minor changes were made in the Securities Act Amendments of 1975 and in later years.

The 1940 act requires that every investment company register with the SEC and imposes restrictions on the activities of such companies and persons connected with them. For the purposes of the act, an investment company is defined as any entity that (1) "is * * * engaged primarily * * * in the business of investing, rein-

23. 15 U.S.C. Sections 80a-1 to 80a-64.

vesting, or trading in securities" or (2) is engaged in such business and has more than 40 percent of its assets in investment securities. Excluded from coverage by the act are banks, insurance companies, savings and loan associations, finance companies, oil and gas drilling firms, charitable foundations, tax-exempt pension funds, and other special types of institutions, such as closely held corporations.

All investment companies must register with the SEC by filing a notification of registration. Each year, registered investment companies must file reports with the SEC. To safeguard company assets, all securities must be held in the custody of a bank or stock-exchange member, and that bank or stock-exchange member must follow strict procedures established by the SEC.

No dividends may be paid from any source other than accumulated, undistributed net income. Furthermore, there are some restrictions on investment activities. For example, investment companies are not allowed to purchase securities on the margin (pay for only part of the total price, borrowing the rest), sell short (sell shares not yet owned), or participate in joint trading accounts.

❖ State Securities Laws

Since the adoption of the 1933 and 1934 federal securities acts, the state and federal governments have regulated securities concurrently. Indeed, both acts specifically preserve state securities laws. Thus, all states have their own corporate securities laws to regulate the offer and sale of securities within state borders.[24] Often referred to as **blue sky laws,** they are designed to prevent "speculative schemes which have no more basis than so many feet of blue sky."

BLUE SKY LAWS
State laws that regulate the offer and sale of securities.

Certain features are common to all state blue sky laws. They have antifraud provisions, many of which are patterned after Rule 10b-5. Also, most state corporate securities laws regulate securities brokers and dealers. Typically, these laws also provide for the registration or qualification of securities offered or issued for sale within the state. Unless an applicable exemption from registration is found, issuers must register or qualify their stock with the appropriate state official, often called a *corporations commissioner.*

There are differences in philosophy among state statutes. Many are like the Securities Act of 1933; they require corporations to make certain disclosures before registration is effective and a permit to sell the securities is issued. Others set fairness standards that a corporation must meet to offer and sell stock in the state. The Uniform Securities Act, which has been adopted in part by several states, was drafted to be acceptable to states with differing regulatory philosophies.

24. These laws are catalogued and annotated in the Commerce Clearing House's *Blue Sky Law Reporter,* a loose-leaf service.

Application

Law and the Entrepreneur—Going Public

Virtually every week, some business "goes public"—that is, begins selling shares to the public. Once a firm has gone public, it is regulated by the Securities and Exchange Commission (SEC) at the federal level, and usually by the state's equivalent to the SEC as well. It may also be regulated by the National Association of Securities Dealers (NASD), depending on the circumstances. If you or anyone you know ever contemplates taking a business public, this checklist indicates clearly what you should do.

Checklist for Going Public

☐ 1. Immediately visit the offices of a qualified securities law attorney.

❖ Key Terms

accredited investor 695
blue sky law 709
bounty payment 705
insider trading 698
investment company 707
mutual fund 708
red herring prospectus 693
Rule 10b-5 697
securities 692
tippee 702
tombstone ad 693

❖ Chapter Summary: Investor Protection

The Securities Act of 1933	Prohibits fraud and stabilizes the securities industry by requiring disclosure of all essential information relating to the issuance of stocks to the investing public. 1. Securities, unless exempt, must be *registered* with the SEC before being offered to the public through the mails or any facility of interstate commerce (including securities exchanges). The *registration statement* must include detailed financial information about the issuing corporation, the intended use of the proceeds of the securities being issued, and certain disclosures, such as interests of directors or officers and pending lawsuits. 2. A *prospectus* must be provided to investors, describing the security being sold, the issuing corporation, and the risk attaching to the security. 3. *Exemptions*—The SEC has exempted certain offerings from the requirements of the Securities Act of 1933. Exemptions may be determined on the basis of the size of the issue, whether the offering is private or public, and whether advertising is involved. Exemptions are summarized in Exhibit 29–1.
The Securities Exchange Act of 1934	Provides for the regulation and registration of securities exchanges, brokers, dealers, and national securities associations (such as the NASD). Maintains a continuous disclosure system for all corporations with securities on the securities exchanges and for those companies that have assets in excess of $5,000,000 and 500 or more shareholders (Section 12 companies). 1. *Insider trading* [*under Section 16(b) of the 1934 act*]—To prevent corporate officers and directors from taking advantage of inside information (information not available to the investing public), the 1934 act requires officers, directors, and shareholders owning 10 percent or more of the issued stock of a corporation to turn over to the corporation all short-term profits (called short-swing profits) realized from the purchase and sale or sale and purchase of corporate stock within any six-month period.

❖ Chapter Summary: Investor Protection—Continued

The Securities Act of 1934—Continued	2. *Rule 10b-5* [*under Section 10(b) of the 1934 act*]: a. Applies to insider trading by corporate officers, directors, majority shareholders, and any persons receiving information not available to the public who base their trading on this information. b. Liability for violation can be civil or criminal. c. May be violated by failing to disclose "material facts" that must be disclosed under this rule. d. Applies in virtually all cases concerning the trading of securities—a firm does not have to have its securities registered under the 1933 act for the 1934 act to apply. e. Applies only when the requisites of federal jurisdiction (such as use of the mails, stock-exchange facilities, or any facility of interstate commerce) are present. 3. *Proxies* [*under Section 14(a) of the 1934 act*]—The SEC regulates the content of proxy statements sent to shareholders by corporate managers of Section 12 companies who are requesting authority to vote on behalf of the shareholders in a particular election on specified issues. Section 14(a) is essentially a disclosure law, with provisions similar to the antifraud provisions of Rule 10b-5.
Regulation of Investment Companies	The Investment Company Act of 1940 provides for SEC regulation of investment company activities. It was altered and expanded by the amendments of 1970 and 1975.
State Securities Laws	All states have corporate securities laws (*blue sky laws*) that regulate the offer and sale of securities within state borders; designed to prevent "speculative schemes which have no more basis than so many feet of blue sky." States regulate securities concurrently with the federal government.

❖ Questions and Case Problems

29-1. Definition of a Security. What are the four elements in the definition of a security? What is the most common form that securities take?

29-2. Securities Laws. What are the essential purposes of the Securities Act of 1933 and the Securities Exchange Act of 1934? How, when, and for what reason was the Securities and Exchange Commission created?

29-3. Registration Requirements. Langley Brothers, Inc., a corporation incorporated and doing business in Kansas, decides to sell $1,000,000 worth of its no-par common stock to the public. The stock will be sold only within the state of Kansas. Joseph Langley, the chairman of the board, says the offering need not be registered with the SEC. His brother, Harry, disagrees. Who is right? Explain.

29-4. Registration Requirements. Huron Corp. had 300,000 common shares outstanding. The owners of these outstanding shares lived in several different states. Huron decided to split the 300,000 shares two for one. Will Huron Corp. have to file a registration statement and prospectus on the 300,000 new shares to be issued as a result of the split? Explain.

29-5. Securities Fraud. Leston Nay owned 90 percent of the stock of First Securities Co. Between 1942 and 1966, Hochfelder sent large sums of money to Nay to be invested in certain accounts of First Securities. The whole investment scheme was a fraud, and Nay converted the money sent by Hochfelder to his own use. When Hochfelder discovered the fraud, he sued Ernst & Ernst, First Securities' auditor, for failing to use proper auditing procedures and thus negligently failing to discover the fraudulent scheme. Was the firm of Ernst & Ernst found guilty of violating Section 10(b) of the 1934 Securities Exchange Act and SEC Rule 10b-5? Explain. [*Ernst & Ernst v. Hochfelder*, 425 U.S. 185, 96 S.Ct. 1375, 47 L.Ed.2d 668 (1976)]

29-6. Rule 10b-5. Campbell was a financial columnist for a Los Angeles newspaper owned by Hearst Corp. He often bought shares in companies on which he was about to give a favorable report and then sold the shares at a profit after the columns appeared. In June of 1969, Campbell interviewed the officers of American Systems, Inc. (ASI). The ASI officers did not disclose to Campbell adverse information concerning the company's financial condition. Campbell relied on the officers' presentation of ASI's financial status, however, and made no independent investigation. Planning to write a favorable report, Campbell purchased 5,000 shares of ASI stock for $2 per share. Following the publication of Campbell's favorable, and misleading, article, ASI's stock rose rapidly in price, and on June 5 Campbell sold 2,000 of his shares at $5 per share. Earlier, in February of 1969, ASI had made an agreement with another corporation, RGC, under which RGC would merge with ASI and ASI would pay RGC stockholders enough ASI stock to equal a market value of $1.8 million on the closing date of June 10, 1969. Zweig and Bruno, each of whom owned one-third of RGC shares, brought suit against Hearst Corp., alleging that because of the artificial rise in ASI stock caused by Campbell's column, they ended up with a smaller percentage of the total outstanding shares of ASI than they would otherwise have received. Explain whether Hearst is liable under Rule 10b-5. [*Zweig v. Hearst Corp.*, 594 F.2d 1261 (9th Cir. 1979)]

29-7. Definition of a Security. The W. J. Howey Co. (Howey) owned large tracts of citrus acreage in Lake County, Florida. For several years, it planted about five hundred acres annually, keeping half of the groves itself and offering the other half to the public to help finance additional development. Howey-in-the-Hills Service, Inc., was a service company engaged in cultivating and developing these groves, including the harvesting and marketing of the crops. Each prospective customer was offered both a land sales contract and a service contract, after being told that it was not feasible to invest in a grove unless service arrangements were made. Of the acreage sold by Howey, 85 percent was sold with a service contract with Howey-in-the-Hills Service, Inc. Howey did not register with the SEC or meet the other administrative requirements that issuers of securities must fulfill. The SEC sued to enjoin Howey from continuing to offer the land sales and service contracts. Howey responded that no SEC violation existed because no securities had been issued. Which party will prevail in court, Howey or the SEC? For what reasons? [*SEC v. W. J. Howey Co.*, 328 U.S. 293, 66 S.Ct. 1100, 90 L.Ed. 1244 (1946)]

29-8. Definition of a Security. Ronald Rodeo's investment group purchased limited partnership interests in certain Illinois apartment buildings. Separately, by contract, it acquired an option to buy out the remaining interests of the general partners. According to the arrangement, the general partners would operate the apartments, and the limited partners would provide essential capital while retaining their limited liability. Rodeo could not actively intervene in the business without losing his limited liability. He therefore had to rely solely upon the general partners for the partnership's profitability. Two years later, Rodeo became disenchanted with the partnership's operation and sued R. Dean Gillman and the other general partners under the Illinois blue sky act. In his claim, Rodeo stated that material misrepresentations and omissions had been made during the negotiation of the limited partnership contracts in violation of the state securities act. The general partners responded that no securities were involved and that, because of the buy-out option, the limited partners actually had ultimate control over the management of the apartments. Discuss the definition of a *security* and whether the limited partnership contracts meet this definition. [*Rodeo v. Gillman*, 787 F.2d 1175 (7th Cir. 1986)]

29-9. Definition of a Security. U.S. News & World Report, Inc., set up a profit-sharing plan in 1962 that allotted to certain employees specially issued stock known as bonus or anniversary stock. The stock was given to the employees for past services and could not be traded or sold to anyone other than the corporate issuer, U.S. News. This special stock was issued only to employees and for no other purpose than as bonuses. Because there was no market for the stock, U.S. News hired an independent appraiser to estimate the fair value of the stock so that the employees could redeem the shares. Charles Foltz and several other employees held stock through this plan and sought to redeem the shares with U.S. News, but Foltz disputed the value set by the appraisers. Foltz sued U.S. News for violation of securities regulations. What defense would allow U.S. News to resist successfully Foltz's claim? [*Foltz v. U.S. News & World Report, Inc.*, 627 F.Supp. 1143 (D.D.C. 1986)]

29-10. Rule 10b-5. In early 1985, FMC Corp. made plans to buy some of its own stock as part of a restructuring of its balance statement. Unknown to FMC management, the brokerage firm FMC employed—Goldman, Sachs & Co.—disclosed information on the stock purchase that found its way to Ivan Boesky. FMC was one of the seven major corporations in whose stock Boesky allegedly traded using inside information. Boesky made purchases of FMC's stock between February 18 and February 21, 1986, and between March 12 and April 4, 1986. Boesky's purchases amounted to a substantial portion of the total volume of FMC stock traded during these periods. The price of FMC stock increased from $71.25 on February 20, 1986, to $97.00 on April 25, 1986. As a result, FMC paid substantially more for the repurchase of its own stock than anticipated. When FMC discovered Boesky's knowledge of its recapitalization plan, FMC sued Boesky for the excess price it had paid—approximately $220 million. Discuss whether FMC should recover under Section 10(b) of the Securities Exchange Act and SEC Rule 10b-5. [*FMC Corp. v. Boesky*, 673 F.Supp. 242 (N.D.Ill. 1987)]

29-11. Short-Swing Profits. Emerson Electric Co. purchased 13.2 percent of Dodge Manufacturing Co.'s stock in an unsuccessful takeover attempt in June of 1967. Less than six months later, when Dodge merged with Reliance Electric Co., Emerson decided to sell its shares. To avoid being subject to the short-swing profit restrictions of Section 16(b) of the Securities Exchange Act of 1934, Emerson decided on a two-step selling plan. First, it sold off sufficient shares to reduce its holdings to 9.96 percent (owners with less than 10 percent are exempt from Section 16(b)), and then it sold the remaining stock—all within a six-month period. Emerson in this way succeeded in avoiding Section 16(b) requirements. Reliance demanded that Emerson return the profits made on both sales. Emerson sought a declaratory judgment from the court that it was not liable, arguing that because at the time of the second sale it had not owned 10 percent of Dodge stock, Section 16(b) did not apply. Does Section 16(b) of the Securities Exchange Act of 1934 apply to Emerson's transactions, and is Emerson liable to Reliance for its profits? [*Reliance Electric Co. v. Emerson Electric Co.*, 404 U.S. 418, 92 S.Ct. 596, 30 L.E.2d 575 (1972)]

29-12. Rule 10b-5. Energy Resource Group, Inc. (ERG), entered into a written agreement with Ivan West by which West was to find an investor willing to purchase ERG stock. West later formed a partnership, called Investment Management Group (IMG), with Don Peters and another person. According to the terms of the partnership agreement, West's consulting work for ERG was excluded from the work of the IMG partnership. West learned through his consulting position with ERG that ERG was to be acquired by another corporation for $6.00 per share. At the time West learned of the acquisition, ERG stock was trading at $3.50 per share. Apparently, Peters learned of the acquisition from papers on West's desk in the IMG office and then shared the information with Ken Mick, his stockbroker. Mick then encouraged several clients to buy ERG stock prior to the public announcement of the acquisition. Mick, in return for leaking this inside information to clients, received a special premium from the enriched investors. Mick then paid a portion of the premium to Peters. The SEC brought an action against Peters for violating Rule 10b-5. Under what theory might Peters be held liable for insider trading in violation of Rule 10b-5? Discuss fully. [*SEC v. Peters*, 735 F.Supp. 1505 (D.Kans. 1990)]

29-13. Securities Fraud. William Gotchey owned 50 percent of the shares of First American Financial Consultants, Inc. (FAFC), an investment company registered with the SEC. In the fall of 1987, Paul Hatfield, a client of FAFC, spoke with Gotchey about investing. As a result of their conversations, Hatfield invested $5,000 with FAFC. In December, Hatfield told Gotchey that he wished to invest $20,000, $15,000 of which he wished to place in a secure investment. Gotchey told Hatfield that he would place this $15,000 in mortgage-backed securities to be invested through a mortgage company. For a time, Hatfield received interest payments from FAFC, purportedly from the mortage-backed investment. He also received statements confirming that the investment had been made. In fact, Gotchey had deposited the entire $20,000 in an FAFC bank account. When Hatfield did not receive the interest payment due at the beginning of July 1988, he confronted Gotchey. Gotchey responded by asking Hatfield to sign an agreement whereby FAFC would repay the $15,000 in monthly installments over ten years. Hatfield refused. To date, Gotchey has not accounted for the $15,000. Hatfield has received no interest payments since June 1988. Has Gotchey violated Section 10b-5 of the Securities Exchange Act? Why or why not? [*SEC v. Gotchey*, 981 F.2d 1251 (4th Cir. 1992)]

A QUESTION OF ETHICS AND SOCIAL RESPONSIBILITY

29-14. *Between 1970 and 1981, Sanford Weill served as the chief executive officer (CEO) of Shearson Loeb Rhodes and several of its predecessor entities (collectively "Shearson"). In 1981, Weill sold his controlling interest in Shearson to the American Express Co., and between 1981 and 1985, he served as president of that firm. In 1985, Weill developed an interest in becoming CEO for BankAmerica and secured a commitment from Shearson to invest $1 billion in BankAmerica if he was successful in his negotiations with that firm. In early 1986, Weill met with BankAmerica directors several times, but these contacts were not disclosed publicly until February 20, 1986, when BankAmerica announced that Weill had sought to become its CEO but that BankAmerica was not interested in his offer. The day after the announcement, BankAmerica stock traded at prices higher than the prices at which it had traded during the five weeks preceding the announcement. Weill had discussed his efforts to become CEO of BankAmerica with his wife, who had discussed the information with her psychiatrist, Dr. Willis, prior to BankAmerica's public announcement of February 20. She had also told Dr. Willis about Shearson's decision to invest in BankAmerica if Weill succeeded in becoming its CEO. Willis disclosed to his broker this material, confidential information and purchased BankAmerica common stock. After BankAmerica's public announcement and the subsequent increase in the price of its stock, Willis sold his shares and realized a profit of approximately $27,500. The court held that Willis was liable for insider trading under the misappropriation theory.* [United States v. Willis, 737 *F.Supp.* 269 *(S.D.N.Y. 1990)*]

1. The court stated in its opinion in this case that "[i]t is difficult to imagine a relationship that requires a higher degree of trust and confidence than the traditional relationship of physician and patient." It then quoted the concluding words of the Hippocratic oath: "Whatsoever things I see or hear concerning the life of men, in my attendance on the sick or even apart therefrom, which ought not be noised abroad, I will keep silence thereon, counting such things to be as sacred secrets." The court held that Willis had violated his fiduciary duty to Mrs. Weill, his patient, by investing in BankAmerica stock. Do you agree that Willis's private investments, which were based on information learned through his sessions with Mrs. Weill, constituted a violation of his duty to his patient? After all, Willis had not "noised abroad" Mrs. Weill's secrets—that is, he had not told others (except for his stockbroker) about the information. If you had been in Willis's shoes, would you have felt ethically restrained from trading on the information?
2. Can you think of any ways in which Willis's trading could have been harmful to Mrs. Weill's interests? Does your answer to this question have a bearing on how you answered Question 1?
3. Do you think that the misappropriation theory of liability imposes too great a burden on outsiders, such as Willis? Why or why not? How might you justify, from an ethical point of view, the application of the misappropriation theory to "outsider trading"?

FOR CRITICAL ANALYSIS

29-15. *Do you think that the tipper/tippee and misappropriation theories extend liability under Rule 10b-5 too far? Why or why not?*

Unit Five

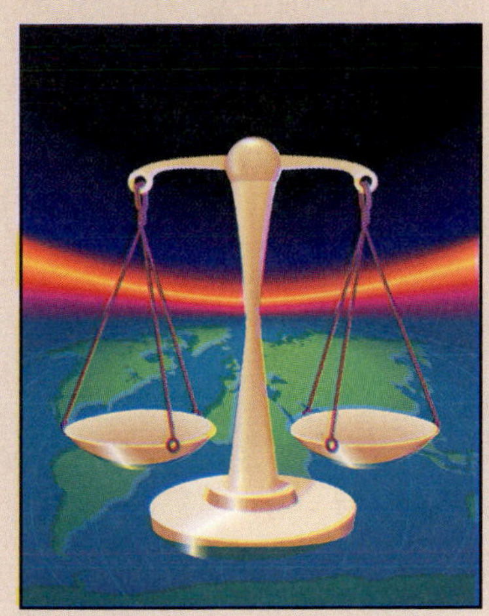

Government Regulation

❖ Why We Study Government Regulation

If this text were being written a hundred years ago, there would be little to say about government regulation. In the 1890s, the beginnings of federal antitrust law were manifested in the form of the Interstate Commerce Act and the Sherman Antitrust Act, but there was little or no legislation affecting consumer protection or environmental issues. And the right of unions to organize had not yet been fully exercised.

Today, in contrast, government regulation permeates the entire business community. A knowledge of what is and is not anticompetitive behavior is critical to the decision making of many businesspersons. State and federal regulations with respect to packaging and labeling, advertising, and the dumping of toxic waste affect numerous businesses; and the issues of employment discrimination, sexual harassment, and safety in the workplace affect virtually every employer in this nation. In this unit, we will examine antitrust issues in Chapter 30, consumer and environmental law in Chapter 31, and employee and labor law in Chapter 32.

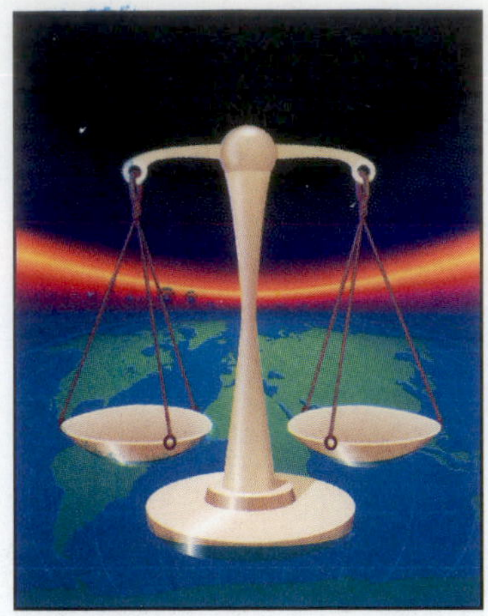

Chapter 30

Antitrust Law

"A rule of such a nature as to bring all trade or traffic into the hands of one company, or one person, and to exclude all others, is illegal."

Sir Edward Coke, 1552–1634
(British jurist and legal scholar)

TRUST
(1) A form of business organization somewhat similar to a corporation. Originally, the trust was a device by which several corporations that were engaged in the same general line of business combined for their mutual advantage to eliminate competition and control the market for their products. The term *trust* derived from the transfer of the voting power of the corporations' shareholders to the committee or board that controlled the organization. (2) An arrangement in which title to property is held by one person (a trustee) for the benefit of another (a beneficiary).

ANTITRUST LAWS
The body of federal and state laws protecting commerce from unlawful restraints, price discrimination, price fixing, and monopolies. The principal federal antitrust statutes are the Sherman Act (1890), the Clayton Act (1914), and the Federal Trade Commission Act (1914).

Today's antitrust laws are the direct descendants of common law actions intended to limit *restraints on trade* (agreements between firms that have the effect of reducing competition in the marketplace). Such actions date to the fifteenth century in England, and the attitude of the courts toward trade restraints is clearly expressed by Sir Edward Coke, an eminent British jurist, in the opening quotation. In America, concern over monopolistic practices arose following the Civil War with the growth of large corporate enterprises and their attempts to reduce or eliminate competition. They did this by legally tying themselves together in **trusts,** legal entities in which trustees hold title to property for the benefit of others. The participants in the most famous trust, the Standard Oil trust (see this chapter's *Landmark in the Law*), transferred their stock to a trustee and received trust certificates in exchange. The trustee then made decisions fixing prices, controlling production, and determining the control of exclusive geographical markets for all of the oil companies in the Standard Oil trust. It became apparent that the trust wielded such economic power that corporations outside the trust could not compete effectively.

Many states attempted to control such monopolistic behavior by enacting statutes outlawing the use of trusts. That is why all of the laws that regulate economic competition today are referred to as **antitrust laws.** At the national level, the government recognized the problem in 1887 and passed the Interstate Commerce Act. The first major federal antitrust law passed was the Sherman Antitrust Act in 1890. In 1914, Congress passed the Clayton Act and the Federal Trade Commission Act to further curb anticompetitive or unfair business practices. Since their passage, the 1914 acts have been amended by Congress to broaden and strengthen their coverage.

This chapter examines these major antitrust statutes, focusing particularly on the Sherman Act and the Clayton Act, as amended, and the types of activities prohibited by those acts. Remember in reading this chapter that the basis of antitrust legislation is the desire to foster competition. Antitrust legislation was initially created—and continues to be enforced—because of our belief that competition leads to lower prices, more product information, and a better distribution of wealth between consumers and producers.

❖ The Sherman Antitrust Act

The author of the Sherman Antitrust Act of 1890, Senator John Sherman, brother of the famed Civil War general and a recognized financial authority, had been concerned for years with the diminishing competition within American industry.

This concern led him to introduce into Congress in 1888, in 1889, and again in 1890 bills designed to destroy the large combinations of capital that were, he felt, creating a lack of balance within the nation's economy. He told Congress that the Sherman Act "does not announce a new principle of law, but applies old and well-recognized principles of the common law."[1] The common law regarding trade regulation was not always consistent. Certainly it was not very familiar to the legislators of the Fifty-first Congress of the United States. The public concern over large business integrations and trusts was familiar, however, and in 1890 Congress passed "An Act to Protect Trade and Commerce against Unlawful Restraints and Monopolies"—commonly known as the Sherman Antitrust Act or, more simply, as the Sherman Act.

Major Provisions of the Sherman Act

Sections 1 and 2 contain the main provisions of the Sherman Act:

> 1: Every contract, combination in the form of trust or otherwise, or conspiracy, in restraint of trade or commerce among the several States, or with foreign nations, is hereby declared to be illegal [and is a felony punishable by fine and/or imprisonment].
>
> 2: Every person who shall monopolize, or attempt to monopolize, or combine or conspire with any other person or persons, to monopolize any part of the trade or commerce among the several States, or with foreign nations, shall be deemed guilty of a felony [and is similarly punishable].

These two sections of the Sherman Act are quite different. Violation of Section 1 requires two or more persons, as a person cannot contract or combine or conspire alone. Thus, the essence of the illegal activity is *the act of joining together.* Section 2 applies both to several people who have joined together and to individual persons, because it specifies, "[e]very person who . . . ." Thus, unilateral conduct can result in a violation of Section 2.

The cases brought to the court under Section 1 of the Sherman Act differ from those brought under Section 2. Section 1 cases are often concerned with finding an agreement (written or oral) that leads to a restraint of trade. Section 2 cases deal with the structure of a monopoly that already exists in the marketplace. The term **monopoly** is generally used to describe a market in which there is a single or a limited number of sellers. Whereas Section 1 focuses on agreements that are restrictive—that is, agreements that have a wrongful purpose—Section 2 looks at the so-called misuse of **monopoly power** in the marketplace. Monopoly power exists when a firm has an extremely great amount of **market power**—the power to affect the market price of its product. We will return to a discussion of these two sections of the Sherman Act after we look at the act's jurisdictional requirements.

MONOPOLY
A term generally used to describe a market for which there is a single seller or a limited number of sellers.

MONOPOLY POWER
The ability of a monopoly to dictate what takes place in a given market.

MARKET POWER
The power of a firm to control the market for its product. A monopoly has the greatest degree of market power.

Jurisdictional Requirements

The Sherman Act applies only to restraints that have a significant impact on commerce. Because Congress can regulate only interstate commerce, in principle only interstate commerce is affected by this act.[2] The Sherman Act also extends to U.S. nationals abroad who are engaged in activities that affect U.S. foreign commerce. The extraterritorial application of U.S. antitrust laws is discussed in Chapter 36. State regulation of anticompetitive practices addresses purely local restraints on competition. Courts have generally held that any activity that substantially affects interstate commerce falls within the ambit of the Sherman Act. As discussed in Chapter 4, courts have construed the meaning of *interstate commerce* more and more broadly,

1. 21 Congressional Record 2456 (1890).
2. See the discussion of the commerce clause in Chapter 4.

bringing even local activities within the regulatory power of the national government. Whether a seemingly local activity touched sufficiently on interstate commerce to come under the purview of the Sherman Act was at issue in the following case.

Case 30.1
SUMMIT HEALTH, LTD. v. PINHAS

Supreme Court of the United States, 1991.
___U.S.___,
111 S.Ct. 1842,
114 L.Ed.2d 366.

HISTORICAL AND POLITICAL SETTING *The record of the congressional debates on the Sherman Act reveals, in Senator Sherman's words, an intent to go "as far as the Constitution permits Congress to go."*[a] *Congress intended to deal comprehensively and effectively with "the evils resulting from contracts, combinations and conspiracies in restraint of trade, and to that end to exercise all the power it possessed."*[b] *Since the passage of the Sherman Act more than a century ago, the U.S. economy has grown, and the federal power over commerce has experienced similar expansion. The United States Supreme Court has long allowed the reach of the Sherman Act to expand with the expanding notions of congressional power. In the words of the Court, "[t]he Act is comprehensive in its terms and coverage, protecting all who are made victims of the forbidden practices by whomever they may be perpetrated."*[c]

FACTS Dr. Simon Pinhas was an ophthalmologist on the staff of Midway Hospital Medical Center (a subsidiary of Summit Health, Ltd.) in Los Angeles. Prior to 1986, most eye surgeries in Los Angeles were performed by a primary surgeon with the assistance of a second surgeon, a practice that significantly increased the cost of eye surgery. In February 1986, the administrators of the Medicare program announced that they would no longer reimburse physicians for the services of assistants, and most hospitals in the area abolished the assistant-surgeon requirement. Midway refused to do so. For Pinhas, who performed numerous surgeries at Midway, this meant he would have to pay $60,000 a year for assistant surgeons that he did not need. He told Midway that if the assistant-surgeon requirement was not eliminated, he would leave. In response, the medical staff initiated peer-review proceedings against Pinhas, terminated his staff privileges, and began preparing an adverse report about Pinhas to distribute to all hospitals in the area. Pinhas filed a complaint under the Sherman Act, alleging that the Midway medical staff had entered into a conspiracy to drive him out of business so that other ophthalmologists would obtain a greater share of the market for ophthalmologic services in Los Angeles. The trial court dismissed his complaint on the ground that interstate commerce was not affected by Pinhas's removal from the Midway medical staff and therefore the Sherman Act did not apply. Pinhas appealed, and ultimately the case was reviewed by the United States Supreme Court.

ISSUE Did the actions of the medical staff against Pinhas fall within the jurisdiction of the Sherman Act (that is, did the actions substantially affect interstate commerce)?

DECISION Yes. The United States Supreme Court held that the medical staff's peer-review proceedings affected interstate commerce and thus their actions against Pinhas fell within the jurisdiction of the Sherman Act.

REASON The Supreme Court found, as had the appellate court, that (1) Midway was involved in interstate commerce because it served out-of-state residents as well as California residents, (2) the peer-review proceedings affected the entire staff at Midway, and therefore (3) the peer-review proceedings affected interstate commerce. The court stated that Midway's argument—that Pinhas's complaint was insufficient because there was no factual connection between the restraint on one particular surgeon's practice and interstate commerce—was flawed for two reasons: First, the "proper analysis focuses, not upon actual consequences, but rather upon the potential harm that would ensue if the conspiracy were successful. * * * Second, if the conspiracy alleged in the complaint is successful, 'as a matter of practical economics,' there will be a reduction in the provision of ophthalmological services in the Los Angeles market." The Court held that the "competitive significance of [Pinhas's] exclusion from the market must be measured, not just by a particularized evaluation of his own practice, but rather, by a general evaluation of the impact of the restraint on other participants and potential participants in the market from which he has been excluded."

ETHICAL CONSIDERATIONS *The substantial disagreement on whether essentially local activities—such as the medical staff's actions against Pinhas—should be subject to the "long arm of federal law" is reflected in the Court's five-to-four decision in this case. The four dissenting jus-*

a. 20 Congressional Record 1167 (1889).
b. *Atlantic Cleaners & Dyers, Inc. v. United States*, 286 U.S. 427, 52 S.Ct. 607, 76 L.Ed. 1204 (1932).
c. *Mandeville Island Farms, Inc. v. American Crystal Sugar Co.*, 334 U.S. 219, 68 S.Ct. 996, 92 L.Ed. 1328 (1948).

Case 30.1—Continued

tices argued that "[t]he complaint does not begin to suggest that the conspiracy at Midway could have even the most trivial effect on interstate commerce." Justice Scalia, who wrote the dissenting opinion, stated, "As I understand the Court's opinion, the test of Sherman Act jurisdiction is whether the entire line of commerce from which Dr. Pinhas has been excluded affects interstate commerce. Since excluding him from eye surgery at Midway Hospital effectively excluded him from the entire Los Angeles market for eye surgery (because no other Los Angeles hospital would accord him practice privileges after Midway rejected him), the jurisdictional question is simply whether that market affects interstate commerce, which of course it does. This analysis tells us nothing[, however,] about the substantiality of the impact on interstate commerce generated by the particular conduct at issue here."

❖ Section 1 of the Sherman Act

The underlying assumption of Section 1 of the Sherman Act is that society's welfare is harmed if rival firms are permitted to join in an agreement that consolidates their market power or otherwise restrains competition. Not all agreements between rivals, however, result in enhanced market power or *unreasonably* restrain trade. Under what is called the **rule of reason,** anticompetitive agreements that allegedly violate Section 1 of the Sherman Act are analyzed with the view that they may, in fact, constitute reasonable restraints on trade.

RULE OF REASON
A test by which a court balances the reasons (such as economic efficiency) for an agreement against its potentially anticompetitive effects. In antitrust litigation, many practices are analyzed under the rule of reason.

The need for a rule-of-reason analysis of some agreements in restraint of trade is obvious—if the rule of reason had not been developed, virtually any business agreement could conceivably be held to violate the Sherman Act. Justice Brandeis effectively phrased this sentiment in *Chicago Board of Trade v. United States,* a case decided in 1918:

> Every agreement concerning trade, every regulation of trade, restrains. To bind, to restrain, is of their very essence. The true test of legality is whether the restraint imposed is such as merely regulates and perhaps thereby promotes competition or whether it is such as may suppress or even destroy competition.[3]

When analyzing an alleged Section 1 violation under the rule of reason, a court will consider several factors, including the purpose of the agreement, the parties' power to implement the agreement to achieve that purpose, and the effect or potential effect of the agreement on competition. Another factor that might be considered is whether the parties could have relied on less restrictive means to achieve their purpose.

Some agreements, however, are so blatantly and substantially anticompetitive that they are deemed illegal *per se* (on their face, or inherently) under Section 1. If an agreement is found to be a ***per se* violation,** a court is precluded from determining whether the agreement's benefits outweigh its anticompetitive effects.

***PER SE* VIOLATION**
A type of anticompetitive agreement—such as a price-fixing agreement—that is considered to be so injurious to the public that there is no need to determine whether it actually injures market competition; rather, it is in itself (*per se*) a violation of the Sherman Act.

The dividing line between agreements that constitute *per se* violations and agreements that should be judged under a rule of reason is seldom clear. Moreover, in some cases, the United States Supreme Court has stated that it is applying a *per se* rule, and yet a careful reading of the Court's analysis suggests that the Court is weighing benefits against harms under a rule of reason. Some have termed this a "soft," or "limited," *per se* rule. Others have called it a "narrow" rule of reason. Perhaps the most that can be said with certainty is that although the distinction between the two rules seems clear in theory, in the actual application of antitrust laws, the distinction has not always been so clear.

We turn now to the types of trade restraints prohibited by Section 1 of the Sherman Act. Generally, these restraints fall into two broad categories: *horizontal*

3. 246 U.S. 231, 38 S.Ct. 242, 62 L.Ed. 683 (1918).

Landmark in the Law

The Standard Oil Co. of New Jersey v. United States (1911)

By 1890, the Standard Oil trust had become the foremost petroleum manufacturing and marketing combination in the United States. Streamlined, integrated, centrally and efficiently controlled, its monopoly over the industry could not be disputed. By the time the Sherman Act was passed in 1890, Standard Oil controlled 90 percent of the U.S market for refined petroleum products, and small manufacturers were incapable of competing with such an industrial leviathan. The increasing consolidation occurring in American industry, and particularly the Standard Oil trust, did not go unnoticed by the American public. In March of 1881, Henry Demarest Lloyd, a young journalist from Chicago, published an article in the *Atlantic Monthly* entitled "The Story of a Great Monopoly," which discussed the success of Standard Oil Company. The article brought to the public's attention for the first time the fact that the petroleum industry in America was dominated by one firm—Standard Oil. Lloyd's article, which was so popular that the issue was reprinted six times, marked the beginning of the American public's growing awareness of and concern over the growth of monopolies, a concern that eventually led to the passage of the Sherman Act of 1890.

Even after the passage of the Sherman Act, however, Standard Oil was able to evade the arm of the new antitrust law for a decade and a half. Technically, the trust confused the government by reorganizing itself from a trust structure into a *holding company* framework in 1892, thus avoiding the Sherman Act's prohibition of the trust device as a means of controlling an industry. Furthermore, for many years, enforcement of the Sherman Act was not a high priority among government officials. In 1905, however, Congress mandated an investigation of the oil industry. James Garfield, the head of the bureau conducting the investigation, was determined to unveil as many facts as possible concerning Standard Oil, and the bureau's 1906 report led eventually to a suit filed by the U.S. government against Standard Oil Company of New Jersey and other corporations involved in the combination. In 1909, the federal court that heard the case rendered a unanimous decision that Standard Oil and the other corporations constituted an illegal monopoly and thus violated the Sherman Act.

The decision was appealed to the United States Supreme Court, and the Court's decision,[a] delivered on May 15, 1911, upheld the verdict of the lower federal court. Thirty-three of the firms involved in the Standard Oil trust were to sever their connections with the parent firm, and the Court forbade Standard Oil to engage in future combinations or conduct in violation of the Sherman Antitrust Act. Chief Justice White, in his decision, summarized how Standard Oil and the other firms in the alliance had gathered control over all phases of petroleum production and marketing, concluding that all of the evidence leads "the mind up to a conviction of a purpose and intent which we think is so certain as practically to cause the subject not to be within the domain of *reasonable* contention [emphasis added]." This *rule of reason* enunciated by the Court in this case has been interpreted and modified many times since in the application of antitrust laws.

a. 221 U.S. 1, 31 S.Ct. 502, 55 L.Ed. 619 (1911).

HORIZONTAL RESTRAINT
Any agreement that in some way restrains competition between rival firms competing in the same market. Price fixing and horizontal market division are examples of horizontal restraints on competition.

PRICE-FIXING AGREEMENT
An anticompetitive agreement between competitors to fix, or render uniform, the prices at which they will sell their products or services.

restraints and *vertical restraints.* Some restraints are *per se* violations of Section 1, but others may be permissible; those that are not *per se* violations are tested under the rule of reason.

Section 1—Horizontal Restraints

The term **horizontal restraint** is encountered frequently in antitrust law. A horizontal restraint is any agreement that in some way restrains competition between rival firms competing in the same market. In the following sections, we look at several types of horizontal restraints.

Price Fixing Any agreement among competitors to fix prices constitutes a *per se* violation of Section 1. Perhaps the definitive case regarding **price-fixing agreements**

remains the 1940 case of *United States v. Socony-Vacuum Oil Co.*[4] In that case, a group of independent oil producers in Texas and Louisiana were caught between falling demand due to the Great Depression of the 1930s and increasing supply from newly discovered oil fields in the region. In response to these conditions, a group of the major refining companies agreed to buy "distress" gasoline (excess supplies) from the independents so as to dispose of it in an "orderly manner." Although there was no explicit agreement as to price, it was clear that the purpose of the agreement was to limit the supply of gasoline on the market and thereby raise prices. The United States Supreme Court recognized the dangerous effects that such an agreement could have on open and free competition. The Court held that the asserted reasonableness of a price-fixing agreement is never a defense; any agreement that restricts output or artificially fixes price is a *per se* violation of Section 1. The rationale of the *per se* rule was best stated in what is now the most famous portion of the Court's opinion. In footnote 59, Justice William O. Douglas compared a freely functioning price system to a body's central nervous system, condemning price-fixing agreements as threats to "the central nervous system of the economy."

Group Boycotts A **group boycott** is an agreement by two or more sellers to boycott, or refuse to deal with, a particular person or firm. Such group boycotts have been held to constitute *per se* violations of Section 1 of the Sherman Act. Section 1 has been violated if it can be demonstrated that the boycott or joint refusal to deal was undertaken with the intention of eliminating competition or preventing entry into a given market. Some boycotts, such as group boycotts against a supplier for political reasons, may be protected under the First Amendment right to freedom of expression, however.

GROUP BOYCOTT
The refusal to deal with a particular person or firm by a group of competitors; prohibited under the Sherman Act.

Horizontal Market Division It is a *per se* violation of Section 1 of the Sherman Act for competitors to divide up territories or customers. For example, manufacturers A, B, and C compete against each other in the states of Kansas, Nebraska, and Iowa. By agreement, A sells products only in Kansas; B sells only in Nebraska; and C sells only in Iowa. This concerted action reduces costs and allows all three (assuming there is no other competition) to raise the price of the goods sold in their respective states. The same violation would take place if A, B, and C simply agreed that A would sell only to institutional purchasers (such as school districts, universities, state agencies and departments, and cities) in all three states, B only to wholesalers, and C only to retailers.

Trade Associations Businesses in the same general industry or profession frequently organize trade associations to pursue common interests. Such an association's activities may include facilitating exchanges of information, representing members' business interests before governmental bodies, conducting advertising campaigns, and setting regulatory standards to govern the industry or profession. Generally, the rule of reason is applied to many of these horizontal actions. For example, if a court finds that a trade association practice or agreement that restrains trade is sufficiently beneficial both to the association and to the public, it may deem the restraint reasonable. Other trade association agreements may have such substantially anticompetitive effects that the court will consider them to be in violation of Section 1 of the Sherman Act. In *National Society of Professional Engineers v. United States*,[5] for example, it was held that the society's code of ethics—which prohibited members from discussing prices with a potential customer until after the customer had chosen an engineer—was a Section 1 violation. The United States Supreme Court found that this ban on competitive bidding was "nothing less than

4. 310 U.S. 150, 60 S.Ct. 811, 84 L.Ed.2d 1129 (1940).
5. 453 U.S. 679, 98 S.Ct. 1355, 55 L.Ed.2d 637 (1978).

a frontal assault on the basic policy of the Sherman Act." In the following case, the court closely scrutinizes an action undertaken by a health-care professional group allegedly for the sole purpose of protecting the public.

Case 30.2
WILK v. AMERICAN MEDICAL ASSOCIATION

United States Court of Appeals, Seventh Circuit, 1990.
895 F.2d 352.

HISTORICAL AND SOCIAL SETTING *In 1898, a German pharmaceutical firm introduced heroin—under the brand name* Heroin*—as a cough suppressant. At the same time,* Lydia Pinkham's Vegetable Compound *was advertised as "The Greatest Medical Discovery Since the Dawn of History." Marketed as a remedy for "woman's weakness and other female complaints," its ingredients included a variety of herbs in a 21 percent alcohol solution. It was outsold in 1898 by* Pe-Ru-Na, *which had a higher alcoholic content. The same year, the Palmer School of Chiropractic was founded in Davenport, Iowa, by Daniel David Palmer. Palmer had previously promoted magnetism as a cure for various ailments. Chiropractic involves the manual manipulation of joints, especially the spine, to prevent or relieve conditions supposedly caused by pressure on the nerve roots.*

FACTS In 1966, the American Medical Association (AMA) passed a resolution labeling chiropractic an unscientific cult. (Chiropractors attempt to cure or relieve bodily ailments by making skeletal adjustments.) In effect, this label prevented physicians from associating with chiropractors, because Principle 3 of the Principles of Medical Ethics—the AMA's code of ethical conduct—provided that a "physician should practice a method of healing founded on a scientific basis; and he should not voluntarily associate with anyone who violates this principle." Medical doctors used Principle 3 to justify their refusal to have anything to do with chiropractors or to allow chiropractors to use hospital diagnostic services or become members of hospital medical staffs. Despite the AMA's efforts, chiropractic became licensed in all fifty states, and in a 1980 revision of the AMA's ethical code, Principle 3 was eliminated. Chester Wilk and four other chiropractors brought an action against the AMA, claiming that the boycott had violated Section 1 of the Sherman Act and seeking injunctive relief from the boycott's "lingering effects" on chiropractors. The trial court, holding that the AMA had violated Section 1 of the Sherman Act by conducting an illegal boycott in restraint of trade, granted an injunction that required the AMA, among other things, to publish widely the trial court's order. The AMA appealed.

ISSUE Had the AMA's boycott of chiropractors violated Section 1 of the Sherman Act?

DECISION Yes. The appellate court affirmed the trial court's decision and its granting of injunctive relief.

REASON The appellate court noted that "the AMA failed to establish that * * * their concern for scientific methods in patient treatment had been objectively reasonable" and "failed to show that it could not adequately have satisfied its concern for scientific method in patient care in a manner less restrictive of competition than a nationwide conspiracy to eliminate a licensed profession." The court concluded that the AMA's illegal boycott, although it had ended a decade before, continued to have adverse lingering effects that threatened the livelihood of licensed chiropractors. The AMA claimed that its exclusionary tactics were motivated by a desire to advise the public to deal only with "scientific" health-care professionals—not "unscientific" chiropractors—but that was not enough to relieve it of liability for anticompetitive behavior designed to " 'destroy a competitor,' namely chiropractors."

Joint Ventures Joint ventures undertaken by competitors are also subject to antitrust laws. As discussed in Chapter 24, a *joint venture* is an undertaking by two or more individuals or firms for a specific purpose. If a joint venture does not involve price fixing or market divisions, the agreement will be analyzed under the rule of reason. Whether the venture will then be upheld under Section 1 depends on an overall assessment of the purposes of the venture, a strict analysis of the potential benefits relative to the likely harms, and in some cases, an assessment of whether there are less restrictive alternatives for achieving the same goals.[6]

6. See, for example, *United States v. Morgan*, 118 F.Supp. 621 (S.D.N.Y. 1953). This case is often cited as a classic example of how to judge joint ventures under the rule of reason.

Business Law in Action

Price Fixing in the Ivy League

In 1989, the Department of Justice (DOJ) undertook an investigation of alleged price-fixing behavior among a group of the nation's most prestigious colleges and universities. The schools involved included the eight Ivy League schools (Brown, Columbia, Cornell, Dartmouth, Harvard, Princeton, the University of Pennsylvania, and Yale) and the Massachusetts Institute of Technology (MIT). The DOJ learned that since 1958, these schools had met twice a year to trade information on the financial aid packages that they would offer to incoming students and their families. The "Ivy Overlap Group" developed methods for analyzing students' financial needs, agreed not to award any merit scholarships, and compared and adjusted proposed family contributions. The goal of each review meeting was to make sure that each of the 10,000 or so students who applied to more than one of the schools in the group would be offered the same basic financial aid package.

The Ivy Group also shared information about proposed tuition increases. Throughout the year, the universities exchanged information on proposed tuition increases for the following year, and they adjusted their tuition rates accordingly. Rates for room and board were also discussed and resulted in similar rates being charged across a wide variety of universities. Room and board at Harvard, for example, located in very expensive Boston, were the same as at Brown, in much less expensive Providence, Rhode Island.

The Ivy schools argued that such meetings were necessary to prevent the schools from engaging in a bidding war for talented students. According to the Ivy Group, if each school offered similar financial aid, students would be free to choose a college based on academic, rather than financial, considerations. The DOJ disagreed. After a two-year investigation, the DOJ charged the colleges with price fixing in violation of Section 1 of the Sherman Act. All of the colleges except MIT eventually entered into "consent decrees," agreeing that they would no longer discuss current financial aid information among themselves. MIT, however, confident in the integrity of its financial aid process, refused to give in and went to trial.

At trial, one of MIT's arguments focused on the fact that educational institutions are not commercial and should not be subject to laws governing the commercial world, including antitrust laws. In response to MIT's contention, the judge stated that he could "conceive of few aspects of higher education that are more commercial than the price charged to students." The court also disagreed with MIT's argument that the Ivy Group's agreements on financial aid were beneficial to students, because the nearly uniform costs left students free to select colleges based on factors other than price. The court found that the agreements "created a horizontal restraint which interfered with the natural functioning of the marketplace by eliminating students' ability to consider price differences when choosing a school and by depriving students of the ability to receive financial incentives which competition between those schools may have generated." "Indeed," said the judge, "the member institutions formed the Ivy Overlap Group for the very purpose of eliminating economic competition for students." Declaring that the court "has no choice but to respect 102 years of our nation's antitrust policy," the judge ruled that the participation of MIT in the Ivy Group's agreements in respect to financial aid violated the antitrust laws.[a]

a. *United States v. Brown University*, 805 F.Supp. 288 (E.D.Pa. 1992). This ruling was later reversed.

Section 1—Vertical Restraints

A **vertical restraint** of trade is one that results from an agreement between firms at different levels in the manufacturing and distribution process. In contrast to horizontal relationships, which occur at the same level of operation, vertical relationships encompass the entire chain of production: the purchase of inventory, basic manufacturing, distribution to wholesalers, and eventual sale of a product at the retail level. For some products, these distinct phases may be carried on by different firms. In other instances, a single firm may carry out two or more of the different functional phases. Such a firm is considered to be a **vertically integrated firm.**

Even though firms operating at different functional levels are not in direct competition with one another, they are in competition with other firms. Thus, agreements between firms standing in a vertical relationship do significantly affect com-

VERTICAL RESTRAINT
Any restraint on trade created by agreements between firms at different levels in the manufacturing and distribution process.

VERTICALLY INTEGRATED FIRM
A firm that carries out two or more functional phases (manufacture, distribution, retailing, etc.) of a product.

petition. Some vertical restraints are *per se* violations of Section 1; others are judged under the rule of reason. Vertical restraints are discussed in the following sections.

Territorial or Customer Restrictions In arranging for the distribution of its product, a manufacturing firm often wishes to insulate dealers from direct competition with other dealers selling the product. In this endeavor, it may institute territorial restrictions, or it may attempt to prohibit wholesalers or retailers from reselling the product to certain classes of buyers, such as competing retailers. There may be legitimate, procompetitive reasons for imposing such territorial or customer restrictions. For example, a manufacturer of copying machines may wish to prevent a dealer from cutting costs and undercutting rivals by providing copiers without promotion or customer service, while relying on a nearby dealer to provide these services. This is an example of the "free rider" problem.

Vertical territorial and customer restrictions are judged under a rule of reason. The following case, *Continental T.V., Inc. v. GTE Sylvania, Inc.*, overturned the United States Supreme Court's earlier stance, which had been set out in *United States v. Arnold, Schwinn & Co.*[7] In *Schwinn*, the Court had held such restrictions to be *per se* violations of Section 1 of the Sherman Act. The *Continental* case has been heralded as one of the most important antitrust cases since the 1940s. It marked a definite shift from rigid characterization of these kinds of vertical restraints to a more flexible, economic analysis of the restraints under the rule of reason.

Case 30.3 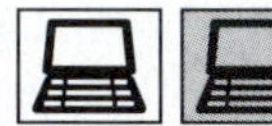

CONTINENTAL T.V., INC. v. GTE SYLVANIA, INC.

Supreme Court of the United States, 1977.
433 U.S. 36,
97 S.Ct. 2549,
53 L.Ed.2d 568.

HISTORICAL AND ECONOMIC SETTING *Since the passage of the antitrust laws around the turn of the century, the courts have been skeptical of any business action that appeared to restrain commerce, having long agreed that the "heart of our national economic policy [is] faith in the value of competition."*[a] *In determining what is and what is not permitted under the antitrust laws, the courts have sometimes applied a rigid standard to business conduct. The trend, however, has been to establish a flexible, rather than a rigid, standard, particularly as to conduct that is considered to have procompetitive benefits. Under a flexible standard, a business practice that is considered a criminal offense in one decade may be judged a corporate virtue in the next. In the mid-1970s, for example, the United States Supreme Court began to qualify or overrule many of its previous decisions that prohibited certain business practices as* per se *violations of the antitrust laws. The Court appeared to be focusing on economic considerations, such as consumer welfare,*[b] *economic efficiency,*[c] *and interbrand versus intrabrand competition.*

FACTS GTE Sylvania, Inc., a manufacturer of television sets, adopted a franchise plan limiting the number of franchises granted in any given geographic area and requiring each franchise to sell Sylvania products only from the location or locations at which they were franchised. A franchise did not constitute an exclusive territory, and Sylvania retained sole discretion to increase the number of retailers in an area, depending on the success or failure of existing retailers in developing their market. Continental T.V., Inc., was a retailer under Sylvania's franchise plan. Shortly after Sylvania proposed a new franchise that would compete with Continental, Sylvania terminated Continental's franchise, and a suit was brought for money owed. Continental claimed that Sylvania's vertically restrictive franchise system violated Section 1 of the Sherman Act. The district court held for Continental, and Sylvania appealed. The appellate court reversed the trial court's decision. Continental appealed to the United States Supreme Court.

ISSUE Was Sylvania's action a *per se* violation of Section 1 of the Sherman Act?

a. *Standard Oil Co. v. Federal Trade Commission*, 340 U.S. 231, 71 S.Ct. 240, 95 L.Ed. 239 (1951).

b. *Reiter v. Sonotone Corp.*, 442 U.S. 330, 99 S.Ct. 2326, 60 L.Ed.2d 931 (1979).

c. *Broadcast Music, Inc. v. Columbia Broadcasting System, Inc.*, 441 U.S. 1, 99 S.Ct. 1551, 60 L.Ed.2d 1 (1979).

7. 388 U.S. 365, 87 S.Ct. 1856, 18 L.Ed.2d 1249 (1967).

Case 30.3—Continued

DECISION No. The United States Supreme Court upheld the appellate court's reversal of the district court's decision. Sylvania's vertical system, which was not price restrictive, did not constitute a *per se* violation of Section 1 of the Sherman Act.

REASON The fact that Sylvania restricted franchise retailers in their locations, even though title in the televisions had passed to the retailers, was a violation of the Sherman Act only if the facts and circumstances indicated that the restrictions were unreasonable. Two facts militated against a *per se* rule here. The restrictions were between a manufacturer and a retailer instead of between two entities on the same level (for example, two retailers or two manufacturers), and no price restrictions were involved. The Court noted that although vertical restrictions may reduce competition, they can also stimulate interbrand competition, because the restrictions may allow the manufacturer "to achieve certain efficiencies in the distribution of his products."

Resale Price Maintenance Agreements An agreement between a manufacturer and a distributor or retailer in which the manufacturer specifies what the retail prices of its products must be is referred to as a **resale price maintenance agreement.** Resale price maintenance agreements, also known as *fair trade agreements*, were authorized for many years under *fair trade laws.* Today, these vertical price-fixing agreements are normally considered to be *per se* violations of Section 1 of the Sherman Act. Although manufacturers can determine the retail prices of their products when they are sold through their own stores or outlets, they may only *suggest* retail prices for their products when the products are sold by independent retailers.

RESALE PRICE MAINTENANCE AGREEMENT
An agreement between a manufacturer and a retailer in which the manufacturer specifies the minimum retail price of its products. Resale price maintenance agreements are illegal *per se* under the Sherman Act.

Refusals to Deal As discussed previously, joint refusals to deal (group boycotts) are subject to sharp scrutiny under Section 1 of the Sherman Act. A single manufacturer acting unilaterally, however, is generally free to deal, or not to deal, with whomever it wishes. For instance, in vertical arrangements, even though a manufacturer cannot set retail prices for its products, it can refuse to deal with retailers or dealers that cut prices to levels substantially below the manufacturer's suggested retail prices. In *United States v. Colgate & Co.,*[8] for example, the United States Supreme Court held that a manufacturer's advance announcement that it would not sell to price cutters was not a violation of the Sherman Act.

There are instances, however, in which a unilateral refusal to deal violates antitrust laws. These instances involve offenses proscribed under Section 2 of the Sherman Act and occur only if (1) the firm refusing to deal has, or is likely to acquire, monopoly power and (2) the refusal is likely to have an anticompetitive effect on a particular market.

"We pray that you will be pleased to make a law ordering [that all doors and windows] should be closed, by which the light of the sun can penetrate into houses, to the injury of the flourishing trade [candle making] with which we have endowed our country."

Frédéric Bastiat, 1801–1850
(French economist)

❖ Section 2 of the Sherman Act

Section 1 of the Sherman Act proscribes certain concerted, or joint, activities that restrain trade. In contrast, Section 2 condemns "every person who shall monopolize, or attempt to monopolize." There are two distinct types of behavior that are subject to sanction under Section 2: *monopolization* and *attempts to monopolize.* In this section, we examine both of these Section 2 offenses.

A tactic that may be involved in either offense is **predatory pricing.** Predatory pricing involves an attempt by one firm to drive its competitors from the market by selling its product at prices substantially *below* the normal costs of production; once the competitors are eliminated, the firm will attempt to recapture its losses and go on to earn very high profits by driving prices up far above their competitive level.

PREDATORY PRICING
The pricing of a product below cost with the intent to drive competitors out of the market.

8. 250 U.S. 300, 39 S.Ct. 465, 63 L.Ed. 992 (1919).

Monopolization

MONOPOLIZATION
The possession of monopoly power in the relevant market and the willful acquisition or maintenance of the power, as distinguished from growth or development as a consequence of a superior product, business acumen, or historic accident. A violation of Section 2 of the Sherman Act requires that both of these elements be established.

In *United States v. Grinnell Corp.*,[9] the United States Supreme Court defined the offense of **monopolization** as involving the following two elements: "(1) the possession of monopoly power in the relevant market and (2) the willful acquisition or maintenance of the power as distinguished from growth or development as a consequence of a superior product, business acumen, or historic accident." A violation of Section 2 requires that both these elements—monopoly power and intent to monopolize—be established.

Monopoly Power The Sherman Act does not define *monopoly*. In economic parlance, monopoly refers to control by a single entity. It is well established in antitrust law, however, that a firm may be a monopolist even though it is not the sole seller in a market. Nor is monopoly a function of size alone (for example, a "mom and pop" grocery located in an isolated desert town is a monopolist if it is the only grocery serving that particular market). Size in relation to the market is what matters, because monopoly involves power to affect prices and output. *Monopoly power*, as mentioned earlier in this chapter, exists when a firm has an extremely great amount of market power. If a firm has sufficient market power to control prices and exclude competition, that firm has monopoly power.

As difficult as it is to define market power precisely, it is even more difficult to measure it. As a workable proxy, courts often look to the firm's percentage share of the "relevant market." This is the so-called **market-share test.**[10] A firm generally is considered to have monopoly power if its share of the relevant market is 70 percent or more. This is not an absolute dictum, however. It is only a loose rule of thumb; in some cases, a smaller share may be held to constitute monopoly power.[11]

MARKET-SHARE TEST
The primary measure of monopoly power. A firm's market share is the percentage of a market that the firm controls.

The relevant market consists of two elements: (1) a relevant product market and (2) a relevant geographic market. What should the relevant product market include? No doubt, it must include all products that, although produced by different firms, have identical attributes, such as sugar. Yet products that are not identical may sometimes be substituted for one another. Coffee may be substituted for tea, for example. In defining the relevant product market, the key issue is the degree of interchangeability between products. If one product is a sufficient substitute for another, the two products are considered to be part of the same product market.

The second component of the relevant market is the geographical boundaries of the market. For products that are sold nationwide, the geographical boundaries of the market encompass the entire United States. If a producer and its competitors sell in only a limited area (one in which customers have no access to other sources of the product), then the geographical market is limited to that area. A national firm may thus compete in several distinct areas and have monopoly power in one area but not in another.

The Intent Requirement Monopoly power, in and of itself, does not constitute the offense of monopolization under Section 2 of the Sherman Act. The offense also requires intent to monopolize. A dominant market share may be the result of business acumen or the development of a superior product. It may simply be the result of historical accident. In these situations, the acquisition of monopoly power is not an antitrust violation. Indeed, it would be counter to society's interest to

9. 384 U.S. 563, 86 S.Ct. 1698, 16 L.Ed.2d 778 (1966).

10. Other measures of market power have been devised, but the market-share test is the most widely used.

11. This standard was first articulated by Justice Learned Hand in *United States v. Aluminum Co. of America*, 148 F.2d 416 (2d Cir. 1945). A 90 percent share was held to be clear evidence of monopoly power. Anything less than 64 percent, said Justice Hand, made monopoly power doubtful, and anything less than 30 percent was clearly not monopoly power. This is merely a rule of thumb, however; it is not a binding principle of law.

condemn every firm that acquired a position of power because it was well managed, efficient, and marketed a product desired by consumers. If, however, a firm possesses market power as a result of carrying out some purposeful act to acquire or maintain that power through anticompetitive means, then it is in violation of Section 2.

In most monopolization cases, intent may be inferred from evidence that the firm had monopoly power and engaged in anticompetitive behavior.

Attempts to Monopolize

Section 2 also prohibits **attempted monopolization** of a market. Any action challenged as an attempt to monopolize must have been specifically intended to exclude competitors and garner monopoly power. In addition, the attempt must have had a "dangerous" probability of success; that is, although actual monopolization is not required, only *serious* threats of monopolization are condemned as violations. The probability cannot be dangerous unless the alleged offender possesses some degree of market power.

ATTEMPTED MONOPOLIZATION
Any actions by a firm to eliminate competition and gain monopoly power.

❖ The Clayton Act

In 1914, Congress attempted to strengthen federal antitrust laws by enacting the Clayton Act. The Clayton Act was aimed at specific anticompetitive or monopolistic practices that were not covered by the Sherman Act. The substantive provisions of the act deal with four distinct forms of business behavior, which are declared illegal but not criminal. With regard to each of the four provisions, the act's prohibitions are qualified by the general condition that the behavior is illegal only if it substantially tends to lessen competition or tends to create monopoly power. The major offenses under the Clayton Act are set out in Sections 2, 3, 7, and 8 of the act.

"The commerce of the world is conducted by the strong, and usually it operates against the weak."

Henry Ward Beecher, 1813–1887
(American abolitionist leader)

Section 2—Price Discrimination

Section 2 of the Clayton Act prohibits **price discrimination,** which occurs when a seller charges different prices to competitive buyers for identical goods. Because businesses frequently circumvented Section 2, Congress strengthened this section by amending it with the passage of the Robinson-Patman Act in 1936. As amended, Section 2 prohibits certain price discrimination that cannot be justified by differences in production, transportation, or other costs due to a particular buyer's purchase. To violate Section 2, the seller must be engaged in interstate commerce, and the effect of the price discrimination must be to substantially lessen competition. Under the Robinson-Patman Act, a seller is prohibited from reducing the price of a product to one buyer below the prices charged the buyer's competitors unless it can justify the reduction by demonstrating that the lower price was charged temporarily "in good faith to meet an equally low price of a competitor." [12]

PRICE DISCRIMINATION
A seller's setting of prices in such a way that two competing buyers pay two different prices for an identical product or service.

Section 3—Exclusionary Practices

Under Section 3 of the Clayton Act, sellers or lessors cannot sell or lease goods "on the condition, agreement or understanding that the * * * purchaser or lessee thereof shall not use or deal in the goods * * * of a competitor or competitors of the seller." In effect, this section prohibits two types of vertical agreements involving exclusionary practices—exclusive-dealing contracts and tying arrangements.

12. *United States v. United States Gypsum Co.,* 438 U.S. 422, 98 S.Ct. 2864, 57 L.Ed.2d 845 (1978).

EXCLUSIVE-DEALING CONTRACT
An agreement under which a producer of goods agrees to sell its goods exclusively through one distributor.

Exclusive-Dealing Contracts A contract under which a seller forbids a buyer to purchase products from the seller's competitors is called an **exclusive-dealing contract.** A seller is prohibited from making an exclusive-dealing contract under Section 3 if the effect of the contract is "to substantially lessen competition or tend to create a monopoly." The leading exclusive-dealing decision was made by the Supreme Court in the case of *Standard Oil Co. of California v. United States.*[13] In this case, the then-largest gasoline seller in the nation made exclusive-dealing contracts with independent stations in seven western states. The contracts involved 16 percent of all retail outlets, whose sales were approximately 7 percent of all retail sales in that market. The Court noted that the market was substantially concentrated because the seven largest gasoline suppliers all used exclusive-dealing contracts with their independent retailers and together controlled 65 percent of the market. Looking at market conditions after the arrangements were instituted, the Court found that market shares were extremely stable, and entry into the market was apparently restricted. Thus, the Court held that Section 3 had been violated because competition was "foreclosed in a substantial share" of the relevant market.

TYING ARRANGEMENT
An agreement between a buyer and a seller under which the buyer of a specific product or service is obligated to purchase additional products or services from the seller.

Tying Arrangements A seller may condition the sale of a product (the tying product) on the buyer's agreement to purchase another product (the tied product) produced or distributed by the same seller. Such an agreement is called a **tying arrangement,** or *tie-in sales agreement.* The legality of such an agreement depends on many factors, particularly the purpose of the agreement and the agreement's likely effect on competition in the relevant markets (there are two markets because the agreement involves both the tying product and the tied product). In 1936, for example, the United States Supreme Court held that International Business Machines and Remington Rand had violated Section 3 of the Clayton Act by requiring the purchase of their own machine cards (the tied product) as a condition to the leasing of their tabulation machines (the tying product). Because only these two firms sold completely automated tabulation machines, the Court concluded that each possessed market power sufficient to "substantially lessen competition" through the tying arrangements.[14]

Section 3 of the Clayton Act has been held to apply only to commodities, not to services. But tying arrangements also can be considered agreements that restrain trade in violation of Section 1 of the Sherman Act. Thus, those cases involving tying arrangements of services have been brought under Section 1 of the Sherman Act. Traditionally, the courts have held tying arrangements brought under the Sherman Act to be illegal *per se.* In recent years, however, courts have shown a willingness to look at factors that are important in a rule-of-reason analysis. This is another example of the "soft" *per se* rule referred to earlier in this chapter.

Section 7—Mergers

Under Section 7 of the Clayton Act, a person or business organization cannot hold stock and/or assets in more than one person or business "where the effect * * * may be to substantially lessen competition." Section 7 is the statutory authority for preventing mergers that could result in monopoly power or a substantial lessening of competition in the marketplace.

MARKET CONCENTRATION
The percentage of a particular firm's market sales in a relevant market area.

A crucial consideration in most merger cases is **market concentration.** Determining market concentration involves allocating percentage market shares among the various companies in the relevant market. When a small number of companies share a larger part of the market, the market is concentrated. For example, if the four largest grocery stores in Chicago accounted for 80 percent of all retail food

13. 37 U.S. 293, 69 S.Ct. 1051, 93 L.Ed. 1371 (1949).

14. *International Business Machines Corp. v. United States,* 298 U.S. 131, 56 S.Ct. 701, 80 L.Ed. 1085 (1936).

sales, the market clearly would be concentrated in those four firms. Competition, however, is not necessarily diminished solely as a result of market concentration, and other factors will be considered in determining whether a merger will violate Section 7. Another concept of particular importance in evaluating the effects of a merger is whether the merger will make it more difficult for potential competitors to enter the relevant market.

We look here at how Section 7 applies to three types of mergers: horizontal mergers, vertical mergers, and conglomerate mergers.

"Combinations are no less unlawful because they have not as yet resulted in restraint."

Hugo L. Black, 1886–1971
(Associate justice of the United States Supreme Court, 1937–1971)

Horizontal Mergers Mergers between firms that compete with each other in the same market are called **horizontal mergers.** If a horizontal merger creates an entity with anything other than a small percentage market share, the merger will be presumed illegal. This is because, according to the United States Supreme Court's interpretation, Congress, in amending Section 7 of the Clayton Act in 1950, intended to prevent mergers that increase market concentration.[15] Three other factors are also considered: overall concentration of the relevant market, the relevant market's history of tending toward concentration, and whether the apparent design of the merger is to establish market power or restrict competition.

HORIZONTAL MERGER
A merger between two businesses or persons competing in the marketplace.

The Court's intense focus on market share in horizontal merger decisions has made the definition of relevant markets especially critical in most Section 7 cases. It also prompted the Federal Trade Commission (FTC) and the Department of Justice (DOJ) to establish guidelines, revised in 1992, indicating which mergers would be challenged.

Under the guidelines, the first factor to be considered in determining whether a merger will be challenged is the degree of concentration in the relevant market. In determining market concentration, the FTC and DOJ employ what is known as the **Herfindahl-Hirschman Index (HHI).** The HHI is the sum of the squares of the percentage market shares of the firms in the relevant market. For example, if there are four firms with shares of 30 percent, 30 percent, 20 percent, and 20 percent, respectively, then the HHI equals 2,600 ($30^2 + 30^2 + 20^2 + 20^2 = 2{,}600$). If the premerger HHI is less than 1,000, then the market is unconcentrated, and the merger will not likely be challenged. If the premerger HHI is between 1,000 and 1,800, the industry is moderately concentrated, and the merger will be challenged only if it increases the HHI by 100 points or more.[16] If the HHI is greater than 1,800, the market is highly concentrated. In a highly concentrated market, a merger that produces an increase in the HHI between 50 and 100 points raises significant competitive concerns. Mergers that produce an increase in the HHI of more than 100 points in a highly concentrated market are deemed likely to enhance the market power of the surviving corporation.

HERFINDAHL-HIRSCHMAN INDEX (HHI)
An index of market power used to calculate whether a merger of two corporations will result in monopoly power and thus violate antitrust laws.

The guidelines stress that determining market share and market concentration is only the starting point in analyzing the potential anticompetitive effects of a merger. Before deciding to challenge a merger, the FTC and the DOJ will look at a number of other factors, including the ease of entry into the relevant market, economic efficiency, the financial condition of the merging firms, the nature and price of the product or products involved, and so on. If a firm is a leading one—having at least a 35 percent market share and twice that of the next leading firm—any merger of that firm with a firm having as little as a 1 percent share will be challenged.

Vertical Mergers A **vertical merger** occurs when a company at one stage of production acquires a company at a higher or lower stage of production. An example

VERTICAL MERGER
A combining of two firms, one of which purchases goods for resale from the other. If a producer or wholesaler acquires a retailer, it is a *forward* vertical merger. If a retailer or distributor acquires its producer, it is a *backward* vertical merger.

15. *Brown Shoe Co. v. United States,* 370 U.S. 294, 82 S.Ct. 1502, 8 L.Ed.2d 510 (1962).

16. Compute the change in the index by doubling the product of the merging firms' premerger market shares. For example, a merger between a firm with a 5 percent share and one with a 6 percent share will increase the HHI by $2 \times (5 \times 6) = 60$.

of a vertical merger is a company merging with one of its suppliers or retailers. Courts in the past have almost exclusively focused on "foreclosure" in assessing vertical mergers. Foreclosure occurs because competitors of the merging firms lose opportunities to either sell or buy products from the merging firms. For example, in *United States v. E. I. du Pont de Nemours & Co.*,[17] du Pont was challenged for acquiring a considerable amount of General Motors (GM) stock. In holding that the transaction was illegal, the United States Supreme Court noted that stock acquisition would enable du Pont to foreclose other sellers of fabrics and finishes from selling to GM, which then accounted for 50 percent of all auto fabric and finishes purchases. Whether a vertical merger has been deemed illegal has depended on several factors, including market concentration, barriers to entry into the market, and the apparent intent of the merging parties. Mergers that do not prevent competitors of either of the merging firms from competing in a segment of the market will not be condemned as foreclosing competition and will be held legal. The foreclosure of an otherwise open segment of the market is the subject of the following case.

Case 30.4
FORD MOTOR CO. v. UNITED STATES

Supreme Court of the United States, 1972.
405 U.S. 562,
92 S.Ct. 1142,
31 L.Ed.2d 492.

HISTORICAL AND ECONOMIC SETTING *In the 1960s, spark plug manufacturers sold spark plugs to automobile manufacturers for about six cents per plug, even when their costs were about eighteen cents per plug. The spark plug manufacturers recouped their losses in the so-called aftermarket. An automobile required, during its useful life, about five replacement sets of plugs. By custom and practice among mechanics, each set was usually replaced with plugs of the brand that the manufacturer had installed.*

FACTS Ford Motor Company purchased Autolite Company, a manufacturer of spark plugs. Ford, Chrysler, and General Motors together produced 90 percent of American automobiles. The spark plug market was dominated by Champion (50 percent), General Motors (30 percent), and Autolite (15 percent). Ford had planned to begin manufacturing its own spark plugs but decided to buy Autolite instead. Following Ford's purchase of Autolite, Champion was the only independent spark plug manufacturer, and five years after Ford's acquisition of Autolite, Champion's share of the spark plug market had been reduced from 50 percent to about 33 percent. The United States brought an action against Ford, claiming that its acquisition of Autolite violated Section 7 of the Clayton Act because it substantially lessened competition in the spark plug market. When the trial court ordered Ford to divest itself of (rid itself of ownership rights in) the Autolite assets, Ford appealed to the United States Supreme Court.

ISSUE Did Ford's acquisition of Autolite violate Section 7 of the Clayton Act by foreclosing a sufficiently large segment of the spark plug market to competition?

DECISION Yes. The acquisition was declared to be unlawful and in violation of Section 7 of the Clayton Act. The ruling of the district court was affirmed.

REASON The United States Supreme Court concluded that if the acquisition were allowed, the spark plug industry would become as concentrated as the automobile industry, and entry into the spark plug market by new firms would be impossible. According to the Court, "[a]s a result of the acquisition of Autolite, the structure of the spark plug industry changed drastically * * *. Ford, which before the acquisition was the largest purchaser of spark plugs from the independent manufacturers, became a major manufacturer. The result was to foreclose to the remaining independent spark plug manufacturers the substantial segment of the market previously open to competitive selling."

CONGLOMERATE MERGER
A merger between firms that do not compete with each other because they are in different markets (as opposed to horizontal and vertical mergers).

Conglomerate Mergers There are three general types of **conglomerate mergers:** market-extension, product-extension, and diversification mergers. A market-extension

17. 353 U.S. 586, 77 S.Ct. 872, 1 L.Ed.2d 1057 (1957).

merger occurs when a firm seeks to sell its product in a new market by merging with a firm already established in that market. A product-extension merger occurs when a firm seeks to add a closely related product to its existing line by merging with a firm already producing that product. For example, a manufacturer might seek to extend its line of household products to include floor wax by acquiring a leading manufacturer of floor wax. Diversification occurs when a firm merges with another firm that offers a product or service wholly unrelated to the first firm's existing activities. An example of a diversification merger is an automobile manufacturer's acquisition of a motel chain. The following case involves a product-extension conglomerate merger.

Case 30.5 

FEDERAL TRADE COMMISSION v. PROCTER & GAMBLE CO.

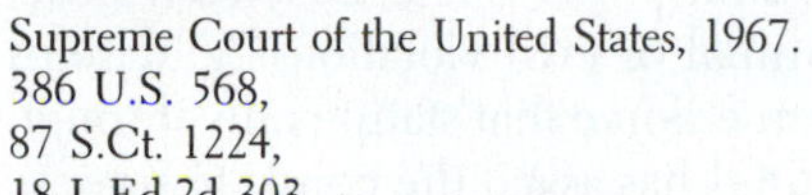

Supreme Court of the United States, 1967.
386 U.S. 568,
87 S.Ct. 1224,
18 L.Ed.2d 303.

HISTORICAL AND SOCIAL SETTING *During the 1960s, corporate mergers—particularly conglomerate mergers—increased significantly in number. Conglomerate mergers presented a special challenge for the courts, because the antitrust laws offered little guidance in regard to these noncompetitive mergers. Rather than formulating a general principle or rule applicable to all conglomerate mergers, the courts have tended to look at the pragmatic, real-world effects of business conglomeration and make their determinations on a case-by-case basis.*

FACTS Procter & Gamble Company (P&G), a large, diversified producer of high-turnover household products, acquired Clorox Chemical Company. At the time, Clorox was the leading manufacturer of household bleach in a highly concentrated market. Purex, the major competitor, did not sell its product in some markets, primarily in the northeastern and mid-Atlantic states. P&G's large advertising budget, along with other factors, allowed it to enjoy economic advantages in advertising its products. The Federal Trade Commission brought an action against P&G claiming that P&G's acquisition of Clorox substantially lessened competition in the market for liquid bleach and thus violated Section 7 of the Clayton Act. Arguing that the merger prevented other bleach products from entering the market, thereby eliminating potential competitors, the FTC ordered P&G to divest itself of the Clorox Company. P&G appealed.

ISSUE Did the merger between P&G and Clorox violate Section 7 of the Clayton Act?

DECISION Yes. The United States Supreme Court held that the merger violated Section 7 of the Clayton Act.

REASON P&G had sought to expand its product line by adding household bleach to it. The Court noted that the markets for the products of P&G and Clorox were highly concentrated; that is, they were already dominated by a few companies. Thus, barriers to entry by potential competitors were already high, and competition was at a minimum. The Court concluded that "[i]n the marketing of soaps, detergents and cleansers, as in the marketing of household liquid bleach, advertising and sales promotion are vital. * * * [T]he substitution of Procter, with its huge assets and advertising advantages, for the already dominant Clorox would dissuade new entrants and discourage active competition from the firms already in the industry due to fear of retaliation by Procter."

Section 8—Interlocking Directorates

Section 8 of the Clayton Act deals with *interlocking directorates*—that is, the practice of having individuals serve as directors on the boards of two or more competing companies simultaneously. Specifically, no person may be a director in two or more competing corporations at the same time if either of the corporations has capital, surplus, or undivided profits aggregating more than $11.37 million or competitive sales of $1.4 million or more. The threshold amounts are adjusted each year by the Federal Trade Commission (FTC). (The amounts given here are those announced by the FTC in 1993.)

❖ The Federal Trade Commission Act

The Federal Trade Commission (FTC) Act was enacted in 1914, the same year the Clayton Act was written into law. Section 5 is the sole substantive provision of the act. It provides, in part, as follows: "Unfair methods of competition in or affecting commerce, and unfair or deceptive acts or practices in or affecting commerce are hereby declared illegal." Section 5 condemns all forms of anticompetitive behavior that are not covered under other federal antitrust laws. The act also created the Federal Trade Commission, an administrative agency with functions that include antitrust enforcement, as well as other duties relating to consumer protection (see Chapter 31).

❖ Enforcement of Antitrust Laws

The federal agencies that enforce the federal antitrust laws are the U.S. Department of Justice (DOJ) and the Federal Trade Commission (FTC). The DOJ can prosecute violations of the Sherman Act as either criminal or civil violations. Violations of the Clayton Act are not crimes, and the DOJ can enforce that statute only through civil proceedings. The various remedies that the DOJ has asked the courts to impose include **divestiture** (making a company give up one or more of its operating functions) and dissolution. The DOJ might force a group of meat packers, for example, to divest itself of control or ownership of butcher shops.

DIVESTITURE
The act of selling one or more of a company's ownership, such as a subsidiary or plant; often mandated by the courts in merger or monopolization cases.

The FTC also enforces the Clayton Act and has sole authority to enforce violations of Section 5 of the Federal Trade Commission Act. FTC actions are effected through administrative orders, but if a firm violates an FTC order, the FTC can seek court sanctions for the violation.

A private party can sue for treble damages and attorneys' fees under Section 4 of the Clayton Act if the party is injured as a result of a violation of any of the federal antitrust laws, except Section 5 of the Federal Trade Commission Act. In some instances, private parties may also seek injunctive relief to prevent antitrust violations. The courts have determined that the ability to sue depends on the directness of the injury suffered by the would-be plaintiff. Thus, a person wishing to sue under the Sherman Act must prove (1) that the antitrust violation either caused or was a substantial factor in causing the injury that was suffered and (2) that the unlawful actions of the accused party affected business activities of the plaintiff that were protected by the antitrust laws.

In recent years, more than 90 percent of all antitrust actions have been brought by private plaintiffs. One reason for this is, of course, that successful plaintiffs may recover three times the damages that they have suffered as a result of the violation. Such recoveries by private plaintiffs for antitrust violations have been rationalized as encouraging people to act as "private attorneys general" who will vigorously pursue antitrust violators on their own initiative.

❖ Exemptions from Antitrust Laws

There are many legislative and constitutional limitations on antitrust enforcement. Most are statutory and judicially created exemptions applying to the following areas:

1. *Labor.* Section 6 of the Clayton Act generally permits labor unions to organize and bargain without violating antitrust laws. Section 20 of the Clayton Act specifies that strikes and other labor activities are not violations of any law of the United

International Perspective

The Growing Popularity of U.S. Antitrust Laws Overseas

Although U.S. courts have not always been consistent or energetic in applying the antitrust laws, they have continued to express their concerns about the allegedly anticompetitive practices of companies operating both here and abroad and the effects of those practices on the American economy. Now other countries have begun adopting their own versions of U.S. antitrust laws to bolster their economies.

Antitrust Rulings in Japan and Europe
In July 1991, the Japan Fair Trade Commission unveiled a new set of guidelines to reduce anticompetitive practices by Japanese companies. These guidelines prohibit companies from agreeing to refuse to sell their products to discounters to eliminate the discounters from a particular market. In addition, companies can no longer give preferential treatment to corporations in which they have significant stockholdings. The rules also purport to address resale price maintenance schemes by prohibiting manufacturers from terminating discount dealers who sell their products for prices below those suggested by the manufacturer. These guidelines were admittedly sought by American trade representatives seeking to reduce Japanese barriers to trade, but their adoption may signal a greater willingness on Japan's part to examine seriously the business practices of its major companies.

The increasing use of American antitrust concepts overseas was also illustrated by a July 1991 decision by the European Court of Justice, upholding a European Commission decision to fine a Dutch chemical company for threatening to engage in below-cost pricing to force a British competitor out of a particular market.[a] Such predatory pricing cases are extremely difficult to prove because of the difficulty of determining whether a particular company is selling above or below cost. The decision was characterized by one European Commission official as a "landmark" because the court established a standard by which predatory pricing may be presumed to exist when prices are set below the cost of production. The standard should make it easier for smaller companies to sue larger companies for using such pricing policies.

Criticisms of the Focus of U.S. Antitrust Policy
Some antitrust specialists have criticized the United States for being far more preoccupied with the business practices of foreign firms than with arguably anticompetitive practices that continue in the United States, such as the ban on foreign airlines' handling domestic routes. Nonetheless, antitrust specialists within the Justice Department and the Federal Trade Commission are increasingly in demand to assist new democracies in Europe, Asia, and Latin America in moving from state monopolies to private enterprise. The collapse of the Soviet Union may well foreshadow requests by the newly independent republics to obtain U.S. technical assistance in revamping their centrally planned economies. Whether U.S. antitrust laws will be palatable when the difficulties of these economic transitions become clear, however, remains to be seen.

a. *AKZO Chemie BV v. Commission of the European Community*, E.C. Ct.Jus., No. C-62/86, July 3, 1991.

States. But a union can lose its exemption if it combines with a nonlabor group rather than acting simply in its own self-interest.
2. *Agricultural associations and fisheries.* Section 6 of the Clayton Act (along with the Capper-Volstead Act of 1922) exempts agricultural cooperatives from the antitrust laws. The Fisheries Cooperative Marketing Act of 1976 exempts from antitrust legislation individuals in the fishing industry who collectively catch, produce, and prepare for market their products. Both exemptions allow members of such co-ops to combine and set prices for a particular product, but they do not allow them to engage in exclusionary practices or restraints of trade directed at competitors.
3. *Insurance.* The McCarran-Ferguson Act of 1945 exempts the insurance business from the antitrust laws whenever state regulation exists. This exemption does not cover boycotts, coërcion, or intimidation on the part of insurance companies.
4. *Foreign trade.* Under the provisions of the 1918 Webb-Pomerane Act, American exporters may engage in cooperative activity to compete with similar foreign asso-

Law in the Extreme

The Singular Status of Baseball

As discussed in this chapter, some activities and organizations, including professional baseball, are exempt from antitrust laws. Why is baseball given this singular status? Why aren't other professional sports also exempted? This perfectly reasonable question has been asked innumerable times, and the answer is always the same: baseball is exempt because in 1922, the United States Supreme Court said that it was.[a] Therefore, a precedent was established to which courts have since adhered.

The 1922 case concerned two baseball leagues, the Federal League and the National League. One of the member clubs in the Federal League (the plaintiff) sued the National League, alleging that the latter had conspired to destroy the Federal League in violation of antitrust laws. According to the plaintiff, the National League bought up some of the Federal League clubs and induced others to leave the league, the result being that the plaintiff was the only club left in the league. The plaintiff also alleged that persons formerly associated with the Federal League, including its president, had joined in the conspiracy.

The trial court found for the plaintiff, but the appellate court reversed the decision, holding that the baseball leagues' activities did not involve interstate commerce and therefore federal antitrust laws did not apply. The United States Supreme Court agreed with the appellate court. Although the Court acknowledged that the clubs were located "in different cities and for the most part different states" and that "constantly repeated travelling on the part of the clubs" was required, the primary business of the clubs was "giving exhibitions of base ball, which are purely state affairs." "It is true," said the Court, "that in order to attain for these exhibitions the great popularity that they have achieved, competitions must be arranged between clubs from different cities and States. But the fact that in order to give the exhibitions the Leagues must induce free persons to cross state lines and must arrange and pay for their doing

a. *Federal Baseball Club of Baltimore, Inc. v. National League of Professional Baseball Clubs*, 259 U.S. 200, 42 S.Ct. 465, 66 L.Ed. 898 (1922).

Law in the Extreme—Continued

The Singular Status of Baseball

so is not enough to change the character of the business." The Court held that these personal efforts were not related to "production" and therefore were not a subject of "commerce." Because neither the state exhibitions nor the interstate travel of the clubs' members involved interstate commerce, the leagues' activities were not within the reach of the antitrust laws.

Under modern interpretations of what constitutes interstate commerce (see, for example, Case 30.1 in this chapter), the Court's decision in the 1922 case would be clearly erroneous. Nonetheless, based on that decision, professional baseball continues to retain its extraordinary status as the only professional sport exempt from antitrust laws.

ciations. Such cooperative activity may not, however, restrain trade within the United States or injure other American exporters. In 1982, the Export Trading Company Act was passed, broadening the Webb-Pomerane Act by permitting the Department of Justice to certify properly qualified export trading companies. Any activity within the scope described by the certificate is exempt from public prosecution under the antitrust laws.

5. *Baseball.* As discussed in this chapter's *Law in the Extreme,* in 1922 the United States Supreme Court held that professional baseball was not within the reach of federal antitrust laws because it did not involve "interstate commerce."

6. *Oil marketing.* The 1935 Interstate Oil Compact allows states to determine quotas on oil that will be marketed in interstate commerce.

7. *Other exemptions.* Other activities exempt from antitrust laws include the following:

   a. Activities approved by the president in furtherance of the defense of our nation (under the Defense Production Act of 1950, as amended).
   b. Cooperative research among small business firms (under the Small Business Administration Act of 1958, as amended).
   c. Research or production of a product, process, or service by joint ventures consisting of competitors (under special federal legislation, including the National Cooperative Research Act of 1984 and the National Cooperative Production Amendments of 1993).
   d. State actions, when the state policy is clearly articulated and the policy is actively supervised by the state.[18]
   e. Activities of regulated industries (such as the transportation, communication, and banking industries) when federal commissions, boards, or agencies (such as the Federal Communications Commission, the Federal Maritime Commission, or the Interstate Commerce Commission) have primary regulatory authority.
   f. Joint efforts by businesspersons to obtain legislative or executive action. This is often referred to as the *Noerr-Pennington doctrine.*[19] For example, video producers might jointly lobby Congress to change the copyright laws, or a video-rental company might sue another video-rental firm, without being

18. See *Parker v. Brown,* 347 U.S. 341, 63 S.Ct. 307, 87 L.Ed. 315 (1943).
19. See *United Mine Workers of America v. Pennington,* 381 U.S. 657, 89 S.Ct. 1585, 14 L.Ed.2d 626 (1965), and *Eastern Railroad Presidents Conference v. Noerr Motor Freight, Inc.,* 365 U.S. 127, 81 S.Ct. 523, 5 L.Ed.2d 464 (1961).

held liable for attempting to restrain trade. Though selfish rather than purely public-minded conduct is permitted, there is an exception: an action will not be protected if it is clear that the action is "objectively baseless in the sense that no reasonable [person] could reasonably expect success on the merits" and it is an attempt to make anticompetitive use of government processes.[20]

20. *Professional Real Estate Investors Inc. v. Columbia Pictures Industries Inc.*, ___ U.S. ___, 113 S.Ct. 1920, 123 L.Ed.2d 611 (1993).

❖ Key Terms

antitrust law 716
attempted monopolization 727
conglomerate merger 730
divestiture 732
exclusive-dealing contract 728
group boycott 721
Herfindahl-Hirschman Index (HHI) 729
horizontal merger 729
horizontal restraint 720
market concentration 728
market power 717
market-share test 726
monopolization 726
monopoly 717
monopoly power 717
***per se* violation 719**
predatory pricing 725
price discrimination 727
price-fixing agreement 720
resale price maintenance agreement 725
rule of reason 719
trust 716
tying arrangement 728
vertical merger 729
vertical restraint 723
vertically integrated firm 723

❖ Chapter Summary: Antitrust Law

Sherman Antitrust Act (1890)	1. *Major provisions:* a. Section 1—Prohibits contracts, combinations, and conspiracies in restraint of trade. (1) Horizontal restraints subject to Section 1 include price-fixing arrangements, group boycotts (joint refusals to deal), horizontal market division, trade association agreements, and joint ventures. (2) Vertical restraints subject to Section 1 include territorial or customer restrictions, resale price maintenance agreements, and refusals to deal. b. Section 2—Prohibits monopolies and attempts or conspiracies to monopolize. 2. *Interpretative rules:* a. Rule of reason—Applied when an anticompetitive agreement may be justified by legitimate benefits. Under the rule of reason, the lawfulness of a trade restraint will be determined by the purpose and effects of the restraint. b. *Per se* rule—Applied to restraints on trade that are so inherently anticompetitive that they cannot be justified and are deemed illegal as a matter of law. 3. *Jurisdictional requirements*—The Sherman Act applies only to activities that have a significant impact on interstate commerce.
Clayton Act (1914)	1. *Major provisions:* a. Section 2—As amended in 1936 by the Robinson-Patman Act, prohibits price discrimination that substantially lessens competition and prohibits a seller engaged in interstate commerce from selling to two or more buyers goods of similar grade and quality at different prices when the result is a substantial lessening of competition or the creation of a competitive injury. b. Section 3—Prohibits exclusionary practices, such as exclusive-dealing contracts and tying arrangements, when the effect may be to substantially lessen competition. c. Section 7—Prohibits mergers when the effect may be to substantially lessen competition or to tend to create a monopoly. (1) Horizontal mergers—The acquisition by merger or consolidation of a competing firm engaged in the same relevant market. Will be unlawful only if a merger results in the merging firms' holding a disproportionate share of the market, resulting in a substantial lessening of competition, and if the merger does not enhance consumer welfare by increasing efficiency of production or marketing.

❖ Chapter Summary: Antitrust Law—Continued

Clayton Act (1914)—Continued	(2) Vertical mergers—The acquisition by a seller of one of its buyers or vice versa. Will be unlawful if the merger prevents competitors of either merging firm from competing in a segment of the market that otherwise would be open to them, resulting in a substantial lessening of competition. (3) Conglomerate mergers—The acquisition of a noncompeting business. Will be unlawful if the merger prevents competitors of either merging firm from competing in a segment of the market that otherwise would be open to them, resulting in a substantial lessening of competition. d. Section 8—Prohibits interlocking directorates.
Federal Trade Commission Act (1914)	Prohibits unfair methods of competition; established and defined the powers of the Federal Trade Commission.
Enforcement of Antitrust Laws	Antitrust laws are enforced by the Department of Justice, by the Federal Trade Commission, and in some cases by private parties, who may be awarded treble damages and attorneys' fees.
Exemptions from Antitrust Laws	1. Labor unions (under Section 6 of the Clayton Act of 1914). 2. Agricultural associations and fisheries (under Section 6 of the Clayton Act of 1914, the Capper-Volstead Act of 1922, and the Fisheries Cooperative Marketing Act of 1976). 3. Insurance—when state regulation exists (under the McCarran-Ferguson Act of 1945, as amended). 4. Export trading companies (under the Webb-Pomerane Act of 1918 and the Export Trading Company Act of 1982). 5. Professional baseball (by 1922 judicial decision). 6. Oil marketing (under the Interstate Oil Compact of 1935). 7. Other activities, including certain national defense actions, special research consortiums, state actions, and actions of certain regulated industries.

❖ Questions and Case Problems

30-1. Sherman Act. An agreement that is blatantly and substantially anticompetitive is deemed a *per se* violation of Section 1 of the Sherman Act. Under what rule is an agreement analyzed if it appears to be anticompetitive but is not a *per se* violation? In making this analysis, what factors will a court consider?

30-2. Clayton Act. The Clayton Act deals with specific practices that are considered to reduce competition or lead to monopoly power but that are not expressly covered by the Sherman Act. What are these practices?

30-3. Antitrust Laws. Assume that the following events take place. Which antitrust law has been *primarily* violated in each event, and why?

(a) Allitron, Inc., and Donovan, Ltd., are interstate competitors selling similar appliances, principally in the states of Indiana, Kentucky, Illinois, and Ohio. Allitron and Donovan agree that Allitron will no longer sell in Ohio and Indiana and that Donovan will no longer sell in Kentucky and Illinois.

(b) The partnership of Alvaredo and Parish is engaged in the oil-wellhead service industry in the states of New Mexico and Colorado. The firm presently has about 40 percent of the market for this service. Webb Corp. competes with the Alvaredo-Parish partnership in the same state area. Webb has approximately 35 percent of the market. Alvaredo and Parish acquire the stock and assets of the Webb Corp.

30-4. Horizontal Restraints. Jorge's Appliance Corp. was a new retail seller of appliances in Sunrise City. Because of its innovative sales techniques and financing, Jorge's caused a substantial loss of sales from the appliance department of No-Glow Department Store, a large chain store with a great deal of buying power. No-Glow told a number of appliance manufacturers that if they continued to sell to Jorge's, No-Glow would discontinue its large volume of purchases from them. The manufacturers immediately stopped selling appliances to Jorge's. Jorge's filed suit against No-Glow and the manufacturers, claiming that their actions constituted an antitrust violation. No-Glow and the manufacturers were able to prove that Jorge's was a small retailer with a small portion of the market. They claimed that because the relevant market was not substantially affected, they were not guilty of restraint of trade. Discuss fully whether there was an antitrust violation.

30-5. Exclusionary Practices. Instant Foto Corp. is a manufacturer of photography film. At the present time, Instant Foto has approximately 50 percent of the market. Instant Foto advertises that the purchase price for Instant Foto film includes photo processing by Instant Foto Corp. Instant Foto claims that its film processing is specially designed to improve the quality of photos taken with Instant Foto film. Is Instant Foto's combination of film purchase and film processing an antitrust violation? Explain.

30-6. **Sherman Act.** In contracts for the 1982–1985 football seasons, the National Collegiate Athletic Association (NCAA), a nonprofit organization, gave the ABC, CBS, and Turner broadcasting networks exclusive rights to negotiate with NCAA colleges to televise games. The contracts limited the number of games that could be televised by the networks, the number of appearances that any one team could make on television, and the amount of money a school could have for televising its games. The NCAA plan also required that a certain number of games between small colleges be televised and prohibited any individual institution from contracting separately for television coverage of its games. Not surprisingly, the NCAA plan drew criticism from major college teams, which felt that they deserved more network appearances and more money than teams from smaller schools. Their efforts to gain a greater voice in the NCAA television policy, though supported by the College Football Association, proved unsuccessful. As a result, the Universities of Oklahoma and Georgia brought an action against the NCAA, alleging that its contracts with the television networks violated Sections 1 and 2 of the Sherman Act. Specifically, the NCAA was charged with price fixing, horizontal limitations on production, group boycott, and monopolization. The NCAA argued, among other things, that as a nonprofit organization with "noneconomic" motives, it should not be subject to antitrust laws. How should the United States Supreme Court rule? [*NCAA v. Board of Regents of the University of Oklahoma*, 468 U.S. 85, 104 S.Ct. 2948, 82 L.Ed.2d 70 (1984)]

30-7. Horizontal Restraints. Radial keratotomy is a surgical procedure to correct myopia (nearsightedness). In 1980, at the recommendation of the National Eye Institute, the American Academy of Ophthalmology, Inc., issued a press release urging "patients, ophthalmologists and hospitals to approach [radial keratotomy] with caution until additional research is completed." Schachar and several other ophthalmologists who specialized in radial keratotomy claimed that the demand for their services declined following the press release. They brought an action against the academy, contending that the press release constituted an illegal horizontal trade restraint. The district court held that the academy had not violated any antitrust law. What will result on appeal? [*Schachar v. American Academy of Ophthalmology, Inc.*, 870 F.2d 397 (7th Cir. 1989)]

30-8. **Sherman Act, Section 1.** To offer a competitive alternative to health maintenance organizations, members of the Maricopa County Medical Society and another medical society established a fee schedule that prescribed the maximum fees that the physicians could charge patients who were insured under specified health insurance plans. The state of Arizona filed a complaint against the medical societies, alleging that the fee schedule constituted a horizontal price-fixing conspiracy and a *per se* violation of Section 1 of the Sherman Act. The medical societies claimed that the *per se* rule should not apply because (1) the medical societies were professional organizations, (2) the agreement fixed maximum prices, not minimum or uniform prices, (3) the judiciary had insufficient experience in the medical industry to justify applying the *per se* rule, and (4) the fee schedule was justified by its procompetitive effects. The district and appellate courts both agreed with the medical societies that the case should not be judged under the *per se* rule. What will the United States Supreme Court decide? [*Arizona v. Maricopa County Medical Society*, 457 U.S. 332, 102 S.Ct. 2466, 73 L.Ed.2d 48 (1982)]

30-9. Tying Arrangements. Dr. Beard, an osteopathic physician specializing in radiology, worked for G. S. Bucholz, Inc. Bucholz was the exclusive provider of radiological services to Parkview Hospital. When Beard resigned from his position at Bucholz, he had every intention of providing radiological services himself to the patients at Parkview, but the Parkview administration informed him that the hospital had an exclusive contract with Bucholz for the provision of radiological services and that Beard would no longer be permitted to work in Parkview's radiology department. Beard sued Parkview, alleging that the exclusive contract between the hospital and Bucholz was a tying arrangement in violation of Section 1 of the Sherman Act. Parkview claimed that its arrangement with Bucholz ensured responsibility and accountability for the radiology department and guaranteed the availability of services when needed. Under the terms of the agreement between Bucholz and Parkview, Bucholz billed patients directly for the services it provided; Parkview did not get a portion of any fees charged by Bucholz. Did the exclusive contract between Parkview and Bucholz violate Section 1 of the Sherman Act? Discuss fully. [*Beard v. Parkview Hospital*, 912 F.2d 138 (6th Cir. 1990)]

30-10. **Sherman Act, Section 2.** For some time, the four major and independently owned downhill skiing facilities in Aspen, Colorado—Ajax, Aspen Highlands, Buttermilk, and Snowmass—offered an "all-Aspen" skiing ticket that could be used at any of the four facilities. The proceeds of the all-Aspen ticket sales were distributed to the four facilities in proportion to the number of skiers using each one. By 1977, Aspen Skiing Co. had acquired ownership of Ajax, Buttermilk, and Snowmass. The company discontinued the all-Aspen ticket, offering instead a ticket that could be used by skiers only at its three facilities. As a result of Aspen Skiing Co.'s activities, Aspen Highlands' share of the skiing market declined from 20 percent in 1977 to only 11 percent by 1981. Aspen Highlands brought an action against Aspen Skiing Co., alleging that the latter had monopolized the Aspen skiing market and that its discontinuation of the all-Aspen ticket sales constituted an intentional attempt to misuse that power in violation of Section 2 of the Sherman Act. Aspen Skiing Co. claimed that its actions represented nothing more than a refusal to participate in a cooperative venture with a competitor and therefore could not possibly be illegal under antitrust laws. Which party will prevail in court, and why? [*Aspen Skiing Co. v. Aspen Highlands Skiing Corp.*, 472 U.S. 585, 105 S.Ct. 2847, 86 L.Ed.2d 467 (1985)]

30-11. Sherman Act, Section 1. Hartwell and Business Electronics Corp. were both authorized by Sharp Electronics to sell Sharp electronic products in the Houston, Texas, area. Business Electronics continuously sold Sharp products at below suggested retail prices. Hartwell complained to Sharp

Electronics about its rival's price-cutting tactics, and Sharp Electronics eventually terminated Business Electronics' dealership. Business Electronics brought an action, claiming that Sharp and Hartwell had conspired together to create a vertical restraint of trade that was illegal *per se* under Section 1 of the Sherman Act. Does Sharp's termination of Business Electronics' dealership constitute a *per se* violation of Section 1, or should the rule of reason apply? Discuss fully. [*Business Electronics Corp. v. Sharp Electronics Corp.*, 485 U.S. 717, 108 S.Ct. 1515, 99 L.Ed.2d 806 (1988)]

30-12. Sherman Act, Section 1. Harcourt Brace Jovanovich Legal and Professional Publications (HBJ), the nation's largest provider of bar review materials and lecture services, began offering a Georgia bar review course in 1976. It was in direct, and often intense, competition with BRG of Georgia, Inc., the other main provider of bar review courses in Georgia, from 1977 to 1979. In early 1980, HBJ and BRG entered into an agreement that gave BRG the exclusive right to market HBJ's materials in Georgia and to use its trade name, Bar/Bri. The parties agreed that HBJ would not compete with BRG in Georgia and that BRG would not compete with HBJ outside of Georgia. Immediately after the 1980 agreement, the price of BRG's course was increased from $150 to over $400. Jay Palmer, a former law student, brought an action against the two firms, alleging that the 1980 agreement violated Section 1 of the Sherman Act. What will the court decide? Discuss fully. [*Palmer v. BRG of Georgia, Inc.*, 498 U.S. 46, 111 S.Ct. 401, 112 L.Ed.2d 349 (1990)]

30-13. Tying Arrangements. Eastman-Kodak Co. has about a 20 percent share of the highly competitive market for high-volume photocopiers and microfilm equipment and controls nearly the entire market for replacement parts for its equipment (which are not interchangeable with parts for other manufacturers' equipment). Prior to 1985, Kodak sold replacement parts for its equipment without significant restrictions. As a result, a number of independent service organizations (ISOs) purchased Kodak parts to use when repairing and servicing Kodak copiers. In 1985, Kodak changed its policy to prevent the ISOs from competing with Kodak's own service organizations. It ceased selling parts to ISOs and refused to sell replacement parts to its customers unless they agreed *not* to have their equipment serviced by ISOs. In 1987, Image Technical Services, Inc., and seventeen other ISOs sued Kodak, alleging that Kodak's policy was a tying arrangement in violation of Section 1 of the Sherman Act. Kodak claimed that its policy was not an illegal tying arrangement. It reasoned that because it had no market power with respect to its equipment, it had no market power with respect to replacement parts. In other words, it could not raise the price of replacement parts and service beyond competitive rates because if it did, it would lose customers, who would purchase other manufacturers' equipment. Assuming that Kodak does not have market power in the market for photocopying and microfilm equipment, does Kodak's restrictive policy constitute an illegal tying arrangement? Does it violate antitrust laws in any way? Discuss fully. [*Eastman Kodak Co. v. Image Technical Services, Inc.*, ___U.S.___, 112 S.Ct. 2072, 119 L.Ed.2d 265 (1992)]

A Question of Ethics and Social Responsibility

30-14. *A group of lawyers in the District of Columbia regularly acted as court-appointed attorneys for indigent defendants in District of Columbia criminal cases. At a meeting of the Superior Court Trial Lawyers Association (SCTLA), the attorneys agreed to stop providing such representation until the district increased their compensation. Their subsequent boycott had a severe impact on the district's criminal justice system, and the District of Columbia gave in to the lawyers' demands for higher pay. After the lawyers had returned to work, the Federal Trade Commission filed a complaint against the SCTLA and four of its officers and, after an investigation, ruled that the SCTLA's activities constituted an illegal group boycott in violation of antitrust laws.* [Federal Trade Commission v. Superior Court Trial Lawyers Association, *493 U.S. 411, 110 S.Ct. 768, 107 L.Ed.2d 851 (1990)*]

1. The SCTLA obviously was aware of the negative impact its decision would have on the district's criminal justice system. Given this fact, do you think the lawyers behaved ethically?
2. On appeal, the SCTLA claimed that its boycott was undertaken to publicize the fact that attorneys were underpaid and that the boycott thus constituted an expression protected by the First Amendment. Do you agree with this argument?
3. Labor unions have the right to strike when negotiations between labor and management fail to result in agreement. Do you think that it is fair for members of the SCTLA to be prohibited from "striking" against their employer, the District of Columbia, simply because the SCTLA is a professional organization and not a labor union?

For Critical Analysis

30-15. *Critics of antitrust law claim that in the long run, competitive market forces will eliminate private monopolies unless they are fostered by government regulation. They cite as an example the decline of International Business Machines Corp. Do you agree with these critics? Why or why not?*

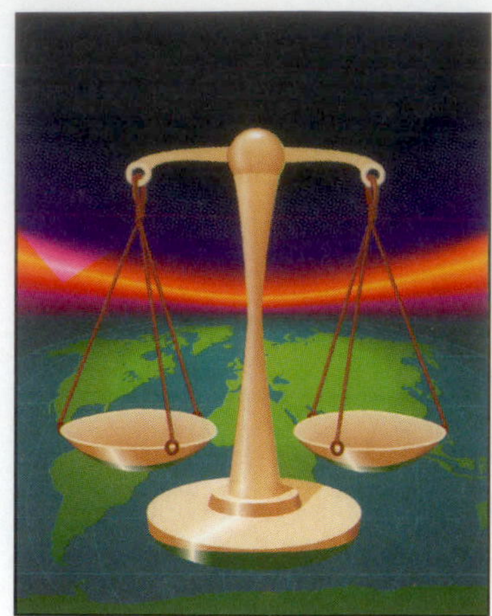

Chapter 31

Consumer and Environmental Law

"Subject to specific constitutional limitations, when the legislature has spoken, the public interest has been declared in terms well nigh conclusive."

William O. Douglas, 1898–1980
(Associate justice of the United States Supreme Court, 1939–1975)

The "public interest" referred to by Justice Douglas in the opening quotation was evident during the 1960s and 1970s in what has come to be known as the consumer movement. Some have labeled the period following the 1960s "the age of the consumer" because so much legislation was passed to protect consumers against purportedly unfair practices and unsafe products of sellers. During the 1980s and early 1990s, the impetus driving the consumer movement lessened, to a great extent because so many of its goals had been achieved. Both state and federal legislation now regulates how businesses may advertise, engage in mail-order transactions, package and label their products, and so on. In addition, numerous local, state, and federal agencies now exist to aid the consumer in settling his or her grievances with sellers and producers. *Consumer protection law* consists of all statutes, agency rules, and common law judicial rulings that serve to protect the interest of consumers. In the first part of this chapter, we will examine some of the sources and some of the major issues of consumer protection.

Environmental protection is an even more recent form of government regulation. The urban industrial society of our century has apparently strained the environment's capacity to handle the pollution being discharged into the air and water. In the last two decades, a growing body of *environmental law* has been created, most of which is statutory or administrative in nature. In the latter part of this chapter, we will examine some of the major federal statutes that seek to protect our environment.

❖ Consumer Protection Laws

Sources of consumer protection exist at all levels of government. At the federal level, a number of laws have been passed to define the duties of sellers and the rights of consumers. Exhibit 31–1 lists the major federal consumer protection statutes. Federal administrative agencies, such as the Federal Trade Commission (FTC), also provide an important source of consumer protection. Nearly every agency and department of the government has an office of consumer affairs, and most states have one or more such offices to assist consumers.

Because of the wide variation among state consumer protection laws, our primary focus here will be on federal legislation—specifically, on legislation governing deceptive advertising, labeling and packaging, sales, health protection, product safety, and credit protection. Realize, though, that state laws often provide more sweeping and significant protections for the consumer than do federal laws, as will be discussed later in this section.

♦ Exhibit 31–1
Federal Consumer Protection Statutes

STATUTE OR AGENCY RULE	PURPOSE
ADVERTISING	
Federal Trade Commission Act (1914/1938)	Prohibits deceptive and unfair trade practices.
Public Health Cigarette Smoking Act (1970)	Prohibits radio and TV cigarette advertising.
FTC Rules of Negative Options (1973)	Federal Trade Commission rules regulating advertising of book and record clubs.
Smokeless Tobacco Health Education Act (1986)	Prohibits radio and TV advertising of smokeless tobacco products; requires special labeling to warn consumers of potential health hazards associated with smokeless tobacco.
CREDIT	
Consumer Credit Protection Act (Truth-in-Lending Act) (1968)	Offers comprehensive protection covering all phases of credit transactions.
Fair Credit Reporting Act (1970)	Protects consumers' credit reputations.
Equal Credit Opportunity Act (1974)	Prohibits discrimination in the extending of credit.
Fair Credit Billing Act (1974)	Protects consumers from credit-card billing errors and in other disputes.
Fair Debt Collection Practices Act (1977)	Prohibits debt collectors' abuses.
Counterfeit Access Device and Computer Fraud and Abuse Act (1984)	Prohibits the production, use, and sale of counterfeit credit cards or other access devices used to obtain money, goods, services, or other things of value.
Fair Credit and Charge Card Disclosure Act (1988)	Requires fuller disclosure of terms and conditions in credit-card and charge-card applications and solicitations.
Home Equity Loan Consumer Protection Act (1988)	Prohibits lenders from changing the terms of a loan after the contract has been signed; requires fuller disclosure in home equity loans of interest-rate formulas and repayment terms.
HEALTH AND SAFETY	
Pure Food and Drugs Act (1906)	Prohibits adulteration and mislabeling of food and drugs sold in interstate commerce.
Meat Inspection Act (1906)	Provides for inspection of meat.
Federal Food, Drug and Cosmetic Act (1938)	Protects consumers from unsafe food products and from unsafe and/or ineffective drugs (superseded Pure Food and Drug Act of 1906).
Flammable Fabrics Act (1953)	Prohibits the sale of highly flammable clothing.
Poultry Products Inspection Act (1957)	Provides for inspection of poultry.
Child Protection and Toy Safety Act (1969)	Requires childproof devices and special labeling.
National Traffic and Motor Vehicle Safety Act (1966)	Requires manufacturers to inform new-car dealers of any safety defects found after manufacture and sale of auto.
Wholesome Meat Act (1967)	Updated Meat Inspection Act of 1906 to provide for stricter standards for plants where red-meat animals are slaughtered.
Consumer Product Safety Act (1972)	Established the Consumer Product Safety Commission to regulate all potentially hazardous consumer products.
Department of Transportation Rule on Passive Restraints in Automobiles (1984)	Requires automatic restraint systems in all new cars sold after September 1, 1990.
Toy Safety Act (1984)	Allows the Consumer Product Safety Commission to quickly recall toys and other articles intended for use by children that present a substantial risk of injury.
Drug-Price Competition and Patent-Term Restoration Act (Generic Drug Act) (1984)	Speeds up and simplifies Food and Drug Administration approval of generic versions of drugs on which patents have expired.
LABELING AND PACKAGING	
Wool Products Labeling Act (1939)	Requires accurate labeling of wool products.
Fur Products Labeling Act (1951)	Prohibits misbranding of fur products.
Textile Fiber Products Identification Act (1958)	Prohibits false labeling and advertising of all textile products not covered under Wool and Fur Products Labeling Acts.

◆ Exhibit 31–1
Federal Consumer Protection Statutes (Continued)

STATUTE OR AGENCY RULE	PURPOSE
LABELING AND PACKAGING (Continued)	
Hazardous Substances Labeling Act (1960)	Requires warning labels on all items containing dangerous chemicals.
Cigarette Labeling and Advertising Act (1965)	Requires labels warning of possible health hazards.
Child Protection and Toy Safety Act (1969)	Requires childproof devices and special labeling.
Fair Packaging and Labeling Act (1966)	Requires that accurate names, quantities, and weights be given on product labels.
Smokeless Tobacco Health Education Act (1986)	Requires labels disclosing possible health hazards of smokeless tobacco; prohibits radio and TV advertising of smokeless tobacco products.
SALES AND WARRANTIES	
Interstate Land Sales Full Disclosure Act (1968)	Requires disclosure in interstate land sales.
Odometer Act (1972)	Protects consumers against odometer fraud in used-car sales.
FTC Door-to-Door Sales Rule (1973)	Federal Trade Commission rule regulating door-to-door sales contracts.
Real Estate Settlement Procedures Act (1974)	Requires disclosure of home-buying costs.
Magnuson-Moss Warranty Act (1975)	Provides rules governing content of warranties.
FTC Vocational and Correspondence School Rule (1980)	Federal Trade Commission rule regulating contracts with these types of schools.
FTC Used-Car Rule (1984)	Federal Trade Commission rule requiring dealers in used-car sales to disclose specified types of information in "Buyer's Guide" affixed to auto.
FTC Funeral Home Rule (1984)	Federal Trade Commission rule requiring disclosure by funeral homes regarding prices and services.

Deceptive Advertising

DECEPTIVE ADVERTISING Advertising that misleads consumers, either by unjustified claims concerning a product's performance or by the omission of a material fact concerning the product's composition or performance.

The increased protection received by consumers during the past two decades against **deceptive advertising** derives more from statutory and administrative sources than from common law. Common law protection is based on fraud and requires proof of intent to misrepresent facts, along with other criteria. Statutory law and administrative regulations focus on whether the advertising is likely to be misleading, regardless of intent. This approach arises from the reasoning that laws against false advertising should attempt to protect the consumer rather than to punish the seller or advertiser.

Numerous government agencies, both federal and state, are empowered to protect consumers from deceptive advertising. At the federal level, the most important agency regulating advertising is the Federal Trade Commission (FTC). The Federal Trade Commission Act (discussed in Chapter 30) empowers the FTC to determine what constitutes a deceptive practice within the meaning of Section 5 of the act.

Defining Deceptive Advertising As defined by the FTC, deceptive advertising generally means advertising that may be interpreted in more than one way, one of which is false or misleading. False or deceptive advertising comes in many forms. Deception may arise from a false statement or claim about a company's own products or competitors' products. The deception may concern a product's quality, effects, price, origin, or availability; or it may arise from an omission of important information about the product.

Some advertisements contain "half-truths," meaning that the presented information is true but incomplete, leading consumers to a false conclusion. For example, the makers of Campbell's soups advertised that "most" Campbell's soups were low in fat and cholesterol and thus were helpful in fighting heart disease. What the ad did not say was that Campbell's soups are high in sodium and high-sodium diets may increase the risk of heart disease. The FTC ruled that Campbell's claims were thus deceptive.

Some states require automobile dealers to include in their advertisements the number of cars available at sale prices.

Other ads contain statements not supported by adequate scientific evidence. These may or may not be considered deceptive. When the claim is incapable of measurement—as in, "When you're out of Schlitz, you're out of beer"—no problem of deception is perceived by the FTC.

An ad may be deceptive even though it is literally true. An ad for "Teak Tables," for example, may be for tables manufactured by a firm named "Teak," and thus the advertiser could claim the ad was truthful. Nonetheless, the ad would probably be considered deceptive because most consumers would be led to assume that the ad referred to teak wood. As a general rule, the test for whether an ad is deceptive is *whether a reasonable consumer would be deceived by the ad.*

Bait-and-Switch Advertising In some cases, the FTC has promulgated specific rules to govern advertising. One of its more important rules is contained in the FTC's "Guides on Bait Advertising."[1] The rule is designed to prohibit advertisements that specify a very low price for a particular item that will likely be unavailable to the consumer, who will then be encouraged to purchase a more expensive item. The low price is the "bait" to lure the consumer into the store. The salesperson is instructed to "switch" the consumer to a different item. According to the FTC guidelines, **bait-and-switch advertising** occurs if the seller refuses to show the advertised item, fails to have adequate quantities of it available, fails to promise to deliver the advertised item within a reasonable time, or discourages employees from selling the item.

BAIT-AND-SWITCH ADVERTISING
Advertising a product at a very attractive price (the "bait") and then informing the consumer, once he or she is in the store, that the advertised product is either not available or is of poor quality; the customer is then urged to purchase ("switched" to) a more expensive item.

FTC Actions against Deceptive Advertising The FTC receives complaints from many sources, including competitors of alleged violaters, consumers, consumer organizations, trade associations, Better Business Bureaus, government organizations, and state and local officials. If enough consumers complain and the complaints are widespread, the FTC will investigate the problem and perhaps take action. If, after its investigations, the FTC believes that a given advertisement is unfair or deceptive, it drafts a formal complaint, which is sent to the alleged offender. The company may agree to settle the complaint without further proceedings.

If the company does not agree to settle a complaint, the FTC can conduct a hearing—which is similar to a trial—in which the company can present its defense. The hearing is held before an administrative law judge (ALJ) instead of a federal district court judge (see the discussion of administrative law in Chapter 1). If the FTC succeeds in proving that an advertisement is unfair or deceptive, it usually issues a **cease-and-desist order** requiring that the challenged advertising be stopped. It might also impose a sanction known as **counteradvertising** by requiring the company to advertise anew—in print, on radio, and on television—to inform the public about the earlier misinformation.

CEASE-AND-DESIST ORDER
An administrative or judicial order prohibiting a person or business firm from conducting activities that an agency or court has deemed illegal.

COUNTERADVERTISING
New advertising that is undertaken pursuant to a Federal Trade Commission order for the purpose of correcting earlier false claims that were made about a product.

When an ALJ rules against a company, the company can appeal to the full commission. The FTC commissioners listen to the parties' arguments and may uphold, modify, or reverse the ALJ's decision. If the commission rules against a company, the FTC's orders can be appealed through judicial channels, but a reviewing court generally accords great weight to the FTC's judgment. This is because

1. 16 C.F.R. Section 288. C.F.R. refers to the Code of Federal Regulations.

the court recognizes that the FTC, as the administrative agency that deals continually with such cases, is often in a better position than the courts to determine when a practice is deceptive within the meaning of the act.

In the following case, the FTC ruled that Kraft, Inc., had engaged in deceptive advertising in marketing its cheese slices and ordered Kraft to cease and desist from such advertising. Kraft appealed the FTC's decision to the Seventh Circuit Court of Appeals.

Case 31.1

KRAFT, INC. v. FEDERAL TRADE COMMISSION

United States Court of Appeals, Seventh Circuit, 1992. 970 F.2d 311.

HISTORICAL AND SOCIAL SETTING *Calcium is an essential component of bones and teeth and is important to human health. Milk and milk products are rich in calcium, and milk is an ingredient in Kraft, Inc.'s Kraft Singles, which are processed cheese food slices. In the making of Kraft Singles, about 30 percent of the calcium contained in the milk is lost. This means that Kraft Singles contain roughly 15 percent of the U.S. Recommended Daily Allowance of calcium per ounce. This is about the same amount contained in imitation cheese slices, which consist primarily of water, vegetable oil, and flavoring and fortifying agents. In the mid-1980s, one Kraft advertisement depicted a group of children having their class picture taken and contained in part the following copy:*

> *Announcer (voice-over): "Can you see what's missing in this picture? Well, a government study says that half the school kids in America don't get all the calcium recommended for growing kids. That's why Kraft Singles are important. Kraft is made from five ounces of milk per slice. So they're concentrated with calcium. Calcium the government recommends for strong bones and healthy teeth!"*

The ad included the disclosure that "one three-quarter-ounce slice has 70 percent of the calcium of five ounces of milk."

FACTS Kraft's individually wrapped cheese slices, or "Singles Slices," which are made from real cheese, cost more than the imitation cheese slices on the market. In the early 1980s, Kraft began losing its market share to an increasing number of producers of imitation cheese slices. Kraft responded with a series of advertisements, collectively known as the "Five Ounces of Milk" campaign. The ads claimed that Kraft Singles cost more than imitation slices because they were made from five ounces of milk rather than less expensive ingredients. The ads also implied that because each slice contained five ounces of milk, Kraft Singles contained a higher calcium content than imitation cheese slices. The FTC filed a complaint against Kraft, charging that Kraft had materially misrepresented the calcium content and relative calcium benefit of Kraft Singles. The administrative law judge (ALJ) ruled that Kraft was misleading consumers because, although Kraft did use five ounces of milk in making each Kraft Single, roughly 30 percent of the calcium contained in the milk was lost during processing—and Kraft had neglected to inform consumers of this fact. Furthermore, the ALJ found that the vast majority of imitation cheese slices sold in the United States contained approximately the same amount of calcium as Kraft Singles. The ALJ ordered Kraft to cease and desist from making these claims. The FTC commissioners affirmed the order, with some modifications, and Kraft appealed.

ISSUE Was Kraft's advertising campaign deceptive and likely to mislead consumers?

DECISION Yes. The court upheld the FTC's ruling.

REASON Kraft's principal argument on appeal was that the FTC erred as a matter of law by not requiring actual evidence that Kraft's advertising had, in fact, misled consumers. In response to this argument, the court stated that the "[c]ourts, including the Supreme Court, have uniformly rejected imposing such a requirement on the FTC." The court also disagreed with Kraft's allegations that "implied claims are inescapably subjective and unpredictable." On the contrary, held the court, "[t]he implied claims Kraft made are reasonably clear from the face of the advertisements, and hence the Commission was not required to utilize consumer surveys in reaching its decision." The court emphasized that although "[t]he Commissioners' personal experiences quite obviously affect their perceptions, * * * it does not follow that they are incapable of predicting whether a particular claim is likely [to mislead] a reasonable number of consumers."

Labeling and Packaging

A number of federal and state labeling and packaging laws have been passed to provide the consumer with accurate information or warnings about the product or its possible misuse. The Fur Products Labeling Act of 1951, the Wool Products Labeling Act of 1939, the Flammable Fabrics Act of 1953, the Federal Food, Drug and Cosmetic Act of 1938, the Fair Packaging and Labeling Act of 1966, and the Smokeless Tobacco Health Education Act of 1986 are a few of the laws that have been enacted, in part, to reduce the amount of incorrect labeling and packaging in consumer products.

In general, labels must be accurate, which means that they must use words as they are ordinarily understood by consumers. For example, a regular-size box of cereal cannot be labeled "giant" if that word would exaggerate the amount of cereal contained in the box. Labels often must specify the raw materials used in the product, such as the percentage of cotton, nylon, or other fibers used in a shirt. The Fair Packaging and Labeling Act requires that consumer goods have labels that identify the product, the manufacturer, the packer or distributor and its place of business, the net quantity of the contents, and the quantity of each serving if the number of servings is stated.[2] This statute also governs package descriptions and savings claims, information disclosure for ingredients in nonfood products, and standards for the partial filling of packages. The provisions are enforced by the Federal Trade Commission and the Department of Health and Human Services.

Sales

A number of statutes that protect the consumer in sales transactions concern the disclosure of certain terms in sales and provide rules governing home or door-to-door sales, mail-order transactions, referral sales, and unsolicited merchandise. The Federal Reserve Board of Governors, for example, has issued **Regulation Z,** which governs credit provisions associated with sales contracts, and numerous states have passed laws governing the remedies available to consumers in home sales. Furthermore, states have adopted a number of consumer protection provisions by incorporating into their statutory codes the Uniform Commercial Code and the Uniform Consumer Credit Code (the latter is discussed later in this chapter).

REGULATION Z
A set of rules issued by the Federal Reserve System's board of governors under the authority of the Electronic Fund Transfer Act to protect users of electronic fund transfer systems.

Door-to-Door Sales Door-to-door sales are singled out for special treatment in the laws of most states. This special treatment stems in part from the nature of the sales transaction. Because repeat purchases are not as likely as they are in stores, the seller has less incentive to cultivate the goodwill of the purchaser. Furthermore, the seller is unlikely to present alternative products and their prices. Thus, a number of states have passed what are known as "**cooling-off" laws** that permit the buyers of goods sold door-to-door to cancel their contracts within a specified period of time, usually two to three days after the sale.

"COOLING OFF" LAWS
Laws that allow buyers a period of time in which to cancel a door-to-door sales contract or a contract for home improvements. Most state statutes and the federal government require that buyers be allowed a three-day cooling-off period during which these types of contracts can be cancelled.

A Federal Trade Commission (FTC) regulation also requires sellers to give consumers three days to cancel any door-to-door sale. Because this rule applies in addition to the relevant state statutes, consumers are given the most favorable benefits of the FTC rule and their own state statutes. In addition, the FTC rule requires that the notification be given in Spanish if the oral negotiations for the sale were in that language.

Mail-Order Sales Heading the list of consumer complaints received by the nation's Better Business Bureaus are problems stemming from product sales by telephone or mail. Consumers typically have been given less protection when they bought from mail-order houses than when they purchased in stores. Many mail-

2. 15 U.S.C. Sections 1451–1461.

REDRESS
Satisfaction for damages incurred through the wrongdoing of another.

order houses are outside the buyer's state, and it is more costly to seek **redress** for grievances in such situations.

In addition to the federal statute that prevents the use of mails to defraud individuals, several states have passed statutes governing certain practices by sellers, including insurance companies, that solicit through the mails. The state statutes parallel the federal statutes governing mail fraud.

The Postal Reorganization Act of 1970 provides that an individual who receives unsolicited merchandise through the U.S. mail may retain, use, discard, or dispose of it in any manner deemed appropriate without incurring any obligation to the sender.[3] In addition, the mailing of unordered merchandise (except for free samples) constitutes an unfair trade practice and is not permitted. (Exceptions are mailings by charitable agencies and those made by mistake.)

FTC Regulation of Specific Industries Over the last decade, the FTC has begun to target certain sales practices on an industry-wide basis. Two examples are the used-car business and the funeral-home trade. In 1984, the FTC enacted a rule that requires used-car dealers to affix a "Buyer's Guide" label to all cars sold on their lots. The label must disclose the following information: (1) the car's warranty or a statement that the car is being sold "as is," (2) information regarding any service contract or promises being made by the dealer, and (3) a suggestion that the purchaser obtain both an inspection of the car and a written statement of any promises made by the dealer.

In 1984, the FTC also enacted rules requiring that funeral homes provide customers with itemized prices of all charges for a funeral. In addition, the regulations prohibit funeral homes from requiring specific embalming procedures or specific types of caskets for bodies that are to be cremated.

Real Estate Sales Various federal and state laws apply to consumer transactions involving real estate. The goal of these laws is to prevent fraud and to provide buyers with certain types of information. Some of these protections mirror those provided for other types of sales. The disclosure requirements of the Truth-in-Lending Act, which will be discussed shortly, apply to a number of real estate transactions. There are differences, however, between the disclosure requirements for real estate transactions and those for other types of transactions. For example, in certain real estate transactions, consumers are given a right to rescind their purchase contracts if certain disclosures are not made to them. Moreover, under certain circumstances—such as the lender's failure to give the borrower the required number of copies of certain loan documents—the Truth-in-Lending Act provides the consumer with a right to cancel the contract even though a creditor has made all of the required disclosures.[4]

Health Protection

In 1906, Congress passed the Pure Food and Drugs Act, which was the first step toward protecting consumers against adulterated and misbranded food and drug products. In 1938, the Federal Food, Drug and Cosmetic Act was passed to strengthen the protective features of the 1906 legislation. These acts and subsequent amendments established standards for foods, specified safe levels of potentially dangerous food additives, and created classifications of foods and food advertising. In addition, drugs must be proved to be effective as well as safe before they can be marketed, and food additives that can be shown to be carcinogenic (cancer causing)

3. 39 U.S.C. Section 3009.
4. 15 U.S.C. Section 1635.

to humans or animals are forbidden. Most of the statutes involving food and drugs are monitored and enforced by the Food and Drug Administration.

Also in 1906, Congress passed the Meat Inspection Act, the beginning of legislation establishing inspection requirements for all meat and poultry sold for human consumption. The Food Safety and Quality Service of the Department of Agriculture enforces statutes relating to meat and poultry inspection.

Congress has enacted a number of other statutes in an attempt to protect individuals from harmful products. In response to public concern over the dangers of cigarette smoking, Congress has required warnings to be placed on cigarette and little-cigar packages, as well as on containers of smokeless tobacco. For years, the statement "Warning: The Surgeon General Has Determined That Cigarette Smoking Is Dangerous to Your Health" was required to appear on cigarette and little-cigar packages. Beginning in 1985, major-brand cigarette producers were required to rotate four warning labels on a quarterly basis. Each warning begins, "Surgeon General's Warning" and then states one of the following:

1. Smoking Causes Lung Cancer, Heart Disease, Emphysema, and May Complicate Pregnancy.
2. Quitting Smoking Now Greatly Reduces Serious Risks to Your Health.
3. Smoking by Pregnant Women May Result in Fetal Injury, Premature Birth, and Low Birth Weight.
4. Cigarette Smoke Contains Carbon Monoxide.

The Smokeless Tobacco Health Education Act of 1986 requires producers, packagers, and importers of smokeless tobacco to label their products conspicuously with one of three warnings:

1. WARNING: This product may cause mouth cancer.
2. WARNING: This product may cause gum disease and tooth loss.
3. WARNING: This product is not a safe alternative to cigarettes.

All advertising, except outdoor billboards, must include these warnings.

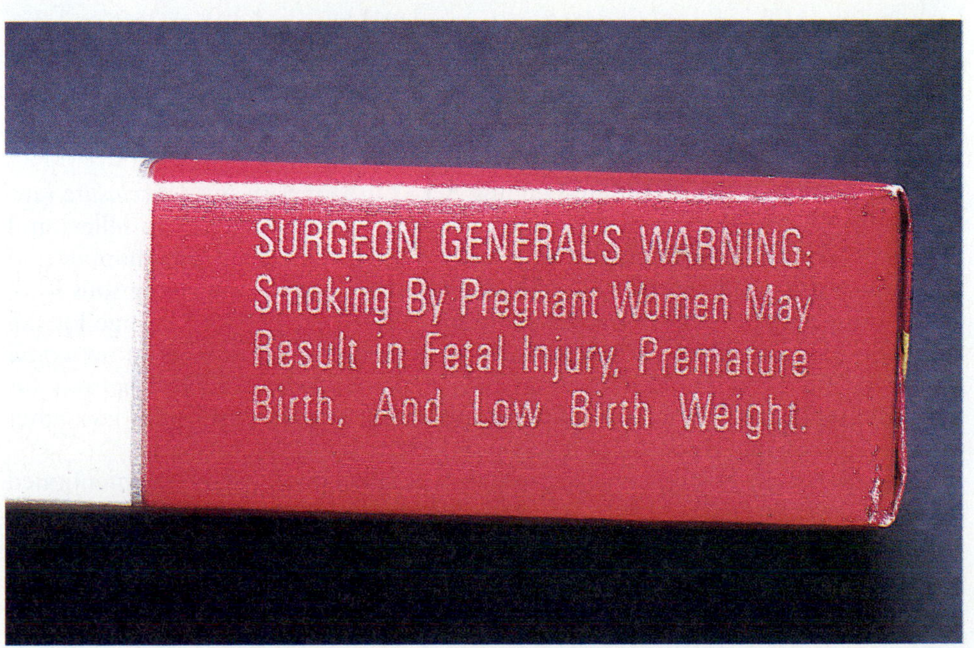

Why is Congress so concerned with protecting consumers against purportedly unsafe products?

Consumer Product Safety

The trend toward increased government regulation in the area of public health has been mirrored in the area of consumer product safety. Legislation in this area began in 1953 with the enactment of the Flammable Fabrics Act, which prohibits the sale of highly flammable clothing or materials. Between 1953 and 1972, Congress enacted legislation regulating specific classes of products or product design or composition, rather than the overall safety of consumer products. Finally, as a result of 1970 recommendations by the National Commission on Product Safety, the Consumer Product Safety Act was passed in 1972 in an attempt to protect consumers from unreasonable risk of injury from hazardous products. The act created the Consumer Product Safety Commission (CPSC). The purpose of the CPSC, as stated in the act, is as follows:

1. To protect the public against unreasonable risk of injury associated with consumer products.
2. To assist consumers in evaluating the comparative safety of consumer products.
3. To develop uniform safety standards for consumer products and to minimize the conflicts between state and local regulations.
4. To promote research and investigation into the causes and prevention of product-related deaths, illnesses, and injuries.

Generally, the CPSC is authorized to set standards for consumer products and to ban the manufacture and sale of any product deemed potentially hazardous to consumers. The commission has the authority to remove products from the market if they are deemed imminently hazardous and to require manufacturers to report information about any products already sold or intended for sale that have proved to be hazardous.

The CPSC also has the authority to administer other acts relating to product safety, such as the Child Protection and Toy Safety Act of 1969, the Hazardous Substances Labeling Act of 1960, and the Flammable Fabrics Act of 1953.

Credit Protection

Because of the extensive use of credit by American consumers, credit protection has become one of the more important areas regulated by consumer protection legislation. One of the most significant statutes regulating the credit and credit-card industry is the Truth-in-Lending Act, the name commonly given to Title 1 of the Consumer Credit Protection Act (CCPA), which was passed by Congress in 1968.

Truth in Lending The Truth-in-Lending Act (TILA) is basically a *disclosure law.* The TILA is administered by the Federal Reserve Board and requires sellers and lenders to disclose credit terms or loan terms so that individuals can shop around for the best financing arrangements. TILA requirements apply only to persons who, in the ordinary course of business, lend money or sell on credit or arrange for the extension of credit. Thus, sales or loans made between two consumers do not come under the protection of the act. Also, only debtors who are *natural* persons (as opposed to the artificial "person" of the corporation) are protected by this law; other legal entities are not.

The disclosure requirements are found in Regulation Z, which, as mentioned previously, was promulgated by the Federal Reserve Board. If the contracting parties are subject to the TILA, the requirements of Regulation Z apply to any transaction involving an installment sales contract in which payment is to be made in more than four installments. These transactions typically include installment loans, retail and installment sales, car loans, home improvement loans, and certain real estate loans if the amount of financing is less than $25,000.

Under the provisions of the TILA, all of the terms of a credit instrument must be fully disclosed. The TILA also provides for contract rescission if a creditor fails to follow *exactly* the procedures required by the act. TILA requirements are strictly enforced.

Equal Credit Opportunity Act In 1974, Congress enacted the Equal Credit Opportunity Act (ECOA) as an amendment to the Consumer Credit Protection Act. The ECOA prohibits the denial of credit solely on the basis of race, religion, national origin, color, sex, marital status, or age. The act also prohibits credit discrimination on the basis of whether an individual receives certain forms of income, such as public assistance benefits. Creditors are prohibited from requesting any information from a credit applicant that could be used for the type of discrimination covered in the act and its amendments. Under the ECOA, a creditor may not require the signature of an applicant's spouse, other than a joint applicant, on a credit instrument if the applicant qualifies under the creditor's standards of creditworthiness for the amount and terms of the credit requested.

Credit-Card Rules The TILA also contains provisions regarding credit cards. One provision limits the liability of a cardholder to $50 per card for unauthorized charges made before the creditor is notified. Another provision prohibits a credit-card company from billing a consumer for any unauthorized charges if the credit card was improperly issued by the company. For example, if a consumer receives an unsolicited credit card in the mail and the card is later stolen and used by the thief to make purchases, the consumer to whom the card was sent will not be liable for the unauthorized charges. Further provisions of the act concern billing disputes related to credit-card purchases. If a debtor thinks that an error has occurred in billing or wishes to withhold payment for a faulty product purchased by credit card, the act outlines specific procedures for both the consumer and the credit-card company in settling the dispute.

Fair Credit Reporting Act To ensure that consumers can determine and alter any inaccurate information in their credit records, Congress passed the Fair Credit Reporting Act (FCRA) in 1970. The FCRA covers all credit bureaus, investigative reporting companies, detective and collection agencies, and computerized information-reporting companies. Under the act, the consumer has the right to be notified of reporting activities, to have access to information contained in reports, and to have corrected any erroneous information upon which a denial of credit, employment, or insurance might have been based. Upon request and proper identification, any consumer is entitled to know the nature and substance of information about him or her that is contained in the agency's file, as well as the sources of the information and the identity of those who have received a consumer credit report, such as businesses that may wish to extend credit to the consumer. Under the act, an investigative report cannot be prepared on an individual consumer unless that person is notified and given the right to request information on the nature and scope of the pending investigation.

Fair Debt Collection Practices Act In 1977, Congress passed the Fair Debt Collection Practices Act (FDCPA) in an attempt to curb what were perceived to be abuses by collection agencies. The act applies only to specialized debt-collection agencies that, usually for a percentage of the amount owed, regularly attempt to collect debts on behalf of someone else. Creditors who attempt to collect debts are not covered by the act unless, by misrepresenting themselves to the debtor, they cause the debtor to believe that they are a collection agency. The act prohibits the following debt-collection practices:

1. Contacting the consumer at his or her place of employment if the employer objects, contacting the consumer at inconvenient or unusual times, or contacting the consumer if he or she is represented by an attorney.
2. Contacting third parties other than parents, spouses, or financial advisers about the payment of a debt unless authorized to do so by a court of law.
3. Using harassment and intimidation, such as abusive language, or using false or misleading information, such as posing as a police officer.
4. Communicating with the consumer after receipt of a notice that the consumer is refusing to pay the debt, except to advise the consumer of further action to be taken by the collection agency.

The FDCPA also requires collection agencies to include a "validation notice" whenever they initially contact a debtor for payment of a debt or within five days of that initial contact. The notice must state that the debtor has thirty days within which to dispute the debt and to request a written verification of the debt from the collection agency. The debtor's request for debt validation must be in writing.

The enforcement of this act is primarily the responsibility of the Federal Trade Commission. The FDCPA allows debtors to recover civil damages, as well as attorneys' fees, in an action against a collection agency that violates provisions of the act.

State Consumer Protection Laws

Some consumer protection at the state level arises from the Uniform Commercial Code (UCC). Consumers are afforded protection by the UCC sections that deal with express and implied warranties. The UCC also restricts the ability of sellers to limit their liability for personal injuries caused by defective products. Perhaps the most significant consumer protection provision of the UCC, however, is the principle of unconscionability expressed in UCC 2–302. That section, as interpreted by the courts, prohibits the enforcement of any contracts that are so one-sided and unfair that they "shock the conscience" of the court.

In 1968, the National Conference of Commissioners on Uniform State Laws promulgated the Uniform Consumer Credit Code (UCCC), which was revised in 1974. The UCCC has been controversial and has been adopted by only a few states, although bits and pieces of it have been extracted for inclusion in numerous state statutes. The UCCC is an attempt to establish a comprehensive body of rules governing the most important aspects of consumer credit. Sections of the UCCC, for example, focus on truth-in-lending disclosures and maximum credit ceilings, as well as door-to-door sales, and certain other types of sales. The UCCC is also concerned with materials contained in fine-print clauses and various provisions of creditor remedies, including deficiency judgments and garnishments. The UCCC applies to most types of sales, including real estate. It also replaces existing state consumer credit laws, as well as acts dealing with installment loans, interest rates, and retail installment sales, in those few states that have adopted it.

Despite the variation among state laws generally, there is a common thread running through most state consumer protection laws. Typically, state consumer protection laws are directed at deceptive trade practices, such as a seller's providing false or misleading information to the consumer. Some of the legislation is quite broad. A prime example is the Texas Deceptive Trade Practices Act of 1973, which forbids a seller from selling to a buyer anything that the buyer does not need or cannot afford. The following case illustrates an application of the Tennessee Consumer Protection Act of 1977.

Case 31.2
MORRIS v. MACK'S USED CARS
Supreme Court of Tennessee, 1992.
824 S.W.2d 538.

HISTORICAL AND SOCIAL SETTING *Sometimes, when consumers are the victims of false advertising and similar practices, their interests can be vindicated by public agencies. Public agencies, however, are often understaffed, underfunded, and overwhelmed with complaints. In that situation, and in other circumstances, consumers may prefer to assert their rights themselves. Whether a consumer can and will sue to uphold his or her rights depends on at least two considerations. First, there must be a legal theory available. Second, there must be an incentive sufficient to make filing the suit worthwhile. As for the first consideration, every state has adopted a statute that is modeled to some degree on the Federal Trade Commission Act. As for the second consideration, many of these statutes provide for awards of treble damages and attorneys' fees.*

FACTS In September 1985, Darrell Morris bought a 1979 Ford truck from Mack's Used Cars & Parts, Inc. He traded in an older truck as a down payment and financed the remainder of the purchase price over a three-year period. The bill of sale contained the following disclaimer: "This unit is sold as is. No warranties have been expressed or implied." After paying the last installment, Morris received the certificate of title and learned that the truck had been previously wrecked and reconstructed. Mack's was aware of this fact but had not disclosed it to Morris at the time of the purchase. Morris sued Mack's, alleging that Mack's had breached express and implied warranties and had violated the Tennessee Consumer Protection Act of 1977, which prohibits unfair or deceptive acts. Mack's contended that the warranty disclaimer in the bill of sale relieved it from any liability for failing to disclose to Morris the fact that the pickup had been wrecked and reconstructed. The trial court agreed with Mack's and dismissed the suit. Morris appealed, contending that the UCC disclaimer did not bar an action for violation of the Tennessee Consumer Protection Act. The appellate court affirmed the dismissal, holding that to hold Mack's liable under the Tennessee Consumer Protection Act "would, in effect, be creating liability under an 'as is' sale which is waived under [UCC] 2–316(3)(a)." Morris appealed the case to the Supreme Court of Tennessee.

ISSUE Did Mack's avoidance of liability under the UCC provisions permitting warranty disclaimers bar Morris's action under the Tennessee Consumer Protection Act?

DECISION No. The Supreme Court of Tennessee reversed the appellate court's decision.

REASON The Supreme Court of Tennessee found that disclaimers permitted by the Uniform Commercial Code "may limit or modify liability otherwise imposed by the code, but such disclaimers do not defeat separate causes of action for unfair or deceptive acts or practices under the [Tennessee] Consumer Protection Act." The court noted that in other jurisdictions, courts hearing cases involving automobile sales had held that an "as is" disclaimer does not bar an action for deceptive trade practices under a state consumer protection statute. The court stressed that the "Tennessee Consumer Protection Act is to be liberally construed to protect consumers and others from those who engaged in deceptive acts or practices. * * * To allow the seller here to avoid liability for unfair or deceptive acts or practices by disclaiming contractual warranties under the UCC would contravene the broad remedial intent of the Consumer Protection Act."

ETHICAL CONSIDERATIONS *Traditionally, in transacting business, superior information and business acumen are legitimate advantages, which lead to no liability. But the continuing development of modern business ethics has limited sellers' attempts to take advantage of ignorance. Thus, if one party knows a fact basic to a transaction, the other party is ignorant of the fact, and under the customs of the trade or other circumstances a disclosure of the fact is reasonably to be expected, the party who does not disclose it may be liable. In that case, good faith and fair dealing require disclosure.*

❖ Environmental Law

To this point, this chapter has dealt with government regulation of business in the interest of protecting consumers. We now turn to a discussion of the various ways in which businesses are regulated by government in the interest of protecting the environment. Concern over the degradation of the environment has increased over time in response to the environmental effects of population growth, urbanization,

"A nuisance may be merely a right thing in the wrong place, like a pig in the parlor instead of the barnyard."

George Sutherland, 1862–1942 (*American jurist*)

and industrialization. But environmental protection is not without a price. For many businesses, the costs of complying with environmental regulations are high, and for some they are too high. There is a constant tension between the desirability of increasing profits and productivity and the need to attain a higher quality in the environment.

To a great extent, environmental law consists of statutes passed by federal, state, or local governments and regulations issued by administrative agencies. Before examining statutory and regulatory environmental laws, however, we look at the remedies available under the common law against environmental pollution.

Common Law Actions

Common law remedies against environmental pollution originated centuries ago in England. In medieval times, for example, the English Parliament passed a number of acts that regulated the burning of soft coal. Moreover, under the common law doctrine of *nuisance*, property owners were given relief from pollution when they could identify a distinct harm separate from that affecting the general public. Thus, if a factory polluted the air and killed a farmer's crops, the farmer could seek an injunction and damages against the factory.

Needless to say, nuisance suits that granted specific relief for individuals were inadequate to protect the public at large. Under the common law, citizens were denied *standing* (access to the courts) unless specific harm to them as individuals could be shown. Therefore, a group of citizens who wished to stop a new factory that would cause significant water pollution would be denied access to the courts on the ground that the harm to them did not differ from the harm borne by the general public.[5] A public authority, however, could sue for public nuisance.

An injured party could—and still may—sue a business polluter in a common law negligence action. The basis for the action is the business's alleged failure to use reasonable care toward the party, when the injury was foreseeable and, of course, caused by the failure. For example, employees might sue an employer whose failure to use proper pollution controls resulted in contaminated air, causing the employees to suffer respiratory illnesses. Injured parties might also recover under a theory of strict liability. Businesses that engage in ultrahazardous activities—such as blasting operations or the transportation of radioactive materials—are liable for whatever injuries the activities cause. In a strict liability action, the injured party does not need to prove that the business failed to exercise reasonable care.

The common law further limited relief from pollution when the harm was caused by two or more independent sources. For example, if a number of firms were polluting the air, a harmed individual could sue any individual firm; however, until early in the twentieth century, the plaintiff was not able to sue all of the factories simultaneously. Consequently, proving damages in individual actions was often impossible. These difficulties in seeking relief in pollution cases, along with the forces creating additional pollution, have been largely responsible for the development of statutory regulation of environmental quality.

State and Local Regulation

Often, environmental controls must take into consideration a geographical area larger than that covered by a local government. In some of these situations, state governments may act. For instance, many states regulate land use, under a master or comprehensive plan, through regional or statewide zoning laws.

Many states regulate the degree to which the environment may be polluted. Thus, for example, even when state zoning laws permit a business's proposed de-

5. *Save the Bay Committee, Inc. v. Mayor of City of Savannah*, 227 Ga. 436, 181 S.E.2d 351 (1971).

velopment, the proposal may have to be altered to change the development's impact on the environment. State laws may restrict a business's discharge of chemicals into the air or water or regulate its disposal of toxic wastes. States may also regulate the disposal or recycling of other wastes, including glass, metal, and plastic containers and paper. Additionally, states may restrict the emissions from motor vehicles.

City, county, and other local governments control some aspects of the environment. For instance, local zoning laws control some land use. These laws may be designed to inhibit or direct the growth of cities and suburbs or to protect the natural environment. Other aspects of the environment may be subject to local regulation for other reasons. Methods of waste and garbage removal and disposal, for example, can have a substantial impact on a community. The appearance of buildings and other structures, including advertising signs and billboards, may affect traffic safety, property values, or local aesthetics. Noise generated by a business or its customers may be annoying, disruptive, or damaging to neighbors. The location and condition of parks, streets, and other publicly used land subject to local control affect the environment and can also affect business.

"Men must turn square corners when they deal with the Government."

Oliver Wendell Holmes, Jr., 1841–1935
(Associate justice of the United States Supreme Court, 1902–1932)

Federal Regulation

Congress has passed a number of statutes to control the impact of human activities on the environment. Some of these have been passed to improve the quality of air and water. Some of them specifically regulate toxic chemicals—including pesticides and herbicides—and hazardous wastes.

The National Environmental Policy Act (NEPA) of 1969 imposes environmental responsibilities on all agencies of the federal government. NEPA requires that all agencies consider environmental factors when making significant decisions. For every major federal action that significantly affects the quality of the environment, an **environmental impact statement (EIS)** must be prepared. An action qualifies as "major" if it involves a substantial commitment of resources, monetary or otherwise. An action is "federal" if a federal agency has the power to control it. For example, building a new nuclear reactor involves federal action because a federal license is required.

ENVIRONMENTAL IMPACT STATEMENT (EIS)
A statement required by the National Environmental Policy Act for any major federal action that will significantly affect the quality of the environment. The statement must analyze the action's impact on the environment and alternative actions that might be taken.

An EIS must analyze (1) the impact on the environment that the action will have, (2) any adverse effects to the environment and alternative actions that might be taken, and (3) irreversible effects the action might generate. If an agency decides that an EIS is unnecessary, it must issue a statement supporting this conclusion. EISs have become instruments by which private citizens, consumer and environmental interest groups, businesses, and others challenge federal agency actions on the basis that the actions improperly threaten the environment. For example, an environmental interest group can use an EIS as evidence in court when challenging a federal agency action on the basis that it violates the Clean Air Act. Today, almost all environmental litigation involves disputes with government agencies rather than disputes between private parties.

In 1970, the Environmental Protection Agency (EPA) was created to coordinate federal environmental responsibilities. The EPA administers most federal environmental policies and statutes. Other federal agencies that have authority to regulate specific environmental matters include the Department of the Interior, the Department of Defense, the Department of Labor, the Food and Drug Administration, and the Nuclear Regulatory Commission.

Air Pollution

Seven main classes of pollutants are emitted into the air. *Carbon monoxide* is a colorless, odorless, poisonous gas that can reduce mental performance and result in death if inhaled in sufficient quantities. *Sulfur oxides* are acrid, corrosive, poisonous gases that are produced when fuel containing sulfur is burned. *Nitrogen oxides* are

Ethical Perspective

Business and the Environment—The Valdez Principles

To what extent is business required to concern itself with the conservation of natural resources? Should a company wait until it is attacked by consumer groups and boycotters of its products before it acts? Must a company wait until a government agency or legislative body prohibits certain environmentally harmful actions before ceasing to engage in those actions? Not according to an environmentally concerned group called the Coalition for Environmentally Responsible Economies (CERES—the acronym spells the name of the Roman goddess of agriculture, Ceres). The CERES group has issued a set of guidelines for socially responsible corporations to follow in attempting to meet environmental goals. The guidelines were motivated in part by the environmental damage caused by the 1989 oil spill that occurred when the *Exxon Valdez* supertanker ran aground on a reef off the coast of Alaska. The guidelines, or "Valdez Principles," as they are called, are reproduced here.

By adopting these principles, we publicly affirm our belief that corporations and their shareholders have a direct responsibility for the environment. We believe that corporations must conduct their business as responsible stewards of the environment and seek profits only in a manner that leaves the Earth healthy and safe. We believe that corporations must not compromise the ability of future generations to sustain their needs.

We recognize this to be a long-term commitment to update our practices continually in light of advances in technology and new understandings in health and environmental science. We intend to make consistent, measurable progress in implementing these principles and to apply them wherever we operate throughout the world.

1. **Protection of the Biosphere.** We will minimize and strive to eliminate the release of any pollutant that may cause environmental damage to the air, water, or earth or its inhabitants. We will safeguard habitats in rivers, lakes, wetlands, coastal zones, and oceans and will minimize contributing to the greenhouse effect, depletion of the ozone layer, acid rain, or smog.
2. **Sustainable Use of Natural Resources.** We will make sustainable use of renewable natural resources, such as water, soils, and forests. We will conserve nonrenewable natural resources through efficient use and careful planning. We will protect wildlife habitats, open spaces, and wilderness, while preserving biodiversity.
3. **Reduction and Disposal of Waste.** We will minimize the creation of waste, especially hazardous waste, and whenever possible recycle materials. We will dispose of all wastes through safe and responsible methods.
4. **Wise Use of Energy.** We will make every effort to use environmentally safe and sustainable energy sources to meet our needs. We will invest in improved energy efficiency and conservation in our operations. We will maximize the energy efficiency of products we produce or sell.
5. **Risk Reduction.** We will minimize the environmental, health, and safety risks to our employees and the communities in which we operate by employing safe technologies and operating procedures and by being constantly prepared for emergencies.
6. **Marketing of Safe Products and Services.** We will sell products or services that minimize adverse environmental impacts and that are safe as consumers commonly use them. We will inform consumers of the environmental impacts of our products or services.
7. **Damage Compensation.** We will take responsibility for any harm we cause to the environment by making

produced when fuel is burned at very high temperatures. (After being emitted into the atmosphere, sulfur dioxides and nitric oxides convert into sulfates and nitrates and return to the earth as acid rain.) *Hydrocarbons* are unburned fuel, an ingredient of smog. *Ozone* is smog, a gas that results from the combination of hydrocarbon vapors and nitrogen oxides in the presence of sunlight. *Lead* is a metallic chemical element that as an environmental contaminant often occurs as lead oxide aerosol or dust. *Particulates* are particles of solid or liquid substances produced by stationary fuel combustion and industrial processes.

Why should business be concerned with the possibility of environmental damage caused by such incidents as the oil spill from the Exxon Valdez?

every effort to fully restore the environment and to compensate those persons who are adversely affected.

8. **Disclosure.** We will disclose to our employees and to the public incidents relating to our operations that cause environmental harm or pose health or safety hazards. We will disclose potential environmental, health, or safety hazards posed by our operations, and we will not take any action against employees who report any condition that creates a danger to the environment or poses health and safety hazards.
9. **Environmental Directors and Managers.** At least one member of the board of directors will be a person qualified to represent environmental interests. We will commit management resources to implement these principles, including the funding of an office of vice president for environmental affairs or an equivalent executive position, reporting directly to the CEO, to monitor and report upon our implementation efforts.
10. **Assessment and Annual Audit.** We will conduct and make public an annual self-evaluation of our progress in implementing these principles and in complying with all applicable laws and regulations throughout our worldwide operations. We will work toward the timely creation of independent environmental audit procedures which we will complete annually and make available to the public.

Federal involvement with air pollution goes back to the 1950s, when Congress authorized funds for air-pollution research. In 1963, the federal government passed the Clean Air Act, which focused on multistate air pollution and provided assistance to states. Various amendments, particularly in 1970, 1977, and 1990, strengthened the government's authority to regulate the quality of air. These laws provide the basis for regulations to control pollution coming primarily from stationary sources, such as industrial plants, or from motor vehicles. The EPA sets air quality standards for major pollutants. General guidelines set out requirements for protecting vege-

After more than thirty years of increasingly strict federal regulation of air quality, why does air pollution continue to be a problem?

tation, climate, visibility, and certain economic conditions. The 1977 amendments to the Clean Air Act established multilevel standards. These standards attempt to prevent the deterioration of air quality—even in areas in which the existing quality exceeds that required by federal law.

"Man, however much he may like to pretend the contrary, is part of nature."

Rachel Carson, 1907–1964 ***(American writer and conservationist)***

Motor Vehicles Regulations governing air pollution from automobiles and other mobile sources specify pollution standards and time schedules. For example, the 1970 Clean Air Act required a reduction of 90 percent in the amount of carbon monoxide and hydrocarbons emitted from automobiles by 1975. (This did not happen, however, and the act was amended to extend the deadline to 1983.) An automobile purchased today emits only about 4 percent as much pollution as a new 1970 model did. Nevertheless, there are so many more automobiles being driven today that urban ground-level ozone, which decreased between the late 1970s and the late 1980s, has risen to former levels. Under the 1990 amendments, automobile manufacturers must cut new automobiles' exhaust emissions of nitrogen oxide by 60 percent and the emissions of other pollutants by 35 percent. Beginning in 1994, increasing numbers of new automobiles must meet these standards. By 1998, all new automobiles must do so.

Regulations were enacted to eliminate lead completely in gasoline sold. In the following case, the court reviewed an EPA order regulating the lead content of gasoline, the validity of which had been challenged by Ethyl Corporation.

Case 31.3 

ETHYL CORP. v. ENVIRONMENTAL PROTECTION AGENCY

United States Court of Appeals, District of Columbia Circuit, 1976. 541 F.2d 1.

HISTORICAL AND ENVIRONMENTAL SETTING *Among the obstacles to effective control of air pollution is the lack of scientific knowledge about the extent of the threat posed by specific pollutants. Sometimes, for example, it is unclear how much of a particular substance can be released into the air before it becomes a hazard to human health. Even when it is known how much of a substance is a health hazard, it can be difficult to regulate the sources of the substance if no single source releases enough of the substance to be hazardous. For instance, it is well known that lead is toxic. Because people are exposed to lead from many sources, however, it can be difficult to determine the negative health effects of an increase in the amount of lead*

Case 31.3—Continued

in the environment from any one source. Notwithstanding these problems, the EPA has a mandate to protect the public health.

FACTS Ethyl Corporation, a leading producer of gasoline additives, sought court review of the Environmental Protection Agency's order that required annual reductions in the lead content of gasoline. The Clean Air Act authorized the agency to regulate gasoline additives that are a danger to public health or welfare. Ethyl Corporation claimed that the EPA had exceeded its authority by requiring annual reductions in the lead content of gasoline.

ISSUE Had the EPA exceeded its authority by requiring a reduction in the lead content of gasoline?

DECISION No. The court found that the EPA had not abused its discretion by requiring a reduction in the lead content of gasoline.

REASON The record in this case was massive—over 10,000 pages. The EPA had relied on this evidence in making its decision, and although the evidence was not wholly unassailable, it did provide a reasonable basis on which to make a decision. The court defined its scope of review as follows: "Our scope * * * requires us to strike 'agency action, findings, and conclusions' [only if] we find [them] to be 'arbitrary, capricious, an abuse of discretion, or otherwise not in accordance with law.' This standard of review is a highly deferential one. It presumes agency action to be valid. Moreover, it forbids the court's substituting its judgment for that of the agency."

Stationary Sources A number of limits have been placed on stationary sources of air pollution. Under the 1990 amendments to the Clean Air Act, 110 of the oldest coal-burning power plants in the United States must cut their sulfur dioxide emissions by 40 percent by the year 2001 to reduce acid rain. Utilities were granted "credits," which allow them to emit certain amounts of sulfur dioxide, and those that emit less than the allowed amount can sell their credits to other polluters. Controls on other factories and businesses are intended to reduce ground-level ozone pollution in ninety-six cities to healthful levels by the year 2005 (Los Angeles has until 2010). Industrial emissions of 189 hazardous air pollutants must be reduced by 90 percent by the year 2000. By 2002, production of chlorofluorocarbons, carbon tetrachloride, and methyl chloroform—used in air conditioning, refrigeration, and insulation and linked to depletion of the ozone layer—must stop.

The 189 hazardous air pollutants just referred to include asbestos, benzene, beryllium, cadmium, mercury, radiation, vinyl chloride, and other cancer-causing materials. Hazardous air pollutants are those likely to cause an increase in mortality or in serious irreversible or incapacitating illness. These pollutants may also cause neurological and reproductive damage. They are emitted by a variety of business activities, including smelting, dry cleaning, house painting, and commercial baking. Instead of establishing specific emissions standards for each hazardous air pollutant, the 1990 amendments require industry to use the best available technology to limit those emissions. The EPA may strengthen this requirement if necessary to protect the public health.

Water Pollution

The major sources of water pollution are industrial, municipal, and agricultural. Pollutants entering streams, lakes, and oceans include organic wastes, heated water, sediments from soil runoff, nutrients (including detergents, fertilizers, and human and animal wastes), and toxic chemicals and other hazardous substances. Certain types of fish cannot live in waters in which organic wastes decompose, turning the water dark and malodorous. Heated water speeds the growth of algae and disrupts fish reproduction. Sediments and nutrients speed the dying of lakes, an otherwise natural process that turns lakes into land. Toxic chemicals and hazardous substances make water and fish, even after treatment, unsafe for human consumption. Laws and regulations governing water pollution relate to the pollution of navigable waters,

"Among the treasures of our land is water—fast becoming our most valuable, most prized, most critical resource."

Dwight D. Eisenhower, 1890–1969
(Thirty-fourth president of the United States, 1953–1961)

drinking water, and ocean water. Each of these areas is discussed in the following sections.

Navigable Waters Federal regulations governing the pollution of water can be traced back to the Rivers and Harbors Appropriations Act of 1899.[6] These regulations required a permit for discharging or depositing refuse in navigable waterways. In 1948, Congress passed the Federal Water Pollution Control Act (FWPCA), but its regulatory system and enforcement proved to be inadequate.

In 1972, amendments to the FWPCA—known as the Clean Water Act—established a new system of goals and standards. These amendments established goals to (1) make waters safe for swimming, (2) protect fish and wildlife, and (3) eliminate the discharge of pollutants into the water. They set forth specific time schedules, which were extended by amendment in 1977 and by the Water Quality Act of 1987. Regulations for the most part specify that the best available technology be installed. The 1972 amendments also required municipal and industrial polluters to apply for permits before discharging wastes into navigable waters. Under the act, injunctive relief and damages can be imposed. The polluting party can be required to clean up the pollution or pay for the cost of doing so. In most cases, explicit penalties are also imposed on parties that pollute the water.

WETLANDS
Areas of land designated by government agencies (such as the Army Corps of Engineers or the Environmental Protection Agency) as protected areas that suppose wildlife and that therefore cannot be filled in or dredged by private contractors or parties.

The Clean Water Act prohibits the filling or dredging of **wetlands** unless a permit has been obtained by the Army Corps of Engineers. The EPA defines *wetlands* as "those areas that are inundated or saturated by surface or ground water at a frequency and duration sufficient to support, and that under normal circumstances do support, a prevalence of vegetation typically adapted for life in saturated soil conditions." In recent years, federal regulatory policy in regard to wetlands has elicited substantial controversy (see, for example, the *Law in the Extreme* in Chapter 1) because of the broad interpretation of what constitutes a wetland subject to the regulatory authority of the federal government. The following case is illustrative.

Case 31.4
HOFFMAN HOMES, INC. v. ADMINISTRATOR, UNITED STATES ENVIRONMENTAL PROTECTION AGENCY

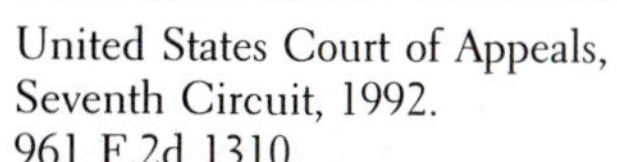

United States Court of Appeals,
Seventh Circuit, 1992.
961 F.2d 1310.

HISTORICAL AND ENVIRONMENTAL SETTING *Wetlands are an important resource. They provide a natural filtration system for water, a spawning ground for a variety of fish and waterfowl, and an important source of recreation. Wetlands appear to be especially necessary for the filtration of water near large urban areas, where pollution is the worst. Without wetlands, the cost to industry and government of abating pollution would be increased because of the additional costs that would be required for technology to take the place of what nature provides. Wetlands that are adjacent to lakes and other open bodies of water also control flooding in those waters. Wetlands are, however, a fragile resource that is constantly in danger of being eliminated by dredge-and-fill operations and the need of developers for more land. Destruction of wetlands degrades the quality of adjacent bodies of water. Thus, the courts agree that navigable waters—including intrastate waters that are used to irrigate crops or support fisheries, or that are visited by interstate travelers—and wetlands adjacent to those waters may be regulated by the EPA. Polluting those waters and their adjacent wetlands affects interstate commerce.*

FACTS Hoffman Homes, Inc., in preparation for the construction of a housing subdivision, filled and graded a bowl-shaped depression with an area of 0.8 acres "(Area A") located on property owned by Hoffman in Hoffman Estates, Illinois. Before Hoffman filled Area A, rainwater periodically collected there. The EPA issued an order stating that Hoffman had filled wetlands without a permit in violation of the

6. 33 U.S.C. Section 401–418.

Case 31.4—Continued

Clean Water Act and ordered Hoffman, among other things, to cease its filling activities and pay a fine of $50,000 for violating the act. In response to Hoffman's protests that the EPA had no regulatory authority over Area A because the area in no way affected *inter*state commerce, the EPA stated that it had authority to regulate discharges of fill materials into *intra*state wetlands that have a "minimal, potential effect" on interstate commerce. The EPA found that Area A had such a minimal, potential effect on interstate commerce because migratory birds could *potentially* use the area. Hoffman appealed the decision to the Seventh Circuit Court of Appeals.

ISSUE Does the EPA have regulatory authority over Area A?

DECISION No. The appellate court held that the EPA had no regulatory authority over Area A and vacated the penalty against Hoffman.

REASON The court found that "the EPA has not even attempted to construct a theory of how filling Area A affects interstate commerce. And, no evidence on the record would support any such theory. For example, there is no evidence that filling Area A would affect navigation. There is no evidence that filling Area A would pollute another open body of water used for irrigation, fishing or recreational activities. There is no evidence that interstate travelers visited Area A (and it is hard to imagine any purpose for their doing so). * * * Not only is there no evidence that interstate travelers came to Area A to watch or photograph birds protected by an international treaty, there is no evidence that migratory birds of any feather actually used Area A. Rather, the EPA claims jurisdiction solely because migratory birds could, potentially, use Area A. Since creation [of the states], migratory birds have flown interstate. But this annual traverse by itself does not affect commerce. The birds obviously do not engage in commerce."

Drinking Water Another statute governing water pollution is the Safe Drinking Water Act. Passed in 1974, this act requires the EPA to set maximum levels for pollutants in public water systems. Public water system operators must come as close as possible to meeting the EPA's standards by using the best available technology that is economically and technologically feasible. The EPA is particularly concerned with contamination from underground sources.

Ocean Dumping The Marine Protection, Research, and Sanctuaries Act of 1972 (popularly known as the Ocean Dumping Act), as amended in 1983, regulates the transportation and dumping of material into ocean waters. It prohibits entirely the ocean dumping of radiological, chemical, and biological-warfare agents and high-level radioactive waste. A violation of any provision may result in a civil penalty of $50,000, and a knowing violation is a criminal offense that may result in a $50,000 fine, imprisonment for not more than a year, or both.

Noise Pollution

Regulations concerning noise pollution include the Noise Control Act of 1972. This act requires the establishment of noise-emission standards (maximum noise levels below which no harmful effects occur due to interference with speech or other activity). The standards must be achievable by the best available technology, and they must be economically within reason. The act prohibits, among other things, distributing products manufactured in violation of the noise-emission standards and tampering with noise-control devices. Either of these activities can result in an injunction or whatever other remedy "is necessary to protect the public health and welfare." Illegal product distribution can also result in a fine and imprisonment.

Categories of products that have been identified as major sources of noise include construction equipment, transportation equipment, motors and engines, and electrical and electronic equipment. Specific products include medium-sized and heavy-duty trucks, portable air compressors, motorcycles, buses, earth-moving equipment, truck transport refrigeration units, and truck-mounted solid waste compactors. Nontransportation sources include forges, foundries, power plants, oil refineries,

Business Law in Action

Interstate Water Pollution

Disputes over interstate waterways often involve the pollution by firms in one state of a waterway that flows into another state. Because states have different water quality standards, a question arises as to which state's laws should govern in this situation. Furthermore, the federal Environmental Protection Agency (EPA) also regulates water pollution under the authority of the Clean Water Act of 1972 and its amendments. Should the states' water quality standards take priority over federal regulation by the EPA, or do the standards issued by the EPA preempt state laws?

In 1992, the United States Supreme Court tackled such questions in *Arkansas v. Oklahoma.*[a] In that case, a Fayetteville, Arkansas, sewage treatment plant had obtained a permit from the EPA to discharge effluent (waste) into a stream that ultimately reached the Illinois River before it flowed into Oklahoma. The state of Oklahoma and other Oklahoma parties challenged the EPA-issued permit, contending that the Fayetteville discharge violated Oklahoma water quality standards, which required that there be "no degradation" of the upper Illinois River, and that the EPA should have taken these standards into consideration. The EPA had, in fact, taken Oklahoma's standards into consideration, but it had decided that Oklahoma's standards would only be violated if the Fayetteville discharge effected an "actually detectable or measurable" change in the water quality of the upper Illinois River in Oklahoma.

After making detailed findings of fact, an EPA administrative law judge (ALJ) found that the Fayetteville discharge would not lead to a detectable change in water quality under any of Oklahoma's four primary measures of water pollution. Therefore, the Fayetteville plant could keep on pouring its wastes into the Arkansas stream. Oklahoma appealed the ALJ's decision to a federal court of appeals, which reversed the ALJ's decision, and ultimately, the case reached the United States Supreme Court.

The Supreme Court first assessed the relative authority of state regulations affecting interstate waterways, concluding that when an interstate waterway is involved and the downstream state objects to an upstream state's discharge, the only state law applicable is the law of the upstream state. Therefore, when a permit to discharge waste into a waterway is being issued by the upstream state's regulatory agency, the downstream state "does not have the authority to block the issuance of the permit if it is dissatisfied with the proposed standards. An affected State's only recourse is to apply to the EPA Administrator, who then has the discretion to disapprove the permit if he concludes that the discharges will have an undue impact on interstate waters. * * * Thus the Act makes it clear that affected States occupy a subordinate position to source States in the federal regulatory program."

The Court then addressed the issue of whether the EPA had the authority to interpret Oklahoma's standard of "no degradation" of its waterways to mean no "detectable or measurable" change in the water quality of its waterways. The Court held that the EPA had such authority. The Clean Water Act "vests in the EPA and the States broad authority to develop long-range area-wide programs to alleviate and eliminate existing pollution." The EPA had validly exercised its discretionary powers when it determined that the Fayetteville discharge had to comply with Oklahoma's water quality standards and also when it determined that Oklahoma's standards would not be violated unless there was a detectable deterioration in the water quality of the upper Illinois River in Oklahoma. The EPA had stressed that "unless there is some method for measuring compliance, there is no way to ensure compliance." The Court agreed with this approach and stated that the EPA's "interpretation of the Oklahoma standards makes eminent sense in the interstate context: if every discharge that had some theoretical impact on a downstream State were interpreted as 'degrading' the downstream waters, downstream States might wield an effective veto over upstream discharges."

a. ___U.S.___, 112 S.Ct. 1046, 117 L.Ed.2d 239 (1992).

cement plants, commercial air-conditioning equipment, and lawn care equipment. By exceeding the noise-emission standards, these sources violate the act. Church bells are not included.

Toxic Chemicals and Toxic Torts

Originally, most environmental clean-up efforts were directed toward reducing smog and making water safe for fishing and swimming. Over time, however, it became clear that chemicals released into the environment in relatively small amounts could pose a threat to human life and health. Control of these toxic chemicals has become an important part of environmental law. The causes of action filed against toxic polluters are referred to as **toxic torts.**

TOXIC TORTS
Failure to use or to clean up properly or where prohibited to use toxic chemicals that cause harm to a person or society.

Pesticides and Herbicides The first toxic chemical problem to receive widespread public attention was that posed by pesticides and herbicides. Using these chemicals to kill insects and weeds has increased agricultural productivity, but their residues remain in the environment. In some instances, accumulations of these residues have killed animals, and scientists have identified potential long-term effects that are detrimental to people.

The federal statute regulating pesticides and herbicides is the Federal Insecticide, Fungicide, and Rodenticide Act (FIFRA) of 1947. Under FIFRA, pesticides and herbicides must be (1) registered before they can be sold, (2) certified and used only for approved applications, and (3) used in limited quantities when applied to food crops. If a substance is identified as harmful, the EPA can cancel its registration after a hearing. If the harm is imminent, the EPA can suspend registration pending the hearing. The EPA, or state officers or employees, may also inspect factories in which these chemicals are manufactured.

It is a violation of FIFRA to sell a pesticide or herbicide that is unregistered, a pesticide or herbicide whose registration has been canceled or suspended, or a pesticide or herbicide with a false or misleading label. For example, it is an offense to sell a substance that is adulterated (that has a chemical strength different from the concentration declared on the label). It is also an offense to destroy or deface any labeling required under the act. The act's labeling requirements include directions for the use of the pesticide or herbicide, warnings to protect human health and the environment, a statement of treatment in the case of poisoning, and a list of the ingredients.

A private party can petition the EPA to suspend or cancel the registration of a pesticide or herbicide. If the EPA fails to act, the private party can petition a federal court to review the EPA's failure. Penalties for registrants and producers for violating FIFRA include imprisonment for up to one year and a fine of no more than $50,000. Penalties for commercial dealers include imprisonment for up to one year and a fine of no more than $25,000. Farmers and other private users of pesticides or herbicides who violate the act are subject to a $1,000 fine and imprisonment for up to thirty days.

Toxic Substances The first comprehensive law covering toxic substances was the Toxic Substances Control Act, which was passed in 1976 to regulate chemicals and chemical compounds that are known to be toxic—such as asbestos and polychlorinated biphenyls, popularly known as PCBs—and to institute investigation of any possible harmful effects from new chemical compounds. The regulations authorize the EPA to require that manufacturers, processors, and other organizations planning to use chemicals first determine their effects on human health and the environment. The EPA can regulate substances that may pose an imminent hazard or an unreasonable risk of injury to health or the environment.

Hazardous Wastes Some industrial, agricultural, and household wastes pose special threats. If not properly disposed of, these toxic chemicals may present a substantial danger to human health and the environment. If released into the environment, they may contaminate public drinking water resources.

Resource Conservation and Recovery Act In 1976, Congress passed the Resource Conservation and Recovery Act (RCRA) in reaction to an ever-increasing concern with the effects of hazardous waste materials on the environment. The RCRA required the EPA to establish regulations to monitor and control hazardous waste

Landmark in the Law

Superfund

In 1980, Congress passed the Comprehensive Environmental Response, Compensation, and Liability Act (CERCLA). The origins of CERCLA, which is commonly referred to as Superfund, can be traced to drafts that the Environmental Protection Agency (EPA) started to circulate in 1978. The EPA wanted the legal power to file a large number of hazardous-waste lawsuits nationwide. The EPA felt that the power it had under the Research Conservation and Recovery Act of 1976 was insufficient and did not adequately address all the relevant issues. EPA officials emphasized the political necessity of new legislation by pointing to what they thought were "ticking time bombs"—dump sites around the country that were ready to explode and injure the public with toxic fumes. The popular press also gave prominence to hazardous-waste dump sites at the time. The New York Love Canal disaster began to make the headlines in 1978 after residents in the area complained about health problems, contaminated sludge oozing into their basements, and chemical "volcanoes" erupting in their yards as a result of Hooker Chemical's dumping of approximately 21,000 tons of chemicals into the canal from 1942 to 1953. The Love Canal situation made the national news virtually every day from the middle of May to the middle of June in 1980. The actress Jane Fonda made a tearful visit there during which she urged the residents to evacuate. Love Canal was featured on *60 Minutes*, *Good Morning America*, and other popular television shows. It was the Love Canal disaster that gave rise to the "ticking time bomb" metaphor and that influenced the tone and direction of the legislation that was to become CERCLA.

Purpose and Basic Provisions of CERCLA

The basic purpose of CERCLA, which was amended in 1986 by the Superfund Amendments and Reauthorization Act, is to regulate the clean-up of leaking hazardous-waste disposal sites. The act has four primary elements:

- CERCLA established an information-gathering and analysis system that allows federal and state governments to characterize chemical dump sites and to develop priorities for appropriate action. This system requires the EPA administrator to designate which substances, when released into the environment, may present substantial danger to the public health.
- CERCLA authorized the EPA to respond to hazardous-substance emergencies and to clean up leaking sites. Such clean-up activities may be carried out by the EPA directly through contractors or through cooperative agreements with the states if the persons responsible for the problem fail to clean up the site.
- CERCLA created a Hazardous Substance Response Trust Fund (Superfund) to pay for the clean-up of hazardous sites. Monies for the fund are obtained through taxes on certain businesses, including those processing or producing petroleum and chemical feed stock. The current size of this fund is about $10 billion.[a]
- CERCLA allows the government to recover the cost of clean-up from the persons who were responsible for hazardous-substance releases (see this chapter's discussion of CERCLA for further detail on liability for clean-up costs).

The Application of CERCLA

Although everybody is in favor of cleaning up America's toxic waste dumps, nobody has the slightest idea what this task will ultimately cost. Much of the problem in determining the ultimate costs of the Superfund program stems from the difficulty of estimating the costs of cleaning up a site. Until excavation has occurred, it is often difficult to assess the extent of contamination. Moreover, there is no agreed-on standard as to how clean these sites need to be before they no longer pose any threat of harm to life. Do you have to remove *all* of the contamination, or would removal of some lesser amount satisfy a reasonable degree of environmental quality? On the cost side of the picture, another question exists: If, say, 90 percent of the waste at a given site could be removed for $50,000, but the removal of the other 10 percent would cost $2 million, is it reasonable to remove that remaining 10 percent?

Perhaps the real question that Congress now needs to ask is how effective the Superfund has been. As of 1992, of the $11 billion paid out by insurance companies for CERCLA liability, about 85 percent went to legal and administrative fees. That means that only 15 percent was used for actual clean-up. The reality today is that there is a multibillion-dollar Superfund industry. This industry comprises thousands of scientists, engineers, government officials, lawyers, lobbyists, and policy specialists. Given the complex nature of CERCLA, as well as the absence of guidance as to what is meant by "clean-up" in the context of hazardous wastes, the industry will only get larger in the future.

a. This amount is not sufficient to cover the cost of cleaning up all hazardous sites. But many of the parties responsible for the costs are unable or unwilling to pay their share. Some have declared bankruptcy; some are involved in litigation with the EPA; others are simply not paying, and an understaffed EPA is too overworked to undertake legal proceedings to collect. Ultimately, it may be the taxpayers who pay for the clean-up.

disposal and to determine which forms of solid waste should be considered hazardous and thus subject to regulation. Under the authority granted by this act, the EPA has promulgated various technical requirements for limited types of facilities for storage and treatment of hazardous waste. It also requires all producers of hazardous waste materials to label and package properly any hazardous waste to be transported.

The RCRA was amended in 1984 and 1986 to add several regulatory requirements to those already monitored and enforced by the EPA. The basic aims of the amendments were to decrease the use of land containment in disposing of hazardous waste and to require compliance with the act by some generators of hazardous waste—such as those generating less than 1,000 kilograms a month—that had previously been excluded from regulation under the RCRA.

Superfund In 1980, Congress passed the Comprehensive Environmental Response, Compensation, and Liability Act (CERCLA), also known as Superfund (described in this chapter's *Landmark in the Law*). Basically, CERCLA provides for clean-up of hazardous-waste disposal sites that threaten environmental health and safety. The act provides that when there is a release or threatened release of hazardous waste from a site (into the soil or groundwater, for example), the EPA can clean up the site and recover the cost of the clean-up from (1) any person who generated the wastes disposed of at the site, (2) any person who transported hazardous wastes to the site, (3) any person who owned or operated the site at the time of the disposal, or (4) the current owner or operator of the site. Liability is joint and several; that is, a person who generated only a fraction of the hazardous waste disposed of at the site may nevertheless be liable for all of the clean-up costs.

Courts often focus on the meaning of the words "owner or operator" to determine who is a potentially responsible party. A parent company has been held liable as an "operator" for clean-up costs for a chemical spill at a plant owned by its subsidiary. The court pointed out that the parent company controlled the subsidiary's finances, real-estate transactions, and contact with the government and that the parent company's personnel held most of the subsidiary's officer and director positions.[7] In other cases, courts have held officers and shareholders liable based on their authority to exercise control over their corporations.[8] A secured creditor of an operator of a facility has also been held liable on the basis that the creditor participated in the financial management of the facility to a degree indicating a capacity to control the corporation's handling of hazardous waste.[9] In the following case, the court considered whether a successor corporation can be held liable under CERCLA.

Case 31.5
ANSPEC CO. v. JOHNSON CONTROLS, INC.
United States Court of Appeals, Sixth Circuit, 1991.
992 F.2d 1240.

HISTORICAL AND TECHNOLOGICAL SETTING *Ultraspherics, Inc., was in the business of manufacturing precision balls made of metal and plastic. Chemicals used in grinding the metal and plastic to form the balls and in degreasing produced by-products of hazardous sludge and liquids. Ultraspherics also used toxic cleaning solvents. On site, the company buried an underground storage tank for the disposal of the hazardous waste. When the underground tank was filled, the company added two aboveground tanks, which, during the life of the corporation, were also filled. The methods used to remove the hazardous waste during the manufacturing process, and to dispose of and store the materials in the tanks, routinely caused substances to be released into the soil and groundwater at the site.*

7. *United States v. Kayser-Roth Corp.*, 910 F.2d 24 (1st Cir. 1990).
8. See, for example, *State of New York v. Shore Realty Corp.*, 759 F.2d 1032 (2d Cir. 1985).
9. *United States v. Fleet Factors Corp.*, 901 F.2d 1550 (11th Cir. 1990).

Case 31.5—Continued

FACTS The Anspec Company purchased a parcel of land from Ultraspherics, Inc., in 1978. After the sale, Ultraspherics merged into the Hoover Group, which was designated as the surviving corporation. Johnson Controls, Inc., was the sole shareholder of the Hoover Group and of Hoover Universal, which was the sole shareholder of Ultraspherics. Prior to the sale of the property to Anspec, Ultraspherics had placed three tanks on the property—one underground and two aboveground—which were used to store hazardous waste materials. Leaks and spills of the hazardous waste contaminated the soil at the site and the groundwater beneath the site. Anspec requested the Hoover Group, as the corporate successor of Ultraspherics, to pay the costs associated with cleaning up the site. When the Hoover Group refused to comply, Anspec brought an action against Ultraspherics and its corporate successors. The trial court held that Ultraspherics could not be liable because it no longer existed. The other defendants—the Hoover Group, Hoover Universal, and Johnson Controls—moved for dismissal. On the grounds that none of them had ever owned, occupied, or stored chemicals on the property and that CERCLA did not provide that successor corporations were liable for clean-up costs, the trial court granted the motion for dismissal, and Anspec appealed.

ISSUE Can the successor corporations be held liable for clean-up costs under CERCLA?

DECISION Yes. The appellate court reversed the trial court's judgment and remanded the case for further proceedings.

REASON The appellate court noted that CERCLA clearly states that liability for clean-up costs are imposed on "any person who[,] at the time of disposal of any hazardous substance[,] owned or operated any facility at which such hazardous substances were disposed of." The court concluded that Congress included successor corporations with other entities that are potentially liable under CERCLA for clean-up costs. The court pointed out that "although the separate existence of every corporation except the surviving corporation in a merger ceases, the surviving corporation has all liabilities of every corporation that was a party to the merger. For purposes of liability, the surviving corporation and the merged corporation are one and the same." Construing CERCLA "in light of [this] universally accepted principle of private corporation law," the court said that "when Congress wrote 'corporation' in CERCLA it intended to include a successor corporation." Thus, "[i]f Ultraspherics is not liable for cleanup costs, it is only because Hoover Group stands in its shoes as the surviving party that became liable for its obligations."

Application

Law and the Businessperson—Keeping Abreast of Environmental Laws

Businesspersons today increasingly face the threat of severe civil or criminal penalties if they violate environmental laws and regulations. It therefore is necessary that every person in the business world be aware of what those laws and regulations are and how to monitor changes in them. At the federal level, approximately five hundred civil and criminal cases are referred by the Environmental Protection Agency (EPA) to the Justice Department each year, and civil judgments in environmental cases are now exceeding one billion dollars annually. At a minimum, knowledge of the changing and complex nature of environmental law will help a businessperson to know when to contact an attorney during the normal course of business.

Consider some areas of concern that affect businesses. Businesspersons often purchase business property. When engaging in such purchases, you must keep in mind the environmental problems that may arise. Purchasers of property must themselves raise environmental issues because sellers, title insurance companies, and real estate brokers will rarely pursue such matters. And only recently have banks begun to worry about the potential environmental hazards of a business property in making loan determinations. A businessperson purchasing property should learn whether there are any restrictions regarding the use of the land, such as whether

Application—Continued

the land can be cleared of trees for construction purposes. The most prominent environmental concern, however, is whether the property has been contaminated by hazardous wastes created by the previous owners. There seems to be an unending number of ways in which purchasers of property can be held liable under the Comprehensive Environmental Response, Compensation, and Liability Act (CERCLA) of 1980 for the clean-up of hazardous wastes dumped by previous property owners. While it is true that current property owners who are sued under CERCLA for clean-up costs can sue the previous owners, such litigation is uncertain and usually costly. Clearly, a more prudent course when purchasing property is to investigate the history of the use of the land. A business property purchaser would certainly be well advised to hire a private environmental site inspector to determine, at a minimum, whether the land has any obvious signs of former contamination.

There is also an incentive for today's companies to discover their own environmental wrongdoings. The Justice Department has issued a new set of guidelines to encourage such corporate activity by allowing those firms that attempt to promptly detect, disclose, and correct environmental crimes to be given lighter penalties. Under the guidelines, a company that regularly conducts comprehensive audits of its compliance with environmental requirements, immediately reports a violation to the government, disciplines the responsible people within the corporation, and provides their names to the government should qualify for leniency.

Checklist for the Businessperson

- ☐ 1. If you are in business or plan to open a business that is going to purchase real estate, use land, or engage in activities that might cause environmental damage, check with your attorney immediately.
- ☐ 2. If you want to avoid liability for violating environmental regulations or statutes, conduct environmental compliance audits on a regular basis. To learn whether you are doing so appropriately, check with your attorney.
- ☐ 3. If you are ever charged with violating an environmental regulation or law, you must check with your attorney.
- ☐ 4. In short, environmental law is sufficiently complex that you should never attempt to deal with it without the help of an attorney.

❖ Key Terms

bait-and-switch advertising 743
cease-and-desist order 743
"cooling-off" law 745
counteradvertising 743
deceptive advertising 742
environmental impact statement (EIS) 753
redress 746
Regulation Z 745
toxic tort 761
wetland 758

❖ Chapter Summary: Consumer and Environmental Law

CONSUMER PROTECTION LAWS	
Advertising	1. *Deceptive advertising*—Advertising that is false or may be misleading to consumers is prohibited by the FTC. 2. *Bait-and-switch advertising*—Advertising a lower-priced product when the intention is not to sell the advertised product but to lure consumers into the store and convince them to buy a higher-priced product is prohibited by the FTC. 3. *FTC actions against deceptive advertising*— a. Cease-and-desist orders—Requiring the advertiser to stop the challenged advertising. b. Counteradvertising—Requiring the advertiser to advertise to correct the earlier misinformation.
Labeling and Packaging	Manufacturers must comply with labeling or packaging requirements for their specific products. In general, all labels must be accurate and not misleading.

❖ Chapter Summary: Consumer and Environmental Law—Continued

Sales	1. *Credit terms*—If certain credit terms pertaining to the purchase of a product are advertised, other relevant credit and sale terms (such as cash price, down payment, payments, other charges, and annual percentage rate of interest) must be included. 2. *Mail-order sales*—Federal and state statutes regulate certain practices of sellers who solicit through the mails and prohibit the use of the mails to defraud individuals. 3. *Unsolicited merchandise sent by U.S. mail*—May be retained, used, discarded, or disposed of in any manner by recipient. Recipient incurs no contractual obligation (under Postal Reorganization Act of 1970). 4. *Door-to-door sales*—The FTC requires all door-to-door sellers to give consumers three days to cancel any sale. 5. *Real estate sales*—Various federal and state laws apply to consumer transactions involving real estate.
Health Protection	Health-protection laws govern the processing and distribution of meat and poultry, poisonous substances, and drugs and cosmetics. For some products (such as cigarettes), explicit warnings about health hazards are required.
Product Safety	The Consumer Product Safety Act of 1972 seeks to protect consumers from risk of injury from hazardous products. The Consumer Product Safety Commission has the power to remove products that are deemed imminently hazardous from the market and to ban the manufacture and sale of hazardous products.
Credit Protection	1. *Consumer Credit Protection Act, Title I (Truth-in-Lending Act)*—A disclosure law regulated by the Federal Reserve Board; requires sellers and lenders to disclose credit terms or loan terms. Transactions covered by the act typically include retail and installment sales and loans, car loans, home-improvement loans, and certain real estate loans. Additionally, the Truth-in-Lending Act provides for the following: a. Equal credit opportunity (prohibits creditors from discriminating on the basis of race, religion, marital status, sex, etc.). b. Credit-card rules (allow credit-card users to withhold payment for a faulty product sold, or for an error in billing, until the dispute is resolved). c. Credit-card protection (limits liability of cardholders prior to notice to $50 for unauthorized charges and protects consumers from liability for unauthorized charges made on unsolicited credit cards). 2. *Fair Credit Reporting Act*—Entitles consumers to be informed of a credit investigation, to request verification of the accuracy of the report, to have unverified information removed from their files, and to add "their side of the story" to their credit files. 3. *Fair Debt Collection Practices Act*—Prohibits debt collectors from using unfair debt-collection practices (such as contacting debtor at place of employment if employer objects or at unreasonable times, contacting third parties about the debt, harassment, intimidation, etc.). 4. *Uniform Consumer Credit Code*—A comprehensive body of rules governing the most important aspects of consumer credit; adopted by only a minority of states.
ENVIRONMENTAL LAW	
Common Law Actions	1. *Nuisance statutes*—Statutes under which early common law actions against pollution-causing activities were brought. An action was permissible only if an individual suffered a harm separate and distinct from that of the general public. 2. *Negligence*—Parties may recover damages for injuries sustained as a result of pollution-causing activities of a firm if it can be demonstrated that the harm was a foreseeable result of the firm's failure to exercise reasonable care. 3. *Strict liability*—Businesses engaging in ultrahazardous activities are liable for whatever injuries the activities cause, regardless of whether the firms exercise reasonable care.
Government Regulation	1. *Local and state regulation*—Activities affecting the environment are controlled at the local and state levels through regulations relating to land use, the disposal and recycling of garbage and waste, and pollution-causing activities in general.

❖ Chapter Summary: Consumer and Environmental Law—Continued

Government Regulation—Continued	2. *Federal regulation*— a. National Environmental Policy Act (1969)—Imposes environmental responsibilities on all federal agencies and requires for every major federal action the preparation of an environmental impact statement (EIS). An EIS must analyze the action's impact on the environment, its adverse effects and possible alternatives, and its irreversible effects on environmental quality. b. Environmental Protection Agency—Created in 1970 to coordinate federal environmental programs; administers most federal environmental policies and statutes. 3. *Air pollution*—Regulated under the authority of the Clean Air Act of 1963 and its amendments, particularly those of 1970, 1977, and 1990. 4. *Water pollution*—Regulated under the authority of the Rivers and Harbors Act of 1886, as amended, and the Federal Water Pollution Control Act of 1948, as amended by the Clean Water Act of 1972. 5. *Toxic chemicals*—Pesticides and herbicides, toxic substances, and hazardous waste are regulated under the authority of the Federal Insecticide, Fungicide, and Rodenticide Act of 1947, the Toxic Substances Control Act of 1976, and the Resource Conservation and Recovery Act of 1976, respectively. The Comprehensive Environmental Response, Compensation, and Liability Act (CERCLA) of 1980, as amended, regulates the clean-up of hazardous waste disposal sites.

❖ Questions and Case Problems

31-1. Credit Protection. What are the major federal statutes providing for consumer protection in credit transactions? Give examples of how each statute protects consumers.

31-2. Environmental Protection. Under what common law theories may businesses be held liable for environmental pollution?

31-3. Environmental Protection. Fruitade, Inc., is a processor of a soft drink called Freshen Up. Fruitade uses returnable bottles and uses a special acid to clean its bottles for further beverage processing. The acid is diluted with water and then allowed to pass into a navigable stream. Fruitade crushes its broken bottles and also throws the crushed glass into the stream. Discuss *fully* any environmental laws that Fruitade has violated.

31-4. Sales. On June 28, a sales representative for Renowned Books called on the Guevaras at their home. After listening to a very persuasive sales pitch, the Guevaras agreed in writing to purchase a twenty-volume set of historical encyclopedias from Renowned Books for a total of $299. An initial down payment of $35 was required, with the remainder of the price to be paid in monthly payments over a one-year period. Two days later, the Guevaras, having second thoughts about the purchase, contacted the book company and stated that they had decided to rescind the contract. Renowned Books said this would be impossible. Has Renowned Books violated any consumer law by not allowing the Guevaras to rescind their contract? Explain.

31-5. Credit Protection. Maria Ochoa receives two new credit cards on May 1. One was solicited from Midtown Department Store, and the other was unsolicited from High-Flying Airlines. During the month of May, Ochoa makes numerous credit-card purchases from Midtown Store, but she does not use the High-Flying Airlines card. On May 31, a burglar breaks into Ochoa's home and steals both credit cards, along with other items. Ochoa notifies the Midtown Department Store of the theft on June 2, but she fails to notify High-Flying Airlines. Using the Midtown credit card, the burglar makes a $500 purchase on June 1 and a $200 purchase on June 3. The burglar then charges a vacation flight on the High-Flying Airlines card for $1,000 on June 5. Ochoa receives the bills for these charges and refuses to pay them. Discuss Ochoa's liability in these situations.

31-6. Deceptive Advertising. Dennis and Janice Geiger saw an advertisement in a newspaper for a Kimball Whitney spinet piano on sale for $699 at McCormick Piano & Organ Co. Because the style of the piano drawn in the advertisement matched their furniture, the Geigers were particularly interested in the Kimball. When they went to McCormick Piano & Organ, however, they learned that the drawing closely resembled another, more expensive Crest piano and that the Kimball spinet looked quite different from the piano sketched in the drawing. The salesperson told the Geigers that she was unable to order the spinet piano in the style requested by the Geigers. When the Geigers asked for the names of other customers who had purchased the advertised pianos, the salesperson became hysterical and said she would not, under any circumstances, sell the Geigers a piano. The Geigers then brought suit against the piano store, alleging that the store had engaged in deceptive advertising in violation of Indiana law. Was the McCormick Piano & Organ Co. guilty of deceptive advertising? Explain. [*McCormick Piano & Organ Co. v. Geiger,* 412 N.E.2d 842 (Ind.App. 1980)]

31-7. Truth in Lending. On July 16, 1982, the Semars signed a loan contract with Platte Valley Federal Savings & Loan

Association, offering a second mortgage on their home as collateral. Under the Truth-in-Lending Act (TILA), borrowers are allowed three business days to rescind, without penalty, a consumer loan that uses their principal dwelling as security. TILA requires lenders in such situations to state specifically the last date on which the borrower can rescind the loan agreement. If they fail to include this date, the borrower may rescind the loan within three years after it was made. Platte Valley's form omitted the exact expiration date of the three-day period, although it stated that the rescission right expired three business days after July 16. The Semars ceased making monthly payments on the loan in September of 1983 and sent a notice of rescission to Platte Valley on February 15, 1984. The Semars claimed that Platte Valley had violated TILA by failing to specify in the loan contract the exact date of the expiration of the three-day rescission period. Because of this violation, the Semars maintained that they had three years in which to rescind the contract. Had Platte Valley violated TILA? Explain. [*Semar v. Platte Valley Federal Savings & Loan Association*, 791 F.2d 699 (9th Cir. 1986)]

31-8. Debt Collection. Swanson owed $262.20 to a hospital in southern Oregon for medical services he had received. When Swanson failed to pay the debt, the hospital turned the account over to a local collection agency, which sent Swanson a letter requesting payment of the bill. Swanson alleged that the letter violated Section 809(a) of the Fair Debt Collection Practices Act (FDCPA), which mandates that any debt collector or agency subject to the act must notify the consumer early in the collection process that the consumer has thirty days within which to request validation of the debt. In the meantime, the consumer may withhold payment on the debt until assured that she or he actually owes the money. The letter did contain notice that the consumer had thirty days in which to demand verification of the debt, but the notice was, according to Swanson, overshadowed and effectively negated by the following statement—which was printed in boldface, underlined, and set in a larger-than-standard typeface: IF THIS ACCOUNT IS PAID WITHIN THE NEXT 10 DAYS IT WILL NOT BE RECORDED IN OUR MASTER FILE AS AN UNPAID COLLECTION ITEM. A GOOD CREDIT RATING IS YOUR MOST VALUABLE ASSET. Had the collection agency violated Section 809(a) of the FDCPA? Explain. [*Swanson v. Southern Oregon Credit Service, Inc.*, 869 F.2d 1222 (9th Cir. 1989)]

31-9. Superfund. During the 1970s, a number of chemical companies disposed of their wastes at a facility maintained by South Carolina Recycling and Disposal, Inc. Hazardous chemical wastes were stored rather haphazardly; some leaked into the ground, and fires occurred on several occasions. Eventually, the Environmental Protection Agency (EPA) conducted clean-up operations under Superfund and sued companies that had used the site for the costs of the clean-up. Five of the defendant companies claimed that they should not be liable for the clean-up costs because there was no evidence that their waste materials had contributed in any way to the leakage problem or to any other hazard posed by the site. The EPA asserted that causation was not required for the companies' liability, only evidence that the companies had sent waste to the site. Will the EPA succeed in its claim? Discuss. [*United States v. South Carolina Recycling and Disposal, Inc.*, 653 F.Supp. 984 (D.S.C. 1986)]

31-10. Superfund. Asarco, Inc., had a copper smelter at Ruston, Washington. As part of its operations, Asarco produced a by-product called slag, a hard, rocklike substance. Industrial Mineral Products (IMP) sold the slag for Asarco to Louisiana-Pacific Corp. and other businesses, which used the slag as a ballast to stabilize the ground at log-sorting yards in the Tacoma, Washington, area. About nine months after IMP stopped selling the slag, it sold substantially all of its assets to L-Bar Products, Inc. Government agencies later discovered that the slag reacted with the acidic wood waste in the log-sorting yards, causing heavy metals from the slag to leach into the groundwater and soil. Louisiana-Pacific and the Port of Tacoma sued Asarco under the Comprehensive Environmental Response, Compensation, and Liability Act (CERCLA), claiming that Asarco was liable for clean-up costs. Asarco brought a third party claim against L-Bar as corporate successor to IMP. L-Bar moved for summary judgment, claiming that it was not the successor to IMP and could not be liable under CERCLA for IMP's actions. Will the court agree with L-Bar? Discuss fully. [*Louisiana-Pacific Corp. v. Asarco, Inc.*, 909 F.2d 1260 (9th Cir. 1990)]

31-11. Equal Credit Opportunity. Sebastian and Maria Shaumyan entered into a home improvement contract with Sidetex Co. Sidetex agreed to install siding, replace windows, and perform other related work at the Shaumyan's home, and the Shaumyans agreed to pay Sidetex a total of $14,800 according to the following schedule: $3,000 as a deposit; $4,000 when Sidetex began the work; $3,900 when the work was half completed; $1,950 on completion of the installation of the siding; and $1,950 on completion of the work on the storm doors and shutters. Although a clause in the agreement referred to the contract as a "consumer credit contract," the Shaumyans' payments were not subject to any finance charges. Sidetex commenced work under the contract, and the Shaumyans made the scheduled payments of $3,000, $4,000, and $3,900. Performance was not completed, however, because a dispute arose concerning the quality of the windows that Sidetex was to install. The Shaumyans brought an action against Sidetex to recover damages, claiming that Sidetex had violated the antidiscrimination provision of the Equal Credit Opportunity Act (ECOA) by requiring the signature of Mrs. Shaumyan on the home improvement contract. The central issue before the court was whether the home improvement contract, which provided for progressive payments by the Shaumyans, constituted a "credit transaction" subject to the antidiscrimination provisions of the ECOA. How should the court rule? Discuss fully. [*Shaumyan v. Sidetex Co.*, 900 F.2d 16 (1990)]

31-12. Equal Credit Opportunity. Mr. and Mrs. Roberts, both African Americans, went shopping at a Walmart store in St. Charles, Missouri, and presented a check to the Walmart cashier to pay for several items that they wanted to purchase. When the Robertses noticed that the cashier was recording their race on the check, they returned the merchandise and retrieved the check. The Robertses then sued the store, claiming in part that the cashier's recording of their race on the check violated the Equal Credit Opportunity Act (ECOA), which prohibits discrimination in consumer credit transactions. The Robertses alleged that the transaction fell under the ECOA because "the exchange of goods and merchandise for a check issued by a customer creates a valid debit or obligation on the part of the purchaser and defers payment until such time as the check is presented for payment to the debtor's bank and thereafter paid." Walmart brought a motion to dismiss the complaint for failure to state a claim upon which relief could be granted. Will the court grant Walmart's motion? Discuss fully. [*Roberts v. Walmart Stores, Inc.*, 736 F.Supp. 1527 (E.D.Mo. 1990)]

31-13. Truth in Lending. Michael and Patricia Jensen purchased a new 1989 Ford Tempo from Ray Kim Ford. The Jensens signed a retail installment contract that provided for an estimated trade-in value of $800 for their old car. When the traded-in car turned out to be worth $1,388.08, Ray Kim prepared a second retail installment contract, without the Jensens' knowledge. The second contract, although it credited the increased trade-in value of the car, compensated for this credit by increasing the interest rate, increasing the sales price of the car, and making other adjustments so that the second contract basically called for future cash payments of about the same amount as the first contract. In effect, the second contract gave the Jensens almost no benefit for the increased value of their traded-in car. The Jensens made payments under the contract until they noticed the five-cent difference in monthly payments, asked for a copy of the contract, and realized that it was not the contract that they had signed. The Jensens sued Ray Kim, alleging that the second contract was a forgery and that Ray Kim had violated the Truth-in-Lending Act by not disclosing to them the credit terms of the second contract. Had Ray Kim violated the Truth-in-Lending Act? If the Jensens chose to adopt the terms of the second contract, despite the forgery, had the act been violated? Discuss fully. [*Jensen v. Ray Kim Ford, Inc.*, 920 F.2d 3 (7th Cir. 1990)]

A Question of Ethics and Social Responsibility

31-14. *In 1979, Paul and John Reardon purchased sixteen acres of land located next to a manufacturing plant in Massachusetts. In 1983, a state environmental agency, responding to a citizen's report, tested soil samples from both properties and discovered extremely high levels of polychlorinated biphenyls (PCBs) on the plant site and on the Reardons' property where it bordered the site. Shortly thereafter, the Environmental Protection Agency (EPA) cleaned up the contaminated areas. In 1985, the EPA notified the Reardons that they might be liable for clean-up costs. An EPA investigation of the property in 1987 revealed that some soil was still contaminated. This time, the Reardons cleaned up the property themselves. In March 1989, the EPA placed a lien for an unspecified amount on all of the Reardons' property to secure payment for any clean-up costs for which the Reardons might be liable. The EPA told the Reardons that they could settle the claims against them for $336,709 but noted that this amount did not limit the Reardons' potential liability. The Reardons filed a motion for a preliminary injunction, arguing, among other things, that filing a lien against their property without any prior notice or hearing violated their due process rights under the Fifth Amendment, which states that no person shall be deprived of life, liberty, or property without due process of law. The trial court dismissed the motion, but the appellate court reversed, holding that the only situation in which "the government's financial well-being may justify the draconian deprivation of its citizens' property" is a federal tax lien.* [Reardon v. United States, 947 *F.2d 1509 (1st Cir. 1991)*]

1. The Superfund statute (the Comprehensive Environmental Response, Compensation, and Liability Act, or CERCLA, of 1980, as amended in 1986) gives the government several powerful tools to use when attempting to collect clean-up costs from responsible parties. Among these tools is the authority to place a lien on a responsible party's property without providing for a reasonable hearing before placing the lien. Do you agree with the court that this practice violates the Fifth Amendment right to due process?
2. The EPA argued that the government's interest in recovering clean-up costs justified placing liens without first conducting hearings. According to the EPA, without that power, the government would lose significant leverage in recovering clean-up costs. Do you agree with this argument? Why or why not?
3. Essentially, this case illustrates a conflict between two major ethical concerns in American society: environmental protection and the constitutional right to due process of law. In 1986, when Congress reauthorized Superfund, it added the lien provision at issue in this case. Assuming that Congress represents the interests of American citizens, do you think that it was right for the court to override this interest by declaring the lien provision unconstitutional (because it failed to provide for the safeguard of prior hearings)?

For Critical Analysis

31-15. This chapter's *Landmark in the Law* raised the following question in regard to cleaning up hazardous-waste sites: "If, say, 90 percent of the waste at a given site could be removed for $50,000, but the removal of the other 10 percent would cost $2 million, is it reasonable to remove that remaining 10 percent?" How would you answer this question?

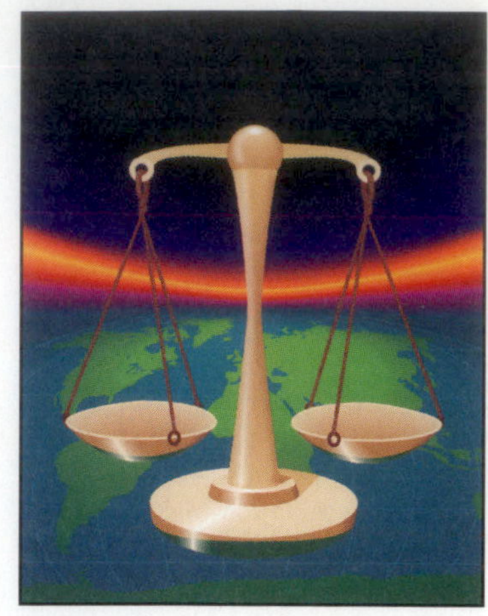

Chapter 32

Employee and Labor Law

"Show me the country in which there are no strikes, and I'll show you the country in which there is no liberty."

Samuel Gompers, 1850–1924 ***(American labor leader)***

Traditionally, employment relationships in the United States were governed by contract, tort, and agency law. Most employer-employee relationships were considered to be "at will." Under the **employment-at-will doctrine,** either party may terminate an employment contract at any time and for any reason. Prior to the Industrial Revolution, the bargaining power between employees and employers was relatively equal, and there was little need for government regulation of the workplace. The industrialization of America during the latter part of the nineteenth century significantly altered traditional employment relationships. Industrialization led to the growth of large factories and corporate employers. Factory employees often worked long hours. If an employee was injured on the job, it was difficult for him or her to recover from the employer, because an employee was considered to have assumed the risks of employment in accepting the job.

EMPLOYMENT-AT-WILL DOCTRINE
A doctrine that permits any employment contract without a definite period of time to be terminated at any time and for any reason by either party without liability.

Until the early 1930s, laws at the federal and state levels generally favored management. Since that time, numerous statutes have been enacted to protect the rights of employees. In this chapter, we look at some of the significant laws that regulate employment relationships, beginning with labor laws. At the heart of labor rights is the right to unionize and bargain with management for improved working conditions, salaries, and benefits. The ultimate weapon of labor is, of course, the strike. As noted in the opening quotation, the labor leader Samuel Gompers concluded that without the right to strike, there could be no liberty.

❖ Unions and Collective Bargaining

COLLECTIVE BARGAINING
The process by which labor and management negotiate the terms and conditions of employment, including such things as hours and workplace conditions.

Most of the early legislation to protect employees focused on the rights of workers to join unions and to engage in **collective bargaining.** Congress protected peaceful strikes, picketing, and boycotts in 1932 in the Norris-LaGuardia Act.[1] In effect, this act declared a national policy permitting employees to organize. The National Labor Relations Act (NLRA) of 1935, which is also known as the Wagner Act,[2] established the rights of employees to engage in collective bargaining and to strike. The act also created the National Labor Relations Board to oversee union elections and to prevent employers from engaging in unfair and illegal union-labor activities and

1. 29 U.S.C. Sections 101–110, 113–115.
2. 29 U.S.C. Sections 151–169.

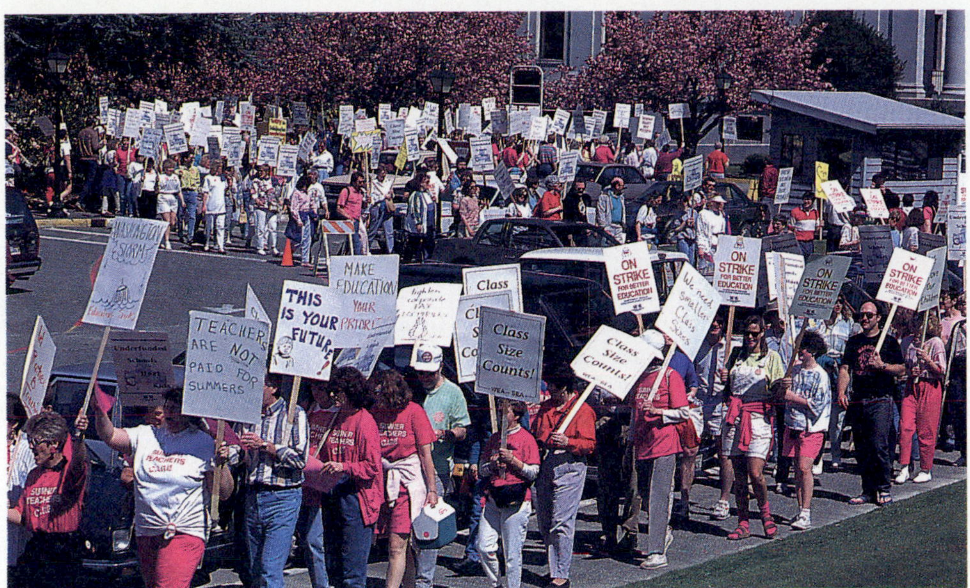

Are there any circumstances under which a strike could be considered an unfair labor practice?

unfair labor practices. The act specifically defined a number of employer practices as unfair to labor:

1. Interference with the efforts of employees to form, join, or assist labor organizations or to engage in concerted activities for their mutual aid or protection.
2. An employer's domination of a labor organization or contribution of financial or other support to it.
3. Discrimination in the hiring or awarding of tenure to employees for reason of union affiliation.
4. Discrimination against employees for filing charges under the act or giving testimony under the act.
5. Refusal to bargain collectively with the duly designated representative of the employees.

"Strong responsible unions are essential to industrial fair play. Without them the labor bargain is wholly one-sided."

Louis D. Brandeis, 1856–1941
(Associate justice of the United States Supreme Court, 1916–1939)

The Labor-Management Relations Act (Taft-Hartley Act)[3] of 1947 contained provisions protecting employers as well as employees. It provided a detailed list of unfair labor activities that unions as well as management were now forbidden to practice. Moreover, a *free-speech* amendment allowed employers to propagandize against unions prior to any union election.

The Labor-Management Reporting and Disclosure Act of 1959 (Landrum-Griffin Act)[4] established an employee bill of rights and reporting requirements for union activities. This act strictly regulates internal union procedures, such as elections, and prohibits so-called *hot-cargo contracts*—agreements in which employers voluntarily agreed with unions not to handle, use, or deal in the non-union-produced goods of other employers.

❖ Employment Discrimination

As mentioned previously, at common law, employment was terminable "at will." An employer could establish all terms and conditions of employment. Labor unions

3. 29 U.S.C. Sections 141–144.
4. 29 U.S.C. Sections 401–531.

Business Law in Action

Teamwork—A Solution or a Problem?

One of the major problems facing any corporation today is how to remain globally competitive in the face of stiff competition from Japan, other Asian countries, Germany, and the rest of Europe. Quality is a serious issue in remaining globally competitive. One of the ways in which many corporations have increased the quality of their products is by using some type of employee-participation program. Such programs are established not only to promote labor-management cooperation but also to incorporate employee input into the decision-making process in order to improve the quality of the products being produced. Some employee-participation programs also help corporations reduce their unit costs.

A typical employee-participation program along these lines was devised by Electromation, Inc., a midwestern electrical-components manufacturer. Electromation set up so-called action committees. The committees were initially established to counter employee dissatisfaction with new employment policies that related to absenteeism, nonsmoking rules, and so on. The workers who participated in these committees involved themselves in developing solutions to these and various other problems, including worker benefits. The Teamsters Union, which was attempting to unionize Electromation's work force, claimed that the committees violated the National Labor Relations Act (NLRA) of 1935 because essentially the committees were labor organizations that were unlawfully "dominated" by the employer.

The National Labor Relations Board (NLRB) supported the union's claims in a decision made on December 16, 1992,[a] in which the NLRB held that Electromation's action committees were essentially the equivalent of labor organizations as defined by Section 2(b) of the NLRA. Under that section, a labor organization is "any organization of any kind, or any agency or employee representation committee or plan, in which employees participate and which exists for the purpose, in whole or in part, of dealing with employers concerning grievances, labor disputes, wages, rates of pay, hours of employment, or conditions of work."

a. *Electromation, Inc.*, 309 NLRB No. 163 (1992).

Because management was a part of the action committees—after all, the committees operated in conjunction with managers, who listened to workers' ideas—the NLRB also determined that management had unlawfully "dominated" the organizations.

Numerous companies throughout the United States use similar action committees. Consequently, the corporate community felt that it had been dealt a severe blow by the NLRB's decision in regard to Electromation. The NLRB tried to make it clear that its December 16, 1992, decision was specific to the facts of the Electromation case and could not be applied generally to all other programs resembling Electromation's action committees. Nonetheless, the decision has alerted employers to the need for caution in establishing and maintaining such employee-participation programs. The problem for employers is that almost any type of employee-participation program could possibly be characterized as a labor organization as defined by Section 2(b) of the NLRA. This means that employers will have to be very careful in the future to minimize the risk of having employee-participation programs declared unlawful.

EMPLOYMENT DISCRIMINATION
Treating employees or job applicants unequally on the basis of race, sex, nationality, religion, or age; prohibited by Title VII of the Civil Rights Act of 1964 as amended.

PROTECTED CLASS
Under Title VII of the Civil Rights Act of 1964, any persons classified because of race, color, national origin, religion, or sex. Age and disability are classifications of protected classes under other acts.

were deemed private associations, so they could determine all membership requirements without oversight of the courts. In the past several decades, however, as a result of judicial decisions, administrative agency actions, and legislation, both employers and unions have been restricted in their ability to discriminate on the basis of race, color, religion, national origin, age, or sex. The most important statute relating to **employment discrimination** is Title VII of the Civil Rights Act of 1964.[5]

Title VII of the Civil Rights Act of 1964

Basically, Title VII of the Civil Rights Act of 1964 and its amendments eliminate job discrimination against employees, applicants, and union members on the basis of race, color, national origin, religion, and sex at any stage of employment. A class of persons defined by one or more of these criteria is known as a **protected class.** Title VII of the act applies to employers who affect interstate commerce and who

5. 42 U.S.C. Sections 2000e–2000e-17.

have fifteen or more employees, labor unions with fifteen or more members, labor unions that operate hiring halls (to which members go regularly to be rationed jobs as they become available), employment agencies, and state and local governing units or agencies. A special section forbids discrimination in most federal government employment.

A person who has suffered discrimination may not simply file a lawsuit under Title VII. Compliance with Title VII is monitored by the Equal Employment Opportunity Commission (EEOC). The EEOC has the power to issue guidelines for interpreting the law and to bring lawsuits against organizations that violate the law. Thus, first the victim must file a claim with the EEOC, which investigates the facts and seeks to achieve a voluntary conciliation through which the employer and the employee settle the dispute. If conciliation does not occur, the EEOC may sue the employer under Title VII. If the EEOC chooses not to sue—for example, if it does not believe that the complaining individual was discriminated against—the victim may bring his or her own lawsuit.

"All men think justice to be a sort of equality. But there still remains a question: equality or inequality of what?"

Aristotle, 384–322 B.C.
(Greek philosopher)

Employer liability under Title VII may be extensive. If the plaintiff successfully proves that unlawful discrimination occurred, he or she may be awarded reinstatement, back pay, retroactive promotions, and, as of 1991, damages (provided for in the 1991 Civil Rights Act's amendments to Title VII, discussed in this chapter's *Landmark in the Law*).

Intentional versus Unintentional Discrimination Title VII prohibits both intentional and unintentional discrimination. Intentional discrimination by an employer against an employee is known as **disparate-treatment discrimination.** Because intent may sometimes be difficult to prove, courts have established certain procedures for resolving disparate-treatment cases. Suppose that a woman applies for employment with a construction firm and is rejected. If she sues on the basis of disparate-treatment discrimination in hiring, she must show that (1) she is a member of a protected class, (2) she applied and was qualified for the job in question, (3) she was rejected by the employer, and (4) the employer continued to seek applicants for the position or filled the position with a person not in a protected class.

DISPARATE-TREATMENT DISCRIMINATION
In an employment context, intentional discrimination against individuals on the basis of color, gender, national origin, race, or religion.

If she can meet these relatively easy requirements, she makes out a ***prima facie* case** of illegal discrimination. Making out a *prima facie* case of discrimination means that the plaintiff has met her initial burden of proof and will win in the absence of an acceptable employer defense. The burden then shifts to the employer-defendant, who must articulate a legal reason for not hiring the plaintiff. For example, the employer might say that the plaintiff was not hired because she lacked sufficient experience or training. The plaintiff must then show that the employer's reason is a pretext (not the true reason) and that discriminatory intent actually motivated the employer's decision.

***PRIMA FACIE* CASE**
A case in which the plaintiff has produced sufficient evidence of his or her conclusion that the case can go to a jury; a case in which the evidence compels the plaintiff's conclusion if the defendant produces no evidence to rebut it.

Employers often find it necessary to use interviews and testing procedures to choose from among a large number of applicants for job openings. Consequently, personnel tests have been used as devices for screening applicants. Minimum educational requirements are also common. Employer practices such as those involving educational or job requirements may have an unintended discriminatory impact on a protected class. **Disparate-impact discrimination** occurs when, as a result of educational or other job requirements or hiring procedures, an employer's work force does not reflect the percentage of nonwhites, women, or members of other protected classes that characterizes qualified individuals in the local labor market. If a person challenging an employment practice having a discriminatory effect can show a connection between the practice and the disparity, he or she makes out a *prima facie* case, and no evidence of discriminatory intent needs to be shown.

DISPARATE-IMPACT DISCRIMINATION
In an employment context, discrimination that results from certain employer practices or procedures that, although not discriminatory on their face, have a discriminatory effect.

Defenses After an employee makes out a *prima facie* case of discrimination, the employer has an opportunity to respond. The employer may attempt to disprove the case, or the employer may use certain defenses to justify the discriminatory practice. For example, an employer may offer a good business reason for a practice that has a discriminatory effect. If requiring a high school diploma, for instance, is shown to have a discriminatory effect, an employer might argue that a high school education is required for workers to perform the job at a required level of competence. If the employer can demonstrate to the court's satisfaction that there exists a definite connection between a high school education and job performance, then the employer will succeed in this **business necessity defense.**

BUSINESS NECESSITY DEFENSE
A showing that an employment practice that discriminates against members of a protected class is required for job performance.

BONA FIDE OCCUPATIONAL QUALIFICATION (BFOQ)
Under Title VII of the Civil Rights Act of 1964, identifiable characteristics reasonably necessary to the operation of a particular business. These characteristics can include gender, national origin, and religion, but not race.

SENIORITY SYSTEM
In regard to employment relationships, a system in which those who have worked longest for the company are first in line for promotions, salary increases, and other benefits; they are also the last to be laid off if the work force must be reduced.

Another defense applies when discrimination against a protected class is essential to a job—that is, when a particular trait is a **bona fide occupational qualification (BFOQ)**. For example, a men's fashion magazine might legitimately hire only male models. Under Title VII, race can never be a BFOQ. The defense applies only to the traits of other protected classes. Much controversy has arisen over this defense, particularly in sex-discrimination cases. Some companies have argued that being male is a BFOQ for jobs requiring heavy lifting,[6] whereas others have contended that being female is a BFOQ for flight attendants.[7] Courts have rejected both these arguments and have generally restricted the BFOQ defense to instances in which the employee's gender is essential to the job. In 1991, the United States Supreme Court held that even a fetal-protection policy that was adopted to protect unborn children from the harmful effects of exposure to lead was an unacceptable BFOQ.[8]

A third defense protects bona fide **seniority systems.** An employer with a history of discrimination may have no members of protected classes in upper-level positions. Even if the employer now seeks to be unbiased, it may face a lawsuit seeking an order that minorities be promoted ahead of schedule to compensate for past discrimination. If no present intent to discriminate is shown, and promotions or other job benefits are distributed according to a fair seniority system, the employer has a good defense against the suit.

Discrimination Based on Race, Color, Religion, and National Origin If a company's standards or policies for selecting or promoting employees have the effect of discriminating against minorities on the basis of race, color, religion, or national origin and do not have a substantial, demonstrable relationship to qualifications for the job in question, they are illegal. Discrimination against employees on the basis of any of these criteria violates Title VII of the Civil Rights Act of 1964 and may violate state human rights statutes or other state laws prohibiting discrimination (state laws prohibiting employment discrimination are discussed later in this chapter).

Discrimination in employment conditions and benefits is also illegal. An employer cannot maintain all-white or all-black crews for no demonstrable reason, nor can an employer grant higher average Christmas bonuses to whites than to blacks. Title VII also prohibits discrimination based on religion. As discussed in Chapter 4, employers must reasonably accommodate the religious needs of their employees.

"The true Republic: men, their rights and nothing more; women, their rights and nothing less."

Susan B. Anthony, 1820–1906
(American reformer)

Sex Discrimination Under Title VII as well as other federal acts, employers are forbidden to discriminate against women in employment. Employers are prohibited from classifying jobs as male or female and from advertising in help-wanted columns that are designated male or female unless sex is a bona fide job qualification. Furthermore, employers cannot have separate male and female seniority lists.

Two areas involving sex discrimination that have become particularly sensitive relate to pregnancy discrimination and sexual harassment. We look here at the law covering both of these types of sex discrimination.

6. *Rosenfeld v. Southern Pacific Co.*, 444 F.2d 1219 (9th Cir. 1971).
7. *Diaz v. Pan American World Airways, Inc.*, 442 F.2d 385 (5th Cir. 1971).
8. *United Automobile Workers v. Johnson Controls, Inc.*, 113 U.S. 158, 111 S.Ct. 1196, 113 L.Ed.2d 158 (1991). This case was presented in Chapter 2 as Case 2.3.

Pregnancy Discrimination The Pregnancy Discrimination Act of 1978,[9] which amended Title VII, expanded the definition of sex discrimination to include discrimination based on pregnancy. Women affected by pregnancy, childbirth, or related medical conditions must be treated—for all employment-related purposes, including the receipt of benefits under employee-benefit programs—the same as other persons not so affected but similar in ability to work.

An employer is required to treat an employee temporarily unable to perform her job owing to a pregnancy-related condition in the same manner as the employer would treat other temporarily disabled employees. The employer must change work assignments, grant paid disability leaves, or grant leaves without pay if that is how other temporarily disabled employees would be treated. Policies concerning an employee's return to work, accrual of seniority, pay increases, and so on must also result in equal treatment.

Sexual Harassment Workers have some protection against **sexual harassment** in the workplace under Title VII provisions. Courts generally distinguish between two kinds of sexual harassment. *Quid pro quo harassment* occurs when job opportunities, promotions, and the like are doled out on the basis of sexual favors. *Hostile-environment harassment* occurs when an employee is subjected to sexual comments, jokes, or physical contact perceived to be offensive. The EEOC guidelines describe hostile-environment harassment as conduct that "has the purpose or effect of unreasonably interfering with an individual's work performance or creating an intimidating, hostile, or offensive working environment."[10]

SEXUAL HARASSMENT
In the employment context, hiring or granting of job promotions or other benefits in return for sexual favors or language or conduct that is so sexually offensive that it creates a hostile working environment.

In a sexual harassment case, the employer may be liable even though an employee did the harassing. If the employee is in a supervisory position, the employer will usually automatically be held liable for the behavior. If a lower-level employee is responsible for the harassment, the employer will be held liable only if it knew, or should have known, about the harassment and failed to take corrective action.

Sexual harassment is often very difficult to prove. Many times, such cases come down to a question of who is more believable—the alleged victim or the alleged offender—because there are no third party witnesses and no written evidence. This sort of situation may present an insurmountable problem for the victim who must prove that the offensive conduct took place. Also, the damages available to plaintiffs in sex-discrimination suits are limited under the Civil Rights Act of 1991 (discussed in this chapter's *Landmark in the Law*). Thus, victims' attorneys may choose to file tort claims against the employers in state courts, alleging such things as intentional infliction of emotional distress and assault, to avoid the federal limits on damages.

As discussed in this chapter's *Ethical Perspective*, one of the difficulties in evaluating sexual harassment claims is the fact that men and women often have different opinions on what constitutes offensive conduct. Because of this, some courts have held that sexual harassment should not be viewed from the gender-neutral "reasonable person" perspective but from a "reasonable woman" perspective.

Affirmative Action

Title VII and equal opportunity regulations were designed to reduce or eliminate discriminatory practices with respect to hiring, retaining, and promoting employees. **Affirmative action** programs go a step further and attempt to "make up" for past patterns of discrimination by giving qualified minorities and women preferential treatment in hiring or promotion. Affirmative action programs have caused much controversy, particularly when they result in what is frequently called "reverse discrimination"—discrimination against "majority" workers, such as white males.

AFFIRMATIVE ACTION
Job-hiring policies that give special consideration or compensatory treatment to minority groups in an effort to overcome present effects of past discrimination.

9. 42 U.S.C. Section 2000e(k).
10. 29 C.F.R. Section 1604.11(a)(3).

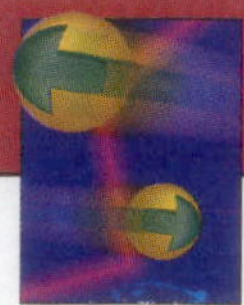

Ethical Perspective

The "Reasonable Woman" Standard

One of the most compelling revelations concerning sexual harassment that has emerged in the 1980s and 1990s is how differently men and women view the issue. Polls indicate that the two genders have widely disparate views as to whether particular types of conduct, such as persisting in unwanted requests for a date, constitute harassment. Some polls have reported that while 75 percent of men say that they would be flattered by sexual advances in the workplace, 75 percent of the women would be offended by the same actions.

The traditional legal standard for determining what is or is not appropriate behavior is the "reasonable person" standard. Conduct is considered to be appropriate if a reasonable person in the same circumstances would have acted or responded similarly. In cases of alleged sexual harassment, however, some critics contend that the gender-neutral reasonable person standard offers little guidance as to how a reasonable man or a reasonable woman might respond to sexually offensive conduct.

This problem has led some courts to adopt a "reasonable woman" standard in sexual harassment cases. In *Ellison v. Brady*,[a] for example, the U.S. Court of Appeals for the Ninth Circuit ruled that whether conduct may be considered sexual harassment should be viewed in light of a reasonable woman standard. The 1991 case concerned an employee who alleged that a fellow employee's persistent and unwelcome love letters and requests for lunch dates created a hostile working environment. The trial court dismissed the claim, calling the behavior "trivial." The appellate court, however, found that the employee made allegations of fact that a reasonable woman would consider to create a hostile working environment. Any other standard, said the court, "tends to systematically ignore the experiences of women." The court held that the employee had established a *prima facie* case and ordered a new trial.

The Michigan Court of Appeals in *Radtke v. Everett* adopted a reasonable woman standard, maintaining that "a standard which views harassing conduct from the 'reasonable person' perspective has the tendency to be male-biased and runs the risk of reinforcing the prevailing level of discrimination which * * * [Title VII was] designed to eliminate." The court also noted that when a man alleges sex discrimination, the proper perspective should be a "reasonable man" standard.[b] On appeal, the Michigan Supreme Court rejected the gender-conscious standard in favor of the reasonable person standard.

Some of the implications of using the gender of the victim to determine the appropriate standard of conduct were raised by the attorneys for both sides in the *Ellison* case. They asserted that the adoption of a reasonable woman standard in sexual harassment cases could lead to adopting, in other cases, other reasonable gender or ethnic standards—a reasonable African-American standard, for example, or a reasonable elderly person standard.

a. 924 F.2d 872 (9th Cir. 1991).

b. Some courts have applied a reasonable man standard to claims of sexual harassment. See, for example, *Daniels v. Essex Group, Inc.*, 937 F.2d 1264 (7th Cir. 1991).

Although affirmative action programs have been under attack in recent years, the United States Supreme Court has generally held that they are legitimate if they are designed to correct existing imbalances in the work force and as long as employers consider factors in addition to race or gender when making employment decisions. Generally, the Supreme Court looks at the special circumstances surrounding each case when determining whether challenged affirmative action plans are legitimate.

Age Discrimination

Age discrimination is potentially the most widespread form of discrimination, because anyone—regardless of race, color, national origin, or gender—could be a victim at some point in life. The Age Discrimination in Employment Act (ADEA) of 1967,[11] as amended, prohibits employment discrimination on the basis of age

11. 29 U.S.C. Sections 621–634.

Under what circumstances could an older worker be discharged without prompting charges of age discrimination?

against individuals forty years of age or older. An amendment to the act prohibits mandatory retirement for nonmanagerial workers. For the act to apply, an employer must have twenty or more employees, and the employer's business activities must affect interstate commerce.

The ADEA is similar to Title VII in that it offers protection against both intentional (disparate-treatment) age discrimination and unintentional (disparate-impact) age discrimination. The burden-shifting procedure under the ADEA is also similar to that under Title VII. For example, if a plaintiff who is discharged can establish that he or she (1) was a member of the protected age group, (2) was qualified for the position from which he or she was discharged, and (3) was discharged under circumstances that give rise to an inference of discrimination, the plaintiff has established a *prima facie* case of unlawful age discrimination. The burden then shifts to the employer, who must articulate a legitimate reason for the discrimination. If the plaintiff can prove that the employer's reason is only a pretext and that the plaintiff's age was a determining factor in the employer's decision, the employer will be held liable under the ADEA.

"To work is to pray."

St. Benedict of Nursia, 480–543 A.D.
(Catholic monk and scholar; founder of the Order of St. Benedict)

Numerous cases of alleged age discrimination have been brought against employers who, to cut costs, replaced older, higher-salaried employees with younger, lower-salaried workers. In one case, for example, a fifty-four-year-old manager of a plant who earned approximately \$15.75 an hour was temporarily laid off when the plant was closed for the winter. When spring came, the manager was replaced by a forty-three-year-old worker who earned approximately \$8.05 an hour. The older manager, who had worked for the firm for twenty-seven years, was given no opportunity to accept a lower wage rate or otherwise accommodate the firm's need to reduce costs. The court, which referred to the firm's dismissal of the manager as an exercise in "industrial capital punishment," held that the manager's dismissal in these circumstances violated the ADEA.[12]

Whether a firing is discriminatory or simply part of a rational business decision to prune the company's ranks is not always clear. Companies will generally defend a decision to discharge a worker by asserting that the worker could no longer perform his or her duties or that the worker's skills were no longer needed. The employee

12. *Metz v. Transit Mix, Inc.*, 828 F.2d 1202 (7th Cir. 1987).

must prove that the discharge was motivated, at least in part, by age bias. Proof that qualified older employees are generally discharged before younger employees or that co-workers continually made unflattering age-related comments about the discharged worker may be enough. The following case is typical of many age-discrimination cases involving companies that try to trim the payrolls and become more cost effective by reorganizing the firm and consolidating various job positions.

Case 32.1

MARESCO v. EVANS CHEMETICS, DIVISION OF W. R. GRACE & CO.

United States Court of Appeals, Second Circuit, 1992.
964 F.2d 106.

HISTORICAL AND SOCIAL SETTING *In 1848, after two years at sea, William Russell Grace, who was then sixteen years old, was hired in Liverpool, England, by a ship chandlery (a firm that buys and sells ships). Two years later, Grace went to work in Callao, Peru, for a similar firm, which he and his brother eventually took over. In 1865, Grace founded W. R. Grace & Company in New York to engage in trade in South America. To help the government of Peru avoid bankruptcy in 1890, Grace assumed the debt of two Peruvian government bond issues in exchange for control of nearly all of the country's resources, including silver mines, oil and mineral rights, and railroads. A year later, Grace founded the New York & Pacific Steamship Company, later adding the Grace Steamship Company. In 1895, at the age of sixty-three, Grace combined his New York and Peruvian holdings into William R. Grace and Company, which ultimately expanded into agricultural, banking, chemical, mercantile, and utility investments in North and South America. In December 1978, the company acquired Evans Chemetics, which became part of the firm's Organic Chemicals Division, with offices in Nashua, New Hampshire; Lexington, Massachusetts; and Darien, Connecticut.*

FACTS Eugene Maresco had worked for Evans Chemetics from 1967 to 1986. In 1986, the company closed its branch office in Darien, Connecticut, in which Maresco worked as an accountant and credit manager, for legitimate cost-saving reasons. All of Darien's accounting functions were transferred to the Lexington, Massachusetts, office. Four of the workers in the Darien office were allowed to relocate to the Lexington office. Of this group, three were nonaccounting employees over the age of forty, and one was an accountant. The accountant was under forty but had more education and experience than Maresco. Maresco, who was sixty years old, and several other employees were discharged, and Maresco's responsibilities were assumed by two accountants in the Lexington office. After the consolidation, the Lexington accounting department consisted of twenty employees, only one of whom was over the age of forty. Maresco sued Evans Chemetics, alleging that his termination constituted age discrimination in violation of the Age Discrimination in Employment Act (ADEA). The trial court granted Evans's motion for summary judgment, holding that Maresco had not established that the circumstances of his discharge gave rise to an inference of age discrimination. Maresco appealed.

ISSUE Did the circumstances surrounding Maresco's discharge give rise to an inference of age discrimination?

DECISION Yes. The trial court's decision was reversed and the case remanded for trial.

REASON The court stated that whether the "evidence proffered by Maresco yields an inference of discrimination depends largely on the vantage from which this case is viewed." Evans viewed the case as involving a simple decision to close the Darien office and to transfer only those with special qualifications or abilities to the Lexington office. Because three of the four persons transferred to the Lexington office were in the protected age group, no inference of discrimination arose. From Maresco's point of view, however, what occurred was a consolidation of the Darien and Lexington offices. "Under this view, upon consolidation there were more employees than available positions," and "there was no valid presumption that layoffs would come from the Darien office." In all, there were twenty-three persons working in the accounting section prior to the consolidation, only three of whom were in the protected age group. The court concluded that "[t]he decision to terminate two of the three older accounting employees, and none of the twenty younger employees, presents circumstances which give rise to an inference * * * that age was impermissibly considered in allocating the post-consolidation employment positions."

ETHICAL CONSIDERATIONS *Laws protecting workers against age discrimination force employers to balance their need to save costs by hiring or retaining younger workers against their duty to treat older employees fairly. In Maresco's case, he had worked for Evans for nearly twenty years, and the evidence indicated that he was fully qualified*

Case 32.1—Continued

for the job he performed. On the face of it, it would appear that Evans was acting unfairly when it discharged Maresco instead of offering him a position in the Lexington office. Certainly, the appellate court felt that there was at least a possibility that age discrimination had been a factor in Evans's decision to terminate Maresco.

Discrimination Based on Disability

In 1990, Congress passed the Americans with Disabilities Act (ADA),[13] which became effective in 1992. The ADA, like earlier civil rights legislation, was designed to eliminate discriminatory hiring and firing practices that prevent otherwise qualified disabled workers from fully participating in the national labor force. It is broadly drafted to define disabled persons as persons with a physical or mental impairment that "substantially limits" their everyday activities.

What Is a Disability? The ADA defines *disability* as "(1) a physical or mental impairment that substantially limits one or more of the major life activities of such individuals; (2) a record of such impairment; or (3) being regarded as having such an impairment." More specifically, the law covers such physical disabilities as heart disease, cancer, muscular dystrophy, cerebral palsy, paraplegia, and diabetes. It excludes from coverage certain conditions, such as homosexuality and kleptomania.

Reasonable Accommodations The ADA prohibits employers from refusing to hire disabled persons who are otherwise qualified for a particular position. It does not, however, require that unqualified disabled applicants be hired. That the employer may have to make some reasonable accommodations for a disabled applicant, such as installing ramps for a wheelchair, will not cause the applicant to be considered unqualified. Reasonable accommodations might also include establishing more flexible working hours, creating new job assignments, and creating or improving training materials and procedures. Employers who do not wish to make such accommodations must demonstrate that the accommodations will cause "undue hardship." The

Why did Congress mandate that employers make reasonable accommodations for disabled employees and job applicants?

13. 42 U.S.C. Sections 12102–12118.

Landmark in the Law

The Civil Rights Act of 1991

On November 21, 1991, President George Bush signed into law the Civil Rights Act of 1991. The act consists primarily of a series of amendments and additions to existing laws protecting persons from employment discrimination.

Historical Background

In 1971, the United States Supreme Court was confronted with a case in which it had to rule on tests and other practices used by an employer in hiring employees. The employer used two qualifications for employment: a high school diploma and an objective ability test. There was no proof that the employer intended to discriminate against any class of persons—that is, the case did not involve *disparate-treatment* discrimination—but the Supreme Court found that the qualifications had a *disparate impact* on African Americans as a class. Further, the Court found that the employer had failed to show how the qualifications related to job performance or job capability.

In this case—*Griggs v. Duke Power Co.*[a]—the Supreme Court held that if an employer appeared more likely to hire or promote people of one sex or race, the employer could be required to justify the practice that caused the disparate impact. The employer could be held liable even if there was no proof that the employer intended to discriminate. The Supreme Court stated that "Congress has placed on the employer the burden of showing that any given requirement must have a manifest relationship to the employment in question." For example, if an employer has a height requirement, and the requirement is challenged, the employer must prove its necessity—by demonstrating that persons below that height cannot operate certain standard machinery at the worksite, for instance.[b] Thus, according to the holding in the *Griggs* case, the plaintiff had only to prove that a specific employment practice constituted disparate-impact discrimination. At that point, it was up to the employer to prove that the practice was justified by business necessity.

Eighteen years later, in 1989, the Supreme Court was confronted with another case in which it had to consider employment practices that caused an imbalance in a work force. In that case—*Wards Cove Packing Co. v. Atonio*[c]—the Supreme Court held that persons challenging an employment practice as discriminatory must prove not only that the practice has a disparate impact on a protected class, but also that the practice was *not* a business necessity. In other words, the *Wards Cove* ruling, by placing a heavier burden of proof on plaintiffs, made it more difficult for persons to obtain remedies for disparate-impact discrimination.

In six other cases decided in 1989 and 1991, the Supreme Court further limited the rights of persons challenging employment practices as discriminatory. These rulings generated substantial concern over the need to clarify the rights of persons alleging employment discrimination and to ensure that these rights were adequately protected.

Congressional Response

Congress responded to this concern with the Civil Rights Act of 1991. The act effectively overruled the seven Supreme Court decisions by amending existing laws related to the type of discrimination involved in each case. For example, it overturned the *Wards Cove* decision by amending Section 703 of Title VII to again place the burden of proving business necessity on the employer, as under the *Griggs* ruling.

The act also provided that damages are recoverable under Title VII of the Civil Rights Act of 1964—the major law protecting employees and potential employees from employment discrimination—as well as under laws prohibiting discrimination based on age or disability. Until the Civil Rights Act of 1991, damages were not available for victims of intentional employment discrimination based on sex, religion, age, or disability.

Under the 1991 act, compensatory damages are available only in cases of intentional discrimination. The statute also stipulates that compensatory damages shall not include back pay, interest on back pay, or other relief already available under Title VII. Punitive damages may be recovered against a private employer only if the employer acted with malice or reckless indifference to an individual's rights. The sum of the amount of compensatory and punitive damages is limited by the statute to specific amounts against specific employers—ranging from $50,000 against employers with one hundred or fewer employees to $300,000 against employers with more than five hundred employees.

When compensatory or punitive damages are sought, either party to the suit can demand a jury trial, but the jury may not be told about the limits on the damages. Prior to the 1991 act, jury trials were not allowed in Title VII cases.

a. 401 U.S. 424, 91 S.Ct. 849, 28 L.Ed.2d 158 (1971).

b. *Boyd v. Ozark Airlines, Inc.*, 568 F.2d 50 (8th Cir. 1977).

c. 490 U.S. 642, 109 S.Ct. 2115, 104 L.Ed.2d 733 (1989).

law offers no uniform standards for identifying what is an undue hardship other than the imposition of a "significant difficulty or expense" on the employer.

Preemployment Physicals Under the ADA, employers are not permitted to ask job applicants about the nature or extent of any known disabilities. Furthermore, they cannot require disabled persons to submit to preemployment physicals unless such exams are required of all other applicants. Employers can condition an offer of employment on the employee's successfully passing a medical examination, but disqualification must result from the discovery of problems that render the applicant unable to perform the job for which he or she is to be hired.

Dangerous Workers An employer may defend a decision not to hire a disabled worker if the applicant would pose a "direct threat to the health or safety" of his or her coworkers. This danger must be substantial and immediate; it cannot be speculative. A worker who suffers from hallucinations that cause him to attack his coworkers would probably be considered such a threat. Federal regulations also permit employers to terminate the employment of qualified workers whose disabilities are such that they may pose a danger to their own personal well-being.

Remedies Disabled persons who wish to file a claim under the ADA may sue for many of the same remedies available under Title VII. They may seek reinstatement, back pay, a limited amount of compensatory and punitive damages (for intentional discrimination), and certain other forms of injunctive relief. Such actions may be commenced only after the plaintiff has pursued the claim through the Equal Employment Opportunity Commission. Repeat violators may be ordered to pay fines of up to $100,000.

State Laws Prohibiting Employment Discrimination

Although the focus of this chapter is on federal legislation, bear in mind that most states have statutes that prohibit employment discrimination. Generally, the kinds of discrimination prohibited under federal legislation are also prohibited by state laws. In addition, state statutes often provide protection for certain individuals, such as homosexuals, who are not protected under Title VII.

Numerous plaintiffs who allege employment discrimination seek relief under state statutes instead of Title VII. In the following case, the plaintiff alleged that he was discriminated against in his employment because of his foreign accent (he was from Cambodia), in violation of a Washington state statute.

Case 32.2
XIENG v. PEOPLES NATIONAL BANK OF WASHINGTON

Supreme Court of Washington, 1993.
120 Wash.2d 512,
844 P.2d 389.

HISTORICAL AND POLITICAL SETTING *During the 1950s, the 1960s, and the 1970s, the United States was militarily involved in actions against the Vietnamese communists, who were attempting to control Southeast Asia. Cambodia (or Kampuchea), which lies between Vietnam and Thailand, attempted to remain neutral. Cambodia's ruler, Prince Norodom Sihanouk, refused to cooperate with either the Vietnamese or the Americans. Despite Sihanouk's policy, U.S. military commanders believed that the Vietnamese communists had command centers in Cambodia. Sihanouk was overthrown in 1970 by Lon Nol, who began persecuting Cambodia's 400,000 ethnic Vietnamese and asked for U.S. aid to prevent a Vietnamese takeover. President Richard Nixon authorized U.S. military forces to move into eastern Cambodia. Meanwhile, Cambodian communists, known as the Khmer Rouge, fought against Lon Nol. As U.S. involvement in Southeast Asia decreased in the early 1970s, the balance of military power shifted. In April 1975, communists seized power by force all over Southeast Asia. Lon Nol's government fell to the Khmer Rouge, who began a systematic program of genocide that eventually resulted in the deaths of more than one million people—a fifth of Cambodia's population.*

Case 32.2—Continued

FACTS Phanna Xieng first came to the United States in 1974, when he was sent here from Cambodia for "advanced military training." When the Cambodian government fell in 1975, Xieng remained in the United States, eventually finding employment with Peoples National Bank of Washington in 1979. In performance appraisals from 1980 through 1985, Xieng was rated by his supervisors as "capable of dealing effectively with customers" and qualified for promotion, although in each appraisal it was noted that Xieng might improve his communication skills to maximize his possibilities for future advancement. Xieng sought job promotions on numerous occasions but was never promoted. In 1986, he filed a complaint against the bank, alleging employment discrimination based on national origin. The trial court found that Xieng was qualified for many of the promotions he applied for, that his accent would not have materially interfered with his job performance in the positions for which he applied, and that the bank's failure to promote him because of his accent constituted discrimination based on national origin. The bank appealed, and the appellate court affirmed the trial court's decision. The bank then appealed to the Supreme Court of Washington.

ISSUE Had the bank discriminated against Xieng on the basis of national origin?

DECISION Yes. The Supreme Court of Washington affirmed the lower courts' decisions.

REASON The court acknowledged that "[t]here is nothing improper about an employer making an honest assessment of the oral communications skills of a candidate for a job when such skills are reasonably related to job performance." But, said the court, "[a]ccent and national origin are inextricably intertwined in many cases. It would therefore be an easy refuge in this context for an employer unlawfully discriminating against someone based on national origin to state falsely that it was not the person's national origin that caused the employment or promotion problem, but the candidate's inability to measure up to the communications skills demanded by the job." The state supreme court concluded, as had the trial court, that Xieng's accent did not interfere materially with job performance and that the bank's allegation that Xieng's accent interfered with his job performance amounted to a mere pretext for discrimination on the basis of national origin.

ETHICAL CONSIDERATIONS *On one of the occasions on which Xieng sought a promotion, he was interviewed by a managerial-level supervisor who threw Xieng's résumé into the wastebasket as soon as Xieng left the office. On another occasion, he was told that he would be promoted if he could guarantee that all of the ethnic Cambodians in the city would become customers of the bank. When he explained that it would be impossible to make that guarantee, the promotion went to someone else. On a third occasion, he was told that he would be promoted automatically as soon as a position became available, but when a position opened, the promotion went to someone less qualified. The bank claimed that it had acted in good faith in rejecting Xieng for promotion because of his "communications skills." The trial court found that "the reason for the rejection [for promotion] was not worthy of credence."*

❖ Privacy Issues

In the 1980s, the law began to protect the privacy of employees in a number of areas. Lie-detector tests, drug tests, electronic monitoring of work and the workplace, preemployment screening procedures, and other practices have been challenged as violations of employees' rights to privacy.

Lie-Detector Tests

At one time, many employers required employees or job applicants to take polygraph examinations in connection with their employment. The results of these lie-detector tests are not admissible as evidence in criminal trials, and many persons consider the tests to be an invasion of privacy.

In 1988, Congress passed the Employee Polygraph Protection Act.[14] The act prohibits certain employers from (1) requiring or causing employees or job applicants to take lie-detector tests or suggesting or requesting that they do so; (2) using,

14. 29 U.S.C. Sections 2001–2009.

accepting, referring to, or asking about the results of lie-detector tests taken by employees or applicants; and (3) taking or threatening negative employment-related action against employees or applicants based on results of lie-detector tests or on their refusal to take the tests.

Employers excepted from these prohibitions include federal, state, and local government employers, certain security service firms, and companies manufacturing and distributing controlled substances. Other employers may use polygraph tests when investigating losses attributable to theft, including embezzlement and stealing of trade secrets.

Drug Testing

Workers whose ability to perform is impaired as a result of drug use can pose a substantial threat to the safety of others. For example, railway or airline employees may seriously endanger the public safety if they perform their jobs under the influence of alcohol or other drugs. Drug and alcohol use also is very costly for employers, who lose billions of dollars each year as a result of absenteeism, impaired performance, and accidents caused by employee drug use. In the interest of public safety and to reduce unnecessary costs, many of today's employers, including the government, require their employees to submit to drug testing.

State laws relating to privacy rights of private-sector employees in this area vary from state to state. Some state constitutions may inhibit private employers' testing for drugs, and state statutes may restrict private drug testing in any number of ways. A collective bargaining agreement may also provide protection against drug testing. In other cases, employees may bring an action for the tort of invasion of privacy (described in Chapter 5).

Constitutional limitations apply to the testing of government employees. The Fourth Amendment provides that individuals have the right to be "secure in their persons" against "unreasonable searches and seizures" conducted by government agents. Drug tests have been held constitutional, however, when there was a reasonable basis for suspecting government employees of using drugs. Also, when drug use in a particular government job could threaten public safety, testing has been upheld. For example, a Department of Transportation rule that requires employees engaged in oil and gas pipeline operations to submit to random drug testing was upheld, even though the rule did not require that before being tested the individual must have been suspected of drug use.[15] The court held that the government's interest in promoting public safety in the pipeline industry outweighed the employees' privacy interests. In the following case, employees of the Department of Labor claimed that drug testing based on the reasonable suspicion of off-duty drug use violated their constitutional rights under the Fourth Amendment.

Case 32.3
AMERICAN FEDERATION OF GOVERNMENT EMPLOYEES, AFL-CIO, LOCAL 2391 v. MARTIN
United States Court of Appeals, Ninth Circuit, 1992.
969 F.2d 788.

HISTORICAL AND POLITICAL SETTING *In the 1980s, President Ronald Reagan was concerned with recovering ground that he felt had been lost in our nation's security and economy, in both a physical and a psychological sense, during the 1970s. To show that the United States' commitment to security was as strong as it had ever been, the president deployed Cruise missiles in Europe and supported the development of the Stealth bomber and a range of laser-guided missiles known as the Strategic Defense Initiative (SDI, or "Star Wars"). In defense of American interests, Reagan authorized the landing of U.S. troops in Grenada and an attack on military headquarters in Libya. Domestically, Reagan supported a restructuring of the fed-*

15. *Electrical Workers Local 1245 v. Skinner*, 913 F.2d 1454 (9th Cir. 1990).

Case 32.3—Continued

eral income tax system and other economic stimulants, including "deregulation"—a reduction in the number of administrative regulations. By the mid-1980s, the greatest threat to domestic tranquility appeared to be an increasing use of illegal drugs. As part of a war on drugs, Reagan issued Executive Order 12564, which prohibited illegal drug use by federal employees both on and off duty.

FACTS In 1986, the president issued an executive order requiring all agencies and departments in the executive branch of the government to "develop a plan for achieving the objective of a drug-free workplace with due consideration of the rights of the government, the employee, and the general public." In 1988, in response to the order, the Department of Labor (DOL) developed a "Drug-Free Workplace Plan." The plan designated certain DOL employment positions to be sensitive positions in regard to public health and safety or national security. The plan provided that employees holding these positions, called "testing-designated positions," or TDPs, could be subjected to drug testing, including drug testing based on a reasonable suspicion of on-duty or off-duty drug use. The American Federation of Government Employees (AFGE) and two individual DOL employees sought to enjoin the DOL from certain types of drug testing, including drug testing based on a reasonable suspicion of on-duty or off-duty drug use. The trial court approved the DOL's drug-testing plan except for testing based on the reasonable suspicion of off-duty use. The court granted an injunction against such testing, holding that the Fourth Amendment permits testing only when it is based on a reasonable suspicion of on-duty, and not off-duty, illegal drug use or impairment. The DOL appealed the court's decision in respect to this issue.

ISSUE Does drug testing based on a reasonable suspicion of off-duty drug use by the DOL employees in TDPs violate the Fourth Amendment?

DECISION No. The appellate court reversed the trial court's ruling in respect to this issue.

REASON The court stated at the outset that "urinalysis drug tests necessarily invade reasonable expectations of privacy rendering [the tests] searches within the meaning of the Fourth Amendment." Whether the government can require its employees to submit to drug testing, and thus intrude on employees' privacy rights, depends on whether these rights are outweighed by "legitimate governmental interests." The court found in the circumstances of this case that the employees' interests in privacy were "outweighed by the DOL's interest in preventing on-duty or off-duty drug use from impairing TDP employees in the performance of their duties." In the court's opinion, the safety-sensitive and security-sensitive nature of TDPs justified the DOL's drug testing of TDP employees based on a reasonable suspicion arising from observed off-duty illegal drug use or impairment. "We are convinced," concluded the court, "that under these limited circumstances the reasonable suspicion requirement of the DOL's Plan adequately protects its TDP employees from arbitrary and unreasonable drug testing."

ETHICAL CONSIDERATIONS *Recall from Chapter 4 that no constitutional right is absolute. Ultimately, the courts, and particularly the United States Supreme Court, interpret constitutional provisions and determine the extent to which rights guaranteed by the Constitution can be limited to protect other interests, such as public health and safety. The case just presented offers a clear illustration of how courts weigh the interests of the individual against the legitimate interests of the government in deciding when and how to limit individuals' constitutional rights.*

Performance Monitoring

In the last decade, many employers have begun to monitor the performance of their employees through electronic means. Some employers electronically monitor their employees' use of computer terminals or company telephones. In some situations, employers use video cameras to evaluate their employees' performance.

Listening to employees' telephone conversations may violate the Omnibus Crime Control and Safe Streets Act of 1968. This act prohibits the intentional interception of a wire or electronic communication or the intentional disclosure of the contents of the interception.[16] Otherwise, there is little specific government regulation of monitoring activities, and an employer may be able to avoid these laws by simply informing employees that they are subject to monitoring. Employers

16. 18 U.S.C. Sections 2510–2521.

should be cautious, however, when monitoring employees because an employee may bring an action for invasion of privacy, and a court may decide that the employee's reasonable expectation of privacy outweighs the employer's need for surveillance. Similarly, an employer should consider alternatives before searching an employee's desk, filing cabinet, or office. If a search is conducted and the employee sues, a court may balance the purposes of the search against its intrusiveness. The court may also consider the availability of less intrusive alternatives that would have accomplished the same purposes.

One monitoring technique that has serious implications for employees' privacy rights is the use of identification badges that signal their wearers' location by sending off infrared signals, which are read by sensors at various locations in a building. Some research centers in the United States, as well as in Europe, require their employees to wear these badges so that the employees can be quickly located when necessary. The badges are efficient in the sense that an employee's co-workers and others can quickly learn whether a particular employee is in his or her office, at a meeting, or not on the premises at all. Using the badges thus saves fruitless phone calls and trips to vacant offices. But whether the use of such badges can withstand challenges based on privacy rights is yet to be seen.

Screening Procedures

An area of concern to potential employees has to do with preemployment screening procedures. What kinds of questions on an employment application or a preemployment test are permissible? What kinds of questions go too far in terms of invading the potential employee's privacy? Is it an invasion of the potential employee's privacy, for example, to ask questions about his or her sexual inclinations or religious convictions? While an employer may believe that such information is relevant to the job for which the individual has applied, the applicant may feel differently about the matter. A key factor in determining whether preemployment screening tests violate the privacy rights of potential employees is whether there exists a nexus, or connection, between the questions and the job for which an applicant is applying. The following case is illustrative in this respect.

Case 32.4
SOROKA v. DAYTON HUDSON CORP.

California Court of Appeal,
First District, Division 4, 1991.
7 Cal.App.4th 203,
1 Cal.Rptr.2d 77.

HISTORICAL AND ECONOMIC SETTING *Traditionally, most lawsuits brought by employees against their employers have been based on federal or state statutes that prohibit discrimination, retaliation, or other employer misconduct in the workplace. In the 1980s, employers saw an increase in the number of employee lawsuits based on common law tort theories. Many of these suits sought relief for the misconduct of a co-worker. Customers and others who deal with an employer's workers are also filing an increasing number of suits against employers for the misconduct of their employees. All of these lawsuits are costly to defend, and a significant number of them have resulted in expensive jury verdicts against the employers. The most practical way for an employer to respond to these challenges is to take preventive measures to minimize the likelihood that an employee will act in a way that forms the basis for a lawsuit. One preventive measure is to screen out unfit applicants for employment. This can substantially minimize the likelihood of lawsuits being brought by those who deal with an employer's work force.*

FACTS Dayton Hudson Corporation owns and operates Target Stores throughout the United States. Target hires store security officers (SSOs) to observe, apprehend, and arrest suspected shoplifters. SSOs are not armed, but they carry handcuffs and may use force, in self-defense, against suspected shoplifters. Target views good judgment and emotional stability as important SSO job skills. To determine whether applicants for SSO positions possess these qualities, Target uses a psychological test that it calls the Psychscreen. All job applicants must take the test as a condition of employment. A number of the questions included in the Psychscreen test are highly personal and intimate. Some of the questions relate to the applicant's re-

Case 32.4—Continued

ligious beliefs ("I believe in the second coming of Christ" and "I believe my sins are unpardonable"); other questions concern the job candidate's sexual orientation ("I have often wished that I were a girl" and "Many of my dreams are about sex matters"). Sibi Soroka and two other applicants (the plaintiffs) found the test objectionable and brought a class-action suit against Dayton Hudson, challenging the test as violating their privacy rights. The trial court found that Target's use of the test was reasonable, and the plaintiffs appealed.

ISSUE Did Target's use of the Psychscreen violate the job applicants' right to privacy?

DECISION Yes. The appellate court reversed the trial court's decision and remanded the case.

REASON Target conceded that its use of the Psychscreen intruded upon the privacy rights of job applicants. The question before the court was therefore whether this intrusion could be justified. The court concluded that it could not: "While Target unquestionably has an interest in employing emotionally stable persons to be SSO's, testing applicants about their religious beliefs and sexual orientation does not further this interest. To justify the invasion of privacy resulting from the use of the Psychscreen, Target must demonstrate a compelling interest and must establish that the test serves a job-related purpose. * * * Target made no showing that a person's religious beliefs or sexual orientation have any bearing on emotional stability or on the ability to perform an SSO's job responsibilities. It did no more than to make generalized claims about the Psychscreen's relationship to emotional fitness and to assert that it has seen an overall improvement in SSO quality and performance since it implemented the Psychscreen. This is not sufficient to constitute a compelling interest, nor does it satisfy the nexus [job-relatedness] requirement. Therefore Target's inquiry into the religious beliefs and sexual orientation of SSO applicants unjustifiably violates the state constitutional right to privacy."

ETHICAL CONSIDERATIONS *Increasingly, states are protecting employees' privacy rights through legislation, amendments to their state constitutions, and court decisions. In this case, for example, the court noted that the California state constitution had been amended to provide that all people have the right to pursue and obtain "happiness" and "privacy," among other things. The court acknowledged that some previous California court decisions had distinguished between the rights of employees and the rights of job applicants. Under this distinction, limitations on employees' rights to privacy could only be justified by a "compelling interest" on the part of the employer, while limitations on job applicants' privacy rights could be justified by a less stringent standard. Significantly, the court in this case held that the same standard should apply to both employees and job applicants.*

❖ Employment at Will

As discussed in this chapter's introduction, under the traditional employment-at-will doctrine, either party may terminate an employment contract at any time and for any reason. Federal statutes have modified this doctrine, and over the last two decades, the doctrine has also been eroded through a series of court rulings that restrict the right of employers to fire workers. Because this is a common law issue, the rules vary from state to state. The trend is to recognize exceptions to the at-will doctrine, however, and some courts have awarded punitive damages against employers in wrongful-discharge litigation. Wise employers will discharge employees only for good cause and will obtain documentation to support their position, in accordance with published company policies. Exceptions to the employment-at-will doctrine include those based on statutes, contract theory, and public policy.

Statutory Exceptions

WHISTLEBLOWING An employee's disclosure to government, the press, or upper-management that his or her employer is engaged in unsafe or illegal activities.

Whistleblowing occurs when an employee tells a government official, upper-management authorities, or the press that his or her employer is engaged in some unsafe or illegal activity. For example, an employee might tell the Environmental Protection Agency (EPA) that his employer has been violating pollution laws.

Employees who blow the whistle often find themselves disciplined or even out of a job. If a state statute protects whistleblowers, however, the employer cannot discharge the employee for informing the EPA. Federal law may also protect a whistleblower. For example, if an employee of a defense contractor reveals overcharges on weapons, the employee is protected. In one such federal case, when trucking-company employees were fired for reporting safety violations, the Department of Labor ordered that the employees be reinstated.[17] In situations in which neither a whistleblowing statute nor an employment contract protects the worker, the case must be decided on the basis of common law doctrine.

Exceptions Based on Contract Theory

Some courts have held that an implied employment contract exists between the employer and the employee. If the employee is fired outside the terms of the implied contract, he or she may succeed in a breach-of-contract action.

For example, an employer's handbook or personnel bulletin may state that, as a matter of policy, workers will be dismissed only for good cause. If the employee is aware of this policy and continues to work for the employer, a court may find that there is an implied contract based on the terms stated in the handbook or bulletin. Promises an employer makes to employees regarding discharge policy may also be considered part of an implied contract. If the employer fires the worker in a manner contrary to the manner promised, a court may hold that the employer has violated the implied contract and is liable for damages. Most state courts will consider this claim and judge it by traditional contract standards.

A few states have gone further and held that all employment contracts contain an implied covenant of good faith. This means that both sides promise to abide by the contract in good faith. If an employer fires an employee for an arbitrary or unjustified reason, the employee can claim that the covenant of good faith was breached and the contract violated.

Public-Policy Exceptions

The most widespread common law exception to the employment-at-will doctrine is the public-policy exception. Under this rule, an employer may not fire a worker for reasons that violate a fundamental public policy of the jurisdiction. For example, a court may prevent an employer from firing a worker who serves on a jury and therefore cannot work scheduled hours. Sometimes, an employer will direct an employee to do something that violates the law. If the employee refuses to perform the illegal act, the employer might decide to fire the worker. Most states have held that firing the worker under these circumstances violates public policy.

Whistleblowers may be protected from wrongful discharge for reasons of public policy. For example, a bank was held to have wrongfully discharged an employee who pressured the employer to comply with state and federal consumer credit laws.[18] In another case, an at-will employee—a probation officer with the police department of the city of Globe, Arizona—discovered that a man had been arrested for vagrancy under an obsolete statute, had been sentenced to ten days in prison, and had been in jail for twenty-one days. The officer pointed out to a magistrate that this was illegal. The magistrate informed the police chief, the chief fired the officer, and the officer sued the city for wrongful discharge. Holding that the discharge violated public policy, the court said, "So long as employees' actions are not merely private or proprietary, but instead seek to further the public good, the decision to expose illegal or unsafe practices should be encouraged * * *. There is no public policy

17. See *Brock v. Roadway Express, Inc.*, 481 U.S. 252, 107 S.Ct. 1740, 95 L.Ed.2d 239 (1987).
18. *Harless v. First National Bank in Fairmont*, 162 W.Va. 116, 246 S.E.2d 270 (1978).

more important or fundamental than the one favoring the effective protection of the lives, liberty, and property of the people. The officer's successful attempt to free the arrestee from illegal confinement was a refreshing and laudable exercise that should be protected, not punished."[19]

Exceptions Based on Tort Theory

In a few cases, the discharge of an employee may give rise to a tort cause of action. Abusive discharge procedures may result in intentional infliction of emotional distress or defamation. In one case, a restaurant had suffered some thefts of supplies, and the manager announced that he would start firing waitresses alphabetically until the thief was identified. The first waitress fired said that she suffered great emotional distress as a result. The state's highest court upheld her claim as stating a valid cause of action.[20]

❖ Injury, Compensation, and Safety

Numerous state and federal statutes are designed to protect employees and their families from the risk of accidental injury, death, or disease resulting from their employment. This section discusses state workers' compensation acts and the Occupational Safety and Health Act of 1970, which are specifically designed to protect employees and their families.

State Workers' Compensation Acts

Workers' compensation laws are state laws that compensate workers for injuries sustained on the job. These laws are usually administered by some administrative agency or board that has quasi-judicial powers. All rulings of such boards are subject to review by the courts. In general, the right to recover under workers' compensation laws is determined without regard to the existence of negligence or fault in the traditional sense. Rather, it is predicated wholly on the employment relationship and the fact that the injury *occurred on the job or in the course of normal employment.* A simple, two-pronged test for determining whether an employee can receive workers' compensation consists of the following two questions:

1. Was the injury accidental?
2. Did the injury occur on the job or in the course of employment?

Intentionally inflicted self-injury, for example, would not be considered accidental and, hence, would not be covered under the workers' compensation laws. In regard to the second question, some states require that just one of the conditions be met, whereas other states require that both be satisfied. In the past, heart attacks and other medical problems arising out of preexisting diseases or physical conditions were not covered, but recently some states have allowed recovery.

Basically, employers are under a system of strict liability. Few, if any, defenses (including the common law defenses of contributory negligence and assumption of risk) exist for them. Therefore, the costs of treating workers' injuries are considered a cost of production and are passed on to consumers.

In exchange for compensation under workers' compensation statutes, workers give up the right to sue in court for on-the-job injuries. Even if an injury is caused

19. *Wagner v. City of Globe*, 150 Ariz. 82, 722 P.2d 250 (1986).
20. *Agis v. Howard Johnson Co.*, 371 Mass. 140, 355 N.E.2d 315 (1976).

by an employer's negligence, the injured worker must normally accept workers' compensation as the sole remedy.

Health and Safety Protection

At the federal level, the primary legislation for employee health and safety protection is the Occupational Safety and Health Act of 1970.[21] This act was passed in an attempt to ensure safe and healthful working conditions for practically every employee in the country. The act requires that businesses be maintained free from recognized hazards.

Three federal agencies were created to develop and enforce the standards set by this act. The Occupational Safety and Health Administration (OSHA) is part of the Department of Labor and has the authority to promulgate standards, make inspections, and enforce the act. The National Institute for Occupational Safety and Health is part of the Department of Health and Human Services. Its main duty is to conduct research on safety and health problems and to recommend standards for OSHA administrators to adopt. Finally, the Occupational Safety and Health Review Commission is an independent agency set up to handle appeals from actions taken by OSHA administrators.

All employers affecting interstate commerce who have one or more employees are covered by the act. Employees can file complaints of OSHA violations. Under the act, an employer cannot discharge an employee who files a complaint or who, in good faith, refuses to work in a high-risk area if bodily harm or death might result. Employers with eleven or more employees are required to keep occupational injury and illness records for each employee. Each record must be made available for inspection when requested by an OSHA inspector. Whenever a work-related injury or disease occurs, employers must make reports directly to OSHA. When an employee is killed in a work-related accident, or when three or more employees are hospitalized in one accident, the Department of Labor must be notified within eight hours. If it is not, the company is fined. Following the accident, a complete inspection of the premises is mandatory.

OSHA compliance officers may enter and inspect facilities of any establishment covered by the act. In the past, warrantless inspections were conducted. As the following case illustrates, however, it is now recognized that such inspections violate the warrant clause of the Fourth Amendment.

Case 32.5 

MARSHALL v. BARLOW'S, INC.

Supreme Court of the United States, 1978.
436 U.S. 307,
98 S.Ct. 1816,
56 L.Ed.2d 305.

HISTORICAL AND SOCIAL SETTING *The Fourth Amendment to the U.S. Constitution provides that, except when there is probable cause supported by oath or affirmation, people have a right to be secure in their persons, houses, papers, and effects against unreasonable searches and seizures. The amendment was adopted to prevent government officers from breaking into homes, unannounced and without warrants, in random sweeps for criminal evidence. As social changes produced circumstances outside the traditional scope of the law, including governmental regulation of business, it became necessary to determine whether Fourth Amendment protections applied to government agents' inspections of regulated business firms. Although such inspections involve searches of business premises by regulatory agency personnel, not searches of homes by police officers, the constitutional principles are still relevant.*

FACTS In 1975, an OSHA inspector entered the customer service area of Barlow's, Inc., an electrical and

21. 29 U.S.C. Sections 553, 651–678.

Case 32.5—Continued

plumbing installation business. After showing his credentials, the inspector informed the president and general manager, Barlow, that he wished to conduct a search of the working areas of the business. Upon inquiry, Barlow learned that no complaint had been received about his company. The inspection was simply the result of a random selection process, and the inspector did not have a search warrant. Barlow refused to permit the inspector to enter the working area of his business, claiming rights guaranteed by the Fourth Amendment of the U.S. Constitution. OSHA filed suit in the district court and received an order compelling Barlow to admit the inspector for purposes of conducting an occupational safety and health inspection. When the OSHA inspector presented himself, however, Barlow again refused admission. Barlow then sought an injunction against the warrantless search on the ground that it violated the Fourth Amendment. A panel of three judges issued a permanent injunction, and OSHA appealed.

ISSUE Was OSHA entitled to make a safety and health inspection of Barlow's work premises without a warrant?

DECISION No. The United States Supreme Court upheld the permanent injunction. The Court held that OSHA inspections conducted without warrants are unconstitutional, because the warrant clause of the Fourth Amendment protects "commercial buildings as well as private homes."

REASON OSHA argued that the search-warrant requirement should not apply to "pervasively regulated businesses" affecting interstate commerce. The Court disagreed that an exception should be granted on this basis, stating that nothing "but the most fictional sense of voluntary consent to later searches [can] be found in the single fact that one conducts a business affecting interstate commerce; under current practice and law, few businesses can be conducted without having some effect on interstate commerce."

❖ Retirement and Security Income

Federal and state governments participate in insurance programs designed to protect employees and their families by covering the financial impact of retirement, disability, death, hospitalization, and unemployment. The key federal law on this subject is the Social Security Act of 1935.[22]

Old Age, Survivors, and Disability Insurance (OASDI)

The Social Security Act provides for old age (retirement), survivors, and disability insurance. The act is therefore often referred to as OASDI. Both employers and employees must "contribute" under the Federal Insurance Contributions Act (FICA)[23] to help pay for the employees' loss of income on retirement. The basis for an employee's contribution is the employee's annual wage base—the maximum amount of the employee's wages that are subject to the tax. Benefits are fixed by statute but increase automatically with increases in the cost of living.

Medicare

A health insurance program, Medicare is administered by the Social Security Administration for people sixty-five years of age and older and for some under sixty-five who are disabled. It has two parts, one pertaining to hospital costs and the other to nonhospital medical costs, such as visits to doctors' offices. People who have Medicare hospital insurance can also obtain additional federal medical insurance if they pay small monthly premiums, which increase as the cost of medical care increases.

22. 42 U.S.C. Sections 301–1397e.
23. 26 U.S.C. Sections 3101–3125.

Profile

Oliver Wendell Holmes, Jr. (1841–1935)

The task of a judge or justice can be awesome—especially a justice on the United States Supreme Court. How do you decide what cases are significant enough to warrant the attention of the Court? How do you decide which precedent to apply when more than one possibility exists? How do you decide at what point justice requires that a well-established precedent be overturned? And finally, how can you be sure that you are making a significant decision on the basis of objective reasoning instead of subjective prejudices and biases?

These kinds of questions escape few jurists, and certainly they were among those that preoccupied Oliver Wendell Holmes during his long tenure as a jurist on the Supreme Judicial Court of Massachusetts (twenty years) and then as a United States Supreme Court justice (thirty years).

Holmes was a man of ideas. He was an intellectual, a scholar, and a prolific writer. He read avidly and even kept a notebook in which he recorded the books he read each year. According to the notebook entries for 1910–1911, Holmes, while serving on the United States Supreme Court, also somehow found the time to read forty-nine books, including works by Plato (in Greek), Dante, and Alfred North Whitehead. During his tenure on the bench, Holmes—who was frequently referred to as the "court scholar"—became celebrated for his pithy philosophical statements concerning law and the human condition in general. He remains probably the most widely quoted of American jurists.

Holmes was greatly influenced by the work of Charles Darwin and by those who transplanted Darwin's "survival of the fittest" principle into a social context. In his view, just as society is in a constant state of evolution, so, too, must the law remain fluid and open to the moral, political, and economic evolution of the times. In *The Common Law*, written in 1881 and one of his best-known works, Holmes wrote of the practical, experiential nature of the law: "The life of the law has not been logic, it has been experience"; it is affected by the "prejudices which judges share with their fellow men" and corresponds, "as far as it goes, with what is * * * understood to be convenient."

His concern with the role played by personal prejudices and biases in judicial decision making was clearly expressed in his dissenting opinion in *Lochner v. New York* (1905).[a] In *Lochner*, the Supreme Court found unconstitutional a New York state law prohibiting bakery workers from working more than ten hours a day. The Court stated that the New York law violated the due process clause of the Fourteenth Amendment, which provides that no state may "deprive any person of life, liberty, or property without due process of law." The law also violated, according to the Court, the constitutionally guaranteed freedom to contract. Holmes pointed out in his dissent that the majority opinion betrayed the personal biases and prejudices of the justices in favor of freedom of contract rather than contributing to objective consistency in judicial reasoning. After all, Holmes argued, the Supreme Court had, only nine years earlier, upheld a Utah law limiting working hours for miners[b]—a precedent "conveniently" overlooked by the majority on the court.

Probably one of Holmes's greatest insights into the common law was that the same legal rules can be manipulated by judges to serve different policies at different times. The task of judges, in Holmes's opinion, must be to keep their own prejudices and biases out of their decisions, insofar as possible, and to be ever vigilant in distinguishing between conclusions based on objective legal reasoning and those stemming from purely subjective biases and attitudes.

a. 198 U.S. 45, 25 S.Ct. 539, 49 L.Ed. 937 (1905).

b. *Holden v. Hardy*, 169 U.S. 366, 18 S.Ct. 383, 42 L.Ed. 780 (1898).

Private Retirement Plans

There has been significant legislation to regulate retirement plans set up by employers to supplement social security benefits. The major federal act covering these retirement plans is the Employee Retirement Income Security Act (ERISA) of

1974.[24] This act empowers the Labor Management Services Administration of the Department of Labor to enforce its provisions to regulate individuals who operate private pension funds.

Unemployment Compensation

The United States has a system of unemployment insurance in which employers pay into a fund, the proceeds of which are paid out to qualified unemployed workers. The Federal Unemployment Tax Act[25] of 1935 created a state system that provides unemployment compensation to eligible individuals. Employers that fall under the provisions of the act are taxed quarterly. Taxes are typically paid by the employers to the states, which then deposit them with the federal government. The federal government maintains an unemployment insurance fund, in which each state has an account.

❖ Other Employment Laws

"Constant employment and well-paid labor produce, in a country like ours, general prosperity, content, and cheerfulness."

Daniel Webster, 1782–1852 ***(American politician, diplomat, and orator)***

In 1931, during the Great Depression, the president signed the Davis-Bacon Act,[26] which requires the payment of "prevailing wages" to employees of contractors and subcontractors working on government construction projects. In 1936, an act that extended the Davis-Bacon Act was put into effect—the Walsh-Healey Act.[27] This act requires a minimum wage as well as overtime pay of time and a half for employees of manufacturers or suppliers entering into contracts with agencies of the federal government.

In 1938, Congress passed the Fair Labor Standards Act[28] (FLSA), which is also known as the Wage-Hour Law. The act covers child labor, maximum hours, and minimum wages. Children under sixteen years of age cannot be employed full-time except by a parent under certain circumstances; nor can children between the ages of sixteen and eighteen be employed in hazardous jobs or in jobs detrimental to their health and well-being. Most states require children under sixteen years of age to obtain work permits. In regard to maximum hours, the FLSA provides that any employee who agrees to work more than forty hours per week must be paid no less than one-and-a-half times his or her regular pay for all hours over forty. Exceptions are made for employees working under the terms of collective bargaining agreements and in some other circumstances.

The FLSA further provides that a minimum wage of a specified amount ($4.25 per hour as of April 1, 1991) must be paid to employees in covered industries. Congress periodically revises the minimum wage. The term *wages* is meant to include the reasonable cost to the employer of furnishing employees with board, lodging, and other facilities if they are customarily furnished by that employer.

24. 29 U.S.C. Section 1001.
25. 26 U.S.C. Sections 3301–3310.
26. 40 U.S.C. Sections 276a–276a-5.
27. 41 U.S.C. Sections 35–45.
28. 29 U.S.C. Sections 201–260.

Application

Law and the Employer—A Rational Approach to Sexual Harassment in the Workplace

Even before the passage of the Civil Rights Act of 1991, the issue of sexual harassment was an important legal—as well as moral, social, and ethical—problem facing employers throughout the United States. Certainly, the problems associated with sexual harassment, such as lost productivity, workplace disruption, and litigation expenses, are sufficiently imposing to require every company to get serious about the issue. Federal and state courts have held that sexual harassment includes sexually offensive conduct ranging from physical contact to subtle hints and suggestions. In most jurisdictions, any of the following actions may be grounds for a lawsuit alleging sexual harassment in the workplace:

- *Unwelcome sexual advances.* These can be made at the office or away from the office. They include any situation in which an employee is repeatedly propositioned by a supervisor or co-worker who wishes to establish an intimate relationship.
- *Coercion.* This includes any situation in which a supervisor asks for a date or sexual favor with the explicit or implicit understanding that the favor will be returned or that reprisal will be made if the date or sexual favor is refused.
- *Favoritism.* This occurs when employees who submit to requests for sexual favors are rewarded while employees who refuse to submit to such requests are not.
- *Indirect harassment.* This may occur when those who witness sexual harassment in the workplace feel that the harassment has created a hostile working environment.
- *Physical conduct.* Such conduct does not have to be actual touching—unseemly gestures may be included.
- *Visual harassment.* Even graffiti written on the walls of men's bathrooms about a female employee may constitute grounds for a claim of sexual harassment.

Checklist for Dealing with Harassment in the Workplace

☐ 1. Just say "knock it off." Employees should be instructed to explicitly ask an offending co-worker, supervisor, or boss to stop any activity that they feel constitutes sexual harassment.

☐ 2. Employers should make it easy and safe for employees to seek help. DuPont, for example, has a twenty-four-hour hotline that offers advice on personal security and sexual harassment. Callers do not need to identify themselves.

☐ 3. If a victim or witness to harassment lodges an official complaint, the company must respond immediately, often with a full-fledged investigation. If the allegations are substantiated, the company must respond appropriately with actions ranging from warnings to reassignment to termination.

☐ 4. Finally, companies that create stable work environments typically report fewer cases of sexual harassment. Companies that treat all employees with sensitivity and respect go a long way toward eliminating the problem.

❖ Key Terms

❖ Chapter Summary: Employee and Labor Law

Unions and Collective Bargaining	1. *Norris-LaGuardia Act (1932)*—Permitted employees to organize into unions and to engage in peaceful strikes. 2. *National Labor Relations Act (Wagner Act) (1935)*—Established the right of employees to engage in collective bargaining and to strike. Created the National Labor Relations Board to oversee elections and to prevent employers from engaging in unfair and illegal union-labor activities and unfair labor practices. 3. *Labor-Management Relations Act (Taft-Hartley Act) (1947)*—Allowed for protection of employers as well as employees by providing a list of unfair labor activities that both unions and management were forbidden to practice. 4. *Labor-Management Reporting and Disclosure Act (Landrum-Griffin Act) (1959)*—Regulated internal union elections and procedures and established reporting requirements for union activities.
Employment Discrimination	1. *Title VII of the Civil Rights Act (1964), as amended*—Prohibits discrimination by most employers, labor unions, employment agencies, and state and local governments against employees, job applicants, and union members on the basis of race, color, national origin, religion, or sex. The Pregnancy Discrimination Act (1978) amended Title VII to prohibit discrimination based on pregnancy. Increasingly, employees are protected against sexual harassment in the workplace. Under Title VII provisions: a. Both intentional (disparate-treatment) discrimination and unintentional (disparate-impact) discrimination are prohibited. b. As defenses, employers may assert that discrimination was required for reasons of business necessity, to meet a bona fide occupational qualification (BFOQ), or to maintain a legitimate seniority system. 2. *Affirmative action*—Programs that give women and minorities preference in hiring and promotion; established to make up for past patterns of discrimination against these groups. These programs are generally held to be legal if they are designed to correct existing imbalances in the work force and as long as employers consider factors in addition to race or gender when making employment decisions. 3. *Age Discrimination in Employment Act (1967), as amended*—Prohibits discrimination on the basis of age against employees or job applicants aged forty or older. 4. *Americans with Disabilities Act (1990)*—Prohibits discrimination on the basis of disability against individuals qualified for a given job. Employers must reasonably accommodate the needs of disabled persons. 5. *State laws*—Most states have statutes or regulations prohibiting employment discrimination; often, in terms of the protections they offer, these laws are broader in scope than federal legislation.
Privacy Issues	The privacy rights of employees in the private sector are often established by state constitutions, legislation, or court decisions. Government employees are protected to some extent under the Fourth Amendment. Major privacy issues relate to lie-detector tests, drug testing, performance monitoring, and preemployment screening tests.
Employment at Will	Traditionally, the employment relationship has been "at will"—that is, the relationship could be terminated at any time for any reason by either the employer or the employee. Because of the harsh results of this doctrine for employees who are fired wrongfully, whistleblowing statutes and court decisions have limited the at-will doctrine in certain circumstances.
Injury, Compensation, and Safety	1. *State workers' compensation acts*—Allows compensation to workers whose injuries arise out of and/or during the course of their employment; regulated by state agency or board. 2. *Health and safety protection*—The Occupational Safety and Health Act of 1970 attempts to ensure safe and healthful working conditions for employees.
Retirement and Security Income	1. *Social Security*—Old Age, Survivors, and Disability Insurance provides retired or disabled employees or their families with income created by mandatory employer and employee contributions. The Social Security Administration, created by the Social Security Act of 1935, also administers Medicare, a health insurance program for people sixty-five years of age and older and for some under sixty-five who are disabled.

❖ Chapter Summary: Employee and Labor Law—Continued

Retirement and Security Income—Continued	2. *Private retirement plans set up by employers*—These plans supplement Social Security income for retired individuals. Most plans are regulated by the Employee Retirement Income Security Act of 1974. 3. *Unemployment compensation*—The Federal Unemployment Tax Act of 1935 created a state system that provides unemployment compensation to eligible individuals; funded by employer-paid taxes.
Other Employment Laws	1. *Fair Labor Standards Act* (1938)—Prohibits oppressive child labor, provides that a minimum hourly wage rate be paid to covered employees, and requires individuals working over forty hours a week to be paid overtime wages of no less than one-and-a-half times the regular pay for hours worked beyond forty hours a week (with some exceptions). 2. *Other minimum-wage laws*—Employees working on government-project contracts must be paid at least a minimum wage (established and periodically revised by the federal government), and employees working on government construction projects must be paid "prevailing wages." Established by the Davis-Bacon Act of 1931 and extended by the Walsh-Healey Act of 1936.

❖ Questions and Case Problems

32-1. Employment at Will. What does "employment at will" mean? What exceptions to this doctrine are made, and why?

32-2. Employment Discrimination. What major federal statute prohibits employment discrimination? In bringing a claim of employment discrimination under this statute, what procedures must be followed, and what remedies are available?

32-3. Labor Laws. Calzoni Boating Co. is an interstate business engaged in manufacturing and selling boats. The company has five hundred nonunion employees. Representatives of these employees are requesting a four-day, ten-hours-per-day workweek, and Calzoni is concerned that this would require paying time and a half after eight hours per day. Which federal law might Calzoni believe would require this? Will this law in fact require paying time and a half for all hours worked over eight hours per day if the employees' proposal is accepted? Explain.

32-4. Employment Discrimination. Chinawa, a major processor of cheese sold throughout the United States, employs one hundred workers at its principal processing plant. The plant is located in Heartland Corners, in which the population is 50 percent white and 25 percent black, with the balance Hispanic, Asian, and others. Chinawa requires a high school diploma as a condition of employment for its clean-up crew. Three-fourths of the white population complete high school, compared with only one-fourth of those in the minority groups. Chinawa has an all-white cleaning crew. Has Chinawa violated Title VII of the Civil Rights Act of 1964? Explain.

32-5. Health and Safety Regulations. Denton and Carlo were employed at an appliance plant. Their jobs required them to do occasional maintenance work while standing on a wire mesh twenty feet above the plant floor. Other employees had fallen through the mesh, and one had been killed by the fall. When Denton and Carlo were asked by their supervisor to do work that would likely require them to walk on the mesh, they refused because they feared bodily harm or death. Because of their refusal to do the requested work, the two employees were fired from their jobs. Was their discharge wrongful? If so, under what federal employment law? To what federal agency or department should they turn for assistance?

32-6. Sex Discrimination. Beginning in June 1966, Corning Glass Works started to open up jobs on the night shift to women. The previously separate male and female seniority lists were consolidated, and the women became eligible to exercise their seniority on the same basis as men and to bid for higher-paid night inspection jobs as vacancies occurred. But on January 20, 1969, a new collective bargaining agreement went into effect; it established a new job evaluation system for setting wage rates. This agreement abolished (for the future) separate base wages for night- and day-shift inspectors and imposed a uniform base wage for inspectors that exceeded the wage rate previously in effect for the night shift. The agreement, however, did allow for a higher "red circle" rate for employees hired prior to January 20, 1969, when they were working as inspectors on the night shift. This "red circle" wage served essentially to perpetuate the differential in base wages between day and night inspectors. Had Corning violated Title VII of the Civil Rights Act of 1964? Discuss. [*Corning Glass Works v. Brennan*, 417 U.S. 188, 94 S.Ct. 2223, 41 L.Ed.2d 1 (1974)]

32-7. Health and Safety Regulations. At an REA Express shipping terminal, a conveyor belt was inoperative because an electrical circuit had shorted out. The manager called a licensed electrical contractor. When the contractor arrived, REA's maintenance supervisor was in the circuit breaker room. The floor was wet, and the maintenance supervisor was using sawdust to try to soak up the water. While the licensed electrical contractor was attempting to fix the short circuit, standing on the wet floor, he was electrocuted. Simultaneously, REA's maintenance supervisor, who was standing on a wooden platform, was burned and knocked unconscious. The Occupational Safety and Health Administration (OSHA) sought to fine REA Express $1,000 for failure to furnish a place of employment free from recognized hazards. Will the court uphold OSHA's decision? Discuss fully. [*REA Express, Inc. v. Brennan*, 495 F.2d 822 (2d Cir. 1974)]

32-8. Employment Discrimination. Duke Power Co. was sued by a number of its African-American employees for practicing racial discrimination in the hiring and assigning of employees at its Dan River plant. The plant was organized into five operating departments: (1) labor, (2) coal handling, (3) operation, (4) maintenance, and (5) laboratory testing. African Americans were employed only in the labor department, in which the highest-paying jobs paid less than the lowest-paying jobs in the other four departments (which employed no African Americans). Promotions were normally made within each department on the basis of seniority. Transferees into a department usually began in the lowest position. In 1955, the company began to require a high school education for an initial assignment into any department except the labor department. In addition, it required a high school education for any transfer from the coal-handling department to any inside department (operations, maintenance, or laboratory). For ten years, this company-wide policy was enforced. In 1965, when the company abandoned its policy of restricting blacks to the labor department, a high school diploma or equivalency test was nevertheless made a prerequisite to transfer from the labor department into any other department. This requirement rendered a markedly disproportionate number of African Americans ineligible for employment advancement in the company. Did these employer practices violate Title VII of the Civil Rights Act? Discuss fully. [*Griggs v. Duke Power Co.*, 401 U.S. 424, 91 S.Ct. 849, 28 L.Ed.2d 158 (1971)]

32-9. Whistleblowing. Richard Winters was an at-will employee for the Houston *Chronicle* from April 1977 to June 1986. Beginning in 1980, he became aware of alleged illegal activities carried out by other employees. He claimed that the *Chronicle* was falsely reporting an inflated number of paid subscribers, that several employees were engaged in inventory theft, and that his supervisor had offered him an opportunity to participate in a kickback scheme with the manufacturers of plastic bags. Winters reported all these activities to upper-level management in January 1986 but made no report to law enforcement agencies. He was fired six months later. He sued the *Chronicle* for wrongful termination. How should the court decide? Discuss fully. [*Winters v. Houston Chronicle Publishing*, 795 S.W.2d 723 (Tex. 1990)]

32-10. Employment at Will. Robert Adams worked as a delivery truck driver for George W. Cochran & Co. Adams persistently refused to drive a truck that lacked a required inspection sticker and was subsequently fired as a result of his refusal. Adams was an at-will employee, and Cochran contended that because there was no written employment contract stating otherwise, Cochran was entitled to discharge Adams at will—that is, for cause or no cause. Adams sought to recover $7,094 in lost wages and $200,000 in damages for the "humiliation, mental anguish and emotional distress" that he had suffered as a result of being fired from his job. Under what legal doctrines discussed in this chapter—or exceptions to those doctrines—might Adams be able to recover damages from Cochran? Discuss fully. [*Adams v. George W. Cochran & Co.*, 597 A.2d 28 (D.C.App. 1991)]

32-11. Whistleblowing. Debra Roxberry supervised the dry-cleaning department for Robertson and Penn, Inc. (R&P), a private contractor to the U.S. government for laundry and dry-cleaning services at Fort Riley, Kansas. Willie Dawson was an employee of another private contractor to the U.S. government, which operated the Central Issue Facility at Fort Riley. On one occasion, when Dawson was picking up some shirts from R&P, Roxberry informed him that the shirts had been washed instead of dry-cleaned, the process for which they had been delivered and which R&P was contractually obligated to perform. Roxberry was fired a short time later, and she sued R&P for wrongful discharge, alleging that she had been fired for "blowing the whistle" on her employer's violation of its contract with the government. Under the relevant state law, at-will employees had a cause of action against an employer for discharge in retaliation for whistleblowing. R&P contended, among other things, that Roxberry was not a whistleblower because she did not report the incident to the proper authorities but only to an employee of a private company. Will the court agree with R&P's conclusion that Roxberry was not a whistleblower? Discuss. [*Roxberry v. Robertson and Penn, Inc.*, 963 F.2d 382 (10th Cir. 1992)]

32-12. Privacy Rights. Newell and Juanita Spears owned a small store near Camden, Arkansas, and lived in a mobile home adjacent to the store. The telephone in the store had an extension in the home, and it was the only phone line into either location. The store was burglarized in April 1990, and approximately $16,000 was stolen. The Spearses, suspecting that their employee, Sibbie Deal, might have been involved, installed a recording device on the extension phone in the mobile home and tape-recorded calls made to or from the store. Deal, who was married at the time, was involved in an extramarital affair with Calvin Lucas, who was also married. Deal talked to Lucas frequently and for long periods of time, using the store's phone. Although Deal never mentioned anything about the burglary, she did indicate in one of her conversations with Lucas that she had sold Lucas a keg of beer at cost, in violation of the store's policy. Newell Spears played a few seconds of the incriminating tape for Deal and then fired her. Deal and Lucas, after learning that their private phone conversations had been recorded without their knowledge or permission, sued the Spearses for violating the Omnibus Crime Control and Safe Streets Act of 1968. Had the Spearses violated this act? Discuss fully. [*Deal v. Spears*, 980 F.2d 1153 (8th Cir. 1992)]

A QUESTION OF ETHICS AND SOCIAL RESPONSIBILITY

32-13. *Hazen Paper Co. manufactured coated, foil-laminated, and printed paper and paperboard for use in such products as cosmetic wrap, lottery tickets, and pressure-sensitive items. Walter Biggins, a chemist hired by Hazen in 1977, developed a water-based paper coating that was both environmentally safe and of superior quality. By the mid-1980s, the company's sales had increased dramatically as a result of its extensive use of "Biggins Acrylic." Because of this, Biggins thought he deserved a substantial raise in salary, and from 1984 to 1986, Biggins's persistent requests for a raise became a bone of contention between him and his employers. Biggins ran a business on the side cleaning up hazardous wastes for various* *companies. Hazen told Biggins that unless he signed a "confidentiality agreement" promising to restrict his outside activities during the time he was employed by Hazen and for a limited time afterward, he would be fired. Biggins said he would sign the agreement only if Hazen raised his salary to $100,000. Hazen refused to do so, fired Biggins, and hired a younger man to replace him. At the time of his discharge in 1986, Biggins was sixty-two years old, had worked for the company nearly ten years, and was just a few weeks away from being entitled to pension rights worth about $93,000. In view of these circumstances, evaluate and answer the following questions.* [Hazen Paper Co. v. Biggins, *___ U.S. ___, 113 S.Ct. 1701, 123 L.Ed.2d 338 (1993).*]

1. Biggins sued Hazen for age discrimination in violation of the Age Discrimination in Employment Act of 1967. If you were the judge, would you hold for Biggins or Hazen? Discuss fully.
2. Did the company owe an ethical duty to Biggins to increase his salary, given the fact that its sales increased dramatically as a result of Biggins's efforts and ingenuity in developing the coating? If you were one of the company's owners, would you have raised Biggins's salary? Why or why not?
3. Generally, what public policies come into conflict in cases involving employers who, for reasons of cost and efficiency of operations, fire older, higher-paid workers and replace them with younger, lower-paid workers? What would you do, and on what ethical premises would you justify your decision, if you were an employer facing the need to cut back on personnel to save costs?

CASE BRIEFING ASSIGNMENT

32-14. *Examine Case* A.12 [Johnston v. Del Mar Distributing Co., *776 S.W.2d 768 (Tex.App.—Corpus Christi 1989)*] *in Appendix A. The case has been excerpted there in great detail. Review and then brief the case, making sure that you include answers to the following questions in your brief.*

1. Why did Del Mar Distributing Co. terminate Nancy Johnston's employment?
2. What defense did Del Mar Distributing raise against Johnston's claim of wrongful discharge?
3. On what case precedent did the appellate court base its reasoning?
4. Why did the appellate court conclude that, given the circumstances of this case, it was irrelevant whether the act that Johnston was asked to perform was legal or illegal?

FOR CRITICAL ANALYSIS

32-15. *Review this chapter's* Ethical Perspective *on the reasonable woman standard. In respect to claims of sexual harassment, do you think that a reasonable woman standard or a reasonable man standard—depending on the gender of the victim—is more appropriate than the traditional reasonable person standard? Why or why not?*

Unit Six

Property and Its Protection

❖ Why We Study Law Relating to Property and Its Protection

Property can be either movable, in which case it is called *personal property*, or not movable, in which case it is called *real property*. The law treats these two separate types of property in distinctly different ways. Consequently, we will discuss each in a separate chapter: personal property in Chapter 33 and real property in Chapter 34. Also included in Chapter 33 is an analysis of a situation in which personal property is temporarily delivered by its owner into the care of another person. This temporary transfer of personal property is called a *bailment*. What happens when you loan this law book to one of your friends and it is destroyed in a fire? You need to know the law of bailments to give an answer. If your car is stolen in an attended parking lot, who is responsible? Again, you need to know the law of bailments to answer this question.

Both personal property and real property are usually insured. In Chapter 35, we examine insurance contracts in general terms. We also look at how property is passed from one generation to another through the use of wills, the application of inheritance laws, or the establishment of trusts.

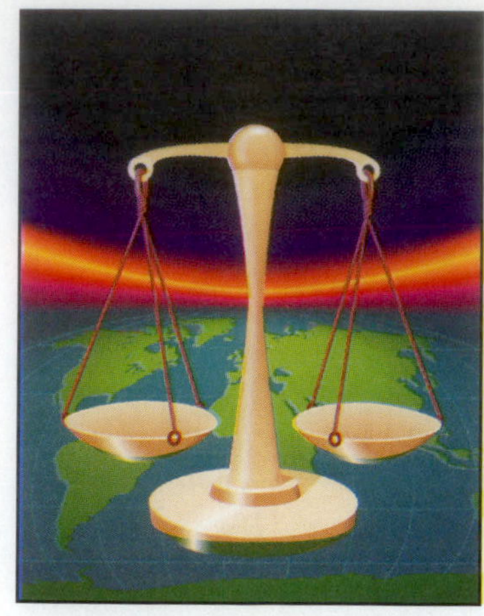

Chapter 33

Personal Property and Bailments

"The great and chief end . . . of men united into commonwealths, and putting themselves under government, is the preservation of their property."

John Locke, 1632–1704
(English political philosopher)

Property consists of the legally protected rights and interests a person has in anything with an ascertainable value that is subject to ownership. Property would have little value (and the word would have little meaning) if the law did not define the right to use it, to sell or dispose of it, and to prevent trespass upon it. In the United States, the ownership of property receives unique protection under the law. The Bill of Rights states that "no person shall * * * be deprived of life, liberty, or property, without due process of law; nor shall private property be taken for public use, without just compensation." The Fourteenth Amendment provides that "no State shall * * * deprive any person of life, liberty, or property, without due process of law." Indeed, John Locke, as indicated in the opening quotation, considered the preservation of property to be the primary reason for the establishment of government.

In the first part of this chapter, we will look at the nature of personal property, property rights and ownership title, the methods of acquiring ownership of personal property, and issues relating to mislaid, lost, and abandoned personal property. In the second part of the chapter, we will look at the bailment relationship, which is created when personal property is temporarily delivered into the care of another without a transfer of title. This is the distinguishing characteristic of a bailment compared with a sale or a gift—there is no passage of title and no intent to transfer title.

❖ The Nature of Personal Property

REAL PROPERTY
Immovable property consisting of land and buildings thereupon, as opposed to personal property, which can be moved. In the absence of a contract, real property includes things growing on the land before they are severed (such as timber), as well as fixtures.

PERSONAL PROPERTY
Property that is movable; any property that is not real property.

CHATTEL
A tangible piece of personal property or an intangible right therein.

As discussed in the introduction to this unit, property is divided into two categories. **Real property** consists of the land and everything permanently attached to the land. When structures are permanently attached to the land, then everything attached permanently to the structures is also real property, or *realty*. All other property is **personal property**, or *personalty*. Attorneys sometimes refer to all personal property as **chattels**, a more comprehensive term than *goods*, because it includes living as well as inanimate property.

Personal property can be tangible or intangible. *Tangible* personal property, such as a TV set or a car, has physical substance. *Intangible* personal property represents some set of rights and interests but has no real physical existence. Stocks and bonds, patents, and copyrights are examples of intangible personal property.

In a dynamic society, the concept of personal property must expand to take account of new types of ownership rights. For example, gas, water, and telephone services are now considered to be personal property for the purpose of criminal prosecution when they are stolen or used without authorization. Federal and state statutes protect against the copying of musical compositions. It is a crime now to engage in the "bootlegging"—illegal copying for resale—of records and tapes. The theft of computer programs is usually considered a theft of personal property.

❖ Property Ownership

Property ownership[1] can be viewed as a bundle of rights, including the right to possession of the property and disposition—by sale, gift, lease, or other means—of the property.

"Private property began the minute somebody had a mind of his own."

e. e. cummings, 1894–1962
(American poet)

Fee Simple

A person who holds the entire bundle of rights to property is said to be the owner in **fee simple.** The owner in fee simple is entitled to use, possess, or dispose of the property as he or she chooses during his or her lifetime, and upon this owner's death, the interests in the property descend to his or her heirs. We will return to this form of property ownership in Chapter 34, in the context of ownership rights in real property.

FEE SIMPLE
A form of property ownership entitling the property owner to use, possess, or dispose of the property as he or she chooses during his or her lifetime. Upon death, the interest in the property descends to the owner's heirs.

Concurrent Ownership

Persons who share ownership rights simultaneously in a particular piece of property are said to be *concurrent* owners. There are two principal types of concurrent ownership: tenancy in common and joint tenancy.

Tenancy in common is co-ownership in which each of two or more persons owns an undivided fractional interest in the property. Upon one tenant's death, that interest passes to his or her heirs. For example, Rosalind and Chad own a rare stamp collection as tenants in common. Should Rosalind die before Chad, one-half of the stamp collection would become the property of Rosalind's heirs. If Rosalind sold her interest to Fred before she died, Fred and Chad would be co-owners as tenants in common. If Fred died, his interest in the personal property would pass to his heirs, and they in turn would own the property with Chad as tenants in common.

TENANCY IN COMMON
Co-ownership of property in which each party owns an undivided interest that passes to his or her heirs at death.

Joint tenancy is co-ownership in which each of two or more persons owns an undivided interest in the property, and a deceased joint tenant's interest passes to the surviving joint tenant or tenants. Joint tenancy can be terminated at any time before a joint tenant's death by gift or by sale. If no termination occurs, then upon the death of a joint tenant, his or her interest transfers to the remaining joint tenants, not to the heirs of the deceased joint tenant. In the preceding example, if Rosalind and Chad held their stamp collection in a joint tenancy, and if Rosalind died before Chad, the entire collection would become the property of Chad. Rosalind's heirs would receive absolutely no interest in the collection. If, prior to Rosalind's death, she sold her interest to Fred, Fred and Chad would become co-owners. Rosalind's sale, however, would terminate the joint tenancy, and Fred and Chad would become owners as tenants in common.

JOINT TENANCY
The ownership interest of two or more co-owners of property whereby each owns an undivided portion of the property. Upon the death of one of the joint tenants, his or her interest automatically passes to the others and cannot be transferred by the will of the deceased.

Concurrent ownership of property can also take the form of a **tenancy by the entirety**—a form of co-ownership between a husband and wife that is similar to a

TENANCY BY THE ENTIRETY
The joint ownership of property by husband and wife. Neither party can alienate or encumber the property without the consent of the other. The property is inherited by the survivor of the two, and dissolution of marriage transforms a tenancy by the entirety into a tenancy in common.

1. The principles discussed in this section apply equally to real property ownership, discussed in Chapter 34.

Business Law in Action

Who Owns Your Body Tissue?

When a patient has an appendectomy, who owns the appendix that is removed from the patient's body? If the appendix is used for medical research that ultimately results in a patented, commercially profitable product, should the patient have any ownership rights in that product? Would it matter if the patient was advised of the research activity but not of the fact that the doctor expected to profit monetarily from it? The California Supreme Court faced questions very similar to these in *Moore v. Regents of the University of California*.[a]

The patient in the case was John Moore. The doctor was Dr. David Golde, who treated Moore at the University of California at Los Angeles (UCLA) Medical Center. Moore was being treated for a special form of leukemia in which Dr. Golde and his associates were interested for research purposes. Golde advised Moore that he should have his spleen removed to slow down the progress of his disease. Moore later moved to Seattle, Washington, but continued to return to the UCLA Medical Center for blood tests, because Golde told him that the procedures had to be performed under Golde's direction and could not be performed in Seattle. In the meantime, Golde used these blood samples in his research and eventually established and patented a cell line from Moore's white blood cells. As a result of his research and patent rights, Golde received substantial profits. Although prior to the splenectomy, Golde had told Moore that research would be conducted on his spleen tissue, Golde had at no time let his patient know of Golde's commercial interests in the research.

When Moore learned of Golde's activities and patent rights in a cell line developed from Moore's body tissues, Moore sued Golde, his colleagues, and the medical center, alleging, among other things, conversion of his spleen. (Recall from Chapter 5 that the intentional tort of conversion occurs when property is wrongfully taken from its rightful owner or possessor and placed in the service of another.) A central issue before the court thus became whether Moore continued to possess ownership rights in his spleen after it had been removed.

The court held that he did not. Although there was no case law on the issue, a California statute providing for the incineration or other disposition of human tissues and remains following scientific use to protect public health and safety drastically limited patients' ownership rights in excised body tissues. The court also pointed out that a ruling in Moore's favor would have serious implications for the future of medical research. According to the court, "the theory of liability that Moore urges us to endorse threatens to destroy the economic incentive to conduct important medical research. If the use of cells in research is a conversion, then with every cell sample a researcher purchases a ticket in a litigation lottery." Although the court concluded that Moore had a cause of action against Golde for breach of a physician's duty to disclose any possible conflict of interest, Moore had no cause of action for conversion. Neither did Moore have any rights in the patented cell line or any products derived from it because "the patented cell line is both factually and legally distinct from the cells taken from Moore's body."

Three of the seven justices deciding the case were not persuaded by the majority's reasoning. One justice stated that the majority had totally overlooked what he thought was the real issue raised by the case—the moral issue of whether the court should "recognize and enforce a right to sell one's own body tissue for profit." Another justice contended that the majority was more concerned with policy implications than with the specific issue in this case. This justice concluded that "although a patient may not retain any legal interest in a body after its removal when he has properly consented to its removal and use for scientific purposes, it is clear under California law that before a body part is removed it is the patient, rather than his doctor or hospital, who possesses the right to determine the use to which the body part will be put after removal. If, as alleged in this case, plaintiff's doctor improperly interfered with the plaintiff's right to control the use of a body part by wrongfully withholding material information from him before its removal, under traditional common law principles plaintiff may maintain a conversion action to recover the economic value of the right to control the use of his body part."

The close, four-to-three, decision in this case indicates the problematic nature and potential implications of the question raised by Moore's claim. Medical research on body tissues and the development of genetic "clones" and cell lines is a growing "industry." Without a doubt, other courts in other jurisdictions will face similar questions in the future.

a. 51 Cal.3d 120, 793 P.2d 479, 271 Cal.Rptr. 146 (1990).

joint tenancy, except that a spouse cannot transfer separately his or her interest during his or her lifetime. Property can also be held as **community property**—in which each spouse technically owns an *undivided* one-half interest in property acquired during the marriage. The latter type of ownership occurs in only a few states.

COMMUNITY PROPERTY
A form of concurrent ownership of property in which each spouse owns an undivided one-half interest in property. This type of ownership applies to most property acquired by the husband or wife during the course of marriage. It generally does not apply to property acquired prior to the marriage or to property acquired by gift or inheritance during the marriage. After a divorce, community property is divided equally in some states and according to the discretion of the court in other states.

❖ Acquiring Ownership of Personal Property

The ownership of personal property can be acquired by possession, purchase, production, gift, will or inheritance, accession, and confusion. Each of these is discussed in the following sections.

Possession

A particularly interesting example of acquiring ownership by possession is the capture of wild animals. Wild animals belong to no one in their natural state, and the first person to take possession of a wild animal normally owns it. The killing of a wild animal amounts to assuming ownership of it. Merely being in hot pursuit does not give title, however. There are two exceptions to this basic rule. First, any wild animals captured by a trespasser are the property of the landowner, not the trespasser. Second, if wild animals are captured or killed in violation of wild game statutes, the capturer does not obtain title to the animals; rather, the state does. Other illustrations of acquiring ownership of personal property by possession are presented later in this chapter (in the section on lost property).

"Possession is nine points of the law."

Thomas Fuller, 1608–1661
(English clergyman and writer)

Purchase or Production

Purchase is one of the most common means of acquiring and transferring ownership of personal property. The purchase or sale of personal property (called *goods*) falls

In their natural state, wild animals belong to no one.

under the Uniform Commercial Code and was discussed in detail in Chapters 14 to 17. Production—the fruits of labor—is another means of acquiring ownership of personal property. For example, writers, inventors, and manufacturers all produce personal property and thereby acquire title to it. (In some situations—for example, when a researcher is hired to invent a new product or technique—the producer does not own what is produced.)

Gifts

GIFT
Any voluntary transfer of property made without consideration, past or present.

A **gift** is another fairly common means of acquiring and transferring ownership of real and personal property. A gift is essentially a voluntary transfer of property ownership. It is not supported by legally sufficient consideration because the very essence of a gift is giving without consideration. Moreover, a gift must be transferred or delivered in the present rather than in the future. For example, if your aunt tells you that she is going to give you a new Mercedes-Benz for your next birthday, this is a promise, not a gift. It does not become a gift until the Mercedes-Benz is delivered to you, the donee (the recipient of the gift).

Three conditions determine whether an effective gift exists: donative intent, delivery, and acceptance.

1. *Donative intent.* There must be evidence of the donor's intent to give the donee the gift. Such donative intent is determined from the language of the donor and the surrounding circumstances. Thus, when a gift is challenged in court, the court may look at the relationship between the parties and the size of the gift in relation to the donor's other assets. A gift to a mortal enemy is viewed with suspicion. Likewise, when a gift represents a large portion of a person's assets, the courts scrutinize the transaction closely to determine the mental capacity of the donor and whether there is any element of fraud or duress present.
2. *Delivery.* An effective delivery requires giving up complete control and **dominion** (ownership rights) over the subject matter of the gift. Delivery is obvious in most cases. But suppose that you want to make a gift of various old rare coins that you have stored in a safe-deposit box. You certainly cannot deliver the box itself to the donee, and you do not want to take the coins out of the bank. In such a case, when the physical object cannot be delivered, a symbolic, or *constructive*, delivery will be sufficient. **Constructive delivery** is a general term for all those acts that the law holds to be equivalent to acts of real delivery. In the preceding example, the delivery of the key to the safe-deposit box constitutes a constructive delivery of the contents of the box. The delivery of intangible property—such as stocks, bonds, insurance policies, contracts, and so on—is always accomplished by symbolic, or constructive, delivery. This is because the documents represent rights and are not, by themselves, the true property.

DOMINION
Ownership in its fullest sense; includes both the ownership rights in property as well as the right to possess the property.

CONSTRUCTIVE DELIVERY
An act equivalent to the actual, physical delivery of property that cannot be physically delivered because of difficulty or impossibility; to illustrate, the transfer of a key to a safe constructively delivers the contents of the safe.

Delivery may be accomplished by means of a third party. If the third party is the agent of the donor, the delivery is effective when the agent delivers the gift to the donee. If the third party is the agent of the donee, then the gift is effectively delivered when the donor delivers the property to the donee's agent.[2] Naturally, no delivery is necessary if the gift is already in the hands of the donee.
3. *Acceptance.* The final requirement of a valid gift is acceptance by the donee. This rarely presents any problems, as most donees readily accept their gifts. The courts generally assume acceptance unless shown otherwise.

In the following case, the court focused on the requirement that a donor must give up complete control and dominion over property given to the donee before a gift can be effectively delivered.

2. *Bickford v. Mattocks,* 95 Me. 547, 50 A. 894 (1901).

Case 33.1
IN RE ESTATE OF PIPER
Missouri Court of Appeals, 1984.
676 S.W.2d 897.

HISTORICAL AND CULTURAL SETTING *The rule that there must be a delivery for a gift to be valid originated at a time when handing over possession of an item was the only method of transferring it. The policy behind the rule is to protect alleged donors and their heirs from fraudulent claims based only on parol evidence. It is too easy for an alleged donee to claim that a gift was made when, in fact, it was not. For this reason, courts are wary of purported gifts that have not been delivered, except when the alleged donee is a member of the family.*

FACTS Gladys Piper died intestate (without a will) in 1982. At her death, she owned miscellaneous personal property worth $5,000 and had in her purse $200 in cash and two diamond rings known as the Andy Piper rings. The contents of her purse were taken by her niece Wanda Brown, allegedly to preserve them for the estate. Clara Kaufmann, a friend of Gladys's, filed a claim against the estate for $4,800 because from October 1974 until Gladys's death, Clara had taken Gladys to the doctor, beauty shop, and grocery store, had written her checks to pay her bills, and had helped her care for her home. Clara maintained that Gladys had promised to pay her for these services and had given her the diamond rings as a gift. The trial court denied her request for payment, finding that her services had been voluntary. Clara then filed a petition for delivery of personal property, the rings, which was granted by the trial court. Wanda, other heirs, and the administrator of Gladys's estate appealed.

ISSUE Had Gladys Piper made an effective gift of the rings to Clara Kaufmann?

DECISION No. The appellate court reversed the judgment of the trial court on the ground that Gladys had never delivered the rings to Clara.

REASON Clara claimed that the rings belonged to her by reason of a "consummated gift long prior to the death of Gladys Piper." Two witnesses testified for Clara at the trial that Gladys had told them the rings belonged to Clara but that she was going to wear them until she died. The appellate court found "no evidence of any actual delivery." The court held that the essentials of a gift are (1) a present intention to make a gift on the part of the donor, (2) a delivery of the property by the donor to the donee, and (3) an acceptance by the donee. The evidence in the case showed only an intent to make a gift. Because there was no delivery—either actual or constructive—a valid gift was not made. For Gladys to have made a gift, her intention would have to have been executed by the complete and unconditional delivery of the property or the delivery of a proper written instrument evidencing the gift. As this did not occur, the court found that there had been no gift.

Gifts *Inter Vivos* and Gifts *Causa Mortis*

Gifts *inter vivos* are gifts made during one's lifetime, whereas **gifts *causa mortis*** (so-called *deathbed gifts*) are made in contemplation of imminent death. A gift *causa mortis* does not become absolute until the donor dies from the contemplated illness, and it is automatically revoked if the donor recovers from the illness. Moreover, the donee must survive to take the gift. To be effective, a gift *causa mortis* must also meet the three requirements discussed earlier—donative intent, delivery, and acceptance by the donee. The question of whether a gift *causa mortis* had been effectively delivered is at issue in the following case.

GIFT *INTER VIVOS*
A gift made during one's lifetime and not in contemplation of imminent death, in contrast to a gift *causa mortis*.

GIFT *CAUSA MORTIS*
A gift made in contemplation of death. If the donor does not die of that ailment, the gift is revoked.

Case 33.2
KESTERSON v. CRONAN
Court of Appeals of Oregon, 1991.
105 Or.App. 551,
806 P.2d 134.

HISTORICAL AND ETHICAL SETTING *Gifts* causa mortis *were accepted by courts of equity before they were accepted by courts of law. The basis for giving effect to these gifts is a religious premise that a person expresses his or her true feelings when facing death and settles debts and disburses property to ease his or her soul. Today, some of the religious basis may be evaporating, and in part for this reason, gifts* causa mortis *are not entirely favored by courts of law. Another reason for the courts' disfavor is that these gifts defeat the purpose of the statutes that require specific forms for the transfer of property at death. Also, because the donor is no longer available to testify,*

Case 33.2—Continued

the donee may be tempted to commit fraud. For these and other reasons, the delivery requirement is a particularly important element of a gift causa mortis.

FACTS James Wilson learned that he had terminal cancer in 1983 or 1984. At about that time, he arranged for a friend, Harold Buell, to have joint access to his safe-deposit box. Wilson gave Buell a key. The box contained, among other things, a copy of a promissory note for $65,000 from Michael Cronan. Wilson told Buell that the debt represented by the note was to be forgiven when he died and that on Wilson's death, Buell was to deliver the copy of the note to Cronan. In 1984, Cronan learned of Wilson's illness, and Wilson told Cronan on at least two occasions that Cronan's debt was to be forgiven on Wilson's death. In the meantime, Cronan continued to make payments on the note. Wilson died in July 1987. On the day after Wilson died, Buell delivered the copy of the note to Cronan, as directed. Wilson's personal representative (a person appointed to look after the deceased's affairs), Carol Kesterson, sought to recover from Cronan the balance owing on the $65,000 note, the original of which was found among Wilson's personal effects after his death. Cronan claimed that the debt had been forgiven, as a gift to Cronan. The trial court held that the gift had not been adequately delivered prior to Wilson's death and therefore Cronan was liable on the debt. Cronan appealed.

ISSUE Had Wilson effectively delivered the gift?

DECISION No. The trial court's decision was affirmed. Wilson's gift to Cronan—the forgiveness of Cronan's debt—was never adequately delivered to Cronan during Wilson's lifetime.

REASON The court stated that "[f]or a gift of personal property * * * to be valid, there must be a donative intent, coupled with the delivery of the subject of the gift to the donee with the intent that the donee have a present interest in it and an acceptance by the donee. * * * The one claiming a gift has the burden to prove the elements by clear and convincing evidence." Cronan argued that Wilson had delivered the copy of the note to Buell and that Buell was acting as Cronan's agent, but the court noted that the evidence did not support the finding that an agency relationship between Buell and Cronan existed. The court found "no evidence that [Cronan] knew that Buell had the key to the safe deposit box or that he had possession of the envelope" that contained the copy of the note or even that Cronan had given instructions to Buell. Because Buell acted on Wilson's instructions and essentially served as Wilson's agent, the court found that there was no delivery of the note to Cronan before Wilson died.

ETHICAL CONSIDERATIONS *Sometimes an aging or ill person intends to make a gift to another, but the gift fails because the proper legal requirements were not met. Here, Wilson intended that Cronan's debt be forgiven on Wilson's death. Yet Cronan never received this "gift" because it was never effectively delivered. Although it may seem unfair that the law should prevent a donor's intention from being realized, strict legal requirements are imposed in such cases to ensure that the donor did indeed intend to make a gift. Effective delivery of a gift by the donor to the donee is an objective indication of the donor's intent.*

Will or Inheritance

Ownership of personal property may be transferred by will or by inheritance under state statutes. These transfers will be discussed in detail in Chapter 35.

Accession

ACCESSION
A principle by which the owner or the improver of personal property becomes entitled to all that the property produces, or all that is added to it, or the property in a changed form.

Accession means "adding on" to something. It occurs when someone adds value to a piece of personal property by either labor or materials. Generally, there is no dispute about who owns the property after accession has occurred, especially when the accession is accomplished with the owner's consent.

When accession occurs without the permission of the owner, the courts will tend to favor the owner over the improver—the one who improves the property—provided the accession is caused wrongfully and in bad faith. In addition, many courts will deny the improver any compensation for the value added; for example, a car thief who puts new tires on the stolen car will obviously not be compensated for the value of the new tires.

If the accession is performed in good faith, however, even without the owner's consent, ownership of the improved item most often depends on whether the accession has increased the value of the property or changed its identity. The greater the increase in value, the more likely it is that ownership will pass to the improver. If ownership so passes, the improver obviously must compensate the original owner for the value of the property prior to the accession. If the increase in value is not sufficient for ownership to pass to the improver, most courts will require the owner to compensate the improver for the value added.

To illustrate, suppose Juárez is walking in a large country field and discovers a huge stone that is shaped approximately like a horse. For twenty-seven weeks, Juárez works on the stone and eventually transforms it into an exact replica of the Lone Ranger's horse, Silver. Juárez's artist friends are very impressed and convince him to move the stone horse to a gallery, which values the sculpture at $50,000. The owner of the field in which Juárez found the stone now wants to claim title to it. Normally, the courts will give Juárez title to the stone because the changes he has made have greatly increased its value and the accession was performed in good faith. But Juárez will have to pay the owner of the field for the reasonable value of the stone before it was altered.

Confusion

Confusion is defined as the commingling (mixing together) of goods so that one person's personal property cannot be distinguished from another's. It frequently occurs when the goods are *fungible*, meaning that each particle is identical with every other particle, as with grain and oil. For example, if two farmers put their Number 2–grade winter wheat into the same storage bin, confusion would occur.

CONFUSION
The mixing together of goods belonging to two or more owners so that the independent goods cannot be identified.

If confusion of goods is caused by a person who wrongfully and willfully mixes the goods for the purpose of rendering them indistinguishable, the innocent party acquires title to the whole. If confusion occurs as a result of agreement, an honest mistake, or the act of some third party, the owners share ownership as tenants in common and will share any loss in proportion to their shares of ownership of the property.

❖ Mislaid, Lost, and Abandoned Property

If you find another's property, it is important to learn whether the owner mislaid, lost, or simply abandoned the property. This is because the legal effect differs in each case. We discuss each of these categories in the following sections.

Mislaid Property

Property that has been placed somewhere by the owner voluntarily and then inadvertently forgotten is **mislaid property.** Suppose you go to the theater and leave your gloves on the concession stand. The gloves are mislaid property, and the theater owner is entrusted with the duty of reasonable care for them. When mislaid property is found, the finder (or the owner of the realty) does not obtain title to the goods but becomes an *involuntary bailee* (to be discussed later in this chapter). This is because it is highly likely that the true owner will return for the property.

MISLAID PROPERTY
Property that the owner has voluntarily parted with and then cannot find or recover.

Lost Property

LOST PROPERTY
Property with which the owner has involuntarily parted and then cannot find or recover.

Property that is involuntarily left and forgotten is **lost property.** A finder of the property can claim title to the property against the whole world, *except the true*

Law in the Extreme

Are "Frozen Embryos" Property?

Unique to our time are disputes over whether certain products available only through applied technology should be classified as property or something else. Perhaps one of the most extraordinary questions to come before the courts in this respect is whether cryogenically preserved pre-embryos (commonly referred to as "frozen embryos") should be classified as persons or property or something in between. These pre-embryos result from a process known as *in vitro* fertilization (IVF), in which a man's sperm and a woman's ova are fertilized outside the human organism for later implantation into the woman's uterus. The IVF process has enabled many couples to have children when they otherwise could not have. Normally, the "frozen life" of an embryo is two years or so; after that time, the embryo loses its potential to develop into a fetus. But during their short lives, the embryos have the potential to develop into human beings, and therefore the question whether they should be treated as persons or property becomes tangled with major ethical implications.

In spite of the fact that over 5,000 IVF babies have been born in the United States and that some 20,000 or more frozen embryos remain in storage, very few courts have had to wrestle with the problem. One case involved a dispute between a couple and the clinic that had assisted them in IVF. The couple wanted to transfer a frozen embryo to a clinic in another state, and the first clinic objected. A federal district court held that the frozen embryo was property and that the clinic was essentially a bailee of this property (bailments are discussed later in this chapter). As a bailee, the clinic had to turn over the frozen embryo on the request of the bailor (the couple).[a]

Another case involved a divorce action brought by Junior Lewis Davis against his wife, Mary Sue Davis. The couple agreed on all terms of the divorce settlement except one: Who should have "custody" of the seven frozen embryos that they had created through IVF with the assistance of a Knoxville, Tennessee, fertility clinic? Mary Davis wanted to donate them to a childless couple. Junior Davis wanted the embryos discarded; he did not want to become the parent of a child whom he would never know and who might end up being raised without a father, as Junior Davis had. The Tennessee Supreme Court held that frozen embryos were neither property nor persons but occupied an intermediate category that entitled them to "special respect." Control over the disposition of the embryos should be left with the couple donating the sperm and ova. But this decision did not help the court decide which of the Davises should have that control.

Ultimately, the court concluded that Junior Davis should have custody of the embryos on the ground that his constitutional right to privacy mandated that he should not have to procreate if he chose not to do so. Weighing Junior's interest in avoiding being forced to beget a child against Mary's interest in donating the embryos to a childless couple, the court held that Junior's interest was the more compelling.[b]

a. *York v. Jones,* 717 F.Supp. 421 (E.D.Va. 1989).
b. *Davis v. Davis,* 842 S.W.2d 588 (Tenn. 1992).

owner.[3] If the true owner demands that the lost property be returned, the finder must return it. If a third party attempts to take possession of lost property from a finder, however, the third party cannot assert a better title than the finder. When a finder knows who the true owner of the property is and fails to return it to that person, the finder is guilty of the tort of *conversion* (see Chapter 5). Finally, many states require the finder to make a reasonably diligent search to locate the true owner of lost property.

To illustrate the preceding rules, suppose Kormian works in a large library at night. In the courtyard on her way home, she finds a piece of gold jewelry set with stones that look like precious stones to her. She takes it to a jeweler to have it appraised. While pretending to weigh the jewelry, an employee of the jeweler removes several of the stones. If Kormian brings an action to recover the stones from the jeweler, she normally will win, because she found lost property and holds valid title against everyone *except the true owner.* Because the property was lost, rather than mislaid, the finder is not the caretaker of the jewelry. Instead, she acquires title good against the whole world (except the true owner).

Many states have **estray statutes** to encourage and facilitate the return of property to its true owner and then to reward a finder for honesty if the property remains unclaimed. Such statutes provide an incentive for finders to report their discoveries by making it possible for them, after the passage of a specified period of time, to acquire legal title to the property they have found. The statute usually requires the county clerk to advertise the property in an attempt to enhance the opportunity of the owner to recover what has been lost. Some preliminary questions must always be resolved before the estray statute can be employed. The item must be lost property, not merely mislaid property. When the situation indicates that the property was probably lost and not mislaid or abandoned, as a matter of public policy, loss is presumed, and the estray statute applies.

ESTRAY STATUTE
Statutes dealing with finders' rights in property when the true owners are unknown.

Abandoned Property

Property that has been discarded by the true owner, who has no intention of reclaiming title to it, is **abandoned property.** Someone who finds abandoned property acquires title to it, and such title is good against the whole world, *including the original owner.* The owner of lost property who eventually gives up any further attempt to find the lost property is frequently held to have abandoned the property. In cases in which the finder is trespassing on the property of another and finds abandoned property, title vests not in the finder but in the owner of the land.

ABANDONED PROPERTY
Property with which the owner has voluntarily parted, with no intention of recovering it.

In the following case, the issue was whether some valuable property found by the plaintiff was lost or abandoned.

Case 33.3 

MICHAEL v. FIRST CHICAGO CORP.

Appellate Court of Illinois, Second District, 1985.
139 Ill.App.3d 374,
487 N.E.2d 403,
93 Ill.Dec. 736.

HISTORICAL AND ECONOMIC SETTING *In the late 1970s, much of the world was suffering from double- and triple-digit inflation. Prices in the United States increased 13.3 percent in 1979, the largest increase in thirty-three years. In that same year, banks raised the prime loan rate to 14.5 percent and the next year to 21.5 percent. Double-digit inflation continued in 1980, and the interest rates that banks paid on certificates of deposit (CDs) rose in response. A CD is a time deposit, usually for one or two years. The depositor gives up the right to withdraw the funds on short notice, and the bank pays a higher rate of interest than it pays on savings accounts. In the early 1980s, a corporation could not draw interest on savings accounts or other demand deposits in commercial banks.*

3. See *Armory v. Delamirie,* 93 Eng.Rep. 664 (K.B. 1722), discussed in this chapter's *Landmark in the Law.*

Case 33.3—Continued

A firm with a temporary excess of cash could invest in a CD, however, as a hedge against inflation.

FACTS In June of 1983, the First National Bank of Chicago (First Chicago) sold some of its used office furniture to Walter Zibton, a dealer in new and secondhand office supplies and furniture. Included among the items of furniture were some file cabinets that were locked and presumed to be empty. No keys for the file cabinets were available. Zibton sold one of the file cabinets to Charles Strayve, throwing in three other file cabinets free of charge. Strayve later gave one of the cabinets to his friend Richard Michael, the plaintiff in this case. About six weeks after Michael had received the cabinet, it fell over in his garage, burst open, and exposed the contents—$6,687,948.85 worth of certificates of deposit. Michael took the certificates to the FBI for safekeeping and brought an action to determine ownership of the certificates, claiming that they were abandoned property and that he, as the finder, was thus the rightful owner. The trial court disagreed with Michael and gave First Chicago possession, holding that the certificates had not been abandoned but were instead lost property. As such, First Chicago was the rightful owner. Michael appealed.

ISSUE Were the certificates abandoned property or lost property?

DECISION The appellate court upheld the trial court's judgment. First Chicago was the rightful owner.

REASON The court noted that if the property was lost property, Michael could claim possession against all others except the rightful owner. If it was abandoned property, however, Michael, as the finder, could claim possession against all others including the owner. According to the court, "As a general rule, abandonment is not presumed, and the party seeking to declare an abandonment must prove the abandoning party intended to do so. * * * Plaintiffs failed to show that First Chicago intended to abandon the certificates of deposit. It is readily apparent from the evidence that the certificates of deposit were to be transferred to other storage and some simply were overlooked and left in the file cabinets. The relinquishment of possession, under the circumstances here, without a showing of an intention to permanently give up all right to the certificates of deposit is not enough to show an abandonment."

❖ Bailments

Virtually every individual or business is affected by the law of bailments at one time or another (and sometimes even on a daily basis). When individuals deal with bailments, whether they realize it or not, they are subject to the obligations and duties that arise from the bailment relationship. A **bailment** is formed by the delivery of personal property, without transfer of title, by one person, called a **bailor,** to another, called a **bailee,** usually under an agreement for a particular purpose (for example, for storage, repair, or transportation). Upon completion of the purpose, the bailee is obligated to return the bailed property to the bailor or to a third person or to dispose of it as directed.

BAILMENT
An agreement in which goods or personal property of one person (a bailor) are entrusted to another (a bailee), who is obligated to return the bailed property to the bailor or dispose of it as directed.

BAILOR
One who entrusts goods to a bailee.

BAILEE
One to whom goods are entrusted by a bailor.

Bailments are usually created by agreement but not necessarily by contract, because in many bailments not all of the elements of a contract (such as mutual assent and consideration) are present. For example, if you loan your bicycle to a friend, a bailment is created, but not by contract, because there is no consideration. Many commercial bailments, such as the delivery of your suit to the cleaners for dry cleaning, are based on contract, however.

The number, scope, and importance of bailments created daily in the business community and in everyday life make it desirable for any person to understand the elements necessary for the creation of a bailment and to know what rights, duties, and liabilities flow from bailments.

Elements of a Bailment

Not all transactions involving the delivery of property from one person to another create a bailment. For such a transfer to become a bailment, the three conditions discussed in the following sections must be met.

Landmark in the Law

The Law of Finders

The well-known children's adage, "finders keepers, losers weepers," is actually written into law—provided that the loser (the rightful owner) cannot be found, that is. A finder may acquire good title to found personal property (that is not abandoned) *against everyone except the true owner.* A number of landmark cases have made this principle clear. An early English case, *Armory v. Delamirie,*[a] is considered a landmark in Anglo-American jurisprudence concerning so-called *actions in trover*—an early form of recovery of damages for the conversion of property. The plaintiff in this case was Armory, a chimney sweep who found a jewel in its setting during the course of his work. He took the jewel to a goldsmith to have it appraised. The goldsmith refused to return the jewel to Armory, claiming that Armory was not the rightful owner of the property. The court held that the finder, as prior possessor of the item, had rights to the jewel superior to those of all others except the rightful owner. The court said, "The finder of a jewel, though he does not by such finding acquire an absolute property or ownership, yet * * * has such a property as will enable him to keep it against all but the rightful owner, and consequently maintain trover."

The *Armory* case illustrates the doctrine of the *relativity of title.* Under this doctrine, if two contestants are before the court, neither of whom can claim absolute title to the property, the one who can claim prior possession will likely have established sufficient rights to the property to win the case.

A curious situation arises when goods wrongfully obtained by one person are in turn wrongfully obtained by another, and the two parties contest their rights to possession. In such a case, does the *Armory* rule still apply—that is, does the first (illegal) possessor have more rights in the property than the second (illegal) possessor? In a case that came before the Minnesota Supreme Court in 1892, *Anderson v. Gouldberg,*[b] the court said yes. In the *Anderson* case, the plaintiffs had trespassed on another's land and wrongfully cut timber. The defendants later took the logs from the mill site, allegedly in the name of the owner of the property on which the timber had been cut. The evidence at trial indicated that both parties had illegally acquired the property. The court instructed the jury that even if the plaintiffs were trespassers when they cut the logs, they were entitled to recover them from later possessors—except the true owner or an agent of the true owner. The jury found for the plaintiffs, a decision affirmed later by the Minnesota Supreme Court. The latter court held that the plaintiffs' possession, "though wrongfully obtained," justified an action to repossess the property from another who took it from them.

In a series of cases involving a shipwrecked galleon, the law of finders was pitted against the claimed ownership rights of both a state government and the federal government. The cases involved a Spanish galleon—one of a fleet of twenty-eight Spanish ships that set sail from Cuba to Spain in the summer of 1622. In the straits of Florida, the ships sailed into a hurricane, and several of them were ripped apart on the reefs. Among them was *Nuestra Senora de Atocha,* the richest ship of the fleet, with more than forty-seven tons of gold and silver on board. In 1968, Treasure Salvors, Inc., began a search for the lost galleons, and in 1971, it found remnants of the *Atocha* forty-five miles off Key West, Florida, which was outside U.S. territorial waters. In 1975, Treasure Salvors discovered the bulk of the wreck, after having spent $2 million in the search and after four members of the search party had lost their lives. The discovery yielded gold, silver, and artifacts valued at more than $6 million. When Treasure Salvors filed suit to confirm its title to the wreck of the *Atocha,* the U.S. government claimed title to the find under the Antiquities Act of 1906 (which primarily concerns the designation of historic landmarks and related activity) and the theory of sovereign prerogative. The district court rejected the government's arguments, however, and applied what it called the law of finders, as the *Atocha* lay beyond U.S. territorial waters and thus was not subject to U.S. control.[c] The state of Florida also claimed ownership of the find, but the state lost, again on the basis that the wreck lay outside U.S. territorial waters.[d]

These decisions helped to clarify the application of the law of finders in relation to shipwrecks. Today, the law is as follows: if the find lies outside U.S. territorial waters, then the law of finders applies. If the find is within U.S. territorial waters, then the property belongs to the sovereign state.[e]

a. 93 Eng.Rep. 664 (K.B. 1722).

b. 51 Minn. 294, 53 N.W. 636 (1892).

c. *Treasure Salvors, Inc. v. Unidentified, Wrecked and Abandoned Sailing Vessel,* 569 F.2d 330 (5th Cir. 1978).

d. *Florida Department of State v. Treasure Salvors, Inc.,* 458 U.S. 670, 102 S.Ct. 3304, 73 L.Ed.2d 1057 (1982).

e. Prior to the Abandoned Shipwreck Act of 1987, ownership of shipwrecks within U.S. territorial waters was sometimes held to rest with the finder and sometimes with the sovereign state, depending on the jurisidiction. The 1987 act specifically provides that "the law of finds shall not apply to abandoned shipwrecks" located on federal or state land, including submerged land. 43 U.S.C. Sections 2101–2106.

Personal Property Bailment involves only personal property; there can be no bailment of persons. Although a bailment of your luggage is created when it is transported by an airline, as a passenger you are not the subject of a bailment. Also, you cannot bail realty; thus, leasing your house to a tenant does not create a bailment.

Delivery of Possession In a voluntary bailment, possession of the property must be transferred to the bailee in such a way that (a) the bailee is given exclusive possession and control over the property and (b) the bailee *knowingly* accepts the personal property. If either of these conditions for effective delivery of possession is lacking, there is no bailment relationship.

To illustrate, suppose that you take a friend out to dinner at an expensive restaurant. Upon arrival, you turn over your car to the parking attendant. Has a bailment of your car been created? Yes. As a general rule, valet parking constitutes a bailment, but self-parking does not. The difference is found in the control of the car keys. If you parked the car yourself, locked it, and kept the keys, this would be considered a lease of space from the restaurant or owner of the parking place. The owner would be a *lessor* and you would be a *lessee* of the space. Now let us carry our example a step further. When you enter the restaurant, your friend checks her coat. In the pocket of the coat is a $20,000 diamond necklace. The bailee, by accepting the coat, does not *knowingly* also accept the necklace; thus, a bailment of the coat exists—because the restaurant has exclusive possession and control over the coat and knowingly accepted it—but a bailment of the necklace does not exist.

Two types of delivery—*physical* and *constructive*—will result in the bailee's exclusive possession of and control over the property. As discussed earlier, in the context of gifts, constructive delivery is a substitute, or symbolic, delivery. What is delivered to the bailee is not the actual property bailed (such as a car) but something so related to the property (such as the car keys) that the requirement of delivery is satisfied.

In certain unique situations, a bailment is found despite the apparent lack of the requisite elements of control and knowledge. In particular, the rental of a safe-deposit box is usually held to create a bailor-bailee relationship between the bank and its customer, despite the bank's lack of knowledge of the contents and its inability to have exclusive control of the property.[4] Another example of such a situation occurs when the bailee acquires the property accidentally or by mistake—as in finding someone else's lost or mislaid property. A bailment is created even though the bailor did not voluntarily deliver the property to the bailee. Such bailments are called *constructive* or *involuntary* bailments.

Bailment Agreement A bailment agreement can be *express* or *implied*. Although a written agreement is not required for bailments of less than one year (that is, the Statute of Frauds does not apply—see Chapter 11), it is a good idea to have one, especially when valuable property is involved.

The bailment agreement expressly or impliedly provides for the return of the bailed property to the bailor or to a third person, or it provides for disposal by the bailee. The agreement presupposes that the bailee will return the identical goods originally given by the bailor. In certain types of bailments, however, such as bailments of fungible goods, the property returned need only be equivalent property.

For example, if Holman stores his grain (fungible goods) in Joe's Warehouse, a bailment is created. But at the end of the storage period, the warehouse is not obligated to return to Holman exactly the same grain that he stored. As long as the warehouse returns goods of the same *type*, *grade*, and *quantity*, the warehouse—the bailee—has performed its obligation.

4. By statute or by express contract, the rental of a safe-deposit box may be regarded as a lease of space or a license instead of a bailment.

Why is this situation a bailment and self-parking is not?

Ordinary Bailments

Bailments are either *ordinary* or *special (extraordinary)*. There are three types of ordinary bailments. The distinguishing feature among them is *which party receives a benefit from the bailment.* Ultimately, the courts may use this factor to determine the standard of care required of the bailee in possession of the personal property, and this factor will dictate the rights and liabilities of the parties. The three types of ordinary bailments are as follows:

1. *Bailment for the sole benefit of the bailor.* This is a gratuitous bailment for the convenience and benefit of the bailor.
2. *Bailment for the sole benefit of the bailee.* This is typically a loan of an article to a person (the bailee) solely for that person's convenience and benefit.
3. *Bailment for the mutual benefit of the bailee and the bailor.* This is the most common kind of bailment, involving some form of compensation for storing items or holding property.

The degree of care that was traditionally required of the bailee in each of these three types of bailments is indicated in Exhibit 33–1. Recently, however, most courts have tended to require a *reasonable standard of care* regardless of the type of bailment arrangement in effect, including involuntary bailments.

Rights of the Bailee Certain rights are implicit in the bailment agreement. A hallmark of the bailment agreement is that the bailee acquires the *right to control*

◆ **Exhibit 33–1**
Degree of Care Required of a Bailee

Bailment for the Sole Benefit of the Bailor — Mutual-Benefit Bailment — Bailment for the Sole Benefit of the Bailee

DEGREE OF CARE →

SLIGHT — REASONABLE — GREAT

and possess the property temporarily. The bailee's right of possession permits the bailee to recover damages from any third person for damage or loss of the property, and if the property is stolen, the bailee has a legal right to regain possession of it or obtain damages from any third person who has wrongfully interfered with the bailee's possessory rights.

Depending on the type of bailment and the terms of the bailment agreement, a bailee also may have a *right to use the bailed property.* In a bailment involving the long-term storage of a car, however, the bailee is not expected to use the car because the ordinary purpose of a storage bailment does not include use of the property. For example, if you borrow a friend's car to drive to the airport, you, as the bailee, would obviously be expected to use the car.

Except in a gratuitous bailment, a bailee has a *right to be compensated* as provided for in the bailment agreement or to be reimbursed for costs and services rendered in the keeping of the bailed property, or both. Even in a gratuitous bailment, a bailee has a right to be reimbursed or compensated for costs incurred in the keeping of the bailed property. For example, Margo loses her pet dog, which is found by Judith. Judith takes Margo's dog to her home and feeds it. Even though she takes good care of the dog, it becomes ill, and she calls a veterinarian. Judith pays the bill for the veterinarian's services and the medicine. Judith is normally entitled to be reimbursed by Margo for all reasonable costs incurred in the keeping of Margo's dog. To enforce the right of compensation, the bailee has a right to place a *possessory lien* (which entitles a creditor to retain possession of the debtor's goods until a debt is paid) on the specific bailed property until he or she has been fully compensated. This type of lien, sometimes referred to as an *artisan's lien* or a *bailee's lien*, was discussed in Chapter 22.

Ordinary bailees have the *right to limit their liability* as long as the limitations are called to the attention of the bailor and are not against public policy. It is essential that the bailor in some way know of the limitation. Even if the bailor has notice, certain types of disclaimers of liability have been considered to be against public policy and therefore illegal. For example, certain exculpatory clauses limiting a person's liability for his or her own wrongful acts are often scrutinized by the courts and, in the case of bailments, are routinely held to be illegal. This is particularly true in bailments for the mutual benefit of the bailor and the bailee—as the following case illustrates.

Case 33.4

BROCKWELL v. LAKE GASTON SALES AND SERVICE

Court of Appeals of North Carolina, 1992.
105 N.C.App. 226,
412 S.E.2d 104.

HISTORICAL AND TECHNOLOGICAL SETTING *Navigation is the science and technology of finding the position, course, and distance traveled by a boat, ship, plane, or other craft. Traditionally, sailors used a magnetic compass and a sextant to plot their courses. Today, sailors and others use highly sophisticated electronic methods employing radio signals transmitted by satellites. Modern navigation satellites enable users to calculate their position to within a few feet. When navigating in deep waters, such as freshwater lakes, or when fishing, sailors use charts that represent underwater depths.*

FACTS R. W. Brockwell took his boat and its motor to Lake Gaston Sales and Service (Gaston) to be repaired. At the time Brockwell delivered the boat to Gaston, the boat contained many items of personal property, including fishing gear, navigation equipment, and electronic equipment. Before the boat could be repaired, Brockwell had to sign a repair order that contained the following disclaimer: "It is understood and agreed that [Gaston] assumes no responsibility whatsoever for loss or damage by theft, fire, vandalism, water or weather related damages, nor for any items of personal property left with the unit placed with [Gaston] for repair, storage or sale." About ten days later, after the boat had been repaired, Brockwell learned that equipment and other personal property worth over $2,000 was missing from the boat. Gaston contended that the disclaimer in the repair order absolved it from any liability for the missing property. Brockwell sued Gaston for negligence. The trial court held for Brockwell and awarded him damages. Gaston appealed.

Case 33.4—Continued

ISSUE Did the disclaimer in the repair order absolve Gaston from liability for the missing property?

DECISION No. The trial court's decision was affirmed. Gaston could not, by contract, disclaim liability for its own negligence.

REASON The court stated that as a general rule, in mutual-benefit bailment contracts, bailees can relieve themselves from the liability imposed on them under the common law so long as contract provisions are not contrary to public policy. The court noted that "[m]any courts hold that where the bailee makes it his business to act as bailee for hire, on a uniform and not an individual basis, it is against the public interest to permit him to exculpate himself from his own negligence. And the decided trend of modern decisions is against the validity of such exculpatory clauses or provisions in behalf of proprietors of parking lots, garages, parcel check rooms, and warehouses, who undertake to protect themselves against their own negligence by posting signs or printing limitations on the receipts or identification tokens delivered to the bailor-owner at the time of bailment." Gaston, the bailee, was in the business of acting as a bailee for hire on a uniform basis and took Brockwell's boat and its contents and attachments "into its sole possession in order to perform repairs on the boat in the regular course of its business, and we hold it was against public policy for [Gaston] to attempt to exculpate itself from the duty of ordinary care it owed to [Brockwell]. We therefore hold the liability disclaimer in the present case is void and unenforceable as a matter of law."

Duties of the Bailee The bailee has two basic responsibilities: (1) to take proper care of the property and (2) to surrender or dispose of the property at the end of the bailment. A bailee's failure to exercise appropriate care in handling the bailor's property results in tort liability. The duty to relinquish the property at the end of the bailment is grounded in both contract and tort law principles. Failure to return the property constitutes a breach of contract or the tort of conversion, and, with one exception, the bailee is liable for damages. The exception is when the obligation is excused because the goods or chattels have been destroyed, lost, or stolen through no fault of the bailee (or claimed by a third party with a superior claim).

Under the law of bailments, a bailor's proof that damage or loss to the property has occurred will, in and of itself, raise a *presumption* that the bailee is guilty of negligence or conversion. In other words, whenever a bailee fails to return bailed property, the bailee's negligence will be *presumed* by the court.

Duties of the Bailor It goes without saying that the rights of a bailor are essentially the same as the duties of a bailee. The major duty of the bailor is to provide the bailee with goods or chattels that are free from known defects that could cause injury to the bailee. In the case of a mutual-benefit bailment, the bailor must also notify the bailee of any hidden defects that the bailor could have discovered with reasonable diligence and proper inspection.

The bailor's duty to reveal defects is based on a negligence theory of tort law. A bailor who fails to give the appropriate notice is liable to the bailee and to any other person who might reasonably be expected to come into contact with the defective article. For example, if an equipment rental firm leases equipment with a *discoverable* defect, and the lessee (bailee) is not notified of such a defect and is harmed because of it, the rental firm is liable for negligence under tort law.

An exception to this rule exists if the bailment was created for the sole benefit of the bailee. Thus, if you loaned your car to a friend as a favor to your friend and not for any direct return benefit to yourself, you would be required to notify your friend of any *known* defect of the automobile that could cause injury but not of a defect of which you were unaware (even if it is a *discoverable* defect). If your friend was injured in an accident as a result of a defect unknown to you, you would normally not be liable.

A bailor can also incur *warranty liability* based on contract law for injuries resulting from the bailment of defective articles. Property leased by a bailor must be *fit for the intended purpose of the bailment.* Warranties of fitness arise by law in sales contracts and leases and by judicial interpretation in the case of bailments for hire.

Special Bailments

To this point, this section has been concerned with ordinary bailments—bailments in which bailees are expected to exercise ordinary care in the handling of bailed property. Some bailment transactions warrant special consideration. These include bailments in which the bailee's duty of care is *extraordinary*—that is, his or her liability for loss or damage to the property is absolute—as is generally true in cases involving common carriers and innkeepers. Warehouse companies have the same duty of care as ordinary bailees; but like carriers, they are subject to extensive coverage of federal and state laws, including the UCC's Article 7.

COMMON CARRIERS
Owners of trucks, railroads, airlines, ships, and other vehicles who offer transportation services to the public generally in return for compensation or a payment.

Common Carriers **Common carriers** are publicly licensed to provide transportation services to the general public. They are distinguished from private carriers that operate transportation facilities for a select clientele. Whereas a private carrier is not bound to provide service to every person or company making a request, a common carrier must arrange carriage for all who apply, within certain limitations.[5]

The delivery of goods to a common carrier creates a bailment relationship between the shipper (bailor) and the common carrier (bailee). Unlike ordinary bailees, the common carrier is held to a standard of care based on *strict liability,* rather than reasonable care, in protecting the bailed personal property. This means that the common carrier is absolutely liable, regardless of negligence, for all loss or damage to goods except damage caused by one of the following common law exceptions: (1) an act of God, (2) an act of a public enemy, (3) an order of a public authority, (4) an act of the shipper, or (5) the inherent nature of the goods. Common carriers cannot contract away this liability for damaged goods; but subject to government regulations, they are permitted to limit their dollar liability to an amount stated on the shipment contract.[6] Even when a carrier's liability is limited on the shipment contract, unless the shipper is fully aware of this provision and its implications when signing the contract, the carrier may still be held liable for property damages by the court.

Warehouse Companies Warehousing is the business of providing storage of property for compensation.[7] A warehouse company is a professional bailee whose responsibility differs from an ordinary bailee's in two important aspects. First, a warehouse company is empowered to issue documents of title—in particular, warehouse receipts.[8] Second, warehouse companies are subject to an extraordinary network of state and federal statutes, including Article 7 of the UCC.

A warehouse company accepts goods for storage and issues a warehouse receipt describing the property and the terms of the bailment contract. The warehouse

---

5. A common carrier is not required to take any and all property anywhere in all instances. Public regulatory agencies, such as the Interstate Commerce Commission, govern commercial carriers, and carriers can be restricted to geographical areas. They can also be limited to carrying certain kinds of goods or to providing only special types of transportation equipment.
6. State and federal laws and Interstate Commerce Commission regulations require common carriers to offer shippers the opportunity to obtain higher dollar limits for loss by paying a higher fee for the transport.
7. UCC 7–102(h) defines the person engaged in the storing of goods for hire as a "warehouseman."
8. A document of title is defined in UCC 1–201(15) as any "document which in the regular course of business or financing is treated as adequately evidencing that the person in possession of it is entitled to receive, hold, and dispose of the document and the goods it covers. To be a document of title, a document must purport to be issued by or addressed to a bailee and purport to cover goods in the bailee's possession."

Can a warehouse company limit the dollar amount of its liability for loss or damage to bailed property?

receipt can be negotiable or nonnegotiable, depending on how it is written. It is negotiable if its terms provide that the warehouse company will deliver the goods "to the bearer" of the receipt or "to the order of" a person named on the receipt.[9]

The warehouse receipt serves multiple functions. It is a receipt for the goods stored; it is a contract of bailment; it also represents the goods (that is, it indicates title) and hence has value and utility in financing commercial transactions. For example, Ossip, a processor and canner of corn, delivers 6,500 cases of corn to Shaneyfelt, the owner of a warehouse. Shaneyfelt issues a negotiable warehouse receipt payable "to bearer" and gives it to Ossip. Ossip sells and delivers the warehouse receipt to a large supermarket chain, Better Foods, Inc. Better Foods is now the owner of the corn and has the right to obtain the cases from Shaneyfelt. It will present the warehouse receipt to Shaneyfelt, who in return will release the cases of corn to the grocery chain.

Like ordinary bailees, a warehouse company is liable for loss or damage to property resulting from *negligence* (and therefore does not have the same liability as a common carrier). Its duty is to use reasonable care to protect and preserve the goods. A warehouse company can limit the dollar amount of its liability, but the bailor must be given the option of paying an increased storage rate for an increase in the liability limit.

Innkeepers At common law, innkeepers, hotel owners, and similar operators were held to the same strict liability as common carriers with respect to property brought into the rooms by guests. Today, only those who provide lodging to the public for compensation as a *regular* business are covered under this rule of strict liability. Moreover, the rule applies only to those who are guests, as opposed to lodgers. A lodger is a permanent resident of the hotel or inn, whereas a guest is a traveler.

"All saints can do miracles, but few of them can keep a hotel."

Mark Twain (Samuel Clemens), 1835–1910 *(American author and humorist)*

In many states, innkeepers can avoid strict liability for loss of guests' valuables and money by providing a safe in which to keep them. Each guest must be clearly notified of the availability of such a safe. Statutes often limit the liability of innkeepers with regard to articles that are not kept in the safe or that are of such a nature that they are not normally kept in a safe. These statutes may limit the amount

9. UCC 7–104.

of monetary damages or even provide for no liability in the absence of innkeeper negligence.

Suppose that Jiminez stays for a night at the Harbor Hotel. When he returns from eating breakfast in the hotel restaurant, he discovers that the people in the room next door have forced the lock on the door between the two rooms and stolen his suitcase. Jiminez claims that the hotel is liable for his loss. The hotel maintains that because it was not negligent, it is not liable. At common law, the hotel would have been liable because innkeepers were actually insurers of the property of their guests, but today state statutes limit the strict liability of the common law. In most states, statutes limit the amount of monetary damages for which the innkeeper is liable and may even provide that the innkeeper has no liability in the absence of negligence. Many statutes require these limitations to be posted or the guest to be notified. Such postings, or notices, are frequently found on the doors of the rooms in the motel or hotel.

Normally, the innkeeper (a motel keeper, for example) assumes no responsibility for the safety of a guest's automobile, because the guest usually retains possession and control over it. If, however, the innkeeper provides parking facilities, and the guest's car is entrusted to the innkeeper or to an employee, the innkeeper will be liable under the rules that pertain to parking-lot bailments (which are ordinary bailments).

In the following case, a hotel patron brought an action against a Marriott Hotel after the disappearance of his cashmere coat, which he had placed on a rack outside a seminar room. As you read through the case, try to determine if the elements of a bailment are present.

Case 33.5
AUGUSTINE v. MARRIOTT HOTEL

Town Court, Town of Amherst, Erie County, 1986.
132 Misc.2d 180,
503 N.Y.S.2d 498.

HISTORICAL AND ECONOMIC SETTING *Founded in 1927 as a root-beer stand, Marriott Corporation opened its first hotel in 1957. In 1980, Marriott had sixty-five hotels with 21,000 rooms. By 1985, the corporation had more than three times as many rooms to rent. No hotel firm manages as many rooms as Marriott, and it is also the world leader in contract food services, operating restaurants and gift shops in fifty-two airports and more than a hundred travel plazas on U.S. highways. Marriott hotels are often used by professional associations for conferences and seminars.*

FACTS Augustine attended a dental seminar held at a Marriott Hotel. The sponsor of the seminar had rented the banquet room in which the seminar was held and had requested the hotel to place a movable coat rack outside the room, in the public lobby. Augustine placed his coat on the rack before entering the seminar room. When he tried to find the coat at the noon recess, however, he noted that the rack had been moved a distance down the lobby and around a corner, near an exit. To his dismay, his cashmere coat was missing. Claiming that the hotel was liable for the loss, Augustine brought an action against it.

ISSUE Was the hotel a bailee of the coat and thus liable to its owner for the loss?

DECISION No. The court held that the hotel was not liable to Augustine for the loss of the coat and dismissed the claim.

REASON The court stated that no bailor-bailee relationship had come into existence here because Augustine had not entrusted his coat to the hotel. There had been no delivery to the hotel, nor had the hotel, in the eyes of the court, ever been in actual or constructive custody of the coat. Furthermore, Augustine had not even been a guest of the hotel directly. The court likened Augustine's status in relation to the hotel to that of a "wedding guest of individuals who rent banquet facilities from a hotel." The court concluded that "a reasonable man would have wondered about the safety of his coat which he hung on a rack in a public lobby of a hotel, without ascertaining if there were a guard." The court could find no evidence that users of the rack were led to assume that the rack would be guarded, and hence users placed their coats there at their own risk.

Application

What to Do with Lost Property

If you are walking down a street in New York City and chance upon a valuable diamond ring lying next to a gutter, what should you do with the ring? The tempting thing would be to keep it or sell it and enjoy the proceeds. But not only would that be unethical, it would also be illegal under New York laws governing the finding of lost property. New York law defines *lost property* to include lost property, mislaid property, abandoned property, "waifs [goods to which all ownership rights have been waived, such as goods that are found but unclaimed] and treasure trove, and other property which is found." Property includes "money, goods, chattels and tangible personal property," with some exceptions. Generally, the finder of property worth $20 or more must deposit it with police authorities (or with the owner of the premises on which the property was found) within ten days. Failure to do so is a misdemeanor, subject to a fine of up to $100 and imprisonment for not more than six months.

Many states have enacted lost-property statutes. The statutes differ significantly from state to state, but typically, they eliminate the distinction between lost, mislaid, and abandoned property or treasure trove, as the New York statute does. Also, many statutes require the finder to deposit found property with local authorities, although the penalty imposed for failure to do so may not be as severe as under New York's statute (in Illinois, for example, a finder who fails to comply with the requirements of that state's lost-property statute may be fined $10). Lost-property statutes also typically require the police to attempt to find the true owner—by calling the owner or person in charge of the premises on which the property was found, for example. Sometimes, the finder must advertise, at the county court, the property and its discovery.

Generally, if the true owner cannot be located within a certain period of time—which varies depending on the value of the property and whether the property is perishable—the finder gets the property. If the finder does not appear after the period of time has lapsed, the property may be sold and the proceeds disposed of as specified by the statute. In California, for instance, the proceeds from such a sale go into a state abandoned-property fund (if the state police had custody of the lost property) or become the property of the city, county, town, or village (if other police had custody).

Every statute has exceptions, of course. In some situations, an employer may have rights to property found by an employee. Property found in a safe-deposit area in a bank may also be subject to different rules.

Checklist for the Finder of Lost Property

☐ 1. To maximize your chances of *legally* keeping lost property, take the found property to the nearest police station.

❖ Key Terms

abandoned property 809
accession 806
bailee 810
bailment 810
bailor 810
chattel 800
common carrier 816
community property 803
confusion 807
constructive delivery 804
dominion 804
estray statute 809
fee simple 801
gift 804
gift *causa mortis* 805
gift *inter vivos* 805
joint tenancy 801
lost property 807
mislaid property 807
personal property 800
real property 800
tenancy by the entirety 801
tenancy in common 801

❖ Chapter Summary: Personal Property and Bailments

PERSONAL PROPERTY	
Definition of Personal Property	Personal property (personalty) is considered to include all property not classified as real property (realty). It can be tangible (such as a TV set or a car) or intangible (such as stocks or bonds). Referred to legally as *chattels*—a term that includes both living and inanimate property.
Common Types of Property Ownership	1. *Fee simple*—Exists when individuals have the right to possess, use, or dispose of the property as they choose during their lifetimes and to pass on the property to their heirs at death. 2. *Concurrent ownership:* a. Tenancy in common—Co-ownership in which two or more persons own an undivided fractional interest in the property; upon one tenant's death, the property interest passes to his or her heirs. b. Joint tenancy—Exists when two or more persons own an undivided interest in property; upon the death of a joint tenant, the property interest transfers to the remaining tenant(s), not to the heirs of the deceased. c. Tenancy by the entirety—A form of co-ownership between a husband and wife that is similar to a joint tenancy, except that a spouse cannot transfer separately his or her interest during his or her lifetime. d. Community property—A form of co-ownership in which each spouse technically owns an undivided one-half interest in property acquired during the marriage. This type of ownership occurs in only a few states.
How Ownership of Personal Property Is Acquired	1. *Possession*—Ownership may be acquired by possession if no other person has ownership title (e.g., wild animals or abandoned property). 2. *Purchase*—The most common means of acquiring and transferring ownership of personal property. 3. *Production*—Any product or item produced by an individual (with minor exceptions) becomes the property of that individual. 4. *Gift*—An effective gift exists when: a. There is evidence of *intent* to make a gift of the property in question. b. The gift is delivered (physically or constructively) to the donee or the donee's agent. c. The gift is accepted by the donee or the donee's agent. 5. *Will or inheritance*—Upon death, the property of the deceased passes to family members or others by will or inheritance laws. 6. *Accession*—When someone adds value to a piece of property by labor or materials, the added value generally becomes the property of the owner of the original property (includes accessions made in bad faith or wrongfully). Good-faith accessions that substantially increase the property's value or change the identity of the property may cause title to pass to the improver. 7. *Confusion*—In the case of fungible goods, if a person wrongfully and willfully commingles goods with those of another in order to render them indistinguishable, the innocent party acquires title to the whole. Otherwise, the owners become tenants in common of the intermingled goods.
Mislaid, Lost, and Abandoned Property	1. *Mislaid property*—Property that is placed somewhere *voluntarily* by the owner and then inadvertently forgotten. A finder of mislaid property will not acquire title to the goods, and the owner of the place where the property was mislaid becomes a caretaker of the mislaid property. 2. *Lost property*—Property that is *involuntarily* left and forgotten. A finder of lost property can claim title to the property against the whole world *except the true owner.* 3. *Abandoned property*—Property that has been discarded by the true owner, who has no intention of claiming title to the property in the future. A finder of abandoned property can claim title to it against the whole world, *including the original owner.*

❖ Chapter Summary: Personal Property and Bailments—Continued

BAILMENTS	
Elements of a Bailment	1. *Personal property*—Bailments involve only personal property. 2. *Delivery of possession*—For an effective bailment to exist, the bailee (the one receiving the property) must be given exclusive possession and control over the property, and in a voluntary bailment, the bailee must knowingly accept the personal property. 3. *The bailment agreement*—Expressly or impliedly provides for the return of the bailed property to the bailor or a third party or for the disposal of the bailed property by the bailee.
Ordinary Bailments	1. *Types of bailments:* a. Bailment for the sole benefit of the bailor—A gratuitous bailment undertaken for the sole benefit of the bailor (e.g., as a favor to the bailor). Only slight care to preserve the bailed property is traditionally required of the bailee. b. Bailment for the sole benefit of the bailee—A gratuitous loan of an article to a person (the bailee) solely for the bailee's benefit. Great care to preserve the bailed property is traditionally required of the bailee. c. Mutual-benefit (contractual) bailment—The most common kind of bailment; involves compensation between the bailee and bailor for the service provided. Reasonable care to preserve the bailed property is traditionally required of the bailee. 2. *Rights of a Bailee (Duties of a Bailor):* a. The right to be compensated and reimbursed for expenses—In the event of nonpayment, the bailee has the right to place a bailee's lien on the bailed property and the right to foreclose. b. The right to limit liability—An ordinary bailee can limit his or her liability for loss or damage, provided proper notice is given and the limitation is not against public policy. In special bailments, limitations on liability for negligence are usually not allowed, but limitations on the monetary amount of liability are permitted. c. The right of possession—Allows actions against third persons who damage or convert the bailed property and allows actions against the bailor for wrongful breach of the bailment. 3. *Duties of a Bailee (Rights of a Bailor):* a. A bailee must exercise reasonable care over property entrusted to him or her. b. Bailed goods in a bailee's possession must be either returned to the bailor or disposed of according to the bailor's directions.
Special Bailments	1. *Common carriers*—Carriers that are publicly licensed to provide transportation services to the general public. A common-carrier contract of transportation creates a mutual-benefit bailment, and the common carrier is held to a standard of care based on *strict liability* unless the bailed property is lost or destroyed due to (a) an act of God, (b) an act of a public enemy, (c) an order of a public authority, (d) an act of a shipper, or (e) the inherent nature of the goods. 2. *Warehouse companies*—Professional bailees that differ from ordinary bailees because they (a) can issue documents of title (warehouse receipts) and (b) are subject to state and federal statutes, including Article 7 of the UCC (as are common carriers). They must exercise reasonable care (a high degree of care) over the bailed property and are liable for loss or damage of property due to negligence. 3. *Innkeepers* (hotel operators)—Those who provide lodging to the public for compensation as a *regular* business. The common law strict-liability standard to which innkeepers were once held is limited today by state statutes, which vary from state to state.

❖ Questions and Case Problems

33-1. Acquisition of Personal Property. What are the three elements required for an effective gift? How else can personal property be acquired?

33-2. Duties of the Bailee. Discuss the standard of care traditionally required of the bailee for the bailed property in each of the following situations and determine whether the bailee breached that duty.

(a) Ricardo borrows Steve's lawn mower because his own lawn mower needs repair. Ricardo mows his front yard. To mow the back yard, he needs to move some hoses and lawn furniture. He leaves the mower in front of his house while doing so. When he returns to the front yard, he discovers that the mower has been stolen.

(b) Alicia owns a valuable speedboat. She is going on vacation and asks her neighbor, Maureen, to store the boat in one stall of Maureen's double garage. Maureen consents, and the boat is moved into the garage. Needing some grocery items for dinner, Maureen drives to the store. She leaves the garage door open while she is gone, as is her custom, and the speedboat is stolen during that time.

33-3. Gifts. Reineken, very old and ill, wanted to make a gift to his nephew, Gerald. He had a friend obtain $2,500 in cash for him from his bank account, placed this cash in an envelope, and wrote on the envelope, "This is for my nephew, Gerald." Reineken then placed the envelope in his dresser drawer. When Reineken died a month later, his family found the envelope, and Gerald got word of the intended gift. Gerald then demanded that Reineken's daughter, the executor of Reineken's estate (the person appointed by Reineken to handle his affairs after his death), turn over the gift to him. The daughter refused to do so. Discuss fully whether Gerald can successfully claim ownership rights to the $2,500.

33-4. Gifts. In 1968, Armando was about to be shipped to Vietnam for active duty with the U.S. Marines. Shortly before he left, he gave an expensive stereo set and other personal belongings to his girlfriend, Sara, saying, "I'll probably not return from this war, so I'm giving these to you." Armando returned eighteen months later and requested that Sara return the property. Sara said that because Armando had given her these items to keep, she was not required to return them. Was a gift made in this instance, and can Armando recover his property? Discuss fully.

33-5. Gifts. Louis Bardozo has a son named Richard. Louis wants to give his son a new car that he has recently purchased. Louis and his son have not gotten along during the past few years, and Louis feels that this is partly his fault. He goes to his son's house, wanting to make amends by giving the car to Richard. When Louis arrives at Richard's house, his daughter-in-law (Richard's wife) tells Louis that Richard is out of town and will return the next day. Louis gives the keys to the new car to his daughter-in-law, tells her to hold the keys for his son, and says that he will return the next day. Two hours later, Louis has second thoughts about giving Richard the car. He retrieves the keys from his daughter-in-law before she can turn them over to Richard. Richard returns from his trip, learns of the events, and demands possession of the car, claiming a gift was made. Is Richard entitled to the car? Explain.

33-6. Gifts. Welton, an experienced businessperson, transferred to Gallagher some bearer bonds. He stated that the bonds were hers with "no strings attached" and that she should place the bonds in her safe-deposit box for safekeeping. Later, Welton wanted Gallagher to return the bonds to him, claiming that he was still the owner. Gallagher refused, claiming that Welton's transfer was a gift. Was it? Discuss fully. [*Welton v. Gallagher*, 2 Hawaii App. 242, 630 P.2d 1077 (1981)]

33-7. Abandoned Property. Leonard Charrier, an amateur archaeologist in Louisiana, uncovered artifacts from a several-hundred-year-old Indian burial ground. The artifacts had been made by the ancestors of the present-day Tunica Indian tribe of Louisiana. The Tunica tribe asked the court to award it custody of the property, which included burial pots, ornaments, and pottery. Charrier claimed that the property had been abandoned and that he had the right to title because he had taken possession of the property. Discuss whether the Tunica tribe, as heirs to the former owners of the property, should succeed in their claim to the artifacts or whether the property was abandoned. [*Charrier v. Bell*, 496 So.2d 601 (La.App. 1st Cir. 1986)]

33-8. Abandoned Property. Danny Smith and his brother discovered a sixteen-foot boat lying beside a roadway in Alabama. Smith informed the police, who immediately impounded the boat and stored it in a city warehouse. Although Smith acquiesced to the police action, he told the police that if the true owner did not claim the boat, he wanted it. When the true owner did not come forward, the police refused to relinquish the boat to Smith and instead told Smith that they planned to auction it to the highest bidder on behalf of the city. Smith sued for custody of the boat. Because Smith never physically held the boat but rather allowed the police to take possession, should Smith succeed in his claim to title as finder? Could Smith defeat a claim if the true owner sought to retake the boat? Discuss fully. [*Smith v. Purvis*, 474 So.2d 1131 (Ala.Civ.App. 1985)]

33-9. Gifts. Before her death, Melanie McCarthy had written and sent or otherwise delivered nine $3,000 checks intended as gifts to various relatives. None of the checks had been cashed prior to Melanie's death. Melanie's son, Daniel, who was one of the administrators of her estate, claimed that the Internal Revenue Service (IRS) should not levy estate taxes on the $27,000 still in Melanie's bank account to cover these checks, because the checks were completed gifts. The IRS contended that the gifts had not been effectively delivered prior to Melanie's death. According to the IRS, Melanie could have ordered the bank to stop payment on the uncashed checks, and therefore she had not relinquished complete dominion and control over the checks. Thus, the gifts had not been completed. What should the court decide? [*McCarthy v. United States*, 806 F.2d 129 (7th Cir. 1986)]

33-10. Duties of the Bailee. Wanda Perry, who had an account with Farmers Bank of Greenwood, wanted to rent a safe-deposit box from the bank. The boxes were available only to bank customers, and no fee was charged. When renting the box, Wanda was asked to sign a signature card that stated as follows: "The undersigned customer holds the Farmers Bank harmless for loss of currency or coin left in the box." A little over four years later, the bank was burglarized, and most of the safe-deposit boxes were broken into. Wanda's box was among those burglarized, and she lost all the currency and coins it contained. At trial, evidence showed that the bank had been negligent in failing to restore a burglar alarm system that had been inoperative for more than a week when the bank was burglarized. Wanda sued the bank to recover the value of the currency and coins, alleging negligence on the part of the bank. Discuss fully whether the bank should be held liable for the loss. [*Farmers Bank of Greenwood v. Perry*, 301 Ark. 547, 787 S.W.2d 645 (1990)]

33-11. Liability of Innkeepers. Marvin Gooden checked into a Day's Inn Motel in Atlanta, Georgia, on March 3, 1988, paying in advance for two days' lodging. The next day, Gooden temporarily left his room, in which he had a paper bag allegedly containing $9,000 in U.S. currency. Shortly after Gooden left the room, Mary Carter, a housekeeper, went into the room to clean it. She found the bag of money and, seeing no other personal effects, concluded that Gooden had checked out. Accordingly, she turned the bag and its contents over to her supervisor, Vivian Clark, who in turn gave the bag to another employee, Dempsey Wilson, to take to the motel office. Wilson had worked for the motel for about three years and had always before returned items of value to the office when asked to do so. This time, however, he decided to abscond with the bag of money. A safe was located on the premises of the motel, and a notice concerning the availability of the safe was posted on the inside of the door of the room occupied by Gooden. In the notice, the motel disclaimed liability for guests' valuables unless they were placed in the safe. Gooden at no time had asked to use the safe. Gooden sued the motel and its employees (Carter and Clark) to recover the $9,000. Can Gooden recover the $9,000 from the motel? Discuss fully. [*Gooden v. Day's Inn*, 196 Ga.App. 324, 395 S.E.2d 876 (1990)]

33-12. Gifts. Mary Blettell owned a residence, which she had acquired before her marriage to Herman Blettell in 1951. Darlene Snider was Mary's daughter by a previous marriage. In 1965, Herman and Mary moved into the residence. Herman's name was never added to the title. In 1974, Mary executed a deed to the property to Darlene but did not deliver or record it. In 1978, Mary informed Darlene about the deed and told her that it was located in Mary and Darlene's joint safe-deposit box. In August 1987, Mary's health was declining, and she told Darlene to get the deed from their safe-deposit box, rent a safe-deposit box in Darlene's name only, and put the deed in it so "nobody can get [it] but you." Darlene removed the deed from the joint safe-deposit box and placed it in her own box. Herman was not aware of these events until shortly before Mary's death in 1989. On the day after Mary died, Darlene recorded the deed. Herman Blettell, as Mary's personal representative (the person appointed in Mary's will to look after her affairs after her death), contended that Mary's transfer of the deed to Darlene was not a valid *inter vivos* gift because the deed was never effectively delivered to Darlene. Darlene argued that there was a valid delivery in 1987, when Mary instructed Darlene to place the deed in her own safe-deposit box. What should the court decide? Explain. [*Estate of Blettell v. Snider*, 114 Or.App. 162, 834 P.2d 505 (1992)]

A QUESTION OF ETHICS AND SOCIAL RESPONSIBILITY

33-13. *George Cook stayed at a Day's Inn Motel in Nashville, Tennessee, while attending a trade show. At the trade show, Cook received orders for 225 cases of his firm's product, representing $17,336.25 in profits to the company. On the third day of his stay, Cook's room was burglarized while he was gone from the room. The burglar took Cook's order lists, as well as $174 in cash and medicine worth about $10. Cook sued the owner of the motel, Columbia Sussex Corp., alleging negligence. The motel defended by stating that it had posted a notice on the door of Cook's room informing guests of the fact that the motel would not be liable for any valuable property not placed in the motel safe for safekeeping. Given these circumstances, evaluate and answer the following questions.* [Cook v. Columbia Sussex Corp., *807 S.W.2d 567 (Tenn.App. 1990)*]

1. The relevant state statute governing the liability of innkeepers allowed motels to disclaim their liability by posting a notice such as the one posted by Day's Inn, but the statute also required that the notice be posted "in a conspicuous manner." The notice posted by Day's Inn on the inside of the door to Cook's room was six by three inches in size. In your opinion, is the notice sufficiently conspicuous? If you were the guest, would you notice the disclaimer? Is it fair to guests to assume that they will notice such disclaimers? Discuss fully.
2. Should hotels or motels ever be allowed to disclaim liability by posting such notices? From a policy point of view, evaluate the implications of your answer.

CASE BRIEFING ASSIGNMENT

33-14. *Examine Case A.13* [Strang v. Hollowell, *387 S.E.2d 664 (N.C.App. 1990)*] in Appendix A. The case has been excerpted there in great detail. Review and then brief the case, making sure that you include answers to the following questions in your brief.

1. Are there any facts in dispute in this case?
2. What was the only issue presented on appeal?
3. How was the bailment contract breached?
4. Why did the defendant, Hollowell, contend that he should not be held personally liable for the damages to the plaintiff's automobile?

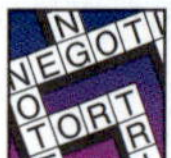

FOR CRITICAL ANALYSIS

33-15. *Review this chapter's* Business Law in Action. *Do you agree with the majority decision that Moore had no cause of action for conversion of personal property (his spleen) by Golde and the others? Why or why not?*

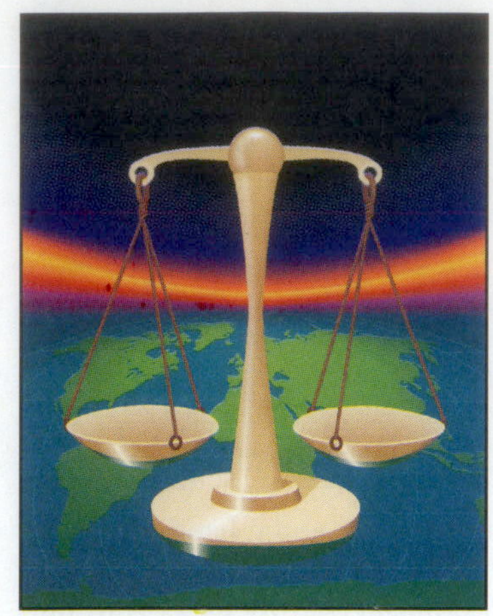

Chapter 34

Real Property

"[T]he right of property is the most sacred of all the rights of citizenship."

Jean Jacques Rousseau, 1712–1778
(French writer and philosopher)

From earliest times, property has provided a means for survival. Primitive peoples lived off the fruits of the land, eating the vegetation and wildlife. Later, as the wildlife was domesticated and the vegetation cultivated, property provided pasturage and farmland. In the twelfth and thirteenth centuries, the power of feudal lords was determined by the amount of land that they held; the more land they held, the more powerful they were. After the age of feudalism passed, property continued to be an indicator of family wealth and social position. In the Western World, the protection of an individual's right to his or her property has become, in the words of Jean Jacques Rousseau, one of the "most sacred of all the rights of citizenship."

In this chapter, we first examine what is meant by the term *real property* as opposed to *personal property*. We then look at the various ways in which real property can be owned and at how ownership rights in real property are transferred from one person to another. We conclude the chapter with a discussion of leased property and landlord-tenant relationships.

❖ The Nature of Real Property

Real property consists of land and the buildings, plants, and trees that it contains. Whereas personal property is movable, real property—also called *real estate* or *realty*—is immovable. Real property usually means land, but it also includes subsurface and air rights, plant life and vegetation, and personal property that has become permanently attached to real property.

Land

Land includes the soil on the surface of the earth and the natural or artificial structures that are attached to it. It further includes all the waters contained on or under the surface and much, but not necessarily all, of the air space above it. The exterior boundaries of land extend down to the center of the earth and up to the farthest reaches of the atmosphere (subject to certain qualifications).

Subsurface and Air Rights

The owner of real property has relatively exclusive rights to the air space above the land as well as the soil and minerals underneath it. Early cases involving air rights dealt with matters such as the right to run a telephone wire across a person's property when the wire did not touch any of the property[1] and whether a bullet shot over a person's land constituted trespass.[2] Today such cases involve the right of commercial and private planes to fly over property and the right of individuals and governments to seed clouds and produce artificial rain. Flights over private land do not normally violate the property owners' rights unless the flights are low and frequent, causing a direct interference with the enjoyment and the use of the land.[3]

In many states, the owner of the surface of a piece of land is not the owner of the subsurface, and hence the land ownership may be separated. Subsurface rights can be extremely valuable, as these rights include the ownership of minerals and, in most states, oil and natural gas. Water rights are also extremely valuable, especially in the West. When the ownership is separated into surface and subsurface rights, each owner can pass title to what he or she owns without the consent of the other. Each owner has the right to use the land owned, and in some cases a conflict arises between a surface owner's use and the subsurface owner's need to extract minerals, oil, and natural gas.

Significant limitations on either air rights or subsurface rights normally have to be indicated on the deed transferring title at the time of purchase. (Deeds and the types of warranties they contain are discussed later in this chapter.)

Plant Life and Vegetation

Plant life, both natural and cultivated, is also considered to be real property. In many instances, the natural vegetation, such as trees, adds greatly to the value of the realty. When a parcel of land is sold and the land has growing crops on it, the sale includes the crops, unless otherwise specified in the sales contract. When crops are sold by themselves, however, they are considered to be personal property or goods. Consequently, the sale of crops is a sale of goods, and it is governed by the Uniform Commercial Code rather than by real property law.[4]

Fixtures

Certain personal property can become so closely associated with the real property to which it is attached that the law views it as real property. Such property is known as a **fixture**—a thing *affixed* to realty, meaning it is attached to it by roots, embedded in it, or permanently attached by means of cement, plaster, bolts, nails, or screws. The fixture can be physically attached to real property, be attached to another fixture, or even be without any actual physical attachment to the land (such as a statue). As long as the owner *intends* the property to be a fixture, it will be a fixture.

FIXTURE
A thing that was once personal property but that has become attached to real property in such a way that it takes on the characteristics of real property and becomes part of that real property.

Fixtures are included in the sale of land if the sales contract does not provide otherwise. The sale of a house includes the land and the house and the garage on it, as well as the cabinets, plumbing, and windows. Because these are permanently affixed to the property, they are considered to be a part of it. Unless otherwise agreed, however, the curtains and throw rugs are not included. Items such as drapes and window-unit air conditioners are difficult to classify. Thus, a contract for the sale of a house or commercial realty should indicate which items of this sort are included in the sale. The following case illustrates the court's interpretation of whether a grain-storage silo became a fixture to the realty or remained personal property.

---

1. *Butler v. Frontier Telephone Co.*, 186 N.Y. 486, 79 N.E. 716 (1906). Stringing a wire across someone's property violates the air rights of that person. Leaning walls or buildings and projecting eave spouts or roofs also violate the air rights of the property owner.
2. *Herrin v. Sutherland*, 74 Mont. 587, 241 P. 328 (1925). Shooting over a person's land constitutes trespass.
3. *United States v. Causby*, 328 U.S. 256, 66 S.Ct. 1062, 90 L.Ed. 1206 (1946).
4. See UCC 2–107(2).

Case 34.1 

METROPOLITAN LIFE INSURANCE CO. v. REEVES

Supreme Court of Nebraska, 1986.
223 Neb. 299,
389 N.W.2d 295.

HISTORICAL AND TECHNOLOGICAL SETTING *As a foundation, one type of grain-storage silo uses a concrete slab that is partially embedded in the ground. The steel structures in which the grain is dried and stored are sometimes transported unassembled to the slab. The structures are then bolted together (with over a thousand bolts in each storage bin), lifted into the air, and hoisted onto the slab, where they are bolted into place. One type of silo consists of three compartments: a dryer and two storage bins. To move the grain from the dryer into either of the bins, it may be necessary to pump air electronically through fifty or more feet of underground tubing. To take the silo apart and remove the steel structures could take more than two weeks.*

FACTS Lawrence Reeves was a landowning farmer whose land was being foreclosed upon by his mortgage holder, Metropolitan Life Insurance Company. Prior to the foreclosure, Reeves had contracted with Production Sale Company to erect a grain-storage facility on the farm. Its total cost was $171,185.30. Prior to the foreclosure, Reeves had paid only $16,137.77. When Metropolitan brought the foreclosure proceedings, the question arose as to whether the grain-storage facility was a fixture to the realty or personal property. If it was considered to be a fixture, Metropolitan would receive the proceeds from the sale; if it was considered to be personal property, the proceeds would go to Production Sale Company. The trial court held that the facility was a fixture, and Production Sale Company appealed to the Supreme Court of Nebraska.

ISSUE Was the facility a fixture to the real property, or was it personal property?

DECISION The Supreme Court of Nebraska reversed the district court's ruling and deemed the storage facility to be personal property.

REASON The court cited three factors that determine whether an article, or combination of articles, is a fixture: (1) whether the article was actually annexed to the realty, (2) whether the article had been appropriated to the use or purpose of that part of the realty with which it was connected, and (3) whether it was the intention of the parties making the contract to affix the article permanently to the land. The last factor was the most important in determining this case, and the court gave much weight to the circumstances of the purchase agreement between Reeves and Production Sale. The court concluded that, under the provisions of that agreement, the parties had not intended the grain-storage facility to become a part of the real property until full payment had been made. Because full payment had not been made, the facility had not become a fixture.

❖ Ownership of Real Property

> *"If a man owns land, the land owns him. Now let him leave home, if he dare."*
>
> **Ralph Waldo Emerson, 1803–1882**
> ***(American essayist and poet)***

Ownership of property is an abstract concept that cannot exist independently of the legal system. No one can actually possess or *hold* a piece of land, the air above it, the earth below it, and all the water contained on it. The legal system therefore recognizes certain rights and duties that constitute ownership interests in real property.

Recall from Chapter 33 that property ownership is often viewed as a bundle of rights. One who possesses the entire bundle of rights is said to hold the property in *fee simple*, which is the most complete form of ownership. When some of the rights in the bundle are transferred to another person, the effect is to limit the ownership rights of both the one transferring the rights and the one receiving them. We look in the following sections first at ownership rights held in fee simple and then at how these rights can be limited through certain types of real property transfers.

Ownership in Fee Simple

FEE SIMPLE ABSOLUTE
An estate or interest in land with no time, disposition, or descendibility limitations.

The most common type of property ownership today is the fee simple. Generally, the term *fee simple* is used to designate a **fee simple absolute,** in which the owner has the greatest possible aggregation of rights, privileges, and power. The fee simple is limited absolutely to a person and his or her heirs and is assigned forever without limitation or condition. The rights that accompany a fee simple include the right to use the land for whatever purpose the owner sees fit, subject to laws that prevent the owner from unreasonably interfering with another person's land and subject to applicable zoning laws. Furthermore, the owner has the rights of *exclusive* possession and use of the property. A fee simple is potentially infinite in duration and can be disposed of by deed or by will (by selling or giving away). When there is no will, the fee simple passes to the owner's legal heirs.

Ownership in fee simple may become limited whenever the property is transferred to another *conditionally*. When this occurs, the fee simple is known as a **fee simple defeasible** (the word *defeasible* means capable of being terminated, or annulled). For example, a **conveyance,** or transfer of real property, "to A and his heirs as long as the land is used for charitable purposes" creates a fee simple defeasible because ownership of the property is conditioned on the land being used for charitable purposes. The original owner retains a *partial* ownership interest because if the specified condition does not occur (if the land ceases to be used for charitable purposes), then the land reverts, or returns, to the original owner. If the original owner is not living at the time, the land passes to his or her heirs.

FEE SIMPLE DEFEASIBLE
An estate that can be taken away (by the prior grantor) upon the occurrence or nonoccurrence of a specified event.

CONVEYANCE
The transfer of a title to land from one person to another by deed; a document (such as a deed or a mortgage) by which an interest in land is transferred from one person to another.

Life Estates

A **life estate** is an estate that lasts for the life of some specified individual. A conveyance "to A for his life" creates a life estate.[5] In a life estate, the life tenant has fewer rights of ownership than the holder of a fee simple defeasible, because the rights necessarily cease to exist on the life tenant's death. The life tenant has the right to use the land provided no waste (injury to the land) is committed. In other words, the life tenant cannot injure the land in a manner that would adversely affect its value to the owner of the future interest in it. The life tenant can use the land to harvest crops or, if mines and oil wells are already on the land, can extract minerals and oil from it, but the life tenant cannot exploit the land by creating new wells or mines. The life tenant has the right to mortgage the life estate and create liens, easements, and leases; but none can extend beyond the life of the tenant. In addition, with few exceptions, the owner of a life estate has an exclusive right to possession during his or her life. Along with these rights, the life tenant also has some duties—to keep the property in repair and to pay property taxes. In short, the owner of the life estate has the same rights as a fee simple owner except that he or she must maintain the value of the property during his or her tenancy, less the decrease in value resulting from the normal use of the property allowed by the life tenancy.

LIFE ESTATE
An interest in land that exists only for the duration of the life of some person, usually the holder of the estate.

Future Interests

When an owner in fee simple absolute conveys the estate conditionally to another (such as with a fee simple defeasible) or for a limited period of time (such as with a life estate), the original owner still retains an interest in the land. The owner retains the right to repossess ownership of the land if the conditions of the fee simple defeasible are not met or when the life of the life-estate holder ends. The residuary (or leftover) interest in the property that the owner retains is called a **future interest** because if it arises, it will only arise in the future.

If the owner retains ownership of the future interest, then the future interest is described as a **reversionary interest** because the property will *revert* to the original owner if the condition specified in a fee simple defeasible fails or when a life tenant

FUTURE INTEREST
An estate that is not at present possessory but will or may be possessory in the future. Remainders and reversions are future estates.

REVERSIONARY INTEREST
A future residuary interest retained in property by the grantor. For example, a landowner who conveys property to another for life creates retains a future interest in the property. When the person holding the life estate dies, the property will revert to the grantor (unless the grantor has transferred the future interest to another party).

5. A less common type of life estate is created by the conveyance "to A for the life of B." This is known as an estate *pur autre vie,* or an estate for the duration of the life of another.

dies. If, however, the owner of the future interest transfers ownership rights in that future interest to another, the future interest is described a **remainder.** For example, a conveyance "to A for life, then to B" creates a life estate for A and a remainder (future interest) for B. An **executory interest** is a type of future interest very similar to a remainder, the difference being that an executory interest does not take effect immediately upon the expiration of another interest, such as a life estate. For example, a conveyance "to A and his (or her) heirs, as long as the premises are used for charitable purposes, and if not so used for charitable purposes, then to B" creates an executory interest in the property for B.

REMAINDER
A future interest in property, held by a person other than the grantor, that occurs at the natural termination of the preceding estate.

EXECUTORY INTEREST
A future interest, held by a person other than the grantor, that either cuts short or begins some time after the natural termination of the preceding estate.

Nonpossessory Interests

In contrast to the types of property interests just described, some interests in land do not include any rights to possess the property. These interests, known as *nonpossessory interests*, include easements, profits, and licenses. Because easements and profits are similar and the same rules apply to both, they are discussed together.

EASEMENT
A nonpossessory right to use another's property in a manner established by either express or implied agreement.

PROFIT
In real property law, the right to enter upon and remove things from the property of another (for example, the right to enter onto a person's land and remove sand and gravel therefrom).

Easements and Profits An **easement** is the right of a person to make limited use of another person's real property without taking anything from the property. An easement, for example, can be the right to travel over another's property. In contrast, a **profit** is the right to go onto land in possession of another and take away some part of the land itself or some product of the land. For example, Akhmed, the owner of Sandy View, gives Carmen the right to go there and remove all the sand and gravel that she needs for her cement business. Carmen has a profit. Easements and profits can be classified as either *appurtenant* or *in gross*.

Easement or Profit Appurtenant An easement or profit appurtenant arises when the owner of one piece of land has a right to go onto (or remove things from) an *adjacent* piece of land owned by another. Suppose Akhmed, the owner of Whiteacres, has a right to drive his car across Green's land, Greenacres, which is adjacent to Whiteacres. This right-of-way over Greenacres is an easement appurtenant to Whiteacres and can be used only by the owner of Whiteacres. Akhmed can convey the easement when he conveys Whiteacres. Now suppose that the highway is on the other side of Black's property, Blackacres, which is on the other side of Greenacres. To reach the highway, Akhmed has an easement across both properties. Whiteacres and Blackacres are not adjacent, but Akhmed has an easement appurtenant nonetheless.

Easement or Profit in Gross An easement or profit in gross exists when one's right to use or take things from another's land does not depend on one's owning an adjacent tract of land. Suppose Akhmed owns a parcel of land with a marble quarry. Akhmed conveys to XYZ Corporation, which owns no land, the right to come onto his land and remove up to five hundred pounds of marble per day. XYZ Corporation owns a profit in gross. When a utility company is granted an easement to run its power lines across another's property, it obtains an easement in gross.

Effect of a Sale of Property When a parcel of land that is *benefited* by an easement or profit appurtenant is sold, the property carries the easement or profit along with it. Thus, if Akhmed sells Whiteacres to Thomas and includes the appurtenant right-of-way across Greenacres in the deed to Thomas, Thomas will own both the property and the easement that benefits it.

When a parcel of land that has the *burden* of an easement or profit appurtenant is sold, the new owner must recognize its existence only if he or she knew or should have known of it or if it was recorded in the appropriate office of the county. Thus, if Akhmed records his easement across Greenacres in the appropriate county office before Green conveys the land, the new owner of Greenacres will have to allow

Akhmed, or any subsequent owner of Whiteacres, to continue to use the path across Greenacres.

Creation of an Easement or Profit Profits and easements can be created by deed or will or by implication, necessity, or prescription. Creation by *deed* or *will* simply involves the delivery of a deed or a disposition in a will by the owner of an easement stating that the grantee (the person receiving the profit or easement) is granted the owner's rights in the easement or profit. An easement or profit, however, may be created by *implication* when the circumstances surrounding the division of a parcel of property imply its creation. If Barrow divides a parcel of land that has only one well for drinking water and conveys the half without a well to Jarad, a profit by implication arises, because Jarad needs drinking water. An easement may also be created by necessity. An easement by *necessity* does not require division of property for its existence. A person who rents an apartment, for example, has an easement by necessity in the private road leading up to it.

Easements and profits by *prescription* are created in much the same way as title to property is obtained by *adverse possession* (discussed later in this chapter). An easement arises by prescription when one person exercises an easement, such as a right-of-way, on another person's land without the landowner's consent, and the use is apparent and continues for a period of time equal to the applicable statute of limitations.

Termination of an Easement or Profit An easement or profit can be terminated or extinguished in several ways. The simplest way is to deed it back to the owner of the land that is burdened by it. Another way is to abandon it and create evidence of intent to relinquish the right to use it. Mere nonuse will not extinguish an easement or profit *unless it is accompanied by an intent to abandon.* Finally, when the owner of an easement or profit becomes the owner of the property burdened by it, then it is merged into the property.

Licenses A **license** is the revocable right of a person to come onto another person's land. It is a personal privilege that arises from the consent of the owner of the land and that can be revoked by the owner. A ticket to attend a movie at a theater is an example of a license. Assume that a Broadway theater owner issues to Carlotta a ticket to see a play. If Carlotta is refused entry into the theater because she is improperly dressed, she has no right to force her way into the theater. The ticket is only a revocable license, not a conveyance of an interest in property.

LICENSE
A revocable right or privilege of a person to come on another person's land.

Leasehold Estates

A **leasehold estate** is created when a real property owner or lessor (landlord) agrees to convey the right to possess and use the property to a lessee (tenant) for a period of time. In every leasehold estate, the tenant has a *qualified* right to exclusive possession (qualified by the right of the landlord to enter upon the premises to assure that no waste is being committed, to make repairs, and the like). The tenant can use the land—for example, by harvesting crops—but cannot injure the land by such activities as cutting down timber for sale or extracting oil. The respective rights and duties of the landlord and tenant that arise under a lease agreement will be discussed in greater detail later in this chapter. Here we look at the types of leasehold estates, or tenancies, that can be created when real property is leased.

LEASEHOLD ESTATE
An estate in realty held by a tenant under a lease. In every leasehold estate, the tenant has a qualified right to possess and/or use the land.

Tenancy for Years A **tenancy for years** is created by an express contract by which property is leased for a specified period of time, such as a month, a year, or a period of years. For example, signing a one-year lease to occupy an apartment creates a tenancy for years. At the end of the period specified in the lease, the lease ends

TENANCY FOR YEARS
A nonfreehold estate/lease for a specified period of time, after which the possession and use of the real property reverts to the grantor.

How does a leasehold estate differ from ownership in fee simple, from a life estate, and from such nonpossessory interests as easements and profits?

(without notice), and possession of the apartment returns to the lessor. If the tenant dies during the period of the lease, the lease interest passes to the tenant's heirs as personal property. Often, leases include renewal or extension provisions.

PERIODIC TENANCY
A lease interest in land for an indefinite period involving payment of rent at fixed intervals, such as week to week, month to month, or year to year.

Periodic Tenancy A **periodic tenancy** is created by a lease that does not specify how long it is to last but does specify that rent is to be paid at certain intervals. This type of tenancy is automatically renewed for another rental period unless properly terminated. For example, a periodic tenancy is created by a lease that states, "Rent is due on the tenth day of every month." This provision creates a tenancy from month to month. This type of tenancy can also extend from week to week or from year to year.

At common law, to terminate a periodic tenancy, the landlord or tenant must give one period's notice to the other party. If the tenancy extends from month to month, for example, one month's notice must be given. State statutes may require a different period for notice of termination in a periodic tenancy, however.

TENANCY AT WILL
A tenancy by consent without a fixed interval for paying rent (not a periodic tenancy). At common law, either party can terminate this tenancy without notice.

Tenancy at Will Suppose a landlord rents an apartment to a tenant "for as long as both agree." In such a case, the tenant receives a leasehold estate known as a **tenancy at will.** At common law, either party can terminate the tenancy without notice (that is, "at will"). This type of estate usually arises when a tenant who has been under a tenancy for years retains possession after the termination date of that tenancy with the landlord's consent. Before the tenancy has been converted into a periodic tenancy (by the periodic payment of rent), it is a tenancy at will, terminable by either party without notice. Once the tenancy is treated as a periodic tenancy, termination notice must conform to the one already discussed for that type of tenancy. The death of either party or the voluntary commission of waste by the tenant will terminate a tenancy at will.

Tenancy at Sufferance The mere possession of land without right is called a **tenancy at sufferance.** It is not a true tenancy. A tenancy at sufferance is not an estate, because it is created when a tenant *wrongfully* retains possession of property. Whenever a tenancy for years, periodic tenancy, or tenancy at will ends and the tenant continues to retain possession of the premises without the owner's permission, a tenancy at sufferance is created.

TENANCY AT SUFFERANCE
Tenancy by one who, after rightfully being in possession of leased premises, continues (wrongfully) to occupy the property after the lease has been terminated. The tenant has no rights to possess the property and occupies it only because the person entitled to evict the tenant has not done so.

❖ Transfer of Ownership

Ownership of real property can pass from one person to another in a number of ways. Commonly, ownership interests in land are transferred by sale, in which case the terms of the transfer are specified in a real estate sales contract. When real property is sold or transferred as a gift, title to the property is conveyed by means of a **deed**—the instrument of conveyance of real property. We look here at transfers of real property by deed, as well as some other ways in which ownership rights in real property can be transferred.

DEED
A document by which title to property (usually real property) is passed.

Deeds

A valid deed must contain the following elements:

1. The names of the buyer (grantee) and seller (grantor).
2. Words evidencing an intent to convey the property (for example, "I hereby bargain, sell, grant, or give").
3. A legally sufficient description of the land.
4. The grantor's (and usually the spouse's) signature.

Additionally, to be valid, a deed must be delivered to the person to whom the property is being conveyed or his or her agent.

Warranty Deeds Different types of deeds provide different degrees of protection against defects of title. A **warranty deed** warrants the greatest number of things and thus provides the greatest protection for the buyer, or grantee. In most states, special language is required to make a general warranty deed; generally, the deed must include a written promise to protect the buyer against all claims of ownership of the property. A sample warranty deed is shown in Exhibit 34–1. Warranty deeds commonly include a number of *covenants*, or promises, that the grantor makes to the grantee.

A **covenant of seisin**[6] and a **covenant of the right to convey** warrant that the seller has title and the power to convey the estate that the deed describes. The covenant of seisin specifically assures the buyer that the grantor has the property in the purported quantity and quality.

A **covenant against encumbrances** is a covenant that the property being sold or conveyed is not subject to any outstanding rights or interests that will diminish the value of the land, except as explicitly stated. Examples of common encumbrances include mortgages, liens, profits, easements, and private deed restrictions on the use of the land.

A **covenant of quiet enjoyment** guarantees that the buyer will not be disturbed in his or her possession of the land by the seller or any third persons. For example, assume that Julio sells a two-acre lot and office building by warranty deed. Subsequently, a third person shows better title than Julio had and proceeds to evict the

WARRANTY DEED
A deed under which the grantor guarantees to the grantee that the grantor has title to the property conveyed in the deed, that there are no encumbrances on the property other than what the grantor has represented, and that the grantee will enjoy quiet possession.

COVENANT OF THE RIGHT OF SEISIN
An assurance to the purchaser that the grantor has the very estate in the quantity and quality that the grantor purports to convey.

COVENANT OF THE RIGHT TO CONVEY
A grantor's assurance that he or she has sufficient capacity and title to convey the property being transferred.

COVENANT AGAINST ENCUMBRANCES
A grantor's assurance that on land conveyed there are no encumbrances—that is, that no third parties have rights to, or interests in, the land that would diminish its value to the grantee.

COVENANT OF QUIET ENJOYMENT
A promise by the grantor (or landlord) that the grantee (or tenant) will not be evicted or disturbed by the grantor or a person having a lien or superior title.

6. Pronounced *see*-zuhn.

◆ **Exhibit 34–1**
A Sample Warranty Deed

Date: May 31, 1995

Grantor: GAYLORD A. JENTZ AND WIFE, JOANN H. JENTZ

Grantor's Mailing Address (including county):
4106 North Loop Drive
Austin, Travis County, Texas

Grantee: DAVID F. FRIEND AND WIFE, JOAN E. FRIEND AS JOINT TENANTS WITH RIGHT OF SURVIVORSHIP

Grantee's Mailing Address (including county):
5929 Fuller Drive
Austin, Travis County, Texas

Consideration:
For and in consideration of the sum of Ten and No/100 Dollars ($10.00) and other valuable consideration to the undersigned paid by the grantees herein named, the receipt of which is hereby acknowledged, and for which no lien is retained, either express or implied.

Property (including any improvements):
Lot 23, Block "A", Northwest Hills, Green Acres Addition, Phase 4, Travis County, Texas, according to the map or plat of record in volume 22, pages 331-336 of the Plat Records of Travis County, Texas.

Reservations from and Exceptions to Conveyance and Warranty:

This conveyance with its warranty is expressly made subject to the following:

Easements and restrictions of record in Volume 7863, Page 53, Volume 8430, Page 35, Volume 8133, Page 152 of the Real Property Records of Travis County, Texas, Volume 22, Pages 335-339, of the Plat Records of Travis County, Texas; and to any other restrictions and easements affecting said property which are of record in Travis County, Texas.

Grantor, for the consideration and subject to the reservations from and exceptions to conveyance and warranty, grants, sells, and conveys to Grantee the property, together with all and singular the rights and appurtenances thereto in any wise belonging, to have and hold it to Grantee, Grantee's heirs, executors, administrators, successors, or assigns forever. Grantor binds Grantor and Grantor's heirs, executors, administrators, and successors to warrant and forever defend all and singular the property to Grantee and Grantee's heirs, executors, administrators, successors, and assigns against every person whomsoever lawfully claiming or to claim the same or any part thereof, except as to the reservations from and exceptions to conveyance and warranty.

When the context requires, singular nouns and pronouns include the plural.

BY: Gaylord A. Jentz
Gaylord A. Jentz

BY: JoAnn H. Jentz
JoAnn H. Jentz

(Acknowledgment)

STATE OF TEXAS
COUNTY OF

This instrument was acknowledged before me on the 31st day of May, 1995
by Gaylord A. and JoAnn H. Jentz

Rosemary Potter
Notary Public, State of Texas
Notary's name (printed): Rosemary Potter

Notary Seal

Notary's commission expires: 1/31/ 1995

buyer. Here, the covenant of quiet enjoyment has been breached, and the buyer can recover the purchase price of the land plus any other damages incurred as a result of the eviction.

Quitclaim Deeds A **quitclaim deed** offers the least amount of protection against defects in the title. Basically, a quitclaim deed conveys to the grantee whatever interest the grantor had; so if the grantor had no interest, then the grantee receives no interest. Quitclaim deeds are often used when the seller, or grantor, is uncertain as to the extent of his or her rights in the property.

QUITCLAIM DEED
A deed intended to pass any title, interest, or claim that the grantor may have in the premises but not professing that such title is valid and not containing any warranty or covenants of title.

Recording Statutes **Recording statutes** are in force in every jurisdiction to provide prospective buyers with a way to check whether there have been earlier transactions creating interests or rights in specific parcels of real property. Hence, recording a deed gives notice to the public that a certain person is now the owner of a particular parcel of real estate. Placing everyone on notice as to the true owner is intended to prevent the previous owners from fraudulently conveying the land to other purchasers. Deeds are generally recorded in the county in which the property is located. Many state statutes require that the grantor sign the deed in the presence of two attesting witnesses before it can be recorded.

RECORDING STATUTE
A statute requiring that deeds, mortgages, and other real property transactions be recorded so as to provide notice to future purchasers, creditors, and encumbrancers of an existing claim on the property.

Will or Inheritance

Property that is transferred on an owner's death is passed either by will or by state inheritance laws. If the owner of land dies with a will, the land passes in accordance with the terms of the will. If the owner dies without a will, state inheritance statutes prescribe how and to whom the property will pass. Transfers of property by will or inheritance are examined in detail in Chapter 35.

Adverse Possession

Adverse possession is a means of obtaining title to land without delivery of a deed. Essentially, when one person possesses the property of another for a certain statutory period of time (three to thirty years, with ten years being most common), that person, called the adverse possessor, acquires title to the land and cannot be removed from it by the original owner. The adverse possessor is vested with a perfect title just as if there had been a conveyance by deed.

ADVERSE POSSESSION
The acquisition of title to real property by occupying it openly, without the consent of the owner, for a period of time specified by state statutes. The occupation must be actual, open, notorious, exclusive, and in opposition to all others, including the owner.

For property to be held adversely, four elements must be satisfied:

1. Possession must be actual and exclusive; that is, the possessor must take sole physical occupancy of the property.
2. The possession must be open, visible, and notorious, not secret or clandestine. The possessor must occupy the land for all the world to see.
3. Possession must be continuous and peaceable for the required period of time. This requirement means that the possessor must not be interrupted in the occupancy by the true owner or by the courts.
4. Possession must be hostile and adverse. In other words, the possessor must claim the property as against the whole world. He or she cannot be living on the property with the permission of the owner.

There are a number of public policy reasons for the adverse possession doctrine. These reasons include society's interest in resolving boundary disputes and determining ownership rights when title to property is in question and in assuring that real property remains in the stream of commerce. More fundamentally, policies behind the doctrine include punishing owners who sit on their rights too long and rewarding possessors for putting land to productive use.

In the following case, the question before the court was whether a couple had obtained title to a certain portion of land by adverse possession.

Case 34.2
KLOS v. MOLENDA
Superior Court of Pennsylvania, 1986.
355 Pa.Super. 399,
513 A.2d 490.

HISTORICAL AND CULTURAL SETTING *After the Second World War ended in 1945, soldiers, sailors, and marines returned to their families, or began families, and the birthrate increased dramatically each year. Many of the former servicepeople went to college, but even those who did not go back to school needed relatively low-cost housing. In 1947, a builder, Abraham Levitt, and his sons developed Levittown—a community on Long Island consisting of inexpensive houses and a playground, shops, and other amenities. Over the next few years, other builders began to imitate Levitt's idea, and by 1950, suburban developments were sprawling across the American landscape.*

FACTS In September 1950, Michael and Albina Klos purchased part of some property in Pennsylvania owned by John and Anne Molenda. The Kloses' lot was 50 feet wide and 135 feet deep. Rather than surveying the property, the seller and buyer paced off the lot and placed stakes in the ground as boundary markers. The Kloses built a house on the lot in 1952 and put in a sidewalk along the full front. They also put in a driveway 30 inches from the stake line. They planted grass in that 30 inches and maintained it until 1984. In 1983, Mr. Molenda died, and his widow hired a surveyor to inventory the landholdings. The survey located the rightful property line between the Molendas' and Kloses' land as being 30 inches closer to the Kloses' house than the line established earlier. This placed the property line right along the Kloses' driveway, instead of 30 inches to the side of the driveway. Upon learning this, Mrs. Molenda erected a fence right along the Kloses' driveway, marking the property line. The Kloses brought an action challenging Mrs. Molenda's conduct, claiming that they held title to the land by adverse possession. The trial court held that the Kloses had title to the land. Mrs. Molenda appealed.

ISSUE Who held title to the 30-inch strip of land?

DECISION The Kloses held rightful title to the land. The appellate court affirmed the trial court's decision.

REASON The rule of adverse possession holds that if a person has actual, continuous, exclusive, visible, notorious, distinct, and hostile possession of land for a long period of time (in Pennsylvania, twenty-one years), that person gains title to the land. This means that the adverse possessor must use the land in a regular, normal, and obvious manner so that the original title owner would know, upon inspection, of the possessor's use. If the original title owner does not evict the possessor or otherwise exercise his or her ownership rights, then the possessor will obtain title once the statutory time period has lapsed. Here, the Kloses were certainly open, hostile, and notorious in their possession of the land in question, and they possessed the land for over thirty years. They therefore obtained title to the land by adverse possession.

Eminent Domain

EMINENT DOMAIN
The power of a government to take land for public use from private citizens for just compensation.

TAKING
The taking of private property by the government for public use and for just compensation.

Even ownership in real property in fee simple absolute is limited by a superior ownership. Just as in medieval England the king was the ultimate landowner, so in the United States the government has an ultimate ownership right in all land. This right is known as **eminent domain,** and it is sometimes referred to as the condemnation power of the government to take land for public use. It gives a right to the government to acquire possession of real property in the manner directed by the Constitution and the laws of the state whenever the public interest requires it. Property may be taken only for public use.

When the government takes land owned by a private party for public use, it is referred to as a **taking,** and the government must compensate the private party. Under the so-called *takings clause* of the Fifth Amendment, private property may not be taken for public use without "just compensation."

The power of eminent domain is generally invoked through condemnation proceedings. For example, when a new public highway is to be built, the government must decide where to build it and how much land to condemn. After the govern-

Under what circumstances can the government require owners to sell their land? What requirement must the government meet when it takes this property?

ment determines that a particular parcel of land is necessary for public use, it brings a judicial proceeding to obtain title to the land. Then, in another proceeding, the court determines the *fair value* of the land, which is usually approximately equal to its market value.

In an attempt to preserve the natural beauty and resources of the land, environmental laws have increasingly prohibited private parties from using certain lands (wetlands and coastal lands, for example) in specific ways. Does imposing such limitations on landowners' rights constitute a "taking" by the government? This question is explored in this chapter's *Business Law in Action.* The following case illustrates another example of an alleged taking in violation of a state constitution.

Case 34.3
WEGNER v. MILWAUKEE MUTUAL INSURANCE CO.
Supreme Court of Minnesota, 1991.
479 N.W.2d 38.

HISTORICAL AND ETHICAL SETTING *Under the doctrine of public necessity, as described in the Restatement (Second) of Torts, Section 196, "One is privileged to enter land in the possession of another if it is, or if the actor reasonably believes it to be, necessary for the purpose of averting an imminent public disaster." As an example, the renowned legal scholar William Prosser stated that "one who dynamites a house to stop the spread of a conflagration that threatens a town * * * is not liable to the owner, so long as the emergency is great enough, and he [or she] has acted reasonably under the circumstances."*[a] *Thus, in a case decided in Minnesota in 1868, involving city officers' destruction of a building to stop the spread of a fire, the city of Red Wing was excused from paying compensation.*[b] *Prosser also commented, however, that "[i]t would seem that the moral obligtion upon the group affected to make compensation in such a case should be recognized by the law."*

FACTS The Minneapolis police department, in trying to apprehend a suspect who had entered and hidden himself in Harriet Wegner's house, severely damaged the house. The police and a SWAT team called in to assist the police were unable to persuade the suspect to come out, so they fired twenty-five rounds of tear gas into the house, as well as three concussion ("flash-bang") grenades. The police finally apprehended the suspect as he crawled out of a basement window. Wegner alleged that these events caused damages of $71,000 to her home. Her insurance carrier, Milwaukee Mutual Insurance Company, paid her about $28,000 but refused to pay for the rest of the damage. Wegner and Milwaukee Mutual both sued the city of Minneapolis, alleging that the police department's actions constituted a compensable taking under the Minnesota constitution. (The insurance company sought reimburse-

a. W. Page Keeton et al., *Prosser and Keeton on Torts*, 5th ed. (St. Paul: West Publishing Co., 1986), p. 146.

b. *McDonald v. City of Red Wing*, 13 Minn. 38 (1868).

Case 34.3—Continued

ment for the money it had paid to Wegner and for possible future liability on her claim.) The trial court granted summary judgment for the city on the taking issue, holding that "[e]minent domain is not intended as a limitation on [the] police power" of the state. The appellate court affirmed. Wegner and the insurance company appealed to the Minnesota Supreme Court.

ISSUE Did the police department's partial destruction of Wegner's home constitute a taking of private property without compensation?

DECISION Yes. The Minnesota Supreme Court reversed the lower courts' decisions.

REASON Article I, Section 13, of the Minnesota constitution provides that "[p]rivate property shall not be taken, destroyed or damaged for public use without just compensation." The court stated that the "purpose of the damage clause is to ensure that private landowners are compensated, not only for physical invasion of their property, but also damages caused by the state where no physical invasion has occurred." In response to the city's contention that there was no taking for a public use "because the actions of the police constituted a legitimate exercise of the police power," the court stated that "simply labeling the actions of the police as an exercise of the police power 'cannot justify the disregard of the constitutional inhibitions.' " The court found that the "plain meaning" of Article I, Section 13, of the Minnesota constitution "requires compensation when property is damaged for a public use." Because Wegner's property was damaged by the police for a public use—to protect the public safety—Wegner was constitutionally entitled to be compensated by the city for the damages.

ETHICAL CONSIDERATIONS *The court noted that basically, the policy considerations in this case centered on notions of fairness and justice. "At its most basic level," said the court, "the issue is whether it is fair to allocate the entire risk of loss to an innocent homeowner for the good of the public. We do not believe the imposition of such a burden on the innocent citizens of this state would square with the underlying principles of our system of justice."*

❖ Landlord-Tenant Relationships

LEASE
A transfer of possession by the landlord/lessor of real or personal property to the tenant/lessee for a period of time for consideration (usually the payment of rent). Upon termination of the lease, the property reverts to the lessor.

Much real property is used by those who do not own it. A **lease** is a contract by which the owner—the landlord—grants the tenant an exclusive right to use and possess the land, usually for a specified period of time, in return for rent or some other form of payment.

In the past century—and particularly in the past two decades—landlord-tenant relationships have become much more complex than they were before, as has the law governing them. Generally, the law has come to apply contract doctrines, such as those providing for implied warranties and unconscionability, to the landlord-tenant relationship. Increasingly, landlord-tenant relationships have become subject to specific state and local statutes and ordinances as well. In 1972, in an effort to create more uniformity in the law governing landlord-tenant relationships, the National Conference of Commissioners on Uniform State Laws issued the Uniform Residential Landlord and Tenant Act (URLTA).

We look here at how a landlord-tenant relationship is created and at the respective rights and duties of landlords and tenants.

Creating the Landlord-Tenant Relationship

A landlord-tenant relationship is established by a lease agreement, which may be oral or written. At common law, an oral lease is valid. As is the case with most oral agreements, however, a party who seeks to enforce an oral lease may have difficulty proving its existence. In most states, statutes mandate that leases be in writing for some tenancies (such as those exceeding one year). To ensure the validity of a lease agreement, it should therefore be in writing and do the following:

1. Express an intent to establish the relationship.

Business Law in Action

Private versus Public Property Rights

Environmental regulations and other legislation to control land use are prevalent throughout the United States. Generally, these laws reflect the public interest in preserving the beauty and natural resources of the land and in allowing the public to have access to and enjoy limited resources, such as coastal areas. While few would disagree with the rationale underlying these laws, the owners of the private property directly affected by the laws may feel that they should be compensated for the limitation imposed on their right to do as they wish with the land. Several cases have been brought by private property owners who allege that regulations limiting their control over the land essentially constitute a taking of private property rights in the public interest. Therefore, they should receive the just compensation guaranteed under the Fifth Amendment.

For example, in Maine, firmly established rules of property law had long dictated that the owners of beachfront property held title to intertidal land—the part of the beach that is submerged at high tide but not at low tide. That intertidal land was subject to an easement permitting public use only for fishing, fowling, and navigation and any other uses reasonably incidental or related to those activities. In 1986, however, the Maine Public Trust and Intertidal Land Act was passed. This act gave the public the right to use, essentially without limitation, the intertidal land for recreation. Members of the public in unrestricted numbers were given the right to come onto this "private property" for boating, sunbathing, walking, ball games or other athletic events, camping, nighttime beach parties, and horseback riding.

One of the beachfront property owners decided to sue, claiming that the new law constituted an unconstitutional taking of private property without compensation and was therefore in violation of the Fifth Amendment. The court, when faced with this question, agreed with the property owner.[a] The court cited a similar case that arose in California and was decided in favor of the landowner.[b] In that case, the United States Supreme Court found that a permanent physical occupation occurs whenever the public is given a permanent and continuous right to pass to and fro on real property. Such permanent physical possession constitutes a taking.

In another case, a landowner claimed that legislation restricting the use of his beachfront property diminished the value of the land dramatically. He claimed that the decrease in the economic value of the property constituted a taking for which he should be compensated. The case was brought by David Lucas, who had paid $975,000 for two residential beachfront lots in South Carolina in 1986. Lucas intended to build single-family homes on the lots and sell them at a profit. In 1988, however, the South Carolina legislature enacted the Beachfront Management Act, which had the effect of prohibiting Lucas from erecting any permanent habitable structures on his two parcels. Lucas contended that the act's effect on the economic value of his lots, which he claimed were now valueless to him, constituted a taking of private property under the Fifth Amendment for which he should be compensated. The trial court agreed with Lucas, but the state supreme court reversed, and ultimately the United States Supreme Court reviewed the case. The Court reversed the state supreme court's judgment and remanded the case with instructions that Lucas must be paid compensation unless narrow exceptions applied, such as if his property would create a public nuisance. (The Court indicated that building a nuclear generating plant astride an earthquake fault or filling a lake and consequently flooding adjacent landowners' property would constitute public nuisances.)[c]

For years, courts evaluating these kinds of claims by private property owners generally sided with the public authorities. Beginning in the 1980s, however, the tide began to turn, and as the cases just discussed illustrate, courts are beginning to give a little more weight to the interests of private property owners.

a. *Bell v. Town of Wells,* 557 A.2d 168 (Me. 1989).
b. *Nollan v. California Coastal Commission,* 483 U.S. 825, 107 S.Ct. 3141, 97 L.Ed.2d 677 (1987).
c. *Lucas v. South Carolina Coastal Council,* __U.S.__, 112 S.Ct. 2886, 120 L.Ed.2d 798 (1992).

2. Provide for the transfer of the property's possession to the tenant at the beginning of the term.
3. Provide for the landlord's reversionary interest, which entitles the property owner to retake possession at the end of the term.
4. Describe the property—for example, give its street address.
5. Indicate the length of the term, the amount of the rent, and how and when it is to be paid.

State or local law often dictates permissible lease terms. For example, a statute or ordinance might prohibit the leasing of a structure that is in a certain physical condition or is not in compliance with local building codes. Similarly, a statute may prohibit the leasing of property for a particular purpose. For instance, a state law might prohibit gambling houses. Thus, if a landlord and tenant intend that the leased premises be used only to house an illegal betting operation, their lease is unenforceable.

The *unconscionability* concept is one of the most important of the contract doctrines applied to leases. Basically, as applied to leases in some jurisdictions, the concept follows the provision of UCC 2–302. Under this provision, a court may declare an entire contract or any of its clauses unconscionable and thus illegal, depending on the circumstances surrounding the transaction and the parties' relative bargaining positions. For example, in a residential lease, a clause claiming to absolve a landlord from responsibility for interruptions in such essential services as central heating or air-conditioning will not shield the landlord from liability if the systems break down when they are needed most.

A property owner cannot legally discriminate against prospective tenants on the basis of race, color, religion, national origin, or sex. Similarly, a tenant cannot legally promise to do something counter to laws prohibiting discrimination. A tenant, for example, cannot legally promise to do business only with members of a particular race. The public policy underlying these prohibitions is to treat all people equally.

Often, rental properties are leased by agents of the landowner. Recall from Chapter 23 that under the theory of *respondeat superior*, a principal (a landlord, with respect to leases) is liable for the wrongful actions of his or her agent if the actions occurred within the scope of employment. At issue in the following case is whether a landlord can be held liable for his agent's discrimination on the basis of sex against a woman who sought to rent a particular apartment.

Case 34.4
WALKER v. CRIGLER
United States Court of Appeals,
Fourth Circuit, 1992.
976 F.2d 900.

HISTORICAL AND SOCIAL SETTING *At common law, a landlord was free to rent, or refuse to rent, to anyone for any reason. For example, a landlord was not required to rent an apartment to someone with a considerable number of unpaid bills. Today, that rule still generally applies: a landlord does not need a particularly good reason to refuse to rent his or her property to someone. Over the last forty years, however, the federal government has recognized that persons have a right* not *to be denied a housing opportunity because of race, color, religion, gender, national origin, mental and physical disability, marital status, or the presence of children. Some states protect against discrimination on the basis of other characteristics as well, such as age.*

FACTS Darlene Walker, a single parent with one son, was looking for an apartment in Falls Church, Virginia. A real estate agent, John Moore, was assisting her in her search and took Walker to view an apartment owned by Frank Whitesell III and managed by Constance Crigler. Walker liked the apartment because it was near a school for her son and near transportation, and Moore called Crigler and told her that he had an applicant for the apartment. Crigler told Moore, and later Walker, that she would never rent to a woman in any circumstances. Walker asked Crigler if she was speaking for the owner, and Crigler said that she was. Walker sued Crigler and Whitesell for violating federal laws prohibiting discrimination in housing. The trial court found Crigler liable for damages in the amount of $5,000 but held that Whitesell was not liable for Crigler's actions because he had previously instructed her, in writing, not to discriminate illegally against any potential renters. Walker appealed. (Shortly after the appeal was filed, Crigler filed for Chapter 7 bankruptcy, and a few months later the $5,000 judgment against her was discharged.)

ISSUE Can Whitesell be held liable for Crigler's discrimination against Walker?

DECISION Yes. The appellate court reversed the trial court's decision on this issue. Whitesell was ordered to pay $5,000 in damages to Walker.

REASON The trial jury had found that Crigler, because she disobeyed Whitesell's instructions, had acted outside the scope of her employment. The appellate court stated

Case 34.4—Continued

that this was an erroneous reading of the law. For one thing, the appellate court doubted whether the "mere act of instructing Crigler not to discriminate would be sufficient to justify a ruling that she was acting outside the scope of employment." But in any event, whether Crigler was acting within the scope of her employment was irrelevant in this case because the duty not to discriminate was nondelegable. The court noted that just as property owners cannot avoid responsibilities for paying taxes and meeting health and safety requirements by delegating those responsibilities to others, neither can owners avoid the duty not to discriminate through delegation of the duty. In sum, said the court, "Whitesell could not insulate himself from liability for sex discrimination in regard to living premises owned by him and managed for his benefit merely by relinquishing the responsibility for preventing such discrimination to another party."

ETHICAL CONSIDERATIONS *The court was aware of the seeming unfairness of holding landlords liable in situations such as the one described in this case. "The central question to be decided in a case such as this," said the court, "is which innocent party, the owner whose agent acted contrary to instruction, or the potential renter who felt the direct harm of the agent's discriminatory failure to offer the residence for rent, will ultimately bear the burden of the harm caused." The court found that because the landlord had the power to control the acts of his or her agent, it was fairer that the landlord should bear the burden.*

Rights and Duties

The rights and duties of landlords and tenants generally pertain to four broad areas of concern—the possession, use, and maintenance of leased property and, of course, rent.

Possession Possession involves the obligation of the landord to deliver possession to the tenant at the beginning of the lease term and the right of the tenant to obtain possession and retain it until the lease expires.

The covenant of quiet enjoyment mentioned previously also applies to leased premises. Under this covenant, the landlord promises that during the lease term, neither the landlord nor anyone having a superior title to the property will disturb the tenant's use and enjoyment of the property. This covenant forms the essence of the landlord-tenant relationship, and if it is breached, the tenant can terminate the lease and sue for damages.

If the landlord deprives the tenant of the tenant's possession of the leased property or interferes with the tenant's use or enjoyment of it, an **eviction** occurs. This is the case, for example, when the landlord changes the lock and refuses to give the tenant a new key. A **constructive eviction** occurs when the landlord wrongfully performs or fails to perform any of the undertakings the lease requires, thereby making the tenant's further use and enjoyment of the property exceedingly difficult or impossible. Examples of constructive eviction include a landlord's failure to provide heat in the winter, light, or other essential utilities.

EVICTION
Depriving a person of the possession of land or rental property that he or she owns or leases by having the person removed from the premises.

CONSTRUCTIVE EVICTION
A landlord's act or failure to act that deprives a person of the possession of rental property that he or she leases by rendering the premises unfit or unsuitable for occupancy.

Use and Maintenance of the Premises If the parties do not limit by agreement the uses to which the property may be put, the tenant may make any use of it, as long as the use is legal and reasonably relates to the purpose for which the property is adapted or ordinarily used and does not injure the landlord's interest.

The tenant is responsible for all damage that he or she causes, intentionally or negligently, and the tenant may be held liable for the cost of returning the property to the physical condition it was in at the lease's inception. Unless the parties have agreed otherwise, the tenant is not responsible for ordinary wear and tear and the property's consequent depreciation in value.

Usually, the landlord must comply with state statutes and city ordinances that delineate specific standards for the construction and maintenance of buildings. Typically, these codes contain structural requirements common to the construction, wiring, and plumbing of residential and commercial buildings. In some jurisdictions, landlords of residential property are required by statute to maintain the premises in good repair.

IMPLIED WARRANTY OF HABITABILITY
A presumed promise by the landlord that rented residential premises are fit for human habitation—including being free of violations of building and sanitary codes.

The **implied warranty of habitability** requires a landlord who leases residential property to furnish the premises in a habitable condition—that is, in a condition that is safe and suitable for people to live in—at the beginning of a lease term and to maintain them in that condition for the lease's duration. Some state legislatures have enacted this warranty into law. In other jurisdictions, courts have based the warranty on the existence of a landlord's statutory duty to keep leased premises in good repair, or they have simply applied it as a matter of public policy.

Generally, this warranty applies to major—or *substantial*—physical defects that the landlord knows or should know about and has had a reasonable time to repair—for example, a large hole in the roof. An unattractive or annoying feature, such as a crack in the wall, may be unpleasant, but unless the crack is a structural defect or affects the residence's heating capabilities, it is probably not sufficiently substantial to make the place uninhabitable.

The following case involves a dispute between a landlord and a tenant over the proper measure of damages for a tenant's failure to maintain the premises as promised in the lease agreement. Although normally the landlord is responsible for basic maintenance of the premises (painting, repairs, and so on), in this case, the tenant had contractually agreed to be responsible for maintaining the premises.

Case 34.5
SDR ASSOCIATES v. ARG ENTERPRISES, INC.

Court of Appeals of Arizona, Division 2, Department B, 1991.
170 Ariz. 1,
821 P.2d 268.

HISTORICAL AND ECONOMIC SETTING *At common law, with respect to the condition of leased property, landlords had no duty to make repairs or to keep the property suitable for tenants' use. Tenants did have a duty, however, to keep the property sealed against the "wind and weather" to prevent the premises from falling into disrepair. During the nineteenth century, as the cities in the United States grew larger, the courts recognized exceptions to these rules in cases involving residential leases. A few states enacted housing codes to regulate the condition of residential property and warranties of habitability to impose on landlords a duty to make major repairs. In the twentieth century, particularly during the 1960s and the 1970s, a revolution in landlord-tenant law occurred, resulting in a landlord having the duty to keep residential property in a habitable condition throughout the term of a lease. Of course, a tenant may still be liable for allowing the premises to fall into disrepair, and leases of commercial property often contain clauses imposing on a tenant the duty of making all repairs. Leases of commercial property are different, because unlike residential property, commercial property often generates cash on a recurring basis to the tenant, usually in the form of sales to customers.*

FACTS ARG Enterprises, Inc., operated a Black Angus restaurant on premises leased from SDR Associates. The lease included a provision that required ARG to return the premises in the condition in which it had received them. In return for ARG's agreeing to maintain the premises, SDR charged lower rent payments than it otherwise would have. About six months before the lease was due to expire, SDR notified ARG of the need to return the premises in good condition if the lease was not renewed. When the lease expired, however, the premises were in disrepair. Extensive repairs were required for the roof as well as for the air-conditioning unit, the exhaust fans, and the parking lot. These problems prevented SDR from renting the premises to anyone else. Before the lease expired, SDR had been negotiating with Toys "Я" Us, Inc., about the possibility of demolishing the building and selling just the land; but SDR's preference was to lease the building as a restaurant. At the time of trial, the structure had not been destroyed. SDR sued ARG, alleging that ARG had breached the lease agreement by failing to return the premises to SDR in good condition. Among other things, SDR sought damages in the amount of $200,000 as the cost for restoring the premises to good condition. The trial court held for SDR, and ARG appealed.

ISSUE Given the fact that SDR was contemplating the demolition of the building, must ARG pay the $200,000 in damages to restore the premises to their earlier condition?

DECISION Yes. The appellate court affirmed the trial court's decision. ARG was ordered to pay $200,000 in damages to SDR.

REASON ARG's main argument on appeal concerned the fact that SDR was contemplating having the building

Case 34.5—Continued

demolished and selling just the land to Toys "Я" Us. The court held, however, that the issue in this case did not concern the future use of the property. Rather, the issue centered solely on ARG's breach of its contract with SDR. ARG had a contractual duty to maintain the premises and had been given a discount on the rent payments in consideration of this duty. ARG failed to maintain the premises and therefore was liable for the difference between the value of the property at the time it was originally leased to ARG and its value at the time that SDR took possession of it at the end of the lease term. The fact that SDR might decide to demolish the premises and sell the land to Toys "Я" Us was not relevant to the measure of damages to be applied in this situation.

Rent *Rent* is the tenant's payment to the landlord for the tenant's occupancy or use of the landlord's real property. Generally, the tenant must pay the rent even if the tenant refuses to occupy the property or moves out, as long as the refusal or the move is unjustifiable and the lease is in force.

At common law, destruction by fire or flood of a building leased by a tenant did not relieve the tenant of the obligation to pay rent and did not permit the termination of the lease. Today, however, state statutes have altered the common law rule. If the building burns down, apartment dwellers in most states are not continuously liable to the landlord for the payment of rent.

In some situations, such as when a landlord breaches the implied warranty of habitability, a tenant is allowed to withhold rent as a remedy. When rent withholding is authorized under a statute (sometimes referred to as a "rent-strike" statute), the tenant must usually put the amount withheld into an *escrow account.* This account is held in the name of the depositor (in this case, the tenant) and an *escrow agent* (in this case, usually the court or a government agency), and the funds are returnable to the depositor if the third person (in this case, the landlord) fails to fulfill the escrow condition. Generally, the tenant may withhold an amount equal to the amount by which the defect rendering the premises unlivable reduces the property's rental value. How much that is may be determined in different ways, and the tenant who withholds more than is legally permissible is liable to the landlord for the excessive amount withheld.

Transferring Rights to Leased Property

Either the landlord or the tenant may wish to transfer his or her rights to the leased property during the term of the lease.

Transferring the Landlord's Interest Just as any other real property owner can sell, give away, or otherwise transfer his or her property, so can a landlord—who is, of course, the leased property's owner. If complete title to the leased property is transferred, the tenant becomes the tenant of the new owner. The new owner may collect subsequent rent but must then abide by the terms of the existing lease agreement.

Transferring the Tenant's Interest The tenant's transfer of his or her entire interest in the leased property to a third person is an *assignment of the lease.* A lease assignment is an agreement to transfer all rights, title, and interest in the lease to the assignee. It is a complete transfer. Many leases require that the assignment have the landlord's written consent, and an assignment that lacks consent can be avoided by the landlord. A landlord who knowingly accepts rent from the assignee, however, will be held to have waived the requirement. A tenant does not end his or her liabilities on a lease upon assignment, because the tenant may assign rights but not duties. Thus, even though the assignee of the lease is required to pay rent, the original tenant is not released from the contractual obligation to pay the rent if the assignee fails to do so.

SUBLEASE
A lease executed by the lessee of real estate to a third person, conveying the same interest that the lessee enjoys, but for a shorter term than that held by the lessee (as compared with an assignment of a lease, in which the lessee transfers the entire unexpired term of the leasehold to a third party).

The tenant's transfer of all or part of the premises for a period shorter than the lease term is a **sublease.** The same restrictions that apply to an assignment of the tenant's interest in leased property apply to a sublease. To illustrate, a student named Derek leases an apartment for a two-year period. Although Derek had planned on attending summer school, he is offered a job in Europe for the summer months and accepts. Because he does not wish to pay three months' rent for an unoccupied apartment, Derek subleases the apartment to Darwin (the sublessee). (Derek may have to obtain his landlord's consent for this sublease if the lease requires it.) Darwin is bound by the same terms of the lease as Derek, but as in a lease assignment, Derek remains liable for the obligations under the lease if Darwin fails to fulfill them.

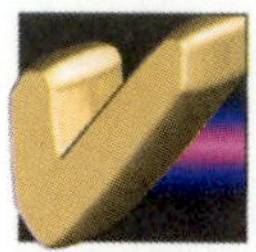
Application

Law and the Entrepreneur— How to Negotiate a Favorable Lease

Generally, an entrepreneur first starting a business is well advised to lease rather than buy property because the future success of the business is uncertain. By leasing instead of purchasing property, persons just starting out in business allow themselves some time to determine whether business profits will warrant the outright purchase of property.

One thing to keep in mind when leasing property is that lease contracts are usually form contracts that favor the landowner. That means that, as a prospective tenant, you need to think about negotiating terms more favorable to you. Before negotiating the terms of the lease, do some comparison shopping to see what other comparable properties in the area rent for. Usually, rental prices for business property are stated as so many dollars per square foot (per month or per year). In commercial leases to retail stores, it is common for part or all of the rent to consist of a percentage of the tenant's sales made on the premises during the term of the lease. Bear in mind, too, that the nature of your business should determine, to a great extent, the location of the leased premises. If you are involved in a mail-order business, for example, you need not pay the extra price for a prime location that might be required for a restaurant business.

When negotiating a lease, you must also determine who will pay property taxes and insurance on the property and who will be responsible for repairs of the property and utility payments. These terms are generally negotiable, and depending on who takes responsibility, the rent payment may be adjusted accordingly. Generally, your success in negotiating favorable lease terms will depend on the market. If the rental market is "good" (that is, if you have numerous other rental options at favorable rates), you may be able to convince the landlord that he or she should be responsible for taxes, insurance, maintenance, and the like, and possibly for improvements to the property necessary for your business. Therefore, it is important to investigate the status of the market before you begin negotations with a potential landlord.

Checklist for the Lessee of Business Property

☐ 1. When you are entering into business, leasing rather than buying property has advantages because it reduces your liability in the event that your business is unsuccessful.

☐ 2. Realize that, although lease contracts normally favor the landlord, you can negotiate favorable terms for your lease of a given premises.

☐ 3. Make sure that the lease contract clearly indicates whether the landlord or tenant is to be responsible for taxes on the property, costs relating to necessary maintenance and repairs, and utility costs. By comparison shopping, you should be able to judge which lease terms are favorable and which are not.

☐ 4. To protect yourself in the event your business is unsuccessful, start with a short-term initial lease, perhaps with an option to renew the lease in the future.

❖ Key Terms

adverse possession 833
constructive eviction 839
conveyance 827
covenant against encumbrances 831
covenant of quiet enjoyment 831
covenant of seisin 831
covenant of the right to convey 831
deed 831
easement 828
eminent domain 834
eviction 839
executory interest 828
fee simple absolute 826
fee simple defeasible 827
fixture 825
future interest 827
implied warranty of habitability 840
lease 836
leasehold estate 829
license 829
life estate 827
periodic tenancy 830
profit 828
quitclaim deed 833
recording statute 833
remainder 828
reversionary interest 827
sublease 842
taking 834
tenancy at sufferance 831
tenancy at will 830
tenancy for years 829
warranty deed 831

❖ Chapter Summary: Real Property

Nature of Real Property	Real property—also called real estate or realty—is immovable. It includes land, subsurface and air rights, plant life and vegetation, and fixtures.
Ownership of Real Property	1. *Fee simple absolute*—The most complete form of ownership. 2. *Fee simple defeasible*—Ownership in fee simple that can end if a specified event or condition occurs. 3. *Life estate*—An estate that lasts for the life of a specified individual; ownership rights in a life estate are subject to the rights of the future-interest holder. 4. *Future interest*—A residuary interest not granted by the grantor in conveying an estate to another for life, for a specified period of time, or on the condition that a specific event does or does not occur. The grantor may retain the residuary interest (which is then called a reversionary interest) or transfer ownership rights in the future interest to another (in which case the interest is referred to as a remainder). 5. *Nonpossessory interest*—An interest that involves the right to use real property but not to possess it. Easements, profits, and licenses are nonpossessory interests. 6. *Leasehold estate*—An interest in real property that is held only for a limited period of time, as specified in the lease agreement. Types of tenancies relating to leased property include the following: a. Tenancy for years—Tenancy for a period of time stated by express contract. b. Periodic tenancy—Tenancy for a period determined by the frequency of rent payments; automatically renewed unless proper notice is given. c. Tenancy at will—Tenancy for as long as both parties agree; no notice of termination is required. d. Tenancy at sufferance—Possession of land without legal right.
Transfer of Ownership Rights in Real Property	1. *By deed*—When real property is sold or transferred as a gift, title to the property is conveyed by means of a deed. A deed must meet specific legal requirements. A *warranty deed* warrants the most extensive protection against defects of title. A *quitclaim deed* conveys to the grantee whatever interest the grantor had; it warrants less than any other deed. A deed may be recorded in the manner prescribed by *recording statutes* in the appropriate jurisdiction to give third parties notice of the owner's interest. 2. *By will or inheritance*—If the owner dies after having made a valid will, the land passes as specified in the will. If the owner dies without having made a will, the heirs inherit according to state inheritance statutes. 3. *By adverse possession*—When a person possesses the property of another for a statutory period of time (three to thirty years, with ten years being the most common), that person acquires title to

❖ Chapter Summary: Real Property—Continued

Transfer of Ownership Rights in Real Property—Continued	the property, provided the possession is actual and exclusive, open and visible, continuous and peaceable, and hostile and adverse (without the permission of the owner). 4. *By eminent domain*—The taking of private land by the government for public use, with just compensation, when the public interest requires the taking.
Landlord-Tenant Relationships	1. *Lease agreement*—The landlord-tenant relationship is created by a lease agreement. State or local law may dictate whether the lease must be in writing and what lease terms are permissible. 2. *Rights and duties*—The rights and duties that arise under a lease agreement generally pertain to the following areas: a. *Possession*—The tenant has an exclusive right to possess the leased premises, which must be available to the tenant at the agreed-on time. Under the covenant of quiet enjoyment, the landlord promises that during the lease term neither the landlord nor anyone having superior title to the property will disturb the tenant's use and enjoyment of the property. b. *Use and maintenance of the premises*—Unless the parties agree otherwise, the tenant may make any legal use of the property. The tenant is responsible for any damage that he or she causes. The landlord must comply with laws that set specific standards for the maintenance of real property. The implied warranty of habitability requires that a landlord furnish and maintain residential premises in a habitable condition (that is, in a condition safe and suitable for human life). 3. *Rent*—The tenant must pay the rent as long as the lease is in force, unless the tenant justifiably refuses to occupy the property or withholds the rent because of the landlord's failure to maintain the premises properly. 4. *Transferring rights to leased property:* a. If the landlord transfers complete title to the leased property, the tenant becomes the tenant of the new owner. The new owner may then collect the rent but must abide by the existing lease. b. Generally, tenants may assign their rights (but not their duties) under a lease contract to a third person. Tenants may also sublease leased property to a third person, but the original tenant is not relieved of any obligations to the landlord under the lease. In either case, the landlord's consent may be required.

❖ Questions and Case Problems

34-1. Ownership of Real Property. What is the difference between a fee simple absolute and a fee simple defeasible? What is the difference between a fee simple defeasible and a life estate?

34-2. Transfer of Real Property. What are the requirements for adverse possession?

34-3. Ownership of Real Property. Antonio is the owner of a lakeside house and lot. He deeds the house and lot "to my wife, Angela, for life, then to my son, Charles." Given these facts, answer the following questions:

(a) Does Antonio have any ownership interest in the lakeside house after making these transfers? Explain.

(b) What is Angela's interest called? Is there any limitation on her rights to use the property as she wishes? Discuss.

(c) What is Charles's interest called? Explain.

34-4. Adverse Possession. Lorenz was a wanderer twenty-two years ago. At that time, he decided to settle down on an unoccupied, three-acre parcel of land that he did not own. People in the area indicated to him that they had no idea who owned the property. Lorenz built a house on the land, got married, and raised three children while living there. He fenced in the land, placed a gate with a sign above it that read "Lorenz's Homestead," and had trespassers removed. Lorenz is now confronted by Joe Reese, who has a deed in his name as owner of the property. Reese, claiming ownership of the land, orders Lorenz and his family off the property. Discuss who has the better "title" to the property.

34-5. Deeds. Iliana and Jorge are neighbors. Jorge's lot is extremely large, and his present and future use of it will not involve the entire area. Iliana wants to build a single-car garage and driveway along the present boundary of the lot. Because of ordinances requiring buildings to be set back fifteen feet from an adjoining property line and because of the placement of her existing structures, she cannot build the garage. Iliana contracts to purchase ten feet of Jorge's property along their boundary line for $3,000. Jorge is willing to sell but will give Iliana only a quitclaim deed, whereas Iliana wants a warranty deed. Discuss the differences between these deeds as they would affect the rights of the parties if the title to this ten feet of land later proved to be defective.

34-6. Leased Property. The landlord of an apartment building leased a building he owned nearby for use as a cocktail lounge. The residential tenants complained to the landlord about the late-evening and early morning music and disturbances coming from the lounge. Although the lease for the lounge provided that entertainment had to be conducted so that it could not be heard outside the building and would not disturb the apartment tenants, the landlord was unsuccessful in remedying the problem. The tenants vacated their apartments. Was the landlord successful in his suit to collect rent from the tenants who vacated? Discuss. [*Blackett v. Olanoff,* 371 Mass. 714, 358 N.E.2d 817 (1977)]

34-7. Easements. In 1882, Moses Webster owned a parcel of land that extended down to the Atlantic Ocean. He conveyed the strip of the property fronting the ocean to another party. The deed included the following statement: "Reserve being had for said Moses Webster the right of way by land or water." The strip of property is now owned by Margaret Williams, and the portion retained by Webster now belongs to Thomas O'Neill. Williams is denying O'Neill access to the ocean. O'Neill has brought an action to establish his title to an easement over Williams's property. What should the court decide? Discuss fully. [*O'Neill v. Williams,* 527 A.2d 322 (Me. 1987)]

34-8. Adverse Possession. As the result of a survey in 1976, the Nolans discovered that their neighbor's garage extended more than a foot onto their property. Nolan requested that his neighbor, Naab, tear down the garage. The Naabs refused to do this, stating that the garage had been built in 1952 and had been on the property when the Naabs purchased it in 1973. In West Virginia, where these properties were located, there is a ten-year statute of limitations covering adverse possession of property. Were the Naabs able to claim title to the land on which the garage was situated by adverse possession? Explain. [*Naab v. Nolan,* 327 S.E.2d 151 (W.Va.1985)]

34-9. Adverse Possession. Paul and Barbara Sue Flanagan owned property in Alma, Arkansas, which was being purchased by the Smiths under an installment land contract. It had been assumed by all owners of the property since 1946 that a fence located at the southern end of the property was in fact the southern boundary of the property. Over the years, all owners had maintained and generally exercised dominion over the property up to the fence. In 1985, when Jerry and Mildred Hicks purchased a lot bordering the southern side of the Flanagan property, a survey showed that the true boundary was approximately eleven feet north of the existing fence. The Hickses asked the Smiths to remove the fence, but they refused to do so. The Hickses then brought an action to compel their neighbors to remove the fence. What will the court decide? Discuss fully. [*Hicks v. Flanagan,* 30 Ark.App. 53, 782 S.W.2d 587 (1990)]

34-10. Leased Property. Tachtronic Instruments, Inc., leased office and warehouse space in a building owned by Provident Mutual Life Insurance Co. The three-year lease ran until October 31, 1985, and specified monthly payments to Provident in the amount of $2,463. During the first year of the lease term, Tachtronic defaulted on its payments. When Provident brought an action to evict Tachtronic, the small firm paid a portion of the rent due, and the action was dismissed. By February 1984, Tachtronic had largely vacated the premises. On March 1, 1984, Tachtronic met with representatives of Provident at the leased premises. The premises were inspected by Provident, and Tachtronic removed its remaining possessions, swept the floor with a broom, and turned over the keys to Provident. Immediately thereafter, Provident sought a new tenant for the premises. A new tenant was found, and a more lucrative lease beginning November 1, 1984, was created between Provident and the new tenant. In June 1984, Provident commenced an action to recover the rent due from Tachtronic prior to its departure from the leased premises and also the rent due and payable for the remainder of the lease. Discuss whether Provident could collect. [*Provident Mutual Life Insurance Co. v. Tachtronic Instruments, Inc.,* 394 N.W.2d 161 (Minn.App. 1986)]

34-11. Leased Property. Inwood North Professional Group—Phase I leased medical office space to Joseph Davidow, a physician. The terms of the five-year lease specified that Inwood would provide electricity, hot water, air-conditioning, janitorial and maintenance services, light fixtures, and security services. During his tenancy, Davidow encountered a number of problems. The roof leaked, and the air-conditioning did not function properly. The premises were not cleaned and maintained by Inwood as promised in the lease agreement, and as a consequence, rodents and pests infested the premises and trash littered the parking area. There was frequently no hot water, and at one point Davidow was without electricity for several days because Inwood had not paid the bill. About a year prior to the lease's expiration, Davidow moved to another office building and refused to pay the remaining rent due under the lease. Inwood sued for the unpaid rent. Must Davidow pay the remaining rent due under the lease? Discuss. [*Davidow v. Inwood North Professional Group—Phase I,* 747 S.W.2d 373 (Tex. 1988)]

34-12. Leased Property. MCM Ventures, II, Inc., leased premises from Rushing Construction Co. on which to operate a restaurant. The lease term covered two years, from January 1, 1987, to December 31, 1988. The lease agreement stated in part that MCM "shall have a continuing option for a period of eight (8) consecutive years to renew this lease." Before the lease term expired on December 31, 1988, MCM did nothing to renew the lease; but it made monthly rent payments in the same amount as before in January and February 1989, after the lease had expired. Then, on February 28, 1989, MCM notified Rushing by mail that it wanted to exercise its option to renew the lease. Rushing refused to renew the lease, contending that MCM had forfeited the option by not exercising it prior to the expiration of the lease agreement in which the option had been given. Discuss fully whether MCM still had a right to exercise the lease renewal option as late as February 28, 1989. [*Rushing Construction Co. v. MCM Ventures, II, Inc.,* 100 N.C.App. 259, 395 S.E.2d 130 (1990)]

34-13. Leased Property. Christine Callis formed a lease agreement with Colonial Properties, Inc., to lease property in a shopping center in Montgomery, Alabama. Callis later alleged that before signing the lease agreement, she had told a representative of Colonial that she wanted to locate in a shopping center that would attract a wealthy clientele and the representative had assured her that no discount stores would be allowed to lease space in the shopping center. The written lease agreement, which Callis signed, contained a clause stating that "[n]o representation, inducement, understanding or anything of any nature whatsoever made, stated or represented on Landlord's behalf, either orally or in writing (except this Lease), has induced Tenant to enter into this lease." The lease also stipulated that Callis would not conduct any type of business commonly called a discount store, surplus store, or other similar business. Later, Colonial did, in fact, lease space to discount stores, and Callis sued Colonial for breach of the lease contract. Will Callis succeed in her claim? Discuss fully. [*Callis v. Colonial Properties, Inc.*, 597 So.2d 660 (Ala. 1991)]

A QUESTION OF ETHICS AND SOCIAL RESPONSIBILITY

34-14. *The Stanards have owned lakeshore property since 1963. In 1969, the Urbans purchased lakeshore property adjoining the Stanards' lot. They used the property for a summer cabin from 1969 through 1974. In 1975, the Urbans converted the summer cabin into a year-round home and moved there permanently. Since 1969, the Urbans have used a grassy area of land—part of which belonged to the Stanards—up to a wooded area between the two houses. Between 1969 and 1988, the Urbans mowed the grassy area and kept the weeds down, let their children and grandchildren play in the grassy area, and in winter stored their boat dock on the grassy area. In 1981, the Urbans constructed a white tin storage shed—mounted on a concrete slab—on the grassy area. Most of the shed was located on the Stanards' property. In 1988, the Stanards brought a lawsuit against the Urbans for trespass and sought removal of the white shed. The Urbans claimed that they had acquired ownership of the property by adverse possession because they had used the property since 1969 (the state's statutory period for adverse possession was fifteen years). The Stanards claimed that the measurement of the statutory period should begin in 1981, when the permanent storage shed was constructed. Given these circumstances, consider the following questions.* [Stanard v. Urban, 453 N.W.2d 733 *(Minn.App. 1990)*]

1. Do you think that the Urbans' use of the Stanards' property *prior to* 1981 (when the shed was built) met the requirements for adverse possession? That is, was the use actual, open, hostile, continuous, and exclusive during those years? Or is this situation similar to many others in which there are no fences between neighboring lots and the owners and their families occasionally trespass on each other's property?
2. Would the fact that the Urbans, sometime between 1980 and 1982, offered to purchase the parcel of property in question from the Stanards affect your answer to the above question?
3. At what point should trespass on another's property constitute adverse possession? For example, if your neighbors customarily store their boat partially on your property, and you do not object, should this circumstance trigger a statutory period for adverse possession? What if your neighbors' children also customarily play on your side of the boundary line between your property and your neighbors' property?
4. Why do you think that state statutes permit people to acquire title to property by adverse possession? What public policy is reflected in these statutes?

FOR CRITICAL ANALYSIS

34-15. *Real property law dates back hundreds of years. What changes have occurred in society, including business and technological changes, that have affected the development and application of real property law? (Hint: Was air space an issue three hundred years ago?)*

Chapter 35

Insurance, Wills, and Trusts

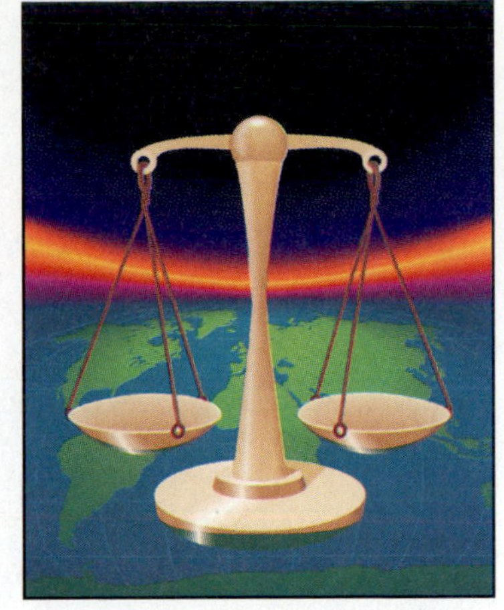

"Insurance is part charity and part business, but all common sense."

Calvin Coolidge, 1872–1933
(Thirtieth president of the United States, 1923–1929)

Most individuals insure both real and personal property (as well as their lives). As Calvin Coolidge asserted, insurance is "all common sense"—by insuring our property, we protect ourselves against damage and loss. After discussing insurance, which is a foremost concern of all property owners, we will examine how property is passed upon the death of its owner. Certainly, the laws of succession of property are a necessary corollary to the concept of private ownership of property. Our laws require that upon death, title to the property of a decedent (one who has recently died) must be delivered in full somewhere. In this chapter we will see that this can be done by will, through trusts, or through state laws prescribing distribution of property among heirs or next of kin.

❖ Insurance

Insurance is a contract by which the insurance company (insurer) promises to pay a sum of money or give something of value to another (either the insured or the beneficiary) in the event that the insured is injured or the insured's property sustains damage as a result of particular, stated contingencies. Basically, insurance is an arrangement for *transferring and allocating risk*. In many cases, **risk** can be described as a prediction concerning potential loss based on known and unknown factors. Insurance, however, involves much more than a game of chance.

INSURANCE
A contract in which, for a stipulated consideration, one party agrees to compensate the other for loss on a specific subject by a specified peril.

RISK
A specified contingency or peril.

There are many precautions that may be taken to protect against the hazards of life. For example, an individual may wear a seat belt to protect against automobile injuries or install smoke detectors to guard against injury from the risk of fire. Of course, no one can predict whether an accident or a fire will ever occur, but individuals and businesses must establish plans to protect their personal and financial interests should some event threaten to undermine their security. This concept is known as **risk management.** The most common method of risk management is the transfer of certain risks from the individual to the insurance company.

RISK MANAGEMENT
Planning that is undertaken to protect one's interest should some event threaten to undermine its security. In the context of insurance, transferring certain risks from the insured to the insurance company.

Risk is transferred to an insurance company by a contractual agreement. The insurance contract and its provisions will be examined in this section. First, however, we look at the concept of risk pooling, insurance classifications, and insurance terminology.

The Concept of Risk Pooling

All types of insurance companies use the principle of risk pooling; that is, they spread the risk among a large number of people—the pool—to make the premiums small

◆ **Exhibit 35–1**
Insurance Classifications

TYPE OF INSURANCE	COVERAGE
Accident	Covers expenses, losses, and suffering incurred by the insured because of accidents causing physical injury and any consequent disability; sometimes includes a specified payment to heirs of the insured if death results from an accident.
All-risk	Covers all losses that the insured may incur except those resulting from fraud on the part of the insured.
Automobile	May cover damage to automobiles resulting from specified hazards or occurrences (such as fire, vandalism, theft, or collision); normally provides protection against liability for personal injuries and property damage resulting from the operation of the vehicle.
Casualty	Protects against losses that may be incurred by the insured as a result of being held liable for personal injuries or property damage sustained by others.
Credit	Pays to a creditor the balance of a debt upon the disability, death, insolvency, or bankruptcy of the debtor; often offered by lending institutions.
Decreasing-term life	Provides life insurance; requires uniform payments over the life (term) of the policy, but with a decreasing face value, or amount of coverage.
Employer's liability	Insures employers against liability for injuries or losses sustained by employees during the course of their employment; covers claims not covered under workers' compensation insurance.
Fidelity or guaranty	Provides indemnity against losses in trade or losses caused by the dishonesty of employees, the insolvency of debtors, or breaches of contract.
Fire	Covers losses caused to the insured as a result of fire.
Floater	Covers movable property, as long as the property is within the territorial boundaries specified in the contract.
Group	Provides individual life, medical, or disability insurance coverage but is obtainable through a group of persons, usually employees; the policy premium is paid either entirely by the employer or partially by the employer and partially by the employee.

compared with the coverage offered. Life insurance companies, for example, know that only a small proportion of the individuals in any particular age group will die in any one year. If a large percentage of this age group pays premiums to the company in exchange for a benefit payment in case of death, there will be a sufficient amount of money to pay the beneficiaries of the policyholders who die. Through the extensive correlation of data over a period of time, insurers can estimate fairly accurately the total amount they will have to pay if they insure a particular group and the rates they will have to charge each member of the group so they can make the necessary payments and still show a profit.

Classifications of Insurance

Insurance is classified according to the nature of the risk involved. For example, fire insurance, casualty insurance, life insurance, and title insurance apply to different types of risk. Furthermore, policies of these types differ in the persons and interests that they protect. This is reasonable, because the types of losses that are expected and the types that are foreseeable or unforeseeable vary with the nature of the activity. See Exhibit 35–1 for a list of insurance classifications.

◆ **Exhibit 35–1**
Insurance Classifications (Continued)

TYPE OF INSURANCE	COVERAGE
Health	Covers expenses incurred by the insured resulting from physical injury or illness and other expenses relating to health and life maintenance.
Homeowners	Protects homeowners against some or all risks of loss to their residences and the residences' contents or liability related to such property.
Key-person	Protects a business in the event of the death or disability of a key employee.
Liability	Protects against liability imposed on the insured resulting from injuries to the person or property of another.
Life	Covers the death of the policyholder. Upon the death of the insured, an amount specified in the policy is paid by the insurer to the insured's beneficiary.
Major medical	Protects the insured against major hospital, medical, or surgical expenses.
Malpractice	Protects professionals (doctors, lawyers, and others) against malpractice claims brought against them by their patients or clients; a form of liability insurance.
Marine	Covers movable property (ships, freight, or cargo) against certain perils or navigation risks during a specific voyage or time period.
Mortgage	Covers a mortgage loan; the insurer pays the balance of the mortgage to the creditor upon the death or disability of the debtor.
No-fault auto	Covers personal injury and (sometimes) property damage resulting from automobile accidents. The insured submits his or her claims to his or her own insurance company, regardless of who was at fault. A person may sue the party at fault or that party's insurer only in cases involving serious medical injury and consequent high medical costs. Governed by state "no-fault" statutes.
Term life	Provides life insurance for a specified period of time (term) with no cash surrender value; usually renewable.
Title	Protects against any defects in title to real property and any losses incurred as a result of existing claims against or liens on the property at the time of purchase.

Insurance Terminology

An insurance contract is called a **policy;** the consideration paid to the insurer is called a **premium;** and the insurance company is sometimes called an **underwriter.**

POLICY
In insurance law, the contract of indemnity against a contingent loss between the insurer and the insured.

PREMIUM
In insurance law, the price for insurance protection for a specified period of time.

UNDERWRITER
In insurance law, the one assuming a risk in return for the payment of a premium; the insurer. In securities law, any person, banker, or syndicate that guarantees a definite sum of money to a business or government in return for the issue of stock or bonds, usually for resale purposes.

Parties The parties to an insurance policy are the *insurer* (the insurance company) and the *insured* (the person covered by its provisions or the holder of the policy). Insurance contracts are usually obtained through an *agent*, who ordinarily works for the insurance company, or through a *broker*, who is ordinarily an *independent contractor*. When a broker deals with an applicant for insurance, the broker is, in effect, the applicant's agent. In contrast, an insurance agent is an agent of the insurance company, not the applicant. As a general rule, the insurance company is bound by the acts of its agents when they act within the agency relationship (discussed in Chapter 23). A broker, however, has no relationship with the insurance company and is an agent of the insurance applicant. In most situations, state law determines the status of all parties writing or obtaining insurance.

Insurable Interest A person can insure anything in which he or she has an **insurable interest.** Without this insurable interest, there is no enforceable contract,

INSURABLE INTEREST
An interest either in a person's life or well-being or in property that is sufficiently substantial that insuring against injury to the person or damage to the property does not amount to a mere wagering (betting) contract.

and a transaction to insure would have to be treated as a wager. In the case of real and personal property, an insurable interest exists when the insured derives a pecuniary benefit (a benefit consisting of or relating to money) from the preservation and continued existence of the property. Put another way, one has an insurable interest in property when one would sustain a pecuniary loss from its destruction. In the case of life insurance, a person must have a reasonable expectation of benefit from the continued life of another in order to have an insurable interest in that person's life. The benefit may be pecuniary (as with so-called *key-person insurance*, which insures the lives of important officers, usually in small companies), or it may be founded upon the relationship between the parties (by blood or affinity). Also, the insurable interest in life insurance must exist at the time the policy is obtained. Conversely, for property insurance, the insurable interest must exist at the time the loss occurs but need not exist when the policy is purchased. The existence of an insurable interest is a primary concern in determining liability under an insurance policy.

The Insurance Contract

An insurance contract is governed by the general principles of contract law, although the insurance industry is heavily regulated by each state. The filled-in application form for insurance is usually attached to the policy and made a part of the insurance contract. Thus, an insurance applicant is bound by any false statements that appear in the application (subject to certain exceptions). Because the insurance company evaluates the risk factors based on the information included in the insurance application, misstatements or misrepresentations can void a policy, especially if the insurance company can show that it would not have extended insurance if it had known the facts.

Several aspects of the insurance contract will be treated here, including when the contract takes effect, important contract provisions, cancellation of the policy, and defenses that can be raised by insurance companies against payment on a policy.

Timing The effective date of an insurance contract is important. In some instances, the insurance applicant is not protected until a formal written policy is issued. In other situations, the applicant is protected between the time the application is received and the time the insurance company either accepts or rejects it. Four facts should be kept in mind:

1. A broker is merely the agent of an applicant. Therefore, until the broker obtains a policy, the applicant normally is not insured.
2. A person who seeks insurance from an insurance company's agent will usually be protected from the moment the application is made, provided—in the case of life insurance—that some form of premium has been paid. Between the time the application is received and either rejected or accepted, the applicant is covered (possibly subject to medical examination). Usually, the agent will write a memorandum, or **binder,** indicating that a policy is pending and stating its essential terms.

BINDER
A written, temporary insurance policy.

3. If the parties agree that the policy will be issued and delivered at a later time, the contract is not effective until the policy is issued and delivered or sent to the applicant, depending on the agreement. Thus, any loss sustained between the time of application and the delivery of the policy is not covered.
4. Parties may agree that a life insurance policy will be binding at the time the insured pays the first premium, or the policy may be expressly contingent on the applicant's passing a physical examination. In the latter case, if the applicant pays the premium and passes the examination, then the policy coverage is in effect. If the applicant pays the premium but dies before having the physical examination,

then to collect, the applicant's estate must show that the applicant would have passed the examination had he or she not died.

Coverage on an insurance policy can begin when a binder is written, when the policy is issued, or, depending on the terms of the contract, after a certain period of time has elapsed. In the following case, the question is whether insurance coverage ever became effective or even existed because, owing to a clerical error, the insured's coverage was not reflected in the computer records.

Case 35.1
HUMANA HEALTH CARE PLANS v. SNYDER-GILBERT
Court of Appeals of Indiana, 1992.
596 N.E.2d 299.

HISTORICAL AND ECONOMIC SETTING *In the marketing of any product or service, economy can be achieved through a high volume of transactions. Insurance is no different. The primary method of attaining economy in the insurance field is through selling group insurance (a single contract that provides coverage for many individuals). In the United States, the first modern group insurance policies were issued by the Equitable Life Assurance Society in 1911. These policies provided life or health insurance coverage for the employees of a single employer. Group insurance is now available for the members of many other groups, including unions, industry organizations that include the employees of more than one employer, and trade and professional associations.*

FACTS Charis Snyder-Gilbert, a school psychologist, enrolled herself and her husband in a group health plan offered through the school system. The insurance was to take effect on October 1, 1989, and thereafter monthly premiums ($1 a month for herself and $150.22 for her husband) were deducted from her paycheck. The insurer, Humana Health Care Plans, entered both names separately into its computer system, but owing to a clerical mistake, the computer entry for Mr. Gilbert indicated that his coverage both began and ended on October 1, 1989. During the following year, Mr. Gilbert submitted two claims totaling $69, but Humana denied both claims. Because of the small amount, the Gilberts chose not to dispute the denials and paid the amount themselves. In October 1990, the clerical error came to light. Humana told the Gilberts that Mr. Gilbert was, in fact, covered under the group plan and had been since October 1, 1989. Charis Snyder-Gilbert, apparently realizing that paying $69 for the two claims was cheaper than paying the $1,807.84 that had been deducted from her paycheck for Mr. Gilbert's coverage, filed suit to recover the premiums. The trial court held that Humana, by denying the two claims, had materially breached the insurance contract, entitling Snyder-Gilbert to a refund of the premiums. Humana appealed.

ISSUE Did the clerical error and the denial of the two claims entitle Snyder-Gilbert to a refund of the premiums?

DECISION No. The appellate court reversed the trial court's judgment.

REASON The court stated that "[i]t is axiomatic that a court cannot award a refund of premiums paid to secure insurance once the insurance company has been put at risk on behalf of the insured." Here, a valid offer (Snyder-Gilbert's enrollment form) and acceptance (entry of the Gilberts into Humana's computer records) had been made, and as a result an insurance contract existed from that point on. Humana was thus at risk for any legitimate claims submitted by Mr. Gilbert after October 1, 1989. "Furthermore," said the court, "we fail to see how Humana's computer error could legally shield it from risk." Although Indiana courts had not directly addressed the issue, the court noted that the Mississippi Supreme Court had consistently held, in similar cases, that "error or mistake does not constitute an arguable reason for failure to honor a just claim." The court concluded that "regardless of its computer error, Humana was still legally at risk for any and all legitimate claims of Mr. Gilbert that occurred after his coverage was erroneously terminated." Because Humana remained at risk, the trial court "erred as a matter of law in awarding a refund of premiums."

Provisions and Clauses Some of the important provisions and clauses contained in insurance contracts are listed and defined in Exhibit 35–2. The courts are increasingly cognizant of the fact that most people do not have the special training

◆ **Exhibit 35–2**
Insurance Contract Provisions and Clauses

Incontestability clause	An incontestability clause provides that after a policy has been in force for a specified length of time—usually two or three years—the insurer cannot contest statements made in the application.
Coinsurance clause	A coinsurance clause provides that if the owner insures his or her property up to a specified percentage—usually 80 percent—of its value, she or he will recover any loss up to the face amount of the policy. If the insurance is for less than the fixed percentage, the owner is responsible for a proportionate share of the loss.
Appraisal clause and arbitration clause	Insurance policies frequently provide that if the parties cannot agree on the amount of a loss covered under the policy of the value of the property lost, an appraisal, or estimate, by an impartial and qualified third party can be demanded. Similarly, many insurance policies include clauses that call for arbitration of disputes that may arise between the insurer and the insured concerning the settlement of claims.
Antilapse clause	An antilapse clause provides that the policy will not automatically lapse if no payment is made on the date due. Ordinarily, under such a provision, the insured has a *grace period* of thirty or thirty-one days within which to pay an overdue premium before the policy is canceled.
Cancellation	Cancellation of an insurance policy can occur for various reasons, depending on the type of insurance. When an insurance company can cancel its insurance contract, the policy or a state statute usually requires that the insurer give advance written notice of the cancellation. An insurer cannot cancel—or refuse to renew—a policy because of the national origin or race of an applicant or because the insured has appeared as a witness in a case against the company.

necessary to understand the intricate terminology used in insurance policies. Thus, the words used in an insurance contract have their ordinary meaning. They are interpreted by the courts in light of the nature of the coverage involved. When there is an ambiguity in the policy, the provision is interpreted against the insurance company. When the written policy has not been delivered and it is unclear whether an insurance contract actually exists, the uncertainty will be resolved against the insurance company. The court will presume that the policy is in effect unless the company can show otherwise.

Cancellation The insured can cancel a policy at any time, and the insurer can cancel under certain circumstances. When an insurance company can cancel its insurance contract, the policy or a state statute usually requires that the insurer give advance written notice of the cancellation to the insured.

Cancellation of an insurance policy can occur for various reasons, depending on the type of insurance. For example, automobile insurance can be canceled for nonpayment of premiums or suspension of the insured's driver's license. Property insurance can be canceled for nonpayment of premiums or for other reasons, including the insured's fraud or misrepresentation, conviction for a crime that increases the hazard insured against, or gross negligence that increases the hazard insured against. Life and health policies can be canceled because of false statements made by the insured in the application. An insurer cannot cancel—or refuse to renew—a policy for discriminatory reasons or other reasons that violate public policy (see this chapter's *Business Law in Action*, for example) or because the insured has appeared as a witness in a case against the company.

The following case involves a group life insurance plan that was canceled because the employer failed to pay the premiums. The question before the court was whether the employer could be held liable for not notifying its employees that the coverage had been canceled.

Case 35.2
McCARTHY v. LOUISVILLE CARTAGE CO.
Court of Appeals of Kentucky, 1990.
796 S.W.2d 10.

HISTORICAL AND ECONOMIC SETTING *Sometimes, the administrator of a group insurance program makes mistakes. For example, an employer that acts as an administrator for a group plan may fail to notify the insurer of a new employee or may fail to pay its part of the premium for the employee's coverage. In those cases, the issue concerns who bears the effect of the mistake—the employer, the insurer, or the employee. When coverage provided under a group plan terminates altogether, notice must generally be given to the individuals who were insured under the plan. In this situation, if an employer who acts as an administrator for a group plan fails to provide that notice, the issue concerns who bears the effect of that failure—the employer or the insured. As insurance costs rise and more employers cancel group insurance policies or allow them to lapse, the number of disputes resulting from termination is also increasing.*

FACTS Ronald McCarthy was employed by Louisville Cartage Company as a truck driver. As part of his employment benefits, McCarthy was covered by a group life insurance plan that was paid for entirely by his employer. When McCarthy died and his wife sought to collect on the policy as her husband's beneficiary, she learned that the employer had let the policy lapse without notifying the employees that they were no longer covered by the life insurance plan. Mrs. McCarthy sued the employer to recover the proceeds under the policy, alleging that the employer was estopped from canceling coverage without notice to the employees, even though the life insurance plan was voluntary on the part of the employer. The trial court directed a verdict for the employer, holding that the employer did not have a legal duty to notify employees of the lapsed coverage and therefore Mrs. McCarthy could not establish an action based on promissory estoppel. Mrs. McCarthy appealed.

ISSUE Could Mrs. McCarthy maintain an action against the employer based on promissory estoppel?

DECISION Yes. The judgment of the trial court was thus reversed and the case remanded for trial.

REASON The court stated that "[t]he whole theory of a promissory estoppel action is that detrimental reliance becomes a substitute for consideration under the facts" and thus the absence of a contract between Mr. McCarthy and the company was irrelevant. It was reasonable for the employer to expect that the employee's continued employment would be induced by virtue of its promise to provide insurance coverage. An unjust result could be avoided only by giving effect to that promise. Consequently, the court found that the true issue in this case was not whether the company should have given notice that the policy was being terminated but instead whether Mrs. McCarthy had "set forth a *prima facie* case of estoppel sufficient to preclude the directed verdict rendered below." The court declared that it was not unreasonable to conclude that the McCarthys would rely on the supposed existence of the coverage. Accordingly, the court remanded the case for trial.

Defenses against Payment In attempting to avoid payment on a policy claim, an insurance company can raise any of the defenses that would be valid in any ordinary action on a contract and some defenses that do not apply in ordinary contract actions. If the insurance company can show that the policy was procured by fraud, misrepresentation, or violation of warranties, it may have a valid defense for not paying on a claim. Improper actions, such as those that are against public policy or that are otherwise illegal, can also give the insurance company a defense against the payment of a claim or allow it to rescind the contract.

An insurance company can be prevented from asserting some defenses that are normally available. For example, if a company tells an insured that information requested on a form is optional and the insured provides it anyway, the company cannot use the information to avoid its contractual obligation under the insurance contract. Similarly, incorrect statements as to the age of the insured normally do not provide the company with a way to escape payment on the death of the insured.

In the following case, an inaccurate answer to a pertinent question on an application for a mortgage life insurance policy was successfully used by the insurance company to deny a claim following the policyowner's death.

Case 35.3 

BERTHIAUME v. MINNESOTA MUTUAL LIFE INSURANCE CO.

Court of Appeals of Minnesota, 1986.
388 N.W.2d 15.

HISTORICAL AND POLITICAL SETTING *Although misrepresentation often arises in connection with claims under insurance policies, the issue seems to arise more frequently in connection with applications for insurance. Insurance involves a considerable amount of money, as well as personal interests and public policy. For this reason, state legislatures have been politically motivated to devote time and effort to drafting statutes that address misrepresentation in insurance claims and applications. There are differences among the statutes, but generally they provide that an insurer has the option to void an insurance contract if it discovers that the insured has willfully misrepresented a material fact and the misrepresentation has materially increased the risk of the insurer.*

FACTS On April 16, 1982, Frances and Michael Berthiaume made a written application for mortgage life insurance with the Minnesota Mutual Life Insurance Company. The policy sought was to provide $44,308.37 in insurance coverage to cover the amount of the Berthiaumes' loan balance on the mortgage for their house, for a monthly premium of $12.42. Mr. Berthiaume did not take a physical examination for the policy, but in filling out the application he answered "no" to a question asking whether he had ever been treated for or had ever been advised that he had high blood pressure. The answer Mr. Berthiaume gave was incorrect; in fact, he had been diagnosed as having hypertension four months before the application was made. In October of 1982, Mr. Berthiaume became ill, and he died two months later. When his widow submitted a claim for the mortgage insurance, the insurance company denied payment, citing Mr. Berthiaume's inaccurate answer on the application. Minnesota Mutual sought summary judgment, which was granted by the trial court. Mrs. Berthiaume appealed.

ISSUE Did Mr. Berthiaume's inaccurate answer on the insurance policy application void Minnesota Mutual's obligation to pay on the policy?

DECISION Yes. The Minnesota Court of Appeals affirmed the trial court's decision to grant summary judgment to the insurance company.

REASON The state law of Minnesota allows an insurer to void an insurance policy issued without a prior medical examination if the insured willfully misstated necessary information or intentionally misled the insurance company. The materiality of a misrepresentation is measured by the extent to which the disclosure influenced the insurer's decision to accept the risk of coverage, not by the degree of causal connection between the false statement and the loss protected by the policy. Here, it is clear that Mr. Berthiaume failed to disclose that he had been advised by his doctor that he had high blood pressure and had been treated by the doctor for that condition. Thus, the court concluded that the insurance company deserved summary judgment in this case.

❖ Wills

"Nothing in his life became him like . . . leaving it."

William Shakespeare, 1564–1616
(English dramatist and poet)

Private ownership of property leads logically to both the protection of that property by insurance coverage while the owner is alive and the transfer of that property upon the death of the owner to those designated by the owner. At common law, people had no way to control the distribution of their property after death. The power of transfer or distribution is derived solely from statutes originating in feudal England that strictly controlled the transfer of property at death. The heir (the one who inherited) was required to pay the feudal lord a sum of money[1] for the privilege of succeeding to his or her ancestor's lands. When a tenant died without heirs, title to the land reverted to the feudal lord of the manor.[2]

Sweeping land reforms in England during the 1920s replaced inheritance payments and reversion of title to the feudal lord with the right of the crown to receive

1. The sum, called a *relief,* was usually equivalent to one year's rent.
2. C. J. Moynihan, *Introduction to the Law of Real Property* (St. Paul: West Publishing Co., 1962), p. 22.

Business Law in Action

An Old Story with a New Twist

Insurance companies have far more resources than most individuals do when it comes to disputing insurance claims, and the courts normally do what they can to make sure that policyholders and their beneficiaries are treated fairly. An insurance company that resorts to unfair tactics to avoid payment on a policy may find less than a warm reception in the courtroom—as New England Mutual Life Insurance Company learned when it attempted to avoid payment to a beneficiary of one of its policyholders.

The policyholder was Jeffrey Duke, who had purchased life insurance from New England Mutual. Duke listed as his beneficiary his lover and business advisor, William Remmelink. On his insurance application, however, Duke had described his beneficiary as merely his business partner. After Duke died of AIDS, the insurance company brought an action against William Johnson, the executor of Duke's estate, to rescind the insurance contract on the ground that Duke had misrepresented his relationship with his beneficiary. The court found that there was no misrepresentation. "Even if there was misrepresentation," stated the court, "it was not material. Plaintiff [New England Mutual] mistakenly likens the description of a beneficiary to a warranty and argues that a mischaracterization of a beneficiary is grounds for rescission, similar to the misrepresentation of a pre-existing health condition."

The court viewed the matter otherwise, reasoning that the relationship between the insured person and his or her beneficiary "is considered to be a description and not a warranty. The instant case involves a description of a non-traditional * * * relationship, not a warranty, which, even if misrepresented, would not invalidate the policy."

The court did not stop there. It went on to say that the insurance company should have to pay attorneys' fees as well. The court noted that "[w]hile attorneys' fees are rarely awarded in actions involving breach of contract, two exceptions exist which are applicable here. First, attorneys' fees can be awarded to insureds forced to defend against an insurer's action to escape coverage. Second, attorneys' fees may be awarded where there has been an unreasonable, bad faith denial of coverage." The court found that New England Mutual's actions evidenced "a gross disregard for its policy obligation." The court said, "Upon learning that Duke had contracted AIDS and that there would, most likely, be a claim asserted under the life insurance policy within a short period of time, plaintiff searched through its files in an effort to determine a way to escape its obligation. * * * Such an investigation to find a bogus basis for disclaiming because the insured was a male homosexual (at higher risk for contracting AIDS than the general public) constitutes discrimination, both on the basis of disability and marital status."[a]

a. *New England Mutual Life Insurance Co. v. Johnson*, 589 N.Y.S.2d 736 (1992).

inheritance taxes and to take property of an **intestate** (one who dies without a valid will) without heirs. Modern legislation has changed the terminology but not the result. In all states, title to land of persons who die intestate and without heirs vests in the state; the right to make a will and the ways to make one are determined by state law. To be valid, wills normally must follow statutory requirements.

INTESTATE
As a noun, one who has died without having created a valid will; as an adjective, the state of having died without a will.

The Purpose of a Will

A **will** is the final declaration of how a person desires to have his or her property disposed of after death. A will is referred to as a *testamentary disposition* of property. It is a formal instrument that must follow exactly the requirements of state law to be effective. The reasoning behind such a strict requirement is obvious. A will becomes effective only after death. No attempts to modify it after the death of the maker are allowed because the court cannot ask the maker to confirm the attempted modifications. (But sometimes the wording of the will must be "interpreted" by the courts.) A will can serve other purposes besides the distribution of property. It can appoint a guardian for minor children or incapacitated adults. It can also appoint a personal representative to settle the affairs of the deceased.

WILL
An instrument directing what is to be done with the testator's property upon his or her death, made by the testator and revocable during his or her lifetime. No interests pass until the testator dies.

Ethical Perspective

Ethics and Insurance—the "Moral Hazard" Problem

A major ethical concern in the area of insurance involves *moral hazard.* In the insurance industry, moral hazard occurs when insurance coverage reduces the incentive of individuals or companies to act cautiously or to guard against destruction or loss that will be paid for by their insurance companies. For example, the businessperson who takes out a large insurance policy on a building has less incentive to take care that the building is protected from fire than an individual without any insurance policy. What is the ethical responsibility of the owner of the building when insurance is in effect? Is he or she exempt from taking precautions against fire?

The same issue arises for insurance policies that cover losses from theft. For example, with insurance in effect, the property owner may have less incentive to install alarm systems, to pay for private patrol service, and so on. Also, the smaller the *deductible* in such policies, the less incentive the property owner has to prevent losses from theft. (The deductible is an amount specified in the insurance contract that the policyholder must pay on a claim—for example, the first $250 of a $500 claim.) Of course, the more claims made on such insurance policies, the higher the average insurance rate per dollar amount insured. Thus, those individuals who are careless about protecting their own property impose costs on all individuals who buy property insurance.

Moral hazard exists with medical insurance as well. The smaller the deductible, the greater the incentive for the individual to neglect the practice of preventive medicine. What is the ethical responsibility of the individual citizen in terms of providing for his or her own well-being? Does the fact that health insurance is available for individuals in the United States mean that these individuals should not be concerned about smoking, being overweight, and so on? It is argued that in the United States, too many resources are devoted to the care of those who are already sick and too few resources to preventive medicine.

TESTATOR
One who makes and executes a will.

PROBATE COURT
A court having jurisdiction over proceedings concerning the settlement of a person's estate.

EXECUTOR
A person appointed by a testator to see that his or her will is administered appropriately.

ADMINISTRATOR
One who is appointed by a court to handle the probate (disposition) of a person's estate if that person dies intestate (without a will).

DEVISE
To make a gift of real property by will.

BEQUEST
A gift by will of personal property (from the verb—*to bequeath*).

Vocabulary of Wills

Every area of law has its own special vocabulary, and the area of wills is no exception. A person who makes out a will is known as a **testator** (from the Latin *testari,* "to make a will"). The court responsible for administering any legal problems surrounding a will is called a **probate court.** When a person dies, a *personal representative* settles the affairs of the deceased. An **executor** is a personal representative named in the will; an **administrator** is a personal representative appointed by the court for a decedent who dies without a will, who fails to name an executor in the will, who names an executor lacking the capacity to serve, or who writes a will that the court refuses to admit to probate. A gift of real estate by will is generally called a **devise,** and a gift of personal property by will is called a **bequest** or **legacy.** The recipient of a gift by will is a **legatee.**

Types of Gifts

Gifts by will can be specific, general, or residuary. A *specific* devise or bequest (legacy) describes particular property that can be distinguished from all the rest of the testator's property (for example, a specific bequest may consist of a gold watch). A *general* devise or bequest (legacy) does not single out any particular item of property to be transferred by will but usually specifies a sum of money to be paid from the remaining assets. If the assets of an estate are insufficient to pay in full all general bequests provided for in the will, an *abatement,* by which the legatees receive reduced benefits, takes place. If a legatee dies prior to the death of the testator or before the legacy is payable, a *lapsed legacy* results. At common law, the legacy failed. Today, the legacy may not lapse if the legatee is in a certain blood relationship to the testator (such as a child, grandchild, brother, or sister) and has left a child or other surviving descendant.

Sometimes a will provides that any assets remaining after specific gifts have been made and debts are paid are to be distributed through a *residuary* clause. This is necessary when the exact amount to be distributed cannot be determined until all other gifts and payouts have been made. A residuary estate can pose problems, however, when the will does not specifically name the beneficiaries to receive the residue. In such a case, if the court cannot determine the testator's intent, the residue passes according to state laws of intestacy.

LEGACY
A gift of personal property under a will.

LEGATEE
A person who inherits property under a will.

Probate versus Nonprobate

To *probate* a will means to establish its validity and to carry the administration of the estate through a court process. Probate laws vary from state to state. In 1969, however, the American Bar Association and the National Conference of Commissioners on Uniform State Laws approved the Uniform Probate Code (UPC). The UPC codifies general principles and procedures for the resolution of conflicts in settling estates and relaxes some of the requirements for a valid will contained in earlier state laws. About a third of the states have adopted some form of the UPC. References to its provisions will be included in the remainder of this chapter when the UPC is consistent with the general practice in most states. Because succession and inheritance laws vary widely among states, one should always check the particular laws of the state involved.[3] The process of probate is time consuming and costly, and the court is involved in every step of the proceedings. Attorneys and personal representatives of decedents' estates often become involved in probate.

Many states have statutes that allow for the distribution of assets without probate proceedings. Faster and less expensive methods are then used. For example, property can be transferred by affidavit, and problems or questions can be handled during an administrative hearing. These methods are frequently referred to as *summary probate*. In addition, some state statutes provide that title to cars, savings and checking accounts, and certain other property can be passed merely by the filling out of forms. This is particularly true when most of the property is held in joint tenancy or when there is only one heir.

"If you want to see a man's true character, watch him divide an estate."

**Benjamin Franklin,
1706–1790**
(American diplomat, author, and scientist)

A majority of states provide for *family settlement agreements*, which are private agreements among the beneficiaries. Once a will is admitted to probate, the family members can agree to settle among themselves the distribution of the decedent's assets. Although a family settlement agreement speeds the settlement process, a court order is still needed to protect the estate from future creditors and to clear the title to the assets involved.

Testamentary Capacity

Not everyone who owns property necessarily qualifies to make a valid disposition of that property by will. *Testamentary capacity* requires the testator to be of legal age and sound mind *at the time the will is made*. The legal age for executing a will varies, but in most states and under the UPC the minimum age is eighteen years [UPC 2–501]. Thus, the will of a twenty-one-year-old decedent written when the person was sixteen is often invalid. The concept of "being of sound mind" refers to the testator's ability to formulate and to comprehend a personal plan for the disposition of property. Further, a testator must intend the document to be his or her last will and testament.

3. For example, California law differs substantially from the UPC.

In the following case, the question before the court was whether the testator had the required testamentary capacity. As the court notes, testamentary capacity will be presumed unless sufficient evidence exists to call such capacity into question.

Case 35.4
BOLAN v. BOLAN
Supreme Court of Alabama, 1993.
611 So.2d 1051.

HISTORICAL AND CULTURAL SETTING *In cases involving contested wills, English courts did not allow trial by jury. In actions of* ejectment *(in which a plaintiff seeks the removal of the defendant from land), English courts did allow trial by jury, even when one of the issues in the case was title to land that had been part of a testamentary disposition. When wills involving title to land came to be probated in the United States, it was believed that if those wills were contested, trial by jury should be allowed. Thus, trial by jury in will-contest cases came to be allowed in many states, including Alabama. Juries answer questions of fact. Incapacity is a question of fact. Because appellate courts do not generally consider questions of fact, an appellate court will normally not overturn the finding of a jury on the issue of incapacity as long as there is evidence to support the finding.*

FACTS Charley Bolan died on October 8, 1990, survived by six children. His will left one dollar to each of three of his children and to each child of his deceased son ("the contestants") and the remainder of his estate to the other three children ("the proponents"). The contestants claimed that the will was invalid, alleging, among other things, that Charley lacked testamentary capacity at the time the will was made. The evidence before the court was conflicting. Witnesses present at the time the will was executed testified that Charley was in sound mental condition on that occasion, and other family members testified to the same effect. But other testimony, including statements made by the contestants, indicated that Charley was "in poor health before the date of execution; that he repeatedly held conversations with his dead wife; that he refused to bathe, change his clothes, or otherwise take care of himself; and that he had rigged up a dangerous spring-gun to protect himself from intruders when no real threat existed." The case was transferred from a probate court to a state trial court, and the trial jury held for the contestants. The proponents appealed.

ISSUE Was there sufficient evidence to support a finding that Charley Bolan lacked testamentary capacity?

DECISION Yes. The trial court's judgment was affirmed.

REASON The court stated that every testator is presumed to have the capacity to make a will and the burden is on the contestant of a will to prove that testamentary capacity is lacking. "The contestant need not show that the testator suffered from permanent insanity," said the court. All that the contestant must do is show that the testator lacked testamentary capacity at the time the will was made. After reviewing the record, the court concluded that "[a]lthough the evidence was conflicting, the contestants presented sufficient evidence of a lack of testamentary capacity to support the submission of the contest to the jury on this ground."

Formal Requirements of Wills

A will must comply with statutory formalities designed to ensure that the testator understood his or her actions at the time the will was made. These formalities are intended to help prevent fraud. Unless they are followed, the will is declared void, and the decedent's property is distributed according to the laws of intestacy of that state. The requirements are not uniform among the jurisdictions. Most states, however, uphold the following basic requirements for executing a will.

1. A *will must be in writing.* A written document is generally required. The writing itself can be informal as long as it substantially complies with the statutory requirements. In some states, a will can be handwritten in crayon or ink. It can be written on a sheet or scrap of paper, on a paper bag, or on a piece of cloth. A will that is completely in the handwriting of the testator is called a **holographic** (or olographic) **will.**

HOLOGRAPHIC WILL
A will written entirely in the signer's handwriting and usually not witnessed.

2. A *will must be signed by the testator.* It is a fundamental requirement that the testator's signature appear, generally at the end of the will. Each jurisdiction dictates by statute and court decision what constitutes a signature. Initials, an X or other mark, and words like "Mom" have all been upheld as valid when it was shown that the testators intended them to be signatures.
3. A *formal (nonholographic) will must be witnessed.* A will must be attested by two and sometimes three witnesses. The number of witnesses, their qualifications, and the manner in which the witnessing must be done are generally set out in a statute. A witness can be required to be disinterested—that is, not a beneficiary under the will. By contrast, the UPC provides that a will is valid even if it is attested by an interested witness [UPC 2–505]. There are no age requirements for witnesses, but they must be mentally competent.

The purpose of witnesses is to verify that the testator actually executed (signed) the will and had the requisite intent and capacity at the time. A witness does not have to read the contents of the will. Usually, the testator and all witnesses must sign in the sight or the presence of one another, but the UPC deems it sufficient if the testator acknowledges his or her signature to the witnesses [UPC 2–502]. The UPC does not require all parties to sign in the presence of one another.
4. *Sometimes a will must be published.* A will is *published* by an oral declaration by the maker to the witnesses that the document they are about to sign is his or her "last will and testament." Publication is becoming an unnecessary formality in most states, and it is not required under the UPC.

In general, strict compliance with the preceding formalities is required before a formal document is accepted as the decedent's will. Holographic wills constitute an exception in some jurisdictions. Nevertheless, holographic wills must be signed by the decedent and their material provisions must be in the testator's handwriting for them to be probated [UPC 2–503].

Nuncupative Wills

A **nuncupative will** is an oral will made before witnesses. It is not permitted in most states. Where authorized by statute, such wills are generally valid only if made during the last illness of the testator and are therefore sometimes referred to as *deathbed wills.* Normally, only personal property (not real property) can be transferred by a nuncupative will. Statutes frequently permit soldiers and sailors to make nuncupative wills when on active duty.

NUNCUPATIVE WILL
An oral will (often called a deathbed will) made before witnesses; usually limited to transfers of personal property.

Undue Influence

A valid will is one that represents the maker's intention to transfer and distribute his or her property. When it can be shown that the decedent's plan of distribution was the result of improper pressure brought by another person, the will is declared invalid. Undue influence may be inferred by the court if the testator ignored blood relatives and named as beneficiary a nonrelative who was in constant close contact and in a position to influence the making of the will. For example, if a nurse or friend caring for the deceased at the time of death was named as beneficiary to the exclusion of all family members, the validity of the will might well be challenged on the basis of undue influence.

Revocation of Wills

An executed will is revocable by the maker at any time during the maker's lifetime. Wills can also be revoked by operation of law. Revocation can be partial or complete, and it must follow certain strict formalities.

Revocation by Act of the Maker Revocation of an executed will by an *act of the maker* can be effected by a physical act such as burning the will or by a writing that revokes the will. The physical acts by which a testator may revoke a will may include, in addition to intentionally burning it, intentionally tearing, canceling, obliterating, or destroying it or having someone else do so in the presence of the maker and at the maker's direction.[4] In some states, partial revocation by physical act of the maker is recognized. Thus, those portions of a will lined out or torn away are dropped, and the remaining parts of the will are valid. In no case, however, can a provision be crossed out and an additional or substitute provision written in. Such altered portions require reexecution (resigning) and reattestation (rewitnessing). To revoke a will by physical act, it is necessary to follow the mandates of a state statute exactly. When a state statute prescribes the exact methods for revoking a will by physical act, those are the only methods that will revoke the will.

CODICIL
A written supplement or modification to a will. Codicils must be executed with the same formalities as a will.

A will may also be wholly or partially revoked by a **codicil,** a written instrument separate from the will that amends or revokes provisions in the will. A codicil eliminates the necessity of redrafting an entire will merely to add to it or amend it. It can also be used to revoke an entire will. The codicil must be executed with the same formalities required for a will, and it must refer expressly to the will. In effect, it updates a will because the will is "incorporated by reference" into the codicil.

A *second* or *new will* can be executed that may or may not revoke the first or a prior will, depending on the language used. To revoke a prior will, the second will must use language specifically revoking other wills, such as, "This will hereby revokes all prior wills." If the second will is otherwise valid and properly executed, it will revoke all prior wills. If the express *declaration of revocation* is missing, then both wills are read together. If any of the dispositions made in the second will are inconsistent with the prior will, the second will controls.

Revocation by Operation of Law Revocation by *operation of law* occurs when marriage, divorce or annulment, or the birth of a child takes place after a will has been executed. In most states, when a testator marries after executing a will that does not include the new spouse, and then dies, the spouse can still receive the amount he or she would have taken had the testator died intestate (without a valid will). In effect, this revokes the will to the point of providing the spouse with an intestate share. The rest of the estate is passed under the will [UPC 2–301, 2–508]. If, however, the new spouse is otherwise provided for in the will (or by transfer of property outside the will), the new spouse will not be given an intestate amount.

At common law and under the UPC, divorce does not necessarily revoke the entire will. A divorce or an annulment occurring after a will has been executed will revoke those dispositions of property made under the will to the former spouse [UPC 2–508].

If a child is born after a will has been executed and if it appears that the deceased parent would have made a provision for the child, then the child is entitled to receive whatever portion of the estate he or she is allowed under state intestacy laws. Most state laws allow a child to receive some portion of a parent's estate if no provision is made in the parent's will, unless it appears from the terms of the will that the testator intended to disinherit the child. Under the UPC, the rule is the same.

"Land was never lost for want of an heir."

(English proverb)

Property Distribution Absent a Will—Intestacy Laws The rules of descent are governed by statutes of descent and distribution. That means each state can regulate

4. The destruction cannot be inadvertent. The maker's intent to revoke must be shown. Consequently, when a will has been burned or torn accidentally, it is normally recommended that the maker have a new document created so that it will not falsely appear that the maker intended to revoke the will.

how the property of a person who dies without a will is to be distributed. State laws attempt to carry out the likely intent and wishes of the decedent. These statutes are called **intestacy laws.**

INTESTACY LAWS
State laws determining the division and descent of the property of one who dies intestate (without a will).

The rules of descent vary widely from state to state. There is, however, usually a special statutory provision for the rights of the surviving spouse and children. In addition, the law provides that first the debts of the decedent must be satisfied out of his or her estate, and then the remaining assets can pass to the surviving spouse and to the children. A surviving spouse usually receives only a share of the estate—one-half if there is also a surviving child and one-third if there are two or more children. Only if no children or grandchildren survive the decedent will a surviving spouse succeed to the entire estate. Assume that Allen dies intestate and is survived by his wife, Della, and his children, Duane and Tara. Allen's property passes according to intestacy laws. After Allen's outstanding debts are paid, Della will receive the homestead (either in fee simple or as a life estate) and ordinarily a one-third to one-half interest in all other property. The remaining real and personal property will pass to Duane and Tara in equal portions.

When there is no surviving spouse or child, the order of inheritance is grandchildren, then brothers and sisters, and, in some states, parents of the decedent are the next in line to share. These relatives are usually called *lineal descendants.* If there are no lineal descendants, then *collateral heirs*—nieces, nephews, aunts, and uncles of the decedent—make up the next group to share. If there are no survivors in any of these groups, most statutes provide for the property to be distributed among the next of kin of the collateral heirs. Under intestacy laws, stepchildren are not considered kin. Legally adopted children, however, are recognized as lawful heirs of their adoptive parents. The degree to which illegitimate children are permitted to inherit is the topic of this chapter's *Landmark in the Law.*

Because state statutes differ so widely, few generalizations can be made about the laws of descent and distribution. It is extremely important to refer to the exact terms of the applicable state statutes when addressing any problem of intestacy distribution.

When an intestate is survived by descendants of deceased children, a question arises as to what share these descendants (that is, grandchildren of the intestate) will receive. ***Per stirpes*** is a method of dividing an intestate share by which, within a class or group of distributees (for example, grandchildren), the children of any one descendant take the share that their deceased parent *would have been* entitled to inherit. For example, assume that Michael, a widower, has two children, Scott and Jonathan. Scott has two children (Becky and Holly), and Jonathan has one child (Paul). Scott and Jonathan die before their father, and then Michael dies. If Michael's estate is distributed *per stirpes*, the following distribution will take place:

PER STIRPES
A Latin term meaning *by the roots.* In the law governing estate distribution, a method of distributing an intestate's estate in which a class or group of distributees take the share to which their deceased ancestor would have been entitled.

1. Becky and Holly: one-fourth each, sharing Scott's one-half share.
2. Paul: one-half, taking Jonathan's share.

Exhibit 35–3 illustrates the *per stirpes* method of distribution.

An estate may also be distributed on a ***per capita*** basis. This means that each person in a class or group takes an equal share of the estate. If Michael's estate is distributed *per capita*, Becky, Holly, and Paul will each receive a one-third share. Exhibit 35–4 illustrates the *per capita* method of distribution.

PER CAPITA
A Latin term meaning *per person.* In the law governing estate distribution, a method of distributing the property of an intestate's estate by which all the heirs receive equal shares.

Under most state intestacy laws and under the UPC, in-laws do not share in an estate. If a child dies before his or her parents, the child's spouse will not receive an inheritance upon the parents' death. Assume that Michael, a widower, has two married children, Scott and Jonathan, and no grandchildren. If Scott predeceases his father, Michael's entire estate will go to Jonathan. Scott's surviving wife will not inherit.

◆ **Exhibit 35–3**
***Per Stirpes* Distribution**
Under this method of distribution, an heir takes the share that his or her deceased parent would have been entitled to inherit, had the parent lived. This may mean that a class of distributees–the grandchildren in this example—will not inherit in equal portions. Note that Becky and Holly only receive one-fourth of Michael's estate, while Paul inherits one-half.

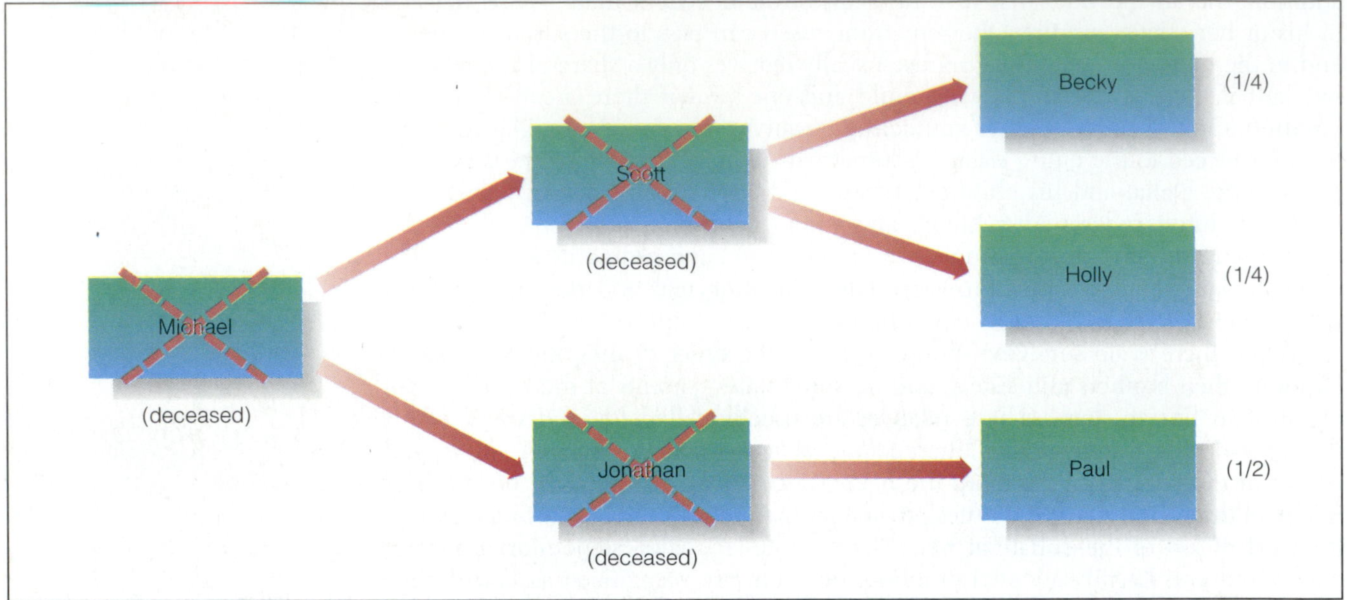

TRUST
(1) A form of business organization somewhat similar to a corporation. Originally, the trust was a device by which several corporations that were engaged in the same general line of business combined for their mutual advantage to eliminate competition and control the market for their products. The term *trust* derived from the transfer of the voting power of the corporations' shareholders to the committee or board that controlled the organization. (2) An arrangement in which title to property is held by one person (a trustee) for the benefit of another (a beneficiary).

"Put not your trust in money, but put your money in trust."

Oliver Wendell Holmes, Jr., 1841–1935
(Associate justice of the United States Supreme Court, 1902–1932)

❖ Trusts

A **trust** is any arrangement through which property is transferred from one person to a trustee to be administered for the transferor's or another party's benefit. It can also be defined as a right or property, real or personal, held by one party for the benefit of another. A trust can be created for any purpose that is not illegal or against public policy. Its essential elements are as follows:

1. A designated beneficiary.
2. A designated trustee.
3. A fund sufficiently identified to enable title to pass to the trustee.
4. Actual delivery by the settlor or grantor to the trustee with the intention of passing title.

If James conveys his farm to the First Bank of Minnesota to be held for the benefit of his daughters, he has created a trust. James is the settlor, the First Bank of Minnesota is the trustee, and James's daughters are the beneficiaries. This arrangement is illustrated in Exhibit 35–5. Numerous types of trusts can be established. In this section, we look at some of the major kinds of trusts and their characteristics.

Express Trusts

An *express trust* is one created or declared in expressed terms, usually in writing. It differs from one that is inferred by law from the conduct or dealings of the parties (an *implied trust*, to be discussed later). The two types of express trusts that will be discussed here are *inter vivos* trusts and testamentary trusts.

◆ **Exhibit 35–4**
***Per Capita* Distribution**
Under this method of distribution, all heirs in a certain class—in this case, the grandchildren—inherit equally. Note that Becky and Holly in this situation each inherit one-third, as does Paul.

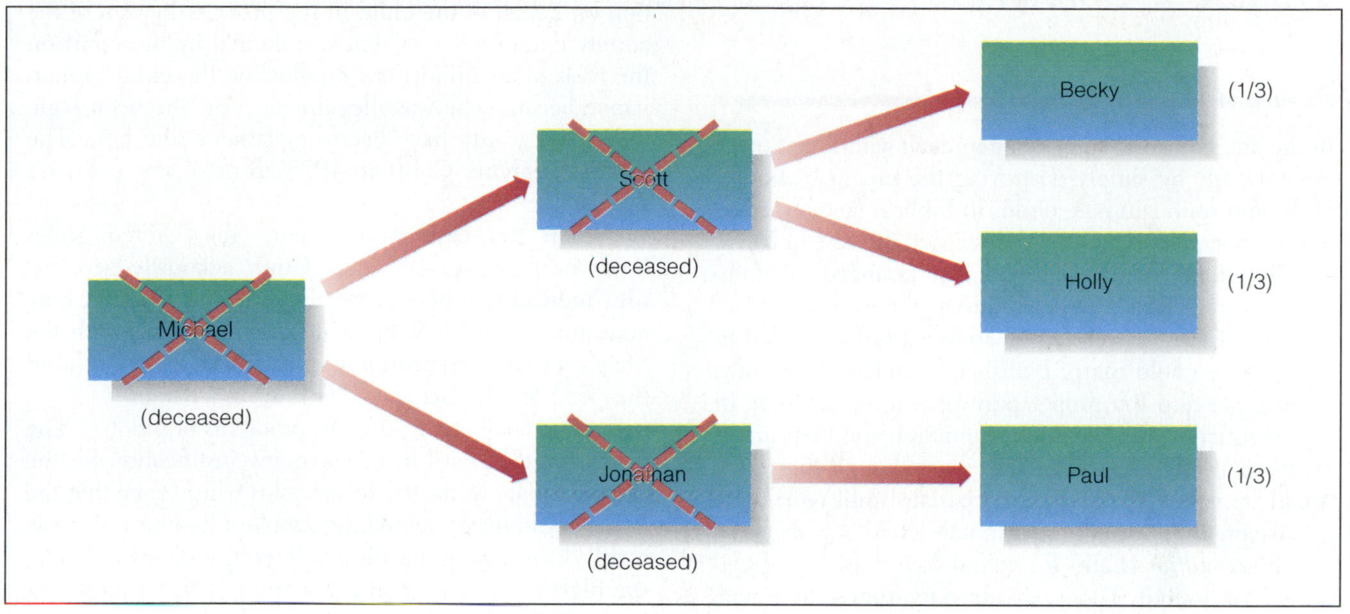

◆ **Exhibit 35–5**
Trust Arrangement
In a trust, there is a separation of interests in the trust property. The trustee takes *legal* title, which is the complete ownership and possession but which does not include the right to receive any benefits from the property. The beneficiary takes *equitable* title, which is the right to receive all benefits from the property.

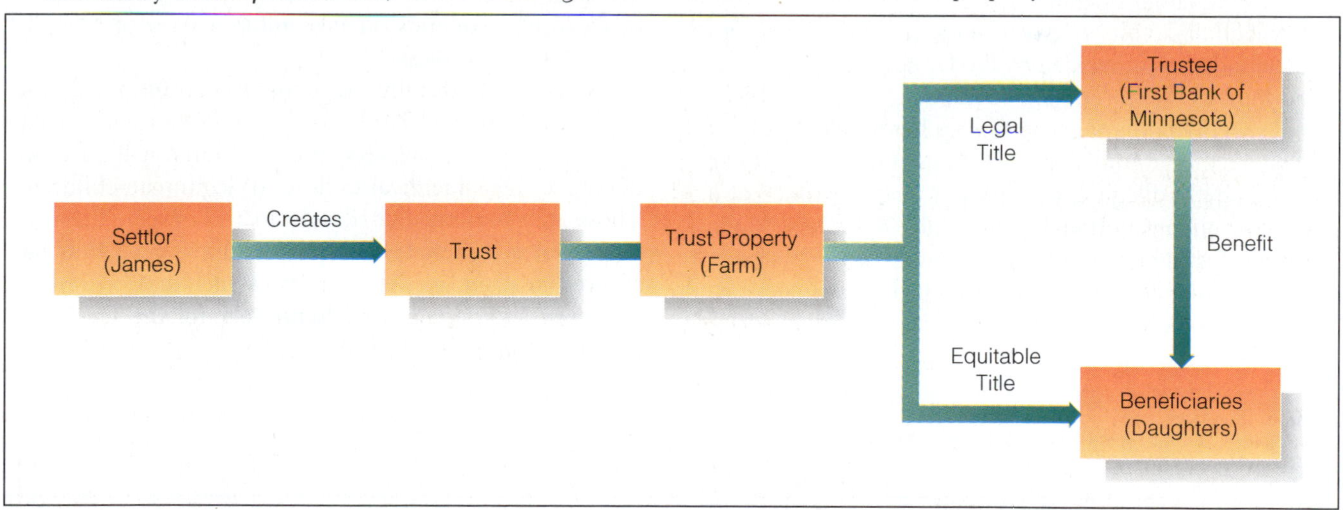

An ***inter vivos* trust** is a trust executed by a grantor during his or her lifetime. The grantor (settlor) executes a *trust deed*, and legal title to the trust property passes to the named trustee. The trustee has a duty to administer the property as directed by the grantor for the benefit and in the interest of the beneficiaries. The trustee must preserve the trust property, make it productive, and, if required by the terms of the trust agreement, pay income to the beneficiaries, all in accordance with the terms of the trust. Once the *inter vivos* trust is created, the grantor has, in effect, given over the property for the benefit of beneficiaries. Often, tax-related benefits exist in setting up this type of trust.

***INTER VIVOS* TRUST**
A trust created by the grantor (settlor) and effective during the grantor's lifetime (that is, a trust not established by a will).

Landmark in the Law

Trimble v. Gordon (1977)

In the ancient world, people often dealt with illegitimacy expeditiously by simply destroying the pregnant mother of the future illegitimate child. In biblical days, an adulteress was stoned to death—unless, as in the case of David and Bathsheba, a marriage could be arranged. In Bathsheba's case, David saved her life at the expense of her husband, Uriah, whom David arranged to have killed in battle so he could marry Bathsheba. Under Islamic law, stoning was also the proper punishment for adultery. In the Christian world, illegitimate children and their mothers were always allowed to live, even though they were usually regarded as outcasts and pariahs until recently.[a]

At common law, the illegitimate child was regarded as a *filius nullius* (Latin for "child of no one") and had no right to inherit. Today, statutes vary from state to state in regard to the inheritance laws governing illegitimate offspring. Generally, an illegitimate child is treated as the child of the mother and can inherit from her and her relatives. The child is usually not regarded as the legal child of the father with the right of inheritance unless paternity is established through some legal proceeding prior to the father's death.

A landmark case in establishing the rights of illegitimate children was decided by the United States Supreme Court in 1977. In *Trimble v. Gordon*,[b] an illegitimate child sought to inherit property from her deceased natural father on the ground that an Illinois statute prohibiting inheritance by illegitimate children in the absence of a will was unconstitutional. The child was Deta Mona Trimble, daughter of Jessie Trimble and Sherman Gordon. The paternity of the father had been established before a Cook County, Illinois, circuit court in 1973. Gordon died intestate in 1974. The mother filed a petition on behalf of the child in the probate division of the county circuit court, which was denied by the court on the basis of an Illinois law disallowing the child's inheritance because she was illegitimate. Had she been legitimate, she would have been her father's sole heir. The Illinois Supreme Court in 1975 affirmed the petition's dismissal.

When the case came before the United States Supreme Court in 1977, the Court acknowledged that the "judicial task here is the difficult one of vindicating constitutional rights without interfering unduly with the State's primary responsibility in this area * * * [a]nd the need for the States to draw 'arbitrary lines * * * to facilitate potentially difficult problems of proof.' " The Court found it hard to perceive any justification for the Illinois statute or for the lower court's insistence that the father could have avoided the problem had he just made a will. In reversing the Illinois Supreme Court decision, the high court stated that the section of the Illinois Probate Act that forbade Deta Mona to inherit her father's property "cannot be squared with the command of the Equal Protection Clause of the Fourteenth Amendment." Even though the Illinois statute rested to some extent on public policy supporting the family unit, the Court "expressly considered and rejected the argument that a State may attempt to influence the actions of men and women by imposing sanctions on the children born of their illegitimate relationships."

By declaring the Illinois statute unconstitutional, the Court invalidated similar laws of several other states. That does not mean that all illegitimate children will have inheritance rights identical to those of legitimate children. Those state statutes that discriminate between the two classes for a legitimate state purpose have been thus far allowed to stand, in the interests of each state's need to create an appropriate legal framework for the legal disposition of property at death.[c]

a. Jenny Teichman, *Illegitimacy: A Philosophical Examination* (Oxford: Blackwell, 1982), pp. 53–55.
b. 430 U.S. 762, 97 S.Ct. 1459, 52 L.Ed.2d 31 (1977).
c. UPC 2–109; *White v. Randolph*, 59 Ohio St.2d 6, 391 N.E.2d 333 (1979).

TESTAMENTARY TRUST
A trust that is created by will and therefore does not take effect until the death of the testator.

A **testamentary trust** is a trust created by a will to come into existence upon the settlor's death. Although a testamentary trust has a trustee who maintains legal title to the trust property, actions of the trustee are subject to judicial approval. This trustee can be named in the will or be appointed by the court. Thus, a testamentary trust does not fail because a trustee has not been named in the will. The legal responsibilities of the trustee are the same as in an *inter vivos* trust. If the will setting up a testamentary trust is invalid, then the trust will also be invalid. The property that was supposed to be in the trust will then pass according to intestacy laws, not according to the terms of the trust.

Implied Trusts

Sometimes a trust is imposed by law, even in the absence of an express trust. Customarily, these *implied trusts* are divided into constructive and resulting trusts.

A **constructive trust** differs from an express trust in that it arises by operation of law. Whenever a transaction takes place in which the person who takes a legal estate in property cannot also enjoy the beneficial interest without violating some established principle of equity, the court will create a constructive trust. In effect, the legal owner becomes a trustee for the parties who, in equity, are actually entitled to the beneficial enjoyment that flows from the trust. One element of a constructive trust is a wrongful action. To illustrate, Kraft and Lattimore are partners in buying, developing, and selling real estate. Kraft learns through the staff of the partnership that a vacant lot will soon come on the market that the staff will recommend that the partnership purchase. Kraft purchases the property secretly in his own name, violating his fiduciary relationship. When these facts are discovered, a court will determine that Kraft must hold the property in trust for the partnership.

CONSTRUCTIVE TRUST
A trust created by operation of law against one who wrongfully has obtained or holds a legal right to property that the person should not, in equity and good conscience, hold and enjoy.

A **resulting trust** arises from the conduct of the parties. Here, the trust results from, or is created by, the *apparent intention* of the parties. Because the trust is created by law, the conduct of the parties evidencing the intent to create a trust relationship is carefully scrutinized. To illustrate, Garrison wants to put one acre of land she owns on the market for sale. Because she is going out of the country for two years and would not be able to deed the property to a buyer during that period, Garrison conveys the property to her good friend Oswald. Oswald can then sell and deed the property with the proceeds to be turned over to Garrison. Because the intent of the transaction to deed the property to Oswald is neither a sale nor a gift, the property will be held in trust (a resulting trust) by Oswald for the benefit of Garrison. Therefore upon Garrison's return, Oswald will be required to either deed back the property to Garrison or if the property has been sold, to turn over the proceeds (held in trust) to Garrison.

RESULTING TRUST
A trust implied in law from the apparent intentions of the parties to a given transaction. A trust in which a party holds actual legal title but for the benefit of another, frequently the grantor.

The following case illustrates the concept of a constructive trust.

Case 35.5
THOMAS v. FALES
Supreme Judicial Court of Maine, 1990.
577 A.2d 1181.

HISTORICAL AND CULTURAL SETTING *English courts began to use the constructive trust as a remedy in the seventeenth century. It was used as a remedy in the eighteenth century under the Statute of Frauds (which was enacted in 1677) to prevent injustice. Since those early cases, the constructive trust has been used mainly to deprive a person in a fiduciary position of a gain obtained through the misuse of the position. In the United States, most courts do not require the existence of a fiduciary relationship to impose a constructive trust. Thus, for the most part, the use of the constructive trust as a remedy to prevent unjust enrichment has occurred in this country.*

FACTS Paula Thomas was formerly married to Charles Fales. During their marriage, Charles sold illegal drugs and frequently had large amounts of cash resulting from those transactions. To avoid the increasing scrutiny of a neighbor (a police officer), Charles decided to purchase a home (the Winslow property) in another area in September 1983. Allegedly to avert suspicion concerning his drug activity, Charles had his brother Steven purchase the property in Steven's name. Charles, however, provided Steven with the money for the down payment, and Charles and Paula lived in the home and paid the mortgage payments and all other expenses. Eventually, Paula separated from Charles; she left the home, and it was rented to a third party. In 1988, Paula and Charles were divorced, and the divorce judgment awarded her all of their right, title, and interest in the Winslow property. Steven refused to convey the property to Paula, contending that he was the legal owner. Paula then brought an action seeking the imposition of a constructive trust on the Winslow property and an order that legal title be conveyed to her. The trial court imposed a constructive trust on the property for the benefit of Paula and ordered that it be conveyed to her. Steven appealed.

ISSUE Should the court have imposed a constructive trust on the Winslow property for the benefit of Paula?

Case 35.5—Continued

DECISION Yes. The trial court's judgment was affirmed. The appellate court could find no clear error in the lower court's findings of fact and no abuse of discretion in its imposition of a constructive trust on the Winslow property for the benefit of Paula.

REASON The appellate court held that "[a] constructive trust may be imposed when a party holding legal title to property stands in a fiduciary relation to another, resulting in an 'equitable duty to convey [the property] on the ground that he would be unjustly enriched if he were permitted to retain it.' " The court held that Steven stood in a fiduciary relation to Charles and Paula and would be unjustly enriched if allowed to retain the house. Because the house was bought by Charles for his own benefit, Steven had an equitable duty to convey the property to Paula, who had been awarded Charles's interest in the house. Among other things, Steven had argued that Paula should not be entitled to the house because it was bought with the proceeds from an illegal activity. In response to this argument, the court noted that there was no evidence that Paula had actively participated in the illegal activity.

CHARITABLE TRUST
A trust in which the property held by a trustee must be used for a charitable purpose.

SPENDTHRIFT TRUST
A trust created to protect the beneficiary from spending all the money to which he or she is entitled. Only a certain portion of the total amount is given to the beneficiary at any one time, and most states prohibit creditors from attaching assets of the trust.

TOTTEN TRUST
A trust created by the deposit of a person's own money in his or her own name as a trustee for another. It is a tentative trust, revocable at will until the depositor dies or completes the gift in his or her lifetime by some unequivocal act or declaration.

Other Kinds of Trusts

Certain trusts are created for special purposes. Three such trusts that warrant discussion are charitable, spendthrift, and totten trusts. A trust designed for the benefit of a segment of the public or of the public in general is a **charitable trust.** It differs from a private trust in that the identities of the beneficiaries are uncertain. Usually, to be deemed a charitable trust, a trust must be created for charitable, educational, religious, or scientific purposes.

A trust created to provide for the maintenance of a beneficiary by preventing his or her improvidence with the bestowed funds is a **spendthrift trust.** Essentially, the beneficiary is permitted to draw only a certain portion of the total amount to which he or she is entitled at any one time. The majority of states allow spendthrift trust provisions that prohibit creditors from attaching such trusts.

A **Totten trust** is created when one person deposits money in his or her own name as a trustee for another. This trust is tentative in that it is revocable at will until the depositor dies or completes the gift in his or her lifetime by some unequivocal act or declaration (for example, delivery of the funds to the intended beneficiary). If the depositor should die before the beneficiary dies and if the depositor has not revoked the trust expressly or impliedly, a presumption arises that an absolute trust has been created for the benefit of the beneficiary. At the death of the depositor, the beneficiary obtains property rights to the balance on hand.

Application

Law and the Partner or Shareholder—Key-Person Insurance

As mentioned in the *Application* in Chapter 25, life insurance on the lives of partners or shareholders may be a valuable tool for you as a participant in a partnership or a closely held corporation. Typically, should one partner or co-shareholder die, the others will want to buy that person's interest, particularly if they wish to continue in the business; and the partnership or corporation may wish to purchase key-person life insurance on each partner or co-shareholder to help fund the buy-out. Problems arise, however, when the partners or co-shareholders are not all the same age or do not all have the same financial interest in the partnership or corporation. How does one arrange an insurance and buy-out agreement that is fair to everyone?

First, you must determine the current value of the business and then provide a method for determining the value of the business when one of the owners dies. There are numerous ways to accomplish such a valuation. The important point is that all partners agree on the method to be used. Each must be satisfied that if he or she is the first to die, the valuation method will provide a fair and equitable way to buy that interest from the estate.

Next, you must determine how much life insurance to purchase. Insurance can be used to fund the entire amount of the purchase price of the deceased's interest in the firm or just a part of that purchase price. Because the premiums for some of the owners may cost more (due to more advanced age or poorer health), an agreement may be reached to buy less insurance for them to reduce the current cost of the life insurance policy. The agreement could specify that the remaining part of the buy-out purchase price would be paid to the deceased's heirs in the form of installments, including interest payments at current interest rates.

Owners can negotiate a variety of payment plans to fit each partner's or co-shareholder's individual needs in the event a buy-out becomes necessary. For example, for an older partner, the payments may be spread over only a few years, and for younger partners, over a longer period of time. All these points are negotiable. It should be possible to draft an agreement that provides for insurance and/or a buy-out purchase plan that protects the interest of each person.

Checklist for Partners and Close Corporation Shareholders

☐ 1. If anyone in your partnership or closely held corporation can be considered a key person, then you should probably buy key-person life insurance on that individual.

☐ 2. Estimate the amount of loss that the partnership or closely held corporation would suffer if a key person died or became incapacitated. Insure for only that amount (the partnership or close corporation should not benefit from a partner's or shareholder's death but rather be left in an equal financial position compared to prior to the death).

☐ 3. Establish a buy-out purchase plan for the partnership or close corporation members in the event of one key person's death.

❖ Key Terms

administrator 856
bequest 856
binder 850
charitable trust 866
codicil 860
constructive trust 865
devise 856
executor 856
holographic will 858
insurable interest 850
insurance 847
***inter vivos* trust** 863
intestacy laws 861
intestate 855
legacy 857
legatee 857
nuncupative will 859
per capita 861
per stirpes 861
policy 849
premium 849
probate court 856
resulting trust 865
risk 847
risk management 847
spendthrift trust 866
testamentary trust 864
testator 856
Totten trust 866
trust 862
underwriter 849
will 855

❖ Chapter Summary: Insurance, Wills, and Trusts

INSURANCE	
Risk Pooling	Insurance is based on the principle of pooling risks—spreading the risk among a large number of people to make the premiums small compared with the coverage offered.
Terminology	1. *Policy*—The insurance contract. 2. *Premium*—The consideration paid to the insurer for a policy. 3. *Underwriter*—The insurance company.

❖ Chapter Summary: Insurance, Wills, and Trusts—Continued

Terminology—Continued	4. *Parties*—Include the insurer (the insurance company), the insured (the person covered by insurance), and an agent (representative of the insurance company) or a broker (ordinarily an independent contractor). 5. *Insurable interest*—Exists whenever an individual or entity benefits from the preservation of the health or life of the insured or the property to be insured.
The Insurance Contract	1. *Laws governing*—The general principles of contract law are applied. 2. *Timing of coverage*—Coverage on an insurance policy can begin when the *binder* (a written memorandum indicating that a formal policy is pending and stating its essential terms) is written, when the policy is issued, or, depending on the terms of the contract, when a certain period of time has elapsed. 3. *Provisions and clauses*—See Exhibit 35–2. Words will be given their ordinary meaning, and any ambiguity in the policy will be interpreted against the insurance company. When the written policy has not been delivered and it is unclear whether an insurance contract actually exists, the uncertainty will be determined against the insurance company. The court will presume that the policy is in effect unless the company can show otherwise. 4. *Defenses against payment to the insured*—Misrepresentation, fraud, or violation of warranties by the applicant.
WILLS	
Laws Governing Wills	1. *State statutes* (probate laws)—Vary from state to state. 2. *Uniform Probate Code (UPC)*—Codifies general principles and procedures concerning wills and probate; adopted in some form by fifteen states.
Types of Wills	1. *Holographic*—A will completely in the handwriting of the testator; valid where permitted by state statute. 2. *Attested*—A written will, signed by the testator, properly witnessed, and, when required, published; one that meets formal statutory requirements for a valid will. 3. *Noncupative*—An oral will made before witnesses during the deathbed illness of the testator; it is valid to transfer only personal property, not real property.
Formal Requirements of a Will	1. A will must be in writing (except for nuncupative wills). 2. A will must be signed by the testator; what constitutes a signature varies from jurisdiction to jurisdiction. 3. A nonholographic will must be witnessed in the manner prescribed by state statute. 4. A will may have to be *published*—i.e., the testator may be required to announce to witnesses that this is his or her "last will and testament." Not required under the UPC.
Methods of Revoking or Modifying a Will	1. *By acts of the maker*: a. Physical act—Tearing up, canceling, obliterating, or deliberately destroying part or all of a will. b. Codicil—A formal separate document to amend or revoke an existing will. c. Second or new will—A new, properly executed will expressly revoking the existing will. 2. *By operation of law*: a. Marriage—Generally revokes part of a will written before the marriage. b. Divorce or annulment—Revokes dispositions made under a will to a former spouse. c. Subsequently born child—It is *implied* that the child is entitled to receive the portion of the estate granted under intestacy distribution laws.
Gifts by Will	1. *Specific*—A devise or bequest of specified property in the testator's estate. 2. *General*—A devise or bequest that does not single out a particular item in the testator's estate; usually a sum of money. 3. *Residuary*—A devise or bequest of any properties left in the estate after all specific and general gifts have been made.

❖ Chapter Summary: Insurance, Wills, and Trusts—Continued

Intestacy Laws (Statues of Descent and Distribution)	1. Vary widely from state to state. Usually, the law provides that the surviving spouse and children inherit the property of the decedent (after the decedent's debts are paid). The spouse usually will inherit the entire estate if there are no children, one-half of the estate if there is one child, and one-third of the estate if there are two or more children. 2. If there is no surviving spouse or child, then, in order, lineal descendants (grandchildren, brothers and sisters, and—in some states—parents of the decedent) inherit. If there are no lineal descendants, then collateral heirs (nieces, nephews, aunts, and uncles of the decedent) inherit.
TRUSTS	
Definition	Any arrangement through which property is transferred from one person to be administered by a trustee for another party's benefit. The essential elements of a trust are (1) a designated beneficiary, (2) a designated trustee, (3) a fund sufficiently identified to enable title to pass to the trustee, and (4) actual delivery to the trustee with the intention of passing title.
Types of Trusts	1. *Express trusts*—Created by expressed terms, usually in writing. a. *Inter vivos* trust—A trust executed by a grantor during his or her lifetime. b. Testamentary trust—A trust created by will and coming into existence upon the death of the grantor. 2. *Implied trusts*—Trusts imposed by law. a. Constructive trust—Arises by operation of law whenever a transaction takes place in which the person who takes title to or possession of the property is in equity not entitled to enjoy the beneficial interest therein. b. Resulting trust—Arises from the conduct of the parties when an *apparent intention* to create a trust is present. 3. *Other kinds of trusts:* a. Charitable trust—A trust designed for the benefit of a public group or the public in general. b. Spendthrift trust—A trust created to provide for the maintenance of a beneficiary by allowing only a certain portion of the total amount to be received by the beneficiary at any one time. c. Totten trust—A trust created when one person deposits money in his or her own name as a trustee for another.

❖ Questions and Case Problems

35-1. Insurable Interest. What is an insurable interest? To obtain life insurance, when must an insurable interest exist—at the time the policy is obtained, at the time the death or the loss occurs, or both? Does the same rule apply to property insurance?

35-2. Timing of Insurance Coverage. On October 10, Joleen Vora applied for a $50,000 life insurance policy with Magnum Life Insurance Co., naming her husband, Jay, as the beneficiary. Joleen paid the insurance company the first year's policy premium upon making the application. Two days later, before she had a chance to take the physical examination required by the insurance company and before the policy was issued, Joleen was killed in an automobile accident. Jay submitted a claim to the insurance company for the $50,000. Can Jay collect? Explain.

35-3. Validity of Wills. Merlin Winters had three sons. Winters and his youngest son, Abraham, had a falling out in 1984 and had not spoken to each other since. Winters made a formal will in 1986, leaving all his property to the two older children and deliberately excluding Abraham. Winters's health began to deteriorate, and by 1987 he was under the full-time care of a nurse, Julia. In 1988, he made a new will expressly revoking the 1986 will and leaving all his property to Julia. Upon Winters's death, the two older children contested the 1988 will, claiming that Julia had exercised undue influence over their father. Abraham claimed that both wills were invalid, because the first one had been revoked by the second will, and the second will was invalid on the ground of undue influence. Is Abraham's contention correct? Explain.

35-4. Wills. Gary Mendel drew up a will in which he left his favorite car, a 1966 red Ferrari, to his daughter, Roberta. A year prior to his death, Mendel sold the 1966 Ferrari and purchased a 1969 Ferrari. Discuss whether Roberta will inherit the 1969 Ferrari under the terms of her father's will.

35-5. Estate Distribution. Benjamin is a widower who has two married children, Edward and Patricia. Patricia has two children, Perry and Paul. Edward has no children. Benjamin dies, leaving a typewritten will that leaves all his property equally to his children, Edward and Patricia, and provides that should a child predecease him, the grandchildren are to take *per stirpes*. The will was witnessed by Patricia and by Benjamin's lawyer and was signed by Benjamin in their presence. Patricia has predeceased Benjamin. Edward claims the will is invalid.

(a) Discuss whether the will is valid.

(b) Discuss the distribution of Benjamin's estate if the will is invalid.

(c) Discuss the distribution of Benjamin's estate if the will is valid.

35-6. Validity of Wills. An elderly, childless widow had nine nieces and nephews. Her will divided her entire estate equally among two nieces and the husband of one of the nieces, who was also the attorney-draftsman of the will and the executor named in the will. The testator was definitely of sound mind when the will was executed. If you were one of the seven nieces or nephews omitted from the will, could you think of any way to have the will invalidated? [*Estate of Eckert*, 93 Misc.2d 677, 403 N.Y.S.2d 633 (Surrogate's Ct. 1978)]

35-7. Insurance Cancellation. Martin A. Gurrentz applied for life insurance from Federal Kemper Life Assurance Co. through an insurance agent named Alfrey. In September 1982, Gurrentz filled out an application but paid no premiums. Between the submission of the application and the delivery of the policy, Gurrentz sought medical advice from a physician about an ear problem. On examination, a throat lesion was noted. A biopsy was done, and Gurrentz was advised that he had a throat malignancy, for which he subsequently received radiation treatments. Upon delivery of the policy, Gurrentz signed a statement stating that there had been no change in his health status and that he had not seen a doctor since filing the application for insurance. In April 1983, Federal learned of Gurrentz's throat problem when he filed a claim under a separate medical health policy. After an investigation, Federal notified Gurrentz in February 1984 that it was canceling the life insurance policy and refunding all premiums paid. Was Federal able to rescind Gurrentz's life insurance policy? Explain. [*Gurrentz v. Federal Kemper Life Assurance Co.*, 513 So.2d 241 (Fla.Dist.App. 1987)]

35-8. Validity of Wills. Louie Villwok died on November 12, 1984, leaving an executed will that left everything to his present wife, Rose. If Rose had predeceased him, according to the will, his three daughters from a previous marriage would have received a general bequest of money and a portion of the residue of the estate. When the will was offered for probate, the decedent's daughters contested the will. They claimed, among other things, that the will was a result of undue influence on the part of Rose. At the hearing, the daughters presented evidence to show that after Rose married the decedent, the relationship between her and the decedent's children deteriorated; that the decedent drank heavily on a daily basis and was intoxicated most of the time; and that Rose made concerted efforts to come between the decedent and his daughters. Each daughter also testified that her father had made statements to her expressly indicating that he did not want Rose or her children to have his property and that he wanted his daughters to receive all of his property. The probate court entered summary judgment in favor of Rose. What will the appellate court decide? Discuss fully. [*In re Estate of Villwok*, 226 Neb. 693, 413 N.W.2d 921 (1987)]

35-9. Revocation of Wills. Myrtle Courziel executed a valid will that provided for the establishment of a scholarship fund designed to encourage the study of corrosion as it affects metallurgical engineering. The recipients were to be students in the upper halves of their classes at the University of Alabama. Subsequently, Myrtle died. John Calhoun, the eventual administrator of her estate, obtained access to Myrtle's safe-deposit box to search for her will. He found the will intact, except that the last page of the will, which had contained Myrtle's signature and the signatures of the witnesses, had been removed from the document and was not in the safe-deposit box or anywhere else to be found. Because Myrtle had had sole control over the will, should it be presumed that her removal of the last page (or her having allowed it to be removed) effectively revoked the will? Discuss. [*Board of Trustees of University of Alabama v. Calhoun*, 514 So.2d 895 (Ala. 1987)]

35-10. Testamentary Trusts. In 1956, Jack Adams executed a will, the terms of which established a charitable trust. The trust income was to go to Prince Edward School Foundation as long as the foundation continued to operate and admit to its schools "only members of the White Race." If the foundation admitted nonwhites to its schools, the trust income was to go to the Miller School, under the same limitation, and so on to two other educational institutions. If all of the successively named educational beneficiaries violated the limitation, the income would go to Hermitage Methodist Homes of Virginia, Inc., without any limitation attending the bequest. In 1968, Adams died. Subsequent to the execution of the will, all of the educational beneficiaries enrolled African-American students. The trustee, uncertain as to how to distribute the trust income under these circumstances, sought counsel from the court. Assuming that the racially discriminatory provisions are unconstitutional and void, which, if any, of the named beneficiaries should receive the trust income? Explain. [*Hermitage Methodist Homes of Virginia, Inc. v. Dominion Trust Co.*, 387 S.E.2d 740 (Va. 1990)]

35-11. Insurer's Defenses. Kirk Johnson applied for life insurance with New York Life Insurance Co. on October 7, 1986. One of the questions on the application form required Johnson to provide information as to his past and present smoking habits. In answer to the question, Johnson stated that he had not smoked in the past twelve months and that he had never smoked cigarettes. In fact, Johnson had smoked for thirteen years, and during the month prior to the insurance application, he was smoking approximately ten cigarettes per day. Johnson died on July 17, 1988, for reasons unrelated to smoking. Johnson's father, Lawrence Johnson, who was the beneficiary of the policy, filed a claim for the insurance proceeds. While investigating the claim, New York Life discovered Kirk Johnson's misrepresentation on the application about his smoking habit. The company denied the claim and sought to cancel the policy by returning to Lawrence Johnson a check for the premiums paid under the policy. Lawrence Johnson refused to accept the check, and New York Life undertook an action for declaratory judgment (a court determination of a plaintiff's rights). What should the court decide?

Discuss fully. [*New York Life Insurance Co. v. Johnson*, 923 F.2d 279 (3d Cir. 1991)]

35-12. Testamentary Trusts. Edwin Fickes died in 1943. His will provided for the creation of a trust, half of which was to be divided, upon the death of Fickes's last surviving child, "in equal portions between [the testator's] grandchildren then living." At the time of the death of Fickes's last surviving child, there were four biological grandchildren and four adopted grandchildren living. Two of the adopted grandchildren, both boys, had been adopted prior to Fickes's death. The other two, both girls, had been adopted after Fickes died. The trustee, Connecticut National Bank and Trust Co., sought a court determination of whether the adopted grandchildren were entitled to share in the trust distribution. The trial court found that the testator, Fickes, had intended to include his adopted grandsons as "grandchildren" within the meaning of his will but could not have intended to include his adopted granddaughters as "grandchildren," so they were not entitled to a share of the trust. What will happen on appeal? Discuss fully. [*Connecticut National Bank and Trust Co. v. Chadwick*, 217 Conn. 260, 585 A.2d 1189 (1991)]

35-13. Interpretation of Insurance Contract Terms. Martha Frances purchased insurance coverage from Nationwide Insurance Co. prior to going on a cruise. The policy covered "accidental bodily injury occurring anywhere in the world which arises solely from accident" and "is not contributed to by sickness, disease or bodily or mental infirmity." The policy also stated that if the injury resulted in the loss of life "within 180 days after the date of the accident," the company would pay the beneficiary $75,000. While on the cruise, Frances fell and broke her hip. She was immediately taken to a Florida hospital for surgery, during which she had a fatal heart attack. The death certificate described the cause of death as "terminal cardiac arrest due to or as a consequence of arteriosclerotic cardiovascular disease due to or as a consequence of previous [heart problems]." Audrey Allison, Frances's beneficary, sought payment under the policy, but Nationwide refused to pay because Frances's death had been caused in part by her preexisting heart condition. Allison then sued Nationwide to collect the death benefit. Assuming that Frances would not have died (at least, at that time) from her heart problems had it not been for the surgery, how should the court decide? Discuss fully. [*Allison v. Nationwide Mutual Insurance Co.*, 964 F.2d 291 (3d Cir. 1992)]

A Question of Ethics and Social Responsibility

35-14. *Heber Burke and his wife Evelyn had spent most of their lives in Ohio and had jointly accumulated a substantial amount of property there. The Burkes, who had been married for fifty-three years, had two children, four grandchildren, and four great-grandchildren. Evelyn died in February 1985. Heber had originally hailed from Pike County, Kentucky, and in June 1985, he returned to Pike County and bought a house there. In the same month, he told his children that he was going to marry Lexie Damron, a widow who attended his church. Lexie and Heber were married on July 20. On July 27, Heber executed a will, which was drawn up by Lexie's attorney, in which he left all of his property to Lexie. Heber died three weeks later. Heber's children, Donald Burke and Beatrice Bates, contested the will, alleging that Heber lacked testamentary capacity and that Heber's will resulted from Lexie's undue influence over him. Friends and relatives of Heber in Pike County testified that they had never known Heber to drink and that, although he seemed saddened by his first wife's death, he was not incapacitated by it. According to the children's witnesses, however, after Evelyn's death, Heber drank heavily and constantly; had frequent crying spells; repeatedly visited his wife's grave; tried to dig her up so that he could talk to her; and had hallucinations, talking to people who were not present and claiming that Evelyn visited him regularly at night, which frightened him into sleeping in the attic. The jury found the will to be invalid on the grounds of undue influence, and Lexie appealed.* [Burke v. Burke, *801 S.W.2d 691 (Ken.App. 1990)*]

1. The appellate court had to weigh two conflicting policies in deciding this issue. What two policies are in conflict here, and what criteria should be used in resolving the issue?
2. Given the circumstances described above, would you infer undue influence on the part of Lexie if you were the judge? Would you conclude that Heber lacked testamentary capacity? What would be the fairest solution, in your opinion?
3. Heber's first wife, Evelyn, contributed substantially to the acquisition of the property subject to Heber's will. A natural assumption would be that Evelyn would want their children to inherit the jointly acquired property. Yet if Heber were found to be of sound mind and not the victim of any undue influence, the court would allow him to totally disregard the children, if he wished, in his will. Is this fair to Evelyn's presumed intentions? To the children? Is there any solution to the possible unfairness that can result from giving people the right to disregard natural heirs in their wills?

For Critical Analysis

35-15. *Statistics show that the extent of risk assumed by insurance companies varies depending on the gender of the insured. Yet many people contend that gender-based insurance rates discriminate against women and therefore should be banned. Do you agree with this contention? Why or why not?*

Unit Seven

The International Legal Environment

❖ Why We Study the International Legal Environment

International trade in the United States, measured as a percentage of annual national output, has increased threefold since the end of World War II in 1945. While it is true that international trade still represents a relatively modest share of annual national output—around 10 percent—the global business community is, in fact, "the tail that wagged the dog." In the case of the United States, the growing economic power of the Pacific Rim (Singapore, Taiwan, South Korea, Thailand, Japan, Hong Kong, and the Guangdong province of mainland China), a united Europe, and some rapidly expanding economies in Latin America (including that of Mexico) has created serious competitive threats to many American businesses. The rapid improvement in communications technology has, in part, been responsible for increased global competition. After all, today information on profitability, interest rates, prices, and the like is virtually instantaneously available in any country of the world at every moment in time.

Certainly, persons who wish to do business in foreign countries or with foreign corporations must know about international law. In addition, because the international context frames so many business decisions and activities carried out by U.S. businesspersons, every potential member of the U.S. business community must have at least a passing understanding of the international legal environment and the principal areas of conflict relating to international trade.

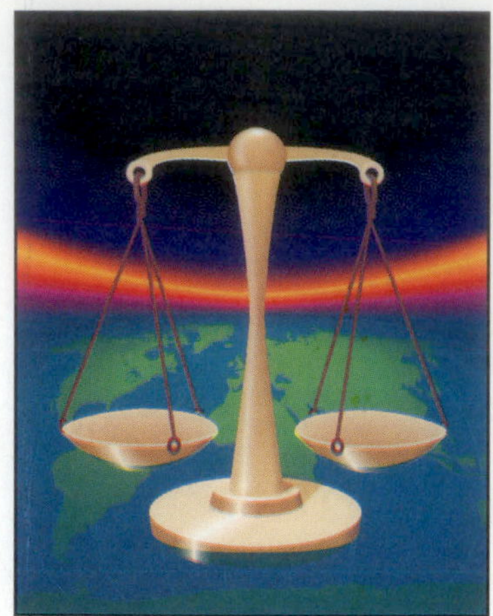

Chapter 36

International Law in a Global Economy

"Our interests are those of the open door—a door of friendship and mutual advantage. This is the only door we care to enter."

Woodrow Wilson, 1856–1924
(Twenty-eighth president of the United States, 1913–1921)

Since ancient times, independent peoples and nations have traded their goods and wares with one another. In other words, international business transactions are not unique to the modern world because people have always found that they can benefit from exchanging goods with others, as suggested by President Woodrow Wilson's statement in the opening quotation. What is new in our time is that, particularly since World War II, business has become increasingly *multinational.* It is not uncommon, for example, for a U.S. corporation to have investments or manufacturing plants in a foreign country, or for a foreign corporation to have operations within the United States.

Transacting business on an international level is considerably different from transacting business within the boundaries of just one nation. Buyers and sellers face far greater risks in the international marketplace than they do in a domestic context because the laws governing such transactions are more complex and uncertain. For example, the Uniform Commercial Code will govern many disputes that arise between U.S. buyers and sellers of goods unless they have provided otherwise in their contracts. But what if a U.S. buyer breaches a contract formed with a British seller? What law will govern the dispute—British or American? Or what if an investor owns substantial assets in a Third World nation and the government of that nation decides to nationalize—assert its ownership over—the property? What recourse does the investor have against the actions of a foreign government? In short, questions that do not normally arise in a domestic context can become pressing, if not crucial, in international business dealings.

Because the exchange of goods, services, and ideas on a global level is now a common phenomenon, it is important for the student of business law to be familiar with the laws pertaining to international business transactions. In this chapter, we first examine the legal context of international business transactions. We then look at some selected areas relating to business activities in a global context, including letters of credit, international sales contracts, civil dispute resolution, and investment protection. We conclude the chapter with a discussion of the application of U.S. antitrust laws in a transnational setting.

❖ The Legal Context of International Business Transactions

INTERNATIONAL LAW
The law that governs relations among nations. International customs and treaties are generally considered to be two of the most important sources of international law.

Recall from our discussion of international law in Chapter 1 that **international law** is a body of written and unwritten laws that are observed by otherwise independent nations and that govern the acts of individuals as well as states. We also discussed in that chapter the major sources of international law, including international customs, treaties between nations, and international organizations and conferences. Here, we look at some other legal principles and doctrines that have evolved over time and that have been employed—to a greater or lesser extent—by the courts of various nations to resolve or reduce conflicts that involve a foreign element. The three important legal principles and doctrines discussed in the following sections are based primarily on courtesy and respect and are applied in the interests of maintaining harmonious relations among nations.

The Principle of Comity

Under what is known as the principle of **comity,** one nation will defer and give effect to the laws and judicial decrees of another country, as long as those laws and judicial decrees are consistent with the law and public policy of the accommodating nation. This recognition is based primarily on courtesy and respect. For example, assume that a Swedish seller and an American buyer have formed a contract, which the buyer breaches. The seller sues the buyer in a Swedish court, which awards damages. But the buyer's assets are in the United States and cannot be reached unless the judgment is enforced by a U.S. court of law. In such a case, if it is determined that the procedures and laws applied in the Swedish court were consistent with U.S. national law and policy, a court in the United States will likely defer to, and enforce, the foreign court's judgment.

COMITY
A deference by which one nation gives effect to the laws and judicial decrees of another nation. This recognition is based primarily upon respect.

The Act of State Doctrine

The **act of state doctrine** is a judicially created doctrine that provides that the judicial branch of one country will not examine the validity of public acts committed by a recognized foreign government within its own territory. As indicated by the court in *Libra Bank, Ltd. v. Banco Nacional de Costa Rica, S.A.*, this doctrine is premised on the theory that the judicial branch should not "pass upon the validity of foreign acts when to do so would vex the harmony of our international relations with that foreign nation." [1]

ACT OF STATE DOCTRINE
A doctrine that provides that the judicial branch of one country will not examine the validity of public acts committed by a recognized foreign government within its own territory.

The act of state doctrine can have important consequences for individuals and firms doing business with and investing in other countries. For example, this doctrine is frequently employed in cases involving expropriation or confiscation. **Expropriation** occurs when a government seizes a privately owned business or privately owned goods for a proper public purpose and awards just compensation. When a government seizes private property for an illegal purpose or without just compensation, the taking is referred to as a **confiscation.** The line between these two forms of taking is sometimes blurred because of differing interpretations of what is illegal and what constitutes just compensation. To illustrate, Tim Flaherty, an American businessperson, owns a mine in Brazil. The government of Brazil seizes the mine for public use and claims that the profits that Tim has realized from the mine in *preceding* years constitute just compensation. Tim disagrees, but the act of state doctrine may prevent Tim's recovery in a U.S. court of law.

EXPROPRIATION
The seizure by a government of privately owned business or personal property for a proper public purpose and with just compensation.

CONFISCATION
A government's taking of privately owned business or personal property without a proper public purpose or an award of just compensation.

When applicable, both the act of state doctrine and the doctrine of sovereign immunity (to be discussed shortly) tend to immunize foreign nations from the jurisdiction of U.S. courts. What this means is that firms or individuals who own property overseas have little legal protection against government actions in the countries in which they operate.

1. 570 F.Supp. 870 (S.D.N.Y. 1983).

The applicability of the act of state doctrine is at issue in the following case.

Case 36.1
W. S. KIRKPATRICK & CO. v. ENVIRONMENTAL TECTONICS CORP., INTERNATIONAL
Supreme Court of the United States, 1990.
493 U.S. 400,
110 S.Ct. 701,
107 L.Ed.2d 816.

HISTORICAL AND POLITICAL SETTING *Once a colony of Great Britain, Nigeria gained its independence in 1960, which was also the year of the first meeting of the Organization of Petroleum Exporting Countries (OPEC). Nigeria, which possesses the greatest oil resources in Africa, later joined OPEC. In 1963, Nigeria became a federal republic, but between 1966 and 1979, the government changed hands four times in military coups. In 1975, the military announced that it would gradually return the government to civilian democratic rule, which finally occurred in 1979. Benefiting from the increase in oil prices during the 1970s, Nigeria began an intense program of modernization and construction. Among other problems that Nigeria has endured since its independence is internal corruption.*

FACTS In 1981, W. S. Kirkpatrick & Company learned that the Republic of Nigeria was interested in contracting for the construction and equipment of a medical center in Nigeria. Kirkpatrick, with the aid of a Nigerian citizen, secured the contract as a result of bribing Nigerian officials. Nigerian law prohibits both the payment and the receipt of bribes in connection with the awarding of government contracts, and the U.S. Foreign Corrupt Practices Act of 1977 expressly prohibits U.S. firms and their agents from bribing foreign officials to secure favorable contracts. Environmental Tectonics Corporation, International (ETC), an unsuccessful bidder for the contract, learned of the bribery and sued Kirkpatrick in a U.S. federal court for damages. The district court granted summary judgment for Kirkpatrick, because resolution of the case in favor of ETC would require imputing to foreign officials an unlawful motivation (the obtaining of bribes) and accordingly might embarrass the government or interfere with the conduct of U.S. foreign policy. ETC appealed, and the court of appeals reversed the judgment of the district court. Kirkpatrick appealed to the United States Supreme Court.

ISSUE Is ETC's action barred by the act of state doctrine?

DECISION No. The United States Supreme Court held that the action was not barred by the act of state doctrine.

REASON The Court stated that in every case in which it had held the act of state doctrine applicable, "the relief sought * * * would have required a court in the United States to declare invalid the official act of a foreign [government] performed within its own territory." In the present case, the Court held that the validity of a foreign government's act was not in question. "The short of the matter is this: Courts in the United States have the power, and ordinarily the obligation, to decide cases and controversies properly presented to them. The act of state doctrine does not establish an exception for cases and controversies that may embarrass foreign governments, but merely requires that, in the process of deciding, the acts of foreign [governments] taken within their own jurisdictions shall be deemed valid. That doctrine has no application to the present case because the validity of no foreign [government] act is at issue."

The Doctrine of Sovereign Immunity

SOVEREIGN IMMUNITY A doctrine that immunizes foreign nations from the jurisdiction of U.S. courts when certain conditions are satisfied.

Under certain conditions, the doctrine of **sovereign immunity** immunizes foreign nations from the jurisdiction of the U.S. courts. In 1976, Congress codified this rule in the Foreign Sovereign Immunities Act (FSIA). The FSIA also modified previous applications of the doctrine in certain respects by expanding the rights of plaintiff creditors against foreign nations.

The FSIA exclusively governs the circumstances in which an action may be brought in the United States against a foreign nation, including attempts to attach a foreign nation's property. One of the primary purposes of the FSIA was to have federal courts, rather than the Department of State, determine claims of foreign sovereign immunity. It was thought that a determination of such immunity by the courts would increase the degree of certainty in the law of sovereign immunity.

Section 1605 of the FSIA sets forth the major exceptions to the jurisdictional immunity of a foreign state or country. A foreign state is not immune from the jurisdiction of the courts of the United States when the state has "waived its immunity either explicitly or by implication" or when the action is "based upon a commercial activity carried on in the United States by the foreign state."[2]

Issues frequently arise as to what entities fall within the category of a foreign state. The question of what is a commercial activity has also been the subject of dispute. Under Section 1603 of the FSIA, a *foreign state* is defined to include both a political subdivision of a foreign state and an instrumentality of a foreign state. A *commercial activity* is broadly defined under Section 1603 to mean a commercial activity that is carried on by the foreign state within the United States. But the particulars of what constitutes a commercial activity are not defined in the act. Rather, it is left up to the courts to decide whether a particular activity is governmental or commercial in nature. In the following case, the court had to determine whether the defense of sovereign immunity was available under the FSIA.

Case 36.2
CHISHOLM & CO. v. BANK OF JAMAICA
United States District Court,
Southern District of Florida, 1986.
643 F.Supp. 1393.

HISTORICAL AND POLITICAL SETTING *Jamaica suffered from high unemployment in the mid-1970s, and the economy deteriorated even further in the second half of the decade. The government, in the control of the People's National Party, advocated economic independence from the developed countries. The 1980 general election campaign was extremely violent, despite calls by political leaders for restraint. Most of the members of the government were replaced by members of the Jamaica Labour Party, which severed links with Cuba and sought a renewal of ties with the United States. The new government emphasized free enterprise.*

FACTS The Bank of Jamaica, which is wholly owned by the government of Jamaica, contracted with Chisholm & Company in January 1981 for Chisholm to arrange for lines of credit from various U.S. banks and to obtain $50 million in credit insurance from the Export-Import Bank of the United States. This Chisholm successfully did, but subsequently the deals arranged by Chisholm were refused by the Bank of Jamaica. The bank had decided to do its own negotiating while having Chisholm work for it as well. When the bank refused to pay Chisholm for its services, Chisholm brought an action to obtain relief for the bank's breach of the implied contract. The Bank of Jamaica brought a motion to dismiss, claiming, among other things, that it was immune from the jurisdiction of U.S. courts under the doctrine of sovereign immunity. The bank argued that the money was needed for a government purpose.

ISSUE Is the Bank of Jamaica immune from Chisholm's action for breach of contract in a U.S. federal court?

DECISION No. The court ruled that although the bank is an arm of a foreign government, its actions here met the requirements for an exception to the Foreign Sovereign Immunities Act (FSIA); therefore, the bank was not immune from Chisholm's action.

REASON The FSIA grants foreign states immunity from suits in U.S. federal and state courts subject to certain exceptions, one being when the foreign state deals in a commercial activity that causes a direct effect in the United States. Commercial activity is defined as a regular course of commercial conduct or a particular commercial transaction or act and includes contracting for lines of credit or credit insurance. Another test for commercial activity is whether the activity is solely within the realm of governing or could be done by any private enterprise. Here, private banks can and do seek lines of credit and credit insurance; so the Bank of Jamaica is not the only party that can perform this activity. Further, a court does not look at the purpose of an activity, only at the activity itself. Thus, although the bank argued that the money was needed for a government purpose, the court ignored this and looked only at the contract itself. It found that the Bank of Jamaica's action was commercial activity and thus met the requirements of an exception to the FSIA.

2. 28 U.S.C. Section 1605(a)(1), (2).

McDonald's has franchised its operations in countries around the world. What benefits can a U.S. domestic firm realize from selling a franchise to an overseas entity?

❖ Doing Business Internationally

EXPORT
The sale or transportation of goods and services from one country to another in the course of trade.

There are a number of ways in which a U.S. domestic firm can engage in international business transactions. The simplest way is to seek out foreign markets for domestically produced products or services. In other words, U.S. firms can look abroad for **export** markets for their goods and services. Alternatively, a U.S. firm can establish foreign production facilities so as to be closer to the foreign market or markets in which its products are sold. The advantages may include lower labor costs, fewer government regulations, and lower taxes and trade barriers. It is also possible to obtain business from abroad by licensing technology developed and owned by the domestic firm to an existing foreign company. Yet another way to expand abroad is by selling franchises to overseas entities. The presence of McDonald's, Burger King, and KFC franchises throughout the world attests to the popularity of franchising.

Exporting

"Commerce is the great equalizer. We exchange ideas when we exchange fabrics."

R. G. Ingersoll, 1833–1899
(American lawyer and orator)

The initial foray into international business by most U.S. companies is through exporting. Exporting can take two forms: direct exporting and indirect exporting. In *direct exporting,* a U.S. company signs a sales contract with a foreign purchaser that provides for the conditions of shipment and payment for the goods. (How payments are made in international transactions is discussed later in this chapter.) If business develops sufficiently in foreign countries, a U.S. corporation may develop a specialized marketing organization that, for example, sells directly to consumers in that country. Such *indirect exporting* can be undertaken by the appointment of a foreign agent or a foreign distributor.

Foreign Agent When a U.S. firm desires a limited involvement in an international market, it will typically establish an *agency relationship* with a foreign firm. In an agency relationship (discussed in Chapter 23), one person (the agent) agrees to act on behalf of, or instead of, another (the principal). The foreign agent is thereby empowered to enter into contracts in the agent's country on behalf of the U.S. principal.

Foreign Distributor When a substantial market exists in a foreign country, a U.S. firm may wish to appoint a distributor located in that country. The U.S. firm and the distributor enter into a **distribution agreement,** which is a contract between the seller and the distributor setting out the terms and conditions of the distributorship—for example, price, currency of payment, guarantee of supply availability, and method of payment. The terms and conditions primarily involve contract law. Disputes concerning distribution agreements may involve jurisdictional or other issues (discussed in detail later in this chapter). In addition, some **exclusive distributorships** have raised antitrust problems.

DISTRIBUTION AGREEMENT
A contract between a seller and a distributor of the seller's products setting out the terms and conditions of the distributorship.

EXCLUSIVE DISTRIBUTORSHIP
A distributorship in which the seller and distributor of the seller's products agree that the distributor has the exclusive right to distribute the seller's products in a certain geographic area.

Manufacturing Abroad

An alternative to direct or indirect exporting is the establishment of foreign manufacturing facilities. Typically, U.S. firms want to establish manufacturing plants abroad if they believe that by doing so they will reduce costs—particularly for labor, shipping, and raw materials—and thereby be able to compete more effectively in foreign markets. Apple Computer, IBM, General Motors, and Ford are some of the many U.S. companies that have established manufacturing facilities abroad. Foreign firms have done the same in the United States. Sony, Nissan, and other Japanese manufacturers have established U.S. plants to avoid possible import duties that the U.S. Congress may impose on Japanese products entering this country.

There are several ways in which an American firm can manufacture in other countries. They include licensing and franchising, as well as investing in a wholly owned subsidiary or a joint venture.

All U.S. automakers have established manufacturing facilities in other countries. Why would a U.S. domestic firm set up a manufacturing facility abroad?

TECHNOLOGY LICENSING Allowing another to use and profit from intellectual property (patents, copyrights, trademarks, innovative products or processes, and so on) for consideration. In the context of international business transactions, technology licensing sometimes is an attractive alternative to the establishment of foreign production facilities.

Licensing It is possible for U.S. firms to license their technologies to foreign manufacturers. **Technology licensing** may involve a process innovation that lowers the cost of production, or it may involve a product innovation that generates a superior product. Technology licensing may be an attractive alternative to establishing foreign production facilities, particularly if the process or product innovation has been patented, because the patent protects—at least to some extent—against the possibility that the innovation might be pirated. Like any licensing agreement, a licensing agreement with a foreign-based firm calls for a payment of royalties on some basis—such as so many cents per unit produced or a certain percentage of profits from units sold in a particular geographical territory.

In certain circumstances, even in the absence of a patent, a firm may be able to license the "know-how" associated with a particular manufacturing process—for example, a plant design or a secret formula. The foreign firm that agrees to sign the licensing agreement further agrees to keep the know-how confidential and to pay royalties. For example, the Coca-Cola Bottling Company licenses firms worldwide to use (and keep confidential) its secret formula for the syrup used in that soft drink, in return for a percentage of the income gained from the sale of Coca-Cola by those firms.

The licensing of technology benefits all parties to the transaction: Those who receive the license can take advantage of an established reputation for quality, and the firm that grants the license receives income from the foreign sales of the firm's products, as well as establishing a worldwide reputation. Also, once a firm's trademark is known worldwide, the demand for other products manufactured or sold by that firm may increase—obviously an important consideration.

Franchising Franchising is a well-known form of licensing. Recall from Chapter 24 that a franchise can be defined as an arrangement in which the owner of a trademark, trade name, or copyright (the franchisor) licenses another (the franchisee) to use the trademark, trade name, or copyright, under certain conditions or limitations, in the selling of goods or services in exchange for a fee, usually based on a percentage of gross or net sales. Examples of international franchises include McDonald's, the Coca-Cola Bottling Company, Holiday Inn, Avis, and Hertz.

Investing in a Wholly Owned Subsidiary or a Joint Venture One way to expand into a foreign market is to establish a wholly owned subsidiary firm in a foreign country. The European subsidiary would likely take the form of the *société anonyme* (S.A.), which is similar to a U.S. corporation. In German-speaking nations, it would be called an *Aktiengesellschaft* (A.G.). When a wholly owned subsidiary is established, the parent company, which remains in the United States, retains complete ownership of all the facilities in the foreign country, as well as complete authority and control over all phases of the operation.

The expansion of a U.S. firm into international markets can also take the form of a joint venture. In a joint venture, the U.S. company owns only part of the operation; the rest is owned either by local owners in the foreign country or by another foreign entity. In a joint venture, responsibilities, as well as profits and liabilities, are shared by all of the firms involved in the venture.

❖ Commercial Contracts in an International Setting

Like all commercial contracts, an international contract should be in writing. The sample form shown in Exhibit 36–1 illustrates the typical terms and conditions that might be contained in an international contract.

Landmark in the Law

The United Nations Convention on Contracts for the International Sale of Goods (CISG)

Although international trade has taken place since at least the beginning of recorded history, the emergence of multinational and global business enterprises is a twentieth-century phenomenon. As early as the 1930s, a number of nations saw the need for—and began to develop—uniform laws to cover contracts for the international sale of goods to facilitate international transactions. The end result of this important legal development was the 1980 United Nations Convention on Contracts for the International Sale of Goods (CISG), which applies to all contracts between firms located in the countries that have ratified the convention. As of 1992, thirty-four countries had ratified the CISG, including the United States, Canada, Mexico, some Central and South American countries, and most of the European nations.

An "International UCC"

Essentially, the CISG is to international sales contracts what Article 2 of the Uniform Commercial Code (UCC) is to domestic sales contracts. Recall that in domestic transactions, the UCC applies when the parties to a contract for a sale of goods have failed to specify in writing some important term concerning price, delivery, or the like. Similarly, whenever the parties to international transactions have failed to specify in writing the precise terms of a contract, the CISG will be applied. The provisions of the CISG, while similar for the most part to those of the UCC, differ from them in some respects. For example, the rules governing offer and acceptance in sales contracts are modified by the CISG for international transactions, and the CISG does not include the formal requirements imposed by the Statute of Frauds. In the event that the CISG and the UCC are in conflict, the CISG applies.

When the CISG Applies

Technically speaking, the CISG applies only to contracts between entities located in countries that have ratified the CISG. The application of the provisions of the CISG is not mandatory, because any U.S. company dealing with a firm located in a signatory country can, by contractual agreement, provide that another law, and not the CISG, will apply. The specific language used in such a provision would have to be as follows:

> The provisions of the Uniform Commercial Code as adopted by the state of [say] California, and *not* the Convention for the International Sale of Goods, apply.

The CISG does not apply to domestic sales or noncommercial sales—that is, it does not apply to consumer sales of goods bought for family, household, or personal use. Nor does it apply to the sale of services. In situations in which the contract calls for both services and goods, if the sale of goods outweighs the sale of services, then the CISG will apply. In these respects, the CISG is very similar to the UCC.

Language and legal differences among nations can create special problems for parties to international contracts when disputes arise. It is possible to avoid these problems by including in a contract special provisions designating the official language of the contract, the legal forum (court or place) in which disputes under the contract will be settled, and the substantive law that will be applied in settling any disputes. Parties to international contracts should also indicate in their contracts what acts or events will excuse the parties from performance under the contract and whether disputes under the contract will be arbitrated or litigated.

Choice of Language

A deal struck between a U.S. company and a company in another country normally involves two languages. The complex contractual terms involved may not be understood by one party in the other party's language. Typically, many phrases in one language are not readily translatable into another. To make sure that no disputes arise out of this language problem, an international sales contract should have a **choice-of-language clause** designating the official language by which the contract will be interpreted in the event of disagreement.

CHOICE-OF-LANGUAGE CLAUSE
A clause in a contract designating the official language by which the contract will be interpreted in the event of a future disagreement over the contract's terms.

◆ **Exhibit 36–1**
Sample International Purchase Order Form (Front)
Caution: This form contains a typical set of terms written from the buyer's point of view, but it is not applicable to all factual situations and the laws of all states. Terms and conditions of sale or purchase must be custom drafted to be appropriate to the type of business and type of goods involved.

Sample International Purchase Order Terms & Conditions*

The ________________ Company, Inc.
International Terms and Conditions of Purchase

1. *Acceptance.* Acceptance of this order is expressly limited to the terms and conditions contained herein, including all terms and conditions set forth on the face hereof. Acceptance of this order by Seller may be made by signing and returning the attached acknowledgement copy hereof, by other express acceptance, or by shipment of goods hereunder. If Seller uses its own order acknowledgement or other form to accept this order, it is understood that said form shall be used for convenience only and any terms or conditions contained therein inconsistent with or in addition to those contained herein shall be of no force or effect whatsoever between the parties hereto.

2. *Warranty.* Seller warrants the goods covered by this Agreement and their packaging and labelling shall be in merchantable condition and shall be free from defects in workmanship and materials and shall be in conformity with the specifications, drawings, samples and descriptions attached hereto or referred to on the face hereof, if any. Seller warrants that the goods covered by this Agreement shall be fit for such particular purposes and uses, if any, as specified by BUYER or otherwise known to Seller. Seller warrants that the goods shall be free and clear of any lien or other adverse claim against title, and to the extent not manufactured to detailed designs furnished by BUYER shall be free from defects in design. All warranties contained herein shall survive inspection, test and acceptance by BUYER. Seller agrees, at its own costs and expense, to defend and hold BUYER harmless from and against any and all claims made against BUYER based upon, relating to, or arising out of any claimed defects in the goods or services ordered hereunder. Seller's warranties (and any consumer warranties, service policies, or similar undertakings of Seller) shall be enforceable by BUYER'S customers and any subsequent owner or operator of the goods as well as by BUYER.

3. *Shipping Instructions.* No charge shall be made to BUYER for draying and packaging unless authorized by BUYER. Merchandise shipped by freight or express shall be packed, marked and described and the carrier shall be selected, so as to obtain the lowest rate possible under freight or express classifications or regulations except when otherwise specified by BUYER, and penalties or increased charges due to failure so to do will be charged to Seller. The foregoing notwithstanding, Seller shall comply with all instructions of BUYER as to packaging, marking, shipping and insurance. Prior to passage of title to BUYER the goods shall be held by Seller without risk or expense to BUYER.

4. *Invoices, Other Documents and Charges.* Seller shall invoice in duplicate. Originals of all invoices, government and commercial bills of lading and air express receipts shall be air mailed to the Purchasing Department of BUYER when goods are shipped. Packing slips must accompany item number, and a complete description of its contents. Except as otherwise provided on the face hereof, the contract price includes all costs and charges to be paid or reimbursed to Seller by BUYER, including without limitation, all applicable taxes and duties and all charges for packing, loading and transportation. Transportation charges and taxes and duties, when applicable, and when agreed on the face hereof to be borne by BUYER shall be billed as separate items on Seller's invoices.

5. *Inspection—Nonconformity.* BUYER may inspect the goods and, with respect to nonconforming goods, may return them or hold them at the Seller's risk and expense, and may in either event charge the Seller with cost of transportation, shipping, unpacking, examining, repacking, reshipping, and other like expense. Promptly upon BUYER's written request, and without expense to BUYER, Seller agrees to replace or correct defects of any rejected goods or other goods not conforming to the warranty set forth above. In the event of failure of Seller to replace or correct defects in nonconforming goods promptly, BUYER after reasonable notice to Seller, may make such corrections or replace such goods and charge Seller for the costs incurred by BUYER in doing so. Time is of the essence in this transaction. In addition to its remedies for breach of contract, BUYER reserves the right to return any or all goods in unopened original packing to Seller if delivered to BUYER more than five (5) days after the delivery date shown in shipping instructions. If the delivery date shown in shipping instructions is revised by BUYER by notification to Seller, then such five (5) day period shall not commence to run until such revised delivery date. Also, BUYER reserves the right to refuse goods delivered contrary to instructions or not in recognized standard containers. BUYER shall be under no duty to inspect goods prior to BUYER's use or resale, and neither retention, use nor resale of such goods shall be construed to constitute an acceptance of goods not in compliance with the requirements of this order.

6. *Changes.* Unless agreed in writing by BUYER, Seller shall not purchase materials, or make material commitments, or production arrangements, in excess of the amount, or in advance of the time necessary to meet BUYER'S delivery schedule. BUYER shall have the right at any time to make changes in drawings, designs, specifications, materials, packaging, time and place of delivery and method of transportation. If any such changes cause an increase or decrease in the cost, or the time required for the performance, an equitable adjustment shall be made and this agreement shall be modified in writing accordingly. Seller agrees to accept any such changes subject to this paragraph. This right to an adjustment shall be deemed waived unless asserted within thirty (30) days after the change is ordered. BUYER reserves the right to terminate this order or any part hereof for its sole convenience. In the event of such termination, Seller shall immediately stop all work hereunder, and shall immediately cause any of its suppliers or subcontractors to cease such work. Seller shall be paid a reasonable termination charge consisting of a percentage of the order price reflecting the percentage of the work performed prior to the notice of termination. Such charge shall be Seller's only remedy for such termination. Seller shall not be paid for any work done after receipt of the notice of termination nor for any work done by Seller's suppliers or subcontractors which Seller could reasonably have avoided.

7. *Default.* BUYER may also terminate this order or any part hereof for cause in the event of any default by the Seller or if the Seller fails to comply with any of the terms and conditions of this offer. Late deliveries, deliveries of goods which are defective or which do not conform to this order, and failure to provide BUYER, upon request, reasonable assurances of future performance shall all be causes allowing BUYER to terminate this order for cause. In the event of termination for cause, BUYER shall not be liable to Seller for any amount and Seller shall be liable to BUYER for any and all damage sustained by reason of the default which gave rise to the termination.

 These sample terms and conditions were used in connection with a presentation with the 21st Annual Uniform Commercial Code Institute. Mr. Sanders is with Latham & Watkins in Los Angeles, CA.

◆ Exhibit 36–1 (Continued) Sample International Purchase Order Form (Back)

8. *Indemnity.* Seller will defend and indemnify BUYER, upon demand, against all claims, actions, liability, damage, loss and expense (including investigative expense and attorney's fees incurred in litigation or because of threatened litigation) as the result of BUYER'S purchase and/or use of the goods and arising or alleged to arise from patent, trademark or copyright infringement; unfair competition; the failure or alleged failure of the goods to comply with specifications or with any express or implied warranties of Seller; the alleged violation by such goods or in its manufacture or sale of any statute, ordinance, or administrative order, rule or regulation; defects, whether latent or patent, in material or workmanship; defective design; defective warnings or instructions; or Seller's negligence.

9. *Price Reductions.* Seller will give BUYER the benefit of any price reductions occurring before the specified shipping date or to actual time of shipment, whichever is later. Likewise, if Seller accepts this order as a commission merchant, Seller shall obtain for BUYER from the manufacturer of such goods the benefit of price reductions to the specified date or to actual time of shipment, whichever is later. Seller warrants that the price for the articles sold BUYER hereunder are not less favorable than those currently extended to any other customer for the same or similar articles in similar quantities.

10. *Information.* Seller shall consider all information furnished by BUYER to be confidential and shall not disclose any such information to any other person, or use such information itself for any purpose other than performing this order unless Seller obtains written permission from BUYER to do so. This confidential requirement shall also apply to drawings, specifications, or other documents prepared by Seller for BUYER in connection with this order. Seller shall provide confidential information only to those of its agents, servants and employees who have been informed of the requirements of this paragraph and have agreed to be bound by them. Upon completion or termination of this order, Seller shall make such disposition of all such information and items as may be directed by BUYER. Seller shall not advertise or publish the fact that BUYER has ordered goods from Seller nor shall any information relating to this order be disclosed without BUYER'S written permission. Unless otherwise agreed in writing, no commercial, financial or technical information disclosed in any manner or at any time by Seller to BUYER shall be deemed secret or confidential and Seller shall have no rights against BUYER with respect thereto except such rights as may exist under patent laws.

11. *Tools, Dies, Etc.* Seller agrees that the information, tools, jigs, dies, etc., drawings, patterns and specifications supplied or paid for by BUYER shall be and remain BUYER'S property, shall be used only on BUYER'S orders, and shall be held by Seller for BUYER unless directed otherwise. Seller will account for such items and keep them in good working condition and fully covered by insurance at all times without expense to BUYER. In the event Seller devises and incorporates any new features design into any goods made under this order, Seller grants to BUYER the right of reproduction of such goods, together with a royalty-free, nonexclusive, irrevocable license to use such new features of design.

12. *General Provisions.*

(a) Seller and BUYER shall be independent contractors. This transaction does not create a principal-agent or partnership relationship between them, and neither one may legally commit the other in any matter.

(b) BUYER may deduct from any payment due to Seller or set-off against any claim by Seller any amount which is due to BUYER by Seller for any reason, including, among other reasons, any excess transportation charges caused by deviations from BUYER'S shipping instructions or the shipping of partial shipments.

(c) Seller shall comply with all laws, regulations and policies applicable to it by any jurisdiction and shall obtain all permits needed to complete this transaction under the laws of the country from which the shipment is made, including among other things, any required export permits and Central Bank approvals.

(d) All billings and payments shall be made in U.S. Dollars.

(e) In the event the importation of the goods results in the assessment of a countervailing duty on BUYER as the importer, Seller shall reimburse such countervailing duty to BUYER, provided such reimbursement is permitted under U.S. laws and regulations,

(f) Goods ordered hereunder to be made with use of BUYER'S confidential information, BUYER'S designs, BUYER'S trademarks or tradenames or BUYER'S customer's trademarks or tradenames shall be furnished by Seller exclusively to BUYER. Any excess of such inventory shall be destroyed by Seller at its own expense.

(g) Seller warrants that it has accepted no gratuities of any kind from any employee of BUYER in connection with placement of this order.

(h) Seller shall cooperate fully with BUYER at Seller's expense in obtaining approvals of the goods requested by BUYER from certifying organizations such as Underwriters Laboratories.

(i) Any goods that are hazardous will be packaged, marked and shipped by Seller to comply with all U.S. federal, state and local regulations and will further comply with all special BUYER requirements. Seller shall furnish BUYER a Material Hazard Data Sheet covering all such goods.

(j) BUYER shall not be liable to Seller for any loss incurred by Seller due to strikes, riots, storms, fires, explosions, acts of God, war, embargo, government boycott or other governmental action or any other causes similar thereto beyond the reasonable control of BUYER. Any failure or delay in performance of any of the foregoing shall not be a default hereunder.

(k) BUYER may waive performance of any condition, but waiver by BUYER of a condition shall not be considered a waiver of that condition for succeeding performance. None of BUYER'S remedies hereunder shall exclude its pursuit of its other legal remedies.

(l) This document and any other documents mentioned on the face hereof, constitute the entire agreement between the parties on this subject. All prior representations, negotiations or arrangements on this subject matter are superseded by these terms and shall not form a basis for interpretation of these terms. All amendments to these terms must be agreed to in writing by BUYER.

(m) If any manufacturer's excise tax, value added tax or other tax measured by selling price is included in or added to the price of the goods paid by BUYER, then, in the event all or any part of that tax shall be refunded to Seller, Seller shall promptly remit such refund in full to BUYER.

(n) This order is nonassignable. Any attempt to assign without BUYER'S written consent is void.

(o) This transaction and all its terms shall be construed in accordance with and all disputes shall be governed by the laws of the State of ___________, U.S.A., specifically including the provisions of the Uniform Commercial Code, as adopted by that state, and excluding the provisions of the Convention on the International Sale of Goods. Seller submits to the jurisdiction of the courts located in the State of ___________ in the event of any proceedings therein in connection herewith.

(p) Any and all disputes arising between BUYER and Seller in connection with this transaction (other than actions for contribution or indemnity with respect to court actions involving third parties) shall be exclusively and finally decided by arbitration in ___________ under the rules of the American Arbitration Association. The arbitration award shall be final and nonappealable. There shall be three arbitrators, one chosen by each party and the third chosen by the first two, or in the event of their failure to agree, by the ___________ state court of general jurisdiction. The arbitrators shall reach their decision, and state it in writing with reason for it, within twelve months after the appointment of the third arbitrator.

(q) This order shall expire in thirty (30) days from the date of issuance by BUYER, unless earlier revoked by BUYER or accepted by Seller. ■

Choice of Forum

When several countries are involved, litigation may be sought in courts in different nations. There are no universally accepted rules regarding the jurisdiction of a particular court over subject matter or parties to a dispute. Consequently, parties to an international transaction should always include in the contract a **forum-selection clause** indicating what court, jurisdiction, or tribunal will decide any disputes arising under the contracts. It is especially important to indicate specifically what court will have jurisdiction. The forum does not necessarily have to be within the geographical boundaries of either of the parties' nations.

FORUM-SELECTION CLAUSE
A provision in a contract designating the forum (the nation, state, or jurisdiction) in which a dispute will be litigated.

Choice of Law

A contractual provision designating the applicable law—such as the law of Germany or England or California—is called a **choice-of-law clause.** Such clauses are typically included in every international contract. At common law (and in European civil law systems), parties are allowed to choose the law that will govern their contractual relationship provided that the law chosen is the law of a jurisdiction that has a substantial relationship to the parties and to the international business transaction. The 1986 Hague Convention on the Law Applicable to Contracts for the International Sale of Goods—often referred to as the Choice-of-Law Convention—allows unlimited autonomy in the choice of law. Whenever a choice of law is not specified in a contract, the Hague Convention indicates that the governing law is that of the country in which the *seller's* place of business is located.

CHOICE-OF-LAW CLAUSE
A clause in a contract designating the law that will govern the contract. For example, two contracting parties from different countries may choose the law of a third country to govern their agreement.

Force Majeure Clause

Every contract, particularly those involving international transactions, should have a ***force majeure* clause.** *Force majeure* is a French term meaning "impossible or irresistible force"—which sometimes is loosely identified as "an act of God." In international business contracts, *force majeure* clauses commonly stipulate that a number of other eventualities, in addition to acts of God, may excuse a party from liability for nonperformance. Consider, for example, the following typical *force majeure* clause:

FORCE MAJEURE CLAUSE
A provision in a contract stipulating that certain unforeseen events—such as war, political upheavals, acts of God, or other events—will excuse a party from liability for nonperformance of contractual obligations.

> The parties hereto shall not be liable for failure of performance hereunder if occasioned by undeclared or declared war, flood, fire, embargo, governmental orders, regulations, restrictions, governmental expropriation, fire, flood, accident, interruptions of transportation facilities, labor strikes and disputes, shortages of materials or production facilities, or any other causes beyond the control of the parties.

Civil Dispute Resolution

Arbitration of civil disputes is becoming an increasingly attractive alternative to costly litigation through the court system. This is true on the international level as well. As already mentioned, arbitration clauses are frequently found in contracts governing the international sale of goods. By means of such clauses, the parties agree in advance to be bound by the decision of a specified third party in the event of a dispute. The third party may be a neutral entity (such as the International Chamber of Commerce), a panel of individuals representing both parties' interests, or some other group or organization. The United Nations Convention on the Recognition and Enforcement of Foreign Arbitral Awards—which has been implemented in more than fifty countries, including the United States—assists in the enforcement of arbitration clauses, as do provisions in specific treaties between nations.

If no arbitration clause is contained in the sales contract, litigation may occur. If forum and choice-of-law clauses are included in the contract, the lawsuit will be heard by a court in the forum country specified and decided according to that country's law. If no forum and choice of law have been specified, however, legal proceedings will be more complex and attended by much more uncertainty. For example, litigation may take place in two or more countries, with each country applying its own choice-of-law rules to determine which substantive law will be applied to the particular transactions. Furthermore, even if a plaintiff wins a favorable judgment in a lawsuit litigated in the plaintiff's country, there is no guaranty that the court's judgment will be enforced by judicial bodies in the defendant's country. As discussed earlier in this chapter, under the principle of comity, the judgment may be enforced in the defendant's country, particularly if the defendant's country is the United States and the foreign court's decision is consistent with U.S. national law and policy. Other nations, however, may not be as accommodating as the United States, and the plaintiff may be left empty-handed.

❖ Making Payment on International Transactions

Currency differences between nations and the geographical distance between parties to international sales contracts add a degree of complexity to international sales that does not exist within the domestic market. Because international contracts involve greater financial risks, special care should be taken in drafting such contracts to specify both the currency in which payment is to be made and the method of payment.

Monetary Systems

While it is true that our national currency, the U.S. dollar, is one of the primary forms of international money, any U.S. firm undertaking business transactions abroad must be prepared to deal with one or more other currencies. After all, just as a U.S. firm wants to be paid in U.S. dollars for goods and services sold abroad, so, too, does a Japanese firm want to be paid in Japanese yen for goods and services sold outside of Japan. Both firms therefore must rely on the convertibility of currencies.

Foreign Exchange Markets Currencies are convertible when they can be freely exchanged one for the other at some specified market rate in a **foreign exchange market.** Foreign exchange markets are a worldwide system for the buying and selling of foreign currencies. At any point in time, the foreign exchange rate is set by the forces of supply and demand in unrestricted foreign exchange markets. The foreign exchange rate is simply the price of a unit of one country's currency in terms of another country's currency. For example, if today's exchange rate is one hundred Japanese yen for one dollar, that means that anybody with one hundred yen can obtain one dollar, and vice versa.

FOREIGN EXCHANGE MARKET
A worldwide system in which foreign currencies are bought and sold.

Correspondent Banking Often, a U.S. company can deal directly with its domestic bank, which will take care of the international money flow problem. Commercial banks sometimes have **correspondent banks** in other countries. Correspondent banking is a major means of transferring funds internationally. Suppose, for example, that a customer of Citibank wishes to pay a bill in French francs to a company in Paris. Citibank can draw a bank check payable in francs on its account in *Crédit Lyonnais,* a Paris correspondent bank, and then send it to the French company to which its customer owes the money. Alternatively, Citibank's customer can request a wire transfer of the funds to the French company. Citibank instructs *Crédit Lyonnais* by wire to pay the necessary amount in French francs. The Clear-

CORRESPONDENT BANK
A bank in which another bank has an account (and vice versa) for the purpose of facilitating fund transfers.

inghouse Interbank Payment Systems (CHIPS) handles about 90 percent of both national and international interbank transfers of U.S. funds. Finally, the Society for Worldwide International Financial Telecommunications (SWIFT) is a communication system that provides banks with messages concerning transactions.

Letters of Credit

LETTER OF CREDIT
A written instrument, usually issued by a bank on behalf of a customer or other person, in which the issuer promises to honor drafts or other demands for payment by third persons in accordance with the terms of the instrument.

Because buyers and sellers engaged in international business transactions are often separated by thousands of miles, special precautions are often taken to ensure performance under the contract. Sellers want to avoid delivering goods for which they might not be paid. Buyers desire the assurance that sellers will not be paid until there is evidence that the goods have been shipped. Thus, **letters of credit** are frequently used to facilitate international business transactions. In a simple letter-of-credit transaction, the *issuer* (a bank) agrees to issue a letter of credit and to ascertain whether the *beneficiary* (seller) performs certain acts. In return, the *account party* (buyer) promises to reimburse the issuer for the amount paid to the beneficiary. There may also be an *advising bank* that transmits information, and a *paying bank* may be involved to expedite payment under the letter of credit. See Exhibit 36–2 for the letter-of-credit "life cycle."

Under a letter of credit, the issuer is bound to pay the beneficiary (seller) when the beneficiary has complied with the terms and conditions of the letter of credit. The beneficiary looks to the issuer, not to the account party (buyer), when it presents the documents required by the letter of credit. Typically, the letter of credit will require that the beneficiary deliver a *bill of lading* to prove that shipment has been made. Letters of credit assure beneficiaries (sellers) of payment while at the same time assuring account parties (buyers) that payment will not be made until the beneficiaries have complied with the terms and conditions of the letter of credit.

◆ **Exhibit 36–2**
The "Life Cycle" of a Letter of Credit

Although the letter of credit appears quite complex at first, it is not difficult to understand. This cycle merely involves the exchange of documents (and money) through intermediaries. The following steps depict the letter-of-credit procurement cycle.

Step 1: The buyer and seller agree upon the terms of sale. The sales contract dictates that a letter of credit is to be used to finance the transaction.

Step 2: The buyer completes an application for a letter of credit and forwards it to his or her bank, which will issue the letter of credit.

Step 3: The issuing (buyer's) bank then forwards the letter of credit to a correspondent bank in the seller's country.

Step 4: The correspondent bank relays the letter of credit to the seller.

Step 5: Having received assurance of payment, the seller makes the necessary shipping arrangements.

Step 6: The seller prepares the documents required under the letter of credit and delivers them to the correspondent bank.

Step 7: The correspondent bank examines the documents. If it finds them in order, it sends them to the issuing bank and pays the seller in accordance with the terms of the letter of credit.

Step 8: The issuing bank, having received the documents, examines them. If they are in order, the issuing bank will charge the buyer's account and send the documents on to the buyer or his or her customs broker. The issuing bank also will reimburse the correspondent bank.

Step 9: The buyer or broker receives the documents and picks up the merchandise from the shipper (carrier).

Source: National Association of Purchasing Management.

The Value of a Letter of Credit The basic principle behind letters of credit is that payment is made against the documents presented by the beneficiary and not against the facts that the documents purport to reflect. Thus, in a letter-of-credit transaction, the issuer does not police the underlying contract; a letter of credit is independent of the underlying contract between the buyer and the seller. Eliminating the need for banks (issuers) to inquire into whether or not actual conditions have been satisfied greatly reduces the costs of letters of credit. Moreover, the use of a letter of credit protects both buyers and sellers.

Compliance with a Letter of Credit In a letter-of-credit transaction, generally at least three separate and distinct contracts are involved: the contract between the account party (buyer) and the beneficiary (seller), the contract between the issuer (bank) and the account party (buyer), and finally the letter of credit itself, which involves the issuer (bank) and the beneficiary (seller). As noted, given that these contracts are separate and distinct, the issuer's obligations under the letter of credit do not concern the underlying contract between the buyer and the seller. Rather, it is the issuer's duty to ascertain whether the documents presented by the beneficiary (seller) comply with the terms of the letter of credit.

If the documents presented by the beneficiary comply with the terms of the letter of credit, the issuer (bank) must honor the letter of credit. Sometimes, however, it is difficult to determine exactly what a letter of credit requires. Moreover, the courts are divided as to whether *strict* or *substantial* compliance with the terms of the letter of credit is required. Traditionally, courts required strict compliance with the terms of a letter of credit, but in recent years, some courts have moved to a standard of *reasonable* compliance.

If the issuing bank refuses to pay the seller (beneficiary) even though the seller has complied with all the requirements of the letter, the seller can bring an action to enforce payment. In the international context, the fact that the issuing bank may be thousands of miles distant from the seller's business location can pose difficulties for the seller—as the following case illustrates.

Case 36.3
PACIFIC RELIANT INDUSTRIES, INC. v. AMERIKA SAMOA BANK
United States Court of Appeals, Ninth Circuit, 1990.
901 F.2d 735.

HISTORICAL AND POLITICAL SETTING *Originally inhabited by Polynesians, Samoa is a group of islands 2,610 miles south of Hawaii. In 1899, the islands were divided into Western Samoa and American Samoa by the Treaty of Berlin, which was signed by Great Britain, Germany, and the United States. Thus, the United States acquired American Samoa. In 1960, American Samoa adopted a constitution, which it revised in 1967, but it remains a non-self-governing, unincorporated territory of the United States. Its currency is the U.S. dollar, its languages are Samoan and English, and it is administered by the U.S. Department of the Interior. The population of American Samoa is less than 50,000.*

FACTS Pacific Reliant Industries, Inc., an Oregon company, sold building materials to Paradise Development Company, a company located in American Samoa. Pacific was reluctant to make several large deliveries, totaling more than $1 million in value, without some protection against nonpayment. Accordingly, representatives from Pacific, Paradise, and Amerika Samoa Bank (ASB) met in American Samoa on two occasions to discuss the supply contract and a letter of credit. Following these negotiations, ASB issued a letter of credit in favor of Pacific on Paradise's account. Later, alleging that ASB had wrongfully dishonored the letter of credit, Pacific brought suit against ASB to recover payment. The United States District Court for the District of Oregon dismissed the suit for lack of personal jurisdiction, holding that ASB lacked sufficient "minimum contacts" (see Chapters 3 and 26) with the state of Oregon to subject it to a lawsuit in that state.[a] Pacific appealed, contending that this case was not typical of other letter-of-credit cases because ASB had participated in forming the underlying contract, had had personal contact with the beneficiary (Pacific), and had known that Pacific would not

a. State law governs some cases that may be brought in a federal court because the parties to the case are citizens of different states or are aliens. In such a case, the federal court must apply the law of the state in which the court is located.

Case 36.3—Continued

extend credit or ship goods from Oregon without the letter of credit.

ISSUE Did ASB have sufficient minimum contacts with the state of Oregon to justify the state's jurisdiction over the dispute?

DECISION No. The appellate court affirmed the lower court's ruling. Pacific could not bring suit against ASB in Oregon.

REASON The court stated that ASB lacked sufficient minimum contacts with Oregon to satisfy jurisdictional requirements. ASB did not initiate the transactions between itself, Paradise, and Pacific, nor did ASB take any significant actions in Oregon. The court noted that "both the negotiations for the underlying contract and the letter of credit occurred in American Samoa." The court reasoned that ASB could not have reasonably expected to be hauled into court in Oregon and "that ASB's conduct as an issuing bank of a letter of credit does not subject it to suit in Oregon."

ETHICAL CONSIDERATIONS *It may appear to be unfair to require a resident to maintain a cause of action in another jurisdiction. If a court could exercise jurisdiction over a nonresident corporation that did not have minimum contacts with the jurisdiction in which the suit was brought, however, the court could exercise jurisdiction over any entity. This would be more than unfair—it would constitute an exercise of unlimited power.*

❖ Regulation of Specific Business Activities

"The notion dies hard that in some sort of way exports are patriotic but imports are immoral."

Lord Harlech (David Ormsley Gore), 1918–1985
(English writer)

Doing business abroad can affect the economies, foreign policy, domestic politics, and other national interests of the countries involved. For this reason, nations impose laws to restrict or facilitate international business. Controls may also be imposed by international agreement. The following sections discuss how different types of international activities are regulated.

Export Restrictions and Incentives

The U.S. Constitution provides in Article I, Section 9, that "No Tax or Duty shall be laid on Articles exported from any State." Thus, Congress cannot impose any export taxes. Congress can, however, use a variety of other devices to control exports. Congress may set export quotas on various items, such as grain being sold abroad. Under the Export Administration Act of 1979, restrictions can be imposed on the flow of technologically advanced products and technical data.

Devices to stimulate exports and thereby aid domestic businesses include export incentives and subsidies. The Revenue Act of 1971, for example, gave tax benefits to firms marketing their products overseas through certain foreign sales corporations, exempting income produced by the exports. Under the Export Trading Company Act of 1982, U.S. banks are encouraged to invest in export trading companies. An export trading company consists of exporting firms joined to export a line of goods. The Export-Import Bank of the United States provides financial assistance, consisting primarily of credit guaranties given to commercial banks that in turn loan funds to U.S. exporting companies.

Import Restrictions

All nations have restrictions on imports, and the United States is no exception. Restrictions include strict prohibitions, quotas, and tariffs. Under the Trading with the Enemy Act of 1917, for example, no goods may be imported from nations that have been designated enemies of the United States. Other laws prohibit the importation of illegal drugs, books that urge insurrection against the United States, and agricultural products that pose dangers to domestic crops or animals.

Quotas are limits on the amounts of goods that can be imported. At one time, the United States had legal quotas on the numbers of automobiles that could be

Although imports cost less than 10 percent of our annual national income, they create intense competition in many markets. Is this why the United States imposes restrictions on some imports?

imported from Japan. Currently, Japan "voluntarily" restricts the numbers of automobiles exported to the United States. Tariffs are taxes on imports. A tariff is usually a percentage of the value of the import, but it can be a flat rate per unit (for example, per barrel of oil). Tariffs raise the prices of goods, causing some consumers to purchase less expensive, domestically manufactured goods.

Restrictions on imports are also known as trade barriers. The elimination of trade barriers is sometimes seen as essential to the world's economic well-being. To minimize trade barriers among nations, most of the world's leading trade nations abide by the General Agreement on Tariffs and Trade (GATT). The GATT has become the principal instrument for regulating international trade. Originally negotiated in 1947, the GATT has gone through seven major tariff and trade renegotiations. Between 1964 and 1967, for example, forty-eight countries negotiated tariff reductions of 50 percent on a broad range of products. Between 1973 and 1979, one hundred countries negotiated nearly a dozen agreements relating to other trade barriers. An eighth round of negotiations began in 1986 (called the Uruguay Round) to consider intellectual property rights, investment policies, dispute resolution, and other topics.

Under Article I of the GATT, each member country agrees to grant **most-favored-nation status** to other member countries. This article obligates each GATT member to treat other GATT members at least as well as it treats that country that receives its most favorable treatment with regard to imports or exports.

MOST-FAVORED-NATION STATUS
A status granted in an international treaty by a provision stating that the citizens of the contracting nations may enjoy the privileges accorded by either party to citizens of the most favored nations. Generally, most-favored-nation clauses are designed to establish equality of international treatment in regard to imports or exports.

The United States has specific laws directed at what it sees as unfair international trade practices. **Dumping,** for example, is the sale of imported goods at "less than fair value." "Fair value" is usually determined by the price of those goods in the exporting country. Foreign firms that engage in dumping in the United States hope to undersell U.S. businesses to obtain a larger share of the U.S. market. To prevent this, an extra tariff—known as an antidumping duty—may be assessed on the imports.

DUMPING
Selling goods in a foreign country at a price below the price charged for the same goods in the domestic market.

Investing

Investing in foreign nations involves a risk that the foreign government may take the investment property. Expropriation, as mentioned, occurs when property is taken and the owner is paid just compensation for what is taken. This does not violate generally observed principles of international law. Confiscation occurs when property is taken and no (or inadequate) compensation is paid. International legal principles are violated when property is confiscated.

International Perspective

Comparative Product Liability Laws

In the *Business Law in Action* in Chapter 5 (on tort reform), we stated that the United States has more lawyers per capita than any other nation on earth. U.S. businesses also face more product liability suits than business firms in any other nation on earth. Why is this? One reason has to do with the fact that the U.S. legal environment is significantly different in some respects from the legal environments of other countries.

In a comparative study of the product liability laws of the United States and ten other countries, Donald G. Gifford, dean of the College of Law of West Virginia University, noted that in many of the foreign countries, victims of injuries caused by defective products need not always go to court to be compensated. Their medical expenses are often covered by national health insurance programs or some combination of private and public health insurance. Gifford also found that in many nations, workers' compensation systems are more extensive, covering more injuries than are covered by U.S. workers' compensation laws.[a] Although many countries impose strict liability for injuries relating to defective products and inherently dangerous activities, such as travel by trains, automobiles, and aircraft, injured claimants cannot recover under strict liability laws for expenses already paid by entitlement programs, such as those just mentioned.

Additionally, in contrast to the United States, many European countries do not allow punitive damages, class-action lawsuits, or contingency fees. (Recall from Chapter 5 that lawyers who charge their clients on a contingency-fee basis receive a specified percentage—such as 30 percent—of whatever the court awards the client as damages.) All of these features of our legal system tend to encourage litigation.

While European businesses who do not deal in the U.S. marketplace may be isolated by their legal systems from product liability litigation to a certain extent, any foreign business firm that manufactures products marketed in the United States is potentially subject to product liability under U.S. laws for defective products that injure American consumers. For example, if a French firm manufactures a toy that is distributed in the United States and is deemed to be unreasonably dangerous by a U.S. court, the French firm may be held liable for damages, including punitive damages.

a. For a discussion of this study, see *American Bar Association Journal*, June 1992, p. 42.

Few remedies are available for confiscation of property by a foreign government. Claims are often resolved by lump-sum settlements after negotiations between the United States and the taking nation. For example, investors whose claims arose out of confiscations following the Russian Revolution in 1917 were offered a lump-sum settlement by the Union of Soviet Socialist Republics in 1974. Still outstanding are $2 billion in claims against Cuba for confiscations that occurred in 1959 and 1960.

To counter the deterrent effect that the possibility of confiscation may have on potential investors, many countries guarantee that foreign investors will be compensated if their property is taken. A guarantee can take the form of national constitutional or statutory laws or provisions in international treaties. As further protection for foreign investments, some countries provide insurance for their citizens' investments abroad.

Bribing Foreign Officials

Giving cash or in-kind benefits to foreign government officials to obtain business contracts and other favors is often considered normal practice. To reduce such bribery by representatives of U.S. corporations, Congress enacted the Foreign Corrupt Practices Act (FCPA)[3] in 1977. This act and its implications for American businesspersons engaged in international business transactions are discussed in detail in the *Landmark in the Law* in Chapter 2.

3. 15 U.S.C. Sections 78m–78ff.

❖ U.S. Laws in an International Setting

The internationalization of business raises questions of the extraterritorial effect of a nation's laws—that is, the effect of the country's laws outside the country. To what extent do U.S. domestic laws affect other nations' businesses? To what extent are U.S. businesses affected by domestic laws when doing business abroad? The following sections discuss these questions in the context of U.S. antitrust, patent, and discrimination laws.

U.S. Antitrust Laws

U.S. antitrust laws (discussed in Chapter 30) have a wide application. They may *subject* persons in foreign nations to their provisions as well as *protect* foreign consumers and competitors from violations committed by U.S. citizens. Consequently, *foreign persons*, a term that by definition includes foreign governments, may sue under U.S. antitrust laws in U.S. courts.

Section 1 of the Sherman Act provides for the extraterritorial effect of the U.S. antitrust laws. The United States is a major proponent of free competition in the global economy, and thus any conspiracy that has a substantial effect on U.S. commerce is within the reach of the Sherman Act. The violation may even occur outside the United States, and foreign governments as well as persons can be sued for violation of U.S. antitrust laws. Before U.S. courts will exercise jurisdiction and apply antitrust laws, it must be shown that the alleged violation had a *substantial effect* on U.S. commerce. U.S. jurisdiction is automatically invoked, however, when a *per se* violation occurs.[4] A *per se* violation may consist of resale price fixing and tying, or tie-in, contracts. If a domestic firm, for example, joins a foreign cartel to control the production, price, or distribution of goods, and this cartel has a *substantial restraining effect* on U.S. commerce, a *per se* violation may exist. Hence, both the domestic firm and the foreign cartel may be sued for violation of the U.S. antitrust laws. Likewise, if foreign firms doing business in the United States enter into a price-fixing or other anticompetitive agreement to control a portion of U.S. markets, a *per se* violation may exist.

An alleged conspiracy on the part of Japanese television manufacturers to gain control of the electronic products market in the United States—in violation of the Sherman Act and other antitrust and tariff legislation—was considered by the United States Supreme Court in the following case.

Case 36.4
MATSUSHITA ELECTRIC INDUSTRIAL CO. v. ZENITH RADIO CORP.

Supreme Court of the United States, 1986.
475 U.S. 574,
106 S.Ct. 1348,
89 L.Ed.2d 538.

HISTORICAL AND ECONOMIC SETTING *Zenith Electronics Corporation began broadcasting with the first all-electronic television station, W9XZV, in 1939. In 1948, Zenith introduced its first television sets. By 1960, there were twenty-seven U.S. companies manufacturing television sets. The technology improved and sales increased. By 1980, virtually every American home had a television set and many had two or three. During the 1970s, however, some of the companies that based their products entirely on U.S. technology had begun losing their market shares to foreign competition. During the early 1980s, purchases of television sets manufactured by U.S. companies fell dramatically. While other U.S. manufacturers ceased selling television sets or sold their brands to foreign companies,*

4. Certain types of restrictive contracts, such as price-fixing agreements, are deemed inherently anticompetitive and thus in restraint of trade as a matter of law. When such a restrictive contract is entered into, there is said to be a *per se* violation of the antitrust laws. See Chapter 30.

Case 36.4—Continued

Zenith fought its foreign competitors in the marketplace, in Congress, and in the United States Supreme Court.

FACTS Zenith Radio Corporation and several other U.S. manufacturers of television sets alleged that Matsushita Electric Industrial Company and other Japanese firms had "illegally conspired to drive American firms from the consumer electronic products market" by means of a "scheme to raise, fix and maintain artificially high prices for television receivers sold by [Matsushita and others] in Japan and, at the same time, to fix and maintain low prices for television receivers exported to and sold in the United States." The alleged conspiracy had begun, according to Zenith, in 1953. The American firms claimed that the Japanese were engaged in a "predatory pricing" arrangement in which the losses sustained by selling at such low prices in the United States were offset by monopoly profits obtained in Japan. Once the Japanese gained control over an overwhelming portion of the American market for electronic products, their monopoly power would enable them to recover their losses by charging artificially high prices in America as well. The district court granted summary judgment in favor of the Japanese firms, and the case was appealed and ultimately heard by the United States Supreme Court.

ISSUE Were the Japanese firms engaging in a price-fixing scheme in violation of U.S. antitrust laws?

DECISION No. The trial court's decision was affirmed.

REASON The United States Supreme Court found the allegation that the Japanese firms were engaging in predatory pricing and other anticompetitive arrangements to be "implausible" and one "that simply makes no economic sense." Citing numerous authorities on predatory pricing, the Court argued that the risk of suffering real, immediate losses in the present in the mere hope of not only establishing monopoly power, but maintaining it for a sufficiently long period to recoup the losses at some point in the distant future, was one rarely, if ever, taken by any firm. For a cartel, or alliance of firms, to undertake such a risk was even more unlikely. The difficulties involved in allocating losses and future profits among a group of firms and in ensuring that none of them cheated on the others—which would be especially tempting given the uncertainty of the future monopoly profits—were unlikely to be overcome. The Court further contended that the "alleged predatory scheme makes sense only if petitioners can recoup their losses. In light of the large number of firms involved here, petitioners can achieve this only by engaging in some form of price-fixing after they have succeeded in driving competitors from the market. Such price-fixing would, of course, be an independent violation of Section 1 of the Sherman Act." Thus, even if the cartel could overcome the difficulties mentioned earlier by consistently pricing below cost, the existence of antitrust legislation in the United States would still make it extremely difficult, if not impossible, to realize the goal of monopoly profits. Finally, and perhaps most persuasively, the Court noted a relevant fact: In 1953, the two leading television producers in the United States, RCA and Zenith, controlled approximately 40 percent of that market. Over the succeeding years during which the Japanese were implementing their alleged plan, that percentage remained approximately constant and had not changed significantly. "The alleged conspiracy's failure to achieve its ends in the two decades of its asserted operation," stated the Court, "is strong evidence that the conspiracy does not in fact exist." It was the Court's opinion that to claim that such a conspiracy exists simply "makes no practical sense."

Patent Laws

In the United States, inventions are protected by patent law, which is intended to prevent others from copying the inventions. U.S. patent laws provide no direct protection overseas, however. To be protected in another country, an invention must be patented under the laws of that country. Internationally, an agreement known as the Paris Convention[5] guarantees nondiscriminatory treatment under the laws of other nations, but it does not provide independent international patent protection. The United States may prohibit the importation of products that infringe on patents registered in the United States.

5. The agreement is known as the Paris Convention because it was signed in Paris (on March 20, 1883). See International Convention for the Protection of Industrial Property, 25 Stat. 1372, T.S. No. 379. A revision of the Paris Convention was signed in Stockholm on July 14, 1967. See International Convention for the Protection of Industrial Property, 21 U.S.T. 1629, T.I.A.S. No. 6923.

Business Law in Action

What's an Employer to Do?

Doing business in a foreign country clearly poses problems unlike those faced within U.S. boundaries. For example, a U.S. firm doing business in Germany must abide not only by U.S. laws but also by German laws. But what if these laws come into apparent conflict? As discussed in this chapter, the "foreign laws exception" to many U.S. discrimination laws addresses this potential problem by excusing U.S. employers from liability under U.S. discrimination laws if adherence to the U.S. laws would violate the law of the host country. Nonetheless, at least one employer has been caught between the proverbial "rock and a hard place" in trying to abide by the laws of two countries simultaneously.

The employer was a U.S. corporation, RFE/RL, Inc., better known under the names of its broadcast services, Radio Free Europe and Radio Liberty. RFE/RL employs more than three hundred U.S. citizens at its principal place of business in Munich, Germany. The concept of a mandatory retirement age is deeply embedded in German labor policy. Unlike U.S. laws, German laws do not prohibit this form of age discrimination, and labor union contracts in Germany frequently include clauses that require workers to be retired when they reach the age of sixty-five. A contract formed in 1982 between RFE/RL and a German labor union contained such a clause.

In 1984, when the U.S. Age Discrimination in Employment Act (ADEA) of 1967 was amended to apply extraterritorially, RFE/RL tried to accommodate the new law by signing individual employment contracts that allowed certain employees to continue working past the age of sixty-five. The company's "works council"—which is bound by German law to give effect to a union contract—rejected the individual contracts because they violated the mandatory retirement provision in the union contract. RFE/RL appealed to the German labor courts with no success. Those courts held that the union contract did not permit a retirement age higher than sixty-five. Thus it was that when William Mahoney and other American employees reached the age of sixty-five, RFE/RL assumed (or so it alleged) that it had a legal obligation to terminate their employment. Thus RFE/RL faced a lawsuit brought by Mahoney and the others (the plaintiffs) for age discrimination in violation of the ADEA, which prohibits mandatory retirement at the age of sixty-five.

For all its purported efforts to avoid illegal age discrimination, RFE/RL did not succeed. In 1992, a U.S. federal court held that in spite of the union contract's provisions and the German labor courts' decisions, German law did not compel RFE/RL to fire the workers. According to the U.S. court, the decisions made by the German labor courts "involved a narrower issue than that addressed here. Those decisions simply held that the union contract did not permit a retirement age higher than 65; they merely enforced the contract upon the parties to it. * * * They did not hold that anything in German law compelled the decisions reached." Therefore, the "foreign laws exception" did not apply to RFE/RL's mandatory retirement of the plaintiffs, and the company's mandatory retirement of the plaintiffs was illegal. The U.S. court clarified the matter by describing a hypothetical situation "in which a foreign country's labor unions came to be controlled by a group committed to the exclusion of a racial minority. It can hardly be doubted that Title VII of the Civil Rights Act of 1964 would not allow a U.S. employer in that country to enforce racist policies under the guise of obeying the foreign labor unions."[a]

In view of the court's instructive opinion, RFE/RL now knows the difference between a German labor practice and German law. But assuming that the company acted in good faith in discharging the employees, one cannot but sympathize with RFE/RL and any other employer facing the challenge of trying to obey two masters, or sets of laws.

a. *Mahoney v. RFE/RL, Inc.*, 1992 W.L. 410037 (D.D.C. 1992). This opinion is not published in the Federal Supplement reporter but may be retrieved from WESTLAW using the citation given here.

Discrimination Laws

As explained in Chapter 32, there are laws in the United States prohibiting discrimination on the basis of race, color, national origin, religion, sex, age, and disability. These laws, as they affect employment relationships, generally apply extraterritorially. Since 1984, for example, the Age Discrimination in Employment Act (ADEA) of 1967 has covered U.S. employees working abroad for U.S. employers. The Americans with Disabilities Act of 1990, which requires employers to accommodate the needs of workers with disabilities, also applies to U.S. nationals working abroad for U.S. firms.

For some time, it was uncertain whether the major U.S. law regulating discriminatory practices in the workplace, Title VII of the Civil Rights Act of 1964, applied extraterritorially. Because the act did not specifically claim that it protected employees outside the boundaries of the United States, courts reached different conclusions. In 1991, the United States Supreme Court concluded that Title VII did not apply extraterritorially.[6] Later that same year, Congress passed the Civil Rights Act of 1991 (described in the *Landmark in the Law* in Chapter 32). Among other things, it provides that Title VII applies extraterritorially to all U.S. employees working for U.S. employers abroad.

U.S. discrimination laws, in regard to their extraterritorial application, generally stipulate that U.S. employers must abide by U.S. discrimination laws *unless* to do so would violate the laws of the country in which their workplaces are located. This "foreign laws exception" allows employers to avoid being subjected to conflicting laws. (But see this chapter's *Business Law in Action*, which discusses a case in which a U.S. employer, acting under the assumption that the law of its host country required mandatory retirement, ended up facing liability for violating the ADEA.)

What happens if a Japanese firm doing business in the United States allegedly discriminates against U.S. employees in favor of Japanese citizens, which is permitted under a treaty between the United States and Japan? Is discrimination on the basis of citizenship the same thing as discrimination on the basis of national origin? These questions were addressed in the following case.

Case 36.5
FORTINO v. QUASAR CO., A DIVISION OF MATSUSHITA ELECTRIC CORP. OF AMERICA

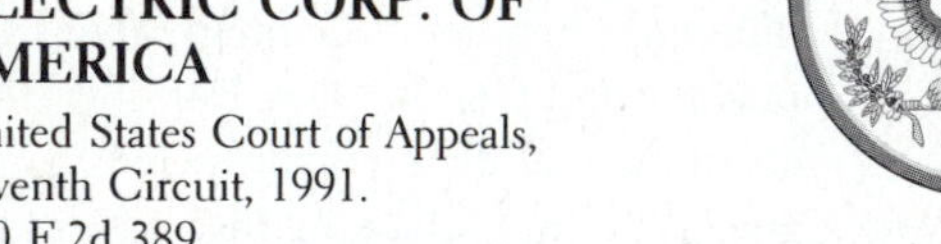

United States Court of Appeals, Seventh Circuit, 1991.
950 F.2d 389.

HISTORICAL AND ECONOMIC SETTING *Motorola, Inc., manufactured automobile radios, police radios, and walkie-talkies before and during the Second World War, which ended in 1945. In the early years of television, Motorola marketed the first television sets priced under $200. By the 1970s, however, Motorola had begun losing its share of the television market to Japanese manufacturers, and in 1974, the company sold its Quasar television manufacturing facilities in Franklin Park, Illinois, to Matsushita Electric Industrial Company, which is based in Osaka, Japan. Matsushita made more than a million television sets in the Quasar plant in 1988. The next year, Matsushita appointed an American, who had worked for Quasar before its sale by Motorola, to Matsushita's second highest executive position in North America.*

FACTS In 1953, the United States and Japan entered into a Treaty of Friendship, Commerce, and Navigation. The treaty provides, among other things, that Japanese companies doing business in the United States and U.S. companies doing business in Japan have the right to choose citizens of their own nations as executives for their firms. Quasar Company, doing business in the United States as a subsidiary of the Japanese company Matsushita Electric Industrial Company, employed U.S. workers and management personnel but was largely controlled by executives of Matsushita. After suffering a $20 million loss in 1985, Matsushita executives restructured Quasar and cut its work force dramatically. Of eighty-nine managers working for the company, sixty-six were fired. None of the company's ten Japanese executives was laid off, and some of them received raises. John Fortino and two other American executives who had been fired (the plaintiffs) sued Quasar for, among other things, discriminating against them on the basis of national origin in violation of Title VII. Quasar defended by asserting that discrimination on the basis of citizenship, as allowed under the treaty, did not violate Title VII. The trial court held for the American executives, and Quasar appealed.

ISSUE Did Quasar's discrimination on the basis of citizenship constitute discrimination on the basis of national origin in violation of Title VII?

DECISION No. The appellate court reversed the trial

6. *Equal Employment Opportunity Commission v. Arabian American Oil Co.*, 499 U.S. 244, 111 S.Ct. 1227, 113 L.Ed.2d 274 (1991).

Case 36.5—Continued

court's decision. The plaintiffs had no cause of action under Title VII.

REASON The court stressed that the discrimination on the basis of citizenship permitted by the treaty is not prohibited by Title VII. Title VII prohibits discrimination on the basis of national origin but not preference based on citizenship. The court conceded that most Japanese citizens are likely to be of Japanese national origin but concluded that discrimination on the basis of citizenship is conceptually distinct from bias based on national origin. Japanese companies were expressly given the right to choose citizens from their own nation as executives of their foreign subsidiaries in the United States. "That right would be empty," said the court, "if the subsidiary could be punished for treating its citizen executives differently from American executives on the ground that, since the former were of Japanese national origin and the latter were not, it was discriminating on the basis of national origin. Title VII would be taking back from the Japanese with one hand what the treaty had given them with the other. This collision is avoided by holding national origin and citizenship separate."

ETHICAL CONSIDERATIONS *The court admitted that its decision might seem "callous" but pointed out that the treaty rights were reciprocal. "There are Americans employed abroad by foreign subsidiaries of U.S. companies who, but for the treaty, would lose their jobs to foreign nationals. Indeed, the treaty provision was inserted at the insistence of the United States. Japan was opposed to it." The court also considered the possibility that a Japanese firm might purchase an American company, fire all of its American executives because it was prejudiced against Americans, and replace them with Japanese citizens. In such a situation, the question "would then arise whether the treaty of friendship in effect confers a blanket immunity from Title VII." The court concluded, however, that it "need not choose sides" on this issue because "there is no evidence of discrimination here [in the present case] save what is implicit in wanting your own citizens to run your foreign subsidiary." Some observers, worried about the implications of this ruling for future cases, contend that perhaps the court should have "chosen sides" on the issue or at least further clarified the distinction between national origin and citizenship in this kind of situation. Others contend that if other courts rule similarly, the issue may require the amendment of Title VII.*

❖ Key Terms

act of state doctrine 875
choice-of-language clause 881
choice-of-law clause 884
comity 875
confiscation 875
correspondent bank 885
distribution agreement 879
dumping 889
exclusive distributorship 879
export 878
expropriation 875
***force majeure* clause** 884
foreign exchange market 885
forum-selection clause 884
international law 874
letter of credit 886
most-favored-nation status 889
sovereign immunity 876
technology licensing 880

❖ Chapter Summary: International Law in a Global Economy

The Legal Context of International Business Transactions	Three important legal principles and doctrines frame international relations and business transactions: 1. *The principle of comity*—Under this principle, nations give effect to the laws and judicial decrees of other nations for reasons of courtesy and international harmony. 2. *The act of state doctrine*—A doctrine developed by American courts to avoid passing judgment on the validity of public acts committed by a recognized foreign government within its own territory. 3. *The doctrine of sovereign immunity*—When certain conditions are satisfied, foreign nations are immune from U.S. jurisdiction under the Foreign Sovereign Immunities Act of 1976.

❖ Chapter Summary: International Law in a Global Economy—Continued

The Legal Context of International Business Transactions—Continued	Exceptions are (a) when the foreign state has "waived its immunity either explicitly or by implication" and (b) when the action is "based upon a commercial activity carried on in the United States by the foreign state."
Doing Business Internationally	Ways in which U.S. domestic firms engage in international business transactions include (a) exporting, which may involve foreign agents or distributors, and (b) manufacturing abroad through licensing arrangements, franchising operations, wholly owned subsidiaries, or joint ventures.
Commercial Contracts in an International Setting	Choice-of-language, forum-selection, and choice-of-law clauses are often included in international business contracts to reduce the uncertainties associated with interpreting the language of the agreement. *Force majeure* clauses are included in most domestic and international contracts. They commonly stipulate that certain events, such as floods, fire, accidents, labor strikes, and shortages, may excuse a party from liability for nonperformance of the contract. Arbitration clauses are also frequently found in international contracts.
Making Payment on International Transactions	1. *Currency conversion*—Because nations have different monetary systems, payment on international contracts requires currency conversion at a rate specified in a foreign exchange market. 2. *Correspondent banking*—Correspondent banks facilitate the transfer of funds from a buyer in one country to a seller in another. 3. *Letters of credit*—Letters of credit facilitate international transactions by ensuring payment to sellers and ensuring to buyers that payment will not be made until the sellers have complied with the terms of the letters of credit. Typically, compliance occurs when a bill of lading is delivered to the issuing bank.
Regulation of Specific Business Activities	In the interests of their economies, foreign policies, domestic policies, or other national priorities, nations impose laws that restrict or facilitate international business. Such laws regulate exporting and importing activities, foreign investments, and, in the United States, the bribery of foreign officials to obtain favorable contracts.
U.S. Laws in an International Setting	1. *Antitrust laws*—U.S. antitrust laws may be applied beyond the borders of the United States. Any conspiracy that has a substantial effect on commerce within the United States may be subject to the Sherman Act, even if the violation occurs outside the United States. 2. *Patent laws*—U.S. patent laws provide no direct protection overseas. To be protected in another country, an invention must be patented under the laws of that country. International treaties provide some protection to U.S. patent holders, however. 3. *Discrimination laws*—The major U.S. laws prohibiting employment discrimination, including Title VII of the Civil Rights Act of 1964, the Age Discrimination in Employment Act of 1967, the Americans with Disabilities Act of 1990, and the Civil Rights Act of 1991, cover U.S. employees working abroad for U.S. firms—*unless* to apply the U.S. laws would violate the laws of the host country.

❖ Questions and Case Problems

36-1. Comity. What is the principle of comity, and why do courts deciding disputes involving a foreign law or judicial decree apply this principle?

36-2. Sovereign Immunity. A foreign nation is not immune from the jurisdiction of U.S. courts if the state waives its immunity. Under the Foreign Sovereign Immunities Act of 1976, on what other basis might a foreign state be considered subject to the jurisdiction of U.S. courts?

36-3. Letters of Credit. James Reynolds entered into an agreement to purchase dental supplies from Tooth-Tech, Inc. Reynolds also secured a letter of credit from Central Bank to pay for the supplies. Tooth-Tech placed sixty crates of dental supplies on board a steamship and received in return the invoices required under the letter of credit. The purchaser, Reynolds, subsequently learned that Tooth-Tech, Inc., had filled the sixty crates with rubbish, not dental supplies. Given the fact that an issuer's obligation under a letter of credit is independent of the underlying contract between the buyer and the seller, would the issuer be required to pay the seller in this situation? Explain. [See UCC 5–114(1), (2).]

36-4. Jurisdictional Requirements. Harris Corp. entered into a contract with National Iranian Radio and Television (NIRT) to manufacture and deliver 144 FM broadcast transmitters to Teheran, Iran. Because of the revolution in Iran, Harris was unable to complete delivery of the transmitters. Harris, the plaintiff, subsequently brought an action in the United States against NIRT, the defendant. Bank Melli Iran, the issuer of a letter of credit relating to the transaction, was also made a defendant. Both defendants alleged that the district court lacked jurisdiction over them. Since 1969, Melli had maintained an office in New York City in which it carried out significant business transactions. Moreover, the contract between NIRT and Harris required performance by Harris in the United States and also the training of NIRT personnel in the United States. Could a U.S. court exercise jurisdiction over the defendants? Was the "minimum contacts" standard discussed in Chapter 3 satisfied? [*Harris Corp. v. National Iranian Radio and Television*, 691 F.2d 1344 (11th Cir. 1982)]

36-5. Sovereign Immunity. Texas Trading & Milling Corp. and other companies brought an action for breach of contract against the Federal Republic of Nigeria and its central bank. Nigeria, a rapidly developing and oil-rich nation, had overbought huge quantities of cement from Texas Trading and others. Unable to accept delivery of the cement, Nigeria repudiated the contract, alleging immunity under the Foreign Sovereign Immunities Act of 1976. Because the buyer of the cement was the Nigerian government, did the doctrine of sovereign immunity remove the dispute from the jurisdiction of U.S. courts? [*Texas Trading & Milling Corp. v. Federal Republic of Nigeria*, 647 F.2d 300 (2d Cir. 1981)]

36-6. Letters of Credit. The Swiss Credit Bank issued a letter of credit in favor of Antex Industries to cover the sale of 92,000 electronic integrated circuits manufactured by Electronic Arrays. The letter of credit specified that the chips would be transported to Tokyo by ship. Antex shipped the circuits by air. Payment on the letter of credit was dishonored because the shipment by air did not fulfill the precise terms of the letter of credit. Should a court compel payment? Explain. [*Board of Trade of San Francisco v. Swiss Credit Bank*, 728 F.2d 1241 (9th Cir. 1984)]

36-7. Act of State Doctrine. Sabbatino, an American, contracted with a Cuban corporation that was largely owned by U.S. residents to buy Cuban sugar. When the Cuban government expropriated the corporation's property and rights in retaliation against a U.S. reduction of the Cuban sugar quota, Sabbatino entered into a new contract to make payment for the sugar to Banco Nacional, a government-owned Cuban bank. Sabbatino refused to make the promised payment, and Banco subsequently filed an action in a U.S. district court seeking to recover payment for the sugar. The issue was whether the act of state doctrine should apply when a foreign state violates international law. (If the doctrine were applied, the Cuban government's action would be presumed valid, and thus Banco's claim would be legitimate.) The district court held that the doctrine did not apply and granted summary judgment for Sabbatino. The case was ultimately appealed to the United States Supreme Court. Will the Supreme Court agree that the act of state doctrine should not be applied in these circumstances? Discuss. [*Banco Nacional de Cuba v. Sabbatino*, 376 U.S. 398, 84 S.Ct. 923, 11 L.Ed.2d 804 (1964)]

36-8. Antitrust Claims. Billy Lamb and Carmon Willis (the plaintiffs) were tobacco growers in Kentucky. Phillip Morris and B.A.T. Industries, PLC, routinely purchased tobacco not only from Kentucky but also from producers in several foreign countries. In 1982, subsidiaries of Phillip Morris and B.A.T. (the defendants) entered into an agreement with La Fundacion Del Niño (the Children's Foundation) of Caracas, Venezuela. The president of the Children's Foundation was the wife of the man who was then president of Venezuela. The agreement provided that the two subsidiaries would donate a total of approximately $12.5 million to the Children's Foundation and, in exchange, the subsidiaries would obtain price controls on Venezuelan tobacco, elimination of controls on retail cigarette prices in Venezuela, tax deductions for the donations, and assurances that existing tax rates applicable to tobacco companies would not be increased. The plaintiffs brought an action, alleging that the Venezuelan arrangement was an inducement designed to restrain trade in violation of U.S. antitrust laws. Such an arrangement, the plaintiffs contended, would result in the artificial depression of tobacco prices to the detriment of domestic tobacco growers, while ensuring lucrative retail prices for tobacco products sold abroad. The trial court held that the plaintiffs' claim was barred by the act of state doctrine. What will result on appeal? Discuss. [*Lamb v. Phillip Morris, Inc.*, 915 F.2d 1024 (6th Cir. 1990)]

36-9. Sovereign Immunity. While in the United States, Scott Nelson was hired as a monitoring systems engineer for the King Faisal Specialist Hospital in Riyadh, Saudi Arabia. Nelson alleged that in the course of performing his duties under his employment contract with the hospital, he was detained and tortured by agents of the Saudi government in Saudi Arabia for reporting safety violations at the hospital. Nelson brought suit for his injuries against Saudi Arabia, the hospital, and Royspec, a corporation owned and controlled by the government of Saudi Arabia (collectively, Saudi Arabia). Saudi Arabia claimed immunity under the doctrine of sovereign immunity. Nelson contended that because his detention and torture resulted from his recruitment within the United States by an agent of the Saudi government as part of a commercial activity, the district court had subject matter jurisdiction under the Foreign Sovereign Immunities Act of 1976. What should the court decide? Discuss fully. [*Nelson v. Saudi Arabia*, 923 F.2d 1528 (11th Cir. 1991)]

36-10. Forum-Selection Clauses. Royal Bed and Spring Co., a Puerto Rican distributor of furniture products, entered into an exclusive distributorship agreement with Famossul Industria e Comercio de Moveis Ltda., a Brazilian manufacturer of furniture products. Under the terms of the contract, Royal Bed was to distribute in Puerto Rico the furniture products manufactured by Famossul in Brazil. The contract contained choice-of-forum and choice-of-law clauses, which designated the judicial district of Curitiba, State of Paraná, Brazil, as the judicial forum and the Brazilian Civil Code as the law to be applied in the event of any dispute. Famossul terminated the exclusive distributorship and suspended the shipment of goods without just cause. Puerto Rican law refuses to enforce forum-selection clauses providing for foreign venues as a matter of public policy. In what jurisdiction should Royal Bed bring suit? Discuss fully. [*Royal Bed and Spring Co. v. Famossul*

Industria e Comercio de Moveis Ltda., 906 F.2d 45 (5th Cir. 1990)]

36-11. Forum-Selection Clauses. Ronald Riley, an American citizen, wanted to underwrite some insurance policies issued by the Society and Council of Lloyd's, a British insurance corporation with its principal place of business in London. In 1980, Riley and Lloyd's entered into an agreement that allowed Riley to underwrite insurance through Lloyd's and provided that if any dispute arose between Lloyd's and Riley, the courts of England would have exclusive jurisdiction and the laws of England would apply. Over the next decade, some of the parties insured under policies that Riley underwrote experienced large losses, for which they filed claims. Instead of paying his share of the claims, Riley filed a lawsuit in a United States district court, seeking, among other things, rescission of his agreement with Lloyd's. The defendants included Lloyd's and those among its managers and directors—all British citizens or entities—with whom Riley had dealt when he began his association with Lloyd's. Riley alleged that the defendants had violated the Securities Act of 1933, the Securities Exchange Act of 1934, and Rule 10b-5. The defendants asked the court to enforce the forum-selection clause in the agreement. Riley argued that if the clause was enforced, he would be deprived of his rights under the U.S. securities laws. The court ruled that the clause was enforceable, and Riley appealed. What will the appellate court decide? Discuss. [*Riley v. Kingsley Underwriting Agencies, Ltd.*, 969 F.2d 953 (10th Cir. 1992)]

A Question of Ethics and Social Responsibility

36-12. *Gordonsville Industries, Inc., located in Virginia, entered into a contract with American Artos Corp., a North Carolina corporation, for the design, construction, and installation of a textile-drying system. Artos, in turn, contracted with GEA Luftkuhlergesellschaft, a German firm, for the design of a hot oil boiler, one of the system's integral parts. GEA subcontracted the actual construction of the boiler to Industrial Boiler Co., a Georgia corporation. A forum-selection clause in the Artos-GEA contract specified that in the event of a lawsuit, "it is agreed that the place for litigation shall be the Amtsgericht [civil court] in Bochum, Germany." Later, Gordonsville Industries, unhappy with the performance of the textile-drying system, filed suit in a U.S. federal court against Artos to recover damages. Artos then filed a complaint, essentially seeking indemnification (reimbursement), against GEA. GEA moved to dismiss the complaint on the grounds that under the forum-selection clause in the Artos-GEA contract, the dispute should be heard in the specified German court. Artos contended that the clause should not be enforced because the construction of the boiler had taken place in the United States, and all of the relevant records and witnesses were located in the United States, not Germany.* [Gordonsville Industries, Inc. v. American Artos Corp., *549 F.Supp. 200 (W.D.Va. 1982)]*

1. Discuss whether the circumstances of this case would justify permitting the case to proceed in the U.S. courts.
2. What arguments might Artos raise against having the dispute heard in the German courts?
3. How would you evaluate the argument that strict enforcement of the forum-selection clause is necessary to promote certainty in international commercial transactions?

For Critical Analysis

36-13. *Business cartels and monopolies that are legal in some countries may engage in practices that violate U.S. antitrust laws. In view of this fact, what are some of the implications of applying U.S. antitrust laws extraterritorially?*

PERSONAL LAW HANDBOOK

Contents

*Note to Student**

Business law and the legal environment do not just consist of theoretical concepts and vague statutes. Rather, you will find that you can use what you have learned from your course in many practical ways throughout your life. In this *Personal Law Handbook* you will discover suggestions for preventing costly legal problems, as well as ideas about how to handle those legal problems that you have not been able to avoid. To a large extent, personal law is preventive—the more you know about the legal consequences of your actions and the actions of those with whom you have dealings, the better you will be able to prevent legal problems.

In no way should you take this *Handbook* to be a substitute for licensed, professional legal assistance. Whenever you think that you have a legal problem, you should consult an attorney.

* This handbook was written by Frank B. Cross of the University of Texas at Austin.

Topic 1 Renting a Home

Like millions of Americans, you may decide not to own your own home. Instead, you may choose to rent a house, an apartment, a mobile home, or some other form of housing. As a tenant, your relationship with your landlord is generally governed by the law of the state in which you live.

❖ Leases

The **lease** is the agreement between you and your landlord that sets out rights and duties regarding the rental property. A written lease is a legal document enforceable in court—a signature on a lease is generally proof that the person who signed it read it and agreed to it. Thus, if you sign a lease, you are bound to do what it says. For this reason, you should read an entire lease carefully before you sign it.

Most leases are written to favor the landlord's interests. If you are unsure of the meaning or effect of any of the terms, before signing the lease you should seek the advice of a lawyer, a tenants' rights organization, a legal aid office, or others experienced with leases.

Oral Leases

In almost all states, an oral lease for a period of less than a year is valid. The basic problem with an oral lease is the same as the basic problem with other oral contracts: it is difficult to prove the terms of the oral agreement. Generally, it is assumed an oral lease that requires rent to be paid monthly creates a **month-to-month tenancy.** This means that, with a month's written notice, a landlord can raise the rent or end the tenancy. Of course, you can also end the tenancy with a month's written notice.

Lease Terms

Leases include such terms as the following items:

1. The names of the parties to the agreement.
2. The address of the rental property.
3. The amount and the due date of the rent.
4. Other fees and charges.
5. The period of time for which the property is rented.
6. The rights and duties of the parties, which relate to use of the premises, alterations, maintenance, repairs, and other areas of responsibility.
7. The amount of a security deposit.
8. The conditions under which the rent can be raised.
9. Provisions for subleasing the property and terminating the lease.

Alterations Can you make changes to rental property after you move in? In most circumstances, the answer depends on the terms of the lease. Most leases include a provision that prohibits alterations without the landlord's written approval. If you do not get the landlord's approval before making alterations, you will violate the lease and may be liable for any presumed destruction of the property. If there is no lease provision concerning alterations, you can make changes to the property that do not reduce the value of the property to the landlord.

If no lease provision applies and you have made a change—for example, if you have added bookshelves or installed new cabinets, who owns the new addition? If you cannot come to an agreement with your landlord, and you ask a court to decide the question, the court will look at the laws of your state to determine who owns what. In some states, the addition may be the property of the landlord; in other states, it may be yours, and you can sell it to the landlord or remove it. If it is your property and you choose to remove it, you should do so carefully to avoid any damage to the rental property. If the property is damaged, you are responsible.

Subleases Normally, a lease contains a provision that prohibits a tenant from **subleasing** the rental property without the landlord's written approval. If the lease does not require the landlord's approval, in most cases you can sublease for whatever period of time you could remain on the property under the lease. A sublease cannot be for a longer period than you could stay on the property. For instance, if you signed a one-year lease that contains no provision regarding subleasing and there are six months left before the lease expires, you could sublease the property for six months or less. As the original tenant, however, you are still liable for the rent and any damage to the property.

Whether or not your lease prohibits subleasing, can you move out before the lease expires? Generally, the answer is yes. You will be liable for the rent for the rest of the lease, however. There may be a limit on how much you pay: in some states, a landlord must make a reasonable effort to find a new tenant for the same amount of rent and the same period of time. If the property can only be rented for a smaller amount of money or a shorter time, you will be liable for the difference.

To minimize your losses, as soon as you know you will be moving out, send the landlord written notice (via certified or registered mail) of your plan to allow as much time as possible to find a new tenant. Keep a copy of the notice. You might also help find a new tenant by advertising that the property will be available.

Renewal Typically, a lease requires that you move out when it expires. A lease can provide, however, that it renews automatically unless you tell the landlord in advance that you plan to move out. If you do not give the landlord this notice, you will be renewing the lease on the same terms for the same period of time. A different lease might provide that if you stay on the property after the lease expires and the landlord accepts a payment of rent, the lease renews according to the original terms.

If the lease does not mention renewal, in some states the landlord does not need to give you notice that the lease is ending. In these states, the reasoning is that you know when the lease expires because you signed it, and thus you must leave the property when the lease ends without additional notice. In other states, if you remain on the property after the lease ends and the landlord accepts a payment of rent, a new month-to-month tenancy is created or, in some states, the lease renews according to its original terms.

Illegal Terms

A landlord cannot legally discriminate against you on the basis of your race, color, religion, national origin, or gender. Also, a landlord cannot discriminate against you if you have a handicap or, in most cases, if you have children. Similarly, as a tenant, you cannot legally promise to do something counter to the laws prohibiting discrimination. The public policy underlying these prohibitions is to treat all people equally.

One of the reasons to read a lease carefully is to look for, and avoid, illegal terms. Generally, any clause that purports to waive your legal rights is unenforceable. For this reason, clauses that attempt to do any or all of the following may be unenforceable in your state:

1. Waiving your right to a jury trial in eviction proceedings.
2. Permitting your landlord to evict you in a court proceeding without your presence.
3. Providing for a nonrefundable security deposit.
4. Limiting your landlord's liability for hazardous conditions that injure you or your guests.
5. Requiring that you pay an unreasonably high fee or penalty for a late rent payment.
6. Requiring that you assume your landlord's responsibility for maintenance and repair.
7. Requiring that you pay your landlord's attorney's fees if the landlord sues to enforce the lease.

A lease is enforceable in most cases even if it contains an illegal clause. A court will strike the illegal clause from the lease and enforce the other terms. For example, some states prohibit a clause under which you agree to pay the landlord's attorney's fees if the landlord sues to enforce the lease. If you fail to pay the rent and the landlord sues, the court could enforce the lease but order the landlord to pay her own attorneys' fees.

❖ Eviction

Eviction is a legal process by which your landlord can get you off the rental property. In most states, the procedure involves a written notice to you and some time in court.

Reasons for Eviction

Your landlord can have you evicted for violating the lease, the law, or other rules that apply to the rental property. Reasons that your landlord might want to evict you include:

1. Failing to pay the rent.
2. Remaining on the property after the lease expires.
3. Damaging the property.
4. Disturbing your neighbors' quiet enjoyment.

The most common reason for eviction is nonpayment of rent. Paying rent late, paying less than is due, and paying it to the wrong person or at the wrong place are related reasons that a landlord might want to evict you. Failing to pay a valid rent increase may justify eviction. If you believe that an increase is not valid, you may defend against an eviction on that ground. Another course of action is to pay the increase under protest and challenge it in court.

Can your landlord refuse to accept rent that is offered on time and evict you for nonpayment of rent? If your landlord refuses to accept your payment, send the landlord a certified, return-receipt-requested letter offering again to pay the rent. Keep a copy of the letter. If your landlord tries to evict you, you can show the copy of the letter and receipt to the court to prove that you offered the rent and it was refused.

Your landlord can evict you for staying on the property after your lease expires. You might avoid an eviction after the last month of the term by offering the landlord the next month's rent. If the landlord accepts the payment, a new month-to-month tenancy begins or, in some states, the lease is renewed.

Eviction Notice

Ordinarily, your landlord has to give you written notice before beginning an eviction, to give you a chance to correct the violation. For example, if you have not paid the rent, you must be given an opportunity to pay it. The notice period is usually short—three days, in most states. Of course, if the lease has expired, in some states the landlord is not required to give notice. Many states have strict requirements about how the notice must be given. Sometimes it must be given to you personally or sent to you by registered or certified mail.

Eviction Proceedings

In most states, eviction requires going to court. An eviction proceeding is generally a brief proceeding in which the court acts quickly to determine who has the right to the rental property. In some states and in some cases, you have the right to a jury trial (ask the clerk of the court). You are not entitled to a lawyer in an eviction proceeding, and you are not required to have one, but it is a good idea because the landlord will probably have an attorney. If you choose to represent yourself, you can do anything an attorney could do, but you will be expected to do it competently. If you do not show up to defend yourself, you normally automatically lose.

In the proceeding, your landlord must prove the truth of what he or she claims and show that what is proved is a cause for eviction. You have a right to prove that the landlord is wrong. For example, if the landlord is attempting to evict you for not paying all of the rent or not paying a rent increase, you might defend yourself on any of the following grounds:

1. You paid the rent.
2. No rent was owed.
3. You deducted the cost of a repair to the property from the amount of the rent.
4. The landlord's motive for the eviction or the rent increase violated the lease or was otherwise illegal.
5. The eviction notice did not give you necessary information within the required time.

The court decides whom to believe and if what is proved is a sufficient cause for eviction or a sufficient defense against it. The court can issue an order to the landlord to leave you alone, or the court can order you to pay the rent. The court can also issue an order to an officer (usually a sheriff) to put you out on the street. The officer may give you notice a few days before acting, depending on local law. In many states, the court can order a **stay of eviction,** which temporarily postpones execution of the judgment, usually on the basis of a hardship such as cold winter weather or the lack of another place to live. The entire process, from the day you receive the notice of eviction to the day the sheriff appears at your door, may take as little as three weeks or as much as three months. Either party may appeal the judgment.

❖ Substandard Housing

Landlords must maintain rental property to meet certain minimum health and safety standards. These standards are generally established in state or local laws known as housing codes. In most states, the **implied warranty of habitability** also guarantees that landlords will provide decent, safe, sanitary, and livable housing, as defined by local housing codes.

Local Housing Codes

Housing codes normally include regulations that cover such details as the following:

1. Room temperature.
2. Water temperature, water pressure, and plumbing.
3. Electrical wiring and fire safety, including smoke alarms.
4. Rodent and insect infestation.
5. The number of garbage cans.
6. Building structure and related features, such as the kind of locks required on apartment doors.

To learn the exact requirements of your local housing code, contact your attorney, a legal aid office, a local tenants' rights organization, or the city or county building inspection department. Your local library may also have a reference copy of the housing code and other state and local laws.

The Implied Warranty of Habitability

The implied warranty of habitability applies whether or not it is mentioned in your lease, and a clause in the lease that attempts to reject the warranty is unenforceable. Generally, this warranty covers only the most serious problems—a lack of heat in the winter, for example, rather than a few ants on the kitchen floor. If your landlord fails to fix a serious problem, you can go to court and charge the landlord with violation of the warranty. Your best evidence to prove the substandard condition of your home is your copy of the building inspection department's report (discussed below).

Steps to Take to Fix the Situation

What can you do if your landlord fails to provide decent, safe, sanitary, and livable housing? You can contact the city or county to enforce your local housing code. There are steps you can take on your own, or with other tenants, to remedy the situation. Possible steps that you can take include moving out; repairing the condition that makes the housing unsafe, unsanitary, or unlivable and deducting the cost of the repair from the rent; reducing the amount of the rent that you pay; getting a court order to have the property repaired; and suing your landlord. Your landlord may challenge what you do, and this challenge may involve court action, but if you choose your remedy carefully and follow the appropriate steps, you should have a good defense.

Contact Your Local Building Inspection Department If you believe that your landlord is in violation of your local housing code, contact your local building inspection department. Explain what you think is wrong and ask for an inspection. When the inspector arrives, point out the conditions that need repair and ask the inspector to check the rest of the building for other violations. When the inspector files a report, get a copy from the building inspection department. If there are mistakes or something is missing, ask for a new inspection.

Your landlord will be given a copy of the report and an order to repair violations within a certain period of time (usually thirty days). The building inspection department and the courts are responsible for seeing that your landlord makes the repairs, but if there will be a hearing, you may want to go to explain what you think is wrong. A landlord who does not make the repairs is subject to a fine. If the violations are very serious, the property may be condemned and the building demolished.

Move Out If the property is essentially uninhabitable, you can move out. Generally, it does not matter what caused the property to become uninhabitable—a fire, a storm, a flood, or your landlord's failure to maintain the property—so long as the cause was not something that you did. Frequently, you can move out without giving the landlord notice and without being liable for future rent. You should be aware, however, that the option to move out was created by the courts as the **doctrine of constructive eviction.** Its availability varies from state to state and from case to case—if you move out and your landlord sues you, the court may decide that the property was habitable, and you can be held liable for unpaid and future rent.

Make Repairs and Deduct the Cost from the Rent In some states, if the rental property includes a defective condition that will affect your health or safety (that is, if the condition violates the warranty of habitability), you can pay for the repairs and deduct the cost from the rent. To use this remedy, take the following steps:

1. Determine that the problem is the landlord's responsibility. This will depend on your local law. In some states, the condition must concern a basic service, such as heat or water.
2. Notify the landlord about the problem in writing, (certified mail), explaining that you intend to use this remedy if repairs are not made within a reasonable time. Normally, thirty days is sufficient. An emergency might warrant less time.
3. Make repairs (or hire someone to make repairs), if the landlord does not take steps to fix the problem. Some states require that you get written estimates first. Save all receipts and other paperwork.

4. Deduct the cost of the repairs from your next rent payment. Give the receipts to the landlord but keep copies. In some states, the deductible amount is restricted to a month's rent or some other fixed amount. To avoid this restriction in making a major repair, you and other tenants might act together and deduct a portion of the cost from each tenant's rent. Before doing so, however, ask your attorney, or someone else familiar with your local law, about this possibility.

If your landlord tries to evict you for nonpayment of rent, you can explain your side of the story in court. Generally, if you have followed the law and used common sense, you should have few problems. If the court decides that you were wrong, you will have to pay the entire rent, regardless of how much you spent on repairs.

Withhold Rent In some states, if the rental property includes a defective condition that violates the warranty of habitability, you can withhold some of the rent. To use this remedy, take the following steps:

1. Determine that the condition violates the warranty of habitability.
2. Notify the landlord of the problem in writing (certified mail).
3. Allow the landlord a reasonable time to make repairs.
4. Withhold all or part of your next rental payment. In some states, you may be able to withhold amounts for past months when the property was uninhabitable and you paid the rent. In a few states, you must deposit any withheld amounts in a special **escrow account.** The money in the account will be returned to you if the landlord does not make the repairs.

The basic difficulty with using this remedy is determining how much rent to withhold. Often, the decision is made by a court because usually, when rent is withheld, a landlord tries to evict the tenant for nonpayment of rent or asks a court to order the tenant to pay back rent. The court reviews the condition of the property and decides whether the amount withheld was correct. Generally, the court considers how much the defective condition affects the habitability of the property. There is no penalty for withholding too much rent if you act in good faith. If the court determines that you withheld too much, you pay the difference.

Sue the Landlord If you decide to withhold rent, you do not have to wait for your landlord to sue you for nonpayment of rent in order that a court determine whether you withheld enough or too much. You can sue your landlord. In your suit, you can ask the court for any of the following remedies.

1. A declaration of your rights and remedies in the relationship with your landlord.
2. An order to the landlord to pay you money for any injury to you or any damage to your property.
3. An order to the landlord to fix the condition of the property or to stop doing whatever it is that makes the property uninhabitable.

Before asking a court for relief, you should be aware that a court will usually declare parties' rights and remedies, but courts are reluctant to order landlords to do something or to stop doing something when constant supervision is required to ensure that the orders are followed. Also, although a lawsuit is always a possible course of action, it is not always economical.

Going to Court

If a serious dispute develops between you and your landlord, and the dispute cannot be resolved, one course of action is to take the matter to court. In some circumstances, this may be required. In most cases and in most states, the appropriate court is a small claims court. When taking a matter to small claims court, you should keep the following points in mind:

1. In many states, no attorney is necessary. In some states, an attorney cannot appear on behalf of a client in small claims court. Assistance can be obtained from the clerk of the court or some other designated official.
2. The proper party must be notified about the suit. You may know only the resident manager of the property, not the actual owner, or you may know the owner only as the name of a corporation. An owner's name may be available through the local tax assessor's office or the county clerk.
3. All relevant documents should be kept available for the court. These may include a copy of the lease, rent receipts, an inventory of the condition of the premises taken before you moved in, canceled checks, receipts and estimates for repairs, and notes taken during any negotiations between you and your landlord.
4. You might be able to recover attorneys' fees, if an attorney was consulted and paid. In some cases, you may recover double or triple the amount of a security deposit wrongfully retained by your landlord. For more information about small claims courts, see Topic 3.

Retaliatory Eviction

Retaliatory eviction occurs if your landlord evicts you for complaining to a government agency about the condition of the property. If you can prove that your landlord's primary purpose in evicting or attempting to evict you is retaliation for reporting violations—of a housing or sanitation code, for example—you may be entitled to stop the eviction proceedings or collect damages. This can be difficult to prove, unless your landlord admits his or her purpose in a note, in a statement to another person, or in testimony to a court.

In many states, a landlord is presumed to be acting in retaliation if the eviction proceedings are begun within a certain period of time (six to twelve months, in some states) after a tenant has contacted a government agency. In this case, the landlord must prove that he or she did not have a retaliatory purpose. If your landlord shows that you did not pay the rent or that you violated the lease, you could be evicted. If you win, however, you can stay on the premises.

When your lease comes up for renewal (which would be the next month in a month-to-month tenancy), the landlord may raise the rent to help cover the cost of the repairs. Your landlord cannot raise the rent simply to punish you for reporting the violations, however. In most of the states that protect tenants from retaliatory eviction, courts would consider this retaliatory and subject to the same limitations as a retaliatory eviction.

❖ Rent

The primary obligation of the tenant is to pay the agreed-upon rent at the time specified. You retain this obligation even after you have subleased the apartment. If the sublessee fails to pay, your lease obliges you to make payment. Rent is typically due on a certain date of the month. If payments are late, the landlord may charge interest for being late. Most leases provide that if rent is late by more than a certain amount, you will be charged a penalty fee. The amount and nature of this fee must be specified in the lease. The amount must also be reasonable. One Vermont case held that a dollar-a-day charge for late rent payments was excessive.

Raising the Rent

As a general rule, your landlord cannot raise your rent during the term of your lease. An exception would exist if the lease itself provides some procedure for rent increases during its term. Such a provision is typically called an **escalation clause,** which permits period increases that usually are based upon rising costs for fuel or building upkeep.

After a lease expires, you may continue renting on a month-to-month basis. This means that the terms of the old lease continue in operation but can be terminated at any time either by you or the landlord (usually with thirty days notice). Alternatively, you may execute a new lease with your landlord, who may require a higher rental payment. This is a matter to be negotiated.

Rent Control While landlords may generally charge whatever the market will bear, many large cities have rent control laws that restrain rent increases. These ordinances place limits on how much rent can be raised by landlords, even after a lease expires. Rent can be increased only by a set percentage, which may be tied to the cost of living.

❖ Security Deposits

Before renting an apartment, you probably will be required to make a **security deposit** in an amount such as one month's rent. The landlord holds this money during your lease to protect against damage that you may do to the property. Theoretically, you recover this deposit when you move out of the apartment. All security deposits must be potentially refundable. If you caused more damage than covered by your security deposit, the landlord may sue you for the remainder.

Use of the Security Deposit

You may lose your security deposit if the landlord requires the money to repair damages that you have done to the premises. The security deposit is not applied to **ordinary wear and tear.** This term applies to ordinary deterioration of an apartment over time, such as fading paint, fingerprints on walls, etc. The landlord may take your security deposit for larger damages, such as permanent stains or cigarette burns in carpeting, broken appliances or window frames, or holes punched in walls. Even a small hole to hang a picture might permit withholding (though repair costs would be quite small). Some landlords might attempt to use your security deposit to recover fees for late payment of rent, but this is illegal in most states.

Protecting Your Security Deposit

When you attempt to recover your security deposit, a dispute may arise over the nature of damages and the condition of the apartment when you moved in. The following steps will help you protect your deposit:

1. Get a receipt for the amount of the deposit.
2. Before moving in, make a list of existing defects or problems and provide a copy of the list to your landlord.
3. Before moving out, clean the apartment and repair damages insofar as possible.
4. Before moving out, inspect the apartment yourself along with the landlord or other witness.

You might also ask your landlord for interest on your deposit during your lease. This is only required in a few states.

Witholding Your Deposit

The landlord may decide to withhold some of your security deposit for repairs. Most jurisdictions require the landlord to provide you with an itemized list of repairs and their cost. You may dispute your landlord's assessment.

You may file suit against your landlord for withholding your deposit, probably in small claims court. The procedures for use of this court are discussed in the Consumer Law topic in this *Handbook*. You can question either the need for the repairs or whether the cost of the repairs was reasonable.

❖ Liability for Injuries

What if a guest of yours is injured while in your apartment? The guest might sue the landlord, or you, or both. Either one of you could be liable.

Common Areas

Liability for injuries in apartments depends on who has legal control over the area in question. **Common areas** are under the control of the landlord, who will be liable for injuries in this area. If your guest trips over a defective stair step on the way to your apartment, the landlord is liable and you probably are not. The landlord may also be responsible for slippery surfaces, inadequate lighting, or rotting wood.

Structural Defects

Even if the injury occurs inside your apartment, the landlord may be liable. A defective water heater or outside railing, for example, are within the landlord's control. Similarly, if the landlord undertakes certain repairs in your apartment and performs the repairs negligently, the landlord is responsible for resultant damages.

Tenant Liability

You are potentially liable for certain injuries occurring within your apartment. You have some control over this area and are responsible for maintaining its safe condition. You are responsible for any injuries resulting from your furnishings or from your misuse of apartment fixtures, such as lights or plumbing.

❖ Lockouts

If a dispute with your landlord has reached an extreme level, your landlord may lock you out of your apartment and seize your possessions. In the vast majority of states, such lockouts are unlawful. The laws provide that a tenant has a right to notice and a hearing, but some landlords continue to conduct illegal lockouts. If you suffer an illegal lockout, you should call the police and complain of a criminal trespass and conversion of your personal property. If the police are unhelpful, you can get an attorney to obtain an order recovering possession. You may recover all your costs from the landlord and may continue to pursue a tort action.

In lieu of a lockout, the landlord may conduct a **utility shutoff,** in an effort to force you off the premises. This action is also illegal, and states provide both civil and criminal penalties against the offending landlord. As with a lockout, you may need to go to court to enforce your rights and get your utilities turned back on.

Topic 2 Family Law

Families ideally work out their relationships internally and settle their own problems without resorting to legal process. In reality, however, courts often become involved in family disputes. Moreover, the law establishes a basic framework through which parties may voluntarily resolve their disputes without going before a judge.

❖ Getting Married

The decision to get married has changed in recent decades. Couples are more frequently living together, or cohabiting, without first marrying. This is generally legal, though some states have normally unenforced laws prohibiting extramarital cohabitation. Many couples still get married and there are some practical advantages to marriage. Unmarried couples may have a more difficult time obtaining insurance, credit, etc. Married couples are more likely to receive child custody or adoption opportunities. Many companies offer health insurance to spouses but not to unmarried partners.

Engagement

There are few legal requirements governing engagement. Traditionally, one left at the altar could sue a fiancé for breach of promise to marry. Today, most states have done away with this cause of action. If an engagement is broken, the law probably would force the party to return certain gifts, such as engagement rings, shower gifts, etc.

Marriage Requirements

States place some limitations upon who may marry. Typically, the betrothed must be man and woman, currently unmarried, not closely related by blood, and over a certain age (often eighteen). State laws differ, and some actually prohibit marriages among those closely related even if the relation is only by marriage. Those who are underage may marry with parental consent or if judicially emancipated from their parents. Below a certain age, such as fourteen or sixteen, marriage may be absolutely prohibited by state law.

Marriage Ceremony

Certain procedures are generally required for a legally recognized marriage. The parties must first obtain a marriage license from the state government involving a blood test, in which the government checks for diseases, such as venereal diseases. States require a waiting period before getting the license or between the time of acquiring the license and officially getting married. In thirteen states and the District of Columbia, this license is the only requirement for a marriage.

In the other thirty-seven states, some form of marriage ceremony is also required. The parties must present the license to someone authorized to perform marriages (a state official or member of the clergy). The ceremony must involve a public statement of agreement to marriage. The remainder of the ceremony is generally within the couple's discretion. After the ceremony, the marriage license must be recorded.

Common Law Marriage

About fifteen states recognize **common law marriage,** a procedure by which parties become married without a license or ceremony. There are four general requirements for a common law marriage:

1. The parties must be eligible to marry.
2. The parties must have a present and continuing intention and agreement to be husband and wife.
3. The parties must live together as husband and wife.
4. The parties must hold themselves out to the public as husband and wife.

There are a number of misapprehensions about common law marriage. Cohabitation alone cannot produce a common law marriage; the parties must additionally hold themselves out to others as husband and wife. There is no minimum time period required for a common law marriage. The parties may become married as soon as they both live as husband and wife and hold themselves out to the public as married.

Duties of Marriage

The law considers marriage to be a form of contract, and historically the marriage contract came complete with a full set of duties for the husband and wife. Formerly, the husband had the duty to be the provider, and could not purchase luxuries for himself until the family was provided with necessities. The wife had certain duties in the home. Times have changed, and courts today enforce few duties arising from the marriage contract. Spouses are generally allowed to arrange their own affairs however they see fit.

The law still holds that a spouse has a duty of financial support, providing such basics as food, shelter, and medical care, insofar as he or she is able. In many states, this duty lasts throughout the marriage, even if the spouses are living apart. Failure to provide support for a child may be a criminal violation. Additional duties may be created by a separate agreement between the spouses. Some decisions have held that a spouse may not deny sexual relations without good cause, though courts are becoming more hesitant to enforce such a requirement.

Traditional common law provided for **interspousal immunity.** This means that one spouse could not sue the other for torts, such as assault and battery. Most states now have modified this law and permit one spouse to sue the other for at least intentional torts. Interspousal immunity still means that one partner may not be required to testify against a spouse in court, though a spouse may voluntarily so testify. An increasing number of states recognizes a crime of marital rape.

It is of course illegal to batter a spouse. Illegal beating is that which inflicts "substantial harm." Unlawful abuse has been extended to include extreme cases of harassment and threats of physical beating or confinement. A victim of spousal battering should call the police and may seek other legal protection against the abuser, including an emergency restraining order, which requires the abusing spouse to stay away from the victim. Many shelters are available to assist an abused spouse.

❖ Financial Aspects of Marriage

Prenuptial Agreements

Brides and grooms are increasingly bringing substantial assets into a marriage, which has led to greater use of the **prenuptial,** or premarital, **agreement.** A prenuptial agreement is a contract between the parties entered into before the wedding occurs. Such an agreement generally provides for disposition of property in the event of the divorce or death of one spouse. One typical use of a prenuptial agreement would be to guarantee that children from a previous marriage receive a certain share of their parent's estate. Prenuptial agreements generally must be in writing to be enforceable.

There are certain advantages to prenuptial agreements. Such contracts enable the parties to settle possible disagreements in advance and provide some long-term financial certainty to the parties. Note, though, that prenuptial agreements are criticized for evincing a lack of mutual trust and for being unromantic. Such agreements may even prove unfair to a spouse in the event of divorce.

As with any contract, prenuptial agreements are presumptively valid but are not always so. While traditional courts refused to recognize prenuptial agreements, most states now uphold such contracts, even if they eliminate financial support in the event of divorce. Courts do look closely at the agreement for evidence of unfairness. There are several circumstances when courts have refused to enforce prenuptial agreements, such as:

- When the agreement would so impoverish the spouse as to make him or her eligible for welfare.
- When there was unfair bargaining at the time of the agreement, such as a failure to disclose all money and property assets.
- When one party was not represented by counsel.
- When the agreement was entered into immediately before the marriage (such agreements should be made weeks or months in advance).

In general, a party must show that the prenuptial agreement was made voluntarily and without threats or unfair pressure.

Property Ownership

Separate property is property that a spouse owned before the marriage, plus inheritances and gifts acquired during the marriage. This property belongs to the spouse personally and not to the marital unit. Upon dissolution of the marriage, separate property is not divided but retained by the owner.

The separate property right may be lost during marriage, however. If the couple combines separate property with that acquired during the marriage, the two properties may be merged into jointly held property. Suppose that a wife owns a lot on which the couple builds a house after their marriage. The wife has lost her separate property rights in the land. Merely renovating a separately held property (e.g., sprucing up a vacation home) may transform the separate property into joint property. Placing separate property into a jointly held bank account may also transform the money into joint property. The separate property issue is important even if the couple is happy and trusting. For example, a wife's creditors may not attach her husband's separate property but may reach at least a portion of jointly held property.

The converse of separate property occurs when one spouse brings debts into the marriage. In most states, you are not liable for your spouse's premarital debts. In community property states (described below), under certain circumstances, a spouse may become liable for premarital debts.

Nine jurisdictions (Arizona, California, Idaho, Louisiana, Nebraska, New Mexico, Texas, Washington and Wisconsin) have the system known as **community property.** These states provide that each spouses share equally in all income earned and property acquired during the marriage. This is true even if one party supplied all the income and assets. The community property system is significant both for creditors and for the parties upon divorce. In community property states, one spouse may encumber the other with debts. In other states, one party generally may not incur debts for the other.

Separation and Divorce

Divorce is generally preceded by a separation period. Such separation may amount to abandonment or may be through mutual consent. States may require a separation period prior to granting a divorce.

A divorce is a formal court proceeding used to legally dissolve a marriage. Divorce laws vary considerably among the states, with some having much easier procedures. All states provide for some form of **no-fault**

divorce. This eliminates the requirement that divorce be justified by some demonstrable reason, such as abuse or abandonment. The most common basis for a no-fault divorce is probably irreconcilable differences. No-fault divorce laws make it practically impossible for one spouse to prevent a divorce desired by the other. Even in these states, courts may look to fault in deciding financial settlements between the parties.

Lawyers are not strictly required for a divorce proceeding. Most states permit "do-it-yourself divorces," sometimes called ***pro se* divorces.** In this process, the individuals handle everything themselves before the court. Couples can obtain the necessary forms at the local courthouse (or in books). If a significant amount of money is at stake, however, the divorcing spouses should obtain professional legal and accounting advice.

Most divorces are not actually tried in court. Only about ten percent of divorces go to trial. The parties typically settle their outstanding claims, though often only after lengthy negotiations. Divorcing spouses increasingly use **mediation** to settle disagreements. A mediator is typically trained and meets with the parties in the absence of lawyers. The mediator does not make decisions but tries to prod the parties into a mutually acceptable agreement.

In a divorce settlement, some written agreement is reached on contested issues, such as property settlement, child custody, continued support, etc. This agreement must be presented to the court for its approval. The court may disapprove the agreement as unconscionable (extremely unfair), though this is very rare. If only one side of the divorce had legal representation, courts will scrutinize settlement agreements more closely.

An **annulment** is more than a divorce and means that the marriage was never effective in the first place. Annulment may be available if the marriage is based upon fraud, if the marriage was unconsummated, if there was **bigamy,** and for a limited set of other reasons. Obtaining an annulment is especially significant for those belonging to certain religions (such as Catholicism) in order for a person to remarry.

Property Division and Alimony

Although most divorcing parties settle their financial disputes, this settlement is colored by the requirements of the law, as established in decisions after trial. Whether the state has community property laws or not, the court may divide marital property without respect to formal papers of ownership. Judges have almost unlimited discretion in deciding which person receives what property, as long as the division is reasonably equitable.

Courts divide marital property and in most circumstances separate property remains with the owner. When deciding how to divide the common property, however, judges consider the existence of the separate property and its effect on the wealth and needs of the divorcing spouses. Retirement benefits are generally considered to be marital property, divided between the spouses. In community property states, the property is presumptively split 50-50. Judges may change this division to suit the circumstances, however. Courts use a variety of standards in considering how to divide property, including the following:

- The duration of the marriage.
- The individuals' occupations and vocational skills.
- The individuals' relative wealth and income.
- The standard of living during the marriage.
- The relative contributions to the marriage, both financially and in homemaker contributions.
- Needs and concerns of any children.
- Tax and inheritance considerations.

Marital debts must also be divided according to similar criteria.

A typical property controversy in divorce cases is over rights to the marital residence. If there are minor children, the house is usually given to the parent with custody of the children. It may be difficult to balance the grant of the house with other property (many families have few substantial assets other than their home). Once the children are grown, the court may order the house to be sold and the proceeds divided.

Alimony is money paid for support of the former spouse. Alimony is now often called *spousal support*. Historically, the husband was the wage earner and was expected to pay alimony to his former wife, to permit her to maintain her standard of living. There are well-known cases involving wealthy entertainers, such as former NBC late-night T.V. host Johnny Carson, who have been directed to pay their ex-wives hundreds of thousands of dollars in alimony. Alimony ends when the recipient remarries.

The law of alimony is changing. One common form of alimony today is called **rehabilitative support.** Rather than providing indefinite support payments, rehabilitative support is designed to provide the ex-spouse with the education, training, or job experience necessary to support himself or herself. This form of alimony assists spouses who devoted their lives to homemaking or who left lucrative opportunities in connection with the marriage. Such rehabilitative support may only last for a limited period, particularly if the spouse finds a good job. Such temporary rehabilitative support has been criticized, since many divorcees are of an age that hampers their prospects of developing a new career. Many courts still award permanent support, if the recipient's earning prospects are far less than those of the wealthier spouse or if the recipient is of relatively advanced age. About half the states also consider fault in the divorce as a factor in awarding spousal support such as alimony. Alimony may be modified as the parties' situations change.

A common controversy involves one spouse supporting another through graduate school (such as law or medical school), followed by a divorce. The supporting spouse may claim a share of the income subsequently earned as a lawyer or a doctor. The supporting spouse has a job, of course, and needs no rehabilitative support. Courts have been hesitant to grant the supporting spouse some property right in the advanced or professional degree obtained but have awarded periodic payments to compensate for the contributions to the education. One New York decision did hold that an academic degree earned by the husband was marital property.

Palimony

Palimony is a common but nonlegal name for claims made by a member of an unmarried couple after they have split up. After cohabiting for years, a partner may claim some interest in the other's property. There is no statutory provision for such a claim, and courts have been somewhat reluctant to recognize an automatic right to palimony. Unmarried couples may enter a contract that specifies legal rights should they break up. Such contracts may be valid, but courts have tended to scrutinize them closely for legality. These contracts should be in writing, although this is not strictly required at law. The California Supreme Court has held that a contract between a cohabiting couple may even be implied from conduct or unspoken understandings. Other states, such as Illinois, are unwilling to recognize palimony actions. Palimony may be especially important for homosexual couples, who are barred from marrying legally.

Child Custody

The most contentious issue in many divorces is child custody—the right to live with and to care for the children on an everyday basis. Traditionally, the mother almost always received custody. Forty-four states have now adopted the Uniform Marriage and Divorce Act, which governs custody determinations. Mothers still usually receive custody, but courts now explicitly consider a list of factors, including:

- The wishes of the child.
- The nature of the relationship and emotional ties with each parent.
- The ability and interest of the parents in providing for the child's needs and education.
- Any required adjustments to a new house or community.
- The stability of the family relationship.

Family stability is probably the most important factor. Some recent decisions have put increased emphasis on whether one parent was a smoker, because secondary smoke may damage the child's lungs. Courts may appoint a **guardian *ad litem*,** usually an attorney, who directly represents the child's interests in court. Custody decisions are not permanent and may be changed by a court.

The noncustodial parent generally receives visitation rights. The parent may get to spend weekends or other time periods with the child. Visitation is denied in extreme cases, such as child abuse or when there is a reasonable fear of child snatching by the noncustodial parent.

The court may provide a system of **joint custody,** which many states now prefer. Joint legal custody means that both parents together make major decisions about the child. Some procedure, such as mediation, is available in the event of disagreement. In some states, including California, mediation is mandatory in child custody disputes. This may also involve joint physical custody, in which both parents maintain a home for the child and have roughly comparable time with the child.

Regardless of the custody arrangements, a court must make some provision for financial **child support.** Child-support obligations arise even if the parents were never married. States have official guidelines to determine child-support duties. These guidelines are often percentage formulas based on parental income. Judges must follow the guidelines, unless special facts justify a departure. Children with particularly large needs (e.g., the disabled) may require a greater support award. A large number of noncustodial parents are failing to make their child-support payments, and states are providing for automatic withholding of support payments from the wages of the parent. Child-support orders may also be revised and adjusted according to need and ability to pay. Large numbers of parents have failed to pay their child-support obligations, which has led to the passage of the Uniform Reciprocal Enforcement of Support Act. This law assists states in recovering support payments from parents living in other states. The failure to make child-support payments is a crime.

❖ Children

The decision whether to have children is a central part of the family relationship. The law of childbearing has become increasingly complex with the advent of new arrangements, such as surrogate parenthood and artificial insemination. The law here is still unsettled. Within a marriage, the decision to have children obviously should be mutually reached. The woman ultimately has the right to use contraceptive devices or to go ahead and bear a child, and she does not need to obtain the husband's permission.

Paternity

If a couple is married, the law presumes that any newborn child is the husband's, and he must support the child unless he can prove that he is not the biological father. Some states do not even allow the husband an opportunity to prove that he is not the biological father. An unmarried mother may file a suit to establish the **paternity** of her child. If the unwed mother is on public welfare aid, the government may file a paternity suit to be reimbursed.

The paternity of a child may be proved scientifically. Science has advanced beyond historically used blood tests and now uses DNA testing or comparable procedures that check for genetic factors. Such tests reportedly are 98 to 99 percent accurate in determining parenthood. The biological father of the child has a legal obligation to provide support, regardless of marital status. These obligations are just as great as for married fathers and are determined by the child-support guidelines of the state. The obligations usually last until the child is no longer a minor. The mother's subsequent marriage to another man does not necessarily extinguish the child-support obligations of the biological father.

While all biological fathers have an obligation to provide child support regardless of marital status, children born out of wedlock still suffer disadvantages. Legally, an illegitimate child has no presumptive right to inherit as an heir of the father. An increasing number of children are born to unmarried parents (about one-third of all first births). In response, the law is evolving to provide added rights and protections to children born out of wedlock. Courts have held that the government cannot discriminate against illegitimate children and that such children have a right to recover damages for the death of their parents. In some states, the eventual marriage of the parents "legitimizes" a previous child of theirs.

Adoption

Adoption is a procedure in which persons become the official legal parents of a child that is not their biological child. Adoption may be contrasted with **foster care,** which is a temporary arrangement in which a family is paid by the state to care for a child over a limited time period, often pending adoption. There are three minimum requirements for an adoption to be legal:

1. The legal rights of the biological parents must have been terminated by death or judicial decree.
2. The adopting parents must follow all procedures required by the state of adoption.
3. The adoption must be formally approved by a judge.

There may be additional requirements in specific circumstances. For example, adopting a teenage child generally requires the child's official consent.

Adoption is often done through a public or private agency that has received authority to agree to the adoption of children in its custody. The biological parents may convey the authority to the agency to find legal parents for their child. The agency investigates potential adopters and chooses a set of parents. In other circumstances, potential parents may employ independent adoption, when a doctor or lawyer or other individual puts adopting parents together with a pregnant woman who must give up her child. These parties make their own private arrangements, which usually involve the adopting parents paying for the legal and medical expenses associated with childbirth and adoption. The intermediary also generally receives a fee. This approach has the potential for abuse and is prohibited by some states. There is a growing number of black market adoptions from impoverished foreign nations (such as China and Romania).

Even entirely independent adoptions must be approved in court. The primary standard for approving an adoption is the best interests of the child. The court (and applicable private agency) considers the financial resources of the adopting parents, their family stability and home environment, their age, religious and racial compatibility, and other factors relevant to the child's future health and welfare. Most states permit single persons to adopt, though married couples are generally preferred.

After the adoption, many states place the new parents on probation for a time. This period is usually from six months to one year. The agency or court appoints an individual to ensure that the adoptive parents are caring appropriately for the child's well-being. If not, the child may be removed and returned to an agency for placement in another home.

Once an adoption is formally completed, the adoptive parents have all the responsibilities of biological parents. Should they divorce, each adoptive parent still has all the child-support obligations associated with biological parents. Depending on the state, the child may retain some legal connection with the biological parents, such as inheritance rights upon their death. The adopted child also has rights of inheritance from the adoptive parents.

Children's Rights

The law has special concern for children. Legally, a child is an unmarried minor (under the age of eighteen), who is not emancipated. **Emancipation** occurs when children leave home to support themselves. Parents have duties toward their children to provide food, shelter, clothing, medical care, and other necessities.

Parents must also ensure that their children attend school (normally until the age of sixteen). Parents are prohibited from abusing or neglecting their children. Parental duties to children generally end at age eighteen, but these duties may continue longer if the child is seriously disabled.

Along with these duties, parents have certain rights of control over children. Parents can direct the upbringing of their children and control where they live, what school they attend, and even what religion they practice. Parents also generally control the medical care to be given, though parents' refusal to provide for such care in life-threatening situations (usually for religious reasons) can be a crime. Parents have broad legal authority to control the behavior of their children, though this lessens as the children age and become more mature. Parents may punish children but not excessively.

Historically, children could not sue their parents for negligence, due to a governmental interest in family harmony. Today, most states permit such lawsuits, which are generally covered by insurance. The traditional common law rule was that parents were not liable for the tortious actions of their children. About half the states now provide partial parental liability for their children's intentional torts, up to a limit of about $10,000 (depending upon the state).

Child Abuse and Neglect

All states have laws that prohibit the abuse and neglect of children by their parents or others. Child abuse primarily covers severe physical beatings and sexual molestation of minors by anyone. Child abuse may even extend to emotional abuse, when a person publicly humiliates a child in an extreme way. Child neglect occurs when parents or legal guardians fail to provide for basic needs, such as food, shelter, clothing, and medical treatment. Laws now require doctors and social workers to report suspected cases of child abuse, in cases such as that of a child with a suspicious pattern of bruises.

In serious cases of child abuse or neglect, the government may remove the child from his or her parents. Ideally, this is temporary and the objective is to reunite the family after the parents' problems have been corrected through counseling or otherwise. If the parents are unrepentant, the state may ask the court to terminate all parental rights and make the children available for adoption.

❖ Wills and Estates

In a marriage, each spouse should have a will. State law automatically provides spouses with financial benefits after death but adds complications. If a spouse dies **intestate** (without a will), the family may still recover but may assume added administrative costs and tax burdens. The adjudication of inheritance rights is known as **probate,** and legal probate battles may be protracted and costly. If there is no will, a court will appoint someone to manage the estate. Couples also should revise the terms of their wills to take advantage of changes in the tax laws and changing needs of their heirs. A will is even more important for unmarried couples. An unmarried partner has no automatic right to assets on death and may depend on a will to recover anything.

In the absence of a will, the deceased property is distributed according to a state's intestate succession law. The surviving spouse has a legal right to a certain share of the estate (usually one-third or one-half, depending upon the state). Children also have a right to a share of the property, though children may be disinherited and thereby denied a share of the deceased parent's estate. A child may be disinherited even while he or she is a minor. Such disinheritance must be clearly intended, however. Mere failure to mention a child in the will does not constitute disinheritance. A spouse cannot be legally disinherited.

When there is a will, the law restricts its terms in order to protect the surviving family. A married person cannot will an entire estate to charity, for example. The surviving spouse has a right to what is known as the **elective share.** The elective share is a certain guaranteed minimum of the deceased's estate. It is called elective, because the spouse may choose to take what is provided in the will or may elect the minimum share specified by state law. A spouse may lose this elective share option if he or she signed the deceased's will. In limited circumstances, the contents of a will may be challenged by potential heirs.

Some families partially avoid probate and wills by using a **living trust.** The living trust is a device in which a person known as the **trustee** holds legal title to property and manages it in the interest of named beneficiaries of the trust. A wife might establish such a trust with herself as beneficiary for life and her husband as the other beneficiary. After her death, her husband may receive the property directly or continue the trust, with himself as beneficiary. The latter option requires appointment of a new trustee, which could be the husband himself. The trust option may allow greater flexibility than a will and also avoid certain taxes.

❖ Homosexual Families

Some of the most controversial family law topics involve gay or lesbian families. Many homosexual couples live in stable, long-term relationships. They may wish to formally recognize their relationships through a wedding ceremony. No state legally recognizes such same-sex marriages. Gays and lesbians may hold what have become known as "commitment ceremonies," which are similar to marriage ceremonies. Such commitment ceremonies do not invoke the legal protections surrounding marriage, however. There is no legal provision for community property or alimony in such cases. Homosexual couples may provide for similar protections through a contract.

Some homosexual couples wish to adopt children, though this can be difficult. Two states, Florida and New Hampshire, have explicitly prohibited homosexual adoptions, but some local Florida courts have struck down that state's law. Even in the absence of such a law, an Ohio judge held in 1988 that gays and lesbians were ineligible to adopt. Despite the roadblocks, over two hundred homosexual couples have successfully adopted children. Gays and lesbians are also at a disadvantage in child-custody battles that follow a divorce.

Topic 3 Consumer Law

The typical American undertakes hundreds of consumer transactions every year. Most such purchases prove ordinary and uncontroversial, but an occasional purchase goes awry. The product may be worthless or even dangerous. In these instances, the consumer may need the protection of the law. The traditional common law embraced the doctrine of *caveat emptor,* meaning "let the buyer beware." Consumers had little recourse when purchases went sour. Today, there is an increasing number of consumer protection laws.

❖ The Consumer Contract

Whenever you purchase groceries or any other product, you enter a contract. Although grocery shopping does not involve a formal written contract, such purchases are contracts and are governed by the principles of contract law. Consumer purchases must meet all of the requirements of a contract in order to be binding on you and the seller. Most purchases easily satisfy the main requirements of contract law and present no loopholes for escaping a deal. An exception exists when a purchaser is a minor. The general rule is that a minor (someone under eighteen years of age) may disavow and escape a contract even after it has been completed.

Fraud

You can escape a contract if you were fraudulently induced into making the contract. **Fraud** requires proof of the following elements:

1. A misrepresentation of material fact.
2. With an intent to deceive.
3. Justifiable reliance.

A seller who lies about the attributes of a product to make a sale may commit fraud. You must distinguish fraudulent lying from **puffing,** which refers to the seller's qualitative statements about the product. A seller who promises that its product is "of great quality" or "fantastic" is merely puffing about the product. To show fraud you would have to demonstrate a more specific statement of fact, such as a false statement about the number of miles on a used car. If you can prove fraud, you may either rescind (escape) the contract or collect the damages that you suffered as a consequence of the fraud.

Unconscionability

The law ordinarily does not look into the fairness of contracts. It is the responsibility of the parties to obtain the best deal for themselves. Courts usually will not strike down contracts simply for unfairness. A limited exception exists for **unconscionability,** which means such extreme unfairness as to "shock the conscience" of a court. Courts can refuse to enforce unconscionable contracts.

Unconscionability may be found when there is a great disparity of bargaining power. Such disparity may arise with **contracts of adhesion.** These exist when a seller presents you with a "take-it-or-leave-it" form contract and refuses to negotiate over the terms on the form. You have little bargaining power in this circumstance. Note that not all contracts of adhesion are unconscionable—you could simply walk away from the deal. If circumstances force you to make a contract and you cannot bargain over the terms, and if those terms seem manifestly unfair to you, the contract may be deemed unconscionable.

❖ Warranties

Most products that you purchase will come with some form of warranty or promise regarding the quality of the product. If the product does not meet the warranted standard, you have a right to a remedy. Generally this remedy is readily provided by the manufacturer or retailer, but in some cases you may need to go to court. Warranties may come in several forms.

Express Warranties

An **express warranty** is any explicit assurance about a product. The express warranty may be a written promise of quality and performance or may be an oral assurance from a salesperson. An express warranty may even be visual. If the retailer shows you a model of the product, it is creating an express warranty that the item purchased will conform to that model. Of course, a written warranty is easier to enforce in court. You should also be aware that puffing does not create a warranty but is merely sales talk.

Many warranties contain a specific remedy should something go wrong with the product. A **full warranty** means that the product will be repaired or replaced free of charge within a reasonable time, or else you will receive a refund. Even a full warranty does not provide absolute protection, because the warranty will also set forth terms and conditions. For example, a microwave may be under full warranty for 180 days. After that time you are unprotected. A limited warranty provides even less protection. A limited warranty might provide for repair but not a refund. Moreover, to take advantage of such a warranty you may have to deliver or mail the product to a designated site.

Beware of disclaimers. Even after a salesperson makes detailed promises about a product, you may be expected to sign a written contract that disclaims all express warranties. Although this may seem unfair, it is a legal practice and can eliminate your warranty protection. Disclaimers are discussed below. Be sure to read any warranty and understand your rights before you make a purchase.

Implied Warranties

Many consumer contracts come with implied warranties that automatically come with the product. These warranties protect you even if the salesperson made no promises about the product. The law implies these warranties in sales by merchants but not by casual sellers. A garage sale purchase does not create implied warranties.

The **implied warranty of merchantability** means that your purchase will be of at least average quality for that type of product and will perform its intended function. This means that if you buy a camera, it will successfully take pictures. The **implied warranty of fitness** applies when the salesperson helps you select a product for a particular purpose. If you inform the retailer of your purpose and rely on him or her to choose a suitable product, the company warrants that the product is suited for that purpose. If you ask for an underwater camera, the product a salesperson picks out must function under water. The **implied warranty of title** simply means that the seller warrants that it is the owner of the item for sale.

Disclaimers

Companies may choose to disclaim warranties in order to limit their potential liability. The disclaimer may bluntly declare that there are no warranties on the product or may state that your only remedy is repair or replacement of the product. Merchants may even disclaim the implied warranties discussed above, but they must use specific language to do so. The implied warranty of merchantability may be disclaimed by declaring that the product is sold "as is." This language is understood to state that the product is being sold with flaws and that the buyer assumes the risk of the flaws.

Most disclaimers are legally effective and prevent you from claiming breach of warranty. Some courts will at least require that the disclaimer be conspicuous (e.g., in capital letters on the front page of the contract) or in clear and understandable language. In any event, you are expected to read the contract and be aware of any disclaimers.

❖ Product Liability

If you are physically injured by a product, you may bring a product liability action. Under modern law, you may sue even if you did not personally purchase the product that injured you. This is the doctrine of **strict product liability.**

Under strict product liability, you need not prove that the manufacturer was negligent or careless, but you must show that the product contained a defect causing an unreasonable danger. Suppose that you received from your toaster a nasty shock that required medical attention. You might recover these damages in strict product liability. You could not get a new toaster, however. You cannot recover if you or anyone else altered the product after it was purchased.

You may recover product liability damages in negligence, though negligence tends to be difficult to prove. A breach of warranty action may also be available for unsafe products. Warranty tends to be limited to the actual purchasers of the product, however. Warranty actions are limited by the scope of the warranty and any disclaimers.

❖ Deceptive Sales Practices

All the protections discussed above developed from common law, and most of these protections are limited by the sales contract. In recent years, many legislatures have passed statutes that provide further protection to consumers against a variety of deceptive sales practices used by merchants.

Bait and Switch

Bait and switch is a sales tactic that has been outlawed. The typical bait-and-switch scheme begins with a store advertising a popular product at an extremely low price. This is the "bait." Consumers see the advertisement and go to the store to purchase the advertised product. The store informs the consumers that it is sold out of the advertised product or otherwise discourages the sale of this product. Salespersons attempt to convince the consumer to purchase an alternative product that has a higher profit margin (the "switch"). The bait-and-switch scheme lures customers into the store, where they can be persuaded to "buy up" by the salesperson.

The federal government has prohibited bait-and-switch tactics. If you believe that a store is using this method, you should complain to the Federal Trade Commission, which enforces the law. Most states and many local government consumer protection agencies also act against unlawful bait-and-switch tactics.

Note the differences between illegal bait-and-switch scams and legal *loss-leader tactics*. Grocery stores may offer a very low price on milk or some other staple to get you into the store. Their theory is that once you buy the milk, you are also likely to purchase other groceries that have higher markups. You should be aware of this tactic, but as long as the milk is available for your purchase, the tactic is a sound business practice and perfectly legal.

Mail-Order Sales

Mail-order sales are growing rapidly, as tens of millions of Americans rely on the convenience of ordering at home. Mail-order purchases obviously represent some risk to consumers, however, because you don't obtain immediate possession of the product. Some laws have been passed to protect against mail-order fraud.

A Federal Trade Commission rule states that the seller must inform you when the purchase will be shipped and must conform to promises about shipping. If no shipping date is given, the merchandise must be sent within thirty days. If the product is not shipped within thirty days, you have a right to cancel the order.

Sometimes, unsolicited products are sent to you by mail. You may treat these as gifts, and you have no obligation to pay for the unrequested merchandise. Sending you a bill for free samples may be mail fraud, which is a federal crime. This rule does not apply if you belong to a club, such as a book-of-the-month club or a record club. When you joined this club, it is likely that you contractually agreed to purchase the month's selection unless you took affirmative action and sent in a card rejecting the selection. If you failed to send in the card, you are legally obligated to pay for the selection shipped.

"Free" Offers

From time to time, you may receive what appear to be remarkable offers for free merchandise. One common form of such offers is a promise that if you visit a condominium complex you will receive one of a selection of valuable-sounding gifts. These offers are seldom as they appear. In one reported case, a person was promised an "all-terrain vehicle," but this proved to be a lawn chair on wheels. You might have a fraud action in response to such an offer, but it is wisest simply to have a healthy skepticism and protect yourself in the first place. Be particularly suspicious if you must pay any money to take advantage of some later offer.

Door-to-Door-Sales

Door-to-door sales occur when a salesperson goes from house to house in a neighborhood offering a product. Today, these sales have been supplanted in part by telephone merchandising (telemarketing). In either case, you are in the privacy of your home when the salesperson makes an offer. The law offers special protections for consumers in these transactions.

The law establishes a three-day **cooling-off period** for sales made in your home or anywhere that is not a fixed place of business for the seller. Under this rule, you may cancel the contract for any or no reason within three days of entering the deal. The three-day period does not begin to run until you have been informed of your cooling-off-period rights. There can be no charge for your canceling the deal. If you have already made payment, the salesperson must refund your money in full within ten business days. If you have received the merchandise, you must make it available to be picked up during this time.

In addition to the cooling-off period, federal and state laws dictate that the door-to-door salesperson provide you with certain information on a receipt or otherwise. This information includes:

- A description of the goods or services sold.
- The seller's identity and place of business.

- The amount of money you paid or the value of the goods delivered to you.
- Your cooling-off-period rights.

❖ Consumer Credit

A large proportion of purchases in today's market is made with credit. While use of credit is convenient, the process creates its own legal issues. Several laws have been passed to settle credit issues.

Credit Cards

Most consumers use credit cards for purchases. These cards may be issued by a specific store or may be all-purpose cards, such as Visa or American Express. While such cards make shopping convenient, be sure that you understand how the cards operate.

Many credit cards, such as Visa and Mastercard and most department store credit cards, use a **revolving credit** system. Each month's purchases are added and a bill is sent to you. Many cards grant you a "free ride period," meaning you need not pay interest during the weeks before you receive the bill. You may pay all or a minimum portion of the bill. The remaining unpaid balance represents a loan to you. Be careful about maintaining an unpaid balance on your charge cards. Interest rates charged on credit cards continue to be high, compared with market rates for bank loans. You may end up paying a considerable premium for use of your credit card. Some companies reserve the right to change their interest rates over time.

Some companies, such as American Express, issue cards that do not permit a revolving credit balance and require you to pay off your debts in full every month. If you fail to pay in full on these cards, you will be charged a contractual penalty that may well exceed the high interest rates of charge cards. Many cards also charge an annual fee for possession of the card. You should compare interest rates and other features before choosing a charge card for regular use.

One concern with credit card ownership is theft. If your card is stolen, the thief could make many purchases and bill them to you. Indeed, a thief does not need your actual card—learning your card number enables such a person to make mail-order purchases on your card. Credit card theft is increasingly common. The law provides some strong protections for the consumer who suffers from credit card theft.

Under the Truth in Lending Act, you have no liability on your credit card unless the granting company has followed required procedures. The credit grantor must prove that you used the card at least once yourself, that the company notified you of your potential liability, and that the company notified you of how to inform the company in the event the card was stolen or lost. Even if the company follows all these requirements, your potential liability is still quite limited.

The law normally restricts your total liability for improper use of your charge cards to $50 per card. Moreover, you have no liability for any charges that occur after you have reported the card as stolen. Consequently, you should report lost or stolen charge cards as soon as you discover them to be missing.

Another potential credit card problem involves **billing errors.** Billing errors could include being charged for products you did not purchase, mistakes in computations, or failure to give credit for your payments or returned purchases. If you believe that you have discovered a billing error, the Fair Credit Billing Act provides procedures for you to use.

First, notify the credit card company in writing soon enough that it can receive the letter within sixty days after the bill was mailed to you. Notification must be in writing—telephone calls do not protect your rights under the statute. Be sure to include your account number, the date of the error, and a specification of the nature of the error. The credit company must acknowledge your letter or correct the error within thirty days. If the error is not corrected, the company must explain to you within ninety days why it believes the bill to be correct. You may continue to correspond with the company. If you protest the company's explanation within ten days, your credit record will reflect the presence of the dispute. The following table summarizes the time limits of the law.

• Notify company of error—*sixty days from error*
• Company acknowledgment to you—*thirty days from notification*
• Company correction or final response—*ninety days from notification*
• Your notice of protest—*ten days from final response*

If the company fails to follow the required legal procedures, it cannot collect the first $50 of the disputed amount or finance charges but can bill you for any remainder. If you fail to pay the remainder, the company may institute collection proceedings against you. At this point, your choice may be to pay or to go to court.

Credit Reports

After using credit cards or paying off other loans, you will establish a **credit record.** It is important to make payments on time, as this will create a good credit record and make it much easier to obtain a loan in the future. If you have a bad credit record, you may face difficulty getting a loan, even if you are gainfully employed.

Your credit record is summarized on **credit reports** that are maintained by credit bureaus and other companies. Despite your best efforts to pay responsibly, there is a risk that an error in your credit report could make you appear to have an unreliable credit record. To help correct this problem, Congress passed the Fair Credit Reporting Act.

The Fair Credit Reporting Act requires that those who deny you credit based on credit bureau information must inform you of the name and address of the credit bureau. If you inquire of the bureau, it must disclose the substance of the information in your file, though you do not have a right to actual copies of the file. If the information in your credit record is inaccurate or incomplete, you can demand that the credit bureau investigate and correct these errors. If the disagreement continues, you can have your position included in your file. If the credit bureau refuses to cooperate at all, you may complain to the Federal Trade Commission which enforces the Act.

Bill Collection Practices

If you have an overdue debt, a company may assign it to a debt collector. This is a person or company that effectively receives a percentage of the debt in exchange for efforts to collect overdue debts. In the past, collection agencies have been quite abusive in their efforts to collect past-due accounts.

In response to past abuses, Congress passed the Fair Debt Collection Practices Act in 1978. This act requires the debt collector first notify you of the following facts:

1. The amount that you owe.
2. To whom you owe the money.
3. That the collector accepts the debt as authentic unless you challenge it within thirty days.
4. What to do if you dispute the debt.

Perhaps you accept that you owe the debt but are simply unable to pay at this time. You may be able to negotiate a payment schedule with the debt collector.

The Act prohibits a specific series of debt collection practices, such as:

- Informing employers or others of the debt.
- Using obscene or harassing language.
- Using threats to harm you or your reputation.
- Making harassing telephone calls at inconvenient times.
- Misrepresenting the amount of the debt or the collector's identity.
- Threatening you with imprisonment or garnishment other than that provided at law.

If the debt collection agency violates these provisions you may sue the collector and recover up to $1000. You should also inform the Federal Trade Commission, any state or local consumer protection departments, and perhaps the telephone company.

You may choose to send a letter to the debt collector telling the agency not to contact you any further. The collector must also stop contacting you if you write within thirty days that you dispute the existence or amount of the debt. The collector may respond by sending you proof of the debt. In any event, the collector still may commence legal collection action against you for the unpaid debt.

If you are sued for an unpaid debt, you should contact a lawyer or go to a legal aid office if you cannot afford an attorney. You may have defenses to the alleged debt, such as your belief that you purchased a defective product. If the problem is particularly serious, you might consider declaring bankruptcy. If the court enters a judgment against you for the debt, it may **attach** your property. Attachment is a court order that enables the creditor to seize your property in the amount owed and sell it to satisfy the debt. Attachment might also be an order forcing your bank to make payment out of your account. In many states, the court might **garnish** your wages. This permits the creditor automatically to receive a portion of your take-home pay from your employer (up to a maximum of 25 percent).

❖ Small Claims Court

Some defective products may cause great harm, such as bodily injury, and these damages should be pursued with a lawyer in a general state court. Many consumer transactions, such as the purchase of a nonfunctioning product, result in only small damages, which make it impractical to hire a lawyer and pursue an ordinary claim. For these smaller harms, every state provides some form of **small claims court** (sometimes called *pro se* courts or magistrates' courts).

There are many advantages to use of small claims court. The cost of bringing an action is much less than in regular court, and you probably will receive a decision much sooner. A typical small claims case is resolved in a couple of months, while ordinary litigation may take years. In small claims court, you will not need to retain a lawyer to represent you; many states prohibit the use of attorneys in small claims court. You will not need complicated forms or special language. You do make some sacrifices, however, such as the absence of a jury trial.

Jurisdictional Limits

Not every case can be filed in small claims court. The court's jurisdiction is limited to truly small claims and varies by state. The typical dollar limit for small claims court is about $2,500, which means you may not bring an action seeking more than that amount in damages. Some states have higher limits—the highest is in Tennessee, which permits small claims court to hear cases for up to $10,000. Other states have lower limits, such as Arizona and Ohio, which limit jurisdiction to claims of under $1,000.

You may voluntarily choose to reduce your claim to slip under the jurisdiction of the small claims court. If you believe that you are owed $3,000, you might file a claim for only $2,500 in small claims court. While you lose the opportunity to recover the $500 difference, you gain the reduced costs of proceeding in small claims court. You cannot split a single claim into two separate cases and then try to bring them both in small claims court. In about half the states, small claims cases are limited to damages and the court cannot issue injunctions or other equitable remedies.

Filing a Claim

As in a general court, a small claims court action begins with the filing of a claim at a specific government office. Before filing this claim, you should notify the prospective defendant through a **demand letter** that states the amount that you believe you are owed. The claim need follow few formalities but must contain certain essential information, such as:

- Your name and address.
- The correct name and address of the person that you are suing.
- The reason that you are owed money, such as when and where your damages arose or a debt was incurred.
- The amount of damages that you are claiming.

Some states give you a form on which you supply this information.

Statutes of limitations apply to small claims actions. This means that you must bring your case within a reasonably prompt time after you suffered damages or learned of your claim. The statutes of limitations vary by state. In most states, the limitations period for actions under a written contract is four years; under an oral contract it is two years; and for a tort action it is two or three years, depending upon the tort.

There is a fee associated with filing a claim in small claims court. The amount of this fee is typically small (about $25 to $50), and the fee may vary based on the amount of your claim. You must pay this fee at the time that you file the claim. If you win, the fee may be refunded.

After the claim is filed, the court will notify the person you are suing. That party will receive a summons to appear before the court. You must provide the court with the correct address, however, which is not always easy for out-of-state corporations. You may obtain this information from your state's secretary of state office, which maintains a roster of companies doing business in the state. In most jurisdictions, the defendant need file no papers in response to your claim.

Pretrial Procedures

In the traditional legal action, trial is preceded by extensive **discovery,** in which the parties exchange documents, question witnesses, etc. The small claims court dispenses with most of this expensive and time-consuming process. As a litigant, you can **subpoena** documents if necessary. While this procedure is seldom used in small claims court, it could be that the defendant or other party has documents that you need for your case. You can require the party to turn over these documents, but don't abuse this authority. If extensive discovery is necessary, you should go to a more traditional court.

You should also identify and arrange for the appearance of relevant witnesses. Go over their testimony with witnesses in advance of trial, so that you are prepared for what they will say. You can have a subpoena issued to uncooperative witnesses. If a question of value is at issue, you may need an expert witness. If you are disputing the efficacy of an automobile repair, you should have your own mechanic render an opinion.

You will probably receive a hearing on your claim within thirty days. In most jurisdictions, this is an informal pretrial hearing without witnesses. The court may try to arrange a settlement between you and the defendant. If the defendant fails to appear, you can win a **default judgment,** which is a victory without a trial. If you fail to appear, your case may be dismissed. In the absence of a settlement, your case will promptly advance to trial.

Trial Procedures

Because you will be presenting the case in small claims court, you should do some preparation. Arrange all your documentary evidence of support (receipts, canceled checks, contracts, etc.) and other physical evidence, such as the damaged product. Outline your case and go over your presentation. You should also consider sitting in on a few cases before your own trial, in order to familiarize yourself with the court's methods. Sitting in can also alert you to potential pitfalls.

When the trial time comes, you will stand up and present your case, along with your documents, witnesses, and other evidence. You and your witnesses can speak freely, without the constraints of the formal rules of evidence. Indeed, your witness need not appear in person but might provide a written statement. You may prepare maps or charts or write on a court blackboard.

The defendant will have an opportunity to present its case to the court as well. The judge will ask questions of both sides.

When presenting your case, stand up. Be clear, organized, and concise. Limit yourself to the facts and treat the defendant with courtesy. Provide only that evidence which is relevant to your particular claim. Present your facts in a conversational manner; do not attempt to read or memorize every word of a prepared statement. Don't act like Perry Mason but simply present your facts in a straightforward fashion.

Judgment and Appeal

After deliberating, the small claims judge will render a decision. If you prevail, you will receive a **final judgment,** which is a document that states that you are authorized to recover a certain amount from the party that you sued. This amount will be whatever the court found you were owed, plus court fees and **prejudgment interest.** The court may provide that the judgment is to be paid out in installments over a period of time.

Even if you win and receive the final judgment, you still must collect the claim. The court does not serve as a collection agency. The court will inform you of how to go about collecting your judgment. If the defendant refuses to pay, you must go back to court to obtain a **writ of execution**—a legal document that you can present to the sheriff, who will seize the defendant's property for you. When payment is complete, you file a **satisfaction of judgment** form with the court.

If you lose your case in small claims court, you may appeal. Some states, including California, do not permit plaintiffs to appeal a small claims judgment. If appeal is allowed, you must file a notice of appeal within a brief time following the judgment, such as thirty days. There will be an additional fee to file an appeal, and attorneys may be used on appeal.

Topic 4 Employment Law

Getting and holding a job is clearly important to your future well-being. In the past, an employer could hire and fire workers with virtually no legal restrictions. Today, many laws have been passed to restrict the employer's discretion and ensure that employees are treated more fairly. These laws do not guarantee fairness in the workplace, but they do prevent certain specific forms of unfairness.

❖ The Civil Rights Act

Until the early 1960s, private employers were free to discriminate openly against minorities, women, or any other group. The Civil Rights Act of 1964 prohibited much of this discrimination against certain groups of **protected classes.** The Equal Employment Opportunity Commission (EEOC) was created to help resolve or prosecute discrimination cases for employees. Only the protected classes are sheltered from discrimination, however, and employers may lawfully discriminate against other unlisted groups (such as homosexuals). The Civil Rights Act applies to all those businesses who have fifteen or more employees.

Protected Classes

The Civil Rights Act prohibits discrimination against five specific protected classes:

- Race
- Sex
- Color
- Religion
- National Origin

With a few minor exceptions, employers may not discriminate based upon any of these factors. Other unlisted groups are not covered by the Civil Rights Act and must seek protection elsewhere in the law. The law has been interpreted broadly to protect ethnic groups that might not fit exactly in a protected class, such as Arabs, Latinos, and those of mixed race. Religion also is defined broadly. The Civil Rights Act does not prohibit discrimination based upon sexual orientation, but a number of states and localities do ban this form of discrimination.

Prohibited Acts

The law shelters the protected classes from all significant forms of employment discrimination. A business may not discriminate in hiring. Contrary to popular belief, the law does not strictly prohibit an employer's questioning of potential workers about their race, religion, marital status, etc. Many employers avoid asking such questions, though, because the interrogation may be viewed as evidence of a discriminatory intent. Questioning should be limited to objectively necessary topics.

An employer may not consider the prohibited factors when firing workers, setting pay scales, or granting promotions. The law also prohibits discrimination regarding the "terms and conditions of employment." This means that an employer cannot expect a given protected class of workers to work longer or suffer less desirable working conditions than other employees. Indeed, employers must be very careful about giving preferential treatment to the members of any protected class. Sexual or racial harassment, which is discussed below, is another prohibited act.

The law does permit employers to have different standards for men and women. For example, a company may have different dress codes, based upon the employee's gender. Such dress codes may become illegal, however, if they require women to wear demeaning, sexist clothing. Employers may not discriminate based upon pregnancy but must provide leave at least equal to that provided to disabled employees who require time off from the job.

Procedures

If you believe that you have suffered unlawful discrimination, you should first file a claim with the EEOC or a state government human rights agency, which will investigate and pursue your case if it is deemed meritorious. The EEOC will also try to reach a voluntary settlement with your employer that protects your interests. If no settlement can be reached, the EEOC will determine whether there is reasonable cause to suspect unlawful discrimination. If so, the Commission will take the case to court for you. If not, the Commission will give you a "right-to-sue" letter, and you can attempt to prove that you suffered illegal discrimination. If the EEOC does not act promptly (within six months), you can seek a right-to-sue letter.

The law also establishes procedural requirements for enforcing your rights. You must file a claim with the EEOC within 180 days of suffering the discrimination and must file your lawsuit within 90 days of obtaining the right-to-sue letter. Even if you have suffered unlawful discrimination in hiring, you should seek out another job, as this can demonstrate your desire to work and strengthen your claim.

Disparate Impact

The initial focus of the Civil Rights Act of 1964 was upon intentional discrimination against protected classes. As the law evolved, courts began to recognize the presence of apparently unintentional discriminatory practices. The doctrine of **disparate impact** discrimination followed.

Illegal disparate impact discrimination arises when an employer has a rule that is superficially neutral and nondiscriminatory, but that rule happens to have a significantly adverse impact upon members of a protected group. For example, suppose that a fire department had a rule requiring all job applicants to be at least six feet tall and weigh at least 175 pounds. Although this rule is applied equally to everyone, the requirements exclude a disproportionate number of women who might want to become firefighters. This rule has a disparate impact.

An employer may justify a rule with a disparate impact if it is a business necessity. The fire department could respond that firefighters need strength and so the rule is necessary for the job. The plaintiff could rebut this by showing that an alternative strength test or other measure could serve the fire department's interests without having a discriminatory impact upon women.

Affirmative Action

The Civil Rights Act of 1964 protects everyone against discrimination, including white males. There is an exception for **affirmative action,** which may in effect create discrimination to a degree against white males or other groups that historically have been successful in employment and promotions. In some circumstances, an employer might favor a minority or woman in hiring.

While theoretically lawful, affirmative action is limited. First, the employer must show a reason or need for an affirmative action program. Such a reason might well be that the company has extremely few minority employees, relative to the community population of qualified workers. Any resultant program must be temporary, limited to correcting the need for affirmative action, restricted to qualified persons, and cannot unduly restrict the opportunities of whites. Courts have upheld affirmative action programs in hiring but have been very reluctant to accept affirmative action programs which might mean white workers could be fired from their positions.

❖ Other Discrimination Laws

The Civil Rights Act of 1964 was followed by laws prohibiting discrimination against other groups of people. These laws generally track the operation of the Civil Rights Act, with some exceptions.

Age Discrimination

The Age Discrimination in Employment Act of 1967 ("ADEA") prohibits age discrimination against anyone forty or older. The protected class is limited to those of forty years of age and older; the law implicitly permits age discrimination against those less than forty years old. As in the Civil Rights Act of 1964, the law prohibits many forms of discrimination, including promotions, and extends to disparate impact discrimination as well. The law extends to businesses with twenty or more employees.

As amended, the law also prohibits mandatory retirement ages. A limited exception exists for corporate management. The ADEA does not mean that an employer cannot fire or force the retirement of an older worker. The law simply requires that the retirement be based on the employee's ability to do the job and not simply his or her age. The ADEA does permit an employer to offer voluntary retirement programs based on the age of the worker. Such a program must be truly voluntary, and the worker cannot be pressured to accept the program.

Disability Discrimination

In 1990, Congress passed the Americans with Disabilities Act (ADA), which expanded protection for persons with disabilities. Protected individuals include those with traditional disabilities (blindness, inability to walk) and other disabilities (AIDS, certain emotional illnesses). The law prohibits most forms of employment discrimination and extends to businesses with fifteen or more employees. The ADA explicitly outlaws an employer's questioning of an employee or potential employee about the presence or extent of a disability. Under the ADA, it is also illegal to avoid potential employees out of a fear that they might generate large health insurance claims.

The ADA requires businesses to make **reasonable accommodations** for disabled workers or job applicants. Such an accommodation is one that enables the disabled person to do a job without being too expensive or difficult for the employer. Larger companies with greater assets will be expected to do more to accommodate qualified disabled workers.

Another provision of the ADA forces employers to grant leaves of absence in excess of company policies, unless the company can show that the extended leave would cause "undue hardship" to the company. If you must take such an extended leave due to disability, the employer must hold your job open, unless the employer can demonstrate such hardship.

Discrimination against the disabled is allowed under certain limited circumstances. If the disabled worker would present a risk to self or others on the job, the employer normally need not hire the worker. For example, while it is illegal to discriminate against AIDS victims in general, an employer may refuse to hire someone with AIDS for a job that presents a realistic risk that the disease will be transmitted to others.

❖ Sexual Harassment

Harassment of employees based upon their membership in a protected class can be illegal under the antidiscrimination laws. The most common and frequent form of such harassment is sexual harassment, which is considered to be discrimination based upon sex.

Quid Pro Quo Harassment

The historically infamous form of sexual harassment is known as **quid pro quo.** This is the "casting couch" scenario where a boss demands sexual favors as a condition of promotion or continued employment. If the employee refuses and suffers adverse employment consequences, he or she may rightfully claim illegal discrimination.

Hostile Environment Harassment

The law also prohibits **hostile environment** harassment, which means the creation of a working environment so tainted by harassment that the worker's terms and conditions of employment are affected. Extreme cases of blatant harassment, such as grabbing parts of the worker's body and making blatantly obscene suggestive remarks clearly qualify as hostile environment harassment. Other circumstances, such as flirting, are less clear-cut. Romance may arise on the job, and sexual relations or advances among workers are only illegal if they are unwelcome.

It can be difficult to draw the line between a hostile environment and either flirtation or episodes of harassment so minor that they do not affect the terms and conditions of employment. A rare off-color joke is not normally illegal harassment. In general, you may ask a co-worker out on a date, but you should not persist if he or she refuses. Posting pornographic pictures at work is certainly questionable. The seriousness of harassment is judged in part by the perceptions of its victim. Because most victims are female, many courts apply the **reasonable woman** standard to test whether a reasonable woman would be seriously offended by the behavior in question.

Under the Civil Rights Act of 1964, only the employer is liable for sexual harassment, not the offending worker. The company is liable for harassment by a coworker if it knew or had reason to know of the harassment and failed to prevent it. For this reason, the victim of harassment should first inform a supervisor or other corporate official and try to resolve the problem internally. If the harasser is a supervisor or a high corporate officer, the court may presume the employer's awareness. In a 1992 case, the chief executive of a company conducted the harassment, and the victim was awarded over $1.3 million in damages, which included **punitive damages.**

❖ Wrongful Discharge

Suppose that you are fired from your job for no reason or because your boss is arbitrary and believed a lie told about you. You were not even given an opportunity to explain your side of the story. You had no right to any prior notice before your discharge. Historically, it would have been virtually impossible for you to file a successful lawsuit over your discharge. Anti-discrimination statutes imposed one important restriction on employer discharges. In recent years, courts have been placing even greater constraints on the employer's discretion to fire a worker, developing the doctrine of **wrongful discharge.**

At-Will Employment

The customary common law recognizes a doctrine called **at-will employment.** This doctrine means that in most employment contracts (not for an explicit term of years), the worker may quit at any time or the employer may discharge the worker at any time. Neither action requires justification. Thus, an employer could fire a worker for no reason or even a bad reason, and courts would not interfere with this choice. This might seem unfair to you, but the law does not second guess the employer's reasoning.

Implied Contract

The employer may yield its at-will employment rights through an explicit or implied contract with the employee. An implied contract may be created through an **employment manual.** Perhaps the employment manual promises that you will not be fired without good cause and a chance to explain yourself. If these promises are expressed in terms of your rights as an employee and then are violated, you might claim that the discharge was an illegal violation of your implied contract. Some employment manuals have disclaimers, however, which state that the employee rights in the manuals are not enforceable. Such a disclaimer might undermine your wrongful discharge claim. Oral assurances by responsible corporate officers may also create an implied contract, though these can be more difficult for you to prove.

Public Policy Exception

Courts also recognize a worker's wrongful discharge action if a firing violates public policy. The public policy standard is limited, however, and simple unfairness does not constitute a wrongful discharge. Rather, you must demonstrate that the firing contravenes a fundamental principle of public policy.

An employee who has a generalized and even admirable concern for public safety is not protected from discharge by public policy. The public policy exception applies in circumstances such as the following:

- You are fired for exercising a civic right or duty, such as jury duty or voting.
- You are fired for refusing to violate the law, such as refusal to participate in an environmental crime.
- You are fired in retaliation for exercising legal rights, such as filing a proper workers' compensation claim.

An employer normally may always fire an employee for good cause, such as absenteeism, incompetence, or disruptiveness.

Whistleblowing

Whistleblowing is a term describing the situation in which an employee notifies management or the press of wrongdoing in the corporation. Perhaps you have discovered that an officer is engaged in an unlawful price-fixing scheme. After you "blow the whistle" on this individual, you are fired by the company.

Whistleblowing is partially protected by state law. Some states have statutes that protect whistleblowers and other states use the public policy exception. In either case, you should be sure of your facts before blowing the whistle. In addition, you should first blow the whistle internally and enable the corporation to correct the problem before airing the issue in the media. Even so, there is no guarantee of protection. In a California case, an employee was fired after informing management that his supervisor was under investigation by the FBI. The court held that the discharge was legal on the ground that an employee has no right to spread even accurate rumors about fellow employees. In some industries, such as defense contracting, whistleblowers are strongly protected by federal law.

Independent Torts

In some cases, even if your firing is legal, the employer may conduct the discharge in a way that provides you with an independent tort action. Imagine that your employer wrongfully accuses you of stealing company property and fires you. If the employer called you a thief in front of other employees or to potential future employers, you may have a strong **defamation** action against the employer. Other possible tort actions are **fraud** or

intentional infliction of emotional distress, if the firing was conducted in a particularly abusive manner.

❖ Employee Privacy

Employee privacy rights are a major new concern of the law. In general, employees have little on-the-job privacy protection under common law. Some statutes have been passed to provide a measure of privacy protection to workers, but this protection is still quite limited.

Lie Detector Tests

Some companies used to conduct polygraph or other lie detector examinations regularly and at random in order to detect employee theft or other problems. Congress was concerned about the widespread utilization of such tests and passed legislation in 1988 to limit their use.

In most occupations you cannot be forced to take a lie detector test and therefore cannot be fired for refusing to take the test. There are some exceptions when polygraph testing is allowed. Workers holding certain sensitive jobs, such as security personnel and production of controlled substances, are subject to lie detector testing. The employer may also force you to take such a test if the company is conducting an ongoing investigation of losses and has reasonable suspicion that you were involved in the losses.

Even when you are lawfully subject to testing, federal law contains further protections. You cannot be asked needlessly intrusive or degrading questions. You must be informed of the purpose for the testing, and disclosure of the test results is limited. The testing must follow accepted standards for accuracy.

Drug Testing

Recent years have seen a significant increase in the use of employer drug testing, as the costs of drug abuse are increasingly recognized. With the exception of a few states, such drug tests are legal. Although drug tests plainly intrude upon your privacy, the tests are generally held to be a reasonable exercise of the employer's rights. Courts may require that steps be taken to ensure the test's accuracy and that the privacy invasion of a drug test be no greater than needed. Employer searches of workers are also generally legal, unless precluded by a collective bargaining agreement or other contract with employees. Other forms of medical tests have been acceptable, but the Americans with Disabilities Act now restricts such testing to cases of necessity.

Employee Monitoring

With the advance of new technologies, employers are increasingly able to monitor the work of their employees. Companies may keep track of the contents of your telephone calls or your computer work. Closed circuit monitors may be installed in the workplace to observe your work habits. Like drug testing, such monitoring is considered a matter between employer and employee and is generally legal. A few states have limited laws restricting such monitoring, such as prohibiting monitoring of non-work areas.

Personnel Records

Federal law provides no right for workers to see their personnel records, though a number of states grant such a right, as do many employers' voluntary policies. Moreover, an employer may lawfully disclose the contents of your personnel file to individuals either inside or outside the company. If the revealed information is false, you may sue for defamation.

❖ Other Employee Protection Laws

In addition to the discrimination and privacy laws discussed above, there are a large number of statutes that provide a variety of protections to workers. Many of these protect the economic and safety interests of workers and are summarized below.

Labor Unions

The first significant law for worker protection was enacted in 1932 and gave legal protection to labor unions. Before federal legislation such as minimum wage or occupational safety laws, workers depended on unions to protect their interests. Today, unions are less significant than in the past but many workforces are still unionized and you always have the right to attempt to form a union and protect your interests.

If you wish to form a union you may enlist the assistance of a well-established, powerful organization such as the AFL-CIO. You then must demonstrate the interest of other workers in unionizing, by getting them to sign authorization cards. If this is successful, you can obtain a vote among the workers over whether to form a union. If you are already represented but dissatisfied with your current union, you may obtain a vote to **decertify** that union. If you don't want to join an existing union, your rights will depend upon state law. Some "right to work" states prohibit a requirement of union membership, while other states allow it.

Once a union is formed, its primary responsibility is **collective bargaining** with the employer. Representatives from the union and the employer confer and seek to hammer out a contract that will govern all the covered workers. If an agreement cannot be reached, the union may call a strike against the employer. Only the union can call a strike, and a walkout by a small group of disgruntled workers will be an illegal wildcat strike. In most strikes, the employer may hire permanent replacement workers, and the unionized employees could lose their jobs.

Fair Labor Standards Act

The Fair Labor Standards Act (FLSA), which dates back to 1938, governs the hours and wages of work. The coverage of the FLSA is very broad and reaches virtually every employer in the country. This law establishes a minimum wage, which is now set at $4.25 per hour. Some states have a higher minimum wage. Employers must pay the applicable minimum wage rate for up to the first forty hours worked in a week. If you work more than forty hours, you are entitled to one and one-half times your regular wage rate (usually called "overtime"). The operative period is a week, and you are not automatically entitled to overtime simply because you worked more than eight hours in any single day.

The FLSA has detailed rules for calculating the number of hours worked. For example, brief coffee breaks of twenty minutes or less are counted as working time. In general, meal time is not counted as hours worked, even if the worker must eat on the premises. Of course, meals are working time if the employee has duties during this period, such as answering the phone. Travel time or "on-call" time may count as hours worked if the employer places material restrictions on the worker's use of this time.

The minimum wage standard is not limited to those employees who are paid by the hour. A salaried worker must be paid a salary equal to at least the number of hours worked multiplied by the minimum wage rate ($170 per fourty-hour week as of 1993). The FLSA gives employers some flexibility, because the measured forty-hour workweek under the law need not begin on a Monday. Moreover, an employer may pay less than minimum wage when the difference is made up in cash tips. In some circumstances, a company may pay less than minimum wage if it provides free meals or lodging to employees.

Not every worker is protected by the FLSA. For example, professional, managerial, and supervisory employees are exempted from the law. The FLSA also has child-labor provisions that generally prevent employment of those younger than fourteen and that restrict the terms of employment of those aged fourteen to seventeen.

ERISA

The Employee Retirement Income Security Act (ERISA) of 1974 was adopted to protect worker interests in pension plans and certain other benefit plans. ERISA is an enormously complicated statute that addresses the administration of such plans. ERISA does *not* require that an employer establish any form of benefit plan for its workers.

If an employer chooses to establish a pension plan or agrees to a plan in negotiations, ERISA regulates the operation of the plan to protect employee interests. ERISA imposes vesting requirements, which mean that the worker obtains an irrevocable interest in his plan benefits after a certain time, such as five years. ERISA also regulates the investments of pension plans and takes other measures to ensure the safety of these investments.

Worker Safety

The Occupational Safety and Health Act of 1970 was enacted to help ensure safe and healthful working conditions on the job. Numerous standards have been set under this law, including limits on exposures to harmful chemicals and numerous workplace standards to avert accidents. In addition, the law contains a **general duty clause,** which obligates employers to keep the workplace free of recognized hazards to health, even in the absence of a standard. Employees can file complaints about unsafe conditions and cannot be required to work when they have a good faith reason to fear that their safety is in jeopardy. Workers also have an OSHA duty to comply with federal safety and health rules.

When an on-the-job accident does occur, the employee may recover **workers' compensation.** Each state has a workers' compensation system that pays benefits for accidents or diseases that arise out of or occur in the course of normal employment. States also require employers to carry insurance to guarantee funds for payment. The worker need not prove any fault on the part of the employer, so recovery is relatively easy. A worker may recover even if his or her own negligence contributed to the injury, but there is no recovery for intentionally self-inflicted harms. The amount of recovery, though, is typically less than what is available in **litigation.** The injured worker may not file suit against the employer but may be able to bring a case against a manufacturer of the product that caused the injury.

Some workers have been afraid to file for compensation, lest they be fired. In most states, a person cannot be discharged in retaliation for filing a legitimate workers' compensation claim. Employers may still fire high-risk employees who have a history of filing many such claims. The scope of workers' compensation has been expanding to cover circumstances such as a heart attack suffered by a white-collar employee.

Family Leave

In 1993, Congress passed the Family and Medical Leave Act, which covers entities that have fifty or more employees. This law requires covered employers to provide up to twelve weeks of unpaid, job-protected leave to "eligible" employees for certain family and medical reasons. You are "eligible" if you worked for the covered employer for at least one year and for 1250 hours in the previous twelve months.

The law requires that this unpaid leave be granted "for the care of the employee's child (birth or placement for adoption or foster care); for the care of the employee's spouse, son or daughter, or parent, who has a serious health condition; or for a serious health condition that makes the employee unable to perform their job." The Department of Labor has prepared a medical certification form to meet the act's requirement that workers certify that the leave requests are related to serious health conditions. Workers must provide thirty days advance notice of their need for leave, if possible.

The Family Leave Act guarantees certain protections to workers who avail themselves of the guaranteed leave time. These workers must be restored to their original job or an equivalent job upon their return from leave. The law also guarantees the protection of employment benefits that were accrued prior to the start of leave and the maintenance of health coverage during the time on leave.

Plant Closing Legislation

In 1988, Congress passed the Worker Adjustment and Retraining Notification Act (WARNA) in order to provide workers with advance notice of certain job losses. WARNA applies to larger companies, such as those with one hundred or more employees. This law covers plant closings and mass layoffs (more than fifty workers and at least 33 percent of the workforce fired). In such circumstances, an employer must provide at least sixty days advance written notice to workers. Failure to provide such notice entitles workers to pay and benefits for the period when the required warning was lacking.

Unemployment Compensation

The United States has an unemployment compensation system, in which employers pay taxes into a fund, and the proceeds are paid out to workers who qualify for such compensation. Each state has authority to set rules determining which workers are entitled to unemployment benefits. Some typical state requirements are as follows:

- The employee must have been fired without good cause or have quit the job with good cause.
- The employee must be unemployed for some minimum amount of time, such as a week.
- The employee must have worked on a reasonably regular basis prior to unemployment.
- The employee must register with a state-run employment agency, seek a new job, and accept any reasonably suitable new job offer.
- The employee must be able to work and not be a striker.

If the worker qualifies for unemployment compensation, he or she will receive regular but temporary benefits based on a formula. The formula is generally based on a fraction of the worker's average wages during a recent period up to a certain maximum. Benefits are available for up to twenty-six weeks, and this has been extended during times of serious unemployment.

Topic 5 Owning and Operating Motor Vehicles

Motor vehicles are a significant part of the average American's life. In many areas of the country, a car or motorcycle is a necessity for commuting, shopping, etc. A car is also one of the most significant expenses that you may have. The laws of owning and operating motor vehicles vary by state jurisdiction, but the state requirements have many common features.

❖ Buying a New Car

When shopping for a new motor vehicle, you will inevitably be drawn to dealer advertising in newspapers or on television. Some states regulate automobile ads, requiring that they state the duration of a sale or the number of vehicles that the dealer has available. Automobile ads may nevertheless mislead you. Published prices often omit necessary or factory-installed option packages, dealer preparation costs, taxes, and other fees.

Once you have settled on a new motor vehicle, its purchase is a fairly standard contractual arrangement in which you obtain title to the vehicle in exchange for cash or loan financing. The contract must be in writing and should clearly set forth all important terms (such as total cost, value for trade-in, terms of financing, etc.). The contract also should set forth the vehicle identification number ("VIN") and any other fundamental understandings between the buyer and seller. For example, the contract should state that the car is in fact new and has not been used as a demonstrator or rental car. Also, be sure to get promised warranties in writing in the contract.

Financing

Most individuals cannot pay cash for a new car and must therefore arrange for financing. You may obtain such financing through a bank, savings and loan, or credit union, but many dealers now offer their own financing, often at a discount rate, in order to attract customers. Compare rates and be aware that dealers may increase the purchase price of the car to compensate for discount financing.

Federal law regulates contracts for financing products such as automobiles. The lender must inform you of the following facts:

1. The annual percentage rate charged.
2. How the lender sets the finance charge.
3. The balance on which the finance charge is computed.
4. The finance charge amount.
5. The amount to be financed.
6. The total dollar amount to be paid.
7. The number, amount and due dates of payments.

Lenders who violate the law owe you any damages you suffered, plus a fine and court costs.

Title

Once financing has been arranged, you obtain the vehicle plus a **document of title** to the vehicle. This title serves as proof of ownership and should be safely kept by the buyer. The title alone does not give you the right to drive the vehicle, however. States require that the car be registered with the state and be issued license plates. The driver also must have a driver's license.

If you fail to make required loan payments, the seller may take back the title and repossess the car. After a car is repossessed, you have a chance to redeem it by making up all overdue payments, plus repossession costs. Some loan contracts may require you to make full payment before recovering a repossessed vehicle.

Warranties

Most new cars come with some form of **express warranty.** This is a promise of quality or service that should be stated in the contract. A typical express warranty would provide that the seller will replace any defective parts without charge, for a certain time period or until the car has been driven a certain number of miles.

Automobile purchasers also automatically receive certain **implied warranties.** These warranties are presumed to be included in all contracts and need not be stated explicitly. The **implied warranty of title** declares that the seller is the true owner of the car and has legal right to transfer that ownership to you. The **implied warranty of merchantability** states that the vehicle at least meets ordinary standards of mechanical efficiency. This assures you that the car won't break down as soon as you drive it off the seller's lot.

While these implied warranties generally accompany any sale of a new car, the seller may avoid such warranties by using a **disclaimer.** A provision in the contract of sale would clearly declare that the seller is making no warranties. The sale of a car "as is" disclaims implied warranties. If you sign such a contract, you lose the legal protections associated with implied warranties.

If a warranty or other contract provision is violated, you may reject the car within a reasonable time after you have obtained it. A reasonable time is no more than a week or two. Alternatively, you may provide the dealer an opportunity to "cure" the defect. Once you reject the car, it is no longer yours and you must stop using it.

If the warranty violation is discovered too late for rejection, you can seek damages. As a general rule, you must continue to make your car payments while seeking legal recourse. If the violation is significant or costly to correct, you may need a lawyer to help you enforce your contractual rights.

Lemon Laws

Forty-five states have passed **lemon laws** to protect those who purchase defective vehicles. These laws provide you protection over and above any warranties. The precise terms of lemon laws vary from state to state. In general, a "lemon" is a vehicle that has a defect substantially affecting its use, value, or safety, even after reasonable efforts at repair. This may mean as many as four repair attempts on the same problem before repair is deemed futile. Alternatively, some states consider a car a lemon if it is out of commission for more than thirty days during the first year of ownership or the term of the express warranty.

In order to take advantage of a lemon law, you must notify the dealer of the defect and keep a copy of all repair records and receipts. In most states, you will be required to take the dispute to **arbitration** before suing. If you win, you may obtain a satisfactory replacement vehicle or a refund of the purchase price plus associated taxes and fees (minus some allowance for the value of your use of the car). The states also provide other consumer protection laws that offer larger damages than those under lemon laws (such as triple the cost of the car), though these laws may require you to prove that the dealer knowingly or willfully sold you a defective vehicle.

❖ Buying or Selling a Used Car

Used vehicles represent a significant percentage of sales, and ordinary individuals may be on both sides of a used car sale. The law provides some basic requirements for such a contract. First, if the price is more than $500, the contract must be in writing to be enforceable in court. Second, the transaction generally must include a written **bill of sale.** The bill of sale should state the amount paid, the method of payment, and identifying details about the car, including its VIN. The bill of sale should be signed and dated and generally must be submitted to a specific government agency for registration. Note that applicable sales tax must be paid on used car sales.

Used car sales are subject to many of the same buyer-protection laws as are new car sales. Lemon laws are increasingly being extended to apply to used car sales. Warranties also apply to many used car sales. If you are selling a car with a material latent defect (one that is not readily discoverable by the buyer), you have a duty to disclose that defect. Otherwise you may be liable for fraud. The implied warranty of merchantability, however, only applies to merchants and does not exist if the sale is by an individual who is not in the business of selling used cars. An individual seller makes no implied warranty of quality, though the seller may make an express warranty of quality. Any and all such warranties may be disclaimed by selling the car "as is."

Additional regulatory requirements apply to dealers in used cars and provide further buyer protection. A dealer is anyone who sells six or more used cars in a twelve-month period. The Federal Trade Commission requires that dealers post a **Buyer's Guide** on the side window of each used car they sell. This includes a warning that oral promises are difficult to enforce as a practical matter and a recommendation that you get all promises in unambiguous writing. The Guide also lists the terms of any warranties provided and supplies details about any service contracts and significant recurrent problems with the car's mechanical or safety systems.

❖ Renting or Leasing a Car

A short-term automobile rental is another form of contractual arrangement subject to the agreement of the parties. Most automobile rental companies require that you have a driver's license and a major credit card, and some require that you be at least twenty-five years old before they will rent you a vehicle. These companies often waive the age requirement if the rental is business related or if you are a member of an established auto club.

The rental agreement contract will contain a variety of detailed terms and provide you some options. The most significant of these options is the **collision damage waiver.** If you pay for this collision protection, you are not liable for accidental damages to the rental car. The coverage does not extend to personal injuries or damage to others' property, however. Accepting the company's collision damage insurance may be unnecessary. Your existing automobile insurance policy may already provide for this coverage, as may your employer's policy (if this is a business rental) or your credit card itself. Even if you are not covered from these sources, you may still consider declining collision coverage. This type of coverage tends to be overpriced.

Automobile leasing is a growing business. While such a lease is a form of longer-term rental, leasing typically substitutes for the purchase of a car. Under a typical lease, you make monthly payments to the dealer for two to four years. These payments are in place of and typically much less than the monthly payments you would make on a new car loan. Unlike such loan payments, however, lease payments do not provide you with an **equity (ownership) interest** in the vehicle. Leasing a car may in some states avoid the need to pay sales tax and avoid a down payment (although one- or two-months' advance lease payments are typically required).

When the lease expires, you return the vehicle to the dealer. You no longer have any obligation or interest in this car. If you want to keep the car, you may buy it from the dealer at the end of the lease. Some leases specify an end-of-lease purchase price. For other leases, you simply must negotiate a price with the dealer.

The terms of a lease are like any other contract. Many leases provide that you must make additional payments if you drive more than 15,000 miles per year or cause some irreparable damage to the vehicle. Other terms may include insurance, maintenance agreements, loaner-car arrangements, etc. These may be negotiated, at least in theory. Some dealers may be unwilling to modify their standard form lease.

In some respects, a lease of a motor vehicle may be as much of a commitment as a purchase. The contract binds you to keep the car for the duration of the lease, unless you can sublease the vehicle. Some lease contracts contain an early termination clause through which you may escape the lease early if you don't like the car. These clauses typically require you to pay a penalty, however. If your leased car is stolen or destroyed, it is considered to be an early termination, and your insurance probably will not cover the early termination penalty. **Gap insurance** is available to cover this possibility.

❖ Insuring a Car

Categories of Insurance

Many states require you to have automobile **liability insurance** and others require you to demonstrate "financial responsibility" (such as obtaining insurance or posting a bond). The laws specify a minimum basic level of coverage that is required. These requirements vary by state. Insurance laws are designed to ensure that you can pay damages if injury occurs to another person as a result of your careless driving. Failure to maintain such insurance is a driving violation that subjects you to a fine and potential loss of your license.

When you acquire liability insurance, your insurance company must pay for the damages that you caused. If you are sued for negligent driving, your insurance company generally will take charge of the suit and supply its own lawyer. You remain personally liable, however, for damages over and above the policy limits (which may be as low as $50,000). The compulsory liability insurance laws also help protect your ability to recover damages if you are injured by others.

When you obtain insurance, your periodic payment rate will be based upon a number of factors. These include type of car, your age, gender, driving record, primary use of car, plus local accident rates. Although it may seem unfair, all young males pay an extra premium, because so many young males get into accidents. You may pay a higher rate if your type of car is particularly expensive to repair or especially likely to be stolen. As with any business deal, you can shop around to find the best rates.

When acquiring insurance, you may obtain **uninsured motorist coverage.** Indeed, seventeen states require you to have such a policy. This uninsured motorist coverage enables you to collect for your damages if you are injured by a negligent driver who lacks his or her own insurance. Even in states in which liability insurance is required, a significant number of drivers lack coverage. Under uninsured motorist coverage, your own insurance company pays for your damages and then attempts to recover this payment in an action against the uninsured driver. You are thus covered even if the negligent driver lacks the ability to pay.

To collect under uninsured motorist coverage, you generally must show that the other driver was at fault and lacked liability insurance. Many uninsured motorist policies provide protection even when the other party has insurance, but the party's policy limits are insufficient to cover all your damages. You can only recover your damages once, however, and cannot duplicate payments from both your own and the other party's insurers.

In addition to liability and uninsured motorist coverage, you have other insurance options. Many individuals purchase **collision insurance,** through which the insurer pays for any damages to your car from a collision, regardless of who was at fault. **Comprehensive insurance** protects against non-collision damage to your vehicle (including theft, vandalization, and hail damage). These policies generally do *not* cover personal items left in your vehicle. These policies also generally contain a **deductible,** which means that you must pay a certain amount of your loss, such as the first $200 of damages. You may also obtain insurance to cover medical payments for you and your passengers after an accident.

About half of the states have a system of **no-fault insurance.** This system largely eliminates lawsuits for negligence and requires every driver to carry insurance to pay for his or her own damages, regardless of who was at fault in the accident. Under this system, parties need not go to court to recover and need not worry that the other driver lacks insurance. Damage compensation in no-fault systems tends to be lower than in traditional jurisdictions.

Insurance Coverage

If you obtain automobile insurance and inform your insurance company that others may drive your car, they too are protected by the policy. An automobile insurance policy typically extends coverage to the following parties:

- You and your spouse.
- Other residents of your household that you have declared to the insurance company.
- Other undeclared persons who drive the car with your permission (though this may be limited to infrequent borrowings).
- Non-drivers who may be liable due to your negligence, such as your employer.

If you fail to inform the insurance company that another party will be a regular driver of your car, that person may not be covered by the insurance.

If you purchase a new car, your old automobile insurance policy continues in effect for at least thirty days, while a new policy may be written and acquired. You should notify your insurance company of your purchase and obtain a new policy promptly in order to ensure continued protection. Your policy will also cover you when you drive an automobile owned by another person. If you go on vacation and have an accident while driving your sister's car, you will probably be covered by both your policy and her policy. In many cases, your policy will not provide coverage for driving in foreign countries (except Canada).

❖ Repairing a Car

When your car is damaged and requires repair, you will need to choose a mechanic. In some areas, auto mechanics are notorious for questionable or fraudulent practices. To defend yourself against such practices, investigate the reputation and past practices of mechanics and negotiate a repair contract that legally protects your interests.

The repair contract is often called a **repair order.** This order is customarily a form standard in the industry that describes the work to be done on your vehicle. Signing the order creates a contract authorizing the mechanic to make the described repairs. The repair order contains necessary identifying information about you and your car but does not generally state a price for the repairs.

It is a good practice to receive a cost estimate for repairs before authorizing the work, though some repair shops will charge for such estimates. At common law, this estimate is not binding, and if the cost proves greater than the estimate, you are still bound to pay the difference. Some states have legislation that provides that actual costs cannot exceed the estimate by more than a certain percentage.

After repair work, complaints may arise over the quality of the work, the cost, or warranties made by the mechanic. Most states have laws requiring that you be provided with a detailed invoice of parts and labor as well as the right to receive parts that have been replaced. If you believe that you have been cheated, you may be able to sue in contract or under a deceptive trade practices statute. If you inform your state attorney general, he or she may take action on your behalf.

If you refuse to pay for the repairs, the mechanic may keep your car. This is done through an **artisan's lien,** which gives the repair shop the right to possession of your car to satisfy your debt. This lien is available only if the shop has complied with legal requirements for repair authorization. If you make payments, the mechanic must return your car.

❖ Driving Violations

A long list of criminal laws govern driving. These laws vary greatly in seriousness and in penalties. For the most significant violations, penalties may include years of prison time.

Stop and Search

The police have a broad right to stop you while you are driving. When you see the police flashing lights in your rearview mirror, you should pull over to the side of the road as promptly and safely as possible. The police have a right to see your driver's license and to have you step out of the car.

After a stop, the officer may want to search your car. The officer need not have a warrant. Your car can only be searched, however, if either (a) you consent or (b) the officer has probable cause to believe that your vehicle contains incriminating evidence. If an illegal item (such as drugs or guns) is in plain view in your car, the officer may seize it without the need for a search warrant. The law defining the scope of police searches is ever changing as new cases are brought. At a minimum, the police may search the area within the driver's reach, including the glove compartment. Under some circumstances, the police can impound your car. If so, they may do a thorough search without a warrant or even probable cause.

Speeding

A common driving violation is excessive speed. If you are caught speeding, you may be subject to a substantial fine. The officer may choose not to arrest you for speeding if you have a particularly good reason (such as a health emergency). Most speeding violations are demonstrated by radar readings of your speed. You may have heard of cases in which radar results were thrown out of court for improper maintenance or other reasons. In the vast majority of cases, however, courts accept the results of radar guns as virtually conclusive evidence that you were speeding. In many jurisdictions, you may take a defensive driving course in lieu of a fine for speeding. Completion of the course may also keep the ticket off your driving record and avoid an increase in insurance rates.

Some people use radar detectors to avoid getting caught speeding. Connecticut and Virginia have outlawed the use of such radar detectors. In a recent New Jersey case, a person was arrested for flashing his headlights to warn oncoming traffic of the presence of a radar trap. The court held that his actions were perfectly legal.

Driving while Intoxicated

Perhaps the most serious driving violation is driving while intoxicated with alcohol or other drugs. Some states call this crime "driving under the influence." Intoxication is typically defined by blood-alcohol level, and different states have different standards for defining intoxication. Drunk driving is responsible for about 20,000 deaths annually.

The blood-alcohol level defining intoxication varies somewhat by state, with most using a .10 standard (meaning one tenth of one percent blood-alcohol concentration). California and some other states have lowered this threshold to .08. Your blood-alcohol level is a function of your weight and alcohol consumption, plus some other factors. Having two regular-sized drinks (one ounce of alcohol each) within one hour may put you in the danger zone of violation.

The police may pull you over if your driving appears erratic, such as weaving from lane to lane. Indeed, the police may establish roadblocks in areas frequented by drinkers and stop cars randomly to check for drunk driving. Once you are stopped they will observe your coordination, your speech, whether you smell of alcohol, and the appearance of your eyes. They may administer a simple test of your ability to walk a straight line or your ability to focus your eyes on a point. If they continue to suspect that you were driving while intoxicated, they will ask you to take a breathalyzer examination.

You are not required to take the breathalyzer test, due to the constitutional protection against self-incrimination. If you refuse, however, states are authorized to suspend your driver's license, usually for several months. Many attorneys advise that you should refuse the breathalyzer if you suspect that you are indeed intoxicated beyond the legal limit. If you fail a breathalyzer test, your attorney may subsequently challenge the results, but the test is often powerful evidence. In many states, you have a right to a second, confirmatory test if you fail the first breathalyzer exam. If you refuse the breathalyzer, the case against you will be built upon the testimony of the police officer and others who observed your condition at the time.

Penalties

The penalty for most driving violations is a fine, ranging from tens to hundreds of dollars. If you have accumulated a number of driving violations, the state may also suspend your license temporarily or revoke your license indefinitely. Revocation is generally limited to serious violations, such as driving while intoxicated, fleeing the police, or using a vehicle to commit a felony crime. You are entitled to notice and a hearing before revocation takes effect.

If you drive without a license (because it has been suspended or revoked), you may be arrested and held in jail until you can post bond. The amount of this bond will depend on your driving record and the nature of any other violation you may have committed to provoke the arrest. In this event, you should find an attorney as promptly as possible.

Particularly serious violations, such as driving while intoxicated, may result in imprisonment. Fourteen states require mandatory imprisonment after the first offense of drunk driving. (The requirement may be only a few days.) Numerous other states require imprisonment after repeat violations and potential penalties include months or years in prison. A drunk-driving conviction also results in a substantial increase in insurance premiums or even insurance cancellation.

❖ Driving Accidents

Liability

Under the law, you have a duty to drive with reasonable care. If your negligent driving injures someone, you and/or your insurance company may be liable for the resultant damages. Negligence is a general term covering any sort of carelessness including driving violations. It is also negligence if you fail to keep your vehicle in good repair. If the accident was unavoidable, you are not liable.

You may be liable even if you were not the driver. The doctrine of **negligent entrustment** applies if you permit an underage, intoxicated, or other incapable person to use your car. In about half the states, parents or guardians are automatically liable if they have signed the driver's license application for their children who subsequently cause an accident. An employer is also typically liable for accidents caused by an employee acting within the scope of employment.

In many accidents, both involved parties were negligent in some manner. In this circumstance, the law provides for **comparative negligence.** Under this doctrine, each party must pay damages in proportion to his or her negligence. In most states, you cannot recover any damages if you were more than 50 percent to blame. Even in these states, the damages you owe will be reduced by the proportion of negligence assigned to the other driver.

You also may be liable to passengers in your own car who are injured in an accident that was your fault. Under traditional law, **guest statutes** meant that you had no liability to such passengers, but the vast majority of states have repealed these guest statutes. Even under guest statutes, you will be liable for grossly negligent driving.

Reporting Requirements

The law requires that you report some driving accidents. A written report is required if the accident causes personal injury or if property damage exceeds a minimum threshold (usually about $250). This report generally must be filed with a specific government agency within five or ten days of the accident, depending on the state. To help ensure the report's accuracy, take careful note of weather and road conditions, speed estimates, time, and other relevant factors.

Failure to file the report is a misdemeanor and may be punishable by suspension of your driver's license. When you submit the report, you are automatically verifying that all the reported facts are true and that you are not omitting any material facts about the accident. Knowingly providing false information may be a felony.

What to Do after Your Accident

If you are in a significant accident, you should first park your car out of traffic, if possible. Driving away from the scene of the accident is illegal. Post warning flares by the side of the road or have a person warn oncoming vehicles. Exchange information with the other driver involved in the accident. This information should include the names and addresses of all passengers, vehicle license number, vehicle registration, and proof of insurance. Today's laws require a person to provide such identification. If police officers arrive on the scene, ask for their names and badge numbers. If you have a camera in your car, take pictures of the scene.

Do not make statements about fault to the other driver, bystanders, or the police. If you have injured someone, you may feel bad. There is nothing to be gained, however, by confessing fault immediately after the accident. At this time, you may well be unaware of the true cause of the accident. After you are familiar with all the relevant facts and you have consulted with your insurance company and an attorney, you may choose to admit fault.

If someone is hurt or killed in the accident, you should alert the police and emergency medical services immediately. Be cautious about attempting to provide medical assistance unless you are qualified—you could aggravate an injury. After emergency concerns have been addressed, you should file required reports, contact your insurance company, and possibly contact an attorney.

Even if you do not seem to be injured, you should see a doctor for possible hidden or delayed conditions. If the insurance claims adjustor for the other party contacts you, refer the adjustor to your attorney. If you don't have an attorney, be careful what you say. Make no settlement until you have sufficiently explored your medical condition and legal opportunities. If you suspect that the accident was caused by a defect in your own vehicle, do not have the car repaired until after consulting with an attorney. In any event, keep careful records of any repairs done following the accident and retain replaced parts.

Rendering Assistance to Others

If you come across an accident while driving, you may consider stopping and rendering assistance. As a general rule, you have no duty to provide assistance if you were uninvolved in the accident. If you were involved in the accident, all states require you to stop and render assistance, even if you do not believe that you were at fault. Rendering assistance may simply involve telephoning the police and emergency medical services.

If you witness an accident, you may render assistance even when it is not legally required. If you stop and provide assistance to an accident victim, theoretically you could subsequently be sued by the victim for negligence in the manner of providing such assistance. The vast majority of states have adopted **Good Samaritan laws,** which shield you from any liability for simple negligence in assisting an accident victim. You could still be sued, though, for extreme or gross negligence in providing assistance.

Topic 6 Criminal Law

It is wise to obey the law and avoid the criminal justice system. Should you be charged with a crime, it is crucial for you to understand the charges and your constitutional rights. Except for the most minor crimes, it is prudent to consult an attorney.

❖ The Nature of Crimes

A criminal act is one that is prohibited by the legislature in a statute. An act does not become criminal simply because it is unethical or reprehensible—it must be specifically outlawed to be a crime.

There is considerable overlap between criminal law and civil law. If a person steals your car, that action is the crime of auto theft and also the civil tort of conversion. The responsible party may be prosecuted for the crime and also sued for the tort in separate judicial actions. The criminal action will be brought by the state government and tried by a **prosecutor** employed by the government. If convicted, the defendant will be required to pay a fine and/or do time in jail. The civil action must be brought by you and litigated by your lawyer. If you win, the defendant must pay you damages. The defendant cannot be sentenced to jail in a civil case. Although the two cases deal with the same action, they are pursued independently and employ different procedures, such as different burdens of proof.

Either the state or the federal legislature may make a certain action criminal. Most crimes are state crimes, prosecuted by the state and heard in state court. Other crimes, such as mail fraud or failure to pay federal income tax, are uniquely federal and enforced by federal authorities. A few crimes, such as possession of illegal drugs and bank robbery, are both federal and state crimes.

Types of Crimes

A wide range of activities have been outlawed as criminal acts. The best known are the most serious and violent crimes, such as murder, rape, and kidnapping. These crimes are punishable by an imprisonment sentence for a period such as twenty years to life. The **felony murder rule** makes a person guilty of murder, even if he did not pull the trigger. Suppose a group undertakes an armed robbery of a convenience store. No violence is planned, but the clerk resists and is killed. Everyone in the group is guilty of murder, even those who did nothing more than drive the "getaway car."

The criminal justice system considers lesser but still severe crimes to include those such as armed robbery and manslaughter (e.g., murder in a moment of passion or through negligence). Careless driving that results in a fatal accident may give rise to a negligent manslaughter prosecution. The sentence for these crimes may be three to five years in prison.

Some crimes against property are also punished severely. For example, arson and extortion may be punished by years of imprisonment. Robbery, the taking of money or property directly from a person, is a more serious crime than burglary, the taking of property from a home in that person's absence. A burglary conviction may have greater penalties if it was conducted with a weapon, at night, or when the home was occupied. Receiving or buying property that you know or should know has been stolen is itself a crime sometimes referred to as obtaining stolen goods.

Crimes against public health, safety, and welfare form another category of criminal action. This category includes the possession, manufacture, or sale of certain prohibited drugs, such as cocaine or heroin. Selling alcohol to a minor is another example of this type of crime. Many of the laws against such crimes are aimed at businesses that may violate environmental laws or food safety laws.

Among the most controversial crimes are those "against public decency and morals." Such crimes include bigamy, prostitution, and illegal gambling. A controversial Supreme Court decision held that it was constitutional to prohibit homosexual sodomy, even in private. A number of states still have statutes that outlaw both homosexual and heterosexual sodomy, but these laws are seldom enforced. By contrast, molestation or other lewd and lascivious behavior toward a child is illegal and strictly enforced.

Misdemeanors v. Felonies

Crimes are deemed to be either **misdemeanors** or **felonies.** A felony is a particularly serious crime. Examples of felonies are homicide, rape, and armed robbery. Misdemeanors are somewhat less serious crimes. Shoplifting, public drunkenness, and mildly resisting arrest are examples of misdemeanors.

The general distinction between felonies and misdemeanors is based upon the potential sentence for the crime. Offenses punishable by a prison sentence of more than one year are considered felonies. Misdemeanors are punishable by sentences of a year or less, and incarceration is in a county jail rather than a state prison. Those convicted of felonies may also lose other significant rights, including the right to vote.

The same basic action may be a misdemeanor or a felony, depending on the circumstances. For example, petty theft involves stealing less than a certain dollar amount and is a misdemeanor. Stealing goods worth more than the statutorily specified dollar amount is grand theft and constitutes a felony. For other crimes, the first offense may be considered a misdemeanor, but subsequent offenses become felonies.

❖ Arrest and Prosecution

Stop and Arrest

The criminal process often commences with a procedure known as **stop and frisk.** This occurs when the police have reason to suspect that you are engaged in a criminal enterprise and that you may be armed. Such suspicion may arise if you were loitering outside a home or business in a manner to suggest that you might be "casing" the place for a break-in. After the police have stopped you, they may ask you questions. They may also conduct a frisk, which is a patting down of the outside of your clothing. If they feel something that might be a weapon, the police are permitted to reach into your pocket and remove it. If they feel something soft that could not be a dangerous weapon, the police generally cannot search for it. In June 1993, the Supreme Court expanded police authority to allow removal and seizure of a package of drugs felt during a frisk.

Except for the stop-and-frisk rule, the police may not search you, unless you are under arrest or the police have a **search warrant.** The police may ask you to consent to a search, but there is no reason for you to agree. Refusal to cooperate with a stop and frisk, however, may represent independent grounds to arrest you.

The stop and frisk may be followed by an **arrest.** An arrest occurs when a suspect is taken into custody. The police may obtain an arrest warrant in advance, then seek out and arrest the suspect. If a person is caught in the act of committing a crime, the police lack time to obtain a warrant and may perform a **warrantless arrest.** A warrantless arrest must be based upon **probable cause.** Probable cause is a concept meaning that the police have a reasonable belief that a specific person has committed a crime. Probable cause is based on more than just a hunch or a stereotype, but involves far less than the evidence required to convict at trial. A tip from an informer is one way of establishing probable cause. Those subjected to warrantless arrest have an opportunity for a prompt hearing on the presence of probable cause.

Warrantless arrests are generally limited to public situations. For the police to seek you out and arrest you in a private place, such as your home, an arrest warrant is generally required. The police may put you under surveillance at your house and then arrest you without a warrant after you leave home.

If you are arrested, you should be very careful of what you say or do. Don't resist the arrest or fingerprinting, and give the police your name and address. Don't say anything about the arrest to the police until after you have consulted with an attorney. If you are held in jail, you will have an opportunity to call a friend or relative. Inform them of the situation and arrange for legal representation. Be scrupulously honest with your lawyer—confessions to your lawyer cannot be used against you, due to the attorney/client privilege. Have your lawyer present at any police questioning or lineups at which you might be identified by the purported crime victim.

The police may seek to question you immediately after the arrest, before you have an opportunity to consult with an attorney. The Constitution guarantees you a right against self-incrimination, so that you cannot be forced to testify against yourself, and you need not respond to such questioning. Historically, the police have sometimes used physical or psychological pressure to coerce confessions even from the innocent. To avoid this scenario, the Supreme Court has required that persons in custody be given a set of **Miranda warnings** (named for the case that created the requirement). Police initially carried a "Miranda card" to remind them of the language, but these warnings are now quite well known to police and many ordinary citizens.

MIRANDA WARNINGS

- You have the right to remain silent. Anything you say can be used against you.
- You have the right to a lawyer and to have one present during questioning.
- If you cannot afford a lawyer, one will be appointed for you before questioning commences.

If the police fail to provide Miranda warnings, a suspect may still be prosecuted and convicted. The Miranda warnings are required only for use at trial of statements by the accused.

Search and Seizure

The Fourth Amendment to the United States Constitution protects the privacy of Americans and restricts the government's ability to conduct searches. The government may search your home if it obtains a *search warrant.* Such a warrant generally must be obtained from a judge. The police go before the court and present evidence of its probable cause to believe that evidence of a crime is present. This warrant must particularly describe the place or person to be searched and the evidence to be seized. With such a warrant, the police may thoroughly search you, your home, your car, your business, or other places.

Under certain defined circumstances, the police may conduct a warrantless search. The stop and frisk is a limited form of such a warrantless search. Some examples of lawful warrantless searches are:

1. When the police are in hot pursuit of a felon trying to escape the scene of a crime.
2. When the police have probable cause to believe that a vehicle contains illegal items, the police may search the vehicle without a warrant.
3. When an item is in plain view of an officer, it may be seized without a warrant.
4. When the police make a proper arrest, they may search the area immediately surrounding the arrested person.
5. When a person consents to the search and seizure.
6. Searches in some special locations, such as at the national border or at an airport.

What if a search is illegal, due to the absence of a warrant or grounds for a warrantless search, and the police then find evidence of a crime? Under the **exclusionary rule,** evidence from the illegal search cannot be introduced at the criminal trial.

❖ Pretrial Procedures

After the arrest, the accused typically is **booked** at the local police station. Booking is the official police processing of the arrest. The accused will be fingerprinted and photographed, and the police may take handwriting specimens or blood samples. The defendant may even be strip-searched.

Hearing Right

Soon after the booking, the accused has a right to a first appearance before a court. At this point, the judge explains the charges to be brought and the defendant's rights. The court will appoint a lawyer for the defendant if necessary. In a felony case, this appearance is often called a **presentment** or **preliminary arraignment.** When the government's case is weak, the judge may throw out the prosecution in this first appearance; this hearing may serve as an **arraignment,** when the defendant is formally advised of the charges and given an opportunity to respond by pleading guilty or not guilty.

Release before Trial

The key aspect of this first-appearance hearing is whether the defendant will be released from custody automatically, or if **bail** will be set. Bail involves the payment of a bond by the defendant in order to secure release from custody. The core function of bail is to ensure that the accused does not go into hiding to avoid trial. In many cases, the defendant may obtain a **release on recognizance.** This occurs when the defendant promises to return for trial and convinces the court that he or she is a good risk.

In some cases, even bail may be denied and the defendant held in custody without prospect for release. Bail may be denied for particularly horrendous crimes, if the defendant is considered a threat to the community. Bail may also be denied if the defendant was already on parole or probation and if the defendant presents a particular danger of flight from the jurisdiction before trial.

The next major step in a criminal prosecution is usually the **preliminary hearing.** This hearing involves a closer investigation of the charges against the defendant. The prosecutor seeks to establish the guilt of the defendant. The accused is represented by counsel and may present witnesses or cross-examine prosecution witnesses. Today, the preliminary hearing generally takes the place of the traditional indictment by the **grand jury.** A grand jury is a large group (about twenty-three persons) of ordinary citizens which historically has made the decision whether or not to indict the accused and send the defendant to trial. Most states have reduced the use of the grand jury, but grand jury indictments are still required in federal prosecutions of felonies.

If the prosecution proceeds and the defendant maintains innocence, the parties then undergo discovery of evidence. Lawyers may file pretrial motions to the court. For example, the defense may contend that the prosecution's evidence is inadmissible and ask the judge to dismiss the action. If the prosecution prevails, the next step is the criminal trial.

❖ Trial and Defenses

Defendants have a right to a speedy trial which must quickly follow the indictment or arraignment. Typically, a state might guarantee that the trial begin within sixty days. It is common, however, for defendants to waive their right to be tried so promptly, in order to obtain more time to prepare their defense.

The Trial

The Constitution gives the defendant the right to a jury trial for significant crimes (punishable by imprisonment of six months or more). The defendant has a right to a jury of peers, but this does not mean individuals in the same financial or social position as the defendant. A jury of peers simply means that the jury is selected from residents of the accused's community and that no groups have been artificially excluded from serving on the jury. If the crime has received extensive pretrial publicity, the defendant may ask for a **change of venue,** so that the trial can be held in another location where jurors may not be so prejudiced by media coverage of the crime.

Eventually, the criminal case will come to trial. The prosecution will present its evidence. Such evidence may be in the form of eyewitness testimony, namely individuals who claim to have seen the defendant commit the crime. The prosecution may present documentary evidence of guilt. The prosecution may also present circumstantial evidence, facts that create a strong inference that the defendant must have committed the crime.

Several constitutional protections extend to the trial of the accused. The Fifth Amendment contains a general right to **due process,** which requires procedural fairness, such as an impartial judge. The Sixth Amendment gives the accused a right to confront and cross-examine the witnesses against them. As noted, the defendant has a right to an attorney and the right not to testify. The defendant also has the **presumption of innocence.** This means that the prosecution has the burden of proof to establish guilt beyond a reasonable doubt.

Defenses

Constitutional defenses are available at a trial. The defendant may seek to exclude some prosecution evidence as inadmissible. The exclusionary rule means that most illegally obtained evidence cannot be introduced against you in trial. This includes evidence from illegal searches and seizures or confessions obtained through coercion or without first giving the accused his or her Miranda warnings.

Criminal defendants may have available other procedural or constitutional defenses. One such defense is known as **entrapment.** Defendants often claim entrapment but seldom succeed. The defense is quite narrow, and the defendant has the burden of proof to demonstrate entrapment. It is not enough to show that government agents suggested the commission of a crime. A police officer offering to sell drugs to a college student is generally not a case of entrapment. Entrapment means that the government somehow induced a person to commit a crime that he or she otherwise would never have considered committing. If the government merely affords a person the opportunity to commit a crime, and the person seizes that opportunity, entrapment is not established.

Entrapment might exist when the government continues at great length in its efforts to catch an individual. Suppose that an undercover agent arrived at your door and offered to sell you a stolen stereo. You declined. The agent then appeared at your door and made the same offer day after day. After you declined to purchase the stereo many times, you finally relented. This degree of government perseverance might constitute entrapment.

In addition to constitutional defenses, the accused may of course maintain that no crime was committed or that he or she is not the guilty party. This defense may involve undermining the testimony of the prosecution witnesses, such as challenging the accuracy of eyewitness testimony. The defendant may also present evidence of his or her innocence. This may consist, for example, of an **alibi,** showing that the defendant was somewhere else at the time of the crime's commission. The defendant may testify but is not required to do so.

Another defense to crime is **self-defense** or the defense of others. It is not unlawful to attack someone in self-defense. To demonstrate self-defense, a defendant must show that he or she had a reasonable fear of an imminent danger of bodily harm from an attacker. This same defense is available if you come to the defense of others endangered by an attack. The force used in self-defense must be reasonable. If the attacker runs away from you, you generally may not pursue him to strike him further. Deadly force (such as a gun or knife) may be used in self-defense only when you are threatened with deadly force. You can also use some force in the defense of your property, but you usually cannot use deadly force in defense of property. Some states have exceptions to this rule. In Texas, you can use deadly force if a person is seeking to escape with your property at night.

Another defense is available if the defendant is not responsible for his or her actions. Extreme cases of intoxication may mean that the defendant lacked the state of mind to commit certain crimes. Slight drunkenness is not a defense, though, and some states hold that voluntary intoxication cannot be a defense, no matter how drunk the defendant is. Another such defense is **insanity.** The insanity defense is actually rather narrow, and even a significant psychological problem may not qualify. Standards differ somewhat by state but a common test is that the defendant be so insane as to lack the ability to appreciate the nature of the criminal act or that the conduct was wrongful. Insanity is judged as pertaining to the time of the crime. If the defendant remains insane, a trial cannot proceed, because due process requires that the defendant be able to understand the charges brought. Such a defendant is typically held in an institution until sanity is regained.

Yet another defense is the passage of too much time between the act and the prosecution. The **statute of limitations** is a law that requires that legal proceedings (such as a complaint) commence within a certain period of time. A typical state statute of limitations would be one year for misdemeanors and three years for felonies. The statute stops running if the defendant is out of the state during this period. For very serious crimes, such as murder, there is no statute of limitations.

❖ Sentencing

After a person is convicted of a crime, the court metes out some form of sentence. Sentencing has a variety of purposes. Some of the objectives of sentencing are rehabilitation of the offender, incapacitation of the offender so that the crime is not repeated, and deterrence of future crimes by the offender and others.

Types of Sentences

The law provides for a broad range of sentencing options, depending upon the nature of the crime. The most severe is capital punishment, in which the defendant is executed. Other serious crimes provide for imprisonment for a specified term, often a number of years. Felony sentences are commonly served in state prison, while misdemeanor sentences are typically served in a local jail. In many other cases, the defendant must pay a fine to the state.

A variety of lesser sentences are also available for less serious crimes or first offenders. **Probation** refers to a sentence by which an offender does not go to jail or prison but is released under the supervision of a probation officer. States prohibit probation for certain especially serious offenses. The offender also agrees to follow certain conditions, such as not carrying a gun, not using drugs, getting a job, and checking in regularly with the probation officer. Probation is for a set period of time, such as one year. If the offender violates the terms of probation during this period, probation may be revoked and he or she may be sent to prison. Revocation of probation requires a hearing to establish the presence of a violation.

In some cases, the convicted criminal may receive a **suspended sentence.** The offender first receives a particular prison sentence (e.g., two years in prison), which is then suspended by the judge. The offender is then released without conditions or supervision by a probation officer. In a suspended sentence, the conviction and sentence is a matter of public record and may hamper the job prospects of the convicted. Another procedure is called **deferred sentencing.** After a conviction, the judge will elect to defer sentencing for a period such as a year. If the offender commits no more violations during that year, the judge imposes no sentence at all.

States are increasingly turning to innovative forms of punishment. Many states have **restitution statutes.** Under such laws the defendant must pay back the victims to compensate for the loss they suffered from the crime. While conceptually appealing, restitution statutes have limits for the reason that many convicted criminals lack the resources to make restitution. Judges have also turned to public humiliation as a sanction. A convicted criminal may be forced to wear a sign or take out an advertisement in the newspaper confessing his or her guilt. Convicted drunk drivers have been compelled to apply bumper stickers declaring themselves guilty of that crime.

The Eighth Amendment to the Constitution prohibits **cruel and unusual punishment.** This typically concerns punishments such as torture, but courts are extending the amendment to unreasonable prison conditions if the government exhibits "deliberate indifference" to the conditions. A 1993 Supreme Court decision held that being confined to a cell with a smoker could be cruel and unusual punishment if the prisoner could show that the secondhand tobacco smoke presented a serious risk to his or her health.

❖ Juvenile Justice

The United States provides a justice system for juveniles separate from that for adults. This system tends to be more lenient and often refers to "delinquent acts" rather than crimes. Sentences are also lighter. As juveniles are increasingly committing heinous crimes, the relative lenience of juvenile courts has fallen into some disfavor.

The Juvenile

Each state sets its own age limit for determination of whether an accused person should be tried as an adult or as a juvenile. In most states the age of maturity is eighteen, but a number of states have reduced this age to sixteen or seventeen. Underage individuals are presumptively treated as youths and tried in juvenile court. Most states provide that some juveniles may be tried in an adult court and subjected to the full range of penalties. The juvenile may be transferred to adult court, depending on certain factors. The relevant factors include the seriousness of the crime, the criminal record of the defendant, the age of the defendant, and the likelihood that juvenile status will better enable the rehabilitation of the defendant.

Pretrial

The apprehension of a juvenile is not called an arrest but a *taking into custody.* Juveniles may be taken into custody for the very same criminal acts that would result in the arrest of an adult. Juveniles may also be taken into custody for **status offenses.** Status offenses are not criminal acts proscribed by the legislature but are problems such as repeated truancy at school or habitual disobedience and may apply to those minors who have run away from home. A single episode of misbehavior does not render a youth a status offender. Consistent misbehavior is required. Juveniles charged with status offenses have basically the same legal protections as those charged with crimes.

As juvenile criminal behavior has grown, status offenses have taken a back seat. Such offenses are still significant, however, as they often reflect an emotionally troubled life that may be amenable to rehabilitation. Various programs, such as youth shelters and counseling, have been established to assist runaways and other troubled youths.

After a juvenile is taken into custody for either a crime or a status offense, the police may choose to file a formal charge, refer the case to social workers, or release the youth to the care of parents. If the police detain the juvenile, a process known as **intake** follows. At this stage the authorities question the juvenile, to assess the seriousness of the problem. Many complaints are eliminated at this stage, also, as the youth may yet be referred to social service or have charges dismissed.

Juvenile Court Procedures

Juveniles in custody must first receive an initial hearing on the validity of their detention. The youth has a right to an attorney and may have one appointed by the court if necessary. Instead of a trial, a juvenile is given an **adjudication hearing.** This functions much like an adult trial, and the juvenile has a constitutional right to due process, including the right to present evidence, cross-examine witnesses, and be represented by an attorney. In contrast to the trial of an adult, a juvenile adjudication hearing is not public.

A juvenile may be found delinquent, rather than guilty. In this event juveniles undergo a *dispositional hearing* in which the judge decides what disposition (sentence) the youth should receive. Juvenile dispositions tend to place more emphasis on rehabilitation and less on deterrence or incarceration as compared to adult sentencing. Probation is a common disposition, and the conditions of probation may be particularly strict, such as a curfew. The juvenile may be sentenced to a juvenile institution for an indeterminate amount of time, up to the maximum statutorily allowed for the violation committed. The youth may instead be sent to a halfway house or foster home for rehabilitation.

Disposition is more limited for status offenders, who have committed no adult crime. Parents may actually take their child to a local prosecutor and ask that a status offender complaint be filed against the juvenile. Such a petition might request that the youth be removed from the home and placed in some sort of government institution or foster home. Many states allow such a ruling for a child who continually refuses to obey the directions of parents or fails to attend school. Such a juvenile might be declared a **person in need of supervision.**

Juveniles have many, but not all, of the constitutional protections afforded adults. The Supreme Court has held that juveniles have the right not to be found in violation of a criminal act without proof beyond a reasonable doubt, though this does not extend to status offenses. Juveniles also have the right to an attorney and to confront their accusers. Juveniles do not have the right to trial by jury, however. An adult can never be tried for status offenses. Most states permit juveniles to appeal their dispositions, but the Supreme Court has never held that this is constitutionally required.

Topic 7 Jury Duty

The jury system is central to the American system of justice. Serving on a jury is both a privilege and a responsibility of citizenship. While such service may be a temporary inconvenience, the willingness of citizens to serve is essential to preserve constitutional rights and is reflective of democracy. Community participation in justice is important to public confidence in the system.

❖ Jury Venire and Selection

The process of jury selection can be lengthy and confusing to the ordinary person. While parts of the process may appear arbitrary, they are designed to help select an impartial jury of the defendant's peers.

Jury Venire

Jury selection must begin with a pool of possible jurors. This pool of potential jurors is often called a jury **venire.** Choosing the individuals in this pool for any given case requires a list of all possible jurors in the community. There is no such convenient list. In the past, some communities used lists of property taxpayers or telephone book listings. Such lists created a bias toward the wealthier citizens, who are more likely to own property and have more telephone lines. Consequently, exclusive reliance on such lists may violate the constitutional requirement of a **jury of peers.**

A defendant's right to a jury of peers does not mean that the jurors must come from the same walk of life as the defendant. A hot rodder charged with drunk driving has no right to a jury composed of automobile fanciers. Rather, the term "jury of peers" simply means that no group in the community has been systematically excluded from the jury. The jury pool must represent a "fair cross section" of the community. Suppose that the jury pool was drawn from all those who voted in the last two presidential elections. The hot rodder might reasonably complain that this unfairly excluded a large number of younger persons in their twenties.

There is no perfect list for a jury venire. Many communities still use phone books but supplement them with lists of registered voters, census rolls, and motor vehicle registration lists. Whatever the list used, the jury pool is selected randomly from the list. The venire may consist of hundreds of names, depending on the number of trials to be covered and the potential difficulty of finding impartial individuals. A highly publicized trial may require a larger initial venire of potential jurors, because many individuals may already have formed a strong opinion of the case.

If you are in the venire of jurors for a given case or cases, you will first receive a card in the mail summoning you to the courthouse. Many people ignore this card—over 50 percent of those summoned to jury duty fail to appear on the designated day and time. It is your civic duty to appear, however, and it is normally a crime if you fail to appear in response to the summons. Failure to appear may result in your arrest, though it is more common for the government to issue a contempt-of-court letter that may result in a fine. Many people on the venire will not actually be selected for a jury. One New Jersey study found that 63 percent of those summoned for jury duty never served.

Jury Selection

After responding to your summons to jury duty, you probably will sit in a large courtroom and listen to a judge lecture you on the importance of jury service and your duties. At this point, some jurors will be removed from the pool because of exemptions from jury service. An exemption is a statutory provision declaring that certain groups need not serve on juries, often because their jobs are considered so important that the individuals cannot be taken away from their employment.

Historically, states provided a large number of exemptions from jury service. Even in this century, women were exempted for a variety of reasons, including their duties to home and family. The exemption for women was deemed unconstitutional, but many professional groups are still excluded. A representative list of exemptions might include the clergy, doctors, lawyers, teachers, pharmacists, firefighters, and even embalmers. These professional exemptions do not mean the the individuals *cannot* serve on a jury. The exemptions mean that the professionals are not required to serve.

There is currently a trend toward abolishing all these exemptions. The exclusion of professionals obviously makes the jury less than representative of the community. In some states, even judges serve on juries when summoned. These states still provide some exemption for individuals who would be removed from work necessary for the public health or safety of the community or who can establish some other good cause for being exempted.

Suppose that you are summoned for jury duty and have no professional exemption. It also happens that the next month is particularly critical to your business and requires your close attention. You probably can receive a deferral of jury service until a later, more convenient date. Such deferrals are routinely granted.

States also provide for other exemptions in addition to the named professions. Felons, minors, noncitizens, and those who cannot understand English are typically exempted. Most states also exempt severely disabled individuals. Single parents with minor children or others with special cause may also be excluded. Fear of losing one's job is not a basis for exemption from jury duty.

Voir Dire

Once the exemption process is completed, the court commences *voir dire.* This is a process of questioning jurors to elicit any prejudices that could preclude the individual's impartiality. In some states, the attorneys conduct *voir dire* and question the potential jurors directly. In other states, the attorneys for the parties submit questions to the judge, who does the direct questioning of the venire.

Voir dire questions might inquire about whether the individual had a strong prejudice against members of a given race or religion. Other questions relate to the facts of the case, such as whether the juror would be willing to consider imposing capital punishment. A common question is whether the potential jurors have read about the case in the papers and formed an opinion about the guilt or innocence of a criminal defendant. Merely reading about a case does not disqualify a juror as biased, but the formation of a strong opinion about guilt will undermine impartiality. The court or lawyers also will ask about education, relevant experiences, family background, and other factors.

If you wish to avoid jury service, you might be tempted to state that you are biased about the case. In addition to being dishonest, this approach might not work. In a Massachusetts case, a doctor openly sought to avoid jury service for financial reasons. He stated that he would be biased in the case. The judge believed that he was lying and ordered the doctor to sit in the courtroom as a spectator for the duration of the trial.

Challenges

After a juror is questioned, the attorneys may accept him or her or they may attempt to challenge the individual. Such a challenge may prevent the person from serving on the jury. Each side of the case may raise an unlimited number of **challenges for cause.** A challenge for cause involves the attorney asking the judge to excuse the juror because of disqualifying bias or lack of competence for jury service. The judge makes the ultimate decision whether the individual should serve or not.

Each side of the case also gets a limited number of **peremptory challenges.** In capital cases, the defendant may have as many as twenty peremptories, while for misdemeanors peremptories may be limited to four. In a peremptory challenge, an attorney may excuse a prospective juror from service without giving any reason at all. Lawyers typically use peremptory challenges when they have a hunch that a juror will favor the other side but cannot establish this bias sufficiently to convince the judge to accept a challenge for cause.

The theory of jury selection is to find an impartial jury. In reality, each side is seeking to identify and seat jurors who favor its case, even if only subconsciously. Some lawyers hire psychologists for jury selection to help choose favorable jurors. The tobacco industry, for example, has discovered that current smokers tend to be unsympathetic to smokers suing cigarette companies for health harms. It is hoped that the efforts of both sides will balance each other out so that the resulting jury will be reasonably impartial.

Lawyers' use of peremptory challenges is limited by the Constitution. Such challenges cannot be used to exclude a given race from the jury. In a case when an African American was on trial for a crime, there might be only a few African Americans in the jury venire. Some prosecutors would use all their peremptory challenges against these African Americans, ensuring an all-white jury. The Supreme Court held that this use of peremptories was unconstitutional and denied the defendant a jury of peers.

Alternate Jurors and Jury Size

The *voir dire* and challenge process continues until a full jury can be seated. In complicated cases, *voir dire* can last for months. Most juries consist of twelve persons, though a court usually selects a couple of alternate jurors as well. The alternates sit in the courtroom and observe the case just like the real jurors. Should a juror fall sick during the trial or become disqualified for other reasons, an alternate juror may sit in. This avoids the waste of restarting the trial from the beginning with a new jury.

The twelve-person jury is historically traditional but not constitutionally required. The court has approved six-person juries but has held that five is too few for a criminal action. The reduced number makes it easier and quicker to empanel a jury.

❖ Trial

Once you are selected for a jury, you sit through the trial in a designated spot in the courtroom. You will likely discover that trials are not as exciting as portrayed on television or in movies. Nevertheless, your close attention is required in order that the parties get a fair verdict.

Trial Procedures

The trial usually will begin with opening arguments from the attorneys for each side in the case. These arguments are not evidence but are persuasive appeals that help you understand the theory of the parties. Each side then will present its evidence in the form of physical exhibits, documents, and witnesses. The witnesses probably will be cross-examined. You must follow this presentation closely and decide which witnesses are believable. It is likely that you will be prohibited from taking notes, so you must struggle to remember key facts. After the evidence, the attorneys will present closing arguments, which are not evidence but which summarize the case and seek to persuade you.

Jury Instructions

At the end of the trial, the judge will give you instructions to help decide the case. These instructions inform you of the law that should be applied to the facts that you find, based upon the testimony. A judge's instruction might tell you that you have to find certain facts before you may decide the case for a given side.

It is the jury's general responsibility to apply the law, even if you disagree with the law. Some juries have been known to ignore the law, a process known as **jury nullification.** Such a jury might decide that marijuana should be legal and therefore refuse to convict a person for possession of that drug. Jury nullification is often criticized, but jury deliberations are secret and there is no known way to prevent a jury from nullifying the law and acquitting a defendant. If the jury obviously ignores the law in a civil case, the decision is more likely to be overturned on appeal.

In addition to instructions, the judge may comment upon the evidence at trial. The judge might say that she found one witness to be particularly credible and another not to be believable. You can consider the judge's opinion, but the decision is ultimately yours, so you are free to disagree with the judge.

Deliberations

Different juries may adopt very different approaches to deliberations. Whatever procedure is chosen, you should speak openly about your views and listen closely to the opinions of fellow jurors. You must decide the case on the evidence presented at trial, not on prejudices or outside sources of information known to you. If you forget something that occurred during the trial, you may ask the judge for information. If you wish to examine an exhibit, it generally will be provided. In contrast, courts commonly deny jury requests for transcripts of trial testimony.

It is expected that there will be disagreement among the jurors. After discussion and give-and-take, the jury is expected to reach a verdict. In some circumstances, the verdict must be unanimous, but other states provide for verdicts by a **supermajority** of the jury, such as a three-fourths vote. If you cannot reach a verdict it is called a hung jury, and the judge must declare a **mistrial**. This means that the trial must be conducted again before a new jury. For obvious reasons, courts try to avoid such deadlocks and will urge you to compromise and reach a verdict.

It is very difficult to challenge a jury verdict after the fact. It is important that verdicts have finality and not be subject to constant reopening. Suppose that a juror evinces extreme racial bias toward the defendant during deliberations. Courts are still unsettled about whether evidence of such bias will even be considered. Some judges have refused even to listen to such evidence of bias. This makes it all the more important that unbiased jurors work to ensure a fair result. Courts are more likely to overturn a verdict if a juror lied in *voir dire* about a significant fact such as that he or she has been convicted of a felony. A $45 million verdict against Lockheed Corporation was overturned because of such a lie.

❖ Juror's Rights

Jury service is a duty that may inconvenience you. In the best case you will lose some time at work. In the worst case, you may be penalized or even fired by your employer for losing this time. The law increasingly provides some protections for jurors.

Employment

In the past under common law, an employer could fire a worker for any reason whatsoever. Today, courts recognize a **wrongful discharge** action that makes it illegal to fire employees for certain public policy reasons. Courts have consistently found that it is wrongful to fire a person for serving on a jury. The juror will, of course, have to prove that jury service was indeed the cause of the termination. In a 1992 Oklahoma case, the juror successfully proved this point and received $175,000 in actual damages for being fired and another $175,000 in punitive damages.

In addition to private wrongful discharge actions, a number of states make it illegal to fire a worker because of jury duty. In Arizona, for example, companies are prohibited from dismissing workers, demoting workers, or taking away seniority rights for time on jury service. This law is punishable by both a fine and imprisonment of the responsible individual.

Pay

Jurors are paid a per diem fee for their service. The rate of pay for jury service is set by state law and is far below the minimum wage. A common per diem is $5 per day of jury duty. There is momentum to increase the per diem, but the most generous states pay only about $30/day.

Firms are not necessarily required to pay wages for employees' time spent on jury service. Most cases last only two or three days, however, and companies often pay for this time. When a Los Angeles law firm refused to pay a worker for extended jury duty in 1992, the federal district court reprimanded the firm for evading its civic responsibility. The judge declared that he would "make them" pay her.

Secrecy

Traditionally, the law provided for the **sequestration** of jurors in order to maintain their objectivity. If a trial was receiving great publicity, the jurors would be confined to hotel rooms and denied access to newspapers and television, to prevent them from reading public accounts of their trial. This helped ensure that the jury decided the case only on the facts presented in court.

Today, a more extreme form of sequestration may occur for a different reason. In organized crime prosecutions, jurors have been bribed or threatened by criminals in order to gain an acquittal. In response, the identities of jurors in such trials is kept secret, and the jury may even sit behind a screen. A similar approach may be used in extremely controversial cases, such as certain police-brutality prosecutions. If such a case may produce rioting, jurors may have concern for their safety or fear public blame for bringing in an unpopular verdict. These jurors also may have their identities shielded by the court.

◆ **Exhibit H-1**
Characteristics of Small Claims Courts in Selected States

State	Maximum Amount of Suit	Lawyers Allowed?	Who Can Appeal? Plaintiff	Defendant	Filing Cost*
Alabama	$ 1,500	yes	yes	yes	$22
Arizona	$ 1,000	no	yes	yes	$ 3
California	$ 5,000	no	no	yes	$ 8
Colorado	$ 3,500	no	yes	yes	$0–$2,000, $17 $2,001–$3,500, $26
Connecticut	$ 2,000	yes	no	no	$25
Washington, D.C.	$ 2,000	yes	yes	yes	$ 1
Florida	$ 2,500	yes	yes	yes	$69
Georgia	$ 5,000	yes	yes	yes	$40
Illinois	$15,000	no	yes	yes	$0–$250, $20 $251–$500, $30 $501–$2,500, $40 $2,501–$15,000, $85
Indiana	$ 6,000	yes	yes	yes	$31
Iowa	$ 2,000	yes	yes	yes	$30
Kansas	$ 1,000	no	yes	yes	$0–$500, $15 $500–$1,000, $35
Kentucky	$ 1,500	yes	yes	yes	$23.90
Louisiana	$ 2,000	yes	no	no	$55
Maine	$ 1,400	yes	yes	yes	$20 per defendant
Maryland	$ 2,500	yes	yes	yes	$5
Massachusetts	$ 1,500	yes	no	yes	$9
Michigan	$ 1,500	no	no	no	$33.50
Minnesota	$ 4,000	yes	yes	yes	$16
Mississippi	$ 1,000	yes	yes	yes	$32.50
Missouri	$ 1,500	yes	yes	yes	$36
New Jersey	$ 1,000	yes	yes	yes	$12
New York	$ 2,000	yes	judge, yes arbitrator, no	yes no	$19
North Carolina	$ 1,500	yes	yes	yes	$19
Ohio	$ 1,000	yes	yes	yes	$21
Oklahoma	$ 1,000	yes	yes	yes	$37
Oregon	$ 2,500	no	no	no	$20
Pennsylvania	$ 5,000	yes	yes	yes	$1–$500, $16 $501–$2,000, $22 $2,000–$5,000, $42
South Carolina	$ 2,500	yes	yes	yes	$30
Tennessee	$10,000	yes	yes	yes	$42.75
Texas	$ 5,000	yes	yes	yes	$50
Virginia	$ 7,000	yes	yes	yes	$10 per defendant
Wisconsin	$ 2,000	yes	yes	yes	$18
Wyoming	$ 2,000	yes	yes	yes	$13

* In most states a serving fee is added to the filing fee. This amount will generally be charged for each defendant served with legal papers. In Mississippi, for example, an extra $8 is charged for each person who is being sued.

Appendix A

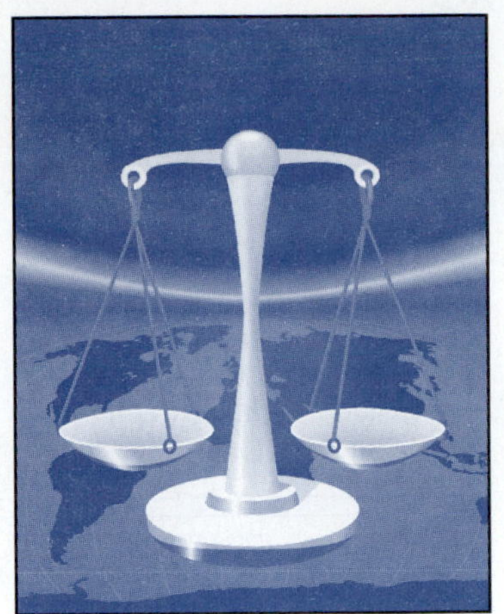

How To Brief A Case and Selected Cases

❖ How to Brief a Case

To fully understand the law with respect to business, you need to be able to read and understand court decisions. To make this task easier, you can use a method of case analysis that is called *briefing.* There is a fairly standard procedure that you can follow when you "brief" any court case. You must first read the case opinion carefully. When you feel you understand the case, you can prepare a brief of it.

Although the format of the brief may vary, typically it will present the essentials of the case under headings such as those listed below.

1. **Citation.** Give the full citation for the case, including the name of the case, the date it was decided, and the court that decided it.
2. **Facts.** Briefly indicate (a) the reasons for the lawsuit; (b) the identity and arguments of the plaintiff(s) and defendant(s), respectively; and (c) the lower court's decision—if appropriate.
3. **Issue.** Concisely phrase, in the form of a question, the essential issue before the court. (If more than one issue is involved, you may have two—or even more—questions here.)
4. **Decision.** Indicate here—with a "yes" or "no," if possible—the court's answer to the question (or questions) in the *Issue* section above.
5. **Reason.** Summarize as briefly as possible the reasons given by the court for its decision (or decisions) and the case or statutory law relied on by the court in arriving at its decision.

When you prepare your brief, be sure you include all of the important facts. But remember that, by definition, the result should be brief.

❖ Selected Cases for Briefing

Court opinions can run from a few pages to hundreds of pages in length. For reasons of space, only the essential parts of the opinions are presented in the cases that follow. A series of three asterisks indicates that a portion of the text—other than citations and footnotes—has been omitted. Four asterisks indicate the omission of at least one paragraph.

Case A.1

BUKOWSKI v. COOPERVISION INC.

New York Supreme Court, Appellate Division, Third Department, 1993.
185 A.D.2d 31,
592 N.Y.S.2d 807.

CREW, Justice.

Appeal from that part of an order of the Supreme Court (Mugglin, J.), entered November 26, 1991 in Broome County, which partially denied the motion

The first part of the court opinion normally summarizes the facts of the case. The facts include the identities of the plaintiff (the party initiating the lawsuit) and the defendant (the party against whom the suit is brought), the reason for the action, and the contentions of the parties.

of defendant CooperVision Inc. for summary judgment dismissing the complaint.

On April 18, 1984, plaintiff purchased from defendant George Roberts, a licensed optometrist, a pair of Permalens XL extended wear contact lenses manufactured by defendant CooperVision Inc. (hereinafter defendant). Plaintiff apparently wore the contact lenses without incident until July 4, 1984, at which time she began experiencing "a lot of dry eye symptoms". On July 7, 1984, plaintiff's eyes became irritated and plaintiff removed the lenses; when she awoke the following morning, plaintiff's left eye was swollen shut. Plaintiff was subsequently diagnosed with a pseudomonas corneal ulcer and abscess of the left eye, which has allegedly resulted in reduced visual acuity and psychological injury.

Discovery is a method by which opposing parties may obtain information from each other in preparation for trial.

Strict liability is liability without fault. It may be imposed on a manufacturer or seller who markets a product that is unreasonably dangerous when in a defective condition.

Negligence is the failure to exercise the standard of care that a reasonable person would exercise in similar circumstances.

A summary judgment is a pretrial judgment that is granted when no facts are in dispute and the only question is what law applies.

The lower court's decision.

These are important legal principles that the court cites in support of its decision.

Plaintiff thereafter commenced this action against defendant on theories of **strict products liability** and **negligence.** Following * * * **discovery,** defendant moved for **summary judgment.** **Supreme Court granted summary judgment dismissing the strict products liability cause of action for a manufacturing defect but denied summary judgment on the remaining theories of liability, finding that questions of fact remained.** Defendant now appeals from so much of Supreme Court's order as denied its motion for summary judgment on the remaining causes of action.

We affirm. **It is well settled that a plaintiff may recover in strict products liability or negligence for a manufacturer's failure to warn of the risks and dangers associated with the use of its product. The manufacturer's duty extends to warning consumers of latent dangers resulting from the foreseeable use of its product of which the manufacturer knew or should have known, and liability may be imposed based upon either the complete failure to warn of a particular hazard or the inclusion of warnings that are insufficient.** "The adequacy of the instruction or warning is generally a question of fact to be determined at trial * * * and is not ordinarily susceptible to the drastic remedy of summary judgment."

Here, defendant argues that the risk of corneal ulceration was unknown or believed to be insignificant prior to plaintiff's injury in 1984 and, hence, it had no duty to warn. In support of this argument, defendant points to the examination before trial testimony of its manager of quality and standards, William Trilsch, who testified that the reported incidence of corneal ulcers in the general population of people wearing contact lenses is less than 1/1000 %. The source of this information is unclear, however, and Trilsch did not specifically know how many pseudomonas corneal ulcers had been reported to defendant.

The court's conclusion on the first part of the issue.

The judgment of the lower court on this part of the issue is affirmed. Summary judgment on the negligence claim was inappropriate because there are questions of fact to be determined at trial.

We are of the view that such proof is insufficient to meet defendant's initial burden on the motion for summary judgment. However, assuming such proof was sufficient, the clinical reports, adverse effect abstracts and internal correspondence submitted by plaintiff in opposition to defendant's motion was sufficient to raise a question of fact as to whether defendant knew or should have known of the risk that corneal ulcers posed for extended wear contact lens users. We are also of the view that the sufficiency of the warnings accompanying the Permalens XL extended wear contact lenses is an issue best resolved by a jury. **Accordingly, Supreme Court properly denied defendant's motion for summary judgment on the failure to warn cause of action.**

Defendant next argues that the **informed * * * intermediary doctrine** should be applied to the facts of this case. This doctrine has evolved in the field of prescription drugs and requires such a manufacturer to warn of all potential dangers of which it knows or should know are associated with its product and, further, to take such steps as reasonably necessary to bring that knowledge to the attention of the medical community. The manufacturer discharges its duty in this regard by providing adequate warnings to the prescribing physician, who then acts as an informed intermediary between the manufacturer and the patient, "assessing the risks and benefits of the drug and advising the patient of its possible risks and side effects."

Under the informed intermediary doctrine, a physician who prescribes a drug or, in some cases, a medical device for a patient acts as an "informed intermediary" between the product's manufacturer and the patient, assessing the risks and benefits and advising the patient.

The informed intermediary doctrine has been extended to apply to certain medical devices, and defendant argues that the nature of the optometrist/patient relationship and the optometrist's expertise in eye-related matters militates in favor of the application of the doctrine to this case. As the parties correctly note, implicit in the application of the doctrine is the existence of a medical professional with the knowledge and expertise to assimilate technical information and, further, the corresponding need for that professional to assess the risks and benefits posed by the drug or device in light of the particular patient's medical history and treatment needs.

Based upon a review of the limited record before us, we are unable to ascertain * * * the nature of the relationship between plaintiff and Roberts and the role each played in the decision to wear and selection of the extended wear contact lenses manufactured by defendant. Additionally, the record is devoid of evidence that an optometrist is possessed of the knowledge and expertise necessary to assimilate technical information and, further, that there was a corresponding need to assess the risks and benefits posed by the Permalens XL to prescribing the device, given plaintiff's medical history and vision needs. **Accordingly, we cannot determine at this juncture whether the informed intermediary doctrine is applicable.** Moreover, the informed intermediary doctrine, to be applicable, presupposes that the medical professional has been sufficiently warned of the risks of the product so that she or he may assess those risks in relation to the patient's needs. Here, we have already determined that the sufficiency of the warnings is an issue to be determined at trial. Consequently, even if we were to extend the informed intermediary doctrine to this case, our determination as to the sufficiency of the warnings precludes a finding that defendant is absolved of liability as a matter of law. **It was therefore proper for Supreme Court to partially deny defendant's motion.** * * *

The court's conclusion on the second part of the issue.

The judgment of the lower court on this part of the issue is affirmed.

ORDERED that the order is affirmed, with costs.

Case A.2 *Reference: Problem 3-14.*

GOELLER v. LIBERTY MUTUAL INSURANCE CO.

Supreme Court of Pennsylvania, 1990.
568 A.2d 176.

McDERMOTT, Justice.

This is an appeal from an order of the Superior Court which reversed an order of the Court of Common Pleas of Philadelphia County. The latter order denied appellee's petition to confirm a decision of a panel of arbitrators. It also mandated the **convention** [a convening; bringing together] of a new panel and re-hearing of appellant's claim under the uninsured motorist provision of an insurance policy. The facts and procedural history of the case are set forth below.

Appellant was injured in an automobile mishap in Connecticut while removing the driver from an overturned automobile. Involved in the accident were two other drivers, one of whom was allegedly uninsured. He entered a claim against appellee, the carrier of his employer's insurance policy, for coverage under an uninsured motorist provision which appellee disputed. The contract provided that disputes would be resolved by arbitration conducted in accordance with the Pennsylvania Arbitration Act * * *.

A panel of three arbitrators was assembled, as provided in the agreement, and presided over hearings on September 12 and 25, 1986. On July 28, 1987, the neutral arbitrator mailed a letter to the attorneys of the parties and each of the other panel members. It stated simply to the effect that appellee's arbitrator and the neutral arbitrator found for appellee and that appellant's arbitrator dissented and found for appellant. The neutral arbitrator's was the solitary signature to the letter. The following day, the letter was filed with the **Prothonotary** [principal court clerk].

Also on the following day, appellant's arbitrator by certified mail, responded with a letter to the neutral arbitrator. In it he made a number of complaints. He stated that he had not agreed to the letter nor had he been consulted. He maintained in effect that the letter misrepresented his opinion. Regarding the deliberations of the panel members, he went on to express shock on learning that the other arbitrators had discussed the case out of his presence. In summary he stated that the letter was absolutely incorrect. He suggested further that the panel withdraw their purported findings and withdraw as the arbitrators in order to allow another panel to take over the matter. He sent courtesy copies to the other addressees of the neutral arbitrator's letter. On August 3, 1987, the neutral arbitrator responded by letter. Its entire text stated, "Because of (sic) you have impugned my integrity, I am withdrawing my award and I am withdrawing from the panel of arbitrators in this case."

On August 7, 1987, appellee filed a petition to confirm the award. On August 24, 1987, appellant answered, and filed new matter, petitioning, *inter alia* [among other things], for an order to convene a new arbitration panel. The court found adequate grounds to conclude that all of the panel members had not participated in the deliberations and that the award was not final in nature. The court therefore denied appellee's petition to confirm the award and ordered the parties to convene a new arbitration panel to try the case.

On appeal, the Superior Court reversed, determining that the lower court erred in its resolution of both the question of whether the panel had issued a final award and that of whether the award was the product of misconduct or other gross irregularity. Appellant petitioned this Court and we granted leave to appeal in order to review the Superior Court's determinations.

With respect to appellant's first contention, he asserts * * * that there was no final award by the arbitrators. The [Pennsylvania Arbitration] Act states in appropriate part:

> Award of Arbitrators
> General Rule—The award of the arbitrators shall be in writing and signed by the arbitrators joining in the award. The arbitrators shall deliver a copy of the award to each party personally or by registered or certified mail or as prescribed in the agreement to arbitrate.

In reply, appellee argues that the neutral arbitrator was without the power to withdraw the award of the arbitrators after it had been issued. We are impressed that the latter argument is non-responsive to the issue raised: whether there was an award in the first instance. We conclude that there was not.

First we note that this arbitration, as agreed by the parties, was to be regulated by the provisions of the Act. The reviewing court is bound to construe the words of the Act according to rules of grammar and according to their common and approved usage. The object of the Court's interpretation is to ascertain and effectuate the intention of the General Assembly [the Pennsylvania legislature]. The word "shall," in the section relied on by appellant, is clearly mandatory [authoritative; compelling] in effect. But it is manifest that a purported award signed by no more than one of the three members of the panel, as herein, does not comply with the plain wording of the Act. The purported award in this case, in failing the formal statutory requirement, failed the requirement of their agreement as well. The "award" was a nullity.

Furthermore we are persuaded that there was no award in this case for another, more substantive, reason. This Court long ago voiced the principle that, "The opportunity to deliberate, and, if possible, to convince their fellows is the right of the minority, of which they cannot be deprived by the arbitrary will of the majority." * * *

The record indicates, and it is not disputed, that one of the members of the panel in this case was denied his opportunity to deliberate. When an arbitrator, properly appointed and entitled to act, is denied access to the deliberations of the other arbitrators, their decision is not a decision. It matters not whose arbitrator he or she may be. What is important is that all viewpoints must at least be heard. Each must be entitled to the opportunity to persuade the others, be permitted to dissent and to maintain his voice in the decision. It is manifest that that principle was violated in this case.

We recognize, as the Superior Court admonishes, that a strong presumption exists in favor of an arbitration panel's final award. However, before the award is paid such deference [courteous submission to another's opinion or judgment] by the courts it must come into existence as a corporate act of the panel. For the reasons set forth above, we conclude that in this case it did not.

Furthermore, the mandate of the trial court, that a new panel be convened and the matter retried, is necessary to afford the parties no less than that to which they agreed, an award by an arbitration panel.

Since we resolve appellant's first contention as we do, it is not necessary to pierce the veil of the panel's deliberations and pass on whether the award was a product of misconduct or other grave irregularity in terms of the Act.

The order of the Superior Court is reversed. The order of the Court of Common Pleas of Philadelphia County is reinstated.

Case A.3 *Reference: Problem 4-15.*

AUSTIN v. BERRYMAN

United States Court of Appeals, Fourth Circuit, 1989.
878 F.2d 786.

MURNAGHAN, Circuit Judge:

We have before us for en banc reconsideration an appeal taken from an action successfully brought by Barbara Austin in the United States District Court for the Western District of Virginia against the Virginia Employment Commission, challenging a denial of unemployment compensation benefits. * * * In brief, Austin charged, *inter alia* [among other things], that the denial of her claim for unemployment benefits, based on a Virginia statute specifically precluding such benefits for any individual who voluntarily quits work to join his or her spouse in a new location, was an unconstitutional infringement upon the incidents of marriage protected by the fourteenth amendment and an unconstitutional burden on her first amendment right to the free exercise of her religion. Her religion happened to command that she follow her spouse wherever he might go and the sincerity of her religious belief was not questioned. The district court found in Austin's favor and awarded injunctive relief and retroactive benefits.

On appeal, Judge Sprouse, writing for a panel majority, found that the denial of benefits did not implicate Austin's fourteenth amendment rights, but that it did unconstitutionally burden Austin's right to the free exercise of her religion. The panel also found, however, that any award of retroactive benefits was barred by the eleventh amendment. One panel member concurred with the panel majority as to the fourteenth and eleventh amendment issues, but dissented as to the existence of a free exercise violation. The panel opinion now, of course, has been vacated by a grant of rehearing *en banc*.

After careful consideration of the additional arguments proffered by both sides, the Court, en banc, is convinced that the panel majority correctly concluded that denying Austin unemployment benefits did not infringe upon fundamental marital rights protected by the fourteenth amendment. To this extent, we adopt the majority panel opinion. We also find, however, that the denial of benefits did not unconstitutionally burden Austin's first amendment right to the free exercise of her religion. We are persuaded that the views expressed on the first amendment, free exercise of religion claim in the opinion dissenting in part from the panel majority are correct, and we hereby adopt that opinion as that of the en banc court. As we find that Austin is not entitled to any relief, we need not address whether the eleventh amendment bars an award of retroactive benefits.

The decisive consideration, as we see it, is that the proximate cause of Austin's unemployment is geographic distance, not her religious beliefs. There is no conflict between the circumstances of work and Austin's religious precepts. Austin's religious beliefs do not "require" her "to refrain from the work in question." Austin is unable to work simply because she is now too far removed from her employer to make it practical. In striking contrast, if one, for genuine religious beliefs, moves to a new residence in order to continue to live with a spouse, and that residence is not geographically so removed as to preclude regular attendance at the worksite, no unemployment, and hence no unemployment benefits, will arise. That amounts to proof that extent of geographical non-propinquity, not religious belief, led to Austin's disqualification for unemployment benefits.

Austin voluntarily decided to quit her job and join her spouse in a new geographic location 150 miles away. Virginia has stated that every individual who follows such a course, no matter what the reason, religious or non-religious, is disqualified for unemployment benefits. To craft judicially a statutory exception only for those individuals who profess Austin's religious convictions, particularly in the absence of a direct conflict between a given employment practice and a religious belief, would, in our view, result in a subsidy to members of a particular religious belief, impermissible under the Establishment Clause.

Accordingly, the judgment of the district court is REVERSED.

Case A.4 *Reference: Problem 10-12.*

MANN v. WETTER

Court of Appeals of Oregon, 1990.
100 Or.App. 184,
785 P.2d 1064.

DEITS, Judge.

Plaintiff, as **personal representative** [a person designated in a will to handle estate matters upon the death of the maker of the will] of the estate of Bruce E. Virkler, brought this **wrongful death action** [a lawsuit, brought on behalf of a deceased person's beneficiaries, that alleges that the deceased person's death was attributable to the willful or negligent act of another] against defendants, alleging negligence in conducting a scuba diving instructional program. The trial court granted defendants' motion for summary judgment, based on a release signed by Virkler. Plaintiff appeals. We reverse as to defendant Wetter.

Horizon Water Sports, Inc. (Horizon) operates a diving school and is a member of NASDS, a nationwide standardized scuba instruction program. Horizon employed Wetter as a NASDS certified diving instructor. Virkler enrolled in one of Horizon's diving instruction programs. He completed a Total Information Card form, supplied by NASDS. The form requires personal and medical information and includes a clause respecting liability. The clause includes a release that states in pertinent part:

> [T]he Undersigned does for him/herself, his/her heirs, executors [persons appointed in wills to carry out the wills' directions] administrators [persons appointed by the court to manage a deceased person's estate] and assigns [those to whom property is or may be assigned (transferred)] hereby release, waive, discharge and relinquish any action or causes of action, aforesaid, which may hereafter arise for him/herself for his/her estate, and agrees that under no circumstances will he/she or his/her heirs, executors, administrators and assigns prosecute, present any claim for personal injury, property damage or wrongful death against N.A.S.D.S. or its member school, or any of its officers, agents, servants or employees for any of said causes of action, whether the same shall arise by the negligence of any of said persons, or otherwise. IT IS THE INTENTION OF THE ABOVE NAMED STUDENT BY THIS INSTRUMENT, TO EXEMPT AND RELIEVE N.A.S.D.S. AND ITS MEMBER SCHOOL FROM LIABILITY FOR PERSONAL INJURY, PROPERTY DAMAGE OR WRONGFUL DEATH CAUSED BY NEGLIGENCE. (Emphasis supplied.)

After Virkler had completed six to eight weeks of classroom and pool instruction, he participated in a required open-water certification dive, which was conducted by Horizon and supervised by Wetter. He died during the dive.

Plaintiff asserts that the trial court erred in granting defendants' motion for summary judgment. She first contends that the release should be held invalid as a matter of public policy because of the parties' unequal bargaining power, particularly because **decedent** [a deceased person; one who has recently died] was asked to sign the release after he had already attended some of the classes, had paid his fees and was fully committed to the program.

Although agreements to limit liability are not favored, neither are they automatically void. An agreement limiting liability is governed by principles of contract law and will be enforced in the absence of some consideration of public policy derived from the nature of the subject of the agreement or a determination that the contract was **adhesionary** [a contract in which the terms are dictated by a party having clearly superior bargaining power]. The [Oregon] Supreme Court has stated:

> There is nothing inherently bad about a contract provision which exempts one of the parties from liability. The parties are free to contract as they please, unless to permit them to do so would contravene the public interest.

Here, there are no public policy considerations that prevent a diving school from limiting liability for its own negligence. The diving school does not provide an essential public service, as was the case in *Real Good Food v. First National Bank*, where the court held that a bank could not limit its liability for the negligence of its own employes. The economic advantage, if any, that a small business that provides a nonessential service may have over its customers will not create unequal bargaining power, because the customers have a multitude of alternatives. Further, although decedent may not have signed the release until after he had paid for and started the program, that did not create unequal bargaining power between the parties that would require us to invalidate the release. He remained free not to continue the diving program.

Plaintiff also argues that the trial court erred when it granted summary judgment for Wetter, because, as a matter of law, the language of the release did not include him. Wetter contends that the language of the release clearly did include him.

As a general rule, the construction of a contract is a question of law for the court. The exception to that rule is that, if the language in a contract is ambiguous, evidence may be admitted as to the intent of the parties, and the determination of the parties' intent then is a question of fact. * * * A contract provision is ambiguous if it is capable of more than one sensible and reasonable interpretation * * *.

The disputed language in the release agreement provides that the release applies to actions "against N.A.S.D.S. or its member school or any of its officers, agents, servants or employees." The reference to "its officers, agents, servants or employees" could be read to refer to the officers, agents, servants or employes of NASDS or to those of Horizon. The language of the agreement is ambiguous, and so the parties are entitled to present evidence as to the intention of the drafters and of those who executed the release agreement. Accordingly, summary judgment in favor of Wetter was error.

Plaintiff also contends that the summary judgment in favor of Wetter should not have been granted, because there was a material question of fact whether Wetter was an officer, agent, servant or employe of NASDS. We agree that, depending on the construction of the language of the release agreement, that may be a material question of fact. Defendant presented evidence that Wetter was a nonvoting member of NASDS. Although it may not necessarily follow that, because of that, he may be an officer, agent, servant or employe of NASDS, plaintiff is entitled to present evidence concerning Wetter's status with NASDS.

Judgment for respondent Wetter reversed and remanded; otherwise affirmed.

Case A.5 *Reference: Problem 11-15.*

WILKIN v. 1ST SOURCE BANK

Court of Appeals of Indiana, Third District, 1990.
548 N.E.2d 170.

HOFFMAN, Judge.

Respondents-appellants Terrence G. Wilkin and Antoinette H. Wilkin (the Wilkins) appeal from the judgment of the St. Joseph Probate Court [a court with jurisdiction over wills and estate administration] in favor of petitioner-appellee 1st Source Bank (Bank). The Bank, as personal representative of the estate of Olga Mestrovic, had filed a petition to determine title to eight drawings and a plaster sculpture owned by Olga Mestrovic at the time of her death but in the possession of the Wilkins at the time the petition was filed. The probate court determined that the drawings and sculpture were the property of the estate, and the court ordered the Wilkins to return the items to the Bank.

At the request of the Bank, the probate court entered findings of fact and conclusions of law. Neither party disputes the validity of the findings of fact. Accordingly, this Court will accept the findings as true. The findings of fact may be summarized as follows.

Olga Mestrovic died on August 31, 1984. Her last will and testament was admitted to probate on September 6, 1984, and the Bank was appointed personal representative of the estate.

At the time of her death, Olga Mestrovic was the owner of a large number of works of art created by her husband, Ivan Mestrovic, an internationally-known sculptor and artist. [FN1] By the terms of Olga's will, all the works of art created by her husband and not specifically devised [bequeathed by will] were to be sold and the proceeds distributed to members of the Mestrovic family.

FN1. Ivan Mestrovic lived from 1883 to 1962. A Yugoslavian sculptor, Mestrovic became internationally known and spent his final working years in the United States. He taught at Syracuse University and at the University of Notre Dame. Much of his instruction as well as his own creative work involved religious themes * * *.

Also included in the estate of Olga Mestrovic was certain **real property** [land and permanent structures attached thereto; immovable property]. In March of 1985, the Bank entered into an agreement to sell the real estate to the Wilkins. The agreement of purchase and sale made no mention of any works of art, although it did provide for the sale of such **personal property** [all property that is not real property; movable property and intangible property, such as stocks and bonds] as the stove, refrigerator, dishwasher, drapes, curtains, sconces and French doors in the attic.

Immediately after closing on the real estate, the Wilkins complained that the premises were left in a cluttered condition and would require substantial cleaning effort. The Bank, through its trust officer, proposed two options: the Bank would retain a rubbish removal service to clean the property or the Wilkins could clean the premises and keep any items of personal property they wanted. The Wilkins opted to clean the property themselves. At the time arrangements were made concerning the cluttered condition of the real property, neither the Bank nor the Wilkins suspected that any works of art remained on the premises.

During their clean-up efforts, the Wilkins found eight drawings apparently created by Ivan Mestrovic. They also found a plaster sculpture of the figure of Christ with three small children. The Wilkins claimed ownership of the works of art, based upon their agreement with the Bank that if they cleaned the real property then they could keep such personal property as they desired.

The probate court ruled that there was no agreement for the purchase, sale or other disposition of the eight drawings and plaster sculpture. According to the lower court, there was no meeting of the minds, because neither party knew of the existence of the works of art.

On appeal, the Wilkins contend that the court's conclusions of law were erroneous. When the error charged is the trial court's application of the law, then this Court must correctly apply the law to the trial court's findings of fact.

Mutual assent is a prerequisite to the creation of a contract. Where both parties share a common assumption about a vital fact upon which they based their bargain, and that assumption is false, the transaction may be avoided if because of the mistake a quite different exchange of values occurs from the exchange of values contemplated by the parties. There is no contract, because the minds of the parties have in fact never met.

The necessity of mutual assent, or "meeting of the minds," is illustrated in the classic case of *Sherwood v. Walker* (1887). The owners of a * * * cow indicated to the purchaser that the cow was barren. The purchaser also appeared to believe that the cow was barren. Consequently, a bargain was made to sell at a price per pound at which the cow would have brought approximately $80.00. Before delivery, it was discovered that the cow was with calf and that she was, therefore, worth from $750.00 to $1,000.00. The court ruled that the transaction was voidable. * * *

Like the parties in *Sherwood*, the parties in the instant case shared a common presupposition as to the existence of certain facts which proved false. The Bank and the Wilkins considered the real estate which the Wilkins had purchased to be cluttered with items of personal property variously characterized as "junk," "stuff" or "trash." Neither party suspected that works of art created by Ivan Mestrovic remained on the premises.

As in *Sherwood*, one party experienced an unexpected, unbargained-for gain while the other party experienced an unexpected, unbargained-for loss. Because the Bank and the Wilkins did not know that the eight drawings and the plaster sculpture were included in the items of **personalty** [personal property] that cluttered the real property, the discovery of those works of art by the Wilkins was unexpected. The resultant gain to the Wilkins and loss to the Bank were not contemplated by the parties when the Bank agreed that the Wilkins could clean the premises and keep such personal property as they wished.

The following commentary on *Sherwood* is equally applicable to the case at bar: "Here the buyer sought to retain a gain that was produced, not by a subsequent change in circumstances, nor by the favorable resolution of known uncertainties when the contract was made, but by the presence of facts quite different from those on which the parties based their bargain."

The probate court properly concluded that there was no agreement for the purchase, sale or other disposition of the eight drawings and plaster sculpture, because there was no meeting of the minds.

The judgment of the St. Joseph Probate Court is affirmed.

Case A.6 *Reference: Problem 13-14.*

POTTER v. OSTER

Supreme Court of Iowa, 1988.
426 N.W.2d 148.

NEUMAN, Justice.

This is a suit in equity brought by the plaintiffs to rescind an installment land contract based on the seller's inability to convey title. The question on appeal is whether, in an era of declining land values, returning the parties to the status quo works an inequitable result. We think not. Accordingly, we affirm the district court judgment for rescission and restitution.

The facts are largely undisputed. Because the case was tried in equity, our review is ***de novo*** [as if the case had not been heard and no decision rendered before]. We give weight to the findings of the trial court, particularly where the credibility of witnesses is concerned, but we are not bound thereby.

The parties, though sharing a common interest in agribusiness, present a study in contrasts. We think the disparity in their background and experience is notable insofar as it bears on the equities of the transaction in issue. Plaintiff Charles Potter is a farm laborer and his wife, Sue, is a homemaker and substitute teacher. They have lived all their lives within a few miles of the real estate in question. Defendant Merrill Oster is an agricultural journalist and recognized specialist in land investment strategies. He owns Oster Communications, a multimillion dollar publishing concern devoted to furnishing farmers the latest in commodity market analysis and advice on an array of farm issues.

In May 1978, Oster contracted with Florence Stark to purchase her 160-acre farm in Howard County, Iowa, for $260,000 on a ten-year contract at seven percent interest. Oster then sold the homestead and nine acres to Charles and Sue Potter for $70,000. Potters paid $18,850 down and executed a ten-year installment contract for the balance at 8.5% interest. Oster then executed a contract with Robert Bishop for the sale of the remaining 151 acres as part of a package deal that included the sale of seventeen farms for a sum exceeding $5.9 million.

These back-to-back contracts collapsed like dominoes in March 1985 when Bishop failed to pay Oster and Oster failed to pay Stark the installments due on their respective contracts. Stark commenced forfeiture proceedings [proceedings to retake the property because Oster failed to perform a legal obligation—payment under the contract—and thus forfeited his right to the land]. Potters had paid every installment when due under their contract with Oster and had included Stark as a **joint payee** [one of two or more payees—persons to whom checks or notes are payable; see Chapter 25] with Oster on their March 1, 1985, payment. But they were financially unable to exercise their right to advance the sums due on the entire 160 acres in order to preserve their interest in the nine acres and homestead. As a result, their interest in the real estate was forfeited along with Oster's and Bishop's and they were forced to move from their home in August 1985.

Potters then sued Oster to rescind their contract with him, claiming restitution damages for all consideration paid. * * *

Trial testimony * * * revealed that the market value of the property had decreased markedly since its purchase. Expert appraisers valued the homestead and nine acres between $27,500 and $35,000. Oster himself placed a $28,000 value on the property; Potter $39,000. Evidence was also received placing the reasonable rental value of the property at $150 per month, or a total of $10,800 for the six-year Potter occupancy.

The district court concluded the Potters were entitled to rescission of the contract and return of the consideration paid including principal and interest, cost of improvements, closing expenses, and taxes for a total of $65,169.37. From this the court deducted $10,800 for six years' rental, bringing the final judgment to $54,369.37.

On appeal, Oster challenges the judgment. * * * [H]e claims Potters had an adequate remedy at law for damages which should have been measured by the actual economic loss sustained * * *

* * * *

Rescission is a restitutionary remedy which attempts to restore the parties to their positions at the time the contract was executed. The remedy calls for a return of the land to the seller, with the buyer given judgment for payments made under the contract plus the value of improvements, less reasonable rental value for the period during which the buyer was in possession. The remedy has long been available in Iowa to buyers under land contracts when the seller has no title to convey.

Rescission is considered an extraordinary remedy, however, and is ordinarily not available to a litigant as a matter of right but only when, in the discretion of the court, it is necessary to obtain equity. Our cases have established three requirements that must be met before rescission will be granted. First, the injured party must not be in default. Second, the breach must be substantial and go to the heart of the contract. Third, remedies at law must be inadequate.

The first two tests are easily met in the present case. Potters are entirely without fault in this transaction. They tendered their 1985 installment payment to Oster before the forfeiture, and no additional payments were due until 1986. On the question of materiality, Oster's loss of equitable title [ownership rights protected in equity] to the homestead by forfeiture caused not only substantial, but total breach of his obligation to insure peaceful possession [an implied promise made by a landowner, when selling or renting land, that the buyer or tenant will not be evicted or disturbed by the landowner or a person having a lien or superior title] and convey marketable title under the Oster-Potter contract.

Only the third test—the inadequacy of damages at law—is contested by Oster on appeal. * * *

Restoring the status quo is the goal of the restitutionary remedy of rescission. Here, the district court accomplished the goal by awarding Potters a sum representing all they had paid under the contract rendered worthless by Oster's default. Oster contends that in an era of declining land values, such a remedy goes beyond achieving the status quo and results in a windfall to the Potters. Unwilling to disgorge the benefits he has received under the unfulfilled contract, Oster would have the court shift the "entrepreneural risk" [the risk assumed by one who initiates, and provides or controls the management of, a business enterprise] of market loss to the Potters by limiting their recovery to the difference between the property's market value at breach ($35,000) and the contract balance ($27,900). In other words, Oster claims the court should have awarded * * * damages. * * *

* * * *

* * * [L]egal remedies are considered inadequate when the damages cannot be measured with sufficient certainty. Contrary to Oster's assertion that Potters' compensation should be limited to the difference between the property's fair market value and contract balance at time of breach, * * * damages are correctly calculated as the difference between contract price and market value at the time for performance. Since the time of performance in this case would have been March 1990, the market value of the homestead and acreage cannot be predicted with any certainty, thus rendering such a formulation inadequate.

Most importantly, the fair market value of the homestead at the time of forfeiture is an incorrect measure of the benefit Potters lost. It fails to account for the special value Potters placed on the property's location and residential features that uniquely suited their family. For precisely this reason, remedies at law are presumed inadequate for breach of a real estate contract. Oster has failed to overcome that presumption here. His characterization of the transaction as a mere market loss for Potters, compensable by a sum which would enable them to make a nominal down payment on an equivalent homestead, has no legal or factual support in this record. * * *

* * * *

In summary, we find no error in the trial court's conclusion that Potters were entitled to rescission of the contract and return of all benefits allowed thereunder, less the value of reasonable rental for the period of occupancy * * *.

AFFIRMED.

Case A.7 *Reference: Problem 14-14.*

GOLDKIST, INC. v. BROWNLEE

Court of Appeals of Georgia, 1987.
182 Ga.App. 287,
355 S.E.2d 733.

BEASLEY, Judge.

The question is whether the two defendant farmers, who as a partnership both grew and sold their crops, were established by the undisputed facts as not being "merchants" as a matter of law, according to the definition in OCGA [Section] 11-2-104(1) [Official Code of Georgia Annotated; Section 11-2-104(1) corresponds to UCC 2-104(1)]. We are not called upon here to consider the other side of the coin, whether farmers or these farmers in particular are "merchants" as a matter of law.

In November 1983, Goldkist sued under OCGA [Section] 11-2-712 for losses arising out of the necessity to cover [a remedy of the buyer in a breached sales contract; if the seller fails to deliver the goods contracted for, the buyer can purchase them elsewhere and recover any additional price paid from the breaching seller (see Chapter 21)] a contract for soybeans. It produced a written confirmation dated July 22 for 5,000 bushels of soybeans to be delivered to it by defendants between August 22 and September 22 at $6.88 per bushel. A defense was that there was no writing signed by either of the Brownlees, as required by OCGA [Section] 11-2-201(1).

* * * [T]he court agreed with the Brownlees that the circumstances did not fit any of the exceptions provided for in Section 201 and granted summary judgment. On appeal, Goldkist asserts that defendants came within subsection (2), relating to dealings "between merchants."

Appellees admit that their crops are "goods" as defined in OCGA [Section] 11-2-105. The record establishes the following facts. The partnership had been operating the row crop farming business for 14 years, producing peanuts, soybeans, corn, milo, and wheat on 1,350 acres, and selling the crops.

It is also established without dispute that Barney Brownlee, whose deposition was taken, was familiar with the marketing procedure of "booking" crops, which sometimes occurred over the phone between the farmer and the buyer, rather than in person, and a written contract would be signed later. He periodically called plaintiff's agent to check the price, which fluctuated. If the price met his approval, he sold soybeans. At this time the partnership still had some of its 1982 crop in storage, and the price was rising slowly. Mr. Brownlee received a written confirmation in the mail concerning a sale of soybeans and did not contact plaintiff to contest it but simply did nothing. In addition to the agricultural business, Brownlee operated a gasoline service station.

In dispute are the facts with respect to whether or not an oral contract was made between Barney Brownlee for the partnership and agent Harrell for the buyer in a July 22 telephone conversation. The plaintiff's evidence was that it occurred and that it was discussed soon thereafter with Brownlee at the service station on two different occasions, when he acknowledged it, albeit reluctantly, because the market price of soybeans had risen. Mr. Brownlee denies booking the soybeans and denies the nature of the conversations at his service station with Harrell and the buyer's manager.

In this posture, of course, the question of whether an oral contract was made would not yield to summary adjudication, as apparently recognized by the trial court, which based its decision on the preliminary question of whether the Brownlee partnership was a "merchant."

Whether or not the farmers in this case are "merchants" as a matter of law, which is not before us, the evidence does not demand a conclusion that they are outside of that category which is excepted from the requirement of a signed writing to bind a buyer and seller of goods. * * *

* * * *

Defendants' narrow construction of "merchant" would, given the booking procedure used for the sale of farm products, thus guarantee to the farmers the best of both possible worlds (fulfill booking if price goes down after booking and reject it if price improves) and to the buyers the worst of both possible worlds. On the other hand, construing "merchants" in OCGA [Section] 11-2-104(1) as not excluding as a matter of law farmers such as the ones in this case, protects them equally as well as the buyer. If the market price declines after the booking, they are assured of the higher booking price; the buyer cannot renege, as OCGA [Section] 11-2-201(2) would apply.

* * * *

We believe this is the proper construction to give the two statutes, OCGA [Sections] 11-2-104(1) and 11-2-201(2), as taken together they are thus further branches stemming from the centuries-old simple legal idea *pacta servanda sunt*—agreements are to be kept. So construed, they evince the legislative intent to enforce the accepted practices of the marketplace among those who frequent it.

Judgment reversed.

Case A.8 *Reference: Problem 16-14.*

TRIAD SYSTEMS CORP. v. ALSIP

United States Court of Appeals, Tenth Circuit, 1989.
880 F.2d 247.

PER CURIAM.

This is a case arising out of the sale of a computer system by Triad Systems Corporation, the appellant, to Mr. Dale Alsip, the appellee, for use in Mr. Alsip's automotive parts supply store, Mr. Automotive of Duncan. Triad brought this action seeking to recover the full purchase price for the system plus payment for its maintenance and service of the system. Mr. Alsip counterclaimed, seeking a refund of the purchase price based on his alleged revocation of acceptance of the system.

After a six-day trial, the jury returned a verdict for Mr. Alsip, awarding him a refund of the amount paid to Triad, less a setoff for the value of his use of the equipment prior to revocation of acceptance. Triad appeals, arguing that Mr. Alsip's attempted revocation of acceptance was ineffective as a matter of law, that the contract for the sale of the system further limited Mr. Alsip's ability to revoke acceptance, and that the court erroneously permitted parol evidence regarding certain statements of Triad's personnel made prior to execution of the contract. We affirm.

Triad's first assertion of error concerns the propriety of submitting the issue of Mr. Alsip's purported revocation of acceptance to the jury. Triad contends that the uncontroverted facts demonstrated, as a matter or law, that Mr. Alsip's revocation was ineffective under [Section] 2-608 of California's Uniform Commercial Code (U.C.C.), because of substantial changes in the equipment prior to revocation and because of Mr. Alsip's pre- and post-revocation use of the equipment. We disagree.

Whether a party's revocation of acceptance is effective in any given case is dependent upon the facts and circumstances surrounding the revocation, and is normally a question for the trier of fact. In order for us to conclude that submission of this case to the jury was improper, we would have to find that reasonable minds could not differ as to whether Mr. Alsip's revocation was proper. Based on the evidence in this case, such a conclusion would be clear error.

Viewing the facts in the light most favorable to Mr. Alsip, there is sufficient evidence to show that Mr. Alsip's use of the Triad system for more than two years after it was first delivered was not unreasonable. The record indicates that the System 5 which Mr. Alsip received never operated as expected. In addition, certain components of it were completely replaced only six months after installation. Further evidence suggests that Mr. Alsip's delay in revoking his acceptance of the system was based on Triad's assurances that certain newly developed software would meet Mr. Alsip's reporting and information requirements, but that Mr. Alsip would have to replace the System 5 with a System 7. Mr. Alsip then purchased the System 7 approximately one year after receiving the original system from Triad, and again certain software malfunctioned or was completely inoperable. Only when Mr. Alsip concluded that the new system simply would not generate the reports he required, after repeated attempts by Triad to correct the problem, did he revoke his acceptance. We think on the basis of this evidence that the jury could conclude that Mr. Alsip's revocation was reasonable under all the circumstances.

Triad also asserts that revocation was barred by Mr. Alsip's continued use of the system after notice of revocation and by certain changes in the condition of the system. The fact that Mr. Alsip may have used the system for certain purposes subsequent to revocation does not as a matter of law bar revocation, as long as such use is reasonable. Based on our review of the record, there is little evidence suggesting unreasonable use. As to Triad's allegations that a substantial change in the condition of the system had occurred, this, too, is an issue for the jury's determination. We believe that the jury could properly conclude that rodent droppings and debris in the equipment and one stolen display terminal was not such a substantial change in the condition of the equipment as to prevent revocation, especially when there is evidence that some of this damage could have been prevented had Triad diligently pursued collection of the equipment.

Triad next contends that express language in its contract with Mr. Alsip precluded his revocation of acceptance of the system. Such language provided, *inter alia* [among other things] that "[a]t any time during the 60-day System Evaluation Period, the Customer may notify Triad in writing of Customer's intent to revoke its purchase of the System. * * * Upon timely receipt by Triad of such notice of revocation, Customer shall promptly return the System to Triad, and Triad shall then promptly refund all sums paid hereunder by Customer to Triad." The contract contained no limitation of basis for revocation during this period; it appears that the customer could return the system for any reason if it were dissatisfied.

In response to Triad's argument that this provision limited Mr. Alsip's right to return the system to only the first 60 days after delivery, the district court ruled that the System Evaluation Period was not a limitation of Mr. Alsip's U.C.C. [Section] 2-608 right to revoke, but an expansion of that right. We are in full agreement. Section 2-608 provides that "[t]he buyer may revoke his acceptance of a lot or commercial unit whose nonconformity substantially impairs its value to him * * *." The Triad contract does not require a nonconformity impairing value to justify revocation of acceptance, only a desire on the part of the customer to return the system. Consequently, we view this contract language as simply expanding upon the customer's normal remedies under the U.C.C., in line with the presumption that clauses prescribing remedies are cumulative rather than exclusive.

Triad's final argument in this appeal is that the district court erred in permitting Mr. Alsip to introduce evidence of pre-contract oral representations and warranties made by Triad salespersons, and that such testimony violated the parol evidence rule. The district court permitted this testimony on the grounds that it was simply an explanation of the equipment and software purchased by Mr. Alsip and that it could be introduced for the purpose of explaining or supplementing the contract's terms, a purpose expressly sanctioned by the rule. We concur with this reasoning.

The judgment of the United States District Court for the Western District of Oklahoma is AFFIRMED.

Case A.9 *Reference: Problem 23-13.*

GREEN v. SHELL OIL CO.

Court of Appeals of Michigan, 1989.
181 Mich.App. 439,
450 N.W.2d 50.

FITZGERALD, Justice.

* * * *

At approximately 6:00 P.M. on December 21, 1981, plaintiff drove into a Shell service station owned and operated by defendant Lanford and leased from defendant Shell Oil Company. Plaintiff filled his gas tank and, as he walked from the self-service island to the station's office to pay for the gasoline, was struck by a slow-moving vehicle plaintiff alleges was driven by Monica Gottwald. Plaintiff slapped the hood of the vehicle with his hand and yelled for Gottwald to stop and to be more careful. Immediately thereafter, Leslie Salgado, an occupant of the Gottwald vehicle and employee of the station, exited from the vehicle and began striking plaintiff. An unidentified station attendant joined Salgado in his attack on plaintiff.

On January 2, 1982, plaintiff filed a complaint in Oakland Circuit Court against defendants and Salgado, as well as others no longer parties to the instant action, alleging [among other things] **vicarious liability** [indirect liability] of defendants for * * * assault and battery and negligence by defendants in failing to provide a safe place for doing business. The case was remanded to district court after mediation.

Defendants moved for and were granted summary disposition. The district court held that defendants could not be held liable for an intentional tort committed by the service station attendant. The court also held that the attendant owed no duty to stop an assault by a third party. * * *

Plaintiff appealed * * * to circuit court. The circuit court reversed the district court's grant of summary disposition * * *.

* * * *

We believe that * * * defendant Lanford's employees were in a position to control the unruly situation, to eject the instigator from the premises and to refrain from increasing plaintiff's injuries. On these facts, a jury could find that defendant Lanford failed to exercise reasonable care for his invitees' protection.

The question * * * becomes whether Shell Oil had apparent authority over the service station so as to make it liable for the assault on plaintiff. In *Johnston v. American Oil Co.*, the plaintiff's decedent was shot during an altercation with the proprietor of a Standard service station, who refused to serve him and his companions. The trial court granted defendant American Oil Company's summary judgment motion based on the proprietor's status as an independent contractor. The plaintiff had pointed to the service station's use of American Oil's trademark and its sale of supplies and products obtained from American Oil. On appeal, the panel concluded:

> American Oil's national advertising campaign promoting the Standard Oil name and products, including the slogans "As you travel ask us" and "You expect more from Standard and you get it," would seem to raise a sufficient question of fact as to the existence of agency by estoppel or by apparent authority to defeat the granting of summary judgment.
>
> * * * * * *
>
> We believe the trial court herein likewise erred in granting the motion for summary judgment. The question, of course, is not whether Murphy is, in fact, an agent of American Oil, the question is whether plaintiff has raised a material issue of fact that requires further proofs before the finding of fact. Here plaintiff has carried that burden.

In his **affidavit** [a written or printed statement confirmed by oath or affirmation], plaintiff stated:

> I always assumed that a Shell gas station was operated by Shell Oil. I cannot state whether I ever actually considered whether the operators of gas stations have an ownership interest in the business or not, but it was my belief at the time of the assault upon me, and prior, that Shell Oil either owned the facilities and operated them directly, or exercised active control over the operations of the gas station so as to ensure uniform standards of quality, reliability and conduct of the employees at the stations.

According to defendants, Shell Oil exercised no control over the hiring, firing and supervision of the service station employees and had no authority over the supervision, management and control of the station. In addition, defendant Lanford was not required to purchase any parts from Shell Oil. As defendants state on appeal, "the most that can be said is that '[Wayne Lanford] displayed [Shell's] brand signs, that he honored [Shell's] credit cards, [and that Shell's] agents from time to time made suggestions as to operation of the station.' "

In light of the foregoing, we cannot say with any degree of certainty that further factual development of plaintiff's theory of apparent authority would be futile. Accordingly, we believe that plaintiff should be given the opportunity to show that Shell Oil had apparent authority over defendant Lanford's employees.

Defendants also argue that they cannot be held vicariously liable for the attendant's participation in the assault. We agree.

An employer is liable for the intentional tort of his employee if the tort is committed in the course and within the scope of the employment. An employer is not liable if the employee's tortious act is committed while the employee is working for the employer but the act is outside his authority, "as where he steps aside from his employment to gratify some personal animosity or to accomplish some purpose of his own."

An employer's liability may also be based upon a finding that the employee acted within the scope or apparent scope of his employment. Generally, the trier of fact determines whether an employee was acting within the scope or apparent scope of his employment. Summary disposition is appropriate, however, where it is apparent that the employee is acting to accomplish a purpose of his own.

Plaintiff testified at a deposition that Salgado struck him on the left side of the head. Plaintiff fell to the ground, dazed by the blow. The next thing he remembered was being kicked, while laying on the ground, by a man in a brown uniform, allegedly the unidentified station attendant. On this testimony, we conclude that the attendant's violent conduct was engaged in for the purpose of assisting Salgado and not for any purpose in furtherance of the employer's business interests. This is not a situation where the employee was attempting to collect plaintiff's payment on behalf of his employer. Nor is it a situation where the attendant's conduct can be reasonably construed as an attempt to end the altercation or eject plaintiff from the employer's establishment in order to restore order. Accordingly, summary disposition on plaintiff's vicarious liability claim was appropriate. The attendant's action could only be construed as an attempt to accomplish his own purpose, not to further his employer's business interests.

* * * *

We affirm in part, reverse in part and remand.

Case A.10 *Reference: Problem 27-14.*

MASCHMEIER v. SOUTHSIDE PRESS, LTD.

Court of Appeals of Iowa, 1989.
435 N.W.2d 377.

HABHAB, Judge.

Defendant Kenneth E. Maschmeier and Charlotte A. Maschmeier created a corporation, Southside Press, Ltd., that did business at 1220 Second Avenue North in Council Bluffs. This building is owned by Kenneth and Charlotte and was leased by them to the corporation.

Kenneth and Charlotte are the majority shareholders, with each having 1300 shares. They are the only officers and directors of the corporation.

They gifted to their two sons [Marty and Larry] each 1200 shares of stock. All the parties were employed by Southside Press until the summer of 1985 when, because of family disagreements, Marty and Larry were terminated as employees. * * *

The parents on August 2, 1985, created a new corporation, Southside Press of the Midlands, Ltd. They are its only officers and directors. As individuals they terminated the lease of their building * * * with Southside and leased the same premises to Midlands. In addition, Kenneth, as president of Southside, entered into a lease with himself as president of Midlands whereby the printing equipment and two of the vehicles were leased to Midlands for $22,372 per year for five years, with an option to buy such assets at the end of the lease term at their fair market value but not to exceed $20,000. In addition, the inventory and two other vehicles owned by Southside were sold by it to Midlands. Notwithstanding the fact that a substantial part of the assets of Southside had been disposed of, the parents still received an annual salary from it of more than $20,000.

After Marty and Larry's employment with Southside had terminated, each obtained employment with other printing companies in the same metropolitan area. The family disagreement continued. All stockholders were employed by companies that were competitive to Southside. Ultimately, the parents, as majority shareholders, offered to buy the sons' shares of stock for $20 per share. Their sons felt that this amount was inadequate. Thus, this lawsuit.

In 1985, Southside Press had gross sales of more than $600,000. The trial court found that in 1985 the corporate assets had a fair market value of $160,745. Shareholders' equity was found to be $236,502.92, and divided by the number of shares equals $47.30 per share. The court found that the majority shareholders had been abusive and oppressive to the minority shareholders by wasting the corporate assets and leaving Southside Press only a shell of a corporation. The court ordered the majority shareholders to pay $47.30 per share to the sons, or $56,760 to each son, plus interest at the maximum legal rate from the date of the filing of the petition.

* * * *

* * * [D]efendants state that the shares were valued at $20 pursuant to the corporate bylaws and should be enforced as an agreement of the shareholders. * * *

* * * *

Whenever a situation exists which is contrary to the principles of equity and which can be redressed within the scope of judicial action, a court of equity will devise a remedy to meet the situation though no similar relief has been granted before. The district court has the power to liquidate a corporation under [Iowa Code] section 496A.94(1). This statute also allows the district court to fashion other equitable relief.

It is contended that, in order for the trial court to have properly invoked the powers under section 496A.94(1), it had to find either the majority shareholders were oppressive in their conduct towards the minority shareholders, or that the majority shareholders misapplied or wasted corporate assets. * * * The alleged oppressive conduct by those in control of a close corporation must be analyzed in terms of "fiduciary duties" owed by majority shareholders to the minority shareholders and "reasonable expectations" held by minority shareholders in committing capital and labor to the particular enterprise, in light of the predicament in which minority shareholders in a close corporation can be placed by a "freeze-out" situation.

* * * The trial court found * * * here [that] the majority shareholders attempted to "freeze out" or "squeeze out" the minority shareholders by terminating their employment and not permitting them to participate in the business.

* * * *

We concur with the trial court's findings that the majority shareholders acted oppressively toward the minority shareholders and wasted corporate assets. In this respect, we further determine that the trial court properly invoked Iowa Code section 496A.94 when it fashioned the remedy requiring the majority shareholders to purchase the shares of the minority.

But that does not resolve the problem, for as stated above. * * * The appellant challenges the method fashioned by the trial court in fixing the value of the stock and payment thereof by asserting it should be governed by the bylaws.

The articles of incorporation of Southside vested in the directors of the corporation the "authority to make provisions in the Bylaws of the corporation restricting the transfer of shares of this corporation." This the board of directors did when they adopted the following bylaw that relates to restrictions on the transferability of stock. * * *

* * * *

Section 3 [of the corporate bylaws] is a restriction on stock transfer. If a shareholder intends to sell his stock, he must first offer it to the corporation at a price "agreed upon by the shareholders at each annual meeting." The shareholders must agree on the value of the stock and if they are unable to do so, each has a right to select an appraiser and the appraisers shall appoint another and in this instance the five appraisers are to act as a Board of Appraisers to value the stock.

* * * Since none of the shareholders requested appraisers, we deem this, as the trial court did, to be a waiver. We concur with this statement from the trial court's ruling: "All parties have left the Court with the burden of evaluating the corporate stock."

* * * *

We agree with the defendants that a contractual formula price is enforceable even if the formula price is less than its fair market value. But here the parties were unable to agree to a price, i.e., at the last meeting of the stockholders. Thus the trial court was called upon to do so.

Courts have generally held that no one factor governs the valuation of shares; but that all factors, such as market value, asset value, future earning prospects, should be considered. In this case, the parties relied rather heavily on what is referred to in the record as book value (shareholders' equity) in arriving at stock value. The trial court likewise used shareholder equity but adjusted that amount by the present day fair market value of corporate assets.

* * * *

We determine that under the circumstances here the valuation per share as fixed by the trial court and the method it employed in arriving at value is fair and reasonable. However, we further conclude that the amount Larry and Marty are to receive must be reduced by the total amount of loans made to them as they appear on the corporate books.

* * * *

We affirm and modify.

Case A.11 *Reference: Problem 28-14.*

GREENLEE v. SHERMAN

New York Supreme Court, Appellate Division, Third Department, 1989.
142 A.D.2d 472,
536 N.Y.S.2d 877.

CASEY, Justice Presiding.

[This action arises] out of a 1980 transaction between Horace and Annie Greenlee, plaintiffs * * * and Philip Sherman, the sole proprietor of Sherman Fuel and Oil Burner Service, whereby Sherman installed a combination wood/oil furnace in the basement of the Greenlees' house. The Greenlees used the furnace until March 30, 1984, when a fire substantially destroyed their house. It is alleged that the fire was caused by the improper installation of the flue pipe from the furnace, which resulted in the exposure of a wooden joist to intense radiant heat while the furnace was operating. This exposure to intense heat allegedly caused a chemical process, known as pyrolyisis, in the wooden joist which ultimately lowered the ignition temperature of the wood to the point where it was ignited by the flue pipe.

* * * [T]he Greenlees seek [among other things] to recover damages based upon Sherman's negligent installation of the furnace. Named as defendants * * * are the executor of Sherman's estate and Main Care Heating Service, Inc. (hereinafter Main Care), as the successor in interest to Sherman Fuel and Oil Burner Service. * * * Main Care moved * * * for summary judgment dismissing the Greenlees' complaint and Supreme Court granted the motion. * * * The Greenlees have appealed * * *.

The issue raised by the appeal in [this action] is whether there exists a triable issue of fact on the question of Main Care's liability as a successor in interest to Sherman's business, pursuant to an agreement between Sherman and Main Care, dated November 19, 1980.

It is the general rule that a corporation which acquires the assets of another is not liable for the torts of its predecessor. * * * There are exceptions. * * * A corporation may be held liable for the torts of its predecessor if (1) it expressly or impliedly assumed the predecessor's tort liability, (2) there was a consolidation or merger of seller and purchaser, (3) the purchasing corporation was a mere continuation of the selling corporation, or (4) the transaction is entered into fraudulently to escape such obligations.

Main Care relies upon this general rule, while the Greenlees contend that the second and third exceptions are applicable. In *Grant-Howard Assoc. v. General Housewares Corp.*, the Court of Appeals noted that these two exceptions "are based on the concept that a successor that effectively takes over a company in its entirety should carry the predecessor's liabilities as a concomitant [something that exists concurrently with something else] to the benefits it derives from the good will purchased." But the court prefaced this remark with the following explanation of the genesis of the successor liability theory:

> Allowing recovery in tort against a successor corporation is merely an extension of the concept of products liability, which calls for the burden of consumer injuries to be borne by the manufacturer, who can transfer the costs to the general public as a component of the selling price. Strict liability assures that a responsible source is available to compensate the injured party.

The case at bar does not involve the concept of products liability. The Greenlees' action is based upon the negligence of Sherman in the installation of the furnace; there is no claim that Sherman manufactured or sold a defective product. The Greenlees contracted directly with Sherman for certain services to be performed by him, and their claim for damages is based upon Sherman's negligence in performing those services. In these circumstances, the public policy considerations underlying the concept of products liability are not present. Therefore, based upon the previously quoted language of the Court of Appeals in *Grant-Howard Assoc. v. General House-*

wares Corp., supra ["above—meaning in this instance the case cited above; the full citation for this case was omitted by the authors when editing this case], it appears that the successor liability theory is not applicable in this case.

In any event, we find no proof in the record to support the Greenlees' contention that there was a consolidation or merger of Main Care and Sherman's business or that Main Care is a mere continuation of Sherman's business. As to the consolidation or merger claim, Sherman, the sole proprietor of the selling business, did not become involved with Main Care, either as a shareholder or as an employee; Main Care did not acquire either the cash on hand or the accounts receivable of Sherman's business; Main Care did not hire any employee of Sherman's business; and Main Care did not install furnaces, which was at least a part of Sherman's business. As to the "mere continuation" claim, that exception refers to corporate reorganization, which did not occur here. Main Care had been in existence for at least 12 years prior to its purchase of Sherman's business and it continued in substantially the same form thereafter, with the addition of Sherman's assets. In short, Main Care cannot be viewed as a "mere continuation" of Sherman's business. Thus, assuming that the successor liability theory is applicable outside the context of products liability, the Greenlees' proof was inadequate to defeat Main Care's motion for summary judgment.

* * * *

ORDERS AND JUDGMENT AFFIRMED.

Case A.12 *Reference: Problem 32-14.*

JOHNSTON v. DEL MAR DISTRIBUTING CO.

Court of Appeals of Texas—Corpus Christi, 1989.
776 S.W.2d 768.

BENAVIDES, Justice.

Nancy Johnston, appellant, brought suit against her employer, Del Mar Distributing Co., Inc., alleging that her employment had been wrongfully terminated. Del Mar filed a motion for summary judgment in the trial court alleging that appellant's pleadings failed to state a cause of action. After a hearing on the motion, the trial court agreed with Del Mar and granted its motion for summary judgment.

* * * *

In her petition, appellant alleged that she was employed by Del Mar during the summer of 1987. As a part of her duties, she was required to prepare shipping documents for goods being sent from Del Mar's warehouse located in Corpus Christi, Texas to other cities in Texas. One day, Del Mar instructed appellant to package a semi-automatic weapon (for delivery to a grocery store in Brownsville, Texas) and to label the contents of the package as "fishing gear." Ultimately, the package was to be given to United Parcel Service for shipping. Appellant was required to sign her name to the shipping documents; therefore, she was concerned that her actions might be in violation of some firearm regulation or a regulation of the United Postal Service. Accordingly, she sought the advice of the United States Treasury Department Bureau of Alcohol, Tobacco & Firearms * * *. A few days after she contacted the Bureau, appellant was fired. Appellant brought suit for wrongful termination alleging that her employment was terminated solely in retaliation for contacting the Bureau.

* * * *

Del Mar asserted in its motion that, notwithstanding the above described facts, appellant's cause of action was barred by the employment-at-will doctrine. Specifically, Del Mar asserted that since appellant's employment was for an indefinite amount of time, she was an employee-at-will and it had the absolute right to terminate her employment for any reason or no reason at all.

It is well-settled that Texas adheres to the traditional employment-at-will doctrine. The Texas Supreme Court [has] held that absent a specific contractual provision to the contrary, either the employer or the employee may terminate their relationship at any time, for any reason.

Today, the absolute employment-at-will doctrine is increasingly seen as a "relic of early industrial times" and a "harsh anachronism." Accordingly, our Legislature has enacted some exceptions to this doctrine * * *.

Recently, the Texas Supreme Court, recognizing the need to amend the employment-at-will doctrine, invoked its judicial authority to create a very narrow common law exception to the doctrine. In [*Sabine Pilot Service, Inc. v. Hauck*] the Texas Supreme Court was faced with a narrow issue for consideration, i.e., whether an allegation by an employee that he or she was discharged for refusing to perform an illegal act stated a cause of action. The Court held that

> public policy, as expressed in the laws of this state and the United States which carry criminal penalties, requires a very narrow exception to the employment-at-will doctrine * * * [t]hat narrow exception covers only the discharge of an employee for the sole reason that the employee refused to perform an illegal act.

Justice Kilgarlin noted in his concurring opinion to *Sabine Pilot* that it is against public policy to allow an employer "to require an employee to break a law or face termination * * *." He elaborated that to hold otherwise "would promote a thorough disrespect for the laws and legal institutions of our society."

* * * *

On appeal, appellant alleges that her petition did state a cause of action pursuant to the public policy exception announced in *Sabine Pilot*. In her brief, appellant contends that since Texas law currently provides that an employee has a cause of action when she is fired for refusing to perform an illegal act, it necessarily follows that an employee states a cause of action where she alleges that she is fired for simply inquiring into whether or not she is committing illegal acts. To hold otherwise, she argues, would have a chilling [inhibiting, discouraging] effect on the public policy exception announced in *Sabine Pilot*. We agree.

It is implicit that in order to refuse to do an illegal act, an employee must either know or suspect that the requested act is illegal. In some cases it will be patently obvious that the act is illegal (murder, robbery, theft, etc.); however, in other cases it may not be so apparent. Since ignorance of the law is no defense to a criminal prosecution, it is reasonable to expect that if an employee has a good faith belief that a required act might be illegal, she will try to find out whether the act is in fact illegal prior to deciding what course of action to take. If an employer is allowed to terminate the employee at this point, the public policy exception announced in *Sabine Pilot* would have little or no effect. To hold otherwise would force an employee, who suspects that a requested act might be illegal, to (1) subject herself to possible discharge if she attempts to find out if the act is in fact illegal; or (2) remain ignorant, perform the act and, if it turns out to be illegal, face possible criminal sanctions.

We hold that since the law recognizes that it is against public policy to allow an employer to coerce its employee to commit a criminal act in furtherance of its own interest, then it is necessarily inferred that the same public policy prohibits the discharge of an employee who in good faith attempts to find out if the act is illegal. It is important to note that we are not creating a new exception to the employment-at-will doctrine. Rather, we are merely enforcing the narrow public policy exception which was created in *Sabine Pilot*.

* * * *

Furthermore, it is the opinion of this Court that the question of whether or not the requested act was in fact illegal is irrelevant to the determination of this case. We hold that where a plaintiff's employment is terminated for attempting to find out from a regulatory agency if a requested act is illegal, it is not necessary to prove that the requested act was in fact illegal. A plaintiff must, however, establish that she had a good faith belief that the requested act might be illegal, and that such belief was reasonable. * * *

* * * *

The judgment of the trial court is reversed and remanded for trial.

Case A.13 *Reference: Problem 33-14.*

STRANG v. HOLLOWELL

Court of Appeals of North Carolina, 1990.
387 S.E.2d 664.

[WELLS, Judge.]

On 2 January 1987 plaintiff met with defendants Hollowell and Jones in Cary, North Carolina to negotiate a consignment agreement for the sale of plaintiff's 1974 Pantera automobile which had an estimated value of $23,000 to $25,000. A written consignment contract was executed between plaintiff and Hollowell Auto Sales. Defendant Jones, then employed by Hollowell Auto Sales, signed the contract on behalf of Hollowell Auto Sales. Plaintiff gave defendants the keys to his automobile and they transported it by flatbed trailer to the Hollowell Auto Sales lot in Morehead City. Defendants Jones and Hollowell were unable to sell the Pantera and it was returned to plaintiff in August 1987. At that time plaintiff discovered that the automobile had been damaged to an extent which reduced its value to between $10,000 and $12,000.

On 23 December 1987 plaintiff sued defendants Jones and Hollowell for negligence in their bailment of his automobile. Plaintiff was unaware that Hollowell Auto Sales was a trade name for Solar Center, Inc., whose principal place of business is in Carteret County. Plaintiff was under the impression that Hollowell Auto Sales was a sole proprietorship operated by defendant Hollowell. On motion of defendant Hollowell in open court, defendant Solar Center, Inc. was added as an additional party prior to trial.

Defendant Jones did not file an answer to plaintiff's complaint and default judgment was subsequently entered against him. At a non-jury trial, judgment in the amount of $11,000 was entered against defendants Jones and Hollowell, jointly and severally. Defendant Gene Hollowell appeals.

* * * *

The only issue presented in this appeal is whether defendant Hollowell can be held individually liable for plaintiff's damages. Defendant contends that he was acting as an agent of Hollowell Auto Sales and therefore cannot be held personally liable. Defendant further asserts that, regardless of the fact that plaintiff was unaware that Hollowell Auto Sales was a trade name for Solar Center, Inc., defendant is nevertheless shielded from individual liability because Solar Center, Inc. fulfilled its legal obligation to disclose its relationship with Hollowell Auto Sales by filing an assumed name certificate in [the appropriate county office]. For the following reasons, we disagree.

When plaintiff gave possession of his automobile to defendant under the consignment contract a bailment for the mutual benefit of bailor and bailee was created. This bailment continued until the automobile was returned to plaintiff in August 1987. Defendant was therefore a bailee of plaintiff's automobile while it was in his custody in Morehead City. A bailee is obligated to exercise due care to protect the subject of the bailment from negligent loss, damage, or destruction. His liability depends on the presence or absence of ordinary negligence. While this obligation arises from the relationship created by the contract of bailment, breach of this contractual duty results in a tort. It is well settled that one is personally liable for all torts committed by him, including negligence, notwithstanding that he may have acted as agent for another or as an officer for a corporation. Furthermore, the potential for corporate liability, in addition to individual liability, does not shield the individual tortfeasor from liability. Rather, it provides the injured party a choice as to which party to hold liable for the tort.

Here there is no dispute that plaintiff's automobile was returned to him in a damaged condition. Defendant does not except to the trial court's findings and conclusions that a bailment was created between plaintiff and defendant and that "defendants were negligent in their care and control of the vehicle while it was in their possession." We therefore hold that the trial court correctly ruled that by failing to exercise due care and allowing the automobile to be damaged while in his custody, defendant committed a tort for which he can be held individually liable.

Because the resolution of this case is in tort for negligence, rather than in contract for breach, we need not reach the issue of whether defendant had sufficiently disclosed his agency with Hollowell Auto Sales or with Solar Center, Inc. However, we note that our Supreme Court has said that use of a trade name is not sufficient as a matter of law to disclose the identity of the principal and the fact of agency.

Likewise, the existence of means by which the fact of agency might be discovered is also insufficient to disclose agency.

* * * *

Affirmed.

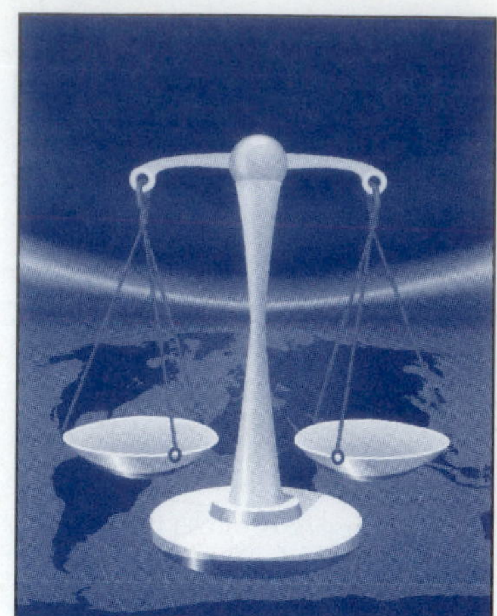

Appendix B

The Constitution of the United States

PREAMBLE

We the People of the United States, in Order to form a more perfect Union, establish Justice, insure domestic Tranquility, provide for the common defence, promote the general Welfare, and secure the Blessings of Liberty to ourselves and our Posterity, do ordain and establish this Constitution for the United States of America.

ARTICLE I

Section 1. All legislative Powers herein granted shall be vested in a Congress of the United States, which shall consist of a Senate and House of Representatives.

Section 2. The House of Representatives shall be composed of Members chosen every second Year by the People of the several States, and the Electors in each State shall have the Qualifications requisite for Electors of the most numerous Branch of the State Legislature.

No Person shall be a Representative who shall not have attained to the Age of twenty five Years, and been seven Years a Citizen of the United States, and who shall not, when elected, be an Inhabitant of that State in which he shall be chosen.

Representatives and direct Taxes shall be apportioned among the several States which may be included within this Union, according to their respective Numbers, which shall be determined by adding to the whole Number of free Persons, including those bound to Service for a Term of Years, and excluding Indians not taxed, three fifths of all other Persons. The actual Enumeration shall be made within three Years after the first Meeting of the Congress of the United States, and within every subsequent Term of ten Years, in such Manner as they shall by Law direct. The Number of Representatives shall not exceed one for every thirty Thousand, but each State shall have at Least one Representative; and until such enumeration shall be made, the State of New Hampshire shall be entitled to chuse three, Massachusetts eight, Rhode Island and Providence Plantations one, Connecticut five, New York six, New Jersey four, Pennsylvania eight, Delaware one, Maryland six, Virginia ten, North Carolina five, South Carolina five, and Georgia three.

When vacancies happen in the Representation from any State, the Executive Authority thereof shall issue Writs of Election to fill such Vacancies.

The House of Representatives shall chuse their Speaker and other Officers; and shall have the sole Power of Impeachment.

Section 3. The Senate of the United States shall be composed of two Senators from each State, chosen by the Legislature thereof, for six Years; and each Senator shall have one Vote.

Immediately after they shall be assembled in Consequence of the first Election, they shall be divided as equally as may be into three Classes. The Seats of the Senators of the first Class shall be vacated at the Expiration of the second Year, of the second Class at the Expiration of the fourth Year, and of the third Class at the Expiration of the sixth Year, so that one third may be chosen every second Year; and if Vacancies happen by Resignation, or otherwise, during the Recess of the Legislature of any State, the Executive thereof may make temporary Appointments until the next Meeting of the Legislature, which shall then fill such Vacancies.

No Person shall be a Senator who shall not have attained to the Age of thirty Years, and been nine Years a Citizen of the United States, and who shall not, when elected, be an Inhabitant of that State for which he shall be chosen.

The Vice President of the United States shall be President of the Senate, but shall have no Vote, unless they be equally divided.

The Senate shall chuse their other Officers, and also a President pro tempore, in the Absence of the Vice President, or when he shall exercise the Office of President of the United States.

The Senate shall have the sole Power to try all Impeachments. When sitting for that Purpose, they shall be on Oath or Affirmation. When the President of the United States is tried, the Chief Justice shall preside: And no Person shall be convicted without the Concurrence of two thirds of the Members present.

Judgment in Cases of Impeachment shall not extend further than to removal from Office, and disqualification to hold and enjoy any Office of honor, Trust, or Profit under the United States: but the Party convicted shall nevertheless be liable and subject to Indictment, Trial, Judgment, and Punishment, according to Law.

Section 4. The Times, Places and Manner of holding Elections for Senators and Representatives, shall be prescribed in each State by the Legislature thereof; but the Congress may at any time by Law make or alter such Regulations, except as to the Places of chusing Senators.

The Congress shall assemble at least once in every Year, and such Meeting shall be on the first Monday in December, unless they shall by Law appoint a different Day.

Section 5. Each House shall be the Judge of the Elections, Returns, and Qualifications of its own Members, and a Majority of each shall constitute a Quorum to do Business; but a smaller Number may adjourn from day to day, and may be authorized to compel the Attendance of absent Members, in such Manner, and under such Penalties as each House may provide.

Each House may determine the Rules of its Proceedings, punish its Members for disorderly Behavior, and, with the Concurrence of two thirds, expel a Member.

Each House shall keep a Journal of its Proceedings, and from time to time publish the same, excepting such Parts as may in their Judgment require Secrecy; and the Yeas and Nays of the Members of either House on any question shall, at the Desire of one fifth of those Present, be entered on the Journal.

Neither House, during the Session of Congress, shall, without the Consent of the other, adjourn for more than three days, nor to any other Place than that in which the two Houses shall be sitting.

Section 6. The Senators and Representatives shall receive a Compensation for their Services, to be ascertained by Law, and paid out of the Treasury of the United States. They shall in all Cases, except Treason, Felony and Breach of the Peace, be privileged from Arrest during their Attendance at the Session of their respective Houses, and in going to and returning from the same; and for any Speech or Debate in either House, they shall not be questioned in any other Place.

No Senator or Representative shall, during the Time for which he was elected, be appointed to any civil Office under the Authority of the United States, which shall have been created, or the Emoluments whereof shall have been increased during such time; and no Person holding any Office under the United States, shall be a Member of either House during his Continuance in Office.

Section 7. All Bills for raising Revenue shall originate in the House of Representatives; but the Senate may propose or concur with Amendments as on other Bills.

Every Bill which shall have passed the House of Representatives and the Senate, shall, before it become a Law, be presented to the President of the United States; If he approve he shall sign it, but if not he shall return it, with his Objections to the House in which it shall have originated, who shall enter the Objections at large on their Journal, and proceed to reconsider it. If after such Reconsideration two thirds of that House shall agree to pass the Bill, it shall be sent together with the Objections, to the other House, by which it shall likewise be reconsidered, and if approved by two thirds of that House, it shall become a Law. But in all such Cases the Votes of both Houses shall be determined by Yeas and Nays, and the Names of the Persons voting for and against the Bill shall be entered on the Journal of each House respectively. If any Bill shall not be returned by the President within ten Days (Sundays excepted) after it shall have been presented to him, the Same shall be a Law, in like Manner as if he had signed it, unless the Congress by their Adjournment prevent its Return in which Case it shall not be a Law.

Every Order, Resolution, or Vote, to which the Concurrence of the Senate and House of Representatives may be necessary (except on a question of Adjournment) shall be presented to the President of the United States; and before the Same shall take Effect, shall be approved by him, or being disapproved by him, shall be repassed by two thirds of the Senate and House of Representatives, according to the Rules and Limitations prescribed in the Case of a Bill.

Section 8. The Congress shall have Power To lay and collect Taxes, Duties, Imposts and Excises, to pay the Debts and provide for the common Defence and general Welfare of the United States; but all Duties, Imposts and Excises shall be uniform throughout the United States;

To borrow Money on the credit of the United States;

To regulate Commerce with foreign Nations, and among the several States, and with the Indian Tribes;

To establish an uniform Rule of Naturalization, and uniform Laws on the subject of Bankruptcies throughout the United States;

To coin Money, regulate the Value thereof, and of foreign Coin, and fix the Standard of Weights and Measures;

To provide for the Punishment of counterfeiting the Securities and current Coin of the United States;

To establish Post Offices and post Roads;

To promote the Progress of Science and useful Arts, by securing for limited Times to Authors and Inventors the exclusive Right to their respective Writings and Discoveries;

To constitute Tribunals inferior to the supreme Court;

To define and punish Piracies and Felonies committed on the high Seas, and Offenses against the Law of Nations;

To declare War, grant Letters of Marque and Reprisal, and make Rules concerning Captures on Land and Water;

To raise and support Armies, but no Appropriation of Money to that Use shall be for a longer Term than two Years;

To provide and maintain a Navy;

To make Rules for the Government and Regulation of the land and naval Forces;

To provide for calling forth the Militia to execute the Laws of the Union, suppress Insurrections and repel Invasions;

To provide for organizing, arming, and disciplining, the Militia, and for governing such Part of them as may be employed in the Service of the United States, reserving to the States respectively, the Appointment of the Officers, and the Authority of training the Militia according to the discipline prescribed by Congress;

To exercise exclusive Legislation in all Cases whatsoever, over such District (not exceeding ten Miles square) as may, by Cession of particular States, and the Acceptance of Congress, become the Seat of the Government of the United States, and to exercise like Authority over all Places purchased by the Consent of the Legislature of the State in which the Same shall be, for the Erection of Forts, Magazines, Arsenals, dock-Yards, and other needful Buildings;—And

To make all Laws which shall be necessary and proper for carrying into Execution the foregoing Powers, and all other Powers vested by this Constitution in the Government of the United States, or in any Department or Officer thereof.

Section 9. The Migration or Importation of such Persons as any of the States now existing shall think proper to admit, shall not be prohibited by the Congress prior to the Year one thousand eight hundred and eight, but a Tax or duty may be imposed on such Importation, not exceeding ten dollars for each Person.

The privilege of the Writ of Habeas Corpus shall not be suspended, unless when in Cases of Rebellion or Invasion the public Safety may require it.

No Bill of Attainder or ex post facto Law shall be passed.

No Capitation, or other direct, Tax shall be laid, unless in Proportion to the Census or Enumeration herein before directed to be taken.

No Tax or Duty shall be laid on Articles exported from any State.

No Preference shall be given by any Regulation of Commerce or Revenue to the Ports of one State over those of another: nor shall Vessels bound to, or from, one State be obliged to enter, clear, or pay Duties in another.

No Money shall be drawn from the Treasury, but in Consequence of Appropriations made by Law; and a regular Statement and Account of the Receipts and Expenditures of all public Money shall be published from time to time.

No Title of Nobility shall be granted by the United States: And no Person holding any Office of Profit or Trust under them, shall, without the Consent of the Congress, accept of any present, Emolument, Office, or Title, of any kind whatever, from any King, Prince, or foreign State.

Section 10. No State shall enter into any Treaty, Alliance, or Confederation; grant Letters of Marque and Reprisal; coin Money; emit Bills of Credit; make any Thing but gold and silver Coin a Tender in Payment of Debts; pass any Bill of Attainder, ex post facto Law, or Law impairing the Obligation of Contracts, or grant any Title of Nobility.

No State shall, without the Consent of the Congress, lay any Imposts or Duties on Imports or Exports, except what may be absolutely necessary for executing its inspection Laws: and the net Produce of all Duties and Imposts, laid by any State on Imports or Exports, shall be for the Use of the Treasury of the United States; and all such Laws shall be subject to the Revision and Controul of the Congress.

No State shall, without the Consent of Congress, lay any Duty of Tonnage, keep Troops, or Ships of War in time of Peace, enter into any Agreement or Compact with another State, or with a foreign Power, or engage in War, unless actually invaded, or in such imminent Danger as will not admit of delay.

ARTICLE II

Section 1. The executive Power shall be vested in a President of the United States of America. He shall hold his Office during the Term of four Years, and, together with the Vice President, chosen for the same Term, be elected, as follows:

Each State shall appoint, in such Manner as the Legislature thereof may direct, a Number of Electors, equal to the whole Number of Senators and Representatives to which the State may be entitled in the Congress; but no Senator or Representative, or Person holding an Office of Trust or Profit under the United States, shall be appointed an Elector.

The Electors shall meet in their respective States, and vote by Ballot for two Persons, of whom one at least shall not be an Inhabitant of the same State with themselves. And they shall make a List of all the Persons voted for, and of the Number of Votes for each; which List they shall sign and certify, and transmit sealed to the Seat of the Government of the United States, directed to the President of the Senate. The President of the Senate shall, in the Presence of the Senate and House of Representatives, open all the Certificates, and the Votes shall then be counted. The Person having the greatest Number of Votes shall be the President, if such Number be a Majority of the whole Number of Electors appointed; and if there be more than one who have such Majority, and have an equal Number of Votes, then the House of Representatives shall immediately chuse by Ballot one of them for President; and if no Person have a Majority, then from the five highest on the List the said House shall in like Manner chuse the President. But in chusing the President, the Votes shall be taken by States, the Representation from each State having one Vote; A quorum for this Purpose shall consist of a Member or Members from two thirds of the States, and a Majority of all the States shall be necessary to a Choice. In every Case, after the Choice of the President, the Person having the greater Number of Votes of the Electors shall be the Vice President. But if there should remain two or more who have equal Votes, the Senate shall chuse from them by Ballot the Vice President.

The Congress may determine the Time of chusing the Electors, and the Day on which they shall give their Votes; which Day shall be the same throughout the United States.

No person except a natural born Citizen, or a Citizen of the United States, at the time of the Adoption of this Constitution, shall be eligible to the Office of President; neither shall any Person be eligible to that Office who shall not have attained to the Age of thirty five Years, and been fourteen Years a Resident within the United States.

In Case of the Removal of the President from Office, or of his Death, Resignation or Inability to discharge the Powers and Duties of the said Office, the same shall devolve on the Vice President, and the Congress may by Law provide for the Case of Removal, Death, Resignation or Inability, both of the President and Vice President, declaring what Officer shall then act as President, and such Officer shall act accordingly, until the Disability be removed, or a President shall be elected.

The President shall, at stated Times, receive for his Services, a Compensation, which shall neither be increased nor diminished during the Period for which he shall have been elected, and he shall not receive within that Period any other Emolument from the United States, or any of them.

Before he enter on the Execution of his Office, he shall take the following Oath or Affirmation: "I do solemnly swear (or affirm) that I will faithfully execute the Office of President of the United States, and will to the best of my Ability, preserve, protect and defend the Constitution of the United States."

Section 2. The President shall be Commander in Chief of the Army and Navy of the United States, and of the Militia of the several States, when called into the actual Service of the United States; he may require the Opinion, in writing, of the principal Officer in each of the executive Departments, upon any Subject relating to the Duties of their respective Offices, and he shall have Power to grant Reprieves and Pardons for Offenses against the United States, except in Cases of Impeachment.

He shall have Power, by and with the Advice and Consent of

the Senate to make Treaties, provided two thirds of the Senators present concur; and he shall nominate, and by and with the Advice and Consent of the Senate, shall appoint Ambassadors, other public Ministers and Consuls, Judges of the supreme Court, and all other Officers of the United States, whose Appointments are not herein otherwise provided for, and which shall be established by Law; but the Congress may by Law vest the Appointment of such inferior Officers, as they think proper, in the President alone, in the Courts of Law, or in the Heads of Departments.

The President shall have Power to fill up all Vacancies that may happen during the Recess of the Senate, by granting Commissions which shall expire at the End of their next Session.

Section 3. He shall from time to time give to the Congress Information of the State of the Union, and recommend to their Consideration such Measures as he shall judge necessary and expedient; he may, on extraordinary Occasions, convene both Houses, or either of them, and in Case of Disagreement between them, with Respect to the Time of Adjournment, he may adjourn them to such Time as he shall think proper; he shall receive Ambassadors and other public Ministers; he shall take Care that the Laws be faithfully executed, and shall Commission all the Officers of the United States.

Section 4. The President, Vice President and all civil Officers of the United States, shall be removed from Office on Impeachment for, and Conviction of, Treason, Bribery, or other high Crimes and Misdemeanors.

ARTICLE III

Section 1. The judicial Power of the United States, shall be vested in one supreme Court, and in such inferior Courts as the Congress may from time to time ordain and establish. The Judges, both of the supreme and inferior Courts, shall hold their Offices during good Behaviour, and shall, at stated Times, receive for their Services a Compensation, which shall not be diminished during their Continuance in Office.

Section 2. The judicial Power shall extend to all Cases, in Law and Equity, arising under this Constitution, the Laws of the United States, and Treaties made, or which shall be made, under their Authority;—to all Cases affecting Ambassadors, other public Ministers and Consuls;—to all Cases of admiralty and maritime Jurisdiction;—to Controversies to which the United States shall be a Party;—to Controversies between two or more States;—between a State and Citizens of another State;—between Citizens of different States;—between Citizens of the same State claiming Lands under Grants of different States, and between a State, or the Citizens thereof, and foreign States, Citizens or Subjects.

In all Cases affecting Ambassadors, other public Ministers and Consuls, and those in which a State shall be a Party, the supreme Court shall have original Jurisdiction. In all the other Cases before mentioned, the supreme Court shall have appellate Jurisdiction, both as to Law and Fact, with such Exceptions, and under such Regulations as the Congress shall make.

The Trial of all Crimes, except in Cases of Impeachment, shall be by Jury; and such Trial shall be held in the State where the said Crimes shall have been committed; but when not committed within any State, the Trial shall be at such Place or Places as the Congress may by Law have directed.

Section 3. Treason against the United States, shall consist only in levying War against them, or, in adhering to their Enemies, giving them Aid and Comfort. No Person shall be convicted of Treason unless on the Testimony of two Witnesses to the same overt Act, or on Confession in open Court.

The Congress shall have Power to declare the Punishment of Treason, but no Attainder of Treason shall work Corruption of Blood, or Forfeiture except during the Life of the Person attainted.

ARTICLE IV

Section 1. Full Faith and Credit shall be given in each State to the public Acts, Records, and judicial Proceedings of every other State. And the Congress may by general Laws prescribe the Manner in which such Acts, Records and Proceedings shall be proved, and the Effect thereof.

Section 2. The Citizens of each State shall be entitled to all Privileges and Immunities of Citizens in the several States.

A Person charged in any State with Treason, Felony, or other Crime, who shall flee from Justice, and be found in another State, shall on Demand of the executive Authority of the State from which he fled, be delivered up, to be removed to the State having Jurisdiction of the Crime.

No Person held to Service or Labour in one State, under the Laws thereof, escaping into another, shall, in Consequence of any Law or Regulation therein, be discharged from such Service or Labour, but shall be delivered up on Claim of the Party to whom such Service or Labour may be due.

Section 3. New States may be admitted by the Congress into this Union; but no new State shall be formed or erected within the Jurisdiction of any other State; nor any State be formed by the Junction of two or more States, or Parts of States, without the Consent of the Legislatures of the States concerned as well as of the Congress.

The Congress shall have Power to dispose of and make all needful Rules and Regulations respecting the Territory or other Property belonging to the United States; and nothing in this Constitution shall be so construed as to Prejudice any Claims of the United States, or of any particular State.

Section 4. The United States shall guarantee to every State in this Union a Republican Form of Government, and shall protect each of them against Invasion; and on Application of the Legislature, or of the Executive (when the Legislature cannot be convened) against domestic Violence.

ARTICLE V

The Congress, whenever two thirds of both Houses shall deem it necessary, shall propose Amendments to this Constitution, or, on the Application of the Legislatures of two thirds of the several States, shall call a Convention for proposing Amendments, which, in either Case, shall be valid to all Intents and Purposes, as part of this Constitution, when ratified by the Legislatures of three fourths of the several States, or by Conventions in three fourths thereof, as the one or the other Mode of Ratification may be proposed by the Congress; Provided that no Amendment which may be made prior to the Year One thousand eight hundred and eight shall in any Manner affect the first and fourth Clauses in the Ninth Section of the first Article; and that no State, without its Consent, shall be deprived of its equal Suffrage in the Senate.

ARTICLE VI

All Debts contracted and Engagements entered into, before the Adoption of this Constitution shall be as valid against the United States under this Constitution, as under the Confederation.

This Constitution, and the Laws of the United States which shall be made in Pursuance thereof; and all Treaties made, or which shall be made, under the Authority of the United States, shall be the supreme Law of the Land; and the Judges in every State shall be bound thereby, any Thing in the Constitution or Laws of any State to the Contrary notwithstanding.

The Senators and Representatives before mentioned, and the Members of the several State Legislatures, and all executive and judicial Officers, both of the United States and of the several States, shall be bound by Oath or Affirmation, to support this Constitution; but no religious Test shall ever be required as a Qualification to any Office or public Trust under the United States.

ARTICLE VII

The Ratification of the Conventions of nine States shall be sufficient for the Establishment of this Constitution between the States so ratifying the Same.

AMENDMENT I [1791]

Congress shall make no law respecting an establishment of religion, or prohibiting the free exercise thereof; or abridging the freedom of speech, or of the press; or the right of the people peaceably to assembly, and to petition the Government for a redress of grievances.

AMENDMENT II [1791]

A well regulated Militia, being necessary to the security of a free State, the right of the people to keep and bear Arms, shall not be infringed.

AMENDMENT III [1791]

No Soldier shall, in time of peace be quartered in any house, without the consent of the Owner, nor in time of war, but in a manner to be prescribed by law.

AMENDMENT IV [1791]

The right of the people to be secure in their persons, houses, papers, and effects, against unreasonable searches and seizures, shall not be violated, and no Warrants shall issue, but upon probable cause, supported by Oath or affirmation, and particularly describing the place to be searched, and the persons or things to be seized.

AMENDMENT V [1791]

No person shall be held to answer for a capital, or otherwise infamous crime, unless on a presentment or indictment of a Grand Jury, except in cases arising in the land or naval forces, or in the Militia, when in actual service in time of War or public danger; nor shall any person be subject for the same offence to be twice put in jeopardy of life or limb; nor shall be compelled in any criminal case to be a witness against himself, nor be deprived of life, liberty, or property, without due process of law; nor shall private property be taken for public use, without just compensation.

AMENDMENT VI [1791]

In all criminal prosecutions, the accused shall enjoy the right to a speedy and public trial, by an impartial jury of the State and district wherein the crime shall have been committed, which district shall have been previously ascertained by law, and to be informed of the nature and cause of the accusation; to be confronted with the witnesses against him; to have compulsory process for obtaining witnesses in his favor, and to have the Assistance of Counsel for his defence.

AMENDMENT VII [1791]

In Suits at common law, where the value in controversy shall exceed twenty dollars, the right of trial by jury shall be preserved, and no fact tried by jury, shall be otherwise re-examined in any Court of the United States, than according to the rules of the common law.

AMENDMENT VIII [1791]

Excessive bail shall not be required, nor excessive fines imposed, nor cruel and unusual punishments inflicted.

AMENDMENT IX [1791]

The enumeration in the Constitution, of certain rights, shall not be construed to deny or disparage others retained by the people.

AMENDMENT X [1791]

The powers not delegated to the United States by the Constitution, nor prohibited by it to the States, are reserved to the States respectively, or to the people.

AMENDMENT XI [1798]

The Judicial power of the United States shall not be construed to extend to any suit in law or equity, commenced or prosecuted against one of the United States by Citizens of another State, or by Citizens or Subjects of any Foreign State.

AMENDMENT XII [1804]

The Electors shall meet in their respective states, and vote by ballot for President and Vice-President, one of whom, at least, shall not be an inhabitant of the same state with themselves; they shall name in their ballots the person voted for as President, and in distinct ballots the person voted for as Vice-President, and they shall make distinct lists of all persons voted for as President, and of all persons voted for as Vice-President, and of the number of votes for each, which lists they shall sign and certify, and transmit sealed to the seat of the government of the United States, directed to the President of the Senate;—The President of the Senate shall, in the presence of the Senate and House of Representatives, open all the certificates and the votes shall then be counted;—The person having the greatest number of votes for President, shall be the President, if such number be a majority of the whole number of Electors appointed; and if no person have such majority, then from the persons having the highest numbers not exceeding three on the list of those voted for as President, the House of Representatives shall choose immediately, by ballot, the President. But in choosing the President, the votes shall be taken by states, the representation from each state having one vote; a quorum for this purpose shall consist of a member or members from two-thirds of the states, and a majority of all states shall be necessary to a choice. And if the House of Representatives shall not choose a President whenever the right of choice shall devolve upon them, before the fourth day of March next following, then the Vice-President shall act as President, as in the case of the death or other constitutional disability of the President.—The person having the greatest number of votes as Vice-President, shall be the Vice-President, if such number be a majority of the whole number of Electors appointed, and if no person have a majority, then from the two highest numbers on the list, the Senate shall choose the Vice-President; a quorum for the purpose shall consist of two-thirds of the whole number of Senators, and a majority of the whole number shall be necessary to a choice. But no person constitutionally ineligible to the office of President shall be eligible to that of Vice-President of the United States.

AMENDMENT XIII [1865]

Section 1. Neither slavery nor involuntary servitude, except as a punishment for crime whereof the party shall have been duly convicted, shall exist within the United States, or any place subject to their jurisdiction.

Section 2. Congress shall have power to enforce this article by appropriate legislation.

AMENDMENT XIV [1868]

Section 1. All persons born or naturalized in the United States, and subject to the jurisdiction thereof, are citizens of the United States and of the State wherein they reside. No State shall make or enforce any law which shall abridge the privileges or immunities of citizens of the United States; nor shall any State deprive any person of life, liberty, or property, without due process of law; nor deny to any person within its jurisdiction the equal protection of the laws.

Section 2. Representatives shall be apportioned among the several States according to their respective numbers, counting the whole number of persons in each State, excluding Indians not taxed. But when the right to vote at any election for the choice of electors for President and Vice President of the United States, Representatives in Congress, the Executive and Judicial officers of a State, or the members of the Legislature thereof, is denied to any of the male inhabitants of such State, being twenty-one years of age, and citizens of the United States, or in any way abridged, except for participation in rebellion, or other crime, the basis of representation therein shall be reduced in the proportion which the number of such male citizens shall bear to the whole number of male citizens twenty-one years of age in such State.

Section 3. No person shall be a Senator or Representative in Congress, or elector of President and Vice President, or hold any office, civil or military, under the United States, or under any State, who having previously taken an oath, as a member of Congress, or as an officer of the United States, or as a member of any State legislature, or as an executive or judicial officer of any State, to support the Constitution of the United States, shall have engaged in insurrection or rebellion against the same, or given aid or comfort to the enemies thereof. But Congress may by a vote of two-thirds of each House, remove such disability.

Section 4. The validity of the public debt of the United States, authorized by law, including debts incurred for payment of pensions and bounties for services in suppressing insurrection or rebellion, shall not be questioned. But neither the United States nor any State shall assume or pay any debt or obligation incurred in aid of insurrection or rebellion against the United States, or any claim for the loss or emancipation of any slave; but all such debts, obligations and claims shall be held illegal and void.

Section 5. The Congress shall have power to enforce, by appropriate legislation, the provisions of this article.

AMENDMENT XV [1870]

Section 1. The right of citizens of the United States to vote shall not be denied or abridged by the United States or by any State on account of race, color, or previous condition of servitude.

Section 2. The Congress shall have power to enforce this article by appropriate legislation.

AMENDMENT XVI [1913]

The Congress shall have power to lay and collect taxes on incomes, from whatever source derived, without apportionment among the several States, and without regard to any census or enumeration.

AMENDMENT XVII [1913]

Section 1. The Senate of the United States shall be composed of two Senators from each State, elected by the people thereof, for six years; and each Senator shall have one vote. The electors in each State shall have the qualifications requisite for electors of the most numerous branch of the State legislatures.

Section 2. When vacancies happen in the representation of any State in the Senate, the executive authority of such State shall issue writs of election to fill such vacancies: *Provided,* That the legislature of any State may empower the executive thereof to make temporary appointments until the people fill the vacancies by election as the legislature may direct.

Section 3. This amendment shall not be so construed as to affect the election or term of any Senator chosen before it becomes valid as part of the Constitution.

AMENDMENT XVIII [1919]

Section 1. After one year from the ratification of this article the manufacture, sale, or transportation of intoxicating liquors within, the importation thereof into, or the exportation thereof from the United States and all territory subject to the jurisdiction thereof for beverage purposes is hereby prohibited.

Section 2. The Congress and the several States shall have concurrent power to enforce this article by appropriate legislation.

Section 3. This article shall be inoperative unless it shall have been ratified as an amendment to the Constitution by the legislatures of the several States, as provided in the Constitution, within seven years from the date of the submission hereof to the States by the Congress.

AMENDMENT XIX [1920]

Section 1. The right of citizens of the United States to vote shall not be denied or abridged by the United States or by any State on account of sex.

Section 2. Congress shall have power to enforce this article by appropriate legislation.

AMENDMENT XX [1933]

Section 1. The terms of the President and Vice President shall end at noon on the 20th day of January, and the terms of

Senators and Representatives at noon on the 3d day of January, of the years in which such terms would have ended if this article had not been ratified; and the terms of their successors shall then begin.

Section 2. The Congress shall assemble at least once in every year, and such meeting shall begin at noon on the 3d day of January, unless they shall by law appoint a different day.

Section 3. If, at the time fixed for the beginning of the term of the President, the President elect shall have died, the Vice President elect shall become President. If the President shall not have been chosen before the time fixed for the beginning of his term, or if the President elect shall have failed to qualify, then the Vice President elect shall act as President until a President shall have qualified; and the Congress may by law provide for the case wherein neither a President elect nor a Vice President elect shall have qualified, declaring who shall then act as President, or the manner in which one who is to act shall be selected, and such person shall act accordingly until a President or Vice President shall have qualified.

Section 4. The Congress may by law provide for the case of the death of any of the persons from whom the House of Representatives may choose a President whenever the right of choice shall have devolved upon them, and for the case of the death of any of the persons from whom the Senate may choose a Vice President whenever the right of choice shall have devolved upon them.

Section 5. Sections 1 and 2 shall take effect on the 15th day of October following the ratification of this article.

Section 6. This article shall be inoperative unless it shall have been ratified as an amendment to the Constitution by the legislatures of three-fourths of the several States within seven years from the date of its submission.

AMENDMENT XXI [1933]

Section 1. The eighteenth article of amendment to the Constitution of the United States is hereby repealed.

Section 2. The transportation or importation into any State, Territory, or possession of the United States for delivery or use therein of intoxicating liquors, in violation of the laws thereof, is hereby prohibited.

Section 3. This article shall be inoperative unless it shall have been ratified as an amendment to the Constitution by conventions in the several States, as provided in the Constitution, within seven years from the date of the submission hereof to the States by the Congress.

AMENDMENT XXII [1951]

Section 1. No person shall be elected to the office of the President more than twice, and no person who has held the office of President, or acted as President, for more than two years of a term to which some other person was elected President shall be elected to the office of President more than once. But this Article shall not apply to any person holding the office of President when this Article was proposed by the Congress, and shall not prevent any person who may be holding the office of President, or acting as President, during the term within which this Article becomes operative from holding the office of President or acting as President during the remainder of such term.

Section 2. This article shall be inoperative unless it shall have been ratified as an amendment to the Constitution by the legislatures of three-fourths of the several States within seven years from the date of its submission to the States by the Congress.

AMENDMENT XXIII [1961]

Section 1. The District constituting the seat of Government of the United States shall appoint in such manner as the Congress may direct:

A number of electors of President and Vice President equal to the whole number of Senators and Representatives in Congress to which the District would be entitled if it were a State, but in no event more than the least populous state; they shall be in addition to those appointed by the states, but they shall be considered, for the purposes of the election of President and Vice President, to be electors appointed by a state; and they shall meet in the District and perform such duties as provided by the twelfth article of amendment.

Section 2. The Congress shall have power to enforce this article by appropriate legislation.

AMENDMENT XXIV [1964]

Section 1. The right of citizens of the United States to vote in any primary or other election for President or Vice President, for electors for President or Vice President, or for Senator or Representative in Congress, shall not be denied or abridged by the United States, or any State by reason of failure to pay any poll tax or other tax.

Section 2. The Congress shall have power to enforce this article by appropriate legislation.

AMENDMENT XXV [1967]

Section 1. In case of the removal of the President from office or of his death or resignation, the Vice President shall become President.

Section 2. Whenever there is a vacancy in the office of the Vice President, the President shall nominate a Vice President who shall take office upon confirmation by a majority vote of both Houses of Congress.

Section 3. Whenever the President transmits to the President pro tempore of the Senate and the Speaker of the House of Representatives his written declaration that he is unable to discharge the powers and duties of his office, and until he transmits to them a written declaration to the contrary, such powers and duties shall be discharged by the Vice President as Acting President.

Section 4. Whenever the Vice President and a majority of either the principal officers of the executive departments or of such other body as Congress may by law provide, transmit to the President pro tempore of the Senate and the Speaker of the House of Representatives their written declaration that the President is unable to discharge the powers and duties of his office, the Vice President shall immediately assume the powers and duties of the office as Acting President.

Thereafter, when the President transmits to the President pro tempore of the Senate and the Speaker of the House of Representatives his written declaration that no inability exists, he shall resume the powers and duties of his office unless the Vice President and a majority of either the principal officers of the executive department or of such other body as Congress may by law provide, transmit within four days to the President pro tempore of the Senate and the Speaker of the House of Representatives their written declaration and the President is unable to discharge the powers and duties of his office. Thereupon Congress shall decide the issue, assembling within forty-eight hours for that purpose if not in session. If the Congress, within twenty-one days after receipt of the latter written declaration, or, if Congress is not in session, within twenty-one days after Congress is required to assemble, determines by two-thirds vote of both Houses that the President is unable to discharge the powers and duties of his office, the Vice President shall continue to discharge the same as Acting President; otherwise, the President shall resume the powers and duties of his office.

AMENDMENT XXVI [1971]

Section 1. The right of citizens of the United States, who are eighteen years of age or older, to vote shall not be denied or abridged by the United States or by any State on account of age.

Section 2. The Congress shall have power to enforce this article by appropriate legislation.

AMENDMENT XXVII [1992]

No law, varying the compensation for the services of the Senators and Representatives, shall take effect, until an election of Representatives shall have intervened.

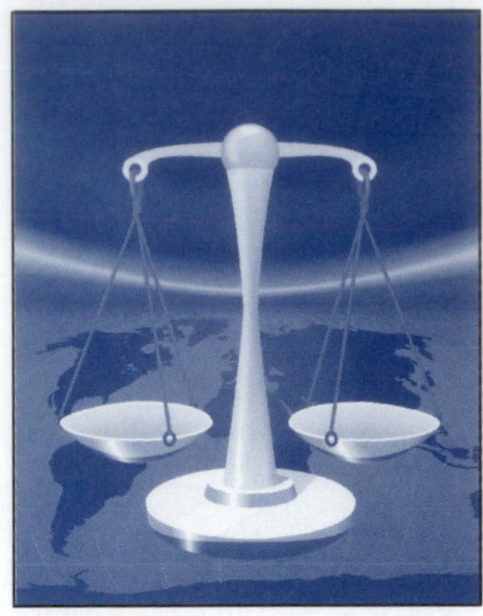

Appendix C

The Uniform Commercial Code (Excerpts)

(Adopted in 52 jurisdictions; all 50 states, although Louisiana has adopted only Articles 1, 3, 4, 7, 8, and 9; the District of Columbia, and the Virgin Islands.)

The Code consists of the following articles:

Art.

1. General Provisions
2. Sales

2A. Leases

3. Commercial Paper
4. Bank Deposits and Collections

4A. Funds Transfers

5. Letters of Credit
6. Bulk Transfers (including Alternative B)
7. Warehouse Receipts, Bills of Lading and Other Documents of Title
8. Investment Securities
9. Secured Transactions: Sales of Accounts and Chattel Paper
10. Effective Date and Repealer
11. Effective Date and Transition Provisions

Article 1
GENERAL PROVISIONS

Part 1 Short Title, Construction, Application and Subject Matter of the Act

§ 1—101. **Short Title.**

This Act shall be known and may be cited as Uniform Commercial Code.

§ 1—102. **Purposes; Rules of Construction; Variation by Agreement.**

(1) This Act shall be liberally construed and applied to promote its underlying purposes and policies.

(2) Underlying purposes and policies of this Act are

(a) to simplify, clarify and modernize the law governing commercial transactions;

(b) to permit the continued expansion of commercial practices through custom, usage and agreement of the parties;

(c) to make uniform the law among the various jurisdictions.

(3) The effect of provisions of this Act may be varied by agreement, except as otherwise provided in this Act and except that the obligations of good faith, diligence, reasonableness and care prescribed by this Act may not be disclaimed by agreement but the parties may by agreement determine the standards by which the performance of such obligations is to be measured if such standards are not manifestly unreasonable.

(4) The presence in certain provisions of this Act of the words "unless otherwise agreed" or words of similar import does not imply that the effect of other provisions may not be varied by agreement under subsection (3).

(5) In this Act unless the context otherwise requires

(a) words in the singular number include the plural, and in the plural include the singular;

(b) words of the masculine gender include the feminine and the neuter, and when the sense so indicates words of the neuter gender may refer to any gender.

§ 1—103. **Supplementary General Principles of Law Applicable.**

Unless displaced by the particular provisions of this Act, the principles of law and equity, including the law merchant and the law relative to capacity to contract, principal and agent, estoppel, fraud, misrepresentation, duress, coercion, mistake, bankruptcy, or other validating or invalidating cause shall supplement its provisions.

§ 1—104. **Construction Against Implicit Repeal.**

This Act being a general act intended as a unified coverage of its subject matter, no part of it shall be deemed to be impliedly repealed by subsequent legislation if such construction can reasonably be avoided.

§ 1—105. **Territorial Application of the Act; Parties' Power to Choose Applicable Law.**

(1) Except as provided hereafter in this section, when a transaction bears a reasonable relation to this state and also to another state or nation the parties may agree that the law either of this state or of such other state or nation shall govern their rights and duties. Failing such agreement this Act applies to transactions bearing an appropriate relation to this state.

(2) Where one of the following provisions of this Act specifies the applicable law, that provision governs and a contrary agreement is effective only to the extent permitted by the law (including the conflict of laws rules) so specified:

Rights of creditors against sold goods. Section 2—402.

Applicability of the Article on Leases. Sections 2A—105 and 2A—106.

Applicability of the Article on Bank Deposits and Collections. Section 4—102.

Governing law in the Article on Funds Transfers. Section 4A—507.

Bulk sales subject to the Article on Bulk Sales. Section 6–103.

Applicability of the Article on Investment Securities. Section 8—106.

Perfection provisions of the Article on Secured Transactions. Section 9—103.

§ 1—106. **Remedies to Be Liberally Administered.**

(1) The remedies provided by this Act shall be liberally administered to the end that the aggrieved party may be put in as good a position as if the other party had fully performed but neither consequential or special nor penal damages may be had except as specifically provided in this Act or by other rule of law.

(2) Any right or obligation declared by this Act is enforceable by action unless the provision declaring it specifies a different and limited effect.

§ 1—107. **Waiver or Renunciation of Claim or Right After Breach.**

Any claim or right arising out of an alleged breach can be discharged in whole or in part without consideration by a written waiver or renunciation signed and delivered by the aggrieved party.

§ 1—108. **Severability.**

If any provision or clause of this Act or application thereof to any person or circumstances is held invalid, such invalidity shall not affect other provisions or applications of the Act which can be given effect without the invalid provision or application, and to this end the provisions of this Act are declared to be severable.

§ 1—109. **Section Captions.**

Section captions are parts of this Act.

Part 2 General Definitions and Principles of Interpretation

§ 1—201. **General Definitions.**

Subject to additional definitions contained in the subsequent Articles of this Act which are applicable to specific Articles or Parts thereof, and unless the context otherwise requires, in this Act:

(1) "Action" in the sense of a judicial proceeding includes recoupment, counterclaim, set-off, suit in equity and any other proceedings in which rights are determined.

(2) "Aggrieved party" means a party entitled to resort to a remedy.

(3) "Agreement" means the bargain of the parties in fact as found in their language or by implication from other circumstances including course of dealing or usage of trade or course of performance as provided in this Act (Sections 1—205 and 2—208). Whether an agreement has legal consequences is determined by the provisions of this Act, if applicable; otherwise by the law of contracts (Section 1—103). (Compare "Contract".)

(4) "Bank" means any person engaged in the business of banking.

(5) "Bearer" means the person in possession of an instrument, document of title, or certificated security payable to bearer or indorsed in blank.

(6) "Bill of lading" means a document evidencing the receipt of goods for shipment issued by a person engaged in the business of transporting or forwarding goods, and includes an airbill. "Airbill" means a document serving for air transportation as a bill of lading does for marine or rail transportation, and includes an air consignment note or air waybill.

(7) "Branch" includes a separately incorporated foreign branch of a bank.

(8) "Burden of establishing" a fact means the burden of persuading the triers of fact that the existence of the fact is more probable than its non-existence.

(9) "Buyer in ordinary course of business" means a person who in good faith and without knowledge that the sale to him is in violation of the ownership rights or security interest of a third party in the goods buys in ordinary course from a person in the business of selling goods of that kind but does not include a pawnbroker. All persons who sell minerals or the like (including oil and gas) at wellhead or minehead shall be deemed to be persons in the business of selling goods of that kind. "Buying" may be for cash or by exchange of other property or on secured or unsecured credit and includes receiving goods or documents of title under a pre-existing contract for sale but does not include a transfer in bulk or as security for or in total or partial satisfaction of a money debt.

(10) "Conspicuous": A term or clause is conspicuous when it is so written that a reasonable person against whom it is to operate ought to have noticed it. A printed heading in capitals (as: NON-NEGOTIABLE BILL OF LADING) is conspicuous. Language in the body of a form is "conspicuous" if it is in larger or other contrasting type or color. But in a telegram any stated term is "conspicuous". Whether a term or clause is "conspicuous" or not is for decision by the court.

(11) "Contract" means the total legal obligation which results from the parties' agreement as affected by this Act and any other applicable rules of law. (Compare "Agreement".)

(12) "Creditor" includes a general creditor, a secured creditor, a lien creditor and any representative of creditors, including an assignee for the benefit of creditors, a trustee in bankruptcy, a receiver in equity and an executor or administrator of an insolvent debtor's or assignor's estate.

(13) "Defendant" includes a person in the position of defendant in a cross-action or counterclaim.

(14) "Delivery" with respect to instruments, documents of title, chattel paper, or certificated securities means voluntary transfer of possession.

(15) "Document of title" includes bill of lading, dock warrant, dock receipt, warehouse receipt or order for the delivery of goods, and also any other document which in the regular course of business or financing is treated as adequately evidencing that the person in possession of it is entitled to receive, hold and dispose of the document and the goods it covers. To be a document of title a document must purport to be issued by or addressed to a bailee and purport to cover goods in the bailee's possession which are either identified or are fungible portions of an identified mass.

(16) "Fault" means wrongful act, omission or breach.

(17) "Fungible" with respect to goods or securities means goods or securities of which any unit is, by nature or usage of trade, the equivalent of any other like unit. Goods which are not fungible shall be deemed fungible for the purposes of this Act to the extent that under a particular agreement or document unlike units are treated as equivalents.

(18) "Genuine" means free of forgery or counterfeiting.

(19) "Good faith" means honesty in fact in the conduct or transaction concerned.

(20) "Holder" with respect to a negotiable instrument, means the person in possession if the instrument is payable to bearer or, in the cases of an instrument payable to an identified person, if the identified person is in possession. "Holder" with respect to a document of title means the person in possession if the goods are deliverable to bearer or to the order of the person in possession.

(21) To "honor" is to pay or to accept and pay, or where a credit so engages to purchase or discount a draft complying with the terms of the credit.

(22) "Insolvency proceedings" includes any assignment for the benefit of creditors or other proceedings intended to liquidate or rehabilitate the estate of the person involved.

(23) A person is "insolvent" who either has ceased to pay his debts in the ordinary course of business or cannot pay his debts as they become due or is insolvent within the meaning of the federal bankruptcy law.

(24) "Money" means a medium of exchange authorized or adopted by a domestic or foreign government and includes a monetary unit of account established by an intergovernmental organization or by agreement between two or more nations.

(25) A person has "notice" of a fact when

(a) he has actual knowledge of it; or

(b) he has received a notice or notification of it; or

(c) from all the facts and circumstances known to him at the time in question he has reason to know that it exists.

A person "knows" or has "knowledge" of a fact when he has actual knowledge of it. "Discover" or "learn" or a word or phrase of similar import refers to knowledge rather than to reason to know. The time and circumstances under which a notice or notification may cease to be effective are not determined by this Act.

(26) A person "notifies" or "gives" a notice or notification to another by taking such steps as may be reasonably required to inform the other in ordinary course whether or not such other actually comes to know of it. A person "receives" a notice or notification when

(a) it comes to his attention; or

(b) it is duly delivered at the place of business through which the contract was made or at any other place held out by him as the place for receipt of such communications.

(27) Notice, knowledge or a notice or notification received by an organization is effective for a particular transaction from the time when it is brought to the attention of the individual conducting that transaction, and in any event from the time when it would have been brought to his attention if the organization had exercised due diligence. An organization exercises due diligence if it maintains reasonable routines for communicating significant information to the person conducting the transaction and there is reasonable compliance with the routines. Due diligence does not require an individual acting for the organization to communicate information unless such communication is part of his regular duties or unless he has reason to know of the transaction and that the transaction would be materially affected by the information.

(28) "Organization" includes a corporation, government or governmental subdivision or agency, business trust, estate, trust, partnership or association, two or more persons having a joint or common interest, or any other legal or commercial entity.

(29) "Party", as distinct from "third party", means a person who has engaged in a transaction or made an agreement within this Act.

(30) "Person" includes an individual or an organization (See Section 1—102).

(31) "Presumption" or "presumed" means that the trier of fact must find the existence of the fact presumed unless and until evidence is introduced which would support a finding of its nonexistence.

(32) "Purchase" includes taking by sale, discount, negotiation, mortgage, pledge, lien, issue or re-issue, gift or any other voluntary transaction creating an interest in property.

(33) "Purchaser" means a person who takes by purchase.

(34) "Remedy" means any remedial right to which an aggrieved party is entitled with or without resort to a tribunal.

(35) "Representative" includes an agent, an officer of a corporation or association, and a trustee, executor or administrator of an estate, or any other person empowered to act for another.

(36) "Rights" includes remedies.

(37) "Security interest" means an interest in personal property or fixtures which secures payment or performance of an obligation. The retention or reservation of title by a seller of goods notwithstanding shipment or delivery to the buyer (Section 2—401) is limited in effect to a reservation of a "security interest". The term also includes any interest of a buyer of accounts or chattel paper which is subject to Article 9. The special property interest of a buyer of goods on identification of those goods to a contract for sale under Section 2—401 is not a "security interest", but a buyer may also acquire a "security interest" by complying with Article 9. Unless a consignment is intended as security, reservation of title thereunder is not a "security interest," but a consignment is

in any event subject to the provisions on consignment sales (Section 2—326).

Whether a transaction creates a lease or security interest is determined by the facts of each case; however, a transaction creates a security interest if the consideration the lessee is to pay the lessor for the right to possession and use of the goods is an obligation for the term of the lease not subject to termination by the lessee, and

(a) the original term of the lease is equal to or greater than the remaining economic life of the goods,

(b) the lessee is bound to renew the lease for the remaining economic life of the goods or is bound to become the owner of the goods,

(c) the lessee has an option to renew the lease for the remaining economic life of the goods for no additional consideration or nominal additional consideration upon compliance with the lease agreement, or

(d) the lessee has an option to become the owner of the goods for no additional consideration or nominal additional consideration upon compliance with the lease agreement.

A transaction does not create a security interest merely because it provides that

(a) the present value of the consideration the lessee is obligated to pay the lessor for the right to possession and use of the goods is substantially equal to or is greater than the fair market value of the goods at the time the lease is entered into,

(b) the lessee assumes risk of loss of the goods, or agrees to pay taxes, insurance, filing, recording, or registration fees, or service or maintenance costs with respect to the goods,

(c) the lessee has an option to renew the lease or to become the owner of the goods,

(d) the lessee has an option to renew the lease for a fixed rent that is equal to or greater than the reasonably predictable fair market rent for the use of the goods for the term of the renewal at the time the option is to be performed, or

(e) the lessee has an option to become the owner of the goods for a fixed price that is equal to or greater than the reasonably predictable fair market value of the goods at the time the option is to be performed.

For purposes of this subsection (37):

(x) Additional consideration is not nominal if (i) when the option to renew the lease is granted to the lessee the rent is stated to be the fair market rent for the use of the goods for the term of the renewal determined at the time the option is to be performed, or (ii) when the option to become the owner of the goods is granted to the lessee the price is stated to be the fair market value of the goods determined at the time the option is to be performed. Additional consideration is nominal if it is less than the lessee's reasonably predictable cost of performing under the lease agreement if the option is not exercised;

(y) "Reasonably predictable" and "remaining economic life of the goods" are to be determined with reference to the facts and circumstances at the time the transaction is entered into; and

(z) "Present value" means the amount as of a date certain of one or more sums payable in the future, discounted to the date certain. The discount is determined by the interest rate specified by the parties if the rate is not manifestly unreasonable at the time the transaction is entered into; otherwise, the discount is determined by a commercially reasonable rate that takes into account the facts and circumstances of each case at the time the transaction was entered into.

(38) "Send" in connection with any writing or notice means to deposit in the mail or deliver for transmission by any other usual means of communication with postage or cost of transmission provided for and properly addressed and in the case of an instrument to an address specified thereon or otherwise agreed, or if there be none to any address reasonable under the circumstances. The receipt of any writing or notice within the time at which it would have arrived if properly sent has the effect of a proper sending.

(39) "Signed" includes any symbol executed or adopted by a party with present intention to authenticate a writing.

(40) "Surety" includes guarantor.

(41) "Telegram" includes a message transmitted by radio, teletype, cable, any mechanical method of transmission, or the like.

(42) "Term" means that portion of an agreement which relates to a particular matter.

(43) "Unauthorized" signature means one made without actual, implied or apparent authority and includes a forgery.

(44) "Value". Except as otherwise provided with respect to negotiable instruments and bank collections (Sections 3—303, 4—208 and 4—209) a person gives "value" for rights if he acquires them

(a) in return for a binding commitment to extend credit or for the extension of immediately available credit whether or not drawn upon and whether or not a chargeback is provided for in the event of difficulties in collection; or

(b) as security for or in total or partial satisfaction of a preexisting claim; or

(c) by accepting delivery pursuant to a preexisting contract for purchase; or

(d) generally, in return for any consideration sufficient to support a simple contract.

(45) "Warehouse receipt" means a receipt issued by a person engaged in the business of storing goods for hire.

(46) "Written" or "writing" includes printing, typewriting or any other intentional reduction to tangible form.

§ 1—202. **Prima Facie Evidence by Third Party Documents.**

A document in due form purporting to be a bill of lading, policy or certificate of insurance, official weigher's or inspector's certificate, consular invoice, or any other document authorized or required by the contract to be issued by a third party shall be prima facie evidence of its own authenticity and genuineness and of the facts stated in the document by the third party.

§ 1—203. **Obligation of Good Faith.**

Every contract or duty within this Act imposes an obligation of good faith in its performance or enforcement.

§ 1—204. **Time; Reasonable Time; "Seasonably".**

(1) Whenever this Act requires any action to be taken within a reasonable time, any time which is not manifestly unreasonable may be fixed by agreement.

(2) What is a reasonable time for taking any action depends on the nature, purpose and circumstances of such action.

(3) An action is taken "seasonably" when it is taken at or within the time agreed or if no time is agreed at or within a reasonable time.

§ 1—205. **Course of Dealing and Usage of Trade.**

(1) A course of dealing is a sequence of previous conduct between the parties to a particular transaction which is fairly to be regarded as establishing a common basis of understanding for interpreting their expressions and other conduct.

(2) A usage of trade is any practice or method of dealing having such regularity of observance in a place, vocation or trade as to justify an expectation that it will be observed with respect to the transaction in question. The existence and scope of such a usage are to be proved as facts. If it is established that such a usage is embodied in a written trade code or similar writing the interpretation of the writing is for the court.

(3) A course of dealing between parties and any usage of trade in the vocation or trade in which they are engaged or of which they are or should be aware give particular meaning to and supplement or qualify terms of an agreement.

(4) The express terms of an agreement and an applicable course of dealing or usage of trade shall be construed wherever reasonable as consistent with each other; but when such construction is unreasonable express terms control both course of dealing and usage of trade and course of dealing controls usage trade.

(5) An applicable usage of trade in the place where any part of performance is to occur shall be used in interpreting the agreement as to that part of the performance.

(6) Evidence of a relevant usage of trade offered by one party is not admissible unless and until he has given the other party such notice as the court finds sufficient to prevent unfair surprise to the latter.

§ 1—206. **Statute of Frauds for Kinds of Personal Property Not Otherwise Covered.**

(1) Except in the cases described in subsection (2) of this section a contract for the sale of personal property is not enforceable by way of action or defense beyond five thousand dollars in amount or value of remedy unless there is some writing which indicates that a contract for sale has been made between the parties at a defined or stated price, reasonably identifies the subject matter, and is signed by the party against whom enforcement is sought or by his authorized agent.

(2) Subsection (1) of this section does not apply to contracts for the sale of goods (Section 2—201) nor of securities (Section 8—319) nor to security agreements (Section 9—203).

§ 1—207. **Performance or Acceptance Under Reservation of Rights.**

(1) A party who with explicit reservation of rights performs or promises performance or assents to performance in a manner demanded or offered by the other party does not thereby prejudice the rights reserved. Such words as "without prejudice", "under protest" or the like are sufficient.

(2) Subsection (1) does not apply to an accord and satisfaction.

§ 1—208. **Option to Accelerate at Will.**

A term providing that one party or his successor in interest may accelerate payment or performance or require collateral or additional collateral "at will" or "when he deems himself insecure" or in words of similar import shall be construed to mean that he shall have power to do so only if he in good faith believes that the prospect of payment or performance is impaired. The burden of establishing lack of good faith is on the party against whom the power has been exercised.

§ 1—209. **Subordinated Obligations.**

An obligation may be issued as subordinated to payment of another obligation of the person obligated, or a creditor may subordinate his right to payment of an obligation by agreement with either the person obligated or another creditor of the person obligated. Such a subordination does not create a security interest as against either the common debtor or a subordinated creditor. This section shall be construed as declaring the law as it existed prior to the enactment of this section and not as modifying it. Added 1966.

Note: *This new section is proposed as an optional provision to make it clear that a subordination agreement does not create a security interest unless so intended.*

Article 2
SALES

Part 1 Short Title, General Construction and Subject Matter

§ 2—101. **Short Title.**

This Article shall be known and may be cited as Uniform Commercial Code—Sales.

§ 2—102. **Scope; Certain Security and Other Transactions Excluded From This Article.**

Unless the context otherwise requires, this Article applies to transactions in goods; it does not apply to any transaction which although in the form of an unconditional contract to sell or present sale is intended to operate only as a security transaction nor does this Article impair or repeal any statute regulating sales to consumers, farmers or other specified classes of buyers.

§ 2—103. **Definitions and Index of Definitions.**

(1) In this Article unless the context otherwise requires

(a) "Buyer" means a person who buys or contracts to buy goods.

(b) "Good faith" in the case of a merchant means honesty in fact and the observance of reasonable commercial standards of fair dealing in the trade.

(c) "Receipt" of goods means taking physical possession of them.

(d) "Seller" means a person who sells or contracts to sell goods.

(2) Other definitions applying to this Article or to specified Parts thereof, and the sections in which they appear are:
"Acceptance". Section 2—606.
"Banker's credit". Section 2—325.
"Between merchants". Section 2—104.
"Cancellation". Section 2—106(4).
"Commercial unit". Section 2—105.
"Confirmed credit". Section 2—325.
"Conforming to contract". Section 2—106.
"Contract for sale". Section 2—106.
"Cover". Section 2—712.
"Entrusting". Section 2—403.
"Financing agency". Section 2—104.
"Future goods". Section 2—105.
"Goods". Section 2—105.
"Identification". Section 2—501.
"Installment contract". Section 2—612.
"Letter of Credit". Section 2—325.
"Lot". Section 2—105.
"Merchant". Section 2—104.
"Overseas". Section 2—323.
"Person in position of seller". Section 2—707.
"Present sale". Section 2—106.
"Sale". Section 2—106.
"Sale on approval". Section 2—326.
"Sale or return". Section 2—326.
"Termination". Section 2—106.

(3) The following definitions in other Articles apply to this Article:
"Check". Section 3—104.
"Consignee". Section 7—102.
"Consignor". Section 7—102.
"Consumer goods". Section 9—109.
"Dishonor". Section 3—507.
"Draft". Section 3—104.

(4) In addition Article 1 contains general definitions and principles of construction and interpretation applicable throughout this Article.

§ 2—104. **Definitions: "Merchant"; "Between Merchants"; "Financing Agency".**

(1) "Merchant" means a person who deals in goods of the kind or otherwise by his occupation holds himself out as having knowledge or skill peculiar to the practices or goods involved in the transaction or to whom such knowledge or skill may be attributed by his employment of an agent or broker or other intermediary who by his occupation holds himself out as having such knowledge or skill.

(2) "Financing agency" means a bank, finance company or other person who in the ordinary course of business makes advances against goods or documents of title or who by arrangement with either the seller or the buyer intervenes in ordinary course to make or collect payment due or claimed under the contract for sale, as by purchasing or paying the seller's draft or making advances against it or by merely taking it for collection whether or not documents of title accompany the draft. "Financing agency" includes also a bank or other person who similarly intervenes between persons who are in the position of seller and buyer in respect to the goods (Section 2—707).

(3) "Between merchants" means in any transaction with respect to which both parties are chargeable with the knowledge or skill of merchants.

§ 2—105. **Definitions: Transferability; "Goods"; "Future" Goods; "Lot"; "Commercial Unit".**

(1) "Goods" means all things (including specially manufactured goods) which are movable at the time of identification to the contract for sale other than the money in which the price is to be paid, investment securities (Article 8) and things in action. "Goods" also includes the unborn young of animals and growing crops and other identified things attached to realty as described in the section on goods to be severed from realty (Section 2—107).

(2) Goods must be both existing and identified before any interest in them can pass. Goods which are not both existing and identified are "future" goods. A purported present sale of future goods or of any interest therein operates as a contract to sell.

(3) There may be a sale of a part interest in existing identified goods.

(4) An undivided share in an identified bulk of fungible goods is sufficiently identified to be sold although the quantity of the bulk is not determined. Any agreed proportion of such a bulk or any quantity thereof agreed upon by number, weight or other measure may to the extent of the seller's interest in the bulk be sold to the buyer who then becomes an owner in common.

(5) "Lot" means a parcel or a single article which is the subject matter of a separate sale or delivery, whether or not it is sufficient to perform the contract.

(6) "Commercial unit" means such a unit of goods as by commercial usage is a single whole for purposes of sale and division of which materially impairs its character or value on the market or in use. A commercial unit may be a single article (as a machine) or a set of articles (as a suite of furniture or an assortment of sizes) or a quantity (as a bale, gross, or carload) or any other unit treated in use or in the relevant market as a single whole.

§ 2—106. **Definitions: "Contract"; "Agreement"; "Contract for Sale"; "Sale"; "Present Sale"; "Conforming" to Contract; "Termination"; "Cancellation".**

(1) In this Article unless the context otherwise requires "contract" and "agreement" are limited to those relating to the present or future sale of goods. "Contract for sale" includes both a present sale of goods and a contract to sell goods at a future time. A "sale" consists in the passing of title from the seller to the buyer for a price (Section 2—401). A "present sale" means a sale which is accomplished by the making of the contract.

(2) Goods or conduct including any part of a performance are "conforming" or conform to the contract when they are in accordance with the obligations under the contract.

(3) "Termination" occurs when either party pursuant to a power created by agreement or law puts an end to the contract otherwise than for its breach. On "termination" all obligations which are still executory on both sides are discharged but any right based on prior breach or performance survives.

(4) "Cancellation" occurs when either party puts an end to the contract for breach by the other and its effect is the same as that of "termination" except that the cancelling party also retains any remedy for breach of the whole contract or any unperformed balance.

§ 2—107. **Goods to Be Severed From Realty: Recording.**

(1) A contract for the sale of minerals or the like (including oil and gas) or a structure or its materials to be removed from realty is a contract for the sale of goods within this Article if they are to be severed by the seller but until severance a purported present sale thereof which is not effective as a transfer of an interest in land is effective only as a contract to sell.

(2) A contract for the sale apart from the land of growing crops or other things attached to realty and capable of severance without material harm thereto but not described in subsection (1) or of timber to be cut is a contract for the sale of goods within this Article whether the subject matter is to be severed by the buyer or by the seller even though it forms part of the realty at the time of contracting, and the parties can by identification effect a present sale before severance.

(3) The provisions of this section are subject to any third party rights provided by the law relating to realty records, and the contract for sale may be executed and recorded as a document transferring an interest in land and shall then constitute notice to third parties of the buyer's rights under the contract for sale.

Part 2 Form, Formation and Readjustment of Contract

§ 2—201. **Formal Requirements; Statute of Frauds.**

(1) Except as otherwise provided in this section a contract for the sale of goods for the price of $500 or more is not enforceable by way of action or defense unless there is some writing sufficient to indicate that a contract for sale has been made between the parties and signed by the party against whom enforcement is sought or by his authorized agent or broker. A writing is not insufficient because it omits or incorrectly states a term agreed upon but the contract is not enforceable under this paragraph beyond the quantity of goods shown in such writing.

(2) Between merchants if within a reasonable time a writing in confirmation of the contract and sufficient against the sender is received and the party receiving it has reason to know its contents, its satisfies the requirements of subsection (1) against such party unless written notice of objection to its contents is given within ten days after it is received.

(3) A contract which does not satisfy the requirements of subsection (1) but which is valid in other respects is enforceable

(a) if the goods are to be specially manufactured for the buyer and are not suitable for sale to others in the ordinary course of the seller's business and the seller, before notice of repudiation is received and under circumstances which reasonably indicate that the goods are for the buyer, has made either a substantial beginning of their manufacture or commitments for their procurement; or

(b) if the party against whom enforcement is sought admits in his pleading, testimony or otherwise in court that a contract for sale was made, but the contract is not enforceable under this provision beyond the quantity of goods admitted; or

(c) with respect to goods for which payment has been made and accepted or which have been received and accepted (Sec. 2—606).

§ 2—202. **Final Written Expression: Parol or Extrinsic Evidence.**

Terms with respect to which the confirmatory memoranda of the parties agree or which are otherwise set forth in a writing intended by the parties as a final expression of their agreement with respect to such terms as are included therein may not be contradicted by evidence of any prior agreement or of a contemporaneous oral agreement but may be explained or supplemented

(a) by course of dealing or usage of trade (Section 1—205) or by course of performance (Section 2—208); and

(b) by evidence of consistent additional terms unless the court finds the writing to have been intended also as a complete and exclusive statement of the terms of the agreement.

§ 2—203. **Seals Inoperative.**

The affixing of a seal to a writing evidencing a contract for sale or an offer to buy or sell goods does not constitute the writing a sealed instrument and the law with respect to sealed instruments does not apply to such a contract or offer.

§ 2—204. **Formation in General.**

(1) A contract for sale of goods may be made in any manner suffıcent to show agreement, including conduct by both parties which recognizes the existence of such a contract.

(2) An agreement sufficient to constitute a contract for sale may be found even though the moment of its making is undetermined.

(3) Even though one or more terms are left open a contract for sale does not fail for indefiniteness if the parties have intended to make a contract and there is a reasonably certain basis for giving an appropriate remedy.

§ 2—205. **Firm Offers.**

An offer by a merchant to buy or sell goods in a signed writing which by its terms gives assurance that it will be held open is not revocable, for lack of consideration, during the time stated or if no time is stated for a reasonable time, but in no event may such period of irrevocability exceed three months; but any such term of assurance on a form supplied by the offeree must be separately signed by the offeror.

§ 2—206. **Offer and Acceptance in Formation of Contract.**

(1) Unless other unambiguously indicated by the language or circumstances

(a) an offer to make a contract shall be construed as inviting acceptance in any manner and by any medium reasonable in the circumstances;

(b) an order or other offer to buy goods for prompt or current shipment shall be construed as inviting acceptance either by a prompt promise to ship or by the prompt or current shipment of conforming or non-conforming goods, but such a shipment of non-conforming goods does not constitute an acceptance if the seller seasonably notifies the buyer that the shipment is offered only as an accommodation to the buyer.

(2) Where the beginning of a requested performance is a reasonable mode of acceptance an offeror who is not notified of acceptance within a reasonable time may treat the offer as having lapsed before acceptance.

§ 2—207. **Additional Terms in Acceptance or Confirmation.**

(1) A definite and seasonable expression of acceptance or a written confirmation which is sent within a reasonable time operates

as an acceptance even though it states terms additional to or different from those offered or agreed upon, unless acceptance is expressly made conditional on assent to the additional or different terms.

(2) The additional terms are to be construed as proposals for addition to the contract. Between merchants such terms become part of the contract unless:

(a) the offer expressly limits acceptance to the terms of the offer;

(b) they materially alter it; or

(c) notification of objection to them has already been given or is given within a reasonable time after notice of them is received.

(3) Conduct by both parties which recognizes the existence of a contract is sufficient to establish a contract for sale although the writings of the parties do not otherwise establish a contract. In such case the terms of the particular contract consist of those terms on which the writings of the parties agree, together with any supplementary terms incorporated under any other provisions of this Act.

§ 2—208. **Course of Performance or Practical Construction.**

(1) Where the contract for sale involves repeated occasions for performance by either party with knowledge of the nature of the performance and opportunity for objection to it by the other, any course of performance accepted or acquiesced in without objection shall be relevant to determine the meaning of the agreement.

(2) The express terms of the agreement and any such course of performance, as well as any course of dealing and usage of trade, shall be construed whenever reasonable as consistent with each other; but when such construction is unreasonable, express terms shall control course of performance and course of performance shall control both course of dealing and usage of trade (Section 1—205).

(3) Subject to the provisions of the next section on modification and waiver, such course of performance shall be relevant to show a waiver or modification of any term inconsistent with such course of performance.

§ 2—209. **Modification, Rescission and Waiver.**

(1) An agreement modifying a contract within this Article needs no consideration to be binding.

(2) A signed agreement which excludes modification or rescission except by a signed writing cannot be otherwise modified or rescinded, but except as between merchants such a requirement on a form supplied by the merchant must be separately signed by the other party.

(3) The requirements of the statute of frauds section of this Article (Section 2—201) must be satisfied if the contract as modified is within its provisions.

(4) Although an attempt at modification or rescission does not satisfy the requirements of subsection (2) or (3) it can operate as a waiver.

(5) A party who has made a waiver affecting an executory portion of the contract may retract the waiver by reasonable notification received by the other party that strict performance will be required of any term waived, unless the retraction would be unjust in view of a material change of position in reliance on the waiver.

§ 2—210. **Delegation of Performance; Assignment of Rights.**

(1) A party may perform his duty through a delegate unless otherwise agreed or unless the other party has a substantial interest in having his original promisor perform or control the acts required by the contract. No delegation of performance relieves the party delegating of any duty to perform or any liability for breach.

(2) Unless otherwise agreed all rights of either seller or buyer can be assigned except where the assignment would materially change the duty of the other party, or increase materially the burden or risk imposed on him by his contract, or impair materially his chance of obtaining return performance. A right to damages for breach of the whole contract or a right arising out of the assignor's due performance of his entire obligation can be assigned despite agreement otherwise.

(3) Unless the circumstances indicate the contrary a prohibition of assignment of "the contract" is to be construed as barring only the delegation to the assignee of the assignor's performance.

(4) An assignment of "the contract" or of "all my rights under the contract" or an assignment in similar general terms is an assignment of rights and unless the language or the circumstances (as in an assignment for security) indicate the contrary, it is a delegation of performance of the duties of the assignor and its acceptance by the assignee constitutes a promise by him to perform those duties. This promise is enforceable by either the assignor or the other party to the original contract.

(5) The other party may treat any assignment which delegates performance as creating reasonable grounds for insecurity and may without prejudice to his rights against the assignor demand assurances from the assignee (Section 2—609).

Part 3 General Obligation and Construction of Contract

§ 2—301. **General Obligations of Parties.**

The obligation of the seller is to transfer and deliver and that of the buyer is to accept and pay in accordance with the contract.

§ 2—302. **Unconscionable Contract or Clause.**

(1) If the court as a matter of law finds the contract or any clause of the contract to have been unconscionable at the time it was made the court may refuse to enforce the contract, or it may enforce the remainder of the contract without the unconscionable clause, or it may so limit the application of any unconscionable clause as to avoid any unconscionable result.

(2) When it is claimed or appears to the court that the contract or any clause thereof may be unconscionable the parties shall be afforded a reasonable opportunity to present evidence as to its commercial setting, purpose and effect to aid the court in making the determination.

§ 2—303. **Allocations or Division of Risks.**

Where this Article allocates a risk or a burden as between the parties "unless otherwise agreed", the agreement may not only shift the allocation but may also divide the risk or burden.

§ 2—304. **Price Payable in Money, Goods, Realty, or Otherwise.**

(1) The price can be made payable in money or otherwise. If it is payable in whole or in part in goods each party is a seller of the goods which he is to transfer.

(2) Even though all or part of the price is payable in an interest in realty the transfer of the goods and the seller's obligations with reference to them are subject to this Article, but not the transfer of the interest in realty or the transferor's obligations in connection therewith.

§ 2—305. **Open Price Term.**

(1) The parties if they so intend can conclude a contract for sale even though the price is not settled. In such a case the price is a reasonable price at the time for delivery if

(a) nothing is said as to price; or

(b) the price is left to be agreed by the parties and they fail to agree; or

(c) the price is to be fixed in terms of some agreed market or other standard as set or recorded by a third person or agency and it is not so set or recorded.

(2) A price to be fixed by the seller or by the buyer means a price for him to fix in good faith.

(3) When a price left to be fixed otherwise than by agreement of the parties fails to be fixed through fault of one party the other may at his option treat the contract as cancelled or himself fix a reasonable price.

(4) Where, however, the parties intend not to be bound unless the price be fixed or agreed and it is not fixed or agreed there is no contract. In such a case the buyer must return any goods already received or if unable so to do must pay their reasonable value at the time of delivery and the seller must return any portion of the price paid on account.

§ 2—306. **Output, Requirements and Exclusive Dealings.**

(1) A term which measures the quantity by the output of the seller or the requirements of the buyer means such actual output or requirements as may occur in good faith, except that no quantity unreasonably disproportionate to any stated estimate or in the absence of a stated estimate to any normal or otherwise comparable prior output or requirements may be tendered or demanded.

(2) A lawful agreement by either the seller or the buyer for exclusive dealing in the kind of goods concerned imposes unless otherwise agreed an obligation by the seller to use best efforts to supply the goods and by the buyer to use best efforts to promote their sale.

§ 2—307. **Delivery in Single Lot or Several Lots.**

Unless otherwise agreed all goods called for by a contract for sale must be tendered in a single delivery and payment is due only on such tender but where the circumstances give either party the right to make or demand delivery in lots the price if it can be apportioned may be demanded for each lot.

§ 2—308. **Absence of Specified Place for Delivery.**

Unless otherwise agreed

(a) the place for delivery of goods is the seller's place of business or if he has none his residence; but

(b) in a contract for sale of identified goods which to the knowledge of the parties at the time of contracting are in some other place, that place is the place for their delivery; and

(c) documents of title may be delivered through customary banking channels.

§ 2—309. **Absence of Specific Time Provisions; Notice of Termination.**

(1) The time for shipment or delivery or any other action under a contract if not provided in this Article or agreed upon shall be a reasonable time.

(2) Where the contract provides for successive performances but is indefinite in duration it is valid for a reasonable time but unless otherwise agreed may be terminated at any time by either party.

(3) Termination of a contract by one party except on the happening of an agreed event requires that reasonable notification be received by the other party and an agreement dispensing with notification is invalid if its operation would be unconscionable.

§ 2—310. **Open Time for Payment or Running of Credit; Authority to Ship Under Reservation.**

Unless otherwise agreed

(a) payment is due at the time and place at which the buyer is to receive the goods even though the place of shipment is the place of delivery; and

(b) if the seller is authorized to send the goods he may ship them under reservation, and may tender the documents of title, but the buyer may inspect the goods after their arrival before payment is due unless such inspection is inconsistent with the terms of the contract (Section 2—513); and

(c) if delivery is authorized and made by way of documents of title otherwise than by subsection (b) then payment is due at the time and place at which the buyer is to receive the documents regardless of where the goods are to be received; and

(d) where the seller is required or authorized to ship the goods on credit the credit period runs from the time of shipment but post-dating the invoice or delaying its dispatch will correspondingly delay the starting of the credit period.

§ 2—311. **Options and Cooperation Respecting Performance.**

(1) An agreement for sale which is otherwise sufficiently definite (subsection (3) of Section 2—204) to be a contract is not made invalid by the fact that it leaves particulars of performance to be specified by one of the parties. Any such specification must be made in good faith and within limits set by commercial reasonableness.

(2) Unless otherwise agreed specifications relating to assortment of the goods are at the buyer's option and except as otherwise provided in subsections (1)(c) and (3) of Section 2—319 specifications or arrangements relating to shipment are at the seller's option.

(3) Where such specification would materially affect the other party's performance but is not seasonably made or where one party's cooperation is necessary to the agreed performance of the

other but is not seasonably forthcoming, the other party in addition to all other remedies

(a) is excused for any resulting delay in his own performance; and

(b) may also either proceed to perform in any reasonable manner or after the time for a material part of his own performance treat the failure to specify or to cooperate as a breach by failure to deliver or accept the goods.

§ 2—312. **Warranty of Title and Against Infringement; Buyer's Obligation Against Infringement.**

(1) Subject to subsection (2) there is in a contract for sale a warranty by the seller that

(a) the title conveyed shall be good, and its transfer rightful; and

(b) the goods shall be delivered free from any security interest or other lien or encumbrance of which the buyer at the time of contracting has no knowledge.

(2) A warranty under subsection (1) will be excluded or modified only by specific language or by circumstances which give the buyer reason to know that the person selling does not claim title in himself or that he is purporting to sell only such right or title as he or a third person may have.

(3) Unless otherwise agreed a seller who is a merchant regularly dealing in goods of the kind warrants that the goods shall be delivered free of the rightful claim of any third person by way of infringement or the like but a buyer who furnishes specifications to the seller must hold the seller harmless against any such claim which arises out of compliance with the specifications.

§ 2—313. **Express Warranties by Affirmation, Promise, Description, Sample.**

(1) Express warranties by the seller are created as follows:

(a) Any affirmation of fact or promise made by the seller to the buyer which relates to the goods and becomes part of the basis of the bargain creates an express warranty that the goods shall conform to the affirmation or promise.

(b) Any description of the goods which is made part of the basis of the bargain creates an express warranty that the goods shall conform to the description.

(c) Any sample or model which is made part of the basis of the bargain creates an express warranty that the whole of the goods shall conform to the sample or model.

(2) It is not necessary to the creation of an express warranty that the seller use formal words such as "warrant" or "guarantee" or that he have a specific intention to make a warranty, but an affirmation merely of the value of the goods or a statement purporting to be merely the seller's opinion or commendation of the goods does not create a warranty.

§ 2—314. **Implied Warranty: Merchantability; Usage of Trade.**

(1) Unless excluded or modified (Section 2—316), a warranty that the goods shall be merchantable is implied in a contract for their sale if the seller is a merchant with respect to goods of that kind. Under this section the serving for value of food or drink to be consumed either on the premises or elsewhere is a sale.

(2) Goods to be merchantable must be at least such as

(a) pass without objection in the trade under the contract description; and

(b) in the case of fungible goods, are of fair average quality within the description; and

(c) are fit for the ordinary purposes for which such goods are used; and

(d) run, within the variations permitted by the agreement, of even kind, quality and quantity within each unit and among all units involved; and

(e) are adequately contained, packaged, and labeled as the agreement may require; and

(f) conform to the promises or affirmations of fact made on the container or label if any.

(3) Unless excluded or modified (Section 2—316) other implied warranties may arise from course of dealing or usage of trade.

§ 2—315. **Implied Warranty: Fitness for Particular Purpose.**

Where the seller at the time of contracting has reason to know any particular purpose for which the goods are required and that the buyer is relying on the seller's skill or judgment to select or furnish suitable goods, there is unless excluded or modified under the next section an implied warranty that the goods shall be fit for such purpose.

§ 2—316. **Exclusion or Modification of Warranties.**

(1) Words or conduct relevant to the creation of an express warranty and words or conduct tending to negate or limit warranty shall be construed wherever reasonable as consistent with each other; but subject to the provisions of this Article on parol or extrinsic evidence (Section 2—202) negation or limitation is inoperative to the extent that such construction is unreasonable.

(2) Subject to subsection (3), to exclude or modify the implied warranty of merchantability or any part of it the language must mention merchantability and in case of a writing must be conspicuous, and to exclude or modify any implied warranty of fitness the exclusion must be by a writing and conspicuous. Language to exclude all implied warranties of fitness is sufficient if it states, for example, that "There are no warranties which extend beyond the description on the face hereof."

(3) Notwithstanding subsection (2)

(a) unless the circumstances indicate otherwise, all implied warranties are excluded by expressions like "as is", "with all faults" or other language which in common understanding calls the buyer's attention to the exclusion of warranties and makes plain that there is no implied warranty; and

(b) when the buyer before entering into the contract has examined the goods or the sample or model as fully as he desired or has refused to examine the goods there is no implied warranty with regard to defects which an examination ought in the circumstances to have revealed to him; and

(c) an implied warranty can also be excluded or modified by course of dealing or course of performance or usage of trade.

(4) Remedies for breach of warranty can be limited in accordance with the provisions of this Article on liquidation or limi-

tation of damages and on contractual modification of remedy (Sections 2—718 and 2—719).

§ 2—317. **Cumulation and Conflict of Warranties Express or Implied.**

Warranties whether express or implied shall be construed as consistent with each other and as cumulative, but if such construction is unreasonable the intention of the parties shall determine which warranty is dominant. In ascertaining that intention the following rules apply:

(a) Exact or technical specifications displace an inconsistent sample or model or general language of description.

(b) A sample from an existing bulk displaces inconsistent general language of description.

(c) Express warranties displace inconsistent implied warranties other than an implied warranty of fitness for a particular purpose.

§ 2—318. **Third Party Beneficiaries of Warranties Express or Implied.**

Note: If this Act is introduced in the Congress of the United States this section should be omitted. (States to select one alternative.)

Alternative A

A seller's warranty whether express or implied extends to any natural person who is in the family or household of his buyer or who is a guest in his home if it is reasonable to expect that such person may use, consume or be affected by the goods and who is injured in person by breach of the warranty. A seller may not exclude or limit the operation of this section.

Alternative B

A seller's warranty whether express or implied extends to any natural person who may reasonably be expected to use, consume or be affected by the goods and who is injured in person by breach of the warranty. A seller may not exclude or limit the operation of this section.

Alternative C

A seller's warranty whether express or implied extends to any person who may reasonably be expected to use, consume or be affected by the goods and who is injured by breach of the warranty. A seller may not exclude or limit the operation of this section with respect to injury to the person of an individual to whom the warranty extends.

§ 2—319. **F.O.B. and F.A.S. Terms.**

(1) Unless otherwise agreed the term F.O.B. (which means "free on board") at a named place, even though used only in connection with the stated price, is a delivery term under which

(a) when the term is F.O.B. the place of shipment, the seller must at that place ship the goods in the manner provided in this Article (Section 2—504) and bear the expense and risk of putting them into the possession of the carrier; or

(b) when the term is F.O.B. the place of destination, the seller must at his own expense and risk transport the goods to that place and there tender delivery of them in the manner provided in this Article (Section 2—503);

(c) when under either (a) or (b) the term is also F.O.B. vessel, car or other vehicle, the seller must in addition at his own expense and risk load the goods on board. If the term is F.O.B. vessel the buyer must name the vessel and in an appropriate case the seller must comply with the provisions of this Article on the form of bill of lading (Section 2—323).

(2) Unless otherwise agreed the term F.A.S. vessel (which means "free alongside") at a named port, even though used only in connection with the stated price, is a delivery term under which the seller must

(a) at his own expense and risk deliver the goods alongside the vessel in the manner usual in that port or on a dock designated and provided by the buyer; and

(b) obtain and tender a receipt for the goods in exchange for which the carrier is under a duty to issue a bill of lading.

(3) Unless otherwise agreed in any case falling within subsection (1)(a) or (c) or subsection (2) the buyer must seasonably give any needed instructions for making delivery, including when the term is F.A.S. or F.O.B. the loading berth of the vessel and in an appropriate case its name and sailing date. The seller may treat the failure of needed instructions as a failure of cooperation under this Article (Section 2—311). He may also at his option move the goods in any reasonable manner preparatory to delivery or shipment.

(4) Under the term F.O.B. vessel or F.A.S. unless otherwise agreed the buyer must make payment against tender of the required documents and the seller may not tender nor the buyer demand delivery of the goods in substitution for the documents.

§ 2—320. **C.I.F. and C. & F. Terms.**

(1) The term C.I.F. means that the price includes in a lump sum the cost of the goods and the insurance and freight to the named destination. The term C. & F. or C.F. means that the price so includes cost and freight to the named destination.

(2) Unless otherwise agreed and even though used only in connection with the stated price and destination, the term C.I.F. destination or its equivalent requires the seller at his own expense and risk to

(a) put the goods into the possession of a carrier at the port for shipment and obtain a negotiable bill or bills of lading covering the entire transportation to the named destination; and

(b) load the goods and obtain a receipt from the carrier (which may be contained in the bill of lading) showing that the freight has been paid or provided for; and

(c) obtain a policy or certificate of insurance, including any war risk insurance, of a kind and on terms then current at the port of shipment in the usual amount, in the currency of the contract, shown to cover the same goods covered by the bill of lading and providing for payment of loss to the order of the buyer or for the account of whom it may concern; but the seller may add to the price the amount of the premium for any such war risk insurance; and

(d) prepare an invoice of the goods and procure any other documents required to effect shipment or to comply with the contract; and

(e) forward and tender with commercial promptness all the documents in due form and with any indorsement necessary to perfect the buyer's rights.

(3) Unless otherwise agreed the term C. & F. or its equivalent has the same effect and imposes upon the seller the same obligations and risks as a C.I.F. term except the obligation as to insurance.

(4) Under the term C.I.F. or C. & F. unless otherwise agreed the buyer must make payment against tender of the required documents and the seller may not tender nor the buyer demand delivery of the goods in substitution for the documents.

§ 2—321. **C.I.F. or C. & F.: "Net Landed Weights"; "Payment on Arrival"; Warranty of Condition on Arrival.**

Under a contract containing a term C.I.F. or C. & F.

(1) Where the price is based on or is to be adjusted according to "net landed weights", "delivered weights", "out turn" quantity or quality or the like, unless otherwise agreed the seller must reasonably estimate the price. The payment due on tender of the documents called for by the contract is the amount so estimated, but after final adjustment of the price a settlement must be made with commercial promptness.

(2) An agreement described in subsection (1) or any warranty of quality or condition of the goods on arrival places upon the seller the risk of ordinary deterioration, shrinkage and the like in transportation but has no effect on the place or time of identification to the contract for sale or delivery or on the passing of the risk of loss.

(3) Unless otherwise agreed where the contract provides for payment on or after arrival of the goods the seller must before payment allow such preliminary inspection as is feasible; but if the goods are lost delivery of the documents and payment are due when the goods should have arrived.

§ 2—322. **Delivery "Ex-Ship".**

(1) Unless otherwise agreed a term for delivery of goods "ex-ship" (which means from the carrying vessel) or in equivalent language is not restricted to a particular ship and requires delivery from a ship which has reached a place at the named port of destination where goods of the kind are usually discharged.

(2) Under such a term unless otherwise agreed

(a) the seller must discharge all liens arising out of the carriage and furnish the buyer with a direction which puts the carrier under a duty to deliver the goods; and

(b) the risk of loss does not pass to the buyer until the goods leave the ship's tackle or are otherwise properly unloaded.

§ 2—323. **Form of Bill of Lading Required in Overseas Shipment; "Overseas".**

(1) Where the contract contemplates overseas shipment and contains a term C.I.F. or C. & F. or F.O.B. vessel, the seller unless otherwise agreed must obtain a negotiable bill of lading stating that the goods have been loaded on board or, in the case of a term C.I.F. or C. & F., received for shipment.

(2) Where in a case within subsection (1) a bill of lading has been issued in a set of parts, unless otherwise agreed if the documents are not to be sent from abroad the buyer may demand tender of the full set; otherwise only one part of the bill of lading need be tendered. Even if the agreement expressly requires a full set

(a) due tender of a single part is acceptable within the provisions of this Article on cure of improper delivery (subsection (1) of Section 2—508); and

(b) even though the full set is demanded, if the documents are sent from abroad the person tendering an incomplete set may nevertheless require payment upon furnishing an indemnity which the buyer in good faith deems adequate.

(3) A shipment by water or by air or a contract contemplating such shipment is "overseas" insofar as by usage of trade or agreement it is subject to the commercial, financing or shipping practices characteristic of international deep water commerce.

§ 2—324. **"No Arrival, No Sale" Term.**

Under a term "no arrival, no sale" or terms of like meaning, unless otherwise agreed,

(a) the seller must properly ship conforming goods and if they arrive by any means he must tender them on arrival but he assumes no obligation that the goods will arrive unless he has caused the non-arrival; and

(b) where without fault of the seller the goods are in part lost or have so deteriorated as no longer to conform to the contract or arrive after the contract time, the buyer may proceed as if there had been casualty to identified goods (Section 2—613).

§ 2—325. **"Letter of Credit" Term; "Confirmed Credit".**

(1) Failure of the buyer seasonably to furnish an agreed letter of credit is a breach of the contract for sale.

(2) The delivery to seller of a proper letter of credit suspends the buyer's obligation to pay. If the letter of credit is dishonored, the seller may on seasonable notification to the buyer require payment directly from him.

(3) Unless otherwise agreed the term "letter of credit" or "banker's credit" in a contract for sale means an irrevocable credit issued by a financing agency of good repute and, where the shipment is overseas, of good international repute. The term "confirmed credit" means that the credit must also carry the direct obligation of such an agency which does business in the seller's financial market.

§ 2—326. **Sale on Approval and Sale or Return; Consignment Sales and Rights of Creditors.**

(1) Unless otherwise agreed, if delivered goods may be returned by the buyer even though they conform to the contract, the transaction is

(a) a "sale on approval" if the goods are delivered primarily for use, and

(b) a "sale or return" if the goods are delivered primarily for resale.

(2) Except as provided in subsection (3), goods held on approval are not subject to the claims of the buyer's creditors until acceptance; goods held on sale or return are subject to such claims while in the buyer's possession.

(3) Where goods are delivered to a person for sale and such person maintains a place of business at which he deals in goods of the kind involved, under a name other than the name of the person making delivery, then with respect to claims of creditors of the person conducting the business the goods are deemed to

be on sale or return. The provisions of this subsection are applicable even though an agreement purports to reserve title to the person making delivery until payment or resale or uses such words as "on consignment" or "on memorandum". However, this subsection is not applicable if the person making delivery

(a) complies with an applicable law providing for a consignor's interest or the like to be evidenced by a sign, or

(b) establishes that the person conducting the business is generally known by his creditors to be substantially engaged in selling the goods of others, or

(c) complies with the filing provisions of the Article on Secured Transactions (Article 9).

(4) Any "or return" term of a contract for sale is to be treated as a separate contract for sale within the statute of frauds section of this Article (Section 2—201) and as contradicting the sale aspect of the contract within the provisions of this Article on parol or extrinsic evidence (Section 2—202).

§ 2—327. **Special Incidents of Sale on Approval and Sale or Return.**

(1) Under a sale on approval unless otherwise agreed

(a) although the goods are identified to the contract the risk of loss and the title do not pass to the buyer until acceptance; and

(b) use of the goods consistent with the purpose of trial is not acceptance but failure seasonably to notify the seller of election to return the goods is acceptance, and if the goods conform to the contract acceptance of any part is acceptance of the whole; and

(c) after due notification of election to return, the return is at the seller's risk and expense but a merchant buyer must follow any reasonable instructions.

(2) Under a sale or return unless otherwise agreed

(a) the option to return extends to the whole or any commercial unit of the goods while in substantially their original condition, but must be exercised seasonably; and

(b) the return is at the buyer's risk and expense.

§ 2—328. **Sale by Auction.**

(1) In a sale by auction if goods are put up in lots each lot is the subject of a separate sale.

(2) A sale by auction is complete when the auctioneer so announces by the fall of the hammer or in other customary manner. Where a bid is made while the hammer is falling in acceptance of a prior bid the auctioneer may in his discretion reopen the bidding or declare the goods sold under the bid on which the hammer was falling.

(3) Such a sale is with reserve unless the goods are in explicit terms put up without reserve. In an auction with reserve the auctioneer may withdraw the goods at any time until he announces completion of the sale. In an auction without reserve, after the auctioneer calls for bids on an article or lot, that article or lot cannot be withdrawn unless no bid is made within a reasonable time. In either case a bidder may retract his bid until the auctioneer's announcement of completion of the sale, but a bidder's retraction does not revive any previous bid.

(4) If the auctioneer knowingly receives a bid on the seller's behalf or the seller makes or procures such as bid, and notice has not been given that liberty for such bidding is reserved, the buyer may at his option avoid the sale or take the goods at the price of the last good faith bid prior to the completion of the sale. This subsection shall not apply to any bid at a forced sale.

Part 4 Title, Creditors and Good Faith Purchasers

§ 2—401. **Passing of Title; Reservation for Security; Limited Application of This Section.**

Each provision of this Article with regard to the rights, obligations and remedies of the seller, the buyer, purchasers or other third parties applies irrespective of title to the goods except where the provision refers to such title. Insofar as situations are not covered by the other provisions of this Article and matters concerning title became material the following rules apply:

(1) Title to goods cannot pass under a contract for sale prior to their identification to the contract (Section 2—501), and unless otherwise explicitly agreed the buyer acquires by their identification a special property as limited by this Act. Any retention or reservation by the seller of the title (property) in goods shipped or delivered to the buyer is limited in effect to a reservation of a security interest. Subject to these provisions and to the provisions of the Article on Secured Transactions (Article 9), title to goods passes from the seller to the buyer in any manner and on any conditions explicitly agreed on by the parties.

(2) Unless otherwise explicitly agreed title passes to the buyer at the time and place at which the seller completes his performance with reference to the physical delivery of the goods, despite any reservation of a security interest and even though a document of title is to be delivered at a different time or place; and in particular and despite any reservation of a security interest by the bill of lading

(a) if the contract requires or authorizes the seller to send the goods to the buyer but does not require him to deliver them at destination, title passes to the buyer at the time and place of shipment; but

(b) if the contract requires delivery at destination, title passes on tender there.

(3) Unless otherwise explicitly agreed where delivery is to be made without moving the goods,

(a) if the seller is to deliver a document of title, title passes at the time when and the place where he delivers such documents; or

(b) if the goods are at the time of contracting already identified and no documents are to be delivered, title passes at the time and place of contracting.

(4) A rejection or other refusal by the buyer to receive or retain the goods, whether or not justified, or a justified revocation of acceptance revests title to the goods in the seller. Such revesting occurs by operation of law and is not a "sale".

§ 2—402. **Rights of Seller's Creditors Against Sold Goods.**

(1) Except as provided in subsections (2) and (3), rights of unsecured creditors of the seller with respect to goods which have been identified to a contract for sale are subject to the buyer's

rights to recover the goods under this Article (Sections 2—502 and 2—716).

(2) A creditor of the seller may treat a sale or an identification of goods to a contract for sale as void if as against him a retention of possession by the seller is fraudulent under any rule of law of the state where the goods are situated, except that retention of possession in good faith and current course of trade by a merchant-seller for a commercially reasonable time after a sale or identification is not fraudulent.

(3) Nothing in this Article shall be deemed to impair the rights of creditors of the seller

(a) under the provisions of the Article on Secured Transactions (Article 9); or

(b) where identification to the contract or delivery is made not in current course of trade but in satisfaction of or as security for a pre-existing claim for money, security or the like and is made under circumstances which under any rule of law of the state where the goods are situated would apart from this Article constitute the transaction a fraudulent transfer or voidable preference.

§ 2—403. **Power to Transfer; Good Faith Purchase of Goods; "Entrusting".**

(1) A purchaser of goods acquires all title which his transferor had or had power to transfer except that a purchaser of a limited interest acquires rights only to the extent of the interest purchased. A person with voidable title has power to transfer a good title to a good faith purchaser for value. When goods have been delivered under a transaction of purchase the purchaser has such power even though

(a) the transferor was deceived as to the identity of the purchaser, or

(b) the delivery was in exchange for a check which is later dishonored, or

(c) it was agreed that the transaction was to be a "cash sale", or

(d) the delivery was procured through fraud punishable as larcenous under the criminal law.

(2) Any entrusting of possession of goods to a merchant who deals in goods of that kind gives him power to transfer all rights of the entruster to a buyer in ordinary course of business.

(3) "Entrusting" includes any delivery and any acquiescence in retention of possession regardless of any condition expressed between the parties to the delivery or acquiescence and regardless of whether the procurement of the entrusting or the possessor's disposition of the goods have been such as to be larcenous under the criminal law.

(4) The rights of other purchasers of goods and of lien creditors are governed by the Articles on Secured Transactions (Article 9), Bulk Transfers (Article 6) and Documents of Title (Article 7).

Part 5 Performance

§ 2—501. **Insurable Interest in Goods; Manner of Identification of Goods.**

(1) The buyer obtains a special property and an insurable interest in goods by identification of existing goods as goods to which the contract refers even though the goods so identified are non-conforming and he has an option to return or reject them. Such identification can be made at any time and in any manner explicitly agreed to by the parties. In the absence of explicit agreement identification occurs

(a) when the contract is made if it is for the sale of goods already existing and identified;

(b) if the contract is for the sale of future goods other than those described in paragraph (c), when goods are shipped, marked or otherwise designated by the seller as goods to which the contract refers;

(c) when the crops are planted or otherwise become growing crops or the young are conceived if the contract is for the sale of unborn young to be born within twelve months after contracting or for the sale of crops to be harvested within twelve months or the next normal harvest season after contracting whichever is longer.

(2) The seller retains an insurable interest in goods so long as title to or any security interest in the goods remains in him and where the identification is by the seller alone he may until default or insolvency or notification to the buyer that the identification is final substitute other goods for those identified.

(3) Nothing in this section impairs any insurable interest recognized under any other statute or rule of law.

§ 2—502. **Buyer's Right to Goods on Seller's Insolvency.**

(1) Subject to subsection (2) and even though the goods have not been shipped a buyer who has paid a part or all of the price of goods in which he has a special property under the provisions of the immediately preceding section may on making and keeping good a tender of any unpaid portion of their price recover them from the seller if the seller becomes insolvent within ten days after receipt of the first installment on their price.

(2) If the identification creating his special property has been made by the buyer he acquires the right to recover the goods only if they conform to the contract for sale.

§ 2—503. **Manner of Seller's Tender of Delivery.**

(1) Tender of delivery requires that the seller put and hold conforming goods at the buyer's disposition and give the buyer any notification reasonably necessary to enable him to take delivery. The manner, time and place for tender are determined by the agreement and this Article, and in particular

(a) tender must be at a reasonable hour, and if it is of goods they must be kept available for the period reasonably necessary to enable the buyer to take possession; but

(b) unless otherwise agreed the buyer must furnish facilities reasonably suited to the receipt of the goods.

(2) Where the case is within the next section respecting shipment tender requires that the seller comply with its provisions.

(3) Where the seller is required to deliver at a particular destination tender requires that he comply with subsection (1) and also in any appropriate case tender documents as described in subsections (4) and (5) of this section.

(4) Where goods are in the possession of a bailee and are to be delivered without being moved

(a) tender requires that the seller either tender a negotiable document of title covering such goods or procure acknowledgment by the bailee of the buyer's right to possession of the goods; but

(b) tender to the buyer of a non-negotiable document of title or of a written direction to the bailee to deliver is sufficient tender unless the buyer seasonably objects, and receipt by the bailee of notification of the buyer's rights fixes those rights as against the bailee and all third persons; but risk of loss of the goods and of any failure by the bailee to honor the non-negotiable document of title or to obey the direction remains on the seller until the buyer has had a reasonable time to present the document or direction, and a refusal by the bailee to honor the document or to obey the direction defeats the tender.

(5) Where the contract requires the seller to deliver documents

(a) he must tender all such documents in correct form, except as provided in this Article with respect to bills of lading in a set (subsection (2) of Section 2—323); and

(b) tender through customary banking channels is sufficient and dishonor of a draft accompanying the documents constitutes non-acceptance or rejection.

§ 2—504. **Shipment by Seller.**

Where the seller is required or authorized to send the goods to the buyer and the contract does not require him to deliver them at a particular destination, then unless otherwise agreed he must

(a) put the goods in the possession of such a carrier and make such a contract for their transportation as may be reasonable having regard to the nature of the goods and other circumstances of the case; and

(b) obtain and promptly deliver or tender in due form any document necessary to enable the buyer to obtain possession of the goods or otherwise required by the agreement or by usage of trade; and

(c) promptly notify the buyer of the shipment.

Failure to notify the buyer under paragraph (c) or to make a proper contract under paragraph (a) is a ground for rejection only if material delay or loss ensues.

§ 2—505. **Seller's Shipment under Reservation.**

(1) Where the seller has identified goods to the contract by or before shipment:

(a) his procurement of a negotiable bill of lading to his own order or otherwise reserves in him a security interest in the goods. His procurement of the bill to the order of a financing agency or of the buyer indicates in addition only the seller's expectation of transferring that interest to the person named.

(b) a non-negotiable bill of lading to himself or his nominee reserves possession of the goods as security but except in a case of conditional delivery (subsection (2) of Section 2—507) a non-negotiable bill of lading naming the buyer as consignee reserves no security interest even though the seller retains possession of the bill of lading.

(2) When shipment by the seller with reservation of a security interest is in violation of the contract for sale it constitutes an improper contract for transportation within the preceding section but impairs neither the rights given to the buyer by shipment and identification of the goods to the contract nor the seller's powers as a holder of a negotiable document.

§ 2—506. **Rights of Financing Agency.**

(1) A financing agency by paying or purchasing for value a draft which relates to a shipment of goods acquires to the extent of the payment or purchase and in addition to its own rights under the draft and any document of title securing it any rights of the shipper in the goods including the right to stop delivery and the shipper's right to have the draft honored by the buyer.

(2) The right to reimbursement of a financing agency which has in good faith honored or purchased the draft under commitment to or authority from the buyer is not impaired by subsequent discovery of defects with reference to any relevant document which was apparently regular on its face.

§ 2—507. **Effect of Seller's Tender; Delivery on Condition.**

(1) Tender of delivery is a condition to the buyer's duty to accept the goods and, unless otherwise agreed, to his duty to pay for them. Tender entitles the seller to acceptance of the goods and to payment according to the contract.

(2) Where payment is due and demanded on the delivery to the buyer of goods or documents of title, his right as against the seller to retain or dispose of them is conditional upon his making the payment due.

§ 2—508. **Cure by Seller of Improper Tender or Delivery; Replacement.**

(1) Where any tender or delivery by the seller is rejected because non-conforming and the time for performance has not yet expired, the seller may seasonably notify the buyer of his intention to cure and may then within the contract time make a conforming delivery.

(2) Where the buyer rejects a non-conforming tender which the seller had reasonable grounds to believe would be acceptable with or without money allowance the seller may if he seasonably notifies the buyer have a further reasonable time to substitute a conforming tender.

§ 2—509. **Risk of Loss in the Absence of Breach.**

(1) Where the contract requires or authorizes the seller to ship the goods by carrier

(a) if it does not require him to deliver them at a particular destination, the risk of loss passes to the buyer when the goods are duly delivered to the carrier even though the shipment is under reservation (Section 2—505); but

(b) if it does require him to deliver them at a particular destination and the goods are there duly tendered while in the possession of the carrier, the risk of loss passes to the buyer when the goods are there duly so tendered as to enable the buyer to take delivery.

(2) Where the goods are held by a bailee to be delivered without being moved, the risk of loss passes to the buyer

(a) on his receipt of a negotiable document of title covering the goods; or

(b) on acknowledgment by the bailee of the buyer's right to possession of the goods; or

(c) after his receipt of a non-negotiable document of title or other written direction to deliver, as provided in subsection (4)(b) of Section 2—503.

(3) In any case not within subsection (1) or (2), the risk of loss passes to the buyer on his receipt of the goods if the seller is a merchant; otherwise the risk passes to the buyer on tender of delivery.

(4) The provisions of this section are subject to contrary agreement of the parties and to the provisions of this Article on sale on approval (Section 2—327) and on effect of breach on risk of loss (Section 2—510).

§ 2—510. **Effect of Breach on Risk of Loss.**

(1) Where a tender or delivery of goods so fails to conform to the contract as to give a right of rejection the risk of their loss remains on the seller until cure or acceptance.

(2) Where the buyer rightfully revokes acceptance he may to the extent of any deficiency in his effective insurance coverage treat the risk of loss as having rested on the seller from the beginning.

(3) Where the buyer as to conforming goods already identified to the contract for sale repudiates or is otherwise in breach before risk of their loss has passed to him, the seller may to the extent of any deficiency in his effective insurance coverage treat the risk of loss as resting on the buyer for a commercially reasonable time.

§ 2—511. **Tender of Payment by Buyer; Payment by Check.**

(1) Unless otherwise agreed tender of payment is a condition to the seller's duty to tender and complete any delivery.

(2) Tender of payment is sufficient when made by any means or in any manner current in the ordinary course of business unless the seller demands payment in legal tender and gives any extension of time reasonably necessary to procure it.

(3) Subject to the provisions of this Act on the effect of an instrument on an obligation (Section 3—802), payment by check is conditional and is defeated as between the parties by dishonor of the check on due presentment.

§ 2—512. **Payment by Buyer Before Inspection.**

(1) Where the contract requires payment before inspection non-conformity of the goods does not excuse the buyer from so making payment unless

(a) the non-conformity appears without inspection; or

(b) despite tender of the required documents the circumstances would justify injunction against honor under the provisions of this Act (Section 5—114).

(2) Payment pursuant to subsection (1) does not constitute an acceptance of goods or impair the buyer's right to inspect or any of his remedies.

§ 2—513. **Buyer's Right to Inspection of Goods.**

(1) Unless otherwise agreed and subject to subsection (3), where goods are tendered or delivered or identified to the contract for sale, the buyer has a right before payment or acceptance to inspect them at any reasonable place and time and in any reasonable manner. When the seller is required or authorized to send the goods to the buyer, the inspection may be after their arrival.

(2) Expenses of inspection must be borne by the buyer but may be recovered from the seller if the goods do not conform and are rejected.

(3) Unless otherwise agreed and subject to the provisions of this Article on C.I.F. contracts (subsection (3) of Section 2—321), the buyer is not entitled to inspect the goods before payment of the price when the contract provides

(a) for delivery "C.O.D." or on other like terms; or

(b) for payment against documents of title, except where such payment is due only after the goods are to become available for inspection.

(4) A place or method of inspection fixed by the parties is presumed to be exclusive but unless otherwise expressly agreed it does not postpone identification or shift the place for delivery or for passing the risk of loss. If compliance becomes impossible, inspection shall be as provided in this section unless the place or method fixed was clearly intended as an indispensable condition failure of which avoids the contract.

§ 2—514. **When Documents Deliverable on Acceptance; When on Payment.**

Unless otherwise agreed documents against which a draft is drawn are to be delivered to the drawee on acceptance of the draft if it is payable more than three days after presentment; otherwise, only on payment.

§ 2—515. **Preserving Evidence of Goods in Dispute.**

In furtherance of the adjustment of any claim or dispute

(a) either party on reasonable notification to the other and for the purpose of ascertaining the facts and preserving evidence has the right to inspect, test and sample the goods including such of them as may be in the possession or control of the other; and

(b) the parties may agree to a third party inspection or survey to determine the conformity or condition of the goods and may agree that the findings shall be binding upon them in any subsequent litigation or adjustment.

Part 6 Breach, Repudiation and Excuse

§ 2—601. **Buyer's Rights on Improper Delivery.**

Subject to the provisions of this Article on breach in installment contracts (Section 2—612) and unless otherwise agreed under the sections on contractual limitations of remedy (Sections 2—718 and 2—719), if the goods or the tender of delivery fail in any respect to conform to the contract, the buyer may

(a) reject the whole; or

(b) accept the whole; or

(c) accept any commercial unit or units and reject the rest.

§ 2—602. **Manner and Effect of Rightful Rejection.**

(1) Rejection of goods must be within a reasonable time after their delivery or tender. It is ineffective unless the buyer seasonably notifies the seller.

(2) Subject to the provisions of the two following sections on rejected goods (Sections 2—603 and 2—604),

(a) after rejection any exercise of ownership by the buyer with respect to any commercial unit is wrongful as against the seller; and

(b) if the buyer has before rejection taken physical possession of goods in which he does not have a security interest under the provisions of this Article (subsection (3) of Section 2—711), he is under a duty after rejection to hold them with reasonable care at the seller's disposition for a time sufficient to permit the seller to remove them; but

(c) the buyer has no further obligations with regard to goods rightfully rejected.

(3) The seller's rights with respect to goods wrongfully rejected are governed by the provisions of this Article on Seller's remedies in general (Section 2—703).

§ 2—603. **Merchant Buyer's Duties as to Rightfully Rejected Goods.**

(1) Subject to any security interest in the buyer (subsection (3) of Section 2—711), when the seller has no agent or place of business at the market of rejection a merchant buyer is under a duty after rejection of goods in his possession or control to follow any reasonable instructions received from the seller with respect to the goods and in the absence of such instructions to make reasonable efforts to sell them for the seller's account if they are perishable or threaten to decline in value speedily. Instructions are not reasonable if on demand indemnity for expenses is not forthcoming.

(2) When the buyer sells goods under subsection (1), he is entitled to reimbursement from the seller or out of the proceeds for reasonable expenses of caring for and selling them, and if the expenses include no selling commission then to such commission as is usual in the trade or if there is none to a reasonable sum not exceeding ten per cent on the gross proceeds.

(3) In complying with this section the buyer is held only to good faith and good faith conduct hereunder is neither acceptance nor conversion nor the basis of an action for damages.

§ 2—604. **Buyer's Options as to Salvage of Rightfully Rejected Goods.**

Subject to the provisions of the immediately preceding section on perishables if the seller gives no instructions within a reasonable time after notification of rejection the buyer may store the rejected goods for the seller's account or reship them to him or resell them for the seller's account with reimbursement as provided in the preceding section. Such action is not acceptance or conversion.

§ 2—605. **Waiver of Buyer's Objections by Failure to Particularize.**

(1) The buyer's failure to state in connection with rejection a particular defect which is ascertainable by reasonable inspection precludes him from relying on the unstated defect to justify rejection or to establish breach

(a) where the seller could have cured it if stated seasonably; or

(b) between merchants when the seller has after rejection made a request in writing for a full and final written statement of all defects on which the buyer proposes to rely.

(2) Payment against documents made without reservation of rights precludes recovery of the payment for defects apparent on the face of the documents.

§ 2—606. **What Constitutes Acceptance of Goods.**

(1) Acceptance of goods occurs when the buyer

(a) after a reasonable opportunity to inspect the goods signifies to the seller that the goods are conforming or that he will take or retain them in spite of their nonconformity; or

(b) fails to make an effective rejection (subsection (1) of Section 2—602), but such acceptance does not occur until the buyer has had a reasonable opportunity to inspect them; or

(c) does any act inconsistent with the seller's ownership; but if such act is wrongful as against the seller it is an acceptance only if ratified by him.

(2) Acceptance of a part of any commercial unit is acceptance of that entire unit.

§ 2—607. **Effect of Acceptance; Notice of Breach; Burden of Establishing Breach After Acceptance; Notice of Claim or Litigation to Person Answerable Over.**

(1) The buyer must pay at the contract rate for any goods accepted.

(2) Acceptance of goods by the buyer precludes rejection of the goods accepted and if made with knowledge of a non-conformity cannot be revoked because of it unless the acceptance was on the reasonable assumption that the non-conformity would be seasonably cured but acceptance does not of itself impair any other remedy provided by this Article for non-conformity.

(3) Where a tender has been accepted

(a) the buyer must within a reasonable time after he discovers or should have discovered any breach notify the seller of breach or be barred from any remedy; and

(b) if the claim is one for infringement or the like (subsection (3) of Section 2—312) and the buyer is sued as a result of such a breach he must so notify the seller within a reasonable time after he receives notice of the litigation or be barred from any remedy over for liability established by the litigation.

(4) The burden is on the buyer to establish any breach with respect to the goods accepted.

(5) Where the buyer is sued for breach of a warranty or other obligation for which his seller is answerable over

(a) he may give his seller written notice of the litigation. If the notice states that the seller may come in and defend and that if the seller does not do so he will be bound in any action against him by his buyer by any determination of fact common to the two litigations, then unless the seller after seasonable receipt of the notice does come in and defend he is so bound.

(b) if the claim is one for infringement or the like (subsection (3) of Section 2—312) the original seller may demand in writing that his buyer turn over to him control of the litigation including settlement or else be barred from any remedy over and if he also agrees to bear all expense and to satisfy any adverse judgment, then unless the buyer after seasonable receipt of the demand does turn over control the buyer is so barred.

(6) The provisions of subsections (3), (4) and (5) apply to any obligation of a buyer to hold the seller harmless against infringement or the like (subsection (3) of Section 2—312).

§ 2—608. **Revocation of Acceptance in Whole or in Part.**

(1) The buyer may revoke his acceptance of a lot or commercial

unit whose non-conformity substantially impairs its value to him if he has accepted it

(a) on the reasonable assumption that its nonconformity would be cured and it has not been seasonably cured; or

(b) without discovery of such non-conformity if his acceptance was reasonably induced either by the difficulty of discovery before acceptance or by the seller's assurances.

(2) Revocation of acceptance must occur within a reasonable time after the buyer discovers or should have discovered the ground for it and before any substantial change in condition of the goods which is not caused by their own defects. It is not effective until the buyer notifies the seller of it.

(3) A buyer who so revokes has the same rights and duties with regard to the goods involved as if he had rejected them.

§ 2—609. **Right to Adequate Assurance of Performance.**

(1) A contract for sale imposes an obligation on each party that the other's expectation of receiving due performance will not be impaired. When reasonable grounds for insecurity arise with respect to the performance of either party the other may in writing demand adequate assurance of due performance and until he receives such assurance may if commercially reasonable suspend any performance for which he has not already received the agreed return.

(2) Between merchants the reasonableness of grounds for insecurity and the adequacy of any assurance offered shall be determined according to commercial standards.

(3) Acceptance of any improper delivery or payment does not prejudice the party's right to demand adequate assurance of future performance.

(4) After receipt of a justified demand failure to provide within a reasonable time not exceeding thirty days such assurance of due performance as is adequate under the circumstances of the particular case is a repudiation of the contract.

§ 2—610. **Anticipatory Repudiation.**

When either party repudiates the contract with respect to a performance not yet due the loss of which will substantially impair the value of the contract to the other, the aggrieved party may

(a) for a commercially reasonable time await performance by the repudiating party; or

(b) resort to any remedy for breach (Section 2—703 or Section 2—711), even though he has notified the repudiating party that he would await the latter's performance and has urged retraction; and

(c) in either case suspend his own performance or proceed in accordance with the provisions of this Article on the seller's right to identify goods to the contract notwithstanding breach or to salvage unfinished goods (Section 2—704).

§ 2—611. **Retraction of Anticipatory Repudiation.**

(1) Until the repudiating party's next performance is due he can retract his repudiation unless the aggrieved party has since the repudiation cancelled or materially changed his position or otherwise indicated that he considers the repudiation final.

(2) Retraction may be by any method which clearly indicates to the aggrieved party that the repudiating party intends to perform, but must include any assurance justifiably demanded under the provisions of this Article (Section 2—609).

(3) Retraction reinstates the repudiating party's rights under the contract with due excuse and allowance to the aggrieved party for any delay occasioned by the repudiation.

§ 2—612. **"Installment Contract"; Breach.**

(1) An "installment contract" is one which requires or authorizes the delivery of goods in separate lots to be separately accepted, even though the contract contains a clause "each delivery is a separate contract" or its equivalent.

(2) The buyer may reject any installment which is nonconforming if the non-conformity substantially impairs the value of that installment and cannot be cured or if the non-conformity is a defect in the required documents; but if the non-conformity does not fall within subsection (3) and the seller gives adequate assurance of its cure the buyer must accept that installment.

(3) Whenever non-conformity or default with respect to one or more installments substantially impairs the value of the whole contract there is a breach of the whole. But the aggrieved party reinstates the contract if he accepts a non-conforming installment without seasonably notifying of cancellation or if he brings an action with respect only to past installments or demands performance as to future installments.

§ 2—613. **Casualty to Identified Goods.**

Where the contract requires for its performance goods identified when the contract is made, and the goods suffer casualty without fault of either party before the risk of loss passes to the buyer, or in a proper case under a "no arrival, no sale" term (Section 2—324) then

(a) if the loss is total the contract is avoided; and

(b) if the loss is partial or the goods have so deteriorated as no longer to conform to the contract the buyer may nevertheless demand inspection and at his option either treat the contract as voided or accept the goods with due allowance from the contract price for the deterioration or the deficiency in quantity but without further right against the seller.

§ 2—614. **Substituted Performance.**

(1) Where without fault of either party the agreed berthing, loading, or unloading facilities fail or an agreed type of carrier becomes unavailable or the agreed manner of delivery otherwise becomes commercially impracticable but a commercially reasonable substitute is available, such substitute performance must be tendered and accepted.

(2) If the agreed means or manner of payment fails because of domestic or foreign governmental regulation, the seller may withhold or stop delivery unless the buyer provides a means or manner of payment which is commercially a substantial equivalent. If delivery has already been taken, payment by the means or in the manner provided by the regulation discharges the buyer's obligation unless the regulation is discriminatory, oppressive or predatory.

§ 2—615. **Excuse by Failure of Presupposed Conditions.**

Except so far as a seller may have assumed a greater obligation and subject to the preceding section on substituted performance:

(a) Delay in delivery or non-delivery in whole or in part by a seller who complies with paragraphs (b) and (c) is not a breach of his duty under a contract for sale if performance as agreed has been made impracticable by the occurrence of a contingency the nonoccurrence of which was a basic assumption on which the contract was made or by compliance in good faith with any applicable foreign or domestic governmental regulation or order whether or not it later proves to be invalid.

(b) Where the causes mentioned in paragraph (a) affect only a part of the seller's capacity to perform, he must allocate production and deliveries among his customers but may at his option include regular customers not then under contract as well as his own requirements for further manufacture. He may so allocate in any manner which is fair and reasonable.

(c) The seller must notify the buyer seasonably that there will be delay or non-delivery and, when allocation is required under paragraph (b), of the estimated quota thus made available for the buyer.

§ 2—616. **Procedure on Notice Claiming Excuse.**

(1) Where the buyer receives notification of a material or indefinite delay or an allocation justified under the preceding section he may by written notification to the seller as to any delivery concerned, and where the prospective deficiency substantially impairs the value of the whole contract under the provisions of this Article relating to breach of installment contracts (Section 2—612), then also as to the whole,

(a) terminate and thereby discharge any unexecuted portion of the contract; or

(b) modify the contract by agreeing to take his available quota in substitution.

(2) If after receipt of such notification from the seller the buyer fails so to modify the contract within a reasonable time not exceeding thirty days the contract lapses with respect to any deliveries affected.

(3) The provisions of this section may not be negated by agreement except in so far as the seller has assumed a greater obligation under the preceding section.

Part 7 Remedies

§ 2—701. **Remedies for Breach of Collateral Contracts Not Impaired.**

Remedies for breach of any obligation or promise collateral or ancillary to a contract for sale are not impaired by the provisions of this Article.

§ 2—702. **Seller's Remedies on Discovery of Buyer's Insolvency.**

(1) Where the seller discovers the buyer to be insolvent he may refuse delivery except for cash including payment for all goods theretofore delivered under the contract, and stop delivery under this Article (Section 2—705).

(2) Where the seller discovers that the buyer has received goods on credit while insolvent he may reclaim the goods upon demand made within ten days after the receipt, but if misrepresentation of solvency has been made to the particular seller in writing within three months before delivery the ten day limitation does not apply. Except as provided in this subsection the seller may not base a right to reclaim goods on the buyer's fraudulent or innocent misrepresentation of solvency or of intent to pay.

(3) The seller's right to reclaim under subsection (2) is subject to the rights of a buyer in ordinary course or other good faith purchaser under this Article (Section 2—403). Successful reclamation of goods excludes all other remedies with respect to them.

§ 2—703. **Seller's Remedies in General.**

Where the buyer wrongfully rejects or revokes acceptance of goods or fails to make a payment due on or before delivery or repudiates with respect to a part or the whole, then with respect to any goods directly affected and, if the breach is of the whole contract (Section 2—612), then also with respect to the whole undelivered balance, the aggrieved seller may

(a) withhold delivery of such goods;

(b) stop delivery by any bailee as hereafter provided (Section 2—705);

(c) proceed under the next section respecting goods still unidentified to the contract;

(d) resell and recover damages as hereafter provided (Section 2—706);

(e) recover damages for non-acceptance (Section 2—708) or in a proper case the price (Section 2—709);

(f) cancel.

§ 2—704. **Seller's Right to Identify Goods to the Contract Notwithstanding Breach or to Salvage Unfinished Goods.**

(1) An aggrieved seller under the preceding section may

(a) identify to the contract conforming goods not already identified if at the time he learned of the breach they are in his possession or control;

(b) treat as the subject of resale goods which have demonstrably been intended for the particular contract even though those goods are unfinished.

(2) Where the goods are unfinished an aggrieved seller may in the exercise of reasonable commercial judgment for the purposes of avoiding loss and of effective realization either complete the manufacture and wholly identify the goods to the contract or cease manufacture and resell for scrap or salvage value or proceed in any other reasonable manner.

§ 2—705. **Seller's Stoppage of Delivery in Transit or Otherwise.**

(1) The seller may stop delivery of goods in the possession of a carrier or other bailee when he discovers the buyer to be insolvent (Section 2—702) and may stop delivery of carload, truckload, planeload or larger shipments of express or freight when the buyer repudiates or fails to make a payment due before delivery or if for any other reason the seller has a right to withhold or reclaim the goods.

(2) As against such buyer the seller may stop delivery until

(a) receipt of the goods by the buyer; or

(b) acknowledgment to the buyer by any bailee of the goods except a carrier that the bailee holds the goods for the buyer; or

(c) such acknowledgment to the buyer by a carrier by reshipment or as warehouseman; or

(d) negotiation to the buyer of any negotiable document of title covering the goods.

(3) (a) To stop delivery the seller must so notify as to enable the bailee by reasonable diligence to prevent delivery of the goods.

(b) After such notification the bailee must hold and deliver the goods according to the directions of the seller but the seller is liable to the bailee for any ensuing charges or damages.

(c) If a negotiable document of title has been issued for goods the bailee is not obliged to obey a notification to stop until surrender of the document.

(d) A carrier who has issued a non-negotiable bill of lading is not obliged to obey a notification to stop received from a person other than the consignor.

§ 2—706. **Seller's Resale Including Contract for Resale.**

(1) Under the conditions stated in Section 2—703 on seller's remedies, the seller may resell the goods concerned or the undelivered balance thereof. Where the resale is made in good faith and in a commercially reasonable manner the seller may recover the difference between the resale price and the contract price together with any incidental damages allowed under the provisions of this Article (Section 2—710), but less expenses saved in consequence of the buyer's breach.

(2) Except as otherwise provided in subsection (3) or unless otherwise agreed resale may be at public or private sale including sale by way of one or more contracts to sell or of identification to an existing contract of the seller. Sale may be as a unit or in parcels and at any time and place and on any terms but every aspect of the sale including the method, manner, time, place and terms must be commercially reasonable. The resale must be reasonably identified as referring to the broken contract, but it is not necessary that the goods be in existence or that any or all of them have been identified to the contract before the breach.

(3) Where the resale is at private sale the seller must give the buyer reasonable notification of his intention to resell.

(4) Where the resale is at public sale

(a) only identified goods can be sold except where there is a recognized market for a public sale of futures in goods of the kind; and

(b) it must be made at a usual place or market for public sale if one is reasonably available and except in the case of goods which are perishable or threaten to decline in value speedily the seller must give the buyer reasonable notice of the time and place of the resale; and

(c) if the goods are not to be within the view of those attending the sale the notification of sale must state the place where the goods are located and provide for their reasonable inspection by prospective bidders; and

(d) the seller may buy.

(5) A purchaser who buys in good faith at a resale takes the goods free of any rights of the original buyer even though the seller fails to comply with one or more of the requirements of this section.

(6) The seller is not accountable to the buyer for any profit made on any resale. A person in the position of a seller (Section 2—707) or a buyer who has rightfully rejected or justifiably revoked acceptance must account for any excess over the amount of his security interest, as hereinafter defined (subsection (3) of Section 2—711).

§ 2—707. **"Person in the Position of a Seller".**

(1) A "person in the position of a seller" includes as against a principal an agent who has paid or become responsible for the price of goods on behalf of his principal or anyone who otherwise holds a security interest or other right in goods similar to that of a seller.

(2) A person in the position of a seller may as provided in this Article withhold or stop delivery (Section 2—705) and resell (Section 2—706) and recover incidental damages (Section 2—710).

§ 2—708. **Seller's Damages for Non-Acceptance or Repudiation.**

(1) Subject to subsection (2) and to the provisions of this Article with respect to proof of market price (Section 2—723), the measure of damages for non-acceptance or repudiation by the buyer is the difference between the market price at the time and place for tender and the unpaid contract price together with any incidental damages provided in this Article (Section 2—710), but less expenses saved in consequence of the buyer's breach.

(2) If the measure of damages provided in subsection (1) is inadequate to put the seller in as good a position as performance would have done then the measure of damages is the profit (including reasonable overhead) which the seller would have made from full performance by the buyer, together with any incidental damages provided in this Article (Section 2—710), due allowance for costs reasonably incurred and due credit for payments or proceeds of resale.

§ 2—709. **Action for the Price.**

(1) When the buyer fails to pay the price as it becomes due the seller may recover, together with any incidental damages under the next section, the price

(a) of goods accepted or of conforming goods lost or damaged within a commercially reasonable time after risk of their loss has passed to the buyer; and

(b) of goods identified to the contract if the seller is unable after reasonable effort to resell them at a reasonable price or the circumstances reasonably indicate that such effort will be unavailing.

(2) Where the seller sues for the price he must hold for the buyer any goods which have been identified to the contract and are still in his control except that if resale becomes possible he may resell them at any time prior to the collection of the judgment. The net proceeds of any such resale must be credited to the buyer and payment of the judgment entitles him to any goods not resold.

(3) After the buyer has wrongfully rejected or revoked acceptance of the goods or has failed to make a payment due or has repudiated (Section 2—610), a seller who is held not entitled to the price under this section shall nevertheless be awarded damages for non-acceptance under the preceding section.

§ 2—710. **Seller's Incidental Damages.**

Incidental damages to an aggrieved seller include any commercially reasonable charges, expenses or commissions incurred in stopping delivery, in the transportation, care and custody of goods after the buyer's breach, in connection with return or resale of the goods or otherwise resulting from the breach.

§ 2—711. **Buyer's Remedies in General; Buyer's Security Interest in Rejected Goods.**

(1) Where the seller fails to make delivery or repudiates or the buyer rightfully rejects or justifiably revokes acceptance then with respect to any goods involved, and with respect to the whole if the breach goes to the whole contract (Section 2—612), the buyer may cancel and whether or not he has done so may in addition to recovering so much of the price as has been paid

(a) "cover" and have damages under the next section as to all the goods affected whether or not they have been identified to the contract; or

(b) recover damages for non-delivery as provided in this Article (Section 2—713).

(2) Where the seller fails to deliver or repudiates the buyer may also

(a) if the goods have been identified recover them as provided in this Article (Section 2—502); or

(b) in a proper case obtain specific performance or replevy the goods as provided in this Article (Section 2—716).

(3) On rightful rejection or justifiable revocation of acceptance a buyer has a security interest in goods in his possession or control for any payments made on their price and any expenses reasonably incurred in their inspection, receipt, transportation, care and custody and may hold such goods and resell them in like manner as an aggrieved seller (Section 2—706).

§ 2—712. **"Cover"; Buyer's Procurement of Substitute Goods.**

(1) After a breach within the preceding section the buyer may "cover" by making in good faith and without unreasonable delay any reasonable purchase of or contract to purchase goods in substitution for those due from the seller.

(2) The buyer may recover from the seller as damages the difference between the cost of cover and the contract price together with any incidental or consequential damages as hereinafter defined (Section 2—715), but less expenses saved in consequence of the seller's breach.

(3) Failure of the buyer to effect cover within this section does not bar him from any other remedy.

§ 2—713. **Buyer's Damages for Non-Delivery or Repudiation.**

(1) Subject to the provisions of this Article with respect to proof of market price (Section 2—723), the measure of damages for non-delivery or repudiation by the seller is the difference between the market price at the time when the buyer learned of the breach and the contract price together with any incidental and consequential damages provided in this Article (Section 2—715), but less expenses saved in consequence of the seller's breach.

(2) Market price is to be determined as of the place for tender or, in cases of rejection after arrival or revocation of acceptance, as of the place of arrival.

§ 2—714. **Buyer's Damages for Breach in Regard to Accepted Goods.**

(1) Where the buyer has accepted goods and given notification (subsection (3) of Section 2—607) he may recover as damages for any non-conformity of tender the loss resulting in the ordinary course of events from the seller's breach as determined in any manner which is reasonable.

(2) The measure of damages for breach of warranty is the difference at the time and place of acceptance between the value of the goods accepted and the value they would have had if they had been as warranted, unless special circumstances show proximate damages of a different amount.

(3) In a proper case any incidental and consequential damages under the next section may also be recovered.

§ 2—715. **Buyer's Incidental and Consequential Damages.**

(1) Incidental damages resulting from the seller's breach include expenses reasonably incurred in inspection, receipt, transportation and care and custody of goods rightfully rejected, any commercially reasonable charges, expenses or commissions in connection with effecting cover and any other reasonable expense incident to the delay or other breach.

(2) Consequential damages resulting from the seller's breach include

(a) any loss resulting from general or particular requirements and needs of which the seller at the time of contracting had reason to know and which could not reasonably be prevented by cover or otherwise; and

(b) injury to person or property proximately resulting from any breach of warranty.

§ 2—716. **Buyer's Right to Specific Performance or Replevin.**

(1) Specific performance may be decreed where the goods are unique or in other proper circumstances.

(2) The decree for specific performance may include such terms and conditions as to payment of the price, damages, or other relief as the court may deem just.

(3) The buyer has a right of replevin for goods identified to the contract if after reasonable effort he is unable to effect cover for such goods or the circumstances reasonably indicate that such effort will be unavailing or if the goods have been shipped under reservation and satisfaction of the security interest in them has been made or tendered.

§ 2—717. **Deduction of Damages From the Price.**

The buyer on notifying the seller of his intention to do so may deduct all or any part of the damages resulting from any breach of the contract from any part of the price still due under the same contract.

§ 2—718. **Liquidation or Limitation of Damages; Deposits.**

(1) Damages for breach by either party may be liquidated in the agreement but only at an amount which is reasonable in the light of the anticipated or actual harm caused by the breach, the difficulties of proof of loss, and the inconvenience or nonfeasibility of otherwise obtaining an adequate remedy. A term fixing unreasonably large liquidated damages is void as a penalty.

(2) Where the seller justifiably withholds delivery of goods be-

cause of the buyer's breach, the buyer is entitled to restitution of any amount by which the sum of his payments exceeds

(a) the amount to which the seller is entitled by virtue of terms liquidating the seller's damages in accordance with subsection (1), or

(b) in the absence of such terms, twenty per cent of the value of the total performance for which the buyer is obligated under the contract or $500, whichever is smaller.

(3) The buyer's right to restitution under subsection (2) is subject to offset to the extent that the seller establishes

(a) a right to recover damages under the provisions of this Article other than subsection (1), and

(b) the amount or value of any benefits received by the buyer directly or indirectly by reason of the contract.

(4) Where a seller has received payment in goods their reasonable value or the proceeds of their resale shall be treated as payments for the purposes of subsection (2); but if the seller has notice of the buyer's breach before reselling goods received in part performance, his resale is subject to the conditions laid down in this Article on resale by an aggrieved seller (Section 2—706).

§ 2—719. **Contractual Modification or Limitation of Remedy.**

(1) Subject to the provisions of subsections (2) and (3) of this section and of the preceding section on liquidation and limitation of damages,

(a) the agreement may provide for remedies in addition to or in substitution for those provided in this Article and may limit or alter the measure of damages recoverable under this Article, as by limiting the buyer's remedies to return of the goods and repayment of the price or to repair and replacement of non-conforming goods or parts; and

(b) resort to a remedy as provided is optional unless the remedy is expressly agreed to be exclusive, in which case it is the sole remedy.

(2) Where circumstances cause an exclusive or limited remedy to fail of its essential purpose, remedy may be had as provided in this Act.

(3) Consequential damages may be limited or excluded unless the limitation or exclusion is unconscionable. Limitation of consequential damages for injury to the person in the case of consumer goods is prima facie unconscionable but limitation of damages where the loss is commercial is not.

§ 2—720. **Effect of "Cancellation" or "Rescission" on Claims for Antecedent Breach.**

Unless the contrary intention clearly appears, expressions of "cancellation" or "rescission" of the contract or the like shall not be construed as a renunciation or discharge of any claim in damages for an antecedent breach.

§ 2—721. **Remedies for Fraud.**

Remedies for material misrepresentation or fraud include all remedies available under this Article for non-fraudulent breach. Neither rescission or a claim for rescission of the contract for sale nor rejection or return of the goods shall bar or be deemed inconsistent with a claim for damages or other remedy.

§ 2—722. **Who Can Sue Third Parties for Injury to Goods.**

Where a third party so deals with goods which have been identified to a contract for sale as to cause actionable injury to a party to that contract

(a) a right of action against the third party is in either party to the contract for sale who has title to or a security interest or a special property or an insurable interest in the goods; and if the goods have been destroyed or converted a right of action is also in the party who either bore the risk of loss under the contract for sale or has since the injury assumed that risk as against the other;

(b) if at the time of the injury the party plaintiff did not bear the risk of loss as against the other party to the contract for sale and there is no arrangement between them for disposition of the recovery, his suit or settlement is, subject to his own interest, as a fiduciary for the other party to the contract;

(c) either party may with the consent of the other sue for the benefit of whom it may concern.

§ 2—723. **Proof of Market Price: Time and Place.**

(1) If an action based on anticipatory repudiation comes to trial before the time for performance with respect to some or all of the goods, any damages based on market price (Section 2—708 or Section 2—713) shall be determined according to the price of such goods prevailing at the time when the aggrieved party learned of the repudiation.

(2) If evidence of a price prevailing at the times or places described in this Article is not readily available the price prevailing within any reasonable time before or after the time described or at any other place which in commercial judgment or under usage of trade would serve as a reasonable substitute for the one described may be used, making any proper allowance for the cost of transporting the goods to or from such other place.

(3) Evidence of a relevant price prevailing at a time or place other than the one described in this Article offered by one party is not admissible unless and until he has given the other party such notice as the court finds sufficient to prevent unfair surprise.

§ 2—724. **Admissibility of Market Quotations.**

Whenever the prevailing price or value of any goods regularly bought and sold in any established commodity market is in issue, reports in official publications or trade journals or in newspapers or periodicals of general circulation published as the reports of such market shall be admissible in evidence. The circumstances of the preparation of such a report may be shown to affect its weight but not its admissibility.

§ 2—725. **Statute of Limitations in Contracts for Sale.**

(1) An action for breach of any contract for sale must be commenced within four years after the cause of action has accrued. By the original agreement the parties may reduce the period of limitation to not less than one year but may not extend it.

(2) A cause of action accrues when the breach occurs, regardless of the aggrieved party's lack of knowledge of the breach. A breach of warranty occurs when tender of delivery is made, except that where a warranty explicitly extends to future performance of the goods and discovery of the breach must await the time of such performance the cause of action accrues when the breach is or should have been discovered.

(3) Where an action commenced within the time limited by subsection (1) is so terminated as to leave available a remedy by another action for the same breach such other action may be commenced after the expiration of the time limited and within six months after the termination of the first action unless the termination resulted from voluntary discontinuance or from dismissal for failure or neglect to prosecute.

(4) This section does not alter the law on tolling of the statute of limitations nor does it apply to causes of action which have accrued before this Act becomes effective.

Article 3
COMMERCIAL PAPER

Part 1 Short Title, Form and Interpretation

§ 3—101. **Short Title.**

This Article shall be known and may be cited as Uniform Commercial Code—Commercial Paper.

§ 3—102. **Definitions and Index of Definitions.**

(1) In this Article unless the context otherwise requires

(a) "Issue" means the first delivery of an instrument to a holder or a remitter.

(b) An "order" is a direction to pay and must be more than an authorization or request. It must identify the person to pay with reasonable certainty. It may be addressed to one or more such persons jointly or in the alternative but not in succession.

(c) A "promise" is an undertaking to pay and must be more than an acknowledgment of an obligation.

(d) "Secondary party" means a drawer or indorser.

(e) "Instrument" means a negotiable instrument.

(2) Other definitions applying to this Article and the sections in which they appear are:
"Acceptance". Section 3—410.
"Accommodation party". Section 3—415.
"Alteration". Section 3—407.
"Certificate of deposit". Section 3—104.
"Certification". Section 3—411.
"Check". Section 3—104.
"Definite time". Section 3—109.
"Dishonor". Section 3—507.
"Draft". Section 3—104.
"Holder in due course". Section 3—302.
"Negotiation". Section 3—202.
"Note". Section 3—104.
"Notice of dishonor". Section 3—508.
"On demand". Section 3—108.
"Presentment". Section 3—504.
"Protest". Section 3—509.
"Restrictive Indorsement". Section 3—205.
"Signature". Section 3—401.

(3) The following definitions in other Articles apply to this Article:
"Account". Section 4—104.
"Banking Day". Section 4—104.
"Clearing House". Section 4—104.
"Collecting Bank". Section 4—105.
"Customer". Section 4—104.
"Depositary Bank". Section 4—105.
"Documentary Draft". Section 4—104.
"Intermediary Bank". Section 4—105.
"Item". Section 4—104.
"Midnight deadline". Section 4—104.
"Payor Bank". Section 4—105.

(4) In addition Article 1 contains general definitions and principles of construction and interpretation applicable throughout this Article.

§ 3—103. **Limitations on Scope of Article.**

(1) This Article does not apply to money, documents of title or investment securities.

(2) The provisions of this Article are subject to the provisions of the Article on Bank Deposits and Collections (Article 4) and Secured Transactions (Article 9).

§ 3—104. **Form of Negotiable Instruments; "Draft"; "Check"; "Certificate of Deposit"; "Note".**

(1) Any writing to be a negotiable instrument within this Article must

(a) be signed by the maker or drawer; and

(b) contain an unconditional promise or order to pay a sum certain in money and no other promise, order, obligation or power given by the maker or drawer except as authorized by this Article; and

(c) be payable on demand or at a definite time; and

(d) be payable to order or to bearer.

(2) A writing which complies with the requirements of this section is

(a) a "draft" ("bill of exchange") if it is an order;

(b) a "check" if it is a draft drawn on a bank and payable on demand;

(c) a "certificate of deposit" if it is an acknowledgment by a bank receipt of money with an engagement to repay it;

(d) a "note" if it is a promise other than a certificate of deposit.

(3) As used in other Articles of this Act, and as the context may require, the terms "draft", "check", "certificate of deposit" and "note" may refer to instruments which are not negotiable within this Article as well as to instruments which are so negotiable.

§ 3—105. **When Promise or Order Unconditional.**

(1) A promise or order otherwise unconditional is not made conditional by the fact that the instrument

(a) is subject to implied or constructive conditions; or

(b) states its consideration, whether performed or promised, or the transaction which gave rise to the instrument, or that the promise or order is made or the instrument matures in accordance with or "as per" such transaction; or

(c) refers to or states that it arises out of a separate agreement or refers to a separate agreement for rights as to prepayment or acceleration; or

(d) states that it is drawn under a letter of credit; or

(e) states that it is secured, whether by mortgage, reservation of title or otherwise; or

(f) indicates a particular account to be debited or any other fund or source from which reimbursement is expected; or

(g) is limited to payment out of a particular fund or the proceeds of a particular source, if the instrument is issued by a government or governmental agency or unit; or

(h) is limited to payment out of the entire assets of a partnership, unincorporated association, trust or estate by or on behalf of which the instrument is issued.

(2) A promise or order is not unconditional if the instrument

(a) states that it is subject to or governed by any other agreement; or

(b) states that it is to be paid only out of a particular fund or source except as provided in this section.

§ 3—106. **Sum Certain.**

(1) The sum payable is a sum certain even though it is to be paid

(a) with stated interest or by stated installments; or

(b) with stated different rates of interest before and after default or a specified date; or

(c) with a stated discount or addition if paid before or after the date fixed for payment; or

(d) with exchange or less exchange, whether at a fixed rate or at the current rate; or

(e) with costs of collection or an attorney's fee or both upon default.

(2) Nothing in this section shall validate any term which is otherwise illegal.

§ 3—107. **Money.**

(1) An instrument is payable in money if the medium of exchange in which it is payable is money at the time the instrument is made. An instrument payable in "currency" or "current funds" is payable in money.

(2) A promise or order to pay a sum stated in a foreign currency is for a sum certain in money and, unless a different medium of payment is specified in the instrument, may be satisfied by payment of that number of dollars which the stated foreign currency will purchase at the buying sight rate for that currency on the day on which the instrument is payable or, if payable on demand, on the day of demand. If such an instrument specifies a foreign currency as the medium of payment the instrument is payable in that currency.

§ 3—108. **Payable on Demand.**

Instruments payable on demand include those payable at sight or on presentation and those in which no time for payment is stated.

§ 3—109. **Definite Time.**

(1) An instrument is payable at a definite time if by its terms it is payable

(a) on or before a stated date or at a fixed period after a stated date; or

(b) at a fixed period after sight; or

(c) at a definite time subject to any acceleration; or

(d) at a definite time subject to extension at the option of the holder, or to extension to a further definite time at the option of the maker or acceptor or automatically upon or after a specified act or event.

(2) An instrument which by its terms is otherwise payable only upon an act or event uncertain as to time of occurrence is not payable at a definite time even though the act or event has occurred.

§ 3—110. **Payable to Order.**

(1) An instrument is payable to order when by its terms it is payable to the order or assigns of any person therein specified with reasonable certainty, or to him or his order, or when it is conspicuously designated on its face as "exchange" or the like and names a payee. It may be payable to the order of

(a) the maker or drawer; or

(b) the drawee; or

(c) a payee who is not maker, drawer or drawee; or

(d) two or more payees together or in the alternative; or

(e) an estate, trust or fund, in which case it is payable to the order of the representative of such estate, trust or fund or his successors; or

(f) an office, or an officer by his title as such in which case it is payable to the principal but the incumbent of the office or his successors may act as if he or they were the holder; or

(g) a partnership or unincorporated association, in which case it is payable to the partnership or association and may be indorsed or transferred by any person thereto authorized.

(2) An instrument not payable to order is not made so payable by such words as "payable upon return of this instrument properly indorsed."

(3) An instrument made payable both to order and to bearer is payable to order unless the bearer words are handwritten or typewritten.

§ 3—111. **Payable to Bearer.**

An instrument is payable to bearer when by its terms it is payable to

(a) bearer or the order of bearer; or

(b) a specified person or bearer; or

(c) "cash" or the order of "cash", or any other indication which does not purport to designate a specific payee.

§ 3—112. **Terms and Omissions Not Affecting Negotiability.**

(1) The negotiability of an instrument is not affected by

(a) the omission of a statement of any consideration or of the place where the instrument is drawn or payable; or

(b) a statement that collateral has been given to secure obligations either on the instrument or otherwise of an obligor on the instrument or that in case of default on those obligations the holder may realize on or dispose of the collateral; or

(c) a promise or power to maintain or protect collateral or to give additional collateral; or

(d) a term authorizing a confession of judgment on the instrument if it is not paid when due; or

(e) a term purporting to waive the benefit of any law intended for the advantage or protection of any obligor; or

(f) a term in a draft providing that the payee by indorsing or cashing it acknowledges full satisfaction of an obligation of the drawer; or

(g) a statement in a draft drawn in a set of parts (Section 3—801) to the effect that the order is effective only if no other part has been honored.

(2) Nothing in this section shall validate any term which is otherwise illegal.

§ 3—113. **Seal.**

An instrument otherwise negotiable is within this Article even though it is under a seal.

§ 3—114. **Date, Antedating, Postdating.**

(1) The negotiability of an instrument is not affected by the fact that it is undated, antedated or postdated.

(2) Where an instrument is antedated or postdated the time when it is payable is determined by the stated date if the instrument is payable on demand or at a fixed period after date.

(3) Where the instrument or any signature thereon is dated, the date is presumed to be correct.

§ 3—115. **Incomplete Instruments.**

(1) When a paper whose contents at the time of signing show that it is intended to become an instrument is signed while still incomplete in any necessary respect it cannot be enforced until completed, but when it is completed in accordance with authority given it is effective as completed.

(2) If the completion is unauthorized the rules as to material alteration apply (Section 3—407), even though the paper was not delivered by the maker or drawer; but the burden of establishing that any completion is unauthorized is on the party so asserting.

§ 3—116. **Instruments Payable to Two or More Persons.**

An instrument payable to the order of two or more persons

(a) if in the alternative is payable to any one of them and may be negotiated, discharged or enforced by any of them who has possession of it;

(b) if not in the alternative is payable to all of them and may be negotiated, discharged or enforced only by all of them.

§ 3—117. **Instruments Payable With Words of Description.**

An instrument made payable to a named person with the addition of words describing him

(a) as agent or officer of a specified person is payable to his principal but the agent or officer may act as if he were the holder;

(b) as any other fiduciary for a specified person or purpose is payable to the payee and may be negotiated, discharged or enforced by him;

(c) in any other manner is payable to the payee unconditionally and the additional words are without effect on subsequent parties.

§ 3—118. **Ambiguous Terms and Rules of Construction.**

The following rules apply to every instrument:

(a) Where there is doubt whether the instrument is a draft or a note the holder may treat it as either. A draft drawn on the drawer is effective as a note.

(b) Handwritten terms control typewritten and printed terms, and typewritten control printed.

(c) Words control figures except that if the words are ambiguous figures control.

(d) Unless otherwise specified a provision for interest means interest at the judgment rate at the place of payment from the date of the instrument, or if it is undated from the date of issue.

(e) Unless the instrument otherwise specifies two or more persons who sign as maker, acceptor or drawer or indorser and as a part of the same transaction are jointly and severally liable even though the instrument contains such words as "I promise to pay."

(f) Unless otherwise specified consent to extension authorizes a single extension for not longer than the original period. A consent to extension, expressed in the instrument, is binding on secondary parties and accommodation makers. A holder may not exercise his option to extend an instrument over the objection of a maker or acceptor or other party who in accordance with Section 3—604 tenders full payment when the instrument is due.

§ 3—119. **Other Writings Affecting Instrument.**

(1) As between the obligor and his immediate obligee or any transferee the terms of an instrument may be modified or affected by any other written agreement executed as a part of the same transaction, except that a holder in due course is not affected by any limitation of his rights arising out of the separate written agreement if he had no notice of the limitation when he took the instrument.

(2) A separate agreement does not affect the negotiability of an instrument.

§ 3—120. **Instruments "Payable Through" Bank.**

An instrument which states that it is "payable through" a bank or the like designates that bank as a collecting bank to make presentment but does not of itself authorize the bank to pay the instrument.

§ 3—121. **Instruments Payable at Bank.**

Note: If this Act is introduced in the Congress of the United States this section should be omitted.
(States to select either alternative)

Alternative A—

A note or acceptance which states that it is payable at a bank is the equivalent of a draft drawn on the bank payable when it falls due out of any funds of the maker or acceptor in current account or otherwise available for such payment.

Alternative B—

A note or acceptance which states that it is payable at a bank is not of itself an order or authorization to the bank to pay it.

§ 3—122. **Accrual of Cause of Action.**

(1) A cause of action against a maker or an acceptor accrues

(a) in the case of a time instrument on the day after maturity;

(b) in the case of a demand instrument upon its date or, if no date is stated, on the date of issue.

(2) A cause of action against the obligor of a demand or time certificate of deposit accrues upon demand, but demand on a time certificate may not be made until on or after the date of maturity.

(3) A cause of action against a drawer of a draft or an indorser of any instrument accrues upon demand following dishonor of the instrument. Notice of dishonor is a demand.

(4) Unless an instrument provides otherwise, interest runs at the rate provided by law for a judgment

(a) in the case of a maker, acceptor or other primary obligor of a demand instrument, from the date of demand;

(b) in all other cases from the date of accrual of the cause of action.

Part 2 Transfer and Negotiation

§ 3—201. **Transfer: Right to Indorsement.**

(1) Transfer of an instrument vests in the transferee such rights as the transferor has therein, except that a transferee who has himself been a party to any fraud or illegality affecting the instrument or who as a prior holder had notice of a defense or claim against it cannot improve his position by taking from a later holder in due course.

(2) A transfer of a security interest in an instrument vests the foregoing rights in the transferee to the extent of the interest transferred.

(3) Unless otherwise agreed any transfer for value of an instrument not then payable to bearer gives the transferee the specifically enforceable right to have the unqualified indorsement of the transferor. Negotiation takes effect only when the indorsement is made and until that time there is no presumption that the transferee is the owner.

§ 3—202. **Negotiation.**

(1) Negotiation is the transfer of an instrument in such form that the transferee becomes a holder. If the instrument is payable to order it is negotiated by delivery with any necessary indorsement; if payable to bearer it is negotiated by delivery.

(2) An indorsement must be written by or on behalf of the holder and on the instrument or on a paper so firmly affixed thereto as to become a part thereof.

(3) An indorsement is effective for negotiation only when it conveys the entire instrument or any unpaid residue. If it purports to be of less it operates only as a partial assignment.

(4) Words of assignment, condition, waiver, guaranty, limitation or disclaimer of liability and the like accompanying an indorsement do not affect its character as an indorsement.

§ 3—203. **Wrong or Misspelled Name.**

Where an instrument is made payable to a person under a misspelled name or one other than his own he may indorse in that name or his own or both; but signature in both names may be required by a person paying or giving value for the instrument.

§ 3—204. **Special Indorsement; Blank Indorsement.**

(1) A special indorsement specifies the person to whom or to whose order it makes the instrument payable. Any instrument specially indorsed becomes payable to the order of the special indorsee and may be further negotiated only by his indorsement.

(2) An indorsement in blank specifies no particular indorsee and may consist of a mere signature. An instrument payable to order and indorsed in blank becomes payable to bearer and may be negotiated by delivery alone until specially indorsed.

(3) The holder may convert a blank indorsement into a special indorsement by writing over the signature of the indorser in blank any contract consistent with the character of the indorsement.

§ 3—205. **Restrictive Indorsements.**

An indorsement is restrictive which either

(a) is conditional; or

(b) purports to prohibit further transfer of the instrument; or

(c) includes the words "for collection", "for deposit", "pay any bank", or like terms signifying a purpose of deposit or collection; or

(d) otherwise states that it is for the benefit or use of the indorser or of another person.

§ 3—206. **Effect of Restrictive Indorsement.**

(1) No restrictive indorsement prevents further transfer or negotiation of the instrument.

(2) An intermediary bank, or a payor bank which is not the depositary bank, is neither given notice nor otherwise affected by a restrictive indorsement of any person except the bank's immediate transferor or the person presenting for payment.

(3) Except for an intermediary bank, any transferee under an indorsement which is conditional or includes the words "for collection", "for deposit", "pay any bank", or like terms (subparagraphs (a) and (c) of Section 3—205) must pay or apply any value given by him for or on the security of the instrument consistently with the indorsement and to the extent that he does so he becomes a holder for value. In addition such transferee is a holder in due course if he otherwise complies with the requirements of Section 3—302 on what constitutes a holder in due course.

(4) The first taker under an indorsement for the benefit of the indorser or another person (subparagraph (d) of Section 3—205) must pay or apply any value given by him for or on the security of the instrument consistently with the indorsement and to the extent that he does so he becomes a holder for value. In addition such taker is a holder in due course if he otherwise complies with the requirements of Section 3—302 on what constitutes a holder in due course. A later holder for value is neither given notice nor otherwise affected by such restrictive indorsement unless he has knowledge that a fiduciary or other person has negotiated the instrument in any transaction for his own benefit or otherwise in breach of duty (subsection (2) of Section 3—304).

§ 3—207. **Negotiation Effective Although It May Be Rescinded.**

(1) Negotiation is effective to transfer the instrument although the negotiation is

(a) made by an infant, a corporation exceeding its powers, or any other person without capacity; or

(b) obtained by fraud, duress or mistake of any kind; or

(c) part of an illegal transaction; or

(d) made in breach of duty.

(2) Except as against a subsequent holder in due course such negotiation is in an appropriate case subject to rescission, the declaration of a constructive trust or any other remedy permitted by law.

§ 3—208. **Reacquisition.**

Where an instrument is returned to or reacquired by a prior party he may cancel any indorsement which is not necessary to his title and reissue or further negotiate the instrument, but any intervening party is discharged as against the reacquiring party and subsequent holders not in due course and if his indorsement has been cancelled is discharged as against subsequent holders in due course as well.

Part 3 Rights of a Holder

§ 3—301. **Rights of a Holder.**

The holder of an instrument whether or not he is the owner may transfer or negotiate it and, except as otherwise provided in Section 3—603 on payment or satisfaction, discharge it or enforce payment in his own name.

§ 3—302. **Holder in Due Course.**

(1) A holder in due course is a holder who takes the instrument

(a) for value; and

(b) in good faith; and

(c) without notice that it is overdue or has been dishonored or of any defense against or claim to it on the part of any person.

(2) A payee may be a holder in due course.

(3) A holder does not become a holder in due course of an instrument:

(a) by purchase of it at judicial sale or by taking it under legal process; or

(b) by acquiring it in taking over an estate; or

(c) by purchasing it as part of a bulk transaction not in regular course of business of the transferor.

(4) A purchaser of a limited interest can be a holder in due course only to the extent of the interest purchased.

§ 3—303. **Taking for Value.**

A holder takes the instrument for value

(a) to the extent that the agreed consideration has been performed or that he acquires a security interest in or a lien on the instrument otherwise than by legal process; or

(b) when he takes the instrument in payment of or as security for an antecedent claim against any person whether or not the claim is due; or

(c) when he gives a negotiable instrument for it or makes an irrevocable commitment to a third person.

§ 3—304. **Notice to Purchaser.**

(1) The purchaser has notice of a claim or defense if

(a) the instrument is so incomplete, bears such visible evidence of forgery or alteration, or is otherwise so irregular as to call into question its validity, terms or ownership or to create an ambiguity as to the party to pay; or

(b) the purchaser has notice that the obligation of any party is voidable in whole or in part, or that all parties have been discharged.

(2) The purchaser has notice of a claim against the instrument when he has knowledge that a fiduciary has negotiated the instrument in payment of or as security for his own debt or in any transaction for his own benefit or otherwise in breach of duty.

(3) The purchaser has notice that an instrument is overdue if he has reason to know

(a) that any part of the principal amount is overdue or that there is an uncured default in payment of another instrument of the same series; or

(b) that acceleration of the instrument has been made; or

(c) that he is taking a demand instrument after demand has been made or more than a reasonable length of time after its issue. A reasonable time for a check drawn and payable within the states and territories of the United States and the District of Columbia is presumed to be thirty days.

(4) Knowledge of the following facts does not of itself give the purchaser notice of a defense or claim

(a) that the instrument is antedated or postdated;

(b) that it was issued or negotiated in return for an executory promise or accompanied by a separate agreement, unless the purchaser has notice that a defense or claim has arisen from the terms thereof;

(c) that any party has signed for accommodation;

(d) that an incomplete instrument has been completed, unless the purchaser has notice of any improper completion;

(e) that any person negotiating the instrument is or was a fiduciary;

(f) that there has been default in payment of interest on the instrument or in payment of any other instrument, except one of the same series.

(5) The filing or recording of a document does not of itself constitute notice within the provisions of this Article to a person who would otherwise be a holder in due course.

(6) To be effective notice must be received at such time and in such manner as to give a reasonable opportunity to act on it.

§ 3—305. **Rights of a Holder in Due Course.**

To the extent that a holder is a holder in due course he takes the instrument free from

(1) all claims to it on the part of any person; and

(2) all defenses of any party to the instrument with whom the holder has not dealt except

(a) infancy, to the extent that it is a defense to a simple contract; and

(b) such other incapacity, or duress, or illegality of the transaction, as renders the obligation of the party a nullity; and

(c) such misrepresentation as has induced the party to sign the instrument with neither knowledge nor reasonable opportunity to obtain knowledge of its character or its essential terms; and

(d) discharge in insolvency proceedings; and

(e) any other discharge of which the holder has notice when he takes the instrument.

§ 3—306. **Rights of One Not Holder in Due Course.**

Unless he has the rights of a holder in due course any person takes the instrument subject to

(a) all valid claims to it on the part of any person; and

(b) all defenses of any party which would be available in an action on a simple contract; and

(c) the defenses of want or failure of consideration, nonperformance of any condition precedent, non-delivery, or delivery for a special purpose (Section 3—408); and

(d) the defense that he or a person through whom he holds the instrument acquired it by theft, or that payment or satisfaction to such holder would be inconsistent with the terms of a restrictive indorsement. The claim of any third person to the instrument is not otherwise available as a defense to any party liable thereon unless the third person himself defends the action for such party.

§ 3—307. **Burden of Establishing Signatures, Defenses and Due Course.**

(1) Unless specifically denied in the pleadings each signature on an instrument is admitted. When the effectiveness of a signature is put in issue

(a) the burden of establishing it is on the party claiming under the signature; but

(b) the signature is presumed to be genuine or authorized except where the action is to enforce the obligation of a purported signer who has died or become incompetent before proof is required.

(2) When signatures are admitted or established, production of the instrument entitles a holder to recover on it unless the defendant establishes a defense.

(3) After it is shown that a defense exists a person claiming the rights of a holder in due course has the burden of establishing that he or some person under whom he claims is in all respects a holder in due course.

Part 4 Liability of Parties

§ 3—401. **Signature.**

(1) No person is liable on an instrument unless his signature appears thereon.

(2) A signature is made by use of any name, including any trade or assumed name, upon an instrument, or by any word or mark used in lieu of a written signature.

§ 3—402. **Signature in Ambiguous Capacity.**

Unless the instrument clearly indicates that a signature is made in some other capacity it is an indorsement.

§ 3—403. **Signature by Authorized Representative.**

(1) A signature may be made by an agent or other representative, and his authority to make it may be established as in other cases of representation. No particular form of appointment is necessary to establish such authority.

(2) An authorized representative who signs his own name to an instrument

(a) is personally obligated if the instrument neither names the person represented nor shows that the representative signed in a representative capacity;

(b) except as otherwise established between the immediate parties, is personally obligated if the instrument names the person represented but does not show that the representative signed in a representative capacity, or if the instrument does not name the person represented but does show that the representative signed in a representative capacity.

(3) Except as otherwise established the name of an organization preceded or followed by the name and office of an authorized individual is a signature made in a representative capacity.

§ 3—404. **Unauthorized Signatures.**

(1) Any unauthorized signature is wholly inoperative as that of the person whose name is signed unless he ratifies it or is precluded from denying it; but it operates as the signature of the unauthorized signer in favor of any person who in good faith pays the instrument or takes it for value.

(2) Any unauthorized signature may be ratified for all purposes of this Article. Such ratification does not of itself affect any rights of the person ratifying against the actual signer.

§ 3—405. **Impostors; Signature in Name of Payee.**

(1) An indorsement by any person in the name of a named payee is effective if

(a) an impostor by use of the mails or otherwise has induced the maker or drawer to issue the instrument to him or his confederate in the name of the payee; or

(b) a person signing as or on behalf of a maker or drawer intends the payee to have no interest in the instrument; or

(c) an agent or employee of the maker or drawer has supplied him with the name of the payee intending the latter to have no such interest.

(2) Nothing in this section shall affect the criminal or civil liability of the person so indorsing.

§ 3—406. **Negligence Contributing to Alteration or Unauthorized Signature.**

Any person who by his negligence substantially contributes to a material alteration of the instrument or to the making of an unauthorized signature is precluded from asserting the alteration or lack of authority against a holder in due course or against a drawee or other payor who pays the instrument in good faith and in accordance with the reasonable commercial standards of the drawee's or payor's business.

§ 3—407. **Alteration.**

(1) Any alteration of an instrument is material which changes the contract of any party thereto in any respect, including any such change in

(a) the number or relations of the parties; or

(b) an incomplete instrument, by completing it otherwise than as authorized; or

(c) the writing as signed, by adding to it or by removing any part of it.

(2) As against any person other than a subsequent holder in due course

(a) alteration by the holder which is both fraudulent and material discharges any party whose contract is thereby changed unless that party assents or is precluded from asserting the defense;

(b) no other alteration discharges any party and the instrument may be enforced according to its original tenor, or as to incomplete instruments according to the authority given.

(3) A subsequent holder in due course may in all cases enforce the instrument according to its original tenor, and when an incomplete instrument has been completed, he may enforce it as completed.

§ 3—408. **Consideration.**

Want or failure of consideration is a defense as against any person not having the rights of a holder in due course (Section 3—305), except that no consideration is necessary for an instrument or obligation thereon given in payment of or as security for an antecedent obligation of any kind. Nothing in this section shall be taken to displace any statute outside this Act under which a promise is enforceable notwithstanding lack or failure of consideration. Partial failure of consideration is a defense pro tanto whether or not the failure is in an ascertained or liquidated amount.

§ 3—409. **Draft Not an Assignment.**

(1) A check or other draft does not of itself operate as an assignment of any funds in the hands of the drawee available for its payment, and the drawee is not liable on the instrument until he accepts it.

(2) Nothing in this section shall affect any liability in contract, tort or otherwise arising from any letter of credit or other obligation or representation which is not an acceptance.

§ 3—410. **Definition and Operation of Acceptance.**

(1) Acceptance is the drawee's signed engagement to honor the draft as presented. It must be written on the draft, and may consist of his signature alone. It becomes operative when completed by delivery or notification.

(2) A draft may be accepted although it has not been signed by the drawer or is otherwise incomplete or is overdue or has been dishonored.

(3) Where the draft is payable at a fixed period after sight and the acceptor fails to date his acceptance the holder may complete it by supplying a date in good faith.

§ 3—411. **Certification of a Check.**

(1) Certification of a check is acceptance. Where a holder procures certification the drawer and all prior indorsers are discharged.

(2) Unless otherwise agreed a bank has no obligation to certify a check.

(3) A bank may certify a check before returning it for lack of proper indorsement. If it does so the drawer is discharged.

§ 3—412. **Acceptance Varying Draft.**

(1) Where the drawee's proffered acceptance in any manner varies the draft as presented the holder may refuse the acceptance and treat the draft as dishonored in which case the drawee is entitled to have his acceptance cancelled.

(2) The terms of the draft are not varied by an acceptance to pay at any particular bank or place in the United States, unless the acceptance states that the draft is to be paid only at such bank or place.

(3) Where the holder assents to an acceptance varying the terms of the draft each drawer and indorser who does not affirmatively assent is discharged.

§ 3—413. **Contract of Maker, Drawer and Acceptor.**

(1) The maker or acceptor engages that he will pay the instrument according to its tenor at the time of his engagement or as completed pursuant to Section 3—115 on incomplete instruments.

(2) The drawer engages that upon dishonor of the draft and any necessary notice of dishonor or protest he will pay the amount of the draft to the holder or to any indorser who takes it up. The drawer may disclaim this liability by drawing without recourse.

(3) By making, drawing or accepting the party admits as against all subsequent parties including the drawee the existence of the payee and his then capacity to indorse.

§ 3—414. **Contract of Indorser; Order of Liability.**

(1) Unless the indorsement otherwise specifies (as by such words as "without recourse") every indorser engages that upon dishonor and any necessary notice of dishonor and protest he will pay the instrument according to its tenor at the time of his indorsement to the holder or to any subsequent indorser who takes it up, even though the indorser who takes it up was not obligated to do so.

(2) Unless they otherwise agree indorsers are liable to one another in the order in which they indorse, which is presumed to be the order in which their signatures appear on the instrument.

§ 3—415. **Contract of Accommodation Party.**

(1) An accommodation party is one who signs the instrument in any capacity for the purpose of lending his name to another party to it.

(2) When the instrument has been taken for value before it is due the accommodation party is liable in the capacity in which he has signed even though the taker knows of the accommodation.

(3) As against a holder in due course and without notice of the accommodation oral proof of the accommodation is not admissible to give the accommodation party the benefit of discharges dependent on his character as such. In other cases the accommodation character may be shown by oral proof.

(4) An indorsement which shows that it is not in the chain of title is notice of its accommodation character.

(5) An accommodation party is not liable to the party accommodated, and if he pays the instrument has a right of recourse on the instrument against such party.

§ 3—416. **Contract of Guarantor.**

(1) "Payment guaranteed" or equivalent words added to a signature mean that the signer engages that if the instrument is not paid when due he will pay it according to its tenor without resort by the holder to any other party.

(2) "Collection guaranteed" or equivalent words added to a signature mean that the signer engages that if the instrument is not paid when due he will pay it according to its tenor, but only after the holder has reduced his claim against the maker or acceptor to judgment and execution has been returned unsatisfied, or after the maker or acceptor has become insolvent or it is otherwise apparent that it is useless to proceed against him.

(3) Words of guaranty which do not otherwise specify guarantee payment.

(4) No words of guaranty added to the signature of a sole maker or acceptor affect his liability on the instrument. Such words added to the signature of one of two or more makers or acceptors create a presumption that the signature is for the accommodation of the others.

(5) When words of guaranty are used presentment, notice of dishonor and protest are not necessary to charge the user.

(6) Any guaranty written on the instrument is enforceable notwithstanding any statute of frauds.

§ 3—417. **Warranties on Presentment and Transfer.**

(1) Any person who obtains payment or acceptance and any prior transferor warrants to a person who in good faith pays or accepts that

(a) he has a good title to the instrument or is authorized to obtain payment or acceptance on behalf of one who has a good title; and

(b) he has no knowledge that the signature of the maker or drawer is unauthorized, except that this warranty is not given by a holder in due course acting in good faith

(i) to a maker with respect to the maker's own signature; or

(ii) to a drawer with respect to the drawer's own signature, whether or not the drawer is also the drawee; or

(iii) to an acceptor of a draft if the holder in due course took the draft after the acceptance or obtained the acceptance without knowledge that the drawer's signature was unauthorized; and

(c) the instrument has not been materially altered, except that this warranty is not given by a holder in due course acting in good faith

(i) to the maker of a note; or

(ii) to the drawer of a draft whether or not the drawer is also the drawee; or

(iii) to the acceptor of a draft with respect to an alteration made prior to the acceptance if the holder in due course took the draft after the acceptance, even though the acceptance provided "payable as originally drawn" or equivalent terms; or

(iv) to the acceptor of a draft with respect to an alteration made after the acceptance.

(2) Any person who transfers an instrument and receives consideration warrants to his transferee and if the transfer is by indorsement to any subsequent holder who takes the instrument in good faith that

(a) he has a good title to the instrument or is authorized to obtain payment or acceptance on behalf of one who has a good title and the transfer is otherwise rightful; and

(b) all signatures are genuine or authorized; and

(c) the instrument has not been materially altered; and

(d) no defense of any party is good against him; and

(e) he has no knowledge of any insolvency proceeding instituted with respect to the maker or acceptor or the drawer of an unaccepted instrument.

(3) By transferring "without recourse" the transferor limits the obligation stated in subsection (2)(d) to a warranty that he has no knowledge of such a defense.

(4) A selling agent or broker who does not disclose the fact that he is acting only as such gives the warranties provided in this section, but if he makes such disclosure warrants only his good faith and authority.

§ 3—418. **Finality of Payment or Acceptance.**

Except for recovery of bank payments as provided in the Article on Bank Deposits and Collections (Article 4) and except for liability for breach of warranty on presentment under the preceding section, payment or acceptance of any instrument is final in favor of a holder in due course, or a person who has in good faith changed his position in reliance on the payment.

§ 3—419. **Conversion of Instrument; Innocent Representative.**

(1) An instrument is converted when

(a) a drawee to whom it is delivered for acceptance refuses to return it on demand; or

(b) any person to whom it is delivered for payment refuses on demand either to pay or to return it; or

(c) it is paid on a forged indorsement.

(2) In an action against a drawee under subsection (1) the measure of the drawee's liability is the face amount of the instrument. In any other action under subsection (1) the measure of liability is presumed to be the face amount of the instrument.

(3) Subject to the provisions of this Act concerning restrictive indorsements a representative, including a depositary or collecting bank, who has in good faith and in accordance with the reasonable commercial standards applicable to the business of such representative dealt with an instrument or its proceeds on behalf of one who was not the true owner is not liable in conversion or otherwise to the true owner beyond the amount of any proceeds remaining in his hands.

(4) An intermediary bank or payor bank which is not a depositary bank is not liable in conversion solely by reason of the fact that proceeds of an item indorsed restrictively (Sections 3—205 and 3—206) are not paid or applied consistently with the restrictive indorsement of an indorser other than its immediate transferor.

Part 5 Presentment, Notice of Dishonor and Protest

§ 3—501. When Presentment, Notice of Dishonor, and Protest Necessary or Permissible.

(1) Unless excused (Section 3—511) presentment is necessary to charge secondary parties as follows:

(a) presentment for acceptance is necessary to charge the drawer and indorsers of a draft where the draft so provides, or is payable elsewhere than at the residence or place of business of the drawee, or its date of payment depends upon such presentment. The holder may at his option present for acceptance any other draft payable at a stated date;

(b) presentment for payment is necessary to charge any indorser;

(c) in the case of any drawer, the acceptor of a draft payable at a bank or the maker of a note payable at a bank, presentment for payment is necessary, but failure to make presentment discharges such drawer, acceptor or maker only as stated in Section 3—502(1)(b).

(2) Unless excused (Section 3—511)

(a) notice of any dishonor is necessary to charge any indorser;

(b) in the case of any drawer, the acceptor of a draft payable at a bank or the maker of a note payable at a bank, notice of any dishonor is necessary, but failure to give such notice discharges such drawer, acceptor or maker only as stated in Section 3—502(1)(b).

(3) Unless excused (Section 3—511) protest of any dishonor is necessary to charge the drawer and indorsers of any draft which on its face appears to be drawn or payable outside of the states, territories, dependencies, and possessions of the United States, the District of Columbia and the Commonwealth of Puerto Rico. The holder may at his option make protest of any dishonor of any other instrument and in the case of a foreign draft may on insolvency of the acceptor before maturity make protest for better security.

(4) Notwithstanding any provision of this section, neither presentment nor notice of dishonor nor protest is necessary to charge an indorser who has indorsed an instrument after maturity.

§ 3—502. Unexcused Delay; Discharge.

(1) Where without excuse any necessary presentment or notice of dishonor is delayed beyond the time when it is due

(a) any indorser is discharged; and

(b) any drawer or the acceptor of a draft payable at a bank or the maker of a note payable at a bank who because the drawee or payor bank becomes insolvent during the delay is deprived of funds maintained with the drawee or payor bank to cover the instrument may discharge his liability by written assignment to the holder of his rights against the drawee or payor bank in respect of such funds, but such drawer, acceptor or maker is not otherwise discharged.

(2) Where without excuse a necessary protest is delayed beyond the time when it is due any drawer or indorser is discharged.

§ 3—503. Time of Presentment.

(1) Unless a different time is expressed in the instrument the time for any presentment is determined as follows:

(a) where an instrument is payable at or a fixed period after a stated date any presentment for acceptance must be made on or before the date it is payable;

(b) where an instrument is payable after sight it must either be presented for acceptance or negotiated within a reasonable time after date or issue whichever is later;

(c) where an instrument shows the date on which it is payable presentment for payment is due on that date;

(d) where an instrument is accelerated presentment for payment is due within a reasonable time after the acceleration;

(e) with respect to the liability of any secondary party presentment for acceptance or payment of any other instrument is due within a reasonable time after such party becomes liable thereon.

(2) A reasonable time for presentment is determined by the nature of the instrument, any usage of banking or trade and the facts of the particular case. In the case of an uncertified check which is drawn and payable within the United States and which is not a draft drawn by a bank the following are presumed to be reasonable periods within which to present for payment or to initiate bank collection:

(a) with respect to the liability of the drawer, thirty days after date or issue whichever is later; and

(b) with respect to the liability of an indorser, seven days after his indorsement.

(3) Where any presentment is due on a day which is not a full business day for either the person making presentment or the party to pay or accept, presentment is due on the next following day which is a full business day for both parties.

(4) Presentment to be sufficient must be made at a reasonable hour, and if at a bank during its banking day.

§ 3—504. How Presentment Made.

(1) Presentment is a demand for acceptance or payment made upon the maker, acceptor, drawee or other payor by or on behalf of the holder.

(2) Presentment may be made

(a) by mail, in which event the time of presentment is determined by the time of receipt of the mail; or

(b) through a clearing house; or

(c) at the place of acceptance or payment specified in the instrument or if there be none at the place of business or residence of the party to accept or pay. If neither the party to accept or pay nor anyone authorized to act for him is present or accessible at such place presentment is excused.

(3) It may be made

(a) to any one of two or more makers, acceptors, drawees or other payors; or

(b) to any person who has authority to make or refuse the acceptance or payment.

(4) A draft accepted or a note made payable at a bank in the United States must be presented at such bank.

(5) In the cases described in Section 4—210 presentment may be made in the manner and with the result stated in that section.

§ 3—505. **Rights of Party to Whom Presentment Is Made.**

(1) The party to whom presentment is made may without dishonor require

(a) exhibition of the instrument; and

(b) reasonable identification of the person making presentment and evidence of his authority to make it if made for another; and

(c) that the instrument be produced for acceptance or payment at a place specified in it, or if there be none at any place reasonable in the circumstances; and

(d) a signed receipt on the instrument for any partial or full payment and its surrender upon full payment.

(2) Failure to comply with any such requirement invalidates the presentment but the person presenting has a reasonable time in which to comply and the time for acceptance or payment runs from the time of compliance.

§ 3—506. **Time Allowed for Acceptance or Payment.**

(1) Acceptance may be deferred without dishonor until the close of the next business day following presentment. The holder may also in a good faith effort to obtain acceptance and without either dishonor of the instrument or discharge of secondary parties allow postponement of acceptance for an additional business day.

(2) Except as a longer time is allowed in the case of documentary drafts drawn under a letter of credit, and unless an earlier time is agreed to by the party to pay, payment of an instrument may be deferred without dishonor pending reasonable examination to determine whether it is properly payable, but payment must be made in any event before the close of business on the day of presentment.

§ 3—507. **Dishonor; Holder's Right of Recourse; Term Allowing Re-Presentment.**

(1) An instrument is dishonored when

(a) a necessary or optional presentment is duly made and due acceptance or payment is refused or cannot be obtained within the prescribed time or in case of bank collections the instrument is seasonably returned by the midnight deadline (Section 4—301); or

(b) presentment is excused and the instrument is not duly accepted or paid.

(2) Subject to any necessary notice of dishonor and protest, the holder has upon dishonor an immediate right of recourse against the drawers and indorsers.

(3) Return of an instrument for lack of proper indorsement is not dishonor.

(4) A term in a draft or an indorsement thereof allowing a stated time for re-presentment in the event of any dishonor of the draft by nonacceptance if a time draft or by nonpayment if a sight draft gives the holder as against any secondary party bound by the term an option to waive the dishonor without affecting the liability of the secondary party and he may present again up to the end of the stated time.

§ 3—508. **Notice of Dishonor.**

(1) Notice of dishonor may be given to any person who may be liable on the instrument by or on behalf of the holder or any party who has himself received notice, or any other party who can be compelled to pay the instrument. In addition an agent or bank in whose hands the instrument is dishonored may give notice to his principal or customer or to another agent or bank from which the instrument was received.

(2) Any necessary notice must be given by a bank before its midnight deadline and by any other person before midnight of the third business day after dishonor or receipt of notice of dishonor.

(3) Notice may be given in any reasonable manner. It may be oral or written and in any terms which identify the instrument and state that it has been dishonored. A misdescription which does not mislead the party notified does not vitiate the notice. Sending the instrument bearing a stamp, ticket or writing stating that acceptance or payment has been refused or sending a notice of debit with respect to the instrument is sufficient.

(4) Written notice is given when sent although it is not received.

(5) Notice to one partner is notice to each although the firm has been dissolved.

(6) When any party is in insolvency proceedings instituted after the issue of the instrument notice may be given either to the party or to the representative of his estate.

(7) When any party is dead or incompetent notice may be sent to his last known address or given to his personal representative.

(8) Notice operates for the benefit of all parties who have rights on the instrument against the party notified.

§ 3—509. **Protest; Noting for Protest.**

(1) A protest is a certificate of dishonor made under the hand and seal of a United States consul or vice consul or a notary public or other person authorized to certify dishonor by the law of the place where dishonor occurs. It may be made upon information satisfactory to such person.

(2) The protest must identify the instrument and certify either that due presentment has been made or the reason why it is excused and that the instrument has been dishonored by nonacceptance or nonpayment.

(3) The protest may also certify that notice of dishonor has been given to all parties or to specified parties.

(4) Subject to subsection (5) any necessary protest is due by the time that notice of dishonor is due.

(5) If, before protest is due, an instrument has been noted for protest by the officer to make protest, the protest may be made at any time thereafter as of the date of the noting.

§ 3—510. **Evidence of Dishonor and Notice of Dishonor.**

The following are admissible as evidence and create a presumption of dishonor and of any notice of dishonor therein shown:

(a) a document regular in form as provided in the preceding section which purports to be a protest;

(b) the purported stamp or writing of the drawee, payor bank or presenting bank on the instrument or accompanying it stating that acceptance or payment has been refused for reasons consistent with dishonor;

(c) any book or record of the drawee, payor bank, or any collecting bank kept in the usual course of business which shows dishonor, even though there is no evidence of who made the entry.

§ 3—511. **Waived or Excused Presentment, Protest or Notice of Dishonor or Delay Therein.**

(1) Delay in presentment, protest or notice of dishonor is excused when the party is without notice that it is due or when the delay is caused by circumstances beyond his control and he exercises reasonable diligence after the cause of the delay ceases to operate.

(2) Presentment or notice or protest as the case may be is entirely excused when

(a) the party to be charged has waived it expressly or by implication either before or after it is due; or

(b) such party has himself dishonored the instrument or has countermanded payment or otherwise has no reason to expect or right to require that the instrument be accepted or paid; or

(c) by reasonable diligence the presentment or protest cannot be made or the notice given.

(3) Presentment is also entirely excused when

(a) the maker, acceptor or drawee of any instrument except a documentary draft is dead or in insolvency proceedings instituted after the issue of the instrument; or

(b) acceptance or payment is refused but not for want of proper presentment.

(4) Where a draft has been dishonored by nonacceptance a later presentment for payment and any notice of dishonor and protest for nonpayment are excused unless in the meantime the instrument has been accepted.

(5) A waiver of protest is also a waiver of presentment and of notice of dishonor even though protest is not required.

(6) Where a waiver of presentment or notice or protest is embodied in the instrument itself it is binding upon all parties; but where it is written above the signature of an indorser it binds him only.

Part 6 Discharge

§ 3—601. **Discharge of Parties.**

(1) The extent of the discharge of any party from liability on an instrument is governed by the sections on

(a) payment or satisfaction (Section 3—603); or

(b) tender of payment (Section 3—604); or

(c) cancellation or renunciation (Section 3—605); or

(d) impairment of right of recourse or of collateral (Section 3—606); or

(e) reacquisition of the instrument by a prior party (Section 3—208); or

(f) fraudulent and material alteration (Section 3—407); or

(g) certification of a check (Section 3—411); or

(h) acceptance varying a draft (Section 3—412); or

(i) unexcused delay in presentment or notice of dishonor or protest (Section 3—502).

(2) Any party is also discharged from his liability on an instrument to another party by any other act or agreement with such party which would discharge his simple contract for the payment of money.

(3) The liability of all parties is discharged when any party who has himself no right of action or recourse on the instrument

(a) reacquires the instrument in his own right; or

(b) is discharged under any provision of this Article, except as otherwise provided with respect to discharge for impairment of recourse or of collateral (Section 3—606).

§ 3—602. **Effect of Discharge Against Holder in Due Course.**

No discharge of any party provided by this Article is effective against a subsequent holder in due course unless he has notice thereof when he takes the instrument.

§ 3—603. **Payment or Satisfaction.**

(1) The liability of any party is discharged to the extent of his payment or satisfaction to the holder even though it is made with knowledge of a claim of another person to the instrument unless prior to such payment or satisfaction the person making the claim either supplies indemnity deemed adequate by the party seeking the discharge or enjoins payment or satisfaction by order of a court of competent jurisdiction in an action in which the adverse claimant and the holder are parties. This subsection does not, however, result in the discharge of the liability

(a) of a party who in bad faith pays or satisfies a holder who acquired the instrument by theft or who (unless having the rights of a holder in due course) holds through one who so acquired it; or

(b) of a party (other than an intermediary bank or a payor bank which is not a depositary bank) who pays or satisfies the holder of an instrument which has been restrictively indorsed in a manner not consistent with the terms of such restrictive indorsement.

(2) Payment or satisfaction may be made with the consent of the holder by any person including a stranger to the instrument. Surrender of the instrument to such a person gives him the rights of a transferee (Section 3—201).

§ 3—604. **Tender of Payment.**

(1) Any party making tender of full payment to a holder when or after it is due is discharged to the extent of all subsequent liability for interest, costs and attorney's fees.

(2) The holder's refusal of such tender wholly discharges any party who has a right of recourse against the party making the tender.

(3) Where the maker or acceptor of an instrument payable otherwise than on demand is able and ready to pay at every place of payment specified in the instrument when it is due, it is equivalent to tender.

§ 3—605. **Cancellation and Renunciation.**

(1) The holder of an instrument may even without consideration discharge any party

(a) in any manner apparent on the face of the instrument or the indorsement, as by intentionally cancelling the instrument or the party's signature by destruction or mutilation, or by striking out the party's signature; or

(b) by renouncing his rights by a writing signed and delivered or by surrender of the instrument to the party to be discharged.

(2) Neither cancellation nor renunciation without surrender of the instrument affects the title thereto.

§ 3—606. **Impairment of Recourse or of Collateral.**

(1) The holder discharges any party to the instrument to the extent that without such party's consent the holder

(a) without express reservation of rights releases or agrees not to sue any person against whom the party has to the knowledge of the holder a right of recourse or agrees to suspend the right to enforce against such person the instrument or collateral or otherwise discharges such person, except that failure or delay in effecting any required presentment, protest or notice of dishonor with respect to any such person does not discharge any party as to whom presentment, protest or notice of dishonor is effective or unnecessary; or

(b) unjustifiably impairs any collateral for the instrument given by or on behalf of the party or any person against whom he has a right of recourse.

(2) By express reservation of rights against a party with a right of recourse the holder preserves

(a) all his rights against such party as of the time when the instrument was originally due; and

(b) the right of the party to pay the instrument as of that time; and

(c) all rights of such party to recourse against others.

Part 7 Advice of International Sight Draft

§ 3—701. **Letter of Advice of International Sight Draft.**

(1) A "letter of advice" is a drawer's communication to the drawee that a described draft has been drawn.

(2) Unless otherwise agreed when a bank receives from another bank a letter of advice of an international sight draft the drawee bank may immediately debit the drawer's account and stop the running of interest pro tanto. Such a debit and any resulting credit to any account covering outstanding drafts leaves in the drawer full power to stop payment or otherwise dispose of the amount and creates no trust or interest in favor of the holder.

(3) Unless otherwise agreed and except where a draft is drawn under a credit issued by the drawee, the drawee of an international sight draft owes the drawer no duty to pay an unadvised draft but if it does so and the draft is genuine, may appropriately debit the drawer's account.

Part 8 Miscellaneous

§ 3—801. **Drafts in a Set.**

(1) Where a draft is drawn in a set of parts, each of which is numbered and expressed to be an order only if no other part has been honored, the whole of the parts constitutes one draft but a taker of any part may become a holder in due course of the draft.

(2) Any person who negotiates, indorses or accepts a single part of a draft drawn in a set thereby becomes liable to any holder in due course of that part as if it were the whole set, but as between different holders in due course to whom different parts have been negotiated the holder whose title first accrues has all rights to the draft and its proceeds.

(3) As against the drawee the first presented part of a draft drawn in a set is the part entitled to payment, or if a time draft to acceptance and payment. Acceptance of any subsequently presented part renders the drawee liable thereon under subsection (2). With respect both to a holder and to the drawer payment of a subsequently presented part of a draft payable at sight has the same effect as payment of a check notwithstanding an effective stop order (Section 4—407).

(4) Except as otherwise provided in this section, where any part of a draft in a set is discharged by payment or otherwise the whole draft is discharged.

§ 3—802. **Effect of Instrument on Obligation for Which It Is Given.**

(1) Unless otherwise agreed where an instrument is taken for an underlying obligation

(a) the obligation is pro tanto discharged if a bank is drawer, maker or acceptor of the instrument and there is no recourse on the instrument against the underlying obligor; and

(b) in any other case the obligation is suspended pro tanto until the instrument is due or if it is payable on demand until its presentment. If the instrument is dishonored action may be maintained on either the instrument or the obligation; discharge of the underlying obligor on the instrument also discharges him on the obligation.

(2) The taking in good faith of a check which is not postdated does not of itself so extend the time on the original obligation as to discharge a surety.

§ 3—803. **Notice to Third Party.**

Where a defendant is sued for breach of an obligation for which a third person is answerable over under this Article he may give the third person written notice of the litigation, and the person notified may then give similar notice to any other person who is answerable over to him under this Article. If the notice states that the person notified may come in and defend and that if the person notified does not do so he will in any action against him by the person giving the notice be bound by any determination of fact common to the two litigations, then unless after seasonable receipt of the notice the person notified does come in and defend he is so bound.

§ 3—804. **Lost, Destroyed or Stolen Instruments.**

The owner of an instrument which is lost, whether by destruction, theft or otherwise, may maintain an action in his own name and recover from any party liable thereon upon due proof of his ownership, the facts which prevent his production of the instrument and its terms. The court may require security indemnifying the defendant against loss by reason of further claims on the instrument.

§ 3—805. **Instruments Not Payable to Order or to Bearer.**

This Article applies to any instrument whose terms do not preclude transfer and which is otherwise negotiable within this Article but which is not payable to order or to bearer, except that there can be no holder in due course of such an instrument.

Revised Article 3
NEGOTIABLE INSTRUMENTS

Part 1 General Provisions and Definitions

§ 3—101. **Short Title.**

This Article may be cited as Uniform Commercial Code—Negotiable Instruments.

§ 3—102. **Subject Matter.**

(a) This Article applies to negotiable instruments. It does not apply to money, to payment orders governed by Article 4A, or to securities governed by Article 8.

(b) If there is conflict between this Article and Article 4 or 9, Articles 4 and 9 govern.

(c) Regulations of the Board of Governors of the Federal Reserve System and operating circulars of the Federal Reserve Banks supersede any inconsistent provision of this Article to the extent of the inconsistency.

§ 3—103. **Definitions.**

(a) In this Article:

(1) "Acceptor" means a drawee who has accepted a draft.

(2) "Drawee" means a person ordered in a draft to make payment.

(3) "Drawer" means a person who signs or is identified in a draft as a person ordering payment.

(4) "Good faith" means honesty in fact and the observance of reasonable commercial standards of fair dealing.

(5) "Maker" means a person who signs or is identified in a note as a person undertaking to pay.

(6) "Order" means a written instruction to pay money signed by the person giving the instruction. The instruction may be addressed to any person, including the person giving the instruction, or to one or more persons jointly or in the alternative but not in succession. An authorization to pay is not an order unless the person authorized to pay is also instructed to pay.

(7) "Ordinary care" in the case of a person engaged in business means observance of reasonable commercial standards, prevailing in the area in which the person is located, with respect to the business in which the person is engaged. In the case of a bank that takes an instrument for processing for collection or payment by automated means, reasonable commercial standards do not require the bank to examine the instrument if the failure to examine does not violate the bank's prescribed procedures and the bank's procedures do not vary unreasonably from general banking usage not disapproved by this Article or Article 4.

(8) "Party" means a party to an instrument.

(9) "Promise" means a written undertaking to pay money signed by the person undertaking to pay. An acknowledgment of an obligation by the obligor is not a promise unless the obligor also undertakes to pay the obligation.

(10) "Prove" with respect to a fact means to meet the burden of establishing the fact (Section 1—201(8)).

(11) "Remitter" means a person who purchases an instrument from its issuer if the instrument is payable to an identified person other than the purchaser.

(b);(c) [Other definitions' section references deleted.]

(d) In addition, Article 1 contains general definitions and principles of construction and interpretation applicable throughout this Article.

§ 3—104. **Negotiable Instrument.**

(a) Except as provided in subsections (c) and (d), "negotiable instrument" means an unconditional promise or order to pay a fixed amount of money, with or without interest or other charges described in the promise or order, if it:

(1) is payable to bearer or to order at the time it is issued or first comes into possession of a holder;

(2) is payable on demand or at a definite time; and

(3) does not state any other undertaking or instruction by the person promising or ordering payment to do any act in addition to the payment of money, but the promise or order may contain (i) an undertaking or power to give, maintain, or protect collateral to secure payment, (ii) an authorization or power to the holder to confess judgment or realize on or dispose of collateral, or (iii) a waiver of the benefit of any law intended for the advantage or protection of an obligor.

(b) "Instrument" means a negotiable instrument.

(c) An order that meets all of the requirements of subsection (a), except paragraph (1), and otherwise falls within the definition of "check" in subsection (f) is a negotiable instrument and a check.

(d) A promise or order other than a check is not an instrument if, at the time it is issued or first comes into possession of a holder, it contains a conspicuous statement, however expressed, to the effect that the promise or order is not negotiable or is not an instrument governed by this Article.

(e) An instrument is a "note" if it is a promise and is a "draft" if it is an order. If an instrument falls within the definition of both "note" and "draft," a person entitled to enforce the instrument may treat it as either.

(f) "Check" means (i) a draft, other than a documentary draft, payable on demand and drawn on a bank or (ii) a cashier's check or teller's check. An instrument may be a check even though it is described on its face by another term, such as "money order."

(g) "Cashier's check" means a draft with respect to which the drawer and drawee are the same bank or branches of the same bank.

(h) "Teller's check" means a draft drawn by a bank (i) on another bank, or (ii) payable at or through a bank.

(i) "Traveler's check" means an instrument that (i) is payable on demand, (ii) is drawn on or payable at or through a bank, (iii) is designated by the term "traveler's check" or by a substantially similar term, and (iv) requires, as a condition to payment, a countersignature by a person whose specimen signature appears on the instrument.

(j) "Certificate of deposit" means an instrument containing an acknowledgment by a bank that a sum of money has been received by the bank and a promise by the bank to repay the sum of money. A certificate of deposit is a note of the bank.

§ 3—105. **Issue of Instrument.**

(a) "Issue" means the first delivery of an instrument by the maker or drawer, whether to a holder or nonholder, for the purpose of giving rights on the instrument to any person.

(b) An unissued instrument, or an unissued incomplete instrument that is completed, is binding on the maker or drawer, but nonissuance is a defense. An instrument that is conditionally issued or is issued for a special purpose is binding on the maker or drawer, but failure of the condition or special purpose to be fulfilled is a defense.

(c) "Issuer" applies to issued and unissued instruments and means a maker or drawer of an instrument.

§ 3—106. **Unconditional Promise or Order.**

(a) Except as provided in this section, for the purposes of Section 3—104(a), a promise or order is unconditional unless it states (i) an express condition to payment, (ii) that the promise or order is subject to or governed by another writing, or (iii) that rights or obligations with respect to the promise or order are stated in another writing. A reference to another writing does not of itself make the promise or order conditional.

(b) A promise or order is not made conditional (i) by a reference to another writing for a statement of rights with respect to collateral, prepayment, or acceleration, or (ii) because payment is limited to resort to a particular fund or source.

(c) If a promise or order requires, as a condition to payment, a countersignature by a person whose specimen signature appears on the promise or order, the condition does not make the promise or order conditional for the purposes of Section 3—104(a). If the person whose specimen signature appears on an instrument fails to countersign the instrument, the failure to countersign is a defense to the obligation of the issuer, but the failure does not prevent a transferee of the instrument from becoming a holder of the instrument.

(d) If a promise or order at the time it is issued or first comes into possession of a holder contains a statement, required by applicable statutory or administrative law, to the effect that the rights of a holder or transferee are subject to claims or defenses that the issuer could assert against the original payee, the promise or order is not thereby made conditional for the purposes of Section 3—104(a); but if the promise or order is an instrument, there cannot be a holder in due course of the instrument.

§ 3—107. **Instrument Payable in Foreign Money.**

Unless the instrument otherwise provides, an instrument that states the amount payable in foreign money may be paid in the foreign money or in an equivalent amount in dollars calculated by using the current bank-offered spot rate at the place of payment for the purchase of dollars on the day on which the instrument is paid.

§ 3—108. **Payable on Demand or at Definite Time.**

(a) A promise or order is "payable on demand" if it (i) states that it is payable on demand or at sight, or otherwise indicates that it is payable at the will of the holder, or (ii) does not state any time of payment.

(b) A promise or order is "payable at a definite time" if it is payable on elapse of a definite period of time after sight or acceptance or at a fixed date or dates or at a time or times readily ascertainable at the time the promise or order is issued, subject to rights of (i) prepayment, (ii) acceleration, (iii) extension at the option of the holder, or (iv) extension to a further definite time at the option of the maker or acceptor or automatically upon or after a specified act or event.

(c) If an instrument, payable at a fixed date, is also payable upon demand made before the fixed date, the instrument is payable on demand until the fixed date and, if demand for payment is not made before that date, becomes payable at a definite time on the fixed date.

§ 3—109. **Payable to Bearer or to Order.**

(a) A promise or order is payable to bearer if it:

(1) states that it is payable to bearer or to the order of bearer or otherwise indicates that the person in possession of the promise or order is entitled to payment;

(2) does not state a payee; or

(3) states that it is payable to or to the order of cash or otherwise indicates that it is not payable to an identified person.

(b) A promise or order that is not payable to bearer is payable to order if it is payable (i) to the order of an identified person or (ii) to an identified person or order. A promise or order that is payable to order is payable to the identified person.

(c) An instrument payable to bearer may become payable to an identified person if it is specially indorsed pursuant to Section 3—205(a). An instrument payable to an identified person may become payable to bearer if it is indorsed in blank pursuant to Section 3—205(b).

§ 3—110. **Identification of Person to Whom Instrument Is Payable.**

(a) The person to whom an instrument is initially payable is determined by the intent of the person, whether or not authorized, signing as, or in the name or behalf of, the issuer of the instrument. The instrument is payable to the person intended by the signer even if that person is identified in the instrument by a name or other identification that is not that of the intended person. If more than one person signs in the name or behalf of the issuer of an instrument and all the signers do not intend the same person as payee, the instrument is payable to any person intended by one or more of the signers.

(b) If the signature of the issuer of an instrument is made by automated means, such as a check-writing machine, the payee of the instrument is determined by the intent of the person who supplied the name or identification of the payee, whether or not authorized to do so.

(c) A person to whom an instrument is payable may be identified in any way, including by name, identifying number, office, or account number. For the purpose of determining the holder of an instrument, the following rules apply:

(1) If an instrument is payable to an account and the account is identified only by number, the instrument is payable to the person to whom the account is payable. If an instrument is payable to an account identified by number and by the name of a person, the instrument is payable to the named person, whether or not that person is the owner of the account identified by number.

(2) If an instrument is payable to:

(i) a trust, an estate, or a person described as trustee or representative of a trust or estate, the instrument is payable to the trustee, the representative, or a successor of either, whether or not the beneficiary or estate is also named;

(ii) a person described as agent or similar representative of a named or identified person, the instrument is payable to the represented person, the representative, or a successor of the representative;

(iii) a fund or organization that is not a legal entity, the instrument is payable to a representative of the members of the fund or organization; or

(iv) an office or to a person described as holding an office, the instrument is payable to the named person, the incumbent of the office, or a successor to the incumbent.

(d) If an instrument is payable to two or more persons alternatively, it is payable to any of them and may be negotiated, discharged, or enforced by any or all of them in possession of the instrument. If an instrument is payable to two or more persons not alternatively, it is payable to all of them and may be negotiated, discharged, or enforced only by all of them. If an instrument payable to two or more persons is ambiguous as to whether it is payable to the persons alternatively, the instrument is payable to the persons alternatively.

§ 3—111. **Place of Payment.**

Except as otherwise provided for items in Article 4, an instrument is payable at the place of payment stated in the instrument. If no place of payment is stated, an instrument is payable at the address of the drawee or maker stated in the instrument. If no address is stated, the place of payment is the place of business of the drawee or maker. If a drawee or maker has more than one place of business, the place of payment is any place of business of the drawee or maker chosen by the person entitled to enforce the instrument. If the drawee or maker has no place of business, the place of payment is the residence of the drawee or maker.

§ 3—112. **Interest.**

(a) Unless otherwise provided in the instrument, (i) an instrument is not payable with interest, and (ii) interest on an interest-bearing instrument is payable from the date of the instrument.

(b) Interest may be stated in an instrument as a fixed or variable amount of money or it may be expressed as a fixed or variable rate or rates. The amount or rate of interest may be stated or described in the instrument in any manner and may require reference to information not contained in the instrument. If an instrument provides for interest, but the amount of interest payable cannot be ascertained from the description, interest is payable at the judgment rate in effect at the place of payment of the instrument and at the time interest first accrues.

§ 3—113. **Date of Instrument.**

(a) An instrument may be antedated or postdated. The date stated determines the time of payment if the instrument is payable at a fixed period after date. Except as provided in Section 4—401(c), an instrument payable on demand is not payable before the date of the instrument.

(b) If an instrument is undated, its date is the date of its issue or, in the case of an unissued instrument, the date it first comes into possession of a holder.

§ 3—114. **Contradictory Terms of Instrument.**

If an instrument contains contradictory terms, typewritten terms prevail over printed terms, handwritten terms prevail over both, and words prevail over numbers.

§ 3—115. **Incomplete Instrument.**

(a) "Incomplete instrument" means a signed writing, whether or not issued by the signer, the contents of which show at the time of signing that it is incomplete but that the signer intended it to be completed by the addition of words or numbers.

(b) Subject to subsection (c), if an incomplete instrument is an instrument under Section 3—104, it may be enforced according to its terms if it is not completed, or according to its terms as augmented by completion. If an incomplete instrument is not an instrument under Section 3—104, but, after completion, the requirements of Section 3—104 are met, the instrument may be enforced according to its terms as augmented by completion.

(c) If words or numbers are added to an incomplete instrument without authority of the signer, there is an alteration of the incomplete instrument under Section 3—407.

(d) The burden of establishing that words or numbers were added to an incomplete instrument without authority of the signer is on the person asserting the lack of authority.

§ 3—116. **Joint and Several Liability; Contribution.**

(a) Except as otherwise provided in the instrument, two or more persons who have the same liability on an instrument as makers, drawers, acceptors, indorsers who indorse as joint payees, or anomalous indorsers are jointly and severally liable in the capacity in which they sign.

(b) Except as provided in Section 3—419(e) or by agreement of the affected parties, a party having joint and several liability who pays the instrument is entitled to receive from any party having the same joint and several liability contribution in accordance with applicable law.

(c) Discharge of one party having joint and several liability by a person entitled to enforce the instrument does not affect the right under subsection (b) of a party having the same joint and several liability to receive contribution from the party discharged.

§ 3—117. **Other Agreements Affecting Instrument.**

Subject to applicable law regarding exclusion of proof of contemporaneous or previous agreements, the obligation of a party to an instrument to pay the instrument may be modified, supplemented, or nullified by a separate agreement of the obligor and a person entitled to enforce the instrument, if the instrument is issued or the obligation is incurred in reliance on the agreement or as part of the same transaction giving rise to the agreement. To the extent an obligation is modified, supplemented, or nullified by an agreement under this section, the agreement is a defense to the obligation.

§ 3—118. **Statute of Limitations.**

(a) Except as provided in subsection (e), an action to enforce the obligation of a party to pay a note payable at a definite time must be commenced within six years after the due date or dates stated in the note or, if a due date is accelerated, within six years after the accelerated due date.

(b) Except as provided in subsection (d) or (e), if demand for payment is made to the maker of a note payable on demand, an action to enforce the obligation of a party to pay the note must be commenced within six years after the demand. If no demand for payment is made to the maker, an action to enforce the note is barred if neither principal nor interest on the note has been paid for a continuous period of 10 years.

(c) Except as provided in subsection (d), an action to enforce the obligation of a party to an unaccepted draft to pay the draft must be commenced within three years after dishonor of the draft or 10 years after the date of the draft, whichever period expires first.

(d) An action to enforce the obligation of the acceptor of a certified check or the issuer of a teller's check, cashier's check, or traveler's check must be commenced within three years after demand for payment is made to the acceptor or issuer, as the case may be.

(e) An action to enforce the obligation of a party to a certificate of deposit to pay the instrument must be commenced within six years after demand for payment is made to the maker, but if the instrument states a due date and the maker is not required to pay before that date, the six-year period begins when a demand for payment is in effect and the due date has passed.

(f) An action to enforce the obligation of a party to pay an accepted draft, other than a certified check, must be commenced (i) within six years after the due date or dates stated in the draft or acceptance if the obligation of the acceptor is payable at a definite time, or (ii) within six years after the date of the acceptance if the obligation of the acceptor is payable on demand.

(g) Unless governed by other law regarding claims for indemnity or contribution, an action (i) for conversion of an instrument, for money had and received, or like action based on conversion, (ii) for breach of warranty, or (iii) to enforce an obligation, duty, or right arising under this Article and not governed by this section must be commenced within three years after the [cause of action] accrues.

§ 3—119. **Notice of Right to Defend Action.**

In an action for breach of an obligation for which a third person is answerable over pursuant to this Article or Article 4, the defendant may give the third person written notice of the litigation, and the person notified may then give similar notice to any other person who is answerable over. If the notice states (i) that the person notified may come in and defend and (ii) that failure to do so will bind the person notified in an action later brought by the person giving the notice as to any determination of fact common to the two litigations, the person notified is so bound unless after seasonable receipt of the notice the person notified does come in and defend.

Part 2 Negotiation, Transfer, and Indorsement

§ 3—201. **Negotiation.**

(a) "Negotiation" means a transfer of possession, whether voluntary or involuntary, of an instrument by a person other than the issuer to a person who thereby becomes its holder.

(b) Except for negotiation by a remitter, if an instrument is payable to an identified person, negotiation requires transfer of possession of the instrument and its indorsement by the holder. If an instrument is payable to bearer, it may be negotiated by transfer of possession alone.

§ 3—202. **Negotiation Subject to Rescission.**

(a) Negotiation is effective even if obtained (i) from an infant, a corporation exceeding its powers, or a person without capacity, (ii) by fraud, duress, or mistake, or (iii) in breach of duty or as part of an illegal transaction.

(b) To the extent permitted by other law, negotiation may be rescinded or may be subject to other remedies, but those remedies may not be asserted against a subsequent holder in due course or a person paying the instrument in good faith and without knowledge of facts that are a basis for rescission or other remedy.

§ 3—203. **Transfer of Instrument; Rights Acquired by Transfer.**

(a) An instrument is transferred when it is delivered by a person other than its issuer for the purpose of giving to the person receiving delivery the right to enforce the instrument.

(b) Transfer of an instrument, whether or not the transfer is a negotiation, vests in the transferee any right of the transferor to enforce the instrument, including any right as a holder in due course, but the transferee cannot acquire rights of a holder in due course by a transfer, directly or indirectly, from a holder in due course if the transferee engaged in fraud or illegality affecting the instrument.

(c) Unless otherwise agreed, if an instrument is transferred for value and the transferee does not become a holder because of lack of indorsement by the transferor, the transferee has a specifically enforceable right to the unqualified indorsement of the transferor, but negotiation of the instrument does not occur until the indorsement is made.

(d) If a transferor purports to transfer less than the entire instrument, negotiation of the instrument does not occur. The transferee obtains no rights under this Article and has only the rights of a partial assignee.

§ 3—204. **Indorsement.**

(a) "Indorsement" means a signature, other than that of a signer as maker, drawer, or acceptor, that alone or accompanied by other words is made on an instrument for the purpose of (i) negotiating the instrument, (ii) restricting payment of the instrument, or (iii) incurring indorser's liability on the instrument, but regardless of the intent of the signer, a signature and its accompanying words is an indorsement unless the accompanying words, terms of the instrument, place of the signature, or other circumstances unambiguously indicate that the signature was made for a purpose other than indorsement. For the purpose of determining whether a signature is made on an instrument, a paper affixed to the instrument is a part of the instrument.

(b) "Indorser" means a person who makes an indorsement.

(c) For the purpose of determining whether the transferee of an instrument is a holder, an indorsement that transfers a security interest in the instrument is effective as an unqualified indorsement of the instrument.

(d) If an instrument is payable to a holder under a name that is not the name of the holder, indorsement may be made by the holder in the name stated in the instrument or in the holder's name or both, but signature in both names may be required by a person paying or taking the instrument for value or collection.

§ 3—205. **Special Indorsement; Blank Indorsement; Anomalous Indorsement.**

(a) If an indorsement is made by the holder of an instrument, whether payable to an identified person or payable to bearer, and the indorsement identifies a person to whom it makes the instrument payable, it is a "special indorsement." When specially indorsed, an instrument becomes payable to the identified person and may be negotiated only by the indorsement of that person. The principles stated in Section 3—110 apply to special indorsements.

(b) If an indorsement is made by the holder of an instrument and it is not a special indorsement, it is a "blank indorsement." When indorsed in blank, an instrument becomes payable to bearer and may be negotiated by transfer of possession alone until specially indorsed.

(c) The holder may convert a blank indorsement that consists only of a signature into a special indorsement by writing, above the signature of the indorser, words identifying the person to whom the instrument is made payable.

(d) "Anomalous indorsement" means an indorsement made by a person who is not the holder of the instrument. An anomalous indorsement does not affect the manner in which the instrument may be negotiated.

§ 3—206. **Restrictive Indorsement.**

(a) An indorsement limiting payment to a particular person or otherwise prohibiting further transfer or negotiation of the instrument is not effective to prevent further transfer or negotiation of the instrument.

(b) An indorsement stating a condition to the right of the indorsee to receive payment does not affect the right of the indorsee to enforce the instrument. A person paying the instrument or taking it for value or collection may disregard the condition, and the rights and liabilities of that person are not affected by whether the condition has been fulfilled.

(c) If an instrument bears an indorsement (i) described in Section 4—201(b), or (ii) in blank or to a particular bank using the words "for deposit," "for collection," or other words indicating a purpose of having the instrument collected by a bank for the indorser or for a particular account, the following rules apply:

(1) A person, other than a bank, who purchases the instrument when so indorsed converts the instrument unless the amount paid for the instrument is received by the indorser or applied consistently with the indorsement.

(2) A depositary bank that purchases the instrument or takes it for collection when so indorsed converts the instrument unless the amount paid by the bank with respect to the instrument is received by the indorser or applied consistently with the indorsement.

(3) A payor bank that is also the depositary bank or that takes the instrument for immediate payment over the counter from a person other than a collecting bank converts the instrument unless the proceeds of the instrument are received by the indorser or applied consistently with the indorsement.

(4) Except as otherwise provided in paragraph (3), a payor bank or intermediary bank may disregard the indorsement and is not liable if the proceeds of the instrument are not received by the indorser or applied consistently with the indorsement.

(d) Except for an indorsement covered by subsection (c), if an instrument bears an indorsement using words to the effect that payment is to be made to the indorsee as agent, trustee, or other fiduciary for the benefit of the indorser or another person, the following rules apply:

(1) Unless there is notice of breach of fiduciary duty as provided in Section 3—307, a person who purchases the instrument from the indorsee or takes the instrument from the indorsee for collection or payment may pay the proceeds of payment or the value given for the instrument to the indorsee without regard to whether the indorsee violates a fiduciary duty to the indorser.

(2) A subsequent transferee of the instrument or person who pays the instrument is neither given notice nor otherwise affected by the restriction in the indorsement unless the transferee or payor knows that the fiduciary dealt with the instrument or its proceeds in breach of fiduciary duty.

(e) The presence on an instrument of an indorsement to which this section applies does not prevent a purchaser of the instrument from becoming a holder in due course of the instrument unless the purchaser is a converter under subsection (c) or has notice or knowledge of breach of fiduciary duty as stated in subsection (d).

(f) In an action to enforce the obligation of a party to pay the instrument, the obligor has a defense if payment would violate an indorsement to which this section applies and the payment is not permitted by this section.

§ 3—207. **Reacquisition.**

Reacquisition of an instrument occurs if it is transferred to a former holder, by negotiation or otherwise. A former holder who reacquires the instrument may cancel indorsements made after the reacquirer first became a holder of the instrument. If the cancellation causes the instrument to be payable to the reacquirer or to bearer, the reacquirer may negotiate the instrument. An indorser whose indorsement is canceled is discharged, and the discharge is effective against any subsequent holder.

Part 3 Enforcement of Instruments

§ 3—301. **Person Entitled to Enforce Instrument.**

"Person entitled to enforce" an instrument means (i) the holder of the instrument, (ii) a nonholder in possession of the instrument who has the rights of a holder, or (iii) a person not in possession of the instrument who is entitled to enforce the instrument pursuant to Section 3—309 or 3—418(d). A person may be a person entitled to enforce the instrument even though the person is not the owner of the instrument or is in wrongful possession of the instrument.

§ 3—302. **Holder in Due Course.**

(a) Subject to subsection (c) and Section 3—106(d), "holder in due course" means the holder of an instrument if:

(1) the instrument when issued or negotiated to the holder does not bear such apparent evidence of forgery or alteration or is not otherwise so irregular or incomplete as to call into question its authenticity; and

(2) the holder took the instrument (i) for value, (ii) in good faith, (iii) without notice that the instrument is overdue or has been dishonored or that there is an uncured default with respect to payment of another instrument issued as part of the same series, (iv) without notice that the instrument contains an unauthorized signature or has been altered, (v) without notice of any claim to the instrument described in Section 3—306, and (vi) without notice that any party has a defense or claim in recoupment described in Section 3—305(a).

(b) Notice of discharge of a party, other than discharge in an insolvency proceeding, is not notice of a defense under subsection (a), but discharge is effective against a person who became a holder in due course with notice of the discharge. Public filing or recording of a document does not of itself constitute notice of a defense, claim in recoupment, or claim to the instrument.

(c) Except to the extent a transferor or predecessor in interest has rights as a holder in due course, a person does not acquire rights of a holder in due course of an instrument taken (i) by legal process or by purchase in an execution, bankruptcy, or creditor's sale or similar proceeding, (ii) by purchase as part of a bulk transaction not in ordinary course of business of the transferor, or (iii) as the successor in interest to an estate or other organization.

(d) If, under Section 3—303(a)(1), the promise of performance that is the consideration for an instrument has been partially performed, the holder may assert rights as a holder in due course of the instrument only to the fraction of the amount payable under the instrument equal to the value of the partial performance divided by the value of the promised performance.

(e) If (i) the person entitled to enforce an instrument has only a security interest in the instrument and (ii) the person obliged to pay the instrument has a defense, claim in recoupment, or claim to the instrument that may be asserted against the person who granted the security interest, the person entitled to enforce the instrument may assert rights as a holder in due course only to an amount payable under the instrument which, at the time of enforcement of the instrument, does not exceed the amount of the unpaid obligation secured.

(f) To be effective, notice must be received at a time and in a manner that gives a reasonable opportunity to act on it.

(g) This section is subject to any law limiting status as a holder in due course in particular classes of transactions.

§ 3—303. **Value and Consideration.**

(a) An instrument is issued or transferred for value if:

(1) the instrument is issued or transferred for a promise of performance, to the extent the promise has been performed;

(2) the transferee acquires a security interest or other lien in the instrument other than a lien obtained by judicial proceeding;

(3) the instrument is issued or transferred as payment of, or as security for, an antecedent claim against any person, whether or not the claim is due;

(4) the instrument is issued or transferred in exchange for a negotiable instrument; or

(5) the instrument is issued or transferred in exchange for the incurring of an irrevocable obligation to a third party by the person taking the instrument.

(b) "Consideration" means any consideration sufficient to support a simple contract. The drawer or maker of an instrument has a defense if the instrument is issued without consideration. If an instrument is issued for a promise of performance, the issuer has a defense to the extent performance of the promise is due and the promise has not been performed. If an instrument is issued for value as stated in subsection (a), the instrument is also issued for consideration.

§ 3—304. **Overdue Instrument.**

(a) An instrument payable on demand becomes overdue at the earliest of the following times:

(1) on the day after the day demand for payment is duly made;

(2) if the instrument is a check, 90 days after its date; or

(3) if the instrument is not a check, when the instrument has been outstanding for a period of time after its date which is unreasonably long under the circumstances of the particular case in light of the nature of the instrument and usage of the trade.

(b) With respect to an instrument payable at a definite time the following rules apply:

(1) If the principal is payable in installments and a due date has not been accelerated, the instrument becomes overdue upon default under the instrument for nonpayment of an installment, and the instrument remains overdue until the default is cured.

(2) If the principal is not payable in installments and the due date has not been accelerated, the instrument becomes overdue on the day after the due date.

(3) If a due date with respect to principal has been accelerated, the instrument becomes overdue on the day after the accelerated due date.

(c) Unless the due date of principal has been accelerated, an instrument does not become overdue if there is default in payment of interest but no default in payment of principal.

§ 3—305. **Defenses and Claims in Recoupment.**

(a) Except as stated in subsection (b), the right to enforce the obligation of a party to pay an instrument is subject to the following:

(1) a defense of the obligor based on (i) infancy of the obligor to the extent it is a defense to a simple contract, (ii) duress, lack of legal capacity, or illegality of the transaction which, under other law, nullifies the obligation of the obligor, (iii) fraud that induced the obligor to sign the instrument with neither knowledge nor reasonable opportunity to learn of its character or its essential terms, or (iv) discharge of the obligor in insolvency proceedings;

(2) a defense of the obligor stated in another section of this Article or a defense of the obligor that would be available if the person entitled to enforce the instrument were enforcing a right to payment under a simple contract; and

(3) a claim in recoupment of the obligor against the original payee of the instrument if the claim arose from the transaction that gave rise to the instrument; but the claim of the obligor may be asserted against a transferee of the instrument only to reduce the amount owing on the instrument at the time the action is brought.

(b) The right of a holder in due course to enforce the obligation of a party to pay the instrument is subject to defenses of the obligor stated in subsection (a)(1), but is not subject to defenses of the obligor stated in subsection (a)(2) or claims in recoupment stated in subsection (a)(3) against a person other than the holder.

(c) Except as stated in subsection (d), in an action to enforce the obligation of a party to pay the instrument, the obligor may not assert against the person entitled to enforce the instrument a defense, claim in recoupment, or claim to the instrument (Section 3—306) of another person, but the other person's claim to the instrument may be asserted by the obligor if the other person is joined in the action and personally asserts the claim against the person entitled to enforce the instrument. An obligor is not obliged to pay the instrument if the person seeking enforcement of the instrument does not have rights of a holder in due course and the obligor proves that the instrument is a lost or stolen instrument.

(d) In an action to enforce the obligation of an accommodation party to pay an instrument, the accommodation party may assert against the person entitled to enforce the instrument any defense or claim in recoupment under subsection (a) that the accommodated party could assert against the person entitled to enforce the instrument, except the defenses of discharge in insolvency proceedings, infancy, and lack of legal capacity.

§ 3—306. **Claims to an Instrument.**

A person taking an instrument, other than a person having rights of a holder in due course, is subject to a claim of a property or possessory right in the instrument or its proceeds, including a claim to rescind a negotiation and to recover the instrument or its proceeds. A person having rights of a holder in due course takes free of the claim to the instrument.

§ 3—307. **Notice of Breach of Fiduciary Duty.**

(a) In this section:

(1) "Fiduciary" means an agent, trustee, partner, corporate officer or director, or other representative owing a fiduciary duty with respect to an instrument.

(2) "Represented person" means the principal, beneficiary, partnership, corporation, or other person to whom the duty stated in paragraph (1) is owed.

(b) If (i) an instrument is taken from a fiduciary for payment or collection or for value, (ii) the taker has knowledge of the fiduciary status of the fiduciary, and (iii) the represented person makes a claim to the instrument or its proceeds on the basis that the transaction of the fiduciary is a breach of fiduciary duty, the following rules apply:

(1) Notice of breach of fiduciary duty by the fiduciary is notice of the claim of the represented person.

(2) In the case of an instrument payable to the represented person or the fiduciary as such, the taker has notice of the breach of fiduciary duty if the instrument is (i) taken in payment of or as security for a debt known by the taker to be the personal debt of the fiduciary, (ii) taken in a transaction known by the taker to be for the personal benefit of the fiduciary, or (iii) deposited to an account other than an account of the fiduciary, as such, or an account of the represented person.

(3) If an instrument is issued by the represented person or the fiduciary as such, and made payable to the fiduciary personally, the taker does not have notice of the breach of fiduciary duty unless the taker knows of the breach of fiduciary duty.

(4) If an instrument is issued by the represented person or the fiduciary as such, to the taker as payee, the taker has notice of the breach of fiduciary duty if the instrument is (i) taken in payment of or as security for a debt known by the taker to be the personal debt of the fiduciary, (ii) taken in a transaction known by the taker to be for the personal benefit of the fiduciary, or (iii) deposited to an account other than an account of the fiduciary, as such, or an account of the represented person.

§ 3—308. **Proof of Signatures and Status as Holder in Due Course.**

(a) In an action with respect to an instrument, the authenticity of, and authority to make, each signature on the instrument is admitted unless specifically denied in the pleadings. If the validity of a signature is denied in the pleadings, the burden of establishing validity is on the person claiming validity, but the signature is presumed to be authentic and authorized unless the action is to enforce the liability of the purported signer and the signer is dead or incompetent at the time of trial of the issue of validity of the signature. If an action to enforce the instrument is brought against a person as the undisclosed principal of a person who signed the instrument as a party to the instrument, the plaintiff has the burden of establishing that the defendant is liable on the instrument as a represented person under Section 3—402(a).

(b) If the validity of signatures is admitted or proved and there is compliance with subsection (a), a plaintiff producing the instrument is entitled to payment if the plaintiff proves entitlement to enforce the instrument under Section 3—301, unless the defendant proves a defense or claim in recoupment. If a defense or claim in recoupment is proved, the right to payment of the plaintiff is subject to the defense or claim, except to the extent the plaintiff proves that the plaintiff has rights of a holder in due course which are not subject to the defense or claim.

§ 3—309. **Enforcement of Lost, Destroyed, or Stolen Instrument.**

(a) A person not in possession of an instrument is entitled to enforce the instrument if (i) the person was in possession of the instrument and entitled to enforce it when loss of possession occurred, (ii) the loss of possession was not the result of a transfer by the person or a lawful seizure, and (iii) the person cannot reasonably obtain possession of the instrument because the instrument was destroyed, its whereabouts cannot be determined, or it is in the wrongful possession of an unknown person or a person that cannot be found or is not amenable to service of process.

(b) A person seeking enforcement of an instrument under subsection (a) must prove the terms of the instrument and the person's right to enforce the instrument. If that proof is made, Section 3—308 applies to the case as if the person seeking enforcement had produced the instrument. The court may not enter judgment in favor of the person seeking enforcement unless it finds that the person required to pay the instrument is adequately protected against loss that might occur by reason of a claim by another person to enforce the instrument. Adequate protection may be provided by any reasonable means.

§ 3—310. **Effect of Instrument on Obligation for Which Taken.**

(a) Unless otherwise agreed, if a certified check, cashier's check, or teller's check is taken for an obligation, the obligation is discharged to the same extent discharge would result if an amount of money equal to the amount of the instrument were taken in payment of the obligation. Discharge of the obligation does not affect any liability that the obligor may have as an indorser of the instrument.

(b) Unless otherwise agreed and except as provided in subsection (a), if a note or an uncertified check is taken for an obligation, the obligation is suspended to the same extent the obligation would be discharged if an amount of money equal to the amount of the instrument were taken, and the following rules apply:

(1) In the case of an uncertified check, suspension of the obligation continues until dishonor of the check or until it is paid or certified. Payment or certification of the check results in discharge of the obligation to the extent of the amount of the check.

(2) In the case of a note, suspension of the obligation continues until dishonor of the note or until it is paid. Payment of the note results in discharge of the obligation to the extent of the payment.

(3) Except as provided in paragraph (4), if the check or note is dishonored and the obligee of the obligation for which the instrument was taken is the person entitled to enforce the instrument, the obligee may enforce either the instrument or the obligation. In the case of an instrument of a third person which is negotiated to the obligee by the obligor, discharge of the obligor on the instrument also discharges the obligation.

(4) If the person entitled to enforce the instrument taken for an obligation is a person other than the obligee, the obligee may not enforce the obligation to the extent the obligation is suspended. If the obligee is the person entitled to enforce the instrument but no longer has possession of it because it was lost, stolen, or destroyed, the obligation may not be enforced to the extent of the amount payable on the instrument, and to that extent the obligee's rights against the obligor are limited to enforcement of the instrument.

(c) If an instrument other than one described in subsection (a) or (b) is taken for an obligation, the effect is (i) that stated in subsection (a) if the instrument is one on which a bank is liable as maker or acceptor, or (ii) that stated in subsection (b) in any other case.

§ 3—311. **Accord and Satisfaction by Use of Instrument.**

(a) If a person against whom a claim is asserted proves that (i) that person in good faith tendered an instrument to the claimant as full satisfaction of the claim, (ii) the amount of the claim was unliquidated or subject to a bona fide dispute, and (iii) the claimant obtained payment of the instrument, the following subsections apply.

(b) Unless subsection (c) applies, the claim is discharged if the person against whom the claim is asserted proves that the instrument or an accompanying written communication contained a conspicuous statement to the effect that the instrument was tendered as full satisfaction of the claim.

(c) Subject to subsection (d), a claim is not discharged under subsection (b) if either of the following applies:

(1) The claimant, if an organization, proves that (i) within a reasonable time before the tender, the claimant sent a conspicuous statement to the person against whom the claim is asserted that communications concerning disputed debts, including an instrument tendered as full satisfaction of a debt, are to be sent to a designated person, office, or place, and (ii) the instrument or accompanying communication was not received by that designated person, office, or place.

(2) The claimant, whether or not an organization, proves that within 90 days after payment of the instrument, the claimant tendered repayment of the amount of the instrument to the person against whom the claim is asserted. This paragraph does not apply if the claimant is an organization that sent a statement complying with paragraph (1)(i).

(d) A claim is discharged if the person against whom the claim is asserted proves that within a reasonable time before collection of the instrument was initiated, the claimant, or an agent of the claimant having direct responsibility with respect to the disputed obligation, knew that the instrument was tendered in full satisfaction of the claim.

§ 3—312. **Lost, Destroyed, or Stolen Cashier's Check, Teller's Check, or Certified Check.**

(a) In this section:

(1) "Check" means a cashier's check, teller's check, or certified check.

(2) "Claimant" means a person who claims the right to receive the amount of a cashier's check, teller's check, or certified check that was lost, destroyed, or stolen.

(3) "Declaration of loss" means a written statement, made under penalty of perjury, to the effect that (i) the declarer lost possession of a check, (ii) the declarer is the drawer or payee of the check, in the case of a certified check, or the remitter or payee of the check, in the case of a cashier's check or teller's check, (iii) the loss of possession was not the result of a transfer by the declarer or a lawful seizure, and (iv) the declarer cannot reasonably obtain possession of the check because the check was destroyed, its whereabouts cannot be determined, or it is in the wrongful possession of an unknown person or a person that cannot be found or is not amenable to service of process.

(4) "Obligated bank" means the issuer of a cashier's check or teller's check or the acceptor of a certified check.

(b) A claimant may assert a claim to the amount of a check by a communication to the obligated bank describing the check with reasonable certainty and requesting payment of the amount of the check, if (i) the claimant is the drawer or payee of a certified check or the remitter or payee of a cashier's check or teller's check, (ii) the communication contains or is accompanied by a declaration of loss of the claimant with respect to the check, (iii) the communication is received at a time and in a manner affording the bank a reasonable time to act on it before the check is paid, and (iv) the claimant provides reasonable identification if requested by the obligated bank. Delivery of a declaration of loss is a warranty of the truth of the statements made in the declaration. If a claim is asserted in compliance with this subsection, the following rules apply:

(1) The claim becomes enforceable at the later of (i) the time the claim is asserted, or (ii) the 90th day following the date of the check, in the case of a cashier's check or teller's check, or the 90th day following the date of the acceptance, in the case of a certified check.

(2) Until the claim becomes enforceable, it has no legal effect and the obligated bank may pay the check or, in the case of a teller's check, may permit the drawee to pay the check. Payment to a person entitled to enforce the check discharges all liability of the obligated bank with respect to the check.

(3) If the claim becomes enforceable before the check is presented for payment, the obligated bank is not obliged to pay the check.

(4) When the claim becomes enforceable, the obligated bank becomes obliged to pay the amount of the check to the claimant if payment of the check has not been made to a person entitled to enforce the check. Subject to Section 4—302(a)(1), payment to the claimant discharges all liability of the obligated bank with respect to the check.

(c) If the obligated bank pays the amount of a check to a claimant under subsection (b)(4) and the check is presented for payment by a person having rights of a holder in due course, the claimant is obliged to (i) refund the payment to the obligated bank if the check is paid, or (ii) pay the amount of the check to the person having rights of a holder in due course if the check is dishonored.

(d) If a claimant has the right to assert a claim under subsection (b) and is also a person entitled to enforce a cashier's check, teller's check, or certified check which is lost, destroyed, or stolen, the claimant may assert rights with respect to the check either under this section or Section 3—309.

Part 4 Liability of Parties

§ 3—401. Signature.

(a) A person is not liable on an instrument unless (i) the person signed the instrument, or (ii) the person is represented by an agent or representative who signed the instrument and the signature is binding on the represented person under Section 3—402.

(b) A signature may be made (i) manually or by means of a device or machine, and (ii) by the use of any name, including a trade or assumed name, or by a word, mark, or symbol executed or adopted by a person with present intention to authenticate a writing.

§ 3—402. Signature by Representative.

(a) If a person acting, or purporting to act, as a representative signs an instrument by signing either the name of the represented person or the name of the signer, the represented person is bound by the signature to the same extent the represented person would be bound if the signature were on a simple contract. If the represented person is bound, the signature of the representative is the "authorized signature of the represented person" and the represented person is liable on the instrument, whether or not identified in the instrument.

(b) If a representative signs the name of the representative to an instrument and the signature is an authorized signature of the represented person, the following rules apply:

(1) If the form of the signature shows unambiguously that the signature is made on behalf of the represented person who is identified in the instrument, the representative is not liable on the instrument.

(2) Subject to subsection (c), if (i) the form of the signature does not show unambiguously that the signature is made in a representative capacity or (ii) the represented person is not identified in the instrument, the representative is liable on the instrument to a holder in due course that took the instrument without notice that the representative was not intended to be liable on the instrument. With respect to any other person, the representative is liable on the instrument unless the representative proves that the original parties did not intend the representative to be liable on the instrument.

(c) If a representative signs the name of the representative as drawer of a check without indication of the representative status and the check is payable from an account of the represented person who is identified on the check, the signer is not liable on the check if the signature is an authorized signature of the represented person.

§ 3—403. Unauthorized Signature.

(a) Unless otherwise provided in this Article or Article 4, an unauthorized signature is ineffective except as the signature of the unauthorized signer in favor of a person who in good faith pays the instrument or takes it for value. An unauthorized signature may be ratified for all purposes of this Article.

(b) If the signature of more than one person is required to constitute the authorized signature of an organization, the signature of the organization is unauthorized if one of the required signatures is lacking.

(c) The civil or criminal liability of a person who makes an unauthorized signature is not affected by any provision of this Article which makes the unauthorized signature effective for the purposes of this Article.

§ 3—404. Impostors; Fictitious Payees.

(a) If an impostor, by use of the mails or otherwise, induces the issuer of an instrument to issue the instrument to the impostor, or to a person acting in concert with the impostor, by impersonating the payee of the instrument or a person authorized to act for the payee, an indorsement of the instrument by any person in the name of the payee is effective as the indorsement of the payee in favor of a person who, in good faith, pays the instrument or takes it for value or for collection.

(b) If (i) a person whose intent determines to whom an instrument is payable (Section 3—110(a) or (b)) does not intend the person identified as payee to have any interest in the instrument, or (ii) the person identified as payee of an instrument is a fictitious person, the following rules apply until the instrument is negotiated by special indorsement:

(1) Any person in possession of the instrument is its holder.

(2) An indorsement by any person in the name of the payee stated in the instrument is effective as the indorsement of the payee in favor of a person who, in good faith, pays the instrument or takes it for value or for collection.

(c) Under subsection (a) or (b), an indorsement is made in the name of a payee if (i) it is made in a name substantially similar to that of the payee or (ii) the instrument, whether or not indorsed, is deposited in a depositary bank to an account in a name substantially similar to that of the payee.

(d) With respect to an instrument to which subsection (a) or (b) applies, if a person paying the instrument or taking it for value or for collection fails to exercise ordinary care in paying or taking the instrument and that failure substantially contributes to loss resulting from payment of the instrument, the person bearing the loss may recover from the person failing to exercise ordinary care to the extent the failure to exercise ordinary care contributed to the loss.

§ 3—405. **Employer's Responsibility for Fraudulent Indorsement by Employee.**

(a) In this section:

(1) "Employee" includes an independent contractor and employee of an independent contractor retained by the employer.

(2) "Fraudulent indorsement" means (i) in the case of an instrument payable to the employer, a forged indorsement purporting to be that of the employer, or (ii) in the case of an instrument with respect to which the employer is the issuer, a forged indorsement purporting to be that of the person identified as payee.

(3) "Responsibility" with respect to instruments means authority (i) to sign or indorse instruments on behalf of the employer, (ii) to process instruments received by the employer for bookkeeping purposes, for deposit to an account, or for other disposition, (iii) to prepare or process instruments for issue in the name of the employer, (iv) to supply information determining the names or addresses of payees of instruments to be issued in the name of the employer, (v) to control the disposition of instruments to be issued in the name of the employer, or (vi) to act otherwise with respect to instruments in a responsible capacity. "Responsibility" does not include authority that merely allows an employee to have access to instruments or blank or incomplete instrument forms that are being stored or transported or are part of incoming or outgoing mail, or similar access.

(b) For the purpose of determining the rights and liabilities of a person who, in good faith, pays an instrument or takes it for value or for collection, if an employer entrusted an employee with responsibility with respect to the instrument and the employee or a person acting in concert with the employee makes a fraudulent indorsement of the instrument, the indorsement is effective as the indorsement of the person to whom the instrument is payable if it is made in the name of that person. If the person paying the instrument or taking it for value or for collection fails to exercise ordinary care in paying or taking the instrument and that failure substantially contributes to loss resulting from the fraud, the person bearing the loss may recover from the person failing to exercise ordinary care to the extent the failure to exercise ordinary care contributed to the loss.

(c) Under subsection (b), an indorsement is made in the name of the person to whom an instrument is payable if (i) it is made in a name substantially similar to the name of that person or (ii) the instrument, whether or not indorsed, is deposited in a depositary bank to an account in a name substantially similar to the name of that person.

§ 3—406. **Negligence Contributing to Forged Signature or Alteration of Instrument.**

(a) A person whose failure to exercise ordinary care substantially contributes to an alteration of an instrument or to the making of a forged signature on an instrument is precluded from asserting the alteration or the forgery against a person who, in good faith, pays the instrument or takes it for value or for collection.

(b) Under subsection (a), if the person asserting the preclusion fails to exercise ordinary care in paying or taking the instrument and that failure substantially contributes to loss, the loss is allocated between the person precluded and the person asserting the preclusion according to the extent to which the failure of each to exercise ordinary care contributed to the loss.

(c) Under subsection (a), the burden of proving failure to exercise ordinary care is on the person asserting the preclusion. Under subsection (b), the burden of proving failure to exercise ordinary care is on the person precluded.

§ 3—407. **Alteration.**

(a) "Alteration" means (i) an unauthorized change in an instrument that purports to modify in any respect the obligation of a party, or (ii) an unauthorized addition of words or numbers or other change to an incomplete instrument relating to the obligation of a party.

(b) Except as provided in subsection (c), an alteration fraudulently made discharges a party whose obligation is affected by the alteration unless that party assents or is precluded from asserting the alteration. No other alteration discharges a party, and the instrument may be enforced according to its original terms.

(c) A payor bank or drawee paying a fraudulently altered instrument or a person taking it for value, in good faith and without notice of the alteration, may enforce rights with respect to the instrument (i) according to its original terms, or (ii) in the case of an incomplete instrument altered by unauthorized completion, according to its terms as completed.

§ 3—408. **Drawee Not Liable on Unaccepted Draft.**

A check or other draft does not of itself operate as an assignment of funds in the hands of the drawee available for its payment, and the drawee is not liable on the instrument until the drawee accepts it.

§ 3—409. **Acceptance of Draft; Certified Check.**

(a) "Acceptance" means the drawee's signed agreement to pay a draft as presented. It must be written on the draft and may consist of the drawee's signature alone. Acceptance may be made at any time and becomes effective when notification pursuant to instructions is given or the accepted draft is delivered for the purpose of giving rights on the acceptance to any person.

(b) A draft may be accepted although it has not been signed by the drawer, is otherwise incomplete, is overdue, or has been dishonored.

(c) If a draft is payable at a fixed period after sight and the acceptor fails to date the acceptance, the holder may complete the acceptance by supplying a date in good faith.

(d) "Certified check" means a check accepted by the bank on which it is drawn. Acceptance may be made as stated in subsection (a) or by a writing on the check which indicates that the check is certified. The drawee of a check has no obligation to certify the check, and refusal to certify is not dishonor of the check.

§ 3—410. **Acceptance Varying Draft.**

(a) If the terms of a drawee's acceptance vary from the terms of the draft as presented, the holder may refuse the acceptance and treat the draft as dishonored. In that case, the drawee may cancel the acceptance.

(b) The terms of a draft are not varied by an acceptance to pay at a particular bank or place in the United States, unless the acceptance states that the draft is to be paid only at that bank or place.

(c) If the holder assents to an acceptance varying the terms of a draft, the obligation of each drawer and indorser that does not expressly assent to the acceptance is discharged.

§ 3—411. **Refusal to Pay Cashier's Checks, Teller's Checks, and Certified Checks.**

(a) In this section, "obligated bank" means the acceptor of a certified check or the issuer of a cashier's check or teller's check bought from the issuer.

(b) If the obligated bank wrongfully (i) refuses to pay a cashier's check or certified check, (ii) stops payment of a teller's check, or (iii) refuses to pay a dishonored teller's check, the person asserting the right to enforce the check is entitled to compensation for expenses and loss of interest resulting from the nonpayment and may recover consequential damages if the obligated bank refuses to pay after receiving notice of particular circumstances giving rise to the damages.

(c) Expenses or consequential damages under subsection (b) are not recoverable if the refusal of the obligated bank to pay occurs because (i) the bank suspends payments, (ii) the obligated bank asserts a claim or defense of the bank that it has reasonable grounds to believe is available against the person entitled to enforce the instrument, (iii) the obligated bank has a reasonable doubt whether the person demanding payment is the person entitled to enforce the instrument, or (iv) payment is prohibited by law.

§ 3—412. **Obligation of Issuer of Note or Cashier's Check.**

The issuer of a note or cashier's check or other draft drawn on the drawer is obliged to pay the instrument (i) according to its terms at the time it was issued or, if not issued, at the time it first came into possession of a holder, or (ii) if the issuer signed an incomplete instrument, according to its terms when completed, to the extent stated in Sections 3—115 and 3—407. The obligation is owed to a person entitled to enforce the instrument or to an indorser who paid the instrument under Section 3—415.

§ 3—413. **Obligation of Acceptor.**

(a) The acceptor of a draft is obliged to pay the draft (i) according to its terms at the time it was accepted, even though the acceptance states that the draft is payable "as originally drawn" or equivalent terms, (ii) if the acceptance varies the terms of the draft, according to the terms of the draft as varied, or (iii) if the acceptance is of a draft that is an incomplete instrument, according to its terms when completed, to the extent stated in Sections 3—115 and 3—407. The obligation is owed to a person entitled to enforce the draft or to the drawer or an indorser who paid the draft under Section 3—414 or 3—415.

(b) If the certification of a check or other acceptance of a draft states the amount certified or accepted, the obligation of the acceptor is that amount. If (i) the certification or acceptance does not state an amount, (ii) the amount of the instrument is subsequently raised, and (iii) the instrument is then negotiated to a holder in due course, the obligation of the acceptor is the amount of the instrument at the time it was taken by the holder in due course.

§ 3—414. **Obligation of Drawer.**

(a) This section does not apply to cashier's checks or other drafts drawn on the drawer.

(b) If an unaccepted draft is dishonored, the drawer is obliged to pay the draft (i) according to its terms at the time it was issued or, if not issued, at the time it first came into possession of a holder, or (ii) if the drawer signed an incomplete instrument, according to its terms when completed, to the extent stated in Sections 3—115 and 3—407. The obligation is owed to a person entitled to enforce the draft or to an indorser who paid the draft under Section 3—415.

(c) If a draft is accepted by a bank, the drawer is discharged, regardless of when or by whom acceptance was obtained.

(d) If a draft is accepted and the acceptor is not a bank, the obligation of the drawer to pay the draft if the draft is dishonored by the acceptor is the same as the obligation of an indorser under Section 3—415(a) and (c).

(e) If a draft states that it is drawn "without recourse" or otherwise disclaims liability of the drawer to pay the draft, the drawer is not liable under subsection (b) to pay the draft if the draft is not a check. A disclaimer of the liability stated in subsection (b) is not effective if the draft is a check.

(f) If (i) a check is not presented for payment or given to a depositary bank for collection within 30 days after its date, (ii) the drawee suspends payments after expiration of the 30-day period without paying the check, and (iii) because of the suspension of payments, the drawer is deprived of funds maintained with the drawee to cover payment of the check, the drawer to the extent deprived of funds may discharge its obligation to pay the check by assigning to the person entitled to enforce the check the rights of the drawer against the drawee with respect to the funds.

§ 3—415. **Obligation of Indorser.**

(a) Subject to subsections (b), (c), and (d) and to Section 3—419(d), if an instrument is dishonored, an indorser is obliged to pay the amount due on the instrument (i) according to the terms of the instrument at the time it was indorsed, or (ii) if the indorser indorsed an incomplete instrument, according to its terms when completed, to the extent stated in Sections 3—115 and 3—407. The obligation of the indorser is owed to a person entitled to enforce the instrument or to a subsequent indorser who paid the instrument under this section.

(b) If an indorsement states that it is made "without recourse" or otherwise disclaims liability of the indorser, the indorser is not liable under subsection (a) to pay the instrument.

(c) If notice of dishonor of an instrument is required by Section 3—503 and notice of dishonor complying with that section is not given to an indorser, the liability of the indorser under subsection (a) is discharged.

(d) If a draft is accepted by a bank after an indorsement is made, the liability of the indorser under subsection (a) is discharged.

(e) If an indorser of a check is liable under subsection (a) and the check is not presented for payment, or given to a depositary bank for collection, within 30 days after the day the indorsement was made, the liability of the indorser under subsection (a) is discharged.

§ 3—416. **Transfer Warranties.**

(a) A person who transfers an instrument for consideration warrants to the transferee and, if the transfer is by indorsement, to any subsequent transferee that:

(1) the warrantor is a person entitled to enforce the instrument;

(2) all signatures on the instrument are authentic and authorized;

(3) the instrument has not been altered;

(4) the instrument is not subject to a defense or claim in recoupment of any party which can be asserted against the warrantor; and

(5) the warrantor has no knowledge of any insolvency proceeding commenced with respect to the maker or acceptor or, in the case of an unaccepted draft, the drawer.

(b) A person to whom the warranties under subsection (a) are made and who took the instrument in good faith may recover from the warrantor as damages for breach of warranty an amount equal to the loss suffered as a result of the breach, but not more than the amount of the instrument plus expenses and loss of interest incurred as a result of the breach.

(c) The warranties stated in subsection (a) cannot be disclaimed with respect to checks. Unless notice of a claim for breach of warranty is given to the warrantor within 30 days after the claimant has reason to know of the breach and the identity of the warrantor, the liability of the warrantor under subsection (b) is discharged to the extent of any loss caused by the delay in giving notice of the claim.

(d) A [cause of action] for breach of warranty under this section accrues when the claimant has reason to know of the breach.

§ 3—417. **Presentment Warranties.**

(a) If an unaccepted draft is presented to the drawee for payment or acceptance and the drawee pays or accepts the draft, (i) the person obtaining payment or acceptance, at the time of presentment, and (ii) a previous transferor of the draft, at the time of transfer, warrant to the drawee making payment or accepting the draft in good faith that:

(1) the warrantor is, or was, at the time the warrantor transferred the draft, a person entitled to enforce the draft or authorized to obtain payment or acceptance of the draft on behalf of a person entitled to enforce the draft;

(2) the draft has not been altered; and

(3) the warrantor has no knowledge that the signature of the drawer of the draft is unauthorized.

(b) A drawee making payment may recover from any warrantor damages for breach of warranty equal to the amount paid by the drawee less the amount the drawee received or is entitled to receive from the drawer because of the payment. In addition, the drawee is entitled to compensation for expenses and loss of interest resulting from the breach. The right of the drawee to recover damages under this subsection is not affected by any failure of the drawee to exercise ordinary care in making payment. If the drawee accepts the draft, breach of warranty is a defense to the obligation of the acceptor. If the acceptor makes payment with respect to the draft, the acceptor is entitled to recover from any warrantor for breach of warranty the amounts stated in this subsection.

(c) If a drawee asserts a claim for breach of warranty under subsection (a) based on an unauthorized indorsement of the draft or an alteration of the draft, the warrantor may defend by proving that the indorsement is effective under Section 3—404 or 3—405 or the drawer is precluded under Section 3—406 or 4—406 from asserting against the drawee the unauthorized indorsement or alteration.

(d) If (i) a dishonored draft is presented for payment to the drawer or an indorser or (ii) any other instrument is presented for payment to a party obliged to pay the instrument, and (iii) payment is received, the following rules apply:

(1) The person obtaining payment and a prior transferor of the instrument warrant to the person making payment in good faith that the warrantor is, or was, at the time the warrantor transferred the instrument, a person entitled to enforce the instrument or authorized to obtain payment on behalf of a person entitled to enforce the instrument.

(2) The person making payment may recover from any warrantor for breach of warranty an amount equal to the amount paid plus expenses and loss of interest resulting from the breach.

(e) The warranties stated in subsections (a) and (d) cannot be disclaimed with respect to checks. Unless notice of a claim for breach of warranty is given to the warrantor within 30 days after the claimant has reason to know of the breach and the identity of the warrantor, the liability of the warrantor under subsection (b) or (d) is discharged to the extent of any loss caused by the delay in giving notice of the claim.

(f) A [cause of action] for breach of warranty under this section accrues when the claimant has reason to know of the breach.

§ 3—418. **Payment or Acceptance by Mistake.**

(a) Except as provided in subsection (c), if the drawee of a draft pays or accepts the draft and the drawee acted on the mistaken belief that (i) payment of the draft had not been stopped pursuant to Section 4—403 or (ii) the signature of the drawer of the draft was authorized, the drawee may recover the amount of the draft from the person to whom or for whose benefit payment was made or, in the case of acceptance, may revoke the acceptance. Rights of the drawee under this subsection are not affected by failure of the drawee to exercise ordinary care in paying or accepting the draft.

(b) Except as provided in subsection (c), if an instrument has been paid or accepted by mistake and the case is not covered by subsection (a), the person paying or accepting may, to the extent permitted by the law governing mistake and restitution, (i) recover the payment from the person to whom or for whose benefit payment was made or (ii) in the case of acceptance, may revoke the acceptance.

(c) The remedies provided by subsection (a) or (b) may not be asserted against a person who took the instrument in good faith and for value or who in good faith changed position in reliance on the payment or acceptance. This subsection does not limit remedies provided by Section 3—417 or 4—407.

(d) Notwithstanding Section 4—215, if an instrument is paid or accepted by mistake and the payor or acceptor recovers payment or revokes acceptance under subsection (a) or (b), the instrument is deemed not to have been paid or accepted and is treated as dishonored, and the person from whom payment is recovered has rights as a person entitled to enforce the dishonored instrument.

§ 3—419. **Instruments Signed for Accommodation.**

(a) If an instrument is issued for value given for the benefit of a party to the instrument ("accommodated party") and another party to the instrument ("accommodation party") signs the instrument for the purpose of incurring liability on the instrument without being a direct beneficiary of the value given for the instrument, the instrument is signed by the accommodation party "for accommodation."

(b) An accommodation party may sign the instrument as maker, drawer, acceptor, or indorser and, subject to subsection (d), is obliged to pay the instrument in the capacity in which the accommodation party signs. The obligation of an accommodation party may be enforced notwithstanding any statute of frauds and whether or not the accommodation party receives consideration for the accommodation.

(c) A person signing an instrument is presumed to be an accommodation party and there is notice that the instrument is signed for accommodation if the signature is an anomalous indorsement or is accompanied by words indicating that the signer is acting as surety or guarantor with respect to the obligation of another party to the instrument. Except as provided in Section 3—605, the obligation of an accommodation party to pay the instrument is not affected by the fact that the person enforcing the obligation had notice when the instrument was taken by that person that the accommodation party signed the instrument for accommodation.

(d) If the signature of a party to an instrument is accompanied by words indicating unambiguously that the party is guaranteeing collection rather than payment of the obligation of another party to the instrument, the signer is obliged to pay the amount due on the instrument to a person entitled to enforce the instrument only if (i) execution of judgment against the other party has been returned unsatisfied, (ii) the other party is insolvent or in an insolvency proceeding, (iii) the other party cannot be served with process, or (iv) it is otherwise apparent that payment cannot be obtained from the other party.

(e) An accommodation party who pays the instrument is entitled to reimbursement from the accommodated party and is entitled to enforce the instrument against the accommodated party. An accommodated party who pays the instrument has no right of recourse against, and is not entitled to contribution from, an accommodation party.

§ 3—420. **Conversion of Instrument.**

(a) The law applicable to conversion of personal property applies to instruments. An instrument is also converted if it is taken by transfer, other than a negotiation, from a person not entitled to enforce the instrument or a bank makes or obtains payment with respect to the instrument for a person not entitled to enforce the instrument or receive payment. An action for conversion of an instrument may not be brought by (i) the issuer or acceptor of the instrument or (ii) a payee or indorsee who did not receive delivery of the instrument either directly or through delivery to an agent or a co-payee.

(b) In an action under subsection (a), the measure of liability is presumed to be the amount payable on the instrument, but recovery may not exceed the amount of the plaintiff's interest in the instrument.

(c) A representative, other than a depositary bank, who has in good faith dealt with an instrument or its proceeds on behalf of one who was not the person entitled to enforce the instrument is not liable in conversion to that person beyond the amount of any proceeds that it has not paid out.

Part 5 Dishonor

§ 3—501. **Presentment.**

(a) "Presentment" means a demand made by or on behalf of a person entitled to enforce an instrument (i) to pay the instrument made to the drawee or a party obliged to pay the instrument or, in the case of a note or accepted draft payable at a bank, to the bank, or (ii) to accept a draft made to the drawee.

(b) The following rules are subject to Article 4, agreement of the parties, and clearing-house rules and the like:

(1) Presentment may be made at the place of payment of the instrument and must be made at the place of payment if the instrument is payable at a bank in the United States; may be made by any commercially reasonable means, including an oral, written, or electronic communication; is effective when the demand for payment or acceptance is received by the person to whom presentment is made; and is effective if made to any one of two or more makers, acceptors, drawees, or other payors.

(2) Upon demand of the person to whom presentment is made, the person making presentment must (i) exhibit the instrument, (ii) give reasonable identification and, if presentment is made on behalf of another person, reasonable evidence of authority to do so, and (. . .) sign a receipt on the instrument for any payment made or surrender the instrument if full payment is made.

(3) Without dishonoring the instrument, the party to whom presentment is made may (i) return the instrument for lack of a necessary indorsement, or (ii) refuse payment or acceptance for failure of the presentment to comply with the terms of the instrument, an agreement of the parties, or other applicable law or rule.

(4) The party to whom presentment is made may treat presentment as occurring on the next business day after the day of presentment if the party to whom presentment is made has established a cut-off hour not earlier than 2 p.m. for the receipt and processing of instruments presented for payment or acceptance and presentment is made after the cut-off hour.

§ 3—502. **Dishonor.**

(a) Dishonor of a note is governed by the following rules:

(1) If the note is payable on demand, the note is dishonored if presentment is duly made to the maker and the note is not paid on the day of presentment.

(2) If the note is not payable on demand and is payable at or through a bank or the terms of the note require presentment, the note is dishonored if presentment is duly made and the note is not paid on the day it becomes payable or the day of presentment, whichever is later.

(3) If the note is not payable on demand and paragraph (2) does not apply, the note is dishonored if it is not paid on the day it becomes payable.

(b) Dishonor of an unaccepted draft other than a documentary draft is governed by the following rules:

(1) If a check is duly presented for payment to the payor bank otherwise than for immediate payment over the counter, the check is dishonored if the payor bank makes timely return of the check or sends timely notice of dishonor or nonpayment under Section 4—301 or 4—302, or becomes accountable for the amount of the check under Section 4—302.

(2) If a draft is payable on demand and paragraph (1) does not apply, the draft is dishonored if presentment for payment is duly made to the drawee and the draft is not paid on the day of presentment.

(3) If a draft is payable on a date stated in the draft, the draft is dishonored if (i) presentment for payment is duly made to the drawee and payment is not made on the day the draft becomes payable or the day of presentment, whichever is later, or (ii) presentment for acceptance is duly made before the day the draft becomes payable and the draft is not accepted on the day of presentment.

(4) If a draft is payable on elapse of a period of time after sight or acceptance, the draft is dishonored if presentment for acceptance is duly made and the draft is not accepted on the day of presentment.

(c) Dishonor of an unaccepted documentary draft occurs according to the rules stated in subsection (b)(2), (3), and (4), except that payment or acceptance may be delayed without dishonor until no later than the close of the third business day of the drawee following the day on which payment or acceptance is required by those paragraphs.

(d) Dishonor of an accepted draft is governed by the following rules:

(1) If the draft is payable on demand, the draft is dishonored if presentment for payment is duly made to the acceptor and the draft is not paid on the day of presentment.

(2) If the draft is not payable on demand, the draft is dishonored if presentment for payment is duly made to the acceptor and payment is not made on the day it becomes payable or the day of presentment, whichever is later.

(e) In any case in which presentment is otherwise required for dishonor under this section and presentment is excused under Section 3—504, dishonor occurs without presentment if the instrument is not duly accepted or paid.

(f) If a draft is dishonored because timely acceptance of the draft was not made and the person entitled to demand acceptance consents to a late acceptance, from the time of acceptance the draft is treated as never having been dishonored.

§ 3—503. **Notice of Dishonor.**

(a) The obligation of an indorser stated in Section 3—415(a) and the obligation of a drawer stated in Section 3—414(d) may not be enforced unless (i) the indorser or drawer is given notice of dishonor of the instrument complying with this section or (ii) notice of dishonor is excused under Section 3—504(b).

(b) Notice of dishonor may be given by any person; may be given by any commercially reasonable means, including an oral, written, or electronic communication; and is sufficient if it reasonably identifies the instrument and indicates that the instrument has been dishonored or has not been paid or accepted. Return of an instrument given to a bank for collection is sufficient notice of dishonor.

(c) Subject to Section 3—504(c), with respect to an instrument taken for collection by a collecting bank, notice of dishonor must be given (i) by the bank before midnight of the next banking day following the banking day on which the bank receives notice of dishonor of the instrument, or (ii) by any other person within 30 days following the day on which the person receives notice of dishonor. With respect to any other instrument, notice of dishonor must be given within 30 days following the day on which dishonor occurs.

§ 3—504. **Excused Presentment and Notice of Dishonor.**

(a) Presentment for payment or acceptance of an instrument is excused if (i) the person entitled to present the instrument cannot with reasonable diligence make presentment, (ii) the maker or acceptor has repudiated an obligation to pay the instrument or is dead or in insolvency proceedings, (iii) by the terms of the instrument presentment is not necessary to enforce the obligation of indorsers or the drawer, (iv) the drawer or indorser whose obligation is being enforced has waived presentment or otherwise has no reason to expect or right to require that the instrument be paid or accepted, or (v) the drawer instructed the drawee not to pay or accept the draft or the drawee was not obligated to the drawer to pay the draft.

(b) Notice of dishonor is excused if (i) by the terms of the instrument notice of dishonor is not necessary to enforce the obligation of a party to pay the instrument, or (ii) the party whose obligation is being enforced waived notice of dishonor. A waiver of presentment is also a waiver of notice of dishonor.

(c) Delay in giving notice of dishonor is excused if the delay was caused by circumstances beyond the control of the person giving the notice and the person giving the notice exercised reasonable diligence after the cause of the delay ceased to operate.

§ 3—505. **Evidence of Dishonor.**

(a) The following are admissible as evidence and create a presumption of dishonor and of any notice of dishonor stated:

(1) a document regular in form as provided in subsection (b) which purports to be a protest;

(2) a purported stamp or writing of the drawee, payor bank, or presenting bank on or accompanying the instrument stating that acceptance or payment has been refused unless reasons for the refusal are stated and the reasons are not consistent with dishonor;

(3) a book or record of the drawee, payor bank, or collecting bank, kept in the usual course of business which shows dishonor, even if there is no evidence of who made the entry.

(b) A protest is a certificate of dishonor made by a United States consul or vice consul, or a notary public or other person authorized to administer oaths by the law of the place where dishonor occurs. It may be made upon information satisfactory to that person. The protest must identify the instrument and certify either that presentment has been made or, if not made, the reason why it was not made, and that the instrument has been dishonored by nonacceptance or nonpayment. The protest may also certify that notice of dishonor has been given to some or all parties.

Part 6 Discharge and Payment

§ 3—601. **Discharge and Effect of Discharge.**

(a) The obligation of a party to pay the instrument is discharged as stated in this Article or by an act or agreement with the party which would discharge an obligation to pay money under a simple contract.

(b) Discharge of the obligation of a party is not effective against a person acquiring rights of a holder in due course of the instrument without notice of the discharge.

§ 3—602. **Payment.**

(a) Subject to subsection (b), an instrument is paid to the extent payment is made (i) by or on behalf of a party obliged to pay the instrument, and (ii) to a person entitled to enforce the instrument. To the extent of the payment, the obligation of the party obliged to pay the instrument is discharged even though payment is made with knowledge of a claim to the instrument under Section 3—306 by another person.

(b) The obligation of a party to pay the instrument is not discharged under subsection (a) if:

(1) a claim to the instrument under Section 3—306 is enforceable against the party receiving payment and (i) payment is made with knowledge by the payor that payment is prohibited by injunction or similar process of a court of competent jurisdiction, or (ii) in the case of an instrument other than a cashier's check, teller's check, or certified check, the party making payment accepted, from the person having a claim to the instrument, indemnity against loss resulting from refusal to pay the person entitled to enforce the instrument; or

(2) the person making payment knows that the instrument is a stolen instrument and pays a person it knows is in wrongful possession of the instrument.

§ 3—603. **Tender of Payment.**

(a) If tender of payment of an obligation to pay an instrument is made to a person entitled to enforce the instrument, the effect of tender is governed by principles of law applicable to tender of payment under a simple contract.

(b) If tender of payment of an obligation to pay an instrument is made to a person entitled to enforce the instrument and the tender is refused, there is discharge, to the extent of the amount of the tender, of the obligation of an indorser or accommodation party having a right of recourse with respect to the obligation to which the tender relates.

(c) If tender of payment of an amount due on an instrument is made to a person entitled to enforce the instrument, the obligation of the obligor to pay interest after the due date on the amount tendered is discharged. If presentment is required with respect to an instrument and the obligor is able and ready to pay on the due date at every place of payment stated in the instrument, the obligor is deemed to have made tender of payment on the due date to the person entitled to enforce the instrument.

§ 3—604. **Discharge by Cancellation or Renunciation.**

(a) A person entitled to enforce an instrument, with or without consideration, may discharge the obligation of a party to pay the instrument (i) by an intentional voluntary act, such as surrender of the instrument to the party, destruction, mutilation, or cancellation of the instrument, cancellation or striking out of the party's signature, or the addition of words to the instrument indicating discharge, or (ii) by agreeing not to sue or otherwise renouncing rights against the party by a signed writing.

(b) Cancellation or striking out of an indorsement pursuant to subsection (a) does not affect the status and rights of a party derived from the indorsement.

§ 3—605. **Discharge of Indorsers and Accommodation Parties.**

(a) In this section, the term "indorser" includes a drawer having the obligation described in Section 3—414(d).

(b) Discharge, under Section 3—604, of the obligation of a party to pay an instrument does not discharge the obligation of an indorser or accommodation party having a right of recourse against the discharged party.

(c) If a person entitled to enforce an instrument agrees, with or without consideration, to an extension of the due date of the obligation of a party to pay the instrument, the extension discharges an indorser or accommodation party having a right of recourse against the party whose obligation is extended to the extent the indorser or accommodation party proves that the extension caused loss to the indorser or accommodation party with respect to the right of recourse.

(d) If a person entitled to enforce an instrument agrees, with or without consideration, to a material modification of the obligation of a party other than an extension of the due date, the modification discharges the obligation of an indorser or accommodation party having a right of recourse against the person whose obligation is modified to the extent the modification causes loss to the indorser or accommodation party with respect to the right of recourse. The loss suffered by the indorser or accommodation party as a result of the modification is equal to the amount of the right of recourse unless the person enforcing the instrument proves that no loss was caused by the modification or that the loss caused by the modification was an amount less than the amount of the right of recourse.

(e) If the obligation of a party to pay an instrument is secured by an interest in collateral and a person entitled to enforce the instrument impairs the value of the interest in collateral, the obligation of an indorser or accommodation party having a right of recourse against the obligor is discharged to the extent of the impairment. The value of an interest in collateral is impaired to the extent (i) the value of the interest is reduced to an amount less than the amount of the right of recourse of the party asserting discharge, or (ii) the reduction in value of the interest causes an increase in the amount by which the amount of the right of recourse exceeds the value of the interest. The burden of proving impairment is on the party asserting discharge.

(f) If the obligation of a party is secured by an interest in collateral not provided by an accommodation party and a person entitled to enforce the instrument impairs the value of the interest in collateral, the obligation of any party who is jointly and severally liable with respect to the secured obligation is discharged to the extent the impairment causes the party asserting discharge to pay more than that party would have been obliged to pay, taking into account rights of contribution, if impairment had not occurred. If the party asserting discharge is an accommodation party not entitled to discharge under subsection (e), the party is deemed to have a right to contribution based on joint and several liability rather than a right to reimbursement. The burden of proving impairment is on the party asserting discharge.

(g) Under subsection (e) or (f), impairing value of an interest in collateral includes (i) failure to obtain or maintain perfection or recordation of the interest in collateral, (ii) release of collateral without substitution of collateral of equal value, (iii) failure to perform a duty to preserve the value of collateral owed, under Article 9 or other law, to a debtor or surety or other person secondarily liable, or (iv) failure to comply with applicable law in disposing of collateral.

(h) An accommodation party is not discharged under subsection (c), (d), or (e) unless the person entitled to enforce the instrument knows of the accommodation or has notice under Section 3—419(c) that the instrument was signed for accommodation.

(i) A party is not discharged under this section if (i) the party asserting discharge consents to the event or conduct that is the basis of the discharge, or (ii) the instrument or a separate agreement of the party provides for waiver of discharge under this section either specifically or by general language indicating that parties waive defenses based on suretyship or impairment of collateral.

ADDENDUM TO REVISED ARTICLE 3

Notes to Legislative Counsel

1. If revised Article 3 is adopted in your state, the reference in Section 2—511 to Section 3—802 should be changed to Section 3—310.

2. If revised Article 3 is adopted in your state and the Uniform Fiduciaries Act is also in effect in your state, you may want to consider amending Uniform Fiduciaries Act § 9 to conform to Section 3—307(b)(2)(iii) and (4)(iii). See Official Comment 3 to Section 3—307.

Article 4
BANK DEPOSITS AND COLLECTIONS

Part 1 General Provisions and Definitions

§ 4—101. Short Title.

This Article shall be known and may be cited as Uniform Commercial Code—Bank Deposits and Collections.

§ 4—102. Applicability.

(1) To the extent that items within this Article are also within the scope of Articles 3 and 8, they are subject to the provisions of those Articles. In the event of conflict the provisions of this Article govern those of Article 3 but the provisions of Article 8 govern those of this Article.

(2) The liability of a bank for action or non-action with respect to any item handled by it for purposes of presentment, payment or collection is governed by the law of the place where the bank is located. In the case of action or non-action by or at a branch or separate office of a bank, its liability is governed by the law of the place where the branch or separate office is located.

§ 4—103. Variation by Agreement; Measure of Damages; Certain Action Constituting Ordinary Care.

(1) The effect of the provisions of this Article may be varied by agreement except that no agreement can disclaim a bank's responsibility for its own lack of good faith or failure to exercise ordinary care or can limit the measure of damages for such lack or failure; but the parties may by agreement determine the standards by which such responsibility is to be measured if such standards are not manifestly unreasonable.

(2) Federal Reserve regulations and operating letters, clearing house rules, and the like, have the effect of agreements under subsection (1), whether or not specifically assented to by all parties interested in items handled.

(3) Action or nonaction approved by this Article or pursuant to Federal Reserve regulations or operating letters constitutes the exercise of ordinary care and, in the absence of special instructions, action or nonaction consistent with clearing house rules and the like or with a general banking usage not disapproved by this Article, prima facie constitutes the exercise of ordinary care.

(4) The specification or approval of certain procedures by this Article does not constitute disapproval of other procedures which may be reasonable under the circumstances.

(5) The measure of damages for failure to exercise ordinary care in handling an item is the amount of the item reduced by an amount which could not have been realized by the use of ordinary care, and where there is bad faith it includes other damages, if any, suffered by the party as a proximate consequence.

§ 4—104. Definitions and Index of Definitions.

(1) In this Article unless the context otherwise requires

(a) "Account" means any account with a bank and includes a checking, time, interest or savings account;

(b) "Afternoon" means the period of a day between noon and midnight;

(c) "Banking day" means that part of any day on which a bank is open to the public for carrying on substantially all of its banking functions;

(d) "Clearing house" means any association of banks or other payors regularly clearing items;

(e) "Customer" means any person having an account with a bank or for whom a bank has agreed to collect items and includes a bank carrying an account with another bank;

(f) "Documentary draft" means any negotiable or nonnegotiable draft with accompanying documents, securities or other papers to be delivered against honor of the draft;

(g) "Item" means any instrument for the payment of money even though it is not negotiable but does not include money;

(h) "Midnight deadline" with respect to a bank is midnight on its next banking day following the banking day on which it receives the relevant item or notice or from which the time for taking action commences to run, whichever is later;

(i) "Properly payable" includes the availability of funds for payment at the time of decision to pay or dishonor;

(j) "Settle" means to pay in cash, by clearing house settlement, in a charge or credit or by remittance, or otherwise as instructed. A settlement may be either provisional or final;

(k) "Suspends payments" with respect to a bank means that it has been closed by order of the supervisory authorities, that a public officer has been appointed to take it over or that it ceases or refuses to make payments in the ordinary course of business.

(2) Other definitions applying to this Article and the sections in which they appear are:

"Collecting bank" Section 4—105.
"Depositary bank" Section 4—105.
"Intermediary bank" Section 4—105.
"Payor bank" Section 4—105.
"Presenting bank" Section 4—105.
"Remitting bank" Section 4—105.

(3) The following definitions in other Articles apply to this Article:

"Acceptance" Section 3—410.
"Certificate of deposit" Section 3—104.
"Certification" Section 3—411.
"Check" Section 3—104.
"Draft" Section 3—104.
"Holder in due course" Section 3—302.
"Notice of dishonor" Section 3—508.
"Presentment" Section 3—504.
"Protest" Section 3—509.
"Secondary party" Section 3—102.

(4) In addition Article 1 contains general definitions and principles of construction and interpretation applicable throughout this Article.

§ 4—105. **"Depositary Bank"; "Intermediary Bank"; "Collecting Bank"; "Payor Bank"; "Presenting Bank"; "Remitting Bank".**

In this Article unless the context otherwise requires:

(a) "Depositary bank" means the first bank to which an item is transferred for collection even though it is also the payor bank;

(b) "Payor bank" means a bank by which an item is payable as drawn or accepted;

(c) "Intermediary bank" means any bank to which an item is transferred in course of collection except the depositary or payor bank;

(d) "Collecting bank" means any bank handling the item for collection except the payor bank;

(e) "Presenting bank" means any bank presenting an item except a payor bank;

(f) "Remitting bank" means any payor or intermediary bank remitting for an item.

§ 4—106. **Separate Office of a Bank.**

A branch or separate office of a bank [maintaining its own deposit ledgers] is a separate bank for the purpose of computing the time within which and determining the place at or to which action may be taken or notices or orders shall be given under this Article and under Article 3.

Note: *The brackets are to make it optional with the several states whether to require a branch to maintain its own deposit ledgers in order to be considered to be a separate bank for certain purposes under Article 4. In some states "maintaining its own deposit ledgers" is a satisfactory test. In others branch banking practices are such that this test would not be suitable.*

§ 4—107. **Time of Receipt of Items.**

(1) For the purpose of allowing time to process items, prove balances and make the necessary entries on its books to determine its position for the day, a bank may fix an afternoon hour of 2 P.M. or later as a cut-off hour for the handling of money and items and the making of entries on its books.

(2) Any item or deposit of money received on any day after a cut-off hour so fixed or after the close of the banking day may be treated as being received at the opening of the next banking day.

§ 4—108. **Delays.**

(1) Unless otherwise instructed, a collecting bank in a good faith effort to secure payment may, in the case of specific items and with or without the approval of any person involved, waive, modify or extend time limits imposed or permitted by this Act for a period not in excess of an additional banking day without discharge of secondary parties and without liability to its transferor or any prior party.

(2) Delay by a collecting bank or payor bank beyond time limits prescribed or permitted by this Act or by instructions is excused if caused by interruption of communication facilities, suspension of payments by another bank, war, emergency conditions or other circumstances beyond the control of the bank provided it exercises such diligence as the circumstances require.

§ 4—109. **Process of Posting.**

The "process of posting" means the usual procedure followed by a payor bank in determining to pay an item and in recording the payment including one or more of the following or other steps as determined by the bank:

(a) verification of any signature;

(b) ascertaining that sufficient funds are available;

(c) affixing a "paid" or other stamp;

(d) entering a charge or entry to a customer's account;

(e) correcting or reversing an entry or erroneous action with respect to the item.

Part 2 Collection of Items: Depositary and Collecting Banks

§ 4—201. Presumption and Duration of Agency Status of Collecting Banks and Provisional Status of Credits; Applicability of Article; Item Indorsed "Pay Any Bank".

(1) Unless a contrary intent clearly appears and prior to the time that a settlement given by a collecting bank for an item is or becomes final (subsection (3) of Section 4—211 and Sections 4—212 and 4—213) the bank is an agent or sub-agent of the owner of the item and any settlement given for the item is provisional. This provision applies regardless of the form of indorsement or lack of indorsement and even though credit given for the item is subject to immediate withdrawal as of right or is in fact withdrawn; but the continuance of ownership of an item by its owner and any rights of the owner to proceeds of the item are subject to rights of a collecting bank such as those resulting from outstanding advances on the item and valid rights of setoff. When an item is handled by banks for purposes of presentment, payment and collection, the relevant provisions of this Article apply even though action of parties clearly establishes that a particular bank has purchased the item and is the owner of it.

(2) After an item has been indorsed with the words "pay any bank" or the like, only a bank may acquire the rights of a holder

(a) until the item has been returned to the customer initiating collection; or

(b) until the item has been specially indorsed by a bank to a person who is not a bank.

§ 4—202. Responsibility for Collection; When Action Seasonable.

(1) A collecting bank must use ordinary care in

(a) presenting an item or sending it for presentment; and

(b) sending notice of dishonor or non-payment or returning an item other than a documentary draft to the bank's transferor [or directly to the depositary bank under subsection (2) of Section 4—212] *(see note to Section 4—212)* after learning that the item has not been paid or accepted as the case may be; and

(c) settling for an item when the bank receives final settlement; and

(d) making or providing for any necessary protest; and

(e) notifying its transferor of any loss or delay in transit within a reasonable time after discovery thereof.

(2) A collecting bank taking proper action before its midnight deadline following receipt of an item, notice or payment acts seasonably; taking proper action within a reasonably longer time may be seasonable but the bank has the burden of so establishing.

(3) Subject to subsection (1)(a), a bank is not liable for the insolvency, neglect, misconduct, mistake or default of another bank or person or for loss or destruction of an item in transit or in the possession of others.

§ 4—203. Effect of Instructions.

Subject to the provisions of Article 3 concerning conversion of instruments (Section 3—419) and the provisions of both Article 3 and this Article concerning restrictive indorsements only a collecting bank's transferor can give instructions which affect the bank or constitute notice to it and a collecting bank is not liable to prior parties for any action taken pursuant to such instructions or in accordance with any agreement with its transferor.

§ 4—204. Methods of Sending and Presenting; Sending Direct to Payor Bank.

(1) A collecting bank must send items by reasonably prompt method taking into consideration any relevant instructions, the nature of the item, the number of such items on hand, and the cost of collection involved and the method generally used by it or others to present such items.

(2) A collecting bank may send

(a) any item direct to the payor bank;

(b) any item to any non-bank payor if authorized by its transferor; and

(c) any item other than documentary drafts to any non-bank payor, if authorized by Federal Reserve regulation or operating letter, clearing house rule or the like.

(3) Presentment may be made by a presenting bank at a place where the payor bank has requested that presentment be made.

§ 4—205. Supplying Missing Indorsement; No Notice from Prior Indorsement.

(1) A depositary bank which has taken an item for collection may supply any indorsement of the customer which is necessary to title unless the item contains the words "payee's indorsement required" or the like. In the absence of such a requirement a statement placed on the item by the depositary bank to the effect that the item was deposited by a customer or credited to his account is effective as the customer's indorsement.

(2) An intermediary bank, or payor bank which is not a depositary bank, is neither given notice nor otherwise affected by a restrictive indorsement of any person except the bank's immediate transferor.

§ 4—206. Transfer Between Banks.

Any agreed method which identifies the transferor bank is sufficient for the item's further transfer to another bank.

§ 4—207. Warranties of Customer and Collecting Bank on Transfer or Presentment of Items; Time for Claims.

(1) Each customer or collecting bank who obtains payment or acceptance of an item and each prior customer and collecting bank warrants to the payor bank or other payor who in good faith pays or accepts the item that

(a) he has a good title to the item or is authorized to obtain payment or acceptance on behalf of one who has a good title; and

(b) he has no knowledge that the signature of the maker or drawer is unauthorized, except that this warranty is not given by any customer or collecting bank that is a holder in due course and acts in good faith

(i) to a maker with respect to the maker's own signature; or

(ii) to a drawer with respect to the drawer's own signature, whether or not the drawer is also the drawee; or

(iii) to an acceptor of an item if the holder in due course took the item after the acceptance or obtained the acceptance without knowledge that the drawer's signature was unauthorized; and

(c) the item has not been materially altered, except that this warranty is not given by any customer or collecting bank that is a holder in due course and acts in good faith

(i) to the maker of a note; or

(ii) to the drawer of a draft whether or not the drawer is also the drawee; or

(iii) to the acceptor of an item with respect to an alteration made prior to the acceptance if the holder in due course took the item after the acceptance, even though the acceptance provided "payable as originally drawn" or equivalent terms; or

(iv) to the acceptor of an item with respect to an alteration made after the acceptance.

(2) Each customer and collecting bank who transfers an item and receives a settlement or other consideration for it warrants to his transferee and to any subsequent collecting bank who takes the item in good faith that

(a) he has a good title to the item or is authorized to obtain payment or acceptance on behalf of one who has a good title and the transfer is otherwise rightful; and

(b) all signatures are genuine or authorized; and

(c) the item has not been materially altered; and

(d) no defense of any party is good against him; and

(e) he has no knowledge of any insolvency proceeding instituted with respect to the maker or acceptor or the drawer of an unaccepted item.

In addition each customer and collecting bank so transferring an item and receiving a settlement or other consideration engages that upon dishonor and any necessary notice of dishonor and protest he will take up the item.

(3) The warranties and the engagement to honor set forth in the two preceding subsections arise notwithstanding the absence of indorsement or words of guaranty or warranty in the transfer or presentment and a collecting bank remains liable for their breach despite remittance to its transferor. Damages for breach of such warranties or engagement to honor shall not exceed the consideration received by the customer or collecting bank responsible plus finance charges and expenses related to the item, if any.

(4) Unless a claim for breach of warranty under this section is made within a reasonable time after the person claiming learns of the breach, the person liable is discharged to the extent of any loss caused by the delay in making claim.

§ 4—208. **Security Interest of Collecting Bank in Items, Accompanying Documents and Proceeds.**

(1) A bank has a security interest in an item and any accompanying documents or the proceeds of either

(a) in case of an item deposited in an account to the extent to which credit given for the item has been withdrawn or applied;

(b) in case of an item for which it has given credit available for withdrawal as of right, to the extent of the credit given whether or not the credit is drawn upon and whether or not there is a right of charge-back; or

(c) if it makes an advance on or against the item.

(2) When credit which has been given for several items received at one time or pursuant to a single agreement is withdrawn or applied in part the security interest remains upon all the items, any accompanying documents or the proceeds of either. For the purpose of this section, credits first given are first withdrawn.

(3) Receipt by a collecting bank of a final settlement for an item is a realization on its security interest in the item, accompanying documents and proceeds. To the extent and so long as the bank does not receive final settlement for the item or give up possession of the item or accompanying documents for purposes other than collection, the security interest continues and is subject to the provisions of Article 9 except that

(a) no security agreement is necessary to make the security interest enforceable (subsection (1)(a) of Section 9—203); and

(b) no filing is required to perfect the security interest; and

(c) the security interest has priority over conflicting perfected security interests in the item, accompanying documents or proceeds.

§ 4—209. **When Bank Gives Value for Purposes of Holder in Due Course.**

For purposes of determining its status as a holder in due course, the bank has given value to the extent that it has a security interest in an item provided that the bank otherwise complies with the requirements of Section 3—302 on what constitutes a holder in due course.

§ 4—210. **Presentment by Notice of Item Not Payable by, Through or at a Bank; Liability of Secondary Parties.**

(1) Unless otherwise instructed, a collecting bank may present an item not payable by, through or at a bank by sending to the party to accept or pay a written notice that the bank holds the item for acceptance or payment. The notice must be sent in time to be received on or before the day when presentment is due and the bank must meet any requirement of the party to accept or pay under Section 3—505 by the close of the bank's next banking day after it knows of the requirement.

(2) Where presentment is made by notice and neither honor nor request for compliance with a requirement under Section 3—505 is received by the close of business on the day after maturity or in the case of demand items by the close of business on the third banking day after notice was sent, the presenting bank may treat the item as dishonored and charge any secondary party by sending him notice of the facts.

§ 4—211. **Media of Remittance; Provisional and Final Settlement in Remittance Cases.**

(1) A collecting bank may take in settlement of an item

(a) a check of the remitting bank or of another bank on any bank except the remitting bank; or

(b) a cashier's check or similar primary obligation of a remitting bank which is a member of or clears through a member of the same clearing house or group as the collecting bank; or

(c) appropriate authority to charge an account of the remitting bank or of another bank with the collecting bank; or

(d) if the item is drawn upon or payable by a person other than a bank, a cashier's check, certified check or other bank check or obligation.

(2) If before its midnight deadline the collecting bank properly dishonors a remittance check or authorization to charge on itself or presents or forwards for collection a remittance instrument of or on another bank which is of a kind approved by subsection (1) or has not been authorized by it, the collecting bank is not liable to prior parties in the event of the dishonor of such check, instrument or authorization.

(3) A settlement for an item by means of a remittance instrument or authorization to charge is or becomes a final settlement as to both the person making and the person receiving the settlement

(a) if the remittance instrument or authorization to charge is of a kind approved by subsection (1) or has not been authorized by the person receiving the settlement and in either case the person receiving the settlement acts seasonably before its midnight deadline in presenting, forwarding for collection or paying the instrument or authorization,—at the time the remittance instrument or authorization is finally paid by the payor by which it is payable;

(b) if the person receiving the settlement has authorized remittance by a non-bank check or obligation or by a cashier's check or similar primary obligation of or a check upon the payor or other remitting bank which is not of a kind approved by subsection (1)(b),—at the time of the receipt of such remittance check or obligation; or

(c) if in a case not covered by sub-paragraphs (a) or (b) the person receiving the settlement fails to seasonably present, forward for collection, pay or return a remittance instrument or authorization to it to charge before its midnight deadline,—at such midnight deadline.

§ 4—212. **Right of Charge-Back or Refund.**

(1) If a collecting bank has made provisional settlement with its customer for an item and itself fails by reason of dishonor, suspension of payments by a bank or otherwise to receive a settlement for the item which is or becomes final, the bank may revoke the settlement given by it, charge back the amount of any credit given for the item to its customer's account or obtain refund from its customer whether or not it is able to return the items if by its midnight deadline or within a longer reasonable time after it learns the facts it returns the item or sends notification of the facts. These rights to revoke, charge-back and obtain refund terminate if and when a settlement for the item received by the bank is or becomes final (subsection (3) of Section 4—211 and subsections (2) and (3) of Section 4—213).

[(2) Within the time and manner prescribed by this section and Section 4—301, an intermediary or payor bank, as the case may be, may return an unpaid item directly to the depositary bank and may send for collection a draft on the depositary bank and obtain reimbursement. In such case, if the depositary bank has received provisional settlement for the item, it must reimburse the bank drawing the draft and any provisional credits for the item between banks shall become and remain final.]

Note: *Direct returns is recognized as an innovation that is not yet established bank practice, and therefore, Paragraph 2 has been bracketed. Some lawyers have doubts whether it should be included in legislation or left to development by agreement.*

(3) A depositary bank which is also the payor may charge-back the amount of an item to its customer's account or obtain refund in accordance with the section governing return of an item received by a payor bank for credit on its books (Section 4—301).

(4) The right to charge-back is not affected by

(a) prior use of the credit given for the item; or

(b) failure by any bank to exercise ordinary care with respect to the item but any bank so failing remains liable.

(5) A failure to charge-back or claim refund does not affect other rights of the bank against the customer or any other party.

(6) If credit is given in dollars as the equivalent of the value of an item payable in a foreign currency the dollar amount of any charge-back or refund shall be calculated on the basis of the buying sight rate for the foreign currency prevailing on the day when the person entitled to the charge-back or refund learns that it will not receive payment in ordinary course.

§ 4—213. **Final Payment of Item by Payor Bank; When Provisional Debits and Credits Become Final; When Certain Credits Become Available for Withdrawal.**

(1) An item is finally paid by a payor bank when the bank has done any of the following, whichever happens first:

(a) paid the item in cash; or

(b) settled for the item without reserving a right to revoke the settlement and without having such right under statute, clearing house rule or agreement; or

(c) completed the process of posting the item to the indicated account of the drawer, maker or other person to be charged therewith; or

(d) made a provisional settlement for the item and failed to revoke the settlement in the time and manner permitted by statute, clearing house rule or agreement.

Upon a final payment under subparagraphs (b), (c) or (d) the payor bank shall be accountable for the amount of the item.

(2) If provisional settlement for an item between the presenting and payor banks is made through a clearing house or by debits or credits in an account between them, then to the extent that provisional debits or credits for the item are entered in accounts between the presenting and payor banks or between the presenting and successive prior collecting banks seriatim, they become final upon final payment of the item by the payor bank.

(3) If a collecting bank receives a settlement for an item which is or becomes final (subsection (3) of Section 4—211, subsection (2) of Section 4—213) the bank is accountable to its customer

for the amount of the item and any provisional credit given for the item in an account with its customer becomes final.

(4) Subject to any right of the bank to apply the credit to an obligation of the customer, credit given by a bank for an item in an account with its customer becomes available for withdrawal as of right

(a) in any case where the bank has received a provisional settlement for the item,—when such settlement becomes final and the bank has had a reasonable time to learn that the settlement is final;

(b) in any case where the bank is both a depositary bank and a payor bank and the item is finally paid,—at the opening of the bank's second banking day following receipt of the item.

(5) A deposit of money in a bank is final when made but, subject to any right of the bank to apply the deposit to an obligation of the customer, the deposit becomes available for withdrawal as of right at the opening of the bank's next banking day following receipt of the deposit.

§ 4—214. **Insolvency and Preference.**

(1) Any item in or coming into the possession of a payor or collecting bank which suspends payment and which item is not finally paid shall be returned by the receiver, trustee or agent in charge of the closed bank to the presenting bank or the closed bank's customer.

(2) If a payor bank finally pays an item and suspends payments without making a settlement for the item with its customer or the presenting bank which settlement is or becomes final, the owner of the item has a preferred claim against the payor bank.

(3) If a payor bank gives or a collecting bank gives or receives a provisional settlement for an item and thereafter suspends payments, the suspension does not prevent or interfere with the settlement becoming final if such finality occurs automatically upon the lapse of certain time or the happening of certain events (subsection (3) of Section 4—211, subsections (1)(d), (2) and (3) of Section 4—213).

(4) If a collecting bank receives from subsequent parties settlement for an item which settlement is or becomes final and suspends payments without making a settlement for the item with its customer which is or becomes final, the owner of the item has a preferred claim against such collecting bank.

Part 3 Collection of Items: Payor Banks

§ 4—301. **Deferred Posting; Recovery of Payment by Return of Items; Time of Dishonor.**

(1) Where an authorized settlement for a demand item (other than a documentary draft) received by a payor bank otherwise than for immediate payment over the counter has been made before midnight of the banking day of receipt the payor bank may revoke the settlement and recover any payment if before it has made final payment (subsection (1) of Section 4—213) and before its midnight deadline it

(a) returns the item; or

(b) sends written notice of dishonor or nonpayment if the item is held for protest or is otherwise unavailable for return.

(2) If a demand item is received by a payor bank for credit on its books it may return such item or send notice of dishonor and may revoke any credit given or recover the amount thereof withdrawn by its customer, if it acts within the time limit and in the manner specified in the preceding subsection.

(3) Unless previous notice of dishonor has been sent an item is dishonored at the time when for purposes of dishonor it is returned or notice sent in accordance with this section.

(4) An item is returned:

(a) as to an item received through a clearing house, when it is delivered to the presenting or last collecting bank or to the clearing house or is sent or delivered in accordance with its rules; or

(b) in all other cases, when it is sent or delivered to the bank's customer or transferor or pursuant to his instructions.

§ 4—302. **Payor Bank's Responsibility for Late Return of Item.**

In the absence of a valid defense such as breach of a presentment warranty (subsection (1) of Section 4— 207), settlement effected or the like, if an item is presented on and received by a payor bank the bank is accountable for the amount of

(a) a demand item other than a documentary draft whether properly payable or not if the bank, in any case where it is not also the depositary bank, retains the item beyond midnight of the banking day of receipt without settling for it or, regardless of whether it is also the depositary bank, does not pay or return the item or send notice of dishonor until after its midnight deadline; or

(b) any other properly payable item unless within the time allowed for acceptance or payment of that item the bank either accepts or pays the item or returns it and accompanying documents.

§ 4—303. **When Items Subject to Notice, Stop-Order, Legal Process or Setoff; Order in Which Items May Be Charged or Certified.**

(1) Any knowledge, notice or stop-order received by, legal process served upon or setoff exercised by a payor bank, whether or not effective under other rules of law to terminate, suspend or modify the bank's right or duty to pay an item or to charge its customer's account for the item, comes too late to so terminate, suspend or modify such right or duty if the knowledge, notice, stop-order or legal process is received or served and a reasonable time for the bank to act thereon expires or the setoff is exercised after the bank has done any of the following:

(a) accepted or certified the item;

(b) paid the item in cash;

(c) settled for the item without reserving a right to revoke the settlement and without having such right under statute, clearing house rule or agreement;

(d) completed the process of posting the item to the indicated account of the drawer, maker or other person to be charged therewith or otherwise has evidenced by examination of such indicated account and by action its decision to pay the item; or

(e) become accountable for the amount of the item under subsection (1)(d) of Section 4—213 and Section 4—302 dealing with the payor bank's responsibility for late return of items.

(2) Subject to the provisions of subsection (1) items may be accepted, paid, certified or charged to the indicated account of its customer in any order convenient to the bank.

Part 4 Relationship Between Payor Bank and Its Customer

§ 4—401. **When Bank May Charge Customer's Account.**

(1) As against its customer, a bank may charge against his account any item which is otherwise properly payable from that account even though the charge creates an overdraft.

(2) A bank which in good faith makes payment to a holder may charge the indicated account of its customer according to

(a) the original tenor of his altered item; or

(b) the tenor of his completed item, even though the bank knows the item has been completed unless the bank has notice that the completion was improper.

§ 4—402. **Bank's Liability to Customer for Wrongful Dishonor.**

A payor bank is liable to its customer for damages proximately caused by the wrongful dishonor of an item. When the dishonor occurs through mistake liability is limited to actual damages proved. If so proximately caused and proved damages may include damages for an arrest or prosecution of the customer or other consequential damages. Whether any consequential damages are proximately caused by the wrongful dishonor is a question of fact to be determined in each case.

§ 4—403. **Customer's Right to Stop Payment; Burden of Proof of Loss.**

(1) A customer may by order to his bank stop payment of any item payable for his account but the order must be received at such time and in such manner as to afford the bank a reasonable opportunity to act on it prior to any action by the bank with respect to the item described in Section 4—303.

(2) An oral order is binding upon the bank only for fourteen calendar days unless confirmed in writing within that period. A written order is effective for only six months unless renewed in writing.

(3) The burden of establishing the fact and amount of loss resulting from the payment of an item contrary to a binding stop payment order is on the customer.

§ 4—404. **Bank Not Obligated to Pay Check More Than Six Months Old.**

A bank is under no obligation to a customer having a checking account to pay a check, other than a certified check, which is presented more than six months after its date, but it may charge its customer's account for a payment made thereafter in good faith.

§ 4—405. **Death or Incompetence of Customer.**

(1) A payor or collecting bank's authority to accept, pay or collect an item or to account for proceeds of its collection if otherwise effective is not rendered ineffective by incompetence of a customer of either bank existing at the time the item is issued or its collection is undertaken if the bank does not know of an adjudication of incompetence. Neither death nor incompetence of a customer revokes such authority to accept, pay, collect or account until the bank knows of the fact of death or of an adjudication of incompetence and has reasonable opportunity to act on it.

(2) Even with knowledge a bank may for 10 days after the date of death pay or certify checks drawn on or prior to that date unless ordered to stop payment by a person claiming an interest in the account.

§ 4—406. **Customer's Duty to Discover and Report Unauthorized Signature or Alteration.**

(1) When a bank sends to its customer a statement of account accompanied by items paid in good faith in support of the debit entries or holds the statement and items pursuant to a request or instructions of its customer or otherwise in a reasonable manner makes the statement and items available to the customer, the customer must exercise reasonable care and promptness to examine the statement and items to discover his unauthorized signature or any alteration on an item and must notify the bank promptly after discovery thereof.

(2) If the bank establishes that the customer failed with respect to an item to comply with the duties imposed on the customer by subsection (1) the customer is precluded from asserting against the bank

(a) his unauthorized signature or any alteration on the item if the bank also establishes that it suffered a loss by reason of such failure; and

(b) an unauthorized signature or alteration by the same wrongdoer on any other item paid in good faith by the bank after the first item and statement was available to the customer for a reasonable period not exceeding fourteen calendar days and before the bank receives notification from the customer of any such unauthorized signature or alteration.

(3) The preclusion under subsection (2) does not apply if the customer establishes lack of ordinary care on the part of the bank in paying the item(s).

(4) Without regard to care or lack of care of either the customer or the bank a customer who does not within one year from the time the statement and items are made available to the customer (subsection (1)) discover and report his unauthorized signature or any alteration on the face or back of the item or does not within three years from that time discover and report any unauthorized indorsement is precluded from asserting against the bank such unauthorized signature or indorsement or such alteration.

(5) If under this section a payor bank has a valid defense against a claim of a customer upon or resulting from payment of an item and waives or fails upon request to assert the defense the bank may not assert against any collecting bank or other prior party presenting or transferring the item a claim based upon the unauthorized signature or alteration giving rise to the customer's claim.

§ 4—407. **Payor Bank's Right to Subrogation on Improper Payment.**

If a payor bank has paid an item over the stop payment order of the drawer or maker or otherwise under circumstances giving a basis for objection by the drawer or maker, to prevent unjust enrichment and only to the extent necessary to prevent loss to the bank by reason of its payment of the item, the payor bank shall be subrogated to the rights

(a) of any holder in due course on the item against the drawer or maker; and

(b) of the payee or any other holder of the item against the drawer or maker either on the item or under the transaction out of which the item arose; and

(c) of the drawer or maker against the payee or any other holder of the item with respect to the transaction out of which the item arose.

Part 5 Collection of Documentary Drafts

§ 4—501. Handling of Documentary Drafts; Duty to Send for Presentment and to Notify Customer of Dishonor.

A bank which takes a documentary draft for collection must present or send the draft and accompanying documents for presentment and upon learning that the draft has not been paid or accepted in due course must seasonably notify its customer of such fact even though it may have discounted or bought the draft or extended credit available for withdrawal as of right.

§ 4—502. Presentment of "On Arrival" Drafts.

When a draft or the relevant instructions require presentment "on arrival", "when goods arrive" or the like, the collecting bank need not present until in its judgment a reasonable time for arrival of the goods has expired. Refusal to pay or accept because the goods have not arrived is not dishonor; the bank must notify its transferor of such refusal but need not present the draft again until it is instructed to do so or learns of the arrival of the goods.

§ 4—503. Responsibility of Presenting Bank for Documents and Goods; Report of Reasons for Dishonor; Referee in Case of Need.

Unless otherwise instructed and except as provided in Article 5 a bank presenting a documentary draft

(a) must deliver the documents to the drawee on acceptance of the draft if it is payable more than three days after presentment; otherwise, only on payment; and

(b) upon dishonor, either in the case of presentment for acceptance or presentment for payment, may seek and follow instructions from any referee in case of need designated in the draft or if the presenting bank does not choose to utilize his services it must use diligence and good faith to ascertain the reason for dishonor, must notify its transferor of the dishonor and of the results of its effort to ascertain the reasons therefor and must request instructions.

But the presenting bank is under no obligation with respect to goods represented by the documents except to follow any reasonable instructions seasonably received; it has a right to reimbursement for any expense incurred in following instructions and to prepayment of or indemnity for such expenses.

§ 4—504. Privilege of Presenting Bank to Deal With Goods; Security Interest for Expenses.

(1) A presenting bank which, following the dishonor of a documentary draft, has seasonably requested instructions but does not receive them within a reasonable time may store, sell, or otherwise deal with the goods in any reasonable manner.

(2) For its reasonable expenses incurred by action under subsection (1) the presenting bank has a lien upon the goods or their proceeds, which may be foreclosed in the same manner as an unpaid seller's lien.

Revised Article 4
BANK DEPOSITS AND COLLECTIONS

Part 1 General Provisions and Definitions

§ 4—101. Short Title.

This Article may be cited as Uniform Commercial Code—Bank Deposits and Collections.

§ 4—102. Applicability.

(a) To the extent that items within this Article are also within Articles 3 and 8, they are subject to those Articles. If there is conflict, this Article governs Article 3, but Article 8 governs this Article.

(b) The liability of a bank for action or non-action with respect to an item handled by it for purposes of presentment, payment, or collection is governed by the law of the place where the bank is located. In the case of action or non-action by or at a branch or separate office of a bank, its liability is governed by the law of the place where the branch or separate office is located.

§ 4—103. Variation by Agreement; Measure of Damages; Action Constituting Ordinary Care.

(a) The effect of the provisions of this Article may be varied by agreement, but the parties to the agreement cannot disclaim a bank's responsibility for its lack of good faith or failure to exercise ordinary care or limit the measure of damages for the lack or failure. However, the parties may determine by agreement the standards by which the bank's responsibility is to be measured if those standards are not manifestly unreasonable.

(b) Federal Reserve regulations and operating circulars, clearing-house rules, and the like have the effect of agreements under subsection (a), whether or not specifically assented to by all parties interested in items handled.

(c) Action or non-action approved by this Article or pursuant to Federal Reserve regulations or operating circulars is the exercise of ordinary care and, in the absence of special instructions, action or non-action consistent with clearing-house rules and the like or with a general banking usage not disapproved by this Article, is prima facie the exercise of ordinary care.

(d) The specification or approval of certain procedures by this Article is not disapproval of other procedures that may be reasonable under the circumstances.

(e) The measure of damages for failure to exercise ordinary care in handling an item is the amount of the item reduced by an amount that could not have been realized by the exercise of ordinary care. If there is also bad faith it includes any other damages the party suffered as a proximate consequence.

§ 4—104. **Definitions and Index of Definitions.**

(a) In this Article, unless the context otherwise requires:

(1) "Account" means any deposit or credit account with a bank, including a demand, time, savings, passbook, share draft, or like account, other than an account evidenced by a certificate of deposit;

(2) "Afternoon" means the period of a day between noon and midnight;

(3) "Banking day" means the part of a day on which a bank is open to the public for carrying on substantially all of its banking functions;

(4) "Clearing house" means an association of banks or other payors regularly clearing items;

(5) "Customer" means a person having an account with a bank or for whom a bank has agreed to collect items, including a bank that maintains an account at another bank;

(6) "Documentary draft" means a draft to be presented for acceptance or payment if specified documents, certificated securities (Section 8—102) or instructions for uncertificated securities (Section 8—308), or other certificates, statements, or the like are to be received by the drawee or other payor before acceptance or payment of the draft;

(7) "Draft" means a draft as defined in Section 3—104 or an item, other than an instrument, that is an order;

(8) "Drawee" means a person ordered in a draft to make payment;

(9) "Item" means an instrument or a promise or order to pay money handled by a bank for collection or payment. The term does not include a payment order governed by Article 4A or a credit or debit card slip;

(10) "Midnight deadline" with respect to a bank is midnight on its next banking day following the banking day on which it receives the relevant item or notice or from which the time for taking action commences to run, whichever is later;

(11) "Settle" means to pay in cash, by clearing-house settlement, in a charge or credit or by remittance, or otherwise as agreed. A settlement may be either provisional or final;

(12) "Suspends payments" with respect to a bank means that it has been closed by order of the supervisory authorities, that a public officer has been appointed to take it over, or that it ceases or refuses to make payments in the ordinary course of business.

(b);(c) [Other definitions' section references deleted.]

(d) In addition, Article 1 contains general definitions and principles of construction and interpretation applicable throughout this Article.

§ 4—105. **"Bank"; "Depositary Bank"; "Payor Bank"; "Intermediary Bank"; "Collecting Bank"; "Presenting Bank".**

In this Article:

(1) "Bank" means a person engaged in the business of banking, including a savings bank, savings and loan association, credit union, or trust company;

(2) "Depositary bank" means the first bank to take an item even though it is also the payor bank, unless the item is presented for immediate payment over the counter;

(3) "Payor bank" means a bank that is the drawee of a draft;

(4) "Intermediary bank" means a bank to which an item is transferred in course of collection except the depositary or payor bank;

(5) "Collecting bank" means a bank handling an item for collection except the payor bank;

(6) "Presenting bank" means a bank presenting an item except a payor bank.

§ 4—106. **Payable Through or Payable at Bank: Collecting Bank.**

(a) If an item states that it is "payable through" a bank identified in the item, (i) the item designates the bank as a collecting bank and does not by itself authorize the bank to pay the item, and (ii) the item may be presented for payment only by or through the bank.

Alternative A

(b) If an item states that it is "payable at" a bank identified in the item, the item is equivalent to a draft drawn on the bank.

Alternative B

(b) If an item states that it is "payable at" a bank identified in the item, (i) the item designates the bank as a collecting bank and does not by itself authorize the bank to pay the item, and (ii) the item may be presented for payment only by or through the bank.

(c) If a draft names a nonbank drawee and it is unclear whether a bank named in the draft is a co-drawee or a collecting bank, the bank is a collecting bank.

§ 4—107. **Separate Office of Bank.**

A branch or separate office of a bank is a separate bank for the purpose of computing the time within which and determining the place at or to which action may be taken or notices or orders shall be given under this Article and under Article 3.

§ 4—108. **Time of Receipt of Items.**

(a) For the purpose of allowing time to process items, prove balances, and make the necessary entries on its books to determine its position for the day, a bank may fix an afternoon hour of 2 P.M. or later as a cutoff hour for the handling of money and items and the making of entries on its books.

(b) An item or deposit of money received on any day after a cutoff hour so fixed or after the close of the banking day may be treated as being received at the opening of the next banking day.

§ 4—109. **Delays.**

(a) Unless otherwise instructed, a collecting bank in a good faith effort to secure payment of a specific item drawn on a payor other than a bank, and with or without the approval of any person involved, may waive, modify, or extend time limits imposed or permitted by this [act] for a period not exceeding two additional banking days without discharge of drawers or indorsers or liability to its transferor or a prior party.

(b) Delay by a collecting bank or payor bank beyond time limits prescribed or permitted by this [act] or by instructions is excused if (i) the delay is caused by interruption of communication or computer facilities, suspension of payments by another bank, war, emergency conditions, failure of equipment, or other circumstances beyond the control of the bank, and (ii) the bank exercises such diligence as the circumstances require.

§ 4—110. **Electronic Presentment.**

(a) "Agreement for electronic presentment" means an agreement, clearing-house rule, or Federal Reserve regulation or operating circular, providing that presentment of an item may be made by transmission of an image of an item or information describing the item ("presentment notice") rather than delivery of the item itself. The agreement may provide for procedures governing retention, presentment, payment, dishonor, and other matters concerning items subject to the agreement.

(b) Presentment of an item pursuant to an agreement for presentment is made when the presentment notice is received.

(c) If presentment is made by presentment notice, a reference to "item" or "check" in this Article means the presentment notice unless the context otherwise indicates.

§ 4—111. **Statute of Limitations.**

An action to enforce an obligation, duty, or right arising under this Article must be commenced within three years after the [cause of action] accrues.

Part 2 Collection of Items: Depositary and Collecting Banks

§ 4—201. **Status of Collecting Bank As Agent and Provisional Status of Credits; Applicability of Article; Item Indorsed "Pay Any Bank".**

(a) Unless a contrary intent clearly appears and before the time that a settlement given by a collecting bank for an item is or becomes final, the bank, with respect to an item, is an agent or sub-agent of the owner of the item and any settlement given for the item is provisional. This provision applies regardless of the form of indorsement or lack of indorsement and even though credit given for the item is subject to immediate withdrawal as of right or is in fact withdrawn; but the continuance of ownership of an item by its owner and any rights of the owner to proceeds of the item are subject to rights of a collecting bank, such as those resulting from outstanding advances on the item and rights of recoupment or setoff. If an item is handled by banks for purposes of presentment, payment, collection, or return, the relevant provisions of this Article apply even though action of the parties clearly establishes that a particular bank has purchased the item and is the owner of it.

(b) After an item has been indorsed with the words "pay any bank" or the like, only a bank may acquire the rights of a holder until the item has been:

(1) returned to the customer initiating collection; or

(2) specially indorsed by a bank to a person who is not a bank.

§ 4—202. **Responsibility for Collection or Return; When Action Timely.**

(a) A collecting bank must exercise ordinary care in:

(1) presenting an item or sending it for presentment;

(2) sending notice of dishonor or nonpayment or returning an item other than a documentary draft to the bank's transferor after learning that the item has not been paid or accepted, as the case may be;

(3) settling for an item when the bank receives final settlement; and

(4) notifying its transferor of any loss or delay in transit within a reasonable time after discovery thereof.

(b) A collecting bank exercises ordinary care under subsection (a) by taking proper action before its midnight deadline following receipt of an item, notice, or settlement. Taking proper action within a reasonably longer time may constitute the exercise of ordinary care, but the bank has the burden of establishing timeliness.

(c) Subject to subsection (a)(1), a bank is not liable for the insolvency, neglect, misconduct, mistake, or default of another bank or person or for loss or destruction of an item in the possession of others or in transit.

§ 4—203. **Effect of Instructions.**

Subject to Article 3 concerning conversion of instruments (Section 3—420) and restrictive indorsements (Section 3—206), only a collecting bank's transferor can give instructions that affect the bank or constitute notice to it, and a collecting bank is not liable to prior parties for any action taken pursuant to the instructions or in accordance with any agreement with its transferor.

§ 4—204. **Methods of Sending and Presenting; Sending Directly to Payor Bank.**

(a) A collecting bank shall send items by a reasonably prompt method, taking into consideration relevant instructions, the nature of the item, the number of those items on hand, the cost of collection involved, and the method generally used by it or others to present those items.

(b) A collecting bank may send:

(1) an item directly to the payor bank;

(2) an item to a nonbank payor if authorized by its transferor; and

(3) an item other than documentary drafts to a nonbank payor, if authorized by Federal Reserve regulation or operating circular, clearing-house rule, or the like.

(c) Presentment may be made by a presenting bank at a place where the payor bank or other payor has requested that presentment be made.

§ 4—205. **Depositary Bank Holder of Unindorsed Item.**

If a customer delivers an item to a depositary bank for collection:

(1) the depositary bank becomes a holder of the item at the time it receives the item for collection if the customer at the time of delivery was a holder of the item, whether or not the customer indorses the item, and, if the bank satisfies the other requirements of Section 3—302, it is a holder in due course; and

(2) the depositary bank warrants to collecting banks, the payor bank or other payor, and the drawer that the amount of the item was paid to the customer or deposited to the customer's account.

§ 4—206. **Transfer Between Banks.**

Any agreed method that identifies the transferor bank is sufficient for the item's further transfer to another bank.

§ 4—207. **Transfer Warranties.**

(a) A customer or collecting bank that transfers an item and receives a settlement or other consideration warrants to the transferee and to any subsequent collecting bank that:

(1) the warrantor is a person entitled to enforce the item;

(2) all signatures on the item are authentic and authorized;

(3) the item has not been altered;

(4) the item is not subject to a defense or claim in recoupment (Section 3—305(a)) of any party that can be asserted against the warrantor; and

(5) the warrantor has no knowledge of any insolvency proceeding commenced with respect to the maker or acceptor or, in the case of an unaccepted draft, the drawer.

(b) If an item is dishonored, a customer or collecting bank transferring the item and receiving settlement or other consideration is obliged to pay the amount due on the item (i) according to the terms of the item at the time it was transferred, or (ii) if the transfer was of an incomplete item, according to its terms when completed as stated in Sections 3—115 and 3—407. The obligation of a transferor is owed to the transferee and to any subsequent collecting bank that takes the item in good faith. A transferor cannot disclaim its obligation under this subsection by an indorsement stating that it is made "without recourse" or otherwise disclaiming liability.

(c) A person to whom the warranties under subsection (a) are made and who took the item in good faith may recover from the warrantor as damages for breach of warranty an amount equal to the loss suffered as a result of the breach, but not more than the amount of the item plus expenses and loss of interest incurred as a result of the breach.

(d) The warranties stated in subsection (a) cannot be disclaimed with respect to checks. Unless notice of a claim for breach of warranty is given to the warrantor within 30 days after the claimant has reason to know of the breach and the identity of the warrantor, the warrantor is discharged to the extent of any loss caused by the delay in giving notice of the claim.

(e) A cause of action for breach of warranty under this section accrues when the claimant has reason to know of the breach.

§ 4—208. **Presentment Warranties.**

(a) If an unaccepted draft is presented to the drawee for payment or acceptance and the drawee pays or accepts the draft, (i) the person obtaining payment or acceptance, at the time of presentment, and (ii) a previous transferor of the draft, at the time of transfer, warrant to the drawee that pays or accepts the draft in good faith that:

(1) the warrantor is, or was, at the time the warrantor transferred the draft, a person entitled to enforce the draft or authorized to obtain payment or acceptance of the draft on behalf of a person entitled to enforce the draft;

(2) the draft has not been altered; and

(3) the warrantor has no knowledge that the signature of the purported drawer of the draft is unauthorized.

(b) A drawee making payment may recover from a warrantor damages for breach of warranty equal to the amount paid by the drawee less the amount the drawee received or is entitled to receive from the drawer because of the payment. In addition, the drawee is entitled to compensation for expenses and loss of interest resulting from the breach. The right of the drawee to recover damages under this subsection is not affected by any failure of the drawee to exercise ordinary care in making payment. If the drawee accepts the draft (i) breach of warranty is a defense to the obligation of the acceptor, and (ii) if the acceptor makes payment with respect to the draft, the acceptor is entitled to recover from a warrantor for breach of warranty the amounts stated in this subsection.

(c) If a drawee asserts a claim for breach of warranty under subsection (a) based on an unauthorized indorsement of the draft or an alteration of the draft, the warrantor may defend by proving that the indorsement is effective under Section 3—404 or 3—405 or the drawer is precluded under Section 3—406 or 4—406 from asserting against the drawee the unauthorized indorsement or alteration.

(d) If (i) a dishonored draft is presented for payment to the drawer or an indorser or (ii) any other item is presented for payment to a party obliged to pay the item, and the item is paid, the person obtaining payment and a prior transferor of the item warrant to the person making payment in good faith that the warrantor is, or was, at the time the warrantor transferred the item, a person entitled to enforce the item or authorized to obtain payment on behalf of a person entitled to enforce the item. The person making payment may recover from any warrantor for breach of warranty an amount equal to the amount paid plus expenses and loss of interest resulting from the breach.

(e) The warranties stated in subsections (a) and (d) cannot be disclaimed with respect to checks. Unless notice of a claim for breach of warranty is given to the warrantor within 30 days after the claimant has reason to know of the breach and the identity of the warrantor, the warrantor is discharged to the extent of any loss caused by the delay in giving notice of the claim.

(f) A cause of action for breach of warranty under this section accrues when the claimant has reason to know of the breach.

§ 4—209. **Encoding and Retention Warranties.**

(a) A person who encodes information on or with respect to an item after issue warrants to any subsequent collecting bank and to the payor bank or other payor that the information is correctly encoded. If the customer of a depositary bank encodes, that bank also makes the warranty.

(b) A person who undertakes to retain an item pursuant to an agreement for electronic presentment warrants to any subsequent collecting bank and to the payor bank or other payor that retention and presentment of the item comply with the agreement. If a customer of a depositary bank undertakes to retain an item, that bank also makes this warranty.

(c) A person to whom warranties are made under this section and who took the item in good faith may recover from the warrantor as damages for breach of warranty an amount equal to the loss suffered as a result of the breach, plus expenses and loss of interest incurred as a result of the breach.

§ 4—210. **Security Interest of Collecting Bank in Items, Accompanying Documents and Proceeds.**

(a) A collecting bank has a security interest in an item and any accompanying documents or the proceeds of either:

(1) in case of an item deposited in an account, to the extent to which credit given for the item has been withdrawn or applied;

(2) in case of an item for which it has given credit available for withdrawal as of right, to the extent of the credit given, whether or not the credit is drawn upon or there is a right of charge-back; or

(3) if it makes an advance on or against the item.

(b) If credit given for several items received at one time or pursuant to a single agreement is withdrawn or applied in part, the security interest remains upon all the items, any accompanying documents or the proceeds of either. For the purpose of this section, credits first given are first withdrawn.

(c) Receipt by a collecting bank of a final settlement for an item is a realization on its security interest in the item, accompanying documents, and proceeds. So long as the bank does not receive final settlement for the item or give up possession of the item or accompanying documents for purposes other than collection, the security interest continues to that extent and is subject to Article 9, but:

(1) no security agreement is necessary to make the security interest enforceable (Section 9—203(1)(a));

(2) no filing is required to perfect the security interest; and

(3) the security interest has priority over conflicting perfected security interests in the item, accompanying documents, or proceeds.

§ 4—211. **When Bank Gives Value for Purposes of Holder in Due Course.**

For purposes of determining its status as a holder in due course, a bank has given value to the extent it has a security interest in an item, if the bank otherwise complies with the requirements of Section 3—302 on what constitutes a holder in due course.

§ 4—212. **Presentment by Notice of Item Not Payable by, Through, or at Bank; Liability of Drawer or Indorser.**

(a) Unless otherwise instructed, a collecting bank may present an item not payable by, through, or at a bank by sending to the party to accept or pay a written notice that the bank holds the item for acceptance or payment. The notice must be sent in time to be received on or before the day when presentment is due and the bank must meet any requirement of the party to accept or pay under Section 3—501 by the close of the bank's next banking day after it knows of the requirement.

(b) If presentment is made by notice and payment, acceptance, or request for compliance with a requirement under Section 3—501 is not received by the close of business on the day after maturity or, in the case of demand items, by the close of business on the third banking day after notice was sent, the presenting bank may treat the item as dishonored and charge any drawer or indorser by sending it notice of the facts.

§ 4—213. **Medium and Time of Settlement by Bank.**

(a) With respect to settlement by a bank, the medium and time of settlement may be prescribed by Federal Reserve regulations or circulars, clearing-house rules, and the like, or agreement. In the absence of such prescription:

(1) the medium of settlement is cash or credit to an account in a Federal Reserve bank of or specified by the person to receive settlement; and

(2) the time of settlement is:

(i) with respect to tender of settlement by cash, a cashier's check, or teller's check, when the cash or check is sent or delivered;

(ii) with respect to tender of settlement by credit in an account in a Federal Reserve Bank, when the credit is made;

(iii) with respect to tender of settlement by a credit or debit to an account in a bank, when the credit or debit is made or, in the case of tender of settlement by authority to charge an account, when the authority is sent or delivered; or

(iv) with respect to tender of settlement by a funds transfer, when payment is made pursuant to Section 4A—406(a) to the person receiving settlement.

(b) If the tender of settlement is not by a medium authorized by subsection (a) or the time of settlement is not fixed by subsection (a), no settlement occurs until the tender of settlement is accepted by the person receiving settlement.

(c) If settlement for an item is made by cashier's check or teller's check and the person receiving settlement, before its midnight deadline:

(1) presents or forwards the check for collection, settlement is final when the check is finally paid; or

(2) fails to present or forward the check for collection, settlement is final at the midnight deadline of the person receiving settlement.

(d) If settlement for an item is made by giving authority to charge the account of the bank giving settlement in the bank receiving settlement, settlement is final when the charge is made by the bank receiving settlement if there are funds available in the account for the amount of the item.

§ 4—214. **Right of Charge-Back or Refund; Liability of Collecting Bank: Return of Item.**

(a) If a collecting bank has made provisional settlement with its customer for an item and fails by reason of dishonor, suspension of payments by a bank, or otherwise to receive settlement for the item which is or becomes final, the bank may revoke the settlement given by it, charge back the amount of any credit given for the item to its customer's account, or obtain refund from its customer, whether or not it is able to return the item, if by its midnight deadline or within a longer reasonable time after it learns the facts it returns the item or sends notification of the facts. If the return or notice is delayed beyond the bank's midnight deadline or a longer reasonable time after it learns the facts, the bank may revoke the settlement, charge back the credit, or obtain refund from its customer, but it is liable for any loss resulting from the delay. These rights to revoke, charge back, and obtain refund terminate if and when a settlement for the item received by the bank is or becomes final.

(b) A collecting bank returns an item when it is sent or delivered to the bank's customer or transferor or pursuant to its instructions.

(c) A depositary bank that is also the payor may charge back the amount of an item to its customer's account or obtain refund in accordance with the section governing return of an item received by a payor bank for credit on its books (Section 4—301).

(d) The right to charge back is not affected by:

(1) previous use of a credit given for the item; or

(2) failure by any bank to exercise ordinary care with respect to the item, but a bank so failing remains liable.

(e) A failure to charge back or claim refund does not affect other rights of the bank against the customer or any other party.

(f) If credit is given in dollars as the equivalent of the value of an item payable in foreign money, the dollar amount of any charge-back or refund must be calculated on the basis of the bank-offered spot rate for the foreign money prevailing on the day when the person entitled to the charge-back or refund learns that it will not receive payment in ordinary course.

§ 4—215. **Final Payment of Item by Payor Bank; When Provisional Debits and Credits Become Final; When Certain Credits Become Available for Withdrawal.**

(a) An item is finally paid by a payor bank when the bank has first done any of the following:

(1) paid the item in cash;

(2) settled for the item without having a right to revoke the settlement under statute, clearing-house rule, or agreement; or

(3) made a provisional settlement for the item and failed to revoke the settlement in the time and manner permitted by statute, clearing-house rule, or agreement.

(b) If provisional settlement for an item does not become final, the item is not finally paid.

(c) If provisional settlement for an item between the presenting and payor banks is made through a clearing house or by debits or credits in an account between them, then to the extent that provisional debits or credits for the item are entered in accounts between the presenting and payor banks or between the presenting and successive prior collecting banks seriatim, they become final upon final payment of the item by the payor bank.

(d) If a collecting bank receives a settlement for an item which is or becomes final, the bank is accountable to its customer for the amount of the item and any provisional credit given for the item in an account with its customer becomes final.

(e) Subject to (i) applicable law stating a time for availability of funds and (ii) any right of the bank to apply the credit to an obligation of the customer, credit given by a bank for an item in a customer's account becomes available for withdrawal as of right:

(1) if the bank has received a provisional settlement for the item, when the settlement becomes final and the bank has had a reasonable time to receive return of the item and the item has not been received within that time;

(2) if the bank is both the depositary bank and the payor bank, and the item is finally paid, at the opening of the bank's second banking day following receipt of the item.

(f) Subject to applicable law stating a time for availability of funds and any right of a bank to apply a deposit to an obligation of the depositor, a deposit of money becomes available for withdrawal as of right at the opening of the bank's next banking day after receipt of the deposit.

§ 4—216. **Insolvency and Preference.**

(a) If an item is in or comes into the possession of a payor or collecting bank that suspends payment and the item has not been finally paid, the item must be returned by the receiver, trustee, or agent in charge of the closed bank to the presenting bank or the closed bank's customer.

(b) If a payor bank finally pays an item and suspends payments without making a settlement for the item with its customer or the presenting bank which settlement is or becomes final, the owner of the item has a preferred claim against the payor bank.

(c) If a payor bank gives or a collecting bank gives or receives a provisional settlement for an item and thereafter suspends payments, the suspension does not prevent or interfere with the settlement's becoming final if the finality occurs automatically upon the lapse of certain time or the happening of certain events.

(d) If a collecting bank receives from subsequent parties settlement for an item, which settlement is or becomes final and the bank suspends payments without making a settlement for the item with its customer which settlement is or becomes final, the owner of the item has a preferred claim against the collecting bank.

Part 3 Collection of Items: Payor Banks

§ 4—301. **Deferred Posting; Recovery of Payment by Return of Items; Time of Dishonor; Return of Items by Payor Bank.**

(a) If a payor bank settles for a demand item other than a documentary draft presented otherwise than for immediate payment over the counter before midnight of the banking day of receipt, the payor bank may revoke the settlement and recover the settlement if, before it has made final payment and before its midnight deadline, it

(1) returns the item; or

(2) sends written notice of dishonor or nonpayment if the item is unavailable for return.

(b) If a demand item is received by a payor bank for credit on its books, it may return the item or send notice of dishonor and may revoke any credit given or recover the amount thereof withdrawn by its customer, if it acts within the time limit and in the manner specified in subsection (a).

(c) Unless previous notice of dishonor has been sent, an item is dishonored at the time when for purposes of dishonor it is returned or notice sent in accordance with this section.

(d) An item is returned:

(1) as to an item presented through a clearing house, when it is delivered to the presenting or last collecting bank or to the clearing house or is sent or delivered in accordance with clearing-house rules; or

(2) in all other cases, when it is sent or delivered to the bank's customer or transferor or pursuant to instructions.

§ 4—302. **Payor Bank's Responsibility for Late Return of Item.**

(a) If an item is presented to and received by a payor bank, the bank is accountable for the amount of:

(1) a demand item, other than a documentary draft, whether properly payable or not, if the bank, in any case in which it

is not also the depositary bank, retains the item beyond midnight of the banking day of receipt without settling for it or, whether or not it is also the depositary bank, does not pay or return the item or send notice of dishonor until after its midnight deadline; or

(2) any other properly payable item unless, within the time allowed for acceptance or payment of that item, the bank either accepts or pays the item or returns it and accompanying documents.

(b) The liability of a payor bank to pay an item pursuant to subsection (a) is subject to defenses based on breach of a presentment warranty (Section 4—208) or proof that the person seeking enforcement of the liability presented or transferred the item for the purpose of defrauding the payor bank.

§ 4—303. **When Items Subject to Notice, Stop-Payment Order, Legal Process, or Setoff; Order in Which Items May Be Charged or Certified.**

(a) Any knowledge, notice, or stop-payment order received by, legal process served upon, or setoff exercised by a payor bank comes too late to terminate, suspend, or modify the bank's right or duty to pay an item or to charge its customer's account for the item if the knowledge, notice, stop-payment order, or legal process is received or served and a reasonable time for the bank to act thereon expires or the setoff is exercised after the earliest of the following:

(1) the bank accepts or certifies the item;

(2) the bank pays the item in cash;

(3) the bank settles for the item without having a right to revoke the settlement under statute, clearing-house rule, or agreement;

(4) the bank becomes accountable for the amount of the item under Section 4—302 dealing with the payor bank's responsibility for late return of items; or

(5) with respect to checks, a cutoff hour no earlier than one hour after the opening of the next banking day after the banking day on which the bank received the check and no later than the close of that next banking day or, if no cutoff hour is fixed, the close of the next banking day after the banking day on which the bank received the check.

(b) Subject to subsection (a), items may be accepted, paid, certified, or charged to the indicated account of its customer in any order.

Part 4 Relationship Between Payor Bank and its Customer

§ 4—401. **When Bank May Charge Customer's Account.**

(a) A bank may charge against the account of a customer an item that is properly payable from the account even though the charge creates an overdraft. An item is properly payable if it is authorized by the customer and is in accordance with any agreement between the customer and bank.

(b) A customer is not liable for the amount of an overdraft if the customer neither signed the item nor benefited from the proceeds of the item.

(c) A bank may charge against the account of a customer a check that is otherwise properly payable from the account, even though payment was made before the date of the check, unless the customer has given notice to the bank of the postdating describing the check with reasonable certainty. The notice is effective for the period stated in Section 4—403(b) for stop-payment orders, and must be received at such time and in such manner as to afford the bank a reasonable opportunity to act on it before the bank takes any action with respect to the check described in Section 4—303. If a bank charges against the account of a customer a check before the date stated in the notice of postdating, the bank is liable for damages for the loss resulting from its act. The loss may include damages for dishonor of subsequent items under Section 4—402.

(d) A bank that in good faith makes payment to a holder may charge the indicated account of its customer according to:

(1) the original terms of the altered item; or

(2) the terms of the completed item, even though the bank knows the item has been completed unless the bank has notice that the completion was improper.

§ 4—402. **Bank's Liability to Customer for Wrongful Dishonor; Time of Determining Insufficiency of Account.**

(a) Except as otherwise provided in this Article, a payor bank wrongfully dishonors an item if it dishonors an item that is properly payable, but a bank may dishonor an item that would create an overdraft unless it has agreed to pay the overdraft.

(b) A payor bank is liable to its customer for damages proximately caused by the wrongful dishonor of an item. Liability is limited to actual damages proved and may include damages for an arrest or prosecution of the customer or other consequential damages. Whether any consequential damages are proximately caused by the wrongful dishonor is a question of fact to be determined in each case.

(c) A payor bank's determination of the customer's account balance on which a decision to dishonor for insufficiency of available funds is based may be made at any time between the time the item is received by the payor bank and the time that the payor bank returns the item or gives notice in lieu of return, and no more than one determination need be made. If, at the election of the payor bank, a subsequent balance determination is made for the purpose of reevaluating the bank's decision to dishonor the item, the account balance at that time is determinative of whether a dishonor for insufficiency of available funds is wrongful.

§ 4—403. **Customer's Right to Stop Payment; Burden of Proof of Loss.**

(a) A customer or any person authorized to draw on the account if there is more than one person may stop payment of any item drawn on the customer's account or close the account by an order to the bank describing the item or account with reasonable certainty received at a time and in a manner that affords the bank a reasonable opportunity to act on it before any action by the bank with respect to the item described in Section 4—303. If the signature of more than one person is required to draw on an account, any of these persons may stop payment or close the account.

(b) A stop-payment order is effective for six months, but it lapses after 14 calendar days if the original order was oral and was not confirmed in writing within that period. A stop-payment order may be renewed for additional six-month periods by a writing given to the bank within a period during which the stop-payment order is effective.

(c) The burden of establishing the fact and amount of loss resulting from the payment of an item contrary to a stop-payment order or order to close an account is on the customer. The loss from payment of an item contrary to a stop-payment order may include damages for dishonor of subsequent items under Section 4—402.

§ 4—404. **Bank Not Obliged to Pay Check More Than Six Months Old.**

A bank is under no obligation to a customer having a checking account to pay a check, other than a certified check, which is presented more than six months after its date, but it may charge its customer's account for a payment made thereafter in good faith.

§ 4—405. **Death or Incompetence of Customer.**

(a) A payor or collecting bank's authority to accept, pay, or collect an item or to account for proceeds of its collection, if otherwise effective, is not rendered ineffective by incompetence of a customer of either bank existing at the time the item is issued or its collection is undertaken if the bank does not know of an adjudication of incompetence. Neither death nor incompetence of a customer revokes the authority to accept, pay, collect, or account until the bank knows of the fact of death or of an adjudication of incompetence and has reasonable opportunity to act on it.

(b) Even with knowledge, a bank may for 10 days after the date of death pay or certify checks drawn on or before the date unless ordered to stop payment by a person claiming an interest in the account.

§ 4—406. **Customer's Duty to Discover and Report Unauthorized Signature or Alteration.**

(a) A bank that sends or makes available to a customer a statement of account showing payment of items for the account shall either return or make available to the customer the items paid or provide information in the statement of account sufficient to allow the customer reasonably to identify the items paid. The statement of account provides sufficient information if the item is described by item number, amount, and date of payment.

(b) If the items are not returned to the customer, the person retaining the items shall either retain the items or, if the items are destroyed, maintain the capacity to furnish legible copies of the items until the expiration of seven years after receipt of the items. A customer may request an item from the bank that paid the item, and that bank must provide in a reasonable time either the item or, if the item has been destroyed or is not otherwise obtainable, a legible copy of the item.

(c) If a bank sends or makes available a statement of account or items pursuant to subsection (a), the customer must exercise reasonable promptness in examining the statement or the items to determine whether any payment was not authorized because of an alteration of an item or because a purported signature by or on behalf of the customer was not authorized. If, based on the statement or items provided, the customer should reasonably have discovered the unauthorized payment, the customer must promptly notify the bank of the relevant facts.

(d) If the bank proves that the customer failed, with respect to an item, to comply with the duties imposed on the customer by subsection (c), the customer is precluded from asserting against the bank:

(1) the customer's unauthorized signature or any alteration on the item, if the bank also proves that it suffered a loss by reason of the failure; and

(2) the customer's unauthorized signature or alteration by the same wrongdoer on any other item paid in good faith by the bank if the payment was made before the bank received notice from the customer of the unauthorized signature or alteration and after the customer had been afforded a reasonable period of time, not exceeding 30 days, in which to examine the item or statement of account and notify the bank.

(e) If subsection (d) applies and the customer proves that the bank failed to exercise ordinary care in paying the item and that the failure substantially contributed to loss, the loss is allocated between the customer precluded and the bank asserting the preclusion according to the extent to which the failure of the customer to comply with subsection (c) and the failure of the bank to exercise ordinary care contributed to the loss. If the customer proves that the bank did not pay the item in good faith, the preclusion under subsection (d) does not apply.

(f) Without regard to care or lack of care of either the customer or the bank, a customer who does not within one year after the statement or items are made available to the customer (subsection (a)) discover and report the customer's unauthorized signature on or any alteration on the item is precluded from asserting against the bank the unauthorized signature or alteration. If there is a preclusion under this subsection, the payor bank may not recover for breach or warranty under Section 4—208 with respect to the unauthorized signature or alteration to which the preclusion applies.

§ 4—407. **Payor Bank's Right to Subrogation on Improper Payment.**

If a payor has paid an item over the order of the drawer or maker to stop payment, or after an account has been closed, or otherwise under circumstances giving a basis for objection by the drawer or maker, to prevent unjust enrichment and only to the extent necessary to prevent loss to the bank by reason of its payment of the item, the payor bank is subrogated to the rights

(1) of any holder in due course on the item against the drawer or maker;

(2) of the payee or any other holder of the item against the drawer or maker either on the item or under the transaction out of which the item arose; and

(3) of the drawer or maker against the payee or any other holder of the item with respect to the transaction out of which the item arose.

Part 5 Collection of Documentary Drafts

§ 4—501. **Handling of Documentary Drafts; Duty to Send for Presentment and to Notify Customer of Dishonor.**

A bank that takes a documentary draft for collection shall present or send the draft and accompanying documents for presentment and, upon learning that the draft has not been paid or accepted in due course, shall seasonably notify its customer of the fact even though it may have discounted or bought the draft or extended credit available for withdrawal as of right.

§ 4—502. **Presentment of "On Arrival" Drafts.**

If a draft or the relevant instructions require presentment "on arrival", "when goods arrive" or the like, the collecting bank need not present until in its judgment a reasonable time for arrival of the goods has expired. Refusal to pay or accept because the goods have not arrived is not dishonor; the bank must notify its transferor of the refusal but need not present the draft again until it is instructed to do so or learns of the arrival of the goods.

§ 4—503. **Responsibility of Presenting Bank for Documents and Goods; Report of Reasons for Dishonor; Referee in Case of Need.**

Unless otherwise instructed and except as provided in Article 5, a bank presenting a documentary draft:

(1) must deliver the documents to the drawee on acceptance of the draft if it is payable more than three days after presentment, otherwise, only on payment; and

(2) upon dishonor, either in the case of presentment for acceptance or presentment for payment, may seek and follow instructions from any referee in case of need designated in the draft or, if the presenting bank does not choose to utilize the referee's services, it must use diligence and good faith to ascertain the reason for dishonor, must notify its transferor of the dishonor and of the results of its effort to ascertain the reasons therefor, and must request instructions.

However, the presenting bank is under no obligation with respect to goods represented by the documents except to follow any reasonable instructions seasonably received; it has a right to reimbursement for any expense incurred in following instructions and to prepayment of or indemnity for those expenses.

§ 4—504. **Privilege of Presenting Bank to Deal With Goods; Security Interest for Expenses.**

(a) A presenting bank that, following the dishonor of a documentary draft, has seasonably requested instructions but does not receive them within a reasonable time may store, sell, or otherwise deal with the goods in any reasonable manner.

(b) For its reasonable expenses incurred by action under subsection (a) the presenting bank has a lien upon the goods or their proceeds, which may be foreclosed in the same manner as an unpaid seller's lien.

Article 4A
FUNDS TRANSFERS

Part 1 Subject Matter and Definitions

§ 4A—101. **Short Title.**

This Article may be cited as Uniform Commercial Code—Funds Transfers.

§ 4A—102. **Subject Matter.**

Except as otherwise provided in Section 4A—108, this Article applies to funds transfers defined in Section 4A—104.

§ 4A—103. **Payment Order—Definitions.**

(1) In this Article:

(a) "Payment order" means an instruction of a sender to a receiving bank, transmitted orally, electronically, or in writing, to pay, or to cause another bank to pay, a fixed or determinable amount of money to a beneficiary if:

(i) the instruction does not state a condition to payment to the beneficiary other than time of payment,

(ii) the receiving bank is to be reimbursed by debiting an account of, or otherwise receiving payment from, the sender, and

(iii) the instruction is transmitted by the sender directly to the receiving bank or to an agent, funds-transfer system, or communication system for transmittal to the receiving bank.

(b) "Beneficiary" means the person to be paid by the beneficiary's bank.

(c) "Beneficiary's bank" means the bank identified in a payment order in which an account of the beneficiary is to be credited pursuant to the order or which otherwise is to make payment to the beneficiary if the order does not provide for payment to an account.

(d) "Receiving bank" means the bank to which the sender's instruction is addressed.

(e) "Sender" means the person giving the instruction to the receiving bank.

(2) If an instruction complying with subsection (1)(a) is to make more than one payment to a beneficiary, the instruction is a separate payment order with respect to each payment.

(3) A payment order is issued when it is sent to the receiving bank.

§ 4A—104. **Funds Transfer—Definitions.**

(1) In this Article:

(a) "Funds transfer" means the series of transactions, beginning with the originator's payment order, made for the purpose of making payment to the beneficiary of the order. The term includes any payment order issued by the originator's bank or an intermediary bank intended to carry out the originator's payment order. A funds transfer is completed by acceptance by the beneficiary's bank of a payment order for the benefit of the beneficiary of the originator's payment order.

(b) "Intermediary bank" means a receiving bank other than the originator's bank or the beneficiary's bank.

(c) "Originator" means the sender of the first payment order in a funds transfer.

(d) "Originator's bank" means (i) the receiving bank to which the payment order of the originator is issued if the originator is not a bank, or (ii) the originator if the originator is a bank.

§ 4A—105. **Other Definitions.**

(1) In this Article:

(a) "Authorized account" means a deposit account of a customer in a bank designated by the customer as a source of payment of payment orders issued by the customer to the bank. If a customer does not so designate an account, any account of the customer is an authorized account if payment of a payment order from that account is not inconsistent with a restriction on the use of that account.

(b) "Bank" means a person engaged in the business of banking and includes a savings bank, savings and loan association, credit union, and trust company. A branch or separate office of a bank is a separate bank for purposes of this Article.

(c) "Customer" means a person, including a bank, having an account with a bank or from whom a bank has agreed to receive payment orders.

(d) "Funds-transfer business day" of a receiving bank means the part of a day during which the receiving bank is open for the receipt, processing, and transmittal of payment orders and cancellations and amendments of payment orders.

(e) "Funds-transfer system" means a wire transfer network, automated clearing house, or other communication system of a clearing house or other association of banks through which a payment order by a bank may be transmitted to the bank to which the order is addressed.

(f) "Good faith" means honesty in fact and the observance of reasonable commercial standards of fair dealing.

(g) "Prove" with respect to a fact means to meet the burden of establishing the fact (Section 1— 201(8)).

(2) Other definitions applying to this Article and the sections in which they appear are:

"Acceptance"	Section 4A—209
"Beneficiary"	Section 4A—103
"Beneficiary's bank"	Section 4A—103
"Executed"	Section 4A—301
"Execution date"	Section 4A—301
"Funds transfer"	Section 4A—104
"Funds-transfer system rule"	Section 4A—501
"Intermediary bank"	Section 4A—104
"Originator"	Section 4A—104
"Originator's bank"	Section 4A—104
"Payment by beneficiary's bank to beneficiary"	Section 4A—405
"Payment by originator to beneficiary"	Section 4A—406
"Payment by sender to receiving bank"	Section 4A—403
"Payment date"	Section 4A—401
"Payment order"	Section 4A—103
"Receiving bank"	Section 4A—103
"Security procedure"	Section 4A—201
"Sender"	Section 4A—103

(3) The following definitions in Article 4 apply to this Article:

"Clearing house"	Section 4—104
"Item"	Section 4—104
"Suspends payments"	Section 4—104

(4) In addition, Article 1 contains general definitions and principles of construction and interpretation applicable throughout this Article.

§ 4A—106. **Time Payment Order Is Received.**

(1) The time of receipt of a payment order or communication cancelling or amending a payment order is determined by the rules applicable to receipt of a notice stated in Section 1—201(27). A receiving bank may fix a cut-off time or times on a funds-transfer business day for the receipt and processing of payment orders and communications cancelling or amending payment orders. Different cut-off times may apply to payment orders, cancellations, or amendments, or to different categories of payment orders, cancellations, or amendments. A cut-off time may apply to senders generally or different cut-off times may apply to different senders or categories of payment orders. If a payment order or communication cancelling or amending a payment order is received after the close of a funds-transfer business day or after the appropriate cut-off time on a funds-transfer business day, the receiving bank may treat the payment order or communication as received at the opening of the next funds-transfer business day.

(2) If this Article refers to an execution date or payment date or states a day on which a receiving bank is required to take action, and the date or day does not fall on a funds-transfer business day, the next day that is a funds-transfer business day is treated as the date or day stated, unless the contrary is stated in this Article.

§ 4A—107. **Federal Reserve Regulations and Operating Circulars.**

Regulations of the Board of Governors of the Federal Reserve System and operating circulars of the Federal Reserve Banks supersede any inconsistent provision of this Article to the extent of the inconsistency.

§ 4A—108. **Exclusion of Consumer Transactions Governed by Federal Law.**

This Article does not apply to a funds transfer any part of which is governed by the Electronic Fund Transfer Act of 1978 (Title XX, Public Law 95—630, 92 Stat. 3728, 15 U.S.C. § 1693 et seq.) as amended from time to time.

Part 2 Issue and Acceptance of Payment Order

§ 4A—201. **Security Procedure.**

"Security procedure" means a procedure established by agreement of a customer and a receiving bank for the purpose of (i) verifying that a payment order or communication amending or cancelling a payment order is that of the customer, or (ii) detecting error in the transmission or the content of the payment order or communication. A security procedure may require the use of algorithms or other codes, identifying words or numbers, encryption, callback procedures, or similar security devices. Comparison of a signature on a payment order or communication with an authorized specimen signature of the customer is not by itself a security procedure.

§ 4A—202. **Authorized and Verified Payment Orders.**

(1) A payment order received by the receiving bank is the authorized order of the person identified as sender if that person authorized the order or is otherwise bound by it under the law of agency.

(2) If a bank and its customer have agreed that the authenticity of payment orders issued to the bank in the name of the customer as sender will be verified pursuant to a security procedure, a pay-

ment order received by the receiving bank is effective as the order of the customer, whether or not authorized, if (i) the security procedure is a commercially reasonable method of providing security against unauthorized payment orders, and (ii) the bank proves that it accepted the payment order in good faith and in compliance with the security procedure and any written agreement or instruction of the customer restricting acceptance of payment orders issued in the name of the customer. The bank is not required to follow an instruction that violates a written agreement with the customer or notice of which is not received at a time and in a manner affording the bank a reasonable opportunity to act on it before the payment order is accepted.

(3) Commercial reasonableness of a security procedure is a question of law to be determined by considering the wishes of the customer expressed to the bank, the circumstances of the customer known to the bank, including the size, type, and frequency of payment orders normally issued by the customer to the bank, alternative security procedures offered to the customer, and security procedures in general use by customers and receiving banks similarly situated. A security procedure is deemed to be commercially reasonable if (i) the security procedure was chosen by the customer after the bank offered, and the customer refused, a security procedure that was commercially reasonable for that customer, and (ii) the customer expressly agreed in writing to be bound by any payment order, whether or not authorized, issued in its name and accepted by the bank in compliance with the security procedure chosen by the customer.

(4) The term "sender" in this Article includes the customer in whose name a payment order is issued if the order is the authorized order of the customer under subsection (1), or it is effective as the order of the customer under subsection (2).

(5) This section applies to amendments and cancellations of payment orders to the same extent it applies to payment orders.

(6) Except as provided in this section and in Section 4A—203(1)(a), rights and obligations arising under this section or Section 4A—203 may not be varied by agreement.

§ 4A—203. **Unenforceability of Certain Verified Payment Orders.**

(1) If an accepted payment order is not, under Section 4A—202(1), an authorized order of a customer identified as sender, but is effective as an order of the customer pursuant to Section 4A—202(2), the following rules apply:

(a) By express written agreement, the receiving bank may limit the extent to which it is entitled to enforce or retain payment of the payment order.

(b) The receiving bank is not entitled to enforce or retain payment of the payment order if the customer proves that the order was not caused, directly or indirectly, by a person (i) entrusted at any time with duties to act for the customer with respect to payment orders or the security procedure, or (ii) who obtained access to transmitting facilities of the customer or who obtained, from a source controlled by the customer and without authority of the receiving bank, information facilitating breach of the security procedure, regardless of how the information was obtained or whether the customer was at fault. Information includes any access device, computer software, or the like.

(2) This section applies to amendments of payment orders to the same extent it applies to payment orders.

§ 4A—204. **Refund of Payment and Duty of Customer to Report with Respect to Unauthorized Payment Order.**

(1) If a receiving bank accepts a payment order issued in the name of its customer as sender which is (i) not authorized and not effective as the order of the customer under Section 4A—202, or (ii) not enforceable, in whole or in part, against the customer under Section 4A—203, the bank shall refund any payment of the payment order received from the customer to the extent the bank is not entitled to enforce payment and shall pay interest on the refundable amount calculated from the date the bank received payment to the date of the refund. However, the customer is not entitled to interest from the bank on the amount to be refunded if the customer fails to exercise ordinary care to determine that the order was not authorized by the customer and to notify the bank of the relevant facts within a reasonable time not exceeding 90 days after the date the customer received notification from the bank that the order was accepted or that the customer's account was debited with respect to the order. The bank is not entitled to any recovery from the customer on account of a failure by the customer to give notification as stated in this section.

(2) Reasonable time under subsection (1) may be fixed by agreement as stated in Section 1—204(1), but the obligation of a receiving bank to refund payment as stated in subsection (1) may not otherwise be varied by agreement.

§ 4A—205. **Erroneous Payment Orders.**

(1) If an accepted payment order was transmitted pursuant to a security procedure for the detection of error and the payment order (i) erroneously instructed payment to a beneficiary not intended by the sender, (ii) erroneously instructed payment in an amount greater than the amount intended by the sender, or (iii) was an erroneously transmitted duplicate of a payment order previously sent by the sender, the following rules apply:

(a) If the sender proves that the sender or a person acting on behalf of the sender pursuant to Section 4A—206 complied with the security procedure and that the error would have been detected if the receiving bank had also complied, the sender is not obliged to pay the order to the extent stated in paragraphs (b) and (c).

(b) If the funds transfer is completed on the basis of an erroneous payment order described in clause (i) or (iii) of subsection (1), the sender is not obliged to pay the order and the receiving bank is entitled to recover from the beneficiary any amount paid to the beneficiary to the extent allowed by the law governing mistake and restitution.

(c) If the funds transfer is completed on the basis of a payment order described in clause (ii) of subsection (1), the sender is not obliged to pay the order to the extent the amount received by the beneficiary is greater than the amount intended by the sender. In that case, the receiving bank is entitled to recover from the beneficiary the excess amount received to the extent allowed by the law governing mistake and restitution.

(2) If (i) the sender of an erroneous payment order described in subsection (1) is not obliged to pay all or part of the order, and (ii) the sender receives notification from the receiving bank that

the order was accepted by the bank or that the sender's account was debited with respect to the order, the sender has a duty to exercise ordinary care, on the basis of information available to the sender, to discover the error with respect to the order and to advise the bank of the relevant facts within a reasonable time, not exceeding 90 days, after the bank's notification was received by the sender. If the bank proves that the sender failed to perform that duty, the sender is liable to the bank for the loss the bank proves it incurred as a result of the failure, but the liability of the sender may not exceed the amount of the sender's order.

(3) This section applies to amendments to payment orders to the same extent it applies to payment orders.

§ 4A—206. **Transmission of Payment Order through Funds-Transfer or Other Communication System.**

(1) If a payment order addressed to a receiving bank is transmitted to a funds-transfer system or other thirdparty communication system for transmittal to the bank, the system is deemed to be an agent of the sender for the purpose of transmitting the payment order to the bank. If there is a discrepancy between the terms of the payment order transmitted to the system and the terms of the payment order transmitted by the system to the bank, the terms of the payment order of the sender are those transmitted by the system. This section does not apply to a funds-transfer system of the Federal Reserve Banks.

(2) This section applies to cancellations and amendments to payment orders to the same extent it applies to payment orders.

§ 4A—207. **Misdescription of Beneficiary.**

(1) Subject to subsection (2), if, in a payment order received by the beneficiary's bank, the name, bank account number, or other identification of the beneficiary refers to a nonexistent or unidentifiable person or account, no person has rights as a beneficiary of the order and acceptance of the order cannot occur.

(2) If a payment order received by the beneficiary's bank identifies the beneficiary both by name and by an identifying or bank account number and the name and number identify different persons, the following rules apply:

(a) Except as otherwise provided in subsection (3), if the beneficiary's bank does not know that the name and number refer to different persons, it may rely on the number as the proper identification of the beneficiary of the order. The beneficiary's bank need not determine whether the name and number refer to the same person.

(b) If the beneficiary's bank pays the person identified by name or knows that the name and number identify different persons, no person has rights as beneficiary except the person paid by the beneficiary's bank if that person was entitled to receive payment from the originator of the funds transfer. If no person has rights as beneficiary, acceptance of the order cannot occur.

(3) If (i) a payment order described in subsection (2) is accepted, (ii) the originator's payment order described the beneficiary inconsistently by name and number, and (iii) the beneficiary's bank pays the person identified by number as permitted by subsection (2)(a), the following rules apply:

(a) If the originator is a bank, the originator is obliged to pay its order.

(b) If the originator is not a bank and proves that the person identified by number was not entitled to receive payment from the originator, the originator is not obliged to pay its order unless the originator's bank proves that the originator, before acceptance of the originator's order, had notice that payment of a payment order issued by the originator might be made by the beneficiary's bank on the basis of an identifying or bank account number even if it identifies a person different from the named beneficiary. Proof of notice may be made by any admissible evidence. The originator's bank satisfies the burden of proof if it proves that the originator, before the payment order was accepted, signed a writing stating the information to which the notice relates.

(4) In a case governed by subsection (2)(a), if the beneficiary's bank rightfully pays the person identified by number and that person was not entitled to receive payment from the originator, the amount paid may be recovered from that person to the extent allowed by the law governing mistake and restitution as follows:

(a) If the originator is obliged to pay its payment order as stated in subsection (3), the originator has the right to recover.

(b) If the originator is not a bank and is not obliged to pay its payment order, the originator's bank has the right to recover.

§ 4A—208. **Misdescription of Intermediary Bank or Beneficiary's Bank.**

(1) This subsection applies to a payment order identifying an intermediary bank or the beneficiary's bank only by an identifying number.

(a) The receiving bank may rely on the number as the proper identification of the intermediary or beneficiary's bank and need not determine whether the number identifies a bank.

(b) The sender is obliged to compensate the receiving bank for any loss and expenses incurred by the receiving bank as a result of its reliance on the number in executing or attempting to execute the order.

(2) This subsection applies to a payment order identifying an intermediary bank or the beneficiary's bank both by name and an identifying number if the name and number identify different persons.

(a) If the sender is a bank, the receiving bank may rely on the number as the proper identification of the intermediary or beneficiary's bank if the receiving bank, when it executes the sender's order, does not know that the name and number identify different persons. The receiving bank need not determine whether the name and number refer to the same person or whether the number refers to a bank. The sender is obliged to compensate the receiving bank for any loss and expenses incurred by the receiving bank as a result of its reliance on the number in executing or attempting to execute the order.

(b) If the sender is not a bank and the receiving bank proves that the sender, before the payment order was accepted, had notice that the receiving bank might rely on the number as the proper identification of the intermediary or beneficiary's bank even if it identifies a person different from the bank identified by name, the rights and obligations of the sender and the receiving bank are governed by subsection (2)(a), as though the sender were a bank. Proof of notice may be made by any admissible evidence. The receiving bank satisfies the burden of proof if it proves that the sender, before the payment order was accepted, signed a writing stating the information to which the notice relates.

(c) Regardless of whether the sender is a bank, the receiving bank may rely on the name as the proper identification of the intermediary or beneficiary's bank if the receiving bank, at the time it executes the sender's order, does not know that the name and number identify different persons. The receiving bank need not determine whether the name and number refer to the same person.

(d) If the receiving bank knows that the name and number identify different persons, reliance on either the name or the number in executing the sender's payment order is a breach of the obligation stated in Section 4A—302(1)(a).

§ 4A—209. **Acceptance of Payment Order.**

(1) Subject to subsection (4), a receiving bank other than the beneficiary's bank accepts a payment order when it executes the order.

(2) Subject to subsections (3) and (4), a beneficiary's bank accepts a payment order at the earliest of the following times:

(a) When the bank (i) pays the beneficiary as stated in Section 4A—405(1) or 4A—405(2), or (ii) notifies the beneficiary of receipt of the order or that the account of the beneficiary has been credited with respect to the order unless the notice indicates that the bank is rejecting the order or that funds with respect to the order may not be withdrawn or used until receipt of payment from the sender of the order;

(b) When the bank receives payment of the entire amount of the sender's order pursuant to Section 4A—403(1)(a) or 4A—403(1)(b); or

(c) The opening of the next funds-transfer business day of the bank following the payment date of the order if, at that time, the amount of the sender's order is fully covered by a withdrawable credit balance in an authorized account of the sender or the bank has otherwise received full payment from the sender, unless the order was rejected before that time or is rejected within (i) one hour after that time, or (ii) one hour after the opening of the next business day of the sender following the payment date if that time is later. If notice of rejection is received by the sender after the payment date and the authorized account of the sender does not bear interest, the bank is obliged to pay interest to the sender on the amount of the order for the number of days elapsing after the payment date to the day the sender receives notice or learns that the order was not accepted, counting that day as an elapsed day. If the withdrawable credit balance during that period falls below the amount of the order, the amount of interest payable is reduced accordingly.

(3) Acceptance of a payment order cannot occur before the order is received by the receiving bank. Acceptance does not occur under subsection (2)(b) or (2)(c) if the beneficiary of the payment order does not have an account with the receiving bank, the account has been closed, or the receiving bank is not permitted by law to receive credits for the beneficiary's account.

(4) A payment order issued to the originator's bank cannot be accepted until the payment date if the bank is the beneficiary's bank, or the execution date if the bank is not the beneficiary's bank. If the originator's bank executes the originator's payment order before the execution date or pays the beneficiary of the originator's payment order before the payment date and the payment order is subsequently cancelled pursuant to Section 4A—211(2), the bank may recover from the beneficiary any payment received to the extent allowed by the law governing mistake and restitution.

§ 4A—210. **Rejection of Payment Order.**

(1) A payment order is rejected by the receiving bank by a notice of rejection transmitted to the sender orally, electronically, or in writing. A notice of rejection need not use any particular words and is sufficient if it indicates that the receiving bank is rejecting the order or will not execute or pay the order. Rejection is effective when the notice is given if transmission is by a means that is reasonable in the circumstances. If notice of rejection is given by a means that is not reasonable, rejection is effective when the notice is received. If an agreement of the sender and receiving bank establishes the means to be used to reject a payment order, (i) any means complying with the agreement is reasonable and (ii) any means not complying is not reasonable unless no significant delay in receipt of the notice resulted from the use of the noncomplying means.

(2) This subsection applies if a receiving bank other than the beneficiary's bank fails to execute a payment order despite the existence on the execution date of a withdrawable credit balance in an authorized account of the sender sufficient to cover the order. If the sender does not receive notice of rejection of the order on the execution date and the authorized account of the sender does not bear interest, the bank is obliged to pay interest to the sender on the amount of the order for the number of days elapsing after the execution date to the earlier of the day the order is cancelled pursuant to Section 4A—211(4) or the day the sender receives notice or learns that the order was not executed, counting the final day of the period as an elapsed day. If the withdrawable credit balance during that period falls below the amount of the order, the amount of interest is reduced accordingly.

(3) If a receiving bank suspends payments, all unaccepted payment orders issued to it are are deemed rejected at the time the bank suspends payments.

(4) Acceptance of a payment order precludes a later rejection of the order. Rejection of a payment order precludes a later acceptance of the order.

§ 4A—211. **Cancellation and Amendment of Payment Order.**

(1) A communication of the sender of a payment order cancelling or amending the order may be transmitted to the receiving bank orally, electronically, or in writing. If a security procedure is in effect between the sender and the receiving bank, the communication is not effective to cancel or amend the order unless the communication is verified pursuant to the security procedure or the bank agrees to the cancellation or amendment.

(2) Subject to subsection (1), a communication by the sender cancelling or amending a payment order is effective to cancel or amend the order if notice of the communication is received at a time and in a manner affording the receiving bank a reasonable opportunity to act on the communication before the bank accepts the payment order.

(3) After a payment order has been accepted, cancellation or amendment of the order is not effective unless the receiving bank agrees or a funds-transfer system rule allows cancellation or amendment without agreement of the bank.

(a) With respect to a payment order accepted by a receiving bank other than the beneficiary's bank, cancellation or amendment is not effective unless a conforming cancellation or amendment of the payment order issued by the receiving bank is also made.

(b) With respect to a payment order accepted by the beneficiary's bank, cancellation or amendment is not effective unless the order was issued in execution of an unauthorized payment order, or because of a mistake by a sender in the funds transfer which resulted in the issuance of a payment order (i) that is a duplicate of a payment order previously issued by the sender, (ii) that orders payment to a beneficiary not entitled to receive payment from the originator, or (iii) that orders payment in an amount greater than the amount the beneficiary was entitled to receive from the originator. If the payment order is cancelled or amended, the beneficiary's bank is entitled to recover from the beneficiary any amount paid to the beneficiary to the extent allowed by the law governing mistake and restitution.

(4) An unaccepted payment order is cancelled by operation of law at the close of the fifth funds-transfer business day of the receiving bank after the execution date or payment date of the order.

(5) A cancelled payment order cannot be accepted. If an accepted payment order is cancelled, the acceptance is nullified and no person has any right or obligation based on the acceptance. Amendment of a payment order is deemed to be cancellation of the original order at the time of amendment and issue of a new payment order in the amended form at the same time.

(6) Unless otherwise provided in an agreement of the parties or in a funds-transfer system rule, if the receiving bank, after accepting a payment order, agrees to cancellation or amendment of the order by the sender or is bound by a funds-transfer system rule allowing cancellation or amendment without the bank's agreement, the sender, whether or not cancellation or amendment is effective, is liable to the bank for any loss and expenses, including reasonable attorney's fees, incurred by the bank as a result of the cancellation or amendment or attempted cancellation or amendment.

(7) A payment order is not revoked by the death or legal incapacity of the sender unless the receiving bank knows of the death or of an adjudication of incapacity by a court of competent jurisdiction and has reasonable opportunity to act before acceptance of the order.

(8) A funds-transfer system rule is not effective to the extent it conflicts with subsection (3)(b).

§ 4A—212. **Liability and Duty of Receiving Bank Regarding Unaccepted Payment Order.**

If a receiving bank fails to accept a payment order that it is obliged by express agreement to accept, the bank is liable for breach of the agreement to the extent provided in the agreement or in this Article, but does not otherwise have any duty to accept a payment order or, before acceptance, to take any action, or refrain from taking action, with respect to the order except as provided in this Article or by express agreement. Liability based on acceptance arises only when acceptance occurs as stated in Section 4A—209, and liability is limited to that provided in this Article. A receiving bank is not the agent of the sender or beneficiary of the payment order it accepts, or of any other party to the funds transfer, and the bank owes no duty to any party to the funds transfer except as provided in this Article or by express agreement.

Part 3 Execution of Sender's Payment Order by Receiving Bank

§ 4A—301. **Execution and Execution Date.**

(1) A payment order is "executed" by the receiving bank when it issues a payment order intended to carry out the payment order received by the bank. A payment order received by the beneficiary's bank can be accepted but cannot be executed.

(2) "Execution date" of a payment order means the day on which the receiving bank may properly issue a payment order in execution of the sender's order. The execution date may be determined by instruction of the sender but cannot be earlier than the day the order is received and, unless otherwise determined, is the day the order is received. If the sender's instruction states a payment date, the execution date is the payment date or an earlier date on which execution is reasonably necessary to allow payment to the beneficiary on the payment date.

§ 4A—302. **Obligations of Receiving Bank in Execution of Payment Order.**

(1) Except as provided in subsections (2) through (4), if the receiving bank accepts a payment order pursuant to Section 4A—209(1), the bank has the following obligations in executing the order:

(a) The receiving bank is obliged to issue, on the execution date, a payment order complying with the sender's order and to follow the sender's instructions concerning (i) any intermediary bank or funds-transfer system to be used in carrying out the funds transfer, or (ii) the means by which payment orders are to be transmitted in the funds transfer. If the originator's bank issues a payment order to an intermediary bank, the originator's bank is obliged to instruct the intermediary bank according to the instruction of the originator. An intermediary bank in the funds transfer is similarly bound by an instruction given to it by the sender of the payment order it accepts.

(b) If the sender's instruction states that the funds transfer is to be carried out telephonically or by wire transfer or otherwise indicates that the funds transfer is to be carried out by the most expeditious means, the receiving bank is obliged to transmit its payment order by the most expeditious available means, and to instruct any intermediary bank accordingly. If a sender's instruction states a payment date, the receiving bank is obliged to transmit its payment order at a time and by means reasonably necessary to allow payment to the beneficiary on the payment date or as soon thereafter as is feasible.

(2) Unless otherwise instructed, a receiving bank executing a payment order may (i) use any funds-transfer system if use of that system is reasonable in the circumstances, and (ii) issue a pay-

ment order to the beneficiary's bank or to an intermediary bank through which a payment order conforming to the sender's order can expeditiously be issued to the beneficiary's bank if the receiving bank exercises ordinary care in the selection of the intermediary bank. A receiving bank is not required to follow an instruction of the sender designating a funds-transfer system to be used in carrying out the funds transfer if the receiving bank, in good faith, determines that it is not feasible to follow the instruction or that following the instruction would unduly delay completion of the funds transfer.

(3) Unless subsection (1)(b) applies or the receiving bank is otherwise instructed, the bank may execute a payment order by transmitting its payment order by first class mail or by any means reasonable in the circumstances. If the receiving bank is instructed to execute the sender's order by transmitting its payment order by a particular means, the receiving bank may issue its payment order by the means stated or by any means as expeditious as the means stated.

(4) Unless instructed by the sender, (i) the receiving bank may not obtain payment of its charges for services and expenses in connection with the execution of the sender's order by issuing a payment order in an amount equal to the amount of the sender's order less the amount of the charges, and (ii) may not instruct a subsequent receiving bank to obtain payment of its charges in the same manner.

§ 4A—303. **Erroneous Execution of Payment Order.**

(1) A receiving bank that (i) executes the payment order of the sender by issuing a payment order in an amount greater than the amount of the sender's order, or (ii) issues a payment order in execution of the sender's order and then issues a duplicate order, is entitled to payment of the amount of the sender's order under Section 4A—402(3) if that subsection is otherwise satisfied. The bank is entitled to recover from the beneficiary of the erroneous order the excess payment received to the extent allowed by the law governing mistake and restitution.

(2) A receiving bank that executes the payment order of the sender by issuing a payment order in an amount less than the amount of the sender's order is entitled to payment of the amount of the sender's order under Section 4A—402(3) if (i) that subsection is otherwise satisfied and (ii) the bank corrects its mistake by issuing an additional payment order for the benefit of the beneficiary of the sender's order. If the error is not corrected, the issuer of the erroneous order is entitled to receive or retain payment from the sender of the order it accepted only to the extent of the amount of the erroneous order. This subsection does not apply if the receiving bank executes the sender's payment order by issuing a payment order in an amount less than the amount of the sender's order for the purpose of obtaining payment of its charges for services and expenses pursuant to instruction of the sender.

(3) If a receiving bank executes the payment order of the sender by issuing a payment order to a beneficiary different from the beneficiary of the sender's order and the funds transfer is completed on the basis of that error, the sender of the payment order that was erroneously executed and all previous senders in the funds transfer are not obliged to pay the payment orders they issued. The issuer of the erroneous order is entitled to recover from the beneficiary of the order the payment received to the extent allowed by the law governing mistake and restitution.

§ 4A—304. **Duty of Sender to Report Erroneously Executed Payment Order.**

If the sender of a payment order that is erroneously executed as stated in Section 4A—303 receives notification from the receiving bank that the order was executed or that the sender's account was debited with respect to the order, the sender has a duty to exercise ordinary care to determine, on the basis of information available to the sender, that the order was erroneously executed and to notify the bank of the relevant facts within a reasonable time not exceeding 90 days after the notification from the bank was received by the sender. If the sender fails to perform that duty, the bank is not obliged to pay interest on any amount refundable to the sender under Section 4A—402(4) for the period before the bank learns of the execution error. The bank is not entitled to any recovery from the sender on account of a failure by the sender to perform the duty stated in this section.

§ 4A—305. **Liability for Late or Improper Execution or Failure to Execute Payment Order.**

(1) If a funds transfer is completed but execution of a payment order by the receiving bank in breach of Section 4A—302 results in delay in payment to the beneficiary, the bank is obliged to pay interest to either the originator or the beneficiary of the funds transfer for the period of delay caused by the improper execution. Except as provided in subsection (3), additional damages are not recoverable.

(2) If execution of a payment order by a receiving bank in breach of Section 4A—302 results in (i) noncompletion of the funds transfer, (ii) failure to use an intermediary bank designated by the originator, or (iii) issuance of a payment order that does not comply with the terms of the payment order of the originator, the bank is liable to the originator for its expenses in the funds transfer and for incidental expenses and interest losses, to the extent not covered by subsection (1), resulting from the improper execution. Except as provided in subsection (3), additional damages are not recoverable.

(3) In addition to the amounts payable under subsections (1) and (2), damages, including consequential damages, are recoverable to the extent provided in an express written agreement of the receiving bank.

(4) If a receiving bank fails to execute a payment order it was obliged by express agreement to execute, the receiving bank is liable to the sender for its expenses in the transaction and for incidental expenses and interest losses resulting from the failure to execute. Additional damages, including consequential damages, are recoverable to the extent provided in an express written agreement of the receiving bank, but are not otherwise recoverable.

(5) Reasonable attorney's fees are recoverable if demand for compensation under subsection (1) or (2) is made and refused before an action is brought on the claim. If a claim is made for breach of an agreement under subsection (4) and the agreement does not provide for damages, reasonable attorney's fees are recoverable if demand for compensation under subsection (4) is made and refused before an action is brought on the claim.

(6) Except as stated in this section, the liability of a receiving bank under subsections (1) and (2) may not be varied by agreement.

Part 4 Payment

§ 4A—401. Payment Date.

"Payment date" of a payment order means the day on which the amount of the order is payable to the beneficiary by the beneficiary's bank. The payment date may be determined by instruction of the sender but cannot be earlier than the day the order is received by the beneficiary's bank and, unless otherwise determined, is the day the order is received by the beneficiary's bank.

§ 4A—402. Obligation of Sender to Pay Receiving Bank.

(1) This section is subject to Sections 4A—205 and 4A—207.

(2) With respect to a payment order issued to the beneficiary's bank, acceptance of the order by the bank obliges the sender to pay the bank the amount of the order, but payment is not due until the payment date of the order.

(3) This subsection is subject to subsection (5) and to Section 4A—303. With respect to a payment order issued to a receiving bank other than the beneficiary's bank, acceptance of the order by the receiving bank obliges the sender to pay the bank the amount of the sender's order. Payment by the sender is not due until the execution date of the sender's order. The obligation of that sender to pay its payment order is excused if the funds transfer is not completed by acceptance by the beneficiary's bank of a payment order instructing payment to the beneficiary of that sender's payment order.

(4) If the sender of a payment order pays the order and was not obliged to pay all or part of the amount paid, the bank receiving payment is obliged to refund payment to the extent the sender was not obliged to pay. Except as provided in Sections 4A—204 and 4A—304, interest is payable on the refundable amount from the date of payment.

(5) If a funds transfer is not completed as stated in subsection (3) and an intermediary bank is obliged to refund payment as stated in subsection (4) but is unable to do so because not permitted by applicable law or because the bank suspends payments, a sender in the funds transfer that executed a payment order in compliance with an instruction, as stated in Section 4A—302(1)(a), to route the funds transfer through that intermediary bank is entitled to receive or retain payment from the sender of the payment order that it accepted. The first sender in the funds transfer that issued an instruction requiring routing through that intermediary bank is subrogated to the right of the bank that paid the intermediary bank to refund as stated in subsection (4).

(6) The right of the sender of a payment order to be excused from the obligation to pay the order as stated in subsection (3) or to receive refund under subsection (4) may not be varied by agreement.

§ 4A—403. Payment by Sender to Receiving Bank.

(1) Payment of the sender's obligation under Section 4A—402 to pay the receiving bank occurs as follows:

(a) If the sender is a bank, payment occurs when the receiving bank receives final settlement of the obligation through a Federal Reserve Bank or through a funds-transfer system.

(b) If the sender is a bank and the sender (i) credited an account of the receiving bank with the sender, or (ii) caused an account of the receiving bank in another bank to be credited, payment occurs when the credit is withdrawn or, if not withdrawn, at midnight of the day on which the credit is withdrawable and the receiving bank learns of that fact.

(c) If the receiving bank debits an account of the sender with the receiving bank, payment occurs when the debit is made to the extent the debit is covered by a withdrawable credit balance in the account.

(2) If the sender and receiving bank are members of a funds-transfer system that nets obligations multilaterally among participants, the receiving bank receives final settlement when settlement is complete in accordance with the rules of the system. The obligation of the sender to pay the amount of a payment order transmitted through the funds-transfer system may be satisfied, to the extent permitted by the rules of the system, by setting off and applying against the sender's obligation the right of the sender to receive payment from the receiving bank of the amount of any other payment order transmitted to the sender by the receiving bank through the funds-transfer system. The aggregate balance of obligations owed by each sender to each receiving bank in the funds-transfer system may be satisfied, to the extent permitted by the rules of the system, by setting off and applying against that balance the aggregate balance of obligations owed to the sender by other members of the system. The aggregate balance is determined after the right of setoff stated in the second sentence of this subsection has been exercised.

(3) If two banks transmit payment orders to each other under an agreement that settlement of the obligations of each bank to the other under Section 4A—402 will be made at the end of the day or other period, the total amount owed with respect to all orders transmitted by one bank shall be set off against the total amount owed with respect to all orders transmitted by the other bank. To the extent of the setoff, each bank has made payment to the other.

(4) In a case not covered by subsection (1), the time when payment of the sender's obligation under Section 4A—402(2) or 4A—402(3) occurs is governed by applicable principles of law that determine when an obligation is satisfied.

§ 4A—404. Obligation of Beneficiary's Bank to Pay and Give Notice to Beneficiary.

(1) Subject to Sections 4A—211(5), 4A—405(4), and 4A—405(5), if a beneficiary's bank accepts a payment order, the bank is obliged to pay the amount of the order to the beneficiary of the order. Payment is due on the payment date of the order, but if acceptance occurs on the payment date after the close of the funds-transfer business day of the bank, payment is due on the next funds-transfer business day. If the bank refuses to pay after demand by the beneficiary and receipt of notice of particular circumstances that will give rise to consequential damages as a result of nonpayment, the beneficiary may recover damages resulting from the refusal to pay to the extent the bank had notice of the damages, unless the bank proves that it did not pay because of a reasonable doubt concerning the right of the beneficiary to payment.

(2) If a payment order accepted by the beneficiary's bank instructs payment to an account of the beneficiary, the bank is obliged to notify the beneficiary of receipt of the order before midnight of the next funds-transfer business day following the payment date. If the payment order does not instruct payment to

an account of the beneficiary, the bank is required to notify the beneficiary only if notice is required by the order. Notice may be given by first class mail or any other means reasonable in the circumstances. If the bank fails to give the required notice, the bank is obliged to pay interest to the beneficiary on the amount of the payment order from the day notice should have been given until the day the beneficiary learned of receipt of the payment order by the bank. No other damages are recoverable. Reasonable attorney's fees are also recoverable if demand for interest is made and refused before an action is brought on the claim.

(3) The right of a beneficiary to receive payment and damages as stated in subsection (1) may not be varied by agreement or a funds-transfer system rule. The right of a beneficiary to be notified as stated in subsection (2) may be varied by agreement of the beneficiary or by a funds-transfer system rule if the beneficiary is notified of the rule before initiation of the funds transfer.

§ 4A—405. **Payment by Beneficiary's Bank to Beneficiary.**

(1) If the beneficiary's bank credits an account of the beneficiary of a payment order, payment of the bank's obligation under Section 4A—404(1) occurs when and to the extent (i) the beneficiary is notified of the right to withdraw the credit, (ii) the bank lawfully applies the credit to a debt of the beneficiary, or (iii) funds with respect to the order are otherwise made available to the beneficiary by the bank.

(2) If the beneficiary's bank does not credit an account of the beneficiary of a payment order, the time when payment of the bank's obligation under Section 4A—404(1) occurs is governed by principles of law that determine when an obligation is satisfied.

(3) Except as stated in subsections (4) and (5), if the beneficiary's bank pays the beneficiary of a payment order under a condition to payment or agreement of the beneficiary giving the bank the right to recover payment from the beneficiary if the bank does not receive payment of the order, the condition to payment or agreement is not enforceable.

(4) A funds-transfer system rule may provide that payments made to beneficiaries of funds transfers made through the system are provisional until receipt of payment by the beneficiary's bank of the payment order it accepted. A beneficiary's bank that makes a payment that is provisional under the rule is entitled to refund from the beneficiary if (i) the rule requires that both the beneficiary and the originator be given notice of the provisional nature of the payment before the funds transfer is initiated, (ii) the beneficiary, the beneficiary's bank, and the originator's bank agreed to be bound by the rule, and (iii) the beneficiary's bank did not receive payment of the payment order that it accepted. If the beneficiary is obliged to refund payment to the beneficiary's bank, acceptance of the payment order by the beneficiary's bank is nullified and no payment by the originator of the funds transfer to the beneficiary occurs under Section 4A—406.

(5) This subsection applies to a funds transfer that includes a payment order transmitted over a funds-transfer system that (i) nets obligations multilaterally among participants, and (ii) has in effect a loss-sharing agreement among participants for the purpose of providing funds necessary to complete settlement of the obligations of one or more participants that do not meet their settlement obligations. If the beneficiary's bank in the funds transfer accepts a payment order and the system fails to complete settlement pursuant to its rules with respect to any payment order in the funds transfer, (i) the acceptance by the beneficiary's bank is nullified and no person has any right or obligation based on the acceptance, (ii) the beneficiary's bank is entitled to recover payment from the beneficiary, (iii) no payment by the originator to the beneficiary occurs under Section 4A—406, and (iv) subject to Section 4A—402(5), each sender in the funds transfer is excused from its obligation to pay its payment order under Section 4A—402(3) because the funds transfer has not been completed.

§ 4A—406. **Payment by Originator to Beneficiary; Discharge of Underlying Obligation.**

(1) Subject to Sections 4A—211(5), 4A—405(4), and 4A—405(5), the originator of a funds transfer pays the beneficiary of the originator's payment order (i) at the time a payment order for the benefit of the beneficiary is accepted by the beneficiary's bank in the funds transfer and (ii) in an amount equal to the amount of the order accepted by the beneficiary's bank, but not more than the amount of the originator's order.

(2) If payment under subsection (1) is made to satisfy an obligation, the obligation is discharged to the same extent discharge would result from payment to the beneficiary of the same amount in money, unless (i) the payment under subsection (1) was made by a means prohibited by the contract of the beneficiary with respect to the obligation, (ii) the beneficiary, within a reasonable time after receiving notice of receipt of the order by the beneficiary's bank, notified the originator of the beneficiary's refusal of the payment, (iii) funds with respect to the order were not withdrawn by the beneficiary or applied to a debt of the beneficiary, and (iv) the beneficiary would suffer a loss that could reasonably have been avoided if payment had been made by a means complying with the contract. If payment by the originator does not result in discharge under this section, the originator is subrogated to the rights of the beneficiary to receive payment from the beneficiary's bank under Section 4A—404(1).

(3) For the purpose of determining whether discharge of an obligation occurs under subsection (2), if the beneficiary's bank accepts a payment order in an amount equal to the amount of the originator's payment order less charges of one or more receiving banks in the funds transfer, payment to the beneficiary is deemed to be in the amount of the originator's order unless upon demand by the beneficiary the originator does not pay the beneficiary the amount of the deducted charges.

(4) Rights of the originator or of the beneficiary of a funds transfer under this section may be varied only by agreement of the originator and the beneficiary.

Part 5 Miscellaneous Provisions

§ 4A—501. **Variation by Agreement and Effect of Funds-Transfer System Rule.**

(1) Except as otherwise provided in this Article, the rights and obligations of a party to a funds transfer may be varied by agreement of the affected party.

(2) "Funds-transfer system rule" means a rule of an association of banks (i) governing transmission of payment orders by means of a funds-transfer system of the association or rights and obligations with respect to those orders, or (ii) to the extent the rule governs rights and obligations between banks that are parties to

a funds transfer in which a Federal Reserve Bank, acting as an intermediary bank, sends a payment order to the beneficiary's bank. Except as otherwise provided in this Article, a funds-transfer system rule governing rights and obligations between participating banks using the system may be effective even if the rule conflicts with this Article and indirectly affects another party to the funds transfer who does not consent to the rule. A funds-transfer system rule may also govern rights and obligations of parties other than participating banks using the system to the extent stated in Sections 4A—404(3), 4A—405(4), and 4A—507(3).

§ 4A—502. **Creditor Process Served on Receiving Bank; Setoff by Beneficiary's Bank.**

(1) As used in this section, "creditor process" means levy, attachment, garnishment, notice of lien, sequestration, or similar process issued by or on behalf of a creditor or other claimant with respect to an account.

(2) This subsection applies to creditor process with respect to an authorized account of the sender of a payment order if the creditor process is served on the receiving bank. For the purpose of determining rights with respect to the creditor process, if the receiving bank accepts the payment order the balance in the authorized account is deemed to be reduced by the amount of the payment order to the extent the bank did not otherwise receive payment of the order, unless the creditor process is served at a time and in a manner affording the bank a reasonable opportunity to act on it before the bank accepts the payment order.

(3) If a beneficiary's bank has received a payment order for payment to the beneficiary's account in the bank, the following rules apply:

(a) The bank may credit the beneficiary's account. The amount credited may be set off against an obligation owed by the beneficiary to the bank or may be applied to satisfy creditor process served on the bank with respect to the account.

(b) The bank may credit the beneficiary's account and allow withdrawal of the amount credited unless creditor process with respect to the account is served at a time and in a manner affording the bank a reasonable opportunity to act to prevent withdrawal.

(c) If creditor process with respect to the beneficiary's account has been served and the bank has had a reasonable opportunity to act on it, the bank may not reject the payment order except for a reason unrelated to the service of process.

(4) Creditor process with respect to a payment by the originator to the beneficiary pursuant to a funds transfer may be served only on the beneficiary's bank with respect to the debt owed by that bank to the beneficiary. Any other bank served with the creditor process is not obliged to act with respect to the process.

§ 4A—503. **Injunction or Restraining Order with Respect to Funds Transfer.**

For proper cause and in compliance with applicable law, a court may restrain (i) a person from issuing a payment order to initiate a funds transfer, (ii) an originator's bank from executing the payment order of the originator, or (iii) the beneficiary's bank from releasing funds to the beneficiary or the beneficiary from withdrawing the funds. A court may not otherwise restrain a person from issuing a payment order, paying or receiving payment of a payment order, or otherwise acting with respect to a funds transfer.

§ 4A—504. **Order in Which Items and Payment Orders May Be Charged to Account; Order of Withdrawals from Account.**

(1) If a receiving bank has received more than one payment order of the sender or one or more payment orders and other items that are payable from the sender's account, the bank may charge the sender's account with respect to the various orders and items in any sequence.

(2) In determining whether a credit to an account has been withdrawn by the holder of the account or applied to a debt of the holder of the account, credits first made to the account are first withdrawn or applied.

§ 4A—505. **Preclusion of Objection to Debit of Customer's Account.**

If a receiving bank has received payment from its customer with respect to a payment order issued in the name of the customer as sender and accepted by the bank, and the customer received notification reasonably identifying the order, the customer is precluded from asserting that the bank is not entitled to retain the payment unless the customer notifies the bank of the customer's objection to the payment within one year after the notification was received by the customer.

§ 4A—506. **Rate of Interest.**

(1) If, under this Article, a receiving bank is obliged to pay interest with respect to a payment order issued to the bank, the amount payable may be determined (i) by agreement of the sender and receiving bank, or (ii) by a funds-transfer system rule if the payment order is transmitted through a funds-transfer system.

(2) If the amount of interest is not determined by an agreement or rule as stated in subsection (1), the amount is calculated by multiplying the applicable Federal Funds rate by the amount on which interest is payable, and then multiplying the product by the number of days for which interest is payable. The applicable Federal Funds rate is the average of the Federal Funds rates published by the Federal Reserve Bank of New York for each of the days for which interest is payable divided by 360. The Federal Funds rate for any day on which a published rate is not available is the same as the published rate for the next preceding day for which there is a published rate. If a receiving bank that accepted a payment order is required to refund payment to the sender of the order because the funds transfer was not completed, but the failure to complete was not due to any fault by the bank, the interest payable is reduced by a percentage equal to the reserve requirement on deposits of the receiving bank.

§ 4A—507. **Choice of Law.**

(1) The following rules apply unless the affected parties otherwise agree or subsection (3) applies:

(a) The rights and obligations between the sender of a payment order and the receiving bank are governed by the law of the jurisdiction in which the receiving bank is located.

(b) The rights and obligations between the beneficiary's bank and the beneficiary are governed by the law of the jurisdiction in which the beneficiary's bank is located.

(c) The issue of when payment is made pursuant to a funds transfer by the originator to the beneficiary is governed by the law of the jurisdiction in which the beneficiary's bank is located.

(2) If the parties described in each paragraph of subsection (1) have made an agreement selecting the law of a particular jurisdiction to govern rights and obligations between each other, the law of that jurisdiction governs those rights and obligations, whether or not the payment order or the funds transfer bears a reasonable relation to that jurisdiction.

(3) A funds-transfer system rule may select the law of a particular jurisdiction to govern (i) rights and obligations between participating banks with respect to payment orders transmitted or processed through the system, or (ii) the rights and obligations of some or all parties to a funds transfer any part of which is carried out by means of the system. A choice of law made pursuant to clause (i) is binding on participating banks. A choice of law made pursuant to clause (ii) is binding on the originator, other sender, or a receiving bank having notice that the funds-transfer system might be used in the funds transfer and of the choice of law by the system when the originator, other sender, or receiving bank issued or accepted a payment order. The beneficiary of a funds transfer is bound by the choice of law if, when the funds transfer is initiated, the beneficiary has notice that the funds-transfer system might be used in the funds transfer and of the choice of law by the system. The law of a jurisdiction selected pursuant to this subsection may govern, whether or not that law bears a reasonable relation to the matter in issue.

(4) In the event of inconsistency between an agreement under subsection (2) and a choice-of-law rule under subsection (3), the agreement under subsection (2) prevails.

(5) If a funds transfer is made by use of more than one funds-transfer system and there is inconsistency between choice-of-law rules of the systems, the matter in issue is governed by the law of the selected jurisdiction that has the most significant relationship to the matter in issue.

Article 9
SECURED TRANSACTIONS; SALES OF ACCOUNTS AND CHATTEL PAPER

Note: *The adoption of this Article should be accompanied by the repeal of existing statutes dealing with conditional sales, trust receipts, factor's liens where the factor is given a nonpossessory lien, chattel mortgages, crop mortgages, mortgages on railroad equipment, assignment of accounts and generally statutes regulating security interests in personal property.*

Where the state has a retail installment selling act or small loan act, that legislation should be carefully examined to determine what changes in those acts are needed to conform them to this Article. This Article primarily sets out rules defining rights of a secured party against persons dealing with the debtor; it does not prescribe regulations and controls which may be necessary to curb abuses arising in the small loan business or in the financing of consumer purchases on credit. Accordingly there is no intention to repeal existing regulatory acts in those fields by enactment or reenactment of Article 9. See Section 9—203(4) and the Note thereto.

Part 1 Short Title, Applicability and Definitions

§ 9—101. **Short Title.**

This Article shall be known and may be cited as Uniform Commercial Code—Secured Transactions.

§ 9—102. **Policy and Subject Matter of Article.**

(1) Except as otherwise provided in Section 9—104 on excluded transactions, this Article applies

(a) to any transaction (regardless of its form) which is intended to create a security interest in personal property or fixtures including goods, documents, instruments, general intangibles, chattel paper or accounts; and also

(b) to any sale of accounts or chattel paper.

(2) This Article applies to security interests created by contract including pledge, assignment, chattel mortgage, chattel trust, trust deed, factor's lien, equipment trust, conditional sale, trust receipt, other lien or title retention contract and lease or consignment intended as security. This Article does not apply to statutory liens except as provided in Section 9—310.

(3) The application of this Article to a security interest in a secured obligation is not affected by the fact that the obligation is itself secured by a transaction or interest to which this Article does not apply.

§ 9—103. **Perfection of Security Interest in Multiple State Transactions.**

(1) Documents, instruments and ordinary goods.

(a) This subsection applies to documents and instruments and to goods other than those covered by a certificate of title described in subsection (2), mobile goods described in subsection (3), and minerals described in subsection (5).

(b) Except as otherwise provided in this subsection, perfection and the effect of perfection or non-perfection of a security interest in collateral are governed by the law of the jurisdiction where the collateral is when the last event occurs on which is based the assertion that the security interest is perfected or unperfected.

(c) If the parties to a transaction creating a purchase money security interest in goods in one jurisdiction understand at the time that the security interest attaches that the goods will be kept in another jurisdiction, then the law of the other jurisdiction governs the perfection and the effect of perfection or non-perfection of the security interest from the time it attaches until thirty days after the debtor receives possession of the goods and thereafter if the goods are taken to the other jurisdiction before the end of the thirty-day period.

(d) When collateral is brought into and kept in this state while subject to a security interest perfected under the law of the jurisdiction from which the collateral was removed, the security interest remains perfected, but if action is required by Part 3 of this Article to perfect the security interest,

(i) if the action is not taken before the expiration of the period of perfection in the other jurisdiction or the end of four months after the collateral is brought into this state, whichever period first expires, the security interest becomes unperfected at the end of that period and is thereafter deemed to have been unperfected as against a person who became a purchaser after removal;

(ii) if the action is taken before the expiration of the period specified in subparagraph (i), the security interest continues perfected thereafter;

(iii) for the purpose of priority over a buyer of consumer

goods (subsection (2) of Section 9—307), the period of the effectiveness of a filing in the jurisdiction from which the collateral is removed is governed by the rules with respect to perfection in subparagraphs (i) and (ii).

(2) Certificate of title.

(a) This subsection applies to goods covered by a certificate of title issued under a statute of this state or of another jurisdiction under the law of which indication of a security interest on the certificate is required as a condition of perfection.

(b) Except as otherwise provided in this subsection, perfection and the effect of perfection or non-perfection of the security interest are governed by the law (including the conflict of laws rules) of the jurisdiction issuing the certificate until four months after the goods are removed from that jurisdiction and thereafter until the goods are registered in another jurisdiction, but in any event not beyond surrender of the certificate. After the expiration of that period, the goods are not covered by the certificate of title within the meaning of this section.

(c) Except with respect to the rights of a buyer described in the next paragraph, a security interest, perfected in another jurisdiction otherwise than by notation on a certificate of title, in goods brought into this state and thereafter covered by a certificate of title issued by this state is subject to the rules stated in paragraph (d) of subsection (1).

(d) If goods are brought into this state while a security interest therein is perfected in any manner under the law of the jurisdiction from which the goods are removed and a certificate of title is issued by this state and the certificate does not show that the goods are subject to the security interest or that they may be subject to security interests not shown on the certificate, the security interest is subordinate to the rights of a buyer of the goods who is not in the business of selling goods of that kind to the extent that he gives value and receives delivery of the goods after issuance of the certificate and without knowledge of the security interest.

(3) Accounts, general intangibles and mobile goods.

(a) This subsection applies to accounts (other than an account described in subsection (5) on minerals) and general intangibles (other than uncertificated securities) and to goods which are mobile and which are of a type normally used in more than one jurisdiction, such as motor vehicles, trailers, rolling stock, airplanes, shipping containers, road building and construction machinery and commercial harvesting machinery and the like, if the goods are equipment or are inventory leased or held for lease by the debtor to others, and are not covered by a certificate of title described in subsection (2).

(b) The law (including the conflict of laws rules) of the jurisdiction in which the debtor is located governs the perfection and the effect of perfection or non-perfection of the security interest.

(c) If, however, the debtor is located in a jurisdiction which is not a part of the United States, and which does not provide for perfection of the security interest by filing or recording in that jurisdiction, the law of the jurisdiction in the United States in which the debtor has its major executive office in the United States governs the perfection and the effect of perfection or non-perfection of the security interest through filing. In the alternative, if the debtor is located in a jurisdiction which is not a part of the United States or Canada and the collateral is accounts or general intangibles for money due or to become due, the security interest may be perfected by notification to the account debtor. As used in this paragraph, "United States" includes its territories and possessions and the Commonwealth of Puerto Rico.

(d) A debtor shall be deemed located at his place of business if he has one, at his chief executive office if he has more than one place of business, otherwise at his residence. If, however, the debtor is a foreign air carrier under the Federal Aviation Act of 1958, as amended, it shall be deemed located at the designated office of the agent upon whom service of process may be made on behalf of the foreign air carrier.

(e) A security interest perfected under the law of the jurisdiction of the location of the debtor is perfected until the expiration of four months after a change of the debtor's location to another jurisdiction, or until perfection would have ceased by the law of the first jurisdiction, whichever period first expires. Unless perfected in the new jurisdiction before the end of that period, it becomes unperfected thereafter and is deemed to have been unperfected as against a person who became a purchaser after the change.

(4) Chattel paper.

The rules stated for goods in subsection (1) apply to a possessory security interest in chattel paper. The rules stated for accounts in subsection (3) apply to a nonpossessory security interest in chattel paper, but the security interest may not be perfected by notification to the account debtor.

(5) Minerals.

Perfection and the effect of perfection or non-perfection of a security interest which is created by a debtor who has an interest in minerals or the like (including oil and gas) before extraction and which attaches thereto as extracted, or which attaches to an account resulting from the sale thereof at the wellhead or minehead are governed by the law (including the conflict of laws rules) of the jurisdiction wherein the wellhead or minehead is located.

(6) Uncertificated securities.

The law (including the conflict of laws rules) of the jurisdiction of organization of the issuer governs the perfection and the effect of perfection or non-perfection of a security interest in uncertificated securities.

§ 9—104. **Transactions Excluded From Article.**

This Article does not apply

(a) to a security interest subject to any statute of the United States, to the extent that such statute governs the rights of parties to and third parties affected by transactions in particular types of property; or

(b) to a landlord's lien; or

(c) to a lien given by statute or other rule of law for services or materials except as provided in Section 9—310 on priority of such liens; or

(d) to a transfer of a claim for wages, salary or other compensation of an employee; or

(e) to a transfer by a government or governmental subdivision or agency; or

(f) to a sale of accounts or chattel paper as part of a sale of the business out of which they arose, or an assignment of accounts or chattel paper which is for the purpose of collection only, or a transfer of a right to payment under a contract to an assignee who is also to do the performance under the contract or a transfer of a single account to an assignee in whole or partial satisfaction of a preexisting indebtedness; or

(g) to a transfer of an interest in or claim in or under any policy of insurance, except as provided with respect to proceeds (Section 9—306) and priorities in proceeds (Section 9—312); or

(h) to a right represented by a judgment (other than a judgment taken on a right to payment which was collateral); or

(i) to any right of set-off; or

(j) except to the extent that provision is made for fixtures in Section 9—313, to the creation or transfer of an interest in or lien on real estate, including a lease or rents thereunder; or

(k) to a transfer in whole or in part of any claim arising out of tort; or

(l) to a transfer of an interest in any deposit account (subsection (1) of Section 9—105), except as provided with respect to proceeds (Section 9—306) and priorities in proceeds (Section 9—312).

§ 9—105. **Definitions and Index of Definitions.**

(1) In this Article unless the context otherwise requires:

(a) "Account debtor" means the person who is obligated on an account, chattel paper or general intangible;

(b) "Chattel paper" means a writing or writings which evidence both a monetary obligation and a security interest in or a lease of specific goods, but a charter or other contract involving the use or hire of a vessel is not chattel paper. When a transaction is evidenced both by such a security agreement or a lease and by an instrument or a series of instruments, the group of writings taken together constitutes chattel paper;

(c) "Collateral" means the property subject to a security interest, and includes accounts and chattel paper which have been sold;

(d) "Debtor" means the person who owes payment or other performance of the obligation secured, whether or not he owns or has rights in the collateral, and includes the seller of accounts or chattel paper. Where the debtor and the owner of the collateral are not the same person, the term "debtor" means the owner of the collateral in any provision of the Article dealing with the collateral, the obligor in any provision dealing with the obligation, and may include both where the context so requires;

(e) "Deposit account" means a demand, time, savings, passbook or like account maintained with a bank, savings and loan association, credit union or like organization, other than an account evidenced by a certificate of deposit;

(f) "Document" means document of title as defined in the general definitions of Article 1 (Section 1—201), and a receipt of the kind described in subsection (2) of Section 7—201;

(g) "Encumbrance" includes real estate mortgages and other liens on real estate and all other rights in real estate that are not ownership interests;

(h) "Goods" includes all things which are movable at the time the security interest attaches or which are fixtures (Section 9—313), but does not include money, documents, instruments, accounts, chattel paper, general intangibles, or minerals or the like (including oil and gas) before extraction. "Goods" also includes standing timber which is to be cut and removed under a conveyance or contract for sale, the unborn young of animals, and growing crops;

(i) "Instrument" means a negotiable instrument (defined in Section 3—104), or a certificated security (defined in Section 8—102) or any other writing which evidences a right to the payment of money and is not itself a security agreement or lease and is of a type which is in ordinary course of business transferred by delivery with any necessary indorsement or assignment;

(j) "Mortgage" means a consensual interest created by a real estate mortgage, a trust deed on real estate, or the like;

(k) An advance is made "pursuant to commitment" if the secured party has bound himself to make it, whether or not a subsequent event of default or other event not within his control has relieved or may relieve him from his obligation;

(l) "Security agreement" means an agreement which creates or provides for a security interest;

(m) "Secured party" means a lender, seller or other person in whose favor there is a security interest, including a person to whom accounts or chattel paper have been sold. When the holders of obligations issued under an indenture of trust, equipment trust agreement or the like are represented by a trustee or other person, the representative is the secured party;

(n) "Transmitting utility" means any person primarily engaged in the railroad, street railway or trolley bus business, the electric or electronics communications transmission business, the transmission of goods by pipeline, or the transmission or the production and transmission of electricity, steam, gas or water, or the provision of sewer service.

(2) Other definitions applying to this Article and the sections in which they appear are:

"Account". Section 9—106.
"Attach". Section 9—203.
"Construction mortgage". Section 9—313(1).
"Consumer goods". Section 9—109(1).
"Equipment". Section 9—109(2).
"Farm products". Section 9—109(3).
"Fixture". Section 9—313(1).
"Fixture filing". Section 9—313(1).
"General intangibles". Section 9—106.
"Inventory". Section 9—109(4).
"Lien creditor". Section 9—301(3).
"Proceeds". Section 9—306(1).
"Purchase money security interest". Section 9—107.
"United States". Section 9—103.

(3) The following definitions in other Articles apply to this Article:

"Check". Section 3—104.
"Contract for sale". Section 2—106.

"Holder in due course". Section 3—302.
"Note". Section 3—104.
"Sale". Section 2—106.

(4) In addition Article 1 contains general definitions and principles of construction and interpretation applicable throughout this Article.

§ 9—106. **Definitions: "Account"; "General Intangibles".**

"Account" means any right to payment for goods sold or leased or for services rendered which is not evidenced by an instrument or chattel paper, whether or not it has been earned by performance. "General intangibles" means any personal property (including things in action) other than goods, accounts, chattel paper, documents, instruments, and money. All rights to payment earned or unearned under a charter or other contract involving the use or hire of a vessel and all rights incident to the charter or contract are accounts.

§ 9—107. **Definitions: "Purchase Money Security Interest".**

A security interest is a "purchase money security interest" to the extent that it is

(a) taken or retained by the seller of the collateral to secure all or part of its price; or

(b) taken by a person who by making advances or incurring an obligation gives value to enable the debtor to acquire rights in or the use of collateral if such value is in fact so used.

§ 9—108. **When After-Acquired Collateral Not Security for Antecedent Debt.**

Where a secured party makes an advance, incurs an obligation, releases a perfected security interest, or otherwise gives new value which is to be secured in whole or in part by after-acquired property his security interest in the after-acquired collateral shall be deemed to be taken for new value and not as security for an antecedent debt if the debtor acquires his rights in such collateral either in the ordinary course of his business or under a contract of purchase made pursuant to the security agreement within a reasonable time after new value is given.

§ 9—109. **Classification of Goods; "Consumer Goods"; "Equipment"; "Farm Products"; "Inventory".**

Goods are

(1) "consumer goods" if they are used or bought for use primarily for personal, family or household purposes;

(2) "equipment" if they are used or bought for use primarily in business (including farming or a profession) or by a debtor who is a non-profit organization or a governmental subdivision or agency or if the goods are not included in the definitions of inventory, farm products or consumer goods;

(3) "farm products" if they are crops or livestock or supplies used or produced in farming operations or if they are products of crops or livestock in their unmanufactured states (such as ginned cotton, wool-clip, maple syrup, milk and eggs), and if they are in the possession of a debtor engaged in raising, fattening, grazing or other farming operations. If goods are farm products they are neither equipment nor inventory;

(4) "inventory" if they are held by a person who holds them for sale or lease or to be furnished under contracts of service or if he has so furnished them, or if they are raw materials, work in process or materials used or consumed in a business. Inventory of a person is not to be classified as his equipment.

§ 9—110. **Sufficiency of Description.**

For purposes of this Article any description of personal property or real estate is sufficient whether or not it is specific if it reasonably identifies what is described.

§ 9—111. **Applicability of Bulk Transfer Laws.**

The creation of a security interest is not a bulk transfer under Article 6 (see Section 6—103).

§ 9—112. **Where Collateral Is Not Owned by Debtor.**

Unless otherwise agreed, when a secured party knows that collateral is owned by a person who is not the debtor, the owner of the collateral is entitled to receive from the secured party any surplus under Section 9—502(2) or under Section 9—504(1), and is not liable for the debt or for any deficiency after resale, and he has the same right as the debtor

(a) to receive statements under Section 9—208;

(b) to receive notice of and to object to a secured party's proposal to retain the collateral in satisfaction of the indebtedness under Section 9—505;

(c) to redeem the collateral under Section 9—506;

(d) to obtain injunctive or other relief under Section 9—507(1); and

(e) to recover losses caused to him under Section 9—208(2).

§ 9—113. **Security Interests Arising Under Article on Sales or Under Article on Leases.**

A security interest arising solely under the Article on Sales (Article 2) or the Article on Leases (Article 2A) is subject to the provisions of this Article except that to the extent that and so long as the debtor does not have or does not lawfully obtain possession of the goods

(a) no security agreement is necessary to make the security interest enforceable; and

(b) no filing is required to perfect the security interest; and

(c) the rights of the secured party on default by the debtor are governed (i) by the Article on Sales (Article 2) in the case of a security interest arising solely under such Article or (ii) by the Article on Leases (Article 2A) in the case of a security interest arising solely under such Article.

§ 9—114. **Consignment.**

(1) A person who delivers goods under a consignment which is not a security interest and who would be required to file under this Article by paragraph (3)(c) of Section 2—326 has priority over a secured party who is or becomes a creditor of the consignee and who would have a perfected security interest in the goods if they were the property of the consignee, and also has priority with respect to identifiable cash proceeds received on or before delivery of the goods to a buyer, if

(a) the consignor complies with the filing provision of the Article on Sales with respect to consignments (paragraph

(3)(c) of Section 2—326) before the consignee receives possession of the goods; and

(b) the consignor gives notification in writing to the holder of the security interest if the holder has filed a financing statement covering the same types of goods before the date of the filing made by the consignor; and

(c) the holder of the security interest receives the notification within five years before the consignee receives possession of the goods; and

(d) the notification states that the consignor expects to deliver goods on consignment to the consignee, describing the goods by item or type.

(2) In the case of a consignment which is not a security interest and in which the requirements of the preceding subsection have not been met, a person who delivers goods to another is subordinate to a person who would have a perfected security interest in the goods if they were the property of the debtor.

Part 2 Validity of Security Agreement and Rights of Parties Thereto

§ 9—201. General Validity of Security Agreement.

Except as otherwise provided by this Act a security agreement is effective according to its terms between the parties, against purchasers of the collateral and against creditors. Nothing in this Article validates any charge or practice illegal under any statute or regulation thereunder governing usury, small loans, retail installment sales, or the like, or extends the application of any such statute or regulation to any transaction not otherwise subject thereto.

§ 9—202. Title to Collateral Immaterial.

Each provision of this Article with regard to rights, obligations and remedies applies whether title to collateral is in the secured party or in the debtor.

§ 9—203. Attachment and Enforceability of Security Interest; Proceeds; Formal Requisites.

(1) Subject to the provisions of Section 4—208 on the security interest of a collecting bank, Section 8—321 on security interests in securities and Section 9—113 on a security interest arising under the Article on Sales, a security interest is not enforceable against the debtor or third parties with respect to the collateral and does not attach unless:

(a) the collateral is in the possession of the secured party pursuant to agreement, or the debtor has signed a security agreement which contains a description of the collateral and in addition, when the security interest covers crops growing or to be grown or timber to be cut, a description of the land concerned;

(b) value has been given; and

(c) the debtor has rights in the collateral.

(2) A security interest attaches when it becomes enforceable against the debtor with respect to the collateral. Attachment occurs as soon as all of the events specified in subsection (1) have taken place unless explicit agreement postpones the time of attaching.

(3) Unless otherwise agreed a security agreement gives the secured party the rights to proceeds provided by Section 9—306.

(4) A transaction, although subject to this Article, is also subject to . . . .*, and in the case of conflict between the provisions of this Article and any such statute, the provisions of such statute control. Failure to comply with any applicable statute has only the effect which is specified therein.

Note: *At * in subsection (4) insert reference to any local statute regulating small loans, retail installment sales and the like.*

The foregoing subsection (4) is designed to make it clear that certain transactions, although subject to this Article, must also comply with other applicable legislation.

This Article is designed to regulate all the "security" aspects of transactions within its scope. There is, however, much regulatory legislation, particularly in the consumer field, which supplements this Article and should not be repealed by its enactment. Examples are small loan acts, retail installment selling acts and the like. Such acts may provide for licensing and rate regulation and may prescribe particular forms of contract. Such provisions should remain in force despite the enactment of this Article. On the other hand if a retail installment selling act contains provisions on filing, rights on default, etc., such provisions should be repealed as inconsistent with this Article except that inconsistent provisions as to deficiencies, penalties, etc., in the Uniform Consumer Credit Code and other recent related legislation should remain because those statutes were drafted after the substantial enactment of the Article and with the intention of modifying certain provisions of this Article as to consumer credit.

§ 9—204. After-Acquired Property; Future Advances.

(1) Except as provided in subsection (2), a security agreement may provide that any or all obligations covered by the security agreement are to be secured by after-acquired collateral.

(2) No security interest attaches under an after-acquired property clause to consumer goods other than accessions (Section 9—314) when given as additional security unless the debtor acquires rights in them within ten days after the secured party gives value.

(3) Obligations covered by a security agreement may include future advances or other value whether or not the advances or value are given pursuant to commitment (subsection (1) of Section 9—105).

§ 9—205. Use or Disposition of Collateral Without Accounting Permissible.

A security interest is not invalid or fraudulent against creditors by reason of liberty in the debtor to use, commingle or dispose of all or part of the collateral (including returned or repossessed goods) or to collect or compromise accounts or chattel paper, or to accept the return of goods or make repossessions, or to use, commingle or dispose of proceeds, or by reason of the failure of the secured party to require the debtor to account for proceeds or replace collateral. This section does not relax the requirements of possession where perfection of a security interest depends upon possession of the collateral by the secured party or by a bailee.

§ 9—206. Agreement Not to Assert Defenses Against Assignee; Modification of Sales Warranties Where Security Agreement Exists.

(1) Subject to any statute or decision which establishes a different rule for buyers or lessees of consumer goods, an agreement by a buyer or lessee that he will not assert against an assignee any claim or defense which he may have against the seller or lessor is enforceable by an assignee who takes his assignment for value,

in good faith and without notice of a claim or defense, except as to defenses of a type which may be asserted against a holder in due course of a negotiable instrument under the Article on Commercial Paper (Article 3). A buyer who as part of one transaction signs both a negotiable instrument and a security agreement makes such an agreement.

(2) When a seller retains a purchase money security interest in goods the Article on Sales (Article 2) governs the sale and any disclaimer, limitation or modification of the seller's warranties.

§ 9—207. **Rights and Duties When Collateral is in Secured Party's Possession.**

(1) A secured party must use reasonable care in the custody and preservation of collateral in his possession. In the case of an instrument or chattel paper reasonable care includes taking necessary steps to preserve rights against prior parties unless otherwise agreed.

(2) Unless otherwise agreed, when collateral is in the secured party's possession

(a) reasonable expenses (including the cost of any insurance and payment of taxes or other charges) incurred in the custody, preservation, use or operation of the collateral are chargeable to the debtor and are secured by the collateral;

(b) the risk of accidental loss or damage is on the debtor to the extent of any deficiency in any effective insurance coverage;

(c) the secured party may hold as additional security any increase or profits (except money) received from the collateral, but money so received, unless remitted to the debtor, shall be applied in reduction of the secured obligation;

(d) the secured party must keep the collateral identifiable but fungible collateral may be commingled;

(e) the secured party may repledge the collateral upon terms which do not impair the debtor's right to redeem it.

(3) A secured party is liable for any loss caused by his failure to meet any obligation imposed by the preceding subsections but does not lose his security interest.

(4) A secured party may use or operate the collateral for the purpose of preserving the collateral or its value or pursuant to the order of a court of appropriate jurisdiction or, except in the case of consumer goods, in the manner and to the extent provided in the security agreement.

§ 9—208. **Request for Statement of Account or List of Collateral.**

(1) A debtor may sign a statement indicating what he believes to be the aggregate amount of unpaid indebtedness as of a specified date and may send it to the secured party with a request that the statement be approved or corrected and returned to the debtor. When the security agreement or any other record kept by the secured party identifies the collateral a debtor may similarly request the secured party to approve or correct a list of the collateral.

(2) The secured party must comply with such a request within two weeks after receipt by sending a written correction or approval. If the secured party claims a security interest in all of a particular type of collateral owned by the debtor he may indicate that fact in his reply and need not approve or correct an itemized list of such collateral. If the secured party without reasonable excuse fails to comply he is liable for any loss caused to the debtor thereby; and if the debtor has properly included in his request a good faith statement of the obligation or a list of the collateral or both the secured party may claim a security interest only as shown in the statement against persons misled by his failure to comply. If he no longer has an interest in the obligation or collateral at the time the request is received he must disclose the name and address of any successor in interest known to him and he is liable for any loss caused to the debtor as a result of failure to disclose. A successor in interest is not subject to this section until a request is received by him.

(3) A debtor is entitled to such a statement once every six months without charge. The secured party may require payment of a charge not exceeding $10 for each additional statement furnished.

Part 3 Rights of Third Parties; Perfected and Unperfected Security Interests; Rules of Priority

§ 9—301. **Persons Who Take Priority Over Unperfected Security Interests; Rights of "Lien Creditor".**

(1) Except as otherwise provided in subsection (2), an unperfected security interest is subordinate to the rights of

(a) persons entitled to priority under Section 9—312;

(b) a person who becomes a lien creditor before the security interest is perfected;

(c) in the case of goods, instruments, documents, and chattel paper, a person who is not a secured party and who is a transferee in bulk or other buyer not in ordinary course of business or is a buyer of farm products in ordinary course of business, to the extent that he gives value and receives delivery of the collateral without knowledge of the security interest and before it is perfected;

(d) in the case of accounts and general intangibles, a person who is not a secured party and who is a transferee to the extent that he gives value without knowledge of the security interest and before it is perfected.

(2) If the secured party files with respect to a purchase money security interest before or within ten days after the debtor receives possession of the collateral, he takes priority over the rights of a transferee in bulk or of a lien creditor which arise between the time the security interest attaches and the time of filing.

(3) A "lien creditor" means a creditor who has acquired a lien on the property involved by attachment, levy or the like and includes an assignee for benefit of creditors from the time of assignment, and a trustee in bankruptcy from the date of the filing of the petition or a receiver in equity from the time of appointment.

(4) A person who becomes a lien creditor while a security interest is perfected takes subject to the security interest only to the extent that it secures advances made before he becomes a lien creditor or within 45 days thereafter or made without knowledge of the lien or pursuant to a commitment entered into without knowledge of the lien.

§ 9—302. **When Filing Is Required to Perfect Security Interest; Security Interests to Which Filing Provisions of This Article Do Not Apply.**

(1) A financing statement must be filed to perfect all security interests except the following:

(a) a security interest in collateral in possession of the secured party under Section 9—305;

(b) a security interest temporarily perfected in instruments or documents without delivery under Section 9—304 or in proceeds for a 10 day period under Section 9—306;

(c) a security interest created by an assignment of a beneficial interest in a trust or a decedent's estate;

(d) a purchase money security interest in consumer goods; but filing is required for a motor vehicle required to be registered; and fixture filing is required for priority over conflicting interests in fixtures to the extent provided in Section 9—313;

(e) an assignment of accounts which does not alone or in conjunction with other assignments to the same assignee transfer a significant part of the outstanding accounts of the assignor;

(f) a security interest of a collecting bank (Section 4—208) or in securities (Section 8—321) or arising under the Article on Sales (see Section 9—113) or covered in subsection (3) of this section;

(g) an assignment for the benefit of all the creditors of the transferor, and subsequent transfers by the assignee thereunder.

(2) If a secured party assigns a perfected security interest, no filing under this Article is required in order to continue the perfected status of the security interest against creditors of and transferees from the original debtor.

(3) The filing of a financing statement otherwise required by this Article is not necessary or effective to perfect a security interest in property subject to

(a) a statute or treaty of the United States which provides for a national or international registration or a national or international certificate of title or which specifies a place of filing different from that specified in this Article for filing of the security interest; or

(b) the following statutes of this state; [list any certificate of title statute covering automobiles, trailers, mobile homes, boats, farm tractors, or the like, and any central filing statute.]; but during any period in which collateral is inventory held for sale by a person who is in the business of selling goods of that kind, the filing provisions of this Article (Part 4) apply to a security interest in that collateral created by him as debtor; or

(c) a certificate of title statute of another jurisdiction under the law of which indication of a security interest on the certificate is required as a condition of perfection (subsection (2) of Section 9—103).

(4) Compliance with a statute or treaty described in subsection (3) is equivalent to the filing of a financing statement under this Article, and a security interest in property subject to the statute or treaty can be perfected only by compliance therewith except as provided in Section 9—103 on multiple state transactions. Duration and renewal of perfection of a security interest perfected by compliance with the statute or treaty are governed by the provisions of the statute or treaty; in other respects the security interest is subject to this Article.

§ 9—303. **When Security Interest Is Perfected; Continuity of Perfection.**

(1) A security interest is perfected when it has attached and when all of the applicable steps required for perfection have been taken. Such steps are specified in Sections 9—302, 9—304, 9—305 and 9—306. If such steps are taken before the security interest attaches, it is perfected at the time when it attaches.

(2) If a security interest is originally perfected in any way permitted under this Article and is subsequently perfected in some other way under this Article, without an intermediate period when it was unperfected, the security interest shall be deemed to be perfected continuously for the purposes of this Article.

§ 9—304. **Perfection of Security Interest in Instruments, Documents, and Goods Covered by Documents; Perfection by Permissive Filing; Temporary Perfection Without Filing or Transfer of Possession.**

(1) A security interest in chattel paper or negotiable documents may be perfected by filing. A security interest in money or instruments (other than certificated securities or instruments which constitute part of chattel paper) can be perfected only by the secured party's taking possession, except as provided in subsections (4) and (5) of this section and subsections (2) and (3) of Section 9—306 on proceeds.

(2) During the period that goods are in the possession of the issuer of a negotiable document therefor, a security interest in the goods is perfected by perfecting a security interest in the document, and any security interest in the goods otherwise perfected during such period is subject thereto.

(3) A security interest in goods in the possession of a bailee other than one who has issued a negotiable document therefor is perfected by issuance of a document in the name of the secured party or by the bailee's receipt of notification of the secured party's interest or by filing as to the goods.

(4) A security interest in instruments (other than certificated securities) or negotiable documents is perfected without filing or the taking of possession for a period of 21 days from the time it attaches to the extent that it arises for new value given under a written security agreement.

(5) A security interest remains perfected for a period of 21 days without filing where a secured party having a perfected security interest in an instrument (other than a certificated security), a negotiable document or goods in possession of a bailee other than one who has issued a negotiable document therefor

(a) makes available to the debtor the goods or documents representing the goods for the purpose of ultimate sale or exchange or for the purpose of loading, unloading, storing, shipping, transshipping, manufacturing, processing or otherwise dealing with them in a manner preliminary to their sale or exchange, but priority between conflicting security interests in the goods is subject to subsection (3) of Section 9—312; or

(b) delivers the instrument to the debtor for the purpose of ultimate sale or exchange or of presentation, collection, renewal or registration of transfer.

(6) After the 21 day period in subsections (4) and (5) perfection depends upon compliance with applicable provisions of this Article.

§ 9—305. **When Possession by Secured Party Perfects Security Interest Without Filing.**

A security interest in letters of credit and advices of credit (subsection (2)(a) of Section 5—116), goods, instruments (other than certificated securities), money, negotiable documents, or chattel paper may be perfected by the secured party's taking possession of the collateral. If such collateral other than goods covered by a negotiable document is held by a bailee, the secured party is deemed to have possession from the time the bailee receives notification of the secured party's interest. A security interest is perfected by possession from the time possession is taken without a relation back and continues only so long as possession is retained, unless otherwise specified in this Article. The security interest may be otherwise perfected as provided in this Article before or after the period of possession by the secured party.

§ 9—306. **"Proceeds"; Secured Party's Rights on Disposition of Collateral.**

(1) "Proceeds" includes whatever is received upon the sale, exchange, collection or other disposition of collateral or proceeds. Insurance payable by reason of loss or damage to the collateral is proceeds, except to the extent that it is payable to a person other than a party to the security agreement. Money, checks, deposit accounts, and the like are "cash proceeds". All other proceeds are "noncash proceeds".

(2) Except where this Article otherwise provides, a security interest continues in collateral notwithstanding sale, exchange or other disposition thereof unless the disposition was authorized by the secured party in the security agreement or otherwise, and also continues in any identifiable proceeds including collections received by the debtor.

(3) The security interest in proceeds is a continuously perfected security interest if the interest in the original collateral was perfected but it ceases to be a perfected security interest and becomes unperfected ten days after receipt of the proceeds by the debtor unless

(a) a filed financing statement covers the original collateral and the proceeds are collateral in which a security interest may be perfected by filing in the office or offices where the financing statement has been filed and, if the proceeds are acquired with cash proceeds, the description of collateral in the financing statement indicates the types of property constituting the proceeds; or

(b) a filed financing statement covers the original collateral and the proceeds are identifiable cash proceeds; or

(c) the security interest in the proceeds is perfected before the expiration of the ten day period.

Except as provided in this section, a security interest in proceeds can be perfected only by the methods or under the circumstances permitted in this Article for original collateral of the same type.

(4) In the event of insolvency proceedings instituted by or against a debtor, a secured party with a perfected security interest in proceeds has a perfected security interest only in the following proceeds:

(a) in identifiable noncash proceeds and in separate deposit accounts containing only proceeds;

(b) in identifiable cash proceeds in the form of money which is neither commingled with other money nor deposited in a deposit account prior to the insolvency proceedings;

(c) in identifiable cash proceeds in the form of checks and the like which are not deposited in a deposit account prior to the insolvency proceedings; and

(d) in all cash and deposit accounts of the debtor in which proceeds have been commingled with other funds, but the perfected security interest under this paragraph (d) is

(i) subject to any right to set-off; and

(ii) limited to an amount not greater than the amount of any cash proceeds received by the debtor within ten days before the institution of the insolvency proceedings less the sum of (I) the payments to the secured party on account of cash proceeds received by the debtor during such period and (II) the cash proceeds received by the debtor during such period to which the secured party is entitled under paragraphs (a) through (c) of this subsection (4).

(5) If a sale of goods results in an account or chattel paper which is transferred by the seller to a secured party, and if the goods are returned to or are repossessed by the seller or the secured party, the following rules determine priorities:

(a) If the goods were collateral at the time of sale, for an indebtedness of the seller which is still unpaid, the original security interest attaches again to the goods and continues as a perfected security interest if it was perfected at the time when the goods were sold. If the security interest was originally perfected by a filing which is still effective, nothing further is required to continue the perfected status; in any other case, the secured party must take possession of the returned or repossessed goods or must file.

(b) An unpaid transferee of the chattel paper has a security interest in the goods against the transferor. Such security interest is prior to a security interest asserted under paragraph (a) to the extent that the transferee of the chattel paper was entitled to priority under Section 9—308.

(c) An unpaid transferee of the account has a security interest in the goods against the transferor. Such security interest is subordinate to a security interest asserted under paragraph (a).

(d) A security interest of an unpaid transferee asserted under paragraph (b) or (c) must be perfected for protection against creditors of the transferor and purchasers of the returned or repossessed goods.

§ 9—307. **Protection of Buyers of Goods.**

(1) A buyer in ordinary course of business (subsection (9) of Section 1—201) other than a person buying farm products from a person engaged in farming operations takes free of a security interest created by his seller even though the security interest is perfected and even though the buyer knows of its existence [subject to the Food Security Act of 1985 (7 U.S.C. Section 1631)].

(2) In the case of consumer goods, a buyer takes free of a security interest even though perfected if he buys without knowledge of

the security interest, for value and for his own personal, family or household purposes unless prior to the purchase the secured party has filed a financing statement covering such goods.

(3) A buyer other than a buyer in ordinary course of business (subsection (1) of this section) takes free of a security interest to the extent that it secures future advances made after the secured party acquires knowledge of the purchase, or more than 45 days after the purchase, whichever first occurs, unless made pursuant to a commitment entered into without knowledge of the purchase and before the expiration of the 45 day period.

§ 9—308. **Purchase of Chattel Paper and Instruments.**

A purchaser of chattel paper or an instrument who gives new value and takes possession of it in the ordinary course of his business has priority over a security interest in the chattel paper or instrument

(a) which is perfected under Section 9—304 (permissive filing and temporary perfection) or under Section 9—306 (perfection as to proceeds) if he acts without knowledge that the specific paper or instrument is subject to a security interest; or

(b) which is claimed merely as proceeds of inventory subject to a security interest (Section 9—306) even though he knows that the specific paper or instrument is subject to the security interest.

§ 9—309. **Protection of Purchasers of Instruments, Documents and Securities.**

Nothing in this Article limits the rights of a holder in due course of a negotiable instrument (Section 3—302) or a holder to whom a negotiable document of title has been duly negotiated (Section 7—501) or a bona fide purchaser of a security (Section 8—302) and the holders or purchasers take priority over an earlier security interest even though perfected. Filing under this Article does not constitute notice of the security interest to such holders or purchasers.

§ 9—310. **Priority of Certain Liens Arising by Operation of Law.**

When a person in the ordinary course of his business furnishes services or materials with respect to goods subject to a security interest, a lien upon goods in the possession of such person given by statute or rule of law for such materials or services takes priority over a perfected security interest unless the lien is statutory and the statute expressly provides otherwise.

§ 9—311. **Alienability of Debtor's Rights: Judicial Process.**

The debtor's rights in collateral may be voluntarily or involuntarily transferred (by way of sale, creation of a security interest, attachment, levy, garnishment or other judicial process) notwithstanding a provision in the security agreement prohibiting any transfer or making the transfer constitute a default.

§ 9—312. **Priorities Among Conflicting Security Interests in the Same Collateral.**

(1) The rules of priority stated in other sections of this Part and in the following sections shall govern when applicable: Section 4—208 with respect to the security interests of collecting banks in items being collected, accompanying documents and proceeds; Section 9—103 on security interests related to other jurisdictions; Section 9—114 on consignments.

(2) A perfected security interest in crops for new value given to enable the debtor to produce the crops during the production season and given not more than three months before the crops become growing crops by planting or otherwise takes priority over an earlier perfected security interest to the extent that such earlier interest secures obligations due more than six months before the crops become growing crops by planting or otherwise, even though the person giving new value had knowledge of the earlier security interest.

(3) A perfected purchase money security interest in inventory has priority over a conflicting security interest in the same inventory and also has priority in identifiable cash proceeds received on or before the delivery of the inventory to a buyer if

(a) the purchase money security interest is perfected at the time the debtor receives possession of the inventory; and

(b) the purchase money secured party gives notification in writing to the holder of the conflicting security interest if the holder had filed a financing statement covering the same types of inventory (i) before the date of the filing made by the purchase money secured party, or (ii) before the beginning of the 21 day period where the purchase money security interest is temporarily perfected without filing or possession (subsection (5) of Section 9—304); and

(c) the holder of the conflicting security interest receives the notification within five years before the debtor receives possession of the inventory; and

(d) the notification states that the person giving the notice has or expects to acquire a purchase money security interest in inventory of the debtor, describing such inventory by item or type.

(4) A purchase money security interest in collateral other than inventory has priority over a conflicting security interest in the same collateral or its proceeds if the purchase money security interest is perfected at the time the debtor receives possession of the collateral or within ten days thereafter.

(5) In all cases not governed by other rules stated in this section (including cases of purchase money security interests which do not qualify for the special priorities set forth in subsections (3) and (4) of this section), priority between conflicting security interests in the same collateral shall be determined according to the following rules:

(a) Conflicting security interests rank according to priority in time of filing or perfection. Priority dates from the time a filing is first made covering the collateral or the time the security interest is first perfected, whichever is earlier, provided that there is no period thereafter when there is neither filing nor perfection.

(b) So long as conflicting security interests are unperfected, the first to attach has priority.

(6) For the purposes of subsection (5) a date of filing or perfection as to collateral is also a date of filing or perfection as to proceeds.

(7) If future advances are made while a security interest is perfected by filing, the taking of possession, or under Section 8—321 on securities, the security interest has the same priority for the purposes of subsection (5) with respect to the future advances as it does with respect to the first advance. If a commitment is made before or while the security interest is so perfected,

the security interest has the same priority with respect to advances made pursuant thereto. In other cases a perfected security interest has priority from the date the advance is made.

§ 9—313. **Priority of Security Interests in Fixtures.**

(1) In this section and in the provisions of Part 4 of this Article referring to fixture filing, unless the context otherwise requires

(a) goods are "fixtures" when they become so related to particular real estate that an interest in them arises under real estate law

(b) a "fixture filing" is the filing in the office where a mortgage on the real estate would be filed or recorded of a financing statement covering goods which are or are to become fixtures and conforming to the requirements of subsection (5) of Section 9—402

(c) a mortgage is a "construction mortgage" to the extent that it secures an obligation incurred for the construction of an improvement on land including the acquisition cost of the land, if the recorded writing so indicates.

(2) A security interest under this Article may be created in goods which are fixtures or may continue in goods which become fixtures, but no security interest exists under this Article in ordinary building materials incorporated into an improvement on land.

(3) This Article does not prevent creation of an encumbrance upon fixtures pursuant to real estate law.

(4) A perfected security interest in fixtures has priority over the conflicting interest of an encumbrancer or owner of the real estate where

(a) the security interest is a purchase money security interest, the interest of the encumbrancer or owner arises before the goods become fixtures, the security interest is perfected by a fixture filing before the goods become fixtures or within ten days thereafter, and the debtor has an interest of record in the real estate or is in possession of the real estate; or

(b) the security interest is perfected by a fixture filing before the interest of the encumbrancer or owner is of record, the security interest has priority over any conflicting interest of a predecessor in title of the encumbrancer or owner, and the debtor has an interest of record in the real estate or is in possession of the real estate; or

(c) the fixtures are readily removable factory or office machines or readily removable replacements of domestic appliances which are consumer goods, and before the goods become fixtures the security interest is perfected by any method permitted by this Article; or

(d) the conflicting interest is a lien on the real estate obtained by legal or equitable proceedings after the security interest was perfected by any method permitted by this Article.

(5) A security interest in fixtures, whether or not perfected, has priority over the conflicting interest of an encumbrancer or owner of the real estate where

(a) the encumbrancer or owner has consented in writing to the security interest or has disclaimed an interest in the goods as fixtures; or

(b) the debtor has a right to remove the goods as against the encumbrancer or owner. If the debtor's right terminates, the priority of the security interest continues for a reasonable time.

(6) Notwithstanding paragraph (a) of subsection (4) but otherwise subject to subsections (4) and (5), a security interest in fixtures is subordinate to a construction mortgage recorded before the goods become fixtures if the goods become fixtures before the completion of the construction. To the extent that it is given to refinance a construction mortgage, a mortgage has this priority to the same extent as the construction mortgage.

(7) In cases not within the preceding subsections, a security interest in fixtures is subordinate to the conflicting interest of an encumbrancer or owner of the related real estate who is not the debtor.

(8) When the secured party has priority over all owners and encumbrancers of the real estate, he may, on default, subject to the provisions of Part 5, remove his collateral from the real estate but he must reimburse any encumbrancer or owner of the real estate who is not the debtor and who has not otherwise agreed for the cost of repair of any physical injury, but not for any diminution in value of the real estate caused by the absence of the goods removed or by any necessity of replacing them. A person entitled to reimbursement may refuse permission to remove until the secured party gives adequate security for the performance of this obligation.

§ 9—314. **Accessions.**

(1) A security interest in goods which attaches before they are installed in or affixed to other goods takes priority as to the goods installed or affixed (called in this section "accessions") over the claims of all persons to the whole except as stated in subsection (3) and subject to Section 9—315(1).

(2) A security interest which attaches to goods after they become part of a whole is valid against all persons subsequently acquiring interests in the whole except as stated in subsection (3) but is invalid against any person with an interest in the whole at the time the security interest attaches to the goods who has not in writing consented to the security interest or disclaimed an interest in the goods as part of the whole.

(3) The security interests described in subsections (1) and (2) do not take priority over

(a) a subsequent purchaser for value of any interest in the whole; or

(b) a creditor with a lien on the whole subsequently obtained by judicial proceedings; or

(c) a creditor with a prior perfected security interest in the whole to the extent that he makes subsequent advances

if the subsequent purchase is made, the lien by judicial proceedings obtained or the subsequent advance under the prior perfected security interest is made or contracted for without knowledge of the security interest and before it is perfected. A purchaser of the whole at a foreclosure sale other than the holder of a perfected security interest purchasing at his own foreclosure sale is a subsequent purchaser within this section.

(4) When under subsections (1) or (2) and (3) a secured party has an interest in accessions which has priority over the claims of all persons who have interests in the whole, he may on default subject to the provisions of Part 5 remove his collateral from the

whole but he must reimburse any encumbrancer or owner of the whole who is not the debtor and who has not otherwise agreed for the cost of repair of any physical injury but not for any diminution in value of the whole caused by the absence of the goods removed or by any necessity for replacing them. A person entitled to reimbursement may refuse permission to remove until the secured party gives adequate security for the performance of this obligation.

§ 9—315. **Priority When Goods Are Commingled or Processed.**

(1) If a security interest in goods was perfected and subsequently the goods or a part thereof have become part of a product or mass, the security interest continues in the product or mass if

(a) the goods are so manufactured, processed, assembled or commingled that their identity is lost in the product or mass; or

(b) a financing statement covering the original goods also covers the product into which the goods have been manufactured, processed or assembled.

In a case to which paragraph (b) applies, no separate security interest in that part of the original goods which has been manufactured, processed or assembled into the product may be claimed under Section 9—314.

(2) When under subsection (1) more than one security interest attaches to the product or mass, they rank equally according to the ratio that the cost of the goods to which each interest originally attached bears to the cost of the total product or mass.

§ 9—316. **Priority Subject to Subordination.**

Nothing in this Article prevents subordination by agreement by any person entitled to priority.

§ 9—317. **Secured Party Not Obligated on Contract of Debtor.**

The mere existence of a security interest or authority given to the debtor to dispose of or use collateral does not impose contract or tort liability upon the secured party for the debtor's acts or omissions.

§ 9—318. **Defenses Against Assignee; Modification of Contract After Notification of Assignment; Term Prohibiting Assignment Ineffective; Identification and Proof of Assignment.**

(1) Unless an account debtor has made an enforceable agreement not to assert defenses or claims arising out of a sale as provided in Section 9—206 the rights of an assignee are subject to

(a) all the terms of the contract between the account debtor and assignor and any defense or claim arising therefrom; and

(b) any other defense or claim of the account debtor against the assignor which accrues before the account debtor receives notification of the assignment.

(2) So far as the right to payment or a part thereof under an assigned contract has not been fully earned by performance, and notwithstanding notification of the assignment, any modification of or substitution for the contract made in good faith and in accordance with reasonable commercial standards is effective against an assignee unless the account debtor has otherwise agreed but the assignee acquires corresponding rights under the modified or substituted contract. The assignment may provide that such modification or substitution is a breach by the assignor.

(3) The account debtor is authorized to pay the assignor until the account debtor receives notification that the amount due or to become due has been assigned and that payment is to be made to the assignee. A notification which does not reasonably identify the rights assigned is ineffective. If requested by the account debtor, the assignee must seasonably furnish reasonable proof that the assignment has been made and unless he does so the account debtor may pay the assignor.

(4) A term in any contract between an account debtor and an assignor is ineffective if it prohibits assignment of an account or prohibits creation of a security interest in a general intangible for money due or to become due or requires the account debtor's consent to such assignment or security interest.

Part 4 Filing

§ 9—401. **Place of Filing; Erroneous Filing; Removal of Collateral.**

First Alternative Subsection (1)

(1) The proper place to file in order to perfect a security interest is as follows:

(a) when the collateral is timber to be cut or is minerals or the like (including oil and gas) or accounts subject to subsection (5) of Section 9—103, or when the financing statement is filed as a fixture filing (Section 9—313) and the collateral is goods which are or are to become fixtures, then in the office where a mortgage on the real estate would be filed or recorded;

(b) in all other cases, in the office of the [Secretary of State].

Second Alternative Subsection (1)

(1) The proper place to file in order to perfect a security interest is as follows:

(a) when the collateral is equipment used in farming operations, or farm products, or accounts or general intangibles arising from or relating to the sale of farm products by a farmer, or consumer goods, then in the office of the .... in the county of the debtor's residence or if the debtor is not a resident of this state then in the office of the .... in the county where the goods are kept, and in addition when the collateral is crops growing or to be grown in the office of the .... in the county where the land is located;

(b) when the collateral is timber to be cut or is minerals or the like (including oil and gas) or accounts subject to subsection (5) of Section 9—103, or when the financing statement is filed as a fixture filing (Section 9—313) and the collateral is goods which are or are to become fixtures, then in the office where a mortgage on the real estate would be filed or recorded;

(c) in all other cases, in the office of the [Secretary of State].

Third Alternative Subsection (1)

(1) The proper place to file in order to perfect a security interest is as follows:

(a) when the collateral is equipment used in farming operations, or farm products, or accounts or general intangibles arising from or relating to the sale of farm products by a farmer, or consumer goods, then in the office of the .... in the county of the debtor's residence or if the debtor is not a resident of this state then in the office of the .... in the county where the goods are kept, and in addition when the collateral is crops growing or to be grown in the office of the .... in the county where the land is located;

(b) when the collateral is timber to be cut or is minerals or the like (including oil and gas) or accounts subject to subsection (5) of Section 9—103, or when the financing statement is filed as a fixture filing (Section 9—313) and the collateral is goods which are or are to become fixtures, then in the office where a mortgage on the real estate would be filed or recorded;

(c) in all other cases, in the office of the [Secretary of State] and in addition, if the debtor has a place of business in only one county of this state, also in the office of .... of such county, or, if the debtor has no place of business in this state, but resides in the state, also in the office of .... of the county which he resides.

Note: *One of the three alternatives should be selected as subsection (1).*

(2) A filing which is made in good faith in an improper place or not in all of the places required by this section is nevertheless effective with regard to any collateral as to which the filing complied with the requirements of this Article and is also effective with regard to collateral covered by the financing statement against any person who has knowledge of the contents of such financing statement.

(3) A filing which is made in the proper place in this state continues effective even though the debtor's residence or place of business or the location of the collateral or its use, whichever controlled the original filing, is thereafter changed.

Alternative Subsection (3)

[(3) A filing which is made in the proper county continues effective for four months after a change to another county of the debtor's residence or place of business or the location of the collateral, whichever controlled the original filing. It becomes ineffective thereafter unless a copy of the financing statement signed by the secured party is filed in the new county within said period. The security interest may also be perfected in the new county after the expiration of the four-month period; in such case perfection dates from the time of perfection in the new county. A change in the use of the collateral does not impair the effectiveness of the original filing.]

(4) The rules stated in Section 9—103 determine whether filing is necessary in this state.

(5) Notwithstanding the preceding subsections, and subject to subsection (3) of Section 9—302, the proper place to file in order to perfect a security interest in collateral, including fixtures, of a transmitting utility is the office of the [Secretary of State]. This filing constitutes a fixture filing (Section 9—313) as to the collateral described therein which is or is to become fixtures.

(6) For the purposes of this section, the residence of an organization is its place of business if it has one or its chief executive office if it has more than one place of business.

Note: *Subsection (6) should be used only if the state chooses the Second or Third Alternative Subsection (1).*

§ 9—402. Formal Requisites of Financing Statement; Amendments; Mortgage as Financing Statement.

(1) A financing statement is sufficient if it gives the names of the debtor and the secured party, is signed by the debtor, gives an address of the secured party from which information concerning the security interest may be obtained, gives a mailing address of the debtor and contains a statement indicating the types, or describing the items, of collateral. A financing statement may be filed before a security agreement is made or a security interest otherwise attaches. When the financing statement covers crops growing or to be grown, the statement must also contain a description of the real estate concerned. When the financing statement covers timber to be cut or covers minerals or the like (including oil and gas) or accounts subject to subsection (5) of Section 9—103, or when the financing statement is filed as a fixture filing (Section 9—313) and the collateral is goods which are or are to become fixtures, the statement must also comply with subsection (5). A copy of the security agreement is sufficient as a financing statement if it contains the above information and is signed by the debtor. A carbon, photographic or other reproduction of a security agreement or a financing statement is sufficient as a financing statement if the security agreement so provides or if the original has been filed in this state.

(2) A financing statement which otherwise complies with subsection (1) is sufficient when it is signed by the secured party instead of the debtor if it is filed to perfect a security interest in

(a) collateral already subject to a security interest in another jurisdiction when it is brought into this state, or when the debtor's location is changed to this state. Such a financing statement must state that the collateral was brought into this state or that the debtor's location was changed to this state under such circumstances; or

(b) proceeds under Section 9—306 if the security interest in the original collateral was perfected. Such a financing statement must describe the original collateral; or

(c) collateral as to which the filing has lapsed; or

(d) collateral acquired after a change of name, identity or corporate structure of the debtor (subsection (7)).

(3) A form substantially as follows is sufficient to comply with subsection (1):

Name of debtor (or assignor) ....
Address ....
Name of secured party (or assignee) ....
Address ....
1. This financing statement covers the following types (or items) of property:
(Describe) ....
2. (If collateral is crops) The above described crops are growing or are to be grown on:
(Describe Real Estate) ....
3. (If applicable) The above goods are to become fixtures on *
*Where appropriate substitute either "The above timber is standing on ...." or "The above minerals or the like (including oil and gas) or accounts will be financed at the wellhead or minehead of the well or mine located on ...."

(Describe Real Estate) ....
and this financing statement is to be filed [for record] in the real estate records. (If the debtor does not have an interest of record) The name of a record owner is ....
4. (If products of collateral are claimed) Products of the collateral are also covered.

(use whichever	.... Signature of Debtor (or Assignor)
is applicable)	.... Signature of Secured Party (or Assignee)

(4) A financing statement may be amended by filing a writing signed by both the debtor and the secured party. An amendment does not extend the period of effectiveness of a financing statement. If any amendment adds collateral, it is effective as to the added collateral only from the filing date of the amendment. In this Article, unless the context otherwise requires, the term "financing statement" means the original financing statement and any amendments.

(5) A financing statement covering timber to be cut or covering minerals or the like (including oil and gas) or accounts subject to subsection (5) of Section 9—103, or a financing statement filed as a fixture filing (Section 9—313) where the debtor is not a transmitting utility, must show that it covers this type of collateral, must recite that it is to be filed [for record] in the real estate records, and the financing statement must contain a description of the real estate [sufficient if it were contained in a mortgage of the real estate to give constructive notice of the mortgage under the law of this state]. If the debtor does not have an interest of record in the real estate, the financing statement must show the name of a record owner.

(6) A mortgage is effective as a financing statement filed as a fixture filing from the date of its recording if

(a) the goods are described in the mortgage by item or type; and

(b) the goods are or are to become fixtures related to the real estate described in the mortgage; and

(c) the mortgage complies with the requirements for a financing statement in this section other than a recital that it is to be filed in the real estate records; and

(d) the mortgage is duly recorded.

No fee with reference to the financing statement is required other than the regular recording and satisfaction fees with respect to the mortgage.

(7) A financing statement sufficiently shows the name of the debtor if it gives the individual, partnership or corporate name of the debtor, whether or not it adds other trade names or names of partners. Where the debtor so changes his name or in the case of an organization its name, identity or corporate structure that a filed financing statement becomes seriously misleading, the filing is not effective to perfect a security interest in collateral acquired by the debtor more than four months after the change, unless a new appropriate financing statement is filed before the expiration of that time. A filed financing statement remains effective with respect to collateral transferred by the debtor even though the secured party knows of or consents to the transfer.

(8) A financing statement substantially complying with the requirements of this section is effective even though it contains minor errors which are not seriously misleading.

Note: *Language in brackets is optional.*

Note: *Where the state has any special recording system for real estate other than the usual grantor-grantee index (as, for instance, a tract system or a title registration or Torrens system) local adaptations of subsection (5) and Section 9—403(7) may be necessary. See Mass.Gen.Laws Chapter 106, Section 9—409.*

§ 9—403. **What Constitutes Filing; Duration of Filing; Effect of Lapsed Filing; Duties of Filing Officer.**

(1) Presentation for filing of a financing statement and tender of the filing fee or acceptance of the statement by the filing officer constitutes filing under this Article.

(2) Except as provided in subsection (6) a filed financing statement is effective for a period of five years from the date of filing. The effectiveness of a filed financing statement lapses on the expiration of the five year period unless a continuation statement is filed prior to the lapse. If a security interest perfected by filing exists at the time insolvency proceedings are commenced by or against the debtor, the security interest remains perfected until termination of the insolvency proceedings and thereafter for a period of sixty days or until expiration of the five year period, whichever occurs later. Upon lapse the security interest becomes unperfected, unless it is perfected without filing. If the security interest becomes unperfected upon lapse, it is deemed to have been unperfected as against a person who became a purchaser or lien creditor before lapse.

(3) A continuation statement may be filed by the secured party within six months prior to the expiration of the five year period specified in subsection (2). Any such continuation statement must be signed by the secured party, identify the original statement by file number and state that the original statement is still effective. A continuation statement signed by a person other than the secured party of record must be accompanied by a separate written statement of assignment signed by the secured party of record and complying with subsection (2) of Section 9—405, including payment of the required fee. Upon timely filing of the continuation statement, the effectiveness of the original statement is continued for five years after the last date to which the filing was effective whereupon it lapses in the same manner as provided in subsection (2) unless another continuation statement is filed prior to such lapse. Succeeding continuation statements may be filed in the same manner to continue the effectiveness of the original statement. Unless a statute on disposition of public records provides otherwise, the filing officer may remove a lapsed statement from the files and destroy it immediately if he has retained a microfilm or other photographic record, or in other cases after one year after the lapse. The filing officer shall so arrange matters by physical annexation of financing statements to continuation statements or other related filings, or by other means, that if he physically destroys the financing statements of a period more than five years past, those which have been continued by a continuation statement or which are still effective under subsection (6) shall be retained.

(4) Except as provided in subsection (7) a filing officer shall mark

each statement with a file number and with the date and hour of filing and shall hold the statement or a microfilm or other photographic copy thereof for public inspection. In addition the filing officer shall index the statement according to the name of the debtor and shall note in the index the file number and the address of the debtor given in the statement.

(5) The uniform fee for filing and indexing and for stamping a copy furnished by the secured party to show the date and place of filing for an original financing statement or for a continuation statement shall be $. . . . . if the statement is in the standard form prescribed by the [Secretary of State] and otherwise shall be $. . . . ., plus in each case, if the financing statement is subject to subsection (5) of Section 9—402, $. . . . . The uniform fee for each name more than one required to be indexed shall be $. . . . . The secured party may at his option show a trade name for any person and an extra uniform indexing fee of $. . . . . shall be paid with respect thereto.

(6) If the debtor is a transmitting utility (subsection (5) of Section 9—401) and a filed financing statement so states, it is effective until a termination statement is filed. A real estate mortgage which is effective as a fixture filing under subsection (6) of Section 9—402 remains effective as a fixture filing until the mortgage is released or satisfied of record or its effectiveness otherwise terminates as to the real estate.

(7) When a financing statement covers timber to be cut or covers minerals or the like (including oil and gas) or accounts subject to subsection (5) of Section 9—103, or is filed as a fixture filing, [it shall be filed for record and] the filing officer shall index it under the names of the debtor and any owner of record shown on the financing statement in the same fashion as if they were the mortgagors in a mortgage of the real estate described, and, to the extent that the law of this state provides for indexing of mortgages under the name of the mortgagee, under the name of the secured party as if he were the mortgagee thereunder, or where indexing is by description in the same fashion as if the financing statement were a mortgage of the real estate described.

Note: *In states in which writings will not appear in the real estate records and indices unless actually recorded the bracketed language in subsection (7) should be used.*

§ 9—404. **Termination Statement.**

(1) If a financing statement covering consumer goods is filed on or after . . . ., then within one month or within ten days following written demand by the debtor after there is no outstanding secured obligation and no commitment to make advances, incur obligations or otherwise give value, the secured party must file with each filing officer with whom the financing statement was filed, a termination statement to the effect that he no longer claims a security interest under the financing statement, which shall be identified by file number. In other cases whenever there is no outstanding secured obligation and no commitment to make advances, incur obligations or otherwise give value, the secured party must on written demand by the debtor send the debtor, for each filing officer with whom the financing statement was filed, a termination statement to the effect that he no longer claims a security interest under the financing statement, which shall be identified by file number. A termination statement signed by a person other than the secured party of record must be accompanied by a separate written statement of assignment signed by the secured party of record complying with subsection (2) of Section 9—405, including payment of the required fee. If the affected secured party fails to file such a termination statement as required by this subsection, or to send such a termination statement within ten days after proper demand therefor, he shall be liable to the debtor for one hundred dollars, and in addition for any loss caused to the debtor by such failure.

(2) On presentation to the filing officer of such a termination statement he must note it in the index. If he has received the termination statement in duplicate, he shall return one copy of the termination statement to the secured party stamped to show the time of receipt thereof. If the filing officer has a microfilm or other photographic record of the financing statement, and of any related continuation statement, statement of assignment and statement of release, he may remove the originals from the files at any time after receipt of the termination statement, or if he has no such record, he may remove them from the files at any time after one year after receipt of the termination statement.

(3) If the termination statement is in the standard form prescribed by the [Secretary of State], the uniform fee for filing and indexing the termination statement shall be $. . . . ., and otherwise shall be $. . . . ., plus in each case an additional fee of $. . . . . for each name more than one against which the termination statement is required to be indexed.

Note: *The date to be inserted should be the effective date of the revised Article 9.*

§ 9—405. **Assignment of Security Interest; Duties of Filing Officer; Fees.**

(1) A financing statement may disclose an assignment of a security interest in the collateral described in the financing statement by indication in the financing statement of the name and address of the assignee or by an assignment itself or a copy thereof on the face or back of the statement. On presentation to the filing officer of such a financing statement the filing officer shall mark the same as provided in Section 9—403(4). The uniform fee for filing, indexing and furnishing filing data for a financing statement so indicating an assignment shall be $. . . . . if the statement is in the standard form prescribed by the [Secretary of State] and otherwise shall be $. . . . ., plus in each case an additional fee of $. . . . . for each name more than one against which the financing statement is required to be indexed.

(2) A secured party may assign of record all or part of his rights under a financing statement by the filing in the place where the original financing statement was filed of a separate written statement of assignment signed by the secured party of record and setting forth the name of the secured party of record and the debtor, the file number and the date of filing of the financing statement and the name and address of the assignee and containing a description of the collateral assigned. A copy of the assignment is sufficient as a separate statement if it complies with the preceding sentence. On presentation to the filing officer of such a separate statement, the filing officer shall mark such separate statement with the date and hour of the filing. He shall note the assignment on the index of the financing statement, or in the case of a fixture filing, or a filing covering timber to be cut, or covering minerals or the like (including oil and gas) or accounts subject to subsection (5) of Section 9—103, he shall index the assignment under the name of the assignor as grantor and, to the extent that the law of this state provides for indexing the assignment of a mortgage under the name of the assignee, he shall

index the assignment of the financing statement under the name of the assignee. The uniform fee for filing, indexing and furnishing filing data about such a separate statement of assignment shall be $. . . . . . if the statement is in the standard form prescribed by the [Secretary of State] and otherwise shall be $. . . . . ., plus in each case an additional fee of $. . . . . . for each name more than one against which the statement of assignment is required to be indexed. Notwithstanding the provisions of this subsection, an assignment of record of a security interest in a fixture contained in a mortgage effective as a fixture filing (subsection (6) of Section 9—402) may be made only by an assignment of the mortgage in the manner provided by the law of this state other than this Act.

(3) After the disclosure or filing of an assignment under this section, the assignee is the secured party of record.

§ 9—406. **Release of Collateral; Duties of Filing Officer; Fees.**

A secured party of record may by his signed statement release all or a part of any collateral described in a filed financing statement. The statement of release is sufficient if it contains a description of the collateral being released, the name and address of the debtor, the name and address of the secured party, and the file number of the financing statement. A statement of release signed by a person other than the secured party of record must be accompanied by a separate written statement of assignment signed by the secured party of record and complying with subsection (2) of Section 9—405, including payment of the required fee. Upon presentation of such a statement of release to the filing officer he shall mark the statement with the hour and date of filing and shall note the same upon the margin of the index of the filing of the financing statement. The uniform fee for filing and noting such a statement of release shall be $. . . . . . if the statement is in the standard form prescribed by the [Secretary of State] and otherwise shall be $. . . . . ., plus in each case an additional fee of $. . . . . . for each name more than one against which the statement of release is required to be indexed.

§ 9—407. **Information From Filing Officer.**

[(1) If the person filing any financing statement, termination statement, statement of assignment, or statement of release, furnishes the filing officer a copy thereof, the filing officer shall upon request note upon the copy the file number and date and hour of the filing of the original and deliver or send the copy to such person.]

[(2) Upon request of any person, the filing officer shall issue his certificate showing whether there is on file on the date and hour stated therein, any presently effective financing statement naming a particular debtor and any statement of assignment thereof and if there is, giving the date and hour of filing of each such statement and the names and addresses of each secured party therein. The uniform fee for such a certificate shall be $. . . . . . if the request for the certificate is in the standard form prescribed by the [Secretary of State] and otherwise shall be $. . . . . . . Upon request the filing officer shall furnish a copy of any filed financing statement or statement of assignment for a uniform fee of $. . . . . . per page.]

Note: *This section is proposed as an optional provision to require filing officers to furnish certificates. Local law and practices should be consulted with regard to the advisability of adoption.*

§ 9—408. **Financing Statements Covering Consigned or Leased Goods.**

A consignor or lessor of goods may file a financing statement using the terms "consignor," "consignee," "lessor," "lessee" or the like instead of the terms specified in Section 9—402. The provisions of this Part shall apply as appropriate to such a financing statement but its filing shall not of itself be a factor in determining whether or not the consignment or lease is intended as security (Section 1—201(37)). However, if it is determined for other reasons that the consignment or lease is so intended, a security interest of the consignor or lessor which attaches to the consigned or leased goods is perfected by such filing.

Part 5 **Default**

§ 9—501. **Default; Procedure When Security Agreement Covers Both Real and Personal Property.**

(1) When a debtor is in default under a security agreement, a secured party has the rights and remedies provided in this Part and except as limited by subsection (3) those provided in the security agreement. He may reduce his claim to judgment, foreclose or otherwise enforce the security interest by any available judicial procedure. If the collateral is documents the secured party may proceed either as to the documents or as to the goods covered thereby. A secured party in possession has the rights, remedies and duties provided in Section 9—207. The rights and remedies referred to in this subsection are cumulative.

(2) After default, the debtor has the rights and remedies provided in this Part, those provided in the security agreement and those provided in Section 9—207.

(3) To the extent that they give rights to the debtor and impose duties on the secured party, the rules stated in the subsections referred to below may not be waived or varied except as provided with respect to compulsory disposition of collateral (subsection (3) of Section 9—504 and Section 9—505) and with respect to redemption of collateral (Section 9—506) but the parties may by agreement determine the standards by which the fulfillment of these rights and duties is to be measured if such standards are not manifestly unreasonable:

(a) subsection (2) of Section 9—502 and subsection (2) of Section 9—504 insofar as they require accounting for surplus proceeds of collateral;

(b) subsection (3) of Section 9—504 and subsection (1) of Section 9—505 which deal with disposition of collateral;

(c) subsection (2) of Section 9—505 which deals with acceptance of collateral as discharge of obligation;

(d) Section 9—506 which deals with redemption of collateral; and

(e) subsection (1) of Section 9—507 which deals with the secured party's liability for failure to comply with this Part.

(4) If the security agreement covers both real and personal property, the secured party may proceed under this Part as to the personal property or he may proceed as to both the real and the personal property in accordance with his rights and remedies in respect of the real property in which case the provisions of this Part do not apply.

(5) When a secured party has reduced his claim to judgment the

lien of any levy which may be made upon his collateral by virtue of any execution based upon the judgment shall relate back to the date of the perfection of the security interest in such collateral. A judicial sale, pursuant to such execution, is a foreclosure of the security interest by judicial procedure within the meaning of this section, and the secured party may purchase at the sale and thereafter hold the collateral free of any other requirements of this Article.

§ 9—502. **Collection Rights of Secured Party.**

(1) When so agreed and in any event on default the secured party is entitled to notify an account debtor or the obligor on an instrument to make payment to him whether or not the assignor was theretofore making collections on the collateral, and also to take control of any proceeds to which he is entitled under Section 9—306.

(2) A secured party who by agreement is entitled to charge back uncollected collateral or otherwise to full or limited recourse against the debtor and who undertakes to collect from the account debtors or obligors must proceed in a commercially reasonable manner and may deduct his reasonable expenses of realization from the collections. If the security agreement secures an indebtedness, the secured party must account to the debtor for any surplus, and unless otherwise agreed, the debtor is liable for any deficiency. But, if the underlying transaction was a sale of accounts or chattel paper, the debtor is entitled to any surplus or is liable for any deficiency only if the security agreement so provides.

§ 9—503. **Secured Party's Right to Take Possession After Default.**

Unless otherwise agreed a secured party has on default the right to take possession of the collateral. In taking possession a secured party may proceed without judicial process if this can be done without breach of the peace or may proceed by action. If the security agreement so provides the secured party may require the debtor to assemble the collateral and make it available to the secured party at a place to be designated by the secured party which is reasonably convenient to both parties. Without removal a secured party may render equipment unusable, and may dispose of collateral on the debtor's premises under Section 9—504.

§ 9—504. **Secured Party's Right to Dispose of Collateral After Default; Effect of Disposition.**

(1) A secured party after default may sell, lease or otherwise dispose of any or all of the collateral in its then condition or following any commercially reasonable preparation or processing. Any sale of goods is subject to the Article on Sales (Article 2). The proceeds of disposition shall be applied in the order following to

(a) the reasonable expenses of retaking, holding, preparing for sale or lease, selling, leasing and the like and, to the extent provided for in the agreement and not prohibited by law, the reasonable attorneys' fees and legal expenses incurred by the secured party;

(b) the satisfaction of indebtedness secured by the security interest under which the disposition is made;

(c) the satisfaction of indebtedness secured by any subordinate security interest in the collateral if written notification of demand therefor is received before distribution of the proceeds is completed. If requested by the secured party, the holder of a subordinate security interest must seasonably furnish reasonable proof of his interest, and unless he does so, the secured party need not comply with his demand.

(2) If the security interest secures an indebtedness, the secured party must account to the debtor for any surplus, and, unless otherwise agreed, the debtor is liable for any deficiency. But if the underlying transaction was a sale of accounts or chattel paper, the debtor is entitled to any surplus or is liable for any deficiency only if the security agreement so provides.

(3) Disposition of the collateral may be by public or private proceedings and may be made by way of one or more contracts. Sale or other disposition may be as a unit or in parcels and at any time and place and on any terms but every aspect of the disposition including the method, manner, time, place and terms must be commercially reasonable. Unless collateral is perishable or threatens to decline speedily in value or is of a type customarily sold on a recognized market, reasonable notification of the time and place of any public sale or reasonable notification of the time after which any private sale or other intended disposition is to be made shall be sent by the secured party to the debtor, if he has not signed after default a statement renouncing or modifying his right to notification of sale. In the case of consumer goods no other notification need be sent. In other cases notification shall be sent to any other secured party from whom the secured party has received (before sending his notification to the debtor or before the debtor's renunciation of his rights) written notice of a claim of an interest in the collateral. The secured party may buy at any public sale and if the collateral is of a type customarily sold in a recognized market or is of a type which is the subject of widely distributed standard price quotations he may buy at private sale.

(4) When collateral is disposed of by a secured party after default, the disposition transfers to a purchaser for value all of the debtor's rights therein, discharges the security interest under which it is made and any security interest or lien subordinate thereto. The purchaser takes free of all such rights and interests even though the secured party fails to comply with the requirements of this Part or of any judicial proceedings

(a) in the case of a public sale, if the purchaser has no knowledge of any defects in the sale and if he does not buy in collusion with the secured party, other bidders or the person conducting the sale; or

(b) in any other case, if the purchaser acts in good faith.

(5) A person who is liable to a secured party under a guaranty, indorsement, repurchase agreement or the like and who receives a transfer of collateral from the secured party or is subrogated to his rights has thereafter the rights and duties of the secured party. Such a transfer of collateral is not a sale or disposition of the collateral under this Article.

§ 9—505. **Compulsory Disposition of Collateral; Acceptance of the Collateral as Discharge of Obligation.**

(1) If the debtor has paid sixty per cent of the cash price in the case of a purchase money security interest in consumer goods or sixty per cent of the loan in the case of another security interest in consumer goods, and has not signed after default a statement renouncing or modifying his rights under this Part a secured party who has taken possession of collateral must dispose of it under

Section 9—504 and if he fails to do so within ninety days after he takes possession the debtor at his option may recover in conversion or under Section 9—507(1) on secured party's liability.

(2) In any other case involving consumer goods or any other collateral a secured party in possession may, after default, propose to retain the collateral in satisfaction of the obligation. Written notice of such proposal shall be sent to the debtor if he has not signed after default a statement renouncing or modifying his rights under this subsection. In the case of consumer goods no other notice need be given. In other cases notice shall be sent to any other secured party from whom the secured party has received (before sending his notice to the debtor or before the debtor's renunciation of his rights) written notice of a claim of an interest in the collateral. If the secured party receives objection in writing from a person entitled to receive notification within twenty-one days after the notice was sent, the secured party must dispose of the collateral under Section 9—504. In the absence of such written objection the secured party may retain the collateral in satisfaction of the debtor's obligation.

§ 9—506. **Debtor's Right to Redeem Collateral.**

At any time before the secured party has disposed of collateral or entered into a contract for its disposition under Section 9—504 or before the obligation has been discharged under Section 9—505(2) the debtor or any other secured party may unless otherwise agreed in writing after default redeem the collateral by tendering fulfillment of all obligations secured by the collateral as well as the expenses reasonably incurred by the secured party in retaking, holding and preparing the collateral for disposition, in arranging for the sale, and to the extent provided in the agreement and not prohibited by law, his reasonable attorneys' fees and legal expenses.

§ 9—507. **Secured Party's Liability for Failure to Comply With This Part.**

(1) If it is established that the secured party is not proceeding in accordance with the provisions of this Part disposition may be ordered or restrained on appropriate terms and conditions. If the disposition has occurred the debtor or any person entitled to notification or whose security interest has been made known to the secured party prior to the disposition has a right to recover from the secured party any loss caused by a failure to comply with the provisions of this Part. If the collateral is consumer goods, the debtor has a right to recover in any event an amount not less than the credit service charge plus ten per cent of the principal amount of the debt or the time price differential plus 10 per cent of the cash price.

(2) The fact that a better price could have been obtained by a sale at a different time or in a different method from that selected by the secured party is not of itself sufficient to establish that the sale was not made in a commercially reasonable manner. If the secured party either sells the collateral in the usual manner in any recognized market therefor or if he sells at the price current in such market at the time of his sale or if he has otherwise sold in conformity with reasonable commercial practices among dealers in the type of property sold he has sold in a commercially reasonable manner. The principles stated in the two preceding sentences with respect to sales also apply as may be appropriate to other types of disposition. A disposition which has been approved in any judicial proceeding or by any bona fide creditors' committee or representative of creditors shall conclusively be deemed to be commercially reasonable, but this sentence does not indicate that any such approval must be obtained in any case nor does it indicate that any disposition not so approved is not commercially reasonable.

Article 10 EFFECTIVE DATE AND REPEALER

§ 10—101. **Effective Date.**

This Act shall become effective at midnight on December 31st following its enactment. It applies to transactions entered into and events occurring after that date.

§ 10—102. **Specific Repealer; Provision for Transition.**

(1) The following acts and all other acts and parts of acts inconsistent herewith are hereby repealed:
(Here should follow the acts to be specifically repealed including the following:

Uniform Negotiable Instruments Act
Uniform Warehouse Receipts Act
Uniform Sales Act
Uniform Bills of Lading Act
Uniform Stock Transfer Act
Uniform Conditional Sales Act
Uniform Trust Receipts Act
Also any acts regulating:
Bank collections
Bulk sales
Chattel mortgages
Conditional sales
Factor's lien acts
Farm storage of grain and similar acts
Assignment of accounts receivable)

(2) Transactions validly entered into before the effective date specified in Section 10—101 and the rights, duties and interests flowing from them remain valid thereafter and may be terminated, completed, consummated or enforced as required or permitted by any statute or other law amended or repealed by this Act as though such repeal or amendment had not occurred.

Note: *Subsection (1) should be separately prepared for each state. The foregoing is a list of statutes to be checked.*

§ 10—103. **General Repealer.**

Except as provided in the following section, all acts and parts of acts inconsistent with this Act are hereby repealed.

§ 10—104. **Laws Not Repealed.**

(1) The Article on Documents of Title (Article 7) does not repeal or modify any laws prescribing the form or contents of documents of title or the services or facilities to be afforded by bailees, or otherwise regulating bailees' businesses in respects not specifically dealt with herein; but the fact that such laws are violated does not affect the status of a document of title which otherwise complies with the definition of a document of title (Section 1—201).

[(2) This Act does not repeal ....*, cited as the Uniform Act for the Simplification of Fiduciary Security Transfers, and if in any respect there is any inconsistency between that Act and the Article of this Act on investment securities (Article 8) the provisions of the former Act shall control.]

Note: *At * in subsection (2) insert the statutory reference to the Uniform Act for the Simplification of Fiduciary Security Transfers if such Act has previously been enacted. If it has not been enacted, omit subsection (2).*

Article 11
(REPORTERS' DRAFT) EFFECTIVE DATE AND TRANSITION PROVISIONS

This material has been numbered Article 11 to distinguish it from Article 10, the transition provision of the 1962 Code, which may still remain in effect in some states to cover transition problems from pre-Code law to the original Uniform Commercial Code. Adaptation may be necessary in particular states. The terms "[old Code]" and "[new Code]" and "[old U.C.C.]" and "[new U.C.C.]" are used herein, and should be suitably changed in each state.

Note: *This draft was prepared by the Reporters and has not been passed upon by the Review Committee, the Permanent Editorial Board, the American Law Institute, or the National Conference of Commissioners on Uniform State Laws. It is submitted as a working draft which may be adapted as appropriate in each state.*

§ 11—101. **Effective Date.**

This Act shall become effective at 12:01 A.M. on ________, 19______.

§ 11—102. **Preservation of Old Transition Provision.**

The provisions of [here insert reference to the original transition provision in the particular state] shall continue to apply to [the new U.C.C.] and for this purpose the [old U.C.C. and new U.C.C.] shall be considered one continuous statute.

§ 11—103. **Transition to [New Code]—General Rule.**

Transactions validly entered into after [effective date of old U.C.C.] and before [effective date of new U.C.C.], and which were subject to the provisions of [old U.C.C.] and which would be subject to this Act as amended if they had been entered into after the effective date of [new U.C.C.] and the rights, duties and interests flowing from such transactions remain valid after the latter date and may be terminated, completed, consummated or enforced as required or permitted by the [new U.C.C.]. Security interests arising out of such transactions which are perfected when [new U.C.C.] becomes effective shall remain perfected until they lapse as provided in [new U.C.C.], and may be continued as permitted by [new U.C.C.], except as stated in Section 11—105.

§ 11—104. **Transition Provision on Change of Requirement of Filing.**

A security interest for the perfection of which filing or the taking of possession was required under [old U.C.C.] and which attached prior to the effective date of [new U.C.C.] but was not perfected shall be deemed perfected on the effective date of [new U.C.C.] if [new U.C.C.] permits perfection without filing or authorizes filing in the office or offices where a prior ineffective filing was made.

§ 11—105. **Transition Provision on Change of Place of Filing.**

(1) A financing statement or continuation statement filed prior to [effective date of new U.C.C.] which shall not have lapsed prior to [the effective date of new U.C.C.] shall remain effective for the period provided in the [old Code], but not less than five years after the filing.

(2) With respect to any collateral acquired by the debtor subsequent to the effective date of [new U.C.C.], any effective financing statement or continuation statement described in this section shall apply only if the filing or filings are in the office or offices that would be appropriate to perfect the security interests in the new collateral under [new U.C.C.].

(3) The effectiveness of any financing statement or continuation statement filed prior to [effective date of new U.C.C.] may be continued by a continuation statement as permitted by [new U.C.C.], except that if [new U.C.C.] requires a filing in an office where there was no previous financing statement, a new financing statement conforming to Section 11—106 shall be filed in that office.

(4) If the record of a mortgage of real estate would have been effective as a fixture filing of goods described therein if [new U.C.C.] had been in effect on the date of recording the mortgage, the mortgage shall be deemed effective as a fixture filing as to such goods under subsection (6) of Section 9—402 of the [new U.C.C.] on the effective date of [new U.C.C.].

§ 11—106. **Required Refilings.**

(1) If a security interest is perfected or has priority when this Act takes effect as to all persons or as to certain persons without any filing or recording, and if the filing of a financing statement would be required for the perfection or priority of the security interest against those persons under [new U.C.C.], the perfection and priority rights of the security interest continue until 3 years after the effective date of [new U.C.C.]. The perfection will then lapse unless a financing statement is filed as provided in subsection (4) or unless the security interest is perfected otherwise than by filing.

(2) If a security interest is perfected when [new U.C.C.] takes effect under a law other than [U.C.C.] which requires no further filing, refiling or recording to continue its perfection, perfection continues until and will lapse 3 years after [new U.C.C.] takes effect, unless a financing statement is filed as provided in subsection (4) or unless the security interest is perfected otherwise than by filing, or unless under subsection (3) of Section 9—302 the other law continues to govern filing.

(3) If a security interest is perfected by a filing, refiling or recording under a law repealed by this Act which required further filing, refiling or recording to continue its perfection, perfection continues and will lapse on the date provided by the law so repealed for such further filing, refiling or recording unless a financing statement is filed as provided in subsection (4) or unless the security interest is perfected otherwise than by filing.

(4) A financing statement may be filed within six months before the perfection of a security interest would otherwise lapse. Any such financing statement may be signed by either the debtor or the secured party. It must identify the security agreement, statement or notice (however denominated in any statute or other law

repealed or modified by this Act), state the office where and the date when the last filing, refiling or recording, if any, was made with respect thereto, and the filing number, if any, or book and page, if any, of recording and further state that the security agreement, statement or notice, however denominated, in another filing office under the [U.C.C.] or under any statute or other law repealed or modified by this Act is still effective. Section 9—401 and Section 9—103 determine the proper place to file such a financing statement. Except as specified in this subsection, the provisions of Section 9—403(3) for continuation statements apply to such a financing statement.

§ 11—107. **Transition Provisions as to Priorities.**

Except as otherwise provided in [Article 11], [old U.C.C.] shall apply to any questions of priority if the positions of the parties were fixed prior to the effective date of [new U.C.C.]. In other cases questions of priority shall be determined by [new U.C.C.].

§ 11—108. **Presumption that Rule of Law Continues Unchanged.**

Unless a change in law has clearly been made, the provisions of [new U.C.C.] shall be deemed declaratory of the meaning of the [old U.C.C.].

OFFICIAL TEXT—UCC—1993

The preceding articles and sections constitute the official text of the Uniform Commercial Code as of 1993.

Appendix D

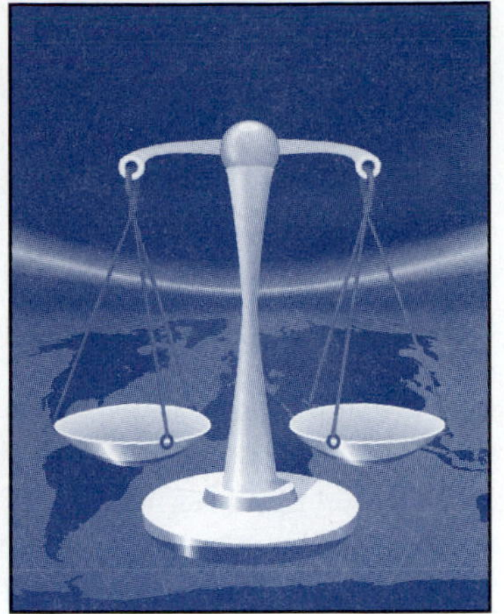

The Uniform Partnership Act

(Adopted in forty-nine states [all of the states except Louisiana], the District of Columbia, the Virgin Islands, and Guam. The adoptions by Alabama and Nebraska do not follow the official text in every respect, but are substantially similar, with local variations.)

The Act consists of 7 Parts as follows:

I. Preliminary Provisions

II. Nature of Partnership

III. Relations of Partners to Persons Dealing with the Partnership

IV. Relations of Partners to One Another

V. Property Rights of a Partner

VI. Dissolution and Winding Up

VII. Miscellaneous Provisions

An Act to make uniform the Law of Partnerships

Be it enacted, etc.:

Part I Preliminary Provisions

Sec. 1. Name of Act

This act may be cited as Uniform Partnership Act.

Sec. 2. Definition of Terms

In this act, "Court" includes every court and judge having jurisdiction in the case.

"Business" includes every trade, occupation, or profession.

"Person" includes individuals, partnerships, corporations, and other associations.

"Bankrupt" includes bankrupt under the Federal Bankruptcy Act or insolvent under any state insolvent act.

"Conveyance" includes every assignment, lease, mortgage, or encumbrance.

"Real property" includes land and any interest or estate in land.

Sec. 3. Interpretation of Knowledge and Notice

(1) A person has "knowledge" of a fact within the meaning of this act not only when he has actual knowledge thereof, but also when he has knowledge of such other facts as in the circumstances shows bad faith.

(2) A person has "notice" of a fact within the meaning of this act when the person who claims the benefit of the notice:

(a) States the fact to such person, or

(b) Delivers through the mail, or by other means of communication, a written statement of the fact to such person or to a proper person at his place of business or residence.

Sec. 4. Rules of Construction

(1) The rule that statutes in derogation of the common law are to be strictly construed shall have no application to this act.

(2) The law of estoppel shall apply under this act.

(3) The law of agency shall apply under this act.

(4) This act shall be so interpreted and construed as to effect its general purpose to make uniform the law of those states which enact it.

(5) This act shall not be construed so as to impair the obligations of any contract existing when the act goes into effect, nor to affect any action or proceedings begun or right accrued before this act takes effect.

Sec. 5. Rules for Cases Not Provided for in This Act.

In any case not provided for in this act the rules of law and equity, including the law merchant, shall govern.

Part II Nature of Partnership

Sec. 6. Partnership Defined

(1) A partnership is an association of two or more persons to carry on as co-owners a business for profit.

(2) But any association formed under any other statute of this state, or any statute adopted by authority, other than the authority of this state, is not a partnership under this act, unless such association would have been a partnership in this state prior to the adoption of this act; but this act shall apply to limited partnerships except in so far as the statutes relating to such partnerships are inconsistent herewith.

Sec. 7. **Rules for Determining the Existence of a Partnership**

In determining whether a partnership exists, these rules shall apply:

(1) Except as provided by Section 16 persons who are not partners as to each other are not partners as to third persons.

(2) Joint tenancy, tenancy in common, tenancy by the entireties, joint property, common property, or part ownership does not of itself establish a partnership, whether such co-owners do or do not share any profits made by the use of the property.

(3) The sharing of gross returns does not of itself establish a partnership, whether or not the persons sharing them have a joint or common right or interest in any property from which the returns are derived.

(4) The receipt by a person of a share of the profits of a business is prima facie evidence that he is a partner in the business, but no such inference shall be drawn if such profits were received in payment:

(a) As a debt by installments or otherwise,

(b) As wages of an employee or rent to a landlord,

(c) As an annuity to a widow or representative of a deceased partner,

(d) As interest on a loan, though the amount of payment vary with the profits of the business,

(e) As the consideration for the sale of a good-will of a business or other property by installments or otherwise.

Sec. 8. **Partnership Property**

(1) All property originally brought into the partnership stock or subsequently acquired by purchase or otherwise, on account of the partnership, is partnership property.

(2) Unless the contrary intention appears, property acquired with partnership funds is partnership property.

(3) Any estate in real property may be acquired in the partnership name. Title so acquired can be conveyed only in the partnership name.

(4) A conveyance to a partnership in the partnership name, though without words of inheritance, passes the entire estate of the grantor unless a contrary intent appears.

Part III Relations of Partners to Persons Dealing with the Partnership

Sec. 9. **Partner Agent of Partnership as to Partnership Business**

(1) Every partner is an agent of the partnership for the purpose of its business, and the act of every partner, including the execution in the partnership name of any instrument, for apparently carrying on in the usual way the business of the partnership of which he is a member binds the partnership, unless the partner so acting has in fact no authority to act for the partnership in the particular matter, and the person with whom he is dealing has knowledge of the fact that he has no such authority.

(2) An act of a partner which is not apparently for the carrying on of the business of the partnership in the usual way does not bind the partnership unless authorized by the other partners.

(3) Unless authorized by the other partners or unless they have abandoned the business, one or more but less than all the partners have no authority to:

(a) Assign the partnership property in trust for creditors or on the assignee's promise to pay the debts of the partnership,

(b) Dispose of the good-will of the business,

(c) Do any other act which would make it impossible to carry on the ordinary business of a partnership,

(d) Confess a judgment,

(e) Submit a partnership claim or liability to arbitration or reference.

(4) No act of a partner in contravention of a restriction on authority shall bind the partnership to persons having knowledge of the restriction.

Sec. 10. **Conveyance of Real Property of the Partnership**

(1) Where title to real property is in the partnership name, any partner may convey title to such property by a conveyance executed in the partnership name; but the partnership may recover such property unless the partner's act binds the partnership under the provisions of paragraph (1) of section 9, or unless such property has been conveyed by the grantee or a person claiming through such grantee to a holder for value without knowledge that the partner, in making the conveyance, has exceeded his authority.

(2) Where title to real property is in the name of the partnership, a conveyance executed by a partner, in his own name, passes the equitable interest of the partnership, provided the act is one within the authority of the partner under the provisions of paragraph (1) of section 9.

(3) Where title to real property is in the name of one or more but not all the partners, and the record does not disclose the right of the partnership, the partners in whose name the title stands may convey title to such property, but the partnership may recover such property if the partners' act does not bind the partnership under the provisions of paragraph (1) of section 9, unless the purchaser or his assignee, is a holder for value, without knowledge.

(4) Where the title to real property is in the name of one or more or all the partners, or in a third person in trust for the partnership, a conveyance executed by a partner in the partnership name, or in his own name, passes the equitable interest of the partnership, provided the act is one within the authority of the partner under the provisions of paragraph (1) of section 9.

(5) Where the title to real property is in the names of all the partners a conveyance executed by all the partners passes all their rights in such property.

Sec. 11. **Partnership Bound by Admission of Partner**

An admission or representation made by any partner concerning partnership affairs within the scope of his authority as conferred by this act is evidence against the partnership.

Sec. 12. **Partnership Charged with Knowledge of or Notice to Partner**

Notice to any partner of any matter relating to partnership affairs, and the knowledge of the partner acting in the particular matter, acquired while a partner or then present to his mind, and the knowledge of any other partner who reasonably could and should have communicated it to the acting partner, operate as notice to or knowledge of the partnership, except in the case of a fraud on the partnership committed by or with the consent of that partner.

Sec. 13. **Partnership Bound by Partner's Wrongful Act**

Where, by any wrongful act or omission of any partner acting in the ordinary course of the business of the partnership or with the authority of his co-partners, loss or injury is caused to any person, not being a partner in the partnership, or any penalty is incurred, the partnership is liable therefor to the same extent as the partner so acting or omitting to act.

Sec. 14. **Partnership Bound by Partner's Breach of Trust**

The partnership is bound to make good the loss:

(a) Where one partner acting within the scope of his apparent authority receives money or property of a third person and misapplies it; and

(b) Where the partnership in the course of its business receives money or property of a third person and the money or property so received is misapplied by any partner while it is in the custody of the partnership.

Sec. 15. **Nature of Partner's Liability**

All partners are liable

(a) Jointly and severally for everything chargeable to the partnership under sections 13 and 14.

(b) Jointly for all other debts and obligations of the partnership; but any partner may enter into a separate obligation to perform a partnership contract.

Sec. 16. **Partner by Estoppel**

(1) When a person, by words spoken or written or by conduct, represents himself, or consents to another representing him to any one, as a partner in an existing partnership or with one or more persons not actual partners, he is liable to any such person to whom such representation has been made, who has, on the faith of such representation, given credit to the actual or apparent partnership, and if he has made such representation or consented to its being made in a public manner he is liable to such person, whether the representation has or has not been made or communicated to such person so giving credit by or with the knowledge of the apparent partner making the representation or consenting to its being made.

(a) When a partnership liability results, he is liable as though he were an actual member of the partnership.

(b) When no partnership liability results, he is liable jointly with the other persons, if any, so consenting to the contract or representation as to incur liability, otherwise separately.

(2) When a person has been thus represented to be a partner in an existing partnership, or with one or more persons not actual partners, he is an agent of the persons consenting to such representation to bind them to the same extent and in the same manner as though he were a partner in fact, with respect to persons who rely upon the representation. Where all the members of the existing partnership consent to the representation, a partnership act or obligation results; but in all other cases it is the joint act or obligation of the person acting and the persons consenting to the representation.

Sec. 17. **Liability of Incoming Partner**

A person admitted as a partner into an existing partnership is liable for all the obligations of the partnership arising before his admission as though he had been a partner when such obligations were incurred, except that this liability shall be satisfied only out of partnership property.

Part IV Relations of Partners to One Another

Sec. 18. **Rules Determining Rights and Duties of Partners**

The rights and duties of the partners in relation to the partnership shall be determined, subject to any agreement between them, by the following rules:

(a) Each partner shall be repaid his contributions, whether by way of capital or advances to the partnership property and share equally in the profits and surplus remaining after all liabilities, including those to partners, are satisfied; and must contribute towards the losses, whether of capital or otherwise, sustained by the partnership according to his share in the profits.

(b) The partnership must indemnify every partner in respect of payments made and personal liabilities reasonably incurred by him in the ordinary and proper conduct of its business, or for the preservation of its business or property.

(c) A partner, who in aid of the partnership makes any payment or advance beyond the amount of capital which he agreed to contribute, shall be paid interest from the date of the payment or advance.

(d) A partner shall receive interest on the capital contributed by him only from the date when repayment should be made.

(e) All partners have equal rights in the management and conduct of the partnership business.

(f) No partner is entitled to remuneration for acting in the partnership business, except that a surviving partner is entitled to reasonable compensation for his services in winding up the partnership affairs.

(g) No person can become a member of a partnership without the consent of all the partners.

(h) Any difference arising as to ordinary matters connected with the partnership business may be decided by a majority of the partners; but no act in contravention of any agreement between the partners may be done rightfully without the consent of all the partners.

Sec. 19. **Partnership Books**

The partnership books shall be kept, subject to any agreement between the partners, at the principal place of business of the partnership, and every partner shall at all times have access to and may inspect and copy any of them.

Sec. 20. **Duty of Partners to Render Information**

Partners shall render on demand true and full information of all things affecting the partnership to any partner or the legal representative of any deceased partner or partner under legal disability.

Sec. 21. **Partner Accountable as a Fiduciary**

(1) Every partner must account to the partnership for any benefit, and hold as trustee for it any profits derived by him without the consent of the other partners from any transaction connected with the formation, conduct, or liquidation of the partnership or from any use by him of its property.

(2) This section applies also to the representatives of a deceased partner engaged in the liquidation of the affairs of the partnership as the personal representatives of the last surviving partner.

Sec. 22. **Right to an Account**

Any partner shall have the right to a formal account as to partnership affairs:

(a) If he is wrongfully excluded from the partnership business or possession of its property by his co-partners,

(b) If the right exists under the terms of any agreement,

(c) As provided by section 21,

(d) Whenever other circumstances render it just and reasonable.

Sec. 23. **Continuation of Partnership beyond Fixed Term**

(1) When a partnership for a fixed term or particular undertaking is continued after the termination of such term or particular undertaking without any express agreement, the rights and duties of the partners remain the same as they were at such termination, so far as is consistent with a partnership at will.

(2) A continuation of the business by the partners or such of them as habitually acted therein during the term, without any settlement or liquidation of the partnership affairs, is prima facie evidence of a continuation of the partnership.

Part V Property Rights of a Partner

Sec. 24. **Extent of Property Rights of a Partner**

The property rights of a partner are (1) his rights in specific partnership property, (2) his interest in the partnership, and (3) his right to participate in the management.

Sec. 25. **Nature of a Partner's Right in Specific Partnership Property**

(1) A partner is co-owner with his partners of specific partnership property holding as a tenant in partnership.

(2) The incidents of this tenancy are such that:

(a) A partner, subject to the provisions of this act and to any agreement between the partners, has an equal right with his partners to possess specific partnership property for partnership purposes; but he has no right to possess such property for any other purpose without the consent of his partners.

(b) A partner's right in specific partnership property is not assignable except in connection with the assignment of rights of all the partners in the same property.

(c) A partner's right in specific partnership property is not subject to attachment or execution, except on a claim against the partnership. When partnership property is attached for a partnership debt the partners, or any of them, or the representatives of a deceased partner, cannot claim any right under the homestead or exemption laws.

(d) On the death of a partner his right in specific partnership property vests in the surviving partner or partners, except where the deceased was the last surviving partner, when his right in such property vests in his legal representative. Such surviving partner or partners, or the legal representative of the last surviving partner, has no right to possess the partnership property for any but a partnership purpose.

(e) A partner's right in specific partnership property is not subject to dower, curtesy, or allowances to widows, heirs, or next of kin.

Sec. 26. **Nature of Partner's Interest in the Partnership**

A partner's interest in the partnership is his share of the profits and surplus, and the same is personal property.

Sec. 27. **Assignment of Partner's Interest**

(1) A conveyance by a partner of his interest in the partnership does not of itself dissolve the partnership, nor, as against the other partners in the absence of agreement, entitle the assignee, during the continuance of the partnership, to interfere in the management or administration of the partnership business or affairs, or to require any information or account of partnership transactions, or to inspect the partnership books; but it merely entitles the assignee to receive in accordance with his contract the profits to which the assigning partner would otherwise be entitled.

(2) In case of a dissolution of the partnership, the assignee is entitled to receive his assignor's interest and may require an account from the date only of the last account agreed to by all the partners.

Sec. 28. **Partner's Interest Subject to Charging Order**

(1) On due application to a competent court by any judgment creditor of a partner, the court which entered the judgment, order, or decree, or any other court, may charge the interest of the debtor partner with payment of the unsatisfied amount of such judgment debt with interest thereon; and may then or later appoint a receiver of his share of the profits, and of any other money due or to fall due to him in respect of the partnership, and make all other orders, directions, accounts and inquiries which the debtor partner might have made, or which the circumstances of the case may require.

(2) The interest charged may be redeemed at any time before foreclosure, or in case of a sale being directed by the court may be purchased without thereby causing a dissolution:

(a) With separate property, by any one or more of the partners, or

(b) With partnership property, by any one or more of the partners with the consent of all the partners whose interests are not so charged or sold.

(3) Nothing in this act shall be held to deprive a partner of his right, if any, under the exemption laws, as regards his interest in the partnership.

Part VI Dissolution and Winding up

Sec. 29. **Dissolution Defined**

The dissolution of a partnership is the change in the relation of the partners caused by any partner ceasing to be associated in the carrying on as distinguished from the winding up of the business.

Sec. 30. **Partnership not Terminated by Dissolution**

On dissolution the partnership is not terminated, but continues until the winding up of partnership affairs is completed.

Sec. 31. **Causes of Dissolution**

Dissolution is caused:

(1) Without violation of the agreement between the partners,

(a) By the termination of the definite term or particular undertaking specified in the agreement,

(b) By the express will of any partner when no definite term or particular undertaking is specified,

(c) By the express will of all the partners who have not assigned their interests or suffered them to be charged for their separate debts, either before or after the termination of any specified term or particular undertaking,

(d) By the expulsion of any partner from the business bona fide in accordance with such a power conferred by the agreement between the partners;

(2) In contravention of the agreement between the partners, where the circumstances do not permit a dissolution under any other provision of this section, by the express will of any partner at any time;

(3) By any event which makes it unlawful for the business of the partnership to be carried on or for the members to carry it on in partnership;

(4) By the death of any partner;

(5) By the bankruptcy of any partner or the partnership;

(6) By decree of court under section 32.

Sec. 32. **Dissolution by Decree of Court**

(1) On application by or for a partner the court shall decree a dissolution whenever:

(a) A partner has been declared a lunatic in any judicial proceeding or is shown to be of unsound mind,

(b) A partner becomes in any other way incapable of performing his part of the partnership contract,

(c) A partner has been guilty of such conduct as tends to affect prejudicially the carrying on of the business,

(d) A partner wilfully or persistently commits a breach of the partnership agreement, or otherwise so conducts himself in matters relating to the partnership business that it is not reasonably practicable to carry on the business in partnership with him,

(e) The business of the partnership can only be carried on at a loss,

(f) Other circumstances render a dissolution equitable.

(2) On the application of the purchaser of a partner's interest under sections 28 or 29 [should read 27 or 28];

(a) After the termination of the specified term or particular undertaking,

(b) At any time if the partnership was a partnership at will when the interest was assigned or when the charging order was issued.

Sec. 33. **General Effect of Dissolution on Authority of Partner**

Except so far as may be necessary to wind up partnership affairs or to complete transactions begun but not then finished, dissolution terminates all authority of any partner to act for the partnership,

(1) With respect to the partners,

(a) When the dissolution is not by the act, bankruptcy or death of a partner; or

(b) When the dissolution is by such act, bankruptcy or death of a partner, in cases where section 34 so requires.

(2) With respect to persons not partners, as declared in section 35.

Sec. 34. **Rights of Partner to Contribution from Co-partners after Dissolution**

Where the dissolution is caused by the act, death or bankruptcy of a partner, each partner is liable to his copartners for his share of any liability created by any partner acting for the partnership as if the partnership had not been dissolved unless

(a) The dissolution being by act of any partner, the partner acting for the partnership had knowledge of the dissolution, or

(b) The dissolution being by the death or bankruptcy of a partner, the partner acting for the partnership had knowledge or notice of the death or bankruptcy.

Sec. 35. **Power of Partner to Bind Partnership to Third Persons after Dissolution**

(1) After dissolution a partner can bind the partnership except as provided in Paragraph (3).

(a) By any act appropriate for winding up partnership affairs or completing transactions unfinished at dissolution;

(b) By any transaction which would bind the partnership if dissolution had not taken place, provided the other party to the transaction

(I) Had extended credit to the partnership prior to dissolution and had no knowledge or notice of the dissolution; or

(II) Though he had not so extended credit, had nevertheless known of the partnership prior to dissolution, and, having no knowledge or notice of dissolution, the fact of dissolution had not been advertised in a newspaper of general circulation in the place (or in each place if more than one) at which the partnership business was regularly carried on.

(2) The liability of a partner under paragraph (1b) shall be satisfied out of partnership assets alone when such partner had been prior to dissolution

(a) Unknown as a partner to the person with whom the contract is made; and

(b) So far unknown and inactive in partnership affairs that the business reputation of the partnership could not be said to have been in any degree due to his connection with it.

(3) The partnership is in no case bound by any act of a partner after dissolution

(a) Where the partnership is dissolved because it is unlawful to carry on the business, unless the act is appropriate for winding up partnership affairs; or

(b) Where the partner has become bankrupt; or

(c) Where the partner has no authority to wind up partnership affairs; except by a transaction with one who

(I) Had extended credit to the partnership prior to dissolution and had no knowledge or notice of his want of authority; or

(II) Had not extended credit to the partnership prior to dissolution, and, having no knowledge or notice of his want of authority, the fact of his want of authority has not been advertised in the manner provided for advertising the fact of dissolution in paragraph (1bII).

(4) Nothing in this section shall affect the liability under Section 16 of any person who after dissolution represents himself or consents to another representing him as a partner in a partnership engaged in carrying on business.

Sec. 36. **Effect of Dissolution on Partner's Existing Liability**

(1) The dissolution of the partnership does not of itself discharge the existing liability of any partner.

(2) A partner is discharged from any existing liability upon dissolution of the partnership by an agreement to that effect between himself, the partnership creditor and the person or partnership continuing the business; and such agreement may be inferred from the course of dealing between the creditor having knowledge of the dissolution and the person or partnership continuing the business.

(3) Where a person agrees to assume the existing obligations of a dissolved partnership, the partners whose obligations have been assumed shall be discharged from any liability to any creditor of the partnership who, knowing of the agreement, consents to a material alteration in the nature or time of payment of such obligations.

(4) The individual property of a deceased partner shall be liable for all obligations of the partnership incurred while he was a partner but subject to the prior payment of his separate debts.

Sec. 37. **Right to Wind Up**

Unless otherwise agreed the partners who have not wrongfully dissolved the partnership or the legal representative of the last surviving partner, not bankrupt, has the right to wind up the partnership affairs; provided, however, that any partner, his legal representative or his assignee, upon cause shown, may obtain winding up by the court.

Sec. 38. **Rights of Partners to Application of Partnership Property**

(1) When dissolution is caused in any way, except in contravention of the partnership agreement, each partner, as against his co-partners and all persons claiming through them in respect of their interests in the partnership, unless otherwise agreed, may have the partnership property applied to discharge its liabilities, and the surplus applied to pay in cash the net amount owing to the respective partners. But if dissolution is caused by expulsion of a partner, bona fide under the partnership agreement and if the expelled partner is discharged from all partnership liabilities, either by payment or agreement under section 36(2), he shall receive in cash only the net amount due him from the partnership.

(2) When dissolution is caused in contravention of the partnership agreement the rights of the partners shall be as follows:

(a) Each partner who has not caused dissolution wrongfully shall have,

(I) All the rights specified in paragraph (1) of this section, and

(II) The right, as against each partner who has caused the dissolution wrongfully, to damages for breach of the agreement.

(b) The partners who have not caused the dissolution wrongfully, if they all desire to continue the business in the same name, either by themselves or jointly with others, may do so, during the agreed term for the partnership and for that purpose may possess the partnership property, provided they secure the payment by bond approved by the court, or pay to any partner who has caused the dissolution wrongfully, the value of his interest in the partnership at the dissolution, less any damages recoverable under clause (2a II) of the section, and in like manner indemnify him against all present or future partnership liabilities.

(c) A partner who has caused the dissolution wrongfully shall have:

(I) If the business is not continued under the provisions of paragraph (2b) all the rights of a partner under paragraph (1), subject to clause (2a II), of this section,

(II) If the business is continued under paragraph (2b) of this section the right as against his co-partners and all claiming through them in respect of their interests in the partnership, to have the value of his interest in the partnership, less any damages caused to his co-partners by the dissolution, ascertained and paid to him in cash, or the payment secured by bond approved by the court, and to be released from all existing liabilities of the partnership; but in ascertaining the value of the partner's interest the value of the good-will of the business shall not be considered.

Sec. 39. **Rights Where Partnership Is Dissolved for Fraud or Misrepresentation**

Where a partnership contract is rescinded on the ground of the fraud or misrepresentation of one of the parties thereto, the party entitled to rescind is, without prejudice to any other right, entitled,

(a) To a lien on, or right of retention of, the surplus of the partnership property after satisfying the partnership liabilities to third persons for any sum of money paid by him for the purchase of an interest in the partnership and for any capital or advances contributed by him; and

(b) To stand, after all liabilities to third persons have been satisfied, in the place of the creditors of the partnership for any payments made by him in respect of the partnership liabilities; and

(c) To be indemnified by the person guilty of the fraud or making the representation against all debts and liabilities of the partnership.

Sec. 40. **Rules for Distribution**

In settling accounts between the partners after dissolution, the following rules shall be observed, subject to any agreement to the contrary:

(a) The assets of the partnership are:

(I) The partnership property,

(II) The contributions of the partners necessary for the payment of all the liabilities specified in clause (b) of this paragraph.

(b) The liabilities of the partnership shall rank in order of payment, as follows:

(I) Those owing to creditors other than partners,

(II) Those owing to partners other than for capital and profits,

(III) Those owing to partners in respect of capital,

(IV) Those owing to partners in respect of profits.

(c) The assets shall be applied in the order of their declaration in clause (a) of this paragraph to the satisfaction of the liabilities.

(d) The partners shall contribute, as provided by section 18(a) the amount necessary to satisfy the liabilities; but if any, but not all, of the partners are insolvent, or, not being subject to process, refuse to contribute, the other partners shall contribute their share of the liabilities, and, in the relative proportions in which they share the profits, the additional amount necessary to pay the liabilities.

(e) An assignee for the benefit of creditors or any person appointed by the court shall have the right to enforce the contributions specified in clause (d) of this paragraph.

(f) Any partner or his legal representative shall have the right to enforce the contributions specified in clause (d) of this paragraph, to the extent of the amount which he has paid in excess of his share of the liability.

(g) The individual property of a deceased partner shall be liable for the contributions specified in clause (d) of this paragraph.

(h) When partnership property and the individual properties of the partners are in possession of a court for distribution, partnership creditors shall have priority on partnership property and separate creditors on individual property, saving the rights of lien or secured creditors as heretofore.

(i) Where a partner has become bankrupt or his estate is insolvent the claims against his separate property shall rank in the following order:

(I) Those owing to separate creditors,

(II) Those owing to partnership creditors,

(III) Those owing to partners by way of contribution.

Sec. 41. **Liability of Persons Continuing the Business in Certain Cases**

(1) When any new partner is admitted into an existing partnership, or when any partner retires and assigns (or the representative of the deceased partner assigns) his rights in partnership property to two or more of the partners, or to one or more of the partners and one or more third persons, if the business is continued without liquidation of the partnership affairs, creditors of the first or dissolved partnership are also creditors of the partnership so continuing the business.

(2) When all but one partner retire and assign (or the representative of a deceased partner assigns) their rights in partnership property to the remaining partner, who continues the business without liquidation of partnership affairs, either alone or with others, creditors of the dissolved partnership are also creditors of the person or partnership so continuing the business.

(3) When any partner retires or dies and the business of the dissolved partnership is continued as set forth in paragraphs (1) and (2) of this section, with the consent of the retired partners or the representative of the deceased partner, but without any assignment of his right in partnership property, rights of creditors of the dissolved partnership and of the creditors of the person or partnership continuing the business shall be as if such assignment had been made.

(4) When all the partners or their representatives assign their rights in partnership property to one or more third persons who promise to pay the debts and who continue the business of the dissolved partnership, creditors of the dissolved partnership are also creditors of the person or partnership continuing the business.

(5) When any partner wrongfully causes a dissolution and the remaining partners continue the business under the provisions of section 38(2b), either alone or with others, and without liquidation of the partnership affairs, creditors of the dissolved partnership are also creditors of the person or partnership continuing the business.

(6) When a partner is expelled and the remaining partners continue the business either alone or with others, without liquidation of the partnership affairs, creditors of the dissolved partnership are also creditors of the person or partnership continuing the business.

(7) The liability of a third person becoming a partner in the partnership continuing the business, under this section, to the creditors of the dissolved partnership shall be satisfied out of partnership property only.

(8) When the business of a partnership after dissolution is continued under any conditions set forth in this section the creditors of the dissolved partnership, as against the separate creditors of the retiring or deceased partner or the representative of the deceased partner, have a prior right to any claim of the retired partner or the representative of the deceased partner against the person or partnership continuing the business, on account of the retired or deceased partner's interest in the dissolved partnership or on account of any consideration promised for such interest or for his right in partnership property.

(9) Nothing in this section shall be held to modify any right of creditors to set aside any assignment on the ground of fraud.

(10) The use by the person or partnership continuing the business of the partnership name, or the name of a deceased partner as part thereof, shall not of itself make the individual property of the deceased partner liable for any debts contracted by such person or partnership.

Sec. 42. **Rights of Retiring or Estate of Deceased Partner When the Business Is Continued**

When any partner retires or dies, and the business is continued under any of the conditions set forth in section 41 (1, 2, 3, 5, 6), or section 38(2b) without any settlement of accounts as between him or his estate and the person or partnership continuing the business, unless otherwise agreed, he or his legal representative as against such persons or partnership may have the value of his interest at the date of dissolution ascertained, and shall receive as an ordinary creditor an amount equal to the value of his interest in the dissolved partnership with interest, or, at his option or at the option of his legal representative, in lieu of interest, the profits attributable to the use of his right in the property of the dissolved partnership; provided that the creditors of the dissolved partnership as against the separate creditors, or the representative of the retired or deceased partner, shall have priority on any claim arising under this section, as provided by section 41(8) of this act.

Sec. 43. **Accrual of Actions**

The right to an account of his interest shall accrue to any partner, or his legal representative, as against the winding up partners or the surviving partners or the person or partnership continuing the business, at the date of dissolution, in the absence of any agreement to the contrary.

Part VII Miscellaneous Provisions

Sec. 44. **When Act Takes Effect**

This act shall take effect on the ___ day of ___ one thousand nine hundred and ___.

Sec. 45. **Legislation Repealed**

All acts or parts of acts inconsistent with this act are hereby repealed.

Appendix E

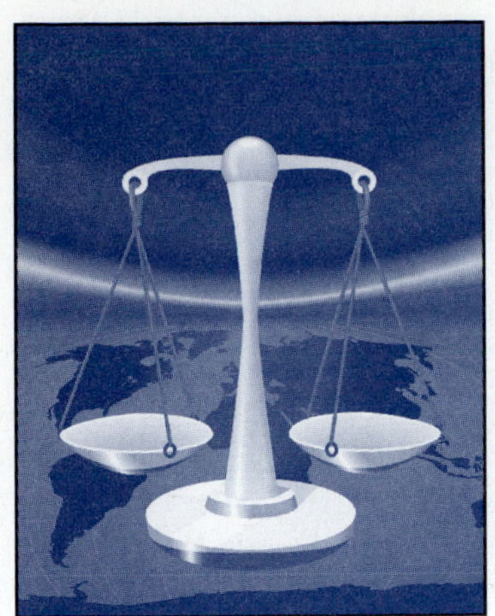

Restatement (Second) of Torts (Excerpts)

Section 402 A. Special liability of seller of product for physical harm to user or consumer.

(1) One who sells any product in a defective condition unreasonably dangerous to the consumer or to his property is subject to liability for physical harm thereby caused to the ultimate user or consumer, or to his property, if

(a) the seller is engaged in the business of selling such a product, and

(b) it is expected to and does reach the user or consumer without substantial change in the condition in which it is sold.

(2) The rule stated in Subsection (1) applies although

(a) the seller has exercised all possible care in the preparation and sale of his product, and

(b) the user or consumer has not bought the product from or entered into any contractual relation with the seller.

Section 402 B. Misrepresentation by seller of chattels to consumer.

One engaged in the business of selling chattels who, by advertising, labels, or otherwise, makes to the public a misrepresentation of a material fact concerning the character or quality of a chattel sold by him is subject to liability for physical harm to a consumer of the chattel caused by justifiable reliance upon the misrepresentation, even though

(a) it is not made fraudulently or negligently, and

(b) the consumer has not bought the chattel from or entered into any contractual relations with the seller.

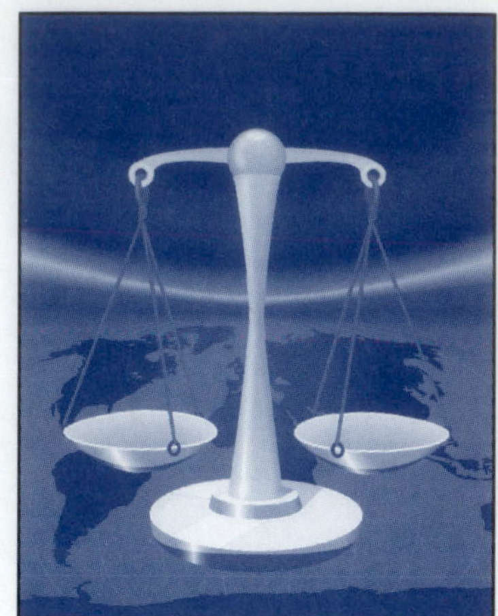

Appendix F

Sherman Antitrust Act of 1890 (Excerpts)

Section. 1 Every contract, combination in the form of trust or otherwise, or conspiracy, in restraint of trade or commerce among the several States, or with foreign nations, is hereby declared to be illegal. Every person who shall make any such contract or engage in any such combination or conspiracy shall be deemed guilty of a felony, and, on conviction thereof, shall be punished by fine not exceeding one million dollars if a corporation, or, if any other person, one hundred thousand dollars or by imprisonment not exceeding three years, or by both said punishments in the discretion of the court.

Section 2. Every person who shall monopolize, or attempt to monopolize, or conspire with any other person or persons, to monopolize any part of the trade or commerce among the several States, or with foreign nations, shall be deemed guilty of a felony, and, on conviction thereof, shall be punished by fine not exceeding one million dollars if a corporation, or, if any other person, one hundred thousand dollars or by imprisonment not exceeding three years, or by both said punishments, in the discretion of the court.

Appendix G

Securities Act of 1933 (Excerpts)

Definitions

Section 2. When used in this title, unless the context requires—

(1) The term "security" means any note, stock, treasury stock, bond, debenture, evidence of indebtedness, certificate of interest or participation in any profit-sharing agreement, collateral-trust certificate, preorganization certificate or subscription, transferable share, investment contract, voting-trust certificate, certificate of deposit for a security, fractional undivided interest in oil, gas, or other mineral rights, any put, call, straddle, option, or privilege on any security, certificate of deposit, or group or index of securities (including any interest therein or based on the value thereof), or any put, call, straddle, option, or privilege entered into on a national securities exchange relating to foreign currency, or, in general, any interest or participation in, temporary or interim certificate for, receipt for, guarantee of, or warrant or right to subscribe to or purchase, any of the foregoing.

Exempted Securities

Section 3. (a) Except as hereinafter expressly provided the provisions of this title shall not apply to any of the following classes of securities:

* * * *

(2) Any security issued or guaranteed by the United States or any territory thereof, or by the District of Columbia, or by any State of the United States, or by any political subdivision of a State or Territory, or by any public instrumentality of one or more States or Territories, or by any person controlled or supervised by and acting as an instrumentality of the Government of the United States pursuant to authority granted by the Congress of the United States; or any certificate of deposit for any of the foregoing; or any security issued or guaranteed by any bank; or any security issued by or representing an interest in or a direct obligation of a Federal Reserve Bank. * * *

(3) Any note, draft, bill of exchange, or banker's acceptance which arises out of a current transaction or the proceeds of which have been or are to be used for current transactions, and which has a maturity at the time of issuance of not exceeding nine months, exclusive of days of grace, or any renewal thereof the maturity of which is likewise limited;

(4) Any security issued by a person organized and operated exclusively for religious, educational, benevolent, fraternal, charitable, or reformatory purposes and not for pecuniary profit, and no part of the net earnings of which inures to the benefit of any person, private stockholder, or individual;

* * * *

(11) Any security which is a part of an issue offered and sold only to persons resident within a single State or Territory, where the issuer of such security is a person resident and doing business within, or, if a corporation, incorporated by and doing business within, such State or Territory.

(b) The Commission may from time to time by its rules and regulations and subject to such terms and conditions as may be described therein, add any class of securities to the securities exempted as provided in this section, if it finds that the enforcement of this title with respect to such securities is not necessary in the public interest and for the protection of investors by reason of the small amount involved or the limited character of the public offering; but no issue of securities shall be exempted under this subsection where the aggregate amount at which such issue is offered to the public exceeds $5,000,000.

Exempted Transactions

Section 4. The provisions of section 5 shall not apply to—

(1) transactions by any person other than an issuer, underwriter, or dealer.

(2) transactions by an issuer not involving any public offering.

(3) transactions by a dealer (including an underwriter no longer acting as an underwriter in respect of the security involved in such transactions), except—

(A) transactions taking place prior to the expiration of forty days after the first date upon which the security was bona fide offered to the public by the issuer or by or through an underwriter.

(B) transactions in a security as to which a registration statement has been filed taking place prior to the expiration of forty days after the effective date of such registration statement or prior to the expiration of forty days after the first date upon which the security was bona fide offered to the public by the issuer or by or through an underwriter after such effective date, whichever is later (excluding in the computation of such forty days any time during which a stop order issued under section 8 is in effect as to the security), or such shorter period as the Commission may specify by rules and regulations or order, and

(C) transactions as to the securities constituting the whole or a part of an unsold allotment to or subscription by such dealer as a participant in the distribution of such securities by the issuer or by or through an underwriter.

With respect to transactions referred to in clause (B), if securities of the issuer have not previously been sold pursuant to an earlier effective registration statement the applicable period, instead of forty days, shall be ninety days, or such shorter period as the Commission may specify by rules and regulations or order.

(4) brokers' transactions, executed upon customers' orders on any exchange or in the over-the-counter market but not the solicitation of such orders.

* * * *

(6) transactions involving offers or sales by an issuer solely to one or more accredited investors, if the aggregate offering price of an issue of securities offered in reliance on this paragraph does not exceed the amount allowed under Section 3(b) of this title, if there is no advertising or public solicitation in connection with the transaction by the issuer or anyone acting on the issuer's behalf, and if the issuer files such notice with the Commission as the Commission shall prescribe.

Prohibitions Relating to Interstate Commerce and the Mails

Section 5. (a) Unless a registration statement is in effect as to a security, it shall be unlawful for any person, directly or indirectly—

(1) to make use of any means or instruments of transportation or communication in interstate commerce or of the mails to sell such security through the use or medium of any prospectus or otherwise; or

(2) to carry or cause to be carried through the mails or in interstate commerce, by any means or instruments of transportation, any such security for the purpose of sale or for delivery after sale.

(b) It shall be unlawful for any person, directly or indirectly—

(1) to make use of any means or instruments of transportation or communication in interstate commerce or of the mails to carry or transmit any prospectus relating to any security with respect to which a registration statement has been filed under this title, unless such prospectus meets the requirements of section 10, or

(2) to carry or to cause to be carried through the mails or in interstate commerce any such security for the purpose of sale or for delivery after sale, unless accompanied or preceded by a prospectus that meets the requirements of subsection (a) of section 10.

(c) It shall be unlawful for any person, directly, or indirectly, to make use of any means or instruments of transportation or communication in interstate commerce or of the mails to offer to sell or offer to buy through the use or medium of any prospectus or otherwise any security, unless a registration statement has been filed as to such security, or while the registration statement is the subject of a refusal order or stop order or (prior to the effective date of the registration statement) any public proceeding of examination under section 8.

Appendix H

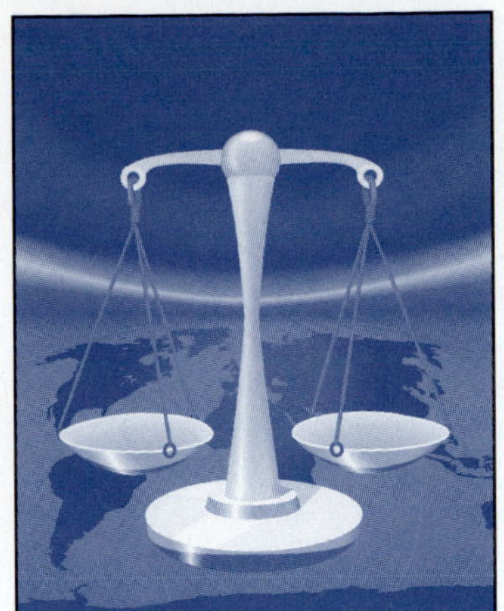

Securities Exchange Act of 1934 (Excerpts)

Definitions and Application of Title

Section 3. (a) When used in this title, unless the context otherwise requires—

* * * *

(4) The term "broker" means any person engaged in the business of effecting transactions in securities for the account of others, but does not include a bank.

(5) The term "dealer" means any person engaged in the business of buying and selling securities for his own account, through a broker or otherwise, but does not include a bank, or any person insofar as he buys or sells securities for his own account, either individually or in some fiduciary capacity, but not as part of a regular business.

* * * *

(7) The term "director" means any director of a corporation or any person performing similar functions with respect to any organization, whether incorporated or unincorporated.

(8) The term "issuer" means any person who issues or proposes to issue any security; except that with respect to certificates of deposit for securities, voting-trust certificates, or collateral-trust certificates, or with respect to certificates of interest or shares in an unincorporated investment trust not having a board of directors or the fixed, restricted management, or unit type, the term "issuer" means the person or persons performing the acts and assuming the duties of depositor or manager pursuant to the provisions of the trust or other agreement or instrument under which such securities are issued; and except that with respect to equipment-trust certificates or like securities, the term "issuer" means the person by whom the equipment or property is, or is to be, used.

(9) The term "person" means a natural person, company, government, or political subdivision, agency, or instrumentality of a government.

Regulation of the Use of Manipulative and Deceptive Devices

Section 10. It shall be unlawful for any person, directly or indirectly, by the use of any means or instrumentality of interstate commerce or of the mails, or of any facility of any national securities exchange—

(a) To effect a short sale, or to use or employ any stop-loss order in connection with the purchase or sale, of any security registered on a national securities exchange, in contravention of such rules and regulations as the Commission may prescribe as necessary or appropriate in the public interest or for the protection of investors.

(b) To use or employ, in connection with the purchase or sale of any security registered on a national securities exchange or any security not so registered, any manipulative or deceptive device or contrivance in contravention of such rules and regulations as the Commission may prescribe as necessary or appropriate in the public interest or for the protection of investors.

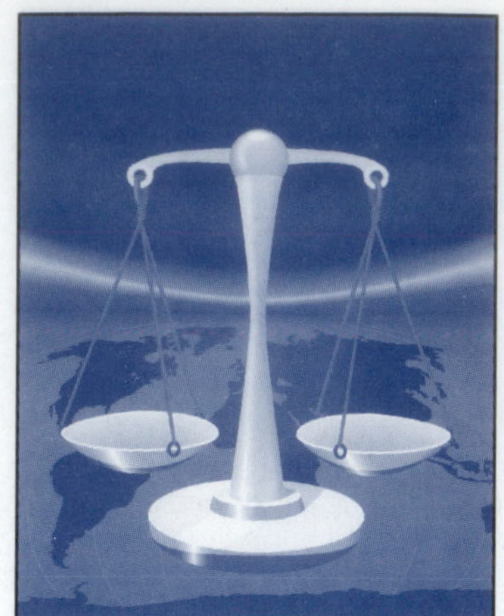

Appendix I

Title VII of the Civil Rights Act of 1964 (Excerpts)

Section 703. Unlawful Employment Practices. (a) It shall be an unlawful employment practice for an employer—

(1) to fail or refuse to hire or to discharge any individual, or otherwise to discriminate against any individual with respect to his compensation, terms, conditions, or privileges of employment, because of such individual's race, color, religion, sex, or national origin; or

(2) to limit, segregate, or classify his employees or applicants for employment in any way which would deprive or tend to deprive any individual of employment opportunities or otherwise adversely affect his status as an employee, because of such individual's race, color, religion, sex, or national origin.

(b) It shall be an unlawful employment practice for an employment agency to fail or refuse to refer for employment, or otherwise to discriminate against, any individual because of his race, color, religion, sex, or national origin, or to classify or refer for employment any individual on the basis or his race, color, religion, sex, or national origin.

(c) It shall be an unlawful employment practice for a labor organization—

(1) to exclude or to expel from its membership, or otherwise to discriminate against, any individual because of his race, color, religion, sex, or national origin;

(2) to limit, segregate, or classify its membership or applicants for membership, or to classify or fail or refuse to refer for employment any individual, in any way which would deprive or tend to deprive any individual of employment opportunities, or would limit such employment opportunities or otherwise adversely affect his status as an employee or as an applicant for employment, because of such individual's race, color, religion, sex, or national origin; or

(3) to cause or attempt to cause an employer to discriminate against an individual in violation of this section.

(d) It shall be an unlawful employment practice for any employer, labor organization, or joint labor-management committee controlling apprenticeship or other training or retraining, including on-the-job training programs to discriminate against any individual because of his race, color, religion, sex, or national origin in admission to, or employment in, any program established to provide apprenticeship or other training.

(e) Notwithstanding any other provision of this subchapter—

(1) it shall not be an unlawful employment practice for an employer to hire and employ employees, for an employment agency to classify, or refer for employment any individual, for a labor organization to classify its membership or to classify or refer for employment any individual, or for an employer, labor organization, or joint labor-management committee controlling apprenticeship or other training or retraining programs to admit or employ any individual in any such program, on the basis of his religion, sex, or national origin in those certain instances where religion, sex, or national origin is a bona fide occupational qualification reasonably necessary to the normal operation of that particular business or enterprise, and

(2) it shall not be an unlawful employment practice for a school, college, university, or other educational institution or institution of learning to hire and employ employees of a particular religion if such school, college, university, or other educational institution or institution of learning is, in whole or in substantial part, owned, supported, controlled, or managed by a particular religion or by a particular religious corporation, association, or society, or if the curriculum of such school, college, university, or other educational institution or institution of learning is directed toward the propagation of a particular religion.

(f) As used in this subchapter, the phrase "unlawful employment practice" shall not be deemed to include any action or measure taken by an employer, labor organization, joint labor-management committee, or employment agency with respect to an individual who is a member of the Communist Party of the United States or of any other organization required to register as a Communist-action or Communist-front organization. * * *

(g) Notwithstanding any other provision of this subchapter, it shall not be an unlawful employment practice for an employer to fail or refuse to hire and employ any individual for any position, for an employer to discharge any individual from any position, or for an employment agency to fail or refuse to refer any individual for employment in any position, or for a labor organization to fail or refuse to refer any individual for employment in any position, if—

(1) the occupancy of such position, or access to the premises in or upon which any part of the duties of such position is performed or is to be performed, is subject to any requirement imposed in the interest of the national security of the United States * * * and

(2) such individual has not fulfilled or has ceased to fulfill that requirement.

(h) Notwithstanding any other provision of this subchapter, it shall not be an unlawful employment practice for an employer to apply different standards of compensation, or different terms, conditions, or privileges of employment pursuant to a bona fide seniority or merit system, or a system which measures earnings by quantity or quality of production or to employees who work in different locations, provided that such differences are not the result of an intention to discriminate because of race, color, religion, sex, or national origin, nor shall it be an unlawful employment practice for an employer to give and act upon the results of any professionally developed ability test provided that such test, its administration or action upon the results is not designed, intended or used to discriminate because of race, color, religion, sex, or national origin. * * *

(j) Nothing contained in this subchapter shall be interpreted to require any employer, employment agency, labor organization, or joint labor-management committee subject to this subchapter to grant preferential treatment to any individual or to any group because of the race, color, religion, sex, or national origin of such individual or group on account of an imbalance which may exist with respect to the total number or percentage of persons of any race, color, religion, sex, or national origin employed by any employer, referred or classified for employment by any employment agency or labor organization, or admitted to, or employed in, any apprenticeship or other training program, in comparison with the total number or percentage of persons of such race, color, religion, sex, or national origin in any community, State, section, or other area, or in the available work force in any community, State, section, or other area.

* * * *

Section 704. Other Unlawful Employment Practices. (a) It shall be an unlawful employment practice for an employer to discriminate against any of his employees or applicants for employment, for an employment agency, or joint labor-management committee controlling apprenticeship or other training or retraining, including on-the-job training programs, to discriminate against any individual, or for a labor organization to discriminate against any member thereof or applicant for membership, because he has opposed any practice made an unlawful employment practice by this subchapter, or because he has made a charge, testified, assisted, or participated in any manner in an investigation, proceeding, or hearing under this subchapter.

(b) It shall be an unlawful employment practice for an employer, labor organization, employment agency, or joint labor-management committee controlling apprenticeship or other training or retraining, including on-the-job training programs, to print or publish or cause to be printed or published any notice or advertisement relating to employment by such an employer or membership or any classification or referral for employment by such a labor organization, or relating to any classification or referral for employment by such an employment agency, or relating to admission to, or employment in, any program established to provide apprenticeship or other training by such a joint-labor-management committee, indicating any preference, limitation, specification, or discrimination, based on race, color, religion, sex, or national origin, except that such a notice or advertisement may indicate a preference, limitation, specification, or discrimination based on religion, sex or national origin when religion, sex, or national origin is a bona fide occupational qualification for employment.

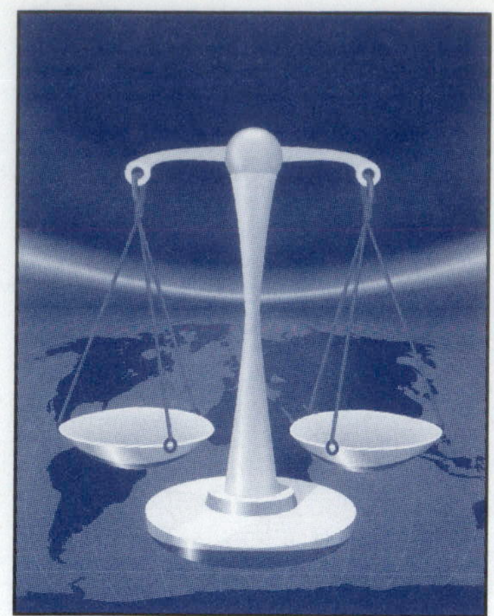

Appendix J

Americans with Disabilities Act of 1990 (Excerpts)

TITLE I—EMPLOYMENT

Sec. 101. Definitions.

As used in this title: * * *

(8) **Qualified individual with a disability.**—The term "qualified individual with a disability" means an individual with a disability who, with or without reasonable accommodation, can perform the essential functions of the employment position that such individual holds or desires. For the purposes of this title, consideration shall be given to the employer's judgment as to what functions of a job are essential, and if an employer has prepared a written description before advertising or interviewing applicants for the job, this description shall be considered evidence of the essential functions of the job.

(9) **Reasonable accommodation.**—The term "reasonable accommodation" may include—

(A) making existing facilities used by employees readily accessible to and usable by individuals with disabilities; and

(B) job restructuring, part-time or modified work schedules, reassignment to a vacant position, acquisition or modification of equipment or devices, appropriate adjustment or modifications of examinations, training materials or policies, the provision of qualified readers or interpreters, and other similar accommodations for individuals with disabilities.

(10) **Undue Hardship.**—

(A) **In general.**—The term "undue hardship" means an action requiring significant difficulty or expense, when considered in light of the factors set forth in subparagraph (B).

(B) **Factors to be considered.**—In determining whether an accommodation would impose an undue hardship on a covered entity, factors to be considered include—

(i) the nature and cost of accommodation needed under this Act;

(ii) the overall financial resources of the facility or facilities involved in the provision of the reasonable accommodation; the number of persons employed at such facility; the effect on expenses and resources, or the impact otherwise of such accommodation upon the operation of the facility;

(iii) the overall financial resources of the covered entity; the overall size of the business of a covered entity with respect to the number of its employees; the number, type, and location of its facilities; and

(iv) the type of operation or operations of the covered entity, including the composition, structure, and functions of the workforce of such entity; the geographic separateness, administrative, or fiscal relationship of the facility or facilities in question to the covered entity.

Sec. 102. Discrimination.

(a) **General Rule.**—No covered entity shall discriminate against a qualified individual with a disability because of the disability of such individual in regard to job application procedures, the hiring, advancement, or discharge of employees, employee compensation, job training, and other terms, conditions, and privileges of employment.

(b) **Construction.**—As used in subsection (a), the term "discriminate" includes—

(1) limiting, segregating, or classifying a job applicant or employee in a way that adversely affects the opportunities or status of such applicant or employee because of the disability of such applicant or employee;

(2) participating in a contractual or other arrangement or relationship that has the effect of subjecting a covered entity's qualified applicant or employee with a disability to the discrimination prohibited by this title (such relationship includes a relationship with an employment or referral agency, labor union, an organization providing fringe benefits to an employee of the covered entity, or an organization providing training and apprenticeship programs);

(3) utilizing standards, criteria, or methods of administration—

(A) that have the effect of discrimination on the basis of disability; or

(B) that perpetuate the discrimination of others who are subject to common administrative control;

(4) excluding or otherwise denying equal jobs or benefits to a qualified individual because of the known disability of an individual with whom the qualified individual is known to have a relationship or association;

(5)

(A) not making reasonable accommodations to the known physical or mental limitations of an otherwise qualified individual with a disability who is an applicant or employee, unless such covered entity can demonstrate that the accommodation would impose an undue hardship on the operation of the business of such covered entity; or

(B) denying employment opportunities to a job applicant or employee who is an otherwise qualified individual with a disability, if such denial is based on the need of such covered entity to make reasonable accommodation to the physical or mental impairments of the employee or applicant;

(6) using qualification standards, employment tests or other selection criteria that screen out or tend to screen out an individual with a disability or a class of individuals with disabilities unless the standard, test or other selection criteria, as used by the covered entity, is shown to be job-related for the position in question and is consistent with business necessity; and

(7) failing to select and administer tests concerning employment in the most effective manner to ensure that, when such test is administered to a job applicant or employee who has a disability that impairs sensory, manual, or speaking skills, such test results accurately reflect the skills, aptitude, or whatever other factor of such applicant or employee that such test purports to measure, rather than reflecting the impaired sensory, manual, or speaking skills of such employee or applicant (except where such skills are the factors that the test purports to measure). * * *

Sec. 104. Illegal Use of Drugs and Alcohol. * * *

(b) **Rules of Construction.**—Nothing in subsection (a) shall be construed to exclude as a qualified individual with a disability an individual who—

(1) has successfully completed a supervised drug rehabilitation program and is no longer engaging in the illegal use of drugs, or has otherwise been rehabilitated successfully and is no longer engaging in such use;

(2) is participating in a supervised rehabilitation program and is no longer engaging in such use; or

(3) is erroneously regarded as engaging in such use, but is not engaging in such use; except that it shall not be a violation of this Act for a covered entity to adopt or administer reasonable policies or procedures, including but not limited to drug testing, designed to ensure that an individual described in paragraph (1) or (2) is no longer engaging in the illegal use of drugs. * * *

Sec. 107. Enforcement.

(a) **Powers, Remedies, and Procedures.**—The powers, remedies, and procedures set forth in sections 705, 706, 707, 709, and 710 of the Civil Rights Act of 1964 (42 U.S.C. 2000e-4, 2000e-5, 2000e-6, 2000e-8, and 2000e-9) shall be the powers, remedies, and procedures this title provides to the Commission, to the Attorney General, or to any person alleging discrimination on the basis of disability in violation of any provision of this Act, or regulations promulgated under section 106, concerning employment.

(b) **Coordination.**—The agencies with enforcement authority for actions which allege employment discrimination under this title and under the Rehabilitation Act of 1973 shall develop procedures to ensure that administrative complaints filed under this title and under the Rehabilitation Act of 1973 are dealt with in a manner that avoids duplication of effort and prevents imposition of inconsistent or conflicting standards for the same requirements under this title and the Rehabilitation Act of 1973. The Commission, the Attorney General, and the Office of Federal Contract Compliance Programs shall establish such coordinating mechanisms (similar to provisions contained in the joint regulations promulgated by the Commission and the Attorney General at part 42 of title 28 and part 1691 of title 29, Code of Federal Regulations, and the Memorandum of Understanding between the Commission and the Office of Federal Contract Compliance Programs dated January 16, 1981 (46 Fed. Reg. 7435, January 23, 1981)) in regulations implementing this title and Rehabilitation Act of 1973 not later than 18 months after the date of enactment of this Act.

Sec. 108. Effective Date.

This title shall become effective 24 months after the date of enactment.

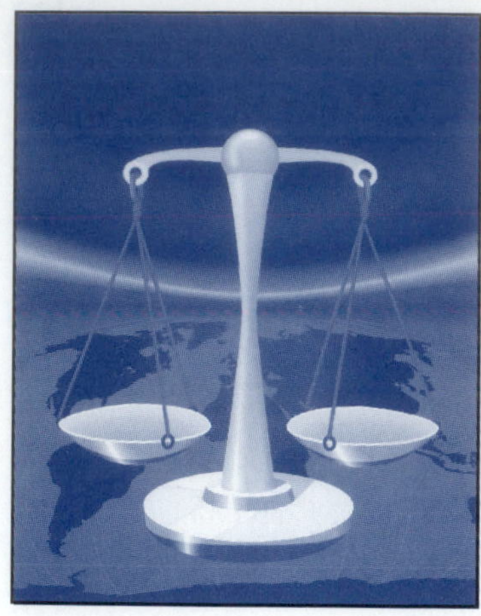

Appendix K

Civil Rights Act of 1991 (Excerpts)

Section 3. Purposes.

The purposes of this Act are—

(1) to provide appropriate remedies for intentional discrimination and unlawful harassment in the workplace;

(2) to codify the concepts of "business necessity" and "job related" enunciated by the Supreme Court in *Griggs v. Duke Power Co.*, 401 U.S. 424 (1971), and in the other Supreme Court decisions prior to *Wards Cove Packing Co. v. Atonio*, 490 U.S. 642 (1989);

(3) to confirm statutory authority and provide statutory guidelines for the adjudication of disparate impact suits under title VII of the Civil Rights Act of 1964 (42 U.S.C. 2000e *et seq.*); and

(4) to respond to recent decisions of the Supreme Court by expanding the scope of relevant civil rights statutes in order to provide adequate protection to victims of discrimination.

Section 101. Prohibition against All Racial Discrimination in the Making and Enforcement of Contracts.

Section 1977 of the Revised Statutes (42 U.S.C. 1981) is amended * * * by adding at the end the following new subsections:

(b) For purposes of this section, the term "make and enforce contracts" includes the making, performance, modification, and termination of contracts, and the enjoyment of all benefits, privileges, terms, and conditions of the contractual relationship.

(c) The rights protected by this section are protected against impairment by nongovernmental discrimination and impairment under color of State law.

Section 102. Damages in Cases of Intentional Discrimination.

The Revised Statutes are amended by inserting after section 1977 (42 U.S.C.1981) the following new section:

Section 1977A. Damages in Cases of Intentional Discrimination in Employment.

(a) Right of Recovery.—

(1) Civil Rights.—In an action brought by a complaining party under section 706 or 717 of the Civil Rights Act of 1964 (42 U.S.C. 2000e-5) against a respondent who engaged in unlawful intentional discrimination (not an employment practice that is unlawful because of its disparate impact) prohibited under section 703, 704, or 717 of the Act (42 U.S.C. 2000e-2 or 2000e-3), and provided that the complaining party cannot recover under section 1977 of the Revised Statutes (42 U.S.C.1981), the complaining party may recover compensatory and punitive damages as allowed in subsection (b), in addition to any relief authorized by section 706(g) of the Civil Rights Act of 1964, from the respondent.

* * * *

(b) Compensatory and Punitive Damages.—

(1) Determination of Punitive Damages.—A complaining party may recover punitive damages under this section against a respondent (other than a government, government agency or political subdivision) if the complaining party demonstrates that the respondent engaged in a discriminatory practice or discriminatory practices with malice or with reckless indifference to the federally protected rights of an aggrieved individual.

(2) Exclusions from Compensatory Damages.—Compensatory damages awarded under this section shall not include backpay, interest on backpay, or any other type of relief authorized under section 706(g) of the Civil Rights Act of 1964.

(3) Limitations.—The sum of the amount of compensatory damages awarded under this section for future pecuniary losses, emotional pain, suffering, inconvenience, mental anguish, loss of enjoyment of life, and other nonpecuniary losses, and the amount of punitive damages awarded under this section, shall not exceed, for each complaining party—

(A) in the case of a respondent who has more than 14 and fewer than 101 employees in each of 20 or more calendar weeks in the current or preceding calendar year, $50,000;

(B) in the case of a respondent who has more than 100 and fewer than 201 employees in each of 20 or more calendar weeks in the current or preceding calendar year, $100,000; and

(C) in the case of a respondent who has more than 200 and fewer than 501 employees in each of 20 or more calendar weeks in the current or preceding calendar year, $200,000; and

(D) in the case of a respondent who has more than 500 employees in each of 20 or more calendar weeks in the current or preceding calendar year, $300,000.

* * * *

Section 105. Burden of Proof in Disparate Impact Cases.

(a) Section 703 of the Civil Rights Act of 1964 (42 U.S.C. 2000e-2) is amended by adding at the end the following new [subsections to 703(k)(1)]—

(A) An unlawful employment practice based on disparate impact is established under this title only if—

(i) a complaining party demonstrates that a respondent uses a particular employment practice that causes a disparate impact on the basis of race, color, religion, sex, or national origin and the respondent fails to demonstrate that the challenged practice is job related for the position in question and consistent with business necessity; or

(ii) the complaining party makes the demonstration described in subparagraph (C) with respect to an alternative employment practice and the respondent refuses to adopt such alternative employment practice.

* * * *

(C) The demonstration referred to by subparagraph (A)(ii) shall be in accordance with the law as it existed on June 4, 1989, with respect to the concept of "alternative employment practice."

* * * *

Section 107. Clarifying Prohibition against Impermissible Consideration of Race, Color, Religion, Sex, or National Origin in Employment Practices.

(a) In General.—Section 703 of the Civil Rights Act of 1964 (42 U.S.C. 2000e-2) (as amended by sections 105 and 106) is further amended by adding at the end the following new subsection:

(m) Except as otherwise provided in this title, an unlawful employment practice is established when the complaining party demonstrates that race, color, religion, sex, or national origin was a motivating factor for any employment practice, even though other factors also motivated the practice.

* * * *

Section 109. Protection of Extraterritorial Employment.

(a) Definition of Employee.—Section 701(f) of the Civil Rights Act of 1964 (42 U.S.C. 2000e(f)) and section 101(4) of the Americans with Disabilities Act of 1990 (42 U.S.C. 12111(4)) are each amended by adding at the end the following: "With respect to employment in a foreign country, such term includes an individual who is a citizen of the United States."

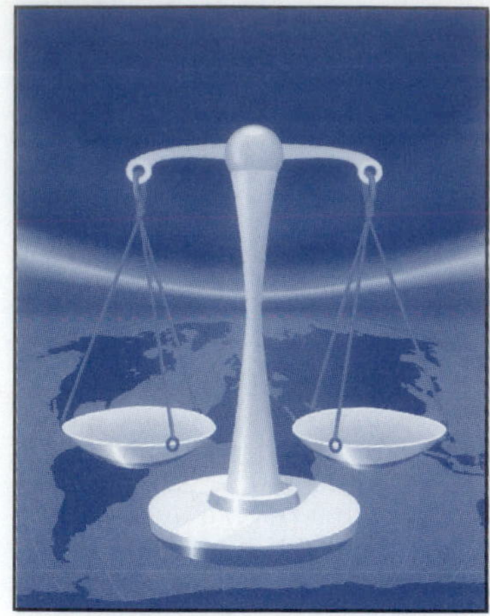

Appendix L

Spanish Equivalents for Important Legal Terms in English

Abandoned property: bienes abandonados
Acceptance: aceptación; consentimiento; acuerdo
Acceptor: aceptante
Accession: toma de posesión; aumento; accesión
Accommodation indorser: avalista de favor
Accommodation party: firmante de favor
Accord: acuerdo; convenio; arregio
Accord and satisfaction: transacción ejecutada
Act of state doctrine: doctrina de acto de gobierno
Administrative law: derecho administrativo
Administrative process: procedimiento o metódo administrativo
Administrator: administrador (-a)
Adverse possession: posesión de hecho susceptible de proscripción adquisitiva
Affirmative action: acción afirmativa
Affirmative defense: defensa afirmativa
After-acquired property: bienes adquiridos con posterioridad a un hecho dado
Agency: mandato; agencia
Agent: mandatorio; agente; representante
Agreement: convenio; acuerdo; contrato
Alien corporation: empresa extranjera
Allonge: hojas adicionales de endosos
Answer: contestación de la demande; alegato
Anticipatory repudiation: anuncio previo de las partes de su imposibilidad de cumplir con el contrato
Appeal: apelación; recurso de apelación
Appellate jurisdiction: jurisdicción de apelaciones
Appraisal right: derecho de valuación
Arbitration: arbitraje
Arson: incendio intencional
Articles of partnership: contrato social
Artisan's lien: derecho de retención que ejerce al artesano
Assault: asalto; ataque; agresión
Assignment of rights: transmisión; transferencia; cesión
Assumption of risk: no resarcimiento por exposición voluntaria al peligro
Attachment: auto judicial que autoriza el embargo; embargo

Bailee: depositario
Bailment: depósito; constitución en depósito
Bailor: depositante
Bankruptcy trustee: síndico de la quiebra
Battery: agresión; física
Bearer: portador; tenedor
Bearer instrument: documento al portador
Bequest or legacy: legado (de bienes muebles)
Bilateral contract: contrato bilateral
Bill of lading: conocimiento de embarque; carta de porte
Bill of Rights: declaración de derechos
Binder: póliza de seguro provisoria; recibo de pago a cuenta del precio
Blank indorsement: endoso en blanco
Blue sky laws: leyes reguladoras del comercio bursátil
Bond: título de crédito; garantía; caución
Bond indenture: contrato de emisión de bonos; contrato del ampréstito
Breach of contract: incumplimiento de contrato
Brief: escrito; resumen; informe
Burglary: violación de domicilio
Business judgment rule: regla de juicio comercial
Business tort: agravio comercial

Case law: ley de casos; derecho casuístico
Cashier's check: cheque de caja
Causation in fact: causalidad en realidad
Cease-and-desist order: orden para cesar y desistir
Certificate of deposit: certificado de depósito
Certified check: cheque certificado
Charitable trust: fideicomiso para fines benéficos
Chattel: bien mueble
Check: cheque
Chose in action: derecho inmaterial; derecho de acción
Civil law: derecho civil
Close corporation: sociedad de un solo accionista o de un grupo restringido de accionistas
Closed shop: taller agremiado (emplea solamente a miembros de un gremio)
Closing argument: argumento al final
Codicil: codicilo
Collateral: guarantía; bien objeto de la guarantía real
Comity: cortesía; cortesía entre naciones
Commercial paper: instrumentos negociables; documentos a valores commerciales
Common law: derecho consuetudinario; derecho común; ley común
Common stock: acción ordinaria
Comparative negligence: negligencia comparada
Compensatory damages: daños y perjuicios reales o compensatorios

Concurrent conditions: condiciones concurrentes
Concurrent jurisdiction: competencia concurrente de varios tribunales para entender en una misma causa
Concurring opinion: opinión concurrente
Condition: condición
Condition precedent: condición suspensiva
Condition subsequent: condición resolutoria
Confiscation: confiscación
Confusion: confusión; fusión
Conglomerate merger: fusión de firmas que operan en distintos mercados
Consent decree: acuerdo entre las partes aprobado por un tribunal
Consequential damages: daños y perjuicios indirectos
Consideration: consideración; motivo; contraprestación
Consolidation: consolidación
Constructive delivery: entrega simbólica
Constructive trust: fideicomiso creado por aplicación de la ley
Consumer-protection law: ley para proteger el consumidor
Contract: contrato
Contract under seal: contrato formal o sellado
Contributory negligence: negligencia de la parte actora
Conversion: usurpación; conversión de valores
Copyright: derecho de autor
Corporation: sociedad anómina; corporación; persona juridica
Co-sureties: cogarantes
Counterclaim: reconvención; contrademanda
Counteroffer: contraoferta
Course of dealing: curso de transacciones
Course of performance: curso de cumplimiento
Covenant: pacto; garantía; contrato
Covenant not to sue: pacto or contrato a no demandar
Covenant of quiet enjoyment: garantía del uso y goce pacífico del inmueble
Creditors' composition agreement: concordato preventivo
Crime: crimen; delito; contravención
Criminal law: derecho penal
Cross-examination: contrainterrogatorio
Cure: cura; cuidado; derecho de remediar un vicio contractual
Customs receipts: recibos de derechos aduaneros

Damages: daños; indemnización por daños y perjuicios
Debit card: tarjeta de dé bito
Debtor: deudor
Debt securities: seguridades de deuda
Deceptive advertising: publicidad engañosa
Deed: escritura; título; acta translativa de domino
Defamation: difamación
Delegation of duties: delegación de obligaciones
Demand deposit: depósito a la vista
Depositions: declaración de un testigo fuera del tribunal
Devise: legado; deposición testamentaria (bienes inmuebles)
Directed verdict: veredicto según orden del juez y sin participación activa del jurado
Direct examination: interrogatorio directo; primer interrogatorio
Disaffirmance: repudiación; renuncia; anulación
Discharge: descargo; liberación; cumplimiento
Disclosed principal: mandante revelado
Discovery: descubrimiento; producción de la prueba
Dissenting opinion: opinión disidente
Dissolution: disolución; terminación
Diversity of citizenship: competencia de los tribunales federales para entender en causas cuyas partes intervinientes son cuidadanos de distintos estados
Divestiture: extinción premature de derechos reales
Dividend: dividendo
Docket: orden del día; lista de causas pendientes
Domestic corporation: sociedad local
Draft: orden de pago; letrade cambio
Drawee: girado; beneficiario
Drawer: librador
Duress: coacción; violencia

Easement: servidumbre
Embezzlement: desfalco; malversación
Eminent domain: poder de expropiación
Employment discrimination: discriminación en el empleo
Entrepreneur: empresario
Environmental law: ley ambiental
Equal dignity rule: regla de dignidad egual
Equity security: tipo de participación en una sociedad
Estate: propiedad; patrimonio; derecho
Estop: impedir; prevenir
Ethical issue: cuestión ética
Exclusive jurisdiction: competencia exclusiva
Exculpatory clause: cláusula eximente
Executed contract: contrato ejecutado
Execution: ejecución; cumplimiento
Executor: albacea
Executory contract: contrato aún no completamente consumado
Executory interest: derecho futuro
Express contract: contrato expreso
Expropriation: expropriación

Federal question: caso federal
Fee simple: pleno dominio; dominio absoluto
Fee simple absolute: dominio absoluto
Fee simple defeasible: dominio sujeta a una condición resolutoria
Felony: crimen; delito grave
Fictitious payee: beneficiario ficticio
Fiduciary: fiduciaro
Firm offer: oferta en firme
Fixture: inmueble por destino, incorporación a anexación
Floating lien: gravamen continuado
Foreign corporation: sociedad extranjera; U.S. sociedad constituída en otro estado
Forgery: falso; falsificación
Formal contract: contrato formal
Franchise: privilegio; franquicia; concesión
Franchisee: persona que recibe una concesión
Franchisor: persona que vende una concesión
Fraud: fraude; dolo; engaño
Future interest: bien futuro

Garnishment: embargo de derechos
General partner: socio comanditario
General warranty deed: escritura translativa de domino con garantía de título
Gift: donación
Gift *causa mortis*: donación por causa de muerte
Gift *inter vivos*: donación entre vivos
Good faith: buena fe
Good-faith purchaser: comprador de buena fe

Holder: tenedor por contraprestación
Holder in due course: tenedor legítimo
Holographic will: testamento olográfico
Homestead exemption laws: leyes que exceptúan las casas de familia de ejecución por duedas generales
Horizontal merger: fusión horizontal

Identification: identificación
Implied-in-fact contract: contrato implícito en realidad
Implied warranty: guarantía implícita
Implied warranty of merchantability: garantía implícita de vendibilidad
Impossibility of performance: imposibilidad de cumplir un contrato
Imposter: imposter
Incidental beneficiary: beneficiario incidental; beneficiario secundario
Incidental damages: daños incidentales
Indictment: auto de acusación; acusación
Indorsee: endorsatario
Indorsement: endoso
Indorser: endosante
Informal contract: contrato no formal; contrato verbal
Information: acusación hecha por el ministerio público
Injunction: mandamiento; orden de no innovar
Innkeeper's lien: derecho de retención que ejerce el posadero
Installment contract: contrato de pago en cuotas
Insurable interest: interés asegurable
Intended beneficiary: beneficiario destinado
Intentional tort: agravio; cuasi-delito intenciónal
International law: derecho internaciónal
Interrogatories: preguntas escritas sometidas por una parte a la otra o a un testigo
***Inter vivos* trust**: fideicomiso entre vivos
Intestacy laws: leyes de la condición de morir intestado
Intestate: intestado
Investment company: compañia de inversiones
Issue: emisión

Joint tenancy: derechos conjuntos en un bien inmueble en favor del beneficiario sobreviviente
Judgment *n.o.v.*: juicio no obstante veredicto
Judgment rate of interest: interés de juicio
Judicial process: acto de procedimiento; proceso jurídico
Judicial review: revisión judicial
Jurisdiction: jurisdicción

Larceny: robo; hurto
Law: derecho; ley; jurisprudencia
Lease: contrato de locación; contrato de alquiler
Leasehold estate: bienes forales
Legal rate of interest: interés legal
Legatee: legatario
Letter of credit: carta de crédito
Levy: embargo; comiso
Libel: libelo; difamación escrita
Life estate: usufructo
Limited partner: comanditario
Limited partnership: sociedad en comandita
Liquidation: liquidación; realización
Lost property: objetos perdidos

Majority opinion: opinión de la mayoría
Maker: persona que realiza u ordena; librador
Mechanic's lien: gravamen de constructor
Mediation: mediación; intervención
Merger: fusión
Mirror image rule: fallo de reflejo
Misdemeanor: infracción; contravención
Mislaid property: bienes extraviados
Mitigation of damages: reducción de daños
Mortgage: hypoteca
Motion to dismiss: excepción parentoria
Mutual fund: fondo mutual

Negotiable instrument: instrumento negociable
Negotiation: negociación
Nominal damages: daños y perjuicios nominales
Novation: novación
Nuncupative will: testamento nuncupativo

Objective theory of contracts: teoria objetiva de contratos
Offer: oferta
Offeree: persona que recibe una oferta
Offeror: oferente
Order instrument: instrumento o documento a la orden
Original jurisdiction: jurisdicción de primera instancia
Output contract: contrato de producción

Parol evidence rule: regla relativa a la prueba oral
Partially disclosed principal: mandante revelado en parte
Partnership: sociedad colectiva; asociación; asociación de participación
Past consideration: causa o contraprestación anterior
Patent: patente; privilegio
Pattern or practice: muestra o práctica
Payee: beneficiario de un pago
Penalty: pena; penalidad
Per capita: por cabeza
Perfection: perfeción
Performance: cumplimiento; ejecución
Personal defenses: excepciones personales
Personal property: bienes muebles
Per stirpes: por estirpe
Plea bargaining: regateo por un alegato
Pleadings: alegatos
Pledge: prenda
Police powers: poders de policia y de prevención del crimen
Policy: póliza
Positive law: derecho positivo; ley positiva
Possibility of reverter: posibilidad de reversión
Precedent: precedente
Preemptive right: derecho de prelación
Preferred stock: acciones preferidas
Premium: recompensa; prima
Presentment warranty: garantía de presentación
Price discrimination: discriminación en los precios
Principal: mandante; principal
Privity: nexo jurídico
Privity of contract: relación contractual
Probable cause: causa probable
Probate: verificación; verificación del testamento
Probate court: tribunal de sucesiones y tutelas
Proceeds: resultados; ingresos
Profit: beneficio; utilidad; lucro
Promise: promesa
Promisee: beneficiario de una promesa
Promisor: promtente
Promissory estoppel: impedimento promisorio
Promissory note: pagaré; nota de pago
Promoter: promotor; fundador
Proximate cause: causa inmediata o próxima
Proxy: apoderado; poder
Punitive, or exemplary, damages: daños y perjuicios punitivos o ejemplares

Qualified indorsement: endoso con reservas
Quasi contract: contrato tácito o implícito
Quitclaim deed: acto de transferencia de una propiedad por finiquito, pero sin ninguna garantía sobre la validez del título transferido

Ratification: ratificación
Real property: bienes inmuebles
Reasonable doubt: duda razonable
Rebuttal: refutación
Recognizance: promesa; compromiso;

reconocimiento
Recording statutes: leyes estatales sobre registros oficiales
Redress: reporacíon
Reformation: rectificación; reforma; corrección
Rejoinder: dúplica; contrarréplica
Release: liberación; renuncia a un derecho
Remainder: substitución; reversión
Remedy: recurso; remedio; reparación
Replevin: acción reivindicatoria; reivindicación
Reply: réplica
Requirements contract: contrato de suministro
Rescission: rescisión
Res judicata: cosa juzgada; res judicata
Respondeat superior: responsabilidad del mandante o del maestro
Restitution: restitución
Restrictive indorsement: endoso restrictivo
Resulting trust: fideicomiso implícito
Reversion: reversión; sustitución
Revocation: revocación; derogación
Right of contribution: derecho de contribución
Right of reimbursement: derecho de reembolso
Right of subrogation: derecho de subrogación
Right-to-work law: ley de libertad de trabajo
Robbery: robo
Rule 10b-5: Regla 10b-5

Sale: venta; contrato de compreventa
Sale on approval: venta a ensayo; venta sujeta a la aprobación del comprador
Sale or return: venta con derecho de devolución
Sales contract: contrato de compraventa; boleto de compraventa
Satisfaction: satisfacción; pago
Scienter: a sabiendas
S corporation: S corporación
Secured party: acreedor garantizado
Secured transaction: transacción garantizada
Securities: volares; titulos; seguridades
Security agreement: convenio de seguridad
Security interest: interés en un bien dado en garantía que permite a quien lo detenta venderlo en caso de incumplimiento
Service mark: marca de identificación de servicios
Shareholder's derivative suit: acción judicial entablada por un accionista en nombre de la sociedad
Signature: firma; rúbrica
Slander: difamación oral; calumnia
Sovereign immunity: immunidad soberana
Special indorsement: endoso especial; endoso a la orden de una person en particular
Specific performance: ejecución precisa, según los términos del contrato
Spendthrift trust: fideicomiso para pródigos
Stale check: cheque vencido
Stare decisis: acatar las decisiones, observar los precedentes
Statutory law: derecho estatutario; derecho legislado; derecho escrito
Stock: acciones
Stock warrant: certificado para la compra de acciones
Stop-payment order: orden de suspensión del pago de un cheque dada por el librador del mismo
Strict liability: responsabilidad uncondicional
Summary judgment: fallo sumario

Tangible property: bienes corpóreos
Tenancy at will: inguilino por tiempo indeterminado (según la voluntad del propietario)
Tenancy by sufferance: posesión por tolerancia
Tenancy by the entirety: locación conyugal conjunta
Tenancy for years: inguilino por un término fijo
Tenancy in common: specie de copropiedad indivisa
Tender: oferta de pago; oferta de ejecución
Testamentary trust: fideicomiso testamentario
Testator: testador (-a)
Third party beneficiary contract: contrato para el beneficio del tercero-beneficiario
Tort: agravio; cuasi-delito
Totten trust: fideicomiso creado por un depósito bancario
Trade acceptance: letra de cambio aceptada
Trademark: marca registrada
Trade name: nombre comercial; razón social
Traveler's check: cheque del viajero
Trespass to land: ingreso no authorizado a las tierras de otro
Trespass to personal property: violación de los derechos posesorios de un tercero con respecto a bienes muebles
Trust: fideicomiso; trust

Ultra vires: ultra vires; fuera de la facultad (de una sociedad anónima)
Unanimous opinion: opinión unámine
Unconscionable contract or clause: contrato leonino; cláusula leonino
Underwriter: subscriptor; asegurador
Unenforceable contract: contrato que no se puede hacer cumplir
Unilateral contract: contrato unilateral
Union shop: taller agremiado; empresa en la que todos los empleados son miembros del gremio o sindicato
Universal defenses: defensas legitimas o legales
Usage of trade: uso comercial
Usury: usura

Valid contract: contrato válido
Venue: lugar; sede del proceso
Vertical merger: fusión vertical de empresas
Voidable contract: contrato anulable
Void contract: contrato nulo; contrato inválido, sin fuerza legal
Voir dire: examen preliminar de un testigo a jurado por el tribunal para determinar su competencia
Voting trust: fideicomiso para ejercer el derecho de voto

Waiver: renuncia; abandono
Warranty of habitability: garantía de habitabilidad
Watered stock: acciones diluídos; capital inflado
White-collar crime: crimen administrativo
Writ of attachment: mandamiento de ejecución; mandamiento de embargo
Writ of *certiorari*: auto de avocación; auto de certiorari
Writ of execution: auto ejecutivo; mandamiento de ejecutión
Writ of mandamus: auto de mandamus; mandamiento; orden judicial

Glossary

A

Abandoned property Property with which the owner has voluntarily parted, with no intention of recovering it.

Accord and Satisfaction An agreement between the parties to allow discharge of a contract by a performance different from the performance originally contracted.

Acceleration clause A clause in an installment contract that provides for all future payments to become due immediately upon the failure to tender timely payments or upon the occurrence of a specified event.

Acceptance (1) In contract law, the offeree's notification to the offeror that the offeree agrees to be bound by the terms of the offeror's proposal. Although historically the terms of acceptance had to be the mirror image of the terms of the offer, the UCC provides that even modified terms of the offer in a definite expression of acceptance constitute a contract. (2) In commercial paper law, the drawee's signed agreement to pay a draft when presented.

Acceptor A drawee who accepts a draft and who engages to be primarily responsible for its payment.

Accession A principle by which the owner or the improver of personal property becomes entitled to all that the property produces, or all that is added to it, or the property in a changed form.

Accommodation party A person who signs an instrument for the purpose of lending his or her credit to another party on the instrument.

Accredited investors In the context of securities offerings, "sophisticated" investors, such as banks, insurance companies, investment companies, the issuer's executive officers and directors, and persons whose income or net worth exceeds certain limits.

Act of state doctrine A doctrine that provides that the judicial branch of one country will not examine the validity of public acts committed by a recognized foreign government within its own territory.

Actionable Capable of serving as the basis of a lawsuit. An actionable claim can be pursued in a lawsuit or other court action.

Actual malice Real and demonstrable evil intent. In a defamation suit, a statement made about a public figure normally must be made with actual malice (with either knowledge of its falsity or a reckless disregard of the truth) for liability to be incurred.

Adjudication The act of rendering a judicial decision. In the administrative process, the proceeding in which an administrative law judge hears and decides on issues that arise when an administrative agency charges a person or a firm with violating a law or regulation enforced by the agency.

Adhesion contract A contract, such as one drafted by a large retailer on a standard form for a consumer signature, in which the stronger party (retailer) dictates the terms.

Administrative agency A federal or state government agency established to perform a specific function. Administrative agencies are authorized by legislative acts to make and enforce rules relating to the purpose for which they were established.

Administrative law Body of law created by administrative agencies—such as the Securities and Exchange Commission and the Federal Trade Commission—in the form of rules, regulations, orders, and decisions in order to carry out their duties and responsibilities. This law can initially be enforced by these agencies outside the judicial process.

Administrative law judge One who presides over an administrative agency hearing and who has the power to administer oaths, take testimony, rule on questions of evidence, and make determinations of fact.

Administrative process The procedure used by administrative agencies in the administration of law.

Administrator One who is appointed by a court to handle the probate (disposition) of a person's estate if that person dies intestate (without a will).

Adverse possession The acquisition of title to real property by occupying it openly, without the consent of the owner, for a period of time specified by state statutes. The occupation must be actual, open, notorious, exclusive, and in opposition to all others, including the owner.

Affidavit A written or printed voluntary statement of facts, confirmed by the oath or affirmation of the party making it and made before a person having the authority to administer the oath or affirmation.

Affirmative action Job-hiring policies that give special consideration or compensatory treatment to minority groups in an effort to overcome present effects of past discrimination.

Affirmative defense A response to a plaintiff's claim that does not deny the plaintiff's facts but attacks the plaintiff's legal right to bring an action. An example is the running of the statute of limitations.

After-acquired property Property of the debtor that is acquired after a secured creditor's interest in the debtor's property has been created.

Agency A relationship between two persons in which, by agreement or otherwise, one is bound by the words and acts of the other. The former is a *principal*; the latter is an *agent*.

Agent A person authorized by another to act for or in place of him or her.

Aggressor The acquiring corporation in a takeover attempt.

Agreement A meeting of two or more minds; often used as a synonym for a contract.

Alien corporation A designation in the United States for a corporation formed in another country but doing business in the United States.

Alienation A term used to define the process of transferring land out of one's ownership (thus "alienating" the land from oneself).

Allonge A piece of paper firmly attached to a negotiable instrument, upon which transferees can make indorsements if there is no room left on the instrument itself.

Alternative dispute resolution (ADR) The resolution of disputes in ways other than those involved in the traditional judicial process. Mediation and arbitration are forms of ADR.

Amend To change and improve through a formal procedure.

American Arbitration Association (AAA) The major organization offering arbitration services in the United States.

Answer Procedurally, a defendant's response to the complaint.

Anticipatory repudiation An assertion or action by a party indicating that he or she will not perform an obligation that the party is contractually obligated to perform at a future time.

Antitrust laws The body of federal and state laws protecting commerce from unlawful restraints, price discrimination, price fixing, and monopolies. The principal federal antitrust statutes are the Sherman Act (1890), the Clayton Act (1914), and the Federal Trade Commission Act (1914).

Appellant The party who takes an appeal from one court to another; sometimes referred to as the petitioner.

Appellee The party against whom an appeal is taken—that is, the party who opposes setting aside or reversing the judgment; sometimes referred to as the respondent.

Appraisal right A dissenting shareholder's right, if he or she objects to an extraordinary transaction of the corporation (such as a merger or consolidation), to have his or her shares appraised and to be paid the fair market value of his or her shares by the corporation.

Appropriate bargaining unit A designation, based on job duties, skills levels, and other occupational characteristics, of the proper entity covered by a collective-bargaining agreement.

Appropriation In tort law, the act of making a thing one's own or exercising or making use of an object to subserve one's own interest. When the act is wrongful, a tort is committed.

Arbitration The settling of a dispute by submitting it to a disinterested third party (other than a court), who renders a legally binding decision.

Arbitration clause A clause in a contract that provides that, in case of a dispute, the parties will determine their rights by arbitration rather than through the judicial system.

Arson The malicious burning of another's dwelling. Some statutes have expanded this to include any real property regardless of ownership and the destruction of property by other means—for example, by explosion.

Articles of incorporation The document filed with the appropriate governmental agency, usually the secretary of state, when a business is incorporated; state statutes usually prescribe what kind of information must be contained in the articles of incorporation.

Articles of partnership A written agreement that sets forth each partner's rights in, and obligations to, the partnership.

Artisan's lien A possessory lien given to a person who has made improvements and added value to another person's personal property as security for payment for services performed.

Assault Any word or action intended to make another person fearful of immediate physical harm; a reasonably believable threat.

Assignment The act of transferring to another all or part of one's rights arising under a contract.

Assumption of risk A doctrine whereby a plaintiff may not recover for injuries or damages suffered from risks he or she knows of and assents to. A defense against negligence that can be used when the plaintiff has knowledge of and appreciates a danger and voluntarily exposes himself or herself to the danger.

Attachment (1) In a secured transaction, the process by which a security interest in the property of another becomes enforceable. (2) The legal process of seizing another's property in accordance with a writ or judicial order for the purpose of securing satisfaction of a judgment yet to be rendered.

Attempted monopolization Any actions by a firm to eliminate competition and gain monopoly power.

Authorization card A card signed by an employee that gives a union permission to act on his or her behalf in negotiations with management once a majority of the employees have signed the cards.

Automatic stay A suspension of all judicial proceedings upon the occurrence of an independent event. Under the Bankruptcy Code, the moment a petition to commence bankruptcy proceedings is filed, all litigation and other actions by creditors against a debtor and the debtor's property are suspended.

Award As a noun, the decision rendered by an arbitrator or other extrajudicial decider of a controversy. As a verb, to give or assign by sentence, judicial determination, or otherwise after a careful weighing of evidence, as when a jury awards damages.

B

Bailee One to whom goods are entrusted by a bailor.
Bailment An agreement in which goods or personal property of one person (a bailor) are entrusted to another (a bailee), who is obligated to return the bailed property to the bailor or dispose of it as directed.
Bailor One who entrusts goods to a bailee.
Bait-and-switch advertising Advertising a product at a very attractive price (the "bait") and then informing the consumer, once he or she is in the store, that the advertised product is either not available or is of poor quality; the customer is then urged to purchase ("switched" to) a more expensive item.
Battery The unprivileged, intentional touching of another.
Beachhead acquisition In military terminology, a beachhead is the establishment of an initial, significant inroad into the heart of the enemy's territory. In the terminology of corporate takeovers, a beachhead acquisition is the purchase by an aggressor corporation of a small but significant number of shares in a target company's stock to establish a position within the company from which the aggressor can launch a full-fledged takeover attempt.
Bearer A person in the possession of an instrument payable to bearer or indorsed in blank.
Bearer instrument In the law of commercial paper, any instrument that is not payable to a specific person, including instruments payable to the bearer or to "cash."
Bequest A gift by will of personal property (from the verb—*to bequeath*).
Bilateral contract A contract that includes the exchange of a promise for a promise.
Bill of Rights The first ten amendments to the Constitution.
Binder A written, temporary insurance policy.
Blank indorsement An indorsement made by the mere writing of the indorser's name on the back of an instrument. Such indorsement causes an instrument, otherwise payable to order, to become payable to bearer and negotiated only by delivery.
Blood-shield statutes State statutes that insulate hospitals and other blood suppliers from warranty liability in the event that the recipient of transfused blood suffers sickness or death as a result of the transfused blood.
Blue laws State or local laws that make the performance of commercial activities on Sunday illegal.
Blue sky laws State laws that regulate the offer and sale of securities.
Bona fide occupational qualification (BFOQ) Under Title VII of the Civil Rights Act of 1964, identifiable characteristics reasonably necessary to the operation of a particular business. These characteristics can include gender, national origin, and religion, but not race.
Bona fide purchaser A buyer who purchases in good faith for value without notice of any defects in the title of the seller.
Bond indenture A contract between the issuer of a bond and the bondholder.
Bond A certificate that evidences a corporate debt. It is a security that involves no ownership interest in the issuing corporation.
Bounty payment A reward (payment) given to a person or persons who perform a certain service—such as informing legal authorities of illegal actions.
Breach of contract The failure, without legal excuse, of a promisor to perform the obligations of a contract.
Brief A written summary or statement prepared by one side in a lawsuit to explain its case to the judge; a typical brief has a facts summary, a law summary, and an argument about how the law applies to the facts.
Burglary The unlawful entry into a building with the intent to commit a felony. (Some state statutes expand this to include the intent to commit any crime.)
Business ethics Ethics in a business context; a consensus of what constitutes right or wrong behavior in the world of business and the application of moral principles to situations that arise in a business setting.
Business invitees Those people, such as customers or clients, who are invited onto business premises by the owner of those premises for business purposes.
Business judgment rule A rule that immunizes corporate management from liability for actions that are undertaken in good faith, when the actions are within both the power of the corporation and the authority of management to make.
Business necessity defense A showing that an employment practice that discriminates against members of a protected class is required for job performance.
Business tort A tort occurring within the business context; typical business torts are wrongful interference with the business or contractual relationships of others and unfair competition.
Bylaws A set of governing rules or regulations adopted by a corporation or other association.

C

Case law Rules of law announced in court decisions. Case law includes the aggregate of reported cases that interpret judicial precedents, statutes, regulations, and constitutional provisions.
Cashier's check A draft drawn by a bank on itself.
Categorical imperative A concept developed by the philosopher Immanual Kant as an ethical guideline for behavior. In deciding whether an action is right or wrong, or desirable or undesirable, a person should evaluate the action in terms of what would happen if everybody else in the same situation, or category, acted the same way.
Causation in fact An act or omission without which an event would not have occurred.

Cause of action A situation or set of facts that entitles a party to sustain a legal action against another and gives the party the right to seek a judicial remedy on his or her behalf.

Cease-and-desist order An administrative or judicial order prohibiting a person or business firm from conducting activities that an agency or court has deemed illegal.

Certificate of deposit An instrument evidencing a promissory acknowledgment by a bank of a receipt of money with an engagement to repay it.

Certificate of incorporation The primary document that evidences corporate existence (referred to as articles of incorporation in some states).

Certificate of limited partnership The basic document filed with a designated state official by which a limited partnership is formed.

Certified check A check drawn by an individual on his or her own account but bearing a signature guaranty (acceptance) by a bank that the bank will pay the check at the time the check is presented.

Charging order In partnership law, an order granted by a court to a judgment creditor that entitles the creditor to attach profits or assets of a partner upon dissolution of the partnership.

Charitable trust A trust in which the property held by a trustee must be used for a charitable purpose.

Chattel paper Any writing or writings that show both a debt and the fact that the debt is secured by personal property. In many instances, chattel paper consists of a negotiable instrument coupled with a security agreement.

Check A draft drawn by a drawer ordering the drawee bank or financial institution to pay a certain amount of money to the holder on demand.

Checks and balances The national government is composed of three separate branches: the executive, the legislative, and the judicial. Each branch of the government exercises a check upon the actions of the others.

Choice-of-language clause A clause in a contract designating the official language by which the contract will be interpreted in the event of a future disagreement over the contract's terms.

Choice-of-law clause A clause in a contract designating the law that will govern the contract. For example, two contracting parties from different countries may choose the law of a third country to govern their agreement.

Chose in action A right that can be enforced in court to recover a debt or to obtain damages.

Citation A citation indicates where a particular constitutional provision, statute, reported case, or article may be found; also an order for a defendant to appear in court or indicating that a person has violated a legal rule.

Civil law The branch of law dealing with the definition and enforcement of all private or public rights, as opposed to criminal matters.

Civil law system A system of law derived from that of the Roman Empire and based on a code rather than case law; the predominant system of law in the nations of continental Europe and the nations that were once their colonies. In the United States, Louisiana is the only state that has a civil law system.

Clearinghouse A system or a place where banks exchange checks and drafts drawn on each other and settle daily balances.

Close corporation A corporation whose shareholders are limited to a small group of persons, often including only family members. The rights of shareholders of a close corporation usually are restricted regarding the transfer of shares to others.

Closing argument An argument made after the plaintiff and defendant have rested their cases. Closing arguments are made prior to the jury charges.

Codicil A written supplement or modification to a will. Codicils must be executed with the same formalities as a will.

Collateral Any property used as security for a loan. Under the UCC, property of a debtor in which a creditor has an interest.

Collateral promise A secondary promise that is ancillary to a principal transaction or primary contractual relationship, such as a promise made by one person to pay the debts or discharge the duties of another if the latter fails to perform. A collateral promise normally must be in writing to be enforceable.

Collecting bank Any bank handling an item for collection, except the payor bank.

Collective bargaining The process by which labor and management negotiate the terms and conditions of employment, including such things as hours and workplace conditions.

Comity A deference by which one nation gives effect to the laws and judicial decrees of another nation. This recognition is based primarily upon respect.

Comment period A period of time following an administrative agency's publication of a notice of a proposed rule during which private parties may comment in writing on the proposal in an effort to influence agency policy. When the agency drafts the final version of the regulation, it considers any comments received.

Commerce clause The provision in Article I, Section 8, of the U.S. Constitution that gives Congress exclusive powers over interstate commerce.

Commercial impracticability A doctrine under which a seller may be excused from performing a contract when (1) a contingency occurs, (2) the contingency's occurrence makes performance impracticable, and (3) the nonoccurrence of the contingency was a basic assumption on which the contract was made. Despite the fact that UCC 2–615 expressly frees only sellers under this doctrine, courts have not distinguished between buyers and sellers in applying it.

Commercial paper Under UCC Article 3, negotiable instruments, including drafts, promissory notes, certificates of deposit, and checks.

Commingle To put funds or goods together into one mass so that the funds or goods are so mixed that they no longer have separate identities.

Common carriers Owners of trucks, railroads, airlines, ships, and other vehicles who offer transportation services to the public generally in return for compensation or a payment.

Common law That body of law developed from custom or judicial decisions in English and U.S. courts, not attributable to a legislature.

Common situs picketing The illegal picketing of a secondary employer's work site by workers who are involved in a labor dispute with a primary employer.

Common stock Shares of ownership in a corporation that are lowest in priority with respect to payment of dividends and distribution of the corporation's assets upon dissolution.

Community property A form of concurrent ownership of property in which each spouse owns an undivided one-half interest in property. This type of ownership applies to most property acquired by the husband or wife during the course of marriage. It generally does not apply to property acquired prior to the marriage or to property acquired by gift or inheritance during the marriage. After a divorce, community property is divided equally in some states and according to the discretion of the court in other states.

Comparative negligence A theory in tort law under which the liability for injuries resulting from negligent acts is shared by all persons who were guilty of negligence (including the injured party), on the basis of each person's proportionate carelessness.

Compensatory damages A money award equivalent to the actual value of injuries or damages sustained by the aggrieved party.

Complaint The pleading made by a plaintiff or a charge made by the state alleging wrongdoing on the part of the defendant.

Computer crime Any wrongful act that is directed against computers and computer parts, or wrongful use or abuse of computers or software.

Concentrated industry An industry in which a large percentage of market sales is controlled by either a single firm or a small number of firms.

Conciliation A form of alternative dispute resolution in which the parties reach an agreement themselves with the help of a neutral third party, called a conciliator, who facilitates the negotiations.

Concurrent conditions Conditions that must occur or be performed at the same time; they are mutually dependent. No obligations arise until these conditions are simultaneously performed.

Concurrent jurisdiction Jurisdiction that exists when two different courts have the power to hear a case. For example, some cases can be heard in a federal or state court.

Condition A qualification, provision, or clause in a contractual agreement, the occurrence of which creates, suspends, or terminates the obligations of the contracting parties.

Condition precedent In a contractual agreement, a condition that must be met before the other party's obligations arise.

Condition subsequent A condition in a contract that, if not met, discharges an existing obligation of the other party.

Confession of judgment A judgment entered against a debtor by a creditor, with the debtor's permission and for an agreed sum, without the use of legal proceedings.

Confiscation A government's taking of privately owned business or personal property without a proper public purpose or an award of just compensation.

Confusion The mixing together of goods belonging to two or more owners so that the independent goods cannot be identified.

Conglomerate merger A merger between firms that do not compete with each other because they are in different markets (as opposed to horizontal and vertical mergers).

Consent Voluntary agreement to a proposition or an act of another. A concurrence of wills.

Consequential damages Special damages that compensate for a loss that is not direct or immediate (for example, lost profits). The special damages must have been reasonably foreseeable at the time the breach or injury occurred in order for the plaintiff to collect them.

Consideration That which motivates the exchange of promises or performance in a contractual agreement. The consideration, which must be present to make the contract legally binding, must result in a detriment to the promisee (something of legal value, legally sufficient, and bargained for) or a benefit to the promisor.

Consignment A transaction in which an owner of goods (the consignor) delivers the goods to another (the consignee) for the consignee to sell. The consignee pays the consignor for the goods sold and returns unsold goods to the consignor.

Consolidation A contractual and statutory process whereby two or more corporations join to become a completely new corporation. The original corporations cease to exist, and the new corporation acquires all their assets and liabilities.

Constructive delivery An act equivalent to the actual, physical delivery of property that cannot be physically delivered because of difficulty or impossibility; to illustrate, the transfer of a key to a safe constructively delivers the contents of the safe.

Constructive eviction A landlord's act or failure to act that deprives a person of the possession of rental property that he or she leases by rendering the premises unfit or unsuitable for occupancy.

Constructive trust A trust created by operation of law against one who wrongfully has obtained or holds a legal right to property that the person should not, in equity and good conscience, hold and enjoy.

Continuation statement A statement that, if filed within six months prior to the expiration date of the original financing statement, continues the effectiveness of the original statement for another five years. The effectiveness of a financing statement can be continued in the same manner indefinitely.

Contract A set of promises constituting an agreement between parties, giving each a legal duty to the other and also the right to seek a remedy for the breach of the promises/duties owed to each. The elements of an enforceable contract are competent parties, a proper or legal purpose, consideration (an exchange of promises/duties), and mutuality of agreement and of obligation.

Contractual capacity The mental capacity required by the law for a party who enters into a contract to be bound by that contract.

Contributory negligence A theory in tort law under which a complaining party's own negligence contributed to or caused his or her injuries. Contributory negligence is an absolute bar to recovery in a minority of jurisdictions.

Conversion The wrongful taking or retaining possession of personal property that belongs to another.

Conveyance The transfer of a title to land from one person to another by deed; a document (such as a deed or a mortgage) by which an interest in land is transferred from one person to another.

"Cooling off" laws Laws that allow buyers a period of time in which to cancel a door-to-door sales contract or a contract for home improvements. Most state statutes and the federal government require that buyers be allowed a three-day cooling-off period during which these types of contracts can be cancelled.

Copyright The exclusive right of "authors" to publish, print, or sell an intellectual production for a statutory period of time. A copyright has the same monopolistic nature as a patent or trademark, but it differs in that it applies exclusively to works of art, literature, and other works of authorship (including computer programs).

Corporate charter The document issued by a state official (usually the secretary of state) granting a corporation legal existence and the right to function.

Corporate social responsibility The concept that corporations can and should act ethically and be accountable to society for their actions.

Corporation A legal entity created under the authority of the laws of a state or the federal government. The entity is distinct from its shareholders/owners.

Correspondent bank A bank in which another bank has an account (and vice versa) for the purpose of facilitating fund transfers.

Cosign The act of signing a document (such as a note promising to pay another in return for a loan or other benefit) jointly with another person and thereby assuming liability for performing what was promised in the document.

Cost-benefit analysis A way to reach decisions in which the costs of a given action are compared with the benefits of the action.

Co-surety A joint surety. One who assumes liability jointly with another surety for the payment of an obligation.

Counteradvertising New advertising that is undertaken pursuant to a Federal Trade Commission order for the purpose of correcting earlier false claims that were made about a product.

Counterclaim A claim made by a defendant in a civil lawsuit that in effect sues the plaintiff; it can be based on entirely different grounds than those given in the plaintiff's complaint.

Counteroffer An offeree's response to an offer in which the offeree rejects the original offer and at the same time makes a new offer.

Course of dealing A sequence of previous conduct between the parties to a particular transaction that establishes a common basis for their understanding.

Course of performance The conduct that occurs under the terms of a particular agreement; such conduct indicates what the parties to an agreement intended it to mean.

Covenant against encumbrances A grantor's assurance that on land conveyed there are no encumbrances—that is, that no third parties have rights to, or interests in, the land that would diminish its value to the grantee.

Covenant not to sue An agreement to substitute a contractual obligation for some other type of action.

Covenant of quiet enjoyment A promise by the grantor (or landlord) that the grantee (or tenant) will not be evicted or disturbed by the grantor or a person having a lien or superior title.

Covenant of the right of seisin An assurance to the purchaser that the grantor has the very estate in the quantity and quality that the grantor purports to convey.

Covenant of the right to convey A grantor's assurance that he or she has sufficient capacity and title to convey the property being transferred.

Cover Under the UCC, a remedy of the buyer that allows the buyer, on the seller's breach, to purchase the goods from another seller and substitute them for the goods due under the contract. If the cost of cover exceeds the cost of the contract goods, the breaching seller will be liable to the buyer for the difference, plus incidental and consequential damages.

Creditors' composition agreement An agreement formed between a debtor and his or her creditors in which the creditors agree to accept a lesser sum than that owed by the debtor in full satisfaction of the debt.

Crime A broad term for violations of law that are punishable by the state and are codified by legislatures. The objective of criminal law is to protect the public.

Criminal law Law that governs and defines those actions that are crimes and that subject the convicted offender to punishment imposed by the government.

Cross-examination The questioning of an opposing witness during the trial.

Cure The right of a party who tenders nonconforming performance to correct his or her performance within the contract period [UCC 3–508].

D

Damages Money sought as a remedy for a breach of contract or for a tortious act.

Debtor A person who owes a sum of money or other obligations to another.

Debtor in possession (DIP) In Chapter 11 bankruptcy proceedings, a debtor who is allowed to continue in possession of the estate in bankruptcy (the business) and to continue business operations.

Deceptive advertising Advertising that misleads consumers, either by unjustified claims concerning a product's performance or by the omission of a material fact concerning the product's composition or performance.

Declaratory judgment A judgment rendered by a court that declares for the parties what their respective rights and duties are in regard to a specific controversy.

Deed A document by which title to property (usually real property) is passed.

Defalcation The misuse of funds.

Defamation Anything published or publicly spoken that causes injury to another's good name, reputation, or character.

Default The failure to observe a promise or discharge an obligation. The term is commonly used to mean the failure to pay a debt when it is due.

Default judgment A judgment entered by a clerk or court against a party who has failed to appear in court to answer or defend against a claim that has been brought against him or her by another party.

Defendant One against whom a lawsuit is brought; the accused person in a criminal proceeding.

Defense That which a defendant offers and alleges in an action or suit as a reason why the plaintiff should not recover or establish what he or she seeks.

Deficiency judgment A judgment against a debtor for the amount of a debt remaining unpaid after collateral has been repossessed and sold or after foreclosure proceedings.

Delegation of duties The act of transferring to another all or part of one's duties arising under a contract.

Demand deposit Funds (accepted by a bank) subject to immediate withdrawal, in contrast to a time deposit, which requires that a depositor wait a specific time before withdrawing or pay a penalty for early withdrawal.

Deposition A generic term that refers to any evidence verified by oath. As a legal term, it is often limited to the testimony of a witness taken under oath before a trial, with the opportunity of cross-examination.

Depository bank The first bank to which an item is transferred for collection, even though it may also be the payor bank.

Derivative suit A suit by a shareholder to enforce a corporate cause of action against a third person.

Destination contract A contract for the sale of goods in which the seller assumes liability for any losses or damage to the goods until they are tendered at the destination specified in the contract.

Devise To make a gift of real property by will.

Direct examination The examination of a witness by the attorney who calls the witness to the stand to testify on behalf of the attorney's client.

Directed verdict A verdict in which the judge takes the decision out of the hands of the jury.

Disaffirmance The repudiation of an obligation.

Discharge The termination of one's obligation. In contract law, discharge occurs when the parties have fully performed their contractual obligations or when events, conduct of the parties, or operation of the law releases the parties from further performance.

Disclosed principal A principal whose identity and existence as a principal is known by a third person at the time a transaction is conducted by an agent.

Discovery A method by which opposing parties may obtain information from each other to prepare for trial. Generally governed by rules of procedure, but may be controlled by the court.

Disparagement of property Economically injurious falsehoods made about another's product or property. A general term for torts that are more specifically referred to as slander of quality or slander of title.

Disparate-impact discrimination In an employment context, discrimination that results from certain employer practices or procedures that, although not discriminatory on their face, have a discriminatory effect.

Disparate-treatment discrimination In an employment context, intentional discrimination against individuals on the basis of color, gender, national origin, race, or religion.

Dissolution The formal disbanding of a partnership or a corporation. It can take place by (1) agreement of the parties or the shareholders and board of directors, (2) the death of a partner, (3) the expiration of a time period stated in a partnership agreement or a certificate of incorporation, or (4) court order.

Distribution agreement A contract between a seller and a distributor of the seller's products setting out the terms and conditions of the distributorship.

Diversity of citizenship Under Article III, Section 2, of the Constitution, a basis for federal court jurisdiction over a lawsuit between citizens of different states.

Divestiture The act of selling one or more of a company's ownership, such as a subsidiary or plant; often mandated by the courts in merger or monopolization cases.

Dividend A distribution to corporate shareholders of corporate profits or income, disbursed in proportion to the number of shares held.

Docket The list of cases entered on a court's calendar and thus scheduled to be heard by the court.

Documents of title Paper exchanged in the regular course of business that evidences the right to possession of goods (for example, a bill of lading or warehouse receipt).

Domestic corporation In a given state, a corporation that does business in, and is organized under the laws of, that state.

Dominion Ownership in its fullest sense; includes both the ownership rights in property as well as the right to possess the property.

Draft Any instrument drawn on a drawee (such as a bank) that orders the drawee to pay a certain sum of money.

Dram shop acts State statutes that impose liability on the owners of bars and taverns, as well as those who serve alcoholic drinks to the public, for injuries resulting from accidents caused by intoxicated persons when the sellers or servers of alcoholic drinks contributed to the intoxication.

Drawee The person who is ordered to pay a draft or check. With a check, a financial institution is always the drawee.

Drawer A person who initiates a draft (including a check), thereby ordering the drawee to pay.

Due diligence A required standard of care that certain professionals, such as accountants, must meet to avoid liability for securities violations. Under securities law, an accountant will be deemed to have exercised due diligence if he or she followed generally accepted accounting principles and generally accepted auditing standards and had, "after reasonable investigation, reasonable grounds to believe and did believe, at the time such part of the registration statement became effective, that the statements therein were true and that there was no omission of a material fact required to be stated therein or necessary to make the statements therein not misleading."

Due process clause The provisions of the Fifth and Fourteenth Amendments to the Constitution provide that no person shall be deprived of life, liberty, or property without due process of law (fair and just reason and procedure). Similar clauses are found in most state constitutions.

Dumping Selling goods in a foreign country at a price below the price charged for the same goods in the domestic market.

Duress Unlawful pressure brought to bear on a person, overcoming that person's free will and causing him or her to do (or refrain from doing) what he or she otherwise would not (or would) have done.

Duty of care The duty of all persons, as established by tort law, to exercise a reasonable amount of care in their dealings with others. Failure to exercise due care, which is normally determined by the "reasonable person standard," constitutes the tort of negligence.

E

Easement A nonpossessory right to use another's property in a manner established by either express or implied agreement.

Economic strike A strike called by a union to pressure an employer to make concessions relating to hours, wages, or other terms of employment.

Emancipation In regard to minors, the act of being freed from parental control. The emancipation of a minor by his or her parents involves the parents' surrender of the right to the care, custody, and earnings of the minor as well as a renunciation of parental duties.

Embezzlement The fraudulent appropriation of money or other property by a person to whom the money or property has been entrusted.

Eminent domain The power of a government to take land for public use from private citizens for just compensation.

Employment-at-will doctrine A doctrine that permits any employment contract without a definite period of time to be terminated at any time and for any reason by either party without liability.

Employment discrimination Treating employees or job applicants unequally on the basis of race, sex, nationality, religion, or age; prohibited by Title VII of the Civil Rights Act of 1964 as amended.

Enabling legislation Statutes enacted by Congress that authorize the creation of an administrative agency and specify the name, composition, and powers of the agency being created.

Entrapment In criminal law, a defense in which the defendant claims that he or she was induced by a public official—usually an undercover agent or police officer—to commit a crime that he or she would otherwise not have committed.

Entrepreneur One who initiates and assumes the financial risks of a new enterprise and who undertakes to provide or control its management.

Environmental impact statement (EIS) A statement required by the National Environmental Policy Act for any major federal action that will significantly affect the quality of the environment. The statement must analyze the action's impact on the environment and alternative actions that might be taken.

Equal dignity rule In most states, a rule stating that express authority given to an agent must be in writing if the contract to be made on behalf of the principal is required to be in writing.

Equal protection clause The provision in the Fourteenth Amendment to the Constitution that guarantees that no state will "deny to any person within its jurisdiction the equal protection of the laws." This clause mandates that the state governments treat similarly situated individuals in a similar manner.

Establishment clause The provision in the First Amendment to the Constitution that prohibits Congress from creating any law "respecting an establishment of religion"

Estate Broadly, all that a person owns, including both real and personal property; in real-estate law, the extent of ownership or interest that one has in realty.

Estopped Barred, impeded, or precluded.

Estray statute Statutes dealing with finders' rights in property when the true owners are unknown.

Ethics Moral principles and values applied to social behavior.

Eviction Depriving a person of the possession of land or rental property that he or she owns or leases by having the person removed from the premises.

Exclusionary rule In criminal procedure, a rule under which any evidence that is obtained in violation of the accused's constitutional rights guaranteed by the Fourth, Fifth, and Sixth Amendments, as well as any evidence derived from illegally obtained evidence, will not be admissible in court.

Exclusive distributorship A distributorship in which the seller and distributor of the seller's products agree that the distributor has the exclusive right to distribute the seller's products in a certain geographic area.

Exclusive jurisdiction Jurisdiction that exists when a case can only be heard in a particular court.

Exclusive-dealing contract An agreement under which a producer of goods agrees to sell its goods exclusively through one distributor.

Exculpatory clause A clause that releases a party (to a contract) from liability for his or her wrongful acts.

Executed contract A contract that has been completely performed by both parties.

Execution An action to carry into effect the directions in a decree or judgment; otherwise stated, an official carrying out of a court's order or judgment.

Executor A person appointed by a testator to see that his or her will is administered appropriately.

Executory contract A contract that has not as yet been fully performed.

Executory interest A future interest, held by a person other than the grantor, that either cuts short or begins some time after the natural termination of the preceding estate.

Export The sale or transportation of goods and services

from one ountry to another in the course of trade.

Express contract A contract that is oral and/or written (as opposed to an implied contract).

Express warranty A promise, ancillary to an underlying sales agreement, that is included in the written or oral terms of the sales agreement under which the promisor assures the quality, description, or performance of the goods.

Expropriation The seizure by a government of privately owned business or personal property for a proper public purpose and with just compensation.

Extension clause A clause in a time instrument extending the instrument's date of maturity. An extension clause is the reverse of an acceleration clause.

F

Featherbedding A requirement that more workers than are necessary be employed to do a particular job.

Federal question A question that pertains to the U.S. Constitution, acts of Congress, or treaties. A federal question provides jurisdiction for federal courts. This jurisdiction arises from Article III, Section 2, of the Constitution.

Federal Reserve System A network of twelve central banks headed by a board of governors, with the advice of the Federal Advisory Council and the Federal Open Market Committee, to give the United States an elastic currency, supervise and regulate banking activities, and facilitate the flow and discounting of commercial paper. All national banks and state-chartered banks that voluntarily join the system are members.

Federalism A system of government in which power is divided by a written constitution between a central government and regional, or subdivisional, governments. Each level must have some domain in which its policies are dominant and some genuine political or constitutional guarantee of its authority. The United States has a federal government in which power is shared between the central government and the state governments.

Fee simple absolute An estate or interest in land with no time, disposition, or descendibility limitations.

Fee simple A form of property ownership entitling the property owner to use, possess, or dispose of the property as he or she chooses during his or her lifetime. Upon death, the interest in the property descends to the owner's heirs.

Fee simple defeasible An estate that can be taken away (by the prior grantor) upon the occurrence or nonoccurrence of a specified event.

Felony A crime—such as arson, murder, rape, or robbery—that carries the most severe sanctions, usually ranging from one year in a state or federal prison to the forfeiture of one's life.

Fictitious payee A payee on a negotiable instrument whom the maker or drawer does not intend to have an interest in the instrument. Indorsements by fictitious payees are not forgeries under negotiable instruments law.

Fiduciary As a noun, a person having a duty created by his or her undertaking to act primarily for another's benefit in matters connected with the undertaking. As an adjective, a relationship founded upon trust and confidence.

Final order The final decision of an administrative agency on an issue. If no appeal is taken, or if the case is not reviewed or considered anew by the agency commission, the administrative law judge's initial order becomes the final order of the agency.

Financing statement A document prepared by a secured creditor, and filed with the appropriate state or local official, to give notice to the public that the creditor claims an interest in collateral belonging to the debtor named in the statement. The financing statement must be signed by the debtor, contain the addresses of both the debtor and the creditor, and describe the collateral by type or item.

Firm offer An offer (by a merchant) that is irrevocable without consideration for a period of time (not longer than three months). A firm offer by a merchant must be in writing and must be signed by the offeror.

Fixture A thing that was once personal property but that has become attached to real property in such a way that it takes on the characteristics of real property and becomes part of that real property.

Floating lien A security interest retained in collateral even when the collateral changes in character, classification, or location.

For value In a sale of goods, legally sufficient consideration (such as a money payment).

***Force majeure* clause** A provision in a contract stipulating that certain unforeseen events—such as war, political upheavals, acts of God, or other events—will excuse a party from liability for nonperformance of contractual obligations.

Foreign corporation In a given state, a corporation that does business in the state without being incorporated therein.

Foreign exchange market A worldwide system in which foreign currencies are bought and sold.

Forgery The false or unauthorized signature of a document, or the false making of a document, with the intent to defraud.

Form The technical manner or order to be observed in creating legal agreements, as opposed to the substance of the agreements.

Formal contracts Agreement or contract that by law requires for its validity a specific form, such as executed under seal.

Forum-selection clause A provision in a contract designating the forum (the nation, state, or jurisdiction) in which a dispute will be litigated.

Franchise A written agreement whereby an owner of a trademark, trade name, or copyright licenses another to use that trademark, trade name, or copyright, under specified conditions in the selling of goods and services.

Franchisee One receiving a license to use another's (the franchisor's) trademark, trade name, or copyright in the sale of goods and services.

Franchisor One licensing another (the franchisee) to use his or her trademark, trade name, or copyright in the sale of goods or services.

Fraud Any misrepresentation, either by misstatement or omission of a material fact, knowingly made with the intention of deceiving another and on which a reasonable person

would and does rely to his or her detriment.
Free exercise clause The provision in the First Amendment to the Constitution that prohibits Congress from making any law "prohibiting the free exercise" of religion.
Fungible goods Goods that are alike by physical nature, by agreement, or by trade usage. Examples of fungible goods are wheat, oil, and wine that are identical in type and quality.
Future interest An estate that is not at present possessory but will or may be possessory in the future. Remainders and reversions are future estates.

G

Gap-filling powers Powers of administrative agencies to create regulations to implement congressional delegations of power that are expressed only in general terms.
Garnishment A legal process whereby a creditor appropriates the debtor's property or wages that are in the hands of a third party.
General partner In a limited partnership, a partner who assumes responsibility for the management of the partnership and liability for all partnership debts.
Generally accepted accounting principles (GAAP) The conventions, rules, and procedures necessary to define accepted accounting practices at a particular time. The source of the principles is the Federal Accounting Standards Board.
Generally accepted auditing standards (GAAS) Standards concerning an auditor's professional qualities and the judgment exercised by him or her in the performance of an examination and report. The source of the standards is the American Institute of Certified Public Accountants.
Gift Any voluntary transfer of property made without consideration, past or present.
Gift *causa mortis* A gift made in contemplation of death. If the donor does not die of that ailment, the gift is revoked.
Gift *inter vivos* A gift made during one's lifetime and not in contemplation of imminent death, in contrast to a gift *causa mortis*.
Good Samaritan statutes State statutes that provide that persons who provide emergency services to, or rescue, others in peril—unless they do so recklessly, thus causing further harm—cannot be sued for negligence.
Good faith purchaser A purchaser who buys without notice of any circumstance that would put a person of ordinary prudence on inquiry as to whether the seller has valid title to the goods being sold.
Greenmail A higher-than-market price paid to repurchase stock that a corporation bought in attempting to take over a target corporation through a gradual accumulation of stock rather than through a tender offer.
Group boycott The refusal to deal with a particular person or firm by a group of competitors; prohibited under the Sherman Act.
Guarantor One who agrees to satisfy the debt of another (the debtor) *only* if and when the debtor fails to pay the debt. A guarantor's liability is thus secondary.

H

Herfindahl-Hirschman Index (HHI) An index of market power used to calculate whether a merger of two corporations will result in monopoly power and thus violate antitrust laws.
Holder A person "who is in possession of a document of title or negotiable instrument or a certificated investment security drawn, issued, or indorsed to him or his order or to bearer or in blank" [UCC 1–201(20)].
Holder in due course (HDC) Any holder who acquires a negotiable instrument for value; in good faith; and without notice that the instrument is overdue, that it has been dishonored, or that any defense or claim to it exists on the part of any person.
Holding company A company that limits its activities to owning stock in and supervising the management of other companies.
Holographic will A will written entirely in the signer's handwriting and usually not witnessed.
Homestead exemption A law allowing an owner to designate his or her home and adjoining land as a homestead and thus exempt it from liability for his or her general debt.
Horizontal merger A merger between two businesses or persons competing in the marketplace.
Horizontal restraint Any agreement that in some way restrains competition between rival firms competing in the same market. Price fixing and horizontal market division are examples of horizontal restraints on competition.
Hybrid rulemaking A set of loosely defined procedures for agency rulemaking that incorporate advantages of both the formal and informal procedures. As in formal rulemaking, a public hearing provides an opportunity for direct participation, but the right of interested parties to cross-examine witnesses is much more restricted. Also, a different standard is applied by an independent court reviewing the agency's procedures.

I

Identification Proof that a thing is what it is purported or represented to be. In the sale of goods, the express designation of the goods provided for in the contract.
Implied warranty A warranty that the law implies through either the situation of the parties or the nature of the transaction.
Implied warranty of habitability A presumed promise by the landlord that rented residential premises are fit for human habitation—including being free of violations of building and sanitary codes.
Implied warranty of merchantability A presumed promise by a merchant seller of goods that the goods are reasonably fit for the general purpose for which they are sold, are properly packaged and labeled, and are of proper quality.
Implied-in-fact contract A contract formed in whole or in part from the conduct of the parties (as opposed to an express contract).
Impossibility of performance A doctrine under which a party to a contract is relieved of his or her duty to perform

when performance becomes impossible or totally impracticable (through no fault of either party).

Imposter One who, with the intent to deceive, pretends to be somebody else.

Incidental beneficiary A third party who incidentally benefits from a contract but whose benefit was not the reason the contract was formed; incidental beneficiaries have no rights in a contract and cannot sue the promisor if the contract is breached.

Incidental damages Damages resulting from a breach of contract, including all reasonable expenses incurred because of the breach.

Independent contractor One who works for, and receives payment from, an employer but whose working conditions and methods are not controlled by the employer. An independent contractor is not an employee but may be an agent.

Independent regulatory agency An administrative agency that is not considered part of the government's executive branch and is not subject to the authority of the president. Agency officials cannot be removed without cause.

Indictment A charge or written accusation, issued by a grand jury, that a named person has committed a crime.

Indorsee The one to whom a negotiable instrument is transferred by indorsement.

Indorsement A signature placed on an instrument or a document of title for the purpose of transferring one's ownership in the instrument or document of title.

Indorser One who, being the payee or holder of a negotiable instrument, signs his or her name on the back of it.

Informal contracts Contracts that do not require a specified form or formality for validity.

Information A formal accusation or complaint (without an indictment) issued in certain types of actions by a prosecuting attorney or other law officer, such as a magistrate. The types of actions are set forth in the rules of states or in the Federal Rules of Criminal Procedure.

Initial order In the context of administrative law, an agency's disposition in a matter other than a rulemaking. An administrative law judge's initial order becomes final unless it is appealed.

Innkeeper's lien A possessory or statutory lien allowing the innkeeper to take the personal property of a guest, brought into the hotel, as security for nonpayment of the guest's bill (debt).

Insider trading Purchasing or selling securities on the basis of information that has not been made available to the public.

Insolvent A term describing a person whose liabilities exceed the value of owned assets *or* a person who "either has ceased to pay his debts in the ordinary course of business or cannot pay his debts as they come due"
[UCC 1–201(23)].

Installment contract A contract in which payments due are made periodically. Also may allow for delivery of goods in separate lots with payment made for each.

Insurable interest An interest either in a person's life or well-being or in property that is sufficiently substantial that insuring against injury to the person or damage to the property does not amount to a mere wagering (betting) contract.

Insurance A contract in which, for a stipulated consideration, one party agrees to compensate the other for loss on a specific subject by a specified peril.

Integrated contract A written contract that constitutes the final expression of the parties' agreement. If a contract is integrated, evidence extraneous to the contract that contradicts or alters the meaning of the contract in any way is inadmissible.

Intended beneficiary A third party for whose benefit a contract is formed; intended beneficiaries can sue the promisor if such a contract is breached.

Intentional tort A wrongful act knowingly committed.

***Inter vivos* trust** A trust created by the grantor (settlor) and effective during the grantor's lifetime (that is, a trust not established by a will).

Intermediary bank Any bank to which an item is transferred in the course of collection, except the depositary or payor bank.

International law The law that governs relations among nations. International customs and treaties are generally considered to be two of the most important sources of international law.

Interpretative rule An administrative agency rule that is simply a statement and opinion issued by the agency explaining how the agency interprets and intends to apply the statutes it enforces. Such a rule is not automatically binding on private individuals or organizations.

Interrogatories A series of written questions for which written answers are prepared and then signed under oath by a party to a lawsuit (the plaintiff or the defendant).

Intestacy laws State laws determining the division and descent of the property of one who dies intestate (without a will).

Intestate As a noun, one who has died without having created a valid will; as an adjective, the state of having died without a will.

Investment company A company that acts on behalf of many smaller shareholders/owners by buying a large portfolio of securities and managing that portfolio professionally.

J

Joint and several liability A doctrine under which a plaintiff may sue, and collect a judgment from, any of several jointly liable defendants, regardless of that particular defendant's degree of fault. In partnership law, joint and several liability means a third party may sue one or more of the partners separately or all of them together, at his or her option. This is true even if the partner did not participate in, ratify, or know about whatever it was that gave rise to the cause of action.

Joint liability Shared liability. In partnership law, partners incur joint liability for partnership obligations and debts. For example, if a third party sues a partner on a partnership debt, the partner has the right to insist that the other partners be sued with him or her.

Joint tenancy The ownership interest of two or more co-owners of property whereby each owns an undivided portion of the property. Upon the death of one of the joint tenants, his or her interest automatically passes to the others and cannot be transferred by the will of the deceased.

Joint venture A joint undertaking of a specific commercial enterprise by an association of persons. A joint venture is normally not a legal entity and is treated like a partnership for federal income tax purposes.

Judgment *n.o.v.* A judgment notwithstanding the verdict; may be entered by the court for the plaintiff (or the defendant) after there has been a jury verdict for the defendant (or the plaintiff).

Judicial process The procedures relating to, or connected with, the administration of justice through the judicial system.

Judicial review The authority of a court to reexamine a previously considered dispute; the process by which a court decides on the constitutionality of legislative acts.

Junk bond In corporate finance, a bond that is subject to such a high degree of risk (the risk being that the borrower will not be able to pay the lender under the terms of the bond) that the bond is referred to as "junk."

Jurisdiction The authority of a court to hear and decide a specific action.

Jurisprudence The science or philosophy of law.

L

Larceny The act of taking another person's personal property unlawfully. Some states classify larceny as either grand or petit, depending on the property's value.

Law A body of rules of conduct with legal force and effect, prescribed by the controlling authority (the government) of a society.

Lease A transfer of possession by the landlord/lessor of real or personal property to the tenant/lessee for a period of time for consideration (usually the payment of rent). Upon termination of the lease, the property reverts to the lessor.

Leasehold estate An estate in realty held by a tenant under a lease. In every leasehold estate, the tenant has a qualified right to possess and/or use the land.

Legacy A gift of personal property under a will.

Legal realism A school of legal thought of the 1920s and 1930s that challenged many existing jurisprudential assumptions, particularly the assumption that subjective elements played no part in judicial reasoning. The legal realists, as the term implies, generally advocated a less abstract and more realistic approach to the law, an approach that would take into account customary practices and the circumstances in which transactions take place. The school left a lasting imprint on American jurisprudence.

Legatee A person who inherits property under a will.

Legislative rule An administrative agency rule that carries the same weight as a congressionally enacted statute.

Letter of credit A written instrument, usually issued by a bank on behalf of a customer or other person, in which the issuer promises to honor drafts or other demands for payment by third persons in accordance with the terms of the instrument.

Leveraged buy-out (LBO) A corporate takeover financed by loans secured by the acquired corporation's assets or by the issuance of corporate bonds, resulting in a high debt load for the corporation.

Levy The obtaining of money by legal process through the seizure and sale of property, usually done after a writ of execution has been issued.

Liability Any actual or potential legal obligation, duty, debt, or responsibility.

License A revocable right or privilege of a person to come on another person's land.

Lien An encumbrance upon a property to satisfy or protect a claim for payment of a debt.

Life estate An interest in land that exists only for the duration of the life of some person, usually the holder of the estate.

Limited liability company (LLC) A hybrid form of business organization or enterprise authorized by a state in which its members have limited liability and taxes on profits are passed through that entity to its members.

Limited partner In a limited partnership, a partner who contributes capital to the partnership but has no right to participate in the management and operation of the business. The limited partner assumes no liability for partnership debts beyond the capital contributed.

Limited partnership A partnership consisting of one or more general partners (who manage the business and are liable to the full extent of their personal assets for debts of the partnership) and of one or more limited partners (who contribute only assets and are liable only up to the amount contributed by them).

Liquidated damages An amount, stipulated in the contract, that the parties to a contract believe to be a reasonable estimation of the damages that will occur in the event of a breach.

Liquidation The sale of the assets of a business or an individual for cash and the distribution of the cash received to creditors, with the balance going to the owner(s).

Lobster trap A defense against a takeover attempt in which holders of convertible securities (corporate bonds or stock that are convertible into common shares) are prohibited from converting the securities into common shares if the holders already own, or would own after conversion, 10 percent or more of the voting shares of stock. Because this defense applies only to holders of large blocks of shares, it is referred to as a lobster trap (which is designed to catch the larger lobsters while allowing the smaller ones to escape).

Long arm statute A state statute that permits a state to obtain personal jurisdiction over nonresident individuals and corporations. Individuals or corporations, however, must have certain "minimum contacts" with that state for the statute to apply.

Lost property Property with which the owner has involuntarily parted and then cannot find or recover.

M

Mailbox rule A rule providing that an acceptance of an offer becomes effective upon dispatch (upon being placed in a mailbox), if mail is, expressly or impliedly, an authorized means of communication of acceptance to the offeror.

Maker One who issues a promissory note or certificate of deposit (that is, one who promises to pay a certain sum to the holder of the note or CD).

Malpractice Professional misconduct or the lack of the requisite degree of skill as a professional or the negligence—the failure to exercise due care—on the part of a professional, such as a physician, is commonly referred to as malpractice.

Market concentration The percentage of a particular firm's market sales in a relevant market area.

Market power The power of a firm to control the market for its product. A monopoly has the greatest degree of market power.

Market-share test The primary measure of monopoly power. A firm's market share is the percentage of a market that the firm controls.

Marshalling assets The arrangement or ranking of assets in a certain order toward the payment of debts. In equity, when two creditors have recourse to the same property of the debtor but one of those two creditors has recourse to other property of the debtor, that creditor must resort first to those assets of the debtor not available to the other creditor.

Mask work A series of images related to the pattern formed by the many layers of a semiconductor chip product.

Mechanic's lien A statutory lien upon the real property of another, created to ensure payment for work performed and materials furnished in erecting or repairing a building or other structure.

Mediation A method of settling disputes outside of court by using the services of a neutral third party, who acts as a communicating agent between the parties; a method of dispute settlement that is less formal than arbitration.

Merchant Under the UCC, a person who deals in goods of the kind involved in the sales contract. (For additional definitions, see UCC 2–104.)

Merger A contractual process by which one corporation (the surviving corporation) acquires all the assets and liabilities of another corporation (the merged corporation). The shareholders of the merged corporation receive either payment for their shares or shares in the surviving corporation.

Mini-trial A private proceeding that assists disputing parties in determining whether to take their case to court. During the proceeding, each party's attorney briefly argues the party's case before the other party and (usually) a neutral third party, who acts as an adviser. If the parties fail to reach an agreement, the adviser renders an opinion as to how a court would likely decide the issue.

Mirror image rule A common law rule that requires, for a valid contractual agreement, that the terms of the offeree's acceptance adhere exactly to the terms of the offeror's offer.

Misdemeanors Lesser crimes than felonies, punishable by a fine or imprisonment for up to one year in other than a state or federal penitentiary.

Mislaid property Property that the owner has voluntarily parted with and then cannot find or recover.

Misrepresentation A false representation created by one party—by a misstatement of facts, by a failure to mention a material fact, or by conduct—with the intention of deceiving another and on which the other reasonably relies to his or her detriment.

Mitigation of damages The rule requiring the party suing to have done whatever was reasonable to minimize the damages caused by the defendant.

Money laundering Falsely reporting income that has been obtained through criminal activity as income obtained through a legitimate business enterprise—in effect, "laundering" the "dirty money."

Monopolization The possession of monopoly power in the relevant market and the willful acquisition or maintenance of the power, as distinguished from growth or development as a consequence of a superior product, business acumen, or historic accident. A violation of Section 2 of the Sherman Act requires that both of these elements be established.

Monopoly A term generally used to describe a market for which there is a single seller or a limited number of sellers.

Monopoly power The ability of a monopoly to dictate what takes place in a given market.

Mortgagee The creditor who takes the security interest under the mortgage agreement.

Mortgagor The debtor who pledges collateral in a mortgage agreement.

Most-favored-nation status A status granted in an international treaty by a provision stating that the citizens of the contracting nations may enjoy the privileges accorded by either party to citizens of the most favored nations. Generally, most-favored-nation clauses are designed to establish equality of international treatment in regard to imports or exports.

Motion to dismiss A pleading in which a defendant admits the facts as alleged by the plaintiff but asserts that the plaintiff's claim fails to state a cause of action (that is, has no basis in law) or that there are other grounds on which a suit should be dismissed. Also called a demurrer.

Mutual fund A specific type of investment company that continually buys or sells to investors shares of ownership in a portfolio.

N

National law Law that pertains to a particular nation (as opposed to international law).

Natural law school The oldest and one of the most significant schools of legal thought. Adherents of the natural law school believe that government and the legal system should reflect universal moral and ethical principles that are inherent in human nature.

Necessaries Necessities required for life, such as food, shelter, clothing, and medical attention; normally, necessaries are also considered to include items or services appropriate to an individual's circumstances and condition in life.

Negligence The failure to exercise the standard of care that a reasonable person would exercise in similar circumstances.

Negligence *per se* An action or failure to act in violation of a statutory requirement.

Negotiable instrument A written and signed unconditional promise or order to pay a specified sum of money on

demand or at a definite time to order (to a specific person or entity) or to bearer.
Negotiation A form of alternative dispute resolution by which the parties informally meet and by themselves resolve their dispute.
No-par shares Corporate shares that have no face value—that is, no specific dollar amount is printed on their face.
Nominal damages A small monetary award (often one dollar) granted to a plaintiff when no actual damage was suffered.
Notary public A person authorized by a state government or the federal government to administer oaths and to attest to the authenticity of signatures.
Notice-and-comment rulemaking A procedure in agency rulemaking that requires (1) notice, (2) opportunity for comment, and (3) a general statement of the basis for, and purpose of, the proposed rule. Also referred to as informal rulemaking.
Notice of proposed rulemaking A notice published (in the *Federal Register*) by an administrative agency describing a proposed rule. The notice must give the time and place for which agency proceedings on the proposed rule will be held, a description of the nature of the proceedings, the legal authority for the proceedings (which is usually the agency's enabling legislation), and the terms of the proposed rule or the subject matter of the proposed rule.
Novation The substitution, by agreement, of a new contract for an old one, with the rights under the old one being terminated. Typically, there is a substitution of a new person who is responsible for the contract and the removal of the original party's rights and duties under the contract.
Nuncupative will An oral will (often called a deathbed will) made before witnesses; usually limited to transfers of personal property.

O

Objective theory of contracts The view taken by American law that contracting parties shall only be bound by terms that can actually be inferred from promises made. Contract law does not examine a contracting party's subjective intent or underlying motive.
Offer An offeror's proposal to do something, which creates in the offeree accepting the offer a legal power to bind the offeror to the terms of the proposal by accepting the offer.
Offeree A person to whom an offer is made.
Offeror A person who makes an offer.
Opinion A statement by the court expressing the reasons for its decision in a case.
Option contract A contract (with consideration) whereby the offeror agrees not to withdraw an offer for a period of time as specified in the contract, or if no time period is specified, for a reasonable period.
Order instrument A negotiable instrument that is payable to the order of a specific person.
Output contract A binding agreement in which a seller agrees to deliver/sell the seller's output of a good (an unspecified amount at the time of agreement) to a buyer, and the buyer agrees to buy all the goods supplied.
Overdraft A check written on a checking account in which there are insufficient funds to cover the check.

P

Par-value shares Corporate shares that have a specific face value, or formal cash-in value, written on them, such as one dollar.
Parol evidence rule A substantive rule of contracts under which a court will not receive into evidence prior statements or contemporaneous oral statements that contradict a written agreement when the court finds that the written agreement was intended by the parties to be a final, complete, and unambiguous expression of their agreement.
Partially disclosed principal A principal whose identity is unknown by a third person, but the third person knows that the agent is or may be acting for a principal at the time the contract is made.
Partnership An association of two or more persons to carry on, as co-owners, a business for profit.
Past consideration An act done before the contract is made, which ordinarily, by itself, cannot be consideration for a later promise to pay for the act.
Patent A government grant that gives an inventor the exclusive right or privilege to make, use, or sell his or her invention for a limited time period. The word *patent* usually refers to some invention and designates either the instrument by which patent rights are evidenced or the patent itself.
Payee A person to whom an instrument is made payable.
Payor bank A bank on which an item is payable as drawn (or is payable as accepted).
Penalty A sum inserted into a contract, not as a measure of compensation for its breach but rather as punishment for a default. The agreement as to the amount will not be enforced, and recovery will be limited to actual damages.
Per capita A Latin term meaning *per person*. In the law governing estate distribution, a method of distributing the property of an intestate's estate by which all the heirs receive equal shares.
***Per se* violation** A type of anticompetitive agreement—such as a price-fixing agreement—that is considered to be so injurious to the public that there is no need to determine whether it actually injures market competition; rather, it is in itself (*per se*) a violation of the Sherman Act.
Per stirpes A Latin term meaning *by the roots*. In the law governing estate distribution, a method of distributing an intestate's estate in which a class or group of distributees take the share to which their deceased ancestor would have been entitled.
Perfection The method by which a secured party obtains a priority by notice that his or her security interest in the debtor's collateral is effective against the debtor's subsequent creditors. Usually accomplished by filing a financing statement at a location set out in the state statute.
Performance In contract law, the fulfillment of one's duties arising under a contract with another; the normal way of discharging one's contractual obligations.
Periodic tenancy A lease interest in land for an indefinite

period involving payment of rent at fixed intervals, such as week to week, month to month, or year to year.

Personal defenses Defenses that can be used to avoid payment to an ordinary holder of a negotiable instrument. Personal defenses cannot be used to avoid payment to a holder in due course (HDC) or (under the shelter principle) to a holder through an HDC.

Personal property Property that is movable; any property that is not real property.

Petitioner The party who presents a petition to a court, initiates an equity proceeding, or appeals from a judgment.

Petty offenses In criminal law, the least serious kind of wrong, such as a traffic or building-code violation. (Not classified as a crime in some states.)

Plaintiff One who initiates a lawsuit.

Plea bargaining The process by which the accused and the prosecutor in a criminal case work out a mutually satisfactory disposition of the case, subject to court approval. Usually involves the defendant's pleading guilty to a lesser offense in return for a lighter sentence.

Pleadings Statements by the plaintiff and the defendant that detail the facts, charges, and defenses. Modern rules simplify common law pleading, often requiring only the complaint, an answer, and sometimes a reply to the answer.

Pledge The bailment of personal property to a creditor as security for the payment of a debt.

Police powers Powers possessed by states as part of their inherent sovereignty. These powers may be exercised to protect or promote public health, safety, or morals, or the general welfare.

Policy In insurance law, the contract of indemnity against a contingent loss between the insurer and the insured.

Positive law The objective laws legally created by a society, as opposed to natural law or the unwritten laws arising from social customs; also called *black-letter law.*

Positivist school A school of legal thought that holds that there can be no higher law than a nation's positive law—law created by a particular society at a particular point in time. In contrast to the natural law school, the positivist school maintains that there are no "natural" rights; rights come into existence only when there is a sovereign power (government) to confer and enforce those rights.

Power of attorney A document or instrument authorizing another to act as one's agent or attorney.

Precedent A court decision that furnishes an example or authority for deciding subsequent cases in which identical or similar facts are presented.

Predatory pricing The pricing of a product below cost with the intent to drive competitors out of the market.

Preemption A doctrine under which certain federal laws preempt, or take precedence over, state or local laws.

Preemptive rights Rights held by shareholders that entitle them to purchase newly issued shares of a corporation's stock, equal in percentage to shares presently held, before the stock is offered to any outside buyers. Preemptive rights enable shareholders to maintain their proportionate ownership and voice in the corporation.

Preferred stock Classes of stock that have priority over common stock both as to payment of dividends and distribution of assets upon the corporation's dissolution.

Premium In insurance law, the price for insurance protection for a specified period of time.

Prenuptial agreement An agreement entered into in contemplation of marriage that specifies the rights and ownership of property brought into the marriage and, where permitted, property acquired during the marriage.

Presentment Occurs when the holder of a negotiable instrument presents it to the maker, acceptor, drawee, or other payor for acceptance or payment.

Presentment warranties Implied warranties, made by any person who seeks payment or acceptance of a negotiable instrument to any person who in good faith pays or accepts the instrument, that the party presenting the instrument has good title to the instrument or is authorized to obtain payment or acceptance on behalf of a person who has good title, has no knowledge that the signature of the maker or the drawer is unauthorized, and has no knowledge that the instrument has been materially altered.

Price discrimination A seller's setting of prices in such a way that two competing buyers pay two different prices for an identical product or service.

Price-fixing agreement An anticompetitive agreement between competitors to fix, or render uniform, the prices at which they will sell their products or services.

***Prima facie* case** A case in which the plaintiff has produced sufficient evidence of his or her conclusion that the case can go to a jury; a case in which the evidence compels the plaintiff's conclusion if the defendant produces no evidence to rebut it.

Principal In agency law, a person who, by agreement or otherwise, authorizes an agent to act on his or her behalf in such a way that the acts of the agent become binding on the principal.

Privilege In tort law, the ability to act contrary to another person's right without being liable for the consequences.

Privity of contract The relationship that exists between the promisor and the promisee of a contract.

Probable cause Reasonable grounds to believe the existence of facts warranting certain actions, such as the search or arrest of a person.

Probate court A court having jurisdiction over proceedings concerning the settlement of a person's estate.

Procedural rule A rule that describes an agency's methods of operation and establishes procedures for dealing with the agency.

Proceeds In secured transactions law, whatever is received when the collateral is sold, exchanged, collected, or otherwise disposed of, such as insurance payments for destroyed or lost collateral. Money, checks, and the like are *cash proceeds*, whereas all other proceeds received are *noncash proceeds*.

Product liability The legal liability of manufacturers and sellers to buyers, users, and bystanders for injuries or damages suffered because of defects in goods. Liability arises when a product has a defective condition that makes it unreasonably dangerous and the product causes damage or injury.

Profit In real property law, the right to enter upon and remove things from the property of another (for example, the right to enter onto a person's land and remove sand and gravel therefrom).

Promise A declaration that binds the person who makes it (promisor) to do or not to do a certain act. The person to whom the promise is made (promisee) has a right to expect or demand the performance of some particular thing.

Promisee A person to whom a promise is made.

Promisor A person who makes a promise.

Promissory estoppel A doctrine that applies when a promisor reasonably expects a promise to induce definite and substantial action or forbearance by the promisee, and that does induce such action or forbearance in reliance thereon; such a promise is binding if injustice can be avoided only by enforcing the promise. *See also* Estoppel.

Promissory note A written instrument signed by a maker unconditionally promising to pay a certain sum in money to a payee or a holder on demand or on a specified date.

Promoter An entrepreneur who participates in the organization of a corporation in its formative stage, usually by issuing a prospectus, procuring subscriptions to the stock, making contract purchases, securing a charter, and the like.

Prospectus A document that contains all material facts about a company and its operations so that those who wish to purchase stock (invest) in the corporation have the basis for making an informed decision.

Protected class Under Title VII of the Civil Rights Act of 1964, any persons classified because of race, color, national origin, religion or sex. Age and disability are classifications of protected classes under other acts.

Protected interests All interests protected by law. Protected interests include civil rights and liberties, freedom from harms resulting from intentional or unintentional torts, harms caused by criminal actions, and so on.

Proximate cause The "next" or "substantial" cause; in tort law, a concept used to determine whether a plaintiff's injury was the natural and continuous result of a defendant's negligent act. If the negligent act of a defendant was the sole cause or a substantial cause of injuries to a plaintiff, the defendant will be liable.

Proxy In corporation law, a written agreement between a stockholder and another under which the stockholder authorizes the other to vote the stockholder's shares in a certain manner.

Proxy fight A battle waged for shareholder proxies; usually, the battle is between corporate directors who want to retain their control over the corporation and others who want to "throw the directors out."

Puffery A salesperson's often exaggerated claims concerning the quality of the goods offered for sale. Such claims involve opinions rather than facts and are not considered to be legally binding promises or warranties.

Punitive (exemplary) damages Compensation in excess of actual or consequential damages. They are awarded in order to punish the wrongdoer and usually will be awarded only in cases involving willful or malicious misconduct.

Purchase-money security interest (PMSI) A security interest to the extent that it is (1) taken or retained by a seller of the collateral to secure all or part of the price of the collateral or (2) taken by a creditor who, by making advances or incurring an obligation, gives value to enable the debtor to acquire rights in, or use of, the collateral, if such value is in fact so used.

Q

Qualified indorsement An indorsement on a negotiable instrument under which the indorser disclaims to subsequent holders secondary liability on the instrument; the most common qualified indorsement is "without recourse."

Quasi contract An obligation or contract imposed by law, in the absence of agreement, to prevent unjust enrichment. Sometimes referred to as an implied-in-law contract (a legal fiction) to distinguish it from an implied-in-fact contract.

Quitclaim deed A deed intended to pass any title, interest, or claim that the grantor may have in the premises but not professing that such title is valid and not containing any warranty or covenants of title.

Quorum The number of members of a decision-making body that must be present before business may be transacted.

R

Race norming Separating the results of a standardized aptitude test into groups on the basis of race or ethnic origin and using the same cut-off percentile for each group, regardless of the individuals' scores.

Ratification The approval or validation of a previous action. In contract law, the confirmation of a voidable act (that is, an act that without ratification would not be an enforceable contractual obligation). In agency law, the confirmation by one person of an act or contract performed or entered into on his or her behalf by another, who assumed, without authority, to act as his or her agent.

Real property Immovable property consisting of land and buildings thereupon, as opposed to personal property, which can be moved. In the absence of a contract, real property includes things growing on the land before they are severed (such as timber), as well as fixtures.

Reasonable doubt The standard used to determine the guilt or innocence of a person charged with a criminal offense. To be guilty of a crime, one must be proved guilty "beyond and to the exclusion of every reasonable doubt." A reasonable doubt is one that would cause prudent or "reasonable" persons to hesitate before acting in matters important to them.

Reasonable person standard The standard of behavior expected of a hypothetical "reasonable person." The standard against which negligence is measured and that must be observed to avoid liability for negligence.

Rebuttal The refutation of evidence introduced by an adverse party's attorney.

Receiver A court-appointed person who receives, preserves, and manages a business or other property that is involved in bankruptcy proceedings.

Recording statute A statute requiring that deeds, mortgages, and other real property transactions be recorded so as to provide notice to future purchasers, creditors, and encumbrancers of an existing claim on the property.

Red herring prospectus A prospectus permitted to be distributed by an issuing corporation after a registration statement is filed and before the sale of securities can take place (during the twenty-day waiting period). The prospectus must have a red legend or mark on it.

Redress Satisfaction for damages incurred through the wrongdoing of another.

Reformation A court-ordered correction of a written contract so that it reflects the true intentions of the parties.

Regulation Z A set of rules issued by the Federal Reserve System's board of governors under the authority of the Electronic Fund Transfer Act to protect users of electronic fund transfer systems.

Rejoinder The defendant's answer to the plaintiff's rebuttal.

Release The relinquishment, concession, or giving up of a right, claim, or privilege, by the person in whom it exists or to whom it accrues, to the person against whom it might have been enforced or demanded.

Remainder A future interest in property, held by a person other than the grantor, that occurs at the natural termination of the preceding estate.

Remedy The relief given to innocent parties, by law or by contract, to enforce a right or to prevent or compensate for the violation of a right.

Replevin An action brought to recover the possession of personal property unlawfully held by another.

Reply Procedurally, a plaintiff's response to a defendant's answer.

Requirements contract An agreement under which a promisor promises to supply the promisee with all the goods and/or services the promisee might require from period to period.

Res ipsa loquitur A doctrine under which negligence may be inferred simply because an event occurred, if it is the type of event that would not occur absent negligence. Literally, the term means *the thing speaks for itself.*

Resale price maintenance agreement An agreement between a manufacturer and a retailer in which the manufacturer specifies the minimum retail price of its products. Resale price maintenance agreements are illegal *per se* under the Sherman Act.

Rescission A remedy whereby a contract is terminated and the parties are returned to the positions they occupied before the contract was made; may be effected through the mutual consent of the parties, by their conduct, or by the decree of a court of equity.

Respondeat superior In Latin, "Let the master respond." A principle of law whereby a principal or an employer is held liable for the wrongful acts committed by agents or employees while acting within the scope of their agency or employment.

Respondent In equity practice, the party who answers a bill or other proceeding. In appellate practice, the party against whom an appeal is taken (sometimes referred to as the appellee).

Restitution An equitable remedy under which a person is restored to his or her original position prior to loss or injury, or placed in the position he or she would have been in had the breach not occurred.

Restrictive indorsement Any indorsement of a negotiable instrument that purports to condition or prohibit further transfer of the instrument. As against payor and intermediary banks, such indorsements are usually ineffective. A restrictive indorsement does not prohibit further transfer or negotiation of the instrument.

Resulting trust A trust implied in law from the apparent intentions of the parties to a given transaction. A trust in which a party holds actual legal title but for the benefit of another, frequently the grantor.

Retained earnings The portion of a corporation's profits that has not been paid out as dividends to shareholders.

Reversionary interest A future residuary interest retained in property by the grantor. For example, a landowner who conveys property to another for life creates retains a future interest in the property. When the person holding the life estate dies, the property will revert to the grantor (unless the grantor has transferred the future interest to another party).

Revocation In contract law, the withdrawal of an offer by an offeror; unless the offer is irrevocable, it can be revoked at any time prior to acceptance without liability.

Right of contribution The right of a co-surety who pays more than his or her proportionate share upon a debtor's default to recover the excess paid from other co-sureties.

Right of first refusal The right to purchase personal or real property—such as corporate shares or real estate—before the property is offered for sale to others.

Right of reimbursement The legal right of a person to be restored, repaid, or indemnified for costs, expenses, or losses incurred or expended on behalf of another.

Right of subrogation The right of a person to stand in the place of (be substituted for) another, giving the substituted party the same legal rights that the original party had.

Right-to-work laws State laws generally providing that employees are not to be required to join a union as a condition of receiving or retaining employment.

Risk A specified contingency or peril.

Risk management Planning that is undertaken to protect one's interest should some event threaten to undermine its security. In the context of insurance, transferring certain risks from the insured to the insurance company.

Robbery Theft from a person, accompanied by force or fear of force.

Rule 10b-5 A rule of the Securities and Exchange Commission that makes it unlawful, in connection with the purchase or sale of any security, to make any untrue statement of a material fact or to omit a material fact if such omission causes the statement to be misleading.

Rule of reason A test by which a court balances the reasons (such as economic efficiency) for an agreement against its potentially anticompetitive effects. In antitrust litigation, many practices are analyzed under the rule of reason.

Rulemaking The actions undertaken by administrative agencies when formally adopting new regulations or amending old ones. Under the Administrative Procedures Act, rulemaking includes notifying the public of proposed rules or changes and receiving and considering the public's comments.

Rulemaking-on-a-record Agency rulemaking that is much more extensive than informal rulemaking and in which a public hearing is conducted in the manner of a trial. After the hearing is concluded, the agency is required to prepare a formal written statement describing its findings based on the evidence presented by both sides. Also referred to as formal rulemaking.

S

S corporation A close business corporation that has met certain requirements as set out by the Internal Revenue Code and thus qualifies for special income-tax treatment. Essentially, an S corporation is taxed the same as a partnership, but its owners enjoy the privilege of limited liability.

Sale The passing of title from the seller to the buyer for a price.

Sales contract A contract by means of which the ownership of goods is transferred from a seller to a buyer for a fixed price in money, paid or agreed to be paid by the buyer.

Sale on approval A type of conditional sale that becomes absolute only when the buyer approves or is satisfied with the good(s) sold. Besides express approval of goods, approval may be inferred if the buyer keeps the goods beyond a reasonable time or uses the goods in any way that is inconsistent with the seller's ownership.

Sale or return A type of conditional sale wherein title and possession pass from the seller to the buyer; however, the buyer retains the option to rescind or return the goods during a specified period even though the goods conform to the contract.

Scienter Knowledge by the misrepresenting party that material facts have been falsely represented or omitted with an intent to deceive.

Searches and seizures The searching or taking into custody of persons or private property by the government. The Fourth Amendment prohibits unreasonable and unwarranted searches and seizures. In the context of administrative law, administrative agencies may undertake searches and seizures to gather information and necessary evidence to prove that a regulation has been violated.

Seasonably Within a specified time period, or if no period is specified, within a reasonable time.

Secured party A lender, seller, or any other person in whose favor there is a security interest, including a person to whom accounts or chattel paper has been sold.

Secured transaction Any debt transaction which creates a security interest in personal property or fixtures, including goods, documents, and other intangibles, guaranteeing payment of the debt.

Securities Stock certificates, bonds, notes, debentures, warrants, or other documents, certificates, or interests given as evidence of an ownership interest in the corporation or as a promise of repayment by the corporation.

Security agreement The agreement that creates or provides for a security interest between the debtor and a secured party.

Security interest Every interest "in *personal property or fixtures* [emphasis added] that secures payment or performance of an obligation" [UCC 1–201(37)].

Self-defense The legally recognized privilege to protect one's self or property against injury by another. The privilege of self-defense only protects acts that are reasonably necessary to protect one's self or property.

Seniority system In regard to employment relationships, a system in which those who have worked longest for the company are first in line for promotions, salary increases, and other benefits; they are also the last to be laid off if the work force must be reduced.

Service mark A mark used in the sale or the advertising of services, such as to distinguish the services of one person from the services of others. Titles, character names, and other distinctive features of radio and television programs may be registered as service marks.

Sexual harassment In the employment context, hiring or granting of job promotions or other benefits in return for sexual favors or language or conduct that is so sexually offensive that it creates a hostile working environment.

Shareholder's derivative suit A suit by a shareholder to enforce a corporate cause of action for a wrong suffered by the corporation committed by a third person.

Shelter principle The principle that the holder of a negotiable instrument who cannot qualify as a holder in due course (HDC), but who derives his or her title through an HDC, acquires the rights of an HDC.

Shipment contract A contract for the sale of goods in which the buyer assumes liability for any losses or damage to the goods on the seller's delivery of the goods to a carrier.

Short-form merger A merger between a subsidiary corporation and a parent corporation that owns at least 90 percent of the outstanding shares of each class of stock issued by the subsidiary corporation. Short-form mergers can be accomplished without the approval of the shareholders of either corporation.

Signature The name or mark of a person, written by that person or at his or her direction. In commercial law, any name, word, or mark used with the intention to authenticate a writing constitutes a signature.

Slander of quality Publication of false information about another's product, alleging it is not what its seller claims; also referred to as trade libel.

Slander of title The publication of a statement that denies or casts doubt upon another's legal ownership of any property, causing financial loss to that property's owner.

Small claims courts Special courts in which parties may litigate small claims (usually, claims involving $2,500 or less). Attorneys are not required in small claims courts, and in many states, attorneys are not allowed to represent the parties.

Sole proprietorship The simplest form of business, in which the owner is the business; thus, anyone who does business without creating a formal business entity has a sole proprietorship. The owner of a sole proprietorship reports business income on his or her personal income tax return and is legally responsible for all debts and obligations incurred by the business.

Sovereign immunity A doctrine that immunizes foreign

nations from the jurisdiction of U.S. courts when certain conditions are satisfied.
Special indorsement An indorsement on an instrument that specifies a specific person to whom or to whose order the instrument is payable.
Specific performance An equitable remedy requiring *exactly* the performance that was specified in a contract. Usually granted only when money damages would be an inadequate remedy and the subject matter of the contract is unique (for example, real property).
Spendthrift trust A trust created to protect the beneficiary from spending all the money to which he or she is entitled. Only a certain portion of the total amount is given to the beneficiary at any one time, and most states prohibit creditors from attaching assets of the trust.
Stakeholder view of corporate social responsibility A view of corporate social responsibility holding that corporations have duties to all individuals or groups who have a "stake" in the corporation, not just to shareholders, employees, and customers. In the stakeholder view of corporate social responsibility, corporations should also consider the needs of lenders, suppliers, the community, and others who will be affected by corporate decision making.
Stale check A check, other than a certified check, that is presented for payment more than six months after its date.
Standing The requirement that an individual must have a sufficient stake in a controversy before he or she can bring a lawsuit. The plaintiff must demonstrate that he or she either has been injured or threatened with injury.
Stare decisis A flexible doctrine of the courts, recognizing the value of following prior decisions (precedents) in cases similar to the one before the court; the courts' practice of being consistent with prior decisions based on similar facts.
Statute of Frauds A state statute under which certain types of contracts must be in a signed writing to be enforceable.
Statute of limitations A federal or state statute setting the maximum time period during which a certain action can be brought or rights enforced. After the time period set out in the applicable statute of limitations has run, no legal action can be brought.
Statutory law Laws enacted by a legislative body (as opposed to constitutional law, administrative law, or case law).
Stock An equity or ownership interest in a corporation, measured in units of shares.
Stock certificate A certificate issued by a corporation evidencing the ownership of a specified number of shares in the corporation.
Stock warrant A certificate that grants the owner the option to buy a given number of shares of stock, usually within a set time period.
Stop-payment order An order by the drawer of a draft or check directing the drawer's bank not to pay the check or draft.
Strict liability Liability regardless of fault. In tort law, strict liability is imposed on a merchant who introduces into commerce a good that is unreasonably dangerous when in a defective condition.
Sublease A lease executed by the lessee of real estate to a third person, conveying the same interest that the lessee enjoys, but for a shorter term than that held by the lessee (as compared with an assignment of a lease, in which the lessee transfers the entire unexpired term of the leasehold to a third party).
Subpoena A document commanding a person to appear at a certain time and place to give testimony concerning a certain matter.
Summary judgment A judgment entered by a trial court prior to trial that is based on the valid assertion by one of the parties that there are no disputed issues of fact that would necessitate a trial.
Summary jury trial (SJT) A relatively recent method of settling disputes in which a trial is held, but the jury's verdict is not binding. The verdict only acts as a guide to both sides in reaching an agreement during the mandatory negotiations that immediately follow the trial. If a settlement is not reached, both sides have the right to a full trial later.
Summons A document informing a person that a legal action has been commenced against him or her and that he or she must appear in court on a certain date to respond.
Supremacy clause The provision in Article VI of the Constitution that provides that the Constitution, laws, and treaties of the United States are "the supreme Law of the Land." Under this clause, state laws that directly conflict with federal law will be rendered invalid.
Surety One who agrees to be primarily responsible for the debt of another, such as a cosigner on a note.
Suretyship A contract in which a third party to a debtor-creditor relationship (the surety) promises that the third party will be primarily responsible for the debtor's obligation.
Symbolic speech Nonverbal conduct that expresses opinions or thoughts about a subject. Symbolic speech is protected under the First Amendment's guarantee of freedom of speech.

T

Taking The taking of private property by the government for public use and for just compensation.
Tangible property Property that has physical existence and can be distinguished by the senses of touch, sight, and so on. A car is tangible property; a patent right is intangible property.
Target corporation The corporation to be acquired in a corporate takeover; a corporation to whose shareholders a tender offer is submitted.
Technology licensing Allowing another to use and profit from intellectual property (patents, copyrights, trademarks, innovative products or processes, and so on) for consideration. In the context of international business transactions, technology licensing sometimes is an attractive alternative to the establishment of foreign production facilities.
Tenancy at sufferance Tenancy by one who, after rightfully being in possession of leased premises, continues (wrongfully) to occupy the property after the lease has been terminated. The tenant has no rights to possess the property and occupies it only because the person entitled to evict the tenant has not done so.
Tenancy at will A tenancy by consent without a fixed in-

terval for paying rent (not a periodic tenancy). At common law, either party can terminate this tenancy without notice.

Tenancy by the entirety The joint ownership of property by husband and wife. Neither party can alienate or encumber the property without the consent of the other. The property is inherited by the survivor of the two, and dissolution of marriage transforms a tenancy by the entirety into a tenancy in common.

Tenancy for years A nonfreehold estate/lease for a specified period of time, after which the possession and use of the real property reverts to the grantor.

Tenancy in common Co-ownership of property in which each party owns an undivided interest that passes to his or her heirs at death.

Tender of delivery A seller's holding out conforming goods in a reasonable manner with notice to enable the buyer to take delivery.

Tender offer An offer to purchase shares made by one company directly to the shareholders of another company; often referred to more simply as a "take-over bid."

Testamentary trust A trust that is created by will and therefore does not take effect until the death of the testator.

Testator One who makes and executes a will.

Third party beneficiary One for whose benefit a promise is made in a contract but who is not a party to the contract.

Tippees Persons who receive inside information from an insider or another tippee.

Tombstone ad An advertisement announcing a sale of securities and informing the prospective investor where and how to obtain a prospectus.

Tortfeasor One who commits a tort.

Torts Civil (as opposed to criminal) wrongs not arising from a breach of contract. A breach of a legal duty owed by the defendant to the plaintiff; the breach must be the proximate cause of harm to the plaintiff.

Totten trust A trust created by the deposit of a person's own money in his or her own name as a trustee for another. It is a tentative trust, revocable at will until the depositor dies or completes the gift in his or her lifetime by some unequivocal act or declaration.

Toxic torts Failure to use or to clean up properly or where prohibited to use toxic chemicals that cause harm to a person or society.

Trade acceptance A draft drawn by the seller of goods on the purchaser and accepted by the purchaser's written promise to pay the draft. Once accepted, the purchaser becomes primarily liable to pay the draft.

Trade name A name used in commercial activity to designate a particular business, a place at which a business is located, or a class of goods. Trade names can be exclusive or nonexclusive. Examples of trade names are Sears, Safeway, and Firestone.

Trade secrets Information or processes that give a business an advantage over competitors who do not know the information or processes.

Trade-off A desired result that one must sacrifice (trade off) to obtain another, equally desired result.

Trademark A word or symbol that has become sufficiently associated with a good (at common law) or has been registered with a government agency. Once a trademark is established, the owner has exclusive use of it and has the right to bring a legal action against those who infringe upon the protection given the trademark.

Transfer warranties Warranties made by the indorser and transferor of a negotiable instrument who receives consideration to subsequent transferees and holders who take the instrument in good faith that (1) the transferor has good title to the instrument or is otherwise authorized to obtain payment or acceptance on behalf of one who does have good title; (2) all signatures are genuine or authorized; (3) the instrument has not been materially altered; (4) no defense of any party is good against the transferor; and (5) the transferor has no knowledge of any insolvency proceedings against the maker, the acceptor, or the drawer of an unaccepted instrument.

Traveler's check An instrument purchased from a bank, express company, or the like, in various denominations, that can be used as cash upon a second signature by the purchaser. It has the characteristics of a cashier's check.

Treaty An agreement, or compact, formed between two independent nations.

Trespass to land Passing over another's land uninvited. Most courts require that to constitute trespass, an intrusion must be intentional, negligent, or the result of an "abnormally dangerous activity."

Trespass to personalty Any wrongful transgression or offense against the personal property of another.

Trust (1) A form of business organization somewhat similar to a corporation. Originally, the trust was a device by which several corporations that were engaged in the same general line of business combined for their mutual advantage to eliminate competition and control the market for their products. The term *trust* derived from the transfer of the voting power of the corporations' shareholders to the committee or board that controlled the organization. (2) An arrangement in which title to property is held by one person (a trustee) for the benefit of another (a beneficiary).

Trust indorsement An indorsement for the benefit of the indorser or a third person; also known as an agency indorsement. The indorsement results in legal title vesting in the original indorsee.

Tying arrangement An agreement between a buyer and a seller under which the buyer of a specific product or service is obligated to purchase additional products or services from the seller.

Type I error An error made as a result of a decision or an action.

Type II error An error made as a result of the failure to make a decision or take action.

U

Ultra vires A Latin term meaning *beyond the powers*. Activities of a corporation's managers that are outside the scope of the power granted them by the corporation's charter or the laws of the state of incorporation are *ultra vires* acts.

Unconscionability A doctrine under which courts may deny enforcement of a contract or clause on the basis of public policy, when one party, as a result of his or her disproportionate bargaining power, is forced to accept terms that are unfairly burdensome and that unfairly benefit the dominating party.

Unconscionable contract or clause A contract or clause that is void on the basis of public policy because one party, as a result of his or her disproportionate bargaining power, is forced to accept terms that are unfairly burdensome and that unfairly benefit the dominating party.

Underwriter In insurance law, the one assuming a risk in return for the payment of a premium; the insurer. In securities law, any person, banker, or syndicate that guarantees a definite sum of money to a business or government in return for the issue of stock or bonds, usually for resale purposes.

Undisclosed principal A principal whose identity is unknown by a third person, and the third person has no knowledge that the agent is acting in an agency capacity at the time the contract is made.

Unenforceable contract A valid contract having no legal effect or force in a court action.

Unilateral contract A contract that includes the exchange of a promise for an act (completion of the contract performance).

Universal defenses Defenses that can be used to avoid payment to all holders of a negotiable instrument, including a holder in due course (HDC) or (under the shelter principle) a holder through an HDC. Also called *real defenses*.

Unreasonably dangerous In product liability, defective to the point of threatening a consumer's health and safety. A product will be considered unreasonably dangerous if it is dangerous beyond the expectation of the ordinary consumer or if a less dangerous alternative was economically feasible for the manufacturer, but the manufacturer failed to produce it.

Usage of trade Any practice or method of dealing having such regularity of observance in a place, vocation, or trade as to justify an expectation that it will be observed with respect to the transaction in question.

Utilitarianism An approach to ethical reasoning in which ethically correct behavior is not related to any absolute ethical or moral values but to an evaluation of the consequences of a given action on those who will be affected by it. In utilitarian reasoning, a "good" decision is one that results in the greatest good for the greatest number of people affected by the decision.

V

Valid contract A properly constituted contract having legal strength or force.

Venue The geographical district in which an action is tried and from which the jury is selected.

Vertical merger A combining of two firms, one of which purchases goods for resale from the other. If a producer or wholesaler acquires a retailer, it is a *forward* vertical merger. If a retailer or distributor acquires its producer, it is a *backward* vertical merger.

Vertical restraint Any restraint on trade created by agreements between firms at different levels in the manufacturing and distribution process.

Vertically integrated firm A firm that carries out two or more functional phases (manufacture, distribution, retailing, etc.) of a product.

Void contract A contract having no legal force or binding effect.

Voidable contract A contract that may be legally annulled at the option of one of the parties.

Voir dire From the French, meaning "to speak the truth." A phrase denoting the preliminary questions that attorneys for the plaintiff and the defendant ask prospective jurors to determine whether potential jury members are biased or have any connection with a party to the action or with a prospective witness.

Voting trust The transfer of title by stockholders of shares of a corporation to a trustee who is authorized to vote the shares on their behalf.

W

Waiver An intentional, knowing relinquishment of a legal right.

Warrant An order granted by a public authority. An arrest warrant authorizes law-enforcement personnel to arrest a particular suspect; a search warrant authorizes law-enforcement personnel to search particular premises or property.

Warranty deed A deed under which the grantor guarantees to the grantee that the grantor has title to the property conveyed in the deed, that there are no encumbrances on the property other than what the grantor has represented, and that the grantee will enjoy quiet possession.

Watered stock Stock issued by a corporation as if fully paid for, when in fact less than par value has been paid.

Wetlands Areas of land designated by government agencies (such as the Army Corps of Engineers or the Environmental Protection Agency) as protected areas that suppose wildlife and that therefore cannot be filled in or dredged by private contractors or parties.

Whistleblowing An employee's disclosure to government, the press, or upper-management that his or her employer is engaged in unsafe or illegal activities.

White-collar crime Nonviolent crime committed by corporations and individuals. Embezzlement and commercial bribery are two examples of white-collar crime.

Will An instrument directing what is to be done with the testator's property upon his or her death, made by the testator and revocable during his or her lifetime. No interests pass until the testator dies.

Winding up The second of two stages involved in the dissolution of a partnership or corporation. Once the firm is dissolved, it continues to exist legally until the process of winding up all business affairs (collecting and distributing the firm's assets) is complete.

Working papers The various documents used and developed by an accountant during an audit. Working papers include notes, computations, memoranda, copies, and other papers that make up the work product of an accountant's services to a client.

Workout A common law or bankruptcy out-of-court negotiation with creditors in which a debtor enters into an agreement with a creditor or creditors for a payment or plan to discharge the debtor's debt(s).

Writ of attachment A writ employed to enforce obedience to an order or judgment of the court. The writ may take the form of taking or seizing property to bring it under the control of the court.

Writ of *certiorari* A writ from a higher court asking the lower court for the record of a case.

Writ of execution A writ that puts in force a court's decree or judgment.

Wrongful discharge An employer's termination of an employee's employment in violation of common law principles or statutory law that protects a specific class of employees.

Table of Cases

The principal cases are in bold type. Cases cited or discussed are in roman type. Cases that can also be retrieved on West's LEGAL CLERK Research Software System are indicated by a colored dot. To determine which of the three versions of LEGAL CLERK a particular case appears on, please turn to the text page cited and refer to the color-coded computer symbol printed with the case citation.

A black computer symbol with a white background indicates that the case appears on *Uniform Commercial Code Article 2 Sales-Version 1.0.* A black computer symbol with a grey background indicates that the case is on *Government Regulation and the Legal Environment of Business-Version 1.0.* A black computer symbol with a light blue background identifies the case as appearing on *Contracts-Version 1.0.*

A

B

I

J

K

L

T

U

V

W

X

Y

Z

Index

C

E

F

G

H

I

J

K

L

M

N

Q

R

S

T

U

V

W

Y

Associate Justices (continued)

NAME	YEARS OF SERVICE	STATE APP'T FROM	APPOINTING PRESIDENT	AGE APP'T	POLITICAL AFFILIATION	EDUCATIONAL BACKGROUND
Lamar, Lucius Quintus C.	1888-1893	Mississippi	Cleveland	63	Democrat	Emory College
Brewer, David Josiah	1890-1910	Kansas	Harrison	53	Republican	Wesleyan University; Yale; Albany Law School
Brown, Henry Billings	1891-1906	Michigan	Harrison	55	Republican	Yale; studied at Yale Law School and Harvard Law School
Shiras, George, Jr.	1892-1903	Pennsylvania	Harrison	61	Republican	Ohio University; Yale; studied law at Yale and privately
Jackson, Howell Edmunds	1893-1895	Tennessee	Harrison	61	Democrat	West Tennessee College; University of Virginia; one year in Legal Dept. of Cumberland University
White, Edward Douglass	1894-1910	Louisiana	Cleveland	49	Democrat	Mount St. Mary's College; Georgetown College (now University)
Peckham, Rufus Wheeler	1896-1909	New York	Cleveland	58	Democrat	Read law in father's firm
McKenna, Joseph	1898-1925	California	McKinley	55	Republican	Benicia Collegiate Institute, Law Dept.
Holmes, Oliver Wendell,Jr.	1902-1932	Massachusetts	Roosevelt, T.	61	Republican	Harvard College; studied law at Harvard Law School
Day, William Rufus	1903-1922	Ohio	Roosevelt, T.	54	Republican	University of Michigan; University of Michigan Law School
Moody, William Henry	1906-1910	Massachusetts	Roosevelt, T.	53	Republican	Harvard; Harvard Law School
Lurton, Horace Harmon	1910-1914	Tennessee	Taft	66	Democrat	University of Chicago; Cumberland Law School
Hughes, Charles Evans	1910-1916	New York	Taft	48	Republican	Colgate University; Brown University; Columbia Law School
Van Devanter, Willis	1911-1937	Wyoming	Taft	52	Republican	Indiana Asbury University; University of Cincinnati Law School
Lamar, Joseph Rucker	1911-1916	Georgia	Taft	54	Democrat	University of Georgia; Bethany College; Washington and Lee University
Pitney, Mahlon	1912-1922	New Jersey	Taft	54	Republican	College of New Jersey (Princeton); read law under father
McReynolds, James Clark	1914-1941	Tennessee	Wilson	52	Democrat	Vanderbilt University; University of Virginia
Brandeis, Louis Dembitz	1916-1939	Massachusetts	Wilson	60	Democrat	Harvard Law School
Clarke, John Hessin	1916-1922	Ohio	Wilson	59	Democrat	Western Reserve University; read law under father
Sutherland, George	1922-1938	Utah	Harding	60	Republican	Brigham Young Academy; one year at University of Michigan Law School
Butler, Pierce	1923-1939	Minnesota	Harding	57	Democrat	Carleton College
Sanford, Edward Terry	1923-1930	Tennessee	Harding	58	Republican	University of Tennessee; Harvard; Harvard Law School
Stone, Harlan Fiske	1925-1941	New York	Coolidge	53	Republican	Amherst College; Columbia University Law School
Roberts, Owen Josephus	1930-1945	Pennsylvania	Hoover	55	Republican	University of Pennsylvania; University of Pennsylvania Law School
Cardozo, Benjamin Nathan	1932-1938	New York	Hoover	62	Democrat	Columbia University; two years at Columbia Law School
Black, Hugo Lafayette	1937-1971	Alabama	Roosevelt, F.	51	Democrat	Birmingham Medical College; University of Alabama Law School
Reed, Stanley Forman	1938-1957	Kentucky	Roosevelt, F.	54	Democrat	Kentucky Wesleyan University; Yale; studied law at University of Virginia and Columbia University; University of Paris